HANDBOOK OF CHILD PSYCHOLOGY

HANDBOOK OF
CHILD
PSYCHOLOGY

Formerly CARMICHAEL'S MANUAL
OF CHILD PSYCHOLOGY

PAUL H. MUSSEN EDITOR

FOURTH EDITION

Volume IV
SOCIALIZATION, PERSONALITY,
AND SOCIAL DEVELOPMENT

E. Mavis Hetherington
VOLUME EDITOR

JOHN WILEY & SONS
NEW YORK CHICHESTER BRISBANE TORONTO SINGAPORE

Library of Congress Cataloging in Publication Data
Main entry under title:

Socialization, personality, and social development.

   (Handbook of child psychology; v. 4)
   Includes index.
   1. Socialization—Addresses, essays, lectures.
2. Child development—Addresses, essays, lectures.
3. Personality—Addresses, essays, lectures.
4. Child psychology—Addresses, essays, lectures.
I. Heterington, E. Mavis (Eileen Mavis), 1926—
II. Series.   [DNLM: 1: Child psychology. WS 105
H2354 (P)]
BF721.H242   1983 vol. 4   155.4s [155.4′18] 83-6552
[HQ783]

ISBN 0-471-09065-4

Printed in the United States of America

10 9 8 7 6 5 4 3

PREFACE TO THE FOURTH EDITION

The *Handbook of Child Psychology* is a direct descendant of three editions of the *Manual of Child Psychology*. The first and second editions, edited by Leonard Carmichael, were published in 1946 and 1954, the third, called *Carmichael's Manual of Child Psychology*, which I edited, was published in 1970. Each of these editions attempted to provide a definitive account of the state of knowledge of child psychology at the time of its publication.

In the 13 years since the publication of the third edition of *Carmichael's Manual*, child psychology has been an extraordinarily lively and productive discipline, expanding in many directions and at a rapid rate. Only a few of the most important of the countless changes will be reviewed here. The volume of the research activity and the annual output of research articles and books have accelerated enormously. As more information accumulates, new questions are generated, new research approaches are invented and older ones are applied in new versions, established theories are challenged and revised, novel theories are proposed, concepts are redefined, and specialized fields of interest and investigation evolve. These changes are closely intertwined and consequently have an impact on one another. Investigation of a new issue (or a revised version of an older one) often requires novel research techniques and approaches. New research findings may evoke questions about the conclusions derived from earlier studies and about underlying theories, and these questions, in turn, lead to further research. These cycles of events are repeated, progress in the field is continuous, and the amount of accumulated data snowballs. Consequently, even an authoritative 1970 publication cannot give an adequate picture of the field in the 1980s. A brand new source book is needed and the present volumes are intended to satisfy this need.

This *Handbook* attempts to reflect the changes in child psychology that have occurred since 1970 and to present as comprehensive, balanced, and accurate a survey of the contemporary field as possible. It is twice the size of the earlier two-volume work and differs from it in many ways. The coverage is broader and more topics are included, discussed in greater depth, and organized according to different principles. Discussions of topics of enduring interest that were presented in chapters in the last edition of *Carmichael's Manual*—for example, Piaget's theory, learning, language, thinking, aggression, sex-typing, socialization in the family and peer group—are reconceptualized and brought up to date in chapters in this *Handbook*.

The reader may get a clearer understanding of the structure and contents of the *Handbook* by noting some of the most significant contrasts between it and the last edition of *Carmichael's Manual*. The *Handbook* includes more chapters on theories and fundamental approaches to research in child psychology (Volume I). The chapter by Piaget on his own theory has been retained. In addition, there are chapters on information processing and systems theories—previously applied to issues in perception, learning, cognition, and social organization—which have proven useful in integrating a substantial body of the data of developmental psychology and in stimulating research. Cross-cultural and field studies have become very fruitful in the last 20 years and these too are discussed in separate chapters, as are the latest advances in general research methodology and assessment. And, as the discipline has matured, there is heightened (or renewed) interest in its philosophical and historical antecedents, so two chapters of Volume I are centered on these issues.

Developmental psychologists have always been interested in the *origins* of behavior, and the factors involved in very early development have become more prominent foci of research attention in the last 10 or 15 years. The psychological study of infants has burgeoned, while advances in research methodology in physiology, ethology, genetics, and neurology have made possible more refined and penetrating explorations of the biological bases of behavior. These research emphases are examined in Volume II of this *Handbook*.

The content area of greatest activity since 1970 has been cognitive development and the results of this activity are apparent in Volume III. For example, the third edition of *Carmichael's Manual* contained one chapter on language development and it dealt almost exclusively with the acquisition of grammar. In contrast, the *Handbook* has separate chapters on grammar, meaning, and communication. Much of the recent research in cognitive development confirms and extends Piaget's conclusions, but the results of other studies challenge aspects of Piagetian theory. Both kinds of findings are included in chapters in Volume III.

Several research areas that were new in 1970 have become well established, vigorous, and fruitful. Among these are social cognitive development, moral reasoning, and prosocial behavior; each of these is the topic of a chapter in this *Handbook*. In addition a number of traditional issues that had been somewhat neglected until recently have become more prominent in the literature of developmental psychology. For example, this *Handbook* contains chapters on representation, on logical thinking, play, the self, and on the school as an agent of socialization. None of these topics was discussed in the 1970 edition of *Carmichael's Manual*.

In response to social needs, developmental psychologists in increasing numbers conduct research on practical problems and attempt to apply their research findings to the solution of urgent problems, spelling out the implications of basic data for such areas as educational practice and social policy (see particularly the chapters on intervention and on risk factors in development in Volume II, on learning, memory, and comprehension in Volume III, and on treatment of children with emotional problems in Volume IV). The results of these activities are highly salutary for advancing the field of child psychology, for they extend the definitions of concepts investigated, test the findings of laboratory research in real-life settings, and illuminate the limitations of available data and theory.

The volume editors (William Kessen of Yale University, Marshall Haith and Joseph Campos of the University of Denver, John Flavell and Ellen Markman of Stanford, and E. Mavis Hetherington of the University of Virginia) and I met to plan and organize this *Handbook* over five years ago. Our objective was clear and straightforward: to prepare a source book that would present as complete, accurate, balanced, and up-to-date view of the field as possible.

Although there is no entirely satisfactory way of subdividing and organizing all of the vast body of theory, methods, and data in a field as large, varied, and ever-changing as developmental psychology, we constructed a table of contents that in our opinion included all the key topics—that is, all the topics that are currently receiving substantial amounts of research and theoretical attention. It soon became obvious that four volumes would be required, and we decided to arrange the material in accordance with the four predominent divisions of the field—theory and methods, biological bases of behavior and infancy, cognitive development, and social and personality development.

Comprehensive coverage was not our only aim; integrative summaries were to be accompanied by new perspectives and insights, critical analyses, and explications of deficiencies in existing data and theoretical orientations. We hoped to produce more than an encyclopedic review of accumulated knowledge; our goal was a source book that would encourage sophisticated thinking about fundamental issues, formulation of questions and hypotheses, and, ultimately, more good research.

We selected and invited a group of distinguished authorities in developmental psychology and related fields who were highly qualified to contribute chapters that would accomplish these goals. Almost all of our invitations were accepted and the assignments were carried out with extraordinary diligence, care, and thoughtfulness. Each working outline, preliminary draft, and final manuscript was reviewed by the volume editor, the general editor, and another authority on the subject, and suggestions for revision were communicated to the author. Although three of the chapters included in the original plan are missing, all the key chapters are included. We are therefore convinced that the *Handbook* provides the most comprehensive picture of contemporary child psychology that exists in one place.

If the objectives of the *Handbook* have been achieved, it is due primarily to the painstaking work, dedication, and creativity of the contributors and the volume editors. The lion's share of the basic work—preparation of scholarly, integrative, and critical chapters—was done by the authors. The contribution of the volume editors was indispensable; in their difficult roles of critic, advisor, and guardian of high standards, they were infinitely wise, patient, and persistent. My debts to all these individuals are incalculable.

Paul H. Mussen

PREFACE TO VOLUME IV

Editing a volume such as this is rather like reading a suspense story; you are never quite sure how it will turn out until it's finished. You select topics that give broad coverage to the most important areas in the field and choose authors who are expert in those areas. As editor, you have some conception of how the chapters are to fit together and complement, enhance, and parallel each other. You have a master plan for developing a creative, comprehensive gestalt. Finally, you present this vision and your goals to the authors; after that it's like herding cats. Authors have their own perspectives on their topics, their own notions about what constitutes significant issues and adequate coverage, and their own preferred styles of organization and presentation. No editor, no matter how dedicated, skilled, supportive, nurturant, opinionated, nagging, coercive, or wheedling can completely control authors. This leads to some topics falling through the cracks and not being dealt with at all, or being covered in a more restricted manner than you had intended, to title changes and redefined topics, as well as to some overlap and redundancy among chapters. However, this is more than compensated for by the unique insights, evaluations, speculations, and projections of some of the most distinguished behavioral scientists working in their fields. A more serious problem occurs when an author is unable to complete a chapter in time to have it appear in the volume. Originally, we planned to include in this volume a chapter on stress and coping in children. It was to have covered such topics as the impact of separation, loss, death, divorce, poverty, and physical and mental illness on families and the development of children. Although these issues are dealt with in other chapters, the last-minute unavailability of this chapter has led to less adequate coverage of these topics than was desired.

How have the perspectives, the interests, and the strategies of behavioral scientists studying the personality and social development of children changed since the publication of the last edition of this Handbook in 1970? There have been some notable shifts in the past years.

First, there has been a marked trend toward "cognizing" social development. The cognitive capacities, processes, and strategies of children of different ages that mediate developmental outcomes are a central focus in many chapters in this volume. Most of the chapters dealing with social development in the previous edition, had a narrowly focused social learning perspective. Reinforcement, punishment, and modeling were seen as the basic processes in social and personality development. In this edition, childrens' concepts, role-taking skills, information-processing abilities, interpretations, and attributions have come to the fore.

Second, the child is no longer viewed as a passive object of socialization. The so-called "social mold" theory has been abandoned in favor of an interactive model of development, with children being active participants in shaping their life experiences and social development. Children are seen not only as targets of socialization, but also as elicitors and processors of life experiences. This emphasis has led to a renewed interest in such topics as individual differences, temperament, attributional styles, the self-system, and self-control.

Third, psychologists are increasingly aware of the complexity of social development. Human development can be understood only in terms of the social, cultural, and historial context of the child's life. Concerns with social change, ecological influences, cultural diversity, and historical transitions are reflected in all the chapters.

A fourth related trend is the shift toward the use of more diverse methods and varied settings in the study of children. Scientific respectability does not rest as exclusively on the experimental method and laboratory studies as it did thirteen years ago. Bronfenbrenner (1977) described the developmental psychology of that time as "the science of the strange behavior of children in strange situations, with strange adults for the briefest possible period of time.''* This move from valuing rigor over relevance has led to an increase in the variety of methods, measures, and settings used in the studies of children and families. Investigators recognize that different methods have different strengths and weaknesses; different methods and measures yield different kinds of information, and the information may not be congruent. Moreover, children's behavior varies in different situations and may even vary in the same situation on different occasions. Researchers are rising to the challenge of questioning and refining old methods and developing new methods to deal with the complexities of the study of social and personality development.

I would like to thank the many people who contributed to this volume. Readers sometimes fail to recognize the enormous effort expended by authors in the review and integration of the literature and in the conceptualization of issues while writing a chapter of this kind. Our authors were open to suggestions and criticism and went through multiple revisions of their chapters.

In addition, we were fortunate to have a group of dedicated reviewers who wrote detailed, constructive commentaries on the chapters. I wish to express my appreciation to: Jeanne H. Block, Wanda C. Bronson, William Damon, Carol O. Eckerman, Nancy Eisenberg-Berg, Robert Emery, Ian W. J. M. Evans, Howard Gardner, Catherine J. Garvey, Donna M. Gelfand, Jean Ann Linney, K. Daniel O'Leary, Ross D. Parke, Charlotte Patterson, David G. Perry, Michael Rutter, Douglas B. Sawin, Daniel Solomon, and Janet T. Spence for their helpful suggestions in revising the chapters.

Finally, I wish to thank all the secretaries and student assistants who labored on these chapters. In my office, Miriam Trogdon played a major role in coordinating the activities of everyone involved in this volume.

It was only with the contributions of this diligent network of participants that the production of this Handbook was possible.

E. MAVIS HETHERINGTON

---

*Bronfenbrenner, U. Toward an experimental ecology of human development. *American Psychologist*, July 1977, 513–531.

CONTENTS

SOCIALIZATION IN THE CONTEXT OF THE FAMILY: PARENT-CHILD INTERACTION | 1

ELEANOR E. MACCOBY, *Stanford University*
JOHN A. MARTIN, *Stanford University*

CHAPTER CONTENTS

INTRODUCTION

The parent-child relationship is unique among human ties. Although it embodies many of the features of any close relationship—companionship, affection, interdependence of action sequences, some degree of meshing of goals, and the potential for considerable conflict—there are several features that distinguish it. The degree of obligation of parent to child is maximal, and in some societies this is balanced later, at least to some degree, by a reciprocal obligation of child to parent in the parent's old age. The tie is an enduring one. Through the years of the child's growth, children are not free to leave the relationship, and parents, though potentially more able than children to break the tie, seldom do. During the child's adulthood, even when the child and parent may not be in frequent contact, the tie is seldom severed completely in the sense that divorce severs a marriage bond.

The parent-child bond is unique in its initial asymmetry, and in the amount of change it must accommodate as the child and parent grow older. Of course, infants influence parents as well as vice versa. But our current enthusiasm for this idea should not cause us to lose sight of the enormous differential in power and competence that exists between an adult and an infant, and the potential for asymmetry that this implies. Inevitably, the functions of the two parties to a parent-infant interaction sequence are quite unlike, and in certain respects the parent must be the more influential. The parent comes to the relationship as a well-formed person who already has a language, preestablished friendships, a vast fund of knowledge and skills, and well-developed tastes and interests. Although these things are influenced by the arrival of the child, to a substantial degree they remain stable. By contrast, the infant's whole milieu is made up of the parents (and other family members) and of the environment they have established. The early development of the infant's affectional bonds, tastes, interests, skills, and knowledge all take place within this milieu and are influenced by it. Thus if we were to think in simplistic terms of the proportion of an individual's developed persona that had been subject to influence by a given interaction partner, within the parent-child dyad the proportion would always be greater for the child than for the parent at any given point in the life cycle. However, focusing more narrowly on the parent-child relationship itself and on the short-term contingencies governing brief bouts of interaction, we would very probably find influence flowing in both directions, with the balance determined by situational factors such as whether the parent is busy with other tasks, whether the parent is attempting to get the child to perform a task, and the child's need state.

In adult relationships, the amount of change in the partner that each participant must accommodate is usually limited. When one member of the dyad changes unpredictably or too dramatically, the partner may break off the relationship (as in divorce, where the complaint might be: ''He is no longer the person I married.''). In the parent-child relationship, dramatic change is endemic and yet the relationship continues and adapts. The enormous developmental changes occurring in the child force changes in the way parents deal with discipline, joint activities, and child care. Within this flow of change, however, there are certain basic parental functions that continue despite alterations in the specific way they are carried out.

Parental functions, of course, include providing protection, food, housing, and clothing for the child. Parents also determine the settings in which young children will spend their time, and they act on behalf of their children in situations where the children are not yet competent to act for themselves. These functions have largely been taken for granted by psychologists, and have entered into theories about the socialization process primarily in terms of any impact they have on specific characteristics of parent-child interaction itself. It is the parental role as educator—using this term broadly—that has been the primary focus of the developmental psychologist's interest. Psychological studies of socialization in the family setting have been concerned with how parental behavior supports children's learning to inhibit behavior that would be irritating or injurious to others, and at the same time fosters the acquisition of the positive behavior that society demands, including helpfulness and thoughtfulness toward others, self-reliance, acceptance of responsibility, and the acquisition of skills that will support successful adult functioning. Underlying such studies is the basic question: To what extent and in what ways are the child's development and adult character influenced by the nature of the interaction with parents during the child's life in the family of origin? To ask this question does not, of course, exclude other questions about the parent-child relationship, such as the influence of individual temperament, or genetically biased response tendencies, on the nature of the relationship or its outcomes.

The Chapter's Coverage

This chapter deals primarily with the role of parent-child interchanges in the socialization of young children. Although parent-child interaction is clearly instrumental in children's development of language and cognitive functions, the focus in this chapter is on the development of social behavior and personality patterns. Social and cognitive development cannot be kept conceptually distinct, however, and this is especially true now that social cognition has emerged as an increasingly active field of study. Furthermore, a major aspect of the socialization process is children's acquisition of the ability to monitor and control their own behavior, and self-regulation involves both cognitive and affective factors. Thus the influence of family interaction patterns on self-regulation and social cognition are topics that will be given some attention in this chapter.

Of course, the family is not the only arena in which socialization occurs. Schools and peer groups, to name only two of many sources of influence, play an important part. However, these influences are dealt with in separate chapters in these volumes. Because the focus of the present chapter is on the interchanges between parent and child, the major concern will be with the period of time during which the child is most closely embedded in the family interaction system—namely, the years up to adolescence.

The family does not function in a vacuum. It exists in a cultural milieu, and recently there has been growing emphasis on the fact that a family's physical, social, and economic situation has a considerable impact on the way parents carry out their parenting functions and on the nature of the parent-child interactions that occur. The factors that influence families have been conceptualized and measured at a number of levels. The most common are the family's socioeconomic level and ethnic background. Within the scope of this chapter, it is not possible to include a review of the research on socialization in different social classes, different ethnic groups, or different societies. The literature is voluminous and would justify a separate chapter. We will try to take account of social ecology and its impact on family functioning at a less generic level. We include a section on factors affecting family functioning (see *Factors Influencing the Interaction Pattern*), referring to research in which some direct assessment has been made of external supports, stressing conditions or situational factors that affect some aspect of parent-child relationships. In other words, we have gone directly to a more proximal level of analysis, searching for factors that may help to explain some of the social class and ethnic differences in socialization patterns that have been ubiquitous in the literature. We have attempted to take social class and ethnicity into account in another way: When there is evidence that a given relationship between parent and child variables holds for one socioeconomic or ethnic group but not another, this will of course be noted.

We have faced similar problems in dealing with sex differences in family interaction. This topic too deserves a chapter. The research has burgeoned during the 1970s, and it is a formidable task to organize and digest what is known about four sex-linked issues: (1) how or whether parents treat boys and girls differently; (2) how or whether there are characteristic differences in the behavior of mothers and fathers; (3) how and whether boys and girls differ in their reaction to a given socialization practice; and (4) how relationships differ in same-sex versus cross-sex parent-child pairs. Research relevant to these questions appears in Huston's chapter (see *vol. IV, chap. 5*). In the present chapter we do not attempt a comprehensive view but do discuss issue (3) above where relevant.

The focus of our chapter is on naturalistic parent-child interactions. A number of studies will be included in which special situations have been set up, including special tasks set for parents and children to perform, where the researcher's purpose is to increase the probability of occurrence of interactive behaviors of special interest. We are including, however, only a few of the experiments that are intended as laboratory analogues of socialization encounters, in which relatively unfamiliar adults play the role of socialization agents. This restricted treatment is not meant to deny the value of laboratory studies. Clearly there are issues concerning the direction of effects that can only be settled by experimental manipulation. In addition, laboratory studies sometimes bear on general features of interaction that are relevant to the parent-child relationship as well as other relationships. Our emphasis on naturalistic studies reflects our belief that despite the insights that can be had from experimental studies, the prior history of the relationship between an adult and a child has a strong impact on the way the two persons interact in any situation, contrived or naturalistic. Our concern in this chapter is with the parent-child relationship, and we think it doubtful that certain important aspects of this relationship can be duplicated to any significant degree in laboratory analogues involving relative strangers.

The point of view that has guided the writing of this chapter is an interactionist one. The implications of this viewpoint will presumably emerge throughout the chapter. For the present, we merely note that it means we will focus on bidirectional or multidirectional influence among the participants to an interaction, and will be concerned with the process of interaction itself rather than solely with "outcomes" of parent-child interaction. Concern with interaction also leads to consideration of the family as a system, a functioning integrated structure that has properties other than those of the individuals who make it up. These matters will be discussed in the next section (see *Theoretical Issues*).

The Choice of Variables and Levels of Analysis

A concern with the process of interaction does not replace, or render unimportant, the study of outcomes. In the long run, most students of parent-child interaction still want to know whether and in what ways the influence of participants on one another extends beyond the framework of the interaction itself. Usually the interest in outcome will focus on some aspect of the child's behavior, such as cognitive competence, sociometric status, initiative in problem solving, or antisocial behavior. If a study relies on naturally occurring variations in behavior rather than on variations produced by an experimental treatment, it will necessarily approach the problem of identifying parental influence on behaviors through an individual-differences paradigm. A group of children known to display the target behavior at high rates can be selected for comparison with a group known to be low or average; or an unselected group of children may be studied who are rank ordered with respect to the target behavior so that relationships between this rank order and characteristics of the parent-child interaction can be studied. These strategies rest on one of two assumptions: Either (1) there is enough similarity between major aspects of a child's situation at home and situations encountered outside the home so that behaviors acquired at home will generalize to many out-of-home situations (e.g., orientations toward parents may be generalized to nonfamilial authority figures); or (2) some significant portion of the variance in children's target behavior reflects stable characteristics of individual children, over and above the variance attributable to situations. The two approaches to personal consistency differ in certain conceptual ways. The first assumption leads to an analysis of similarities and dissimilarities between home and other situations. The second assumption involves factoring the variation in behavior into two components (the "situation" component and the "person" component) and looking for stability in the rank order of individuals even under situational changes that raise or lower the base rates of a target behavior for the whole population being studied. Clearly, the issues are complex, and they are currently under active debate. We cannot deal with them directly in this chapter, though they will emerge at several points in the discussion of other issues. All we wish to point out at present is that if family interaction patterns do have any impact on the nature of a child's skills and behavior tendencies as displayed outside the home, the effect must be on a portion of the behavioral variance that has some stability across time or situations or both. Perhaps the most important aspect of the design of any study, then, is the choice of target behaviors that are worth studying, in the sense that they reflect something more than momentary situational pressures.

Choosing the most meaningful level of analysis remains one of the most challenging problems in studies of parent-child interaction. Studies to be discussed in this chapter range from those choosing highly molecular variables (e.g., the frequency of mothers and infants smiling at one another) to those in which sets of specific behaviors have been clustered together into more molar categories (e.g., Patterson's "coercive" behavior; Ainsworth's "secure attachment"). Few issues have been more hotly debated in psychology than the validity of studying personality in terms of traitlike molar clusters. In developmental psychology the problem is particularly pressing, because developmental change occurs in the frequency, topography, and cognitive concomitants of every specific overt behavior, with change being especially rapid during the early years of life. If prediction from parent behaviors to later characteristics of children is to be attempted, it is almost inevitable that some clustering be attempted—clustering that reflects presumptions about what behaviors at one age are linked in meaningful ways to topographically different behaviors at a later age. Many researchers have gone about the clustering task empirically, through factor analysis; others have done so deductively, on the basis of psychological constructs (e.g., Ainsworth, Bell, & Stayton, 1971; Sears et al., 1965; Sroufe & Waters, 1977a). Either approach involves decisions about how broad a cluster to look for. Among the most molar clusters that have been studied are such personality characteristics as "competence," "ego control," and "coping."

Just as children's characteristics can be described in terms of either specific behavior or more global personality traits, so parents' socialization goals may be seen as encompassing a parallel range from specific to general. Parents attempt to shape their children's behavior toward very specific outcomes: They want them to use their table utensils in a certain way, say "please" and "thank you," or hang up their clothes. These specific behavior goals can be clustered into more general objectives: They want their children to be "polite," or "neat," or "to have good manners." Their socialization efforts may also be thought of in quite general terms: as aimed at fostering *optimal functioning* in children. The meaning of this global outcome varies with the child's age, sex, and cultural milieu. However, we may assume that any definition includes the child's (1) being as effective as possible in pursuing whatever goals are appropriate to the child's age and current situation, and (2) growing up to be a well-functioning adult. This too has many meanings, depending on what is valued in a particular culture, but usually implies taking up a productive work role, being free from obvious disabling pathologies, and having the ability to form bonds of some minimum degree of intimacy and stability with other persons.

It will not be easy to integrate findings from studies that examine moment-to-moment interchanges of specific behavioral acts with those that look for more global outcomes over more extended periods of time. The reader is warned that certain disjunctions will be inevitable, but attempts will be made to bridge them.

THEORETICAL ISSUES

Several points of view have influenced the psychological research on parent-child interaction. Psychoanalytic theory—in some instances reformulated in learning-theory terms—was a dominant theme in the work of the 1950s and 1960s, and the theory and its derivations have been summarized in several writings (cf. Erikson, 1950; Miller, 1969; Sears, Rau, & Alpert, 1965). Ethological theory has been most influential with respect to the work on attachment and parent-infant bonding (Bowlby, 1969, 1973; Hinde, 1976), and although most of the research emanating from their theory has dealt with the attachment of infants and young children to their caretakers, the theory also posits reciprocal predispositions for parents (perhaps particularly mothers) to bond to their infants (Klaus & Kennell, 1976). The implications of cognitive-developmental theory for the socialization process were discussed in detail by Kohlberg (1966), but this theory has so far had only a tangential influence on the body of research on parent-child interaction that will be reviewed in this chapter. Social learning theory has provided the predominant set of constructs with which most American students of child rearing have worked, and this theory has undergone considerable restructuring. Early versions of the theory, as it relates to socialization within the family, may be found in Patterson and Cobb (1971), Gewirtz (1969), and Bandura (1969). The more recent version, incorporating cognitive processes to a greater degree, is set forth in Bandura (1977) and Mischel and Mischel (1976).

Detailed presentations of these theories may be found in the cited sources, and we will not attempt to present them once again. Rather, we will discuss some recent formulations of the parent-child interaction process that supplement, integrate, or challenge these points of view, with special emphasis on the emerging body of theory about interaction itself.

Developments in Social Learning Theory

Reinforcement

Social learning theorists have long stressed that reinforcement is not necessary for learning. Indeed this is probably the primary respect in which they diverged from the theories of Hull and Skinner. However, they do emphasize the importance of contingencies in determining whether a response, once learned, will be produced; in this sense, reinforcement figures strongly in the theory. The effects of reinforcement are by no means seen as automatic, however. In current cognitive social learning theory, the effect of reinforcement depends on how the relationship between an act and its consequence is perceived by the subject, and how the probabilities of consequences are assessed.

It has never been simple to determine what response is being reinforced. We can illustrate the problem by referring to mother-child interaction. As will be noted below, the mother's responsiveness and sensitivity are powerful variables predicting the infant's development of a secure attachment. These aspects of maternal behavior can, of course, easily be conceptualized in reinforcement terms. When a parent holds and soothes an infant who is afraid, feeds a hungry infant, removes a source of pain or discomfort, or even merely entertains an infant who would otherwise be bored, all these actions can be seen as rewards. Parental sensitivity is important in that it reflects a parent's accuracy in diagnosing what is the cause of the child's distress, and consequently how rewarding the remedial action is likely to be. Also, it reflects how close the linkage in time will be between the child's signal and the parent's contingent response. In earlier writings on reinforcement, it was usually taken for granted that the nature of the response being reinforced was known. In parent-child interaction, however, the answer to this presumably simple question is not always clear. When a mother picks up a crying infant, is she reinforcing (a) crying? (b) the child's act of communicating (signaling)? (c) the child's attentiveness to and approach tendencies toward herself? (d) some rudimentary sense of efficacy, accompanying an infant's learning that it can produce signals that will have an ameliorative effect? (e) basic trust in the mother? If (b), then we may expect that as the child grows old enough to use noncrying kinds of signals, these may be substituted for the infantile crying that was previously reinforced (see Bell & Ainsworth, 1972; and a challenge to the Ainsworth position by Gewirtz & Boyd, 1977). If (c), then it would be expected that the children of the more responsive mothers would stay closest to their mothers. The fact that, on the contrary, it is these children who are better able to move *away* from their mothers to explore a novel environment has been used by Sroufe and Waters (1977a) to argue against a view that secure attachment results from the reinforcement of specific responses. If one were to view the process in reinforcement terms at all (which Sroufe and Waters do not do), one would have to turn to a much more global definition of the nature of the response being reinforced, for example, (e) above.

These issues return us to some of the questions raised in our introduction, concerning the most useful level of behavior—on the dimension running from molecular to molar—for analysis in studies of parent-child interaction. There can be no question that parents do teach specific molecular responses through reinforcement, and there is every reason to be interested in such teaching. It will become clear in our review, however, that many aspects of parent-child relationships cannot be captured if one thinks only of the acquisition of specific responses. As children's behavior becomes more highly organized, so that sets of responses become alternatives for one another and plans are superimposed, it is likely that parents begin to have an influence on the child's organization and planning processes, not only on the behavioral elements of which action sequences are composed. Our view is that one need not choose one level of analysis as more valuable than another, but only that researchers should be aware that (1) there are changes, with children's development, in the complexity of the levels of functioning likely to be affected by parental inputs; (2) that a number of levels, from molecular to molar, may be affected at the same time by a parental input such as reinforcement; and (3) the effects at different levels may not be fully compatible.

A second issue for reinforcement theory has to do with adaptation level. In some early work, Stevenson (1965) investigated the at-home child-rearing characteristics that were associated with a child's being responsive or unresponsive to social reinforcement in laboratory situations. The single variable that proved to be significant was the parents' use of praise: The more praise used at home, the *less* effective was praise as a form of reinforcement for learning a laboratory task. A likely interpretation of this finding is that children become accustomed to a given level of praise and pay less and less attention to praise that falls within the bounds of their adaptation level. If parental praise is to get an effect, then, it must either be used sparingly, or must be escalated in intensity or frequency so as to exceed a gradually rising adaptation level. Similar problems attend the use of rewards. If they are given regularly, they come to be expected, and their absence is experienced as punishment whereas their presence may no longer stand out as rewarding. Parents attempt to counteract this trend by reminding their children that a given event or gift is a special treat, something not to be expected routinely. Nevertheless, they may find themselves forced to escalate the value of treats in order to maintain their efficacy as rewards. Perhaps it is partly their awareness of the problems of adaptation level that lead to a certain amount of parental wariness concerning both praise and rewards: Many report they believe children should behave properly simply because they know they should, without "bribes" (Sears, Maccoby, & Levin, 1957).

A third issue in reinforcement theory concerns certain negative motivational effects of rewards. It has now been shown in a variety of studies that children who are initially spontaneously interested in an activity may lose interest in it if they are explicitly rewarded for it (see Lepper & Greene, 1978, for a review). This work and its implications is discussed in some detail below. For the present, it is sufficient to point out that the problem seems to be bound up with children's resistance to being externally controlled or manipulated. Despite all the demonstrations of the efficacy of positive reinforcement for response production, then, it is necessary to be alert to the side effects.

A final issue has to do with developmental change. Students of moral development describe a preconventional period in which children are hedonistic, conceiving of right and wrong in terms of what they will be rewarded or punished for. With development, however, many children shift away from this orientation. This formulation suggests that explicit contingencies should be more important in shaping the behavior of young children than of older persons. Part of the developmental change no doubt has to do with the increasing awareness of long-term as well as short-term consequences, and an increasing ability to think of contingencies in probabilistic terms and conduct a complex cost-benefit analysis. But probably even more important, there are changes in children's conceptions of what constitutes a positive outcome. Also, positive outcomes for others, or for one's group, may increasingly acquire positive weight.

Observational Learning

Observational learning plays a central role in social learning theory. Through observing the behavior of others, children can acquire novel behaviors, can discover ways to recombine elements in their existing repertoires, and can become aware of the consequences of behaviors. Although the term "observation" seems to imply watching, other sensory modalities, notably listening, are also clearly involved, and in the acquisition of language, exposure to models plays an essential role. Though the social learning theorists of the 1950s and 1960s said little about the cognitive aspects of observational learning, in more recent years they have stressed that such learning operates through its informational function (Bandura, 1972). A model need not be physically present for the model's behavior to be acquired; under certain circumstances, all that is necessary is that the subject *know* (e.g., through reading) what the model has done. Cognitive representations of others' behavior and its consequences are like other elements in thought, in that selective attention operates at initial intake of information, and there are constraints on storage and retrieval. It may be seen that through these modifications social learning theory has lost much of its status as a distinct theory, and is merging into the general body of psychological science.

Despite the strong emphasis on cognitive processes, social learning theorists have not brought cognitive *development* into a central role in their theory of modeling and its effects. The more recent book by Yando and colleagues (Yando, Seitz, & Zigler, 1978) attempts to repair the omission. It is evident that there are enormous developmental changes in the way in which information about a model's behavior is utilized. Though there is controversy concerning how early in infancy imitation can be reliably observed (see Uzgiris, 1981, for a review), there is no doubt that infants will imitate simple acts, such as tongue protrusions or hand movements, early in their first year. By the beginning of the second year, imitation becomes more complex; a sequence of several elements may be imitated, and the child enters into games of reciprocal imitation. Both Guillaume (1971, first published in 1926) and Piaget (1962, first published in English in 1951) have stressed the importance of delayed imitation, which appears during the second year, and indicates the formation of representations of others' behavior. The importance of such representations for the acquisition of language is highlighted in Weir's book *Language in the Crib* (1962), in which a young child is overheard correcting himself so as to bring his own pronunciation into conformity with that of a model who is no longer present.

Most studies of imitation after the second year have involved either situations in which the child is instructed to imitate, or situations in which the child needs the information provided by a model's actions in order to know how to utilize novel materials or behave in novel situations. The accuracy of such imitations increases with age (Yando et al., 1978). We know little about developmental change in uninstructed imitation that is not required for skill acquisition, except that it occurs, and more so in some children than in others.

In their longitudinal study of aggression, Lefkowitz, Eron, Walder, and Huesmann (1977) assessed "identification" by administering the *Expressive Behavior Profile* to both parents and children. The subjects rated aspects of their own expressive behavior (e.g., walking, talking) on a set of bipolar scales such as fast-slow, loud-soft. The extent of match between each child and the child's parents was calculated. Individual differences in the closeness of the match was a good predictor of the child's later aggressiveness: The closer the match, the lower the aggression at a later age. Thus not only is it true that children differ with respect to their tendency to adopt their parent's stylistic mannerisms, but this tendency appears to be linked to other aspects of personality development.

There can be little doubt that simple parrot-like imitation of what another person does or says becomes very rare after the first 2 years. Instead, a child acquires a large fund of knowledge, through observation and by many other means, concerning possible ways to behave and what the outcomes of actions are likely to be. The child then picks and chooses among possible courses of action on the basis of current motives and the way an action would fit in with a progressively more complex set of nested, coordinated plans. Elements acquired from several different models may be combined into a novel sequence.

What determines whether a child will or will not utilize the information previously obtained from observing the actions of other persons? A long series of experiments, many by Bandura and colleagues (Bandura, 1969, 1971), have shown that imitation is most probable if the model is powerful or prestigious, nurturant, and skillful relative to the child's preexisting level of skill. (See Yando et al., 1978, for a summary of studies.) Furthermore, there is evidence that when children are under the influence of dependency motives—as inferred from frequent seeking of reassurance from and contact with an adult—they are more likely to imitate task-irrelevant as well as task-relevant elements of the adult's behavior (Ross, 1966).

It is evident from the foregoing that parents should be powerful models for children. Games of mutual imitation play a role in the establishment of mutually understood interactive scripts in early childhood. From infancy on, parents are highly available; they are powerful, and thus able to command attention; they are skillful in performing many activities about which the child needs to learn; and they are nurturant, and the child's continuing attachment to them and need for their emotional support should foster the acquisition of incidental elements of parental behavior. Thus it is no surprise that young children may be seen to adopt similar gestures, or similar styles of speech, as well as similar instrumental activities, to those of their parents.

Yet we must be wary of predicting too much. Children of immigrant parents seldom speak with their parents' strong accents. And attempts to show better than chance similarity between a number of personality characteristics of parents and their children have proved disappointing (Scarr, Webber, Weinberg, & Wittig, 1981). Although it can be shown that children grow up to share a number of their parent's attitudes, including political or religious orientation, much of the similarity can be explained by the similar sociocultural milieu in which both parents and children live. Within a given social class, ethnic group, and sex, it has proved extraordinarily difficult to show that children are any more similar to their own parents than they are to other children's parents. More recent work has confirmed the lack of matching (Bryant & Crockenberg, 1980, with respect to teaching style; Loeb, Horst, & Horton, 1980, with respect to self-esteem). An interesting example is found in Haan (1977), who has assessed both the coping and defense mechanisms characteristically utilized by individual parents and children. She finds (p. 225) that use of the same mechanism by a parent and child is rare. This does not mean that the coping and defensive processes of different family members are unrelated, however. Rather, they tend to be in complementary or reciprocal relationship. It seems clear that this aspect of the children's personality structures is *not* formed by imitation.

The work on the acquisition of sex-typed behavior yields some interesting insights into factors determining children's choice of models. Freud's theory, as interpreted and modified by Sears and colleagues (Sears et al., 1965), was that early sex-typing is acquired primarily through identification

with the same-sex parent. Yet Maccoby and Jacklin (1974), reviewing a number of studies, reported that children's sex-typing did not match that of the same-sex parent. A more recent study by Smith and Daglish (1977) also finds no mother-daughter or father-son correlations for sex-typing measures. When given a choice between a single same-sex model and a single opposite-sex model, children (at least those under the age of about 10) typically do not show either more task-oriented or more incidental imitation of one over the other (Maccoby & Jacklin, 1974). An important study by Perry and Bussey (1979), however, shows that if one action is modeled by *several* female models, and another by several male models, 8-year-old children will copy the same-sex models. And a preliminary report by Bussey (1981) suggests that the same result may be found with younger children. This work points to inferential processes, whereby children use a number of instances to determine what behavior is typicaly for their sex. A single model is not enough to make such an inference, and hence it is not surprising that a child's mother's or father's behavior should not be taken as prescriptive for sex-role behavior. The child needs to build a prototype, and indeed if the behavior of the parent does not correspond to the prototype that emerges from observation of many exemplars of male and female behavior, we may expect that the parent's behavior will be discarded as a model for this class of behaviors.

This work raises some issues of general importance. Under what conditions do children build a prototype and then use it for adaptation of their own actions to the prototypical behaviors? Blue-eyed children do not ordinarily try to determine how blue-eyed persons act and then behave accordingly. A first requirement must be that the category is an important one, in that it accounts for a significant portion of the variance in other people's behavior. Eye color is not important in this sense, whereas sex is. However, we must ask whether all categories that differentiate groups behaviorally are adopted for use as a basis for self-monitoring and selective imitation. Behavior differs to some degree by race, social class, and country of origin, as well as sex, yet individuals probably do not give these equal weight in guiding their own behavior. Undoubtedly the consequences that are contingent on adopting or not adopting the stereotyped behavior of one's group are relevant. Kohlberg (1966) suggested that knowledge of the permanence of one's membership in a group was important, and that it was only when children became aware of the lifelong permanence of their sex identity that they would begin to attempt to discover and adopt the typical behaviors for their sex. Bussey's recent work suggests that sex constancy is not so powerful a factor as Kohlberg thought, while the work by Ruble et al. (1981) suggests that it may be. In any case, children must have some knowledge of their sex identity, *and attach some value to it*, before they would begin to pattern themselves on their emerging prototypes. We suggest that the matter of value is central. It was shown some years ago (Maccoby & Wilson, 1957) that school-aged children were likely to notice and remember more accurately the behavior of a filmed character who was of their own social class, *provided that they expected to remain in that social class*. But working-class children who wanted to go to college focused on the middle-class filmed hero, rather than the working-class one. Clearly we are dealing with matters of identity here, including aspects of the ego ideal. We suggest, then, that the extent to which parents will remain powerful models for their children as the children reach school age and adolescence will depend on the child's developing identity and aspirations, and the extent to which the parent is perceived as similar to what the child is and wants to be.

In thinking about such *identity-based imitation* (i.e., conscious or unconscious matching of self to other), we appear to have come full circle, back to some form of the concept of identification. And we are led to the view that, as Kohlberg suggested, certain forms of imitation are a consequence of identity-formation processes, rather than being their cause. In fact, however, we may have encountered another instance of circular process here. Perhaps through early imitations, occurring when the child is too young for the imitations to be identity based, the child acquires characteristics that later become incorporated into the child's concept of self, are valued, and hence become part of the basis for later identity-based selection of certain other persons as models.

Attribution Theory

Attribution theory can be applied to the process of children's internalization of parental values. The classic attitude-change situation is one in which an external agent applies pressure to get a subject to change a preexisting belief or value. Students of this process (e.g., Kelman, 1958) have made distinctions between several different processes that can be involved in such changes. The first is "mere" compliance, in which the individual expresses changed attitudes publicly in situations where to do so will gain rewards or avoid punishment, but reverts to the original attitude otherwise. In a second process, which has been called "identification," the individual's attitudes change both publicly and privately, but the private change holds only so long as the relationship with the change agent remains salient. The third process, "internalization," involves change that is more lasting, is uncoupled from the subject's relationship to the influence source, and is independent of the immediate instrumental value of holding or expressing the attitude.

In a recent review article, Lepper (1982) notes that children's acquisition of prosocial values in the context of interaction with adult socialization agents may be seen as analogous to what happens in attitude-change experiments. That is, in socialization, the adult agents make influence attempts. Children may or may not conform, with conformity taking one of two forms: verbalizing the values that have been presented or adopting the behaviors that are required by the values. If children do conform, the change in behavior may be based either on pragmatic considerations of expected reward or punishment, or on the internalization of the values so that they guide behavior in the absence of external sanctions. It is the latter kind of change that is the ultimate goal of most socialization efforts, although mere compliance is frequently the short-term goal.

Several sets of attitude-change experiments are relevant. One involves *objectively insufficient* pressure to change. A change agent applies pressure to get the subject to do or believe something, or *not* to do or believe something; but the pressure is insufficient, and the individual does not comply, even overtly (e.g., a religious zealot is pressured to recant, but continues to preach the gospel publicly despite threats of dire punishment). The studies of this phenomenon find that pressure that does not result in compliance produces increased strength of belief in the subject's original position, and the greater the pressure, the farther the subject moves *away* from the position the change agent is attempting to inculcate.

A different phenomenon occurs under pressure that is *objectively sufficient* but *psychologically insufficient*. The classic experiment (Festinger & Carlsmith, 1959) puts subjects into a situation where they must defend in public a position at variance with their own initial views. When the subjects were paid relatively large amounts of money to do this, their own attitudes remained unchanged. It was the subjects who received very little reward for their behavior who changed in the direction of their public statements—who showed the "saying is believing" effect. An analogous process has been shown to occur when the subject receives pressure *not* to engage in a forbidden action. The stronger and more salient the pressure (threat of punishment), the less likely is the individual to abide by the prohibition when there seems little danger of getting caught. With mild pressure, greater resistance to temptation in the absence of surveillance is achieved (Aronson & Carlsmith, 1963).

When external pressure is a great deal stronger than would be needed to bring about compliance, the subject's initial attitudes begin to move in a contrary direction, as they did under objectively insufficient pressure. A series of experiments on the *psychological overjustification effect* have shown that when pressure considerably exceeds the compliance-producing level, subjects begin to disvalue the behavior or attitude that is being required. Lepper's experiments on intrinsic motivation are relevant here. He and his colleagues (Lepper & Greene, 1978; Lepper, Greene, & Nisbett, 1973) have shown that when children have an initial interest in an activity—interest that is sufficient to get them to engage in it—then applying salient external pressure (in the form of reward) for engaging in the activity reduces the children's spontaneous interest at times when reward is not expected. Lepper (1982) now interprets these findings as showing that such loss of interest depends on whether children perceive the situation as implying that they are being externally controlled. Not only the promise of rewards, but unnecessarily close surveillance, the expectation of external evaluation, or superfluous deadlines, will reduce children's interest in an activity. A similar phenomenon may be seen when pressure is applied for the child *not* to engage in activity, rather than to engage in it. In a forbidden toy experiment, in which the arrangements were such that the child would, in fact, not deviate, children received either mild or severe threats about the consequences of deviation. As predicted on the basis of the psychological insufficiency of the mild threats, the children in the mild-threat condition subsequently devalued the prohibited activity more. More interesting for our present purposes is the behavior that occurred 2 weeks later in a more traditional temptation situation where deviation was possible. The children who had previously resisted temptation under strong threats were more likely to deviate than children who had resisted under mild threats. Thus compliance in the face of sufficient but weak external pressure increased internalization, whereas sufficient but strong pressure decreased it.

Lepper interprets this body of research in terms of the *minimal sufficiency principle* of social control. Maximum internalization of whatever standard of behavior the influence agent is attempting to teach will occur under conditions where the agent's pressure is just sufficient to bring about compliance. This is true both for pressures to perform actions that would not be carried out spontaneously, or pressure to inhibit proscribed actions. Influence attempts will be counterproductive—that is, produce rejection of, and alienation from, the values that the socialization agent is attempting to transmit—under two conditions: when pressure is fairly strong, but not quite strong enough to induce compliance (objectively insufficient); or when pressure is much stronger than the level needed to produce compliance.

Lepper interprets the findings of several socialization studies in light of the minimal sufficiency principle. The use of unqualified power assertion (Hoffman, 1960) or authoritarian parenting (Baumrind, 1971) are seen as examples of children's being subject to "direct, salient, and psychologically unambiguous" techniques of external control. "Authoritative" parenting approaches the point of optimal internalization, in that pressure is sufficient to produce compliance, but not oversufficient. Permissive parenting is often not objectively sufficient.

The Lepper formulation has two central themes. The first is the extraordinary importance of compliance itself. The maximum shift from rejection of parental requirements to internalization of them comes just at the compliance point. The second theme concerns the child's causal attribution for compliance, given that it has occurred. (Note that if a child does not comply, attributional processes function to explain *non*compliance.) Internalization is equated with a child's sense of having complied willingly rather than because of external pressure.

How can parents obtain compliance with minimal pressure? How can they foster self-attribution in their children? Several possibilities come to mind, some of which are drawn from sociopsychological studies of social control: labeling a subject's behavior as the consequence of free choice, even when it is not; using diffuse social pressure instead of explicit rewards and punishments; creating an illusion of choice by offering alternatives on minor aspects of *how* to comply while offering none on the question of *whether* to comply; modeling a desired action rather than merely dictating that it shall be done; offering to share a task with a child. Grusec (1982), applying an attributional model to children's acquisition of altruistic behavior, places great stress on the concealment of the iron hand within the silken glove. She says: "A socializing agent who applies negative consequences for misbehavior but who helps the child to make an attributional error by accompanying these consequences with verbal statements will be successful in producing internalization of altruism.'' Maccoby (1982) notes that children undoubtedly learn to see through parental misattribution rather quickly, particularly as they grow older, and that probably the most reliable way to get children to believe that they have exercised free choice is to allow them a degree of real free choice.

The attributional model has been criticized on the grounds that it does not take into account the amount of pressure needed to secure compliance. Maximum internalization is expected to occur when just-sufficient pressure has been applied, even if this pressure is very great. Maccoby (1982) presents a modification in which the amount of pressure needed for compliance is entered as a variable, and in which strong pressure, even if it is just sufficient, will not produce internalization. Only mild pressure that achieves compliance will have this effect. Thus, in this formulation, the child's readiness to comply with mild pressure becomes crucial. The social influence literature points to compliance as a self-fostering process over time. The ''foot in the door'' studies show that once having complied to a mild request, subjects are readier to comply to a stronger one; and once having refused, they are less ready to comply even to a lesser demand. Thus a child's readiness to comply must depend substantially on the previous interactive history of the parent-child pair, and the skill with which parents have presented their demands in ways and at times that optimize the chances of getting compliance.

In concluding our discussion of attribution theory, we should note an intriguing suggestion by Hoffman (1982). Hoffman draws from the attitude-change literature that deals with remembering or forgetting the source of information. It has been shown that recipients of persuasive messages sometimes accept the content of the message and change their own attitudes accordingly, but forget the source of the communication. In fact, there are sometimes delayed effects of a message when the source is mistrusted; it is only after the source has been forgotten that the subject's resistance to the message dwindles and acceptance can occur. Hoffman suggests that power-assertive parental behaviors keep the source of persuasive communications salient to children. They cannot forget where the influence attempt came from, and continue to make an external attribution. Therefore, especially if they feel that their own interests do not coincide with those of their parents, they maintain their defenses against accepting (''in-

ternalizing'') the message. Mild or subtle influence attempts, by contrast, are less likely to be ''tagged'' with their source in the child's encoding of the message content, so that when the messages are retrieved, they do not have the quality of an external imposition but seem like the child's own conclusions or beliefs.

Interaction Theory

Social learning theory as applied to the family was primarily a ''shaping'' theory—a view of how parents formed the personalities of their children via their own behavior as agenda setters, reinforcers, and models. The realization that children are active participants in the socialization process, and that they influence socialization agents as well as vice versa, led to increasing interest in reciprocal processes and efforts to describe them. Coming out of the social learning tradition, some conceptualizations of interaction focused on mutual reinforcement and punishment. But interaction theorists go beyond the analysis of specific contingencies that partners provide for one another's specific responses. They study extended interchanges—chains of responses (Raush, 1965). Cairns (1979) points to continuing reverberations between members of an interacting pair. He notes that the concept of social interaction points attention to the properties of the feedback process by which organisms influence each other. That is, one does not merely act in a social relationship; one reacts. The reaction, according to Cairns, may have been stimulated, in part, by one's own earlier actions and the repercussions that the actions produced. Thus in interaction theory there has been increasing attention to circular processes; in addition, families have been increasingly conceptualized as *systems* with mutually dependent parts, whose interrelationships could be described independently of the individual characteristics of the persons forming them. Conceptualizations of this sort called for measurements that characterized dyads or larger groups—measurements that could be used to distinguish well-functioning from malfunctioning families and that would permit the tracing of changes in the functioning of families over time.

Some roots of interaction theory can be traced to the work of James Mark Baldwin (1906). Baldwin stressed the child's embeddedness in an interactional network, and argued that the child's personality in general, and self-concept in particular, underwent continuous modification as a result of the feedback from significant others. This point of view was later modified and expanded by G. H. Meade (1934) in the theory of the ''looking-glass self.''

The concept of interaction in these theories goes much beyond the simple fact of children being involved in relationships of mutual influence with others. Put in extreme and rather simplistic form, it implies that although children's bodies and brains are unique and separate entities, their social selves do not have an independent existence apart from the relationships in which they are involved. An example of this distinction may be found in Youniss' (1980) discussion of altruistic behavior in children (p. 236). He points out that, from a traditional viewpoint, a child, in behaving altruistically, acts as an independent person to benefit another in a situation where there will be no obvious payoff to the self. An interactive perspective would be that the actor and recipient belong to a joint unit, wherein actors initiate altruistic acts so as to support a mutually understood system of exchange. The thing that is expressed in such an exchange is the *relationship*, not the characteristic of an individual actor. In discussing the interactionist implications of the theories of Piaget and Harry Stack Sullivan, Youniss says that a basic tenet for both these theorists was that "actions can have reliable meaning only when they are understood as reciprocal to the actions of other persons" (1980, p. 234).

In its strongest form, such a theory would appear to deny the existence of a single, organized personality. Individuals would be chameleon-like, having as many selves as they have familiar partners. To understand the formation of a coherent personality, one needs to move beyond the concept of specific relationships, and to think in terms of a kind of distillate or percipitate derived from many relationships. This is the essence of Meade's (1934) concept of the *generalized other*. On the basis of such a core of relational understandings, the individual could take up a relation of obligation or reciprocity with a stranger, or with a whole category of others (as in anonymous donations to charity). Here we are entering the familiar territory of role or script theory, where an individual's social behavior is differentiated according to the category to which other persons belong. The interactionist, however, would continue to insist that different parties to any interaction must be acting from roughly the same script.

Presumably, no two persons ever have identical scripts, and it would seem that it must be difficult for an interacting pair composed of an adult and young child to achieve even similar scripts, considering the vastly greater fund of knowledge and the sophisticated set of expectations any adult brings to an interaction. Thus a developmental psychologist interested in interaction will be concerned with such

questions as these: What mutually understood scripts are possible between adults and children of different ages? Is there any respect in which early-acquired scripts feed into later ones, so that there are some constraints on the order in which scripts are acquired by children? The observations by Stern, to be discussed later in this chapter, bear on these questions. Mothers and infants are shown adapting their behavior to one another through mutual imitation, so that an alternating pattern emerges at least briefly. Such a pattern can be seen (as Bruner has claimed) as an example of the acquisition of one of the most rudimentary of social scripts, one that facilitates the development of more differentiated linguistic and social interactional patterns at a later time.

Schaffer, Collis, and Parsons (1977) hold that the concept of a *dialogue* is essential to the understanding of interactions. They suggest that two acquisitions in early childhood are vital to the child's ability to participate in dialogues: *reciprocity* and *intentionality*. Reciprocity is stressed by other students of interaction (see Gottman, 1979a, and Raush, 1965, for a review). Schaffer (1977) adds to it the notion that in the initial interactions between mother and infant reciprocal behaviors are really only pseudodialogues, because the mother is sustaining a sequence by replying to infant behavior *as though* it had communicative significance, when initially it does not. He says:

> It is not until the end of the first year that the infant will learn that dialogues are two-sided, that they are based on roles which are both reciprocal and interchangeable (actor-spectator, giver-taker, speaker-auditor), and that the playing of these roles and their periodic exchange are managed according to certain rules to which both partners must adhere . . . action patterns of a *joint* nature cannot appear until the infant has mastered the idea of reciprocity. (p. 10)

They argue further that dialogue depends on each partner behaving intentionally—that is, using action in the expectation that a reciprocal partner action will occur. As infants discover that their smiles, vocalizations, and gestures produce contingent responses in others, they will begin to use these behaviors purposefully to generate and maintain an interactive sequence. The work of Bates, Camaioni, and Volterra (1975) also supports the view that this aspect of the skill needed for dialogue is not reliably present before the end of the first year. A feature of maternal behavior that Schaffer (1977) considers crucial to building up these two aspects of infants' understanding of dialogue is imitation. He says:

By repeating the infant's response, the mother not only reflects back to him his own behavior but also produces a stereotyped and therefore predictable form of interaction. And let us also note the extent to which the mother ensures that the infant gets maximum benefit of the information content of her behavior by exaggerating, repeating, and slowing down her actions. (p. 12)

What binds interactors together, and maintains them in a relationship to one another? This is a question that has been a central concern of sociologists and social psychologists for decades, and the literature is of course much too extensive to be covered here. Much of it is not relevant, in that it deals with voluntary associations, rather than relationships that are biological in origin and socially obligatory. Nevertheless there are approaches growing out of this work that may be, and have been, applied to interaction within the family. Aldous (1977) reviews some of the main trends in this work. The points of greatest relevance for our present purposes are as follows: For many years, family interactions were conceptualized in terms of power and exchange relationships. Power was seen as a function of the control of resources. The person in the family who has the most resources to contribute has the most power over other family members. Persons low in the power structure must accept the influence of those higher up because they need the resources controlled by powerful persons. And they must offer something in exchange for the resources they receive: namely, obedience and services. The relative power or dominance of husbands and wives within the marital relationship has been conceptualized in terms of the resources each brings to the marriage, so that for example, working wives are found to share decision making more fully than wives who do not bring money to the family resource pool. Of course, monetary resources are not the only ones involved in the exchange: The control of sexual access and of prestige are others frequently mentioned.

The reader will note the kinship of exchange theory with the principles of dyadic functioning enunciated by Sears in 1951. Sears said:

A dyadic situation exists whenever the actions of Beta produce the (sought-after) environmental events for Alpha, and vice versa. The behavior of each person is essential to the other's successful completion of his goal directed sequence of actions. The drives of each are satisfied only when the motivated actions of the other are carried through to completion. (p. 479)

Thus although Sears did not explicitly conceptualize the dyadic relationship in power terms, he did emphasize that it was the mutual satisfaction of needs, or in other words an exchange of benefits, that sustained the interaction and created a relationship between two persons.

More recently, Foa and Foa (1974) have conceptualized relationships in terms of exchange processes, but have provided a classification scheme for the resources that are being exchanged, and have suggested that exchanges have different meanings and consequences, depending on the class of resources being exchanged. Some exchanges are zero-sum games, as in the case of money, where payment involves a gain by one person matched by an equivalent loss by the other. Affectional interchanges are obviously very different in quality, and hence, presumably, in meaning to the participants.

An example of exchange theory as applied to family interaction may be found in the field of family therapy, in the work originated by D. D. Jackson and colleagues. Jackson suggests that well-functioning families operate in terms of an unspoken quid pro quo rule. If one person asks and receives a favor from a partner, that creates a right on the part of the partner to ask a favor in return, and an obligation on the part of the original asker to reciprocate the favor (Jackson, 1965). Gottman (1979a), reviewing the research literature growing out of the quid pro quo hypothesis, finds no support for the proposition that well-functioning spousal pairs are characterized by an exchange of "favors" (positive reinforcers).

Critics of power and exchange theories have noted that family members who have power, in the sense that they control resources, frequently appear to choose not to exercise their power. When they do exercise it they tend to encounter overt compliance but covert resistance, a fact that imposes limits on its value. A second point is that exchange theory posits a pair-by-pair bargaining process where participants react fairly immediately to one another's demands. In families, exchange processes, if they operate at all, do not require that when one person benefits another, reciprocation will occur in a short time, or even necessarily from the person benefited. Families generally operate as groups where persons may assume that their needs will be met eventually by someone. But between parents and children, the exchange of resources probably never balances out. As Aldous says:

When family members start using a strictly *quid pro quo* mode of calculating rights in exchange for resource contributions, an outside observer might be justified in using this as an indicator of the breakdown of family solidarity. The bonds of sentiment have lost their capacity to insure non-contingent giving. (1977, p. 109)

A study of adolescents by T. E. Smith (1970) illustrates the limitations of power theory couched in terms of resource exchanges. Smith began with the hypothesis that the amount of influence parents could exert over their adolescent children would be a function of the degree of control the parents had over the adolescents' economic resources (and the lack of adolescent access to alternative resources). This hypothesis was not sustained. Instead, parental influence was shown to be a function of the adolescents' willingness to rely on parental guidance, their acceptance of the parents' right to exercise control, and their assessment of the parents' skill, knowledge, and competence with respect to a particular domain of influence. Findings such as these have led students of the family to turn away from conceptualizing family interaction in terms of power and the exchange of resources. Aldous points out that current work has shifted attention from studies of interaction outcomes to efforts to delineate the interaction process itself. The quality of family interaction is under study, and involves such issues as distinguishing between constructive and destructive conflict (Coser, 1956; Deutch, 1969) and relationship-supportive versus relationship-weakening modes of conflict resolution (Barry, 1970; Glick & Gross, 1975; Raush, Barry, Hertel, & Swain, 1974). Attention is also being focused on mutual perceptions among family members—that is, on the understanding of one another's needs and sources of satisfaction (Neidhart, 1976) and the congruence among family members in their perceptions of the causes and possible remedies for conflict (Klein & Jorgeson, 1976). And finally, the need for taking into account the affectional and commitment relationships among family members is now widely recognized. In analyzing interaction processes, students of the family have turned away from simple cross-sectional and correlational methods and have begun to make greater use of sequential data. Although much of this work deals with interspousal conflict, the concepts would appear to be applicable to relationships between parents and children. It appears that the trends that have been occurring in sociological studies of the family have been very similar to those occurring in psychological studies of parent-child interaction, which will be reviewed later in this chapter, though the two streams of research have grown up in relative isolation from one another.

In both research traditions, the need for better description of relationships has become paramount. The task of theory building that deals with the characteristics of pairs or groups is only in its infancy. As Hinde (1976, 1978c) says, the first step must be to identify the important characteristics of dyadic functioning and define them in measurable terms. In an analysis derived from observational studies of subhuman primates, Hinde distinguishes among three levels of relatedness: simple interactions, relationships, and social structures. Interactions are the elements or building blocks of more complex relationships. In Hinde's terms, to describe an interaction, one needs only describe the content and quality (manner) of the moment-to-moment other-directed behavior of each party to an interaction. Relationships involve a succession of interactions between specific individuals, and to describe a relationship it is necessary to describe not only the content of the interaction elements, but how they are patterned relative to one another and in time. The social structure of a group, in turn, is constructed from the relationships of the members.

One of the major concerns of students of parent-child interaction has been to find means of describing and tracing how interactions are patterned through time, and to use information on moment-to-moment actions and reactions to derive adequate descriptions of relationships. To this end, temporal series of the actions and reactions of a parent-child pair have been examined for cycles (e.g., phases of escalation and deescalation), for similarity or complementarity, for simultaneity or alternation, and for degree of integration or meshing. As Hinde (1979) notes, it would be desirable to be able to describe relationships in terms of the commitment of the partners to each other, in the sense of the readiness of each to act for the benefit of the other without regard to recompense. To date, this aspect of relatedness has not been isolated for study.

The description of relationships is an extremely important item on the agenda for interaction research. But it is obviously not enough for theory building. Hinde (1978c) has suggested several classes of principles that need to be the focus of theory and research. One concerns the presence of social constraints, and their effect on the relationships that are subject to them. A second has to do with how interactions at one time affect those that occur subsequently in the same pair or group. Dyads may be thought of as entities that are capable of learning; possibly the changes occurring through time could be analyzed in terms of principles of acquisition and performance similar to those that have been utilized in the study of changes in individuals. Psychologists, however, will not want to leave the individual buried in the dyad. Their central concern remains with individual development. So for them, an enterprise of primary importance is to conceptualize and test the ways in which a child's participation in a parent-child dyad with certain properties affects the individual child's subsequent functioning outside the confines of that dyad.

We cannot conclude a discussion of interaction theory as it applies to parent-child interaction without including some reference to general systems theory, although so far it has rarely been incorporated into research operations. A central idea in this theory is that systems function to maintain themselves in equilibrium. Raush (1965) maintained that among well-functioning persons, participants to an interaction act in order to "rescue" an interaction when it shows signs of deteriorating. Malfunctioning persons, however—in Raush's case, hyperaggressive boys—either cannot anticipate what is happening to the interaction or lack the skills to correct it.

Bell and Harper (1977) propose a version of control systems theory similar to that employed by Bowlby (1969) in his analysis of attachment. Bell and Harper (1977) suggest that each member of the parent-child dyad establishes a permissible range for the intensity, frequency, or situational appropriateness of the behavior shown by the other. When that range is exceeded in either direction the individual is impelled to take action that will return the interaction to the permissible range. For parents, there is an upper bound of intensity or frequency of certain child behaviors that they will tolerate; when the bound is exceeded, they act so as to reduce the intensity or frequency of the behavior. There is also a lower bound, and if the frequency or intensity of the given child behavior is too low, the parent will act so as to increase it. [This mechanism was seen in operation in the work of Jones (1977) with retarded children, where the parents were found to take more initiative than parents of normal children to stimulate their children into interaction.] On the child's side, a reciprocal situation prevails such that if parental pressure is beyond the child's permissible range, the child acts so as to evade or stop it; if the parent is too inaccessible, however, the child will make attempts to goad the parent into resumption of interaction. If the initial attempts by either parent or child to guide the partner's behavior back into the acceptable range are not successful, pressure to this end will be escalated until it either succeeds or drives the participants apart. The behavioral repertoires of each participant are thus organized sequentially and

hierarchically, elements being activated in a predictable order depending on the intensity of the partner's pressure, and on the partner's response to prior control attempts.

This formulation has the limitation that it does not attempt to deal with variations in the nature of the interactions that occur when both participants are operating within the acceptable bounds set by the other. We must assume that such variations do affect both the long-term course of a relationship and the generalization of social behavior from the parent-child relationship to other relationships. Nevertheless the theory does raise a number of important issues that have only begun to be addressed in research. A major one is this: What determines the nature of the bounds set by each participant? In seeking answers to this question, we will no doubt need to have recourse to adaptation-level theory. Olweus, as we shall see, finds that parents of aggressive children tend to become more "permissive" toward aggression over time. In short, in Bell's terms, they appear to acquire a higher upper bound for the level of child behavior that will be tolerated before they instigate counteraction. We do not know whether this higher bound antedated their children's aggressiveness. It is a reasonable hypothesis, however, that the parents of aggressive children have adapted themselves to their own child's behavior in such a way that they react to deviations from the child's own norm, rather than (or in addition to) deviations from a societal norm. In a similar way, we might expect that children who receive unusually frequent and intense pressure from their parents would come to see this as "normal," and would set fairly high upper bounds (and perhaps lower bounds as well) for parental behavior that they will accept without counteraction. If these adaptation-level phenomena prove to be powerful, they may reduce the proportion of variance in long-term outcomes that can be explained by control systems theory. At least they call attention to the importance of knowing what the absolute bounds are, how they are arrived at, and the limits (if any) of their adaptation—issues to which control systems theory has not so far addressed itself.

Sameroff (1982) draws on general systems theory, applying an analysis of the levels of structural organization within systems to the ontogeny of the human child. He points to the increasing complexity of the organization of the developing person, and stresses the self-stabilizing properties of systems. He notes that such properties permit persons to minimize environmental effects, but also points to the adaptive processes that are involved in the reorganization of systems in response to changes in the environment (readers will note echoes of Piaget's *assimilation* and *accommodation* here). Sameroff notes that in considering persons within their environments, we are dealing with hierarchical arrangements of systems. Thus the individual child, who is himself an organized system, exists within a higher level system (the family) that has its own system properties. Although arguing that higher level systems do not necessarily have control over all lower level functions within their parts, he gives us few clues that could guide the search for the ways in which families as systems might be related to the functioning of the individual family members who compose the family system. For our present purposes, the important point is the allegation—not a new one—that families have their own systems properties. Family therapists have noted that families may have self-stabilizing properties such that they resist the perturbations that emanate from the interventions of change agents. The intersection of roles within families is highlighted in instances where the mental health of one member of a family improves under treatment, but where this improvement seems to trigger a breakdown on the part of another family member (see review by Satir, 1967). Theoretical analyses of such instances have led to the view that certain families are organized in such a way that they "need" some form of deviance on the part of at least one member. More in the mainstream of family research is the work on role relationships between the two parents: the degree of role differentiation and the amount of support given by each to the child-rearing functions of the other. On the whole, however, the systems properties of families, particularly as they involve the intersection of roles among siblings, have received little attention in the socialization literature.

METHODS OF STUDY

At various points in the history of work by developmental psychologists, certain methods of study have been preferred by a majority of investigators studying family interaction. Each major type of methodology has identifiable advantages and disadvantages, and experience with these has been one of the sources of secular trends in the popularity each type of methodology has enjoyed at various times. In this section, we will briefly describe the major methodologies that have at various times dominated the research conducted by students of family socialization, and touch on some of the major advantages and disadvantages of each method.

Subjects as Informants

Most of the early studies of the relationship between parental practices and various child outcomes used parents' introspective and descriptive reports as a primary source of data (Newson & Newson, 1968; Schaefer & Bell, 1968; Sears et al., 1957; Sears, Whiting, Nowlis, & Sears, 1953), although in some cases parent reports were supplemented by home observations (Baldwin, Kalhorn, & Breese, 1945). Techniques of interviewing and designing questionnaires grew out of several disciplines: clinical psychology, social work, and public opinion survey methodology.

Using parents as informants has great potential advantages. For assessment of behavior that varies considerably across situations, or behavior that is usually not displayed in public, reliable observational data are difficult to obtain and parent interviews are often the only viable alternative. Parents have an opportunity to observe their children and the patterns of interaction in their families over extended periods of time in a broad range of situations. Thus, by virtue of their daily participation in the family system, parents have access to a truly unique body of information about the family, and it is reasonable to tap into this information by questioning them. For the most part, mothers have been the principal informants in this kind of research; however, both fathers and children have also provided family interaction information to researchers on occasion. Similar to the use of interviews is researchers' application of questionnaire methods. Here, too, parents or children act as the informants, with the additional advantage that questionnaires require less training to administer and are less costly to code than interviews. (See Maccoby & Maccoby, 1954, for a fuller discussion of the relative merits of interviews and questionnaires.)

Despite the obvious strengths of subject-as-informant methods, questionnaire and interview data came under strong attack during the 1960s and subsequently (see, e.g., Brekstad, 1966; Chess, Thomas, & Birch, 1966; Haggard, Brekstad, & Skard, 1960; Mednick & Schaffer, 1963; Robins, 1963; Wenar, 1961; Wenar & Coulter, 1962). The criticisms were mounted on a variety of bases. A frequently noted problem is that parents may not be aware of certain aspects of their own behavior. They may be able to report accurately on the occurrence of salient events such as spanking. But some aspects of parental response, such as the withdrawal of parental affection following a child's misbehavior, are much more subtle, and parents are often unaware of such reactions, especially of the nonverbal components.

Measures that call for the identification of close contingencies, such as the proportion of a child's bids that are noticed and responded to by the parent, are obviously beyond the reach of parent report.

A further major issue in the use of parent report data has to do with subject-to-subject variation in the subjective anchor points for descriptive terms. When a particular mother calls her child "fussy," it is difficult to know what she means, and a child called fussy by one mother might be called good-natured by another. These problems become even more serious when the principal information about both socialization "antecedents" and child "outcomes" are obtained from the same informant source. Here there is especially great danger that the informant's "theories" about child rearing and child development might influence the informant's anchor points and derived descriptive statements. In the worst case our findings might then represent little more than documentation of common parental theories of socialization.

Perhaps the most powerful criticism that was levied against parent report data in the 1960s relates to the reliability of parental retrospective reports (cf. Robins, 1963; Yarrow, Campbell, & Burton, 1968). It has been repeatedly demonstrated that mothers' reports of such matters as the age at which they had weaned or toilet trained their children are highly inaccurate, although there are some items of information for which later reports match fairly well the reports that are made concurrently. Unfortunately, there seems to be no general principle that would distinguish retrospective reports that can be relied on from those that cannot.

The criticisms leveled against interviews and questionnaires have been responded to in a number of ways. Parent reports are now used primarily for obtaining concurrent, not retrospective, information about family interaction. To move further in the direction of obtaining information that is highly accessible to parents because of its recency, the Patterson group have developed the Parent Daily Report (PDR) instrument (Patterson, 1982), a checklist based on a telephone interview in which the parent is asked to report which, if any, of a list of child behaviors had occurred within the preceding 24 hrs. Good short-term stability has been obtained with the PDR (e.g., Chamberlain, 1980). Use of parent diaries, in which parents record in 15-, 30-, or 60-min. intervals the occurrence of a set of easily identified behaviors, similarly minimizes the problems of retrospection in reporting.

Another adaptation in interview methodology has been to distinguish between parent attitudes or values and parental reports of what is presumably their own or their children's actual behavior. For certain research purposes, it may be important to know whether parents regard their children as difficult or fussy, whatever the children's actual position on these dimensions in terms of objective comparisons with other children. If the research objectives call for using the parents' reports as a basis for assessing objective individual differences among parents or children, however, the problem of subjective anchor points becomes paramount. One solution has been to employ Q-sorts (Baumrind, 1967, 1971, 1979, 1982; Block, 1971), in which, rather than being asked to rate the child on a scale running from high to low on a given characteristic—a procedure that implicitly calls for comparing this child with other children—parents compare children with themselves. In a Q-sort, the parent must decide which among a set of trait adjectives, such as "aggressive" or "adventurous" or "helpful," best describes the child. There is evidence that such "ipsative" procedures yield scores that correlate quite well with observer ratings of the more usual sort (Block, 1957).

Another approach to the problem of variable anchor points has been to move away from trait descriptions altogether toward asking parents to give detailed descriptions of events: what the child did or said, and what the parent did or said. Subsequently, the researcher applies rating scales, using the same anchor points for the whole sample of interviews, in order to obtain a valid rank ordering of children or parents on traits, such as "coerciveness" or "permissiveness," for purposes of correlational analysis. The "critical incident" interview recommended by Hoffman (1957) is an example of this kind of data gathering.

Asking parents to describe recent events entails certain problems, even if the events being described are such presumably objective matters as how many hours the child spent viewing television, or what the child's food intake was. There may be biases that result in serious underreporting of the occurrence of certain events, even for recent periods of time. Greenberg and colleagues (Greenberg, Ericson, & Vlahos, 1972) find that 10-year-old children report considerably more hours spent viewing TV than their mothers report for them, and this is especially true for violent programs. Schramm, Lyle, and Parker (1961) find fuller (and presumably more accurate) reporting of TV viewing with the use of aided recall than when family members are simply asked to report what programs they watched. (Aided recall involves providing the respondent with a list of programs that were available at a given time, and asking them to check the ones they saw.) And joint family reports yield fuller reports than interviews with each family member individually. These findings remind us of the superiority of recognition over recall memory, and the need for providing as many memory clues as possible.

An additional problem with diary-type reports has to do with the representativeness of the particular day or week chosen for report. Clearly it is desirable to obtain a sampling of several time periods, to even out the effects of unusual circumstances. The method developed by Zahn-Waxler, Radke-Yarrow, and King (1979) goes farther to reduce or eliminate the behavior-sampling problem than other methods that rely on parents for detailed behavior reports. In this method, mothers of young children are trained as observers. The mothers are asked to look for and report *all* of certain specified types of incidents occurring in the home over a period of weeks or months. The mothers write a brief but specific narrative report of the events preceding and following each incident, giving the details of the behavior and describing affective reactions of both mother and child. These reports can then be coded subsequently for the frequency of selected responses of each partner to the other, and can also be employed for limited sequence analyses. An example of the kind of raw data obtained through this procedure is given in our section, *Withdrawal of Love*.

Probably the most widespread change in method following the criticisms leveled at the parent interview was a shift to a focus on observational methods, to which we turn now.

Observational Methods

Proponents of observational methods have argued for their superiority from a variety of perspectives. Observers may be trained to be reliable recorders of carefully specified behavioral events, using uniform comparison standards. When all of the children in a particular study are observed under constant circumstances and with uniform coding criteria, sources of variation in child behavior resulting from the observational situation or variously defined coding categories can be minimized.

Frequently, however, observational methods may provide researchers with a false sense of objectivity. Observers are in most research projects trained up to an acceptable level of interobserver reliability; yet, following this initial training period, there is considerable variation over research projects in how closely observers are monitored during the course of a study. Even during the initial training period, "training up" may simply amount to a (reliable)

perpetuation of a *mis*perception of some part of the behavioral reality being observed, so that observers may agree closely with one another but be uniformly incorrect in their inferences about the behavior being observed. Moreover, reliability assessments are generally made when observers are aware that they are being monitored for reliability; conceivably, observers may be more attentive and more "reliable" when they know they are being evaluated than when they are not, so that reliability figures based on such instances may be overestimates of "true" reliability. Taplin and Reid (1977) studied this issue by comparing the reliability of three different groups of observers: (1) those who were told that they would be "spot-checked" for reliability on a random basis throughout the course of a study; (2) those who were told that they would be checked at regular intervals; and (3) those who were told that they would not be monitored. There was a gradual decay of reliability in all three groups over time, but this was less pronounced (although not significantly so) in the random-check group. Finally, Reid (1970) has also pointed to the issue of *intra*observer reliability in which groups of observers may consensually but unwittingly change their definitions of certain classes of coded behavior over the course of a study, so that they remain quite reliable with one another but unreliable *with themselves*.

Similarly, whether observations are conducted in the home, at school, or in the laboratory using naturalistic, seminaturalistic, or contrived observational scenarios, the representativeness and ecological validity of the conditions of observation deserve serious consideration. Concerns about ecological validity may be thought of as part of a more general set of concerns about specifying the sources and degree of within-subject variability in behavior.

Sampling over Time and Situations

There is no need for concern about sampling situations when one is measuring an individual characteristic (e.g., height) that does not vary across situations. But the behavioral characteristics of both parents and children that are of interest to students of socialization do vary considerably from one time to another and from one situation to another. In some instances, researchers may be interested in the sources of cross-situational variation, in which case their experimental design involves comparison of subjects' behavior in more than one controlled and standardized setting. More commonly, however, researchers are interested in identifying a "person" component of either parents or children that stably differentiates individuals despite situational or moment-to-moment variance. Clearly it is difficult to justify making generalizations about such individual characteristics when behavior is observed only once in a single setting. The issue becomes one of how widely a researcher wishes to generalize about an individual characteristic. Consider, for example, the differences in children's behavior at home and at school. If a given behavior occurs more frequently in the one setting than the other, it might still be legitimate to take observations in only one of the settings if it is known that children's rank order is maintained across settings despite the change in base rates. If the correlation is low, however (as is commonly the case), the researcher must decide whether to narrow the definition of the variable so that it applies to only one setting, or to take observations in both settings. Usually it is difficult to know in advance how high the cross-situational correlations will be. Assuming they will be low, the next issue becomes which and how many situations need to be sampled in order to provide an adequate representation of the variable the researcher has in mind. These and other issues are discussed at length in Cronbach, Gleser, Nanda, and Rajartnam (1972).

A partial solution to problems of cross-situational variability is to focus one's attention on understanding behavior occurring in situations that are highly representative of some class of settings of particular theoretical interest. For example, the general class of situations in which the parent is busy and the young child in the family has little or nothing to do may be of considerable theoretical interest owing to its naturalistic frequency and its potential for eliciting demanding, coercive encounters. If so, one or more observational scenarios can be constructed to approximate this common interpersonal situation, and generalization from an observation will occur only to other similar mother-busy/child-not-busy situations. A good deal of research has been conducted in this way using carefully structured, "contrived" laboratory situations (set up both in the laboratory and in families' homes). By and large, the point of this work is to attempt to bring the effects of situational variance under control by eliminating it as fully as possible.

Even within such controlled settings, a number of problems with observational research persist. For example, regardless of how meticulous the researcher has been in contriving a laboratory situation that mirrors some circumscribed aspects of social reality for the person(s) being observed, the presence of an observer and the knowledge by the subjects that they are being observed may have large and unspecifiable influences on salient components of behavior. Yet, a research strategy that takes this fact into account is necessarily a costly one, since it calls for enough observational sessions for subjects to become adapted to the observer's presence.

Epstein (1980) has proposed a different kind of solution to the situational variance issue that amounts to proceeding from an opposite extreme. That is, instead of carefully specifying the nature of a single interpersonal situation and duplicating the salient characteristics of that situation as closely as possible via a single contrived observational scenario, the idea here is to sample over many occasions and over a large number of diverse situations. The hope is that one's sample of situations will be representative enough of the range of situations families regularly encounter that the impact of situation variance can be eliminated by averaging over situations. This approach assumes, of course, that some characteristics of individuals are sufficiently stable and consistent across time and situations that computing an average over time and situations is a psychologically meaningful operation. The validity of this assumption is a matter of active current debate.

Separate from these issues are questions concerning how best to apply data-analytic procedures to observational data of any sort. Two categories of approaches have dominated the field of study of observational data on parent-child relations: the construction of frequency scores and the microanalysis of behavior sequences.

Frequency Scores

The majority of observational studies of the relationship between the behavior of parents and that of their children have conceptualized various aspects of interaction in frequency terms. The events of interest (e.g., the occurrence of a child's crying) are determined in advance, and then either time-sampled or event-sampled occurrences of the event are recorded. Summary measures are derived by summing scores for individuals over the recording period, and reporting the overall frequency of the events of interest. Individuals may then be compared with one another according to the frequency with which certain behaviors occur, and the total scores for parent and child behaviors can be correlated.

Frequency methods, although by far the commonest and least complex approach to interaction data, cannot reflect certain aspects of interaction. In collapsing data over time (or events), the sequential component of the interaction, and the idea of behavior flowing and interlocking through time, cannot be incorporated into analysis. One solution to this problem has been to define behavioral events in such a way that their contingency on the actions of a partner is preserved. For example, if the selected characteristics include infant bidding to the mother, as well as mother responses to infant bidding, a score for mother responsiveness may be calculated in terms of the proportion of the infant's bids to which the mother responds (Clarke-Stewart, 1973).

In their study of mother-infant interaction among rhesus monkeys, Hinde and Hermann (1977) have differentiated among three major classes of frequency measures: (1) *duration* measures (e.g., the amount of time the infant spends off the mother); (2) *occurrence* measures (e.g., the number of infant approaches); and (3) *derived* measures (e.g., the proportion of mutual approaches that were initiated by the infant). A responsiveness or compliance score taken as a proportion of opportunities presented by a partner would be a derived score in this sense. Hinde and Herman found no differences in the reliability of the three kinds of measures, and thus expressed a strong preference for derived measures, because the behaviors of both individuals could be included. We would add that derived measures may also reflect simple contingencies in the interaction, and as such provide an especially useful application of frequency measures to the study of interactive processes. However, there is reason to believe that the problems of reliability and stability in derived measures may be greater than for simple occurrence and duration measures. Derived scores have at least two sources of unreliability that combine to reduce the reliability of stability of the derived score. Furthermore, they may require more extended periods of observation, an issue we discuss below.

Eckerman (1979) makes a similar point in her discussion of how the relatedness of the behaviors of two actors can be reflected in a coding system. She notes that it is possible to reflect such relatedness in the initial coding (e.g., by coding as ''initiations'' only those instances in which a child's contacting of an object follows another's contacting of the same object within a specified period of time). She warns against this kind of early data reduction, however, on two grounds: It precludes an investigation of the chance level at which the behavior occurs irrespective of a partner's behavior, and it prejudges the nature of the social influence on a given behavior that may occur (e.g., perhaps one individual reacts to another by doing a complementary rather than a similar thing). Such considerations, of course, do not argue against computing scores for imitation or other relational characteristics of behavior once the more detailed initial codes are available.

Microanalyses of Behavior Sequences

In recent years, with the growing accessibility of videotape and high-speed computers, researchers have increasingly employed microscopic methods in their studies of interaction. These microscopic methods are aimed at specifying the nature of the moment-to-moment contingencies during some more or less circumscribed period of interaction between parents and children. Because these methods are relatively new and may be unfamiliar to some readers, we will describe in some detail the nature of the issues involved in the choice of procedures, and the nature of the procedures themselves.

First, before analyzing interactions sequentially, a choice must be made regarding how to encode the sequential events. Two approaches are possible: time sequential and event sequential. Time-sequential data are obtained by coding the behavior of the participants in each successive time interval (usually 3–10 sec. long), whereas for event-sequential data, a new observation is coded only when the behavior of one or both partners changes. The effects of the partner as distinct from the effects of the self are easier to detect with event-coded sequential data (this issue is discussed in greater detail below). There are, however, several advantages to time-sequential coding. Among these are the following:

1. Sequential analysis is often not the only kind of analysis to be done with a body of data on parent-child interaction. Certain ''count'' (or base-rate) scores may also be of interest. Time-interval coding provides an opportunity to create a variety of scores that have comparable units—namely, the number of time intervals in which a behavior occurs.

2. For many aspects of interaction, it is difficult to obtain agreement among coders on the boundaries of events. The problem is not very troublesome (although it exists) in the analysis of conversations (e.g., Jaffe & Feldstein, 1970), where a strong turn-taking convention prevails. However, the beginning and ending of events is less clear for many aspects of parent-child interaction, where the behavior of the participants often occurs simultaneously.

If time-sequential data are employed, the choice of how long a time interval to use as a period of observation is an important one, particularly when studying the effect of an actor's prior behavior on his or her ensuing behavior. Certain behaviors tend to perseverate once begun, and certain others tend *not* to succeed themselves. Consider, for example, a mother changing her infant's diaper. In this case, the time interval chosen by the researcher will crucially affect the conclusions on perseverance. If a 15-min. interval were chosen, we would probably conclude that diaper-changing in one interval suppresses the behavior in a succeeding interval. However, with 5-sec. intervals, perseveration for this activity will be high and will swamp whatever "refractory phase" exists following its completion.

With either time or event data, choices must be made as to which behaviors, if any, to combine. The most microscopic approach is to analyze each individual behavior in relation to each partner behavior. Thus one could study the effect of each infant behavior on the mother: infant smiling on mother's smiling, mother's vocalizing, and mother's gazing (each taken separately); then infant vocalizing on mother's smiling, vocalizing, and gazing, and so on. Then, the effect of each maternal behavior in turn on the infant's fuss-crying, smiling, vocalizing, or proximity-seeking, and so on, could be examined. Clearly when a number of behaviors are coded for each participant, the number of possible pairs for separate analysis mounts rapidly. This is especially true as the children grow beyond infancy and engage in a greater variety of behaviors, thus calling into play a larger repertoire of maternal behaviors. Accompanying the proliferation of classes of behavior is a relatively low frequency of occurrence of many behaviors, so that a very large number of intervals of observation is needed to accumulate enough instances of each behavior so that the sequential contingencies can be examined.

Researchers have differed in how they have dealt with the twin problems of the huge number of mutual contingency tables that could be generated from sequential records and the lengthy observation periods required to amass enough instances of rare behaviors. One solution is to select only the most frequent behaviors for analysis, or the ones in which the researcher has a theoretical interest, and to regard these as prototypes of what must be happening with respect to the behaviors not analyzed. Another (Martin, 1981; Thomas & Martin, 1976; Tronick, Als, & Brazelton, 1980) is to scale behaviors along a single dimension, giving each behavior or combination of behaviors a numerical value along this scale. In the work by Tronick and colleagues, scores range from maximum negative to maximum positive. In the studies by Thomas and Martin, and Martin, the dimension chosen is intensity. Other continuous variables might be used. A limitation of continuous methods is that an underlying dimension cannot always be found in the contexts in which interaction is to be studied. Moreover, even if such dimensions can be found, and they make sufficient theoretical sense, the matter of scaling behavior along the dimension is not trivial. And finally, any mutual influences that are not associated with variations in the selected dimension are automatically excluded from the analysis. Thus these continuous methods may be appropriate only in the interactions between parents and either infants or very young children; even then, they involve a large number of simplifying assumptions about the nature of the interaction.

Another solution is to combine behaviors that are considered to be equivalent on some basis. The occurrence of any of these behaviors is then taken as a criterial instance of a larger, more global behavioral cluster. The most carefully worked out application of this approach may be seen in the work of Patterson and his colleagues (Patterson, 1982; Patterson & Cobb, 1973), who have identified a set of behaviors all of which they class as "coercive." Conditional probability analyses can then be performed for the occurrence of *any* coercive behavior (singly or in combination) contingent on prior events.

Another decision concerns whether to compute scores for individual subject pairs or to pool cases and consider the contingencies in the body of data taken as a whole. There are strengths and weaknesses associated with each approach. It is possible to derive contingency scores for each pair. Scores of this kind have principally been used for purely descriptive purposes and to make qualitative comparisons among pairs (Brazelton, Koslowski, & Main, 1974; Gottman, 1979b; Patterson, 1979; Patterson & Moore, 1979; Stern, 1974; Stern, Beebe, Jaffe, & Bennett, 1977; Suomi, 1976). A number of methodological problems arise with individual scores, however, centering around the fact that individuals vary in the number of instances recorded and hence in the reliability of their scores. This raises questions about the usual statistical tests for group differences.

Alternately, it is possible to pool data across subjects, and thereby make statements about the contingencies that prevail in a group of parents and children taken as a whole. By pooling, one typically obtains a very large sample of criterial instances for contingency analyses. It is also possible to aggregate data separately for subgroups (e.g., by age, sex, or birth order of the child) and have several substantial data bases for group comparisons. Because of these and other considerations, the pooling of data over parent-child pairs has been a common approach in analyses of sequential interaction data (Bakeman & Brown, 1977; Fogel, 1977; Gottman & Bakeman,

1979; Kaye, 1977; Lewis & Lee-Painter, 1974; Lytton, 1979; Martin, Maccoby, Baran, & Jacklin, 1981; Patterson, 1979; Patterson & Cobb, 1973; Thomas & Martin, 1976). Pooling entails the disadvantage that the contribution of individual cases to the pool is lost. However, tests of significance may still be done by assuming that the pooled data represent a prototypical interaction involving "the" mother and "the" child and using simple probability methods to test whether particular contingencies are significantly different from zero.

Once the relevant decisions have been made, the researcher proceeds to code each interval (or event segment) so as to indicate whether the selected behaviors are present or absent for each of the partners involved in the interaction. Markov models may be used to summarize information from the coded record. These models provide a relatively simple and concise descriptive technique for investigating certain kinds of relationships between the behavior of two persons. Markov analysis begins with the concept of *states*. Given a single behavior or behavior combination of interest, and two interacting persons, four states are possible at any given point in time: State (0,0), in which neither person is exhibiting the selected behavior; State (0,1), in which the second person (e.g., the child) acts, but the first (the mother) does not; and likewise, State (1,0) and State (1,1). Simple Markov models concern themselves with describing the *probability of transition* in and out of states from one time period to the next. It is important to note that the unit of analysis for Markov models is not the behavior of the individual partners in interaction, but rather the *state of the interacting system*. Thus a Markov analysis traces changes in joint states. It does not attempt to isolate the contribution of, or the consequences for, either participant separately.

A second and more widely used microanalytic technique for analyzing discrete sequential data is the analysis of conditional probabilities. Conditional probability analysis is very similar in structure to Markov analysis: Both methods code behavior during interaction as present or absent for a given time interval, and both involve the computation of conditional probabilities. The major difference is that the two techniques use different units of analysis. Conditional probability methods focus not on the probability of the interacting pair being in a particular joint state, but rather on the probability of a particular behavior by a single person. Thus these methods do attempt to identify the effects of one partner on the other, and either participant may be taken as the target of the analysis.

There are modifications of the basic conditional probability methods. For example, Sackett's (1979) lag-sequential method traces probabilities conditional on events that occurred several intervals prior to the target behavior. The general concept for all conditional probability methods is, however, the same: Conditional probabilities (conditional, that is, on partner behavior) are compared to unconditional, base line probabilities. This comparison is presumed to show the magnitude of the effect that the partner's behavior has on the subject's behavior. When conditional probabilities are computed on time-sampled data, however, such an interpretation is questionable (Gottman & Ringland, 1981; Martin et al., 1981). A major problem is that when behaviors perseverate over several time intervals (e.g., when an infant continues to cry for several intervals), behavior of the partner that occurred in response to this behavior (e.g., mother touching and holding) may be mistaken for a cause rather than an effect of the infant's behavior. The confounding occurs because the subject's behavior is already elevated prior to the partner behavior that is taken as the criterial event. Another way of putting this is to say that the overall subject base line is not the valid level with which to compare the probability of a subject's behavior following a given partner behavior. One solution is to analyze only the *onset* of behavior as influenced by the behavior of the partner. Analyzing only onsets—the first of a series of time intervals through which a behavior persists—is in a sense equivalent to converting time-series analysis into event-series analysis. Another approach is to incorporate perseverative acts—the "self" component—directly into the analysis.

The Self Component. During bouts of interaction partners are never completely responsive to one another. Streams of behavior are never completely meshed. Individuals begin a series of actions that have their own time course; the individual's behavior constitutes a practiced string of actions that trigger one another, so that the impulse to carry out the self-generated sequence is strong and, in a sense, competes with the partner's pressure to modify the behavior so as to coordinate it with, or respond to, the partner's actions. In the case of a child's starting to cry, crying usually generates some degree of momentum, and although a mother's efforts to soothe may have the effect of shortening the crying bout, they seldom stop it instantly. In the study of interaction, researchers face a dual problem: Not only must they trace the direction of influence between partners, but they must also attempt to distinguish between the influence of a partner and the momentum of the individual's own autonomous behavioral cycles. This is an additional problem over and above the problem of bidirectionality of influence, and causes us to reformulate the question we attempt to answer through microscopic analysis. The new question becomes: How much of the variance in an individual's behavior can be explained by previous characteristics of the person's own behavior, and how much can be explained by characteristics of the partner after the influence of the self has been taken into account? To answer this question, models of interactive behavior are needed that include both the behavior of the self and the behavior of the partner. A recently employed solution is to use multiple regression. The self's prior behavior is entered as one predictor, and the partner's behavior as the other predictor, the subject's current behavior being the outcome measure (Martin et al., 1981; Thomas & Martin, 1976). In such analyses, although there is still evidence for significant effects of mothers on children and of children on mothers, the size of the effect is greatly attenuated compared to simple sequential probability findings.

Thomas and Martin (1976) referred to the contribution of the self's prior behavior as the *self-regulatory* component, and to the contribution of the partner as the *interactive* component. Thomas and Malone (1979) reanalyzed several existing data sets using a variety of models for interaction, each of these models having in common both a self-regulatory and an interactive component. They found weak evidence for an interdependency in the behavior of interacting partners. In all cases, the size of the interactive component was quite small, substantially smaller than the size of the self component. Hayes' (1978) analyses of interactions between mothers and young infants employed a "shuffling" procedure, which amounts essentially to comparing observed transition probabilities in a Markov analysis to a chance model for the transition probabilities. He came to the same conclusion: that the evidence for the effect of the partner, although present, was miniscule compared to the impact of one's own behavior on subsequent behavior. A further confirming bit of evidence comes from Martin's (1981) analysis of changes in intensity in the interactions between 10-month-old infants and their mothers, providing estimates of several different self and partner effects. In data for an individual subject (appendix to Martin's monograph, 1981), the F-tests on the self components were in all cases larger (up to 50 times larger) than the F-tests on the various partner components.

Can we conclude that the self component must always be greater than the influence of a partner?

Not in any general sense. The magnitude of the self component in the studies reviewed above is in part a function of the fact that time sequences, rather than event sequences, were chosen for study; moreover, as noted above, its magnitude is partly dependent on the length of the time interval chosen. The use of time intervals involves the imposition of arbitrary segmentation on a continuous stream of behavior; the intervals fractionate continuous acts, and it is not surprising that there should be a tendency to complete an act once begun, and hence for behavior to perseverate across time boundaries, creating a large self component. If one chooses to analyze event sequences, the self component shrinks or even disappears. But here too, the choice of unit determines the outcome. In analyzing conversation, for example, if the stream of utterances is broken up into sentences, the tendency for a speaker to continue talking—as opposed to yielding the floor to the partner—would be less than if the units were phrases, and less still than if the units were words. In the extreme case, one can consider a unit of analysis to be the segment of speech by one speaker that occurs between the ending of the partner's preceding utterance and the partner's resuming speech. With this choice of unit, the self component goes to zero by definition. The same applies when acts other than speech acts are being analyzed. Some aspects of the relative merits of time sampling and event sampling have already been discussed. We would add that time sampling will in general yield a larger self component than event sampling. However, this is not necessarily an argument for event sampling. The tendency of individuals to respond to their own prior behavior—to behave autonomously—while presumably engaged in interaction with others may be an important aspect of their behavior to be measured and understood. Indeed, autonomous functioning by mothers and infants (as measured by the size of individuals' self components) has proved to be a significant predictor of subsequent characteristics of the pair (Martin, 1981). Such a finding argues for assessing the self component and making use of it as a variable of some significance, rather than ruling it out by definition through the choice of event units.

Extension of Issues to Longitudinal Analysis

The importance of considering the self component is not confined to microscopic analyses of moment-to-moment interactions. In attempting to understand long-term effects, one may compute a correlation between a parent behavior at time 1 and a child behavior at time 2. If a significant correlation emerges, this fact alone does not, of course, justify an inference of cross-time causal relationship between the two measures. The correlation may reflect the outcome of simple perseveration of the child's behavior from time 1 to time 2, with the parent's behavior at time 1 being an effect of the child's time 1 behavior. It is this kind of issue that has led to the use of panel designs, in which the behavior of both participants is assessed at both measurement periods. Cross-lagged panel correlation has been widely used to assess the effects of early socialization events on later outcomes, but this method has been broadly criticized (Rogosa, 1980) and is now in disrepute. Structural modeling (e.g., Duncan, 1975) has been applied to panel data, using both measured variable and latent variable (e.g., Joreskog, 1980) approaches. These methods are promising, but there are many methodological problems yet to be solved in this controversial area, a major one being that they call for larger samples and more stable measures than are usually employed in parent-child interaction studies (Clarke-Stewart & Hevey, 1981). The important point in the present context is that panel models incorporate both prior self scores and prior partner scores in longitudinal research. Panel data thus permit the use of multiple regression to partial out the self component while searching for partner effects in a way that is conceptually equivalent to the procedures discussed above for doing so in analyses of moment-to-moment effects.

Much of the research summarized in this chapter employs a simple correlational design. The difficulties of making causal inferences from such data are well known. Even designs that employ the comparison of extreme groups—abusive parents versus nonabusers, depressed or alcoholic parents versus "normals," parents of children with behavior problems compared with those of well-adjusted children—do not free the findings from ambiguities of interpretation (e.g., we cannot tell whether oppositional behavior in a child makes a parent depressed, or whether parental depression makes a child oppositional). More and more, it seems evident that circular processes, in which the influence flows in both directions, are the rule. But determining the weights of the various interactive components is difficult indeed. As researchers have become more aware of this fact, some have turned to analysis of immediate interactive process for their own sake, in an effort to understand the dynamics of interaction, meanwhile setting aside the issue of longer lasting effects on individual participants. Others have taken an experimental approach, either through therapeutic interventions into family process, or through contrived simulations where the behavior of one person is ar-

tificially fixed. These experimental procedures enable the researcher to see the effects of a given partner behavior on a subject, but do so at the sacrifice of the interpersonal history that would normally have led to this behavior on the part of the partner. Longitudinal designs present an opportunity to preserve this history, while nevertheless permitting modest testing of causal hypotheses concerning the effect of partners on one another's behavior.

Multimethod Approaches and the Revival of Ratings

So far, we have discussed some of the advantages and disadvantages of subject-as-informant (interviews and questionnaires) and of observational (both frequency and microscopic) data. It appears that some sorts of information can more reliably be obtained from one type of data than the other. In response to known strengths and weaknesses of subject-as-informant as well as of observational data, many researchers—including the Blocks (cf. Block & Block, 1979); Baumrind (cf. Baumrind, 1971); Patterson (1982); Hetherington, Cox, and Cox (1982); Radke-Yarrow and Zahn-Waxler (see *vol. IV, chap. 6*); and ourselves—have opted for an approach to the study of family interaction that derives information from a variety of data sources. Parents may be interviewed, or given questionnaires or Q-sorts to complete; children may be included as informants via paper-and-pencil tests or interviews; and parents and children may be observed both together and separately in both naturalistic settings and the laboratory. In a sense, such an approach amounts to "covering one's bets": To the extent that distortions and incorrect inferences are drawn from any single data source, such problems can be minimized by using several data sources. The intention is to make use of the best that each method has to offer in constructing scores.

As part of these multimethod packages, there has been a renaissance of interest in the use of ratings. Cairns and Green (1979) note that frequency counts (obtained from time-interval observations) and ratings (also based on behavior observation) have different strengths and weaknesses and are adapted to different objectives. They point out that raters tend to report the central tendency of an individual's behavior, averaging out the moment-to-moment changes in situations or eliciting conditions. Thus in ratings, the situational component of behavior is minimized and the person component highlighted. Behavior-count observations, on the other hand, give maximal information on situational variability, with the result that the person component may be obscured. Evidence is accumulating (Clark-Stewart & Hevey, 1981; Waters, 1978) that ratings yield higher cross-time stability than frequency-count scores.

However, raters may do more than simply average out behavior over time and situations. They may also adjust their ratings in relation to an assumed group base line. Cairns and Green (1979) note that, for example, sex differences are more frequently found in behavior-count data than in ratings. Presumably, in rating a behavior such as aggression, raters may unconsciously rate a boy as being high or low in aggression *for a boy,* and may use a different subjective base line for girls. Such adaptations of the anchor points of ratings clearly weaken group comparisons. Nevertheless, the ability of raters to cumulate information across time and situations may be a considerable asset if the research objectives call for detecting stable within-group individual differences for purposes of correlational analysis.

Bakeman and Brown (1980) discuss the relative usefulness of ratings versus microanalytic scores. From videotapes, they did time-interval coding; in addition, the observers rated mother and infant on more global characteristics, such as responsiveness of infant and responsiveness of mother. Significant correlations were found between certain ratings made during the infant's first 3 months and the child's social competence at age 3 years. The microanalytic scores, by contrast, did not predict the child's subsequent social characteristics, either rated or observed. Bakeman and Brown comment on their findings as follows:

> We think it may be more fruitful to think of characteristics of early interaction, like responsiveness, not as frequencies or sequences of particular acts, but rather as a disposition which permeates all of the mother's and/or all of the baby's interactive behavior. And in that case, global rating scales, and not sequential recording of minute particular behaviors followed by various microanalyses, might be the method of choice. Or perhaps most fruitful, would be an approach which combines features of molar (rating-scale) and micro methods. (p. 445)

They suggest that the frequency, duration, and emotional tone of interactive bouts might be more predictive measures than detailed analysis of (for example) onsets and offsets. We are reminded that Patterson and colleagues have found that most of the moment-to-moment contingencies applied by family members to one another's behavior do not reliably distinguish normal from distressed families, whereas base rates, and the duration of mutually coercive bouts, do distinguish them. Thus the level of analysis appears to be of great importance in determining the utility of scores.

We do not wish to imply at this time that microanalytic methods ought to be abandoned in favor of more global, macroscopic ratings. Microanalytic scores themselves vary considerably in level of analysis. Studies of the sequential probabilities governing mutual gazing (e.g., Stern, 1974) are clearly different from the equally microanalytic study of content-free mutual "activity" employed by Bakeman and Brown, and each of these approaches is quite distinct from microanalytic methods that focus on more global characteristics of behavior such as positive/negative (Martin et al., 1981) or "intensity" (Martin, 1981; Thomas & Martin, 1976). The Bakeman and Brown (1980) work is unique in that it compares the utility of one form of microanalytic method with a more molar method; however, many more comparisons of the various forms of microanalytic and molar methodologies are needed before any generalizations can be made about the predictive value of these methods. It seems likely that the form of analysis needs to be conceptually matched to the sorts of predictions that are sought. Clearly no single approach should be advocated as appropriate for all research questions.

The Independence of Parent and Child Scores

In observations of the interaction of parent and child pairs, scores derived from the interaction of two persons are often presumed to describe a characteristic of one person. For example, when a mother picks up a crying infant, the length of time needed for the child to stop crying may be recorded, and this datum may then be labeled either as the infant's "soothability" score or the mother's "skill in soothing" score. Or, from accumulated instances in which a parent makes demands and a child does or does not comply, the level of either parent control or child compliance may be scored. Similarly, from instances in which the child makes a demand and the parent does or does not respond, we can get a parent responsiveness score; we could presumably also get a score on "child dominance" or "child control," although the child's side of the interaction is less often conceptualized in this way. That the scores of the two persons actually pertain to the dyad rather than to either individual is easily seen if we consider findings from several diverse research settings.

Dunn (1977) showed that the proportion of signals by 14-month-old infants that mothers respond to depended on what proportion of those signals were demands for objects or help. And Bronson (1974) found that mothers showed an increasing proportion of responses to infant bidding through the second year, as the infants' demands became more focused and more articulate. Thus what is scored as maternal responsiveness reflects the child's skills in bidding as well as maternal readiness to respond. As we will see, there are similar confoundings in scores for parental control. This variable is often treated in terms of the degree to which parents follow through on a demand until they obtain compliance. Thus the parent with the more compliant child is scored as having a high degree of control. Similar difficulties are found in scores for children's compliance. Schaffer and Crook (1980) showed that parents of 18-month-old children had a greater likelihood of obtaining compliance to an object-oriented demand if they either waited till they had the child's attention, or used an attention-getting signal before making the object-oriented demand. We may assume that similar parental skills are involved in getting compliance from older children as well, so that at any age, a child's compliance is as much a reflection of the parent's skill in synchronizing demands to the child's state of readiness to receive them as it is a reflection of the child's readiness to comply.

It would appear that in many instances there is no alternative but to recognize the inherent interdependence of interactors and to combine the behaviors of the two participants into a dyadic score that reflects the functioning of the pair. This does not, however, imply that there are *no* behaviors that distinctively describe individuals during interaction. Nor does the fact that the behaviors of two participants may be functionally related invalidate individual scores. For example, the frequency of mother smiling and infant smiling may be positively correlated and sequentially dependent, but the frequency of smiles by each remain individual characteristics. The issue here concerns *relational* scores that, we suggest, cannot be defined independently. This means that scores that are necessarily dyadic should be labeled and conceptualized as such, and that the nature of theories about interaction should reflect this conceptualization. Thus a hypothesis such as "controlling parents will tend to have compliant children" becomes meaningless. But a hypothesis in which a dyadic score is taken as either the antecedent or the outcome of a parent or child characteristic *measured outside the framework of the interaction itself* retains its value.

ESTABLISHING THE PARENT-CHILD RELATIONSHIP

Bonding, Reciprocity, and Pair Integration

At birth, healthy infants have reflexes and tropisms that equip them for the rapid establishment of interactive behavior patterns with caretakers. They can turn their heads toward the source of a voice, fixate their eyes on a face, and calm when touched or held. Their cries are vigorous and related to their need states. Adults, for their part, are equipped to be drawn into reciprocal relations with infants. Infantile cries are highly arousing to adults, and certain infantile characteristics are strong positive attractants. Thus both participants in an adult-newborn encounter are in a state of readiness for bonding to take place. The development of attachment bonds is included in the chapter by Campos, Goldsmith, and Svejda (see *vol. II, chap. 10*), so for the purposes of this chapter we have selected only that portion of the research on parent-infant bonding that documents the flow of mutual influence between the interacting pair and shows how the initial responses of parent and infant become coordinated (meshed) to a greater or lesser degree through the first 18 months of life.

The First Stage of Bonding: A Critical Period?

Ethologists' studies of the interactions between mammals or birds and their newborn young have revealed a variety of synchronized instinctive behavior patterns that bring about bonding between the individuals in the parent and offspring generations. There are chemical effects on the mother that, in some species, stem from the maternal licking of the newborn and the ingestion of the placenta; there are pheromones emitted by the mother that are strong attractants to the young, the degree of this attraction being governed by a timetable that is linked to the locomotor stage of the young (Leon, 1977). In birds, there are certain periods during which individuals are particularly sensitive to certain specific stimuli emanating from the partner. Drawing on ethological studies and concepts, Klaus and Kennell (1976) propose that the first few hours following birth of an infant are critical for the facilitation of mother-infant bonding. During the decade since the appearance of the first Klaus and Kennell work, there has been an extensive set of studies by these and other investigators, and several detailed reviews are available (Leiderman, in press; Minde, 1980; Richards, 1978). The following generalizations appear justified. There is consistent evidence that extending the close physical contact between a mother and a newborn infant fosters the early development of close bonding between the pair. The effects are strongest when the child is a firstborn, when the infant is at risk (e.g., premature), or when the mother is especially young or from a disadvantaged population group. Although it has been shown that stimulation of low-birthweight infants by nurses has positive effects on the infants' subsequent development, infant stimulation alone probably does not account for all the effects of providing early mother-infant contact. There are probably important aspects of maternal bonding that are fostered by such contact and that contribute to the subsequent development of the relationship. A consistent effect of early contact is on the incidence and duration of breast-feeding, but additional effects may be seen in the amount of affectionate touching (including the closeness with which the infant is held), the sensitivity of the mother to the infant's signals, and the amount of *en face* interaction. The effects are fairly clearly demonstrable over the first several months of the infant's life, and in several cases effects are seen at age 12 or 18 months. Relatively few studies have followed the mother-infant pairs for a sufficient period to determine the extent and nature of long-term effects, and among those that have, the results are not consistent. However, there are enough positive findings in recent studies (deChateau, Frankenhaeuser, Lundberg, Wiberg, & Winberg, 1981; O'Connor, Vietze, Sandler, Sherrod, & Altemeier, 1980) to warrant continued openness to the hypothesis that, at least for certain mother-infant pairs who might otherwise be at some risk, the provision of early close physical contact helps to get the mother-infant relationship off to a good start, and that this good start may be important in the subsequent development of the relationship.

We do not believe, however, that the positive findings of the studies on augmented contact between mother and newborn should be taken as evidence that exclusively supports the idea that the bonding processes are instinctive and qualitatively similar to the processes that occur in lower animals. Although the readiness of both mother and infant for bonding undoubtedly does reflect the presence of certain biologically dictated reflexes and tropisms on both sides, and although early close physical contact may indeed foster the activation of such biological processes, we would like to emphasize that there is probably a nonbiological component to the bonding. A nurse caring for a newborn in a nursery and providing regular stimulation for it may become somewhat attached to it, but her response does not compare with that of the child's parent. An adopting parent, as well as a biological one, does enter into a close bond. Both know that this is the beginning of a lifelong, deep relationship. Richards (1978) notes that mothers who are separated from infants because the infants must be placed in special-care units often comment that they do not feel as though the infant really "belongs" to them. What determines whether a mother feels that the infant belongs to her? Surely this must involve the sociostructural factors that have to do with who has responsibility for the care of the infant, whose name it will have, and what the future relationship of the adult and child (as determined, e.g., by the society's kinship system) will be. Thus biological and social elements are interwoven from the beginning of the parent-child relationship.

Mutual Contingency

Although it is clear that a parent who ministers to a crying infant is behaving contingently, it is not so obvious that the newborn's behavior is contingent on the adult's behavior in the sense of adapting to the adult's immediately prior behavior. Perhaps the infant merely emits behavior in accordance with its internal states, so that the only way in which the adult can influence a newborn's behavior is by modifying those need states (e.g., by feeding or by covering with a warm blanket). Observations of the interactions of newborns (2, 3, or 4 days old) with their mothers provide qualified evidence for the infant's ability to be influenced by adult behavior in a more interactive sense. When a quiescent state prevails, in which neither party is directing social behavior toward the other, mothers are more likely to break the quiescent state, and infants are more likely to break off interaction and return the pair to a quiescent state (Bakeman & Brown, 1977; Rosenthal, 1982). In this sense, mothers appear to be "driving" the interaction. However, once interaction has begun, newborns play a more active role; for example, they have been seen to synchronize their subtle body movements with maternal speech sounds (Condon, 1977). Furthermore, both mother and infant are more likely to begin to direct behavior toward the partner when the partner is directing behavior toward them than when the partner is not engaged in such social action; thus each is capable of capturing the other's attention, and the behavior of each appears to be controlled at least in part by the perceived interactive readiness of the partner (Bakeman & Brown, 1977).

The interaction of mother and infant has been likened to a dance or a behavioral dialogue, in which the successive actions of the partners are closely coordinated. The coordination can take the form simply of mutual contingency or synchrony—that is, where each person's action depends on the partner's prior action—or it can be reciprocal in a narrower sense: The actions of the two persons can be qualitatively matched, as in the case of imitation or mutual smiling. A number of students of the details of the early mother-infant interaction have dealt with the interchange of specific similar acts: the exchange of gaze, of vocalizations, or of smiles. Bakeman and Brown (1977) have suggested that all these things (and perhaps other actions as well) can be regarded as communicative acts, and that it may be more meaningful to trace dialogue (i.e., the mutual contingencies that prevail between communicative acts of any kind) rather than to look for same-act exchanges. We begin with an overview of the research that has dealt with the exchange of specific acts, and then turn to the studies of dialogue where clusters of social behavior have been analyzed.

The Exchange of Specific Behaviors. One of the simplest and most compelling aspects of interactive behavior is the direction of each partner's visual attention during interaction. Mutual gazing, or eye contact, is a prerequisite for many forms of adult social interaction, most notably conversation (Stern, 1974). Microanalytic studies of gazing allow us to examine the function of visual attention in interactions between parents and children. These studies make it clear that mutual visual regard is a central part of the interactive process. In describing the interactions of two mother-infant pairs analyzed in detail from videotapes, Stern et al. (1977) discuss "episodes of maintained engagement" and point out that both mother and infant tend to emit a variety of behavioral acts while they are looking at each other; by contrast, when either participant looks away, the rate of other behaviors subsides. Thus mutual gazing seems to provide a context for sustaining a complex set of interactive behaviors. Fogel (1977) makes a similar point in noting that mothers gaze at their infants in long spurts that are coordinated to the up and down rhythms of the infant's behavior. Sequential analyses (Jaffe, Stern, & Peery, 1973; Stern, 1974; Stern et al., 1977) have shown that when either member of the mother-infant pair gazes at the other, the probability of the partner's *en face* gazing is increased, as though one person's gaze acts as a magnet for the other person's eyes and initiates a mutuality (reciprocity), which then spreads to other modalities of behavior (vocalizing, touching, mutual imitation). Mutuality of gazing at external objects can also be demonstrated: Collis and Schaffer (1975) showed that when a variety of objects were present, mothers and infants tended to look at the same object—primarily because mothers tracked and imitated their infants' line of regard. The importance of such coordination in permitting the mother to contribute to the infant's development of referential language is clear.

We see, then, that mutual gazing is a common component of interaction between parents and children, and both parents and children are likely to follow the lead of the other in creating the dyadic state of mutual gazing. We should be aware, however, that the existing findings on the role of mutual gazing in parent-child interaction may be culture-bound. There are societies in which children are taught to avert their gaze from an adult's face as a sign of respect for the adult's authority. We do not know at what age gaze aversion begins or what the significance of such a custom is for the development of meshing of the behaviors of a parent-child pair, but must beware of assuming that direct eye contact is an essential element in such development.

In a sense, the exchange of vocalizations presents a different problem to mother and infant than the exchange of visual regard. Two persons can gaze at one another simultaneously, and simultaneous gazing continues to be a central component of interaction from infancy into adulthood. By contrast, one cannot easily receive vocal signals from a partner at the same time that one is sending them; thus talking occurs primarily in a turn-taking mode. In adult conversation (see, e.g., Jaffe & Feldstein, 1970), vocal onsets of one member of an interacting pair are most likely when the partner has paused, resulting in a switch of who "has the floor."

Anderson, Vietze, and Dokecki (1977), Stern, Jaffe, Beebe, and Bennett (1975), and Parke and Sawin (1977) have all sampled vocalizations in 3- to 4-month-old infants and their mothers. Although the findings of the three studies are not entirely consistent, in general they show that the signal for each participant to begin vocalizing is the onset, rather than the offset, of the partner's vocalization. This is especially true for infant vocalizing. Stern et al. (1975) found that, in the mother-infant dyads, coacting—that is, both partners vocalizing together—was more common than alternating. Thus, at this young age at least, it does not seem that infants have acquired the convention of alternating for vocal acts. Mothers, though clearly aware of the adult rules of conversation, may or may not adhere to these rules when interacting with their infants. At least in the Anderson et al. (1977) study, they employ vocal acts in their interactions with their infants in the same way that they employ gazing—namely, to maintain attention.

By the time the infant is 1 year old, the nature of vocal interchanges has undergone drastic changes (Schaffer, Collis, & Parsons, 1977). Now the mother and child do take turns in their vocalizing, and seldom interrupt one another. Schaffer and his colleagues find some evidence for the proposition that the child sets the pace and the mother does the adapting in the interchange of vocalizations. That is, the child tends to initiate and the mother to reply; and the mother waits for pauses in the infant's vocalizations to make her own contributions to the exchange.

There is a possibility that some mothers initiate the alternation convention at an earlier age than had previously been thought. A recent study of 4-month-olds and their mothers (Ver Hoeve, Stevenson, Leavitt, & Roach, 1981) found that whereas maternal vocalization increased very briefly (for one time lag) following the infant's vocalization, it returned to a low level thereafter, as though the mother was waiting for the infant to vocalize again. The mother's visual regard following an infant's gaze, however, was maintained for a much longer time, so that the maternal signals appropriate for alternation included maintaining visual attention in addition to creating an auditory pause.

Studies of the mutual contingencies that prevail between infant smiling and maternal smiling have had equivocal results. Etzel and Gewirtz (1967) showed that if infants' smiles are responded to contingently by positive adult behaviors (smiling, head nodding, verbal praise), the rate of infant smiling increases. This does not mean, however, that the infant's smile is contingent on the adult having smiled. Thomas and Martin (1976) found from a sequential analysis that the probability of an infant's smiling was only minimally affected by whether the mother had smiled in a prior interval, although the mother's smiling was somewhat more contingent (but not highly contingent) on the infant's having smiled. And, in fact, Parke and Sawin (1977) report that in their sample of 3-month-olds, parental smiling had an inhibitory effect on infant smiling in the ensuing interval.

The Etzel and Gerwirtz study (1967) might be seen as a straightforward instance in which a specific response—smiling—is "learned" through reinforcement. However, an alternative explanation becomes possible if we consider a different conditioning situation used by Papousek and Papousek (1977). They used a reinforcement paradigm in which infant head turning was conditioned to an acoustic signal and rewarded with the delivery of milk. The infants were 5 months old. These researchers found that the probability of the infant's

displays of positive affect increased when maternal stimulation was highly contingent on the infant's own behavior. Thus it appears that maternal responsiveness is enjoyable to the infant, and the child's smiling may be an expression of this fact, rather than (or in addition to) being a class of responses that has been specifically selected for reinforcement by the mother.

More and more, students of adult-infant interaction have questioned the wisdom of analyzing specific responses, believing that there are clusters of responses within which the specific behaviors are readily substituted for one another. Some of the methodological issues surrounding the choice of which behaviors to "cluster" together were discussed earlier. For the present, we turn to some of the substantive findings that have emerged from studies that do aggregate specific behaviors into sets.

Affective Reciprocity. Though smiles may not be answered specifically with smiles, or frowns with frowns, there is considerable evidence that mothers and infants do match the general affective tone of one another's behavior. M. Lewis (1972) found that the amount of affectively positive maternal behavior was positively correlated with the amount of positive behavior of their 3-month-old infants, and negatively correlated with the amount of infant negative behavior. Tronick et al. (1980), in their study of "monadic phases" in the interaction of mothers and 3-month-old infants, also found matching of positive with positive affective states, and negative with negative. Martin and colleagues (Martin et al., 1981), observing the interaction of mothers and 18-month-old children, also grouped a variety of behaviors into positive and negative clusters, and found that both positive and negative behaviors were influenced by the behavior of the partner, and that the greatest influences were those in which there was a response *in kind* (that is, affectively matched). Most especially, behavior *onsets* tended to be qualitatively matched in this way.

Bronson (1974) combined a variety of manifestations of positive affective behavior into more molar clusters, called "positive bids" on the part of the child, and "positive responses" on the part of the mother. She studied 10 mother-child pairs, with observations being conducted approximately every 2½ weeks between the child's first and second birthdays. The data were collapsed into 12-, 18-, and 24-month summaries. She reports increasing synchronization between the positive states of mother and child; thus the probability that an infant positive bid would elicit a mother positive response increased from .57 to 1.00. Whether a child's behavior has a positive or negative affective sign, then, seems to be a powerful determinant of maternal response.

The overall picture of the studies taken together is one of reciprocation of affect. And there is some indication that this reciprocation may become stronger as the child grows older.

Synchrony at a Molar Level. A number of studies of mother-infant interaction have not focused on the exchange of narrowly defined responses or classes of matched responses, but have examined the coordination of behaviors across response classes or in more comprehensive clusters. For example, as noted above, Bakeman and Brown (1977) have used Markov analyses to trace the exchange of *any* form of interactive behavior between newborns and their mothers, employing the strongly reductive convention of regarding each partner as being in an "on" or "off" state at any given moment, and studying transitions from mutual quiescence through activity of only one partner to coacting states. Rosenthal (1982) warns that this may be too global an approach, and that important contingencies of specific behavior on specific partner behavior may be missed through such radical clustering. Nevertheless, it is becoming clear that meaningful patterns can be identified through exceedingly global clustering. As we noted above in the discussion of mutual gazing, other social behaviors occur along with eye contact and subside when eye contact is broken. Stern and colleagues (1977) use the term "kinesic phases" to describe the up-and-down movement of a set of social behaviors linked to gazing, and showed that the cycling of these phases was coordinated between the two members of the mother-infant pair.

In a few studies, changes in the intensity of interactive behaviors (rather than merely changes from "on" to "off" states or vice versa) have been studied. Working with 9- and 10-month-old infants, respectively, Thomas and Martin (1976) and Martin (1981) coded each combination of observed mother-directed infant behaviors (e.g., look at mother while smiling and vocalizing) occurring in a particular time interval according to its intensity, and a similar coding was done of the intensity of the mother's infant-directed behavior. Effects were analyzed sequentially taking into account the intensity of both the self's and the partner's prior behavior. Martin (1981) estimated values for these effects separately (using multiple-regression models) for every mother-child pair. Thus, for example, the degree to which the intensity of a given mother's behavior was contingent on her infant's prior intensity level, and the degree to which her intensity represented an effect of her own prior intensity, was reflected in her individual regression weights taken from the regression of these two predictors on her current behavior. Individual regression weights were then used as scores for purposes of distinguishing among individuals and predicting subsequent characteristics of the mother-infant relationship. There was wide individual variability in the extent to which various components of the interaction influenced changes in intensity for the mother or for the infant, but over the sample as a whole there was clear evidence that the two participants did indeed influence one another during interaction. The findings indicated that interactions at this age may be understood as a process of resolving discrepancies in intensity. Both mothers and infants worked to resolve these discrepancies, but did so in somewhat different ways. Infants tended to intensify when there was a discrepancy between mother and infant intensity in the prior observation interval, regardless of the direction of that discrepancy (i.e., mother greater than infant or infant greater than mother). Mothers, by contrast, either intensified or deintensified to bring about a closer match between their own intensity and that of their infants.

Who Is Influencing Whom?

Taken as a whole, the body of research reviewed above documents that the behaviors of mothers and infants are linked. That is, behaviors such as gazing, vocalizing, touching, and smiling are synchronized, and affective states tend to be reciprocal. And levels of intensity cycle synchronously. However, as we noted earlier, it could be the case that mothers are doing most of the work in achieving synchrony, by being alert to their infants' states and adapting their behavior to the infant's specific responses.

There are some surprising complexities in arriving at an answer concerning who is "driving" the interaction. Mothers can facilitate interaction in several ways: They can initiate it, by emitting signals that capture the infant's attention when the infant is quiescent; they can convert infants' nonsocial behavior into social behavior by joining in when the infant has begun a sequence of behaviors that probably were not initially social (such as babbling); and they can sustain an interactive sequence once begun, by responding in attention-maintaining ways to behavior initiated by the infant. Maternal responsiveness of the latter two kinds could be considered as merely another term for infant control. If the mother's behavior is contingent on the infant's but the infant's is not contingent on the mother's (e.g., in mutual smiling, see Thomas and Martin, 1976), can we say that the infant is in control? In one sense yes, because the infant's behavior is determining what the mother does. However, the mother is selective in her response. She does not smile at everything the infant does, and if her response shapes the infant's behavior by maintaining a sequence of responses, then we can say that she is influencing the infant at the same time that she is being influenced.

We have listed a number of ways in which mothers can facilitate infants' behavior. Infants could presumably facilitate interaction in the same ways. There is reason to believe that when the infant is quite young, the mother is doing considerably more facilitating than the infant. We saw that among newborns, the mother is more likely to break the quiescent state, the infant more likely to break the coacting state (i.e., to withdraw from interaction). Through the first year and probably into the second, maternal joining in with an infant's ongoing nonsocial behavior is more common than the infant's joining the mother's behavior (Bronson, 1974; Schaffer, Collis, & Parsons, 1977; Stern et al., 1975; Thomas & Martin, 1976). Pawlby (1977) reports that throughout the age range from 11 to 43 weeks, mothers are significantly more likely to imitate their infants than vice versa. Even in cases where it might seem that the infant is setting the pace for interaction, as in the case of vocal exchanges between mothers and year-old children (Schaffer et al., 1977), the mother is creating the occasion for the child to speak, by first speaking and then pausing expectantly. Clarke-Stewart and Hevey (1981) also stress the predominance of the mother's contribution to the detachment process whereby children become more autonomous during the second year.

Before concluding that mothers are taking a more active role in all these aspects of facilitation, however, it is important to note that most studies of mother-infant interaction—especially those done with infants younger than 6 months of age—involve situations where the mother is feeding the infant, or where the mother has been asked to play with the infant or get the infant involved in interaction in some way. It is to be expected that in such situations the mother would take more initiative, and the infant less, than in situations where the mother is busy and the infant is, say, hungry. In the relatively rare situations where interaction was studied when the mother was busy with another task, sequential analysis has shown infants taking quite an active role in initiating interaction (Martin, 1981; Martin et al., 1981; Thomas & Martin, 1976). Probably there is no general answer to the question of which member of the pair is more likely to initiate interaction, because the balance depends so heavily on the situational constraints. However, although the point has not been empirically demonstrated as yet, it is a good hypothesis that there is a shift toward the end of the first year in the infant's ability to produce interaction by joining in. We should be aware, however, that the mother's tendency to join the child's stream of spontaneous actions depends on the development of the child's interactive capacities. Thus Pawlby showed that even though the mother did more imitating of the infant's behavior throughout the 17- to 43-week period than the infant did of the mother's, there was an increase in maternal imitation when the infant reached the age of about 26 weeks, and this increase appeared to be accounted for by an increase in the infant's rate of interaction at this time.

Rosenblum and Youngstein (1974) make an interesting point concerning the relative contribution of mother and infant to their interaction in bonnet macaques. They find that both mother and infant decline in their active elicitation of response from the other over the first several months of life, but that the mothers decline faster. (Note the congruence of this finding with that of Clarke-Stewart and Hevey with human mother-infant pairs.) Furthermore, they have studied the ability of each member of the dyad to compensate for the other's lack of response when the partner is somehow incapacitated for interaction. They have conducted experiments in which either the mother or the infant is briefly anesthetized. They find that if the experiment is done when the infant is 6–7 months old, either infant or mother will maintain considerable contact with an unconscious partner, whereas when the infant is older (16–19 months), infants maintain a moderate level of contact with unconscious mothers but mothers make little effort to contact an unconscious infant. The authors suggest that the tendency of an infant or mother to compensate for the partner's unresponsiveness falls off rapidly with the increasing age of the infant, and that the mother's tendency declines more rapidly than the infant's. Their analysis suggests that with increasing age, the infant must do an increasingly greater proportion of the contact-maintaining work. (See also Hinde, 1975.)

There are some serious methodological flaws in a number of the attempts that have been made so far to identify quantitatively the contribution of each member of the mother-infant pair to an interaction. We have discussed these issues in an earlier section (see *Methods of Study*). Here, we merely remind the reader that much of the work on the mutual responsiveness of mothers and infants has involved computing simple sequential probabilities. Researchers have seldom analyzed the impact of one person on the other after partialing out the self or perseverational component. To the extent that existing studies have failed to do this, we are at best left with an incomplete picture of the impact of parents and children on one another.

Pair-to-Pair Variations in the Developing Relationship

So far, we have been considering the interactive patterns occurring in groups of mothers and infants, giving little attention to the variation among mother-infant pairs in the nature of the relationship that develops. Such variation can be considerable, however, and is apparent very early in life. Osofsky and Danzger (1974), for example, studied 51 mothers and their newborn infants, and found considerable variation in the way the pair related to one another from the very onset of the relationship. Some pairs showed high levels of both attentiveness in the infants and responsiveness in the mothers; other pairs were at the opposite extreme. A correlation between the attentiveness of the infant and the responsiveness of the mother reflected the fact that the pairs could be rank ordered fairly well along a dimension of mutuality.

What determines how a pair will begin their relationship? There is evidence (to be summarized later) that preexisting maternal attitudes contribute to the quality of the initial relationship. The mother's decision to breast-feed may be an important element as well. Dunn and Richards (1977), studying mother-infant pairs over the first 8 weeks of the infants' lives, focused on the feeding situation. Mothers who were breast-feeding kissed, stimulated, touched, and smiled at their infants more frequently and were more responsive to certain infant signals than mothers who were bottle-feeding. Breast-fed infants showed more initiative in both maintaining and terminating feedings. We do not know whether these differences are traceable to the process of breast-feeding itself, or to preexisting characteristics of the mother that led to the decision to breast-feed. It is likely that both factors are involved in sequential fashion: The decision to breast-feed reflects such factors as maternal attitudes (including self-confidence about motherhood) and the mother's working situation; but once the decision to breast-feed has been made, the process itself may make its own contribution to the dynamics of interaction.

The infant's characteristics, as well as the mother's, undoubtedly play a role in the nature of the relationship that evolves. To the extent that the smoothness of adult behavior in interaction with infants is dependent on the predictability of the infants' movements, parents are likely to have a more difficult time "locking in" to the rhythms of an infant whose movements are poorly coordinated or unstable, as they are in a variety of infantile disorders and developmental delays.

Goldberg (1978) summarized six studies in which the interactions of mothers with premature infants have been studied. In five of these studies, there was a comparison group of full-term infants. Taken together, the studies show that preterm infants are less alert and responsive than full-term infants. Parents of preterm infants, in comparison with those with full-term infants, do less talking, touching, smiling, and mutual gazing with their infants during the period immediately following the infant's birth. When the infants are somewhat older, parents are generally more active in stimulating preterm infants than full-term ones, whereas the infants tend to remain relatively inattentive, and to be fussy, especially if they had been ill during the neonatal period. The affective relationship between parent and child tends to be more positive with full-term infants, at least over a period of the first several months.

Among full-term infants, variations in the condition of the newborn also have their effects. Osofsky (1976) observed 134 mothers and their newborns in feeding and semistructured nonfeeding situations, and found that infants who had been rated as alert and mature on the Brazelton neonatal scale received more maternal stimulation than low scorers on the Brazelton scale. Infants rated as irritable received less maternal auditory stimulation.

Infantile irritability is often a relatively temporary condition, and it is likely that under normal conditions, when an infant has been irritable during the first few months but then stabilizes in its emotional reactions, the mother-infant pair will recover from their slow start, although we have regrettably little information concerning the extent to which early-established patterns of interaction persist over time.

In a later section, we deal more fully with the characteristics of parent and child, and the living conditions of the family, that have an impact on the way family members interact with one another (see *Factors Influencing the Interaction Pattern*). For the present, we merely note that the characteristics that both mother and infant bring to the interaction help to determine the joint relationship that will develop. Some of these characteristics have self-maintaining qualities (stemming from either biological or social sources) and will not readily yield to the daily give-and-take of the parent-child encounters. Others are much more subject to modification from this interaction.

Focused Attachment

During the first year, the enormous developmental changes occurring in the infant bring about important changes in the ways parents and infants respond to one another. The infant becomes mobile, and capable of choosing a proximity level befitting its own current need state; the infant develops a focused attachment to the parents, begins to protest separation from them, and may resist the ministrations of strangers. The frequency of crying diminishes and the infant acquires a repertoire of other means of getting the parents' attention and involving them in interaction. Though researchers in this field recognize fully that attachment is a two-way bond, most of the existing studies have focused on characterizing the infant's bond to the mother. Those that have been concerned with antecedents deal primarily with the question of what attributes or behaviors of the mother determine the quality of the infant's attachment. The reciprocal link from early infant characteristics to subsequent maternal attachment has been only lightly sketched in, and studies of the sequences involved in father-infant bonding are conspicuously missing.

Our primary evidence concerning the evolution of attachment out of prior mother-infant interactions comes from studies by Ainsworth and her colleagues, by Sroufe and colleagues, and one by Clarke-Stewart. The Ainsworth group observed the interactions of mothers and infants in their homes on several occasions during the infants' first year. Then, at age 12 months, the infants and their mothers came to a laboratory where the nature of the infant's attachment was assessed through the Strange Situation procedure (see Ainsworth et al., 1971). Children were classified as either Type A (avoidant), Type B (securely attached), or Type C (resistant). Ainsworth and Bell (1969) report relationships between mothers' feeding styles during the first 3 months of the infants' lives and the pattern of attachment behavior exhibited by the infants at age 12 months. The 23 infants in the study were divided into two groups: those whose mothers had been relatively sensitive during feeding (responsive to the infant's signals, adaptive to the infant's states) and those whose mothers had been insensitive. Among the group designated sensitive, all the infants were classified as Type B (securely attached) at age 12 months, whereas the majority of the group who had been insensitively fed were classified as either Type A or Type C.

Observations were made of the same mother-infant pairs during the last half of the first year, and the mothers were rated on four aspects of responsiveness: sensitivity/insensitivity, acceptance/rejection, cooperation/interference, and accessibility/ignoring (Ainsworth et al., 1971). Scores on the four scales were positively interrelated. Once again, relationships were found between the mothers' interaction styles and the children's subsequent attachment rating. The mothers of Type B infants were above the median on all four of the responsiveness scales. Types A and C children tended to have mothers who had been rated below the median on all four scales, and although there were some differences in the maternal patterns associated with Type A and Type C, these did not emerge as clearly as the differences between the mothering styles associated with Type B and those associated with the other two attachment groups.

Replication of a kind is provided by the Clarke-Stewart (1973) study. A group of infants and their mothers were observed at home when the infants were 11 months old. On the basis of their interactions with their infants, mothers were scored on their responsiveness (percentage of infant bids responded to), their frequency of expression of positive affect, and the amount of social stimulation given the child (scored as a proportion of the child's waking time during which the mother vocalized to, smiled at, imitated, or touched the child). Once again, the three dimensions were intercorrelated and Clarke-Stewart labels the cluster "optimal caretaking." When the children were 12 months old, they were observed in the Strange Situation, and rated on a five-point scale ranging from unattached through securely attached to malattached. Mothers of children rated at the midpoint of the scale—as securely attached—scored higher on all three of the maternal dimensions assessed a month earlier than did the mothers of either unattached or malattached infants.

Egeland and Sroufe (1981a,b) contrasted a group of abused children with a group who had received no known maltreatment. When brought into the Strange Situation at 12 and 18 months of age, the abused children showed exceptionally high rates of resistant and avoidant behaviors toward their mothers, in contrast to the normal control group, three fourths of whom were securely attached. Taken together, these studies provide strong evidence for the role of supportive and nonpunitive maternal behaviors in the development of secure attachment.

The Second Year

A small but growing body of research charts changes in the elements and contingencies in parent-infant interchanges during the second year of life. Clarke-Stewart's early study, as we have seen, finds some continuities in the midst of the changes that are occurring at this time. In the study of vocal interchanges mentioned earlier (Schaffer et al., 1977), where it was found that turn-taking in vocalization was already well established by the beginning of the second year, little change in this respect was found between ages 1 and 2 years. Among adults, there is synchronization between vocalizing and looking during conversations. A speaker uses a visual check to pick up signals that the partner wants the floor, and a listener watches for signs that the speaker is ready to yield the floor. The data in the study by Schaffer and colleagues indicate that by the end of the second year children were more likely to accompany mother-directed talk with a mother-directed gaze than they were at the beginning of the year. However, neither child nor mother seemed to be using visual information as a basis for a switch in who has the floor. Mothers' visual attention to the child was at a high level regardless of who was speaking; the child maintained lower visual attentiveness to the mother, and did not appear to watch her, while she was talking, for signs that a good moment had arrived for beginning to speak. The major cue for beginning to speak during this age period was the other person's silence. Thus it appears that although a major element of the conventions for conversation—namely, turn-taking—has been adopted, children in their second year are using only a portion of the information that adults use in regulating a turn-taking system.

Turn-taking in speech, of course, is not the only way in which children are learning to integrate their behavior temporally with that of a coactor. In fact, Bruner (1975) has argued that the achievement of integration in speech grows out of some earlier developed skill acquired during action games. He reports detailed observations of six infants seen with their mothers at 2-week intervals from the age of 7 months to 13 months. At about 11 months, the beginnings of give-and-take games appear, wherein the child offers an object and then takes it back (the mother cooperating), or where, as in games of peek-a-boo, the child is both the recipient and the agent of acts of face-covering. Bruner suggests that such interpersonal actions help infants to differentiate perceptually and behaviorally among agents, objects, and actions, and thus foster differentiation of these elements in speech. Whether or not this is true, we see the very young child developing a repertoire of interactive schemas that may be used in sustained interactive sequences with a partner who knows the reciprocal or matching role. It may be adults' greater skill in discovering the effective matching behavioral schemas that permits them to sustain interaction with a young child more effectively than can a

peer (see Holmberg, 1980). Even though by the age of 18 months a child can signal to an age mate that it is time for a change of turns, there is considerable difficulty at this age in waiting through the necessary time for the partner to carry out a reciprocal action, and a same-age partner often misses signals by the child that would be adequate to guide the cooperative behavior of a familiar adult partner (Ross & Goldman, 1977). It is a reasonable hypothesis, then, that in the prelinguistic period simple joint play with toys, mutual imitation, interactive games, and exchanges of smiles and vocalizations serve to develop some rudimentary social skills in children that make it possible for them to integrate their behavior with that of others in a cooperative way.

Clarke-Stewart and Hevey (1981) report an increase in children's responsiveness (though not in maternal responsiveness, which remains high throughout) during the period from 18 to 24 months. And they find a substantial increase during this time in the amount of verbalization directed by both mother and child toward the partner, with increasing correlations between the two. Thus, as the authors say, "the net result was that the child became a more equal participant in conversation and partner in interaction" (p. 143).

Bronson (1974) observed a group of children and their mothers at frequent intervals through the second year, conducting some of the observations at the families' homes, some in play groups, and some in structured laboratory situations. Although there was little change over the year in the affective quality of interchanges (mothers continuing to be highly positive), there was a clear improvement in the efficiency of the dyad. Infant signals became clearer in terms of specifying what the infants wanted; infants also became more insistent, in the sense that they became less likely to turn away if the mother had not responded to an initial bid. Mothers, perhaps as a consequence of greater infant clarity and forcefulness, responded to a higher proportion of infant bids. Reciprocally, infants ignored fewer maternal suggestions, and made greater use of the information their mothers provided them in adapting their responses to the situations they faced. Bronson sees the changes as reflecting in part a process whereby the infants, with their growing repertoire of cognitive and social skills, become able to train their mothers into a closer meshing of responses.

In this connection, a finding by Ainsworth and Bell (1974) should be noted. They report that maternal responsiveness and sensitivity during the first year, especially when coupled with the mother's giving her infant ample opportunity to explore the environment, was associated with the infants becoming especially clear signal givers to their caretakers during the second year. Clarke-Stewart also reports fairly strong correlations between a cluster of maternal behaviors labeled "optimal caretaking" and children's "competence" (a measure including cognitive ability, motivation to perform in new situations, language skill, frequent expressions of positive affect, and positive interest in and attachment to the mother). Thus it would appear that there were aspects of maternal behavior that were "training" the children into a more competent meshing of responses, as well as vice versa.

It is interesting that at the end of the second year, the children studied by Bronson "visually checked" their mothers only half as often as they had done at the beginning of the year. This fact may be taken in conjunction with a study by Mahler, Pine, and Bergman (1975), who report that in a group of infants aged 15 to 16 months, "shadowing" of the mother (staying close to her as she moved from one place to another) was fairly common, and had diminished several months later. Kopp (1982) attributes such changes to cognitive growth, suggesting that the acquisition of the ability to maintain a symbolic representation of the mother enables the child to dispense with continuous assurance of the mother's physical proximity.

The work of Clarke-Stewart and Hevey (1981) suggests an additional mediator for the changes that occur during this age period. They report that mother and child were becoming more distant physically between 12 and 24 months, at the same time they were becoming closer conversationally. They interpret these changes as reflecting growing autonomy on the part of the child, and note that the shift from proximal to distal modes of interaction occurred primarily among securely attached children. For the insecurely attached, physical contacting continued to be an integral part of their attachment behavior. Thus secure attachment can be seen as a condition that permits cognitive growth to produce increases in the child's autonomy.

The important role played by the child's cognitive growth in permitting better communication and closer integration of behavior sequences in mother and child is shown in a report by Falender and Heber (1975). The subjects were black, low-socioeconomic status, high-risk children and their mothers. The experimental group had been enrolled in an intervention program outside the home since approximately the age of 6 months. By the time the children were 4 to 5 years old, the experimental children clearly had superior verbal skills compared

to the nonintervention controls. When seen in interaction with their mothers, these children exercised more verbal initiative on a joint task, and both mother and child gave one another more positive and less negative feedback than was seen in the control pairs. Most important for the present point: There was a higher level of what the researchers called *information association*—that is, a closer relationship between the information being transmitted by the mother and child—among the experimental pairs. Though these results were seen at ages 4 and 5, it is likely that the cognitive and social stimulation provided daily to the children in their first 2 years would have had an impact on the nature of the mother-child interaction at these earlier ages as well.

Regulation: Its Nature and Beginnings

A major change that occurs during the second year is a qualitative one: the onset of socialization pressure. Of course, children are still indulged and waited on well into the third and fourth years (and, to a lesser degree, beyond). Parents tend to be child-centered whereas children are self-centered (cf., Pakizegi, 1978) and relatively unaware of their parents' reactions and plans (Marvin, 1977). Nevertheless, in being socialized, children must learn to inhibit disruptive antisocial behavior; they must also learn to engage in socially required or approved behavior, even if this means effort or the sacrifice of some immediate personal objectives. These are not all-or-none requirements. It is difficult to identify any behavior that is either *wrong* or *required* under any and all circumstances. Training children not to engage in specified disapproved behavior is seldom a matter of implanting total inhibition. It is part of a larger process of fostering children's abilities to regulate and control their behavior so that it will be appropriate to the situation prevailing at the time.

The distinction between external and internal controls of behavior is often made, but in a sense it is misleading. A child who starts to touch a forbidden object and then pulls back, remembering a previous spanking, is exercising self-regulation. The only way in which an external agent can directly control a child's behavior without relying on the child's self-regulatory processes is physically to move the child away from a tempting or dangerous situation, confine the child in a playpen, or in some other way impose physical restraint on the child's movements. During early childhood, socialization agents move rapidly away from such external constraints, relying instead on the child's own inhibitory processes. Inhibition that is based on external commands or fear of punishment (frequently called external control), as well as inhibition that is based on a child's self-accepted prosocial values (frequently called internal controls), call on a common nexus of self-regulatory processes, including the ability to start and stop behavior on the basis of situational requirements, to postpone the pursuit of a given goal, and to regulate the intensity of both overt action and affective arousal.

In the first year, the infant's capacity for self-regulation is limited but does expand considerably. A very young infant is capable, for example, of moderating its level of arousal by sucking its fingers; or it can buffer itself against strong stimulation by turning away or even going to sleep. Inhibitory control of motor movements, however, is very poorly developed in the first half of the first year. Schaffer (1974) has documented a change occurring about the age of 8 months in the ability to inhibit reaching movements. Before this age, infants reach out for an unfamiliar object even though their facial expression shows wariness. Shortly after the age of 8 months, the reaching movement is inhibited at least briefly. Kopp (1982) uses the term *modulation* to refer to the controls that develop during roughly the first year, to distinguish them from the next two phases, which she calls self-control and self-regulation.

It is unclear to what degree self-control during the second and third years of life involves children's increasing capacity for symbolic representation. Kopp (1982) reports that 2-year-olds who are advanced in their language development are not above average in impulse control. However, work on deferred imitation has shown that during the age range of 18–36 months, children's symbolic representation of the prior actions of others plays an increasing role among the many factors affecting the current output of behavior (McCall, Parke, & Kavanaugh, 1977). Presumably, a child's knowing how parents would react if they were present is not enough to produce self-restraint in situations where there are opportunities for immediate self-gratification. The ability to plan one's own actions in relation to longer range goals, to weigh alternatives, and to control frustration during periods of delay—processes that Kopp includes in the self-regulation category—all become increasingly important after the age of about 3 years. Later, a concept of how one wishes to be seen by others enters in. Thus the development of metacognitive skills that permit children to assess how well their behavior fits a network of goals is clearly implicated in self-regulation.

The factors affecting the early development of self-regulatory processes are not well understood. There is reason to believe they are in part neurologi-cal. It has been widely argued that the nature of children's interactions with caretakers also plays a role. Psychoanalytic writers have stressed both physiological and social factors in their analyses of the development of ego functions, most specifically in their discussions of impulse controls (see Fenichel, 1945; Rexford, 1978). In such writings, adult care givers are seen as providing the structure and the predictable contingencies for the child's behavior that make the development of self-regulatory mechanisms possible. Although not usually conceptualized in this way, it is also possible to see the adult behavior as an outcome of the young child's lack of inhibitory controls. Parents must carry out for their children some of the ego functions that are not yet adequately developed in the children. And to a greater or lesser degree, they must pace their demands on children in accordance with their understanding of the children's self-regulatory skills. Parents normally do not begin toilet training, or attempt to teach their children a set of ''don't's,'' until they believe the children have become capable of understanding prohibitions and learning to control their own behavior to some degree. Thus the relationship between parent-child interaction and a child's self-regulatory abilities may be seen as a bidirectional one.

Minton, Kagan, and Levine (1977) studied disciplinary encounters in the homes of 90 2-year-olds (mean age, 27 months). Home visitors recorded *violation sequences,* noting the mother's response to a violation and the child's response to the mother's actions. Violations included children's physical or verbal aggression, temper tantrums, actions that damaged (or threatened damage to) household objects, or other behaviors that provoked maternal reprimands or maternal efforts to redirect the child's behavior. Violation sequences were fairly common. They occurred, on the average, about nine times per hour, and took up nearly half the mother-child interaction time. Relatively few of the violations could be classified as aggression; most had to do with protection of household objects. Mothers' initial responses were typically mild in tone. Pressure on the child was escalated to a more active, more forceful level if the child did not comply to the initial effort. The forcefulness of the mother's initial intervention was shown to depend on the recent history of the interaction of the pair. That is, a mother's first response to a violation was shown to be more severe if the child had not obeyed in the previous sequence; stronger initial pressure was also used if, in the previous violation sequence, the child had complied but only after the mother had used force. The mothers' behavior was thus being shaped by their children's responses, as well as vice versa.

Even at this early age, it is clear that children's behavior is controlled not only by explicit commands and instructions being issued by their mothers, but by the children's self-regulation based on some understanding of what is allowed and what is not. A study by Lytton (1980) with 2-year-old boys is illustrative. Although the study focused primarily on the children's compliance to explicit demands, and will be discussed later (see *Children's Readiness to Be Socialized*), it also included a rating of the degree to which the children had internalized parental standards. The rating was based on two sources of information: parental reports concerning whether the child obeyed rules without having to be reminded, and observers' reports of instances of self-restraint, in which the child was seen to begin a forbidden action and then stop the behavior spontaneously without parental intervention. The frequency of such self-controlling behavior was related to maternal control techniques. Lytton scored maternal behavior on a variety of dimensions, one of which was *encouraging mature action*, defined as helping the child to do things competently and independently, and approving independent behavior. High maternal ratings on this dimension, and low amounts of maternal scolding, were significantly correlated with the children's internalization scores.

There is a virtual absence of studies with children older than Lytton's 2-year-olds in which researchers have asked what aspects of parental behavior might foster or impede the child's acquisition of self-regulating processes. No doubt the gap exists partly because of the difficulty of measuring these processes reliably. But the area appears to be ripe for research efforts in the near future.

The increasing demands that parents place on young children are accompanied by many demands being placed by children on parents. Families vary greatly in the nature of the balance they achieve between these often conflicting sets of demands. We turn now to a discussion of how parents differ in the way they impose socialization requirements on their children and the way they respond to their children's needs, focusing on the relationship between those variations and characteristics being developed by children.

CHILD-REARING VARIATIONS AND THEIR EFFECTS

Dimensions of Parenting: A Historical Overview

Much of the work on child rearing and its effects has sought to identify characteristics whereby parents differ stably from one another. These charac-teristics have then been related to relatively stable individual differences in children, either through simple correlations or more complex forms of multivariable and longitudinal analysis. Multidimensional assessments of parents' child-rearing behaviors, attitudes, and values yield batteries of scores that are not independent of one another. A number of early studies of parenting used interviews, questionnaires, or attitude scales to gather information from parents on their disciplinary techniques, typical reactions to specified child behaviors, and values concerning the child-rearing process. Several factor analyses were done of parents' scores on these batteries of items or questions (Becker, Peterson, Luria, Shoemaker, & Hellmer, 1957; Cline, Richards, & Needham, 1963; Lorr & Jenkins, 1953; Nichols, 1962; Sears et al., 1957; Slater, 1962). Schaefer (1959) analyzed the intercorrelations of variables from a number of studies, showing that they could be ordered in a circumplex pattern with respect to two orthogonal variables: warmth/hostility and control/autonomy. Becker (1964) proposed two very similar variables: warmth (acceptance) versus hostility (rejection); restrictive versus permissive.

Becker classified the outcomes of a variety of studies in terms of a fourfold typology of parenting based on his two major dimensions (see Figure 1). We will discuss the "outcome" entries below, but continue now to consider the two primary parent variables. Although Becker's two dimensions accounted for a good deal of the variance in parental activities, there were additional factors that emerged in individual studies, such as responsible child-rearing orientation (Sears et al., 1957), and calm detachment versus anxious emotional involvement (Becker, 1964). In these early studies, techniques of discipline tended to be classified under two major headings: (1) power-assertive discipline, including physical punishment, yelling, shouting, forceful commands, and threats; and (2) "love-oriented" discipline, including showing disappointment, isolation, withdrawal of love, praise, contingent giving of affection, and reasoning.

It should be noted that the dimensions that emerged from these early factor analyses were only weakly related to the theories that had guided the formulation of the studies. Warmth could be seen as somewhat relevant to psychoanalytic theory, because parental warmth was conceptualized as a factor that would lead children to inhibit aggressive impulses toward the parents and to identify with them. It also related to learning theory in that it could be seen as representing a general tendency of parents to reward desired behavior in their children, but it

	Restrictiveness	Permissiveness
Warmth	Submissive, dependent, polite, neat, obedient (Levy)	Active, socially outgoing, creative, successfully aggressive (Baldwin)
	Minimal aggression (Sears)	Minimal rule enforcement, boys (Maccoby)
	Maximum rule enforcement, boys (Maccoby)	Facilitates adult role taking (Levin)
	Dependent, not friendly, not creative (Watson)	Minimal self-aggression, boys (Sears)
	Maximal compliance (Meyers)	Independent, friendly, creative, low projective hostility (Watson)
Hostility	"Neurotic" problems (clinical studies)	Delinquency (Gluecks, Bandura, & Walters)
	More quarreling and shyness with peers (Watson)	Noncompliance (Meyers)
	Socially withdrawn (Baldwin)	Maximal aggression (Sears)
	Low in adult role taking (Levin)	
	Maximal self-aggression, boys (Sears)	

Figure 1. Interactions in the consequences of warmth versus hostility and restrictiveness versus permissiveness. From Becker (1964), p. 198.

was not nearly so central to the theory as more specific contingency of parental reward or punishment on specific desired or undesired behavior in children. The restrictive/permissive or control/autonomy dimension simply emerged repeatedly with little theoretical rationale as a dimension with respect to which parents differed reliably. It could be incorporated post hoc by learning theory on the grounds that high control or restriction represented parents' setting tasks for children to learn, but in practice the dimension did not fit this formulation very clearly.

The early work of Baldwin and colleagues (summarized in A. L. Baldwin, 1955) differed from the factor-analytic studies summarized above in that it made use of home visits, so that parent interviews were supplemented by the visitors' observational ratings. Analysis of parental variables in these studies also revealed a major warmth/coldness dimension, but two other orthogonal dimensions emerged neither of which clearly corresponded to the restrictive/permissive dimension: democracy versus autocracy, and emotional involvement versus detachment. "Democratic" parenting reflected the de-

gree to which the parents merely communicated information regarding the requirements of the real world in which the child operates, rather than making themselves the source of requirements. As Baldwin puts it, "When the parent makes himself the source of the controls upon the child, he is following an authoritarian technique; when he merely communicates to the child the rules that exist, he is following a democratic technique" (p. 447). Included under democratic parenting were parents' efforts to justify their actions or policies. This dimension had its theoretical origin in the writings of Lewin (see especially Lewin, Lippitt, & White, 1939).

Since the early work described above, concepts concerning the salient dimensions of parenting have undergone considerable change. The use of children's reports and observations of parent-child interaction to supplement or replace parent interviews and questionnaires has provided a more differentiated dimensional picture. Work with infants on the aspects of parenting related to bonding has contributed to the differentiation. Parker and colleagues (Parker, Tupling, & Brown, 1979), in their analysis of the Parental Bonding Instrument, identify two dimensions: (1) caring and empathic versus rejecting or indifferent; and (2) an overprotection dimension that involves encouraging dependency, controlling, intruding, and infantilizing. The influential work of Ainsworth and colleagues (cf. Ainsworth et al., 1971) has emphasized *responsiveness,* a dimension that is related to, but not synonymous with, the warmth/hostility dimension (see also Clarke-Stewart, 1973). Responsiveness, as used by Ainsworth and colleagues, comes out of ethological theory and emphasizes the linking or meshing of parent and child behaviors. From the standpoint of learning theory, responsiveness (i.e., contingency of parent responses on prior child behavior), may be viewed as reinforcement, broadly defined, although it includes responses that are not rewards in the usual sense. J. S. Watson (1969) has emphasized the importance of contingency in an infant's environment in keeping the infant engaged, active, and responsive; Cairns (1979) provides evidence from animal experiments that the *ratio* of contingent to noncontingent social reinforcements determines whether an organism continues to be highly responsive to social reinforcement over succeeding periods of time. Patterson (1982) analyzes the interaction between parents and aggressive children in the same terms. The emphasis on parental contingent responsiveness may also be seen as linked to the large body of work on "learned helplessness" (Seligman, 1975). When parents respond contingently they may be seen as providing children with control over their environment, and thus fostering the development of efficacy as distinct from helplessness. Whether parental responsiveness be viewed as contingent reinforcement (meaning, presumably, that the parents are ''shaping'' the child by responding differentially to desired and undesired behavior), as providing control to the child, or merely as parental sensitivity and adaptation to the child's signals, states, and needs, the concept differs importantly from that of warmth, which includes affection or praise when they are given contingently but also when they are given on the parent's impulse regardless of the concurrent state, signals, and behavior of the child.

Following the early factor-analytic studies, the control/autonomy (or restrictive/permissive) dimension also began to break down and be redefined. Studies based on children's reports of their parents' child-rearing attitudes and behavior differentiated two dimensions: (1) psychological autonomy-giving versus psychological control (i.e., control through arousing guilt or instilling anxiety); and (2) firm versus lax control (Burger & Armentrout, 1971; Schaefer, 1965). Baumrind and Black (1967), working with scores based on both observations and interviews, identified four dimensions that were surprisingly orthogonal: consistent discipline, maturity demands, restrictiveness, and encouragement of independent contacts. In a tripartite classification of patterns of parenting, Baumrind (1967, in preparation) included consistent discipline and high maturity demands, but not simple restrictiveness, with the pattern of authoritative parenting. In Baumrind's most recent conceptualization, a parenting classification is employed representing the intersection of two dimensions: parental *demandingness* and parental *responsiveness*.

In a number of studies, the degree of parental involvement—high amounts of either positive or negative interaction versus ''diminished,'' inactive, or indifferent parenting—has emerged as a characteristic of parenting worthy of attention. Martin (1981) distinguished mothers of infants as being either involved or ''autonomous'' (i.e., driven mainly by their own prior behavior rather than by that of their infants); Pulkkinen (1982) differentiated among parents according to whether they were child-centered or parent-centered. Wallerstein and Kelly (1981) point to ''diminished'' parenting occurring after a divorce.

A Fourfold Scheme

Figure 2 is a representation of the clusters of parental characteristics that result from the cross-

	Accepting Responsive Child-centered	Rejecting Unresponsive Parent-centered
Demanding, controlling	Authoritative-reciprocal High in bidirectional communication	Authoritarian Power assertive
Undemanding, low in control attempts	Indulgent	Neglecting, ignoring, indifferent, uninvolved

Figure 2. A two-dimensional classification of parenting patterns.

classification of a more expanded and differently defined dual-dimensional system than the one employed by Becker (1964). In the sections that follow, we will summarize findings that at least roughly relate to the four patterns of parental behavior shown in the four cells of the diagram, as well as to the main dimensions taken one at a time.

The classification scheme shown in Figure 2 will prove to be a procrustean bed for some studies that were not designed to fit it, but we will attempt to draw out the major themes related to the fourfold picture. To anticipate, we will argue that the set of outcomes that can be assigned to the cells will present quite a different picture from the one that emerged from the Becker classification.

Readers will note that whereas one of the traditional dimensions of disciplinary techniques—power assertiveness—can be subsumed fairly well under the heading of authoritarian parenting, there is no place in the diagram for induction or other forms of reasoning, for causal attributions made by parents, or for withdrawal of love. We have clustered these aspects of parenting loosely in a separate section (*The Content of Parent-Child Communication*).

The Authoritarian-Autocratic Pattern

In the authoritarian pattern, parents' demands on their children are not balanced by their acceptance of demands from their children. Although it is understood that children have needs that parents are obligated to fulfill, power-assertive parents place strict limits on allowable expression of these needs by children. Children are expected to inhibit their begging and demanding, and in extreme cases they may not even speak before being spoken to. Parents' demands take the form of edicts. Rules are not discussed in advance or arrived at by any consensus or bargaining process. Parents attach strong value to the maintenance of their authority, and suppress any efforts their children make to challenge it. When children deviate from parental requirements, fairly severe punishment (often physical) is likely to be employed. Some studies have attempted to assess only selected elements of the authoritarian cluster, others the cluster as a whole. Whichever approach is taken, it has been assumed that even within the group of parents who may be roughly classified as authoritarian in their parenting style, there are variations in degree and in the weighting of the component elements.

One of the earliest studies to examine authoritarian parenting and its relation to children's personality development was that by Baldwin and his colleagues (Baldwin, 1948, 1949; Baldwin et al., 1945). Child behaviors were rated by an observer in a variety of settings, and parent characteristics were assessed from interviews and observers' ratings. Two major parent dimensions emerged as predictive of children's characteristics: the *democratic/autocratic* dimension and the *permissive/controlling* dimension. The major findings related to the democratic/autocratic dimension were as follows: Children of autocratic parents were low in social interaction with peers and tended to be dominated by their peers during the interactions that did occur. These children also tended to be obedient, and neither quarrelsome nor resistive. They seemed to lack spontaneity, affection, curiosity, and originality.

Authoritarian Parenting and Children's Competence. Baumrind (1967, 1971, 1977, 1979; Baumrind & Black, 1967) has identified several clusters of parental behaviors, one of which is labeled authoritarian parenting. Parents included in this cluster are those who have relatively high scores on several or all of the following characteristics:

1. Attempting to shape, control, and evaluate the behavior and attitudes of their children in accordance with an absolute set of standards
2. Valuing obedience, respect for authority, work, tradition, and preservation of order
3. Discouraging verbal give-and-take between parent and child

Low scores on encouraging the child's independence and individuality were also part of the authoritarian cluster. In an early study with a relatively small sample (Baumrind, 1967; Baumrind & Black, 1967), it was found that a group of children who were unhappy and socially withdrawn in nursery school tended to have parents who fit the authoritarian pattern. In a later longitudinal study with a larger sample (initial $n = 134$), parents were assigned to either the authoritarian, authoritative, per-

missive, or "nonconforming" categories, depending on their dominant mode of interaction with their children. The children's characteristics were studied at several ages, through observations made at home, at school, and in contrived laboratory situations. At preschool age, the children of authoritarian parents showed relatively little independence, and obtained middle-range scores on "social responsibility," which is defined as the communal (as opposed to agentic) component of social behavior. These relationships were stronger for boys than girls, and boys also showed higher rates of anger and defiance, a correlate of authoritarian parenting not found in girls.

Baumrind's analyses of the Time 2 (ages 8–9) data are in progress and are currently incomplete. From preliminary reports, (Baumrind, in preparation) however, it appears that she has begun to shift the central focus of the study away from the analysis of parenting types to the analysis of two orthogonal dimensions of parenting (which are thought to underlie the parenting types): demandingness and responsiveness. Authoritarian child rearing may be thought of as involving high levels of demandingness and low levels of responsiveness. However, as of this writing, no analyses have yet been reported that involve explicit investigation of the impact of the earlier identified parenting types on Time 2 child behavior.

At Time 2, the children in Baumrind's study were evaluated in terms of behavioral characteristics that formed three major clusters:

Social assertiveness: positive loadings on social participation with peers, leadership in group activities, social approach and initiation; negative loadings on anxiety or apprehension in peer interaction
Social responsibility: positive loadings on friendly and cooperative interaction with peers and adults, social maturity, facilitation of adult-directed activities, altruism toward peers, and reciprocal orientation with peers and adults
Cognitive competence: positive loadings on setting standards and striving to meet them, liking and responding positively to intellectual challenge, showing originality in thought, clear sense of identity

With repeated observations in a variety of situations and over a considerable span of time, highly reliable and stable scores on these three clusters were obtained.

What is the impact of previous and concurrent authoritarian child rearing on Time 2 child behavior? We can speculate about this from the major findings concerning the long-term and concurrent impact of parental demandingness and responsiveness. These major findings are as follows. At both Time 1 and Time 2, high parental demandingness is associated with higher social assertiveness in girls, higher social responsibility in boys, and somewhat higher cognitive competence in children of both sexes. High parental responsiveness is associated with higher cognitive competence and somewhat higher social assertiveness in boys, and higher social responsibility in children of both sexes. The relative magnitudes of these various effects allow us to guess that if parents are high in demandingness but *low* in responsiveness (the authoritarian pattern), girls should be somewhat lower in social responsibility and somewhat higher in both social assertiveness and cognitive competence than their peers, but that boys of authoritarian parents should be lower both in social assertiveness and in cognitive competence. It appears, then, that the evidence in this study points toward the negative impact of authoritarian child rearing being somewhat stronger for boys than for girls.

A number of studies have focused on the relationship between power-assertive or authoritarian parenting and specific outcome characteristics of children, such as prosocial behavior, self-esteem, aggression, and moral judgment or moral behavior. Because these topics are the subjects of several chapters in this volume, and detailed coverage is given there to the relevant research, we will give only a general overview here, citing specific studies only when they are especially relevant to the general issues dealt with in this chapter.

Authoritarian Parenting and Moral Development. Studies concerned with the relationship of authoritarian parenting to children's moral development have assessed several aspects of children's moral behavior and used a variety of methods. (See reviews by Burton, 1976; Hoffman, 1970; Salzstein, 1976.) Studies attempting to predict children's resistance to temptation in contrived laboratory situations from aspects of parenting have had weak and inconsistent results, and no conclusions can be drawn at this time concerning the impact of authoritarian parenting on such behavior measured in this way. Studies of "conscience," or "guilt," have had somewhat better success, although the amount of variance accounted for by parental attributes is small. In some studies, parents have been asked how frequently a child will confess when the misdeed might not have been discovered, will admit guilt rather than lie when charged, will show guilt (self-blame or self-criticism). In other studies, these kinds of reactions are assessed from the children through projective measures such as story completions. Hoffman (1970) summarizes data from eight studies having such measures, where relationships with child-rearing variables have been studied. There are differences among studies in the way in which aspects of child rearing are classified and defined; studies also differ in whether information is obtained from both parents or only the mother, and in whether the findings are similar for the two sexes. Hoffman shows that in about half the tests made, no significant relationship is found between child-rearing variables and measures of conscience. When relationships are found, however, the direction is quite consistent: Power-assertive child-rearing techniques are associated with low scores on measures of conscience. We know of no studies done since Hoffman's summary that would change this conclusion.

Studies of moral development have dealt extensively with moral cognitions, but relatively little research has considered the way in which parent-child interaction relates to children's moral judgment or moral reasoning. The work of Hoffman and Saltzstein in the early 1960s (reported in Hoffman, 1970, 1976; Hoffman & Saltzstein, 1967; Saltzstein, 1976) remains one of the most extensive studies of the subject. Their work included measures of moral cognitions. The relation of "unqualified power assertion" to the children's internal or external moral orientation (as measured by their responses to moral judgment stories) was examined. Internal moral judgments, as distinct from external ones, were more common among children whose mothers used power assertion infrequently.

Self-Concepts. In a study of fifth- and sixth-grade boys, Coopersmith (1967) found that authoritarian parenting was associated with low self-esteem in sons. Loeb and colleagues (Loeb et al., 1980) deal with one aspect of authoritarian parenting, namely the use of a directive teaching style (physically taking over, or giving direct verbal orders or directions), as distinct from offering suggestions that leave the child some freedom of choice. The directive style was more often found among parents of fourth- and fifth-grade children with low self-esteem than among the parents of children whose self-esteem was high. In an earlier study, Loeb also showed that a directive parenting style was associated with an external, rather than internal, locus of control among fourth- and fifth-grade children. Loeb interprets these results as supporting the hypothesis that high levels of parental authoritarian control will impart to children a sense that they are not trusted to undertake activities independently—

that they are not considered competent. Hence a controlling parental style is thought to be a negative factor in the development of self-esteem.

Authoritarian Child Rearing and Aggression. A number of studies have dealt with the relation between children's concurrent aggression, either at home or at school, and parents' punitiveness or frequent use of power-assertive techniques (cf. Becker et al., 1962; Eron, Walder, & Lefkowitz, 1971; Feshbach, 1974; Hoffman, 1960; Patterson, 1982; Radke, 1946; Sears et al., 1953, 1965; Yarrow et al., 1968). The bulk of the evidence points to a tendency for power-assertive, punitive parenting to be associated with above-average levels of aggression in children, although the strength of the relationship varies greatly according to the nature of the sample, the setting in which measurements are taken, and the methods of assessment used.

Studies that have examined the relationship between children's aggression and the parents' punishment of aggression itself (as distinct from a generally punitive style directed toward a wide range of behaviors) also show a generally positive relationship between punishment for aggression and children's aggressiveness, although findings are not consistent in whether the relationship generalizes from home to school. As many writers have noted, one cannot determine from these correlations alone whether punishment arouses or strengthens aggressive tendencies in children, or aggressiveness in children elicits punitive reactions in their caretakers, or both. Longitudinal studies help to identify causal direction by providing the opportunity to examine whether high punishment for suggestion at one time is associated with aggressiveness in children at a later time. In three longitudinal studies (Johannesson, 1974; Lefkowitz et al., 1977; Sears, 1961), it was found that, although there were positive concurrent relationships between parental punishment and children's aggression, no relationships emerged between frequent punishment in the child's early years and aggression at a later time. If punishment does have a direct stimulating effect on aggression, then, it appears to be a brief one, and the more likely explanation of the concurrent correlations is that they reflect parental reactions to the child's aggression.

Patterson and colleagues (Patterson, 1976, 1979, 1980, 1982; Patterson & Cobb, 1971, 1973) have carried out sequential analyses of parent-child interaction in an effort to discover what aspects of interaction distinguish aggressive, "out of control" children from normal controls. We describe this work in some detail because it provides a much richer picture than is normally available of the fami-

ly interaction patterns that are involved in the reactions of aggressive children and their parents to one another. At the outset it should be said that there is some question as to where the Patterson work should be classified in our fourfold diagram (Figure 2). Patterson does not use the term authoritarian in describing the parents of aggressive children. We have included them in this section on the grounds that they are coercive, and also lacking in positive responsiveness. However, as we shall see, they do not exercise firm control in the sense of establishing clear standards of expected behavior and maintaining consistent, effective discipline. In these respects, they resemble the uninvolved-inattentive parental pattern to some degree.

The Patterson studies illustrate how truly bidirectional family interaction patterns are. The sample of aggressive children is made up of children identified as "out of control" either by their families, by school authorities, or by the courts. These children, along with a normal comparison group, have been repeatedly visited at their homes, and the moment-to-moment interchanges of these children with their parents and siblings have been observed in detail in an effort to discover what family processes, if any, distinguish the families of these "acting-out" disturbed children from normal families. As part of this 10-year project, interventions have been undertaken to see whether any changes could be brought about in the maladaptive processes that appear to be at work.

In-home observations have focused on each family member in turn. Using a set of preestablished behavioral categories, the observer codes the target person's behavior every 5 sec. For our present purposes, we will consider the data for a subgroup of the clinical population of children: those identified as socially aggressive. In his more recent writing Patterson (1982), compares a group of socially aggressive boys and their families with a group of normal boys and their families, the two groups being matched on a variety of background characteristics and on the age of the target child. The first point to note is that home observation confirms the diagnosis of the clinical sample as aggressive. Summing a variety of aversive behaviors into a single score for coercive behavior, Patterson shows that younger aggressive children (age range 3 through 8½) are involved in an average of 26.3 coercive episodes per hour when at home with their families, compared to 9.7 for same-age normals. Older deviant children (aged 8½ through 13½ years) are involved in 22.9 episodes per hour compared to 8.4 for their controls. A second point that has emerged repeatedly from the Patterson observations is that in the families of aggressive children, other family members employ coercive behaviors at a higher than normal rate. This is particularly true of the identified child's siblings.

The Patterson data show that aversive behavior, within the family or outside it, is not a single action. It forms part of an interactive chain, and once it has begun, partners may serve either to cool one another's hurtful behavior or to exacerbate it, so that a mildly coercive encounter may or may not escalate into a serious fight. In the families of aggressive boys, mutual coercion seems to operate to prolong aggressive encounters. The length of coercive chains is longer in the family interactions involving aggressive children. And it is also the case that a higher proportion of the aggressive child's coercion (compared to that of normal boys) represents counterattack toward another family member who has initiated an attack—a further illustration of the fact that aggressive children live in an aversive milieu in their homes.

The Patterson group has asked the question: Precisely what are other family members, particularly parents, doing that serves to maintain the target children's aversive behavior? Their first hypotheses dealt with the immediate consequences children experienced for such behavior. Three kinds of consequences have been examined: (1) reinforcement that occurs when a child initiates a successful attack on another person, and thereby gets some desired result (e.g., attention, another child's toy); (2) reinforcement that occurs when a child counterattacks following another person's aversive behavior, and causes that other person to stop his or her harassment; (3) punishment, in which the child's coercive behavior is followed by countercoercion from other family members. The initial predictions were that either kind of reinforcement would strengthen aggression, and that punishment would weaken it. In early reports it appeared that the second factor was an important process distinguishing aggressive from normal children. More recent reports (Patterson, 1982), however, involving larger numbers of children and more precise controls on age, sex, and the nature of the child's clinical symptoms, have shown that consequences (1) and (2) above do not reliably distinguish parents of aggressive from those of normal children. That is, aggressive children do not receive higher rates* of either kind of reinforcement for their aggressive behavior. Coercive actions of aggressive children are slightly more likely to be

---

*Rate here means a proportion; that is, it represents the probability that once a given behavior has occurred, a given consequence will follow. Of course, for aggressive children, the absolute frequency of both reinforcement and punishment are higher than for normals.

followed by countercoercion (punishment). The probability of such a reaction from some member of the family is .25 for the sample of normal boys, compared to .34 for the aggressive boys. Considering the response of each family member separately, the difference in rates of countercoercion is significant only for mothers. Furthermore, the boys' just-preceding level of aversive behavior was not partialed out. The difference in rates of punishment, then, is borderline, and in any case runs opposite to the predicted effect, being slightly associated with high, not low, aggression.

It is Patterson's observation that the parents of normal boys are somewhat more likely to ignore their children's aversive behavior, but once they do react, they do so forcefully in such a way as to stop it. They appear to be employing effective means of discipline that prevent extended, acrimonious interchanges of the sort that are frequently seen in the coercive families. However, the rates of reinforcement and punishment appear not to provide an adequate description of the normal families' more successful techniques.

There are some interesting differences between coercive and normal families with respect to the behavior by other family members that accompanies a child's aggression. In a coercive child's family, if another family member has initiated an attack, that attack tends to continue no matter what the target child's reaction is; and if the target child has initiated an attack when the partner was behaving pleasantly, the partner tends to continue behaving pleasantly somewhat longer into the child's aggressive chain than would be the case in a normal family. These findings suggest that the behavior of other family members is self-responsive in coercive families, and lacks sensitivity to the behavior of the subject child.

An important finding of the Patterson group is that aggressive children react in an unusual way to punishment. When a normal child's aggression is punished by a parent, the probability of the child's continuing to be aggressive is reduced. With aggressive children, the probability is *increased* (Patterson, 1982; Patterson & Cobb, 1971). Furthermore, there is a body of literature indicating that aggressive children are less responsive than normals to social reinforcement, and the findings of the Patterson group are consistent with this conclusion (Patterson, 1976, 1982). Thus it appears that aggressive children may be underresponsive to social stimuli of all kinds, whether positive or negative. But this fact merely tells us more about the characteristics of aggressive children. It does not tell us how or why their characteristics developed as they did. Of course, the possibility exists that there are genetically biased temperamental factors that either exert an influence directly on children's behavior or interact with parental behavior to maintain aggression. But it is also likely that there are aspects of parental behavior that have contributed to the child's hyporesponsiveness, and the remaining challenge is to discover what they are.

To summarize what has been presented concerning authoritarian parenting, a number of child characteristics have proved to be correlated with this pattern of parenting. Children of authoritarian parents tend to lack social competence with peers: They tend to withdraw, not to take social initiative, to lack spontaneity. Although they do not behave differently from children of other types of parents on contrived measures of resistance to temptation, on projective tests and parent reports they do show lesser evidence of "conscience" and are more likely to have an external, rather than internal, moral orientation in discussing what is the "right" behavior in situations of moral conflict. In boys, there is evidence that motivation for intellectual performance is low. Several studies link authoritarian parenting with low self-esteem and external locus of control.

Whereas the parents of aggressive children tend to be authoritarian, children of authoritarian parents may or may not be aggressive, and so far the aspects of family interaction that are important in determining whether a child of authoritarian parents will be subdued or "out of control" have not been satisfactorily identified.

The Indulgent-Permissive Pattern

Any parent who is functioning in any degree in the parental role exercises *some* control over children. Thus permissiveness is a relative matter. In Baumrind's work, parents labeled as permissive are those who take a tolerant, accepting attitude toward the child's impulses, including sexual and aggressive impulses; who use little punishment, and avoid, whenever possible, asserting authority or imposing controls or restrictions; they make few demands for mature behavior (e.g., manners or carrying out tasks); they allow children to regulate their own behavior and make their own decisions when at all possible, and have few rules governing the child's time schedule (bedtime, mealtime, TV watching).

In Baumrind's first study (1967), permissive parents were relatively warm, at least by comparison with the authoritarian group. In the later work, however, a good many of the permissive parents were also cool or uninvolved. This group of parents, then, includes both an indulgent subgroup and a subgroup who are closer to the indifferent-neglecting cell of our fourfold classification. Definitions used in a variety of studies describe parents at the nonpermissive end of the permissive/restrictive continuum, by contrast, as people who impose many rules, restrictions, and demands, and regulate many aspects of the child's daily life.

In the early studies by Baldwin and colleagues, already referred to, the permissive/controlling dimension emerged as a strong factor. In addition to the above characteristics defining a restricting parent, the Baldwin group added as a criterion of restrictiveness that there was little conflict over discipline in the home—that is, the parents succeeded in getting the children to conform to the restrictions. The children of restrictive parents, when observed in nursery school, were obedient and nonaggressive, but also rather passive and colorless in their interactions with peers. Baldwin argued that a fairly heavy price was paid for parental restrictiveness: That obedience was obtained at the expense of the children's spontaneity, creativity, and the more active aspects of social competence. Consistent with the Baldwin point of view are the reports by Qadri and Kaleem (1971) and Apolonio (1975) that restrictive, nonpermissive parenting is associated with children's low self-esteem.

Baumrind, on the other hand, has emphasized the price to be paid for parental failure to exercise controls and make maturity demands. In the early small-sample study (Baumrind, 1967), it was found that children whose behavior was immature, in the sense that they lacked both impulse control and self-reliance, tended to have permissive parents. In the later study (Baumrind, 1971), children of nursery-school age who had permissive parents tended to lack both social responsibility and independence. The follow-up of these children at ages 8 to 9 years reveals that the children whose parents had been permissive at an earlier age are low in both cognitive and social agency.

The issue of permissiveness hardly comes up with respect to behaviors that are socially approved or desired. Thus permissiveness is a dimension of parental variation that is brought to the fore when the child engages in some form of behavior that disturbs or threatens others, or otherwise contravenes some social norm. It is not surprising, then, that permissiveness for aggression has been the focus of considerable research effort. Summarizing a number of studies, Yarrow and colleagues (1968) conclude that permissiveness for aggression is positively correlated with children's aggression when aggression toward the parent or toward other family members in the parent's presence is the outcome variable, but that permissiveness could not be shown to have this effect with respect to aggression outside the home. One difficulty in assessing the effects of permissiveness is that it tends to be negatively correlated with punishment for the same behavior. As Schuck (1974) has pointed out, permissiveness and punishment for aggression tend to mask each other's effects; when one is partialed out, the other acquires a stronger positive correlation with the child's aggression, whether at home or school.

Olweus (1980) presents a more complex causal model. He studied boys' aggressiveness outside the home (as assessed by peer nominations and teachers' ratings), at two time periods: when the boys were in the sixth grade, and again in the ninth grade. He interviewed the mothers at the sixth-grade time period, including retrospective questions concerning the child's earlier temperamental characteristics and the mother's earlier attitudes. Two scores were derived for the early period: maternal negativism, defined as the mother's basic emotional attitude toward the child; and the boy's temperament, ranging from easy going to strong-willed and hot-tempered. Scores for the sixth-grade time period reflected the parents' use of power-assertive discipline, and their permissiveness for aggression. Olweus developed a structural model from the data, computing path coefficients across the three time periods. He found that boys' early temperament appeared to make both a direct and an indirect contribution to later aggression. Strong-willed, hot-tempered boys had some (slight) tendency to become aggressive later regardless of what their mothers did, but in addition such children seemed to generate permissiveness for aggression in their mothers, and permissiveness in its turn led to increased aggression. Early negative mother attitudes toward the child were associated with the use of power-assertive discipline at grade six, and this was slightly associated with higher ninth-grade aggression.

The Olweus model presents a picture that is consistent with the data from other studies. It is necessary to be aware, however, that the data for the earlier time period are retrospective, and it is possible that the mothers' recall of aspects of their earlier relationship with their sons is selective, biased to some degree by their current relationship. A further problem is that the child's initial aggression level was not assessed, and was not partialed out in the prediction of subsequent aggression. (For discussion of this issue see *Methods of Study*.)

As we noted earlier, in the Patterson studies it was found that the parents of normal boys acted effectively to stop their children's aversive behavior once it crossed a certain criterial threshold, whereas parents of aggressive boys did not do so. Thus it appears that the parents of the unaggressive boys were not permissive toward aversive behavior. The behavior of the parents of aggressive boys is more difficult to place along a permissive/nonpermissive dimension. They did not have an accepting attitude toward their children's aversive behavior; indeed, it made them angry and countercoercive. Their reactions were not effective in stopping the behavior, however, and in that sense they were permissive. The ineffectiveness can be attributed either to the failure of the child to respond to the parents' attempted restraints, or to deficiencies in the parental efforts, or both.

The Olweus study, along with several of the studies that preceded it, underlines the importance of parental permissiveness for aggression as one of the factors contributing to children's aggressiveness. What precisely does permissiveness entail? There is considerable variation in how this parental characteristic is defined and measured. In the work by Sears and colleagues (1957), permissiveness usually stemmed from an ideological stance by parents. Permissive parents tended to believe that it was ''right'' or ''natural'' for children to show anger toward their parents, and thought that such emotions in children ought not to be repressed. However, certain parents who said they frequently allowed their children to be aggressive also reported that they would occasionally find themselves unable to tolerate their children's continued outbursts and would react with harsh punitiveness. Thus it appears that permissiveness, at least in some parents, is part of a complex and conflicted set of parental attitudes and behaviors. In some cases it undoubtedly reflects parental inattention and indifference, rather than commitment to children's rights. Children are allowed to fight because it takes too much effort from tired, depressed, or preoccupied parents to stop them. Interesting in this regard is the Olweus report that boys who are described as having been strong-willed and hot-tempered when young have mothers who are more permissive toward aggression. As noted earlier, it may be that such children have changed their parents' adaptation level. What is unacceptable behavior to some parents seems ''normal'' to parents whose children show frequent and intense outbursts of temper; such parents may be likely to reserve their counterpressure for what they have come to regard as the more serious episodes.

To summarize our brief review on the correlates of the permissive pattern of parenting, it appears on the whole to have more negative than positive effects, in the sense that it is associated with children's being impulsive, aggressive, and lacking in independence or the ability to take responsibility.

The Authoritative-Reciprocal Pattern

It is inevitable that parents have more power than children. Parents have more knowledge and skill, control more resources, and ultimately have the physical power (at least while the children are young) to pick their children up, move them from one place to another, and physically restrain them from starting or continuing a forbidden action. Children's power depends on their ability to produce both distress and pleasure in their parents, but ultimately it also depends on parental consent, in the sense that it reflects a parental acceptance of an obligation to be responsive to children's needs, desires, and persuasive arguments. A pattern of family functioning in which children are required to be responsive to parental demands, and parents accept a reciprocal responsibility to be as responsive as possible to their children's reasonable demands and points of view, has been labeled ''authoritative'' by Baumrind. We use this term and also the label ''reciprocal.''

Authoritative Parenting and Children's Competence. Baumrind's work (Baumrind, 1967, 1971) has dealt centrally with this pattern of parenting. The pattern Baumrind calls authoritative includes the following elements:

1. Expectation for mature behavior from child and clear standard setting
2. Firm enforcement of rules and standards, using commands and sanctions when necessary
3. Encouragement of the child's independence and individuality
4. Open communication between parents and children, with parents listening to children's point of view, as well as expressing their own; encouragement of verbal give-and-take
5. Recognition of rights of both parents and children

In Baumrind's samples, children of authoritative parents have proved to be more competent than the children of either authoritarian or permissive parents. At preschool age, daughters of authoritative parents were as socially responsible as other girls, and more independent. Sons were as independent as other boys, and more socially responsible. From Baumrind's preliminary reports concerning the relationship between parental characteristics at Time 1

(when the child is of preschool age) and the children's characteristics at Time 2 (ages 8–9), we have once again estimated the effects of a parental cluster—here the authoritative one—from the correlates of two parental characteristics: high demandingness and high responsiveness. This combination appears to be related positively to high levels of competence in both the communal (social responsibility) and agentic (social and intellectual self-assertion) spheres in children of both sexes.

Catherine Lewis (1981) has raised a number of questions concerning the role Baumrind claims for firm parental control in the authoritative parenting cluster. Lewis argues that each of Baumrind's measures of parental firm control includes items that reflect whether the parent succeeds in obtaining obedience. Thus they may be regarded as measures of the parent's control, of the child's obedience, or both jointly. In short, they reflect a characteristic of the dyad—low parent-child conflict—and the contribution of prior parental practices to the low-conflict state remains undetermined. A second point in Lewis' critique is that if firm control is subtracted from the pattern of behaviors characterizing authoritative parenting, the children do not become less competent. Working from the data presented in Baumrind (1971), Lewis shows that for each sex, there is a pattern of parenting that is like the authoritative pattern in all respects save that firm control is absent (for girls, the ''harmonious'' cluster; for boys, the ''nonconforming'' pattern). Lewis argues that the children in these groups of families do not differ from children of authoritative parents on any of the seven child-behavior dimensions measured. This critique is recent, and we do not yet have a formal commentary or clarification from Baumrind. The issue is not settled, but the discussion does point to the complexity of measuring parental control independently of child compliance, and draws our attention to the difficulty of knowing which components of clusters are responsible for relationships between parent and child behavior. At the very least, however, the Baumrind work would appear to show that firm parental control does not detract from children's competence.

Authoritative Parenting and Self-Esteem. A second major study that highlights a cluster of parental characteristics that fit a picture of reciprocal demands and responsiveness is that by Coopersmith (1967) with fifth- and sixth-grade boys. Coopersmith reports that the parents of high self-esteem boys (by contrast with parents of the low self-esteem group) set high standards for competence and obedience, and consistently enforced these standards. In addition, they tended to favor inductive over coercive methods, and fostered a democratic style of family decision making in which children participated and were allowed to question parental viewpoints. Furthermore, their sons reported that when the parents administered punishment, the boy usually felt that the punishment had been deserved. In short, parental control was exercised in such a way that it appeared fair and reasonable to the child. As C. C. Lewis (1981) notes, however, one component of Coopersmith's measure of control is the parents' statement that their discipline was generally effective. Thus once more we are faced with the question of whether it is parental control or child compliance that is being measured, and whether the differences in parental practices are causal or whether they merely reflect variations that are made possible by (or necessitated by) characteristics of the children.

Considering the body of work on self-esteem as a whole, we see that there is only equivocal support for the hypothesis that high parental control implies lack of trust in the child and hence fails to foster the child's self-esteem. As we saw earlier, Coopersmith's study found that power-assertive parenting was associated with low self-esteem, whereas firm rule enforcement (when accompanied by warmth and democratic family decision making) was associated with high self-esteem. Loeb et al. (1980) found that a directive rather than suggestive style of parental "helping" was also associated with low self-esteem in children. And two other studies report positive relationships between permissive (low-restrictive) parenting and high self-esteem in children (Apolonio, 1975; Qadri & Kaleem, 1971). However, Comstock (1973) reports that high self-esteem children tend to perceive their parents as exercising fairly high levels of firm control, and McEachern (1973) reports a similar relationship. These last two studies are consistent with Coopersmith. The weight of the evidence would appear to be that neither authoritarian control nor unalloyed freedom and permissiveness is the key to the development of high self-esteem in children. Rather, a pattern of interaction in which parents make reasonable and firm demands that are accepted as legitimate by the children, but in which parents do not impose unreasonable restrictions but make demands and give directions in ways that leave a degree of choice and control in the hands of the children, is the control pattern most likely to foster high self-esteem.

Authoritative Parenting and Moral Development. Moral development is another area in which reciprocation appears to foster mature functioning in children. The work by Hoffman (1970) and Hoff-

man and Saltzstein (1967) was discussed earlier, and we noted that although they found that unqualified power assertion was negatively associated with measures of conscience and with mature moral judgments, the parents of "humanistic" children (children who were concerned with the effects of misbehavior on others, rather than merely with conformity to rules) did exercise firm control, in the sense of following through on parental demands, at the same time that they showed a good deal of warmth and were not punitive.

Yarrow, Waxler, and Scott (1971) also found, in an experimental situation, an interaction between nurturance and demandingness in the acquisition of prosocial behaviors. They found that a 2-week period of interaction with a nurturant adult (as contrasted with experience with a nonnurturant adult) had no effect on the overall level of the children's prosocial behavior. However, when the adult conducted sessions involving teaching the child prosocial responses (via demonstration), the teaching by the nurturant adult was more effective. In fact, the training in prosocial behavior generalized to real-life situations *only* if the training was done by a previously nurturant adult.

Training for Authoritative Parenting. In 10 years of working with distressed families in a treatment program, the Patterson group has identified a number of processes they regard as central to the etiology of family distress, and a number of remedial measures that they have shown to be effective in changing patterns of family interaction and alleviating familial malfunction. In their view, the problem of aggressive children's lack of compliance to parental requirements occupies a central role. The treatment program is oriented around the view that the parents must reestablish their authority—their power to get compliance to their wishes—and to this end a program of child management is instituted that has several facets:

1. Clear understandings of what is to be considered acceptable and unacceptable behavior are established.
2. Children's behavior is closely monitored so that both compliance and noncompliance with the understood rules can be noted quickly and consistently.
3. Consistent contingencies for such behavior are established. In the case of unacceptable behavior, many parents of aggressive children have fallen into patterns of what Patterson calls "sibling parenting." That is, they respond to the children's aversive behavior as though they were children themselves.

They allow themselves to be drawn into bickering, and are diverted from the initial socialization issue that started the aversive cycle. Therapists train these parents not to respond in kind when the children resist parental demands with whining and yelling, but to carry through with their demands and adopt a more dispassionate system of consequences external to the interpersonal relationship (e.g., withdrawal of privileges) if the child does not comply.

4. Positive consequences for the child's prosocial behavior are emphasized. In distressed families, when parents do show affection or give praise, their positive behavior seems to be occasioned more by the parent's mood than the child's behavior. The researchers argue that this may be one of the reasons that the children have become insensitive to social approval. Their sensitivity needs to be reestablished. In the view of the Patterson group, this can be done by recoupling parent approval with good behavior, and by backing up approval with tangible rewards.

Once the parents have established their power to get compliance from their child, they are then in a position to teach some of the elementary self-help skills and prosocial behaviors that aggressive children usually lack. With the acquisition of these skills gradually comes acceptance from other children and adults outside the family, and the subject children are less often the targets of other people's hostility, so that some of the maintaining conditions for their aggression are weakened.

It is evident that in their therapeutic program the Patterson group are training parents to adopt many elements of the authoritative-reciprocal pattern. Although much of the emphasis is on strengthening the firm control and enforcement side of the picture, the emphasis on using nonpunitive discipline and responding positively to good behavior makes the recommended pattern more authoritative than authoritarian.

To summarize, the information presented on the joint effects of parents' being both controlling (demanding) and responsive presents a considerably different picture from the one given in Becker's summary (Figure 1). At least, the entries for dependency and submissiveness given there do not correspond with the picture emerging from the work cited here. We have seen that the authoritative-reciprocal pattern of parenting is associated with children's being independent, "agentic" in both the cognitive and social spheres, socially responsible, able to control aggression, self-confident, and high in self-esteem. We hasten to add that in none of the studies cited does the pattern of parenting account for a high proportion of the variance in child behavior. Nev-

ertheless, there are some striking consistencies in the direction of relationships found across studies and across domains of child behavior.

The Indifferent-Uninvolved Pattern

By involvement, we mean the degree to which a parent is committed to his or her role as a parent, and to the fostering of "optimal child development." Except for certain extreme cases of dysfunction in parent-child relations, the decision to maintain a child as a member of the household involves at least some base line level of emotional commitment of the parent to the child, and of involvement by the parent in the child's welfare and development. However, variability in involvement above and beyond this base level is considerable, ranging from the parent who is completely consumed by the parenting role to the parent who is heavily involved in other activities and has little time or attention to spare for the child. The uninvolved parent is likely to be motivated to do whatever is necessary to minimize the costs in time and effort of interaction with the child.

Parental involvement is orthogonal to many of the dimensions of parenting we have discussed thus far in this chapter. An abrasive, unresponsive, unsupportive parenting style can be coupled with either high or low levels of involvement. Likewise low demands and low enforcement are compatible both with high and low commitment to the child, representing a child-centered orientation toward child rearing on the one hand and an orientation toward expedience on the other. A highly involved parent need not be intrusive or dominating, but on the contrary may grant the child considerable autonomy; such a parent, however, is by definition unlikely to ignore or neglect the child. In general, the parenting styles that are associated with low levels of involvement are likely to reflect a desire to keep the child at a distance. The parenting styles that are associated with high levels of involvement probably cover a broader range, being reflections of parents' differential hypotheses about optimal parenting. A more general point is that involvement may in fact be unrelated to optimal parenting. Some kinds of high-level involvement—that is, some of the parenting styles associated with considerable commitment to the child—may, though motivated by the best interests of the child, be incompatible with optimal child development.

With decreasing involvement (and concomitantly decreasing levels of interaction between parent and child), some parenting functions will correspondingly decrease in importance or drop out altogether, whereas others will be maintained. That is, some parenting functions can probably be dropped more easily than others, and the rank order ought to be to some degree predictable. In a relationship characterized by very low parental involvement, parents will tend to orient their behavior primarily toward the avoidance of inconvenience. Thus they will respond to immediate demands from the children in such a way as to terminate them. Certain components of the parenting role, however, have little to do with the parent's immediate comfort and more to do with the long-range developmental trajectory of the child—for example, establishing and enforcing rules about homework; setting standards for the acceptability of agonistic encounters with other children; and exposing the child to various principles that underlie a range of interpersonal exchanges. These parental functions may be greatly reduced or simply disappear, and the minimally functional relationship can still survive. It would be useful to know whether and to what extent some parenting functions do indeed drop out more readily than others for relatively uninvolved parents, and if they do, whether the order of dropping out is invariant across families or within certain clusters of families.

Egeland and Sroufe (1981a,b) have documented some of the more extreme implications of low levels of parent involvement, in their study of a group of abusive parents. They distinguished several aspects of these parents' behavior: physical abuse, hostile verbal abuse, neglect, and psychological unavailability. The latter pattern involved a parent's being detached, emotionally uninvolved, often depressed, and uninterested in the child. Children of the psychologically unavailable mothers showed clear disturbances in their attachment relationships to the mother. Of special importance, they also showed increasing deficits in all aspects of psychological functioning by the age of 2—greater deficits than occurred with the other patterns of parental maltreatment.

What are the correlates of high or low parental involvement in a more normal sample? In a microanalytic study of parent-child interaction involving 10-month-olds and their mothers, Martin (1981) defined involvement as the extent to which the mother's behavior fluctuated with respect to her infant's activity rather than with respect to her own prior level of activity. Follow-up studies were subsequently conducted when the children were 22 and 42 months old. At 42 months, mother *non*involvement was measured with an autonomy questionnaire, designed to determine the extent to which mothers ignored the child's needs and preferences in setting

and enforcing socialization rules and goals. It was found that involved mothers (at 10 months) tended to have children who were high in compliance at both 22 and 42 months, and who (at 42 months) were willing to let the mother leave the room briefly without a fuss. It was also found, using a two-wave panel model, that maternal involvement was associated with a decrease in child demandingness and coerciveness in the interval from 10 to 42 months, but that child demandingness had no detectable influence on maternal involvement in that interval.

Other researchers have studied involvement via observer ratings. Baldwin et al. (1945) found that emotional involvement on the part of the parent (a factor-analytically derived measure) was associated with the emotional development of the child. Loeb et al. (1980) found that involvement was positively correlated with the child's self-esteem, and Gordon, Nowicki, and Wickern (1981) report a positive relationship between observed maternal involvement and inner locus of control in second graders. Hatfield, Ferguson, and Alpert (1967) studied parent-child interaction in 4- to 5½-year-olds, and found a negative relationship between a global rating of maternal involvement and behavioral measures of aggression and disobedience in the children. Seegmiller and King (1975) found that maternal involvement at 14, 18, and 22 months was correlated positively with scores on the Bayley Mental scale at 22 months.

Uninvolved Parenting and Ego Processes. Parental involvement was critical in a classic study of personality development by Block (1971). One focus of this study was on what Block called "ego control," defined as "the individual's characteristic mode of monitoring impulse . . . representing excessive containment of impulse and delay of gratification at one end (over-control) versus insufficient modulation of impulse and inability to delay gratification at the other end (under-control)" (p. 261). The subjects were taken from the two major Berkeley longitudinal studies: the Oakland Growth Study and the Guidance Study. Data were available on the parents and their relationships with their children at two points in time: when the children were between the ages of 21 and 36 months of age, and later when the children were preadolescent and adolescent. The early family ratings were based both on observations during home visits, and on parent interviews. The second set of ratings were based on mother interviews. In most cases, three interviews were obtained, one at age 11, one at 14, and one at 15. Personality data on the children were derived from Q-sorts completed by a team of clinical psychologists who worked from extensive case files. The files included a wide range of test data (both cognitive and personality tests being represented), attitude checklists, teachers' ratings, observers' ratings, and sociometric data. Independent "case-assembly" files were created for two periods of time: the junior high school period and the senior high school period, and Q-sorts were completed for both time periods. The Q-sort scores were combined for the two time periods and factor-analyzed, separately by sex of subject. Subjects were then grouped into personality types on the basis of the factor loadings derived from an inverted factor-analytic procedure. Among the male subjects, there was a group (Type E) that clearly differed from other subjects in their low level of ego control. The factor analysis of scores for the female subjects did not reveal so clear an "impulsivity" dimension, but two types—Types X and Y—shared the characteristic of being undercontrolled during adolescence, although the clusters of characteristics and the family histories of the two types were somewhat different.

Parental involvement figures heavily as a determinant in all three types. Type E males ($n = 10$), and both Type X ($n = 11$) and Type Y ($n = 10$) females all had parents who were atypically uninvolved. Mothers were rated as (for example) unhappy as homemakers, unconcerned about their children's education, and more generally as unmaternal, distant, and indifferent. Likewise fathers were uninterested in their children, discontented with home life, and did not want to have more children.

A recent longitudinal study, done in Finland with a considerably larger sample (Pulkkinen, 1982), likewise underscores the importance of parental involvement. The children were assessed through teacher ratings, peer nominations, and self-reports, at the ages of 8, 14, and 20 years, with the focus of the assessment being on several aspects of self-control. At the 14-year assessment, depth interviews were conducted with a sample of parents; either the father or the mother was interviewed, according to the parents' own choice. Interview scores were factor-analyzed, and a major dimension emerged, labeled *child-centered guidance versus parent-centered (selfish) child rearing*. Scales contributing to a child-centered guidance score included the following:

Parent knows child's whereabouts, activities, and associates when child is away from home.

Parent is interested in events at child's school.

Daily conversation occurs between parent and child.

Parent considers child's opinion.

In addition, the child-centered parents trusted their children, were consistent and firm in their demands, employed just (as distinct from capricious) restrictions and sanctions, rarely or never used physical punishment, and maintained a generally democratic atmosphere. Thus it may be seen that high parental involvement was usually embedded in a context of reciprocal or authoritative parenting.

At the age of 14, children of the child-oriented parents were on the average responsible, achievement oriented, competent in social relationships, and likely to maintain good relationships with their parents. By contrast, the children of parent-centered parents were impulsive (in the sense of lacking concentration, being moody, spending money quickly rather than saving it, and having difficulty controlling aggressive outbursts), uninterested in school, likely to be truant and spend time on the streets and at discos; in addition, their friends were often disliked by the parents. The children of parent-centered families also tended to start drinking, smoking, and heterosexual dating at earlier ages. Continuities to the age of 20 were found: At this age, the children from parent-centered families were more likely than those from child-centered homes to be hedonistic and lack frustration tolerance and emotional control; they also lacked long-term goals, drank to excess, and more often had a record of arrests. The children from child-centered homes were more likely to have strong achievement motives and be oriented toward the future.

No doubt there are circular effects at work in the families Pulkkinen has studied. Impulsive children may have made it difficult for their parents to remain closely and democratically involved. We can only assume that some portion of the parent-child correlations stems from parent-to-child effects as well.

Work by Patterson (1976, 1982), discussed in detail elsewhere in this chapter, provides further insights into the sorts of family dysfunctions that may co-occur with low levels of parent involvement. When cycles of mutual coercion become embedded in the family interaction process, Patterson finds that family members habitually avoid one another. Mutual avoidance implies that certain essential socialization processes, such as joint problem solving, seldom take place in these families. This deficit in turn leads to intensification of the mutually coercive patterning. Like Pulkkinen, Patterson finds that one aspect of low parental involvement—the failure to monitor where the children are and what they are doing—is a factor carrying particularly strong risk of subsequent delinquent behavior in the children.

In summary, it appears that parental involvement is positively associated with a number of aspects of optimal development in children. We do not know from the correlational evidence whether the major effect of this dimension occurs at the high or low end. It may be that the low end of the scale accounts for more of the variance—that is, that there is a threshold level that needs to be achieved, but that variations beyond this point have little effect. It is possible, too, that there is such a thing as too much involvement—a point when involvement becomes intrusive and overcontrolling. We may suppose that the optimal levels of parental involvement must be linked to the child's developmental level, being high when the child is immature and decreasing as the child becomes able to function more independently. As Thoman (1974) has argued, a truly optimal parent-child system is one that, from the start, is set up to lead to its own demise. We know little about the ways in which the parent-child relationship is restructured over time. It is a reasonable hypothesis that the lessening of parental involvement will be a supportive process to the degree that the new, less controlling relationship is built on a foundation of relatively close interaction and high parental commitment at earlier ages. There is reason to believe, however, that there is a positive function to be played by continued parental involvement in the child's life and decisions, and by continued monitoring well into adolescence (Patterson, 1982; Pulkkinen, 1982).

The Content of Parent-Child Communication

Parents vary in how much they talk to their children, in what they say, and how bidirectional communication is. Baumrind (1971) included "open communication" as one of the criteria that distinguished authoritative from authoritarian child rearing, the distinction resting primarily on whether parents were willing to listen and be responsive to their children's point of view, rather than merely promulgating their own. In this sense, the nature of the communicative pattern has already been discussed under the responsiveness dimension. Although there is little research dealing with the *clarity* of parental communications, we can only assume that this is an important aspect of the ability of parents to be effective in setting standards and following through on their enforcement; thus clarity becomes relevant to the demanding-controlling dimension.

There are other aspects of parental communication that cannot so easily be subsumed under the fourfold classification discussed above. In some early research (e.g., Sears et al., 1957), "reasoning" was listed as a training technique, along with several kinds of positive and negative sanctions. But it was an amorphous category, and there have been a number of efforts to identify meaningful dimensions of variation among parents in their discussions with, and didactic communications to, their children. Some writers have distinguished between the information-giving function (in which parents teach children that action x will lead to consequence y) and parental communications that have a moralistic or value-stating component (Henry, 1980; Hoffman, 1970; Zahn-Waxler et al., 1979). Within the domain of value statements, distinctions have been made concerning the source of moral authority to which children's attention is being drawn. Still other distinctions concern the nature of the damage that will be done by the child's undesired action: whether or not the damage is interpersonal; and if it is, whether the action involves hurting the parents, hurting others (especially peers), or doing injury to the child's self-interests. In problem-solving situations, a distinction has been made between *directive* and *suggestive* parental teaching strategies. Most of these distinctions stem from theoretical views concerning the parenting conditions that should be most conducive to internalization in children—that is, to the development in children of the ability to regulate their own behavior, with little external monitoring or sanctioning, with respect to a set of self-accepted prosocial values. Several components in the development of internalization can be identified: development of self-regulatory functions, including self-monitoring, impulse control, and a variety of executive skills; acquisition of a set of moral values, accompanied by sufficient ability to take the perspective of others so that these values can be sensitively employed; and an inner locus of control, so that prosocial behavior seems to spring from inner intention rather than fear of punishment or hope of reward. In addition, the motivational component that has most frequently been pointed to in internalized responding has been empathy. In the next section, we will summarize some of the work dealing with the distinctions among types of parental communicative inputs, and their relation to some of these aspects of internalized responding in children.

Induction

In his chapter on moral development for the third edition of these volumes, Hoffman (1970) included under the heading of *Induction* the use of explanations or reasons by parents, their appeals to the child's pride or desire to be grown up, and appeals to their concern for others. He singled out "other-oriented'' induction—namely, the implications of the child's behavior for other persons—as especially important in relation to moral development. A more recent review by Rollins and Thomas (1979) has also highlighted induction as an aspect of parental functioning that relates strongly to various aspects of children's competence. In the studies reviewed below, induction is variously defined, but there appears to be a common core of meaning that links the studies together.

Induction and Prosocial Behavior. The work by Radke-Yarrow and Zahn-Waxler on the development of prosocial behavior is covered in detail in their chapter (see *vol. IV, chap. 6*). We will therefore give only a very brief account of the research, selecting here the aspects most relevant to the use of inductive parent techniques. In a study of children in their second year, these investigators (Zahn-Waxler et al., 1979) trained a group of mothers as observers. The mothers kept diary records of incidents in which another person showed distress in the child's presence. The mothers' reports were supplemented by in-home observations of mother-child interactions conducted by research personnel. During their visits the observers not only recorded spontaneous events, but occasionally staged simulated distress incidents. Records showed that these very young children responded with offers of objects, help, or comfort to distressed persons in about a third of the distress incidents they witnessed, but there were great individual differences among children in their tendency to respond in this way, and the rank order of children was quite stable over a period of 9 months. Mothers' responses to incidents in which the child had caused distress to others were coded, and related to (1) frequency of the child's offering reparation in child-caused incidents, and (2) the tendency to offer help or comfort in bystander incidents. It was found that maternal use of reasoning and explanation was important, in that the use of unexplained prohibitions correlated *negatively* with children's prosocial behavior in both kinds of incidents. However, the affective tone of any explanations that were offered by the mother was also important. The frequency of mothers' use of affectively neutral explanations (e.g., ''Tom is crying because you pushed him'') was unrelated to children's prosocial actions, whereas affectively toned moralizing and statements of principle related positively to reparations, help giving, and comfort giving.

With considerably older children, Hoffman (1975a) has studied the child-rearing correlates of altruism. In this work, the aspect of induction studied is ''victim-centered discipline,'' by which is meant encouraging the child to do something to repair the damage the child has done, requiring the child to apologize, or expressing concern for the victim's feelings. Parental reliance on victim-centered discipline was assessed through ''critical incident'' interviews. Children's altruism was assessed by means of peer nominations. Parental use of victim-centered discipline was positively related to children's altruism; at least, significant correlations were found for mothers and sons ($r = .50$), and fathers and daughters ($r = .53$).

The importance of other-oriented induction, as compared with other forms of reasoning, is documented in a recent experiment by Kuczynski (in press). Children aged 9 and 10 years were asked to do a repetitive and onerous task in the presence of attractive toys. Three treatments were used: (1) Looking at or playing with the toys was prohibited without explanation; (2) prohibition was based on the warning that if the children did not do their work now they would have to do it later and might not have a chance to play with the toys (self-oriented); and (3) if the child did not help now, the experimenter would have to finish the work later (an other-oriented prohibition). Children's attention to task, and task persistence, was assessed under both experimenter-present and (later) experimenter-absent conditions. The results were that the other-oriented induction (treatment 3 above) was more effective than either treatment 1 or 2, but the differences emerged only in the experimenter's absence, when external controls were reduced.

The work by Zahn-Waxler and colleagues suggests that in early childhood, other-oriented induction is especially effective (or perhaps *only* effective) if accompanied by strong expressions of parental affect. The Hoffman work with older children suggests that victim-centered induction may be enough, although these researchers did not study such affective elements as the amount of moral indignation displayed by parents in applying victim-centered discipline. Cheyne (1972) comments on possible developmental changes in the relation between affect and cognition in the outcome of disciplinary encounters. He proposes that there are two processes underlying the effect of punishment: the arousal of fear or anxiety, and the communication of a rule concerning what behavior is acceptable. He suggests further that the latter component becomes relatively more important with age.

Induction and Moral Development. There are documented changes with age in the nature of the adult reasoning that is effective in inhibiting children's deviations. As Parke (1974) has shown, 3-

year-olds are more deterred from touching a forbidden object if its fragility is stressed; they are relatively impervious to appeals to property rights. Five-year-olds, by contrast, respond more to the information that the object belongs to someone else.

In his review of the research on socialization and moral development, Hoffman (1970) reported that in nearly half the groups studied, induction proved to be a significant and positive correlate of several aspects of children's moral development. Negative correlations were rare. Rollins and Thomas (1979), including some additional studies, similarly conclude that induction is a clear positive factor in moral development. In their own work, Hoffman and Saltzstein (Hoffman, 1970; Hoffman & Saltzstein, 1967; Saltzstein, 1976) have distinguished between parent-oriented induction and peer-oriented induction. They found that the parents of internally oriented children were more likely than parents of children with external moral orientations to call attention to the effect of a child's behavior on *peers,* rather than on parents.

Bearison and Cassel (1975) carried out a study that is relevant to the development of moral judgment, though not directly focused on it. They investigated children's ability to take the perspective of another person in a communication game, and related this ability to aspects of child rearing. The mothers were interviewed and asked how they would react to several common disciplinary situations. Their answers were scored according to whether they were *person oriented* or *position oriented*. Person-oriented appeals included regulatory statements that draw attention to the feelings, thoughts, needs, or intentions of the mother, the child, or a third person who may be affected by the child's action. Position-oriented appeals referred to rules or statuses (e.g., "Eight-thirty is your bedtime"; "All children have to go to school"). Children whose mothers were more given to the use of person-oriented arguments, rather than position-oriented ones, were more successful in taking the perspective of another person in a game that required them to do so. Insofar as perspective-taking is instrumental in the development of moral judgment—and Kohlberg, Selman, and others have argued that it is—then person-oriented reasoning by parents should foster this development.

Considering the work on moral cognition as a whole, the role of parental use of *induction* emerges as a strong theme. Although Hartshorne and May (1929) concluded many years ago that traditional moral training—such as membership in the Boy Scouts or attendance at Sunday school—were ineffective in fostering children's honesty, we see from the work reported above that a certain amount of moral exhortation on the part of parents does seem to have some effect. At least, repeated parental stress on the consequences (especially consequences for others) of children's actions seems to move them toward more mature levels of thought when they are asked to consider moral issues.

The work on induction has carried us considerably beyond the parental use of reasoning as an undifferentiated category. It is now clear that reasoning is too global a category to be useful in socialization research. The nature of the reasoning used is of paramount significance. The work reviewed above indicates that it makes a difference whether the parent refers to effects on others rather than the child's self. Furthermore, distinctions between parent and peer have proved important. We noted that there are developmental changes in children's responsiveness to different categories of adult reasoning about the consequences of their actions. This may be especially true of other-oriented induction. There must be systematic changes in the identity of the others whose welfare the child is most likely to consider, and concerning whom inductive reasoning will have the greatest effect. But such changes have not yet been explored.

The fact that some parental techniques are more effective than others in producing internalization—that is, voluntary compliance by the child when there is no adult surveillance—is something that seems to be understood to some degree, though perhaps not consciously, by parents. Grusec and Kuczynski (1980) point out that most parents say they would use multiple methods in their child rearing. They tend to use power-assertive methods to achieve short-term objectives (such as stopping a fight between children, controlling excessively noisy behavior, or dealing with a child who is throwing a ball in the living room), but would use reasoning and explanations in such situations as the following: A parent learns after the fact that the child has been teasing an old man; that the child has stolen from the mother's purse; or that the child has run carelessly into the street. Thus it would seem that if a parent wants to influence the behavior of the child in situations where the parent will not be present, inductive techniques tend to be invoked.

A recent experiment by Kuczynski (1981) is relevant here. Parents' methods of dealing with children were studied in a situation where the child must do an onerous, repetitive task in the presence of attractive toys. In one condition the parents did not know in advance that the child's task persistence would be monitored after the parent had left the room; in another condition, they did know. Preliminary analyses indicate that when parents know that their control of their children's behavior must carry over to a forthcoming situation where they themselves will not be present, they increase their use of reasoning (including induction) and also their use of character attribution ("You are certainly nice and helpful"). For boys, there was also a decrease in negative power-assertive control techniques.

In concluding our comments on induction, we should note that the effect of this technique undoubtedly depends on the context of other socialization practices in which it occurs. In Hoffman's study of prosocial behavior toward peers, it was found that mothers' use of reasoning was positively associated with the children's prosocial score *if* the mothers were low in power assertion; in families where the mothers were high in power assertion, reasoning was negatively associated with the children's prosocial behavior toward peers. In most studies of the effects of induction, such interactions have not been looked for. If examined more widely, they might prove to be pervasive.

Attribution

Earlier (see *Theoretical Issues*) we discussed the current emphases on attribution as a process closely related to internalization. Hoffman (1982), Grusec (1982), and Lepper (1982) have argued that power-assertive parenting leads children to make external attributions, and hence is inimical to internalization. These accounts are mainly reinterpretations of existing socialization studies, and there are few studies in which the nature of the attributions explicitly made by adults, or the nature of children's spontaneous attributions, have been directly studied. As we noted earlier, Baldwin and associates did obtain empirical data concerning the correlates of their democratic/autocratic dimension (findings already discussed; see *The Authoritarian-Autocratic* pattern). Because the Baldwin group conceived of democratic parenting as a pattern in which the parents go to some pains not to make themselves the source of authority, we may assume that this work, too, bears on the attribution issue. That is, when parents avoid making themselves the source of authority, but instead draw their children's attention to the realistic constraints imposed on their behavior by the natural environment, we may assume that they are training their children to make internal rather than external attributions. And the Baldwin group found that this pattern of parenting was associated with children's being spontaneous, exploratory, and creative.

As noted above, Kuczynski reports that when parents attribute good, helpful qualities to the child, there is more compliance to the parent's directives under conditions when the parent is no longer present. The important study by Dienstbier and associates (Dienstbier, Hillman, Lehnhoff, Hillman, & Valkenaar, 1975) conveys a similar message. In this study, a child was left alone to maintain attention on experimental equipment, in the presence of distracting stimulation. Deviation was experimentally produced: The equipment malfunctioned when the child looked away. The experimenter, returning and discovering the malfunction, made one of two attributions concerning the child's emotional disturbance over the accident: "You feel bad because I caught you," or "You feel bad because you did something you knew was wrong." In a subsequent test for compliance in the absence of surveillance, the children who had received the internal attribution showed stronger resistance to temptation.

In a similar study, Grusec, Kuczynski, Ruston, and Simutis (1978) told children who had just donated to a charity either that they had done so because they enjoyed helping people, or that they had done so because they were expected to (there was also a "no reason" control condition). When the initial donation had been stimulated by observing a model (rather than by direct instruction), the internal-attribution children not only donated more time to charity on delayed tests, but generalized their altruism to sharing with schoolmates.

Although there have been many studies of the consequences for children's functioning of their making internal attributions—that is, for their having an inner rather than external locus of control—little is known concerning the parental behaviors that are associated with locus-of-control scores. There is evidence that allowing children certain autonomous activities at a relatively early age as well as training them for independence are associated with an internal locus in the child (Chance, 1972; Crandall, 1973; Wichern & Nowicki, 1976). And Loeb (1975) reported that a suggestive, rather than directive, teaching style was associated with inner locus in children. However, Chandler and colleagues (Chandler, Wolf, Crook, & Dugovics, 1980) found that parents of internal-locus children reported themselves as being more restrictive than parents of externals. These results would be reconcilable if the parents of inner-control children were restrictive in the sense of setting clear standards, enforcing them firmly, and requiring mature behavior (including *independent* behavior), but were permissive in the sense that they allowed their children considerable freedom to make their own decisions and to find problem solutions for themselves; however, the existing research does not enable us to be sure whether these distinctions do in fact underlie the inconsistencies between Chandler's and other studies.

Withdrawal of Love

The affectional tie between parent and child creates a powerful motive for acting so as to please and gratify one another; it also creates the potential for powerful sanctions. Students of socialization have long been aware of the power that parents have to manipulate children through their need for parental affection and approval, and their fears of loss of the parents' emotional support. We include the work on this aspect of parenting in the present section first of all because we regard it as an important aspect of the content of parent-child communication (both verbal and nonverbal), but also because it is an aspect of communication that has been assumed to be especially relevant to internalization (cf. Sears et al., 1957).

Since Hoffman's 1970 review, in which withdrawal of love was found to have only weak and inconsistent relationships with indices of children's moral development, the withdrawal-of-love dimension has dropped out of favor as an aspect of child rearing that is worthy of study. A few studies have included it, however, and the findings suggest that this loss of interest may have been premature. We therefore devote brief attention to it mainly to remind readers of it, and to reflect the fact that in our view it is still viable.

Coopersmith (1967), in his study of self-esteem in fifth- and sixth-grade boys, questioned mothers concerning the disciplinary methods they commonly employed when their children violated rules. Although withdrawal of love was a low-frequency choice in the sample as a whole, mothers of low self-esteem boys were more likely than other mothers to say that they used it. It is worth noting that the mothers of low self-esteem boys, by comparison with other mothers, were more likely to say that their disciplinary methods were ineffective.

Hoffman and Saltzstein (Hoffman, 1970; Saltzstein, 1976), in their work on internalized moral values, initially divided their seventh-grade subjects into two groups: those with an external, and those with an internal moral orientation. The internally oriented group was then further subdivided into two groups, who were labeled "conventional" or "humanistic." The conventional children's responses to the moral judgment stories took the form of adherence to a fairly rigid set of rules; the humanistic children were more concerned with the effects of misbehavior on other people, and their rules were

applied more flexibly, balancing various consequences and taking extenuating circumstances into account. These two kinds of internalized moral judgments were associated with somewhat different patterns of parenting. In one of the situations that the parents and children were asked to discuss, a child "talked back" to, or defied, a parent. The parents of conventional children, when asked how they handled such incidents, gave responses that the researchers classified as parent-oriented induction. That is, they called attention to the effect of such behavior on the parents' feelings. Parent-oriented induction may be thought of as implying withdrawal of love. The parents of humanistic children, on the other hand, when their children were defiant, firmly insisted that the children do what was asked, though they were likely to explain their reasons in the process of asserting their authority. More important for our present purposes, they did not allow the incident to become focused on parental anger or hurt feelings over the child's anger. These findings thus suggest that withdrawal of love may not be associated with internalization per se, but rather with the kind of internalized responses—whether guilt or empathy—that accompany a child's deviation.

The power of withdrawal of love at younger ages is illustrated in some recent work by Chapman and Zahn-Waxler (1981). These investigators have used mothers' tape-recorded reports of day-to-day disciplinary encounters as they occur in the homes of children in their second and third year of life. An example of one such report, from the mother of a 67-week-old boy, illustrates the nature of the raw data:

> He woke up about 4:30 and began crying. Absolutely nothing would make him happy. Even when I was holding him, he was still crying and climbing all over me. Finally, after about a solid hour of crying, I succumbed to my frustration and lost patience with him. I was sitting on the sofa holding him, and it seemed he was trying to climb up to the top of my head. Anyway, he scratched my nose with his fingernail, and it made me so angry that I very harshly put him down on the floor. He seemed really hurt and screamed much louder. All I needed at that point was more screaming, so I picked him up and carried him upstairs and put him in his bed. When I put him in bed he screamed even more, but at that point I was so angry that I just didn't want to be near him anymore. So I left him in bed and closed the door and came downstairs.

This incident exemplifies incidents given high scores for withdrawal of love, a category defined as involving withdrawing affection or attention, and including enforced separations. A number of other disciplinary techniques were also coded from the mother reports, including physical coercion, verbal prohibitions, explanation, and teaching. Most episodes involved more than one disciplinary technique, and withdrawal of love was almost never used alone. For each episode, the child's response to the mother's disciplinary action was coded, the major categories being compliance, noncompliance, and avoidance. It was found that withdrawal of love was more powerful than any of the other techniques, taken singly or in combination, in that children were more likely to comply when withdrawal of love was one element in the set of techniques used. It did not matter which of the other techniques withdrawal of love was combined with, and the other techniques did not differ significantly from one another. Withdrawal of love was associated not only with compliance, but with avoidance (a relatively rarer response), and the authors suggest that the higher rates of avoidance indicate that withdrawal of love is an especially aversive event for children of this age.

This work reminds us of the affective intensity of withdrawal of love, and its power to generate anxiety in children. It seems that the anxiety may motivate compliance, at least immediate compliance. Whereas earlier theorizing emphasized the role of withdrawal of love in internalization of parental strictures and the building of conscience, it now appears that at least when used with very young children, it may be similar to physical punishment in being a technique whereby parents buy desired behavior in the short term. It remains to be seen whether this is achieved at the expense of longer term cooperation.

THE FAMILY AS A SYSTEM: THE ROLE OF FATHERS

In our review thus far, we have discussed the relationships between "the parent" and the child, seldom distinguishing between fathers and mothers. We have proceeded on the assumption that the dynamics and impact of interaction would not depend on the sex of the parent who was involved with the child. A number of the major studies we have described in detail have included fathers as well as mothers (e.g., Baumrind; Lytton; Patterson), but in fact the majority of research on parent-child interaction has focused exclusively on mother-child rather

than father-child relationships. The last decade has, however, seen an increasing interest in the father-child relationship (e.g., see books by Benson, 1968; Biller, 1971; Green, 1976; Hamilton, 1977; Lamb, 1976b, 1981b; Lynn, 1974; Pedersen, 1980). Much of this recent work has been motivated by an interest in changing sex roles and the effects of those changes, specifically with questions concerning to what degree, in what ways, and with what effects, child-rearing functions can be more equally shared between mothers and fathers than has traditionally been the case. Most of the research can be subsumed under one of three categories. The first is descriptive and comparative, dealing with the quantitative and qualitative differences and similarities between male and female care givers in their modes of interaction with children. The second category studies the impact of individual differences among fathers on a variety of child outcomes. The third group of studies, far fewer in number, consider the mother-father-child triad as a system, and consider the interplay of an interlocking set of familial subsystems.

Father Characteristics: Description and Outcomes

A number of recent reviews have summarized the results of the descriptive-comparative studies (Biller, 1981; Hoffman, 1981; Lamb, 1981a; Radin, 1981). Major themes emerging from these reviews are as follows: (1) Both mothers and fathers are psychologically salient to the developing child in infancy as attachment figures (Kotelchuk, 1976), and to older children as importantly involved in the socialization process; and (2) mothers and fathers may adopt somewhat different roles with respect to certain parenting functions. Studies by Clarke-Stewart (1978), Lamb (1977), and Parke (1979) find that mothers tend to be more nurturant, to engage in more "conventional" play, and to perform more routine physical child care than fathers, whereas fathers tend to be more involved in *active* social play with their children than mothers. It is possible, however, that at least some of these mother-father differences are attributable to the three-person observation setting. There are circumstances—for example, at the end of the day after the father has returned home from work; or in a laboratory setting in which parents may feel the need to "perform" for the experimenter—in which mothers may to some extent withdraw and give center stage to their husbands. This conjecture is supported by Clarke-Stewart's finding (1978) that mothers initiate more play with their children when the father is not present. Thus a mother's relatively low level of playful interaction with her child during triadic sessions may not reflect her general level of playfulness.

The higher levels of maternal nurturance have been of special interest in that they may reflect either the social shaping of girls and women into maternal behavior, or a genetic bias in females toward nurturant responding to the young, or some combination of the two kinds of factors. Thus there has been great interest in the outcomes of the adoption of primary-caretaker roles by men. As samples of men who have assumed such roles become available, research is beginning to appear that examines whether the differences between male and female care givers tend to disappear when men carry out the primary care-giving functions. A recent study by Lamb, Frodi, Hwang, Frodi, and Steinberg (1982) with Swedish families suggests, that they do not. They found that the amount of nurturant interaction with infants was higher for mothers than for fathers even when both were primary care givers. But additional studies are needed with additional populations before this issue can be clarified.

With respect to the second category of studies, it has been shown that child outcomes are clearly related to individual differences in father characteristics in a number of behavioral domains (Hoffman, 1981; Radin, 1981). Sex-typing in children of both sexes has been found to be particularly responsive to parental inputs (Hetherington, 1967). And, at the descriptive-comparative level, it has become clear that fathers, more than mothers, differentiate between sons and daughters in their interaction (Jacklin, Di-Pietro, & Maccoby, in press; Langlois & Downs, 1980; and see summaries in Maccoby, 1980; see also Huston *vol. IV, chap. 5*).

Of greater interest to our present chapter is the third category of studies, those on the family as a system. Throughout this chapter, we have conceptualized the parent-child dyad as a relationship characterized by reciprocal influence; that is, a relationship between two persons in which the behavior of each person is influenced both by internal processes specific to the person and by partner or "relationship" factors. Clearly such reciprocal influences are not confined to the mother-child dyad, even though most of the work demonstrating them has focused on this pair. We previously made the point that existing socialization research for the most part has failed to take into account the idea that the mother-child dyad itself exists in a larger social system of reciprocal influences. A review by Lewis, Feiring, and Weinraub (1981) suggests that, if our aim is to understand the sources of children's social development, an approach is needed in our research that adequately conceptualizes and assesses the impact of the child's *social network*—involving both mother and father as well as siblings, grandparents, aunts, uncles, neighbors, friends, and others. Though it is certainly true that conceptual and methodological problems increase substantially when an attempt is made to study reciprocal influences in relationships involving more than two persons (Lamb, Suomi, & Stephenson, 1979), the study of *family* socialization must at least include an acknowledgment of the distinct role of the father in family interaction. Pedersen (1981) has argued that when the study of family socialization is confined to mother-child relations, the researcher creates a "fiction of convenience"; because no relationship exists in a psychological vacuum, descriptions and studies of the outcomes of mother-child relationships taken out of the family context in which they are embedded may be misleading. We cannot say a great deal about this issue in the present chapter because research relevant to family systems and the role of fathers in family systems is scarce. However, the little work that has been done in this area raises some interesting issues that are relevant to our concern with socialization in the family.

Most of the existing work on family systems may be thought of as falling into a category of thinking that Bronfenbrenner (1974) described as the study of "second-order effects." That is, research on fathering in the family has generally focused on questions regarding how the interactions between mothers and children influence and are influenced by fathers. Some of this work has documented changes in the nature of mother-child interaction brought about by father presence. For example, Lytton (1979) demonstrated, in his study of 2-year-old children, that fathers' presence increased mothers' effectiveness in controlling their young children. Studies comparing the nature of interactions involving two-person (mother-child or father-child) and three-person (mother-father-child) interactions (e.g., Belsky, 1979; Clarke-Stewart, 1978; Lamb, 1976a; Parke & O'Leary, 1976; Pedersen, Anderson, & Cain, 1980) demonstrate that, at least under some circumstances, less interaction takes place for any particular pair (mother-child; father-child; mother-father) when the third person is present. However, these studies do *not* necessarily imply that, on the whole, the child is interacting less in a three-person group than in a two-person group. It could be, for example, that each parent talks only two-thirds as much to the child as he or she would do when alone with the child; however, if this were true, the child would nevertheless be involved in more verbal interaction in a three-person group than in either two-person group. Moreover, some behaviors (such as smiling—see Parke & O'Leary, 1976) are more commonly engaged in by *both* parents when the spouse is present.

A study by Pedersen, Yarrow, Anderson, and Cain (1979) attempted to clarify changes associated with the addition of the second parent. In this study, observations were conducted of interactions involving mothers, fathers, and their 5-month-old infants. The researchers found that during periods of active communication between mother and father, the frequency of certain parent-child interactions that involved focused attention by the parent on the child decreased (including eye contact with, talking with, smiling at, and playing with the child). However, mother-father communication did not influence the rate of less-focused parent-child interaction. These differences can be attributed both to parent and to child behavior: Both parents *and* children directed fewer behaviors to the other when parents were involved in active communication with one another. A single exception emerged: Mothers tended to nurse and to bottle-feed their infants *more* frequently during episodes of active engagement with their husbands, perhaps because of the quieting effect feeding tends to have on infants. Furthermore, there were some differences in child behavior that appeared to be specific to one parent (e.g., when mother-father interaction ceased, infants gazed significantly more frequently at mothers than at fathers). These findings suggest the emergence of a rather complex coordination of infant behavior at this early age with the parents' behavior toward one another. Children may therefore have unique opportunities to learn and practice certain social interactive skills in three-person mother-father-child groups. It should be noted that observational studies on second-order effects have so far involved parents interacting with infants or very young children. These effects may be different in important ways with older children.

Although fathers do appear to be increasingly involved in child rearing in the United States (Glick, 1977; Pleck, 1979; Smith & Reid, 1980), there is little evidence that very many families are opting for a nontraditional family structure in which fathers take the primary responsibility for child rearing while the mother works or goes to school. Field (1978) and Russell (1978) have studied these rare families. Moreover, as indicated in a recent study (Feldman, Nash, & Aschenbrenner, 1982), even

when parents plan to implement a nontraditional division of labor in the home prior to the birth of a child, they rarely succeed in doing so after the child is born. However, women have increasingly entered the work force in recent years. Hoffman (1977), in a review of research on the role of fathers in families having working mothers, finds that although fathers rarely completely take over primary care-giving functions from the mother, fathers do tend to be more actively involved in routine child rearing of school-aged children when the mother is employed. However, it is unlikely that mothers are ready to give up major responsibility for mothering despite the increasing number of mothers who work: Studies by Lamb, Frodi, Hwang, and Frodi (1982) in Sweden, and by Pedersen, Cain, Zaslow, and Anderson (1982) in the United States have shown that working mothers had higher rates of interaction with babies than nonworking mothers during the after-dinner hours. Likewise, fathers interacted *less* with their children in non-child-care settings when their wives worked. These findings might be explained by working mothers, being out of the house most of the day, feeling the need to establish for themselves a primary role in child care during the time they *are* at home with the child, and fathers' willingness under the circumstances to fade, at least to some extent, into the psychological background.

An important aspect of the family system is the quality of the mother-father relationship. In his review of the work on the effects of loss of a parent, Rutter (1981) shows that loss of a parent through death is not associated with the subsequent development of antisocial behavior in children, whereas loss through divorce or desertion is. Furthermore, interparental discord and disharmony is associated with children's subsequent antisocial behavior when there has been no marital breakup, as well as when there has. Thus Rutter points to marital discord, rather than loss of a parent, as the key predictive factor. Hetherington, Cox, and Cox (1982) have found that if divorced parents continue to quarrel openly in front of the children on the occasions when they meet, the behavior of the children is more disrupted over a longer period than if parental conflict is either low or hidden. Lamb (1981a) reviews work on husband-wife discord, and concludes that it is associated with a range of adverse effects on children's psychosocial adjustment. We know little, however, about the dynamics of the process. Do children imitate a father's irritable, noncooperative reactions toward their mother? Do parents displace their anger and frustration from spouse to children? Is it a matter of mood induction? This latter possibility is highlighted by some recent work by Radke-Yarrow and colleagues (Radke-Yarrow & Kuczynski, in press). Young children who were exposed to the sound of unfamiliar adults' quarreling in a neighboring room became less helpful toward their mothers than children in a control group. We can only assume that open parental quarreling generates anxiety in children, and that this may disrupt the more positive aspects of their interaction with their parents; if this occurs, it would be an additional factor, over and above the effect of marital discord on the performance of each parent's child-rearing functions.

If marital discord disrupts child-rearing functions, there is another side of the coin—namely, that support from a spouse facilitates them. For example, Shereshefsky and Yarrow (1973) showed that emotional supportiveness of the father was correlated with successful maternal adaptation to pregnancy. Henneborn and Cogan (1975) demonstrated that mothers reported more positive reactions to the birth experience when their husbands were present during delivery. A longitudinal study by Barnard (1980) showed a relationship between mothers' reports of father involvement during pregnancy and observational measures of maternal involvement and responsiveness throughout the first 4 years of the children's lives. Similarly, Switsky, Vietze, and Switsky (1979), Price (1977), and Pedersen (1975) showed that father encouragement and supportiveness were related to successful breast-feeding in mothers. Rutter (1979), studying the impact of divorce on children, found that in a sample of inner-city families, the negative effects of familial disruption on the children's future behavior were mitigated if the mother remarried or otherwise entered into a supportive relationship with an adult partner.

Not only do many parents give support to one another's child-rearing activities; they also serve to shield the child from negative effects that might otherwise stem from a spouse's weaknesses. Hetherington, Cox, and Cox (1982) and Rutter (1979) report a "buffering" process whereby the impact of an emotionally unstable or otherwise incompetent parent on a child is moderated by the presence and availability of a more stable parent. Thus if either parent is functioning well, the child is unlikely to show disturbances in development.

The implications of the work on family systems is clear: Research that attempts to understand child outcomes entirely from the perspective of mother-child interaction is leaving out an important influence on child development.

BIDIRECTIONAL PROCESSES

In an earlier section (see *Child-Rearing Variations and Their Effects*) we described patterns of parental behavior and considered them in relation to child outcomes. We adopted this unidirectional mode of organization because the bulk of the psychological research on socialization within the family—at least the work done with children beyond infancy—has been conceptualized as a flow of influence from parent to child. Even so, we repeatedly encountered evidence of circular processes. We now move to a more explicitly interactive perspective.

The article by Bell (1968) on the reinterpretation of the direction of effects in socialization studies focused attention on bidirectionality, as did the later book on this subject (Bell & Harper, 1977). During the 1970s, a limited amount of research accumulated in which the effects of child characteristics on parental behaviors were directly assessed. In the present section, we first review research in which such effects have been examined. Next, we discuss the cumulative mutual cognitions within parent-child pairs. We then turn to a discussion of the sequential steps whereby aspects of the early parent-child relationship influence the development of a specific child characteristic: the child's readiness to accept influence from parents. Finally, we suggest a scheme whereby the child's socialization readiness can be linked as a mediator with the more traditional parenting typologies.

Children's Influence on Parents

It is obvious that a great deal of what parents do is determined by their children's prior actions. As Bell and Harper (1977) note, young children are highly effective in using their signaling and executive capabilities to bring their parents into proximity when needed. Children initiate a large proportion of the interactions with parents (Wright, 1967). And disciplinary encounters occur primarily when the child does something that violates rules or limits; thus the frequency of occurrence of such encounters may be seen as a reflection of the frequency with which the child creates the occasion for them. We saw that highly aggressive children tend to receive higher than average levels of concurrent punishment, but that time-lagged correlations did not reveal a tendency for punishment to strengthen aggression. We concluded that the concurrent correlations probably reflect parental responses to the children's aggression, rather than vice versa. In a similar vein, Patterson reports that hyperaggressive boys tend to be unresponsive to punishment, and that their unresponsiveness is a major factor bringing about escalation and perseveration in the coercive encounters between parent and child. The fact (to be discussed more fully below) that different children within the same family develop different relationships with their parents points strongly to the impact of individual children's characteristics on the relationship.

Children with Impairments

We know from microanalytic studies of parent-infant interaction, reviewed above, that the spontaneous behavior of infants is transformed into interactive behavior by a mother who responds contingently to infant behavior that may not be initially social. By and large, it is the infant's behavior that is being responded to in the dyad, rather than the mother's. We can get a glimpse of the way mothers adapt themselves to the individual characteristics of infants by studying extreme cases in which infants have some form of impairment in their ability to initiate or respond to social behavior. (See Cantwell, Baker, & Rutter, 1978, for a detailed review.) Certain anomalous conditions—such as blindness, deafness, mental retardation, low birthweight, or neonatal illness—can be identified at birth, and when this is possible, we are on strong ground for inferring child causality when relationships are found between the infant's characteristics and the nature of parent-child interactions; prior socialization is not implicated. We should note that infantile impairments can affect parent-child interaction in two ways: via the infant's own behavior in stimulating and reacting to the parent or failing to do so; and via the assumptions that parents make about what the child is capable of perceiving or doing. The latter kind of effect is not, strictly speaking, a child effect at all. It is an effect of parental cognitions, which mediate between a child's characteristics and parental behavior. It will not always be possible to separate these two kinds of effects, but some data are available that address the issue.

Earlier, we reviewed the work on low-birthweight infants, showing that mothers were initially less interactive with such infants than with full-term infants. We turn now to other kinds of impairments, some much more profound.

Jones (1977) studied the interactions in 8- to 19-month-old infants and their mothers in a group of six children with Down's syndrome (DS) and six controls. Overall, the DS infants were less effective

communicators: They used fewer "referential looks" in their interactions with their mothers, and were engaged in less mutual eye contact. Their use of vocalizations during interaction was erratic and noncontingent, and their vocal turn-taking was poor compared to normals. In turn, the mothers of the DS infants were more controlling of their infants' behavior during interaction. We may surmise that mothers' use of control with these DS infants is a result, to a large extent, of the disorganization of the behavior of the infants.

In general, when faced with a child with some profound handicapping condition, parents must make different kinds of accommodations to their children than parents of normal children, and similarly adjust their expectations about their children so as to be in line with their children's special needs and competencies. Walker and Kershman (1981), for example, found that deaf-blind infants were less predictable in their interactions with their parents and that parents, in turn, employed more repetition of simple behavioral sequences with their children than did matched controls. Fraiberg's work with blind infants and their parents (1974, 1975, 1977) points to some of the problems in parent-child relations, but she also describes high levels of adaptation. She reports that, in the general population of blind children, a large proportion have severe problems in their social relationships. The mothers in her study showed considerable anxiety about their ability to deal effectively with their blind babies. However, careful study of the development of attachment between blind infants and their mothers through the second year of life indicated that, on the whole, the developmental course of attachment relations between blind infants and mothers was similar to that between mothers and sighted babies, although the development of the concept of mother-as-object was somewhat delayed in the blind group. The major difference between blind and sighted infants was the greater attachment-eliciting power of the mother's voice in the blind sample. Also, even though the blind infants were in most respects quite similar to their sighted counterparts, mothers were having difficulty interpreting the "foreign language" of their blind infants when they entered the study. With guidance and reassurance most were able to achieve relationships with their infants that were, in overall quality, indistinguishable from parent-child relationships with sighted infants. In this context, it is interesting to note that Meadows' work with deaf children and their parents (1975) indicates that deaf children seem to make better progress in various areas of development when the parents themselves are also deaf and use sign language.

A study by Lederberg (1981) highlights this point. Lederberg observed interactions between adult women and unfamiliar children who were either hearing impaired or normal. When dealing with a hearing-impaired child, the women used shorter utterances and a higher proportion of attentional utterances, and their questions were of a simpler "yes/no" variety. Overall, they spoke less and used more stock phrases when they did speak, but *they did not use gestures* more than when interacting with normal children. Thus we see that the real and perceived characteristics of the deaf children were such as to disrupt the adults' normal patterns of interacting with children, but the adults lacked some of the substitute skills needed for adaptation to deaf children so that interaction was impaired.

Two other studies illustrate the difficult problems certain kinds of children can present to their parents. Frodi and Lamb (1978) studied parents of 5-month-old infants. The parents were shown videotapes of infants in various states. One group viewed full-term infants, and another saw infants who were premature. During the situations in which the infants cried, the sound tracks were counterbalanced so that half of the videotapes of premature infants were paired with the sound tracks of full-term infants crying, and vice versa. The cry of the premature infants, whether associated with premature or full-term videotapes, was judged to be more aversive by the parents and elicited more physiological arousal than the cry of full-term infants. It would appear that differences in the quality of infants' cries may have considerable impact on parents and in turn on the quality of parent-child interaction. In a similar study, Sagi (1981) exposed 132 adults to the recorded cries of normal and abnormal infants (including infants diagnosed as Down's syndrome and maladie du cri du chat). The abnormal cries were rated as much more aversive on 10 rating scales.

A less extreme example of preexisting child characteristics comes from the literature on physical attractiveness. It is well established that adults treat preschool-aged children who are independently rated as physically unattractive quite differently from children who are rated as physically attractive. (See Langlois, 1981, for a review of this work.) Some (although probably not all) of these differences have been shown to be attributable to differences in the actual behavior of physically attractive and physically unattractive children. Where do these differences in behavior come from? Do *par-ents* treat physically attractive children differently from unattractive ones? A study of Langlois and Sawin (1981) suggests that this is so from very early in life. Infant physical attractiveness was rated by experimenters when infants were 2 days old. Physically attractive infants were held close and given more cuddly ventral contact by their mothers than unattractive infants. When attractive infants were held by their mothers, the mothers shifted their infants' positions less often. Mothers of attractive infants were more sensitive in feeding interactions, and the interactions themselves were rated as more effective and relaxed. Less attractive infants were looked at less by their mothers and given more distal (relative to proximal) stimulation than attractive infants. Here we have a case where maternal perceptions are clearly implicated. It is difficult to imagine that the behavior of a 2-day-old infant depends on its physical attractiveness.

To what extent are the influences of children on the development of parent-child relations a result of real variations in their appearance, their behavior, and their perceptual capacities, and to what extent are these influences mediated by parental expectations and perceptions concerning their children? Children with profound handicaps are of course different from other children, but in addition, their parents are probably selectively attentive to those specific characteristics of their children that they believe *must be* present. These parental beliefs may, in turn, influence the behavior of the parents toward the children and on the development of their relationship. In a study of low-birthweight infants, Minde, Brown, and Whitelaw (1981) observed the behavior of mothers toward their infants during visits to the intensive care nursery. They found that most of the components of mother behavior they studied were more highly correlated with maternal *perceptions* of the severity of their infants' illnesses than with the actual severity, and that 60% of the mothers to some extent overestimated this severity. In other handicapping conditions it is likely that parents' perceptions of their children, and their theories about what the children's characteristics imply, may also be at least as important to the developing parent-child relationship as the actual behavioral differences among children. Thus our understanding of the impact of preexisting characteristics of children on parents would be greatly enhanced by information about parents' theories of child development and their beliefs regarding the potential impact of various forms of socialization.

On the whole, the studies of impaired children,

and comparisons of the parents of these children to parents of normals, provide evidence that parental expectations, parental perceptions, *and* differences in the actual behavior of the children all can influence parental behavior in interaction with their children. There appear to be kinds of child characteristics that take precedence over expectations, but there are probably other areas in which expectations obscure the reality of the child's behavior to a substantial degree.

Children's Temperament

In considering the impact of child characteristics on the parent, we can draw on the literature on temperament. Although this term, in its usual definition, is meant to refer to that portion of a designated behavioral characteristic that is controlled by genetic (or at least congenital) factors, in practice one cannot identify what portion of a temperamental characteristic (e.g., a child's activity level, emotional reactivity, or sociability) is a function of innate endowment. Because several of the major temperamental dimensions cannot be reliably assessed at birth, some portion of the variance in these dimensions must be assumed to be a product of the child's experiences, including the history of parent-child interaction, up to the time of measurement.

The most comprehensive study of the relations between infant temperament and the nature of the interaction that develops with parents is the one currently being conducted by Bates and colleagues (Bates, 1980a and b), and we will use this study to illustrate both the great potential of such studies and the difficulties in their interpretation. A fairly large group of families ($n = 168$ mother-infant pairs at the time of first measurement) have been assessed at infant ages 6 months, 13 months, and 24 months. Follow-up work is currently being done at 36 months. An initial screening was done to permit selecting a sample that would include a substantial number of "difficult" as well as "easy" babies. The primary device for assessing infant temperament is the Infant Characteristics Questionnaire (ICQ). Factor analysis identified the "fussy-difficult" dimension as the first factor, and the infant characteristics that contribute most clearly to it are the amount of fussing and crying and the intensity of crying, as well as the mother's overall rating of infant difficultness. Social demandingness is also a contributor (Bates, 1979). Validation studies have been done in which parent reports of infant difficultness have been related to (1) spectral analyses of infant cries; (2) assessments by other mothers of the aversiveness of infants' tape-recorded cries; and (3) home visitors' moment-to-moment records of infants' behavior. It has been found that infant difficulty as measured by the ICQ is related to all three kinds of validation measures. The correlations are significant but low (in the .30 range). Thus the parental report of infant difficultness represents a composite of "real" infant characteristics and parental reactions to, or perceptions of, infantile characteristics in which the tolerance of individual parents for an infant's cries or demands is implicated.

Infant difficultness, as measured by the ICQ, shows considerable stability from one measurement period to the next. Nevertheless there are some changes over time: Children who are "easy" at the earlier ages tend to remain so. Quite a few children who are initially difficult become easier to manage with time. There is a fairly even sex distribution among "difficult" infants at 6 months, but by age 24 months, the most difficult children are almost all boys. Surprisingly, at 6 and 13 months there are few relationships between infant difficultness, as measured by the ICQ, and maternal responsiveness, teaching, or affection-giving, even though observations of interaction show a close and increasing meshing between mother positive control and child positivity (willing compliance). By 24 months, however, relationships between the main child temperamental dimension and interactive characteristics have emerged. A preliminary analysis by Lee (reported in Bates, 1980a) based on a segment of the data from the Bates project, shows that the mothers of the more difficult children were engaging in more control behaviors, and that there was more conflict in control situations. These mothers used more repetitions of prohibitions or warnings, removed objects from their children more frequently, and used power assertion; the difficult children, on the other hand, though not actually initiating "trouble" behavior significantly more than other children, tended to persist in it once begun. They tended to ignore maternal control attempts, or to react to such attempts with fussing or protests.

At the time of this writing, the only relationships that have been reported from the Bates study between infant temperament and the nature of the mother-infant interaction have been based on concurrent measures. Thus we do not know whether the children scored as difficult at 24 months have become more difficult (or remained more difficult) over time because their mothers have been using power-assertive techniques, or whether the mothers have been driven into these methods by the negative reactions of their children to milder forms of control. The longitudinal nature of the Bates project's data provides an opportunity for path analyses and predictive multiple regressions that will begin to differentiate these possibilities.

In a recent study (reported in Maccoby & Jacklin, in press) Maccoby, Snow, and Jacklin make use of a composite measure of difficultness that is conceptually comparable to the Bates dimension. Difficult infants were defined as infants for whom the frequency of fussing and crying is high; who are difficult to soothe; who resist routine caretaking operations, such as diapering; and who are difficult to distract from undesired activity. A group of infants were studied longitudinally at age 12 and 18 months, and assessment of difficult temperament was made at both ages. Duplicating Bates, it was found that the behavior of the mothers toward their infants was generally unrelated to the children's scores on the difficulty dimension, with the exception that there was a tendency for mothers to do more holding and physical comforting with difficult children. There was evidence, however, that the child's difficulty was influencing some aspects of the mother's behavior over the 12- to 18-month period. Mothers of difficult boys exerted less teaching pressure, over this period. Thus it appeared that a number of mothers of difficult boys reacted to their children's temperaments by backing away from socialization efforts. It is worth noting that mothers who exerted relatively little teaching pressure at 12 months had sons who had become somewhat more difficult at 18 months, suggesting the beginning of a destabilizing circular process.

A further suggestion that difficult temperament in boys leads mothers, over time, to reduce their socialization pressure comes from the previously discussed work by Olweus with older boys. Olweus reports that when boys had been hot-tempered and strong-willed in early childhood (according to their mothers' retrospective reports), their mothers tended to be permissive toward aggression at a later point in time, and that maternal permissiveness was associated with increasing levels of aggression. Although, as we noted earlier, there is a problem in interpreting the mothers' retrospective reports, the data are consistent with the view that, at least with boys, the children's early temperamental qualities made it difficult for the mothers to exercise firm control, and that this maternal "backing off" in turn interfered with the normal socialization of aggression. Further longitudinal data are badly needed, including measures of both fathers and mothers, and children of several different ages, to trace out the mutual adaptations occurring over time between parents and children with different early dispositions.

Cumulative Cognitions of Partners

We have seen many instances of circular process in our review of the effects of parental or child characteristics on the interaction of the pair in naturalistic situations. Some recent studies have underlined a theme that complicates the picture: Participants in an interaction do not merely react to what their partner is doing at the moment. They react to their *interpretation* of what the partner is doing, or to their anticipation of what the partner may do. Each participant brings a cognized history to any interaction with a familiar partner. Each attributes traits to the other, and evaluates these traits. Such processes are evident in a study by Halverson and Waldrop (1970), who found that a mother's use of controlling statements in an interaction with her son at nursery school was correlated with independent assessment of the child's hyperactivity. Her use of controlling statements with an unfamiliar same-age boy, however, was not related to his hyperactivity, even though his objectively observed impulsive behavior was equally frequent when with his own or another child's mother. Thus mothers, when with their own sons, were reacting to their accumulated knowledge about the child's characteristics rather than to the specific acts occurring in the immediate situation. The process may be part of the explanation of the finding by Cunningham and Barkley (1979) that mothers of hyperactive boys were less likely than other mothers to respond positively to their sons' compliant behavior when it did occur.

Chapman (1979) makes a similar point, noting that when children are supposed to be following their mothers' instructions, and a distracting videotape is introduced, the mothers change their directing style. With boys, the mothers increase their use of commands. However, their commands are not contingent on specific instances of the boys' loss of attention. Evidently, the commands are being increased *in anticipation* of the boys' response to a distracting stimulus. An impressionistic report by Paton, reported in Bell (1977), is relevant in this connection. Observing the reactions of mothers to medicated and nonmedicated hyperactive boys, he observed that improvement in the impulse control of a medicated child was likely not be followed immediately by a more benign relationship with his mother. There was a lag, during which the mother reorganized her perceptions of the child and gradually readjusted her own behavior toward a changed partner.

Parents' cumulative self-cognitions also have a bearing on their reactions to children. Bugenthal and colleagues (Bugenthal, Caporael, & Shennum, 1980; Bugenthal & Shennum, 1981) have noted that the effect of a child's behavior on an adult depends on the adult's self-cognitions and general attitudes about the competency of children. In the first study, 7- to 9-year-old confederates worked on a joint construction task with adults. One condition involved the child being uncooperative. The child did not respond to the adult until asked several times, and spent relatively little time engaged with the joint task. Under these conditions of child non-compliance, adults on the average became more negative in their comments to the child, and more assertive in their tone of voice. However, there was a subgroup of adults who became *less* voice-assertive rather than more so when dealing with an uncooperative child, and these were people who obtained relatively low scores on a measure of internal locus of control.

A preliminary report (Bugenthal & Shennum, 1981) describes a study in which children, as confederates, were trained to behave in a manner that was either shy or assertive. Adults' tones of voice were assessed in terms of whether they were "condescending" (similar to baby talk) or respectful. Shyness in the confederate led adults to speak in a condescending way *if* the adults attributed low social competence to children in general. An assertive child, on the other hand, increased the adult's respectful tones *if* the adults believed that children of this age were generally quite competent.

Children's Readiness to Be Socialized

The idea that parents differ in responsiveness, and that this is a critically important dimension affecting the progress of the parent-child relationship, is a familiar one, and has heavily influenced the research reviewed so far. The idea that the responsiveness of the child is also of great importance is less familiar, and has only recently come to prominence in the research literature. Our assumption in the present section is that children do differ in their positive interest in their parents, and their readiness to accept influence attempts from them. The child's receptiveness may thus be seen as a mediating variable that affects not only how the child will react to a given parental pressure, but also what kind of pressure the parent will be led to apply. An issue of great interest then becomes this: What child-rearing conditions are associated with a child's adopting a receptive stance toward parental influence attempts? The aspect of this question that has received most research attention has been children's *compliance*.

We turn now to a consideration of this research, but will find, not surprisingly, that not all acts of compliance on the part of children stem from a positive receptive state. We will therefore find it necessary to distinguish among the conditions under which compliance occurs.

In our earlier discussion of the study by Minton et al. (1971), we noted the high rate of incidents in which the behavior of 2-year-olds at home called for mothers' imposing restriction or direction on the child. As these incidents occur, parents inevitably begin to communicate rules of conduct to their children, via a graduated series of demands and requests. The unfolding of the parent-child relationship from this point on depends to a considerable extent on the child's readiness to learn the rules and accept the demands. As Minton et al. (1971) showed, compliance is often not a matter of a single act by a parent followed by a single act by a child; rather, there is a sequence of events, later elements being determined by what happened at earlier points. Thus if the child complied to the parent's initial mild pressure, that tended to be the end of the sequence; but if the child failed to comply, the mother escalated the level of her pressure until compliance was obtained. From these observations it follows that if excessive family conflict is to be avoided, compliance to mild pressure becomes in itself a norm about which children must learn. It is reasonable to suppose that certain parental behaviors either enhance or diminish children's orientation toward paying attention to, and making an effort to adapt their behavior to, what their parents are trying to teach.

Compliance and obedience serve to circumvent conflict in the family and elsewhere. Furthermore, a generalized disposition to cooperate with others' requirements indicates that the child is on the way to learning how interpersonal rules function. In this connection, Lytton (1977a) and others have suggested that early compliance is the first in a long series of steps toward the acquisition of conscience. An indication that a compliant (or cooperative) stance toward parents can be an indicator of the development of self-regulatory processes comes from the study by Gordon, Nowicki, and Wichern (1981), who found that second graders high in inner locus of control were more likely than external-locus children to cooperate with their mothers' directions and suggestions, while being *less* likely to seek help. As children grow older, of course, automatic compliance with the demands of others would hardly be an indication of internalization; it is to be expected that as children grow older they will learn how to bargain for a reasonable balance between the demands of others and their own needs, and how to evaluate the demands of others in terms of a set of internalized moral values before deciding whether to comply or refuse. For our present purposes, however, the main point is that during early and middle childhood, children's learning to adapt themselves to the requirements of others (specifically other family members) is part of the more general process of learning to participate effectively in social interaction.

We saw earlier that during the second year of life, children become more efficient in expressing their desires to their mothers, whereupon the mothers become more responsive (Bronson, 1974). Concurrently, the children become more attentive to, and responsive to, their mother's requests and directions. As we have seen, no general statement can be made concerning which member of a parent-child pair is more likely to make attempts to influence the partner. The balance is highly situationally specific. In situations where the parent is attempting to teach the child something, or obtain the child's cooperation in a task, parents of course do more of the suggesting and demanding, and children more of the complying (or refusing). When the parent is busy with a task that does not involve the child, and there are few competing activities available for the child, the child makes relatively many bids for interaction and the parent makes few. Beyond infancy, parental compliance has been studied mainly in the parent-busy situation, and is labeled as responsiveness or accessibility. Child compliance has been studied primarily in the parent teaching or task-oriented situation, where the child is being pressed by the parent to do something that the child would not do spontaneously, rather than during cooperative play where both are presumably willing participants. Such studies can be highly informative, but they may present a somewhat distorted picture, underrepresenting the degree of *mutual* compliance that actually prevails within parent-child pairs.

Whatever the balance in terms of the number of influence attempts parents and children direct toward one another, there can be no doubt that the frequency of such attempts by parents toward children increases in the second year. Parents begin to perceive increased intentionality and competence in their children as the second birthday approaches. No doubt these perceptions are involved in parents becoming less indulgent, more willing to refuse a child's demand, and more likely to expect that children will display at least nominal amounts of cooperation and obedience.

The cognitions that are involved on the child's side are not so well understood. C. F. Schmidt (1976), in a chapter on social cognition in adults, discusses the amount of inference that is involved in even the simplest cognitions of others' actions. As an illustration, he compares two descriptions of a football play that would be given by two persons. An inexperienced observer reports that player No. 10 is holding the ball and moving backwards. An experienced observer says that the quarterback is dropping back to pass. With experienced observers, cognitions about others' behavior always involve inferences concerning the others' plans of action. The subject's own behavior is always geared to these understandings of plans, rather than to the details of the others' overt actions. Furthermore, such beliefs about plans are *recursive,* in the sense that the observer not only believes that the other person has plans, but believes that others share in this belief. Thus in an exchange involving one person giving an order and another person obeying it, the person giving the order has a plan that involves the other person's following directions; more importantly, the existence of this plan is common knowledge to both members of the pair. In Schmidt's words, "One person cannot really give an order to another unless that other recognizes that an order is being given" (1976, p. 51).

To what extent can young children recognize that orders are being given? Anyone who has tried to give an order to a child of 18 months will recognize the problem. The child may attend with interest, may appear to be cheerful, and may even do what is asked; but something is missing that would be present in an older child, namely the mutual awareness that the parent expects to be obeyed and that the child has some kind of obligation to follow directions. We know very little about the way young children cognize their parents' intents, much less their own obligations. We can only assume that such cognitions must be involved in the development of compliant and cooperative interchanges.

In the discussion that follows, we make a rough distinction between compliance that stems from immediate situational pressures and compliance that seems to stem from a more generalized willingness to cooperate with (or perhaps to "exchange compliances with") a partner. The distinction cannot be a clear one because it has not been one that has explicitly guided research on compliance to date. Nevertheless, we feel that the distinction helps to explain some of the inconsistencies in existing findings. We begin with a discussion of the second variety: "receptive" compliance. The research under this rubric will be discussed in terms of two presumed mediating processes: (1) the development of a relationship of positive emotional bonding and trust between parent and child, including a secure attachment on the part of the child; and (2) the use by parents of socialization techniques that emphasize children's individuality and their responsibility for their own actions, as distinct from techniques that rely on parental power. "Situational" compliance will be discussed in terms of the immediate socialization pressures present during the situation where compliance is demanded.

Receptive Compliance

Secure attachment is unique among the intervening processes listed above in that it is the only area in which researchers have actually attempted to measure the intervening process. Matas, Arend, and Sroufe (1978), for example, conducted a short-term longitudinal study of 48 mothers and their children. When the children were 18 months old, the authors utilized the Ainsworth Strange Situation (Ainsworth et al., 1971) in order to rate the children as securely attached, conflicted, or avoidant. Six months later, the mothers and children were observed in a variety of laboratory situations, including a mother-initiated cleanup of the experimental room and several problem-solving tasks. Children who were rated as securely attached at 18 months were found to be more compliant to their mothers at 24 months than were the other two groups of children.

Secure attachment, as defined by Ainsworth and her colleagues, is a characteristic of the child that reflects something about the relationship between the mother and child. As we saw earlier, the maternal behaviors that Ainsworth and her colleagues have identified as antecedents of secure attachment during the child's first year include sensitivity, cooperation, acceptance, accessibility, sociability, and displays of positive affect. We may ask whether any of these maternal characteristics are directly associated with a child's compliance, without recourse to attachment as a mediating process. Stayton, Hogan, and Ainsworth (1971) found direct relationships between compliance in 12-month-old infants and the mothers' sensitivity, cooperation, and acceptance. Martin (1981) found a relatively strong relationship between maternal responsiveness, measured when a sample of children were 10 months old, and children's compliance at both ages 22 and 42 months, but the relationship was found in boys and not in girls.

More recent work by Schaffer and Crook (1980) provides a fine-grained account of mechanisms that may underlie such correlations. Schaffer and Crook observed children of 15 months and 24 months with their mothers in a laboratory playroom. To ensure that mother-child interaction would occur, the mothers were asked to try to see to it that the children played with each of the different toys provided. The mother's directives were classified into three categories: *orientation* (e.g., "look here"), *contact* (child is directed to establish contact with an object), and *task* (child is asked to carry out a specific action with an object). The children's compliance was categorized according to whether orientation, contact, or task compliance had been demanded. Compliance was shown to depend on the child's just-preceding state. A child not oriented toward a given object would attend to it about half the time when given an orientation directive. However, if the mother issued a contact or task directive when the child was not already oriented to the object, the chances of compliance were very low. Indeed compliance was almost never obtained from the 15-month-old children under these conditions. Verbal directives designed to attract the child's attention were much more effective in doing so if accompanied by gestures. If the child was already oriented to an object, the chances of getting contact compliance were much improved. The success of task demands, in turn, depended partly (at least for 15-month-olds) on having already brought the child into contact.

These findings point clearly to an important aspect of parental sensitivity. Those parents who closely monitor the attentional state of their children, and adapt the nature of their demand to it, sequencing their demands so as to obtain orientation first and then narrowing down the demands toward the more specific action required, will have more success in obtaining compliance than parents who issue directives that are not geared to the child's initial state of orientation and involvement.

Hatfield, Ferguson, and Alpert (1967) studied a group of 40 4- to 5½-year-old children and their mothers, and found that mothers who were highly involved with their children and who freely expressed positive emotion during various laboratory situations and joint mother-child tasks had children who were generally low in disobedience—that is, predisposed toward cooperation. Martin (1981) similarly found that, independent of children's level of demandingness toward their mothers, when mothers were identified as "involved" at age 10 months, they tended to be more effective in exacting compliance from their children 12 and 32 months later. In Clarke-Stewart's longitudinal study (1978) of 14 children and their parents (observed when the children were between ages 15 and 30 months), fathers were more involved in play and showed more positive emotion than mothers. The children, in turn, were more cooperative with their fathers than with their mothers during play. These studies all point to a linkage between parental involvement with their children and the children's willing compliance. To the extent that emotional relationships are disrupted during the interval closely following divorce, the study by Hetherington, Cox, and Cox (1979) may be taken as evidence for the same point: Children from intact families were more compliant toward their parents than were children whose parents were recently divorced.

Lytton and his colleagues have studied various aspects of parental emotional bonding and trust and the relationship between these characteristics and compliance. (See Lytton, 1980, for a summary.) The sample employed in all three studies discussed below consisted of 90 to 136 2½-year-old boys, a subsample of whom were twins. Parents and children were observed in the home, where parent behavior and children's compliance were recorded and rated by observers; also, parents kept "compliance diaries." It was found that consistent enforcement of rules (Lytton, 1979), parental use of psychological as opposed to material rewards (Lytton, 1977a), and frequency of joint play and cooperative activities (Lytton, 1979) were related to high levels of compliance in these 2½-year-old boys. In sharp contrast, parental characteristics that may be thought of as fostering *mistrust*—namely the use of withdrawal of love and other forms of psychological punishment (Lytton, 1979) were associated with low levels of compliance. Support for this relationship comes from a study (Newson & Newson, 1968) of 600 4-year-olds, in which it was found that the use of unfulfilled, idle threats was associated with high levels of disobedience.

The frequent occurrence of cooperative play in the families of compliant children deserves to be highlighted. We suggested earlier that playful interchanges during the first and second years foster the development of mutual scripts that make cooperative activity possible. Some recent work with older children and their parents makes a similar point. At-home observations of the free play of 45-month-old children with either the mother or father (Stanford Longitudinal Project, unpublished) indicates that much of the interaction is verbal, and involves suggestions, demands, or questions by each partner complied to or answered by the other. Refusal by either partner is rare. In most cases, the pattern is one of more suggestions by the parent and compliance by

the child than vice versa, although in many families, there is a close balance between parent and child in terms of the level of demanding and complying by the two partners. (In a few cases, the child "drives" the interaction.) For many pairs, part of a play session moves into thematic joint play, a more fully meshed form of play where the partners play roles and act out an imaginary episode with toys, and where it becomes difficult to tell who is initiating and who is responding. Such integrated play is more likely to occur if at other times during the session (1) the child has fairly often given directions or made demands, with the parent complying; the frequency of parental suggesting or demanding and child complying is *not* related to thematic play; and (2) the child has seldom or never shown refusal to comply with a parental demand or suggestion. These findings support the proposition that mutual responsiveness (compliance) provides the conditions in which genuinely cooperative interaction can occur, and that allowing the child to share with the parent the role of initiating joint action may be especially important.

The importance of an adult's signaling "I am willing to cooperate with you" is further highlighted in a study by Cox (1974), in which it was found that when an adult had just complied to a child's request, the child was more likely to comply to the adult's request than if the prior adult compliance had not taken place. The possibility that a child's cooperative behavior generalizes to other partners when the parent has been compliant is suggested by a finding by Bryant and Crockenburg (1980). Sisters were seen to be more helpful toward one another if their mothers were helpful *when asked for help*. Unsolicited maternal helpfulness was unrelated to helpfulness between sisters.

The child's signaling readiness to cooperate is equally important. Minton et al. (1971) found that mothers were more likely to grant a 2-year-old's request if the child had obeyed her prior request or command.

The work on mutuality of compliance, discussed above, leads us into the second possible mediating process, namely parental emphasis on the child's individuality and freedom of choice. This process is much more inferential at this time. There is little research that bears directly on it. We wish to suggest that there are certain parental techniques that contribute to the child's sense of cooperating in family interactions voluntarily, whereas other techniques convey the feeling that the child is being forced to cooperate—that is, that compliance is not internally motivated, but is instead externally manipulated.

The use of physical control (Lytton, 1979; Lytton & Zwirner, 1975), physical punishment (Lytton, 1977a; Minton et al., 1971), and negative action in general toward the child (Lytton & Zwirner, 1975) as techniques for exacting compliance may be viewed as an overriding of the child's individual opinions, needs, and desires. Relatively low levels of compliance have been found to be associated with all these parent variables. On the other hand, respect for the child's competence and individuality, manifested by encouraging mature action (Lytton, 1977a), using explanations (Minton et al., 1971), and the use of induction (Baumrind & Black, 1967; Lytton, 1979), have been shown to be associated with high levels of compliance.

Hetherington, Cox, and Cox (1982) studied immediate compliance by children to the directives of their recently divorced mothers and fathers. They did not find that the use of reasoning and explanation by the parents was any more likely to obtain compliance than other more peremptory parental demands. However, parental use of reasoning and explanation were related to longer term positive outcomes: to increasing self-control and prosocial behavior. If these behavioral characteristics can be seen as according with parental desires for their children's behavior, we may interpret these findings as providing an instance in which children's receptive or spontaneous compliance is enhanced by inductive techniques.

Along slightly different lines, Cunningham and Barkley (1979) found that hyperactive children complied less than normal children; they found further that parents of hyperactive children, consistent with the notion of deindividuation, issued more commands and were less contingently responsive to their children than were parents of normal children. Here, of course, the issue of the direction of effects is particularly apparent, and we may suspect that a circular process is under way. It is likely that when children comply to mild pressure, their parents increasingly do the very things—involve themselves in affectively positive interchanges, comply to the child's requests—that foster further compliance in the child. A propos of this point, Yarrow, Waxler, and Scott (1971) found that when a nursery school child has complied to an adult request, the probability is increased that the adult will return to that child and initiate positive contact.

In summary, when researchers have measured compliance in such a way that the compliance could indicate the presence of a cooperative, receptive style in the children, the following are shown to be associated with compliance: parental behaviors that antecede secure attachment (sensitivity, cooperation, acceptance, etc.); secure attachment itself; parental emotional bonding and the fostering of trust; high levels of playful, affectively positive interaction with the child; frequent joint task-related activity; and the parents' use of non-power-assertive techniques emphasizing the child's individuality.

Damon (1977) has described the development of cooperative behavior and conceptions of authority in children in terms of the child's developing understanding of the notion of reciprocity in interaction with parents. Research on the correlates of compliance, in this regard, suggests that parents may play a role in this aspect of conceptual development. Parents who are themselves cooperative with their children's needs tend to have children who are cooperative with theirs; parents who are trustworthy tend to have children who trust them and thus cooperate with them; parents who themselves legitimize their children's needs and desires tend to have children who treat their parents' needs and desires as legitimate, as well. Regarding receptive compliance, then, there is fairly strong and consistent evidence for reciprocal cooperation in families. That is, a style of cooperation tends to co-occur in parents and children. In the absence of strong longitudinal evidence, it is of course difficult to know how these styles of mutual cooperation are initiated and maintained in families. It is tempting to argue that the attachment literature points toward a predominant influence of parents on children. Yet, because some children may become attached more easily than others independent of parental treatment, it is quite possible that some children are temperamentally more predisposed than others to establish cooperative styles with their parents.

Situational Compliance

We now turn to a body of research that presents a very different picture than the one just described. A classic study by Landauer, Carlsmith, and Lepper (1970) sets the stage. Preschool-aged children were asked to carry out an onerous task (pick up 100 tennis balls). They were asked to do this either by their own mothers or another child's mother. Their compliance (as measured by the number of balls picked up) was much less when the request came from their own mothers. Thus the history of attachment and trust that we may assume characterized the relationship with the mother more than it did with a strange woman did not have the effect of enhancing compliance. On the contrary, it seems to have had an opposite effect. We will discuss below the subsequent studies by these researchers in which they attempted to explain their initial finding. For the present, the study serves to alert us to the fact that there is more than one way to obtain compliance from children. One involves calling on a preestablished relationship that implies mutual cooperation; the other is more difficult to define. It may involve some form of actual or implied coercion. Under direct coercion we include the use of direct requests and commands, punishment for transgression, and rewards for cooperation. Most parents undoubtedly mix both approaches, although the proportions in the mixture will vary from family to family.

There can be no doubt that direct pressure, varying in degree of coerciveness, is immediately effective. Patterson (1976) studied compliance and noncompliance in a microanalytic framework, and found that in his control sample of normal boys, mothers' use of counterpressure when their children attempted to coerce them reduced the children's uncooperative behavior in the ensuing brief time intervals. Yet the overall correlations between parent coerciveness and children's cooperativeness are negative. Lytton and Zwirner (1975) conducted a microanalysis of rates of compliance, and found that compliance increased (over base line levels) immediately following instances of parental physical control and negative action. Additional microanalytic studies by Lytton (1979) similarly demonstrated that commands increased the probability of compliance, although it should be noted that the commands were most effective when coupled with positive actions and least effective when accompanied by physical control techniques. And as was the case with the Patterson work, the moment-to-moment relationships are different from the more long-term correlations: In the same Lytton studies where coercive pressures led to immediate compliance, overall levels of compliance (base rates) were associated with the opposite parental behaviors—with *low* rates of material rewards for compliance, physical punishment for transgression, physical prohibition, and frequent demands and suggestions.

A study by Chapman (1979) yields similar apparently paradoxical findings. Children of either 4 or 6 years of age were brought to a laboratory room. The mothers were asked to get the children to work on tasks that were presented to the children as a way of earning money for a deaf child, or for a poor child who wanted to go to summer camp. During a portion of the session, the children were subjected to distraction in the form of an easily visible cartoon movie. At the end of the session, the mothers left the room, asking the children to continue working on the task alone. During this portion of the procedure, the distracting film was not present. Sequential analysis showed that during the distraction portion of the session, the probability that the children would maintain task concentration (not glance at the screen and away from their task) was higher if the mother had issued an imperative command in the preceding interval than if she had been using an inductive teaching style. By contrast, the children who worked most persistently at the task during the final portion of the session when they were alone were the children whose mothers had made more frequent use of inductive teaching methods. Taken together, these studies suggest that power-assertive methods work to obtain compliance in the short run, but that affection-based and inductive methods are more effective in establishing a willingness on the part of the child to comply to mild pressure, and increase the likelihood that compliance will generalize to situations where children are outside the reach of immediate parental pressure.

It is a reasonable hypothesis that the immediate effectiveness of power-assertive methods depends in part on generating some degree of fear in children. Landauer et al. (1970) considered the possibility that the reason children obeyed other children's mothers more readily than their own was that they were afraid of the strange adult, not of their mothers. In subsequent studies (Carlsmith, Lepper, & Landauer, 1974), they varied the fear-producing properties of a strange adult by allowing the child to see videotapes of strangers, one showing an adult who acted beneficently toward a group of children and another who acted in harsh, unfriendly ways. An additional feature of the experiment was to vary the mood of the children. Before the obedience session, some children saw a benign film designed to induce a happy mood, whereas others saw a frightening film (one chosen from standard Saturday morning TV fare!). The children were then brought into an experimental room where they encountered either the kindly adult they had seen on videotape, or the harsh adult; the adult directed them to do an onerous task. Children who were in a happy mood were more likely to obey the kindly adult. Children who had seen the frightening film were more likely to obey the harsh adult. This experiment illustrates the two different motive systems involved in compliance. Judging from the experiments reported above, we may predict that if generalization tests were done, children would be more likely to continue working on an assigned task in the absence of immediate surveillance, and would be readier to respond to mild suggestions, when in a happy mood and receiving suggestions from a person known to be kindly, and that the power of the harsh adult to exact compliance would erode rapidly under low-surveillance conditions. But this remains to be shown empirically.

We can see the possibility of both vicious and benign cycles here. Parents find that they can obtain immediate compliance by raising their voices and issuing orders rather than requests. However, in so doing they may be reducing their children's readiness to be cooperative on subsequent occasions. Thus if they have used power-assertive methods they must resort to them more and more frequently as time goes on. Ultimately power-assertive methods may lose their capacity to exact even immediate compliance unless pressures are escalated to very fear-producing levels indeed. The possibility of benign cycles quite clearly also exists. If parents succeed in obtaining compliance with inductive methods and cooperation-based appeals (partly by timing their requests to coincide with moments when they have the child's attention and have induced a positive mood), then the chances for obtaining willing compliance on subsequent occasions should be improved.

It remains to be seen what the relationship is, if any, between a cooperative attitude toward parents and the outcome of the child's later socialization encounters. Is there generalization of a cooperative attitude to the school setting, so that children who have become receptive to parents will be more ready to adapt themselves to schoolroom routines and persist at the learning tasks set for them by teachers? We have only the most tangential evidence on this subject. We know that children who are exceptionally resistive at home are likely to have poor relationships with teachers and peers at school, and to do poor academic work (Patterson, 1982). We know further that during the time following divorce, those children who show the most disrupted, noncompliant reactions to their mothers are the same children whose schoolwork deteriorates (Hetherington, Cox, & Cox, 1982). However, these pieces of information do not tell us whether the child's defiant attitude at home contributes independently in the complex causal nexus involved in such cases. It remains merely a strong hypothesis that the connections are meaningful.

An Alternative Dimensional Scheme

Firm parental control is usually only exercised when it needs to be—that is, when children do not readily respond to low-pressure requirements, or set appropriate requirements for themselves. The frequent occurrence of situations calling for firm con-

trol implies that socialization is already off to a bad start, in the sense that the parent-child pair frequently have conflicting objectives, and the two are not responsive to one another's subtle signals as to what is desired or expected by the partner. Much attention has been given to the means whereby family conflicts are resolved once they arise—that is, whether parents obtain compliance democratically or autocratically, openly or subtly, and whether the needs of both parents and children are met when the two conflict. Much less attention has been given to the factors that affect the amount and intensity of conflict that arises and requires resolution. It would be naive to believe that the parent-child relationship could ever be free of conflict. But families vary in the degree to which members feel that they have conflicting interests that must be bargained out, fought over, or pursued despite family opposition, as opposed to feeling that they are engaged in cooperative efforts in pursuit of common objectives. In some relationships, too, partners are motivated to please one another, so that the partner's goal quickly becomes the subject's goal even if it requires some effort or postponement of personal gratification on the subject's part.

Maccoby (1979) has argued that two orthogonal dimensions of family functioning need to be considered: (1) the direction of conflict resolution between parent and child, and (2) the frequency of occurrence of conflicts in which issues of control arise (see Figure 3). If the parent-child dyad is operating in Region D on the diagram, each participant is in a state of readiness to comply willingly to the other's moderately expressed demands. And the demands made are in the range already known to be acceptable to the partner. In the words of Edmund Muir, "Each asks from each what each most wants to give." The need for bargaining, or for dominance of one person over another, or for escalation of pressure by one person to obtain compliance from the other, seldom occurs, and thus the A-B-C dimension is not called into play. Moving from Region D toward B in the diagram, it may be seen that the more frequent and intense the conflict, the more salient does the conflict-resolution dimension become. In our view, the understanding of family processes will be greatly enhanced if serious consideration is given to the conditions that determine a family's ability to operate in Region D, and to the consequences, for the child's later development, of having been involved in the type of low-conflict interactions implied for this portion of the diagram.

In analyzing this kind of family functioning, we will not be able to do without the time-honored con-

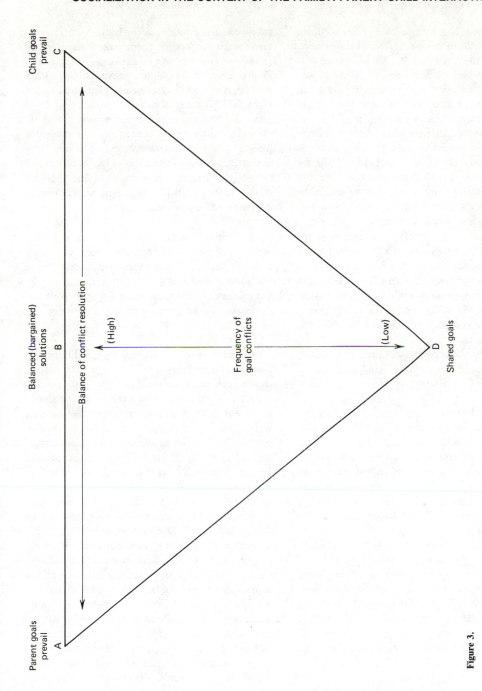

Figure 3.

cepts of warmth and identification, each no doubt redefined. A fresh perspective on identification comes from Abelson's work (1975) on observer perspectives. Abelson asked viewers of a filmed scene to imagine either that they were standing on a balcony watching an actor walk through a path, or to imagine that they were in the actor's place. The reactions to the scene, and the nature of the details recalled, differed according to the perspective taken. (See also Taylor, Etcoff, Fiske, & Laufer, 1979, for further demonstration of this phenomenon.) We suggest that in some families, members invest their egos in one another's activities in just this sharing-of-perspectives sense. If they take another family member's perspective, they participate vicariously in that other person's experiences. The construction of shared scripts, the sharing of goals, and the possibility of cooperative action, no doubt depend in part on such mutual identification. Thus identification—using the term in this more restricted sense—becomes both a consequence and a cause of operating in Region D.

We suggest some hypotheses concerning factors that may influence the ability of families to operate in the low-conflict region:

1. External stressors impinging on the family usually increase the salience of individual (as distinct from all-family) goals, and hence move the interaction away from Region D.

2. The increasing cognitive competence of the child is an enabling condition that permits, but does not require, more mutuality and fewer conflicts among family members' individual goals.

We base the second hypothesis on the fact that, in most families, episodes of overt parent-child conflict occur on the average much more frequently when children are young. For many families, then, the pattern is one of moving from the high-conflict to the lower conflict regions as the child grows older, with considerable interfamily variation in the rate and degree to which this movement takes place, and perhaps some reversal at adolescence.

3. At each developmental period of the parent-child relationship, the region in which the family operates will depend on the amount of conflict and the nature of its resolution at earlier periods.

Hypothesis 3 would imply, e.g., that early parental responsiveness, and the parent-sustained pseudodialogues in infancy—which can then become real (though limited) dialogues in the second

year—constitute money in the bank, on which parents can draw as it becomes more necessary for them to impose controls and refuse some of their children's demands. As children move into the middle childhood and adolescent years, their attitudes toward the legitimacy of parental authority no doubt plays an increasing role in whether conflicts are escalated and maintained. At each stage, the quality of prior relationship must have an impact on the quality of the relationships that can grow out of the child's developing capacities for interaction. But the nature of the cross-age linkages is something that is only beginning to be explored.

4. Frequent cooperative activity, in which the activities of each family member clearly contribute to group goals, will foster the subsequent readiness of all family members to function in Region D. The more salient the group goal (e.g., cooperative food-getting needed for group survival), the stronger the effect.

We have been considering the conditions that permit families to pursue joint goals through cooperative actions that involve the meshing of the streams of behavior of the individual participants. We should not overlook the possibility that there are costs as well as benefits associated with this mode of functioning. The tension between the need for relatedness to others and the need for individual autonomy pervades the writings of many personality theorists: See, for example, Erikson (1950) on intimacy versus isolation; Bakan (1966) on agency versus community. Baumrind (in preparation), in her emphasis on agency and communion as the dual goals of socialization, calls attention to the need for balancing objectives that may not be fully compatible. Our analysis has not solved the dilemma nor provided a formula for where the emphasis ought to go. We would like to suggest, however, that the two poles may not be so opposite as has been supposed. We have seen a number of indications that successful self-assertion in children is positively, not negatively, related to interactive skills and ability to operate within a reciprocal cooperative social system.

FACTORS INFLUENCING THE INTERACTION PATTERN

We have been considering the various ways in which parents carry out—or fail to carry out—their parental functions. So far, our primary concern has been with the mutual influences prevailing within the parent-child dyad, and with the impact the parent-child relationship has on various aspects of the child's development. Now we wish to consider some of the external factors that help to determine the nature of the parent-child interaction that occurs. By external, we mean factors arising outside the dyad, and the major factors we will consider in this section are (1) preexisting characteristics of the parents, and (2) external stressors and supports.

Characteristics of the Parents

To what extent do attitudes and characteristics of parents that existed before the birth of the child relate to the quality of the interaction that occurs with the child following its birth and to other components of the child's cognitive and social development? An early study by Becker et al. (1962) assessed a variety of parent personality characteristics which were assumed to have antedated the arrival of the child, and correlated these with child characteristics. They found that child conduct problems were most likely when both parents were maladjusted, when they frequently gave vent to unbridled emotions, and when the mothers were rated as tense. Shy, maladjusted, withdrawn, and insecure children tended to have fathers who were themselves maladjusted. Although we may assume that some of these parental characteristics had their origins in the parents' own youth, it is likely that some proportion also resulted from a history of difficult interactions with their problem children. In other studies, information about the parents' own socialization histories has been sought. Minde (1980), in his study of low-birthweight infants, found that two groups of mothers could be identified: those who were high-rate interactors, and those who interacted little with their infants. He found that mothers in the low-interaction group tended to have had low-quality relationships with their own mothers, according to their own retrospective report. Likewise, Morris (1981) found that infants who were insecurely attached tended to have mothers who had had disturbed relationships in their own families of origin, particularly with their fathers. These studies support the view that there is integenerational transmission of the forms family relationships might take. However, they do not entirely escape the chicken-and-egg problem. It is conceivable that, at least to some extent, parents rewrite their own histories when faced with a difficult child or difficult parent-child relations.

A more convincing argument can be made for parent effects when characteristics of the parents are actually measured before the birth of the child. Moss and Robson (1968) assessed the degree to which a

group of pregnant women looked forward positively to the birth of the infant and anticipated affectionate contact with it. They subsequently observed mother-infant interaction when the infants were 13 weeks old. They found that the prenatal maternal measures were positively related to the amount of mutual eye contact during interaction.

Moss and Jones (1977) similarly found that positive attitudes toward parenting, assessed prenatally, were correlated with mother responsiveness when the infants were 3 months old (although the relationship between attitudes and behavior was specific to a high-socioeconomic status group in this study). Shereshefsky and Yarrow (1973) found that nurturance, ego strength, and ability to visualize oneself as a mother, measured early in pregnancy, were related to overall adaptation to pregnancy, and that adaptation to pregnancy, along with interest in and experience with children, were in turn related to maternal adaptation after the birth of the child. Likewise, Leifer (1977) found that various characteristics of maternal personality, measured early in pregnancy, related to maternal psychological growth throughout pregnancy and through the early months of parenthood.

If these attitudes toward pregnancy and toward the birth of the child influence maternal adaptation and behavior after the birth of the child, we would expect the children of mothers with positive attitudes to benefit accordingly. In the Shereshefsky and Yarrow (1973) study, it was found that acceptance of the maternal role and confidence in the maternal role were related positively to various indices of infant physiological and psychological development through age 6 months. Davids, Holden, and Gray (1963) identified two groups of mothers during pregnancy: high- and low-anxiety mothers. The mothers in the high-anxiety group had infants who at 8 months had lower cognitive and motor scores, who were rated lower in general emotional tone, and who had poorer quality interactions with their mothers than infants with mothers in the low-anxiety group. Likewise, Heinecke and Diskin (1981) found that certain subscales from prenatally administered MMPIs correlated with infant Motor and Mental scores on the Bayley scale at both 6 and 12 months. Specifically, mother ego strength, attention, endurance, and basic trust were positively related to Bayley Mental scores, and mother persecutory ideas and "exquisite sensitivity" scores were negatively related to Bayley Motor scores. Kaplan, Eichler, and Winickoff (1980) studied both mothers and fathers during the mother's pregnancy, and did child assessments at birth, 2 months, and 1 year. Mother prenatal anxiety and depression were associated with infant irritability, low alertness, and low motor maturity at birth. The prenatal anxiety and depression of the mother, as well as her general life adaptation, were related to infant adaptation at age 2 months. Up to 2 months, there were no correlations with father measures. By age 1 year, however, infant cognitive, social, and motor development, as measured by a variety of indices, were correlated with a number of mother-father *relationship* scores obtained prenatally—particularly assessments of the quality of the sexual relationship between the parents.

A consistent picture emerges from these studies. Mothers who are well-adjusted adults and who look forward to the role transition to motherhood tend to adapt better to the period of pregnancy, and in turn tend to exhibit interest in and adaptation to their infants when they are born. This is a case, then, in which expectations about mothering result in real differences in behavior. (It should be noted that most of the studies described above involved primiparous mothers, so that the women were not drawing on their own previous experiences with the mothering role to form their expectations.) In addition, there is reason to believe that parent-infant relations are freer from tensions in families in which the parents recall having had good relationships with their own parents. Thus a mother's expectations about the experience of mothering appear to come, at least to some extent, from her own family of origin.

Mothers who have positive expectations about mothering and who act on these expectations by good adaptation to being a mother tend to have children with high levels of cognitive, social, and motor maturity. On the other hand, mothers who, before the child's birth were depressed or anxious, and who had poor relationships with their husbands, tended to have relatively immature children. It is at this point that we may presume the feedback loop gets under way: Mothers who have high expectations about the rewards of mothering adapt well to mothering, which in turn impacts on the course of their children's development; evidence of success—a happy, mature child—is likely to increase mothers' sense of efficacy, further reinforcing their expectations and adaptive behavior with respect to their children. In these cases, we see that maternal expectations very likely helped to get the relationship off to a good start,* but once under way, the nature of the parent-

child system makes it impossible to differentiate cause from effect.

External Stressors and Supports

Family interaction does not occur in a vacuum. It exists in a surround of social and ecological forces that impact on it in many ways. Bronfenbrenner, in his recent book *The Ecology of Human Development* (1979), has conceptualized family environments, and distinguishes between mesosystems and exosystems. Mesosystems refer to the relationships between two or more systems in which family members function, such as those between home and school or home and work place, and Bronfenbrenner suggests that members' participation in a variety of settings outside the home can have positive effects on family functioning and individual development so long as role demands and goals are compatible across settings. Exosystems are systems or settings in which family members do not participate directly, but that nevertheless establish some of the conditions of family life. Examples are the political and economic characteristics of the society in which the family lives, the program content of the available television fare, and the quality of the physical environment: air, water, or levels of noise. Aspects of the exosystem can have either positive or negative impacts on families.

The amount of research on the impact of external conditions on family function is limited, and what there is tends to emphasize stressors rather than growth-fostering conditions. There is an extensive body of sociological research on stressful conditions affecting families, and the moderators that determine the impact of such conditions. In much of this work, the outcome variables have to do with family functioning, such as incidence of marital conflict or divorce, levels of physical and mental health, or children's success or failure in school. We cannot hope to do justice to this literature, and the reader is referred to McCubbin et al. (McCubbin, Cauble, Patterson, & Comeau, 1981; McCubbin, Joy, Cauble, Comeau, Patterson, & Needle, 1980), Cobb (1976), Burke and Weir (1977), and to *Contemporary Theories about the Family* (1979, edited by Burr, Hill, Nye, & Reiss) for references and thoughtful discussion of some of this work. We will select for discussion here studies from both the sociological and psychological literature that directly examine parent-child interaction and relate it to varieties of stresses emanating from outside the parent-child relationship itself.

We begin with a very minor stress imposed experimentally, and then move to studies of stressors

---

*We cannot be entirely confident about the timing of the causal event, because the possibility exists that prenatal maternal anxiety has a direct effect on the fetus that carries over into the neonatal period, contributing to fussiness in the infant and consequent distress in the mother (see Thompson et al., 1962).

occurring naturalistically. Zussman (1980) worked with families having both a preschool child and a toddler. Either the mother or the father brought both children to an observation room, where there were play materials as well as opportunities for the children to get into mischief. In one condition, the parent was given a competing cognitive task, using no external materials (such as paper and pencil) that might signal the parent's preoccupation to the children. Compared to the control condition where the parent was not preoccupied, the parents under the competing cognitive task condition reduced their level of interaction with the preschool-aged children. They played with them less, gave less stimulation and support, and were less responsive to their bids for attention or help. With the toddlers, the preoccupied parents did not interact less, on the whole, but the quality of the interaction changed: They became more peremptory, more critical, more interfering. This "stress" is, of course, very mild and temporary, but it may serve as an indicator of the kinds of changes in parental behavior that may occur when parents become preoccupied with concerns that have nothing directly to do with the children; it also suggests that the nature of the change may depend on the developmental level of the child.

Forgatch and Wieder (reported in Patterson, 1982) obtained daily reports from a group of mothers concerning the occurrence of crises of varying magnitudes, including an unexpectedly large bill, a car breaking down, illness of a family member, quarrels between spouses. Mothers were also asked to report their moods. And on a number of occasions, observations were made of family interaction. One of the measures from the observations was the mother's *probability of continuance* of aversive behavior toward the child (also called "maternal irritability"). This measure reflects the likelihood that a mother who has behaved aversively (e.g., hit, scolded, yelled at, or refused to comply with her child) will do so again in the next interval of time, and is a measure that has been shown to differentiate the families of aggressive boys from those in a control sample. Forgatch and Wieder found that in some families, the mother's probability of continuance is substantially and significantly correlated with the day-to-day variations in the incidence of crises. In other families it is not. Indeed there are families in which the correlation is significantly negative—meaning, Patterson suggests, that there are some mothers who, under stress, withdraw from interaction. On the whole, however, the number of crises was a positive predictor of maternal irritability.

Patterson points to a circular process. He suggests that if a mother's reaction to crises is an increased probability of aversive behavior (irritability), this reaction interferes with competent family problem solving, and the lack of such problem solving means that unsolved problems accumulate and lead to an increased rate of crises. One study in which several sessions of family problem solving were videotaped permitted evaluating the quality of the problem solution arrived at by the family and also provided a frequency count of such negative behaviors as blame, command, complain, criticize, disagree, and impute guilt to others. The sum of such behaviors by the mother correlated negatively with the quality of the family's problem solving. And the mothers' negative behavior during the problem-solving sessions had a significant relationship to the current frequency of crises. (Patterson, 1982, p. 279).

It comes as no surprise that the frequency of crises is greater in poor families than well-to-do ones (Brown, Ni Bhrolchain, & Harris, 1975). The work described above linking the frequency of crises to deterioration in the quality of family problem solving strengthens the hypothesis that crises originating outside the family constitute one factor underlying social class differences in family problem-solving skills.

Divorce, of course, imposes major stress upon all members of the family system. Hetherington, Cox, and Cox (1976, 1979, 1982) have followed a group of families during several years following divorce, observing the interactions of each parent with the children on several occasions. The study was initiated at the time the legal divorce took place, usually following a period of marital separation. At this time the target children were 4 years old; in all the families included in the study, mothers were the custodial parent and fathers had visiting rights. The initial reports of the study deal primarily with the first 2 years following divorce, and chart a deteriorating relationship between parents and children. During the first year following divorce, mothers, on the average, became more authoritarian, increasing their number of direct commands and prohibitions and decreasing their responsiveness and affection-giving. The children, especially the boys, became less compliant and more aggressive. There was also a breakdown in family organization and routine: Meals were more haphazard, bedtime irregular, baths omitted, and so on. The children's relationship with the fathers changed, but in a different way. The fathers tended to withdraw from participation in rule enforcement, discipline, and management of the children's routines. There was an increase in indulgence and gift-giving. By the time 2 years had passed since the legal divorce, there was evidence of restoration of the balance in parent-child relationships. Fathers were becoming stricter, mothers more patient and communicative, children more cooperative. Routines were reestablished at home and during visiting periods with the noncustodial parent. But the restoration occurred at greatly varying rates in different families, the rate depending on a variety of factors such as the formation of new intimate relationships by one or both the parents, the mothers' employment, and the economic stability of her household.

Wallerstein and Kelley, too (1975, 1976, 1981), have documented what they call "diminished parenting" occurring at the time of divorce. They show that parents' intense preoccupation with their marital conflicts, and the emotional depression and agitated distress that frequently accompanies the divorce, reduce parents' ability to sustain interaction and communication with their children. Constructive problem-solving efforts directed toward the solution of parent-child conflicts are short-circuited, no doubt with the result Patterson has pointed to: the accumulation of unsolved problems that feed into increased conflict.

In both the work by Hetherington et al. and that by Wallerstein and Kelley, the question has been raised as to whether it is the stress of divorce that is responsible for the effects, or whether there is a selective factor such that people who divorce were poor problem solvers, and weak in parent-child communication and interaction, before the divorce. Hetherington et al. report that in their sample of "control" families, there are some who subsequently divorced; they say that on the average such families do not show, before their divorce, the pattern of disrupted parent-child interaction that characterizes families during the year following divorce. Wallerstein and Kelley, too, believe on the basis of their clinical evidence that divorce itself is an additional stressor for all family members, beyond the stresses imposed by the marital discord that led to the divorce.

It has become clear that crises do not always disrupt family functioning. Some families have effective means of coping with difficulties, others do not. Considerable research effort has been devoted to identifying the factors that affect family reactions to stressors, and social support systems have emerged as important. Wahler, Leske, and Roberts (1978) report that the families of antisocial children are "insular," by comparison with normal families. Members of such families have fewer contacts per day with persons outside the family, and the contacts they do have are less often with friends. Brown et al. (1975) report that the impact of crises on working-class women is modified if they have a close friend, relative, or husband with whom the problems can be supportively discussed. We should note, however, that such correlations mask a great deal of variation in the importance of external support. Patterson (in press) reports on a small number of families studied intensively, and finds that the patterns of covariation with the mother's irritability were unique to each family. For some mothers, it was the child's coerciveness, and no other factor, that appeared to influence her irritability. For other mothers, the number of community contacts significantly covaried with reactions to the child.

Relations with a spouse or lover appear to be of special significance in a mother's ability to sustain effective parental behavior. Earlier, we summarized several studies on the effects of fathers' attitudes toward mothers. Crnic and colleagues (Crnic, Ragozin, Robinson, & Basham, 1981) report that the presence of positive support in the form of an intimate spousal relationship during the first month following an infant's birth predicted positive affective responses between mother and infant several months later when their interaction was observed. Hetherington et al. (1976, 1979) report that even following divorce, the continuing support of the former husband matters: The mother-child relationship deteriorates less if the father not only provides economic support to the family but visits the children frequently and participates actively in their upbringing. If the contacts that do occur between the formerly married pair are relatively free of continuing conflict, this too is associated with higher levels of parent-child communication and lessened parent-child conflict. Rutter (1981) reports that in one sample, "broken homes" were not associated with antisocial behavior in children, whereas in a second sample, they were; in this second sample, the family breakup was less often followed by remarriage, so that more mothers were attempting to raise the children alone; and finally, the remarriages that did occur were less harmonious. These studies, and work by Colletta (1981), point to the importance of social supports in ameliorating the stress of divorce.

Child Abuse: An Illustration of Multiple-Risk Conditions

Research on child abuse provides researchers interested in the family a microcosm of extreme problems in parent-child relations. Typically, families of abused children are families in which the usual balance between reward and punishment, and between discipline and emotional bonding, have broken down; thus they are families that have ceased to function as effective media for the support of a child's social and cognitive development and as an arena for socialization.

A great deal has been written about the conditions that contribute to and maintain child abuse. (See a review by Parke & Collmer, 1975, for more detail on this research.) For the most part, researchers have attempted to describe characteristics of children and characteristics of parents in abusing families with an eye to learning something about "cause." The questions have been: What sorts of parents are most likely to be abusers, and what sorts of children are most likely to be abused?

Steele (1975) examined a group of case reports of abusing parents. He found that parents who abused their children were typically immature, were low in self-esteem, had a poor sense of their own competence, and were socially isolated without environmental support. In addition, they held a large number of misconceptions about children, had an orientation toward punishment as a remedy for family problems, and were generally unable to perceive or to understand their children's needs. Terr (1970) found that abusing parents reported that they were afraid of their children—specifically of perceived child helplessness and seductiveness. The parents also felt disappointed in their children's inability to meet their own preconceptions about what children are like and about what to expect in their relationships with their parents. Likewise, deLissovoy (1973) found that abusing parents were socially isolated, had little knowledge of child development, and had unrealistic expectations about their children. Bee, Disbrow, Johnson-Crowley, and Barnard (1981) studied abused children and their parents in a teaching situation, and compared them to a control group of parents and children. The abusing parents were less sensitive to their children's cues, and scored lower on fostering their children's socioemotional and cognitive functioning. Many researchers (e.g., Curtis, 1963; Fontana, 1973; Steele & Pollack, 1968) have noted that abusing parents are much more likely to have been abused themselves as children than are nonabusing parents.

Children may also contribute to abuse. In a study by Ounsted, Oppenheimer, and Lindsay (1974), abusing parents described their children as clingy, irritable, and likely to have sleep difficulties, to cry excessively, and to vomit frequently. Milowe and Lourie (1964) found that abused children were diffi-cult to manage, that they cried excessively, and that they were generally unappealing. Gil (1971) factor-analyzed descriptions of 1381 child-abuse cases, and found a "child-oriented abuse" factor to be dominant in 25% of the cases. This factor involved items that Gil described as "persistently behaviorally atypical": For example, the children were hyperaggressive, hyperactive, and had a high potential for annoyance. The deLissovoy study (1973) found that the abused children were restless, colicky and irritable, and that parents very frequently used the phrase "she (he) won't stop crying" in their descriptions of their abused children. Similarly, the Bee et al. (1981) study found that abused children's social cues were unclear, and that they were low in responsiveness to their parents. Parke and Collmer (1975) report that child abuse not only clearly reflects the adverse social and economic conditions in which many families live, but also that abuse is frequently an outcome of the demands that children place on their care givers, and that abused children are likely to be less physically attractive, have more aversive temperaments, and react less well to discipline than nonabused children. They report very strong evidence that low-birthweight children are more likely to be abused than normals, and cite the appearance and slow maturation of low-birthweight infants as possible explanations.

Their summary suggests that a wide variety of parent, child, and societal characteristics can contribute to abuse. Hay and Hall's (1981) study of 2- to 6-year-old abused and nonabused children and their mothers documents a wide range of differences in the mothers' behavior toward their children, in mother personality characteristics, and in child competence; and in their book on abused children, Steinmetz and Straus (1974) describe child abuse as part of a general pattern of violent interactions among family members.

The problem with the research we have described so far is that most of the studies involve descriptions of parents and of children already known to be involved in abusive interactions. Parents of abused children have personality difficulties and unrealistic views of their children; abused children are fussy, irritable, and unresponsive. But all of these characteristics of parents and children are plausible *outcomes,* as well as plausible causes, of a persistent pattern of abuse in the family. Even the finding that abusing parents tend to have come from abusing families is marred by the problems with retrospective data: Abusing parents may well exaggerate or otherwise distort their memories about discipline and violence in their families of origin. Is there any work that allows less ambiguous causal interpretation?

The physical appearance of abused children and the preponderance of low-birthweight children in abused samples surely qualifies. Johnson and Moore (1968) studied the case reports of children before the first report of abuse, and found that children who were later abused were described as fussy, whiny, listless, demanding, stubborn, unresponsive, and fearful. We cannot be completely certain in this last study, however, that these child characteristics did not result from differences in parental treatment— probably something less severe than full-blown abuse—before the first *report* of abuse.

Studies by Egeland and colleagues have shed light on the impact on abuse of parent characteristics that were measured before the birth of the child. They began with a sample of 267 economically disadvantaged expectant mothers, a group identified as being at risk for child abuse. Of these, 32 were identified later as abusers, and 33 as providing ''excellent'' care. They focused on these two extremes of the distribution, and examined differences in their prenatal assessments of the mothers in the two groups. Egeland, Breitenbucher, and Rosenberg (1980) found that, under conditions of high stress, mothers who were defensive, anxious, low in succor, low in social desirability, and high on expressed desire to control their infants turned out to be abusers. Brunnquell, Crichton, and Egeland (in press) report that the abusing mothers were less intelligent, more aggressive, more defensive, less socially desirable, and more anxious than the excellent-care mothers, that they had lower expectations about their infants and about themselves in the role of mothering, that they advocated inappropriate severity for the control of aggression in their children, and that they had low expectations about reciprocity in their relationship with their children.

Egeland and Sroufe (1981a) found differences in the quality of the mother-child relationship in the abused group, using Ainsworth's Strange Situation. They found that 50% of the children in the abused sample were categorized as resistant, compared to 10% in normals. For normal families, attachment patterns from 12 to 18 months were highly stable; in the abused group, attachment patterns were highly unstable, with much movement into the avoidant category.

From this work, it seems that child abuse is, indeed, a multidetermined phenomenon. External stresses and preexisting characteristics of the parents, of the children, or of both may spark patterns of abuse in the family, and it appears that little is needed to maintain the patterns of abuse once they are under way.

OVERVIEW, COMMENTARY, AND QUESTIONS

Interaction and Developmental Change

The emphasis on interaction has led us away from viewing parental behavior as something that is done *to* children, or *for* children, toward the view that it is done *with* children. The emphasis on the child's contribution to the interactive pattern has led to questions about the sequence of events that determine the path a parent-child relationship will follow over time. That is, the relationship established at an early point appears to have some bearing on the readiness of the child to enter into a cooperative relationship with parents as the subsequent steps in socialization are undertaken. However, work on the links between sequential phases of the parent-child relationship is only in its infancy.

The idea that developmental changes in the parent-child relationship involve a shift of regulatory functions from the parent to the child is a venerable one. We do not doubt that this transfer occurs. It also seems clear that there must be great differences among families in the rate and degree to which the transfer occurs, and in whether the child, in becoming self-controlling, monitors the self with respect to a set of criteria that are compatible with those the parents have used. We would like to suggest, however, that the developmental changes in regulatory functions can be seen in a different way: as a shift from parental regulation to *co*regulation. Thomas Weisner (personal communication, 1982) has argued that even in adulthood, individuals are seldom self-regulating. Rather, they are always embedded in social systems in which they must accept some degree of regulation from others while simultaneously exercising influence on these others. We saw that some degree of coregulation between the members of the parent-child dyad occurs even in infancy, but the degree to which the child is capable of participating in a coregulating system increases greatly with age. And as the child becomes increasingly capable of functioning outside the parent-child dyad, the shift in regulation that is occurring is only partly one of increases in self-regulation. In part, developmental change involves a shift from coregulated relationships within the family to coregulated relationships with persons outside the family.

The field of parent-child interaction research has been revitalized by contact with the methods and concepts of related disciplines, particularly social and cognitive psychology. But the potential benefits from these sources has only begun to be realized, and in our view they will not be realized until a more strongly developmental perspective is brought to bear. We need to give deeper thought to the way in which parents and children conceptualize one another: the mutual imputation of intent, and the level of understanding that they achieve concerning one another's plans and perspectives, and each person's rights and obligations. Surely such understandings determine their ability to construct linked social scripts from which both can act in an integrated way. And surely the nature of the mutually understood content must depend heavily on the level of cognitive development the child has achieved. Thus the work of students of social cognition, particularly in its developmental aspects, is of great and direct relevance to parent-child interaction, although its impact has only just begun to be felt.

Varieties of Parental Power Assertion

Our review of the research on the effects of various patterns of child rearing has revealed a picture that is fairly coherent in its broad outlines, though important questions remain. The picture is different in important ways from the one shown in Becker's (1964) fourfold table (see Figure 1). We have seen that immediate impacts and long-range impacts of certain parental behaviors may be different. Longer term impacts of children's interactions with parents have to do with the degree to which such interactions impede or foster the development of skills, the internalization of values, and processes of self-regulation. It has become clear that the development of children's autonomous competency is not maximally fostered by their parents' simply granting them autonomy. The family is the primary arena in which both social skills and aspects of self-regulation are learned, at least early in life. And not surprisingly, children's learning appears to be supported best by parents who quite explicitly take on the task of teaching. Fairly high levels of parent-child involvement, rather than disengagement, appear to be needed for the optimal development of social skills and ultimately for successful functioning independently of parents.

The parenting pattern that involves setting clear (and sometimes rather stringent) requirements for mature behavior, along with firm enforcement of these demands, is associated with self-reliance and high self-esteem, as well as with cooperative and prosocial behavior in children, so long as the high parental demands and firm control are accompanied by parental affection, attentiveness and responsiveness to the child's needs, and open communication with the child during family problem solving. Both theory and evidence point to the importance of parents' obtaining compliance to reasonable demands, and not yielding to children's coercive resistance, if children are to acquire acceptable and effective patterns of social behavior.

A dilemma is posed by the attribution theorists, however. They argue that the firmer and more salient parental control becomes, the more it is associated with loss of children's initiative, low internalization of values, and poor self-regulation. And indeed, we saw evidence that the use of power-assertive techniques, such as the issuance of imperative commands, was associated with children's complying with parental wishes so long as the parent was present, but that "softer" techniques such as induction were more likely to induce compliance when the child was presumably not under surveillance.

The solution to the dilemma that is offered by the attribution theorists is to suggest that warm, reasonable, and democratic parents usually employ just enough power assertion to secure compliance, whereas authoritarian parents are likely to employ more than is needed. In so doing, they make their power assertion highly salient, so that children inevitably attribute their own actions to external pressure. By contrast, the children of authoritative-reciprocal parents are able to believe (because parental pressure was mild) that they are behaving in desired ways because they wish to. We have agreed with this position in some respects, but have reformulated it. We have agreed that authoritative-reciprocal parents use milder pressure, on the average, but have argued that this occurs, at least in part, because they are able to get compliance with milder pressure than autocratic parents require. Probably mild pressure *is* less salient, and more compatible with internal attribution, than is strong pressure. Nevertheless, we must express some skepticism as to how often children of either kind of parents fail to perceive external pressure for what it is. Surely clear and firmly enforced directives, even when issued by affectionate and responsive parents, are rightly perceived as emanating from outside the child. Perry and Perry (in press) make a similar point, and argue that there is nothing to prevent behavior that was originally clearly required by external authority, and perceived as such, from becoming habitual and eventually forming part of the child's self-regulated and intrinsically motivated action patterns. We suggest an additional point: that when authoritative-reciprocal parents impose demands, these are less likely to arouse antagonistic responses than is the case when authoritarian parents impose demands of the same strength. We are suggesting that intrinsic motivation to behave as the parent wishes need not be based on internal attribution. Clearly we need more information on the way in which children growing up in families with different parenting styles perceive the locus of their own behavior and the legitimacy of their parents' demands.

The Role of Affect

Zajonc's recent article (1980) on the relation of feeling and thinking has focused the attention of psychologists once more on the importance of emotions. Zajonc presents evidence that emotions take priority over thought, in the sense that emotional reactions to stimuli tend to occur faster than most cognitions about these stimuli, and that cognitions are often brought to bear only to rationalize or justify emotional reactions that have already occurred. He argues that affect and cognition are "under the control of separate and partially independent systems that can influence each other in a variety of ways, and that both constitute independent sources of effects in information processing" (p. 151).

Recent work by Bower (1980) on state-dependent memory further underscores the influence of the emotional aspects of experience on cognitive processes. He shows that under conditions of positive mood induction, pleasant past experiences are brought to the forefront of current thinking, whereas past experiences having to do with failure are more likely to be retrieved during depressed or pessimistic moods. This work and that of Zajonc implies that experiences are tagged with affective labels, and that these labels have a great deal to do with the way in which past experience is brought to bear on current functioning.

Studies of mood induction similarly point to the importance of affective states. They indicate, among other things, that when either children or adults are in a positive mood, they are more likely to be concerned about the perspectives and needs of others. In negative mood states, they become more self-centered. Clearly, one implication is that children's emotional responses to parental behavior may be as important as, or more important than, the cognitive lessons they are learning during bouts of interaction. In discussing parental responsiveness to children,

we suggested that its importance lay in the fact that providing consistent contingencies for children's behavior fostered their sense of being able to control the events that impinge on them. In discussing children's compliance, we stressed its contribution to children's learning about mutual give-and-take, and emphasized the importance of a prior history of cooperative activities in building a repertoire of social skills. All these discussions had something of a cognitive bias. But it may be that the crucial element in all these interchanges is the children's emotional reactions to parental nonresponse or to parental pressures for compliance. What determines a child's emotional reactions to parental socialization pressures? In our review of compliance, we saw that parental warmth was a factor in children's willing acceptance of parental directive. Perhaps the crucial element in parental warmth is its role in establishing and maintaining a positive mood during interaction with children. How do parents establish positive moods? Through humor? Play? Making light of difficulties? Using affectionate tones and gestures? Stressing positive rather than negative outcomes? A small clue appears in the recent work of Campos and Goldsmith (1981), who showed that an infant's willingness to venture out onto a risky surface depended on the mother's facial expression of fear or confidence. We know little about how parents go about inducing positive moods, but surely it is an aspect of parental functioning that deserves more attention than it has received. And, of course, the induction of negative mood states ought to matter greatly as well. We saw evidence for the strong emotional loading of withdrawal of love, and its importance when it accompanies other socialization techniques. Parents' communication of being worried or depressed (even if children cannot understand the reasons for these states) ought to pin negative affective labels on a variety of early experiences and make them salient for the child's later functioning whenever a matching mood state occurs. We suggest a hypothesis: It may be parents' own affective reactions, rather than the cognitive content of their communications, that have the greatest impact on their children's affective reactions, particularly in early childhood. Malatesta and Haviland (1981) have reported that as early as ages 3 to 6 months, mothers high in emotional expressiveness have infants who are unusually prone to displays of joy and excited interest.

Two venerable psychoanalytic hypotheses are relevant here: (1) that affective reactions are strong and highly resistant to change; and (2) that one consequence of the arousal of strong negative affect is repression. The second hypothesis implies that certain areas of experience become to some degree shut away from rational thought and rational problem solving, but that the emotional reactions connected with these areas remain strong and continue to have an influence on behavior. Indeed, repression is assumed to contribute to the enduring quality of certain emotional reactions, by protecting them from being accessible to developmentally changing cognitive processes. Although current research has turned away from these hypotheses, the Zajonc article reminds us that they have never been refuted, and indeed, that they are alive and well. One could take an extreme position that it is precisely in the area of emotional reactions that early parent-child interactions should have their most enduring effects. If affect and cognitions are indeed independent systems to some degree, then the possibility exists that they are subject to different degrees of developmental change. We know that cognitions undergo enormous transformations in the course of normal development. It could be argued that emotions change much less. Thus specific emotional reactions that a child learns early in life have a chance of enduring in a way that would be impossible for specific cognitions.

We do not believe that an extreme position of this kind can be unreservedly accepted. Emotions *do* undergo developmental change. At least the frequency of episodes of intense emotional disturbance declines rapidly with age, and there is reason to believe that the acquisition of the ability to regulate emotional states—to control impulses—is closely linked to cognitive development. Furthermore, despite later counterevidence, Schachter and Singer's claim (1962)—that the nature of an emotion (even its positive versus negative direction) depends on cognitive labeling—still contains a kernel of truth, at least in its insistence that affect is influenced by cognition as well as vice versa. Thus if cognitions change developmentally, so must the emotional reactions that depend on them.

Nevertheless, it may be valid to make some distinctions between emotional and cognitive development, and to consider the possibility that in some degree different conditions (and therefore different aspects of socialization) govern acquisition and developmental change in the two systems. It must also be true that the balance between them changes with age. It is reasonable to believe, for example, that the contribution of affective reactions to the total "meaning" of an interaction with another person, relative to the contribution of cognition, is greater in early childhood than it will be later. Parke (1974) found that among children of ages 3–6, the rationale

accompanying punishment made a difference in its effect. It is likely that it would make considerably less difference for younger children. And it becomes quite reasonable that Zahn-Waxler et al. (1979) found, with 2-year-olds, that it was the degree of affective intensity accompanying the mothers' verbal reactions to the children's distress-producing behavior, rather than the use of explanations per se, that influenced the amount of sympathetic arousal and helpful action that the children displayed over other persons' distress.

What kind of affective learning might children be doing during their early interaction with their parents? In discussing the interaction of parents and infants, we emphasized the function of these interactions in teaching the child some simple mini-scripts (e.g., alternation) that could be made use of later in a variety of sociointeractional contexts. But it is likely that in these early interactions, infants are learning something else as well: namely, the sharing of affect. A major finding of the research on parent-child interaction in the first 2 years is that affective matching occurs. When children repeatedly experience situations in which their affective state is matched to, or shared with, that of another person, this provides the conditions for the acquisition of conditioned empathic emotional responses. All we need to assume, in order to know that empathic learning must be taking place, is that children are innately capable of having their emotions classically conditioned. If they are, then under conditions of repeated affective matching, the signs of certain emotional states in familiar other persons will soon acquire the power to elicit similar emotional states in the child. The frequency and consistency with which parents do match their children's emotional states, and the parents' emotional expressiveness, thus become important aspects of parental behavior that may explain some of the variance in children's readiness to respond empathically.

What about the affective "tags" that parental reactions may help to attach to children's experiences and hence to their stored record of these experiences? We have seen that being held by an adult who is a primary attachment object for the child can reduce the child's physiological distress reactions. At the very least, such experiences should cause the child to attach the marker "good," "pleasant," or "comforting" to close physical contact with another human being. In addition, the label "fearful" might be less likely to be attached, say, to novel settings. On the negative side, parents produce states of fear and anxiety in their children through the pain of physical punishment and the threat of such punishment, through yelling, through the more subtle manipulations involved in withdrawal of love, and perhaps simply through the sheer amount of anger expressed. What kind of long-term residues might result? Surely anxiety over arousing the displeasure of a loved person is a likely outcome; perhaps also, wary reactions to authority figures of all kinds could be predicted. We do not know what the patterns of generalization are, and surely these will be affected by cognitive level in that they must depend on the nature of children's classification systems. The main point, however, is that parents undoubtedly play a crucial role in establishing some emotional reactions that are primary in the Zajonc sense. The exact nature of the connections, however, and whether they transform themselves in any systematic way with children's development, are matters that are poorly understood.

It has proved to be extraordinarily difficult to put these questions to empirical test. We still do not know, for example, whether there are fears engendered through early-childhood socialization experiences that persist in phobia-like fashion and are highly resistant to modification through subsequent experience. Whiting and Child (1953), using cross-cultural evidence amassed by anthropologists, found that in societies that use considerable punishment in connection with weaning, adults tend to have higher than average levels of "oral anxiety," as manifested by their attributing disease to food ingestion. Psychologists, however, are not likely to be satisfied with such societal levels of analysis. There have been a few demonstrations of long-term emotional effects using individual measures: Sears (1961) showed that a high level of punishment for aggression when children were of kindergarten age was moderately associated with these children's having high anxiety over aggression several years later. Hoffman and Saltzstein (as reported in Hoffman, 1970) found that parents' frequent use of withdrawal of love and their strong reactions to children's parent-directed aggression were associated with children's showing strong guilt reactions over the arousal of their own impulses. Furthermore, children treated in these ways tended to push their own impulses out of awareness. On the whole, however, psychologists have not been notably successful in finding ways to trace the long-term effects of early anxiety induction by parents. Here, we merely wish to call attention to the fact that, although these issues have gone out of fashion and are currently rarely studied, they still hold considerable promise as powerful predictive factors.

How Much Variance is Being Accounted for?

In our review, many studies were cited in which significant relationships were found between aspects of parental functioning and characteristics of children. However, we have given more attention to the positive findings than to the studies in which no significant relationships have emerged. And in most cases, the relationships that have appeared are not large, if one thinks in terms of the amount of variance accounted for. Many studies involve the measurement of a fairly large number of characteristics of both parents and children, so that the question must be raised as to whether the number of significant correlations exceeds the number to be expected by chance. In the long run, the only way to pick out the robust findings is replication. Although explicit replication studies are rare, certain consistent themes have appeared in many studies involving different methods of assessment and different outcome variables, so that a picture of what constitutes "competent" or "skillful" parenting is beginning to emerge. Nevertheless, the trends are sufficiently weak that it is evident that there must be a very large number of exceptions to them. There are many cases in which either authoritarian or permissive parenting seems to work as well as the authoritative-reciprocal pattern that emerged as optimal in a number of studies.

A sobering set of findings has been emerging from studies of intrafamilial correlations in personality characteristics. Biologically unrelated children growing up in the same households are shown to be quite unlike (i.e., their scores are uncorrelated) with respect to personality characteristics measured by standardized personality scales (Rowe & Plomin, 1981; Scarr et al., 1981). Even for biologically related siblings, correlations are low.

These findings imply strongly that there is very little impact of the physical environment that parents provide for children and very little impact of parental characteristics that must be essentially the same for all children in a family: for example, education, or the quality of the relationship between the spouses. Indeed, the implications are either that parental behaviors have no effect, or that the only effective aspects of parenting must vary greatly from one child to another within the same family.

We do not doubt that there is a great deal of variance within families in the quality of the relationships parents have with each individual child. Some of the variance is accounted for by birth order (cf. Lasko, 1954; Rothbart, 1971; Snow, Jacklin, &

Maccoby, 1981) and by the sex of the child (Block, 1979; Maccoby & Jacklin, 1974); other factors, such as the temperamental match between parent and child, no doubt enter in as well. We have woefully little information on intrafamilial variation in the nature of the parent-child relationship, and what we do have has looked for differences rather than similarities. Thus the birth-order studies give mean differences between the treatment of firstborns and later borns, but it is rare indeed to find a report of the correlations, over a group of mothers or fathers, in the child-rearing techniques they use with two or more children. The isolated bits of information available on such relationships show some congruence in child-rearing techniques used with the different children within a family. Rowe and Plomin (1981) show significant congruence between the reports by twins concerning how psychologically controlling or how firm (vs. lax) in discipline their parents are. Patterson (1982) reports that, within the families of aggressive children, all family members tend to be coercive toward one another; and Bryant and Crockenburg (1980) report consistency in the observed maternal behavior toward two daughters. The correlations in this study range from .26 for the degree of control exercised by the mother, to .49 for maternal sensitivity-responsiveness, to .78 for unsolicited disapproval. These findings alert us to the likelihood that parents may treat their different children similarly in some respects and differently in others; we ought to expect therefore that insofar as parental inputs are important in children's development, siblings ought to be similar in some respects and different in others. We must delve beneath the global personality scores derived from standardized self-administered personality tests to look for more differentiated aspects of behavior and development that bear closer theoretical relationships to the aspects of parenting that are or are not congruent across siblings. Even more important, however, we need longitudinal tracing of the parent-child relationships of two or more children within the same family (Scarr & Grajek, 1982), in order to elucidate the contributions of individual characteristics of parent and child. Also we need to consider aspects of family structure, such as the role differentiation that is presumed to occur among children. Meanwhile, the data on sibling correlations remind us that the contributions of parental practices to children's personality development may not be very great if parental behaviors are taken in isolation; rather, it is when they are considered as part of an interactive system between parent and child—a system that is in some respects unique to each parent-child relationship, even within the same family—that their impact can be understood.

Cross-Cultural Generality

It is possible that the impact of individual parental characteristics on individual children may depend on the cultural setting in which families function. In their article on egoism and altruism (1973), Whiting and Whiting report that a group of children of a given age in a given society may differ consistently from a like-age group of children in a different culture with respect to an observed characteristic such as sharing or helping, and that the differences are related to aspects of the socialization training the children receive. At the same time, within-culture correlations (relating the characteristics of children to the child-rearing or living conditions of their individual parents) are not found. In a summary article, Beatrice Whiting (1980) suggests that children learn to adapt behaviorally to the specific demands of the various settings they are in, and that the primary way in which parents "shape" their children is by assigning them to specific settings (to places, tasks, and the company of other persons of a specific age and sex). Children then develop primarily the characteristics that are elicited by the major settings in which they have participated.

We have presented evidence that children's optimal functioning is associated with fairly high levels of mutual involvement between parent and child, with mutual responsiveness and compliance, accompanied by a negotiating (rather than power-assertive) style of conflict resolution when conflicts arise. Among American middle-class families, and perhaps among middle-class families in other industrialized societies as well, this appears to be the pattern that carries a relatively low risk of deviance in the children. In making such generalizations we are, of course, glossing over enormous variations in family styles and in the individual personalities that emerge from the family system. In stressing the familial origins of deviance, we are dealing with only the most molar outcomes. But even on this level, one must ask whether the generalizations are valid for other times, for other societies, and for all subcultural groups within the societies that have been studied.

The observations of the Whitings and their colleagues (Whiting & Whiting, 1973, 1975) indicate that in small, fairly homogeneous, nonindustrialized social groups the picture may be very different indeed. In these societies, there is relatively little interaction between adults and children after the infancy and toddler periods. Adults seldom negotiate with children over the merits of the adults' demands or the children's responses. It appears to be understood by both adults and children that the adults are in command and have a right to be so; a fair amount of indulgence may be shown toward children during their first 2 or 3 years, but after this point, fairly heavy demands (at least, heavy by middle-class American standards) may be placed on children, and if they resist, adults become power assertive. Effective control is exercised over the children's behavior, and with rare exceptions children grow up competent to step into the adult roles the society provides.

Clearly the nature of the parent-child interaction that occurs, and the nature of its outcomes, depends on the social structure within which a family is functioning. What are the societal conditions that determine whether it is the middle-class American pattern of frequent close and democratic interaction, or a more authoritarian pattern, that will prove best adapted to turning out well-socialized individuals? A number of possibilities come to mind:

1. *The degree of congruence between a given family's values and expectations and those of other parents in the society.* Presumably, more negotiation of rights and obligations is required when there are no societywide standards taken for granted by everyone. Explicit age-grading, perhaps accompanied by initiation rites or other clear markers of passage from one status to another, probably contribute to a clear definition of the rights and obligations of children of different ages vis-à-vis adults, and produce a high degree of uniformity within the members of a social group in their understanding of how children and adults are expected to behave toward one another.

2. *The degree of social surveillance to which children are subject both inside and outside the home.* Presumably, if children operate anonymously for a significant portion of time, it is more important that they be socialized in such a way that behavior patterns are internalized—that is, self-regulated. In some societies, where many family members share one or two rooms, and where dwellings are closely clustered with those of other families, children are seldom out of the sight or earshot of a potential socializing agent.

3. *The degree to which a child's future depends on the approval of parents and other members of the adult generation.* When the adults control the choice of a spouse, the inheritance of land, access to certain occupations, and other factors, it becomes necessary for children to conform to whatever authority structure the adults see fit to maintain. On the other hand, if members of a new generation succeed or fail "on their own," their compliance to adult demands must have a larger component of willing obedience based on affection or respect for the individual qualities of the adult making the demand. And once again, more negotiation must occur.

4. *The importance of all members cooperating with the authority structure of the group.* The value of the authority structure is much more salient in some social groups than others. No musician doubts the importance of all members of the orchestra following the conductor's beat. In a similar way, a group's success in obtaining food or defending its borders may quite obviously depend on the existence of a chain of command and on all members cooperating within this structure. We may assume that the sense of "shared fate" is greater in small face-to-face social groups than it is in large, complex societies where functions are highly differentiated and where the relation of an individual's conformity or effort to the viability of the society as a whole is often quite unclear.

No doubt readers will think of other considerations that might be added to this list. But the above list should be sufficient to call our attention to a basic point: Explicit social constraints can, in a sense, take the place of certain aspects of self-regulation. And further, the pattern of child rearing we have described as optimal—that is, firm control accompanied by high levels of cooperative parent-child interaction, democratic decision making, and mutual affection—is one primarily adpated to fostering children's self-regulation, and it therefore is of greatest value in those societies that lack the kind of strong external constraints listed above. Much less is known about the optimal socialization patterns in societies that do have such constraints, but we may hazard the guess that the child-rearing practices of individual parents may account for less of the variance among individuals in such societies.

Parents and Peers: Comparison of Their Roles in Socialization

In his familiar distinction between the morality of constraint and the morality of cooperation, Piaget (1965) argued that parents, by the very nature of their hierarchical relationship with the child, are limited in the influence they can have on the development of mature levels of moral understanding. He said (p. 36): "The very nature of the relations which the child sustains with the adults around him prevents this socialization from reaching the state of equilibrium which is propitious to the development of reason"—meaning, more specifically, the ability to take, in thought, the perspective of others. In a recent book, Youniss (1980) links the Piagetian view with that of Harry Stack Sullivan, showing that in both theories it is the relationship with peers (and *only* this relationship) that permits the occurrence of status-symmetrical exchange processes. These processes, which for Piaget included "continuous comparison, opposition, discussion, and mutual control," are thought to introduce children to new forms of interpersonal relationships—relationships that are qualitatively different from relationships with adults, in that they allow for the progressive redefinition of a relationship through democratic process, and yield a level of mutual understanding that is not possible between children and adults.

Early tests of Piaget's theory involved determining whether children who were subject to little adult constraint (and were presumably more heavily involved in the peer culture than in the family) achieved a higher level of moral reasoning (Johnson, 1962). The answer was negative. Indeed, children who continued to be closely involved with their parents had, on the average, higher levels of moral judgment. Youniss' own recent work takes a more sophisticated approach and asks a different question. He does not assess levels of moral judgment, but instead queries children concerning their understanding of social relationships, specifically their concepts of acts of kindness or unkindness as they occur in child-child pairs as compared with adult-child pairs. He shows a developmental progression through the age range 6–14, in which younger children stress giving, sharing, and playing together as reflecting kindness between persons, whereas older children add helping and mutual understanding, and begin to deemphasize simple sharing. He also shows some clear differences between child-child and child-adult relationships: In the former, sharing and play are paramount, whereas in the latter, kindness by a child to an adult is likely to involve being obedient, polite, or "good" (i.e., conforming to adult standards of behavior); and kindness by an adult to a child more often involves granting favors or giving permission. In his analysis of such protocols, Youniss distinguishes between two forms of reci-

procity. The first refers to the exchange of kindnesses or unkindnesses with a status equal:

> In a game, my friend let me go first. (Then) I let him sometimes use my ball.

or

> One kid says, "I will not walk to school with you." (Then) the other said, "I won't walk to school with you."

Such exchanges are contrasted with parent-child exchanges such as the following:

> When my mother asked, I swept the floor. (Then) she gives you a big dinner.

As children develop through the age range studied, Youniss shows that reciprocation with friends takes on a more differentiated form, where exchanges can involve differentiated roles (e.g., one offers comfort to the other who is sad) but where the expectation is that mutual support will balance out over time.

Youniss stresses that friendships are *voluntary:* Either party is free to withdraw, so that both parties must accept some obligation to act in ways that will sustain the friendship. Relationships between parents and children are powerfully constrained by societal obligations that do not need to rest on willing association.

Youniss shows that as children move into adolescence, elements of symmetrical reciprocity emerge between parents and children, though such elements continue to be mixed with the elements of respect-obedience and evaluation-control that characterize the authority relationship. He suggests that a certain amount of symmetrical reciprocation can occur between parent and adolescent, but argues that this occurs because the child has learned these modes of interaction earlier, through peer friendships. The implication is that such developments could not occur as part of the evolution of the parent-child relationship itself. In attributing the occurrence of symmetrical reciprocation between parents and children to the influence of the children's out-of-home learning, he agrees with Sullivan, both regarding the peer relationship as primary in certain respects. Youniss says: "Friendship is the originating source of adult intimate relations" (p. 233), and in discussing the value of adult guidance, he says:

> The present findings suggest that the norms which make intimacy possible may be logically

seen to arise from peers' conjoint efforts. By working together to establish and maintain relationships, peers can on their own evolve those principles which supply the logical material of what one would ordinarily call the backbone of mature morality. They are cooperation and equality. This is not to deny that child-adult relations may be a necessary background or context for development within the world of peers. It is, however, to suggest that they are causally secondary. (p. 234)

Youniss clearly documents qualitative differences in the adult-child versus the child-child relationship as conceived by children. Nevertheless a reader only partially committed to the Piaget-Sullivan thesis will note a surprising degree of overlap in children's conceptions of the two kinds of interchanges. Children often see themselves doing favors for adults rather than merely obeying. Certain child-adult interchanges involve sharing and play. Children often believe, when they do things they know will please their parents, that they are doing them *willingly* and not because of expected rewards or feared punishments. And many child-child interchanges are complementary rather than symmetrical, having the quality of currying favor from a status superior. Thus the protocols presented in the book can be interpreted as showing both differences and similarities in the way children conceive their interactions with the two categories of other persons. Elements of reciprocity of the kind that, according to the Piaget-Sullivan thesis, ought to be unique to the peer relationship can be found in the adult-child relationship, although authority-oriented elements are strongly present as well. Although Youniss does not deal with variations among families in the nature of the parent-child relationship, there is good reason to believe that considerable variation does exist in the degree of mix between authority-oriented and more status-equal forms of reciprocity. If this is so, the interesting questions become: In what way, and to what degree do some families succeed in blending these disparate elements? Is the blending necessarily age linked? Can certain reciprocal relationships with parents have similar effects to the effects of peer relationships? When egalitarian elements are present in the parent-child relationship, are these indeed the outcome of the child's peer experience?

A book by Elder (1980) bears on these issues. Elder's book reports the major finding of the Adolescent Project, conducted under the direction of Charles Bowerman, using data that were collected at the University of North Carolina during the late 1950s and early 1960s. Elder also reviews findings from other studies. He points out that the early studies of adolescents' relationships to parents and peers placed the two classes of relationships in opposition. Peer relationships were thought to develop at the expense of closeness with parents. Movement into the youth culture was thought to be an inevitable fact of adolescent development, with a concomitant weakening of the parent-child bond, and an ascendancy of peers as a source of influence on the adolescent's value system. Subsequent research, however, led to a more differentiated picture. It was found that the strong shift to dependence on peers for value orientation occurred primarily among youth whose parents were uninvolved, inattentive, and unsympathetic toward their children. Indeed, for some such children, there was alienation from *both* parental values and the predominant peer culture.

It began to appear that despite the adolescent's striving to gain progressive freedom from parental authority, for most adolescents there was considerable continuity in the relationship with parents, and acceptance of their values. Furthermore, it was not necessarily the case that peer norms conflicted with parental norms. Youths who had close relationships with their parents tended to choose friends whose values were congruent with those of their parents. School achievement formed part of the picture. Adolescents who were doing poorly in school, including eventual dropouts, tended to rely heavily on the values of a subgroup of similar peers. Those performing at or above average academically remained bound into the parental value system. This did not preclude their being active in peer interaction, but on the contrary seemed to foster their social competence. The characteristics of parents that were associated with adolescents' continued acceptance of parental values included a combination of independence fostering and continued guidance. Control was relaxed but not abandoned during the adolescent years, and when parents did exercise control they felt the obligation to justify and explain their actions, rather than merely to impose controls arbitrarily. Furthermore, there continued to be joint activities that all family members enjoyed and participated in. And in families where the parents and adolescents were positively oriented toward one another, decision making tended to be shared between the parents, rather than dominated by either mother or father.

Congruent results were obtained by Kandel and Lesser (1972), who studied large numbers of secondary school students in the United States and Denmark. Youth in both countries reported greater reliance on parents than on peers in developing personal standards for conflict resolution, and the sense of autonomy—of being able to exercise valid independent judgment—was greater among youth whose parents used frequent explanations, who relaxed parental control during adolescence (by comparison with preadolescent levels), and who employed a democratic structure of decision making within the family.

The familiar issue of circular process must be raised once more in connection with these studies. Successful governance of adolescents by parents depends heavily on the consent of the governed. In modern societies, particularly in the United States, there are few forces other than mutual goodwill keeping parents and adolescents in contact with one another. Youth usually have free access to the refrigerator, so that many adolescents can avoid sitting down to meals with their parents, thus eliminating one of the major settings in which joint decision making or parental control traditionally occurred. The adolescent's future seldom depends on inheriting family land or taking a place in a family business, so that access to a desirable life path is only minimally controlled by parents (except for parental willingness to finance college education). Thus the conclusion that joint family activities, parental democratic practices, and parental use of explanations contribute to adolescents' developing values that are congruent with those of their parents could just as well be rephrased as follows: Children who have similar values to their parents' are more willing to join them in activities, listen to their explanations, and participate with them in democratic decision making.

We conclude our chapter, then, by restating a question that has arisen repeatedly during our review. When events impinge on a family, to what extent does the effect on the family depend on the history of the relationship among the family members? We have argued for the power of cumulative cognitions and expectations developed by parents and children about one another. We have also claimed that as families encounter new socialization issues that are appropriate to new phases of the child's development, a family's success in handling the issues will depend on the already developed willingness of the partners to accept influence from one another. Yet we know that the family is an open system, subject to change. Are there critical events, or forms of intervention, that can radically alter the mutual cognitions and mutual receptiveness among family members? Clearly we need to know much more than we do about the conditions that determine both stability and change in family relationships,

and these issues deserve a high priority on our research agenda.

REFERENCES

Abelson, R. P. Does a story understander need a point of view? In R. C. Schank & B. Nash-Webber (Eds.), *Theoretical issues in natural language processing.* Cambridge, Mass.: Bolt, Beranek & Newman, 1975.

Ainsworth, M. D. S., & Bell, S. M. Some contemporary patterns of mother-infant interaction in the feeding situation. In A. Ambrose (Ed.), *Stimulation in early infancy.* New York: Academic Press, 1969.

Ainsworth, M. D. S., & Bell, S. M. Mother-infant interaction and the development of competence. In K. Connolly & J. Bruner (Eds.), *The growth of competence.* London: Academic Press, 1974.

Ainsworth, M. D. S., Bell, S. M., & Stayton, D. J. Individual differences in strange situation behavior of one-year-olds. In H. R. Schaffer (Ed.), *The origins of human social relations.* London: Academic Press, 1971.

Aldous, J. Family interaction patterns. *Annual Review of Sociology,* 1977, *3,* 105–135.

Anderson, B. J., Vietze, P., & Dokecki, P. R. Reciprocity in vocal interactions of mothers and infants. *Child Development,* 1977, *48,* 1676–1681.

Apolonio, F. J. Preadolescents' self-esteem, sharing behavior, and perceptions of parental behavior. *Dissertation Abstracts,* 1975, *35,* 3406B.

Aronson, E., & Carlsmith, J. M. The effect of severity of threat on the devaluation of forbidden behavior. *Journal of Abnormal and Social Psychology,* 1963, *66,* 584–588.

Bakan, D. *The duality of existence: Isolation and communion in western man.* Boston: Beacon Press, 1966.

Bakeman, R., & Brown, J. V. Behavioral dialogues: An approach to the assessment of mother-infant interaction. *Child Development,* 1977, *48,* 195–203.

Bakeman, R., & Brown, J. V. Early interaction: Consequences for social and mental development at three years. *Child Development,* 1980, *51,* 437–447.

Baldwin, A. L. Socialization and the parent-child relationship. *Child Development,* 1948, *19,* 127–136.

Baldwin, A. L. The effect of home environment on nursery school behavior. *Child Development,* 1949, *20,* 49–62.

Baldwin, A. L. *Behavior and development in childhood*. New York: The Dreyden Press, 1955.

Baldwin, A. L., Kalhoun, J., & Breese, F. H. Patterns of parent behavior. *Psychological Monographs*, 1945, *58*(3).

Baldwin, J. M. *Social and ethical interpretations in mental development*. New York: Macmillan, 1906.

Bandura, A. Social learning theory of identificatory processes. In D. A. Goslin (Ed.), *Handbook of socialization theory and research*. New York: Rand-McNally, 1969.

Bandura, A. Analysis of modeling processes. In A. Bandura (Ed.), *Psychological modeling?* Chicago: Aldine-Atherton, 1971.

Bandura, A. Modeling theory: Some traditions, trends and disputes. In R. D. Parke (Ed.), *Recent trends in social learning theory*. New York: Academic Press, 1972.

Bandura, A. *Social learning theory*. Englewood Cliffs, N.J.: Prentice-Hall, 1977.

Barnard, K. E. *Maternal involvement and responsiveness: Definition and developmental course*. Paper presented at the Second International Conference on Infant Studies, New Haven, Conn., 1980.

Barry, W. A. Marriage research and conflict: An integrative review. *Psychological Bulletin*, 1970, *73*, 41–54.

Bates, E., Camaioni, L., & Volterra, V. The acquisition of performatives prior to speech. *Merrill-Palmer Quarterly*, 1975, *21*, 205–226.

Bates, J. E., Freeland, C. A. B., and Lounsbury, M. L. Measurement of infant difficulties. *Child Development*, 1979, *50*, 794–803.

Bates, J. E. Detailed progress report on ''Difficult Infants and their Mothers''. Unpublished report, Indiana University, 1980 (a).

Bates, J. E. The concept of difficult temperament. *Merrill-Palmer Quarterly*, 1980(b), *26*, 299–319.

Baumrind, D. Child care practices anteceding 3 patterns of preschool behavior. *Genetic Psychology Monographs*, 1967, *75*, 43–88.

Baumrind, D. Current patterns of parental authority. *Developmental Psychology Monograph*, 1971, *4*(1, Pt. 2).

Baumrind, D. *Socialization determinants of personal agency*. Paper presented at the meeting of the Society for Research in Child Development, New Orleans, March 27–30, 1977.

Baumrind, D. *Sex-related socialization effects*. Paper presented at the meeting of the Society for Research in Child Development, San Francisco, 1979.

Baumrind, D. *Family socialization and developmental competence in middle childhood*. Book in preparation.

Baumrind, D., & Black, A. E. Socialization practices associated with dimensions of competence in preschool boys and girls. *Child Development*, 1967, *38*, 291–327.

Bearison, D. J., & Cassel, T. Z. Cognitive decentration and social codes: Communication effectiveness in young children from differing family contexts. *Developmental Psychology*, 1975, *11*, 29–36.

Becker, W. C. Consequences of different kinds of parental discipline. In M. L. Hoffman & L. W. Hoffman (Eds.), *Review of child development research* (Vol. 1). New York: Russell Sage Foundation, 1964.

Becker, W. C., Peterson, D. R., Luria, Z., Shoemaker, D. J., & Hellmer, L. A. Relations of factors derived from parent-interview ratings to behavior problems of five-year-olds. *Child Development*, 1962, *33*, 509–535.

Bee, H. L., Disbrow, M. A., Johnson-Crowley, N., & Barnard, K. *Parent-child interactions during teaching in abusing and non-abusing families*. Paper presented at the meeting of the Society for Research in Child Development, Boston, 1981.

Bell, R. Q. A reinterpretation of the direction of effects in studies of socialization. *Psychological Review*, 1968, *75*, 81–95.

Bell, R. Q. Research strategies. In R. Q. Bell & L. V. Harper (Eds.), *Child Effects on adults*. Hillsdale, N.J.: Erlbaum, 1977.

Bell, R. Q., & Harper, L. V. (Eds.). *Child effects on adults*. Hillsdale, N.J.: Erlbaum, 1977.

Bell, S. M., & Ainsworth, M. D. S. Infant crying and maternal responsiveness. *Child Development*, 1972, *43*, 1171–1190.

Belsky, J. Mother-father-infant interaction: A naturalistic observational study. *Developmental Psychology*, 1979, *15*, 601–607.

Benson, L. *Fatherhood: A sociological perspective*. New York: Random House, 1968.

Biller, H. B. *Father, child and sex role*. Lexington, Mass.: Heath, 1971.

Biller, H. B. The father and sex role development. In M. E. Lamb (Ed.), *The role of the father in child development* (2nd ed.). New York: Wiley, 1981.

Block, J. A comparison between ipsative and normative ratings of personality. *Journal of Abnormal and Social Psychology*, 1957, *54*, 50–54.

Block, J. *Lives through time*. Berkeley, Calif.: Bancroft Books, 1971.

Block, J. H. Another look at sex differentiation in

the socialization behavior of mothers and fathers. In J. Sherman & F. L. Denmark (Eds.), *Psychology of women: Future directions of research*. New York: Psychological Dimensions, 1979.

Block, J. H., & Block, J. The role of ego-control and ego-resiliency in the organization of behavior. In W. A. Collins (Ed.), *Development of cognitive affect, and social relations,* Minnesota Symposium on Child Psychology (Vol. 13). Hillsdale, N.J.: Erlbaum, 1980.

Bower, G. *Emotional mood and memory*. Address to the American Psychological Association, Montreal, 1980.

Bowlby, J. *Attachment and loss,* vol. 1, *Attachment*. New York: Basic Books, 1969.

Bowlby, J. *Attachment and loss,* vol. 2, *Separation, anxiety and anger*. New York: Basic Books, 1973.

Brazelton, T. B., Koslowski, B., & Main, M. The origins of reciprocity: The early mother-infant interaction. In M. Lewis & L. A. Rosenblum (Eds.), *The effect of the infant on its caregiver*. New York: Wiley, 1974.

Brekstad, A. Factors influencing the reliability of anamestic recall. *Child Development*, 1966, *37*, 603–612.

Bronfenbrenner, U. Developmental research, public policy and the ecology of childhood. *Child Development*, 1974, *45*, 1–5.

Bronfenbrenner, U. *The ecology of human development*. Cambridge, Mass.: Harvard University Press, 1979.

Bronson, W. C. Mother-toddler interaction: A perspective on studying the development of competence. *Merrill-Palmer Quarterly,* 1974, *20*, 275–301.

Brown, G. W., Ni Bhrolchain, M., & Harris, T. O. Social class and psychiatric disturbance among women in an urban population. *Sociology,* 1975, *9*, 225–254.

Bruner, J. S. The ontogenesis of speech acts. *Journal of Child Language*, 1975, *2*, 1–19.

Brunnquell, D., Crichton, L., & Egeland, B. Maternal personality and attitude in disturbances of child-rearing. *Journal of Orthopsychiatry,* in press.

Bryant, B. K., & Crockenberg, S. B. Correlates and dimensions of presocial behavior: A study of female siblings with their mothers. *Child Development*, 1980, *51*, 529–544.

Bugenthal, D. B., Caporael, L., & Shennum, W. A. Experimentally produced child uncontrollability: Effects on the potency of adult communication patterns. *Child Development*, 1980, *51*, 520–528.

Bugenthal, D. B., & Shennum, W. A. *Adult attributions as moderators of the effects of shy vs. assertive children*. Paper presented at the meeting of the Society for Research in Child Development, Boston, 1981.

Burger, G. R., & Armentrout, J. A. A factor analysis of 5th and 6th graders' reports of parental child-rearing behavior. *Developmental Psychology,* 1971, *4,* 483.

Burke, R. J., & Weir, T. Marital helping relationships: The moderators between stress and well-being. *Journal of Psychology,* 1977, *95,* 121–130.

Burr, W. R., Hill, R., Nye, F. I., & Reiss, I. L. (Eds.). *Contemporary theories about the family,* vol. 1, *Research-based theories*. New York: Free Press, 1979.

Burton, R. V. Honesty and dishonesty. In T. Lickona (Ed.), *Moral development and behavior*. New York: Holt, Rinehart & Winston, 1976.

Bussey, K. *The role of beliefs about self and others in the sex-typing process*. Paper presented at the meeting of the Society for Research in Child Development, Boston, April 1981.

Cairns, R. B. Social interactional methods: An introduction. In R. B. Cairns (Ed.), *The analysis of social interactions: Methods, issues and illustrations*. Hillsdale, N.J.: Erlbaum, 1979.

Cairns, R. B., & Green, J. A. How to assess personality and social patterns: Observations or ratings? In R. B. Cairns (Ed.), *The analysis of social interactions*. Hillsdale, N.J.: Erlbaum, 1979.

Campos, J. J., & Goldsmith, H. *A longitudinal twin study of infant temperament and emotionality*. Paper presented at the meeting of the International Society for the Study of Behavioural Development, Toronto, August 1981.

Cantwell, D., Baker, L., & Rutter, M. Family factors in the syndrome of infantile autism. In M. Rutter & E. Schloper (Eds.), *Autism: A reappraisal of concepts and treatment*. New York: Plenum, 1978.

Carlsmith, J. J., Lepper, M. R., & Landauer, T. K. Children's obedience to adult requests: Interactive affects of anxiety arousal and apparent punitiveness of adults. *Journal of Personality and Social Psychology,* 1974, *30*, 822–828.

Chance, J. E. Academic correlates and maternal antecedents of children's belief of internal control of reinforcement. In J. B. Rotter, J. E. Chance, & E. J. Phares (Eds.), *Applications of a social learning theory of personality*. New York: Holt, Rinehart & Winston, 1972.

Chandler, T. A., Wolf, F. M., Crook, B., & Dugovics, D. A. Parental correlates of locus of control in fifth-graders: An attempt at experimentation in the home. *Merrill-Palmer Quarterly*, 1980, *26*, 1183–1195.

Chapman, M. Listening to reason: Children's attentiveness and parental discipline. *Merrill-Palmer Quarterly*, 1979, *25*, 251–263.

Chapman, M., & Zahn-Waxler, C. *Young children's compliance and noncompliance to parental discipline in a natural setting*. Unpublished manuscript, 1981.

Chess, S., Thomas, A., & Birch, H. G. Distortions in developmental reporting made by parents of behaviorally disturbed children. *Journal of the American Academy of Child Psychiatry*, 1966, *5*, 226–234.

Cheyne, A. Punishment and reasoning in the development of self-control. In R. D. Parke (Ed.), *Recent trends in social learning theory*. New York: Academic Press, 1972.

Clarke-Stewart, K. A. Interactions between mothers and their young children: Characteristics and consequences. *Monographs of the Society for Research in Child Development*, 1973, *38*(6 & 7, Serial No. 153).

Clarke-Stewart, K. A. And daddy makes three: The father's impact on mother and young child. *Child Development*, 1978, *49*, 466–478.

Clarke-Stewart, K. A., & Hevey, C. M. Longitudinal relations in repeated observations of mother-child interactions from 1 to 2½ years. *Developmental Psychology*, 1981, *17*, 127–145.

Cline, V. B., Richards, J. M., & Needham, W. E. A factor-analytic study of the father form of the parental attitude research instrument. *Psychology*, 1963, *13*, 65–72.

Cobb, S. Social support as a moderator of life stress. *Psychosomatic Medicine*, 1976, *38*, 300–314.

Colletta, N. D. *The influence of support systems on the maternal behavior of young mothers*. Paper presented at the meeting of the Society for Research in Child Development, Boston, 1981.

Collis, G. M., & Schaffer, H. R. Synchronization of visual attention in mother infant pairs. *Journal of Child Psychology and Psychiatry*, 1975, *16*, 315–320.

Comstock, M. L. C. Effects of perceived parental behavior on self-esteem and adjustment. *Dissertation Abstracts*, 1973, *34*, 465B.

Condon, W. S. A primary base in the organization of infant responding behavior. In H. R. Schaffer (Ed.), *Studies in mother-infant interaction*. London: Academic Press, 1977.

Coopersmith, S. *The antecedents of self-esteem*. San Francisco: W. H. Freeman & Co., 1967.

Coser, L. A. *The functions of social conflict*. Glencoe, Ill.: Free Press, 1956.

Cox, N. Prior help, ego development and helping behavior. *Child Development*, 1974, *45*, 594–663.

Crandall, V. C. *Differences in parental antecedents of internal-external control in children and in young adulthood*. Paper presented at the meeting of the American Psychological Association, Montreal, 1973.

Crnic, K., Ragozin, A., Robinson, N., & Basham, R. *The effects of stress and social support on maternal attitudes and the mother-infant relationship*. Paper presented at the meeting of the Society for Research in Child Development, Boston, 1981.

Cronbach, L. J., Gleser, G. C., Nanda, H., & Rajartnam, N. *The dependability of behavioral measurements: Theory of generalizability for scores and profiles*. New York: Wiley, 1972.

Cunningham, C. E., & Barkley, R. A. The interactions of normal and hyperactive children with their mothers in free play and structured tasks. *Child Development*, 1979, *50*, 217–224.

Curtis, G. Violence breeds violence. *American Journal of Psychiatry*, 1963, *120*, 386–387.

Damon, W. *The social world of the child*. San Francisco: Jossey-Bass, 1977.

Davids, A., Holden, R. H., & Gray, G. B. Maternal anxiety during pregnancy and adequacy of mother and child adjustment eight months following childbirth. *Child Development*, 1963, *34*, 993–1002.

deChateau, P., Frankenhaeuser, M., Lundberg, M., Wiberg, B., & Winberg, J. *Three-year follow-up of early post-partum skin-to-skin contact*. Paper presented at the meeting of the Society for Research in Child Development, Boston, 1981.

deLissovoy, V. Child care by adolescent parents. *Children Today*, 1973, *14*, 22.

Deutch, M. Conflict: Productive and destructive. *Journal of Social Issues*, 1969, *25*, 7–41.

Dienstbier, R. A., Hillman, D., Lehnhoff, J., Hillman, J., & Valkenaar, M. C. An emotion-attribution approach to moral behavior: Inferfacing cognitive and avoidance theories of moral development. *Psychological Review*, 1975, *82*, 299–315.

Duncan, O. D. *Introduction to structural equation models*. New York: Academic Press, 1975.

Dunn, J. B. Patterns of early interaction: Continuities and consequences. In H. R. Schaffer (Ed.), *Studies in mother-infant interaction*. London: Academic Press, 1977.

Dunn, J. B., & Richards, M. P. M. Observations on the developing relationship between mother and baby in the neonatal period. In H. R. Schaffer (Ed.), *Studies in mother-infant interaction*. London: Academic Press, 1977.

Eckerman, C. O. The human infant in social interaction. In R. B. Cairns (Ed.), *The analysis of social interactions: Methods, issues and illustrations*. Hillsdale, N.J.: Erlbaum, 1979.

Egeland, B., Breitenbucher, M., & Rosenberg, D. Prospective study of the significance of life stress in the etiology of child abuse. *Journal of Consulting and Clinical Psychology*, 1980, *48*, 195–205.

Egeland, B., & Sroufe, L. A. Attachment and early maltreatment. *Child Development*, 1981, *52*, 44–52. (a)

Egeland, B., & Sroufe, L. A. Developmental sequelae of maltreatment in infancy. *New Directions for Child Development*, 1981, *11*, 77–92. (b).

Elder, G. *Family structure and socialization*. New York: Arno Press, 1980.

Epstein, S. The stability of behavior: II. Implications for psychological research. *American Psychologist*, 1980, *35*, 790–806.

Erikson, E. H. *Childhood and society*. New York: Norton, 1950.

Eron, L. D., Walder, L. O., & Lefkowitz, M. M. *Learning of aggression in children*. Boston: Little, Brown & Co., 1971.

Etzel, B. C., & Gewirtz, J. L. Experimental modification of caretaker-maintained high-rate operant crying in a 6- and a 20-week-old infant (Infans tyrannotearus): Extinction of crying with eye contact and smiling. *Journal of Experimental Child Psychology*, 1967, *5*, 303–317.

Falender, C. A., & Heber, R. Mother-child interaction and participation in a longitudinal intervention program. *Developmental Psychology*, 1975, *4*, 830–836.

Feldman, S. S., Nash, S. C., & Aschenbrenner, B. G. *Antecedents of fathering*. Manuscript submitted for publication, 1982.

Fenichel, O. Neurotic acting out. *Psychoanalytic Review*, 1945, *32*, 197–206.

Feshbach, N. D. The relationship of child-rearing factors to children's aggression, empathy and related positive and negative social behaviors. In J. deWitt & W. W. Hartup (Eds.), *Determinants and origins of aggressive behavior*. The Hague: Mouton, 1974.

Festinger, L., & Carlsmith, J. M. Cognitive consequences of forced compliance. *Journal of Abnormal and Social Psychology*, 1959, *58*, 203–210.

Field, T. Interaction behaviors of primary versus secondary caretaker fathers. *Developmental Psychology*, 1978, *14*, 183–184.

Foa, U. G., & Foa, E. B. *Societal structures of the mind*. Springfield, Ill.: Charles C. Thomas, 1974.

Fogel, A. Temporal organization in mother-infant face-to-face interaction. In H. R. Schaffer (Ed.), *Studies in mother-infant interaction*. London: Academic Press, 1977.

Fontana, V. J. *Somewhere a child is crying*. New York: Macmillan, 1973.

Fraiberg, S. Blind infants and their mothers: An examination of the sign system. In M. Lewis & L. A. Rosenblum (Eds.), *The effect of the infant on its caregiver*. New York: Wiley, 1974.

Fraiberg, S. The development of human attachments in infants blind from birth. *Merrill-Palmer Quarterly*, 1975, *21*, 315–334.

Fraiberg, S. *Insights from the blind*. New York: Basic Books, 1977.

Frodi, A. M., & Lamb, M. Sex differences in responsiveness to infants: A developmental study of psychophysiological and behavioral responses. *Child Development*, 1978, *49*, 1182–1188.

Gewirtz, J. L. Levels of conceptual analysis in environment: Infant interaction research. *Merrill-Palmer Quarterly*, 1969, *15*, 7–47.

Gewirtz, J. L., & Boyd, E. F. Does maternal responding imply reduced infant crying? A critique of the 1972 Bell & Ainsworth report. *Child Development*, 1977, *48*, 1200–1207.

Gil, D. G. Violence against children. *Journal of Marriage and the Family*, 1971, *33*, 637–648.

Glick, B. R., & Gross, S. J. Marital interaction and marital conflict. *Journal of Marriage and the Family*, 1975, *37*, 505–512.

Glick, P. C. Social change and the American family. In *The Social Welfare Forum*, 1977. (Official Proceedings, 104th Annual Forum, National Conference on Social Welfare. Chicago: May 15–18, 1977, pp. 43–62.)

Goldberg, S. Prematurity: Effects on parent-child interaction. *Journal of Pediatric Psychology*, 1978, *3*, 137–144.

Gordon, D., Nowicki, S., & Wichern, F. Observed maternal and child behavior in a dependency-producing task as a function of children's locus of control orientation. *Merrill-Palmer Quarterly*, 1981, *27*, 43–51.

Gottman, J. M. *Marital interaction: Experimental investigations*. New York: Academic Press,

1979. (a)

Gottman, J. M. Time series analysis of continuous data in dyads. In M. E. Lamb, S. J. Suomi, & G. R. Stephenson (Eds.), *Social interaction analysis: Methodological issues*. Madison: University of Wisconsin Press, 1979. (b)

Gottman, J. M., & Bakeman, R. The sequential analysis of observational data. In M. E. Lamb, S. J. Suomi, & G. R. Stephenson (Eds.), *Social interaction analysis: Methodological issues*. Madison: University of Wisconsin Press, 1979.

Gottman, J. M., & Ringland, J. T. The analysis of dominance and bidirectionality in social development. *Child Development*, 1981, *52*, 393–412.

Green, M. *Fathering*. New York: McGraw-Hill, 1976.

Greenberg, B., Ericson, P. M., & Vlahos, M. Children's television behavior as perceived by mothers and children. In E. A. Rubenstein, G. A. Comstock, & J. P. Murray (Eds.), *Television and social behavior*, vol. 4, *Television in day to day life: Patterns of use*. Washington, D.C.: U.S. Government Printing Office, 1972.

Grusec, J. E. Training altruistic dispositions: A cognitive analysis. In E. T. Higgins, D. N. Ruble, & W. W. Hartup (Eds.), *Social cognition and social behavior: Developmental perspectives*. Cambridge, Eng.: Cambridge University Press, 1982.

Grusec, J. E., & Kuczynski, L. Direction of effect in socialization: A comparison of the parent vs. the child's behavior as determinants of disciplinary techniques. *Developmental Psychology*, 1980, *16*, 1–9.

Grusec, J. E., Kuczynski, L., Ruston, J. P., & Simutis, Z. M. Modeling direct instruction and attributions: Effects on altruism. *Developmental Psychology*, 1978, *14*, 51–57.

Guillame, P. *Imitation in children*. Chicago: University of Chicago Press, 1971. (Originally published, 1926.)

Haan, N. *Coping and defending*. New York: Academic Press, 1977.

Haggard, E. A., Brekstad, A., & Skard, A. G. On the reliability of the anamnestic interview. *Journal of Abnormal Social Psychology*, 1960, *61*, 311–318.

Halverson, C. F., & Waldrop, M. F. Maternal behavior toward own and other preschool children: The problem of "owness." *Child Development*, 1970, *41*, 838–845.

Hamilton, M. L. *Father's influences on children*. Chicago: Nelson-Hall, 1977.

Hartshorne, H., & May, M. A. *Studies in deceit*

(Book 1). New York: Macmillan, 1929.

Hatfield, J. S., Ferguson, L. R., & Alpert, R. Mother-child interaction and the socialization process. *Child Development*, 1967, *38*, 365–414.

Hay, T. F., & Hall, D. K. *Behavioral, psychological and developmental differences between abusive and control mother-child dyads*. Paper presented at the meeting of the Society for Research in Child Development, Boston, 1981.

Hayes, A. *Facial gaze and vocalization in mother-infant interactions. An examination of the contingency involved*. Paper presented at the fifth Experimental Psychology Conference, LaTrobe University, Bundoora, Victoria, Australia, May 1978.

Heinecke, C. M., & Diskin, S. *Pre-birth parent characteristics and family development in the first year of life*. Paper presented at the meeting of the Society for Research in Child Development, Boston, 1981.

Henneborn, W. J., & Cogan, R. The effect of husband participation on reported pain and probability of medication during labor and birth. *Journal of Psychosomatic Research*, 1975, *19*, 215–222.

Henry, R. M. A theoretical and empirical analysis of "reasoning" in the socialization of young children. *Human Development*, 1980, *23*, 105–125.

Hetherington, E. M. The effects of familial variables on sex-typing, on parent-child similarity, and on imitation in children. In J. P. Hill (Ed.), *Minnesota Symposium on Child Psychology* (Vol. 1). Minneopolis: University of Minnesota Press, 1967.

Hetherington, E. M., Cox, M., & Cox, R. Divorced fathers. *The family Coordinator*, 1976, *25*, 415–428.

Hetherington, E. M., Cox, M., & Cox, R. Stress and coping in divorce: A focus on women. In J. E. Gullahorn (Ed.), *Psychology and women: In transition*. Washington, D.C.: V. H. Winston & Sons, 1979.

Hetherington, E. M., Cox, M., & Cox, R. Effects of divorce on parents and children. In M. Lamb (Ed.), *Nontraditional families*. Hillsdale, N.J.: Erlbaum, 1982.

Hinde, R. A. Mothers' and infants' roles: Distinguishing the questions to be asked. *Ciba Foundation Symposium*, 1975, *33*, 5–13.

Hinde, R. A. Interactions, relationships and social structure. *Man*, 1976, *11*, 1–17.

Hinde, R. A. Interpersonal relationships: In quest of a science. *Psychological Medicine*, 1978, *8*, 373–386.

Hinde, R. A. *Towards understanding relationships*.

New York: Academic Press, 1979.

Hinde, R. A., & Herrmann, J. Frequencies, durations, derived measures and their correlations in studying dyadic and triadic relationships. In H. R. Schaffer (Ed.), *Studies in mother-infant interaction*. London: Academic Press, 1977.

Hoffman, L. W. Changes in family roles, socialization, and sex differences. *American Psychologist*, 1977, *32*, 644–657.

Hoffman, M. L. An interview method for obtaining descriptions of parent-child interaction. *Merrill-Palmer Quarterly*, 1957, *3*, 76–83.

Hoffman, M. L. Power assertion by the parent and its impact on the child. *Child Development*, 1960, *31*, 129–143.

Hoffman, M. L. Moral development. In P. H. Mussen (Ed.), *Carmichael's manual of child psychology* (Vol. 2). New York: Wiley, 1970.

Hoffman, M. L. Altruistic behavior and the parent-child relationship. *Journal of Personality and Social Psychology*, 1975, *31*, 937–943. (a)

Hoffman, M. L. Moral internalization, parental power and the nature of parent–child interaction. *Developmental Psychology*, 1975, *11*, 228–239. (b)

Hoffman, M. L. Empathy, role-taking, guilt, and development of altruistic motives. In T. Lickona (Ed.), *Moral development and behavior*. New York: Holt, Rinehart & Winston, 1976.

Hoffman, M. L. The role of the father in moral internalization. In M. E. Lamb (Ed.), *The role of the father in child development* (2nd ed.). New York: Wiley, 1981.

Hoffman, M. L. Affective and cognitive processes in moral internalization. In E. T. Higgins, D. N. Ruble, & W. W. Hartup (Eds.), *Social cognition and social behavior: Developmental perspectives*. Cambridge, Eng.: Cambridge University Press, 1982.

Hoffman, M. L., & Saltzstein, H. D. Parent discipline and the child's moral development. *Journal of Personality and Social Psychology*, 1967, *5*, 45–57.

Holmberg, M. C. The development of social interchange patterns from 12 to 42 months. *Child Development*, 1980, *51*, 448–456.

Jacklin, C. N., DiPietro, J. A., & Maccoby, E. E. Sex-typing behavior and sex-typing pressure in child-parent interaction. *Archives of Sexual Behavior*, in press.

Jackson, D. D. Family rules: Marital quid-pro-quo. *Archives of General Psychiatry*, 1965, *12*, 1535–1541.

Jaffe, J., & Feldstein, S. *Rhythms of dialogue*. New York: Academic Press, 1970.

Jaffe, J., Stern, D. N., & Peery, J. C. Conversation coupling of gaze behavior in pre-linguistic human development. *Journal of Linguistic Research*, 1973, *2*, 321–329.

Johannessen, I. Aggressive behavior among school children related to maternal practices in early childhood. In J. deWitt and W. W. Hartup (Eds.), *Determinants and origins of aggressive behavior*. The Hague: Mouton, 1974.

Johnson, B., & Moore, H. A. Injured children and their parents. *Children*, 1968, *15*, 147–152.

Johnson, R. C. A study of children's moral judgments. *Child Development*, 1962, *33*, 327–354.

Jones, O. H. M. Mother-child communication with pre-linguistic Down's Syndrome and normal infants. In H. R. Schaffer (Ed.), *Studies in mother-infant interaction*. London: Academic Press, 1977.

Joreskog, K. G. Statistical estimation of structural models in longitudinal-developmental investigations. In J. R. Nesselroade & P. B. Baltes (Eds.), *Longitudinal research in the study of behavior and development*. New York: Academic Press, 1980.

Kandel, D. B., & Lesser, G. S. *Youth in two worlds*. San Francisco: Jossey-Bass, 1972.

Kaplan, F. K., Eichler, L. S., & Winickoff, S. A. *Pregnancy, birth and parenthood*. San Francisco: Jossey-Bass, 1980.

Kaye, K. Toward the origin of dialogue. In H. R. Schaffer (Ed.), *Studies in mother-infant interaction*. London: Academic Press, 1977.

Kelman, H. C. Compliance, identification and internalization: Three processes of opinion change. *Journal of Conflict Resolution*, 1958, *2*, 51–60.

Klaus, M. H., & Kennell, J. H. *Maternal-infant bonding*. St. Louis: Mosby, 1976.

Klein, D., & Jorgeson, S. Evaluating research strategies: A reply to Glick and Gross. *Journal of Marriage and the Family*, 1976, *38*, 216–219.

Kohlberg, L. A. A cognitive-developmental analysis of children's sex-role concepts and attitudes. In E. E. Maccoby (Ed.), *The development of sex differences*. Stanford, Calif.: Stanford University Press, 1966.

Kopp, C. B. Antecedents of self-regulation: A developmental perspective. *Developmental Psychology*, 1982, *18*, 199–214.

Kotelchuk, M. The infant's relationship to the father: Experimental evidence. In M. Lamb (Ed.), *The role of the father in child development*. New York: Wiley, 1976.

Kuczynski, L. Mother's strategies for immediate and long-term compliance. Unpublished manuscript, 1981.

Kuczynski, L. Intensity and Orientation of Reasoning: Motivational Determinants of Children's Compliance to Verbal Rationales. *Journal of Experimental Child Psychology*, 1982, *34*, 357–370.

Lamb, M. E. Effects of stress and cohort on mother- and father-infant interaction. *Developmental Psychology*, 1976, *12*, 435–443. (a)

Lamb, M. E. *The role of the father in child development*. New York: Wiley, 1976. (b)

Lamb, M. E. Father-infant and mother-infant interaction in the first year of life. *Child Development*, 1977, *48*, 167–181.

Lamb, M. E. The effects of the social context on dyadic social interaction. In M. E. Lamb, S. J. Suomi, & G. R. Stephenson (Eds.), *Social interaction analysis: Methodological issues*. Madison: University of Wisconsin Press, 1979.

Lamb, M. E. Fathers and child development: An integrative overview. In M. E. Lamb (Ed.), *The role of the father in child development* (2nd ed.). New York: Wiley, 1981. (a)

Lamb, M. E. *The role of the father in child development* (2nd ed.). New York: Wiley, 1981. (b)

Lamb, M. E., Frodi, A. M., Hwang, C. P., & Frodi, M. Varying degrees of paternal involvement in infant care. In M. E. Lamb (Ed.), *Nontraditional families*. Hillsdale, N.J.: Erlbaum, 1982.

Lamb, M. E., Frodi, A. M., Hwang, C. P., Frodi, M., & Steinberg, J. Mother- and father-infant interaction involving play and holding in traditional and non-traditional Swedish families. *Developmental Psychology*, 1982, *18*, 215–221.

Lamb, M. E., Suomi, S. J., & Stephenson, G. R. *Social interaction analysis: Methodological issues*. Madison: University of Wisconsin Press, 1979.

Landauer, T. K., Carlsmith, J. M., & Lepper, M. Experimental analysis of the factors determining obedience of four-year-old children to adult females. *Child Development*, 1970, *41*, 601–611.

Langlois, J. H. Beauty and the beast: The role of physical attractiveness in the development of peer relations and social behavior. In S. S. Brehm, S. M. Kassin, & F. X. Gibbons (Eds.), *Developmental social psychology: Theory and research*. New York: Oxford University Press 1981.

Langlois, J. H., & Downs, A. C. Mothers, fathers and peers as socialization agents of sex-typed play behaviors in young children. *Child Development*, 1980, *51*, 1217–1247.

Langlois, J. H., & Sawin, D. B. *Infant physical attractiveness as an elicitor of differential parenting behaviors*. Paper presented at the meeting of the Society for Research in Child Development, Boston, 1981.

Lasko, J. K. Parent behavior towards first and second children. *Genetic Psychology Monographs*, 1954, *49*, 97–137.

Lederberg, A. R. *Adult communication to hearing vs. hearing impaired children*. Paper presented at the meeting of the Society for Research in Child Development, Boston, 1981.

Lefkowitz, M. M., Eron, L. D., Walder, L. O., & Huesmann, L. R. *Growing up to be violent*. New York: Pergamon, 1977.

Leiderman, P. H. Human mother to infant social bonding: Is there a sensitive phase? In G. Barlow, K. Immelmann, M. Main, & L. Petrinovich (Eds.), *Ethology and child development*. London: Cambridge University Press, in press.

Leifer, M. Psychological changes accompanying pregnancy and motherhood. *Genetic Psychology Monographs*, 1977, *95*, 55–96.

Leon, M. Pheremonal mediation of maternal behavior. In T. Alloway, P. Pliner, & L. Krames (Eds.), *Attachment behavior* (Vol. 3). New York: Plenum, 1977.

Lepper, M. R. Social control processes, attributions of motivation, and the internalization of social values. In E. T. Higgins, D. N. Ruble, & W. W. Hartup (Eds.), *Social cognition and social behavior: Developmental perspectives*. Cambridge, Eng.: Cambridge University Press, 1982.

Lepper, M. R., & Greene, D. (Eds.). *The hidden costs of reward*. Hillsdale, N.J.: Erlbaum, 1978.

Lepper, M. R., Greene, D., & Nisbett, R. E. Undermining children's intrinsic interest with extrinsic rewards: A test of the "overjustification" hypothesis. *Journal of Personality and Social Psychology*, 1973, *28*, 129–137.

Lewin, K., Lippitt, R., & White, R. Patterns of aggressive behavior in experimentally created social climates. *Journal of Social Psychology*, 1939, *10*, 271–299.

Lewis, C. C. The effects of parental firm control: A reinterpretation of findings. *Psychological Bulletin*, 1981, *90*, 547–563.

Lewis, M. State as an infant-environment interaction: An analysis of mother-infant interaction as a function of sex. *Merrill-Palmer Quarterly*, 1972, *18*, 95–121.

Lewis, M., Feiring, C., & Weinraub, M. The father as a member of the child's social network. In M. E. Lamb (Ed.), *The role of the father in child development* (2nd ed.). New York: Wiley, 1981.

Lewis, M., & Lee-Painter, S. An interactional approach to the mother-infant dyad. In M. Lewis and L. A. Rosenblum (Eds.), *The effect of the infant on its caregiver*. New York: Wiley, 1974.

Loeb, R. C. Concomitants of boys' locus of control examined in parent-child interactions. *Developmental Psychology*, 1975, *11*, 353–358.

Loeb, R. C., Horst, L., & Horton, P. J. Family interaction patterns associated with self-esteem in preadolescent girls and boys. *Merrill-Palmer Quarterly*, 1980, *26*, 203–217.

Lorr, M. G., & Jenkins, R. L. Three factors in parent behavior. *Journal of Consulting Psychology*, 1953, *17*, 306–308.

Lynn, D. B. *The father: His role in child development*. Monterey, Calif.: Brooks/Cole, 1974.

Lytton, H. Correlates of compliance and the rudiments of conscience in 2-year-old boys. *Canadian Journal of Behavioral Sciences*, 1977, *9*, 242–251.

Lytton, H. Disciplinary encounters between young boys and their mothers: Is there a contingency system? *Developmental Psychology*, 1979, *15*, 256–268.

Lytton, H. *Parent-child interaction: The socialization process observed in twin and singleton families*. New York: Plenum, 1980.

Lytton, H., & Zwirner, W. Compliance and its controlling stimuli observed in a natural setting. *Developmental Psychology*, 1975, *11*, 769–779.

Maccoby, E. E. *Parent-child interaction*. Paper presented at the meeting of the Society for Research in Child Development, San Francisco, March 1979.

Maccoby, E. E. *Social development: Psychological growth and the parent-child relationship*. New York: Harcourt Brace Jovanovich, 1980.

Maccoby, E. E. Let's not over-attribute to the attribution process. In E. T. Higgins, D. N. Ruble, & W. W. Hartup (Eds.), *Social cognition and social behavior: Developmental perspectives*. Cambridge, Eng.: Cambridge University Press, 1982.

Maccoby, E. E., & Jacklin, C. N. *The psychology of sex differences*. Stanford, Calif.: Stanford University Press, 1974.

Maccoby, E. E., & Jacklin, C. N. The ''person'' characteristics of children and the family as environment. In D. Magnusson & V. Allen (Eds.), *Human development: An interactional perspective*. New York: Academic Press, in press.

Maccoby, E. E., & Maccoby, N. The interview: A tool of social science. In G. Lindzey (Ed.), *Handbook of social psychology* (Vol. 1). Cambridge, Mass.: Addison-Wesley, 1954.

Maccoby, E. E., & Wilson, W. C. Identification and observational learning from films. *Journal of Abnormal and Social Psychology*, 1957, *55*, 76–87.

Mahler, M. S., Pine, F., & Bergman, A. *The psychological birth of the human infant*. New York: Basic Books, 1975.

Malatesta, C. Z., & Haviland, J. M. *Age- and sex-related changes in infant affect expression*. Paper presented at the meeting of the Society for Research in Child Development, Boston, 1981.

Martin, J. A. A longitudinal study of the consequences of early mother-infant interaction: A microanalytic approach. *Monographs of the Society for Research in Child Development*. 1981, *46* (3, Serial No. 190).

Martin, J. A., Maccoby, E. E., Baran, K. W., & Jacklin, C. N. The sequential analysis of mother-child interaction at 18 months: A comparison of microanalytic methods. *Developmental Psychology*, 1981, *17*, 146–157.

Marvin, R. S. An ethological-cognitive model for the attenuation of mother-child attachment behavior. In T. Alloway, P. Pline, & L. Krames (Eds.), *Advances in the study of communication and affect: Attachment behavior* (Vol. 3). New York: Plenum, 1977.

Matas, L., Arend, R. A., & Sroufe, L. A. Continuity of adaptation in the second year: The relationship between quality of attachment and later competence. *Child Development*, 1978, *49*, 547–556.

McCall, R. B., Parke, R. D., & Kavanaugh, R. D. Imitation of live and televised models by children one to three years of age. *Monographs of the Society for Research in Child Development*, 1977, *42*(5, Serial No. 173).

McCubbin, H. I., Cauble, A. E., Patterson, J. M., & Comeau, J. K. Family coping and social support in the management of stress: A review. In H. I. McCubbin, A. E. Cauble, & J. M. Patterson (Eds.), *Family stress, coping and social support*. Springfield, Ill.: Charles C. Thomas, 1982.

McCubbin, H. I., Joy, C. B., Cauble, A. E., Comeau, J. K., Patterson, J. M., & Needle, R. H. Family stress and coping: A decade in review. *Journal of Marriage and the Family*, 1980, *42*, 825–840.

McEachern, L. V. H. An investigation of the relationships between self-esteem, the power motives and democratic, authoritarian, or laissez-faire home atmosphere. *Dissertation Abstracts*,

1973, *34*, 572A.

Meade, G. H. *Mind, self and society*. Chicago: University of Chicago Press, 1934.

Meadows, K. P. The development of deaf children. In E. M. Hetherington (Ed.), *Review of child development research* (Vol. 5). Chicago: University of Chicago Press, 1975.

Mednick, S. A., & Schaffer, B. P. Mothers' retrospective reports in child-rearing research. *American Journal of Orthopsychiatry*, 1963, *33*, 457–461.

Miller, D. R. Psychoanalytic theory of development: A re-evaluation. In D. Goslin (Ed.), *Handbook of socialization theory and research*. Chicago: Rand-McNally, 1969.

Milowe, J. D., & Lourie, R. S. The child's role in the battered child syndrome. *Journal of Pediatrics*, 1964, *65*, 1079–1081.

Minde, K. M. Bonding of parents to premature infants: Theory and practice. In P. M. Taylor (Ed.), *Parent-infant relationships*. New York: Grune & Stratton, 1980.

Minde, K. M., Brown, J., & Whitelaw, A. *The effect of severe physical illness on the behavior of very small premature infants and their parents*. Paper presented at the meeting of the Society for Research in Child Development, Boston, 1981.

Minton, C., Kagan, J., & Levine, J. A. Maternal control and obedience in the two-year-old. *Child Development*, 1971, *42*, 1873–1894.

Mischel, W., & Mischel, H. A cognitive social-learning approach to morality and self-regulation. In T. Lickona (Ed.), *Moral development and behavior*. New York: Holt, Rinehart & Winston, 1976.

Morris, D. *Mothers' family histories: Relations to attachment and dependency in their toddlers*. Paper presented at the meeting of the Society for Research in Child Development, Boston, 1981.

Moss, H. A., & Jones, S. J. Relations between maternal attitudes and maternal behavior as a function of social class. In P. H. Leiderman, S. R. Tulkin, & A. Rosenfeld (Eds.), *Culture and infancy*. New York: Academic Press, 1977.

Moss, H. A., & Robson, K. S. Maternal influences in early social visual behavior. *Child Development*, 1968, *39*, 401–498.

Neidhart, F. *Stemeigenschaften der Familie*. Munchen: Deutsches Jugendienst, 1976.

Newson, J.; & Newson, E. *Four years old in an urban community*. London: Allen & Unwin, 1968.

Nichols, R. C. A factor analysis of parental attitudes of fathers. *Child Development*, 1962, *33*, 791–802.

O'Connor, S. M., Vietze, P. M., Hopkins, J. B., & Altemeier, W. A. *Post partum extended maternal-infant comfort: Subsequent mothering and child health*. Paper presented at the meeting of the Society for Pediatric Research, San Francisco, 1977.

O'Connor, S. M., Vietze, P. M., Sandler, H. M., Sherrod, K. B., & Altemeier, W. A. Quality of parenting and the mother-infant relationship. In P. M. Taylor (Ed.), *Parent-infant relationships*. New York: Grune & Stratton, 1980.

Olweus, D. Familial and temperamental determinants of aggression behavior in adolescents—A causal analysis. *Developmental Psychology*, 1980, *16*, 644–660.

Osofsky, J. D. Neonatal characteristics and mother-infant interaction in two observational situations. *Child Development*, 1976, *47*, 1138–1147.

Osofsky, J. D., & Danzger, B. Relationships between neonatal characteristics and mother-infant interaction. *Developmental Psychology*, 1974, *10*, 124–130.

Ounsted, C., Oppenheimer, R., & Lindsay, J. Aspects of bonding failure: The psychopathology and psychotherapeutic treatment of families of battered children. *Developmental Medicine and Child Neurology*, 1974, *16*, 447–452.

Pakizegi, B. The interaction of mothers and fathers with their sons. *Child Development*, 1978, *49*, 479–482.

Papousek, H., & Papousek, M. Mothering and the cognitive head-start: Psychological considerations. In H.R. Schaffer (Ed.), *Studies in mother-infant interaction*. London: Academic Press, 1977.

Parke, R. D. Rules, roles and resistance to deviation: Recent advances in punishment, discipline and self-control. In A. D. Pick (Ed.), *Minnesota Symposium on Child Psychology* (Vol. 8). Minneapolis: University of Minnesota Press, 1974.

Parke, R. D. Perspectives of father-infant interaction. In J. D. Osofsky (Ed.), *Handbook of infant development*. New York: Wiley, 1979.

Parke, R. D., & Collmer, C. W. Child abuse: An interdisciplinary analysis. In E. M. Hetherington (Ed.), *Review of child development research* (Vol. 5). Chicago: University of Chicago Press, 1975.

Parke, R. D., & O'Leary, S. Father-mother-infant interaction in the newborn period: Some findings, some observations, and some unresolved issues. In K. A. Riegel & J. Meacham (Eds.), *The developing individual in a changing world*, vol. 2, *Social and environmental issues*. The Hague: Mouton, 1976.

Parke, R. D., & Sawin, D. B. *The family in early infancy: Social interactional analysis*. Paper presented at the meeting of the Society for Research in Child Development, New Orleans, March 1977.

Parker, G., Tupling, H., & Brown, L. B. A parental bonding instrument. *British Journal of Medical Psychology,* 1979, *52,* 1–10.

Patterson, G. R. The aggressive child: Victim and architect of a coercive system. In L. A. Hamerlynck, L. C. Handy, & E. J. Mash (Eds.), *Behavior modification and families: I. Theory and research*. New York: Brunner-Mazell, 1976.

Patterson, G. R. A performance theory for coercive family interactions. In R. B. Cairns (Ed.), *The analysis of social interactions: Methods, issues and illustrations*. Hillsdale, N.J.: Erlbaum, 1979.

Patterson, G. R. Mothers: The unacknowledged victims. *Monographs of the Society for Research in Child Development*. 1980, *45*(5, Serial No. 186).

Patterson, G. R. *Coercive family process*. Eugene, Ore.: Castalia Press, 1982.

Patterson, G. R. Stress: A change agent for family process. In N. Garmezy & M. Rutter (Eds.), *Stress, coping and development*. New York: McGraw-Hill, in press.

Patterson, G. R., & Cobb, J. A. A dyadic analysis of ''aggressive'' behavior. In J. P. Hill (Ed.), *Minnesota Symposium on Child Psychology* (Vol. 5). Minneapolis: University of Minnesota Press, 1971.

Patterson, G. R., & Cobb, J. A. Stimulus control for classes of various behaviors. In J. F. Knutson (Ed.), *The control of aggression: Implications from basic research*. Chicago: Aldine Press, 1973.

Patterson, G. R., & Moore, D. R. Interactive patterns as units. In S. J. Suomi, M. E. Lamb, & G. R. Stephenson (Eds.), *Social interaction analysis: Methodological issues*. Madison: University of Wisconsin Press, 1979.

Pawlby, S. J. Imitative interaction. In H. R. Schaffer (Ed.), *Studies in mother-infant interaction*. London: Academic Press, 1977.

Pedersen, F. A. *Mother, father and infant as an interactive system*. Paper presented at the meeting of the American Psychological Association, Chicago, 1975.

Pedersen, F. A. *The father-infant relationship: Observational studies in the family setting*. New York: Praeger, 1980.

Pedersen, F. A. Father influences viewed in a family context. In M. E. Lamb (Ed.), *The role of the father in child development* (2nd ed.). New York: Wiley, 1981.

Pedersen, F. A., Anderson, B. J., & Cain, R. L. Parent-infant and husband-wife interactions observed at age five months. In F. A. Pedersen (Ed.), *The father-infant relationship: Observational studies in the family setting*. New York: Praeger, 1980.

Pedersen, F. A., Cain, R. L., Zaslow, M. J., & Anderson, B. J. Variation in infant experience associated with alternative family roles. In L. Laosa & I. Sigel (Eds.), *Families as learning environments for children*. New York: Plenum, 1982.

Pedersen, F. A., Yarrow, L. J., Anderson, B. J., & Cain, R. L. Conceptualization of father influences in the infancy period. In M. Lewis & L. Rosenblum (Eds.), *The child and its family*. New York: Plenum, 1979.

Perry, D. G., & Bussey, K. The social learning theory of sex differences: Imitation is alive and well. *Journal of Personality and Social Psychology,* 1979, *37,* 1699–1712.

Perry, D. G., & Perry, L. C. Social learning, causal attribution, and moral internalization. In J. Bisanz, G. L. Bisanz, & R. V. Kail, Jr. (Eds.), *Learning in children; progress in cognitive development research*. New York: Springer-Verlag, in press.

Piaget, J. *Play, dreams and imitation in childhood*. New York: Norton, 1962. (Originally published, 1951.)

Piaget, J. *The moral judgment of the child*. New York: Free Press, 1965. (Original publication in English by Routledge and Kegan Paul, London, 1932.)

Price, G. *Factors influencing reciprocity in early mother-infant interaction*. Paper presented at the meeting of the Society for Research in Child Development, New Orleans, March 1977.

Pulkkinen, L. Self-control and continuity from childhood to adolescence. In P. B. Baltes & O. G. Brim (Eds.), *Life-span development and behavior* (Vol. 4). New York: Academic Press, 1982.

Qadri, A. J., & Kaleem, G. A. Effect of parental attitudes on personality adjustment and self-esteem of children. *Behaviorometric,* 1971, *1,* 19–24.

Radin, N. The role of the father in cognitive, academic, and intellectual development. In M. E. Lamb (Ed.), *The role of the father in child development* (2nd ed.). New York: Wiley, 1981.

Radke, M. The relation of parental authority to children's behavior and attitudes. *University of Minnesota Institute of Child Welfare Monograph,* 1946, (22).

Radke-Yarrow, M., Campbell, J. D., & Burton, R. V. Reliability of maternal retrospection: A preliminary report. In K. Danziger (Ed.), *Readings in child socialization.* Oxford: Pergamon, 1970.

Radke-Yarrow, M., & Kuczynski, L. Perspectives and strategies in childrearing research: Studies of rearing by normal and depressed mothers. In D. Magnusson & V. Allen (Eds.), *Human development: An interactional perspective.* New York: Academic Press, in press.

Raush, H. L. Interaction sequences. *Journal of Personality and Social Psychology,* 1965, *2,* 487–499.

Raush, H. L., Barry, W. A., Hertel, R. K., & Swain, M. A. *Communication, conflict, and marriage.* San Francisco: Jossey-Bass, 1974.

Reid, J. B. Reliability assessment of observational data: A possible methodological problem. *Child Development,* 1970, *41,* 1143–1150.

Rexford, E. N. *A developmental approach to problems of acting out* (rev. ed.). New York: International Universities Press, 1978.

Richards, M. P. M. Possible effects of early separation on later development of children—A review. In F. S. W. Brimblecombe, M. P. M. Richards, & N. R. C. Robertson (Eds.), *Separation and special-care baby units.* Clinics in Developmental Medicine (No. 68). London: Heinemann, 1978.

Robins, L. N. The accuracy of parental recall of aspects of child development and child-rearing practices. *Journal of Abnormal and Social Psychology,* 1963, *33,* 261–270.

Rogosa, D. A critique of cross-lagged correlation. *Psychological Bulletin,* 1980, *88,* 245–258.

Rollins, B. C., & Thomas, D. L. Parental support, power, and control techniques in the socialization of children. In W. R. Burr, R. Hill, F. I. Nye, & I. L. Reiss (Eds.), *Contemporary theories about the family,* vol. 1, *Research based theories.* New York: Free Press, 1979.

Rosenblum, L. A., & Youngstein, K. P. Developmental change in compensatory dyadic response in mother and infant monkeys. In M. Lewis & L. A. Rosenblum (Eds.), *The effect of the infant on its caregiver.* New York: Wiley, 1974.

Rosenthal, M. K. *Mother-infant reciprocity during the neonatal period.* Unpublished manuscript, 1982.

Ross, D. M. Relationship between dependency, intentional learning, and incidental learning in pre-school children. *Journal of Personality and Social Psychology,* 1966, *4,* 374–381.

Ross, H. S., & Goldman, B. D. Establishing new social relations in infancy. In T. Alloway, P. Pliner, & L. Krames (Eds.), *Attachment behavior.* New York: Plenum, 1977.

Rothbart, M. K. Birth order and mother-child interaction in an achievement situation. *Journal of Personality and Social Psychology,* 1971, *17,* 113–120.

Rowe, D. C., & Plomin, R. The importance of nonshared (E_1) environmental influence in behavioral development. *Developmental Psychology,* 1981, *17,* 517–531.

Ruble, D. N., Balaban, T., & Cooper, J. Gender constancy and the effects of sex-typed televised toy commercials. *Child Development,* 1981, *52,* 667–673.

Russell, G. The father role and its relation to masculinity, femininity, and androgyny. *Child Development,* 1978, *49,* 1174–1181.

Rutter, M. Protective factors in children's response to stress and disadvantage. In M. W. Kent and J. E. Rolf (Eds.), *Primary prevention of psychopathology: Vol. 3. Social competence in children.* Hanover, N. H.: University Press of New England, 1979.

Rutter, M. *Maternal deprivation reassessed* (2nd ed.). New York: Penguin Books, 1981.

Rutter, M. Epidemiological-longitudinal approaches to the study of development. In W. A. Collins (Ed.), *The concept of development. Minnesota Symposium on Child Development* (Vol. 15). Hillsdale, N.J.: Erlbaum, 1982.

Sackett, G. P. The lag sequential analysis of contingency and cyclicity in behavioral interaction research. In J. Osofsky (Ed.), *Handbook of infant development.* New York: Wiley, 1979.

Sagi, A. *Adults' responses to normal and pathological cries.* Paper presented at the meeting of the Society for Research in Child Development, Boston, 1981.

Saltzstein, H. D. Social influence and moral development: A perspective on the role of parents and peers. In T. Lickona (Ed.), *Moral development and behavior.* New York: Holt, Rinehart & Winston, 1976.

Sameroff, A. J. Development and the dialectic: The need for a systems approach. In W. A. Collins (Ed.), *The concept of development. Minnesota Symposium on Child Psychology* (Vol. 15). Hillsdale, N.J.: Erlbaum, 1982.

Satir, V. *Conjoint family therapy.* Palo Alto, Calif.: Science and Behavior Books, 1967.

Scarr, S., & Grajek, S. Similarities and differences among siblings. In M. E. Lamb & B. Sutton-Smith (Eds.), *Sibling relationships*. Hillsdale, N.J.: Erlbaum, 1982.

Scarr, S., Webber, P. L., Weinberg, R. A., & Wittig, M. A. Personality resemblance among adolescents and their parents in biologically related and adoptive families. *Journal of Personality and Social Psychology*, 1981, *40*, 885–898.

Schachter, S., & Singer, J. E. Cognitive, social and psychological determinants of emotional state. *Psychological Review*, 1962, *69*, 379–399.

Schaefer, E. S. A circumplex model for maternal behavior. *Journal of Abnormal and Social Psychology*, 1959, *59*, 226–235.

Schaefer, E. S. Children's reports of parental behavior: An inventory. *Child Development*, 1965, *36*, 413–424.

Schaefer, E., & Bell, R. Development of a parental attitude research instrument. *Child Development*, 1958, *29*, 339–361.

Schaffer, H. R. Cognitive components of the infant's response to strangeness. In M. Lewis & L. A. Rosenbaum (Eds.), *The origins of fear*. New York: Wiley, 1974.

Schaffer, H. R. Early interactive development. In H. R. Schaffer (Ed.), *Studies in mother-infant interaction*. New York: Academic Press, 1977.

Schaffer, H. R., Collis, G. M., & Parsons, G. Verbal interchange and visual regard in verbal and preverbal children. In H. R. Schaffer (Ed.), *Studies in mother-infant interaction*. London: Academic Press, 1977.

Schaffer, H. R., & Crook, C. K. Child compliance and maternal control techniques. *Developmental Psychology*, 1980, *16*, 54–61.

Schmidt, C. F. Understanding human action: Recognizing the plans and motives of other persons. In J. S. Caroll & J. W. Payne (Eds.), *Cognition and social behavior*. Hillsdale, N.J.: Erlbaum, 1976.

Schramm, W., Lyle, J., & Parker, E. B. *Television in the lives of our children*. Stanford, Calif.: Stanford University Press, 1961.

Schuck, J. R. The use of causal nonexperimental models in aggression research. In J. DeWitt, & W. W. Hartup (Eds.), *Determinants and origins of aggressive behavior*. The Hague: Mouton, 1974.

Sears, R. R. A theoretical framework for personality and social behavior. *American Psychologist*, 1951, *6*, 476–483.

Sears, R. R. Relation of early socialization experiences to aggression in middle childhood. *Journal of Abnormal and Social Psychology*, 1961, *63*, 466–492.

Sears, R. R., Maccoby, E. E., & Levin, H. *Patterns of child rearing*. Evanston, Ill.: Row Peterson, 1957.

Sears, R. R., Rau, L., & Alpert, R. *Identification and child rearing*. Stanford, Calif.: Stanford University Press, 1965.

Sears, R. R., Whiting, J. W. M., Nowlis, V., & Sears, P. S. Some child-rearing antecedents of aggression and dependency in young children. *Genetic Psychology Monograph*, 1953, *47*, 135–234.

Seegmiller, B. R., & King, W. L. Relations between behavioral characteristics of infants, their mothers' behavior, and performance on the Bayley mental and motor scales. *Journal of Psychology*, 1975, *90*, 99–111.

Seligman, M. *Helplessness*. San Francisco: W. H. Freeman & Co., 1975.

Shereshefsky, P. M., & Yarrow, L. J. *Psychological aspects of a first pregnancy and early postnatal adaptation*. New York: Raven Press, 1973.

Slater, P. E. Parental behavior and the personality of the child. *Journal of Genetic Psychology*, 1962, *101*, 53–68.

Smith, A. D., & Reid, W. J. *The family role revolution*. Paper presented at the program meeting of the Council on Social Work Education, Los Angeles, March 1980.

Smith, P. K., & Daglish, L. Sex differences in parent and infant behavior in the home. *Child Development*, 1977, *48*, 1250–1254.

Smith, T. E. Foundations of parental influence upon adolescents: An application of social power theory. *American Sociological Review*, 1970, *35*, 860–873.

Snow, M. E., Jacklin, C. N., & Maccoby, E. E. Birth order differences in peer sociability at 33 months. *Child Development*, 1981, *52*, 589–595.

Sroufe, L. A., & Waters, E. Attachment as an organizational construct. *Child Development*, 1977, *48*, 1184–1199. (a)

Sroufe, L. A., & Waters, E. Heart rate as a convergent measure in clinical and developmental research. *Merrill-Palmer Quarterly*, 1977, *23*, 3–25. (b)

Stayton, D., Hogan, R., & Ainsworth, M. D. S. Infant obedience and maternal behavior: The origins of socialization reconsidered. *Child Development*, 1971, *42*, 1057–1069.

Steele, B. F. *Working with abusive parents from a psychiatric point of view* [U.S. Department of

Health, Education and Welfare Publication No. (OHD) 75-70]. Washington, D.C.: U.S. Government Printing Office, 1975.

Steele, B. F., & Pollack, D. A psychiatric study of parents who abuse infants and young children. In R. E. Helfer & C. H. Kempe (Eds.), *The battered child*. Chicago: University of Chicago Press, 1968.

Steinmetz, S. K., & Straus, M. A. *Violence in the family*. New York: Harper & Row, 1974.

Stern, D. N. Mother and infant at play: The dyadic interaction involving facial, vocal and gaze behaviors. In M. Lewis & L. A. Rosenblum (Eds.), *The effect of the infant on its caregiver*. New York: Wiley, 1974.

Stern, D. N., Beebe, B., Jaffe, J., & Bennett, S. L. The infant's stimulus world during social interaction: A study of caregiver behaviours with particular reference to repetition and timing. In H. R. Schaffer (Ed.), *Studies in mother-infant interaction*. London: Academic Press, 1977.

Stern, D. N., Jaffe, J., Beebe, B., & Bennett, S. L. Vocalizing in unison and in alternation: Two modes of communication within the mother-infant dyad. *Annals of New York Academy of Science*, 1975, *263*, 89–99.

Stevenson, H. W. Social reinforcement of children's behavior. In L. P. Lipsitt and C. C. Spiker (Eds.), *Advances in child development and behavior* (Vol. 2). New York: Academic Press, 1965.

Strayer, F. F. Social ecology of the preschool peer group. In W. A. Collins (Ed.), *Children's language and communication*. Minnesota Symposium on Child Psychology (Vol. 12). Minneapolis: University of Minnesota Press, 1981.

Sullivan, K., & Sullivan, A. Adolescent-parent separation. *Developmental Psychology*, 1980, *16*, 93–99.

Suomi, S. J. Mechanisms underlying social development: A reexamination of mother-infant interaction in monkeys. In A. D. Pick (Ed.), *Minnesota Symposium on Child Psychology* (Vol. 10). Minneapolis: University of Minnesota Press, 1976.

Switsky, L. T., Vietze, P., & Switsky, H. Attitudinal and demographic predictors of breast-feeding and bottle-feeding behavior in mothers of six-week-old infants. *Psychological Reports*, 1979, *45*, 3–14.

Taplin, P., & Reid, J. B. Changes in parent consequences as a function of family intervention. *Journal of Consulting and Clinical Psychology*, 1977, *45*, 973–981.

Taylor, S., Etcoff, N., Fiske, S., & Laufer, J. Imaging empathy and causal attribution. *Journal of Experimental Social Psychology*, 1979, *15*, 356–377.

Terr, L. C. A family study of child abuse. *American Journal of Psychiatry*, 1970, *127*, 665–671.

Thoman, E. B. Some consequences of early mother-infant interaction. *Early Child Development and Care*, 1974, *3*, 249–261.

Thomas, E. A. C., & Malone, T. W. On the dynamics of two-person interactions. *Psychological Review*, 1979, *86*, 331–360.

Thomas, E. A. C., & Martin, J. A. Analyses of parent-infant interaction. *Psychological Review*, 1976, *83*, 141–156.

Thompson, W. R., Watson, J., & Charlesworth, W. R. The effects of prenatal maternal stress on offspring behavior in rats. *Psychology Monographs*, 1962, *76*(38, Whole No. 557).

Tronick, E., Als, H., & Brazelton, T. B. Monadic phases: A structural descriptive analysis of infant-mother face to face interaction. *Merrill-Palmer Quarterly*, 1980, *26*, 3–24.

Uzgiris, I. C. Two functions of imitation during infancy. *International Journal of Behavioral Development*, 1981, *4*, 1–12.

Ver Hoeve, J. N., Stevenson, M. B., Leavitt, L. A., & Roach, M. A. *Patterns of mother-infant communication at four months*. Paper presented at the meeting of the Society for Research in Child Development, Boston, 1981.

Wahler, R. G., Leske, G., & Roberts, E. J. *The insular family: A dominance support system for oppositional children*. Unpublished manuscript, 1978.

Walker, J. A., & Kershman, S. M. *The deaf-blind in social interaction*. Paper presented at the meeting of the Society for Research in Child Development, Boston, 1981.

Wallerstein, J. S., & Kelly, J. B. The effects of parental divorce: Experiences of the preschool child. *Journal of the American Academy of Child Psychiatry*, 1975, *14*, 600–616.

Wallerstein, J. S., & Kelly, J. B. The effects of parental divorce: Experiences of the child in later latency. *American Journal of Orthopsychiatry*, 1976, *46*, 256–269.

Wallerstein, J. S., & Kelley, J. B. *Surviving the breakup: How children and parents cope with divorce*. New York: Basic Books, 1981.

Waters, E. The reliability and stability of individual differences in infant-mother attachment. *Child Development*, 1978, *49*, 483–494.

Watson, J. S. Operant conditioning of visual fixation in infants under visual and auditory reinforcement. *Developmental Psychology*, 1969, *1*, 508–516.

Weinsten, E. A., & Deutschberger, P. Some dimensions of altercasting. *Sociometry*, 1963, *26*, 454–466.

Weir, R. H. *Language in the crib*. The Hague: Mouton, 1962.

Wenar, C. The reliability of mothers' histories. *Child Development*, 1961, *32*, 491–500.

Wenar, C., & Coulter, J. B. A reliability study of developmental histories. *Child Development*, 1962, *33*, 453–462.

Whiting, B. Culture and social behavior: A model for the development of social behavior. *Ethos*, 1980, *8*, 95–116.

Whiting, B. B., & Whiting, J. W. M. *Children of six cultures: A psychocultural analysis*. Cambridge, Mass.: Harvard University Press, 1975.

Whiting, J. W. M., & Child, I. R. *Child training and personality: A cross-cultural study*. New Haven, Conn.: Yale University Press, 1953.

Whiting, J. W. M., & Whiting, B. B. Altruistic and egoistic behavior in six cultures. In L. Nader & T. W. Maretzki (Eds.), *Cultural illness and health: Essays in human adaptation*. Washington, D.C.: American Anthropological Association, 1973.

Wichern, F., & Nowicki, S. Independence training practices and locus of control orientation in children and adolescents. *Developmental Psychology*, 1976, *12*, 77.

Wright, H. F. *Recording and analyzing child behavior*. New York: Harper & Row, 1967.

Yando, R., Seitz, V., & Zigler, E. *Imitation: A developmental perspective*. Hillsdale, N.J.: Erlbaum, 1978.

Yarrow, M. R., Campbell, J. D., & Burton, R. *Child rearing, an inquiry into research and methods*. San Francisco: Jossey-Bass, 1968.

Yarrow, M. R., Waxler, C. Z., & Scott, P. M. Child effects on adult behavior. *Developmental Psychology*, 1971, *5*, 300–311.

Youniss, J. *Parents and peers in social development: A Sullivan-Piaget perspective*. Chicago: University of Chicago Press, 1980.

Zahn-Waxler, C., Radke-Yarrow, M., & King, R. A. Child-rearing and children's prosocial initiations toward victims of distress. *Child Development*, 1979, *50*, 319–330.

Zajonc, R. B. Feeling and thinking: Preferences need no inferences. *American Psychologist*, 1980, *35*, 151–175.

Zussman, J. U. Situational determinants of parental behavior: Effects of competing cognitive activity. *Child Development*, 1980, *51*, 792–800.

PEER RELATIONS* | 2

WILLARD W. HARTUP, *University of Minnesota*

CHAPTER CONTENTS

New investigations demonstrate that peer relations contribute uniquely to the growth of the individual—to the capacity to relate to others, to the development of social controls, and to the acquisition of social values. In this chapter, peer relations will be discussed with an emphasis on child-child interactions and their changes with age, the emergence of friendships and their significance, group formation and functioning, and the role of peer experience in the socialization of the individual child.

In most cultures, the significance of peer relations as a socialization context is rivaled only by the family. In both hunter-gatherer and contemporary Western societies, access to other children and opportunities to learn from them are almost unlimited.

*The bibliographic assistance of Van Pancake, Michael D. R. Lougee, and Wendy Pradt Lougee is gratefully acknowledged. Preparation of this chapter was facilitated by Grant No. 5 P01-05027, National Institute of Child Health and Human Development.

The circumstances surrounding these contacts vary from culture to culture, but most children receive extensive exposure to other children during the course of their socialization. Much variation exists also in the timing of the child's earliest contacts with peers. In some instances, babies are members of mixed-age enclaves supervised by child nurses or sibling caretakers. In other cultures, regular contact with other children begins only in the third or fourth year of life. But, whatever the age of onset and whatever the circumstance, none of the world's cultures rears its children solely through interaction with adults.

Isolating the variance in children's socialization that derives from contact with other children is extremely difficult. Peer interaction affects behavioral development in conjunction with experience occurring within other social networks. Neither contrived experiments nor experiments of nature provide very good opportunities for studying the developmental contributions that derive directly from peer interaction. The investigator must always tease this information from data confounded by organismic changes, stimulation from the nonsocial environment, and stimulation from adults. Nevertheless, contemporary methods enable us to speculate about the nature of these conjunctions and the manner in which child-child relations augment adult-child relations in the course of socialization.

The unique elements in child-child relations would appear to be the developmental equivalence of the participants and the egalitarian nature of their interaction. These elements do not necessitate theoretical formulations orthogonal to the laws governing the child's experience with other individuals. Peers are merely a subset among the many individuals to whom the child is exposed during the course of growing up, and it is reasonable to assume that behavior with other children will bear some of the hallmarks of behavior within other social networks. But the challenges presented to the child when interacting with another immature individual may differ substantially from the challenges presented by adult caretakers. The manner in which these accommodations are made, cycle through time, and leave their mark on the individual are thus the relevant issues.

This chapter is divided into six sections: (1) an historical overview; (2) an examination of what constitutes a peer; (3) a normative analysis of child-child interaction; (4) a consideration of peer relationships, including friendships and their emergence; (5) an analysis of the literature on children's groups; and (6) a discussion of peer influences on the individual child.

The most detailed treatment will be given to the empirical literature on peer relations that has appeared since 1970. After 20 near-dormant years, the study of peer relations resumed with new enthusiasm shortly after the last edition of the *Manual* appeared. A large number of monographs and edited volumes have been published within the last 10 years and have had wide circulation: *Friendship and peer relations* (Lewis & Rosenblum, 1975); *Friendship and social relations in children* (Foot, Chapman, & Smith, 1980); *The social world of the child* (Damon, 1977); *Youth in two worlds* (Kandel & Lesser, 1972); *Children's friendships* (Rubin, 1980); *Issues in childhood social development* (McGurk, 1978); *The development of children's friendships* (Asher & Gottman, 1981); *Parents and peers in social development* (Youniss, 1980); *The growth of interpersonal understanding* (Selman, 1980); *Peer relationships and social skills in childhood* (Rubin & Ross, 1982). Review articles are now too numerous to mention.

HISTORICAL OVERVIEW

Scientific interest in children's peer relations arose within the context of general interest in the effects of social groups on human behavior. Between 1830 and 1930, there was an outpouring of speculative and theoretical literature that dealt with two major propositions: (1) Group experiences are among the most significant determinants of human nature and (2) social phenomena are amenable to scientific investigation.

During this early period, these propositions were debated by numerous scientists. Some of the most influential were Emile Durkheim, Charles Cooley, George H. Mead, Sigmund Freud, and, in later years, Jean Piaget. The empirical basis for these contributions was idiosyncratic in the sense that data collection was nonsystematic according to modern standards. Nevertheless, these men laid out most of the fundamental hypotheses on which research workers have concentrated their efforts up to, and including, the present. For example, they were interested in the formation and maintenance of social groups and in the group as an agent of social control. Indeed, a long-standing emphasis in both social and developmental psychology has been the role of the group in establishing, maintaining, and changing the behavior of the individual. It is also noteworthy that, in these early writings, it was recognized that early social experience—not merely with adults but with other youngsters—is centrally important to ontogenesis in many species.

Among the early writers, Cooley (1909) probably gave the most explicit attention to the role of peer relations in child development. Even so, he was principally interested in the general effects of group experience on human behavior rather than the particular contributions of peer interaction to the growth of social competence. The following passage reveals some of the hypotheses that were (and, in some cases, still are) debated in this field.

> The view maintained is that human nature is not something existing separately in the individual, but a group nature or primary phase of society. It is the nature which is developed and expressed in those simple, face-to-face groups that are somewhat alike in all societies; groups of the family, the playground, and the neighborhood. In the essential similarity of these is to be found the basis, in experience, for similar ideas and sentiments in the human mind. In these, everywhere, human nature comes into existence. Man does not have it at birth; he cannot acquire it except through fellowship, and it decays in isolation. (pp. 29–30)

In this passage, the child's peer group is given parity with other groups as a source of social norms. Note also that the peer group is recognized as a universal factor in socialization but not an immutable one, even though the time dependencies associated with change and dissolution are not discussed.

The absence of an extensive empirical basis for these suppositions did not prevent their utilization in the applied fields. Intrinsic in most forms of "progressive education" in the 1920s and 1930s was an increased reliance on child-child relations in educational management—on group work, cooperative activities, common study, and self-government—even in the elementary school. These observations, coupled with work in applied psychoanalysis (cf. Isaacs, 1933), also produced an upsurge of interest in peer socialization as a central component of nursery education.

One issue that was frequently debated during the early years of this century was whether groups constitute legitimate objects of scientific inquiry. In addition, many natural scientists thought that the child was an inappropriate target for systematic investigation (Bradbury & Stoddard, 1933). There were heated arguments during this period (see Allport, 1954) concerning the "reality" of social phenomena, as well as arguments that revolved around concepts such as "group mind," "the collective unconscious," and "institutions." While it is not possible to specify the causal factors that finally terminated these debates, Cartwright and Zander (1960) pointed

out that, during the 1930s, the decline in publications concerning these questions occurred simultaneously with the advent of new and improved techniques for gathering "hard data" concerning social behavior.

At least two of the three major advances in the technology of social psychology originated in work with children. The first of these was the invention of systematic methods for observing the behavior of individuals in groups. Participant observation was utilized with notable effectiveness in the late 1920s by Thrasher (1927) in his studies of the formation, location, membership, and behavior of adolescent gangs. But more systematic methods were needed and, late in the decade, categories were devised that were based on overt behavior, sampling methods were worked out, and standards were established for determining reliability of measurement. Scores stemming from this early work tended to be rate measures, that is, frequency of social acts per unit time, and such measures continue to dominate contemporary research. Many child psychologists contributed to this effort, but the major benchwork must be credited to Dorothy Thomas (1929) and her colleagues as well as to Florence Goodenough (1928) and her collaborators. A more detailed account of this early work has been written by Renshaw (1981).

A second methodological advance came in 1936 when Lewin and his colleagues began their experimental work on the "social climate" of children's groups. A major purpose of this research was to isolate, by means of experimental techniques, some of the consequences of variations in leadership style. It is true that experimental (i.e., manipulative) strategies were used in research on peer relations long before. Most writers cite Triplett's (1897–98) study as the first experiment to deal with peer relations.[1] And even at the Iowa Child Welfare Research Station, where Lewin conducted his experiments, earlier studies were designed to discover appropriate interventions for children who were insufficiently assertive in their interactions with other children (Jack, 1934; Page, 1936). But the Lewin studies were associated with the theoretical notions known as field theory, and their subject matter was closely related to political issues. These characteristics, in addition to the utilization of newly developed observational techniques and quantitative methods, gave this work a catalytic quality that influenced countless investigators in the ensuing years.

A third advance occurring in the 1930s involved sociometric methods. Although many investigators had experimented with methods for studying the social choices of children, it was Moreno's (1934) work that popularized the "sociometric test." Moreno began his work with adults (prison inmates and psychiatric patients), but no invention has had a greater impact on students of the social psychology of childhood. Although Moreno was primarily interested in sociometry as a means of illuminating various facets of group structure, other investigators employed this technique to assess individual differences in social acceptance and competence. Indeed, such uses of sociometric instruments are preeminent today. Most commonly, sociometric tests are based on simple interviews and are particularly appropriate for studies of interpersonal attraction, group cohesiveness, and time dependencies in group interaction. Work with children can be traced to the research of Jennings (1937–1938) and Criswell (1939). Other investigators devised sociometric measures based on direct observation of children's interactions with their companions (cf. Challman, 1932; Hagman, 1933; Wellman, 1926). Paired comparison techniques were also employed in the early years (Koch, 1933).

Except for a series of sociometric studies (Bonney, 1943a, 1943b; Northway, 1943, 1944), the study of peer relations passed into eclipse with the advent of World War II. When the preoccupations of the war years were over, child psychologists became interested mainly in the neo-Freudian and social learning theories of personality development with their concomitant emphasis on parent-child relations. Observational studies in nursery schools continued, but with the purpose of testing the contemporary family-oriented theories of aggression and dependency (Sears, Whiting, Nowlis, & Sears, 1953). Most of the postwar research in group dynamics was done with adults. Work with children languished except for three outstanding exceptions: (1) the seminal work of M. Sherif and his co-workers on group formation and intergroup relations (Sherif, Harvey, White, Hood, & Sherif, 1961); (2) the ecological studies of Roger Barker and his colleagues (Barker & Wright, 1951, 1955); and (3) the observational studies of social organization by Ronald Lippitt and his associates (Lippitt, Polansky, & Rosen, 1952).

Throughout the 1960s, relatively little research was conducted in peer relations—either studies devoted to the emergence of peer interactions or to changes occurring as age increases. Advances were made during this decade in demonstrating the efficacy of peer reinforcement, punishment, and modeling (see Hartup, 1964; Patterson, Littman, & Bricker, 1967; Wahler, 1967), but few investigators were interested in exploring the long-term significance of peer relations in child development.

Although the winds of change were detectable when the third edition of *Carmichael's manual of child psychology* was prepared in 1969, no one could have anticipated the surge of interest in peer relations that marked the 1970s. Much of this work was reminiscent of the research of the 1930s: (1) Descriptive studies appeared in abundance, including attempts to obtain information on certain children previously overlooked (e.g., toddlers). (2) New techniques in observational recording and data reduction (e.g., sequential analysis) began to be used for identifying behavior changes that occur as a consequence of interaction with other children. (3) The significance of special relationships (e.g., friendships) were examined, and behavior profiles of friendship interaction were derived from direct observation. (4) Group structures were again being scrutinized, especially in groups of young children. (5) New strategies for enhancing social skills were invented. In addition, the linkages among individual differences in social competence, cognitive skills, and affective development were being explored. Today speculations are becoming more specific about the conjunctions that exist between family relations and peer relations as well as their respective roles in childhood socialization. Indeed, the record of the last decade is astonishing, considering the low level of activity marking research in this area at the time the last *Manual* was prepared.

PEERS AND OTHERS

In English usage, the word *peer* denotes "equal standing" and emanates from the tradition that an individual should be judged in a court of law by persons of equivalent rather than higher or lower rank. Peer status, then, ordinarily means equivalence between individuals and their associates. But equivalence in what sense? In most societies, social ranks are not ascribed to children other than the rankings associated with chronological age. Consequently, among both laypersons and social scientists, it has become conventional to use the word peer to refer to a child who is similar in age to some other child. It is not difficult to understand how a word meaning "equal standing" became generalized to mean "equal age"—especially in the English language. Consider that the English-speaking nations are among the most age-graded social systems in the world in their treatment of children.

The literature on peer relations bears the marks of these semantic conventions. Approximately 90% of the existing studies on child-child relations deal with the interaction among agemates, that is, children within 12 months of one another in chronological age. Usage alone, however, did not bring about this state of affairs. Children have been most accessible to social scientists in schools and other institutions which, as mentioned, are age-graded. Unable to track children on the playground, in city streets, and in farmyards, psychologists have unwittingly generated an age-graded data base.

Although school children, in fact, spend great amounts of time with agemates, our data are constrained in two ways: First, equivalence in chronological age does not mean that children are necessarily equivalent in other attributes—for example, intellectual abilities, social skills, socioeconomic status, athletic skill, physical beauty, and so on. Every graduate student knows that chronological age is a "summary variable" and that individual scores on age-related traits may vary enormously around mean values. Plainly, children who are agemates are not always equivalent—in either psychological or social terms. For this reason, Lewis and Rosenblum (1975) suggested that peer status should mean "interaction at similar levels of behavioral complexity." One can extend this argument to mean equivalence in any socially significant attribute.

Second, by emphasizing same-age interaction, child psychologists may have overemphasized these experiences in their theories of socialization. Although it is widely assumed that a child's time is mostly spent with agemates, systematic observations tell us that this is not true. In *Midwest and its children* (Barker & Wright, 1955), it was discovered that approximately 65% of children's interactions with other children involved individuals who differed in age by more than 12 months. Some of these interactions occurred between siblings but, even excluding sibling experiences, 52% of the child-child contacts involved associates who were not agemates. In other cultures, in which children are not segregated by chronological age in school classes, athletic teams, and clubs, interaction with nonagemates is even more common. Observations of the !Kung San culture revealed that child-child relations occur almost entirely in small mixed-age enclaves (Konner, 1975). Hunter-gatherer social units are so small that the existence of more than one or two children of a given age is unusual. Thus, not all cultures provide children with the same limits on choosing associates from among agemates and nonagemates.

Child Associates Versus Adult Associates

The proportion of social activity occurring with other children and with adults changes with age. Observations of infants and children going about their everyday activities have been used to establish both the quantities and qualities of these experiences. In two cases, the *Midwest* study (Barker & Wright, 1955) and studies of the !Kung San culture (Konner, 1975), 10% of the social interactions observed among 2-year-old children involved other children. Most frequently, these exchanges were between the infant and older children, particularly among the Bushmen. In other preliterate societies (as well as certain literate ones), extended contact with older children includes caretaking by "child nurses."

In *Midwest,* the children observed ranged in age up to 11 years. The proportion of the child's social activity with adults decreased steadily throughout childhood, while contact with child associates increased. By age 11, nearly 50% of the child's social activity involved other children. More extensive studies of socialization experiences with children as contrasted with adults are not available, although there is little reason to doubt the generality of these results. Even in nursery schools, an increase has been observed between the ages of 2 and 4 in the utilization of peers as targets of dependency and a corresponding decrease in the direction of such acts to adults (Heathers, 1955).

Children can distinguish photographs of infants as "baby" and pictures of adults as "Daddy" or "Mommy" in the second year of life (Brooks & Lewis, 1978); the distinction between "children" and "grown-ups" is made between the ages of 3.5 and 5 years (Edwards & Lewis, 1979). Young children refer to individuals older than 13 years as "grown-ups" and they cannot assign absolute ages to individuals. But the conceptual distinction between "adult" and "child" clearly emerges at an early age.

Behavioral differentiation involving child and adult targets also becomes evident in the early years. Several investigators have observed more positive social reactions by babies to preschool-age strangers than to strange adults (Greenberg, Hillman, & Grice, 1973; Lewis & Brooks, 1975). Preschool children also discriminate between adult and child associates in terms of social content. Using incomplete stories in which the children were asked to attribute social functions to either child or adult dolls (or photographs), Edwards and Lewis (1979) found that "help" was more commonly ascribed to adults than to agemates, whereas "play" was ascribed to agemates more regularly than to adults. Other functions, for example, "demonstrating" and "sharing," were not consistently differentiated between child and adult figures.

These differentiations continue in middle childhood. Barker and Wright (1955) found that adult-child relations, in general, are based on the child's dependency and the adult's need to control the child. Children's actions toward adults consist mainly of appeals and submission; the adult's actions toward the child consist of dominance and nurturance. On the other hand, the most common actions of children toward children are sociability, dominance, and resistance. These observations nicely confirm interview results with children in which it has been found that high power functions (e.g., depriving, controlling, blaming) are assigned to parents, while low power functions (e.g., demanding, conforming, asking) are assigned to child figures (Emmerich, 1959; Youniss, 1980). From babyhood to adolescence, then, the adult-child and child-child social systems are differentiated both cognitively and socially.

Same-Age Versus Mixed-Age Interaction

It has already been shown that peer relations include children of a wide variety of ages. Beginning in the preschool years, children utilize categorical boundaries distinguishing a "big boy" from "a boy like you" and "a baby boy." Not only are dolls and photographs appropriately labeled with terms like "big girl" and "baby girl," but different functions are ascribed to these individuals. Edwards and Lewis (1979) found that: (1) Giving help was more often ascribed to older children than to agemates and almost never to babies; (2) assistance through demonstration and sharing was differentiated in the same manner; and (3) play was most often ascribed to agemates and older associates.

Observations conducted in six cultures on three continents (Whiting & Whiting, 1975) showed that social activity is concordant with these distinctions. First, help-giving and sympathy occurred most frequently among children who were engaged in social activity with younger children—especially babies—in each of the six cultures.[2] Second, seeking assistance and other dependent behaviors were most commonly directed by children to associates who were older than themselves (suggesting that the young child, to some extent, views older children and grown-ups similarly). Third, both "sociable" acts (e.g., conversation) and aggression were more likely to occur between children who were similar in chronological age than between children who differed in age by more than a year or two.

Laboratory studies elucidate some of the more subtle contributions that same- and mixed-age experiences may make to socialization. In social communication, 4-year-olds use longer and more complex utterances when they talk to 4-year-olds than when they talk to 2-year-olds; indeed, utterance complexity with agemates is similar to that used with adults (Shatz & Gelman, 1973). Moreover, 4-year-old utterances are adjusted according to the verbal ability of their 2-year-old partners; longer utterances and more complex syntactic constructions are used with more responsive companions (Masur, 1978). Retarded children (Hoy & McKnight, 1977) and adults (Snow, 1972) make similar accommodations. Other studies suggest that the greater facility for decoding messages manifested by older children than by younger ones enhances the communicative performance of the latter in mixed-age interaction as compared with same-age interaction (Fishbein & Osborne, 1971). Even 18-month-olds use vocalizations, imitation, and object-mediated social actions more often when playing with 24-month-olds than with other 18-month-olds (Brownell, 1982).

Other dimensions of social interaction also vary according to the similarity between individuals in chronological age. Examining same- and mixed-age dyads of preschool children, Lougee, Grueneich, and Hartup (1977) observed that social interaction was least frequent between two 3-year-olds (strangers), intermediate between 3-year-olds and 5-year-olds, and most frequent between two 5-year-olds. Accommodation to the mixed-age situation by individual children was evident among both the younger and older children, although this accommodation was extremely variable. Other observations, using preschool children who were familiar with each other, show somewhat different results; social and object-directed behavior (including amount of verbal communication) was more frequent in same-age dyads than in mixed-age dyads among *both* 3- and 5-year-olds (Langlois, Gottfried, Barnes, & Hendricks, 1978). Familiarity thus may override age asymmetries in certain circumstances, but other observations confirm that the age difference existing between children affects the quality and quantity of their interaction even when they are well acquainted (Brownell, 1982).

Interpersonal attitudes also vary according to the age difference between children. In one study (Graziano, Musser, & Brody, 1980), 73 first- and third-grade children were asked to attribute trait names to children identified as 2 years older, the subject's own age, or 2 years younger. More positive traits (e.g., "best," "strong," "smart," "fast") were attributed to older children than to either same-age or younger children; more negative traits (e.g., "dumb," "worst," "silly," "weak") were assigned to younger children than to same-age or older children. In this instance, the social desirability of many trait names was confounded with age-related abilities, increasing the likelihood that the positive traits would be more readily assigned to older than to younger children. But certain negative attributes indicating power and assertiveness turned out to be *positively* related to peer age—for example, "mean," "bossy," and "show off." The results thus show that power-related attributes are the ones most likely to be assigned differentially according to relative age. Consistent with these results are observations that, in peer tutoring, children prefer to be taught by older children than by children of their own age (Allen & Feldman, 1976). Within mixed-age classrooms, children also allocate sociometric nominations more commonly to their older classmates than to their younger associates. Whether in mixed-age day care centers covering a 4-year age span (Flotre, 1980) or in elementary school "pods" (Ahlbrand & Reynolds, 1972), positive choices tend to favor the older children. Age differences in rejection choices are not as clearly evident.

Thus, to summarize, some social actions occur with younger children more frequently than with older children (e.g., nurturance), some with age-mates rather than with nonagemates (e.g., aggression), and some with older children rather than with younger children (e.g., dependency). Social accommodation is not the same in same- and mixed-age interaction. Mixed-age interaction can be viewed as a context for the socialization of assertiveness (both prosocial and antisocial) and for seeking assistance from others. Same-age socialization can be viewed as a context for acquiring skills needed in "give-and-take"—both pleasant social exchanges and aggressive ones. Since social competence in most cultures consists of effectiveness in both symmetrical and asymmetrical interactions, it can be argued that both same- and mixed-age socialization contain constructive challenges for the individual child.

Same-Sex Versus Mixed-Sex Interaction

The existence of a sex cleavage in peer interaction is much too well-known to require extensive comment. Children of all ages associate more frequently with members of their own sex than with members of the opposite sex and like them better. It is not clear that sex cleavages are evident in social interaction before the first birthday, but observations of toddlers show the beginnings of behavioral dimorphism (Hutt & Hutt, 1970). From the age of 3, same-sex assortments are evident as measured by associative or cooperative interactions (Charles-

worth & Hartup, 1967; Clark, Wyon, & Richards, 1969; McCandless & Hoyt, 1961; Parten, 1932; Serbin, Tonick, & Sternglanz, 1977) and by sociometric analysis (Abel & Sahinkaya, 1962; Marshall & McCandless, 1957a; Moore & Updegraff, 1964). Same-sex contacts in parallel play are twice as frequent among preschool children as instances of opposite-sex play; instances of same-sex cooperative interaction are nearly four times as frequent as similar interactions between opposite-sex children (Serbin et al., 1977). Finally, reinforcing interactions are experienced by children more frequently from same-sex than from opposite-sex associates (Charlesworth & Hartup, 1967). An increase in the incidence of same-sex assortments occurs in middle childhood, which peaks in early adolescence: "At this age, by almost world-wide consent, boys and girls separate for a time, and lead their lives during this most critical period more or less apart . . ." (Hall, 1904, p. 617).

What are the forces that underlie this sex cleavage? Most investigators believe that the basis for sex segregation is a combination of encouragement from adults, the compatibilities intrinsic in same-sex play, and sex-role stereotypes that eventually operate within peer interaction itself. Parents begin this process at home by supplying different toys to boys and girls (Rheingold & Cook, 1975) and by seeking out same-sex playmates for their toddlers more often than opposite-sex playmates (Lewis, Young, Brooks, & Michalson, 1975). Next, teachers are known to be responsive to sex-appropriate activities at the same time that the child is in the vicinity of same-sex children (Fagot, 1977a). This is well illustrated by one attempt to increase mixed-sex cooperative play among 4-year-olds through alteration of teacher reactions (Serbin et al., 1977). After baseline observations which showed that cross-sex contacts occurred infrequently, the teachers were asked to make a special effort to comment approvingly, before the entire class, each time a mixed-sex pair or group of children played together. Over a 2-week period, the rate of mixed-sex play increased by 20% without decreasing the rate of same-sex play. Later, when the teacher reactions were stopped, cross-sex interactions declined to their previous level. Whether contingency changes could permanently erase the sex cleavage is doubtful, but the extensiveness of such cleavages is clearly sensitive to adult reactions.

Play may undergird the sex cleavage in at least two ways: (1) through the attraction that similarity in interests between oneself and others carries with it; and (2) through avoidance that emanates from dissimilarities. Boy-boy and girl-girl interactions differ in many ways. Young boys' interactions center on blocks and movable toys, while girls' interactions center on dramatic play and table activities (Charlesworth & Hartup, 1967; Shure, 1963). It is even possible to identify areas in the nursery school playroom that are "boys' places" and "girls' places," and one team of investigators employed time spent in such areas as a measure of early sex-typing (Sears, Rau, & Alpert, 1965). Although overall sociability does not differ greatly in young boys' and girls' interactions (Howes & Rubenstein, 1979; Vandell, Wilson, & Buchanan, 1980), interaction among boys, as compared to girls, is likely to be more boisterous, to involve rough-and-tumble play (DiPietro, 1981), to occur outdoors, to be more competitive, and to last longer (Lever, 1976). Definitive evidence is scarce, but there is a strong suggestion in several studies that young girls actively avoid contact with boys owing to their roughness (e.g., Haskett, 1971). No observer would question the fact that children avoid the opposite sex in middle childhood and early adolescence.

Sex cleavages extend to differences in male and female social networks. Girls can be observed in pairs more often than boys, and boys congregate in large cohesive groups more often than girls. These differences are noticeable from the preschool years through middle childhood and adolescence (Lever, 1976; Omark, Omark, & Edelman, 1973; Savin-Williams, 1980a, 1980b). Boys' interactions are more likely to involve mixed-age contacts than girls', even though school-age girls more frequently engage in mixed-sex contact in organized games ("You're better off with even a girl in the outfield than no one at all"; Lever, 1976).

Other sex differences have been noted in the "intensiveness" and "extensiveness" of child-child interactions. In a factor analytic study of 61 children between the ages of 7 and 8, Waldrop and Halverson (1975) found that intensiveness in social activity (as rated from the mother's mentions of best friends and their importance to the child) loaded highly on a peer-orientation factor only for girls. In contrast, ratings of extensiveness (the degree to which the child participated in group activities and games) loaded on the peer-orientation factor only among boys. Intensive girls also were more socially competent than less intensive girls, and extensive boys were more socially at ease than less extensive boys.

Eder and Hallinan (1978) subsequently predicted that sociometric tests with preadolescents would show that girls, more commonly than boys, are involved in triads in which a single dyadic friendship

exists to the exclusion of the remaining member. Sociometric choices were obtained in five classrooms, and all same-sex triads in each classroom were examined for the existence of mutual choices. Next, the number of triads encompassing an exclusive dyadic friendship were divided by the total number of same-sex triads existing in the class. The proportion of exclusive friendship dyads was greater for girls than for boys in four of the classrooms. On the other hand, nonmutual choices within same-sex triads were more common among boys than among girls. Girls' choices became more exclusive as the school year progressed; boys' choices either became more nonexclusive or did not change. The determinants of these differences are obscure, but it is reasonable to suppose that the character of children's play, beginning in early childhood, brings them about. And some observers have posited that the social extensiveness of male enclaves supports a quest for autonomy and rebellion against authority, while the intensiveness of female enclaves supports a need for close, intimate friendships—a dimorphism in socialization that is concordant with traditional sex-role stereotypes (Douvan & Adelson, 1966).

Although boy-boy and girl-girl relations are distinctive, comparisons between same-sex interaction and opposite-sex interaction are rare. Jacklin and Maccoby (1978) studied ninety 33-month-old children, most without nursery school experience. More social behavior—both positive and negative—was directed toward same-sex partners than toward opposite-sex partners. Girls also evidenced more frequent instances of passivity in the presence of boys than in the presence of girls, but the corresponding difference was not significant for boys. Since certain indicators of the children's gender were not obvious (e.g., modes of dress), more subtle behavior cues or labeling by the children must have mediated the results. While it is not possible to conclude that same-sex contacts were better "meshed" than opposite-sex contacts, it is clear that same-sex situations set in motion more vigorous social interactions.

Similar results were obtained by Langlois, Gottfried, and Seay (1973) using subjects who were acquainted with one another. Five-year-olds showed more smiling, talking, nonword verbalizations, and body contact in same-sex pairs than in opposite-sex pairs. Aggression also occurred more frequently in the same-sex condition indicating that sociability, in general, was facilitated by that condition. Three-year-old girls showed similar tendencies, although boys of this age were more sociable with girls than with other boys. The authors attribute the reversal for the younger boys to the arousing influence of their highly social female partners. Nevertheless, the discrepancy in results for 3-year-old children must be noted in these two studies—along with the observation that the pair members differed in their familiarity with one another.

In general, then, strong incentives exist for children to interact with others of their own sex, probably deriving from intrinsic gratifications contained in their play activities as well as reactions from both adults and other children. Rejection of the opposite sex also occurs, although avoidance of the opposite sex may be a more salient feature of social organization in middle childhood than in earlier years. These assortments are associated with distinctive modes of interaction among males and among females, differences in social organization, and differences between same- and mixed-sex interaction.

Race and the Peer System

Racial Awareness and Racial Attitudes

Most of the early data on the emergence of racial awareness were American. Evidence of discrimination by young children according to skin color was elicited in the form of responses to line drawings (Horowitz, 1936), dolls (Clark & Clark, 1939), and photographs (Radke, Sutherland, & Rosenberg, 1950). Preselection of such stimulus materials must be carefully done (e.g., with regard to relative attractiveness), but the results have been generally consistent across geographic locations, across integrated and segregated settings (much of the early work was completed in the latter), and across time. Both black and white children show an awareness of racial differences as early as the fourth year (Clark & Clark, 1939; 1947) and this appears to increase with age (Spencer, 1981). Awareness of ethnic differences among Hispanic children, Native American children, and other racial groups is also manifest in the early years (Durrett & Davy, 1970) but some investigators have reported later segregation by skin color in the last-named groups (Werner & Evans, 1968).

Most investigators have observed that white children display prowhite/antiblack biases when asked to choose between black and white dolls, for example, or when given the hypothetical choice of living with families pictured as black or white. These same biases have been observed in some instances among young black children (Asher & Allen, 1969; Morland, 1963; Spencer, 1981), although problack biases have sometimes been noted (cf. Hraba & Grant, 1970). Actually, in most investigations, the choices of young black children do not depart significantly from chance (Banks, 1976). But prowhite/antiblack choices are fewer among black preschoolers than among white preschoolers (Williams & Morland, 1976) and, among school-age black children, they decline with age (Spencer, 1981).

A number of investigators (e.g., Williams, Boswell, & Best, 1975) have contrasted children's ratings of black and white animals, in positive and negative terms, to determine the extent to which children evidence generalized negative attitudes toward the color black. By themselves, these studies are of limited interest since, in most Western societies, black is associated with a variety of negative moods. It helps some to know, however, that validation studies show correlations between color attitudes on these tests and attitudes about skin color in the range of .50 in various United States samples and in France, Germany, Italy, and Japan (Best, Field, & Williams, 1976; Best, Naylor, & Williams, 1975; Iwawaki, Sonoo, Williams, & Best, 1978). A light skin bias was observed in each culture, although it is stronger among American white children than among American black children and the other cultural groups.

Race and Social Interaction

What are the concomitants of racial awareness and attitudes in child-child interaction? The vast majority of studies dealing with this question have been sociometric investigations. Observations in mixed-race situations show that same-race contacts are more frequent than cross-race contacts, the results showing continuity from the preschool years (McCandless & Hoyt, 1961) through early adolescence. In a study of seating patterns in the cafeteria of an integrated junior high school, Schofield and Sagar (1977) found that race was a significant grouping criterion even though the students and their families had chosen attendance at the integrated school rather than attendance at segregated ones. A typical observation in this study, on one day, involved 138 white and 109 black students. Random distribution of these students within the occupied seats in the cafeteria would have resulted in 67 side-by-side and 41 face-to-face interracial adjacencies. Only 13 and 9 of the respective adjacencies were actually found. Notable in both preschool observations and junior high school observations is the lesser significance of race as a grouping criterion compared to sex. In both instances, associative contact was more likely to be same sex rather than same race (see also Asher, Singleton, & Taylor, 1982).

A large literature shows that own-race sociometric choices are more common than other-race nominations. Among American children, race cleavages in this form were noted in the 1930s (Criswell, 1939), the 1940s (Radke et al., 1950), and throughout the 1950s and 1960s (Morland, 1966; Springer, 1953). This situation still prevails and is not changing very much, as revealed by a comparison of own- and other-race choices among third-grade children in 12 integrated schools studied in 1973, 1976, and 1980 (Asher et al., 1982; Singleton & Asher, 1979). In this instance, children were asked to rate their associates as preferred playmates or work companions as well as "best friends." Children gave rather positive ratings to other-race classmates as companions, perhaps indicating a secular trend, even though own-race choices were more frequent than other-race choices. Cleavages were much more evident in friendship choices than in choices as playmates or work associates.

In several instances, age differences in same- and cross-race choices have been examined. The results indicate increasing solidification of racial cleavages in child-child relations. Singleton and Asher (1979) included a longitudinal component in their study showing that stronger own-race preferences existed at the sixth-grade level than at the third-grade level, particularly among black children. Own-race preferences as playmates or work companions did not increase further in adolescence, although the race cleavage in choices of "best friends" did (Asher et al., 1982). These age trends are concordant with a national sample study of 4300 British students ranging in age from 8 to 14 (Jelinek & Brittan, 1975) in schools that enrolled from 18 to 84% minority children, including Middle Eastern ethnic groups and those of Afro-Caribbean and Asian origin. Low levels of cross-ethnic friendship choices occurred among the youngest children and declined progressively in the older cohorts; the largest decrease occurred at entrance to secondary school. No ethnic differences in the increased ethnocentrism of the children's choices were found.

It is obviously time for a more differentiated analysis of age functions in the ethnicity of children's peer relations. The extent to which these changes are based on the increased salience of interpersonal similarity and on increased avoidance owing to prejudicial attitudes needs to be better understood. It is easy to deplore the increased race cleavage in child-child relations that occurs with age and to castigate the schools and other social institutions for not reversing these developments. On the other hand, the realities of social pluralism are such that other-race friendship choices may disadvantage both majority and minority children in certain ways.

Policy arguments would be better grounded if the psychological processes underlying these developmental changes were better understood.

Few differences have been reported in the play interactions of black and white preschool children except for aggression (usually more frequent among black children; Hartup, 1974). Relatively little research attention has been given to mixed-race interaction in comparison to same-race interaction, but a microanalysis of proxemic behavior was completed in two studies. Jones and Aiello (1973) observed same-sex interactions in segregated classrooms and found that first-grade black males interacted with each other more closely but less frontally than whites. Fifth-grade black males, however, were more physically distant in their interactions than white males even though the interaction remained less frontal. These racial differences were not evident among females who, overall, were more direct in their interactions than were males. A second study (Zimmerman & Brody, 1975), with consistent results, was conducted with fifth- and sixth-grade dyads (strangers). In general, then, the proxemics of social interaction among elementary school children become more and more like the proxemics that mark interaction between black adults and between white adults (Baxter, 1970).

Zimmerman and Brody also included mixed-race dyads in their study and found that biracial situations produced intermediate social distance, talk, and body axis. Although no direct evidence was obtained, it appears that biracial interaction involved an averaging of each ethnic group, with each boy attempting to act in accordance with the proxemic norms of his own racial group. Accommodations in talk, however, were evident: The white boys' conversations tended to diminish owing to the brevity of the black youngsters' utterances. Hostile interactions, though, were not apparent.

To summarize, race cleavages in child-child relations are ubiquitous in many mixed-race cultures and become more pervasive as children grow older. Negative attitudes toward other-race children are present in early childhood, especially among majority group children. Various ethnic groups may interact according to different norms governing both proxemics and interaction content, although not much is known about the development of these differences in children.

INTERACTION

Child-child interaction evolves from loosely differentiated "interacts" to differentiated social interaction and from primitive awareness of the needs of others to social reciprocities. Elements in the social/cognitive dimensions of child-child interaction (e.g., synchronization, complexity, differentiation) are described in this section along with various instrumental actions (e.g., prosocial behavior and aggression). The competencies of the young child will be examined as well as changes in peer interaction among older children. Continuities, however, are sometimes difficult to trace since intentions and measurements differ in investigations with infants, children, and adolescents.

Classification systems used in the study of child-child interaction vary enormously. Some investigators are taxonomic ''lumpers'' and use large, inclusive categories; others are taxonomic ''splitters'' and use classification systems based on smaller, noninclusive units. Thus, ''social acts'' in one case may consist of actions accompanied by visual orientation to the companion and an observable consequence; these may be divided in other instances into ''proximal'' and ''distal'' actions according to whether the action occurs near to the companion or at a distance. These, too, may be subdivided—into ''coordinated'' units (when more than one behavior element is involved), ''reciprocated'' units (when the companion reacts to the target child's actions), or ''synchronous'' units (when the target child's actions are functionally concordant with those of the companion).

No ''user's guide'' can be constructed to assist the novice in sorting out these categorical conventions; indeed, no conventional taxonomy exists. Moreover, the tie between the classification scheme used by the investigator and the purpose of the investigation is often tenuous. Many investigators measure the *amount* of social interaction on the assumption that it varies with age or the nature of the situation. Others measure *qualities* of the interaction or its content, again because these are believed to be theoretically relevant. Readers must be aware that enormous variations mark this literature and that the terms contained in this section must be carefully mapped onto the measures used in the studies themselves.

Developmental Course

The First Year

For many children, peer relations begin in the first year of life. Sizable numbers of babies in both Western and non-Western cultures have regular contacts with other babies and young children. Authoritative studies are not available, but anecdotal accounts show that from 20% to 40% of 6- to 12-month-old American babies see other babies more than once a week. Including babies who have once-a-week contacts, the number increases to over 50%; about 30% of mothers of 6-month-old babies report that their offspring have no contact with other babies (Vandell & Mueller, 1980). These figures may not be the same in non-Western cultures, particularly in societies where people live in small and scattered enclaves. Sibling caretaking, however, enhances the likelihood of infant-infant contact and, in Western societies, the utilization of day care increases early encounters with other children.

The earliest data concerning infant-infant interaction were derived from observations of babies from poor families that were taken by their mothers to a milk station (Bühler, 1927) and from observations of infants in institutions (Bridges, 1933). Although these babies oriented toward others who were active or crying as early as 2 months of age, responsivity was relatively unpredictable. One early investigator (Bühler) characterized the young infant as ''socially blind'' to other children during the first months of life; contemporary observations (Vincze, 1971) confirm these early assessments. Reaching and touching occur in infant-infant contacts at about 3 or 4 months; smiles and vocalizations by 6 months (Durfee & Lee, 1973; Maudry & Nekula, 1939; Shirley, 1933; Vincze, 1971). When crawling emerges, babies may follow one another and older infants mutually explore eyes, mouths, and ears. Increasingly, throughout the early months, looking at the other baby's face accompanies actions like smiling and reaching, convincing many investigators that these activities are true social behaviors (Vandell & Mueller, 1980).

Between 6 and 12 months, the elements of child-child interaction change both in frequency and complexity. Vandell et al. (1980) observed 32 infants (initially strangers) in pairs at 6, 9, and 12 months in the presence of their mothers. Social actions were identified, consisting of either single acts (e.g., a smile) or coordinated acts accompanied by visual regard of the other baby's face. In some instances, approximately once every 4 minutes, these actions were followed within 5 seconds by social actions from the other baby. ''Semisocial'' acts (e.g., Child A offers a toy to Child B who touches the toy without looking at Child A) also occurred about once every 4 minutes at 6 months and about once every 3 minutes at 9 and 12 months. One-way social acts (unreciprocated) occurred as frequently as the social and ''semisocial'' sequences combined—at every age. Although nonsocial activity was not coded, it is clear that much more time was used nonsocially than socially by the babies in these sessions. Age differences did not occur in the overall frequency of social actions or social sequences. Certain elements, however, increased from 6 to 12 months, including vocalization, cries, smiles, agonistic acts, object-related social acts, gesturing, and touching. Within social sequences, vocalizations, smiles, and touching were the most frequent actions used to initiate, maintain, and terminate the interaction.

Several comments concerning infant-infant interaction can be made. First, interactive elements emerge in a more or less invariant order: Looking appears first, followed by touching and reaching, and, later, coordinated social acts. To a considerable extent, the appearance of these social elements parallels changes occurring in the baby's reactions to the mother as well as to inanimate objects. Early child-child interaction is thus embedded in more general developmental change. Coordinations involving visual fixation of another baby's face, however, do not indicate a discriminant "peer affectional system" (Harlow, 1969); nor does the emergence of complementary actions, such as peek-a-boo and rudimentary imitations (Eckerman, Whatley, & Kutz, 1975). More convincing evidence for the emergence of a "peer repertoire" emanates from observations of infants brought together as strangers in the presence or absence of toys and from observations with mothers as contrasted to activity with other babies. Without toys available in the room, older infants contact each other more often, smile and imitate each other, and engage in longer and more frequent social exchanges (Eckerman & Whatley, 1977; Vandell et al., 1980). When mothers and other babies are both available, looking and vocalization are more commonly directed to the baby; touching is more commonly directed to the mother (Lewis et al., 1975; Vandell, 1980). These contextual differentiations in social reactions provide the best evidence for the emergence of a specific peer repertoire by the end of the first year.

Second, infant-infant social contacts are relatively infrequent even in "intense" circumstances. The "baby party" (i.e., situating two babies in a play pen, crib, or playroom with their mothers close by) is an extremely focused, intensive social situation. Under these conditions, social contacts occur between once and twice a minute according to some investigators (Becker, 1977; Eckerman et al., 1975) or once every 2 minutes according to others (Vandell et al., 1980). These frequencies increase slightly when the babies have become acquainted with one another but do not change markedly through the twelfth month. In day care centers, contact rates are also modest, that is, slightly more than once every 2 minutes (Finkelstein, Dent, Gallagher, & Ramey,

1978). Especially noteworthy is the relative number of contacts made with other babies, mothers, and teachers in these situations. In the laboratory, contact with the mother occurs at about the same rate as contact with another infant (Eckerman et al., 1975; Vandell, 1980) but, in the day care center, contacts with adults are seven times as frequent as contacts with other babies (Finkelstein et al., 1978). Clearly, when competition exists for the infant's attention from adults and from toys, peer socialization is not extensive.

Third, many overtures made by one infant to another are not reciprocated. Reciprocation rates vary according to the investigation, but it seems that 6- to 12-month-old babies do not respond to actions directed at them by another baby from 38% (Vandell et al., 1980) to 50% (Maudry & Nekula, 1939) to 60% (Becker, 1977; Lee, 1973). Familiarity increases reciprocities in infant-infant interaction, but most of the interactions among 6- to 12-month-olds consist of a single overture and a response; multiple alternations are rare until the second year.

How, then, does one describe child-child interaction among infants? The answer obviously depends on whether one emphasizes what babies *do* or *do not do*. Social interest is evident, but the skills necessary for sustained social interaction are not. Reciprocities sometimes occur in infant-infant interaction, but single "interacts" are more salient than sustained interaction. Individual differences are well documented (Bronson, 1975; 1981) and situational constraints apparent. Peer relations exist in babyhood in only the loosest sense.

The Second Year

Child-child social skills remain relatively rudimentary in the second year of life, but both quantitative and qualitative changes occur. The data base on toddler interaction has been augmented considerably in the last decade based on observations in laboratories, play groups, and homes. The level of analysis varies in these studies, but it is clear that the amount and complexity of interaction increase as well as affective concomitants. Eckerman et al. (1975) observed 30 pairs of same-age toddlers: 10 to 12, 16 to 18, and 22 to 24 months of age. The children, who were not previously acquainted, met together for 20 minutes in the presence of their mothers. Attentiveness to the other child was observed in 60% of the 15-second observation intervals and did not change with age; neither did the occurrence of distance contacts (e.g., smiling and vocalizing) and physical contact. Age differences, however, were noted in the simultaneous use of play materials (which increased mainly between 18 and 24 months) and play involvement (which increased gradually throughout the year). These trends were in marked contrast to that of social involvement with the mother, which occurred less frequently among the older children than among the younger ones.

Mueller and Brenner (1977) conducted observations of social interaction in two small groups of male toddlers, one at intervals between 12 and 18 months and another at intervals between 17 and 23 months. Again, the amount of social interaction increased with age in both instances. The effects of increased acquaintance and increases in chronological age are confounded in these analyses, but comparisons between the groups indicate that these changes are associated with *both* acquaintance and age. Most importantly, the age changes centered on the complexity of the social interaction: (1) Both simple and coordinated actions accompanied by looking at another child increased, as did reciprocated interactions (see also Brownell, 1982); (2) both two-unit exchanges and longer ones were observed more frequently as the children grew older; and (3) isolated acts were common but did not change much with age, indicating that unreciprocated overtures remain in the child's experience. Bronson (1981) also reported a higher incidence of isolated social contacts than "contact chains" in observations of toddlers in four-person groups. The proportion of isolated incidents, however, declined between 12 and 24 months (from 73 to 58%) and a corresponding increase was observed in the proportion of contact chains (from 6 to 13%). The highest incidence of peer interaction observed among toddlers was reported by Rubenstein and Howes (1976) in a group of 19-month-old, well-acquainted toddlers observed in their own homes. Socially directed activity accounted for more than 50% of the observation time.

Even though year-old babies smile and laugh at each other, the vast majority of their interactions are emotionally neutral. Several investigators (e.g., Mueller & Brenner, 1977; Rubenstein & Howes, 1976) have shown that as many as 70% of the social contacts in play groups of toddlers are serious (i.e., neutral) in tone. Ross and Goldman (1976), however, found that the incidence of positive affect was more common among 2-year-olds than among 1-year-olds, suggesting that emotional coloring becomes an important qualitative element in social interaction in the second year (see also Mueller and Rich, 1976). Ross and Goldman (1976) argue that these changes in emotionality support or sustain the social interaction through signaling that "this is a

game" or "this is O.K." Through these sustained interactions, it is argued, the child experiences the gratifications contained in play. Negative affect becomes more evident in the second year also, with agonistic exchanges increasing in frequency through the middle of this period (Bridges, 1933; Maudry & Nekula, 1939). Nonaggressive contacts and positive interaction predominate, however (Rubenstein & Howes, 1976).

Peer interaction among 2-year-olds, then, is more complex and more common than among 1-year-olds. Sustained social exchanges are embedded in the child's repertoire by the end of this time. In "intensive" situations, orientation and commerce with other children may even exceed attention to adults, especially when the children are well acquainted with one another. In less intense situations, however, peer socialization may not consume the majority of the child's attention and activity. It is reasonable to suppose that utilization of the mother as a "secure base" for exploration (Ainsworth, 1972) underlies the increased interaction with other children by the end of the second year; social/cognitive maturation also seems manifest in these exchanges. But there is no evidence that children are extensively sought out as social objects at this time nor that they serve necessary or unique functions in socialization. Without minimizing the significance of the changes in child-child interaction occurring in the first 2 years, one can assert that social skills are mainly nascent.

The Preschool Years

Most commonly, child-child relations between the ages of 2 and 5 have been studied in nursery schools and day care centers—either in classrooms or laboratories. Observations in other situations, for example, homes, are extremely rare. Overall, the frequency of both positive and negative social interaction continues to increase. Social contacts occur in dyadic situations more often among 5-year-olds than among 3-year-olds (Lougee et al., 1977) and also in group situations (Charlesworth & Hartup, 1967). Indeed, Parten (1932) obtained a correlation of .61 between chronological age and social participation across this age range. Positive interactions occur more frequently than agonistic exchanges in a ratio of approximately 7:1 or 8:1 (Walters, Pearce, & Dahms, 1957). Although frequencies of aggressive interaction and rough-and-tumble play increase during these years, decreases in the *proportion* of aggressive exchanges to friendly interactions have been noted, especially among middle-class boys. Such decreases apparently do not characterize lower class boys or girls from either middle or lower socioeconomic backgrounds (Schroeder & Flapan, 1971).

Four types of positive exchanges were studied in an investigation of 70 3- and 4-year-old children (Charlesworth & Hartup, 1967): giving positive attention and approval, affection and personal acceptance, submission, and giving tangible objects. Higher rates of these actions occurred among the 4-year-olds than among 3-year-olds, even though exchange rates varied from classroom to classroom and from activity to activity. The initiation of positive overtures was correlated with rates of receiving such overtures (see also Kohn, 1966), and the most reinforcing children were found to scatter their reinforcements widely.

Sharing and sympathy increase only slightly in the preschool years even though spontaneous sharing can be observed among toddlers. Both laboratory observations (Hartup & Coates, 1967) and nursery school observations (Hartup & Keller, 1960; Strayer, Wareing, & Rushton, 1979; Walters et al., 1957) show that altruism remains at a relatively low level among preschool children; sharing occurs about seven times an hour and helping about once an hour in some observational studies.

Although positive social interaction increases in the preschool years, competition and rivalry also increase. Leuba (1933) compared performance on a peg-inserting task when the child worked alone with performance when working with another child. Two-year-olds were not affected by the working conditions, 3-year-olds performed less well in the social situation (seeming to be distracted by the presence of the other child), and 4-year-olds performed better in the presence of another child than when working alone. Greenberg (1932) also discovered large differences in amount of rivalrous competition shown by children between the ages of 2 and 7 when working in an induced competitive atmosphere.

Quarreling changes in several respects during early childhood (Dawe, 1934). Older preschoolers engage in fewer, but longer, quarrels, similar to the increases noted in the length of other social exchanges (Garvey, 1974). Disputes occur most frequently between children of the same sex; and boys engage in more quarreling than girls. Most quarreling is object oriented even though the incidence of such struggles declines in relation to other forms of agonism. Total frequencies of aggressive peer interaction increase between the ages of 2 and 4 years and then decline (Blurton Jones, 1972; Hartup, 1974; Walters et al., 1957). Sex differences, however, become more pronounced and modes of aggression change. For example, screaming, weeping, hitting, and physical attack decline but verbal aggression increases.

Much evidence suggests that the course of child-child interaction cannot be summarized in terms of superordinate measures such as altruism and aggression. Smith and Connolly (1972) observed social interaction in 40 children ranging in age from 2 years 9 months to 4 years 9 months in three day nurseries. Staring, crying, sucking, pointing, and submissive-flight behaviors occurred less frequently among the older children, while talking and social play were increasingly common. Similar results were obtained from observations of 12 2-year-olds and 13 4-year-olds (Blurton Jones, 1972): The older children engaged more frequently in talking, playing with other children (including rough-and-tumble play), smiling, and laughing; the younger children more often cried, watched other children, relinquished toys, and oriented to the teacher. Mueller (1972) also observed that talking tends to be more common in dyads of 5-year-olds than in dyads of 3-year-olds even though the "success" of these verbal interchanges was roughly the same at both ages (about 62%).

Overall, these results indicate that children tend to abandon immature or inefficient social actions with increasing age, while maintaining or acquiring more mature ones. Indeed, Mueller (1972) found that successful replies to verbal messages emitted by preschool children could be most readily predicted by the same characteristics as adult communication successes—for example, the technical quality of the message and the visual attention of the listener at the beginning of the exchange. Other observations suggest that the proxemics of child-child interaction in the preschool years begin to resemble adult social behavior—for example, eye contact and vocalization are positively correlated in social interaction as well as eye contact and body axis (Savitsky & Watson, 1975).

Various social coordinations can be observed in preschool children that are not observable in younger children. Speaker-listener accommodations in relation to the children's ages were mentioned previously (cf. Shatz & Gelman, 1973). Collaborations also begin to emerge in social problem solving. Cooper (1977) observed 32 pairs of agemates, ranging in age from 3 to 5, in a collaborative balancing task. No age differences occurred in problem-solving attempts or time spent with the materials, but successful collaborations were more common among the older children and exchange efficiency was more evident (i.e., the ratio of successes to attempts at coordinated action).

Earlier studies (Parten, 1932) suggest that a more

or less unidimensional movement occurs between the ages of 2 and 5 from asocial or one-way social interaction to associative or coordinated activity. These observations showed that *unoccupied, solitary,* and *onlooker* activities decline between 3 and 4 years of age, *parallel* activities decline between 4 and 5 years, and *associative* and *cooperative* activities increase in this time. Consequently, the social skills of the very young child, for the most part, have been characterized in textbooks as solitary or parallel, and the emergence of associative interaction has been noted as one of the great achievements in peer socialization during the preschool years.

Close examination, however, indicates that the developmental course of child-child interaction is more complex. First, solitary activity (and also parallel play) remains at relatively high levels throughout these years (Clark, Wyon, & Richards, 1969). Solitary play may decline among 3- and 4-year-olds (Smith, 1978) but it still occurred more frequently among 5-year-olds than cooperative activity in the observations conducted by Parten (1932) and Tieszen (1979) and only a bit less frequently in observations by Barnes (1971). Parallel play, too, occurs among 5-year-olds as frequently as cooperative or associative activity according to Barnes (1971), a bit less frequently according to Parten (1932), and more frequently according to Tieszen (1979). It is incorrect, then, to describe the qualitative changes in social interaction as involving the elimination of "nonsocial" and "semisocial" acts from the repertoire. To the contrary, preschool children spend considerable amounts of time by themselves or in noninteractive contact with other children.

What does change seems to be the task involvement or the cognitive maturity of nonsocial and semisocial activity. Rubin, Watson, and Jambor (1978) observed 4- and 5-year old children, distinguishing three kinds of solitary activity: functional involvement with objects, constructive involvement, and dramatic play (Smilansky, 1968). Much less functional, solitary activity was evident among the older subjects than among the younger ones; on the other hand, no age differences were observed in the other two categories of solitary activity. Parallel play also did not generally decline: Functional parallel activity decreased with age, but constructive and dramatic parallel play actually increased. Cognitively mature nonsocial and semisocial actions, then, remain in the repertoire and may not decline in substantial degree for many years. But cognitively immature actions increasingly disappear.

A factor analytic investigation (Roper & Hinde, 1978) further illuminates the structure of social interaction in the preschool years. Using 22 measures derived from observations of two groups of children between the ages of 3 years 2 months and 4 years 10 months, factor analyses were conducted separately for each group and each term of the school year, thus providing multiple replications. Results were consistent in indicating two dimensions of social interaction rather than one: (1) a "group-to-parallel" dimension defined by positive loadings on group activity, talk, and large muscle activities as well as negative loadings on parallel activity; and (2) solitary play. In addition, a third factor emerged that was orthogonal to the two social dimensions—"not playing at all." Clearly, social participation alone does not adequately describe individual differences in child-child interaction; solitary play once again emerges as distinct from social interaction.

Do increases in coordinated social activity in the preschool years mean that children are merely becoming more responsive to people *in general* and more adept in coping with any social situation? Not necessarily. The evidence suggests that social differentiation, as well as increases in sociability, is a major achievement. For example, bids for attention are more commonly directed toward peers and less commonly directed toward teachers and adults by older children than by younger ones, and earlier forms of affection-seeking are replaced by attention-seeking (Heathers, 1955; Stith & Connor, 1962). Immature social actions are replaced by more efficient, smooth interactions. More and more time is spent in peer interaction, but socialization cannot be described solely in terms of the quantity of social activity. Solitary activities are maintained in the repertoire even though the qualitative characteristics of these activities change. Altogether, it is the increasingly differentiated utilization of more sophisticated social skills that marks the preschool years.

Childhood and Adolescence

Qualitative changes in child-child interaction continue beyond the preschool years. With school entrance, children increase their contacts with other children and begin to recognize that other individuals have ideas and points of view that are different from their own. Peer interaction undoubtedly profits from the decline in egocentrism as well as contributes to it, although individual differences in role-taking abilities are not strongly correlated with observational measures of effectiveness in social interaction.

Various experiments reveal that communication skills increase in effectiveness in middle childhood. Encoding of cues commonly found in social interaction (e.g., facial expression, vocal intonation, and movements) increases in proficiency between the sixth and tenth years, although accuracy in detecting similarities between social stimuli does not increase as much as accuracy in apprehending differences (Girgus & Wolf, 1975). Visual attention in interpersonal situations is utilized differentially as children mature. In one investigation (Levine & Sutton-Smith, 1973), conversation and a block construction task were used to compare children across a wide range of ages and adults on various measures of visual attention to an agemate. An increase was noted in social gazing, mutual visual regard, and proportions of gazing in speaking and listening from 4, 5, and 6 years to 7, 8, and 9 years; a slight decrease at 10, 11, and 12 years was found; and another increase for the adults. No age differences were observed in the construction task. Accounting for the nonmonotonic movement toward adult modes of utilizing visual attention is not easy since studies dealing with these developmental trends are rare. The decline in person-directed visual regard noted among the preadolescent subjects could be associated with a general awkwardness in communication prevailing in this period, although the children were acquainted with one another and were observed in same-sex pairs. Unfortunately, preadolescence is such an understudied era in peer interaction that clarification of these results must await additional investigation.

A substantial literature reveals that communication exchanges among agemates increase in effectiveness during the elementary school years. Krauss and Glucksberg (1969) studied kindergarten, first-, third-, and fifth-grade children, asking them to describe a series of novel block designs to an agemate equipped with similar blocks but who sat behind a screen. In telling the listener how to duplicate the child's own stack of blocks, the kindergarten children made many errors, from first trial to last, indicating a general lack of proficiency in assuming the perspective of the listener. In contrast, errors among the older children decreased markedly from trial to trial, with the greatest decrease occurring among the fifth-grade children. Cognitive deficiencies thus were evident among the younger children in role-taking as well as in sensitivity to the communication demands of the situation. These limitations were less evident among the older children.

In studies of speaker-listener interaction (e.g., Alvy, 1968; Dittman, 1972; Karabenick & Miller, 1977), age differences in the speaker's ability to transmit information about simple problem-solving situations have been confirmed, and younger speakers were found to be not very efficient in supplying

additional information in response to queries from their listeners—even though they are responsive to these queries. Although younger listeners show some awareness of the need to provide the speaker with feedback in the form of questions and confirmations, the incidence of such responses varies according to the situation and the feedback many times is inappropriate. Gains in listener utilization of feedback occur more noticeably in later childhood. Abilities to infer motivation and intent in the actions of other children also increase in middle childhood, and an extensive literature now documents these changes (see *Shantz, vol. III, chap. 8*).

Other advances occur in children's utilization of feedback from their encounters with other children. Numerous studies have shown that, in social problem-solving situations, the promise of shared rewards for successful performance will result in cooperative interaction, whereas "winners take all" will result in competition (Brownell & Hartup, 1981; French, Brownell, Graziano, & Hartup, 1977). In these studies, the rules of the games were established by an adult experimenter, and cooperation and competition were observed during the children's interactions on the task. Age differences have been documented, too, in the utilization of *two* sources of information—the companion's behavior as well as the rules of the game as defined by the adult (Hartup, Brady, & Newcomb, 1983). In this instance, bogus feedback was supplied to the child indicating that the companion was playing either cooperatively or competitively. As a result, some companions seemed to be acting consistently with the adult-established rules while others seemed to act inconsistently. First-grade children were limited in the extent to which they could utilize both types of information; their social orientation reflected only the behavior of the companion. Third- and fifth-graders, however, were cooperative or competitive according to both sources of information. More extensive pretraining on the task and more explicit recording of the activity during the game were shown to enhance the utilization of the two sources of information among the first-graders. Younger children, then, experience considerable difficulty in translating the rules of "social games" into action, whereas the older children can do this for themselves, combining this information with feedback from the other child's actions.

Certain characteristics of group interaction undergo change during middle childhood and adolescence. Smith (1960) set up 20 groups, each including four individuals, from nursery schools, elementary schools, and university classes, asking the subjects to create stories based on pictures. Chronological age was positively correlated with both amount of social activity ($r = .81$) and amount of task-related behavior ($r = .64$). The groups of 5-year-olds were less interactive in introducing new ideas than were the groups of older children and adolescents, as well as less cooperative and more individualistic. The younger children behaved like aggregates of independent individuals, whereas the older children manifested more synchronous and co-ordinated interactions. In another investigation (Smith, 1973) five-person same-age groups ranging in age from 4 to 21 years were studied while the members made interpretations for a Rorschach card. Once again, interaction and task-related behavior increased with age, mainly through early adolescence. But the social interaction became more mature in several other ways: (1) Within-group variance in the interaction was lower in the older aggregates; (2) simultaneous verbalizations were less frequent; and (3) behaviors such as unifying actions, use of acknowledgments, signaling that one understands, asking for opinions, and exchanges of questions were more common in adolescents' groups than in the children's groups. Both studies suggest that problem solving involving the coordinated utilization of multiple sources of feedback increases with age.

Child-child interaction increasingly functions in conjunction with social norms. Hartup et al. (1983) observed a cooperative bias among fifth-grade children that transcended the utilization of both adult-induced game rules and feedback from the companion; one indication favoring cooperation from either source elicited as much cooperative activity as concordant information from both sources. Other investigations (Piché, Rubin, & Michlin, 1978) reveal that the content of persuasive messages changes with age according to the identity of the target (e.g., friends versus strangers; high authority figures versus low authority figures). Specifically, imperatives ("If you don't subscribe to it, I might punch you out") were more common among ninth-grade subjects than fifth-grade subjects, especially to friends; position appeals ("We ought to do things for each other") were also more common among the older subjects, especially when directed to adults rather than peers; and personal appeals ("If I get enough subscriptions it's really gonna mean a lot to me") were differentiated more among the older children than among the younger children according to the intimacy of the target—parent and friend versus teacher and peer stranger.

Sharing and other forms of altruism increase in middle childhood (Handlon & Gross, 1959; Ugurel-Semin, 1952). Once again, however, gross amounts do not completely describe the developmental changes. For example, Melburg, McCabe, and Kobasigawa (unpublished) asked 40 kindergarten and third-grade boys to describe the manner in which they would assist another child with a difficult task. Kindergartners selected direct intervention most frequently, while the older children differentiated their assistance according to situational constraints: Suggestions or assistance were *offered* before being given and, sometimes, intervention was withheld altogether.

Overall, aggression decreases in amount among both boys and girls in middle childhood, although modes as well as content change. Quarreling also decreases through adolescence (Venkatramaiah & Barathi, 1977). Abusive language is utilized more commonly, while physical tussles decrease; the latter, however, remain more common among boys than among girls. Aggressive outbursts include "after reactions," such as sulking, brooding, and whining, that are not evident in early childhood (Goodenough, 1931), and the aftermath of quarrels among adolescents can also include feelings of guilt and unhappiness. Older children and adolescents typically engage in instrumental aggression (directed toward retrieving objects, territories, or privileges) less frequently than younger children. Hostile aggression (person directed), on the other hand, increases. Insults, derogation, and other threats to self-esteem occupy a relatively small role in the aggressive activity of preschoolers but assume a major role among older children and among adolescents (Hartup, 1974). Physical beatings are concomitants of hostile aggression among adolescent boys, whereas girls engage more commonly in accusations and teasing (Venkatramaiah & Barathi, 1977).

Theoretical Considerations

Changes in child-child interaction during infancy and childhood are undoubtedly linked to changes in sensorimotor capacities, cognitive skills, and the development of impulse controls. First, early constraints on the understanding of means-ends relations would seem to have obvious concomitants in infant-infant interaction. Second, egocentrism would seem to constrain coordinated interaction among preschool children. Role-taking is intrinsic in cooperative activity and altruistic interaction, inviting the speculation that age changes in role-taking abilities and age changes in child-child interaction are causally linked or derive from common sources. Third, the child's understanding of intentionality and the ability to cope with complex social messages increase in middle childhood and almost certainly underlie changes in social interaction. Finally, social knowledge, itself, becomes more extensive with experience. Nevertheless, the connections between cognitive and social development (e.g., between role-taking and social abilities) are not well documented. It is important to note, however, that age changes in these domains occur in tandem and it is reasonable to suppose that they are functionally related.

Socialization experiences undoubtedly induce changes in both the elements of the social repertoire and their organization. Contingencies of adult and peer reinforcement are known to affect children's assertiveness, aggression, and associative behavior. Contingencies in adult attentiveness, for example, affect sociability, modify frustration reactions, and change the character of children's play (see Harris, Wolf, & Baer, 1967). Exposure to adult models also affects both the prosocial and antisocial dimensions of children's interactions with agemates. Moreover, reinforcement and modeling within the peer system are determinants of child-child interaction, as we will see below. Unfortunately, the extant studies do not show how frequently children of various ages are exposed to altruistic or aggressive models, to self-reinforcement contingencies, or to effective strategies in social communication. Nor does this literature demonstrate that these contingencies change systematically with age in children's everyday lives. The experimental evidence demonstrates only that certain contingencies *can* change child-child interaction. Discriminant feedback for cooperation, competition, altruism, and aggression *may* change as the child grows older; almost certainly this happens. But detailed evidence cannot be retrieved from the ecological literature.

Taken together, both cognitive and social learning studies provide a rudimentary theory accounting for developmental trends in child-child interaction. Convergences can be established between exposure to certain kinds of social models and transformations in social interaction; similar ones can be traced between children's cognitive abilities and their social interactions. But child-child interaction develops *in context;* consequently, these developmental convergences must be examined similarly. Only in this manner can our "best guesses" about the sources of age differences in child-child interaction become a more clearly articulated theory.

Summary

Child-child interaction changes from simple "interacts" to more complex and coordinated interac-tions, from loosely coordinated exchanges to coordinated interaction, and from primitive awareness of the needs of others to reciprocities based on complex attributions and the utilization of multiple sources of information. Children spend more and more time in peer interaction until, by adolescence, time spent with peers exceeds time spent with other agents of socialization (Medrich, Rosen, Rubin, & Buckley, 1982). Why? Children themselves say simply, "It is fun. . . . Your friends don't tell you to wash your hands all the time, clean up your room, or apologize to your little brother" (Hetherington & Morris, 1978). The social demands of child-child interaction are intense, however, requiring the utilization of many finely tuned social skills.

Setting Conditions

Toys

Some observers believe that toys are basic social mediators—that is, that babies are drawn to each other as a by-product of their interest in novel objects. This conclusion is difficult to verify since most infant-infant encounters, even in impoverished circumstances, occur with toys. The reactions of babies to one another in the absence of toys (see section titled *The First Year*) suggest an intrinsic interest in agemates but, in everyday experience, toys are involved in most of the young child's interactions with other children.

Constraints are evident in the second 6 months of the first year. Vandell et al. (1980) observed that small toys changed both individual actions and ongoing interaction. First, coordinated social acts (both reciprocated and unreciprocated) were more common without toys than with them; smiling, vocalizing, touching, and gestures each occurred more frequently in the absence of toys than in their presence. Second, social interaction was more sophisticated in the absence of toys; both two-unit exchanges and longer contact chains were more common in the absence of toys. Another investigation (Eckerman & Whatley, 1977) demonstrated that toys not so much lower the incidence of peer interaction (although mean differences were obtained in this direction) as change the nature of it. Without toys, for example, the 10- to 12-month-old babies contacted one another, smiled and gestured to one another, and duplicated each other's actions. With toys, the babies showed the objects to one another and exchanged them, and synchronously manipulated the play material. Similar differences in social interaction, with and without toys, were observed among children between 22 and 24 months of age.

The number of toys available affects both the quality and quantity of child-child interaction. Maudry and Nekula (1939) alternately presented 0, 1, 2, or 3 toys to 12-month-old babies who had been placed in close proximity to each other. Few negative reactions, but much social contact, occurred with no toy; a mixture of positive and negative interactions was observed when both babies had toys. Negative reactions and conflicts were most evident when only one toy was available (see also Bühler, 1930).

Certain toys influence child-child interaction differently from others. In one investigation (DeStefano & Mueller, 1980), a small group of toddler males was observed when: (1) no toys were present, (2) small manipulable toys (e.g., small balls, trucks) were available; (3) large "move through" toys (e.g., a slide, a rocking boat) were accessible; and (4) both types of toys were available. Contact continuations were less common and negative actions more common with small toys than in the other conditions, although negative actions were also relatively common in the "no toys" condition. Object exploration consumed more time than social exploration in the "small objects" condition only.

The presence of another child also changes the individual child's interactions with his or her own toys. In comparing toddlers' behaviors with toys in peer-present and peer-absent conditions (with mothers available in both instances), Rubenstein and Howes (1976) found that the children's use of objects was more mature in the peer-present condition. Mouthing and passive contacts with the toys were less frequent in this condition than when the child was alone; active manipulation of the objects occurred in roughly the same amounts under the two conditions but creative, unusual uses of the objects (e.g., imaginative play or goal-directed problem solving) were more common with another child in the room. The more mature behaviors with the toys occurred most commonly when both children were involved with the toy, suggesting that the peer interaction was responsible for the more advanced play behavior. Thus, elaborations of previously acquired skills (or the integration of them at more complex levels) may be primary outcomes of peer interaction in relation to toy behavior.

Play materials are also related to child-child interaction in the preschool years. First, positive and negative contacts simultaneously increase in nursery situations when the availability of toys is reduced (Johnson, 1935). Second, toys constrain the nature of the interaction. For example, solitary and parallel activity are most common in art and book locations in nursery schools, while coordinated social interaction occurs most frequently in doll corners and in dramatic play (Charlesworth & Hartup, 1967; Rubin, 1977). Outdoor activities, games, and interaction in "large muscle" areas also encourage coordinated interaction, especially in large groups (Vandenberg, unpublished). Since nursery school activities are sex-linked (Melson, 1977), these observations mean that coordinated social activity among girls is more likely to occur in dyadic interaction with art materials and in dramatic play; among boys, such social contacts tend to occur in larger groups and in the context of highly motoric play.

Factor analytic studies have been conducted on four data sets, based on toddlers and preschool children, to illuminate "toy involvement" as a dimension on which individual differences among children can be ordered (Blurton Jones, 1972; Smith & Connolly, 1972, 1977). Employing between 32 and 40 behavior categories, each investigator found one major component to consist of social participation and another to consist of toy involvement. In these studies, toy involvement was not equivalent to solitary play, so this dimension is not the same one identified by Roper and Hinde (1978). Instead, this source of individual variation is the degree to which children manipulate or hold toys in contrast to contact with an immovable apparatus, general physical activity, and rough-and-tumble play. Would toy involvement be salient in observations conducted in other settings? Probably. The factor structure obtained in the existing studies undoubtedly reflects, to some degree, the physical arrangements of the contemporary nursery school. But it is reasonable to suppose that "toy involvement" would be found as a salient dimension in individual differences in any setting that includes toys and play equipment—including the home.

Similar studies dealing with toys and their role in social interaction are not available for older children. Nevertheless, observations of preadolescent boys attending summer camps are strikingly similar to the results for nursery school children. Gump, Schoggen, and Redl (1957) reported that "robust" interactions, including assertive behavior, blocking attempts, and attack responses, occurred more frequently during swimming than during crafts. On the other hand, helping occurred more frequently during the crafts activities. Also, while expressive actions occurred more frequently in swimming, utilitarian behavior was noted with equal frequency in the two types of activities. When desired goals were delayed or in short supply, competitiveness increased. When the setting diverted attention to individual tasks, child-child interaction declined. That toys constrain social interaction in middle childhood is made clear in a single episode from *One Boy's Day* (Barker &

Wright, 1951).

Stewart and Raymond simultaneously seemed to
get the idea of putting Clifford into the crate.
Raymond climbed up on the crate, which was
quite wobbly from having fallen so many times,
and demonstrated how to get inside. Stewart
said, "Now, see how Raymond does it,
Clifford?" After Raymond stepped aside,
Clifford followed his example. Stewart turned
to Clifford and said, "Now, you get like Raymond. Get just like him, see? Put your feet here;
put your hands here." He showed Clifford exactly how to get situated in the crate. Then he
said to Clifford, "When I turn it over, what are
you going to say?" Clifford said in a high voice,
"Yippeeeeee!" Raymond smiled. (pp.
367–368)

Adults

Young children are rarely left unsupervised by
adults, especially when playing together. A small
literature indicates that adults are important setting
conditions for child-child interaction—along with
toys and the physical arrangements. First, studies
dealing with infant and toddler interaction (see
above) indicate that mothers receive considerable
social attention from their children even though interest in the other child may be evident. Second,
nursery observations indicate that 12-month-olds
more frequently looked, smiled, and offered toys to
their agemates when the mother was not in the room
than when she was. Taking toys away from other
children was also less common in the mother's absence (Field, 1979). In some ways, then, the mother
resembles a toy; she is a competitor for the attention
of the young child. Clearly, there is no indication
that social interaction is facilitated by her presence—at least in familiar settings. Rubenstein and
Howes (1979) also reported that 19-month-old subjects were more socially active and more mature in
the actions directed toward their agemates in the
absence of the *agemate's* mother. Thus, any adult is
a potential competitor for the child's attention even
though strange mothers may not be very salient in
this regard (Eckerman et al., 1975).

The more selective use of social actions and the
greater sociability of children in the absence of their
mothers should not be taken to mean that the mother
contributes little to child-child interaction. Maternal
decisions precipitated the child's enrollment in the
nursery in the first place, and the environment was
familiar to the child by the time the observations
were conducted. Without the sanctions and security
offered by the mother, no child-child interaction

would have occurred at all. Once the child is comfortable with agemates in a familiar situation, the
mother's presence may "interfere" with child-child
interaction; but this does not mean that she plays no
role in its beginnings.

Space

Crowding effects on social interaction among
children have been extremely difficult to establish,
owing to the number of variables that are confounded in studies dealing with the matter (e.g.,
novelty of crowded and less-crowded conditions,
number of resources available to each child, and
group size). Smith and Connolly (1977) have pointed out that evidence of two kinds must be utilized in
studies of crowding: (1) variations associated with
increasing the number of individuals in a constant
space; and (2) variations associated with increases or
decreases in the space made available to a constant
number of individuals. In addition, novelty and resource densities must be kept constant, and behavior
categories must be used that do not confuse rough-
and-tumble activity with aggression. Especially
important is allowance for the long-term adjustment
to crowded conditions. For example, Fagot (1977b)
found both more positive social interaction and
fewer instances of solitary play in Dutch nursery
schools allowing 1.16^2 meter per child compared to
American nurseries allowing 10.46 square meters.

Experimental studies, as might be anticipated,
present a welter of conflicting results. Most investigators have expected decreases in social interaction
with increased crowding and concomitant increases
in aggression. Several studies must be discounted
because number of subjects, spatial density, and resource density were varied simultaneously (Bates,
1970; Hutt & Vaizey, 1966; McGrew, 1970;
McGrew, 1972—Study 1). In some instances, reductions in social activity and increases in aggression were found but can be accounted for by the
fewer resources available in the high density
conditions.

In a number of other instances, spatial density
was varied by altering the room size while maintaining group size and resource densities (Aiello, Nicosia, & Thompson, 1979; Arnote, 1970; Gilligan,
1970; Loo, 1972; McGrew, 1972—Study 2; Preiser,
1972; Price, 1971; Rohe & Patterson, 1974; Smith &
Connolly, 1977). In those instances in which the
highest densities were no more than 25 square feet
per child, crowding had very little effect on either
amount of social interaction or aggression. Densities
above 20 square feet per child, however, more regularly reduced frequencies of social interaction (Loo,
1972; McGrew, 1970; Price, 1971). Rough-

and-tumble play among nursery school children decreases as densities increase beyond 50 square feet per child, and increases in aggression, attributable to spatial densities alone, have not been regularly reported except at very high densities, for example, 20 square feet per child or less (Arnote, 1970; Smith & Connolly, 1977). Two investigators (Loo, 1972; Price, 1971) obtained *decreases* in aggressive activity under very high density conditions, but this seems to have resulted from decreases in rough-and-tumble play that were classified as aggression.

In other studies, increases in aggression have been observed under high density conditions only when resources have been simultaneously limited (Rohe & Patterson, 1974). Indeed, when resource densities and spatial densities have been varied independently, as well as other confounded variables removed (e.g., Smith & Connolly, 1977), the availability of resources seems to account for more of the variance in social interaction and aggressive behavior than spatial density—except under severely crowded conditions.

Under severe crowding, there is very little question that children and adolescents feel crowded, tense, annoyed, and uncomfortable. Both self-reports and skin conductance measures revealed these outcomes among fourth-, eighth-, and twelfth-graders who were crowded, four individuals at a time, into spaces containing only 2½ square feet per child for 30 minutes (Aiello, Nicosia, & Thompson, 1979). Emotional arousal continued for some time following the experience as indicated by greater competitiveness among the subjects who had been crowded compared to those who were not. Extreme spatial densities have not been studied with younger children for obvious reasons.

Group Size

A considerable literature suggests that child care facilities for infants and toddlers should not include more than 8 to 12 children, that classes for preschool children should include no more than 18 to 20 children, and that elementary school classrooms should not contain more than 25 pupils. These traditions derive mainly from management considerations, that is, the limits of an adult's ability to supervise adequately or instruct a number of children. Very little information is available on child-child interaction in relation to group size, although it is well known that toddlers and preschool-age children interact in twosomes more frequently than in larger groups (Bronson, 1975; Vandell, 1977).

One-to-one situations seem to many observers to maximize mutual attention and focus the interaction;

several studies demonstrate that dyadic interaction contains especially strong instigation for increasing sociability and task orientation among young children (Furman, Rahe, & Hartup, 1979; Peters & Torrance, 1972; Torrance, 1970). Dyadic interaction accounts for most of the child's social encounters throughout the preschool years, although larger enclaves can be observed more commonly with increasing age. The occurrence of three-child (and larger) enclaves increases during middle childhood as revealed by observations conducted on school playgrounds (Eifermann, 1971; Hertz-Lazarowitz, Feitelson, Zahavi, & Hartup, 1981). Even so, dyadic interaction remains most common in children's games.

Does social interaction vary as a function of group size? The evidence is very sketchy. Vandell and Mueller (1977) examined the social interaction of 6 male toddlers between the ages of 16 and 22 months, in both dyadic and polyadic situations. During the 6 months that the children were observed, the maturity of the social interaction increased only in dyadic situations; increases occurred in the number of interactions as well as in their complexity. Vocalizations and coordinated actions were used more commonly in twosomes, suggesting that the larger setting diffuses social attention and responsiveness. Howes and Rubenstein (1979) similarly observed more conversational exchanges in family day care homes (typically enrolling only 3 or 4 children) than in day care centers (typically enrolling 10 or more children).

Otherwise, studies of group size in relation to social activity among preschool children are in short supply. Torrance (1970) found that the frequency of asking questions about Mother Goose pictures varied inversely in groups of 5-year-olds ranging in size from 4 to 24 children. Questions were asked even more frequently in dyads (Endsley & Gupta, 1978). Since the number of adults in these situations did not vary (one experimenter was present), the adult-child ratio was confounded with group size. When this variable remains constant, as in a series of comparisons made in a nursery school with 8 or 16 children present, fewer differences in social activity are observed (Asher & Erickson, 1979). Comparisons among nursery school classes ranging in size from 10 to 35 individuals, however, show that friendship structures (including cross-sex choices) and imaginative play are more common in small situations than in large ones (Smith & Connolly, 1981).

More intense and cohesive interaction was demonstrated among preadolescents in 5-member than in 12-member discussion teams (Hare, 1953). Results indicated that: (1) Consensus was greater in the smaller groups; (2) the leader's skill was more necessary to obtain consensus in the larger groups; (3) the leader's opinions carried greater weight in the smaller groups; (4) members of the smaller groups felt their opinions were more important; and (5) factions were more noticeable in the larger groups. Other studies show that children enrolled in classrooms using small study groups are more cooperative than students in classrooms conducted with whole-class instruction (Hertz-Lazarowitz, Sharan, & Steinberg, 1980).

Surely, it is difficult to connect the toddler's preference for dyadic interaction and the greater cohesiveness of smaller, as opposed to larger, discussion groups of preadolescents. And yet, similarities are evident. The smaller, more focused situation promotes greater intensity, vigor, and cohesiveness in child-child interaction. Whether one-on-one contact precipitates noteworthy developmental functions, as suggested in Vandell and Mueller's (1977) research, is a most intriguing but unverified hypothesis.

Familiarity

Mother-child interaction varies according to the familiarity of the setting (Sroufe, Waters, & Matas, 1974), but only three studies address this question in terms of child-child interaction. In one investigation (Becker, 1977), 9-month-old strangers were observed together on 10 occasions (alternating) in each others' homes. First, the babies directed more social activity in their own homes toward *all* social targets, including the other baby, the mother, the other baby's mother, and the observer. Second, the subjects attended more closely to the toys when they were in the other child's residence. Interpretation of these effects is not easy. Wariness, for example, could be elicited in strange environments, thereby suppressing social activity. But, at the same time, the presence of a strange agemate in a familiar environment could stimulate increased social activity. Examination of the results does not confirm either explanation; it can thus be posited that both wariness in strange locations and arousal stemming from the addition of a novel element to a familiar setting underlie these results. Both mechanisms may also have been involved in Fischoff's (1974) observations of kibbutz-reared infants who were more peer-oriented in the infant house (where most time was spent) than in their parents' houses or in strange houses (also located in the kibbutz).

One investigation with nursery school children (Jeffers & Lore, 1979) buttresses these results, although does not explain them. Children, strangers to each other, were observed in two sessions—once in the experimenter's home and once in the home of one of the children. Although individual differences in sociability were stable across the two observations, 31 of 32 children were more socially active when they were observed in their own homes, a situation not prevailing among the children who were observed in strange environments. Initiation of interaction, engagement in extended interchange, and aggression were more frequent among the children observed in their own residences suggesting that, when "at home," children exert a stronger influence over social activities than when "away from home." Especially noteworthy is the increase in aggressive tactics observed among the children in familiar environments. Once again, the mechanisms underlying these setting effects are not known. At home, children have better knowledge of the environment; territorial sensitivities also may be evident. In these observations, however, proprietary comments, questions, and possession fights were not more common in the "at home" observations in comparison to those made at the experimenter's house. But the data are too thin to advance an hypothesis concerning the cognitive and affective concomitants of social interaction in familiar and unfamiliar situations.

Summary

Spatial arrangements constrain social arrangements and, in turn, social interaction. Quantity and quality of social commerce vary according to the amount of space available, resources (both social and nonsocial), and the child's familiarity with the situation. Other situational determinants of child-child interaction are discussed elsewhere—for example, acquaintance and friendship relations; age, sex, and race; and experience with adults.

The psychological impact of these variations is not as well understood as the existence of the ecological constraints themselves. An integrative view of the ecology of child-child interaction is not evident in most of the literature. But investigators are extremely interested in the manner in which setting conditions affect child-child interaction and new work in this area is increasing exponentially.

RELATIONSHIPS

Popularity and Social Status

Peer acceptance consists of two attributes—popularity and status. *Popularity* means likability, that is, the extent to which a child is sought by others for associative contact. *Status* means standing, that is, the extent to which a child is thought to be a worthy or valuable member of a group. Other terms referring to status dimensions in child-child relations include *leadership, social power,* and *prestige.* In many situations, popularity and status are positively correlated, but the magnitude of these correlations may be modest and, sometimes, extremely low (cf. Lippitt, Polansky, & Rosen, 1952).

Neither popularity nor status is a unidimensional attribute. Children may "like" some children, "dislike" others, and be "indifferent" to still more. "Liking" does not mean an absence of "dislike," or vice versa. In fact, the avoidance or the negative evaluation of a child is only related moderately and negatively to the number of positive evaluations received (Gottman, 1977; Moore & Updegraff, 1964; Roff, Sells, & Golden, 1972); in some cases, these correlations are not significant (Hartup, Glazer, & Charlesworth, 1967). Social acceptance and rejection are also correlated with different child characteristics (see section below).

It has thus become customary in research on social attraction to focus on three categories: *stars* (who receive many positive choices from other children), *isolates* (chosen neither positively nor negatively), and *rejects* (who are actively disliked). But several investigators have shown that it may be better to discriminate among children even more precisely—for example, in terms of both likability and social salience. Peery (1979) used two dimensions to assess individual differences in social standing: *impact* (number of nominations, both positive and negative, received on a sociometric test) and *preference* (the difference between the number of positive and negative choices received). Distributions based on observations of preschool children suggest four categories: *populars* (both high impact and highly preferred); *amiables* (low impact but highly preferred); *isolates* (low impact and nonpreferred); and *rejects* (high impact but nonpreferred). Gottman's (1977) sociometric classifications resemble this two-dimensional scheme in some ways: By using observations of preschool children and interviews with their teachers, this investigator identified *stars* (liked by many and rejected by few), *mixers* (who received both positive and negative choices), *isolates* (seldom chosen, either positively or negatively), *teacher negatives* (moderately well liked by peers but negative in their relations with teachers), and *rejects* (disliked by many and liked by few). In both investigations, children ignored in the nominations were markedly different from rejected children.

Frames of reference used in sociometric assessment have varied widely. Choices are sometimes obtained for seating companions, play companions, work partners, or simply "best friends." Most measures consist of the number of nominations received by a child from other children—either positive or negative. Nomination techniques have been used with children ranging in age from as young as 3 years (McCandless & Marshall, 1957a) to adolescence. Usually, nomination scores are based on a small number of questions asked of each child: "Who in the class is your best friend?" "Who is your next-best friend?" The small number of items constituting these nominations attenuate the reliability of the resulting scores, although the concurrent validity of these devices has been well established. At other times, likability ratings on modified Likert-type scales constitute the sociometric instrument, or a complete set of forced-choice comparisons are used that pit each child against every other child in a class. (For methodological reviews, see Asher & Hymel, 1981; Gottman, 1977; Hartup, 1970; and Vaughn & Waters, 1980.)

Stability of Peer Acceptance and Rejection

The stability of sociometric scores has been assessed by means of successive administrations of the relevant tests at intervals ranging from a few days to several years. The test-retest method produces a conservative estimate of the reliability of sociometric scores owing to the fluctuations in peer preferences that occur along with imperfections in the sociometric instruments themselves. Nevertheless, peer preferences remain relatively stable over time.

Five statements summarize most of the significant observations that have accumulated over the years on the stability of sociometric assessments. First, stability estimates vary according to the sociometric device employed. Paired comparison devices, infrequently used because of their ungainliness, have stability coefficients in the range of .75 with preschool children, based on test intervals of one week (Vaughn & Waters, 1980); peer-rating techniques produce test-retest correlations ranging between .74 and .81 with preschoolers tested at 4-week intervals (Asher, Singleton, Tinsley, & Hymel, 1979). Nomination procedures, on the other hand, yield more variable, and generally lower, stability coefficients with young children: .22 to .74 at 3-week intervals (McCandless & Marshall, 1957a) and .38 to .56 at 4-week intervals (Asher et al., 1979). Negative nominations generally have even lesser stability than positive nominations (Asher et al., 1979; Hartup et al., 1967), perhaps because of the greater likelihood that environmental pressures will be brought to bear on aversive behaviors between testing sessions than on prosocial behaviors.

Second, test-retest stability varies inversely with the time interval between tests—stability is highest when the interval is a few days or weeks and lowest when the interval consists of several years. Long-term stability has not been examined in early childhood, but Roff et al. (1972), using a sample of 15,300 school children between the ages of 9 and 12, obtained test-retest correlations of about .50 based on "like most" nominations at 1-year intervals and correlations of .40 at 3-year intervals. Negative nominations ("like least") dropped from .40 across a 1-year interval to about .35 over a 3-year interval.

Third, stability is directly related to the age of the children. With samples of both urban and rural children, less fluctuation in friendship nominations was found among 16- to 19-year-olds than among 11- to 15-year-olds (Horrocks & Thompson, 1946; Thompson & Horrocks, 1947). The younger children chose the same individual as a best friend about 50% of the time when sociometric tests were separated by a 2-week interval, whereas the older children chose the same individuals between 60% and 90% of the time.

Fourth, stability is directly related to degree of acquaintanceship; that is, fluctuations in social status are more marked during the early stages of group formation than after the group has become established (Sherif et al., 1961; Sherif & Sherif, 1964). It is also the case that early acquaintance fluctuations are more marked among children occupying middle sociometric positions as compared to either high or low positions.

Fifth, stability of sociometric scores bears a direct relation to number of sociometric criteria used, sample size, and number of test items, as would be the case with any psychometric instrument (e.g., Gronlund & Barnes, 1956). Weighting of positive and negative choices according to the order in which nominations are made does not affect the stability of sociometric choices (Moore & Updegraff, 1964; Witryol & Thompson, 1953).

Correlates of Peer Acceptance and Rejection

What determines a child's acceptance or rejection by other children? The relevant literature consists almost entirely of correlational studies. The typical strategy has been to administer sociometric tests concurrently with personality and intelligence tests or with ratings and rankings made by teachers, children, or naive observers. The two sets of measures are then correlated. Unfortunately, the inferences to be drawn from these studies are extremely limited. "To know that popular children perform a preponderance of friendly behaviors is not to say that their friendliness is the 'cause' of their popularity" (Moore, 1967).

Little use has been made of experimental strategies even though these can be employed with certain issues (e.g., the influence of positive evaluations by others on the child's evaluations of those doing the evaluating). Nor has sufficient use been made of longitudinal analysis—especially to study social differentiation at critical times (e.g., when new groups are being formed, new associations are made, or major developmental transitions occur). Longitudinal studies can be valuable in studying the role of certain characteristics that cannot be varied experimentally and about which little can be learned cross-sectionally (e.g., physical attractiveness and its role in social attraction). We continue to be constrained by an overuse of cross-sectional correlational strategies applied to children within a restricted range of ages.

Most investigators report modest correlations between peer acceptance and child characteristics. No single trait is of overriding importance in determining children's popularity with their peers. In general, positively valued characteristics—ranging from physical attractiveness to intelligence—account for significant amounts of variance in peer acceptance, whereas negatively valued characteristics—ranging from components of endomorphic physique to antisocial behavior—account for significant variation in peer rejection.

Nonbehavioral Correlates. Birth Order. Schachter (1964) found that later-born college students were more popular than first-borns. Furthermore, first-borns assigned their sociometric choices to fewer individuals and to more popular persons than did later-born children. Other investigators have sometimes not replicated these results, yet many studies have been carried out without sufficient control over major confounding variables (e.g., social class, family size, and parents' ages). In two instances, however, design issues were minimized and the results confirmed that youngest-born children, compared to middle-born or first-born children, are chosen more consistently as friends, seat mates, and playmates (Miller & Maruyama, 1976; Sells & Roff, 1964).

Two theories have been advanced to account for the relation between birth order and sociometric status. First, Schachter (1964) believed that the key mediator in this relation is the greater dependency of the first-born compared to the later-born—a difference presumed to derive from the less consistent parental handling of first-born children compared to later-born children. Some evidence, mainly with adults, suggests that first-borns are indeed more dependent in various ways than later-borns; other studies indicate that dependency itself is negatively related to sociometric status in children. But measuring independence or dependence directly in school-age subjects does not predict birth order or popularity (Miller & Maruyama, 1976).

An alternative hypothesis suggests that later-born children are forced, in family interaction, to develop finely tuned interpersonal skills (e.g., powers of negotiation, accommodation, tolerance, and a capacity to accept less favorable outcomes) to a degree not required of first-borns. By virtue of their primogeniture, the first-born accommodates successfully to social demands using less social skill than may be necessary for later-borns. Miller and Maruyama (1976) found that later-born subjects manifest greater sociability, less demandingness, less jealousy, and more friendliness than the first-born subjects—suggesting that the later-borns were indeed more socially skilled.

The interpretation of these results still remains in doubt. According to the Miller-Maruyama hypothesis, "only" children should resemble first-borns in social competence and, in their investigation, they did. Sells and Roff (1964), however, found that "only" children showed a greater resemblance to later-borns than to first-borns, leaving us with an inconsistent data base. Whatever the antecedents, though, the evidence is increasingly strong that later-born children are somewhat favored in terms of social acceptance.

What's in a Name? McDavid and Harari (1966) asked four classes of 10- to 12-year-olds to rate the attractiveness of a large group of first names, including the names of the children themselves. Later, popularity ratings were obtained, and a positive relation was found between the ratings of the names and the popularity of the children. Ratings of these same names were made by other children (who did not know the children studied), and these too were found to be positively correlated with the popularity ratings. Names have also been found to be modest predictors of teachers' achievement expectations (Harari & McDavid, 1973). Discounting the significance of an "oddball" name is thus difficult.

Does an offbeat name condemn a child to ridicule by other children, thereby lowering self-esteem and popularity? Or, do parents who give their children offbeat names behave in offbeat ways toward them,

restricting opportunities for their children to learn the social skills necessary for effectiveness in peer interaction? Each of these possibilities is plausible, but relevant data are not available. And the writer (a possessor of an offbeat name) can offer no insights.

Physical Attractiveness. Two variations in physical attractiveness have been studied as predictors of social acceptance: facial attractiveness and body build. Neither facial features nor body conformation can be reduced to single dimensions, but both young children and adults can rate the attractiveness of these characteristics reliably. Indeed, children between the ages of 3 and 5 manifest facial stereotypes that match those of adults when choosing the "prettier" or "cuter" of two photographs (Dion, 1973). Rank-ordering of photographs, particularly full-length likenesses, may be more difficult for young children (Cavior & Lombardi, 1973), but even these discriminations can be accomplished by the age of 8. Sufficient studies have been conducted to assert that facial stereotypes among preschool children are the same as those used by adults.

Children have different expectations of attractive and unattractive children—especially children who are not known to them. Preschool children, for example, attribute friendliness and nonaggressiveness to attractive children more readily than to unattractive children and attribute negative social behaviors more commonly to unattractive children (Adams & Crane, 1980; Dion, 1973; Dion & Berscheid, 1974). Similar results have been obtained with school-age children. Langlois and Stephan (1977) showed 6- and 10-year-old black, Anglo-American, and Mexican-American children photographs of attractive and unattractive children from each of the three ethnic groups. The stimulus materials had been rated previously by undergraduates from each of the ethnic groups for facial attractiveness, and the children were asked to rate the individuals shown on various characteristics. Attractive children were rated as smarter, more prosocial, and less antisocial than the unattractive children—within and across the three ethnic groups. Although scattered interactions between attractiveness and the ethnicity of rater and ratee were obtained, ethnicity effects were generally minor—especially in relation to the effects of physical attractiveness. Attractive children are considered to be better prospects as friends than unattractive children as judged by preschoolers (Dion, 1973; Langlois & Stephan, 1977), elementary school children, and adolescents (Cavior & Dokecki, 1973). But facial attractiveness is also correlated with popularity among children who are well acquainted with one another. Dion and Berscheid (1974) found that, at the end of the school term, attractive preschoolers were nominated as best friends more often than unattractive children. And, among fourth-grade children, Lerner and Lerner (1977) found correlations of .31 and $-.34$ between facial attractiveness (rated by a group of adult judges) and positive and negative peer evaluations, respectively. Children's own ratings of their peers' attractiveness also correlate very highly with sociometric nominations—near .90 among same-sex fifth-graders and between .47 and .64 among same-sex eleventh-graders (Cavior & Dokecki, 1973), in part because of halo effects. Although these correlations were lower for the older children than the younger ones, social attraction and physical attractiveness are also correlated among adults (Dion, Berscheid, & Walster, 1972). There is thus little reason to believe that facial attractiveness declines, with age, in its importance in interpersonal relations.

Attractiveness may be involved in social attraction in more complicated ways when children are well acquainted than when unacquainted with one another. The role of facial attractiveness in the social relations of boys, especially, becomes less predictable. Styczynski and Langlois (1977), for example, contrasted expectations of attractive and nonattractive preschool children (based on adult judgments) by same age acquaintances and strangers. Attractive boys, as compared with unattractive ones, were nominated more frequently by strangers as prosocial and competent rather than antisocial and incompetent; the same was true for girls. Acquaintances, however, nominated attractive boys, compared to unattractive ones, as both more prosocial and antisocial, more incompetent, and no different in terms of competent characteristics. In a subsequent study (Langlois & Styczynski, 1979), the relation between facial attractiveness (as judged by adults) and social attraction was examined among acquaintances between the ages of 3 and 10. Attractive males were better liked among the 3-year-olds, but more disliked by older children. The attractive males, especially the older ones, were identified more commonly with antisocial characteristics and social incompetence, but were also identified as being more prosocial and competent. Preference for attractive agemates did not emerge among girls until the age of 8; attractive girls were not more prosocial than their unattractive companions, although they were less antisocial and, in the oldest group, more competent according to their agemates' attributions.

One other study also suggests that attractiveness, rated according to the criteria used by both children and adults, may relate to social effectiveness differently in males and females. Dion and Stein (1978) studied persuasion success among attractive and unattractive fifth- and sixth-graders, showing both attractive males and females to be more successful than their unattractive counterparts with targets of the opposite sex. With same-sex targets, however, unattractive males were more successful. Examination of these children's actions showed that unattractive males relied extensively on aggressive commands, whereas their attractive counterparts were more assertive and coaxing. Apparently, a more direct, aggressive, and persuasive style works better, among males, than a more indirect, pleading style, thus favoring the unattractive male. The style proving most effective among females was the same style used by the attractive males.

Gender differences in the behavioral concomitants of facial attractiveness and their implications for sociometric status need further exploration. The findings clearly suggest that attractiveness has social advantages for girls—both social acceptance and positive behavioral attributions are identified with being pretty. But it is too soon to assert that attractiveness has either advantages or disadvantages for males. The social relations of attractive boys are marked by a mixture of prosocial and antisocial behavior, "competence" and "incompetence." The behavioral attributions made to attractive boys *could* disadvantage them with agemates, but it remains that attractiveness and popularity are positively correlated in most studies. It may be that the "mixed" social styles of attractive males would be better interpreted as "social intrusiveness" or "social lability" rather than "antisocial" or "socially incompetent." Physical attractiveness may not disadvantage the young male so much as be associated with different social dynamics than those seen among females.

Are attractive and unattractive children different in their social behavior? The evidence is scant. Langlois and Downs (1979) examined this issue with preschoolers during play sessions composed of either two attractive children, two unattractive children, or one attractive and one unattractive child. The observational records varied according to age: (1) Relatively few differences between attractive and unattractive children were disclosed among the younger children; (2) unattractive older children were more aggressive toward their companions than attractive children, engaged in fewer low-key social activities, and were generally more active during the play sessions; (3) attractive and unattractive children did not differ in the frequency of affiliative actions, although this activity was more common in dyads comprised of either both attractive or unattractive children than in mixed-attractiveness dyads. By the age of 5, then, unattractive children showed some of the behavioral characteristics attributed to them by other children and adults; for example, they were more aggressive. Yet these children were also more socially active. No clear methodological or theoretical reason exists for this failure to confirm the attributional data. But there is a basis, even in these data, for the stereotype that unattractive children act in a more socially negative fashion than attractive children.

Bodies, like faces, are socially regarded as "desirable" or "undesirable." Children, as well as adults, agree that mesomorphic body builds (broad shoulders, large muscles, and strong legs) are more desirable than ectomorphic (thin, linear builds) or endomorphic bodies (rounded, chubby physiques). In one study, children looked longer at silhouettes of mesomorphic individuals than the two other body types and attributed more positive characteristics to them—for example, brave, strong, neat, and helpful. Among the children themselves, it was discovered that the mesomorphs were most popular and the endomorphs least popular (Staffieri, 1967). Earlier studies showed similar results—especially for boys (Clarke & Greene, 1963). Adult stereotypes also attribute more positive attributes to individuals with mesomorphic physiques than to those with the other two body types, and personality studies confirm that there is some empirical basis for this. Even 2- and 4-year-old children differ in social activity according to body type (Walker, 1962).

These differences are accentuated among adolescents, especially among early maturing boys (Jones & Bayley, 1950). Among boys, those reaching puberty earliest are more popular and generally more socially advanced than late maturers. Early maturers are more poised, self-confident, and masculine. This cycle is so consistent that early maturers have been found to be better adjusted socially than late maturers when they reach their early forties (Jones, 1965). Among girls, the relation between rate of maturation and social acceptance is more complicated. The best studies (Faust, 1960) indicate that, in early adolescence, the late maturer is more favored—both in social adjustment and peer acceptance. In late adolescence, however, the situation is reversed—early maturers are more socially advantaged. When girls move into an age bracket in which heterosexual attraction is important, early maturing is associated with greater popularity. Well done as these studies were, they badly need to be redone using contemporary adolescents. Secular trends in rate of physical maturation and changing social mores could well mean that these interrelations are different among today's youth. Even so, there is no reason to question the general conclusion that maturation rates are correlated with children's social standing—both with the same and the opposite sex.

What are the origins of the interrelations that exist among stereotypes, behavior, and social acceptance involving physical attractiveness and rate of maturation? Clearly, the evidence shows that "beauty is good" is a social stereotype existing from a very early age and, within United States culture, it is not restricted to white ethnic groups. Behavioral differences associated with physical attractiveness suggest that a self-fulfilling prophecy begins to affect children's social relations at an early age.

Much evidence shows that both parents and teachers have different expectations about children according to their attractiveness. Such expectations are evident even in attitudes about neonates (Corter, Trehub, Boukydis, Ford, Celhoffer, & Minde, 1978). Attractiveness ratings, based on a small sample of premature infants, were highly correlated (r_s = .90) with intellectual prognosis by nursery nurses. Parents and teachers of preschool-age children exhibit "beauty-is-good" expectations in evaluating unfamiliar children (cf. Adams, 1978) but also display these same expectations toward their own children. Adams and Crane (1980) asked adults to compare pictures of attractive and unattractive children and, then, to predict which child their own children would designate as "nicest" and would choose as a playmate. Mothers, fathers, and teachers consistently indicated that they expected their children to attribute a more pleasing personality to the more attractive individuals and to choose them as prospective playmates. (The children, indeed, made choices in this direction when they were examined.) Other analyses showed that the expectations of mothers and teachers, but not fathers, were correlated with the children's use of the beauty-is-good stereotype. For girls, the attribution concordances were .57, .39, and −.08, respectively; for boys, .48, .47, and .11, respectively. Correlations between adult expectations and children's peer preferences were: for girls, .70, .27, and .00, respectively; for boys, .81, .41, and .11, respectively. Note especially the high covariation between mothers' expectations that their children would choose to play preferentially with an attractive child and the child's own choices.

Through the elementary school years, there is ample evidence that adults make different attributions to attractive and unattractive children—both with respect to academic achievement and social adjustment. When provided with photographs attached to report cards, teachers anticipated that attractive children would get better marks than unattractive children (Clifford & Walster, 1973). Teachers also perceived attractive children in their own classrooms as better achievers than unattractive children from the preschool years through the fourth grade (Styczynski & Langlois, 1980). Attractive children also received higher ratings on classroom adjustment, emotional adjustment, social behavior, and intellectual adjustment than did unattractive children. Underlying these expectations were, in fact, higher achievement test scores that were garnered by the attractive children at the fourth-grade level, even though no IQ differences were evident. In other work (Algozzine, 1977) it has been found that attractive children actually engage in more positive interactions with teachers than unattractive children as well as fewer negative interactions.

But what are the origins of the beauty-is-good stereotype? Does the caregiver begin this process in the nursery, with attitudes and actions formed during the course of the caregiver's socialization released according to the attractiveness of the infant? Is there sufficient continuity in facial attractiveness, across early childhood, middle childhood, and adolescence, to establish stable patterns of self-attitude and social behavior in individuals according to their facial features? Answers to these questions are not available except in fragments. Adams (1977) found correlations between attractiveness ratings, based on photographs, between adolescence and young adulthood of .87 for women and .63 for men; between second grade and fifth grade of .50 for girls and .41 for boys. But no information exists on the continuity of facial attractiveness from infancy and the preschool years through later childhood. It is not unreasonable to argue that "cuteness" in young children elicits differential expectations in adults which, in turn, affects the adult's behavior toward the child and the child's self-attitudes and social actions. Increasingly, as the beauty-is-good stereotype operates among children themselves, the two sources of the stereotype must act in concert (Adams, 1977; Langlois & Stephan, 1981). Whether these stereotypes operate as extensively in non-Western cultures as in Western cultures is not known; nor does cross-cultural research confirm the ontogenetic model described here. But the pervasiveness of facial discrimination in children's social relations is well established.

Handicaps. Until recently, one could say very little about the social status of handicapped children. Almost never enrolled in classrooms with unhandicapped children, the relative isolation and exclusion of the handicapped could only be verified from case studies and individual records. Personal accounts, too numerous to mention, make the social isolation of the physically and mentally handicapped painfully clear; children's societies reserve very little positive attention and social glory for the handicapped child.

One can speculate that similar dynamics underlie the social exclusion of both the handicapped and the "ugly duckling," and that negative expectations and self-fulfilling prophecies also occur in the socialization of the handicapped child. But the socialization of the handicapped must be more complicated than the experience of the child who merely has jug ears, a bulbous nose, or oversized eyes (except, of course, for severe disfigurements that, perforce, are handicapping conditions). Sensory and locomotor handicaps arouse anxiety and defensiveness in nonhandicapped persons; these dynamics must be intermixed with the other negative expectations, negative self-attitudes, and the lack of social skill that characterize handicapped children. Indeed, when a severely handicapped individual achieves successful socialization, the nonhandicapped world sometimes treats them as superior beings—for example, think of Helen Keller.

Within the last decade, handicapped children have been "mainstreamed" in American schools in increasing numbers. Of interest to both educators and social psychologists is the acceptance of these children into the peer system. By now, a number of empirical works have appeared in this area and it is possible to make some preliminary statements about handicaps and social acceptance.

First, learning disabled (LD) children, who have learning dysfunctions but are not otherwise classified as handicapped, are usually less well-accepted than their regular classmates. The evidence supporting this conclusion is based on studies of LD children who are "mainstreamed," that is, who spend most of their school time in regular classrooms (Bruininks, 1978; Bryan, 1974). This situation does not change even when the LD children are transferred, after one year, to new classrooms and new teachers (Bryan, 1976). It is also known that LD children are less accurate in self-perceptions of peer status, believe themselves to be no different from their classmates, and are more intrusive in their social interactions than other children. More revealing, perhaps, is a study of young elementary school children, having reading difficulties, and their social acceptance (McMichael, 1980). Poor readers were accepted less and rejected more often than good readers were, but reading ability itself seemed to have very little to do with the sociometric results. On the contrary, when poor readers were rejected, it was because of their antisocial behavior rather than because of their difficulties in reading. Poor readers who conformed to classroom requirements were no more rejected than good readers of equivalent behavior.

Second, educable mentally retarded (EMR) children are not well accepted, as revealed in a large number of studies dating back several years (Gottlieb, 1975). Although many advocates of mainstreaming believe that improvements in social acceptance would be registered among EMR children enrolled in regular classrooms, this has not proved to be the case. The literature is very large and exceptions have been noted (e.g., Renz & Simensen, 1969), but the weight of the evidence shows that EMR children are not well accepted—regardless of class placement. An analysis of the social behaviors of EMR children in integrated classrooms shows numerous differences, beginning in the preschool years. Young children with low developmental level scores (severely retarded) engage in more unoccupied and less onlooker, associative, and cooperative play than less retarded children or nonhandicapped ones (Guralnick, 1981). Concordantly, the most severely handicapped children engage in less constructive play and communicate less effectively with each other than less severely retarded children or normal children. Among school children, both a higher incidence of classroom misbehavior and academic failure mark the EMR child as compared with normal classmates. Gottlieb, Semmel, and Veldman (1978) administered a sociometric device, eliciting both positive and negative nominations, and discovered that academic failure was predictive of low social acceptance among EMR children but had no bearing on their social rejection. Misbehavior, on the other hand, predicted rejection but not acceptance. Thus the correlates of acceptance and rejection among EMR children resemble those among LD children.

Third, "hyperactive" children generally have poorer peer relations than other children. Since an inordinately large number of preschool children (especially boys) are labeled "hyperactive" by their mothers and teachers, we will consider only those investigations in which pediatric or other referrals serve as selection criteria. In mainstreamed groups, preschool hyperactive children have been observed to be no different from nonhyperactive children in sociability and cooperation, but to be more noncompliant and aggressive (Campbell & Levine, 1980; Schleifer, Weiss, Cohen, Elman, Cvejic, & Kruger, 1975). Teacher ratings and maternal reports also emphasize difficulties with aggression and peer relations among young hyperactive children. Among school-age children, hyperactivity has been shown to be highly correlated (r_{pb} = .74) with negative sociometric nominations and closely associated with nominations for negative roles in a class play (Klein & Young, 1979; Mainville & Friedman, 1976; Pelham & Bender, 1982). In one study (Milich, 1980), including hyperactive, hyperactive/aggressive, and aggressive children, it was discovered that hyperactivity was more closely associated with sociometric status than was aggression. Since hyperactivity is associated with a variety of attentional, affective, and communication difficulties (Whalen, Henker, Collins, McAuliffe, & Vaux, 1979), the low social status of hyperactive children may well be mediated by bizarre and inappropriate social behaviors rather than aggressive manifestations. Again, the evidence suggests that behavior disorders tend to be associated with social rejection rather than social isolation, and that unusual, aversive social behaviors may be related more closely to social status than physical aggression.

Fourth, children are able to differentiate among one another in terms of symptoms that are associated with emotional disturbance, becoming better able to do this toward the end of the elementary school years (Hoffman, Marsden, & Kalter, 1977; Marsden & Kalter, 1976). Indeed, this is not surprising since, in comparisons of a national sample of children referred to child guidance clinics with a matched sample of nonreferred children, disturbances in peer relations were among the most commonly reported behaviors differentiating the two groups (Achenbach & Edelbrock, 1981). Parents of disturbed children reported more often than parents of nondisturbed children: "poor peer relations," "loneliness," "fighting," "is teased," "hangs around with kids who get into trouble," "not liked," "shy or timid," "has few friends," "prefers older or younger children," "does not participate in organizations." No other cluster of symptoms differentiated these two groups more clearly.

When examining the sociometric status of emotionally disturbed children, it is once again necessary to distinguish acceptance from rejection. When this is done, at least one investigative team (Vacc & Rajpal, 1975) found no difference in acceptance scores between disturbed and normal children, but greater rejection of the disturbed children. Samples were drawn from both the United States and India; the sociometric patterns were the same in both countries. Again, the relatively low status of the handicapped child apparently can be traced to negative characteristics, that is, behavioral ones. Adolescents "at risk" for schizophrenia are more impulsive and less popular than matched individuals who are not at risk (Grubb & Watt, 1979). Moreover, the relative degree of maladjustment is inversely related to popularity in residential and school situations in which all the children have been classified as behaviorally disturbed (Davids & Parenti, 1958; Kaplan & Kaufman, 1978); maladjustment is also greater among antisocial "externalizing" children than among withdrawn, "internalizing" children (Rolf, 1972).

Fifth, multihandicapped and orthopedically handicapped children have considerably different socialization experiences beginning in early childhood. Gralewicz (1973), for example, studied parents' diary records covering 3 days for 10 multihandicapped children and 11 nonhandicapped ones, ranging in age between 2 years 7 months and 4 years 10 months. The handicapped children had less play time with others and fewer playmates, although the groups did not differ in time spent playing alone. Play with adults was more common, too, among the handicapped children. By the preschool years, an awareness of orthopedic and other handicaps is evident among nonhandicapped children, varying with the visibility of the handicapping condition. Thus, Gerber (1977), using interviews in an integrated preschool, found that 88% of the children mentioned something different in their descriptions of an autistic, hyperactive child; 68% mentioned something different about a child in a body brace, and 50% noted a difference in a child with cerebral palsy. Sociometric scores based on positive and negative nominations (invitations or exclusions from a birthday party) revealed slightly greater lack of acceptance of the handicapped children but a markedly higher incidence of rejection. Once again, the difference leads to social avoidance and disengagement with the handicapped child rather than to mere ignoring of the child. Data on the social adjustment of older children with orthopedic handicaps are similar (Richardson, Goodman, Hastorf, & Dornbusch, 1961).

Social Class. In the United States, many children attend elementary schools that are segregated in terms of socioeconomic status. Neighborhood geography determines the enrollment in public schools, making them homogeneous rather than heterogeneous in social class; private schools are also segregated owing to the necessity for parents to pay tuition. These conditions mean that, inevitably, children resemble their friends in social class background. There may be insufficient variation within classrooms on this variable, however, to show more than attenuated relations between socioeconomic indicators and popularity.

In fact, there are relatively few studies of preschool and elementary school children that clearly trace significant variance in popularity to social class. Early investigators (e.g., Cannon, 1957) who explored this relation in small town schools (where enrollments would be more heterogeneous) did not conduct their analyses separately for children of varying levels of intelligence. Similar flaws mar a number of other studies in this area. One exception (Grossman & Wrighter, 1948) showed that, when sixth-grade children were divided into three IQ levels, the higher the economic level of the father's occupation, the more popular the child at each level.

Perhaps more interesting than the issue of covariation between social class and peer popularity is the question of whether socioeconomic variations are evident in values associated with social standing. For example, behavioral variations were observed among popular and unpopular children attending working-class and middle-class schools, respectively, but in different directions (Gottman, Gonzo, & Rasmussen, 1975). Popularity in the middle-class school was correlated with positive verbal initiations but, in the working-class schools, with positive nonverbal initiations. Middle-class children who engaged in nonverbal interaction, even though it was positive, actually tended to be more disliked than children not using these techniques.

Feinberg, Smith, and Schmidt (1958) conducted a survey of peer attitudes among male adolescents in lower-, middle-, and upper-income schools determining that individuals from all income groups characterized accepted peers as bright, fair, able to take a joke, good company, athletic, conscientious, and honest; whereas rejected individuals were characterized as pesty, noisy, conceited, silly, and effeminate. Boys from low- and middle-income families, however, also stressed the importance of common interests, ability to talk well, and minding one's own business as factors in acceptance; fighting was commonly given as a reason for rejection. In contrast, adolescents from high-income groups stressed cooperativeness, leadership, participation in activities, and scholarship in acceptance; low IQ, lack of leadership, failure to participate in activities, and immaturity were stressed in rejection. Peer status may thus be ascribed on the basis of certain values held in common by children from various social classes while, at the same time, a certain amount of discordance exists across socioeconomic levels. Thus whatever variance in social acceptance may be attributable to social class may rest on value differences such as the ones mentioned here. Even so, the commonality that is seen in values associated with popularity that cuts across social class is noteworthy.

Behavioral Characteristics. *Friendliness and Sociability*. Many studies show that peer acceptance is directly associated with friendliness and social visibility (Hartup, 1970). Measurement strategies vary from study to study, including direct observations of social interaction, assessments based on ratings and interviews with teachers and other children, and measures drawn from situational tests and paper-and-pencil devices. Direct observations are the method of choice among investigators working with preschool children, partly owing to the verbal constraints apparent among young children and partly owing to the relatively unconstrained environments that exist in nursery schools. Observations are less frequently employed with older children and adolescents, except in classrooms, and these have obvious limitations as predictors of social status. Nevertheless, a consistent picture emerges: The popular child, as compared to less popular individuals, is friendly and socially adept in initiating and maintaining social interaction with other children. The rejected child is not less sociable or less friendly than the nonrejected child, but displays more antisocial, disruptive, and inappropriate behaviors in interaction with other children.

In observations of infants, social preferences seem to be more closely related to the quality of interaction than to quantity. Lee (1973) studied five babies, between 8 and 10 months of age, who attended a day care center. One baby was more consistently approached than the other members of the group, and one was more consistently avoided. Most evident were qualitative differences between them: The preferred infant was a responsive social partner who interacted nonassertively with the other babies and whose social involvements were reciprocal. Both the intensity and extensiveness of the avoided infant's involvements depended on whether he had initiated the interaction, and terminations of contact were almost invariably his doing.

Among nursery school children, sociability (i.e., total social contacts) may not be the best predictor of either acceptance or rejection. The available evidence is not extensive, but three studies (Deutsch, 1974; Gottman, 1977; Rosén, 1978) revealed zero-order correlations based on observed sociability and sociometric status. On the other hand, an extensive number of studies show that positive sociometric nominations are predicted from individual differences in "friendly approach" and "associative" behaviors (Marshall & McCandless, 1957b); social visibility, as measured by means of a "Guess Who" test (Clifford, 1963); the frequencies with which the child initiates positive social contacts (Abramovitch, 1979; Hartup et al., 1967) and receives attention from others (Vaughn & Waters, 1980; 1981); and even engagement in neutrally toned interactions (Masters & Furman, 1981). Other prosocial actions are also positively correlated with acceptance among young children—these actions include compliance with routines and "acceptance of the situation" (Koch, 1933); adjustment to, and cooperation with, group rules (Lippitt, 1941); peer perceptions of conformity (Moore, 1967); and possession of "social knowledge" (Jennings, 1975). The relation between popularity and communicative egocentrism at these ages remains in doubt (Deutsch, 1974; Jennings, 1975; Rubin, 1972).

Similar results have been reported for elementary school children. Peer acceptance has been found to be positively related to friendliness and outgoing behavior (Bonney, 1944; Bonney & Powell, 1953); lack of withdrawal as perceived by peers (Winder & Rau, 1962); expressing "kindness" to peers (Smith, 1950); distributing and receiving positive peer reinforcement in the classroom (Gottman et al., 1975); knowing how to "make friends" (Gottman et al., 1975); use of conventional rather than unconventional modes of help-giving (Ladd & Oden, 1979); willingness to give and receive friendly overtures, as well as willingness to respond positively to the dependent behavior of peers (Campbell & Yarrow, 1961); friendliness, assurance, and enthusiasm (Pope, 1953); being neat and tidy and a good sport (Klaus, 1959); and acceptance of others (Reese, 1961).

Scattered data for adolescents are concordant with the data for younger children. Social acceptance between the ages of 12 and 17 is positively associated with being perceived as helpful, good-natured, the "life of the party," and conforming to peer group norms (Elkins, 1958); friendly and enthusiastic (Gronlund & Anderson, 1957); sensitive to the feelings of others (Loban, 1953); and accepted by the peer group (Singer, 1951). Somewhat more evidence exists for adolescents than for children that popularity has a basis in social mobility (Feinberg et al., 1958; Keislar, 1953; Marks, 1954) but, because of the nature of the data, we cannot tell whether the popular adolescent is socially "busier" than the less popular individual or merely that his or her social activities are more valued and, hence, more visible than the activities of less popular individuals.

One experiment suggests that positive interaction directly affects social attraction. Karen (1965), using a small sample, demonstrated in the laboratory that increases in the distribution of reinforcers to other members of the group increased the sociometric evaluation of the donor. It is also the case that, when two children receive positive reinforcers simultaneously for cooperating with each other, mutual sociometric evaluation increases (Blau & Rafferty, 1970).

Self-esteem. If positive evaluation by others is accomplished by effective socialization, we can hypothesize that self-esteem and peer acceptance should be positively correlated. That is, we would predict that popular children have more positive self-concepts than less popular children. The evidence, however, suggests that the relation between self-attitudes and social acceptance is more complicated than this.

With children, several investigators have obtained small, but significant, correlations between self-esteem and popularity (Cox, 1966; Helper, 1958; Horowitz, 1962; Sears, 1964; Withycombe, 1973). Reese (1961) found this relation to be curvilinear. That is, children with moderately high self-concepts were more accepted by their peers than children with either low or very high self-esteem. Intuitively, the curvilinear relation between these variables makes sense, since high self-esteem may be associated with certain behaviors that "put off" other children. In fact, both sixth-grade children and college students with high self-esteem have been shown to make more extreme statements about the likability of others based on information about attitude similarity than subjects with low self-esteem (Cook, Goldman, & Olczak, 1978). Furthermore, the extent to which a subject believes one's evaluations of others are reciprocated is a positive function of self-esteem. Thus far, then, the role of self-attitudes in determining a child's peer status is not well understood; these dynamics require more study than available at this time.

Aggression and Antisocial Behavior. The relation between aggression and sociometric status cannot be easily described. First, it is necessary to differentiate fighting from "negative reinforcement," "negative peer interaction," "peer punishment," and the like. Second, little attention has been given to the role of rough-and-tumble play or "pseudoaggression" in any investigation. Third, the measure of sociometric status must be specified, that is, as positive peer nominations (acceptance) or negative ones (rejection).

Studies that use measures weighted with fighting and physical attack generally show little relation to either social acceptance or rejection. With preschool children, two investigations show no relation between popularity and aggression (Lippitt, 1941; McCandless & Marshall, 1957b); one showed a positive relation (Marshall, 1961); and one a negative relation (Koch, 1933). Among school-age children, peer ratings of "who starts fights" and "who answers back" were not significantly correlated with popularity in a large-scale longitudinal study involving two groups of boys (Olweus, 1977) and in several studies involving "guess who" assessments (Bonney & Powell, 1953; Pope, 1953). Whether fighting is "provoked" and "direct" may make the difference in the prediction of popularity: Lesser (1959) reported a positive relation ($r = .31$) between provoked attack and popularity, but a negative relation ($r = -.69$) between popularity and indirect aggression in fifth- and sixth-grade boys. Campbell and Yarrow (1961) also found that popular children showed more friendly aggression than unpopular children.

By using measures that are weighted with attentuated aggression (i.e., "negative reinforcement"), more consistent relations with sociometric status have been obtained. Negative interactions of this kind, however, are not strongly predictive of *positive* nominations among preschool children (Gottman, 1977; Hartup et al., 1967; Wagner & Asarnow, 1980) or elementary school children (Gottman et al., 1975). Instead, considerable evidence suggests that the child who both initiates and receives negative interactions obtains many *negative* nominations. For example, "negative reinforcements" distributed by preschoolers were positively correlated with rejection scores on picture sociometric tests (Gottman, 1977; Hartup et al., 1967), as were negative acts received (Hymel, Tinsley, Geraci, & Asher [cited in Asher & Hymel, 1981]; Masters & Furman, 1981). In addition, rejected preschool children are perceived by their peers as more antisocial (Moore, 1967) and show more bizarre aggressive patterns in doll play (Dunnington, 1957).

Similar relations prevail among school-age children. (1) Butler (1979) discovered that children with low social reputations both gave and received more negative reinforcements in the classroom; (2) Wagner and Asarnow (1980) found males with low reputations to evidence frequent hostile/submissive actions toward their agemates as opposed to hostile/dominant actions; and (3) Dor and Asher (cited in Asher & Hymel, 1981) found that third- and sixth-graders differentiated between liked and rejected classmates largely in terms of deviant but nonaggressive behaviors (e.g., dishonest, irritating, or immature actions). Winder and Rau (1962) and Goertzen (1959) have also reported positive correlations between rejection and inappropriate, disruptive aggressive behavior, and two other investigators found rejection to be positively associated with "objectionable behavior" (Davids & Parenti, 1958; Elkins, 1958). Consistent with these trends are responses of school children on the *Rosenzweig Picture Frustration Test* (Coons, 1957). Medium- and low-popular children, as contrasted with highly popular children, were more readily blocked, more likely to minimize or deny frustration, less likely to direct hostility to the environment or to others, and more impunitive.

Sex differences in the relation between aggressive/antisocial behavior and popularity have not been extensively explored. Major differences are not apparent among preschool children—where data are most readily available. It should be noted, however, that the studies of fighting and antisocial behavior among school children have mostly dealt with males.

Intelligence. The relation between intelligence and sociometric status has been explored in countless studies dating back to the 1920s (Almack, 1922). The strategy in most investigations has been to correlate IQ scores with sociometric indexes in unselected populations of school children. In these instances, though, the variance attributable to social class could also be considerable; hence most of the literature showing the predictability of popularity from intelligence test scores will not be cited. Roff et al. (1972), however, conducted two studies with large samples in which the relation between IQ and sociometric status was examined separately within social class levels. In one of these investigations, popular children were significantly brighter than less popular children within each of four socioeconomic levels; mean differences varied from 12 to 20 points. Correlational analysis was used with the second sample—computed separately within social class groups. These coefficients ranged between .22 and .39.

Academic performance is also positively correlated with sociometric status. Roff et al. (1972), using their samples of fourth- to seventh-grade children, found an overall correlation of .33 between school marks and acceptance; separate analyses for the various school classes indicated that the magnitude of this correlation dropped with increasing age, ranging from .43 for fourth-graders to .28 for seventh-graders. Part of this attenuation, of course, is attributable to the high dropout rates of children with low peer status.

The relation between specific abilities and peer status depends on the sociometric criterion. Arithmetic ability and reading skill are associated with general popularity (Davis, 1957; McMichael, 1980), although these skills themselves are most closely related to choice of work partners in tasks requiring the skill. Keislar (1953) has also shown that school marks are more highly correlated with prestige than with popularity. Athletic prowess remains as strong a predictor of popularity among adolescent males as it has been for many years in American society (Eitzen, 1975).

Success and failure, generally, affect children's social status. Heber and Heber (1957) studied high and low status groups under conditions of success, failure, or neutral outcome. Regardless of the initial status of the groups, success experiences caused a positive shift in peer evaluations that was particularly long-lasting. Failure experiences, however, varied according to initial status: High status children shifted toward more negative evaluations of each other, whereas no change occurred among the low status subjects. Individual success or failure also has an impact on a child's social status, especially when other children know about it. Praise from teachers directed toward individual students enhances the attraction of others to those individuals (Flanders & Havumaki, 1960). Other studies show that, when success occurs in the company of another child, attraction to that child shifts in a positive direction; nonreward, in contrast, produces no change (Lott & Lott, 1960).

Summary. Social acceptance and rejection have different correlates. In general, to possess an attractive face and a beautiful body is a social advantage as well as it is to be a later-born child in a middle- or upper-class family. It doesn't hurt to have an ordinary name as compared with an offbeat one. A repertoire of friendly, prosocial, and competent social behaviors is clearly predictive of social acceptance, while devious, aversive reactions to other children enhance one's chances of social rejection. Intelligence and achievement—in both school and sports—also contribute significant variance in social status. The role of physical aggression, on the other hand, is not entirely clear.

Acquaintanceship

Acquaintanceship is a significant issue in peer relations for two reasons: First, the familiarization process has significance for the study of social relations in its own right. The more familiar that two individuals become with one another, the more likely they will find themselves attractive and desirable as friends (Berscheid & Walster, 1978). "Mere exposure" (Zajonc, 1968) has been advanced as a hypothesis to account for these effects, and an extensive number of studies with adults demonstrate that the repeated exposure to persons enhances liking and promotes positive interaction. Second, familiarity may be an unsuspected confound in certain kinds of research on agemate interaction—particularly longitudinal studies. Increased maturity in social interaction, over time, in naturalistic studies of infants, toddlers, and preschool children could represent acquaintance effects—or, at once, derive from familiarization, socialization, *and* cognitive development.

Familiarity may enhance social interaction in a number of ways—none of them well understood with children. As two individuals become acquainted with one another, their social repertoires may become enriched and better "meshed," thereby promoting smooth, sophisticated interaction as compared to the interaction seen among strangers (Lewis et al., 1975). Behavioral and attitudinal similarity, in turn, may increase liking and attraction (Byrne & Griffitt, 1966). It is also possible that familiarization has affective concomitants; that is, the presence of a familiar social stimulus may be less arousing than the presence of a stranger, thereby paving the way for more effective intercourse. Familiar peers may also come to function as "secure bases" in a manner resembling the way that mothers serve as "secure bases" for exploration of the environment. If so, interaction with toys and the inanimate environment, as well as interaction with the social environment, should be more vigorous and competent than when strangers dominate the social landscape.

The literature thus far demonstrates the existence of acquaintance effects at virtually every age, ranging from infancy through preadolescence. The underlying dynamics are not well understood, but the effects themselves are evident. First, Young and Lewis (1979) studied seven babies who were observed once with familiar babies and once with strangers. The familiar children ranged in age between 7 and 20 months and had visited the subject at least once each week during the previous 2 months and twice each week for 2 weeks prior to the observation. Strangers were matched with the friends according to sex and age. Proximal activities—body contact, proximity, and touching—were more frequently directed toward familiar babies than toward strangers, as were gesturing and imitative interactions. Looking at the other child did not differ according to familiarity, and differences in play and affective interaction were minimal. These investigators also studied the interactions of babies before and after several play exposures. Effects were not as

extensive as in the earlier study, but proximity-seeking was again found to be enhanced by acquaintance—as was gesturing.

The familiarity of babies with one another affects not only their actions toward each other but generalizes to interaction with strange babies as well. Becker (1977) arranged for 16 pairs of 9-month-old infants to meet for 10 play sessions, followed by an 11th session with a new partner. Control pairs met twice, at intervals matching the beginning and ending sessions of the experimental pairs. Peer-oriented behavior increased in quantity, complexity, and degree of social engagement (i.e., reciprocated initiations) among the experimental subjects but not among the controls. Social exposure effects were observed with the new infant in addition to the familiar infant, thus suggesting a general learning of more advanced social behavior rather than the acquisition of a behavior repertoire associated with a specific infant.

The effects of acquaintanceship on social interaction among preschool children are similar (Doyle, Connolly, & Rivest, 1980). Fifty-minute observations of pairs of children ranging in age from 36 to 46 months of age (with a nursery school classmate and with a child from another school in successive sessions) were analyzed to assess: (1) sociability, (2) cognitive maturity of play interactions, (3) ratings of affective tone (e.g., positive, neutral, and negative), and (4) incidence of specific social acts. With a familiar child, social interaction was more frequent and the cognitive maturity of the social play was enhanced. Positive and successful peer-directed actions were also more frequent between familiar peers than unfamiliar peers, although the affective tone of the interchange was not different in the two conditions. The affective measure is not a very stable one (it was a one-item test), but the results indicate that the major events associated with acquaintance are the shared response repertoires acquired through experience in the same classrooms and with each child in that context.

In another investigation (Ipsa, 1981), children enrolled in Soviet nursery schools were matched with either a classmate or another child enrolled in a different nursery. Observations were conducted in the presence and absence of a responsive, strange woman. Children in the familiar peer condition displayed very little distress at the departure of the adult, whereas children paired with unfamiliar peers were upset by her departure. Older children were less upset by the adult's absence than were the younger children, but the effects of peer familiarity were observed at all ages. Hence, there is an indication that familiar peers exert an affective influence on their associates, serving as a sort of "secure base" in distress situations.

The literature on familiarity and social attraction in middle childhood is not extensive and not entirely consistent. Observational studies of social interaction can be aligned with the studies of younger children. For example, Brody, Graziano, and Musser (in press) assembled triads of first- and third-grade children from different classrooms who indicated they did not know one another and, in some instances, were different in age. Following a baseline experience with a tower-building task, five familiarization sessions were arranged, focusing on activities such as puppets, cutouts, drawing, and dramatic play. In postfamiliarization performance, verbal interaction and group performance improved significantly in the experimental groups but not the control groups, indicating a better "meshing" of individual contributions to the task. Goldberg and Maccoby (1965) also contrasted tower building among second-grade children who spent four sessions working with the same partners and who were then transferred to a new group with children who had worked on the task in four *different* groups. No differences were observed in the performance of the stable and changing groups during training but, on the posttest, children who had worked in a stable group outperformed those who had worked in changing groups. The repeated experience with the same partners provided the children with an opportunity to develop smooth, equalitarian interaction techniques that generalized to the posttest conditions. The changing groups also showed more frequent instances of dominance and coercion during the training sessions, seemingly preventing them from learning techniques that would maximize well-synchronized performance in new groups. Familiarization experiences among children, then, produce generalizable effects that are similar in some ways to those found with babies.

Sometimes social attraction is positively associated with familiarity among school-age children and sometimes negatively. It has been especially difficult to demonstrate the "mere exposure" effect based on attraction ratings as a function of brief exposure to children's photographs in the laboratory. In fact, much of this evidence is negative: Children seem to prefer nonfamiliar photographs to ones with which they have been familiarized (Cantor, 1968; Cantor & Kubose, 1969), although the reverse was reported when white subjects were exposed to pictures of black children (Cantor, 1972). Other data, based on children's preferences for peers of the same or opposite sex (Kail, 1977), demonstrate that the effects of familiarity interact with individual differences in *both* the target children and their acquaintances. Among children in the first through sixth grades, those with strong sex-typed preferences showed increased liking for same-sex faces as a function of familiarity but decreased liking for opposite-sex faces. Among less strongly sex-typed children, however, familiarity did not affect attraction.

In summary, the evidence does not support the contention that familiarity breeds contempt in child-child interaction. Familiarity, in observational studies, has consisted of much more than "mere exposure," so that it is difficult to establish links between the various parts of this literature. What are the salient elements in "familiarity" that emerge in the course of acquaintanceship? Mere exposure is involved, but other experiences occur that could affect subsequent attitudes and behavior. Processes of impression formation, initial interactions among children, and acquaintanceship are too understudied to supply answers here.

Friends

Interviewer: Why is Caleb your friend?

Tony: Because I like him.

Interviewer: And why do you like him?

Tony: Because he's my friend.

Interviewer: And why is he your friend?

Tony (with mild disgust): Because . . . I . . . choosed . . . him . . . for . . . my friend. (Rubin, 1980)

For most children, social relations are concentrated on their friends. Children want the company of Hope, Grant, or Barry, not just any child: Friendships are dyadic. A child may have affectionate and trusting relations within a larger group, but friendships are specific attachments that, in some ways, resemble the attachments existing between children and their mothers. Friendships maintain proximity or contact with the other person; separation is disturbing. Friends provide a sense of security in strange situations that acquaintances do not (Schwartz, 1972); children enjoy their friends, trust them, and receive pleasure from them. The friendship dyad, however, is extremely vulnerable and, unlike the child's attachment to the mother, is not protected by legal safeguards. Friends cannot rely on sanctions against abuse or neglect and can claim no special rights or obligations. Children expect to be obliged to their friends, but friendships can be terminated quickly. Friendships require continuous affirmation, a process in which both parties must participate. In spite of their fragility, though, the affective experience, intellectual reciprocities, and social experimentation occurring within friendships may be as intense and significant in the child's development as the events occurring within familial attachments:

> All of you who have children are sure that your children love you; when you say that, you are expressing a pleasant illusion. But if you look very closely at one of your children when he finally finds a chum—somewhere between 8½ and 10—you will discover something very different in the relationship—namely, that your child begins to develop a real sensitivity to what matters to another person . . . . The developmental epoch of preadolescence is marked by the coming of the integrating tendencies which, when they are completely developed, we call love, or to say it another way, by the manifestation of the need for interpersonal intimacy. (Sullivan, 1953, pp. 245–246)

Friendship has not been studied as extensively as it should be. We know too little about friendship formation other than the attributes associated with children's initial attraction to one another. Age-related vicissitudes are better documented with regard to children's conceptions of friendship than the manner in which friends behave with one another. The characteristics of children who have many mutual friends, as compared to those who do not, have been studied less extensively than similarities in attitudes and behavior between friends.

Conceptions of Friendships

Children's ideas about friendship can be explored through the way they talk or write about their associates. A number of studies reveal that both the conceptual system used by children to describe their friends, as well as specific expectations, undergo changes from the preschool years through adolescence. A summary statement based on this material is included here; for a more extensive analysis, the reader is referred to the chapter on social cognitive development contained elsewhere in this *Handbook* (see *Shantz, vol. III, chap. 8*).

The vignette used to open this section reveals that preschool children are limited in the extent to which they can discuss friendships in terms that are meaningful to adults. "Friend" is a consensual concept among preschoolers, but most investigators have not been more successful than Rubin (1980) in eliciting information from young children about the qualities that friends are expected to have. Through patient questioning of 4-year-old children, however, Hayes (1978) was able to elicit at least one reason from each of 40 children for liking their best friends and one reason from 32 of the children for disliking a particular child. Common activities (47%), general play (43%), propinquity (28%), and possession of interesting things (25%) were the most commonly mentioned bases for liking; aggression (46%), aberrant behavior (32%), and rule violations (28%) were most commonly cited in association with disliking. The concordance of these friendship expectations with the attributions associated with social attraction are striking.

Considerable agreement exists in the literature on middle childhood and adolescence: With age, increases occur in the number of interpersonal constructs used, the flexibility and precision with which they are used, the complexity and organization of information and ideas about one's friends, and the recognition of certain attributes as characteristic of friends distinguished from acquaintances. Most investigators are agreed that age differences in children's conceptions of their friends derive from more general changes in cognitive and language development as well as social experience.

Bigelow and La Gaipa (1975) coded essays written by 480 Canadian school children in the first through the eighth grades on 21 dimensions of friendship expectations. The categories were bounded by different levels of abstraction and different conditions favoring social attraction. Coding focused on "onset" (i.e., the grade level at which a given expectation appeared in the children's essays with an incidence greater than zero). A cross-validation study was also conducted with 480 Scottish children (Bigelow, 1977) with concordant results: Onset of 11 expectations was noted at about the same age in both samples, along with subsequent increases. These included (onset grade in parentheses): friend as helpgiver (2), common activities (2), propinquity (3), evaluation (3), acceptance (4), admiration (4), increasing prior interaction (4), loyalty and commitment (5), genuineness (6), intimacy (7), and common interests (7). Close examination of these changes suggests a movement from egocentric to sociocentric notions about friendship, and from sociocentric to empathic expectations and more intimate relations. Ego reinforcement and reciprocity (not mentioned in the list above) were mentioned frequently at all ages, indicating their basic significance in friendship relations.

Cluster analyses (Bigelow, 1977) suggested that

the ontogeny of friendship expectations occurs in three loose "stages": (1) a *reward-cost stage*, marked by the emergence of common activities, propinquity, and similar expectations, at about the second or third grade; (2) a *normative stage* in which sharing is evident—occurring at about the fourth or fifth grade; and (3) an *empathic stage* in which understanding, self-disclosure, and shared interests emerge—about the fifth to seventh grade. In other investigations (e.g., Berndt, 1979b), correlational analysis has not supported the thesis that transformations in expectations occur to the extent that one should speak of "stages" in this area. (Indeed, many of the correlations in the Canadian/Scottish studies were not significant.) Longitudinal studies have not been conducted either, so that the invariance of individual progression in friendship expectations has not been well established. But other studies corroborate the developmental outline limned in the Canadian and Scottish studies.

Berndt (1981c) interviewed kindergarten, third-, and sixth-grade children using cartoons depicting either friends or acquaintances as stimulus material. Separate interviews were also used to assess the children's friendship expectations. To the cartoons, children of all ages more commonly attributed sharing and helping to friends than to acquaintances; quarreling was less often ascribed to friends. Responses to the friendship interview also revealed an emphasis on shared activities, sharing of possessions, helping, and the absence of fighting. The most noteworthy increase occurring with age in these interviews was stress on intimacy and loyalty, especially among girls.

In most studies, the subjects' ages have ranged only across middle childhood and early adolescence. Older adolescents and adults, however, were included in one study (Reisman & Shorr, 1978) to extend our developmental perspective on friendship expectations. Scoring their interview protocols according to the method of Bigelow and La Gaipa (1975), these investigators showed that intimacy potential, common activities, and loyalty commitments increased until about the eighth grade, but were mentioned less frequently by adults. Play was mentioned less and less often, decreasing from the second grade through adulthood. There was an indication that pleasure, in general, figures as less important in friendship expectations with increasing age, while utilitarian expectations increase. Children's expectations that friends are sources of pleasure or entertainment thus seem to be supplanted by adolescent and adult expectations that friends are useful.

Selman (1980) has striven to assess the child's meaning and understanding of interpersonal relations in terms of general cognitive development; his methods have entailed clinical interviewing rather than the analysis of verbal content in the manner of the other investigators. The notion being tested is that "friendship awareness" is embedded in stage-like progressions, including more general transformations in self-awareness and other-awareness as well as awareness of group relations. Assuming that children's conceptualizations within these domains are tied to perspective-taking and its development, it is argued that friendship awareness emerges in a series of stages differing qualitatively from one another and occurring in a hierarchical sequence. These stages range, with age, across: (1) momentary play, (2) one-way assistance, (3) "fairweather cooperation," (4) intimacy and mutual sharing, and (5) autonomous interdependence (Selman & Jaquette, 1977). These studies indicate substantial correlations among "awareness domains," longitudinal advances across stages rather than random fluctuations, and two-stage increases (on the average) across the years from 6 to 15. Content changes closely resemble those obtained by the other investigators: (1) Certain expectations (e.g., sharing and reciprocity) appear early in the child's conceptions of interpersonal affairs and remain; (2) other attributions (e.g., loyalty, sensitivity, and intimacy) appear at a later time. Given the cognitive complexity of the expectations emerging in later development, parallels between general cognitive development and the development of interpersonal relations are evident.

The development of friendship conceptions in children and adolescents may not consist of a mere "clocking in" of new and unrelated notions at various ages. Reciprocity underlies friendship expectations at all ages. It may be better to view developmental change as a series of transformations and elaborations of the child's understanding of these reciprocities rather than the "adding on" of distinct and different ideas about friendship. Building on the views of Piaget (1932) and Sullivan (1953), Youniss (1980) conducted a series of four studies on children's definitions of friendship, notions about their natural history, and ideas about norms governing violations in friendship interaction. Over 300 children were interviewed in these studies, ranging in age from 6 to 14, revealing the emergence of elements in conceptions of friendship that are similar to those reported elsewhere in the literature. But, through detailed analysis of the interview protocols, the case is made that most of the major changes occur in the way the child uses notions about reciprocities in social relations. For example, among the 6- to 8-year-olds, reciprocity was conceived naively and concretely: A friend's contribution to social interaction was believed to match the contributions of one's companion; positive exchanges bring children together as friends, whereas negative ones drive them apart. Between 9 and 11, the children's understanding of reciprocities extended to cooperation. Indeed, cooperation becomes a norm: Interpersonal adjustments were conceived as mutual, and friends were believed to practice equality and equal treatment in their relations with each other. The children also began to emphasize the importance of "personhood" in the reciprocities they attributed to friends. Finally, the transition to adolescence was accompanied by an expansion of these equity norms to include a sense that friends share identities, merging themselves into a near unit: "I and You" become a "We." Quite possibly, then, the developmental history of children's conceptions of friendship is the elaboration of their notions about reciprocity and its ramifications in interpersonal relations—not merely the accumulation of a diffuse collection of norms governing the relations between individuals.

Individual differences in friendship expectations remain largely unexplored, although recent work by Selman (1980) helps to remedy this situation. More troublesome is the lack of information about links between the development of children's conceptualizations of friendship and their actual interactions with friends. Parallels can be traced between friendship expectations and friendship interaction, but few investigators have been able to demonstrate correlations, within time periods, in modes of perceiving one's friends and modes of interacting with them. In fact, Berndt (1981c) has noted a general failure among school-age children to link their expectations about friends to predictions about the manner in which their own friends might behave. Predicting social interaction from social cognition, of course, has not been easy in any social domain, but this issue needs more concentrated research attention than it has received heretofore.

Resemblance Between Friends

Similarities between individuals have been widely assumed to underlie their attraction for one another. Concordant attitudes, personality traits, abilities, physical characteristics, and behavior have all been believed to furnish a basis for mutual friendships. First, such similarities are assumed to determine the *selection* of one's friends. That is, assortments may be made that enhance closeness and identification with another individual—especially in preadolescence. Second, similarities may *maintain* relationships over time through a continuing validation of one's social identity, which maximizes one's chances for supportive social interaction and minimizes interactions that are contentious and ego deflating. Third, similarities may be an *outcome* of friendship interactions; reciprocities existing between two individuals may generate attitudinal and behavioral concordances. Given that young children's notions about friendship are based on constructions of naive reciprocity and those of adolescents on shared identity, one would predict that attitudinal and behavioral similarities should be more evident among older than younger subjects. But there is no reason to believe that demographic similarities (e.g., age, race, and sex) would not be implicated in the friendship relations of both younger and older children.

The most common strategy for examining these issues has been to correlate the scores of mutual friends on relevant attributes, sometimes contrasting these correlations with comparable data obtained from "nominal associates." Usually, the investigator conducts a cross-sectional study at only one point in time, thus providing little basis for evaluating the developmental and socializing notions mentioned above. As a consequence, a coherent picture of the role of similarity in children's friendships, especially in developmental perspective, is difficult to extract. Nevertheless, a number of recent studies have bolstered our knowledge about similarities and their role in real-life friendships.

The two attributes most extensively shared by friends are age and gender. Age concordances are only modest between friends within classrooms, owing to the small age range in most of them (Challman, 1932; Furfey, 1927). Indeed, Tuma and Hallinan (1977), in a study of fourth-, fifth-, and sixth-graders, found that the average age difference between friendship dyads and nonfriend dyads was only 3 days (about 6 months in both cases). Nevertheless, within entire elementary or secondary school systems, the ages of children and their friends are highly correlated. Among a large number of high school students (Kandel, 1978b), similarity estimates (kappas) within friendship dyads were .84 and .64 for school grade and age, respectively. Similar evidence does not exist for elementary school children but it is unlikely that the pertinent studies would yield different results.

Growing out of children's preferences for associating with same-sex children is a strong tendency for friends to be of the same sex. Indeed, mixed-sex "best friends" are rare. Among 97 friendship choices registered in one study (Duck, 1975), only two unreciprocated cross-sex choices were counted. Similar results have been reported in many instances, although Tuma and Hallinan (1977) found 25% of their best-friend choices to be cross-sex friendships. Frequency counts in these studies, however, were not of mutual friendship pairs. Gender concordance in adolescent friendship dyads was found to be .81, more clearly indicating the significance of gender in the selection of friends (Kandel, 1978b).

Fewer cross-race friendship selections are made in integrated classrooms than would be expected on the basis of chance (Criswell, 1939; Singleton & Asher, 1979; Tuma & Hallinan, 1977), and it has already been mentioned that this proportion declines with age. Ethnic concordance in Kandel's (1978b) adolescent research was .66, indicating the high salience of racial similarity in friendship relations. Changes over time in friendship choice may be more likely among minority children in integrated school settings (e.g., white children's choices were less stable than black children's in schools with more black pupils than white ones; Tuma & Hallinan, 1977), but this occurs within a general tendency for friends to be similar in ethnic background.

Behavioral and attitudinal similarities are not as great as similarity between best friends in sex, age, and race. (1) Positive correlations between best friends' IQs have been reported by some investigators but not others (Hartup, 1970). The concordance among adolescent friends in self-reported grade point averages in Kandel's (1978b) study was .29. (2) Sociability appears to be more similar among pairs of school children who are friends than among pairs of nonfriends. The capacity for organized cooperative activity is particularly evident in boys' friendships; general social participation is more salient in girls' friendships (Challman, 1932). Concordance in peer activity among adolescent friends is similarly low (.28), according to Kandel (1978b). (3) Sociometric status has not been established as more similar among friends than among nonfriends (Thorpe, 1955), although disentangling the effects of social status among "choosers" and "chosens" is not easy. Tagiuri, Kogan, and Long (1958) found a positive relation between the status of chooser and chosen, using roommate preferences among students in a private school as the status criterion, and Savin-Williams (1979) reported that friends were similar in dominance rankings in a summer camp. But Roff and Sells (1967) found zero-order correlations between the peer status scores of over 10,000 children and the children whom the subjects chose as

"liked most." Choosers' status was negatively correlated with the status of children chosen as "liked least," but these were very low in magnitude. Stability across time in friendship choices is greater when status is similar than when not (Tuma & Hallinan, 1977), but no strong evidence exists that friends occupy similar status levels in the peer group. (4) Similarity in attitudes and values is related to social attraction in laboratory studies (Byrne & Griffitt, 1966), but these are difficult to relate to real-life friendship dyads. Davitz (1955) found preferences for camp activities to be similar between children and their sociometric nominees, even though perceived similarity was greater than actual similarity. Adolescents whose friends aspire to college are more likely to want to attend college themselves, even with social class held constant (Duncan, Featherman, & Duncan, 1972). Other studies have also shown modest concordances in the educational and occupational aspirations of friends, especially when supported by parental values (Haller & Butterworth, 1960; Kandel, 1978b). (5) Personal construct systems are more similar between friends than between nominal pairs (Duck, 1975), but age differences occur with respect to the constructs on which the similarity is evident: Among boys, a shift from early to mid-adolescence was noted from the use of factual constructs to an emphasis on interaction and physical factors; among girls, the shift occurred from factual and physical constructs to a mixture of physical and psychological constructs.

The most comprehensive analysis of similarity in the friendship relations of young people is Kandel's (1978b) study of various attributes in a sample of 1879 adolescent best friends drawn from five public high schools in New York State. Subject selection and methods of procedure were extremely sophisticated, and the concordances obtained tie together the disparate studies mentioned above. Similarity was greatest on sociodemographic factors such as age, sex, and ethnicity; next greatest was specific behaviors, especially the use of illicit drugs (on which the study was focused), and least on psychological factors, attitudes, and interpersonal relations. No sex differences were evident.

Measurement at only a single point in time, as characteristic of most studies in this area, may miss some of the most important features in the role played by similarity in peer relations. Kandel (1978a) thus used the data base from her studies of adolescents longitudinally; two testings were conducted— at the beginning and the end of the school year. Three types of dyads could be compared in terms of demographic and behavioral concordance: (1)

friendship pairs that remained stable over time; (2) those that dissolved over time; and (3) children who were not initially friends but who became friends by the end of the year. The role of similarity in the *selection* of friends was indicated by: (1) the greater similarity in behavior and attitudes (Time 1) between children who subsequently remained friends than children who did not; (2) the lesser similarity (Time 1) between children who did not remain friends over time than between children who become friends subsequently; and (3) the lesser similarity (Time 2) between former friends and children who remained friends over the entire year. That friendship exerts a *socializing* effect is revealed by: (1) the greater similarity between stable friends at Time 2 than at Time 1; and (2) the greater similarity among newly formed friends at Time 2 than was true between them—even though not friends—at Time 1. Similarity between friends, then, cannot be attributed entirely to the mutual influence of friends on each other (Duncan et al., 1972) but rests also on assortative processes. Kandel's (1978a) work indicates that these conjunctive processes are especially important in adolescent drug use, although the general pattern was also evident for educational aspirations, political orientation, and minor delinquencies. Given the possibility that friendship relations change developmentally as well as with acquaintanceship, investigators need to extend this line of research to include other age periods and longer longitudinal spans.

Behavior with Friends

It is nearly impossible to specify an age when friendships first become visible in social interaction. Mothers label infants with whom their own babies have regular contact as ''friends'' (Lewis et al., 1975), and they may have good reasons for doing so. In these instances, however, the baby has not *chosen* the other baby from among many associates, and some of the friendship qualities observed by the mother may be in her eyes rather than in the activities of the youngsters.

Among preschoolers, children spend more time in social interaction with individuals labeled as ''friends'' than with others (Challman, 1932; McCandless & Marshall, 1957b), although individual differences may be considerable. Only 27% of one group of 4-year-olds was observed to interact most with their stated ''best friend'' in the classroom (Chapman, Smith, Foot, & Pritchard, 1979). Observations of elementary school children are scarce, and there may be reason to question that sociometric choices are strongly related to playground interac-

tions (Chapman et al., 1979) in this period. But time-use studies indicate that out-of-school time with child associates is primarily spent with friends among both children and adolescents (Medrich et al., 1982). Associative contact thus seems to be more evident between children and their friends than between children and more nominal associates.

Are qualitative differences observable in the interaction between friends and nonfriends? Overall, positive exchange and mutuality are found among friends to a greater extent than among nonfriends at all ages. Masters and Furman (1981) observed the social interactions of 94 preschool children and classified them according to three categories: (1) positive reinforcement (given to others and received from others); (2) neutral actions (given and received); and (3) punishing actions (also given and received). Rates of these social acts were then contrasted in terms of the child's contacts with friends, disliked children, and nominal others. Children both gave and received more positive reinforcements and neutral behaviors in their interactions with friends than with disliked or unselected children. These rates were twice as great with friends as with either category of nonfriends; this did not extend to negative, punitive interactions. Friendship interaction among preschool children also has affective overtones in novel situations, as contrasted to interaction among nonfriends. Schwartz (1972) observed more positive affect, greater mobility, and more frequent verbalizations in a strange situation between children designated by their teachers as friends than between unacquainted children. Friends, like acquaintances (Ipsa, 1981), thus seem to reduce anxiety and promote exploration in novel environments.

Comparisons between the behavior of school-age friends and nonfriends have not been made using observations in natural settings; instead, simulated conditions have been arranged in the laboratory. In one investigation, friends were more talkative in their interactions than nonfriends and chose to work under cooperative conditions more often; task performance, however, did not differ according to whether the partner was a friend or a stranger (Philp, 1940). Other studies also show that the nature of the interaction, rather than the task success, may be the major difference between friends and nonfriends. Newcomb, Brady, and Hartup (1979) observed 6- and 8-year-old children performing a block-building task under competitive and cooperative conditions with friends and nominal others. Task success did not vary according to friendship status under either incentive condition, but the nature of the interaction did. Friends were more interactive, more affective, paid closer attention to equity rules ("If we take turns we'll both make more points"), and their conversational strategies were mutually directed ("Let's do it this way") rather than directed at each other as individuals ("Put your block over there"). Similar differences were observed in an exploratory task (Newcomb & Brady, 1982). In this instance, the behavior of school-age friends was more synchronous, affectively tuned, and mutually directed than the behavior of nonfriends, and it also led to more extensive exploration of the experimental materials and acquisition of information about them.

Consolidation of cooperation in friendship relations increases in middle childhood (Berndt, 1981a) and among adolescents in the prisoner's dilemma situation (Swingle & Gillis, 1968). Ninth- and tenth-grade children were exposed to either highly cooperative or highly competitive strategies attributed to partners whom they liked, disliked, or had no special feelings about. Following a number of trials, strategies were changed to the opposing condition. Subjects were more cooperative when playing with partners whom they liked than other partners and were also more influenced by strategy changes attributed to them.

Social responsiveness among school-age friends in interactive humor situations also differs from the interchanges of nonfriends (Foot, Chapman, & Smith, 1977; Smith, Foot, & Chapman, 1977). When children watched "Tom and Jerry" cartoons or listened to humorous records, both the duration and frequency of laughing, smiling, looking, and talking were greater between friends than between strangers. In addition, response matching, a measure of behavioral concordance between the two children, was greater between friends than between nonfriends. Finally, Gottman and Parkhurst (1980) found that, in conversations, the exchanges of school-age friends are more telescoped and less empathic than the exchanges of preschool-age friends. In one sense, this means that communication is *less* efficient among friends as the children grow older but, in another, it indicates that older friends may be more sensitive and attentive to more subtle cues in communication than are younger children.

More competitiveness can sometimes be observed in the interaction between friends than between nonfriends. Children are especially generous with strangers who are believed to be in greater need than their friends (Fincham, 1978) or with strangers who are relatively generous to begin with (Floyd, 1964). Also, more competition occurs between friends than between nonfriends when property rights are clearly understood (Staub & Noerenberg,

1981) and, among males, when the atmosphere is competitive (Berndt, 1981b). On the other hand, when the task does not involve rewards for the children's work, more sharing occurs between friends than between nonfriends (Staub & Sherk, 1970). Seemingly, the sensitivity and spontaneity characterizing friendship interaction may encourage *either* competition or cooperation, depending on task conditions.

Summary

Current research on children's friendships is beginning to converge in developmental outline. Changes in friendship expectations occur with increasing age, but reciprocity is prominent at all ages. Cooperation and intimacy emerge in childhood and adolescence; personal support is especially strong in adolescence. Similarities in demographic characteristics are especially strong determinants of friendship selection, although behavioral similarities determine both selection and socialization outcomes among adolescents. Observations of children with their friends and with nonfriends confirm that reciprocity and mutuality characterize friendship relations at all ages, but synchrony, smoothness, and cooperation become increasingly evident in middle childhood.

Long-term studies, designed to elucidate the functions of friendship interaction in human development, have not been conducted. Effective adult social relations require reciprocal interaction—for example, in work relations and marital relations. Give-and-take is necessary to effective outcomes for each partner. But individual differences and continuities, from childhood to adolescence and then to adulthood, in friendships have not been charted, especially in relation to these questions.

GROUPS

As the Eagles walked down the road, they discussed the reasons for their victory. Mason attributed it to their prayers. Myers, agreeing heartily, said the Rattlers lost because they used cusswords all the time. Then he shouted, "Hey, you guys, let's not do any more cussing, and I'm serious, too." All the boys agreed on this line of reasoning. Mason concluded that since the Rattlers were such poor sports and such "bad cussers," the *Eagles should not even talk to them anymore*. (Sherif et al., 1961, p. 106)

Children band together in collectives that range from two or three individuals to a dozen or more. In some instances, these collectives are short-lived, lasting only a few minutes or several hours. At other times, children interact on a more-or-less regular basis sharing attitudes, values, and a strong desire to belong to the unit. Collectives become groups when: social interaction occurs regularly, values are shared over and above those maintained in society at large, individual members have a sense of belonging, and a structure exists to support the attitudes that members should have toward one another.

The term *membership group* is used to refer to any enclave to which the individual belongs, whether or not membership in it is actively sought. Sex, age, school status, and ethnicity determine membership in some groups; membership status can also be bestowed on the basis of an infinite number of other attributes. The internal functioning of groups and their impact on the individual, however, vary according to the degree to which the membership group serves *reference functions*—that is, according to the strength of the member's identification with the group or desire to belong to it. In short, reference groups are "the we of me."

Structured interviews reveal that children's conceptions of group relations change with age. Preschool and kindergarten children have very little sense of "groupness" (Margolin, 1969), while 7- and 8-year-olds commonly conceive of the peer group as a series of unilateral relations. Nine- to 12-year-olds, however, think of group relations in bilateral terms—as interlocking twosomes. The notion that the peer group is a homogeneous community appears rarely in children's thinking before adolescence and coexists in adulthood with the idea that groups are pluralistic entities (Jaquette, 1976). In some ways, then, the child's understanding of group relations changes in concert with notions about friendship and other interpersonal relations.

Group Formation

Peer groups do not emerge instantaneously, even though some collectives acquire their structures in a very short time. Cooperative work on classroom projects can be organized quickly, but most peer groups come into existence on the basis of observations, interactions, and evaluations that cumulate over time. Social standards and codes of conduct are elaborated as time passes; statuses change over time. In order to understand the processes of group formation, it is thus necessary to study peer interaction in a time-dependent sense. Group formation cannot be understood fully through observations of groups that already exist.

Group formation has been studied mainly with preadolescents or adolescents, and more often with boys than with girls. One well-known experiment was conducted by Sherif and Sherif (1953) to test three major hypotheses: (1) When individual children are brought together in physical proximity and perceive that they share common goals, the collective will acquire a hierarchical structure—leader and follower positions, friendship patterns, and divisions of labor will emerge. (2) The group will acquire reference functions—social norms will become evident. (3) If two or more groups are brought into contact under conditions of competition and frustration, relations within groups will change and intergroup hostility will result. A second experiment, commonly called the Robbers Cave (Sherif et al., 1961), replicated and extended the earlier work to include a fourth hypothesis: (4) If two hostile groups work cooperatively under superordinate goal conditions, intergroup hostility will decline.

The Robbers Cave experiment best exemplifies the Sherif *oeuvre* including their use of both anecdotal and quantitative methods. Twenty-two fifth-grade boys (initially strangers) were recruited for summer camp, divided into two aggregates, and removed to separate campsites in the Oklahoma woods. Neither aggregation was aware of the other's presence. The boys lived closely together, engaged in enjoyable activities such as hiking and crafts, built "hideouts," and organized games. To encourage the formation of group structures, the investigators arranged a series of situations requiring cooperative activity. One evening, for example, the boys appeared for dinner to find that the staff had not prepared the meal. Only the raw ingredients were available (e.g., meat, Kool-Aid, and watermelon); the boys were left to their own devices. A division of labor occurred immediately and cooperative problem solving ensued. Some boys cooked, others mixed drinks, and others organized the food services. Different members assumed different statuses; leaders and followers emerged. Later, both groups adopted names—Rattlers and Eagles. The children, unacquainted at the beginning, thus became groups defined by common goals, names, a sense of belonging, and a structure.

In the next phase of the experiment, the relations *between* the Rattlers and Eagles were studied along with the interactions and structures *within* them. The counselors first arranged for the groups to discover each other "accidentally," then talked the groups into a series of "friendly" competitions—baseball games, tugs-of-war, and so forth. Unknown to the boys, the counselors manipulated these competitions so that neither group would experience more frequent failures than the other. The immediate effects of losing a competition were dramatic. Within each group, grousing, blaming one another, and scapegoating were common. For example, the Eagles lost their first baseball game and Mason, their best athlete, threatened to beat up certain members if they didn't "try harder." Later, Craig, the acknowledged leader of the Eagles, was actually overthrown because of his failure to work hard in the competitions. Thus, the social structures were changed as a consequence of the competition, and the groups passed through a period of internal disharmony and decreased cohesiveness.

With time, however, the shakedown instigated by the competitions ceased, and both Eagles and Rattlers became more cohesive than ever before. New norms developed (they're the "cussers," we're the "pray-ers"), and increased solidarity was displayed in various ways, especially through verbal abuse of the other group at games and retaliations following losses. After loosing one series, the Eagles stole the Rattler's flag and burned it; then, when they won the next series, their verbal abuse of the Rattlers was unrelenting. In turn, the Rattlers decided that the Eagles had used unfair tactics and organized a raid on their campsite. They stole comic books and a pair of jeans that they painted orange and displayed as a flag. Armed with rocks for a counterattack, the Eagles were interrupted by the counselors before any serious damage could be done. Thus, both internal structures and solidarity were altered by the competition. "We" and "they" were the most salient dimensions in group relations along with pervasive intergroup hostility. Aggression toward the outgroup was characteristic of both high- and low-status members, even though it had been anticipated that the low-status boys might manifest more of this behavior.

The final episodes in this experiment involved attempts by the experimenters to engineer circumstances that would reduce the intergroup conflict. The first strategy to be tried was to bring the boys together in pleasant, noncompetitive circumstances—for example, for movies, a meal, and fireworks. These were disasters. If anything, hostility between the groups was more intense; squabbling, name-calling, fights, and pelting each other with food were common. (Exhortations in the name of cooperation and brotherly love also failed to reduce intergroup conflict in the earlier study; Sherif & Sherif, 1953.) But one tactic worked to establish more harmonious relations: a series of events requiring cooperative effort. For example, the water supply "broke down" on a hot day. Told that there must

be something wrong with the pipes leading from the water tank, the boys from both groups immediately began a long and intensive search for the trouble. At another time, when everybody was hungry, the truck used to transport food supplies "developed" engine trouble. There was no alternative but for the boys to pull together to get the engine started. Finally, a movie couldn't be shown unless both groups pooled their money. These experiences, involving superordinate goals, produced sharp reductions in intergroup conflict and stereotyping as well as concomitant increases in friendship choices across group lines.

The Eagles and the Rattlers teach us many lessons: (1) Peer groups coalesce on the basis of common motivations; (2) interactions within the group are primary sources of gratification; (3) if satisfaction does not develop or diminishes, the cohesiveness of the group may be reduced; (4) intergroup competition for resources promotes stereotyping and hostility between groups; (5) intergroup conflict can promote solidarity within groups; and (6) superordinate goals can reduce deep-seated animosities. These experiments have wide social applicability—to the arms race as well as to ethnic tensions. In fact, the failure of many "contact" interventions to reduce group tensions is consonant with these findings; the better record of interventions that involve mutually shared norms and cooperative activity in reducing tensions (Aronson, 1978) would also be expected on the basis of these studies.

Self-generated informal groups are common in the social lives of American youngsters throughout childhood, assuming great significance in adolescence (Burk, Zdep, & Kushner, 1973). Studies of these groups confirm the field experiments: First, social structures are always visible, with leader and low-status positions the easiest to identify. Leadership and popularity may covary differently in different groups; some groups are more diffuse in social structure than others. But social structures based on power relations, that is, the effectiveness of members in initiating activities over time, are ubiquitous (Sherif & Sherif, 1964; 1969). The functioning of norms in intact groups is also clearly visible.

Group Norms

Standards of conduct, sometimes called *norms*, govern the actions of group members. Certain norms emanate from the culture as a whole—for example, sex-role stereotypes, attitudes toward authority, and equity considerations. But peer groups generate their own norms, applying them only to themselves.

Best known to outsiders are the norms that emanate from adolescent peer groups: How many buttons should be open on one's shirt? What music should be listened to? What language should be used? Is one a "wimp" or a "zoid"?

Constellations of these social norms create broad divisions in children's societies. *Sporties,* for example, are adolescents of both sexes who engage in sports, who attend sports activities, and who drink beer. *Workers* are students who have jobs, who are motivated to accumulate money, who own cars, and whose social lives revolve mostly around the automobile. *Crispies* are students who use drugs on other than a one-time basis, who are the best football players, and who do not work very hard at school. *Musicians* are students who spend much time in the music room, who attend or assist with performance activities of one type or another, and who drink alcoholic beverages. *Debaters* are those who read a lot, get good grades, participate in clubs focused on intellectual activities and who drink Pepsi-Cola at their parties. Normative constellations and their nomenclatures vary from time to time and place to place (these categories were used *only* in one Minnesota high school in the mid-1970s), but the normative regulators that segment the peer system are extremely visible.

According to Fine (1980), five conditions must exist in order for norms to become established within the peer group. First, someone must "know." That is, someone must possess a specific bit of social information and introduce it to the group before normative activity can evolve. Second, members must find the information usable. Dirty jokes, for example, may become embedded in the "idioculture," but only if situations exist in which telling dirty jokes is possible. Third, normative elements must be functional; that is, they must satisfy some common need. Fourth, social norms must support the group's social structure, and vice versa. Finally, circumstances must exist to trigger the normative activity. When normative elicitors cease, for whatever reason, changes in social interaction will inevitably occur. This framework can be used to examine the introduction, maintenance, and termination of normative activity across time, although it has not been used extensively to do so.

Do social norms govern peer interaction at all age levels? Excluding infancy, the answer to this question is probably yes. "We" and "they" distinctions have been noted among toddlers reared together in Israeli *kibbutzim* as manifested in their adherence to elementary social rules and defense of one another when quarrels developed with children from other groups (Faigin, 1958). An especially elaborate normative network surrounds the social categories of "boy" and "girl," although children's notions about gender do not have great stability across time and situation until the preschool years (Slaby & Frey, 1975). Other social conventions—including seating orders, ownership rules, ceremonies connected with the use of toys, and game rituals—can be seen (Merei, 1949), but the cognitive elaborations of these rules are not likely to be obvious and their enforcement is inconsistent.

Normative activity becomes increasingly visible in the preschool years. Lakin, Lakin, and Costanzo (1979) studied normative behavior in various Israeli settings within same-age groups: 1½ to 2 years; 2 to 2½; 2½ to 3; and 3 to 3½. Assignment and execution of clear-cut roles, rule enforcement and rehearsal, and helping behavior were observed more frequently in the older groups than in the younger ones, although setting differences were also apparent. No clear relation between setting characteristics and normative activity is evident, but structured classroom situations (with clear-cut rules established by adult authorities), as compared to less structured classrooms, seem to favor children's expectations that their social interactions are governed by rules (Margolin, 1969).

Certain social conventions are not evident among preschool children unless adults demand adherence to them. The distribution of rewards according to one's own success relative to the success of one's companions (i.e., equity norms) is not evident unless children are told explicitly to use such norms or apply them to others rather than to themselves (Lane & Coon, 1972; Nelson & Dweck, 1977). Explicit sanctions from adults, though, may merely be the conditions required for normative activity in the preschool years; it is more significant to know that social norms are evident *to some degree* than to overemphasize the inability to apply such norms to the children themselves. In other words, primitive norms are emergent in the preschool years, even though they may be derived from, and reinforced by, adults.

One investigation (Nucci & Turiel, 1978) shows that preschool children are likely to engage spontaneously in certain kinds of normative interaction more often than others. Observations revealed that "moral events," involving the welfare or rights of individuals, were more likely to elicit responses from other children than were "conventional events" that concerned use of work and play spaces, appropriate conduct, and the like. When queried about these two kinds of events, however, the children could distinguish them in the same manner as adults; two normative domains thus existed among these young children at a conceptual level. The conventional events, which originated with the adults and were arbitrary in nature, were left by these children to be enforced by adults. But moral norms for governing social behavior were beginning to be evident in the interactions of the children themselves.

Primary school children are apparently able to generate much more formal, moralistic norms than are groups of younger children. Turner (1957) described a quasilegal procedure for handling disputes that was generated over a 3-year period by children themselves and resembled, in many ways, conventional adult sanctions. Since the teacher was unobtrusive in the children's deliberations, the results suggest that the interactions occurring within the group were the principal sources of the norms that emerged. Piaget's (1932) observations concerning the generation of consensual norms among school-age children are concordant with these school-based observations. Margolin (1969) obtained interviews from school-age children about social rules and conventions and concluded that school entrance is associated with a temporary disruption in children's recognition of social conventions. These observations, however, have not received further attention.

Social norms concordant with the core culture proliferate in peer interaction during middle childhood. Among kindergartners, reciprocated prosocial and antisocial actions are evaluated differently from nonreciprocated actions, resembling the evaluations of adults (Berndt, 1977). Among 5- to 8-year-olds, reward distribution is based on self-interest or equality norms when one's own performance is compared to another; equity norms are invoked, however, when self-interest is removed (Lane & Coon, 1972; Lerner, 1974; Leventhal & Anderson, 1970; Leventhal, Popp, & Sawyer, 1973; Streater & Chertkoff, 1976). By preadolescence, equality norms are used in reward distribution in both bargaining and nonnegotiable situations (Benton, 1971; Morgan & Sawyer, 1967; Streater & Chertkoff, 1976), unless intentional norm violations are detected (Garett & Libby, 1973). Such trends are consistent with Piaget's observations (1932) on the increasing use of equality as a basis for evaluating disobedience and transgression. Both cognitive constraints and the vicissitudes of social experience underlie these changes, although individual differences have not been widely explored. Sex differences favoring males in the use of equity norms have been reported (Benton, 1971; Leventhal & Anderson, 1970; Leventhal et al., 1973), but gender differences have not been found in every instance.

Numerous studies, both field experiments and laboratory investigations, confirm the salience of self-generated norms in peer group functioning during middle childhood (Hallworth, 1953; Polansky, Lippitt, & Redl, 1950). Normative activity does not seem to be more pervasive in adolescent peer interaction than in middle childhood, but this transition has not been studied extensively. The norm taxonomy shifts, of course, but most investigators have studied this taxonomy within adolescence rather than before and after pubescence.

Normative constellations vary tremendously from enclave to enclave. Adolescent drug users tend to associate with one another, for example, indicating that the social norms surrounding the use of these substances are significant determinants of social affiliation. Drug users, however, do not appear to form subcultures that are distinguishable from non-user subcultures, except in drug use (Huba, Wingard, & Bentler, 1979). Similarly, soccer players associate with one another, but there is no evidence to support the notion that soccer-playing collectives can be normatively distinguished from other collectives based on automobile use, grooming standards, or dating rules. Knowing that drug users and soccer players associate, respectively, with one another thus indicates the importance of these activities among some adolescents but predicts little else. Normative variations may be more significant to the social scientist than normative similarities.

Various studies indicate that norms determine both the assortments worked out by children and adolescents (i.e., the selection of one's associates) and the negotiations between individuals once interaction begins. Norms are both exogenous and endogenous with respect to the individual. One's own norms about physical appearance, drinking, or drug use may determine one's associates (Dembo, Schmeidler, & Burgos, 1979; Littrell & Eicher, 1973), but longitudinal studies reveal that whether one drinks also influences the drinking habits of the individuals selected as one's friends. "Whatever exogenous determinants of drinking there might be, there is an active social animal at work constructing a compatible normative structure and supportive peers by changing the former and selecting the latter" (Britt & Campbell, 1977, p. 546). Group members then become similar to one another through both normative selection and normative socialization.

There is little evidence concerning the stability of group-negotiated norms during childhood and adolescence or variations in their exogenous magnitude. Wilson (1963) reported that ethnic attitudes become more stable and less variable from early to late adolescence, but the normative constellations characterizing specific groups have not been examined from this perspective. Once again, there are interesting developmental issues that need to be explored more extensively than they have been.

Group Structures

Group members are seldom equivalent in *social power;* one or more always emerge with greater power than others. Social power may not be transferable from one group to another nor, within groups, be vested in the same individual(s) in all situations. But group members inevitably differentiate themselves on this dimension, assorting themselves into hierarchical organizations.

What is social power? In the simplest sense, social power is *effectant initiative* (Sherif & Sherif, 1964), that is, actions that direct, coordinate, and sanction the activities of others. Some writers (see Omark, Strayer, & Freedman, 1980) emphasize dominance as the construct most central to the power dimension since aggression and assertiveness seem intrinsic in social control and sanctions. Increasingly, however, it is recognized that leaders are not necessarily "tough" or "mean," and considerable evidence exists to show that powerful individuals infrequently use physical aggression, coercion, or aversive pressures in order to exert their influence. Similarly, popularity does not always characterize individuals with social power, nor does social skill. "The leader need not have the best car, be the smoothest operator, the biggest lady killer, nor the toughest, as the case may be. In fact, usually he is not" (Sherif & Sherif, 1964, p. 159).

Social power may best be conceived as a constellation of attributes that facilitates the attainment of group objectives. Since every group possesses a unique normative structure, it follows that social power will accrue to individual members on different bases in different groups. In some instances, individual differences in aggressiveness or assertiveness may be relevant to the attainment of group objectives and, if so, dominance structures based on these attributes will be salient in the social organization. Leaders will be assertive individuals and followers will be submissive. In other instances, social sensitivity and Machiavellian adroitness may best serve the group's objectives; individuals with these characteristics will then emerge as "dominant" rather than individuals who are assertive. Survival skills may even underlie leadership in adolescent gangs that operate in dangerous environments (Krisberg, 1974).

Hierarchical structures are evident in the social organization of many species, particularly the primates, leading to considerable interest in the role of these structures in phylogeny. The basic notion is that social structures serve adaptive functions, maximizing access to food, to individuals from whom problem-solving skills can be learned, and, ultimately, to individuals with whom reproduction can occur. Since aggression and assertiveness (or quasiaggression in the form of threats) are evident among many species in association with these objectives, social organization has been studied most extensively in terms of dominance hierarchies, that is, social orders based on "winning versus losing." Even among nonhuman primates, however, aggressiveness may not be the only attribute associated with social power. Nonaggressive competencies, both cognitive and social, also contribute to an animal's effectiveness, and these competencies sometimes delineate group structures better than aggression. Indeed, more subtle markers of social structure, such as the distribution of social attention (Chance & Larsen, 1976), may tell us more about certain groups than aggressive indicators.

Group structures have received considerable attention among child psychologists working within an evolutionary perspective. Most of this work concerns structures emerging in classrooms—that is, aggregates of nursery school children or elementary school children that were not established spontaneously by the children themselves. Group structures in classrooms and summer camps, though, may differ from the structures existing in informal groups, since normative activity in formal and informal groups may not be the same. While much can be deduced about social organization through the study of classrooms, it is not appropriate to generalize these observations to the entire peer system.

Significantly missing in many studies is a consideration of the interrelations between social norms and social organization. A large number of investigators have worked with social structures that emerge in groups of preschool children among whom social norms are nascent. Even when dominance relations have been considered in adolescent groups (cf. Savin-Williams, 1980a, 1980b), these interrelations are not emphasized except in relation to the hypothesis that social structures exist to reduce the amount of aggression occurring between group members. In nearly every respect, group structures have been considered divorced from their normative functions, and normative functions have been studied mainly apart from social structures. The earlier studies of the Sherifs, of course, stand in exception to this statement.

Social structures in nursery school classrooms

have been examined mainly in relation to physical attack, struggles over objects, threats, teasing, and sometimes in terms of conflict outcomes (i.e., winning a fight or an object struggle). Strayer and Strayer (1976) observed attack-submission exchanges, threat-submission instances, and object-position struggles in a group of eighteen 4-year-olds, discovering that linearity and rigidity (both parameters of transitivity) varied according to the dominance criterion. Attack-submission occurred with complete transitivity; threats occurred with 88% linearity and 96% rigidity; and objects struggles at 82% and 90%, respectively. Linearity in aggressive relations and in object struggles has been observed in a number of other nursery school classrooms, although the social orders based on these two criteria consistently appear to be somewhat different (Strayer, 1980a; Vaughn & Waters, 1980). Dominance hierarchies based on the *initiation* of attacks and threats are as linear as hierarchies based on the *outcomes* of agonistic encounters (who wins) but, again, the social structure is somewhat different as viewed from each of these perspectives (Sluckin & Smith, 1977). The number of nursery school groups observed in these studies is, as yet, rather small so that group differences in dominance assortments are not well documented. It is likely that dominance hierarchies are not uniformly linear and rigid, although the current evidence suggests that some form of social order based on aggressive relations probably exists in every group.

The social system in nursery schools has also been examined in terms of "attention structures," the extent to which children look at one another. Clearly, some children receive more attention from their companions than do others (Abramovitch, 1976; Hold, 1977; Vaughn & Waters, 1980), but attention gradients are not linear even though high-ranking and low-ranking children can be differentiated from the other children (Hold, 1977). Children who receive the most attention from their peers also tend to look at each other more often than they receive attention from low-ranking children (Vaughn & Waters, 1980).

Superimposed on the social networks described by dominance and attention are structures based on affiliation and altruism. Preschool children who make affiliative overtures to others receive many such overtures, and the same exists for altruistic activity (Furman & Masters, 1980a; Hartup et al., 1967; McCandless & Marshall, 1957b; Strayer, 1980b). But the structures involved are not hierarchical in the sense that group structures based on agonism and attention are. Affiliative structures in most nursery school groups consist of subgroupings, each organized around a focal dyad and including other children on the periphery; several networks are visible in most classrooms. Since affiliative networks are not composed of children with similar dominance rankings, social organization does not approximate a linear arrangement when agonism and affiliation are combined in the analysis (Abramovitch & Strayer, 1978). Similarly, altruism does not seem to define hierarchical structures.

Assuming that dominance and attention structures both represent power dimensions in young children's groups, considerable interest has been evidenced in the correlates of these two attributes. Does attention distribution correlate with social dominance? Are other social status indicators related to either dimension? First, the concordance between dominance and attention structures depends on the dominance measure selected and the strategy used in the measurement of attention. Object struggles (winning) are positively correlated with looks and glances received from other children. These correlations are considerable (.73 to .96) when the attention measures are derived from interactive instances (excluding object struggles themselves as well as onlooker behavior). Correlations are modest (.43 to .48) when the attention measure is heavily weighted with onlooker activity (Abramovitch & Strayer, 1978; Vaughn & Waters, 1980). Second, physical attack is not consistently correlated with the attention structure. Correlations obtained in four classrooms were .56, −.03, .42, and .13, respectively, with only the first of these being statistically significant (Abramovitch & Strayer, 1978; Strayer, 1980a; Vaughn & Waters, 1980). Attention to others also does not seem to be distributed in accordance with aggression rankings of the "looker" (Strayer, 1980a; Vaughn & Waters, 1980). Although the total number of classrooms used in these studies is not large, the current evidence suggests, then, that some concordance exists between social structures delineated in terms of attention and object struggles but not between structures delineated in terms of attention and hostile aggression.

Since toys and games are central in the social interaction of young children, it is not surprising to note these outcomes. The preschool classroom seems to be organized in one way with respect to access to objects and in another way with respect to hostile attacks and threats. Further indications that the attention structure is a derivative of commerce with toys and games are positive correlations obtained between being looked at and being imitated (Abramovitch & Grusec, 1978; Strayer, Chapeskie,

& Strayer, 1978), "starting a game," "proposing a game," and "being an organizer" (Hold, 1977). Coupled with the correlation between the attention structure and sociometric status (Vaughn & Waters, 1980), this evidence makes clear that social structures based on competence dimensions are different from those based on the utilization of brute force.

Among preschool children, group structures are visible mainly to the observer; the children themselves cannot agree on "who is the toughest" to the extent that transitivity is evident in their perceptions. Selection of the "toughest" or "strongest" child from arrays of photographs seldom produces agreement beyond chance within pairs of preschool children (Edelman & Omark, 1973; Sluckin & Smith, 1977; Strayer et al., 1978). Young children overestimate their own toughness relative to other children, and their nominations bear little relation to status as determined by direct observation. Agreement about the "toughness" of one's companions, however, increases with age—from 62% among kindergarten children to 73% among fourth-graders (Edelman & Omark, 1973). Since social hierarchies do, in fact, exist among young children, it is evident that the emergence of social structures does not depend entirely on children's seriation abilities with respect to the construct of "toughness." Studies of social structures among elementary school children are too limited at this point to say much more about cognitive constraints on social organization from a developmental perspective.

Among elementary school children, attacks, threats, and object struggles converge in social orderings (Strayer & Strayer, 1976). The Robbers Cave experiment demonstrates that social structures among school children may also be based on being good at games, knowing how to organize activities, and social skill—competencies that have relevance to group norms. Similarly, in classrooms containing a mixture of high- and low-ability children, social status has been found to correlate mainly with academic ability whereas, in homogeneous classrooms, status correlates primarily with social power and affect regulation (Schunke, 1978). Among low-ability children in particular, individual differences in assertiveness are closely associated with social status (Zander & Van Egmond, 1958). Individual differences in attributes that facilitate a group's objectives are thus the primary basis for the social order; power structures based on social dominance may or may not vary concordantly.

Group structures have been studied most extensively among young adolescents in camp settings. Savin-Williams (1979) conducted daily observations for 5 weeks on 8 cabin groups, each including 4 to 6 boys or girls. The observations were centered on suggestions, arguing, ridicule, recognition, ignoring, physical assertiveness, taking objects, and threats. Both the individual indexes and a summary measure showed that a systematic ranking with fewer than 20% reversals marked each cabin group. Sociometric nominations, based on dominance criteria, also approximated linearity in the male groups, although not consistently in the female ones. Linearity increased over the 5-week period but, more important, the rank orderings were stable. Rank ordering was also stable across behavior settings including cabin interactions, meals, and athletic events, although stability across time was greater in athletic events than in the other settings.

For both sexes, ridicule was the most frequent dominance behavior, while threats were the least frequent. Thus, the trading of insults may be more salient in leader-follower relations among young adolescents than physical coercion. Boys were more likely to manifest physical dominance than girls; the girls were more likely to compliment, ask favors, imitate, and solicit advice. Dominance activity declined, in general, over the 5-week period more in boys' enclaves than in girls', but the dominance hierarchies among the girls fluctuated more on a day-to-day basis and from setting to setting in comparison to the boys. The decrease in dominance interactions over time supports the thesis that these social structures restrained agonism. Significant correlations, for both sexes, of dominance rankings with athletic ability, sexual maturation, and leadership indicate that the social structures also served other functions: to divide labor and distribute resources so that the group could function effectively in the camp milieu. Unlike preschool children, the dominance interactions of young adolescents did not focus on toys or similar objects, but on other salient resources: the biggest piece of cake at meals, the choice seat during discussions, and sleeping places near the fire on a campout.

In a similar study of two groups of older adolescents (14- to 17-year-olds), Savin-Williams (1980a; 1980b) also found stable dominance structures emerging in cabin groups. In these situations, however, sexual maturation, athletic ability, and physical fitness no longer predicted dominance rank. Instead, variations in intelligence, creativity, skill at crafts, popularity, and camp experience were concordant with the power structure. Once the transition to adolescence is made, then, the power structure seems less likely to depend on attributes associated with early maturation, and more on other characteristics perceived by the group as relevant to their normative activities.

To summarize, group structures emerge in social interaction beginning in the preschool years. Dominance hierarchies are evident in early childhood, middle childhood, and adolescence, although group structures are based on somewhat different constellations of attributes at various ages. Individuals who can keep possessions and know how to use them are likely to possess the greatest social power in early childhood; individuals who are adroit in directing play and games emerge as leaders in middle childhood; individuals who are early maturers and have athletic and social skills are invested with social power in early adolescence, and individuals who are bright and well-liked hold high-status positions in later adolescence. These structural dimensions, however, have been studied in a limited number of settings, mostly in classrooms and summer camps, so it is not known whether social power accrues on these bases in every social situation. But the stability of the social organization across settings in these studies suggests that group structures have some generality, as long as the structure guides the individual members in what they should do. Dominance, in the form of physical aggression, is not central in children's social organizations unless it facilitates attainment of group goals. Social power is always a derivative of the social norms around which a group has coalesced and supports the group in its normative activities.

Setting Conditions

Research workers have been ingenious in constructing experimental situations in order to study situational factors in group functioning. Ecological variations were mentioned in several earlier sections; others will now be discussed: (1) adult leaders and their influence; (2) children as leaders; (3) goal structures; and (4) group composition. This research consists primarily of studies conducted with ad hoc groups rather than spontaneously formed ones.

Adult Leaders

In many situations, adults are members of children's groups. In classrooms, especially, the teacher is a key figure in the social system. It is not surprising, therefore, that the actions of adult members should bear a relation to the qualities of social interaction occurring among the children. The classic studies were conducted by Lewin, Lippitt, and White (1938; see also Lippitt & White, 1943, 1958) to examine the effects on social interaction of "group atmosphere" or "social climate." These studies, using groups of 11-year-old boys, demonstrated that varying styles of adult behavior produced marked differences according to whether the leaders were "democratic," "authoritarian," or "laissez-faire." The components of these leadership styles are well known and thus not reviewed here.

The following discussion is a brief summary of some of the major results of these studies. (1) Authoritarian leadership produced two major types of social climate—aggressive or apathetic. (2) In the atmospheres created by authoritarian leadership, as well as in the atmosphere created by laissez-faire leadership, expressions of irritability and aggressiveness toward fellow group members occurred more frequently than in the democratic climates. (3) In at least one group, authoritarian leadership created high interpersonal tension and scapegoating; in others, authoritarian leadership produced aggressiveness that was channeled toward outgroups or toward the leader. (4) Requests for attention and approval from fellow members were more frequent in the democratic and laissez-faire climates than in the autocratic climates. (5) Friendliness did not vary as a function of leadership style, although "we-feeling" tended to be lower in the authoritarian groups than in the others. (6) Task-related suggestions by the children were less frequent in the authoritarian groups. (7) When the authoritarian leaders were absent for brief periods, work motivation dropped quickly or did not develop; absence of the democratic leader produced little change in amount of task-oriented effort. (8) There was a wider range of individual differences, particularly in ascendant reactions, in the democratic atmospheres than in the authoritarian or laissez-faire climates.

The data from these studies are, of course, far richer than this brief summary indicates. Of major importance is the general finding that leadership style bears directly on group interaction. These studies are somewhat less convincing in specifying the outcomes that result from particular styles of leadership. First, the experimenter-leaders were, as a group, equalitarian adults. As a consequence, the studies do not furnish information concerning group functioning under authoritarian leadership imposed by committed authoritarian adults. Second, most of the subjects came from "democratic" homes. Thus clues concerning interaction effects between differences in family background of the subjects and differences in leadership style are absent. Finally, it should be mentioned that the studies embraced only a small number of leadership styles. For example, the authoritarian climates were based on rather distant, cold leadership. It has long been regretted by researchers in this field that no good data exist concerning children's interactions within a "benevolent autocracy." The results of this research have been applied widely, to fields such as education, without full recognition of the limitations mentioned here. Even so, these studies and others (see Hartup, 1970) indisputably accomplished their primary objective: testing the hypothesis that leadership style is one determinant of social interaction in children's groups.

Child Leaders

Child leaders differ from one another according to the kinds of activities the group engages in and the qualities that count in their scheme of things. Consequently, it is not possible to draw a composite picture of child leaders except to show that their intellectual abilities and social competencies are notable in meeting group objectives. Within these limitations, however, child leaders are active and vigorous in participation with their peers as well as successful in their attempts to influence other children (Rosen, Levinger, & Lippitt, 1961).

Children are quick to perceive deficiencies in children who are arbitrarily assigned to leadership positions and who do not possess the requisite social skills. On the other hand, being perceived by the other children as competent confirms the legitimacy of the assignment as does sincere motivation to assist in meeting the group's objectives (Hollander & Julian, 1970). The leader's legitimacy also derives from the source of his or her authority, that is, whether the leader usurps authority, obtains it by appointment from some external source, or derives it from the group members themselves. Read (1974) assembled four-person groups of high school students, always designating the same "stooge" as the supervisor of a series of mock juries but varying the means of selection. Leaders for some groups were selected by the members; others were appointed by a "lawyer" who helped with the study (an experimenter dressed in a three-piece suit and carrying an attaché case) or by an undergraduate (an English literature major who wore blue jeans); still others usurped the group's balloting and independently took over as the leader. Both the usurpers and the leaders appointed by the nonexpert were perceived as less legitimate, less competent, and less well-liked than were the elected leaders or those appointed by the expert. Evaluations of the leaders' performance and the group's willingness to continue with them followed a similar pattern. Both source of au-

thority and personal attributes thus appear to determine the leader's effectiveness. The manner in which these variables emerge to determine leader effectiveness in groups of younger subjects, however, is not known.

Performance outcomes must match expectations in order for social interaction to remain harmonious under designated leaders. Among Boy Scouts, the designation of individuals (by the adult experimenter) who were already leaders produced an increase in self-esteem, whereas the appointment of nonleaders led to decreased élan (Klinger & McNelly, 1976). In another investigation, boys whose leadership status was either high or low were exposed to success or failure and then asked to divide a sum of money with another child. High-status individuals who lost to low-status individuals were less generous than low-status boys who had lost to high-status ones. Parallel results were obtained among the winners (White, 1974), consistent with other investigations showing that successful leadership experiences increase positive assessments of group experience and enhance self-esteem (Borgatta, Cottrell, & Wilker, 1959).

Goal Structures

Children coordinate their actions with one another beginning in early childhood. The emergence of cooperative problem solving in the second year of life has been documented (Brownell, 1982; Getz, 1977) and it is evident that reward contingencies are significant in the acquisition of discriminative cooperation (Azrin & Lindsley, 1956; Vogler, Masters, & Morrill, 1970). Younger children achieve such coordinations more consistently if a verbal rationale accompanies the reinforcement (Biron, Ramos, & Higa, 1977) and punishment, in the form of loosing points, has been observed to decrease cooperative responding once it has been established in the repertoire (Weingold & Webster, 1964). Finally, social attributions indicating that a child is either "cooperative" or "competitive" have been shown to produce concordant changes in social interaction (Jensen & Moore, 1977). Overall, then, coordinated social activity seems to be related to social contingencies in a manner similar to other behaviors.

Sometimes, one member of a group can obtain a reward only if others do; at other times, "winners take all" or the individual's attainments may be independent of the attainments of others. These goal structures are salient factors in group interaction; even in their absence, children assume an implicit structure and interact accordingly (Brownell & Hartup, 1981). In general, more friendly and facilitative interaction occurs when rewards are group-administered than when "winners take all." Nelson and Madsen (1969) observed pairs of 4-year-old children in a game requiring coordinated action in order to move a marker over target spots on a board. On one series of trials, rewards were given to both children if the marker reached the designated spots; in other instances, rewards were given to only one individual, depending on whether the marker reached the spot designated for that child. The children assisted each other in moving the marker when rewards were given to both, but their interaction was different when only one reward was given on each trial; the children then took longer to assist each other and did not take turns, even though turn-taking would have maximized the accumulation of rewards for each player across trials (see also Richmond & Weiner, 1973). Competitive structures, in contrast to cooperative ones, are also marked by more frequent aggression and task interference, especially among children predisposed to be aggressive (Rocha & Rogers, 1976). Rewards must be perceived by children as more probable, however, under cooperative structures than under competitive structures in order for differences in social interaction to occur and for children to prefer working under cooperative rather than under competitive conditions (Mithaug, 1969).

Classroom observations are concordant with these laboratory observations. Stendler, Damrin, and Haines (1951) contrasted social interaction during art classes when: (1) each child was promised a prize, and (2) a prize was promised to the child who painted the best picture. Friendly conversation, sharing, and helping exceeded negative interaction during the cooperative work sessions, while the reverse was true under competitive conditions. More boasting and depredation occurred in the competitive conditions and less time was spent on the task. Other studies have shown that peer tutoring occurs more frequently under cooperative conditions than under competitive ones (DeVries & Edwards, 1972) and that children evaluate the sharing of information differently. Seeking information, for example, is valued more positively than volunteering information under cooperative conditions; these evaluations are reversed in competitive conditions (Johnson, Falk, Martino, & Purdie, 1976).

Relatively little is known about the carry-over of cooperative and competitive experiences to other situations. Stendler et al. (1951) observed no differences in children's classroom conversations following the experimental sessions. On the other hand, Altman (1971) found that preschool children who were successful in learning to cooperate in a laboratory task subsequently engaged in more friendly interaction and less hostile interaction in the classroom compared to children who did not learn the task. Among elementary school children, altruism has been observed to occur more frequently following cooperative than individualistic classroom experience (Johnson, Johnson, Johnson, & Anderson, 1976). The carry-over from cooperative and competitive experience, however, may vary according to the outcomes of the interaction. Crockenberg, Bryant, and Wilce (1976) found that the giving of rewards to one another occurred equally among cooperative subjects, competitive subjects who were winners, and competitive subjects who were losers. On the other hand, children who were unsuccessful competitors gave more prizes to the winners than cooperating subjects gave to each other. Boys who were successful in competition also took away prizes more frequently than boys who worked under cooperation.

Attitudes toward oneself and one's co-workers are more positive as a consequence of cooperative experience than competitive experience. Bryant (1977) observed 8- to 10-year-old children in four conditions: (1) *cooperative*—working together in three-child groups with prizes awarded to each child; (2) *competitive*—working independently with prizes awarded only to one randomly chosen individual who was identified as writing the best story; (3) *individualistic with self-evaluation*—working independently with no mention of rewards or incentives; and (4) *individualistic with external evaluation*—working independently with the promise of a reward for each child, depending on performance. Subsequent to the experimental sessions, the children were observed and their conversations recorded while they completed a series of mazes. Self-enhancement that did not relate to the other children ("Look how many I've done") occurred equivalently across conditions. Self-enhancement at the expense of others ("I've done a lot more than you") occurred more frequently among children in the competitive condition than among the other subjects. Encouragement of others ("Keep going") occurred most frequently among children who had worked under cooperative conditions. Children thus engage in enhancement at the expense of others in competitive environments, enhancement of both self and others in cooperative environments, and enhancement of self with neither enhancement nor abuse of others in individualistic circumstances.

Cooperative classroom structures, as compared with individualistic ones, also affect attitudes toward self and others. Among fifth- and sixth-grade students working cooperatively on arithmetic lessons for 50 days, increases in perceptions of personal worth were greater than among students working individualistically (Johnson, Johnson, & Scott, 1978). Concurrently, sociometric evaluations of classmates and attitudes toward conflict resolution were more positive following cooperative than individualistic experiences. In a similar study (Johnson et al., 1976), children in the cooperative conditions believed that their peers liked them better than did children in individualized conditions, as well as believed that their classmates were more motivated to render them assistance. But, once again, the outcomes of competition determine its effects on social attitudes. Competition engenders self-punishment, unfavorable social comparisons, and negative affects among "losers" but not among "winners"; cooperative experience attenuates these differences (Ames, Ames, & Felker, 1977).

Cooperative groups are more cohesive units than competitive ones. Phillips and D'Amico (1956) compared the effects of group versus individual rewards on the cohesiveness of small groups of fourth-grade children. Sociometric ratings were used to assemble four cohesive groups and four noncohesive groups (i.e., groups containing few mutual friends). The game of "Twenty Questions" was then played with two cohesive groups and two noncohesive groups being told that each child would share the rewards according to the relative contributions made to the game. Significant increases in cohesiveness were found in three of the four groups that worked under these conditions. On the other hand, the effects of competition were more variable: No changes in cohesiveness occurred in two groups, an increase occurred in one, and a decrease occurred in the remaining group. In the competitive groups that increased in cohesiveness or that did not change, interaction during the game eventuated in a more equitable distribution of rewards than in the group whose cohesiveness declined. The results thus indicate that a cooperative adjustment to a competitive goal structure *made by the children themselves* can minimize the effects of competition on group solidarity. In classrooms, too, social isolates have been found to be more readily integrated into friendship networks under cooperative than under competitive conditions (DeVries & Mescon, 1974; Kinney, 1953).

Concordant results have emerged from studies of racial desegregation in the schools. In general, interracial contact involving individualistic or competitive goal structures does not enhance self-esteem among minority students or their social acceptance;

in fact, social relations are often worsened by these circumstances (Schofield, 1978). More reliable gains in the social acceptance of minority children and greater increases in the cohesiveness of integrated classrooms have been demonstrated when cooperative goal structures prevail over a period of time. For this to happen, though, the contributions of the minority children must be recognized as essential to the group's success in the cooperative task (Aronson, 1978; Johnson et al., 1978; Martino & Johnson, 1979).

Performance outcomes under cooperative and competitive goal structures vary according to the nature of the task. Winners-take-all conditions evoke better performance than cooperative ones on simple tasks that do not require coordinated interaction—for example, winding fishing reels, sorting pegs, or carrying marbles (Sorokin, Tranquist, Parten, & Zimmerman, 1930; Triplett, 1897–1898). On tasks requiring social coordination, even though the cognitive demands are not complex, cooperative conditions generally lead to more positive outcomes. On a block construction task, for example, elementary school children working in three-person groups performed better when rewards were shared equally than when the only child to be rewarded was the one who contributed most (French et al., 1977). When rewards were distributed in proportion to each individual's contribution (an individualistic goal structure), performance levels were lower than under cooperative structures but higher than under competitive ones. Finally, when goal structures were changed from competitive to either cooperative or individualistic, performance improved. Similar effects were obtained with adolescents in a card game (Workie, 1974).

Evidence collected in classrooms suggests that academic achievement may be superior in cooperative conditions than in competitive or individualistic ones (Johnson & Johnson, 1975). In most of the relevant studies, work arrangements and goal structures were covaried—that is, group rewards were used when children worked together and individual rewards were used when children worked independently. Since group problem solving may be superior to independent problem solving, the outcomes of these studies might reflect work arrangements rather than the goal structures used.[3] Nevertheless, Woderski, Hamblin, Buckholdt, and Ferritor (1971) compared student achievement in mathematics under cooperative, individualistic, and "mixed" (partly cooperative and partly individualistic) structures. Daily assessments revealed that performance was best under cooperative conditions, next best under mixed conditions, and worst under individualistic ones. Postexperimental assessment, however, does not yield such clear-cut results. In two studies (Hudgins, 1960; Johnson, Johnson, Johnson, & Anderson, 1976) outcomes varied according to the assessment conditions used. With individualistic assessments, children whose initial experience was cooperative did not differ from those whose initial experience was competitive. On the other hand, when achievement outcomes were measured themselves under cooperative conditions (i.e., subjects were told that their scores would be averaged with those of their classmates), children who learned originally under competitive conditions were superior to children who both learned and were tested under individualistic conditions. Since no children with individualistic experience were assessed under cooperative circumstances, it is difficult to disentangle the effects of the original learning conditions from the effects of the test conditions. While the weight of the evidence supports the contention that cooperative goal structures facilitate classroom learning as compared to competitive ones, certain issues still need clarification.

Age differences occur in children's uses of altruistic and rivalrous strategies under certain goal structures, especially quasicompetitive ones. For example, Kagan and Madsen (1971) established game conditions that involved winners-take-all on individual trials but that permitted the sharing of rewards across trials. In this situation, 7- and 9-year-olds were more competitive than 4- to 5-year-olds. Similar age differences have been reported in the use of competitive strategies, as contrasted with cooperative ones, when prizes are awarded in proportion to the number of points accumulated in the game (Avellar & Kagan, 1976) or simply when points are tallied (McClintock, 1974). Under these conditions, competitive actions are even more common among 10- to 12-year-olds than among younger children, with similar age gradients evident in a variety of cultures.[4] Age differences are less evident when individual gain is not compromised by competition. In fact, with outcome controlled, preferences for competitive strategies in these situations do not change much with increasing age (Kagan, Zahn, & Gealy, 1977), and there is some indication that cooperation actually increases as adolescence approaches—especially when one's own gains and the gains of others are not in conflict (Skarin & Moely, 1976).

The clearest demonstration of an interaction between chronological age and goal structure is contained in two studies contrasting strategic choices in the *Maximizing Differences Game* under indi-

vidualistic, competitive, and cooperative conditions (McClintock & Moskowitz, 1976; McClintock, Moskowitz, & McClintock, 1977). First, increases in competition under the winners-take-all settings occurred between the ages of 4 and 5 whether such strategies maximized the child's own gain, the child's gain relative to other players, or their joint gain; competition did not increase between the ages of 6 and 8. Second, cooperation under shared reward conditions did not increase between the ages of 4 and 5, but did between 6 and 8. Third, the individualistic conditions were marked by age differences that varied according to the manner in which the child's own gains were linked to the gains of others. Between the ages of 4 and 5, children would forgo their own gains in order to produce a competitive advantage in some situations but not in others. In these instances, however, competition increased between the ages of 6 and 8. With time, then, children learn to use strategies that are consistent with the goal structures controlling the achievement of valued outcomes; children are not simply more competitive or cooperative as they grow older. That cooperation under shared rewards emerges somewhat later than competition under winners-take-all is not surprising considering that coordinated social interaction requires a delay of gratification, perspective-taking, and an understanding of complex social interdependencies. Indeed, empirical evidence confirms that young children understand cooperative situations less fully than they understand competitive ones (Feigenbaum, Geiger, & Crevoshay, 1970).

Group Composition

Children's enclaves vary in the extent to which age, sex, attitudes, and abilities are distributed within them; the extent to which members are attracted to one another also varies from group to group. These between-group variations can be measured in several ways, for example, by using: (1) *discrepancies*— that is, the difference between the most extreme members; (2) *variances*—that is, the average variation around a mean score; or (3) *asymmetries*—that is, the skewness or kurtosis of the frequency distribution for the characteristic being studied. Distributional asymmetries are especially important since they reveal the presence of majority and minority subgroups as well as other imbalances. Compositional analysis has been used only sporadically in studies with children. A small number of investigations indicate, however, that heterogeneities in age, sex, race, attitudes, and friendship relations have an important bearing on social interaction.

The effects of age mixture have been demonstrated in one or two instances. Tower-building performance was studied in same- and mixed-age triads of first- and third-grade children (Graziano, French, Brownell, & Hartup, 1976). Considered as units, the mixed-age triads performed as well as the same-age triads whether the latter consisted exclusively of first- or third-graders. On the other hand, the mixed-age triads (either two first-graders working with a third-grader or one first-grader working with two third-graders) were marked by different contributions from the individual members; greater task activity was evident among the older children and reduced activity among the younger ones. Mixed-age conditions, as contrasted with same-age conditions, thus elicited complementarities rather than reciprocities in social interaction. Whether these processes characterize mixed-age interaction in adolescence, however, is still open to question (Lohman, 1969).

Good studies of social interaction in mixed-age and same-age classrooms are in short supply. Parent selection almost always determines a child's enrollment in one or the other type of classroom, imposing design limitations on comparative investigations. Nevertheless, Goldman (1981) observed three classes of 3-year-olds, three classes of 4-year-olds, and three mixed-age classes. Three-year-olds in mixed-age situations engaged in more solitary play, less parallel play, and less teacher-directed activity than those 3-year-olds in same-age classrooms. The 4-year-olds in mixed-age classes also spent more time in solitary play and less time in parallel activity and teacher-directed work. Assuming that solitary play is more "mature" than parallel play (see *Rubin, Fein, & Vandenberg, vol. IV, chap. 9*), it appears that social activity in mixed-age situations may be more mature than in same-age classrooms.

Mixed-sex and same-sex interaction have seldom been compared except in dyadic situations. In mixed-sex triads, however, interaction varies according to whether males or females are the majority members and according to their age. Sgan and Pickert (1980) examined assertive bids in a cooperative task using mixed-sex triads of kindergarten, first-, and third-grade children. First, in male majority situations, kindergarten and first-grade boys made more assertive bids toward each other than toward the girls, as well as more bids than girls made to boys; in female majority situations, the younger boys were more assertive toward girls than the reverse or than girls were toward each other. Second, interaction was more symmetrical among the third-grade children: In male majority situations, girls were more assertive toward the boys than in the younger triads and boys were equally assertive to-

ward their male and female companions. In female majority situations, the third-grade boys were less assertive than in the younger triads and girls were more assertive toward each other than in the younger triads. With age, then, boys made proportionally fewer cross-sex assertive bids in mixed-sex triads and the girls made more; concomitantly, same-sex assertion increased among girls but decreased among boys. Whether these sex and age differences in reaction to the mixed-sex situation would prevail in competitive or individualistic tasks is not known, but the results underscore the importance of compositional analysis in conjunction with contextual demands and developmental trends.

Gender also affects coalition formation. Using both same-sex and mixed-sex triads, Leimbach and Hartup (1981) examined coalition formation in a bargaining game in which the individuals also varied in their capacities to determine the outcome. Coalitions were established equally in same- and mixed-sex triads but, in the latter case, the children formed same-sex coalitions more frequently than cross-sex coalitions, especially when individuals of the same sex possessed relatively low social power. Both gender mixture and power relations thus lead to asymmetries in social organization.

Social interaction varies in same-race and mixed-race situations. In one investigation, preschool children in mixed-race situations (four individuals) were observed to initiate both positive and negative overtures less frequently than in same-race situations. Also, responsiveness to initiations from the other children occurred less frequently in the mixed-race groups than in the same-race groups. Since no differences were evident between the homogeneous groups of black and white children, it seems that social activity was inhibited by the mixed-race condition (Harrison, Messe, & Stollak, 1971). In another instance (Cohen, 1972), initiation patterns among young adolescent males were observed to vary *within* mixed-race four-member groups. Whites were more likely to initiate social interaction than blacks and to influence the group's final decision, especially when decisions were contested. The social awkwardness that marks the mixed-race situation, then, may be closely linked to the discomfort of the minority child. But, since racial differences in social behavior seem to decline with the passage of time in cooperative interracial situations (Aronson, 1978; Stevenson & Stevenson, 1960), it is important to conduct future analyses over many rather than a few sessions.

Homogeneity versus heterogeneity in social attitudes also affects social interaction. Altman and McGinnies (1960) assigned 500 high school boys to five different kinds of groups on the basis of scores on the California *E Scale:* (1) low scorers, (2) high scorers, (3) low scorers in the majority, (4) high scorers in the majority, and (5) equal numbers of high and low scorers. After viewing a film dealing with ethnic minorities, group discussion revealed that the most heterogeneous groups (equal numbers of high and low scorers) were less spontaneous, made fewer comments, and communicated fewer oppositional comments than did the other groups. Furthermore, the members of these groups were less attracted to one another, were least accurate in their perceptions of the opinions held by other members, and were least attracted to other members who held the same opinions as themselves. Not only does heterogeneity reduce reciprocity in communication, but it also reduces interpersonal attraction.

Friends and nonfriends differ in group interaction as well as dyadic interaction. Scofield (1960) found that ad hoc groups of seventh-graders who were nonfriends spent more time in arriving at a consensus concerning appropriate stories for TAT pictures than did groups of friends. Presumably, the heterogeneous groups required a longer time to resolve differences of opinion than did homogeneous ones. Shaw and Shaw (1962) also found that cohesiveness (defined sociometrically) was positively related to democratic, friendly, and cooperative interaction during a series of spelling lessons. Cohesiveness was positively correlated with learning outcomes in the first study session, but not in subsequent encounters (the more cohesive groups felt free to stop studying altogether). Lott and Lott (1966) also reported that cohesiveness impinges on group performance, but in conjunction with the abilities of the children in the group. Among fourth- and fifth-graders with high IQs, cohesive groups did better than noncohesive groups on a verbal learning task. Among low-IQ children, however, cohesiveness was not related to group performance. The incentive motivation deriving from interpersonal attraction thus seems to determine problem-solving efficacy in relation to the difficulty of the task (high among low-IQ children but low among high-IQ children).

Summary

Setting conditions account for considerable variance in social interaction in children's groups. Social exchanges are more harmonious and productive when adults are interactive rather than retiring, and supportive rather than coercive, in their contacts with group members. Child leaders contribute significantly to social interaction according to group expectations, the source of their authority, and the nature of the exchanges occurring between themselves and their followers. Cooperative goal structures, as compared to competitive or individualistic ones, induce friendlier and more facilitative interaction, more positive attitudes toward self and others, and greater productivity—in most circumstances. Social relations are generally more cohesive under cooperative conditions and, with increasing age, children better discriminate between cooperative and competitive situations. Finally, compositional analysis shows that homogeneous groups are marked by greater reciprocity in their social exchanges than heterogeneous ones.

PEER RELATIONS AND THE SOCIALIZATION OF THE INDIVIDUAL CHILD

In August 1945, six 3-year-old German-Jewish children were brought from a Moravian concentration camp to Britain where they were placed in a residential nursery. The children had been in concentration camps and separated from their mothers since before their first birthdays. Passed from camp to camp, they had essentially reared themselves; contacts with adults were minimal. With the relocation, their behavior toward adults was bizarre:

> They showed no pleasure in the arrangements which had been made for them and behaved in a wild, restless, and noisy manner. . . . They destroyed all the toys and damaged the furniture. . . . Toward the staff they behaved either with cold indifference or with active hostility. . . . At times they ignored the adults completely. . . . [The children] cared greatly for each other and not at all for anybody or anything else. They had no other wish than to be together and became upset when they were separated. When separated, a child would constantly ask for the other children, while the group would fret for the missing member. (Freud & Dann, 1951, pp. 130–131)

On the other hand,

> they were neither deficient, delinquent, nor psychotic. They had found an alternative placement for their libido and, on the strength of this, had mastered some of their anxieties, and developed social attitudes. That they were able to acquire a new language in the midst of their upheavals, bears witness to a basically unharmed contact with their environment. (p. 168)

Now, 35 years later, Sophie Dann writes (personal communication) that these children are leading effective lives as adults. No more graphic account exists in the literature to demonstrate resilience in social development and to display that peer interaction can contribute importantly to the socialization of the individual child.

Peer relations have been discussed thus far largely in terms of their dynamics and development. In this section, socialization mechanisms will be examined as these occur in peer interaction; conformity will be discussed as a special issue. Peer experience will be considered in relation to individual differences in the growth of social competence. Finally, concordances and discordances between family and peer socialization will be examined.

Processes of Socialization

Peer Reinforcement

Naturalistic demonstrations of reinforcement effects have been difficult to achieve because of the complexities in establishing connections between stimuli and responses in ongoing interaction. Searching for those stimuli that, in fact, maintain aggression among nursery school children, Patterson et al. (1967) observed one set of reactions thought to be positively reinforcing (e.g., passivity, crying, making defensive postures) and a second set thought to be punishing (e.g., tattling, recovering property, and retaliation). When victims reacted with one of the acts assumed to be a positive reinforcer, aggressors made similar responses toward their victims in ensuing observations. When victims counterattacked, the aggressors changed their actions, their victims, or both. On the other hand, so-called positive reinforcers (talk, approval, compliance, and dependency) may not predict whether aggression will reoccur immediately (Kopfstein, 1972). Among seven children, three nonaggressive ones were *more* likely to aggress following negative consequences (noncompliance, counterattack) and *less* likely to aggress following positive consequences. Concordant with these results are certain observations from Patterson et al.: When a victim counterattacked, over time, these counterattacks increased. These fragments suggest that negative reinforcement (i.e., cessation of an aversive event) may be another mechanism controlling aggression in peer interaction.

Peer interaction is discriminative in relation to sex-appropriate and sex-inappropriate behavior. One investigator (Fagot, 1977a) recorded eight sex-typed activities occurring among nursery school children (e.g., use of transportation toys, doll play) and three types of peer reactions (positive, critical,

and neutral). The largest proportion of the children's reactions to each other was neutral, but boys received proportionally greater criticism than girls when engaged in doll play and dressing up, as well as more positive reactions to hammering and play in the sandbox. On the other hand, girls exceeded boys in the extent to which positive reactions were received in "domestic" activities.

Of course, discovering that "positive" and "negative" reactions occur discriminatively in sex-typed activities does not demonstrate reinforcement effects. To do so, contingencies in social interaction must be accompanied by acceleration or deceleration of the activity over time. Consequently, Lamb and Roopnarine (1979) observed sex-typed activities among preschool children, the reactions of their classmates to these activities, and the number of half-minute time units that the activity persisted. Positively reinforced activities continued longer than punished activities especially when the activity was appropriate for the child's sex. Results were similar in a second investigation (Lamb, Easterbrooks, & Holden, 1980), suggesting that child-child exchanges affect activity according to preexisting response strength or inhibition. Given the nature of these data (the target child's actions and the classmates' reactions were observed within the same 10-minute observation interval), it is difficult to know whether the children's actions constituted "reinforcement" or merely served as cognitive reminders of sex-role prescriptions already in the child's repertoire. Nevertheless, the correlation between the occurrence of events thought to be reinforcing and continuation of the activity is consonant with a reinforcement interpretation.

To determine whether certain social stimuli function as reinforcers in ongoing interaction, Furman and Masters (1980a) examined the affective reactions of children to whom the presumed reinforcers were directed. First, base rates were computed for positive (e.g., laughter, praise), negative (e.g., crying, physical attack, disapproval), and neutral affects (i.e., not coded in the other categories). Second, conditional probabilities were calculated showing the co-occurrence of positive, neutral, and negative events and the affective reactions. Behaviors classified as positive reinforcements according to the a priori criteria were almost twice as likely to be succeeded by concordant affective reactions as the base rates; punishments were more than five times as likely to be classified in this manner, and a significant but more modest increase was noted in the classification of neutral acts. Such increments were evident among more than 90% of the 101 children observed. Although the effects of these social events on behavior maintenance and change are not known, the concordance of the affective reactions among the target children and the social initiations directed toward them suggest that a priori classification of reinforcing events may be valid.

Experimental analysis remains the only way to determine whether a social stimulus is a reinforcing event. To do this, investigators must first train children to provide feedback to each other according to prearranged contingencies. This can be done. Young children can be trained to notice a variety of social acts, ranging from articulation errors to aggressiveness, and to ignore or react to them in accordance with adult instructions to bring about selective change in the target child (Bailey, Timbers, Phillips, & Wolf, 1971; Johnston & Johnston, 1972; Wahler, 1967). Selective use of peer rewards can also be used to modify disruptive activity in sixth-grade classrooms (Solomon & Wahler, 1973) and to change study behaviors (Surratt, Ulrich, & Hawkins, 1969).

Taken together, the evidence suggests that peer interaction consists of events that are reinforcing, that children use these events with increasing deliberateness as they grow older, and that these contingencies can be modified by adult intervention. Consequently, one must assume that peer interaction is a context that promotes behavior change and maintenance through selective reinforcement. Just what is learned and how much is learned in this manner remains difficult to say. Considering the complexities of conducting contingency analyses over extended time periods (even with the most sophisticated techniques), these specifics may long elude us.

Peers as Models

Imitation consists of events in which the actions of one person become similar to the actions of some other person as a consequence of direct or symbolic observation. Imitation in situ has been examined in terms of immediate matching-to-sample (i.e., model and observer performing the same act within very short intervals). Deferred imitation, like long-term reinforcement effects, has been difficult to demonstrate owing to methodological limitations. Nevertheless, Abramovitch and Grusec (1978) observed two classes of nursery school children during free play and three classes of elementary school children (ranging from 5 to 10 years of age) during "activity periods." Immediate imitation consisted of behavior matching that was observed within a 10-second interval. Imitative acts occurred: (1) 14.6 and 11.8 per hour in the preschool classes; (2) 6.0 and 4.6 per

hour in the younger elementary school classes; and (3) 1.8 per hour in the oldest elementary school class. Although peer imitation decreased with age, no changes were evident in the events imitated; the proportion of verbal to motor behavior imitated was constant over the three age groups, and judges were not able to differentiate examples of imitative behavior according to age. Among the preschool children, boys imitated others and were themselves imitated more often than girls; being imitated was positively correlated with imitating others. These trends, however, were not observed among the elementary school children.

In some ways, this investigation raises more questions than it answers. Does the decrease in imitation with age reflect differences in the classroom ecologies in which the observations were made? Does the decrease in immediate imitation indicate that, in general, imitation occurs less frequently as children grow older? Or, is immediate imitation replaced by more subtle and deferred imitations with increasing age? Social sanctions against "copying" could underlie the decline in children's use of immediate imitation; yet, at the same time, socialization may increasingly favor deferred imitation and nonobvious forms of observational influence. These issues have considerable significance, granting that naturalistic methods are notoriously difficult to use in studying them.

Experimental studies demonstrate that peer models possess strong and diverse potential for affecting behavior change in children. O'Connor (1969) selected severely withdrawn nursery school children, showing some a movie in which peer interaction began quietly (with the sharing of toys), then increasing in tempo and in the number of children involved. Control children saw a film of equal length about dolphins. After returning to their classrooms, the children who had viewed the peer interaction were more sociable than earlier, whereas the children who had watched the movie about dolphins were not. In another experiment (Peck, Apolloni, Cooke, & Raver, 1978), a training technique consisting of adult-delivered prompts and social reinforcement was used to increase retarded children's imitation of their nonretarded classmates. Observations indicated maintenance of these imitations under nontraining conditions as well as increases in social interaction between the retarded and nonretarded children.

Prosocial actions are sensitive to modeling influences. For example, imitation plays a role in determining whether preschool children will laugh and smile in humorous situations (Brown, Wheeler, &

Cash, 1980) and whether sharing will be evidenced (Canale, 1977; Elliott & Vasta, 1970; Hartup & Coates, 1967). Criteria for administering self-rewards can be induced through exposure to peer models (Bandura & Kupers, 1964), and other studies demonstrate that peer models can induce behavior that is either consonant or counter to a prohibition (Grosser, Polansky, & Lippitt, 1951; Ross, 1971; Slaby & Parke, 1971). Both live and televised peer models are effective in this way, although models who transmit these norms through verbalization are not as effective as those who enact them (Wolf & Cheyne, 1972). Role-playing (another kind of modeling enactment) has also been demonstrated to be effective in the induction of delay of gratification (Atwood, Ruebush, & Everett, 1978), although there is some evidence to suggest that model verbalizations assist in transmitting conformity norms to a greater extent than deviation norms. In the latter instance, peer models who actually display the prohibited behavior seem to be more effective (Wolf, 1973a).

Peer modeling extends to sex-role stereotypes. Kobasigawa (1968) demonstrated with kindergarten children that exposure to models engaged with sex-inappropriate toys had disinhibitory effects on observers, although boys evidenced disinhibition only when the model was a male. Observation of models who inhibited inappropriate sex-role behavior, on the other hand, enhanced the observers' own control over inappropriate behavior; models who were observed to choose neutral toys also reduced the observers' subsequent interaction with sex-inappropriate materials. Studies with older children are consistent in demonstrating the effectiveness of peer models in disinhibiting play with sex-inappropriate toys although, for both sexes, these effects are mainly evident with same-sex models (Wolf, 1973b). Girls seem to disinhibit more readily following exposure to same-sex models than boys, whether the exposure involves televised (Wolf, 1975) or live models (Wolf, 1973b). Throughout, then, there is indication that disinhibition induced through peer modeling varies according to the original strength of the inhibition (assumed to be stronger among males than among females).

Since children do not imitate same- and opposite-sex models differentially in every situation (Maccoby & Jacklin, 1974), the foregoing results must indicate that the children perceived the activity as sex-inappropriate, recognized the model's sex as congruent with the child's own, and then integrated this information to determine his or her own behavior. One investigation with nursery school children suggests that an integration of this kind indeed oc-

curs (Masters, Ford, Arend, Grotevant, & Clark, 1979). Children were exposed to a modeling sequence including toys that are ordinarily not sex-typed but that were labeled by the experimenter as sex-appropriate or sex-inappropriate toys, or else not labeled. When the toys were labeled as sex-inappropriate but manipulated by a model of the same sex, the subject was more likely to disinhibit than when the model was of the opposite sex. On the other hand, when the toys were labeled as sex-appropriate, viewing a same-sex model did not add to the subjects' preferences for them. In this instance, the children seemed not to need model confirmation that it was permissible to play with the toys. The work in this area is especially illuminating because it indicates that children integrate peer modeling cues within a growing normative framework rather than respond simplistically to single elements in the modeling situation.

Emotional disinhibition can also be brought about through peer modeling. Bandura, Grusec, and Menlove (1967) selected children between the ages of 3 and 5 who were identified as afraid of dogs and exposed them to either "fearless" 4-year-old models, a dog with no model present, or play materials with neither the model nor the dog present. On both immediate and delayed posttests, subjects who observed the model interact with the dog showed a reduction in avoidance behavior greater than among the children assigned to the other two groups. Multiple modeling may be required, however, to effect reductions in avoidance behavior in threatening circumstances (Bandura & Menlove, 1968).

Problem-solving behavior can be modified by observation of peer models. Miller and Dollard (1941) demonstrated that the solution of a two-choice discrimination problem could be learned by observation of such models, and Clark (1965) found that performance in such situations could be enhanced provided the model was observed to be rewarded contingently. Geshuri (1972) observed that correct responses in a problem-solving situation occurred more frequently among children who observed a peer model receive clear-cut approval but not among children who saw the model receive less relevant information. Peer modeling effects have also been demonstrated on memory tasks (Walters, Parke, & Cane, 1965) and in conceptual tempo as measured in problem-solving situations (Ridberg, Parke, & Hetherington, 1971). The utility of peer modeling among disabled children has been demonstrated in following instructions (Talkington, Hall, & Altman, 1973) as well as in problem solving (Barry & Overmann, 1977).

Several studies show that the personal characteristics of models and observers influence imitation. Sex of the subject and the model has already been mentioned. It is also the case that perceived similarity in terms of personal background and interests enhances imitation of other children (Rosekrans, 1967), as do friendly relations between model and observer (Grosser et al., 1951; Hartup & Coates, 1967) and the opportunity to share emotional experiences (Aronfreed, 1968). The ages of model and subject make a difference, too. In two studies, children were observed to imitate older children (or children perceived to be older) more readily than they imitated children of their own age (Peifer, 1971; Wolf, 1975).

The effects on children of *being imitated* should not be overlooked. Toner, Moore, and Ashley (1978) contrasted resistance to deviation in three groups of elementary school boys: those asked to serve as self-controlling models and who were given an opportunity to do so, those asked to serve as models but prevented from doing so, and those who were given no responsibility. Resistance to deviation subsequently varied directly across these conditions. Thelen and Kirkland (1976) examined the effects of being imitated on the child's tendency to reciprocate—that is, the tendency to imitate someone who imitates onself. Some subjects in the experiment were imitated by children 1 year older than themselves, while others were imitated by children 1 year younger (the experimenter's confederates in both cases). Comparisons centered on imitation that was reciprocated versus imitation of a nonimitating individual, showing that reciprocal imitation was more frequent than nonreciprocal imitation when the confederates were older but not when they were younger children. Also, subjects who interacted with older confederates chose the imitator over the nonimitator on measures of interpersonal attraction.

Finally, imitation is used spontaneously *to influence others*. When children were urged to influence a potential model, they were observed to imitate that individual more extensively than children receiving no induction (Thelen, Frautschi, Fehrenbach, & Kirkland, 1978). Overall, there is little doubt that imitation is a basic mechanism in peer interaction although, once again, it is not possible to specify its exact contributions to naturalistic socialization.

Conformity

Normative conflict (e.g., to act in accordance with sex-appropriate or sex-inappropriate norms) is ubiquitous in everyday life, and children use modeling cues in an effort to reduce it. In some cases, exposure to a model actually generates normative conflict (e.g., when a boy is observed to play with feminine toys) as well as supplies the observer with behavioral examples for reducing it. In other situations, normative conflict may exist prior to exposure and the modeling cues merely suggest plausible coping strategies. In either case, the ensuing similarities between observers and their models are usually called *conformity*. Most of the imitation described in the previous section can be called conformity since the changes in attitudes and actions of the observers occurred within a normative frame of reference.

Conformity may occur when children are passive observers of one another or when they engage in active discussion of ideas and viewpoints. *Imitation* and *conformity* have been the terms most commonly used to refer to the passive events; *suggestion* and *persuasion* are used most commonly in reference to the active events. Although the processes and outcomes of peer influence may not be the same in these situations, each nevertheless refers to shifts in behavior occurring concomitantly as an outcome of normative conflict and exposure to the actions of other individuals. For this reason, it may be desirable to link these forms of social influence together under some common rubric such as *behavior contagion* (Wheeler, 1966).

Most often, conformity in children and adolescents has been studied in contrived situations (e.g., the Asch paradigm) on the assumption that generalized notions about the origins and applications of social rules are being measured. These situations have been widely used to test the theory that: (1) conformity increases in middle childhood as egocentrism declines and the child comes to believe that social rules require rigid and explicit imitation of others, and (2) conformity decreases in late childhood as individuals begin to perceive that rules are human artifacts, constructed by themselves through interaction with one another (Piaget, 1932). Although it seemed for a time that laboratory experimentation might document these trends (Hartup, 1970), it has become increasingly evident that conformity is a complex mixture of one's understanding of the origins and nature of social rules, one's motives (e.g., the need to be correct or the need for social approval), and the nature of the social organizations to which one belongs (Allen & Newtson, 1972). Contrived situations serve only moderately well to specify the nature of these interactions. Too often, one can only guess about the meaning of age differences, sex differences, or task differences in conformity. Does an increase in early adolescence on one task reflect increases in the need to be correct and to receive social approval (Hoving, Hamm, & Galvin, 1969)? Does a decrease in other tasks over the same ages reflect changes in the individual's understanding of consensus (Allen & Newtson, 1972)? It is virtually impossible to tell. And it is doubtful that the most careful analysis, using these situations, will supply the answers.

The weight of the evidence suggests that in easy tasks (in which the subject is exposed to peer judgments that are obviously erroneous) conformity becomes evident at about 5 or 6 years of age and then declines. Preschool children have not been studied extensively but their actions in these situations seem essentially to be egocentric rather than conforming (Aboud, 1981; Hunt & Synnerdale, 1959; Starkweather, 1964). In middle childhood, decreases in conformity have been noted across ranges both narrow and wide (Allen & Newtson, 1972; Berenda, 1950; Cohen, Bornstein, & Sherman, 1973; Hamm, 1970; Hoving, 1964; Hoving et al., 1969; Weinheimer, 1972). Beyond puberty, decreases sometimes have been observed (Cohen et al., 1973; Landsbaum & Willis, 1971; Pasternack, 1973; Patel & Gordon, 1960) but not always (Allen & Newtson, 1972; Hamm, 1970; Hoving et al., 1969). Beyond puberty, in the instances when decreases are not observed, it is usually the case that further decreases could not be demonstrated because of "floor effects." On easy tasks, then, children become less and less amenable to peer suggestion as they grow older.

On more difficult tasks, age gradients are not consistent. In some instances, increases in conformity have been observed from middle childhood through early adolescence (Hamm & Hoving, 1969; Hoving et al., 1969) or no changes with age were observed (Cohen et al., 1973). In each of these studies, the task was insoluble (e.g., numerosity comparisons involving exactly the same number of dots on a card or apparent movement in the autokinetic situation) and peer norms were conveyed to the subject in a creditable manner.[5] With increasing age, individuals thus seem willing to utilize peer information when the task is impossibly difficult. Since increased conformity is evident only in these circumstances, we can posit that age changes in the need to be correct and the need for social approval are involved (Hoving et al., 1969).

On difficult tasks that seem soluble (e.g., comparing lines obviously varying in length, counting metronome clicks, or making numerosity judgments between slightly varying arrays), the age gradient either rises to a peak in middle childhood and then declines (Costanzo & Shaw, 1966; Hoving et al., 1969; Iscoe, Williams, & Harvey, 1964) or declines continuously (Allen & Newtson, 1972; McConnell, 1963). While it is not possible to establish the reasons for the inconsistency in these results, it is noteworthy that decreasing conformity in adolescence was observed in every case—similar to the gradient on easy tasks. The evidence thus consistently supports the proposition that adolescents behave in accordance with an "anticonformity" norm in soluble situations but to correctness and approval norms in other situations.

Numerous studies demonstrate that situational factors impinge on conformity among children and adolescents: (1) Competent individuals generally exert greater influence than noncompetent ones (Gelfand, 1962; Harvey & Rutherford, 1960; Landsbaum & Willis, 1971; Patel & Gordon, 1960); (2) the presence of a nonconforming individual will reduce conformity to otherwise uniform social pressure (Allen & Newtson, 1972); (3) difficult tasks generally induce greater conformity than less difficult ones (Berenda, 1950; Hamm, 1970; Hoving et al., 1969), although this may not be true across every type of task (Iscoe et al., 1964); and (4) achievement-oriented instructions induce greater conformity than neutral ones (Wyer, 1966).

Subject differences also account for significant variance in conformity: (1) Self-esteem or self-evaluations of competence generally lead to reduced conformity (Gelfand, 1962; Kogan & Wallach, 1966; Landsbaum & Willis, 1971; Lesser & Abelson, 1959; Yuferova, 1975); (2) social status impinges on conformity in relation to the social power of both subject and the source of influence (Harvey & Consalvi, 1960; Lippitt et al., 1952; MacNeil & Pace, 1973); and (3) orientation toward the *source* of a message rather than its *content* (McDavid, 1959), being socially accommodative (Wilson, 1960), and being dependent rather than independent in peer interaction (Jakubczak & Walters, 1959), all increase conformity. Birth-order differences and sex differences in conformity have been noted but are beyond the scope of this essay (Hartup, 1970; Maccoby & Jacklin, 1974; also see *Huston, vol. IV, chap. 5*).

Peer Tutoring[6]

Considerable interest has been expressed in peer tutoring—the utilization of children as teachers in schools and other contexts. Peer tutoring has a long history in educational practice (Allen, 1976), acquiring new popularity in recent years. Thought to benefit both tutor and tutee, these experiences are believed to be cost-effective instructional supplements to traditional classroom settings and are core elements in childhood socialization in some cultures (Bronfenbrenner, 1970b).

Among United States educators, benefits to the tutor have been believed to include increases in motivation and task involvement and, in turn, increases in academic achievement. The empirical evidence, however, is inconsistent. Scores on standardized tests have been increased in some instances (Cloward, 1967; Guarnaccia, 1973; Lakin, 1971; Mollod, 1970; Morgan & Toy, 1970), but a substantial number of investigations show no benefits or extremely limited ones (Arkell, 1975; Paoni, 1971; Robertson, 1971; Rogers, 1969; Snapp, Oakland, & Williams, 1972; Stainback, 1971; Strodtbeck, Ronchi, & Hansell, 1976; Willis & Crowder, 1974). Although the conditions separating "successful" from "unsuccessful" tutoring are not clear, it seems that tutor benefits are more likely to occur if the intervention lasts for an extended time, if the tutors are underachievers who are several years older than the tutees, and if the tutors themselves are trained carefully and supervised regularly.

Tutor benefits are also thought to include increases in self-esteem, increases in prosocial behavior, and more positive attitudes toward school since the tutor role carries social status, attention from adults, and deference from other children. Again, the evidence is not consistent. Staub (1975) reported that, after a single tutoring session, fifth- and sixth-grade girls wrote more letters to hospitalized children than did girls who did not tutor. Other investigators have demonstrated improved attitudes toward oneself, toward subject matter, and toward teachers as well as improved school attendance. It is not certain, however, that tutoring is responsible for these changes since similar benefits accrue to children given experiences in "interdependent learning" (Blaney, Stephan, Rosenfield, Aronson, & Sikes, 1977; Frager & Stern, 1970; Paoni, 1971; Robertson, 1971). In addition, a number of well-constructed interventions have not changed self-esteem, school attitudes, or personal and social adjustment (Arkell, 1975; Cloward, 1976; Morgan & Toy, 1970; Stainback, 1971). There is no obvious reason for the inconsistent appearance of these benefits but it is clear, on the basis of some studies (e.g., Strodtbeck et al., 1976), that tutoring may sometimes be less than a pleasure for the tutor.

Substantial benefits for those tutored have been reported both in mastery of the tutored content and in performance on standardized tests (Cloward, 1967; East, 1976; Guarnaccia, 1973; Mollod, 1970; Paoni, 1971; Rogers, 1970; Willis, Morris, & Crowder, 1972). Reading skills, especially, can be improved in this manner, but quantitative skills can, too. Tutees benefit most from long-lasting, well-maintained, one-to-one tutoring, although gains can also be achieved with short-term experiences (East, 1976). Thus, children can teach each other. Even so, it is not clear that the efficacy of peer tutoring is greater than individualized adult instruction. Furthermore, the number of investigations showing tutee changes in social attitudes and aspirations does not outweigh the number showing no effects. "Successful" and "unsuccessful" tutoring demonstrations do not differ in any systematic way. Moreover, tutoring associated with achievement increases is neither more nor less likely to be accompanied by changes in attitudes and aspirations.

Outcome considerations aside, several generalizations can be made about the peer tutoring situation. First, children prefer to teach younger children and to be taught by older ones. Achievement gains are more common when the tutor is somewhat older than the tutee, although same-age tutoring can sometimes be effective (Guarnaccia, 1973; Hamblin & Hamblin, 1972; Linton, 1972; Thomas, 1970). Second, children prefer same-sex situations to opposite-sex situations, although there is no evidence that tutoring is more effective in one rather than in the other situation. Third, tutors do not like to participate in the evaluation of their tutees, especially if the evaluation will determine something that really matters to the tutee. Finally, children's attitudes about tutoring and its effectiveness are related to the competence of both tutor and tutee and to their motivation. For example, when tutors believe that their tutees are responsible for their failures but not for their successes, both verbal and nonverbal cues will be used more frequently in the tutoring (Medway, 1977).

Peer tutoring most commonly involves teaching modes that are modeled on adult pedagogics. Training, in general, increases the tutor's effectiveness, although sometimes the mere assignment as a tutor is enough (Page, 1975). Indeed, the method used to train prospective tutors can have adverse effects. Garbarino (1975), for example, compared the tutoring of sixth-graders who were promised movie tickets for successful teaching with the tutoring of children who were not promised a reward. In the reward condition, tutors were more critical, more demanding, and used time less efficiently compared to the no-reward condition. Social interaction was more positive and learning was quicker in the no-reward condition. Reward expectations thus may generate an instrumental orientation among tutors that has deleterious effects on those they are tutoring.

Children spontaneously instruct one another on many occasions. Classroom observations of kindergarten and second-grade children indicate that most of these are instigated by the learners, although approximately 30% are instigated by the tutors themselves (Cooper, Ayers-Lopez, & Marquis, 1982). Issuing directives, describing the task, and evaluative comments were the techniques most commonly employed, but demonstration, labeling, pointing, questioning, praise, and criticism occurred in these exchanges as well. When asked to become a tutor, kindergarten children were more directive and intrusive than second-graders but, since these observations were conducted in same-age situations, it is not clear whether the age differences occurred as a function of the capacities of the tutors, the tutees, or a combination of the two. Comparing same-age and mixed-age tutoring demonstrates that such differences may be primarily attributable to the *tutee's* age. Ludeke (1978) observed 9- and 11-year-olds teaching other children who were either their own age or 2 to 4 years younger. Younger tutees performed as effectively on the task as older ones, but their tutors engaged in more cognitive structuring (focusing attention, pointing out workable strategies, and supplying redundant information) as well as affective support (praise, assessing the learner's progress, and helping). Since both the 9- and 11-year-old tutors made these accommodations, it can be concluded that children's instruction is sensitively adjusted according to their tutees' capabilities.

Children are thus effective teachers of one another. The evidence does not consistently demonstrate that peer instruction benefits the tutor to the same degree that it benefits the tutee, especially in situations contrived by adults. But tutor benefits deriving from *self-instigated* instruction have not been evaluated and it is difficult to believe that these do not contribute to socialization. Although the cost-effectiveness of peer tutoring in American classrooms may thus be open to question, this may not be an issue in many cultures. When demonstration of early competence in peer instruction is highly valued in its own right, cost-effectiveness may not matter. Children *can* teach one another; to deliberately utilize these social skills involves policy considerations that must take other objectives into account.

Summary

The available evidence supports the contention that child-child interaction exerts a variety of socializing effects on the individual child. Both reinforcing and modeling contingencies can be observed and are associated with behavior maintenance and change in the individuals toward whom they are directed. Situational and subject factors interact in determining the outcomes of both informal and formal peer exchanges, but there is little doubt that children exert powerful influences over one another beginning in early childhood. One cannot specify the processes that account for variations among individual children, but the evidence clearly supports the contention that peer interaction is a socializing context, not merely the reflection of repertoires acquired in other settings.

Individual Differences

Peer Relations and Social Adaptation

Beginning in the 1960s, Harlow (1969) examined the development of rhesus monkeys raised: (1) with peers and without mothers and (2) with mothers and without contact with other infants. Those animals raised with agemates developed strong attachments to one another and manifested intense proximity-seeking similar to the "peer-reared" infants described by Freud and Dann (1951). When early experience involved two or three same-age animals, affective and instrumental disturbances in subsequent encounters with other animals were not evident. Social competencies were more generalized among these animals than among others reared with a single associate, although marked deficiencies were not shown under either condition. Maternal rearing without peer contact, on the other hand, produced animals showing both contemporaneous disturbances in play behavior and long-term disturbances in affective development; wariness and hyperaggressiveness were especially apparent. Derivatives of peer experience thus seem to include the emotional and instrumental capacities needed to engage in give-and-take with other, similar individuals.

Engagement with other children is, indeed, associated with emotional security and an active orientation toward the environment. In one investigation (Bronson, 1966), social reservedness among boys was associated with an egocentric social orientation, anxiety, and low activity from age 5 through 16. Correlates of social reservedness in early adolescence also included vulnerability, submissiveness, nonadventuresomeness, and instability. Correlates of social reservedness among girls were not substantially different. Remember, too, that sociometric studies indicate the correlates of popularity to include friendliness, moderate self-esteem, and low anxiety.

Scattered evidence suggests that aggressive socialization occurs in child-child interaction as well as in adult-child interaction. Both aggression and reactions to others' aggression are socialized within this context (Patterson et al., 1967). Sociometric status varies with appropriate, as contrasted with inappropriate, aggression, and other investigations underscore the centrality of "poor peer relations" in the emergence of conduct disorders (see next section).

Third, gender-typing occurs in the earliest interactions between the child and its parents, but the peer culture extends and elaborates this process through selective reinforcement and modeling (see preceding section). Sexual knowledge and sexual experimentation also derive from contacts with other children, adult contributions notwithstanding (Kinsey, Pomeroy, & Martin, 1948). Parents may sanction the sexual activity of their children but dating, the onset of sexual intercourse, and the circumstances under which it takes place are eventually determined in agemate interaction (Miller & Simon, 1980). Opposite-sex associations increase in adolescence, especially among girls (Blyth, Hill, & Thiel, 1981), contributing simultaneously to sexual socialization and intimacy. Same-sex associations contribute, too, through the sharing of dating and sexual experiences among girls (Douvan & Adelson, 1966) and perhaps through braggadocio among boys (Hill & Lynch, in press).

No evidence exists to show that peer relations contribute to intelligence or school achievement in the early years. Among girls and among boys, however, achievement expectations diverge in early adolescence (Hill & Lynch, in press). Peer interaction may contribute to this state of affairs through differentiated socialization with same-sex and opposite-sex others. Coleman (1961), for example, discovered that social status with same-sex associates was believed to involve good grades and school activities, but that status with opposite-sex associates was based on attributes associated with dating success.

Children's conversations modify their moral judgments (Berndt, Caparulo, McCartney, & Moore, 1980), and some evidence suggests that effectiveness in child-child relations is associated with a mature moral orientation. Keasey (1971) found that preadolescents who belonged to relatively many clubs and social organizations received higher moral judgment scores than ones belonging to fewer organized groups. In addition, child leaders display more sophisticated social ideologies than nonleaders, show good moral judgment according to their associates, and exemplify core-culture values (see Hartup, 1970). Overall, then, effectiveness in peer relations occurs in tandem with the effective internalization of social norms.

The weight of the evidence thus suggests that good peer relations occur together with sociability

and friendliness, the regulation of aggression and sex, and the internalization of social standards. The meaning of these results is not always clear, since characteristics enabling one to enter into the peer interaction may, in turn, be socialized within it. Longitudinal studies strengthen these arguments and reveal that poor peer relations are prognostic indicators of various disorders in adolescence and adulthood. We turn now to these studies.

Longitudinal Studies

Juvenile Delinquency. Delinquency among adolescents and young adults can be predicted mainly from one dimension of early peer relations—"not getting along with others." In one investigation (Roff, 1961), clients in child guidance clinics were tracked through adolescence and into the armed services. As adolescents, delinquency rates were higher among those individuals who were not accepted earlier by their peers than among those who were. As adults, those men receiving "bad conduct" discharges were more likely to have been rated by their childhood counselors as having poor peer adjustment than men with successful service records. Significant correlations between childhood peer rejection and delinquency in adolescence also occur among less selected individuals (Roff & Sells, 1968; Roff et al., 1972). Overall, the children in these studies who were "at risk" for delinquency were not socially withdrawn but were "actively unpleasant youngsters" (Roff, 1970).

The centrality of child-child relations in the etiology of delinquency is underscored in another investigation of 184 male delinquents and 184 nondelinquents matched in terms of age, social class, IQ, school, and ethnicity; subjects were tracked through elementary and secondary school (Conger & Miller, 1966). School records for those cases that were available from kindergarten through third grade showed future delinquents to be differentiated from nondelinquents in their regard for the rights and feelings of others and their acceptance of social responsibilities and obligations. The delinquents-to-be exhibited "more difficulty in getting along with peers, both in individual one-to-one contacts and in group situations, and they were less willing or able to treat others courteously, tactfully, and fairly. In return, they were less well liked and accepted by their peers" (p. 68). Between the fourth and sixth grades, the future delinquents were less empathic, more aggressive, and less well liked by other children, and these differences remained in early adolescence. Self-evaluations revealed that the delinquents did not enjoy close personal relations with other adolescents as much as the nondelinquents; the delinquents were also less interested in organized parties and school organizations and were more immature. Differentiation between these samples was no greater in adolescence than in middle childhood, suggesting that poor peer relations emerge early in the social histories of future delinquents and persist through time.

Participation in a delinquent subculture is a prognostic indicator of adult crime and sociopathic personality, but it is not clear that such involvement extends from childhood. Robins (1966) examined over 400 adults who had been referred to child guidance clinics for antisocial behavior (only 29% under the age of 11), finding that 28% could be diagnosed as sociopathic personalities in contrast to 2% of a matched control group. Aggression, sexual deviation, staying out late, and associating with "bad companions" were common among the sociopathic personalities, with more than 30% of the cases showing these antecedents. "Difficulties with contemporaries" were also common but occurred in closer association with certain other adult diagnoses (e.g., chronic brain syndrome) than with sociopathic personality. Sociopathic cases, however, differed from the other clinical groups in the extent to which early antisocial behavior was directed toward contemporaries outside the individual's immediate circle of friends rather than within it; violence against strange contemporaries marked the histories of 43% of these cases, whereas violence against companions occurred in only 26% of them.

Although concordance in criminality is relatively low among unselected adolescents and their friends (Kandel, 1978b), considerable concordance is evident between delinquents themselves and their associates (Jessor & Jessor, 1977); participation in delinquent gangs is also common (Glueck & Glueck, 1950; McCord, McCord, & Zola, 1959). But certain findings contradict the notion that bad companions are significant in the early etiology of delinquency. Glueck and Glueck (1950), for example, found that 48% of their delinquents engaged in criminal behavior before the age of 8 and before extensive participation in delinquent gangs. Exposure to criminal violence within the family and the community also occurs in the early years among future delinquents (McCord et al., 1959); thus social clusters in adolescence may partly result from self-selection. While friendship networks may dispose the individual adolescent toward more adult forms of crime and maintain criminal behavior through the adolescent period (Kandel, 1978b), these associations may not be implicated as prognostic indicators of delinquency in early and middle childhood.

Criminal behavior thus seems to emerge developmentally from disturbed family relations, followed by troubled peer relations, and finally by exposure to delinquent norms. The association between early difficulties in peer relations and delinquent outcomes is difficult to interpret, although these difficulties seem to imply an insidious conjunction between early socialization failures within the family and subsequent socialization within an explicitly criminal context. Recent evidence suggests that the failure to form effective social relationships within the family disposes the individual child to trouble in peer relations (Waters, Wippman, & Sroufe, 1979), and it is reasonable to imagine that these difficulties contribute to a further lowering of self-esteem, more alienation, and less social effectiveness which, in turn, increase the motivation to seek self-enhancement outside the core culture.

Behavior Disorders. Peer difficulties and antisocial behavior are associated with other disorders in emotional and social adjustment. Early childhood assessments have not proved to be strong predictors of later emotional adjustment (e.g., Richman, Stevenson, & Graham, 1982), and few studies extend across a large number of years. But, using adult males who were seen as children in child guidance clinics, Roff (1963; 1965; 1966) found that poor peer relations in middle childhood were predictive of adult neurotic and psychotic disturbances of a variety of types as well as disturbances in sexual behavior and adjustment. Childhood and adolescent peer relations have proved to be prognostic indicators in other longitudinal studies as well (Cowen, Pederson, Babijian, Izzo, & Trost, 1973; Havighurst, Bowman, Liddle, Matthews, & Pierce, 1962; Robins, 1966; Sundby & Kreyberg, 1968). For example, Cowen et al. obtained a variety of measures on a sizable sample of third-grade children, including IQ scores, school grades, achievement test scores, school attendance, teacher ratings, and peer ratings (i.e., nominations by other children for positive and negative roles in a class play). Eleven years later, community mental health registers were examined to locate those individuals then consulting a mental health professional. Of the measures secured in the third grade, the best predictor of adult mental health status was the peer rating. Subjects listed in the mental health registers were 2.5 times as likely to have been nominated for the negative roles in the third-grade class play as those not appearing in these registers.

Prediction of schizophrenic breakdown from peer status in childhood has not been successful because social withdrawal and isolation are themselves not stable through time (see Michael, Morris, & Sorokor, 1957); moreover, identification of target cases in early clinical records is often unsystematic. Sometimes the premorbid social history appears to be relatively good, sometimes not. For the most part, differentiation between preschizophrenic individuals and their matched controls in terms of peer relations is not evident until adolescence. Watt and Lubensky (1976), for example, compared elementary and secondary school records for 54 schizophrenic cases and 163 matched controls. Only information from the high school records discriminated between the samples—irritability, aggressiveness, and negativistic behavior were more common among the premorbid individuals than among the controls, especially among males. Concordant results were obtained in a prospective study of 20 cases "at risk" for schizophrenia (i.e., they had schizophrenic mothers) who subsequently became psychotic. These individuals, as adolescents, had been more irritable and aggressive toward their classmates than those not experiencing a later psychotic episode (Grubb & Watt, 1979; Mednick & Schulsinger, 1970).

Taken together, these results are not easily interpreted. Do adolescent social relations predict schizophrenic breakdown better than childhood social relations because of an intensification of social isolation at puberty? Of, is social isolation among younger children simply not a visible and worrisome marker to teachers and parents? Perhaps conventional assessment strategies do not lend themselves to prediction across long periods of time; especially in "follow back" studies, information about early social relations is likely to be sketchy (Rodnick & Goldstein, 1974). We can conclude only that the evidence does not yet support the thesis that there are broadly generalized precursors of schizophrenia in peer relations in early and middle childhood, although patterns become evident in adolescence that are associated with ultimate breakdown.

Summary. Poor peer relations are embedded in the life histories of individuals who are "at risk" for emotional and behavioral disturbance. Conduct disorders, especially, are marked by difficulties with contemporaries that extend from middle childhood, if not earlier. Affective disorders are presaged by troubled peer relations, although these are not evident until adolescence when they have their basis in antisocial behavior. Not one study exists, however, to show that social relations among individuals "at risk" for psychopathy are extraordinarily good. There is every reason, then, to conclude that poor peer relations are centrally involved in the etiology of a variety of emotional and social maladjustments.

But what does this mean? Correlational evidence is awkward to use as a basis for causal inference.

Childhood indicators of adult maladjustment include somatic disturbances, troubled family relations, and failure to adjust to school as well as problems with contemporaries. "Not getting along" with other children may simply reflect general difficulties in life course development and not contribute directly to individual vulnerability. It is difficult to believe, however, that trouble with contemporaries does not contribute its own variance to the etiology of psychopathology.

The Family and the Peer Culture

Synergistic Systems

The comparative literature contains numerous investigations supporting the view that family relations and peer relations interact synergistically in social development. For example, Goy and Goldfoot (1973) separated infant rhesus monkeys from their mothers at 3 months of age and then exposed them daily to other infants for half an hour. Other animals were reared in larger groups, having unrestricted access to both mothers and infants. Major differences marked their development: (1) Mature sexual behavior developed in the combined social environment in approximately 6 months but not in the peer environment for 2 to 3 years; (2) aggression/submission interactions predominated in the social behavior of the animals reared with only peer exposure, whereas these behaviors were rarely shown by the animals reared in the combined environment. Peer-rearing itself may bring about a superficially adequate adaptation in adulthood, but the behaviors associated with such rearing conditions are not identical with the actions of animals reared with *both* mothers and other infants (see Suomi, 1978).

Other observations suggest the manner in which the synergism between the family and the peer culture begins (Hinde, 1974). First, attachment to the mother provides the child with a "secure base" that reduces fear in strange situations and promotes exploration of the environment. Among the consequences of this exploration are encounters with other individuals. Some of these individuals are adults, many of whom show little interest in the youngster. Exploration, however, also brings about contacts with agemates and sustained interaction with them. Second, mothers maximize the chances that their offspring will enter into these social engagements with other youngsters. Beginning in the second year (earlier among most nonhuman primates), mothers increasingly ignore or reject play overtures from their offspring; contacts with other youngsters are arranged instead. Monkey mothers secure these contacts by remaining close to the members of a larger social unit—the troop. Human mothers develop contacts by arranging home visits with other mothers and their infants or through group care. Third, secure social relations within the family promote individuation and the growth of self-esteem, attributes that maximize chances of success in peer interaction once it begins. In summary, the conjunctions between family interaction and peer interaction seem to be mediated by the basic trust and autonomy acquired by the child in the first 2 years of life (Erikson, 1950).

In a study of 3-year-olds, Lieberman (1977) found children whose attachments to their mothers were rated as "secure" to be more responsive to other children and to engage in more protracted social interactions than children who were not securely attached. The security of the attachment was mainly correlated with nonverbal dimensions of peer interaction, while verbal maturity in these interactions was associated with the extent to which the mother arranged home visits with other children. Other evidence (Easterbrooks & Lamb, 1979) shows that 18-month-olds whose interactions with their mothers were characteristically "distal" (i.e., more mature) were more likely to engage a strange baby in social interaction than were babies whose contacts with their mothers were marked by intense proximity-seeking (i.e., less mature).

Longitudinal studies constitute the most convincing documentation of the early synergism between family and peer socialization. Waters et al. (1979) found that "secure" versus "anxious" attachments assessed from videotape records at 15 months of age were predictive of peer interaction assessed on the basis of 5 weeks of observer experience with the children when they were enrolled in nursery school (i.e., when their average age was 42 months). Compared with the anxiously attached children, the securely attached youngsters were socially active rather than withdrawn, sought out by the other children, active in making suggestions, sympathetic to peer distress, and reactive to overtures from other children. Concordant results have been obtained in more recent studies covering the first 2 years in the lives of children "at risk" for social maladjustment owing to various kinds of life stress (Pastor, 1981).

Cross-sectional studies with older children are consistent with the results for younger children. Using interview and sociometric methods with elementary school boys, Winder and Rau (1962) found that both mothers and fathers of "likable" children were emotionally supportive, infrequently frustrating and punitive, and discouraging of antisocial behavior. Earlier, Hoffman (1961) reported that a number of parent measures, especially those relating to the father's role in the family, were predictive of boys' peer relations. For example, boys with dominant fathers (not necessarily punitive) were forceful and intrusive in initiating contacts with other children. Paternal affection was also associated with the child's being liked, liking others, self-confidence, assertiveness, and effectiveness in social exchange. Maternal affection was associated with good peer adjustment among both boys and girls, but maternal dominance was associated with aggressiveness and unfriendliness only in their sons. Other studies show that sociometric status is positively associated with parental affection and absence of family tension (Cox, 1966), parental satisfaction with their offspring, and children's own satisfaction with their home lives (Elkins, 1958). Considerable support thus exists for the theory that the child's relations with its parents provide emotional and instrumental bases for success in peer relations.

Secure early attachments do not necessarily immunize the child against subsequent stress and ensure good peer relations forever. To illustrate, in an investigation of 24 boys and 24 girls from divorced families, Hetherington (1979) conducted observations in nursery schools 2 months, 1 year, and 2 years after divorce. At 2 months after the divorce, both boys and girls exhibited less imaginative play, less associative constructive play, less cooperative constructive play, and more functional play than did the children from matched nuclear families; affective disturbances with other children were also more common. One year after divorce, the only differences remaining among girls were lower scores for imaginative play among those from divorced families; 2 years afterward, these differences were gone. Among boys, though, differences were observed between those from divorced families and those from nuclear families at all three time periods. These changes, over time, are consistent with a synergistic view of family and peer relations. First, conflict and stress in the home situation induce affective insecurity, constrict exploration of the environment, constrain engagements with other children, and retard play development. Second, the restoration of stable home conditions and the provision of extra emotional support (especially evident among girls in the Hetherington data) are associated with improvement in peer relations. Clearly, then, the interdependencies between family socialization and peer socialization consist of more than the transfer of specific social skills from one situation to the other. Instead, an integrative coherence in ego development would seem to mediate the quality of the child's adaptation across social systems (Sroufe, 1979).

Consonance and Dissonance

Common stereotypes assert that, in Western Europe and America, the synergism existing between family and peer relations dissolves into opposition in middle childhood, with this opposition becoming acute in adolescence. In United States culture, adult norms center around conformity, work, and achievement, and it is believed that peer norms center around having a good time, nonconformity, and doing as you please. Certain investigators have warned of overexposure to agemates among American and British youth, assuming a concomitant erosion in family orientation (Bronfenbrenner, 1970b; Coleman, 1961). Surveys and questionnaires, however, do not establish that normative opposition is as intense as portrayed by this stereotype and that adolescence, in particular, is probably not the stormy period of normative dissonance that tradition suggests.

The transition to adolescence may be better described in terms of transformations in normative expectations of others. In one investigation (Emmerich, Goldman, & Shore, 1971), involving individuals from 8 to 17 years of age, norms regulating conduct in four areas (agreeing with others, helping others, seeking help, and arguing) were differentiated by younger subjects as well as by older ones. The children, however, believed that parents and peers both expect higher conduct standards to be used in interpersonal relations with adults than with agemates, a view that the adolescents attributed only to their parents. With respect to peer expectations, the adolescents actually believed that higher standards would be used with agemates than with adults. Normative differentiation, then, suggests that younger children conceive of a unitary social world in which conduct obligations are based mainly on generation. Adolescents, on the other hand, conceive of two social worlds—one with parents and one with peers—each marked by high moral standards. Consequently, the notion that parent-child relations are understood by adolescents to require self-control while peer relations are based on self-indulgence and unbridled instinctual activity is not upheld.

In addition, most parents and their children do not disagree about fundamental moral principles, aspirations, goals, and standards of self-control. Disagreements occur over many issues but these "normative conflicts," in most instances, are socially trivial. Arguments about musical tastes may be carried to great lengths but do not indicate dissonance in commitments to honesty, work, education, or the control of aggression. Even instances of basic normative dissonance (e.g., standards of sexual conduct) are likely to involve less conflict than the media suggest. Tacit agreements are worked out whereby, "The parents know, and the children know that the parents know, that the child 'makes out,' more or less, with an occasional prayer or hope on the parents' part. . . . Parents look the other way and hope for the best" (Douvan & Adelson, 1966, p. 81). Violations of these tacit agreements may be explosive but, more important, parents and the peer culture have worked out many ways to avoid these explosions. In a national survey of adolescents between the ages of 14 and 18 (Douvan & Adelson, 1966), approximately 25% reported no disagreements with parents and, when disagreements were reported, they most commonly involved control of movements, dating, and clothing. Disagreements concerning work, friends, sibling relations, ideas, money, and cars were each sources of parent-child disagreement in less than 6% of the sample.

On certain issues, parents may exceed peers in normative control—for example, with respect to educational aspirations and job expectations (Kandel & Lesser, 1972; Sandis, 1970). In other instances, peers exceed parents, as in the use of marijuana (Kandel, 1973). But the evidence does not support the contention that discord and alienation are pervasive, and that adolescents experience inordinate normative opposition as a consequence of their involvement in both the family and the peer culture. Douvan and Adelson (1966) attribute the persistent belief in normative conflict during adolescence to the tendency by media and social scientists alike to generalize from a narrow and verbal segment of the population whose conflicts are more visible and dramatic than parent-peer concordance.

Synergistic effects of parent and peer influences have been reported by a number of investigators. For example, among United States adolescents whose mothers want them to go to college, only 49% have college plans if their best friends intend to discontinue their educations after high school. On the other hand, 83% intend on pursuing postsecondary education if mothers and friends are both college-oriented. Even when mothers prefer that their children not go beyond high school, the percentage indicating an interest in college rises from 8% to 21% if best friends are college-bound (Kandel & Lesser, 1972). Similarly, Haller and Butterworth (1960) discovered that concordance between friends in occupational and educational aspirations was very low unless both adolescents experienced at least moderate pressure from their parents in seeking high-status jobs and postsecondary education.

Social norms deriving mainly from peer interaction are also modulated by parent influence. For example, concordance between friends in the use of marijuana is much greater (.49) than concordance between parents' use of psychotropic drugs and adolescents' drug use (.08). Even so, when best friends use drugs, children of nonusing parents are less likely to use drugs themselves (56%) than children of drug-using parents (67%; Kandel, 1973). A similar synergism exists in the situations of adolescents who smoke (Bewley & Bland, 1977) or who engage in delinquency (Glueck & Glueck, 1950).

These synergisms, to some extent, depend on existing "reference relations." Rosen (1955), in a study of the attitudes of Jewish adolescents toward the use of kosher meat, observed that: (1) when either parents or peers observed the practice of using kosher products, the subject was more likely to be observant than when both groups were not; (2) the strongest relation between group and adolescent norms occurred when the attitudes of parents and peers were concordant—either for or against the food practice; (3) when parents and peers conflicted, the adolescent was most likely to conform to the source that served a reference function; and (4) when parents or peers were not consistent among themselves, the child was likely to agree with the alternative source—especially when peers were consistent and parents were not.

Since children spend increasing amounts of time with other children in middle childhood and adolescence, considerable attention has been given to *cross-pressures,* that is, situations in which parents endorse one course of action and peers endorse an alternative. Thus, Brittain (1963) administered an inventory to a group of adolescent girls on two occasions, reversing parent and peer norms in each of the two administrations. Control subjects also took the test twice, but parent and peer pressures were associated with the same norms both times. Choice changes from the first to the second test were greater among the experimental than the control subjects on most of the items. When status and identity issues were salient, there was a drift toward peer endorsement; when future aspirations and achievement in school were salient, the subjects followed adult endorsements.

Some writers regard these results as an indication that adolescents remain oriented toward the attitudes of their parents in situations with implications for future status but incline toward their peers in situations with implications for current needs. Situational salience, however, may not function so straightforwardly. Using a four-item inventory, Larson (1972) showed greater parent than peer influence in decisions about club membership and social activities as

well as in choosing between alternative school curricula. In these situations, however, an even larger number of subjects chose to follow their own inclinations than those of *either* parents or peers. This "situation compliance" occurred among nearly three-quarters of the subjects, suggesting that content accounts for most of the variance in these situations, parent and peer pressures notwithstanding. Cross-validation using more varied item content is needed since most of the items in the inventory were related to important cultural norms with which the subjects were undoubtedly familiar. Nevertheless, we can conclude that the relative degree of parent and peer influence depends on the situation in more complex ways than earlier studies suggested.

Developmental changes in reactions to cross-pressures must be examined with this situational variation in mind. It is unlikely, for example, that peer conformity to prosocial norms follows the same developmental course as conformity to antisocial norms. In a first attempt to place the cross-pressure issue in developmental perspective, Utech and Hoving (1969) used a series of hypothetical dilemmas (each involving two attractive, socially approved alternatives administered twice). No breakdown by situational content was made, although about 60% of the children's reactions from the third to the eleventh grade represented situation compliance rather than conformity. Even so, parent conformity in relation to peer conformity decreased according to age, with most of the decline occurring in early adolescence; additional decline did not occur after seventh grade. Using a different measure of social influence, Bowerman and Kinch (1959) explored the child's general orientation toward the family and toward peers among students in the fourth to the tenth grade. Results were concordant with the age gradient in conformity; 87% of fourth-graders were family-oriented, and about 50% of the eighth-graders and 32% of the tenth-graders were family-oriented. The greatest shift, however, occurred in decisions concerning who should be chosen as best friends, supporting the hypothesis that developmental changes occur in interaction with situational effects.

More extensive developmental investigations were conducted by Berndt (1979a) in which situational content was varied systematically across inventory items; two types of parent conformity items were included (prosocial and neutral) and two types of peer situations (prosocial and antisocial). The most striking results were: (1) small decrements in prosocial conformity to parents or peers; (2) a gradual decline in conformity to parents in neutral situations from third grade to senior high school; and (3) a marked increase in peer conformity to antisocial norms extending from the third to the ninth grade but not beyond. These data, then, suggest that children maintain some orientation to both parents and peers as anchors of prosocial activity, perhaps with peer norms serving to validate or "filter" parent norms (Siman, 1977). Although parents gradually loose their influence as normative anchors in neutral situations, one of the experiments reveals that peer conformity in these situations increases slightly with age and then decreases (Berndt, 1979a). Together with the increased peer conformity in antisocial situations, it is apparent once again that the transition to adolescence is marked by a differentiation in the social worlds of the child.

Changes with age also were obtained in the correlations between parent and peer conformity (Berndt, 1979a). Negative correlations (indicating opposition) were not evident until early adolescence (ninth grade), decreasing thereafter. Since maximum opposition occurred at the time of maximum peer conformity in antisocial situations, the evidence suggests that early adolescence may be the only developmental era in which cross-pressures are at all intense.

Age changes in general attitudes toward parents and peers are concordant with these results. Based on the responses of 3000 children, from the third to the twelfth grade, Harris and Tseng (1957) found that: (1) attitudes toward both parents and peers were more favorable than unfavorable at all ages; (2) the number of subjects reporting positive attitudes toward parents declined somewhat during middle childhood, with an increase occurring once again in middle adolescence (especially toward fathers); and (3) there was no general increase in the favorability of attitudes toward peers. Thus, other than a "dip" in the popularity of parents in preadolescence, there was no indication of increasing rejection of parents or increasing general acceptance of peers during the middle childhood and adolescent years.

The foregoing studies suggest that the major age changes occurring in response to parent or peer cross-pressures involve antisocial behavior and that these changes are coincident with the onset of puberty. To better understand these cross-pressures, Bronfenbrenner and his colleagues (Bronfenbrenner, 1967, 1970a; Devereux, 1970) devised a dilemmas test consisting of about 30 conflict situations, each of which pits peer-endorsed misconduct against parent-endorsed, socially acceptable conduct. Although these dilemmas cannot be compared directly to dilemmas that pit *approved* adult and peer norms against each other or *disapproved* norms against

each other, the stories nevertheless resemble those social situations that most observers believe are the major sources of conflict between children and their parents. Using this cross-pressure test, investigators can derive measures of adult or peer orientation by comparing subjects' responses under three conditions: (1) a *base condition,* in which the experimenter tells the subject that the answers will be confidential; (2) an *adult-exposure condition,* in which subjects are told that responses will be posted on a chart to be seen later by their parents and teachers; and (3) a *peer-exposure condition,* in which responses will be posted for viewing by classmates.

Classroom, school, and cultural differences are common in children's responses to these exposure conditions. Children in the United States, for example, shift significantly in the direction of peer-endorsed misconduct under the peer-exposure condition, whereas Russian children shift toward socially approved values under *either* adult or peer exposure (Bronfenbrenner, 1967). These differences have been interpreted as reflecting the autonomy of the peer culture in the United States and the fact that the peer group is a more direct extension of adult socialization in Russian society than it is in the United States. Indeed, among students attending Soviet boarding schools, where the emphasis on the role of the collective is especially strong, peer exposure produces even greater endorsement of accepted values compared to students in Soviet day schools (Bronfenbrenner, 1970a).

In certain instances, cultural differences in peer orientation on the dilemmas test seem to be attributable to differences in time spent with parents and peers. These variations, for example, would account for differences between English children (very peer-oriented) and United States children (moderately peer-oriented). Within U.S. culture, too, peer experience may be related to misconduct endorsement. Condry and Siman (1974), for example, found that peer-oriented males reported spending less time with parents and more time with friends than "resistant" boys, even though the same differences were not significant among girls. In addition, peer orientation was correlated with the number of associates seen outside of school, the time spent with them, and the time engaging in "undesirable" activities (e.g., playing hooky, smoking, doing something illegal) or "affiliative" ones (e.g., going to the movies, listening to records). In addition, children ascribing to peer-endorsed misconduct tend to be "followers" rather than "leaders" (Devereux, 1970) and to have attitudes toward adults that are less favorable than those who ascribe to adult-endorsed conventional norms (Bixenstine, DeCorte, & Bixenstine, 1976). This pattern of alienation from adults and misconduct with friends outside of school is similar to the histories of "bad associates" observed among predelinquents. Significantly, having friends and displaying effectiveness with other children, in themselves, do *not* predict conformity to peer-endorsed misconduct in these dilemmas.

Most of the studies by Bronfenbrenner and his colleagues were conducted with fifth- and sixth-grade children who, according to other evidence, may be experiencing more opposition in parent and peer relations than older or younger individuals. Bixenstine et al. (1976) examined age differences on the dilemmas test, observing that endorsement of peer-sponsored misconduct increased from the third to the sixth grade and from the sixth to the eighth grade, but not beyond. The data, then, conform generally to age changes that occur in antisocial conformity on inventory items not confounding the source of influence with acceptability of the behavior described (Berndt, 1979a).

Summary

Secure family relations are the basis for entry into the peer system and success within it. Family breakdown tends to interfere with adaptation to the peer culture, and good family relations are needed throughout childhood and adolescence as the basis for peer relations. Parent and peer values are mainly concordant, especially on issues "that matter." Normative opposition is probably more acute in early adolescence than before or after, with the most intense oppositional experience surrounding antisocial behavior. Most adolescents remain attuned to parental norms even though much time is spent with other children. Dissonance may be considerable when adolescents are alienated from their parents and associate with agemates who endorse misconduct, but the majority of adolescents are able to synthesize their understandings and expectations of their families and their peers.

CONCLUSION

A major objective for the contemporary psychologist is to better understand the role of peer relations in the socialization of the individual child. We seek not only to describe peer interaction at various ages and the processes underlying change from age to age, but also to understand the functions of child-child interaction in social adaptation. What accommodative demands are experienced with agemates or co-equals that are different from the demands experienced with individuals who do not share one's own status? What does the child carry forward into adulthood—in instrumental dispositions, affective biases, and interpersonal expectations—that enhances the probabilities of social success as an adolescent or an adult? The salience of the peer culture is obvious. By the end of the second decade of life, most of the individuals with whom one interacts are near agemates. What, then, are the derivatives of early peer interaction in human development as found in later life? What "human" attributes originate within peer interaction in childhood? Answers to these questions are beginning to emerge—mainly in broad outline.

Contemporary studies, as described in this chapter, have six characteristics. First, investigators are increasingly aware of the necessity for examining peer interactions across time. New interest is evident in psychogenesis, that is, developmental time dependencies. Although data on peer relations in infancy do not articulate very well with data concerning adolescence, a comprehensive picture of peer relations in childhood is nevertheless emerging, partly as a consequence of new studies that close certain gaps in the literature (e.g., the second year of life). Other gaps remain: (1) only two or three attempts have ever been made to chart changes in small group interaction as a function of the age of the group members, (2) few longitudinal studies look at peer interactions and relationships, and (3) too little is known about peer relations in middle childhood. Temporal considerations, however, are the essence of friendships and group experience; the time-dependent dimensions of these phenomena cannot continue to be ignored.

Second, contemporary research on peer relations is beginning to acquire a comparative base. The world provides very few opportunities for studying children's development in the absence of peer experience. The nonhuman primates, however, have become available to students of human development as analogues for experimentation dealing with conditions that cannot be observed with human children—for example, "peer deprivation." By and large, studies with the nonmammalian species have been less useful in contributing to our understanding of peer interaction, although the developmental literature is replete with interesting exceptions (Rajecki, Lamb, & Suomi, 1978).

Third, an ecological or situational perspective is characteristic of current work being done on the role of peer relations in child development. One of the major themes in this chapter is the pervasive role played by contextual factors in determining the nature of peer relations in childhood. Even when cultural variations are set aside, few aspects of peer interaction are free from situational constraint—for example, group composition, physical space, the task at hand, and other circumstantial variations. The nature of the peer group's norms, the difficulty of the social task, the age of the interacting children, and the personalities of the children making up the group are also modifiers of the general principles that affect peer interaction.

Fourth, the cultural context constrains the role of peer relations in the development of the child. Peer contacts vary enormously from culture to culture—both among cultures in which peer relations contribute informally to socialization (e.g., the United States) and among cultures in which peer relations function more formally in education and child-rearing (e.g., the Soviet Union). It remains the case that more is known about peer relations among American children than among children in any other culture; few universal assertions can be made with confidence. On some issues (e.g., cultural similarities and differences in cooperation and competition), interesting comparisons can be made. Clearly, more extensive cross-cultural studies are needed than are now available.

Fifth, systems considerations are emerging in the study of peer interaction. Peer relations may lack some of the properties of a formal social system but not others. The peer network is structured and governed by rules. Most important, though, is the recognition that peer relations contribute to child development in conjunction with other social systems (e.g., the family and the school) rather than independently. Emphasis on the interdependencies existing between the ''peer system'' and other social systems has supplanted more simplistic additive or elaborative models of social development (Hartup, 1980).

Sixth, contemporary views make clear that the developing child must be viewed as an integrated ''whole'' and not as an organism inhabited by social, cognitive, and emotional homunculi. Cognitive dimensions of peer interaction received little attention in the literature a decade ago; no topic interests contemporary investigators more. Similarly, the affective bases of peer interaction were previously ignored but are assuming a new prominence in studies of friendship interaction and the child's use of other children as ''havens of support.'' More than a mere exercise in theoretical integration, this holistic view of the child reflects the current enthusiasm for elucidating the adaptive functions of peer experience. It goes without saying that cognitions, affects, and social actions serve these functions simultaneously, and any description of social adaptation must reference the psychological organization of the whole child rather than elemental fragments.

The complexities of the peer culture constitute our greatest challenge. To document the extent to which child-child relations contribute to social competence would seem to be an easy task but—in fact—it is not. Fortunately, methodologies remain diverse and our interests remain scattered across a wide range of issues—both descriptive and explanatory. Fortuitous, too, are the continuing commitments of investigators to the analysis of both molecular and molar elements in social relations. Only through a better command of these diversities are we likely to achieve the same appreciation of peer relations that children themselves possess.

NOTES

1. He found that children were more energetic and performed better at winding fishing reels when they worked in groups than when they worked alone.

2. Such interactions are more common among girls than among boys (Frodi & Lamb, 1978), but sex differences are not evident in the nature of the interchange.

3. Group problem solving may be more efficacious than individual problem solving because the presence of one able person in the group ensures that all individuals will be able to perform the task. One investigation, however, shows that the effectiveness of group problem solving depends on the nature of the task and whether the most able member of the group is perceived as such. Hudgins and Smith (1966) found that, when the most competent member was perceived as unusually able, group problem solving was not better than independent problem solving. When the most able member was not perceived as unusually competent, group problem solving was better than independent problem solving in arithmetic but not in social studies problems.

4. Cultural differences have been observed under these conditions at every age; children in certain cultures are especially competitive (e.g., Japanese and Greek children), others somewhat less competitive (e.g., Anglo-American children), and others notably noncompetitive (e.g., Mexican-American, black American, rural Native American, Israeli, and Kenyan children). The documentation is extensive (Avellar & Kagan, 1976; Kagan & Madsen, 1971, 1972; Kagan, Zahn, & Gealy, 1977; Knight & Kagan, 1977; McClintock, 1974; Miller & Thomas, 1972; Munroe & Munroe, 1977; Richmond &

Vance, 1974–1975; Shapira, 1976; Shapira & Madsen, 1974; Toda, Shinotsuka, McClintock, & Stech, 1978).

5. When peer norms are not creditable, conformity declines with age, even on insoluble tasks (Hamm, 1970).

6. The assistance of Russell J. Ludeke with this section is gratefully acknowledged.

REFERENCES

Abel, H., & Sahinkaya, R. Emergence of sex and race friendship preferences. *Child Development*, 1962, *33*, 939–943.

Aboud, F. E. Egocentrism, conformity, and agreeing to disagree. *Developmental Psychology*, 1981, *17*, 791–799.

Abramovitch, R. The relation of attention and proximity to rank in preschool children. In M. R. A. Chance & R. R. Larsen (Eds.), *The social structure of attention*. London: Wiley, 1976.

Abramovitch, R. *Proximity, prosocial and agonistic behaviors of preschool children: An observational study*. Unpublished manuscript, University of Toronto, 1979.

Abramovitch, R., & Grusec, J. E. Peer imitation in a natural setting. *Child Development*, 1978, *49*, 60–65.

Abramovitch, R., & Strayer, F. Preschool social organization: Agonistic, spacing, and attentional behaviors. In L. Krames, P. Pliner, & T. Alloway (Eds.), *Advances in the study of communication and affect: Aggression, dominance and individual spacing* (Vol. 4). New York: Plenum Press, 1978.

Achenbach, T. M., & Edelbrock, C. S. Behavioral problems and competencies reported by parents of normal and disturbed children aged 4 through 16. *Monographs of the Society for Research in Child Development*, 1981, *46*(1, Whole No. 188).

Adams, G. R. Physical attractiveness research: Toward a developmental social psychology of beauty. *Human Development*, 1977, *20*, 217–239.

Adams, G. R. Racial membership and physical attractiveness effects on preschool teachers' expectations. *Child Study Journal*, 1978, *8*, 29–41.

Adams, G. R., & Crane, P. An assessment of parents' and teachers' expectations of preschool children's social preference for attractive or unattractive children and adults. *Child Development*, 1980, *51*, 224–231.

Ahlbrand, W. P., & Reynolds, J. A. Some social

effects of cross-age grouping. *Elementary School Journal*, 1972, *73*, 327–332.

Ahlgren, A., & Johnson, D. W. Sex differences in cooperative and competitive attitudes from the 2nd through the 12th grades. *Developmental Psychology*, 1979, *15*, 45–49.

Aiello, J. R., Nicosia, G., & Thompson, D. E. Physiological, social, and behavioral consequences of crowding on children and adolescents. *Child Development*, 1979, *50*, 195–202.

Ainsworth, M. D. S. Attachment and dependency: A comparison. In J. L. Gewirtz (Ed.), *Attachment and dependency*. New York: Wiley, 1972.

Algozzine, O. Perceived attractiveness and classroom interactions. *Journal of Experimental Education*, 1977, *46*, 63–66.

Allen, V. L. *Children as teachers: Theory and research on tutoring*. New York: Academic Press, 1976.

Allen, V., & Feldman, R. S. Studies on the role of tutor. In V. Allen (Ed.), *Children teaching children: Theory and research in tutoring*. New York: Academic Press, 1976.

Allen, V. L., & Newtson, D. Development of conformity and independence. *Journal of Personality and Social Psychology*, 1972, *22*, 18–30.

Allport, G. W. The historical background of modern social psychology. In G. Lindzey (Ed.), *Handbook of social psychology* (Vol. 2). Cambridge, Mass.: Addison-Wesley, 1954.

Almack, J. C. The influence of intelligence on the selection of associates. *School and Society*, 1922, *16*, 529–530.

Altman, I., & McGinnies, E. Interpersonal perception and communication in discussion groups of varied attitudinal composition. *Journal of Abnormal and Social Psychology*, 1960, *60*, 390–395.

Altman, K. Effects of cooperative response acquisition on social behavior during free-play. *Journal of Experimental Child Psychology*, 1971, *12*, 387–395.

Alvy, K. T. Relation of age to children's egocentric and cooperative communication. *Journal of Genetic Psychology*, 1968, *112*, 275–286.

Ames, C., Ames, R., & Felker, D. W. Effects of competitive reward structure and valence of outcome on children's achievement attributions. *Journal of Educational Psychology*, 1977, *69*, 1–8.

Arkell, R. N. Are student helpers helped? *Psychology in the Schools*, 1975, *12*, 111–115.

Arnote, T. E. Variations in amount of indoor play space as associated with certain physical aggressive contacts of young children in group settings. *Dissertation Abstracts International,* 1970, *31*(3-A), 1396.

Aronfreed, J. *Conduct and conscience.* New York: Academic Press, 1968.

Aronson, E. *The jigsaw classroom.* Beverly Hills, Calif.: Sage Publications, 1978.

Asher, K. N., & Erickson, M. T. Effects of varying child-teacher ratio and group size on day care children's and teacher's behavior. *American Journal of Orthopsychiatry,* 1979, *49*, 518–521.

Asher, S. R., & Allen, V. L. Racial preference and social comparison processes. *Journal of Social Issues,* 1969, *25*, 157–166.

Asher, S. R., & Gottman, J. M. *The development of children's friendships.* New York: Cambridge University Press, 1981.

Asher, S. R., & Hymel, S. Children's social competence in peer relations: Sociometric and behavioral assessment. In J. D. Wine & M. D. Smye (Eds.), *Social Competence.* New York: Guilford Press, 1981.

Asher, S. R., Singleton, L. C., & Taylor, A. R. *Acceptance versus friendship: A longitudinal study of racial integration.* Paper presented at the meeting of the American Educational Research Association, New York, 1982.

Asher, S. R., Singleton, L. C., Tinsley, B. R., & Hymel, S. A reliable sociometric measure for preschool children. *Developmental Psychology,* 1979, *15*, 443–444.

Atwood, M. D., Ruebush, B. K., & Everett, F. L. The effects of modeling and role playing on children's delay of gratification behavior. *Child Study Journal,* 1978, *8*, 149.

Avellar, J., & Kagan, S. Development of competitive behaviors in Anglo-American and Mexican-American children. *Psychological Reports,* 1976, *39*, 191–198.

Azrin, N. H., & Lindsley, O. R. The reinforcement of cooperation between children. *Journal of Abnormal and Social Psychology,* 1956, *52*, 100–102.

Bailey, J. S., Timbers, G. D., Phillips, E. L., & Wolf, M. M. Modification of articulation errors of pre-delinquents by their peers. *Journal of Applied Behavior Analysis,* 1971, *4*, 265–281.

Bandura, A., Grusec, J. E., & Menlove, F. L. Vicarious extinction of avoidance behavior. *Journal of Personality and Social Psychology,* 1967, *5*, 16–23.

Bandura, A., & Kupers, C. J. Transmission of patterns of self-reinforcement through modeling. *Journal of Abnormal and Social Psychology,* 1964, *69*, 1–9.

Bandura, A., & Menlove, F. L. Factors determining vicarious extinction of avoidance behavior through symbolic modeling. *Journal of Personality and Social Psychology,* 1968, *8*, 99–108.

Banks, W. C. White preference in blacks: A paradigm in search of a phenomenon. *Psychological Bulletin,* 1976, *83*, 1179–1186.

Barker, R. G., & Wright, H. F. *One boy's day.* New York: Harper Brothers, 1951.

Barker, R. G., & Wright, H. F. *Midwest and its children.* New York: Harper & Row, 1955.

Barnes, K. E. Preschool play norms: A replication. *Developmental Psychology,* 1971, *5*, 99–103.

Barry, N. J., Jr., & Overmann, P.B. Comparison of the effectiveness of adult and peer models with EMR children. *American Journal of Mental Deficiency,* 1977, *82*(1), 33–36.

Bates, B. C. *Effects of social density on the behavior of nursery school children.* Unpublished doctoral dissertation, University of Oregon, 1970.

Baxter, J. C. Interpersonal distancing in natural settings. *Sociometry,* 1970, *33*, 444–456.

Becker, J. M. T. A learning analysis of the development of peer-oriented behavior in nine-month-old infants. *Developmental Psychology,* 1977, *13*, 481–491.

Benton, A. A. Productivity, distributive justice, and bargaining among children. *Journal of Personality and Social Psychology,* 1971, *18*, 68–78.

Berenda, R. W. *The influence of the group on the judgments of children.* New York: King's Crown Press, 1950.

Berndt, T. J. The effect of reciprocity norms on moral judgment and causal attribution. *Child Development,* 1977, *48*, 1322–1330.

Berndt, T. J. Developmental changes in conformity to peers and parents. *Developmental Psychology,* 1979, *15*, 608–616. (a)

Berndt, T. J. *The reliability and validity of social-cognitive measures of friendship.* Unpublished manuscript, Yale University, 1979. (b)

Berndt, T. J. Age changes and changes over time in prosocial intentions and behavior between friends. *Developmental Psychology,* 1981, *17*, 408–416. (a)

Berndt, T. J. Effects of friendship on prosocial intentions and behavior. *Child Development,* 1981, *52*, 636–643. (b)

Berndt, T. J. Relations between social cognition, nonsocial cognition, and social behavior: The case of friendship. In J. H. Flavell & L. Ross (Eds.), *Social cognitive development.* Cambridge: Cambridge University Press, 1981. (c)

Berndt, T. J., Caparulo, B. K., McCartney, K., & Moore, A. *Processes and outcomes of social influence in children's peer groups.* Unpublished manuscript, Yale University, 1980.

Berscheid, E., & Walster, E. H. *Interpersonal attraction* (2nd ed.). Reading, Mass.: Addison-Wesley, 1978.

Best, D. L., Field, J. T., & Williams, J. E. Color bias in a sample of young German children. *Psychological Reports*, 1976, *38*, 1145–1146.

Best, D. L., Naylor, C. E., & Williams, J. E. Extension of color bias research to young French and Italian children. *Journal of Cross-cultural Psychology*, 1975, *6*, 390–405.

Bewley, B. R., & Bland, J. M. Academic performance and social factors related to cigarette smoking by school children. *British Journal of Preventive and Social Medicine*, 1977, *31*, 18–24.

Bigelow, B. J. Children's friendship expectations: A cognitive developmental study. *Child Development*, 1977, *48*, 246–253.

Bigelow, B. J., & La Gaipa, J. J. Children's written descriptions of friendship: A multidimensional analysis. *Developmental Psychology*, 1975, *11*, 857–858.

Biron, A., Ramos, F., & Higa, W. R. Cooperation in children: Social and material rewards. *Psychological Reports*, 1977, *41*, 427–430.

Bixenstine, V. E., DeCorte, M. S., & Bixenstine, B. A. Conformity to peer-sponsored misconduct at four grade levels. *Developmental Psychology*, 1976, *12*, 226–236.

Blaney, N. T., Stephan, C., Rosenfield, D., Aronson, E., & Sikes, J. Interdependence in the classroom: A field study. *Journal of Educational Psychology*, 1977, *69*, 121–128.

Blau, B., & Rafferty, J. Changes in friendship status as a function of reinforcement. *Child Development*, 1970, *41*, 113–121.

Blurton Jones, N. Categories of child-child interaction. In N. Blurton Jones (Ed.), *Ethological studies of child behavior.* Cambridge, England: The University Press, 1972.

Blyth, D. A., Hill, J. P., & Thiel, K. S. *Early adolescents' significant others: Grade and gender differences in perceived relationships with familial and non-familial adults and young people.* Unpublished manuscript, Boys Town Center for the Study of Youth Development, 1981.

Bonney, M. E. Personality traits of socially successful and socially unsuccessful children. *Journal of Educational Psychology*, 1943, *34*, 449–472. (a)

Bonney, M. E. The relative stability of social, intellectual, and academic status in grades II to IV, and the interrelationships between various forms of growth. *Journal of Educational Psychology*, 1943, *34*, 88–102. (b)

Bonney, M. E. Relationships between social success, family size, socioeconomic home background, and intelligence among school children in grades III to V. *Sociometry*, 1944, *7*, 26–39.

Bonney, M. E., & Powell, J. Differences in social behavior between sociometrically high and sociometrically low children. *Journal of Educational Research*, 1953, *46*, 481–495.

Borgatta, E. F., Cottrell, L. S., & Wilker, L. Initial expectation, group climate, and assessment of leaders and members. *Journal of Social Psychology*, 1959, *49*, 285–296.

Bowerman, C. E., & Kinch, J. W. Changes in family and peer orientation of children between the fourth and tenth grades. *Social Forces*, 1959, *37*, 206–211.

Bradbury, D., & Stoddard, G. *Pioneering in child welfare: A history of the Iowa Child Welfare Research Station 1917–1933.* Iowa City: University of Iowa, 1933.

Bridges, K. M. B. A study of social development in early infancy. *Child Development*, 1933, *4*, 36–49.

Britt, D. W., & Campbell, E. Q. Assessing the linkage of norms, environments, and deviance. *Social Forces*, 1977, *56*, 532–550.

Brittain, C. V. Adolescent choices and parent-peer cross-pressures. *American Sociological Review*, 1963, *28*, 385–391.

Brody, G. H., Graziano, W. G., & Musser, L. M. Familiarity and children's behavior in same-age and mixed-age peer groups. *Developmental Psychology*, in press.

Bronfenbrenner, U. Response to pressure from peers versus adults among Soviet and American school children. *International Journal of Psychology*, 1967, *2*, 199–207.

Bronfenbrenner, U. Reaction to social pressure from adults versus peers among Soviet day school and boarding school pupils in the perspective of an American sample. *Journal of Personality and Social Psychology*, 1970, *15*, 179–189. (a)

Bronfenbrenner, U. *Two worlds of childhood.* New York: Russell Sage, 1970. (b)

Bronson, W. C. Central orientations: A study of behavior organization from childhood to adolescence. *Child Development*, 1966, *37*, 125–155.

Bronson, W. C. Developments in behavior with age mates during the second year of life. In M. Lewis and L. A. Rosenblum (Eds.), *Friendship and peer relations*. New York: Wiley, 1975.

Bronson, W. C. *Toddlers' behaviors with agemates: Issues of interaction, cognition, and affect*. Norwood, N.J.: Ablex, 1981.

Brooks, J., & Lewis, M. Early social knowledge: The development of knowledge about others. In H. McGurk (Ed.), *Childhood social development*. London: Methuen, 1978.

Brown, G. E., Wheeler, K. J., & Cash, M. The effects of a laughing versus a nonlaughing model on humor responses in preschool children. *Journal of Experimental Child Psychology*, 1980, *29*, 334–339.

Brownell, C. A. *Peer interaction among toddler aged children: Effects of age and social context on interactional competence and behavioral roles*. Unpublished doctoral dissertation, University of Minnesota, 1982.

Brownell, C. A., & Hartup, W. W. Indeterminate and sequential goal structures in relation to task performance in small groups. *Child Development*, 1981, *52*, 651–659.

Bruininks, V. L. Actual and perceived peer status of learning-disabled students in mainstream programs. *Journal of Special Education*, 1978, *12*, 51–58.

Bryan, T. H. Peer popularity of learning disabled children. *Journal of Learning Disabilities*, 1974, *7*, 621–625.

Bryan, T. H. Peer popularity of learning disabled children: A replication. *Journal of Learning Disabilities*, 1976, *9*, 307–311.

Bryant, B. K. The effects of the interpersonal context of evaluation on self- and other-enhancement behavior. *Child Development*, 1977, *48*, 885–892.

Bühler, C. Die ersten sozialen Verhaltungsweisen des Kindes. In C. Bühler, H. Hetzer, & B. Tudor-Hart (Eds.), *Soziologische und psychologische Studien uber sdas erste Lebensjahr*. Jena, Germany: Gustav Fischer, 1927.

Bühler, C. *The first year of life*. Rahway, N.J.: John Day, 1930.

Burk, B. A., Zdep, S. M., & Kushner, H. Affiliation patterns among American girls. *Adolescence*, 1973, *8*, 541–546.

Butler, L. J. *Social and behavioral correlates of peer reputation*. Paper presented at the meeting of the Society for Research in Child Development, San Francisco, April 1979.

Byrne, D., & Griffitt, W. B. A developmental investigation of the law of attraction. *Journal of Personality and Social Development*, 1966, *4*,

699–702.

Campbell, J. D., & Yarrow, M. R. Perceptual and behavioral correlates of social effectiveness. *Sociometry*, 1961, *24*, 1–20.

Campbell, S. B., & Levine, P. C. *Peer interactions of young "hyperactive" children in preschool*. Paper presented at the meeting of the American Psychological Association, Montreal, September 1980.

Canale, J. R. The effect of modeling and length of ownership on sharing behavior of children. *Social Behavior and Personality*, 1977, *5*, 187–191.

Cannon, K. L. The relationship of social acceptance to socioeconomic status and residence among high school students. *Rural Sociology*, 1957, *22*, 142–148.

Cantor, G. N. Children's "like-dislike" ratings of familiarized and nonfamiliarized visual stimuli. *Journal of Experimental Child Psychology*, 1968, *6*, 651–657.

Cantor, G. N. Effects of familiarization on children's ratings of pictures of whites and blacks. *Child Development*, 1972, *43*, 1219–1229.

Cantor, G. N., & Kubose, S. K. Preschool children's ratings of familiarized and non-familiarized visual stimuli. *Journal of Experimental Child Psychology*, 1969, *8*, 74–81.

Cartwright, D., & Zander, A. *Group dynamics* (2nd ed.). Evanston, Ill.: Row, Peterson, 1960.

Cavior, N., & Dokecki, P. R. Physical attractiveness, perceived attitude similarity, and academic achievement as contributors to interpersonal attraction among adolescents. *Developmental Psychology*, 1973, *9*, 44–54.

Cavior, N., & Lombardi, D. A. Developmental aspects of judgment of physical attractiveness in children. *Developmental Psychology*, 1973, *8*, 67–71.

Challman, R. C. Factors influencing friendships among preschool children. *Child Development*, 1932, *3*, 146–158.

Chance, R. A., & Larsen, R. R. *The social structure of attention*. New York: Wiley, 1976.

Chapman, A. J., Smith, J. R., Foot, H. C., & Pritchard, E. Behavioural and sociometric indices of friendship in children. In M. Cook & G. D. Wilson (Eds.), *Love and attraction*. Oxford: Pergamon, 1979.

Charlesworth, R., & Hartup, W. W. Positive social reinforcement in the nursery school peer group. *Child Development*, 1967, *38*, 993–1002.

Clark, A. H., Wyon, S. M., & Richards, M. P. M. Free play in nursery school children. *Journal of*

Child Psychology and Psychiatry, 1969, *10*, 205–216.

Clark, B. S. The acquisition and extinction of peer imitation in children. *Psychonomic Science*, 1965, *2*, 147–148.

Clark, K. B., & Clark, M. K. The development of consciousness of self and the emergence of racial identification in Negro preschool children. *Journal of Social Psychology*, 1939, *10*, 591–599.

Clark, K. B., & Clark, M. Racial identification and preference in Negro children. In T. M. Newcomb & E. L. Hartey (Eds.), *Readings in social psychology*. New York: Holt, 1947.

Clarke, H. H., & Greene, W. H. Relationships between personal-social measures applied to 10-year-old boys. *Research Quarterly of the American Association of Health & Physical Education*, 1963, *34*, 288–298.

Clifford, E. Social visibility. *Child Development*, 1963, *34*, 799–808.

Clifford, M. M., & Walster, E. The effects of physical attractiveness on teacher expectations. *Sociology of Education*, 1973, *46*, 248–258.

Cloward, R. Studies in tutoring. *Journal of Experimental Education*, 1976, *36*, 14–25.

Cohen, E. Interracial interaction disability. *Human Relations*, 1972, *25*, 9–24.

Cohen, R., Bornstein, R., & Sherman, R. C. Conformity behavior of children as a function of group makeup and task ambiguity. *Developmental Psychology*, 1973, *9*, 124–131.

Coleman, J. S. *The adolescent society*. New York: The Free Press, 1961.

Condry, J., & Siman, M. L. Characteristics of peer- and adult-oriented children. *Journal of Marriage and the Family*, 1974, *36*, 543–554.

Conger, J. J., & Miller, W. C. *Personality, social class and delinquency*. New York: Wiley, 1966.

Cook, T. P., Goldman, J. A., & Olczak, P. V. The relationship between self-esteem and interpersonal attraction in children. *Journal of Genetic Psychology*, 1978, *132*, 149–150.

Cooley, C. H. *Social organization*. New York: Scribners, 1909.

Coons, M. O. Rosenzweig differences in reactions to frustration in children of high, low, and middle sociometric status. *Group Psychotherapy*, 1957, *10*, 60–63.

Cooper, C. R. *Collaboration in children: Dyadic interaction skills in problem solving*. Paper presented at the meeting of the Society for Research in Child Development, New Orleans, March 1977.

Cooper, C. R., Ayers-Lopez, S., & Marquis, A.

Children's discourse during peer learning in experimental and naturalistic situations. *Discourse Processes*, 1982, *5*, 177–191.

Corter, C., Trehub, S., Boukydis, C., Ford, L., Celhoffer, L., & Minde, K. Nurses' judgments of the attractiveness of premature infants. *Infant Behavior and Development*, 1978, *1*, 373–380.

Costanzo, P. R., & Shaw, M. E. Conformity as a function of age level. *Child Development*, 1966, *37*, 967–975.

Cowen, E. L., Pederson, A., Babijian, H., Izzo, L. D., & Trost, M. A. Long-term follow-up of early detected vulnerable children. *Journal of Consulting and Clinical Psychology*, 1973, *41*, 438–446.

Cox, S. H. *Family background effects on personality development and social acceptance*. Unpublished doctoral dissertation, Texas Christian University, 1966.

Criswell, J. H. Social structure revealed in a sociometric test. *Sociometry*, 1939, *2*, 69–75.

Crockenberg, S. B., Bryant, B. K., & Wilce, L. S. The effects of cooperatively and competitively structured learning environments on inter- and intra- personal behavior. *Child Development*, 1976, *47*, 386–396.

Damon, W. *The social world of the child*. San Francisco: Jossey-Bass, 1977.

Davids, A., & Parenti, A. N. Time orientation and interpersonal relations of emotionally disturbed and normal children. *Journal of Abnormal and Social Psychology*, 1958, *57*, 299–305.

Davis, J. A. Correlates of sociometric status among peers. *Journal of Educational Research*, 1957, *50*, 561–569.

Davitz, J. R. Social perception and sociometric choice in children. *Journal of Abnormal and Social Psychology*, 1955, *50*, 173–176.

Dawe, H. C. Analysis of two hundred quarrels of preschool children. *Child Development*, 1934, *5*, 139–157.

Dembo, R., Schmeidler, J., & Burgos, W. Factors in the drug involvement of innercity junior high school youths: A discriminant analysis. *International Journal of Social Psychology*, 1979, *25*, 92–103.

DeStefano, C. T., & Mueller, E. *Environmental determinants of peer social activity in 18 month old males*. Unpublished manuscript, Boston University, 1980.

Deutsch, F. Observational and sociometric measures of peer popularity and their relationship to egocentric communication in female preschoolers. *Developmental Psychology*, 1974,

10, 745–747.

Devereux, E. C. The role of peer-group experience in moral development. In J. P. Hill (Ed.), *Minnesota Symposia on Child Psychology* (Vol. 4). Minneapolis: University of Minnesota Press, 1970.

DeVries, D. L., & Edwards, K. J. *Learning games and student teams: Their effects on classroom processes.* Johns Hopkins University, Maryland: Center for Social Organization of Schools, Report No. 142, 1972.

DeVries, D. L., & Mescon, I. T. *Teams-games-tournament: An effective task and reward structure in the elementary grades.* Johns Hopkins University, Maryland: Center for Social Organization of Schools, Report No. 189, 1975.

Dion, K. K. Young children's stereotyping of facial attractiveness. *Developmental Psychology*, 1973, *9*, 183–198.

Dion, K. K., & Berscheid, E. Physical attractiveness and peer perception among children. *Sociometry*, 1974, *37*, 1–12.

Dion, K. K., Berscheid, E., & Walster, E. What is beautiful is good. *Journal of Personality and Social Psychology*, 1972, *24*, 285–290.

Dion, K. K., & Stein, S. Physical attractiveness and interpersonal influence. *Journal of Experimental Social Psychology*, 1978, *14*, 97–108.

DiPietro, J. A. Rough and tumble play: A function of gender. *Developmental Psychology*, 1981, *17*, 50–58.

Dittman, A. T. Developmental factors in conversational behavior. *Journal of Communication*, 1972, *22*, 404–423.

Douvan, E., & Adelson, J. *The adolescent experience.* New York: Wiley, 1966.

Doyle, A., Connolly, J., & Rivest, L. The effects of playmate familiarity on the social interactions of young children. *Child Development*, 1980, *51*, 217–223.

Duck, S. W. Personality similarity and friendship choices by adolescents. *European Journal of Social Psychology*, 1975, *5*, 351–365.

Duncan, O. D., Featherman, D. L., & Duncan, B. *Socioeconomic background and achievement.* New York: Seminar Press, 1972.

Dunnington, M. J. Behavioral differences of sociometric status groups in a nursery school. *Child Development*, 1957, *28*, 103–111.

Durfee, J. T., & Lee, L. C. *Infant-infant interaction in a daycare setting.* Paper presented at the meeting of the American Psychological Association, Montreal, August 1973.

Durrett, M. E., & Davy, A. I. Racial awareness in young Mexican-American, Negro and Anglo children. *Young Children*, 1970, *26*, 16–24.

East, B. A. Cross-age tutoring in the elementary school. *Graduate Research in Education and Related Disciplines*, 1976, *8*, 88–111.

Easterbrooks, M. A., & Lamb, M. E. The relationship between quality of infant-mother attachment and infant peer competence in initial encounters with peers. *Child Development*, 1979, *50*, 380–387.

Eckerman, C. O., & Whatley, J. L. Toys and social interaction between infant peers. *Child Development*, 1977, *48*, 1645–1656.

Eckerman, C. O., Whatley, J. L., & Kutz, S. L. The growth of social play with peers during the second year of life. *Developmental Psychology*, 1975, *11*, 42–49.

Edelman, M. S., & Omark, D. R. Dominance hierarchies in young children. *Social Science Information*, 1973, *12*, 103–110.

Eder, D., & Hallinan, M. T. Sex differences in children's friendships. *American Sociological Review*, 1978, *43*, 237–250.

Edwards, C. P., & Lewis, M. Young children's concepts of social relations: Social functions and social objects. In M. Lewis & L. A. Rosenblum (Eds.), *The child and its family: Genesis of behavior* (Vol. 2). New York: Plenum, 1979.

Eifermann, R. R. *Determinants of children's game styles.* Jerusalem: Israel Academy of Sciences, 1971.

Eitzen, D. S. Athletics in the status system of male adolescents: A replication of Coleman's *The adolescent society. Adolescence*, 1975, *10*, 267–276.

Elkins, D. Some factors related to the choice status of ninety eighth-grade children in a school society. *Genetic Psychology Monographs*, 1958, *58*, 207–272.

Elliott, R., & Vasta, R. The modeling of sharing: Effects associated with vicarious reinforcement, symbolization, age, and generalization. *Journal of Experimental Child Psychology*, 1970, *10*, 8–15.

Emmerich, W. Young children's discriminations of parent and child roles. *Child Development*, 1959, *30*, 403–419.

Emmerich, W., Goldman, K. S., & Shore, R. E. Differentiation and development of social norms. *Journal of Personality and Social Psychology*, 1971, *18*, 323–353.

Endsley, R. C., & Gupta, S. Group size as a determinant of preschool children's frequency of asking questions. *Journal of Genetic Psychology*,

1978, *132*, 317–318.

Erikson, E. H. *Childhood and society.* New York: Norton, 1950.

Fagot, B. I. Consequences of moderate cross-gender behavior in preschool children. *Child Development,* 1977, *48,* 902–907. (a)

Fagot, B. I. Variations in density: Effect on task and social behaviors of preschool children. *Developmental Psychology,* 1977, *13,* 166–167. (b)

Faigin, H. Social behavior of young children in the kibbutz. *Journal of Abnormal and Social Psychology,* 1958, *56,* 117–129.

Faust, M. S. Developmental maturity as a determinant of prestige in adolescent girls. *Child Development,* 1960, *31,* 173–184.

Feigenbaum, K. D., Geiger, D., & Crevoshay, S. An exploratory study of the 3-, 5-, and 7-year-old female's comprehension of cooperative and uncooperative social interaction. *Journal of Genetic Psychology,* 1970, *116,* 141–148.

Feinberg, M. R., Smith, M., & Schmidt, R. An analysis of expressions used by adolescents of varying economic levels to describe accepted and rejected peers. *Journal of Genetic Psychology,* 1958, *93,* 133–148.

Field, T. Games parents play with normal and high-risk infants. *Child Psychiatry and Human Development,* 1979, *10,* 41–48.

Fincham, F. Recipient characteristics and sharing behavior in the learning disabled. *Journal of Genetic Psychology,* 1978, *133,* 143–144.

Fine, G. A. The natural history of preadolescent friendship groups. In H. Foot, A. Chapman, & J. Smith (Eds.), *Friendship and social relations in children.* New York: Wiley, 1980.

Finkelstein, N. W., Dent, C., Gallagher, K., & Ramey, C. T. Social behavior of infants and toddlers in a daycare environment. *Developmental Psychology,* 1978, *14,* 257–262.

Fischoff, A. *A comparison between peer-oriented social behavior of Kibbutz and city infants in different settings.* Unpublished master's thesis, Hebrew University, 1974.

Fishbein, H. D., & Osborne, M. The effects of feedback variations on referential communication of children. *Merrill-Palmer Quarterly,* 1971, *17,* 243–250.

Flanders, N. A., & Havumaki, S. The effect of teacher-pupil contacts involving praise on the sociometric choices of students. *Journal of Educational Psychology,* 1960, *51,* 65–68.

Flotre, K. E. *Peer acceptance and rejection in a mixed-age preschool group.* Unpublished manuscript, Early Childhood Teachers College, Oslo, Norway, 1980.

Floyd, J. M. K. *Effects of amount of reward and friendship status of the other on the frequency of sharing in children.* Unpublished doctoral dissertation, University of Minnesota, 1964.

Foot, H. C., Chapman, A. J., & Smith, J. R. Friendship and social responsiveness in boys and girls. *Journal of Personality and Social Psychology,* 1977, *35,* 401–411.

Foot, H. C., Chapman, A. J., & Smith, J. R. *Friendship and social relations in children.* New York: Wiley, 1980.

Frager, S., & Stern C. Learning by teaching. *The Reading Teacher,* 1970, *23,* 403–405.

French, D. C., Brownell, C. A., Graziano, W. G., & Hartup, W. W. Effects of cooperative, competitive, and individualistic sets on performance in children's groups. *Journal of Experimental Child Psychology,* 1977, *24,* 1–10.

Freud, A., & Dann, S. An experiment in group upbringing. In R. S. Eisler, A. Freud, H. Hartmann, & E. Kris (Eds.), *The psychoanalytic study of the child* (Vol. 6). New York: International Universities Press, 1951.

Frodi, A. M., & Lamb, M. Sex differences in responsiveness to infants: A developmental study of psychophysiological and behavioral responses. *Child Development,* 1978, *49,* 1182–1188.

Furfey, P. H. Some factors influencing the selection of boys' "chums." *Journal of Applied Psychology,* 1927, *11,* 47–51.

Furman, W., & Masters, J. C. Affective consequences of social reinforcement, punishment, and neutral behavior. *Developmental Psychology,* 1980, *16,* 100–104. (a)

Furman, W., & Masters, J. C. Peer interactions, sociometric status, and resistance to deviation in young children. *Developmental Psychology,* 1980, *16,* 229–336. (b)

Furman, W., Rahe, D. F., & Hartup, W. W. Rehabilitation of socially withdrawn preschool children through mixed-age and same-age socialization. *Child Development,* 1979, *50,* 915–922.

Garbarino, J. The impact of anticipated reward upon cross-age tutoring. *Journal of Personality and Social Psychology,* 1975, *32,* 421–428.

Garett, J., & Libby, W. L. Role of intentionality in mediating responses to inequity in the dyad. *Journal of Personality and Social Psychology,* 1973, *28,* 21–27.

Garvey, C. Some properties of social play. *Merrill-Palmer Quarterly,* 1974, *20,* 163–180.

Gelfand, D. M. The influence of self-esteem on rate

of verbal conditioning and social matching behavior. *Journal of Abnormal and Social Psychology,* 1962, *65,* 259–265.

Gerber, P. J. Awareness of handicapping conditions and sociometric status in an integrated pre-school setting. *Mental Retardation,* 1977, *15,* 24–25.

Geshuri, Y. Observational learning: Effects of observed reward and response patterns. *Journal of Educational Psychology,* 1972, *63,* 374–380.

Getz, S. K. *Components and characteristics of early spontaneous play among preschool children.* Unpublished doctoral dissertation, University of Minnesota, 1977.

Gilligan, M. C. *The effects of varied playground space on certain behavioral aspects of four- and five-year-old children.* Unpublished doctoral dissertation, New York University, 1970.

Girgus, J. S., & Wolf, J. Age changes in the ability to encode social class. *Developmental Psychology,* 1975, *11,* 118.

Glueck, S., & Glueck, E. *Unraveling juvenile delinquency.* New York: The Commonwealth Fund, 1950.

Goertzen, S. M. Factors relating to opinions of seventh grade children regarding the acceptability of certain behaviors in the peer group. *Journal of Genetic Psychology,* 1959, *94,* 29–34.

Goldberg, M. H., & Maccoby, E. E. Children's acquisition of skill in performing a group task under two conditions of group formation. *Journal of Personality and Social Psychology,* 1965, *2,* 898–902.

Goldman, J. A. The social interaction of preschool children in same-age versus mixed-age groupings. *Child Development,* 1981, *52,* 644–750.

Goodenough, F. L. Measuring behavior traits by means of repeated short samples. *Journal of Juvenile Research,* 1928, *12,* 230–235.

Goodenough, F. L. *Anger in young children.* Minneapolis: University of Minnesota Press, 1931.

Gottlieb, J. Public, peer and professional attitudes toward mentally retarded persons. In M. J. Begab & S. A. Richardson (Eds.), *The mentally retarded and society: A social science perspective.* Baltimore, Md.: University Park Press, 1975.

Gottlieb, J., Semmel, M. I., & Veldman, D. J. Correlates of social status among mainstreamed mentally retarded children. *Journal of Educational Psychology,* 1978, *70,* 396–405.

Gottman, J. M. Toward a definition of social isolation in children. *Child Development,* 1977, *48,* 513–517.

Gottman, J., Gonzo, J., & Rasmussen, B. Social interaction, social competence, and friendship in children. *Child Development,* 1975, *45,* 709–718.

Gottman, J. M., & Parkhurst, J. A developmental theory of friendship and acquaintanceship processes. In W. A. Collins (Ed.), *Minnesota symposia on child psychology* (Vol. 13). Hillsdale, N.J.: Lawrence Erlbaum, 1980.

Goy, R. W., & Goldfoot, D. A. Experimental and hormonal factors influencing development of sexual behavior in the male rhesus monkey. In *The neurosciences, third study program.* Cambridge, Mass.: M.I.T. Press, 1973.

Gralewicz, A. Play deprivation in multihandicapped children. *American Journal of Occupational Therapy,* 1973, *27,* 70–72.

Graziano, W., French, D., Brownell, C., & Hartup, W. W. Peer interaction in same- and mixed-age triads in relation to chronological age and incentive condition. *Child Development,* 1976, *47,* 707–714.

Graziano, W. G., Musser, L. M., & Brody, G. H. *Children's social cognitions and preferences regarding younger and older peers.* Unpublished manuscript, University of Georgia, 1980.

Greenberg, D. J., Hillman, D., & Grice, D. Infant and stranger variables related to stranger anxiety in the first year of life. *Developmental Psychology,* 1973, *9,* 207–212.

Greenberg, P. J. Competition in children: An experimental study. *American Journal of Psychology,* 1932, *44,* 221–248.

Gronlund, N. E., & Anderson, L. Personality characteristics of socially accepted, socially neglected and socially rejected junior high school pupils. *Education Administration and Supervision,* 1957, *43,* 329–338.

Gronlund, N. E., & Barnes, F. P. The reliability of social-acceptability scores using various sociometric choice limits. *Elementary School Journal,* 1956, *57,* 153–157.

Grosser, D., Polansky, N., & Lippitt, R. A laboratory study of behavioral contagion. *Human Relations,* 1951, *4,* 115–142.

Grossman, B., & Wrighter, J. The relationship between selection-rejection and intelligence, social status, and personality among sixth-grade children. *Sociometry,* 1948, *11,* 346–355.

Grubb, T., & Watt, N. F. *Longitudinal approaches to promoting social adjustment through public school programs.* Paper presented at the meeting of the Society for Research in Child Development, San Francisco, April 1979.

Guarnaccia, V. J. *Pupil tutoring in elementary math*

instruction. Unpublished doctoral dissertation, Columbia University, 1973.

Gump, P., Schoggen, P., & Redl, F. The camp milieu and its immediate effects. *Journal of Social Issues,* 1957, *13,* 40–46.

Guralnick, M. J. The social behavior of preschool children of different developmental levels: Effects of group composition. *Journal of Experimental Child Psychology,* 1981, *31,* 115–130.

Hagman, E. P. The companionships of preschool children. *University of Iowa Studies in Child Welfare,* 1933, *4,* 1–69.

Hall, G. S. *Adolescence* (Vol. 2). New York: Appleton, 1904.

Haller, A. O., & Butterworth, C. E. Peer influences on levels of occupational and educational aspiration. *Social Forces,* 1960, *38,* 289–295.

Hallworth, H. J. Group relationships among grammar school boys and girls between the ages of eleven and sixteen years. *Sociometry,* 1953, *16,* 39–70.

Hamblin, J. A., & Hamblin, R. L. On teaching disadvantaged preschoolers to read: A successful experiment. *American Educational Research Journal,* 1972, *9,* 2209–2216.

Hamm, N. A partial test of a social learning theory of children's conformity. *Journal of Experimental Child Psychology,* 1970, *9,* 29–42.

Hamm, N., & Hoving, K. Age and sex differences in the perception of autokinesis in children. *Perceptual and Motor Skills,* 1969, *28,* 317–318.

Handlon, B. J., & Gross, P. The development of sharing behavior. *Journal of Abnormal and Social Psychology,* 1959, *59,* 425–428.

Harari, H., & McDavid, J. W. Teachers' expectations and name stereotypes. *Journal of Educational Psychology,* *65,* 1973, 222–225.

Hare, A. P. Small group discussions with participatory and supervisory leadership. *Journal of Abnormal and Social Psychology,* 1953, *48,* 273–275.

Harlow, H. F. Age-mate or peer affectional system. In D. S. Lehrman, R. A. Hinde, & E. Shaw (Eds.), *Advances in the study of behavior* (Vol. 2). New York: Academic Press, 1969.

Harris, D. B., & Tseng, S. Children's attitudes towards peers and parents as revealed by sentence completions. *Child Development,* 1957, *28,* 401–411.

Harris, F. R., Wolf, M. M., & Baer, D. M. Effects of adult social reinforcement on child behavior. In W. W. Hartup & N. L. Smothergill (Eds.), *The young child.* Washington, D.C.: National Association for the Education of Young Children, 1967.

Harrison, M. G., Messe, L. A., & Stollak, G. E. Effects of racial composition group size on interactional patterns in preschool children. *Proceedings of the 79th Annual Convention of the American Psychological Association,* 1971, *6* (Pt. 1), 325–326.

Hartup, W. W. Friendship status and the effectiveness of peers as reinforcing agents. *Journal of Experimental Child Psychology,* 1964, *1,* 154–162.

Hartup, W. W. Peer interaction and social organization. In P. H. Mussen (Ed.), *Carmichael's Manual of Child Psychology* (Vol. 2). New York: Wiley, 1970.

Hartup, W. W. Aggression in childhood: Developmental perspectives. *American Psychologist,* 1974, *29,* 336–341.

Hartup, W. W. Two social worlds: Family relations and peer relations. In M. Rutter (Ed.), *Scientific foundations of developmental psychiatry.* London: Heinemann, 1980.

Hartup, W. W., Brady, J. E., & Newcomb, A. F. Social cognition and social interaction in childhood. In E. T. Higgins, D. N. Ruble, & W. W. Hartup (Eds.), *Social cognition and social development.* New York: Cambridge University Press, 1983.

Hartup, W. W., & Coates, B. Imitation of a peer as a function of reinforcement from the peer group and rewardingness of the model. *Child Development,* 1967, *38,* 1003–1016.

Hartup, W. W., Glazer, J. A., & Charlesworth, R. Peer reinforcement and sociometric status. *Child Development,* 1967, *38,* 1017–1024.

Hartup, W. W., & Keller, E. D. Nurturance in preschool children and its relation to dependency. *Child Development,* 1960, *31,* 681–690.

Harvey, O. J., & Consalvi, C. Status and conformity to pressures in informal groups. *Journal of Abnormal and Social Psychology,* 1960, *60,* 182–187.

Harvey, O. J., & Rutherford, J. Status in the informal group: Influence and influencibility at differing age levels. *Child Development,* 1960, *31,* 377–385.

Haskett, G. J. Modification of peer preferences of first-grade children. *Developmental Psychology,* 1971, *4,* 429–433.

Havighurst, R. J., Bowman, P. H., Liddle, G. P., Matthews, C. V., & Pierce, J. V. *Growing up in River City.* New York: Wiley, 1962.

Hayes, D. S. Cognitive bases for liking and disliking among preschool children. *Child Development,*

1978, *49*, 906–909.

Heathers, G. Emotional dependence and independence in nursery school play. *Journal of Genetic Psychology*, 1955, *87*, 37–57.

Heber, R. F., & Heber, M. E. The effect of group failure and success on social status. *Journal of Educational Psychology*, 1957, *48*, 129–134.

Helper, M. M. Parental evaluations of children and children's self-evaluations. *Journal of Abnormal and Social Psychology*, 1958, *56*, 190–194.

Hertz-Lazarowitz, R., Feitelson, D., Zahavi, S., Hartup, W. W. Social interaction and social organization of Israeli five- to seven-year-olds. *International Journal of Behavioral Development*, 1981, *4*, 143–155.

Hertz-Lazarowitz, R., Sharan, S., & Steinberg, R. Classroom learning style and cooperative behavior of elementary school children. *Journal of Educational Psychology*, 1980, *72*, 99–106.

Hetherington, E. M. Divorce: A child's perspective. *American Psychologist*, 1979, *34*, 851–858.

Hetherington, E. M., & Morris, W. M. The family and primary groups. In W. H. Holtzman (Ed.), *Introductory psychology in depth: Developmental topics*. New York: Harper's College Press, 1978.

Hill, J. P., & Lynch, M. E. The intensification of gender-related role expectations during early adolescence. In J. Brooks-Gunn & A. Peterson (Eds.), *Female puberty*. New York: Plenum, in press.

Hinde, R. A. *Biological bases of human social behavior*. New York: McGraw-Hill, 1974.

Hoffman, E., Marsden, G., & Kalter, N. Children's understanding of their emotionally disturbed peers: A replication. *Journal of Clinical Psychology*, 1977, *33*, 949–953.

Hoffman, L. W. The father's role in the family and the child's peer-group adjustment. *Merrill-Palmer Quarterly*, 1961, *7*, 97–105.

Hold, B. Rank and behavior: An ethological study of preschool children. *Homo*, 1977, *28*, 158–188.

Hollander, E. P., & Julian, J. W. Studies in leader legitimacy, influence and innovation. In L. Berkowitz (Ed.), *Advances in Experimental Social Psychology* (Vol. 5). New York: Academic Press, 1970.

Horowitz, E. L. The development of attitudes toward the Negro. *Archives of Psychology*, 1936, *194*, 47.

Horowitz, F. D. Incentive value of social stimuli for preschool children. *Child Development*, 1962, *33*, 111–116.

Horrocks, J. E., & Thompson, G. G. A study of the

friendship fluctuations of rural boys and girls. *Journal of Genetic Psychology*, 1946, *69*, 189–198.

Hoving, K. L. *Some parameters of yielding in children*. Paper presented at the meeting of the Midwestern Psychological Association, St. Louis, April 1964.

Hoving, K. L., Hamm, N., & Galvin, P. Social influence as a function of stimulus ambiguity at three age levels. *Developmental Psychology*, 1969, *1*, 631–636.

Howes, C., & Rubenstein, J. L. *Influences on toddler peer behavior in two types of daycare*. Unpublished manuscript, Harvard University, 1979.

Hoy, E. A., & McKnight, J. R. Communication style and effectiveness in homogeneous and heterogeneous dyads of retarded children. *American Journal of Mental Deficiency*, 1977, *81*, 587–598.

Hraba, J., & Grant, G. Black is beautiful: A reexamination of racial preference and identification. *Journal of Personality and Social Psychology*, 1970, *16*, 398–402.

Huba, G. J., Wingard, J. A., & Bentler, P. M. Beginning adolescent drug use and peer and adult interaction patterns. *Journal of Consulting and Clinical Psychology*, 1979, *47*, 265–276.

Hudgins, B. B. Effects of group experience on individual problem solving. *Journal of Educational Psychology*, 1960, *51*, 37–42.

Hudgins, B. B., & Smith, L. M. Group structure and productivity in problem-solving. *Journal of Educational Psychology*, 1966, *57*, 287–296.

Hunt, R. G., & Synnerdale, V. Social influences among kindergarten children. *Sociological Social Research*, 1959, *43*, 171–174.

Hutt, C., & Vaizey, M. J. Differential effects of group density on social behaviour. *Nature*, 1966, *209*, 1371–1372.

Hutt, S. J., & Hutt, C. *Direct observation and measurement of behavior*. Springfield, Ill.: Charles C. Thomas, 1970.

Ipsa, J. Peer support among Soviet day care toddlers. *International Journal of Behavioral Development*, 1981, *4*, 255–269.

Isaacs, S. *Social development in young children: A study of beginnings*. London: Routledge, 1933.

Iscoe, I., Williams, M., & Harvey, J. Age, intelligence, and sex as variables in the conformity behavior of Negro and white children. *Child Development*, 1964, *35*, 451–460.

Iwawaki, S., Sonoo, K., Williams, J. E., & Best, D. L. Color bias among young Japanese children. *Journal of Cross-cultural Psychology*, 1978, *9*, 61–73.

Jack, L. M. An experimental study of ascendant behavior in preschool children. *University of Iowa Studies in Child Welfare*, 1934, *9*, 7–15.

Jacklin, C. N., & Maccoby, E. E. Social behavior at thirty-three months in same-sex and mixed-sex dyads. *Child Development*, 1978, *49*, 557–569.

Jakubczak, C. F., & Walters, R. H. Suggestibility as dependency behavior. *Journal of Abnormal and Social Psychology*, 1959, *59*, 102–107.

Jaquette, D. *Developmental stages in peer group organization: A cognitive-developmental analysis of peer group concepts in childhood and adolescence*. Unpublished manuscript, Harvard University, 1976.

Jeffers, V. W., & Lore, R. K. Let's play at my house: Effects of the home environment on the social behavior of children. *Child Development*, 1979, *50*, 837–841.

Jelinek, M. M., & Brittan, E. M. Multiracial education: I. Inter-ethnic friendship patterns. *Educational Research*, 1975, *18*, 44–53.

Jennings, H. Structure of leadership: Development and sphere of influence. *Sociometry*, 1937–38, *1*, 99–143.

Jennings, K. D. People versus object orientation, social behavior, and intellectual abilities in preschool children. *Developmental Psychology*, 1975, *11*, 511–519.

Jensen, R. E., & Moore, S. G. The effect of attribute statements on cooperativeness and competitiveness in school-age boys. *Child Development*, 1977, *48*, 305–307.

Jessor, R., & Jessor, S. L. *Problem behavior and psychosocial development*. New York: Academic Press, 1977.

Johnson, D. W., Falk, D., Martino, L., & Purdie, S. The evaluation of persons seeking and volunteering information under cooperative and competitive conditions. *Journal of Psychology*, 1976, *92*, 161–165.

Johnson, D. W., & Johnson, R. T. *Learning together and alone*. Englewood Cliffs, N.J.: Prentice-Hall, 1975.

Johnson, D. W., Johnson, R. T., Johnson, J., & Anderson, D. Effects of cooperative versus individualized instruction on student prosocial behavior, attitudes toward learning, and achievement. *Journal of Educational Psychology*, 1976, *68*, 446–452.

Johnson, D. W., Johnson, R. T., & Scott, L. The effects of cooperative *vs.* individualized instruction on student attitudes and achievement. *Jour-nal of Social Psychology*, 1978, *104*, 207–216.

Johnson, M. W. The effect on behavior of variation in the amount of play equipment. *Child Development*, 1935, *6*, 56–68.

Johnston, J. M., & Johnston, G. T. Modification of consonant speech-sound articulation in young children. *Journal of Applied Behavior Analysis*, 1972, *5*, 233–246.

Jones, M. C. Psychological correlates of somatic development. *Child Development*, 1965, *36*, 899–911.

Jones, M. C., & Bayley, N. Physical maturing among boys as related to behavior. *Journal of Educational Psychology*, 1950, *41*, 129–148.

Jones, S. E., & Aiello, J. R. Proxemic behavior of black and white first-, third-, and fifth-grade children. *Journal of Personality and Social Psychology*, 1973, *25*, 21–27.

Kagan, S., & Madsen, M. C. Cooperation and competition of Mexican, Mexican-American, and Anglo-American children of two ages under four instructional sets. *Developmental Psychology*, 1971, *5*, 32–39.

Kagan, S., & Madsen, M. C. Rivalry in Anglo-American and Mexican children of two ages. *Journal of Personality and Social Psychology*, 1972, *24*, 214–220.

Kagan, S., Zahn, G. L., & Gealy, J. Competition and school achievement among Anglo-American and Mexican-American children. *Journal of Educational Psychology*, 1977, *69*, 432–441.

Kail, R. V. Familiarity and attraction to pictures of children's faces. *Developmental Psychology*, 1977, *13*, 289–290.

Kandel, D. Adolescent marihuana use: Role of parents and peers. *Science*, 1973, *181*, 1067–1070.

Kandel, D. Homophily, selection, and socialization in adolescent friendships. *American Journal of Sociology*, 1978, *84*, 427–436. (a)

Kandel, D. B. Similarity in real-life adolescent friendship pairs. *Journal of Personality and Social Psychology*, 1978, *36*, 306–312. (b)

Kandel, D., & Lesser, G. S. *Youth in two worlds*. San Francisco: Jossey-Bass, 1972.

Kaplan, H. K., & Kaufman, I. Sociometric status and behaviors of emotionally disturbed children. *Psychology in the Schools*, 1978, *15*, 8–15.

Karabenick, J. D., & Miller, S. A. The effects of age, sex, and listener feedback on grade school children's referential communication. *Child Development*, 1977, *48*, 678–683.

Karen, R. L. *Operant conditioning and social preference*. Unpublished doctoral dissertation, Arizona State University, 1965.

Keasey, C. B. Social participation as a factor in the moral development of preadolescents. *Developmental Psychology*, 1971, *5*, 216–220.

Keislar, E. R. A distinction between social acceptance and prestige among adolescents. *Child Development*, 1953, *24*, 275–284.

Kinney, E. E. A study of peer-group social acceptability at the fifth grade level in a public school. *Journal of Educational Research*, 1953, *47*, 57–64.

Kinsey, A. C., Pomeroy, W. B., & Martin, C. E. *Sexual behavior in the human male*. Philadelphia: Saunders, 1948.

Klaus, R. A. *Interrelationships of attributes that accepted and rejected children ascribe to their peers*. Unpublished doctoral dissertation, George Peabody College for Teachers, 1959.

Klein, A. R., & Young, R. D. Hyperactive boys in the classroom: Assessment of teacher and peer perceptions, interactions, and classroom behaviors. *Journal of Abnormal Child Psychology*, 1979, *7*, 425–442.

Klinger, E., & McNelly, F. W. Self states and performances of preadolescent boys carrying out leadership roles inconsistent with their social status. *Child Development*, 1976, *47*, 126–137.

Knight, G. P., & Kagan, S. Acculturation of prosocial and competitive behaviors among second- and third-generation Mexican-American children. *Journal of Cross-cultural Psychology*, 1977, *8*, 273–284.

Kobasigawa, A. Inhibitory and disinhibitory effects of models on sex-inappropriate behavior in children. *Psychologia*, 1968, *11*, 86–96.

Koch, H. L. Popularity in preschool children: Some related factors and a technique for its measurement. *Child Development*, 1933, *4*, 164–175.

Kogan, N., & Wallach, M. A. Modification of a judgmental style through group interaction. *Journal of Personality and Social Psychology*, 1966, *4*, 165–174.

Kohn, M. The child as a determinant of his peers' approach to him. *Journal of Genetic Psychology*, 1966, *109*, 91–100.

Konner, M. Relations among infants and juveniles in comparative perspective. In M. Lewis & L. A. Rosenblum (Eds.), *Friendship and peer relations*. New York: Wiley, 1975.

Kopfstein, D. Effects of accelerating and decelerating consequences on the social behavior of trainable retarded children. *Child Development*, 1972, *43*, 800–809.

Krauss, R. M., & Glucksberg, S. The development of communication: Competence as a function of age. *Child Development*, 1969, *40*, 255–266.

Krisberg, B. Gang youth and hustling: The psychology of survival. *Issues in Criminology*, 1974, *9*, 115–131.

Ladd, G. W., & Oden, S. The relationship between peer acceptance and children's ideas about helpfulness. *Child Development*, 1979, *50*, 402–408.

Lakin, D. S. Cross-age tutoring with Mexican-American pupils. Unpublished doctoral dissertation, University of California at Los Angeles, 1971.

Lakin, M., Lakin, M. G., & Costanzo, P. R. Group processes in early childhood: A dimension of human development. *International Journal of Behavioral Development*, 1979, *2*, 171–183.

Lamb, M. E., Easterbrooks, M. A., & Holden, G. W. Reinforcement and punishment among preschoolers: Characteristics, effects, and correlates. *Child Development*, 1980, *51*, 1230–1236.

Lamb, M. E., & Roopnarine, J. L. Peer influences on sex-role development in preschoolers. *Child Development*, 1979, *50*, 1219–1222.

Landsbaum, J. B., & Willis, R. H. Conformity in early and late adolescence. *Developmental Psychology*, 1971, *4*, 334–337.

Lane, I. M., & Coon, R. C. Reward allocation in preschool children. *Child Development*, 1972, *43*, 1382–1389.

Langlois, J. H., & Downs, A. C. Peer relations as a function of physical attractiveness: The eye of the beholder or behavioral reality? *Child Development*, 1979, *50*, 409–418.

Langlois, J. H., Gottfried, N. W., Barnes, B. M., & Hendricks, D. E. The effect of peer age on the social behavior of preschool children. *Journal of Genetic Psychology*, 1978, *132*, 11–19.

Langlois, J. H., Gottfried, N. W., & Seay, B. The influence of sex of peer on the social behavior of preschool children. *Developmental Psychology*, 1973, *8*, 93–98.

Langlois, J. H., & Stephan, C. The effects of physical attractiveness and ethnicity on children's behavioral attributions and peer preferences. *Child Development*, 1977, *48*, 1694–1698.

Langlois, J. H., & Stephan, C. Beauty and the beast: The role of physical attractiveness in the development of peer relations and social behavior. In S. S. Brehm, S. H. Kassin, and F. X. Gibbons (Eds.), *Developmental social psychology*. New York: Oxford University Press, 1981.

Langlois, J. H., & Styczynski, L. E. The effects of physical attractiveness on the behavioral attributions and peer preferences of acquainted children. *International Journal of Behavioral Development*, 1979, *2*, 325–342.

Langworthy, R. L. Community status and influence in a high school. *American Sociological Review*, 1959, *24*, 537–539.

Larson, L. E. The influence of parents and peers during adolescence: The situation hypothesis revisited. *Journal of Marriage and the Family*, 1972, *34*, 67–74.

Lee, L. C. *Social encounters of infants: The beginnings of popularity*. Paper presented at the meeting of the International Society for the Study of Behavioral Development, Ann Arbor, Michigan, August 1973.

Leimbach, M. P., & Hartup, W. W. Forming cooperative coalitions during a competitive game in same-sex and mixed-sex triads. *Journal of Genetic Psychology*, 1981, *139*, 165–171.

Lerner, M. J. The justice motive: ''Equity'' and ''parity'' among children. *Journal of Personality and Social Psychology*, 1974, *29*, 539–550.

Lerner, R. M., & Lerner, J. V. Effects of age, sex, and physical attractiveness on child-peer relations, academic performance, and elementary school adjustment. *Developmental Psychology*, 1977, *13*, 585–590.

Lesser, G. S. The relationships between various forms of aggression and popularity among lower-class children. *Journal of Educational Psychology*, 1959, *50*, 20–25.

Lesser, G. S., & Abelson, R. P. Personality correlates of persuasibility in children. In C. I. Hovland & I. L. Janis (Eds.), *Personality and persuasibility*. New Haven: Yale University Press, 1959.

Leuba, C. An experimental study of rivalry in young children. *Journal of Comparative Psychology*, 1933, *16*, 367–378.

Leventhal, G. S., & Anderson, D. Self interest and the maintenance of equity. *Journal of Personality and Social Psychology*, 1970, *15*, 57–62.

Leventhal, G. S., Popp, A., & Sawyer, L. Equity or equality in children's allocation of reward to other persons? *Child Development*, 1973, *44*, 753–763.

Lever, J. Sex differences in the games children play. *Social Problems*, 1976, *23*, 479–487.

Levine, M. H., & Sutton-Smith, B. Effects of age, sex, and task on visual behavior during dyadic interaction. *Developmental Psychology*, 1973, *9*, 400–405.

Lewin, K., Lippitt, R., & White, R. K. Patterns of aggressive behavior in experimentally created

''social climates.'' *Journal of Social Psychology*, 1938, *10*, 271–299.

Lewis, M., & Brooks, J. Infants' social perception: A constructivist view. In L. Cohen & P. Salapatek (Eds.), *Infant perception: From sensation to cognition* (Vol. 2). New York: Academic Press, 1975.

Lewis, M., & Rosenblum, L. A. *Friendship and peer relations*. New York: Wiley, 1975.

Lewis, M., Young, G., Brooks, J., & Michalson, L. The beginning of friendship. In M. Lewis & L. A. Rosenblum (Eds.), *Friendship and peer relations*. New York: Wiley, 1975.

Libby, R. W., Gray, L., & White, M. A test and reformulation of reference group and role correlates of premarital sexual permissiveness theory. *Journal of Marriage and the Family*, 1978, *40*, 79–92.

Lieberman, A. F. Preschoolers' competence with a peer: Relations with attachment and peer experience. *Child Development*, 1977, *48*, 1277–1287.

Linton, T. *Effects of grade displacement between students tutored and student tutors*. Unpublished doctoral dissertation, University of Cincinnati, 1972.

Lippitt, R. Popularity among preschool children. *Child Development*, 1941, *12*, 305–322.

Lippitt, R., Polansky, N., & Rosen, S. The dynamics of power: A field study of social influence in groups of children. *Human Relations*, 1952, *5*, 37–64.

Lippitt, R., & White, R. K. The ''social climate'' of children's groups. In R. G. Barker, J. S. Kounin, & H. F. Wright (Eds.), *Child Behavior and Development*. New York: McGraw-Hill, 1943.

Lippitt, R., & White, R. K. An experimental study of leadership and group life. In E. E. Maccoby, T. M. Newcomb, & E. L. Hartley (Eds.), *Readings in Social Psychology*. New York: Holt, 1958.

Littrell, M. B., & Eicher, J. B. Clothing opinions and the social acceptance process among adolescents. *Adolescence*, 1973, *8*, 197–212.

Loban, W. A. A study of social sensitivity (sympathy) among adolescents. *Journal of Educational Psychology*, 1953, *44*, 102–112.

Lohman, J. E. *Age, sex, socioeconomic status and youths' relationships with older and younger peers*. Unpublished doctoral dissertation, University of Michigan, 1969.

Loo, C. M. The effects of spatial density on the social behavior of children. *Journal of Applied Social Psychology*, 1972, *2*, 372–381.

Lott, A. J., & Lott, B. E. Group cohesiveness and individual learning. *Journal of Educational Psychology*, 1966, *57*, 61–73.

Lott, B. E., & Lott, A. J. The formation of positive attitudes towards group members. *Journal of Abnormal and Social Psychology*, 1960, *61*, 297–300.

Lougee, M. D., Grueneich, R., & Hartup, W. W. Social interaction in same- and mixed-age dyads of preschool children. *Child Development*, 1977, *48*, 1353–1361.

Ludeke, R. J. *Teaching behaviors of 11-year-old and 9-year-old girls in same-age and mixed-age dyads*. Unpublished doctoral dissertation, University of Minnesota, 1978.

Maccoby, E. E., & Jacklin, C. N. *The psychology of sex differences*. Stanford, Calif.: Stanford University Press, 1974.

MacNeil, M. K., & Pace, D. Differential adoption of norms by high-status and low-status members of informal groups. *Perceptual and Motor Skills*, 1973, *36*, 1275–1283.

Mainville, F., & Friedman, R. J. Peer relations of hyperactive children. *The Ontario Psychologist*, 1976, *8*, 17–20.

Margolin, E. What do group values mean to young children? *Elementary School Journal*, 1969, *69*, 250–258.

Marks, J. B. Interests, leadership, and sociometric status among adolescents. *Sociometry*, 1954, *17*, 340–349.

Marsden, G., & Kalter, N. Children's understanding of their emotionally disturbed peers: I. The concept of emotional disturbance. *Psychiatry*, 1976, *39*, 227–238.

Marshall, H. R. Relations between home experiences and children's use of language in play interactions with peers. *Psychological Monographs*, 1961, *7*(Whole No. 509).

Marshall, H. R., & McCandless, B. R. A study in prediction of social behavior of preschool children. *Child Development*, 1957, *28*, 149–159. (a)

Marshall, H. R., & McCandless, B. R. Relationships between dependence on adults and social acceptance by peers. *Child Development*, 1957, *28*, 413–419. (b)

Martino, L., & Johnson, D. W. Cooperative and individualistic experiences among disabled and normal children. *Journal of Social Psychology*, 1979, *107*, 177–183.

Masters, J. C., Ford, M. E., Arend, R., Grotevant, H. D., & Clark, L. V. Modeling and labeling as integrated determinants of children's sex-typed imitative behavior. *Child Development*, 1979, *50*, 364–371.

Masters, J. C., & Furman, W. Popularity, individual friendship selections, and specific peer interaction among children. *Developmental Psychology*, 1981, *17*, 344–350.

Masur, E. F. Preschool boys' speech modifications: The effect of listeners' linguistic levels and conversational responsiveness. *Child Development*, 1978, *49*, 924–927.

Maudry, M., & Nekula, M. Social relations between children of the same age during the first two years of life. *Journal of Genetic Psychology*, 1939, *54*, 193–215.

Mazur, A. A cross-species comparison of status in small established groups. *American Sociological Review*, 1973, *38*, 513–530.

McCandless, B. R., & Hoyt, J. M. Sex, ethnicity and play preferences of preschool children. *Journal of Abnormal and Social Psychology*, 1961, *62*, 683–685.

McCandless, B. R., & Marshall, H. R. A picture sociometric technique for preschool children and its relation to teacher judgments of friendship. *Child Development*, 1957, *28*, 139–148. (a)

McCandless, B. R., & Marshall, H. R. Sex differences in social acceptance and participation of preschool children. *Child Development*, 1957, *28*, 421–425. (b)

McClintock, C. G. Development of social motives in Anglo-American and Mexican-American children. *Journal of Personality and Social Psychology*, 1974, *29*, 348–354.

McClintock, C. G., & Moskowitz, J. M. Children's preferences for individualistic, cooperative, and competitive outcomes. *Journal of Personality and Social Psychology*, 1976, *34*, 543–555.

McClintock, C. G., Moskowitz, J. M., & McClintock, E. Variations in preferences for individualistic, competitive, and cooperative outcomes as a function of age, game class, and task in nursery social children. *Child Development*, 1977, *48*, 1080–1085.

McConnell, T. R. Suggestibility in children as a function of chronological age. *Journal of Abnormal Psychology*, 1963, *67*, 286–289.

McCord, W., McCord, J., & Zola, I. K. *Origins of crime*. New York: Columbia University Press, 1959.

McDavid, J. W. Personality and situational determinants of conformity. *Journal of Abnormal and Social Psychology*, 1959, *58*, 241–246.

McDavid, J. W., & Harari, H. Stereotyping of names and popularity in grade-school children.

Child Development, 1966, *37*, 453–459.

McGrew, P. L. Social and spatial density effects on spacing behaviour in preschool children. *Journal of Child Psychology and Psychiatry*, 1970, *11*, 197–205.

McGrew, W. C. *An ethological study of children's behaviour*. New York: Academic Press, 1972.

McGurk, H. *Issues in childhood social development*. London: Methuen, 1978.

McMichael, P. Reading difficulties, behavior, and social status. *Journal of Educational Psychology*, 1980, *72*, 76–86.

Mednick, S. A., & Schulsinger, F. Factors related to breakdown in children at high risk for schizophrenia. In M. Roff & D. F. Ricks (Eds.), *Life history research in psychopathology*. Minneapolis: University of Minnesota Press, 1970.

Medrich, E. A., Rosen, J., Rubin, V., & Buckley, S. *The serious business of growing up*. Berkeley: University of California Press, 1982.

Medway, F. J. Attributional determinants of teaching and learning in cross-age tutoring. *Psychological Reports*, 1977, *41*, 71–76.

Melburg, V., McCabe, A. E., & Kobasigawa, A. *Young boys' selection of helping strategies under situational constraints*. Unpublished manuscript, University of Windsor, 1980.

Melson, G. F. Sex differences in use of indoor space by preschool children. *Perceptual and Motor Skills*, 1977, *44*, 207–213.

Merei, F. Group leadership and institutionalization. *Human Relations*, 1949, *2*, 23–39.

Michael, C., Morris, D. P., & Sorokor, E. Follow-up studies of shy, withdrawn children: II. Relative incidence of schizophrenia. *American Journal of Orthopsychiatry*, 1957, *27*, 331–337.

Milich, R. *Hyperactivity, aggression, and peer status*. Paper presented at the meeting of the American Psychological Association, Montreal, September 1980.

Miller, A. G., & Thomas, R. Cooperation and competition among Blackfoot Indian and urban Canadian children. *Child Development*, 1972, *43*, 1104–1110.

Miller, N., & Maruyama, G. Ordinal position and peer popularity. *Journal of Personality and Social Psychology*, 1976, *33*, 123–131.

Miller, N. E., & Dollard, J. *Social learning and imitation*. New Haven, Conn.: Yale University Press, 1941.

Miller, P. Y., & Simon, W. The development of sexuality in adolescence. In J. Adelson (Ed.), *Handbook of Adolescent Psychology*. New York: Wiley, 1980.

Mithaug, D. E. The development of cooperation in alternative task situations. *Journal of Experimental Child Psychology*, 1969, *8*, 443–460.

Mollod, R. W. *Pupil tutoring as part of reading instruction in the elementary grades*. Unpublished doctoral dissertation, Columbia University, 1970.

Moore, S. G. Correlates of peer acceptance in nursery school children. In W. W. Hartup & N. L. Smothergill (Eds.), *The young child*. Washington, D.C.: National Association for the Education of Young Children, 1967.

Moore, S. G., & Updegraff, R. Sociometric status of preschool children as related to age, sex, nurturance-giving, and dependence. *Child Development*, 1964, *35*, 519–524.

Moreno, J. L. *Who shall survive?* Washington, D.C.: Nervous and Mental Disease Publishing Company, 1934.

Morgan, R. F., & Toy, T. B. Learning by teaching: A student to student compensatory tutoring program in a rural school system and its relevance to the educational cooperative. *Psychological Record*, 1970, *20*, 159–169.

Morgan, W. R., & Sawyer, J. Bargaining, expectations and the preference for equality over equity. *Journal of Personality and Social Psychology*, 1967, *6*, 139–149.

Morland, J. K. Racial self-identification: A study of nursery school children. *The American Catholic Sociological Review*, 1963, *24*, 231–242.

Morland, J. K. A comparison of race awareness in northern and southern children. *American Journal of Orthopsychiatry*, 1966, *36*, 22–31.

Morris, W. N., Marshall, H. M., & Miller, R. S. The effect of vicarious punishment on prosocial behavior in children. *Journal of Experimental Child Psychology*, 1973, *85*, 317–318.

Mueller, E. The maintenance of verbal exchanges between young children. *Child Development*, 1972, *43*, 930–938.

Mueller, E., & Brenner, J. The origins of social skills and interaction among playgroup toddlers. *Child Development*, 1977, *48*, 854–861.

Mueller, E., & Rich, A. Clustering and socially-directed behaviors in a play-group of 1-year-old boys. *Journal of Child Psychology and Psychiatry*, 1976, *17*, 315–322.

Munroe, R. L., & Munroe, R. H. Cooperation and competition among East African and American children. *Journal of Social Psychology*, 1977, *101*, 145–146.

Nelson, L., & Madsen, M. C. Cooperation and competition in four-year-olds as a function of reward. *Developmental Psychology*, 1969, *1*, 340–344.

Nelson, S. A., & Dweck, C. S. Motivation and competence as determinants of young children's reward allocation. *Developmental Psychology*, 1977, *13*, 192–197.

Newcomb, A. F., & Brady, J. E. Mutuality in boy's friendship relations. *Child Development*, 1982, *53*, 392–395.

Newcomb, A. F., Brady, J. E., & Hartup, W. W. Friendship and incentive condition as determinants of children's task-oriented social behavior. *Child Development*, 1979, *50*, 878–881.

Northway, M. Social relationships among preschool children: Abstracts and interrelationships of three studies. *Sociometry*, 1943, *6*, 492–433.

Northway, M. Outsiders: A study of the personality patterns of children least acceptable to their age mates. *Sociometry*, 1944, *7*, 10–25.

Nucci, L. P., & Turiel, E. Social interactions and the development of social concepts in preschool children. *Child Development*, 1978, *49*, 400–407.

O'Connor, R. Modification of social withdrawal through symbolic modeling. *Journal of Applied Behavior Analysis*, 1969, *2*, 15–22.

Olweus, D. Aggression and peer acceptance in adolescent boys: Two short-term longitudinal studies of ratings. *Child Development*, 1977, *48*, 1301–1313.

Omark, D. R., Omark, M., & Edelman, M. S. *Formation of dominance hierarchies in young children*. Paper presented at the IXth International Congress of Anthropological and Ethological Sciences, Chicago, 1973.

Omark, D. R., Strayer, F. F., & Freedman, D. G. *Dominance relations*. New York: Garland, 1980.

Page, I. A. *The effects of peer tutoring on sight word gains of primary pupils*. Unpublished doctoral dissertation, University of Illinois at Urbana-Champaign, 1975.

Page, M. L. The modification of ascendant behavior in preschool children. *University of Iowa Studies in Child Welfare*, 1936, *12*(3), 1–69.

Paoni, F. J. *Reciprocal effects of sixth-graders tutoring third-graders in reading*. Unpublished doctoral dissertation, Oregon State University, 1971.

Parten, M. B. Social participation among preschool children. *Journal of Abnormal and Social Psychology*, 1932, *27*, 243–269.

Pasternack, T. Qualitative differences in development of yielding behavior by elementary school children. *Psychological Reports*, 1973, *32*, 883–896.

Pastor, D. L. The quality of mother-infant attachment and its relationship to toddlers' initial sociability with peers. *Developmental Psychology*, 1981, *17*, 326–335.

Patel, H. S., & Gordon, J. E. Some personal and situational determinants of yielding to influence. *Journal of Abnormal and Social Psychology*, 1960, *61*, 411–418.

Patterson, G. R., Littman, R. A., & Bricker, W. Assertive behavior in children: A step toward a theory of aggression. *Monographs of the Society for Research in Child Development*, 1967, *32*(5, Serial No. 113).

Peck, C. A., Apolloni, T., Cooke, T. P., & Raver, S. A. Teaching retarded preschoolers to imitate the free play behavior of nonretarded classmates: Trained and generalized effects. *Journal of Special Education*, 1978, *12*, 195–207.

Peery, J. C. Popular, amiable, isolated, rejected: A reconceptualization of sociometric status in preschool children. *Child Development*, 1979, *50*, 1231–1234.

Peifer, M. *The effects of varying age-grade status of models on the imitative behavior of six-year-old boys*. Unpublished doctoral dissertation, University of Delaware, 1971.

Pelham, W. E., & Bender, M. E. Peer relationships in hyperactive children: Description and treatment. In K. D. Gadow & I. Bialer (Eds.), *Advances in learning and behavior disabilities*. Greenwich, Conn.: JAI Press, 1982.

Peters, R. W., & Torrance, E. P. Dyadic interaction of preschool children and performance on a construction task. *Psychological Reports*, 1972, *30*, 747–750.

Phillips, B. N., & D'Amico, L. H. Effects of cooperation and competition on the cohesiveness of small face-to-face groups. *Journal of Educational Psychology*, 1956, *47*, 65–70.

Philp, A. J. Strangers and friends as competitors and co-operators. *Journal of Genetic Psychology*, 1940, *57*, 249–258.

Piaget, J. *The moral judgment of the child*. Glencoe, Ill.: Free Press, 1932.

Piché, G. L., Rubin, D. L., & Michlin, M. L. Age and social class in children's use of persuasive communicative appeals. *Child Development*, 1978, *49*, 773–780.

Polansky, N., Lippitt, R., & Redl, F. An investigation of behavior contagion in groups. *Human Relations*, 1950, *3*, 319–348.

Pope, B. Socioeconomic contrasts in children's peer

culture prestige values. *Genetic Psychology Monographs*, 1953, *48*, 157–220.

Preiser, W. F. E. Work in progress: Behavior of nursery school children under different spatial densities. *Man-environment Systems*, 1972, *2*, 247–250.

Price, J. M. *The effects of crowding on the social behavior of children*. Unpublished doctoral dissertation, Columbia University, 1971.

Radke, M., Sutherland, J., & Rosenberg, P. Racial attitudes of children. *Sociometry*, 1950, *13*, 154–171.

Rajecki, D. W., Lamb, M. E., & Suomi, S. J. Effects of multiple peer separation in domestic chicks. *Developmental Psychology*, 1978, *14*, 379–387.

Read, P. B. Source of authority and the legitimation of leadership in small groups. *Sociometry*, 1974, *37*, 189–204.

Reese, H. W. Relationship between self-acceptance and sociometric choice. *Journal of Abnormal and Social Psychology*, 1961, *62*, 472–474.

Reisman, J. M., & Shorr, S. I. Friendship claims and expectations among children and adults. *Child Development*, 1978, *49*, 913–916.

Renshaw, P. D. The roots of peer interaction research: A historical analysis of the 1930's. In S. R. Asher & J. M. Gottman (Eds.), *The development of children's friendships*. New York: Cambridge University Press, 1981.

Renz, P., & Simensen, R. J. The social perception of normals toward their EMR grade-mates. *American Journal of Mental Deficiency*, 1969, *74*, 405–408.

Rheingold, H. L., & Cook, K. V. The content of boys' and girls' rooms as an index of parents' behavior. *Child Development*, 1975, *46*, 459–463.

Richardson, S. A., Goodman, U., Hastorf, A. H., & Dornbusch, S. A. Cultural uniformity in reaction to physical disabilities. *American Sociological Review*, 1961, *26*, 241–247.

Richman, N., Stevenson, J. E., & Graham, P. J. *Preschool to school: A behavioural study*. London: Academic Press, 1982.

Richmond, B. O., & Vance, J. J. Cooperative-competitive game strategy and personality characteristics of black and white children. *Interpersonal Development*, 1974–1975, *5*, 78–85.

Richmond, B. O., & Weiner, G. P. Cooperation and competition among young children as a function of ethnic grouping, grade, sex, and reward condition. *Journal of Educational Psychology*, 1973, *64*, 329–334.

Ridberg, E. H., Parke, R. D., & Hetherington, E. M. Modification of impulsive and reflective cognitive styles through observation of film-mediated models. *Developmental Psychology*, 1971, *5*, 369–377.

Robertson, D. J. *The effects of intergrade tutoring experience on tutor attitudes and reading achievement*. Unpublished doctoral dissertation, University of Oregon, 1971.

Robins, L. *Deviant children grown up*. Baltimore: Williams and Wilkins, 1966.

Rocha, R., & Rogers, R. W. Ares and Babbitt in the classroom: Effects of competition and reward on children's aggression. *Journal of Personality and Social Psychology*, 1976, *33*, 588–593.

Rodnick, E. H., & Goldstein, M. J. A research strategy for studying risk for schizophrenia during adolescence and early adulthood. In J. Anthony & C. Koupernick (Eds.), *The child in his family: Children at psychiatric risk* (Vol. 3). New York: Wiley, 1974.

Roff, M. Childhood social interactions and young adult bad conduct. *Journal of Abnormal and Social Psychology*, 1961, *63*, 333–337.

Roff, M. Childhood social interaction and young adult psychosis. *Journal of Clinical Psychology*, 1963, *19*, 152–157.

Roff, M. *Some developmental aspects of schizoid personality*. U.S. Army Medical Research and Developmental Command, Report No. 65-4, March 1965.

Roff, M. *Some childhood and adolescent characteristics of adult homosexuals*. U.S. Army Medical Research and Developmental Command, Report No. 66-5, May 1966.

Roff, M. Some life history factors in relation to various types of adult maladjustment. In M. Roff & D. F. Ricks (Eds.), *Life history research in psychopathology* (Vol. 1). Minneapolis: University of Minnesota Press, 1970.

Roff, M., & Sells, S. B. The relation between the status of chooser and chosen in a sociometric situation at the grade school level. *Psychology in the Schools*, 1967, *4*, 101–111.

Roff, M., & Sells, S. B. Juvenile delinquency in relation to peer acceptance-rejection and socioeconomic status. *Psychology in the Schools*, 1968, *5*, 3–18.

Roff, M., Sells, S. B., & Golden, M. M. *Social adjustment and personality development in children*. Minneapolis: University of Minnesota Press, 1972.

Rogers, M. S. *A study of an experimental tutorial reading program in which sixth-grade under-*

achievers tutored third-grade children who were experiencing difficulty in reading. Unpublished doctoral dissertation, University of Alabama, 1969.

Rohe, W. M., & Patterson, A. H. The effects of varied levels of resources and density on behavior in a day care center. Paper presented at the conference of the Environmental Design Research Association, Milwaukee, April 1974.

Rolf, J. E. The social and academic competence of children vulnerable to schizophrenia and other behavior pathologies. Journal of Abnormal Psychology, 1972, 80, 225–243.

Roper, R., & Hinde, R. A. Social behavior in a play group: Consistency and complexity. Child Development, 1978, 49, 570–579.

Rosekrans, M. A. Imitation in children as a function of perceived similarity to a social model and vicarious reinforcement. Journal of Personality and Social Psychology, 1967, 7, 307–315.

Rosen, B. C. Conflicting group membership: A study of parent-peer group cross-pressures. American Sociological Review, 1955, 20, 155–161.

Rosén, L. A. Sociometric effects of a peer interaction therapy for social isolation. Unpublished undergraduate thesis, University of Minnesota, 1978.

Rosen, S., Levinger, G., & Lippitt, R. Perceived sources of social power. Journal of Abnormal and Social Psychology, 1961, 62, 439–441.

Ross, H. S., & Goldman, B. M. Establishing new social relations in infancy. In T. Alloway, L. Krames, & P. Pliner (Eds.), Advances in communication and affect (Vol. 4). New York: Plenum Press, 1976.

Ross, S. A. A test of the generality of the effects of deviant preschool models. Developmental Psychology, 1971, 4, 262–267.

Rubenstein, J., & Howes, C. The effects of peers on toddler interaction with mothers and toys. Child Development, 1976, 47, 597–605.

Rubenstein, J. L., & Howes, C. Effects of presence of peer's mother on toddler-peer interaction. Unpublished manuscript, Tufts University, 1979.

Rubin, K. H. Relationship between egocentric communication and popularity among peers. Developmental Psychology, 1972, 7, 364.

Rubin, K. H. The social and cognitive value of preschool toys and activities. Canadian Journal of Behavioral Science/Review of Canadian Science, 1977, 9, 382–385.

Rubin, K. H., & Ross, H. S. (Eds.). Peer relation-ships and social skills in childhood. New York: Springer-Verlag, 1982.

Rubin, K. H., Watson, K. S., & Jambor, T. W. Free-play behaviors in preschool and kindergarten children. Child Development, 1978, 49, 534–536.

Rubin, Z. Children's friendships. Cambridge, Mass.: Harvard University Press, 1980.

Sandis, E. The transmission of mothers' educational ambitions, as related to specific socialization techniques. Journal of Marriage and the Family, 1970, 32, 204–211.

Savin-Williams, R. C. Dominance hierarchies in groups of early adolescents. Child Development, 1979, 50, 142–151.

Savin-Williams, R. C. Dominance hierarchies in groups of middle to late adolescent males. Journal of Youth and Adolescence, 1980, 9, 75–85. (a)

Savin-Williams, R. C. Social interactions of adolescent females in natural groups. In H. C. Foot, A. J. Chapman, & J. R. Smith (Eds.), Friendship and social relations in children. New York: Wiley, 1980. (b)

Savitsky, J. C., & Watson, M. J. Patterns of proxemic behavior among preschool children. Representative Research in Social Psychology, 1975, 6, 109–113.

Schachter, S. Birth order and sociometric choice. Journal of Abnormal and Social Psychology, 1964, 68, 453–456.

Schleifer, M., Weiss, G., Cohen, N., Elman, M., Cvejic, H., & Kruger, E. Hyperactivity in preschoolers and the effect of methylphenidate. American Journal of Orthopsychiatry, 1975, 45, 38–50.

Schofield, J. W. School desegregation and intergroup relations. In D. Bar-Tal & L. Saxe (Eds.), Social psychology of education. New York: Wiley, 1978.

Schofield, J. W., & Sagar, H. A. Peer interaction patterns in an integrated middle school. Sociometry, 1977, 40, 130–138.

Schroeder, R., & Flapan, D. Aggressive and friendly behaviors of young children from two social classes. Child Psychiatry and Human Development, 1971, 2, 32–41.

Schulz, B., Bohrnstedt, G. W., Borgatta, E. F., & Evans, R. R. Explaining pre-marital sexual intercourse among college students: A causal mode. Social Forces, 1977, 56, 148–165.

Schunke, G. M. Social effects of classroom organization. Journal of Educational Research, 1978, 11, 303–307.

Schwartz, J. C. Effects of peer familiarity on the behavior of preschoolers in a novel situation. *Journal of Personality and Social Psychology*, 1972, *24*, 276–284.

Scofield, R. W. Task productivity of groups of friends and non-friends. *Psychological Reports*, 1960, *6*, 459–460.

Sears, P. S., & Sherman, V. S. *In pursuit of self-esteem*. Belmont, Calif.: Wadsworth, 1964.

Sears, R. R., Rau, L., & Alpert, R. *Identification and child rearing*. Stanford, Calif.: Stanford University Press, 1965.

Sears, R. R., Whiting, J. W. M., Nowlis, V., & Sears, P. S. Some child-rearing antecedents of aggression and dependency in young children. *Genetic Psychology Monographs*, 1953, *47*, 135–234.

Sells, S. B., & Roff, M. Peer acceptance—rejection and birth order. *Psychology in the Schools*, 1964, *1*, 156–162.

Selman, R. L. *The growth of interpersonal understanding*. New York: Academic Press, 1980.

Selman, R. L., & Jaquette, D. Stability and oscillation in interpersonal awareness: A clinical-developmental analysis. In C. B. Keasey (Ed.), *Nebraska Symposium on Motivation* (Vol. 25). Lincoln: University of Nebraska Press, 1977.

Serbin, L. A., Tonick, I. J., & Sternglanz, S. H. Shaping cooperative cross-sex play. *Child Development*, 1977, *48*, 924–929.

Sgan, M. L., & Pickert, S. M. Cross-sex and same-sex assertive bids in a cooperative group task. *Child Development*, 1980, *51*, 928–931.

Shapira, A. Developmental differences in competitive behavior of Kibbutz and city children in Israel. *Journal of Social Psychology*, 1976, *98*, 19–26.

Shapira, A., & Madsen, M. C. Between- and within-group cooperation and competition among Kibbutz and non-Kibbutz children. *Developmental Psychology*, 1974, *10*, 140–145.

Shatz, M., & Gelman, R. The development of communication skills: Modification in the speech of young children as a function of listener. *Monographs of the Society for Research in Child Development*, 1973, *38*(Whole No. 152).

Shaw, M. E., & Shaw, L. M. Some effects of sociometric grouping upon learning in a second grade classroom. *Journal of Social Psychology*, 1962, *57*, 453–458.

Sherif, M., Harvey, O. J., White, B. J., Hood, W. R., & Sherif, C. W. *Inter-group conflict and cooperation: The Robbers Cave experiment*. Norman: University of Oklahoma Press, 1961.

Sherif, M., & Sherif, C. W. *Groups in harmony and tension*. New York: Harper, 1953.

Sherif, M., & Sherif, C. W. *Reference groups*. New York: Harper & Row, 1964.

Sherif, M., & Sherif, C. W. Adolescent attitudes and behavior in their reference groups within differing sociocultural settings. In J. P. Hill (Ed.), *Minnesota Symposia on Child Psychology* (Vol. 3). Minneapolis: University of Minnesota Press, 1969.

Shirley, M. *The first two years: A study of twenty-five babies* (Vol. 2). Minneapolis: University of Minnesota Press, 1933.

Shure, M. B. Psychological ecology of a nursery school. *Child Development*, 1963, *34*, 979–992.

Siman, M. L. Application of a new model of peer group influence to naturally existing adolescent friendship groups. *Child Development*, 1977, *48*, 270–274.

Singer, A. J. Certain aspects of personality and their relation to certain group modes, and constancy of friendship choices. *Journal of Educational Research*, 1951, *45*, 33–42.

Singleton, L. C., & Asher, S. R. Racial integration and children's peer preferences: An investigation of developmental and cohort differences. *Child Development*, 1979, *50*, 936–941.

Skarin, K., & Moely, B. E. Altruistic behavior: An analysis of age and sex differences. *Child Development*, 1976, *47*, 1159–1165.

Slaby, R. G., & Frey, K. S. Development of gender constancy and selective attention to same-sex models. *Child Development*, 1975, *46*, 849–856.

Slaby, R. G., & Parke, R. D. Effect on resistence to deviation of observing a model's affective reaction to response consequences. *Developmental Psychology*, 1971, *5*, 40–47.

Sluckin, A. M., & Smith, P. K. Two approaches to the concept of dominance in preschool children. *Child Development*, 1977, *48*, 917–923.

Smilansky, S. *The effects of sociodramatic play on disadvantaged children*. New York: Wiley, 1968.

Smith, A. J. A developmental study of group processes. *Journal of Genetic Psychology*, 1960, *97*, 29–39.

Smith, G. H. Sociometric study of best-liked and least-liked children. *Elementary School Journal*, 1950, *51*, 77–85.

Smith, H. W. Some developmental interpersonal dynamics through childhood. *American Sociological Review*, 1973, *38*, 543–352.

Smith, J. R., Foot, H. C., & Chapman, A. J. Nonverbal communication among friends and strangers sharing humor. In A. J. Chapman & H. C. Foot (Eds.), *It's a funny thing, humor.* Oxford, England: Pergamon, 1977.

Smith, P. K. A longitudinal study of social participation in preschool children: Solitary and parallel play reexamined. *Developmental Psychology,* 1978, *14,* 517–523.

Smith, P. K., & Connolly, K. Patterns of play and social interaction in preschool children. In N. Blurton Jones (Ed.), *Ethological studies of child behavior.* Cambridge, England: Cambridge University Press, 1972.

Smith, P. K., & Connolly, K. J. Social and aggressive behaviour in preschool children as a function of crowding. *Social Science Information,* 1977, *16,* 601–620.

Smith, P. K., & Connolly, K. J. *The ecology of preschool behaviour.* Cambridge, England: Cambridge University Press, 1981.

Snapp, M., Oakland, T., & Williams, F. C. A study of individualizing instruction by using elementary school children as tutors. *Journal of School Psychology,* 1972, *10,* 1–8.

Snow, C. E. Mother's speech to children learning language. *Child Development,* 1972, *43,* 549–565.

Solomon, R. G., & Wahler, R. Peer reinforcement control of classroom problem behavior. *Journal of Applied Behavior Analysis,* 1973, *6,* 49–56.

Sorokin, P. A., Tranquist, M., Parten, M., & Zimmerman, C. C. An experimental study of efficiency of work under various specified conditions. *American Journal of Sociology,* 1930, *35,* 765–782.

Spencer, M. B. *Personal-social adjustment of minority children.* Emory University, final report, Project No. 5-R01-MH 31106, 1981.

Springer, D. National-racial preferences of fifth-grade children in Hawaii. *Journal of Genetic Psychology,* 1953, *83,* 121–136.

Sroufe, L. A. The coherence of individual development: Early care, attachment, and subsequent developmental issues. *American Psychologist,* 1979, *34,* 834–841.

Sroufe, L. A., Waters, E., & Matas, L. Contextual determinants of infant affective response. In M. Lewis & L. Rosenblum (Eds.), *The origins of fear.* New York: Wiley, 1974.

Staffieri, J. R. A study of social stereotypes of body image in children. *Journal of Personality and Social Psychology,* 1967, *7,* 101–104.

Stainback, W. C. *Effects of pupil-to-pupil tutoring on arithmetic achievement and personal and so-cial adjustment.* Unpublished doctoral dissertation, University of Virginia, 1971.

Starkweather, E. K. *Conformity and nonconformity as indicators of creativity in preschool children.* United States Office of Education, Cooperative Research Project, No. 1967, 1964.

Staub, E. To rear a prosocial child: Reasoning, learning by doing, and learning by teaching others. In D. DePalma & J. Foley (Eds.), *Moral development: Current theory and research.* Hillsdale, N.J.: Lawrence Erlbaum, 1975.

Staub, E., & Noerenberg, H. Property rights, deservingness, reciprocity, friendship: The transactional character of children's sharing behavior. *Journal of Personality and Social Psychology,* 1981, *40,* 271–289.

Staub, E., & Sherk, L. Need approval, children's sharing behavior, and reciprocity in sharing. *Child Development,* 1970, *41,* 243–253.

Stendler, C. B., Damrin, D., & Haines, A. C. Studies in cooperation and competition: I. The effects of working for group and individual rewards on the social climate of children's groups. *Journal of Genetic Psychology,* 1951, *79,* 173–198.

Stevenson, H. W., & Stevenson, N. Social interaction in an interracial nursery school. *Genetic Psychology Monographs,* 1960, *61,* 37–75.

Stith, M., & Connor, R. Dependency and helpfulness in young children. *Child Development,* 1962, *33,* 15–20.

Stone, L. H., Miranne, A. C., & Ellis, G. J. Parent-peer influence as a predictor of marijuana use. *Adolescence,* 1979, *14,* 115–122.

Strayer, F. F. Current problems in the study of human dominance. In D. Omark, F. Strayer, & D. Freedman (Eds.), *Dominance relations.* New York: Garland, 1980. (a)

Strayer, F. F. The nature and organization of altruistic behavior among preschool children. In J. P. Rushton & R. M. Sorrentino (Eds.), *Altruism and helping behavior* (Vol. 2). Hillsdale, N.J.: Lawrence Erlbaum, 1980. (b)

Strayer, F. F., Chapeskie, T. R., & Strayer, J. The perception of preschool social dominance. *Aggressive Behavior,* 1978, *4,* 183–192.

Strayer, F. F., & Strayer, J. An ethological analysis of social agonism and dominance relations among preschool children. *Child Development,* 1976, *47,* 980–989.

Strayer, F. F., Wareing, S., & Rushton, J. P. Social constraints on naturally occurring preschool altruism. *Ethology and Sociobiology,* 1979, *1,* 3–11.

Streater, A. L., & Chertkoff, J. M. Distribution of

rewards in a triad: A developmental test of equity theory. *Child Development,* 1976, *47,* 800–805.

Strodtbeck, F., Ronchi, D., & Hansell, S. Tutoring and psychological growth. In V. L. Allen (Ed.), *Children as teachers: Theory and research in tutoring.* New York: Academic Press, 1976.

Styczynski, L. E., & Langlois, J. H. The effects of familiarity on behavioral stereotypes associated with physical attractiveness in young children. *Child Development,* 1977, *48,* 1137–1141.

Styczynski, L. E., & Langlois, J. H. *Judging the book by its cover: Children's attractiveness and achievement.* Unpublished manuscript, University of Texas at Austin, 1980.

Sullivan, H. S. *The interpersonal theory of psychiatry.* New York: Norton, 1953.

Sundby, H. S., & Kreyberg, P. C. *Prognosis in child psychiatry.* Baltimore: Williams and Wilkins, 1968.

Suomi, S. J. Differential development of various social relationships by Rhesus monkey infants. In M. Lewis & L. A. Rosenblum (Eds.), *The social network of the developing infant.* New York: Plenum, 1978.

Surratt, P. E., Ulrich, R. E., & Hawkins, R. P. An elementary student as a behavioral engineer. *Journal of Applied Behavior Analysis,* 1969, *2,* 85–92.

Swingle, P. G., & Gillis, J. S. Effects of the emotional relationship between protagonists in the prisoner's dilemma. *Journal of Personality and Social Psychology,* 1968, *8,* 160–165.

Tagiuri, R., Kogan, N., & Long, L. M. K. Differentiation of sociometric and status relations in a group. *Psychological Reports,* 1958, *4,* 523–526.

Talkington, L. W., Hall, S. M., & Altman, R. Use of a peer modeling procedure with severely retarded subjects on a basic communication response skill. *Training School Bulletin,* 1973, *69,* 145–149.

Thelen, M. H., Frautschi, N. M., Fehrenbach, P. A., & Kirkland, K. D. Imitation in the interest of social influence. *Developmental Psychology,* 1978, *14,* 429–430.

Thelen, M. H., & Kirkland, K. D. On status and being imitated: Effects on reciprocal imitation and attraction. *Journal of Personality and Social Psychology,* 1976, *33,* 691–697.

Thomas, D. Introduction: The methodology of experimental sociology. *Child Development Monographs: Teachers College, Columbia University,* (1) 1929, 1–21.

Thomas, J. L. *Tutoring strategies and effectiveness:*

A comparison of elementary age tutors and college age tutors. Unpublished doctoral dissertation, University of Texas at Austin, 1970.

Thompson, G. G., & Horrocks, J. E. A study of the friendship fluctuations of urban boys and girls. *Journal of Genetic Psychology,* 1947, *70,* 53–63.

Thorpe, J. G. A study of some factors in friendship formation. *Sociometry,* 1955, *18,* 207–214.

Thrasher, F. M. *The gang.* Chicago: University of Chicago Press, 1927.

Tieszen, H. R. Children's social behavior in a Korean preschool. *Journal of Korean Home Economics Association,* 1979, *17,* 71–84.

Toda, M., Shinotsuka, H., McClintock, C. G., & Stech, F. J. Development of competitive behavior as a function of culture, age, and social comparison. *Journal of Personality and Social Psychology,* 1978, *36,* 825–839.

Toner, I. J., Moore, L. P., & Ashley, P. K. The effect of serving as a model of self-control on subsequent resistance to deviation in children. *Journal of Experimental Child Psychology,* 1978, *26,* 85–91.

Torrance, E. P. Influence of dyadic interaction on creative functioning. *Psychological Reports,* 1970, *26,* 391–394.

Triplett, N. The dynamogenic factors in pacemaking and competition. *American Journal of Psychology,* 1897–98, *9,* 507–533.

Tuma, N. B., & Hallinan, M. T. *The effects of similarity and status on change in schoolchildren's friendships.* Unpublished manuscript, Stanford University, 1977.

Turner, M. E. *The child within the group: An experiment in self-government.* Stanford, Calif.: Stanford University Press, 1957.

Ugurel-Semin, R. Moral behavior and moral judgment of children. *Journal of Abnormal and Social Psychology,* 1952, *47,* 463–474.

Utech, D. A., & Hoving, K. L. Parents and peers as competing influences in the decisions of children of differing ages. *Journal of Social Psychology,* 1969, *78,* 267–274.

Vacc, N. A., & Rajpal, P. L. Comparison of social positions of school children in India and the United States. *Psychological Reports,* 1975, *37,* 208–210.

Vandell, D. L. *Boy toddlers' social interaction with mothers, fathers, and peers.* Unpublished doctoral dissertation, Boston University, 1977.

Vandell, D. L. Sociability with peer and mother during the first year. *Developmental Psychology,* 1980, *16,* 355–361.

Vandell, D. L., & Mueller, E. C. *The effects of group size on toddler's social interactions with peers*. Paper presented at the meeting of the Society for Research in Child Development, New Orleans, March 1977.

Vandell, D. L., & Mueller, E. C. Peer play and friendships during the first two years. In H. C. Foot, A. J. Chapman, & J. R. Smith (Eds.), *Friendship and social relations in children*. New York: Wiley, 1980.

Vandell, D. L., Wilson, K. S., & Buchanan, N. R. Peer interaction in the first year of life: An examination of its structure, content, and sensitivity to toys. *Child Development*, 1980, *51*, 481–488.

Vandenberg, B. *Environmental and cognitive factors in social play*. Unpublished manuscript, University of Missouri, 1980.

Vaughn, B. E., & Waters, E. Social organization among preschool peers: Dominance, attention and sociometric correlates. In D. Omark, F. Strayer, & D. Freedman (Eds.), *Dominance relations*. New York: Garland, 1980.

Vaughn, B. E., & Waters, E. Attention structure, sociometric status and dominance: Interrelations, behavioral correlates and relationships to social competence. *Developmental Psychology*, 1981, *17*, 275–288.

Venkatramaiah, S. R., & Barathi, K. K. Socio-psychological analysis of children's quarrels: Empirical investigation—Results and discussion. *Child Psychiatry Quarterly*, 1977, *10*, 1–7.

Vincze, M. The social contacts of infants and young children reared together. *Early Child Development and Care*, 1971, *1*, 99–109.

Vogler, R. E., Masters, W. M., & Morrill, G. S. Shaping cooperative behavior in young children. *Journal of Psychology*, 1970, *74*, 181–186.

Wagner, E., & Asarnow, R. *The interpersonal behavior of preadolescent boys with high and low peer status*. Unpublished manuscript, University of Waterloo, 1980.

Wahler, R. G. Child-child interactions in five field settings: Some experimental analyses. *Journal of Experimental Child Psychology*, 1967, *5*, 278–293.

Waldrop, M. F., & Halverson, C. F. Intensive and extensive peer behavior: Longitudinal and cross-sectional analyses. *Child Development*, 1975, *46*, 19–26.

Walker, R. N. Body build and behavior in young children: I. Body build and nursery school teachers' ratings. *Monographs of the Society for Research in Child Development*, 1962, *27* (3, Whole No. 84).

Walters, J., Pearce, D., & Dahms, L. Affectional and aggressive behavior of preschool children. *Child Development*, 1957, *28*, 15–26.

Walters, R. H., Parke, R. D., & Cane, V. A. Timing of punishment and the observation of consequences to others as determinants of response inhibition. *Journal of Experimental Child Psychology*, 1965, *2*, 10–30.

Waters, E., Wippman, J., & Sroufe, L. A. Attachment, positive affect, and competence in the peer group: Two studies in construct validation. *Child Development*, 1979, *50*, 821–829.

Watt, N., & Lubensky, A. Childhood roots of schizophrenia. *Journal of Consulting and Clinical Psychology*, 1976, *44*, 363–375.

Weingold, H. P., & Webster, R. L. Effects of punishment on a cooperative behavior in children. *Child Development*, 1964, *35*, 1211–1216.

Weinheimer, S. Egocentrism and social influences in children. *Child Development*, 1972, *43*, 567–578.

Wellman, B. The school child's choice of companions. *Journal of Educational Research*, 1926, *14*, 126–132.

Werner, N. E., & Evans, I. M. Perception of prejudice in Mexican-American preschool children. *Perceptual and Motor Skills*, 1968, *27*, 1039–1046.

Westley, W., & Elkin, F. The protective environment and adolescent socialization. *Social Forces*, 1956, *35*, 243–249.

Whalen, C. K., Henker, B., Collins, B. E., McAuliffe, S., & Vaux, A. Peer interaction in a structured communication task: Comparisons of normal and hyperactive boys and of methylphenidate (ritalin) and placebo effects. *Child Development*, 1979, *50*, 388–401.

Wheeler, L. Toward a theory of behavioral contagion. *Psychological Review*, 1966, *73*, 179–192.

White, J. H. Justice and generosity in social exchange: An experimental study of reactions to winning or losing a game. *British Journal of Social and Clinical Psychology*, 1974, *13*, 369–371.

Whiting, B. B., & Whiting, J. W. M. *Children of six cultures*. Cambridge, Mass.: Harvard University Press, 1975.

Williams, J. E., Boswell, D. A., & Best, Q. L. Evaluative responses of preschool children to the colors white and black. *Child Development*, 1975, *46*, 501–508.

Williams, J. E., & Morland, J. K. *Race, color, and*

the young child. Chapel Hill: University of North Carolina Press, 1976.

Willis, J., & Crowder, J. Does tutoring enhance the tutor's academic learning? *Psychology in the Schools,* 1974, *11,* 68–70.

Willis, J., Morris, B., & Crowder, J. A remedial reading technique for disabled readers that employs students as behavioral engineers. *Psychology in the Schools,* 1972, *6,* 67–70.

Wilson, R. S. Personality patterns, source attractiveness, and conformity. *Journal of Personality,* 1960, *28,* 186–199.

Wilson, W. C. Development of ethnic attitudes in adolescence. *Child Development,* 1963, *34,* 247–256.

Winder, C. L., & Rau, L. Parental attitudes associated with social deviance in preadolescent boys. *Journal of Abnormal and Social Psychology,* 1962, *64,* 418–424.

Withycombe, J. S. Relationships of self-concept, social status, and self-perceived social status and racial differences of Paiute Indian and white elementary school children. *Journal of Social Psychology,* 1973, *91,* 337–338.

Witryol, S. L., & Thompson, G. G. A critical review of the stability of social acceptability scores obtained with the partial-rank-order and the paired-comparison scales. *Genetic Psychology Monographs,* 1953, *48,* 221–260.

Woderski, J. S., Hamblin, D., Buckholdt, D., & Ferritor, D. *Effects of individual and group contingencies on arithmetic performance.* Paper presented at the meeting of the American Educational Research Association, New York, 1971.

Wolf, T. M. Effects of televised modeled verbalizations and behavior on resistance. *Developmental Psychology,* 1973, *8,* 51–56. (a)

Wolf, T. M. Effects of live modeled sex-inappropriate play behavior in a naturalistic setting. *Developmental Psychology,* 1973, *9,* 120–123. (b)

Wolf, T. M. Response consequences to televised modeled sex-inappropriate play behavior. *Journal of Genetic Psychology,* 1975, *127,* 35–44.

Wolf, T. M., & Cheyne, J. A. Persistence of effects of live behavioral, televised behavioral, and live verbal models on resistance to deviation. *Child Development,* 1972, *43,* 1429–1436.

Workie, A. The relative productivity of cooperation and competition. *Journal of Social Psychology,* 1974, *92,* 225–230.

Wyer, R. S. Effects of incentive to perform well, group attraction, and group acceptance on conformity in a judgmental task. *Journal of Personality and Social Psychology,* 1966, *4,* 21–26.

Young, G., & Lewis, M. Effects of familiarity and maternal attention on infant peer relations. *Merrill-Palmer Quarterly,* 1979, *25,* 105–119.

Youniss, J. *Parents and peers in social development: A Sullivan-Piaget perspective.* Chicago: The University of Chicago Press, 1980.

Yuferova, T. I. The behavior of ''affective'' children in conflict situations. *Voprosy Psikhologii,* 1975, *2,* 113–123.

Zajonc, R. B. Attitudinal effects of mere exposure. *Journal of Personality and Social Psychology Monographs,* 1968, *9*(2, Pt. 2), 1–27.

Zander, A., & Van Egmond, E. Relationship of intelligence and social power to the interpersonal behavior of children. *Journal of Educational Psychology,* 1958, *49,* 257–268.

Zimmerman, B. J., & Brody, G. H. Race and modeling influences on the interpersonal play patterns of boys. *Journal of Educational Psychology,* 1975, *67,* 591–598.

THE SCHOOL AS A CONTEXT FOR SOCIAL DEVELOPMENT

3

PATRICIA P. MINUCHIN, *Temple University*
EDNA K. SHAPIRO, *Bank Street College*

CHAPTER CONTENTS

INTRODUCTION

The school is a social institution, reflecting the culture of which it is part and transmitting to the young an ethos and a world view as well as specific skills and knowledge. Although psychologists are often preoccupied with the school's effect on cognition and achievement, other social scientists have taken a broader and more socially oriented perspec-tive. Critics of the educational system often protest the social values, the character of personal interac-tion, and attitudes about teaching and learning in the schools. They also attack the schools for their role in maintaining the status quo. Colin Greer (1972), for example, challenges the widely shared image that the public schools were a vehicle for social mobility, enabling the children of America's immigrants to achieve middle-class status, and Bowles and Gintis (1976) argue that the educational system perpetuates social stratification and the values that have maintained the prevailing class structure. These visions of the school as an institutional medium for social rigidity have a pessimistic as well as angry cast. Others, however, have been more optimistic about the potential of the school for creating positive change. Following Dewey (1899/1956; 1916/1966), they have argued that if schools encourage critical reasoning and offer democratic paradigms to the growing child, the school culture can prepare the young to function as agents of social change as well as responsible and knowledgeable adults. Both perspectives are valid. At any given time, the zeitgeist of the culture and the characteristics of the local community and particular school determine whether it will transmit established forms or provide a context for change.

As psychologists, we look at the school not only as a social institution with general functions in relation to the acculturation of the young, but as an environment for individual development. Children spend years in school as members of a small society in which there are tasks to be done, people to relate to, and rules that define the possibilities of behavior. Such experiences presumably affect aspects of social behavior and development that concern developmental psychologists: the sense of self, the belief in one's own competence, images of life possibilities as a male or female, relationships to other people, views of justice and morality, and conceptions of how a social system beyond the family functions and of how self and system interact. It is the research and theory about such aspects of social development in relation to the school that form the content of this chapter.

The Basic Framework

Certain ideas form the framework for our treatment of the material: schools have an impact on behavior and growth; the context of the school varies with developmental stage; the conceptualization and study of social behavior in school is shaped by underlying scientific paradigms.

The Impact of Schools

It seems odd to question whether school makes a difference. How could it not? The research task would seem to be a matter of documentation: to detail the effects of different educational environments on development and on specific kinds of children. There is considerable research of this kind, and a

major section of the chapter describes both the educational alternatives and studies of their impact.

One aspect of school impact, however, that has broad social implications—the school's capacity to overcome the negative effects of poverty—has generated controversial research challenging the very assumption that schools make a difference. The argument that schools do not matter is rooted in the work of Coleman and Jencks and their colleagues (Coleman, Campbell, Hobson, McPartland, Mood, Weinfeld, & York, 1966; Jencks, Smith, Acland, Bane, Cohen, Gintis, Heyns, & Michelson, 1972; see also Stephens, 1967). In this work, characteristics of schools are pitted against family and economic background variables as predictors of school achievement and subsequent success. Coleman and Jencks interpret their data as evidence that schools have little influence and point to the capacities, expectations, and support systems that students bring with them as causal explanations of outcome.

These studies have had a powerful impact on social theory and social policy; yet many have faulted Coleman's methodology and data base. They have considered it inappropriate that schools rather than classrooms were the unit of analysis; that the data were cross-sectional; that certain kinds of resources were counted while others were not; and that both schools and their effects were handled as distal variables. These studies do not deal with what happens inside the schools. Recent investigations, also focusing on achievement in school and after, have reached different conclusions. Researchers have compared the differential effectiveness of schools and classrooms that serve students from similar socioeconomic backgrounds and have identified characteristics associated with more successful outcomes (cf. Brookover, Beady, Flood, Schweitzer, & Weisenbaker, 1979; Edmonds, 1979; Klitgaard & Hall, 1975; Rutter, Maughan, Mortimore, & Ouston, with Smith, 1979). Their findings highlight the qualities of the school as a social system. The schools identified as producing high achievement were characterized not only by certain features of curriculum and academic procedure but by the climate of the school, the nature of teachers' expectations, and the patterns of interaction between teachers and students.

It does not seem fruitful to focus on schooling as more or less influential than families or socioeconomic realities. These are interacting systems, and experiences in any system may either confirm or modify experiences in other contexts. It seems essential to accept the fact that the school is a major social institution with inevitable impact on individual development and social attitudes. It is from this point of view that we present and evaluate research on school impact, paying particular attention to variations in school climate, social organization, and educational practice as these may affect social behavior and growth.

School Context and Developmental Stage

Another kind of variation among schools is of particular interest to developmental psychologists because it is associated with age and growth. Schools are different social contexts at preschool, elementary, and secondary levels. They are organized differently, children perceive them differently, and different aspects of social behavior are expressed in school as a function of children's changing capacities and needs.

As children grow older, the school environment increases in scope and complexity. The preschool is a protected environment, bounded by the classroom and limited in scope. If our understanding of development is correct, preschool children have little concept of the classroom as an organized society. They interact with one or two classroom teachers, usually female, who are particularly significant figures for the young child, and with individual peers or in small groups. Preschool children are finding ways to make and maintain social contact, communicate needs and express frustrations. Patterns of behavior based on family experience are modified in the school environment as children move toward social patterns that are mutually established with other people and viable for this setting.

For elementary school children the classroom is still the major context, but it is experienced now as a social unit, and the network of social expression and learning is more complex. Children in the middle years are involved equally with teachers and peers. Teachers represent authority and leadership, establishing the climate of the classroom, the conditions of possible contact among class members, and a set of relationships with individuals and the class as a group. The peer group, however, is the social frontier in the classroom, as well as elsewhere in the lives of middle years children. It functions as a social group independent of adults, with norms and a structure of its own. Within this group, the concern is for friendship, belonging, and status. It is also a learning community, under adult supervision, in which social paradigms for working and accomplishment are formed.

For the high school student, the social field becomes the school as a whole, rather than a particular self-contained classroom. The adolescent student comes into contact with a variety of teachers and peers, is likely to have both male and female instructors, and is offered a choice of activities outside the classroom. Social behavior is oriented toward peers, toward extra curricular events and activities, and toward the community. At this stage, the student is often aware of the school as a social organization and may either adapt and participate or challenge the system.

Since both the context and social behavior change as children grow older, studies related to schooling focus on somewhat different variables at different stages. Research on the social behavior of young children in school is often limited to immediate interpersonal contacts. Investigators study the sheer amount of social interaction or the conditions that foster prosocial or negative behavior. Studies of elementary school children reflect broader aspects of social development, including concepts of the self, changing relationships with peers and teachers, and concepts of social convention and morality. Some studies relate social behavior to learning, examining, for instance, the social correlates of cooperative learning structures, while others focus on purely social matters, such as the sociometric structure of the classroom peer group. Studies of social behavior at the high school level concern participation in school activities, moral attitudes, tolerance and prejudice among subgroups, and antisocial behavior. These are considered to have implications for society at large, partly because adolescent protest and antisocial behavior have power, and partly because the attitudes of students who are almost adults may translate directly from the school context to the larger social order.

Linear and Systemic Scientific Paradigms

Traditional scientific paradigms have been linear, assuming direct cause-effect connections that can be tested and verified. Most developmental research is in this tradition. In studying the effect of parental attitudes on empathic behavior, for instance, it is assumed that these are separable units that can be measured independently, and that a direct line of influence can be drawn from one to the other. Science, however, has been moving toward new paradigms that challenge concepts of linear causality and discretely measurable units. This change in thinking is pervasive, appearing in physics, biology, economics, ecology, and agriculture, as well as in the study of human relationships (e.g., Ackoff & Emery, 1972; Bateson, 1972; Bertalanffy, 1968; Kuhn, 1962; Miller, 1978; Prigogine, 1973; Schumacher, 1973; Sutherland, 1973; Thomas,

1974; Wiener, 1950). New paradigms stress the context of events and the organization of relationships within unified systems. From this point of view, the appropriate scientific search is for recurrent patterns that describe the characteristics of a system rather than for linear causal chains of events. No unit is considered separable from its context, and no part of a system is either the inevitable source of influence or the sole recipient of impact. Input at any point may challenge the pattern of organization, affecting all units in the system as well as the system as a whole.

Such paradigms have been influential in clinical fields, moving the focus of psychotherapy, for instance, from the individual to larger social units such as the family and affecting theories of etiology and therapeutic change (Haley, 1976; Hoffman, 1981; S. Minuchin & Fishman, 1981). The concepts are not well worked out for normally functioning human systems, however, and they have barely touched the field of child development. How will we conceptualize sex role development, or similar developmental phenomena, when mother, father, the relationship between them, the sibling group, and the individual child are all seen as interacting parts of an organized whole, whose patterns shape and are shaped by each member of the system? Such a paradigm requires wider definitions of the relevant social unit, a vocabulary for describing growth in complex interacting systems, and a way of conceptualizing individuals who are both separate entities and inseparable from their context.

A paradigm change has both conceptual and methodological implications. If phenomena occur in patterned systems, a methodology is required for investigating the way patterns are formed and sustained. There is little developmental research of this kind. The prevailing methodology in psychology is impressively sophisticated within the paradigms of traditional science, yet would be regarded as proceeding from false assumptions and therefore inadequate from the perspective of systems theorists. Almost all the material reviewed in this chapter has been based on traditional paradigms, with an underlying assumption of linear causality and a methodology that follows from this viewpoint. There are, however, some new trends. A growing body of ecological or ethnographic studies, for instance, investigates phenomena in natural settings, including classrooms. Locating research in such settings, where the social unit is realistic and recurrent patterns can be documented, is more compatible with a systems framework than laboratory studies that take the individual out of context. In a startling twist of the conventional hierarchy of scientific respectability, Bronfenbrenner (1979) has suggested that laboratory research may serve to generate interesting hypotheses which must then be verified in natural field settings.

While psychology has not made major progress toward systemic concepts, some psychologists have been critical of conventional ways of conceptualizing human behavior and organizing research (for example, Baumrind, 1980; Bronfenbrenner, 1979; Cole, Hood, & McDermott, 1978; Gibbs, 1979; Kessen, 1979; McCall, 1977; Petrinovich, 1979; Riegel, 1976; Sarason, 1971; Urban, 1978). It is our assumption that during the next decades paradigms for developmental theory will move toward the systems concepts that prevail in modern science. In keeping with the changing paradigm, it is probable that research will more often be located in natural settings, employ observational methods, and focus on systematic descriptions of complex patterns. In this chapter we review research within the framework that has guided the investigations. However, we have tried to raise questions about how patterns are developed and maintained, and how scientific phenomena studied in a cause-effect paradigm may fit into larger systems that sustain or reorganize their meaning.

The Conceptions of Context and Social Development

The School as Context

Our conception of the school as context draws on the work of ecologically oriented psychologists, such as Barker and his associates, who have been working within such a framework since the 1950s (Barker, 1968; Barker & Wright, 1955; Wright, Barker, Null, & Schoggen, 1955) and Bronfenbrenner (1979), who has more recently formulated an ecological approach to the understanding of human development. Barker and Wright were among the first researchers to call attention to the setting as a necessary focus both in studying and explaining behavior. Their concept of behavior settings identifies the ecological niches within which people tend to function in predictable ways. Thus, the classroom, the playground, and the home, as well as smaller units such as a math lesson, constitute different behavior settings in the child's life. These investigators contend that behavior settings elicit and organize certain kinds of behavior, and define a setting to include both the tangible properties of the environment and the behavior patterns associated with it. Their theoretical approach offers a useful way of looking at different aspects of the school environment as different behavior settings or contexts.

Bronfenbrenner contributes a framework and vocabulary that can be applied to describing school contexts at different levels, and a theoretical viewpoint about the connections among them. He distinguishes among the immediate context in which one participates (the microsystem); the relation between two or more contexts in which the person participates (the mesosystem); the broader contexts that affect an individual's experience, even though he or she does not participate directly at this level (the exosystem); and the philosophical and organizational contexts that govern a network, constituting a common thread among the subsystems within it (the macrosystem). In school relevant terms, the classroom, the playground, and subunits within these are all microsystems for the child. The relationship between home and school is a mesosystem, involving the linkage between two of the child's immediate settings; similarly, the relationship between the teacher-child context in any classroom and the peer group context in that same setting is also a mesosystem.

Exosystems are at a community or societal level and determine policies about such issues as busing, bilingual education, or teacher pay. Such matters are remote from the child's daily experience, but may affect the nature of schooling in tangible ways. The same can be said for patterns in the macrosystem. Cultural values, for instance, are responsible for the idea that education should be compulsory until age 16, or that elementary and secondary students should be educated in separate institutions. Macrosystems in different cultures are distinct, making the role of the school in social development different in China, America, or on the Israeli kibbutzim. The macrosystems of particular schools and school systems are also distinct, even within American culture. Some schools are guided by traditional principles of education, while others are organized around a more open educational philosophy. In each case, principles of the macrosystem give coherence to subsystems within the school, so that educational content, teaching styles, and the physical and social organization of the classrooms have elements in common.

Social Development

Two questions about the concept of social development deserve discussion since they involve some theoretical assumptions: What are the goals of social development, and what is the relation between experience in school and long-term social functioning?

In formulating the goals of social development we draw on concepts from the field of human development and the mental health profession that identify relevant variables, suggest directions of growth, and provide descriptions of the healthy social personality, at least within the value system of modern Western society. These conceptions focus attention on the capacity to establish meaningful and sustained relationships with other people—loving, empathic, flexible, and with viable mechanisms for resolving conflict; the ability to work cooperatively with others; a differentiated and positive sense of self; a humanitarian value system; and a capacity for productive effort and active participation in the social order. Are school experiences relevant to these goals? There is no common point of view among educators, who differ not only in the way they choose to socialize students but in their judgment of what aspects of social development are legitimately part of the school's domain. Our own assumption, however, is that school is relevant to all these aspects of development, simply because it is a major and continuing context for social experience.

The way in which school experience is relevant to subsequent behavior is also subject to different conceptions. Many personality theorists view the individual as a consistent being whose internal organization determines behavior in a variety of situations. They might see school as influencing the formation of certain personality traits which would then mediate future social behavior. Others, however, see behavior as situation-specific. From their point of view, the generalization of behavior learned in school would depend on the similarity of situations encountered in later life. These fundamentally different positions have generated considerable controversy (cf. Mischel, 1979). The issues can be only partially resolved empirically because each position inevitably regards different data as critical. Our own view, somewhat different from both, is that behavior cannot be separated from the context in which it occurs, and that it is neither totally specific to the setting nor totally an expression of enduring personality traits. People bring a repertoire of possibilities into new situations, and both contribute and adapt to the new patterns that are formed. The teacher and children in a fourth-grade classroom, for instance, bring their past into the classroom, but together they create a new system that stabilizes over time and defines the ways in which different members will behave in that particular setting.

Then what does a person carry out of high school in the way of "social development" after some 12 years in school? Neither an immutable social personality nor a completely open response, but a propensity to approach new situations in certain ways. School matters for social development, in our view, because it affects the kinds of social paradigms a person carries forth, even though these will change as the individual becomes part of new contexts.

Scope of the Chapter

We have marked the territory of this chapter by eliminating studies focused on school achievement and cognitive development. We have been struck, however, by the essentially social nature of almost everything that takes place in school. Much of school learning occurs through interactions between teachers and children, or between child and child. The rules of how to behave in classrooms are social rules. Furthermore, achievement has consequences for social interaction as well as for feelings of personal competence. For example, the composition of first-grade reading groups has social as well as academic antecedents and affects the nature of the child's contacts with both teachers and other children. Although we have not covered literally hundreds of studies that focus on achievement as outcome, we have paid attention to research in which the connections between learning and social development are made explicit. We have included school-related studies that concern concepts at the core of the child development field: prosocial behavior, peer relations, self-concept, sex-role development, and moral judgment. We have looked also at studies of what goes on in classrooms—the fine-grained descriptions of social interchange in the school context. These investigations document the ways in which children learn to be social beings in school, to function in a learning situation, to read the messages of how they are evaluated, and to take their place in the social system.

Inevitably, some important topics are left out or treated too briefly. We have not considered the school as a social context for children of particular groups, such as the handicapped, bilingual, or gifted, nor have we dealt with cross-cultural education or the relationship between homes and schools. We have omitted certain important social issues, such as violence in schools or dropping out, and have handled others, such as integration or drug and alcohol abuse, with less detail than they deserve.

Plan of the Chapter

The chapter is organized around the concept of contexts. School as context can be thought of in various ways: as a physical setting; as a system of educational philosophy; as a series of behavior settings in the classroom; as a microcosm of the larger society. The first section, *The School as a Social Unit*, deals with the school as a microsystem, a series of behavior settings in which the student participates directly. It has four subdivisions: the school as a *physical setting;* the school as a *philosophical context,* including the rationale and effects of alternative educational models; the *classroom context,* including teacher-child interaction and classroom social pressures; and *socially oriented curricula and learning structures,* including curricula for affective education and moral development and the organization of cooperative learning environments. The second section, *The School in Society,* considers the school in relation to broader social contexts. Programs and research presented in this section are located in the school but stem from the concerns of other systems, such as the family or community. This section includes *desegregation, sex-role stereotyping, substance use and abuse,* and *divorce.*

THE SCHOOL AS A SOCIAL UNIT

The Physical Setting

People make everyday assumptions about the importance of the physical environment, believing that the design of their homes and the characteristics of cities and landscapes affect their comfort, mood, and relations with other people. Such assumptions have come in for scientific scrutiny. Ethologists who study the behavior of a species gather data about the terrain in which their subjects function, assuming that the territory facilitates or inhibits particular kinds of behavior. Are such assumptions valid for children in school? Do children relate differently to others because space is ample rather than restricted, or because classrooms are organized in certain ways? In modern times, at least, educational planners have given considerable thought to school architecture, assuming that there is an important relationship between the setting and the behavior within it (e.g., *Harvard Educational Review,* 1969; Proshansky, Ittelson, & Rivlin, 1976). Research testing this assumption has established some connections between environment and behavior. At the same time, it is clear that the physical setting is not independent of other features; it contributes to child behavior in the school context but is by no means a final determinant.

Research on the physical setting covers the span from preschool through the secondary school. Since both the environmental variables and social behavior are conceptualized differently at successive levels, the material will be reviewed in three sections.

The Preschool Setting. Since the beginning of the nursery school movement, educators have considered the classroom setting a potential force for growth. They have made careful decisions about appropriate space, classroom design, numbers of children, and play equipment. Such decisions had two characteristics: they were embedded in a framework of goals for children and they were generally evaluated through informal observation. When social scientists entered the preschool classroom, they brought with them the psychologist's focus on the factors that influence behavior, the ethologist's methodology for documenting behavior (Blurton Jones, 1972; McGrew, 1972), and a general orientation toward scientific investigation. We now have systematic studies of the impact of physical settings, though the studies are often fragmented and must be reconnected to educational goals and to broader definitions of context.

Preschool research has some identifiable characteristics. The scope of the context is the single classroom; the focus is on small social units, such as dyads or small groups; and all studies are observational, since preschool children are poor sources of self-report data. Studies on the impact of the preschool physical setting usually investigate positive social interaction, productive play, conflict, or aggression. The context variables most frequently studied are space, room arrangement, materials, and activity settings.

Space and Density. A large number of preschool studies addresses the question of density—the ratio of people to space—assessing the effects of crowded conditions on social interaction. The impetus for this work comes not only from educational issues but from a body of sociological research on crowding that has reflected social concern about urban density. This research, conducted principally with adults, has produced some contradictory data, but has also indicated possible connections between crowded conditions and social withdrawal, increased conflict, and a sense of stress (Freedman, 1975; Lawrence, 1974; Stokols, 1976; Sundstrom, 1975). Studies of preschool children have generally tested hypotheses along the same lines.

A number of studies supports the suggested linkage between density and social withdrawal—children show less social interaction and cooperative play under conditions of high density (Bates, 1970; Loo, 1972; Price, 1971; Rohe & Nuffer, 1977). Other studies, however, do not support this finding (Berk, 1971; Fagot, 1977c; Gilligan, 1970;

McGrew, 1972; Smith & Connolly, 1977). Studies of aggression are also equivocal. Some suggest that aggression increases under crowded conditions, while others show no change or contradictory data (Aiello, Nicosia, & Thompson, 1979; Bates, 1970; Gump, 1978; Jersild & Markey, 1935; Loo, 1972; McGrew, 1972; Price, 1971; Rohe & Nuffer, 1977; Smith & Connolly, 1972, 1977). In a thorough review of this work, Smith and Connolly suggest that methodological problems may account for some of the discrepancies. In their own program of studies, the Sheffield Project, these English investigators conducted a series of carefully controlled experiments in a preschool established for their purposes (Smith & Connolly, 1981). They worked with two groups of 3- and 4-year-old boys and girls of mixed socioeconomic background, systematically varying space, size of group, and amount and kind of play equipment. Findings from the project serve as a reasonable summary of knowledge in this area.

In general, Smith and Connolly found that social play among preschool children is hardy. Children interacted under a wide variety of physical conditions, and the incidence of desirable or undesirable behavior did not vary much with simple changes in space, group size, or equipment. Aggression increased under two conditions, however. One was extreme density. While most variations in density had no systematic effects, reduction of space to less than 15 square feet per child led to greater aggression. The second condition was the combination of density with other sources of stress. Failure to increase the amount of play material when social density increased, for instance, led to more aggression, though there was no rise in conflict if toys were increased proportionately. These findings were similar to those of Rohe and Patterson (1974), who found the greatest incidence of conflict when conditions were crowded and resources limited.

Smith and Connolly stress the importance of considering physical factors in combination. They also make a point of differentiating social variables that are often combined, distinguishing aggressive behavior—intentional hurting or conflict—from what the ethologists have called "quasiagonistic" or rough-and-tumble play, which has no harmful intent (Blurton Jones, 1972; McGrew, 1972). Ethologists have described the adaptive nature of rough-and-tumble play among young animals, and the distinction is certainly pertinent to the question of what social behavior shall be controlled or allowed expression in the preschool setting. Smith and Connolly found that physical changes in the preschool environment may not have identical effects on aggression and rough-and-tumble play. Under conditions of extreme density, for instance, aggression increases but roughhouse decreases.

Room Arrangement. Preschool educators have usually balanced open space and sheltered corners in the classroom, separating areas for noisy activities such as block building from areas for puzzles, looking at books, and other quiet activities. The goal has been to facilitate both concentration and sociability, and to allow a flow of movement around the room that is not at cross purposes with ongoing activity. Specific studies of room arrangement have tested the effects of classroom organization on social play, constructive activity, and disruptive behavior. Rogers (1976) found, for instance, that the social play of 4- and 5-year-olds was active whether the room was well organized, with open pathways and protected play space, or cluttered. However, maximum organization fostered the most desirable pattern: children were significantly more verbal than physical, and their physical behavior was more productive than disruptive.

Spatial boundary-making in the classroom has been studied by Krantz and Risley (1977) as part of the research program conducted by the Living Environments Group (Risley, 1977). They were interested in increasing ''on task'' behavior and reducing inattentive or disruptive behavior during teacher-directed activities, such as storytelling time. Since they considered inattentive behavior a byproduct of customary classroom procedures in which children are allowed to sit at will around the teacher, they created a bounded area for each child by marking the floor with masking tape. They found significantly more focal attention and less peer contact and distraction under these conditions. The physical rearrangement produced the same effect as teacher reinforcement of attention, and the investigators concluded that manipulation of the physical environment may sometimes be a simpler way to generate desirable behavior. Of course, not all theorists would agree that for preschool children, on-task behavior and the acquisition of academic responses have priority over peer contact and spontaneous behavior, or that sociability is incompatible with learning. There would probably be more theoretical agreement about the value of boundaries around activity areas than about boundaries around children. Educators often create well-defined activity centers on the assumption that physical clarity helps the child understand spatial order, find equipment, and make choices. The impact of such spatial boundaries has been studied by Rohe and Nuffer (1977) who partitioned activity areas and found that cooperative

behavior increased. Partitions were especially effective in fostering constructive activity under conditions of high density, when distractions were potentially most compelling.

Play Materials and Activity Settings. According to the research, social interaction, cooperative play, and conflict vary with the amount and nature of the available material, and the same materials can generate both sociability and conflict. The research also confirms a pattern of gender differences in the use of certain materials and activity settings.

Both Smith and Connolly and the Risley group have looked at the social effects of limited play resources. Montes and Risley (1975) required children to check their toys out one at a time, and found that under these conditions children were likely to combine their materials in cooperative play. Smith and Connolly (1977) also found that limited supplies led to sharing of equipment, the spontaneous formation of relatively large subgroups, fewer loners, and increased competition, while plentiful equipment reversed the pattern. They note that each of the environmental conditions involves both advantages and disadvantages: plentiful equipment reduces conflict but creates less need for sharing, while limited equipment produces the reverse. Decisions about physical arrangements should therefore be made with awareness of these tradeoffs and consideration of the educational goals for a particular group.

Studies of the effects of different materials and activities have produced consistent and logical findings. They suggest that social interchange is most characteristic of activities that involve shared space and equipment or that require other people and are enriched by their participation. The classic studies of Shure (1963) and Charlesworth and Hartup (1967) documented the fact that activities such as block building, housekeeping, or dramatic play generate more complex social interaction and more social reinforcement among peers than activities such as painting, looking at books, puzzles, and other table activities. Later studies carry the same import (Doyle, 1975; Quilitch & Risley, 1973). Of course, this well-documented association does not dictate automatic policy for providing play equipment. As Hartley, Frank, and Goldenson (1952) pointed out some years ago and as others continue to suggest (e.g., McIntyre, Lounsbury, Hamilton, & Mantooth, 1980), activities that generate little cooperation or sociability, such as puzzles and art, may serve important developmental purposes, allowing for the expression of feeling, consolidation of skills, and the pleasure of mastery or a unique product.

One program of studies, directed by Kounin, has

taken an ecological perspective, assessing the effects of different behavior settings on children's attention span and on expressions of conflict and positive emotion (Kounin & Sherman, 1979). Rosenthal (1973) found that art, the sandbox, and books hold children longer than other activities such as play with vehicles, possibly because these materials allow for varied behavior and the child is not easily satiated. The expression of contagious pleasurable feeling, or "group glee," appeared in large lesson formats, mixed gender groups, and especially in connection with music and movement (Sherman, 1975), a context remarkably similar to the mixed gender, large group, musical milieu in which adolescents also express strong feeling. Conflict was associated with block building, the climber, and housekeeping play rather than with art or routines (Houseman, 1972), and this finding is consistent with that of other investigators (Patterson, 1976; Shure, 1963). Activities that invite social interaction, such as block building, logically generate some conflict, since conflict is an inevitable part of social exchange. However, Houseman suggests that some activities are particularly conflict-prone because they involve shared space and equipment which must be negotiated, and because they create a subgroup of participants who may exclude other children.

If materials call out different social behavior and children are differentially involved with the available materials, are their social experiences different? Systematic study of differences in play patterns has focused on comparison between girls and boys. Such studies suggest that boys spend more time with blocks, transportation toys, carpentry, and hammering, while girls are more involved in housekeeping and doll play, dress-up and art activities (e.g., Etaugh, Collins, & Gerson, 1975; Fagot, 1977a; Hartley et al., 1952; Maccoby & Jacklin, 1974; Patterson, 1976; Shure, 1963). Harper and Sanders (1975; Sanders & Harper, 1976) found also that boys favor outdoor settings for their fantasy activities, using space, climbers, and vehicles as props, while girls favor indoor settings, expressing fantasy with crafts and housekeeping materials. It seems unlikely that the play of boys and girls differs in the sheer amount of social exchange; both blocks and housekeeping play generate social interaction. There may be some qualitative difference, however. Block building, for instance, has been associated with more conflict than other activities. The structuring activities involved in block play may also have different cognitive implications than the imitation and repetition associated with housekeeping play

(Block, 1981). If so, typical gender differences in play activities may have both social and cognitive consequences.

In summary, research on the physical aspects of the preschool environment suggests three points. First, it is possible to describe a socially negative setting. If the preschool classroom is crowded, disorganized, and inadequately provided with play equipment, productive social play will be jeopardized and aggressive behavior is likely. There will also be minimal social contact if the equipment is consistently restricted to materials such as books, puzzles, and art, which call for focused individual attention. A wide variety of physical settings appears compatible with constructive social play, however. Research supports the value of selecting conditions that serve the needs of the group and of providing variation in the environment so that multiple goals are served, allowing the child to play cooperatively in some situations and autonomously in others.

Second, the social goals for preschool children have not been thoroughly examined, at least by researchers. In most studies of the physical context, an optimal setting is implicitly defined as maximizing positive contact and eliminating conflict. The value of social contact and cooperative play seems well established, but the assumptions about conflict are worth more consideration. For small children, social competence includes not only the ability to play with others but the development of skill for negotiating clashes. Incessant unresolved tension is not helpful for social growth, but the preschool is an important setting for learning modes of conflict-resolution and need not be organized to eliminate such situations. Probably the crucial factor in determining the social outcome of conflict is the behavior of adults in the classroom. The third point, in fact, is that the physical context of the school is not a given. It is created and mediated by people, who largely determine the effects of the setting. The research establishes connections between tangible features of the preschool context and children's social behavior, but these features are tied to program, adult behavior, and the patterns established for social interaction. This is perhaps the broadest generalization concerning the physical context, and holds equally for elementary and secondary school settings.

Elementary School. In the elementary school, the child's physical context is still the self-contained classroom. The predominant method for studying the impact of the environment is still through classroom observation, though some effort has also been made to tap the child's subjective sense of space.

The study of environmental design is often associated with the goal of facilitating learning, but some studies also consider social and affective variables.

Innovations in elementary school architecture and classroom design have been widespread in recent decades, stemming from the surge of interest in open education. When the idea of open education crossed the Atlantic from Great Britain and spread across the United States, a palpable feature of this innovation was the new physical layout for classrooms. In place of the traditional design with its rows of fixed desks, open classrooms were characterized by large open areas and by activity centers rather than immovable furniture. The open education movement spread rapidly during the 1960s, and new school construction in some sections of the country consisted almost exclusively of innovative architecture and large open-space classrooms (Gump, 1975).

For sophisticated educators, the physical setting was related to the educational philosophy. Proshansky and Wolfe (1974) indicate, for instance, that to meet the goals of independent activity, materials should be easily accessible to the children, and small, bounded areas provided so that children can work without interruption. To encourage cooperation, work space should be organized for face-to-face contact, so children can share information. They also suggest that children should have an active role in planning classroom design and in monitoring how it is working. Such participation is consistent with several goals: to give meaning to the idea that responsibility for learning is shared by teachers and children; to help children develop a problem-solving relation to classroom issues, such as crowding and privacy; and to help them understand that the relation of the physical setting to human needs changes over time, requiring flexible attitudes and reorganization.

It is not inevitable, of course, that educators who inhabit open-space classrooms will share these goals. The trajectory of the open education movement, in fact, raises an intriguing question about the fit between physical milieu and program. There is some evidence that the popularity of the movement peaked in the 1960s and declined in the next decade (Gump, 1978; Myers, 1974). Once constructed, however, open-space schools remain in place whether or not they fit the prevailing educational philosophy, and Gump and Ross (1977) found a sizeable proportion of open architecture schools in a midwest area operating without open programs. What happens if the classroom is physically open and the orientation is traditional? Essentially, teachers who do not want an open program close what is open in any way they can: by walling off open areas with cabinets or bookcases (Gump, 1978), or by establishing traditional rules for behavior that restrict the social possibilities of the space and design. In most instances, however, teachers who work in open space classrooms attempt to implement an open program. Furthermore, some teachers who work in schools with traditional architecture opt for an open program, redesigning classrooms to provide more flexibility and using corridors or other areas in unconventional ways (Weber, 1971). Since the advent of these more flexibly designed classrooms, a body of research has been devoted to describing the environments and the way in which they are used by teachers and children. In a later section we review open education as a complex educational model. Here we review studies on the effects of open-space settings (e.g., Beeken & Janzen, 1978; Brunetti, 1972; Durlack, Beardsley, & Murray, 1972; Evans & Lovell, 1979; Gump, 1974, 1975, 1978; Rivlin & Rothenberg, 1976; Weinstein, 1977).

In this research some problems of the open setting have been identified which are probably inevitable, since they are directly associated with the physical structure. Noise level is a major example, although Brunetti (1972) reports that the extent to which noise is actually distracting depends on individuals, the nature of the activity, and whether conditions are also crowded. Other problems are not inevitable, however. In an observational study of eight open elementary settings, Rivlin and Rothenberg (1976) found that teachers made few changes in classroom arrangement during the year, though patterns of use were not optimal. These investigators and Weinstein (1977) found that children used space unevenly, clustering in some activity centers and neglecting others. The pattern created problems of crowding and ran counter to the goal of providing experience with different materials. Weinstein identified other patterns that would not be considered optimal: a limited variety of behavior within areas and some gender differences in the use of the environment, in that girls used science and game areas less than boys.

Almost all comparative studies find certain patterns for using the environment that are consistent with educational goals, such as more active movement and more interaction among children in open settings than in traditional classrooms (Beeken & Janzen, 1978; Gump, 1974; Horwitz, 1979). However, the effects cannot be attributed exclusively to classroom design, as Gump's (1974) study illustrates. He found that children in open classrooms were spending more time in "nonsubstantial" behavior, such as waiting for the teacher to start an activity, than children in traditional classrooms. In the classrooms he observed children were not given a choice of activities, and it seems evident that they were not permitted to begin work on their own. Their behavior, therefore, seems a function of teaching style and rules for behavior in those settings. The pattern might not hold in other open classrooms with identical physical features but different rules.

The clearest data concerning physical design come from studies in which the teachers, program, and educational attitudes remain constant, while the design is modified. In Weinstein's (1977) study, problems in an open classroom were identified and discussed with the teacher and the setting was modified to provide shelving, work surfaces, and more attractive design in neglected areas of the room. As hypothesized, there was a significant shift in behavior: a more even distribution of children around the room, a higher incidence of girls in the science and game areas, and a wider variety of behavior within areas. Evans and Lovell (1979) report positive effects in a similar study at the high school level. They suggest that design modifications can reduce excessive stimulation, create privacy, and allow a sense of jurisdiction over parts of the setting. Research of this kind is probably a productive line for the future, since it does not confound program with setting and has direct implications for teachers.

Studies of the physical setting in conventional classrooms focus on specific variables. Research on windowless environments connects this feature with increased student aggression or more negative feelings toward school (Karmel, 1965; Romney, 1976), and studies of classroom seating arrangements indicate that students seated across the front and down the middle of the room are involved in most of the teacher-student interaction (Adams & Biddle, 1970; Gump, 1978; Koneya, 1976; Sommer, 1967). According to Smith and Glass (1979), research on class size has established an inverse relationship between size and achievement. Their analysis has been challenged on methodological grounds, however, and the relationship is considered debatable once classes contain 15 or 20 students (Educational Research Service, 1980). Some studies find more friendships and more cliques in large classes (Hallinan, 1977), and more individualization, group activity, positive student attitudes, and teacher satisfaction in small classes, as well as less time spent in misbehavior and discipline, but effects depend on whether teachers structure small classes differently from large ones (Filby, Cahen, McCutcheon, & Kyle, 1980; Olson,

1970; Smith & Glass, 1979). As in open classroom research, the physical setting is often confounded with program and classroom rules, and inferences must be drawn with caution.

An interesting research development is the effort to assess the child's subjective reactions to physical conditions. This kind of research becomes possible beyond the preschool level because of the child's increased ability to report experience and respond to questionnaires. In an experimental study by Aiello et al. (1979), fourth-, eighth-, and eleventh-grade children were placed in either uncrowded or extremely crowded spaces in groups of four, and were required to sit without talking for 30 minutes. It might be noted that the crowded condition was denser than the conditions associated with increased aggression in the preschool studies of Smith and Connolly. In the study of Aiello et al., crowded subjects reported significantly greater tension and annoyance and more discomfort with the proximity of others. They also showed greater physiological arousal than noncrowded subjects and significantly higher levels of competition in a game situation. Males were particularly susceptible to crowding, a finding characteristic of research in this area (Guardo, 1969, Tennis & Dabbs, 1975) but there were no consistent age differences. Since some studies have suggested that young children require less interpersonal distance than older children or adults, the question of age variation in the sense of personal space remains unresolved (Aiello & Aiello, 1974; Bass & Weinstein, 1971; Guardo, 1969; Tennis & Dabbs, 1975). In general, this study supports the suggestion that extremely crowded conditions are associated with conflict and competition. It indicates, as well, that such conditions generate a subjective experience of distress and a sense that one's personal space has been invaded.

In a study more directly relevant to the classroom, Brody and Zimmerman (1975) found that children from open classrooms develop a different sense of personal space than children from traditional classrooms. They compared third- and fourth-grade children from open and traditional classrooms, using an instrument developed by Meisels and Guardo (1969). The children were asked to place models of figures relevant to the classroom situation in relation to the self. The two groups did not differ in the placement of teachers or best friends, but children from open settings placed visitors, bullies, and other negative or unfamiliar figures at shorter distances from themselves, suggesting a tolerance of physical proximity over a wider range of people. Open settings provide more frequent experience with close physical contact, and this may influence the perception of essential personal space. However, the experience of proximity must presumably be positive as well as frequent in order to be valued. If so, the tolerance for closeness learned in the classroom must depend on classroom atmosphere as well as on the sheer experience of physical proximity.

The High School. High school students are no longer in self-contained classrooms; their physical context is the school as a whole. Data about social behavior is frequently based on student self-report in the form of questionnaires and interviews or on information from school records. Observational research is rare. Some studies investigate the relationship between the school's physical features and antisocial behavior, while others concern the effect on constructive participation in the social system of the school.

No consistent relationships have been found between most aspects of the physical plant and pupil outcome (e.g., Rutter et al., 1979) but research on school size has produced systematic findings. This variable is important. A combination of factors has led to an increase in the number of large secondary schools: the growing concentration of students in urban areas, budget factors, retention of marginal students who formerly would have left school, and an educational rationale stressing the possibilities for academic stimulation in consolidated institutions (Conant, 1959; Garbarino, 1980). Although no systematic association has been found between school size and academic achievement (e.g., Coleman et al., 1966; Rutter et al., 1979), there is evidence of more prosocial behavior and perhaps less antisocial behavior in smaller schools. In making the latter generalization it is important to note that increase in school size appears to make little difference beyond a certain point; small reductions in very large schools would have few social benefits. Five hundred has been suggested as a threshold, though investigators have set the optimal size at different points under 1000 (Garbarino, 1980; Paskal & Miller, 1973; Rosenberg, 1970; Turner & Thrasher, 1970).

The relationship of school size to antisocial behavior is more equivocal than the relationship to prosocial behavior. Some investigators find no association between size and truancy, dropout rate, discipline problems or delinquency (e.g., Burkhead, 1967; Galloway, 1976; Rutter et al., 1979). Even in studies with significant correlations, account must be taken of school population and neighborhood, since certain conditions may generate both large schools and antisocial behavior. Nonetheless, a body of research suggests that large schools tend to have a higher incidence of negative behavior than small schools (Duke & Perry, 1979; McPartland & McDill, 1977; Plath, 1965; Reynolds, Jones, St. Leger, & Murgatroyd, 1980; Rubel, 1977; Ruchkin, 1977). Various explanations have been offered. It has been suggested that large schools have more difficulty in creating a personalized climate or system of social control, and that students may therefore feel alienated and irresponsible rather than accountable for their behavior. This may be especially true for unsuccessful students, who do not have much academic identification with the school and who may become part of oppositional peer groups (Garbarino, 1978; Wilson, 1976; Wynne, 1977). School responsiveness may also be a mediating factor. In their work on crime in the schools, McPartland and McDill (1976) defined responsiveness in terms of rewards for desirable behavior, penalties for misbehavior, and student access to decision making, finding that smaller schools were more responsive and had less crime. The fact that small schools are generally more flexible and responsive to change than large ones (Averch, Carroll, Donaldson, Kiesling, & Pincus, 1974; Ford Foundation, 1972) may also mediate the incidence of negative social behavior, albeit indirectly. In the review of innovative programs throughout this chapter, the point is made that schools can either undermine or support the effects of programs introduced for specific purposes, such as curbing drug and alcohol use or reducing ethnic and gender stereotyping. Since large schools are more resistant to change than small ones, they may make poor use of programs aimed at alleviating social problems. Studies relating school size to negative behavior should take account of the fact that conditions are potentially more pressured and impersonal in large groups. Further, academic ability and the homogeneous or mixed ethnic nature of the student population should be considered in drawing conclusions, since optimal school size may vary with these characteristics.

Research on the relationship between school size and prosocial behavior has produced straightforward findings: small schools offer more opportunity for participating in school activities, and more students are active and identified. The key to the finding is the ratio of people to available school functions. The classic study was conducted by Barker and Gump

(1964), who studied behavior settings and their effects in 13 schools, ranging in size from 35 to over 2,000 students. The settings were defined as discernible units with associated behavior, including both tangible locations, such as the library, and school functions, such as the drama club. There were more behavior settings in larger schools, but the possibilities are not infinite and the increase was not proportional to the number of students. The largest school had many more students than the smallest but only five times the number of settings. Given this fact, it is logical that a higher proportion of students in small schools participated in extracurricular functions and held positions of responsibility, a finding confirmed by Baird (1969). In small schools, activities are often "undermanned," so that even marginal students are mobilized by the social group and feel a sense of responsibility to the school (Wicker, 1968; Willems, 1967). In large institutions these students are usually part of the population described as "redundant," or as "tribe members" instead of "citizens"; citizens are involved in activities and satisfied with school, while tribe members are inactive and alienated or oppositional (Todd, 1979). Factors such as social class, personality, gender, and self-concept determine who become the citizens (Winne & Walsh, 1980; Yarworth & Gauthier, 1978), but there will be a smaller percentage in large schools, simply because most students are not needed to make the society work. In Barker and Gump's study, students in small schools reported satisfaction in terms of challenge, involvement in activities, and the development of competence, while the satisfactions of students in large schools were more vicarious and impersonal. Both the possibility for gaining experience in productive social roles and the feeling of identification with the institution in smaller settings appear to be positive social gains, increasing the students' pleasure and serving as a paradigm for later participation in the culture.

Of course, no feature of the physical setting, whether size or some aspect of design, is independent of the school's social structure, which determines how the setting is used. In Kelly's (1979) study of two high schools, social behavior and attitudes were more positive in the school that had, among other features, a lounge for students where they could socialize with each other and with teachers. The presence or absence of this behavior setting provided students in the two schools with different social experiences. However, different school policies created a lounge in one school and not in the other, so that the effects reflected both climate and setting.

It is evident that future research should further delineate size and population variables and that both social and academic criteria must be employed. Statements that school size makes little difference are often based solely on academic measures, though the effects on antisocial behavior and participation in school activities appear equally important. Furthermore, it would be a step forward if investigators included both antisocial and prosocial measures in studying the effects of physical settings. With rare exceptions, studies focus on one aspect or the other. The data can be set side by side as we have done in this chapter, but a fuller perception of the social effects depends on binocular vision in the primary sources.

Summary

Research on the school as a physical setting suggests that some aspects of space, size, materials, and physical arrangement are systematically related to social behavior. While the facts may be clear, the import may depend on the theoretical perspective of the viewer, especially concerning the relative importance of academic and social behavior. For example, different implications may be drawn from the fact that certain room arrangements facilitate social contact but reduce the amount of autonomous involvement in academic tasks. The resolution of such issues may depend partly on clarifying the school's developmental goals for children and partly on determining which conditions produce a developmentally appropriate balance. The relationship between physical setting and social behavior varies with developmental stage. Different aspects of the context matter to preschool, middle-years, and adolescent students, and social consequences take age-appropriate form. Both preschool and high school research, for instance, identify the importance of the ratio between pupils and resources. However, limited resources in the preschool means less play equipment and may result either in increased cooperation or, if conditions are also crowded, more aggressive behavior. The problem can be alleviated by providing more toys. For high school adolescents limited resources may be functional rather than concrete, taking the form of finite possibilities for participation in social activities within large schools. The result may be a division between those who are active, reaping the social benefits, and those who are not, and the problem cannot be remedied by purchasing more resources. Finally, the physical setting is never independent of school policy and orientation. School settings are created or chosen by people and use of the setting is determined by educational viewpoint.

The Philosophical Context: Alternative Models of Education

The physical setting of a school is palpable, but the educational ideology is not. Nonetheless, the ideas that govern a school are basic to its operation and form an important part of the educational context. The philosophy of a school, whether implicit or explicit, determines its social organization and curricular content, as well as the quality of academic and social experience for the students. We review different educational models, efforts to assess their implementation, and comparative research concerning effects on children's social development.

Rationale: Different Philosophies of Education

How to educate? The question has generated considerable rhetoric and controversy. Both Plato and Confucius gave it their attention, and they had earlier opinions to draw on. In America during the twentieth century, education has been characterized both by basic changes in ideas about learning and by highly publicized short-term fads. Change and exploration are as typical as resistance and inertia. The development of nontraditional approaches goes back at least to John Dewey (1938/1963; 1899/1956), whose ideas—heralded, discounted, and bowdlerized—continue to have influence, though not always acknowledged. The history of progressive education, which stemmed directly from his work, has been documented by Cremin (1961), who connects the rise and fall of the movement to changes in American society from the 1870s to the 1950s.

In the mood of reevaluation that characterized the 1960s, the schools, like other social institutions, were examined and found to be dreary. Bruner's (1960, 1966) challenge to conventional definitions of intellectual growth sparked a major effort to revise curricula and ways of teaching. At the same time, the discovery of the "other America" led to federal funding of programs for children and families of the poor, especially those from minority backgrounds. Social scientists conceptualized the rationale for these programs and designed their implementation and evaluation. Some of the conceptions were based on naive notions about ameliorating poverty through education or repairing "cultural deficits" in the development of young minority children (see Baratz & Baratz, 1970). Although these concepts have been modified, there has been a continuing preference for working with young children, partly because they are considered more malleable than older children and partly as a strategy to prevent cumulative school problems. Consequently, preschool and primary education have more variants than elementary or secondary education, although there are alternative designs at each level.

In this chapter we concentrate on the programs most closely tied to psychological theory and most systematically studied. Among programs that meet these criteria are those that were part of the Head Start and Follow Through Planned Variation experiment, progressive or open elementary schools, and alternative forms of secondary education. There are shared goals in all these models. Developers want children to become competent, to feel positive about themselves, capable of doing well in school, and able to take advantage of opportunities. Differences among models should be seen against this common background. It is the differences, however, that are the focus of comparative research.

We do not describe programs in detail; the reader should consult sources such as Day and Parker (1977); Deal and Nolan (1978); Duke (1978); Franklin and Biber, 1977; Hodges and Sheehan, 1978; Maccoby and Zellner (1970); Palmer and Anderson (1981); Rhine (1981); Stanley (1972); White, Day, Freeman, Hantman, and Messenger (1973); and Zigler and Valentine (1979).

Preschool and Early Educational Alternatives. Preschool education has its roots in the nursery school movement, which primarily served children of middle class families. Such schools usually had multiple developmental goals. They fostered interaction with peers, trusting relationships with adults, the expression of ideas and feelings through language and other media, the development of motor skills, and expansion of the child's knowledge of the environment (Biber, 1972; Swift, 1964). In the 1960s, federal funding made it possible to extend early education to children who were poor and from minority backgrounds. The psychologists and educators who created the programs had a mixture of elements to draw on: a variety of psychological theories considered relevant to education (e.g., Piagetian, behavioral, psychodynamic); the nursery school movement, with its concern for personal and social development; a prevailing emphasis on preparing children for effective learning in elementary school; and different ideas about how to connect educational environments with goals. Since they represented a diversity of viewpoints they made quite different recipes out of these ingredients, and the result was a proliferation of models.

The models represent fundamentally different approaches to children's development and learning. They differ principally in the scope of their developmental goals (academic preparation, social and emotional growth, or both); their conceptions of how children learn (by direct instruction or active experience); in the amount of autonomy given to the child; conceptions of the teacher's role; and the provision of possibilities for learning from peers. A number of schemes have been proposed to classify the models. They follow from the intellectual challenge to order the array and the practical necessity to define coherent groups so that effects on children can be measured and generalized. Maccoby and Zellner (1970) classified Follow Through programs into four sets: those oriented toward behavior modification, toward cognitive growth, toward self-actualization, or toward changing the locus of control over the schools. Stanford Research Institute, charged with evaluating the effectiveness of Follow Through, sorted programs into five groups: Structured Academic, Discovery, Cognitive-Discovery, Self-Sponsored (designed by people in local school districts), and Parent-Implemented (Emrick, Sorensen, & Stearns, 1973). Abt Associates categorized thirteen models into three groups: Basic Skills, Cognitive-Conceptual, and Affective-Cognitive (Stebbins, St. Pierre, Proper, Anderson, & Cerva, 1977). The parallels and overlap among these systems are obvious, but the agreement is not necessarily a test of their viability. Weaknesses of the Abt classification system, which governed subsequent comparison of effects, have been pointed out by House, Glass, McLean, and Walker (1978) in their comprehensive critique of the Abt evaluation of Follow Through.

A more fundamental criterion for classifying early educational programs, and one more appropriate for studying their psychological consequences, is in terms of their view of children's development. White and his colleagues (1973, v. II) derived a taxonomy from developmental concepts in the three major schools of psychology: the behaviorist, which leads to preacademic programs; the cognitive-developmental, which leads to cognitive enrichment programs; and the psychodynamic, which leads to a focus on social and emotional development. Kohlberg's (1968) scheme is based on a slightly dif-

ferent reading of the streams of thought governing educational programs. He identifies a maturationist view that originated with Rousseau and is currently represented by Neill's Summerhill and by followers of Gesell and Freud, a somewhat uneasy alliance. Kohlberg sees this approach as romantic because it stresses the need to allow the inner "good" of the child to unfold and to control the inner "bad," without adult cultural pressure. A contrasting view sees education as a process of transmitting cultural content. This is the view that guides traditional education, and contemporary examples in early education include behavior modification programs, the Direct Instruction model (Bereiter & Engelmann, 1966; Becker, Engelmann, & Thomas, 1971), and the Behavior Analysis model (Bushell, 1973; Sherman & Bushell, 1975). As Sherman and Bushell note, "The first assumption is that the primary function of the schools and the teachers is to produce changes in student performance—to teach specifiable skills considered desirable by society" (pp. 452–453). The third view is the cognitive-developmental, based on Piagetian concepts, and represented by a number of models (Kamii & DeVries, 1977; Lavatelli, 1970; Schwebel & Raph, 1973; Weikart, Rogers, Adcock, & McClelland, 1971). The basic premise is that structural change in the child's cognitive development follows from the interaction between the child and the environment, when conditions foster such interaction.

Other approaches to early education cut across certain of these boundaries. The developmental-interaction approach, for example, emphasizes cognitive, affective, and social development. It is interactional in two senses: the assumption that cognitive and affective growth are interdependent, and the focus on the interaction of child and environment. It is developmental in its concern for matching the educational environment with the characteristics of the developing child (Biber, 1977; Franklin & Biber, 1977; Shapiro & Biber, 1972; Shapiro & Weber, 1981).

The classification schemes have obvious parallels, but they force a number of marginal categorizations. The need to group models into a feasible number of categories may have jeopardized the more subtle task of capturing critical dimensions of difference and the internal complexities of each approach. The classification schemes serve more than a heuristic purpose, since they govern comparative research.

Elementary School. Current formulations of alternatives for grade school children usually contrast traditional and open education, but nontraditional philosophies, such as progressive education, have a long history in this country. Although the progressive movement was considered defunct by the 1950s, certain of its principles continued to have power and some schools with this general orientation survived and evolved. During this period, the authors and their colleagues at Bank Street College conducted a comparative study of children in traditional and alternative elementary schools (Minuchin, Biber, Shapiro, & Zimiles, 1969). Differences in the educational environments of the schools were operationalized and rated in accordance with a set of governing ideas.

The *traditional* orientation, as described in this study, emphasized socialization of the child toward culturally approved forms of behavior and levels of achievement. The school's major task was to convey an established body of knowledge, seen as the intellectual content of the culture. Adults carried the authority role as one with fixed prerogatives for decisions of right and wrong. Child behavior and achievement were evaluated according to general standards, and the school fostered competition among children, regarding other aspects of peer interaction as distractions.

Alternative schools followed what was called a *modern* philosophy. It emphasized a balance between the requirements of socialization and the needs of the individual child. The goals of the school stressed intellectual competence, exploration and depth of understanding, the capacity to live and work with others, and individual development. Adults carried a flexible authority role, tolerating challenge and sharing authority as developmentally appropriate. Child behavior and achievement were evaluated primarily against a profile of individual strength and weakness, and secondarily against group norms. The school regarded the peer group as a vital force for learning and social growth, and saw the teacher-child relationship as pivotal (adapted from Minuchin et al., 1969, pp. 7–8).

The description of traditional education is still basically accurate and applies to the bulk of elementary schools. On the other hand, the concepts of modern or progressive education bear a strong resemblance to those of the open education movement (Engstrom, 1970). Formulations of open education stress certain principles that distinguish this orientation from traditional education. There are different assumptions about the process of learning, sources of motivation, the teaching role, and appropriate models of evaluation. Bussis and Chittenden (1970), for instance, take the relative contributions of teacher and child as a twofold system for categorizing

differences between open and traditional approaches. In open education, both children and teachers are active agents in creating the educational setting and determining content, sequence, and pacing, whereas in traditional education the teacher's contribution is high but that of the children is low. There are differences in emphasis among the formulations, however; some theorists stress open space and student choice, while others include the teacher's role and mutuality in student relationships (Marshall, 1981). A sizeable literature further explicates the rationale and principles of open education (e.g., Barth, 1972; Bussis & Chittenden, 1970; Featherstone, 1971; Plowden, 1967; Rathbone, 1971; Sealey, 1976; Spodek & Walberg, 1975; Stodolsky, 1975; Weber, 1971).

The High School. Alternative programs for secondary schools are not so thoroughly delineated as those for early and elementary education. Perhaps this is because the high school alternatives that arose in the 1960s and early 1970s were predominantly a response to adolescent unrest. Alternative forms of education for younger children are thought through by adults who are concerned with theoretical goals and work out programs to achieve them. The children themselves generally sit still for whatever system they find themselves in. In contrast, adolescents have the power to challenge the environment and can be direct catalysts for change through antisocial behavior, leaving school, or critical protest. Alternative high schools of this era served varied populations, including disaffected or rebellious middle-class students and low achieving, alienated students from black ghettos (Deal & Nolan, 1978; Duke, 1978). The schools were public and private, and existed both as separate institutions and as self-contained units within conventional high schools. What they had in common was their effort to meet adolescent needs. They were less connected to theory, to the history of educational experiments, or to clear educational goals than were alternative models for younger children.

The curricular approach of these high schools usually involved student choice of subjects, a problem-solving orientation, and an emphasis on learning experiences that would be considered "relevant" by students. Most analysts, however, point to the authority structure and social organization of these schools as their critical features (Argyris, 1974; Deal, 1975; Deal & Nolan, 1978; Duke, 1978; Epstein & McPartland, 1979; Singleton, Boyer, & Dorsey, 1972; Swidler, 1979). Deal has described six aspects of the learning environment that distinguish between conventional and alternative secondary schools: *who* is involved (roles), *what* is learned (curriculum), *why* it is learned (where authority resides), *how* it is learned (methods), *where* learning takes place, and *when* it takes place. He sees the shift in authority and decision making as a particularly important feature, involving informal relations between staff and students and considerable student authority for making instructional decisions, developing rules, and influencing school governance. Deal also traces the experience of students and staff in these new humanistic schools through stages of euphoria, psychic upheaval, and dissatisfaction. At that point, schools either dissolved, reverted to conventional authority structures, or resolved their difficulties by finding an organizational middle ground where roles and decision-making processes were clarified. The alternative high schools that survived have been judged not so much by their academic effects as by social criteria, such as their ability to prevent alienation, hold students in school, and reduce the incidence of stealing, drug abuse, discipline problems, and violence. According to a Gallup survey, communities are sometimes more concerned about high school students' behavior than about their academic progress (Gallup, 1977, cited in Perry & Duke, 1978), and studies of crime in the schools have suggested that the social climate of secondary schools can exacerbate or reduce such problems (McPartland & McDill, 1977).

Alternatives to traditional secondary education do not necessarily involve dramatic reorganization of the school's social structure and may not be governed by a comprehensive, explicit rationale. Some empirical research has focused on organizational alternatives in secondary schools, starting not from theoretical definitions about models of education but from an interest in identifying the structures that maximize student progress. These studies have identified dimensions of difference among schools, and at least one such study (Rutter et al., 1979) arrived inductively at the conception of an overall "school ethos." Since this dimension was correlated better with academic and behavioral effects than specific variables were, empirical work of this kind may generate new philosophical formulations concerning secondary educational alternatives.

Assessing the Educational Environment: The Relation Between Theoretical Model and Program Implementation

An educational model is a set of ideas. It governs the nature of classroom practice, but the goodness of fit between theory and reality in any given situation is an empirical question. Surprisingly, many studies

purporting to assess the impact of different approaches have not looked at programs in detail, or have accepted the label given by school authorities. Assessing the correspondence between a model and its exemplars requires delineation of the critical dimensions of the model and a methodology for measuring them; this is a prerequisite to interpreting the effects of comparative studies. In her analysis of open education research, Marshall (1981) points out that investigators often do not examine either the degree to which teachers implement a model or the dimensions that they do implement, and that this may account for discrepant findings. There has been some progress in the last decade, however, in the methodology of environmental assessment. Two comprehensive comparative studies of early education, those of Miller and Dyer (1975) and Stallings (1975), identify dimensions of similarity and difference among models, assess the programs as exemplars, and link programs with effects on the children.

Miller and Dyer selected four Head Start models that were relatively clear about goals and methods and trained teachers to implement them (Bereiter-Engelmann; Darcee, an acronym; Montessori; and an "enrichment" program labeled Traditional). Consultants familiar with each model rated the correspondence of program to model. Miller and Dyer also observed in the classrooms and analyzed videotapes of teacher-child interactions. Teachers and children behaved differently in the classrooms representing different models. Some dimensions were different for each of the four programs, but in other respects there were two rather than four discriminably different programs: "two teacher-directed, fast-paced, didactic treatments in a group format, involving high amounts of positive reinforcement (Bereiter-Engelmann and Darcee), and . . . two child-centered, slower-paced treatments in an individualized format . . . (Montessori and Traditional)" (pp. 60–62). The analyses are generally congruent with the descriptions of the models. There were some surprises, however. For instance, there was more emphasis on the control of social behavior in the Traditional program than in the others, a finding Miller and Dyer consider similar to that of Soar and Soar (1972), who report a negative relation between classroom structure and teacher control. That is, if the children's behavior is less controlled by teacher's rules, there are more occasions when the teacher has to intercede.

Stallings, in a study of seven Follow Through models, adopted a different strategy. Sponsors identified variables they considered critical to their program. Stallings then created the Classroom Observation Instrument to assess classroom arrangements and events. The instrument distinguished among programs, enabling Stallings to say with some confidence that the programs were discriminably different. Resnick and Leinhardt, however, critique her approach as atheoretical: "Her strategy was to collect large amounts of process data, essentially measuring everything possible that might differentiate models or relate to outcomes. . . . A large amount of data—over 500 separate variables—in this case yields a relatively small number of interpretable and significant patterns" (1975, pp. 130–131).

Although these studies are an advance over past research, there are major questions about the scope and centrality of the dimensions used to describe the different approaches and to assess the correspondence between models and programs. Stallings notes that "the critical list of variables describes a sponsor's model only in part. The observation instrument employed in this study is not designed to capture the important subtle process of some of the programs" (p. 22). In both studies it is clear that the descriptive dimensions are more successful in capturing significant aspects of behavioral programs than of developmental programs. In an effort to measure the essential dimensions of their models more effectively, some sponsors of developmental programs have created their own assessment techniques. These include observational instruments to assess child and teacher behavior in Weikart's Cognitively Oriented program, and to document communication and individual child behavior in classrooms of the Bank Street model (Bowman & Mayer, 1976; Ross, Zimiles, & Gerstein, 1974; Weikart, Hohmann, & Rhine, 1981; see also Rhine, 1981). These instruments have generally been used to assess implementation of the particular approach, and to differentiate Follow Through exemplars from classrooms following traditional practices. There has been little effort to study distinctions among programs sharing a common orientation.

The open education movement has also led to various procedures for identifying and describing open settings. These have included identification by administrators, teacher questionnaires, and classroom observations. The two most widely used instruments are the Dimensions of Schooling (DISC), a teacher questionnaire (Traub, Weiss, Fisher, & Musella, 1972), and an instrument devised by Walberg and Thomas, which serves both for classroom observation and as a questionnaire for teachers. The Walberg-Thomas scale has been used to differentiate between open and traditional environments on

such dimensions as materials provided, individualization of program, and opportunities to choose activities and work companions (Walberg & Thomas, 1972). The various instruments and procedures, however, emphasize different though overlapping criteria (Marshall, 1981). The Walberg and Thomas scale, for instance, has many more items about provisioning the environment than does the DISC, and other investigators focus on yet other dimensions, such as children's development of responsibility (Blumenfeld, Hamilton, Wessels, & Falkner, 1979).

In an interesting study of the correspondence among three different measures, Marshall, Weinstein, Middlestadt, & Brattesani (1980) correlated administrators' nominations of teachers as open or traditional, teacher ratings of their beliefs on the Walberg-Thomas scale, and teacher estimates of the extent to which they implemented each statement on the scale in their classrooms. Nominations correlated significantly with teachers' beliefs but not with reported implementation, and teachers' beliefs about the importance of a statement were not significantly correlated with their own reports of implementation; the latter finding is consistent with that of Kremer (1978). Furthermore, studies of the correspondence between teacher reports and observer ratings often show discrepancies, with teachers generally rating themselves as more open than observers do (Evans, 1971; Groobman, Forward, & Peterson, 1976; Hook & Rosenshine, 1979; Klass & Hodge, 1978; Marshall, 1981). Such findings may seem discouraging, but they also represent progress. There is now sufficient research to highlight the nature of the problems and the need for careful specification of the environmental features that serve as independent variables in comparative studies.

The most systematically developed and widely tested instrument for assessing environments in junior and senior high schools is the Classroom Environment Scale (CES), a 90-item questionnaire administered to students or teachers (Moos & Trickett, 1974). The scale assesses nine dimensions of the classroom grouped in three areas: personal relationships, academic goal orientation, and structural dimensions. The scale has been used to create a typology of classrooms, describe normative trends, and compare alternative methods of environmental assessment (Ellison & Trickett, 1978; Kaye, Trickett, & Quinlan, 1976; Moos, 1978; Trickett, 1978). It also has been used to compare environments in traditional and alternative high schools. In a study of over 400 classrooms, Trickett (1978) found that students described the alternative high school classrooms on the CES as less competitive, more innovative, and characterized by stronger peer affiliation, teacher support, and student involvement than traditional classrooms. The alternative settings were lowest in teacher control but, more surprising, were also reported to be significantly higher than traditional classes in rule clarity, organization, and order. While the latter characteristics may be more typical of the Connecticut public schools in this sample than some other alternative settings, the data support the idea that environments where teachers are not in tight control are not necessarily inhospitable to order and clarity.

As Ellison and Trickett point out, the CES is limited in that the qualities of a school must be inferred from data about classrooms. Other researchers working at the secondary level have attempted to assess the climate and structure of the school as a whole. They usually create their own instruments, which take the form of students' self-report on questionnaires (Epstein & McPartland, 1979; Kelly, 1979), or interviews with staff, students, and sometimes parents (Duke, 1978). In a comprehensive approach to assessing administrative features and school processes in 12 London secondary schools, Rutter and his colleagues employed a combination of techniques, including interviews with staff, pupil questionnaires, and direct observation in classrooms (Rutter et al., 1979). Although all of these studies attempt to describe the total school environment, they differ in their handling of the data, some focusing more on single variables, others on combinatory concepts and descriptions. The issue of how to describe the characteristics of environments with many interactive features is far from settled. The conceptual and methodological difficulties have ramifications for testing school effects, since such research requires analysis of both the setting and the behavior of the students within it.

The Effects of Different Educational Approaches

Research on the effects of different school environments started with systematic work before and during the 1960s (e.g., Baker et al., 1941; Gardner, 1966; Leonard & Eurich, 1942; Minuchin et al., 1969), and escalated thereafter. The task has proven complex and the accumulating data are sometimes contradictory, although there are some reliable findings.

Problems in comparative research are cumulative. As indicated, the method of classifying and describing educational settings is sometimes careless and certainly varies from one study to another.

Comparisons of different approaches may be based on what Charters and Jones (1973) have called a non-event, in that essential components of the models are not actually implemented. Furthermore, dependent measures are often fallible, or tap the goals of some models better than others. Programs have different criteria for intellectual mastery and the conventional standardized measures of cognitive growth are not uniformly appropriate. The broad goals for personal and social development characteristic of some approaches often receive only perfunctory attention, and meaningful measures of affective growth have generally been difficult to create. This is particularly acute when the subjects are young children (see Walker, 1973). Social measures obtained from young children are often unreliable because behavior is fluid and because self-report instruments that call for introspective material are essentially age-inappropriate. The results of comparative research, especially at preschool and primary levels, must be viewed in the light of these limitations.

Preschool and Primary Programs.   A great deal of evaluation research at preschool and primary levels has been spurred by federal funding and has focused primarily on programs for children of poor and minority families. This research has had two major characteristics: a heavy stress on IQ and cognitive gain, and equivocal findings.

The cognitive data are not within our province but can be briefly summarized. Miller and Dyer (1975) found that at the end of the preschool year, children in the four programs they studied (Bereiter-Engelmann, Darcee, Montessori, and "enrichment") were superior to controls on the Stanford-Binet; the didactic Bereiter-Engelmann program, in particular, led to cognitive and academic gains. In a follow up of the children, however, early advances in IQ and achievement were not maintained whether the kindergarten program was continuous or discontinuous with the preschool model. Stallings (1975) found reading and math scores to be higher for children in more behavioral models, reflecting time spent in academic activities, but the subsequent Follow Through evaluation by Abt Associates, based on the same SRI data, presented a more complex picture (Stebbins et al., 1977). The Abt group found that no model was more successful than others in enhancing cognitive-conceptual growth but that the basic skills programs succeeded better than others in helping children gain those skills. Their most significant finding, however, was that the effectiveness of each model varied substantially from one site to another. The variation among models was small in comparison to this internal variability, thus high-lighting the importance of local contextual variables.

There is convincing data that preschool programs can have beneficial effects for children from low-income backgrounds, almost regardless of program specifics. A Consortium of twelve research groups who had conducted early education programs in the 1960s followed up on their graduates in 1976–1977. The original programs varied considerably in the age of the children involved, whether or not they worked with parents, and in the sheer amount of program time, but all demonstrated staying power. For in-stance, fewer program children were assigned to special classes than controls, and fewer were held back in grade (Lazar, Darlington, Murray, Royce, & Snipper, 1982; see also Schweinhardt & Weikart, 1981). No one suggests that the programs served to inoculate children against school failure. The im-plication, rather, is that the mechanisms are social; that the programs either had a direct influence on the child's sense of competence or an influence on par-ent interests, expectations, and relationships with the child. Certainly these speculations warrant fur-ther study.

In evaluation studies of the national programs, data on social behavior were relatively sparse. Com-parisons of children in Follow Through programs with controls yielded some contradictory findings (e.g., Abelson, Zigler, & DeBlasi, 1974; Shapiro, 1973). Miller and Dyer found, at the end of the preschool year, that Darcee effects were most evi-dent in areas of motivation and attitude, including inventiveness; that an enriched program appeared to increase curiosity and school participation; and that Montessori children were high on inventiveness and curiosity. They note that it is difficult to trace the antecedents of such patterns. Since curiosity and in-ventiveness were not taught directly in any program, it was considered likely that ecological or interac-tional factors indirectly affected these aspects of development.

In her study of Follow Through children, Stall-ings found lower absence rates among children in the open, flexible programs, interpreting this as evi-dence of more positive attitudes toward school. She also found higher scores on the Intellectual Achieve-ment Responsibility Scale (IAR), though this find-ing is not easy to interpret since these children ac-cepted more responsibility for their successes than other children but not for their failures. The Abt analysis, however, suggested that basic skills pro-grams led to higher scores on responsibility for

achievement as well as greater self-esteem. The Abt evaluation raised considerable controversy, per-haps inevitably, since the Follow Through evalua-tion was beset by political pressures from the begin-ning and no evaluation could have satisfied all the constituents (see Elmore, 1976; Haney, 1977; Rhine, 1981; Stebbins et al., 1977). The Ford Foun-dation commissioned an evaluation of the evaluation to be conducted by four impartial experts. Their cri-tique, entitled *No Simple Answer* (House, Glass, McLean, & Walker, 1978), criticized the categori-zation of the models, the choice of measures, and the analytic strategy. They found the classification of programs simplistic and unclear, with too many marginal cases, and the measures both biased toward the basic skills programs and inappropriate. They note that the IAR scale and Coopersmith Self Esteem Index are not suitable to the age levels studied, that both depend on reading skills, and that measures show low intercorrelations. Finally, they criticized the handling of the data and pointed out that the report presents only one method of data analysis. On reanalyzing the data, they found no important dif-ferences among models.

Comparative evaluation at preschool and early primary levels, then, has been relatively disappoint-ing. Despite vast efforts at evaluative research, we have little certainty about the comparative effects of different educational models on the social develop-ment of young school children. It seems evident that the spread of preschool education to children who are poor and of different ethnic groups has been generally beneficial to the children and their fami-lies, and the Consortium findings substantiate this impression. The effects of different approaches, however, have been subject to washout or open to different interpretations. It is unlikely that the very different school contexts created by the various models have no differential impact on the social ex-perience and expectations of the young child. It is possible, however, that there are limitations on com-parative assessment of young children, especially through conventional testing. As White et al. (1973) have noted, preschool evaluation must probably move toward observational techniques and forma-tive rather than summative research. It is also possi-ble that we will need to look to the data on older children in order to understand the relationship be-tween different educational approaches and chil-dren's development.

Elementary School.   The data gathered from elementary school children are generally more de-pendable than preschool data and tap a broader range of dimensions. The behavior of these older pupils is more stable and reflects several years of experience within the school context.

There have been several reviews of comparative research on elementary education (e.g., Gatewood, 1975; Gump, 1978; Horwitz, 1979; Walberg, 1979), as well as some discussion about alternative methods for synthesizing the cumulative findings (Marshall, 1981; Peterson, 1979). Horwitz prepared a ''box score'' of the results of approximately 200 studies comparing traditional and open education, noting that positive effects are more frequently associated with open settings but that in some areas most studies find no significant differences. He concludes that ''the open classroom sometimes has measurable advantages for children, and . . . sometimes appears to make no measurable difference, but . . . rarely appears to produce evidence of measurable harm'' (p. 80). Peterson integrated data from many of the same studies considered by Horwitz, but took into account the size of the effects as well as the sheer number of significant findings in each direction. Her conclusions were not basically different from those of Horwitz, nor could she draw definite inferences from attempts to explain inconsistencies between studies by considering student characteristics. Nevertheless, such efforts to refine the analysis and synthesis of cumulative research findings are probably crucial for clarifying the nature of comparative effects (see also Marshall, 1981).

Most comparative studies of elementary school children test academic variables. In their study of over 7,000 children, Epstein and McPartland (1979) conclude that, ''at the elementary and secondary levels, students neither gain nor lose in their performance on standardized achievement tests as a consequence of attending open schools'' (p. 302). Horwitz also reports that three quarters of 102 studies concerning achievement found either no significant differences or mixed results, while the remaining studies were evenly divided. In future research, it may be more productive to study learning patterns in different contexts than to continue global assessments of comparative achievement.

In reviewing the findings concerning social development, we consider four clusters: attitude toward school, self-concept, social relationships, and learning behavior and style.

Attitudes Toward School. It has been assumed that the atmosphere of open settings and the opportunity to choose activities would make children in open classrooms more appreciative of their schools than children in traditional settings. The research

data have generally borne out this expectation. Children in open classrooms reported more positive attitudes toward school in 40% of the studies reviewed by Horwitz; traditional school children were more positive in only 4%. While the trend is clear, approximately half the studies found no consistent difference. Discrepancies in the findings may reflect both variability in defining the environment, as already discussed, and differences in the methods for assessing children's attitudes, which ranged from informal questionnaires to standardized scales. Also, some studies focus on early grades while others assess older children.

Perhaps the most convincing studies are those that define the environment clearly, gather material from children at least 8 or 9 years old, and describe specific instruments (e.g., Groobman et al., 1976; Minuchin et al., 1969; Ruedi & West, 1973; Traub, Weiss, & Fisher, 1974; Tuckman, Cochran, & Travers, 1974; Wilson, Langevin, & Stuckey, 1972). Several of these studies suggest that cumulative experience in alternative environments is an important determinant of attitude. Traub, Weiss, and Fisher (1974), assessing the attitudes of 8- and 11-year-olds, found that only the older children in open and traditional classrooms were significantly different from each other. Further evidence of cumulative effect comes from the investigations of Groobman et al. (1976) and Epstein and McPartland (1979). In the former study, attitudes of sixth-grade students in their first year at informal schools were comparable to those of students in traditional schools, but positive feelings about school were stronger for sixth graders in their second year, and most positive for those with three years of experience in the informal setting.

Self-Concept. Self-concept is the focus of many comparative studies, despite persistent difficulties of definition and measurement. Most studies investigate self-esteem through such instruments as the Sears Self Concept Inventory, the Piers-Harris Children's Self Concept Scale, or the Coopersmith Self Esteem Inventory. Self-concept is often treated as a unitary dimension, and children are scaled according to the way they present their sense of competence and satisfaction. The issue of whether such data represent the child's perception of self or a defensive communication has not been resolved.

The underlying assumption is that children in open classrooms will have higher self-esteem because they live in more supportive school environments and have more satisfying experiences of mastery. In an earlier publication, the authors and their colleagues questioned the assumption that growth-supporting environments necessarily generate a constant sense of self-satisfaction. Like many investigators since, we found no difference in the sheer self-confidence of modern and traditional school children (Minuchin et al., 1969). Horwitz's review of 61 studies indicates that almost three-quarters did not find significant differences. When differences were found, however, 16 of 18 studies favored open classrooms (e.g., Abelson et al., 1974; Heimgartner, 1974; Purkey, Graves, & Zellner, 1970; and Wilson, Langevin, & Stuckey, 1972).

Aspects of self-concept other than self-esteem in relation to schooling have drawn little research attention since the Bank Street study in the 1960s, which investigated self-knowledge as a function of different school environments. It was our assumption that varied learning experiences, personalized contact with teachers, and more opportunities for interaction with peers would provide children in modern schools with more differentiated feedback about themselves, and that the style of intellectual inquiry would extend to ways of thinking about the self. We found that children from the modern schools were more personalized and differentiated in describing themselves than children from traditional schools. It is unclear whether children from current open classrooms would show similar effects, since the open-classroom philosophy has focused less directly on the individuality of teacher-child relationships. Nevertheless, it might be assumed that children in open classrooms are exposed to experiences that give differentiated feedback, and this assumption should be tested further. Such research should keep in mind developmental findings that children in the early grades do not readily take multiple perspectives or regard the self objectively. Comparative research on the self-differentiation of younger children may only generate data that are contradictory and difficult to interpret.

Another aspect of self-concept relevant to school experience is the child's conception of self as female or male. Open and traditional environments provide different experiences and models for children, with implications for their learning of gender-associated roles. In our study of fourth-grade children, we tested the effects of different school settings on this area of development. The most modern school presented an almost paradoxical set of attitudes. It encouraged a differentiated view of the self as an individual but a less differentiated view of male and female characteristics and roles than was typical of the culture. The children's attitudes reflected both aspects. Their self-concepts were more differentiated than those of children from traditional schools but girls, in particular, had less conventional and dichotomized perceptions of males and females, both as children and in future roles. Their play behavior was also less sex-typed, and they had some tendency to make more cross-gender friendship choices (Minuchin, 1965; Minuchin et al., 1969).

The amount of subsequent research in this area has been surprisingly small, given the interest in the topic, but some studies have confirmed the findings. Berk and Lewis (1977) and Bianchi and Bakeman (1978) found typical patterns of same-sex play among young children in traditional schools, but a high incidence of cross-gender play in open settings. Epstein (1978) tested friendship choices among children in middle and secondary schools, finding that males and females chose each other more frequently in open than traditional settings. Findings in open classrooms range from those in which a majority of peer interaction takes place in mixed groups (Berk & Lewis, 1977; Bianchi & Bakeman, 1978, 1980) to those in which most contacts are with children of the same sex, even though the incidence of cross-gender interaction is higher than in traditional classrooms (Minuchin, 1976; Minuchin et al., 1969; Travis, 1974). Such discrepancies, which may partly reflect age differences, require further investigation. In general, the data suggest that conventional descriptions of gender-related behavior are tied to the traditional environments in which behavior is usually investigated. When environments vary, behavior appears to vary as well. Documenting the environmental conditions associated with different patterns of behavior should lead to a more differentiated theory of gender development.

Social Relationships. There is no question that the patterns of social interaction in open and traditional classrooms are different. Many studies have documented the wider variety of interactions in open classrooms and the existence of more cross-gender contact, more cooperative work behavior, and more varied bases for forming friendships and achieving popularity. Some investigators who document behavior in open classrooms have distinguished between on-task behavior, meaning work activity, and off-task behavior, or social interchange. Minuchin's (1976) observations of children in first-grade open classrooms, however, indicate that spontaneous interchange includes both work-oriented and social matters, often occurring simultaneously. Treating social interaction as off-task ignores the fact that children learn from each other as well as from teachers and material.

Comparisons of peer interaction include research

on friendship and cooperative behavior, as well as the cross-gender contact discussed earlier. Studies of friendship have generally been based on sociometric data from children in elementary or junior high grades. The assumption has been that children in open classrooms are more apt to find friends of different kinds and less likely to adopt the teacher's value system. Typically, children who have high status with peers also meet the teacher's norms for academic achievement and social behavior (Glidewell, Kantor, Smith, & Stringer, 1966). In comparative studies, however, investigators find more diffuse, less hierarchical patterns of friendship in open classrooms, with fewer stars and fewer children who are isolated or scapegoated. They also find a higher incidence of friendships among children with dissimilar qualities or levels of ability (Barker-Lunn, 1970; Epstein, 1978; Hallinan, 1976; Signatur & Reiss, 1974).

Hallinan (1976) analyzed sociometric data from 51 classrooms, grades 5 to 8, classified according to the Walberg-Thomas scale. She found a fixed hierarchy of choices in traditional classrooms with clear consensus concerning popular and isolated children, while patterns in the open classrooms were less focused. She also found that unreciprocated choices were less frequent in open classrooms and were more quickly dissolved than in traditional classrooms, where they persisted over time. Hallinan suggests that children in open classrooms have more opportunity for reality testing and for reorganizing their friendships toward greater psychological comfort. Her findings are supported by Epstein's (1978) large-scale study at upper elementary and high school levels. More students were selected and fewer neglected as best friends in open settings, and choices were more reciprocal. Students in open schools chose more friends from outside their own classes, and their choices were more heterogeneous.

Studies of cooperation in the classroom usually focus on learning activities, bridging the domains of social and academic behavior. Open and traditional environments provide different opportunities for cooperative work. In traditional environments teachers generally teach to the whole class and children work individually; sharing information is seen as cheating. In open classrooms there is considerable small group effort, and an emphasis on developing a cooperative work ethic. Although some comparative studies gather observational data in the classroom where the incidence of cooperation is partially a function of opportunity, most studies compare the performance of children on experimental tasks that require cooperation (e.g., Downing & Bothwell,

1979; Duckworth, 1971; Feeney, Hochschild, Joy, & Sadow, 1974; Minuchin et al., 1969; Solomon & Kendall, 1976; Traub et al., 1972). Of the comparative studies reviewed by Horwitz, 67% show that children in open classrooms cooperate more effectively; in none of the studies were children from traditional classrooms more cooperative. Downing and Bothwell (1979) paired eighth-grade students of the same sex for a game in which more points accrue from greater cooperation between partners. Students from open schools anticipated more peer interaction than those from traditional schools, as indicated by the way they seated themselves near their partners, and they played the game more cooperatively.

Some studies have also suggested that cooperative behavior may vary with gender, ethnicity, and age. In Downing and Bothwell's study, females were more cooperative in matched than in mixed racial pairs, while white males were generally more cooperative and less competitive than black males. In an observational study of prosocial behavior among 5- to 8-year-olds in a vertical open classroom, Roth (1981) found that older girls were more often involved in cooperative behavior than boys or younger children. Since open classrooms may communicate values and generate behavior not usually considered typical in the middle years (e.g., cross-gender contact and cooperation), it becomes important to clarify the parameters of change and the details of interaction between developmental trends and environmental settings.

Learning Style.   Some aspects of learning style such as creativity, curiosity, locus of control, and autonomous behavior are part of personal and social development. Comparison of children in open and traditional classrooms suggests that open settings are more conducive to favorable development on all these dimensions, but findings concerning creativity, curiosity, and locus of control tend to be equivocal (Horwitz, 1979). Findings concerning autonomy, on the other hand, are clear. Of 23 studies, 78% report greater autonomy in open classrooms (Horwitz, 1979), including those by Bleier, Groveman, Kuntz, & Mueller, 1972; Epstein & McPartland, 1979; Myers, 1971; Sullivan, 1974; and Traub et al., 1974. Only 18% report mixed or nonsignificant findings.

In the study of Traub et al. (1974), 11-year-olds in open schools reported initiating their own work and acting in terms of their own values more often than their traditional school counterparts. Epstein and McPartland (1979) found similar differences in students' self-reliance in their large-scale study of 39 open and traditional elementary, middle, and secondary schools. Their data are based on information from a self-report scale measuring the individual's need for social approval and explicit direction. The scale successfully identifies those named by teachers and peers as independent students, lending external validity to the self-report data. It also shows developmental validity in that older children score higher on self-reliance. Student satisfaction, school adjustment, and prosocial task-related behavior, as well as self-reliance, were more clearly related to the informal relations between teachers and students than to the formal organization of the classroom, suggesting that effective exemplars of open education are characterized not only by open organization but by a nonauthoritarian atmosphere and decision-making style on the part of the teacher.

In the comparative research on elementary schools a pattern of findings emerges, in spite of problems of conception, measurement, environmental definition, and research design. It seems generally established that children in open settings are more positive in their attitudes toward schools and teachers than children in traditional classrooms, and are part of a peer system in which they are more likely to find friends and make nonstereotyped cross-gender contacts. They also engage in more cooperative work with others and show more self-reliant behavior—an important combination of autonomy and mutuality in learning situations. There is little evidence that different school environments affect self-esteem, but the self-conceptions of children in open classrooms appear more differentiated. If we look at this pattern, Horwitz's conclusion that open classrooms do not produce measurable harm seems unduly parsimonious.

Future research should be directed toward more refined analysis of environmental conditions and detailed study of the interaction between child and setting. A small body of studies has examined person-environment interaction in different elementary school settings, focusing on variations in such child characteristics as anxiety, curiosity, locus of control, compliance, ability, and self-concept, as well as on the socioeconomic background of the children (e.g., Arlin, 1975; Bennett, 1976; Brophy & Evertson, 1976; Grimes & Allinsmith, 1961; Minuchin, 1976; Minuchin et al., 1969; Peterson, 1979; Solomon & Kendall, 1979). The findings in most of these areas are not yet clear and are sometimes contradictory, but the move toward more differentiated study is positive. Optimal settings are by definition flexible, and increased knowledge should permit adaptations within the setting so that different kinds of children can function well.

High School. Most·research on the alternative high schools that flourished in the 1960s is methodologically flawed, seldom including comparative data, and it is difficult to draw firm conclusions about effects. However, Duke and Muzio's (1978) summary of 19 studies of alternative public secondary schools provides some tentative conclusions. The schools served mixed populations, including students with poor academic and behavioral records in previous schools. No clear findings about academic progress emerged from the data but social patterns were clearer, though they can only be regarded as suggestive. Students in alternative schools had positive attitudes about their schools and teachers and showed some growth in self-confidence. They also appeared to engage in less antisocial behavior and fighting than was typical in traditional secondary schools. Among the more tangible data were those reporting low dropout rates, indicating at least a minimal sense of fit between the student and the school.

In order to investigate further the relation between alternative high schools and problems of discipline, Duke and a colleague studied 18 "schools within schools" in California (Duke & Perry, 1978). Staff and students were asked to rate a series of behavior problems and compare their incidence in alternative and conventional schools. Both teachers and students reported fewer and less serious problems in alternative schools. These data are hardly objective and may be considered as much a measure of loyalty as a report of social reality. However, Duke and Perry's observations confirmed the findings; they noted that fighting, stealing, and vandalism were rare in alternative schools, though smoking, profanity, cutting class, and drug use were more evident. They suggest that personalized teacher-student relations, student participation in school governance, and a nonauthoritarian rule structure contributed to the low rate of discipline problems. The conventional high schools often had a large number of minutely defined rules and rigid ways of dealing with infractions. Other relevant characteristics of the alternative schools were their small size and the skill of their teachers, though neither is an inevitable feature of the alternative setting.

Duke and Perry also gathered data on the perceived characteristics of students who do well in alternative settings. Findings highlight the combination of intrinsic motivation and participation in school activities. Students who needed direction and were not socially involved were seen as unsuccessful. There is a striking correspondence between this pattern and the qualities of autonomy and cooperation encouraged by open elementary schools. Students who bring this paradigm into the open high school setting seem to fare well.

Among studies that compare the effects of different high school environments, two are noteworthy for their scope and design. One is the work of Epstein and McPartland, referred to earlier (Epstein, 1978; Epstein & McPartland, 1979). Their study employs a large sample and a sophisticated system for data analysis, though it is limited by the dependence on self report data for assessing social development and coping skills. The more varied and reciprocal friendship pattern and the greater self reliance reported for students in open elementary classrooms were also generally characteristic of students from open high schools. These students were more positive in their evaluation of teachers than students in traditional settings, and the longer students had been attending open schools the more they valued the school and its personnel. Longitudinal data suggested that ''students with adjustment problems one year had fewer problems the next year in more open schools, while in traditional schools more students continued to have discipline problems from one year to the next'' (Epstein & McPartland, 1979, p. 303).

Rutter and his associates assessed the effects of differences among schools although they did not conceptualize the schools as exemplars of an integrated approach (Rutter et al., 1979). It is a conclusion rather than an assumption of their study that schools have an ''ethos.'' Rutter and his group studied 12 inner city London schools, documenting their administrative and social nature and measuring four kinds of pupil outcomes: behavior, attendance, delinquency, and academic attainment. They found that the behavior and attainments of students in different schools were distinct, but that these differences did not primarily reflect the background and characteristics of the school population; rather, they reflected in large part the experiences of the secondary years. Rutter and his colleagues point out that variations in outcome were not associated with physical or administrative features of the schools, but were systematically related to social organization, including the degree of academic emphasis, teacher behavior, the system of rewards and punishments, and student roles. The combined measures of ''school process'' related more significantly to outcome variables than did individual measures. The correlation was especially high with student behavior, which included simple breaches of the rules such as lateness or talking in class, and more serious matters such as truancy, disruptive class behavior, and damage to school property. School process variables were also related to the other three outcome measures, although ability and background variables were also influential.

Certainly Rutter's investigation of English schools is not concerned with open-traditional contrasts. The schools in his study varied in social organization but it is evident from descriptive data that lessons were quite formal, teacher praise was not extensive, and student responsibility took conventional forms, such as official school positions, rather than involvement in school governance, as in American alternative schools. Nevertheless, more positive student behavior in the English schools was associated with more praise from teachers, greater academic independence, and more possibilities for participating in school activities. The direction of these findings is notably consistent with that of American studies, despite marked differences in the alternatives being compared.

Summary

The state of the art in comparative research is different at preschool, elementary, and secondary levels. Preschool research has produced little definitive data about the sustained effects of different models. Most studies, however, have dealt with only a narrow band of variables. It is possible that different educational approaches have different effects on such qualities as empathy, curiosity, and interpersonal relationships with peers and adults. These are in development during the preschool years, but have had little comparative study. Research on elementary programs has produced more definitive findings, indicating that children in open environments have more varied social contacts and more positive attitudes toward school; they also show both self-reliant and cooperative behavior in learning situations. The findings from high school research on alternative schools are less firmly based. They suggest, however, that in schools that are not authoritarian in organization, students participate more in school activities, have more varied social relationships, and create fewer discipline problems than students in traditionally organized schools. Recent well-designed studies have also demonstrated the positive effects of clear standards, praise, non-authoritarian teacher attitudes, opportunities for student independence, and a coherent social organization in the school.

While comparative research has been methodologically uneven, recent work has built on accumulated findings, combining data from multiple sources and clarifying the nature of the independent variable. We have reviewed the field in the dichotomous "open-traditional" terms that have characterized thinking and research, but this gross distinction may have outlived its usefulness. Both positive and inconclusive findings point to the need for more refined descriptions of the context.

Productive lines for comparative research include the study of person-environment interaction, focused on the ways in which different kinds of children cope with different school environments; the use of ethnographic methods to document social processes in different educational settings; and the study of consonance and dissonance in home and school environments, as these affect the child's social behavior in school.

The Classroom Context: Teacher-Child Interaction and the Classroom as a Society

The classroom is the child's immediate context in school. If we see the classroom as a social system defined by the interactions among teachers and children, then most of what takes place is irrefutably social. Research on classroom processes reflects the orientation of the investigators, and the literature varies widely in focus and methodology. We review five approaches to classroom research: quantification of teacher-child interaction; ethnographic study of classroom processes; analysis of classroom conventions and social rules; documentation of teachers' responses to different children; and children's perceptions of teacher behavior.

Quantifying Teacher-Child Interaction

This approach, characteristic of educational researchers, seeks to provide a "scientific basis for the art of teaching" (Gage, 1978). The underlying concept has been that of the teacher as leader, the one who makes the rules and determines the climate of the classroom. A model for this work was Lewin, Lippitt, and White's (1939) classic study comparing the effects of authoritarian, democratic, and laissez-faire leadership styles on 10-year-old boys in after-school clubs. Anderson and his colleagues (e.g., Anderson, 1939; Anderson & Brewer, 1946) adapted these concepts to the classroom, defining teaching styles with less political overtone as *dominative* and *integrative*. Withall (1956) devised a method of measuring the "social-emotional" climate of the classroom on a continuum from *teacher-centered* to *learner-centered,* and Flanders and his colleagues developed a system of interaction analysis for observing classroom behavior (Amidon & Flanders,

1963; Amidon & Hough, 1967; Flanders, 1966, 1970). The latter system, widely used in research, focuses on verbal behavior, primarily that of the teacher. Seven categories differentiate "teacher talk," two concern "student talk," and one is a code for "silence or confusion." This emphasis reflects the fact that verbal behavior is easier to code reliably than nonverbal communication, but it also reflects a traditional concept of teaching in which the teacher's primary role is to give information, evaluate performance, and manage classroom procedures.

Coding methods in these systems are objective, but the systems do have a value orientation. The expectation has been that children will learn more and have more positive attitudes toward school in an atmosphere that is integrative rather than dominative, learner-centered rather than teacher-centered, or indirect rather than direct. Many researchers have tallied interactions in many classrooms, but findings have been disappointing and it has been argued that this line of research should be abandoned (e.g., Anderson, 1959). It has continued, however, and Simon and Boyer's 1974 anthology of observational instruments contains dozens that are used in classroom research.

We do not review these studies, partly because they focus on achievement as the primary outcome and partly because there have been several careful summary reviews (e.g., Bennett, 1978; Brophy, 1979; Dunkin & Biddle, 1974; Good, 1979; Rosenshine, 1979; Rosenshine & Furst, 1973). The Dunkin and Biddle review, like others over the years, came to a dismaying conclusion: that the mass of research on teaching has produced inconclusive and inconsistent findings. They note that the single greatest omission in the research had to do with context variables. Many researchers simply had not taken account of the situation, the age or grade of the children, or their ethnic and socioeconomic characteristics. These variations are now being studied, and there is greater awareness that "appropriate teaching behavior" needs to be defined differently in different contexts. Many studies also used an inadequate data base, sometimes only a few hours of observation, and some purported to study teaching without entering a classroom, using the school or district as their unit of analysis. Finally, the bulk of studies has been conducted in traditional classrooms. While such classrooms are prevalent, they are not the only way of organizing classroom life, and findings obtained in these settings cannot be generalized to other contexts.

Recent summaries of research on teaching emphasize the efficacy of direct instruction, or time engaged; student achievement is reliably correlated with the amount of instruction and students' involvement in work. The teacher's managerial skills mediate effective teaching (e.g., Brophy & Evertson, 1976; Good & Power, 1976; Kounin, 1970). At the least, in order for the children to learn and work, the teacher has to be in charge of the classroom to provide the conditions that make work possible.

How one summarizes this work is largely a matter of point of view and the level of analysis considered fruitful. Much of the research has dealt with the teaching of basic skills in the early grades. By and large, it is atheoretical, or aims to test a model of teaching that takes little account of the child as learner (cf. Barr & Dreeben, 1978). The focus on cognitive outcomes, with achievement test scores the almost universal measure, ignores social and emotional development. The search for *the* effective teaching technique has only occasionally taken account of contextual variables. Coding particular types of teacher behavior divorced from context is not enough, as Brophy and Evertson's (1976) analysis of the different functions of teacher praise shows. Gage (1978), in his review of the reviews, argues that the dismal summations of research on teaching may be committing a Type II error, dismissing a relationship that does exist. He advocates a method of statistically summing the results of studies that bear on the same issue. Each study may be flawed and inconclusive, but if their flaws do not coincide, the results can be integrated. Gage's synthesis is more cheerful than that of other reviewers, but still depressing. "Thus the path to increasing certainty becomes not the single excellent study that is nonetheless weak in one or more respects, but the convergence of findings from many studies that are also weak but in many different ways." (p. 233). It may be, but it may also be that what is needed is a reexamination of the basic orientation underlying much of this research: the focus on one-way verbal communication from teacher to child, while paying little attention to child response, the processes of group functioning, or the context in which communications and actions are embedded.

Ethnographic Study of Classroom Processes

The research approach of ecologists, ethnographers, and other field workers shares certain features. The concept of context is central in their work, they are interested in fine-grained descriptive analysis, and they focus on environmental influence, patterns of interaction, and the communication of expectations about appropriate behavior, both through verbal and nonverbal means. They look closely at behavior that typically has been taken for granted in

psychological and educational research. On the other hand, they pay little attention to phenomena that have been central for many psychologists, such as individual characteristics, and are not interested in developmental phenomena; terms such as age, stage, or level seldom appear in their work. The "structures" they are concerned with are those that govern relations between people and between person and environment.

The primary focus of the ecological approach is to link environmental variables and behavior. Ecological psychologists assume that a similarity of shape (or synomorphy) develops between the milieu and standing patterns of behavior, and this requires description and analysis of both milieu and behavior (Gump, 1975). These investigations eschew manipulation of the situation being studied and the analysis of data at a high level of inference. The concept of behavior settings, attempts to analyze the stream of behavior, and the ecological research methods employed by Barker, Wright, Kounin, Gump, and others have influenced many investigators, both in and outside of psychology. This work is not reviewed here, however, since relevant material has been discussed in the earlier section on physical settings, and Gump (1975, 1978, 1980) has recently reviewed research on school environments.

The observational or fieldwork approach attempts to capture the richness and sequential flow of events in classrooms and schools. The anthropological tradition is evident. Some years ago, Henry (1955, 1966) drew attention to the implicit cultural messages that children receive in everyday classroom encounters—the need to be docile and to give the answer that the teacher wants. Such accounts are especially pertinent when one looks at the impact of school on social development, since they elaborate the essentially social and interactive nature of classroom events. The work of Jackson (1968) and of Smith and Geoffrey (1968) clarifies the intricate interplay of events and communication between teachers and children, and the skills required of both to sustain classroom life.

Smith and Geoffrey (1968), in an unusual collaborative effort, documented the "complexities of an urban classroom." Geoffrey was the teacher and Smith the observer of a sixth-seventh grade classroom in a slum neighborhood. Smith recorded events for a full school year, producing a detailed picture of the social structure of the classroom and the children's roles and belief systems. Their analysis of the evolution of individual student roles—the "court jester," the "nonworker"—highlights the contribution of both teacher and children in crystallizing such roles. Their data and concepts make it clear that patterns of classroom social interaction are developed and maintained as a complex system.

Rist's (1970) case study of children in a ghetto school also focuses on the expectations and social interactions that create social organization in the classroom. Rist observed a class of black children and their teacher from the first day of school through the first half of second grade. He describes the process by which the kindergarten teacher, on the eighth day of school, sorts the 30 children into three reading groups; from then on they sit at three different tables.

> The organization of the kindergarten classroom according to the expectation of success or failure after the eighth day of school became the basis for the differential treatment of the children for the remainder of the school year. From the day that the class was assigned permanent seats, the activities in the classroom were perceivably different. . . . The fundamental division of the class into those expected to learn and those expected not to permeated the teacher's orientation to the class. (p. 423)

The children came to adopt the teacher's attitude: "fast learners" make belittling remarks about children at the lower status tables, who withdraw and express hostility among themselves. The system is self-perpetuating, continuing through second grade. Rist convincingly demonstrates that the kindergarten teacher's criteria for a "fast learner" had to do with middle-class status—speaking standard English, being neat and clean, being at ease with adults, coming from a family that has more education and is not on welfare. These judgments determined the children's future academic placement and their opportunities for social interaction.

Rist (1978) also studied an urban middle-class white school during its first year of racial integration. Approximately 30 black children were bused to a school with a white enrollment of approximately 500. The prevailing concept of integration, he concluded, was to absorb the black children into the school with as little recognition of their difference as possible. The idea was to be "fair," and to make the black students just like the white students; the consequence was to render them invisible. The processes through which integration is or is not achieved are social. The children's academic chances and the social consequences are intertwined.

These studies, like the reports of teachers, evoke the immediacy of classroom life. They are often crit-icized because of the anecdotal nature and questionable generalizability of the data (e.g., Brophy, 1979; Mehan, 1979), but the anecdotes are often telling, and resonate with the experience of anyone who has spent time in schools. When these researchers tally teacher or child behaviors, they do not lose sight of the context. Aside from offering a fare richer than the rather thin gruel provided by strictly quantitative studies, they can be viewed as sourcebooks for the more methodologically oriented researcher, since they describe phenomena that research is supposed to account for.

Another group of researchers specifically labels its work as ethnographic. Ethnographers share with ethnomethodologists (e.g., Garfinkel, 1967) a resolute desire to keep the analysis of social phenomena as close as possible to the participants' perception (Erickson, 1979; McDermott, 1977; Mehan, 1979). Edward Hall's (1959, 1966) ideas are evident here, and Dell Hymes' (1974) concept of communicative competence is at the core. Ethnographic work entails the detailed analysis of interactional behavior and language. It often uses an advanced video technology that allows for the repeated viewing of events, and has been greatly facilitated by the development of the wireless microphone. These researchers tend to locate their work in the early grades, since this is when children learn the how, what, when, and where of appropriate behavior.

Within this group, researchers focus on different aspects of the classroom system. McDermott (1977), for example, is interested in the ways people work to "make sense" of each other's behavior. As an example of failure to develop the necessary trusting relations, he describes Rosa, a failing student in a first-grade classroom. She seems to be constantly trying to get a chance to read but is never called on. Analysis of filmed material shows that she in fact conspires with the teacher, asking for a turn just when the teacher has called on someone else, or calling for a turn but looking away from the teacher, who feels she does not know how to reach this child. The interaction is a nice example of what systems theorists would identify as the maintenance of a dysfunctional system.

Shultz and Florio (1979) deal with the development of social competence, which requires the capacity to monitor the context and know when it changes (cf. Erickson & Shultz, 1977). They studied first-grade classroom work periods and the junctures between them, considering that one of the teacher's major functions is to communicate to students what context they are in and how to understand transitions, so that they know what is expected of them. They note that some of the teacher's communication is verbal, but that the teacher signals the children also by posture, movement, and gestures.

In a similar effort to understand the structure of classroom sequences, Mehan (1979) concentrated on the analysis of lessons, finding a recurrent sequence of events: teacher initiation, child response, and (often but not always) teacher evaluation. Further analysis of these sequences demonstrated the rhythmic cooperative activity of children and teacher, which created and maintained procedures for turn-allocation and for getting and holding the floor. Mehan notes that successful students must learn not only the academic content but the appropriate form for presenting their knowledge. His analysis of extended sequences of classroom discourse also showed change during the school year, demonstrating that the appropriate forms are learned by the children in the course of interaction with the teacher and each other (see also Griffin & Humphrey, 1978).

The detailed analysis of classroom events highlights the complexity of communications hitherto dismissed as routine. Green and Harker (1982) delineate the communicative processes involved when a teacher reads a story to children. Other studies in this mode focus on the teacher's communication of rules such as "only one person speaks at a time" (Wallat & Green, 1979), on the verbal and nonverbal behavior of children and teachers that create the conditions for "first circle time" (Bremme & Erickson, 1977), and on similarities and differences in discourse at school and at home (Florio & Shultz, 1979; Shultz, Florio, & Erickson, 1982).

It is important to realize that children are not taught these rules of the classroom. Of course, teachers make certain rules explicit (no running, yelling, or chewing gum; raise your hand if you want to talk). For the most part, however, the rules governing the forms of social interaction in the classroom are tacit.

Analysis of Classroom Conventions and Social Rules

Another group of researchers also studies the normative rules that govern classroom life, but they are more interested in demonstrating the existence and application of social norms than in uncovering the strategic acts that create them. Further, this set of studies uses more traditional techniques, relying on narrative records or interviews. LeCompte's (1978) analysis of how children learn to work in school, and

Blumenfeld et al.'s (1979) study of how children learn the student role, focus on the normative rule structure generated and communicated by the teacher.

Another kind of rule-governed behavior is examined by Much and Shweder (1978). They analyze what they call *situations of accountability;* that is, situations in which one is asked to give an account of why someone has done something. They are interested in the messages associated with such situations. For example:

Everett has brought a box to school. Adelle takes it to use. Everett asks to have it back, but Adelle won't give it to him.

Everett: Well, it's my box and I can do whatever I want with it.
Adelle: *Not if you bring it to school it isn't.* (Adelle keeps the box)

Cultural Control Message: If you bring toys to school, they become property for common use. (p. 25)

Much and Shweder classify different kinds of cultural rules—regulations, conventions, moral truths, and instructions—and analyze the breach recognition patterns of 2- to 6-year-olds. These young children recognize such breaches, demonstrating an awareness of expected behavior and distinguishing among different kinds of rules.

Their analysis links directly with the recent work of Turiel and his coworkers. Turiel's primary aim is to distinguish concepts of social convention from concepts of morality, and to demonstrate that children and adults recognize the difference (Turiel, 1978a, 1978b, 1979). Much of the data that he and his collaborators have collected concern judgments of infractions in school.

Nucci and Turiel (1978) observed social transgressions in preschool classrooms. A social conventional transgression might be working or playing in the wrong place at the wrong time, and a moral transgression might be hitting a child or taking something that belongs to another. When children were interviewed about incidents that had occurred in their school, their classifications of conventional and moral transgressions agreed with adults' judgment in 60 of the 72 instances. However, teachers responded to more social conventional transgressions than did children, who were likely to consider as moral what teachers took to be conventions or rules. In spite of some disparities between the Much-

Shweder and Nucci-Turiel findings, it seems clear that children of preschool age respond differently to different kinds of transgressions in the school context. Older children (second-, fifth-, and seventh-graders) also make this distinction (Nucci & Nucci, 1979). When dealing with a violation of social convention, they comment on the rules, reserving arguments about the intrinsic consequences of events for infractions of morality.

Weston and Turiel (1979) examined children's evaluation of school rules. Do children think that a school can establish any kind of rule, and must all rules be followed? Children 5 to 11 years old were told hypothetical stories in which a child engaged in certain actions—hitting, undressing on the playground, leaving toys on the floor. They were asked what the teacher would say and to evaluate the teacher's response. Most children thought the teacher would act in accord with school policy, but many thought that the teacher should reprimand a child for hitting even if the school did not have a rule against such behavior. They did not assume all policies are right, and distinguished between rules about harming others and those having to do with conventions such as dress codes and messiness.

Much of the rule-governed behavior identified by various researchers, such as LeCompte (1978) and Blumenfeld et al. (1979), belongs to what Turiel and his colleagues have called the "domain of social convention." Teachers, however, often confuse the issue and treat such transgressions as if they were moral. Nucci (1979) notes that it is "domain inappropriate" for teachers to moralize about acts children view as conventional, or to justify moral acts in terms of social organization. The children may or may not be confused, but the teacher's lack of differentiation may erode her or his credibility as knowledgeable adult.

Documenting Teachers' Responses to Different Children

In much of the research on classrooms, effects have been considered unidirectional, flowing from teacher to child, with an underlying assumption that the teacher has equivalent impact on all children in the class. Any description of classroom life, however, throws into relief the particularity of the teacher's interaction with different children. This has been apparent in some of the studies described earlier; for instance, in Rist's analysis of the allocation of children in reading groups, Smith and Geoffrey's elucidation of how certain children come to fill special roles in the classroom, and McDermott's description of a child's dysfunctional behavior. Jackson's

(1968) description of "life in classrooms," and study of communication in sixth-grade classrooms (Jackson & Lahaderne, 1967) demonstrated the variation as well as the uniformities in the experiences of different children in the same classroom. More recently, Carew and Lightfoot (1979) have developed profiles of the dispersal of teacher attention in four first-grade classrooms, showing that teachers give demonstrably more attention to some children than to others. The assertion that different children are treated differently often meets with considerable resistance, for it seems to go against the ethos of teaching. The teacher should be fair and differential treatment suggests bias. At the same time the teacher is exhorted to respond to children's individual needs, and to adapt curriculum and teaching method to individual ability, pace, and style. Some teachers may be aware of the bases of their differential responsiveness and, as in Carew and Lightfoot's study, "when [they] treat children dissimilarly, they may be responding rationally and sensitively to manifest differences" (p. 16). Others, however, may not. Further, we have little data about the cumulative or long-term impact of teachers' differential ways of responding to different children (see, however, Pedersen, Faucher, & Eaton's (1978) provocative analysis).

In this section we examine studies that have dealt with teachers' reactions to children's personal characteristics, their expectations of children's performance, and their responses to children's social class, ethnic background, and gender.

Teachers' Responses to Children's Personal Characteristics. Silberman (1969, 1971), working with third-grade teachers and children, identified four qualitatively different relationships that teachers might have with children. He called these attachment, concern, indifference, and rejection. Silberman's categorization has been used in several studies, some of which modified the original methodology and added to the range of age and SES backgrounds (e.g., Good & Brophy, 1972; Jenkins, 1972). Findings have been quite consistent. Teachers are generally attached to students who are achieving, conforming, and make few demands. They show concern for students who make demands appropriate to classroom activity, but are indifferent to invisible and silent children and have little interaction with them. They reject children who make many demands considered illegitimate or who tend to be "behavior problems." In a similar vein, N. Feshbach (1969) investigated the kinds of personality characteristics preferred by female education majors, finding that they preferred students described as rigid, conforming, and orderly, and rated last those described as independent, active, and assertive. This study was replicated with student teachers, psychology majors, and Teacher Corps interns, and the pattern appeared only among the student teachers (Beigel & Feshbach, 1970). Nevertheless, Good and Grouws (1972) found that the pattern applied to male as well as female student teachers, and Levitin and Chananie (1972) showed that female primary school teachers favor dependent behavior in both boys and girls. There seems to be general support for the idea that teachers are more receptive to conforming children. Perhaps what is most important in these studies is the demonstration that teacher time, attention, and involvement is differentially distributed among the children in the classroom.

Teachers' Expectations of Children's Performance. The most widely known study concerning teachers' expectations of children's academic performance is Rosenthal and Jacobson's *Pygmalion in the Classroom* (1968). The findings suggested a self-fulfilling prophesy and appealed both to the knowledgeable and the naive. It seemed reasonable to suppose that what teachers expect from children will influence how they treat them, and that this will affect how the children actually perform. *Pygmalion* created considerable furor. The study has been severely criticized on methodological grounds (e.g., Snow, 1969; Thorndike, 1968), and has been replicated with methodological improvements (e.g., Fleming & Anttonen, 1971). Reviews of this literature indicate that the original approach to manipulating teachers' expectations (by providing fictional aptitude scores) oversimplifies the issues. A mass of variables is involved and the notion of the self-fulfilling prophecy is not always warranted (see Braun, 1976; Brophy & Good, 1974; Cooper, 1979; Good, 1980). The fact that teachers have different expectations for different children, however, is not usually questioned.

Recent formulations suggest that, because teachers expect certain kinds of behavior from high achievers and different behavior from low achievers, they treat them differently and thereby sustain the patterns (e.g., Cooper, 1979; Good, 1980). High achievers are given more opportunities to participate in class and more time to respond. They receive more praise for giving the right answers and less criticism than low achievers. Low achievers are expected not to know and not to participate, and are given less opportunity and encouragement for doing so. Cooper's hypothesis, based on attribution theory (Weiner, 1979), is that the teacher initiates more interaction with successful students because their behavior is more predictable. He also posits that students for whom teachers have high expectations are criticized when the teacher thinks they have not tried and praised when they do try, while students for whom the teacher has low expectations are treated less logically. They are less often praised and are both praised and criticized for reasons irrelevant to their effort. To our knowledge, this hypothesis has not been tested. However, it is of interest because it moves beyond counts of praise and blame to the analysis of contingencies, and suggests processes that may mediate teachers' expectations.

Teachers' Responses to Children's Ethnic and Social Class Backgrounds. The American school has been characterized as a mainstream, middle-class, white institution, in which conventional attitudes hold sway. The fact that teachers respond differently to children from different backgrounds is not necessarily cause for alarm; discrimination is not inherently biased. Some studies indicate that differential treatment is consistent with students' needs or teachers' preferences for different kinds of children, but does not systematically adhere to racial or class lines (e.g., Carew & Lightfoot, 1979). However, the bulk of the evidence points to teachers' stereotyped and negative response to children from poor and nonmainstream backgrounds. Leacock (1969) found, for example, that teachers' like/dislike ratings conformed to social stereotypes; blacks were rated lower than whites, and children from low-income backgrounds were rated lower than middle-class children. Teachers were also likely to reject children who were black and of low socioeconomic background who had higher IQs. Leacock's study documents the decline in low-income black children's involvement in school from second to fifth grade, and their decreasing confidence in their ability.

Rist's studies, described earlier, underline the powerful social consequences of teachers' confounding SES with judgments of potential competence. Children of minority groups traditionally have been treated as candidates for assimilation, and teachers often have been ignorant of different cultural meanings that non-mainstream children have learned in their communities. The difficulties experienced in conventional schools by children from Mexican-American, Puerto Rican, Native American and other nonwhite families have been often described or studied (e.g., Castañeda, Ramirez, Cortés, & Barrera, 1971; Cuffaro, Ginsberg, Mack, Sample, Shapiro, Wallace, & Zimiles, 1976; Dumont, 1972; Fuchs & Havighurst, 1972; Indian Education, 1969; Phillips, 1972; U.S. Commission on Civil Rights, 1967, 1972). In a later section we review some of the issues in relation to desegregation, but it is pertinent to note here that the social development of minority children in the classroom depends on the interplay of a number of variables: culturally determined variations in teacher expectations; teachers' preparation for working with children from diverse backgrounds; the white middle-class nature of the standard curriculum; the presence of viable role models in school for minority students; the quality of the relations between school personnel and parents from different ethnic, economic, and educational backgrounds; and the liaison between the school and the community (see Lightfoot, 1978).

Any kind of discrimination that is based on a tag such as race, ethnicity, welfare status, or gender has deleterious effects that are not limited to the persons being discriminated against. Because interaction is reciprocal and perception is guided by expectations, discriminatory behavior serves to strengthen conscious or unconscious stereotypes in the teacher. Further, what happens to one child happens to all. The classroom is a public place, and when one child is treated unfairly the event is everybody's data for the construction of social reality.

Teachers' Responses to Boys and Girls. That teachers treat boys and girls differently in school has been well documented. The data base is exceptionally sturdy; the inferences to be drawn about causal linkages are more problematic. This set of data is a paradigm of the reciprocal influence of teacher and students on each other's behavior, and of the enmeshment between the schoolroom and other social contexts.

Until the 1970s, studies concerning the differential treatment of girls and boys in school focused on the negative effects such treatment might have on boys. The elementary school was seen as a female province. The prevailing modes of conduct, the decorum, and the hours of enforced physical inactivity were considered consonant with the propensities of young girls but antithetic to those of boys. A number of investigators have shown that children see school and school paraphernalia as matching the feminine stereotype (cf. Kagan, 1964; Kellogg, 1969; Stein & Smithells, 1969). The concern was that boys were being "feminized" (cf. Sexton, 1969). In recent years the same facts have been turned to a different issue: How is it that girls, who do better than boys in the elementary grades, falter later on? They do less well than boys in science and math, and continue to be underrepresented in careers that do not conform to conventional concepts of appropriate female roles. The new concern is for "sex equity."

Studies of teachers' reactions to girls and boys document recurrent differences, but it is not immediately clear where the advantages lie. Elementary school teachers interact more with boys than girls, but this interaction is also more often critical. Meyer and Thompson (1956) observed three sixth-grade classrooms, tallying teachers' expressed approval and disapproval of children's behavior. Boys' behavior was disapproved significantly more than girls', on the order of 5:1, and boys also received more approval. Some years later, classroom observation and teacher interviews confirmed that boys received both more instructional and controlling messages from teachers, who also expressed more negative involvement with the boys in their classes (Jackson & Lahaderne, 1967; Jackson, Silberman, & Wolfson, 1969). On the surface, greater teacher attention to boys may suggest an advantage, but the negative critical content does not.

A sizeable body of work has been directed toward gender-related differences in children's and teacher's behavior in preschools. A primary interest has been to demonstrate that boys and girls come to the preschool with different interests and act differently. An equally pertinent question is how teachers respond to boys and girls, and how gender-related patterns are maintained and modified. Fagot and Patterson's (1969) study has been a base for a number of others (e.g., H. Biber, Miller, & Dyer, 1972; Etaugh, Collins, & Gerson, 1975; Fagot, 1973, 1977a, 1977b). They observed 3-year-olds in two nursery groups during free play, systematically coding children's behavior and the responses made by teachers and other children. The behavior of boys and girls fit conventional stereotypes, but they found that teachers reinforce both sexes for "feminine" behavior. Nevertheless, boys maintained their boy-like choices of what to do in school. Fagot and Paterson suggest that peers reinforce sex-typical behavior.

Serbin, O'Leary, Kent, and Tonick (1973) first took account of different frequencies in girl and boy behaviors and then analyzed teacher reactions. Teachers were more responsive to the disruptive behavior of boys than girls and more likely to reprimand boys loudly. When children solicited attention the teacher responded to boys with instructions, giving girls fewer directions but more nurturance. Girls received most attention when they were close to the teacher, whereas boys were contacted at a distance. Thus, the girls were encouraged to stay close to the teacher and seek attention rather than becoming involved in activities. Both Fagot (1977a) and Serbin et al. observe that when boys engage in what the teacher considers task-relevant behavior she or he gives them more positive attention than that given to girls engaged in similar activities. The implication is that the teacher expects such behavior from girls but thinks it requires encouragement in boys.

It should be noted that patterns of sex-typed behavior and of teachers' differential reactions to girls and boys have been established primarily in traditional classrooms. As reported earlier, some research suggests that conventional attitudes, interests, and peer contacts are less evident among the children in nontraditional classrooms. Such issues require further study, however, and the question of teacher behavior with girls and boys in alternative settings has hardly been touched.

When one puts all the research together, one is confronted by a basic paradox. The school is perceived as a female institution; teachers prefer children with "feminine" characteristics; girls "do better" in grade school, and boys are consistently reprimanded more than girls; yet boys not only maintain their boyishness, they are more confident and persistent, while girls' success in the earlier years fades in high school. Working with the concept of learned helplessness, Dweck and her associates have conducted a series of imaginative studies that have bearing on these paradoxical facts. First, Dweck and Bush (1976) established that girls more than boys attribute their failure in achievement situations to lack of ability rather than to lack of effort. If one lacks ability, there is no recourse; if failure follows lack of effort, one needs to try harder. Dweck, Davidson, Nelson, and Enna (1978) then observed and coded teachers' feedback to boys and girls in fourth- and fifth-grade classrooms. The differences were as expected: boys and girls received the same amount of "correctness feedback," but feedback on the intellectual quality of the work was reliably greater for boys than for girls. Boys received considerable criticism for failing to obey the rules, while almost all the work-related criticism of girls referred to intellectual aspects of performance. Teachers also attributed success or failure to different causes: lack of motivation was predominantly attributed to boys, seldom to girls. In an experimental follow-up, the investigators gave children soluble and insoluble anagrams, arranging the feedback to simulate classroom conditions experienced by boys and by girls. Both boys and girls in the teacher-boy simulation later attributed failure to lack of effort; those in the teacher-girl simulation attributed failure to lack of ability. These studies make a strong case that the *pattern* rather than the sheer amount of evaluative feedback affects children's attributions of failure. It seems to us that these studies represent an advance over earlier work. Dweck and her associates have

verified the facts, differentiated the antecedents, and tested the ideas by creating analogous conditions in a controlled situation. This paradigm has seldom been followed in research relevant to schooling.

Another line of research relevant to the classroom experience of boys and girls has looked at the attitudes and behavior of male and female teachers. While there are scattered findings of difference, most studies suggest that male and female teachers do not have very different expectations for gender-related behavior in school. In Etaugh and Hughes' (1975) study, both male and female teachers (grades 5–8) were found to approve of dependency more than aggression for both boys and girls, although this was more pronounced for male than female teachers. In a study of fifth- and sixth-grade boys and girls and male and female teachers, Etaugh and Harlow (1975) found little difference in the children's behavior, but both male and female teachers scolded boys much more often than girls. Fagot (1977b) found some differences between male and female teachers of preschool children, with male teachers showing more physical affection and more often joining the children's play—a finding that may reflect self-selection of nurturant men among preschool teachers. The major finding, however, was that experience was more critical than gender. Both male and female inexperienced teachers responded positively when children behaved in sex-typed ways, while teachers with at least three years of experience responded favorably to the "feminine" behavior of both boys and girls. A good deal of research supports the idea that social roles are powerful and that the gender of the teacher makes less difference in the classroom than might be expected (cf. Brophy & Good, 1974).

In our view, much of the confusion in the research on teachers' differential responses to girls and boys follows from labeling the children's behavior as "feminine" and "masculine." Teachers are undoubtedly influenced by their ideas about what is appropriate for boys and girls, but they are also responding to what they think is appropriate to the schoolroom. The concept of masculinity-femininity is confounded with activity that is task-related and quiet as opposed to that which is large-scale, noisy and potentially disruptive. The fact that these concepts are confused in school is no reason why they should be confused in the research.

Children's Perceptions of Teachers' Behavior

How children learn to decode the messages that teachers send is an important part of social learning in school. Further, different teachers send different messages. We know anecdotally that children are well aware of differences among teachers, but we have little systematic knowledge of how they perceive their teachers, what their expectations are, or the consequences for social development.

Takanishi and Spitzer (1980) investigated children's perception of teachers and peers. They interviewed children of ages 4 to 12 in multiage rooms taught by teaching teams. Children were asked whom they would go to for different purposes (e.g., If you need to spell a word, whom would you ask? If you were feeling sad, who would understand the way you felt?). The children discriminated among the teachers and among peers. Teachers may be perceived differently by different children or, as the investigators note, teachers may offer different resources to different children. Fiedler (1975), working with deCharms' concept of the importance of feeling oneself as an origin, observed classroom interactions and asked students to assess the extent to which their teacher encouraged them to feel in control of their own behavior. The perceptions of these seventh- and eighth-graders related to the amount of influence they actually had.

Elementary school children move from one classroom to another, and teachers, like children, have reputations. We are not aware of any recent studies of what kind of expectations children have of teachers (see, however, Biber & Lewis, 1949). In secondary schools it is likely that students will have different teachers for different subjects, creating the conditions that invite judgment and comparison. We know little about how different teacher and student expectations interact. As in research on parent-child relationships, it has taken a long time for the interaction between teacher and children to be viewed as reciprocal. The suggestion that the observer and the child may not interpret classroom events in the same way has major implications for research (Clark & Creswell, 1978; Weinstein, Middlestadt, Brattesani, & Marshall, 1980).

Summary
The shift from studying teacher behavior per se to studying interactions and the sequences of classroom processes is uncovering some new findings. We see that the classroom is a place for participating in a social system and that all children learn its social rules. Relatively recent data document the processes by which such rules are established, focusing on rules that govern academic and social interchange. No classroom provides a uniform environment for all the children in it. The teacher-child relationship forms a different social experience for each child.

Teacher preferences and expectations and the characteristics of both teacher and child enter into this relationship, and teacher and child together form a pattern of social interaction that stabilizes in the classroom context.

Methods for classroom study are moving from more linear and atomistic studies of teacher influence on children to studies of more complex, interactional, and systemic processes. Current observational and ethnographic studies are both broader in concept and more detailed in focus than earlier work, building a natural history of socialization in the classroom. The field requires both methodological work and more substantive information, but the direction is promising.

Socially Oriented Curricula and Learning Structures

A number of specific curricula have been devised in a direct effort to influence children's personal and social development. In this section we consider educational approaches to promoting moral development and affective growth, and the nature and effects of cooperative learning structures. The latter have usually been created to facilitate academic learning, but they often have social goals as well and are sometimes tested for social effects.

Moral Education
Developmental psychologists have given considerable attention to moral attitudes and behavior. We focus this review on moral education, delimiting the scope to nonparochial schools and defining moral education as the organization of experiences to affect the moral reasoning or behavior of the students.[1] For the most part, such efforts have taken the form of specific programs. However, some educators and psychologists have seen the school itself as an ethical system, and have attempted to create a positive moral environment and encourage the active participation of students in school issues.

Programs in Moral Education. Underlying differences in theory have created diversity in moral education programs. Some conceptions emphasize appropriate moral attitudes and behavior, while others focus on the development of increasingly principled moral reasoning, regardless of content. The emphasis on specific moral content stems from the social learning approach (e.g., Mischel & Mischel, 1976) and has had a research tradition built around the control of unacceptable behavior. The current orientation toward prosocial behavior is in the same social learning tradition but stresses positive aspects of helping, altruism, and cooperation (e.g., Mussen

& Eisenberg-Berg, 1977; Staub, 1978a; Yarrow and Zahn-Waxler, *Vol. IV, Chap*. 6).

Programs based on this orientation and directed to moral education in the schools are rare. A discussion of the prosocial theorists' approach to moral citizenship education, for instance, involves almost no material specifically relevant to the school (Staub, 1978b). One of the few curricula based on social learning theory and developed for school use, Skills for Ethical Action, is directed toward promoting ethical action in daily life (Chapman & Davis, 1978). It consists of 38 sequenced lessons for junior high students, providing instruction in a six-step strategy: identifying value problems, thinking up action ideas, considering self and others, and judging, acting, and evaluating effects. Programs of this nature will probably increase, since the emphasis on teaching definite moral concepts typifies not only social learning theorists but some educators interested in moral education. Peters (1963), for instance, has maintained that basic values must be taught and become habitual before reasoning can be expected to lead to moral ideas or behavior. Leming (1980) also considers that there are certain moral givens and that ''the emphasis on process and ways of decision making ignores the social imperative within which any choice necessarily takes place'' (p. 27). His comment is partly a reaction to the predominant orientation in the field, which stems from the Piaget-Kohlberg tradition and is geared to the enhancement of moral reasoning rather than specific values or behavior. Kohlberg's influential stage theory of moral development will not be reviewed here (see Kohlberg, 1981), but it is pertinent to note that evaluation research has usually employed either Kohlberg's Moral Judgment Interview (MJI), which yields a Moral Maturity Score (MMS) that assesses the individual's level of moral reasoning (Kohlberg, Colby, Gibbs, Speicher-Dubin, Power, & Candee, 1978), or Rest's (1979) Defining Issues Test (DIT).

Some programs based on Kohlberg's thinking incorporate the discussion of moral issues into subject matter curricula. In such cases the material comes from the content of the subject but procedures reflect Kohlberg's ideas about the discussion of moral issues (e.g., Kohlberg & Turiel, 1971). One such program, designed by Biskin and Hoskisson (1977) for fourth- and fifth-grade children, uses moral dilemmas inherent in children's literature and involves the children in role-playing and discussion. The investigators found significant changes in the experimental group as compared to controls, especially in the longer program (18 instead of 7 weeks). Other efforts to combine moral education with subject mat-

ter curricula include programs in *social studies* (e.g., Colby, Kohlberg, Fenton, Speicher-Dubin, & Lieberman, 1977; Fenton, Colby, & Speicher-Dubin, 1974; Galbraith & Jones, 1976, 1977; Lieberman, 1975); *history or current events* (e.g., Black, 1977; Boulogne, 1978; Duffey, 1975); *environmental studies* (e.g., Allen, 1975); and *literature* (e.g., Garrod & Bramble, 1977; Mackey, 1975).

Most moral education programs have been designed as curricula in their own right. They focus on moral issues as the subject matter and test effects on moral reasoning. In Blatt's study, classroom discussions with sixth- and tenth-grade students were based on hypothetical dilemmas, involved the Socratic method, and encouraged cognitive conflict. Approximately one-third of the students in experimental classes moved fully or partially to the next stage, while students in control groups showed no change (Blatt & Kohlberg, 1975). Other studies have also tested the assumptions of cognitive-developmental moral education—that moral reasoning develops through dialogue among peers rather than didactic instruction, and that teachers should facilitate the dialogue by providing stimulating material, probing student reasoning, and offering examples one stage above the student's level (e.g., Adams, 1977; Beck, Sullivan, & Taylor, 1972; Colby et al., 1977; Enright, 1975; Fendel, 1970; Harris, 1977; Harvard, 1974; Lieberman & Selman, 1974; Sapp & Dossett, 1977). Variations in format have included the use of videotapes (Fendel, 1970), gaming (Boulogne, 1978), student role-playing of advanced moral reasoning (Wilkins, 1976), and the use of student leaders for cross-age training (Enright, 1975) or with peers (Wilcox, 1976). In the Wilcox study, trained student leaders appeared more effective than teachers in eliciting discussion from preadolescent inner-city students.

In his review of moral education research, Lockwood (1978) faults some studies on the basis of sample selection, data-gathering techniques, and problems of validity, but he finds others to be well designed (e.g., Blatt & Kohlberg, 1975; Paolitto, 1976) and considers that certain effects have been reasonably well established. The direct discussion of moral dilemmas appears to produce significant advances of approximately half a stage in reasoning, though there is variability among students. Programs mixing moral discussion with psychological education (empathy, communication) have similar though less certain effects. Lockwood points to some limitations, however. Advances are more consistently obtained at lower stages (2, 3, and 4) than at postconventional levels, either because the assessment instrument is differentially sensitive at different levels or because interventions more readily affect less advanced forms of reasoning. There is also some question about the persistence and behavioral meaning of the small measured gains, and there has been criticism of Kohlberg's concepts and assessment techniques (e.g., Gilligan, 1977; Kurtines & Greif, 1974; Turiel, 1979). By the mid-1970s, Kohlberg (1980) reported his own dissatisfaction with the discussion approach to moral education. He was influenced by the fact that teachers in a successful project, when followed up one year later, were not continuing the procedures. He also thought that attempts to induce principled morality in adolescents may be unrealistic since, according to accumulating research, most people do not reach principled levels of moral reasoning even when their logical operations are formal and abstract (Kohlberg, 1979). In addition, he felt that the ethos of the late 1970s was characterized by a preconventional "privatism" focused on the self, rather than a concern with principles of constitutional democracy (stage 5) or even a conventional orientation toward law and order (stage 4). His concepts of moral education shifted, therefore, to an interest in the school as a social system and in the creation of moral school communities.

The School as a Moral System. Schools, like families, are contexts for moral development. Teachers are models of ethical behavior; the classroom peer group conveys attitudes about cheating, lying, and aggression; and the school expresses a value system concerning justice and social regulation through its rules and policies. Schools have not been thoroughly studied in these terms, but the conception has a long history, stemming from the theories of John Dewey and the organization of his laboratory school early in the century. It was Dewey's idea that participation in an egalitarian school community would enable the child to internalize democratic mores and become a contributing citizen of society (Dewey, 1916/1966). Progressive or modern schools established thereafter usually shared this conception.

Though there has been little systematic evaluation of these schools, the comparative study of fourth-grade children described in an earlier section assessed the moral concepts of children from modern and traditional schools through interviews and dilemma situations (Minuchin et al., 1969). Children from traditional schools were preoccupied with issues of obedience and transgression in school, while children from modern schools were concerned with broader issues of morality and self-restraint.

The functional nature of the rule structure in the modern schools, it appeared, allowed the children to think beyond the immediate pressures of external school authority.

More contemporary work on the moral atmosphere of elementary schools has been conducted by Lickona (1977) who worked with teachers to create "just communities" in the classroom. He stresses open teacher attitudes, the use of naturally occurring classroom issues as a basis for moral discussions, and class meetings to create a sense of community. He notes that ethical behavior is primarily acquired in the context of cooperative learning activities, where issues of fairness and responsibility come to the fore. The effect of this program on children has not been documented, and it is evident that such efforts require both more research and more consideration of developmental issues. Second- and sixth-grade children, for instance, are differentially capable of grasping moral issues, understanding the concept of a unified social system, and dealing with the competing perspectives of individuals and the group. In establishing moral classroom communities, the appropriate balance of responsibility between teachers and children would have to be different at different ages.

At the secondary level, conceptions of moral behavior may encompass the incidence of crime and disciplinary problems among students, as well as the extent of active student responsibility toward the school community. There are some data associating small schools and alternative schools with greater student involvement and lesser problems of crime, discipline, and alienation (e.g., Duke & Perry, 1978; Garbarino, 1978; McPartland & McDill, 1976). However, some of the phenomena considered in these studies, such as participation in extracurricular activities, alienation, or minor breaches of discipline, are not clearly moral issues. We focus on the small body of research concerning the moral reasoning of students in democratically and traditionally organized schools.

One such study demonstrated clear differences associated with school experience (Clinchy, Lief, & Young, 1977). Seniors in a progressive high school were more advanced in moral reasoning (MMS) than seniors in a traditional school or sophomores from either school. Sophomores and traditional school seniors reasoned no higher than stage 3, while 40% of the progressive school seniors reasoned at least at stage 4, with a surpising proportion (one-third) at principled levels. The general maturity of the seniors appeared to be a *sine qua non* for such advances, but it did not ensure significant moral growth without accompanying cumulative experiences of participation in the school community. A study of junior high students from traditional and alternative programs did find greater gains after a year in the alternative setting, even though these students were relatively young, but the gains were no greater than those produced by brief interventions (Crockenberg & Nicolayev, 1979). This finding is similar to that of Power (1979), who assessed changes in students of the Cluster School, which was established by Kohlberg as a ''just community.''

The Cluster School, established in 1974 with black and white students from different socioeconomic backgrounds, embodied Kohlberg's changing view of moral education. It shared with other alternative schools an emphasis on self-governance, mutual caring, and group solidarity, but focused specifically on moral issues and the creation of a democratic community. Goals for moral development were aimed at increasing students' responsibility to the community (stage 4) rather than at principled reasoning. In contrast to Kohlberg's earlier educational techniques, which involved discussion of hypothetical dilemmas, moral reasoning, and a facilitating role for teachers, the emphasis here was on considering realistic issues that arise in the school, the nature of moral behavior as well as moral thought, and an active role for teachers as moral advocates. In this orientation Kohlberg drew closer to prosocial theorists and to educators concerned with the moral givens of social life. The experience of Cluster School has been reported by Hersh, Paolitto, & Reimer, 1979; Kohlberg, 1980; Power, 1979; Power & Reimer, 1978; and Wasserman, 1976.

Power's (1979) four-year longitudinal study is the first systematic study of Cluster School. He tested the expectations that environmental norms would move toward higher levels, and that individual moral development would be affected by school values and would advance more than the reasoning of students in other programs. He found that community norms advanced over time toward stages 3 and 4, and that students adhered increasingly to the rules they had established. However, they were better able to maintain a sense of trust in the community and to keep to rules about stealing and attending class than to maintain consistent racial integration or restrain the use of alcohol and drugs. The latter were consensual school values but remained sources of tension and *de facto* violation, presumably reflecting social pressures beyond the school.

The moral reasoning of Cluster students advanced over time, but not in excess of gains achieved through moral discussion programs. In discussing this unexpected finding, Kohlberg and Power, as well as Crockenberg and Nicolayev (1979), point to the problems of measurement. They note that the usual assessment instrument (MJI) presents hypothetical dilemmas and may not register observed changes in students' ability to recognize the moral implications of daily events and to deal with them. They also note that, in the case of Cluster students, there were significant gains for particular students: those who had been in difficulty in previous schools (Wasserman, 1976), and those who had entered the school reasoning at preconventional levels but were reasoning at conventional (stage 4) levels when they graduated.

These investigators have produced interesting data about the possible effects of democratic or ''just'' school communities, but there are many open questions. Can more relevant standardized measures be developed for assessing their effects? Should research in such schools concentrate on ethnographic techniques, since the schools offer a rare opportunity to document naturalistic moral discussions, decision making, and behavior? Does the involvement in realistic moral issues generalize beyond these educational settings? And does experience in such schools differentially affect students from different socioeconomic backgrounds? More and less active participants? Males and females? Research on such issues is sparse, and some theorists have challenged the basic formulations and data base that might be applied to these questions. Gilligan (1977), for instance, considers both the formulation of moral stages and the findings on gender difference to be questionable, since they take little account of the humanistic and relational values that characterize the development of women. By the usual measures, females show stage 3 reasoning, described in terms of social expectations and the need for approval (Holstein, 1976), but Gilligan's interpretation suggests that women are concerned with responsibility and caring. She conceptualizes a developmental sequence reflecting organized understanding of the relationship between self and others and of the moral conflict between selfishness and responsibility. Theoretical challenges of this kind have implications for any approach to moral education and for the definition and assessment of associated gains.

It is difficult to summarize the state of moral education at the beginning of the 1980s. The field has unresolved issues but offers various alternatives for further exploration. The movement of Kohlberg and his group toward establishing ''just'' school communities is a particularly interesting development, since his work on moral development has been so influential. The problems of establishing and maintaining a moral school community, of course, are considerable. Schools of this kind have generally been small, allowing for face-to-face contact, close relationships, and active participation by all students in school affairs. How large a school can be transformed into a "just community," even with determined effort? What are the possibilities for the large urban high schools that may be most in need of such efforts? How must school adults be trained in order to ensure successful implementation of the ideas? And how much does the success of the school depend on charismatic leaders, the support of interested parents, economic conditions, and the temper of the times? Despite practical problems, this conception of moral education is worth careful study. In fact, the moral quality of the school as a social system is probably relevant to the fate of any program of moral education based in the school.

Affective Education

Affective education includes a variety of programs that use different terminology but have overlapping goals: humanistic education, confluent education, values clarification, group dynamics for the classroom, and affective education per se. Those who implement such programs stress the development of self-awareness, direct communication, and supportive relationships, and they view the school as a significant locale for the education of such qualities. Although they have much in common with educational philosophies discussed earlier (open, modern, developmental-interaction, alternative schools), the programs are generally more circumscribed. Some versions, such as humanistic or confluent education, stress the creation of a pervasive atmosphere or the melding of intellectual and affective learning, but the hallmark of affective education has been the creation of specific techniques. In the 1960s and early 1970s, affective education expanded rapidly and proponents developed a variety of exercises for classroom use, providing teachers with specific techniques for processing classroom events and encouraging constructive interaction.

We describe three programs as examples of different approaches to affective education. For further details readers are referred to other reviews (e.g., Allender, 1982; Lockwood, 1978), and to the extensive descriptive literature (e.g., Bany & Johnson, 1964; Brown, 1971, 1975; Castillo, 1974; Clark & Kadis, 1971; Gazda, 1973; Johnson & Johnson, 1975; Jones, 1967; Kahn & Weiss, 1973; Miller,

1976; Morse & Munger, 1975; Raths, Harmin, & Simon, 1966; Schmuck & Schmuck, 1974; Simon, Howe, & Kirschenbaum, 1978; Thayer, 1976; Weinstein & Fantini, 1970).

The *Human Development Program,* created by Bessell and Palomares (1969, 1970), is an example of a specific affective curriculum with broad goals and sequenced exercises for children at different grade levels. The program is focused on the development of awareness, self-confidence, and mastery, and on the understanding of social interaction. Planned for children from preschool through sixth grade or beyond, the curriculum is considered developmental in that the experiences at each grade level prepare the child for the next. Games and exercises are provided to cover a 20-minute period daily for the school year. Activities include discussions of selected topics (e.g., "It made me feel good when . . .") and take place in a "magic circle," in which there are rules about attentive listening, mutual respect, and the noncritical acceptance of each child's contribution.

Teachers feel that children profit from these experiences but evaluation has not been systematic and there are unanswered questions about the meaning and effects of the program. The curriculum has a predetermined sequence and is not connected with interpersonal events or learning experiences in the classroom. One may question whether it is meaningful, especially for young children, to deal with affective and interpersonal topics when they are scheduled rather than when they occur naturally, and whether such exercises can have lasting effects if they are inconsistent with the teacher's style or the climate of classroom and school.

Of course, evaluation research does not always solve such issues. There is an accumulation of research on the effects of values clarification, which also has affective goals and employs specific classroom strategies, but findings have generally been inconclusive (Kirschenbaum, 1975; Lockwood, 1978). Evaluators of such programs have claimed positive effects over a wide range of variables but these claims are not well substantiated. Applying rigorous methodological criteria, Lockwood reports some confidence in studies that show positive changes in classroom behavior and small improvements in reading ability but does not consider that studies have demonstrated a systematic impact on such crucial variables as self-esteem, self-concept, personal adjustment or student values. The problems lie partly in matters of research design, but the research has also been hampered by the lack of appropriate measures. Given the difficulties of the research task, it may not be surprising that programs have often been implemented on the basis of intent and evaluated informally through teacher impressions.

The *Affective Education Program (AEP)*, established as a separate office within the Philadelphia School District, is a more comprehensive program and includes a structure for inhouse evaluation. It is an example of a program that is interdependent with a large educational system and must thus negotiate its place within that system. Program functions have included the training of teachers in the use of affective techniques, the development of affective materials, and the creation of particular humanistic projects such as an intergenerational school (Newberg, 1980). As in other affective programs, the emphasis in the first years of work was on the social and emotional aspects of school experience. Newberg points to familiar problems in measuring the effects, but internal evaluations showed some positive changes. High school students in affective classes, for instance, reported more positive attitudes toward school, better problem-solving skills, and more interpersonal competence, indicating that the students at least felt they had gained from the program.

In the 1970s, the local school system focused on basic skills and the AEP adapted its program toward goals of academic competence, working with schools that were attempting to improve reading levels. The affective approach included relaxation techniques, as well as exercises focused on positive imagery and experiences of competence in relation to reading. Students in affective programs made significantly greater gains than control groups on standardized tests of reading and other academic skills. While it is not clear what specific factors account for the effects, it was apparently important that teachers trained in affective techniques combined these with their usual approach to the teaching of skills.

The *Empathy Training Project*, developed by Norma and Seymour Feshbach for elementary school children, would be among the most familiar and convincing programs to developmental psychologists, since it has a strong theoretical substructure and is accompanied by rigorous evaluation (N. Feshbach, 1979). The Feshbachs define empathy as ''a shared emotional response which the child experiences on perceiving another person's emotional reaction.'' Empathy is seen as a mediating variable with social implications, since it tends to reduce aggression and increase prosocial behavior. The three components of empathy are the ability to discriminate affect, the capacity to take other perspectives, and emotional responsiveness. Activities in the

training program are directed at these three capacities and take place in a small group of children over a period of several weeks.

The material has been tested in a pilot project with elementary school children of mixed backgrounds (black, white, and Chicano) who also differed in aggressiveness, as rated by teachers. To evaluate effects, the investigators used measures they had developed for assessing the three aspects of empathy, as well as measures of aggression, prosocial behavior, and cognition. They found significantly greater decreases in rated aggression for children in the program, and cognitive gains among those whose prosocial and aggressive behavior had improved most. The program has been modified and continues to be evaluated. The investigators bring an admirable sophistication to the field which would profit from more systematic theory, definition, and research of this nature. The solidity of the work, however, does not guarantee that demonstrated effects will take place under all conditions. Stable changes in children's behavior depend not only on the value of a curriculum as an independent unit, but on the quality of the educational setting within which it is conducted.

Reviews of the history of affective education through the 1960s and 1970s stress the correspondence between the general social framework and the programs accepted into the schools (Nash, 1980). During the 1960s such programs required no justification. The worth of focusing on self-development and social relationships seemed self-evident, as was the idea that the learning mechanisms should be experiential. In the late 1970s, however, the educational establishment moved to an emphasis on basic skills and a new concern for cost effectiveness. Many affective programs were phased out, but those that survived usually demonstrated their worth in one of two ways: by connecting with the academic goals that were of major concern to the school system, or by redirecting their focus to the social problems that beset the schools and the community. The AEP program in Philadelphia is an example of the former. As the program proved its value by hardcore demonstration of gains in reading scores, it was integrated into the mainstream of the city system and better able to influence the schools toward other humanistic concerns (Newberg, 1980). A variety of programs illustrates the integration with social issues (e.g., Alschuler, Phillips, & Weinstein, 1977). As is apparent in the later discussion of social problems and the school, programs geared toward the prevention of drug and alcohol abuse, discipline problems, or racial integration have often used techniques developed within the affective education movement. Even the empathy project of the Feshbachs may have had more ready acceptance in the schools because of the theoretical connection between increased empathy and decreased aggression, since violence is an acknowledged problem of contemporary society.

During the period of active growth, affective education progressed far enough to make an impact on the educational field. Affective techniques have increased the options for classroom teaching and continue to be available, even if the peak of enthusiasm has passed. Further, the movement has had time to generate internal criticism concerning attitudes of anti-intellectualism, excessive orientation toward technique, and some imbalance between concentration on self and sensitivity to others (Allender, 1982; Au, 1977; Divoky, 1975). Such criticism often prepares a field for more effective programs.

Neither the rise of affective education nor changes in the field have been guided much by research, which has been sparse and inconclusive. It has been suggested, with reason, that research evaluations of impact in an area characterized by such fallible measures should depend on sizeable differences rather than the attainment of statistical significance, and that researchers should consider whether demonstrated effects have actual significance for classroom behavior (Lockwood, 1978). The integration of affective techniques with learning situations and social problem-solving programs may represent progress rather than retreat. Such integrated programs may affect social development and behavior in school more substantially than self-contained curricula with specifically affective goals.

Cooperative Learning Programs

Cooperative learning structures are an integral part of open environments, but circumscribed approaches to cooperative learning have been introduced into a variety of settings, where they may constitute only part of the child's school experience. Such programs have often had their roots in social psychological theory concerning cooperation and competition (Deutsch, 1949) and in studies suggesting that cooperative situations generate positive social effects. Investigators who adapted these ideas to the educational setting were often interested in advancing academic progress through changes in the learning situation, but they were also interested in the social byproducts of the structures they created.

Studies of cooperative learning environments have usually been conducted in the elementary grades, though the range is from third grade through senior high school. The research is generally experimental in design. Programs are introduced into traditional settings, where they are conducted on a regular schedule and continue for some weeks or months. Experimental groups are then compared with control groups, often on both academic and social variables. Research in this area is relatively advanced; two comprehensive review articles describe and compare the major programs and summarize the research findings (Sharan, 1980; Slavin, 1980).

Techniques for creating cooperative environments always involve small groups of students who work together on learning material. A point is often made of forming heterogeneous groups that mix children of different ability, sex, and ethnic background. The goal is to maximize the learning of all students and to increase the mutuality of their relationships with children different from themselves. Programs vary on a number of important dimensions, including the amount of teacher input and control, whether or not there is competition between groups as well as cooperation within them, and the emphasis placed on individual or group products and rewards. Sharan (1980) has dichotomized the major programs into peer tutoring and group investigation techniques. Peer tutoring techniques are closer to the traditional format. They usually contain informational material organized in advance by the teacher. In the jigsaw method (Aronson, Stephan, Sikes, Blaney, & Snapp, 1978), the material is divided into segments, and each member of a small group is responsible for one segment. Students work with members of other teams who are responsible for the same segment, then teach the material to other members of their original group. Students are thus highly interdependent for their learning, but each is responsible for all the parts of the ''jigsaw'' and pupils are tested individually. They do not produce a group product or compete with other teams. In similar techniques developed by investigators at Johns Hopkins, students also learn through peer tutoring but teams compete with each other (DeVries & Slavin, 1978; Slavin, 1978).

Group investigation methods give students more autonomy relative to the teacher and usually involve more complex tasks in which material must be searched out, integrated, and interpreted by the group. Teams often work on different aspects of the material and coordinate their knowledge. Thus both the small group and the total classroom constitute cooperative social units; the learning product is often collective and the content less predetermined by the teacher than in peer tutoring methods. Examples of such programs include the Small Group Teaching method of Sharan and Sharan (1976) and the work of Johnson and Johnson (1975), and Joyce and Weil (1972).

Distinctions among these methods may have implications for the social experience of the children, since they differ with respect to outgroup competition and the amount of child initiative allowed within the small group. However, the various techniques have been compared primarily with traditional classroom structures, and findings, which have been fairly consistent, will be reviewed together.

Most studies of cooperative learning environments have demonstrated a positive impact on self-esteem, helping behavior, interpersonal liking, mutual concern among peers, cooperation, and attitudes toward school and learning (e.g., Blaney, Stephan, Rosenfield, Aronson, & Sikes, 1977; Bryant & Crockenberg, 1974; DeVries & Slavin, 1978; Johnson, Johnson, Johnson, & Anderson, 1976; Johnson, Johnson, & Scott, 1978; Lazarowitz, Sharan, & Steinberg, 1980; Sharan, 1980; Slavin, 1978, 1980; Wheeler & Ryan, 1973). The studies of Crockenberg and her associates, however, have contributed a more differentiated picture of possible effects. Their study of children from cooperatively and competitively structured classrooms established a relationship between cooperative experience and the tendency to help and share with other children (Bryant & Crockenberg, 1974). Crockenberg reasoned, however, that cooperative learning might also lead to greater cohesiveness, susceptibility to peer influence, and an unwillingness to risk disagreement. In an experimental study, she found that for third- and fourth-grade children the more cooperative the experience the greater the conformity (Crockenberg, 1979). Children identified by teachers as conformists were most influenced by others under any conditions, but experience in a group that followed cooperative processes generated more conformity among its members than other conditions. Since the study found less conformity in groups composed of children with preexisting friendships, the short experimental situation may have tapped only the early parts of a process. Loyalty to peer values is generally tenacious among middle-years children, and the establishment of a balance between loyalty and independence takes time (Minuchin, 1977). The issue is important since mutual exchange, helpful relationships, and group cohesiveness are desirable effects, but consistent conformity and the avoidance of conflict are not.

In another study, Crockenberg, Bryant, and Wilce (1976) found striking gender differences in the reactions of children to winning and losing in competitive and cooperative situations. Girls generally gave more prizes to others and accepted the evaluations built into the situation, but boys' behavior varied under different conditions. Boys who did not win were dissatisfied, vindictive, and self-rewarding. Boys who won in competitive situations were interested and satisfied, but boys who won in cooperative groups did not take pleasure in the accomplishment. The researchers suggest that this kind of success may not have been meaningful for boys, since they are competitively socialized and may need the satisfaction that comes from competition more than girls do. It is possible to conclude that competitive elements should be built into cooperative situations in order to mobilize the boys. It is also possible, and perhaps more constructive, to temper the need for competitive individual achievement by developing alternative incentives. Gender differences in motivation and satisfaction should be assessed in school situations that create and reinforce sustained naturalistic experiences of cooperative learning. As suggested in the discussion of alternative educational models, such environments may generate a different pattern of gender-related behavior than either traditional settings, experimental situations, or short-term programs.

Considerable research on cooperative learning has focused on cross-ethnic relationships in desegregated schools (e.g., Aronson, Bridgeman, & Geffner, 1978; Blaney et al., 1977; DeVries, Edwards, & Slavin, 1978; DeVries & Slavin, 1978; Sharan, 1980; Slavin, 1979, 1980; Slavin & Madden, 1979; Weigel, Wiser, & Cook, 1975). These studies will be reviewed in the section on desegregation as a school-related social issue. It can be stated here, however, that this research has frequently demonstrated positive effects. Cooperative learning experiences appear more promising than most mechanisms for fostering positive contact between students from different backgrounds.

This area of theory and research is challenging. The organization of learning structures determines the proportion of contact a child will have with authorities and peers and the quality of such contacts. If the learning structure is traditional, the contact is primarily with teachers and the relationship with peers is organized for competition. If the structure is cooperative, the child has more academic-social contact with peers. The quality of that contact depends on the specific organization of the learning task, the reward system, the particular children, and teacher attitudes. We need more research information on these contingencies, as well as more emphasis on practical applications. Johnson (1981) points out that the educational establishment pays little attention to theoretical and research knowledge in this field and that competitive, individualistic learning dominates most classrooms, despite evidence that cooperative goal structures are more effective.

THE SCHOOL IN SOCIETY

As major cultural institutions, the schools both reflect and affect contemporary social problems. Social ills are not created by schools, but society has often looked to the schools for positive solutions. In this section we review selected problems in relation to the schools. Our goals are limited. We do not discuss the background or causality of any issue. Rather, we review efforts by the schools to take positive action, and research associated with such efforts.

Problems associated with the schools include discrimination, substance abuse, violence, alienation, dropping out, teenage pregnancy, and the special needs of handicapped, bilingual, or disturbed children. From among these, we have selected issues with particular characteristics. *Ethnic discrimination* and *gender stereotyping* have a long history in the culture and the schools. Social pressure and federal legislation have made these issues especially acute in recent decades, focusing attention on the schools as carriers of discrimination and potential forces for change. *Substance use and abuse* is a problem with crisis characteristics. Hardly a concern for the schools before the 1960s, drug and alcohol use reached serious proportions in the last two decades and has been of concern to parents, educators, and the community. *Divorce* is an example of a social phenomenon that is located outside the schools but one that affects many school children. It raises questions about the scope of the school's responsibilities, and about viable methods for handling transitional difficulties in the lives of individual students.

In general, school-related research in these areas is not advanced. It is essential, however, to see the schools and the students in their broad social context, and to consider the implications for research and social policy. The era we review has been one of major social and political change, moving from social upheaval, federal legislation, and the funding of school-based programs and research in the 1960s and 1970s to political and economic constrictions and the withdrawal of support at the beginning of the 1980s. Programs and research in the decade to come will continue to reflect changing realities in the larger social context.

Desegregation

One of the most profound social issues of the century, racial inequality, has touched the schools directly. The Supreme Court decision of 1954 (*Brown* v. *Board of Education of Topeka*), affirming the inherent inequality of separate educational facilities, was largely based on the social and psychological consequences of segregation. Robert Coles' (1967) portraits of the children who pioneered in crossing racial lines as desegregation began documented the deep emotional currents on both sides. By now, a huge literature has accumulated, including a spate of books attempting to analyze where things stood a quarter century after the Supreme Court decision (e.g., Bell, 1980; Friedman, Meltzer, & Miller, 1979; Harris, Jackson, & Rydingsword, 1975; Hughes, Gordon, & Hillman, 1980; St. John, 1975; Stephan & Feagin, 1980). Much of this work is outside our scope, but it is worth noting that desegregation efforts appear to have slowed in the late 1970s and early 1980s as a result of conservative Supreme Court decisions, the reduction of federal involvement in education, continuing segregation in housing patterns, and growing opposition among middle-class whites, as well as decreasing consensus among blacks about the value of desegregated schools (e.g., Bell, 1980; Feagin, 1980). Some analysts comment, also, that there has been an unfortunate shift from social to academic goals, limiting the national evaluation of progress to academic gains (Orfield, 1978). We briefly survey different efforts to desegregate and integrate schools, and research bearing most directly on children's social development.

Approaches to Desegregation and Integration

For the general public as well as much of the social science literature, a focus of desegregation has been on improving the ratio of black and white children attending the same school. Given *de facto* neighborhood segregation, efforts to improve the ratio have often involved busing students, usually the minority children, from home neighborhoods to more distant schools.

An underlying assumption has been that bringing different groups together would reduce stereotyped attitudes and foster positive intergroup relations. This hypothesis has been tested in a number of studies. Busing, however, tells us nothing about what happens inside the school. Black children bused to a predominantly white school are often resegregated in the classroom and *de facto* segregation is often recreated by seating patterns, so-called ability grouping, and tracking systems in high schools (e.g., Epstein, 1980; Rist, 1970, 1978, 1979; Rosenbaum, 1978). Reviews of this literature by Amir (1976), Carithers (1970), St. John (1975), and Schofield (1978), point to the atheoretical nature of most studies and the inadequacy of criterion measures, which often employ simple sociometric questions purporting to tap changes in deeply rooted attitudes. Research findings have not been impressive, but the different approaches to improving group relations are not equally disheartening. When positive effects appear, they seem to depend on active efforts to affect teaching practices, content, and attitudes, rather than the sheer fact of physical proximity between students from different backgrounds.

In a comprehensive national study of factors contributing to positive interracial relations, Forehand, Ragosta, and Rock (1976) surveyed over 5,000 fifth-grade students in more than 90 elementary schools and over 400 tenth graders in 72 high schools, as well as principals, teachers, and guidance counselors in the same schools. Their results suggest that multiethnic curricula, projects focused on racial issues, and mixed work groups lead to positive changes, and that improved relationships are also associated with the presence of supportive principals and teachers. These data have been reworked, bringing to light some limitations, such as the fact that student and teacher information could not be linked, but also reinforcing some of their conclusions. Epstein's (1980) correlational analysis of the fifth-grade data indicates that active learning programs, curricula promoting concepts of equal racial status, and assigning work to integrated groups do facilitate positive attitudes among elementary school children. At the same time, some teacher and school characteristics are associated with resegregation. Reanalysis of the high school data (Slavin & Madden, 1979) raises questions about the effectiveness of certain efforts (teacher workshops, multiethnic texts, minority history courses, heterogeneous grouping, and classroom discussion of race relations) but indicates strong and consistent improvement in race relations when secondary students are assigned to work together or participate in multiracial sports teams.

Another kind of effort to increase positive contact within the educational setting has been the creation of "magnet" schools, which are designed to attract children of different backgrounds by offering enriched programs for students with special talents. They have been seen as a natural meeting ground for children of different ethnic groups who share particular interests and skills. There is little systematic research on the effects of such schools, but Rosenbaum and Presser's (1978) case study of a magnet junior high illustrates the difficulties of achieving the goals. Set in a black urban neighborhood, the school began in a spurt of enthusiasm with an initial enrollment of 70% white students, but soon ran into multiple problems. The proportion of blacks and whites in the different specialty areas was unbalanced; for instance, few blacks were enrolled in math or science. In spite of the consensually agreed upon school policy, academic classes became segregated into ability groups because teachers were not prepared to cope with the wide disparity in student preparation. In music, art, and drama, however, the groups were heterogeneous and the plan worked well. The fact that the magnet plan showed some success and peacefully desegregated a formerly black school was seen as positive in the light of the many problems confronted (see also Metz, 1980).

The Social Effects of Desegregation

Though there has been voluminous research on the effects of desegregation, the findings have been disappointing (see Amir, 1976; Carithers, 1970; Cohen, 1975; St. John, 1975; Schofield, 1978; Stephan & Feagin, 1980). Contradictory results may stem both from the prevalent definition of desegregation, which relies on simple black-white ratios in school, and from the fact that investigators often have not taken account of surrounding conditions. Most investigators take the school rather than the classroom as a criterion for desegregation and say nothing about grouping practices or the racial composition of either the student body or the faculty. They seldom note whether desegregation has come about through natural demographic changes, busing, or school board rezoning, and do not report whether there was controversy in the community, how school personnel viewed the changes, or whether desegregation was accompanied by changes in teaching methods. Further, student attitudes and behavior are often measured at a single point in time. Without information about how students scored earlier on dependent measures, later patterns cannot safely be attributed to the effects of desegregation.

The bulk of the research deals with academic achievement. St. John's (1975) summary of more than 120 studies conducted in elementary and secondary schools up to 1973 indicates that there are no definitive positive findings concerning achievement, but that desegregation has not usually lowered achievement for either black or white children. Other studies focus either on self-concept or intergroup attitudes.

Self-Concept. Studies of self-esteem test the hypothesis that black children in desegregated schools will develop more confidence and self-appreciation than they would in segregated situations. St. John reviews 40 studies employing a broad range of self-concept measures, some of which separate general and academic self-esteem. The evidence is mixed, but there is little support for the idea that desegregation per se contributes significantly to enhancing the self-esteem of minority students. There are some suggestive findings concerning subgroups, however, Children of higher social status respond more positively than lower-class children, and boys respond more positively than girls.

The circumstances surrounding desegregation and the composition of the school's student body also appear to affect the black child's sense of confidence. Studies incorporating the context of desegregation are rare, but one investigator found that children in a school that was integrated peacefully showed *lower* self-esteem than those in a segregated school or one desegregated under stressful circumstances. The author suggests that children in the latter school may have gained from the high morale in the black community following a successful desegregation battle (Meketon, 1966; cited in Amir, 1976, and St. John, 1975).

Studies on the effects of different black-white ratios in the schools are more numerous, and the findings are interesting but not consistent. Some studies, such as that of Coleman and his associates (1966), suggest an advantage for blacks when the percentage of white students in the school is high. While noting that the academic self-concept of black children was generally lower than that of whites, Coleman reported that black students in such schools had a stronger sense of control over the environment. McPartland's (1968) reanalysis of the data, taking account of socioeconomic status, also suggests that early school integration and a higher proportion of white students in the classroom contribute significantly to this sense of effectiveness. In contrast, Rosenberg and Simmons (1971) reported that there were no appreciable racial differences in self-esteem between black and white students in a sizeable sample of elementary and secondary schools, and self-esteem was lower among black high school seniors in predominantly white schools than among those in predominantly black schools. The latter pattern also holds for black student aspirations. In most studies, black and white youth of comparable socioeconomic status are found to have comparable educational and occupational aspirations, but the aspirations of black students in all black schools tend to be higher than those of blacks in mixed situations (St. John, 1975).

Discrepant findings concerning desegregation and self-esteem may be mediated by a host of features in the community, school, and classroom that are not usually reported. They may also reflect problems of measurement. Measures applied to black children have either adapted techniques designed for whites or taken preference for whiteness, or a white standard of attractiveness, as indicators of self-rejection. Such measures do not honor the complexities. It has been argued that blacks, and possibly other minorities, have a dual-reference group orientation—to their own culture and to the majority white culture; a stated preference for white standards, therefore, may indicate knowledge of prevailing cultural norms rather than a rejection of self. Young black children's self-concepts can be differentiated as Eurocentric or Afrocentric, as Spencer (1981) has shown. Valid assessment of the impact of environmental manipulations of the self-esteem of black children requires further exploration of these fundamental distinctions.

Intergroup Relations. One kind of effort to improve intergroup relations has been the development of structured cooperative learning situations (e.g., Aronson, Bridgeman, & Geffner, 1978; Blaney et al., 1977; DeVries, Edwards, & Slavin, 1978; DeVries & Slavin, 1978; Sharan, 1980; Slavin, 1979, 1980; Slavin & Madden, 1979; Weigel, Wiser, & Cook, 1975). In tabling the results of 12 studies, Slavin (1980) noted that ten found significant differences between experimental and control groups, while two found no difference. Relationships in the classroom are particularly likely to improve with cooperative experiences. In the study of Weigel et al., mixed groups of white, black, and Mexican-American students in newly integrated secondary schools were involved in cooperative learning programs; members divided their labor and helped each other toward common goals and rewards, while competing with other groups. Harmonious relationships were evident in experimental classrooms, which were characterized by significantly more cross-racial helping and less interracial conflict than the control settings. In a similar investigation, Slavin (1980) found greater interracial contact both during the task and in other situations in classrooms with cooperative learning structures.

Examination of cross-ethnic sociometric choices and student attitudes in cooperative situations also indicates significant increases, but the findings are not as consistent and do not necessarily apply equally to all ethnic groups. In the Weigel study, white students in experimental classes expressed increased liking for Mexican-American classmates, but there were no significant differences between experimental and control groups in white attitudes toward blacks, or in friendship choices of black and Mexican-American students toward whites and toward each other. The investigators felt that the essentially traditional nature of the school environment may have outweighed the effects of cooperative programs and that the competition between teams, introduced to increase motivation, may have worked against the social purposes.

Research on desegregation and interethnic attitudes usually focuses on black and white students but the study of Weigel et al. also included Mexican-Americans and there is a small body of research relevant to this population. Stephan and Rosenfield (1978a, 1978b) studied schools with a mixed population of whites (65%), blacks (20%), and Mexican-Americans (15%). They measured the self-esteem of fifth and sixth graders who attended segregated or naturally integrated schools, and gathered data again eight months after the schools were officially desegregated. Both before and after desegregation students had most contact with members of their own group and each group evaluated itself most positively, though Mexican-Americans scored lower on self-esteem than either black or white students. The only notable effect of desegregation was that blacks from segregated backgrounds showed lower self-esteem after desegregation. The authors comment that positive effects, if they occur, probably take time to evolve.

Other specific studies of cooperative learning situations with black, white, and Mexican-American children suggest the same kind of positive changes in interracial tension and group liking as those found by Weigel et al., and they also draw attention to subgroup differences. Blaney et al. (1977) found that under cooperative conditions only Anglos and blacks developed more positive attitudes toward school, while the attitudes of Mexican-Americans improved significantly less than those of children in control groups. In later research (Aronson, Bridgeman, & Geffner, 1978), the attitudes of Mexican-Americans in cooperative situations followed the same pattern as other groups. The investigators suggest that Mexican-American children in the latter study were more comfortable in small groups because they constituted about one-half of the student population and were well established in the school.

However, some studies indicate more positive outcomes when classes have either small or large minority groups rather than racially balanced situations (Sharan, 1980), and the importance of the variable is more evident than is the optimal pattern. In general, too little is known about intergroup relationships and attitudes involving school children who are neither black nor white. In a country that contains many minorities, including Native Americans and the recent wave of Southeast Asian and Caribbean immigrants, the need for differentiated research is evident.

Much research on desegregation treats events in the school as encapsulated. We know that both children and teachers come to school with prior attitudes about other groups (Goodman, 1964; Katz, 1976), and that explosive schools are often in explosive communities, but we have little systematic research on the interaction among family, community, and school experience. One relevant study is Stephan and Rosenfield's (1978a,b) investigation of the relationship between parental variables and the attitudes of children in a multiethnic school situation. They gave a questionnaire to mothers of fifth- and sixth-grade students, tapping authoritarian attitudes, punitiveness, and attitudes toward integration. Two years later they followed up a subsample of the students, 41 of whom had been in segregated schools and 24 in triethnic schools. Their findings suggest that increased ethnic contact and positive self-esteem are associated, and that both are negatively related to parental punitiveness and authoritarian child-rearing practices. It is not clear, of course, whether increased contact leads to more positive attitudes or the reverse, but the study is important in its effort to study change over time and to connect student attitudes in school with family variables.

The assumption in desegregating schools is that desegregation is an unmitigated good. Yet, as Gordon Allport (1954) noted long ago, contact between different groups may lead to hostility and the intensification of stereotypes unless the contact is long-term, institutionally sanctioned, and organized between groups of equal status pursuing shared goals. These conditions are difficult to meet. For many minority children, the school may be the first social institution they encounter that represents the values of the dominant white society. The modes of speech, dress, and behavior that are expected may be alien to their early experience. If students first attend segregated schools, they may be unprepared for contacts with white students and teachers and find the move into desegregated situations difficult. Rosenberg and Simmons (1971) note that black students in desegregated schools often experience racial prejudice, conflicting cultural values, and stiff academic competition. Their observations are borne out by Noblit and Collins' (1980) ethnographic study of a Southern high school that had served as an all white college preparatory school before it was desegregated in 1972. In order to keep the school integrated and hold white students, the principal had to maintain a core of accelerated courses, for which few blacks were qualified. The student council, clubs, and honors remained in the control of an elite white student body. Those blacks who wanted to succeed had to "act white" and were rejected by many of their black peers. The competing demands of peers and teachers—and the resulting conflict—are hardly conducive to increased self-esteem or harmonious group relationships. It seems likely that the pressures described by these researchers are more general concomitants of desegregation than much of the research literature has indicated.

Sex-Role Stereotyping

Researchers and educators have long been interested in gender-related patterns of behavior in school, but it is only recently that the school's role in creating or perpetuating stereotypes has been acknowledged. We describe documentation of bias in the educational context, efforts to change practices and attitudes, and research on the effects of these efforts.

Documenting Bias in the Schools

Even the youngest children come to school with concepts about girls and boys and ideas of gender-appropriate behavior; furthermore, role socialization continues in the culture and the family while the children are going to school (Huston, *Vol. IV, Chap. 5*; Weinraub & Brown, 1983). Still, the literature suggests that schools have been major contributors to stereotyping and bias through teacher interactions with boys and girls, inequality of access to activities and training, the representation of males and females in learning materials, and the distribution of male and female role models in the school system.

Relationships in School: Teacher Interaction with Boys and Girls. Research on this aspect of sex typing has a long history and considerable bulk (see the section *Teachers' Responses to Boys and Girls*). While there are some contradictory findings, certain points stand out. Especially in the early grades, most teachers tend to "feminize" children of both sexes, perhaps because such behavior fits the convention of acceptable behavior in school. Girls seem to adapt more readily than boys to the expected

pattern. Boys are less academically effective and have more learning difficulties in the grade school years, but do not forfeit their independence like the girls (Frazier & Sadker, 1973; Guttentag & Bray, 1976; Stockard, Schmuck, Kempner, Williams, Edson, & Smith, 1980). Some observers have commented that "males suffer especially in the early years of school, and females in the later years" (Stockard et al., p. 185).

Research on teacher attitudes suggests that conventional expectations underlie their interactions with children. In the early grades they expect boys to be more unruly and to have more learning problems. As the children grow older, teachers expect female and male students to have divergent interests and skills and to be headed toward different kinds of adult lives. In one study, 50 high school teachers were given essentially identical descriptions of ideal male and female students. They expected the males to go on to further accomplishments, but did not expect the females even to go to college (Gaite, 1977). This study was conducted in a small town and the attitudes can hardly be typical of American teachers, but more subtle forms of the same bias are prevalent. Such expectations are, to some extent, based on reality. What the data indicate is a stable system: male and female behavior maintains teacher expectations and teacher expectations maintain the behavior.

Equality of Opportunity: Access to Material, Activities, and Vocational Training. Differential experience with materials begins in the preschool, where gender differences in the selection of play materials have been amply demonstrated, though whether the pattern is already ingrained or subtly influenced in the school remains controversial (e.g., Fagot & Patterson, 1969; Fling & Manosevitz, 1972; Harper & Sanders, 1975; Weinraub & Brown, 1983). In recent research at older age levels, differential access to sports activities has been documented in detail: sports for boys are more varied and extensive and have larger budgets than sports for girls. Participation in school teams has also depended on gender. The pattern has been considered detrimental in that girls have not had the same opportunities for physical training, for developing competitive skills, or for the experience of team cooperation and camaraderie as boys, while boys have suffered from excessive emphasis on competition rather than on the pleasures of participation and mastery (The Editors, *Harvard Educational Review*, 1979; Stockard et al., 1980).

Another well-documented form of discrimination has occurred in vocational training (Pottker & Fishel, 1977; Saario, Jacklin, & Tittle, 1973; Stockard et al., 1980). Saario et al. suggest that discrimination is particularly evident in metropolitan areas where there are specialized vocational high schools. These often have served only one sex, usually male; females were not admitted or needed to meet more stringent requirements. In comprehensive high schools a similarly skewed sorting has sent students into vocational tracks and courses considered "sex appropriate." Saario, Jacklin, and Tittle (1973) note that a 1970 listing of courses in New York City public high schools included 77 technical courses restricted to males and 36 designed for females. Males generally are not offered training related to homemaking, health, or office work, and females are not offered training in agriculture, trade, or industry.

Even when training is available, stereotyped counseling of high school students has blocked both males and females from nonconventional courses and careers. Both female and male counselors tend to give conventional advice and do not give materials or encouragement for exploring new fields, though some research has found more traditional assumptions among male counselors (Donahue & Costar, 1977; Harway, 1977; Pottker & Fishel, 1977). Constriction in school counseling is especially regrettable because counseling provides an opportunity for expanding students' horizons beyond the views and examples offered by parents (Steinmann, 1977).

Presentation of Males and Females in Textbooks, Curriculum Materials, and Course Content. Gender-related stereotyping in learning materials was more or less unsuspected until the late 1960s, but subsequent documentation has been startling in its scope and consistency, demonstrating bias in readers, curriculum materials, the items on standardized tests, and textbooks across a wide range of topics from social studies to math (e.g., Child, Potter, & Levine, 1946; Frasher & Walker, 1972; Frazier & Sadker, 1973; Jay & Schminke, 1975; Kingston & Lovelace, 1977-1978; Oliver, 1974; Pottker & Fishel, 1977; Saario et al., 1973; Scott & Feldman-Summers, 1979; Shirreffs, 1975; Stockard et al., 1980; U'ren, 1971; Weitzman & Rizzo, 1974; Women on Words and Images, 1972). The language, illustrations, and depictions of roles, as well as the ratio of male to female figures, reflect conventional assumptions and, in the opinion of many, a clear bias against females. The generic "he" is consistently used to refer to girls as well as boys.

Little nurturance or social and emotional complexity are associated with men and boys in these materials, and little strength, skill, or capacity for making decisions with women and girls. Occupational roles are more evident and varied for men than women, who are usually shown as homemakers or as engaged in a limited and conventional set of occupations. Women are seldom portrayed as both working and raising families. Since a significant proportion of women are currently carrying both roles, such portrayals indicate, at the least, a lag between educational materials and social reality (Saario et al., 1973). In addition, the content of history and social studies have typically bypassed the activities of women. Trecker's (1977) detailed analysis of U.S. history texts shows that women are inadequately discussed in all periods, and that the length of skirts may receive more attention than the contribution of female intellectuals or those who worked against slavery, for the labor movement, or for other social and legal reforms.

Role Models in School: Males and Females in the Educational Hierarchy. The distribution of males and females in the educational system is well known: most teachers are women, most administrators are men. There are more male teachers in secondary schools than in the early grades, but many teach science and math, while female teachers more often teach English and foreign languages (Stockard et al., 1980). Issues about gender imbalance in administration or the rights of pregnant teachers filter through the system but are not directly experienced by the children. On the other hand, distinctions in status between male principals and female teachers and the clustering of female and male teachers in certain subjects are part of the immediate school context. They may have a direct impact on children's identification with teaching adults and on what they learn about the distribution of power in the adult world. We do not know of any research that examines children's perceptions of these phenomena.

Since American education has not been uniform, it would be interesting to know if these biases have been as characteristic of alternative settings as of traditional schools. Comparative research reported earlier indicates that sex-role behavior is less stereotyped in open settings, but alternative environments have not been systematically examined from this point of view. A close look at teacher interaction with boys and girls and at curriculum materials in nontraditional settings might well uncover some conventional patterns. Detailed analysis of equity and bias in alternative settings offers an interesting arena for investigation.

In considering the research on bias in the schools, it is important to regard the children themselves as part of a self-perpetuating system, since they have internalized the same assumptions as those appearing in school material and held by school personnel. Children have clear images of gender-associated occupations, reinforce each other for sex-typed behavior, and may resist possibilities for new directions and nonstereotyped careers (e.g., Garrett, Ein, & Tremaine, 1977; Guttentag & Bray, 1976; Mitchell, 1978; Papalia & Tennent, 1975; Pottker & Fishel, 1977; Schlosberg & Goodman, 1975; Stockard et al., 1980; Weinraub & Brown, 1983; Williams, Bennett, & Best, 1975). Efforts to change materials, opportunities, and relationships in the school setting are essential if equity is desired, but it is simplistic to postulate immediate modifications in children's behavior and development.

Changing the School Context

Since the early 1970s many projects have attempted to reduce bias in the schools, concentrating on one or another of the areas described above. The most direct and probably the most successful have focused on changing curriculum materials and providing equal access to activities and courses. Teacher attitudes and power hierarchies in the school are more resistant to change since they involve ingrained viewpoints, matters of status, and economic realities.

Federal legislation concerning sex equity in schools has played a prominent role in bringing about change. Title IX of the Education Amendments Act of 1972 prohibited discrimination on the basis of sex in any educational program or activity receiving federal financial assistance. The legislation triggered action by local school boards and community groups, providing increased equity in high school sports and broader access to vocational training. Reviews of the first years of implementation describe both progress and resistance to change, and indicate that concerted efforts by educators, parents, and students are required to assure compliance (Pottker & Fishel, 1977; Stockard et al., 1980; The Editors, *Harvard Educational Review,* 1979).

Interestingly, Title IX was judged not to apply to textbooks or other curricular material because of possible conflict with First Amendment guarantees of freedom of speech (Dunkle & Sandler, 1974). Nonetheless, publishers now have guidelines for authors concerning nonsexist language, and many publications describe resources for nonsexist literature and materials (e.g., Adell & Klein, 1976; Cohen & Martin, 1976; Davis, 1977; Educational Challenges, 1975; Guttentag & Bray, 1976; Kalamazoo Public Schools, 1976; PEER, 1978; Sprung, 1978). Guidelines for implementing Title IX appeared in 1976,

and the Women's Educational Equity Act (WEEA) provided funds and a rubric for projects to improve sex equity. These have included training for teachers and guidance personnel, development and distribution of sex fair materials, and new nondiscriminatory tests. A variety of programs has been aimed at providing teachers with specific skills for reducing bias in the classroom and at affecting the attitudes of teachers, counselors, and students from preschool through college (e.g., Evenson & O'Neil, 1978; Kalunian, 1975; Klinman, Gollub, Mulvihill, Shulkin, & Sloan, 1979; Maple Heights City Schools, Ohio, 1977; Romero & Romero, 1978; Wangen & Wagner, 1977; Woolever, 1977).

Stockard and her colleagues, drawing on social psychological theory, argue that behavioral change must precede a change in values, and that legislative action has therefore been crucial, since it forces behavioral modifications at an acceptable level of militancy. They question the impact of projects aimed directly at changing stereotyped attitudes. Guttentag and Bray (1976), on the other hand, report that what determined the effectiveness of material they introduced into schools was the attitude of the teacher. The process is, of course, reciprocal. If concrete changes are mandated, they can be maintained only if school personnel support them; at the same time, only a sustained change in concrete experience will stabilize new attitudes in children and teachers.

Research Findings

There are new materials available to the schools, new mandates concerning equal opportunity, and a variety of programs to change the attitudes of school personnel. When there is less stereotyping in school, do children have less stereotyped images of themselves and others, and do their career plans expand?

One line of evaluation research has focused on adolescent females, exploring changes in career plans and training. Vocational plans are seen as an expression of female students' attitudes toward women's rights, their place in society, and their sense of confidence and aspiration, which has consistently been documented as lower than that of males. Some studies find that consciousness raising and career development interventions create more positive attitudes (e.g., Abernathy, 1977), but others find that adolescent women may continue to hold conventional views and make stereotyped choices even when they know that possibilities are changing (Mitchell, 1978), or that intervention is more likely to increase knowledge than to affect attitudes and behavior (Woodcock & Herman, 1978). Mitchell urges attention to the conditions and inducements necessary to bring adolescents into career training that is not conventional and to support their continued participation. An important issue for adolescent females is the realistic fear of negative feedback from male peers. One study found that girls integrated into male shop classes reported more concern about reactions from their shopmates than about handling the work (Snell, 1977). Some data suggest that resistance to the expansion of female aspirations and training may be stronger among white middle-class males than among black and working-class males. The latter are more accepting of economic realities and less threatened by heightened female ambition (Pottker & Fishel, 1977). Such patterns require further study.

When attitudes do change, it is not inevitable that the changes will be maintained. Wirtenberg (1979) studied the impact of Title IX implementation among junior high school students. Immediately after coed placement in previously segregated courses, such as industrial arts or cooking, experimental subjects, especially girls, expressed a significantly greater sense of competence in non-stereotyped domains and less perception of differences between males and females than control subjects. Differences were not so evident at the end of the school year, however. Observations in the classrooms and questionnaire data from teachers and parents indicated many conventional attitudes on the part of both adults and students, subtle sex segregation within coed classes, and some stereotyping in materials and teacher-student interaction. It is evident that, as in all areas of discrimination, technical implementation of legislative mandates is not enough.

One study took a comprehensive approach, fostering a variety of experimental changes in the schools and giving teachers special training (Lockheed & Harris, 1978). The investigators found significant differences between 400 fourth and fifth graders in the experimental groups and their controls. Children whose school experiences included work, sports, and club activities in coeducational groups, who were exposed to adults in nonstereotyped roles, and whose parents supported cross-gender friendships, had more positive attitudes about interaction between the sexes, made more cross-gender choices for work partners and friends, and had more egalitarian views about social and occupational roles. The pattern is similar to that reported in comparisons between alternative and traditional settings, which are sustained environments rather than experimental interventions. It is also similar to the findings that connect shared goal-directed experiences with more positive contact among different subgroups. There are consistencies, therefore, in the research, though the importance of parental support in this study is a reminder that the conditions for change in such deeply ingrained patterns involve more than one social system.

The most comprehensive, developmentally oriented study of school intervention was conducted by Guttentag and Bray (1976). Their project focused on kindergarten, fifth- and ninth-grade children in three school systems during a six-week intervention period and entailed a sequence of activities: a survey of children's attitudes, the construction of nonsexist teacher-child interaction methods and curriculum materials appropriate to each developmental level, a teacher training workshop, and assessment of change through classroom observations and measures of sex-role attitudes. Objectives for kindergarten children reflected the form and limits of their cognitive and social functioning, while those for children in the middle years drew on their greater capacity to think objectively about a broader world. Objectives for high school students aimed to extend their critical capacities to socialization processes they had themselves experienced. Children of all ages were encouraged to consider adults and themselves in multiple roles, but only the two older groups were made aware of current stereotyping in literature, the media, and the social environment, and only the curriculum for adolescents incorporated historical examination of socialization processes.

The preintervention survey produced some interesting data. For instance, fifth graders were less dogmatic in their sex-role attitudes than either kindergarten or adolescent subjects, contrary to developmental expectations concerning middle-years conformity. Children of all ages were less stereotyped about themselves than about other children. They also had more stereotyped ideas about the opposite sex than about their own, though there was more variation concerning female than male roles. The investigators suggest that the male role is more "tightly defined" and that in any intervention special attention should be directed toward the benefits of androgynous qualities in men.

Postintervention findings included the following: Change was difficult to accomplish, occurring in some classrooms more than others and varying by age and gender, though ethnic background, socioeconomic status, and maternal employment were not relevant factors. Girls at all ages were more open to nonstereotyped perspectives. The contrast between sexes was most notable among ninth graders, confirming the suggestion that adolescent girls may be at the same time most vulnerable to peer discouragement of unpopular attitudes and most receptive to broadened possibilities (see Pottker & Fishel). Ninth-grade boys had more stereotyped ideas after the intervention, drawing attention to the possible threat in such issues for adolescent boys. One of the most powerful predictors of change was the attitude and enthusiasm of the teacher. The classroom context was also influential in determining the nature of change. Girls in open settings more frequently initiated interactions, while girls in traditional classrooms became more active in responding to teachers' questions. According to the investigators, these data support theories that emphasize multiple environmental influences, rather than theories that view gender development as a function of internal processing and cognitive change. They agree with Stockard et al. (1980), who stress the relationship among the school, the family, the economy, and the larger social scene as determinants of gender attitudes and of the possibility for change.

Many forces operate to maintain a stereotyped system. Indifference, resistance, economic retrenchment, and the dwindling of federal support have been discouraging to proponents of sex equity in the schools. At the same time there have been certain gains. In some schools unbiased learning materials are available, access to school sports and vocational training is more equitable, and students are exposed to wider career options. If these gains are supported by less stereotyped ideas, models, and pathways in the broader culture, as they increasingly seem to be, the possibilities for sustained effects are enhanced.

Changes in well-established systems, however, do not occur rapidly. The literature corroborates the difficulty of changing the school environment and indicates that children may not take advantage of new opportunities. Teachers and students hold deep-rooted stereotypes, and the values of colleagues, families, and peers may sustain their biases. Attitudes concerning males appear even more intransigent than those concerning females, and the acceptance of androgynous qualities is apparently more difficult for children than the acceptance of ideas about nonstereotyped occupational roles. There is also a gender difference in receptivity to change, with males more resistant than females. The conventional wisdom is that females have more to gain from changing circumstances, but there is increasing attention to the constricting effects of stereotyped expectations on male development. Efforts to modify the school context should be focused on increasing the options and encouraging the expression of potential for all children, regardless of gender.

Substance Use and Abuse

In junior and senior high schools, drug use and drinking are often an accepted fact of social life. For the community, however, such behavior is often a matter of concern, since in some forms it involves a risk to health and to functioning. Schools are involved because they are a locus for the peer culture that often initiates and maintains substance use, because some students who drink or use drugs cannot learn or function effectively in school, and because preventive programs find their target population congregated in schools as in no other locale. It is not our purpose to deal either with the causes of substance use or the specific definition of abuse. Causality is complex, and definitions of abuse range from those that delineate excessive use and unacceptable substances to those that equate abuse with any drinking and any use of any drug. While the definitions may not be equally valid, any conception held by school administrators or parents affects the policies of the school and must be reckoned with. In this section we review material on the prevalence of substance use among students, school intervention and prevention programs, and research on such programs.

Systematic information about drug and alcohol use among teenagers is available from several sources (e.g., Fagerberg & Fagerberg, 1976; Johnston, Bachman, & O'Malley, 1979; Single, Kandel, & Faust, 1974; Walker, Jasinska, & Carnes, 1978). Working with a national sample of over 15,000 high school seniors, Johnston et al. collected survey data on drug use, opinions about the harmfulness of alcohol and different drugs, and perceptions of parent and peer attitudes. Almost all seniors reported some drinking and over half had smoked marihuana. About one-third had used more potent drugs and, as others have also reported, multiple drug use was not uncommon (Milman & Su, 1973; Single et al., 1974; Wechsler, 1976). Ten percent of the seniors reported daily use of marihuana and half that number reported daily drinking. Daily use of other substances was less than 1%, although the report points out that this apparently soothing figure involves about 30,000 adolescents. Substance use and initial contact with drugs occurs principally among students of 15 or older, but a significant minority reported trying inhalants and marihuana before tenth grade. Males reported heavier and more frequent use of drugs and alcohol than females, except for tranquilizers. This pattern of age and gender differences has been reported by others, though gender differences appear to be decreasing (Milman & Su, 1973; Wechsler & McFadden, 1976). Seniors not bound for college reported twice as much daily drinking and heavier drug use than those expecting to continue their schooling.

Most seniors regarded heavy drinking (4–5 drinks a day), heavy smoking (a pack a day), and the daily use of most drugs as potentially harmful. A majority disapproved of daily use of marihuana but it was not considered a harmful drug; only one-third disapproved of occasional use, and most believed that use or sale should be legalized or considered a minor crime. Respondents' perceptions of peer attitudes closely paralleled their own, an expected and important finding, but seniors perceived parents as more disapproving of all substance use. The greatest gap in attitudes concerned marihuana. Only 33% of the seniors disapproved of some experimentation, but 83% said their parents would disapprove.

Given these data some kind of school policy and action is indicated, partly because there is evidence of early and extensive drug use and partly because parents and the community expect an active stance. In addition to policies about substance use on the school premises, therefore, many schools have developed or hosted drug prevention and intervention programs. These programs changed character during the 1970s. Earlier programs stressed detection, discipline, and scare tactics and, like similar approaches to venereal disease or smoking, they proved ineffective (Brecher, 1972; Nowlis, 1976; Randall & Wong, 1976). Subsequent programs stressed relevant information and often dealt with psychological issues, such as self-awareness, values clarification, communication skills, decision making, and peer relationships. Programs often incorporated affective experiential techniques and worked with students in small groups, using medical and psychological experts, ex-addicts, school counselors, teachers, and students as leaders. Most programs were relatively short-term, ranging from one or two days to a semester. Information on such programs appears in Bandt, Hammond, Wisdo, and Mitzel (1976); Charlotte Drug Education Center (1973); Cohen (1973); Eddy (1973); Far West Laboratory for Education Research and Development (1972); Johnson (1980); Langmeyer (1976); McClellan (1975); National Clearinghouse for Mental Health Information (1971); Nowlis (1976); Randall and Wong (1976); Rose and Duer (1978); Shalom, Inc. (1980); and Volpe (1977).

It is difficult to judge the effectiveness of most programs described in the literature, since a large proportion have no associated research. Randall and Wong (1976) examined over 200 published accounts and found that only 23 included systematic evaluation. From the studies available, however, it is evi-

dent that some programs increase student knowledge without demonstrable positive effects on attitudes or substance use (Lewis, Gossett, & Phillips, 1972; Randall & Wong, 1976; Swisher & Crawford, 1971; Swisher, Warner, & Herr, 1972). Swisher, Warner, and Herr compared the effects on ninth and eleventh graders of four six-week programs of drug education: three kinds of counseling groups (stressing relationships, reinforcement by a role model, and verbal reinforcement of positive student statements, respectively) and a control group exposed to a standard health unit on drugs. The study employed random assignment, pre- and post-testing for knowledge, attitudes, and self-reported drug use, and training and rotation of counselors. All approaches were equally effective in increasing knowledge about drugs, but none led to a change in attitudes or use. Increases in knowledge after drug education programs have sometimes been associated with effects contrary to intent (Randall & Wong, 1976). Stuart (1973), for instance, found that increased drug use occurred when greater knowledge was accompanied by a decrease in worry.

Some studies do report positive program effects. An affectively oriented alternative program in a Milwaukee high school led to reductions in the use of drugs and some shift toward drugs with lower abuse potential (McClellan, 1975). A broad-based program in high risk New York City public high schools resulted in decreased drug-related activities, less absence from school, and a decline in disruptive antisocial behavior (reported in Nowlis, 1976). Among programs for younger students, a multimedia project for junior high students combining information and experiential techniques influenced approximately one-fourth of former drug users against continued use and about one-half of the subjects against experimentation, at least according to self-report data (Kline, 1972). A program for sixth and eighth graders, in which teachers were trained in group skills, values clarification, moral development theory, and decision-making strategies, found significant differences between experimental and control groups on attitudes about the self and about drug use and drinking (Rose & Duer, 1978). There has been some suggestion that programs are more effective with elementary school students than those in high school (Warner, Swisher, & Horan, 1973) but there are contrary findings, such as those of Langmeyer (1976), who reports that an affective educational strategy aimed at drug abuse prevention had no systematic effects on fourth-grade children.

This body of studies suggests that some programs, at the least, increase student knowledge and change reported attitudes or behavior, but it is difficult to draw more specific conclusions. Many studies have classic design problems (no control group, no pretesting), or take little account of student characteristics. The criteria for change are often attitudinal rather than behavioral, and both aspects are usually assessed by self-report data, though a few studies use such criteria as hospital admissions or discipline problems related to drug use. Reports do not always separate substance users from other respondents in describing effects, and measures are often global, though substances differ widely in their potential for harm and it is important to measure the specific referents of change. Furthermore, there is little or no study of long-term effects. At best, there are inherent limitations on the stability of attitude change, especially among younger students; sixth graders who retain positive attitudes from a fifth-grade program may need to make their decisions at age 16 within a totally different and unpredictable peer system. Nonetheless, it would be useful to check the residual effects of such programs.

In their review of research on drug education, Randall and Wong criticize the fact that few researchers delineate the specific aspects responsible for the positive effects observed. Their point is well taken. As in many areas, however, it seems necessary both to clarify the useful elements and to approach the school as an integrated system. One long-range project, located in a dozen Catholic high schools and one elementary school, was conceptualized as a comprehensive intervention and prevention program (Klee, 1980, 1981). The project provided information about health and the implications of substance use; group experiences and leadership training for students; intervention services for students with known drug or alcohol problems and those at risk; referral services for families; and work with faculty.

The impact of intervention was studied through a three-year cohort design. Participants were compared with controls on baseline and yearly measures obtained from a student survey that tapped self-concept, social competence, knowledge about drugs and alcohol, and substance use, as well as attendance patterns, conduct, and academic grades. Attendance was higher and disruptive behavior lower among participants, who gained significantly more than controls in self-concept and social competence. The two groups did not differ in academic grades and self-reported substance use, but the program affected an important subgroup: there was a significant reduction in drug use among heavy users. Analysis by schools indicated that positive student change was most characteristic of institutions that made extensive use of the project and in which there were institutional changes in attitudes and policy. According to a survey of school staff, these changes included revisions in suspension policies, more use of intervention services, and increased staff knowledge about drug abuse and about dealing with students. The most effective schools appeared to be those in which project staff worked with the whole system from the beginning, establishing working mechanisms with administrators and teachers rather than focusing primarily on service to individual students.

It is likely that drugs and alcohol will continue to be available, that schools will continue to prohibit their use on the premises, and that many secondary students will continue to perceive these substances as a source of pleasure and a means of challenging authority (Brecher, 1972; Randall & Wong, 1976). School programs designed to influence students against the use of harmful or illicit substances have, by and large, been only marginally successful. The most promising have taken a comprehensive, long-term approach, not only providing specific information and services but affecting the social organization of the school as a whole.

Divorce

Until recently, divorce has been considered a private family matter. Because the divorce rate has risen steadily, however, it has become important to consider the implications for other social systems. In the late 1970s, some 9 to 11 million children living in one-parent families were in the schools (Houts, 1979; Kohn, 1979). Those whose situation was the result of divorce had evidently been going to school through a period of major family upheaval, raising a question about the effects of divorce on children's functioning in school. We review what is known about the children and what the schools are doing, noting in advance that systematic material is limited.

The effects of living in a one-parent family on the academic functioning of children has been thoroughly reviewed by Hetherington, Featherman, and Camara (1981). This survey suggests that children from one-parent households are not different from children in homes with two parents in intellectual ability or academic aptitude, but that they are ''absent from school more frequently, are more disruptive in the classroom, and may have less effective study styles in their school work'' (p. 87). Their grades are lower and teachers rate them as less motivated and academically effective, a perception that may affect as well as reflect the students' behavior.

Children from divorced families, who constitute a sizeable proportion of this group, have been specifically studied by Hetherington, Cox, and Cox (1979; 1981), and Wallerstein and Kelly (1980). In the comprehensive and well-designed Hetherington project, the play and social interaction of young children were studied in the preschool setting at the time of divorce and one and two years later. School-related measures included systematic observations, teacher ratings, and peer nominations. Wallerstein and Kelly's work dealt with children from preschool through adolescence, employing interview and clinical analysis. Data related to school came from teacher interviews soon after the divorce and one and four years later. Material from these two studies indicates that distress associated with the process of transition may last a year or more, that gender and the child's stage of development are associated with different reaction patterns, and that differences in coping and resilience depend partly on parent-child relationships, the reestablishment of stable family patterns, and economic and social realities.

In school-related data from the Hetherington study, children from recently divorced families were more disturbed in their play and social relations than children in the control group. Negative reactions were stronger among boys. Over the succeeding two years, girls' behavior became increasingly like that of their peers, but boys continued to show immaturity in their play and were demanding with female teachers. Teachers rated girls from divorced families as dependent and rated boys as aggressive and lacking in task orientation, perceiving them as less socially and academically competent than other children. As 4-year-olds, these boys were physically aggressive playmates in school. Two years later their aggressive behavior had changed and they made positive overtures to male peers, but other boys still perceived them as aggressive and excluded them. They were observed playing more with girls and younger children than is typical for males their age. Such play patterns may have developed not because the boys were disturbed or poorly identified with males, but because the male peer group at school continued to shut them out and alternative groups had developed. The findings present an interesting example of equilibrium in a classroom system, suggesting that teachers and peers may maintain a particular pattern even after a child is ready for change. The investigators note that boys who moved to another school between the first and second year follow-ups were perceived and responded to more positively by both teachers and peers than children who remained in the setting, and that the advantages

of a fresh start in a new situation, especially for children who have been negatively labeled, may outweigh the difficulties of coping with change.

In their study of school-aged children, Wallerstein and Kelly suggest that school can provide emotional support for children from divorced families simply because routines are predictable, children are expected to work, and there are social contacts. However, their data indicate that some children used the school more effectively than others. Older children had broader possibilities than the younger ones, and some found satisfaction in extracurricular activities. Academically competent children also tended to use the school productively, despite stress at home. Friendly relationships with teachers were often helpful to a child, providing not only support and reassurance but a continuing model of consistent adult authority at a time when parents may have been uncertain, preoccupied, or not available. The capacity to establish relationships with teachers was often part of a more general pattern: those who could draw support from teachers could also draw support from their mothers or make active contact with other children. Some children could not mobilize others at all, and teacher data suggest that some children alienated their peers during periods of stress. As in Hetherington's study, the reactions of peers may persist beyond the period of crisis. Children from families that have divorced may not find acceptance in the classroom peer group at a later point, even though they have adjusted to new family circumstances and are better able to relate to peers. The possibility suggests both a task for follow-up research and a role for teachers in the mediation of transitional difficulties.

School recognition of the possible implications of divorce has been rare, and efforts to develop policy or programs have been informal. However, educational journals have begun to deal with the topic as a school concern (e.g., *National Elementary Principal,* 1979), and there have been some reports of school interventions. Direct efforts to help children from divorcing families in school usually take the form of group counseling, either conducted by guidance specialists or through supervised peer counseling (Berkovitz, 1975). Clarkin and Clarkin (1980) describe a program in which trained professionals conducted groups for 6 to 10 children over a period of 10 weeks. Some children were considered at "high risk" because of poor predivorce adjustment or difficult family situations, and some were considered at "low risk" even though distressed. The groups were aimed at stimulating open discussion, increased self-awareness, and positive peer support. Low-risk children were judged to profit from the groups, while high-risk children required additional help.

Reported efforts to sensitize the school system to the implications of divorce have concentrated on white, upper-middle-class populations. Description of a program in a primarily black, low-income elementary school whose children predominantly lived in single-parent families is therefore of particular interest. The school set up training programs for teachers concerning the social and psychological needs of the students, attempted to provide for student contact with male teachers, and closely monitored the behavior and progress of the children (Kohn, 1979). Such programs are important, but other aspects of the school environment also require change. Conventional assumptions about typical family structures dominate textbooks, curricular content, and teachers' attitudes, just as conventional ideas about white middle-class culture and gender roles have been dominant, and these aspects have hardly been touched.

The relationship between schools and divorced parents has usually been marked by poor communication and unhelpful policies. School personnel often do not know whether one or both parents have custodial rights or should have access to school records, and the school often proceeds with conventional parent events, with little acknowledgment that many children have only one available parent or that "father and son" night may present a problem. Parents, for their part, traditionally protect their privacy. They often do not inform the school about the divorce, and may be surprised to learn that the child has told the teacher or that the school is concerned about the child's behavior. The issues are not simple. Families are entitled to privacy, and they may be realistically concerned that labeling a "child of divorce" can create more problems than it solves. Since home and school are the crucial mesosystem for the child, however, some communication should help the child's adjustment, and some adaptations in school policy should help both families and children. Suggestions have included flexible timing for parent conferences, cooperative arrangements for child care when school is not in session, recognizing that fathers are responsible parents, organizing activities so that either parent may attend, changing the wording of school forms, and establishing mechanisms for informing noncustodial parents about children's progress in school (Clay, 1981; *National Elementary Principal*, 1979). Some of these adaptations meet the needs of families in which both parents work, as well as those of single and divorced parents.

In general, the school's task is to support the children and mobilize their capacity to cope during a period of profound but not abnormal crisis. Children react differently, depending on their stage of development, particular circumstances, and resilience, and schools need to be sensitive to such differences, avoiding labels that outlive the crisis and offering services where needed. Peer group counseling, flexible policies in relation to parents, and the acknowledgment of many varieties of family life should all be helpful. Some change in school materials and in teacher assumptions about normality is required (see Santrock & Tracy, 1978), so that young children from varied family structures can find matter-of-fact acceptance in school, and older children can deal with realistic curriculum material about social trends and the issues of marriage and family life in contemporary society.

Research on the functioning of children from divorced families in different classroom settings would be particularly informative. Active classrooms with opportunity for cooperative work might well provide an antidote for these children's reported distractibility and poor study habits. On the other hand, Hetherington, Cox, and Cox (1981) have found that a predictable, organized school environment with consistent standards, responsible roles for students, and a nuturant responsive atmosphere facilitates adaptive, self-controlled behavior in young children from divorced families, and is associated with a low rate of behavior disorders. Structure appears particularly important for boys; warmth, responsiveness, and expectations of maturity for girls. Further research along these lines is indicated, with extensions to older children and to the investigation of consistency between school and family styles of relating to the child. It should also be productive to study the classroom processes that either rigidify the child's maladaptive behavior or support positive adaptation. Research of this kind may have implications for other transitional situations such as moving, illness, or death in the family, in which the child's school behavior reflects temporary difficulties but may be extended beyond the crisis by rigidities in peer and teacher expectations.

Summary

While the schools have always reflected the nature of society and its problems, efforts to use schools as pathways for change have been particularly active in the last two decades, especially in relation to discrimination and socially threatening phenomena such as substance abuse or violent behavior.[2] Evaluative research on the many forms of intervention has produced few definite conclusions, but does suggest that children may become more knowledgeable without necessarily changing either attitudes or behavior, and that short-term interventions are unlikely to produce sturdy new patterns. Simple modifications in curriculum material or social grouping also have limited effects. Interventions that approach the school and its personnel as a system appear to have more impact, and research that takes multiple factors into consideration appears to produce more useful data.

The probability of sustained effects depends not only on the nature and scope of the intervention, but on realities in the larger social context. The areas we have reviewed, and some that we have not, continue to be social problems. It is arguable, however, that social gains have been greater in some areas than others; that women, for instance, have made more progress than blacks and other minorities. If so, educational efforts to reduce gender stereotyping and foster equal opportunities for females and males in the schools may more readily be maintained and create more lasting impact than efforts to improve opportunities for minority students. Efforts to modify violent behavior, enhance moral development, or reduce corporal punishment in schools may have the poorest prognosis, since they must work against negative models and counteractive social forces. This does not imply that school interventions are pointless, but does direct simultaneous attention to the larger social system. The interdependence of school and culture also underscores the importance of specifying cohorts in the presentation and interpretation of research. Data gathered during different social eras may not be interchangeable. Considering the major social changes that have occurred during the last half of this century, research on socially relevant problems in the schools must be considered relatively specific to its time and place.

SOCIAL DEVELOPMENT AND THE SCHOOL: SUMMARY AND IMPLICATIONS

The chapter has been organized in terms of the educational context. The summary is organized in terms of social development, and considers the relationship between the educational context and self-concept, gender role, interpersonal relations, and the child's participation in the social system of the school.

The School and Self-Concept

Studies of the relationship between educational environments and self-concept focus on *self-esteem*. "Low self-esteem" has been implicated in the poor academic performance of minority children, antisocial behavior, and drug abuse. Specific interventions and affective curricula, as well as some comprehensive educational models, have been aimed at enhancing the child's sense of self-worth, although the methods have varied greatly. Evaluation research has sometimes verified the impact of these efforts, but there are numerous contradictory and nonsignificant findings. It has been difficult to demonstrate increases in children's self-esteem as a result of Head Start, racial integration, open classrooms, or affective curricula.

Studies have often been conducted under conditions in which changes in self-image should not have been expected; for instance, when short-term programs are inserted into classrooms with unknown properties, or when the grouping practices in desegregated classrooms nullify the intent to integrate. It has been generally agreed in the literature that both the concept and the existing measures of self-esteem are inadequate. It is also possible that positive self-esteem—conceptualized as a stable, affective attribute of the person—is not a useful concept for assessing educational effects. Internalized feelings about the self may not be stable, and global measures may not have clear meaning in relation to school experience. More specific formulations of aspects of the self-system—self-differentiation, academic self-concept, or locus of control—may lead to more meaningful data. Self-differentiation, for instance, concerns the quality of knowledge children have about themselves, rather than whether they regard themselves more or less favorably. It should be enhanced by educational environments that provide varied experiences, individualized feedback, and a problem-solving style of thinking. Measures of locus of control and attribution patterns are seldom viewed as tapping self-concept, but actually concern the child's assessment of self in relation to authority. They yield data on how the child views the location of power and responsibility, and should relate to effort, accomplishment and feedback in the learning situation. Such measures may offer more pertinent indicators of the effects of different environments than undifferentiated assessments of self-esteem.

Observational studies are an additional source of information about self-concept. Such studies document the cycles of expectation and behavior to which teacher, child, and the classroom peer group contribute, forming stable patterns that define the class clown, achievers and nonachievers, and troublesome children. Observational studies also document the processes through which the child internalizes an image of self in the classroom context, and seem especially suitable for study of how such cycles are formed, sustained, and changed.

The School and Gender

It is through the school in particular that the child builds a sense of competence and of possibilities for finding relevant occupational directions. The school also functions to sustain or modify cultural messages concerning the expected behavior of females and males. Documentation of gender stereotyping in school has been extensive, and considerable effort has been invested in changing biased materials and curricula and in modifying the attitudes of teachers and children. Research on less stereotyped educational settings has suggested that children in these environments hold less conventional, dichotomous images of males and females, and have more contact with children of the opposite gender. As classroom environments, adult models, and specific interventions broaden children's experience, traditional tenets of child development may need to change. Sex-typed play in the preschool and same-sex peer groups in the elementary classroom may be no more inevitable than the association of girls with secretarial careers and fear of math or the affinity of boys for aggression and science. It is still unclear how dramatic the changes will be or what patterns would be developmentally optimal. Perhaps some mixture of same- and mixed-sex peer groups would best serve developmental purposes at certain stages. Research will need to clarify the relationship among changing social mores, the gender-related messages of the school, and developmental patterns.

In evaluating the impact of the school, it is always essential to consider the larger social environment. With respect to gender stereotyping, the direction of change in the schools and the social milieu appear to be consistent. Progress may be considered significant by some and minimal by others, but there is little question that American children are growing up in a society in which male and female models are more diverse than they were twenty years ago, and there are support systems and more varied career possibilities for those exploring nontraditional pathways. Because of this framework, changes in gender-related concepts and behavior fostered by the schools can be expected to persist.

The School and Interpersonal Relations

There are different views of the school's responsibility for the development of attitudes about and behavior with peers and adults. A distinction is often made between negative aspects of interpersonal behavior such as fighting, that interfere with learning or classroom decorum, and prosocial behaviors such as the development of friendships or cooperative work patterns, which are not traditionally considered the province of the school. Psychologists may have given implicit support to this orientation by focusing on achievement, anxiety, aggression, and behavior problems in school. Some educational theorists, however, have deliberately structured the setting, the learning experiences, and the relations between teachers and students to foster interpersonal contacts and cooperative work patterns, and the effects of different structures have been investigated.

The Individual Child in Relation to Others

Research has documented a fact that probably needs no documentation: when classroom conditions permit contact among students, children have a wider variety of interpersonal experiences. Open structures, cooperative learning situations, certain preschool materials, and space for socializing on the high school premises provide some of these conditions. Increased contact can be positive or conflictual. Except for some studies in the preschool, research on peer group tension and conflict resolution in the classroom setting has been sparse. On the other hand, there is a body of research on friendship, status, cooperation, and moral development.

These studies show that children in open settings make more varied friendship choices, have more cross-gender contact, and experience less rigid status in the classroom peer group than children in traditional settings. Elementary school children in open settings are also more cooperative as well as more autonomous, suggesting a desirable balance in qualities sometimes considered antithetical. Programs of moral education have demonstrated small gains in moral reasoning but little evidence of sustained effects. Relatively recent interventions have been directed toward influencing the moral atmosphere of the educational environment and involving students in realistic issues that arise in the school. Given the immoral realities of the larger society, it seems apparent that short-term circumscribed programs have little chance of creating sustained effects. As programs become more comprehensive and multifaceted, however, it is more difficult to conduct traditional evaluative research and alternative forms of assessment must be developed.

Intergroup Relations

A classroom that has a mixture of different kinds of children seems relevant to the democratic ideal, allowing for increased understanding and possibilities for friendship. Nevertheless, concern has been expressed about the potential increase in intergroup tension, and the negative effects on children who enter the classroom with less preparation and status than others. The largest body of research on this topic has accompanied the desegregation of public schools, and the findings have not been encouraging. They have shown that desegregation per se does not guarantee improved relations, and that positive consequences depend on what happens inside the schools once the children are there.

It would be naive to ignore the cultural environment in assessing the relationships among ethnic groups in a school. However, research suggests certain conditions in the school that may increase the possibility of intergroup tolerance and friendship, such as school personnel who support the advancement of minority students, curricula that acknowledge pluralism, and the involvement of the students in cooperative activities and learning situations. Gordon Allport's formulation, offered some years ago, may still be relevant, although difficult to achieve. He posited that reduction of hostility and stereotyping depends on long-term contact, institutional sanctions, and the organization of groups with equal status pursuing shared goals.

The Child and School Authority

The relationship of students to authority is often conceptualized in terms of discipline and the acceptance of school rules. The research is not definitive, but some connections have been established between the social organization of the school and student behavior. Fewer problems of student discipline and antisocial behavior, as well as greater student satisfaction, are associated with opportunities to participate in decision making, small school size, informal contacts between teachers and students, and consistent expectations. Research on students' identification with teachers and other school personnel has been relatively neglected. Given the increasing emphasis in developmental theory on the power of experiences beyond the early years, it is no longer reasonable to ignore the impact of significant figures outside the family. The schools offer an untapped

potential for studying the child's relationship to nonparental authorities at different developmental stages.

The School as a Social System: The Child as Participant

Recent research has focused on the way that tacit rules of social behavior in school are learned, such as how to participate in a lesson or how the social system of the classroom works. Much of this research is located in the early grades, where children are first being inducted into the school world. What the work uncovers is a network of social norms for interaction that defines the meaning of school and of being a student in the classroom. Young elementary school children, it appears, can learn the implicit social forms, and distinguish between social conventions that establish how things are done and moral issues that involve some consideration of fairness and justice. This line of research, which has begun to test developmental trends, appears fruitful.

Other investigations, conducted primarily in secondary schools, concern the relationship between different forms of social organization and the commitment and behavior of the students. We know that students in small high schools are more likely to be active participants than those in large schools. Beyond this, the findings are less certain, but schools with less authoritarian social structures mobilize more student identification and fewer students drop out. The fact that the high school dropout rate approaches 50% in many urban settings suggests a poor match between the social organization of many schools and the developmental needs of their students.

Participation in the school as a social organization is relatively understudied. We know little about the effects of different authority structures on the student's internalized sense of responsibility, not only for his or her own progress but for the well-being of others in the school and for the school as a community. We also know little about variations in the child's social participation as she or he moves from one classroom to another, or about the effects of discrepancies between the social organization of family and school.

The School and Social Development: Directions for Future Research

The body of research on social development in the school is neither unified nor easily summarized. In many areas findings are inconclusive, reflecting the well-known dearth of social measures, inadequate research design, and the sheer number and complexity of relevant variables. Nevertheless, we can say with certainty that schools have an impact, that all children learn social forms in the educational setting, and that schools with broad goals and a flexible, coherent social organization are likely to foster positive social behavior. A context that provides opportunity for social experience and feedback is indispensable for optimal growth, but we know that the nature and quality of those experiences are crucial determinants of the effects. It seems fair to say that research about schooling is making progress toward documenting what happens to whom under specified conditions.

While almost all the topics we have reviewed would profit from more research, certain aspects of the research enterprise are relatively neglected and merit attention over the next decade. The observational study of children's spontaneous social behavior is one. Studies that focus on input-outcome variables or use school children as experimental subjects are legion, but studies that regard classrooms and schools as the child's natural habitat and look simultaneously at the behavior setting and the child's social functioning are uncommon. As children move through the grades, the school environment presents a mixture of continuity and changing situations, providing an unparalleled opportunity for the longitudinal study of developmental change in naturalistic settings. Another frontier for research concerns the relationships between schools and other social systems, as these affect behavior in school and development thereafter. Studies of home and school interaction require a social as well as academic focus, and more detailed analysis of the effects of the fit between the social patterns of the family and those of the school. Studies of the school in the larger social system also require a cohort orientation that takes account of the spirit of the time and its significance for the conduct and interpretation of research.

Recommendations for improvements in the methodology of research based in schools depend on one's orientation. Taking the prevailing viewpoint first, there is an evident need for the development of better measures of both context and behavior; for more fastidiously designed studies; for research that relates the voluminous self-report data to actual behavior; and for studies that use a multivariate approach. From a systems point of view, the need is for more observational research in continuing systems such as the classroom, with an emphasis on documentation of recurrent patterns and clarification of the forces that maintain the system or create change. Innovative approaches in the material we have reviewed appear to be moving in two potentially fruitful directions: toward detailed documentation of ongoing events, and toward comprehensive approaches to the school as an organized system. The challenge is to invent and refine scientific procedures for the study of social development in complex natural systems.

NOTES

1. Additional material on basic concepts, developmental studies, and moral education can be found in DePalma & Foley, 1975; Hersh, Paolitto, & Reimer, 1979; Hill, Klafter, & Wallace, 1976; Hoffman, 1979; Kohlberg, 1976, 1981; Lickona, 1976; Mosher, 1980; National Institute of Education, 1976; Purpel & Ryan, 1976; Rest, 1979; *Handbook, vol. III, ch. 9;* Scharf, 1978.

2. For material on violence and corporal punishment in the schools, see *Contemporary Education,* 1980; Feshbach & Feshbach, 1973; Hyman & Wise, 1979; McPartland & McDill, 1976, 1977; National Institute of Education, 1978; Reitman, Follman, & Ladd, 1972; among others.

REFERENCES

Abelson, W. D., Zigler, E., & DeBlasi, C. L. Effects of a four-year Follow Through program on economically disadvantaged children. *Journal of Educational Psychology,* 1974, *66,* 756–771.

Abernathy, R. W. The impact of an intensive consciousness-raising curriculum on adolescent women. *Psychology of Women Quarterly,* 1977, *2,* 138–147.

Ackoff, R. L., & Emery, F. E. *On purposeful systems.* Chicago: Aldine, 1972.

Adams, D. Building moral dilemma activities. *Learning,* 1977, *5,* 44–46.

Adams, R., & Biddle, B. J. *Realities of teaching: Explorations with video tape.* New York: Holt, Rinehart & Winston, 1970.

Adell, J., & Klein, H. D. *A guide to non-sexist children's books.* Chicago: Academy, 1976.

Aiello, J. R., & Aiello, T. D. The development of personal space: Proxemic behavior of children 6 through 16. *Human Ecology,* 1974, *2,* 177–189.

Aiello, J. R., Nicosia, G., & Thompson, D. E. Physiological, social, and behavioral consequences of crowding on children and adolescents. *Child Development,* 1979, *50,* 195–202.

Allen, R. But the earth abideth forever: Values in environmental education. *Resources in Education,* January-June, 1975, 438.

Allender, J. Affective education. In H. E. Mitzel (Ed.), *Encyclopedia of educational research* (5th ed.). New York: The Free Press, 1982.

Allport, G. *The nature of prejudice*. Cambridge, Mass.: Addison-Wesley, 1954.

Alschuler, A., Phillips, K., & Weinstein, G. Self-knowledge education as an approach to drug abuse education. In *Humanizing preservice teacher education: Strategies for alcohol and drug abuse prevention*. Washington, D.C.: Eric Clearinghouse on Teacher Education, 1977.

Amidon, E. J., & Flanders, N. *The role of the teacher in the classroom: A manual for understanding and improving teachers' classroom behavior*. Minneapolis, Minn.: 1963.

Amidon, E. J., & Hough, J. B. (Eds.). *Interaction analysis theory, research and application*. Reading, Mass.: Addison-Wesley, 1967.

Amir, Y. The role of intergroup contact in change of prejudice and ethnic relations. In P. Katz (Ed.), *Towards the elimination of racism*. New York: Pergamon, 1976.

Anderson, H. H. Domination and social integration in the behavior of kindergarten children and their teachers. *Genetic Psychology Monographs*, 1939, *21*, 287–385.

Anderson, H. H., & Brewer, H. M. Studies of teachers' classroom personalities. II. Effects of teachers' dominative and integrative contacts on children. *Applied Psychology Monographs*, 1946, *8*, 33–122.

Anderson, R. C. Learning in discussions: A resume of the authoritarian-democratic studies. *Harvard Educational Review*, 1959, *29*, 201–215.

Argyris, C. Alternative schools: A behavioral analysis. *Teachers College Record*, 1974, *72*, 429–453.

Arlin, M. The interaction of locus of control, classroom structure, and pupil satisfaction. *Psychology in the Schools*, 1975, *12*, 279–286.

Aronson, E., Bridgeman, D. L., & Geffner, R. The effects of a cooperative classroom structure on student behavior and attitudes. In D. Bar-Tal & L. Saxe (Eds.), *Social psychology of education, theory and research*. Washington, D.C.: Hemisphere, 1978.

Aronson, E., Stephan, C., Sikes, J., Blaney, N., & Snapp, M. *The jigsaw classroom*. Beverly Hills, Calif.: Sage, 1978.

Au, W. Confluent education: A critical evaluation. *Confluent Education Journal*, 1977, *5*, 54–75.

Averch, H., Carroll, S., Donaldson, T., Kiesling, H., & Pincus, J. *How effective is schooling? A critical review of research*. Englewood Cliffs,

N.J.: Educational Technology Publications, 1974.

Baird, L. Big school, small school: A critical examination of the hypothesis. *Journal of Educational Psychology*, 1969, *60*, 253–260.

Baker, G. D. et al. *New methods vs. old in American education: An analysis and summary of recent comparative studies*. New York: Teachers College, Columbia University, 1941.

Bandt, P., Hammond, M., Wisdo, T., & Mitzel, H. *A follow-up study of teachers trained in affective classroom approaches to primary prevention of drug and alcohol abuse*. University Park, Pa.: Addictions Prevention Laboratory, The Pennsylvania State University, 1976.

Bany, M., & Johnson, L. *Classroom group behavior: Group dynamics in education*. New York: Macmillan, 1964.

Baratz, S. S., & Baratz, J. C. Early childhood intervention: The social science basis of institutional racism. *Harvard Educational Review*, 1970, *40*, 29–50.

Barker, R. G. *Ecological psychology: Concepts and methods for studying the environment of human behavior*. Stanford, Calif.: Stanford University Press, 1968.

Barker, R. G., & Gump, P. V. *Big school, small school: High school size and student behavior*. Stanford, Calif.: Stanford University Press, 1964.

Barker, R. G., & Wright, H. F. *Midwest and its children*. New York: Harper & Row, 1955.

Barker-Lunn, J. C. *Streaming in the primary school*. Slough, Bucks., England: National Foundation for Educational Research in England & Wales, 1970.

Barr, R., & Dreeben, R. Instruction in classrooms. In L. Shulman (Ed.), *Review of research in education* (Vol. 5). Itasca, Ill.: Peacock, 1978.

Barth, R. S. *Open education and the American school*. New York: Schocken, 1972.

Bass, M. H., & Weinstein, M. S. Early development of interpersonal distance in children. *Canadian Journal of Behavioral Science*, 1971, *3*, 368–376.

Bates, B. C. *Effects of social density on the behavior of nursery school children*. Unpublished doctoral dissertation, University of Oregon, 1970.

Bateson, G. *Steps to an ecology of mind*. New York: Ballantine, 1972.

Baumrind, D. New directions in socialization research. *American Psychologist*, 1980, *35*, 639–652.

Beck, C., Sullivan, E., & Taylor, N. Stimulating

transition to postconventional morality: The Pickering High School study. *Interchange,* 1972, *3,* 28–37.

Becker, W. C., Engelmann, S., & Thomas, D. R. *Teaching: A course in applied psychology.* Chicago: Science Research Associates, 1971.

Beeken, D., & Janzen, H. L. Behavioral mapping of student activity in open-area and traditional schools. *American Educational Research Journal,* 1978, *15,* 507–517.

Beigel, A., & Feshbach, N. D. *A comparative study of student teacher, teacher corps, and undergraduate preferences for elementary school pupils.* Paper presented at the annual meetings of the California Educational Research Association, 1970.

Bell, D. (Ed.). *Shades of Brown: New perspectives on school desegregation.* New York: Teachers College Press, 1980.

Bennett, S. N. *Teaching styles and pupil progress.* London: Open, 1976.

Bennett, S. N. Recent research on teaching: A dream, a belief, and a model. *British Journal of Educational Psychology,* 1978, *48,* 127–147.

Bereiter, C., & Engelmann, S. *Teaching disadvantaged children in the preschool.* Englewood Cliffs, N.J.: Prentice-Hall, 1966.

Berk, L. E. Effects of variations in the nursery school setting on environmental constraints and children's modes of adaptation. *Child Development,* 1971, *42,* 839–869.

Berk, L. E., & Lewis, N. G. Sex role and social behavior in four school environments. *The Elementary School Journal,* 1977, *77,* 205–217.

Berkovitz, I. H. (Ed.). *When schools care.* New York: Brunner/Mazel, 1975.

Bertalanffy, L. von. *General system theory.* New York: George Braziller, 1968.

Bessell, H., & Palomares, V. *Methods in human development* (lesson guide level B). San Diego, Calif.: Human Development Training Institute, 1969.

Bessell, H., & Palomares, V. *Methods in human development: Theory manual* (Revised). San Diego, Calif.: Human Development Training Institute, 1970.

Bianchi, B. D., & Bakeman, R. Sex-typed affiliation preferences observed in preschoolers: Traditional and open school differences. *Child Development,* 1978, *49,* 910–912.

Bianchi, B. D., & Bakeman, R. *Sex-typed affiliation preferences: Mixed sex play in an open school.* Paper presented at the meetings of the American Psychological Association, Montreal, 1980.

Biber, B. The "whole child," individuality and values in education. In J. R. Squire (Ed.), *A new look at progressive education.* ASCD Yearbook. Washington, D.C.: Association for Supervision and Curriculum Development, 1972.

Biber, B. The developmental-interaction point of view: Bank Street College of Education. In M. C. Day & R. K. Parker (Eds.), *The preschool in action.* Boston: Allyn & Bacon, 1977.

Biber, B., & Lewis, C. An experimental study of what young school children expect from their teachers. *Genetic Psychology Monographs,* 1949, *40,* 3–97.

Biber, H., Miller, L., & Dyer, J. Feminization in preschool. *Developmental Psychology,* 1972, *7,* 86.

Biskin, D. S., & Hoskisson, K. An experimental test of the effects of structured discussions of moral dilemmas found in children's literature on moral reasoning. *The Elementary School Journal,* 1977, *77,* 407–416.

Black, H. Moral judgments and history teaching. *Australian Journal of Education,* 1977, *21,* 34–40.

Blaney, N. T., Stephan, S., Rosenfield, D., Aronson, E., & Sikes, J. Interdependence in the classroom: A field study. *Journal of Educational Psychology,* 1977, *69,* 121–128.

Blatt, M. M., & Kohlberg, L. The effects of classroom moral discussion upon children's level of moral judgment. *Journal of Moral Education,* 1975, *4,* 129–161.

Bleier, M., Groveman, H., Kuntz, N., & Mueller, E. A comparison of yielding to influence in open and traditional classrooms. *Childhood Education,* 1972, *49,* 45–50.

Block, J. H. Gender differences in the nature of premises developed about the world. In E. K. Shapiro & E. Weber (Eds.), *Cognitive and affective growth: Developmental interaction.* Hillsdale, N.J.: Lawrence Erlbaum, 1981.

Blumenfeld, P. C., Hamilton, V. L., Wessels, K., & Falkner, D. Teaching responsibility to first graders. *Theory into Practice,* 1979, *18,* 174–180.

Blurton Jones, N. (Ed.). *Ethological studies of child behaviour.* Cambridge, England: Cambridge University Press, 1972.

Boulogne, J. Simulation games in moral education. *History and Social Science Teacher,* 1978, *13,* 202–203.

Bowles, S., & Gintis, H. *Schooling in capitalist America.* New York: Basic, 1976.

Bowman, G. W., & Mayer, R. S. Behavior ratings and analysis of communication in education (BRACE). In O. G. Johnson (Ed.), *Tests and measurements in child development: Handbook II* (Vol. 2). San Francisco: Jossey-Bass, 1976.

Braun, C. Teacher expectation: Sociopsychological dynamics. *Review of Educational Research,* 1976, *46,* 185–213.

Brecher, M. *Licit and illicit drugs: The Consumers Union report on narcotics, stimulants, depressants, inhalants, hallucinogens, and marijuana—including caffeine, nicotine, and alcohol.* Boston: Little, Brown, 1972.

Bremme, D. W., & Erickson, F. Relationships among verbal and nonverbal classroom behavior. *Theory into Practice,* 1977, *16,* 153–161.

Brody, G. H., & Zimmerman, B. J. The effects of modeling and classroom organization on the personal space of third and fourth grade children. *American Educational Research Journal,* 1975, *12,* 157–168.

Bronfenbrenner, U. *The ecology of human development.* Cambridge, Mass.: Harvard University Press, 1979.

Brookover, W., Beady, C., Flood, P., Schweitzer, J., & Wisenbaker, J. *School social systems and student achievement: Schools can make a difference.* New York: Praeger, 1979.

Brophy, J. E. Teacher behavior and its effects. *Journal of Educational Psychology,* 1979, *71,* 733–750.

Brophy, J. E., & Evertson, C. *Learning from teaching: A developmental perspective.* Boston: Allyn & Bacon, 1976.

Brophy, J. E., & Good, T. L. *Teacher-student relationships: Causes and consequences.* New York: Holt, Rinehart & Winston, 1974.

Brown, G. *Human teaching for human learning: An introduction to confluent education.* New York: Viking, 1971.

Brown, G. *The live classroom: Innovation through confluent education and gestalt.* New York: Viking, 1975.

Bruner, J. S. *The process of education.* Cambridge, Mass.: Harvard University Press, 1960.

Bruner, J. S. *Toward a theory of instruction.* Cambridge, Mass.: Harvard University Press, 1966.

Brunetti, F. A. Noise, distraction and privacy in conventional and open school environments. In W. J. Mitchell (Ed.), *Environmental design: Research and practice.* Proceedings of Environmental Design Research Conference. Los Angeles: University of California Press, 1972.

Bryant, B., & Crockenberg, S. Cooperative and competitive classroom environments. *JSAS Catalog of Selected Documents in Psychology,* 1974, *4,* 53.

Burkhead, J. *Input and output in large-city high schools.* Syracuse, N.Y.: Syracuse University Press, 1967.

Bushell, D. Jr. The behavior analysis classroom. In B. Spodek (Ed.), *Early childhood education.* Englewood Cliffs, N.J.: Prentice-Hall, 1973.

Bussis, A. M., & Chittenden, E. A. *Analysis of an approach to open education.* Princeton, N.J.: Educational Testing Service, 1970.

Carew, J. V., & Lightfoot, S. L. *Beyond bias: Perspectives on classrooms.* Cambridge, Mass.: Harvard University Press, 1979.

Carithers, M. W. School desegregation and racial cleavage, 1954–1970: A review of the literature. *Journal of Social Issues,* 1970, *26,* 25–47.

Castañeda, A., Ramirez, M., Cortés, C. E., & Barrera, M. (Eds.), *Mexican-Americans and educational change.* A Symposium at the University of California, Riverside, 1971. (Mimeo)

Castillo, G. A. *Left-handed teaching: Lessons in affective education.* New York: Praeger, 1974.

Chapman, M. L., & Davis, F. V. Skills for ethical action: A process approach to judgment and action. *Educational Leadership,* 1978, *35,* 457–458, 460–461.

Charlesworth, R., & Hartup, W. Positive social reinforcement in the nursery school peer group. *Child Development,* 1967, *38,* 993–1002.

Charlotte Drug Education Center. *Teachers guide.* National Institute of Law Enforcement Assistance Administration, 1973.

Charters, W. W. Jr., & Jones, J. E. On the risk of appraising non-events in program evaluation. *Educational Researcher,* 1973, *2,* 5–7.

Child, I., Potter, E., & Levine, E. Children's textbooks and personality development: An exploration in the social psychology of education. *Psychological Monographs,* 1946, *60*(3, Whole No. 279).

Clark, B. M., & Creswell, J. L. *Participants' versus nonparticipants' perception of teacher nonverbal behavior.* Paper presented at the meetings of the American Educational Research Association, Toronto, March 1978.

Clark, D., & Kadis, A. *Humanistic teaching.* Columbus, Ohio: Charles E. Merrill, 1971.

Clarkin, A. J., & Clarkin, J. F. *Intervention with children of divorce within the school system.* Paper presented at the meetings of the American Orthopsychiatric Association, 1980.

Clay, P. L. *Single parents and the public schools. How does the partnership work?* Columbia, Md.: National Committee for Citizens in Education, 1981.

Clinchy, B., Lief, J., & Young, P. Epistemological and moral development in girls from a traditional and a progressive high school. *Journal of Educational Psychology,* 1977, *69,* 337–343.

Cohen, A. Y. *Alternatives to drug abuse: Steps toward prevention.* Rockville, Md.: National Clearinghouse for Drug Abuse Information, 1973.

Cohen, E. G. The effects of desegregation on race relations. *Law and Contemporary Problems,* 1975, *39,* 271–299.

Cohen, M. D., & Martin, L. P. (Eds.). *Growing free: Ways to help children overcome sex role stereotypes.* Washington, D.C.: Association for Childhood Education International, 1976.

Colby, A., Kohlberg, L., Fenton, E., Speicher-Dubin, B., & Lieberman, M. Secondary school moral discussions programs led by social studies teachers. *Journal of Moral Education,* 1977, *6,* 90–111.

Cole, M., Hood, L., & McDermott, R. P. Concepts of ecological validity: Their differing implications for comparative cognitive research. *Newsletter of the Institute for Comparative Human Development,* 1978, *2,* 34–37.

Coleman, J. S., Campbell, E. Q., Hobson, C. J., McPartland, J., Mood, A. M., Weinfeld, F. D., & York, R. L. *Equality of educational opportunity.* Washington, D.C.: U.S. Government Printing Office, 1966.

Coles, R. *Children of crisis.* Vol. I: *A study of courage and fear.* Boston: Little, Brown, 1967.

Conant, J. B. *The American high school today: A first report to interested citizens.* New York: McGraw-Hill, 1959.

Contemporary Education, 1980, *52,* 1–62 (Whole). Crime and violence in public schools: Emerging perspectives of the 1980s.

Cooper, H. M. Pygmalion grows up: A model for teacher expectation, communication and performance influence. *Review of Educational Research,* 1979, *49,* 389–410.

Cremin, L. A. *The transformation of the school.* New York: Knopf, 1961.

Crockenberg, S. B. The effects of cooperative learning environments and interdependent goals on conformity in school-age children. *Merrill-Palmer Quarterly,* 1979, *25,* 121–132.

Crockenberg, S. B., Bryant, B. K., & Wilce, L. S. The effects of cooperatively and competitively structured learning environments on inter- and intrapersonal behavior. *Child Development,* 1976, *47,* 386–396.

Crockenberg, S. B., & Nicolayev, J. Stage transition in moral reasoning as related to conflict experienced in naturalistic settings. *Merrill-Palmer Quarterly,* 1979, *25,* 185–192.

Cuffaro, H. K., Ginsberg, S., Mack, G., Sample W., Shapiro, E., Wallace, D., & Zimiles, H. *Young Native Americans and their families: Educational needs and recommendations.* New York: Bank Street College of Education, 1976.

Davis, E. *The Liberty Cap: A catalogue of nonsexist materials for children.* Chicago: Academy, 1977.

Day, M. C., & Parker, R. K. (Eds.). *The preschool in action: Exploring early childhood programs* (2nd ed.). Boston: Allyn & Bacon, 1977.

Deal, T. E. An organizational explanation of the failure of alternative secondary schools. *Educational Researcher,* 1975, *4,* 10–16.

Deal, T. E., & Nolan, R. R. (Eds.). *Alternative schools: Ideologies, realities, guidelines.* Chicago: Nelson-Hall, 1978.

DePalma, D., & Foley, J. *Moral development: Current theory and research.* Hillsdale, N.J.: Lawrence Erlbaum, 1975.

Deutsch, M. A theory of co-operation and competition. *Human Relations,* 1949, *2,* 129–152.

DeVries, D. L., Edwards, K. J., & Slavin, R. E. Biracial learning teams and race relations in the classroom: Four field experiments using teams—games—tournaments. *Journal of Educational Psychology,* 1978, *70,* 356–362.

DeVries, D. L., & Slavin, R. E. Teams—games—tournaments (TGT): Review of ten classroom experiments. *Journal of Research and Development in Education,* 1978, *12,* 28–38.

Dewey, J. *The school and society.* Chicago: Phoenix, 1956. (Originally published, University of Chicago Press, 1899.)

Dewey, J. *Experience and education.* New York: Macmillan, 1963. (Originally published, 1938.)

Dewey, J. *Democracy and education.* New York: Free, 1966. (Originally published, Macmillan, 1916.)

Divoky, D. Affective education: Are we going too far? *Learning,* 1975, *4,* 20–27.

Donahue, T., & Costar, J. W. Counselor discrimination against young women in career selection. *Journal of Counseling Psychology,* 1977, *24,* 481–485.

Downing, L. L., & Bothwell, K. H. Open-space schools: Anticipation of peer interaction and development of cooperative interdependence. *Journal of Educational Psychology,* 1979, *71,* 478–484.

Doyle, P. H. *The efficacy of the ecological model: A study of the impact of activity settings on the social behavior of preschool children.* Unpublished doctoral dissertation, Wayne State University, 1975.

Duckworth, E. *A comparison study for evaluating primary school science in Africa.* Newton, Mass.: Education Development Center, 1971.

Duffey, R. V. Moral education and the study of current events. *Social Education,* 1975, *39,* 33–35.

Duke, D. L. *The retransformation of the school.* Chicago: Nelson-Hall, 1978.

Duke, D. L., & Muzio, I. How effective are alternative schools? A review of recent evaluations and reports. *Teachers College Record,* 1978, *79,* 462–464.

Duke, D. L., & Perry, C. Can alternative schools succeed where Benjamin Spock, Spiro Agnew and B. F. Skinner have failed? *Adolescence,* 1978, *13,* 375–392.

Duke, D. L., & Perry, C. What happened to the high school discipline crisis? *Urban Education,* 1979, *14,* 182–204.

Dumont, R. V., Jr. Learning English and how to be silent: Studies in Sioux and Cherokee classrooms. In C. B. Cazden, V. P. John, & D. Hymes (Eds.), *Functions of language in the classroom.* New York: Teachers College Press, 1972.

Dunkin, M. J., & Biddle, B. J. *The study of teaching.* New York: Holt, Rinehart & Winston, 1974.

Dunkle, M. C., & Sandler, B. Sex discrimination against students: Implications of Title IX of the Education Amendments of 1972. *Inequality in Education,* October 1974, 12–35.

Durlack, J. T., Beardsley, B. E., & Murray, J. S. Observation of user activity patterns in open and traditional plan school environments. In W. J. Mitchell (Ed.), *Environmental design: Research and practice.* Proceedings of Environmental Design Research Conference. Los Angeles: University of California Press, 1972.

Dweck, C. S., & Bush, E. S. Sex differences in learned helplessness: I. Differential debilitation with peer and adult evaluators. *Developmental Psychology,* 1976, *12,* 147–156.

Dweck, C. S., Davidson, W., Nelson, S., & Enna, B. Sex differences in learned helplessness: II. The contingencies of evaluative feedback in the classroom; and III. An experimental analysis. *Developmental Psychology,* 1978, *14,* 268–276.

Eddy, J. *The teacher and the drug scene.* Bloomington, Ind.: Phi Delta Kappa Educational Foundation, 1973.

Edmonds, R. Some schools work and more can. *Social Policy,* 1979, *9,* 28–32.

Educational Challenges, Inc. *Today's changing roles: An approach to non-sexist teaching. Teacher resources with curriculum related activities: 1. Elementary 2. Intermediate 3. Secondary.* Washington, D.C.: Resource Center on Sex Roles in Education, 1975.

Educational Research Service. *Class size: A critique of recent meta-analyses.* Arlington, Va.: Educational Research Service, 1980.

Ellison, T. A., & Trickett, J. Environmental structure and the perceived similarity-satisfaction relationship: Traditional and alternative schools. *Journal of Personality,* 1978, *46,* 57–71.

Elmore, R. E. *Follow Through: Decision-making in a large-scale social experiment.* Unpublished doctoral dissertation, Harvard University, 1976.

Emrick, J. S., Sorensen, P. H., & Stearns, M. S. *Interim evaluation of the national Follow Through program, 1969–1971.* Menlo Park, Calif.: Stanford Research Institute, 1973.

Engstrom, G. (Ed.). *Open education: The legacy of the progressive movement.* Washington, D.C.: National Association for the Education of Young Children, 1970.

Enright, R. D. *A social-cognitive developmental intervention with sixth and first graders.* Paper presented at the meetings of the American Psychological Association, Chicago, 1975.

Epstein, J. L. *Friends in school: Patterns of selection and influence in secondary schools* (Report No. 266). Baltimore: The Johns Hopkins University Center for Social Organization of Schools, 1978.

Epstein, J. L. *After the bus arrives: Resegregation in desegregated schools.* Paper presented at the meetings of the American Educational Research Association, Boston, 1980.

Epstein, J. L., & McPartland, J. M. Authority structures. In H. J. Walberg (Ed.), *Educational environments and effects.* Berkeley, Calif.: McCutchan, 1979.

Erickson, F. Mere ethnography: Some problems in its use in educational practice. *Anthropology and Education Quarterly,* 1979, *10,* 182–188.

Erickson, F., & Shultz, J. When is a context? Some issues and methods in the analysis of social competence. *Quarterly Newsletter of the Institute for*

Comparative Human Development, 1977, *1*, 5–10.

Etaugh, C., Collins, G., & Gerson, A. Reinforcement of sex-typed behaviors of two-year-old children in a nursery school setting. *Developmental Psychology*, 1975, *11*, 255.

Etaugh, C., & Harlow, H. Behaviors of male and female teachers as related to behaviors and attitudes of elementary school children. *Journal of Genetic Psychology*, 1975, *127*, 163–170.

Etaugh, C., & Hughes, V. Teachers' evaluations of sex-typed behaviors in children: The role of teacher sex and school setting. *Developmental Psychology*, 1975, *11*, 394–395.

Evans, G. W., & Lovell, B. Design modification in an open-plan school. *Journal of Educational Psychology*, 1979, *71*, 41–49.

Evans, J. *Characteristics of open education: Results from a classroom observation rating scale and a teacher questionnaire*. Newton, Mass.: Education Development Center, 1971.

Evenson, J. S., & O'Neil, M. L. Current perspectives on the role of career education in combatting occupational sex-role stereotyping. *Research in Education*, December 1978.

Fagerberg, S., & Fagerberg, K. Student attitudes concerning drug abuse education and prevention. *Journal of Drug Education*, 1976, *6*, 141–152.

Fagot, B. I. Influence of teacher behavior in the preschool. *Developmental Psychology*, 1973, *9*, 198–206.

Fagot, B. I. Consequences of moderate cross gender behavior in preschool children. *Child Development*, 1977a, *48*, 902–907.

Fagot, B. I. *Preschool sex stereotyping: Effect of sex of teacher vs. training of teacher*. Paper presented at the meetings of the Society for Research in Child Development, 1977b.

Fagot, B. I. Variations in density: Effect on task and social behaviors of preschool children. *Developmental Psychology*, 1977c, *13*, 166–167.

Fagot, B. I., & Patterson, G. R. An in vivo analysis of reinforcing contingencies for sex-role behaviors in the preschool child. *Developmental Psychology*, 1969, *1*, 563–568.

Far West Laboratory for Educational Research and Development: Drug Education Information Unit. *Drug education: An overview of current efforts*, 1972.

Feagin, J. R. School desegregation: A political-economic perspective. In W. G. Stephan & J. R. Feagin (Eds.), *School desegregation: Past, present and future*. New York: Plenum, 1980.

Featherstone, J. *Schools where children learn*. New York: Liveright, 1971.

Feeney, G., Hochschild, R., Joy, A., & Sadow, J. *Consequences of different modes of classroom organization*. Buffalo, N.Y.: Open Education Center, State University of New York at Buffalo, 1974.

Fendel, M. Videotape for presenting ethical dilemmas. *Educational Television*, 1970, *2*, 32–34.

Fenton, E., Colby, A., & Speicher-Dubin, B. *Developing moral dilemmas for social studies classes*. Cambridge, Mass.: Harvard University Moral Education Research Foundation, 1974.

Feshbach, N. D. Student teacher preferences for elementary school pupils varying in personality characteristics. *Journal of Educational Psychology*, 1969, *60*, 126–132.

Feshbach, N. D. Empathy training: A field study in affective education. In S. Feshbach & A. Fraczek (Eds.), *Aggression and behavior change: Biological and social processes*. New York: Praeger, 1979.

Feshbach, S., & Feshbach, N. D. Alternatives to corporal punishment: Implications for training and control. *Journal of Clinical Child Psychology*, 1973, *11*, 46–48.

Fiedler, M. L. Bidirectionality of influence in classroom interaction. *Journal of Educational Psychology*, 1975, *67*, 735–744.

Filby, N., Cahen, L., McCutcheon, G., & Kyle, D. *What happens in smaller classes? A summary report of a field study*. San Francisco: Far West Laboratory for Educational Research and Development, 1980.

Flanders, N. A. *Interaction analysis in the classroom: A manual for observers* (Rev. ed.). Ann Arbor: School of Education, University of Michigan, 1966.

Flanders, N. A. *Analyzing teaching behavior*. Reading, Mass.: Addison-Wesley, 1970.

Fleming, E. S., & Antonnen, R. G. Teacher expectancy as related to the academic and personal growth of primary age children. *Monographs of the Society for Research in Child Development*, 1971, *36* (145).

Fling, S., & Manosevitz, M. Sex typing in nursery school children's play interests. *Developmental Psychology*, 1972, *7*, 146–152.

Florio, S., & Shultz, J. Social competence at home and at school. *Theory into Practice*, 1979, *18*, 234–243.

Ford Foundation. *A foundation goes to school*. New York: Author, 1972.

Forehand, G., Ragosta, J., & Rock, D. *Conditions and processes of effective school desegregation*.

Final Report, U.S. Office of Education, Department of Health, Education & Welfare. Princeton, N.J.: Educational Testing Service, 1976.

Franklin, M. B., & Biber, B. Psychological perspectives on early childhood education: Some relations between theory and practice. In L. G. Katz (Ed.), *Current topics in early childhood education* (Vol. 1). Norwood, N.J.: Ablex, 1977.

Frasher, R., & Walker, A. Sex roles in early reading textbooks. *The Reading Teacher*, 1972, *25*, 741–749.

Frazier, N., & Sadker, M. *Sexism in school and society*. New York: Harper & Row, 1973.

Freedman, J. L. *Crowding and behavior*. San Francisco: Freeman, 1975.

Friedman, M., Meltzer, R., & Miller, C. (Eds.), *New perspectives on school integration*. Philadelphia: Fortress, 1979.

Fuchs, E., & Havighurst, R. J. *To live on this earth*. New York: Anchor, 1973.

Gage, N. L. The yield of research on teaching. *Phi Delta Kappan*, 1978, *59*, 229–235.

Gaite, A. J. H. Teachers' perceptions of ideal male and female students: Male chauvinism in the schools. In J. Pottker & A. Fishel (Eds.), *Sex bias in the schools: The research evidence*. Cranbury, N.J.: Associated University Presses, 1977.

Galbraith, R. E., & Jones, T. M. *Moral reasoning*. Anoka, Minn.: Greenhaven, 1976.

Galbraith, R. E., & Jones, T. M. Teaching for moral reasoning in the social studies: A research report. *Counseling Psychologist*, 1977, *6*, 60–63.

Galloway, D. Size of school, socio-economic hardship, suspension rates and persistent unjustified absence from school. *British Journal of Educational Psychology*, 1976, *46*, 40–47.

Garbarino, J. The human ecology of school crime: A case for small schools. In *School crime and disruption: Prevention models*. Washington, D.C.: National Institute of Education, U.S. Department of Health, Education and Welfare, 1978.

Garbarino, J. Some thoughts on school size and its effects on adolescent development. *Journal of Youth and Adolescence*, 1980, *9*, 19–31.

Gardner, D. E. M. *Experiment and tradition in primary schools*. London: Methuen, 1966.

Garfinkel, H. *Studies in ethnomethodology*. Englewood Cliffs, N.J.: Prentice-Hall, 1967.

Garrett, C., Ein, P., & Tremaine, L. The development of gender stereotyping of adult occupations in elementary school children. *Child Development*, 1977, *48*, 507–512.

Garrod, A. C., & Bramble, G. A. Moral develop-

ment and literature. *Theory into Practice*, 1977, *16*, 105–111.

Gatewood, T. E. How effective are open classrooms: A review of the research. *Childhood Education*, 1975, *51*, 170–179.

Gazda, G. M. *Human relations development*. Boston: Allyn & Bacon, 1973.

Gibbs, J. The meaning of ecologically oriented inquiry in contemporary psychology. *American Psychologist*, 1979, *34*, 127–140.

Gilligan, C. In a different voice: Women's conceptions of self and morality. *Harvard Educational Review*, 1977, *47*, 481–517.

Gilligan, M. C. *The effects of varied playground space on certain behavioral aspects of four- and five-year-old children*. Unpublished doctoral dissertation, New York University, 1970.

Glidewell, J., Kantor, M., Smith, L., & Stringer, L. Socialization and social structure in the classroom. In M. L. Hoffman & L. W. Hoffman (Eds.), *Review of research in child development* (Vol. 2). New York: Russell Sage Foundation, 1966.

Good, T. L. Teacher effectiveness in the elementary school. *Journal of Teacher Education*, 1979, *30*, 52–64.

Good, T. L. *Teacher expectations, teacher behavior, student perceptions and student behavior: A decade of research*. Paper presented at the meetings of the American Educational Research Association, 1980.

Good, T. L., & Brophy, J. Behavioral expression of teacher attitudes. *Journal of Educational Psychology*, 1972, *63*, 617–624.

Good, T. L., & Grouws, D. Reaction of male and female teacher trainees to descriptions of elementary school pupils. Technical Report No. 62, Center for Research in Social Behavior, University of Missouri at Columbia, 1972. Described in Brophy, J. E., & Good, T. L., *Teacher-student relationships: Causes and consequences*. New York: Holt, Rinehart & Winston, 1974.

Good, T. L., & Power, C. Designing successful classroom environments for different types of students. *Journal of Curriculum Studies*, 1976, *8*, 1–16.

Good, T. L., Sikes, J., & Brophy, J. Effects of teacher sex and student sex on classroom interaction. *Journal of Educational Psychology*, 1973, *65*, 74–87.

Goodman, M. E. *Race awareness in young children*. New York: Collier, 1964.

Green, J. L., & Harker, J. O. Reading to children: A communicative process. In J. Langer & M.

Smith-Burke (Eds.), *Reader meets author: Bridging the gap*. Washington, D.C.: International Reading Association, 1982.

Greer, C. *The great school legend*. New York: Basic, 1972.

Griffin, P., & Humphrey, F. Task and talk at lesson time. In R. Shuy & P. Griffin (Eds.), *The study of children's functional language and education in the early years*. Final Report to the Carnegie Corporation of New York. Arlington, Va.: Center for Applied Linguistics, 1978.

Grimes, S. W., & Allinsmith, W. Compulsivity, anxiety and school achievement. *Merrill-Palmer Quarterly*, 1961, *7*, 247–271.

Groobman, D., Forward, J., & Peterson, C. Attitudes, self-esteem and learning in formal and informal schools. *Journal of Educational Psychology*, 1976, *68*, 32–35.

Guardo, C. J. Personal space in children. *Child Development*, 1969, *40*, 143–151.

Gump, P. V. Operating environments in open and traditional schools. *School Review*, 1974, *84*, 575–593.

Gump, P. V. Ecological psychology and children. In E. M. Hetherington (Ed.), *Review of child development research* (Vol. 5). Chicago: University of Chicago Press, 1975.

Gump, P. V. School environments. In I. Altman & J. F. Wohlwill (Eds.), *Children and the environment*. New York: Plenum, 1978.

Gump, P. V. The school as a social situation. In M. R. Rosenzweig & L. W. Porter (Eds.), *Annual review of psychology*. Palo Alto, Calif.: Annual Reviews, 1980.

Gump, P. V., & Ross, R. *What's happened in schools of open design?* Department of Psychology, University of Kansas, 1977. (Mimeo)

Guttentag, M., & Bray, H. *Undoing sex stereotypes: Research and resources for educators*. New York: McGraw-Hill, 1976.

Haley, J. *Problem-solving therapy*. San Francisco: Jossey-Bass, 1976.

Hall, E. T. *The silent language*. New York: Doubleday, 1959.

Hall, E. T. *The hidden dimension*. New York: Doubleday, 1966.

Hallinan, M. T. Friendship patterns in open and traditional classrooms. *Sociology of Education*, 1976, *49*, 254–265.

Hallinan, M. T. *The development of children's friendship cliques*. Paper presented at the meetings of the American Sociological Association, Chicago, 1977.

Haney, W. *The Follow Through evaluation: A tech-* *nical history* (Vol. 5). Washington, D.C.: Office of Education, U.S. Department of Health, Education and Welfare, 1977.

Harper, L. V., & Sanders, K. M. Pre-school children's use of space: Sex differences in outdoor play. *Developmental Psychology*, 1975, *11*, 119.

Harris, D. A curriculum sequence for moral development. *Theory and Research in Social Education*, 1977, *5*, 1–21.

Harris, N., Jackson, N., & Rydingsword, C. E. (Eds.), *The integration of American schools: Problems, experiences, solutions*. Boston: Allyn & Bacon, 1975.

Hartley, R. F., Frank, L., & Goldenson, R. M. *Understanding children's play*. New York: Columbia University Press, 1952.

Harvard, L. C. Questions from the classroom. *Journal of Moral Education*, 1974, *3*, 235–240.

Harvard Educational Review, 1969, *39*, 4–147 (Whole). Architecture and Education.

Harway, M. et al. Sex discrimination in guidance and counseling. Annotations (Vol. 2). *Research in Education*, May 1977.

Heimgartner, N. L. A comparative study of self-concept: Open space vs. self-contained classrooms. In H. S. Doob (Ed.), *Summary of research on open education*. Arlington, Va.: Educational Research Service, 1974.

Henry, J. Docility, or giving teacher what she wants. *Journal of Social Issues*, 1955, *11*, 33–41.

Henry, J. *On education*. New York: Random House, 1966.

Hersh, R., Paolitto, D., & Reimer, J. *Promoting moral growth*. New York: Longman, 1979.

Hetherington, E. M., Cox, M., & Cox, R. Play and social interaction in children following divorce. *Journal of Social Issues*, 1979, *35*, 26–49.

Hetherington, E. M., Cox, M., & Cox, R. Effects of divorce on parents and children. In M. Lamb (Ed.), *Nontraditional families*. Hillsdale, N.J.: Lawrence Erlbaum, 1982.

Hetherington, E. M., Featherman, D. L., & Camara, K. A. *Intellectual functioning and achievement of children in one-parent households*. Unpublished manuscript written for the National Institute of Education, 1981.

Hill, R., Klafter, M., & Wallace, J. *A bibliography on moral/values education*. Philadelphia: Research for Better Schools, 1976.

Hodges, W. L., and Sheehan, R. Follow Through as ten years of experimentation. *Young Children*, 1978, *34*, 4–14.

Hoffman, L. *Foundations of family therapy*. New York: Basic, 1981.

Hoffman, M. L. Development of moral thought, feeling and behavior. *American Psychologist*, 1979, *34*, 958–966.

Holstein, C. B. Irreversible stepwise sequence in the development of moral judgment: A longitudinal study of males and females. *Child Development*, 1976, *47*, 51–61.

Hook, C., & Rosenshine, B. Accuracy of teacher reports of their classroom behavior. *Review of Educational Research*, 1979, *49*, 1–12.

Horwitz, R. A. Psychological effects of the "open classroom." *Review of Educational Research*, 1979, *49*, 71–86.

House, E. R., Glass, G. V., McLean, L. D., & Walker, D. F. No simple answer: Critique of the Follow Through evaluation. *Harvard Educational Review*, 1978, *48*, 128–160.

Houseman, J. *An ecological study of interpersonal conflict among preschool children*. Unpublished doctoral dissertation, Wayne State University, 1972.

Houts, P. L. The American family minus one. *National Elementary Principal*, 1979, *59*, 10–11.

Hughes, L. W., Gordon, W. M., & Hillman, L. W. *Desegregating America's schools*. New York: Longman, 1980.

Huston, A. C. Sex-typing. This volume, Chap. 5, 1983.

Hyman, I. A., & Wise, J. H. *Corporal punishment in American education*. Philadelphia: Temple University Press, 1979.

Hymes, D. H. *Foundations in sociolinguistics: An ethnographic approach*. Philadelphia: University of Pennsylvania Press, 1974.

Indian education: A national tragedy—a national challenge. Report of the Special Subcommittee on Indian Education of the Committee on Labor and Public Welfare of the United States Senate, Washington, D.C.: U.S. Government Printing Office, 1969.

Jackson, P. W. *Life in classrooms*. New York: Holt, Rinehart & Winston, 1968.

Jackson, P. W., & Lahaderne, H. M. Inequalities of teacher-pupil contacts. *Psychology in the Schools*, 1967, *4*, 201–211.

Jackson, P. W., Silberman, M., & Wolfson, B. Signs of personal involvement in teachers' descriptions of their students. *Journal of Educational Psychology*, 1969, *60*, 22–27.

Jay, W., & Schminke, C. Sex bias in elementary school mathematics texts. *Arithmetic Teacher*, 1975, *22*, 242–246.

Jencks, C. S., Smith, M., Acland, H., Bane, M. J., Cohen, D., Gintis, H., Heyns, B., & Michelson, S. *Inequality: A reassessment of the effects of family and schooling in America*. New York: Basic, 1972.

Jenkins, B. *Teachers' views of particular students and their behavior in the classroom*. Unpublished doctoral dissertation, University of Chicago, 1972. Described in Brophy, J. E., & Good, T. L., *Teacher-student relationships: Causes and consequences*. New York: Holt, Rinehart & Winston, 1974, pp. 133–136.

Jersild, A., & Markey, F. V. Conflicts between preschool children. *Child Development Monographs*, 1935, *21*, 1–181 (Whole).

Johnson, D. W. Constructive peer relationships, social development, and cooperative learning experiences: Implications for the prevention of drug abuse. *Journal of Drug Education*, 1980, *10*, 7–24.

Johnson, D. W. Student-student interaction: The neglected variable in education. *Educational Researcher*, 1981, *10*, 5–10.

Johnson, D. W., & Johnson, R. T. *Learning together and alone*. Englewood Cliffs, N.J.: Prentice-Hall, 1975.

Johnson, D. W., Johnson, R. T., Johnson, J., & Anderson, D. Effects of cooperative versus individualized instruction on student prosocial behavior, attitudes toward learning and achievement. *Journal of Educational Psychology*, 1976, *68*, 446–452.

Johnson, D. W., Johnson, R. T., & Scott, L. The effects of cooperative and individualized instruction on student attitudes and achievement. *The Journal of Social Psychology*, 1978, *104*, 207–216.

Johnston, L. D., Bachman, J. G., & O'Malley, P. M. *Drugs and the class of '78: Behaviors, attitudes, and recent national trends*. Rockville, Md.: National Institute on Drug Abuse, Division of Research, 1979.

Jones, R. *Contemporary educational psychology*. New York: Harper & Row, 1967.

Joyce, B., & Weil, M. *Models of teaching*. Englewood Cliffs, N.J.: Prentice-Hall, 1972.

Kagan, J. The child's sex-role classification of school objects. *Child Development*, 1964, *35*, 1051–1056.

Kahn, S. B., & Weiss, J. The teaching of affective responses. In R. M. W. Travers (Ed.), *Second handbook of research on teaching*. Chicago: Rand McNally, 1973.

Kalamazoo Public Schools. *180 plus: A framework*

for non-stereotyped human roles in elementary media center materials. Kalamazoo, Mich.: Instructional Media Department, Kalamazoo Public Schools, 1976.

Kalunian, P. Changing sex role stereotypes through career development. *Psychology in the Schools*, 1975, *12*, 230–233.

Kamii, C., & DeVries, R. Piaget for early childhood education. In M. C. Day & R. K. Parker (Eds.), *The preschool in action* (2nd ed.). Boston: Allyn & Bacon, 1977.

Karmel, L. J. Effects of windowless classroom environments on high school students. *Perceptual and Motor Skills*, 1965, *20*, 277–278.

Katz, P. A. The acquisition of racial attitudes in children. In P. A. Katz (Ed.), *Toward the elimination of racism*. New York: Pergamon, 1976.

Kaye, S., Trickett, E. J., & Quinlan, D. M. Alternative methods for environmental assessment: An example. *American Journal of Community Psychology*, 1976, *4*, 367–377.

Kellogg, R. A direct approach to sex-role identification of school-related objects. *Psychological Reports*, 1969, *24*, 839–841.

Kelly, J. G. *Adolescent boys in high school*. Hillsdale, N.J.: Erlbaum, 1979.

Kessen, W. The American child and other cultural inventions. *American Psychologist*, 1979, *34*, 815–820.

Kingston, A., & Lovelace, T. Sexism and reading: A critical review of the literature. *Reading Research Quarterly*, 1977–1978, *13*, 133–161.

Kirschenbaum, H. Recent research in values clarification. In J. Meyer, B. Burnham, & J. Cholvat (Eds.), *Values education: Theory/practice/problems/prospects*. Waterloo, Ontario, Canada: Wilfrid Laurier University Press, 1975.

Klass, W., & Hodge, S. Self-esteem in open and traditional classrooms. *Journal of Educational Psychology*, 1978, *70*, 701–705.

Klee, T. *Drug and alcohol abuse prevention in a high risk population: An assessment of intervention activities of the Shalom, Inc. program*. Reports to the National Institute on Drug Abuse, Research Grant No. 1 EO7 DA01874-02, 1980, 1981.

Kline, J. A. Evaluation of a multimedia drug education program. *Journal of Drug Education*, 1972, *2*, 229–239.

Klinman, D., Gollub, W., Mulvihill, A., Shulkin, S., & Sloan, E. *Teacher skill guide for combatting sexism*. Newton, Mass.: Educational Development Center, 1979.

Klitgaard, R. E., & Hall, G. R. Are there unusually effective schools? *Journal of Human Resources*, 1975, *10*, 90–106.

Kohlberg, L. Early education: A cognitive-developmental view. *Child Development*, 1968, *39*, 1013–1062.

Kohlberg, L. Moral stages and moralization: The cognitive-developmental approach. In T. Lickona (Ed.), *Moral development and behavior*. New York: Holt, Rinehart & Winston, 1976.

Kohlberg, L. *The meaning and measurement of moral development*. Heinz Werner Memorial Lecture. Worcester, Mass.: Clark University Press, 1979.

Kohlberg, L. High school democracy and educating for a just society. In R. Mosher (Ed.), *Moral education: A first generation of research and development*. New York: Praeger, 1980.

Kohlberg, L. *The philosophy of moral development: Moral stages and the idea of justice*. San Francisco, Calif.: Harper & Row, 1981.

Kohlberg, L., Colby, A., Gibbs, J. C., Speicher-Dubin, B., Power, C., & Candee, D. *Assessing moral stages: A manual*. Cambridge, Mass.: Moral Education Research Foundation, 1978.

Kohlberg, L., & Turiel, E. Moral development and moral education. In G. S. Lesser (Ed.), *Psychology and educational practice*. Glenview, Ill.: Scott Foresman, 1971.

Kohn, S. Coping with family change. *National Elementary Principal*, 1979, *59*, 40–50.

Koneya, M. Location and interaction in row-and-column seating arrangements. *Environment and Behavior*, 1976, *8*, 265–282.

Kounin, J. S. *Discipline and group management in the classroom*. New York: Holt, Rinehart & Winston, 1970.

Kounin, J. S., & Sherman, L. W. School environments as behavioral settings. *Theory into Practice*, 1979, *18*, 145–151.

Krantz, P. J., & Risley, T. R. Behavioral ecology in the classroom. In K. D. O'Leary & S. G. O'Leary (Eds.), *Classroom management: The successful use of behavior modification* (2nd ed.). N.Y.: Pergamon Press, 1977.

Kremer, L. Teachers' attitudes toward educational goals as reflected in classroom behavior. *Journal of Educational Psychology*, 1978, *70*, 993–997.

Kuhn, T. S. *The structure of scientific revolutions*. Chicago: University of Chicago Press, 1962.

Kurtines, W., & Greif, E. The development of moral thought: Review and evaluation of Kohlberg's approach. *Psychological Bulletin*, 1974, *81*, 453–470.

Langmeyer, D. *Value sharing's effect on the self*

esteem of fourth grade students. University Park, Pa.: Addictions Prevention Laboratory, The Pennsylvania State University, 1976.

Lavatelli, C. S. *Piaget's theory applied to an early childhood curriculum*. Boston: American Science and Engineering, 1970.

Lawrence, J. Science and sentiment: Overview of research on crowding and human behavior. *Psychological Bulletin*, 1974, *81*, 712–720.

Lazar, I., Darlington, R. B., Murray, H., Royce, J., & Snipper, A. Lasting effects of early education: A report from the consortium for longitudinal studies. *Monographs of the Society for Research in Child Development*, 1982, *47* (195).

Lazarowitz, R., Sharan, S., & Steinberg, R. Classroom learning style and cooperative behavior of elementary school children. *Journal of Educational Psychology*, 1980, *72*, 97–104.

Leacock, E. B. *Teaching and learning in city schools*. New York: Basic, 1969.

Le Compte, M. D. Learning to work: The hidden curriculum of the classroom. *Anthropology and Education Quarterly*, 1978, *9*, 22–38.

Leming, J. S. *On the limits of contemporary moral education: Psychological and sociological perspectives*. Paper presented at the meetings of the American Educational Research Association, Boston, 1980.

Leonard, J. P., & Eurich, A. C. *An evaluation of modern education*. A report sponsored by the Society for Curriculum Study. New York: Appleton-Century-Crofts, 1942.

Levitin, T., & Chananie, J. Responses of female primary school teachers to sex-typed behaviors in male and female children. *Child Development*, 1972, *43*, 1309–1316.

Lewin, K., Lippitt, R., & White, R. K. Patterns of aggressive behavior in experimentally created "social climates." *Journal of Social Psychology*, 1939, *10*, 271–299.

Lewis, J. M., Gossett, J., & Phillips, V. A. Evaluation of a drug prevention program. *Hospital and Community Psychiatry*, 1972, *23*, 124–126.

Lickona, T. Creating the just community with children. *Theory into Practice*, 1977, *16*, 97–104.

Lickona, T. (Ed.). *Moral development and behavior: Theory, research and social issues*. New York: Holt, Rinehart & Winston, 1976.

Lieberman, M. *Evaluation of a social studies curriculum based on an inquiry method and a cognitive-developmental approach to moral education*. Paper presented at the meetings of the American Educational Research Association, Washington, D.C., 1975.

Lieberman, M., & Selman, R. *An evaluation of a cognitive-developmental values curriculum for primary grade children*. Paper presented at the meetings of the American Educational Research Association, Chicago, 1974.

Lightfoot, S. L. *Worlds apart: Relationships between families and schools*. New York: Basic, 1978.

Lockheed, M. E., & Harris, A. M. *The effects of equal status cross-sex contact on students' sex stereotyped attitudes and behavior*. Paper presented at the meetings of the American Educational Research Association, Toronto, 1978.

Lockwood, A. The effects of values clarification and moral development curricula on school age subjects: A critical review of recent research. *Review of Educational Research*, 1978, *48*, 325–364.

Loo, C. M. The effects of spatial density on the social behavior of children. *Journal of Applied Social Psychology*, 1972, *2*, 372–381.

Maccoby, E. E., & Jacklin, C. N. *The psychology of sex differences*. Stanford, Calif.: Stanford University Press, 1974.

Maccoby, E. E., & Zellner, M. *Experiments in primary education: Aspects of Project Follow Through*. New York: Harcourt Brace Jovanovich, 1970.

Mackey, J. Discussing moral dilemmas in the classroom. *English Journal*, 1975, *64*, 28–30.

Maple Heights City Schools, Ohio. Equity career education: Curriculum guide. *Research in Education*, April 1977.

Marshall, H. Open classrooms: Has the term outlived its usefulness? *Review of Educational Research*, 1981, *51*, 181–192.

Marshall, H., Weinstein, R., Middlestadt, S., & Brattesani, K. *"Everyone's smart in our class": Relationships between classroom characteristics and perceived differential teacher treatment*. Paper presented at meetings of the American Educational Research Association, Boston, 1980.

McCall, R. B. Challenges to a science of developmental psychology. *Child Development*, 1977, *48*, 333–344.

McClellan, P. The Pulaski Project: An innovative drug abuse prevention program in an urban high school. *Journal of Psychedelic Drugs*, 1975, *7*, 355–362.

McDermott, R. P. Social relations as contexts for learning. *Harvard Educational Review*, 1977, *47*, 198–213.

McGrew, W. C. *An ethological study of children's behavior*. New York: Academic Press, 1972.

McIntyre, A., Lounsbury, K. R., Hamilton, M. L., & Mantooth, J. M. Individual differences in preschool object play: The influences of anxiety proneness and peer affiliation. *Journal of Applied Developmental Psychology*, 1980, *1*, 149–161.

McPartland, J. M. *The segregated student in desegregated schools: Sources of influence on Negro secondary students*. Center for the Study of Social Organization of Schools, Baltimore: The Johns Hopkins University, Report No. 21, 1968.

McPartland, J. M., & McDill, E. L. *The unique role of schools in the causes of youthful crime*. Baltimore: The Johns Hopkins University, 1976.

McPartland, J. M., & McDill, E. L. Research on crime in schools. In J. M. McPartland & E. L. McDill (Eds.), *Violence in schools*. Lexington, Mass.: Lexington, 1977.

Mehan, H. *Learning lessons*. Cambridge, Mass.: Harvard University Press, 1979.

Meisels, M., & Guardo, C. J. Development of personal space schemata. *Child Development*, 1969, *40*, 1168–1178.

Meketon, B. F. *The effect of integration upon the Negro child's response to various tasks and upon his level of self-esteem*. (Unpublished doctoral dissertation, University of Kentucky, 1966. Ann Arbor, Mich.: University Microfilm No. 69-20, 406).

Metz, M. H. *Questioning the centipede: Sources of climate in a magnet school*. Paper presented at meetings of the American Educational Research Association, Boston, April 1980.

Meyer, W. J., & Thompson, G. G. Sex differences in the distribution of teacher approval and disapproval among sixth-grade children. *Journal of Educational Psychology*, 1956, *47*, 385–396.

Miller, J. G. *Living systems*. New York: McGraw-Hill, 1978.

Miller, J. P. *Humanizing the classroom: Models of teaching in affective education*. New York: Praeger, 1976.

Miller, L. B., & Dyer, J. L. Four preschool programs: Their dimensions and effects, with commentary by H. Stevenson and S. H. White. *Monographs of the Society for Research in Child Development*, 1975, *40*(162).

Milman, D. H., & Su, W. Patterns of illicit drug and alcohol use among secondary school students. *Behavioral Pediatrics*, 1973, *83*, 314–320.

Minuchin, P. Sex-role concepts and sex typing in childhood as a function of school and home environments. *Child Development*, 1965, *36*, 1033–1048.

Minuchin, P. *Differential use of the open classroom: A study of exploratory and cautious children*. Final Report, National Institute of Education, 1976.

Minuchin, P. *The middle years of childhood*. Monterey, Calif.: Brooks/Cole, 1977.

Minuchin, P., Biber, B., Shapiro, E., & Zimiles, H. *The psychological impact of school experience*. New York: Basic, 1969.

Minuchin, S., & Fishman, C. *Family therapy techniques*. Cambridge, Mass.: Harvard University Press, 1981.

Mischel, W. On the interface of cognition and personality: Beyond the person-situation debate. *American Psychologist*, 1979, *34*, 740–753.

Mischel, W., & Mischel, H. A cognitive-social learning approach to morality and self-regulation. In T. Lickona (Ed.), *Moral development and behavior: Theory, research and social issues*. New York: Holt, Rinehart & Winston, 1976.

Mitchell, M. H. Attitudes of adolescent girls toward vocational education. *Research in Education*, January 1978.

Montes, F., & Risley, T. R. Evaluating traditional day care practices. *Child Care Quarterly*, 1975, *4*, 208–215.

Moos, R. H. A typology of junior high and high school classrooms. *American Educational Research Journal*, 1978, *15*, 53–66.

Moos, R. H., & Trickett, E. J. *Classroom Environment Scale manual*. Palo Alto, Calif.: Consulting Psychologists Press, 1974.

Morse, W. C., & Munger, R. L. *Affective development in schools: Resource programs and persons*. Ann Arbor, Michigan, 1975. (Mimeo)

Mosher, R. (Ed.). *Moral education: A first generation of research and development*. New York: Praeger, 1980.

Much, N. C., & Shweder, R. A. Speaking of rules: The analysis of culture in the breach. In W. Damon (Ed.), *New directions for child development*, Vol. 2: *Moral development*. San Francisco: Jossey-Bass, 1978.

Mussen, P., & Eisenberg-Berg, N. *Roots of caring, sharing, and helping: The development of prosocial behavior in children*. San Francisco: W. H. Freeman, 1977.

Myers, D. Why open education died. *Journal of Research and Development in Education*, 1974, *8*, 60–71.

Myers, R. A comparison of the perceptions of elementary school children in open area and self-contained classrooms in British Columbia. *Jour-*

nal of Research and Development in Education, 1971, *4,* 100–106.

Nash, P. *Humanism and humanistic education in the eighties: The lessons of two decades.* Paper presented at the meetings of the American Educational Research Association, Boston, 1980.

National Clearinghouse for Mental Health Information. *Resource book for drug abuse education.* Washington, D.C.: Department of Health, Education, and Welfare, 1971.

National Elementary Principal, 1979, *59* (1).

National Institute of Education. *Moral development in children: An abstract bibliography.* Urbana, Ill.: University of Illinois, 1976.

National Institute of Education. *Violent schools— safe schools* (2 vols.). The Safe School Study report to the Congress, Washington, D.C., National Institute of Education, 1978.

Newberg, N. *Affective education addresses the basics.* Paper presented at the meetings of the American Educational Research Association, Boston, 1980.

Noblit, G. W., & Collins, T. W. Cultural degradation and minority student adaptation: The school experience and minority adjustment contingencies. In M. Sugar (Ed.), *Responding to adolescent needs.* Jamaica, N.Y.: Spectrum, 1980.

Nowlis, H. H. Strategies for prevention. *Contemporary Drug Problems,* 1976, *5,* 5–20.

Nucci, L. *Conceptual development in the moral and social-conventional domains: Implications for social education.* Paper presented at the meetings of the American Educational Research Association, San Francisco, 1979.

Nucci, L., & Nucci, M. S. *Social interactions and the development of moral and societal concepts.* Paper presented at the meetings of the Society for Research in Child Development, San Francisco, March 1979.

Nucci, L., & Turiel, E. Social interactions and the development of social concepts in pre-school children. *Child Development,* 1978, *49,* 400–408.

Oliver, L. Women in aprons. The female stereotype in children's readers. *Elementary School Journal,* 1974, *74,* 253–259.

Olson, M. N. *Identifying predictors of institutional quality: An examination of eleven internal classroom variables in relation to a school system criterion measure.* Unpublished doctoral dissertation, Teachers College, Columbia University, 1970.

Orfield, G. *Must we bus? Segregated schools and national policy.* Washington, D.C.: The Brook-

ings Institute, 1978.

Palmer, F., & Anderson, L. Early intervention programs which have been tried, documented and assessed. In M. J. Begab, H. Garber, & J. C. Haywood (Eds.), *Psychosocial influences in retarded performance: Strategies for improving competence.* Baltimore: University Park Press, 1981.

Paolitto, D. *Role-taking opportunities for early adolescents: A program in moral education.* Unpublished doctoral dissertation, Boston University, 1976.

Papalia, D. E., & Tennent, S. S. Vocational aspirations in preschoolers: A manifestation of early sex role stereotyping. *Sex Roles,* 1975, *1,* 197–199.

Paskal, D., & Miller, W. C. Can options work in smaller school districts? *NASSP Bulletin,* 1973, *57,* 47–54.

Patterson, D. S. *Social ecology and social behavior: The development of the differential usage of play materials in preschool children.* Paper presented at the biennial Southeastern Conference on Human Development, Nashville, Tennessee, 1976.

Pedersen, E., Faucher, T. A., & Eaton, W. W. A new perspective on the effects of first-grade teachers on children's subsequent adult status. *Harvard Educational Review,* 1978, *48,* 1–31.

PEER. *Resources for ending sex bias in the schools.* Washington, D.C.: NOW Project on Equal Education Rights, 1978.

Perry, C., & Duke, D. Lessons to be learned about discipline from alternative high schools. *Journal of Research and Development in Education,* 1978, *11,* 77–91.

Peters, R. S. Reason and habit. The paradox of moral education. In W. R. Niblett (Ed.), *Moral education in a changing society.* London: Faber & Faber, 1963.

Peterson, P. L. Direct instruction reconsidered. In P. L. Peterson & H. J. Walberg (Eds.), *Research on teaching.* Berkeley, Calif.: McCutchan, 1979.

Pettigrew, T. F. Racially separate or together? *Journal of Social Issues,* 1969, *25,* 43–70.

Pettigrew, T. F. The racial integration of the schools. In T. F. Pettigrew (Ed.), *Racial discrimination in the United States.* New York: Harper & Row, 1975.

Petrinovich, L. Probabilistic functionalism: A conception of research method. *American Psychologist,* 1979, *34,* 373–390.

Philips, S. U. Participant structures and communicative competence: Warm Springs children in community and classroom. In C. B. Cazden, V. P. John, & D. Hymes (Eds.), *Functions of language in the classroom*. New York: Teachers College Press, 1972.

Plath, K. *Schools within schools: A study of high school organization*. New York: Teachers College, Bureau of Publications, 1965.

Plowden, Lady B. *Children and their primary schools*. A report of the Central Advisory Council for Education (Vol. 1). London: H.M.S.O., 1967.

Portuges, S. H., & Feshbach, N. D. The influence of sex and socioeconomic factors upon imitation of teachers by elementary school children. *Child Development*, 1972, *43*, 981–989.

Pottker, J., & Fishel, A. *Sex bias in the schools: The research evidence*. Cranbury, N.J.: Associated University Presses, 1977.

Power, C. *The moral atmosphere of a just community high school: A four year longitudinal study*. Unpublished doctoral dissertation, Harvard University, 1979.

Power, D., & Reimer, J. Moral atmosphere: An educational bridge between moral judgment and action. In W. Damon (Ed.), *New directions for child development*, Vol. 2: *Moral development*. San Francisco: Jossey-Bass, 1978.

Price, J. M. *The effects of crowding on the social behavior of children*. Unpublished doctoral dissertation, Columbia University, New York, 1971.

Prigogine, I. Time, irreversibility, and structure. In J. Mehra (Ed.), *The physicist's conception of nature*. Dordrecht & Boston: D. Reidel, 1973.

Proshansky, E., & Wolfe, M. The physical setting and open education. *School Review*, 1974, *84*, 557–574.

Proshansky, H., Ittelson, W., & Rivlin, L. (Eds.), *Environmental psychology: People and their physical settings* (2nd ed.). New York: Holt, Rinehart & Winston, 1976.

Purkey, W. W., Graves, W., & Zellner, M. Self-perceptions of pupils in an experimental elementary school. *Elementary School Journal*, 1970, *71*, 166–171.

Purpel, D., & Ryan, K. (Eds.). *Moral education . . . It comes with the territory*. Berkeley, Calif.: McCutchan, 1976.

Quilitch, H. R., & Risley, T. R. The effects of play materials on social play. *Journal of Applied Behavior Analysis*, 1973, *6*, 573–578.

Randall, D., & Wong, M. R. Drug education to date: A review. *Journal of Drug Education*, 1976, *60*, 1–21.

Rathbone, C. H. *Open education: The informal classroom*. New York: Citation, 1971.

Raths, L., Harmin, M., & Simon, S. *Values and teaching*. Columbus, Ohio: Charles E. Merrill, 1966.

Reitman, A., Follman, J., & Ladd, E. T. *Corporal punishment in the public schools: The use of force in controlling student behavior*. New York: American Civil Liberties Union, 1972.

Resnick, L. B., & Leinhardt, G. Commentary. In J. Stallings, Implementation and child effects of teaching practices in Follow Through classrooms. *Monographs of the Society for Research in Child Development*, 1975, *40*(163).

Rest, J. Developmental psychology as a guide to value education: A review of Kohlbergian programs. *Review of Educational Research*, 1974, *44*, 241–259.

Rest, J. *Development in judging moral issues*. Minneapolis: University of Minnesota Press, 1979.

Rest, J. Moral development. In P. H. Mussen (Ed.), *Handbook of child psychology* (4th ed.), Vol. III. New York: Wiley, 1983.

Reynolds, D., Jones, D., St. Leger, S., & Murgatroyd, S. School factors and truancy. In L. Hersov & I. Berg (Eds.), *Out of school: Modern perspectives in truancy and school refusal*. New York: Wiley, 1980.

Rhine, W. R. (Ed.). *Making schools more effective: New directions from Follow Through*. New York: Academic, 1981.

Riegel, K. F. The dialectics of human development. *American Psychologist*, 1976, *31*, 689–700.

Risley, T. R. The ecology of applied behavior analysis. In A. Rogers-Warren & S. Warren (Eds.), *Ecological perspectives in behavioral analysis*. Baltimore: University Park Press, 1977.

Rist, R. C. Student social class and teacher expectations: The self-fulfilling prophecy in ghetto education. *Harvard Educational Review*, 1970, *40*, 411–451.

Rist, R. C. *Invisible children: School integration in American society*. Cambridge, Mass.: Harvard University Press, 1978.

Rist, R. C. (Ed.). *Desegregated schools: Appraisals of an American experiment*. New York: Academic, 1979.

Rivlin, L., & Rothenberg, M. The use of space in open classrooms. In H. Proshansky, W. Ittelson, & L. Rivlin (Eds.), *Environmental psychology: People and their physical settings* (2nd ed.). New York: Holt, Rinehart & Winston, 1976.

Rogers, C. *The relationship between the organiza-*

tion of play space and children's behavior. Unpublished masters thesis, Oklahoma State University, 1976.

Rohe, W. M., & Nuffer, E. L. The effects of density and partitioning on children's behavior. Paper presented at the meetings of the American Psychological Association, San Francisco, 1977.

Rohe, W. M., & Patterson, A. H. The effects of varied levels of resources and density on behavior in a day care center. Paper presented at the annual conference of the Environmental Design Research Association, Milwaukee, 1974.

Romero, P. L., & Romero, D. Toward self discovery and life option: Non-stereotyped career counseling. Paper presented at the meetings of the American Personnel and Guidance Association, Washington, D.C., 1978.

Romney, B. M. The effects of windowless classrooms on the cognitive and affective behavior of elementary school students. Unpublished masters thesis, University of New Mexico, 1976.

Rose, S. E., & Duer, W. F. Drug/alcohol education: A new approach for schools. Education, 1978, 99, 198–202.

Rosenbaum, J. E. The structure of opportunity in school. Social Forces, 1978, 57, 236–256.

Rosenbaum, J. E., & Presser, S. Voluntary racial integration in a magnet school. School Review, 1978, 86, 156–186.

Rosenberg, M., & Simmons, R. G. Black and white self esteem: The urban school child. Rose Monograph Series, American Sociological Association, Washington, D.C., 1971.

Rosenberg, N. E. School size as a factor of school expenditure. Journal of Secondary Education, 1970, 45, 135–142.

Rosenshine, B. Content, time, and direct instruction. In P. L. Peterson & H. J. Walberg (Eds.), Research on teaching: Concepts, findings and implications. Berkeley, Calif.: McCutchan, 1979.

Rosenshine, B., & Furst, N. The use of direct observation to study teaching. In R. Travers (Ed.), Handbook of research on teaching (2nd ed.). Chicago: Rand McNally, 1973.

Rosenthal, B. An ecological study of free play in a nursery school. Unpublished doctoral dissertation, Wayne State University, 1973.

Rosenthal, R., & Jacobson, L. Pygmalion in the classroom: Teacher expectation and pupils' intellectual development. New York: Holt, Rinehart & Winston, 1968.

Ross, S., Zimiles, H., & Gerstein, D. The Differentiated Child Behavior observational system. In M. C. Wang (Ed.), The use of direct observation to study instructional-learning behaviors in school settings. Pittsburgh: Learning Research and Development Center, University of Pittsburgh, 1974.

Roth, J. Prosocial behaviors among first-second grade children in an open classroom: A field study. Unpublished doctoral dissertation, Temple University, 1981.

Rubel, R. The unruly school. Lexington, Mass.: D. C. Heath, 1977.

Ruchkin, J. Does school crime need the attention of policemen or educators? Teachers College Record, 1977, 79, 225–244.

Ruedi, J., & West, C. K. Pupil self-concept in an "open" school and in a "traditional" school. Psychology in the Schools, 1973, 10, 48–53.

Rutter, M., Maughan, B., Mortimore, P., & Ouston, J. with Smith, A. Fifteen thousand hours: Secondary schools and their effects on children. Cambridge, Mass.: Harvard University Press, 1979.

Saario, T. N., Jacklin, C. N., & Tittle, C. K. Sex role stereotyping in the public schools. Harvard Educational Review, 1973, 43, 386–416.

St. John, N. H. School desegregation: Outcomes for children. New York: Wiley, 1975.

Sanders, K. M., & Harper, L. V. Free play fantasy behavior in pre-school children: Relations among gender, age, season and location. Child Development, 1976, 47, 1182–1185.

Santrock, J. W., & Tracy, R. L. The effects of children's family structure status on the development of stereotypes by teachers. Journal of Educational Psychology, 1978, 70, 754–757.

Sapp, G. L., & Dossett, E. The utility of a cognitive-developmental model in stimulating moral reasoning. Paper presented at the meetings of the American Educational Research Association, New York, 1977.

Sarason, S. The culture of the school and the problem of change. Boston: Allyn & Bacon, 1971.

Scharf, P. (Ed.). Readings in moral education. Minneapolis: Winston, 1978.

Schlosberg, N., & Goodman, J. A woman's place: Children's sex stereotyping of occupations. Vocational Guidance Quarterly, 1975, 20, 266–270.

Schmuck, R. A., & Schmuck, P. A. A humanistic psychology of education: Making the school everybody's house. Palo Alto, Calif.: Mayfield, 1974.

Schofield, J. W. School desegregation and intergroup relations. In D. Bar-Tal & L. Saxe

(Eds.), *Social psychology of education: Theory and research*. Washington, D.C.: Hemisphere, 1978.

Schumacher, E. F. *Small is beautiful*. New York: Harper & Row, 1973.

Schwebel, M., & Raph, J. (Eds.). *Piaget in the classroom*. New York: Basic, 1973.

Schweinhardt, L. J., & Weikart, D. P. *Young children grow up: The effects of the Perry Preschool program on youth through age 15*. Monographs of the High/Scope Educational Research Foundation, No. 27, Ypsilanti, Mich., 1981.

Scott, K. P., & Feldman-Summers, S. Children's reactions to textbook stories in which females are portrayed in traditionally male roles. *Journal of Educational Psychology*, 1979, *71*, 396–402.

Sealey, L. Open education: Fact or fiction? *Teachers College Record*, 1976, *77*, 615–630.

Serbin, L. A., O'Leary, K. D., Kent, R. N., & Tonick, I. J. A comparison of teacher response to the preacademic and problem behavior of boys and girls. *Child Development*, 1973, *44*, 796–804.

Sexton, P. *The feminized male: Classrooms, white collars and the decline of manliness*. New York: Random House, 1969.

Shalom, Inc. *Manual of primary prevention and early intervention programs*. Philadelphia: Shalom, 1980.

Shapiro, E. Educational evaluation: Rethinking the criteria of competence. *School Review*, 1973, *81*, 523–549.

Shapiro, E., & Biber, B. The education of young children: A developmental-interaction approach. *Teachers College Record*, 1972, *74*, 55–79.

Shapiro, E. K., & Weber, E. (Eds.). *Cognitive and affective growth: Developmental interaction*. Hillsdale, N.J.: Lawrence Erlbaum, 1981.

Sharan, S. Cooperative learning in small groups: Recent methods and effects on achievement, attitudes, and ethnic relations. *Review of Educational Research*, 1980, *50*, 241–271.

Sharan, S., & Sharan, Y. *Small-group teaching*. Englewood Cliffs, N.J.: Educational Technology Publications, 1976.

Sherman, J. A., & Bushell, D. Jr. Behavior modification as an educational technique. In F. D. Horowitz, E. M. Hetherington, S. Scarr-Salapatek, & G. M. Siegel (Eds.), *Review of child development research* (Vol. 4). Chicago: University of Chicago Press, 1975.

Sherman, L. An ecological study of glee in small groups of preschool children. *Child Development*, 1975, *46*, 53–61.

Shirreffs, J. Sex role stereotyping in elementary school health education textbooks. *Journal of School Health*, 1975, *45*, 519–529.

Shultz, J. J., & Florio, S. Stop and freeze: The negotiation of social and physical space in a kindergarten/first grade classroom. *Anthropology and Education Quarterly*, 1979, *10*, 166–181.

Shultz, J. J., Florio, S., & Erickson, F. "Where's the floor?": Aspects of cultural organization and social relationships in communication at home and at school. In P. Gilmore & A. Glatthorn (Eds.), *Ethnography and education: Children in and out of school*. Washington, D. C.: Center for Applied Linguistics, 1982.

Shure, M. Psychological ecology of a nursery school. *Child Development*, 1963, *34*, 979–992.

Signatur, D. J., & Reiss, S. Friendship patterns. In S. Reiss (Ed.), *Educational and psychological effects of open space education in Oak Park, Illinois*. Oak Park, Ill., 1974.

Silberman, M. Behavioral expression of teachers' attitudes toward elementary school students. *Journal of Educational Psychology*, 1969, *60*, 402–407.

Silberman, M. Teachers' attitudes and actions toward their students. In M. Silberman (Ed.), *The experience of schooling*. New York: Holt, Rinehart & Winston, 1971.

Simon, A., & Boyer, E. (Eds.). *Mirrors for behavior: An anthology of classroom observation instruments, continued*. Philadelphia: Research for Better Schools, 1974.

Simon, S., Howe, L., & Kirschenbaum, H. *Values clarification: A handbook of practical strategies for teachers and students* (Rev. ed.). New York: Hart, 1978.

Single, E., Kandel, D., & Faust, R. Patterns of multiple drug use in high schools. *Journal of Health and Social Behavior*, 1974, *15*, 344–357.

Singleton, S., Boyer, D., & Dorsey, P. Xanadu: A study of the structure of crises in an alternative school. *Review of Educational Research*, 1972, *42*, 525–531.

Slavin, R. E. Student teams and achievement divisions. *Journal of Research and Development in Education*, 1978, *12*, 39–49.

Slavin, R. E. Effects of biracial learning teams on cross-racial friendships. *Journal of Educational Psychology*, 1979, *71*, 381–387.

Slavin, R. E. Cooperative learning. *Review of Educational Research*, 1980, *50*, 315–342.

Slavin, R. E., & Madden, N. A. School practices that improve race relations. *American Educational Research Journal*, 1979, *16*, 169–180.

Smith, L. M., & Geoffrey, W. *The complexities of an urban classroom*. New York: Holt, Rinehart & Winston, 1968.

Smith, M. L., & Glass, G. V. *Relationship of class size to classroom processes, teacher satisfaction and pupil affect: A meta-analysis*. San Francisco: Far West Laboratory for Educational Research and Development, 1979.

Smith, P. K., & Connolly, K. Patterns of play and social interaction in preschool children. In N. Blurton Jones (Ed.), *Ethological studies of child behaviour*. Cambridge, England.: Cambridge University Press, 1972.

Smith, P. K., & Connolly, K. Social and aggressive behaviour in preschool children as a function of crowding. *Social Sciences Information*, 1977, *16*, 601–620.

Smith, P. K., & Connolly, K. *The behavioural ecology of the preschool*. Cambridge, England.: Cambridge University Press, 1981.

Snell, M. Trying out male roles for size. *American Vocational Journal*, 1977, *52*, 59–60.

Snow, R. Unfinished Pygmalion. *Contemporary Psychology*, 1969, *14*, 197–199.

Soar, R. S., & Soar, R. M. An empirical analysis of selected Follow Through programs: An example of a process approach to evaluation in early childhood education. In I. Gordon (Ed.), *71st Yearbook of the National Society for the Study of Education* (Part II). Chicago: University of Chicago Press, 1972.

Solomon, D., & Kendall, A. J. Individual characteristics and children's performance in "open" and "traditional" classroom settings. *Journal of Educational Psychology*, 1976, *68*, 613–625.

Solomon, D., & Kendall, A. J. *Children in classrooms: An investigation of person-environment interaction*. New York: Praeger, 1979.

Sommer, R. Classroom ecology. *Journal of Applied Behavioral Science*, 1967, *3*, 489–503.

Spencer, M. B. *Personal-social adjustment of minority group children*. Final Report to the National Institutes of Mental Health, 1981. (Mimeo)

Spodek, B., & Walberg, H. (Eds.). *Studies in open education*. New York: Agathon, 1975.

Sprung, B. (Ed.). *Perspectives on non-sexist early childhood education*. New York: Teachers College Press, 1978.

Stallings, J. Implementation and child effects of teaching practices in Follow Through classrooms. *Monographs of the Society for Research in Child Development*, 1975, *40*(163).

Stanley, J. C. (Ed.). *Preschool programs for the disadvantaged: Five experimental approaches to early childhood education*. Baltimore: The Johns Hopkins University Press, 1972.

Staub, E. *The development of positive social behavior and morality*. New York: Academic, 1978(a).

Staub, E. The development of prosocial behavior: Directions for future research and applications to education. In *The prosocial theorists' approach to moral citizenship education*. Philadelphia: Research for Better Schools, 1978(b).

Stebbins, L. B., St. Pierre, R. G., Proper, E. C., Anderson, R. B., & Cerva, T. R. *Education as experimentation: A planned variation model, IV-A, An evaluation of Follow Through*. Cambridge, Mass.: Abt Associates, 1977. (Also issued by the U.S. Office of Education as *National evaluation: Patterns of effects*, Vol. II.A of the Follow Through Planned Variation Experiment series.)

Stein, A., & Smithells, J. Age and sex differences in children's sex-role standards about achievement. *Developmental Psychology*, 1969, *1*, 252–259.

Steinmann, A. Female-role perception as a factor in counseling. In J. Pottker & A. Fishell (Eds.), *Sex bias in the schools: The research evidence*. Cranbury, N.J.: Associated University Presses, 1977.

Stephan, W. G., & Feagin, J. R. *School desegregation: Past, present and future*. New York: Plenum, 1980.

Stephan, W. G., & Rosenfield, D. Effects of desegregation on racial attitudes. *Journal of Personality and Social Psychology*, 1978(a), *36*, 795–804.

Stephan, W. G., & Rosenfield, D. Effects of desegregation on race relations and self-esteem. *Journal of Educational Psychology*, 1978(b), *70*, 670–679.

Stephens, J. M. *The process of schooling*. New York: Holt, Rinehart & Winston, 1967.

Stockard, J., Schmuck, P., Kempner, K., Williams, P., Edson, S., & Smith, M. A. *Sex equity in education*. New York: Academic, 1980.

Stodolsky, S. S. Identifying and evaluating open education. *Phi Delta Kappan*, 1975, *57*, 113–117.

Stokols, D. The experience of crowding in primary and secondary environments. *Environment and Behavior*, 1976, *8*, 49–86.

Stuart, R. B. Teaching facts about drugs: Pushing or preventing. *Journal of Educational Psychology*, 1973, *66*, 189–201.

Sullivan, J. Open-traditional—What is the difference? *The Elementary School Journal*, 1974,

74, 493–500.

Sundstrom, E. Toward an interpersonal model of crowding. *Sociological Symposium*, 1975, *14*, 129–144.

Sutherland, J. W. *A general systems philosophy for the social and behavioral sciences*. New York: George Braziller, 1973.

Swidler, A. *Organization without authority: Dilemmas of social control in free schools*. Cambridge, Mass.: Harvard University Press, 1979.

Swift, J. W. Effects of early group experience: The nursery school and day nursery. In M. L. Hoffman & L. W. Hoffman (Eds.), *Review of child development research* (Vol. 1). New York: Russell Sage Foundation, 1964.

Swisher, J. D., & Crawford, J. L. Jr. An evaluation of a short-term drug education program. *School Counselor*, 1971, *18*, 265–272.

Swisher, J. D., Warner, R., & Herr, E. An experimental comparison of four approaches to drug education. *Journal of Counseling Psychology*, 1972, *19*, 328–332.

Takanishi, R., & Spitzer, S. Children's perceptions of human resources in team-teaching classrooms: A cross-sectional developmental study. *The Elementary School Journal*, 1980, *80*, 203–212.

Tennis, G. H., & Dabbs, J. M. Jr. Sex, setting, and personal space: First grade through college. *Sociometry*, 1975, *38*, 385–394.

Thayer, L. (Ed.). *Affective education: Strategies for experiential learning*. La Jolla, Calif.: University Associates, 1976.

The Editors. An interview on Title IX with Shirley Chisholm, Holly Knox, Leslie R. Wolfe, Cynthia G. Brown, and Mary Kaaren Jolly. *Harvard Educational Review*, 1979, *49*, 504–526.

Thomas, L. *The lives of a cell: Notes of a biology watcher*. New York: Viking, 1974.

Thorndike, R. L. Review of *Pygmalion in the classroom* by R. Rosenthal & L. Jacobson. *American Educational Research Journal*, 1968, *5*, 708–711.

Todd, D. M. Contrasting adaptations to the social environment of a high school: Implications of a case study of helping behavior in two adolescent subcultures. In J. G. Kelly (Ed.), *Adolescent boys in high school*. Hillsdale, N.J.: Lawrence Erlbaum, 1979.

Traub, R. E., Weiss, J., & Fisher, C. W. Studying openness in education: An Ontario example. *Journal of Research and Development in Education*, 1974, *8*, 47–59.

Traub, R. E., Weiss, J., Fisher, C. W., & Musella, D. Closure on openness: Describing and quantifying open education. *Interchange*, 1972, *3*, 69–84.

Travis, C. An ethological study of an open classroom. *Education*, 1974, *94*, 282–286.

Trecker, J. L. Women in U.S. history high-school textbooks. In J. Pottker & A. Fishel (Eds.), *Sex bias in the schools: The research evidence*. Cranbury, N.J.: Associated University Presses, 1977.

Trickett, E. J. Toward a social-ecological conception of adolescent socialization: Normative data on contrasting types of public school classrooms. *Child Development*, 1978, *49*, 408–414.

Tuckman, B. W., Cochran, D. W., & Travers, E. J. Evaluating open classrooms. *Journal of Research and Development in Education*, 1974, *8*, 14–19.

Turiel, E. Social regulation and domains of social concepts. In W. Damon (Ed.), *New directions for child development*. Vol. 1: *Social cognition*. San Francisco: Jossey-Bass, 1978(a).

Turiel, E. The development of concepts of social structure. In J. Glick & K. A. Clarke-Stewart (Eds.), *The development of social understanding*. New York: Gardner Press, 1978(b).

Turiel, E. Distinct conceptual and developmental domains: Social convention and morality. *Nebraska Symposium on Motivation* (Vol. 25), 1977. Lincoln: University of Nebraska Press, 1979.

Turner, C., & Thrasher, M. *School size does make a difference*. San Diego, Calif.: Institute for Educational Management, 1970.

United States Commission on Civil Rights. *Racial isolation in the public schools*. Washington, D.C.: U.S. Government Printing Office, 1967.

United States Commission on Civil Rights. *Mexican-American Educational Study* (Report V). Washington, D.C.: Superintendent of Documents, 1972.

Urban, H. B. The concept of development from a systems perspective. In P. B. Baltes (Ed.), *Lifespan development and behavior* (Vol. 1). New York: Academic, 1978.

U'ren, M. The image of women in textbooks. In V. Gornick & G. B. Moran (Eds.), *Women in sexist society: Studies in power and powerlessness*. New York: Basic, 1971.

Volpe, R. Feedback facilitated relaxation training as primary prevention of drug abuse in early adolescence. *Journal of Drug Education*, 1977, *7*, 179–194.

Walberg, H. J. (Ed.). *Educational environments and effects: Evaluation, policy and productivity*. Berkeley, Calif.: McCutchan, 1979.

Walberg, H. J., & Thomas, S. C. Open education: A classroom validation in Great Britain and the United States. *American Educational Research Journal*, 1972, *9*, 197–207.

Walker, B. A., Jasinska, M. D., & Carnes, E. F. Adolescent alcohol abuse: A review of the literature. *Journal of Alcohol Education*, 1978, *23*, 51–65.

Walker, D. K. *Socioemotional measures for preschool and kindergarten children*. San Francisco: Jossey-Bass, 1973.

Wallat, C., & Green, J. L. Social rules and communicative contexts in kindergarten. *Theory into Practice*, 1979, *18*, 275–284.

Wallerstein, J. S., & Kelly, J. B. *Surviving the breakup: How children and parents cope with divorce*. New York: Basic, 1980.

Wangen, N. R., & Wagner, S. *Choices: Learning about changing sex roles*. Minneapolis: Jenny, 1977.

Warner, R. W., Swisher, J. D., & Horan, J. J. Drug abuse prevention: A behavioral approach. *The Bulletin of National Association of Secondary School Principals*, 1973, *57*, 372.

Wasserman, E. R. Implementing Kohlberg's "just community concept" in an alternative high school. *Social Education*, 1976, *40*, 203–207.

Weber, L. *The English infant school and informal education*. Englewood Cliffs, N.J.: Prentice-Hall, 1971.

Wechsler, H. Alcohol intoxication and drug use among teenagers. *Journal of Studies on Alcohol*, 1976, *37*, 1672–1677.

Wechsler, H., & McFadden, M. Sex differences in adolescent alcohol and drug use: A disappearing phenomenon. *Journal of Studies on Alcohol*, 1976, *37*, 1291–1301.

Weigel, R. H., Wiser, P. L., & Cook, S. W. The impact of cooperative learning experiences on cross-ethnic relations and attitudes. *Journal of Social Issues*, 1975, *31*, 219–245.

Weikart, D., Hohmann, C. F., & Rhine, W. R. High/Scope cognitively oriented curriculum model. In W. R. Rhine (Ed.), *Making schools more effective: New directions from Follow Through*. New York: Academic, 1981.

Weikart, D., Rogers, L., Adcock, C., & McClelland, D. *The cognitively oriented curriculum*. Washington, D.C.: National Association for the Education of Young Children, 1971.

Weiner, B. A theory of motivation for some classroom experiences. *Journal of Educational Psychology*, 1979, *7*, 3–25.

Weinraub, M., & Brown, L. M. The development of sex role stereotypes in children: Crushing realities. In V. Franks & E. Rothblum (Eds.), *The stereotyping of women: Its effects on mental health*. New York: Springer, 1983.

Weinstein, C. S. Modifying student behavior in an open classroom through changes in the physical design. *American Educational Research Journal*, 1977, *14*, 249–262.

Weinstein, G., & Fantini, M. D. (Eds.). *Toward humanistic education: A curriculum of affect*. New York: Praeger, 1970.

Weinstein, R. S., Middlestadt, S. E., Brattesani, K. A., & Marshall, H. H. *Student perceptions of differential teacher treatment*. Paper presented at the meetings of the American Educational Research Association, Boston, 1980.

Weitzman, L., & Rizzo, D. *Biased textbooks: Images of males and females in elementary school textbooks in five subject areas*. Washington, D.C.: National Foundation for Improvement of Education, 1974.

Weston, D. R., & Turiel, E. *Act-rule relations: Children's concepts of social rules*. Unpublished manuscript, University of California at Berkeley, 1979.

Wheeler, R., & Ryan, F. L. Effects of cooperative and competitive classroom environments on the attitudes and achievement of elementary school students engaged in social studies inquiry activities. *Journal of Educational Psychology*, 1973, *65*, 402–407.

White, S. H., Day, M. C., Freeman, P. K., Hantman, S. A., & Messenger, K. P. *Federal programs for young children: Review and recommendations* (4 vols.). Washington, D.C.: U.S. Government Printing Office, 1973.

Wicker, A. W. Undermanning, performances and students' subjective experiences in behavior settings of large and small high schools. *Journal of Personality and Social Psychology*, 1968, *10*, 255–261.

Wiener, N. *Human use of human beings: Cybernetics and society*. Boston: Houghton Mifflin, 1950.

Wilcox, M. When children discuss: A study of learning in small groups. *The Elementary School Journal*, 1976, *76*, 302–309.

Wilkins, R. The use of role playing to induce "plus one" dissonance in moral education. *Social Studies Journal*, 1976, *5*, 11–15.

Willems, E. P. Sense of obligation to high school activities as related to school size and marginality of student. *Child Development*, 1967, *38*, 1247–1260.

Williams, J., Bennett, S., & Best, D. Awareness and expression of sex stereotypes in young children. *Developmental Psychology*, 1975, *11*, 635–642.

Wilson, F., Langevin, R., & Stuckey, T. Are the pupils in the open plan school different? *Journal of Educational Research*, 1972, *66*, 115–118.

Wilson, J. Crime in society and school. *Educational Researcher*, 1976, *5*, 3–6.

Winne, P., & Walsh, J. Self-concept and participation in school activities reanalyzed. *Journal of Educational Psychology*, 1980, *72*, 161–166.

Wirtenberg, J. *A case study of Title IX implementation: Some unexpected effects*. Paper presented at the meetings of the American Psychological Association, New York, 1979.

Withall, J. An objective measurement of a teacher's classroom interactions. *Journal of Educational Psychology*, 1956, *47*, 203–212.

Women on Words and Images. *Dick and Jane as victims: Sex stereotyping in children's readers*. Princeton, N.J.: 1972.

Woodcock, P. R., & Herman A. Fostering career awareness in tenth-grade girls. *School Counselor*, 1978, *25*, 252–263.

Woolever, R. Expanding elementary pupils' occupational and social role perceptions: An innovative federal project. *Research in Education*, May 1977.

Wright, H. F., Barker, R. G., Null, J., & Schoggen, P. Toward a psychological ecology of the classroom. In A. Coladarci (Ed.), *Readings in educational psychology*. New York: Holt, Rinehart & Winston, 1955.

Wynne, E. *Growing up suburban*. Austin: University of Texas Press, 1977.

Yarworth, J. S., & Gauthier, W. J. Jr. Relationship of student self-concept and selected personal variables to participation in school activities. *Journal of Educational Psychology*, 1978, *70*, 335–344.

Zigler, E., & Valentine, J. (Eds.). *Project Head Start: A legacy of the war on poverty*. Riverside, N.J.: The Free Press, 1979.

DEVELOPMENTAL PERSPECTIVES ON THE SELF- SYSTEM*

SUSAN HARTER, *University of Denver*

4

CHAPTER CONTENTS

*Preparation of this chapter was facilitated by Grant # HD-09613 from the National Institute of Child Health and Human Development, U.S.P.H.S. I am particularly grateful to Kurt Fischer, Phil Shaver, Jim Connell, and Sybillyn Jennings for their many thoughtful suggestions on earlier drafts of this manuscript. In addition, I would like to thank Mavis Hetherington and her reviewers for their valuable input and constructive criticism. Alison Adams and Mari Jo Renick also deserve several rounds of applause for their editorial assistance, as do Lucia Wainwright and Denise Hall for their valiant struggles with the word processor. Finally, I would like to thank A. H. and P. P. for providing the most critical ingredient, unconditional positive regard!

ISSUES IN THE STUDY OF THE SELF: A DEVELOPMENTAL FRAMEWORK

Historically, during the days of introspection, topics concerning the psyche and the self represented legitimate, if not popular, domains of inquiry. However, with the radical behaviorist purge, such constructs were excised from our scientific vocabularies and we allowed William James and company to gather dust on the shelf. The pedagogical pendulum has swung again, with a resurgence of interest in the self and self-systems. With tumultuous applause, the self has been welcomed back into the fold of legitimate constructs within almost every branch of psychology. These include mainstream developmental psychology, life-span approaches, social psychology, adult cognition, social learning theory, cognitive-behavior modification, personality theory, and educational psychology.

An examination of these literatures, however, leads one to conclude that the ''self'' functions more as a prefix than as a legitimate construct in its own right. Moreover, the diversity of such prefix usage is mildly overwhelming. We encounter self-recognition, self-concept, self-image, self-theory, self-esteem, self-control, self-regulation, self-monitoring, self-evaluation, self-criticism, self-reward, self-perception, self-schematas, self-referent thought, self-consciousness, self-awareness, and self-actualization, to name the most prevalent exemplars. For the most part, these hyphenated constructs have not been examined from a developmental perspective. The challenge of this chapter, therefore, will be to select from this diverse literature those constructs that can be meaningfully cast into a developmental mold, and to suggest new directions for theory and research on the developing sense of self.

As a conceptual framework, there will be two major themes around which the material will be organized. The *first* theme involves a distinction initially articulated by William James in 1890. James contrasted *two fundamental aspects* of the self, the self as actor or *subject*, the ''I,'' and the self as an *object* of one's knowledge, the ''Me.'' The relevance of this distinction for our understanding of the self at different developmental levels will be explored. The second major theme involves the *self in relationship to others*. Emphasis will be placed on how knowledge of the self is necessarily related to one's pattern of social interactions and to one's developing knowledge of others, at each developmental level.

In attempting to explore these issues, a constructivist view will be adopted (see Lewis, 1979; Lewis & Brooks-Gunn, 1979a, 1979b; Sarbin, 1962). For Sarbin, the self is a cognitive structure or inference which is empirically derived; as with many cognitive structures around which behavior is organized, the self undergoes progressive change as the result of experience. Lewis and Brooks-Gunn adopt an even stronger cognitive-developmental perspective in the tradition of Piaget (1963) and Bartlett (1932), which emphasizes the interaction of the organism and the environment in the development of sensorimotor schemas and cognitive structures. Their position highlights the very active role that the infant and developing child play in constructing their view of the world as well as of the self. Lewis and Brooks-Gunn contrast this position with a more mechanistic analysis in which the child is viewed as the relatively passive recipient of surrounding biological and social forces. In advocating a constructivist approach, Lewis (1979) points out that one does not have to discard either the biological imperatives that exist or the necessary social constraints shaping behavior. Instead, one can think of the biological and social forces as potential building material for the construction of cognitive and affective structures. In turn, one can address the question of how these structures, including the self, serve to organize behavior.

Self as Subject Versus Self as Object

The majority of scholars who have devoted thoughtful attention to the topic of the self have come to a similar conclusion: two distinct but intimately intertwined aspects of self can be meaningfully identified, the self as *subject* and the self as *object*. For James, the self as subject was essentially the ''I'' as *knower,* in contrast to the ''Me'' which represented ''an empirical aggregate of things objectively known'' (1890/1963, p. 197). James' analysis was intended to apply to the *adult* self. Moreover, he focused primarily on the ''Me,'' further differentiating the empirical self into the ''material Me,'' the ''social Me,'' and the ''spiritual Me.'' Both Mead (1934) and Cooley (1902) also devoted major attention to the ''Me,'' emphasizing how the social self in particular emerges through interaction with significant others.

A similar distinction has been articulated by more recent writers. Dickstein (1977), for example, has contrasted the ''dynamic'' self, that possesses a sense of personal agency, control, and power, with the self as an object of one's knowledge and evaluation. For Dickstein, this distinction may be applied to children as well as adults. Lewis and Brooks-Gunn (1979b), in setting the stage for their studies on the infant's acquisition of self, define this duality of selves in terms of its relevance for infancy. Thus, they make the distinction between the *existential* self and the *categorical* self.

For Lewis and Brooks-Gunn, the task of the infant self as *subject* is to develop the realization that it is "existential" in the sense that it *exists* as separate from others in the world. Self as *object* is referred to as the categorical self in that the infant must develop categories by which to define himself or herself vis-à-vis the external world. Thus, the female infant must learn, for example, that she belongs to the category of baby or child, not adult, and that she is a girl, not a boy.

Wylie (1974, 1979) summarizes the essence of these distinctions, contrasting the self as active agent or process with the self as the object of one's knowledge and evaluation. The "I," then, is the active observer, whereas the "Me" is the observed, the product of the observing process when attention is focused on the self. This distinction has proved amazingly viable, and appears as a recurrent theme in theoretical treatments of the self. Empirically, however, major attention has been devoted to the study of the self as an object of one's knowledge and evaluation, as witnessed by the myriad number of studies on self-concept and self-esteem (see Wylie, 1961, 1974, 1979). The self as subject, process—as active agent—has received far less attention, particularly from a developmental perspective.

A major question to be addressed in this chapter involves how the "I" as well as the "Me" are to be conceptualized at different developmental levels. How do the cognitive structures of self as subject and self as object change with age? This general framework leads in turn to the following more specific questions:

1. How does the infant develop a sense of self as an active agent, an entity that exists separate from other objects and people in the world? How does this "existential" self (Lewis & Brooks-Gunn, 1979a, 1979b) emerge?

2. How does the child then learn to identify the characteristics and categories that define the self, and how do these defining features of the "Me," the self as observed, change with age?

3. How do the changing cognitive processes that define the "I" as knower and observer influence the nature of the self-theory which the child is constructing? Moreover, how do the changing cognitive structures in the mind of the developing child affect the *content* of the defining features of the self as well as the organization or *structure* of these self-descriptors?

4. Relatedly, to what extent are the defining features of the self as object experienced as an *integrated coherent whole*, in contrast to an aggregate of *multiple roles* or selves? What affective reactions might accompany each of these perceptions at different developmental levels?

5. In what sense is the self as subject, the "I," *aware* of the self as object, the "Me?" How does self-awareness change with development? Why does the self appear to be more *salient* at some stages during the life span, in the sense that the self as observer seems preoccupied with the self as observed?

6. How is *self-evaluation* to be viewed from a developmental perspective? Furthermore, how are the evaluative judgments that the "I" makes about the "Me" related to one's sense of *self-esteem?*

7. How does the concept of self serve as an organizer and regulator of *behavior* at different developmental levels? How are the processes involved in *self-control* to be viewed from a developmental perspective?

Self in Relation to Others: The Social Context

Historically, the content for the development of self has been social interaction with others (Baldwin, 1897; Cooley, 1902; Mead, 1925). For Baldwin, the real self was the bipolar self. He viewed the self as one pole, with the other person, the "alter," as the opposite pole. His general thesis is often quoted: "My sense of myself grows by imitation of you, and my sense of yourself grows in terms of my sense of myself. Both ego and alter are thus essentially social; each is a socius, and each is an imitative creation" (1897, p. 7).

For Cooley (1902), the role of others was analogous to a social mirror. He contended that what becomes the self is what we imagine that others think of us, of our appearance, aims, deeds, character, and so on. A social self of this sort, he writes, might be called the "reflected or looking glass self." He emphasized his point with the following couplet:

Each to each a looking glass
Reflects the other that doth pass.

Cooley identified three components of this "self-idea": the imagination of our appearance to the other person; the imagination of that person's judgment of our appearance; and some sort of "self-feeling" such as pride or mortification.

In Mead (1925), we find an elaboration of the themes identified by Cooley as well as Baldwin. He described "self-consciousness" as follows: "We appear as selves in our conduct insofar as we ourselves take the attitude that others take toward us. . . . We take the role of what may be called the 'generalized other.' And in doing this we appear as social objects, as selves" (p. 270).

More recent writers have echoed the theme of self in relation to other. Bannister and Agnew (1977) frame the general issue as follows: "The ways in which we elaborate our construing of self must be essentially those ways in which we elaborate our construing of others, for we have not a concept of self but a bipolar construct of self—not self or self-others" (p. 99). This general distinction between the self and the not-self has also been put forth by Bugenthal (1949), L'Ecuyer (1981), Symonds (1951), and Ziller (1973).

Lewis and Brooks-Gunn (1979b) elaborate on this distinction, placing considerable emphasis on how knowledge of others is related to the development of the categorical self. They cite, as one of their three general principles of social cognition, the following: "What can be demonstrated to be known about the self can be said to be known about the other and what is known about the other can be said to be known about the self" (p. 231). They draw on Piaget in support of their claim that the knowledge that the developing child possesses about self versus other is a consequence of social interaction. "The human being is immersed right from birth in a social environment. Society, even more, in a sense, than the physical environment, changes the very structure of the individual, because it not only compels him to recognize facts, but also provides him with a ready-made system of signs, which modify his thoughts; it presents him with new values and it imposes on him an infinite series of obligations" (Piaget, 1960, p. 156).

We do not yet have an integrated picture, however, of precisely how the developmental course of social knowledge influences the acquisition of a bipolar sense of self. There are several lines of inquiry that can be brought to bear on this issue, leading to the following specific questions that will be addressed throughout this chapter:

1. How and when does the *infant* develop a sense that he or she is an entity *separate and distinct from other people* and objects in the world? This process of differentiating self from other applies to both the self as subject and the self as object. With regard to self as subject, the infant must first learn that his or her actions and perceptions are experientially separate from the actions and thoughts of oth-

ers, that he or she is an active causal agent distinct from others in the environment. Following the development of this "existential self" (Lewis & Brooks-Gunn, 1979a, 1979b), the infant must then learn to identify the characteristics and categories that define the self as object, the "categorical self" in the terminology of Lewis and Brooks-Gunn. This acquisition process requires an appreciation of which characteristics are distinct or unique to the self, as well as which characteristics one has in common with others.

The issue of differentiation is not restricted to the period of infancy. For example, the young child must come to learn that there is a separate self comprised of private thoughts and experiences that are not shared by others. Later in development, during the period of identity formation, the adolescent must attempt to separate his or her thoughts, emotions, and defining characteristics from those of the significant others in the adolescent's social environment, at a more complex level of analysis.

2. Which comes *first, knowledge of self* or of other? Although this issue has been debated, are we perhaps asking the wrong question? Might the answer depend on the particular type of knowledge in interaction with the skill level of the child such that, in certain instances, knowledge of self is acquired before knowledge of others, whereas in other situations knowledge of other precedes self-knowledge?

3. How do the *judgments of significant others* affect one's concept of self? To what extent do the particular significant others who are most important, for example, parents and peers, *change* with development?

4. What role does *perspective-taking* play in the development of self? How do the cognitive-developmental processes involved in taking the perspective of another influence one's understanding of self?

5. How does *social comparison* affect the development of the self? In particular, how do possible developmental differences in the social comparison process influence the nature of *self-observation* and *self-evaluation?*

Organization of This Chapter

In addressing the two major themes, self as subject versus self as object and self in relation to other, we will begin with the infant. The specific questions that are most salient during this period include the differentiation of self as an active, independent, causal agent, and the emergence of skills involving the infant's initial recognition of those physical features and categories that define the self. The treatment will then shift to the development of self as a cognitive construction during childhood and early adolescence, where the focus will be on changes in the content and structure of the child's self-theory. The issues of perspective-taking and social comparison become paramount during this period, particularly as they relate to self-awareness and self-evaluation. The chapter will then turn to a discussion of identity formation as a major period in the development of the future adult self. In keeping with a life-span perspective, theories relevant to the self during adulthood will then be reviewed. An appreciation of the self during adolescence and adulthood requires a definitional shift of focus in that the self becomes more than a cognitive construction. As discussed in this literature, the self takes on the look of a dynamic personality system that serves to buffer the interactions of the individual with his or her environment.

The next section will turn to the topic of self-esteem, its meaning and measurement. In this literature the ''Me'' self takes center stage under the evaluative scrutiny of the ''I.'' The last major section will deal with self-control, and how the concept of self serves as an organizer and regulator of behavior. We will see that, for some self-control theorists, the controlling self is inbued with trait-like characteristics, whereas for others emphasis is placed on the situation-specific processes through which overt behavior is controlled. A concluding section will attempt to provide an integrative summary and to keep our developmental hopes high.

THE DEVELOPMENT OF THE SELF DURING INFANCY

The infant's first task is the development of a sense of self as subject. Thus, the infant must come to appreciate that he or she exists as an active causal agent, a source and controller of actions, separate from other persons and objects in the world. Once this ''existential'' self (Lewis & Brooks-Gunn, 1979a, 1979b) has been differentiated from others, the infant must learn to recognize those particular features, characteristics, and categories that define the self as object. A representation of self that the infant can identify must be developed. As we will see, the self as subject has been given somewhat more theoretical attention, whereas the self as object has received more direct empirical support.

The Infant Self as Subject

We first need to imagine the Jamesian ''self as knower'' as a young infant who is developing sen-

sorimotor knowledge of his or her world without the benefit of representational skills or language. How does such an infant apply these sensorimotor schemas to an understanding of how the self exists as an active agent, distinct from others in the environment?

Lewis and Brooks-Gunn (1979a, 1979b) have provided the most compelling analysis of the development of the existential self. They propose that the key to this process is the infant's experience of regular and consistent contingencies between one's actions and the outcomes they produce. Kinesthetic feedback produced by the infant's actions provides an important first source of such contingent information. Thus, when one's eyelids close, the world becomes dark. When one bangs one's foot against the bars of the crib, pain results. The contingency between self-generated action and outcome is immediate and consistent.

Contingent feedback is also provided by the external environment, by objects, and by people. Thus, if the infant releases a rattle from the hand, it falls. If the infant cries, mother comes. For Lewis and Brooks-Gunn, regular and consistent contingency feedback provides the basis for establishing generalized expectancies about the infant's control of its world. Such expectancies should help the infant to differentiate its actions from the actions of others.

Lewis and Brooks-Gunn contend that contingency feedback provided by the social world, notably the primary caretakers, is more critical than feedback from the world of inanimate objects. Interactions with objects are considered to be less predictable—less regular—during the early months of infant life, whereas in the social realm caretakers intend for their responses to be contingent on the infant's actions. According to the generalized expectancy model (see also Lewis, 1977; Lewis & Goldberg, 1969), the consistency, as well as timing, and the quality of the mother's responsiveness to her infant's cues create powerful expectancies for the infant about its control of the social environment, in particular.

Recent evidence suggests that social contingency learning based on the pairing of infant action and caretaker response is not limited to situations in which the parent attempts to meet the infant's basic homeostatic needs. Parental imitation of the infant's actions is another important source. It is becoming well documented (see Bretherton & Bates, 1979; Field, 1977; McCall, Parke & Kavanaugh, 1977; Papousek & Papousek, 1974) that parents tend to imitate a variety of infant behaviors from a very early age, and that such imitation is probably the most effective elicitor of social interaction from the baby throughout the first two years.

While there are numerous sources of specific feedback from the social and nonsocial environment, Lewis and Brooks-Gunn contend that mirrors, or similar light-reflecting surfaces, provide a unique type of information. In the mirror, one's actions are reproduced simultaneously and identically in the sense that when the infant moves its hand, the hand in the mirror matches these actions. This one-to-one correspondence between one's actions, which provide proprioceptive information, and the reflection of these actions offers valuable feedback. The immediacy of this contingency would appear to facilitate the emerging understanding of self as an independent agent, as the one who is "making that happen."

Furthermore, an appreciation of this contingency exemplifies an important developmental step in the differentiation of self from other, since the infant learns that "other people do not produce behavior sequences identical to theirs and that only a reflective image of themselves does" (Lewis & Brooks-Gunn, 1979b, p. 200). The infant comes to learn, then, that a reflection is not another person but is the "self," the product of one's own actions.

Through these various developmental acquisitions, the sense of self as subject, as an independent causal agent, emerges. This knowledge, in turn, would appear to be a prerequisite to the development of an understanding of self as object, with recognizable features and specific characteristics. In the following section, the empirical evidence for this analysis will be reviewed.

Visual Self-Recognition

At the outset, it is important to emphasize that the empirical efforts to study the emerging self have focused primarily on the *visual* recognition of self. The self as experienced through other sensory modalities, for example, proprioceptive, tactile, auditory, has not been systematically investigated. In addition, the primary emphasis has been on the analysis of the infant's emerging ability to recognize his or her own facial features, to appreciate the self as an object whose visual image is unique, in short, to "know what one looks like." There is less evidence bearing on the rudimentary self as an active independent agent, although recent studies (Bertenthal & Fischer, 1978; Lewis & Brooks-Gunn, 1979b) have begun to address this issue.

The focus on facial recognition is not the invention of infancy research. Throughout the history of civilization, the face seems to have been the primary representation of the self. In Goffman's (1955) treatise on "facework" he carefully analyzes the many psychological devices we learn to "save face." The face, as an embodiment of the self, can also be found in other metaphorical expressions, for example, "I won't be able to face myself in the mirror in the morning," "I'll challenge him face to face." Thus, there is a sociohistorical rationale for choosing to study the ontogenetic emergence of an appreciation of the face as evidence for the existence of the self.

Studies with Subhuman Primates

The emphasis on the recognition of one's physical features is also due, in part, to the fact that certain infancy investigators built on some fascinating research demonstrating self-recognition in primates (see Gallup, 1968, 1970, 1977, 1979). In a series of studies examining the chimpanzee's reactions to mirrors, Gallup found that, after only three days of experience with such reflective surfaces, chimps demonstrated self-directed behavior such as examining the grooming parts of their own bodies. (During the first few days, the chimpanzees had treated the images as if they represented another chimp, making threatening gestures and vocalizations.) In an ingenious attempt to determine whether the chimpanzees actually recognized their own facial features, Gallup next anesthetized the animals, placing red odorless nonirritating dye on the ridge of one eyebrow and on the opposite ear. When they were subsequently confronted with their mirror image, they immediately began to explore the marked portions of their face. Other chimpanzees, similarly marked but with no prior mirror experience, did not engage in mark-directed or self-directed behavior.

In another study (Gallup & McClure, 1971), the investigators tested the hypothesis that social interaction is a necessary precondition for self-recognition. Chimpanzees raised in social isolation did not exhibit self-directed behavior toward the marks placed on their face, but continued to treat the mirror image as if it were another animal. Precisely how social experience facilitates the recognition of one's facial features has not been adequately explained. One possibility may be that the social isolate has had no opportunity to develop the general schema of a chimpanzee face with which he could subsequently compare and contrast the features of his own face when given mirror experience. We do know, however, that for those few species that demonstrate facial self-recognition, namely the great apes and humans (see Gallup, 1968, 1977), interaction with others in the social environment appears to be essential.

Baby Biographies and Infant Intelligence Tests

When we turn to the human infant literature on visual recognition of the self, the earliest reports of responses to a mirror come from baby biographies compiled by Preyer (1893), Darwin (1877), and later Zazzo (1948). Both Preyer and Darwin documented their infant's interest in the mirror image. Darwin further noted that his 9-month-old son would turn toward the mirror when his name was called, as if he recognized himself. Zazzo was the first to examine the infant's ability to recognize himself in pictures and home movies, focusing primarily on verbal indications of self-recognition, for example, "That's me," or "That's Johnnie."

Mirror behavior also found its way into many of the early infant intelligence tests (Bayley, 1969; Buhler, 1930; Cattell, 1940; Gesell, 1928; Griffiths, 1954). Lewis and Brooks-Gunn (1979b) summarize the mirror test items from these five infant scales. Items appearing within the five- to ten-month period include smiling at the mirror image, vocalizing, patting it, and "playing" with it. Items for subsequent months tap search behavior for objects or people whose image also appears in the mirror. During the 15- to 17-month period on the Buhler scale, behavioral criteria include reaching toward the adult, not the reflection, suggesting that the infants are learning the reflective properties of mirrors. Clear indications of self-recognition, tapped by items in which the infant refers to himself or herself by name, appear between 24 and 26 months.

There is a lack of consensus across these tests with regard to the age at which the infant displays these various mirror behaviors. However, this may well reflect different criteria employed for inclusion of an item at a given level, for example, modal response at a given age versus percentage of children passing the item, different percentage values, and so on. Despite the inconsistencies and the lack of any theoretical rationale for including these particular mirror behaviors, taken as a whole the findings from the infant intelligence tests do suggest a crude developmental sequence. Though these psychometricians were not interested in self-recognition per se, the normative data do provide a general descriptive backdrop for more recent experimental studies.

Research Studies on Infant Self-Recognition

In two of the first studies documenting infants' reactions to mirrors (Amsterdam, 1972; Dixon, 1957), developmental sequences were postulated. Dixon identified four stages. The infant first enjoys watching the *mother's* movement. In the second stage, between 5 and 6 months, the infant responds to the image as if it were a playmate. Then, between 6 and 12 months, the infant manifests an interest in the image of actions performed. Finally, the fourth stage is characterized by coy, shy, or fearful behavior in front of the mirror.

Employing a technique similar to Gallup's procedure with chimps, Amsterdam included a mark-recognition task in her study, placing rouge on the infant's nose. She identified three stages. In the first, the infant smiled, vocalized, and patted the mirror image. In the second stage, the infant responded with coy, shy, or seemingly self-conscious behavior. Only the third stage, which appeared between 20 and 24 months, was characterized by self-recognition operationally defined as mark-directed behavior toward the rouge on the infant's own nose. In touching one's nose, the infant appears to recognize that the image in the mirror is of the self, and that the rouge violates the schema that has been developed for its face. Self-recognition, so defined, refers primarily to the infant's earliest knowledge of the self as *object*, in the sense that one can identify one's unique physical features.

As Lewis and Brooks-Gunn (1979b) and Bertenthal and Fischer (1978) note, these findings, while intriguing, are difficult to interpret. The stages have been defined rather vaguely, and there is not clear theoretical rationale for predicting a particular sequence. Furthermore, small sample sizes with restricted age ranges have posed problems, along with other procedural difficulties (see Lewis and Brooks-Gunn critique).

The most systematic investigations of self-recognition in infancy have been performed by Bertenthal and Fischer (1978) and by Lewis and Brooks-Gunn (1979b). Although the former investigators have restricted their study to mirror behavior, the latter researchers have also examined infants' self-recognition in photographs and on videotape. By looking at different representational modes, Lewis and Brooks-Gunn have been able to separate the knowledge of the direct contingency between one's actions and the mirror image from the featural recognition of oneself in noncontingent situations such as a picture or videotape. As these investigators note (Lewis & Brooks-Gunn, 1979a), contingency cues allow the infant to learn that the self-image "acts like me," while feature cues allow the infant to learn that a self representation "looks like me." Thus, their procedures allow one to distinguish between the infant's appreciation of self as subject or active agent and self as an object with recognizable features.

Lewis and Brooks-Gunn have conducted an impressive array of cross-sectional studies with infants between the ages of 5 and 24 months, employing a variety of measures including attention, affect, imitation, contingency play, use of mirror to locate objects, mark-directed behavior, pointing at the self, and labeling of the self. From their own programmatic series of studies, as well as those of other investigators (e.g., Amsterdam, 1972; Amsterdam & Greenberg, 1977; Bertenthal & Fischer, 1978; Bigelow, 1975; Dickie & Strader, 1974; Dixon, 1957; Papousek & Papousek, 1974; Schulman & Kaplowitz, 1977), these authors cull evidence for the following ontogenetic trends:

Between 5 and 8 months, infants show a wide range of self-directed behaviors in both mirrors and videotape contingent situations, for example, they smile at their image, watch themselves intently, touch their bodies, and engage in rhythmic movements such as bouncing, waving, and clapping. However, there is no evidence for self-other differentiation or feature recognition. Between 9 and 12 months infants begin to use mirrors to reach for the actual object; they will touch their own body and turn toward other persons or objects that are reflected in the mirror. During this stage, they are beginning to acquire an understanding of the reflective nature of mirrors and an appreciation that the self is separate from other people and objects.

Between 15 and 18 months of age, the new advance is the appearance of mark-directed behavior in contingency situations, both mirror and contingent videotape representations. Self-conscious behaviors also occur. There is some evidence for emerging featural self-recognition in noncontingent situations, for example, some infants can label and point to pictures of themselves. By 21 to 24 months, these emerging behavioral trends have become clearly solidified, with the large majority of infants exhibiting mark-directed behavior, differentiating between themselves and others in both contingent and noncontingent situations. They also systematically use their own name and appropriate personal pronouns in both conditions. For Lewis and Brooks-Gunn, "it is the ability to recognize and respond to self *independent* of contingency which represents the important developmental milestone in self-recognition" (1979b, p. 218).

Bertenthal and Fischer (1978) are the only investigators who have specifically designed their study to demonstrate a theoretically derived *acquisition sequence* of infants' responses to the mirror. The five stages in this sequence, formalized in Fischer's theory of cognitive development (Fischer, 1980), are defined in terms of the type and complexity of coordinated actions that the infant can perform. Bertenthal and Fischer derived a different self-recognition task for each stage, and each task was administered to 48 infants drawn from six age groups: 6, 8, 10, 12, and 24 months. The results indicated that 46 of the 48 infants fit the predicted developmental acquisition sequence, that is, for a given infant each stage prior to his or her own highest stage was performed correctly.

The five tasks were (1) *Tactile exploration:* the infant is placed in front of the mirror and observed to look at and touch some part of its mirror image. (2) *Hat task:* the infant is suited in a vest that holds a hat above its head on a rod attached to the vest, and is placed in front of the mirror. In this task the infant must locate the object in space by first looking in the mirror, and then turning to grasp the real hat, the movement of which is contingent on the movement of its own body. (3) *Toy task:* a toy is lowered from behind the infant's head while the infant is looking in the mirror, and the infant must turn and look at the real toy. (4) *Rouge task:* rouge is placed on the infant's nose, and when placed in front of the mirror the infant must touch its nose or verbalize that something is different about it. (5) *Name task:* the mother points to the child's image in the mirror asking, "Who's that?" and the infant has to state its name or use an appropriate personal pronoun.

The Bertenthal and Fischer findings, taken together with those of Lewis and Brooks-Gunn as well as other investigators, can be interpreted as a documentation of the emergence of self as subject—as an active, independent causal agent—and the ensuing emergence of self as object. Table 1 summarizes the hypothesized sequential nature of the processes underlying the development of self during infancy.

In the first stage, although interest in the mirror is demonstrated, there is no evidence that the self is perceived as an independent causal agent, nor is there any indication that the infant differentiates self from other. In the second stage, the infant demonstrates its awareness of the self as an active agent in space, and appreciates the cause and effect relationship between its own movements and a contingent moving visual image. For example, on the *hat* task, the infant uses mirrors to locate objects in space, demonstrating an appreciation of the contingency between its own body movements and the movements of the hat which is attached. It is as if the infant were saying, through its search behavior, "It must be attached to me over my head since when *I*

Table 1. The Emergence of Self as Subject and Self as Object During Infancy: Proposed Acquisition Sequence Based on Studies of Visual Recognition

Behaviors	Approximate Age in Months	Interpretation
EMERGENCE OF SELF AS SUBJECT, AS ACTIVE, INDEPENDENT, CAUSAL AGENT		
I. Interest in mirror image; regards, approaches, touches, smiles, vocalizes. Does not differentially respond to self vs. other in mirror, videotape, or pictorial representation.	5–8	No evidence that self is perceived as a causal agent, independent of others. No featural differentiation between self and other.
II. Understands nature of reflective surface: contingency play, imitation, rhythmic movements, bouncing, waving; can locate objects in space, attached to body. Differentiates between contingent and noncontingent videotape representations of self.	9–12	Active agent in space emerges, awareness of cause-effect relationship between own body movements and moving visual image.
III. Uses mirror to locate people/objects in space. Reaches toward person, not image, and reaches toward object not attached to body. Distinguishes between self movement and movement of others on videotape.	12–15	Self-other differentiation with regard to agency. Appreciates self as an active, independent, agent separate from others, who can also cause their own movements in space.
EMERGENCE OF SELF AS AN OBJECT OF ONE'S KNOWLEDGE		
IV. In mirror and videotape, demonstrates mark-directed behavior, sees image and touches rouge on nose. Points to self. Distinguishes between self and other in pictorial representation and videotape.	15–18	Featural recognition of self; internal schema for own face that can be compared to external visual image.
V. Verbal labeling: infant can state name, attach appropriate personal pronoun to own image in mirror. Can distinguish self from same-gender infant in pictures and can label self.	18–24	Appreciation that one has unique featural attributes that can be verbally labeled as the self.

move, it moves with me.'' Further evidence for this awareness of self as active agent comes from Lewis and Brooks-Gunn's findings that infants can differentiate contingent from noncontingent videotape representations of the self.

In the third stage of this sequence, there is a further advance in the development of self as active agent. The infant can differentiate between movement that is contingent on the *self* and movement that is produced by *other* objects or people, clearly demonstrating self-other differentiation. In the *toy* task, for example, the infant must appreciate that the toy's movement is independent of the infant, that the

toy and the self are each separate active agents in space. In both mirror and videotape tasks, the infant also differentiates between the contingent movement of the self and the movement of other *people*.

The fourth step of the sequence signals the first demonstrable evidence for the sense of self as *object,* defined in terms of the recognition of one's facial features. Performance on the rouge task requires that the infant has a schema for what one's face normally looks like in the mirror, an internal image to which an external tableau can be compared. Lewis and Brooks-Gunn have also demonstrated that the infant can distinguish between self and others in pictorial, as well as noncontingent videotape, representations.

The advance in the fifth stage represents the infant's ability to verbally label the self and to attach the appropriate personal pronoun to one's image. Additionally, the infant can distinguish between pictoral representations of the self and same-gender infants (Lewis & Brooks-Gunn, 1979b). Here, the infant appreciates that it has unique featural attributes; that the self as object can be defined in terms of specific verbal labels. The postulated acquisition sequence during infancy, therefore, delineates three stages in the development of self as subject, followed by two stages of the emerging self as object.

The ages provided in Table 1 are only approximations. As Lewis and Brooks-Gunn point out, there are discrepancies across studies in the ages at which particular behaviors are reported. It would appear, however, that these reflect methodological and data-analytic differences that do not cast doubt on the proposed developmental sequence. For example, when the mean or modal age is employed, these values will be influenced by the range of ages selected for study. Proportion of infants demonstrating the behavior at a particular age level has been utilized in other studies, although the value taken to indicate that a behavior is representative of that age period differs across studies. Finally, certain investigators cite the youngest age at which a particular behavior was observed, an index that is difficult to interpret. On balance, some measure of sequence is probably the most sensitive to the developmental phenomena in question, although it leaves much to be answered in terms of the individual differences observed in the age at which a given behavior is manifest.

One final caution is in order. The findings interpreted here on the emergence of the self draw exclusively on data of visual recognition and the coordination of visual-motor schemas. We should not fall into the trap of equating "self" with visual self-recognition, which in turn is defined as an acknowledgment that the red marks applied to one's face are foreign. To grow accustomed to one's face represents an important developmental advance, but this constitutes only one means of self-understanding. At a more practical level, we should not mislead well-meaning parents into thinking that the mirror is the sine qua non of sociocognitive development. (One has visions of mirror sales soaring, much like the mobile craze a decade ago, such that a mirror in every crib will become touted as the latest panacea to ensure a stable self-identity!) The mirror studies do provide a compelling experimental paradigm. A cogent analysis of the processes underlying the infant's responses to mirrors offers the clearest example of how the self might develop. However, those of us who wish to understand the development of the self during infancy should not be caught staring too long at our own reflection!

Knowledge of Self and Knowledge of Other

As the introduction indicated, a major theme to be traced through this chapter is the relationship between self and other. The bipolar nature of the self-other construct has been highlighted by many (e.g., Baldwin, 1897; Bannister & Agnew, 1977); most recently Lewis and Brooks-Gunn (1979b) have emphasized, as one of their principles of social recognition, that what is known about the self is known about the other, and what is known about the other is known about the self. These assertions lead to the following questions: Does knowledge of self and other arise simultaneously? Does knowledge of self precede knowledge of other or does knowledge of other come first? The scant evidence to date suggests that these questions can only be meaningfully addressed within the context of a particular developmental task or skill domain. In certain situations, knowledge of self will come first. In other situations, knowledge of other will first be acquired.

During infancy, the process through which self-knowledge is acquired would appear to involve three related components, knowledge of self, differentiation of self from other, and knowledge of other. Thus, with regard to the development of the self as *subject*, the infant must learn that it is an active causal bodily agent, separate from others, who are also active causal bodily agents. The evidence and analysis just presented suggests that in this realm, knowledge of *self* precedes knowledge of other. During the second stage the infant demonstrates an understanding of self as an active agent, but it is not until the third stage that the infant appears to appreciate that others are also independent agents. Watson and Fischer (1977), in a developmental study involving a doll-play technique, have also demonstrated that the toddler understands the self as active controlling agent before appreciating this attribute in others.

When we examine the earliest mastery of self as *object*, we find that the infant must learn that there are recognizable physical features that define the "Me,"—that differentiate "Me" from others, who also have unique definable features. Thus the infant not only develops a schema or internal representation for "Me," but for others as well. In this realm, knowledge of *other* would appear to precede knowledge of self. The infant learns to recognize Mommy and Daddy before it can recognize the self, and learns the labels "Mommy" and "Daddy" before learning its own name.

Fischer (personal communication), in applying his skill analysis to this phenomenon, has suggested that feature invariance is easier to learn about *others* than about the self, particularly with those features that must be visually recognized. Not only does the infant not have as much opportunity to observe himself or herself, but it is more difficult to discriminate oneself from the environment. In contrast, Mommy is there, and then not there; she separates herself from the infant, making it easier for the infant to discriminate her and her features from the environment. To oneself, one is "always there."

This analysis applies primarily to an understanding of why *visual recognition* of the self would be more difficult. These same conditions may be hypothesized to *enhance* one's sense of proprioceptive or bodily self, to facilitate one's understanding of self as a physically active agent. Thus, it will be important to extend our investigations to modalities involving tactile and auditory recognition of self as well as others in order to broaden our understanding of how and when such knowledge is acquired developmentally.

Another aspect to be learned about the self as object involves self-definitions in the form of category labels, for example, "I am a girl, not a boy" (gender), "I am an infant or child, not an adult" (age categories). While there is very little direct evidence on whether these category labels are learned for self before other, findings by Van Parys (1980) suggest that these labels may first be applied to the *self* and then to others. In summary, the evidence suggests that self as *agent* is acquired *before* other as agent, whereas self as a recognizable *object* is acquired *after* other as a recognizable object. It is further hypothesized that category labels about the self are acquired before these labels are systematically applied to others. In subsequent treatments of the development of self during childhood, adolescence, and adulthood, the issue of knowledge of self versus other will continue to be addressed.

Separation and Individuation: The Psychoanalytic Perspective

The differentiation of self from other and the infant's emerging awareness of self as an autonomous agent has had a prominent place in psychoanalytic theory as well. Sigmund Freud (1950, 1955) initially

discussed the general process by which the infant must come to recognize that the self is separate from mother. The rudimentary ego was seen to develop from the realization that the mother does not automatically fulfill the infant's every need. Ego psychologists, notably Hartmann (1952, 1964) and Anna Freud (1946, 1965) then developed this theme in relation to the infant's development of *object constancy,* a term that embraces both the libidinal and cognitive aspects of the infant's attachment to its mother. The work of Margaret Mahler (1963, 1965, 1968, 1975), however, has been the most comprehensive in delineating the *developmental phases* through which object constancy is attained, and will therefore be the focus of this section. By object constancy Mahler means "that the maternal image has been intrapsychically available to the child in the same way as the actual mother had been libidinally available—for sustenance, comfort, and love" (Mahler, 1968, p. 222).

Separation-individuation is the process through which object constancy is developed. Separation refers primarily to the process of self-object differentiation whereby the mother comes to be perceived as separate from the self. Individuation encompasses the infant's growing realization of its capabilities as an independent and autonomous entity who can function effectively in the absence of mother. According to Mahler, each new developmental advance in the process toward establishing object constancy is accompanied by a new level of self-object differentiation. She identifies four phases of separation-individuation that unfold over the period from 5 to 36 months of age. These are: (1) differentiation, (2) practicing, (3) rapprochement, and (4) consolidation of individuality and beginning emotional constancy.

Although Mahler describes four phases in the differentiation process, her major focus is on the infant's development of a stable internal representation of the *mother* as the constant object. There is virtually no emphasis on the infant's emerging representation of *self,* in contrast to the cognitive-developmental studies reviewed in the previous section. Nevertheless, her stage-descriptions provide a very compelling picture of the dynamic interpersonal context in which the infant must ultimately develop a sense of both self and other.

Prior to the first stage of differentiation, the newborn is considered to be in a "normal autistic phase" where the major goal is to maintain homeostatic equilibrium, with no differentiation between self and other. After the first few weeks, the infant moves into a phase of "normal symbiosis," a need-satisfying relationship in which self and maternal intrapsychic representations have not yet been differentiated (Mahler, 1968).

Differentiation, the first phase of the actual separation-individuation process, occurs between approximately 5 and 10 months. By the fifth month, a libidinal attachment to the mother has been established. The infant distinguishes mother from other people, smiles and vocalizes at her more readily, and quiets sooner after crying when picked up by the mother. From the infant's reactions to separation, for example, distress, distractibility, gazing toward the door where the mother left (Mahler, 1968; McDevitt, 1975), it is inferred that the infant is beginning to develop the ability to differentiate self from mother. From Mahler, these observations suggest a rudimentary memory of the absent mother, primarily during the infant's need states; however, it is too unstable to comfort the infant during the mother's absence (see also Fraiberg, 1969).

In the *practicing* phase (approximately 10 to 16 months), the infant devotes considerable energy to practicing locomotor skills and exploring the environment. Early in this period, the infant will search for the absent mother or repeat "Mama," suggesting a more differentiated image of the mother. Later in this period, the infant shows a greater tolerance for separation, moving away from mother and seemingly unconcerned with her whereabouts. From these behaviors, Mahler infers that the infant has a more stable mental representation of mother that is comforting in her absence. However, when a need does arise, the infant seeks to reestablish bodily contact with the mother, what Mahler terms a "refueling" process that restores the infant's energy to practice its newfound skills and to explore the environment.

During the third phase, *rapprochement* (16 to 24 months), there is a growing realization of separateness. The cheerful mood of the previous period is replaced by concern for the mother's absence, increased separation distress, and feelings of loneliness, depression, and helplessness (Mahler, 1961, 1965, 1966). The infant appears to experience a "rapprochement crisis" in which realization of separateness is acute, belief in one's attempt to coerce the environment is frustrated, and ambivalence is often intense. The toddler wants to be united with, but at the same time separate from, mother. Temper tantrums, whining, sad moods, and intense separation reactions are at their peak (Mahler, 1968). The "terrible twos" have arrived.

The mental image of mother during the rapprochement stage is considered to be unstable, buf-

feted by feelings of anger and severe separation anxiety. Since there is no maternal image of mother to comfort the toddler in mother's absence, he or she needs repeated contact and often clings to the mother. Mahler proposed that the toddler attempts to maintain an image of the "good" mother, and therefore often displaces anger onto another caretaker who becomes the "bad" object. Through this mechanism of "splitting" the object representation, the longed-for image of mother as love object is separated from the hated image (Mahler, 1967, 1968, 1975).

During the fourth phase of *consolidation* and resolution (24 to 36 months), disappointment, frustration, and the mother's absence are better tolerated, and the young child begins to engage in activities independent of the mother. From these behaviors, it is inferred that mother is clearly perceived as a separate person in the outside world, while at the same time she has an existence in the child's internal representational world. Since the child seems increasingly able to "neutralize" aggression toward the mother, it is assumed that the "good" and "bad" aspects of the mother are more solidly integrated into a single representation. During mother's absence, the child can be comforted with this more secure and stable mental representation of mother. This security, in turn, enables the infant to pursue independent interests and to begin to acquire a distinct sense of his or her own individuality.

Evaluation of Mahler's Theory

At first glance, Mahler's goal appears to be similar to that of the cognitive theorists who are investigating the development of self during infancy. Both groups are concerned with how the self becomes differentiated from "other," how the infant develops a sense of self as an active, independent agent, and how characteristics unique to the self come to be appreciated. However, the cameos of the infants suggested by the cognitive-developmental and the psychoanalytic positions present a marked contrast. In contemplating the visual self-recognition studies, we are full of admiration for the inquisitive young infant scientist who is preoccupied with the serious business of understanding the reflective properties of mirrors, locating objects and people in space, coordinating sensorimotor schemas, developing internalized schemas to promote featural recognition, and mastering linguistic labels that signify the self.

The budding terrible two as described by Mahler is faced with different developmental hurdles, and tends to evoke more sympathy. The infant is wrenched from the blissful stage of need gratification, must endure separation distress, struggle to create a soothing image of mother, tolerate the fickleness of an environment that initially seems to yield to the infant's every whim only to frustrate the infant in a subsequent developmental hour of need; and, finally, to make matters worse, the toddler is greeted with social approbation for throwing himself or herself, red-faced and screaming, on the super-market floor!

The richness of Mahler's behavioral description of the separation-individuation process is extremely compelling, based on her extensive observations in both controlled and naturalistic settings. She portrays a vivid picture of the primary context of this process, namely the mother-infant interaction. The emphasis on the *affective* reactions of the infant provides a realistic account of how this struggle is subjectively experienced. Moreover, her detailed description of the separation-individuation process as a developmental progression that unfolds over several phases represents an advance over earlier theorists who tended to focus on one period of development (see Fraiberg, 1969).

On balance, however, Mahler's account tells us more about the importance of the *mother* as an emotional object in the infant's life than about the infant's sense of self. There are few specifics about the individuation component; how the infant develops an image of self as distinct and unique. Furthermore, the inferences concerning the precise nature of the infant's developing internal representations of the mother are problematic, given the degree of extrapolation from the data. Mahler's findings provide a more compelling documentation of the *emotional constancy* of the mother than of the cognitive representations that accompany this process. An examination of Mahler's phases, in light of recent work on person permanence (see Bell, 1970; Jackson, Campos, & Fischer, 1978), would be a welcome convergence.

In addition, the singular emphasis on *mother* in Mahler's account offers little sense of the infant's own contribution to the interaction. An emphasis on the transactional nature of the mother-infant relationship (see Sameroff & Chandler, 1975; Sander, 1975) offers a promising avenue that should enhance our understanding of the development of the infant self during the separation-individuation process. Finally, while Mahler describes a fascinating normative developmental sequence, there is virtually no discussion of individual differences in the rate of development through these phases, nor is much attention devoted to how differences in the nature or quality of the mother-infant relationship might facil-

itate or interfere with separation and individuation. Mahler (1968) and McDevitt (1975) do observe that infants who appear to have the most positive relationship with their mothers are more likely to make independent forays into the environment, show less hostility, and cling less to the mother during the rapprochement stage. However, these observations on the role of the mother-child relationship have not been systematically documented. One must turn to those representing the ethological approach for a comprehensive treatment of this issue.

The Ethological Approach

Those proponents of the ethological approach who have studied attachment provide the clearest convergence and extension of Mahler's account (see Ainsworth, 1972, 1973, 1974, 1979; Ainsworth, Blehar, Waters, & Wall, 1978; Bowlby, 1969, 1973; Sroufe & Waters, 1977). Since this body of work has not been specifically directed toward the infant's sense of self, only a few findings most relevant to the preceding discussion will be highlighted.

Normative-Developmental Sequence

It was Bowlby who first distinguished between four phases in the development of child-mother attachment, and Ainsworth and her colleagues have elaborated on this sequence. The initial *preattachment* phase corresponds to Mahler's description of the period of normal "autistic" and "symbiotic" behavior prior to the first phase of differentiation. The infant can engage in behaviors representing signals to the caretaker that promote proximity and contact; however, the infant cannot discriminate the mother figure from others. Ainsworth's second phase, *attachment in the making*, corresponds to Mahler's phase of *differentiation*. The infant discriminates between mother and other people, is more likely to direct its proximity-promoting behaviors toward mother, and is comforted more readily by her when distressed.

The third phase of *clear-cut attachment* encompasses Mahler's next two phases, *practicing* and *rapprochement*. Locomotion now serves the attachment system, and the infant follows, greets, and actively seeks proximity and contact with the mother. The infant also begins to actively explore its environment, when attachment behavior is at a low level of activation. For Ainsworth, attachment figures thus provide "a secure base" from which the infant can move out to explore its world. However, the interlocking of the attachment system and the exploration system prevents the infant from straying too far or for too long. Here one sees an obvious convergence with Mahler, who describes the "refueling process" whereby the exploring infant returns to the mother for emotional supplies.

During this third phase of clear-cut attachment, separation distress is particularly likely to occur, a behavior that is viewed as very adaptive for the active, mobile child. Person permanence is well established and, from the behavior manifest during this period, Ainsworth infers that the infant has an inner representation of the attachment figures and of the self in relation to them. The cognitive advance of this period allows the infant to anticipate how its mother is likely to act in certain situations, and to adjust its proximity accordingly; however, there are limits to the infant's ability to understand and control those maternal behaviors that are not directed toward its own egocentric needs. Thus distress, frustration, and anger are often the result.

The fourth phase of *goal-corrected partnership* approximates Mahler's last phase of resolution and consolidation. The child has developed a greater understanding of factors that influence the mother's behavior, and can more skillfully induce her to accommodate her plans to the child's own desires, or reach some compromise.

Individual Differences in Attachment

A major contribution of the Ainsworth group is the documentation of individual differences in patterns of attachment (see Ainsworth, Bell, & Stayton, 1971; Ainsworth et. al., 1978), an issue Mahler does not address. These attachment patterns have been revealed in an impressive programmatic effort in which infants' reactions to the "Strange Situation" have been the primary data base. This experimental situation was devised to capture several clinically and theoretically derived indices of attachment, for example, use of mother as a secure base for exploration, preference for mother versus a stranger, and use of the mother as a haven of safety. This situation consists of a series of episodes involving a preseparation phase, the entrance of a stranger, mother's departure leading to separation, and reunion. Behaviors observed during the separation phase include proximity and contact with the stranger, and search for mother. Behaviors observed during the reunion include proximity and contact with the mother, distancing, resistance, and avoidance of mother.

Based on infants' reactions to the strange situation, in particular the reunion episodes, three general types of attachment patterns have been identified:

Type A—Avoidant: These infants are not particularly stressed by the separation and on reunion tend to look at or move away from the mother.

Type B—Securely Attached: These infants do not remain particularly close to the mother during a preliminary phase of play and exploration, show distress during separation, and when the mother returns, go to her immediately, seeking contact, after which they are able to resume play.

Type C—Resistant: These infants are fussy during the separation phase, and do not easily use the mother as a secure base for exploration. On reunion they simultaneously seek contact but resist, manifesting anger. While they may reach to be picked up, they then struggle to be released.

The major thrust of this research program has been to demonstrate the stability of these typologies longitudinally during the period of infancy and early childhood and to examine how differences in mother caretaking style affect the particular pattern of attachment. For example, mothers have been rated on the following dimensions: sensitivity–insensitivity, acceptance–rejection, cooperation–interference, accessibility–ignoring (see Ainsworth, Bell, & Stayton, 1971). The general pattern suggests that mothers of securely attached (Type B) infants score above the midpoint on all four dimensions, whereas mothers of avoidant (Type A) infants tend to be insensitive and rejecting, while mothers of resistant (Type C) infants tend to be either interfering or ignoring.

Of what relevance are these findings for students of the self? They clearly provide a general framework for considering self in relation to other, and they suggest that differences in the quality of the mother-infant relationship may influence the young child's emerging sense of self. However, to date, investigators have not yet examined how these typologies, and the interactive categories upon which they are based, are specifically related to the development of self. Sroufe and his colleagues (see Sroufe & Waters, 1977) have begun to address this issue, in terms of how individual differences in attachment might predict certain behaviors in early childhood, particularly behaviors within the peer context. They suggest that securely attached infants would be expected to manifest competence, confidence in their relationships with others, and positive self-esteem. Avoidant infants, they hypothesize, might be expected to be self-isolates, whereas resistant infants would be expected to have low self-esteem and low social acceptance from peers.

A recent scale which our own group has developed, The Pictorial Scale of Perceived Competence and Acceptance for Young Children (Harter & Pike, 1981), may allow for an even more differentiated pattern of predictions. This scale taps four domains: cognitive competence, physical competence, peer acceptance, and maternal acceptance. A two-factor solution best describes the scale structure with a *competence* factor (cognitive and physical competence subscales) and an *acceptance* factor (peer and maternal acceptance). However, each subscale has a sufficiently high reliability to be considered separately, if desired.

Of the three attachment types, one would predict that the children who had been *securely* attached (Type B) would perceive themselves to be relatively competent and well accepted by mother and peers. The positive mother-infant bond should lead to perceived acceptance by mother, and the security of this social relationship should facilitate the establishment of peer friendships. The Type B's early pattern of exploring and manipulating the environment, from the secure base provided by the mother, should enhance the infant's effectance motivation and resulting feelings of competence (see Harter, 1978, 1980; White, 1959). Perceived competence may also serve to enhance the child's popularity with peers.

Children who had been typed as *avoidant* infants, Type A, would be expected to score particularly low on the maternal acceptance scale, given that this type of mother has been found to be relatively insensitive and rejecting. However, since such infants seem able to engage in some positive exploration of their environment, scores on the competence dimension may not be attenuated as much as scores on the acceptance dimension, although they would be expected to be lower than those of the securely attached Type B infant. Peer social acceptance is somewhat difficult to predict for this group, though one would expect it to suffer.

Children who had been typed as *resistant*, Type C, would be expected to have feelings of low competence as well as low acceptance. Given that they were unable to use the mother as a secure base for exploration, coupled with the tendency for their mothers to be interfering or ignoring, this constellation would be expected to undermine their sense of efficacy and competence. The ambivalent nature of the mother-infant bond would lead to the prediction of low perceived mother acceptance. Low mother acceptance coupled with low perceived competence may both serve to influence one's feelings of low peer acceptance.

This is but one suggestion for the direction in which we might proceed in examining the relationship between early mother-infant interaction patterns and the child's sense of self. At the suggestion of Connell and Goldsmith (1981), we may do well to extend our inquiry beyond an examination of how typologies alone predict other variables of interest. These investigators have discussed the limitations of typological systems, and have urged a more multidimensional conceptualization of those processes related to attachment. They have presented a structural equation model in which the analyses of scores tapping separate dimensions, for example, proximity-seeking toward mother, distance interaction with mother, contact-maintaining with mother, resistance toward mother, reveal various latent constructs of interest. For example, proximity-seeking toward mother and distance interaction with mother define a construct that they label "initial proximity-seeking," whereas contact-maintaining with mother and resistance toward mother both define a latent construct that they label "resistance/ambivalence."

Scores can be derived for these latent constructs, then, rather than a typological classification, and can be related to other variables of interest. It may well be, for example, that particular constructs such as proximity-seeking and resistance/ambivalence may relate more highly to subsequent perceived *acceptance* by mother, whereas other constructs, for example, exploration using mother as a secure base, would relate more highly to subsequent perceived *competence*. This type of an approach appears to be a fruitful avenue to pursue in furthering our understanding about the relationship between early mother-infant interaction patterns and dimensions of the self.

Sander's Model of Mother-Infant Interaction and the Emerging Self

Sander (1964, 1969, 1975) has formulated what he considers to be an epigenetic sequence of the adaptive issues negotiated in the mother-infant interaction, during the first three years of life. In doing, he places considerably more emphasis on the *infant's* role in the interactional process than does Mahler, and explores the implications for the infant's developing sense of self. Sander's data base comes from an extensive longitudinal study that included home observations, interviews with mothers, infant examinations, and play interviews extending into the third year of life.

Each of the seven stages is defined by an issue

associated with particular behaviors that mother and infant must coordinate. During stage 1 (1–3 months), the issue of *initial regulation* is manifest in the establishment of a predictable, comfortable pattern of sleeping, feeding, elimination, quieting, and arousal. The second stage of *reciprocal exchange* (4–6 months) marks the first coordinated back-and-forth exchanges between mother and infant during feeding, dressing, and simple play. During the third stage of infant *initiative* (7–9 months), the infant chooses or initiates activities in order to secure a reciprocal social exchange with the mother. *Focalization* defines the major issue of the fourth stage (10–13 months) in that the infant now focuses its need-meeting demands on the mother. The infant's activities appear to be concerned with the active, intentionally directed manipulation of the mother, as well as with the limits she sets. If these limits are consistent and constructive, they provide a basis for the infant to turn toward a wider mastery of the world beyond the mother.

In describing the latter stages, 5 through 7, Sander specifically highlights the implications for the developing sense of self. During the fifth stage of *self-assertion* (14–20 months), the infant, now able to explore and manipulate its world, begins to determine goals and activities independent of the mother, at times in opposition to the mother's wishes. Sander notes the convergence between his account of the infant's budding sense of autonomy and Spitz's (1957) description of the toddler's heightened awareness of his or her own intentionality, which may be thwarted by the constraints of socializing agents. For Spitz, this initiates the emergence of the "I" experience.

During the sixth stage of *recognition*, beginning at about 18 months, new advances in representational skills and language allow the toddler to develop some appreciation for her or his "inner" intentions, fantasies, and wishes. For Sander, the coordination of verbal communication between mother and toddler constitutes "a first level in the experience of self-recognition, namely realization that another can be aware of what one is aware of in oneself, that is, a shared awareness" (1975, p. 142). Negotiations of this issue set the stage for the seventh and final step in this epigenetic sequence, the development of a sense of continuity or "*self*" constancy.

Consistent with Mahler, Sander describes the directed aggressive behavior during this period; however, he attaches a more cognitive interpretation to the provocations of the terrible two. For Sander, the

disruption and subsequent restoration of a coordinated relationship between toddler and caretaker is necessary in order to experience a " 'reversal' in regard to self-constancy" (p. 143). That is, the toddler learns that he or she can take a stance contrary to that of the caretaker, but that one's "good self" will still be recognized by the caretaker such that the facilitative pattern of interaction can be restored. According to Sander's analysis, this type of reversibility is necessary in order that the toddler develop self-schemata based on a sense of self-constancy, namely, that self as active initiator or organizer is "conserved."

Sander's model provides a welcome addition to the existing stage theories of infancy, which have tended to highlight either the cognitive implications of the child's interactions with the inanimate world of objects (Piaget, 1954, 1963) or the role that mother-infant interaction plays in the child's emotional development (Mahler, 1968). Of utmost relevance for this chapter is Sander's description of a sequence of coordinated mother-infant interactions that provide the social context for the infant's emerging sense of self. Self, in this model, refers primarily to the development of internalized schemata or cognitive operations for the self as an active agent who is constant and continuous, conserved, as it were, across a variety of behaviors and situations. Thus, Sander focuses more on the emerging awareness of the self as subject, the "I," than the self as object, the "Me." His analysis of the role of aggressive behaviors in promoting a reversible self-concept is particularly intriguing, although it represents quite an extrapolation from his data. One would like to see his model stimulate a more specific empirical attack on those parameters of the self that his stage descriptions imply.

Summary of the Self During Infancy

In discussing the various approaches to the emergence of self during infancy, emphasis was placed on the gradual nature of this process. Table 2 summarizes in comparative fashion the phases postulated by the major theoretical positions presented.

The visual recognition studies provide evidence of a sequence of self-other differentiation in which the infant first develops a sense of the self as subject, as an active agent independent of other active agents. Subsequent to this developmental acquisition, the infant comes to appreciate the self as a physical object with invariant features that it can recognize and differentiate from others as recogniz-

Table 2. Summary of Stage Models Related to the Infant's Development of Self

Approximate Ages	Visual Recognition Studies	Mahler's Phases of Separation–Individuation	Ainsworth's Phases of Attachment	Sander's Stages of Mother–Infant Interaction
0–5	(1) No self-other differentiation	(1) Normal, autistic and symbiotic phases	(1) Preattachment phase	(1) Initial regulation
5–10	(2) Awareness of bodily self as cause of movement	(2) Differentiation	(2) Attachment in the making	(2) Reciprocal exchange
10–15	(3) Differentiation of self as active agent from others	(3) Practicing	(3) Clear-cut attachment	(3) Initiative (4) Focalization
15–20	(4) Featural recognition of self	(4) Rapprochement		(5) Self-assertion
18+	(5) Verbal labeling of the self	(5) Resolution and consolidation	(4) Goal-corrected partnership	(6) Recognition (7) Self-constancy

able objects. It was suggested that self as *agent* is learned *prior* to other as agent, whereas self as a recognizable *object* is learned *after* other as a recognizable object, at least with regard to the visual modality. The singular emphasis on the infant's response to the self as a visual image presented in mirrors or depicted in video and pictorial representations limits the generalizability of these findings, however. We may be learning more about the infant's developing understanding of reflective surfaces and pictorial modes of representation than about the infant's emerging sense of self, more broadly defined and experienced.

Margaret Mahler's stage descriptions of separation and individuation provide a model of self-other differentiation with a more socioemotional thrust. Mother takes center stage in this analysis, where the infant's ultimate developmental task is the development of maternal object constancy. That is, the infant must develop a stable or constant intrapsychic representation of mother that can be emotionally comforting to the infant in the mother's absence. Given this focus, Mahler's theory deals more with the infant's developing representations of mother than of the self. The stage descriptions of the attachment process as presented by those proponents of the ethological approach, notably Bowlby and the Ainsworth group, provide clear points of convergence. Beyond this, the major contribution of this group would appear to be the delineation of individual differences in the pattern or nature of the attachment bond. These differences may have critical implications for the child's developing sense of self, an issue investigators are now beginning to explore.

Although the visual recognition studies present quite a different picture of the infant compared to those formulations that emphasize emotional attachment to the mother, we do not have to theoretically adjudicate the case of mirror versus mother. Both are reflective surfaces, each of which provides different sources of feedback aiding the infant's understanding of self. We do, however, eventually need to integrate these frameworks in order to provide a comprehensive model of the development of self-understanding.

Sander's model would appear to take a first step in this direction, indicating how the particular features of the mother-infant interaction provide the impetus for the infant's emerging sense of self. His focus is primarily on those cognitive representations that come to define the self as an active agent, schemata that form the basis for one's sense of self-constancy. Ultimately, a synthesis must also incorporate the infant's developing awareness of self as an object with numerous features and characteristics that can be recognized, labeled, and evaluated. In the next section, we will deal with those few studies that have attempted to examine the young child's first self-definitions, charting the elaborations that self-descriptions undergo with development.

THE CONSTRUCTION OF THE SELF DURING CHILDHOOD

The orientation of this chapter highlights the self as an active cognitive construction, continually undergoing developmental change. Within this context, we can ask how the changing cognitive processes that define the "I" as knower and observer influence the nature of the self-theory the child is constructing. We can also address how the characteristics and categories that define the self as the "Me," the self as observed, also change with age. The "I" question deals primarily with the *structure* of the self-theory, whereas the "Me" question focuses on the *contents* of one's self-description. With this as a framework, we can further consider in what sense the self as subject, the "I," is *aware* of the self as object, the "Me," and how self-awareness changes with development.

These questions must necessarily be raised within the social context of examining the self in relation to other. As noted in the introduction, the differentiation of self and other is not a developmental task restricted to the period of infancy, but takes on new dimensions during childhood. Another salient issue involves how the judgments of significant others affect one's concept of self. This, in turn, involves an examination of the interface between cognitive-developmental factors and social influences, in the form of perspective-taking. As we will see, the ability to take the perspective of the other has important implications for the development of self-awareness.

The Self as a Self-Theory

The general view that the self can be likened to theory, constructed to organize one's thinking about one's relationship to the social world, has had many proponents (e.g., Brim, 1976a; Epstein, 1973; Kelly, 1955; Sarbin, 1962). The analogy has been drawn for adults, for the most part.

Kelly's (1955) theory of personal constructs is a prime example. Constructs, for Kelly, represented one's personal version of reality, and "the self is, when considered in the appropriate context, a proper concept or construct" (p. 131). In Kelly's formulation, the self-system is hierarchically organized into core constructs—those by which a person maintains identity and existence—and peripheral constructs that can be altered without serious modifications of the core structure. These self-constructs function as postulates in a theory that serves to organize and guide behavior.

Brim (1976a) takes the analogy further. "What humans learn during life are axioms, concepts, and hypotheses about themselves in relation to the world around them. We can think of the sense of self as a personal epistemology, similar to theories in science in its components and its operations, but dealing with a specific person" (p. 242). Brim favors the term self-*theory* to self-concept, a sterile notion that, in his opinion, has impeded our understanding of the processes that define the self.

Sarbin (1962) shares the focus on process, emphasizing the self as an empirically derived cognitive structure or inference. "The self (in common with other cognitive structures) is subject to continual and progressive change, usually in the direction from lower-order inferences about simple perception to higher-order inferences about complex cognitions" (p. 12).

Recent adult information-processing models have also been brought to bear on the self. Markus has explicitly proposed (1977; 1980) that attempts to organize, summarize, or explain one's *own* behavior will result in the formation of cognitive structures about the self, what she terms *self-schemata*. "Self-schemata are cognitive generalizations about the self, derived from past experience, that organize and guide the processing of self-related information contained in the individual's social experience" (p. 64). She traces the historical roots of this particular term to the work of Bartlett (1932), Kelley (1972), Kelly (1955), and Piaget (1965).

The self-schemata Markus has focused on involve traits such as independent versus dependent (1977), sex-role schemata (Markus, Crane, & Siladi, 1979), and self-schemata involving creativity as well as body weight (see Markus, 1980). Her experimental paradigm allows her to distinguish between adults with strong self-schemata and those she labels as "aschematics," people for whom a given dimension is not particularly relevant to their self-concept. She has demonstrated that those with well-articulated self-schemata for a particular trait or dimension can more readily process information about the self, retrieve behavioral evidence, predict their future behavior, resist counter-schematic information about the self, and evaluate the relevance of new information, all with regard to that dimension.

Markus has concentrated primarily on the manner in which isolated self-schemata in the form of single-trait labels affect how information is processed and retrieved. Others, notably Cantor and Mischel (1979), have turned their attention to the manner in which trait terms are hierarchically organized into "person prototypes," which are created to describe *other* people. These investigators suggest that information about the *self* may be organized in similar fashion; however, they have yet to determine how person prototypes and hierarchical taxonomies specifically apply to self-description, nor has this issue been investigated from a developmental perspective.

Lynch (1981) has provided a promising developmental framework, viewing the self-concept as a set of rules for processing information that in turn regulates behavior. The task of the developmentalist, then, is to look for age differences in the formation and validation of rules that apply not only to the child's beliefs about the external world, but about the self as well. Lynch suggests several general developmental shifts that occur over the periods of early and middle childhood. In particular, he has directed his attention to the affective consequences for the child when rules about the self are not validated, for example, frustration, anxiety, aggression, and apathy, which may eventually lead to alterations in the self-concept.

Epstein (1973) provides the most elaborate analysis of the self as a theory: "I submit that the self-concept is a self-theory. It is a theory that the individual has unwittingly constructed about himself as an experiencing, functioning individual, and is part of a broader theory which he holds with respect to his entire range of significant experience. Accordingly, there are major postulate systems for the nature of the world, for the nature of the self, and for their interaction" (p. 407). Self-theory, in Epstein's view, possesses all the formal characteristics of a hypothetico-deductive system. It can be evaluated, therefore, by the degree to which it is extensive, parsimonious, empirically valid, internally consistent, testable, and useful. Epstein also sees the self-theory as obeying an inherent growth principle, since one characteristic of a theory, of a *good* theory, is to increase in scope with exposure to new data.

Epstein's formulation appears to go beyond those of other theorists in specifying the purpose of self-theory as a conceptual tool. Its most fundamental purpose is to optimize the pleasure/pain balance of the individual over the course of a lifetime. Two related functions are to maintain self-esteem and to organize the data of experience in a manner that can be coped with effectively. The central importance assigned to affect is one feature that distinguishes Epstein's view from others who have translated the term "self-concept" into self-theory.

Greenwald's (1980) recent position comes the closest to Epstein's in delineating the functions that are served by the self as an organization of knowledge. He notes that the self is characterized by cognitive biases that are strikingly analogous to totalitarian information-control strategies that function to preserve the organization of the structure. He identifies three such biases: (a) egocentricity, wherein the self is perceived as the axis of cause and effect, and therefore is assigned a more central role than is true in reality; (b) beneffectance, a neologism compounding beneficience and effectance (White, 1959), which refers to one's perception of the self as selectively responsible for desired, but not undesired, outcomes; and (c) conservatism, namely, resistance to cognitive change. Greenwald brings considerable evidence to bear on his argument, drawing on recent models of information-processing and self-perception.

Cognitive-Developmental Implications

For the most part, theorists who have described the self as a theory or cognitive construction have not been developmentally oriented. Sarbin (1962) has postulated a sequence during the first two years of life marking the transition from the somatic to the social self, and Epstein has considered the sequential emergence of three self subsystems, the bodily self, the inferred inner or psychological self, and the moral self. However, these theorists do not deal with the implications of how the child's changing cognitive structures might alter the very fabric of the self-theory. For example, the nature of the self-theory as described by Epstein would not be observed developmentally until adolescence at best, during the period of formal operations. Thus, in this section, the implications of cognitive-developmental changes in the child theorist will be examined from a Piagetian perspective, beginning with the period of preoperational thought.

During infancy the emergence of representational thought and the development of language make featural recognition and the labeling of concrete characteristics such as gender and age grouping possible (Lewis & Brooks-Gunn, 1979b). During the preoperational period, we would anticipate the proliferation of categories the child can use to define the self. However, we would not expect these to be logically ordered or hierarchically arranged, nor would we expect them to have any stability, from the child's perspective. While the young female child may insist that today she is a girl, she may also maintain that she could change genders and become a boy in the future, as Kohlberg's (1966) work on the lack of gender conservation has demonstrated.

The preoperational child would also not be expected to systematically test hypotheses about those characteristics that define the self. Isolated attributes may well be documented, for example, "I'm strong, look at me, I can lift this block." However, if the child could not lift a chair in a subsequent life episode, the child would not be troubled by the contradiction in logic. On balance, our young theorist's construction of self would fail to meet most of Epstein's criteria, with the possible exception of usefulness. In addition, the preoperational child does not yet possess the role-taking skills necessary to cognitively construct Cooley's "looking glass self" or to invoke Mead's "generalized other."

During the concrete operational period, the emergence of logical thinking should produce qualitative changes in the nature of the child's self-theory. The child's ability to hierarchically classify, and the penchant for logically organizing, the concrete events, objects, and people in one's life may also be extended to attempts to define the attributes of the self. Thus, the child would be expected to consolidate and verify certain contents of the self, primarily one's concrete, observable characteristics. Attributes in the self-theory would also show some hierarchical organization, for example, "I'm smart (higher-order trait) because I'm good at reading, spelling, and math" (lower-order behavioral characteristics). We would expect the child of this stage to proceed *inductively,* however, piecing together bits of data from experience in order to construct a puzzle of the self. He or she does not yet possess the capabilities to test more formal hypotheses in a highly systematic, deductive manner. The child should be able to test isolated postulates in the self-theory primarily through the ability to make social comparisons, to treat oneself as an object of knowledge and simultaneously compare one's own characteristics to those of others. The concrete operational child, therefore, has self-knowledge in the form of attributes and categories that apply to the self. However, the child cannot yet think about either one's own thinking, or the process of theory-building itself.

Newfound perspective-taking skills also equip the concrete operational child with the ability to imagine what *other* people are thinking, and in particular what they are thinking of him or her. Therefore, the child can begin to construct a rudimentary "generalized other" (Mead, 1934) or in Cooley's (1902) terms, a "self-idea." All three components of this self-idea would appear to emerge during the period of concrete operations: the imagination of how one appears to others, how they judge or evaluate that appearance, and an affective reaction or "self-feeling" such as pride or embarrassment. For Mead, the term "self-consciousness" captures this process whereby one is conscious of being judged by others, which in turn causes one to be conscious of the self that is being evaluated. Thus, the child's self-theory is marked by a new skill in the emergence of the ability for self-evaluation.

During adolescence, formal operational thought appears and with it the capacity for hypothetico-deductive reasoning. These skills not only imply the powers of deduction, but a preoccupation with the hypothetical. As Flavell (1963) has noted, reality becomes only a small subset of the concerns the adolescent confronts. Moreover, the adolescent is capable of introspection; one can reflect on one's own thoughts, feelings, and motives, which emerge as powerful new constructs in theorizing about the self and one's "personality." Self-theory, à la Epstein, would appear to emerge full-blown during this period.

The adolescent's theory of self most certainly meets Epstein's criterion for being extensive, if not expansive, with increasing awareness of one's feelings, abilities, and personality characteristics. The criterion involving empirical validation may be somewhat problematic. As Epstein notes, higher-order postulates assimilate lower-order constructs that represent generalizations derived from experience. However, he describes a potential hazard in that it is also possible for one to misrepresent reality, particularly when inferences extend beyond data. The newly acquired abilities for abstraction, which may not yet be completely under the adolescent's cognitive control, may well result in such overgeneralizations.

Epstein also notes that one's experiences are not the only factors that determine whether a concept will be assimilated into an individual's self-theory. One also must consider the "need for internal consistency and a need to maintain the organization of the self-system. To satisfy these other conditions, it is at times necessary to sacrifice empirical validity" (p. 409). Empirical validity will also suffer if the organization of a self-theory is under stress and defenses are inadequate. This constellation may well characterize the conditions under which the adolescent is struggling to achieve a coherent self-definition and a stable identity.

This type of developmental analysis appears promising, particularly in suggesting that we consider the self as *subject,* as knower and theorist, to be a legitimate domain of psychological inquiry. The vast majority of studies in the literature have equated the self-concept with the "Me" as an *object* of one's knowledge, investigating the attributes, schemas, motives, and affects people ascribe to themselves (see Wylie, 1979). Far less attention has been directed to the characteristics of the "I," the active agent who constructs this knowledge. In part, we have William James to blame. James (1890/1963) wrestled with the question of precisely what was the thinker, ultimately rejecting numerous definitions including any notion of a soul, ego, or spirit. He finally concluded that there is no knower as such, no substantive self distinguishable from our experiences, but only a stream of consciousness. James reached what he considered to be the final word on the self as subject: "the thoughts themselves are the thinker" (p. 198).

Our understanding of the developing child's sense of self, however, can only be complete if we resurrect the "I." As Gordon (1968) notes, "If it is assumed that this *I,* or continuing process of individual experience, establishes the perspective and contextual ground for much of the person's perception and interpretation, the features of the self-as-experiencer offer almost unlimited opportunities for the student of cognitive processes" (p. 115). Unfortunately for students of development, Gordon goes on to state that "The Me, or self-as-experienced, is of more direct social-psychological concern." He does not urge that we examine the manner in which the "I" as a cognitive process serves to structure and define the "Me," but focuses on how the individual's socialization experiences shape one's self-conceptions. As the preceding cognitive-developmental analysis suggests, we need to do both.

Developmental Differences in Self-Description: Empirical Evidence

We have relatively little empirical evidence pertaining to how the self is constructed or how, from a cognitive-developmental perspective, it changes in content and structure. Those few studies that have been conducted focus on the child's description of those characteristics perceived to be central to the self. As such, these descriptions primarily illuminate developmental changes in the self as observed, the "Me."

In the chapter section on infancy, we saw how the infant first develops a sense of self as an independent sensorimotor agent. Subsequently, the infant learns to recognize certain physical characteristics that define this bodily self. The first self-descriptions that apply to the "categorical self," in the terminology of Lewis and Brooks-Gunn (1979b), are category labels that refer to age groupings (baby, child, adult) and gender, as well as race (see Van Parys, 1980; Wylie, 1979). There are relatively few data, however, that specifically bear on the cognitive-developmental analysis presented, particularly during the toddler and preschool years.

Gender Identity

Children's understanding of their gender has received the most attention. The learning of one's own gender label is accomplished by the end of the second year (see Lewis & Brooks-Gunn, 1979b; Thompson, 1975). However, as Kohlberg (1966) initially demonstrated, *constancy* of gender is not complete before the ages of 5 to 7. Other investigators have documented this finding (deVries, 1969; Marcus & Overton, 1978) and have also found support for Kohlberg's suggestion that gender constancy for self precedes that for others (see also Gouze & Nadelman, 1980). The cognitive-developmental interpretation relates children's initial lack of gender constancy to their inability to solve conservation tasks, which requires an appreciation of constancy in the physical world. There is some support for a relationship between conservation of physical quantities and "conservation of gender" (Kohlberg, 1966), with more recent evidence indicating that conservation of physical quantities developmentally precedes gender constancy (Marcus & Overton, 1978).

It could be argued that conservation of one's gender may well require a learning process more complex than an appreciation of conservation in the physical world. In the typical conservation task, the actual amount, weight, or volume of the substance does not, in fact, change, even though it may *appear* to change to the young child. The task for the child is to learn not to base his or her judgments on the mere perceptual appearance of objects. In contrast, most of the physical characteristics that define the young child's bodily self actually *do* change. One changes dramatically in height, weight, volume, strength, and may also undergo changes in hair length, hair color, or even skin color with exposure to sun. Body proportions change, as do certain features such as the shape of the nose. Thus, there is no psychological set for the constancy of one's physical characteristics; for any continuity in the bodily self, so defined.

Furthermore, socializing agents appear to under-

score, to value change, and to communicate this to their young children. We commonly overhear parents, grandparents, and teachers utter approvingly: "My, what a big boy you're getting to be!" "You weren't that tall last time Grandma saw you!" "You're getting prettier every day." "Look how strong you are, you didn't use to be able to do that!" "You're getting so smart, you know your letters now!" We not only reinforce changes in physical characteristics and attributes of skill, but single out certain membership categories as well, for example, "Now you're a big first grader!" With this tremendous emphasis on change, it isn't surprising that the young child may assume that gender may also undergo transformation. Why should one believe otherwise?

Developmentalists have tended to put the onus on the characteristic fluidity of preoperational thought that they view as primarily responsible for the conceptual instabilities we have documented. The above analysis suggests that we also take account of the inconstancies in the physical and social environment, especially inconstancies that pertain to the defining features of the self. The cognitive task for the child is to learn which characteristics are constant and therefore do not undergo change, and which characteristics can be expected to change. He or she must also learn to discriminate between those characteristics that define categories such as age (e.g., height, facial features, voice) and those characteristics that unequivocally define gender (e.g., genitals at all ages, secondary sex characteristics for adolescents and for adults). Finally, the child must integrate this information in order to appreciate the fact that the majority of physical characteristics that define *age do* change with age, whereas the *primary* characteristics that define gender do not. With this knowledge comes the awareness that gender is constant, whereas age is not.

Self-Identity

Guardo and Bohan (1971) have taken a broader look at the dimensions of what they term "self-identity," employing children between the ages of 6 and 9. Based on Guardo's (1968) earlier work, they devised a semi-structured Piagetian-type interview that assessed four facets of self-identity: (a) the child's perception of his or her humanness (as distinguished from lower animals), (b) his or her gender identity, (c) his or her perception of himself as an individual distinct from other same-gender children, and (d) his or her sense of self as continuous from the past to the future. The term *self-identity* is analogous to the term *constancy,* as Kohlberg and others have used it.

The large majority of children between the ages of 6 and 9 demonstrated such constancy. That is, the children felt that they could not change and become an animal, a child of the opposite gender, or even a different child of the same gender.

However, developmental differences were observed in the reasons given by children for these constancy judgments. The younger children, ages 6 and 7, tended to base their conclusions on externally observable perceptual or behavioral features, whereas the older children cited more covert differences in feelings, thoughts, and interests. The fourth issue of "continuity" involved the child's perception of whether she or he had always been the same person and would continue to be the same person in the future. Of interest was the finding that young children frequently cited their unchanging name as the basis of self-sameness, a finding the authors related to Piaget's concept of nominal realism (Piaget, 1965). Older children seemed to recognize that names were arbitrary designations, and cited other characteristics as the basis for their sameness over time. The results of this study suggest that self-identity or constancy of one's sense of self becomes crystallized during the concrete operational period. However, it would be interesting to determine how these constancies are first established during the transition from preoperational to concrete operational thought.

Defining Features of the Self: Cross-sectional Evidence

The few studies attempting to document age changes in children's self-descriptions have been relatively recent (Bannister & Agnew, 1977; McGuire, 1981; McGuire & McGuire, 1980; McGuire & Padawer-Singer, 1976; Montemayor & Eisen, 1977; Mullener & Laird, 1971; Rosenberg, 1979). One strategy has been to apply traditional classification systems for coding the contents of one's self-conceptions (e.g., Gordon, 1968) to the responses of children at different developmental levels. Both Gordon and McGuire have been critical of adult self-concept scales that they view as restrictive, since they force adults to react to dimensions of adjective checklists preselected by the investigator. In addition to a narrow focus on the "reactive" as opposed to the "spontaneous" self, McGuire has also been concerned that the preponderance of dimensions selected forces subjects to evaluate "how *good* I am" and not "*what* I am."

As a methodological alternative, both Gordon and McGuire have allowed subjects to represent themselves in any manner possible through their responses to the open question "Who am I?" In so doing, they have built on the tradition of earlier investigators, notably Bugenthal and Zelen (1950) and Kuhn and McPartland (1954). An elaborate content coding system has been developed by Gordon that taps such dimensions as ascribed characteristics, roles and membership, abstract identifications, interests and activities, personality characteristics, sense of moral worth, and of self-determination, competence, and sense of unity. For adult samples, Gordon has analyzed the frequency distribution depicting spontaneous mention of responses that could be coded into these categories and subcategories, thereby providing a picture of the dimensions perceived as most relevant to adults' self-representation.

Montemayor and Eisen (1977) have performed the most widely quoted study in which this task, as well as Gordon's coding system, was employed with children. These investigators found that over the 10- to 18-year-old range there are *increases* in the use of the following categories: occupational role, existential self, ideological and belief references, sense of self-determination, sense of unity, interpersonal style, and psychic style (how one typically feels and thinks). Developmental *decreases* were found for three categories: territoriality and citizenship; possessions; and the physical self, or body image. Curvilinear relationships, typically with a dip in the middle age groups (12 through 16), were found for gender, name, kinship role, membership in an abstract category, and judgments, tastes, or likes. They interpret their findings as support for the general hypothesis that with increasing age an individual's self-concept becomes more abstract and less concrete. They conclude: "The children in this study primarily describe themselves in terms of concrete, objective categories such as their address, physical appearance, possessions, and play activities, while the adolescents use more abstract and subjective descriptions such as personal beliefs, motivational and interpersonal characteristics" (p. 317).

This general conclusion is certainly plausible. However, there are potential problems when an adult category system is employed, and responses from different developmental levels are placed into these existing categories and then interpreted in similar fashion for children of every developmental level. The author's perplexity over the curvilinear relationships obtained highlights the interpretive hazards. Gender is one such category. Why might gender take a dip during those middle years or, conversely, why should it assume greater importance for the younger and older subjects? Any interpretation rests on the meaning of gender as a defining characteristic at each of these ages. It may well be that for the younger ages, its mention reflects the consolidation of one's gender identity or constancy (see Guardo & Bohan, 1971) that can then be put to rest for some years as a central issue. Its resurgence at 18 undoubtedly signals a very different concern, best interpreted within the context of one's social and sexual relationships.

We find a similar problem with the category entitled "membership in an abstract category," where the investigators register surprise at the peaks and valleys in their developmental curve. Consider the fact that any of the following responses were coded in this category: a person, a human, a speck in the universe. For the 10-year-old, the term "person" is, in all likelihood, not abstract at all but a very concrete designation that one now has an identity that is unique and distinct from that of others (see Bannister & Agnew, 1977). Guardo and Bohan (1971) employ the term "personeity" to describe this awareness, which they feel becomes consolidated at about this age. In Gesell and Ilg's (1946) norms on the self, the first use of the term "person" occurs at age 6 with the recognition that one is a separate entity, similar to others but unique in oneself. Gesell and Ilg quote the musings of one 6-year-old: "Mommy is a person, Daddy is a person, I am a person. Three persons." At later developmental stages, the term "person" seems to make greater reference to membership in the common club of humanity. One would undoubtedly attach yet another interpretation to a comment such as "a speck in the universe," which conveys a much more philosophical, existential outlook. It would seem, then, that the most thoughtful developmental analysis would attempt to probe the psychological meaning of these verbal responses at different developmental levels rather than to lump them together as a single category and describe changes in the frequency of use at different ages.

Montemayor and Eisen sought to find evidence that self-concept development could be described according to Werner's orthogenetic principle in which there is "increasing differentiation, articulation, and hierarchic integration" with age (Werner, 1957, p. 126). They would like to conclude from their data that, during adolescence, "earlier notions drop out or are integrated into a more complex picture" (p. 318). Their results, as analyzed, do not warrant such a conclusion, nor have they really addressed their goal squarely, "to extend the cognitive-structural perspective to the area of self-concept development" (p. 315). That is, their data do not

bear directly on issues of the differentiation, integration, and organization of these self-descriptors. What they have documented are developmental differences in the frequency with which separate *content* categories, derived from an adult coding system, are utilized. Issues involving the appropriateness of this system for children—its meaning at different age levels as well as possible cognitive-structural changes with age—have yet to be addressed. The purpose of this critique is not to indict these particular investigators. However, since their study is one of the few in this literature, it has been discussed in some detail in order to highlight very critical conceptual and methodological issues that we must take seriously in our efforts to understand the developmental parameters of one's sense of self.

In two studies (Keller, Ford, & Meacham, 1978; Rosenberg, 1979) the issue of choice of categories has been addressed by asking relatively open-ended questions and then examining the data to determine which categories naturally emerge. In the Keller et al. study of 3- to 5-year-olds, nine categories of self-descriptions could be identified. There were: actions, relationships with others, body image, possessions, personal labels, gender, age, evaluation, personal characteristics, and preferences. More specifically, their study was an attempt to determine the relative salience of two particular categories, action and body image. Their findings revealed that in this comparison as well as overall, *activity,* which could represent competencies, helping behaviors, or habitual actions, was the most salient dimension in the self-concept of preschool children. This finding was anticipated in light of the importance of instrumental action in the self-definition of the young child as emphasized in the theories of Erikson (1968), Piaget (1954), and Cooley (1902).

Rosenberg (1979) has perhaps come closest to a thoughtful cognitive-developmental analysis of the child's changing self-theory between the ages of 10 and 18. Utilizing an open-ended interview technique, children were asked a series of questions about what the person who knows them best knows that others don't, questions on points of pride and shame, on how they were different from other children they know, as well as the same, and what kind of person they would like to be when they grow up. Based on the pool of responses, content categories were then constructed that most meaningfully captured the sense of the data, and the developmental differences in the frequency of category usage were examined.

Across Rosenberg's questions, there is evidence for the following general developmental trends. The younger children direct their gaze "outward" toward observables and tend to respond in terms of a social exterior. Thus, they describe a world of behavior, objective facts, overt achievements, manifested preferences, possessions, physical attributes, and membership categories. For Rosenberg, the child at this level functions very much like a demographer and radical behaviorist in that the child's self-descriptors are limited to characteristics that could potentially be observed by others.

With development comes the emergence and increasing use of dispositions and traits to define the self. Rosenberg cites Murphy (1947) in this regard: "the vocabulary of the self becomes, so to speak, less and less visual and in general less and less sensory. . . . The child forms general ideas of himself. In short, the self becomes less and less a pure perceptual object, and more and more a conceptual trait system" (pp. 505–506). Bannister and Agnew's (1977) findings also support this general shift from self-descriptions based on physical features and activities among younger children to self-descriptions emphasizing traits and "personality constructs."

Rosenberg's results indicate that there are several types of traits that can be identified. The earliest trait descriptions tend to focus on qualities of character (brave, honest), emotional characteristics (happy, cheerful), and emotional control (don't get into fights or lose my temper). With increasing age, there is greater emphasis on *interpersonal* traits, for example, friendly, outgoing, shy, sociable, well-liked, kind, considerate, traits that include being attracted to others, being attractive to others, and possessing interpersonal virtues. The child at this level now functions primarily as a trait theorist in his or her self-descriptions.

The oldest subjects in Rosenberg's sample, extending to age 18, typically described themselves in terms of their "psychological interior," a world of emotions, attitudes, wishes, and secrets. The self-reflective gaze is turned inward toward the private and invisible, toward abstract response tendencies and potentials. For Rosenberg, therefore, the adolescent at this level is functioning very much like the Freudian clinician, probing the inner world of thoughts and feelings, both real and hypothetical.

In summary, across the few developmental studies that exist, there is general support for a gradual progression from self-descriptions based on concrete, observable characteristics such as physical attributes, material possessions, behaviors and preferences to trait-like constructs, and eventually to more abstract self-definitions based on psychological processes such as inner thoughts, emotions, attitudes,

and motives. These findings will be integrated into a broader theoretical framework in the last part of this section, which deals with the construction of the self.

Developmental Differences in Children's Understanding of Bipolar Attributes and Traits

Other investigators have emphasized that, within such broad categories of self-description, there is a developmental shift from all-or-none thinking to a more differentiated picture of the self. For example, when trait labels such as smart and dumb first become available to the child, he or she describes the self as all smart or all dumb (Harter, 1977; 1982a). One cannot be both smart and dumb simultaneously, although one may vacillate from one to the other.

This developmental phenomenon has been more systematically documented with regard to children's understanding of how emotion labels are applied to the self (Harter, 1982a). Young children, ages 3 to 5, typically deny that one can have two opposing feelings, for example, happy and sad or loving and mad, at the same time. When children first acknowledge that two such feelings can co-occur, they place them in temporal order or sequence, that is, one feeling is initially experienced, followed by the other. By about age 8, children will report that two opposing feelings can coexist simultaneously. However, at this age they typically attach the positive feeling to one event or person and the negative feeling to another. It is not until the age of 10 or later that children acknowledge that one can simultaneously have both a positive and negative feeling toward the same situation or person.

The work of certain investigators in the area of children's person perception converges on a similar observation (see Livesley & Bromley, 1973; Rogers, 1978). Young children not only describe others in terms of concrete characteristics, but their descriptions appear to be "univalent," for example, one is either all good or all bad. In applying this all-or-none thinking, the child does not qualify his or her statements or recognize seemingly conflicting elements in another person's makeup.

Selman (1980) has incorporated this dimension into his stage model of interpersonal relations. He describes how the child first believes that both self and others are incapable of having more than one feeling, motive, or attribute at a time. When children first acknowledge the co-occurrence of such bipolar attributes, they direct them to different events or situations. It is not until adolescence that positive and negative feelings or motives can be integrated to form an abstraction such as ambivalence.

Hand's (1981) research has provided the most systematic documentation of how this phenomenon applies to self-descriptions involving trait labels. Building on the cognitive-developmental theory of Fischer (1980), Hand tested a nine-step scalable sequence involving children's understanding of how they could be both nice and mean. The derivation of this sequence is quite complex. However, her findings provide compelling support for the hypothesis that the youngest children deny the possibility that they can simultaneously be nice and mean. Children's understanding of the co-occurrence of these trait labels gradually develops through a predictable sequence, culminating with a stage in which the abstract concept of intention is invoked to account for the simultaneous occurrence of both nice and mean characteristics in the self.

These findings, like those documenting the shifts from concrete attributes to traits to abstractions, merely provide descriptive norms for relatively gradual developmental progressions. There are few data, however, that illuminate the specific processes that account for these developmental shifts. In particular, there is very little evidence that bears on the theoretical analysis and speculation concerning how knowledge of the self is dependent on one's social interactions with others. In the next subsection, this topic will be discussed, followed by a treatment of the implications for the development of self-awareness. In the final subsection, an integrative framework will be proposed.

Social Processes in the Construction of the Self

Differentiation of Self from Other

In the section on infancy, we observed how a major developmental task was the differentiation of one's *bodily* self from others. The next hurdle for the young child requires the *psychological* differentiation of self from other. Piaget's (1962) findings reveal that one feature of preoperational egocentrism involves the young child's assumption that others are aware of the child's thoughts and dreams. Coming to appreciate that one has a *private* self, therefore, requires that the young child distinguish between one's *own* thoughts and the thoughts of others. Flavell, Shipstead, and Croft (1978) have pursued this issue more systematically than Piaget, and their findings indicate that, around age 3, young children begin to develop a rudimentary notion that one's thoughts belong to a private self that is not observable by others.

Our own research (Harter & Barnes, 1981) reveals that young children must also learn to differ-

entiate their *emotional* reactions from others. Three- and 4-year-olds reported that in the presence of parental happiness, sadness, anger, or fear, they would experience identical emotions. Furthermore, the *causes* of parental emotions were identical to the causes of their own emotions, for example, "Daddy would be sad if he couldn't stay up and watch 'Hulk' on television," a response the child had previously given for the self. With increasing age, children's reactions to parental emotions became differentiated, for example, responses to parental anger switched from child anger to child fear. Furthermore, the perceived *causes* of parental emotions became increasingly more realistic with age, suggesting that children gradually learn to differentiate causes of their own emotions from events that provoke feelings in others.

Bannister and Agnew (1977) have specifically addressed the question of the differentiation of *self* from other in their treatment of the bipolar nature of the self. They report some fascinating narratives from adults who were asked to describe how, as children, they first became aware of themselves as individuals. Various themes emerged, such as experiences involving separation from others, awareness of the privacy of one's own consciousness, sense of causality and control, an understanding of the difference between one's own possessions and those of others, and the awareness of how one is perceived by others. As Bannister and Agnew stress, common to virtually all the passages was the essential quality of *contrast* between self and other expressed by either a comparison with, or a judgment by, others. While these reconstructive accounts are intriguing, they do not bear directly on the developmental emergence of an awareness of self in contrast to other.

Bannister and Agnew's studies with children are more pertinent. They represent an interesting empirical twist on whether and how one distinguishes oneself from someone else. From children between the ages 5 and 9, Bannister and Agnew first recorded statements these subjects made in response to questions about favorite activities, friends, teachers, grownups, and themselves. The children were in groups of six when they made these statements. The statements were then rerecorded using a single adult voice. Their order was randomized within groups, and clues to the identity of the speaker (proper names, addresses, etc.) were removed. Four months later they presented these tapes to the children asking them which statements they had uttered. Thus, the task required that they discriminate previous verbal productions of their own from those of others. For the 5-year-olds, only 40% of their statements were correctly identified, with this value rising steadily to 60% for the 9-year-olds. Bannister and Agnew cite this as evidence for their "elaboration" hypothesis, that the child will be able to more readily recognize the self as distinct from other people with age.

The actual dimensions utilized by Bannister and Agnew's subjects to identify their verbal statements tell us something about the changing self-structure. In analyzing the different strategies used to identify "me" and "not me" statements, they found that the *younger* children frequently based their judgments on whether or not they typically undertook the activity described. They also claimed with great frequency that they *remembered* that the statement was theirs. In contrast, the three most common recognition strategies among the *older* children were references to an aspect of the statement that the child liked or disliked; judgments about its psychological appropriateness for the self; and the (logical) possibility that the event or statement applied for the self.

Bannister and Agnew also directly questioned the children about how they were different from others. The general tendency was for the younger children to focus on different physical features, activities or behaviors, whereas the older children were more apt to cite "personality" constructs, often of a trait-type, for example, "I'm not quiet," "I have different thoughts."

These investigators speculate that one might analyze such developmental changes from the viewpoint of personal construct theory (Kelly, 1955). They hypothesize, for example, that the network of constructs not only becomes elaborated with age but that younger children are more likely to use "preemptive" and "constellatory" constructs, whereas older children use more "propositional" constructs. That their data suggest intriguing developmental differences for further study is obvious. Whether the construct typology employed by Kelly to describe adult construct formation is the most appropriate remains to be seen. Too often in our developmental investigations we attempt to superimpose existing adult classification schemes onto the responses of children at different ages or stages, forcing a fit. The result is often a distortion of the adult category, a misinterpretation of the child's responses, or both. We would do well to consider development as a forward progression of changing structures, each with their own age-appropriate integrity, rather than employ the regressive model of the downward extension where children must, by definition, be conceptualized as miniature adults. Through the use of such a strategy, we can better come to appreciate

how the self-structure is actually formed, and how the self becomes differentiated from the other.

More attention must be paid to the role of socializing agents whose labeling of the child's behavior becomes a source of self-descriptors. In his self-perception theory, Bem (1967, 1972, 1978) argues that the labels we utilize in describing our emotions, inner states, and attitudes actually reflect past training and instruction in applying these labels to overt observable behavior. Early in the socialization process, adults play what Bem terms the "original word game," labeling the child's feelings, states, and attitudes on the basis of their observations of the child's behavior. Comments such as "You ate two helpings, you must be hungry" or "You're really dragging around this evening, you're tired, aren't you?" signal behavioral events that are attached to descriptors. The child comes to learn these labels and to identify feelings and attitudes by observing his or her own behavior and applying the appropriate self-descriptor. Bem's position leads to the conclusion that the basis for applying self-descriptive statements to one's internal states is not essentially different from the inferences others would make based on their observations of the same behavior.

Although Bem's supporting evidence is restricted to adult populations, this theory does have an appeal for understanding the developmental acquisition of self-descriptors that involve behaviors, for example, competencies and preferences, as well as traits. Those self-descriptions based on the more abstract references to one's psychological interior that emerge during adolescence (Rosenberg, 1979), may be more difficult to handle. However, Bem (1978) does specify conditions under which self-perception and the perceptions others hold about the self may differ. The individual does have sole access to internal stimuli, as well as the most comprehensive knowledge of one's own personal history, which may lead to differences in self-perceptions and the perceptions of others about the self.

One of the more intriguing differences between attributions made by the self and by others involves the actor-observer phenomenon (see Jones & Nisbett, 1971; Taylor & Fiske, 1975). When one (as actor) makes attributions about the self, the basis tends to be situational cues, whereas attributions made by others about the self (or by the self about others) tend to involve stable dispositions or trait labels (see Mischel, 1973). Thus, the reason I give for why this chapter is overdue is that I had other conflicting commitments, whereas my editor's attribution may be that I am a procrastinator. Jones and Nisbett (1971) suggest that differences in perspective leading to the differential salience of cues may be responsible. The actor's attention is directed outward, on situational cues, instead of inward on behavior. For the observer, however, the actor's behavior is the figural stimulus against the ground to the situation, leading one to attribute the actions to stable dispositions of the actor (see also Taylor & Fiske, 1975).

These issues have not been addressed developmentally; however, given that trait labels are not utilized until middle childhood and beyond, one would not expect to obtain such effects with young children. There are a number of fascinating developmental questions that emerge from a consideration of the perceptions of self compared to the perceptions of others, as well as to one's perception of how others view the self. In part, these issues involve the degree to which children can adopt the perspective of others. This topic will be treated in the following section.

Perspective-taking in the Formation of the Self

Historical scholars placed heavy emphasis on the role of others in forming one's sense of self. As noted in the introduction, Baldwin (1897) highlighted the bipolar nature of the self. Cooley's (1902) concept of the "looking glass self" was based on the assumption that the self is basically what we imagine that others think of us. In Mead's (1934) concept of the "generalized other," there is more focus on the developmental process whereby children come to be able to take the perspective of others, a prerequisite for the internalization of the opinions that others hold about the self.

Baldwin emphasized the imitative process. Attributes once ascribed to others are taken over and incorporated into one's thinking about the self. In Baldwin's words, "the acts now possible to himself, and so used by him to describe himself in thought to himself, were formerly only possible to the other; but by imitating the other he has brought them over to the opposite pole, and found them applicable, with a richer meaning and a modified value, as true predicates of himself also" (p. 8). Baldwin considered the young child to be imitative by nature, a "veritable copying machine" who divided his time between imitating others and practicing through play what he learned through his imitations.

Mead postulated a two-stage developmental process through which the child adopted the attitudes of others toward the self, labeling these stages as "the play" and "the game." The "play" for Mead was

the imitation of adult roles, which he documented in his description of the young child "continually acting as a parent, a teacher, a preacher, a grocery man, a policeman, a pirate, or an Indian" (1925, p. 270). The following stage is characterized by *games* in which there are specified procedures and rules. "The child must not only take the role of the other, as he does in the play, but he must assume the various roles of all the participants in the game and govern his action accordingly. If he plays first base, it is as the one to whom the ball will be thrown from the field or from the catcher. Their organized reaction becomes what I have called the "generalized other" that accompanies and controls his conduct. And it is this generalized other in his experience which provides him with a self" (1925, p. 271).

For more recent students of the self, the internalization of the evaluative judgment of others in one's social environment is dependent on the emergence of cognitive-developmental skills in the form of perspective taking. As Rosenberg (1979) notes of the young child, "Not yet viewing himself from the perspective of the others, the child has only a rudimentary propensity to view himself from the perspective of the 'Me,' to see himself as an object" (p. 254). Rosenberg applies this analysis to his data documenting the emergence of the self-concept as a language of interpersonal traits. Not only must the child have developed the ability to think in terms of higher-order concepts, but must be able to see the world, including the self, from the viewpoint of others. Rosenberg writes: "It is only when the child is able to get beyond his own narrow view of the world that he can succeed in seeing himself as an object of observation by others, as one who arouses in other people's minds a definite set of thoughts and feelings. By taking the role of other, the individual comes to *define* himself in terms of the reactions he arouses in the minds of others—as well-liked, popular, easy to get along with, and other looking glass traits" (p. 222).

Rosenberg's interview procedure provides some evidence on the sources of the "looking glass self" and "the generalized other." Children were asked how much they cared about what a variety of people thought of them, including parents, teachers, siblings, kids in their class, and friends. His findings indicate the need to qualify Mead's original expression of the principle of reflected appraisals: "We are more or less unconsciously seeing ourselves as others see us" (Mead, 1934, p. 68). Rosenberg raises the question "Which significant others?" His developmental data indicate that not all significant others are equally significant at every age. The younger child's conclusion about what he or she is like rests heavily on the perceived judgments of external authority, particularly adult authority. Knowledge of the self is regarded as absolute and resides in those with superior wisdom, a conclusion consistent with Piaget's (1932) observations of children's understanding of rules and the sources of moral judgment. With development, respect for parental knowledge declines, and peer evaluations rise in importance. During adolescence, the truth about the self becomes vested in those who are deliberately chosen, one's best friends.

For Rosenberg, it is the "perceived self," what we *think* others think of us, that affects our self-attitudes, and his findings clearly indicate that the particular others change with age. Thus, he amends Mead's statement to reflect these qualifications: "We are more or less unconsciously seeing ourselves as we think others who are important to us and whose opinion we trust see us" (p. 97). Rosenberg's analysis is compelling, although it does not speak directly to the process whereby the child comes to see himself as an object of observation by significant others. The gradual nature of various developmental trends suggests that the capacity for self-awareness and self-evaluation unfolds during the period of concrete operations and into formal operations. In the next section, possible substages in the self-awareness process will be examined.

Stages in the Emergence of Self-Awareness

In order to fully understand how self-awareness arises, we must consider developmental changes in the relationship between the "I," the "Me," and the "Other." Such an analysis will be applied to two sources of evidence, the normative-developmental descriptions of the self proposed by Gesell and Ilg (1946) and the more recent stage-theory of interpersonal relations proposed by Selman (1980). The Gessellian approach is typically criticized as being atheoretical and lacking in empirical rigor. Despite these problems, Gesell and Ilg's norms on the self provide rich descriptive material that suggests hypotheses well worth pursuing.

Across the 6- to 9-year-old age range, Gesell and Ilg describe the following acquistion sequence. The 6-year-old seems preoccupied with the conduct and correctness of his or her *friends'* behavior, frequently criticizing them on this account. In contrast, 7-year-olds worry about what others might think of them, and are careful not to expose themselves to criticism. They are concerned about their actions, ashamed of their mistakes, and cringe when they are laughed at or made fun of.

Gesell and Ilg describe the 8-year-old as "increasingly aware of himself as a person" (p. 176) and "more conscious of himself in the ways in which he differs from other people" (p. 176). He is "interested in evaluating his own performance . . . and he wishes to live up to his notion of the standard that other people have for him. . . . Since his performance is often only mediocre and his notion of other's standards are extremely high, there is often a discrepancy here which leads to tears and temporary unhappiness" (p. 176).

It is not until age 9 that Gesell and Ilg observe the capacity for self-criticism. They describe the 9-year-old as anxious to please, but also apprehensive, sensitive to correction, and very susceptible to embarrassment. At this age "they may underrate themselves as persons, lack confidence, and remark: 'Oh, am I stupid,' or 'I'm the dumbest.'' Nine "tosses off self-critical remarks, though one has to be careful not to take them too seriously" (p. 208).

These observations can be interpreted in terms of developmental changes in the relationship between the "I," the "Me," and others. At age 6, the "I" as knower seems to be able to judge or critically evaluate *others*, but not the self, the "Me." Moreover, with regard to the issues of knowledge of self versus other, it would appear that one can more readily identify faults in others than in the self. An analysis of age 7 behavior suggests that the "I" can observe the action of *others* judging and critically evaluating the "Me." However, the "I" *cannot* yet directly evaluate the "Me." This stage seems to portray the beginning of the looking glass self process during which others function as the reflective surface providing appraisals that will eventually be incorporated into one's self-definition, the "Me." The affective correlates of worry and shame are also noteworthy in light of Cooley's observation that one aspect of the "self-idea" is a "self-feeling." It would appear that the affective reactions that the judgment of others arouse in the self also become incorporated in the sense that eventually they are evoked by the "I's" judgment of the "Me."

At age 8, the "I" now appears to be able to observe not only others but the "Me" as well. The implication here is that the "Me" has now come to be defined on the basis of the reflected appraisals of others. Furthermore, the "I" can *compare* others with the "Me." Standards are becoming incorporated and, through social comparison, the "I" can determine whether the "Me" as observed matches those standards.

The age 8 process implies observation, whereas the advance at age 9 is the "I's" ability to critically *evaluate* the "Me" based on the standards that have become internalized. While the "I" retains the earlier ability to criticize *others,* Gesell and Ilg's descriptions suggest that the "I" is preoccupied with judging the "Me" to the point of extreme self-criticism.

There are no data that speak to these observations as a scalable developmental sequence. There are findings that address potential pieces of the puzzle. The literature on internalization (see Aronfreed, 1969) is convincing in its demonstration of how children incorporate values and performance standards; however, it does not bear directly on self-awareness. Aronfreed (1968) has also demonstrated that children often independently react to their own transgressions by reproducing the verbal criticisms they have experienced as part of the punishment employed by socializing agents. This internalization of self-criticism, however, has not been studied from a developmental perspective, but has been more specifically related to issues involving self-control (see last section of this chapter). The recent literature on social comparison (also to be discussed in that section) suggests that the ability to make use of such information for the purposes of self-evaluation is not presented in the very young child, but emerges in middle childhood. For the most part, however, these studies involve judgments of performance, instead of general evaluations of the self. Loevinger's model of ego development (Loevinger, 1966; Loevinger & Wessler, 1970) places the emergence of introspection and self-criticism at the transition between the Conformist and the Conscientious stages. In this model, growing self-awareness involves an internalization of the behavioral guidelines of one's social group. However, Loevinger's model has been developed around levels of adult functioning, and she does not wish to make specific claims about ages or stages during which these capacities emerge in childhood.

Some of our own data on children's understanding of emotion labels (Harter, 1982) involve changes in the affective component of self-awareness. Among the emotions we asked children to define (happy, sad, mad, scared, worried) were two potential self-affects; ashamed and proud. For both emotions, a four-stage sequence was documented. Our youngest subjects (ages 3 to 4) were unable to define these terms, although they could give adequate definitions of emotions such as happy, sad, mad, and

scared. At the next age level (4 to 5), children reported that ashamed is a "bad" feeling and proud is a "good" feeling, though beyond that they could not define them. The first adequate definitions to emerge (ages 5 to 7) focused on how *others* could be ashamed or proud of the *self*. Sample responses were: "My mom was ashamed of me for doing something I wasn't supposed to," "Dad was proud of me when I took out the trash."

It was not until the age of 8 and older that children described how you could be ashamed or proud of *yourself*. Their responses indicated that children experience these feelings in the absence of observation or surveillance from others, for example, "When you throw milk at someone, the next day you're ashamed of yourself"; "Like when you pass a test or do a good deed, you feel proud of yourself"; "When I thought about how I hurt someone's feelings, I was ashamed of myself." These data suggest that, in the formation of a self-feeling defined as the "I" adopting an emotional attitude toward the "Me," there is an intermediate step. The "I" first perceives the emotional reaction of *others* toward the "Me," *their* shame or pride, and then incorporates these affective standards that are later applied directly to the self. This analysis does *not* imply that younger children cannot *experience* shame and pride, since obviously observations indicate that they do. Instead, it implies that the self as observer is unable to step back and make affective judgments about the self as observed until middle childhood.

Selman's (1980) model of interpersonal understanding formalizes certain of these observations in a five-stage model that focuses primarily on perspective-taking. At his first level, 0, there is virtually no differentiation between the perspectives of self and other. At Level 1, the young child comes to understand that others feel differently, but does not yet understand that others also know how the self feels. The "I," as it were, can observe others, but doesn't yet realize that others can also observe the self. At Level 2, the child (age 7–12) comes to appreciate that others also know how the self might be feeling. In I-Me-Other terminology, the "I" not only observes the "Me" of others but observes the "I" of others observing the "Me" of the self. That is, the "I" can observe the other as both actor and object, and can observe that the actor component of the other is observing the self. This level, then, sets the stage for the looking glass self in that the child becomes aware that others are appraising the self.

At Level 3 (ages 10–15), Selman notes that the child can observe the self as both actor and object simultaneously, and can adopt the position of the "generalized other." In the terminology of this chapter, it is as if a new agency of the self is formed, a "super-I," which is aware of the "I" as observer and actor as well as the "Me" as observed; at the same time, this "super-I" is also aware of *others* as both observers and objects. An appreciation of the generalized other, therefore, would arise in consolidating the evaluations of others as observers of the self, incorporating these judgments into one's self-definition. (Selman's fourth and final level adds another layer of complexity in that the adolescent becomes aware of unconscious processes in the self and others.)

The I-Me-Other terminology may be compelling to some, perhaps superfluous to others. The point is that there is a dearth of evidence bearing on how such cognitive-developmental skills as perspective-taking collaborate with input from the social environment to form one's self-definition, as well as one's capacity for self-observation and self-evaluation. Many questions must be answered. For example, evidence put forth in this section suggests that "true" self-awareness, in the form of the "I"'s ability to take the "Me" as an object of observation, does not emerge until middle childhood. Yet there are those who would argue that it is not until the period of formal operations that one has the capacity to introspect and therefore treat oneself as an object of reflection.

However, to return to our analysis of the period of infancy, it was noted in the discussion of self-recognition that, around 18 months of age, the infant "I" becomes aware of what the infant "Me" looks like, and in subsequent months and years develops a clear "awareness" of the self in terms of such attributes as gender, age categories, and race. Moreover, one can interpret the findings revealing age differences in self-definition as evidence that the developing child is "aware" of attributes that define the self. It would appear that in each case we are employing somewhat different definitions of "self-awareness." Our task, then, is to reconcile these various views of self-knowledge and self-awareness within a single developmental framework. In the next section, some initial steps toward integration will be suggested.

Developmental Differences in the Self-Theory: A Possible Integrative Framework

The developmental data on children's changing self-descriptions suggest the following general pattern: young children focus on concrete, observable aspects of the self such as physical attributes and behaviors, whereas older children increasingly couch their self-descriptions in terms of traits. With the advent of adolescence, there is a further shift toward the use of abstractions and psychological processes such as thoughts, attitudes, and emotions in defining the self. This sequence, however, seems to confound dimensions based on *content*, for example, particular behaviors or emotions, with the *structure* of the self-theory, namely how these contents are organized into traits, abstractions, hierarchies, networks, and so on. A clearer picture might emerge if we distinguished between content and structure and then examined their interaction. The matrix in Table 3 depicts such a framework.

In the leftmost column are hypothesized *content* dimensions, ordered to suggest one possible developmental trajectory. The first two categories represent *observable* dimensions: (1) *Physical attributes* such as size, age, gender, race, possessions, territory, and so on, and (2) *Behaviors,* for example, actions, skills, preferences, and so on. The three categories that follow denote *psychological* dimensions: (1) emotions or affects, (2) motives and intentions, and (3) thoughts and the thought process itself. Thus, with development, children's self-descriptions can be hypothesized to shift from a focus on observable physical and behavioral dimensions to more psychological constructs, although the observable characteristics do not necessarily drop out of one's self-concept.

The *structural* dimensions, or how these contents are organized, are developmentally ordered along the top. These are cast into a sequence of four "stages," each with two levels. I have relied heavily on Fischer's (1980) cognitive-developmental theory in hypothesizing this sequence, and have drawn on Selman's formulation (1980) as well. There are approximate correspondences between these stages and the Piagetian stages described earlier in this chapter. The first stage roughly corresponds to preoperational thought, the second stage to concrete operational thought, and the third stage to early formal operational thought. The fourth stage represents further development during adulthood.

During Stage I, self-descriptions are couched in terms of *specific* attributes, behaviors, emotions, and so on. At Stage II, these are integrated into *traits*. At Stage III, traits become integrated into *single abstractions*. At Stage IV, single abstractions are combined into *higher-order abstractions*. Thus, movement to a new *stage* involves *integration*.

The two levels within each stage represent distinctions not articulated in Piaget's theory. Movement from the first to the second level *within* each

Table 3. **Hypothesized Dimensions of Developmental Change in the Self-concept**

STRUCTURAL CHANGES

CONTENT / Dimensions	STAGE I: Simple Descriptions		STAGE II: Trait Labels		STAGE III: Single Abstractions		STAGE IV: Higher-Order Abstractions	
	Level 1	Level 2	Level 1	Level 2	Level 1	Level 2	Level 1	Level 2
Observable Dimensions	GLOBAL Descriptions, all-or-none thinking	Differentiation, temporal shifts, vacillation	Descriptions integrated into TRAIT LABELS, overgeneralized, all-or-none thinking	Trait labels differentiated, situation-specificity	Trait labels globally integrated into SINGLE ABSTRACTIONS and overgeneralized	Single abstractions differentiated, then reintegrated	Single abstractions globally integrated into HIGHER-ORDER ABSTRACTIONS and overgeneralized	Higher-order abstractions differentiated, then reintegrated
PHYSICAL ATTRIBUTES (size, age, gender, race appearance possessions)								
BEHAVIORS, (actions, skills, preferences)	Good at drawing, puzzles, climbing, singing, running, know numbers, alphabet, colors	Good at drawing, puzzles ¦ Not good at knowing alphabet, numbers	All dumb because bad at math, science, social studies	Smart in creative writing, art, music ¦ Dumb in math, science, social studies	Low intelligence since dumb at conventional indicators of IQ	Artistic, creative, poetry, stories, painting ¦ modest conventional intelligence	Bohemian who rejects conventional values of society	Bohemian ¦ Political radical
Psychological Dimensions								
EMOTIONS (feeling states, affects)								
MOTIVES (intentions, causes of behavior)								
COGNITIONS (the thought process, attitudes)								

stage involves *differentiation*. Thus, at the first level of a given stage the attributes, traits, or abstractions are typically global and often overgeneralized. Self-descriptions at the first level are not necessarily stable, however; one may vacillate from one pole of the dimension, for example, smart, to the other pole, dumb. These descriptions become more differentiated and situation-specific at the second level, such that one may feel smart in one situation but dumb in another. At higher levels, this differentiation is combined with a reintegration of the components, weighting them in a more balanced fashion. It should be noted that this model differs from those that postulate that self-concept develops according to a linear progression represented by increasing differentiation and hierarchic integration (Montemayor & Eisen, 1977; Norem-Hebeisen, 1981) as well as progressive stability (Norem-Hebeisen, 1981). To illustrate the structural changes hypothesized by this model, an example from the *behavioral* content domain will be traced across these stages and levels, with a focus on skills and competence.

Stage I

At the first level, the young child who thinks he or she is good at drawing will also tend to think he or she is good at puzzles; good at knowing the alphabet, numbers, colors; good at climbing, running, singing, and so on. One is all good (or possibly all bad) across a wide range of specific skills (see Harter & Pike, 1981). At level two, these judgments become more differentiated. The child comes to acknowledge that one is good at certain skills, for example, drawing, puzzles, knowing one's colors, but not so good at knowing one's alphabet or numbers. Alternatively, a given skill may be acknowledged in one particular situation or point in time, but will not be consistently maintained or conserved across situation or time.

Stage II

During this stage, the first level involves an integration of specific behaviors into trait labels, for example, smart and dumb. (In Piagetian terminology, this involves the classification skills necessary to construct a hierarchy.) One is dumb because one does poorly at math, science, and social studies. However, within any given domain, where trait labels can be viewed as opposites, the child is only able to cognitively control one trait label in the pair, thereby concluding that she or he is either all smart or all dumb. Opposites cannot coexist at this first level, and through this all-or-none thinking, the trait

is overgeneralized across situations. Thus, the school child may feel that he or she is all *dumb*, based on the fact of doing poorly in math, science, and social studies. In constructing the unidimensional trait of dumb, the child ignores that she or he is simultaneously doing well in art, music, and creative writing. There may also be vacillation, from one trait label to its opposite. Since the child can only control one trait label at a time, when the focus is on dumb one is all dumb. If events subsequently cause smart to be more salient, then one is all smart. However, the two cannot exist simultaneously.

At Level 2 trait labels become differentiated, such that the child comes to appreciate that while one is dumb with regard to math, science, and history one can simultaneously be smart at art, music, and creative writing. The advance of this level, then, is greater differentiation in terms of the situation specificity of the trait labels. However, these self-concepts exist side by side, as it were, each restricted to a separate skill domain. They are not yet integrated.

Stage III

A more advanced type of integration is achieved during the third stage in the emergence of single abstractions (Fischer, 1980). The budding adolescent attempts to combine or integrate the existing trait labels. For example, in constructing the single abstraction of "intelligence," the adolescent may conceptually wrestle with the traits of smart and dumb. One may overgeneralize at this level, as well, and conclude that one is of low intelligence because one is dumb at the more conventional indicators of intellect, namely stellar performance at such school subjects as math and science. Thus, one's talents at writing, art, and music are not integrated into the single abstraction of intelligence.

During the second level, single abstractions become more differentiated. Thus, this same adolescent may combine a perception of himself or herself as a skilled writer of poetry and short stories with perceived talents at drawing and painting to form a separate single abstraction of herself or himself as an artistic, creative person. Although this second abstraction is now differentiated from the abstraction concerning his or her intelligence, the adolescent may not yet be able to integrate these two abstractions. At some point, he or she may become confused or perplexed about what seems to be a contradiction: how can one be of only low intelligence in conventional areas of knowledge but seemingly very gifted in other spheres?

Reintegration at this level might involve the formation of higher-order abstractions so that there is no longer an apparent contradiction, and the self no longer seems fragmented. For example, the young adult may come to define himself or herself as a Bohemian, one who rejects the conventional intellectual values of the society in favor of the pursuit of his or her artistic endeavors.

Stage IV

Initially, the higher-order abstraction of Bohemian may be overgeneralized such that the young adult ignores a possible contradiction, for example, an avid interest in politics. Thus, at Level 2 another higher order abstraction may be differentiated, such as political radical, which will co-exist with one's self-concept of a Bohemian. Further reintegration would lead to a portrait of the self as an iconoclast.

This structural analysis has been applied primarily to one content dimension, behavioral skills. It is hypothesized that, at any given point in development, a child or adolescent may be at a particular structural stage and level for one content domain, but at a different structural stage and level for another content domain. Thus, one may be at a more advanced structural stage of self-description with regard to the dimension of *behaviors* than of motives; for example, a child may have adopted the trait label of smart, but not yet have come to the conclusion, based on the intention to do well, that he or she is also hard-working.

Given the type of décalage predicted by this model, it is not possible to construct a *single* developmental sequence incorporating both content and structural dimensions. One can postulate that *within* any given *content* domain, for example, behavioral competence, the structural sequence will be manifest, as the previous examples illustrated. One might *also* predict developmental shifts *within* a particular *structural* level, for example, Stage II traits, *across* the sequence of *content* dimensions. For example, a child may initially base his or her judgment of smartness on behavioral criteria but subsequently add new content dimensions. In incorporating the psychological dimension of *emotions*, one might extend one's concept to the affect of pleasure one derives from challenge and mastery. "Smart" might later incorporate *motivational* dimensions, for example, hard-working. At some subsequent point in development, the trait label may be extended further to one's *thought processes*, for example, "I'm smart because I can logically think through problems and deduce answers."

According to this analysis, then, the formation of trait labels can occur with regard to any content domain, such that we can think of physical traits, behavioral traits, emotional traits, motivational traits, and cognitive-psychological traits that focus on thought processes. One can consider *abstractions* in this same light. Abstractions can be based on physical characteristics (e.g., masculine), behaviors (e.g., intelligent), emotions (e.g., depressed), motives (e.g., determined), and thought processes (e.g., introspective).

It is hypothesized, however, that the level of structural usage and content category usage are correlated to some degree. With development, one is more likely to use higher structural stages in conjunction with more advanced categories. This raises an interesting question regarding the nature of these proposed developmental sequences. Are they to be viewed primarily as acquisition-deletion sequences in which, as higher levels are attained, earlier levels drop out? Alternatively, do they represent a sequence in which earlier levels are retained, or are they subsumed as they are hierarchically integrated? One hypothesis is that the structural levels undergo a process of hierarchical integration such that the manifest forms of the earlier stages and levels drop out as this information is organized at increasingly more abstract levels. However, the *content* dimensions may be retained and continue to be utilized. Thus, as my earlier examples of different types of abstractions indicated, one can have abstractions based on any one of the content dimensions. Or, an abstraction may combine *several* content dimensions. Thus, a Machiavellian may be described as one who engages in unscrupulous *behavior,* who is callous *emotionally,* who is deviously *motivated* by selfish greed, and whose *thought processes* involve the premeditated manipulation of others.

As with any developmental sequence, we also must eventually specify what transition rules govern the shifts from one stage and level to another, as well as from one content category to another. There was a suggestion, in describing the adolescent with two separate single abstractions for intelligence and artistic talent, that at some point these might appear to represent a contradiction, producing cognitive conflict. In order to resolve such conflict, the adolescent may reach for a higher level of abstraction whereby these two single abstractions can be integrated. The general notion that conflict, in some form, moves one to higher stages of development has been popular in both cognitive-developmental and psychoanalytic theorizing. However, there are many questions to be answered with regard to the specific processes involved and how internal conflict operates to promote developmental reorganization in one's concept of self. Moreover, we need to know what external factors in the social environment might serve to provoke the initial experience of conflict.

Despite these unknowns, the type of framework proposed here may help to reconcile what seem to be differing claims regarding the age at which children develop self-knowledge and self-awareness. The toddler can be said to possess self-knowledge in that the I-self has knowledge of specific physical characteristics and certain categories, for example, age grouping (baby vs. adult) and gender, which define the Me-self. The developing child extends these self-descriptions to a new content domain, behaviors, for example, "I can run fast." Moreover, when the child moves into the second level of Stage I, there may be vacillation from one situation to another or one time period to another. That is, these descriptions are not viewed as enduring or stable characteristics of the self. This lack of conservation, as it were, is best documented by the lack of gender constancy in the young child. Therefore, the young child may be said to have self-knowledge in that at any particular point in time he or she can describe the most salient physical and behavioral characteristics at that moment. However, the young child cannot yet see the self as others see it, and thus does not have the capacity for self-awareness, so defined.

The "I" of the *older* child comes to define the self in terms of traits, a structural advance at Stage II. In addition to traits based on observable characteristics (e.g., smart, athletic, nice) self-descriptions may also include traits based on such psychological dimensions as emotions (e.g., cheerful, brave) and motives (e.g., one's moral worth) as defined in terms of intentions (Piaget, 1954). Presumably, it is during Stage II that the child develops the capacity for self-awareness, in that the specific trait labels adopted reflect the appraisals that significant others have made about the self. This particular framework, however, does not address the social *process* through which the "looking glass self" or the "generalized other" is formed.

During adolescence, self-awareness is marked by another advance. Not only are abstractions possible, but these can be directed toward a new content category, the process of thought itself. The adolescents' self-descriptions will still include behaviors, emotions, and motives. However, the ability to think about one's thinking allows one to hypothesize, to reflect on how emotions, motives, and behavior patterns might have been formed; as a result, one's self-awareness at this stage becomes much more analytical.

In summary, the consideration of both the con-tent and structure of the self-theory appears to be a potential framework for integrating our existing knowledge of the construction of the self, pointing the way toward further empirical and theoretical efforts. While this framework provides for a systematic *description* of developmental changes in the self-theory, its limitation is that it does not speak to the biological, cognitive, and social *processes* that bring about such change. This is the challenge that must be met in illuminating our understanding of the developing self.

ADOLESCENCE AND BEYOND: A LIFE-SPAN PERSPECTIVE

In the previous section, the period of adolescence was characterized by cognitive-structural advances in the form of abstractions. These not only allow the adolescent to think abstractly about his or her attributes, behaviors, emotions, and motives, but to reflect on thought itself. The term "introspection," therefore, carries with it the implication that the "I" can direct its analytic gaze toward the very process through which the self-theory is constructed. These cognitive advances occur at a time when the adolescent self is also facing a dramatic physiological revolution, as well as the expectation that one make a commitment to a particular societal role. Self-awareness, therefore, is heightened.

Unfortunately, there is relatively little in the way of theory that guides us through the vicissitudes of self-concept development during adolescence. Erikson's description of the period of identity formation represents the most cogent and comprehensive analysis, a point Peterson (1981) also underscores. For Erikson (1950, 1959, 1968), the task of this period is the establishment of a sense of ego identity, which involves three components: a sense of *unity* among one's self-conceptions, a sense of *continuity* of these self-attributes over time, and a sense of the *mutuality* between the individual's conceptions of the self and those that significant others hold of the self. While these themes are particularly intense during adolescence, they may resurface during subsequent periods of adulthood (see also Levinson, 1978).

Self-Awareness

Self-awareness, in the form of self-consciousness, becomes particularly acute during adolescence, in contrast to the period of late childhood when the self-concept appears relatively stable (Rosenberg, 1979). According to Rosenberg's findings, the period of unreflective self-acceptance vanishes, and the self becomes more volatile and evanescent. "What were formerly unquestioned self-truths now become problematic self-hypotheses and the search for the truth about the self is on" (p. 255).

Erikson also describes the tortuous self-consciousness of this period, although from a somewhat different perspective. He observes that adolescents, in their search for a coherent, unified self, are often morbidly preoccupied with what they appear to be in the eyes of others and with the question of how to connect earlier-cultivated roles and skills with the ideal prototypes of the day. In this statement we see a developmental resurgence of the looking glass self. After a period of self-stability during later childhood, the adolescent is drawn to the social mirror in a new, often tortured, preoccupation with the imagined judgments of the generalized other. The "I" must once again look to others for assistance in redefining the "Me." Of interest in this regard is Maslow's (1971) observation that the very intensity of self-consciousness during adolescence precludes the ultimate attainment of identity or selfhood. For Maslow, such selfhood involves a state of "egolessness" that requires the *suspension* of self-observation and self-awareness. From Erikson, we would infer that the adolescent does not yet have a sufficiently solid, integrated ego to suspend.

Self-awareness in the form of acute self-consciousness would appear to abate as one's identity becomes established and one moves into adulthood. For the most part, however, those studying self-awareness in adulthood have not yet adopted a life-span perspective. Loevinger and her colleagues (Loevinger & Wessler, 1970; Loevinger, Wessler, & Redmore, 1970) treat self-awareness as one dimension of their model of ego development that extends into adulthood. Self-awareness in the form of self-criticism begins to emerge during the transition from the conformist and conscientious stages, and comes to characterize the conscientious stage. However, these investigators have not elaborated on the role of self-criticism in their developmental model.

Wicklund and his colleagues (Duval & Wicklund, 1972; Wicklund, 1975) have been the most productive investigators to study self-awareness in adults. In Wicklund's model, the term "objective self-awareness" refers to the process through which the self becomes an object of one's observation. In a series of fascinating experiments, Wicklund and his colleagues have documented a number of mechanisms whereby self-focused attention can be enhanced. The presence of a mirror is perhaps the most

dramatic in its effects on self-criticism. Hearing one's voice on a tape recorder or performing a task in the presence of an audience also heightens self-consciousness. Wicklund's mirror manipulation, in particular, operationalized the "I" as subject observing the "Me" as an object of reflection, and provides a very vivid analogue of the looking glass self for adults.

While Wicklund's research has primarily addressed the experimental conditions under which self-awareness can be enhanced for adults in general, Snyder's (1979) work on self-monitoring focuses on individual differences. His findings document two groups of adults who can be classified as high and low self-monitors. The prototypical high self-monitor "is particularly sensitive to the expression and self-presentation of relevant others in social situations and uses these cues as guidelines for monitoring (that is, regulating and controlling) his or her own verbal and nonverbal self-presentation" (p. 89). In contrast, the low self-monitoring person is not nearly "so vigilant to social information about situationally appropriate self-presentation." (See also Carver & Scheier's, 1981, integration of the research on self-awareness, in terms of a cybernetic or information-processing model.)

The work of Wicklund and Snyder is quite provocative, and raises intriguing questions from a life-span perspective. For example, are there periods other than adolescence, as in later adulthood, when heightened self-awareness becomes a natural, stage-appropriate response? In addition, to what socialization experiences might we attribute the marked individual differences in self-monitoring among adults? What are the antecedents of one's adult preoccupation with the reactions of others, why must some polish the looking glass so fervently? Some of these questions will be addressed in a subsequent subsection dealing with the life-span models of Erikson and Levinson.

The ability to observe the self, to be self-aware, is highly touted by many clinicians as the primary avenue through which insight about the self can be obtained. For theorists such as Maslow (1971), however, the greatest attainment of identity or selfhood involves transcending the self, in becoming relatively egoless. Such egolessness is characterized by the total loss of self-consciousness or self-observation. Here, Maslow's contention converges with a central tenet of those Eastern philosophies that emphasize the need to destroy the illusion of the ego or self. As one Master of Tibetan Buddhism writes, "we build up an idea, a preconception, that self and other are solid and continuous. And once we have this idea, we manipulate our thoughts to confirm it, and are afraid of any contrary evidence" (Trungpa, 1976, p. 13).

Trungpa goes on to describe two stages of egolessness toward which one should aspire. "In the first stage we perceive that the ego does not exist as a solid entity, that it is impermanent, constantly changing, that it was our concepts that made it seem solid" (p. 13). But there is still a "watcher of the egolessness, a watcher to identify with it and maintain his existence. The second stage is seeing through this subtle concept and dropping the watcher. So true egolessness is the absence of the concept of egolessness" (p. 13). Trungpa (1973) notes that one type of ignorance in the Buddhist tradition is "self-observing ignorance," namely, watching oneself as an external object. Thus, while much of the current chapter has focused on the distinction between the self as observer and the self as observed, for those in the Humanistic and Eastern traditions, the most mature identity involves a phenomenological integration of these two selves.

When self-awareness *is* acute, there would appear to be three focal points of concern, most salient during the period of adolescent identity formation as described by Erikson. As noted earlier, these are: *continuity* of the self over time; a sense that the attributes that define the self are *unified*, not fragmented; and a sense that one's self-concept and the concept others hold of the self are *mutual*. Each of these topics will be treated, in that order.

Continuity of the Self over Time

William James (1890/1963) was one of the first scholars to analyze self-conceptions in terms of a temporal perspective. His distinctions were rather global in that he contrasted the "potential social Me" to the "Me" of the immediate present and the "Me" of the past. James emphasized how the *continuity* of these different "Me"'s is an important aspect of one's sense of personal identity. Despite differences across time in many concrete aspects of the self, one perceives that one is the same person, the same self. In many ways, James writes, "I am the same, and we may call these the essential ways. My name and profession and relations to the world are identical, my face, my faculties and store of memories, are practically indistinguishable, now and then. Moreover, the Me of now and the Me of

then are *continuous;* the alterations were gradual and never affected the whole of me at once" (p. 186). For James, "the *commonest* element of all, the most uniform, is the possession of some common memories" (1890/1963, p. 189).

Bannister and Agnew (1977) highlight the importance of the organization of such memories, pointing out that in order to "entertain the notion of our own continuity over time, we possess our biography and live in relation to it" (p. 102). Events in which we are involved are codified in the form of such a biography and thus provide proof of our continuity. Bannister and Agnew observe that the desperation with which we struggle to maintain our sense of continuity when it is threatened is itself an acknowledgment of its importance.

As Erikson's analysis indicates, this desperation becomes particularly intense during adolescence, when the continuity of the self is threatened. Unlike James' reconstruction of the self as continuous with gradual changes, the adolescent's experience is one of dramatic discontinuity, given marked physical changes, cognitive advances, and shifting societal expectations. For Erikson, a major aspect of the identity crisis involves a search for inner sameness and continuity that will bridge what one was as a child and what one is about to become as an adult. The heightened self-consciousness of this period is characterized by shame over what one is and doubt over what one will become. He quotes a slogan on a wall hanging that he once observed in this regard: "I ain't what I ought to be, I ain't what I'm going to be, but I ain't what I was" (1959, p. 19). The inability to settle on an occupational identity is, according to Erikson, one of the most unsettling experiences of this period. As we will see in the discussion of both Erikson's and Levinson's stages of adulthood, there are subsequent life stages and crises during which one's sense of continuity is again threatened.

The Unified Self Within the Context of Multiple Roles

In addition to the self's awareness of its continuity over time, there is a concern with continuity or consistency across situations, which typically involves an integration of roles. A number of self-theorists, primarily from the fields of clinical psychology and personality, place major emphasis on the integrated, unified self (Allport, 1955, 1961; Horney, 1950; Jung, 1928; Lecky, 1945; Maslow, 1954, 1961, 1971; Rogers, 1950). For Allport, the "proprium," his term for the self, "includes all aspects of personality that make for a sense of inward unity" (1955, p. 38). Allport identifies a particular motive, "propriate striving," which seeks such a unification.

Lecky (1945) has fashioned an entire theory around the theme of self-consistency, emphasizing how behavior expresses the effort to maintain the integrity and unity of the self. Like later writers (Brim, 1976a; Epstein, 1973; Kelly, 1955), Lecky observed that the individual organizes ideas about the self into a personal theory, much like a scientist. Ideas that are inconsistent create disturbances in the system and thus must be expelled or rejected. Rogers (1950) also views the self-structure as an organized configuration of perceptions about the self. He echoes Lecky's theme, noting that negative feelings about the self arise when the organization is threatened by experiences viewed as inconsistent with that structure. Epstein (1981) has recently formalized many of these observations under the rubric of the unity principle, emphasizing that one of the most basic needs of the individual is to maintain the unity and coherence of the conceptual system that defines the self. For the most part, however, these formulations are derived from clinical observations instead of more systematic empirical investigation.

Other theorists (Baldwin, 1897; Gergen, 1968; James, 1890/1963; Jourard, 1971) have focused on the integration of multiple selves that reside within the person. James first emphasized this multiplicity of the self, claiming that a man has as many social selves as there are individuals who carry an image of him in their mind, as well as groups of people about whose opinion he cares. In documenting the division of the man into several selves, James writes: "Many a youth who is demure enough before his parents and teachers, swears and swaggers like a pirate among his 'tough' young friends" (1890/1963, p. 169). James notes that this multiplicity can be harmonious, as in the case where one who is tender to his children is also stern to the soldiers under his command. Alternatively, there may be a "discordant splitting" if one is afraid to let one group of acquaintances observe his behavior in a different setting.

For James, the "conflict of the different Me's" can also be observed in the incompatibility of potential roles one might wish to adopt in adulthood. He fantasizes about his desires to be handsome, athletic, rich, witty, a bon vivant, lady-killer, philospher, philanthropist, statesman, warrior, African explorer, as well as a tone-poet and a saint! He knowingly concludes that since all these roles could not possibly coexist in the same person, one must selectively choose, suppressing the alternatives. In raising this issue, James anticipates one of the most difficult struggles in the adolescent's search for identity: "So the seeker of his truest, strongest, deepest self must review the list carefully, and pick out the one on which to stake his salvation" (p. 174).

More recently, Gergen (1968) has argued that the most fruitful theory of self must take account of multiple roles, and the conditions under which each occurs. He cites historical resistance to such a stance in the form of a "consistency ethic," that is, we assume personal consistency on the part of others in our social environment, despite the fact that the empirical evidence does not support such an assumption. Gergen contends that the "popular notion of the self-concept as a unified, consistent, or perceptually 'whole' psychological structure is possibly ill-conceived" (p. 306). As an alternative, he suggests that people adjust their behavior in accord with the specific nature of the interpersonal relationship and its situational context. In a close relationship, founded on mutual trust, personal consistency should be expected *within* that relationship. However, consistency would not necessarily be expected or desired *across* relationships; in fact, most likely it would be damaging.

Gergen's general thesis finds considerable support in more recent literature emphasizing situational differences in self-perceptions and behavior (see Gergen, 1971; Mischel, 1968, 1973; Vallacher, 1980). Vallacher's conclusion is very similar to Gergen's. He asserts that the association of different self-views with different roles represents *differentiation* instead of inconsistency. It is only when one has differing self-definitions *within* a role, for example when one feels that he or she has been insensitive to a close friend, that inconsistency is experienced.

For the adolescent, a formidable developmental task is the selection of suitable roles that will lead to a stable sense of identity or self-definition. Erikson describes this period as a psychological moratorium during which the adolescent engages in role experimentation, including occupational, ideological, social, and sexual roles. The potential hazards of this period involve identity defusion and role confusion, manifested by the adolescent's inability to select and integrate the roles he or she wishes to pursue.

In support of his formulation, Erikson himself draws on a rich repository of personal observations, clinical case material, and biographical analyses. Keniston's (1968) description of the alienated student syndrome provides somewhat more systematic observations of the psychological hazards of the identity crisis. Keniston's data come from a series of questionnaires that tapped several interrelated psychological dimensions that define the alienated youth. He notes that many of these students can aptly be described in terms of the Eriksonian identity crisis in that they appear to be in a state of intense diffusion. "Their sense of themselves seems precarious and disunified, they often doubt their own continuing capacity to cope; they have little positive sense of relatedness to other people; the boundaries of their own egos are diffuse and porous" (p. 409).

Several investigators (Constantinople, 1969; LaVoie, 1976; Marcia, 1964, 1966; Waterman, Geary, & Waterman, 1974; Waterman & Goldman, 1976; Waterman & Waterman, 1971) have attempted to investigate Erikson's theory directly. Constantinople reports on both a cross-sectional and longitudinal sample of students at each of the four college year levels, freshmen through seniors. Her longitudinal data are the most informative. With regard to the conflict between identity and identity diffusion, she found consistent increases in the successful resolution of identity issues over the four-year period for both males and females. Decreases in identity diffusion scores were significant for males only.

Marcia (1964, 1966) has conducted some of the most intriguing work on identity, building on Erikson's formulation. Specifically, he has evaluated college students' levels of crisis and role commitment with regard to occupational choice, religion, and political ideology, employing a semistructured interview. His results provide evidence for four types of potential identity statuses. The first two reflect the poles of Erikson's central conflict for this period, Identity versus Identity Diffusion. There were those students who had *achieved* some sense of identity after a period of crisis, and thus manifested a sense of commitment to an occupation or ideology. There were those showing *identity diffusion,* characterized by lack of commitment as well as a negligible concern over this stance. The third type, which Marcia labeled as *moratorium,* represented those in a crisis-like condition, actively searching for an occupation or ideology toward which they could make a commitment. The fourth group was identified as *foreclosure* (see Erikson, 1959). They had adopted the identities prescribed by parents, primarily, with a keen sense of commitment but no obvious experience of crisis.

Subsequent studies have sought to validate these four types (Marcia, 1966) and to investigate sex differences in the correlates of each type (Marcia, 1967; Marcia & Friedman, 1970; Toder & Marcia, 1973). Other investigators, for example, Waterman,

Geary, and Waterman (1974), have studied changes in these identity statuses during college, longitudinally. They found that the frequency of identity achievers increased significantly between the freshman and senior years. Moratorium subjects showed the greatest amount of movement into other categories, shifting to either identity achievement or identity diffusion (see also Marcia, 1976). In a follow-up study several years after college, Waterman and Goldman (1976) reported additional increases in the frequency of identity achievers as well as decreases in moratorium and diffusion subjects. The overall pattern of findings in this literature indicates that, while there seems to be a general movement toward the attainment of a relatively stable integrated identity, not all subjects reach this goal, nor do these identity statuses define a developmental sequence as such. The individual differences are marked, both in the particular endpoint attained as well as the rate of movement through a given identity status group.

There is considerably less evidence on the pattern of individual differences in later adulthood. At best, we have clinical accounts of adults who seem unable to integrate their various self-definitions into a unified sense of self. Allport (1955), for example, notes that many mental patients seem to suffer from what he terms the proliferation of unrelated subsystems that define the self. Rogers (1950) also describes patients who experience inconsistencies and partial disorganization of the self. For Maslow (1971), multiple personalities can best be described in terms of a failure of communication within the self-system. Horney (1950) has focused on a somewhat different barrier in the struggle toward an integrated sense of self, describing the symptoms that characterize a person's alienation from what she terms the *real* self. Self-alienation may involve active movement *away* from the real self, active movement *against* the real self, depersonalization, and depletion of energy. The *real* self for Horney involves "genuine integration and a sound sense of wholeness, oneness" (p. 156) although the description of how this is achieved is rather vague.

Jourard (1971) is somewhat more specific about the meaning of one's *real* self. It pertains to the person's *communication* of what he or she thinks, feels, believes, wants, worries—information one could never know about a person unless one were told. For Jourard, such personal self-disclosure puts one in touch with one's real self and is thus a manifestation of psychological health. Horney's self-alienated individual is cited by Jourard as an example of the type of person who may not know her or his real self. Reisman, Glazer, and Denney's (1950) "lonely crowd" depicts the pervasiveness of this symptom at the societal level. Jourard also includes the acceptance of multiple roles as part of his definition of psychological health. Thus, the healthy person is one who not only can integrate and derive satisfaction from the many roles prescribed by society, but who has an intimate knowledge of the real self who enacts them.

Self in Relation to Other

There has been much less treatment of the mutuality of the judgments of self and other, another concern that becomes salient during adolescence. A more prevalent theme involves the *differentiation* of self from others. For example, the clannishness and commonality in tastes and preferences during adolescence is viewed by Erikson (1959) as a defense against the inability to forge an independent identity. He also observes that for the youth, confused about identity, any physical closeness with either sex arouses at the same time both an impulse to merge with the other person and a fear of losing autonomy and individuation. Before true intimacy can be achieved much of the young person's sexual life, according to Erikson, is "of the self-seeking, identity-hungry kind; each partner is really trying only to reach himself" (1968, p. 137).

Laing's (1960) description of ontological insecurity further documents the problems young people have in differentiating the self from others. For Laing, this takes the form of a sense of engulfment. The individual uncertain about his or her identity dreads relatedness with others, since it threatens one's precarious sense of autonomy. For both Laing and Erikson, the defense against such engulfment is *isolation*. The youth unable to establish intimate relationships may settle for highly stereotyped interpersonal relationships with others, or may distance himself or herself, repudiating others, which may lead to even further estrangement.

There has been little systematic empirical support for this formulation, although the clinical observations are quite compelling. Moreover, they document how the problem of differentiating self from other, first faced during infancy and later in childhood, recurs in a slightly different form during adolescence and early adulthood. Separation-individuation, therefore, is a process that characterizes a number of major developmental transitions. Levinson (1978) argues persuasively that it can be extended to developmental change during later adulthood as well.

In the preceding subsections, several themes involving the concerns of the self during adolescence and adulthood have been treated: the continuity of the self over time and the sense of self as unified, in addition to the theme of the self in relation to other. Data in support of the salience of these themes as different developmental stages are scant, at best. Gordon's (1968) efforts to delineate the categories by which people define themselves holds some promise as an empirical avenue for investigating these issues. In addition to the categories that specify roles, memberships, attributes, preferences, values, and so on, his coding system also includes four categories referring to what he terms "systemic senses of the self." One such system specifically involves a sense of unity and personal integration. Gordon builds directly on Erikson and includes references to all three of the themes just reviewed, continuity over time, unity, and a sense of mutuality between self and other. Self-descriptions such as "in harmony," "mixed up," "a whole person," and so forth, are coded under this category. All such responses are coded under one single category, however: sense of unity. It may well be that a more comprehensive picture of the development of self during adolescence and adulthood would emerge if these themes were assessed separately and traced throughout the life span.

The Implications of Cognitive-Developmental Change During Adolescence and Adulthood

The factors typically considered the most critical in provoking the identity crisis are societal pressures concerning role choices and physiological changes associated with puberty. Much less attention has been devoted to the implications of the cognitive-developmental advances ushered in during the period of formal-operational thought. In the earlier chapter section on the construction of the self it was suggested that several new capabilities would influence the nature of adolescent self-theory: the ability to think abstractly, to reason about the hypothetical, and to introspect, to think about one's thoughts, feelings, and motives. For the most part, however, there has been only lip service paid to the notion that somehow the emergence of formal operational thought will substantively affect the adolescent's self-concept (see Lerner & Spanier, 1980).

Holmes (1980) has conducted one of the few empirical studies on this topic assessing the relationship between formal operational thought and self-theory. In so doing, she administered Lunzer's (1966) test of formal reasoning, which consists of verbal analogies and problems involving quantitative relations. To assess self-concept, she administered Kuhn and McPartland's (1954) Twenty Statements Problem in which subjects write down twenty self-definitions in response to the question "Who am I?" She then categorized these responses into references to the body self, the social self, and the psychological self, categories that others have viewed as a continuum of abstraction (Hartley, 1970; McPartland & Cumming, 1958).

Holmes was particularly interested in the relationship between formal operational thinking and the frequency of references to the inner or psychological self. However, she obtained only a moderate relationship between these two indices. In interpreting these findings, she suggests that perhaps the tasks were not of equivalent difficulty. She further posits that formal operations is not an all-or-none accomplishment, a single skill that generalizes across all content domains, but one that develops progressively. This assumption is consistent with Inhelder and Piaget's (1958) description of the development of adolescent thought and has found recent empirical and theoretical support (Fischer, 1980; Flavell & Wohlwill, 1969; Martorano, 1977; Moshman, 1977; Roberge, 1976). Thus, it is unlikely that a single measure of formal operational thought would bear a strong relationship to a single index of the self-concept.

Another potential fallacy regarding the impact of formal operational thought on the self-concept involves the assumption that the newfound abilities of abstraction result in a "better" theory of self. Formal operational thought is a double-edged sword in many respects, with advantages as well as limitations. Elkind (1967) has identified one limitation in the form of adolescent egocentrism. During adolescence one's own thought processes become a major target of interest and concern. This preoccupation with one's thoughts, with one's self, often causes the adolescent to fail to distinguish between what he or she is thinking and what others are thinking. As Elkind has noted, often the adolescent concludes that others are as preoccupied with his or her appearance, behavior, and feelings as he or she is. The construction of this *imaginary audience* reflects the convergence of intense self-consciousness, the heightened importance of the looking glass self, and problems in differentiating the thoughts of self and others. Moreover, the adolescent would appear to construct an *over*generalized other.

The second feature of adolescent egocentricism identified by Elkind involves the tendency to feel that, because one's own experiences are unique and novel, historically this must also be the case. The adolescent constructs a *personal fable,* as it were, in which he or she as the protagonist has singular feelings and thoughts experienced uniquely by the self. The first adolescent love affair provides a vivid example. Lerner and Spanier (1980) give us the flavor of this melodrama, noting the tendency for the adolescent to assert that no one else has ever loved as deeply, as totally, as intensely. When such a torrid affair is over, the adolescent is convinced that no one else has ever suffered as deeply or has been so wrongfully abused, so spitefully crushed by unrequited love. Furthermore, if concerned parents question what is wrong, the inevitable adolescent answer is: "You can't possibly understand! What do you know about love!"

Fortunately (for many), the egocentrism of this period declines as the adolescent begins to decenter. Such decentration is presumably the result of interactions with peers and adults, and is facilitated by the adoption of more adult roles and responsibilities. For Inhelder and Piaget (1958) occupational choice is especially critical. "The focal point of the decentering process is the entrance into the occupational world or the beginning of serious professional training. The adolescent becomes an adult when he undertakes a real job" (p. 346). Their point converges nicely with Erikson's emphasis on the importance of commitment to an occupational role, in that the inability to select such a role is viewed as the most potentially disturbing outcome of adolescence. The gradual nature of this decentration process again attests to the fact that we should not consider formal-operational thought to appear full-blown, ushering in miraculous powers of deduction and self-discovery.

Levels of Abstraction During Adulthood

Fischer (1980) has articulated the most differentiated theory of cognitive development during adulthood, including implications for one's sense of identity. In this model, four levels of abstraction are identified, each of which define a specific level of adult cognitive development. Prior to the period of adolescence, Fisher's theory delineates six levels of intellectual functioning during childhood. Level 7 marks the first appearance of abstract thought. At Level 7, the adolescent can now construct what Fischer terms a "simple abstract set" in which two representational systems about the self can be coordinated. Thus, one can construct a single abstraction about one's occupational identity, for example.

As an illustration, Fischer describes the youth

who wishes to become a psychologist like his father. He has a concept of himself which he can compare with, or relate to, his father, based on an identification with this parent. In addition, the adolescent has a representational system for what he knows of his own talents in working with people. He can also relate this to his perceived scientific skills, and appreciate the relationship between these capabilities and his representation of the occupational skills required of a psychologist: they employ a scientific approach to the study of people and their problems. The single abstraction involved in constructing an occupational identity requires that the adolescent coordinate these representations about the self with those representations that define the occupational role.

The limitation of Level 7 thinking is that the adolescent can only control one abstraction at a time. That is, he cannot yet relate this newly formed occupational identity concerning the self to another abstraction that involves the identity of someone else. The first indications of the next advance occur at Level 8.

At Level 8, the adolescent can begin to relate one abstract identity—his own, to that of another person, though only in a very rudimentary manner. Fischer labels this an abstract *mapping*. For example, he may consider certain relationships between his own career identity and his concept of his potential spouse's career identity; he may feel that his own career identity requires that his spouse be in a closely related career, or that his spouse be primarily a homemaker. However, there is a rather rigid, undirectional, and egocentric flavor to this cognitive mapping in that its focus is on what *his* career requires of another. One abstraction is mapped onto another, but the relationship is not truly reciprocal.

At Level 9 there is much more reciprocity and differentiation in relating the two identities. As Fischer notes, the person can relate several aspects of both his and his spouse's identity, such as career and parental identities. In so doing, he can also develop a more differentiated, flexible, and sensitive picture of what his own identity requires of his spouse's identity, as well as what his spouse's identity requires of his own identity. Fischer labels this advance at Level 9 a truly *abstract system*. At Level 10, the person can relate *two* abstract *systems* to one another reciprocally. To follow Fischer's example, he might relate his own and his spouse's career and parental identities now (one Level 9 system) to their career and parental identities 10 years ago, when they were first married (a second Level 9 system). Thus, these identities are placed in a temporal perspective, implying a sense of continuity over time.

Fischer's model clearly implies that the tasks involved in forming one's identity cannot be solved all of a piece. Different facets of identity formation require cognitive skills of differing levels of complexity, and these various abstraction skills emerge gradually over the period of adolescence and adulthood. The levels identified by Fischer also provide interesting parallels with the stages of adulthood outlined by Erikson (see Fischer & Lazerson, in press). The limitations of Level 7 thinking in early adolescence allow one to appreciate why the attempt to form one's identity might be characterized by role confusion and lack of a sense of unity. Since the adolescent can only handle one single abstraction at a time, efforts to coordinate the various roles that are the basis for one's emerging new identity are greatly hindered.

Erikson's subsequent stage of Intimacy versus Isolation would appear to require Fischer's Level 8 skills, at a minimum. It is at this level that the young adult can first begin to relate his or her own abstract identity to that of another person. It is likely that the kind of mature mutuality required of true intimacy would necessitate the utilization of Level 9 skills wherein the identities of oneself and another are truly reciprocal. Level 9 skills would also be required to deal successfully with Erikson's crisis of Generativity versus Stagnation, which would entail the meaningful coordination of one's own occupational and parental identities with those of one's spouse.

Finally, in successfully coping with Erikson's last crisis, Ego Integrity versus Despair, Fischer's model implies that Level 10 skills would be required. At this level, one can put his or her various identities into a larger perspective, not only coordinating these identities with those of others, but considering them within a temporal context, as one reviews one's life. For Erikson, successful resolution of this crisis involves even more, in terms of appreciating one's place within the context of society, culture, history, and humankind. Clearly, a system of abstract systems would be required to achieve this feat. In conclusion, there remains much to be worked out in the integration of Fischer's cognitive levels and the stages Erikson has described; however, the initial convergences are extremely promising (see Table 4).

Identity and Beyond: Toward a Life-Span Approach to the Self

For many years Erikson's theory has stood alone as the most compelling account of development throughout the period of adulthood. While he has not

Table 4. Stage Models of Adult Development with Implications for a Life-Span Approach to the Self

Age Period	Fischer's Levels of Abstractions	Erikson's Life Crises During Adulthood	Back & Gergen's Model of Life Space Extensivity and Bodily Well-Being	Levinson's Model of Developmental Periods During Adulthood
Adolescence	Level 7. Identity defined in terms of Single Abstractions.	Identity versus Role Confusion.	Life Space Extensivity relatively restricted. Physical well-being at its peak.	
Young Adulthood	Level 8. Abstract Mapping of one's own identity onto that of another person.	Intimacy versus Isolation.	Life Span Extensivity expands, Physical well-being sound.	EARLY ADULT TRANSITION (a) Entering the Adult World (b) Age 30 Transition (c) Settling Down MIDLIFE TRANSITION
Middle Adulthood	Level 9. Abstract System. Reciprocal coordination of one's own identities with those of significant others, and with societal expectations.	Generativity versus Stagnation.	Life Space at its peak in terms of Extensivity. Physical well-being declines. Maximum discrepancy between potential life space and bodily capabilities.	(a) Entering Middle Adulthood (b) Age 50 Transition (c) Culmination of Middle Adulthood LATE ADULT TRANSITION
Late Adulthood	Level 10. System of Abstract Systems. Coordination of one's own identities over a lifetime, with those of others and with cultural values, so as to form a meaningful whole.	Ego Integrity versus Despair.	Life Space Extensivity and physical well-being both decline, undergo further restrictions.	(a) Entering Late Adulthood

formulated a theory of self per se, he has identified central issues and related developmental conflicts that provide the basis for many self-definitions. Just as each stage of childhood builds on the resolution of previous conflicts, so do the three stages of adulthood rely heavily on the manner in which one's identity crisis is or is not resolved. There is certainly the potential in Erikson's theory for a model of the development of the self, one that would not only target stage-appropriate conflicts but allow for the systematic study of how individual differences, in the degree to which conflicts are experienced and resolved, affect one's self-definition.

However, relatively little attention has been devoted to a comprehensive developmental theory of self that would give thoughtful consideration to the stability and change in one's self-percepts during adulthood. Brim (1976a) outlines several reasons for this neglect. He notes that traditionally we have focused on those developing attributes that would appear to be near completion by early adolescence. Moreover, he contends, for too long we have overemphasized childhood experiences as predictors of adulthood personality. In particular, we have been overly influenced by infantile determinists for whom constructs such as the Oedipal conflict are given too much predictive power. Allport came to a similar insightful conclusion 25 years ago: "People, it seems, are busy leading their lives into the future, whereas psychology, for the most part, is busy tracing them in the past" (Allport, 1955, p. 50).

Within the past decade we have witnessed a proliferation of theoretical speculation, empirical investigation, and methodological commentary on the study of aging, the elderly, and the need for life-span approaches (see Barrow & Smith, 1979; Bromley, 1974; Butler & Lewis, 1973; Hendricks & Hendricks, 1977; Horn & Donaldson, 1976; Nesselroade & Reese, 1973; Seligman, 1975). Many of these contain provocative hypotheses for the study of the self during adulthood, for example, Seligman's hypotheses concerning the increase in learned helplessness among the elderly. However, self-concept development has not been studied in any systematic manner, and for those constructs most relevant to self-definition the focus has primarily been on the aged, not on the changes throughout the lifespan.

Several investigators have put forth modest models of the development of the self during adulthood (see Back & Gergen, 1968; Brim, 1966, 1976a, 1976b). For example, Back and Gergen trace the potential fate of two aspects of the self, the bodily self, and what they term the "extensivity" of one's life space (see Table 4). This latter concept refers to the range of time and space—both physical and psychological—in which one perceives himself or herself to operate and have influence. Although this space is somewhat restricted during adolescence, it expands during the 20s, generally, as the young person expands his or her horizons. However, it peaks somewhere between 30 and 50, and then declines. Bodily well-being, they hypothesize, shows a gradual decline during the adult years.

The degree of convergence or discrepancy between these two projected adulthood curves forms the basis for some speculation on the part of Back and Gergen. For example, they suggest that the low point of morale seems to be reached during the 50s, since this is the point of maximum discrepancy between one's life space and bodily well-being. The life space remains extended, whereas the bodily self undergoes more obvious decline. After this stage a new balance point may be achieved.

It is the relationship between these two selves that most concerns Back and Gergen. Interestingly, they note that the aged seem to be less concerned with the way they present themselves to others. The looking glass begins to collect dust, it would appear. However, it is the constriction of the life space and accompanying lack of concern for present and future relationships that these theorists feel mediates this lack of interest in one's appearance. They view this model as one that must ultimately be expanded, and tested throughout a variety of research methods.

Brim (1976a) has focused on more psychological constructs, particularly one's perceptions of control as a critical determinant of one's self-concept. He draws on research by Gurin and Gurin (1976) revealing that there is a steady increase in the sense of personal control up to age 50, after which there is a clear decline through age 70 and beyond. Brim puts the control issue within a broader context, postulating a constellation of characteristics and perceptions that define the "male midlife crisis." He posits that a number of self-theory changes are required in this period of life in the face of declining personal control, shifting beliefs about one's body capacities, and changing hypotheses about one's future achievements; if these changes are demanded too suddenly or simultaneously they will yield a crisis in one's self-theory.

Levinson's Model of Adult Development in Men

Levinson (1978) has provided a more differentiated stage-model of the events leading up to and following the male midlife crisis. Levinson focuses on changes in the "individual life structure" that involves one's concept of the self in relation to the social world in which one must live and function. Levinson emphasizes the interrelated processes of separation and individuation that characterize developmental transitions in adulthood as well as in childhood. He notes that these transitions require that one review and evaluate the past in order to determine which aspects to keep and which to reject as one moves into the future. In facing this developmental hurdle, one is suspended between past and future, struggling to overcome the gap that separates them, which threatens the continuity of the self.

Levinson's determination of the stages in his model was based on biographical interview procedures with a rather select group of 40 men from the Northeast corridor. These men, between the ages of 35 to 45 at the outset of the study, were drawn from four occupational categories: business executives, university biologists, novelists, and hourly workers in industry. His findings provide evidence for ten identifiable stages of adulthood for this group of men, each of which can be characterized by specific developmental tasks or hurdles (see Table 4).

During the *Early Adult Transition* (ages 17 to 22), the youth must terminate preadulthood and begin to move into the world of the adult. In the course of finding one's place in the world of new relationships and societal institutions, one must reappraise and modify the self in an attempt to consolidate an initial adult identity. The second stage (ages 22 to 28) of *Entering the Adult World* involves the formation of the "first adult life structure." During this period, the novice adult makes and tests a variety of initial choices regarding occupation, love relationships, peer relationships, values, and life style. In so doing, the young man must establish some balance between what Levinson considers to be two antithetical tasks: he must keep his options open, maximize alternatives, and avoid strong commitments while at the same time create a stable life structure.

During the next stage, the *Age Thirty Transition* (28 to 33), the primary task is to work on the flaws and limitations of the first adult life structure. For some men the modifications involved in this transition are handled smoothly, whereas for others, this is a time of stress and crisis. The subsequent period of *Settling Down,* involves the formation of the second life structure. There is now a focus on establishing oneself more firmly. While the life goals may potentially involve occupation, family, friendship, community, and so forth, in Levinson's sample, the primary concern of this period was striving to advance in one's profession. Climbing the ladder of success

became critical, as defined by social rank, income, power, fame, creativity, and so on.

The *Midlife Transition* typically occurs between 40 to 45, during which the life structure is again called into question. The meaning, value, and direction of one's life are reevaluated. This is the period others have labeled the "midlife crisis," in that the person sees the need for major changes in life style. Levinson also notes that during this period previously neglected aspects of the self more urgently seek expression and stimulate modifications in the existing self-structure. In *Entering Middle Adulthood*, at approximately 45, new choices are acted on in the formation of a new life structure. For some there is a crucial marker event such as a drastic change in job or occupation, a change in one's marriage, social relationships, or one's location, though for others the change is not that conspicuous. Levinson's findings highlight the individual differences in the satisfactions this new life structure offers. For some men it is the fullest and most creative season of their life cycle to date, whereas for others it provides little in the way of meaningful self-fulfillment.

Given the age range of his sample, Levinson's findings bear less directly on the remaining four stages he has identified. During the *Age Fifty Transition*, he speculates on certain features in common with the age 30 transition. One continues to modify the new life structure adopted in the previous period. The *Culmination of Middle Adulthood* (55 to 60) that follows is often marked by a rejuvenation of the self in the sense that one attempts to enrich one's life. The period of *Late Adult Transition* (60 to 65) terminates middle adulthood and creates a basis for starting *Late Adulthood*, the specifics of which have yet been investigated by Levinson.

Although Levinson has not constructed an adult developmental model of the self explicitly, his differentiated sequence of stages identify concerns that would inevitably heighten self-awareness. The many major life decisions he articulates, including occupational choices and changes, the selection of a living partner, parenting, disruptions in the family unit, and alterations in one's social network, may well point to situations that force the introspective beacon to beam back on the self as an object of reflection. At such times, the "I" would appear to take a harder look at the "Me."

In addition, Levinson identifies four "polarities" or dimensions of the self that must be redefined and integrated during each transitional period: Young/Old, Destruction/Creation, Masculine/Feminine, and Attachment/Separation. The Young/Old and Masculine/Feminine polarities are especially interesting, since they represent the very first dimensions the young child utilizes in defining the self. For Levinson, movement through the stages of adulthood involves increasing individuation in the sense that these dimensions, once construed as opposites, are not considered to be so antithetical. Archetypes are dissolved, as one can appreciate both the youthful and mature qualities of the self and can more freely integrate both masculine and feminine tendencies. For students of the self, Levinson provides a general framework that may be extended to numerous other polarities that may undergo developmental change as the adult redefines the self during periods of transition.

A major limitation of Levinson's work to date is the restrictive nature of the sample. His findings do not speak to the issue of adult development in women, nor do they apply to a very broad spectrum of men. Levinson and his collaborators are aware of these limitations, and are appropriately cautious about the generalizability of the model. There is much to be pursued, therefore, in following Levinson's lead. His periods provided a general framework that may serve as a model for studying women and other populations. Toward this end, there should be sufficient conceptual and methodological flexibility to allow for the possibility that a somewhat different sequence might emerge. In addition, procedures need to be developed whereby systematic developmental change can be assessed more rigorously.

Finally, for those specifically interested in the self-system, there is the challenge to pursue how the type of stages Levinson has identified have a specific impact on both the content and structure of adult's self-perceptions. Not only might certain categories become more salient at particular ages, but the contents of the self undoubtedly undergo more complex forms of reorganization. While some of these changes may be dictated by the need to adapt to changing social demands, they should also be influenced by the type of cognitive-developmental shifts described by Fischer (1980). Thus, any comprehensive life-span perspective must attempt to integrate the more differentiated models of adult development that have recently been put forth.

SELF-ESTEEM

Just What Is Self-Esteem?

The discussion thus far has focused primarily on issues involving the content and structure of the self, and how the categories or dimensions that define the self might change with age. In turning to the issue of self-esteem, the focus shifts to the value or worth that people attach to these self-descriptors. How does the "I" evaluate the components as well as the totality of the "Me?" Unfortunately, in most treatments of the topic, self-esteem is never clearly defined, but merely taken as a given; presumably there is some common referent of which we are all intuitively aware. William James (1890/1963) represents a historical exception.

It was James who explicitly addressed the meaning of self-esteem in his now famous formula:

$$\text{Self-Esteem} = \frac{\text{Success}}{\text{Pretensions}}$$

Thus, one's feelings of worth were determined by the ratio of one's actual accomplishments to one's supposed potentialities. The dimension of achievement, therefore, was implicit in James' concept of self-esteem.

The affect resulting from such evaluations was an important element of self-esteem for James, as well as for others. For both James and Cooley (1902) the emotions that are aroused by one's self-definition, for example, pride and vanity, as well as shame and mortification, were critical components of the self-evaluative process. In the clinical literature, the affective component of self-esteem has also been highlighted, particularly among neo-Freudians (e.g., Adler, 1927; Horney, 1945, 1950; Sullivan, 1953). In Horney's theory of neurosis, self-demeaning feelings are at the root of one's basic anxiety. To cope with this anxiety, the neurotic must construct an idealized image in an attempt to enhance his or her self-esteem. Sullivan also emphasized the individual's need to ward off anxiety provoked by threats to one's self-esteem caused by rejection or negative evaluation by others. For Adler, one's sense of inferiority, as a result of organ deficiencies and bodily weaknesses, was the major threat to self-esteem.

Epstein's (1973) more recent treatment of self-esteem also emphasizes affect. He contends that the major functions of one's self-theory are to optimize the pleasure/pain balance and to maintain self-esteem. Epstein notes that in childhood we begin to observe how threats to the child's sense of self clearly cause emotional "pain," though how such hurt or injury to the psychological self comes to be experienced is a thorny issue. Phenomenologically, Epstein points out that the feeling is perceived as something in the body that appears to have an identity all its own. For this reason he concludes that ''it is not surprising that the self is conceptualized as a spiritual homunculus rather than as a hierarchical organization of concepts that assimilates experience and guides behavior'' (p. 414). Self-esteem, almost by definition, is elusive given this interpretation.

Other theorists have couched the preservation of one's self-esteem in more motivational language. The operation of defenses as mechanisms cleverly designed to protect or enhance the ego is a convincing testimonial (see Allport, 1955; Hilgard, 1949; Murphy, 1947). Kaplan (1975) has explicitly referred to self-esteem as a universal motive, claiming it to be ''a dominant motive in the individual's motivational system'' (p. 10).

When one turns to those psychometric attempts to *assess* self-esteem, the definitions are equally as vague. As Wylie (1974) comments: ''The basic constructs as defined in the writings of self-concept theorists frequently seem to point to no clear empirical referents'' (p. 8). Coopersmith's (1967) widely quoted investigations of self-esteem in children provides a typical example: ''By self-esteem we refer to the evaluation which the individual makes and customarily maintains with regard to himself; it expresses an attitude of approval or disapproval, and indicates the extent to which the individual believes himself to be capable, significant, successful, and worthy. In short, self-esteem is a *personal* judgment of worthiness that is expressed in the attitudes the individual holds toward himself'' (p. 5).

Given the generality of such a conceptual definition, it is difficult to imagine how one might arrive at a precise *operational* definition of self-esteem. This problem has not stood in the way of efforts to assess this psychological commodity, however. The potpourri of items included within as well as across these scales is a reflection of the failure to clearly define self-esteem. Certain self-esteem measures concentrate heavily on skills and achievements, whereas others include items tapping morality, physical appearance, likeability, and acceptance by parents. While certain items are couched in specific evaluative language, for example, ''I am good at schoolwork,'' others merely describe behavioral tendencies from which evaluative inferences must be made, for example, ''I cry easily'' or ''I spend a lot of time daydreaming.'' Moreover, there is generally a mix with regard to how items are worded. Some items are phrased as activities or behaviors, others refer to observable characteristics, trait labels, perceived response of others toward the self, subjectively experienced affects, and inner thoughts. Typically, there is little rationale for the

range of item contents, nor is it possible to reconstruct the underlying construct supposedly tapped.

As Wylie remarks, ''An examination of empirical studies makes it apparent that ambiguities in the measuring instruments can be traced partly to inadequacies in the theorists' definitions of their terms'' (1968, p. 4). One has to concur with Wylie that ''We cannot attempt . . . systematically to review, compare, criticize, or put in order the various non-operational definitions in common use'' (p. 4). However, neither can we be content to accept the premise that self-esteem is what self-esteem scales measure, and proceed to review this literature in piecemeal fashion. Thus, in the next section a number of general issues will first be addressed, followed by a more detailed review of the most popular psychometric instruments in use. The correlates and antecedents of self-esteem will then be discussed.

Issues in the Study of Self-Esteem

A number of issues will be identified in this section, and, where relevant, the developmental implications will be explored. For the most part, however, the topic of self-esteem has been given little developmental attention. These issues include: (1) the discrepancy between one's real and one's ideal self-esteem; (2) the distinction between self-esteem and self-confidence, and the effect of importance of success on self-esteem; (3) the question of whether self-esteem is more appropriately considered to be a global construct or a more differentiated aggregate of self-evaluations; and (4) the degree to which self-esteem represents a hierarchical organization of the dimensions of self-evaluation.

Real Versus Ideal Self-Esteem

A popular framework for conceptualizing self-esteem has been an examination of the discrepancy between one's *actual* or *real* self-evaluation and one's *ideal* self. Historically, this concept was captured by James in his formula for self-esteem, which emphasized the ratio of one's successes to one's pretensions. This construct later found its way into the clinical literature through the efforts of Rogers and his colleagues (Rogers & Dymond, 1954). In Rogers' view, the magnitude of the disparity between one's real and ideal self was a primary index of maladjustment. This construct was operationalized in a number of measures for adults, the most popular instrument being a Q-sort task designed by Butler and Haigh (1954). With regard to children, Lynch (1981) has recently suggested that it is not until the ages of 6 to 9 that the idealized self develops and when measures can be employed reliably. He suggests that this may be because younger children do not yet have rules for setting expectations about the idealized self, although this hypothesis has not been put to an empirical test.

Zigler and his colleagues (Achenbach & Zigler, 1963; Katz & Zigler, 1967; Katz, Zigler, & Zalk, 1975; Zigler, Balla, & Watson, 1972) have challenged Rogers' assumption that one's self-image disparity is necessarily indicative of maladjustment, and have suggested an alternative developmental framework. Their empirical research support their claim that when viewed from a cognitive-developmental perspective, such a discrepancy is an index of maturity. While the pattern of results differs somewhat from study to study, the general finding on which they base this conclusion indicates that the self-image discrepancy scores for older children are larger than for younger children.

Presumably developmental differences in level of guilt, as well as cognitive differentiation, are responsible. With increasing maturity, there is a parallel process in the capacity to experience guilt as the individual becomes better able to incorporate social demands, morals, and values. "The high developmental person, then, makes greater self-demands, is more often unable to fulfill them, and consequently experiences more guilt than the low developmental person" (Phillips & Rabinovitch, 1958; Phillips & Zigler, 1961; Zigler, Balla, & Watson, 1972, p. 81). With regard to cognitive differentiation, individuals at higher developmental levels "should employ a greater number of categories and should make finer distinctions within each category than an individual at a lower developmental level. The use of a larger number of categories should increase the probability of a greater disparity between any two complex judgments, including those regarding real and ideal self-images" (pp. 81–82). In this research, the role of guilt and cognitive differentiation have been inferred from the pattern of findings; these variables have not been assessed directly. However, these studies represent one of the few attempts to consider the meaning of the self-disparity score from a developmental perspective.

In her treatment of this topic, Wylie (1974) notes that many of the studies employing such a discrepancy score may be introducing a possible "theoretical confusion." By this, she refers to the fact that one's reported ideal may represent a cultural stereotype of the ideal person. Rosenberg (1979) raises a related consideration. He notes that the distinction between one's idealized image and what he terms one's "committed" image is frequently overlooked. The committed image is one which we take seriously; it is not simply a pleasant fantasy. On scales such as the popular Butler and Haigh measure (1954), subjects are asked to rate statements according to what they would "ideally" like to be. As Rosenberg points out, we have no way of knowing how the subject interprets the term "ideally." Does it refer to the "self," unrestricted by any bound of reality, little more than a playful fantasy, or as the self he earnestly wishes to become, or something in between?" (p. 41).

For Rosenberg, this distinction is relevant for children, as well as adults. He cites Piaget (1928) whose observations suggest that by age 3 children can distinguish between two kinds of ideas: those that are true (pour de vrai) and those that are simply imagined (pour s'amuser). Rosenberg's own procedures for eliciting children's ideal self include asking them whether they would *really* like to be that sort of person or is it just a *nice idea*. From the abashed smiles of many who indicated that it was "just a nice idea," he has inferred that children can recognize the difference between a pleasant fantasy and a serious commitment to a desired self.

While Rosenberg's general point is well taken, one would need a more convincing documentation that there indeed was a commitment to a *realistic* desired self. Given that the young child has not even established the basic constancies, for example, gender, one would question the meaning of any seemingly serious desire to become a particular type of person. The alleged desires of the preschool boy to become a policeman or football hero may well have a ring of commitment at that age; however, later in development he may realize that he has neither the desire nor the potential. Thus, the distinction between commitment and ideal self-image is certainly worthy of attention, but it may have different implications for self-esteem at different developmental levels.

Self-Esteem Versus Self-Confidence, and the Role of Importance of Success

For some, self-esteem is contrasted with what it is *not*. One such distinction is drawn between self-esteem and self-confidence (see Dickstein, 1977; Rosenberg, 1979). Rosenberg contends that a good deal of confusion abounds because of the failure to appreciate this distinction. He articulates what he views as the major difference: "Self-confidence essentially refers to the anticipation of successfully mastering challenges or overcoming obstacles or, more generally, to the belief that one can make things happen in accord with inner wishes. Self-esteem, on the other hand, implies self-acceptance, self-respect, feelings of self-worth'' (p. 31). Self-confidence, then, is very much akin to self-efficacy as Bandura (1977a) has recently defined it, namely the conviction that one can successfully execute the behavior required to produce a desired outcome.

For Dickstein (1977), ''Self-confidence involves carrying off a particular task or fostering a role. Level of self-confidence at any one moment may be unrelated to an overall level of self-esteem'' (p. 136). Dickstein speculates that this is probably what is tapped in experiments such as Coopersmith's where subjects are requested to estimate the probability of their success at a particular skill or game. She contends that ''Without measuring self-confidence over a wide variety of situations, or determining the importance of a particular activity for the subject, the results of such studies may be misleading with regard to the role of various factors associated with self-esteem'' (p. 136). Empirical evidence in support of this distinction is provided by Maccoby and Jacklin (1974) in their review of the sex-difference literature; the findings suggest that girls suffer from lack of self-confidence but not self-esteem.

In Dickstein's reference to the *importance* of a particular activity, she raises another central issue that has its origins in James' conceptual formula describing the critical parameters of self-esteem. For Dickstein as well, the importance of an activity will determine the degree to which success and failure affect overall self-evaluation. She has incorporated the dimensions of both perceived importance and perceived competence into her own measure of self-esteem (Dickstein, 1977). A similar argument has been advanced in our own theorizing (Harter, 1978), and has recently found empirical support (Harter & Engstrom, 1981).

Rosenberg has investigated the role of importance under the rubric of psychological centrality, focusing on individual differences in the centrality of one particular characteristic of the self-definition: likeability. His findings reveal that the strength of the relationship between global self-esteem and likeability depends on how important or central the characteristic of likeability is to the individual. ''Among those who *cared about* being likeable, the relationship of the self-estimate to global self-esteem was very strong, whereas among those to whom *this quality mattered little*, the relationship was much weaker'' (1979, p. 73).

In Rosenberg's reference to ''global self-esteem'' we encounter perhaps the most equivocal issue in this literature. Does global self-esteem exist as a legitimate psychological construct, or are feelings of self-worth better characterized in terms of a more differentiated picture of one's self-evaluations across different domains? In discussing the issue, a third possibility will be raised: Is there a place for both, not only in our theorizing but in our phenomenological experience?

Global Self-Esteem Versus a Differentiated Evaluation of the Self

Precious few aspects of the self escaped the intellects of James and Cooley, and this topic is no exception. In elaborating on self-esteem, James (1890/1963) rejected the associationist interpretation that self-satisfaction merely constitutes an aggregate of represented pleasures from success or that the sum total of one's pains or failures is synonymous with one's feelings of shame. Over and above these perceptions James contended that ''there is a certain average tone of self-feeling which each one of us carried about with him, and which is independent of the objective reasons we may have for satisfaction or discontent.'' (p. 171). Cooley (1902) voiced a similar sentiment. The person with a balanced self-respect has ''stable ways of thinking about the image'' of self, and ''cannot be upset by passing phases of praise or blame'' (p. 201). For both of these theorists, something akin to global self-esteem is seen to exist in conjunction with more discrete evaluations of particular behaviors at any given point.

Among certain more recent theorists, however, there is a tendency to emphasize either the global nature of self-esteem or to view it as a differentiated aggregate of evaluations. Coopersmith (1967) can be counted among the proponents of the global nature of self-esteem. Initially, he had considered the possibility that one's self-esteem might vary across different areas of experience, and designated four such domains for which questionnaire items were constructed: school, family, peers, and general references to the self. In analyzing the data from a sample of 56 10- to 12-years-old children, Coopersmith did not find that they systematically differentiated between these four areas. Therefore, he concluded: ''either preadolescent children make little distinction about their worthiness in different areas of experience or, if such distinctions are made, they are made within the context of the over-all, general appraisal of worthiness that the children have already made'' (p. 6). Unfortunately, as we will see in our section on psychometric considerations, such a conclusion is not warranted for several reasons: inadequacies in the model on which this instrument was based, problems with item and domain selection as well as with the question format, and clear evidence to the contrary by other investigators.

Mullener and Laird (1971) have focused on assessing domain-specific components, suggesting that self-esteem undergoes increasing differentiation with age. In a study of seventh graders, high school seniors, and college students, these investigators found increasing differentiation among five domains: achievement traits, intellectual skills, physical skills, interpersonal skills, and sense of social responsibility. They contend that while a single global self-concept may exist at one point in development, it dissolves into a variety of different self-evaluations with increasing age.

Their findings do not provide strong support for this interpretation, however. No clear operationalization of global self-esteem independent of the relationship among the five domains was employed. Proving the null hypothesis, as it were, by demonstrating that domain differences are negligible in seventh grade does not necessarily imply that these pupils have crystallized a sense of global self-esteem. Other factors, for example, inadequacies in the measuring instrument or the inability of adolescents at this age to make realistic judgments about their competencies (see Connell, 1980; Harter, 1982b; Rosenberg, 1979) may simply have precluded the demonstration of domain differences. The issue is an interesting one to pursue, however. Additionally, one would want to see a much broader developmental sample, extending downward into middle childhood. If the analysis suggested in the section on the construction of the self has merit, seventh grade may well represent a period in which seemingly global self-evaluations, not present in the previous stage, emerge as a result of the tendency to overgeneralize single abstractions.

Rosenberg (1979) offers the most compelling argument for why we should both retain the notion of global self-esteem and focus on the constituent parts of this whole. He asserts that the two are not identical. "Both exist within the individual's phenomenal field as separate and distinguishable entities, and each can and should be studied in its own right" (p. 20). He claims that the failure to recognize this point has led to a number of misleading inferences in the literature. As an example, he cites those studies that have inferred that minorities have lower self-esteem merely because they report negative attitudes toward their own skin color or race (Brody, 1964; Clark & Clark, 1947; Goodman, 1952; Kardiner & Ovesey,

1951; Proshansky & Newton, 1968). Rosenberg also points to those educational programs that have attributed the poor achievement of underprivileged children to their perception that they are not smart enough, and then have advocated measures designed to improve the child's global self-esteem. As he notes, the assumption that a potential change in global self-attitude will transfer to a specific self-attitude is neither logically nor empirically warranted. He concludes that "The assessment of one's academic ability and the view of one's general self-worth are two separate attitudes whose relationship must be investigated, not assumed" (p. 21). He cites data by Bachman (1970) indicating that the correlation between "self-concept of school ability" and global self-esteem is .33, highlighting the fact that while there is overlap, the two are far from identical.

Our own approach to this issue (see Harter, 1978, 1982a, 1982b) is very consistent with Rosenberg's. In constructing the Perceived Competence Scale for Children, three specific competence domains were isolated: cognitive, physical, and social skills. In addition, the scale includes a general self-worth subscale that taps the degree to which the child likes the way he or she is, feels good about the way one acts, thinks he or she is a good person, and so forth. While there are moderate correlations among the subscales, a large portion of the variance of the self-worth subscale is unaccounted for by the other three subscales.

Minton (1979) has empirically pursued the bases on which children make judgments concerning their general self-worth, as tapped by this subscale. Her analysis of the reasons elementary school children give revealed four factors, none of which had to do with competence per se. These were: (1) *Parental Relationship,* whether or not they obeyed, and received approval from parents; (2) *Control of Anger,* whether or not they got angry; (3) *Self-Acceptance,* whether or not they were happy with themselves; and (4) *Social Appropriateness,* whether or not they got along with others and were helpful and good in school.

It is interesting that these factors do not involve competence. However, in what sense do they illuminate the construct of general self-worth or global self-esteem? It may well be that we have simply isolated several other dimensions of self-evaluation without convincingly demonstrating that children indeed have a superordinate concept of their overall self-worth. To pursue this issue, therefore, we must shift to a conceptual framework in which the dimensions of self-evaluation are somehow hierarchically organized and perhaps differentially weighted. This issue will be considered next.

Self-Esteem and the Hierarchical Organization of the Dimensions of Self-Evaluation

A number of theorists have posited hierarchical models of the self-concept that have implications for self-esteem. Shavelson, Hubner, and Stanton (1976), for example, have identified two broad classes, academic and nonacademic self-concepts, with further distinctions within these classes. The nonacademic self-concept is subdivided into social, emotional, and physical self-concepts. L'Ecuyer (1981) has proposed an even more differentiated picture of the constituents of the self-concept. He first identifies what he terms "structures," listing five: the material self, the personal self, the adaptive self, the social self, and self-non-self. Within each of these, there are further subcategories. The material self is composed of the somatic self and the possessive self; the personal self is subdivided into self-image and self-identity; the adaptive self is comprised of self-esteem and self-activity; the social self refers to preoccupations and social activities as well as reference to sex; and the self-non-self construct includes reference to others and others' opinion of self. Within each of these substructures there are further divisions or categories. To date, L'Ecuyer has attempted to chart changes in the lowest order categories across the life span. Thus, his model is more multidimensional than it is hierarchical, although it has the potential to identify how the components might be hierarchically arranged. It should be noted that self-esteem, in this model, is considered a substructure under the adaptive self, and is further divided into feelings of competence and personal worth.

In Epstein's (1973) treatment of the self as self-theory, he suggests that the postulates one has about the self are hierarchically arranged. However, self-esteem represents the superordinate construct under which other subcategories are organized. He suggests that

Under a postulate evaluating overall self-esteem, there will be second-order postulates relating to general competence, moral self-approval, power, and love worthiness. . . . Lower order postulates organized under competence include assessments of general mental and physical ability. The lowest order postulates under compe-

tence include assessments of specific abilities. As one moves from lower order to higher order postulates, the postulates become increasingly important to the maintenance of the individual's self-theory. (p. 411)

Of particular interest here is the convergence between Epstein's second-order postulates and the four dimensions of self-evaluation that have been isolated by Coopersmith (1967). Corresponding to competence, moral self-approval, power, and love worthiness in Epstein's scheme are the following for Coopersmith: (1) *competence* (success in meeting achievement demands); (2) *virtue* (adherence to moral and ethical standards); (3) *power* (which involves the ability to control and influence others); and (4) *significance* (the acceptance, attention, and affection of others).

An examination of the literature reveals that these various dimensions have been given differing degrees of emphasis, depending on the particular theorist or investigator. In Coopersmith's (1967) research he has focused on two of the four dimensions he isolated, competence (within the academic setting) and social acceptance, by both parents and peers. White (1959, 1960, 1963) has highlighted these same two dimensions, within a broader theoretical framework. He emphasizes the importance of the early experience of efficacy during infancy. "From this point onward self-esteem is closely tied to feelings of efficacy, and as it develops, to the more general cumulative sense of competence" (1963, p. 134). Efficacy, for White, is only one source of self-esteem. The other source, "the esteem in which we are held by others, begins to assume importance as soon as the child attains a clear enough conception of others to sense them as the sources of attitudes" (1963, p. 135).

Hales (1979a, 1979b) has recently built on such a distinction, emphasizing the two sources of information children utilize in making self-esteem judgments. These constitute an inner source, defined as one's sense of competence or efficacy, and an outer source based on approval by others. Hales also implicates the evaluation of one's morality. She notes that another major component of self-esteem is a sense of "moral integrity" defined as the appraisal of congruence between one's own internalized moral standards and one's actual behavior.

In our own theoretical and empirical efforts (Harter, 1978, 1981a; Harter & Connell, 1982), we have also attempted to isolate several self-evaluative dimensions. These include the dimensions of competence (both cognitive and physical), social acceptance, and sense of control over the outcomes in one's life, in addition to the assessment of feelings of general self-worth. To date we have been interested in the relationships among these dimensions, however, and have not yet cast them into a hierarchical model.

Rosenberg (1965, 1979), in contrast to each of these theorists, has focused exclusively on global self-esteem, which he conceptualizes as a unidimensional construct. He has demonstrated numerous theoretically derived correlates of global self-esteem including depressive affect, anxiety and psychosomatic symptoms, interpersonal insecurity, participation in extracurricular activities among high school students, parental disinterest, and participation in Upward Bound programs (see also Wylie, 1974).

Thus, in addition to global self-esteem, each of the four dimensions of self-esteem identified by Epstein and Coopersmith has found its way into the theorizing as well as the scale construction efforts of researchers. The fact that different investigators have focused on different dimensions, at different levels of specificity, is in part what accounts for the diverse findings subsumed under the rubric of self-esteem. Nevertheless, these four dimensions, in conjunction with the construct of global self-esteem, would appear to provide an appealing framework on which we can begin to build a comprehensive developmental theory of self-esteem.

In postulating a hierarchical structure, global self-esteem appears at the top, as a superordinate construct. Under self-esteem we can then consider the four dimensions: competence, power or control, moral worth, and acceptance. Beneath each of these dimensions will be the more specific domains in which these constructs may be manifest. For example, under competence our own work has isolated three meaningful domains for children, cognitive, social, and physical skills (Harter, 1981a, 1982b).

The "power" dimension of Epstein and Coopersmith seems more cogently translated into one's sense of *control*. A burgeoning literature on the topic of locus of control suggests the fruitfulness of considering the degree to which the child feels internally responsible for outcomes in one's life or attributes these events to sources beyond one's control. Content domains such as cognitive, social, and physical have been found to be appropriate for this construct as well (Connell, 1980).

The dimension of moral worth may also be subdivided into domains. Minton's (1979) data suggest that two critical arenas are home and school. Within each, children appear to be concerned with engaging in positive moral behavior (helping, obeying) as well as curtailing or controlling behaviors that are morally unacceptable (e.g., aggression toward others). The fourth dimension, worthiness of love and acceptance, also dictates certain obvious subdivisions, for example, family, both parents and siblings, versus others, both adults and peers. The various subcategories suggested here are primarily examples of the direction in which one might proceed, and are not meant to be exhaustive.

Affect as a Component of Self-Esteem

Self-esteem typically makes reference to how one "feels" about one's worth across the evaluative dimensions just described. However, little attention has been devoted to the specific role of affect, despite the historical precedent in the works of James and Cooley. Cooley (1902), for example, addressed the varieties of self-feeling, differentiating between such positive affects as pride, vanity, self-respect, reverence, confidence, hope, and the negative affects of shame, mortification, guilt, contrition, self-abnegation, and resentment. Certain items on measures of self-esteem for children are couched in affective language, for example, "I get upset at home," "I worry about my schoolwork," "I am often afraid." However, these items are typically given no particular conceptual or empirical status but are merely averaged in with more evaluative items, for example, "I am smart," "I have a lot of friends." Our own research suggests the fruitfulness of distinguishing between one's evaluation or *judgment* of one's worth on a given dimension and one's *affective* reaction to this judgment (Harter & Connell, 1982). Within the cognitive realm, our data indicate the following predictive chain: one's actual achievement predicts one's evaluation of one's academic competence, which in turn directly influences one's affective reactions. It is the affective component, in turn, that mediates or predicts one's motivational orientation toward engaging in school-related tasks.

We have yet to differentiate the specific types of affective reactions. It may well be that these vary as a function of the particular dimension. For example, in the domain of cognitive competence, positive evaluations may evoke pride, whereas negative evaluations may evoke anxiety or self-anger. Affects such as shame and guilt may be more closely linked with judgments of one's moral worth. Judgments about the degree to which one is in control of one's life may pull for affects such as frustration or depression. It is unlikely that such direct correspondences will be obtained, given the individual differences that would also be anticipated. However, attention to the affective component of self-esteem may well be an important direction to pursue, given the implication that it is the affective reaction that mediates behavior. Buss' (1980) recent formulation of self-consciousness is gratifying to witness in this regard, although, given his focus on social anxiety, his treatment is largely restricted to such negative affects as embarrassment, shame, audience anxiety, and shyness.

A Developmental Approach to Self-Esteem

Within this framework emphasizing the hierarchical organization of the components of self-esteem, the following developmental questions can be raised: (1) How are each of the four second-order dimensions to be defined at different developmental levels? For example, what are the most salient issues involving competence, moral worth, sense of control, and acceptability that form the basis for self-evaluation at different ages? Here one might be guided by the theorizing of Erikson (1950, 1968) and White (1963) with regard to competence, and Kohlberg (1969, 1976) in the realm of morality. (2) What is the relative weighting given to each of these dimensions at different developmental levels? Is sense of control, for example, more critical to one's self-evaluation at certain developmental periods than at others? Is moral worth? (3) What are the relationships among these four dimensions, and how might these change with age? For example, is sense of control or perceived competence more intimately related to one's acceptance and lovability at certain periods than at others? (4) To what extent do children at different developmental levels even base their evaluations of self on this type of hierarchical model? We speculated earlier that the capacity and penchant of the concrete operational child for hierarchically ordering objects and events in the nonpsychological realm might also be observed with regard to self-constructs. However, there are no data on this question. (5) At what point in development is the child capable of constructing a sense of global self-esteem, a superordinate construct dependent on, but detached from, the more discrete self-evaluations of the second-order dimensions? What function does such a global self-concept fulfill, over and above the second-order dimensions? (6) What are the affective reactions to one's domain-specific evaluative judgments as well as one's sense of global self-esteem, and to what extent do these affects mediate behavior? (7) Finally, what are the antecedents of both the second-order dimensions, as well as the more global feeling of self-esteem, and how might

this help us to understand the individual differences observed?

Such an approach to the development of self-esteem is no small challenge. How we measure one's global sense of self-esteem is perhaps the stickiest of problems. Investigators have had considerable success in measuring the second-order dimensions, as we will see. However, we cannot be content merely to infer global self-esteem from some combination of measurable self-evaluations at the second or third levels, though this has tended to be the strategy. Rosenberg (1979) provides an excellent analysis of this problem. He concurs that one cannot simply assess an individual's attitude toward his or her specific characteristics and then add up these responses in order to arrive at a global self-esteem score.

> The critical drawback to this procedure is that it overlooks the extent to which the self-concept is a structure whose elements are arranged in a complex hierarchical order. Hence, simply to add up the parts in order to assess the whole is to ignore the fact that the global attitude is the product of an enormously complex synthesis of elements which goes on in the individual's phenomenal field. It is not simply the elements per se but their relationship, weighting, and combination that is responsible for the final outcome. (p. 21)

Wylie (1974) is also critical of those test constructors who combine responses to items reflecting diverse content, and then conclude that the total score represents general (content-free) self-worth.

The empirical roadblock, however, inheres in the fact that in all likelihood the individual is not *aware* of the beta weights that make up this delicate equation. Rosenberg (1979) acknowledges the problem, but is more hopeful about a solution. "The subject himself may be as ignorant as the investigator about how this complex synthesis of elements has been achieved, but he is in a unique position to recognize, as a matter of immediate experience, the final result. He alone can experience whether he has a generally favorable or unfavorable, positive or negative, pro or con feeling toward himself as a whole" (p. 21).

Thus, for Rosenberg, the individual's inability to reconstruct the hierarchy on which a self-esteem judgment is based should not hinder us from assessing its phenomenological expression as a feeling of general, overall self-worth. How one proceeds along this particular path, fraught with conceptual and methodological perils, is easier said than done. (I am reminded here of our own empirical fumblings as we have attempted to measure global self-esteem. One 10-year-old subject helped us immensely; after we had tried any number of devious questions designed to tap this overall evaluation, with exasperation she asked: "Are you trying to find out how I feel about myself *in general?*") In the next section we will review the more widely used self-esteem instruments for children and adolescents and will evaluate the problems as well as the successes encountered in these assessment efforts.

Psychometric Considerations in the Assessment of Self-Esteem

This discussion will concentrate on those instruments that have either enjoyed popular use or illuminate critical issues that have been raised. Comprehensive critiques can be found in Wylie (1974) and in Robinson and Shaver (1973). Thus, this section is not meant to be an exhaustive review of the studies on self-esteem that abound in the literature. Wylie has performed a thankless but admirable task of this, particularly from a methodological perspective. The intent here will be to highlight representative studies that pertain to issues in scale construction; the consideration of self-esteem as a global versus a differentiated construct; developmental differences in self-esteem; correlates of self-esteem; the stability of this construct; and possible antecedents.

The Coopersmith Self-Esteem Inventory

The two most widely employed instruments with children are the Coopersmith Self-Esteem Inventory (Coopersmith, 1959, 1967) and the Piers-Harris Children's Self-Concept Scale (Piers & Harris, 1969). On both of these self-report instruments, a total score is calculated across items tapping diverse content, and this total score is considered to reflect the child's global self-esteem.

Coopersmith's measure is particularly disappointing, for a number of reasons. His thoughtful introduction to the possible dimensions of self-esteem in children is not paralleled in the actual construction of the measure. The original item pool was drawn from an *adult* scale (see Rogers & Dymond, 1954), and items were reworded for children. Coopersmith initially identified four potential domains across which self-evaluations might differ: school, peers, parents, and general references to the self. However, on the basis of an unspecified analysis of the responses of 56 children 10- to-12-years-old, he concluded that children of this age do not

make differentiations among these domains, and therefore one is justified in calculating a total score. This score is interpreted as an index of the child's global feeling of self-esteem, which can then be generalized to any domain.

Subsequent factor-analytic studies (e.g., Kokenes, 1974), demonstrate that this conclusion is simply unwarranted, as do the findings with other instruments that demonstrate that children make clear distinctions between domains that have been meaningfully derived, for example, the Piers and Harris Self-Concept Scale, and the Perceived Competence Scale for Children (Harter, 1982b). The use of an adult self-esteem scale as a model for the Coopersmith measure may in part be responsible.

The reported split-half and test-retest reliabilities are quite respectable (see Robinson & Shaver, 1973; Wylie, 1974), although it is difficult to determine precisely what is being reliably assessed. For example, the Coopersmith Self-Esteem Inventory has been found to be highly correlated with social desirability scores (see Robinson & Shaver, 1973). While the original scale included a separate 8-item lie scale, nowhere does Coopersmith present any data on these lie items. In our own experience with this instrument, we have found that the self-esteem items are moderately and significantly correlated with the lie items as well as with scores on the Social Desirability Response Scale for Children (Crandall, Crandall, & Katkovsky, 1965). At best, the scale would seem to be tapping the child's idealized self across a variety of diverse content areas. Wylie (1974) raises a number of other concerns, and on balance concludes that the Coopersmith is "not the instrument of choice for self-concept research on child subjects." (p. 174).

Recently, there have been attempts to re-examine the subscale structure of the Coopersmith through factor-analytic procedures (Drummond & McIntire, 1977; Kokenes, 1974; McIntire & Drummond, 1976). The data provided by Kokenes are the most readily interpretable, and represent separate factor analyses on approximately 1,500 pupils each in grades four through eight. Her findings reveal more factors than the original four domains identified by Coopersmith, that is, self, family, peers, and school. For example, the original domain of self breaks down into three separate factors, Perceived Inadequacy of Self, Perceived Adequacy of Self, and Rejection of Self. The items tapping family relationships result in two separate factors, Good Parent Relationships and Poor Parent Relationships. The school domain was also best represented by two factors, one involving academic success and a second tapping school failure. Finally, the peer items tended to cluster together to form one factor involving social success with peers.

One purpose of Kokenes' study was to examine possible grade differences in the factors of self-esteem. Her findings indicate basically the same factor structure at each of the grade levels tested, although there are a few differences in the amount of variance accounted for by a given subscale at different ages. For example, Rejection of Self accounts for slightly more than 50% of the variance for sixth graders, whereas the variance values for the other grades range between 10% and 13%. Unfortunately, the author misinterprets the meaning of these differences. She concludes that "sixth graders were more rejecting of themselves than were children in other grade levels" (p. 958). Differences in factor variance say nothing about the mean level of rejection expressed at a given age level. Instead, they point to the individual differences on this factor, which may suggest that the issue of rejection is a topic of particular concern in the sixth grade, one better coped with by some students than others.

In our own exploratory studies with the Coopersmith, we have found that a four-factor solution is the most interpretable for children in the fourth through sixth grades (Harter & Ward, 1978). Factors tapping academic performance, parental acceptance, and peer relations emerge, though these are not clearly defined by those items Coopersmith designated for these domains. The most interesting factor, however, which accounted for the most variance, was defined by an amalgam of items from each of Coopersmith's four areas. It shares many items in common with Kokenes' first factor, labeled Perceived Inadequacy of the Self. However, what struck us as common among the items defining our first factor was the prevalence of *negative affects* associated with self-evaluations across the different domains. Some of the highest loading items were "I get upset easily at home," "I'm often sorry for the things I do," "I often get discouraged in school," "I often feel ashamed of myself," "Things usually don't bother me," "I get upset easily when I'm scolded." While these findings need to be pursued more systematically, they are intriguing in light of the previous discussion of the role of affect. It would be interesting to determine, for example, whether the affective factor is the best predictor of behaviors hypothesized to be related to self-esteem.

The Piers-Harris Self-Concept Scale

The Piers-Harris measure, and the assumptions underlying its construction, provide an interesting contrast to the Coopersmith Self-Esteem Inventory. Unlike the Coopersmith measure, which was modeled after an adult scale, the Piers-Harris items were adapted from a pool of statements collected by Jersild (1952) who asked children to comment on features about themselves which they liked and didn't like. For Piers and Harris, self-concept refers to "a set of relatively stable self-attitudes" which are "not only descriptive but also evaluative" (Piers, 1976, p. 1). Unlike Coopersmith, Piers and Harris seem to have begun their endeavor to construct a scale under the assumption that the self-concept was relatively unidimensional. However, their initial factor analysis of the scale, with a sample of sixth graders, revealed the existence of six interpretable factors: behavior, intellectual status, physical appearance and attributes, anxiety, popularity, and happiness/satisfaction.

Since the initial factor analysis in 1963, a number of investigators have performed factor analyses employing different populations and age groups, and these findings are reported in Piers (1976). Piers summarizes these studies that seem to suggest that the first three factors are strongly supported. The fourth factor, anxiety, seems to emerge consistently across different samples, though the loadings are small. The fifth and sixth factors, popularity and happiness/satisfaction, appear to be the weakest factors, even though Piers concludes that they are probably worth retaining.

The Piers-Harris instrument receives better marks from reviewers than the Coopersmith Inventory (see Buros, 1970; Robinson & Shaver, 1973; Wylie, 1974), although there has been some question about its reliability for low scorers (see Wylie, 1974; Smith & Rogers, 1977). It is unfortunate, however, that investigators have clung to the overall score as the metric of choice. There is the suggestion that the cluster scores will somehow add something to our understanding of self-concept, but to date this has not been systematically pursued. Furthermore, the thrust of factors analytic studies that have been performed seems to be to demonstrate the existence or nonexistence of the original six factors across a variety of age groups and populations. Little attention has been given to the possibility that the factor structure might change for different developmental levels or in different populations, either in terms of the numbers of factors or their interpretation.

However, one may question the very use of factor-analytic procedures in illuminating our understanding of the developmental processes underlying self-evaluation. In this literature, researchers seem to take as a given fact that the Coopersmith or the

Piers-Harris (depending on one's preference) measure is synonymous with self-esteem or evaluative self-concept, and that further factor—or cluster—analyses at different ages will shed light on developmental change in this construct. What seems to be ignored in this strategy is an appreciation basic to factor analysis, that you can only get out a finite number of variations on what you put in. If the dimensions and items initially included were not based on developmental considerations, one would not expect factor-analytic procedures to produce any compelling results regarding meaningful ontogenetic change.

No scale has yet to adopt a developmental framework. Such an approach would not only need to attend to the dimensions and domains outlined earlier, but it would also require some sensitivity to the nature of self-descriptions at different developmental levels. In the earlier section on the construction of the self it was argued that the child shifts his or her focus, from specific behaviors to trait labels to abstractions. Psychological dimensions such as emotions, motives, and inner thoughts were also postulated. Thus a developmentally based scale must ultimately be able to tap the changing nature of these descriptions.

In conclusion, if the intent of factor-analytic studies is merely to determine if a particular structure of clearly defined dimensions built into the scale exists for a given age group, then this goal can be accomplished. If our intent is to understand the developmental process through which self-evaluations are constructed and manifest, then our strategy must be very different indeed.

Rosenberg's Self-Esteem Scale

Although Rosenberg's (1965) self-esteem scale is of interest in light of the issue of how one best taps global self-esteem, it was initially designed for adolescents and adults. As discussed earlier, Rosenberg argues strongly for the phenomenological experience of general self-worth, over and above one's evaluations of more discrete characteristics and attributes. Based on this assumption, he constructed a unidimensional measure that taps this global perception. His 10-item scale taps content involving the degree to which one is satisfied with his or her life, feels he or she has a number of good qualities, has a positive attitude toward oneself, feels useless, desires more self-respect, or thinks one is a failure.

Wylie's (1974) review of this instrument is quite favorable. She notes that one merit of its brief, direct approach is that it does not assume that a group of items with heterogeneous content, chosen by the experimenter, and of variable and unknown salience to subjects may be summed to indicate global self-regard. She goes on to note that the reliability is impressive for a 10-item scale, and that it has yielded numerous relationships that support its construct validity. In his more recent studies (Rosenberg, 1979), grade-school children as well as adolescents have been included. Rosenberg has documented the effects of ethnicity, religiosity, and social class of self-esteem. He has found, for example, that it is primarily contextual dissonance which damages self-esteem, not one's ethnic or religious identifications per se. Thus, if one must function in a dissonant comparison reference group, for example, a black child attending a primarily white school, self-esteem may suffer because one's abilities or achievements compare unfavorably with the majority members of the group. Rosenberg's data provide a very thoughtful analysis of how the psychological processes of self-evaluation are affected by one's sociological context.

Rosenberg has not yet devoted his attention to the possible developmental parameters of global self-esteem. Nor is it clear whether his downward extension to elementary school children is tapping the same general construct as is measured during adolescence. If one assumes, as does Rosenberg, that the subject may be ignorant of the factors that go into the judgments of one's global self-esteem, then we are faced with both a conceptual and empirical dilemma. How do we ever determine what this index taps? Rosenberg has been content to focus on the construct validity of his instrument; however, this leaves many questions for the developmentalist who wishes to understand the process through which this evaluation comes to be made.

Perceived Competence Scale for Children

In our own theorizing and research, we have grappled with the question of whether to consider self-esteem to be a global evaluation or whether to focus on the evaluations in discrete domains (Harter, 1978, 1981a, 1982b). Our solution has been to do both. The purpose for constructing the Perceived Competence Scale for Children was twofold: (1) to provide an instrument that would be sensitive to domain-specific perceptions of competence, yet (2) allow for a determination of one's global self-esteem over and above one's perception of competence. The focus on the competence dimension was dictated by our desire to test certain predictions derived from our theoretical model of the development of intrinsic mastery motivation. For example, the model predicts that one correlate of an intrinsic mastery orientation in a given skill domain is a feeling of competence at that skill. The four-factor structure of this instrument reveals that, across the age span from third to tenth grades, pupils make clear distinctions between cognitive, social, and physical competence, as well as what we have labeled general self-worth. This structure, which has now been replicated in numerous samples, is characterized by extremely high loadings on the designated factors, with no systematic cross-loadings. In addition, a new question format, designed to offset the tendency to give socially desirable responses, has proved extremely successful.

Given the repeated demonstration of this stable factor structure, we cannot concur with Winne, Marx, and Taylor (1977), who find little evidence that children make distinctions between the physical, social, and academic facets of the self-concept. They base this conclusion on their findings from a multitrait, multimethod analysis of three self-concept inventories; the Piers-Harris scale (1969), the Sears Self-Concept Inventory (1966), and the Gordon "How I See Myself" scale (1968). In this study they found very little evidence for the discriminant validity of these three facets of self-evaluation. Their results also suggest that there were strong influences attributable to method, for example, item content and response format. Given that on each of these three instruments there was little a priori attention given to the construction of items that represented meaningful domains, the lack of divergent validity is not particularly surprising. As Wylie (1974) reminds us, the model of the majority of self-concept scales with children is based on the assumption that global self-regard can be inferred from a diverse assortment of item content. In contrast, the assumption underlying our construction of the Perceived Competence Scale for Children was that children do make distinctions among competence domains if care is taken to select specific items that meaningfully tap these domains.

Furthermore, Minton (1979) has demonstrated that children utilize different sources of information in making judgments in these four domains. Her factor-analysis of the reasons elementary school children give for their competence and self-worth indicate domain differences in the sources of information. Children's judgments of cognitive competence are based on (1) Speed of Performance (how quickly one gets one's work done); (2) Effort (how hard one works or studies); and (3) Authority Evaluation (what teachers and parents tell the child). In the physical domain, the three factors emerge: (1) Picked by Peers (to play on teams); (2) Authority

Evaluation (teacher or coach tells one) and (3) Concrete Ability and Liking (how fast one learns skills and rules, and how much one enjoys it). In the realm of social acceptance the criteria involve: (1) Feedback from Peers (how other children respond); and (2) Personal Attributes (friendly, nice, shy, easy to like). The four bases for judgments of general self-worth were described earlier in this section.

These findings are interesting in light of those theoretical treatments of the sources of information children utilize in making judgments of competence and self-worth. We noted earlier that White (1963) and Hales (1979a) have stressed two sources, the information one gleans from the success of one's efforts toward efficacy and competence, and an external source that involves the evaluations of significant others. Minton's data indicate that both sources are operative, although they vary according to domain. For example, Authority Evaluation is more critical in the cognitive realm, whereas Peer Feedback is important in the physical and social domains. Domain-specific efficacy information is utilized in both the cognitive and physical realms, whereas personal attributes are more salient in the social realm.

Although the Perceived Competence Scale is not a developmentally based instrument, the attempts to devise a pictorial version for younger children, ages 4 to 7, have revealed some interesting ontogenetic differences (Harter, 1981a; Harter & Pike, 1981). The subscales included were cognitive competence, physical competence, and social acceptance by peers, in addition to a fourth subscale, which tapped social acceptance by one's mother. General self-worth was not included based on our assumption, supported by pilot data, that young children do not have a sense of the self in general; that is, they can only evaluate specific behaviors. Furthermore, it was necessary to devise separate forms for 4- to 5-year-olds and for 6- to 7-year-olds, given that a number of the activities defining competence and acceptance change across these ages. Factor analyses revealed that a two-factor solution best describes this scale. The first, defined by the cognitive and physical subscales, has been labeled "general competence," and the second, comprised of the peer and mother acceptance subscales, has been labeled "social acceptance."

Several developmental considerations are noteworthy. Not only do young children not possess a concept of general self-worth, but they do not make a distinction between cognitive and physical skills. One is either competent or incompetent across these activities. Furthermore, a follow-up study (Harter & Chao, 1981) reveals that, at this age level, peer acceptance is not perceived in terms of competence. Instead, one is accepted by others or one is not, and there is little that one can do of a skill nature to obtain this acceptance. In contrast, for both cognitive and physical items, practice and learning are mentioned as the route to competence. These findings indicate the fruitfulness of adopting a developmental perspective in that the specific activities, the number of underlying dimensions, as well as the bases on which evaluations are made appear to change with age.

In looking ahead, given the diversity in the assumptions and models underlying the construction of the various instruments employed, it is difficult to present an integrated picture of those studies purporting to examine the stability correlates, and antecedents of, self-esteem. A few of these studies will next be reviewed in order to convey a sense of this literature. The reader is referred to Wylie (1979) for a comprehensive critique.

Stability of Self-Esteem

The typical psychometric approach to the question of stability has been test-retest correlational data. For each of the major scales reviewed, test-retest reliability coefficients over a period of several weeks or a few months are quite respectable, typically between .70 and .90 (see Wylie, 1979). Coopersmith (1967) has made the strongest claim for the stability of self-esteem, based on a test-retest correlation of .70 over a three-year period. From this he seems to conclude that self-esteem so measured is a relatively enduring judgment on the part of the child.

It should be noted, however, that Coopersmith's subjects were elementary school children between the ages of 10 and 12, a period in which the self-concept appears to be relatively stable (see Rosenberg, 1979). In contrast, the transition to adolescence and junior high school seems to bring about potentially dramatic changes. Simmons, Rosenberg, and Rosenberg (1973) found a decrease in self-esteem between the ages of 12 and 13, and have hypothesized that the shift to junior high school was the primary factor responsible. Their evidence suggests that this environmental change puts demands on the adolescent that heighten self-consciousness, instability of self-image, and lowered self-esteem. Our own findings bolster this conclusion, in that scores on the perceived competence scale take a dip during the first year of junior high (Connell, 1981; Harter & Connell, 1982). Moreover, while the cor-

relation between perceived cognitive competence and achievement test scores increases steadily across grades three through six, this relationship plummets in the seventh grade and then increases in magnitude across the eighth and ninth grades (Harter, 1982b). These findings suggest that the seventh grader has difficulty in adjusting to the novel demands and expectations of the junior high environment, which in turn affects one's ability to make realistic evaluations of one's cognitive competence.

These results suggest that we consider the issue of stability from a developmental perspective, taking account not only of age changes but differences in the environmental context. One would expect more stability in self-esteem during the later elementary school years to the extent that environmental demands, performance expectations, and one's social comparison group are all relatively stable. The shift to junior high school brings about changes for each of these factors, with accompanying alterations in one's self-evaluation. Exploratory data (Harter & Pike, 1981) suggest that a similar disruption in perceived competence and social acceptance occurs as a result of the transition from kindergarten to first grade. If one extends his interpretation into adulthood, one would predict similar periods of instability as one enters a new academic environment, for example, college, or adopts a new occupational or interpersonal role.

Another potential area for research involves a developmental consideration of the reasons children give for their feelings of worth and competence. While Minton (1979) found these to be relatively stable during the later elementary school years, it is highly likely that in junior high school there would be changes in both the nature of these categories and their salience. The degree to which the sources of information are relatively extrinsic, for example, reliance on the judgment of others in evaluating the self, would be of interest in light of the renewed importance of the looking glass self during adolescence, as well as during subsequent stages of adult development.

Correlates and Predictors of Self-Esteem

Subject Characteristics

An encounter with Wylie's (1979) most recent review of the self-concept literature is somewhat overwhelming given the hundreds of studies that have attempted to examine a particular correlate or predictor of self-esteem. Wylie's lack of enthusiasm for the majority of instruments employed with children, and her trenchant critique of these studies, leads us to question the value of reviewing this literature even in summary fashion. We will attempt to convey a few highlights (as well as low points).

In Wylie's treatment of these studies, she first considers the relationship between self-concept and such variables as age, sex, socioeconomic class, and race. When one delimits the topic to studies of self-regard in children and adolescents, there is very little in the way of systematic documentation of significant relationships. In reviewing the developmental studies of self-regard, Wylie is lead to conclude that these studies are "so diverse and respectively inconclusive, they will sustain no integrated, substantive summary" (p. 39).

The failure to find gender differences is supported by Maccoby and Jacklin's review (1974). Wylie cites a number of possible reasons for null findings, including the practice of summing across items in order to obtain a global self-regard score. She speculates that "perhaps males and females obtain equivalent total scores by endorsing different sets of items" (p. 272) and suggests that item and factor-analyses be performed separately for each gender. This would allow for the possibility that "perhaps the factor structures of over-all self-regard are similar for the two sexes, but females obtain higher scores on some factors, males on others" (p. 272). Support for this contention comes from an analysis of the Perceived Competence Scale, which consistently reveals that boys report perceptions of greater physical competence at sports and outdoor games than girls do (Harter, 1982b).

The relationship between self-regard and socioeconomic status is more complex, but Wylie concludes that there is no support for the hypothesis of a direct relationship between self-regard and socioeconomic status: "In short, we know so little about what all the relevant class-linked factors might be, their relative importance, and their possible ways of interacting that no single functional relationship is clearly implied by extant theoretical suggestions" (1979, p. 65). She reaches a similar conclusion concerning those studies examining self-regard in different racial groups. One theme throughout her treatment of this topic involves the mistaken impression that blacks' self-esteem is inferior to that of whites. Wylie thoughtfully suggests that in order to make sense out of this literature one must "differentiate among the development of: (a) the general concept of race as a category; (b) more sophisticated knowledge about such a category; (c) evaluative attitudes toward racial groups, one's own

and others'; (d) a cognitive sense of one's own racial identity; (e) an evaluation of oneself, as this is dependent on one's sense of racial identity" (p. 160).

Self-Esteem and Achievement

For the most part, self-esteem has been related to subject characteristics and to other psychological constructs such as locus of control rather than behavior per se. There is relatively little research directed toward behavioral correlates (see Wylie, 1979). One exception to this pattern is the research relating self-esteem to achievement. Wylie reviews numerous studies in which achievement test scores have been related to self-regard in children. Across these studies she finds that the correlations tend to range from .10 to .50, and more typically fall within the .30s and low .40s. When the self-concept measures involve skills more specific to one's academic performance, then these correlations tend to be somewhat higher. Overall, however, she concludes that it is difficult to interpret the various findings in this literature caused by uncontrolled factors such as socioeconomic level and intellectual ability.

In the educational literature, the issue has been more than correlational. The question of cause has been of primary concern, given the implications for remediation. There are those traditionalists who feel that achievement success leads to enhanced self-esteem, although the more popular view to emerge in the 1960s emphasized the impact of self-esteem enhancement on one's academic performance. In summarizing this literature, Purkey (1970) concluded that "enhancing the self-concept is a vital influence in improving academic performance" (p. 27). This attitude was also adopted by those who have supported desegregation (e.g., Coleman, Campbell, Hobson, McPartland, Mood, Weinfeld, & York, 1966). Coleman and his colleagues took the position that desegregation of the schools would enhance the self-esteem of minority children, which in turn would result in their improved academic achievement. As Calsyn and Kenny (1977) note, however, "the debate between self-enhancement and skill development theorists has been largely rhetorical for both conceptual and methodological reasons" (p. 136). (See also Spears & Deese, 1973.)

More recently, this question has been addressed by investigators intent on testing causal models of the relationship between self-esteem and achievement. In one such longitudinal study, Bachman and O'Malley (1977) examined the relation between the self-esteem of high school males and their post-high school educational and occupational achievements.

They found no evidence that high school self-esteem bore any causal relationship to subsequent education or occupational attainment. Their data do suggest, however, that academic ability and achievement exert a causal influence on self-esteem.

Another recent study takes issue with this claim (Rubin, Maruyama, & Kingsbury, 1979). These investigators sought to test a causal model involving the following variables: ability at age 7 (tapped by the WISC), achievement tapped at ages 9, 12, and 15, and self-esteem, as defined by Coopersmith total scores obtained at age 12. In order to examine the relationships among these variables, they estimated the parameters of their model using a maximum-likelihood structural equation analysis (Joreskog, 1973). The influence of ability on achievement appears early such that intelligence at age 7 predicts achievement at age 9, but does not strongly affect achievement at ages 12 and 15. The best causal predictor of achievement during these later years is previous achievement. Of particular interest is their finding that *ability* at age 7 predicts self-esteem at age 12, whereas *achievement* does not exert a causal influence on self-esteem. Nor does self-esteem at age 12 influence subsequent achievement at age 15.

Based on their failure to find a relationship between self-esteem and achievement, these investigators concluded that there is no support for the development of intervention programs designed to improve academic achievement by enhancing self-esteem. They are undoubtedly correct, if by self-esteem we mean a diverse array of specific self-evaluations that are masked by the total score calculated on the Coopersmith. What is unfortunate, given the longitudinal data available to these investigators, is that they did not include a more specific measure of the pupils' self-evaluations in the area of academic performance. Presumably, however, their intent was to demonstrate that those educational practices designed to enhance the rather vague and global construct of self-esteem are ill-founded.

Recent data which indicate that one can establish causal links between achievement and self-evaluations if these judgments are specific to academic competence (Calsyn & Kenny, 1977; Connell, 1981; Harter & Connell, 1982). In order to examine the causal relationship between achievement and self-concept, Calsyn and Kenny employed a cross-lagged panel correlation technique (see Kenny, 1975). Their measures, taken from eighth-grade to twelfth-grade students at two time periods, included: self-concept of ability, the student's perception of the evaluations of parents, teachers, and friends, as well as grade-point average, which was the major index of achievement. Several rival models of the predictive relationships among these variables were tested. They summarize their findings as follows:

> The results are clearly more supportive of a skill development model in which academic achievement is causally predominant over self-concept of ability as well as perceived evaluation of others, rather than a two-stage self-enhancement model in which perceived evaluations of others are causally predominant over self-concept of ability, which in turn is causally predominant over academic achievement. (p. 142)

These patterns of causal predominance were much stronger in females than males.

In our cross-sectional research (Connell, 1981; Harter & Connell, 1982) we have employed structural-equation models to predict the relationships among achievement, perceived competence, and intrinsic versus extrinsic motivational orientation in the classroom (see also Harter, 1981b). For a sample of third through ninth graders, it was found that achievement is causally prior to perceived cognitive competence. Perceived competence, in turn, predicted one's motivational orientation: the greater one's sense of cognitive competence, the more intrinsically motivated one is to perform academically.

Two studies have sought to examine the relationship between self-judgments and classroom behavior directly. Shiffler, Lynch-Sauer, and Nadelman (1977) found that self-concept predicted children's observed task orientation in the classroom. Bierer and Harter (1981) have determined that the relationship among academic achievement, perceived cognitive competence, and a behavioral measure of preference for challenge depends on the degree to which children accurately perceive their competence. For accurate raters (defined in terms of the congruence between self-ratings and teacher's ratings of competence), achievement predicts perceived competence, which in turn predicts preference for challenge. For those who *underrate* their competence, actual achievement is negatively related to perceived competence; however, perceived competence does predict preference for challenge. For overraters, there are no significant relationships among these variables, suggesting that not only are their judgments of competence unrealistic, but these perceptions do not mediate their behavior. Moreover, their reported competence is relatively high; overraters prefer the less challenging tasks.

Overall, the results on the relationship between achievement and self-evaluation suggest that achievement impacts one's self-evaluation, provided that judgments focus on the academic domain. This relationship may be strongest for children who accurately perceive their competence. To the extent that achievement or cognitive competence is an *important* dimension of one's more general sense of self, then one might speculate that achievement would predict self-esteem on a measure such as Rosenberg's or our general self-worth subscale (Harter, 1982b). However, one would not expect to find such a relationship with self-esteem as defined by the Coopersmith or the Piers-Harris instruments. The conclusion of Bachman and O'Malley (1977) seems warranted, therefore; attempts to enhance a child's self-esteem, as defined by these scales, in order to increase academic performance may be a fruitless endeavor.

Efficacy and Locus of Control as Dimensions of Self-Evaluation

The content tapped by self-concept and self-esteem scales deals, for the most part, with relatively static characteristics or attributes of the self. One judges that one is athletic, popular, competent, attractive, morally good, and so on. A more dynamic theme can be observed in several lines of theorizing and empirical research that have recently converged on the hypothesis that one's sense of efficacy and active control is also a critical dimension of self-evaluation. It was noted earlier that for White (1963), the roots of self-esteem lie in the developing infant's sense of efficacy. From personality and social learning theorists, we find increasing emphasis on constructs such as locus of control (Rotter, 1975), learned helplessness (Seligman, 1975), self-efficacy (Bandura, 1977a, 1981) and self-determination (deCharms, 1968; Deci, 1975).

Interestingly, it was Cooley who, in 1902, scooped all these modern-day theorists. For Cooley, self-esteem, or "self-feeling" to use his term,

> appears to be associated chiefly with ideas of the exercise of power, of being a cause. . . . The first definite thoughts that a child associates with self-feeling are probably those of his earliest endeavors to control visible objects—his limbs, his playthings, his bottle, and the like. Then he attempts to control the actions of the persons about him, and so his circle of power and self-feeling widens without interruption to the most complex of mature ambition. (pp. 145–146)

Groos (1898), writing at about the same period, also emphasized the "joy in being a cause."

Recent writers have echoed these observations. Bannister and Agnew (1977) view the personal sense of cause as one of the definite features of the self. "We entertain a notion of ourselves as causes, we have purposes, we intend, we accept a partial responsibility for the effects of what we do. The construing of ourselves as agent is clearly a superordinate contribution toward a total construction of a self" (p. 102). Brim (1976a) also considers this construct to be central to one's self-theory. "One's sense of personal control is in fact a system of belief, i.e., a theory about oneself in relation to one's environment, and a concern with causality, whether outcomes are a consequence of one's own behavior or tend to occur independently of that behavior" (p. 243).

There is a burgeoning literature on locus of control and its correlates, particularly with adults. The task here is to explore the implications of this construct for one's self-esteem. In the section of this chapter on infancy, sense of efficacy and control were introduced as the defining features of the earliest *I*-self, the self as *actor*. In the present context, one's sense of efficacy and control are treated as characteristics of the *Me,* the self as observed and evaluated. There has been relatively little *developmental* attention given to the construct of control and its relationship to self-concept and self-esteem. In the wake of the popularity of this construct in the adult literature, a number of measures have been constructed for children. The two most widely used instruments are the locus of control scale devised by Nowicki and Strickland (1973) and the Intellectual Achievement Responsibility Questionnaire (Crandall, Katkovsky, & Crandall, 1965). Both of these scales assess control on the dimension of internal to external, following in the theoretical footsteps of Rotter (1966) who viewed this as a relatively unidimensional trait. The Nowicki and Strickland instrument provides an index of the child's general or global sense of control along this dimension. In contrast, the Crandall et al. measure focuses on the academic domain, and allows for a separate assessment of one's sense of control over successes and failures.

Connell (1980) has recently introduced a new measure, the Multidimensional Measure of Children's Perceptions of Control, in which there is an attempt to recast locus of control into a more developmentally relevant and situationally-specific construct that he labels "perceptions of control." Three sources of control are independently assessed: Internal (I am responsible); External—powerful others (someone else is responsible); and Unknown (I don't know who or what is responsible). The Unknown subscale emerged during the construction of this measure. Connell found that children, unlike adults, do not make systematic attributions on the basis of chance or luck, whereas the degree to which children know who or what is in control is a very salient dimension. Items for each source of control tap successes and failures separately in the same four domains that were included on the Perceived Competence Scale for children; cognitive, social, physical, and general.

From the social learning theory perspective, we have Bandura's (1977a, 1981) concept of self-efficacy. Bandura notes that, among the different facets of self-knowledge, perhaps none is more central to people's everyday lives than the conception of their personal efficacy. In defining self-efficacy, Bandura distinguishes between *outcome* expectancies and *efficacy* expectations. An outcome expectancy is the person's estimate that a given behavior will lead to certain outcomes, whereas *efficacy* expectation is the conviction that one can successfully execute the behavior required to produce the outcome. For Bandura, self-efficacy is primarily concerned with judgments about how well one can execute actions in specific *prospective* or future situations, whereas the locus of control construct typically refers to a more generalized attribution of one's control over outcomes in the past, present, or future.

Bandura identifies four sources of efficacy information: feedback from performance accomplishments, vicarious experience (observing others' ability to execute an action competently), verbal persuasion by others, and emotional arousal (in that high arousal typically debilitates performance and thus leads to lower expectancy of success).

Bandura (1981) traces several factors that influence the developmental course of self-efficacy, including experience within the family and peer contexts. He notes that during the critical formative period of children's lives, the school functions as the primary setting for the cultivation and social validation of cognitive efficacy. The ability to make use of social comparison information is particularly critical to the development of self-appraisal skills. As Bandura notes (and as will be discussed further in a subsequent section under self-control), with increasing age, children become progressively more accurate in assessing their own competence in relation to their peers. In addition, Bandura reviews the evidence indicating that young children have difficulty in simultaneously attending to multiple efficacy cues, in distinguishing between important and minor indicants, and in processing sequential efficacy information. As a result, their self-appraisals are likely to be heavily dependent on immediate, salient outcomes and hence they are relatively unstable. Bandura and his colleagues have focused primarily on the process variables that might influence the relative strength of one's sense of self-efficacy, as well as various parameters and dimensions of self-efficacy that may affect performance in particular situations. These dimensions have yet to be systematically investigated within a developmental framework, a topic that will be the challenge to those interested in ontogenetic change.

Relationship Between Self-Esteem and Locus of Control

Several studies with children have examined the relationship between locus of control and self-esteem or its components. Prawat, Grissom, and Parish (1979) administered the Coopersmith Self-Esteem Inventory and the Nowicki-Strickland locus of control scale to samples of elementary school, middle school, and high school pupils. The relationship between self-esteem and locus of control was found to be consistently high for both males and females at each of these three educational levels, with correlations ranging from .58 to .66. The global nature of both of these instruments did not allow for a more differentiated pattern in the relationship among these variables.

In another study by Cunningham and Berberian (1976), the Coopersmith Self-Esteem Inventory and the Intellectual Achievement Responsibility Scale (Crandall et al., 1965) were administered to third and fourth graders. Children were first divided into high and low self-esteem groups. Their findings revealed that high self-esteem children assumed more personal responsibility for successful outcomes than failures. In examining the total responsibility score they found that high self-esteem boys were more internal than low self-esteem boys. However, the pattern was the reverse for the girls: high self-esteem girls were *less* internal than low self-esteem girls. They interpret the somewhat counterintuitive findings for the girls in terms of societal sex-role expectations. Since an internal orientation for girls may conflict with these expectations, such children do not receive approval for their efforts, which may in turn undermine their self-esteem.

Two studies report on the relationship between the Piers-Harris self-concept scale and the Intellectual Achievement Responsibility Scale. Felker and Thomas (1971) found that self-concept was related to responsibility for success for girls, but was related to responsibility for failure in boys. Piers (1977), however, found that for both boys and girls self-concept was significantly related to responsibility for success, but not failure.

These studies provide some evidence for a relationship between self-esteem and locus of control, although there are certain inconsistencies when one considers the dimensions of gender and the extent to which responsibility is assumed for successes and failures. Measurement problems may also mask the underlying processes contributing to these effects. Since self-concept is defined by the total score across items tapping diverse content, it is difficult to determine the precise meaning of these self-evaluations. One problem with the locus of control measures employed is that they do not allow for separate measures of internal and external orientations, given the assumption that this is a unidimensional trait. Thus, it becomes difficult to interpret scores that are not extreme, but fall within the midrange.

On Connell's (1980) measure, independent scores for the three sources of control, Internal, Powerful Others, and Unknown, are calculated. Furthermore, the domain-specific nature of this scale allows one to test more precise hypotheses about the relationship between one's sense of control and one's perceived competence in the same domain. The cognitive domain has received the most attention. In two different samples, it has been demonstrated that the Unknown subscale is the most powerful predictor of one's perceived cognitive competence (Connell, 1981; Harter & Connell, 1982). The less children say they know about what controls their successes and failures in school, the lower their perceived competence. Recent findings (Harter, 1980) suggest that in the domain of sports competence, the powerful others dimension is the primary predictor for boys, where relative internality is more critical for girls.

In an earlier section, it was suggested that we examine the relationship between each of the second-order dimensions (competence, control, acceptance by others, and morality) and self-esteem as a superordinate construct. Our own data speak to the relationship of the first three dimensions to general self-worth, for one sample of sixth-grade girls and boys. For girls, perceived cognitive competence (both evaluative and affective components), and social acceptance by peers were related to general self-worth; however, perceived control was not. For boys, cognitive competence (the evaluative component only), physical competence and peer acceptance as well as the Unknown control dimension in the cognitive realm predicted general self-worth. With regard to control, the boy who says he does not know what is responsible for his successes and failures in the academic realm seems to question his self-worth. Sex-role expectations to the effect that males should be in control, excel at sports, and should not display affect may be responsible for these gender differences; however, these hypotheses remain to be tested.

Although these relationships are interesting, a much more systematic approach to testing the model of self-esteem put forth must be adopted, within a meaningful developmental framework. The affective concomitants of each of the second-order dimensions should also be assessed as potential determinants of one's self-esteem. Moreover, the *importance* of each dimension must be addressed; our own data (Harter & Engstrom, 1981) reveal that the relative importance of success in the cognitive, social, and physical domains affects the relationship between perceived competence in a given domain and general self-worth. In future research, it is urged that investigators test more comprehensive models of the dimensions of self-esteem, instead of proceeding in piecemeal fashion by examining the correlations between two or three variables.

The Antecedents of Self-Esteem

It is admittedly difficult to address the antecedents of a construct that is as conceptually elusive as self-esteem. The most frequently cited empirical work on this topic is that of Coopersmith (1967), who sought to study the antecedents of self-esteem as defined by his Self-Esteem Inventory. Coopersmith focused on the child's acceptance and concerned treatment by others, examining parental attitudes and child-rearing techniques. Subjects were 10- to 12-year-old boys.

The major sources of information were in-depth interviews with the mothers in conjunction with an administration of the Parent Attitudes Research Instrument (Schaeffer & Bell, 1958). Data analytic procedures were rather complex; however, Coopersmith reduced this information to 58 family variables, of which 38 were significant. Maccoby (1980) provides a nice summary of the major findings that are difficult to dig out of the Coopersmith volume. Parents of boys with high self-esteem more often had the following attitudes and behavioral practices: (1) They were accepting, affectionate, and involved, treating the child's interests and problems as meaningful, and showing genuine concern; (2) They were strict in the sense that they enforced rules carefully and consistently, and sought to encourage children to uphold high standards of behavior. (3) They preferred *noncoercive* kinds of discipline, for example, denial of privileges and isolation, and typically discussed the reasons why the child's behavior was inappropriate; (4) They were democratic in the sense that the child's opinions were considered in decisions such as the hour of their bedtime, and the child participated in making family plans.

Most theorists would agree that acceptance, or unconditional positive regard, to use Rogers' (1951) term, is an essential prerequisite to positive self-esteem. Coopersmith attempts to speculate on why well-defined limits are also associated with high self-esteem. He suggests that well-defined limits assist the child in evaluating performance, as they facilitate comparisons and help to clarify many of the ambiguities in the realm of social behavior. For Coopersmith, limits enhance the child's self-definition in highlighting the restrictions and demands imposed by the real world, thereby clarifying one's role in the social environment.

Coopersmith's analysis is certainly plausible and has been accepted by many as the most compelling treatment of the effects of parental attitudes and child-rearing techniques on self-esteem. As Wylie (1979) notes, however, there are numerous methodological problems with this study. For example, the sample size is small and is restricted to boys within a narrow age range, 10 to 12. The measuring instruments have many inadequacies, particularly the Self-Esteem Inventory. The usefulness of the PARI scale has also been questioned (Becker & Krug, 1965). No information is available from fathers, a decided limitation in Wylie's opinion. She also notes complications in the formation of the groupings of subjects. Furthermore, there were undoubtedly numerous statistical tests performed, though the number is unspecified. One also questions the complex configurational interpretation of parental attitudes and behaviors when the data are treated in a more univariate fashion, with Chi Squares as the primary statistical metric. On balance, Wylie concludes that this study is extremely difficult to follow or to critically analyze. "It is such a potpourri of subjective variables and behavior variables, full of such confusing and conflicting statements, that the reader will find it practically impossible to assess" (p. 349). This reader concurs.

Wylie (1979) devotes an entire chapter to a review of studies examining the relationships between family variables and self-concept. Problems with unclear definitions of constructs, experimental design, correlational techniques employed to infer causal links, and inadequate measuring instruments limit the conclusions one can draw from this literature. Wylie concludes that there is some evidence for the claim that a child's level of self-regard is associated with the parent's reported level of regard for the child. A stronger relationship appears to hold between the child's self-perceptions and his perception of parental attitudes toward him. There is little evidence that birth order or father-absence significantly affects self-esteem.

Wylie registers some surprise that so few studies exist on the relationship between family variables and self-concept, given the extent of the lip service paid to the importance of the family context. She notes one major drawback in this area, namely the lack of any attempt to conceptualize a model of the relationships among the variables as has been done in other areas of the child-rearing literature, for example, Baumrind's (1971) model of the seven axes of parental authority. "Such a proposed model would make it possible, perhaps, to formulate more clearly the rationale concerning the psychologically relevant variables in identification and self-concept development and could serve as a focal point from which empirical research might be designed" (Wylie, 1979, p. 352).

There are a few recent attempts to put the self-esteem construct into a broader network of family-related variables. Hales (1979a, 1979b), for example, has attempted to look at the implications of Baumrind's parent typology for self-esteem. Her findings indicate that for girls self-esteem is higher if they have parents who exhibit warmth and acceptance, encourage independence, stress firm enforcement of rules and regulations, use clear directives, and require the child to assume responsibility at home. This constellation is very consistent with Coopersmith's observations, with one glaring exception. Hales only finds this influence for girls, while Coopersmith reports an effect for boys. Hales suggests that boys' self-esteem appears to be more strongly related to peer approval.

While these advances are promising, the use of a total score derived from the Coopersmith Inventory makes it difficult to interpret such findings in any precise manner. It would seem we not only need a more articulated theory of potentially relevant parenting variables, but an equally differentiated model of self-esteem, in keeping with our earlier suggestions. It is highly likely, for example, that the many facets of parental response would differentially affect the four dimensions of self-esteem that were identified as competence, control, moral worth, and worthiness of acceptance.

Moral worth, as a dimension of self-esteem, has been given the least attention. In Hales' theorizing, she takes an important step in urging that we give more weight to one's sense of moral integrity in the self-esteem equation. She notes that one can experience pride and satisfaction of moral achievement through exertion of self-control and resistance to temptation when pressures to transgress are strong. There is some convergence here with the work of Rosenberg (1979) and Minton (1979), both of whom have found that the dimension of self-control is mentioned by middle and late elementary school children as a factor contributing to their feelings of self-esteem. Hales has not yet incorporated these constructs into her empirical attack on parental antecedents. Nevertheless, her formulations, and related research, do provide a bridge between the literature on self-esteem and self-control. Typically, these constructs have been treated independently of one another, and each has received the attention of very different branches of the field. We next turn to the topic of self-control, in an attempt to integrate the treatment of self-control with our previous discussion of both the formation of the self-concept and the evaluative dimension of self-esteem.

SELF-CONTROL

Overview

The preceding sections have focused primarily on the self as a cognitive construction that changes with age and is the object of evaluative scrutiny. We now turn to another major function of the self, the control of its own *behavior*. Throughout the history of civilization, societies have devised training procedures whereby certain forms of external social control are supplanted by internal personal control, as the most efficient means of ensuring that the social and moral order is upheld. Thus, the developing child must learn to control impulses, postpone immediate gratification, impose delays of reward, and tolerate frustration, either by refraining from socially prohibited behaviors or engaging in prosocial behaviors.

Philosophers from ancient to modern times have wrestled with this issue within the context of "will," debating both the existence of a spirit or homunculus that is the source of will power, as well as the concept of free will. While this debate has continued for some, others (see Kanfer & Karoly,

1972; Thoreson & Mahoney, 1974) emphasize that from a psychological viewpoint, the important point is that most people act as if they do have free will. This, they claim, is more important than the philosophical issue itself. Within the realm of academic psychology, self-theorists have speculated on the importance of the self in the socialization process. However, three intellectual traditions have specifically paved the way for the more current theorizing and research on self-control: psychoanalytic thought (Freud, 1922), learning theory (Skinner, 1953), and Soviet neuropsychology (Luria, 1961; Vygotsky, 1962).

For Freud, self-control was linked to the development of ego strength, specifically the ego's adherence to the Reality Principle in order to ensure self-preservation. The Reality Prinicple "demands and enforces the postponement of satisfaction, the renunciation of the manifold possibilities of it, and the temporary endurance of 'pain' on the long circuitous road to pleasure" (1922, p. 6). Resistance to temptation was further facilitated by the development of the superego, the internalization of parental values that provided standards whereby the self could control its own conduct and moral behavior. For Freud, various vicissitudes along the path of development would come to determine the degree of self-control exhibited by a given individual. Moreover, there is the implication in Freud that while self-control is an individual difference variable, within a given individual it is assumed to be a relatively stable personality characteristic that operates across a variety of situations.

Out of this tradition, two major theoretical contributions have emerged. In the work of the Blocks (see J. Block, 1971; J. H. Block & J. Block, 1980), two major personality constructs, ego control and ego resiliency, have been studied longitudinally. Loevinger (see Loevinger & Wessler, 1970; Loevinger, Wessler, & Redmore, 1970), on the other hand, has cast the notion of ego or impulse control into a more general stage model of ego development. In this approach, adult behavior is characterized in terms of a modal stage that reflects the person's general orientation to the self and the world. (Each of these positions will be reviewed in a subsequent section.)

Within the learning theory tradition, Skinner (1953) first approached the issue of self-control in terms of the principles of operant conditioning. Self-control was viewed as a *process* through which an individual alters the probability of a response by altering the variables of which that response is a function. Self-control was particularly evident in situations where a response has conflicting consequences, for example, short-term rewarding consequences but long-term aversive consequences. For Skinner, one "controls himself precisely as he would control the behavior of anyone else—through the manipulation of variables of which behavior is a function. His behavior in doing so is a proper object for analysis, and eventually it must be accounted for with variables lying outside the individual himself" (1953, p. 4). As self-control procedures, he suggested physical restraint, the modification of discriminative stimuli, aversive self-stimulation, self-reinforcement, and "doing something else."

While Skinner acknowledged certain ambiguities in his formulation, his framework set the stage for a proliferation of theoretical models which have addressed the *processes* involved in self-control (cf. Bandura, 1971a, 1976, 1977b, 1978; Kanfer, 1971, 1977, 1980; Kanfer & Karoly, 1972; Karoly, 1977, 1982; Mahoney & Thoresen, 1974; Mischel, 1974; Mischel & Patterson, 1978; Thoresen & Mahoney, 1974). In contrast to the theories that have followed from a more psychoanalytic orientation, those based on the principles of social learning and behavior modification emphasize or allow for the situation-specificity of self-controlling and self-controlled responses. That is, self-control is not viewed as a trait or disposition. Moreover, there has been increasing emphasis on the role of cognitive processes as mediators in the self-control process.

A major impetus for the use of self-instructional programs with impulsive children has come from the theories of the Soviet psychologists Luria (1959, 1961) and Vygotsky (1962). Problems in lack of impulse control were related to children's inability to use verbal self-instruction as a means of inhibiting behavior. Luria specifically proposed a three-stage developmental sequence whereby inhibition as well as initiation of voluntary motor behaviors come under the child's verbal control. In the first stage, behavior is largely controlled by the speech of caretakers. In the second stage, the child's overt speech becomes an effective regulator of behavior. Finally, in stage three, the child's covert or inner speech is capable of assuming a self-governing role. Based on this model, Meichenbaum and his colleagues (Meichenbaum, 1975, 1976, 1977, 1978; Meichenbaum & Goodman, 1971) have developed a treatment program to train impulsive children to talk to themselves as a method for developing self-control. Others, notably Camp and her colleagues (Camp, 1980; Camp & Bash, 1982; Camp, Blom, Hebert & Van Doornick, 1977), have developed an extensive program for aggressive boys, utilizing self-instructional and interpersonal problem-solving techniques as a means of facilitating self-control.

There are some, for example, Goldiamond (1976), who continue to argue that constructs such as self-control and self-reinforcement are merely "explanatory fictions," and that all behavior is ultimately to be attributed to environmental events (see Brownell, 1978). Others (Rachlin, 1974) have claimed that self-control is a convenient mediating construct that is invoked when there is a large temporal gap between behavior and observable reinforcement. A somewhat stronger stance has been taken by Stuart (1972), who suggests that self-control is introduced as a mediating construct when the behavior of a person contradicts more direct predictions based on learning theory. As an example, he cites the behavior of an obese person who chooses to eat cottage cheese after an observable history of consuming cake. While we may interpret this behavior as a demonstration of self-control or willpower, Stuart would have us search for environmental contingencies not readily apparent that actually control such behavior. Catania (1975), in writing about the myth of self-reinforcement, shares the view that the individual is ultimately not in control of his or her behavior.

Karoly (1982), in discussing the metatheoretical aspects of self-management, agrees with the notion that such constructs are fictions. But as he cogently points out, the truly important question is whether it is a *useful* fiction. For many, it obviously is; it ranges from those who view self-control as an intrapsychic agent, a trait or dispositional construct, a moral orientation, a motivational orientation, to those who view it as a learned set of behaviors (Karoly, 1982). As Karoly goes on to point out, each of these orientations implies a person at the center. However, "The *self* in self-management implies not an independent or ultimate source of control, not a homunculus, not a formless entity existing in hyperspace, but the point of origin of an extended series of actions and reactions and the source of continuity that ties contemporary actions to distant goals and outcomes" (p. 81). Bandura (1978) makes a similar point with regard to the social learning perspective, noting that "the self-system is not a psychic agent that controls behavior. Rather, it refers to cognitive structures that provide reference mechanisms and to a set of subfunctions for the perceptions, evaluation, and regulation of behavior" (p. 348). In reviewing the self-control literature, the organization in this major section will be as follows. The importance of the self in the self-control process, as discussed by self-theorists, will first be noted. For the most part, however, these general formulations have not lead to empirical investigation. Next, the theories emphasizing ego control as a relatively stable personality characteristic will be reviewed. Discussion will then turn to those formulations within the social learning theory tradition, as well as the behavior modification tradition. The sequential models that have evolved from these literatures will be described. In their emphasis on self-monitoring, self-evaluation, and self-reward, these models provide the most convergence with topics discussed in previous sections of this chapter. Finally, there will be an attempt to put the self-control work within a developmental framework, suggesting hypotheses for future research.

Self-theorists' Formulations Concerning Self-Control

For the most part, self-theorists have offered only general theoretical speculations on the importance of self-control in maintaining the social and moral order. As a starting point, we must once again pay intellectual homage to James (1890/1963). For James, the self was not only defined in terms of its constituent components and the emotions they arouse, but by *behavior* as well, namely the self-seeking and self-preserving acts these emotions prompt. In describing this behavioral dimension he constructed a ''hierarchy of the Me's'' with the Me of biological impulses at the bottom, the social-self-seeking Me in the middle, and the spiritual self-seeking Me at the top. Implicit in this formulation is the progress toward the intellectual, moral, or spiritual Me, which presumably can only be accomplished if the self exercises some control over its bodily and social impulses.

Self-control within the social context is a more explicit theme in the writings of many others in the self literature. For example, in Kelly's (1955) theory, personal constructs are viewed as ''the controls that one places upon life—the life within him as well as the life which is external to him'' (p. 126). The self is one such superordinate construct in his system. According to Kelly,

When the person begins to use himself as a datum in forming constructs, exciting things begin to happen. He finds that the constructs he forms operate as rigorous controls upon his behavior. His behavior in relation to other people is particu-

larly affected. It is, of course, the comparison *he* sees or construes which affects his behavior. Thus, much of his social life is controlled by the comparisons he has come to see between himself and others. (p. 131)

Other writers, notably Sullivan (1953), find this prospect much less exciting. For Sullivan, the origins of the self-system rest on the irrational character of culture and society. ''Were it not for the fact that a great many prescribed ways of doing things have to be lived up to, in order that one shall maintain workable, profitable, satisfactory relations with his fellows; or were the prescriptions for the types of behavior in carrying on relations with one's fellows perfectly rational—then, for all I know, there would not be evolved, in the course of becoming a person, anything like the sort of self-system that we always encounter'' (p. 168).

For Sullivan, the self-system represented ''an organization of educative experiences called into being by the necessity to avoid or to minimize incidents of anxiety'' (p. 165). According to Sullivan, the infant introjects the forbidding gestures of the mother, directed toward relief of zonal tensions, initially. That is, the child incorporates the values and standards and prohibitions of the significant others in the culture, and learns to control behavior in order to obtain their approval and satisfaction. Introjections are organized into schemas representing the ''good me'' and the ''bad me,'' and behavior directed toward adhering to the ''good me'' is largely motivated by the avoidance of anxiety.

The ramifications of Cooley's (1902) and Mead's (1934) formulations are a bit more sanguine. As we have seen, for both Cooley and Mead, in their respective treatments of the ''looking glass self'' and the ''generalized other,'' the self arises out of social interaction. One internalizes the evaluations of others that then serve as a source of self-regulation to guide one's behavior in the absence of immediate external consequences. There is the further implication, in Mead, that an appreciation for how others view the self is basic to the development of one's sense of *moral* responsibility. (See also Hallowell, 1959; McDougall, 1908.) We will return to this issue in the subsequent discussion of the internalization process.

Baldwin (1897) focuses more on the social origins of the developing child's ethical self, and is more explicit about how the socialization process induces self-control. For Baldwin, the child ''finds himself stimulated constantly to deny his impulses, his desires, even his irregular sympathies, by conforming to the will of another'' (p. 334). The child obeys the prohibitions laid down by others and imitates the model provided by others, even though he or she does not understand the capriciousness of the standards to which one must adhere. According to Baldwin, the child does not yet own this emerging self; it is a ''copy for imitation'' not yet experienced as the true self, but the child is motivated to obey these standards and to mold himself or herself into the ''Me'' he or she is to become. It is as if the child were saying: ''Here is my ideal self, my final pattern, my 'ought' set before me'' (p. 335). Through this imitative process that stimulates action on the child's part, one's character is molded into conformity and the sense of a moral ideal is established.

The concept of a moral ideal is even more central in Freud's theory of superego formation, although his treatment is much more psychodynamic. As in Sullivan's theory, the major motivation for the development of a sense of morality arises from an attempt to avoid anxiety. Freud's analysis was most clearly articulated for the boy child in the throes of the Oedipal struggle, for whom thoughts of possessing the mother and the imagined retaliation of the father produced anxiety that could only be prevented by identification with the parental values.

For Freud, however, somewhat unlike Baldwin, ''the super-ego of the child is not really built up on the model of the parents, but on that of the parent's super-ego; it takes over the same content, it becomes the vehicle of tradition and of all the age-long values which have been handed down in this way from generation to generation'' (1933, p. 95).

Within this context Freud referred to the ''ideologies of the super-ego,'' which in his subsequent theorizing became refashioned as the ego ideal. Thus, the superego came to be viewed as two related structures or processes: the conscience was the more dynamic moral agent, the watchguard who was critical, punitive, and induced feelings of guilt. The ego ideal, on the other hand, represented the positive aspirations one incorporated from significant others. (The empirical attempts to assess these contentions will be reviewed in the section on internalization.)

While Freud's focus was largely on the significant others who defined the nuclear family constellation, others, for example, Shibutani (1961) have emphasized the wider societal context. Human society, he writes, ''exists in concerned action, which rests upon the self-control exercised by those who share a common perspective'' (p. 461). The task of the developing child is to learn to curb one's impulses and to recognize as an obligation the duties others expect the child to perform.

Shibutani gives considerable weight to the process of role-taking in his analysis, elaborating on the formulations of Baldwin, Cooley, and Mead. He contends that ''Self-control by those who partake in concerted action depends upon their ability to respond to themselves. Before a man can inhibit and redirect impulses that are likely to be troublesome, he must get outside of himself, imagine his plan of action as others are likely to see it, and respond to this perceptual object. He must be able to experience and identify himself as a unit'' (p. 503). For Shibutani, this is a complex developmental process, born out of the ''dialectic of personal growth,'' to employ Baldwin's (1897) terminology.

Although it is not his intent to offer a detailed developmental analysis of this process, Shibutani's formulation has interesting developmental implications. For example, he notes that initially the young child resists parental control, though gradually one learns to temper one's outbursts. ''At this point there is no self-control as such, only compliance with the demands of people recognized as capable of enforcing them'' (p. 509). Thus, Shibutani has chosen to restrict the emergence of ''self-control'' to that period in development when the child can take the perspective of another, can treat himself or herself as an object of evaluation, which in turn provokes the control of one's own behavior. We will return to this issue in the final section, where it will be suggested that one can identify different forms of self-control at different developmental levels. In so doing, we will also address the question: Where is the self, in self-control? The self as controller would appear to be the I, the self as actor and observer. How does this self change developmentally in the controlling process? The self as controlled would appear to be the Me, which also undergoes developmental change. The implications of these changes will thus be explored in the final section.

Loevinger's Model of Ego Development and Impulse Control

Although the general speculations of self-theorists have not lead to empirical work, those pursuing the concept of ego control have made a significant contribution. In Loevinger's theory of ego development (Loevinger, 1966; Loevinger & Wessler, 1970), impulse control is an important developmental trajectory as well as a dimension of individual differences. These trajectories, which are described in terms of an invariant hierarchical sequence of stages, are concerned with "impulse control and character development, with interpersonal relations, and with cognitive preoccupations, including self-concept" (Loevinger & Wessler, 1970, p. 3). Although her stages represent a developmental sequence, the primary purpose is to generate a typology of character or personality types applicable to adults. The sequence has not been validated with children at different developmental levels, and Loevinger is quick to point out that the stages are defined conceptually, *independent* of chronological age, although they may be correlated with age. Loevinger's primary emphasis, therefore, has been the measurement of individual differences among adults, and she has devoted considerable energy toward the construction of a sentence completion test that she considers to be psychometrically sound (for an excellent review of these efforts, see Hauser, 1976).

In her earlier theorizing, five stages were postulated, although subsequently Loevinger has found it necessary to add transitional periods between the major stages. The original five stages will be described here with regard to the dimension of impulse control. The first differentiated stage is the *impulsive* stage, during which control of impulses is generally lacking. Rules are not yet understood, and actions are either performed because they are rewarded or inhibited because they lead to punishment. Pragmatically, one controls oneself out of fear of retribution. In the following stage, the *opportunistic* or *self-protective* stage, rules are understood; however, they are largely obeyed out of self-interest or immediate advantage. At this stage one appears self-controlled not because of moral considerations, but for reasons of situational experience. There is a conscious preoccupation with control, lest one get into trouble or be dominated by others.

In the *conformist* stage that follows, rules are obeyed because they are rules. Impulses are controlled lest one encounter condemnation from the social environment. In particular, the individual is concerned with potential disapproval or shame from others. In the subsequent *conscientious* stage, there is a shift toward inner rules or moral imperatives that take precedence over those rules externally enforced by authority or through peer pressure. The sanction for failing to control one's behavior at this stage is self-criticism or guilt. Moreover, there is a concern with obligations to others such that behavior that might hurt others is held in check since such behavior would, in turn, lead to guilt.

In the *autonomous* stage, the individual more directly copes with inner *conflict*, with conflicting needs, or with conflicts between needs and ideals or duties. Interestingly, there may be increased manifest expression of impulses at this stage; however, it is not the unmodulated expression of the opportunistic stage, but is differentiated and principled in that the individual realizes the need to express certain impulses for one's own gain, as long as they do not impinge on others.

The highest stage is the *integrated* stage, in which one is able to reconcile, rather than merely cope with, conflicting demands. This involves a certain renunciation of the unattainable and the achievement of a sense of integrated identity. The empirical description of this stage is meager, given that relatively few individuals attain this level of integration.

As a general framework, Loevinger's theory is quite impressive, although there are also limitations (see Hauser, 1976). Many have suggested that scores on the sentence completion test are highly predicted by intelligence as well as verbal fluency. Although such correlations have been obtained, Hauser urges that we consider the nature of the relationship of these variables to ego development. Are intelligence and verbal fluency necessary but not sufficient conditions for passage into higher stages or, conversely, does the attainment of higher levels facilitate the development of IQ and verbal fluency?

From a developmental perspective, one may also question the assumption that Loevinger's stages represent an invariant sequence. A number of studies (reviewed in Hauser, 1976) report significant correlations with age. However, the sequential nature of these stages has yet to be demonstrated. Given that these stages have primarily been assessed in adults and adolescents, there is little sense of how this sequence might more naturally evolve during childhood, nor what might be the transition rules governing such a sequence. Certain studies have found that Loevinger's stages are substantially correlated with Kohlberg's stages of moral development (1969). These relationships are to be expected, however, given that the content and form of Kohlberg's stages provided one of the models on which Loevinger based her theory.

Troublesome to some is the fact that Loevinger's stages are not assumed or predicted to correlate highly with overt behavior. A relationship has been obtained between ego developmental level among adolescents and street fighting (see Hauser, 1976). There is also some evidence that ego development predicts behaviors such as role playing (Blasi, 1972)

and conformity (Hoppe, 1972) when these constructs are behaviorally defined separately for each
stage. Attempts, however, to relate ego development levels to general behaviors such as helping
others (Cox, 1974) have been less successful. Cox's
findings do suggest an interaction between a situational variable (whether one had received prior help)
and level of ego development in predicting behavior.
Thus, while Loevinger's model was based on certain
assumptions involving relatively global personality
types, future efforts should be directed toward determining how these types interact to predict behaviors
in particular situations designed to elicit self-
control.

The Blocks' Work on Ego Control and Ego Resiliency

A major contribution to the personality literature
has been the Blocks' programmatic effort to examine the constructs of ego control and ego resiliency
(see J. Block, 1971; J. H. Block & J. Block, 1980).
Initially, these investigators attempted to integrate
the psychoanalytic theory of impulse control (as sys-
tematized by Fenichel, 1945) and the theorizing of
Lewin, who sought to describe the motivational dynamics within the individual (Lewin, 1935, 1936,
1938, 1951). The concept of ego control, as they
have formalized it, found its roots in those ego structures that evolved under the dictates of the reality
principle, for example, delay of gratification, inhibition of aggression, anticipation of consequences,
and caution in ambiguous situations. Each of these
structures involves the control of impulses.

The construct of ego control was also derived
from Lewin, who described the psychological system in terms of a system of needs separated from one
another by boundaries. One property of these boundaries was their permeability, which referred to the
capacity to contain or control needs and tensions.
Boundaries could be relatively permeable, such that
tensions would spill into other psychological systems, or they could be relatively impermeable, isolating or compartmentalizing subsystems.

As dimensionalized by the Blocks, therefore, the
ends of the continuum are defined by overcontrol
and undercontrol. The excessive boundary imper-
meability of the overcontroller results in the containment of impulses, delay of gratification, and inhibition of action and affect, all of which lead to a high
modal threshold for response. Undercontrollers, on
the other hand, with excessive boundary permeability, manifest poorly modulated impulses, an
inability to delay gratification, immediate and direct
expression of motivations and affects, and a low
modal threshold for responding.

The concept of ego resiliency was derived from
another property of boundaries posited by Lewin,
namely *elasticity*. "Elasticity refers to the capacity
of the boundary to change its characteristic level of
permeability-impermeability depending upon impinging psychological forces, and to return to its
original modal level of permeability after the temporary, accommodation-requiring influence is no longer pressing" (1980, pp. 47–48). The end points of
this continuum are defined by resourceful adaptation
to changing circumstances and flexible problem-
solving strategies at one end, and ego-brittleness on
the other. Ego-brittleness implies that there is little
adaptive flexibility, often manifested by perseveration or disorganization of behavior when change or
stress is encountered.

The Blocks' original empirical attack on this
problem involves a comprehensive assessment
effort to measure these constructs in adults, to establish typologies, and to examine the antecedents of
these individual differences. The sophistication and
sensitivity of their data-analytic techniques are impressive, although they cannot be described here in
detail. Their adult sample, in their mid-30s, were
drawn from a longitudinal population on which measures of a variety of personality characteristics were
available from both the junior and senior high school
years. Thus, one thrust of their research has been to
investigate continuity over time. Impulsivity, the
variable most relevant to the present discussion, was
among the highest in terms of its stability across the
age range from junior high to adulthood.

A major contribution of this work is the identification of a number of typologies of both men and
women, based on the dimensions of ego control and
ego resiliency, in conjunction with other personality
and cognitive measures. Particularly noteworthy is
the pattern of parental characteristics and child-rearing techniques that were found to predict lack of
impulse control, that is, to be associated with those
typologies characterized by undercontrol. As children, undercontrollers tended to be neglected by parents. Mothers were typically self-indulgent and nar-
cissistic, while fathers were often self-absorbed and
indifferent. Given the selfishness of parents, little
effort was taken to teach age-appropriate skills or
encourage, much less demand, achievement. The
home situation was often unpredictable and frantic.
There was little investment in parenthood, and typically little agreement between parents about child-
rearing values. There was often a tendency to invoke
discipline when the parents themselves were angry.

From their pattern of findings, the investigators
infer that not only does parenting require considerable effort, but perhaps the most crucial element is

the proper *timing* of that effort. As they note, it is troublesome and onerous to have to discipline a child and to have to invest the time and exhibit the constancy needed to deliver the ''precepts of self-regulation'' to children. It is much easier to ignore those situations requiring instruction or discipline.

The parental antecedents of *over*controllers were clearer for men than women. The adult overcontrolling male typically experienced a childhood family environment that was authoritarian, joyless, and constraining. Parents were usually conservative and inhibited, with a brittle, controlling mother who dominated the household while the father pursued his own masculine interests. Compliance and responsibility for chores were enforced, and guilt induction was often the method employed by the mother to impose punishment. These sons, for the most part, were overcontrolled from an early age, and continued this pattern into adulthood, manifesting little expression of impulses.

The Blocks have also investigated the parental and child-rearing antecedents leading to individual differences along the ego-resiliency dimension. Those individuals characterized as ego-resilient have tended to come from families with mothers who were loving, patient, competent, and who encouraged the discussion of feelings and problems; in addition, there was generally agreement between parents on child-rearing values, sexual compatibility, and a mutual concern with moral and philosophical issues. Individuals characterized at the opposite end of the ego-resiliency dimension, as ego-*brittle*, tended to come from family situations that were conflictful, discordant, with anxious, neurotic mothers ambivalent about their maternal role, and who had few intellectual or philosophic interests (see J. Block, 1971).

More recently, the Blocks have turned their attention to the relevance of the dimensions of ego control and ego resiliency to the period of early adulthood. Thus, they embarked on a longitudinal study in which children underwent extensive individual assessment at ages 3, 4, 5, and 7 (Block & Block, 1980). At the time of that publication, they were assessing the children who were then 11. As with their adult study, a detailed description of their many converging measures, tailored to each age level, cannot be given here. Four sources of data, however, were included: (1) subject characteristics, demographic data, and other real-life situation data, (2) observational data, (3) self-report data, and (4) responses to standardized, objective tests.

Patterns reflecting both the ego-control and the ego-resiliency dimensions can be identified in 3-year-olds that are highly replicable at age 4. Under-

controllers can be described as ''more active, assertive, aggressive, competitive, outgoing, attention-seeking, extrapunitive, overreactive to frustration, jealous, exploiting, and as less compliant, orderly, yielding, and private than children scoring in the overcontrolled direction on the experiment-based ego-control indices'' (Block & Block, 1980, p. 68).

With regard to the ego-resiliency dimension, those characterized as highly ego-resilient were assessed by teachers as ''more empathic, able to cope with stress, bright, appropriate in expressions of emotion, self-accepting, novelty-seeking, fluent, self-reliant, competent, creative, and as less anxious, conflicted, suspicious, sulky, imitative and seeking of reassurance'' (pp. 68–71).

Thus, the dimensions, initially identified as relevant for adults, have clearly found their counterparts during childhood. Moreover, the conjunction of the ego control and the ego resilient dimensions yield four measurable types during childhood. Resilient undercontrollers are found to be energetic, active, curious, explorative, interested, arresting, and tend to recoup easily. Resilient overcontrollers, as a group, tend to be compliant, calm, relaxed, and empathic. Brittle undercontrollers are described as restless, fidgety, lacking in impulse control, tending to externalize, to be vulnerable, brittle with a narrow margin of integration, and manipulative. Brittle overcontrollers have been found to be inhibited, anxious, constricted, reserved, intolerant of ambiguity, rigidly repetitive or withdrawn under stress, and, moreover, they tend to manifest inappropriate affect and behavioral mannerisms.

Although their strategy focuses on the search for consistencies in personality over time, this does not necessarily preclude an analysis of developmental differences in the manner in which ego control and ego resiliency are manifest at different levels. In their sensitivity to measurement issues, the Blocks have found it necessary to operationalize these constructs somewhat differently at different age levels, in order that the tasks be age appropriate. A careful look at these differences may well tell us something about the changing manifestations of ego control and ego resiliency with development. This may be particularly critical in the future examination of the longitudinal data from the 11-year-olds.

On balance, the work of the Blocks provides a welcome antidote to the overemphasis on cognitive processes that has dominated the field for the last two decades. As they note, ''The psychological world of the individual is surprisingly seldom occupied by the purely cognitive problems with which psychologists have been prone to concern themselves'' (1980, p. 95). With regard to development, they observe that the feedback experienced by the child in the social realm is considerably more limited, indirect, delayed, and ambiguous than in the physical world. Thus, in order to deal with the interpersonal world, "the child must evolve and apply 'not-so-cognitive-structures' functional enough or sufficient for the prediction of behavior" (p. 96). Within this context they suggest that concepts akin to ego control and ego resiliency may be found useful.

Self-Control from a Social Learning Theory Perspective

The basic self-control processes that have been explored by social learning theorists have involved resistance to temptation in the absence of surveillance, self-imposed delay of gratification or expression of impulses for the sake of future consequences, the tolerance of self-initiated frustration, and delay of self-imposed rewards. In contrast to those formulations of ego control that highlight the dispositional qualities of one's ability to engage in these behaviors, social learning theory proponents emphasize that self-control patterns within an individual are often highly discriminative and situation-specific (Mischel, 1973; Mischel, 1974). As Mischel points out, the data on the discriminativeness of self-control and moral behavior provide "little support for the belief in a unitary intrapsychic moral agency like the super-ego, nor for a unitary trait entity of conscience or honesty" (1974, p. 256). In general, it has been those within the social learning theory tradition who have been most vocal about the need to consider the processes of self-control from an interactionist position (Bandura, 1977b, 1978; Coates & Thoresen, 1979; Kanfer, 1977; Karoly, 1982; Mahoney, 1974; Mischel, 1973, 1974; Staats, 1975).

Within this general context, there have been shifts in emphasis over the past two decades during which these processes have received increasing empirical attention. Much of the earliest work during this period emphasized the role of punishment and the resultant aversive affective states that subsequently mediated the control of one's behavior. In the self-control literature, the effects of instructions and/or prohibitions that were modeled increasingly came to the fore. Most recently, the emphasis has been on models, paradigms, and formulations that highlight the role of cognitive mediators in the self-control process.

Within this context, certain researchers have turned their attention to the components of the self-control process, as postulated by Bandura (1977b, 1978) and Kanfer (1970, 1971, 1980), for example, self-monitoring, self-evaluation, and self-reward. Bandura has been particularly instrumental in encouraging this line of research. As he has noted: "Theory and research related to the process of internalization and self-control have generally focused on *resistance to deviation* and the occurrence of *self-punitive responses* following transgression. Perhaps an even more prevalent and important behavioral manifestation of self-control is the manner in which a person regulates the self-administration of highly rewarding resources" (Bandura & Kupers, 1964). Each of these lines of research will be reviewed in the following sections.

It should be noted that, while some seem to employ the terms "self-control" and "self-regulation" synonymously, others have made clear distinctions between them. For Karoly (1982), "self-regulation refers to a set of aroused processes through which an individual consciously and consistently contributes to maintaining the course of goal-directed behavior in the relative absence of external supports or when external supports are of limited utility" (p. 88). The processes involved in self-control, in contrast, involve "changing the likelihood of engaging in a behavior with conflicting temporal contingencies" (p. 88). The behavior in question either may result in immediate reward but have eventual aversive consequences, or may involve immediately unpleasant consequences but long-range pleasant outcomes.

Patterson (1982) also makes a distinction between self-regulation and self-control. Self-regulated activity involves effective, intentional action, where relatively little effort is required. When there is a breakdown in the normal stream of self-regulated behavior, when an achievement or goal is blocked, then there is often the need for self-control. Although Kanfer's model conveys a similar process in that the disruption of a smooth chain of reactions triggers self-processes designed to correct the situation, he prefers to employ the terms self-regulation and self-management to this process of correction. In the empirical efforts to be reviewed next, the behaviors in question typically fall under Karoly's definition of self-control. (See Thoresen & Mahoney, 1974, for a discussion of the various definitions that have been employed in the literature.)

The Effects of Punishment on Self-Control

Aronfreed (1968, 1969, 1976) has been primarily responsible for integrating many of the early self-control studies around the theme of punishment and affective mediators. He points to two major channels of socialization that bring about internalized control. The first involves the shaping of behavior through positive or aversive outcomes that are contingent on the child's overt acts. The second channel of socialization is observational learning or modeling. Aronfreed (1976) has emphasized the role of punishment in bringing about internalized control that he hopes will "dilute a long-standing and uncritical ideological conviction that children do not learn well under its dominion" (p. 57). (Also see Johnston, 1972; Parke, 1977, for reviews of the effects of punishment.)

By "punishment" Aronfreed does not simply refer to physical forms of discipline, but to rejection, disapproval, and other "psychological" methods. Aronfreed concludes that the clearest picture of the child's acquisition of internalized control has emerged from empirical studies of the effects of punishment on the child's initially predominant behavioral dispositions (see also Aronfreed & Reber, 1965; Parke & Walters, 1967; Walters, Parke, & Cane, 1965).

Many of his own studies demonstrate the child's internalization of control over conduct, without having provided any verbal or moral evaluation of the child's transgression. These Aronfreed explains through a conditioning process in which affective mediation plays a central role. As aversive affective state is conditioned to those cognitive representations that are initially contiguous with the occurrence of punishment. A variety of aversive states may be experienced, for example, fear, shame, guilt, although the common denominator appears to be anxiety and its motivational properties.

Aronfreed has also described those studies that indicate that children show better internalized control when their transgressions are also accompanied by verbal explanation, particularly if the explanation sensitizes the child to his or her intentions (see LaVoie, 1974; Parke, 1974, 1977). However, Aronfreed contends that anxiety is still the mediator of the subsequent suppression of an incipient transgression. In emphasizing affective mechanisms, Aronfreed does not wish to underplay the significance of moral cognition. However, as he notes, "there has been so much recent (and justifiable) investment in the child's capacity to represent the world in thought, and to form complex rules and concepts, that we are in some danger of overlooking the affective learning which is also required to translate knowledge into social behavior" (1976, p. 63).

A number of studies have now demonstrated that punishment is more effective in suppressing the future incidence of the punished behavior if it is accompanied by an explicit rationale (see Blackwood, 1970; Cheyne & Walters, 1969; LaVoie, 1973; MacPherson, Candee, & Hohman, 1974; Parke, 1969, 1970). Moreover the effectiveness of particular types of rationales has been found to vary with the age of the child (see Parke, 1970, 1974, 1977). The general pattern of findings suggests that emphasis on the physical consequences of one's actions are particularly effective with younger children. A number of studies, reviewed in Pressley (1979), have found that rationales based on empathy and an appreciation for the feelings of others, as well as rationales emphasizing the property rights of others, are more effective with children over the age of 7 or 8 than with preschoolers (see Cheyne, 1972; Jensen & Buhanan, 1974; Parke & Murray, 1971; Parke & Sawin, 1975). As Pressley notes, rationales emphasizing the rights and feelings of others require more cognitive sophistication, and this pattern is in keeping with the moral stages articulated by Kohlberg (1969, 1976). See Parke (1970, 1974, 1977), who has developed the argument for how the effectiveness of a particular type of rationale is mediated by the child's cognitive-developmental level.

The Effects of Modeling

There is a growing body of research demonstrating that the child's observation of the behavior of others, and in some cases the consequences of their behavior, function to elicit prosocial behavior or to suppress behavior deemed undesirable. With regard to the control of impulses, when social models are observed to be punished for aggression children tend to become more inhibited about displaying such behavior (see Bandura, 1973; Bandura, Ross, & Ross, 1963). With very young children or children who are exceptionally impulsive, it has been found that the contingencies modeled must be extremely clear (Ross & Ross, 1976). Laboratory modeling studies have also demonstrated that self-control is enhanced if the child is allowed to practice the modeled response (White, 1972) or emit task relevant verbalizations (Wolf, 1973).

Studies designed to model resistance to temptation have had moderate success. Stein (1967) found that a self-indulgent model influenced children's behavior in the direction of imitating the model, that is, they also yielded to temptation; however, children who observed a model who did not yield to temptation showed no more resistance than a control group who observed no model. More promising results have been obtained by other investigators. Both Ross (1971) and Rosenkoetter (1973) found that when children observed a model who did not yield to temptation their own resistance was also increased, compared to a control group that did not observe a model. In another study, Wolf and Cheyne (1972) also demonstrated that a virtuous model who did not yield to temptation led to increases in children's ability to resist temptation; moreover, the effects were observed one month later.

The effects of modeling in a delay of reward situation have also been demonstrated by Bandura and Mischel (1965). In the pretest phase, children were requested to select either a small reward that could be obtained immediately, or a more valued reward for which they would have to wait. Children who had preferred to wait showed an increased preference for an immediate reward if they had observed an adult model who favored immediate gratification; conversely, children who had initially observed a preference for immediate reward showed more willingness to wait for the more valuable, delayed reward if they had observed a model displaying such high-delay behavior. Moreover, these results were maintained over a one-month period.

Other studies have demonstrated that certain characteristics of the model, as well as the model's relationship to the child, will influence the degree to which the child will adopt the model's behavior (e.g., Grusec & Mischel, 1966; Mischel & Grusec, 1966; Mischel & Liebert, 1966, 1967). For example, children are more likely to adopt the performance standards of models who are powerful and rewarding, but will reject these same standards if the models are not perceived as powerful or rewarding (Mischel & Grusec, 1966).

The standards of a model have also been manipulated to be either consistent or inconsistent with the behavior which that model is trying to impart to the child, that is, the model may or may not practice what she or he preaches (see Mischel & Liebert, 1966; Rosenhan & White, 1967). When standards and behaviors are consistent, the child is most likely to adopt those standards. If there are discrepancies, however, children are more likely to adopt the least stringent standards. Mischel and Liebert found that when both the standards and behaviors modeled, as well as imposed, were stringent, the children adopted high standards. When the standards encouraged for children were lenient, the children adopted lenient standards, even though the behavior modeled matched the high standards set for the model. These findings are not only intriguing in terms of their implications for childrearing, but serve to bolster the point that various situational determinants clearly affect children's self-control.

In other studies (e.g., Ebbesen & Zeiss, 1973; Fry, 1977), success and failure manipulations have been employed prior to an assessment of resistance to temptation. Children experiencing success have been shown to be better able to resist subsequent temptation more effectively than those in a prior failure condition. Fry (1975, 1977) has emphasized the role of affect as a mediator in producing this outcome: in one study he found that the child in a state of positive affect was better able to resist temptation than the child experiencing negative affect. He has further demonstrated that positive and negative affects linked with success and failure experiences, respectively, predict a child's resistance to temptation. Other investigators have also manipulated affect and have generally found that children instructed to "think happy thoughts" exhibit greater delay or persistence behavior in temptation situations than those thinking "sad" thoughts or those in a control condition with no instructions concerning what to think (see Masters & Santrock, 1976; Mischel, Ebbesen, & Zeiss, 1972; Moore, Clyburn, & Underwood, 1976; Santrock, 1976).

Other Determinants of Delay of Gratification

In the typical choice paradigm employed by Mischel and his colleagues (see Mischel, 1968; Mischel & Ebbesen, 1970; Mischel, Ebbesen, & Zeiss, 1972) young children are allowed to select a highly desirable reward (marshmallows or a large candy bar) if they choose to wait or delay, or they can select a less desirable reward (a pretzel or a small candy bar) that they can have immediately. Other determinants of the child's willingness or ability to delay gratification in this situation are the age of the child, the length of the waiting period, the child's faith in the fact that the delayed reward will actually be delivered, prior success or failure, and affect. In one developmental study (Mischel & Metzner, 1962) a steady decrease in the choice of the less desirable reward was obtained across the kindergarten through the sixth-grade range, indicating that children were increasingly able to delay gratification in anticipation of the more desirable reward. Weisz (1978) has obtained a similar pattern of findings indicating that children's impulsive choices decline over the age range of 5 to 10. In two studies (Mischel & Grusec, 1967; Mischel & Metzner, 1962) ease of waiting was directly related to the length of the delay. Mischel and Grusec also varied the probability that the more desirable reward would be obtained, telling children it would be definite, 50–50, or even less likely, finding that the choice of the larger reward was inversely related to these conditions.

Individual differences in children's perceptions of control over successes and failures have also been related in the delay paradigm. Mischel, Zeiss, and Zeiss (1974) administered the Stanford Preschool Internal-External Scale to determine the degree to which children perceived themselves in control (internal) or external forces in control of their successes as well as failures. The relationship between an overall score of internality (summed across successes and failures) and an overall delay score was negligible. However, a more complex pattern emerged when separate scores of internal responsibility were related to the different delay conditions employed. Internal responsibility for *success* predicted persistence when the child's behavior resulted in a *positive* outcome, whereas internal responsibility for *negative* events predicted persistence behavior that could prevent the occurrence of a *negative* outcome. As Mischel (1974) notes, while individual differences among children were partial determinants of their goal-directed behavior, the relationships are dependent on specific interactions between type of situation and the nature of the child's perceptions of control with regard to success versus failure.

Cognitive and Attentional Processes That Facilitate Self-Control

A major emphasis in the recent research of Mischel and his colleagues has been an examination of how attentional and cognitive-representational processes influence children's ability to delay gratification and to resist temptation. There is certainly historical precedent for addressing such issues. James, for example, concluded that the essence of "will," as the mechanism through which one controls one's behavior, is "attention with effort." He goes on to observe that "The essential achievement of will is to attend to a difficult object" (1963, p. 393). Mischel (1974) also notes that Freudian thought provides another general theoretical guide. In psychoanalytic theory, it is postulated that the infant's first attempts to withstand delay of gratification involve the construction of a hallucinatory image of the desired object (Freud, 1959). The specific processes mediating such effects, however, have not been clearly elaborated within the psychoanalytic literature. As will be seen in the following brief review, the programmatic research of Mischel and his colleagues provides no support for the contentions of either James or Freud (see Mischel, 1974).

In their initial investigation of the role of attention, Mischel and Ebbesen (1970) employed a paradigm in which preschool children could either wait for a more preferred reward or summon the experimenter to return to give them a less preferred reward. To test the prediction that attention to rewards would facilitate delay, four conditions were employed: *both rewards* could be viewed by the child during the delay period, the *delayed reward only* was observable, the *immediate reward only* was observable, or *no rewards* were observable. Contrary to expectations, the presence of the reward inhibited their delay behavior, such that the shortest waiting time was in the condition where both rewards were observable, and the longest waiting was in the no-rewards condition, with the two single reward conditions falling in between. It appeared, therefore, that attention to the rewards provided an additional source of frustration, making delay even more aversive.

This reasoning lead the investigators to hypothesize that delay of gratification and frustration tolerance should be facilitated by overt or covert activities that would *distract* one from the rewards. Observations of children employing their own ingenious methods of distracting themselves bolstered this hypothesis. Direct support for this prediction was obtained in findings (Mischel, Ebbesen, & Zeiss, 1972) indicating that instructions to think about "fun things" facilitated delay in the presence of the rewards, compared to "think about rewards" and "no ideation" conditions. In addition, delay was found to be minimal under a condition where the rewards were *not* present, but children were instructed to think about them.

The precise nature of children's cognitions during the delay period was the focus of a follow-up study by Mischel and Moore (1973a). Children were presented with "images" of the rewards or irrelevant objects through the use of slides. The findings revealed that the symbolic presentations of the rewards actually facilitated delay. Mischel and Moore have drawn on the distinction between the informational and motivational properties of rewards in interpreting this finding. It was reasoned that the symbolic slide presentation served an informational function, reminding the child of what he or she will receive if they delay, whereas the presence of the actual reward object had a more powerful motivational effect. This arousal function would serve to increase the child's frustration, which in turn would decrease the child's ability to delay.

In a related study, Mischel and Baker (1975) examined the extent to which cognitive transformations of the reward might influence length of delay. One group of children was asked to focus on the consummatory (motivational) qualities of the food rewards (marshmallows are sweet and chewy, pretzels are salty and crunchy); the other group was instructed to think about nonconsummatory qualities, to transform them into nonedible imagery (e.g., marshmallows are like white, puffy clouds and pretzels are like thin, brown logs). Children in the nonconsummatory condition manifested significantly longer delay times. In subsequent studies (see Mischel & Moore, 1973b; Moore, Mischel, & Zeiss, 1976) it has also been demonstrated that in the presence of either rewards or pictures of rewards, it is the cognitive representation that is the critical determinant in that children instructed to focus on the realistic qualities of the reward have the greatest difficulty engaging in delay. Thus, these studies demonstrate that the nature of the cognitive representation appears to be the major determinant of the young child's ability to control delay behavior, and that cognitive transformations that minimize motivational arousal are likely to be the most effective in promoting self-control (see Mischel, 1974).

Self-Instructional Plans

In their more recent work, Mischel and his colleagues (see Mischel & Patterson, 1976, 1978; Patterson, 1982; Patterson & Mischel, 1975, 1976) have turned their attention to children's ability to make use of self-instructional plans, as a further demonstration of how cognitive and linguistic processes facilitate resistance to temptation. The tempter, in their laboratory experiments, is "Mr. Clown Box" who is distracting by virtue of his cheerful comments, distinctive noises, and occasional lighted display of attractive toys within. In one study (Patterson & Mischel, 1976), preschool children were given the opportunity to win attractive rewards by working on a repetitive task in the face of these distractions. The effectiveness of two types of self-instructional plans were examined, a temptation-inhibition plan directing attention away from the clown, and a task-facilitating plan directing the subjects' attention toward the repetitive task. Their findings revealed that the temptation-inhibiting plan was the more effective. Moreover the temptation-inhibiting plan alone was just as effective as a combination of the two types of plans. The effectiveness of temptation-inhibition plans is a finding that has not been observed by other investigators (e.g., Hartig & Kanfer, 1973). Patterson and Mischel cite one possible situational interpretation, namely that the temptation in their experiment was extremely powerful, whereas in other task situations one might not observe the effect they report.

In a subsequent study (Mischel & Patterson, 1976, see also 1978) these investigators added a third type of self-instructional plan in which the child concentrated on the rewarding consequences of successful self-control. In addition to the manipulation of the *content* of the plan, they also sought to vary the *structure* of the plan. Thus they compared the effectiveness of elaborated plans, where they provided the verbal script for the child, with unelaborated plans where the intent of the particular plan was described but no specific content was offered. Temptation-inhibiting plans were found to be most effective, followed by reward-oriented plans, while task-facilitating plans were relatively ineffective. Furthermore, the children's ability to sustain continued work in the face of temptation was facilitated by elaborated plans that focused on temptation-inhibition as well as on reward-orientation, but such plans did not enhance the effectiveness of the task-facilitation manipulation. Thus, the findings support their general expectation that both the content or substance of the plan as well as its structure or organization influence its effectiveness.

Carter, Patterson, and Quasebarth (1979) have begun to pursue children's use of plans developmentally. They have found that fully elaborated plans are necessary to sustain the goal-directed work behavior of preschool children, whereas by the age of second grade children's performance was unaffected by the presence of plans. This finding for the second graders however, may be the result of the ease of the particular task for children of that age, since all children were given the same task. Had a more difficult task been employed, it is possible that plans might have had some effect. Thus, in future research, it would seem necessary to look for task difficulty by plan effectiveness interactions.

The programmatic research effort of Mischel and his colleagues certainly attests to the role that attention and linguistic processes play in the control of behavior, and their findings provide compelling evidence for a cognitive-mediational interpretation. More recently, these investigators have turned to the study of children's *knowledge* about the self-control process itself (see Mischel, Mischel & Hood, 1978a, 1978b; Patterson, 1982; Yates & Mischel, 1979). Their findings suggest that young children are unable to choose or predict which of several conditions would facilitate delay of gratification based on the types of paradigms these researchers have employed. For example, young children do not recognize the advantages of hiding the reward or thinking about its nonconsummatory aspects. As Patterson (1982) notes, these results suggest that the young child's failure to employ effective self-control strategies in naturalistic settings may be caused by their lack of knowledge about relevant strategies (see Glucksberg, Krauss, & Higgins, 1975; Patterson & Kister, in press). Two promising directions in this area would involve the investigation of the effectiveness of plans at different developmental levels, as well as an examination of children's natural plans and preferences.

W. Mischel and H. Mischel (1977) have reported on some pilot work in which they have interviewed children of different ages regarding their understanding of plans. By the age of 8, children can discuss the concept of ''plans'' articulately and can give good examples of how and when they employ plans to structure and organize their behavior. By ages 9 to 10, children also report on how they can utilize strategies or self-instructional plans to control undesirable affect, for example, anger, or antisocial behavior, for example, aggression. In addition, by age 10 some children can also articulate distinctions between the intentional aspects of a plan, its informative function, and its execution.

Mischel and Mischel's data also suggest that, at somewhat older ages, children are not only aware of cognitive and social strategies for devising and implementing plans, but that these eventually become ''more automatic, abbreviated, and rapid, without requiring extensive or explicit self-instructions for each step in an increasingly complex organizational hierarchy'' (1977, p. 53). In this proposition, there is an obvious convergence with the concept of ''scripts'' (Abelson, 1976; Shank & Abelson, 1977); scripts represent cognitive constructions that specify a sequence of predictable events that require minimal monitoring on the part of the adult. The work of the Mischels suggests that it may be fruitful to pursue the developmental precursors of the ability to construct and effectively utilize such scripts.

Sawin and Parke (1979), building on the empirical work of Mischel and Patterson, have sought to test the notion that as the child's verbal mediational skills develop, the specific semantic content of self-instructions should come to have increasingly more regulatory control over behavior. Their study employed first- and second-grade boys. Two types of self-instructions were compared, those focusing on prohibition of deviant behavior and those facilitating a redirection of attention. Their findings revealed that the prohibitive self-verbalizations were effective for boys at both age levels; the redirective self-verbalizations, however, were effective for the older group only, and actually were counterproductive for the younger boys. Their interpretation focuses on the distracting effects of the forbidden toy for the younger group, whereas the older children were better able to focus on more features of the instructions and to discriminate more elements, which in turn facilitated self-regulation. While this general analysis is plausible, future research will need to be directed toward identifying and operationalizing these processes more precisely, as well as examining their effects across a wider age range.

Self-Instructional Training Within the Domain of Cognitive-Behavior Modification

The use of self-instructional techniques in the control of one's behavior has also become prevalent in recent years within the field of behavior modification, as cognitive factors have been given increasing emphasis. Meichenbaum's research, which began in an attempt to treat hyperactive, impulsive children, has provided a major impetus (Meichenbaum, 1976, 1977, 1978; Meichenbaum & Genest, 1980; Meichenbaum & Goodman, 1971). The self-instructional program he has devised was initially grounded in the theoretical formulations of Luria (1959, 1961) in particular, as well as of Vygotsky (1962). His cognitive-behavioral program is modeled after the three stages proposed by Luria, whereby the initiation and inhibition of voluntary motor behaviors come under one's own verbal control. During the first stage, behavior is controlled primarily through the speech of others, typically adults. In the second stage, the child's overt speech becomes an effective regulator of behavior. In stage three, the child's covert or inner speech is capable of assuming a self-governing role. Based on this sequence, Meichenbaum and Goodman (1971) have devised a treatment program to train impulsive children to talk to themselves as a method for developing self-control over overt behavior. Children are typically identified as impulsive based on Kagan's (1966) Matching Familiar Figures test, which taps the dimension of impulsivity-reflectivity.

Meichenbaum has employed this training procedure with a variety of tasks, varying from simple sensorimotor abilities to more complex problem-solving abilities. During the earlier phases of training, sensorimotor tasks, for example, copying line patterns and coloring figures within the boundaries, have been employed. In subsequent phases of the training children are required to follow sequential instructions, reproduce designs, place pictures in a meaningful series, and solve conceptual tasks such as Raven's Matrices. For each task, appropriate self-verbalizations are modeled by the experimenter, and then followed by a fading procedure in which the child's utterances become increasingly covert. It is reported (Meichenbaum & Genest, 1980) that this training procedure leads to significantly improved performance (relative to placebo and control groups) on the Porteus Mazes, and the WISC performance IQ, and increased cognitive reflectivity on the Matching Familiar Figures Test (Kagan, 1966).

Meichenbaum and Genest (1980) report that this cognitive-behavioral paradigm has now been successfully utilized to establish inner speech control over: the disruptive behavior of hyperactive children (Douglas, Parry, Martin, & Garson, 1976); aggressive children (Camp, Blom, Hebert, & Van Doorninck, 1977); disruptive preschoolers (Bornstein & Quevillon, 1976); cheating behavior of kindergarten and first graders (Monahan & O'Leary, 1971); Porteus maze performance of hyperactive boys (Palkes, Stewart, & Freeman, 1972; Palkes, Stewart & Kahana, 1968); and the conceptual tempo of emotionally disturbed boys (Finch, Wilkinson, Nelson, & Montgomery, 1975) as well as that of normal children (Bender, 1976; Meichenbaum & Goodman, 1971).

For reviews of the treatment efficacy of cognitive-behavior modification see also Craighead, Craighead-Wilcoxin, and Meyers, 1978; Karoly, 1977; Kendall, 1977; Kendall and Finch, 1979; Mash and Dalby, 1978; Meichenbaum and Asarnow, 1982; Pressely, 1979; Rosenthal, 1979.

Although there have been favorable reports of this type of self-instruction program, reviews also voice several concerns. The training appears to improve performance on visual-motor tasks, yet there is little evidence across the studies conducted that such effects generalize to other task situations (see Glenwick, 1976; Guralnick, 1976; Kagen, 1977; Meichenbaum & Goodman, 1971). Other questions involve the precise nature of the processes that mediate the more specific effects. The particular training program instituted by Meichenbaum includes a number of components, most notably self-instruction and focusing of attention. Other studies (reviewed in Pressley, 1979) indicate that training in attention alone can serve to reduce impulsivity. Pressley raises the possibility that self-verbalization may be epiphenomenal in that while it may modify the deployment of attention, attention modification can occur without self-verbalization. On the other hand, he notes that attention training may produce self-verbalizing children whose modified attention is the result of self-verbalizations. Thus, he urges more research in order to tease apart the relevant effect of the various components included in these training packages.

Certain training programs have included an even greater variety of skills as the focus of instruction. Camp's Think Aloud Program for young aggressive boys (Camp; 1980; Camp & Bash, 1982; Camp & Ray, in press; Camp et al., 1977) combines elements of self-guiding speech with features of the Spivack and Shure (1974) program devised to enhance interpersonal skills. The Spivack and Shure program was designed for use with disadvantaged young children who seem to have difficulties in considering alternative solutions to interpersonal problems. Their program trains children in a series of social reasoning exercises designed to encourage them to generate alternative solutions in peer-conflict situations, anticipate the consequences of particular solutions, and, in general, to apply cause-and-effect thinking to social situations. Camp's rationale for including elements from both types of programs was based on the assumption that merely inhibiting aggressive behavior is not likely to lead to more desirable behavior unless there is a repertoire of alternative social behaviors that can be substituted.

In addition to measures of aggressive behavior, Camp's assessment approach taps a wide variety of verbal and nonverbal skills. Her findings indicate that young aggressive boys show deficiencies on performance subtests but not on verbal mediation tasks per se. However, she claims that these children seem unable to employ their verbal skills in situations requiring the control of their aggressive behavior. Part of their impulsivity involves more task-irrelevant speech during problem solving, compared to a normal, nonaggressive peer group.

Specifically, the Think Aloud program is directed toward: using verbalization to inhibit initial responses in a problem situation, developing an organized approach to problem solving, increasing the repertoire of alternative response solutions, and developing a language for understanding cause and effect. In order to promote the spontaneous use of skills, adults model cognitions, stimulate overt verbalization on the part of the child followed by fading to covert levels, and promote independence in the use of these skills as well as generalization to other contexts.

The results of one study (Camp, et al., 1977) indicate that the Think Aloud group showed significant gains in cognitive functioning as well as prosocial behavior, compared to a group of aggressive control children. Both groups showed a decrease in aggressive responses, with a slightly greater effect for the Think Aloud boys. In other studies (see Camp, 1980; Camp & Bash, 1982) children in a Think Aloud program have been compared to those in a program designed to enhance self-esteem. Boys in the Think Aloud Program showed improvement in cognitive skills, relative to those in the comparison program, and on follow-up, between 6 and 12 months, these differences were even greater. Both groups show significant improvement in prosocial behavior, however, the Think Aloud boys made greater gains in the reduction of aggressive behaviors.

In a follow-up refresher program for the Think Aloud boys, comparisons were made between boys who had made good progress versus those who had made moderate or poor progress, as judged by the Think Aloud instructor. Independent ratings from teachers of classroom behavior revealed significant improvement for the good progress boys on extroversion, friendliness, and (reduction of) hyperactivity, whereas the poor progress boys showed no change or got worse. This pattern was noteworthy, since the two groups had not differed on these variables at the outset of the program. These findings further highlight the need to consider individual difference variables that might predict the success of a given program for some children compared to others. As Camp and Ray (in press) point out, the clinical subject populations employed in cognitive-behavioral studies, even within a descriptive category such as aggression, are still quite heterogeneous. They urge that client characteristics be specified more clearly in order to improve those program evaluation attempts designed to evaluate treatment outcome. Moreover, as was noted in the review of Meichenbaum's program, more attention needs to be given to which particular elements of the program are responsible for the specific gains reported.

The Understanding of Rules and Contingencies in Self-Control

One feature of intervention programs such as Camp's Think Aloud program and the program designed by Spivack and Shure is the emphasis on teaching the child to employ cause-and-effect thinking. Children are instructed to identify the various contingencies in social situations, and to reason through the possible alternative strategies one could adopt. As the recent work of Mischel and his colleagues reveals, young children have definite limitations with regard to their understanding of what might constitute effective strategies or conditions that would facilitate self-control (see Mischel, Mischel, & Hood, 1978a, 1978b; Patterson, 1982; Yates & Mischel, 1979).

Other theorists and investigators have underscored the importance of understanding the rules and contingencies in self-control situations. As Karoly notes: ''Surely, in almost every experimental study of children's self-control (e.g., delay of gratification) or self-regulation (e.g., self-reinforced academic performance) the experimenter has obviated what would be a major part of the child's job in the natural environment, that is, identifying the rules, recognizing the temporal conflict, and specifying the value and relevance of the available response options'' (1982, p. 90). In his most recent model of self-management, therefore, two critical components are rules discrimination and perceptual-cognitive tuning. With regard to rules discrimination, Karoly urges that we assess children's (1) sensitivity to self-management rules, (2) acceptance of the content and logic of rules, (3) memory for rules, and (4) ability to recognize the generalized utility of certain codes of conduct.

By perceptual-cognitive tuning, Karoly is referring to children's selective awareness of short- and long-run consequences. Thus, in instituting any self-management program, he urges that one also assess the child's awareness of both the short-term and long-term nature and effects of his or her behavior, the child's recognition of the problematic aspects of the short-run behavioral patterns, and the child's awareness of the potential impact (both short- and long-term) of his or her behavior on significant others.

Lopatto and Williams (1976) have also emphasized the role of rule acquisition that they feel aids in understanding the trans-situational generalizability that occurs with self-control behavior. They posit that, in acquiring self-control for a given behavior, the individual is also acquiring a more general rule or strategy with regard to the contingency requirements that have been established by the controlling agent. These investigators have tested the role of rule acquisition in one study with 8-year-old children, using a delay of gratification paradigm. Children were given different amounts of training in which the immediate choice of a least-preferred toy would allow them to play with their most-preferred toy after a period of delay. Children with three days of such experience, in which different toys were employed in each session, showed significantly more delay behavior on tests of self-denial and self-exertion than did those with only one day of experience. The authors suggest that extensive rule acquisition training may be analogous to learning-set formation and thus would tend to strengthen an individual's self-control in new situations.

Findings by Harter and Connell (1982) also highlight the importance of the child's understanding of perceived contingencies in mediating achievement behavior. Connell's perceptions of control scale (Connell, 1980, 1981) include a subscale tapping the extent to which the child *knows* who or what is responsible for the outcomes in her or his life, in addition to subscales tapping internal and external (powerful others) control. It is the level of knowledge score that best predicts achievement, which in turn predicts the child's feelings of competence and mastery motivation. Although this study is not a direct test of self-control behavior, it does suggest that in self-control programs designed to improve academic performance, to promote feelings of competence and increase motivation toward mastery, an important component will involve the child's appreciation for the contingencies involved.

Perceived Contingencies and Locus of Control

The findings by Harter and Connell further suggest that it is not merely knowledge of the contingencies, but knowledge coupled with the belief that one is primarily responsible for one's successes and failures, that influence one's achievement behavior, feelings of competence, and motivation. In a number of formulations of self-control, the reinforcing effects of being able to control one's own environment and behavior have been emphasized (see Bandura & Mahoney, 1974; Thoresen & Mahoney, 1974). From the locus of control literature, there is evidence that one's perceived control over one's environment can motivate one to act (Lefcourt, 1966; Rotter, Chance, & Phares, 1972). In addition, studies with children have indicated that *choice* is a powerful reinforcer (Brigham & Bushell, 1972; Brigman & Sherman, 1973; Montgomery & Parton, 1970).

Logan (1973) has offered an interesting motivational formulation with regard to the issue of control that focuses more on the affective consequences of the absence of control. He hypothesizes that self-control is a learned drive, based on a pattern of association of fear or frustration with lack of self-control. This hypothesis is interesting in light of recent attempts by Weiner and his colleagues (see Weiner, Kun, & Benesh-Weiner, 1980) to document the particular affects that result from people's attributions concerning internal versus external control.

In Karoly's (1982) recent model of self-management, he suggests that one parameter of the effectiveness of a given program may be the child's belief in his or her ability to engage successfully in self-management, which he views as similar to Bandura's self-efficacy concept (Bandura, 1977a, 1978). Fostering a child's sense of control or self-efficacy has not been a primary target variable in self-control programs, although it is certainly implied in the components of most. Consider those cognitive-behavior modification programs in which children go through a training sequence in which overt self-instruction designed to guide behavior gradually becomes more covert (Meichenbaum, 1976, 1977, 1979). One could hypothesize that it is not merely the ability to make use of covert self-instruction in the form of private speech that is the critical factor, but the accompanying knowledge that one can have an effect, and that one is responsible for the ensuing successes or failures. That is, such a procedure not only teaches the skill of using covert speech to guide behavior, but conveys the message that "I am in control or responsible."

If this analysis has merit, one would expect that scores on a perceived control scale such as Connell's (1980) would predict individual differences in the efficacy of such programs. Two specific predictions could be advanced. Children who are relatively high on both internality and level of knowledge concerning what controls the outcomes in the domain tapped by the program would acquire the skills of the training program most readily. Second, children who are relatively low in internality and level of knowledge concerning control at the beginning of such a program should shift toward greater internality and knowledge of control as a result of the training.

Individual differences in attributions of control may also differentially predict the efficacy of specific programs. A recent study by Bugenthal, Whalen, and Henker (1977) emphasizes the importance of matching the treatment program to the child's particular attributional style. In a study of hyperactive boys two such styles were identified, those attributing outcomes to "luck" and those making attributions to "effort." Two treatment programs were instituted, one based on self-instruction and a second that employed an operant, social reinforcement paradigm. The findings revealed that children making attributions on the basis of effort showed more improvement in the self-instruction program, whereas those attributing outcomes to luck did better in the self-reinforcement program. Given the current appeal of constructs such as locus of control and self-efficacy, it is likely that the field will witness the emergence of many such studies in the coming decade.

Sequential Models of the Components in the Self-Control Process

The role of cognitive and verbal mediational processes has increasingly found its place in theoretical formulations and intervention programs with children. Another major contribution to our understanding of the relationship between cognition and behavior can be found in those models that specify the components of the self-control process. While these models were initially devised with adult subjects or clients in mind, there have been recent attempts to apply these models to the behaviors of children. The models of Kanfer (1970, 1971, 1980) and Bandura (1977b, 1978) have emerged from the behavioral literature that is placing increasing emphasis on the importance of cognitive mediation. Within the social psychological literature, a model of self-awareness with similar component processes has been proposed by Wicklund (Duval & Wicklund, 1972; Wicklund, 1975; Wicklund & Frey, 1980).

The essential components of these models involve a chain beginning with self-observation or self-monitoring, followed by self-evaluation, and then self-reward or self-punishment, which in turn mediates further behavior. It should be noted that the components of these models are relevant to many of the processes discussed in previous sections of the chapter, for example, self-awareness, self-evaluation, and self-esteem. After examining each of the models, the research on children's use of these components in the service of self-control will be reviewed. Following this review there will be an attempt to integrate these issues with those raised earlier in the chapter.

Kanfer's Model

For Kanfer (1970, 1971, 1980; Kanfer & Phillips, 1970) the self-regulation process begins when some normally smooth chain of reactions becomes disrupted and the individual must therefore pay closer attention to behavior and its context. Such a situation touches off a sequence in which three distinct stages can be identified. The first stage Kanfer labels as self-observation or *self-monitoring*, in which the person observes his or her behavior carefully. Generally this occurs when the individual encounters an unexpected circumstance and needs to

make a decision about how to proceed. Kanfer notes that this typically occurs when one is in a new learning situation, in a strange situation, or when an environmental reaction has changed. At the decision point, the person asks, "What am I doing?" In responding to this question, he or she calls on previous performance criteria or standards.

This ushers in the second stage labeled *self-evaluation*, in which the person discriminates between what he or she is doing and what he or she *should* be doing. That is, one compares one's present performance with one's standards of performance. If the discrepancy is large, one may experience dissatisfaction with oneself and one's behavior, whereas if there is a close match between performance feedback and performance criteria, one will be relatively satisfied.

The outcome of this evaluation prepares the way for stage three, *self-reinforcement*, contingent on the magnitude of the match or the discrepancy. If the self-reinforcement is positive, the behavior chain should continue; if it is negative, corrective action may be taken.

Kanfer notes that most self-management programs combine techniques that involve self-monitoring, self-evaluation, and self-reinforcement. However, prior to engaging in any program of self-change and self-regulation the individual has to make a commitment to alter behavior and must set a standard of behavior change as a goal. Self-control, within this framework, is a special case of self-management, and is reserved to describe behavior in a particular situation, not a personality trait. For Kanfer, "when a person exercises self-control we talk about the fact that, in the absence of immediate external constraint or urging, he engages in the behavior (the controlling response) that originally had a lower probability than that of a more tempting behavior (the controlled response), in such a way that the controlled response is less likely to occur" (1980, p. 343). This formulation is very similar to that proposed by Thoresen and Mahoney (1974), although the latter investigators place more emphasis on the various mediational processes, for example, contingency rules, which are involved in each phase.

Kanfer (1977) further distinguishes between two types of self-control: decisional self-control and protracted self-control. Decisional self-control occurs when the individual is faced with making a momentary decision in a situation where two or more alternatives are available. Protracted self-control refers to the operation of self-monitoring, self-evaluation, and self-reinforcement over a longer time frame, based on the individual's commitment to change his or her behavior.

As clinicians, Kanfer and his colleagues are primarily interested in the parameters of protracted self-control, and have identified numerous techniques to facilitate the operation of the processes they have postulated (see Kanfer, 1980). For the most part, these clinical techniques have been employed with various adult populations, although there have been recent attempts to study these processes in children, which will be discussed shortly.

Bandura's Model

Bandura's (1978) most recent statement of the self-system emphasizes the principle of reciprocal determinism among three elements: behavior, the cognitive and other internal events that can affect perceptions and actions, and the external environment. He notes that for the radical behaviorist, cognitive determinants have typically been excised from an analysis of causal processes. However, in contemporary theorizing and research, internal determinants of behavior are gaining increasing attention and self-referent processes have come to occupy a central position in social learning theory (Bandura, 1977b, 1978).

Within this context, Bandura outlines the component processes involved in self-regulation: self-observation, a judgmental process, and a self-response that involves an evaluative reaction and tangible self-consequences such as reward or punishment. Behavior is first observed according to a number of dimensions, depending on the person's value orientation and the functional significance of a given activity. Examples of these performance dimensions are the quality, rate, quantity, and originality of the behavior. However, behavior can only produce a self-reaction through a judgmental process that includes several subsidiary processes; self-observation is not sufficient. Whether a given performance is judged as commendable or dissatisfying depends on the personal standards against which it is evaluated. These standards, in turn, are developed through a process of social comparison. However, it is self-comparison with one's previous performance that results in the actual judgment of the adequacy of the behavior.

Bandura notes that this judgmental process also involves an evaluation of how significant the activity is to them, commenting that it is largely in "areas affecting one's welfare and self-esteem that favorable performance appraisals activate personal consequences" (1978, p. 349). Furthermore, attributions regarding the determinants of one's behavior enter into his equation. Bandura writes: "People take pride in their accomplishments when they ascribe their success to their own abilities and efforts. They do not derive much self-satisfaction, however, when they view their performances as heavily dependent upon external factors" (1978, p. 349). Thus, the locus of control construct plays a critical role in Bandura's formulation, as does affect: "Much human behavior is regulated through self-evaluative consequences in the form of self-satisfaction, self-pride, self-dissatisfaction, and self-criticism" (p. 350).

Although Wicklund's theory of objective self-awareness (Duval & Wicklund, 1972; Wicklund, 1975; Wicklund & Frey, 1980) comes out of a different literature and has not yet led to research with children, it has features in common with Bandura's and Kanfer's models. In this formulation, attention must first be focused on an attribute or a performance of the self. This awareness of the self as an object in turn provokes a process of evaluation, and the attribute or behavior is then compared to a standard. Depending on the direction and magnitude of the discrepancy, the person will experience either a negative or positive evaluation. Affects, correspondingly negative or positive, are intimately attached to these judgments and in turn mediate behavior: negative affect results in avoidance of the situation, whereas positive affect will lead the person to maintain or seek out the circumstances prompting such an evaluation. Wicklund has devoted major empirical attention to the conditions that promote such self-awareness in adults.

Studies of the Components of the Self-Control Process in Children

Studies of children's acquisition and use of the self-reinforcement component were among the first to be conducted, notably by Bandura and his colleagues (Bandura, Grusec, & Menlove, 1967; Bandura & Kupers, 1964; Bandura & Perloff, 1967; Bandura & Whalen, 1966). These studies demonstrate that children between the ages of 7 and 10 tend to adopt the standards modeled by others, judge their own performance relative to these standards, and reinforce themselves accordingly. In the typical paradigm, the child observes a model performing a bowling task in which he or she adopts either a high performance standard or a relatively low criterion for self-reinforcement. When the model attains or exceeds the self-imposed demand, he or she rewards himself or herself with candy or a token and expresses positive verbal self-evaluations; if performance falls short of the self-imposed standards, the model denies the available rewards and reacts in a self-derogatory manner.

In the study by Bandura and Kupers (1964), 7- to 9-year-old children who observed either an adult or peer model setting a high standard of self-reinforcement later rewarded themselves sparingly and only when their own performance was superior; in contrast, children exposed to models with relatively low performance standards reinforced themselves generously for mediocre performance. The effects of the adult model were somewhat stronger than the effects of the peer model (see also Bandura & Whalen, 1966).

Mischel and Liebert (1966) have also demonstrated that self-reward patterns can be transmitted through a series of models. Children who adopted the standards of reinforcement modeled by adults subsequently modeled the same self-rewarding behavior with peers and applied the same standards to their own behavior. More recent studies have also revealed that children who adopt high performance standards of self-rewarding through modeling tend to apply similar standards on later occasions to somewhat different activities in dissimilar situations (Lepper, Sagotsky, & Mailer, 1975; Sagotsky & Lepper, 1976).

If children are at liberty to select a performance level deserving of self-reward, they often set extremely difficult standards (Bandura & Perloff, 1967). In this study, no child selected the lowest standard, many selected the highest level, and others raised their initial standard to a higher level without a commensurate increase in self-reward, thereby making the task more demanding. These authors have suggested that this particular situation sets up a conflict between the maximization of material rewards and the tendency to negatively evaluate one's worth or self-esteem if one opts to reward devalued behavior; thus, both aspects must be considered in interpreting such a pattern.

The Bandura and Perloff study also found that self-monitored and externally applied reinforcement were equally effective, a finding that has generally been replicated (see Bolstad & Johnson, 1972; Brownell, 1978; Felixbrod & O'Leary, 1973, 1974; Glynn, 1970). It should be noted that most of these studies involved academic tasks or were performed in classroom settings. Given the strong contingencies in the typical classroom setting that encourage an extrinsic reward orientation, these findings are not surprising. It would be interesting to further examine such effects, taking into account the individual differences in intrinsic versus extrinsic orientation (Harter, 1981b) as well as comparing the efficacy of external and self-reward for domains other than academic performance.

When one compares self-reward to other components of the self-control process, its relative effectiveness has more clearly been demonstrated. Children who self-reward their behavior perform at higher levels than those who receive no reinforcement, those who are rewarded noncontingently, or those who do not reinforce their own behavior but who monitor their behavior, set goals, or engage in self-instruction (Bandura & Perloff, 1967; Bolstad & Johnson, 1972; Felixbrod & O'Leary, 1973; Glynn, 1970; Johnson, 1970; Masters & Santrock, 1976; Nelson & Birkimer, 1978; Switzky & Haywood, 1974).

Bandura (1971) has emphasized the importance of *verbal* self-evaluation as an important defining component of self-reinforcing events. One's verbal reaction of self-commendation or self-derogation evokes an affective response that in turn mediates one's future performance. Others (Harter, in press-d; Harter & Connell, 1982; Masters & Santrock, 1976; Rosenhan, 1972) have made a similar point. Masters and Santrock (1976) report findings with children that suggest that it is the affect associated with the evaluations instead of the content of the evaluations per se that motivates behavior. Findings reported in an earlier section of this chapter (Harter & Connell, 1982) demonstrated that the affective component of children's self-evaluations influenced their motivational orientation to engage in classroom behavior.

Another major element of the self-evaluation component involves *social comparison*. For the most part, those studies by Bandura and others that have demonstrated such effects have involved children aged 7 and older. Several recent developmental studies provide evidence that social comparison for the purpose of self-evaluation is not utilized by the young child, but emerges in middle childhood around the age of 8 (Nicholls, 1978; Ruble, Boggiano, Feldman, & Loebl, 1980; Ruble, Parsons, & Ross, 1976). (See also Boggiano & Ruble, 1979; Spear & Armstrong, 1978.) The findings of Ruble et al. (1980) are among the most compelling. In a thoughtfully designed pair of studies of first through fourth graders, these investigators examined children's use of social comparison information in a problem-solving achievement situation. Their methodology attempted to maximize the possibility for social comparison. In sum, their findings revealed that "the impact of social comparison information was weak and in fact did not consistently and systematically affect self-evaluations until surprisingly late (i.e., fourth grade)'' (p. 113).

In their discussion, Ruble et al. attempt to reconcile these findings with earlier reports that children as young as 4, 5, and 6 show an interest in comparing their performance with others' (Dinner, 1976; Masters, 1971; Ruble, Feldman, & Boggiano, 1976). Their analysis suggests that there are different motivations for attending to the information provided through social comparison, which may well pursue a developmental course. Thus, the earliest interest in social comparison is not concerned with self-evaluation or self-definition but with making sure one is getting one's fair share and is being treated like the other children. The investigators conclude that ''until children recognize that the outcomes have deeper implications for the self, competition or comparative evaluation may have little long-lasting effect'' (p. 114).

These findings can be interpreted within the context of a number of developmental processes discussed earlier. The young child has not yet sufficiently consolidated a sense of self defined by attributes that must be proven or defended in a social situation. Moreover, while the experimental situation employed by Ruble et al. was structured to tap ''achievement,'' the mastery process itself may be the most salient element for younger children, not the evaluative implications of the *product* of one's accomplishment (see Harter, 1980). Finally, until the young child can take the perspective of another and recognize the significance of others' evaluation in shaping one's own self-definition, social comparison information should not dramatically or systematically affect his or her performance estimates.

Certain intervention studies have attempted to train children in *several* components of the self-control process. Glynn and his colleagues (Ballard & Glynn, 1975; Glynn & Thomas, 1974; Glynn, Thomas, & Shee, 1973) have designed a program to enhance ''on task'' behavior in the classroom through the use of a package including self-monitoring, self-evaluation, and self-reward. Evaluation and reward were only partially self-determined since the teacher set the standards of conduct and determined the types and amounts of reinforcement. Moreover, in one study, the teacher also ''cued'' the children as to when to return to on-task behavior, if they had been interrupted because of other instructional requirements in the classroom. The gains in terms of on-task behavior, compared to a base-rate period, were quite impressive. As with any study compounding these various elements, it is difficult to determine which components are the most effec-

tive, or whether all, in fact, are necessary to promote this type of self-regulation in the classroom. As Karoly (1977) notes in his review, there were other incidental features in this setting, for example, cooperative teachers, little disruption in normal classroom routine, and valued activity reinforcers, that may eventually prove to be essential to the success of such programs. Karoly suggests certain alternative strategies that might be pursued. Nevertheless, the compounding strategy employed by Glynn and his colleagues has certainly reaped positive practical benefits and merits further, more systematic, study.

Another series of studies (Litrownik & Steinfeld, 1982) has attempted to train the various components of the self-regulation process in retarded children and adolescents. Of interest in one study was their finding that, with retarded adolescents, self-evaluative statements did not have a reinforcing effect, although training in the self-administration of rewards (pennies) did enhance performance. The authors speculate that this may be a result of the absence of affect associated with self-evaluations. They suggest that inconsistency in the administration of rewards to retarded children during their socialization may preclude the establishment of meaning or secondary reinforcing value attached to self-evaluative statements. If this were true, they go on to suggest that one would need to institute a training program in which self-evaluative statements are repeatedly paired with rewards in order for the self-evaluative statements to become meaningful and therefore functional. A similar argument has been made by Harter (1981d) in suggesting how verbal self-rewards are acquired in the child's naturalistic environment. There is another possible explanation, however, for the failure of self-evaluative statements to influence the behavior of the retarded children in this study. It may be the case that, given the Mental Age levels of these individuals, namely 4 to 8, they were incapable of making use of self-evaluative statements because of their inability to engage in social comparison. That is, developmentally, they may be functioning below the mental age range in which social comparison information can be effectively translated into meaningful self-evaluative appraisals. Thus, there are intriguing avenues for further study, both with regard to the role of affect as well as social comparison, in understanding developmental change as well as individual differences in self-control.

In another study of arithmetic learning of normal first graders, Spates and Kanfer (1977) examined the relative contribution of each of the components in the self-control process, criterion-setting, self-monitoring, self-evaluation, and self-reinforcement. Children were trained to generate self-instructions for each component. Their findings revealed that the single most important component in this context was criterion-setting, and that the addition of self-monitoring and self-reinforcement did not appreciably reduce arithmetic errors.

Other studies have concerned themselves primarily with the components of goal-setting and/or self-monitoring. A provocative study by Broden, Hall, and Mitts (1971) reported dramatic changes in the study habits of two eighth graders after implementing a relatively straightforward self-monitoring procedure. As others (e.g., Sagotsky, Patterson, & Lepper, 1978) have noted, however, it is difficult to determine whether other processes such as criterion setting, self-evaluation, and/or self-reinforcement may have contributed to the effects reported.

Sagotsky, Patterson, and Lepper (1978) sought to examine certain of the processes in a study of goal-setting and self-monitoring on the math performance of fifth- and sixth-grade pupils. Exposure to self-monitoring procedures produced significant increases in both appropriate study behavior and actual math achievement, while exposure to goal-setting procedures had no such effect on either class of behaviors. In interpreting these findings, the authors suggest that the effectiveness of the self-monitoring technique may have been because it contained both an implicit evaluative component in the recording of positive and negative behavior, as well as a general "plan" for maintaining on-task behavior (see also Kazdin, 1974; Lipinski, Black, Nelson, & Ciminero, 1975). That is, the negative connotations of recording off-task behavior might have served as a cue to return to the appropriate on-task behaviors. The emphasis on plans or strategies is consistent with the work of Patterson and Mischel (reviewed earlier in this chapter). The authors also suggest that the failure to find a facilitating effect for the goal-setting procedure may have resulted from the complicated mathematics program to which it was applied.

It is difficult to summarize or reconcile the findings to date that bear on the effectiveness of the various components of self-control with children. The situational, task, and domain differences employed or sampled across studies may well account for some of the apparent discrepancies. The difficulty of controlling or assessing the use of covert monitoring, evaluation, or self-rewarding processes also poses problems in this research. Children of different ages have also been employed across the various studies. It may be that different components

of the self-evaluative process are more critical than others at different developmental levels. Alternatively, they may be equally critical but assume qualitatively different forms and roles at different ages. Thus, more attention to developmental issues may be warranted.

For example, it has recently been suggested (Harter, 1982d) that the order in which the critical component processes of self-regulation are *acquired* developmentally may be just the *reverse* of the order in which they are postulated to *operate* in adulthood—self-monitoring, self-evaluation, and self-reinforcement. That is, children first learn to imitate verbal approval and apply it to their own behavior before they are capable of self-evaluation, and the processes of self-evaluation must be acquired before they can fully appreciate those situations in which they should monitor their behavior.

The naturalistic example given for such a developmental acquisition process (see Harter, 1982d) was of a young child whose mother is attempting to teach her to pick up her clothes, a socialization venture that necessitates the training of self-control. The daughter has previously learned to imitate the mother's approval in the form of "good girl," which leads to an experience of positive affect. However, she next must learn to discriminate between good and bad actions, to evaluate her own behavior. Mother initially serves as the discriminating evaluator, labeling her behavior as "good" when she puts her dirty clothes in the hamper and "not good" when she doesn't. On this basis the child internalizes these standards for self-evaluation. Mother next sets the stage for self-monitoring by initially monitoring the child's behavior. Mommy as monitor says things like: "Now *you* know what you are supposed to do with your dirty shirt," thus modeling the monitoring conditions for the child. Eventually, this process comes to be internalized such that the child can monitor her own behavior. Thus the developmental acquisition sequence postulated is self-reward, self-evaluation, and then self-monitoring.

There is no necessary contradiction here between this analysis of how such processes might be developmentally acquired and how they operate in adulthood. In models such as those of Kanfer and Bandura, particular events or conditions trigger the chain of processes, beginning with self-monitoring and leading to self-evaluation and to self-reward (or punishment). The sequence can only operate in this manner if each of the component processes is available in one's repertoire, and thus the developmental study of their acquisition would appear to be a question of interest.

This analysis also implies that in intervention strategies with certain populations designed to foster self-control we may need to begin at the beginning, as defined by the developmental sequence postulated; thus, one may need to first establish the secondary reinforcing properties of self-reward and verbal approval, a suggestion consistent with the conclusions of Litrownik and Steinfeld (1982) in their work with the retarded. Instruction in the use of self-evaluation would follow, after which procedures designed to teach self-monitoring would then be instituted.

Developmental Considerations in the Study of Self-Control

Until quite recently, there has been relatively little attention directed toward developmental factors involved in self-control (see Karoly, 1977). One must concur with Bandura (1977b) that an application of broad stage models will not suffice, but that one must conduct a more detailed developmental analysis of the specific processes involved in self-control. It is obvious from the preceding discussion that the processes of self-control take many forms. As Meichenbaum (1979) has observed: "It should be apparent that self-control does *not* represent a unitary process, but instead represents a multi-dimensional process involving situational, perceptual, cognitive, behavioral, attitudinal and motivational components" (p. 9). Each of these components must ultimately be considered from a developmental perspective. In attempting to structure the state of our current knowledge of developmental differences, as well as suggest future directions for research, this section will consider three themes: (1) basic cognitive and attentional processes, (2) internalization processes, and (3) motivational and affective processes.

Basic Cognitive and Attention Factors

Kopp (1981) has been one of the few investigators to adopt a developmental perspective from the outset. Specifically, she has focused on the first three years of life in an attempt to chart a stage model of the emergence of self-control. In her model, self-control first emerges around the age of 24 months, when the toddler can behave according to certain social expectations in the absence of external monitors. Prior to this phase, however, Kopp outlines three preceding stages leading up to the manifestation of self-control, identifying the particular perceptual, attentional, motoric, and cognitive processes that are responsible for the behaviors in the infant's repertoire. The very first phase, from birth to about 3 months, is designated as *neurophysiological modulation,* in which arousal states are modulated and reflex movements are exhibited as organized patterns of functional behavior. During the second phase of *sensorimotor modulation,* from 3 to 9 or 12 months, the infant demonstrates the ability to engage in voluntary motor acts (e.g., reaching and grasping), and can change such an act in response to events that arise. However, such modulation does "not involve consciousness, prior intention, or awareness of the *meaning* of the situation" (p. 8).

The third phase, labeled *control* (between 9 to 12 months and 18 to 24 months), is characterized by the child's emerging ability to manifest an awareness of social or task demands defined by caregivers, and to initiate, maintain, modulate, or cease physical acts, communication, and emotional signals accordingly. Compliance to parental commands is a hallmark of this stage, and Kopp discusses the development of the cognitive and motor processes which make these new skills possible.

The advance of the fourth phase, *self-control,* beginning at 24 months, is the ability to comply, delay, or behave according to the caregiver's social expectations in the absence of external monitors. The development of representational thinking and evocative (recall) memory facilitate this transition. Kopp identifies a fifth phase, that she terms *self-regulation,* beginning at about 36 months, which primarily differs from the previous phase in degree. During the prior stage of self-control, the toddler has limited flexibility in adapting acts to meet new situational demands and a limited capacity for waiting or delay. However, in the fifth phase the young child is more adaptive to changes and can make use of strategies to facilitate delay.

Kopp's cross-sectional research with three age groups, 18-, 24-, and 36-month-olds, has demonstrated clear developmental differences on a number of laboratory tasks. In one task, the child is instructed not to touch an attractive toy telephone in front of her or him; in another, raisins are hidden under cups and the child is instructed to wait for a cue to search for them; in a third task, the child is asked to engage in a boring task in the presence of a gift that she or he will ultimately receive. Across the ages sampled, clear developmental progressions are obtained for such measures as latency to touch the telephone, number of raisins eaten, latency to eat raisins, and latency to touch the gift. Kopp has been particularly interested in the spontaneous strategies that children employ, particularly among the oldest group. Tactics such as sitting on one's hands, averting one's gaze, singing, and talking were all diversions children seem to employ in order to maximize delay. Interestingly, her observations of handicapped children, for example, those with Down's syndrome, indicate that such children do not seem to possess such diversionary strategies in their behavioral repertoire.

Kopp's work is particularly interesting in outlining many of the developmental precursors of the cognitive-attentional mechanisms identified by Mischel, Patterson, and their colleagues (see Mischel & Patterson, 1978; Patterson, 1982). As noted previously, their research with preschoolers has identified a number of strategies that facilitate delay, including the cognitive construction of distractors, cognitive transformations that minimize the arousal characteristics of a delayed reward, and the use of self-instructional plans that focus on temptation-inhibition. Moreover, they have begun to pursue the use of such plans developmentally. Most recently, they have turned their attention to children's understanding and use of such strategies in the absence of specific training. Thus, while young children can be instructed to utilize such strategies, they do not appear to do so naturally.

Sawin and Parke (1979) have found some support for the notion that as children's verbal mediational skills develop they can make use of redirective self-verbalizations in resistance to temptation situations, whereas at younger ages only prohibitive self-verbalizations appear to be effective. They suggest that with age, children become better able to focus on more features of the instructions and to discriminate more elements, which in turn facilitates self-regulation. These effects have not yet been studied over a broad age range, however.

The verbal-mediational work of Meichenbaum and his colleagues (see Meichenbaum, 1976, 1977, 1978) on the self-governing role of covert speech was initially based on the developmental model of Luria. However, there has been very little developmental thrust to the research that has followed from the training program he has devised. For the most part, these techniques have been employed with clinical populations, typically with impulsive or aggressive children. Given that the training package contains numerous elements, it is unclear at this point precisely which processes are responsible for changes in the self-control of behavior. Some have suggested, for example, that the self-instructional component per se may be less critical than the focusing of attention on situationally relevant factors. Thus, there is much to be pursued with regard to the isolation of the specific processes and skills respon-

sible for gains in self-regulation, as well as the examination of developmental differences in the ability to engage these processes, with special attention to delays or deficiencies in particular clinical populations.

In his latest model of self-management, Karoly (1982) has urged that we take a more differentiated look at the many skills required for both the acquisition and maintenance of self-regulated responses. He has identified the following skill components: (1) self-observation, (2) self-recording, (3) self-evaluation and standard setting, (4) the self-administration of rewards and punishment, (5) verbal self-instructional control of attention and motor repertoires, (6) informational-processing style (e.g., different modes of encoding, storage, retrieval, and organization of experience in memory), (7) planning and problem-solving style, (8) imaginal control of thought and affect, (9) self-perception and causal attribution, and (10) the deliberate manipulation of stimulus-response, response-outcome, and self-efficacy expectancies.

There is much to be examined with regard to developmental differences in these abilities. With regard to self-observation, for example, an earlier section of this chapter suggested that we have used this term to represent different processes at different developmental levels. With regard to self-control, we need to be more precise about which particular self-awareness skills are required. Is it sufficient to be *aware* of the physical attributes, competencies, and behaviors that the young child uses to define the self in order to engage in the types of self-monitoring processes postulated in models like those of Kanfer and Bandura? Or must one have developed an awareness of self based on the ability to see the self as others see one, must one have reached the stage of Cooley's looking glass self or Mead's generalized other? Are there different forms of self-control that require self-awareness skills from different developmental levels?

A similar question can be raised with regard to the process of self-evaluation. What self-evaluation skills are possible at different developmental levels? Certain studies reviewed earlier suggest, for example, that the young child cannot effectively utilize social comparison information for the purpose of self-evaluation. Young children clearly use evaluative labels, however, in making reference to the self. On what bases are children making such judgments, and of what relevance is this process of self-control? Furthermore, recent evidence (Chao, 1981; Harter & Pike, 1981) suggests that while young children can make reliable judgments concerning their competence and social acceptance, these judgments are less than realistic when compared to teacher's ratings of the child's competence. These are but a few of the developmental issues to be pursued with regard to differences in the self-evaluative process that may have implications for self-control.

Bierer's (1981) research has also revealed individual differences among elementary school children in the degree to which they can make realistic judgments about their competence. Certain children vastly overemphasize their competence, while others seriously underrate their abilities. Thus, accuracy of judgment may be an important individual difference variable influencing the effectiveness of self-monitoring and self-evaluative components in a self-control program. (Each of the other skills outlined by Karoly would require a similar developmental analysis in order to further our understanding of self-management.)

Internalization Processes

In a sense, most of the processes involved in the various formulations of self-control can be viewed in terms of some form of internalization, broadly defined. That is, behavior originally evoked or suppressed by external factors comes under internal control or self-regulation. Aronfreed (1969, 1976) has integrated most of the earlier self-control studies under the rubric of ''internalization.'' For Aronfreed, this term does not merely refer to a process whereby behavior once public and overt becomes an internal cognitive representation. It also encompasses a broader array of affective and cognitive mechanisms that can translate the child's social learning into internalized control over one's behavior. In organizing this literature, Aronfreed points to two major channels of socialization that bring about such internalized control. The first involves the shaping of behavior through positive or aversive outcomes that are contingent on the child's overt acts. The second channel of socialization is observational learning or modeling.

Historically, the psychoanalytic model provided the first developmental perspective on the internalization of parental values through the formation of the superego. The intense pressures and anxieties of the Oedipal conflict were presumed to impel the young child toward identification with parental values, resulting in an internalizing ego ideal. The social learning theory literature in its emphasis on modeling (see also Bandura, 1969a; Mischel, 1970) provides for a more specific mechanisms through which parental values can be adopted, including an acquisition process which is considerably less

fraught. However, more attention must be devoted to the possible developmental parameters of the modeling process. In particular, it may be important to investigate possible age differences in the ability to acquire performance standards, rules, and the contingencies under which to administer self-reward. The most convincing demonstrations of such modeling involved children above the ages of 7 or 8. While younger children have been shown to imitate aggressive and/or prosocial behaviors, the extent to which they can imitate more complicated rules and standards relevant to the processes involved in self-regulation has yet to be systematically explored.

As discussed in an earlier section, recent investigators (e.g., Karoly, 1982) have emphasized the importance of the internalization of rules in the self-management process. As Karoly observes, ''In the absence of constant reminders, the only efficient mode of behavior control is to teach children to be rule carriers, rule detectors, rule formers, and rule users'' (p. 88). As he goes on to note, there is not a single theoretical position on self-management that does not either explicitly or implicitly concern itself with children's conformity to rules.

For the most part, however, the developmentalist's approach to rule conformity has been the postulation of broad stage models (e.g., Kohlberg, 1969, 1976; Loevinger, 1966; Loevinger & Wessler, 1970) that do not assume that rule knowledge is necessarily related to behavior, much less to behavior within a particular situational context. Thus, Loevinger's *self-protective* and *conformity* stages, as well as Kohlberg's stages of *Good Boy/ Good Girl Morality* and *Law and Order*, would lead to the general expectation that children or individuals so typed would follow conventional rules. However, these stage characterizations would only be expected to provide a general backdrop against which one would have to assess the more specific rule understanding required by a given program on self-control. The developmental assessment of specific rule understanding would provide some additional guidelines.

One can also consider *self-reward* in terms of a developmental process of internalization (see Harter, 1982d). How do external rewards in the form of parental approval and praise naturally come to be incorporated into a self-approving voice that can then aid in the control of the child's behavior? How does the child come to be a rewarder of the self as well as the rewardee? A learning analysis would emphasize the early pairing of primary reinforcement (e.g., a hug) with verbal praise, for example, ''good girl,'' accompanied by positive affect on the part of the child. Thus, verbal approval comes to take on secondary reinforcing properties and will evoke pleasure in the child, which in turn will mediate the desired behavior. A general modeling analysis can handle the emergence of the child's own "good girl" utterances. She has not only observed herself as the object of parental reward—the rewardee—but she can also imitate the rewarding process itself and be her own rewarder. These self-approving utterances are accompanied by positive affect that mediates and maintains behavior.

Within this framework, one can examine the specific functions of external reward and explore their implications for self-reward. The initial distinction between two general functions of reward, motivational and informational functions (Aronfreed, 1969; Bandura, 1971; Estes, 1972), is useful in this context. Within each of these functions, one can make further distinctions (see Harter, 1981a, 1982d). For example, with regard to the *informational* function, reward can provide information about which behaviors are *important* to perform; it defines a set of mastery goals. In addition, information is provided with regard to *evaluative criteria* by which the success or failure of a given response or behavior can be judged. With regard to the *motivational* dimensions, reward functions as an *incentive* to engage in the behavior in anticipation of future rewards; and it also leads to the experience of positive *affect*.

It seems likely, furthermore, that socialization agents vary with regard to which reward functions their praise or approval may emphasize. The message "That's good, I'll bet you can do it again" may highlight the *incentive* function, encouraging the child to engage in the behavior. Approval in the form of "That's good, and you seem really happy that you can do that" may call attention to the *affective* properties of reward and the pleasure derived from success. The parent who tells her child "I'm really glad that you did your homework because it's important for you to learn as much as you can" places emphasis on the *importance* of learning as a mastery goal. The parental utterance "I'm pleased that you got every one of your spelling words right, except this one, which has a letter missing" is highlighting the *correctness* of the rewarded response and the *criteria* for making such a determination.

Although a given reinforcer may serve more than one or even all these functions simultaneously, it seems fruitful to make these conceptual distinctions and to examine their implications for the internalization process. If the child internalizes the external rewarding message and develops the capacity to re-ward herself, perhaps these same functions can be examined as they apply to *self*-reward. One can then ask how these informational and motivational functions operate within a given child, within different situational contexts. One can also examine individual differences as well as developmental change in order to provide a normative backdrop.

In our own research, we have begun to address this issue empirically. In one developmental study (Harter, 1981b) we have documented how two informational functions, knowledge about classroom rules and regulations and evaluative criteria for judging successes and failures, show a dramatic shift from extrinsic sources to internalized understanding across the ages sampled, grades 3 through 9. We are currently devising an instrument to tap the relative strength of external reward versus internalized self-reward for each of the subfunctions identified above, in two different mastery domains, schoolwork and sports. We feel that this type of approach will complement the laboratory studies of self-reward that have been performed, and that our self-report measures may be useful in predicting a variety of behaviors, including individual differences in the potential effectiveness of self-control programs utilizing self-reward. In future research on the antecedents of individual differences in self-reward use, it would also be of interest to determine parental patterns in the types of reward functions emphasized, as well as the consistency with which they were employed.

Motivational and Affective Processes

In the preceding discussion, it was suggested that not only could informational functions of reward be internalized—the more traditional viewpoint—but that motivational functions can also undergo internalization with development. Thus, while the young child performs a given behavior in order to obtain extrinsic reward, gradually one appears to become "self-motivated." Within that general framework, we can now address the more specific question of what motivates the child to engage in self-controlling behavior. Toward what goals and consequences is this type of behavior directed? There are some who would emphasize the child's desire to please the parents. Others, for example, Premack and Anglin (1973), have utilized an avoidance paradigm to explain why children engage in self-control, suggesting that they do so to avoid the withdrawal of the parent's affection. Aronfreed notes that there are a number of different reasons why a child might come to control his or her conduct; these can be conceptualized along a continuum of "internal versus external orientation'' (p. 268). For example, ''a child's conduct may be governed by its anticipation of later positive or aversive outcomes for itself, or by its cognitive representation of how other people may have reacted to its behavior in the past'' (p. 268). However, there has been little developmental research indicating that at different developmental levels children may be at different points along such a continuum.

From a developmental perspective, we do have broad stage models (e.g., Loevinger's and Kohlberg's), which indicate that there is a general shift from external to internal control. While Kohlberg's theory is typically described as a cognitive-developmental theory of moral judgment, its stage descriptions contain clear indications of the motivations for why individuals would perform behaviors at different stages. These converge with Loevinger's in part, since she drew on Kohlberg's formulation in devising her model. Thus, the developmentally earliest motivation for exhibiting self-control would be to avoid punishment. Loevinger's Opportunistic stage, which dovetails with Kohlberg's second stage of Naive/Instrumental Hedonism, would add a more willful component to this orientation in that there is also a focus on meeting one's own egocentric needs.

At the next level, Kohlberg's Good Boy/Good Girl stage, which parallels Loevinger's stage of Conformity to some extent, self-control would be motivated by the desire to please others or to avoid their condemnation. At this stage, in Kohlberg's model, the child must be aware of his or her social role and be motivated to perform it in order to please significant others in one's life. Kohlberg goes on to note, moreover, that the child must be able to put himself or herself in the other person's shoes. The motivation for engaging in stereotypically ''good'' behavior is not only one's care and concern for others but ''the need to be a good person in your own eyes and those of others'' (p. 34).

This analysis is reminiscent of earlier discussions about the developmental achievement of perspective-taking, the looking glass self (Cooley, 1902), and the internalization of the generalized other (Mead, 1934). For some, for example, Shibutani (1961), it is not until the child can take the perspective of others that self-control is manifest. Prior to that point, the child is primarily motivated to exhibit control in compliance with the demands of people who could enforce them. The ''self,'' therefore, in this particular analysis is based on the reflected appraisals of others that have come to be incorporated into the child's definition of the ''Me.'' The point, however, is not to argue about what constitutes ''true self-control'' but to chart the developmental course of motivations responsible for causing a child to control behavior.

There would appear to be considerable convergence on the general developmental progression, although there is little systematic evidence. A major developmental shift seems to occur when the young child is motivated to control his or her behavior in order to please the significant others in his or her life, to garner their approval and avoid their disapproval. Concomitantly, the child would be highly motivated to internalize the values and standards whereby appropriate behavior could be controlled and maintained. The developmental shift toward the effectiveness of rationales for punishment that emphasize others' feelings and property rights (see Parke, 1977; Pressley, 1979) is consistent with the analysis. One would also expect that the particular values and standard for appropriate behaviors could be expected to shift with development as the specific significant others undergo changes. As Rosenberg's (1979) findings suggest, there is a shift from parents to peers to close friends with regard to those whose opinion of the self is critical.

It is also noteworthy, in this regard, to recall the findings of Rosenberg (1979) and Minton (1979), which indicate that the very characteristic of self-control itself emerges as a dimension of the self-concept during middle childhood and becomes an important determinant of their sense of self-esteem. Children report that control of verbal and physical aggression and the expression of negative emotions such as anger is critical to their sense of self. Thus, it would be interesting to examine whether changes in one's motivation to engage in self-controlled behavior would parallel changes in the dimensions that define the child's self-concept and would be related to his or her level of self-esteem.

If pleasing *others* represents one developmental advance in a general sequence of motivations to control one's behavior, a further step would be self-control in order to please the *self* and to preserve the self-image that one has constructed. There is a certain convergence here with Loevinger's autonomous stage and Kohlberg's levels of principled moral thought. However, the process undoubtedly begins well before the ages at which Loevinger and Kohlberg place these stages. However, the key to this advance is the ability to be pleased with oneself or displeased with oneself in the absence of external feedback from others. This level, as intended here, implies that one has a clear sense of self based on the reflected appraisals of others: the child has developed a third-person awareness of the self (see Selman, 1980) and the related ability to express such affects as self-pride and self-shame. The developmental studies reviewed in the section on the construction of the self suggest that these processes begin to be consolidated around the age of 8. The "Me" at this point in time has also become sufficiently crystallized that the child can make global judgments about his or her overall worth or self-esteem. In Bandura's (1978) model of self-regulation an important component of the self-evaluative process involves one's feelings of self-satisfaction and self-esteem. The present analysis suggests that it would be interesting to determine at what point in development these self-feelings emerge as critical.

The claim here is not that pride or shame cannot be experienced in younger children, but rather that at earlier ages it requires external support. Once self-pride and self-shame are internalized such that the "I" is proud or ashamed of the "Me" in the absence of the reaction of others, then these self-affects should become capable of mediating behavior directly.

There is little systematic research on the proposed developmental shifts in the motivations underlying children's self-control behaviors. There is some evidence in a recent study by Chandler (1981). Children ranging from 6 to 12 years in age were asked to explain the reasons why they engaged in chore behaviors that they claimed they didn't like to do, for example, cleaning one's room, going to bed on time, doing what mom asks without talking back or arguing. Children's responses could be coded according to the following types of reasons offered for why they performed these activities.

1. *Anticipation of external reward or approval, avoidance of disapproval,* these included gaining or maintaining adult approval, avoiding adult disapproval or punishment, gaining or maintaining peer approval, avoiding peer disapproval, and the anticipation of a specific tangible reward.
2. *Following an explicit rule,* for example, "I'm supposed to clean my room."
3. *Invoking either a positive or negative maxim,* for example, "Your body needs a good night's beauty sleep." "If you don't brush your teeth the yellow sets in."

4. *Achievement of goals set by and for the self,* for example, "I clean my room so I'll be able to find things easily." "I go to bed so I'll feel good in the morning."

Chandler's findings indicate that the use of reasons emphasizing external approval or disapproval, and explicit rules, decreases over the age range sampled, whereas use of internalized reasons in the form of goals set by and for the self show a predicted increase with development. Chandler has postulated that maxims may represent a transitional category, although her cross-sectional design and open-ended interview technique did not permit a compelling test of this hypothesis. Nevertheless, it is an intriguing issue to pursue with regard to the internalization of motivations for controlling one's behavior.

This particular developmental analysis of motivational shifts reflects relatively general classes of motivation. Clearly, in any given situation requiring the establishment of self-control, a much more specific analysis must be performed. Karoly (1982) has articulated this point, and has included motivation as one of the four major components in his model of self-management. For Karoly, motivation refers to both effort and commitment. He notes that the self-managing child must be "affectively aroused to the degree that he or she is willing to work for self-change or self-directed maintenance of behavior." Karoly observes that a major task for those instituting self-management programs is to understand why children and adolescents cannot mobilize the commitment to exercise self-control or self-regulation. Thus, he urges that in addition to an assessment of the child's understanding of rules, awareness of the short and long-run consequences, and skills for executing self-managed responses, we need to pay careful attention to the specific motivational parameters that may govern the child's ability to engage in self-control. The suggestion in this section is that developmental research may provide some general guidelines; however, our assessment techniques ultimately need to focus on the individual child.

With regard to each of the general classes of variables discussed, cognitive-attentional, internalization processes, and motivational factors, a developmental analysis must also be accompanied by an examination of those environmental factors that account for individual differences within as well as across developmental levels. The Blocks' work (see J. H. Block & J. Block, 1980) is of interest in this regard, given their description of the parental and child-rearing antecedents leading to different typologies involving ego control and ego resiliency. However, for the majority of those who are interested in more situation-specific predictability, the search for the antecedents of self-control must necessarily be conducted at a more specific level of analysis.

CONCLUDING REMARKS AND FUTURE DIRECTIONS

The return of the self as a legitimate psychological construct is not only a welcome tonic to many but represents many new directions and exciting convergences that characterize the field at large. For example, we can no longer be content with our former compartmentalizations of traditional topics, where investigator A studies cognition, investigator B focuses on affect, investigator C examines self-perceptions, and investigator D covers the realm of overt behavior. As our treatment of each topic has indicated, issues involving the self require that we bridge these domains and examine the interaction of these psychological systems. For example, in the discussion of infancy there is a fascinating new literature describing a progression of cognitive advances whereby the infant comes to develop a sense of self. The more socioemotional aspects of the differentiation of self from mother have also been described with some precision. There has been some attempt to begin to integrate these lines of development; however, there is much to be accomplished in achieving such a synthesis.

The discussion of the self as a cognitive construction was underscored. However, here too there is a need to consider the construction of the self as a social process, as well. Although many find Cooley's notion of the ''looking glass self'' and Mead's concept of the ''generalized other'' very compelling, there is virtually no research that examines the interaction of cognitive and social processes in the formation of the self-concept.

There are other promising convergences with regard to the interaction of cognition and affect. As the treatment of self-esteem indicated, self-evaluative judgments do not merely represent cold cognitive appraisals but provoke an affective reaction, which in turn may mediate behavior. The links in such a chain are also apparent in many of the recent models of self-control, where one's affective reaction to a cognitive self-appraisal triggers one's behavioral response. The discussion of the self during aolescence also highlights the need to think of this period in terms of a complex interaction involving physical, emotional, social, and cognitive change. The challenge will be to capture these complexities in our theoretical models and research designs.

Another major trend revealed in the treatment of the self is the proliferation of models of development that provide a more differentiated picture of the stages or phases involved in a given process. For example, the treatment of the infant's emerging sense of self was described as a gradual process, marked by a series of developmental advances that build upon previous acquisitions. In the discussion of the construction of the self, an eight-stage model was suggested as a framework for understanding the gradual process of self-concept formation with development. This model relied heavily on Fischer's theory of cognitive development, which has not only articulated a more differentiated picture of development during childhood than has formerly been suggested but also describes four levels of abstraction, beginning with adolescence and continuing through the adult life-span. Convergences of this model with Erikson's theory of adult development provide another exciting arena for research. The emphasis on increasingly differentiated stage models can also be seen in the work of Levinson, who has attempted to characterize the many levels and transitions during adult development.

There has been less developmental attention paid to the topics of self-esteem and self-control. Within the self-esteem literature, individual differences have been the primary focus. Thus, there is a need to consider the evaluation of the self from a developmental perspective. Among those interested in the topic of self-control, there is an increasing awareness of the need to examine the possible developmental parameters of the processes involved. Developmental differences in cognitive-attentional mechanisms, in processes making internalization possible, in motivation, and in the ability to engage in self-reward represent arenas in which there are many challenging avenues to pursue. The increasing popularity of the term cognitive-behavior modification also reflects this outlook.

The study of the self also represents an arena in which a variety of interactionists can find a welcome conceptual niche. Debates between the trait theorists and those opting for a more situation-specific approach have waned, and there is increasing emphasis on the interaction between the nature of the situation and the characteristics of the self that an individual brings to that situation. This emphasis on the interaction between the self and the environment is particularly evident within the fields of cognitive development as well as social learning theory. Within developmental psychology, we can no longer be content to describe normative-developmental sequences but must also look to the environment for transition rules and mechanisms of ontogenetic change. Moreover, we must give more thoughtful attention to the possible antecedents of individual differences within a given developmental level.

Recent approaches to self-esteem also reflect the need to dissolve the myth that trait concepts cannot coexist with those emphasizing situation-specificity. It has been suggested that one can possess a global concept of self-worth and simultaneously make domain-specific evaluations of one's competence, acceptance, morality, and sense of control. Each of these trends reveals that, *conceptually,* the study of the self has become very interactionist in nature; however, *empirically* there is much to be accomplished.

Finally, students of the self appear to be genuinely interested in particular *phenomena* rather than the demonstration that a particular theoretical orientation is the most compelling. Topics such as self-concept, self-awareness, self-esteem, self-evaluation, and self-control can and should be investigated from a variety of perspectives. No one holds a theoretical corner on the market of the self. Moreover, there are still many corners yet to be explored. In so doing, we can advance our understanding of a range of fascinating phenomena, and perhaps even learn a little something about ourselves!

REFERENCES

Abelson, R. P. A script theory of understanding, attitude, and behavior. In J. S. Carrol & J. Payne (Eds.), *Cognition and social behavior*. Hillsdale, N.J.: Erlbaum, 1976.

Achenbach, T., & Zigler, E. Social competence and self-image disparity in psychiatric and non-psychiatric patients. *Journal of Abnormal and Social Psychology*, 1963, 67, 197–205.

Adler, A. *The practice and theory of individual psychology*. New York: Harcourt, 1927.

Ainsworth, M. Attachment and dependency: A comparison. In J. Gewirtz (Ed.), *Attachment and dependency*. Washington, D.C.: Winston, 1972.

Ainsworth, M. The development of infant-mother attachment. In B. Caldwell & H. Ricciuti (Eds.), *Review of child development research* (Vol. 3). Chicago: University of Chicago Press, 1973.

Ainsworth, M. Infant-mother attachment and social development: Socialization as a product of reciprocal responsiveness to signals. In M. Richards (Ed.), *The integration of the child into the social world*. Cambridge, Mass.: Cambridge University Press, 1974.

Ainsworth, M. Infant-mother attachment. *American Psychologist*, 1979, 34, 932–937.

Ainsworth, M. D. Object relations, dependency, and attachment: A theoretical review of the infant-mother relationship. *Child Development*, 1969, 40, 969–1026.

Ainsworth, M. D. S. *Infancy in Uganda: Infant care and the growth of attachment*. Baltimore, Md.: The Johns Hopkins Press, 1967.

Ainsworth, M. D. S., Bell, S. M., & Stayton, D. J. Individual differences in strange-situation behavior of one-year-olds. In H. R. Schaffer (Ed.), *The origins of human social relations*. London: Academic Press, 1971.

Ainsworth, M., Bell, S., & Stayton, D. J. Individual differences in the development of some attachment behaviors. *Merrill-Palmer Quarterly*, 1972, 18, 123–143.

Ainsworth, M. D. S., Blehar, M. C., Waters, E., & Wall, S. *Patterns of attachment: A psychological study of the strange situation*. Hillsdale, N.J.: Lawrence Erlbaum Associates, 1978.

Allport, G. W. *Becoming: Basic considerations for a psychology of personality*. New Haven: Yale University Press, 1955.

Allport, G. W. *Pattern and growth in personality*. New York: Holt, Rinehart & Winston, 1961.

Ames, L. B. The sense of self for nursery school children as manifested by their verbal behavior. *Journal of Genetic Psychology*, 1952, 81, 193–232.

Amsterdam, B. K. Mirror self-image reactions before age two. *Developmental Psychology*, 1972, 5, 297–305.

Amsterdam, B., & Greenberg, L. M. Self-conscious behavior of infants: A videotape study. *Developmental Psychobiology*, 1977, 10, 1–6.

Angyl, A. *Foundations for a science of personality*. New York: Commonwealth Fund, 1941.

Aronfreed, J. *Conduct and conscience: The socialization of internal controls over behavior*. New York: Academic Press, 1968.

Aronfreed, J. The concept of internalization. In D. A. Goslin (Ed.), *Handbook of socialization theory and research*. New York: Rand McNally, 1969.

Aronfreed, J. Moral development from the standpoint of a general psychological theory. In T. Lickona (Ed.), *Moral development and behavior*. New York: Holt, Rinehart and Winston, 1976.

Aronfreed, J., & Reber, A. Internalized behavioral

suppression and the timing of social punishment. *Journal of Personality & Social Psychology*, 1965, *1*, 3–16.

Bachman, J. G. Youth in transition, Volume II: *The impact of family background and intelligence on tenth-grade boys*. Ann Arbor, Mich.: Survey Research Center, Institute for Social Research, 1970.

Bachman, J. G., & O'Malley, P. M. Self-esteem in young men: A longitudinal analysis of the impact of educational and occupational attainment. *Journal of Personality and Social Psychology*, 1977, *35*, 365–380.

Back, K. W., & Gergen, K. J. The self through the latter span of life. In C. Gordon & K. J. Gergen (Eds.), *The self in social interaction*. New York: Wiley, 1968.

Bain, R. The self-and-other words of a child. *American Journal of Sociology*, 1936, *41*, 767–775.

Baldwin, J. M. *Social and ethical interpretations in mental development*. New York: Macmillan, 1897.

Ballard, K. D., & Glynn, T. Behavioral self-management in story writing with elementary school children. *Journal of Applied Behavior Analysis*, 1975, *8*, 387–398.

Bandura, A. Social learning theory of identificatory processes. In D. A. Goslin (Ed.), *Handbook of socialization theory and research*. New York: Rand McNally, 1969. (a)

Bandura, A. *Principles of behavior modification*. New York: Holt, Rinehart & Winston, 1969. (b)

Bandura, A. Vicarious and self-reinforcement processes. In R. Glaser (Ed.), *The nature of reinforcement*. New York: Academic Press, 1971. (a)

Bandura, A. Analysis of modeling processes. In A. Bandura (Ed.), *Psychological modeling: Conflicting theories*. Chicago: Aldine-Atherton, 1971. (b)

Bandura, A. Aggression: A social learning analysis. Englewood Cliffs, N.J.: Prentice-Hall, 1973.

Bandura, A. Behavior theory and the models of man. *American Psychologist*, 1974, *29*, 859–869.

Bandura, A. Self-reinforcement: Theoretical and methodological considerations. *Behaviorism*, 1976, *4*, 135–155.

Bandura, A. Self-efficacy: Toward a unifying theory of behavioral change. *Psychological Review*, 1977, *84*, 191–215. (a)

Bandura, A. *Social learning theory*. Englewood Cliffs, N.J.: Prentice-Hall, 1977. (b)

Bandura, A. The self system in reciprocal determin-ism. *American Psychologist*, 1978, *33*, 344–358.

Bandura, A. Self-referent thought: The development of self-efficacy. In J. H. Flavell & L. D. Ross (Eds.), *Development of social cognition*. New York: Cambridge University Press, 1981.

Bandura, A., Grusec, J. E., & Menlove, F. L. Some social determinants of self-monitoring reinforcement systems. *Journal of Personality and Social Psychology*, 1967, *5*, 449–455.

Bandura, A., & Kupers, C. J. Transmission of patterns of self-reward through modeling. *Journal of Abnormal and Social Psychology*, 1964, *69*, 1–9.

Bandura, A., & Mahoney, M. J. Maintenance and transfer of self-reinforcement functions. *Behavior Research and Therapy*, 1974, *12*, 89–97.

Bandura, A., & McDonald, F. J. The influence of social reinforcement and the behavior of models in shaping children's moral judgments. *Journal of Abnormal and Social Psychology*, 1963, *67*, 274–281.

Bandura, A., & Mischel, W. Modification of self-imposed delay of reward through exposure to live and symbolic models. *Journal of Personality and Social Psychology*, 1965, *2*, 698–705.

Bandura, A., & Perloff, B. Relative efficacy of self-monitored and externally imposed reinforcement systems. *Journal of Personality and Social Psychology*, 1967, *7*, 111–116.

Bandura, A., Ross, D., & Ross, S. A. Vicarious reinforcement and imitative learning. *Journal of Abnormal and Social Psychology*, 1963, *67*, 601–607.

Bandura, A., & Whalen, C. K. The influence of antecedent reinforcement and divergent modeling cues on patterns of self-reward. *Journal of Personality and Social Psychology*, 1966, *3*, 373–382.

Bannister, D., & Agnew, J. The child's construing of self. In J. Cole (Ed.), *Nebraska Symposium on Motivation*. Lincoln: University of Nebraska Press, 1977.

Barrow, G. M., & Smith, P. A. *Aging, ageism, and society*. St. Paul, Minn.: West, 1979.

Bartlett, F. C. *Remembering*. Cambridge: Cambridge University Press, 1932.

Baumrind, D. Current patterns of parental authority. *Developmental Psychology Monographs*, 1971, *1* (Part 2), 1–103.

Bayley, N. *Bayley scales of infant development*. New York: The Psychological Corporation, 1969.

Becker, W., & Krug, R. S. Parent attitude research

instrument: A research review. *Child Development*, 1965, *36*, 329–365.

Bell, S. M. The development of the concept of object as related to infant-mother attachment. *Child Development*, 1970, *41*, 291–311.

Bem, D. Self-perception: An alternative interpretation of cognitive-dissonance phenomena. *Psychological Review*, 1967, *74*, 183–200.

Bem, D. Self-perception theory. In L. Berkowitz (Ed.), *Advances in experimental social psychology* (Vol. 6). New York: Academic Press, 1972.

Bem, D. J. Self-perception theory. In L. Berkowitz (Ed.), *Cognitive theories in social psychology*. New York: Academic Press, 1978.

Bem, S. The measurement of psychological androgyny. *Journal of Consulting and Clinical Psychology*, 1974, *42*, 155–162.

Bender, N. Self-verbalization versus tutor verbalization in modifying impulsivity. *Journal of Educational Psychology*, 1976, *68*, 347–354.

Bertenthal, B. I., & Fischer, K. W. Development of self-recognition in the infant. *Developmental Psychology*, 1978, *14*, 44–50.

Bierer, B. *Motivational and behavioral correlates of children's accuracy in judging their cognitive competence*. Unpublished doctoral dissertation, University of Denver, 1981.

Bierer, B., & Harter, S. *Accuracy of self-perceptions of competence as a predictor of behavior*. Unpublished manuscript, University of Denver, 1981.

Bigelow, A. *A longitudinal study of self-recognition in young children*. Paper presented at the meetings of the Canadian Psychological Association, Quebec, June 1975.

Blackwood, R. The operant conditioning of verbally mediated self-control in the classroom. *Journal of School Psychology*, 1970, *8*, 257–258.

Blasi, A. *A developmental approach to responsibility training*. Unpublished doctoral dissertation, Washington University, 1972.

Block, J. *Lives through time*. Berkeley, Calif.: Bancroft Books, 1971.

Block, J. H., & Block, J. The role of ego-control and ego-resiliency in the organization of behavior. In W. A. Collins (Ed.), *Minnesota Symposium on Child Psychology* (Vol. 13). Hillsdale, N.J.: Lawrence Erlbaum, 1980.

Bobrow, D. G., & Norman, D. Some principles of memory schemata. In D. G. Bobrow & A. Collins (Eds.), *Representation and understanding: Studies in cognitive science*. New York: Academic Press, 1975.

Boggiano, A. K., & Ruble, D. N. Competence and the overjustification effect: A developmental study. *Journal of Personality and Social Psychology*, 1979, *37*, 1462–1468.

Bolsted, O. D., & Johnson, S. M. Self-regulation in the modification of disruptive classroom behavior. *Journal of Applied Behavior Analysis*, 1972, *5*, 443–454.

Bornstein, P., & Quevillon, R. The effects of a self-instructional package on overactive preschool boys. *Journal of Applied Behavior Analysis*, 1976, *9*, 176–188.

Boulanger-Balleyguier, G. Premiers reactions devant le miroir. *Enfance*, 1964, *1*, 51–67.

Bowlby, J. *Attachment and loss* (Vol. 1), Attachment. New York: Basic, 1969.

Bowlby, J. *Attachment and loss* (Vol. 2), Separation: Anxiety and anger. New York: Basic, 1973.

Bretherton, I., & Bates, E. The emergence of intentional communication. In I. C. Uzgiris (Ed.), *Social interaction and communication during infancy*. San Francisco: Jossey Bass New Directions for Child Development, 1979, No. 4.

Brigham, T. A., & Bushell, D. *Notes on autonomous environments: Student selected versus teacher selected rewards*. Unpublished manuscript, University of Kansas, 1972.

Brigham, T. A., & Sherman, J. A. Effects of choice and immediacy of reinforcement on single response and switching behavior of children. *Journal of Experimental Analysis of Behavior*, 1973, *19*, 425–435.

Brim, O. G. Socialization through the life cycle. In O. G. Brim & S. Wheeler (Eds.), *Socialization after childhood: Two essays*. New York: Wiley, 1966.

Brim, O. G. Life span development of the theory of oneself: Implications for child development. In H. W. Reese (Ed.), *Advances in child development and behavior* (Vol. 11). New York: Academic Press, 1976. (a)

Brim, O. G. Theories of the male mid-life crisis. *Counseling Psychologist: Counseling Adults*. Special Issue, 1976. (b)

Broden, M., Hall, R. V., & Mitts, B. The effect of self-recording on the classroom behavior of two eighth-grade students. *Journal of Applied Behavior Analysis*, 1971, *4*, 191–199.

Brody, E. B. Color and identity conflict in young boys. *Archives of General Psychiatry*, 1964, *10*, 354–360.

Bromley, D. B. *The psychology of human aging*, (2nd ed.). London, England: Penguin, 1974.

Brownell, K. D. Theoretical and applied issues in self-control. *The Psychological Record*, 1978,

28, 291–298.

Bugenthal, D., Whalen, C., & Henker, B. Causal attributions of hyperactive children and motivational assumptions of two behavior-change approaches: Evidence for an interactionist position. *Child Development*, 1977, *48*, 874–884.

Bugenthal, J. F. T. An investigation of the relationship of the conceptual matrix to the self-concept. Abstract doctoral dissertation, 1949, *57*, 27–33.

Bugenthal, J. F. T., & Zelen, S. L. Investigations into the "self-concept." I. The W-A-Y technique. *Journal of Personality*, 1950, *18*, 483–498.

Buhler, C. *The first year of life*. New York: John Day, 1930.

Buros, O. K. (Ed.). *Personality tests and reviews*. Highland Park, N.J.: Gryphon Press, 1970.

Buss, A. H. *Self-consciousness and social anxiety*. San Francisco: W. H. Freeman, 1980.

Butler, J. M., & Haigh, G. V. Changes in the relation between self-concepts and ideal concepts consequent upon client-centered counseling. In C. R. Rogers and R. F. Dymond (Eds.), *Psychotherapy and Personality Change*. Chicago: University of Chicago Press, 1954.

Butler, R. N., & Lewis, M. T. *Aging and mental health: Positive psychosocial approaches*. St. Louis: C. V. Mosby, 1973.

Calsyn, R. J., & Kenny, D. A. Self-concept of ability and perceived evaluation of others: Cause or effect of academic achievements? *Journal of Educational Psychology*, 1977, *69*, 136–145.

Camp, B. W. Two psychoeducational treatment programs for young aggressive boys. In C. K. Whalen & E. Henker (Eds.), *Hyperactive children: The social ecology of identification and treatment*. New York: Academic Press, 1980.

Camp, B. W., & Bash, M. A. *The think aloud program: Background research and program guide*. Champaign, Ill.: Research Press, 1982.

Camp, B., Blom, G., Hebert, F., & Van Doorninck, W. "Think aloud": A program for developing self-control in young aggressive boys. *Journal of Abnormal Child Psychology*, 1977, *5*, 157–169.

Camp, B. W., & Ray, R. S. Aggression. In A. Meyers & W. E. Craighead (Eds.), *Cognitive behavior therapy with children*. New York: Plenum, in press.

Cantor, N., & Mischel, W. Prototypes in person perception. In L. Berkowitz (Ed.), *Advances in Experimental Social Psychology* (Vol. 12). New York: Academic Press, 1979.

Carlson, R. Stability and change in the adolescent's self-image. *Child Development*, 1965, *36*, 659–666.

Carter, D. B., Patterson, C. J., & Quasebarth, S. J. Development of children's use of plans for self-control. *Cognitive Therapy and Research*, 1979, *4*, 407–413.

Carver, C. S., & Scheier, M. F. *Attention and self-regulation: A control-therapy approach to human behavior*. New York: Springer-Verlag, 1981.

Catania, C. A. The myth of self-reinforcement. *Behaviorism*, 1975, *3*, 192–199.

Cattell, P. *The measurement of intelligence of infants and young children*. New York: The Psychological Corporation, 1940.

Chandler, C. *The effects of parenting techniques on the development of motivational orientations in children*. Unpublished doctoral dissertation, University of Denver, 1981.

Chao, C. *A competence model of the function of children's imaginary friends*. Unpublished doctoral dissertation, University of Denver, 1981.

Cheyne, J. A. Punishment and reasoning in the development of self-control. In R. D. Parke (Ed.), *Recent trends in social learning theory*. New York: Academic Press, 1972.

Cheyne, J. A., & Walters, R. H. Intensity of punishment, timing of punishment, and cognitive structure as determinants of response inhibition. *Journal of Experimental Child Psychology*, 1969, *7*, 231–244.

Clark, K. B., & Clark, M. P. Racial identification and preference in Negro children. In T. M. Newcomb & E. Hartley (Eds.), *Readings in social psychology*. New York: Holt, 1947.

Coates, T. J., Thoresen, C. E. Self-control and educational practice, or do we really need self-control? In D. Berlinger (Ed.), *Review of research in education*. Itasca, Ill.: Praeger, 1979.

Coleman, J. S., Campbell, E. Q., Hobson, C. J., McPartland, J., Mood, A. M., Weinfeld, F. D., & York, R. L. *Equality of educational opportunity*. Washington, D.C.: U.S. Government Printing Office, 1966.

Connell, J. P. *A multidimensional measure of children's perceptions of control*. Unpublished masters thesis, University of Denver, 1980.

Connell, J. P. *A model of the relationships among children's self-related cognitions, affects and academic achievement*. Unpublished doctoral dissertation, University of Denver, 1981.

Connell, J. P., & Goldsmith, H. H. A structural modeling approach to the study of attachment and strange situation behaviors. In R. Emde & R. Harmon (Eds.), *Attachment and affiliative systems: Neurological and psychobiological aspects*. New York: Plenum Press, 1981.

Constantinople, A. An Eriksonian measure of personality development in college students. *Developmental Psychology*, 1969, *1*, 357–372.

Cooley, C. H. *Human nature and the social order*. New York: Charles Scribner's Sons, 1902.

Cooley, C. H. A study of the early use of self-words by a child. *Psychological Review*, 1908, *15*, 339–357.

Coopersmith, S. A method for determining types of self-esteem. *Journal of Abnormal and Social Psychology*, 1959, *59*, 87–94.

Coopersmith, S. *The antecedents of self-esteem*. San Francisco: W. H. Freeman, 1967.

Corrigan, R. Language development as related to Stage 6 object permanence development. *Journal of Child Language*, 1978, *5*, 173–189.

Corrigan, R. Cognitive correlates of language: Differential criteria yield differential results. *Child Development*, 1979, *50*, 617–631.

Cox, N. Prior help, ego development, and helping behavior. *Child Development*, 1974, *45*, 594–603.

Craighead, E., Craighead-Wilcoxin, L., & Meyers, A. New directions in behavior modifications with children. In M. Hersen, R. Eisler, & P. Miller (Eds.), *Progress in behavior modification* (Vol. 6). New York: Academic Press, 1978.

Crandall, V. C., Crandall, V. J., & Katkovsky, W. A children's social desirability questionnaire. *Journal of Consulting Psychology*, 1965, *29*, 27–36.

Crandall, V. C., Katkovsky, W., & Crandall, V. J. Children's beliefs in their own control of reinforcement in intellectual academic achievement situations. *Child Development*, 1965, *36*, 91–109.

Crowne, W. J., & Marlowe, D. *The approval motive: Studies in evaluative dependence*. New York: Wiley, 1964.

Cunningham, T., & Berberian, V. *Sex differences in the relationship of self-concept to locus of control in children*. Unpublished manuscript, St. Lawrence University, 1976.

Darwin, C. A biographical sketch of an infant. *Mind*, 1877, *2*, 285–294.

Decarie, T. G. *Intelligence and affectivity in early childhood*. New York: International Universities Press, 1965.

deCharms, R. *Personal causation: The internal affective determinants of behavior*. New York: Academic Press, 1968.

Deci, E. L. *Intrinsic motivation*. New York: Plenum, 1975.

DeVries, R. Constancy of gender identity in the years three to six. *Monographs of the Society for Research in Child Development*, 1969, *34*(3, Serial No. 127).

Dickie, J. R., & Strader, W. H. Development of mirror image responses in infancy. *Journal of Psychology*, 1974, *88*, 333–337.

Dickstein, E. Self and self-esteem: Theoretical foundations and their implications for research. *Human Development*, 1977, *20*, 129–140.

Dinner, S. H. *Social comparison and self-evaluation in children*. Unpublished doctoral dissertation, Princeton University, 1976.

Dixon, J. C. Development of self-recognition. *Journal of Genetic Psychology*, 1957, *91*, 251–256.

Douglas, V., Parry, P., Martin, P., & Garson, C. Assessment of a cognitive training program for hyperactive children. *Journal of Abnormal Child Psychology*, 1976, *4*, 389–410.

Drummond. R. J., & McIntire, W. G. Evaluating the factor structure of "self-concept" in children: A cautionary note. *Measurement and Evaluation in Guidance*, 1977, *9*, 172–176.

Duval, S., & Wicklund, R. A. *A theory of objective self-awareness*. New York: Academic Press, 1972.

Elkind, D. Egocentrism in adolescence. *Child Development*, 1967, *38*, 1025–1034.

Engel, M. The stability of the self-concept in adolescence. *Journal of Abnormal and Social Psychology*, 1959, *58*, 211–215.

Epstein, S. The self-concept revisited or a theory of a theory. *American Psychologist*, 1973, *28*, 405–416.

Epstein, S. The unity principle versus the reality and pleasure principles, or the tale of the scorpion and the frog. In M. D. Lynch, A. A. Norem-Hebeisen, & K. Gergen (Eds.), *Self-concept: Advances in theory and research*. Cambridge, Mass.: Ballinger, 1981.

Erikson, E. H. *Childhood and society*. New York: Norton, 1950.

Erikson, E. Identity and the life cycle. *Psychological Issues*, 1959, *1*, 18–164.

Erikson, E. *Identity, youth and crisis*. New York: Norton, 1968.

Estes, W. K. Reinforcement in human behavior. *American Scientist*, 1972, *60*, 723–729.

Felixbrod, J. J., & O'Leary, K. D. Effects of reinforcement on children's academic behavior as a function of self-determined and externally imposed contingencies. *Journal of Applied Behavior Analysis,* 1973, *6,* 241–250.

Felixbrod, J. J., & O'Leary, K. D. Self-determination of academic standards by children. *Journal of Educational Psychology,* 1974, *66,* 845–850.

Felker, D. W., & Thomas, S. B. Self-initiated verbal reinforcement and positive self-concept. *Child Development,* 1971, *42,* 1285–1287.

Fenichel, O. *The psychoanalytic theory of neurosis.* New York: Norton, 1945.

Festinger, L. A theory of social comparison processes. *Human Relations,* 1954, *7,* 117–140.

Field, T. M. Effects of early separation, interactive deficits, and experimental manipulations on infant-mother face-to-face interaction. *Child Development,* 1977, *48,* 763–771.

Finch, A., Wilkinson, M., Nelson, W., & Montgomery, L. Modification of an impulsive cognitive tempo in emotionally disturbed boys. *Journal of Abnormal Child Psychology,* 1975, *3,* 49–52.

Fischer, K. W. A theory of cognitive development: The control and construction of hierarchies of skills. *Psychological Review,* 1980, *87*(6), 477–531.

Fischer, K. W., & Lazerson, A. *Developmental psychology,* New York: Worth, in press.

Flavell, J. H. *The developmental psychology of Jean Piaget.* Princeton, N.J.: Van Nostrand, 1963.

Flavell, J. H., Shipstead, S. G., & Croft, K. *What young children think you see when their eyes are closed.* Unpublished manuscript, Stanford University, 1978.

Flavell, J. H., & Wohlwill, J. F. Formal and functional aspects of cognitive development. In D. Elkind & J. H. Flavell (Eds.), *Studies in cognitive development.* New York: Oxford University Press, 1969.

Fraiberg, S. Libidinal object constancy and mental representation. *Psychoanalytic Study of the Child* (Vol. 24). New York: International Universities Press, 1969.

Freud, S. *Beyond the pleasure principle.* London: Hogarth Press, 1922.

Freud, S. *New introductory lectures on psychoanalysis.* New York: Norton, 1933.

Freud, S. *The ego and mechanisms of defense.* New York: International Universities Press, 1946.

Freud, S. Instincts and their vicissitudes. *Collected papers,* London: Hogarth Press, 1950.

Freud, S. *A general introduction to psychoanalysis.* New York: Washington Square Press, 1952.

Freud, S. *Beyond the pleasure principle. Standard Edition.* London: Hogarth Press, 1955.

Freud, S. Formulations regarding the two principles in mental functioning. In *Collected papers* (Vol. 4). New York: Basic, 1959.

Freud, S. *Normality and pathology in childhood.* New York: International Universities Press, 1965.

Fry, P. S. Affect and resistance to temptation. *Developmental Psychology,* 1975, *11,* 466–472.

Fry, P. S. Success, failure, and resistance to temptation. *Developmental Psychology,* 1977, *13,* 519–520.

Gallup, G. G., Jr. Mirror image stimulation. *Psychological Bulletin,* 1968, *70,* 782–793.

Gallup, G. G., Jr. Chimpanzees: Self-recognition. *Science,* 1970, *167,* 86–87.

Gallup, G. G., Jr. Self-recognition in primates: A comparative approach to the bidirectional properties of consciousness. *American Psychologist,* 1977, *32,* 329–338.

Gallup, G. G., Jr. Self-recognition in chimpanzees and man: a developmental and comparative perspective. In M. Lewis and L. Rosenblum (Eds.), *The child and its family: The genesis of behavior* (Vol. 2). New York: Plenum, 1979.

Gallup, G. G., Jr., & McClure, M. K. Preference for mirror-image stimulation in differentially reared rhesus monkeys. *Journal of Comparative and Physiological Psychology,* 1971, *75,* 403–407.

Gergen, K. J. Personal consistency and the presentation of self. In C. Gordon & K. J. Gergen (Eds.), *The self in social interaction.* New York: Wiley, 1968.

Gergen, K. J. *The concept of self.* New York: Holt, Rinehart & Winston, 1971.

Gesell, A. *Infancy and human growth.* New York: Macmillan, 1928.

Gesell, A., & Ilg, F. *The child from five to ten.* New York: Harper & Row, 1946.

Gesell, A., & Thompson, N. *Infant behavior: Its genesis and growth.* New York: McGraw-Hill, 1934.

Glenwick, D. S. Training impulsive children in verbal self-regulation by use of natural change agents (doctoral dissertation, University of Rochester, 1976). *Dissertation Abstracts International,* 1976, *37,* 459-B (University Microfilms No. 76-14, 758).

Glucksberg, S., Krauss, R. M., & Higgins, E. T. The development of referential communication skills. In F. D. Horowitz (Ed.), *Review of child development research* (Vol. 4). Chicago: University of Chicago Press, 1975.

Glynn, E. L. Classroom applications of self-determined reinforcement. *Journal of Applied Behavior Analysis,* 1970, *3,* 123–132.

Glynn, E. L., & Thomas, J. D. Effect of cueing on self-control of classroom behavior. *Journal of Applied Behavior Analysis,* 1974, *7,* 299–306.

Glynn, E. L., Thomas, J. D., & Shee, S. M. Behavioral self-control of on-task behavior in an elementary classroom. *Journal of Applied Behavior Analysis,* 1973, *6,* 105–111.

Goffman, E. On facework: An analysis of ritual elements in social interaction. *Psychiatry: Journal for the Study of Interpersonal Processes, 1955, 18,* 213–231.

Goffman, E. *The presentation of self in everyday life* (Rev. ed.). New York: Doubleday, 1959.

Goldiamond, I. Self-reinforcement. *Journal of Applied Behavior Analysis,* 1976, *9,* 509–514.

Goodman, M. E. *Race awareness in young children.* Cambridge, Mass.: Addison-Wesley, 1952.

Gordon, C. Self-conceptions: Configurations of content. In C. Gordon & K. J. Gergen (Eds.). *The self in social interaction.* New York: Wiley, 1968.

Gordon, C., & Gergen, K. J. (Eds.). *The self in social interaction.* New York: Wiley, 1968.

Gouze, K. R., & Nadelman, L. Constancy of gender identity for self and others in children between the ages of three and seven. *Child Development,* 1980, *51,* 275–278.

Greenwald, A. G. The totalitarian ego: Fabrication and revision of personal history. *American Psychologist,* 1980, *7,* 603–618.

Griffiths, R. *The abilities of babies.* London: University of London, 1954.

Groos, K. *The play of animals.* New York: Appleton, 1898.

Grusec, J., & Mischel, W. Model's characteristics as determinants of social learning. *Journal of Personality and Social Psychology,* 1966, *4,* 211–215.

Guardo, C. J. Self-revisited: The sense of self-identity. *Journal of Humanistic Psychology,* 1968, *8,* 137–142.

Guardo, C. J., & Bohan, J. B. Development of a sense of self-identity in children. *Child Development,* 1971, *42,* 1909–1921.

Guralnick, M. J. Solving complex perceptual discrimination problems: Techniques for the development of problem-solving strategies. *American Journal of Mental Deficiency,* 1976, *81,* 18–25.

Gurin, G., & Gurin, P. Personal efficacy and the ideology of individual responsibility. In B. Strumpel (Ed.), *A system of social indicators of economic well-being.* Ann Arbor, Mich.: Survey Research Center, Institute of Social Research, 1976.

Hales, S. *A developmental theory of self-esteem based on competence and moral behavior.* Paper presented at the Society for Research in Child Development, San Francisco, California. March 15–18, 1979. (a)

Hales, S. *Developmental processes of self-esteem.* Paper presented at the Society for Research in Child Development, San Francisco, California. March 15–18, 1979. (b)

Hall, C. S., & Lindzey, G. *Theories of personality.* New York: Wiley, 1970.

Hallowell, A. E. Behavioral evolution and the emergence of the self. In *Evolution and anthropology: A centennial appraisal.* Anthropological Society of Washington, Washington, 1959.

Hand, H. *The development of concepts of social interaction: Children's understanding of nice and mean.* Unpublished doctoral dissertation, University of Denver, 1981.

Hann, N., Stroud, J., & Holstein, J. Moral and ego stages in relation to ego processes: A study of "hippies." *Journal of Personality,* 1973, *41,* 596–612.

Harakal, C. *Ego maturity and interpersonal style: A multivariate study of Loevinger's theory.* Unpublished doctoral dissertation, Catholic University, 1971.

Harter, S. A cognitive-developmental approach to children's expression of conflicting feelings and a technique to facilitate such expression in play therapy. *Journal of Consulting and Clinical Psychology,* 1977, *45,* 417–432.

Harter, S. Effectance motivation reconsidered: Toward a developmental model. *Human Development,* 1978, *1,* 34–64.

Harter, S. The development of competence motivation in the mastery of cognitive and physical skills: Is there still a place for joy? *Psychology of Motor Behavior and Sport,* 1980, 3–29.

Harter, S. A model of intrinsic mastery motivation in children: Individual differences and developmental change. In W. A. Collins (Ed.), *Minnesota Symposium on Child Psychology* (Vol. 14). Hillsdale, N.J.: Lawrence Erlbaum, 1981. (a)

Harter, S. A new self-report scale of intrinsic versus extrinsic orientation in the classroom; motivational and informational components. *Devel-*

opmental Psychology, 1981, *17*, 300–312. (b)

Harter, S. *Developmental differences in children's understanding of self-affect labels*. Unpublished manuscript, University of Denver, 1982.

Harter, S. Children's understanding of multiple emotions: A cognitive-developmental approach. In W. F. Overton (Ed.), *The relationship between social and cognitive development*. Hillsdale, N.J.: Lawrence Erlbaum, 1982. (a)

Harter, S. The perceived competence scale for children. *Child Development*, 1982, *53*, 87–97. (b)

Harter, S. A cognitive-developmental approach to children's use of affect and trait labels. In F. Serafica (Ed.), *Social cognition and social relations in context*. New York: Guilford Press, 1982. (c)

Harter, S. A developmental perspective on some parameters of the self-regulation process in children. In F. Kanfer & P. Karoly (Eds.), *The psychology of self-management: From theory to practice*. Pergamon Press, 1982. (d)

Harter, S., & Barnes, R. *Children's understanding of parental emotions: A developmental study*. Unpublished manuscript, University of Denver, 1981.

Harter, S., & Chao, C. *Dimensions underlying young children's evaluation of peer acceptance*. Unpublished manuscript, University of Denver, 1981.

Harter, S., & Connell, J. P. A comparison of alternative models of the relationships between academic achievement and children's perceptions of competence, control, and motivational orientation. In J. Nicholls (Ed.), *The development of achievement-related cognitions and behaviors*. Greenwich, Conn.: J. A. I. Press, 1982.

Harter, S., & Engstrom, R. *The relationship between importance of success, perceived competence, and self-esteem*. Unpublished manuscript, University of Denver, 1981.

Harter, S., & Pike, R. *The pictorial perceived competence scale for young children*. Unpublished manuscript, University of Denver, 1981.

Harter, S., & Ward, C. *A factor-analysis of Coopersmith's Self-Esteem Inventory*. Unpublished manuscript, University of Denver, 1978.

Hartig, M., & Kanfer, F. The role of verbal self-instructions in children's resistance to temptation. *Journal of Personality and Social Psychology*, 1973, *25*, 259–267.

Hartley, W. S. *Manual for the twenty-statements problem (Who Am I?)*. Department of Research,

Greater Kansas City Mental Health Foundation, 1970.

Hartmann, H. The mutual influences in the development of Ego and Id. *The Psychoanalytic Study of the Child* (Vol. 8). New York: International Universities Press, 1952.

Hartmann, H. *Essays on ego psychology: Selected problems in psychoanalytic theory*. New York: International Universities Press, 1964.

Hartshore, H., & May, M. *Studies in deceit*. New York: Macmillan, 1928.

Hauser, S. Loevinger's model and measure of ego development: A critical review. *Psychological Bulletin*, 1976, *83*, 928–955.

Hendricks, J., & Hendricks, C. D. *Aging in mass society*. Cambridge, Mass.: Winthrop, 1977.

Hilgard, E. Human motives and the concept of the self. *American Psychologist*, 1949, *4*, 374–382.

Hoffman, M. Empathy, role-taking, guilt, and development of altruistic motives. In T. L. Lickona (Ed.), *Moral development and behavior*. New York: Holt, Rinehart & Winston, 1976.

Holmes, M. *Formal operations and self-theory in adolescents*. Unpublished manuscript, 1980.

Hoppe, C. *Ego development and conformity behavior*. Unpublished doctoral dissertation, Washington University, 1972.

Horn, J., & Donaldson, G. On the myth of intellectual decline in adulthood. *American Psychologist*, 1976, *31*, 701–719.

Horney, K. *Our inner conflicts*. New York: Norton, 1945.

Horney, K. *Neurosis and human growth* New York: Norton, 1950.

Inhelder, B., & Piaget, J. *The growth of logical thinking from childhood to adolescence*. New York: Basic, 1958.

Jackson, E., Campos, J., & Fischer, K. The question of decalage between object performance and person performance. *Developmental Psychology*, 1978, *14*, 1–10.

James, W. *Psychology*. New York: Fawcett, 1963 (originally published, 1890).

Jensen, L., & Buhanan, K. Resistance to temptation following three types of motivational instructions among four-, six-, and eight-year-old female children. *The Journal of Genetic Psychology*, 1974, *125*, 51–59.

Jersild, A. T. *In search of self: An exploration of the role of the school in promoting self-understanding*. New York: Teachers College, 1952.

Johnson, S. M. Self-reinforcement in behavior modification with children. *Developmental Psychol-*

ogy, 1970, *3*, 147–148.

Johnston, J. M. Punishment of human behavior. *American Psychologist*, 1972, *27*, 1033–1054.

Jones, E. E., & Nisbett, R. E. *The actor and the observer: Divergent perceptions of the causes of behavior*. Morristown, N.J.: General Learning Press, 1971.

Joreskog, K. G. A general method for estimating a linear structural equation system. In A. S. Goldberger & O. D. Duncan (Eds.), *Structural equation models in the social sciences*. New York: Seminar Press, 1973.

Jourard, S. M. *Self-disclosure: An experimental analysis of the transparent self*. New York: Wiley, 1971.

Jung, C. G. *Two essays on analytical psychology*. New York: Dodd, Mead, 1928.

Kagan, J. Reflection-impulsivity: The generality and dynamics of conceptual tempo. *Journal of Abnormal Psychology*, 1966, *71*, 17–24.

Kagen, R. M. Generalization of verbal self-instructional training in cognitively impulsive children (doctoral dissertation, University of Texas at Austin, 1976). *Dissertation Abstracts International*, 1977, *37*, 4148B (University Microfilms No. 77-3926).

Kanfer, F. H. Self-regulation: Research, issues, and speculations. In C. Neuringer & J. L. Michael (Eds.), *Behavior modification in clinical psychology*. New York: Appleton-Century-Crofts, 1970.

Kanfer, F. H. Maintenance of behavior by self-generated stimuli and reinforcement. In A. Jacobs & L. B. Sacks (Eds.), *Psychology of private events*. New York: Academic Press, 1971.

Kanfer, F. The many faces of self-control or behavior modification changes its focus. In R. Stuart (Ed.), *Behavioral self-management*. New York: Bruner/Mazel, 1977.

Kanfer, F. H. Self-management methods. In F. H. Kanfer & A. P. Goldstein (Eds.), *Helping people change: A textbook of methods* (2nd ed.). New York: Pergamon Press, 1980.

Kanfer, F., & Duerfeldt, P. Age, class standing and commitment as determinants of cheating in children. *Child Development*, 1968, *39*, 545–557.

Kanfer, F., & Karoly, P. Self-control: A behavioristic excursion into the lion's den. *Behavior Therapy*, 1972, *3*, 398–416.

Kanfer, F. H., & Phillips, J. S. *Learning foundations of behavior therapy*. New York: Wiley, 1970.

Kaplan, H. B. *Self-attitudes and deviant behavior*.

Pacific Palisades, California: Goodyear, 1975.

Kardiner, A., & Ovesey, L. *The mark of oppression*. New York: Norton, 1951.

Karoly, P. Behavioral self-management in children: Concepts, methods, issues and directions. In M. Hersen, R. Eisler, & P. Miller (Eds.), *Progress in behavior modification* (Vol. 5). New York: Academic Press, 1977.

Karoly, P. Self-management problems in children. In E. J. Mash & L. Terdal (Eds.), *Behavioral assessment of childhood disorders*. New York: Guilford Press, 1982.

Katz, P., & Zigler, E. Self-image disparity? A developmental approach. *Journal of Personality and Social Psychology*, 1967, *5*, 186–195.

Katz, P. A., Zigler, E., & Zalk, S. R. Children's self-image disparity: The effects of age, maladjustment, and action-thought orientation. *Developmental Psychology*, 1975, *11*, 546–550.

Kazdin, A. E. Self-monitoring and behavior change. In M. J. Mahoney & C. E. Thoresen (Eds.), *Self-control: Power to the person*. Monterey, Calif.: Brooks/Cole, 1974, 218–246.

Keller, A., Ford, L. H., & Meacham, J. A. Dimensions of self-concept in preschool children. *Developmental Psychology*, 1978, *14*, 483–489.

Kelley, H. H. *Attribution in social interaction*. New York: General Learning Press, 1972.

Kelly, G. A. *The psychology of personal constructs*. New York: Norton, 1955.

Kendall, P. On the efficacious use of verbal self-instructional procedures with children. *Cognitive Therapy and Research*, 1977, *1*, 331–341.

Kendall, P. C., & Finch, A. Developing non-impulsive behavior in children: Cognitive behavioral strategies for self-control. In P. C. Kendall & S. D. Hollon (Eds.), *Cognitive-behavioral interventions: Theory, research, and procedures*, New York: Academic Press, 1979.

Keniston, K. *Young radicals: Notes on committed youth*. New York: Harcourt Brace Jovanovich, 1968.

Kenny, D. A. Cross-lagged panel correlations: A test for spuriousness. *Psychological Bulletin*, 1975, *82*, 887–903.

Kernberg, O. F. *Borderline conditions and pathological narcissism*. New York: Aronson, 1975.

Kohlberg, L. A cognitive-developmental analysis of children's sex-role concepts and attitudes. In E. Maccoby (Ed.), *The development of sex differences*. Stanford, Calif.: Stanford University Press, 1966.

Kohlberg, L. Stage and sequence: The cognitive-developmental approach to socialization. In D. A. Goslin (Ed.), *Handbook of socialization theory and research*. Chicago: Rand McNally, 1969.

Kohlberg, L. Moral stages and moralization. In T. Lickona (Ed.), *Moral development and behavior*. New York: Holt, Rinehart & Winston, 1976.

Kohlberg, L., & Gilligan, C. The adolescent as a philosopher: The discovery of the self in a postconventional world. *Deadelus*, 1971, *100*, 1051–1086.

Kokenes, B. Grade level differences in factors of self-esteem. *Developmental Psychology*, 1974, *10*, 954–958.

Kopp, C. B. *The antecedents of self-regulation: A developmental perspective*. Unpublished manuscript, University of California, Los Angeles, 1981.

Kuhn, M. H., & McPartland, T. An empirical investigation of self-attitudes. *American Sociological Review*, 1954, *19*, 68–76.

Laing, R. D. *The divided self*. London: Tavistock Publications, 1960.

Langer, E. J. The illusion of control. *Journal of Personality and Social Psychology*, 1975, *32*, 311–328.

Langer, E. J. Rethinking the role of thought in social interaction. In J. H. Harvey, W. Ickes, & R. F. Kidd (Eds.), *New directions in attribution research* (Vol. 2). Hillsdale, N.J.: Erlbaum, 1978.

LaVoie, J. C. Punishment and adolescent self-control. *Developmental Psychology*, 1973, *8*, 16–24.

LaVoie, J. C. Cognitive determinants of resistance to deviation in seven-, nine-, and eleven-year-old children of low and high maturity or moral judgment. *Developmental Psychology*, 1974, *10*, 393–403.

LaVoie, J. C. Ego identity formation in middle adolescence. *Journal of Youth and Adolescence*, 1976, *5*, 371–385.

Lecky, P. *Self-consistency: A theory of personality*. New York: Island Press, 1945.

L'Ecuyer, R. The development of the self-concept through the life span. In M. D. Lynch, A. A. Norem-Hebeisen, & K. Gergen (Eds.), *Self Concept: Advances in theory and research*. Cambridge, Mass.: Ballinger, 1981.

Lefcourt, H. M. Internal versus external control of reinforcement: A review. *Psychological Bulletin*, 1966, *65*, 206–220.

Lepper, M. B., Sagotsky, J., & Mailer, J. Generalization and persistence of effects of exposure to self-reinforcement models. *Child Development*, 1975, *46*, 618–630.

Lepper, M. R., & Greene, D. Overjustification research and beyond: Toward a means-end analysis of intrinsic and extrinsic motivation. In M. R. Lepper & D. Greene (Eds.), *The hidden costs of reward*. Hillsdale, N.J.: Erlbaum, 1978.

Lerner, R. M., & Spanier, G. *Adolescent development*. New York: McGraw-Hill, 1980.

Levenson, H. *Distinction within the concept of internal-external control*. Paper presented at the American Psychological Association Convention, Washington, D.C., 1972.

Levinson, D. J. *The seasons of a man's life*. New York: Ballantine, 1978.

Lewin, K. *A dynamic theory of personality*. New York: McGraw-Hill, 1935.

Lewin, K. *Principles of topological psychology*. New York: McGraw-Hill, 1936.

Lewin, K. *The conceptual representation and the measurement of psychological forces*. Durham, N.C.: Duke University Press, 1938.

Lewin, K. *Field theory in social science*. New York: Harper, 1951.

Lewis, M. *The infant and its caregiver: The role of contingency*. Paper presented at a conference on Infant Intervention programs, The University of Wisconsin, Milwaukee, June 1977.

Lewis, M. The self as a developmental concept. *Human Development*, 1979, *22*, 416–419.

Lewis, M., & Brooks-Gunn, J. Toward a theory of social cognition: The development of the self. In I. Uzgiris (Ed.), *New directions in child development: Social interaction and communication during infancy*. San Francisco: Jossey-Bass, 1979. (a)

Lewis, M., & Brooks-Gunn, J. *Social cognition and the acquisition of self*. New York: Plenum Press, 1979. (b)

Lewis, M., & Goldberg, S. The acquisition and violation of expectancy: An experimental paradigm. *Journal of Experimental Child Psychology*, 1969, *7*, 70–80.

Lickona, T. (Ed.). *Moral development and behavior*. New York: Holt, Rinehart & Winston, 1976.

Lipinski, D. P., Black, J. L., Nelson, R. O., & Ciminero, A. R. Influence of motivational variables on the reactivity and reliability of self-recording. *Journal of Consulting and Clinical Psychology*, 1975, *43*, 637–646.

Litrownick, A. J., & Steinfeld, B. I. Developing self-regulation in retarded children. In P. Karoly & J. J. Steffen (Eds.), *Advances in child behavior analysis and therapy*. New York: Gardner Press, 1982.

Lively, W. J., & Bromley, D. B. *Person perception in childhood and adolescence*. London: Wiley, 1973.

Loevinger, J. The meaning and measurement of ego development. *American Psychologist*, 1966, *21*, 195–206.

Loevinger, J., & Wessler, R. *Measuring ego development* (Vol. 1). San Francisco: Jossey-Bass, 1970.

Loevinger, J., Wessler, R., & Redmore, C. *Measuring ego development* (Vol. 2). San Francisco: Jossey-Bass, 1970.

Logan, F. A. Self-control as habit, drive, and incentive. *Journal of Abnormal Psychology*, 1973, *81*, 127–136.

Lopatto, D., & Williams, J. L. Self-control: A critical review and an alternative interpretation. *The Psychological Record*, 1976, *26*, 3–12.

Lunzer, E. A. Problems of formal reasoning in test situations. In P. Mussen (Ed.), *European research on cognitive development. Monographs of the Society for Research in Child Development*, 1966, *30* (2, Whole No. 100).

Luria, A. The directive function of speech in development. *Word*, 1959, *15*, 341–352.

Luria, A. *The role of speech in the regulation of normal and abnormal behaviors*. New York: Liveright, 1961.

Lynch, M. D. Self-concept development in childhood. In M. D. Lynch, A. A. Norem-Hebeisen, & K. Gergen (Eds.), *Self-concept: Advances in theory and research*. Cambridge, Mass.: Ballinger, 1981.

McCall, R. B., Parke, R. D., Kavanaugh, R. D. Imitation of live and televised models by children one to three years of age. *Monographs of the Society for Research in Child Development* (Vol. 42), No. 5, Serial No. 173, 1977.

McDevitt, J. B. Separation, individuation, and object constancy. *Journal of the American Psychoanalytic Association*, 1975, *23*, 713–739.

McDougall, W. *An introduction to social psychology*. London: Methuen, 1908.

McGuire, W. The spontaneous self-concept as affected by personal distinctiveness. In A. A. Norem-Hebeisen & M. Lynch (Eds.), *Self-concept*. Cambridge, Mass.: Ballinger, 1981.

McGuire, W., & McGuire, C. V. Significant others in self-space: Sex differences and developmental trends in the social self. In J. Suls (Ed.), *Social psychological perspectives on the self*. Hillsdale, N.J.: Erlbaum, in press, 1980.

McGuire, W., & Padawer-Singer, A. Trait salience in the spontaneous self-concept. *Journal of Personality and Social Psychology*, 1976, *33*, 743–754.

McIntire, W., & Drummond, R. The structure of self-concept in second and fourth grade children.

Educational and Psychological Measurement, 1976, *36*, 529–536.

McPartland, T. S., & Cumming, J. Self-conception, social class, and mental health. *Human Organization*, 1958, *17*, 24–29.

MacPherson, E., Candee, B., & Hohman, R. A comparison of three methods of eliminating disruptive lunchroom behavior. *Journal of Applied Behavior Analysis*, 1974, *7*, 287–297.

Maccoby, E. *Social development*. New York: Wiley, 1980.

Maccoby, E. E., & Jacklin, C. N. *The psychology of sex differences*. Stanford, Calif.: Stanford University Press, 1974.

Mahler, M. S. On sadness and grief in infancy and childhood: Loss and restoration of the symbiotic love object. *Psychoanalytic Study of the Child* (Vol. 16). New York: International Universities Press, 1961, 307–324.

Mahler, M. S. Thoughts about development and individuation. *Psychoanalytic Study of the Child* (Vol. 18). New York: International Universities Press, 1963, 307–324.

Mahler, M. S. On the significance of the normal separation-individuation phase: With reference to research in symbiotic child psychosis. In M. Schur (Ed.), *Drives, affects, behavior* (Vol. 2). New York: International Universities Press, 1965, 161–169.

Mahler, M. S. Notes on the development of basic moods: The depressive affect. In R. M. Loewenstein, L. M. Newman, M. Schur, & A. J. Solnit (Eds.), *Psychoanalysis—A general psychology: Essays in honor of Heinz Hartmann*. New York: International Universities Press, 1966, 152–168.

Mahler, M. S. On human symbiosis and the vicissitudes of individuation. *Journal of the American Psychoanalytic Association*, 1967, *15*, 740–763.

Mahler, M. S. *On human symbiosis and the vicissitudes of individuation* (Vol. 1). *Infantile psychosis*. New York: International Universities Press, 1968.

Mahler, M. S., Pine, F., & Bergman, A. *The psychological birth of the infant*. New York: Basic, 1975.

Mahoney, M. J. *Cognition and behavior modification*. Cambridge, Mass.: Ballinger, 1974.

Mahoney, M. J., & Thoresen, C. E. (Eds.). *Self-control: Power to the person*. Monterey, Calif.: Brooks-Cole, 1974.

Mandler, G. *Mind and emotion*. New York: Wiley, 1975.

Marcia, J. E. *Determination and construct validity*

of ego identity status. Unpublished doctoral dissertation, Ohio State University, 1964.

Marcia, J. E. Development and validation of ego-identity status. *Journal of Personality and Social Psychology*, 1966, 551–558.

Marcia, J. E. Ego identity status: Relationship to change in self-esteem, "general maladjustment," and authoritarianism. *Journal of Personality*, 1967, *1*, 118–133.

Marcia, J. Identity six years after: A follow-up study. *Journal of Youth and Adolescence*, 1976, *5*, 145–160.

Marcia, J. E., & Friedman, M. L. Ego identity status in college women. *Journal of Personality*, 1970, *38*, 249–263.

Marcus, D. E., & Overton, W. F. The development of cognitive gender constancy and sex role preferences. *Child Development*, 1978, *49*, 434–444.

Markus, H. Self-schemata and processing information about the self. *Journal of Personality and Social Psychology*, 1977, *35*, 63–78.

Markus, H. The self in thought and memory. In D. M. Wegner & R. R. Vallacher (Eds.), *The self in social psychology*. New York: Oxford University Press, 1980.

Markus, H., Crane, M., & Siladi, M. *Cognitive consequences of androgyny*. Unpublished manuscript, University of Michigan, 1979.

Martorano, S. C. A developmental analysis of performance of Piaget's formal operations tasks. *Developmental Psychology*, 1977, *13*, 666–672.

Mash, E., & Dalby, J. Behavioral interventions for hyperactivity. In R. Trites (Ed.), *Hyperactivity in children: Etiology, measurement and treatment implications*. Baltimore, Md.: University Park Press, 1978.

Maslow, A. *Motivation and personality*. New York: Harper & Row, 1954.

Maslow, A. H. Peak-experiences as acute identity-experiences. *American Journal of Psychoanalysis*, 1961, *21*, 254–260.

Maslow, A. H. *The farther reaches of human nature*. New York: Viking, 1971.

Masters, J. E. Social comparison by young children. *Young Children*, 1971, *27*, 37–60.

Masters, J. C., & Santrock, J. W. Studies in the self-regulation of behavior: Effects of contingent cognitive and affective events. *Developmental Psychology*, 1976, *12*, 334–348.

Mead, G. H. The genesis of the self and social control. *International Journal of Ethics* (*XXXV*, April 1925, No. 3), 251–273.

Mead, G. H. *Mind, self, and society*. Chicago: University of Chicago Press, 1934.

Meichenbaum, D. Theoretical and treatment implications of developmental research on verbal control of behavior. *Canadian Psychological Review*, 1975, *16*, 22–27.

Meichenbaum, D. Toward a cognitive theory of self-control. In G. Schwartz & D. Shapiro (Eds.), *Consciousness and self-regulation* (Vol. 1). New York: Plenum, 1976.

Meichenbaum, D. *Cognitive-behavior modification: An integrative approach*. New York: Plenum, 1977.

Meichenbaum, D. Teaching children self-control. In B. Lahey & A. Kazdin (Eds.), *Advances in child clinical psychology* (Vol. 2). New York: Plenum, 1978.

Meichenbaum, D. Teaching children self-control. In B. Lahey & A. Kazdin (Eds.), *Advances in child clinical psychology* (Vol. 2). New York: Plenum, 1979.

Meichenbaum, D., & Asarnow, J. Cognitive-behavior modification and metacognitive development: Implications for the classroom. In P. Kendall & S. Hollon (Eds.), *Cognitive behavioral interventions: Theory, research and procedures*. New York: Academic Press, 1982.

Meichenbaum, D., & Genest, M. Cognitive-behavior modification: An integration of cognitive and behavioral methods. In F. H. Kanfer & A. P. Goldstein (Eds.), *Helping people change* (2nd ed.). New York: Pergamon Press, 1980.

Meichenbaum, D., & Goodman, J. Training impulsive children to talk to themselves: A means of developing self-control. *Journal of Abnormal Psychology*, 1971, *77*, 115–126.

Minsky, M. A framework for representing knowledge. In P. Winston (Ed.), *The psychology of computer vision*. New York: McGraw-Hill, 1975.

Minton, B. *Dimensions of information underlying children's judgments of their competence*. Unpublished master's thesis, University of Denver, 1979.

Mischel, W. *Personality and assessment*. New York: Wiley, 1968.

Mischel, W. Continuity and change in personality. *American Psychologist*, 1969, *24*, 1012–1018.

Mischel, W. Sex typing and socialization. In P. H. Mussen (Ed.), *Carmichael's manual of child psychology* (Vol. II). New York: Wiley, 1970.

Mischel, W. Toward a cognitive social learning reconceptualization of personality. *Psychological*

Review, 1973, *80,* 252–283.

Mischel, W. Processes in delay of gratification. In L. Berkowitz (Ed.), *Advances in experimental social psychology* (Vol. 7). New York: Academic Press, 1974.

Mischel, W., & Baker, N. Cognitive appraisals and transformations in delay behavior. *Journal of Personality and Social Psychology,* 1975, *31,* 254–261.

Mischel, W., & Ebbesen, E. B. Attention in delay of gratification. *Journal of Personality and Social Psychology,* 1970, *16,* 329–337.

Mischel, W., Ebbesen, E. B., & Zeiss, A. Cognitive and attentional mechanisms in delay of gratification. *Journal of Personality and Social Psychology,* 1972, *21,* 204–218.

Mischel, W., Ebbesen, E. B., & Zeiss, A. Selective attention to the self: Situational and dispositional determinants. *Journal of Personality and Social Psychology,* 1973, *27,* 129–142.

Mischel, W., & Grusec, J. Determinants of the rehearsal and transmission of neutral and aversive behaviors. *Journal of Personality and Social Psychology,* 1966, *3,* 197–205.

Mischel, W., & Grusec, J. Waiting for rewards and punishments: Effects of time and probability on choice. *Journal of Personality and Social Psychology,* 1967, *5,* 24–31.

Mischel, W., & Liebert, R. M. Effects of discrepancies between observed and imposed reward criteria on their acquisition and transmission. *Journal of Personality and Social Psychology,* 1966, *3,* 45–53.

Mischel, W., & Liebert, R. M. The role of power in the adoption of self-reward patterns. *Child Development,* 1967, *38,* 673–683.

Mischel, W., & Metzner, R. Preference for delayed reward as a function of age, intelligence, and length of delay interval. *Journal of Abnormal and Social Psychology,* 1962, *64,* 425–431.

Mischel, W., & Mischel, H. N. A cognitive social-learning approach to morality and self-regulation. In T. Lickona (Ed.), *Moral development and behavior.* New York: Holt, Rinehart & Winston, 1976.

Mischel, W., & Mischel, H. N. Self-control and the self. In T. Mischel (Ed.), *The self: Psychological and philosophical issues.* Totowa, New Jersey: Rowan and Littlefield, 1977.

Mischel, W., Mischel, H. M., & Hood, S. Q. *The development of knowledge about self-control.* Unpublished manuscript, Stanford University, 1978. (a)

Mischel, W., Mischel, H. N., & Hood, S. Q. *The development of knowledge of effective ideation to delay gratification.* Unpublished manuscript, Stanford University, 1978. (b)

Mischel, W., & Moore, B. Effects of attention to symbolically presented rewards upon self-control. *Journal of Personality and Social Psychology,* 1973, *28,* 172–179. (a)

Mischel, W., & Moore, B. *Cognitive transformations of the stimulus in delay of gratification.* Unpublished manuscript, Stanford University, 1973. (b)

Mischel, W., & Patterson, C. J. Substantive and structural elements of effective plans for self-control. *Journal of Personality and Social Psychology,* 1976, *34,* 942–950.

Mischel, W., & Patterson, C. J. Effective plans for self-control in children. In W. A. Collins (Ed.), *Minnesota Symposium on Child Psychology* (Vol. 11). Hillsdale, N.J.: Erlbaum, 1978.

Mischel, W., Zeiss, R., & Zeiss, A. R. Internal-external control and persistence: Validation and implications of the Stanford Preschool Internal-External Scale. *Journal of Personality and Social Psychology,* 1974, *29,* 265–278.

Monahan, J., & O'Leary, D. Effects of self-instruction on rule-breaking behavior. *Psychological Reports,* 1971, *29,* 1059–1066.

Montemayor, R., & Eisen, M. The development of self-conceptions from childhood to adolescence. *Developmental Psychology,* 1977, *13,* 314–319.

Montgomery, G. T., & Parton, D. H. Reinforcing effect of self-reward. *Journal of Experimental Psychology,* 1970, *84,* 273–276.

Moore, B., Clyburn, A., & Underwood, B. The role of affect in delay of gratification. *Child Development,* 1976, *47,* 273–276.

Moore, B., Mischel, W., & Zeiss, A. Comparative effects of the reward stimulus and its cognitive representation in voluntary delay. *Journal of Personality and Social Psychology,* 1976, *34,* 419–424.

Moore, K. C. The mental development of a child. *Psychological Monographs,* 1896, *1*(3).

Moshman, D. Consolidation and stage formation in the emergence of formal operations. *Developmental Psychology,* 1977, *13,* 523–524.

Mullener, N., & Laird, J. D. Some developmental changes in the organization of self-evaluations. *Developmental Psychology,* 1971, *5,* 233–236.

Murphy, G. *Personality.* New York: Harper & Row, 1947.

Neisser, U. *Cognition and reality: Principles and*

implications of cognitive psychology. San Francisco: Freeman, 1976.

Nelson, W., & Birkimer, J. Role of self-instruction and self-reinforcement in the modification of impulsivity. *Journal of Consulting and Clinical Psychology*, 1978, *46*, 183.

Nesselroade, J. R., & Reese, H. W. *Life-span developmental psychology: Methodological issues*. New York: Academic Press, 1973.

Nicholls, J. G. The development of the concepts of effort and ability, perception of academic attainment, and the understanding that difficult tasks require more ability. *Child Development*, 1978, 800–814.

Nisbett, R. E., & Wilson, T. D. Telling more than we can know: Verbal reports on mental processes. *Psychological Review*, 1977, *84*, 231–259.

Norem-Hebeisen, A. A. A maximization model of self-concept. In M. D. Lynch & K. Gergen (Eds.), *Self-concept: Advances in theory and research*. Cambridge, Mass.: Ballinger, 1981.

Nowicki, S., & Strickland, B. A locus of control scale for children. *Journal of Consulting and Clinical Psychology*, 1973, *40*, 148–154.

O'Leary, D. The effects of self-instruction on immoral behavior. *Journal of Experimental Child Psychology*, 1968, *6*, 297–301.

Osgood, C. E., Suci, G. J., & Tannenbaum, P. H. *The measurement of meaning*. Urbana, Ill.: University of Illinois Press, 1957.

Palkes, H., Stewart, M., & Kahana, B. Porteus maze performance after training in self-directed verbal commands. *Child Development*, 1968, *39*, 817–826.

Palkes, H., Stewart, M., & Freeman, J. Improvement in maze performance on hyperactive boys as a function of verbal training procedures. *Journal of Special Education*, 1972, *5*, 237–342.

Papousek, H., & Papousek, M. Mirror-image and self-recognition in young human infants: I. A new method of experimental analysis. *Developmental Psychobiology*, 1974, *7*, 149–157.

Parke, R. D. Effectiveness of punishment as an interaction of intensity, timing, agent nurturance and cognitive structuring. *Child Development*, 1969, *40*, 213–236.

Parke, R. D. The role of punishment in the socialization process. In R. A. Hoppe, G. A. Milton, & E. C. Simmel (Eds.), *Early experiences and the process of socialization*. New York: Academic Press, 1970.

Parke, R. D. Rules, roles, and resistance to deviation in children: Explorations in punishment, discipline and self-control. In A. Pick (Ed.), *Minnesota symposium on child psychology* (Vol. 8). Minneapolis: University of Minnesota Press, 1974.

Parke, R. D. Punishment in children: Effects, side effects, and alternative strategies. In H. L. Hom, Jr. & P. A. Robinson (Eds.), *Psychological processes in early education*. New York: Academic Press, 1977.

Parke, R. D., & Murray, S. *Reinstatement: A technique for increasing stability of inhibition in children*. Unpublished manuscript, University of Wisconsin, 1971.

Parke, R. D., & Sawin, D. B. *The impact of fear and empathy-based rationales on children's response inhibition*. Unpublished manuscript, Fels Research Institute, 1975.

Parke, R. D., & Walters, R. H. Some factors influencing the efficacy of punishment training for inducing response inhibition. *Monographs of the Society for Research in Child Development*, 1967, *32*(1, Serial No. 109).

Patterson, C. J. Self-control and self-regulation in childhood. In T. Field, & A. Huston-Stein (Eds.), *Review of human development*. New York: Wiley, 1982.

Patterson, C. J., & Kister, M. C. Development of listener skills for referential communication. In W. P. Dickson (Ed.), *Children's oral communication skills*. New York: Academic Press, in press.

Patterson, C. J., & Mischel, W. Plans to resist distraction. *Developmental Psychology*, 1975, *11*, 369–378.

Patterson, C., & Mischel, W. Effects of temptation-inhibiting and task-facilitating plans on self-control. *Journal of Personality and Social Psychology*, 1976, *33*, 209–217.

Peterson, A. C. The development of self-concept in adolescence. In M. D. Lynch, A. A. Norem-Hebeisen, & K. Gergen (Eds.), *Self-concept: Advances in theory and research*. Cambridge, Mass.: Ballinger, 1981.

Phillips, L., & Rabinovitch, M. S. Social role and patterns of symptomatic behavior. *Journal of Abnormal and Social Psychology*, 1958, *57*, 181–186.

Phillips, L., & Zigler, E. Social competence: The action-thought parameter and vicariousness in normal and pathological behavior. *Journal of Personality and Social Psychology*, 1961, *63*, 137–146.

Piaget, J. *The language and thought of the child*. New York: Harcourt, Brace, 1926.

Piaget, J. *Judgment and reasoning in the child*. London: Routledge and Kegan Paul, 1928.

Piaget, J. *The moral judgment of the child*. New York: Harcourt, Brace, & World, 1932.

Piaget, J. *The construction of reality in the child*. New York: Basic, 1954.

Piaget. J. *The psychology of intelligence*. Paterson, N.J.: Littlefield, Adams, 1960.

Piaget, J. *Play, dreams, and imitation in childhood*. New York: Norton, 1962.

Piaget, J. *The origins of intelligence in children*. New York: Norton, 1963.

Piaget, J. *The child's conception of the world*. Paterson, N.J.: Littlefield, Adams, 1965.

Piaget, J. *Six psychological studies*. New York: Vintage, 1967.

Piers, E. V. *Manual for the Piers-Harris Children's Self-Concept Scale*. Nashville, Tenn.: Counselor Recordings and Tests, 1969.

Piers, E. V. *The Piers-Harris children's self-concept scale*. Research Monograph No. 1. Nashville, Tennessee: Counselor Recordings and Tests, 1976.

Piers, E. V. Children's self-esteem, level of esteem certainty, and responsibility for success and failure. *Journal of Genetic Psychology*, 1977, *130*, 295–304.

Piers, E., & Harris, D. *The Piers-Harris Children's Self-Concept Scale*. Nashville, Tenn.: Counselor Recordings and Tests, 1969.

Pine, F. Libidinal object constancy: A theoretical note. In *Psychoanalysis and contemporary science* (Vol. 3). New York: International Universities Press, 1975.

Prawat, R. S., Grissom, S., & Parish, T. Affective development in children, grades 3 through 12. *Journal of Genetic Psychology*, 1979, *135*, 37–49.

Premack, D., & Anglin, B. On the possibilities of self-control in man and animals. *Journal of Abnormal Psychology*, 1973, *81*, 137–151.

Pressley, G. M. Increasing children's self-control through cognitive interventions. *Review of Educational Research*, in press, 1979.

Preyer, W. Mind of the child. *Development of the intellect* (Vol. 2). New York: Appleton, 1893.

Proshansky, H., & Newton, P. The nature and meaning of Negro self-identity. In M. Deutsch, I. Katz, & A. R. Jensen (Eds.), *Social class, race, and psychological development*. New York: Holt, Rinehart & Winston, 1968.

Purkey, W. W. *Self-concept and school achievement*. Englewood Cliffs, N.J.: Prentice-Hall, 1970.

Rachlin, H. Self-control. *Behaviorism*, 1974, *2*, 94–107.

Redmore, C., & Waldman, K. Reliability of a sentence completion measure of ego development. *Journal of Personality Assessment*, 1975, *39*, 236–243.

Reese, H. Verbal mediation as a function of age level. *Psychological Bulletin*, 1962, *59*, 502–509.

Reisman, D., Glazer, N., & Denney, R. *The lonely crowd*. New Haven: Yale University Press, 1950.

Roberge, J. J. Developmental analysis of two formal operational structures: Combinatorial thinking and conditional reasoning. *Developmental Psychology*, 1976, *12*, 563–564.

Robinson, J. P., & Shaver, P. R. *Measures of social psychological attitudes*. Ann Arbor, Mich.: Institute for Social Research, 1973.

Rogers, C. R. The significance of the self-regarding attitudes and perceptions. In M. L. Reymert (Ed.), *Feelings and emotions: The Mooseheart Symposium*. New York: McGraw-Hill, 1950.

Rogers, C. R. *Client-centered therapy*. Boston: Houghton Mifflin, 1951.

Rogers, C. R. *On becoming a person: A therapist's view of psychotherapy*. Boston: Houghton Mifflin, 1961.

Rogers, C. The child's perception of other people. In H. McGurk (Ed.), *Issues in childhood social development*. London: Methuen, 1978.

Rogers, C., & Dymond, R. *Psychotherapy and personality change*. Chicago: University of Chicago Press, 1954.

Rogers, T. B., Kuiper, N. A., & Kirker, W. S. Self-reference and the encoding of personal information. *Journal of Personality and Social Psychology*, 1977, *35*, 677–688.

Rosenberg, M. *Society and the adolescent self-image*. Princeton: Princeton University Press, 1965.

Rosenberg, M. *Conceiving the self*. New York: Basic, 1979.

Rosenhan, D. L. Learning theory and prosocial behavior. *Journal of Social Issues*, 1972, *28*, 151–163.

Rosenhan, D. L., & White, G. M. Observations and rehearsal as determinants of prosocial behavior. *Journal of Personality and Social Psychology*, 1967, *5*, 424–431.

Rosenkoetter, L. I. Resistance to temptation: Inhibitory and disinhibitory effects of models. *Developmental Psychology*, 1973, *8*, 80–84.

Rosenthal, T. L. Applying a cognitive behavioral

view to clinical and social problems. In G. J. Whitehurst & B. J. Zimmerman (Eds.), *The functions of language and cognition*. New York: Academic Press, 1979, 265–293.

Ross, D. M., & Ross, S. A. *Hyperactivity: Research, theory, and action*. New York: Wiley, 1976.

Ross, S. A. A test of the generality of the effects of deviant preschool models. *Developmental Psychology*, 1971, *4*, 262–267.

Rotter, J. B. Generalized expectancies for internal versus external control of reinforcement. *Psychological Monographs*, 1966, *80*(1, Whole No. 609).

Rotter, J. B. Some problems and misconceptions related to the construct of internal vs. external control of reinforcement. *Journal of Consulting and Clinical Psychology*, 1975, *43*, 56–67.

Rotter, J. B., Chance, J. E., & Phares, E. J. (Eds.), *Applications of social learning theory to personality*. New York: Holt, Rinehart & Winston, 1972.

Rubin, R. A., Maruyama, G., & Kingsbury, G. G. *Self-esteem and educational achievement: A causal-model analysis*. Paper presented at the Annual Meeting of the American Psychological Association, New York, September, 1979.

Ruble, D. N., Boggiano, A. K., Feldman, N. S., & Loebl, J. H. Developmental analysis of the role of social comparison in self-evaluation. *Developmental Psychology*, 1980, *16*, 105–115.

Ruble, D. N., Feldman, N. S., & Boggiano, A. G. Social comparison between young children in achievement situations. *Developmental Psychology*, 1976, *12*, 192–197.

Ruble, D. N., Parsons, J. E., & Ross, J. Self-evaluative responses of children in an achievement setting. *Child Development*, 1976, *47*, 990–997.

Sagotsky, G., & Lepper, M. R. *Generalization of changes in children's preferences for easy or difficult goals induced by observational learning*. Unpublished manuscript, Stanford University, 1976.

Sagotsky, G., Patterson, C. J., & Lepper, M. R. Training children's self-control: A field experiment in self-monitoring and goal-setting in the classroom. *Journal of Experimental Child Psychology*, 1978, *25*, 242–253.

Sameroff, A., & Chandler, M. Reproductive risk and the continuum of caretaker causality. In F. Horowitz (Ed.), *Review of child development research* (Vol. 4). Chicago: University of Chicago Press, 1975.

Sander, L. W. Adaptive relationships in early mother-child interaction. *Journal of the American Academy of Child Psychiatry*, 1964, *3*, 231–264.

Sander, L. W. The longitudinal course of early mother-child interaction: Cross case comparison in a sample of mother-child pairs. In B. M. Foss (Ed.), *Determinants of infant behavior* IV. London: Methuen, 1969.

Sander, L. W. Infant and caretaking environment: Investigation and conceptualization of adaptive behavior in a system of increasing complexity. In J. Anthony (Ed.), *Explorations in child psychiatry*, 1975, 129–165.

Santrock, J. W. Affect and facilitative self-control: Influence of ecological setting, cognition, and social agent. *Journal of Educational Psychology*, 1976, *68*, 529–535.

Sarbin, T. R. A preface to a psychological analysis of the self. *Psychological Review*, 1962, *59*, 11–22.

Sarbin, T. R. A preface to a psychological analysis of the self. In C. Gordon & K. J. Gergen (Eds.), *The self in social interaction*. New York: Wiley, 1968.

Sawin, D. B., & Parke, R. D. Development of self-verbalized control of resistance to deviation. *Developmental Psychology*, 1979, *15*, 120–127.

Schaeffer, E. S., & Bell, R. Q. Development of a parental attitude research instrument. *Child Development*, 1958, *29*, 339–361.

Schank, R. C., & Abelson, R. P. *Scripts, plans, goals, and understanding*. Hillsdale, N.J.: Erlbaum, 1977.

Schulman, A. H., & Kaplowitz, C. Mirror-image responses during the first two years of life. *Developmental Psychobiology*, 1977, *10*, 133–142.

Sears, P. S. *Memorandum with respect to the use of the Sears Self-Concept Inventory*. Unpublished manuscript, Stanford University, 1966.

Sears, R. R., Rau, L., & Alpert, R. *Identification and child training*. Stanford, Calif.: Stanford University Press, 1965.

Seligman, M. E. P. *Helplessness: On depression, development, and death*. San Francisco: Freeman, 1975.

Selman, R. *The growth of interpersonal understanding*. New York: Academic Press, 1980.

Sgan, M. L. Social reinforcement, socioeconomic status, and susceptibility to experimenter influence. *Journal of Personality and Social Psychology*, 1967, *5*, 202–210.

Shantz, C. U. The development of social cognition. In M. E. Hetherington (Ed.), *Review of Child Development Research* (Vol. 5). Chicago: University of Chicago Press, 1975.

Shavelson, R. J., Hubner, J. J., & Stanton, G. C. Self-concept: Validation of construct interpretations. *Review of Educational Research,* 1976, *46,* 407–441.

Shibutani, T. *Society and personality.* Englewood Cliffs, N.J.: Prentice-Hall, 1961.

Shiffler, N., Lynch-Sauer, & Nadelman, L. Relationship between self-concept and classroom behavior in two informal elementary classrooms. *Journal of Educational Psychology,* 1977, *69,* 349–359.

Simmons, R. G., Rosenberg, F., & Rosenberg, M. Disturbance in the self-image at adolescence. *American Sociological Review,* 1973, *38,* 553–568.

Skinner, B. F. The operational analysis of psychological terms. *Psychological Review,* 1945, *52,* 270–294.

Skinner, B. F. *Science and human behavior.* New York: Macmillan, 1953.

Skinner, B. F. *Verbal behavior.* New York: Appleton, 1957.

Smith, M. D., & Rogers, C. M. Item instability on the Piers-Harris Children's Self-Concept Scale for academic underachievers with high, middle, or low self-concepts. *Educational and Psychological Measurement,* 1977, *37,* 553–558.

Smith, T., & Dalenberg, C. *Social recognition theory: An experimental test of an alternative to dissonance and self-perception theories.* Unpublished manuscript, University of Denver, 1980.

Snyder, M. Self-monitoring processes. In L. Berkowitz (Ed.), *Advances in experimental social psychology* (Vol. 12). New York: Academic Press, 1979.

Snygg, D., & Combs, A. W. *Individual behavior: A new frame of reference for psychology.* New York: Harper, 1949.

Spates, C., & Kanfer, F. Self-monitoring, self-evaluation and self-reinforcement in children's learning: A test of a multistage self-regulation model. *Behavior Therapy,* 1977, *8,* 9–16.

Spear, P. S., & Armstrong, S. Effects of performance expectancies created by peer comparison as related to social reinforcement, task difficulty, and age of child. *Journal of Experimental Child Psychology,* 1978, *25,* 254–266.

Spears, W. D., & Deese, M. E. Self-concept as

cause. *Educational Theory,* 1973, *23,* 144–152.

Spitz, R. A. *No and yes—On the genesis of human communication.* New York: International Universities Press, 1957.

Spivack, G., & Shure, M. *Social adjustment of young children: A cognitive approach to solving real-life problems.* San Francisco: Jossey Bass, 1974.

Sroufe, L. A., & Waters, E. Attachment as an organizational construct. *Child Development,* 1977, *48,* 1184–1199.

Staats, A. W. *Social behaviorism.* Homewood, Ill.: Dorsey, 1975.

Stein, A. H. Imitation of resistance to temptation. *Child Development,* 1967, *38,* 157–159.

Stotland, E., & Canon, L. K. *Social Psychology: A cognitive approach.* Philadelphia: Saunders, 1972.

Stuart, R. B. Situational versus self-control. In R. D. Rubin, H. Fersterheim, J. D. Henderson, & L. P. Ullmann (Eds.), *Advances in behavior therapy.* New York: Academic Press, 1972.

Sullivan, H. S. *Conceptions of modern psychiatry.* New York: Norton, 1947.

Sullivan, H. S. *The interpersonal theory of psychiatry.* New York: Norton, 1953.

Switzky, H. N., & Haywood, H. C. Motivational orientation and the relative efficacy of self-monitored and externally imposed reinforcement systems in children. *Journal of Personality and Social Psychology,* 1974, *30,* 360–366.

Symonds, P. M. *The ego and the self.* New York: Appleton-Century-Crofts, 1951.

Taylor, S. E., & Fiske, S. T. Point of view and perceptions of causality. *Journal of Personality and Social Psychology,* 1975, *32,* 439–445.

Thompson, S. K. Gender labels and early sex role development. *Child Development,* 1975, *46,* 339–347.

Thoresen, C., & Mahoney, M. *Behavioral self-control.* New York: Holt, Rinehart & Winston, 1974.

Toder, N. L., & Marcia, J. E. Ego identity status and response to conformity pressure in college women. *Journal of Personality and Social Psychology,* 1973, *26,* 287–294.

Trungpa, C. *Spiritual materialism.* Berkeley: Shambhalla Books, 1973.

Trungpa, C. *The myth of freedom.* Berkeley: Shambhalla Books, 1976.

Uzgiris, I. C., & Hunt, J. McV. *Assessment in infancy: Ordinal scales of psychological development.* Chicago: University of Illinois Press,

1976.

Vallacher, R. R. An introduction to self-theory. In D. M. Wegner & R. R. Vallacher (Eds.), *The self in social psychology*. New York: Oxford University Press, 1980.

Van Parys, M. *Preschool children's understanding of self in relation to racial and gender labels.* Unpublished master's thesis, University of Denver, 1980.

Vygotsky, L. *Thought and language.* New York: Wiley, 1962.

Walters, R. H., & Parke, R. D. Influence of response consequences to a social model on resistance to deviation. *Journal of Experimental Child Psychology,* 1964, *1,* 269–280.

Walters, R. H., Parke, R. D., & Cane, V. Timing of punishment and the observation of consequences to others as determinants of response inhibition. *Journal of Experimental Child Psychology,* 1965, *2,* 10–30.

Waterman, A. S., & Goldman, J. A. A longitudinal study of changes in ego identity development at a liberal arts college. *Journal of Youth and Adolescence,* 1976, *5,* 361–370.

Waterman, A. S., & Waterman, C. K. A longitudinal study of changes in ego identity states during the freshman year at college. *Developmental Psychology,* 1971, *5,* 167–173.

Waterman, G., Geary, P., & Waterman, C. Longitudinal study of changes in ego identity status from the freshman to the senior year at college. *Developmental Psychology,* 1974, *10,* 387–392.

Watson, M. W., & Fischer, K. W. A developmental sequence of agent use in late infancy. *Child Development,* 1977, *48,* 828–836.

Webster, M., & Sobieszek, B. *Sources of self-evaluation.* New York: Wiley, 1974.

Wegner, D. M., & Vallacher, R. R. *Implicit Psychology: An introduction to social cognition.* New York: Oxford University Press, 1977.

Wegner, D. M., & Vallacher, R. R. (Eds.). *The self in social psychology.* New York: Oxford University Press, 1980.

Weiner, B., Kun, A., & Benesh-Weiner, M. The development of mastery, emotions and morality from an attributional perspective. In W. A. Collins (Ed.), *Development of cognition, affect, and social relations.* The Minnesota Symposium on Child Psychology (Vol. 13). Hillsdale, N.J.: Lawrence Erlbaum, 1980.

Weiner, P. S. Personality correlates of self-appraisal in four-year-old children. *Genetic Psychology Monographs,* 1964, *70,* 329–365.

Weisz, J. R. Choosing problem-solving rewards and Halloween prizes: Delay of gratification and preference for symbolic reward as a function of development, motivation, and personal investment. *Developmental Psychology,* 1978, *14,* 66–78.

Werner, H. The concept of development from a comparative and organismic point of view. In D. B. Harris (Ed.), *The concept of development.* Minneapolis: University of Minnesota Press, 1957.

White, G. Immediate and deferred effects of model observations and guided and unguided rehearsal on donating and stealing. *Journal of Personality and Social Psychology,* 1972, *21,* 139–148.

White, R. W. Motivation reconsidered: The concept of competence. *Psychological Review,* 1959, *66,* 297–333.

White, R. W. Competence and the psychosexual stages of development. *Nebraska Symposium on Motivation.* Lincoln: University of Nebraska Press, 1960.

White, R. W. Ego and reality in psychoanalytic theory. *Psychological Issues,* Monograph 3, 1963.

Wicklund, R. A. Objective self-awareness. In L. Berkowitz (Ed.), *Advances in experimental social psychology* (Vol. 8). New York: Academic Press, 1975.

Wicklund, R. A. Three years later. In L. Berkowitz (Ed.), *Cognitive theories in social psychology.* New York: Academic Press, 1978.

Wicklund, R. A., & Frey, D. Self-awareness theory: When the self makes a difference. In D. M. Wegner & R. R. Vallacher (Eds.), *The self in social psychology.* New York: Oxford University Press, 1980.

Winne, P. H., Marx, R. W., & Taylor, T. D. A multitrait-multimethod study of three self-concept inventories. *Child Development,* 1977, *48,* 893–901.

Wolf, T. Effects of televised modeled verbalizations and behavior on resistance to deviation. *Developmental Psychology,* 1973, *8,* 51–56.

Wolf, T. M., & Cheyne, J. A. Persistence of effects of live behavioral, televised behavioral, and live verbal models on resistance to temptation. *Child Development,* 1972, *43,* 1429–1436.

Wolff, P. H. The developmental psychologies of Jean Piaget and psychoanalysis. *Psychological Issues,* 1960, Monograph 5.

Wylie, R. *The self-concept: A critical survey of pertinent research literature.* Lincoln, Nebraska: University of Nebraska Press, 1961.

Wylie, R. The present status of self-theory. In E. F. Borgatta & W. E. Lambert (Eds.), *Handbook of personality theory and research.* Chicago: Rand McNally, 1968.

Wylie, R. *The self-concept: A review of methodological considerations and measuring instruments* (Rev. ed., Vol. 1). Lincoln, Nebr.: University of Nebraska Press, 1974.

Wylie, R. *The self-concept,* Volume 2. *Theory and research on selected topics.* Lincoln, Nebr.: University of Nebraska Press, 1979.

Yates, B. T., & Mischel, W. Young children's preferred attentional strategies for delaying gratification. *Journal of Personality and Social Psychology,* 1979, *37,* 286–300.

Zazzo, R. Images du corp et conscience du soi. *Enfance,* 1948, *1,* 29–43.

Zigler, E., Balla, D., & Watson, N. Developmental and experimental determinants of self-image disparity in institutionalized and noninstitutionalized retarded and normal children. *Journal of Personality and Social Psychology,* 1972, *23,* 81–87.

Zigler, E., & Phillips, L. Social effectiveness and symptomatic behaviors. *Journal of Abnormal and Social Psychology,* 1960, *61,* 231–238.

Ziller, R. C. *The social self.* New York: Pergamon, 1973.

SEX-TYPING* | 5

ALETHA C. HUSTON, *University of Kansas*

CHAPTER CONTENTS

*I wish to thank Sandra Bem, Beth Crandall, Virginia Crandall, E. Mavis Hetherington, Lawrence Kohlberg, and John C. Wright for reading and commenting on various parts of this chapter. I am deeply grateful to Jeanne Block for doing a careful, thorough, and helpful review of the chapter during a period of ill health when she had many pressing obligations of her own. She was an important contributor to the field, distinguished by her innovative theory development, substantial contributions of new and valuable data, and courageous willingness to challenge conventional wisdom. She has been in the forefront of the ''new look'' at sex-typing, while avoiding faddish oversimplification. Her suggestions have contributed to the quality of this chapter, although I, of course, take responsibility for its shortcomings.

Ten years ago, when the last edition of this volume appeared, sex-typing was considered a desirable goal of socialization by most psychologists, educators, and parents.[1] In the interim, that assumption has been reversed with the explicit rejection by many people of traditional sex-typing as a goal of socialization and with the espousal of non-sex-typed rearing for both boys and girls. This change is largely the result of the Women's Movement and the concomitant recognition that traditional sex-typing is a vehicle for discrimination against women. At a more subtle level, many advocates of the new view argue that sex-typed roles restrict personal fulfillment for *both* males and females by limiting the options that each can pursue. Because of this political and conceptual about-face, sex-typing research, more than most topics in social and developmental psychology, demonstrates the influence of social values on psychological theory and research. In some respects, it is fortunate that values have changed so dramatically because it is now easier to detect the influence of unstated and often unrecognized assumptions on the questions selected for study, the methods of study, and the interpretation of findings. Ravanna Helson (1972) presents an enlightening example of the changing interpretations of data about career-oriented women from the 1940s to the late 1960s. Personality characteristics that were viewed negatively as "masculine," aggressive, and maladjusted in the earlier period are later described positively as assertive, competent, and functional. Let us be clear that no psychological research area is free of guiding values, biases, and assumptions. There is no such thing as "objective" research. The new wave of sex-typing research is no more value-free than the old. And the same cautions apply to all other topics covered in this volume as well.

DEFINITION OF THE AREA

Some authors treat all sex differences as indicators of sex-typing. Others focus on characteristics that are socially defined as appropriate for one gender or the other, regardless of whether there are mean differences between the sexes. The second approach has guided the selection of topics for this chapter more than the first, though material on sex differences is often included. The literature reviewed covers infancy through adolescence, but does not include systematic coverage of studies using college students or adults. Occasional studies

---

[1]Certain language conventions have been followed in an effort to avoid both sexism and awkwardness. Following Bernard's (1976) suggestion that the term "opposite sex" builds an assumption of polarity, I have used the term "other sex" or "other gender" when contrasting males and females. Similarly, Bernard (1976) suggests that descriptions of differences between mean levels of an attribute for males and females should be stated as "More females than males have high levels of X" rather than "Females have higher levels of X than males." The former phrasing makes clear the overlap in distributions; the latter suggests that all females are higher than all males. I have elected to call prepubescent children "boys" and "girls"—the belittling connotations of these terms when they are applied to adults hardly seem to apply to children, and it is more than slightly ridiculous to call them young men and women. Finally, following the cautions of Spence and Helmreich (1978), I have reserved the term "sex role" for those activities, interests, and tasks that are socially prescribed for males and females. The substantive basis for this usage is discussed in the text.

of those age groups are cited where they are important to a particular theory or issue.

Dimensions of Sex-Typing

Sex-typing is multidimensional. Some theorists have proposed sets of constructs that define different dimensions of sex-typing in children. Kagan (1964a) suggested that children's sex role standards, or knowledge of cultural expectations for males and females, be distinguished from sex role identity, the degree to which the children perceived themselves as conforming to the cultural norm for their own gender. Others (Biller, 1971; Lynn, 1966) proposed three constructs: (1) sex role orientation or identity—the person's belief or perception that he or she possesses sex-typed characteristics; (2) sex role preference—the person's preference for activities or characteristics that are sex-typed; and (3) sex role adoption—the behavioral manifestation of sex-typed characteristics as observed by others. These distinctions are useful, but they do not provide for differentiations among the diverse content areas included under the rubric of sex-typing. Spence and Helmreich (1978) proposed that sex roles, defined by the activities and tasks socially prescribed for men and women, must be separated from instrumental and expressive personality traits. Each of these is relatively independent of erotic partner preferences. Constantinople (1973) made a strong case for multidimensionality of the content included in many widely used measures. She argued that serious conceptual errors had resulted from including personality characteristics, interests, attitudes, and empirically derived attributes, such as preference for showers or baths, as part of a single scale.

The issue of what dimensions best describe sex-typing is by no means settled, but it seems clear that two sets of distinctions are involved: distinctions among *constructs* and distinctions among *content areas*. For heuristic and organizational purposes, the constructs and content areas used by different investigators have been arranged in a matrix shown in Table 1. The rows in the matrix are categories of *content* that have been included by at least some investigators in measures or conceptions of sex-typing. The five *content areas* are: (1) biological gender, (2) activities and interests, (3) personal-social attributes, (4) gender-based social relationships, and (5) stylistic and symbolic characteristics. *Biological gender* is self-explanatory. *Activities and interests* include toys and play activities, occupations, household tasks, and areas of achievement such as verbal, math, and spatial skills. *Personal-social attributes*

include personality traits and patterns of social behavior such as aggression, dominance, dependence, and nurturance. *Gender-based social relationships* include the gender of one's friends, one's sexual partners, the persons one chooses to imitate or to identify with, and the persons one selects as attachment figures, all of which have been used as indexes of sex-typing (e.g., Green, 1974; Kohlberg & Zigler, 1967). The common feature in this grouping is that a relationship to another person depends on that person's gender. *Stylistic and symbolic contents* of sex-typing include gestures and nonverbal behavior (Frieze & Ramsey, 1976; Rekers, Amaro-Plotkin, & Low, 1977), speech and language patterns (Fillmer & Haswell, 1977; Haas, 1979), symbolic patterns or attributes such as tempo, size, pitch, open versus closed, angular versus round (e.g., Franck & Rosen, 1949), and patterns of fantasy or play (e.g., Cramer & Hogan, 1975; Erikson, 1963; May, 1971).

The columns in the matrix represent *constructs* that describe an individual's relationship to the content categories. They are (1) concepts or beliefs, (2) identity or self-perception, (3) preference or attitudes, and (4) behavioral enactment.

Concepts or beliefs include social stereotypes or expectations for males and females as well as the child's level of understanding or sophistication about the necessity of such stereotypes. In Table 1, concepts about biological gender are exemplified by measures of gender constancy—children's understanding of the consistency and stability of gender (Cell A1). Concepts about the other four content areas are typically measured by assessing sex stereotypes about interests, activities, abilities, personal social attributes, or beliefs about sex-appropriate behavior (Cells A2 through A5).

Identity or self-perception includes the perception of oneself as masculine or feminine (Kagan, 1964a) or the perception of oneself as possessing characteristics or interests that are sex-typed, whether or not they are labeled that way. The concept *gender identity* is used by some theorists to describe a person's core perception of self as male or female (e.g., Money & Ehrhardt, 1972). For most people, gender identity is congruent with biological gender, but "true" transsexuals are reported to have a gender identity that is incongruent with biological gender (Green, 1974). Gender identity in this case is a psychological construct in the cell where identity and biological gender are crossed (B1). A second type of gender identity, perception of self as masculine or feminine (Storms, 1979), may fall in this cell. Self-perception of activities and interests (B2)

Table 1.   A Matrix of Sex-Typing Constructs by Sex-Typed Content (all entries are examples)

	Construct			
Content Area	A. Concepts or beliefs	B. Identity or self-perception	C. Preferences, attitudes, values (for self or for others)	D. Behavioral enactment, adoption
1. *Biological gender*	A1. Gender constancy.	B1. Gender identity as inner sense of maleness or femaleness. Sex role identity as perception of own masculinity or femininity	C1. Wish to be male or female *or* gender bias defined as greater value attached to one gender than the other.	D1. Displaying bodily attributes of one gender (including clothing, body type, hair, etc.).
2. *Activities and interests:* Toys Play activities Occupations Household roles Tasks Achievement areas	A2. Knowledge of sex stereotypes *or* sex role concepts *or* attributions about others' success and failure.	B2. Self-perception of interests, abilities; *or* sex-typed attributions about own success and failure.	C2. Preference for toys, games, activities; attainment value for achievement areas; attitudes about sex-typed activities by others (e.g., about traditional or nontraditional roles for women).	D2. Engaging in games, toy play, activities, occupations, or achievement tasks that are sex-typed.
3. *Personal-social attributes:* Personality characteristics Social behavior	A3. Concepts about sex stereotypes *or* sex-appropriate social behavior.	B3. Perception of own personality (e.g., on self-rating questionnaires).	C3. Preference or wish to have personal-social attributes *or* attitudes about others' personality and behavior patterns.	D3. Displaying sex-typed personal-social behavior (e.g., aggression, dependence).

includes not only self-descriptions but also expectancies of success and attributions about the reasons for success or failure. Self-perception of personal-social characteristics (B3) includes self-ratings on adjectives or self-descriptions of personality traits and social behavior. In the other two content areas (B4 and B5), self-perceptions could be measured, but there are few efforts to do so with children. Self-perceptions of erotic partner preferences have been measured for adults (Storms, 1980).

Preferences and attitudes include sex role preference as defined by Biller (1971)—a person's desire to possess sex-typed characteristics—as well as values or positive attitudes about having such characteristics. Preferences and attitudes about biological gender are manifested in stated wishes to be one gender or the other and in gender bias, a child's

tendency to perceive one sex as better or more valuable than the other (C1). Preferences for play activities and interests constitute the most frequent content of sex-typing measures used with children (C2). Children are less often asked how much they would like to possess personal-social attributes (C3), but preferences for male or female playmates, adult models, or attachment figures are occasionally assessed (C4). Attitudes about others' sex-typed behavior are reflected in children's approval or disapproval of sex-typed interests and activities or of sex-typed personal-social attributes (e.g., Emmerich, 1979a). It would be possible to study their attitudes about sex-typing in the other content areas listed.

Behavioral enactments consist of behavioral manifestations that can be objectively assessed by others. Literal "adoption" of biological gender is

Table 1.—Continued

Content Area	Construct			
	A. Concepts or beliefs	B. Identity or self-perception	C. Preferences, attitudes, values (for self or for others)	D. Behavioral enactment, adoption
4. *Gender-based social relationships:* Gender of peers, friends, lovers, preferred parent, models, attachment figures	A4. Concepts about sex-typed norms for gender-based social relations.	B4. Self-perception of own patterns of friendship, relationship, or sexual orientation.	C4. Preference for male or female friends, lovers, attachment figures, or wish to be like male or female, or attitudes about others' patterns.	D4. Engaging in social or sexual activity with others on the basis of gender (e.g., same-sex peer choice).
5. *Stylistic and symbolic content:* Gestures, Nonverbal behavior Speech and language patterns Styles of play Fantasy Drawing Tempo Loudness Size Pitch	A5. Awareness of sex-typed symbols or styles.	B5. Self-perception of nonverbal, stylistic characteristics.	C5. Preference for stylistic or symbolic objects or personal characteristics *or* attitudes about others' nonverbal and language patterns.	D5. Manifesting sex-typed verbal and nonverbal behavior, fantasy, drawing patterns.

demonstrated only in the extreme case of surgical gender change—not a frequent occurrence among children—but adopting sex-typed clothing, hairstyles, and makeup also fall in Cell D1. In the other content areas, enactment is defined as a behavioral manifestation of the relevant characteristics (D2 through D5). In the final content category (D5), symbol and style, examples include gestural patterns such as "limp wrist," "arm flutters," and "flexed elbow while walking" (Rekers, Amaro-Plotkin, & Low, 1977), speech patterns (Haas, 1979), fantasy styles (Cramer & Hogan, 1975), and stylistic features of children's drawings, for example, rounded versus angular lines (Franck Drawing Completion Test; Franck & Rosen, 1949). In practice, operational definitions of preference and enactment often overlap, particularly in studies of very young children. For example, measures titled "sex role preference" are sometimes based on children's behavioral choices in a free play setting and sometimes on their

choices among pictured toys. Although it may be justified to assume that a behavior reflects a preference, the two are not necessarily congruent. Therefore, they are maintained as separate constructs in this discussion.

The matrix in Table 1 can be useful for organizing the following discussion and for clarifying conflicting arguments or findings in the literature. In many instances, different conclusions or findings may result from the fact that different constructs or content areas are being studied. A second purpose of the matrix is to focus attention on those components of sex-typing that have been neglected in the literature. For example, nonverbal stylistic attributes may be important social cues about gender, but they are generally ignored in the literature. A man who has a high, nasal voice and "prissy" gestures may encounter considerably more social stigma than one who likes to cook or one who is nurturant. Another purpose served by this classification system is its identification of instances where studies or measures contain a mixture of constructs and content areas or where theorists are attempting to generalize from one part of the matrix to another. Finally, Table 1 suggests an orderly progression in the effort to investigate dimensions of sex-typing. Relations among items within a cell might logically come first, then relations across rows or columns, and finally relations among cells that fall in different rows and columns.

Bipolarity

Within any of the construct-content domains defined in Table 1, masculinity and femininity may be defined as the opposite poles of one dimension or as two separate, independent dimensions. Early conceptions of sex-typing generally assumed bipolarity, but that assumption has been repeatedly challenged in recent years (Bem, 1974; Block, 1973; Constantinople, 1973). Certain aspects of sex-typing, particularly gender identity, are by definition bipolar, but many others are not.

Interests and Activities

Logically, interests and activities associated with masculinity do not preclude those associated with femininity. An interest in sewing or in poetry does not prevent an interest in football or science. Until recently, however, bipolarity was assumed in the construction of most measures, so that assumption could not be tested. In the few studies of children where preferences for masculine and feminine activities have been assessed separately, the two have been independent of one another (Hall & Halberstadt, 1980; Simms, Davis, Foushee, Holahan, Spence, & Helmreich, 1978; Stein, 1971; Stein, Pohly, & Mueller, 1971, Sutton-Smith, 1965). Hence, there is no basis for assuming that masculine and feminine interests and activities are bipolar opposites.

Personal-Social Attributes—Self-Perception

In the mid-1970s, the assumption of bipolarity received its most serious challenge from psychologists who demonstrated that masculine and feminine personality attributes constituted at least two independent dimensions. Empirical demonstration of independence was made possible by the development of several new instruments; the two most widely used are the Bem Sex Role Inventory or BSRI (Bem, 1974) and the Personal Attributes Questionnaire or PAQ (Spence, Helmreich, & Stapp, 1975).

Although there were differences in the processes by which the two tests were constructed, both began with sets of adjectives that were considered sex-stereotyped by samples of college students or adults. Because earlier studies of sex-stereotypes (Broverman, Broverman, Clarkson, Rosenkrantz, & Vogel, 1970) indicated that masculine attributes were more likely than feminine attributes to be socially desirable, both the BSRI and the PAQ were initially intended to be limited to socially desirable characteristics. Recent analyses (Locksley & Colten, 1979; Pedhazur & Tetenbaum, 1979) have raised questions about the desirability of some feminine adjectives on the BSRI, but the conceptual objective was to sample adaptive characteristics associated with both gender stereotypes. The BSRI and PAQ correlate highly with each other. In large samples, the correlations of the two masculine scales were .75 and .73 for males and females, respectively, and of the two feminine scales, .57 and .59 (Spence & Helmreich, 1978).

The data for adults and children alike fail to support the bipolar assumption (Bem, 1974, 1977; Hall & Halberstadt, 1980; Spence & Helmreich, 1978). Correlations between the masculine and feminine scales for the BSRI, the PAQ, and the Children's PAQ are universally low and sometimes positive for samples ranging from third grade through college. That is, when masculinity and femininity are independently defined, they do not in any sense preclude one another.

Spence and Helmreich (1978) did argue for a different kind of bipolarity on the basis of a third scale, the *Mf* scale, included in the original PAQ. In order to understand their argument, further explanation of the instrument and its construction is necessary. All items on the PAQ are bipolar Semantic Differential adjective pairs, but each pair is included on only one scale. Items were selected on the basis of ratings for the ideal and typical man and woman on these adjective pairs. The masculine and feminine scales consist of adjectives on which the ideal for both sexes was above the midpoint of the scale (i.e., the attribute was desirable for both), but the rating for one gender was significantly higher than for the other. The *Mf* scale consists of items for which the rating for the ideal male was above the midpoint and for the ideal female was below the midpoint—hence, it was an attribute considered desirable for one gender, but not the other. Spence and Helmreich (1978) argue that the *Mf* scale is bipolar, but they mean simply that the socially desirable attributes for males and females fall at different ends of the continuum. They do not mean that two independently defined attributes are negatively correlated.

The original BSRI and PAQ were restricted to socially desirable characteristics in order to avoid confounding masculinity and femininity with social desirability. In order to gain a more complete picture of sex-typing, the Texas research team (Helmreich, Spence, & Wilhelm, 1981; Spence, Helmreich, & Holahan, 1979) recently constructed parallel scales of socially *un*desirable masculine and feminine attributes. They appear in the lower half of Table 2. The feminine adjectives formed two scales: weakness (negative communality) and verbal aggression. Again, there is no evidence for bipolarity among college students. The "negative" scales had very low associations with one another except that the masculine scale was positively related to the feminine verbal aggression scale ($rs = .40$ and .45; see Spence et al., 1979).

The adjectives on the six scales of the adult and adolescent PAQ appear in Table 2, arranged so that social desirability forms a vertical axis and masculinity-femininity forms a horizontal axis. The intercorrelations among the six scales suggest some bipolarity when both sex-typing and social desirability are taken into account. For both males and females, the desirable feminine scale ($F+$) was negatively related to the undesirable masculine scale ($M-$) (correlations ranging from $-.33$ to $-.47$). The undesirable feminine scales, particularly extreme self-negation ($Fc-$), were negatively correlated with the desirable masculine scale (correlations ranging from $-.28$ to $-.38$). It appears that the negative aspects of masculinity are associated with low levels of positive expressive personality attributes, and the negative components of femininity, particularly self-negation, are associated with low levels of positive instrumental characteristics.

Enactment of Sex-Typed Behavior

Parallel patterns appear in many observational studies of preschool children. Behaviors such as aggression, sympathy, helpfulness, and independence are uncorrelated or positively correlated with one another (Friedrich-Cofer, Huston-Stein, Kipnis, Susman, & Clewett, 1979; Stein & Friedrich, 1972; Wright, 1960). Moreover, circumplex models derived from behavior ratings of children bear a striking similarity to the fourfold table generated from the self-ratings on the PAQ. In Figure 1, an amalgam

---

Table 2. **Adjectives on the Personal Attributes Questionnaire (PAQ)**

Mf	*MASC +*	*FEM +*
Aggressive	Independent*	Emotional
Dominant	Active	Able to devote self completely to others*
Not excitable in major crisis	Competitive*	
Worldly	Can make decisions easily*	Gentle*
Indifferent to approval	Never gives up easily*	Helpful*
Feelings not easily hurt*	Self-confident*	Kind*
Never cries*	Feels superior*	Aware of others' feelings*
Little need for security.*	Stands up well under pressure	Understanding of others
		Warm to others
	MASC −	*FEM C −*
	Egotistical	Servile
	Arrogant	Spineless
	Boastful	Gullible
	Greedy	Subordinates self to others
	Dictatorial	*FEM VA −*
	Hostile	
	Cynical	Whiny
	Unprincipled	Complaining
		Nagging
		Fussy

*On child PAQ.
+ = Socially Desirable.
− = Socially Undesirable.
FEM C − = Negative Communality.
FEM VA − = Verbal Aggression.

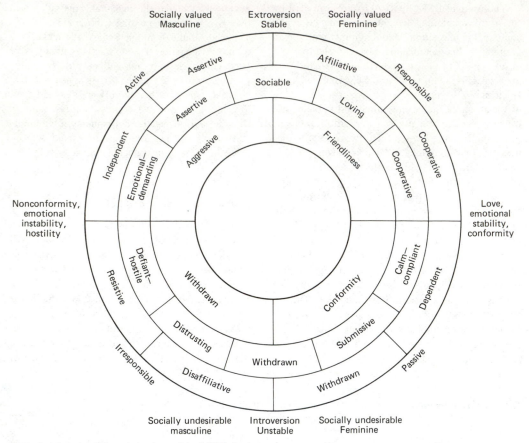

Figure 1. Adaptation of three circumplex models of child behavior from Maccoby and Masters (1970, p. 119) to illustrate parallels with masculine and feminine personal-social behaviors.

of three circumplex models is adapted from Maccoby and Masters (1970, p. 119). All are based on adult ratings of children's behavior using bipolar adjectives or Q-sort procedures (Baumrind, 1973; Baumrind & Black, 1967; Becker & Krug, 1964; Schaefer, 1961). One could relabel the two major axes as social desirability (vertical) and masculine-feminine (horizontal) without doing a great deal of violence to those concepts. The correspondence between the adjectives falling in the four quadrants and those in the four quadrants of Table 2 is striking. Characteristics in the upper right quadrant are positive expressive behavior—helpfulness, cooperation, caring about others, friendliness; those in the upper left quadrant are positively valued instrumental behaviors, such as assertiveness and independence. Behaviors in the lower left quadrant correspond to the negative communal feminine adjectives on the PAQ—submissiveness and conformity to others.

Those in the lower left quadrant partially correspond to the negative masculine PAQ characteristics—resistive, unruly, and the like.

In short, self-ratings by adults and children, behavior observations of young children, and adult ratings of children, all demonstrate the multidimensional character of sex-typed personal-social characteristics. The issue of bipolarity is a special case of multidimensionality. Socially valued aspects of masculinity and femininity are not polar opposites; they are independent dimensions. Socially undesirable aspects of masculinity and femininity are also fairly independent of one another. However, there is some evidence of bipolarity between socially valued masculine qualities and socially undesirable feminine characteristics, on the one hand, and between socially valued feminine attributes and socially undesirable masculine characteristics, on the other.

Androgyny

As the old views and assumptions were discarded, a new concept, *androgyny*, representing an amalgam of masculinity and femininity, arose almost simultaneously in several different theoretical camps (Bem, 1974; Block, 1973; Rebecca, Hefner, & Oleshansky, 1976; Spence et al., 1975). The concept of androgyny swept the field like a fire on a dry prairie, probably because earlier conceptions had become sterile, and also because the Women's Movement had led many investigators to reject the values that were implicit in theories that assumed that males and females should develop as polar opposites or at least with complementary attributes. There were a variety of conceptual definitions, which will be elaborated in the next section, but two basic operational definitions. Bem (1974) originally classified individuals as androgynous when their scores were similar on the two scales, regardless of whether the scores were high or low. She later argued (Bem, 1981) that this procedure was based on the assumption that an androgynous person is one for whom masculinity and femininity are relatively unimportant in behavioral decisions. In contrast, Spence et al. (1975) argued that androgyny should be defined by high scores on both masculine and feminine scales; those with low scores were classified as undifferentiated. By this definition, then, androgyny is the presence of particular personality traits. Most subsequent research has followed this pattern.

Returning to Table 2, one is left with the slightly uncomfortable feeling that the second definition of androgyny reduces to social desirability. The androgynous person has socially desirable traits, regardless of their sex-typed connotations. Yet, far from suggesting that androgyny is a trivial construct, this conclusion supports Bem's (1975) original argument that *both* masculine and feminine attributes are healthy and adaptive for *both* males and females. One of the crucial contributions of this research to social application has been to permit parents, educators, and psychologists to separate those sex-typed characteristics that are psychologically adaptive and socially valued from those that are not, rather than assuming, as is still often the case, that all feminine attributes are healthy for females and all masculine attributes are healthy for males.

Measurement Issues

Many measures of sex-typing have been based on erroneous assumptions of unidimensionality or bipolarity. Beere (1979) has recently reviewed measures for both children and adults. Out of 30 measures designed for children, 25 were scored in a bipolar way. In addition, the great majority of them were toy preference measures. Although it is probably desirable to restrict the content of a measure to one domain, or at least to assess domains separately, these measures are often assumed to represent all aspects of sex-typing. Very few studies in the literature use multiple measures, a practice that is needed to deal with the multidimensionality of sex-typing. Measures that are bipolar or unidimensional can misclassify people with mixtures of patterns. For example, subjects who were androgynous or undifferentiated on the BSRI or PAQ scored somewhere between masculine and feminine subjects when they were given the MMPI and the CPI (Betz & Bander, 1980).

Many measures have inadequate reliability and validity information (see Beere, 1979). In particular, very few measures have evidence of test-retest reliability, an issue of considerable importance when assessing young children. Validity is most often demonstrated by showing that the sexes differ. While absence of such differences might raise questions about validity, the mere presence of sex differences is not sufficient. More recent measures have used social stereotypes or ratings of ideal males and females as criteria for test construction, but some investigators have argued that social stereotypes do not correspond to the organization of either personality characteristics or behavior (Locksley & Colten, 1979).

Still another problem concerns how one obtains an honest answer from a person rather than one that is socially acceptable. Projective techniques, such as asking the child to answer for IT (a supposedly neuter child), were popular in earlier measures (e.g., Brown, 1956). Several methodological studies suggested, however, that some children perceived IT as a boy and answered accordingly (Hartup & Zook, 1960; Lansky & McKay, 1963). In any case, the projective assumption was difficult to verify. The IT scale also demonstrates the problem of historical and social change. Items and pictures become obsolete over time, making comparisons difficult.

Overview of Chapter

With the organizational framework and the methodological cautions described above, I will now discuss the state of developmental research on sex-typing. Current theories are described first; then data on developmental patterns and correlates of various dimensions of sex-typing are presented. Where possible, data are organized to address theoretical issues, but empirical work in this field is often atheoretical or only loosely guided by specific theoretical questions. In the subsequent sections, possible antecedents or influences on sex-typing are examined—first biological variables, then socialization by observational learning (including mass media), parental treatment, sibling interactions, school and peer experiences. Finally, some more general comments on future directions for research and ethical problems involved in social application are discussed.

THEORIES

Two major theoretical traditions form the basis for most of the research conducted in the past 10 years: social learning theory and cognitive developmental theory. Even though the two theories have grown closer over time, they do have fundamentally different roots somewhat like two trees growing on opposite sides of a road and having their branches reach across to meet one another. Social learning theories are based primarily on a mechanistic model (Reese & Overton, 1970). Some include cognitive processes as mechanisms for organizing information and guiding behavior, but the origins of those processes and the means of changing them are generally conceptualized in learning theory terms. Cognitive developmental theories are based primarily on an organismic model (Reese & Overton, 1970). Not only are cognitive processes viewed as active and constructive, but ongoing processes of change within the organism are emphasized. A new hybrid set of theories are based on information-processing constructs that emphasize schemas as cognitive mechanisms for organizing, transforming, and constructing the child's world. Although schemas in this theoretical tradition are constructive and active, these theories differ from cognitive developmental approaches in that they do not emphasize developmental processes as the source of schemas or as the means of changing them.

Social Learning Theory

An extensive statement of social learning theory was presented by Mischel (1970) in the last edition of this Handbook. In that theory, sex-typing is defined primarily by sex differences in behavior (i.e., by *enactment* in the matrix of Table 1). Sex-typed behavior has no special theoretical status; it is learned by the same mechanisms that apply to all kinds of social behavior. Behavior is sex-typed by

virtue of the fact that reinforcement contingencies are dependent on the sex of the responder; that is, girls and boys are reinforced or punished for different kinds of behavior, or male and female models regularly display different kinds of behavior. These two basic learning processes, operant conditioning and observational learning, form the core of virtually all social learning explanations of sex-typing.

One major tenet of the social learning approach is the situation specificity of behavior. Mischel (1968, 1970) has argued cogently that many social behaviors that are sex-typed, such as aggression, dependence, and independence, are not consistent in all situations. Children learn these behaviors as responses to particular stimulus situations; for example, a child may be very aggressive toward a younger sibling at home, but show little aggression in nursery school. This position implies that one should not assume that children acquire global attributes of masculinity or femininity that have cross-situational generality. To the degree that sex-typing occurs, boys probably acquire "masculine" behavior patterns *in more situations* than girls do, and vice versa. The assumption of situation specificity does not imply absence of regularity in behavior. Unless new learning conditions arise, a child should be consistent from one occasion to the next in a particular situation. What it does imply is that the same child may show quite different patterns of behavior in different situations, and that behavior patterns can change within situations fairly rapidly if contingencies of reinforcement or other learning conditions are altered.

Cognitive Social Learning

The social learning theory described thus far is the fundamental behaviorism accepted by a wide range of researchers in the broad camp that resides under that title. Within the camp, however, are divisions about how much one needs to employ additional constructs representing the internal mental processes that mediate learning and behavior. Bandura (1977) and Mischel (1973, 1977, 1979) have both formed cognitive social learning theories in which internal mental processes play an important role. Both proposed that when children experience response consequences, they form *expectancies* about the likely consequences in the future. Reinforcement and punishment do not have an automatic effect on a response, but their effects occur through the establishment of expectancies, which in turn guide future response choices. A reinforcer may influence behavior primarily because it conveys information (e.g., your answer to the math problem was right or wrong), or because it is an incentive (as when the child works to get adult praise (see Bandura, 1977).

Observational learning is also affected by cognitive processes at the level of both attention and retention of observed behavior. In Bandura's formulation, when a child is exposed to a model, there are four component processes that influence the outcome of that observation: attention, retention, motoric reproduction, and motivational variables. *Attention* is influenced by a variety of motivational variables and expectancies generated from previous experience. For purposes of this discussion, the most pertinent of these variables are the sex of the model and the sex of the child. The theory predicts that children will attend more closely to same-sex models than to other-sex models, primarily because of previous reinforcement for imitating same-sex people. *Retention* of the model's behavior occurs through symbolic coding or representation. The form in which the model's behavior is coded depends on the child's level of cognitive development and on already existing mental constructs. As a result, the child may fail to retain aspects of the model's behavior that do not fit preexisting concepts or that are difficult to encode. These retention processes act to *select* some modeled behaviors for retention while dropping others, but the theory does not predict transformations or reorganizations of those behaviors in memory as clearly as do cognitive developmental theories. Once the modeled behavior is stored in memory, imitation depends on the child's capacity for *motor reproduction* and on the child's motivation to reproduce the behavior. *Motivation*, in turn, is a function of both vicarious and direct reinforcement, that is, of the child's expectancies about reinforcement consequences for imitating behavior. Similarity to the model (e.g., same sex) makes it likely that the child will imitate, except when the model is punished, because the child will expect similar consequences to those received by the model.

In *summary*, both the radical behaviorist and cognitive social learning theorist conceptualize sex-typing as a set of *behavioral* responses; cognitions and stereotypes are secondary if they are discussed at all. Social definitions of ''masculine'' and ''feminine'' behavior are conveyed to the child through different patterns of reinforcement and punishment and through different patterns of behavior by male and female models. The bases of sex-typing are in the social environment, not the organism, and changes can occur relatively rapidly if learning conditions are altered.

Cognitive and Developmental Theories

Cognitive developmental theories generally define the core of sex-typing as the child's *concepts* about masculinity, femininity, sex-appropriate behavior and the like, rather than the child's sex-typed *behavior*. Behavior is secondary to thought, whereas the reverse priority occurs in learning theories. The child's concepts or schemas about sex-typing are viewed as organizing rubrics that not only lead to selection of information from the environment, but to active organization, construction, and transformation of that input to fit the schemas. Developmental changes in sex-typing are thought to parallel more general developmental changes in cognitive processes or personality functioning. To the degree that such developmental changes are inherent in the organism, the changes in sex-typing are also governed by maturational, internal variables in interaction with the social environment. Therefore, these theories generally posit organismic as well as environmental antecedents of sex-typing, and most of them suggest some limits on the degree or speed with which sex-typing can be changed.

Kohlberg's Theory

Cognitive developmental theory was first applied to sex-typing by Kohlberg (1966). He proposed that the basis for sex-typing is the child's cognitive organization of the social world in a manner that parallels the cognitive organization of the physical world. The first step in this organization is *gender identity*, a self-categorization as boy or girl, which then serves as an organizer of incoming information and attitudes. Gender identity arises from a judgment of physical reality that males are different from females. The genital difference between the sexes, stressed in psychoanalytic theory, is not, however, the primary basis for the young child's discrimination of gender. Differences in physical size, hairstyle, and clothing are much more apparent to young children than genital differences. As these cues distinguish adult males and females more clearly than they do children, the theory implies that the initial concept of gender may be formed by classifying adults, then assimilating children into the classes of male and female on the basis of verbal labels.

Kohlberg proposed that gender identity, or the correct labeling of the child's own gender, is acquired by about age 3, but that the development of a complete concept of gender as a constant, unchanging attribute occurs gradually between ages 2 and 7. As the child's thinking about the physical world progresses into concrete operations, so does the understanding of social categories such as gender. *Gender constancy* consists of understanding that gender cannot change over time (stability), that gender is not altered by transformations of observable characteristics such as clothing, activities, or hairstyle (consistency), and that gender is not altered by wishing. That is, the young child first forms gender classes on the basis of criteria that are irrelevant correlates of gender. Over time, she or he must learn to discount those correlated attributes—hairstyle, clothing, and activities—as definitions of gender. This process involves understanding that certain properties of people are unchanging despite perceptual evidence to the contrary—a parallel to understanding identity in conservation of physical substances.

As gender becomes a stable, significant organizer of social information, children learn societal sex stereotypes by observing the actions and social roles of males and females around them. Parents can serve as examples of masculine and feminine behavior, but they do not have primary importance. Children will gather information from mutliple sources and form a concept that represents the modal and predominant pattern rather than the pattern manifested by any particular person. Hence, children in one culture are likely to acquire the social stereotypes that are shared in that culture. The concepts formed by children will depend on what they observe, but idiosyncratic sex role concepts are less likely than would be expected from theories that emphasize the nuclear family as the primary source of sex-typing.

Kohlberg's predictions about developmental changes in children's thinking about sex stereotypes have often been misinterpreted. The theory does not predict a linear or monotonic increase in stereotyped thought throughout development, but instead a curvilinear pattern. Stereotypes are expected to be increasingly rigid during the period of 2 to 7 years, when gender constancy is developing. However, once concrete operational thinking is established and the child understands clearly that gender is not altered by superficial changes, adherence to sex stereotypes and rigidity of stereotypes are likely to be *reduced*. When children realize that superficial attributes such as clothing and activities are not essential to gender, then they also understand that a departure from stereotypes can occur without alteration of basic gender. Furthermore, concrete operational thinking should permit more ready understanding of the possibility that males and females can share attributes. Therefore, the theory predicts that sex stereotypes will increase during the period between 2 and 7 years, in association with the development of gender constancy. After age 7, the child may continue to acquire information about social stereotypes, but will recognize that they are flexible, nonuniversal, and subject to change. Some fluctuations in rigidity and flexibility during later childhood and adolescence were suggested in an expansion of the theory based on interviews with children from 6 through 18. By age 8, children understood that social roles and behavior were not necessitated by physical differences between the sexes, but 10-year-olds believed that masculine and feminine roles were inherent and necessary for the social system. Twelve-year-olds understood that such roles were arbitrary, but young adolescents argued the necessity of sex roles for psychological functioning in a marriage and family. Older adolescents viewed sex-typed traits as independent of necessary qualities for psychological adaptation (Kohlberg & Ullian, 1974; Ullian, 1976).

Given cognitive stereotypes, why should the child adopt sex-typed characteristics? Kohlberg argued that the basic motives to acquire sex-typed attributes are effectance motives—the need for self-consistency and for self-esteem. Five interrelated mechanisms were proposed as the means by which sex role concepts lead to positive values and attitudes about sex-appropriate characteristics. (1) The tendency to schematize interests and respond to new interests that are consistent with old ones. (2) The tendency to make value judgments that are consistent with a self-enhancing identity, that is, to value things and people that are similar to oneself. (3) The tendency for values of prestige, competence, or goodness to be associated with sex stereotypes. (4) The tendency to view conformity to one's own role as moral, as part of a conformity to the general sociomoral order, at least until the individual reaches postconventional and relativistic moral thinking. (5) The tendency to imitate people who are valued because of prestige, competence, or similarity to the self. Although these mechanisms are congruent for males in that all should lead to valuing masculine attributes, they are contradictory for females. The feminine role has less prestige and competence associated with it than the masculine role. Nevertheless, Kohlberg thought that the female role had sufficient positive value that girls' competence striving would be channeled into feminine role values.

Block's Theory

Block (1973) proposed a developmental sequence in the acquisition of sex role identity based on Loevinger's (1976) stages of ego development. In her discussion, masculinity and femininity are defined as manifestations of two components of personality, agency and communion (Bakan, 1966). *Agency* is the tendency to be individualistic, self-assertive, and self-expansive. *Communion* is the tendency to focus on harmony with the group, to suppress self-interest in favor of group welfare, to cooperate, and to seek group consensus. In Block's view, very young children of both sexes are primarily agentic; they are primarily concerned with assertion, extension of self, and independence from parental restriction. The next stage is one in which conformity to rules and roles becomes important for both sexes. During this period, there is a critical bifurcation of sex roles because of different socialization pressures on boys and girls. Boys are encouraged to control and suppress tender feelings; girls are encouraged to suppress assertiveness and aggression. Next, children reach a level where introspection and self-consciousness are possible. For the most part, it is a period when sex roles are maintained, though they may be modulated. In the last two stages, presumably occurring for most people in adulthood, the person becomes autonomous and self-aware, and polarities are resolved with the result that masculine and feminine elements of the self are integrated. This state of integration is defined as *androgyny*.

In this theory, as in most other cognitive developmental theories, the *content* of sex roles is determined by the child's cultural and social environment. However, maturational variables play a role in the *structure* of thought about sex-typed content. That is, the level at which the individual responds to the cultural messages and socialization pressures about sex-typing is a function of overall ego development that is, in turn, partially determined by maturational, developmental processes. Like Kohlberg's theory, however, Block's position implies that quite different patterns of sex-typed content might emerge if the child were exposed to different cultural definitions and socialization practices, and cross-cultural data are presented to support this prediction (Block, 1973).

Models Based on Stages of Moral Development

Somewhat parallel changes are predicted in a three-phase model described by Pleck (1975) and elaborated by Rebecca et al. (1976). This model is derived from the three broad phases of moral judgment proposed by Kohlberg: the premoral phase in which moral thinking is dominated by concerns about external reward and punishment; the conventional role conformity phase in which morality is defined by conformity to socially prescribed rules

and norms; and a postconventional phase in which moral judgments are made on the basis of self-accepted moral principles. The parallel model for sex-typing consists of an initial phase of undifferentiated sex roles in which the child begins to learn about cultural expectations for boys and girls. In the second phase, sex roles are polarized, and children come to believe that masculinity and femininity are mutually exclusive. The third phase is described as sex role transcendence, a period in which individual values, choices, and concerns take priority over socially prescribed rules and roles. This third phase is called *androgyny* by Rebecca et al. (1976), but they emphasize that their meaning is different from others' definition of that term. Sex role transcendence is a phase in which gender-related prescriptions become irrelevant; the person makes choices on grounds other than gender. In that sense, it is closest to Bem's (1979, 1981) concept of androgyny as low gender salience and distinct from Spence and Helmreich's (1978) view of androgyny as a set of personality traits or Block's (1973) view of androgyny as an integration of personality traits.

Similarities Among Cognitive Developmental Theories

All these theories posit a curvilinear pattern of adherence to socially defined sex roles and sex-typed expectancies. In each theory, the child moves from a disorganized, undifferentiated initial state into a pattern of conformity to socially imposed values about sex-typing, and then to flexibility, individually based choices, integration of masculine and feminine elements, or androgyny. This curvilinearity was posited in Kohlberg's (1966) initial discussion, before most investigators considered sex-typing a negative outcome, though it has been expanded in recent developmental theories.

Information Processing—Schema Theories

Two models of sex-typing based on information-processing models have been recently proposed, one by Bem (1981) and one by Martin and Halverson (1981). The primary construct used is the *schema*, a cognitive structure consisting of a set of expectations or a network of associations that guide and organize an individual's perception. A schema functions as an anticipatory structure that leads the individual to search for certain information or to be ready to receive information consistent with the schema. Perceptual information that is inconsistent with the schema may be ignored or transformed.

Martin and Halverson (1981) suggest that sex

stereotypes serve as schemas to organize and structure social information. Of all the possible schemas that children might learn, sex stereotypes are heavily used because they relate to the self and because they are salient in the child's environment. Sex stereotypes function at two levels: The child evaluates incoming information as "appropriate or inappropriate for me"; that is, as "appropriate or inappropriate for my gender." At this level, then, schemas for both masculine and feminine stereotypes are formed rather than simply a schema for one's own gender. The second level occurs when an environmental stimulus is judged appropriate for the self. The child explores it further, searches out information about it, and the like. Therefore, schemas about gender-appropriate areas should be more elaborated than those about inappropriate areas. For example, a girl would know that football is for boys and sewing is for girls, but she would have considerably more information about sewing than about football.

Bem (1979, 1981) also proposes that gender-based schemas are important organizers of information. Her thesis, however, is that there are individual differences in the salience or functional importance of gender-related schemas. For highly sex-typed people, gender is a dominant schema applied to many situations in everyday life. The threshold for organizing social information according to gender-related concepts is low. For those who are androgynous, gender-related schemas are present and well-ingrained, but they are less dominant in the individual's overall set of social constructs. Other bases for classification and judgment are relatively more potent than is the case for sex-typed people. Hence, Bem argues that *androgyny is not a combination of masculine and feminine characteristics, but a relative freedom from gender-based judgments*. This, she says, was the original reason for using the difference between masculine and feminine scales as the basis for classifying people as androgynous; the assumption was that people who scored similarly on the two scales did not distinguish their own personality characteristics on the basis of cultural stereotypes of gender-appropriateness (Bem, 1979, 1981).

Although Bem has focused on individual differences in the salience of gender-based schemas, situations probably also differ in the degree to which they arouse such schemas. For example, 3-year-old girls who received a stereotype measure in which they were asked which toys were appropriate for boys and girls subsequently made sex-typed choices on a preference test. Those who received the preference measure first did not choose sex-typed toys (Blakemore, LaRue, & Olejnik, 1979). It appears that responding to the stereotype measure made the sex-typed aspects of the toys salient to these children.

A second implication of the theory is that masculine and feminine attributes and interests ought to be more closely related to one another for sex-typed individuals than for androgynous individuals. If gender is a more important organizing schema for sex-typed people than for androgynous people, then they should group gender-related attributes and behaviors together, whereas androgynous people should have other bases for classifying and organizing similar characteristics.

Although schema theories are similar to cognitive developmental theories in their focus on an active, constructive cognitive process, they differ to some degree in their proposals about the origins of gender-based schemas. Bem (1981) argues that the cultural emphasis on gender makes it a salient dimension; she disputes the cognitive developmental contention that gender is inherently salient because of physical sex differences. In a world where children were not divided by gender and gender was socially unimportant, gender-based schemas would also be relatively unimportant.

Feminist Psychoanalytic Theory

In classical Freudian theory, masculinity and femininity are acquired through a process of identification, which results from castration fear on the part of the male child and castration anxiety on the part of the female child. The Freudian formulations of female development, never very satisfactory, have undergone some radical changes among many psychoanalytic theorists during the past several years. In earlier psychoanalytic thinking, "penis envy" was emphasized as the dynamic that led female children to feel inferior to males, to desire a submissive role in relation to an active man, and to want to bear children (particularly male children) as a substitute for their missing organ.

Some psychoanalytic formulations have turned the tables to discuss envy of women—particularly breast envy and envy of childbearing capacity (Horney, 1932; Klein, 1957; Lerner, 1974, 1978). Lerner suggests that envy of women occurs partially because the young child lives in a psychological matriarchy where the mother is perceived as an all-powerful dispenser of gratifications and punishments. Her primary role in caretaking leads to positive forms of dependency and to the child's fear and anger about her power. The envy, fear, and anger resulting from the child's early feeling of powerlessness and helplessness lead to a devaluation of the mother in particular and women in general. In adulthood, males assure themselves of control in their relations with women, while maintaining the positive aspects of dependency by establishing a paternalistic relationship with a woman in which the male dominates. Women share in creating and "desiring" such relationships because they have accepted devaluation of their own gender. This early, dynamic basis for sex-differentiated adult roles can be reversed by shared caretaking of young children. If the father or other males shared caretaking, then they would receive some of the dependency and some of the fear and anger that is inevitable in adult-child interactions, and the resulting defensive devaluation would not be directed solely at women. This formulation suggests that it is not sufficient to have the mother share caregiving with other females (as is typical in most current day care programs); males must be important caregivers to produce a substantial change in societal views about male and female roles.

Social Structural Hypotheses

Sociological thinking about sex-typing is derived largely from Parsons' (1970) social structural hypotheses based on the instrumental-expressive dichotomy. Using these basic notions, Johnson (1963) proposed that the father plays a more important role than the mother in the sex-typing of both boys and girls. She proposed that fathers serve as models of instrumentality for their sons, but they also train their daughters in feminine expressiveness by playing the complementary instrumental part in interactions with them. This notion was elaborated (Johnson, 1975) by defining two major components of femininity, the maternal role and heterosexual behavior. The maternal role consists of nurturing, caretaking, and elements of expressiveness. Both boys and girls experience that role from their mothers in infancy, and both form an initial identification with the maternal role. The paternal role involves bringing to the child some of the norms and expectations of the outside world, Fathers differentiate between boys and girls more than mothers do. In so doing, they respond to their daughters' sexuality by being mildly seductive, or conveying in subtle ways the message that females are sexually attractive beings. Therefore, fathers influence girls' learning of the heterosexual aspects of femininity, but not their learning of the nurturant, maternal aspects of femininity.

Mothers do not play the same role in training heterosexuality in boys because the basic dependency and attachment relationship to the mother would be too threatened by introducing sexually tinged interactions. Because the affectional tie with the father is secondary (in time, not importance), there is less threat to the child's basic security when a sexual element is introduced. One manifestation of the father's view of the daughter as a sexual being is the pattern, particularly in traditional cultures, of guarding her "honor" and viewing the daughter's sexuality as "capital" to be exchanged. The theory is more specific for female than for male development. The father is thought to teach the boy both the "paternal role" (conceived as instrumental, male role expectations) and the heterosexual aspects of masculinity, but the mechanisms by which the boy shifts from his initial identification with the mother and is socialized by the father are not clearly spelled out.

Summary and Trends in Theories About Sex-Typing

The theories described here are very different from those that were influential 10 years ago. The old timer in the field will be struck by the absence of identification. Although imitation and observational learning are still viewed as important means of learning sex-typing, virtually all theorists have deemphasized parental identification. Parents are viewed as only one of many socializing influences. A related trend is the expansion of the age range considered important for the acquisition of sex-typing (or becoming free of it). The psychoanalytic emphasis on the first 5 years, with a brief recapitulation at puberty, has given way to the thinking that developmental changes occur at least into adulthood and often throughout the life span. One reason for the change has been the increased effort to understand processes by which people become free of gender-based definitions of "sex-appropriate behavior." Many theories are more concerned with androgyny, sex role transcendence, or departures from traditional sex-typing than they are with the acquisition of socially prescribed sex-typed behaviors and attitudes. Recent theories have also given more attention to female development than did earlier theories, a compensation for the fact that early theories often centered on male development or at least provided more complete and well-documented explanations of male sex-typing than of female development.

Perhaps the most striking contrast between current and past theory is the shift away from global, all-encompassing efforts to explain large domains of human behavior. Current theories tend to be specific to particular problems, groups, or issues; they often seem more like a set of hypotheses culled from empirical literature or observation rather than a system of constructs and propositions that form a coherent explanatory structure. Most scholars have been humbled by the difficulties in understanding even a slice of human social development; few are willing to venture the grand vision that will integrate and explain it all. Instead, the modal pattern seems to be an inductive process in which chunks of information and empirical data are gradually integrated; tentative explanations are constructed, tested, and sometimes rejected; and small parts of the puzzle are assembled a bit at a time.

DEVELOPMENTAL CHANGES AND CORRELATES OF SEX-TYPING

The burgeoning of cognitive developmental theory has led to an empirical concentration on developmental changes and on children's cognitions about sex-typing as an influence on self-perception, preference, and behavior. In this section, available data on the developmental course of various components of sex-typing are examined. Although monotonic increases with age are often apparent, there is some support for the curvilinear hypotheses suggested by cognitive developmental theory, particularly for increasing flexibility and departure from rigid sex-typing in middle childhood. The relationships among different components of sex-typing are examined with particular attention to whether cognitive constructs such as gender constancy and sex stereotypes predict self-perceptions and behavior.

Developmental Patterns

Children's Understanding of Gender

Between ages 2 and 3, most children learn to label themselves correctly as boys or girls, and they can classify themselves with others of the same gender (Slaby & Frey, 1975; Thompson, 1975). Measures of gender constancy, however, have three additional components: (1) Motives for change assessed by asking, "Could you be a _____ (other gender) if you wanted to?" (2) Stability of gender assessed by questioning what gender the child was at birth and will be as an adult, *and* whether the child ever has been or ever can be the other gender. (3) Consistency of gender assessed by asking whether the child or a stimulus figure is a boy or girl when hair, clothing, or play activities are changed from masculine to feminine or the reverse. Consistency questions are often accompanied by pictures on which transformations are demonstrated. Marcus and Overton (1978) argue that such pictures are essential for a true test of the child's understanding of constancy because the essence of concrete operational thinking is the ability to maintain a concept in the face of conflicting perceptual evidence. In one study, the pictured children were shown with genitals visible to assure that the test measured the child's knowledge that genitals rather than hair length or clothing were the critical criterion for defining gender (McConaghy, 1979). In spite of these differences, the results of most studies indicate that gender constancy follows a developmental sequence in which the child first understands that motives or wishes do not determine gender, then understands stability, and finally understands consistency of gender even with changes in appearance or activity (DeVries, 1969; Marcus & Overton, 1978; McConaghy, 1979; Slaby & Frey, 1975).

Children from 2 to 9 are included in these studies, and most report a monotonic increase in gender constancy with age. One set of investigators, however, has argued for a curvilinear developmental pattern beginning with "pseudo-constancy" around age 4. In large samples of urban children, 4- and 7-year-olds gave more correct answers to gender constancy questions than 5- and 6-year-olds, though the proportions of correct answers were low for all age groups. When the children were asked for explanations of their answers, the 7-year-olds more often gave justifications based on concrete operational reasoning whereas the 4-year-olds provided little relevant justification (Emmerich, 1981; Emmerich, Goldman, Kirsh, & Sharabany, 1977; Emmerich & Shepard, 1982).

Activities and Interests

Toys and Activities in Preschool Years. By age 3, American children know the sex stereotypes for toys, clothing, tools, household objects, games, and work. Studies of children between 24 and 36 months are inconsistent, suggesting this age period as the time in which such knowledge is initially acquired. Two-year-olds often respond at chance levels (Blakemore et al., 1979; Myers, Weinraub, & Shetler, 1979; Thompson, 1975; Weinraub & Leite, 1977) but, at age 2½, several investigations have shown better-than-chance responding (Kuhn, Nash, & Brucken, 1978; Meyers et al., 1979; Thompson, 1975; Venar & Snyder, 1966). Children age 3 and older know sex stereotypes well (Blakemore et al., 1979; Carter & Patterson, 1979; Edelbrock & Sugawara, 1978; Faulkender, 1980; Flerx, Fidler, & Rogers, 1976; Kuhn et al., 1978; Marantz & Mansfield, 1977; Masters & Wilkinson, 1976; Nadelman, 1970, 1974; Schau, Kahn, Diepold, & Cherry, 1980; Thompson, 1975). Preschool and elementary school children also know the more obvious sex-typed adult occupations (Garrett, Ein, & Tremaine, 1977; Kleinke & Nicholson, 1979; Marantz & Mansfield, 1977; Nemerowicz, 1979; Papalia & Tennent, 1975; Thornburg & Weeks, 1975). The literature on sex stereotypes of children and adults is reviewed in depth by Ruble and Ruble (1980).

Parallel patterns appear in children's toy and game preferences and in their behavioral choices. Sex-typed toy choices appear very early in life—often by age 2 and certainly by age 3. Even children between 1½ and 2 often select and play with same-sex stereotyped toys more than toys typed for the other gender. These patterns have been found in home observations (Fagot, 1974), laboratory settings (Fein, Johnson, Kosson, Stork, & Wasserman, 1975; Weinraub & Leite, 1977), and in free play in a school setting (O'Brien, 1980). By age 3, children show sex-typed toy choices in free play or laboratory observations consistently (Connor & Serbin, 1977; Maccoby & Jacklin, 1974) and they avoid playing with toys stereotyped for the other gender, even when there are few alternatives (Hartup, Moore, & Sager, 1963). Similar findings occur when toy preference is measured by presenting children with pictures of sex-typed toys and asking them to choose those they would like to play with (Beere, 1979; Blakemore et al., 1979; Edelbrock & Sugawara, 1978; Maccoby & Jacklin, 1974; Mischel, 1970). By age 4 or 5, children also have highly stereotyped occupational preferences and expectations—girls expect to be nurses, teachers, and secretaries; boys expect to have "masculine" occupations.

The reasons for these very early sex-typed toy preferences are not clear. Maccoby and Jacklin (1974) entertained and discarded the hypothesis that girls and boys are differentially attracted by toys with faces or by soft toys. In one study, masculine, feminine, and neutral toys were equated for number of pieces, moving parts, and size, but toddlers continued to play with same-sex toys (O'Brien, Huston, & Risley, 1981). However, the fact that behavioral patterns and preferences arise so early does raise questions about the hypothesis that cognitive stereotypes precede preferences and enactment. In later sections, we will see that adults socialize sex-typed toy and activity choices very early. Both behavior and stereotypes may be directly trained; or social stereotypes may result from behavioral differences as well as contributing to them.

Activities and Occupations in Middle Child-

hood and Adolescence. After about age 7, children's *awareness* of societal stereotypes continues to increase monotonically with age well into adolescence. That is, when they are asked whether activities, interests, or achievement areas are socially defined as masculine or feminine, older children's responses typically correspond to adult stereotypes more closely than those of younger children (e.g., Stein, 1971; Stein & Smithells, 1969). However, their *acceptance* of stereotypes as immutable, inflexible, or morally right appears to decline during the elementary and adolescent years. When items can be classified as equally appropriate for both sexes rather than forcing assignment to one or the other, late elementary school children evidence less stereotyped notions about adult occupations than early elementary aged children (Garrett et al., 1977; Kleinke & Nicholson, 1979; Marantz & Mansfield, 1977; Meyer, 1980; Nemerowicz, 1979). Junior and senior high school students also have less pronounced occupational stereotypes than elementary school children (Cummings & Taebel, 1980; Emmerich, 1979a). However, when asked about contemporary peer activities, older children do not express less stereotyped views than younger ones (Emmerich, 1979a; Kleinke & Nicholson, 1979). In one study, the patterns of increasing awareness and increasing flexibility were demonstrated jointly. Children from kindergarten to eighth grade were asked who usually engaged in an activity (stereotype knowledge). Then they were asked whether boys and/or girls *can* engage in an activity and whether there might be a country where this would be an activity only for the gender opposite the stereotype (stereotype flexibility). Older children knew the stereotypes more accurately, but they were also more aware of exceptions and understood better that sex-typed patterns are culturally relative (Carter & Patterson, in press).

Although there is the possibility of increasing cognitive flexibility in middle childhood and adolescence, boys' and girls' preferences follow different developmental paths, suggesting that the differential value attached to male and female roles influences children's preferences and adoption of those attributes that they consider sex-typed. Males show a monotonic age increase in preference for masculine activities, but girls do not. Girls' preference for feminine activities increases until age 5 or 6 (Blakemore et al., 1979; Hartup & Zook, 1960; Kohlberg & Zigler, 1967; Venar & Snyder, 1966), but during the elementary school years, girls often decline in their preference for feminine activities and become increasingly interested in masculine activities (Brown,

1956; Huesmann, Fischer, Eron, Mermelstein, Kaplan-Shain, & Morikawa, 1978; Huston-Stein & Higgins-Trenk, 1978; Kohlberg, 1966; Kohlberg & Zigler, 1967; Sutton-Smith, Rosenberg, & Morgan, 1963). Exceptions to this generalization have occasionally been found (DeLucia, 1963; Nadelman, 1974; Venar & Snyder, 1966) but it is clear that female children do not have the same attraction to sex-appropriate activities and interests that males do. Data are sparce for adolescents. In one study, ninth-grade girls endorsed some sex-appropriate interests more clearly than sixth graders, but did not differ on others (Stein, 1971). However, in Kohlberg and Zigler's (1967) reanalysis of the Terman longitudinal data, females' masculine interests increased between ages 14 and 20.

Achievement Areas. In the 1960s, many educators believed that one reason that more boys than girls performed poorly in school was that school was a feminine environment. Slight support for this notion was provided by studies of early elementary school children, showing that school-related objects were classified as feminine more often than masculine (Hill, Hubbs, & Verble, 1974; Kagan, 1964b). When different types of achievement were examined, however, children considered some as feminine and some as masculine. Studies of children from second through twelfth grades have demonstrated that athletic, spatial, and mechanical skills are viewed as masculine while verbal, artistic, and social skill are considered feminine. Math and science are not consistently stereotyped by elementary school children, but adolescents consider them masculine (Boswell, 1979; Emmerich 1979a; Fennema & Sherman, 1977; Kaczala, 1981; Stein, 1971; Stein & Smithells, 1969).

A more subtle form of stereotyping occurs in the attributions made about other people's abilities and the reasons for their success and failure. Rather consistently children view *success* in an activity stereotyped for the other sex as a result of unstable factors that could easily change, whereas failure in a sex-*in*appropriate activity is an indicator of deficiencies that are not easily altered. In addition, female failure, even in sex-appropriate activities, is viewed as an indicator of a long-term deficiency in ability. For example, in interviews with elementary school children who were asked why men and women did not perform work and activities stereotyped for the other sex, children thought men lacked skill in cooking and domestic activities primarily because they had not learned the skills (a remediable deficit), but they often said women lacked skill in masculine activities because they lacked physical strength or ability, deficiencies that cannot readily be changed (Nemerowicz, 1979).

Similar patterns appear in laboratory tasks; children attribute success on mechanical or other masculine tasks to ability for males and to effort for females. Failure at a mechanical task is attributed to lack of ability for females (Etaugh & Hadley, 1977; Etaugh & Rose, 1975), as is male failure on a sex-inappropriate task (Bond, 1979). This pattern does not appear, however, for athletic skill, perhaps because sports are less rigidly stereotyped than other skill areas measured (Bird & Williams, 1980; Etaugh & Rose, 1975). A more general stereotype of achievement as a masculine norm was suggested by the finding that children evaluated a male who failed on a masculine task very negatively; females who failed did not receive such negative evaluations (Hawkins & Pingree, 1978).

In real-world achievement situations, boys' and girls' expectancies of success, attainment values, minimum standards, and achievement effort are generally greater in domains stereotyped as appropriate for their gender than in "inappropriate" domains. Boys' attainment values and standards are higher than those of girls in masculine areas such as athletic and mechanical skills, and girls' values and standards are higher than boys' in feminine areas such as artistic, verbal, and social skills (Stein, 1971). These differences are most well-documented in "core" school subjects—language arts and math. Girls perceive math as more difficult than boys do and have lower expectancies of success even when their performance is objectively equivalent (Brush, 1979; Kaczala, Futterman, Meece, & Parsons, 1979). Perceived competence and value for math appear to be important mediators of sex differences in electing advanced math courses in high school (Brush, 1979; Kaczala et al., 1979; Sherman & Fennema, 1977; Steel & Wise, 1979). Adolescent females have higher expectancies of success and attainment values in English than their male counterparts (Kaczala, 1981), but these patterns must be placed in a context of sex differences in expectancy that cross most achievement areas.

Girls generally have lower expectancies of success, lower levels of aspiration, greater anxiety about failure, greater tendency to avoid risking failure, and greater acceptance of responsibility for failure than boys (Battle, 1966; Parsons, Ruble, Hodges, & Small, 1976; Stein & Bailey, 1973). These sex differences appear in some studies as early as age 4 (Crandall, 1978). Girls also tend to attribute failure to their lack of ability, and success to unstable causes such as effort; whereas boys more often attribute success to ability, and failure to effort or to external causes (Parsons, 1981; see also Dweck, vol. IV, chap. 8). Nevertheless, the patterns of expectancy, value, and course choice suggest that children are affected by the cultural stereotypes for achievement in different domains.

Sex differences in performance generally parallel social stereotypes. Maccoby and Jacklin (1974) concluded that there was consistent evidence supporting female superiority in verbal skills and male superiority in spatial and mathematical skills. The difference in verbal skills appears early in development, and differences in reading skill are evident from the beginning of the school years (Dwyer, 1973; Terman & Tyler, 1954). Sex differences in performance on mathematics do not appear until adolescence, and some recent studies have not found differences even then (Brush, 1979; Sherman & Fennema, 1977). Although Maccoby and Jacklin (1974) concluded that sex differences in spatial visualization did not emerge consistently until adolescence, some studies with large samples and good measures have found such differences in middle childhood (Harris, 1978; Richmond, 1980; Vandenberg & Kuse, 1979). Sex differences on tasks with visual-spatial components—field independence and Piagetian concepts of horizontality and verticality (Liben, 1978; Ray, Georgiou, & Ravizza, 1979; Thomas & Jamison, 1975)—have also been found in middle childhood. In the preschool years, however, a majority of studies have found girls performing better than boys on tests of field independence (Coates, 1974).

Although the direction of mean differences between the sexes is fairly consistent, the magnitude of the differences is very small. In the studies with large samples reviewed by Maccoby and Jacklin (1974), sex accounted for about 1 to 2% of the variance in reading performance and 4% of the variance in math performance (Plomin & Foch, 1981). Not only are the magnitudes of mean differences small, but the variability between studies, even when sample sizes are in the thousands, suggests that the patterns of sex differences may be different for different populations. Cross-cultural and cross-national comparisons also suggest considerable cultural variation in the patterns of sex differences in cognitive performance. In a comparison of six ethnic groups, Lesser, Fifer, and Clark (1965) found significant interactions between sex and ethnic group for both verbal and spatial tasks. More recently, a comparison of ninth-grade Hispanic, black, and white children demonstrated that Hispanic girls performed better than Hispanic boys on both spatial and mathematical

tasks; black adolescents showed a nonsignificant trend in the same direction; white males were slightly better performers than white females. No sex differences were found for any ethnic group in the third to fifth grades (Schratz, 1978). Other investigators have reported that Eskimo girls performed as well as, or better than, boys on spatial tasks, and that German and English boys typically perform better than girls on reading (Nash, 1979).

Personal-Social Attributes

Concepts and Stereotypes. Children acquire knowledge about sex-typed personal-social attributes later than they learn concepts about activities and interests. One reason may be that personal-social characteristics represent abstractions from behavior rather than concrete, observable activities and play behaviors. In most measures, children are presented with brief descriptions of behavior, such as "strong," "whiny," "emotional," that are sometimes accompanied by pictures but usually not, and they are asked whether that adjective is more typical of males or females. Hence, the child is asked to respond to an abstract, verbal label for behavior. Personal-social characteristics also carry with them a tag of social desirability or the stigma of undesirability. Because young children often manifest a same-sex bias (the tendency to classify positive attributes as appropriate for their own gender), the bias of social desirability can present serious assessment problems (Silvern, 1977). Nevertheless, by middle childhood, children share many adult stereotypes about personal-social behavior. Finally, sex differences in personal-social behavior are much less clear-cut than sex differences in activities and interests, so young children may not readily observe them.

In most studies, children under 5 showed little awareness of sex-typed personal-social characteristics (Baruch, no date; Etaugh & Riley, 1979; Flerx et al., 1976; Katz & Rank, 1981; Kuhn et al., 1978), but preschoolers in one study did think infant girls and boys differed on adjectives such as quiet/loud, fast/slow, or nice/mean (Haugh, Hoffman, & Cowen, 1980). Perhaps the latter study provided a more concrete judgment task for the child than most others have used. Five-year-olds in the United States and Europe display the beginnings of adult stereotypes about personality, but knowledge continues to increase throughout the elementary school years and perhaps during adolescence as well. Much of the information on children in middle childhood comes from a series of studies using the Sex Stereotype Questionnaire, a 32-item instrument in which masculine adjectives (e.g., strong, aggressive, boastful, dominant) and feminine adjectives (e.g., weak, appreciative, gentle, sentimental) are assigned by the child to a male or female stimulus figure (Best, Williams, Cloud, Davis, Robertson, Edwards, Giles, & Fowles, 1977). American 5-year-olds classified 61% of the items "correctly." The frequencies for children in other countries were similar. Eight-year-old Americans assigned 77% of the attributes as expected, and 11-year-olds had not quite reached the level of agreement shown by the college students on whom the measure was standardized (Best et al., 1977; Williams, Bennett, & Best, 1975; Williams, Best, Tilquin, Keller, Voss, Bjerke, & Baarda, 1979).

The Personal Attributes Questionnaire has been used to assess stereotypes by asking the subject to decide whether the behavior is more typical of males or females. Elementary school-age children (5+) know most of the expected stereotypes (Crandall, 1978; Greer, 1980; Sims et al., 1978). Children's perceptions of mother and father roles have also been measured on the assumption that the parents serve as prototypes of more general social roles. By age 6 or 7, children consider nurturance a maternal characteristic and competence, dominance, power, and punitiveness as paternal characteristics (Emmerich, 1961; Gold & St. Ange, 1974; Kagan, Hosken, & Watson, 1961; Nadelman, 1975).

The cognitive developmental prediction that both knowledge and flexibility should increase after age 7 is not as clearly supported for personal attributes as for activities and interests, but relevant evidence is scanty. When forced-choice techniques are used, there is a pattern of greater stereotyping the older the child during middle childhood and adolescence (Best et al., 1977; Greer, 1980; Tucker & Friedrich-Cofer, 1980; Urberg, 1979b). Stereotyping of attributes that are socially assigned to the other gender appears to increase with age more than stereotyping of attributes assigned to one's own gender, largely because of the same-sex bias of younger children. For example, Rothbaum (1977) found no age differences among 7- to 14-year-olds in girls' stereotyping of nurturance or boys' stereotyping of dominance. However, the older girls rated dominance more masculine than younger girls, and older boys rated nurturance more feminine than younger boys. Young children may begin by assuming that many attributes are appropriate for their own gender; what is learned during the elementary and adolescent years is what to exclude. The few studies that provide opportunities to assign traits to "both" males and females have produced conflicting results

(Gold, Brush, & Sprotzer, 1979; Marantz & Mansfield, 1977; Urberg, 1979b).

Self-perception.   Two available studies of age differences or age changes in self-perception both indicate that females' masculine self-perceptions *increase* with age. In a one-year longitudinal study of elementary age children, both boys' and girls' masculine self-perceptions increased over time; but girls' feminine scores declined (Hall & Halberstadt, 1980). Cross-sectional comparisons of early and late adolescents showed that same-sex preferences by late adolescents were lower than those of early adolescents (Leahy & Eiter, 1980). These trends parallel the findings on activities and interests—females become more masculine with age or over time.

Enactment.   A thorough discussion of children's behavioral enactment of sex-typed personality characteristics and social behavior could include the entire literature on sex differences, a task well beyond the scope of this chapter. In their comprehensive review of the literature on psychological sex differences, Maccoby and Jacklin (1974) concluded that there was clear evidence for sex differences in aggression (boys more prone than girls). There was tentative evidence that girls are often more anxious, timid, compliant to adults, and nurturant than boys, while boys are often more physically active, competitive, and dominant in their peer groups than girls. They asserted that there is no evidence for sex differences in sociability, suggestibility, conformity, self-esteem, or achievement motivation. Despite the encyclopedic scope of their work, Block (1976) criticized the book for excluding many relevant sources and for ignoring evidence of consistent patterns of sex differences. Many of the sex differences considered tentative by Maccoby and Jacklin are supported more firmly in the additional literature presented by Block. She suggests that one reason for Maccoby and Jacklin's negative conclusions may be that much of the literature involves preschool children. Many sex differences may appear gradually with age. Indeed, significant differences are more frequent for older children and adolescents than for very young children. From the other flank, Tieger (1980) challenged the one firm conclusion in favor of sex differences drawn by Maccoby and Jacklin—the difference in aggression. In particular, Tieger (1980) argued that the data do not support sex differences in aggression for children under 6. A rejoinder (Maccoby & Jacklin, 1980) presents extensive evidence that this difference is reliable.

For purposes of this review, it is not possible to settle the issues of whether and when significant sex differences in behavior appear. What is clear is that the sex-typing of personality characteristics and social behavior is less pronounced and appears later developmentally than the sex-typing of toy and activity choices. It is now possible to present a summary outline of some broad developmental patterns for different aspects of sex-typing during early and middle childhood.

Summary of Developmental Trends

Although some sex-typed learning probably takes place during the first 18 months of life, it is difficult to measure. The period from approximately 1½ to 3 years is one in which children begin to show pronounced sex-typing of play activities and interests. They select sex-typed activities in spontaneous play; they classify themselves and others according to gender; and they classify many of the concrete objects and activities around them according to culturally defined sex-appropriateness. By age 3, all of these trends are clearly and consistently evident, though children's knowledge of cultural stereotypes and their adherence to them continue to increase with age.

During the years between about 3 and 7, children gradually acquire an understanding of gender constancy and they increasingly prefer same-sex peers (Hartup, 1970; see also vol. IV, chap. 2). They begin to understand sex stereotypes about personal-social attributes, and some behavioral differences begin to appear. There is some tendency for an increasing preference for same-sex models and attachment figures during this period (Kohlberg & Zigler, 1967). Full gender constancy is almost the final event in this sequence.

The early learning of stereotypes and sex-typed behavior precedes even the rudimentary understanding of gender constancy. It appears that, for the young child who lacks an understanding of gender constancy, gender is an overgeneralized class that includes many correlated roles and activities. Between about 3 and 8, the child gradually refines that category and distinguishes those attributes that are critical for defining gender from those attributes that are correlated, but not critical to being female or male. At the same time, children are gaining a more detailed knowledge about cultural definitions of masculinity and femininity. The developmental pattern, then, is to gain an increasingly refined awareness of societal sex stereotypes, while also learning that most of the activities and behaviors prescribed by stereotypes are *not* crucial to being male or female.

Gender constancy does not precede conceptual knowledge about sex-typing—quite the reverse. In fact, a full understanding of gender constancy marks a turning point that permits (but does not guarantee) a decrease in rigidity and an increase in flexibility of children's concepts about sex-typing. During middle childhood, two divergent trends co-occur. On the one hand, a conceptual understanding of culturally defined expectations for males and females increases with age for all content areas. Boys also increasingly prefer and adopt behaviors and attitudes congruent with masculine sex-typing. On the other hand, both sexes become more flexible in their understanding of sex stereotypes; they recognize that such stereotypes are not absolute and that exceptions are possible. Furthermore, females *do not* increase their preference for feminine activities and interests during middle childhood. In fact, most studies suggest that girls shift toward preferring masculine activities and perceiving masculine personality traits in themselves during this period. These findings are not an outcome of the social changes of the 1970s; they appear in studies from the 1920s, 1950s, and 1960s as well.

Throughout childhood, play activities, social roles, and occupations are sex-typed more clearly than personality and social behaviors. It is surprising, therefore, that much of the psychological literature has focused on personal-social behaviors as the core of sex-typing. We will see later that parents and other socialization agents also stress sex-typed interests and activities more than they emphasize personal-social sex differences. Yet, sex-typing of play activities and the resulting segregation of peer groups have often been dismissed as obvious (and therefore uninteresting) while investigators searched for more subtle personality traits and social behaviors or their antecedents in the process of socialization. I do not mean to suggest that personal-social behaviors are unimportant, but that we have not paid enough attention to the most obvious, earliest, and most well-documented differences in expectations and experiences of young girls and boys.

Subgroup Patterns

Sex Differences. When sex differences are found, boys consistently hold more stereotyped views than girls (Emmerich, 1979a; Etaugh & Rose, 1975; Fennema & Sherman, 1977; Gold & Andres, 1978a, 1978b; Gold, Andres, & Glorieux, 1979; Nemerowicz, 1979). One reason for the absence of sex differences in some studies of younger children is the tendency for both sexes to assign positive attributes to their own gender and negative attributes to the other gender. Girls are particularly prone to rate negative characteristics as masculine (Baruch, no date; Parish & Bryant, 1978; Silvern, 1977; Zalk & Katz, 1978). Quite consistently, boys' choices are more extremely sex-typed than those of girls. This pattern occurs in both forced-choice tasks (where masculine and feminine choices are the only ones available) and in tasks where neutral toys or activities are available.

Cultural and Subcultural Differences. Cross-national comparisons for the United States, England, Ireland, Italy, West Germany, Norway, the Netherlands, and France have been carried out using adapted and translated versions of the Sex Stereotype Questionnaire (Best et al., 1977; Williams, Best, et al., 1979). Although there are some differences between children of different nations, the similarities are much more striking. In a comparison of all eight countries, the stereotype scores of the 5-year-old Americans were second only to the English; at age 8, the American children had higher scores than any other country. This pattern for 5-year-olds is consistent with Nadelman's (1974) report that American girls had less stereotyped views of activities than English children. These findings should, however, be interpreted cautiously because language differences can easily affect mean scores. More persuasive evidence of cross-cultural similarity arises from comparisons of the attributes stereotyped. For each pair of countries, the mean "scores" (percent of stereotyped responses) for each of the 32 adjectives were intercorrelated. The correlations among items for American, English, and Irish were high—all above .64. That is, children in all three countries agreed on which items were most and least clearly stereotyped. Correlations for the western European countries were lower, particularly for 5-year-olds. Among the 8-year-olds, the correlations ranged from .25 to .88, indicating some agreement on the certainty of stereotyping for particular adjectives (Williams, Best, et al., 1979).

Within American society, some data suggest that black children have less stereotyped views of women's roles than white children. Black children, particularly black girls, gave less stereotyped answers than white children to questions about whether girls and women could engage in nontraditional activities (Kleinke & Nicholson, 1979) and about parent characteristics (Gold & St. Ange, 1974). However, minority children had slightly more stereotyped beliefs about occupations than whites (Cummings & Taebel, 1980); so firm conclusions await further study.

Social class differences might also be expected on the grounds that lower social status groups are commonly assumed to hold more rigid stereotypes

than middle-class individuals, but the data consistently fail to show them for stereotypes about activities (Nadelman, 1970; 1974), concepts about parents (Nadelman, 1975), concepts about achievement (Stein, 1971), and occupational attitudes and knowledge (Cummings & Taebel, 1980; Nemerowicz, 1979).

Correlations Among Components of Sex-Typing

In cognitive developmental theories, intellectual development is one important antecedent for children's understanding of sex-typing. Cognitive constructs about sex-appropriate behavior, in turn, are considered an important antecedent of valuing and adopting sex-typed attributes for oneself. Social learning theory, on the other hand, suggests that concepts and behaviors are learned concomitantly, probably in interaction. Different components of sex-typing, particularly different content areas, are expected to be relatively independent of one another. Spence and Helmreich (1978), though arguing from a trait model, also propose independence of different content areas and independence of self-perceptions from overt behavior. In this section, data on the relationships among different components of sex-typing are examined, with particular attention to the issues raised by different theoretical perspectives.

Intellectual Development and Gender Concepts

According to cognitive developmental theory, gender constancy is acquired as a part of concrete operational thought. When children can conserve physical qualities, they can conserve qualities of living beings. Virtually all the available research supports that proposition. Before age 6 or 7, children rely on obvious and superficial perceptual attributes of people to determine their gender. When given an explicit choice among using hair length, genitals, or body type to determine the gender of dolls, a majority of preschool children use hair length as the relevant criterion (McConaghy, 1979; Thompson & Bentler, 1971).

Direct measures of concrete operational thought (i.e., performance on conservation measures) predict gender constancy well (DeVries, 1974; Kohlberg, 1966; Marcus & Overton, 1978). In one study, a Guttman Scalogram analysis suggested that conservation precedes gender constancy (Marcus & Overton, 1978). Measures of general intellectual functioning such as IQ, mental age, or vocabulary are also correlated positively with gender constancy

(Emmerich, 1979b; Gouze & Nadelman, 1980; Kohlberg, 1966; Thompson, 1975) with one exception (DeVries, 1974). These data support Kohlberg's assertion that the child's understanding of gender constancy or identity is a function of more general cognitive development and is consolidated only when principles of identity and equivalence of physical substances are understood. They also support his contention that genital differences between the sexes are of minor importance in the young child's understanding of gender.

During middle childhood and adolescence, children's social-cognitive development, rather than their understanding of physical laws, predicts concepts about sex-typing. For children from kindergarten to eighth grade, flexibility of thought about social conventions was related to flexibility of sex stereotypes; neither was related to concepts about physical laws (Carter & Patterson, in press). Among older subjects, postconventional moral thinking was related to androgynous self-perceptions (Leahy & Eiter, 1980).

Gender Constancy as a Predictor. Children's understanding of gender identity and gender constancy is remarkably independent of other components of sex-typing in most of the literature. Among very young children (ages 2 to 3), gender labels are correlated with knowledge of sex stereotypes (Kuhn et al., 1978), but this relationship is probably a function of verbal abilities that influence both measures. During the period from 3 to 7, a number of studies have found no relationship between the child's level of gender constancy and understanding of sex stereotypes (Baruch, no date; Katz & Rank, 1981) or attraction to same-sex activities and same-sex models (Emmerich, 1981; Katz & Rank, 1981; Marcus & Overton, 1978). There is some tendency for children with high gender constancy to be more attentive to, or influenced by, same-sex models, as evidenced in a series of studies using televised stimuli (Frey & Ruble, 1981; Ruble, Balaban, & Cooper, 1981; Slaby & Frey, 1975), but the findings are inconsistent and occur primarily for boys.

There is some hint in the literature that the final stages of gender constancy provide a context for the child to develop flexible concepts about sex-typed activities and roles. In one study, for 5-year-olds and particularly 7-year-olds, gender constancy was positively related to the number of attributes considered appropriate for both sexes (Urberg, 1979a). In another, children with high gender constancy showed reduced stereotypes after seeing films portraying counterstereotyped play; children with low gender constancy were less influenced by such films

(Frey & Ruble, 1981). One reason for these findings may be that gender constancy leads the child to focus on the sex of a peer or a model rather than on the activity as the criterion for choosing sex-appropriate behavior (Emmerich, 1981).

Sex Stereotypes and Concepts as Predictors. Among preschool children, there are weak associations between children's sex stereotypes and other aspects of sex-typing, but the literature does not support the proposition that concepts about gender *precede* preferences or behavioral enactment (Blakemore et al., 1979; Edelbrock & Sugawara, 1978; Weinraub & Leite, 1977). The stereotypes of elementary school children failed to predict their self-perceptions of personality traits in one investigation (Sims et al., 1978), a finding similar to those for adolescents and adults (Spence & Helmreich, 1978). However, in using a different method of analysis, Davis, Williams, and Best (in press) found that traits that were most consistently stereotyped as masculine or feminine were also the traits on which girls' self-descriptions were most sex-typed. This relationship did not occur for boys. These data suggest that individual variations in stereotypes are relatively small or unimportant, but that the culturally shared pattern of stereotypes does correspond to sex-typed self-perceptions.

Individual variations in stereotypes about achievement are often related to preferences and performance during elementary and adolescent years but, again, the evidence is not entirely consistent. Some strong evidence for the early importance of stereotypes comes from a one-year longitudinal study of children from 4 to 6 years old. Stereotypes about intellectual achievement were related to children's expectancy of success at each time of measurement. More important, stereotypes at the first time of measurement predicted changes in expectancy during the subsequent year (Crandall, 1978). Among older children, sex role concepts are sometimes related to attainment value, expectancy, and performance in various sex-typed achievement areas (Boswell, 1979; Dwyer, 1974; Stein, 1971).

The influence of sex stereotypes on achievement has been explored most extensively in studies designed to illuminate the antecedents of sex differences in mathematics performance. At the end of the high school years, one major reason for male superiority in math is that males take more elective math courses than females (Meece & Parsons, 1982). Therefore, these investigations have focused on the determinants of course selection.

Among junior and senior high school students, perceiving math as a male domain is negatively correlated with girls' plans to take elective math courses in some samples (Sherman, 1980; Sherman & Fennema, 1977) but not in others (Brush, 1979; Kaczala, 1981). Girls who consider math useful for their own future career take more math than those who do not, suggesting greater stereotyping of math as "not for me" by the latter group (Brush, 1979; Steel & Wise, 1979). None of these studies has found correlations for boys. These findings suggest that stereotypes about achievement areas may influence children's motivation, effort, and, ultimately, performance, particularly in areas that are culturally defined as appropriate for the other gender. However, correlational findings might also be interpreted as demonstrating that people adjust their stereotypes to fit their behavior.

Experimental Tests of Sex-Typed Activities. Several experimental studies demonstrate that sex stereotyping can have a causal effect on self-perception, preference, and adoption of sex-typed achievement interests. Expectancy of success and attainment values were affected by labeling tasks as masculine, feminine, or neutral (equally appropriate for both sexes) in one study of sixth-grade children (Stein et al., 1971). Younger children (6- to 8-year-olds) also expressed a greater preference for a game presented as sex-appropriate than for a game labeled as appropriate for the other sex (Montemayor, 1974), but another study using the same procedure with 8- and 10-year-olds failed to replicate the finding, perhaps because the game, a mechanical clown, was immature for the older age levels (Etaugh & Ropp, 1976).

The rate of performance or effort is greater for tasks labeled as sex-appropriate than for those labeled as appropriate for the other sex (Gold & Berger, 1978; Helper & Quinlivan, 1973; Krauss, 1977; Montemayor, 1974; Stein et al., 1971). Two studies (Gold & Berger, 1978; Stein et al., 1971) found effects only for boys. Two others did not show effects (Etaugh & Ropp, 1976; Lanktree & Hamilton, 1980), perhaps because of task or instruction differences. In an early series of studies, however, high school and college students solved logical-mathematical problems more accurately when problem content (e.g., counting cakes vs. counting bolts) was sex-appropriate than when it was not (Milton, 1958; Stein & Bailey, 1973). The age range spanned by these studies is preschool through college; there is no discernible age difference in the impact of sex-typed labels and content, though older children may respond to more subtle cues than younger ones. On the whole, these findings in conjunction with cor-

relational data provide strong support for the influence of sex stereotypes on children's self-perceptions of competence, preference and attraction to tasks, and behavioral adoption in the form of effort and performance.

Self-perception as a Predictor

The major focus of recent theory and research on sex-typed identity has been the degree to which measures of masculine and feminine personality characteristics predict other components of personality, attitudes, and behavior. The principal contenders in this discussion have been Bem, on the one hand, and Spence and Helmreich, on the other.

Self-esteem. Both sets of investigators have demonstrated that measures of psychological androgyny are positively correlated with self-esteem, supporting the claim that individuals who combine the positive elements of masculinity and femininity are best adapted for healthy psychological functioning. However, masculinity is more highly correlated with self-esteem than is femininity (Bem, 1977; Spence & Helmreich, 1978). This finding may reflect the fact that masculine attributes are more highly valued in society than feminine attributes, but it may also be the result of an overlap in the content of the scales measuring self-esteem and masculinity. Masculine adjectives such as "confident" and "feels superior" are similar to characteristics assessed by self-esteem scales. Using a multidimensional measure of self-esteem, Flaherty and Dusek (1980) demonstrated that masculinity was related to self-esteem concerning achievement and leadership, but that androgyny and femininity were related to other components of self-esteem.

More recently, Spence et al. (1979) investigated the relationship of self-esteem to negatively valued masculine and feminine attributes. Negative masculinity was not correlated with self-esteem, but both negative femininity scales were related to low self-esteem. Negative feminine traits are more detrimental to self-esteem than negative masculine traits, and positive feminine traits are less enhancing for self-esteem than positive masculine traits. This dual pattern supports the proposition that a self-perception of masculinity (or at least instrumentality) contributes more and detracts less from self-esteem than does femininity or expressiveness.

Personal-Social Behavior. In Bem's initial work on androgyny, several experiments were designed to test the hypothesis that scores on the BSRI would predict instrumental and expressive behavior. As expected, people scoring as androgynous and masculine were more independent of group pressure in a conformity situation (an instrumental behavior) than those classified as feminine (Bem, 1975). It was also expected that androgynous and feminine individuals would be more nurturant and sympathetic than masculine people. That prediction was confirmed for men, but masculine and androgynous women behaved similarly, and both these groups of women were *more* nurturant than the feminine women. However, feminine women did excel on sympathetic listening (Bem, 1976; Bem, Martyna, & Watson, 1976). Bem suggested that feminine sextyping for women led to extreme caution about taking the initiative in a situation where the expected behaviors were not clear; only in a situation where the adaptive behavior was primarily passive would feminine women show superior functioning.

Activities and Interests. Spence and Helmreich (1978) have argued that sex-typed instrumental and expressive personality traits are theoretically and empirically separate from both "sex role" and behavior. In the framework of our matrix (Table 1), they argue that personal-social attributes are not highly related to sex-typed activities, interests, and roles. Therefore, they suggest it is unreasonable to expect measures such as the BSRI or the PAQ to predict sex-typed interests, attitudes about sex roles, or other content areas that are distant from instrumental and expressive personality traits. In their work, scores on the PAQ generally have low correlations with the Attitudes Toward Women Scale, a measure of attitudes about traditional and nontraditional roles for women.

Two experiments have tested the relationship of sex-typed identity (personality) to subjects' choices of masculine or feminine tasks. In the first, androgynous individuals were more willing to perform cross-sex activities than sex-typed individuals (Bem & Lenney, 1976). Storms (1979) has argued that sex role identity (i.e., perception of oneself as masculine or feminine) may account for the association between sex-typed personality attributes and activity preferences. The BSRI contains the adjectives "masculine" and "feminine." Self-ratings on these adjectives are relatively independent of self-ratings on the personality characteristics represented by the other adjectives on the scale (Pedhazur & Tetenbaum, 1979). Storms (1979) suggests that the relationship between the BSRI and sex-typed task choices perhaps resulted because the BSRI measures sex role identity rather than being a "pure" measure of instrumental and expressive personality attributes.

Both experimental and correlational studies suggest, however, that sex-typed personal-social characteristics are associated with other components of sex-typing. The PAQ measures self-perceptions of instrumental and expressive personality attributes without the confound of sex role identity. In one study, sex-typing on the PAQ predicted sex-typed activity choices for males, but not females, though the authors emphasized that the association was a weak one (Helmreich, Spence, & Holahan, 1979). In correlational studies, female varsity athletes and female scientists had masculine or androgynous patterns on the PAQ more often than did control groups. Homosexuals rarely showed the "conventional" pattern of scores for their own gender (i.e., masculine for men and feminine for women). Gay men most often scored as undifferentiated or as feminine. Lesbians most often scored as undifferentiated or androgynous (Spence & Helmreich, 1978). In one sample of sixth- and ninth-grade children, girls who said they would like being boys gave more masculine self-descriptions on a set of adjectives describing their personalities than did girls who preferred being girls (Nash, 1975). All of these data together suggest that one's own perception of sex-typed personality traits is related to adoption of sex-typed behaviors in a variety of content areas. Nevertheless, sex-typing is multidimensional, and one cannot assume that one component necessarily implies others.

Achievement. Self-perceptions of masculine or feminine characteristics fare moderately well as predictors of sex-typed achievement patterns. For individuals from fifth grade through college, masculine and androgynous self-perceptions characterize people of both sexes who hold high expectancies and value for mathematics (Kaczala, 1981) and who perform well on masculine sex-typed achievement areas such as math (Ferguson & Maccoby, 1966), logical problems with masculine content (Milton, 1958), field independence (Signorella & Jamison, 1978), Piagetian logical concepts (Jamison & Signorella, 1980; Signorella & Jamison, 1978), and spatial skill (Nash, 1975). Less consistently, feminine and androgynous self-perceptions characterize students who have high expectancies and value for achievement in English (Kaczala, 1981).

In two samples of college females, Welch (1981) found that those with androgynous scores manifested a "masculine" pattern of attribution and performance when confronted with success or failure on a sex-neutral task. Androgynous women responded to success with improved performance and to failure with little performance decrement; feminine women showed little improvement when they succeeded, but considerable decrement when they failed. Androgynous women also attributed their success to ability and their failure to causes other than ability more than did feminine women.

In summary, people who perceive themselves as masculine or feminine on instruments such as the BSRI or the PAQ do exhibit patterns of achievement, personal-social behavior, and interests that are consistent with their self-perceptions, though the relationships among these variables are typically somewhat low in magnitude (see Nash, 1979, for a more extensive review). The existence of correlations does not, however, shed very much light on the causal relationships involved. There is fairly consistent evidence that adolescent and adult women who enter male domains of career involvement perceive themselves as more "masculine," though not necessarily less feminine, than those who follow traditional female life patterns (Huston-Stein & Higgins-Trenk, 1978; Spence & Helmreich, 1978; Stein & Bailey, 1973). Self-perceptions may be a result of undertaking nontraditional activities rather than a cause. Undoubtedly, there is a complex interaction over time that probably involves a number of small shifts in self-perception of "masculinity," perceptions of "appropriate" activities, and success or involvement in various kinds of behavior. This writer has previously argued (Huston-Stein & Higgins-Trenk, 1978) that we need research that explores the ongoing interactions of such variables during the course of development (at any age) to ferret out the complex patterns that probably exist.

Preferences as Predictors of Behavior

In Mischel's review of the literature in 1970, the weight of the evidence indicated that sex-typed toy preference measures did not predict behavior well. A recent investigation with preschool children supports the conclusion that toy preference, same-sex peer preference, and nursery school behavior are independent dimensions (Brush & Goldberg, 1978). One reason for the negative findings in earlier studies may have been the inadequacy of the measures. Most used the IT Scale or other unidimensional, bipolar indices of toy preference. When preferences for masculine and feminine toys or activities are assessed independently, there is some evidence that masculine preferences predict aggression (Huesmann et al., 1978), persistence on masculine tasks (Stein et al., 1971), and math performance (Boswell, 1979) among elementary school-age children.

In nursery school settings, behaviorally defined toy preferences are related to play with same-sex peers, probably because a child who chooses masculine activities is likely to encounter boys, while children who play in feminine activities will be associated more often with girls. For example, among 2½ to 4-year-old girls, preference for feminine toys was correlated with the percent of same-sex peer play, but was not related to the type of clothing worn (dresses vs. pants), activity level, or percent of outdoor play (Eisenberg-Berg, Boothby, & Matson, 1979). In another study, boys with masculine toy preferences engaged in more cooperation with other boys, and boys with feminine preferences cooperated with girls more often. For girls, feminine activity choices were associated with task persistence, probably because feminine activities are more sedentary (Connor & Serbin, 1977).

Summary of Correlational Patterns

A great deal of information about gender constancy and sex stereotypes has accumulated in the past 10 years. Contrary to many expectations, gender constancy appears to be relatively independent of the child's acquisition of sex stereotypes or sex-typed preferences and behavior. There is weak evidence that the attainment of gender constancy may lead children to attend to same-sex models or peers, perhaps because they understand that a person's gender rather than appearance or behavior is a critical attribute. Gender constancy may also provide the cognitive background that permits children to understand and accept counterstereotypical information. For the most part, however, gender constancy is unrelated to other aspects of sex-typing.

Sex stereotypes are also somewhat weak predictors of individual differences in preference or behavior. In the preschool years, developmental patterns may be so predominant that there is relatively little room for individual differences to be manifested, but even among older children, correlations are small. Many intervention efforts have focused on changing children's sex stereotypes; these findings suggest that such changes cannot be assumed to generalize to values or behavior. They also raise questions about the central role given to children's concepts about gender in many recent theories. Certainly, experimental studies have demonstrated that sex-typed concepts *can* influence behavior, but we do not know how well such studies reflect real-world processes. Behavior and values can also influence sex stereotypes. In any case, there has been a disproportionate emphasis on studying children's sex stereotypes without putting such constructs in a broader context. We do not need more studies showing that children know sex stereotypes; we need studies using multiple measures of multiple dimensions to determine how such stereotypes fit in the broader framework of children's acquisition of sex-typing.

Chicken-and-egg questions can also be raised about self-perceptions of masculine and feminine personality attributes. Independent assessments of masculinity, femininity, and their combinations do predict self-esteem, social behavior, and achievement behavior, particularly for females. But again, one must ask to what degree masculine and feminine self-perceptions arise from participation in activities or behaviors and to what extent they serve as determinants of behavior. Androgyny, as the combination of socially desirable masculine and feminine attributes, has reached the phase in its scientific life cycle where the glow of newness has worn off and the critics are chipping away at the paint. Much of the available literature suggests that masculine instrumentality is the most important and adaptive component of androgyny. Masculinity predicts self-esteem, social behavior, and achievement in many areas about as well as androgyny, especially for females. This conclusion does not negate the importance of measuring masculinity and femininity separately. The recent measures have obtained more coherent and "pure" measures because they did not force masculinity and femininity to covary. On the whole, the correlations among self-perception, preference, and behavior, while modest, provide somewhat more consistent support for relations among different dimensions of sex-typing than the arguments of Mischel (1970) or Spence and Helmreich (1978) might lead one to expect. As we turn to an examination of the antecedents of sex-typing, we will continue to treat it multidimensionally, but one can have a modicum of confidence that its various components do relate to one another.

BIOLOGICAL COMPONENTS OF SEX-TYPED BEHAVIOR

Because the sexes differ genetically and biochemically, many theorists have proposed that sex differences in behavior are at least partially the result of genetic or hormonal influences. Taking the argument one step farther, this approach leads to the prediction that within-sex differences in sex-typed behavior might be associated with biochemical variations among people or within the same person over time. Much of the research testing biological bases of sex-typed behavior has been done with animals,

particularly rats and mice, because it is possible to do experimental manipulations of hormone exposure and anatomical structures that would be unethical in human subjects. The resulting body of literature consists of replicated and well-documented causal relationships for animals. To generalize these findings and apply them to humans, however, is problematic because the relationship of genetic and biochemical factors to behavior in humans is generally much more variable and tempered by experience than is the case for the white rat. The animal studies do suggest a biological substrate that probably operates in humans as well; the issue is how much, if any, importance that substrate has relative to the effects of environmentally produced experience.

Advocates of *nature* often lock horns with proponents of *nurture* when discussing biological contributions to sex differences. Yet, an "either-or" controversy is obviously oversimplified. One useful framework in which to discuss biological contributions to sex-typing is the "continuum of indirectness" proposed by Anastasi (1958) in her classic article on heredity and environment. No one disputes the existence of genetic, biochemical, and anatomical differences between the sexes. Even the proponents of an environmental basis for sex differences in behavior recognize that the environment treats boys and girls differently because they are born with physically different genitals and different potential roles in the reproduction of the species. Therefore, the importance of biological sex differences is not at issue; what is at issue is the directness or indirectness of the influence of biological variables on social behavior. If high levels of androgen influence the central nervous system to make a person more prone to be active, then the influence is fairly direct. If androgen leads to large muscle development, which in turn leads other people to expect a person to be a good athlete, which in turn leads to participation in sports, then the effects of androgen on participation in sports is more indirect.

Two brief cautions apply to an evaluation of this literature. First, the most extreme behavioral departures from sex-typed societal norms do not have any known biological basis. For example, "gender-deviant" boys, who have extreme patterns of feminine preferences and behavior, have shown no chromosomal or physical abnormality on physical examination (Green, 1976; Rekers, Crandall, Rosen, & Bentler, 1979). Second, associations between biochemical and behavioral variables are not one-way causal chains; social and sexual stimuli can influence physiological states, particularly hormone levels (Hoyenga & Hoyenga, 1979; Rogers, 1976; Rose, Gordon, & Bernstein, 1972).

Prenatal Sex Differentiation

The major effect of an XX or XY chromosome combination is to produce differentiation of the primitive gonadal tissue into ovaries or testes. In males, testes are formed around the sixth week of gestation; female ovaries are formed around the third month of gestation. During the remainder of gestation, sexual differentiation is accomplished by hormonal secretions from the infant's own gonads, particularly secretions of androgen. Male infants secrete considerably more androgen than do female infants (though androgens are present in both genders). For human infants, males have higher levels of testosterone in their bloodstream at birth than do females, but there are no differences in the concentrations of estrogens or progesterone (Maccoby, Doering, Jacklin, & Kraemer, 1979). Differentiation of external sexual organs other than the gonads is accomplished primarily as a result of high or low exposure to androgen. If the developing fetus is exposed to high concentrations of androgen, even if there are normal female gonads, it will develop a penis and closed scrotum. If it is not exposed to sufficiently high concentrations of androgens, the genitalia will have the appearance of a normal female, regardless of the child's genetic sex. This fact—that female features are developed in the absence of appropriate hormones—has led some to say that nature makes a female. More detailed treatments of sex differences in prenatal development can be found in Hoyenga and Hoyenga (1979) and Money and Ehrhardt (1972). In most cases, gonadal secretions produce physical characteristics consistent with genetic sex, but the rare exceptions provide experiments of nature that can be used to evaluate the effects of hormone exposure at different points in development.

Genetic Influences

Although a direct genetic basis for most sex-typed behavior has not been proposed, some investigators have advanced the hypothesis that sex differences in visual-spatial skill might result from a sex-linked recessive trait. Because a male has only one X chromosome, a recessive gene on that chromosome will be expressed, whereas a female would have to receive two recessive genes (on both X chromosomes) to have the trait fully expressed. This hypothesis has been tested by examining family re-

semblance in scores on spatial and performance tasks. Because a boy always receives his one X chromosome from his mother, the expected correlation between fathers and sons is .00 for any X-linked trait. The expected correlation between mothers and daughters is also lower than the correlations expected for mothers with sons and fathers with daughters. Expected correlations between sisters are higher than correlations between brothers, which in turn are higher than brother-sister correlations. Although some early studies found family correlations that were consistent with this model, more recent studies using larger samples have found patterns that contradict the hypothesis of an X-linked recessive gene transmitting spatial ability (Boles, 1980; McGee, 1979; Vandenberg & Kuse, 1979; Wittig, 1976).

Individuals with Turner's syndrome, a genetic anomaly in which the individual has only one X chromosome and no corresponding X or Y chromosome (XO), also pose a problem for a simple recessive gene hypothesis. Such individuals have normal intellectual skills in other areas, particularly verbal skills, but are typically poor performers on spatial tasks (Reinisch, Gandelman, & Spiegel, 1979; Rovet & Netley, 1982; Vandenberg & Kuse, 1979). The simple recessive gene hypothesis would, of course, predict the reverse. The advocates of a genetic explanation have proposed, therefore, that some exposure to internally produced androgen or other hormones may be essential for the activation or realization of genetic potential if the recessive X-linked hypothesis is correct (Bock & Kolakowski, 1973; Harris, 1978).

Another prediction from the X-linked genetic hypothesis is that 25% of the females tested should perform above the male median (i.e., the proportion of females showing superior performance should be the square of the proportion of males). While several studies have found distributions of scores consistent with the hypothesis (McGee, 1979; Vandenberg & Kuse, 1979) others have failed to find such distributions (Sherman & Fennema, 1978). In addition, other interpretations have been offered for the former findings (Vandenberg & Kuse, 1979).

Finally, the hypothesis has been tested through linkage analysis. The rationale for linkage analysis is that brothers who are alike on traits known to be controlled by genes located on the X chromosome, called "marker" variables, are more likely to have received the same X chromosome from their mothers than are brothers who have different phenotypes on the marker variables. If spatial ability is controlled by an allele on the X chromosome, the brothers who are alike on the marker variables should be more similar in spatial performance than brothers who differ on the marker variables. Such an analysis was performed on males from 67 Italian families that had at least three sons (Goodenough, Gandini, Olkin, Pizzamiglio, Thayer, & Witkin, 1977). The marker variables were color blindness and Xg(a) blood groups. Nine tests of field independence, spatial performance, and verbal ability were administered. Of 18 correlations, 2 were statistically significant. The authors interpreted the findings as being suggestive of significant results, blaming the small number of subjects for an absence of more significant differences. However, most of the non-significant correlations failed to show any trend in the predicted direction. It appears more parsimonious to interpret the findings as clear *lack* of support for X-linkage of spatial performance or field independence.

In summary, several well-controlled studies have failed to support the hypothesis that visual-spatial skill is influenced by a recessive X-linked gene. (See Boles, 1980; Vandenberg & Kuse, 1979, for reviews; see Harris, 1978, for a review supporting the hypothesis.)

Hemispheric Specialization

In adults, the left cerebral hemisphere is specialized for verbal and analytic processing; the right hemisphere is specialized for visual, spatial, and global processing. One technique for assessing hemispheric specialization is a dichotic listening task in which two types of material are presented simultaneously to the two ears. Easy-to-verbalize material presented to the right ear (hence to the left hemisphere) is reported more accurately than such material presented to the left ear. The reverse pattern occurs for difficult-to-verbalize material such as music (Bryden, 1979; Harris, 1978; McGee, 1979). Similar hemispheric differences have been demonstrated using visual and haptic sensory modalities.

A plethora of conflicting hypotheses about sex differences in the amount of hemispheric specialization have been presented in an effort to explain male superiority in spatial processing. Among adults, the weight of the evidence now suggests that males have more hemispheric specialization and less bilateral processing activity than females (Bryden, 1979; McGee, 1979). This finding is interpreted by some authors as indicating that females tend to use verbal modes of processing for all types of material; hence, they try to solve spatial problems using relatively inefficient verbal methods (Bryden, 1979; Harris, 1978).

For children, however, there is less agreement about the timing and development of sex differences in hemispheric specialization. Specialized functioning has occasionally been demonstrated in infants (Waber, 1979), but most data suggest that lateralization increases gradually during the preschool years and early school years (Maccoby & Jacklin, 1974); still other data suggest changes as late as adolescence (Harris, 1978; McGee, 1979; Waber, 1979). One problem in such studies is that differences between two ears or visual fields may result from the subject's strategies or patterns of attention deployment rather than from true patterns of hemispheric functioning, particularly among children. Perhaps more important, there is presently little consistent evidence of sex differences in the rate of hemispheric specialization. Buffery and Gray (1972) cited several studies showing earlier specialization for girls; McGee (1979) and Harris (1978) concluded that a bulk of the evidence supported earlier specialization by boys; Bryden (1979) argued that most investigations have found no sex differences at all. Any conclusion about the role of hemispheric specialization is premature. Furthermore, there is little evidence about how well hemispheric specialization predicts cognitive performance on tasks where the sexes differ or are thought to differ. Maccoby and Jacklin (1974) pointed out, for example, that the "packages" of skills localized in each hemisphere do not correspond in detail to those on which sex differences typically occur. Left-hemisphere processing is described as verbal, analytic, sequentially detailed, and computerlike. Right-hemisphere processing is global, intuitive, and synthetic. The sexes do not differ on all or even most tasks involving these attributes.

Prenatal Hormone Exposure: Animal Studies

Several sets of well-controlled experiments with rats, mice, and other rodents have demonstrated that prenatal exposure to high concentrations of androgen influences patterns of adult sexual behavior and adult aggression. Animals who are exposed to androgen during the critical, prenatal period of sexual development show male patterns of sexual behavior—mounting, intromission, and ejaculation—when appropriately stimulated as adults. Animals of both sexes who are not exposed to masculinizing levels of androgen in the prenatal period tend to show the feminine pattern of lordosis in adult sexual behavior (Goy, 1975; Hoyenga & Hoyenga, 1979; Ward, 1974). Although female rodents typically manifest nurturing and maternal behaviors to infants more readily than males do, the effects of prenatal hormones on maternal behavior have not been established, perhaps because the critical period is too early to be detected with available experimental techniques (Hoyenga & Hoyenga, 1979; Quadagno, Briscoe, & Quadagno, 1977).

Similar experiments have been conducted with monkeys by injecting pregnant mothers with testosterone during the middle part of the gestation period. Female fetuses, therefore, were exposed to high levels of testosterone and, when not aborted, were born with masculinized genitalia. In one study, these masculinized females showed more play initiation, threatening behavior, rough and tumble play, and pursuit play than normal females, but less than normal males (Goy, 1975; Phoenix, 1974). Masculinized females also manifested male patterns of sexual behavior. It might be noted in this context that normal female monkeys reared in the wild frequently show male patterns of mounting, whereas normal males do not display female sexual behavior very often (Michael, Wilson, & Zumpe, 1974).

How can these results be interpreted? Many theorists have argued that prenatal hormones affect the development of brain structures, with the result that the adult has differential sensitivity to biochemical or environmental stimulants. There is some dispute whether the structural effect is in the brain or in more peripheral organs. In particular, animals not exposed to prenatal androgen have incomplete penile development, making adult sexual behaviors such as intromission and ejaculation mechanically and physically difficult to perform. Even in the few experiments that controlled structural differences in external genitalia, it is possible that neural sensitivity in the genital region is affected by prenatal androgen (Quadagno et al., 1977).

Although the lasting effects of prenatal androgen are of particular interest, animal data also provide information about more immediate effects of hormone levels on the behavior of adults. In general, testosterone levels are positively correlated with aggressive and dominant behavior in males, but the evidence is less consistent for dogs and primates than for rodents. In one experiment, long-term administration of high doses of androgen led to increased levels of aggression and dominance in females, but some of this effect might be the result of increased physical strength. Estrogen administered to adult rodents leads to high activity levels. This pattern is consistent with the fact that females are more active and less timid in experimental testing situations than males (Hoyenga & Hoyenga, 1979). In any case, it is well established that prenatal exposure to testicular hormones has a lasting effect on the sexual behavior of certain animal species and on some aspects of aggressive and physically active social behavior.

Prenatal Androgens and Human Behavior

Information about the effects of early hormone exposure on humans is drawn from cases of disorders in hormone secretions and cases in which hormones have been administered to women during pregnancy for therapeutic reasons. One disorder of the infant's own hormone secretions, the adrenogenital syndrome (AGS), has received considerable attention because it provides biochemical circumstances that are similar to experimental administration of prenatal androgen to animals. Adrenogenital syndrome occurs when the infant's adrenal cortex secretes high concentrations of androgen because of a failure to synthesize cortizone. Female infants with this disorder are often born with fully or partially masculinized genitalia, even though their gonads are normal and female. If untreated, these children will continue to have high concentrations of androgen, resulting in premature puberty for boys and continuing masculinization for girls. However, cortisone therapy is now used to control androgen levels and females' external sexual organs can be surgically "corrected."

Two groups of females with AGS were studied by Money and Ehrhardt (1972) and Ehrhardt and Baker (1974). Samples were small and the ages ranged from preschool to young adult, but all subjects had received cortisone replacement therapy and had been surgically feminized. The first study included a small group of girls who had been masculinized by prenatal administration of a particular type of synthetic progestin, which was apparently converted into androgen in the mothers' bodies. The progestin-exposed girls, of course, required no chemical treatment after birth. Behavioral data were based on interviews with the girls and their mothers. In comparison to the controls, the prenatally androgenized girls were more often tomboys; they preferred active outdoor games including sports; they preferred boys as playmates; they preferred masculine toys; and they preferred pants to dresses. They were less interested in play and fantasy about maternalism (doll play, interest in infants, daydreams of pregnancy and motherhood) and about marriage, but they did not differ in fantasy about dating and romance. They did not differ from controls on aggression or heterosexual orientation. Boys with AGS also differed from the normal boys in liking activities involving intense energy expenditure. They did not differ in preferences for male sex-typed toys, or for fantasy about babies and marriage (Ehrhardt & Baker, 1974).

In one study, girls with adrenogenital syndrome had higher IQs than average, but that finding was not replicated when subjects' siblings were used as a control group. The most parsimonious explanation appears to be sampling bias—children who reach research-based treatment centers are from families with above average education and income (Quadagno et al., 1977; Reinisch, Gandelman, & Spiegel, 1979).

These studies have been widely cited as evidence for central nervous system effects of prenatal androgen in humans, paralleling those found in animals. They have also been criticized on a number of grounds with suggestions of alternative interpretations (Archer, 1976). First, the adrenogenital syndrome requires life-long maintenance on cortisone, and one side effect of cortisone is high activity level. The fact that both boys and girls with the disorder liked high energy play more than their normal siblings suggests that the cortisone treatment rather than the early androgen may have been a causal agent (Quadagno et al., 1977). Second, regulation of androgen levels cannot be perfectly maintained, and it is likely that treated adrenogenital children were exposed to higher-than-normal amounts of androgen at some points in their childhood. Three of the 17 girls in the Ehrhardt and Baker study did not receive cortisone therapy until after the first year of life. Long-term physical effects were evident in the fact that adrenogenital girls tended to have late menarche—about a year older than average. Third, masculinized girls may have been perceived by their parents and older siblings as deviant, "malelike," and unfeminine. These children did have ambiguous or masculinized genitalia at birth, and many of them were not surgically corrected until after they were well beyond infancy. In the second study, 6 were corrected during the first year of life, 7 between 1 and 3 years, and the other 4 "later in life" (Ehrhardt & Baker, 1974). It would not be surprising if people around them thought of them as boys, or at least as "boyish," and treated them accordingly.

Fourth, all were aware that they had a disorder of sexual functioning, and many were told that they might have delayed puberty and possible difficulties in becoming pregnant as adults. One critic has suggested that their lack of interest in maternalism may have resulted from realistic doubts about the possibility of having children. However, clinical data on two other disorders that produce infertility—Turner's syndrome and androgen insensitivity—raise questions about this interpretation. In both disorders, individuals' external genitalia are female, but they are not genetically female and they do not have female gonads. With estrogen replacement therapy, they develop normal secondary sexual characteristics. Clinical samples of both groups displayed patterns of feminine interests, such as concern about maternalism and marriage, that were similar to normal female controls (Money & Ehrhardt, 1972). Given the fact that these females are definitely infertile, one cannot attribute the lack of interest in dolls and babies by AGS girls to anticipations of difficulty in having children. Neither can one attribute it to direct effects of prenatal androgen on the central nervous system. Both Turner's syndrome and androgen-insensitive children look like normal females at birth. The androgen-exposed girls have abnormal genital characteristics that may have important social implications for their families and for themselves.

Prenatal Exposure to Estrogens and Progestins

In animal studies, few if any clear effects of prenatal exposure to estrogens or progestins have been demonstrated. A few studies of human infants whose mothers have been given synthetic progestins, estrogens, or both, have been carried out in an effort to detect long-term effects on behavior or intellect. None of the children studied had physical or genital abnormalities. Interpretation of these studies is complicated by the fact that all infants are exposed to very high levels of progesterone accompanying normal pregnancies and to relatively high levels of certain estrogens as well. When synthetic hormones are administered, the purpose is usually to avert miscarriage for a mother who is at risk, either because of accompanying diseases or complications, such as diabetes or toxemia, or because she has a history of obstetrical problems. Little is known about how much is added to the normal volume of hormones, how different those amounts might be in mothers who are at risk and those who are not, or what amounts might make an important difference.

The small amount of available data provides little evidence of personality or intellectual correlates of prenatal exposure to progesterone or estrogen. In a well-controlled study, Reinisch & Karow (1977) compared children whose mothers had been given three different types of hormones in pregnancy to one another and to their siblings who had not been exposed to synthetic hormones. There were a few personality differences for one of the three groups, but the personality traits on which they differed were not stereotypic masculine or feminine characteristics. Longitudinal follow-ups have been conducted in England, comparing children whose mothers were treated with progestins for toxemia or diabetes to normal control groups. Again, few reliable personality differences emerged, and those that did appear were not correlated with the dosage of estrogen received by the mothers (Lynch, Mychalkiw, & Hutt, 1978; Reinisch et al., 1979; Yalom, Green, & Fisk, 1973). Ehrhardt and Meyer-Bahlburg (1981) reported that females whose mothers had been treated with progesterone or estrogen showed some evidence of less masculine and more feminine interests than control groups, but the differences were scattered. These authors pointed out that the negative results obtained by other investigators might be the result of the personality tests used that do not assess sex-typed behavior patterns. Therefore, no definite conclusion can be drawn.

Prenatal progesterone has little or no influence on intellectual development. Although Dalton (1968, 1976) reported that children of progestin-treated mothers had more advanced educational attainment than untreated controls, other studies, using more precise and extensive measures of intellectual functioning, have found no relationship between progestin exposure and general intelligence or specific sex-typed skills, such as verbal fluency or spatial relationships (Lynch et al., 1978; Reinisch & Karow, 1977).

Hormones and Sex-Typed Behavior in Adolescence

Social and Affective Functioning

Because hormone levels are low and similar for boys and girls during childhood, it makes little sense to attribute behavioral sex differences to hormonal bases. With the onset of puberty, however, both genders experience an increase in sex-appropriate hormones as well as bodily changes that define them as adult, sexual beings in most societies. Perhaps because these biological changes are so inextricably confounded with social and environmental changes, little good evidence exists for the influence of sex hormones on sex-typed behavior. In a review of the available literature, Hoyenga and Hoyenga (1979) concluded that there was some evidence that testosterone levels were correlated with aggression in adolescent males, but they also emphasized that environmental factors can modify any hormonal effect extensively. One group of investigators (Imperato-McGinley, Peterson, Gautier, & Sturla, 1979) re-

ported on a group of male pseudohermaphrodites in rural villages of the Dominican Republic. Many of these individuals were raised as girls, albeit with awareness of genital abnormality, but most identified themselves as male after puberty. The investigators attribute this transformation in gender identity to the direct effects of androgen, but it seems equally likely that it resulted from social perceptions of anatomical changes in the genitalia and secondary sexual characteristics that were clearly male rather than female.

Most of the research on female hormonal changes at puberty has been focused on the emotional and psychological symptoms thought to accompany menstruation. Dysphoric moods, depression, and the like, are irrelevent to sex-typing, and the evidence for their association with hormonal changes is tenuous in any case (Clark & Ruble, 1978; Messent, 1976; Parlee, 1973). There is some evidence that postmenarcheal girls prefer the female gender and have more positive attitudes to female bodily characteristics than premenarcheal girls (Koff, Rierdan, & Silverstone, 1978). These findings can more reasonably be attributed to the social meaning of menarche as an indicator of adult female status than to any direct influence of hormones.

Intellectual Functioning

Waber (1977, 1979) proposed that sex differences in verbal and spatial abilities might be a function of the rate of physical maturation and the timing of puberty. She tested 80 boys and girls, classified as early and late maturers at two age levels (ages 10½ and 13½ for girls; ages 13½ and 15–16 for boys), for verbal fluency and spatial ability. Late maturers of both sexes at both age levels performed better than early maturers on spatial skills; there were no differences on verbal fluency. Tests of dichotic listening were also given to assess brain lateralization. For older children only, late maturers had more clear patterns of lateralization than early maturers. Sherman (1979) also found that the spatial test scores of high school females were positively correlated with self-reported age of greatest growth; girls with high spatial scores had their period of rapid growth later than those with low spatial scores.

In a related study, boys and girls from the Fels longitudinal study were rated for indirect signs of androgen and estrogen levels (muscle/fat, overall shape, genital or breast development, pubic hair). At ages 16 and 18, but not at 13, boys with low spatial scores and high verbal fluency had more signs of masculine physical development than those with the reverse pattern. For girls, feminine body types were negatively related to spatial skills; fluency was not related to body type (Petersen, 1976). An attempted replication for individuals from 18 through early adulthood yielded very weak support for the hypothesis that somatic characteristics were related to cognitive abilities (Berenbaum & Resnick, 1982).

Broverman and his associates (Broverman, Klaiber, Kobayashi, & Vogel, 1968) argued that sex differences in verbal fluency and spatial skills resulted from the neurological effects of sex hormones. They proposed that estrogen facilitated performance on tasks involving "automatization"— quick fluent, repetitive responses—and androgen enhanced performance on tasks involving "inhibition" of automatic responses so that complex processing could occur. Contrary to the hypothesis, adolescent and adult males with body types suggesting high androgen levels (short, heavy, hairy) performed better on automatized tasks and less well on spatial and perceptual restructuring tasks than did those with less evidence of androgen exposure (tall, thin, little body hair) (Broverman, Broverman, Vogel, Palmer, & Klaiber, 1964; Broverman et al., 1968; Petersen, 1979). More recent studies have shown some correlations between direct assessments of testosterone levels and automatization (Petersen, 1979). Researchers have interpreted these results as indicating that high levels of *either* androgen or estrogen may activate neurological functions that favor automatized responding, but all of the adult research has been performed on men. Their hypotheses have been severely criticized on the grounds that incorrect assumptions were made about the neurological equivalence of sympathetic nervous system activation and central nervous system functioning (Parlee, 1972; Petersen, 1979).

In interpreting these findings, it is difficult to disentangle the timing of maturity, the history of hormone exposure, and body type. Each of these variables has both biochemical and social significance; currently available data do not permit clear inferences about how or why the observed patterns occur. Certain empirical generalizations appear to be reasonably solid: Spatial ability relative to verbal fluency appears to be associated with late rather than early maturing and with relatively nonmasculine (for males) or nonfeminine (for females) body types. It may also be associated with relatively low levels of sex-appropriate hormones, but most of the evidence involves body types rather than direct assessment of hormone levels. There is no evidence of cyclical fluctuations in cognitive performance associated with the female menstrual cycle, as would be expected if estrogen levels influenced cognitive functioning (Dan, 1979; Persky, 1974). Furthermore, if androgen is inimical to spatial skill, it is paradoxical that the male superiority in spatial skill increases during adolescence, the period when androgen concentrations increase many times over those experienced in childhood.

The relation of spatial and verbal fluency to timing of maturity is also open to both neurological and social interpretations. Waber (1979) suggests that physical maturing at adolescence produces some types of neurological reorganization, but she is cautious about specifying the nature of that process. Early maturing might terminate mental growth (e.g., hemispheric specialization) just as it ends physical growth. As a result, those that mature later have more time to develop before termination of growth by adult hormones. However, if the analogy to physical growth is taken further, it is possible that the rate of mental growth could be more rapid for early than for late maturers, at least in the few years preceding puberty, so that the end point reached is equivalent. If, as Waber (1979) argues, girls are 1 to 2 years ahead of boys in neuromotor development during childhood, then the fact that girls reach puberty earlier than boys do would not explain the sex differences in spatial and verbal skill. Other investigators have pointed out the social impact of puberty and have suggested that certain kinds of cognitive processing may occur less efficiently during a time when a child is preoccupied with body changes, increased sexual interest, and changing social relationships.

Summary

Biological influences have been investigated most extensively for sex-typed intellectual functioning—spatial and verbal skills—and for sex-typed interests and behavior. The hypothesis that spatial skill is inherited as a recessive gene located on the X chromosome, though supported by some early work, has been seriously questioned and rejected by many investigators. Sex differences in hemispheric specialization have also been suggested; but the data for children are wildly contradictory. There is some agreement that adult females have less pronounced lateralization of the hemispheres and may therefore experience more difficulty in exercising spatial reasoning without verbal mediation or interference. For children, however, there appears to be no clear evidence of sex differences in hemispheric specialization. There is little or no evidence that prenatal hormone exposure influences cognitive functioning. Among adolescents and adults, however, males with relatively nonmasculine body types and females with relatively nonfeminine body types perform better on spatial tasks (relative to verbal fluency) than individuals with highly sex-typed body characteristics. In addition, late maturing boys and girls perform relatively better on spatial skills than early maturing children.

Girls who are exposed to prenatal androgens appear to have more masculine and less feminine interests than normal females, but these widely cited findings rest on a slim data base. Human patterns are partially consistent with experimental demonstrations that prenatal androgen can influence the sexual behavior and activity level of rodents and primates, but more refined and well-controlled studies are needed before we conclude that human sex-typed behavior is affected by early exposure to androgen. Even less evidence of the influence of prenatal progestin and estrogen is currently available. None of the available studies provides evidence for prenatal hormone effects on heterosexual or homosexual orientation or on personality characteristics.

With the upsurge of psychobiology and sociobiology in both scholarly and popular literature, there is an urgent need for refined and methodologically sophisticated studies in which teams of biologically trained investigators collaborate with psychologically oriented researchers. Many available studies suffer from serious problems of inadequate measurement, poor control groups, and other methodological deficiencies, particularly for the psychological and behavioral variables measured. Definite conclusions are often drawn from very weak data. When significant findings occur, biologically oriented investigators often conclude that there is a direct causal effect of hormones on behavior; psychologically oriented collaborators could temper that enthusiasm with alternative hypotheses about intervening psychological and social processes. Perhaps such interdisciplinary efforts could produce a more sophisticated and articulated understanding of the complex interactions of biological and social variables. The information generated would be important not only for basic knowledge, but for practical purposes such as counseling expectant parents about the likely outcomes of prenatal hormone treatments. I was recently asked for advice by a woman who had taken birth control pills during the first three months of a pregnancy because she was unaware that she was pregnant. Although she wanted the baby, her family and friends were strongly advising her to have an abortion because the baby would be abnormal. To make an intelligent decision, she needed sound scientific evidence that is not currently available.

SOCIALIZATION AND SEX-TYPING

Two major processes are posited by almost all theories as the means by which children are taught the sex-typed norms and expectations of their culture: presentation of models for observational learning and direct instruction (often through reinforcement and punishment). The principal agents of socialization are parents, siblings, teachers, peers, and the mass media. In the sections that follow, we first examine the process of observational learning as it applies to sex-typing. Then, the patterns of more direct training by various agents of socialization are discussed.

Observational Learning

Every person with whom a child has contact is a potential model of sex-typed behavior because every person is male or female. Early theories, based on the psychoanalytic concept of identification, assumed that the parents were the principal models of masculinity and femininity. More recent social learning and cognitive developmental theories postulate that children learn sex-typing from observing a wide variety of adults and children in their immediate environments and in the wider world presented through the mass media. To assess the importance of observation, one must first ask to what extent children are exposed to males and females manifesting sex-typed characteristics. Then, one can ask whether such exposure is an important influence in socializing attitudes and behaviors.

Do Children Observe Sex-Stereotyped Behavior?

Although American society has changed to some degree, most adults continue to manifest sex-stereotyped patterns of household responsibility, occupational activity, recreational interests, and achievement. The average child sees women cooking, cleaning, and sewing; working in "female" jobs such as clerical, secretarial, sales, teaching, nursing; choosing to dance, sew, or play bridge for recreation; and achieving in artistic or literary areas more often than in science and engineering. That same child sees men mowing the lawn, washing the car, or doing household repairs; working in "male" occupations; choosing team sports, fishing, and nights with "the boys" for recreation; and achieving in math, science, and technical areas more often than in poetry or art. In school, the teachers of young children are women; the teachers of older students and the administrators with power are usually men. Peers and siblings pursue sex-stereotyped activities, games, and interests more often than they engage in cross-sex activity. Hence, although there are some individual differences, most children are exposed continually in their own environments to models of sex-stereotyped activities, interests, and roles.

Mass Media Content. Even more consistent and extreme presentations of traditional male and female roles appear in most mass media. Television is a monolith of stereotypes. Children of every age spend much more time with television than they do with any other mass medium. The average child spends more time watching television than in any other single activity except sleep (Comstock, Chaffee, Katzman, McCombs, & Roberts, 1978; Gross & Jeffries-Fox, 1978). Partly for that reason, television programming has been subjected to careful scrutiny for its portrayals of males and females.

Content analysis of virtually every category of programming demonstrates consistently that (1) females are underrepresented and males are overrepresented in comparison to their numbers in the real world, (2) adult males and females are very often shown performing sex-stereotyped occupational and domestic roles; and (3) sex-stereotyped personal-social behavior abounds. Males compose approximately two-thirds to three-fourths of the major characters in prime-time drama, Saturday morning programming, advertisements directed at adults or children, spot announcements on Saturday morning, adult programming on public television, and even most educational programs designed for children (Aronoff, 1974; Barcus, 1977; Busby, 1975; Cantor, 1978; Courtney & Whipple, 1974; Dohrmann, 1975; Franzwa, 1978; Lemon, 1977; McArthur & Eisen, 1976b; Schuetz & Sprafkin, 1978; Stein & Friedrich, 1975; Streicher, 1974; Tedesco, 1974; United States Commission on Civil Rights, 1977). In programming where minority characters appear, females are an even smaller percent relative to male members of the same minority group (Lemon, 1977; United States Commission on Civil Rights, 1977). Certain categories of programs, such as situation comedies and soap operas, have more balanced proportions of the two sexes, but there is no program category where females form the majority (Lemon, 1977; Stein & Friedrich, 1975). The overrepresentation of males is interpreted by many as a symbol of the status, value, and power attached to the male role in society and as an indication that males can participate in a wider variety of activities and settings than females. Family dramas include both males and females, but cartoon adventures, crime dramas, news, and public affairs are male domains if one is to believe the messages of television.

The activities, occupations, toy preferences, and domestic roles of most television characters follow sex-typed patterns. In many cases, television presents a more extreme picture than is true in the real world. For example, from 1960 to the late 1970s, the proportion of adult women characters who were employed outside their homes gradually increased, but it remained well below the actual percentage of women who were employed in the American population (DeFleur, 1964; Tedesco, 1974; United States Commission on Civil Rights, 1977). Employed women typically perform female jobs such as nursing, teaching, and clerical work, or they assist a male character in some way. Professional, managerial, and law enforcement occupations are usually occupied by men. In fact, sex is a more reliable correlate of occupational status than race in television drama; black males have higher status occupations than white females (Busby, 1975; Tedesco, 1974; United States Commission on Civil Rights, 1977). In advertisements and in children's programs, adult females are often shown in domestic and parenting roles, and they are shown indoors or at home (Courtney & Whipple, 1974; McArthur & Eisen, 1976b). Males are presented as authority figures. The great majority of "voice-overs" (spoken narration by an off-screen character) on advertisements are male voices even when the product is feminine (Courtney & Whipple, 1974; Stein & Friedrich, 1975).

Males demonstrate masculine personal-social characteristics on television more than females do, but there are few identifiable behaviors that are exhibited more often by females than male characters. In one analysis of children's Saturday morning programs, males more often manifested activity, autonomy, attempts at problem solving, and discord with others (McArthur & Eisen, 1976b). In another, males were more aggressive, constructive, and more helpful (Sternglanz & Serbin, 1974). Females did not show *any* behavior more than males except deference and passivity (McArthur & Eisen, 1976b; Sternglanz & Serbin, 1974; Streicher, 1974). Males also received more consequences for their actions, positive and negative. However, females were often punished for activity (Sternglanz & Serbin, 1974). Television communicates "masculine" attributes of dominance, aggression, autonomy, and activity as clearly sex-typed. In contrast, the image of femininity is largely a vacuum; females do very little except follow the lead of their active male companions.

An almost identical picture emerges from an analysis of children's storybooks and textbooks designed for nearly all age levels; males compose the great majority of central characters (Busby, 1975;

Child, Potter, & Levin, 1946; Key, 1975; Weitzman, Eifler, Hokada, & Ross, 1972). Males and females are shown in traditional domestic and occupational roles. Male characters engage in more activity, and females tend to be passive onlookers or followers. Some analyses have found less stereotyped patterns (Davis, 1979), but the majority concur that girls and women are underrepresented in children's literature and textbooks, and that their activities, interests, and behaviors are either traditionally female or nonexistent.

Mass Media Form. Much of the sex-typed content in the mass media is obvious, but messages about male-female patterns also exist at a more subtle level in the form or composition of the media. In an analysis of magazine advertisements Goffman (1979) demonstrated that messages concerning authority, dominance, and the like, are conveyed through features such as the arrangement of characters (e.g., males are placed higher than women by being taller or by standing while the woman sits), visual and body orientation, and childlike postures of women that have little to do with the product being advertised.

Similarly, television toy commercials aimed at boys and girls contain different patterns of production features. Commercials aimed at boys have more variability of scenes, active toys, rapid cuts, loud music, and more sound effects than neutral or feminine advertisements. Commercials aimed at girls are characterized by camera fades, dissolves, and background music (Welch, Huston-Stein, Wright, & Plehal, 1979). These production features appear to mimic some of the culturally shared symbolic associations with masculinity (e.g., fast, sharp, loud) and femininity (gradual, soft, fuzzy). They may convey messages about sex-typing at a level considerably more subtle and, therefore, more difficult to detect or alter than the content messages.

Social Change and Media Content. An alert reader will by now be saying that television and book content may have changed in response to an increasing social awareness of sexism. In one sense, there has been change in the past 10 years. Many children's books with a specific intent of portraying the sexes equally have been published. One television series, *Freestyle,* was produced with the goal of counteracting sex stereotypes, and several others have shown females taking active, nontraditional roles. However, these are small drops in a large bucket. The overall pattern of media portrayal is changing very slowly if at all. For example, analyses of the winners of the Caldecott Prize for children's literature from 1941 to 1971 showed a decline in the

percent of female characters from 1950 to 1970 (Key, 1975). Content analyses of television from 1967 to 1977 indicated very little change (see Gerbner, 1972; Lemon, 1977). Furthermore, old television programs and books disappear very slowly. Much of children's programming consists of reruns made perhaps 20 years ago. Many mass media lag behind other parts of our society in responding to social change. Unfortunately, the portraits of males and females they present are more stereotyped than the ones that would emerge from a wide sampling of American society.

Media Presentations and Children's Sex-Typing

Sex-Typing and Media Content. Given the content of television, one might expect heavy viewers to absorb highly stereotyped views of sex roles. Correlational studies, however, show very modest associations between the amount of television children watch and their sex-typed beliefs or attitudes. In one study of children from first through sixth grades, those who watched heavy doses of Saturday morning and after-school television had more stereotyped views of male and female personality attributes than did light viewers. Prime time viewing was not related to stereotypes (Greer, 1980). In two other studies, there was no correlation between the amount of television viewed and children's sex stereotypes or sexist attitudes (Gross & Jeffries-Fox, 1978; Perloff, 1977). Sex-typed self-perceptions and preferences (as opposed to stereotypes) are weakly correlated with the amount of television viewed (Beuf, 1974; Frueh & McGhee, 1975; Leary, Greer, & Huston, 1982).

Another approach is to examine correlates of exposure to particular television programs. In one survey, children who watched programs containing nontraditional women characters also considered nontraditional occupations more appropriate for women than children who did not watch those programs (Miller & Reeves, 1976). Of course, correlations do not demonstrate a causal influence of television; they may indicate that individual differences among children lead to a differential selection of television programs. The latter interpretation is supported by the finding that female adolescents who scored high on a measure of androgyny had positive attitudes toward a popular assertive female television character, whereas feminine adolescents often disapproved of her behavior (Friedrich-Cofer, Tucker, Norris-Baker, Farnsworth, Fisher, Hannington, & Hoxie, 1978).

Comprehension of Sex-Typed Media Form. By

elementary school age, children understand the sex-typed connotations of television forms, although their initial and predominant impressions are guided by content. Children from the first through sixth grades were exposed to three different types of stimuli containing the formal features that were identified as masculine or feminine by Welch et al. (1979): commercially made advertisements for sex-neutral products, experimentally made ''pseudocommercials'' with meaningless content, and verbal descriptions of the features without associated content. For all three types of stimuli, children classified those with masculine and feminine features as expected. For the commercially made advertisements, they did not identify the sex-typed forms unless they were instructed to attend to the music or camera techniques rather than the content (Greer, Huston, Wright, Welch, & Ross, 1981). Children in the elementary school age range also come to understand sex-typed forms in spoken language but, again, content cues sometimes override their awareness of form (Edelsky, 1977; Fillmer & Haswell, 1977). At least two interpretations might be given for the fact that children's conscious awareness of sex-typing is guided by content cues. Children may be influenced primarily by content, or the influence of form could be difficult to recognize and therefore potentially more insidious than content. Nevertheless, they perceive and recognize sex-typed forms fairly readily if given a set to do so.

Investigations of the Process of Observational Learning

Direct assessments of the role of observational learning in the acquisition of sex-typed knowledge, attitudes, and behavior can be obtained by examining the experimental literature on modeling as well as experimental investigations of the impact of particular media portrayals. One prediction derived from several major theories is that children will be more likely to imitate a model of their own gender than one of the other gender. However, in a review of a large number of experimental studies incorporating models and children of both genders, there was little evidence that children imitate same-sex models preferentially (Maccoby & Jacklin, 1974). These authors concluded that modeling probably does play a part in the genesis of sex-typed differences, but that the simplistic notion of generalized imitation of same-sex models was not supported.

Yet neither social learning nor cognitive developmental theory necessarily implies such a simplistic prediction. According to social learning theory,

many variables can affect imitative learning and performance. Model nurturance, power, prestige, competence, vicarious reward and punishment, similarity between model and child on many dimensions other than gender are only a few demonstrated determinants of imitation. The real issue is: When is the model's gender sufficiently important in relation to other variables to influence the child's attention, comprehension, recall, or imitative behavior? When is gender sufficiently salient to have an effect? Situational cues emphasizing gender or sex-typing—for example, labeling activities as sex-typed—may attune children to that dimension. Their own previously learned concepts may make them notice the gender of an actor when a behavior is stereotypically associated with masculine or feminine roles more than they do when a behavior is relatively neutral. Therefore, one would expect same-sex imitation to occur in situations where gender is emphasized or when the behavior exhibited is culturally sex-typed. Furthermore, as Bem proposes, individuals may differ in the degree to which gender is salient to them in a wide variety of settings. Highly sex-typed individuals should show more same-sex imitation than individuals with less sex-typed self-perceptions.

The role of same-sex models in cognitive developmental and schema theories is to provide the child with exemplars of the societal expectations congruent with the child's own gender. The child constructs concepts of masculinity and femininity by extracting common features from the observed behavior of many models. Therefore, children learn and recall the most common, obvious, and consistent patterns associated with male and female models. Behavior that is incongruent with the child's gender schemas may go unnoticed, be forgotten quickly, or be assimilated into those schemas by cognitive transformations. Therefore, children may recall the behavior of male or female models as fitting sex-typed concepts even when the original behavior differed in some respect. These theories do imply that children will attend more closely to members of their own gender and learn the roles associated with their own gender more extensively than they learn the other gender's role. The theories also predict differential imitation of same-sex models, but such imitation would probably be most likely when the model exhibits behavior that fits the child's gender role concepts. That is, same-sex imitation should occur most reliably when the child perceives the model as an exemplar of the gender role to which the child aspires.

The investigations reviewed in the following sections do not represent a comprehensive survey of studies in which boys and girls observed male and female models. Instead, they represent studies where gender or sex-typing might be salient to the child. The effect of the model's gender or the sex-typing of the model's behavior is examined in the various steps of the observational learning process, from selective attention through comprehension to imitative behavior.

Selective Attention.   There is little support for the prediction that children attend differentially to same-sex models, even when gender cues are apparent, but the data base is small and somewhat contradictory. In one study, when preschool children saw a male and female simultaneously, boys looked at males more than females, but the trend for girls attending to female models was not significant (Slaby & Frey, 1975). Elementary school children, for whom attention was assessed by feedback electroencephalography, did not attend differentially on the basis of model gender or on the basis of the sex-typed content of the task being performed (Bryan & Luria, 1978). Another study failed to support an extrapolation of the social learning hypothesis that children should attend to same-sex models because of a history of differential reinforcement for imitating same-sex models. Children were reinforced for imitating one male model, but not another; in a subsequent task, there were no differences in attention to the two models (Grusec & Brinker, 1972). In contrast to these generally negative results from laboratory stimuli, Sprafkin and Liebert (1978) found that children did attend to television programs featuring a central character of their own gender more than one featuring the other gender, but only when the theme of the program dealt with sex-typed content.

The evidence for selective attention to sex-typed models is shaky, and more investigation is needed. In particular, available studies deal with only one aspect of attention—children's responses to stimuli that are presented to them. In the real world, selective attention involves choosing the stimuli to which one exposes oneself, as well as attending differentially once the stimuli are present. Boys and girls, or children with masculine or feminine interests, may tune the television to different programs; however, once the program is on, they may not differ greatly in attentional patterns to different components of the program.

Comprehension and Recall.   Studies of recall, designed to measure what children have encoded from an observed stimulus, are strikingly consistent in showing that children recall behavior that fits sex stereotypes, performed by either male or female models, better than they do counterstereotypic behavior. In some cases, they transform information to fit sex stereotype schemas by recalling the sex of the model incorrectly. There is some tendency to recall the behavior of a same-sex model better than that of the other sex, but primarily when that behavior conforms to sex stereotypes. On the whole, there is little evidence that the sex of the model alone determines what children encode and retain; instead, the consistency between the model's sex and the sex-typing of the behavior is the important variable.

The tendency to recall sex-stereotyped behavior is slightly more consistent for children in elementary school than for preschoolers (see Martin & Halverson, 1981, for review). Fifth graders remembered more stereotyped than counterstereotyped behaviors from stories; in particular, they were unlikely to recall feminine traits of male characters (Koblinsky, Cruse, & Sugawara, 1978). In two experiments, Bryan and Luria (1978) found that children remembered activities appropriate for their gender better than those suited for the other gender, regardless of the model's sex. In both stories and films, preschool boys recalled masculine behavior by a male model particularly well, but the results were less consistent for girls (McArthur & Eisen, 1976a, 1976b). One exception was the finding that preschool children remembered more from a story with atypical behavior than they did from a story with sex-typical actions (Jennings, 1975).

Three studies support the cognitive developmental prediction that children not only encode sex-typed behavior more readily than atypical actions, but they *transform* counterstereotypical information to fit gender schemas. In two studies, children saw toy commercials in which child actors played with stereotyped or counterstereotyped toys. When asked afterward whether the children in the commercial were boys or girls, about half of the children who had seen counterstereotyped advertisements recalled the sex of the child actors incorrectly. By contrast, almost all of the children who saw a stereotyped version recalled the actors' gender correctly (Atkin, 1975; Frey & Ruble, 1981; see Martin & Halverson, 1981). Similar distortions occurred when young children saw one of four films depicting a doctor and nurse with all possible combinations of males and females in the two roles. When the children were shown photographs of the actors and asked whether each was a doctor or nurse, all who had seen the male doctor and female nurse answered correctly. By contrast, only 22% of those who saw the female doctor and male nurse identified both roles correctly. Over half of the subjects in that group said they had seen a male doctor and female nurse. There was a stronger tendency to relabel the male nurse than the female physician. Children who had had personal experience with male nurses were more accurate on the task than those who had not (Cordua, McGraw, & Drabman, 1979).

Bem's (1981) hypothesis that individual differences in gender salience affect children's patterns of learning also has some empirical support. In one investigation both boys and girls with masculine sex role preferences remembered a male model's actions better than those of a female, whereas children with feminine preferences recalled both models equally well (Perry & Perry, 1975). Liben and Signorella (1980), studying first- and second-grade children, used a measure of sex stereotyping to divide children into those who considered many activities and behaviors equally appropriate for both sexes or those who considered many appropriate only for one sex. On a recognition memory task, children with highly stereotyped sex role concepts remembered pictures showing males performing traditional activities, but there was no difference for pictures of female actors. For incorrect pictures in the recognition set, children gave false recognition responses to pictures of males in traditional activities more often than to males in nontraditional activities; again, there were no differences for pictures of female actors.

In another investigation (Kail & Levine, 1976), girls' sex-typed toy preferences predicted their tendency to encode and recall information in sex-typed categories. (There was too little variation in boys' toy preferences to test individual differences.) Children's patterns of encoding and recall were measured by observing release from proactive inhibition when the child was given a series of word pairs with masculine or feminine connotations (names of sex-typed objects). After a series of word pairs from one category (masculine or feminine), experimental subjects were given a pair from the other category. Memory for the pair from the new category improved (in comparison to earlier trials), indicating that subjects did encode the words in sex-typed categories. Girls with feminine sex-typed toy preferences showed this release from proactive inhibition when the word category changed, but girls with masculine preferences did not.

These findings support the position that children's concepts about sex roles and stereotypes guide their selection and encoding of information from the behavior of models. Although the behavior of same-sex models is sometimes recalled better than that of other-sex models, this is much more likely when the behavior fits a sex stereotype. Counterstereotypical behavior may be ignored or transformed to fit gender schemas. Children whose concepts or preferences are highly sex-typed are likely to encode and remember information on the basis of the model's gender or the sex-typing of the behavior more often than those children showing less sex-typed patterns. What emerges most clearly from these studies is that both social learning and cognitive developmental theory are slightly off target in emphasizing the child's learning of *same*-sex patterns through observation. What children appear to learn (and then to use in encoding further observations) are the stereotyped patterns for *both* genders, not just for their own. They form concepts of masculinity and femininity, not just concepts of "what is appropriate for me," which they use to encode and remember the behavior of others. They do not simply learn and recall the actions of a model of their own gender. These basic concepts form a substrate on which, as Martin and Halverson (1981) suggest, schemas for one's own gender, or for the gender role which one prefers, are elaborated. Although there is some tendency for children, particularly boys, to remember behavior appropriate to their own gender, regardless of the sex of the model, it appears that the selection of sex-typed behavior patterns occurs not at the level of initial acquisition, but at the level of cognitive elaboration and performance. Children learn and understand social expectations for both genders; attitudinal and motivational factors probably account for behavioral conformity (or the lack of it) to learned patterns prescribed for one's own gender.

Beliefs and Attitudes. In the studies of comprehension discussed above, children were asked to recall what they had just seen and heard. Another approach is to ask children what they believe is true about males and females (stereotypes), or what they approve and disapprove of (attitudes). Despite the general tendency for children to encode and recall information according to sex stereotypes, a few studies suggest that those concepts or stereotypes can be altered by exposure to counterstereotypical models. The modeling stimuli in these studies have typically consisted of real storybooks or television programs that are considerably richer and more complex than the slides, pictures, and laboratory-constructed films used to measure recall, perhaps accounting for the greater impact of counterstereotypical models. Both preschool and elementary school children exposed to nontraditional media portrayals expressed egalitarian views about adult occupational and parenting roles, children's activities, and personal-social attributes more often than children who saw neutral or traditional sex role portrayals (Atkin, 1975; Davidson, Yasuna, & Tower, 1979; Flerx et al., 1976).

Although counterstereotypical models may change children's beliefs about what is possible or true, there is less clear evidence that such models change their attitudes or meet with their full approval. Two studies demonstrated that children approved of storybook characters who behaved in sex-stereotyped ways more often than those who behaved in counterstereotyped ways (Connor, Serbin, & Ender, 1978; Jennings, 1975). By contrast, third- and eighth-graders who saw the counterstereotyped television commercials expressed less traditional attitudes about women's roles than those who saw the stereotyped commercials, but only under certain sets of experimental conditions. Furthermore, the eighth-grade boys "boomeranged" and expressed more traditional attitudes about women's roles after the counterstereotyped commercials than after the traditional ones (Pingree, 1978).

A much more extensive and intensive exposure to counterstereotyped portrayals occurred during the semester-long classroom use of the television series *Freestyle*. The series was designed to portray nontraditional activities, personal-social behaviors, and adult occupations in ways that would change children's sex-typed beliefs, attitudes, and interests, particularly with regard to future careers. The summative evaluation, carried out in several sites with various ethnic groups, indicated that the series did produce changes in children's beliefs and attitudes, changes in the direction of accepting nontraditional behaviors. Children who saw the series developed less stereotyped beliefs and more accepting attitudes about childhood activities, such as girls' participation in athletics and mechanical activities or boys' involvement in helping roles, and about adult occupational and domestic roles. There were fewer changes in stereotypes and attitudes about sex-typed behavior such as independence, assertiveness, and risk taking, but children did come to accept the idea that girls could be leaders. Most of these changes in belief and attitude were retained 9 months after the TV series ended; hence, they appear to have been fairly durable. The only areas in which the series affected children's *own* interests or stated preferences were athletics and mechanical activities— girls expressed more interest in these areas after

seeing the series (Johnston, Ettema, & Davidson, 1980).

Imitative Behavior. There is some tendency for children to imitate same-sex models but, again, the sex-typed nature of the behavior exhibited is even more important than the sex of the model. Imitation is generally greatest when a same-sex model exhibits "sex-appropriate" behavior or when a behavior is labeled as appropriate for the child's gender. Similarly, children's preferences for objects or activities are most clearly affected by a model manifesting sex-appropriate behavior or by sex-typed labels (Liebert, McCall, & Hanratty, 1971; White, 1978). In several studies, children have seen films or heard stories portraying sex-typed behavior such as play with airplanes, task persistence, play with dolls, and affectionate behavior. With one exception (McArthur & Eisen, 1976b), boys imitated masculine behavior, particularly when the model was male. Somewhat less consistently, girls imitated feminine behavior, primarily when the model was female (Barkley, Ullman, Otto, & Brecht, 1977; Franzini, Litrownik, & Blanchard, 1978; Frey & Ruble, 1981; Fryrear & Thelen, 1969; McArthur & Eisen, 1976a; Zimmerman & Koussa, 1975). In these studies, children were presumed to encode the model's behavior in gender-based schemas, but one experiment directly tested the relative importance of the sex-typed labels versus the sex of the model. Neutral play activities were labeled as appropriate for males or females or were not labeled. Children's preferences and imitative behavior were most clearly influenced by the sex-typed labels, but were slightly more extreme when the sex of the model was consistent with the label (Masters, Ford, Arend, Grotevant, & Clark, 1979).

These studies demonstrate that children use already existing concepts about sex-typing in determining the influence of models on preferences and behavior, but they do not demonstrate that children *acquire* those concepts from observing models. The process of acquisition has been demonstrated in a few studies where initially neutral behaviors were sex-typed experimentally by associating them consistently with male or female models. In an extension of social learning theory, Perry and Bussey (1979) proposed that children form concepts of sex-typed behavior from observing the commonalities among males or females or the frequency with which males and females perform various behaviors to arrive at general concepts of sex-appropriate behavior. They exposed children to eight models—four males and four females. In one experiment, the degree of consensus among models of each sex varied. When all males performed one behavior and all females another, children showed significant same-sex imitation. When there was little consensus, same-sex imitation did not occur. In a second study, children imitated a model of their own sex if that person's behavior agreed with the majority of the models of his or her gender; they did not imitate a same-sex model whose behavior differed from the majority. A similar effect occurred for preschool children who saw a television "commercial" for a neutral toy in which the actors were either two boys or two girls. Children later played with the advertised toy more often when they had seen members of their own gender than when they had seen the other gender in the commercial (Ruble et al., 1981).

Summary

The observational learning data support the hypothesis that children form concepts of sex-typed behavior to which they assimilate the behavior of individual models. They learn schemas for *both* masculine and feminine sex-typing, not simply a concept of what is expected for their own gender. A selection of patterns "appropriate" for their own gender occurs more clearly at the level of performance than at the level of acquisition. When observed behavior fits the sex-typed concept or when situational information such as sex-typed labels suggests that a model is an exemplar of sex-appropriateness, children imitate the behavior. The model's gender is one cue for the appropriateness of imitation, but only when it is consistently and frequently associated with a particular behavior. What role can modeling play in encouraging non-sex-stereotyped behavior? Exposure to one model behaving in a counterstereotyped way may change children's stated beliefs about what is masculine and feminine, but it does not lead to powerful imitative effects or changes in preference, attitude, and affective reactions to nonstereotyped behavior. Thus, brief exposure to one model is not likely to produce a very powerful effect. Perry and Bussey's (1979) study suggests that exposure to several counterstereotyped models, particularly if they are in the majority, could produce imitation of nontraditional behavior. The *Freestyle* evaluation indicates that continuing exposure may have wide-ranging and lasting effects. Experimental studies provide limited information because the models are strangers or media characters, not people who are important in the child's life. In the section on parent socialization, I will discuss indirect evidence that parents who follow coun-

terstereotypical life patterns (e.g., mothers who are employed) do influence their children's behavior as well as their beliefs about sex-typing.

SOCIALIZATION OF SEX-TYPING IN THE FAMILY

In recent years efforts to determine the parents' roles in their children's acquisition of sex-typing have focused primarily on the issue of whether parents treat boys and girls differently, particularly in ways that would lead to sex-typed differences in behavior. However, differential treatment, if it exists, could be a response to sex differences in children's behavior as well as a cause. Therefore, most of the earlier studies designed to discover the effects of childrearing on children's sex-typing focused on within-sex examinations of correlations between parent practices and child characteristics. Although these studies also suffer from ambiguity about the direction of effects, they at least avoid some of the possible alternate explanations that arise when males and females are compared. Furthermore, the conclusions that arise from a confluence of findings from the two approaches are stronger than from either independently. In the following section, recent data on sex differences in parent treatment are examined first. Then, evidence on parent socialization practices, parent role participation, and sibling constellation as predictors of within-sex variations is presented. In later sections, differential treatment of the sexes by nonfamily adults, particularly teachers, is discussed and compared to the information about parents.

Do Adults Treat Boys and Girls Differently?

Maccoby and Jacklin (1974) examined differential socialization of boys and girls primarily by determining whether different types of childrearing practices were directed to the two sexes and concluded that there were surprisingly few differences in parents' treatment of boys and girls. During infancy, there were no differences in total interaction or verbal interaction; the only difference that emerged consistently was that boys were given more gross motor stimulation and encouragement in physical activity (p. 309). For preschool and elementary school age groups, there was little evidence from observational studies that boys and girls receive different amounts of parent warmth, restriction, or achievement pressure, but there was a clear pattern indicating that boys received more punishment, particularly physical punishment. Boys also tended to receive more praise than girls. The literature indicated no evidence that parents responded differently to boys' and girls' dependency or aggression.

These authors noted several limitations on the evidential base for their conclusions. One problem, also discussed extensively by Block (1978), is that most of the studies reported involved preschool children. Sex differentiation may increase with age as role-related expectations become more important to parents. A second problem, not addressed by Maccoby and Jacklin, is that the behaviors assessed were almost all limited to the personal-social aspects of sex-typing. Virtually no attention was given to the differential socialization of activities and interests. In one small section, the authors stated that "of course" parents encourage the "superficial" aspects of sex-typing, that is, sex-typed toy and activity choices, though only a few studies are cited, one of which does not support this assertion (Maccoby & Jacklin, 1974, pp. 327–329). Given the evidence that activities and interests are some of the earliest and most clear-cut manifestations of sex-typing, they should not be dismissed as superficial. Personal-social behaviors, such as dependency and aggression, are not stereotyped by gender as early or as clearly as activities or even sex-differentiated adult occupations. A third problem is that most studies focused on mothers, whereas recent data demonstrate fairly consistently that fathers are more likely than mothers to treat boys and girls differently and to emphasize appropriate sex-typing, particularly for their sons. The literature reviewed here, accumulated since 1973, indicates specific areas of sex-differentiated treatment, some of which are apparent very early in children's lives.

Adult Perceptions of Boys and Girls

One means of determining whether adults respond differently to male and female children, independently of any real differences in the children's behavior, is to manipulate the adult's belief about the gender of a young child. In several studies, adults watched a videotape of a young child (9 months to 3 years) whom they were told was a boy or girl. Students made ratings of the child according to sets of presumably sex-typed characteristics, usually personal-social attributes or symbolic characteristics, such as strong-weak, active-inactive, and the like. In these studies, boys and girls were perceived as very similar. However, there was some tendency for male raters to perceive children in slightly more stereotyped ways than female raters did. Raters who had personal experience with young children were sometimes less stereotyped, but not consistently so

(Condry & Condry, 1976; Gurwitz & Dodge, 1975; Meyer & Sobieszek, 1972; Sobieszek, 1978).

By contrast, real parents of newborns rated daughters as smaller, with more fine features, softer, and less alert than sons, despite the fact that there were no physical differences between the male and female infants. In addition, fathers perceived sons as stronger and hardier than daughters. Again, fathers perceived more sex differences than mothers (Rubin, Provenzano, & Luria, 1974). The earlier studies reviewed by Maccoby and Jacklin (1974, pp. 309–311) also indicate that parents perceive girls as more fragile than boys and worry more about their well-being, and several studies demonstrate that parents of preschool children have sex stereotyped perceptions, expectations, and values for their children (Atkinson & Endsley, 1976; Fagot, 1981; Marcus & Corsini, 1978; Schau et al., 1980).

Adult Behavior with Male and Female Infants: Experimental Studies

A more sensitive index of the effect of child sex on adult reactions is obtained in studies where adults are observed interacting with infants whose gender they believe to be male or female. In several studies, the same infants have been labeled as boys or girls for different adult subjects. Most of the adults in these studies were parents themselves, so they had more experience with young children than the students assessed in the studies of perceptions. The infants ranged from 3 to 14 months old. In each case, masculine and feminine sex-typed toys as well as neutral toys were available. With one exception (Bell & Carver, 1980), both male and female adults offered dolls to children they believed to be girls more often than to children they thought were boys. Male sex-typed toys, such as hammers, were offered more often to boys than girls in some studies, but not in others (Frisch, 1977; Seavey, Katz, & Zalk, 1975; Sidorowicz & Lunney, 1980; Smith & Lloyd, 1978; Will, Self, & Datan, 1976).

In two of the most thorough studies (Frisch, 1977; Smith & Lloyd, 1978), adults also encouraged more motor activity for boys than for girls and responded to motor activity from boys more often with whole-body stimulation. Frisch (1977) also found that girls were given interpersonal stimulation and encouraged in "nurturance play" (with dolls and puppets) more often than boys. A parallel finding in a small sample was that girls received more smiling than boys, but there were no differences in touching or holding the child (Will et al., 1976). Females sought help for a crying infant sooner when they believed it was female than when it was male; males waited equally long for both sexes (Condry, Condry,

& Pogatshnik, 1978). When 2-year-old children were labeled as male or female, adults provided more goal-directed reinforcements and held higher expectations for boys, while they gave girls more compliments and encouragement in a task (Day, cited by Block, 1979).

The experimental manipulation of infant "gender" in these studies demonstrates that sex differences in treatment occur independently of differences in the child's behavior. Adults offer sex-typed toys to girls and boys, and they encourage gross motor activity for boys. They sometimes encourage interpersonal play activity and more often offer help and reassurance to girls. However, experimental studies in which adults interact with a strange infant may elicit more stereotyped behavior than parents show with their own children. If gender is one of the few things one knows about a child, it may have more influence on behavior than it would when the child's individual characteristics are well known.

Parents' Treatment of Their Own Children

During the first year of life, parents apparently engage in similar patterns of social interaction with boys and girls—smiling, touching, talking, and the like (Field, 1978; Lamb, 1977), although some earlier studies suggest more verbalization directed toward girls than boys (e.g., Goldberg & Lewis, 1969). However, fathers play with male infants differently than they do with female infants and differently than mothers play with either gender. When fathers play with boys, they are more physically rough, play more gross motor games, and use toys less (Parke & Suomi, 1980; Power & Parke, in press). One of the most consistent sex differences emerging from the earlier literature as well is that physical stimulation and gross motor play are directed toward male infants more often than female infants (see Block, 1979; Maccoby & Jacklin, 1974).

During the second year of life, when some sex-differentiated play patterns first emerge, there is more evidence of differences in parent treatment. Home observations of infants 18 to 24 months old with both parents present were conducted in two studies by Fagot (1974, 1978b) and in one study of English families (Smith & Daglish, 1977). In both U.S. samples, parents interacted with girls more than boys (i.e., boys were left to play alone more). Perhaps as a result, girls received more praise and more criticism than boys. However, parents joined the play of their sons more often than that of their daughters. Using similar methods in English working- and middle-class families, Smith and Daglish

(1977) failed to replicate most of these differences. Boys were more often stopped or punished than girls, but boys also engaged in more forbidden behavior. The differences between the two studies could be a function of different populations (the American sample was largely made up of academic parents), or the fact that the American studies involved 5 hours of observation whereas the English study entailed only 1 hour, making significant differences less likely to emerge. The finding that boys received more punishment than girls was consistent with another set of observations that involved American 27-month-olds and focused specifically on situations where the child violated maternal standards (Minton, Kagan, & Levine, 1971). Boys violated standards and received interaction from their mothers about such violations more often than girls did. There were no sex differences in frequency of maternal commands, maternal anticipations of violations, or child requests to the mother.

A true test of social learning theory requires more than simply showing differences in overall patterns of parent behavior; the theory predicts different contingencies for boys and girls. Total praise and criticism might be equal, but might be contingent on different behaviors. In one study of toddlers (Fagot, 1978b) parents' positive and negative responses to children's sex-typed behavior were recorded in the home. Parents reacted favorably when children engaged in activities typically preferred by their own sex more than when they engaged in cross-sex activities or interpersonal behavior. Specifically, parents responded differentially to block play, manipulating objects, playing with dolls, asking for help, following an adult around, helping with an adult task, running, jumping, and climbing—that is, they responded positively to sex-stereotyped behaviors. There were no sex differences in response to aggression. In a laboratory study of slightly older preschool children, parents' reactions to their children's play with preselected masculine or feminine stereotyped toys were observed. Fathers rewarded sex-appropriate play and punished sex-inappropriate play, particularly for boys. Mothers rewarded sex-inappropriate play for girls, but were inconsistent with boys (Langlois & Downs, 1980). For elementary school children in laboratory play sessions, parents more often engaged in physically active play with boys and sociable play with girls. Fathers reacted more positively to physical activity by boys than girls, and mothers responded more positively to girls seeking physical contact than to boys (Tauber, 1979b). These findings indicate that parents encourage boys in active, gross motor, and manipulative play; they encourage girls in dependent behavior and feminine sex-typed play. Moreover, fathers emphasize sex-typed play more than mothers do.

Both laboratory and naturalistic data suggest that parents, particularly fathers, may interact more with same-sex children than with cross-sex children. This pattern has been observed in laboratory studies of toddlers (Cherry & Lewis, 1976; Lamb, 1977; Weinraub & Frankel, 1977) and in home observations of elementary school age children (Margolin & Patterson, 1975). Fathers' greater involvement with sons than with daughters is also indicated by interviews with parents of young children. When asked whether they would treat boys and girls differently, parents of girls generally said they would not, but parents of boys frequently said that they thought the father should play a special role as model and play companion to his son. Fathers also said they would treat a girl more gently and encourage more active play in a boy (Fagot, 1974). Parents may feel a greater commonality and a greater responsibility for the socialization of children of their own gender compared to children of the other gender. This hypothesis is consistent with earlier findings that parents are more restrictive and controlling with children of their own sex (Rothbart & Maccoby, 1966) and with recent findings that parents use more individualized appeals when exhorting same-sex children and more status-oriented appeals with cross-sex children (Bearison, 1979). Because mothers typically assume primary responsibility for the socialization of all of their children, they may show less difference in response to male and female children. Fathers may be more influenced by a sense that they have a special responsibility for their sons' masculine development.

In the few studies of children beyond the preschool age reviewed by Maccoby and Jacklin (1974), girls reported receiving more parental warmth than boys. Block (1978) compared reports of parent practices by parents of children between 3 and 18 with reports of young adults recalling their own parents' practices during their childhood. Samples from several northern European countries as well as from the United States were included. The following differences in the treatment of sons and daughters were consistently reported by four groups: mothers, fathers, adult sons, and adult daughters. All reported that males more often than females were encouraged to compete, were taught not to cry or express feelings, were threatened with punishment, were pressured to conform socially, and were the target of suppressed anger. Females exceeded males in receiving warmth and affection, being trusted, and having parents who kept track of their whereabouts, worried about them, and hated to see them

grow up. It is difficult to determine whether the discrepancies between these data and the observations of younger children are because of true age changes or because self-reports by parents or ratings by children are more influenced by cultural stereotypes than is directly observed behavior.

Although parents value intellectual accomplishment and school achievement for both sexes, they have higher expectations and standards for their boys' long-range achievement than for that of their daughters. These differences are manifested in styles of teaching and encouraging children when they are performing difficult tasks. Parents consider college completion and advanced occupational attainment a more important goal for their sons than for their daughters (Barnett, 1979; Hoffman, 1977; Maccoby & Jacklin, 1974, p. 337). They value achievement in mathematics less, consider it less important for future life, and have lower estimates of competence in math for their daughters than for their sons (Fennema & Sherman, 1977; Fox, Tobin, & Body, 1979; Parsons, Adler, & Kaczala, 1982). Parents from homes of lower socioeconomic status verbalize discrepant goals for their sons and daughters more often than do middle-class parents (Barnett, 1979; Maccoby & Jacklin, 1974), but direct behavioral observation shows that middle-class parents also socialize achievement in boys and girls differently.

In three studies of preschool children, the teaching behaviors of parents were directly observed. Parents communicated higher expectations and more demands for independent task performance to boys while, for girls, they were more likely to provide help quickly and to focus on the interpersonal aspects of the teaching situation. These patterns occurred for both mothers and fathers (Block, 1979; Golden & Birns, 1975; Rothbart, 1971; Rothbart & Rothbart, 1976), although fathers showed more pronounced differentiation than mothers (Block, 1979). These studies again suggest the importance of examining contingencies in the parent-child interaction rather than simply measuring total amounts of behavior. In the Rothbart studies, there were no overall differences in encouragement, praise, or criticism to boys and girls, but the child behaviors to which mothers responded were different. Mothers responded more quickly to requests for help and to mistakes with daughters than with sons.

When parents respond quickly to a girl's request for help, they may communicate their low evaluations of the child's competence; when they demand independent effort from a boy, this may signify confidence in the child's ability. Another subtle means of communicating a sense of competence and importance occurs in the socialization of sex-typed language patterns, specifically the adult pattern in which males interrupt and talk simultaneously with others more often than females do. Preschool children were observed in play sessions with each parent. The sample was small, so the differences were of borderline significance but were consistent. Fathers interrupted and talked simultaneously with their children more often than mothers did, and both parents interrupted and talked simultaneously with their daughters more often than with their sons (Greif, 1979).

Beginning in middle childhood, parents allow boys more freedom to be away from home or without adult supervision than they do girls. Parents of 8-year-olds stated that they valued independence more for sons than daughters; they were willing to give their sons more choice in a "life organization plan"; and they discouraged emotional dependence more in their sons (Baumrind, 1979). Canadian mothers who were employed more often left their sons unsupervised after school than they did their daughters (Gold & Andres, 1978b). Black ghetto mothers, however, left their daughters without supervision more often than their sons, suggesting some subcultural differences in attitudes about independence (Woods, 1972). Perhaps the most persuasive data appear in a longitudinal study of 700 children in Nottingham, England, whose mothers were interviewed when the children were 4 and 7. At age 7, there were few differences between boys and girls, in reported socialization, but a very consistent pattern of greater "chaperonage" for females. Girls, in comparison to boys, were more often picked up at school or required to go home directly; they were less often left at home without an adult; more often brought playmates to the house rather than "playing in the street"; more often could be found outdoors when the parent called; had more restrictive rules about how far from home they could go alone and how much they were to inform their parents of their whereabouts; and less often were allowed to go alone to parks, recreation areas, libraries, or other public places (Newson & Newson, 1976).

The restriction on the freedom of girls is clearly not based on their level of maturity or their competence to deal with situations independently. Newson and Newson (1976) suggest a plausible explanation that has long-term implications for the experiences and opportunities available to the two sexes.

English parents in a contemporary urban setting are not alone in placing a certain emphasis upon what might be called "the chaperonage of females." Among human societies all over the world and throughout recorded time, it has been a fairly universal cultural preoccupation to place restrictions upon the geographical mobility of women and girls, and, in particular, to limit the possibility of chance encounters between dependent daughters and adult male strangers. The evidence we have discussed clearly indicated that in our own culture, too, the chaperonage factor exerts an important influence upon the daily life experience of girls as compared with boys even by the tender age of seven, ensuring that girls lead a more sheltered and protected existence. This in itself is of interest; but the implications are of greater consequence, since children who are kept under closer and more continuous surveillance must inevitably *come under consistently greater pressure towards conformity with adult standards and values.* (Newson & Newson, p. 101).

Children who are kept under close surveillance may also miss opportunities to develop a sense of their own competence and may incorporate their caregivers' fears of venturing out into the wider world. Obviously, there are long-term consequences that result when freedom of movement is restricted for adult women. Recently this was highlighted in the refrain of a feminist song, "A lady don't go out alone at night."

Summary

Although gaps exist, the current literature provides stronger support for differential treatment of boys and girls than it did in 1973. Two sets of convergent data—experimental studies in which the child's gender label is manipulated and observational studies of parents with their own children—support the conclusion that boys and girls are encouraged in different types of play activities from infancy onward. Adults promote sex-typed toy choices, particularly the exclusive use of dolls by girls. Boys are encouraged in gross motor activity more often than girls are. Adults play more actively with male infants (or infants they believe to be male), and parents respond more positively to physical activity in boys than in girls. Among older children, parents assign household chores according to sex-typed roles (Duncan, Schuman, & Duncan, 1973) and they have different educational and occupational goals for their daughters and sons.

Differences in the socialization of sex-typed personal and social behavior are found less consistently than differences in activities and interests, but several studies suggest that girls receive encouragement to show dependency, affectionate behavior, and expression of tender emotions more than boys do. There is little evidence that aggression elicits different parental reactions for boys and girls. However, boys are given more opportunities for play away from home and freedom from adult supervision, which may provide an important context for learning independence. In achievement contexts, parents also expect and demand more of boys, while they provide help more readily for girls.

Do Parent Practices Predict Children's Behavior?

The whole body of literature examining parents' socialization of agentic characteristics such as aggression, competitiveness, independence, and achievement and of communal characteristics such as cooperation, helpfulness, empathy, and prosocial behavior could conceivably be discussed here. However, such a task is well beyond the scope of this review. This discussion will be restricted to studies relating parent practices to various indexes of identity, preference, and adoption when these indexes were constructed using some theoretical construct pertaining directly to sex-typing.

Studies Based on Identification Theory

Earlier studies testing identification theories produced remarkably consistent findings, though they do not necessarily support the hypothesis that identification is the underlying process that best explains the findings. In brief, for both boys and girls, "appropriate" sex-typing and imitation of the same-sex parent are most likely to be observed in children who receive high levels of warmth, acceptance, and nurturance from the same-sex parent. For boys, paternal dominance and social power also correlate with masculinity (Biller & Borstelmann, 1967; Hetherington, 1967; Mussen, 1969). Parental encouragement of sex-typed behavior is associated with appropriate sex-typing, particularly when it comes from the other-sex parent (Biller & Borstelmann, 1967; Fling & Manosevitz, 1972; Mussen, 1969). Permissiveness about aggression, sex, and the like, is correlated with masculine activity preferences and with masculine personal-social characteristics such as independence for both boys and girls in many studies of child-rearing (Becker, 1964; Martin, 1975; Sears, Rau, & Alpert, 1965). Most of these studies were guided by unidimensional, bipolar conceptions of sex-typing and by the assumption that "appropriate" sex-typing was a positive goal of socialization. Despite recent changes in both of those assumptions, the basic findings have been replicated sufficiently

often that they stand as empirical generalizations even when the theory crumbles.

Studies Based on Recent Conceptions of Sex-Typing

Research attempting to relate parent practices to androgyny—nontraditional patterns of sex-typing or other multidimensional constructs—is sparse. Parental attitudes about sex stereotypes are generally poor predictors of children's sex-typed behavior, though they sometimes predict children's sex stereotypes (Barry, 1980; Crandall, 1978; Lott, 1978; Meyer, 1980; Perloff, 1977). Parents' expectancies about their children's sex-typed behavior are also poor predictors of play interests (Schau et al., 1980) or achievement behavior (Sherman, 1979, 1980). However, Fagot (1974) found little relationship between parents' attitudes and their behavior toward their children, so attitudes may not be the appropriate variables to examine.

Several dimensions of sex-typing were included in a recent longitudinal investigation of children 4 to 6 years old (Hetherington, Cox, & Cox, 1978): orientation (measured by the Draw-a-Person test), toy activity preferences, participation in sex-preferred activies, play with same- and other-sex peers, and ratings of personal-social behavior such as aggression and dependency. For children in nuclear families, parental correlates of "sex-appropriate" patterns were similar to those found in earlier studies. Boys' masculine preferences and adoption of masculine behavior were positively correlated with paternal availability, warmth, dominance, and maturity demands. Girls' feminine sex-typing was positively related to maternal warmth, paternal reinforcement for feminine behavior, paternal restrictiveness, and to the father's masculine score on a personality test. Boys who were androgynous (i.e., showed masculine *and* feminine behavior) had similarly dominant, decisive fathers, but their fathers were also emotionally expressive and supported a close mother-son relationship. Girls who were androgynous had fathers who were warm, but encouraged early independence and achievement. Their mothers also encouraged independence and were often employed.

Similar patterns of parental behavior were found in the histories of androgynous adults in the Berkeley longitudinal data. Men and women who were nonconforming to traditional sex roles, but otherwise were well socialized into societal values, had parents who offered a wide range of attitudinal and behavioral possibilities to their children and manifested nontraditional sex role differentiations

(Block, Von der Lippe, & Block, 1973). The high school and college students studied by Spence and Helmreich (1978) also perceived their parents as having patterns of masculinity and femininity similar to their own. However, the parents' actual scores were not related to the students' scores.

Girls who are independent, assertive, and achievement oriented often have parents who are moderately warm and permissive, and who encourage independence while holding high expectations for mature and achievement-oriented behavior. In an earlier review, Peggy Bailey and I (Stein & Bailey, 1973) assembled a considerable amount of data from both naturalistic and experimental studies, demonstrating that moderately low levels of maternal warmth were associated with girls' achievement orientation, independence, and competitiveness. In addition, mothers of independent, achievement-oriented girls were permissive, but demanded high levels of mature and achievement-related behavior from their daughters. Similar patterns appeared among the 8-year-olds studied by Baumrind (1979). Girls who were assertive, socially confident, and showed leadership had parents who demanded mature behavior and exerted control over the child during interactions. Feminine behavior, such as compliance to adults and prosocial interactions with peers, was highest among girls whose parents were both warm and demanding or controlling. In a study of 4-year-old, predominantly black Head Start children, girls' assertiveness was associated with maternal control and a tendency to use negative feedback in a teaching situation. Socially outgoing behavior (friendliness and the like) was positively correlated with both maternal warmth and control (Emmerich, 1977).

For boys, both prosocial and assertive behavior appear to be associated with parents who are warm and demanding, whereas rejection and lack of control appear to be associated with social withdrawal (Emmerich, 1977). In Baumrind's sample, the boys who manifested the highest levels of prosocial behavior and compliance to adults had parents who were responsive in warm, loving, rational ways and who demanded that their children conform to their standards. Assertiveness was related to moderate parental responsiveness, both positive and negative.

These findings support some global associations found in the socialization practices involved in the acquisition of feminine and masculine personal-social attributes. Feminine, communal behavior appears to be associated with fairly high levels of warmth from both parents and with moderate to high control. For boys, maternal warmth appears to play a particularly important role. Agentic patterns of assertiveness, leadership, and social confidence seem to be associated with high demands, control, and encouragement of independence in a context of moderate warmth. Some studies suggest that control facilitates assertiveness while others point to permissiveness, a paradox that may result from different definitions and different observational contexts. For girls, the "optimal" level of warmth to promote agentic patterns may be lower than it is for boys.

Single-Parent Families

Families with only one resident parent provide one means of evaluating the role of the absent parent in children's development. The great majority of investigations have dealt with mother-only families in which the father was "absent" or at least not in residence. Very recently, some efforts to examine father-only families have been undertaken. Obviously, single-parent families may differ from two-parent families in many ways, but evidence about them provides some broad indicators of the importance of the parents in children's acquisition of sex-typed behavior. Theories that emphasize parental identification, imitation, or reciprocal interaction predict that children without a parent of each gender will lack an important socializing influence. Theories that emphasize cognitive developmental patterns and the broader culture as major influences predict little difference between single-parent and two-parent families (see Kohlberg, 1966).

Overall, the data support the hypothesis that fathers play an important, though not irreplaceable, role in boys' development of masculinity, in girls' acquisition of heterosexual interaction skills, and in the development of sex-typed intellectual skills for both genders. Much scantier evidence supports the notion that mothers are important for girls' femininity, self-confidence, and adjustment. Several studies in the late 1960s (see Biller, 1970; Biller & Weiss, 1970, for reviews) included separate measures of sex role orientation or identity, preference, and adoption or enactment. Children from father-present and father-absent homes were carefully matched on age, IQ, demographic variables, sibling constellation, and other potentially confounding variables. Boys from father-absent homes generally obtained less masculine scores than boys from father-present homes on measures of sex role orientation and preference for sex-typed activities (e.g., the IT scale, toy preference scales, self-ratings, Draw-a-Person, and the Franck Drawing Completion Test) (Beere, 1979; Biller, 1971; Drake & McDougall, 1977;

Hetherington, 1966). Differences in sex role enactment were less clear among young boys. Ratings of classroom and free play aggression, independence, passivity, competitiveness, physical prowess, timidity, and other personal-social characteristics were used as the indexes of enactment in most of these studies. Hence, the preference tasks sampled interests and activities; the adoption measures sampled personal-social attributes. For boys from 5 to about 8, no differences in ratings of adoption were obtained in several studies (Biller, 1971; Drake & McDougall, 1977). Among boys 9 to 12 years old, Hetherington (1966) found that those whose fathers had been absent since their preschool years were less aggressive and less likely to participate in activities involving competition and physical contact than father-present boys or father-absent boys whose fathers had left when the boys were older than age 5.

In a longitudinal study of families with divorced parents (Hetherington, 1979; Hetherington et al., 1978), boys in divorced families did not differ from boys in two-parent families for the first year after the divorce, but they did have less masculine scores on measures of orientation, activity preference, and sex role adoption at the end of two years when they were 6 years old. Specifically, boys from divorced families had less masculine and more feminine toy and activity preferences, more feminine orientation on the Draw-a-Person, played more with female and younger children, and were more dependent and more verbally aggressive than boys from nuclear families.

Girls have been studied less often than boys, largely because it has been assumed that they would be less affected than boys by a father's absence. This assumption is justified if sex-typing results from identification with the same-sex parent, but other theories, particularly those based on reciprocal interaction processes (e.g., Johnson, 1975), predict that a father's absence should affect girls. On the whole, however, the literature is consistent in showing few effects of father absence on sex-typed self-perception, orientation, preferences, or adoption in childhood (Biller & Weiss, 1970; Hainline & Feig, 1978; Hetherington, 1972; Hetherington et al., 1978). However, father-absent girls do show problems in social interactions with males. Observations and interview assessments were carried out on girls between ages 13 to 17 whose fathers were dead or divorced. Neither group differed from father-present girls on measures of personality and sex-typed identity, but both groups manifested deviant patterns of interaction with male peers and adults. The daughters of divorced mothers were flirtatious and sexu-

ally precocious, while the daughters of widows were withdrawn and avoided interacting with males (Hetherinton, 1972). The author suggested that both groups of father-absent girls lacked experience in relating to males in comfortable ways. An attempt to replicate some of these findings with college-age women did not produce the same results (Hainline & Feig, 1978), but the difference may be because of differences in population, age, or other subject variables. Hetherington's sample was from a working-class and lower middle-class neighborhood. In follow-up contacts with the sample, she found that the daughters of divorcées married earlier than the other groups and continued their patterns of precocious heterosexual interaction (Hetherington & Parke, 1979). These girls would probably not get to college; hence, a college sample of father-absent females might be biased in favor of girls who were not affected by divorce in the way the younger girls in Hetherington's study were.

At a more subtle level, performance of both boys and girls in quantitative skills seems to be related to the regular presence of a father or father figure in the home, particularly in the early years. In a comprehensive review of the literature on father absence and cognitive skills, Shinn (1978) reported that quantitative skills were reported as adversely affected more often than verbal skills (though many studies indicate that father-absent children show poorer overall intellectual performance than father-present children). These deficits appear to be partially alleviated by a substitute or stepfather in the home (Chapman, 1977; Shinn, 1978). A small number of studies of middle-class children reported that father-absent children performed *better* than father-present children on verbal skills. The latter findings must be regarded as tentative because of small numbers, but the detrimental effect of a father's absence on quantitative performance is reasonably well established.

For boys, and to some extent for girls, the effects of father absence depend on the age at which the father left. Boys whose fathers left when they were of preschool age show more effects than those whose fathers left after the preschool period (Biller, 1970; Biller & Bahm, 1971; Hetherington, 1966, 1972). Maternal encouragement of masculine behavior is also an important predictor in father-absent boys. When mothers encourage assertive, aggressive, and independent behavior, boys show more masculine preferences and adopt more masculine behavior than when the mother is less encouraging (Biller, 1970; Biller & Bahm, 1971). This finding reflects the more general trend found in the longitudinal study of divorced families (Hetherington et al., 1978). When children live with their mothers, their fathers' attributes and childrearing practices have less effect on them than is the case in father-present families. Correspondingly, the mother's behavior and child rearing practices are more closely related to the child's behavior than is the case in two-parent families. It follows that her encouragement of masculine behavior is more important in boys' behavioral adoption than it is in two-parent families. In divorced families, boys' masculine attributes were positively related to the father's availability, but not to other characteristics that predict masculinity in nuclear families. Boys' masculine attributes were positively correlated with maternal reinforcement for sex-typed behavior, encouragement of independence and exploration, low anxiety, and a positive attitude toward the father.

Maternal behavior was also a more important correlate of girls' sex-typing in single-parent families than in nuclear families. Girls' feminine attributes were positively correlated with maternal warmth and encouragement of sex-typed activity in divorced families. They were not related to any paternal attribute measured. This pattern contrasted sharply with the finding in nuclear families that several paternal characteristics predicted girls' sex-typing (Hetherington et al., 1978). These findings suggest that females can acquire sex-typed attributes through alternate paths. When the father is present, his personality and response to the daughter influence her; when he is not present, the mother's response becomes a strong influence. Both paths serve equally well (or poorly, depending on your view of feminine sex-typing) to produce sex-typed characteristics in daughters—there were no overall differences between the two groups in the longitudinal study. Unfortunately, there is little information in this report about parental correlates of androgyny or nontraditional sex-typing in divorced families.

Why does father absence produce the effects that have been demonstrated? Something about the availability of a father is important in children's acquisition of masculine characteristics and quantitative skills. The effect could result because of the importance of an adult male model, but other literature suggests that this variable is not crucial. To the extent that fathers treat boys differently than mothers do, father-absent children, especially boys, may experience different childrearing practices than father-present boys. They may lack exposure to rough-and-tumble play; they may not get encouragement to be independent, and companionship in male sex-typed activities often provided by fathers may not exist.

Their mothers may also be more restrictive and less likely to encourage independence than mothers who have a male adult around to help them with childrearing. Divorced mothers seem to have difficulty establishing an appropriate level of control and affection for their boys, while also permitting and encouraging independence and assertiveness. Father-absent children may live with a different pattern of maternal behavior than father-present boys, and that difference may be greater for boys than for girls.

The one available study of father-custody families with reasonably good methodological controls suggests that girls' sex-typing and general adjustment are affected by maternal absence more than that of boys. Father-custody girls were rated as less feminine, less independent, and more demanding than mother-custody girls. By contrast, father-custody boys were rated more mature and sociable than mother-custody boys (Santrock & Warshak, 1979).

These patterns, like those from earlier investigations, suggest that the absence of the same-sex parent has some pervasive effects on children's emotional development, not just on sex-typing. The outcomes may reflect generalized adjustment problems that are manifested in failure to adopt the culturally valued and accepted behavior patterns, some of which are sex-typed. It would be misguided to applaud such liberation from cultural strictures, however, because children whose same-sex parent is absent appear to lack self-esteem, social confidence, and other positive attributes associated with either masculinity or femininity. It will be clear in the next section that counterstereotypical socialization is more effective when a child is living with a same-sex parent who departs from traditional roles than when the same-sex parent is absent altogether.

Parental Role Behavior—Maternal Employment and Paternal Home Roles

One potential determinant of children's sex-typed role adoption is the degree to which their parents enact traditionally prescribed sex roles in the areas of earning the family living, performing household and domestic tasks, and taking care of children. One of the major social changes of the twentieth century, particularly the last half of the century, is the increase in maternal employment. Two social trends are co-occurring. Married women with children are entering the labor market in increasing numbers, and they are doing so at an earlier stage in their children's development (Huston-Stein & Higgins-Trenk, 1978). In 1979, over half the mothers with school-age children, 42% of mothers of preschool children, and 33% of mothers with children under 3 who lived with their husbands were employed at least part-time (Hoffman, 1979).

Maternal employment is associated with some changes in parental role enactment. Specifically, husbands help with domestic chores more often when the mother is employed than when she is not, although the mother still performs most of the cooking, cleaning, and child care (Hoffman & Nye, 1974; Huston-Stein & Higgins-Trenk, 1978). Therefore, children whose mothers are employed typically have parent role models who are somewhat less traditional and whose functions overlap more than children whose mothers are full time homemakers.[2]

One consistent finding is that children's concepts about sex-typing are less stereotyped when their mothers are employed than are the concepts of children with nonemployed mothers. This generalization holds true for children ranging from age 3 through adolescence and has been found consistently in studies spanning the last 20 to 25 years. Several studies of young children (approximately 4 to 6) from varying cultural and nationality groups have demonstrated that children have less sex-differentiated notions of personal-social attributes and parental task divisions when their mothers are employed than when they are not (Cordua et al., 1979; Gold & Andres, 1978c; Gold et al., 1979; Marantz & Mansfield, 1977; Miller, 1975; Urberg, 1979a). Older children and adolescents with employed mothers also have broader concepts of appropriate personality traits, behaviors, activities, occupations, relations with adults, and relations with peers than do sons and daughters of nonemployed women (Gold & Andres, 1978a, 1978b; Hartley, 1970; Hoffman, 1974, 1977, 1979; Marantz & Mansfield, 1977; Nemerowicz, 1979; Perloff, 1977). The rare exceptions have occurred among young boys (Urberg, 1979a), adolescent boys from working-class families (Gold & Andres, 1978a), and working-class girls in middle childhood (Meyer, 1980). One investigation suggests a similar loosening of traditional concepts for children whose fathers engage in nontraditional activity. Four-year-old girls had less pronounced sex stereotypes when their fathers assumed responsibility for some aspects of child care

than when fathers did not do so (Baruch & Barnett, 1981).

Although maternal employment affects concepts about sex-typing for both sexes, it affects sex-typed preferences and adoption almost exclusively for girls. On the whole, maternal employment is associated with an androgynous (as opposed to strictly feminine) pattern of interests, activities, and personal-social attributes in daughters. Girls with employed mothers generally have higher educational aspirations, more often expect to have a career themselves, are more achievement oriented, and have higher self-esteem than those with nonemployed mothers (Etaugh, 1974; Gold & Andres, 1978a, 1978b, 1978c; Gold et al., 1979; Hoffman, 1974, 1977, 1979; Woods, 1972). Girls with employed or career-oriented mothers also have masculine or androgynous behavior patterns (Hetherington et al., 1978; Miller, 1975) and engage in physically active play (Tauber, 1979a; 1979b). However, self-descriptions of masculine and feminine personality traits are inconsistently related to maternal employment for adolescents and college students (Baruch, 1973; Broverman et al., 1970; Hansson, Chernovetz, & Jones, 1977; Klecka & Hiller, 1977; Stein, 1973).

Sex-typed patterns in boys are not consistently influenced by maternal employment. In two studies, boys in nursery school made fewer same-sex choices (and, therefore, more cross-sex choices) on the IT Scale when their mothers were employed than when they were not (Gold & Andres, 1978c; Gold et al., 1979). I know of no evidence about whether sex-typed preferences and adoption in boys are affected by fathers performing nontraditional roles in the home. This question has considerable social import and should be explored.

Reasons for Parental Role Influences

One obvious reason for the observed effects of maternal employment is role modeling; children observe a mother who combines traditionally feminine domestic and maternal behavior with earning money—a traditionally masculine function. To some degree, they also see fathers combining the masculine, instrumental, "provider" role with traditionally feminine domestic work. The sex differences in the correlates of maternal employment certainly suggest that maternal role modeling is one basis for these effects. In addition, daughters of employed mothers more often say they want to be like their mothers or that they consciously use their mothers as models when compared to daughters of nonemployed mothers (Hoffman, 1974; Miller, 1975). Employed

---

[2]This discussion is limited to sex-typed outcomes of maternal employment. The reader interested in effects on children's psychological adjustment, intellectual functioning, and parental relationships is referred to Etaugh (1974), Hoffman and Nye (1974), and Hoffman (1979).

mothers not only exemplify androgyny, but are especially attractive models for their daughters.

By contrast, there is some slight evidence that the potency fathers have as models for boys is weaker, at least in working-class families, when the wife is employed than when she is not (Hoffman, 1979). For some children, maternal employment may signify paternal inadequacy in the male "provider" role—a perception that has some factual basis. On the average, employed women have husbands who earn less money than those of nonemployed wives (Hoffman & Nye, 1974). The devaluation of the father by his sons probably does not result from increased child care and domestic responsibilities; these changes in paternal functioning are more prevalent in middle-class families than in lower-class families. Devaluation of the father probably results from the assumption that the father cannot provide sufficient income for the family.

A second possible basis for the correlation of maternal employment with children's sex role concepts and behavior may be parental attitudes about sex roles. Both mothers and fathers display more pro-feminist attitudes in families where the wife is employed or the father assumes child care responsibilities in comparison to families with more traditional patterns (Baruch & Barnett, 1981; Gold & Andres, 1978a, 1978b). Personality differences between employed and nonemployed women may also contribute to the outcomes for their children. Married women who are employed in professional, managerial, and relatively high-status occupations are generally more assertive, independent, and achievement-oriented, though not necessarily less feminine than married women who are not employed (Hock, 1978; Hoffman & Nye, 1974; Huston-Stein & Higgins-Trenk, 1978; Welch, 1979). Whether these differences are determinants or outcomes of the choice to work is not clear. What is clear is that many employed mothers have more masculine personal-social characteristics than nonemployed mothers; these attributes may affect their children through modeling and child-rearing practices.

Child-rearing practices of families with employed mothers may also differ from those with nonemployed mothers. Employed mothers generally encourage independence more often than nonemployed mothers, especially for their daughters (Hoffman, 1974). Parents of adolescents in one study expressed less rejection and said they exerted less achievement pressure when the mother was employed than did parents in families of nonemployed mothers. These differences were especially pronounced in working-class families (Gold & Andres,

1978a). Older children (10 years and above) are left on their own without supervision more when their mothers work outside the home than when mothers do not do so (Gold & Andres, 1978b).

Summary

The manner in which parents adopt the instrumental "provider" role and the domestic role that includes child care and household tasks influences the sex stereotypes accepted by boys and girls. When mothers are employed or fathers assume some child care and domestic responsibility, children's concepts of interests, activities, occupations, personality traits, and behaviors are less sex-differentiated than they are when parents follow a traditional division of roles. For girls, maternal employment is also associated with achievement orientation, masculine as well as feminine personal-social behavior, and acceptance of the mother as a model. Boys' sex-typed preferences and behaviors are usually not affected by maternal employment. These effects of parental roles may be due to role modeling, attitudes about sex roles, parent personality differences, or associated childrearing practices.

Sibling Effects

Two diametrically opposed hypotheses have been proposed regarding sibling influences on sex-typing. One hypothesis, based on social learning theory, is that siblings of one's own gender encourage same-sex stereotyped interests and behavior through modeling and reinforcement. Older siblings are expected to have more effect than younger siblings. Many of the studies supporting the social learning position were carried out by Sutton-Smith and Rosenberg (1970). Male and female college students obtained more "sex-appropriate" scores on personality tests (such as the Gough and the MMPI) when they had same-sex siblings than when their siblings were the other sex (Rosenberg & Sutton-Smith, 1968; Sutton-Smith, Roberts, & Rosenberg, 1964; Sutton-Smith & Rosenberg, 1965, 1970). For the most part, these studies were limited to two-child families. In some cases, the scores of same-sex siblings on interest or personality inventories were positively correlated, while the correlations for opposite-sex siblings were near zero (Munsinger & Rabin, 1978; Rosenberg & Sutton-Smith, 1968).

Some studies with younger children also support the hypothesis that children learn same-sex stereotypes from their siblings, especially older siblings. In Brim's (1958) re-analysis of Koch's data, girls with brothers had higher levels of instrumental behavior than girls with sisters, but they did not differ in expressive characteristics. Boys with brothers were also more instrumental and less expressive than boys with sisters. This early study is one of the few that measured masculine and feminine characteristics independently. Other studies partially support the hypothesis that children learn sex-typed activity preferences (Rosenberg & Sutton-Smith, 1964) and social behavior (Wohlford, Santrock, Berger, & Liberman, 1971), but findings are inconsistent (Barry, 1980; Vroegh, 1971).

These findings provide modest support for the hypothesis that personal-social behavior, interests, and activity preferences may be influenced by sibling sex. One problem in evaluating these data is the fact that most studies used bipolar measures of masculine and feminine characteristics. It is possible that a sibling of the other sex may help children to add some dimensions to their repertoires without reducing characteristics considered appropriate to their gender.

The opposite hypothesis is based on concepts of contrast, "deidentification," and needs for individuation. In a psychoanalytic framework, Schachter and her colleagues (Schachter, Shore, Feldman-Rotman, Marquis, & Campbell, 1976) proposed that the first child identifies with the same-sex parent. The second child will tend to fill the remaining slot—identification with the remaining parent. If the two children are the same gender, then the second child will need to establish his or her "difference" from the first by "deidentifying."

In one study of college students and another in which mothers rated their preschool and school age children, global estimates of whether two siblings were the "same or different" were obtained. Same-sex siblings were rated as "different" more often than opposite-sex siblings, particularly when they were first and second born (Schachter, Gilutz, Shore, & Adler, 1978; Schachter et al., 1976).

Other investigators (e.g., Grotevant, 1978) have proposed that siblings need to establish individual identities by developing interests or behaviors that are distinctively different from their same-sex siblings, particularly in large families. The latter hypothesis predicts more divergence from traditional roles for members of large families with several same-sex children than for small families, whereas the psychoanalytic hypothesis predicts the greatest "deidentification" for the first- and second-born children. In observations of children 8 and 9 years old, cross-sex play occurred more for children whose siblings were their own gender than for other sibling groups. Girls with sisters were also more active and aggressive than girls with brothers (Tau-

ber, 1979a). In three-child families, Rosenberg and Sutton-Smith (1964) found that boys with brothers made less masculine game choices than other groups. One possible reason for these patterns could be the novelty of cross-sex toys and games for children with same-sex siblings who probably do not have many such toys in their homes. Among adolescents, some evidence for the contrast hypothesis appeared for girls, but not boys. On the Strong Vocational Interest Inventory, interests of girls were more feminine in families with brothers than in families with sisters, particularly when there were several sisters (Grotevant, 1978).

No clear conclusion concerning the issue of similarity versus contrast emerges from these fragmentary data. Male and female siblings may have different effects on children, but not necessarily because they are consistent models of masculine or feminine attributes. One clear difference between one-sex and two-sex families is that the latter households are likely to have both male- and female-stereotyped toys, and children in two-sex families probably also have contact with peers of the other gender who play with their siblings. To the degree that an older sibling has sex-typed activity interests or personal-social behavior, the younger child is at least exposed to those as alternatives. On the other hand, siblings may attempt to be different, or younger children may hesitate to compete with older siblings in those activities where the older child already has considerable competence. Parents may also encourage more diverse behavior among their girls if there are no boys, or vice versa. Sibling relations and associated parent socialization patterns have been neglected in the literature despite the widespread recognition of their importance. The information available is tantalizing, but certainly not conclusive. More direct assessments of patterns of interaction and experience for children in one- and two-sex families would provide some important information about sibling effects on sex-typing.

Summary of Family Socialization Influences

Sex-typed socialization in the family proceeds along several different paths. Parents treat boys and girls differently in ways that appear to have long-term implications for interests, skills, independence, achievement, and interpersonal relationships in their children. At least some of these parent practices appear to be antecedents rather than consequences of sex differences in behavior. Adults respond differently to the same infant depending on whether they believe it is a boy or a girl, and parents' perceptions and expectations about their own children's behavior are much more sex stereotyped than the child's behavior would warrant. Individual differences in parents' attitudes about sex-typing do predict children's sex stereotypes and attitudes, but their relationship to behavior is subtle and indirect.

Fathers play an important role in sex-typed socialization, particularly for boys. In our society and many others, fathers feel a special responsibility for masculinizing their sons. They differentiate between boys and girls more than mothers do, and their absence from a family has a clear impact on boys' masculine development. Although fathers emerge from much of the literature as enforcers of traditional sex-typing, they can also encourage flexible sex-typing for their sons by socialization practices that provide the socially positive elements of masculinity along with more feminine qualities of interpersonal sensitivity and positive attitudes toward women. Androgyny for males seems most likely to result from combining a secure sense of masculinity with feminine qualities.

To what extent can parents and families socialize their children to accept nontraditional patterns of sex-typing? One means is by enacting nontraditional household and employment roles. Another is by encouraging children to develop interests, activities, and personal-social behaviors that cross the boundaries of masculine and feminine definitions. This encouragement happens not so much at the level of liberal attitudes about sex-typing, but at the level of contingent behavioral responses of which the parent is probably often unaware. If each parent engaged in equal amounts of gross motor play, encouraged similar toys and games, demanded equal amounts of effort and gave equal amounts of help, allowed equal amounts of independence and freedom from supervision, and encouraged equal amounts of dependency, perhaps their boys and girls would show similar patterns of development. Because many of these parent behaviors are probably not directly linked to the parents' own concepts of sex-typing (i.e., they do not label the child's behavior or their actions as masculine or feminine), these sex-typed socialization patterns may be somewhat independent of cognitions and attitudes about sex-typing. Studies are needed that examine both cognitive and behavioral variables for parents and children and that go beyond documenting sex differences to examining contingencies between parent and child behavior.

SOCIALIZATION OUTSIDE THE FAMILY
School Influences

In many societies, schools are intended as socializing institutions, second in importance only to the home. For the most part, however, the influences of school on sex-typing are unintentional rather than being planned interventions. Children acquire patterns of sex-typed toy and activity preferences by age 3 or earlier, before most of them are in any type of school. When they enter preschool, teachers and peers apparently increase or at least maintain such preferences by differential reinforcement, punishment, and modeling. Curriculum materials, school activities, and classroom organization also affect children's sex-typed social behavior.

Do Teachers Treat Boys and Girls Differently?

Teachers and counselors, like other adults, perceive female students as having feminine characteristics and male students as having masculine characteristics (Fox et al., 1979; Petro & Putnam, 1979; Wise, 1978). Some critics have been concerned that teachers evaluate masculine behavior negatively and that boys feel a conflict between the demands of the male role and the school role. They have suggested that school is a feminine environment where quiet, passive obedience is approved, and active, independent behavior is disapproved. Some evidence supports the contention that teachers perceive females and feminine qualities more positively than their counterparts. In one study of fourth- and fifth-grade children, boys who perceived themselves as having feminine personality attributes were rated by teachers as better adjusted than those whose self-perceptions were more masculine. The reason appeared to lie in the boys' behavior—"feminine" boys were more task-oriented in class whereas "masculine" boys more often sought adult attention, disrupted class, and interacted with peers (Silvern, 1978). In another study, teachers estimated that girls had higher levels of self-esteem than boys, whereas the children's own ratings fell in the reverse pattern—boys higher than girls (Loeb & Horst, 1978). What has not been emphasized by critics concerned about the negative effects on boys is that a "feminine bias" by teachers may be at least as harmful to girls. The cultivation of passive obedience in school may have long-term deleterious effects on girls' independence and self-esteem.

With one exception (Parsons, Kaczala, & Meece, 1982), direct observations of teacher behavior in both preschool and elementary school classes indicate that boys receive more disapproval, scolding, and other forms of negative attention from teachers than girls do (Cherry, 1975; Etaugh & Harlow, 1975; Lee & Wolinsky, 1977; Meyer & Thompson, 1956; Serbin, O'Leary, Kent, & Tonick, 1973; Yarrow, Waxler, & Scott, 1971). In some cases, teachers treat the sexes differently even though the behavior of boys and girls is similar (e.g., Etaugh & Harlow, 1975). The higher rate of teacher scolding and disapproval for boys appears to result from generalized expectations that boys will misbehave, which are based partially on objectively observable patterns and partially on stereotypical beliefs about the sexes.

Findings are more mixed for positive teacher responses to children. In some studies of preschool children, teachers gave more positive attention to girls (Fagot, 1973, 1981); in others, they were more attentive to boys (Cherry, 1975; Etaugh & Harlow, 1975; Meyer & Thompson, 1956; Serbin et al., 1973). One reason for the discrepancy may be that girls spend more time than boys in instructional activities where adults are closely involved, so that girls may have more opportunities for adult contact. For example, in several types of Head Start programs, girls received more instructional contacts and more positive reinforcements from teachers than boys did, but there was no sex difference in the number of positive reinforcements per instructional contact (Biber, Miller, & Dyer, 1972).

Do Teachers Reinforce Sex-Stereotyped Behavior?

In preschool, teachers often reinforce both boys and girls for ''feminine'' activity choices. That is, those activities preferred by girls receive more positive reinforcement in the form of attention and approval from teachers than those preferred by boys (Etaugh, Collins, & Gerson, 1975; Fagot & Patterson, 1969; Robinson & Canaday, 1978). Exceptions occurred in a study of Dutch preschools where teachers reinforced boys for masculine activities and girls for feminine activities (Fagot, 1977b), and in one study of American preschools where boys were reinforced in block play as well as art (Fagot, 1977a). Teachers do not generally disapprove of children with marked cross-gender activity preferences (Fagot, 1977a), but they are relatively unresponsive to children who are uninvolved in both masculine and feminine activities, perhaps because those children are simply inactive (Fagot, 1978d). These findings have sometimes been interpreted as showing that female teachers differentially reinforce feminine behavior for both sexes—a support for the contention that school is a feminized environment.

Teachers do not consistently reinforce sex-typed personal-social behavior. They generally approve of task-oriented achievement behavior and disapprove of aggression for both sexes (Etaugh & Hughes, 1975; Levitin & Chananie, 1972; Smith & Green, 1975; Yarrow et al., 1971). In one case, they responded negatively more often to aggression from boys than from girls (Serbin et al., 1973). Serbin et al. argued that attention of any kind might reinforce boys' aggression and destructive behavior, but Smith and Green (1975) question this interpretation. They point out that most aggression in preschools involves disputes over property; that most aggressive incidents are not seen or influenced by an adult; and that a high percent of aggressive behaviors are reinforced by peers (Patterson, Littman, & Bricker, 1967). In fact, aggressive incidents in which adults intervened were less often successful than those in which adults did not intervene (Smith & Green, 1975). Therefore, the higher rate of aggressive behavior in boys does not appear to be a function of teacher attention.

Teachers encourage some kinds of dependent behavior for girls more often than boys, but not all kinds. In observations of preschool classrooms, teachers attended to girls more when they were close than when they were far away, but their attention to boys did not vary with distance. On the other hand, boys received more positive responses than girls when they solicited the teacher's attention (Serbin et al., 1973). Other observations indicated that teachers punished dependent behavior in boys more often than girls (Yarrow et al., 1971). Ratings of dependent boys and girls by elementary school teachers are inconsistent (Etaugh & Hughes, 1975; Levitin & Chananie, 1972).

Male Versus Female Teachers

One response to the alleged ''feminine'' environment of the preschool or elementary school has been to include male teachers. Male teachers could influence children in at least two ways. (1) They might respond differently than females to children's behavior, and (2) they might serve as nurturant, nontraditional male models. Even if they behave like female teachers, they might convey a nonstereotypic image of maleness to young children. Most of the available literature is focused on the first possibility—that males will behave differently than females. However, the modeling function of male teachers may be more important and more generic to questions of children's learning about sex roles.

Early studies generally indicated that male preschool teachers spent more time in masculine activities and were more attentive to boys than female teachers were (Etaugh et al., 1975; Lee & Wolinsky, 1977; Mueller & Cooper, 1972; Perdue & Connor, 1978). Fagot (1978c, 1981), however, has demonstrated that many of these differences between male and female teachers are probably a function of differences in teaching experience rather than the sex of the teacher. Inexperienced teachers of both sexes more often join children's activities and less often initiate activities than experienced teachers. The activities that teachers join tend to be sex-typed, whereas the activities initiated by teachers are "instructional" and oriented to school-related skills. As a result, inexperienced teachers of both sexes reward children for same-sex stereotyped activities. Experienced teachers of both sexes reinforce children primarily in "feminine" (i.e., female-preferred) instructional activities, such as art and fine·motor activities. These findings suggest that males and females behave similarly when they have acquired skill in teaching. Similar conclusions were reached after reviewing the studies of male elementary school teachers (Brophy & Good, 1974).

At the elementary level, male adults may communicate slightly different orientations than females in subtle ways. Undergraduate students were told to provide rewards to pairs of children who had contributed unequally to a group project. Males and people with high masculine scores on the BSRI administered rewards more on the basis of equity (i.e., divided according to the amount contributed by each child), whereas females and high feminine scorers rewarded on the basis of equality (equal amounts to both children). Males used equity most consistently when rewarding boys who were performing the task in a competitive rather than a team context (Olejnik, Tompkins, & Heinbuck, in press).

Little information exists about the possible role modeling effects of male teachers. In a study comparing all-male, all-female, and mixed-sex teaching teams, 4-year-old children's stereotypes about school-related objects and activities did appear to be differentially affected. At the end of the school year, the children in the all-female teacher class viewed school objects as more feminine than did children in the other two classes (Mueller & Cooper, 1972).

Teacher Behavior as an Agent of Change

The studies discussed thus far have demonstrated some differences in the ways teachers react to boys and girls, but they have not demonstrated a direct effect of teacher behavior on children's learning of sex-typed behavior. In a series of experimental studies conducted in preschool classrooms, Serbin and her colleagues have demonstrated that teachers' reinforcement contingencies and cues about sex-typing of activities can increase or change the behavior of young children. In the first of these studies, teachers reinforced children who played in mixed-sex groups. During the two weeks of reinforcement, the rate of cooperative mixed-sex play increased considerably, but it returned to baseline levels when the contingencies were discontinued (Serbin, Tonick, & Sternglanz, 1977). A replication and extension of this study demonstrated increases in both cross-sex and same-sex play. When the intervention was carried out over six weeks, there was some generalization to the subsequent time period (Serbin, 1980). In another experimental study, teachers reinforced novel behavior and independent task persistence, while ignoring helpseeking and proximity. Attention seeking was affected by these manipulations, but again this result was not carried over to the regular classroom situation (Serbin, Connor, & Citron, 1978). Because observations indicated that teachers often introduced new toys with sex-typed cues, an experiment was conducted comparing toy introductions that were sex-typed (i.e., the toy was described as being used by one sex and members of one gender were asked to demonstrate it) with introductions that suggested the toy was appropriate for both genders. Following the non-sex-typed introductions, children's play with the toys was less sex differentiated than after the sex-typed introductions (Serbin, Connor, & Iler, 1979). Several investigations demonstrated that the presence of a teacher in an activity and active modeling of the activity by the teachers increased children's participation in both masculine and feminine activities. The effects of teacher presence were especially pronounced for girls (Serbin, Connor, & Citron, 1981). Similar effects of sex-typed labeling of toys occurred in an experimental study in which exploration and recall were assessed (Bradbard & Endsley, 1979).

All of these studies indicate that children's sex-typed behavior is readily influenced by adult reinforcement contingencies and cues. Serbin et al. point out that changes are rapid. When contingencies are introduced, behavior changes quickly; when they are removed, behavior returns quickly to baseline levels with little generalization. Rapid shifts of this kind suggest that nonstereotyped behaviors are already in the children's repertoires and that the changes in behavior are a function of discriminating contingencies rather than new learning. Similarly, the rapid decline and lack of generalization following termination of the experimental treatments indicate discrimination of cues rather than extinction. These studies clearly suggest that children's sex-typed behavior is readily controlled by feedback from teachers. In a similar vein, Parsons, Kaczala,

& Meece (1982) found that teachers in math class-rooms, where boys had higher expectancies of suc-cess than girls, praised boys more than girls. In classrooms where expectancies were equal, teachers praised girls more than boys.

School Structure and Curriculum

Children in schools with different educational philosophies have different patterns of sex-typed be-havior and perceptions about sex roles. Open schools stressing nonsexist education and indi-vidualized instruction have less segregated play, less gender bias, less stereotyped sex role concepts, and less sex-typed play than traditional schools (Bianchi & Bakeman, 1978, 1980; Minuchin, 1965). Of course, such differences could be partially the result of self-selection by parents and teachers with differ-ent philosophies, but open schools may also provide different opportunities, cues, and reinforcement contingencies as well as less structured activities than traditional schools.

A deliberate effort to create a school curriculum to counteract sex stereotyping was reported by Gut-tentag and Bray (1976). It was a year-long curricu-lum implemented in kindergarten, fifth-grade, and ninth-grade classrooms involving books, discussion materials, and classroom exercises. A variety of open-ended measures of children's attitudes and preferences was administered before and after ex-posure to the curriculum, but there was no untreated control group. The results were reported descrip-tively rather than quantitatively, so it is difficult to evaluate the curriculum. Comparison of the three age levels indicated that the most clear changes in the direction of nonstereotyped attitudes and prefer-ences occurred for the fifth graders, and the least favorable results occurred for the ninth graders, part-ly because negative group reactions occurred in some classrooms. Several other curriculum efforts have been funded by the Women's Educational Equity Act.

Peer Influences

Children's awareness of peer sex differences ap-pears to develop early. Jacklin and Maccoby (1978) observed 2-year-old, unacquainted, same-sex and mixed-sex pairs of children whose gender cues were minimized. There was more social interaction be-tween same-sex than between mixed-sex pairs. Girls were more passive and more often exhibited social withdrawal when they had a male partner than when their partner was female. Boys were less responsive to a verbal prohibition from a girl than from a boy

partner. Similar patterns occurred for 2-year-olds observed in nursery school free play. Children were more attentive to same-sex peers than peers of the other gender. Even more interesting, positive and negative reactions by same-sex peers appeared to have more impact on behavior than reactions by other-sex peers. Children tended to continue a be-havior when a same-sex peer reacted positively and discontinue it when the reaction was negative; there was no such difference when feedback was received from peers of the other gender (Fagot, 1982).

By age 3, children reinforce one another for sex-typed play and punish each other for deviations from sex stereotypes. Both boys and girls who play in "sex-appropriate" activities are likely to find that other children play with them, respond positively to them, and the like. These patterns occur even when teachers are primarily attending to children in female-preferred activities (Fagot, 1978a; Fagot & Patterson, 1969; Lamb & Roopnarine, 1979). Chil-dren who play in cross-sex activities receive fewer positive peer interactions and more criticism from peers; they are often socially isolated. For example, boys who played in doll, housekeeping, and dress-up activities received more criticism and less posi-tive interaction than girls playing in those areas; these boys were also left alone even when they en-tered masculine activities. Girls also received some ostracism in the form of low rates of interaction in the sandbox and hammer activities, but they were not rejected and left alone to the same degree that boys with cross-gender play patterns were (Fagot, 1977a). Children who play frequently in both same-sex and cross-sex activities receive more criticism from peers than other children, but also experience positive interactions (Fagot, 1978a). Other studies have demonstrated that children inhibit "sex-inap-propriate" play in the presence of a peer, particu-larly a peer of a different gender (Serbin, Connor, Burchardt, & Citron, 1979).

Clinical studies of older children with extreme cross-gender patterns support the same conclusion. Boys with feminine play and behavior patterns are rejected by their peers and spend a considerable amount of time playing alone. Girls with extreme masculine play interests and behavior are not so os-tracized by their peers but experience some disap-proval (Green, Williams, & Harper, 1979).

Why do peers adopt these patterns of reinforce-ment so early and so adamantly? In many respects, children narrow the range of options for one another and define male and female roles more rigidly than adults do. The most reasonable explanation appears to lie in the rigid and absolutist nature of preoperational thought that is manifested in young children's sex role concepts. The peer culture of the preschool reflects cognitive developmental patterns of stereotype acquisition during the early years. If this hypothesis is correct, then the increasing flexibility of thought during the elementary school years may lead to the potential for more tolerance of deviations from sex stereotypes. Whether such tolerance is manifested in patterns of peer acceptance and approval remains to be demonstrated.

We do know that sex segregation of peer groups reaches extreme proportions in middle childhood. This segregation is probably integrally related to participation in sex-typed activities—when boys join other boys, they usually play in masculine activities, and girls who play in feminine activities often find other girls there. On the other hand, under some circumstances, sex segregation may permit more flexibility in sex-typed behavior. For example, girls perform better in all-female math classes and boys perform better at reading in all-male classes than in mixed-sex classes (Fox et al., 1979; McCracken, 1973). Similarly, several studies have shown that both male and female students in single-sex colleges more often take nontraditional majors than those attending coeducational schools (Block, 1981). There is no ready resolution for these paradoxical effects of sex segregation—in some instances, segregation produces more pronounced sex-typing; in others, it appears to facilitate flexibility.

Play Activities and Tasks

Sex-typed activities may provide an environmental context for learning personal-social behaviors such as dependence and independence. For example, Edwards and Whiting (in press) proposed that sex differences in social behavior across cultures are learned through differential exposure to particular social contexts and tasks. In cultures where girls have more contact with infants than boys, girls show more nurturant behavior, but there is no difference in cultures where infant contact does not differ. On the average, girls are more frequently given such responsibility, so that sex differences in nurturance are facilitated.

In the tradition of ecological psychology, environmental contexts are considered determinants of the range and type of behavior displayed by people in those contexts. The home environments for young boys and girls consist of different objects, toys, and room decorations (Rheingold & Cook, 1975). Several studies of preschools have demonstrated that

aggression, interpersonal conflict, and social exchange occur frequently during block play (an activity preferred by boys). Art and table activities, usually preferred by girls, are characterized by low levels of peer interchange and social conflict (Gump, 1975). In these studies, however, it is not possible to determine whether the behaviors associated with activities are the result of different sex ratios (e.g., boys are aggressive and play in blocks; girls are quiet and play in art) or a result of the activities themselves.

More recent investigations (Carpenter & Huston-Stein, 1980) have demonstrated that activities were associated with similar behavior patterns for the boys and girls who entered them, eliminating the possibility that activity differences resulted simply because of generalized sex differences. These investigations also contained an analysis of the properties of these activities that might cultivate sex-typed behavior. One major dimension used was the amount of structure (i.e., information about the rules, parameters, and procedures to be followed in an activity) that is provided by adult feedback to the child or by adult models (Carpenter & Huston-Stein, 1980). Highly structured activities may encourage children to adopt the structures suggested by others and may foster compliance and dependence on adults. Activities with little structure may require children to create their own structures (i.e., to decide how and what to do) and may foster independence, initiative, and novel uses of materials. In three studies of preschool classrooms, girls selected more structured activities than boys during free play (i.e., activities where teacher feedback was frequent or activities that paralleled adult role behaviors). The specific activities with high or low levels of teacher feedback differed from one classroom to another, so that the sex differences in preference appeared to result from the adult-imposed structure rather than from other qualities of particular activities. Children of both sexes showed more compliance and bids for recognition in highly structured activities and more initiative, leadership, and aggression when they played in low structure activities (Carpenter, Huston, & Neath, 1981; Carpenter & Huston-Stein, 1980). Subsequent experimental studies in both laboratory and classroom settings demonstrated that high and low levels of feedback by adults produce consistent differences in children's social behavior (Carpenter, Huston, & Holt, 1981). These findings implicate activity structure as one antecedent of sex-typed social behavior. Because girls and boys elect activities with different levels of adult involvement and structure, boys experience more opportunities for leadership and initiative with peers, while girls have more opportunities for compliance and for seeking recognition from adults.

Sex-typed play activities have also been suggested as antecedents of sex differences in intellectual skills, particularly visual-spatial processing. Sherman (1967) proposed some time ago that blocks, transportation toys, and other play activities that are typically preferred by boys may provide important experience with three-dimensional spatial relationships and other aspects of visual-spatial skills. To the extent that girls are more occupied with dolls, social interaction with adults, and fine motor activities, they may have more opportunities to develop verbal and fine motor skills. Several observational studies of preschool children support the proposition that participation in "masculine" play activities predicts performance in spatial tasks (Coates, Lord, & Jakabovics, 1975; Connor & Serbin, 1977; Serbin & Connor, 1979). Long-term correlates of early play experiences were found in a follow-up of children whose play in nursery school had been observed. Although the sample was small, there were significant correlations of masculine play interests in preschool with field independence at ages 6 and 10 for both sexes. In addition, girls whose play interests had been masculine were rated higher in all areas of achievement compared to those with feminine play interests (Fagot & Littman, 1976). In a longitudinal study of adolescents, spatial skill in the eleventh grade was predicted by "spatial experience, recreational games involving spatial relations, and the like" originally assessed in eighth grade (Sherman, 1980).

Training and Formal Instruction

As children grow older, formal instruction and training gradually replace informal play activity as a potential influence on intellectual functioning. In junior and senior high school, when math becomes an elective, boys take advanced math courses more often than girls do. Several studies have demonstrated that much of the male-female performance difference in math can be accounted for by this differential training; they disagree on whether sex differences remain after controlling for course enrollment (Meece et al., 1982; Steel & Wise, 1979). Although it is possible that course selection is affected by visual-spatial skills and other requisite abilities, such selections are also a function of social and attitudinal variables that lead girls to consider math less important for their own lives than boys do (see earlier discussion). Whatever the reasons for course selection, exposure to instruction is an important determinant of intellectual skills, particularly at advanced levels.

The effects of instruction have been investigated experimentally by attempting to train children on spatial tasks. Some researchers have argued that, if lack of relevant experience accounts for girls' relative deficits in visual-spatial performance, then girls should benefit more than boys from training (see Sherman, 1967). In three studies of young children, girls' performance on embedded figures or mental rotations did improve more than boys' after training or exposure (Connor, Schackman, & Serbin, 1978; Connor, Serbin, & Schackman, 1977; Vandenberg, 1975). Among older children and adolescents, however, girls did not benefit more than boys from experimental aids designed to reduce confusion or to enhance performance (Liben & Golbeck, 1980; Vasta, Regan, & Kerley, 1980).

It is not the case, on the other hand, that females receive no benefit from training—a conclusion reached in a widely cited series of studies by Thomas, Jamison, and Hummel (1973). These researchers attempted to train college females on the water level task by providing opportunities to observe the actual level of water in bottles set at various angles. They concluded that women were untrainable because a very small proportion of their subjects attained a perfect performance or learned the principle that still water is always horizontal. Inspection of their data indicates, however, that training led to a considerable reduction in the magnitude of error, suggesting that the subjects were learning *something* about the patterns they were observing, but were not abstracting a universal principle. In another investigation, twelfth-grade students, most of whom were female, showed significant improvement on a water level task after training in which they observed a bottle containing water slowly rotated, but they were not asked to verbalize the principle involved (Liben, 1978).

The inconsistencies among these findings may be partially the result of differences in training procedures. The successful training in the Connor et al. (1977) study entailed gradual disembedding of a hidden figure by removing a series of overlays; the overlays were then replaced serially, so that the process of embedding could also be observed. Simple practice in locating hidden figures did not improve children's performance. The training used by Liben (1978) also involved the opportunity to observe a moving, changing object that presented transformations in the irrelevant bottle angle while the water remained level, whereas the Thomas et al. (1973)

training procedure allowed the subject to observe static instances (e.g., uncovering the bottle for examination at each angle). Effective training may require active manipulation or transformation of materials rather than simple observation of static outcomes.

In retrospect, it seems a little naive to think that one or two training sessions could eliminate a deficit that is presumably accumulated over several years. The fact that training is successful with young children and less so with college students supports the hypothesis that the difficulties females have with visual-spatial problems are accumulated during childhood. A true test of the potential influence of experience would require a long period of instruction or training for adolescents and adults.

Summary

Teachers of young children do have sex stereotypes about children, but they do not necessarily train sex-typed behavior. Experienced teachers reinforce both boys and girls for "feminine" (i.e., female-preferred) activities. Activities such as art and fine motor activities are the instructional components of the preschool; these activities are the ones to which a teacher's attention is most often directed and the ones preferred by girls. Male teachers who are experienced behave similarly to female teachers. Inexperienced teachers of both sexes tend to join children's activities rather than initiating activities and, as a result, reinforce both boys and girls in sex-typed activity participation.

Children's sex-typed behavior is readily influenced by teachers' patterns of reinforcement as well as environmental cues. Rates of mixed-sex play and play with cross-sex activities change quickly with changes in teacher behavior. More long-term effects appear in children who attend schools with differing philosophies. Activities and classrooms that are relatively unstructured by adults facilitate a departure from rigid sex stereotypes and cultivate novel behavior and independence.

Peers in the preschool are a conservative force, exerting pressure toward sex-typed activity choices. Children who play in "sex-appropriate" activities are reinforced by the company and approval of other children; those who play in cross-sex activities receive criticism or are left to play alone. Children differentiate peers on the basis of sex very early. The patterns of response to other children's behavior appear to be a manifestation of preschool children's increasing knowledge of sex stereotypes.

Play activities also provide an environmental context for masculine or feminine personal-social behavior. In free play, girls gravitate toward activities that are structured and directed by adults, and boys select less structured play environments. Highly structured activities cultivate compliance and attention-seeking; activities without adult structure encourage independence and leadership. Male-preferred activities may also provide opportunities to learn visual-spatial skills.

The importance of early socialization to play with different types of toys has been underrated in the literature. Many psychologists have ignored the obvious (and, to a layperson, the more important) content of play activities, household chores, and occupational role play in favor of personal-social attributes that are considerably more subtle and abstract. Sociologists and anthropologists take seriously the socializing function of activities, interests, and roles. Thus, research in the field could benefit greatly from a more interdisciplinary collaboration of people from these various disciplines. Such an effort could provide an integrated picture of the interactions that exist among social institutions, social environments, and individuals that would benefit our understanding of the sex-typing process.

CLINICAL INTERVENTION

Efforts to intervene in sex-typed patterns take two diametrically opposed directions—they either help "gender deviant" children to become more appropriately sex-typed, or they help normal children to become free of rigid sex-typed patterns. Several groups of clinicians have diagnosed and treated children whose identity and behavior are extremely deviant from that expected for their gender. On the other hand, many educators and psychologists have tried to reduce children's sex stereotypes, attitudes, and behavior, usually on the assumption that traditional sex roles and personality patterns are maladaptive. Both types of intervention raise ethical issues and also provide some information about the etiology and consistency of sex-typing.

Gender Deviance

Most clinical studies of gender deviance have been carried out with boys. Boys are diagnosed as deviant when they play primarily with feminine sex-typed toys, dress up in women's clothes and cosmetics, prefer girls as playmates, play maternal and women's roles, fantasize about being a girl, and use feminine gestures and nonverbal behavior (Green, 1974; Rekers, 1977, 1979). In some cases, these boys wish to be girls or think of themselves as girls. Not only do these boys prefer feminine play activities and roles, but they avoid traditionally masculine activities, sometimes vehemently and compulsively (Rekers, 1979). In particular, they seem to find the rough-and-tumble play of other boys aversive or frightening (Green, 1974). Thus, such boys cannot be described as androgynous. They are feminine.

Gender deviance by girls has received less clinical attention than that of boys, perhaps because the society permits girls greater latitude in dress, play activities, and sex-typed interests than it does boys. In fact, a majority of junior high school girls defined themselves as being ''sort of a tomboy,'' and a majority of adult women reported being tomboys in childhood (Hyde, Rosenberg, & Behrman, 1977). One case of a masculine girl referred for treatment was recently reported (Rekers & Mead, in press), but a sample of tomboy girls needed for research purposes had to be recruited through advertisements (Williams, Green, & Goodman, 1979). The criteria used to diagnose extremes of masculinity in girls are similar to those used for boys: preference for masculine play activities, preference for boys as playmates, taking male roles in fantasy play, fantasies of being a boy, and dressing in masculine clothing. These girls also avoid feminine clothing, activities, and playmates (Rekers & Mead, in press; Williams et al., 1979).

Diagnostic procedures for gender deviance have been spelled out carefully by Rekers and his colleagues (Rekers, 1979; Rekers, Willis, Yates, Rosen, & Low, 1977). Extensive observations, structured and unstructured tests, and interviews with child and parents are recommended. One point emphasized by these investigators was that gender deviant behavior was linked to situational cues. Particularly for children over about 7, the deviant behavior or thoughts may not be manifested in play situations or interviews with an adult present, but will occur when the child plays alone. No doubt they have learned the aversive consequences of admitting their ''deviant'' interests and fantasies.

Both behavioral and psychodynamic treatment procedures have been used with gender deviant children, primarily boys. Self-monitoring, token reinforcement, prompts, and other procedures have been employed to teach boys to play with masculine sex-typed toys (and forsake feminine toys), to stop cross-dressing, and to modify feminine mannerisms and gestures. The gestures and mannerisms are more difficult to change than toy choice, possibly because children have trouble discriminating the gestures and mannerisms that other people consider feminine (Rekers, 1977, 1979). Treatment procedures have produced changes in children's play patterns, but those changes have often been specific to the situation where treatment occurred. Clinic treatment has been supplemented, therefore, by direct interventions at home and in school. Parents have been trained to administer token reinforcement regimes, and teachers have been taught to use behavior modification techniques. Young male adults have acted as home or school visitors to teach boys athletic skills (Rekers, 1977, 1979). These procedures have produced changes that have remained 1 to 3 years after the termination of treatment for a small sample followed by Rekers (1977).

In spite of the efforts at diagnosis and treatment for gender deviance, little information about the etiology of such patterns has been generated. Green (1974) proposed that one common theme for many cases was parental indifference to deviant play patterns in very early childhood. Parents often thought it was cute that little boys dressed up in women's clothing and did not consider doll play a cause for concern. Other variables that appeared in some case histories were cross-dressing of a little boy by an older girl, maternal overprotection and inhibition of rough-and-tumble play, excessive maternal attention, absence of an adult male or a distant relationship with a father, physical beauty on the part of a little boy that caused him to be treated like a girl, lack of male playmates, and maternal dominance. However, little evidence beyond clinical impressions exists.

Ethical Issues

Intervention with gender deviant children has raised a variety of ethical questions, many of which are more general questions regarding any intervention in psychological functioning. It has been criticized on the grounds that traditional sex roles are being forced on children who deviate from the expected pattern of the society (Nordyke, Baer, Etzel, & LeBlanc, 1977; Winkler, 1977). The individual who deviates from a social norm is being blamed when in fact the norm is at fault. These critics argue that clinicians should support children's individual patterns rather than using the tools of behavioral therapy to make them conform to traditional patterns. This issue is a special case of a more general problem in clinical intervention—whether one should change the individual to conform to society or change the society to accept variability in individual behavior. In the case of sex-typing, the deviance does not threaten other people's welfare or have any obvious maladaptive consequences beyond the negative reactions of other people. Hence, individuals ought not to be pressured for change by the clinical establishment.

Proponents of treatment agree that efforts to change society should be made, but they also point out that gender deviance, particularly for males, often results in considerable social isolation, unhappiness, and long-term social deviance. Gender deviant boys are rejected by their peers. In Green's investigations, a large percentage of such boys were considered loners and had few playmates of either sex. Masculine girls, by contrast, are not often loners. In fact, they are likely to be leaders and to be accepted by girls as well as by boys (Green, 1974; Green et al., 1979).

Another argument for intervention in gender deviance is the probability that such children will become transsexuals, transvestites, or homosexuals as adults. In retrospect, adults with such patterns report gender deviant childhood play patterns, peer preferences, and fantasies, but there are not yet extensive prospective studies. In one longitudinal study, of 21 feminine boys followed to adolescence, 10 were found "more than incidentally homosexual." None of the masculine boys were homosexual. No follow-up data are yet available for girls in this study (Green et al., 1979).

Gay activists and others would in turn argue that adult transsexualism, transvestitism, and homosexuality are not inherently abnormal and undesirable, but suffer from the same social stigma that affects childhood gender deviance. Again, they argue that society, not the individual with deviant preferences, should be changed. Proponents of intervention argue, however, that these adult patterns are associated with frequent depression, dysphoria, and social isolation. One source reports that 25% of a sample of adult transsexuals had seriously considered suicide (Green, 1974). Such patterns are extremely difficult to treat in adulthood, so intervention during the formative period of gender identity could spare people a great deal of unhappiness later (Green, 1974; Rekers, 1979). This argument is particularly potent for transsexualism because of the serious difficulties in adult gender change (see Green, 1974), but it does not appear as compelling for homosexuality. Adult homosexuals often do not manifest serious psychological disturbance or depression when samples are recruited outside clinical settings (Bell & Weinberg, 1978).

Still another argument for intervention is the assertion that parental wishes provide ethical grounds for intervention in children's behavior. If parents regard the child's behavior as undesirable and wish it to be changed, then it is ethical for the clinician to respect those wishes and to attempt some change. Informed consent from a child is difficult to determine but, in most instances, some limited agreement by the child that change is desirable should be obtained as well. However, there is some danger that extensive efforts at informed consent could lead children to regard themselves as "queer," or otherwise make children feel more deviant than they did before (Rekers, Bentler, Rosen, & Lovaas, 1977). These justifications for intervention hinge partly on the long-term consequences of treatment. It is clear that behavioral treatment can be successful in teaching children to inhibit their cross-sex interests and play patterns, but we do not know how deep or lasting such changes are. We also know little about the psychological consequences of suppressing a strong and fairly fundamental preference or identity. Virtually all transsexuals and homosexuals have made some efforts to suppress their preferences because of the social consequences they have experienced, but often at considerable psychological cost. There is no evidence at present that changes in gender deviance lead to a lower likelihood of depression and psychological distress than would be the case if such people followed the preferences that appear early and are strong.

Finally, attempting to teach traditional sex-typed patterns of play flies directly in the face of the argument that traditional roles are psychologically maladaptive. Gender deviant children are no more androgynous than traditionally sex-typed children, but the interventions used with them are not geared to teach a wider range of interests or behavior patterns. Instead, boys are taught to play with trucks, soldiers, and other masculine sex-typed toys and are taught to avoid dolls, cosmetics, and dress-up clothes. The underlying conception is a bipolar view of sex-typing, and most treatment procedures appear designed to substitute one pole for the other rather than promoting freedom from rigid sex-typing. Serious psychological consequences could follow the exchange of one maladaptive pattern for another.

One can also raise ethical questions about trying to teach children to depart from socially approved behavior patterns, particularly when there is no evidence of extreme sex-typing in the groups of children to whom the interventions are applied. Proponents of these interventions argue that traditional sex-typing is psychologically harmful and maladaptive for all children, and that it has served as the means for preventing women, in particular, from having equal rights and opportunities. A more careful examination of the argument that sex-typing is maladaptive suggests two basic issues. (1) Arbitrarily limiting the options of any person through socializing them to believe that certain activities, interests, friends, sex partners, or thoughts are inappropriate to their gender is by definition inhibiting the opportunity for full development, and (2) the extremes of some sex-typed attributes are antithetical to good psychological functioning. Little quarrel can be raised with the first argument. In a society that values individualism and the fullest development of each individual's potential, it is maladaptive to proscribe whole areas of endeavor or interest on the basis of a person's gender. This argument applies particularly well to interests, activities, social relationships, and stylistic characteristics. When personality and social behavior are discussed, the second argument comes into play—some sex-typed characteristics may simply be maladaptive for any person in modern society. Extremes of aggression or passivity are obviously unhealthy for anyone, and instrumentality and expressiveness are probably adaptive for anyone. Nevertheless, one cannot ignore the evidence that masculinity has more advantages and fewer disadvantages than femininity. Socially desirable masculine characteristics are more highly related to self-esteem than corresponding feminine attributes, and undesirable aspects of masculinity are less deleterious to self-esteem than socially disapproved feminine characteristics (Spence et al., 1979). Feminine behavior in boys is greeted by extreme social censure; masculine girls are treated fairly tolerantly. In Bem's studies examining behavioral correlates, it was difficult to find a task on which feminine individuals excelled. These data have led some authors to question the glib assumption that androgyny is socially adaptive and have led many others to suggest that real social change will occur when gender becomes irrelevant to definitions of appropriate personal, social, and task-oriented behavior.

CONCLUSION

The last 10 years have witnessed an about-face in the value attached to traditional sex-typing and a resulting elaboration and refinement of concepts in the area. It is now clear that masculinity and femininity are not unidimensional, nor are they usually polar opposites of one another. The matrix in Table 1 is one attempt to organize the wide variety of contents and constructs subsumed under the rubric of sex-typing. It includes activities, interests, occupations, and areas of achievement; personality at-

tributes and social behaviors; the gender of one's friends, attachment figures, and sexual partners; and stylistic, symbolic elements of masculinity and femininity. Obviously, one's level of masculinity or femininity on these different components may vary considerably, but there is some consistency across areas, particularly when people at the extremes of the distribution are examined.

Theories about children's acquisition of sex-typing have shifted from the motivational emphasis embodied in the psychoanalytic tradition to a cognitive developmental focus—a shift that has characterized all areas of social development. This emphasis is reflected in social learning conceptions as well as those based on cognitive developmental theory, though there are still major differences in the underlying models guiding the two approaches. The cognitive emphasis in recent research has led to evidence that children organize the world according to gender very early, with relatively little direct tuition from socialization agents. They form concepts of male and female by age 2 or 3, and they readily incorporate stereotyped views of play activities, adult roles, and occupational pursuits. They do not, as suggested in earlier versions of the theory, simply learn behaviors appropriate for their own gender. They learn concepts of both masculine and feminine behavior. The selection of behaviors appropriate to their own gender occurs more at the level of performance than acquisition. Although children readily classify their social world into male and female, the content they associate with those constructs is, of course, given by their cultural environment. The family and other institutions of the society tell the child *what* is masculine and feminine. They also can influence the degree to which the child views male and female as bipolar, mutually exclusive, or salient categories. That is, in virtually all known societies, children form concepts of gender, but those concepts are more or less rigid, differentiated, or overlapping depending on the models and teachings presented in the child's social surroundings.

Although cognitive constructs are acquired by children and undergo predictable developmental patterns, the relationship between cognition and behavior is less clear. Some people appear to assume that changing children's sex role concepts or stereotypes will change their preferences, attitudes, or behavior. These links between cognition and adoption are not clearly demonstrated. Intervention efforts that focus on stereotypes may have little effect on the child's choices of interests or activities. Furthermore, very early aspects of sex-typed behavior may develop independently of cognitions about gender. There is a real possibility that cognition and behavior develop along somewhat separate tracks, perhaps becoming integrated when the child reaches middle childhood or in a later period of development.

One striking shift in recent years has been a deemphasis on parents as crucial socialization agents for sex-typing with a corresponding increase in emphasis on other socializing influences such as schools, peers, mass media, and other family members. Parents are just one of many sources through which children learn sex-typed concepts and behavior. Yet, we must guard against swinging too far in the other direction and ignoring the influence of parents, particularly when searching for sources of nontraditional sex-typing. For one thing, recent research has supported earlier hints that fathers play a particularly important role in the acquisition of sex-typed behavior by both boys and girls. The absence of a father, especially in the early years, is associated with low levels of masculinity for boys and for girls a relative difficulty in interacting with males. When fathers are present, they differentiate between boys and girls more often than mothers do, often providing gross motor and physical play and other experiences that contribute to masculine development for both sexes. Nontraditional role enactment by parents appears to influence children to have less stereotyped concepts of sex roles compared to peers whose parents follow traditional paths; nontraditional sex role enactment also influences children to pursue nontraditional paths themselves. Other socializing agents—schools and media—can also teach nontraditional sex-typing, but parents appear to have an important influence, even when other socializing institutions convey traditional ideas.

Of all the content areas that are subsumed under sex-typing, psychologists have overemphasized personality attributes and social behavior while paying relatively little attention to play activities, social and occupational roles, interests, the sex of peers and mates, and stylistic qualities. The developmental literature clearly indicates that sex-typing of activities, interests, and roles is acquired earlier and more definitely than sex-typing of personal and social behavior. Children learn that trucks, trains, and active games are masculine while dolls, dishes, and housecleaning toys are feminine almost before they can label such items. Boys and girls engage in different kinds of play and express different occupational preferences very early. By contrast, sex-typed concepts of social behavior are acquired later, and sex differences in personal-social behavior appear much later if at all (with the exception of aggression). Par-

ents also evidence more clear sex-typed training of play activities and interests than they do of behaviors such as dependency, aggression, or achievement effort. Perhaps developmental psychologists should consider more carefully the environmental circumstances generated by early differences in play activities that could have many implications for other aspects of sex-typed development.

The gender of preferred peers is another aspect of sex-typing that has received relatively little attention, and yet it seems to have important implications for socialization. Sex segregation of peer groups has been commonplace knowledge for so long that many people assume it is an innate social pattern. However, the amount of sex-segregated play a child experiences can vary considerably depending on school environment or other circumstances. Obviously, sex segregation in play is closely linked to sex-typed play activities, but it can also facilitate nonstereotyped activities.

Integration may have long-term implications for equality of the sexes just as it does for equality of the races. When boys and girls are separated, it is easy for them to receive different treatment. Athletics is the most blatant example of the differential value attached to male and female groups, but there are probably many others. Integration may prevent such differential treatment, but it may also promote other problems if, as is suggested by a fairly large body of social psychology literature, males tend to dominate mixed groups. Even in the family, there is some hint in the literature that girls are more often interrupted than boys, perhaps indicating at a subtle level the lower value given to girls when a group is mixed.

Stylistic and symbolic aspects of sex-typing have also been relatively neglected. Recent behavioral documentation of gestures, postures, mannerisms, and voice intonations fits the popular conceptions of masculinity and femininity. These "expressive behaviors," as Allport (1961) called them, are important signals of sex-typing for many people in our society. One has only to survey adult reactions to "Mr. Rogers," a favorite children's television program, to be persuaded that expressive behaviors are important social cues. Furthermore, people are less aware of them and have more difficulty changing them than they do play activities or some other aspects of sex-typing.

Androgyny became a byword for proponents of change in sex roles during the 1970s. There are two separate meanings for the term. Androgyny can describe freedom from gender as an important construct. Choices of interests, activities, mates, or behaviors are made on grounds other than gender;

masculine or feminine labels are irrelevant to these choices. This definition is represented by Bem's (1981) notion of gender salience and the concept of sex role transcendence introduced by Rebecca et al. (1976). Androgyny can be applied to any content area discussed as part of sex-typing. For example, one would be androgynous if one chose one's friends for their personal qualities without regard to gender or if one chose one's occupation without regard to its sex-typing.

A second meaning of androgyny, which is more familiar in the empirical literature, describes a combination of masculine and feminine qualities. This meaning has been applied almost exclusively to personality attributes, and the more refined versions have restricted it to socially desirable personality attributes. Hence, Spence and Helmreich (1978) and Block (1973) suggested that an androgynous person is one who combines or integrates both masculine and feminine personality attributes. In Block's developmental view, androgyny is the result of a mature level of ego development that entails the integration of various aspects of self and the freedom from a strong need to conform socially. A careful examination of these definitions suggests that androgyny is essentially a description of psychological health or maturity and involves most of the personal-social qualities that form the core of previous theories of social development. This approach is related to the first definition in that proponents of this type of androgyny are essentially arguing that certain personal-social qualities are desirable for humans, regardless of their gender. Hence, gender is irrelevant to healthy personality functioning. In the aura of optimism created by these new approaches and the social visions that accompany them, however, one is somewhat sobered by the repeated evidence that masculine attributes are more often socially valued and more often associated with self-esteem and adaptive functioning for both males and females than are feminine attributes.

In an area undergoing as much social and conceptual change as this one has in the past 10 years, prognostications about the future are probably foolhardy. Some glib souls might wish that sex-typing would be eliminated as an area of study in 10 years because gender would have become irrelevant to understanding children's development. I consider such a possibility unlikely and probably undesirable. Gender is a basic biological fact. We know very little at this point about how directly the biological correlates of gender influence behavior, but it is clear that gender is a fundamental social classification that is unlikely to disappear. We need considerably more information about the ways in which chemical, hormonal, and other biological variables may affect behavior. Such investigations are not inherently sexist; if males and females do have somewhat different predispositions for certain kinds of behavior, then socializing influences could be designed to compensate for those tendencies. Perhaps, more important, we will continue to deal with the less direct effects of biological gender differences. Females can bear children, and males cannot. The social responsibility of women for children that results (though not inevitably) has clear implications for many aspects of men's and women's lives.

In studies of biological variables as well as other aspects of sex-typing, interdisciplinary research is badly needed. Each discipline approaches the problem with a set of assumptions, constructs, and blinders that lead to research that is either narrow or is methodologically unsound. Studies of biological variables and behavior need both biologists and psychologists. Studies of social influences could benefit greatly from combining sociological and anthropological approaches with those generated by social and developmental psychologists. Research is also needed in which the multidimensionality of sex-typing is taken seriously. Every study should include mutliple indexes of different constructs or content areas unless the research question is clearly limited to one component. Interpretations of research results also need to be less global and more attentive to the particular components of sex-typing that have been measured. For example, many people interpret findings from scales measuring self-perceptions of personal-social characteristics as though such scales encompassed all aspects of masculinity, femininity, or androgyny. A more careful examination of the multiple dimensions of sex-typing would lead to a more well defined and conceptually sophisticated view of the phenomena being studied.

Sex-typing as a topic of inquiry is only beginning a period of expansion and refinement that has been made possible by throwing off the constraints of earlier assumptions. Although the strong social commitments and values of many investigators may occasionally interfere with a critical scientific approach, those same commitments and values can help to guide the field in directions that challenge old theories and assumptions and to produce research findings with real social importance.

REFERENCES

Allport, G. W. *Pattern and growth in personality*. New York: Holt, Rinehart and Winston, 1961.

Anastasi, A. Heredity, environment, and the question, "How?" *Psychological Review*, 1958, *65*, 197–208.

Archer, J. Biological explanations of psychological sex differences. In B. B. Lloyd & J. Archer (Eds.), *Exploring sex differences*. London: Academic Press, 1976.

Aronoff, C. E. Sex role and aging on television. *Journal of Communication*, 1974, *24*(4), 86–87.

Atkin, C. *Effects of television advertising on children* (second year experimental evidence). Michigan State University, Department of Communication, 1975.

Atkinson, J., & Endsley, R. C. Influence of sex of child and parent on parental reactions to hypothetical parent-child situations. *Genetic Psychology Monographs*, 1976, *94*, 131–147.

Bakan, D. *The duality of human existence*. Chicago: Rand McNally, 1966.

Baker, S. W., & Ehrhardt, A. A. Prenatal androgen, intelligence, and cognitive sex differences. In R. C. Friedman, R. M. Richart, & R. S. Vande Wiele (Eds.), *Sex differences in behavior*. New York: Wiley, 1974.

Bandura, A. *Social learning theory*. Englewood Cliffs, N.J.: Prentice-Hall, 1977.

Barcus, E. *Children's television*. New York: Praeger, 1977.

Barkley, A., Ullman, G., Otto, L., & Brecht, M. The effects of sex typing and sex appropriateness of modeled behavior on children's imitation. *Child Development*, 1977, *48*, 721–725.

Barnett, R. C. *Parent child-rearing attitudes: Today and yesterday*. Paper presented at the meeting of the Society for Research in Child Development, San Francisco, March 1979.

Barry, R. J. Stereotyping of sex role in preschoolers in relation to age, family structure, and parental sexism. *Sex Roles*, 1980, *6*, 795–796.

Baruch, G. K. Feminine self-esteem, self-ratings of competence, and maternal career commitment. *Journal of Counseling Psychology*, 1973, *20*, 487–488.

Baruch, G. K. *Own-sex bias, sex-role stereotyping, and gender constancy in preschool girls*. Unpublished manuscript, Brandeis University, Waltham, Massachusetts, no date.

Baruch, G. K., & Barnett, R. C. Fathers' participation in the care of their preschool children. *Sex Roles*, 1981, *7*, 1043–1056.

Battle, E. Motivational determinants of academic competence. *Journal of Personality and Social Psychology*, 1966, *4*, 634–642.

Baumrind, D. The development of instrumental competence through socialization. In A. D. Pick (Ed.), *Minnesota symposia on child psychology* (Vol 7). Minneapolis: University of Minnesota Press, 1973.

Baumrind, D. *Gender-differences and sex-related socialization effects*. Unpublished manuscript, University of California, 1979.

Baumrind, D., & Black, A. E. Socialization practices associated with dimensions of competence in preschool boys and girls. *Child Development*, 1967, *38*, 291–328.

Bearison, D. J. Sex-linked patterns of socialization. *Sex Roles*, 1979, *5*, 11–18.

Becker, W. C. Consequences of parental discipline. In M. L. Hoffman & L. W. Hoffman (Eds.), *Review of child development research* (Vol. 1). New York: Russell Sage, 1964.

Becker, W. C., & Krug, R. S. A circumplex model for social behavior in children. *Child Development*, 1964, *35*, 371–396.

Beere, C. A. *Women and women's issues. A handbook of tests and measures*. San Francisco: Jossey-Bass, 1979.

Bell, A. P., & Weinberg, M. S. *Homosexualities*. New York: Simon & Schuster, 1978.

Bell, N. J., & Carver, W. A reevaluation of gender label effects: Expectant mothers' responses to infants. *Child Development*, 1980, *51*, 925–927.

Bem, S. L. The measurement of psychological androgyny. *Journal of Consulting and Clinical Psychology*, 1974, *42*, 155–162.

Bem, S. L. Sex role adaptability: One consequence of psychological androgyny. *Journal of Personality and Social Psychology*, 1975, *31*, 634–643.

Bem, S. L. Probing the promise of androgyny. In A. G. Kaplan & J. P. Bean (Eds.), *Beyond sex-role stereotypes. Readings toward a psychology of androgyny*. Boston: Little, Brown, 1976, 47–62.

Bem, S. L. On the utility of alternative procedures for assessing psychological androgyny. *Journal of Consulting and Clinical Psychology*, 1977, *45*, 196–205.

Bem, S. L. Theory and measurement of androgyny: A reply to the Pedhazur-Tetenbaum and Locksley-Colten critiques. *Journal of Personality and Social Psychology*, 1979, *37*, 1047–1054.

Bem, S. L. Gender schema theory: A cognitive account of sex typing. *Psychological Review*, 1981, *88*, 354–364.

Bem, S. L., & Lenney, E. Sex typing and the avoidance of cross-sex behavior. *Journal of Personality and Social Psychology*, 1976, *33*, 48–54.

Bem, S. L., Martyna, W., and Watson, C. Sex-typing and androgyny: Further explorations in the expressive domain. *Journal of Personality and Social Psychology,* 1976, *34,* 1016–1023.

Berenbaum, S. A., & Resnick, S. Somatic androgyny and cognitive abilities. *Developmental Psychology,* 1982, *18,* 418–423.

Bernard, J. Sex differences: An overview. In A. G. Kaplan & J. P. Bean (Eds.), *Beyond sex-role stereotypes: Readings toward a psychology of androgyny.* Boston: Little, Brown, 1976, 9–26.

Best, D. L., Williams, J. E., Cloud, J. M., Davis, S. W., Robertson L. S., Edwards, J. R., Giles, H., & Fowles, J. Development of sex-trait stereotypes among young children in the United States, England, and Ireland. *Child Development,* 1977, *48,* 1375–1384.

Betz, N. E., & Bander, R. S. Relationships of MMPI Mf and CPI Fe Scales to fourfold sex role classifications. *Journal of Personality and Social Psychology,* 1980, *39,* 1245–1248.

Beuf, A. Doctor, lawyer, household drudge. *Journal of Communication,* 1974, *24*(2), 142–145.

Bianchi, B. D., & Bakeman, R. Sex-typed affiliation preferences observed in preschoolers: Traditional and open school differences. *Child Development,* 1978, *49,* 910–912.

Bianchi, B. D., & Bakeman, R. *Sex-typed affiliation: Mixed sex play in an open school.* Paper presented at the meeting of the American Psychological Association, Montreal, September 1980.

Biber, H., Miller, L. B., & Dyer, J. L. Feminization in preschool. *Developmental Psychology,* 1972, *7,* 86.

Biller, H. B. Father absence and the personality development of the male child. *Developmental Psychology,* 1970, *2,* 181–201.

Biller, H. B. *Father, child, and sex role.* Lexington, Mass.: Heath Lexington Books, 1971.

Biller, H. B., & Bahm, R. M. Father absence, perceived maternal behavior, and masculinity of self-concept among junior high school boys. *Developmental Psychology,* 1971, *4,* 178–181.

Biller, H. B., & Borstelmann, L. J. Masculine development: An integrative review. *Merrill-Palmer Quarterly,* 1967, *13,* 253–294.

Biller, H. B., & Weiss, S. D. The father-daughter relationship and the personality development of the female. *Journal of Genetic Psychology,* 1970, *116,* 79–93.

Bird, A. M., & Williams, J. M. A developmental-attributional analysis of sex role stereotypes for sport performance. *Developmental Psychology,* 1980, *16,* 319–322.

Birns, B. The emergence and socialization of sex differences in the earliest years. *Merrill-Palmer Quarterly,* 1976, *22,* 229–254.

Blakemore, J. E. O., LaRue, A. A., & Olejnik, A. B. Sex-appropriate toy preference and the ability to conceptualize toys as sex-role related. *Developmental Psychology,* 1979, *15,* 339–340.

Block, J. H. Conceptions of sex role: Some cross-cultural and longitudinal perspectives. *American Psychologist,* 1973, *28,* 512–526.

Block, J. H. Issues, problems, and pitfalls in assessing sex differences: A critical review of *The psychology of sex differences. Merrill-Palmer Quarterly,* 1976, *22,* 285–308.

Block, J. H. Another look at sex differentiation in the socialization behaviors of mothers and fathers. In J. Sherman & F. L. Denmark (Eds.), *The psychology of women: Future directions of research.* New York: Psychological Dimensions, 1978.

Block, J. H. *Personality development in males and females: The influence of differential socialization.* Paper presented as part of the Master Lecture Series at the meeting of the American Psychological Association, New York, September 1979.

Block, J. H. *Gender differences and implications for educational policy.* Unpublished manuscript, University of California at Berkeley, 1981.

Block, J., Von der Lippe, A., & Block, J. H. Sex-role and socialization patterns: Some personality concomitants and environmental antecedents. *Journal of Consulting and Clinical Psychology,* 1973, *41,* 321–341.

Bock, R. D., & Kolakowski, D. Further evidence of sex-linked major-gene influence on human spatial visualizing ability. *American Journal of Human Genetics,* 1973, *25,* 1–14.

Boles, D. B. X-linkage of spatial ability: A critical review. *Child Development,* 1980, *51,* 625–635.

Bond, L. A. *The development of causal attributions for success and failure of males and females.* Paper presented at the meeting of the Society for Research in Child Development, San Francisco, March 1979.

Boswell, S. L. *Sex roles, attitudes and achievement in mathematics: A study of elementary school children and Ph.D's.* Paper presented as part of a symposium on Gender Differences in Participation in Mathematics at The Society for Research in Child Development, San Francisco, March 1979.

Bradbard, M. R., & Endsley, R. C. *The effects of sex-typed labeling on preschool children's infor-*

mation-seeking and retention. Paper presented at the meeting of the Society for Research in Child Development, San Francisco, March 1979.

Brim, O. G. Family structure and sex role learning by children: A further analysis of Helen Koch's data. *Sociometry,* 1958, *21,* 1–16.

Brophy, J. E., & Good, T. L. *Teacher-student relationships: Causes and consequences.* New York: Holt, Rinehart and Winston, 1974.

Broverman, D. M., Broverman, I. K., Vogel, W., Palmer, R. D., & Klaiber, E. L. The automatization cognitive style and physical development. *Child Development,* 1964, *35,* 1343–1359.

Broverman, D. M., Klaiber, E. L., Kobayashi, Y., & Vogel, W. Roles of activation and inhibition in sex differences in cognitive abilities. *Psychological Review,* 1968, *75,* 23–50.

Broverman, I. K., Broverman, D. M., Clarkson, F. E., Rosenkrantz, P. S., & Vogel, S. R. Sex-role stereotypes and clinical judgments of mental health. *Journal of Consulting and Clinical Psychology,* 1970, *34,* 1–7.

Brown, D. G. Sex role preferences in young children. *Psychological Monographs,* 1956, *70,* (Whole No. 421).

Brush, L. R. *Why women avoid the study of mathematics: A longitudinal study.* Report to the National Institute of Education, Abt Associates, Inc., Cambridge, Massachusetts, November 1979.

Brush, L. R., & Goldberg, W. A. The intercorrelation of measures of sex-role identity. *Journal of Child Psychology and Psychiatry,* 1978, *19,* 43–48.

Bryan, J. W., & Luria, A. Sex-role learning: A test of the selective attention hypothesis. *Child Development,* 1978, *49,* 13–23.

Bryden, M. P. Evidence of sex-related differences in cerebral organization. In M. A. Wittig & A. C. Petersen (Eds.), *Sex-related differences in cognitive functioning.* New York: Academic Press, 1979, 121–143.

Buffery, A. W. H., & Gray, J. A. Sex differences in the development of spatial and linguistic skills. In C. Ounstead & D. C. Taylor (Eds.), *Gender differences: Their ontogeny and significance.* London: Churchills, 1972, 123–157.

Busby, L. J. Sex-role research on the mass media. *Journal of Communication,* 1975, *25*(4), 107–131.

Cantor, M. S. Where are the women in public broadcasting? In G. Tuchman, A. K. Daniels, & J. Benet (Eds.), *Hearth and home: Images of women in the mass media.* New York: Oxford University Press, 1978, 78–89.

Carpenter, C. J., Huston, A. C., & Holt, W. The Use of selected activity participation to modify sex-typed behavior. Paper presented as part of the symposium on *Analysis of Children's Play Activities as Antecedents for Sex-typed Behaviors* at the Annual Convention of the Association for Behavior Analysis, Milwaukee, Wisconsin, May 1981.

Carpenter, C. J., Huston, A. C., & Neath, J. *Preschool masculine and feminine behavior associated with activity structure.* Paper presented at the meeting of the Association for Behavior Analysis, Milwaukee, May 1981.

Carpenter, C. J., & Huston-Stein, A. Activity structure and sex-typed behavior in preschool children. *Child Development,* 1980, *51,* 862–872.

Carter, D. B., & Patterson, C. J. Sex roles as social conventions: The development of children's conceptions of sex-role stereotypes. *Developmental Psychology,* in press.

Chapman, M. Father absence, stepfathers, and the cognitive performance of college students. *Child Development,* 1977, *48,* 1152–1154.

Cherry, L. The preschool teacher-child dyad: Sex differences in verbal interaction. *Child Development,* 1975, *46,* 532–535.

Cherry, L., & Lewis, M. Mothers and two-year-olds: A study of sex-differentiated aspects of verbal interaction. *Developmental Psychology,* 1976, *12,* 278–282.

Child, I., Potter, E., & Levine, E. Children's textbooks and personality development. An exploration in the social psychology of education. *Psychological Monographs,* 1946, *60*(Whole No. 3).

Clark, A. E., & Ruble, D. N. Young adolescents' beliefs concerning menstruation. *Child Development,* 1978, *49,* 231–234.

Coates, S. Sex differences in field independence among preschool children. In R. C. Friedman, R. M. Richart, & R. L. Vande Wiele (Eds.), *Sex differences in behavior.* New York: Wiley, 1974.

Coates, S., Lord, M., & Jakabovics, E. Field dependence-independence, social-non-social play and sex differences in preschool children. *Perceptual and Motor Skills,* 1975, *40,* 195–202.

Comstock, G., Chaffee, S., Katzman, N., McCombs, M., & Roberts, D. *Television and human behavior.* New York: Columbia University Press, 1978.

Condry, J., & Condry, S. Sex differences: A study of the eye of the beholder. *Child Development,*

1976, *47*, 812–819.

Condry, S. M., Condry, J. C., & Pogatshnik, L. W. *Sex differences: A study of the ear of the beholder*. Paper presented at the meeting of the American Psychological Association, Toronto, August 1978.

Connor, J. M., Schackman, M., & Serbin, L. A. Sex-related differences in response to practice on a visual-spatial test and generalization to a related test. *Child Development*, 1978, *49*, 24–29.

Connor, J. M., & Serbin, L. A. Behaviorally based masculine- and feminine-activity-preference scales for preschoolers: Correlates with other classroom behaviors and cognitive tests. *Child Development*, 1977, *48*, 1411–1416.

Connor, J. M., & Serbin, L. A. Children's responses to stories with male and female characters. *Sex Roles*, 1978, *4*, 637–646.

Connor, J. M., Serbin, L. A., & Ender, R. A. Responses of boys and girls to aggressive, assertive, and passive behaviors of male and female characters. *Journal of Genetic Psychology*, 1978, *133*, 59–69.

Connor, J. M., Serbin, L. A., & Schackman, M. Sex differences in children's response to training on a visual-spatial test. *Developmental Psychology*, 1977, *13*, 293–294.

Constantinople, A. Masculinity-femininity: An exception to a famous dictum? *Psychological Bulletin*, 1973, *80*, 389–407.

Cordua, G. D., McGraw, K. O., & Drabman, R. S. Doctor or nurse: Children's perceptions of sex typed occupations. *Child Development*, 1979, *50*, 590–593.

Courtney, A. E., & Whipple, T. W. Women in TV commercials. *Journal of Communication*, 1974, *24*(2), 110–118.

Cramer, P., & Hogan, K. A. Sex differences in verbal and play fantasy. *Developmental Psychology*, 1975, *11*, 145–154.

Crandall, V. C. *Expecting sex differences and sex differences in expectancies*. Paper presented at the meeting of the American Psychological Association, Toronto, August 1978.

Cummings, S., & Taebel, D. Sexual inequality and the reproduction of consciousness: An analysis of sex-role stereotyping among children. *Sex Roles*, 1980, *6*, 631–644.

Dalton, K. Ante-natal progesterone and intelligence. *British Journal of Psychiatry*, 1968, *144*, 1377–1382.

Dalton, K. Prenatal progesterone and educational attainments. *British Journal of Psychiatry*, 1976, *129*, 438–442.

Dan, A. J. The menstrual cycle and sex-related differences in cognitive variability. In M. A. Wittig & A. C. Petersen (Eds.), *Sex-related differences in cognitive functioning*. New York: Academic Press, 1979, 241–260.

Davidson, E. S., Yasuna, A., & Tower, A. The effects of television cartoons on sex-role stereotyping in young girls. *Child Development*, 1979, *50*, 597–600.

Davis, A. *Sex roles in children's literature*. Paper presented at the meeting of the Society for Research in Child Development, San Francisco, March 1979.

Davis, S. W., Williams, J. E., & Best, D. L. Sex-trait stereotypes in the self and peer descriptions of third grade children. *Sex Roles*, in press.

DeFleur, M. L. Occupational roles as portrayed on television. *Public Opinion Quarterly*, 1964, *28*, 57–74.

DeLucia, L. A. The toy preference test: A measure of sex-role identification. *Child Development*, 1963, *34*, 107–117.

DeVries, R. Constancy of generic identity in the years three to six. *Monographs of the Society for Research in Child Development*, 1969, *34* (Serial No. 127).

DeVries, R. Relationships among Piagetian, IQ, and achievement assessments. *Child Development*, 1974, *45*, 746–756.

Dohrmann, R. D. A gender profile of children's educational TV. *Journal of Communication*, 1975, *25*(4), 56–65.

Drake, C. T., & McDougall, D. Effects of the absence of a father and other male models on the development of boys' sex roles. *Developmental Psychology*, 1977, *13*, 537–538.

Duncan, O. D., Schuman, H., & Duncan, B. *Social change in a metropolitan community*. New York: Russell Sage, 1973.

Dwyer, C. A. Sex differences in reading: An evaluation and a critique of current methods. *Review of Educational Research*, 1973, *43*, 455–461.

Dwyer, C. A. Influence of children's sex role standards on reading and arithmetic achievement. *Journal of Educational Psychology*, 1974, *66*, 811–816.

Edelbrock, C., & Sugawara, A. I. Acquisition of sex-typed preferences in preschool-aged children. *Developmental Psychology*, 1978, *14*, 614–623.

Edelsky, C. Acquisition of an aspect of communicative competence: Learning what it means to talk like a lady. In S. Ervin-Tripp & C. Mitchell-Kernan (Eds.), *Child discourse*. New York: Academic Press, 1977.

Edwards, C. P., & Whiting, B. B. The inadequacy of current study of differential socialization of girls and boys, in the light of cross-cultural research. In C. Super (Ed.), *Anthropological contributions to theories of child development*. San Francisco: Jossey-Bass, in press.

Ehrhardt, A. A., & Baker, S. W. Fetal androgens, human central nervous system differentiation, and behavior sex differences. In R. C. Friedman, R. M. Richart, & R. L. Vande Wiele (Eds.), *Sex differences in behavior*. New York: Wiley, 1974, 33–51.

Ehrhardt, A. A., & Meyer-Bahlburg, H. F. L. Effects of prenatal sex hormones on gender-related behavior. *Science*, 1981, *211*, 1312–1318.

Eisenberg-Berg, N., Boothby, R., & Matson, T. Correlates of preschool girls' feminine and masculine toy preferences. *Developmental Psychology*, 1979, *15*, 354–355.

Emmerich, W. Family role concepts of children ages six to ten. *Child Development*, 1961, *32*, 609–624.

Emmerich, W. Structure and development of personal-social behaviors in economically disadvantaged preschool children. *Genetic Psychology Monographs*, 1977, *95*, 191–245.

Emmerich, W. *Developmental trends in sex-stereotyped values*. Paper presented at the meeting of the Society for Research in Child Development, San Francisco, March 1979.

Emmerich, W. Non-monotonic developmental trends in social cognition: The case of gender constancy. In S. Strauss (Ed.), *U-Shaped behavioral growth*. New York: Academic Press, 1981.

Emmerich, W. *Development of gender constancy and sex-typed preferences*. Paper presented at the meeting of the Society for Research in Child Development, Boston, April 1981.

Emmerich, W., Goldman, K. S., Kirsh, B., & Sharabany, R. Evidence for a transitional phase in the development of gender constancy. *Child Development*, 1977, *48*, 930–936.

Emmerich, W., & Shepard, K. Development of sex-differentiated preferences during late childhood and adolescence. *Developmental Psychology*, 1982, *18*, 406–417.

Erikson, E. H. *Childhood and society* (2nd ed.). New York: Norton, 1963.

Etaugh, C. Effects of maternal employment on children: A review of recent research. *Merrill-Palmer Quarterly*, 1974, *20*, 71–98.

Etaugh, C., Collins, G., & Gerson, A. Reinforcement of sex-typed behaviors of two-year-old children in a nursery school setting. *Developmental Psychology*, 1975, *11*, 255.

Etaugh, C., & Hadley, T. Causal attributions of male and female performance by young children. *Psychology of Women Quarterly*, 1977, *2*, 16–23.

Etaugh, C., & Harlow, H. Behaviors of male and female teachers as related to behaviors and attitudes of elementary school children. *The Journal of Genetic Psychology*, 1975, *127*, 163–170.

Etaugh, C., & Hughes, V. Teachers' evaluations of sex-typed behaviors in children: The role of teacher sex and school setting. *Developmental Psychology*, 1975, *11*, 394–395.

Etaugh, C., & Riley, S. Knowledge of sex stereotypes in preschool children. *Psychological Reports*, 1979, *44*, 1279–1282.

Etaugh, C., & Ropp, J. Children's self-evaluation of performance as a function of sex, age, feedback, and sex-typed task label. *The Journal of Psychology*, 1976, *94*, 115–122.

Etaugh, C., & Rose, S. Adolescents' sex bias in the evaluation of performance. *Developmental Psychology*, 1975, *11*, 663–664.

Fagot, B. I. Influence of teacher behavior in the preschool. *Developmental Psychology*, 1973, *9*, 198–206.

Fagot, B. I. Sex differences in toddlers' behavior and parental reaction. *Developmental Psychology*, 1974, *10*, 554–558.

Fagot, B. I. Consequences of moderate cross-gender behavior in preschool children. *Child Development*, 1977, *48*, 902–907. (a)

Fagot, B. I. Teachers' reinforcement of sex-preferred behaviors in Dutch preschools. *Psychological Reports*, 1977, *41*, 1249–1250. (b)

Fagot, B. I. *The consequences of same-sex, cross-sex, and androgynous preferences in early childhood*. Paper presented at the Western Psychological Association, San Francisco, April 1978. (a)

Fagot, B. I. The influence of sex of child on parental reactions to toddler children. *Child Development*, 1978, *49*, 459–465. (b)

Fagot, B. I. Reinforcing contingencies for sex-role behaviors: Effect of experience with children. *Child Development*, 1978, *49*, 30–36. (c)

Fagot, B. I. *Sex determined consequences of different play styles in early childhood*. Paper presented at the American Psychological Association, Toronto, Canada, August 1978. (d)

Fagot, B. I. Male and female teachers: Do they treat boys and girls differently? *Sex Roles*, 1981, *7*, 263–272. (a)

Fagot, B. I. Stereotypes versus behavioral judgments of sex differences in young children. *Sex Roles*, 1981, *7*, 1093–1096. (b)

Fagot, B. I. Adults as socializing agents. In T. Field, A. Huston, H. Quay, L. Troll, & G. Finley (Eds.), *Review of human development*. New York: Wiley, 1982.

Fagot, B. I., & Littman, I. Relation of preschool sex-typing to intellectual performance in elementary school. *Psychological Reports*, 1976, *39*, 699–704.

Fagot, B. I., & Patterson, G. R. An *in vivo* analysis of reinforcing contingencies for sex-role behaviors in the preschool child. *Developmental Psychology*, 1969, *1*, 563–568.

Faulkender, P. J. Categorical habituation with sex-typed toy stimuli in older and younger preschoolers. *Child Development*, 1980, *51*, 515–519.

Fein, G., Johnson, D., Kosson, N., Stork, L., & Wasserman, L. Sex stereotypes and preferences in the toy choices of 20-month-old boys and girls. *Developmental Psychology*, 1975, *11*, 527–528.

Fennema, E., & Sherman, J. Sex-related differences in mathematics achievement, spatial visualization, and affective factors. *American Educational Research Journal*, 1977, *14*, 51–71.

Ferguson, R., & Maccoby, E. Interpersonal correlates of differential abilities. *Child Development*, 1966, *37*, 549–571.

Field, T. Interaction behaviors of primary versus secondary caretaker fathers. *Developmental Psychology*, 1978, *14*, 183–184.

Fillmer, H. T., & Haswell, L. Sex-role stereotyping in English usage. *Sex Roles*, 1977, *3*, 257–263.

Flaherty, J. F., & Dusek, J. B. An investigation of the relationship between psychological androgyny and components of self-concept. *Journal of Personality and Social Psychology*, 1980, *38*, 984–992.

Flerx, V. C., Fidler, D. S., & Rogers, R. W. Sex role stereotypes: Developmental aspects and early intervention. *Child Development*, 1976, *47*, 998–1007.

Fling, S., & Manosevitz, M. Sex typing in nursery school children's play interests. *Developmental Psychology*, 1972, *7*, 146–152.

Fox, L. H., Tobin, D., & Body, L. Sex-role socialization and achievement in mathematics. In M. A. Wittig & A. C. Petersen (Eds.), *Sex-related differences in cognitive functioning*. New York: Academic Press, 1979, 303–332.

Franck, K., & Rosen, E. A projective test of masculinity-femininity. *Journal of Consulting Psy-*

chology, 1949, *13*, 247–256.

Franzini, L. R., Litrownik, A. J., & Blanchard, F. H. Modeling of sex-typed behaviors: Effects on boys and girls. *Developmental Psychology*, 1978, *14*, 313–314.

Franzwa, H. The image of women in television: An annotated bibliography. In G. Tuchman, A. K. Daniels, & J. Benet (Eds.), *Hearth and home: Images of women in the mass media*. New York: Oxford University Press, 1978, 272–300.

Frey, K. S., & Ruble, D. N. *Concepts of gender constancy as mediators of behavior*. Paper presented at the meeting of the Society for Research in Child Development, Boston, April 1981.

Friedrich-Cofer, L. K., Huston-Stein, A., Kipnis, D. M., Susman, E. J., & Clewett, A. S. Environmental enhancement of prosocial television content: Effects on interpersonal behavior, imaginative play, and self-regulation in a natural setting. *Developmental Psychology*, 1979, *15*, 637–646.

Friedrich-Cofer, L. K., Tucker, C. J., Norris-Baker, C., Farnsworth, J. B., Fisher, D. P., Hannington, C. M., & Hoxie, K. *Perceptions by adolescents of television heroines*. Paper presented at the meeting of the Southwestern Psychological Association, New Orleans, April 1978.

Frieze, I. H., & Ramsey, S. J. Nonverbal maintenance of traditional sex roles. *Journal of Social Issues*, 1976, *32*(3), 133–142.

Frisch, H. L. Sex stereotypes in adult-infant play. *Child Development*, 1977, *48*, 1671–1675.

Frueh, T., & McGhee, P. E. Traditional sex role development and amount of time spent watching television. *Developmental Psychology*, 1975, *11*, 109.

Fryrear, J. L., & Thelen, M. H. Effects of sex of model and sex of observer on the imitation of affectionate behavior. *Developmental Psychology*, 1969, *1*, 298.

Garrett, C. S., Ein, P. L., & Tremaine, L. The development of gender stereotyping of adult occupations in elementary school children. *Child Development*, 1977, *48*, 507–512.

Gerbner, G. Violence in television drama: Trends and symbolic functions. In G. A. Comstock & E. A. Rubinstein (Eds.), *Television and social behavior. Media content and control*. (Vol. 1). Washington: Government Printing Office, 1972, 28–187.

Goffman, E. *Gender advertisements*. New York: Harper & Row, 1979.

Gold, A. R., Brush, L. R., & Sprotzer, E. R. *The importance of a "neutral" category in research on sex stereotypes*. Paper presented at the meeting of the Society for Research in Child Development, San Francisco, March 1979.

Gold, A. R., & St. Ange, M. C. Development of sex role stereotypes in black and white elementary school girls. *Developmental Psychology*, 1974, *10*, 461.

Gold, D., & Andres, D. Comparisons of adolescent children with employed and nonemployed mothers. *Merrill-Palmer Quarterly*, 1978, *24*, 243–254. (a)

Gold, D., & Andres, D. Developmental comparisons between ten-year-old children with employed and nonemployed mothers. *Child Development*, 1978, *49*, 75–84. (b)

Gold, D., & Andres, D. Relations between maternal employment and development of nursery school children. *Canadian Journal of Behavioural Science*, 1978, *10*, 116–129. (c)

Gold, D., Andres, D., & Glorieux, J. The development of Francophone nursery-school children with employed and nonemployed mothers. *Canadian Journal of Behavioural Science*, 1979, *11*, 169–173.

Gold, D., & Berger, C. Problem-solving performance of young boys and girls as a function of task appropriateness and sex identity. *Sex Roles*, 1978, *4*, 183–194.

Goldberg, S., & Lewis, M. Play behavior in the year-old infant: Early sex differences. *Child Development*, 1969, *40*, 21–32.

Golden, M., & Birns, B. Social class and infant intelligence. In M. Lewis (Ed.), *Origins of intelligence: Infancy and early childhood*. New York: Plenum, 1975, 299–351.

Goodenough, D. R., Gandini, E., Olkin, I., Pizzamiglio, L., Thayer, D., & Witkin, H. A. A study of X-chromosome linkage with field dependence and spatial visualization. *Behavior Genetics*, 1977, *7*, 373–388.

Gouze, K., & Nadelman, L. Constancy of gender identity for self and others in children between the ages of three and seven. *Child Development*, 1980, *51*, 275–278.

Goy, R. W. Early hormonal influences on the development of sexual and sex-related behaviors. In R. K. Unger & F. L. Denmark (Eds.), *Woman: Dependent or independent variable?* New York: Psychological Dimensions, 1975, 447–472.

Green, R. *Sexual identity conflict in children and adults*. New York: Basic Books, 1974.

Green, R. One-hundred ten feminine and masculine boys: Behavioral contrasts and demographic similarities. *Archives of Sexual Behavior*, 1976,

5, 425–446.

Green, R., Williams, K., & Harper, J. *Cross-sex identity: Peer group integration and the double standard of childhood sex typing*. Paper presented at the Childhood and Sexuality Symposium, Montreal, Canada, September 1979.

Greer, L. D. *Children's comprehension of formal features with masculine and feminine connotations*. Unpublished master's thesis, Department of Human Development, University of Kansas, 1980.

Greer, L. D., Huston, A. C., Wright, J. C., Welch, R., & Ross, R. *Children's comprehension of television forms with masculine and feminine connotations*. Paper presented at the meeting of the Society for Research in Child Development, Boston, April 1981.

Greif, E. B. *Sex differences in parent-child conversations: Who interrupts who?* Paper presented at the meeting of the Society for Research in Child Development, San Francisco, March 1979.

Gross, L., & Jeffries-Fox, S. What do you want to be when you grow up, little girl? In G. Tuchman, A. K. Daniels, & J. Benet (Eds.), *Hearth and home: Images of women in the mass media*. New York: Oxford University Press, 1978, 240–265.

Grotevant, H. D. Sibling constellations and sex typing of interests in adolescence. *Child Development*, 1978, *49*, 540–542.

Grusec, J. E., & Brinker, D. B., Jr. Reinforcement for imitation as a social learning determinant with implications for sex-role development. *Journal of Personality and Social Psychology*, 1972, *21*, 149–158.

Gump, P. Psychological ecology and children. In E. M. Hetherington, J. Hagen, R. Kron, & A. H. Stein (Eds.), *Review of child development research* (Vol. 5). Chicago: University of Chicago Press, 1975, 75–126.

Gurwitz, S. B., & Dodge, K. A. Adults' evaluations of a child as a function of sex of adult and sex of child. *Journal of Personality and Social Psychology*, 1975, *32*, 822–828.

Guttentag, M., & Bray, H. *Undoing sex stereotypes. Research and resources for educators*. New York: Mcgraw-Hill, 1976.

Haas, A. Male and female spoken language differences: Stereotypes and evidence. *Psychological Bulletin*, 1979, *86*, 616–626.

Hainline, L., & Feig, E. The correlates of childhood father absence in college-aged women. *Child Development*, 1978, *49*, 37–42.

Hall, J. A., & Halberstadt, A. G. Masculinity and femininity in children: Development of the Children's Personal Attributes Questionnaire. *Developmental Psychology*, 1980, *16*, 270–280.

Hansson, R. O., Chernovetz, M. E., & Jones, W. H. Maternal employment and androgyny. *Psychology of Women Quarterly*, 1977, *2*, 76–78.

Harris, L. J. Sex differences in spatial ability: Possible environmental, genetic, and neurological factors. In M. Kinsbourne (Ed.), *Asymmetrical functions of the brain*. Cambridge, England: Cambridge University Press, 1978.

Hartley, R. E. American core culture: Changes and continuities. In G. H. Seward & R. C. Williamson (Eds.), *Sex roles in changing society*. New York: Random House, 1970.

Hartup, W. W. Peer interaction and social organization. In P. H. Mussen (Ed.), *Carmichael's manual of child psychology* (Vol. 2, 3rd ed.). New York: Wiley, 1970, 361–458.

Hartup, W. W., Moore, S. G., & Sager, G. Avoidance of inappropriate sex-typing by young children. *Journal of Consulting Psychology*, 1963, *27*, 467–473.

Hartup, W. W., & Zook, E. A. Sex-role preferences in three and four-year-old children. *Journal of Consulting Psychology*, 1960, *24*, 420–426.

Haugh, S. S., Hoffman, C. D., & Cowan, G. The eye of the very young beholder: Sex typing of infants by young children. *Child Development*, 1980, *51*, 598–600.

Hawkins, R. P., & Pingree, S. A developmental exploration of the fear of success phenomenon as cultural stereotype. *Sex Roles*, 1978, *4*, 539–547.

Helmreich, R. L., Spence, J. T., & Holahan, C. K. Psychological androgyny and sex role flexibility: A test of two hypotheses. *Journal of Personality and Social Psychology*, 1979, *37*, 1631–1644.

Helmreich, R. L., Spence, J. T., & Wilhelm, J. A. A psychometric analysis of the Personal Attributes Questionnaire. *Sex Roles*, 1981, *7*, 1097–1108.

Helper, M. M., & Quinlivan, M. J. Age and reinforcement value of sex-role labels in girls. *Developmental Psychology*, 1973, *8*, 142.

Helson, R. The changing image of the career woman. *Journal of Social Issues*, 1972, *28*(2), 33–46.

Hetherington, E. M. Effects of paternal absence on sex-typed behaviors in Negro and white preadolescent males. *Journal of Personality and Social Psychology*, 1966, *4*, 87–91.

Hetherington, E. M. The effects of familial variables on sex typing, on parent-child similarity, and on imitation in children. In J. P. Hill (Ed.),

Minnesota symposia on child psychology (Vol. 1). Minneapolis: University of Minnesota Press, 1967, 82–107.

Hetherington, E. M. Effects of father absence on personality development in adolescent daughters. *Developmental Psychology*, 1972, *7*, 313–326.

Hetherington, E. M. Divorce: A child's perspective. *American Psychologist*, 1979, *34*, 851–858.

Hetherington, E. M., Cox, M., & Cox, R. *Family interaction and social, emotional and cognitive development of children following divorce*. Paper presented at the Symposium on the Family: Setting Priorities, sponsored by the Institute for Pediatric Service of the Johnson & Johnson Baby Company, Washington D. C., May 1978.

Hetherington, E. M., & Parke, R. D. *Child psychology: A contemporary viewpoint* (2nd ed.). New York: McGraw-Hill, 1979.

Hill, C. E., Hubbs, M. A., & Verble, C. A developmental analysis of the sex-role identification of school-related objects. *Journal of Educational Research*, 1974, *67*, 205–206.

Hock, E. Working and nonworking mothers with infants: Perceptions of their careers, their infants' needs, and satisfaction with mothering. *Developmental Psychology*, 1978, *14*, 37–43.

Hoffman, L. W. Effects on child. In L. W. Hoffman & F. I. Nye (Eds.), *Working Mothers*. San Francisco: Jossey-Bass, 1974, 126–168.

Hoffman, L. W. Changes in family roles, socialization, and sex differences. *American Psychologist*, 1977, *32*, 644–657.

Hoffman, L. W. Maternal employment: 1979. *American Psychologist*, 1979, *34*, 859–865.

Hoffman, L. W., & Nye, F. I. *Working mothers*. San Francisco: Jossey-Bass, 1974.

Horney, K. The dread of women. *International Journal of Psychoanalysis*, 1932, *13*, 348–360.

Hoyenga, K. B., & Hoyenga, K. T. *The question of sex differences*. Boston: Little, Brown, 1979.

Huesmann, R., Fischer, P., Eron, L., Mermelstein, R., Kaplan-Shain, E., & Morikawa, S. *Children's sex-role preference, sex of television model, and imitation of aggressive behaviors*. Paper presented at the third meeting of the International Society for Research on Aggression, Washington, September 1978.

Huston-Stein, A., & Higgins-Trenk, A. Development of females from childhood through adulthood: Career and feminine role orientations. In P. B. Baltes (Ed.), *Life-span development and behavior* (Vol. 1). New York: Academic Press, 1978, 258–296.

Hyde, J. S., Rosenberg, B. G., & Behrman, J. Tomboyism. *Psychology of Women Quarterly,* 1977, *2,* 73–75.

Imperato-McGinley, J., Peterson, R. E., Gautier, T., & Sturla, E. Androgens and the evolution of male-gender identity among male pseudohermaphrodites with 5-reductase deficiency. *The New England Journal of Medicine,* 1979, *300,* 1234–1237.

Jacklin, C. N., & Maccoby, E. E. Social behavior at 33 months in same-sex and mixed-sex dyads. *Child Development,* 1978, *49,* 557–569.

Jamison, W., & Signorella, M. L. Sex-typing and spatial ability: The association between masculinity and success on Piaget's Water-Level Task. *Sex Roles,* 1980, *6,* 345–353.

Jennings, S. A. Effects of sex typing in children's stories on preference and recall. *Child Development,* 1975, *46,* 220–223.

Johnson, M. M. Sex role learning in the nuclear family. *Child Development,* 1963, *34,* 319–333.

Johnson, M. M. Fathers, mothers and sex typing. *Sociological Inquiry,* 1975, *45,* 15–26.

Johnston, J., Ettema, J., & Davidson, T. *An evaluation of Freestyle: A television series to reduce sex-role stereotypes.* Report from Center for Research on Utilization of Scientific Knowledge, Institute for Social Research, University of Michigan, Ann Arbor, Michigan, 1980.

Kaczala, C. M. *Sex-role identity, stereotypes and their relationships to achievement attitudes.* Paper presented at the meeting of the Society for Research in Child Development, Boston, April 1981.

Kaczala, C., Futterman, R., Meece, J., & Parsons, J. E. *Developmental shifts in expectancies and attributions for performance in mathematics.* Presented as part of a symposium on Gender Differences in Participation in Mathematics at the meeting of the Society for Research in Child Development, San Francisco, March 1979.

Kagan, J. Acquisition and significance of sex typing and sex role identity. In M. L. Hoffman & L. W. Hoffman (Eds.), *Review of child development research* (Vol. 1). New York: Russell Sage, 1964, 137–168. (a)

Kagan, J. The child's sex role classification of school objects. *Child Development,* 1964, *35,* 1051–1056. (b)

Kagan, J., Hosken, B., & Watson, S. Child's symbolic conceptualization of parents. *Child Development,* 1961, *32,* 625–636.

Kail, R. V., & Levine, L. E. Encoding processes and sex-role preferences. *Journal of Experimental Child Psychology,* 1976, *21,* 256–263.

Katz, P. A., & Rank, S. A. *Gender constancy and sibling status.* Paper presented at the meeting of the Society for Research in Child Development, Boston, April 1981.

Key, M. R. The role of male and female in children's books—Dispelling all doubt. In R. K. Unger & F. L. Denmark (Eds.), *Woman: Dependent or independent variable?* New York: Psychological Dimensions, Inc., 1975, 55–70.

Klecka, C. O., & Hiller, D. V. Impact of mothers' life style on adolescent gender-role socialization. *Sex Roles,* 1977, *3,* 241–255.

Klein, M. *Envy and gratitude.* New York: Basic Books, 1957.

Kleinke, C. L., & Nicholson, T. A. Black and white children's awareness of de facto race and sex differences. *Developmental Psychology,* 1979, *15,* 84–86.

Koblinsky, S. G., Cruse, D. F., & Sugawara, A. I. Sex role stereotypes and children's memory for story content. *Child Development,* 1978, *49,* 452–458.

Koff, E. K., Rierdan, J., & Silverstone, E. Changes in representation of body image as a function of menarcheal status. *Developmental Psychology,* 1978, *14,* 635–642.

Kohlberg, L. A cognitive-developmental analysis of children's sex-role concepts and attitudes. In E. E. Maccoby (Ed.), *The development of sex differences.* Stanford: Stanford University Press, 1966, 82–172.

Kohlberg, L. K., & Ullian, D. Z. Stages in the development of psychosexual concepts and attitudes. In R. C. Friedman, R. M. Richart, & R. L. Vande Wiele (Eds.), *Sex differences in behavior.* New York: Wiley, 1974, 209–222.

Kohlberg, L., & Zigler, E. The impact of cognitive maturity on the development of sex-role attitudes in the years 4 to 8. *Genetic Psychology Monographs,* 1967, *75,* 89–165.

Krauss, I. K. Some situational determinants of competitive performance on sex-stereotyped tasks. *Developmental Psychology,* 1977, *13,* 473–480.

Kuhn, D., Nash, S. C., & Brucken, L. Sex role concepts of two- and three-year-olds. *Child Development,* 1978, *49,* 445–451.

Lamb, M. E. The development of parental preferences in the first two years of life. *Sex Roles,* 1977, *3,* 495–497.

Lamb, M. E., & Roopnarine, J. L. Peer influences on sex-role development in preschoolers. *Child Development,* 1979, *50,* 1219–1222.

Langlois, J. H., & Downs, A. C. Mothers, fathers,

and peers as socialization agents of sex-typed play behaviors in young children. *Child Development*, 1980, *51*, 1237–1247.

Lanktree, C. B., & Hamilton, M. L. Sex-typed instructions and sex-role preference in young children's task performance. *Sex Roles*, 1980, *6*, 463–474.

Lansky, L. M., & McKay, G. Sex role preferences of kindergarten boys and girls: Some contradictory results. *Psychological Reports*, 1963, *13*, 415–421.

Leahy, R. L., & Eiter, M. Moral judgment and the development of real and ideal androgynous self-image during adolescence and young adulthood. *Developmental Psychology*, 1980, *16*, 362–370.

Leary, M. A., Greer, D., & Huston, A. C. *The relation between TV viewing and gender roles*. Paper presented at the meeting of the Southwestern Society for Research in Human Development, Galveston, Texas, April 1982.

Lee, P. C., & Wolinsky, A. L. Male teachers of young children: A preliminary empirical study. In E. M. Hetherington & R. D. Parke (Eds.), *Contemporary readings in child psychology*. New York: McGraw-Hill, 1977, 392–400.

Lemon, J. Women and blacks on prime-time television. *Journal of Communication*, 1977, *27*(4), 70–79.

Lerner, H. E. Early origins of envy and devaluation of women: Implications for sex role stereotypes. *Bulletin of the Menninger Clinic*, 1974, *38*, 538–553.

Lerner, H. E. Adaptive and pathogenic aspects of sex-role stereotypes: Implications for parenting and psychotherapy. *American Journal of Psychiatry*, 1978, *135*, 48–52.

Lesser, G. S., Fifer, G., & Clark, D. H. Mental abilities of children from different social-class and cultural groups. *Monographs of the Society for Research in Child Development*, 1965, *30* (4, Serial No. 102).

Levitin, T. E., & Chananie, J. D. Responses of female primary school teachers to sex-typed behaviors in male and female children. *Child Development*, 1972, *43*, 1309–1316.

Lewis, M., & Weinraub, M. Origins of early sex-role development. *Sex Roles*, 1979, *5*, 135–153.

Liben, L. Performance on Piagetian spatial tasks as a function of sex, field dependence, and training. *Merrill-Palmer Quarterly*, 1978, *24*, 97–110.

Liben, L. S., & Golbeck, S. L. Sex differences in performance on Piagetian spatial tasks: Differences in competence or performance? *Child Development*, 1980, *51*, 594–597.

Liben, L. S., & Signorella, M. L. Gender-related schemata and constructive memory in children. *Child Development*, 1980, *51*, 11–18.

Liebert, R., McCall, R., & Hanratty, M. Effects of sex-typed information on children's toy preferences. *Journal of Genetic Psychology*, 1971, *119*, 133–136.

Locksley, A., & Colten, M. E. Psychological androgyny: A case of mistaken identity. *Journal of Personality and Social Psychology*, 1979, *37*, 1017–1031.

Loeb, R. C., & Horst, L. Sex differences in self- and teachers' reports of self-esteem in preadolescents. *Sex Roles*, 1978, *4*, 779–788.

Loevinger, J. *Ego development. Conceptions and theories*. San Francisco: Jossey-Bass, 1976.

Lott, B. Behavioral concordance with sex role ideology related to play areas, creativity, and parental sex typing of children. *Journal of Personality and Social Psychology*, 1978, *36*, 1087–1100.

Lynch, A., Mychalkiw, W., & Hutt, S. J. Prenatal progesterone I. The effect on development and on intellectual and academic achievement. *Early Human Development*, 1978, *2*, 305–322.

Lynn, D. B. The process of learning parental and sex role identification. *Journal of Marriage and the Family*, 1966, *28*, 466–470.

Maccoby, E. E., Doering, C. H., Jacklin, C. N., & Kraemer, H. Concentrations of sex hormones in umbilical-cord blood: Their relation to sex and birth order of infants. *Child Development*, 1979, *50*, 632–642.

Maccoby, E. E., & Jacklin, C. N. *The psychology of sex differences*. Stanford, California: Stanford University Press, 1974.

Maccoby, E. E., & Jacklin, C. N. Sex differences in aggression: A rejoinder and reprise. *Child Development*, 1980, *51*, 964–980.

Maccoby, E. E., & Masters, J. C. Attachment and dependency. In P. Mussen (Ed.), *Carmichael's manual of child psychology* (Vol. 2, 3rd ed.) New York: Wiley, 1970, 73–158.

Marantz, S. A., & Mansfield, A. F. Maternal employment and the development of sex-role stereotyping in five- to eleven-year-old girls. *Child Development*, 1977, *48*, 668–673.

Marcus, D. E., & Overton, W. F. The development of cognitive gender constancy and sex role preferences. *Child Development*, 1978, *49*, 434–444.

Marcus, T. L., & Corsini, D. A. Parental expectation of preschool children as related to child gender and socioeconomic status. *Child Development*, 1978, *49*, 243–246.

Margolin, G., & Patterson, G. R. Differential consequences provided by mothers and fathers for their sons and daughters. *Developmental Psychology*, 1975, *11*, 537–538.

Martin, B. Parent-child relations. In F. D. Horowitz, E. M. Hetherington, S. Scarr-Salapatek, & G. M. Siegel (Eds.), *Review of child development research* (Vol. 4). Chicago: University of Chicago Press, 1975, 463–540.

Martin, C. L., & Halverson, C. F., Jr. A schematic processing model of sex typing and stereotyping in children. *Child Development*, 1981, *52*, 1119–1134.

Masters, J. C., Ford, M. E., Arend, R., Grotevant, H. D., & Clark, L. V. Modeling and labeling as integrated determinants of children's sex-typed imitative behavior. *Child Development*, 1979, *50*, 364–371.

Masters, J. C., & Wilkinson, A. Consensual and discriminative stereotypy of sex-type judgments by parents and children. *Child Development*, 1976, *47*, 208–217.

May, R. R. A method for studying the development of gender identity. *Developmental Psychology*, 1971, *5*, 484–487.

McArthur, L. Z., & Eisen, S. V. Achievements of male and female storybook characters as determinants of achievement behavior by boys and girls. *Journal of Personality and Social Psychology*, 1976, *33*, 467–473. (a)

McArthur, L. Z., & Eisen, S. V. Television and sex-role stereotyping. *Journal of Applied Social Psychology*, 1976, *6*, 329–351. (b)

McConaghy, M. J. Gender permanence and the genital basis of gender: Stages in the development of constancy of gender identity. *Child Development*, 1979, *50*, 1223–1226.

McCracken, J. H. Sex typing of reading by boys attending all male classes. *Developmental Psychology*, 1973, *8*, 148.

McGee, M. G. Human spatial abilities: Psychometric studies and environmental, genetic, hormonal, and neurological influences. *Psychological Bulletin*, 1979, *86*, 889–918.

Meece, J. L., & Parsons, J. E. Sex differences in math achievement: Toward a model of academic choice. *Psychological Bulletin*, 1982, *91*, 324–348.

Messent, P. R. Female hormones and behavior. In B. B. Lloyd & J. Archer (Eds.), *Exploring sex differences*. London: Academic Press, 1976, 185–212.

Meyer, B. The development of girls' sex-role attitudes. *Child Development*, 1980, *51*, 508–514.

Meyer, J. W., & Sobieszek, B. Effect of a child's sex on adult interpretations of its behavior. *Developmental Psychology*, 1972, *6*, 42–48.

Meyer, W. J., & Thompson, G. G. Sex differences in the distribution of teacher approval and disapproval among sixth-grade children. *Journal of Educational Psychology*, 1956, *47*, 385–396.

Michael, R. P., Wilson, M. I., & Zumpe, D. The bisexual behavior of female rhesus monkeys. In R. C. Friedman, R. M. Richart, & R. L. Vande Wiele (Eds.), *Sex differences in behavior*. New York: Wiley, 1974, 399–412.

Miller, M. M., & Reeves, B. B. Children's occupational sex-role stereotypes: The linkage between television content and perception. *Journal of Broadcasting*, 1976, *20*, 35–50.

Miller, S. M. Effects of maternal employment on sex role perception, interests, and self-esteem in kindergarten girls. *Developmental Psychology*, 1975, *11*, 405–406.

Milton, G. A. *Five studies of the relation between sex-role identification and achievement in problem solving* (Tech. Rep. 3). New Haven, Conn.: Department of Industrial Administration and Department of Psychology, Yale University, December 1958.

Minton, C., Kagan, J., & Levine, J. A. Maternal control and obedience in the two-year-old. *Child Development*, 1971, *42*, 1873–1894.

Minuchin, P. Sex-role concepts and sex typing in childhood as a function of school and home environments. *Child Development*, 1965, *36*, 1033–1048.

Mischel, W. *Personality and assessment*. New York: Wiley, 1968.

Mischel, W. Sex typing and socialization. In P. H. Mussen (Ed.), *Carmichael's manual of child psychology* (Vol. 2, 3rd ed.). New York: Wiley, 1970, 3–72.

Mischel, W. Toward a cognitive social learning reconceptualization of personality. *Psychological Review*, 1973, *80*, 252–283.

Mischel, W. On the future of personality measurement. *American Psychologist*, 1977, *32*, 246–254.

Mischel, W. On the interface of cognition and personality: Beyond the person-situation debate. *American Psychologist*, 1979, *34*, 740–754.

Money, J., & Ehrhardt, A. A. *Man & woman. Boy & girl*. Baltimore: Johns Hopkins University Press, 1972.

Montemayor, R. Children's performance in a game and their attraction to it as a function of sex-typed labels. *Child Development*, 1974, *45*, 152–156.

Mueller, E., & Cooper, B. *The effect of preschool teacher's sex on children's cognitive growth and sexual identity*. Final Report to the U.S. Office of Education, Department of Psychology, Boston University, 1972.

Munsinger, H., & Rabin, A. A family study of gender identification. *Child Development*, 1978, *49*, 537–539.

Mussen, P. H. Early sex-role development. In D. A. Goslin (Ed.), *Handbook of socialization theory and research*. Chicago: Rand McNally, 1969, 707–732.

Myers, B. J., Weinraub, M., & Shetler, S. *Preschoolers' knowledge of sex role stereotypes: A developmental study*. Paper presented at the meeting of the American Psychological Association, New York, September 1979.

Nadelman, L. Sex identity in London children: Memory, knowledge, and preference tests. *Human Development*, 1970, *13*, 28–42.

Nadelman, L. Sex identity in American children: Memory, knowledge, and preference tests. *Developmental Psychology*, 1974, *10*, 413–417.

Nadelman, L. *Perception of parents by London five-year-olds*. Paper based on presentation at conference on New Research on Women and Sex Roles II, Ann Arbor, Michigan, March 1975.

Nash, S. C. The relationship among sex-role stereotyping, sex-role preference and the sex difference in spatial visualization. *Sex Roles*, 1975, *1*, 15–32.

Nash, S. C. Sex role as a mediator of intellectual functioning. In M. A. Wittig & A. C. Petersen (Eds.), *Sex related differences in cognitive functioning*. New York: Academic Press, 1979, 263–302.

Nemerowicz, G. M. *Children's perceptions of gender and work roles*. New York: Praeger, 1979.

Newson, J., & Newson, E. *Seven years old in the home environment*. London: Allen & Unwin, 1976.

Nordyke, N. S., Baer, D. M., Etzel, B. C., & LeBlanc, J. M. Implications of the stereotyping and modification of sex role. *Journal of Applied Behavior Analysis*, 1977, *10*, 553–557.

O'Brien, M. *Sex differences in toy and activity preferences of toddlers*. Unpublished master's thesis, University of Kansas, Department of Human Development, 1980.

O'Brien, M., Huston, A. C., & Risley, T. *Emergence and stability of sex-typed toy preferences in toddlers*. Paper presented at the meeting of the Association for Behavior Analysis, Milwaukee, May 1981.

Olejnik, A. B., Tompkins, B., & Heinbuck, C. Sex differences, sex role orientation, and reward allocations. *Sex Roles*, in press.

Papalia, D. E., & Tennent, S. S. Vocational aspirations in preschoolers: A manifestation of early sex role stereotyping. *Sex Roles*, 1975, *1*, 197–199.

Parish, T. S., & Bryant, W. T. Mapping sex group stereotypes of elementary and high school students. *Sex Roles*, 1978, *4*, 135–140.

Parke, R. D., & Suomi, S. J. Adult male-infant relationships: Human and nonprimate evidence. In K. Immelmann, G. Barlow, M. Main, & L. Petrinovitch (Eds.), *Behavioral development: The Bielefeld interdisciplinary project*. New York: Cambridge University Press, 1980.

Parlee, M. B. Comments on "Roles of activation and inhibition in sex differences in cognitive abilities." *Psychological Review*, 1972, *79*, 180–184.

Parlee, M. B. The premenstrual syndrome. *Psychological Bulletin*, 1973, *80*, 454–476.

Parsons, J. E. Attributions, learned helplessness and sex differences in achievement. In S. R. Yussen (Ed.), *The development of reflection*. New York: Academic Press, 1982.

Parsons, J. E., Adler, T. F., & Kaczala, C. Socialization of achievement attitudes and beliefs: Parental influences. *Child Development*, 1982, *53*, 310–321.

Parsons, J. E., Kaczala, C., & Meece, J. L. Socialization of achievement attitudes and beliefs: Classroom influences. *Child Development*, 1982, *53*, 322–339.

Parsons, J. E., Ruble, D. N., Hodges, K. L., & Small, A. W. Cognitive-developmental factors in emerging sex differences in achievement-related expectancies. *Journal of Social Issues*, 1976, *32*(3), 47–61.

Parsons, T. *Social structure and personality*. New York: Free Press, 1970.

Patterson, G. R., Littman, R. A., & Bricker, W. Assertive behavior in children: A step toward a theory of aggression. *Monographs of the Society for Research in Child Development*, 1967, *32* (Serial No. 113).

Pedhazur, E. J., & Tetenbaum, T. J. Bem Sex Role Inventory: A theoretical and methodological critique, *Journal of Personality and Social Psychology*, 1979, *37*, 996–1016.

Perdue, V. P., & Connor, J. M. Patterns of touching between preschool children and male and female teachers. *Child Development*, 1978, *49*, 1258–1262.

Perloff, R. M. Some antecedents of children's sex-role stereotypes. *Psychological Reports*, 1977,

40, 463–466.

Perry, D. G., & Bussey, K. The social learning theory of sex differences: Imitation is alive and well. *Journal of Personality and Social Psychology*, 1979, *37*, 1699–1712.

Perry, D. G., & Perry, L. C. Observational learning in children: Effects of sex of model and subject's sex-role behavior. *Journal of Personality and Social Psychology*, 1975, *31*, 1084–1088.

Persky, H. Reproductive hormones, moods, and the menstrual cycle. In R. C. Friedman, R. J. Richart, & R. L. Vande Wiele (Eds.), *Sex differences in behavior*. New York: Wiley, 1974, 455–476.

Petersen, A. C. Physical androgyny and cognitive functioning in adolescence. *Developmental Psychology*, 1976, *12*, 524–533.

Petersen A. C. Hormones and cognitive functioning in normal development. In M. A. Wittig & A. C. Petersen (Eds.), *Sex-related differences in cognitive functioning*. New York: Academic Press, 1979, 189–214.

Petro, C. S., & Putnam, B. A. Sex-role stereotypes: Issues of attitudinal changes. *Sex Roles*, 1979, *5*, 29–39.

Phoenix, C. H. Prenatal testosterone in the nonhuman primate and its consequences for behavior. In R. C. Friedman, R. M. Richart, & R. L. Vande Wiele (Eds.), *Sex differences in behavior*. New York: Wiley, 1974, 19–32.

Pingree, S. The effects of nonsexist television commercials and perceptions of reality on children's attitudes about women. *Psychology of Women Quarterly*, 1978, *2*, 262–277.

Pleck, J. H. Masculinity-femininity: Current and alternate paradigms. *Sex Roles*, 1975, *1*, 161–178.

Plomin, R., & Foch, T. T. Sex differences and individual differences. *Child Development*, 1981, *52*, 386–388.

Power, T. G., & Parke, R. D. Play as a context for early learning: Lab and home analyses. In I. E. Sigel & L. M. Laosa (Eds.), *The family as a learning environment*. New York: Plenum, in press.

Quadagno, D. M., Briscoe, R., & Quadagno, J. S. Effect of perinatal gonadal hormones on selected nonsexual behavior patterns: A critical assessment of the nonhuman and human literature. *Psychological Bulletin*, 1977, *84*, 62–80.

Ray, W. J., Georgiou, S., & Ravizza, R. Spatial abilities, sex differences, and lateral eye movements. *Developmental Psychology*, 1979, *15*, 455–457.

Rebecca, M., Hefner, R., & Oleshansky, B. A model of sex-role transcendence. *Journal of Social Issues*, 1976, *32*(3), 197–206.

Reese, H. W., & Overton, W. F. Models of development and theories of development. In L. R. Goulet & P. B. Baltes (Eds.), *Life-span developmental psychology. Research and theory*. New York: Academic Press, 1970, 115–145.

Reinisch, J. M., Gandelman, R., & Spiegel, F. S. Prenatal influences on cognitive abilities: Data from experimental animals and human genetic and endocrine syndromes. In M. A. Wittig & A. C. Petersen (Eds.), *Sex-related differences in cognitive functioning*. New York: Academic Press, 1979, 215–240.

Reinisch, J. M., & Karow, W. G. Prenatal exposure to synthetic progestins and estrogens: Effects on human development. *Archives of Sexual Behavior*, 1977, *6*, 257–288.

Rekers, G. A. Atypical gender development and psychosocial adjustment. *Journal of Applied Behavior Analysis*, 1977, *10*, 559–571.

Rekers, G. A. Psychosexual and gender problems. In E. J. Mash & L. G. Terdal (Eds.), *Behavioral assessment of childhood disorders*. New York: Guilford Press, 1979.

Rekers, G. A., Amaro-Plotkin, H. D., & Low, B. P. Sex-typed mannerisms in normal boys and girls as a function of sex and age. *Child Development*, 1977, *48*, 275–278.

Rekers, G. A., Bentler, P. M., Rosen, A. C., & Lovaas, O. I. Child gender disturbances: A clinical rationale for intervention. *Psychotherapy: Theory, Research, and Practice*, 1977, *144*, 2–11.

Rekers, G. A., Crandall, B. F., Rosen, A. C., & Bentler, P. M. Genetic and physical studies of male children with psychological gender disturbances. *Psychological Medicine*, 1979, *9*, 373–375.

Rekers, G. A., & Mead, S. Early intervention for female sexual identity disturbance: Self-monitoring of play behavior. *Journal of Abnormal Child Psychology*, in press.

Rekers, G. A., Willis, T. J., Yates, C. E., Rosen, A. C., & Low, B. P. Assessment of childhood gender behavior change. *Journal of Child Psychology and Psychiatry*, 1977, *18*, 53–65.

Rheingold, H. L., & Cook, K. V. The contents of boys' and girls' rooms as an index of parents' behavior. *Child Development*, 1975, *46*, 459–463.

Richmond, P. G. A limited sex difference in spatial test scores with a preadolescent sample. *Child Development*, 1980, *51*, 501–502.

Robinson, B. E., & Canaday, H. Sex-role behaviors and personality traits of male day care teachers.

Sex Roles, 1978, *4*, 853–865.

Rogers, L. Male hormones and behaviour. In B. B. Lloyd & J. Archer (Eds.), *Exploring sex differences*. London: Academic Press, 1976.

Rose, R. M., Gordon, T. P., & Bernstein, I. S. Plasma testosterone levels in the male rhesus: Influences of sexual and social stimuli. *Science*, 1972, *178*, 643–645.

Rosenberg, B. G., & Sutton-Smith, B. The measurement of masculinity and femininity in children: An extension and revalidation. *Journal of Genetic Psychology*, 1964, *104*, 259–264.

Rosenberg, B. G., & Sutton-Smith, B. Family interaction effects on masculinity-femininity. *Journal of Personality and Social Psychology*, 1968, *8*, 117–120.

Rothbart, M. K. Birth order and mother-child interaction in an achievement situation. *Journal of Personality and Social Psychology*, 1971, *17*, 113–120.

Rothbart, M. K., & Maccoby, E. E. Parents' differential reactions to sons and daughters. *Journal of Personality and Social Psychology*, 1966, *4*, 237–243.

Rothbart, M. K., & Rothbart, M. Birth order, sex of child, and maternal helpgiving. *Sex Roles*, 1976, *2*, 39–46.

Rothbaum, F. Developmental and gender differences in the sex stereotyping of nurturance and dominance. *Developmental Psychology*, 1977, *13*, 531–532.

Rovet, J., & Netley, C. Processing deficits in Turner's syndrome. *Developmental Psychology*, 1982, *18*, 77–94.

Rubin, J. Z., Provenzano, F. J., & Luria, Z. The eye of the beholder: Parents' views on sex of newborns. *American Journal of Orthopsychiatry*, 1974, *44*, 512–519.

Ruble, D. N., Balaban, T., & Cooper, J. Gender constancy and the effects of sex-typed television toy commericals. *Child Development*, 1981, *52*, 667–673.

Ruble, D. N., & Ruble, T. L. Sex stereotypes. In A. G. Miller (Ed.), *In the eye of the beholder: Contemporary issues in stereotyping*. New York: Holt, Rinehart and Winston, 1980.

Santrock, J. W., & Warshak, R. A. Father custody and social development in boys and girls. *Journal of Social Issues*, 1979, *35*(4), 112–125.

Schachter, F. F., Gilutz, G., Shore, E., & Adler, M. Sibling deidentification judged by mothers: Cross-validation and developmental studies. *Child Development*, 1978, *49*, 543–546.

Schachter, F. F., Shore, E., Feldman-Rotman, S.,

Marquis, R. E., & Campbell, S. Sibling deidentification. *Developmental Psychology*, 1976, *12*, 418–427.

Schaefer, E. S. Converging conceptual models for maternal behavior and for child behavior. In J. C. Glidewell (Ed.), *Parental attitudes and child behavior*. Evanston, Ill.: Thomas, 1961.

Schau, C. G., Kahn, L., Diepold, J. H., & Cherry, F. The relationships of parental expectations and preschool children's verbal sex typing to their sex-typed toy play behavior. *Child Development*, 1980, *51*, 266–270.

Schratz, M. A developmental investigation of sex differences in spatial (visual-analytic) and mathematical skills in three ethnic groups. *Developmental Psychology*, 1978, *14*, 263–267.

Schuetz, S., & Sprafkin, J. N. Spot messages appearing within Saturday morning television programs. In G. Tuchman, A. K. Daniels, & J. Benet (Eds.), *Hearth and home: Images of women in the mass media*. New York: Oxford University Press, 1978, 69–77.

Sears, R. R., Rau, L. R., & Alpert, R. *Identification and child rearing*. Stanford, Calif.: Stanford University Press, 1965.

Seavey, C. A., Katz, P. A., & Zalk, S. R. Baby X: The effect of gender labels on adult responses to infants. *Sex Roles*, 1975, *1*, 103–109.

Serbin, L. A. Sex role socialization: A field in transition. In B. Lahey & A. Kazkin (Eds.), *Advances in clinical child psychology* (Vol. 3). New York: Plenum, 1980.

Serbin, L. A., & Connor, J. M. Sex-typing of children's play preferences and patterns of cognitive performance. *Journal of Genetic Psychology*, 1979, *134*, 315–316.

Serbin, L. A., Connor, J. M., Burchardt, C. J., & Citron, C. C. Effects of peer presence on sextyping of children's play behavior. *Journal of Experimental Child Psychology*, 1979, *27*, 303–309.

Serbin, L. A., Connor, J. M., & Citron, C. C. Environmental control of independent and dependent behaviors in preschool girls and boys: A model for early independence training. *Sex Roles*, 1978, *4*, 867–875.

Serbin, L. A., Connor, J. M., & Citron, C. C. Sexdifferentiated free play behavior: Effects of teacher modeling, location, and gender. *Developmental Psychology*, 1981, *17*, 640–646.

Serbin, L. A., Connor, J. M., & Iler, I. Sex-stereotyped and nonstereotyped introductions of new toys in the preschool classroom: An observational study of teacher behavior and its effects.

Psychology of Women Quarterly, 1979, *4,* 261–265.

Serbin, L. A., O'Leary, K. D., Kent, R. N., & Tonick, I. J. A comparison of teacher response to the preacademic and problem behavior of boys and girls. *Child Development,* 1973, *44,* 796–804.

Serbin, L. A., Tonick I. J., & Sternglanz, S. H. Shaping cooperative cross-sex play. *Child Development,* 1977, *48,* 924–929.

Sherman, J. A. Problems of sex differences in space perception and aspects of intellectual functioning. *Psychological Review,* 1967, *74,* 290–299.

Sherman, J. A. Predicting mathematics performance in high school girls and boys. *Journal of Educational Psychology,* 1979, *71,* 242–249.

Sherman, J. A. Mathematics, spatial visualization and related factors: Changes in girls and boys, Grades 8–11. *Journal of Educational Psychology,* 1980, *72,* 476–482.

Sherman, J. A., & Fennema, E. The study of mathematics by high school girls and boys: Related variables. *American Educational Research Journal,* 1977, *14,* 159–168.

Sherman, J. A., & Fennema, E. Distribution of spatial visualization and mathematical problem solving scores: A test of Stafford's X-linked hypotheses. *Psychology of Women Quarterly,* 1978, *3,* 157–167.

Shinn, M. Father absence and children's cognitive development. *Psychological Bulletin,* 1978, *85,* 295–324.

Sidorowicz, L. S., & Lunney, G. S. Baby X revisited. *Sex Roles,* 1980, *6,* 67–73.

Signorella, M. L., & Jamison, W. Sex differences in the correlations among field dependence, spatial ability, sex role orientation, and performance on Piaget's water-level task. *Developmental Psychology,* 1978, *14,* 689–690.

Silvern, L. E. Children's sex-role preferences: Stronger among girls than boys. *Sex Roles,* 1977, *3,* 159–171.

Silvern, L. E. Masculinity-femininity in children's self-concepts: The relationship to teachers' judgments of social adjustment and academic ability, classroom behaviors, and popularity. *Sex Roles,* 1978, *4,* 929–949.

Simms, R. E., Davis, M. H., Foushee, H. C., Holahan, C. K., Spence, J. T., & Helmreich, R. L. *Psychological masculinity and femininity in children and its relationship to trait stereotypes and toy preference.* Paper presented at the meeting of the Southwestern Psychological Association, New Orleans, April 1978.

Slaby, R. G., & Frey, K. S. Development of gender constancy and selective attention to same-sex models. *Child Development,* 1975, *46,* 849–856.

Smith, C., & Lloyd, B. Maternal behavior and perceived sex of infant: Revisited. *Child Development,* 1978, *49,* 1263–1266.

Smith, P. K., & Daglish, L. Sex differences in parent and infant behavior in the home. *Child Development,* 1977, *48,* 1250–1254.

Smith, P. K., & Green M. Aggressive behavior in English nurseries and play groups: Sex differences and response of adults. *Child Development,* 1975, *46,* 211–214.

Sobieszek, B. I. Adult interpretations of child behavior. *Sex Roles,* 1978, *4,* 579–588.

Spence, J. T., & Helmreich, R. L. *Masculinity and femininity: Their psychological dimensions, correlates, and antecedents.* Austin, Texas: University of Texas Press, 1978.

Spence, J. T., Helmreich, R. L., & Holahan, C. K. Negative and positive components of psychological masculinity and femininity and their relationships to self-reports of neurotic and acting-out behaviors. *Journal of Personality and Social Psychology,* 1979, *37,* 1673–1682.

Spence, J. T., Helmreich, R. L., & Stapp, J. Ratings of self and peers on sex-role attributes and their relation to self-esteem and conceptions of masculinity and femininity. *Journal of Personality and Social Psychology,* 1975, *32,* 29–39.

Sprafkin, J. N., & Liebert, R. M. Sex-typing and children's television preferences. In G. Tuchman, A. K. Daniels, & J. Benet (Eds.), *Hearth and home: Images of women in the mass media.* New York: Oxford University Press, 1978.

Steel, L., & Wise, L. L. *Origins of sex differences in high school mathematics achievement and participation.* Paper presented at the Convention of the American Educational Research Association, San Francisco, March 1979.

Stein, A. H. The effects of sex-role standards for achievement and sex-role preference on three determinants of achievement motivation. *Developmental Psychology,* 1971, *4,* 219–231.

Stein, A. H. The effects of maternal employment and educational attainment on the sex-typed attributes of college females. *Social Behavior and Personality,* 1973, *1,* 111–114.

Stein, A. H., & Bailey, M. M. The socialization of achievement orientation in females. *Psychological Bulletin,* 1973, *80,* 345–366.

Stein, A. H., & Friedrich, L. K. Television content and young children's behavior. In J. P. Murray,

E. A. Rubinstein, & G. A. Comstock (Eds.), *Television and social behavior* (Vol. 2). *Television and social learning.* Washington: Government Printing Office, 1972, 202–317.

Stein, A. H., & Friedrich, L. K. Impact of television on children and youth. In E. M. Hetherington, J. W. Hagen, R. Kron, & A. H. Stein (Eds.), *Review of child development research* (Vol. 5). Chicago: University of Chicago Press, 1975, 183–256.

Stein, A. H., Pohly, S. R., & Mueller, E. The influence of masculine, feminine, and neutral tasks on children's achievement behavior, expectancies of success, and attainment values. *Child Development,* 1971, *42,* 196–207.

Stein, A. H., & Smithells, J. Age and sex differences in children's sex-role standards about achievement. *Developmental Psychology,* 1969, *1,* 252–259.

Sternglanz, S. H., & Serbin, L. A. Sex role stereotyping in children's television programs. *Developmental Psychology,* 1974, *10,* 710–715.

Storms, M. D. Sex role identity and its relationships to sex role attributes and sex role stereotypes. *Journal of Personality and Social Psychology,* 1979, *37,* 1779–1789.

Storms, M. D. Theories of sexual orientation. *Journal of Personality and Social Psychology,* 1980, *38,* 783–792.

Streicher, H. W. The girls in the cartoons. *Journal of Communication,* 1974, *24*(2), 125–129.

Sutton-Smith, B. Play preference and play behavior: A validity study. *Psychological Reports,* 1965, *16,* 65–66.

Sutton-Smith, B., Roberts, J. M., & Rosenberg, B. G. Sibling associations and role involvement. *Merrill-Palmer Quarterly,* 1964, *10,* 25–38.

Sutton-Smith, B., & Rosenberg, B. G. Age changes in the effects of ordinal position on sex-role identification. *Journal of Genetic Psychology,* 1965, *107,* 61–73.

Sutton-Smith, B., & Rosenberg, B. G. *The sibling.* New York: Holt, Rinehart and Winston, 1970.

Sutton-Smith, B., Rosenberg, B. G., & Morgan, E. F., Jr. Development of sex differences in play choices during preadolescence. *Child Development,* 1963, *34,* 119–126.

Tauber, M. A. Parental socialization techniques and sex differences in children's play. *Child Development,* 1979, *50,* 225–234. (a)

Tauber, M. A. Sex differences in parent-child interaction styles during a free-play session. *Child Development,* 1979, *50,* 981–988. (b)

Tedesco, N. S. Patterns in prime time. *Journal of Communication,* 1974, *24*(2), 118–124.

Terman, L. M., & Tyler, L. E. Psychological sex differences. In L. Carmichael (Ed.), *Manual of child psychology.* New York: Wiley, 1954, 1064–1114.

Thomas, H., & Jamison, W. On the acquisition of understanding that still water is horizontal. *Merrill-Palmer Quarterly,* 1975, *21,* 31–44.

Thomas, H., Jamison, W., & Hummel, D. D. Observation is insufficient for discovering that the surface of still water is invariantly horizontal. *Science,* 1973, *181,* 173–174.

Thompson, S. K. Gender labels and early sex role development. *Child Development,* 1975, *46,* 339–347.

Thompson, S. K., & Bentler, P. M. The priority of cues in sex discrimination by children and adults. *Developmental Psychology,* 1971, *5,* 181–185.

Thornburg, K. R., & Weeks, M. O. Vocational role expectations of five-year-old children and their parents. *Sex Roles,* 1975, *1,* 395–396.

Tieger, T. On the biological basis of sex differences in aggression. *Child Development,* 1980, *51,* 943–963.

Tucker, C. J., & Friedrich-Cofer, L. *Age-related differences in adolescents' judgments of masculine and feminine stereotypes.* Unpublished manuscript, University of Houston, 1980.

Tyron, B. W. Beliefs about male and female competence held by kindergartners and second graders. *Sex Roles,* 1980, *6,* 85–97.

Ullian, D. Z. The development of conceptions of masculinity and femininity. In B. Lloyd & J. Archer (Eds.), *Exploring sex differences.* London: Academic Press, 1976, 25–48.

United States Commission on Civil Rights. *Window dressing on the set: Women and minorities in television.* Washington: Government Printing Office, 1977.

Urberg, K. A. *The development of androgynous sex-role concepts in young children.* Paper presented at the meeting of the Society for Research in Child Development, San Francisco, March 1979. (a)

Urberg, K. A. Sex role conceptualizations in adolescents and adults. *Developmental Psychology,* 1979, *15,* 90–92. (b)

Vandenberg, S. G. Sources of variance in performance of spatial tests. In J. Eliot & N. J. Salkind (Eds.), *Children's spatial development.* Springfield, Ill.: Thomas, 1975.

Vandenberg, S. G., & Kuse, A. R. Spatial ability: A critical review of the sex-linked major gene hypothesis. In M. A. Wittig & A. C. Petersen

(Eds.), *Sex-related differences in cognitive functioning*. New York: Academic Press, 1979, 67–95.

Vasta, R., Regan, K. G., & Kerley, J. Sex differences in pattern copying: Spatial cues or motor skills? *Child Development*, 1980, *51*, 932–934.

Venar, A. M., & Snyder, C. A. The preschool child's awareness and anticipation of adult sex roles. *Sociometry*, 1966, *29*, 159–168.

Vroegh, K. The relationship of birth order and sex of siblings to gender role identity. *Developmental Psychology*, 1971, *4*, 407–411.

Waber, D. P. Sex differences in mental abilities, hemispheric lateralization, and rate of physical growth at adolescence. *Developmental Psychology*, 1977, *13*, 29–38.

Waber, D. P. Cognitive abilities and sex-related variations in the maturation of cerebral cortical functions. In M. A. Wittig & A. C. Petersen (Eds.), *Sex-related differences in cognitive functioning*. New York: Academic Press, 1979, 161–186.

Ward, I. L. Sexual behavior differentiation: Prenatal hormonal and environmental control. In R. C. Friedman, R. M. Richart, & R. L. Vande Wiele (Eds.), *Sex differences in behavior*. New York: Wiley, 1974, 3–18.

Weinraub, M., & Frankel, J. Sex differences in parent-infant interaction during free play, departure, and separation. *Child Development*, 1977, *48*, 1240–1249.

Weinraub, M., & Leite, J. *Knowledge of sex-role stereotypes and sex-typed toy preference in two-year-old children*. Paper presented at the meeting of the Eastern Psychological Association, Boston, April 1977.

Weitzman, L. J., Eifler, D., Hokada, E., & Ross, C. Sex role socialization in picture books for preschool children. *American Journal of Sociology*, 1972, *77*, 1125–1150.

Welch, R. L. Androgyny and derived identity in married women with varying degrees of non-traditional role involvement. *Psychology of Women Quarterly*, 1979, *3*, 308–315.

Welch, R. L. *The effects of perceived "task gender" and induced success/failure upon subsequent task performance of psychologically androgynous and highly feminine women*. Unpublished doctoral dissertation, University of Kansas, 1981.

Welch, R. L., Huston-Stein, A., Wright, J. C., & Plehal, R. Subtle sex-role cues in children's commercials. *Journal of Communication*, 1979, *29*(3), 202–209.

White, D. G. Effects of sex-typed labels and their source on the imitative performance of young children. *Child Development*, 1978, *49*, 1266–1269.

Will, J., Self, P., & Datan, N. Maternal behavior and perceived sex of infant. *American Journal of Orthopsychiatry*, 1976, *46*, 135–139.

Williams, J. E., Bennett, S. M., & Best, D. L. Awareness and expression of sex stereotypes in young children. *Developmental Psychology*, 1975, *11*, 635–642.

Williams, J. E., Best, D. L., Tilquin, C., Keller, H., Voss, H. G., Bjerke, T., & Baarda, B. *Traits associated with men and women by young children in France, Germany, Norway, the Netherlands, and Italy*. Unpublished manuscript, Wake Forest University, 1979.

Williams, K., Green, R., & Goodman, M. Patterns of sexual identity development: A preliminary report on the "tomboy." *Research in Community and Mental Health*, 1979, *1*, 103–123.

Winkler, R. C. What types of sex-role behaviour should behaviour modifiers promote. *Journal of Applied Behaviour Analysis*, 1977, *10*, 549–552.

Wise, G. W. The relationship of sex-role perception and levels of self-actualization in public school teachers. *Sex Roles*, 1978, *4*, 605–617.

Wittig, M. A. Sex differences in intellectual functioning: How much difference do genes make? *Sex Roles*, 1976, *2*, 63–74.

Wohlford, P., Santrock, J. W., Berger, S. E., & Liberman, D. Older brother's influence on sex-typed, aggressive and dependent behavior in father-absent children. *Developmental Psychology*, 1971, *4*, 124–134.

Woods, M. B. The unsupervised child of the working mother. *Developmental Psychology*, 1972, *6*, 14–25.

Wright, H. F. Observational child study. In P. H. Mussen (Ed.), *Handbook of research methods in child development*. New York: Wiley, 1960.

Yalom, I. D., Green, R., & Fisk, N. Prenatal exposure to female hormones. *Archives of General Psychiatry*, 1973, *28*, 554–561.

Yarrow, M. R., Waxler, C. Z., & Scott, P. M. Child effects on adult behavior. *Developmental Psychology*, 1971, *5*, 300–311.

Zalk, S. R., & Katz, P. A. Gender attitudes in children. *Sex Roles*, 1978, *4*, 349–357.

Zimmerman, B. J., & Koussa, R. Sex factors in children's observational learning of value judgments of toys. *Sex Roles*, 1975, *1*, 121–133.

CHILDREN'S PROSOCIAL DISPOSITIONS AND BEHAVIOR* | 6

MARIAN RADKE-YARROW, *National Institute of Mental Health*
CAROLYN ZAHN-WAXLER, *National Institute of Mental Health*
MICHAEL CHAPMAN, *Max Plank Institute for Human Development and Education*
(*Berlin, West Germany*)

CHAPTER CONTENTS

*We wish to acknowledge our gratitude to our colleagues in the Laboratory of Developmental Psychology who helped us in the process of assembling the research literature and in preparing the manuscript for publication. We especially thank Christine Grewell, Anna Marsh, Barbara Hollenbeck, Lawson Sebris, Cynthia Schellenbach, Eunice Kennelly, Bertha LeCompte, and Anna Williams.

Behavior that is carried out for the benefit of others is essential for the life of the individual and the group. The young do not survive unless there has been caring behavior by someone. Societies in many ways are built on customs and institutions that foster and protect the welfare of others. At the same time, behavior is directed to self-interests that often compete or conflict with the needs of others. If concerns for self and concerns for others are not integrated into compatibly patterned behaviors, the individual of any age is likely to encounter difficulties.

The focus of this chapter is on child behavior that expresses caring or concern for others. Children are interested in others and have the capabilities of positive behavior toward others. The purpose here is to bring together existing knowledge regarding the nature of these positively oriented dispositions and how they develop and coexist interdependently in the behaviors of children.

Our subject matter is an age-old issue concerning the fundamental goodness of human nature, an issue with which philosophers and laypersons of ancient and modern times have wrestled and reached varying conclusions. Altruism has been accepted as a human attribute, rejected as a human possibility, regarded as a weakness, and extolled as an ideal. Thus, prosocial behavior as a focus of study does not belong exclusively to psychology or to the modern era of research. There is a rich heritage of thought regarding empathy, sympathy, cooperation, compassion, and altruism. This legacy is an essential context for viewing the attempts in psychology to make the goodness of human behaviors an object of scientific study—to capture it in psychological concepts, investigate its origins within the individual, quantify it, and shape it.

Therefore, in undertaking a review of what is known about prosocial behavior from empirical research, it is important to recognize the antecedents in philosophy and social thought across time and across cultures. To a large extent, the nature of current research hinges upon conceptions of prosocial behavior drawn from these traditions. Yet, contemporary research in psychology has often been quite unmindful of historical and cultural contexts. We will briefly consider this background from a long-term view before we turn to the more immediate history and theories within psychology and then finally turn to the data from empirical studies of prosocial behavior.

ROOTS IN PHILOSOPHY AND SOCIAL THOUGHT

Philosophical discussion of the nature of positive social behavior has centered around two major questions: What is human nature? How should one behave toward one's fellows?

A positive view of human nature was espoused in Confucianism, the dominant Chinese philosophy until the 20th century. According to Mencius, the 4th century B.C. Confucian philosopher, "All men have the mind which cannot bear to see the suffering of others" (Chan, 1963, p. 65). For Mencius, human beings were innately endowed with feelings of compassion or "human-heartedness." If these feelings were cultivated, they would be strengthened and a harmonious society would result.

Western thinking on these issues can be traced to Greek philosophy and the Judaic religious tradition. For Plato, human beings were moved by passions both good and bad but the will could also be guided by reason (Plato *Phaedrus* 253d). The question of right action was addressed by Aristotle. The definition of virtue included doing justice and developing friendships. He stressed the importance of childhood education in the formation of such good habits: "It makes no small difference, then, whether we form habits of one kind or another from our very youth; it makes a very great difference, or rather *all* the difference" (Aristotle *Nicomachean Ethics* 1103b).

Compassion for those in need occupies a prominent place in the Judaic heritage:

> When thou cuttest down thine harvest in thy field, and hast forgot a sheaf in the field, thou shalt not go again to fetch it; it shall be for the stranger, for the fatherless, and for the widow. (Deut. 24:19, King James version)

This ideal was carried on by the early Christians. Jesus taught his followers to "love thy neighbor." When one inquisitive listener asked him, "Who is my neighbor?" he replied with the familiar story of the good Samaritan (Luke 10:30–35). In the 13th century, St. Thomas Aquinas (1952) attempted to synthesize Christian religion and Greek philosophy. In addition to the virtues of prudence, justice, temperance, and fortitude taken from Plato, St. Thomas prescribed three theological virtues: faith, hope, and charity (or love).

Modern moral philosophy has also struggled with the question of human nature. In one view, human nature is dominated by selfish motives. Thus, for Hobbes (1651/1952), mankind in the state of nature lived in a war of all against all, each human being in perpetual danger of being killed or robbed by neighbors. Civil society was established by social contract as a means of self-preservation. Social cooperation was, thus, based on rational self-interest. Adam Smith (1776/1952) carried this notion into the idea of an "invisible hand" guiding a competitive capitalist economy that turned private greed into public good.

A more amiable view of human nature has also been espoused. According to Locke (1690/1952), mankind is guided by the natural law of human reason to respect each other's person and property. Hume (1740/1952) denied that reason played any role in morality, arguing instead that moral behavior was motivated by a sentiment of benevolence. Rousseau (1755/1952) believed that human beings in the state of nature were moved by sympathy and compassion but that their originally good nature had been corrupted by civilization. For Schopenhauer (1819/1966), sympathy in the form of pity was the most basic of moral motives; pity was understood as the apprehension of the suffering shared with all living things. A thorough analysis of the phenomenon of sympathy is undoubtedly that of Scheler in *The Nature of Sympathy* (1923/1954). In this work, sympathy is seen not as the result of putting oneself in another's place or otherwise sharing the suffering of others but as taking a particular attitude toward the joy or suffering of others. Scheler's views are of interest because they contain an implicit theory of development, a progression from emotional contagion, in which self and other are not clearly distinguished, to sympathy, in which there is recognition of others' experiences as belonging uniquely to them.

A third perspective holds that, because human beings are moved by both selfish and benevolent passions, only reason can be a reliable guide to moral behavior (Kant 1785/1952; Spinoza, 1677/1952). The essence of morality is acting according to a principle. Actions motivated by feelings or sentiments are not truly moral even if they benefit other persons.

In summary, human nature has been variously interpreted by philosophers as being selfishly motivated, positively social, or morally ambivalent. Despite the historical concern of psychology as a discipline to sever its ties with philosophy, it is evident that moral philosophy remains relevant to, and in many ways has anticipated, present-day issues in the psychological study of prosocial motives and behavior. The views of philosophers find their way into the total fabric of culture, influencing the scientists who study prosocial behavior as well as the children and adults whose behavior is studied.

PSYCHOLOGICAL AND BIOLOGICAL THEORIES

Although moral behavior has been of interest to many theorists in psychology, it has not always been a core issue in the discipline. The individual's prosocial concerns for others have been incorporated variously in psychological theories as instincts or general tendencies, need systems, traits, reaction forma-

tions, socialization imperatives, and so on. We will review the theories briefly in terms of their relevance for prosocial development.

Psychoanalytic Theory

Implicit in psychoanalytic theory is the premise that human beings have the potential to use self-knowledge toward betterment of their condition. Although emphasizing the innate tendency of humankind toward aggression and destruction, Freud maintained that the love and death instincts were inseparable and that they were equally essential parts of human nature.

Freud's most direct discourse on altruism, in *Civilization and Its Discontents*, bears repeating:

> The incorporation of the individual as a member of a community, or his adaptation to it, seems like an almost unavoidable condition which has to be filled before he can attain the objective of happiness. . . . Individual development seems to us a product of the interplay of two trends, the striving for happiness, generally called "egoistic," and the impulse towards merging with others in the community, which we call "altruistic." (S. Freud, 1930/1953, p. 98)

The psychoanalytic concept of identification, the means by which societal values are thought to be internalized, has been widely employed in research on prosocial behavior. Freud believed that identification underlay empathic relations with other persons in general: "[Identifications] result among other things in a person limiting his aggressiveness toward those with whom he has identified himself, and in his sparing them and giving them help" (S. Freud, 1921/1953, p. 110). Freud hypothesized that the process of identification resulted in the development of the superego, which Lewis (1971) describes as comprising both a "sense of guilt" and an "ego-ideal." The child may acquire prosocial behaviors either through feelings of guilt inflicted by the conscience for moral transgressions (Hoffman, 1976) or through the internalization of ego ideals that develop into autonomous value systems (Wolff, 1978).

The clinical milieu in which psychoanalysis is practiced has brought a recognition of pathological altruism. Anna Freud (1936/1946) describes altruistic surrender, in which the individual's interests are subordinated to the interests of others, as a way of resolving inner conflict, leading ultimately to symptom formation. Ekstein (1978) reviews cases of pathological altruism, some of which are described as reaction formations against greed. It would be incorrect to conclude from these reports, however, that the psychoanalytic view of altruism is confined to pathological types. Sperling (1955) suggests that, in genuine social-mindedness, a highly sublimated form of love is directed toward society as a whole or toward the underprivileged.

From Freud's 1895 comment that "the original helplessness of human beings is the primal source of all moral motives" (S. Freud, 1954, p. 379), Ekstein elaborates:

These first preverbal cues between mother and infant, this first struggle between waiting and satisfying one's self, are the external organizers of later empathic understanding and of sympathy and altruism. Good mothering, analysts maintain, makes for good empathy. Empathy is the forerunner of the capacity for imitation, for identification and for internalization. (1978, p. 169)

Cognitive-Developmental Theory

Cognitive-developmental theory emphasizes children's understanding of themselves and others as mediating the development of prosocial behavior. Origins of present-day formulations are to be found in early social science writings. One of the first contributors was J. M. Baldwin (1897) who distinguished successive developmental stages in children's understanding of other persons. He argued that children learn first to distinguish one person from another and persons as a class from inanimate objects, then to distinguish themselves from others within the class of persons. This latter differentiation is accomplished through imitation and the experience of effort that accompanies children's own actions but not those of others. The alternating imitation and analogy to self, in which the understanding of self and other grows mutually, form the basis for the development of positive social behavior.

Piaget (1932/1965) accepted Baldwin's idea that the awareness of self only arises in relation to other selves, but he argued that Baldwin did not take into account the young child's egocentrism. Egocentrism is compatible with a sense of the general difference between the self and others; what is lacking is an understanding of particular differences, especially differences in perspective. According to Piaget, the experience of reciprocal interaction between equals leads the child out of egocentrism. Piaget recognized a rudimentary sense of self and other even in very young children, as evidenced in their capacity for jealousy and sympathy.

The sociologist and philosopher G. H. Mead (1934/1974), another important influence on cognitive-developmental theory, saw the understanding of self and other developing in interaction involving symbolic communication. In Mead's terms, the sender of a message must "take the role" of the recipient of the message; the sender calls out in herself the anticipated response to the communication.

The convergence in the writings of these three men is striking. It is Piaget's formulations regarding children's thinking about rules, justice, and morality that are most familiar. According to Piaget, children progress through stages in moral reasoning as a result of interaction between maturational changes in mental functions and active experience with the physical and social environments. These are assumed to be hierarchical developmental stages beginning with the absolutism of external authority anchored in egocentrism and moral realism and progressing through egalitarianism to moral relativism. Kohlberg (1969), influenced by G. H. Mead and Piaget, elaborated a stage-developmental progression of moral reasoning. Neither Piaget's nor Kohlberg's theory is particularly concerned with behavior however. Instead, their theories deal with the ideas that presumably guide behavior. With few exceptions, cognitive theorists have generally not dealt in detail with the links between children's understanding of themselves and others (i.e., their role-taking abilities and stages in moral reasoning) and their moral or prosocial acts (Blasi, 1980). Thus, Wolff (1978) reviewed Kohlberg's theory and queried whether moral reasoning is "a necessary condition for moral acts, or simply a rationalization for actions that are caused or motivated by entirely different psychological but nonmoral factors" (p. 97). Mussen and Eisenberg-Berg (1977) observed that Piaget and Kohlberg have been mainly concerned with moral reasoning pertaining to laws, rules, authority, responsibility, equality, and justice. Prosocial issues, such as personal sacrifice and conflicts between one's own needs and those of others, are not tapped in Piaget's or Kohlberg's procedures. Mussen and Eisenberg-Berg suggest that there is no a priori reason to assume that the same reasoning is used in resolving dilemmas in the two domains.

Learning Theories

In marked contrast to cognitive theory, learning theories traditionally have not been concerned with the ideas, intentions, and reasoning of the child but with the overt observable positive social behavior.

Prosocial behavior, according to learning theory, is acquired just as any other behavior—through direct reinforcements and modeling. In the classical operant learning view (Skinner, 1953), social behavior is controlled by environmental contingencies. The idea that a person's behavior is determined by his emotions, intentions, or other internal dispositions is not accepted. Such internal states do not cause behavior. Instead, both the behavior and the concomitant internal state are controlled by reinforcement contingencies:

> In working for the good of others a person may feel love or fear, loyalty or obligation, or any other condition arising from the contingencies responsible for the behavior. A person does not act for the good of others because of a feeling of belongingness or refuse to act because of feelings of alienation. His behavior depends upon the control exerted by the social environment. (Skinner, 1971, p. 105)

The fact that many altruistic acts do not appear to result in any reinforcement for the altruist and that some extreme examples actually seem to contradict the reinforcement contingencies of the altruist's environment is not viewed as especially problematic for this theoretical position. It is not necessary to assume that the altruist is reinforced for every altruistic act. The altruistic behavior may be maintained if it is only reinforced intermittently.

Conceptions of learning processes have been modified over the years. Bandura and Walters (1963) questioned whether most social behaviors are acquired through operant learning. To be reinforced, the behavior or some approximation to it must first occur. They argued that even approximations of some social behaviors are unlikely to occur often enough by chance to explain their relatively quick acquisition in early childhood. Children have ample opportunity to observe other persons' social behavior however. It is through observation and imitation that children may acquire these behaviors for themselves.

Mowrer (1960) also described observational learning, which is of particular relevance to prosocial behavior. In his empathetic learning, the model both produces the response and is reinforced for it. In observing the model being reinforced, the subject experiences some vicarious reinforcement that provides her with a motive for reproducing the response at a later time. So defined, empathetic learning requires some mechanism whereby reinforcement value is transmitted from one person to another. According to Aronfreed (1970), such transmission may occur either through affective expression or through a cognitive representation.

Increasingly, in social learning theory, the role of cognition has been taken into account. This is evidenced in the writings of such authors as Aronfreed (1970), Bandura (1977), Mischel and Mischel (1976), and Rosenthal and Zimmerman (1978).

Biological Theories

In the 1960s and 1970s, biological, particularly evolutionary, theories of social behavior gained new prominence. In the controversial discipline of sociobiology, the idea was put forth that genes account for complex human social behaviors and an attempt was made to explain altruistic behavior in evolutionary terms (Barash, 1977; Wilson, 1975). In Darwin's (1859) original formulation, a species of organisms gradually comes to assume the characteristics of those individuals within it who are best adapted to their environment. Because each individual is implicitly competing with every other individual for available resources, evolution would seem to favor selfish and competitive behaviors. Many animal behaviors, such as territorial defense, are so interpreted (Ardrey, 1966; Lorenz, 1966). Reasoning analogously to human behavior, the hypothesis that evolution selected human beings to be naturally selfish and aggressive fits well with the Hobbesian view of the war of all against all in the state of nature.

Classical Darwinism was challenged by 20th century ethologists who discovered apparent altruism among numerous animal species (e.g., warning calls in certain species of birds and rodents; helper birds who defend another bird's nest). Several hypotheses have been developed to explain how such behaviors may have evolved: group selection (Wynne-Edwards, 1962), kin selection (Hamilton, 1964), and reciprocal altruism (Trivers, 1971). Trivers goes furthest in attempting to relate sociobiology to human psychology, suggesting that certain emotions and dispositions may have evolved specifically because of the role they play in the regulation of reciprocal altruism.

There are formidable problems and tremendous leaps of reasoning in attempting to explain specific human behaviors in sociobiological terms (Sahlins, 1977; Sociobiology Study Group of Science for the People, 1976). Some of the predictions of sociobiological hypotheses may be equally well explained by psychological or sociological hypotheses. In addition, evolutionary explanations of human altruism must take into account cultural diversity of behavior. Finally, to explain social behavior, sociobiologists must translate terms originating in social interaction to terms amenable to population analysis, (Cairns, 1977). In sociobiology, altruism refers to behavior that promotes the genetic fitness of another at the expense of one's own fitness. How this is related to altruism in the ordinary sense remains conjectural.

A related biological perspective on determinants of social behavior is found in the research on brain evolution. One such effort is represented in Mac-Lean's work (1973) in which he attempts to provide a neural basis for empathy and altruism, relating specific brain structures (the neocortex and the limbic system) to such behaviors. Although his account is highly speculative, it is an intriguing beginning to the search for neural foundations of prosocial behavior.

Summary

In approaching research on children's prosocial behavior by the long road of philosophy and grand theory, a major purpose has been to stress the complexity of the topic and the diversity of thought about it. There is a need in empirical research to proceed with better understanding of the broad background of thought to which a specific study relates and from which the investigator's assumptions and interpretations derive. In his introduction to *Morality as a Biological Phenomenon,* Stent (1978), a molecular biologist, sets a good stage for our review of scientific studies of children's prosocial behavior. He opts for open minds, theoretically and methodologically, to explore this complex issue, and he makes the special point that priority and encouragement be given to a developmental approach in research. He concludes that far too little attention has been given to ontogenetic processes:

> This traditional neglect of childhood by moral philosophers seems surprising, since the ontogeny of moral competence is a phenomenon that, from the technical point of view, has always been empirically accessible . . . it is the study of childhood development that can presently offer one of the potentially most fruitful meeting grounds for biology and moral philosophy. (p. 20)

We would add that it can offer potentially fruitful information for the understanding of prosocial development and behavior from a psychological perspective.

THE HISTORY OF RESEARCH ON CHILDREN'S PROSOCIAL BEHAVIOR

In the history of scientific child study, the nurturing behaviors of caring and responsibility with regard to others have had considerably less attention than have other aspects of child development. Although empirical study of children's affiliative behaviors (dependency, attachment) has been an extensive endeavor, prosocial behaviors have not had the same sustained attention. This is not to say that these behaviors have always been ignored. Social behavior and emotional development were of particular interest among the early students of child behavior. Sympathy and reactions to others' distress were carefully observed by Antipoff (1928) in France and by Stern (1924) in Germany. Blanton (1917), Bühler and Hetzer (1928), and Bridges (1931) devised various standard stimulus situations to assess infants' and very young children's reactions to emotional events around them. In nursery school studies, systematic observations were made of children's responses to signs of suffering in others (e.g., Bathurst, 1933; Berne, 1930; Bridges, 1931; Isaacs, 1933; Murphy, 1937). Influential texts of the period, such as Arlitt (1928), Jersild (1933), and Valentine (1942), devoted considerable attention to these behaviors. Interpretations of the behavior varied. Some writers viewed early sympathetic responses as evidence of innate tendencies, pointing to McDougall's (1908/1960) theory of instincts (e.g., Valentine, 1942). Jersild (1933) stressed conditioning. Isaacs (1933) interpreted sympathy, cooperation, and friendliness in a psychoanalytic framework. Almost all of the research touching on prosocial variables was either on infants or on preschool children. An exception was the monumental work of Hartshorne, May, and Maller (1929), which examined the character, including service to others, of 11,000 school-age children. These early studies were substantial samplings of child behavior. Thus, in an era when child study was on the periphery of academic psychology, much evidence was collected on young children's positive social interactions and sensitivities to others' feelings.

In the 1940s and 1950s when children became favored subjects in experimental psychology, only occasional investigators (e.g., Ugurel-Semin, 1952; Wright, 1942) dealt with questions of children's prosocial behavior. There was little attention to prosocial behavior until the late 1960s. Our present research-based information on children's prosocial behavior draws heavily on studies coming out of the 1960s and 1970s. It is important, therefore, to have a sense of the influences that led to this revival of interest and helped to shape this research.

Social Psychological Forerunners

Social psychology ushered in the new research on the positive social behaviors. In 1965, Campbell called attention to altruism as a subject for psychological study. He argued for the innate bases of both egoistic and altruistic motives, drawing upon both animal data and social (in-group solidarity) data for support. Campbell's paper in setting the stage for this area of "new" inquiry might have inspired developmental and ethological studies as well as social psychological investigations, but the field did not develop so broadly. The emphasis that predominated was a social psychological one without grand theoretical underpinnings (as indicated in the 1970 reviews by Krebs and by Bryan & London). This research is not developmental in nature, yet it set a model that was to dominate the field for a number of years and for many studies of children.

It is usual to refer to the beginning of social psychological studies as a reaction to several well-publicized cases of violent assaults in which bystanders watched passively without coming to the aid of victims. Perhaps the famous study by Darley and Latane (1968) was so triggered. Why did so many studies follow? On the American scene, at least, it was a period of national trauma on many fronts that brought into the limelight examples of human behavior that were inhumane by traditional standards. If it is the case that research interests in psychology often reflect contemporary societal issues, this was an instance. However, no less relevant in viewing the prosocial studies is the fact that the decade of the 1960s was part of an historical epoch that social critics (e.g., Lasch, 1978; Slater, 1970) described as reflecting an excessive preoccupation with self. It was in this historical-cultural milieu that research questions, hypotheses, and interpretations regarding prosocial behavior were formulated.

Despite the crescendo in research activity concerning prosocial behavior, one senses a kind of discomfort or uncertainty on the part of investigators of this period: How would behavioral science accommodate the study of such behaviors as helping, generosity, and compassion? Were these acceptable topics for scientific study (Wispe, 1972)? As if to suggest that the investigators might not be taking the subject too seriously, there were titles, such as "The fallen woman," "The broken-bag caper," "Their money isn't where their mouths are," and "A lady in distress."

This period in psychology was one in which learning theory commanded the field. In this milieu, the ancient topic of altruism (Comte, 1875/1968) acquired a modern identity as prosocial behavior, a label that fitted into the nomenclature of topics in psychology. It is a term known mainly to researchers, and it is virtually without lineage. The dictionaries do not list it (see Wispe, 1972, for the origin of the label). Prosocial behaviors were defined as those behaviors directed toward another person that promote or sustain positive benefit to that person—a definition that serves to establish a zone of research and to homogenize a great variety of actions (helping, generosity, sacrifice, rescue, fairness, honesty, respect for others' rights and feelings, being socially responsible, cooperation, protecting, sharing, sympathizing, comforting, nurturing, being concerned for another's welfare, attempting to undo injustices, kindness). The label carries little theoretical commitment.

Experimental social psychologists fashioned the approach and also the theory. Prosocial behavior was viewed in terms of equity theory, the ratio of outcomes to inputs, or the relative costs and gains for the altruist. Situational determinants were a major focus. Adult prosocial acts were sometimes interpreted as internalized social norms that had been learned in childhood but the processes of acquisition were not investigated.

Many of the social psychological experiments of the 1960s stand out in historical perspective for the realistic and sometimes drastic stimulus situations that were manipulated (watching someone deliver an electric shock to someone, feigning a fire or a seizure—on the street, in the subway, in the classroom). The reality and ecological validity that such experiments accomplished had to be balanced against the possible lingering consequences to the participants. This presented difficult ethical problems that came under increasing scrutiny and criticism in the years following.

It was clear that many of the findings from the social psychological experiments had implications for child behavior. Transfer of the research paradigms to child subjects was, therefore, simply a matter of time. In short order, child research—which, for a quarter of a century, had been virtually without reference to sharing, helping, or rescuing behavior—broke out with innumerable laboratory studies of prosocial behavior. This new experimental research had certain characteristics: The experiments involved far less compelling manipulations than those that had been used with adult subjects. Instead, prosocial actions were built into game contexts, reflecting, perhaps, a cultural view of the roles and realities of children. The prosocial concept was mainly dealt with as a unitary construct. Because many developmental psychologists were interested in children's learning, the time was ripe for prosocial behavior to become the object of studies of modeling and reinforcement influences. In general, the studies in these frameworks were not developmental in orientation.

Although experimental studies of prosocial behavior became a mainstream of research, there were other streams as well. Rosenhan (1969), with a more clinical bent, was investigating "autonomous altruism" (i.e., the very considerable sacrifice and risk taking of persons on behalf of others) and was asking questions about childhood antecedents. Altruism manifested in social movements and in natural and personal calamities was being investigated. Unfortunately, neither the naturalistic designs nor the motivational components of prosocial acts suggested in the Rosenhan research were pursued in child research of the early 1970s.

There were still other currents of research interest in children's moral development: resistance to temptation and the development of conscience and self-control were important themes in the research of Sears, Maccoby, and Levin (1957), Aronfreed (1970), and others. In these studies, psychoanalytic and learning theory influences were evident. Also parallel in time was the growth of interest in children's modes of moral thinking, with obvious origins in Piaget, followed by Kohlberg (1969) (see Hoffman's, 1970, review).

Thus, for a time, researchers investigating moral behavior in terms of conscience and guilt, those studying moral reasoning, and those investigating helping and sharing were making their separate ways in theory and in empirical studies of children. Only later did the interrelations of these processes begin to enter into formulations of research problems (Aronfreed, 1970; Hoffman, 1975b; Mussen, Harris, Rutherford, & Keasey, 1970; Zahn-Waxler, Radke-Yarrow, & King, 1979).

During the decade of the 1970s, a surprising number of reviews, books, and collections of papers appeared, many of which (in part or in whole) concerned children (Bar-Tal, 1976; Bryan, 1970, 1975; Cook & Stingle, 1974; DePalma & Foley, 1975; Hoffman, 1970, 1975b; Krebs, 1970; Macaulay & Berkowitz, 1970; Mussen & Eisenberg-Berg, 1977; Rushton, 1976; Rushton & Sorrentino, 1981; Staub, 1978, 1979; Wispe, 1972, 1978). The abundance of the literature is perhaps somewhat misleading because empirical findings are not as substantial as the prolificacy of writing would suggest. However, its appearance reflects the enormous interest and activity in this "new" field of study.

Toward the end of the 1970s, significant shifts in issues, problem formulations, and research methods became discernible. The face of the research literature took on new expressions as questions of prosocial phenomena were absorbed into many of the issues, methodologies, theoretical controversies, and applications of developmental psychology. Interests of developmental psychologists in cognitive processes began to extend into social cognition, perspective taking, role taking, cognitive empathy, interpersonal inference, and sensitivity. In social learning, cognitive processes were being taken into account. Research was moving away from an orientation in which a prosocial *act* alone was of interest. Research involving the affective and motivational dimensions of prosocial behavior was appearing increasingly. Research in socialization influences indicated the incorporation of the prosocial dimension into the traditional childrearing interests of developmental psychology. By 1980, the research literature had become extensive and diverse. Prosocial behavior had moved from a marginal, hardly permissible topic of research to one that was vigorously investigated. Findings were providing significant beginnings to an understanding of the origins and maintenance of prosocial behavior in children.

The Nature of the Raw Data

As a final overview before reviewing the empirical research, we will examine the raw events that comprise the data on which research information about children's prosocial behavior rests. Whose prosocial behaviors have been researched? What samples of behavior have been used? Which of the many kinds of behaviors under the rubric of prosocial (sharing, sympathy, etc.) have been studied? In response to what kinds of stimulus events? By what methods have the data been obtained?

Who Has Been Studied?

The children who have been studied are predominantly of preschool age through 12 years. Relatively few studies until recent years have been carried out with children under the age of 3 or with children in the adolescent years. This leaves obvious gaps in information regarding early propensities and early learning, and regarding the significant period of the teens when cognitive changes, identity conflicts, and emotional intensities would lead one to expect critical developments in prosocial orientations and behavior.

Most of the studies have been conducted on white, middle class, urban children in the United States and Canada; some studies are from other countries and cultures. The available data do not adequately represent cultural and subcultural differences on prosocial behavior. Further, the children who have been studied are mainly at the norms of society; they are not children known for problems or exceptionalities of person or life circumstances. Parent/child interactions mainly and peer interactions occasionally have been studied, but the influences of other personal socializers (such as teachers, clergy, neighbors, or police) or of social institutions on children's prosocial behavior have had little attention. Television is the single impersonal socializer to which much research has been directed.

Which Prosocial Behaviors Have Been Studied?

Without question, sharing or donating and acts of helping have been the behaviors most often investigated. In over half of several hundred experimental studies surveyed, prosocial behavior was represented in donations of modest material commodities (tokens, candies, nuts, marbles, pennies). Few studies have dealt with compassion and serious aid or rescue. The helping behaviors that have been tested in laboratory settings have tended to be small helps to the experimenter or responses to the cry of an unseen child. Cooperative behavior in games and laboratory tasks has been studied relatively frequently. Laboratory studies of sharing, helping, and cooperation do not provide circumstances in which much personal investment or sacrifice is required or in which much affect is involved. The broader range of prosocial behaviors and the more compelling circumstances in which personal commitment might be expected have been dealt with mainly in hypothetical situations (pictures and stories) and in a small number of field studies.

In most experiments and, obviously, in those studies making use of pictures, videotapes, or stories, the prosocial initiatives by children are toward recipients who are not physically present. Children, real or hypothetical, have been the recipients in most of the studies, as if prosocial interaction belonged primarily to behavior with one's agemates. Interestingly, the recipients have often been an abstract group of children (the poor, orphans, the crippled, and the like). How children of the ages generally studied (between 6 and 11) comprehend these abstract groups is an unknown that complicates interpretations. The prosocial acts in much of the research are impersonal acts (e.g., giving away a just-acquired commodity); they do not involve personal interaction and, therefore, they leave us without information about interactive effects of recipient and giver upon one another.

To share candies, to rescue a child from a burning house, to cooperate with peers in playing a game, to express sympathy to a grieving person, to protect an underdog child from the attacks of a bully—all are prosocial behaviors. Yet, it seems reasonable to assume that these behaviors involve children in very different ways; require differing sensitivities, motives, and skills; interact with different personal attributes; and probably have different antecedents (Staub, 1979). The types of prosocial involvements that have been investigated, whether in behavior, moral reasoning, or affective expression, are, thus, an important factor in shaping the evidence; they are a vital consideration in interpreting the research of the field.

What Are the Behavior Samples in Studies of Prosocial Behavior?

The difficulties for researchers are many in this field: one is dealing with acts that do not occur with high frequency over short periods of time. Situations in which help, sympathy, generosity, and so on, are needed do not happen routinely. The experimental creation of plausible opportunities for a child to behave prosocially is difficult. Research access to children's behaviors in natural circumstances is limited.

Investigators have dealt with these difficulties in a variety of ways:

1. By utilizing game settings on which are grafted occasions for children's cooperation, sharing, or helping.
2. By using hypothetical or absent persons as the recipients of children's generosity or compassion.
3. By using hypothetical events in story form to probe sensitivities and propensities to respond.
4. By contriving realistic minor distresses and observing child behavior.
5. By naturalistic observing of children.
6. By training caregivers to observe and record events of children's prosocial behavior in their daily lives.
7. By using retrospective reports.

The samples of behavior in many of the studies have the handicap of being very small samples of behavior (single acts) obtained over very short periods of time, often in very special contrived situations. There are only a small number of longitudinal and follow-up studies in which there are more substantial data bases.

In summary, there are many kinds of data that tell us a great deal about the capacities of children to relate to other persons with positive concern for their welfare. At the same time there are shortcomings in the data base; most telling of these are:

1. The narrow band of behaviors that has been studied.
2. The heavy emphasis upon a materialistic, impersonal interchange of relatively trivial commodities as the criterion of prosocial actions.
3. The limited and fragmented information on individual children in both a contemporaneous and a longitudinal sense.
4. The relative scarcity of research in which cognitive, affective, and behavioral aspects of response are dealt with integratively.

The Construct of Prosocial Behavior

A definition of prosocial behavior that is least committing theoretically is action that aids or benefits another person. Children, by this definition, are prosocial. They are helpful to others. They can show consideration for others' feelings and indignation over cruelty. They engage in cooperative ventures and share possessions. They may risk their own welfare to protect or rescue another. The unity that joins these different behaviors is their positive consequences for the recipients. To this definition is sometimes added the condition that aiding or benefiting actions are done without anticipation of external reward. Prosocial behavior has also been viewed as an action both having a net cost to the individual and being intrinsically rewarding. Thus, in the same external forms of a child's generosity, there are possibilities of an ingenuous joy of giving, a self-serving manipulation of another person, a calculated but painful decision to share, or a principled response out of a sense of duty. Which of these qualify as prosocial behavior? Some investigators assume an underlying egoism in prosocial behavior, whereas others believe egoism and prosocial behavior to be inherently contradictory. Still others are unconcerned about motives. The diversities and complexities of philosophical positions and scientific theories (described earlier) linger in researchers' conceptual uncertainties. An awareness that great minds over the centuries have struggled with the nature of altruism should be a humbling experience for the investigator who sets forth, with clinching certainty, his theory and its proof.

Research is, thus, built on differing premises and conceptualizations. Behavior, its motives, intentions, and consequences are involved. Motives, it should be noted, do not necessarily fall neatly into egoistic and altruistic categories; there are also impure or mixed motives. Such complexities of construct create serious difficulties in attempting to integrate research findings. Problems arise not only from the complicating factors within the construct but also from the rather casual attention that has been given to these matters in empirical work. Research has often proceeded apace with little deliberation concerning the prosocial acts themselves—what they are, what they require of the child, and what they represent in the personal and cultural contexts in which they are observed. The domains of action (sharing, helping, etc.) and the specific indices of prosocial behavior (dividing candies, picking up papers, providing comfort) have been chosen quite arbitrarily without sufficient conceptual grounding.

It seems of considerable importance to recognize that the organization and interpretation of evidence is necessarily fashioned by the definitions and indices of prosocial behavior in existing studies. What is the concept of prosocial behavior in a given study? How meaningful or constraining are the indices? What is known of the underlying motivations for the behaviors performed?

Our review of the research on children's prosocial behavior has three major organizing considerations:

1. What is the nature of *development* of prosocial behavior? What are its origins and transformations over the course of childhood? And what are the mechanisms underlying developmental change?
2. What are the processes and the conditions through which prosocial orientations and behavior are *learned*? This is not fully separable from development.
3. How is prosocial behavior *organized* within the personality of the child?

DEVELOPMENT AND PROSOCIAL BEHAVIOR

The theories described earlier set up various expectations regarding the genesis and development of prosocial behaviors in children. Evolutionary and biological theories steer us to issues of innateness. Cognitive theories assume that children must be capable of rather high-level cognitive and reasoning processes before prosocial interactions are possible. Orthodox psychoanalytic theories would lead us to developmental formulations in which guilt motivations play a core role. Learning theories formulate no particular developmental expectations. The empirical evidence does not provide sufficient basis for choosing from these theories. Existing data do not systematically describe the nature of children's prosocial behavior over the course of development. For the most part, studies have been conducted on different children at different points in development, using measures and procedures that are not readily comparable from sample to sample. We begin, therefore, by piecing together these disparate studies in an effort to form a picture of the development of prosocial behavior.

Studies of Early Development: Up to 2 Years of Age

Interest in the early years centers on children's initial manifestations of sensitivity to others' emotions and their early prosocial responses to others. This topic was of considerable interest to a number of the early pioneers in developmental psychology. Well over 50 years ago, Stern (1924), from observations of his own and his colleagues' children, came to the conclusion that:

> Even the two year old child has the power of feeling another's sorrow, not only in the sense that, infected by the other's feelings, he grows sad and anxious with him and cries in response to the other's tears (i.e., suggested emotion), but in the higher sense of putting himself in the other's place, identifying himself with his sorrow, pain or fear, and trying to comfort, help, or even avenge him. (p. 521)

In 1932, Piaget wrote similarly of the experience of sympathy in late infancy:

> Jealousy . . . appears extremely early in babies: infants of 8 to 12 months often give signs of violent rage when they see another child seated on their mother's knee, or when a toy is taken from them and given to another child. On the other hand, one can observe in conjunction with imitation and the ensuing sympathy, altruistic reactions and a tendency to share, which are of equally early date. An infant of 12 months will hand his toys over to another child, and so on. (1932/1965, p. 318)

Gesell, Halverson, Thompson, Ilg, Castner, Ames, and Amatruda (1940) also observed that by the time children are 1 year of age, they are seen to repeat others' performances, to begin to understand others' emotions, and to show unmistakable emotions of their own. Lewin (1942) described a form of social sensitivity in children by the age of 18 months:

"Social sensitivity in the sense of awareness of social facts is an oustanding characteristic of the young child" (p. 54). Lewin provided illustrations of children sharing (food) and helping in the first years of life. Guillaume (1926/1968) provided examples of sympathy in very young children. Sullivan (1940), too, described children of an early age as remarkably sensitive to the needs of others and as showing signs of empathy. It was, for Sullivan, an empathic involvement or contagion of affect, a sensing of others' moods and emotions, particularly those of the mother, that formed the cornerstone for much of the child's early and continuing (pro)social relations. These consistent observations of early presence of affective sensitivity are not easily dismissed for there is every reason to assume that these investigators knew children well and were discriminating and astute observers.

Although systematic studies of empathy and sympathy in very young children were not numerous, a small stream of research over the years kept the topic alive. The studies have been of two kinds—those concerned with early affective arousal in the child in response to the emotions of others and those concerned with children's capacities for discriminating among different affective expressions in others.

In the first group are investigations of infants' responses to the cries of other infants. Early baby biographies gave accounts of such arousal. To check out this possibility, Blanton (1917) undertook an experiment in which she played a gramophone recording of an infant's cry in the presence of quiet 2-week-old infants. She found no consistent influences. Bühler and Hetzer (1928), however, reported that over 80% of their 2-week-old infants cried in response to a crying baby. They cautioned that the high frequency of responding by the other babies might be indicative of a distress reaction to a loud, aversive sound. Bühler (1930) then gathered data on infants at 2 months of age. Only 10% responded with crying if the crying baby was not seen, but 32% responded if the infant was seen. The issue was not seriously addressed again until Simner (1971) studied the reflexive crying of newborns under a variety of standard stimulus conditions (computer-synthesized crying, white noise, a silent control, a newborn's cry, a 5½-month-old's cry). His main conclusions were that the vocal properties of the newborn's cry promote crying in other newborns. Sagi and Hoffman (1976) basically replicated Simner's (1971) findings. There is, then, some evidence for special sensitivity and responsiveness to the human infant cry in the early days of life.

Similar research on arousal has followed the infant into the second half of the first year. Bridges (1932) reported that children 10 months and older cried or whined in response to another child's cry when they themselves were uncomfortable, but they were more likely to call or babble in a pitch similar to other babies' cries when their own mood was happy. Infants 6-months-old who were observed with peers in a "naturalistic" laboratory setting (Hay, Nash, & Pederson [1981]) showed little evidence of empathic or reflexive crying in the presence of peer distress. Based on mothers' observational records, distress crying by the infant by the end of the 1st year is a common reaction to emotional distress signals in others (Radke-Yarrow & Zahn-Waxler, in press). Likewise, Weston and Main (1980) studying children in the 2nd year of life report that a significant number of the children observed in a laboratory setting showed concerned attending to the crying of an adult actor.

These studies add up not only to a conclusion of early sensitivity to emotional signals but also to an awareness of individual differences in affective arousal. Not all infants respond; some respond in the extreme. This issue has been given little attention, yet one might speculate that such differences in thresholds could underlie later developmental differences in empathy and altruism (Murphy, 1937).

We turn then to the second type of studies, those concerned with young children's abilities to differentiate the emotions of other persons. Bühler and Hetzer (1928) reported that infants can discriminate between angry and smiling faces by the 6th or 7th month. Lewin (1942) found that children as young as 3 months respond differently to a friendly and an unfriendly adult. Later laboratory studies (Kreutzer & Charlesworth's data, 1973; LaBarbera, Izard, Vietze, & Parisi, 1976; Wilcox & Clayton, 1968) have corroborated these observations. Bretherton, McNew, and Beeghly-Smith (1981) conclude that very soon after children begin to use language, their verbalizations reflect comprehension and inferences regarding a variety of internal states of another person's wants and intentions (e.g., "Her eyes are crying—her sad," at 26 months; "Janie crying, want mommy," at 24 months; "Poor Johnny [brother] owie [hurt]," at 20 months).

The 1970s witnessed a renewed interest in the early manifestations of prosocial behaviors. Two groups of researchers investigated the emergence of prosocial behaviors in the first two years. The research of Rheingold and her associates (Hay & Rheingold, 1979; Rheingold & Hay, 1978; Rheingold, Hay, & West, 1976; Ross & Goldman, 1977) was directed to behaviors of helping, sharing, cooperation, and caregiving without the elements of acute distress in the stimulus circumstances. The work of Radke-Yarrow and Zahn-Waxler (in press) and Zahn-Waxler and Radke-Yarrow (1982) was primarily concerned with young children's prosocial responses when emotional distress is expressed by another person.

Early Sharing, Helping, and Cooperation

According to Rheingold, many behaviors of young children that have been conceptualized as manifestations of dependency, approval-seeking, and attention-seeking are, instead, indications of children's early ability to *give* to others and to *share* with others. Rheingold has made the general point that showing and giving objects to other people are common activities of children as they pass their first birthday and that such behaviors have been reported in the literature at least since Tiedemann's observations in 1787 (cited in Murchison & Langer, 1927). Rheingold et al. (1976) observed 15- to 18-month-old children in interaction with their parents or another adult in a homelike laboratory setting. Sharing was defined as showing objects, giving objects, and attempting to engage another person in play by using a toy or other objects. Almost all of the children were observed to share on one or more occasions. They shared with parents and with a relatively unfamiliar person. The greater range of sharing behaviors was observed in the older children: only 1 out of 12 of the younger but 7 out of 12 of the older children showed all three types of sharing.

Using the same research approach, Rheingold (1979) also investigated helping behaviors. The laboratory contained some ordinary undone household tasks, for example, laundry to fold, scraps to sweep up, a table to set. Mothers were told not to request help from their children. Yet, in a 25-min. session, all of the 2-year-olds helped their mothers; in another session, 18 of the 20 children helped an unfamiliar woman. Some helping behaviors were imitative but many were innovative or complementary to the adult's completion of a task.

Observational studies of German children, too, contradict the notion that children under 2 years of age engage only in egocentric manipulation of toys. Using settings such as a waitingroom or a playroom, Stanjek (1978) reported children's spontaneous sharing with children and with unfamiliar adults. Spontaneous gift giving occurred especially frequently during the 2nd and 3rd years. The youngest children used gift giving as a means of initiating and mediating social contact, although the material content of the gifts—sometimes pieces of wood or stones—seemed less important than their symbolic value.

Cooperative games were used by Hay (1979) to observe for early forms of cooperation between children and parents. In a 20-min. session, one of eight 12-month-olds, seven of eight 18-month-olds, and seven of eight 24-month-olds participated in at least one cooperative interchange. The research of Ross and Goldman (1977) and of Eckerman et al. (1975) provides similar evidence.

Early Responding to Others' Emotional Distress

Children's reactions to the distress of others were studied longitudinally by Zahn-Waxler and Radke-Yarrow (1982). Three age cohorts, 10, 15, and 20 months of age, were observed for a 9-month period. Mothers were trained to provide detailed observational records of distress incidents occurring in the child's immediate environment. The investigators and the mothers also simulated mild emotional distresses.

Between 10 and 12 months of age, incidents of emotional distress brought no discernible response or simple attending in about a third of the instances. In approximately half of the incidents, the response was a frown, a sad face, cries, or visual checking with the caregiver (e.g., "S somberly watched; tears welled in her eyes and she began to cry. She looked to her mother."). Over the next six to eight months the behavior changed. General agitation began to wane, concerned attending remained prominent, and positive initiations to others in distress began to appear. The latter included tentative pattings or touching the person, which might be interpreted as the child's establishing the emotional state as part of the other person. Such contacts became increasingly differentiated and frequent by 18 to 24 months of age. These progressions from early "involuntary" empathic distress to differentiated discriminations and expressions fit nicely the transitions described in Hoffman's (1975b) developmental theory.

By 2 years of age, children bring objects to the person who is suffering, make suggestions about what to do, verbalize sympathy, bring someone else to help, aggressively protect the victim, and attempt to evoke a change in affect in the distressed person. Children also try alternative interventions when one attempt fails. Such means-ends behavior implies that children can keep in mind the other's distress as a problem to be solved. Young children are not always appropriately or positively responsive to the expressive cues of someone's suffering. These cues lead at times to escape, avoidance, or attack. The frequency of such responses is low in comparison to the positive reactions. Zahn-Waxler (1980) also videotaped children's responding to mothers' simulated emotional distress. Many of the positive interventions in these records reproduce the findings from the mothers' naturalistic observations.

Similar data on the early appearance of comforting responses are reported by Dunn and Kendrick (1979). They describe younger siblings, in a few instances as early as 14 months, showing concern for their older brothers and sisters and demonstrating considerable understanding of how to comfort them. Mahler, Pine, and Bergman (1975) in a clinical, psychoanalytically oriented study of individuation followed five infants from 5 months to 3 years of age. These authors point out that early sensitivity to others' suffering does not have uniform behavioral consequences. Although a given 1 ½-year-old is observed to fetch and give his own bottle to another baby when that baby is crying, this same child on another occasion may be unable to bear the other's emotional distress and may respond in an aggressive, attacking mode.

In summary, studies of the early years lead to the conclusion that prosocial behaviors are present before 3 years.

> As infants are not necessarily egocentric, so they are not necessarily egoistic. Theories of dependency portrayed infants and young children as attention-seeking, help-seeking creatures. The observations of prosocial behavior indicate, in contrast, that infants freely *offer* their own attention, affection, sympathy, help, and possessions to others. (Rheingold & Hay, 1978, p. 119)

We now have to ask: What are the processes involved in the early appearance of prosocial behaviors? Hay and Rheingold (1979) speculate that there are numerous occasions for prosocial learning as recipient infants observe their own caregivers tending to their basic needs, comforting them when they are distressed, showing and giving them interesting objects, and helping them solve problems. Parents' intermittent reinforcement of children's prosocial behaviors undoubtedly serve to maintain these responses once they have become established (Grusec, 1982), although the prosocial behaviors may also be intrinsically rewarding. Hay and Rheingold (1979) note: "The task-oriented, yet gleeful, manner in which infants and young children offer their prosocial acts bespeaks the rewarding properties of the acts themselves" (p. 23).

In the longitudinal data reported above by Radke-

Yarrow and Zahn-Waxler (in press), there are indications of various processes by which children come to understand others' feelings and to offer aid to others. Some children imitate others' emotional expressions almost reflexively. Other imitations are more like thoughtful deliberations, as if the child is studying the other's emotion and is trying it on to find out how it feels. This imitative, cognitive approach is less apparent in those children for whom affective arousal floods their reactions. For example, a child at 12 months when confronted with a peer's cries responds with a primitive distress cry of her own and turns to her mother to be nestled and stroked. A few weeks later, when her mother has scalded her hand, the child cries, nestles into her mother but also hugs her mother—now giving some comfort as well as getting comfort. At 17 months, in the presence of a crying baby, her expression is concerned and tearful, but she strokes the baby's head, hugs and pats him, offers toys, and finally tries to bring her mother to the rescue. Here, as in less affective imitation, the child appears to be separating self from other, attempting to comprehend the internal states of the other, finding ways to aid another person. The cognitive and the affective components have differing prominence for different children.

The significance of these early behaviors for later prosocial behaviors remains mainly unexplored. J. McV. Hunt (1979) concludes that:

> In human beings, the early years of life, especially the first three, appear to be highly important for the later development and achievement of initiative as opposed to helplessness, of trust (or readiness and skill in eliciting help from adults and others), and of *compassion* (or readiness to appreciate the needs of and come to the aid of others). (p. 136)

The validity of these predictions needs to be further investigated.

Studies of Early Development: From 2 to 6 Years of Age

Information about prosocial behavior in the years from 2 to 6 is primarily about children in nursery schools—benign, child-centered settings with same-age peers, abundant play materials, and watchful adults. Over these same years, there is little evidence about children whose experiences are primarily in adult environs, with older children, in less caring group settings or institutions, or on the city-street "playground." Lacking this broader sampling, we do not know the range of behavior of which young children are capable, or the variety of circumstances and motives involved in the development of prosocial behavior or its absence. Nevertheless, from these nursery school studies we learn a great deal.

One study of this age group that predates the nursery school research is a questionnaire study in Germany in 1909. Boeck (reported by Stern, 1924) asked parents for descriptions of definite sympathy expressed by their 2- to 6-year-old children. From 408 replies, 66 were cases of sympathy in children of 2 years of age; 95 at 3 years; 94 at 4 years; 93 at 5 years, and 60 at 6 years. Although information about Boeck's methodology is scanty, the high frequencies of parental reports of children's sympathy suggest that this form of social interaction is not uncommon.

Between this study and the first major nursery school study of children's sympathy (Lois Murphy, 1937), there is a large gap of years. Murphy's study is a classic in conception and implementation. It follows the mode of observational research done in the 1930s, a hallmark of which is the impressively extensive sampling of behavior used in assessing social and emotional characteristics of children (e.g., Bridges' 1931 study was based on two years of observing in the nursery school. Murphy's data are from more than 100 days of direct naturalistic observation as well as from a variety of "framed" situations in the natural context). Her definition of sympathy includes the wide range of positive behaviors now labeled prosocial.

Keeping in mind the developmental focus of this discussion, Murphy on the preschool years should be viewed in light of the data we have reviewed on younger children. In this regard, what is very compelling is the continuity in the descriptions of prosocial behaviors of children under 2 years with Murphy's descriptions of prosocial behavior in nursery school children. In other words, much of what is occurring in peer life in nursery school has already been occurring in the family in preceding years. The range and complexity of children's prosocial actions are well communicated by Murphy's coding scheme; namely, children were observed to help as an assistant, help another in distress, comfort, punish the cause of someone's distress, protect and defend, warn of danger, ask an adult for help for a peer, inquire of a child who seems to be in trouble, give something, become visibly anxious. (There are instances, also, in which children laugh at a child's distress, attack, and attend only.) Murphy reports considerable individual variation in prosocial responding. Of 70 children studied, 18 were never observed to show sympathy. Some children were frequent recipients of sympathy when in distress; the distresses of some children were ignored. The relation between frequencies of giving and of receiving sympathy was negligible. Murphy concludes, much as did Hay and Rheingold (1979) and Zahn-Waxler & Radke-Yarrow (1982) on the child of 2, that the child under 4 is not "an overwhelmingly self-centered person."

Using a very different sampling of children's prosocial behavior from that used by Murphy, Sawin (1980) carried out a naturalistic study of the responses of 3- to 7-year-olds to peer distress. Observations were done on playgrounds of child care centers, in which there was relatively little adult supervision, and in which children of mixed ages were present. Sawin limited his observations to instances of full-blown crying by a child. Reactions of the children who were in close proximity to the crying child were recorded. It was rare for the bystander children to show no response (7%). Empathic (concerned) facial expression occurred in nearly half of the children witnessing the incidents; 17% attempted directly to console the distressed child. When consoling acts occurred, they led to reduced crying. Other sympathetic acts included seeking aid from an adult (10%) and threatening the child who had caused the distress (5%). But 12% of the children withdrew and 2% made explicit unsympathetic responses. Overall, Sawin's descriptions of children's reactions are similar to those reported by Murphy (1937).

Numerous studies attest to the preschool child's ability to cooperate with peers to attain common goals (e.g., Barnes, 1971; Berne, 1930; Marcus, Telleen, & Roke, 1979; Parten, 1932; see also review by Cook & Stingle, 1974). In these observational studies, cooperative acts show increased frequency over the preschool years.

The frequency of prosocial interactions has been examined by a number of investigators. Based on 3 hrs. of observation of each child, Murphy (1937) found that 2- to 4-year-olds averaged slightly less than one sympathetic act per hour. She compared these data with findings from a study of aggressive behavior done in the same nursery school by Jersild & Markey (1935). They had reported an average of eight aggressive or conflictful interactions per hour.

In a naturalistic study of 4- to 5-year-olds, Eisenberg-Berg and Hand (1979) reported a mean frequency of .09 prosocial incidents per 2 min. of sampling. Based on 40 min. of observations of free play per child, sampled over several days, Yarrow and Waxler (1976) found an average of two acts of shar-

ing or comforting by 3- to 5-year-olds. Over the same period, for boys, acts of physical and verbal aggression were 5.1 and 4.0 respectively and for girls, 2.1 and 2.7 respectively. When acts of cooperation were included in the domain of prosocial interaction, the frequencies of prosocial and aggressive acts were very similar. Nearly all children (87%) expressed at least one prosocial act toward a peer and nearly all (93%) expressed at least one aggressive act. Strayer, Wareing, and Rushton (1979), from a 30-hr. observational study of preschool children, report an average of 15.5 prosocial acts per hour when a wide range of positive behaviors was included. It becomes clear that generalizations about frequencies of prosocial and antisocial acts by preschool children are hazardous unless care is taken to specify the criteria for both classes of actions and the circumstances under which the behaviors are observed.

From the studies cited, little information can be gleaned about young children's motives for behaving or not behaving prosocially. What evidence there is comes either from direct questioning of children about their own prosocial actions, from inference based on nonverbal behavior, or from children's reasoning about story situations. Eisenberg-Berg and Neal (1979) observed spontaneous sharing, helping, and comforting over a 12-week period in a nursery school setting. When a prosocial act occurred, the child was asked, for example, "Why did you do that?" or "How come you gave that to John?" Children explained their behavior with reference to needs of the other person ("He's hungry") or as their "wanting to" do it. Other reasons included reasons of friendship, gaining approval, and mutual benefits from the act. None referred to authority demands or punishment.

In the study cited earlier of 1- to 6-year-old children's gift-giving behavior, Stanjek (1978) comments on children's apparent motives. The sharing behaviors of the older children appeared sometimes to have a controlling, self-serving quality, done to attain a dominant position. Bar-Tal, Raviv, and Shavit (1980) and Bryant and Crockenberg (1980), too, have inferred that helping is not always altruistic in motive, nor does nonhelping have a single meaning. Staub (1970b) and Yarrow and Waxler (1976) provide anecdotal information about children's reasons for not helping: their verbalizations and actions, when they do not intervene, suggest fear of disapproval from the adult, embarrassment over intrusion, and feelings of fear for themselves.

In summary, research on prosocial development from 2 to 6 years provides evidence of children's complex responsiveness to others' needs and distress and of children's individualistic ways of dealing with these situations. Developmental progression—with regard to the nature of affective arousal, the kinds of prosocial responses, and the motives involved—has not been fully delineated. Naturalistic data begin to expose the substance of children's verbalizations, affects, and actions. What is much needed are detailed analyses of the characteristics of children's responses, the circumstances in which they occur, and their cognitive and motivational components. From the sum of data on preschool-age children, one must conclude that children of these ages are not only egocentric, selfish, and aggressive; they are also exquisitely perceptive, have attachments to a wide range of others, and respond prosocially across a broad spectrum of interpersonal events in a wide variety of ways and with various motives.

Development from 6 to 16 Years of Age

The focus of this discussion remains developmental, even though it becomes ever more difficult over the years of middle childhood and adolescence to find developmental data. In contrast to what can be said about developmentally changing cognitive abilities, there are few data on which to base developmental profiles of prosocial behaviors. Most of the evidence on older children is from laboratory studies.

More often than not, prosocial behavior is measured in terms of only one dimension—frequency—and the developmental question is narrowed to whether there is increased or decreased frequency as children get older. A common and unqualified generalization in the research literature and in textbooks is that prosocial behavior increases with age. Both the formulation of the question of age change and the answer to this question need some examination however. The question seems to imply a unitary concept of prosocial behavior and the answer to suggest an expected increase in any type of prosocial behavior. Neither is a tenable position. Does the generalization mean that children become more sacrificial as they get older? Are their prosocial actions more principled or norm dictated? Are children responding with more affect or more guilt? Are they more discriminating or selective in prosocial responding with age? Are their prosocial actions more effective? Is the assumed increase a linear trend? When does the increase stop? Before reviewing the research evidence on age, one might follow this developmental prediction to its conclusion—unqualified, the generalization that prosocial behavior increases with age

suggests that 13-, 14-, and 15-year-olds are more generous, kind, empathic, socially responsible, helpful, and compassionate than are 6-, 8-, or 10-year-olds. All of which would point to late childhood and adolescence as the golden years for interpersonal relationships in the family, the school, and the community—a conclusion that would seem somewhat to fly in the face of reality. On the other hand, it *is* among adolescents that one finds selfless dedication to protesting or righting social injustices.

Because many studies of school-age children include several ages, there are extensive data with which to examine the frequency of certain kinds of prosocial responses in relation to age. The findings are summarized in Table 1. Change or lack of change with age is indicated according to type of prosocial response, type of data source, and span of ages covered. The preschool years are also included.

As can be seen in Table 1, most studies of children's comforting, caregiving, and sympathy have been done in settings that involve interaction with real persons or animals. In these studies, age trends are not at all consistent. Gottman and Parkhurst (1980) observed pairs of friends (ages 2 to 9 years of age) in play and found that distress in one child was followed by sympathy from the other child with significant frequency only among the youngest children. Yarrow and Waxler (1976), studying 3- to 7 ½ -year-olds, found that older children showed significantly less comforting of a hurt adult than did younger children. In Staub's (1970b) laboratory study of children's responses to a crying child in an adjacent room, there was a curvilinear association with age. The oldest children (sixth graders) showed significantly less prosocial behavior than the middle age groups and behaved like the kindergarten and first-grade children. In an experimental study by Berman, Sloan, & Goodman (1979), acts of caregiving toward younger children increased from preschool ages through elementary grades among girls, whereas among boys of the same ages there was nonsignificant decline. Feldman & Nash (1979) studied adolescents' interactions with, and caring for, infants. Girls showed no changes from high school to college years but boys (although less interested than girls) increased their interaction and caring.

In the studies of helping behavior, frequency is either unrelated to age or is higher in older children. Age trends in cooperative behavior are difficult to interpret because findings are confounded by differences in research method. Most investigations of preschool-age children have been naturalistic observational studies; in these studies, cooperation as well as competition increase with age (Greenberg, 1932;

Table 1. Frequency of Prosocial Behaviors: Comparison of Children of Different Ages

	Method: Laboratory (L) or Naturalistic (N)	Recipient: Real (R) or Hypothetical (H)	Ages of Children[a]	Direction of Difference with Age[b]
Comfort, Sympathy, Caregiving				
Zahn-Waxler & Radke-Yarrow, 1982	N	R	1–2½	+
Berne, 1930	N	R	2–4	0
Boeck (cited in Stern, 1924)	N	R	2–6	0
Gottman & Parkhurst, 1980	N	R	2–9	−
Yarrow, Scott, & Waxler, 1973	L	R,H	3–5½	0
Berman, Sloan, & Goodman, 1979	L	R	3½–5½	+ and 0
Sawin, 1980	N	R	3–7	0
Yarrow & Waxler, 1976	L,N	R	3–7½	− and 0
Whiting & Whiting, 1973	N	R	3–11	+
Staub, 1970b	L	H	5–11	+ and −
Feldman, Nash, & Cutrona, 1977	L	R	8–15	+ and 0
Help, Aid				
Stith & Conner, 1962	N	A	3–5	+
Yarrow, Scott, & Waxler, 1973	L	R,H	3–5½	0
Yarrow & Waxler, 1976	L,N	R	3–7½	0
Eisenberg-Berg & Hand, 1979	N	R	4–5	0
Grusec & Redler, 1980	L	R	5–8	+
Green & Schneider, 1974	L	R,H	5–14	0 and +
Chapman, 1979	L	H	4–6	+
Zahn-Waxler, Friedman, Cummings, in press	L	R	4–11	+
Skarin & Moely, 1976	L	R	5–12	+ and 0
Ladd, Lange, & Stremmel, 1981	L	H	6–9	+
Collins & Getz, 1976	L	H	9–16	+
Cooperation				
Berne, 1930	N	R	2–4	+
Parten, 1932	N	R	2–5	+
Barnes, 1971	N	R	2–5	+
Gottschalt & Franzhoff-Zeiger, (cited in Cook and Stingle, 1974)	N	R	2–6	+
Marcus, Telleen, & Roke, 1979	N	R	3–5	+ and 0
Zak (cited in Cook & Stingle, 1974)	N	R	3–7	+
Silverman & Sprafkin, 1979	L	R	3–7	−
Hirota (cited in Cook & Stingle, 1974)	N	R	4–7	+
Kagan & Madsen, 1971	L	R	4–9	−
Madsen, 1971	L	R	4–11	+ and −
Kagan & Madsen, 1972b	L	R	5–10	−
Madsen & Conner, 1973	L	R	6–12	−

Notes: [a]In studies that report age in terms of school grade, conversions to age have been made for the table.   (*continued*)
[b]+ = significant (*p* < .05) increase with age; − = significant decrease; 0 = no significant age change.

Table 1. (*Continued*)

	Method: Laboratory (L) or Naturalistic (N)	Recipient: Real (R) or Hypothetical (H)	Ages of Children[a]	Direction of Difference with Age[b]
Cooperation (*cont'd*)				
Rushton & Wiener, 1975	L	R	7–11	−
Meister, 1956	L	R	7–12	+
Thomas, 1975	L	R	7–12	+
Sharing				
Rheingold, Hay, & West, 1976	L,N	R	1–2	+
Stanjek, 1978	L,N	R	1½–6	− and 0
Eisenberg-Berg & Hand, 1979	L	R	4–5	+
Presbie & Kanereff, 1970	L	R,H	3–7	0
Yarrow & Waxler, 1976	L,N	R	3–7½	0
Bar-Tal, Raviv, & Leiser, 1980	L	R	4½–9½	+ and 0
Ugurel-Semin, 1952	L	R	4–16	+ and 0
Gelfand, Hartmann, Cromer, Smith, & Page, 1975	L	H	5–7	0
Elliott & Vasta, 1970	L	H	5–7	+
Leiman, 1978	L	H	5–7	+
Peterson, Hartmann, & Gel- fand, 1977	L	H	5–8	+ and 0
Grusec & Redler, 1980	L	H	5–8	0
Dyson-Hudson & Van Dusen, 1972	N	R	5–8	0
Knight & Kagen, 1977b	L	R,H	5–9	+ and −
Willis, Feldman, & Ruble, 1977	L	H	5–9	+
Handlon & Gross, 1959	L	R	4–11	+
Froming, Allen, & Clawson- Marsh, 1981	L	H	5–10	+ and −
Hull & Reuter, 1977	L	H	5–11	+
Green & Schneider, 1974	L	H	5–14	+
Fay, 1971	L	R,H	6–8	+
Midlarsky & Bryan, 1967	L	H	6–9	+ and 0
Underwood, Froming, & Moore, 1977	L	H	6–10	+ and −
Dreman, 1976	L	H	6–13	+
Moore, Underwood, & Rosen- han, 1973	L	H	7–8	0
Barnett & Bryan, 1974	L	H	7–10	+
Grusec, Kuczynski, Rushton, & Simutis, 1978	L	H	7–10	0
Rushton & Wiener, 1975	L	R,H	7–11	+
Rushton, 1975	L	H	7–11	0 and +
Barnett, King, & Howard, 1979	L	H	7–11	+
Emler & Rushton, 1974	L	H	7–13	+
Eisenberg-Berg & Geisheker, 1979	L	H	8–9	+
Grusec & Skubiski, 1970	L	H	8–10	0
Harris, M. B., 1971	L	R,H	8–10	+
Rushton & Teachman, 1978	L	H	8–11	0
Grant, Weiner, & Rushton, 1976	L	H	8–11	+

(*continued*)

Table 1. *(Continued)*

	Method: Laboratory (L) or Naturalistic (N)	Recipient: Real (R) or Hypothetical (H)	Ages of Children[a]	Direction of Difference with Age[b]
Sharing (cont'd)				
Israely & Guttmann, 1980	L	H	8–11	+
Midlarsky & Bryan, 1972	L	H	9–10	+ and −
Staub, 1968	L	H	9–11	+ and −
White & Burnam, 1975	L	H	9–11	+
Dlugokinski & Firestone, 1974	L	H	10–13	0

Leuba, 1933; McClintock & Nuttin, 1969; McKee & Leader, 1955). Most investigations of children past preschool age have been in structured situations of a task or a game that provides opportunities for the child to act cooperatively or competitively with an agemate or near agemate. Data based on this kind of measure almost uniformly indicate a significant decrease in cooperation as a function of age, with corresponding increases in competitive and sometimes individualistic behaviors in the older children.

Sharing behavior in a laboratory task is the prosocial index on which age-frequency comparisons have most often been made. In over half of the reports reviewed, there are age differences in sharing in the middle years of childhood, almost always in the direction of more sharing by older children. One caution is needed. In the majority of laboratory studies in which there are increases with age in sharing responses, there is no interaction with the persons in need. Sharing is with a hypothetical needy group. The positive age trend is, thus, linked to a particular experimental situation. Children of different ages may have different understandings of the identity of the group of needy recipients and may also interpret the demands of the situation differently. One is left with the question whether the age change is one of substance or method.

Investigations of school-age children's sharing with real peers show less consistent age trends. In a study of food-sharing behaviors done in a camp setting, Dyson-Hudson and Van Dusen (1972) found that 5- through 8-year-olds showed similar levels of sharing. Also using food sharing, Ugurel-Semin (1952) found that children (4 to 16 years) became progressively more egalitarian and less selfish but not consistently more generous with age. Handlon and Gross (1959), using a similar design, reported a shift from selfish behavior to unselfish sharing between preschool and elementary school age. An opposite finding is reported by Stanjek (1978) in a naturalistic study of children 1 to 6 years of age. Sharing of objects was most likely to be seen in the younger children. In several studies, increases in sharing with age occur only under some training or modeling conditions (Midlarsky & Bryan, 1967; Skarin & Moely, 1976), only on some measures (Rushton, 1975), or only for one sex (Skarin & Moely, 1976).

Adults, understandably, have considerable investment in believing that children become more civilized in their social interactions with others as they grow older. When findings run counter to such expectations, there is a tendency to explain the findings away. Kagan and Madsen (1971)—comparing cooperation in 4- to 5-year-olds and 7- to 9-year-olds—and Underwood, Froming, and Moore (1977)—comparing donations of first and fifth graders—found a higher incidence of these prosocial behaviors among the younger children. This finding was attributed to irrationality, or to the fact that the younger children did not know the value of what they were giving away. Green and Schneider (1974) found that helping (volunteering to help the poor) occurred with equal frequency among young and older children (5 to 14 years). The authors interpreted this to indicate that the behavior of the young children resulted from their failure to understand fully the implications of their volunteering. A study by Marcus et al. (1979), although not designed as research on adult expectation, contains data relevant to this issue. In naturalistic observations of 3- to 5-year-olds, children's cooperation was rated by teachers and observers; frequencies of cooperative acts were also obtained from an observational scheme in which specific cooperative acts were recorded. Ratings showed significant increases in cooperation with age. There were no differences between children in the two age groups in the systematically recorded acts of cooperation.

In summary, it appears that more caution is warranted regarding generalizations about changes in frequency of prosocial behavior as a function of age. The data from existing research do not support a simple unidirectional trend. There are increases, no changes, and decreases, depending on the prosocial behavior, the research methods, and the ages studied. There are virtually no data that permit a conclusion about age trends from preadolescent through adolescent years.

Turning, then, to more qualitative dimensions of prosocial behavior in relation to age, it is possible to piece together only a few strands of evidence over the school years. We learn something from existing research about the cues to which children respond and something about the repertoires of their helping behavior up to the middle-school years. Pearl (1979) investigated the subtlety of distress cues to which children react, using a series of vignettes in which cues varied in degree of explicitness. Children 4 and 8 years old were equally likely to note distress when the cues were explicit; 4-year-olds were less likely to see a problem or to suggest help when the cues were subtle. Findings reported by Radke-Yarrow, Zahn-Waxler, Cummings, Strope, and Sebris (1981) are in line with Pearl's (1979) results. The same children were studied at 2 and at 7 years of age. Categories of prosocial responses at the two ages show very similar repertoires of prosocial interventions. The 7-year-olds, however, were better able to deal with more abstract kinds of distresses and subtle cues and to take into account feelings other than those expressed in the immediate situation, as illustrated by a child's response after viewing a TV report of a family killed in a fire: "I hope those children weren't so young so they had a chance to have some life before having to die."

An indirect assessment of children's repertoires of prosocial conduct comes from a study by Ladd and Oden (1979). Children 8 to 10 years old were asked to suggest possible helping behavior in circumstances in which a child was experiencing difficulty. The stimuli were a series of cartoons. Children's suggestions included consoling, distracting, instructing, interpreting, mediating, moralizing, attacking the cause, and soliciting adult help. There were almost no age differences in the suggested modes of helping. The children were also asked to evaluate each other's helpfulness. The 10-year-olds rated their peers less helpful then did the 8-year-olds.

Children's deliberations about personal altruistic sacrifice were obtained in an interesting study (Lewis, Lewis, & Ifekwunigue, 1978) designed to analyze the process of informed consent in research. Children (6- to 9-year-olds) who had volunteered to be innoculated with flu vaccine were observed in group discussions about their volunteering. More (although not significantly more) of the older children than the younger children asked questions about future benefits and personal risks. These children were openly weighing alternatives in making altruistic decisions. This kind of study involving real-life decisions would seem to offer opportunities for investigating prosocial reasoning and prosocial decisions.

The literature on late childhood and early adolescence furnishes few developmental data on prosocial behavior, yet these periods are especially important from a developmental perspective—in cognitive growth, emotional investments, and social influences. In developmental periods of transition and emotional turmoil about self, one would anticipate heightened struggles with egoistic and altruistic responding. Also, these are periods when peer life and peer influences are of critical importance. Research offers little information on the kinds of sympathy, help, and personal sacrifice that occur among peers in late childhood. We know little of the developmental forerunners of the expanded empathy and investment in humanitarian causes that sometimes find expression in late adolescence and young adulthood.

In summary, we have placed considerable emphasis in this review on the *descriptive* side of prosocial development. The overwhelming concentration in the research literature has been on *processes* of acquisition. This has left far behind our knowledge of *what* it is that is acquired. With so little information about the nature and variety of the prosocial behaviors in children's repertoires, we are in a relatively disadvantageous position in investigating underlying developmental processes. Processes of what? Choices of prosocial indices seem to have been somewhat arbitrary with little consideration given to the bases of these choices. This practice has seriously weakened the knowledge base in this area of research and is particularly troublesome in studying development. Are sharing candy, helping in card sorting, cooperating on a game in the laboratory, and picking up an experimenter's dropped papers good indices; are they equally appropriate or meaningful at successive ages? Are they samples of significant interpersonal behaviors? It would seem that research on processes would be much enriched by an expanded knowledge of the substance of children's prosocial interactions. We turn now to a review of studies specifically concerned with underlying processes.

Cognitive Capacities in Relation to Prosocial Behavior

The assumptions and expectations that have shaped studies concerned with relations between cognitive abilities and prosocial behavior have been the following: As children develop capacities to understand others' experience, their ability to respond appropriately to inferred experience of others should be correspondingly increased. Perspective-taking and role-taking ability have been suggested as cognitive precursors of prosocial behavior. The relation is usually phrased as a unidirectional influence, although it is also possible that these cognitive abilities are influenced by the child's experiences of prosocial responding. Although children's abilities to understand the experiences of others are, in some sense, a necessary condition to acting on others' behalf, it is not assumed that such understanding will necessarily motivate the child to enter into positive interaction. Understanding can as well facilitate manipulative and aggressive behavior. In no current theory is it proposed that cognitive abilities—perspective taking, role taking, moral reasoning, belief systems—are sole determinants of whether an individual aids another person. Researchers, thus far, have mainly set for themselves the task of investigating associations between cognitive variables and prosocial variables.

Perspective Taking and Role Taking

Studies relating children's prosocial behavior to their abilities to take the perspective of another person have included perceptual, cognitive, social, and affective perspective-taking tasks. Mostly, acts of sharing and helping have been the measures of prosocial behavior. Generally, one or several types of perspective taking are examined in relation to one or several indices of prosocial behavior. Children from preschool age to early adolescence have been studied. There has not been a definitive yield. Significant correlations have not consistently been found; when correlations have been found, they are positive. Significant positive associations between perspective taking and prosocial responses were found by Buckley, Siegel, and Ness (1979), Gilbert (1969), Johnson (1975a), Krebs and Sturrup (1974), Olejnik (1975), and Rubin and Schneider (1973). There were no significant associations in studies by Eisenberg-Berg and Lennon (1980), Emler and Rushton (1974), Kurdek (1978b), Rushton and Wiener (1975), and Zahn-Waxler, Radke-Yarrow, and Brady-Smith (1977). Other investigators (Ahammer and Murray, 1979; Barrett and Yarrow, 1977; Green, cited in Kurdek, 1978a; Iannotti, 1978; Johnson, 1975b; Leckie, cited in Kurdek, 1978a; Rothenberg, 1970; Strayer, 1980; and Wentink, cited in Kurdek, 1978a) report both significant positive correlations and nonsignificant correlations for differing indices of perspective taking. In many of these studies, nonsignificant results predominate.

Several investigators have stepped somewhat outside the mold of most studies by giving children role-taking training (N. Feshbach, 1979; Iannotti, 1978; Staub, 1971c), thus attempting to increase interpersonal sensitivities. In Staub's (1971c) study with kindergarten children, girls who received role training were more likely to respond to a child's cry than were children in the control group; boys with role training more often than boys in the control group shared candy with a hypothetical child. There were no effects of training on helping an adult. In Iannotti's (1978) study, training resulted in higher donation rates among 6-, but not 9-year-old boys. *How* one best teaches a child to take another's role then becomes a critical issue. A program that is underway with school-age children (Feshbach, 1979) provides explicit training in identifying affect, assuming the perspective of another person, and playing the role of another. As we will see later in reviewing socialization studies, some parental techniques are attempts to teach the child to take the perspective of the other person.

In the 20 or more reviewed studies of perspective taking and role taking, there is no obvious developmental or other pattern to explain why some associations with prosocial behavior are positive and others are not. In the view of Kurdek (1978a), who has done a comprehensive review and analysis of this field of studies, both conceptual and methodological problems account for the relatively chaotic state of knowledge. One of Kurdek's major points is that there has been a lack of rationale for the selection of particular perspective-taking tasks in relation to particular prosocial behaviors as well as inadequate conceptualizations of the processes and requirements involved in both sets of responses. The relation of perspective taking to children's prosocial behavior remains an important area needing research that deals more adequately with the complex nature of both the cognitive and behavioral dimensions. Similar conclusions have been reached by other reviewers (Krebs & Russell, 1981).

Moral Reasoning

Questions regarding moral reasoning are much the same as those we have asked with respect to perspective taking: How is moral reasoning related to prosocial behavior? How do relationships change with development? The vast literature on children's moral reasoning, as Mussen and Eisenberg-Berg (1977) have pointed out, has been concerned more with prohibition-oriented dilemmas than with dilemmas in which a choice must be made between self and others' needs or between helping or not helping. Children's reasoning regarding both kinds of dilemmas has been studied in relation to their prosocial behavior. Studies have been of three types. There are those in which children's prosocial behavior is observed and children are questioned about their own behavior. Ugurel-Semin's study (1952), described earlier, is of this type: After children had responded selfishly, egalitarianly, or generously in sharing nuts with a peer, they were asked to give reasons for their behavior. Of the children who gave egocentric reasons, 75% had acted predominantly selfishly; of those who gave reasons based on sociocentrism, awareness of social reactions, or altruism, over 80% had behaved generously. All children who gave reasons based on justice had exhibited egalitarian behavior. In a similar study, Dreman and Greenbaum (1973) reported similar findings. Whether the reasons given by the children were antecedent to, or rationalizations for, the sharing or the selfishness cannot be ascertained from the evidence.

In a second type of study, children were presented with prosocial dilemmas in story form, and their reasoning about the stories was examined in relation to their prosocial behavior. Positive associations were often found. At each grade level (kindergarten to sixth grade), Seegmiller and Suter (1977) found that kindness choices on the *Baldwin Kindness Picture Story Instrument* (1970) were significantly positively related to tests of cooperation but unrelated to tests of helping. Damon (1977) obtained positive justice reasoning from 4- to 10-year-old children on a story and also in a real-life positive-justice situation that involved small groups of children deciding on the distribution of candy. Children's levels of reasoning in the real-life situation, but not in the hypothetical situation, related positively to teacher ratings of children's prosocial behavior. Levin and Bekerman-Greenberg (1980) had preschoolers, and second, fourth, and sixth graders play a game in which the winner had an opportunity spontaneously to share the prize with the loser. Moral reasoning was obtained on story dilemmas that differed in degree from the real-life sharing situation. The magnitude of the positive relation between sharing and reasoning was smaller to the degree that the story

dilemmas differed from the dilemma posed in the actual sharing situation. Rubin and Schneider (1973) found level of reasoning by 7-year-olds on stories involving prosocial dilemmas significantly positively related to their donating to "poor children" and their helping of a younger child with an unfinished task. Moreover, by using stories of social dilemmas, Eisenberg-Berg and Hand (1979) found that nursery school children's sharing was significantly positively associated with needs-oriented reasoning (e.g., "because crippled children's legs hurt"), and negatively related to hedonistic reasoning (e.g., "the child wouldn't share because he likes games"). Helping/comforting was unrelated to moral reasoning.

In a third type of study, moral reasoning on distributive justice stories has been investigated in relation to children's donations to "needy" children. Here the findings are mixed. Children (7 to 13 years of age) at high levels in moral judgment donated significantly more tokens than children at low levels in moral judgment, with age as a covariate (Emler & Rushton, 1974). Rushton (1975) found this association, with age as a covariate, immediately after children (7 to 11 years of age) had participated in a modeling study, but the association was not present 8 weeks later. In two other similar studies (Grant, Wiener, & Rushton, 1976; Santrock, 1975), no significant associations were found between moral reasoning and donating. Harris, Mussen, and Rutherford (1976), on the other hand, reported significant positive correlations between levels of reasoning on Kohlberg's (1969) stories and sociometric measures of altruism in fifth-grade boys.

Summarizing, in studies relating reasoning and prosocial behavior, significant correlations in the .20 to .40 range have frequently been found; but, almost as often, no associations have been found. Significant associations have been somewhat more likely when the story content reasoned about has been highly similar to the situations in which behavior was assessed. It appears that this area of study suffers from conceptual and methodological problems like those discussed by Kurdek (1978a) with regard to perspective taking. It seems relevant, too, to take into consideration the fact that reasoning takes place in contexts of varied motivational and situational conditions. Undoubtedly, research on the interactive influences of reasoning on behavior as well as behavior on reasoning is needed to provide a more informative picture (Blasi, 1980).

Intelligence

The role of intelligence in prosocial behavior has not greatly interested researchers. Although intelligence is positively associated with perspective-taking ability and level of moral reasoning in many studies (see Kurdek's review, 1978a), the findings with prosocial behavior are less consistent. Krebs and Sturrup (1974) reported a significant correlation of +.34 between IQ and altruism in second and third graders. In other studies (Rubin & Schneider, 1973; Rushton & Wiener, 1975), significant associations were not found. Rosenn (1976) found sharing with a partner, in 7- and 8-year-olds, to be related to performance on the Raven Progressive Matrices but not to verbal IQ or Peabody Picture Vocabulary Test scores. Sprafkin and Rubinstein (1979) found academic achievement to be significantly related to peer ratings of prosocial behavior. Spivack and Shure (1974) reported that the extent to which intelligence level predicts ratings of children's concern for others is determined by the extent to which IQ measures interpersonal problem-solving thinking. Concern for others was totally unaffected by IQ once the capacity to conceptualize alternative solutions to interpersonal problems was accounted for. Thus, there is not a strong case to be made for general intelligence as a predictor of prosocial behavior.

Empathy as a Mediator of Prosocial Behavior

There are two concepts of empathy in the research literature relating to prosocial behavior in children. There is a cognitive concept, recognition of feeling states of another person, and an affective concept, vicarious emotional arousal and response to another's state. Having drawn so sharp a dichotomy, it is important to recognize the interactive components of cognition and affect (Iannotti, 1979). To date, however, research has generally proceeded along one or the other line, thereby nourishing the kinds of arguments about children's capacities for empathy that result from differing conceptual and procedural bases. In the research on empathy in children, two kinds of questions predominate: How are empathy (however defined) and prosocial behavior related? What are the developmental patterns in the kinds and extent of empathy?

The Feshbach and Roe (1968) test of empathy has been a central instrument in this research. Children are shown slide sequences of happy, sad, fearful, and angry situations and are asked how these events make them feel. If their reported feelings match those of the story character, they are credited with an empathic response. This measure of empathy has been found to be inversely related to aggression in 7- to 9-year-old boys (Feshbach & Feshbach, 1969), and to competitiveness (Barnett, Matthews, & Howard, 1979), but no consistent pattern of associations with prosocial behavior emerges from the research. Levine and Hoffman (1975) reported non-

significant correlations between empathy and cooperation in preschool children. Marcus et al. (1979) also found nonsignificant associations when preschoolers' empathy was correlated with cooperation scores based on observational measures; however, teacher ratings on cooperation were positively correlated with a subscale measure of empathic pleasure. Correlations between empathy and generosity were nonsignificant for 5-year-olds (Strayer, 1980), 6- to 8-year-old children (Fay, 1971), and 9- to 10-year-old boys (Miller, 1977). Correlations were positive for 9- to 10-year-old girls in the Miller study and for first graders on a subscale of empathy for sadness (Sawin, 1979). Correlations were negative for third graders in the Sawin study and for preschoolers in a report by Eisenberg-Berg and Lennon (1980). Iannotti (1975) found donating behavior positively related to 6- and 9-year-old children's empathic reactions to situational cues of stories but negatively related to the story character's expression when the two sets of cues were incongruent. Eisenberg-Berg and Mussen (1978) found that on an affective empathy questionnaire volunteering help was positively related to adolescent boys' empathy scores, but not to adolescent girls' empathy scores.

In the array of findings just reviewed, no consistent relation between empathy and age is apparent. Fay (1971) and Marcus et al. (1979) found a positive association with age. Iannotti (1978) found a negative association. No significant age differences were found by Feshbach and Feshbach (1969) for 4- to 5- and 6- to 7-year-olds; Adams, Schvaneveldt, and Jenson (1979) for 7th to 9th graders; and Eisenberg-Berg and Mussen (1978) for 9th to 12th graders.

Gnepp, Klayman, and Trabasso (1982) examined age differences in the sources of information that individuals use for making emotional inferences. The responses of preschool children, second graders, and college students were compared. Stories were presented verbally, and the subjects were asked to infer the emotional response of the protagonist to a specific event in each story. Subjects chose one of three drawings of faces (happy, upset, afraid) to indicate the inferred emotions. Sources of information—which occurred singly, in congruence, or in conflict—were the social or physical situation in which the event occurred, normative information about the group to which the protagonist belonged, or personal dispositions of the protagonist. When age groups were compared, there was no evidence of any systematic developmental change in the patterns of information used. A hierarchy of information sources was found at all ages, with personal information preferred over normative information, which, in turn, was preferred over situational information. When personal or normative information was in conflict with situational information, the preschoolers, like the college students, did not rely on projection for their emotional inferences but rather on the information that most indicated the other person's perspective. The findings of this study contradict the earlier view (Chandler & Greenspan, 1972) that young children are incapable of nonegocentric inferences (empathy) concerning others' emotions, that is, that they rely mainly on situational information, using projection and stereotypy.

Some researchers have turned to nonverbal, affective indices of empathy, such as facial or vocal expressions in response to emotional states of others. Leiman (1978) presented kindergartners and first graders with a videotape of a peer's sad experience (her favorite collection of marbles was stolen). Children's facial expressions during the viewing were rated. Children were then given an opportunity to turn a crank on a machine that released marbles into a container designated as belonging to the sad peer. Children whose facial expressions had been rated as more empathic provided significantly more marbles for the peer. These findings were not replicated by Sawin (1979) who rated children's facial and vocal expressions as they responded to the Feshbach (1968) test of empathy. There was a moderate correlation ($+.31$) between ratings of arousal and empathy test scores, but neither measure had a consistent correlational pattern with prosocial behavior. In a naturalistic study in a playground context, Sawin (1980) again found that children whose facial expressions showed concern were no more likely to display consoling behavior to a crying peer than were children who showed no facial signs of empathic arousal.

The inconsistent results on empathy in relation to prosocial responding have led to reexaminations of the concept and the techniques of measurement (Emler & Rushton, 1974; Feshbach & Kuchenbecker, 1974; Marcus & Roke, 1980; Sawin, 1979). First, the usefulness of a unitary concept of empathy has been questioned. Second, the assumption that affect matching expresses feeling for the other person may be open to question. Although such matching may be empathy, it may be fear for self, revulsion, and so on. Third, the use of short story elicitors may not involve the child sufficiently to evoke affective empathy. Fourth, indices of prosocial behavior have been employed in studies of empathy with little attention to the empathy-demands that are involved in the particular prosocial response. For example, children's sharing and helping in the laboratory may be in response to demand characteristics of an experimental situation or in response to social norms or formalized rules. In these cases, empathy may have little or no bearing on the response. In other circumstances, such as seeing a grieving child, empathic arousal would appear to be more likely.

The research on empathy as a mediator of prosocial behaviors has generally been nondevelopmental, and few studies have dealt systematically with cognition and affect. An integrative theory and a developmental theory of empathy could be significant stimulus in this area of research. Beginnings along these lines have been made. Feshbach and Kuchenbecker (1974) have distinguished three components of empathy: the cognitive ability to discriminate affects, the perspective-taking ability to comprehend the other person's experience, and the feelings or emotions aroused within the self. Hoffman (1975b, 1976, 1977a, 1981) has dealt seriously with empathy at a theoretical level, integrating affect and cognition and formulating a developmental model for viewing the origins and transformations of empathy. This model has forerunners and other contributors, such as Aronfreed, 1970; N. Feshbach, 1975a; Hogan, 1973; Iannotti, 1979; Isaacs, 1933; and Stern, 1924. But it is well articulated and elaborated by Hoffman. In his formulation, he describes various kinds of empathic arousal. Arousal may be reflexive and, in this sense, innate. (Recall the earlier descriptions of infants' arousal by the cries of other infants [Sagi & Hoffman, 1976; Simner, 1971].) Arousal may be conditioned (Aronfreed, 1970). It may be an associative response—as a distress cue reminds the individual of past personal experience. It may involve the observer's imagining how the stimuli causing pain to other persons would be experienced if they were his own. Just as the mechanisms of arousal of empathy vary, so too the experiences of empathy vary, influenced by the cognitive capabilities and experiences of the child. Although stagelike development is implied in Hoffman's model, it is neither a necessary nor a primary interpretation. There is no necessity, in this view, of striving to discover a particular time in development when empathy and empathic distress and empathically motivated behavior can first occur. Instead, this formulation opens the door for empathic arousal at any age, with cognitive capabilities modifying the empathic experience. Some modes of empathic arousal and experience (e.g., voluntary symbolic representations) are beyond the capabilities of the very young child, others are not. Also, earlier or more primitive modes of empathic arousal or experience are not assumed to be replaced in the course of development. They can occur (e.g., involuntary affective response) throughout life.

Hoffman attempts to relate what is hypothesized

or known about early self/other differentiations in the first years (e.g., development of person permanence, role-taking development) to the kinds of empathy, cognition, and actions that occur in children of these ages. The evidences of affective (sympathetic) arousal in infancy described by Stern (1924), Guillaume (1926/1968), and Piaget (1932/1965) fit the scheme outlined by Hoffman. So do the longitudinal data on this age period reported by Radke-Yarrow and Zahn-Waxler (in press) and by Zahn-Waxler and Radke-Yarrow (1982) as well as the laboratory observations of Weston and Main (1980).

Continuing in Hoffman's framework of developmental progression, as role-taking abilities evolve in young children, imagining the other's feelings becomes a possible mode of empathic arousal. Again, the mainly naturalistic data cited earlier document the transformation from rudimentary empathy to complex empathic role taking. Hoffman (1975b) places in late childhood or early adolescence children's abilities to be aware of others' personal identities and life experiences beyond the immediate situation. Naturalistic data do not entirely support this late arrival. A 4-year-old, upon hearing about the death of his friend's mother, said solemnly, "You know, when Bonnie grows up, people will ask her who was her mother and she will have to say 'I don't know.' You know, it makes tears come in my eyes" (Murphy, 1980). This young child was dealing with a future-time perspective, going well beyond the here and now. More systematic data are needed on children's empathy in real-life situations before we have a good understanding of how far empathic distress arousal extends for children at various developmental levels, how empathy is molded and moderated by cognitions, and how empathy enters into prosocial behavior in later childhood and adolescence.

Guilt as a Mediator of Prosocial Behavior

Guilt as a mediator of prosocial behavior has not received the research attention that one would have anticipated, given the familiar and traditional psychoanalytic emphasis on guilt as a basis for altruism (A. Freud, 1936/1946).

Orthodox Freudian theory holds a strong grip on guilt and on a sense of duty as necessarily neurotic in origin. But there are, also, the more reality-based negative feelings and blame of self that can come from harm done to another person and a feeling of responsibility for righting the harm. This distinction may not always be firm, however. Investigations of guilt in children have rarely appeared in the research of developmental psychology. The reluctance on the part of developmental psychologists to investigate guilt feelings in normal children may stem partly from the complexities and theoretical trappings surrounding the concept of guilt and partly from procedural difficulties anticipated in systematically measuring feelings of guilt. In the child-rearing studies of the 1950s (Sears, Maccoby, & Levin, 1957), the development of conscience in preschool-age children was a major focus, and, in this context, children's guilt feelings were examined. Various behavioral indicators of guilt about transgressions were identified (the child's confession, hiding, looking sheepish), but the development and nature of guilt were not investigated. When interest in studies of conscience and resistance to temptation in young children waned, interest in guilt waned also. In the decades following, studies of parental disciplinary techniques brought renewed attention to guilt.

The kinds of cognitive and affective reactions engendered by the discipline were examined as possible contributors to the child's feelings of responsibility and guilt (Hoffman & Saltzstein, 1967). There is some evidence that strong blaming and moralizing discipline may be guilt-inducing and may lead to reparative or altruistic behavior (Hoffman, 1981; Zahn-Waxler et al., 1979). Very little is known, however, concerning guilt in relation to altruism in normal children and in children with problems.

In his writings on the development of empathy as a mediator of prosocial actions, Hoffman (1975b, 1976, 1981; Thompson & Hoffman, 1980) has considered the possible role of guilt, and he has speculatively sketched a developmental progression: (1) Rudimentary guilt feelings may appear early. Because the very young child does not clearly separate self and other, when observing distress in another person, she may be unsure about the causal agent. The child may experience a vague sense of being the cause of distress by virtue of proximity to the person in distress and show what appears to be guiltlike reactions. (2) Later in development, when the child is better able to differentiate self and other, causal attributions can more readily be made. When the child is able to take the perspective of the person and can view her own actions as the cause of the other person's plight, feelings of guilt may result. (3) At still later ages, with the development of abstract thinking and the extension of empathy to groups of people, the child (adolescent) may view her actions as the cause of harm in ways that extend beyond the immediate situation. This may include guilt feelings about anticipated harm, about prosocial actions not carried out, or about her own advantaged position contrasted with that of the state of disadvantaged others. This formulation is at least a starting point for investigation into possible contributions of empathy to guilt and guilt to altruism. The concept of guilt is especially complex from a developmental point of view, involving as it does an interplay of cognitive and affective elements, of motivational conflicts, and of positively integrative social behavior and quasi-neurotic behavior.

Social Factors in the Development of Prosocial Behavior

In considering mechanisms underlying prosocial behavior, we have looked to processes within the child—cognition, empathy, and guilt feelings. To fill out the picture, social factors outside the child need to be brought into explanatory models of prosocial development. Social factors can be viewed at three levels: social influences via direct interaction, as in the child's interactions with parent or peer; the settings in which behavior takes place, which facilitate or interfere with prosocial actions; and the influences of society on modes of thinking, norms of behavior, and conditions of life. In many ways, these social influences have developmental stages, a fact neatly phrased by Murphy, Murphy, and Newcomb (1937, p. 325), "To be at a given age level is to be in a certain social situation." The adults and peers available to a child at various ages, the interpersonal responsibilities assigned or assumed, and the home, school, or societal settings imposed all provide predictably different developmental pressures and opportunities for prosocial behavior.

To complicate the picture of interacting social and developmental influences, many social conditions are unstable, both within the span of childhood and from one generation to the next. Thus, secular changes in the family and in society at large may keep research findings in a fluid state. For example, for the 2-year-old in the traditional middle class family setting of Western societies, mothers are the predominant influence on the child. Therefore, research with a mother-child focus is likely to contribute a great deal to our understanding of the prosocial behavior of 2-year-olds. However, social change has altered this configuration markedly for many 2-year-olds. As daycare centers and nursery schools have entered the picture and as women increasingly work outside the home, a new generation of 2-year-olds may have evolved—with multiple adult attachments and expanded peer relationships and with possible consequences for learning prosocial behavior. There is justification for believing that other than maternal factors may have become increasingly influential in shaping the young child's positive interactions with others.

The social influences entering into the development and maintenance of prosocial behavior in the individual child are, thus, vastly complex sets of variables. The traditionally valued unit of study in developmental psychology is the individual; concepts and variables of research are geared to this unit. Beyond this individual terrain, research is relatively ill equipped with concepts and strategies of investigation. To address issues of prosocial values and behavior of children and adolescents or of prosocial or antisocial actions of groups of children, research orientations will need to be modified to include units other than the individual. It is quite obvious, for example, that attempting to understand expanded empathy and altruism in adolescent years (concerns for human suffering, existential guilt, and so on), we will have to come to grips with very difficult research issues regarding the ways in which individual factors and variables of group and society interact in producing prosocial or nonprosocial children, adolescents, and adults.

SOCIALIZATION OF PROSOCIAL BEHAVIOR

In reviewing research on the development of prosocial behavior, socialization influences have intentionally been ignored. Now the focus shifts to questions of how children acquire prosocial orientations and behavior. Parents, as the socializing agents in the life of the child, have the special impact that attaches to early experience as well as to continuity. It is not unreasonable, therefore, that much of the socialization research has centered on relationships and interactions of parent and child (or, in laboratory analogue studies, of experimenter and child). But parents and families are never without the influences of the historical and contemporaneous contexts in which they function; they are influenced by the institutions, values, and conditions of society. We will review the research findings from the vantage points of parents and culture to try to clarify their separate and conjoint influences on children's prosocial development.

Socialization by Culture and Society

For a number of reasons, one would expect societal factors to have especially strong influences on children's prosocial development. First, the traditions of social, political, and religious philosophies (described earlier) pertain directly to how altruistic and egoistic social actions are regarded. Second, the way life is lived (the organization of work, community life, family structure, age and sex roles, and so on) in many respects regulates in what activities children participate, the models available to them, their goals and challenges, and the systems of rewards and punishments they experience. Third, the specific techniques of parents occur within larger contexts that affect the form of parental practices and also the successes and failures of parents in accomplishing their childrearing objectives.

The socialization research of developmental psychologists has been criticized for not being sufficiently attuned to the fact that children are reared by both family and society (Bronfenbrenner, 1979). Current socialization theories and research could benefit, too, from an historical cultural perspective on rearing. For example, in the not too distant past in Western societies, children were to be seen and not heard, father's word was law, and caning was an acceptable disciplinary practice. Children performed many family work functions, not the least of which were childcare responsibilities. The views about children differed from those held by many adults today. In these earlier periods, did children develop less prosocial behavior than in presently advocated or practiced rearing environments? Would one have found reasoning and power-assertive techniques differently effective in different social cultural circumstances? Are children's motives for prosocial acts more or less guilt derived as a result of socialization in one era than in another? Do the makings of prosocial children reside in the same parental rearing techniques in any era?

There are many challenges for research on rearing prosocial and nonprosocial children. The complexity and multiplicity of influences make it unlikely that any one rearing condition, process, or analytic framework will have singularly strong explanatory power at all times for all children.

Norms of Culture and Society

Good studies of socialization processes at the level of culture are extraordinarily difficult from both scientific and practical standpoints. Few studies of cultures have specifically involved socialization of prosocial behavior. In one such early study, Margaret Mead (1937/1961) investigated 13 nonliterate cultures. She classified them as individualistic, competitive, or cooperative on the basis of the mechanisms of distribution of goods and the ends toward which the activities of its members were typically directed. Certain characteristic features of cooperative and competitive groups could be discerned despite great cultural diversity. Cooperative cultures were characterized by relatively fixed and secure interpersonal relationships, prescribed roles, little emphasis on rising in status, and faith in an ordered

universe. Competitive cultures, in contrast, were characterized by an emphasis on rising in status, a social structure depending on individual initiative, valuation of property for individual ends, and strong ego development. Theoretically, the features that differentiated these cultures might be expected to translate into different experiences and pressures in the daily lives of children that would, in turn, establish different kinds of interpersonal behavior and relationships. These kinds of analyses were not made, however.

A study that comes much closer to an examination of socialization is one by Whiting and Whiting (1973, 1975). They used a method of investigation by which individual behavior and cultural characteristics were examined directly. Conditions of socialization and child behaviors in six cultures were compared. In each of six communities, six boys and six girls between 3 and 6 and equal numbers of children between 7 and 11 were observed over a period of several months to a year. Naturalistic observations were made of each child across predetermined settings and conditions. The communities were towns in India, Kenya, Mexico, Okinawa, the Philippines, and the United States. The thousands of "interacts" obtained were converted into categories and the scores for each child on each category were converted into a proportion of the child's total interacts. Scaling procedures were used to develop broad dimensions of behavior. The dimension of interest here is altruism. When individual children's scores on altruism were compared with scores on the total cross-cultural sample, 100% of the children in Kenya were above the median, 73% in Mexico, 63% in the Philippines, 29% in Okinawa, 25% in India, and 8% in the United States. These differences in children's behavior were linked to observed differences in specific rearing practices. Responsible family chores were assigned very differently in different cultures, particularly those of value to the economy of the family and those involving care of younger siblings. Cultures in which children had high responsibilities in task assignments were cultures in which the children had significantly higher altruism scores. These patterns tended to hold also at the level of individual analysis within a culture and applied similarly at the younger and older age levels. Age and altruism tended to be positively related across cultures. The Whitings cite a 1957 study by Barry, Bacon, and Child showing that in many societies there is more pressure on girls than on boys for nurturant and responsible behavior, a finding that was borne out in their own study as well.

The anthropological studies provide developmental psychologists with some models for investigating the culture-family complex as an influence on children's behavior in our own society. In these studies, the practices of the cultures have been *measured* as normative, practiced behaviors. This is quite a different approach from that used in the research of social and developmental psychology. In the latter, societal norms of responsibility, reciprocity, cooperation, competition, and the like are assumed. These presumed norms become the explanation of behavior. The actual practices and values of the society are not (as in Whitings' research) assessed directly. If we are interested in understanding how in our own society children's prosocial behavior is influenced by societal standards and pressures, research questions and methods will need more clearly to determine society's verbalized standards and accepted practices regarding prosocial behavior.

In psychological research, cultural influences have been studied by comparing children of various cultural groups on tasks involving cooperation and competition. Typically, following the lead of Madsen (1967), cooperation has been assessed in the context of games such as the Prisoner's Dilemma or the Madsen Cooperation Board. The general findings of these studies are easily summarized: Children from white Western cultures are least cooperative. Differences in the norms of the adult cultures are inferred. Various cultural comparisons have been made: Mexican, Mexican-American, and Anglo-American (Avellar & Kagan, 1976; Kagan & Madsen, 1971, 1972a, 1972b; Kagan, Zahn, & Gealy, 1977; Knight & Kagan, 1977a, 1977b; Madsen, 1971; Madsen & Shapira, 1970; McClintock, 1974); Indian and urban Canadian (Miller & Thomas, 1972); Australian aborigine and European (Sommerlad & Bellingham, 1972); Kikuyu and United States (Munroe & Munroe, 1977); Zambian and European (Bethlehem, 1973). Generally, the closer a cultural group is to the Western mold, the less cooperatively the children behave (Knight & Kagan, 1977b). These findings are certainly compatible with those reported by the Whitings (1973, 1975).

In a second set of laboratory studies dealing with influences of social norms on children's behavior, investigators have manipulated expectations or have created situations in which the principles governing behavior could be observed or inferred. In the main, these studies have been of reciprocity and responsibility principles. Staub (1970a) varied situational expectations to increase the salience of responsibility. In a laboratory setting, he told kindergartners and first graders that they were in charge of things when he left the room. He said that if anything happened, the children were to take care of it. After a few moments, a cry was heard from the next room. Under conditions of assigned responsibility, there were more attempts at responding to the cry than when no responsibility had been given.

With an interest in the principle of reciprocity in children's prosocial behavior, Staub and Sherk (1970) brought pairs of fourth graders into the laboratory. One of the pair was given an obvious opportunity to share candies with the other. Later, the child who had been the recipient of the peer's sharing or selfishness was given the one available crayon in circumstances in which both children were assigned a drawing task. The preceding experience of having or not having received candies from a partner was not significantly related to subsequent sharing of a crayon. In other words, reciprocity was not a generally prevailing principle for these 9- to 10-year-olds.

Also interested in reciprocity, Dreman and Greenbaum (1973) presented Israeli kindergartners with an opportunity to share candies with their peers. Under one experimental condition, children were told that their identity would be known to the recipient; under the other condition, children were told that their identity would not be known. If reciprocity were a consideration, one would anticipate more sharing when the child's identity was known. This was generally not the case. When the children were asked their reasons for sharing, only 4% were coded under reciprocity ("I gave so he'll play with me"), whereas 29% were coded under social responsibility ("It's nice to give"), 17% under altruistic ("So he'll be happy"), and 14% under affiliative reasons ("He's my friend," "I like him"). The remaining were unclassifiable.

Peterson, Hartmann, and Gelfand (1977) devised an interesting study in which children's responses could be compared according to principles of social responsibility and reciprocity. Kindergartners and third graders were asked about the relative praiseworthiness of donating and helping when behavior (portrayed in stories) was guided by the fact that the recipient had shared with the donor (reciprocity) or by the fact that the recipient was needy (social responsibility). The children judged donating on the basis of the recipient's need as the more meritorious, and this evaluation increased with age. These investigators then observed children under conditions in which reciprocity considerations could be relevant. Generous children (those who shared in a marble-dropping game) experienced either an unseen helpful or an unhelpful peer in a joint endeavor.

Generosity in the game context continued following the helpful peer conditions but dropped following the unhelpful peer conditions. The results were interpreted in terms of reciprocity. The third graders were significantly less retaliatory than the kindergartners after exposure to the unhelpful peer. These age differences are consistent with results in an earlier study by Durkin (1961). The inconsistency between children's principles and their behavior illustrates that children's knowing a norm does not mean that their behavior will be in line with it.

It is apparent from the preceding studies that social norms and their influence on children's behavior are issues that can not easily be brought into the laboratory. How one determines a child's awareness of given norms or principles and how one determines how norms influence a child's behavior present difficulties of considerable magnitude. It is not at all clear that findings based on situations of one-to-one influence, as in the preceding studies, can be interpreted as data on social norms. Nor is it clear that norms or internalized guides in children's prosocial behavior are recoverable and reportable in response to direct questioning, for example, "Why did you divide the candies this way?" One is reminded of an early study by Kalhorn (1944) concerning children's conceptions of the shoulds and should nots of behavior. Mennonite children and non-Mennonite children in Iowa were interviewed. Among the should nots, the Mennonite children rarely mentioned the strict moral religious values held by family and community (regarding stealing, lying, killing, etc.); instead, they mentioned issues of cleanliness and the like. The author interpreted the findings as indicating that the ingrained norms were so much taken for granted that they were not even in the discourse of issues. Only rules that presented some problems or were unresolved in the children's minds were mentioned. In investigating norms and motives regarding prosocial behavior, we may be dealing with something similar. To learn about ingrained guides of behavior, the art of in-depth interviewing may have to be recovered.

Many questions remain for research in this area: How do social norms interact with other motives in determining a child's altruistic actions? How are norms transmitted? What kinds of societal norms regarding altruism or egoism are actually transmitted? How do children deal with conflicting norms?

Society as Socialization Agent

In private interchanges within the family, children experience parents' moral orientations and values, learn what is required or expected specifically of them as individuals, and participate in the just and unjust relationships that the parents provide. In direct encounters with society, children also experience, learn, and participate. Although a society is not always self-aware of the content or the methods by which it is socializing its children in human relationships, it reveals itself clearly in its organization of living; its work and leisure; its literature, arts, products, and laws; and in its records of itself. There are characteristic and institutionalized messages repeated over and over that concern human needs, distress, justice and injustice, and approved and disapproved reactions in human relationships. For a child growing into a society, exposure is almost automatic.

In the early 1970s during the last days of the Mao era in the Peoples' Republic of China, when the country was first opened to Western visitors, American psychologists and psychiatrists (Cohen, 1977; Kessen, 1975) observed a remarkable network of synchronized societal messages directed to children. These messages had the aim of submerging the individual self for the good of the other and the group. In drama, dance, music, art, stories and essays, posters and slogans, the themes were consistent: finding the lost sheep, avenging the cruelty of the landlord, giving away the big apple and keeping the little one, giving the seat to the old man on the bus, praising the selfless dedication of the youth hero. If the child's words or behavior deviated, there were immediate, uniform pressures to conform. To the visitor, the prosocial norm was obvious; it was a single, explicit, and self-conscious message. It seems a good hypothesis that this societal expectation exerted significant control over children's reasoning and interpersonal behavior. The uniformity in this particular network of media made it easy to observe a "norm." In a society in which children are exposed to multiple and conflicting messages, the processes of influence are far more difficult to assess. The difficulty does not diminish the need to identify significant societal influences that affect prosocial development. By and large, the strategies and methods for this kind of investigation have hardly begun to come off the drawing board of research planning.

One societal institution that has been investigated in relation to children's prosocial development is TV. When the number of hours that children of all ages spend watching TV became a public concern, investigators added TV to the variables of childrearing. Following the research model that had been used to study the influences of TV violence on children's aggression, investigators have explored the possible effects of prosocial program content (Murray & Kippax, 1979; Rushton, 1979). In a number of studies, nursery school and kindergarten children were given considerable exposure to children's programs that varied in aggressive and prosocial interpersonal content (e.g., "Mister Rogers' Neighborhood" for prosocial content, "Batman" and "Superman" for aggression, "Sesame Street" for both prosocial and aggression content, and several neutral programs). Generally, base-line rates of children's prosocial and aggressive interaction were obtained in naturalistic (preschool) settings; TV programs were introduced into the schedule and rates of behavior were reassessed in a postviewing period. The work of Friedrich and Stein and their colleagues (Friedrich & Stein, 1973; Friedrich, Stein, & Susman, 1975; Friedrich-Cofer, Huston-Stein, Kepnis, Susman, & Clewett, 1979) is representative. Friedrich and Stein (1973) measured prosocial behavior (cooperation, nurturance, and verbalization of feelings), aggression, rule obedience, and tolerance of delay in the free-play behavior of preschoolers. The viewing of programs with high prosocial content resulted in increased prosocial interactions only in the samples of lower socioeconomic families. These increases in prosocial behavior were not accompanied by decreases in aggressive behavior. In the 1975 study with Headstart children, Friedrich et al. (1975) found that positive effects of prosocial TV programs were more likely when other aspects of the environment were supportive. Children whose prosocial interactions increased after viewing were those who not only watched the programs but also rehearsed the program themes through verbal labeling or through enacting parts of the program or a similar theme of interaction. In their 1979 study, Headstart classrooms were assigned to (1) neutral TV with unrelated play materials, (2) prosocial TV with unrelated play materials, (3) prosocial TV with play materials related to the programs, or (4) prosocial TV with related materials and teachers trained for rehearsal activities. Prosocial TV alone had few effects on behavior. Groups 3 and 4 showed significantly more prosocial interaction after training than did the groups in which the TV content was not related to the children's activities.

In a considerable number of studies, children have been exposed to programs like those in the preceding research and also to commercial serials involving prosocial content (Ahammer & Murray, 1979; Coates, Pusser, & Goodman, 1976; Collins & Getz, 1976; Cosgrove & McIntyre, 1977; Drabman & Thomas, 1975; Sprafkin, Liebert, & Poulos,

1975). The totality of evidence shows small increases in prosocial behavior, but it by no means suggests that prosocial interaction increases automatically from exposure to TV-portrayed positive behavior. Neither dramatic nor lasting effects have been demonstrated. As the investigators point out, socialization histories of children, personal variables, kind of program, and environmental context in which the viewing takes place, all have modifying effects.

As Roberts and Bachen (1981) have noted, emphasis in TV research have shifted from main effects of (prosocial) program content to consideration of variables of presentation and person. Commenting on the possible effects of the formal and technical properties of various media, Mander (1978) for example, has suggested that commercial TV as a low-definition medium with high emphasis on arresting visual effects might portray the action-packed sequences characteristic of violent content more readily than the more subtle cues characteristic of prosocial interactions.

In their review of mass media effects on children, Roberts and Bachen (1981) have indicated that newscasts are a major source of children's knowledge regarding world affairs and political events, beginning in early elementary school years. What children learn from the newscasts (and newspaper reports as well) concerning normative, sanctioned, or punished human relationships would seem to be important socialization influence deserving of research attention. The news frequently depicts events of human distress and need and the individual and national responses to such events (Hyman, 1973). These events are often viewed in a flow of program content that is emotionally incompatible with feelings of concern about human suffering. Human problems are preceded and followed by content in commercials, entertainment, and news that brings forth positive emotions or focuses on the viewer's personal interests. This configuration has many things in common with effective desensitizing procedures (Hartmann, Gelfand, Smith, Paul, Cromer, Page, & Lebenta, 1976).

Television has been our example of society as a socialization agent. It would be very much in error however to assume that TV is the most or only influential medium socializing children's values and behavior relating to prosocial development. There are many media, events, and practices in a society that affect children (e.g., child and youth groups, churches, sports events, Humane Societies, clean-up campaigns, political movements, human conditions). To ignore these factors leaves much to the unknown with regard to influences on children's prosocial development.

Social Class

As the long history of sociological research has shown, the social-class concept organizes a relatively stable cluster of life conditions, behavior settings, and psychological properties of parents and families. A given class represents a set of central tendencies on these dimensions. Many of the conditions or properties that distinguish among classes are those that define the context of childrearing—parents' education, parents' work lives, neighborhood and housing, economic plenty or scarcity. These dimensions translate into psychological variables, such as parental interests, values, goals, anxieties and so on, that one can assume influence the experiences that parents provide for their children, the principles and practices they rely on in childrearing, and the views they have of the world.

Most often in studies of children's prosocial behavior, social class has been used as a classificatory variable only, without intervening bridges from the broad sociological grouping to the personal and interpersonal derivatives. This kind of classification has not led to informative results. When children of the middle classes and lower classes have been compared on prosocial characteristics, the findings are mixed. Three studies, all of which involve prosocial training of preschool children, illustrate the inconclusive evidence. These studies have three different kinds of results. Doland and Adelberg (1967) found significantly less sharing in a group of welfare children (described as dependent and neglected) than in an upper middle class group. These differences held after the children had received reinforcement and modeling training for sharing. Yarrow, Scott, and Waxler (1973) trained children in helping behavior, using modeling procedures. Children from an upper middle class group and children from a low-income group showed similar increases in prosocial behavior after training by a nurturant model. In the Friedrich and Stein (1973) study reported earlier, preschoolers of low-economic backgrounds increased in prosocial behaviors after exposure to prosocial TV programs, but there was no similar increase occurring in children of middle class background.

Class comparisons on laboratory measures of donations show equally inconsistent results. Among Israeli kindergarten children there were no overall class differences, although reciprocity conditions

differently affected children from backgrounds described as academic and nonacademic (Dreman & Greenbaum, 1973). Children in the latter group were influenced more by reciprocity. DePalma (1974) found no class differences in donations by 7- to 10-year-old boys. Knight and Kagan (1977a) found middle class Anglo-American children (5 to 9 years old) more selfish and less egalitarian than lower class Anglo-American children. Ugurel-Semin (1952) also found rich children more selfish and less egalitarian than poor children. When the Cooperation Board Task was used as the prosocial index (Nelson & Madsen, 1969), there were no differences between a Headstart and a middle class group, but on the same task (Madsen, 1967), Mexican urban middle class children were significantly more competitive than Mexican urban poor or rural poor. Madsen, interpreted the cooperation by the rural poor as reflecting the cooperation characteristic of the adult community, an essential for the survival of the rural Mexican family. Inferentially, then, an acquisition process is suggested in this study.

Adolescent boys of differing social-class backgrounds were observed under experimental conditions that were intended analogues of adult work conditions (Berkowitz, 1966; Berkowitz & Friedman, 1967). In the first of two situations, a boy acted as supervisor of a fictitious worker peer. For half of the subjects, the workers were portrayed as having low productivity; for the other half as having high productivity. The supervisor received a prize based on the worker's performance. Then roles were reversed and the supervisor became the worker. Did the productivity of the new worker follow a reciprocity principle? Reciprocity was somewhat more common among boys whose fathers belonged to the entrepreneurial middle class than among boys from middle class bureaucratic or working class backgrounds. However, when the same procedures were used with British middle class and working class boys (there was no entrepreneurial group), the findings were not replicated.

The continuing instabilities and inconsistencies in findings suggest need for changed research approaches to social-class influences. In a few studies, class has been used only as a first level of classification. Then, class-linked conditions, such as occupational life, have been conceptualized in terms of critical interpersonal dimensions (such as supervision on the job, required subservience, or required self-control). In this way, the macro social-class conditions begin to be operationalized at levels that are similar to the individual outcome variables. The research of Kohn (1969/1977) and Kohn and Schooler (1973) are examples. Parents were interviewed about their values and their childrearing practices. Middle class parents were twice as likely as working class parents to select self-control as an important child characteristic; working class more than middle class parents chose obedience as an important characteristic. Much of this class difference could be explained by characteristics of fathers' occupations. Both within and between classes, fathers whose work was closely supervised were more likely to choose obedience as a valued characteristic for their children, whereas fathers whose work was loosely supervised and highly self-directed were more likely to choose children's self-control as a valued characteristic. Fathers were more likely to report using physical punishment the more closely they were supervised at work. Kohn's results are reminiscent of Rühle's (1924/1974) comment on the behavior of the workers who become, "as soon as they have taken off their working clothes, bourgeois too in their behavior. They treat wives and children as they are treated by their bosses, demand subjection, service, authority" (pp. 41–42). The effect of occupational self-direction on parental values has been replicated in a number of countries (reviewed in Kohn, 1969/1977).

In these data, possible mechanisms or routes of influence are discernible—from workplace to parental values, to disciplinary practices, and (presumably) to the development of differing kinds of behavior and controls by the child. Although there were no direct measures of parental and child behavior in these studies and no information specifically on prosocial dimensions, the studies are methodologically important (1) in the rather successful conversion of class-linked variables to data of the same level (or unit size) as data on child behavior and (2) in the identification of a theoretically meaningful network of social and personal interdependencies. This research strategy would be applicable to investigations of prosocial behavior. Although parents' occupational lives have been the focus, it is likely that other class-linked conditions of life could be similarly investigated in relation to the prosocial values and behavior of children.

Another study that takes us part of the way toward a process approach to social-class and prosocial socialization is by Hoffman and Saltzstein (1967). They obtained seventh-grade children's reports on the disciplinary practices of their mothers and fathers, peer ratings of the children's altruism, and projective measures of children's guilt feelings. What is interesting in this study is the finding that parents' disciplinary techniques and children's pro-

social behavior were related in different ways in the middle and the lower class groups. Reasoning as a method of control by middle class mothers and fathers was positively related to children's reputations as altruistic, but reasoning and altruism were unrelated in the lower class, except for mothers' reasoning with girls. Reported power assertion by mothers was negatively related to guilt feelings in middle class girls and unrelated in lower class families. Power assertion by fathers was unrelated to child measures in the middle class and negatively related to guilt in boys in the lower class. In other words, a given parental technique may be positively influential, negatively influential, or not significant in relation to children's altruism, depending on the class context. If this generalization is supported by other studies, a number of questions are suggested. Do patterns of techniques and values differ in the middle and lower classes, thereby modifying the influence of a specific technique? A given parental technique or value may represent the norm in one class but deviance in another. Does this fact influence the meaning and effectiveness of the technique? Are techniques of the same label different techniques or differently used by parents of middle and lower class backgrounds?

Overall, the research findings with respect to social-class influences are distressingly unclear. We cannot generalize about kinds and frequencies of prosocial behavior by children of different class backgrounds. We have scanty data on how parental values and behaviors relating to prosocial behavior are patterned and expressed in different classes. Hoffman and Saltzstein's (1967) study tells us that we cannot ignore the class context in predicting the effectiveness of specific parental influence techniques. We need now to obtain data to understand why this is the case. A promising research approach is hinted at in the Kohn and Schooler (1973) studies, namely, the analysis of significant class-linked conditions outside the family in terms of interpersonal relationships and systems of rewards and punishments that are then also played out in family interactions. In this way, we begin to get a grasp of social forces as individual socializers of the child. The basic research in this area has yet to be done.

Behavior Settings

The topography of children's behavior is interesting to contemplate: where behavior takes place, with whom, with what distribution of time. When Barker (1968) spoke of a "stream of behavior," he also called our attention to "behavior settings" and conveyed very eloquently the force and manner by which the structure and dynamics of such settings regulate behavior. He was concerned not so much with momentary situations but with settings that occur repeatedly in children's experience. His locale for research was small-town middle America (the street corner, church pew, classroom, bowling alley, etc.). A behavior-setting analysis of socialization raises interesting questions about the kinds of settings that are imposed on children or made available to them and about the settings from which children are excluded. With particular regard to prosocial behavior, one might ask how settings govern opportunities for children's helping and sharing and impose demands, constraints, and controls on prosocial interaction. Certain behavior settings that are shared by large numbers of children, like the classroom, are undoubtedly a homogenizing influence with respect to children's standards and motivations regarding prosocial behavior. Differences among families and societies in the distribution of settings in which children engage with others may help to explain the bases of differences in children's prosocial development and may also shed some light on the reasons for differences in the effectiveness of any given parental technique that is intended to influence prosocial behavior.

Bronfenbrenner (1962) has called attention to a characteristic of behavior settings in American culture, namely, that of age stratification. Children's (and adults') social experiences outside the family occur largely within age-homogeneous groups, which means that much of what is learned interpersonally is taught by agemates and reflects the needs and interests of agemates. One can conjecture about possible implications for interpersonal behavior. In a very few studies, this variable has been examined in relation to children's prosocial behavior. In Murphy's (1937) study, sympathetic interactions were fewer and unsympathetic actions were more frequent in a nursery school group with a narrow age distribution than in a group with age heterogeneity (a 2½-year span). In the homogeneous group, the ratio of sympathetic to unsympathetic responses was 1.63:1, whereas in the heterogeneous group, the ratio was 6.63:1. Also, the most self-centered responses, such as "*I* don't cry" (when a peer was crying) occurred most often in the group of homogeneous age. More protective and caregiving acts as well as more patronizing helping took place in the heterogeneous groups. Consistent with these results are findings in a study by Bizman, Yinon, Mivtzari, and Shavit (1978). Children in age-heterogeneous groups were significantly more altruistic than were children from age-homogeneous classes on a test of sharing with peers and in resolutions to moral dilemmas presented in stories. In Sawin's (1980) study of

distress on the playground, there was a marginally significant tendency for greater affective involvement when the child witnessing and the child feeling distress were different in age.

The school (classroom and total school) is a major candidate for analyses in terms of a variety of settings in which social behaviors—competition, cooperation, helping, empathy—are played out. One example of setting is the kind of goal structure in the school—cooperative, competitive, or individualistic. The research reviewed by Johnson and Johnson (1974) indicates that participation in cooperative instructional situations encourages positive interpersonal relations among students, whereas competitive goal structures tend to have more negative interpersonal consequences. A study by Crockenberg, Bryant, and Wilce (1976) presents a more complex picture, with the effects of goal structure interacting with individual success or failure. Besides goal structures, Crockenberg and Bryant (1978) have noted four other factors in the school environment that they hypothesize as contributing to the development of prosocial behavior, namely, the general modeling of prosocial acts, the rewarding of prosocial acts, an environment permitting one to convey one's own feelings and to recognize the feelings of others, and appropriate use of control by the teacher. Given the fact that children spend a high proportion of their time in school, it becomes important to identify those characteristics of the school environment that contribute to their socialization (see *Minuchin & Shapiro, vol. IV, chap. 3*).

The practical obstacles to good field studies of children's prosocial learning in behavior settings, such as sports events, neighborhoods, playgrounds, youth gatherings, and so on, are very real. The conceptual capabilities for such research are available however, and the challenges are to develop research strategies and methods that adequately address socialization where it takes place.

Socialization in the Family

A consideration of the traditional childrearing domain of parents as socialization agents has come late in our review of children's prosocial behavior. We intended, first, to see children from a developmental perspective, to understand something of the cognitive and affective mediators of prosocial behavior, and to place parents' and children's behavior in social contexts. Now, in turning attention to parents, we can take these factors into consideration in the questions we ask and in the interpretations we give to parental rearing influences.

In theories of childrearing, parental behavior is

assumed to have effects on children through a history of experiences. There is faith that, over time, parental influences lead to generalized behavioral tendencies that have some durability. Research on rearing in relation to prosocial child behavior follows along this path of assumptions. Most attention has been given to techniques of parents—with an implied unidirectional influence, with a primary stress on uniform relationships and outcomes, and with little interest in differing outcomes for different children. The reminder that child characteristics are potentially significant modifiers of parental effects on prosocial development (Chapman, 1979; Keller & Bell, 1979) has not materially changed the nature of the socialization studies.

We review the research on childrearing by examining (1) the parent as a model of prosocial behaviors, (2) affective relationships between parent and child, (3) parental teaching and control techniques, and (4) family structure and functioning.

Parents as Models

The parent as a model for the child's behavior has long been appreciated—an awareness that antedates psychological study by many centuries. One might consider the question closed if it were not for the fact that we know that child behavior does not always reflect the parental model. Research over the past years has turned to serious inquiry into how parent-modeled behavior fits into the scheme of the child's learning. Here we are asking specifically about prosocial learning.

In major childrearing studies of the 1950s (e.g., Sears et al., 1957), theories of identification with the loved or feared parent were the framework for interpreting behavior by the child that indicated adoption of the parent's behavior. In the 1960s when modeling theory came into prominence (Bandura & Walters, 1963), the child's imitation of the adult was investigated in a host of experimental studies of observational learning. If, as the studies showed, the frequency of neutral and aggressive acts was increased by the child's observing an adult's performance of these acts, would not prosocial behaviors be similarly influenced? Based on this premise there followed extensive research into the effects of adult-modeled generosity and helping on children's behavior.

Because these studies have been reviewed frequently and in detail (Bryan, 1975; Rushton, 1980; Staub, 1978), we will examine and assess only the major outcomes of this large body of research. In the prototypic prosocial modeling experiment, a bowling game is used in which contrived winning scores bring tokens that can be exchanged for prizes of the child's choosing. An experimenter, after explaining the game to an adult (who will become the model) and to the child, suggests that the players may want to give some of the tokens that they win to charity. Charity may be represented by a box on which there is a picture of a "needy" child. When the experimenter leaves, the adult plays the game, wins in a predetermined way, and gives (or does not give) to charity. The model departs and the child is left alone to play the game and to donate or not. Prosocial behavior is indexed by the number of tokens that the child gives away. The child's interpretation of the procedure has not been examined.

Findings from these studies generally show group differences in the generous behavior of children who have observed a model and those who have not. Generosity is enhanced after observing the generous model (Bryan & Walbek, 1970a, 1970b; Elliott & Vasta, 1970; Grusec & Skubiski, 1970; M. B. Harris, 1970; Presbie & Coiteux, 1971; Rosenhan & White, 1967; Rushton, 1975). There is decreased donating following a selfish model (Bryan & Walbek, 1970a, 1970b; M. B. Harris, 1970; Midlarsky & Bryan, 1972; Presbie & Coiteux, 1971; Rushton, 1975). Children of 7 to 11 years have been the usual subjects, and at all of these ages, modeling has been effective to some degree. Similar modeling influences have also been demonstrated in the few experiments of helping behavior in preschool-age and kindergarten-age children (Fukushima & Kato, 1976; Staub, 1971c; Yarrow et al., 1973).

The positive effect of modeling in influencing prosocial acts is an important finding. Nevertheless, the other side of the coin should also interest us. The amount of donating after observing a model is often quite low, and not all children adopt the model's behavior. For example, 40% to 50% of the children failed to donate after seeing the model do so in studies by Rosenhan and White (1967) and Bryan and Walbek (1970b). In the experiment by Poulos and Liebert (1972) in which a model said, "I think I'll give four tokens to the children [who won't have a chance to earn any]," only 12.5% of the children from second and third grades gave four tokens; however, 80% donated at least one token. Some children acted counter to the behavior of the model, that is, they donated after observing a selfish model (Bryan & Walbek, 1970b). There is not much information regarding the noneffects and the contrary effects of modeling. We know that some children will donate without a model. Do differences in rearing histories explain differences in responding in the laboratory situation? Clearly children do not imitate indiscriminately, even in an experimental situation in which modeling is made as salient as possible and in which the choices open to the child are limited.

If prosocial modeling experiments are to be taken seriously as demonstrations of an important socialization (parental) influence, the model's behavior must have some lasting effects and some generalizability. A number of experiments of sharing and helping have included measures of stability, and effects have been found several days to several months after the experimental modeling (Grusec, Kuczynski, Rushton, & Simutis, 1978; Midlarsky & Bryan, 1972; Rice & Grusec, 1975; Rosenhan, 1969; Rushton, 1975; White, 1972; Yarrow et al., 1973). Evidence of generalization has also been reported. In Elliott and Vasta's (1970) study, children (ages 5 to 7) observed a model sharing candies with a hypothetical poor little boy. Children were tested on sharing of candies, sharing of pennies, and giving away (to a hypothetical child) the more attractive of two toys. Children shared candies and pennies but did not give up the attractive toy. In a preschool study by Yarrow et al. (1973), generalization of modeling effects was assessed 2 weeks after training. The adults in this experiment modeled a variety of prosocial acts of sharing, helping, and sympathy in the training sessions. In the testing, the kinds of opportunities to help differed from those in which the child had observed the model and occurred in a different locale with different personnel. There was significant helping on the new tasks but only by those children whose training had been by nurturant models. Rushton (1975) also investigated generalization. He retested children 2 months after experimental training under conditions somewhat different from training. Children who had donated immediately after seeing the model tended to donate on retest; those who had not donated initially tended also not to donate on retest. By and large, then, experiments on modeling have provided evidence of some continuing effect and some generalization of effect.

Although laboratory studies of modeling have been at center stage, a number of naturalistic studies of prosocial behavior have also dealt with modeling effects. The latter studies take us back slightly in research history, antedating the experiments just summarized. These studies (London, 1970; Rosenhan, 1969, 1970; Rutherford & Mussen, 1968) provide evidence of associations between altruistic behavior of parents and altruism in their children. The indices of parental behavior in these studies are indirect. Rutherford and Mussen (1968) obtained preschool boys perceptions of their parents through semistructured doll play. They selected the most and the least generous nursery school boys—as assessed by teacher ratings and by a test of sharing. They

interpreted as modeling influences the fact that the generous boys more often than the selfish boys portrayed their fathers as generous and sympathetic.

Data from a very different context also make the link between parental model and child behavior. London (1970) found that in their retrospective accounts of childhood, Christians who rescued Jews from the Nazis revealed a strong identification with moralistic, principled parents. Rosenhan (1969) provides data in a study of youth who were involved in the Civil Rights movement. He classified the youth either as fully committed altruists (i.e., with sustained personal involvement in work with the underprivileged) or as partially committed (i.e., with participation in one or several freedom rides). From detailed life-history interviews, Rosenhan characterized parental behavior. Parents of the fully committed youth had themselves been involved in altruistic, social causes of considerable magnitude. They had given their children many opportunities for observing and participating in these causes. They were described as having strongly held humanitarian principles. Positive and warm experiences with their parents were recalled by 12 of the 15 fully committed youth and by 3 of the 21 partially committed. It appeared that the fully committed youth had learned "by loving precept and percept to respond easily to the needs of others" (Rosenhan, 1970, p. 266). Parents of the partially committed youth had moral principles, but what they preached and what they actually practiced were often discrepant. Rosenhan speculated that the children of these latter parents would have little basis for internalizing altruism.

It is interesting to follow Rosenhan's work at this point because it illustrates a nice interplay of naturalistic and experimental research. Taking his direction from the clinical evidence and impressions gained in the retrospective study, he embarked on a series of experiments in which the several parental dimensions were translated into experimental manipulations. The nurturant, altruistic, activist parents who involved their children in their own altruistic causes were represented in the experimenter-model (in the laboratory paradigm described) as (1) donating to orphans, (2) being nurturant (friendly) to the child, and (3) having the child participate (rehearse the generosity) with the model (Rosenhan & White, 1967). As we have seen, observing a generous model fostered children's donating. Rehearsal combined with observing the model was an additional impetus to donating in the absence of the model. Nurturance had no special impact. Unfortunately, nurturance was weakly implemented in this forerunner study. A 5-min. pleasant or unpleasant period of questioning and conversing with the child occurred before the modeling. After the fact, Rosenhan and White raised doubts about these manipulations, seeing them as "too brief" and "innocuous" and not faithful to parental nurturance. Their disenchantment, however, did not dissuade later investigators from using these same manipulations.

The inconsistencies of the parents of the partially committed youth were also represented in experimental analogues. Modeled behavior and stated principles were paired to be either consistent or inconsistent with one another. Rosenhan, Frederick, and Burrowes (1968) found words more important than modeled actions in developing self-denial behavior. In other studies in which the separate or combined effects of modeling and preaching on donations have been compared (Bryan & Walbek, 1970a, 1970b; Eisenberg-Berg, 1979; Grusec, Saas-Kortsaak, & Simutis, 1978; Grusec & Skubiski, 1970; Midlarsky & Bryan, 1972; Poulos & Liebert, 1972; Rushton, 1975) results have been inconsistent. This is not altogether surprising because the kinds of verbal communications and endorsements of prosocial behavior have varied in content and administration. We will return to the variable of the adult's verbal influences in later discussions of rearing techniques.

In summary, experimental and naturalistic research into modeling influences on prosocial behavior has demonstrated that, for many children, observing prosocial behavior in a model increases some kinds of prosocial behaviors. There is insufficient evidence from this research to say how modeling affects a broad range of prosocial responses, particularly affective responses, such as empathic feelings toward a victim or personal sacrifice and intervention in direct encounters with a needy or a distressed person. Another limitation exists in the data from the laboratory studies in which a single adult models a single dimension of behavior: there are no competing models and no competing behaviors. Because the child's learning in everyday life takes place with multiple potential models who offer a variety of behavior, a central issue is the determination of factors affecting which models and which modeled behaviors are selectively adopted and rejected by the child. An inquiry that lies ahead for research on modeling is how this potential influence conjoins with other parental qualities and techniques in influencing prosocial behavior in the child.

Affective Relationships in Childrearing

Parental acceptance/rejection and warmth/coldness are classical dimensions in theories of child development. A positive bond or relationship between parent and child is deemed an essential condition for healthy development, at least in the early years. The assumed relevance of this relationship for prosocial development depends on the conception of prosocial behavior that one holds. If empathy is emphasized as an important mediator of prosocial behavior (Hoffman, 1975b) and if the child's feeling good about herself is seen as facilitating prosocial responding (Staub, 1971a), one would anticipate a positive effect of parental nurturance. On the other hand, if prosocial responses are viewed primarily as reasoned choices or as learned norms (Rushton, 1976), then nurturance is not likely to be seen as relevant. If a child's prosocial responses are made to gain adult approval, then adult contingent reinforcement, not a nurturant parent/child relationship, is important for maintaining prosocial behavior.

An affective relationship is not easily investigated, and not readily established experimentally. A nurturant relationship is a matrix of behaviors that are expressive of attentive care, support, and feelings of love and acceptance (noncontingent *and* contingent). Such a relationship develops over time and extends into many experiences. Although it is quite possible for a neutral or a rejecting parent to reinforce a child for specific conduct (perhaps compliance) or, on occasion (with manipulative purposes) to shower friendly attention on the child, such purely contingent and situational attentions do not qualify for a nurturant relationship.

There have been many studies of nurturance in relation to children's prosocial development, with many different indices of nurturance. A review of the findings destroys a simple generalization of positive associations. Hoffman (1963) found no relation between a global measure of nurturance based on interviews with mothers and prosocial behavior of 3-year-olds as observed in nursery school. In the Rutherford and Mussen (1968) study described earlier, paternal nurturance, as portrayed in the child's doll play, was significantly positively related to generosity in 4 ½-year-old boys. In Feshbach's study (1978), maternal and paternal behavior reflective of positive affect (assessed by Block Q-sort, 1965) was significantly positively related to the generosity of 6- to 8-year-old boys but not to the generosity of girls. Baumrind (1971), basing nurturance assessments on extensive home observations and ratings, reported no significant correlation with preschool children's social-responsibility scores. However, she found that in the patterns of parental behaviors related to children's social responsibility, nurturance was a significant component. Baumrind's naturalistic findings were replicated in an experiment by Yarrow et al., (1973). Nurturant or nonnurturant (i.e., aloof) caregiving provided to preschool children over a 2-

week period left prosocial behavior unchanged over base-line levels. However, when the conditions were continued into a 2-week period that included extensive modeling of prosocial behavior and explanations of the consequences of prosocial acts for the recipients, children with the nurturant models were significantly more helpful and sympathetic than children with the aloof models. In a laboratory study, Staub (1971a) found that a preceding period of nurturance increased the likelihood of kindergartners' responding to a child's distress cry.

Naturalistic studies of older children (10 to 13 years of age) have yielded mixed results. Hoffman and Saltzstein (1967) obtained mothers' and fathers' reports of their expressions of affection toward their children and also children's perceptions of their parents' affection. Only a few positive associations were found between parental affection and peer ratings of the child's consideration for others, and these associations varied by social class, sex of parent, and sex of child. In a later study (Hoffman, 1975a) with the same procedures, the findings were repeated. With children of the same age, Mussen et al. (1970) also found weak and variable correlations. Eisenberg-Berg and Mussen (1978) found positive associations between empathy in boys of high school age and mothers' warm, egalitarian childrearing practices; there was no relation for girls.

The findings continue to waver in the experimental work in which nurturance has been introduced as an attribute of the adult model. In the modeling procedures described earlier, adult and child spend a brief period together before the adult plays the bowling game and donates to needy children. The period is either one in which there is friendly interaction or the adult is aloof (absorbed in his own interests) or somewhat critical in questioning the child. By this manipulation, nurturance has had neither consistently facilitating nor inhibiting effects on children's donating behaviors (Grusec, 1971; Grusec & Skubiski, 1970; Rosenhan & White, 1967; Weissbrod, 1976). In the studies by Grusec and by Weissbrod, donating was less when modeling was preceded by friendly interaction ($p < .07$ in both studies). One interpretation that has been offered is that the unfamiliar adult's friendliness was seen by the child as conveying permission of any behavior. Weissbrod's study also included measures of helping behavior. Friendly interaction preceding the modeling of helping behavior resulted in significantly shortened latency for a helping response. Thus, within the same study, the effects of nurturance differed for different prosocial indices.

In the studies reviewed, nurturant and nonnurturant models have performed only prosocial acts. In one study (Yarrow & Scott, 1972), the adults modeled both prosocial and aggressive actions, thereby permitting analysis of both the amount of, and selectivity in, imitation. Two adults, each of whom had established a nurturant or nonnurturant (aloof) relationship with different groups of preschool children, modeled according to script, both nurturant and aggressive caregiving behavior with toy farm animals. Each child then had an opportunity to play alone with the animals. Nurturance variations in the models' prior relationships with the children made no difference in the total amount of imitation appearing in the play, however, the substance of imitations differed and in directions congruent with the prior nurturance or nonnurturance of the model.

In all of the preceding research, nurturance has been dealt with as the parents' generally accepting and supportive behavior. It is possible to look more analytically into the child's experience for circumstances in which parental nurturance is especially critical. One such class of experiences is situations in which the child is distressed. One might hypothesize that how the parent deals with a child's own feelings of distress may have consequences for the child's capacities for empathy and concern for others. Tomkins (1963) suggested that when parents respond openly, sympathetically, and nurturantly to their child's feelings of helplessness and distress, the child learns to express distress without shame and to respond sympathetically to the distress of others. On the other hand, if parents respond to their child's distress with anger or contempt, the child will learn to suppress his own feelings and to avoid distress in others. Lenrow (1965), in a study inspired by this reasoning, found that preschoolers who expressed their own distress overtly were the most likely to give verbal support and help to a thwarted character in a puppet show. Related evidence comes from a study of young children by Zahn-Waxler et al. (1979). Mothers' empathic or nonempathic handling of their toddlers' needs and distress was observed. Children whose mothers were rated high in empathic expression were more altruistic to persons in distress than were children of less empathic mothers. This would appear to be an area worthy of further research.

Research on affective relationships between parent and child in relation to the child's prosocial development has dwelt on nurturance. Unloving, punitive, depressed, or affectless parents are socializing agents too. We have few insights into the kinds of influences that these complicated affective relationships may have on children's empathy and prosocial behavior. The effect of a punitive socializing agent on children's sharing was investigated in an experimental modeling study by Morris, Marshall, and Miller (1973). First- and second-grade girls who observed a child model being punished for nonsharing, shared significantly more than girls in a control group—as one would expect. Increased sharing occurred also in children who observed a model receiving a strong verbal reprimand that was not contingent upon any specific behavior. The children had no way of knowing what had triggered the punishment. The authors reasoned that because, in most children's learning histories, prosocial behaviors have not led to punishment, such behaviors are apt to be performed in circumstances in which the environment is threatening. Further studies could help to clarify these influences.

Clinicians have observed that some children who are reared by an affectively disturbed parent manifest very helpful, responsible, and sympathetic behavior. No systematic studies have been found that examine the development of prosocial behavior in children growing up under these kinds of parental affective disturbance. The clinical observations strongly suggest, however, that socialization processes other than, or in addition to, those that are usually considered in child developmental research are very relevant to how children acquire the cognitive, affective, and motivational bases for dealing with helplessness and need in other persons.

In summarizing the many studies relating affective (nurturant) behavior of the adult to prosocial behavior of the child, it is clear that nurturance, by itself, has not been a strong predictor of the child's prosocial behavior. When investigators have identified patterns of parental techniques that are positively related to prosocial outcomes, these patterns tend to include parental nurturance as a component. It is probable that nurturance is inherently associated with certain rearing behaviors and not others and that the persisting thread of positive relations between nurturance and prosocial indices that appear in the studies reflects these associated configurations of rearing variables.

Investigators (Staub, 1979; Underwood et al., 1977) have speculated as to the avenues by which adult nurturance and nonnurturance can affect children's prosocial behaviors. It may be through the direct modeling effects of parents' empathy or callousness in caring for the child herself. It may be that the child's feelings about self (influenced by parental nurturance) make it easier for the child to be sensitive and responsive to others. The affective relationship may influence the child's feelings toward, and conceptions of, the caregiver, thereby modifying not only the effectiveness of the caregiver's reinforcement and prohibitions but also the child's receptivity to direct teaching by the caregiver.

Several essential extensions are needed in research on parents' affective relationship with the child. The first is careful conceptualization of affective caretaker characteristics and adequate indexing of affective variables in research procedures. The second is an extension of research to include a broader range of variation on affective dimensions. Third is the need to differentiate kinds of prosocial actions and motivations related to different affective rearing conditions. Fourth is to deal with the affective relationship as one dimension in patterns of configurations of rearing techniques.

Parental Teaching and Control Practices

"Adult caretakers will play a determining role in the way their children develop, either consciously and conscientiously or by default" (Baumrind, 1978, p. 239). In the last decade, there have been renewed research efforts to understand this role by investigating the kinds of teaching and control techniques that parents use. Obviously, modeling and affect can and do teach and control child behavior and, therefore, the distinction made here is somewhat arbitrary. Didactic instruction, reasoning, and punishment all have tones of affect and modeling.

There have been some advances in conceptualizations and methods in rearing research, making research more difficult but giving it a better chance of explaining some of the determinants of complex child behaviors: investigators have persevered at the essential task of conceptualizing specific techniques of teaching and control and identifying their impact on children's prosocial behavior. At the same time, there has been slowly increasing attention to the contexts in which specific techniques are used and to the interactive and combined effects of various techniques used by parents.

In research on parental practices in relation to children's prosocial behavior, parents have been viewed primarily as disciplinarians, and discipline has been dealt with in terms of a dichotomy of power assertion (the use or threat of physical punishment, withholding, and depriving) and reasoning or induction (explanations, pointing out physical requirements of the situation or harmful consequences for the child or others). Hoffman (1963, 1970) elaborated a theory of parental influences on children's moral development in which he compared the effects of power-assertive and reasoning techniques. Induction, he reasoned, should bring out empathic feelings and promote internalized altruism. In contrast, parental power assertion would be expected to arouse fear and anger in the child because it relies on, and theoretically remains, an external source of motivation. Its use would not be expected to foster altruism. This formulation has been the guiding orientation of much of the research. Dienstbier, Hillman, Lehnhoff, Hillman, and Valkenaar (1975) have proposed an attributional analysis of discipline that is in keeping with this approach. According to them, negative emotional arousal, although associated with any disciplinary techniques, is probably less with reasoning than with other punishment techniques. Emotional arousal will have different effects depending on the child's attributions: with punishment that is power assertive, it is assumed that the child will attribute the cause of negative arousal to the external punisher; with reasoning, the child is more likely to attribute the cause to his own transgression. A perceived external cause is assumed to result in less internalized control than perceived internal cause. Thus, negative associations are predicted between the use of power-assertive techniques and an altruistic orientation and positive associations are predicted between inductive methods and empathic feelings and altruistic behavior. Because a sizable number of investigations have been addressed to the comparison of these techniques, it is possible to arrive at some evaluation of the evidence.

Assertion of Power. From seven studies in which power assertion and prosocial behavior have been investigated, the findings are variable. In a study by Hoffman and Saltzstein (1967), parental disciplinary techniques were inferred from their responses to stories of disciplinary encounters. There were six scores: each parent was given a list of techniques from which to select those that he or she recalled as techniques that would have been used when the child was 5 or 6 years old as well as those that would be used now when the child was in seventh grade. With the same procedures, the child reported on each parent's current techniques. Assessments of the child included (1) altruism, based on peer nominations, (2) guilt about wrongdoing, based on story interpretations and on mothers' assessments, and (3) moral reasoning about transgressions. Correlations between reported parental power assertion and the several measures of moral development varied and also differed for boys and girls. Power assertion by mothers was significantly negatively correlated with middle class girls' altruism but significantly positively correlated with boys' altruism in both middle and lower social-class groups. Power assertion by middle class fathers was also significantly positively correlated with boys' altru-

ism. When significant associations appeared between power assertion and children's moral judgments and guilt feelings, they were negative. Thus, associations with the cognitive and affective measures tended to be in the predicted direction; associations of power assertion with prosocial behavior were generally not in the predicted direction.

Dlugokinski and Firestone (1974), with similar research objectives, obtained children's perceptions of their mothers' disciplinary practices by following Hoffman and Saltzstein's (1967) procedures. Power assertion was measured in relation to hypothetical situations involving parent/child conflict. Situations involving unkind behavior with peers were the bases for scores on induction. Other-centeredness in children was measured by a self-report of values, a scale of concept of kindness, sharing with UNICEF the money received for participation in the study, and peer ratings of considerateness. The children were fifth and eighth graders of lower middle class families. Children's perceptions of maternal power assertion correlated negatively (small but statistically significant coefficients) with children's sharing, their understanding of kindness, and their other-centered values, but they were unrelated to peer ratings of altruism. Perceptions of mothers' use of power and use of reasoning were negatively related ($-.32$). When partial correlations were computed to remove the influence of induction from correlations, there were no reliable associations between power assertion and the measures of other-centeredness.

Also, with lower middle class children of the same ages, Mussen et al. (1970) found nonsignificant associations between mothers' power-assertive methods and children's cooperation on the Prisoner's Dilemma and on peer nominations regarding consideration of others. Feshbach (1975b) measured empathy and generosity in middle class 6- and 8-year-olds in relation to mothers' and fathers' use of power. Except for a negative association between girls' empathy and mothers' power assertiveness, associations were nonsignificant. Mothers' use of physical punishment was unrelated to prosocial behavior in 1 ½- and 2 ½-year-olds (Zahn-Waxler et al., 1979). Consistent negative associations were found by Block, Haan, and Smith (1969) between college students' recollections of power-assertive punishment from parents and their own current involvements in humanitarian causes.

Overall, positive, negative, and no associations have been found between power-assertive techniques and prosocial behaviors. One can imagine several sources of these inconsistencies. The many qualities of power assertion have not been specified in the research. Power assertion can vary in form, severity, and rationality and in the kinds of transgressions for which it is used. Parents may use it arbitrarily, it may express a parent's angry state, or it may be an expected price for given serious misbehaviors. The consequences of power assertion may depend on the use of this technique as part of a total pattern of parental characteristics and techniques. Baumrind's (1978) longitudinal work provides a lead in this regard. Parents of children who were most socially responsible were high in the exercise of authoritative control over their children's behavior (which did not preclude power techniques); parents of children who were withdrawn and distrustful were high in authoritarian control. Parents of children who were least socially responsible were low in control techniques. As with Baumrind's (1971) findings on nurturance, (cited earlier), it is necessary to look to the pattern of control techniques to arrive at stable relationships between rearing conditions and prosocial behavior.

Techniques of Explanation and Reasoning. Adults rely mightily on verbal threats, judgmental labeling of the child, communication of principles, values, and rules—all are common verbal interventions. "A brave, kind boy like you helps his sister" is attribution. A scout's pledge of "I will try to do my duty to God and my country, to help other people at all times" would appear to be self-instruction derived from social norms and values. A parent's plea, "Kevin, can't you see how you hurt Jamey when you called him 'shrimp?' Would you like someone to say something mean to you?" is intended to make Kevin aware of Jamey's feelings and arouse empathy. It is apparent that there are many ways of attempting verbally to induce change in a child's behavior. As of now, there are not clear differentiations that permit a sorting out of these methods and their effects. Induction or reasoning has been used globally as a contrast to power assertion.

Despite the variations that are caught up under the label of reasoning, there is a reappearing note of positive association between reasoning and prosocial characteristics in the child—amid many more findings of no association. Investigators who have examined the effects of power assertion have made parallel assessments of reasoning techniques. In the research by Hoffman and Saltzstein (1967), cited above, in addition to power-assertion, other-oriented reasoning as a reported disciplinary approach was also investigated. Reasoning was found to be sometimes positively related to peer ratings of altruistic behavior of girls, although associations var-

ied by class, sex of parent, sex of child, and source of reports on discipline. In Hoffman's study (1975a), parents' use of victim-centered reasoning and child's peer-rated altruism were again positively correlated, but only for mothers and boys and for fathers and girls. Dlugokinski and Firestone (1974) found positive correlations between children's perceptions of mothers' use of consequence reasoning and peer ratings of the children's altruism and children's donations to UNICEF. Inductive techniques and altruism were unrelated in most comparisons in the studies by Mussen et al. (1970) and Feshbach (1975b).

A number of investigators have approached the issue of induction and prosocial behavior experimentally. Staub (1971c) brought pairs of kindergartners together and discussed how one could help someone who needed help and the positive consequences of such behavior. This induction had little effect on subsequent tests of sharing and helping. In a similar study by Staub (1975) with fifth and sixth graders, effects of reasoning on helping behavior were again limited. Several other experimental studies show more positive results. In a study of Russian children, Nevrovich in 1974 (described in Izard, 1977) brought groups of 4- to 6-year-olds into a playroom that was in disarray and asked them to help put it in order. Children were exposed to one of three kinds of induction: (1) they were told that if they did not help, their friends would not be able to play and would be sad, (2) pictures of children with sad faces looking at the disarray were added to the preceding description, (3) pictures were added of children who were both sad and sick. The children worked 20 min. and were then given a choice of finishing the cleanup or engaging in an enjoyed activity. The number of children who elected to finish the job increased progressively from (1) to (2) to (3) procedures. Findings were interpreted as a function of how much distress was induced by the verbal communications. Also working with the notion of intensity of appeal, Eisenberg-Berg and Geisheker (1979) compared the effects on anonymous sharing of verbal communications that had a neutral, a normative, or an empathic message. Empathic messages but not normative messages about sharing with poor children were more effective than neutral messages in inducing third and fourth graders to be generous.

Beyond Power or Reasoning. Recognizing that many parents use both power and reasoning techniques, in combination or in different situations (Grusec & Kuczynski, 1980; Zahn-Waxler & Chapman, 1982), investigators have examined the combined or interactive effects of these techniques.

Hoffman (1963) classified mothers, on the basis of interviews, as high or low on use of power-assertive discipline. No association was found between the use of reasoning techniques and preschool children's prosocial peer behavior unless power-assertive techniques were taken into account. For mothers low in power assertion, there was a significant positive association between other-oriented discipline and prosocial peer behavior; for mothers high in power assertion, there was a significant negative association.

In the previously cited study by Dlugokinski and Firestone (1974), an experimental situation was included in which two kinds of appeals for charity were made. In one appeal, the humanitarian work of UNICEF was described (an inductive appeal), in the other, authority was the source (the teacher says you should give). There was a significant interaction between the type of rearing history and the type of effective appeal; children tended to be more persuaded by the kind of appeal that was consistent with their perception of their mothers' disciplinary style. Children for whom a reasoning style was predominant in their histories donated more under the inductive appeal than under the power appeal. An opposite effect was suggested ($p < .10$) for children accustomed to power assertion. (Parenthetically, these findings are important methodologically in bringing to attention the significance of childrearing histories as potentially strong [and unknown and confounding] factors in children's responses in experimental analogue-rearing studies [Sawin & Parke, 1979]).

In the naturalistic and observational studies of childrearing, *patterns* of parental methods have been emphasized. Block, Haan, and Smith (1969) studied adolescents who were or were not involved in humanitarian causes. There was some tendency for the parents of the youth who were involved to be described, retrospectively, as stressing a rational approach in controlling child behavior, as being low in the use of anxiety- and guilt-inducing techniques of control, and as using mild discipline. In Baumrind's (1971, 1978, 1979) assessments of rearing patterns, high responsiveness by mothers coupled with high demandingness by fathers and high responsiveness and demandingness by both parents were predictive of social responsibility, particularly in boys, at preschool and 9 years. Girls and boys were low in socially responsible behavior when both parents were highly authoritarian and punitive. A childrearing pattern that facilitated the development of social responsibility in girls was one that did not focus on control issues: the parents are described as almost never exercising control, yet appearing to have control, in the sense that the child took pains to try to do what the parents wanted. These families are described as achieving a quality of harmony and rationality.

Consistent with the findings from Baumrind's samples of middle and upper middle class families are data from Mussen et al. (1970) on a lower middle class sample of preadolescents. Again, different socialization techniques were related to prosocial behavioral outcomes in girls and in boys. Boys who were altruistic in peer relations were those whose mothers were not highly permissive, made strong demands, required high standards, and were relatively nonpunitive. The boys experienced these mothers as nurturant and considerate. Girls who were most altruistic were those whose mothers described themselves as affectionate, nonpunitive, permissive, using reasoning, and stressing high standards of personal responsibility.

Cooperative behavior in 21-month-old children was investigated by Londerville and Main (1981) in relation to mothers' control techniques. Mother and child were observed in a laboratory play session. Their verbal commands, physical interventions, voice tone in commands, and amount of force in physical intervention were recorded. Children's cooperation with mother and with other adults was positively related to mothers' use of warm tones and gentle physical interventions. Freely translated, this appears to point to nurturance as an important qualitative dimension of the parent's control methods. These data, obtained in parent/child interaction in a play context, together with data on children of the same age, obtained when the mother was under the stress of disciplining her child who had just hurt someone (Zahn-Waxler et al., 1979), provide informative replicative evidence on the affective dimension of control techniques. Effective discipline was clear verbal messages (reprimands, explanations, expectations) which conveyed the mothers' own negative emotions. However, these sometimes harsh interchanges were embedded in a broad context of generally empathic caregiving by those mothers whose children were the more altruistic.

In summary, the research evidence on power-assertive and reasoning techniques leads away from unqualified predictions about the effects of either technique on the child's altruism, guilt, or selfishness. The effects of each technique on prosocial behavior are conditional. If power assertion is linked negatively with children's prosocial behaviors, it is likely to be associated at the same time with negative attitudes on the part of the parent and, most likely, with punitive power assertion (Olweus, 1980b). In the context of a positive and responsive parent, power assertion may relate quite differently to prosocial behavior by children. The influence of induction on prosocial behavior is similarly modified by rearing context, particularly affective contextual factors, and is modified as well by the content and form of the reasoning.

Although much of the research groundwork has been laid, research on power assertion and reasoning is now ready for the kinds of critiques and reconceptualizations that characterize research progress. There are confusions in the concepts; there has been no thoroughgoing analysis of given kinds of power and reasoning. In a theoretical review, Henry (1980) challenges the posited opposition between reasoning and power procedures, arguing that all reasoning is authoritarian and that the source of authority in the reasoning is an important consideration. Reasoning has come to stand for parental influence based on humanistic values of universal justice. Neither reasoning that informs the child of violation of an obligation to a legitimate authority nor nonmoralistic reasoning has been considered. From her interview study, Henry reports that different types of reasoning are used by mothers for different kinds of transgressions (harm to peers, aggression to parents, etc.). Hence, content and area of control need to be specified in investigating the effects of this technique. She argues, too, that reasoning and love withdrawal are not to be viewed as mutually exclusive modes of discipline. Reasoning may also be conditionally loving:

> The two variables are of different orders. One refers to cognitive aspects of socialization, the other to motivational pressures toward change. "Reasoning" is the verbal mechanism through which the parent may express moral values to the child. (Henry, 1980, p. 106)

The need for content analyses of reasoning techniques has also been discussed by Kuczynski (1982, 1983). Among the issues to be considered is the cognitive content of reasoning in relation to the child's cognitive level and the motivational aspects of the verbal communications to the child. Children's motivations following the parent's use of reasoning, in part, depend on the context of reasoning, such as tone of voice and accompanying disciplinary techniques, and, in part, on the nature of the explanation offered by reasoning. Variations in the content of reasoning can determine both the kind of motivation for prosocial behavior—internal or external—that is aroused as well as the intensity of the

motivation. These many differences underline the problems in treating reasoning or power assertion as unitary concepts and in seeking a single predictable relation between one or the other technique and children's prosocial behaviors.

Advances in our understanding of the roles of power assertion and reasoning in prosocial learning can be along several lines. One is the refinement in conceptualization and measurement. A second is the pursuit of two contrasting research strategies, namely, a closer look at these variables under controlled laboratory conditions, and also a naturalistic approach to patterns of control practices. Some of the control factors that have been investigated experimentally are reviewed in the following discussion.

Experimental Studies of Contingent Praise and Punishment. A control technique that cuts across issues of power and induction is the use of contingent praise and reward or punishment to influence children's generous and selfish behaviors. Experimental results on positive reinforcement in relation to children's generosity have been inconsistent. In a study by Fischer (1963), material rewards from a stranger increased sharing by preschool children, but praise had no effect. Adult praise for peer-modeled sharing resulted in increased donations by 5-year-old girls in a study by Ascione and Bueche (1977). Reward consisting of social and material components plus an explanation of the reward increased preschoolers' cooperation (Biron, Ramos, & Higa, 1977). In an experiment by Gelfand, Hartmann, Cromer, Smith, and Page (1975), praise and prompting had highly variable effects on children's donations. If verbal approval for the child's donating came from a model who herself had been selfish, Midlarsky, Bryan, and Brickman (1973) found that the adult's approving reactions resulted in *less* donating than if no approval had been expressed. Praise given to a generous model in M. B. Harris's (1970) study did not contribute to fourth- and fifth-grade children's generosity. It had no effect on children's sharing in a study by Elliott and Vasta (1970) until content was added to the praise (a normative or an attributional statement, such as "doing something good is nice and makes you a good boy"). There were then marginally enhancing effects. When a model praised her own behavior and expressed happiness over being generous or being selfish with her tokens, children's generosity or selfishness was significantly influenced in the expected directions (Presbie & Coiteux, 1971).

Hartmann et al. (1976) designed a laboratory procedure to study the effect of aversive conditioning on children's generosity. Children (6 to 10 years) were given repeated opportunities to donate a penny to an unseen peer while they were playing a game in which they earned prizes. Children low in initial donating were either fined 2 pennies for not donating or were fined and also told of the contingency between the fine and not donating. Explanation of the contingency was necessary for the donating to increase. When children were told that fines were no longer in effect, their generosity sagged markedly.

These studies do not lead to closure. Prosocial behavior is sometimes enhanced by positive reinforcement. Simple conditioning is often ineffective in bringing changes in prosocial responding. The provision of verbal explanations along with reinforcement or punishment increases the effectiveness. Little is known about the durability of prosocial responses acquired in this way. To an extent, some prosocial actions can be brought under control, the success depending on conditions that apply generally to the conditioning of social behavior. The use of positive or aversive conditioning in encouraging or suppressing prosocial response has rarely been systematically investigated in the repertoire of parents' methods, and it deserves naturalistic study (Grusec, 1982).

Self-instruction in Prosocial Behavior. An old-time discipline that was practiced in many a schoolroom was to assign a culprit a task in self-instruction—to write over and over again his better intentions: "I will not pull Jane's hair again," "I will get to school on time," "I will help my classmates." This approach has come under scrutiny in research as a control of behavior. Although the extensive literature on self-instruction is not within the scope of this review, the technique has relevance for children's learning of prosocial behavior (Kanfer, 1979). Experiments in which this kind of control technique has been studied catch the child in a temptation or a sin of commission. In studies of young children, when prohibiting kinds of self-instructions have been introduced ("I will not . . ."), there have been reductions in forbidden behaviors (Patterson & Mischel, 1976; Sawin & Parke, 1979). When the self-instructions have directed attention not to the forbidden action but to alternative actions as a means of inhibiting the undesirable behavior, this approach has tended to be less effective, although not always. In the Sawin and Parke study, such redirection of attention to an alternative behavior was as effective as the inhibitory self-instruction with second-grade boys, not with first-graders. This finding was interpreted by the authors as possibly indicating that different cognitive capacities are required for utilizing the redirection of behavior as a self-instructional approach.

A pair of studies involving verbal self-instruction of sharing behavior was carried out by Rogers-Warren and Baer (1976) and Rogers-Warren, Warren, and Baer (1977). For a number of days, pairs of adults participated in the group play of preschool children (play consisted of art materials and constructions). They modeled sharing and praising of others' accomplishments. At the end of each period, participants reported on what they had been doing. The adults took the lead. When one described instances in which she had shared, she was reinforced by the other adult. Then each child was queried and reinforced for reporting appropriately. The combination of modeling, children's reporting of their own sharing, and the reinforcement of true reports of actual sharing increased subsequent sharing. These investigators found that adult modeling alone done in a nondemanding way and modeling in combination with the experimenter's reinforcement of the model's report did not increase sharing. Most sharing was achieved by a combination of components that included self-report. It would be interesting to know whether in natural settings parents teach their children to use self-instruction to inhibit harm or neglect of others or to redirect their behavior to an alternative prosocial action, and with what success.

Attributions and Prosocial Behavior. "You are a good girl," "You're really tough," "You are mother's helper," "If only all the boys were as conscientious as you are." Socialization is full of attributions. Among rearing techniques that have an influence on children's inclinations to behave prosocially, adults' verbal communications that suggest to the child that he or she is indeed cooperative or helpful or sympathetic probably play a role. One kind of support of this hypothesis is found in experimental studies in which cooperation, helping, and sharing have been modified through the mechanism of attribution. With behavior-problem boys (7 to 12 years of age), Jensen and Moore (1977) provided either a cooperative attribution ("It shows that you are willing to share, . . . work well with others") or a competitive one ("You're a real winner"). This manipulation led to corresponding differences in the boys' cooperative and competitive approaches to a tower-building task performed in pairs. Miller, Brickman, and Bolen, 1975, attempted to reduce littering by fifth graders by telling them each day that they were tidy. This attribution decreased the undesirable behavior. Children were induced to donate (in a bowling game) either by a modeling procedure or direct instruction or a combination of both (Grusec, Kuczynski, Rushton, & Simutis, 1978). After donating, they were told either that they had done so because they were the kind of person who liked to help others (self-attribution) or because they thought their experimenter expected it or they were given no reason. Amount of donating in the experimenter's absence was significantly greater in the self-attribution condition than in the external-attribution conditions if the initial inducement to donate had been a modeling procedure. If the child had been induced to donate by direct instructions ("Now I want you to share") and was then told, "You shared because you are the kind of person who enjoys sharing," self-attribution was not effective. Self-attribution (with modeling) had a tenuous advantage in a delayed test and an advantage in a generalization test of sharing. The least amount of donating occurred in the external-attribution modeling condition. With a similar experimental procedure, Grusec and Redler (1980) found that donations increased following reinforcement and self-attribution and also that self-attribution contributed to generalization in other tests of altruism in 8- and 10-year-olds but not in 5-year-olds. Rushton and Teachman (1978) found no differences in 7- to 10-year-old children's donating associated with internal, external, or no attribution. Because strong positive reinforcement was also used, it may in itself have provided a positive self-attribution for all of the children.

It is clear that attributions can have an effect on prosocial behavior; the research questions to be further explored are what kinds of attribution and under what conditions do attributions have lasting effects. It is reasonable to suppose that the adult's attribution of generosity or some other prosocial characteristic must appear credible to the child if the child is to accept it. If it is seen as manipulative or inappropriate, one would anticipate no effect or a negative one. Parental skill in sensing receptive circumstances for positive attributions would undoubtedly be a critical factor in the effectiveness of this technique. Very little is known about children's self-assessments with regard to altruism or about the processes by which children arrive at altruistic self-attributions in the course of socialization.

Managing the Situation. The techniques discussed thus far have generally involved practices that bring specific parent behaviors into focus or question. But the skilled parent or teacher does not depend solely on such strategies. Parents intentionally or unintentionally create or manage situations in which prosocial or antisocial behavior is possible, expected, or encouraged—or in which it is not. A good teacher or parents plans children's experiences to bring out desired behavior in children. The researcher who has sat in a nursery school waiting, in vain, for aggressive interactions finds that these interactions almost never occur because the teacher has averted them by altering the situation in ways that make aggression incompatible with the new behavioral possibilities. In a similar vein, a naturalistic study of helping among preschoolers is thwarted by the attentive staff who are ever present to intervene where helping between children might have occurred. The parallels in parental practices are obvious. Parents (of young children particularly) have a significant degree of control over the kinds of experiences to which the child is exposed, including events that involve exposure to the needs and distress of others. The range of such experiences is undoubtedly very different in the lives of different children. It follows that parental techniques—of modeling, power assertion, reasoning, reinforcement, and so on—operate across quite diverse events, and it seems highly likely that the effectiveness of given techniques is dependent on the kinds of situations in which they are customarily applied. Parents are, then, socialization agents at two levels: controlling children's social learning environments and in those environments or settings controlling specific child behaviors.

It is somewhat curious that the strong emphasis on situational factors in social psychological studies of adults' prosocial behavior has not carried over into studies of children and their rearing environments. Instead, there are a few speculations and a very few relevant data. For example, Hoffman (1976) is considering management of the child's experiences when he recommends that rather than shield a child from distress experiences, parents should allow the child to be exposed to the range of natural events to foster the child's sensitivity to the feelings of others. In discussing the impact of participation in the prosocial activities of parents, Staub (1979) also refers to situational provisions for child behavior. By engineering a situation in which the child will be receptive to helping or sharing (M. B. Harris, 1972; Staub, 1979), there is an increased likelihood that the child will engage in another prosocial act. From a scattering of studies, there is tangentially relevant evidence of the effectiveness of having children participate in ongoing social activities of the adults. This idea is conveyed in recollections of childhood by youth in the civil rights movement. They recalled being taken with their parents to participate in various humanitarian causes (Rosenhan, 1969). In two experiments, Staub and Fotta (1978) and Staub, Leavy, and Shortsleeves (1975), having children participate in making puzzles for sick children or in teaching younger children first-aid techniques, increased the likelihood of later prosocial acts by girls, although not by boys.

The most relevant evidence, however, is not available. Specifically, how are the situations that comprise the rearing environment and the specific socialization techniques interrelated? Inquiry into these questions is not readily made with current methods of investigation. It is a viable hypothesis that a significant parental influence on prosocial behavior comes from the kinds of experiences or situations that parents provide either on a principled basis or by virtue of their own life conditions. Until the *situations* of rearing are integrated into investigations of parental techniques, we will remain in a relatively handicapped position in predicting rearing influences on prosocial characteristics of children.

The Family as a Unit of Socialization

It is much more difficult to investigate family qua family influences on child behavior than to deal with dyadic interactions between parent and child. There are conditions and interactions, however, that cannot be reduced to the dyad. These include family structure, family dialogue and communication, and relationships within the family. These factors deserve more study in relation to children's prosocial behavior.

In the present period of social history, the family is undergoing alterations in group structure and parental roles that can be expected to influence children's sensitivities to others and their inclinations to act prosocially. For example, what are the consequences of living in a small family group? Of having few or no siblings? Of living in a one-parent household? Of having a father engaged in nurturing the young? If the family peer group is absent, are many opportunities for learning reciprocity and cooperation and sensitivity to others' perspectives lost? If outside-the-home work takes increased time from both parents, are children acquiring a greater sense of responsibility and of individual worth in the family enterprise? Or are they deprived of needed teaching and discipline? Are the processes of value transmission from parents to child eroded? There are, to our knowledge, no studies geared to studying these social changes in relation to children's prosocial development.

In a few studies, family size and sibling order have been examined in relation to prosocial behavior. Children from larger families were more generous than only children in a laboratory study of sharing by Ugurel-Semin (1952). This finding has not been upheld in later laboratory studies involving helping or sharing. Negative associations with family size were found by Staub (1971a). No significant associations were found by Dreman and Greenbaum (1973), Gelfand et al. (1975), Handlon and Gross (1959), and L. A. Harris (1967). These studies also revealed no significant relation between birth order and prosocial behavior. To do justice to issues of the influences of family structure on children's social development, it will be necessary to investigate directly the socialization that takes place in the daily lives of children in families of various compositions. One of the rare studies of prosocial behavior in which a unit larger than the parent/child dyad has been considered was conducted by Bryant and Crockenberg (1980). These investigators videotaped the behavior of 50 mothers toward their first- and later-born daughters as well as the behavior of the siblings toward each other in a seminaturalistic play setting. Each child's behavior toward the other, including helping and supportive behavior, was related to the ways the mother treated both children. When there were discrepancies in the mother's treatment of the two children, there was increased negative behavior between siblings. These findings point to the importance of addressing rearing practices in terms of the system of social relations in the family.

Other family structural factors, such as the distribution of responsibilities in the daily operation of the family and the nature of authority are relevant to prosocial development. There have been hints in the literature of effects of responsibility assignments in the family. Assignment to children of specific caregiving responsibilities for their younger siblings appears to increase children's caregiving responses generally (Whiting & Whiting, 1975). Bathurst (1933) found that preschool children who had the responsibility of taking care of a pet showed more sympathetic responses to peers than children who had no pet. With regard to family authority structures, in Baumrind's (1978) work, we saw that authoritative, authoritarian, and permissive patterns had consequences for children's characteristics of social responsibility. In a classic experiment (Lewin, Lippitt, & White, 1939) on the influences of adult authority patterns on the interpersonal behavior of children, we have, in a sense, an analogue study of family authority structure. Clubs of 11-year-old boys were conducted under three types of adult leadership: autocratic, democratic, or laissez faire. Children's friendly approaches to the adults and spontaneous sharing of confidences were most frequent in the democratic structure. Irritability and aggressiveness toward peers were more frequent in the autocratic and laissez faire clubs than in the democratic groups. Although neither the Baumrind (1978) nor the Lewin et al. (1939) study provides data directly on empathy or altruism, their findings indicate that variables at the level of group organization have measurable impact on children's modes of relating to other persons, and they suggest the value of investigating family authority and affectional structures in relation to children's learning of cooperation and other positive interpersonal behaviors.

Family rearing environments have cognitive properties that impinge on most if not all of family and child functioning. The categories in which families structure their world, their strategies for problem solving, their beliefs and opinions, and their manner of reasoning about moral dilemmas are only somewhat less tangible than family variables of roles and interactions that investigators have learned to cope with conceptually if not too well empirically. Many of the cognitive properties, it would seem, could materially influence the child's prosocial development. For example, the likelihood of feeling empathy and being moved to act prosocially is influenced (Feshbach, 1978; Reykowski, 1977) by the extent to which the person in need or distress is perceived as similar to the self. Support for this position comes from a variety of sources: Children and adults are more likely to help if the other person is perceived as sharing common opinions or membership in common social categories (Hornstein, 1972; Karylowski, 1976; Zwolinski, 1974, described in Reykowski, 1977). This being the case, parents' cognitive structures in viewing persons and groups, in classifying others in society, and in placing the family in relation to these others should be important for children's prosocial behavior. About whom will the child feel similar or different? How large and inclusive or exclusive are the categories of commonalities that the child is taught? The content of the social information that is transmitted in the family would be expected to influence the child's feelings of empathy and the generality of such feelings. Burton (1976) is explicit about parents' potential contributions to the development of children's cognitive structures. He suggests that parents teach social information in ways that will help children to perceive a variety of moral situations as belonging to the same class of events and behavior and that will help them to comprehend contradictions in norms and values. Among the dimensions of rearing that are thoroughly missed in research are the content and nature of family discourse about human events and relationships.

A small number of investigators have attempted to assess family value orientations in relation to prosocial development. Olejnik and McKinney (1973) classified parents of 4-year-olds as prescriptive or as proscriptive in their value orientation in rewarding and punishing their children. Children whose parents had prescriptive value orientations were more generous (donated more candies to poor children) than children whose parents stressed a proscriptive orientation. When value orientation was controlled, the relative emphasis of rewards and punishments as control techniques made no difference in generosity. In a study of middle class fifth graders, Hoffman (1975a) measured parents' hierarchy of values, disciplinary techniques, and affection for the child. The most influential parental attribute in relation to peer assessments of the children's altruism was found to be parental espousal of altruistic values. Bryan and London (1970) note in their review of research that family values of social status and competition are negatively associated with children's altruism and that values favoring emotional expression are positively related to altruism.

From this short account of findings on family variables, it is quite apparent that families as systems influencing children's prosocial development have not captured much research interest. Parents' influences are indeed multidimensional, they include specific acts directed to the child, continuing attachment relationships with the child, conditions and patterns of daily living, and parental conceptions and values of human behavior. The data of developmental psychology only begin to identify contributory rearing conditions for the development of children's prosocial orientations and behavior. Research is needed in which consideration is given to a broader view of parent and family influences and strategies and methods are shaken loose from old paradigms to meet more adequately the demands of significant socialization questions.

Peers in the Socialization Process

The role of peer relationships in moral development has been the subject of theory for a longer time than it has been investigated empirically. Piaget (1932/1965) emphasized the equality of relationships and the reciprocity in interactions among peers as children's education "out of egocentrism" into cooperative interchange. From a psychoanalytic position, Sullivan (1953) stressed close, intimate friendship as the ground for the development of a real sense of the perspectives and feelings of another person for the development of altruistic sentiments and caring. He suggested that in a close chum relationship a child acquires a sense of humanity, and that the sensitivity and compassion developed and experienced with the chum extend to others beyond.

In many of the studies we have reviewed, peer interactions of sharing and helping and peer ratings of peers have been the dependent variables, the indices of prosocial behavior. Peer interactional systems, however, have not themselves been studied as learning environments in which empathy and altruism develop. To paraphrase Hartup (1970), there is challenge and difficulty in isolating the variance in children's prosocial socialization that derives from interactions with peers.

Peer influences are not a unitary phenomenon. There are peers as agemates, as siblings, as close friends, as in- and out-group peers. There are peers in small face-to-face contacts and in the diffuse peer culture. As the contexts of interaction and intimacy of relationships vary, one would expect the processes of peer influence to vary and to be differentially relevant in the socialization of prosocial behavior. In all of these contexts, there are at least three issues. One concerns the kinds of prosocial learning that takes place in reciprocal interchange between equals or near equals. A second question concerns the interaction of individual child characteristics and peer influences. The two edges to this question are: (1) How do personal variables affect the child's influence as a socializer within the peer group? and (2) How do personal characteristics modify the effects that peers have on the child's prosocial characteristics? A third issue involves adults in relation to peer socialization: How do individual adults and adult society influence peer interactions by virtue of the kinds of peer-life circumstances they make available for children? How do socialization conditions in the family interface with the child's peer socialization?

Peer Interaction

Research on the sociability of very young children provides data on how children educate each other in social relationships. An example of one such study is that by Eckerman et al. (1975). Children between 10 months and 2 years were observed with unfamiliar peers when their mothers were in the room. Present at all ages were the social behaviors out of which prosocial interaction is made: imitating, offering a toy, struggling over an object, coordinating activities with the toys, smiling, and touching. Eckerman et al. observe that peers and adults offer the child something different in identical play situations and that peer life, beginning very early, provides the opportunities for learning to deal with the needs of self and others.

A methodologically refreshing study that deals with prosocial learning among peers was carried out by Gottman and Parkhurst (1980). They investigated verbal communications between pairs of best friends (ages 2 to 9) in a naturalistic setting. Of interest here are children's responses to friends' requests for clarification. Contrary to expectation, the younger children (under 5 years) were not less likely than the older children to respond helpfully with messages of clarification, and they did not lag behind older friends in responding to feelings expressed by peers. Both findings indicate the early development of sensitive, nonegocentric social skills and of capabilities of responsiveness to affective cues in peer interaction.

A very different source of insight into peer relationships is the work with young rhesus monkeys by Harlow (1974) and his associates. Their research provided the stimulus for investigations of human children, in this instance demonstrating the significance of peer affectional relations for normal development. Young monkeys deprived of maternal care and comfort found the needed affective support from peers. The study by Novak and Harlow (1975) using young monkeys as "therapists" is demonstration of affective, supportive interaction among peers.

A dramatic illustration of the operation of peer affectional systems among human children comes in the descriptions of the orphaned German-Jewish preschool-age children brought to hostels in England during World War II (Freud & Dann, 1951). These children showed high dependency on one another, especially in the early months in their new environment when adults had little affective significance for them. Daily logs kept on the children document the children's keen awareness of one another's conditions and needs:

> On walks they were concerned for each other's safety in traffic, looked after children who lagged behind, helped each other over ditches. . . . In the nursery they picked up each other's toys. . . . Behavior of this kind was the rule, not the exception. (p. 134)

The sensitivities of these 3-, 4-, and 5-year-olds in comprehending and ministering to peers demonstrate capacities that are rarely exposed in laboratory research. Here were children at very "high risk," who had experienced brutally extreme circumstances in the first years of life but who were generous, sympathetic, and helpful. One must account for the origins of their behavior in ways at variance from the familiar theories. In this instance, the interdependence of the peers, all under severe stress, provided the ground for empathy and altruism.

There seems little doubt, based on the preceding studies and observations, that young children can provide and withhold from each other in fundamental ways that affect their attitudes about themselves and their feelings about others. The absence of studies with such interactional analyses for older children does not allow one to say how these kinds of peer processes change with age.

Friendship has been given special attention in both theory and empirical study relating to prosocial development. Sullivan's (1953) writings were the inspiration for a study of friendship by Mannarino (1976) in which sixth-grade boys who had a stable and close-chum relationship were compared with a comparable group of boys who were without an intimate friend. Two measures of altruism, an attitude scale of social responsibility and a prisoner's dilemma game were used. As a group, boys with a chum were significantly more altruistic than those without a chum. However, one cannot judge the direction of influence in this association: Did the close friendship provide the relationship in which empathy and altruism were fostered or were empathic and altruistic children those who became close friends? Berndt (1981), too, has drawn upon hypotheses from Sullivan (1953) in a study of children's prosocial intentions and behavior with friends and nonfriends. Kindergarten, second-grade, and fourth-grade children were paired with a friend or a neutral classmate (determined sociometrically). Each child was interviewed about situations, such as helping in cleaning up the classroom or sharing a new bike, and was also observed with a partner in sharing a single available crayon in a competitive task. Girls said that they would share and help friends more than neutral classmates; for boys, friendship made no difference. Children's intentions and their actual sharing, however, were unrelated. Friendship had no effect on girls' sharing, but boys shared the crayon less with friends.

Other investigators have paired friends and nonfriends in laboratory tasks of sharing and helping, with conflicting results. Staub and Sherk's (1970) and Mann's (1974) studies of young children show more sharing between friends than between nonfriends. Floyd (1964) found no differences. Wright (1942), Fincham (1978), and Sharabany and Hertz-Lazarowitz (1981) found more generosity with nonfriends than with friends. One can hardly conclude from these brief laboratory encounters that empathy and altruism are less likely and less significant in close friendships than in interactions with casual or unfamiliar peers. Several problems seem to run through the laboratory studies. One is with regard to the determination of friendship. Only Mannarino (1976) made a detailed assessment of close chumship. Sociometric choices within the confines of a classroom may often not locate close friends. A second problem is one of research procedures. How well does a momentary situation of sharing under the constraints of unfamiliar circumstances and the uncertainties of experimenter/expectations, sample interpersonal processes among friends and nonfriends? The critical issue of identifying mechanisms by which sensitivity to the other person's need is generated and sustained within a friendship relationship cannot easily be addressed in the single laboratory observation.

With procedures that are illuminating, Youniss (1980) learned a good deal about the ways in which children (ages 6 to 12) conceptualize kindness and unkindness in relationships with peers and with adults by asking children to tell stories of kindness (and unkindness) involving child to adult, adult to child, and child to child. The content of kindness differed depending on the interactors. Kindness from adult to child consisted of themes of giving, teaching, being nice; kindness from child to adult more often included themes of doing chores; and kindness from child to child involved common themes of teaching, giving, and assisting one another. To other child subjects, Youniss presented stories of kindness and asked them if the person was being kind, and why. The age trends, although not strong, were of increasing verbal recognition of need in the recipient and sacrifice in the interaction. Children 6- to 8-years-old were more likely than the older children to express their reasons in unqualified terms of sharing is kind. Recognition of need in the recipient occurred somewhat earlier with regard to peers than with regard to adults. When asked what the recipient of kindness (or unkindness) does, children of all ages expected reciprocation between children. Only among older children was there an expectation of reciprocation by the adult in response to the child's kindness. The asymmetry of relationships is also evident in responses to stories of adult kindness or unkindness to a child. The expectation of reciprocation by a child was rarely given.

From the same set of studies, we get a glimpse of children's views of peer processes. Children were questioned about how one becomes a friend, and how one stops being a friend. These are difficult questions at any age, and answers are difficult to put into words. However, for the youngest children, becoming a friend is playing together and sharing; for older children, it is getting to know one another. These responses may be expressing similar sentiments, namely, mutual understanding and related-ness are involved in both. These studies of children's perceptions now need to be joined with behavioral studies of friendship in which attention is given to the experiences among friends that are important for the development of empathic and sympathetic concerns for the peer and for an enlarging prosocial concern.

Personal Variables in Peer Socialization

The influences of peers on peers' prosocial behavior have a more individual side. Children have radically different experiences with peers; socialization by agemates is not uniform and not always benign. Hence, the interchange with equals has different potentials with regard to the learning of prosocial behavior. We know that some children more than others have an impact on the behavior of their peers; some children more than others are influenced by peers. Why? Further, the composition of children's groups affects the social learning that occurs for different individuals in the groups. Research is scanty on all of these issues with respect to prosocial behavior. Individualities in peer socialization were noted in Murphy's (1937) study of sympathy. Certain children consistently, over many months, received unsympathetic responses when they were in distress. Certain children who were highly sympathetic appeared to have the effect of engaging other children in sympathetic interactions. Murphy noted that friends, younger children in the group, and group favorites received peers' sympathetic attention disproportionately.

The child's popularity in relation to his influences on the prosocial behavior of peers has been the subject of a number of studies. The findings on preschool-age children are quite consistent, indicating a tendency (although not overwhelming) for popular, compared with unpopular, children to be more reinforcing of their peers and more cooperative (Lippitt, 1941, Moore, 1967, and Hartup, Glazer, and Charlesworth, 1967). The findings are similar with sixth graders (Raviv, Bar-Tal, Ayalon, & Raviv, 1980). In the latter report, children generally preferred to give help to, and to receive help from, popular peers. A study by Hampson (1979) somewhat complicates the picture. Eighth graders who were not recognized by their peers as either popular or unpopular had the highest overall scores on helping on an impressive battery of prosocial measures. Those who were most unpopular had the lowest helping scores. Hampson suggests that different peer statuses may be related to different modes of helping, and he offers some tentative evidence. The kinds of helping done by the popular children are the visible peer-oriented kinds of help, which are experienced as reinforcing by givers and receivers alike. In contrast, the helping by children who are not high in popularity is less peer-related helping, such as volunteering, picking up papers, and so on. Hampson's idea is provocative and worth pursuing.

The development of new paradigms and reconceptualizations of peer interactions will help to advance knowledge regarding peer influences on children's moral values and moral behaviors. In this sphere of socialization, the individuality of peer effects needs special attention, namely, we need to understand the children and adolescents who are particularly influential peer figures and conversely the children and adolescents who are most susceptible to peer influences.

Techniques of influence in peer circles might be investigated by borrowing from concepts and techniques of parental influence. For example, are the control techniques that have been reviewed in relation to parental practices (i.e., power assertion, love and guilt manipulation, reasoning, etc.) relevant in peer socialization? Or are quite different concepts relevant for understanding the effects of peers on peers? Two research strategies would seem to offer good possibilities for investigating the contribution of peers to prosocial development. One is to investigate certain very special circumstances in which peers have functioned successfully (altruistically) as "therapists" in helping troubled peers (as in peer counseling [Hamburg, 1974], in the war-refugee orphans cited previously [Freud & Dann, 1951], and in socializing the withdrawn peer [Furman, Rahe, & Hartup, 1979]). A second useful research approach is one of detailed longitudinal observations of cohorts of peers.

Adult and Peer Socialization Systems

The parental and peer socialization systems in which children grow up interact with each other, with unique kinds of influences. The present stage of knowledge about this interaction has not advanced very far however. A commonly held view is one of opposing parental and peer pulls on the child (Devereaux, 1970). However, neither dissonance nor consonance conveys the nature of the conjoint influence processes from the two systems. How do children integrate the several sources of models for behavior, of rewards and punishments? How is the child better or less able to develop peer attachments and to interact constructively in peer groups as a consequence of attachments to parents and other family-rearing experiences?

One study that illustrates an important approach to the interface of parent rearing and peer socialization in the early years is that of Waters, Wippman, and Sroufe (1979). Children were observed at intervals between 15 months and 3 ½ years of age. The quality of infant-mother relationship was determined using the "strange situation" from research on attachment. Interpersonal behaviors, such as seeking contact, resisting or avoiding contact, attempting positive distant contact by smiling, vocalizing, or gesturing distinguished babies with secure attachment to the mother from those with anxious attachment. In successive appraisals over time, the children's behavior with peers was also assessed. Peer behavior varied in relation to early attachment. Securely and anxiously attached infants differed significantly and in expected directions in their sympathy for peers in distress, leadership with peers, being sought by peers, and so on. By careful age-wise changes in behavioral indices, these investigators succeeded in tapping into a developmental course, observing continuities in children's abilities "to generate and coordinate flexible adaptive responses to demands and to generate and capitalize on opportunities for interaction and learning" (Waters et al., 1979, p. 828). One begins here to have the kinds of data on children's motivations and skills that develop out of parental socialization, that predispose them to different qualities of peer interaction. The mapping of linkages between parent and peer worlds is a most significant research venture.

A final comment on the role of peers in the socialization of prosocial behavior is from a social psychological perspective. Adults (not parents only) influence the possible kinds of socialization by peers that can enter children's lives by virtue of the circumstances in which children are placed together (in daycare, organized youth groups, cooperative or competitive learning environments, sex and age stratified groups, shrinking sibling groups). Regarding these "experiments" of society, our knowledge is most incomplete. Our expectation is that the conditions of child group life and teen-age group life that are specifically engineered by society and those that are the consequences of social-political events and conditions are as significant as individual parental influences in affecting children's norms of human relationships and capacities to behave prosocially.

PERSON CHARACTERISTICS

Common sense tells us that some children are more sympathetic, helpful, and generous than other children. It is reasonable to ask why. Research on prosocial behavior, although focused on general principles of development and learning, elegantly demonstrates individual differences in its findings. Not all children are influenced by the same technique or experience and they do not develop along a single course. In turning now to person variables, some of these differences are examined.

Prosocial Behavior of Girls and Boys

In studies of children's prosocial behavior, data have been routinely reported for boys and girls. Few studies, however, have been specifically designed to investigate sex differences, that is, variables have not been systematically chosen in relation to sex-related hypotheses. Cultural expectations lead to predictions of greater sensitivity and empathy and compassion from girls than from boys. Traditional socialization pressures have emphasized competitive, assertive, brave, achieving, and nonemotional behavior from boys and men; compliant, dependent, subjective, person-rather-than-thing-oriented interests from girls and women. Likewise, childbearing and childrearing foster nurturing and caregiving behaviors in females. Also, males appear more aggressive than females—another reason to expect opposite findings on compassion and nurturance. For many reasons, then, armchair wisdom tells us that boys and girls should differ in empathy and altruism.

The question of sex differences has a number of components:

1. Are there innate differences?
2. Are similar kinds of prosocial behavior exhibited by boys and girls, and with similar likelihood?
3. Are the stimuli or circumstances that elicit prosocial behavior similar for both sexes?
4. Are there sex differences in mediating factors?
5. How are girls and boys socialized for empathy and altruism?
6. For all of these questions, what are the changes with development?

The studies reported in preceding discussions are reexamined now for sex differences. A very large number of investigations contribute to the summary presented in Table 2 in which boys and girls are compared on prosocial behaviors.

In most of the laboratory studies of sharing, there are no differences in frequency or amount of sharing by boys and girls. In a few of these studies and under some conditions, girls have shared more than boys; for other studies and other conditions, the reverse is

Table 2. Prosocial Behaviors by Boys and Girls

Sex Differences[a]	Method: Laboratory (L) or Naturalistic (N)	Authors
Comfort, Sympathy, Caregiving		
No sex differences	L	Yarrow, Scott, & Waxler, 1973
	N	Eisenberg-Berg & Hand, 1979; Zahn-Waxler, Radke-Yarrow, & King, 1979; Eisenberg-Berg & Lennon, 1980; Sawin, 1980
Girls > boys[b]	N	Friedrich & Stein, 1973; Whiting & Whiting, 1973
Boys > girls[b]	N	Marcus & Jenny, 1977
Interaction for girls[c]	L	Barrett & Yarrow, 1977 (age); Feldman, Nash & Cutrona, 1977 (age); Berman, Sloan & Goodman, 1979 (age)
	N	Hoffman, 1975a (socialization); Whiting & Whiting, 1975 (age); Sawin, 1980 (prosocial stimulus)
Interaction for boys[c]	L	Yarrow & Waxler, 1976 (personality)
	N	Hoffman, 1975a (socialization)
Help, Aid		
No sex differences	L	Stith & Connor, 1962; Staub, 1970b, 1971b; Rubin & Schneider, 1973; Yarrow, Scott, & Waxler, 1973; Krebs & Sturrup, 1974; Sprafkin, Liebert, & Poulos, 1975; Collins & Getz, 1976; Yarrow & Waxler, 1976; Chapman, 1979; Grusec, Kuczynski, Rushton, & Simutis, 1979
Girls > boys[b]	L	Hartshorne, May, & Maller, 1929; O'Bryant & Brophy, 1976; Sprafkin & Rubinstein, 1979; Shigetomi, Hartmann, Gelfand, Cohen, & Montemayor, 1979; Grusec & Redler, 1980
Boys > girls[b]	L	Ahammer & Murray, 1979
	N	Marcus & Jenny, 1977
Interaction for girls[c]	L	Hartshorne, May, & Maller, 1929 (prosocial response); Staub, 1971c (treatment conditions); Shigetomi, Hartmann, Gelfand, Cohen, & Montemayor, 1979 (prosocial response)
	N	Marcus & Jenny, 1977 (prosocial stimulus); Lewis, Lewis, & Ifekwunigue, 1978 (personality)
Interaction for boys[c]	L	Staub, 1971c (treatment conditions); Eisenberg-Berg & Mussen, 1978 (prosocial response); Ahammer & Murray, 1979 (treatment conditions)
	N	Marcus & Jenny, 1977 (prosocial stimulus)
Cooperation		
No sex differences	L	Muste & Sharpe, 1947; Madsen, 1967; Nelson & Madsen, 1969; Madsen & Shapira, 1970; Kagan & Madsen, 1971; Madsen, 1971; Miller & Thomas, 1972;

Notes: [a]It is possible for a study to be categorized in more than one place.

[b]Girls sex is more frequently prosocial than the other ($p < .05$).

[c]Interactions or interrelations of sex with other variables exist for one sex and not the other ($p < .05$). The variables that interact with sex are listed in parentheses following each study.

(*continued*)

Table 2.   (*Continued*)

Sex Differences[a]	Method: Laboratory (L) or Naturalistic (N)	Authors
Cooperation (cont'd)		
		Kagan & Madsen, 1972a; Richmond & Weiner, 1973; Madsen & Conner, 1973; McClintock, 1974; Shapira & Madsen, 1974; Levine & Hoffman, 1975; Madsen & Yi, 1975; Vance & Richmond, 1975; Bryant, 1977; DeVoe, 1977; Knight & Kagan, 1977a; Madsen & Shapira, 1977; Kagan & Knight, 1979; Silverman & Sprafkin, 1979
Girls > boys[b]	L	Sibley, Senn, & Epanchin, 1968; Kagan & Madsen, 1972b
	N	Baumrind, 1980
Boys > girls[b]	L	Wasik, Senn, & Epanchin, 1969; Shapira & Lomranz, 1972; Thomas, 1975
	N	Friedrich & Stein, 1973; Shapira & Madsen, 1974; Marcus, Telleen, & Roke, 1979
Interaction for girls[c]	L	Harford & Cutter, 1966 (race); Sibley, Senn, & Epanchin, 1968 (race); Shapira & Madsen, 1969 (culture); Mussen, Harris, Rutherford, & Keasey, 1970 (socialization/personality); Miller & Thomas, 1972 (race); Shapira & Lomranz, 1972 (social context); Kagan & Madsen, 1972a (culture); Kagan & Madsen, 1972b (culture/treatment conditions); Pepitone, 1977 (treatment conditions)
Interaction for boys[c]	L	Shapira & Madsen, 1969 (culture); Madsen & Shapira, 1970 (culture); Mussen, Harris, Rutherford, & Keasey, 1970 (socialization/personality); Kagan & Madsen, 1972a (culture); Miller & Thomas, 1972 (race); Shapira & Lomranz, 1972 (social context); Shapira & Madsen, 1974 (culture/social context); Pepitone, 1977 (treatment conditions); Knight & Kagan, 1977b (age); Crockenberg & Bryant, 1979 (treatment conditions)
Sharing		
No sex differences	L	Ugurel-Semin, 1952; Handlon & Gross, 1959; Madsen, 1967; Staub, 1968; Wasik, Senn, & Epanchin, 1969; Bryan & Walbek, 1970b; Madsen & Shapira, 1970; Fay, 1971; Grusec, 1971; M. B. Harris, 1971; Masters, 1971; Isen, Horn, & Rosenhan, 1973; Rubin & Schneider, 1973; Dlugokinski & Firestone, 1974; Emler & Rushton, 1974; Rosenhan, Underwood, & Moore, 1974; Masters & Pisarowicz, 1975; Rushton, 1975; Rushton & Owen, 1975; Rushton & Weiner, 1975; O'Bryant & Brophy, 1976; Rheingold, Hay, & West, 1976; Barnett & Andrews, 1977; Hull & Reuter, 1977; Parish, 1977; Peterson, Hartmann, & Gelfand, 1977; Underwood, Froming, & Moore, 1977; Bryant & Hansen, 1978; Grusec, Kuczynski, Rushton, & Simutis, 1978; Barnett, King, & Howard, 1979; Eisenberg-Berg & Gesheker, 1979; Grusec, Kuczynski, Rushton, & Simutis, 1979; Israely & Guttmann, 1980; Grusec & Redler, 1980; Bar-Tal, Raviv, & Leiser, 1980
	N	Yarrow & Waxler, 1976; Eisenberg-Berg & Hand, 1979

(*continued*)

Table 2.   (Continued)

Sex Differences[a]	Method: Laboratory (L) or Naturalistic (N)	Authors
Sharing (cont'd)		
Girls > boys[b]	L	Midlarsky & Bryan, 1972; Moore, Underwood, & Rosenhan, 1973; Harris & Siebel, 1975; Crockenberg, Bryant, & Wilce, 1976; Willis, Feldman, & Ruble, 1977; Knight & Kagan, 1977b; Nadler, Romek, & Shapira-Friedman, 1979
	N	Dyson-Hudson & Van Dusen, 1972
Boys > girls[b]	L	Bond & Phillips, 1971; Leiman, 1978; Shigetomi, Hartmann, Gelfand, Cohen, & Montemayor, 1979
Interaction for girls[c]	L	Rosenhan & White, 1967 (treatment conditions); Grusec & Skubiski, 1970 (treatment conditions); Elliott & Vasta, 1970 (prosocial stimulus); Midlarsky & Bryan, 1972 (personality/prosocial response); Crockenberg, Bryant & Wilce, 1976 (treatment conditions); Skarin & Moely, 1976 (treatment conditions); Barnett & Andrews, 1977 (treatment conditions)
	N	Eisenberg-Berg & Hand, 1979 (prosocial stimulus)
Interaction for boys[c]	L	Elliott & Vasta, 1970 (prosocial stimulus); Bryan & Walbek, 1970b (treatment conditions/race); Leventhal & Anderson, 1970 (treatment conditions); Staub & Sherk, 1970 (personality); Bond & Phillips, 1971 (personality); Fay, 1971 (treatment condition/age); Staub, 1971c (treatment conditions); Midlarsky & Bryan, 1972 (personality/prosocial response); Dreman & Greenbaum, 1973 (social class/treatment conditions); Rheingold, Hay, & West, 1976 (prosocial response); Skarin & Moely, 1976 (treatment conditions); Barnett & Andrews, 1977 (treatment conditions); Bryant & Hansen, 1978 (treatment conditions); Grusec, Kuczynski, Rushton, & Simutis, 1978 (treatment conditions); Nadler, Romek, & Shapira-Friedman, 1979 (social context/treatment conditions)
	N	Stanjek, 1978 (prosocial response); Eisenberg-Berg & Hand, 1979 (prosocial stimulus)
Empathy		
No sex differences	L	Borke, 1971; Fay, 1971; Leiman, 1978; Mood, Johnson, & Shantz, 1978; Marcus, Telleen, & Roke, 1979; Sawin, 1979
Girls > boys[b]	L	Borke, 1973; Levine & Hoffman, 1975; Hoffman & Levine, 1976; Eisenberg-Berg & Mussen, 1978; Ahammer & Murray, 1979; Baumrind, 1980
Boys > girls[b]	L	Eisenberg-Berg & Lennon, 1980
Interaction for girls[c]	L	Feshbach & Roe, 1968 (prosocial stimulus); Fay, 1971 (treatment condition); Roe, 1977 (culture); Sawin, 1979 (prosocial response/age)
Interaction for boys[c]	L	Feshbach & Roe, 1968 (prosocial stimulus); Fay, 1971 (treatment condition); Roe, 1977 (culture); Eisenberg-Berg & Mussen, 1978 (socialization); Barnett, Matthews, & Howard, 1979 (personality); Sawin, 1978 (prosocial response/age)

true. For example, Rosenhan and White (1967) found that girls donated more than boys while in the presence of a male model, but they gave less than boys under conditions of model absence. The conditions distinguishing donating by boys and girls may be informative regarding the meaning of the laboratory procedure for each sex. In a study of affect induction by Moore, Underwood, and Rosenhan (1973), in which girls donated more than boys, the role of the male experimenter is quite dominant: to maintain the child's continued practice of the induction procedure (i.e., "think sad [or happy] thoughts"), the experimenter sat looking at the child during this period. If girls are more sensitive to these demand characteristics, their higher rate of donating could reflect greater conformity to experimental requirements.

A review of the research on cooperative behavior of preschool-age and school-age children (Cook & Stingle, 1974) concluded that there were no consistent sex differences in frequencies of cooperative acts. This conclusion is not changed in the present evaluation. In studies of prosocial behavior in which comfort or help are the indices, there are also no clear indications of consistent sex differences. For each of these measures (cooperation, comfort, sharing, help) prosocial behaviors of boys and girls sometimes interact differently with other variables (see Table 2).

Sex differences in empathy, which is sometimes considered a prosocial response and sometimes a mediator, were also examined. A review by Hoffman (1977b) revealed that in the majority of studies of children's self-reports of their own emotions in relation to the emotions of others (affect matching) there were no statistically significant sex differences. When significant differences and nonsignificant differences in cognitive empathy were counted, girls were more empathic than boys. The present review does not change these conclusions.

In the reviews by Maccoby and Jacklin (1974) and by Underwood and Moore (1982), overall sex differences in frequencies of various kinds of observed prosocial behavior are small and not patterned. In her review of sex differences in responsiveness to the young, Berman (1980) adds a note of methodology. Most consistent support for the hypothesis that females are more responsive than males comes from self-report studies. Experiments that employ physiological measures of responsiveness generally find no sex differences; results in studies that use behavioral indices of responsiveness are mixed.

Shigetomi et al. (1979) also address a meth-

odological issue and present a significant substantive finding as well. These investigators replicated the Hartshorne et al. (1929) study of children's service behavior. In the original study, teachers' perceptions of fifth- and sixth-graders' generosity, friendliness, and helpfulness as well as an elaborate series of behavioral measures (collecting pictures for hospitalized children, working cooperatively, donating, etc.) were obtained. Correlations between composite behavior scores and reputation scores were approximately +.50. Girls behaved only slightly more altruistically than boys, but they had far better reputations than boys for altruism. The findings were very similar 50 years later. In the Shigetomi et al. (1979) study, composite behavior scores and reputation scores correlated at only +.11, with no differences by sex of child. However, as in the Hartshorne et al. (1929) study, teachers as well as peers judged girls more altruistic than boys. On behavioral measures, sex differences in favor of girls were slight. In other words, *reputation* for altruism is strongly influenced by sex of the child. There may be other factors that make girls appear to be more prosocial than boys. For example, Ahlgren and Johnson (1979) found that girls express more positive attitudes toward cooperation than boys. Zahn-Waxler, Friedman, & Cummings (in press) found that in listening to a recording of a crying infant, girls expressed significantly more verbal sympathy then boys. But when confronted with a real infant whose apparent distress they had heard (a recorded cry), girls were no more likely than boys to make prosocial interventions. Girls may manifest facial expressions and ritualized verbal expressions that are not in themselves altruistic but which cause others to see them in an altruistic light. It might be revealing to study boys' and girls' rescue and helping behaviors when the same prosocial acts are labeled differently—as bravery in one condition and as compassion in another condition.

Quite aside from issues of possible sex-linked expectations, the Hartshorne et al. (1929) and the Shigetomi et al. (1979) findings on reputations (peer or teacher ratings) raise some questions about the data base that has been used in much of prosocial research. Peer ratings of altruism (reputations) have been used as stand-ins for observed behavior. If the ratings of reputation and direct interactional measures are tapping different aspects of prosocial response, it may be necessary to reinterpret some of the present findings on prosocial development and socialization. Clearly, ratings and behavioral observations, in general, are indexing different aspects of the child (Cairns, 1979); one is not necessarily more accurate than the other, but they cannot be assumed to be interchangeable.

In summary, we would hazard the hypothesis that there are differences between boys and girls in how and when and why they perform prosocial acts and that such qualitative differences are more revealing of the nature and nurture of sex differences in prosocial behavior than are quantitative differences in frequency.

Personality Variables Relating to Prosocial Behavior

Personality theory has not figured large in research on children's prosocial behavior. Moreover, the theoretical bases for investigating particular personality dimensions in relation to prosocial behavior have not always been explicit. The range of mechanisms and psychological conditions presumed to underlie prosocial actions includes a wide diversity: ego strength, empathy, guilt, anxiety, approval seeking, cost-benefit considerations, adherence to norms, and affective states. Each of these conceptions suggests different dimensions of personality as antecedents or correlates.

Aggression has received more attention than most personality dimensions—without explicit guiding theory. Guilt over aggression and, hence, reparative or generally altruistic behavior might be one explanatory framework. Murphy (1937) reported a positive correlation in preschoolers between aggression and sympathy in nursery school children that she interpreted quite differently—as possibly reflecting an outgoing sociability underlying both aggressive and sympathetic behavior. Muste and Sharpe (1947) provided some confirmatory evidence, finding that preschoolers with the lowest frequencies of aggression had the lowest scores on social participation. These authors followed the children's prosocial and antisocial interactions to obtain more information on when and with whom the behaviors appeared:

For some children frequent aggressions are combined with a variety of other types of social responses and give a pattern of high social sensitivity and responsiveness. For such children there may be intense conflict in their own reactions and there may early appear evidence of feelings of anxiety and guilt concerning their own aggressions, e.g., in the conflicting responses of aggression and sympathy which follow each other in close succession. (p. 19)

By observing with whom the child was aggressive or altruistic, the authors attempted analyses of the origins and functions of each child's pattern of behavior. An example is a boy who was "picked on" by a handicapped older brother. When the child was with peers with whom he had secure relationships, he was frequently very aggressive, but with submissive or much smaller children, he showed little aggression and was very sympathetic and helpful. The authors made the link between the boy's own experiences in his family and his interactions with peers.

There have been other correlational studies of aggression and prosocial behavior, with variable results. Friedrich and Stein (1973) reported positive associations in preschool children. Feshbach and Feshbach (1969) found a positive relation between aggression and responses on the Feshbach and Roe (1968) test of empathy in 4- to 5-year-old boys, but not girls. For 6- to 7-year-old boys, the direction of difference was the converse of that found in the younger boys. There were no associations for girls. In an observational study of 3- to 7 ½-year-olds, Yarrow and Waxler (1976) found positive correlations for girls only. When level of social interaction was controlled, aggressive and prosocial behaviors were unrelated. It was reasoned that high frequencies of aggressive acts might indicate qualitative as well as quantitative differences in children's hostility. Accordingly, girls and boys were classified as above or below the group mean on aggression. Prosocial and aggressive acts were positively related for boys who were generally low in aggression but negatively related for highly aggressive boys. The pattern did not hold for girls, whose general level of aggression was well below that of boys. Marginal negative associations between aggressive and prosocial behavior were reported by Rutherford and Mussen (1968) and by Harris and Siebel (1975), whereas Bryant and Crockenberg (1980) reported no associations. A study by O'Connor, Dollinger, Kennedy, and Pelletier-Smetko (1979) is of special interest because it involves preadolescent emotionally disturbed boys. Negative relations between measures of sharing and parent and teacher ratings of aggression were found.

On the basis of a good deal of research evidence, it appears that a simple conclusion of a positive association between aggression and prosocial behavior is not warranted. Level of aggression, origins of aggression, and context of interaction, sex of child as well as kinds of prosocial behavior (generosity, protecting the underdog, sympathy) are among the modifiers of the magnitude and the direction of relationships.

Another broad personality domain that has been

investigated in relation to prosocial behavior and generally found to be positively related is social competence. The particular indices of competence vary: emotional stability and social adjustment were positively related to ratings of altruism in adolescent boys (Turner, 1948). Peer ratings of altruism and high ego strength were related in a study by Mussen et al. (1970). In Block's (1971) longitudinal study, significant positive relations appear between ego resiliency and children's helpful, cooperative, and considerate behaviors. Moreover, ego strength at age 4 predicted generosity at age 5. Positive traits, such as social responsibility, affiliativeness, and emotional stability, were related to various prosocial indices in studies by Bond and Phillips (1971), Hampson (1979), and Midlarsky & Bryan (1972).

Assertive and expressive children were found to have the higher scores on prosocial indices in studies by Aronfreed (1968), Barrett and Yarrow (1977), Lenrow (1965), and Staub (1971a). In the Barrett and Yarrow (1977) study, children's level of inferential ability mediated the relation between assertiveness and prosocial behavior. Children 6 to 8 years old were classified as high or low in inferential ability based on interpretations of videotaped social interaction episodes. Assertiveness and prosocial behavior were significantly positively related for children with high inferential ability but not for those with low inferential ability.

Lorr, More, and Harnett (1980) proceeded very differently to try to identify personality variables predisposing children to behave prosocially. Junior and senior high school students were given an inventory of items intended to tap personality attributes and also to assess prosocial and antisocial inclinations. Among the best predictors of the self-reports of prosocial behavior were self-assessments of conscientiousness, approval seeking, responsibility, independence, and guilt.

Findings do not always link a confident personality with prosocial behavior. Cox (1974) found no association between Loevinger's (1970) measure of ego development and a behavioral measure of helping. Teacher ratings of kindergarten girls' competence and the girls' helping behavior were negatively related (Staub, 1971a). In Hartup and Keller's (1960) study of preschool children, seeking help and nurturance was positively associated with giving nurturance to peers. In emotionally disturbed boys, O'Connor et al. (1979) found that the more anxious, inhibited, and sensitive boys were the more prosocial.

In summary, associations between personality variables and a multidetermined class of prosocial behaviors have been explored. Out of these explorations emerges a pattern of modest relationships between a broad band of positive, outgoing, and socially competent behaviors and the narrower band of prosocial behaviors that are also positive and outgoing. However, contradictory personality findings require equal consideration. In some studies, anxiety, inhibition, aggression, and guilt have also been linked with empathy and altruism—evidence of varied motivations underlying helping, sharing, and prosocial behavior. Not only may the altruism of different children be differently motivated but also the same children may be differently motivated under different circumstances. Personality studies have not been in-depth investigations. As a result, there is little information about the etiologies and functional significance of prosocial behaviors of various kinds. The predominant emphasis has been a search for universal relationships.

Affective State

There has been little exploration of temperament and long-term mood states in research on altruism, yet it seems highly likely that predisposing factors lie in the "toughmindedness" or "tendermindedness" of the individual and in the predominantly happy, depressed, or angry mood states characteristic of the person. One naturalistic study of normal preschool children is a beginning in this direction. Strayer (1980) observed children over an 8-week period of time, recording their affective displays in play with other children. Angry, sad, hurt, and happy expressions were noted, as were the children's empathic interventions. Significant rank-order correlations were found between persisting affective state (expressed in frequencies) and frequency of empathic behavior. Children who ranked high in incidence of happy emotions also ranked high in empathic behavior toward peers, whereas children who ranked high on expressed sad emotions ranked low in empathy. Probably one can interpret these "happy" and "sad" frequencies as expressions of normal mood differences among children. It would be an important extension of this study to investigate how such enduring moods interact with momentary emotional states in influencing the child's responding in a prosocial opportunity: Is it in happy moments in the sad child's life that she is likely to respond with empathy? Is it happy (or sad) momentary states, regardless of the predominant persisting mood, that are the releasers or inhibitors of empathic behavior?

There has been vigorous research activity in relation to the effects of momentary affective states on children's prosocial responses. Momentary mood has been experimentally induced in a number of ways. In one group of experiments, in which success and failure on a game were manipulated, the findings were inconclusive, but they favored success. In Staub's (1968) study, fourth graders shared more candy after failure, but fifth graders shared marginally more after success. In the studies by Isen, Horn, and Rosenhan (1973), success brought more donating in one sample; in a second sample, children in success and failure conditions did not differ in donating but both shared more than children in a control condition. Barnett and Bryan (1974) and Rushton and Littlefield (1979) reported more donating after success than after failure.

Affective states have also been induced by asking the child to think or talk about happy or sad experiences; then, the child is given an opportunity to share or help. Moore et al. (1973) asked second and third graders to take part in a test that was described to them as helping the adult. They received 25 pennies for helping and were also told about other children, with whom they might share, who would not be able to participate. The children were assigned to one of two conditions in which they were asked to think about sad or happy experiences for 30 sec. or they were assigned to a neutral condition. There was a linear increase in amount of contributions from children in the sad affect condition to the control condition to the happy affect condition. Underwood et al. (1977) replicated this study with first through fifth graders and found the same linear trends. In three other studies, however, the findings were not replicated. Rosenhan, Underwood, and Moore (1974) found that children in the positive affect condition shared more than children in the control condition but that children in the negative affect condition were not different from controls. Harris and Siebel (1975) reported no significant differences in amount of donations related to affect. Cialdini and Kenrick (1976) compared negative or neutral affective states in children 6 to 8, 10 to 12, 15 to 18 years of age. Only in the oldest group, were there differences related to affect. Children with negative affect were significantly more generous than children with neutral affect.

The inconsistencies in results stimulated analysis of the procedures being employed. Barnett, King, and Howard (1979) introduced an important refinement by controlling the source of the affect, namely, whether the children's happy, sad, or neutral thoughts were about themselves or about another child. Donating behavior varied as a function of the source of the affect. Children (second through sixth graders) whose sad events had occurred to themselves were significantly less generous than children whose distressing events related to someone else. They were also less generous than children who thought of positive events. Children whose thoughts had been directed to another person's distress were more generous than children who had been thinking about happy experiences.

The findings of Barnett et al. were replicated by Thompson, Cowan, and Rosenhan (1980) with adult subjects. Here, too, sad affect that was focused on the experiences of the other person enhanced helping behavior. These findings are consistent with an interpretation of altruism mediated by empathy. As Thompson et al. suggest, the distinction in focus of affect begins to reconcile some of the inconsistencies in the literature on the effects of temporary mood. It is especially interesting to note the compatibility of the findings of Barnett et al. with the literature reviewed earlier on the positive effects on altruism of parents' use of other-oriented discipline. When the parent focuses the child's attention on the distress that his misdeed has caused another person, one can assume that the child's momentary affective state is altered and he is brought to experience vicariously the sadness or pain of the other person. This concordance in the findings from different research sources is encouraging.

The relation between altruism and momentary mood must be placed in the broader framework of personality. Particularly relevant are the characteristic or chronic affective states of the individual as moderators of behavior involving the needs of others. Thus far the experimental data on temporary affect are based on a very limited band of prosocial behaviors. It will be important to extend these studies to a range of prosocial actions that make differing demands on the respondent. This area of study brings long-overdue attention to the role of children's affective lives in their social behavior and development.

Consistency and Continuity

The hypothesis in sociobiology that altruism is innate implies some degree of generality in this behavior. Likewise, socialization theories that view social norms or parental practices as major underpinnings of the child's prosocial behavior project general tendencies that become part of the child's makeup. On the other hand, situational specificity in prosocial behavior has been stressed, especially by social psychologists. It is beyond the scope of this review to discuss the many issues regarding consistency and continuity in personality. Complexities of concepts and difficulties in measurement have received much attention (e.g., Bem & Allen, 1974; Block, 1977; Brim & Kagan [eds.], 1980; Epstein, 1979; Gergen, Gergen, & Meter, 1972; Mischel, 1969; Olweus, 1980a). In these studies, evidence is offered of specificity and of generality of behavioral characteristics. The same arguments are extended to children's prosocial actions—whether altruistic behavior is governed by situational and momentary factors or is a broad-based behavioral tendency. Research in this vein has led not so much to the triumph of one or the other position as it has given impetus to explorations of new perspectives concerning consistency. From the lives around us, we know that there are impressive constancies as well as unpredictabilities in individuals. We know this to be the case with prosocial behavior. To try to establish a generalization regarding the degree of consistency in prosocial responding seems to engage us in games that we win or lose depending on how we play them (with what methods, research subjects, and analyses).

One might better proceed to ask questions about consistency and inconsistency in the individual's prosocial behavior from a range of perspectives. Most simply, one can examine the degree of concordant responding in two, three, or n different situations or the comparability of rates of prosocial responding across time. Consistency can better be viewed in terms of the form or quality of the prosocial response, the kinds of stimuli that regularly elicit prosocial actions, and the principles or conditions that underlie responding.

Knowing that one child has shared her pennies with a classmate, whereas her companion has not, may or may not help us in predicting which of these children will come to the rescue of a frightened puppy. If we are given information that our first hypothetical child has almost always responded prosocially in many opportunities to share, help, comfort, and so on, whereas her classmate has only rarely intervened prosocially, we are probably in a stronger position to predict their prosocial actions on yet another opportunity. By this illustration, we are but confirming that children vary in their consistency and that essential questions for research concern the determinants of these individual differences.

Children in all their variety provide the best starting points for formulating such questions. There are children who have been socialized into highly principled orientations for whom social rules, religious commandments, and ethical (or unethical) codes have high salience in their lives. There are children

without standards who have been taught or have learned to live by expediencies. Children develop intense and sometimes conflicting loyalties that may dictate quite different altruistic behaviors for family, friends, clan, and so on. The children who are William James's "tenderminded" ones are probably those easily and generally empathically aroused. Predictions on the nature of consistency of prosocial behavior by these children would no doubt vary.

In existing studies of consistency, investigators have concentrated on issues of concordance in rates or ratings of prosocial responding across situations. A child is consistent if he shares on each of the tested occasions. Sometimes one class of prosocial actions is compared across situations or in response to different stimuli. Also composites of prosocial responses are compared with composites in other settings or at a later time.

What follows is an inventory of findings on the level of associations found in these kinds of comparisons: In many (mostly laboratory) investigations comparing prosocial responses on one task or occasion with responses on another, significant positive associations are in the low to moderate range ($+.20$ to $+.40$) (Ahammer & Murray, 1979; Dlugokinski & Firestone, 1973, 1974; Dyson-Hudson & Van Dusen, 1972; Eisenberg-Berg & Lennon, 1980; Green & Schneider, 1974; Hartshorne et al., 1929; Krebs & Sturrup, 1974; Marcus et al., 1979; Midlarsky & Bryan, 1972; Mussen et al., 1970; O'Connor et al., 1979; Rubin & Schneider, 1973; Rushton & Wiener, 1975; Rutherford & Mussen, 1968; Staub, 1971c; Yarrow & Waxler, 1976). In a few studies, there has been almost no consistency across measures (Bryant & Crockenberg, 1980; Eisenberg-Berg & Hand, 1979; Grusec, Kuczynski, Rushton, & Simutis, 1978; Strayer, 1980; Weissbrod, 1976). In a study by Bar-Tal & Raviv (1979), moderate and significant negative associations were obtained between volunteering to help needy children (the measure most frequently used in studies of sharing) and four measures of helping. When the form of prosocial behavior and the measurement setting have been quite similar, correlations tend to be higher, for example, sharing of candies and sharing of pennies by 5- to 7-year-olds correlated $+.65$ (Elliott & Vasta, 1970); two measures of volunteering correlated $+.70$ (Bar-Tal & Raviv, 1979), and various forms of cooperation in preschool children related $+.63$ in a study by Ahammer and Murray (1979).

A number of investigators have used composite measures of prosocial responses (Dlugokinski & Firestone, 1973; Krebs & Sturrup, 1974; Yarrow & Waxler, 1976). Generally, the correlations are higher between composite measures than between single-item measures. In the original Hartshorne et al. (1929) research on service and self-control, the average correlations between specific prosocial tasks were in the +.30s—findings that have been of tremendous influence, cited repeatedly as evidence for specificity of prosocial behaviors. When the specific behavioral measures in the Hartshorne et al. studies were combined into a composite score and compared with teachers' ratings of children's altruism, the correlation was +.61 (Rushton, 1980). Supporting this finding are data from a number of naturalistic studies. In these studies, composites of prosocial interactions were based on observations of children extending over weeks or months: Strayer et al. (1979) found correlations in the +.50s and +.60s between different types of prosocial behavior (sharing, helping, cooperation, etc.). Friedrich and Stein (1973) found a correlation of +.54 between cooperation and nurturance for boys but a positive, nonsignificant relation for girls. Zahn-Waxler et al. (1979) reported a correlation of +.55 between a composite of children's prosocial responses following distress they had caused and a composite of prosocial reactions when they were bystanders to others' distress that they had not caused. In Murphy's (1937) yearlong assessments of preschool children, sympathy and cooperation were highly related (+.79). In Whiting and Whiting's cross-cultural study (1975), the correlation between children's caretaking of other children and other measures of their altruism was +.82.

There have been a few longitudinal or follow-up studies of children's prosocial behavior. The Blocks (described in Mussen & Eisenberg-Berg, 1977) found that the 5-year-olds who were generous on a test of sharing had been rated by teachers the year before as generous, cooperative, empathic, dependable, considerate, responsible, and helpful. Baumrind (described in Mussen & Eisenberg-Berg, 1977) reported stability between assessments of social responsibility made in the nursery school and assessments made five to six years later (+.60 for boys; +.36 for girls). In the study by Radke-Yarrow, Zahn-Waxler, Cummings, Strope and Sebris (1981), consistent themes of prosocial responding at 2 and at 7 years characterized the altruism of two thirds of the children.

Although informative to a degree, this catalogue of associations does not answer many of the questions posed at the beginning of this discussion. It is well established in personality research that there are extreme variations in individual consistency and continuity (Block, 1971)—a fact that reminds us that group averages and correlations fail us in many respects. From the research reviewed on the relation of cognition, affect, socialization, and personality to prosocial development, one should expect variations in degree and pattern of behavioral consistency in different children and at different times in development. Research on consistency and continuity needs now to be directed to identifying the conditions and experiences that shape the generality and selectivity of children's prosocial behavior at a given time in development and that determine continuity and change in this behavior over the course of development.

CONCLUSIONS

There is an assumption that maturing capacities and socialization experiences significantly influence the nature of children's prosocial behavior regardless of whatever innate readiness there may be for acting on behalf of another. The objective of behavioral research is the explication of these developmental and learning influences. In looking back over the literature that has been reviewed, to summarize where the field is and along which routes it is progressing, it may be illuminating to take into consideration not only the body of cumulative knowledge but the *process* of research as well.

Research process refers to factors in the discipline and in society that influence the directions of inquiry, the course that new investigators are likely to follow, and the ways in which research questions, procedures, and analyses are structured. It is zeitgeist, fashion, dogma, science. Two decades ago, research on prosocial behavior was very much a matter of a "new" variable slipping uncertainly into the predominant activities of the discipline—social learning theory, laboratory designs, rate measures, and, later, cognitive developmental theory. Prosocial research was more influenced by, than influencing, the discipline. The prosocial data themselves had little basic impact on conceptions of children or of child development. The research then and in years following has had a strong imprint of Western 20th-century philosophy and culture. This is evident in the operations by which prosocial behavior has been indexed (e.g., material exchange, impersonal charity) and in the individualistic theories and analytic orientations applied to prosocial development and behavior.

In the preceding review, we have seen how research has filled in many of the questions posed within the frameworks of social learning theory and social-cognitive development. We have seen how the findings and also the inconsistencies in the findings have pressed for change: New issues have grown out of the research. Certain questions have remained unsolved. Changing interests, theories, and methods in the discipline have resulted in a good deal of rethinking of issues. By 1983, although research generally continued in earlier molds, diverse theoretical formulations and methodologies were being articulated and wide-ranging questions were being posed.

Perhaps the most important general change in perspectives has been the inclusion of empathy and altruism in the conception of the child. This changed view comes about at the insistence of the prosocial data themselves, which have demonstrated that sharing, cooperating, helping, feeling empathy, and caring for others are as much a part of children's behavioral repertoires as are other kinds of social interactions. An investigative view now attaches to these behaviors, with awareness of the multidetermined nature of children's overt prosocial behavior and the varied motives that can be served by such actions. In principle (although less in practice), there has been growing recognition that prosocial behavior cannot be dealt with as one undifferentiated class of behaviors. Studies of prosocial behavior have become an integral part of research on social and emotional development at a time when social development and the direct observation of children's social interactions have become major research interests in developmental psychology.

Changed perspectives are also evident concerning relationships between cognition and prosocial conduct. For a long time, research was focused on *levels* of cognitive ability—in perspective taking, role taking, and moral reasoning—in relation to prosocial behavior. Certain levels of abilities were viewed as gatekeepers or prerequisites for children's empathy, sympathy, and helping. This position has become less firm or defensible. Because, after many studies, processes linking cognition and prosocial behavior have not been impressively clarified, theoretical and methodological redirection has been urged by a number of writers. As Kurdek (1978a) has pointed out in his review, conceptual cleanup and specification could change problem formulations and the nature of the findings. A search for *a* necessary cognitive level for prosocial behavior has begun to give way to more sophisticated orientations. As one example, the developmental theory offered by Hoffman (1975b; described earlier) begins to articulate some of the changing cognitive

involvements and requirements in different empathic and prosocial reactions at different developmental levels. Likewise, at any age level, different cognitive involvements would be expected for different types of prosocial behaviors (e.g., contrast responding to the anguish of seeing a child who has been hit by a car with responding to a peer's request for equal time with a toy).

In a view that is shared by other investigators, Aronfreed (1976) has expressed concern about the research procedures that have predominated in this area of study. He comments that young children sometimes show understanding not only of

> the consequences of their actions, but also their obligations to particular other people, and even of the relevance of their intentions—when these components are being considered with respect to their own concrete actions, rather than from the perspective of the more hypothetical and abstract situations that Piaget (1932) and others have posed to them. (p. 63)

The increased attention to affective processes is evident also with regard to prosocial behavior. Aronfreed (1970), Dienstbier et al. (1975), Feshbach (1974), Hoffman (1975b), and others have emphasized the conjoint influences of affective and cognitive mechanisms on the child's prosocial actions. Their formulations stress the importance of affective orientations acquired in early socialization experiences and also the interaction of affect with changing cognitive capabilities and content. Although these formulations are mainly descriptive at this time, they provide direction to research on mediators of prosocial behavior.

In at least one other major regard, research perspectives on prosocial development have changed since the 1960s. This is with respect to socialization influences. There is increasing appreciation of the configurations of rearing factors affecting the child's behavior and of the need to deal with the complex of techniques and conditions rather than with single variables (Baumrind, 1980; Block, 1976; Bryant & Crockenberg, 1980; Cairns, 1979; Dlugokinski & Firestone, 1974; Mussen, 1977; Yarrow et al., 1973).

None, or almost none, of the perspectives described was present to any extent in research discussions of prosocial behavior a decade and a half ago. In this sense, change in the field is considerable. It remains, however, an area of research in which theoretical development is needed and in which there are discrepancies between the perspectives and the paradigms and procedures in practiced research. Research craft has often prevailed over theoretical and conceptual considerations.

One of the most serious limitations in research on children's prosocial behavior is a problem referred to earlier—namely, how prosocial behavior has been indexed in empirical investigations. There has been a tendency to lose sight of the phenomenon. The concept of prosocial behavior embraces behaviors that differ enormously in the psychological processes, properties, and capacities that are involved. The overt behaviors are of many kinds: sharing of goods or opportunities, participating in cooperative endeavors, giving help in relation to objects, giving help in rescuing or protecting a dependent or endangered person, giving sympathy and comfort. These behaviors can also be graded in intensity, benefit, degree of sacrifice (e.g., from picking up paper clips to searching the park for a lost child). They can be differentiated in terms of underlying motives (e.g., love, fear, duty, personal gain). If this is an approximation of the domain, it is apparent that a very narrow band of actions has been manipulated or observed in research. Many of the indices are trivial, without reality in children's experiences with others, and generally without appreciable affective or serious dimensions. Rarely is prosocial behavior evaluated in terms other than frequency. The in vivo successive experiences of encountering need or distress in someone, of having feelings aroused, of interacting with the person or animal in need, of deciding on a solution through some action, and of experiencing the consequences of the prosocial actions are not often investigated intact, either in natural or standard situations.

Concern about the kinds of procedures on which developmental psychologists rely in investigating children's social development is not new. A. Baldwin (1967) is an early critic who described developmental researchers as building a "mythology of childhood" in which effects obtained in laboratory settings are assumed to provide accurate accounts of processes by which the child is socialized. Mussen (1977) criticized the experimental model as it has been used in studying children's prosocial behavior for violating the natural complexity of the phenomenon, defining relevant dimensions in artificial ways, and excluding from consideration many essential issues, such as the interaction of donor and recipient. Baumrind (1980) rejects the manner in

which a complex psychological concept is reduced to "manageable but miniscule proportions, as though it were exhausted by the trivial operations by which it is measured" (p. 646).

To build on the already considerable research evidence on children's prosocial development and to contribute information that is vital and significant for understanding and helping children, a number of research directions seem to be particularly deserving of attention in future investigation:

1. There is need for descriptive data on the kinds of prosocial behavior that children actually manifest, the circumstances in which prosocial behavior occurs, to whom it is directed, how help and generosity are sought, and the interactions that take place between the giver and receiver. Descriptive information on children throughout childhood is in short supply. Such data would have three valuable benefits:

They would provide hypothesis generating data on which systematic studies could build.

They could be the basis for interviewing children in the clinical model of early Piagetian interviews. From this we would learn about children's thinking, feelings, and reasoning relating to others' needs and about their own motivations for, or resistance to, responding prosocially.

They would prevent errors of the kind that settle into the literature from unsubstantiated extrapolations downward in age from adult social psychological models and from an uncritical view of development as evolving into more and better altruism (see Gottman & Parkhurst, 1980).

A call for more descriptive data is not a minimization of the importance of theory.

2. The separate study of learning, cognition, and affect was perhaps necessary before an integrative theory or approach was possible. Beyond a point, however, the separate approach is subject to diminished returns; further progress depends on relating these several domains to each other.

3. There is a body of rich data on childrearing variables in relation to prosocial behavior. The value of configural analyses—that is, analyses of patterns of variables—has been documented repeatedly in the reviewed studies. This approach needs to be developed further.

4. More often than not in research, we learn

about the child's reputation as considerate or inconsiderate, as cooperative or uncooperative, or her status on a test of prosocial behavior. We do not learn how prosocial responding is rooted in the child's personality and personal-life experiences. There is need for truly developmental studies and for systematic clinical investigations of prosocial behavior and personality with attention not only to the development and functions of prosocial behavior but to the converse as well, that is, to the failure of development of empathy and positive social responses (Feshbach & Feshbach, 1969).

5. Research on children's altruism has an overriding orientation of "self-contained individualism" (Sampson, 1977) that is apparent in the theoretical perspectives, the procedures, and the analytic categories of the field. Authors at the end of the 1970s (Mussen & Eisenberg-Berg, 1977; Staub, 1979; Rushton, 1980) concluded their books on a note of social concern, resting the quality of life and the welfare of present and future generations on children's learning of other-oriented positive social relationships. Although they placed major responsibility on the individual child's altruism, each author pointed to the strong influences of society and culture as well. It will be difficult but essential to incorporate into research the considerable interdependencies between the individual and the larger societal units and systems in which the child functions.

This review has been confined mainly to research within the domain of developmental psychology. Across a broader range of disciplines, there are widely variant frameworks regarding altruism—in biological, cross-species, and evolutionary terms. Later reviews of children's prosocial behavior may well benefit from investigations that will include these broader orientations. The present period in developmental research is one in which there is high interest in children's social development and social interactions. Such attention is bound to broaden inquiry and provide a firmer base of evidence, all of which augurs well for future research and understanding of prosocial behavior in children.

REFERENCES

Adams, G. R., Schvaneveldt, J. D., & Jenson, G. O. Sex, age and perceived competency as correlates of empathic ability in adolescence. *Adolescence,* 1979, *14,* 811–818.

Ahammer, I. M., & Murray, J. P. Kindness in the kindergarten: The relative influence of role playing and prosocial television in facilitating altru-

ism. *International Journal of Behavioral Development,* 1979, *2,* 133–157.

Ahlgren, A., & Johnson, D. W. Sex differences in cooperative and competitive attitudes from the 2nd through the 12th grades. *Developmental Psychology,* 1979, *15,* 45–49.

Antipoff, H. Observations on compassion and a sense of justice in the child. *Archives de Psychologie,* 1928, *21,* 208–214.

Aquinas, St. Thomas. *Summa theologica.* In R. M. Hutchins (Ed.), *Great books of the Western world* (Vol. 20). Chicago: Encyclopaedia Britannica, 1952.

Ardrey, R. *The territorial imperative.* New York: Atheneum, 1966.

Aristotle. *Nicomachean ethics.* In R. M. Hutchins (Ed.), *Great books of the Western world* (Vol 9). Chicago: Encyclopaedia Britannica, 1952.

Arlitt, A. *Psychology of infancy to early childhood.* New York: McGraw-Hill, 1928.

Aronfreed, J. *Conduct and conscience.* New York: Academic Press, 1968.

Aronfreed, J. The socialization of altruistic and sympathetic behavior: Some theoretical and experimental analyses. In J. R. Macaulay & L. Berkowitz (Eds.), *Altruism and helping behavior.* New York: Academic Press, 1970.

Aronfreed, J. Moral development from the standpoint of a general psychological theory. In T. Lickona (Ed.), *Moral development and behavior: Theory, research, and social issues.* New York: Holt, Rinehart & Winston, 1976.

Ascione, F. R., & Bueche, N. *The effects of peer modeling and praise on children's donating to charity.* Paper presented at the meeting of the Rocky Mountain Psychological Association, Albuquerque, N. Mex., May 1977.

Avellar, J., & Kagan, S. Development of competitive behaviors in Anglo-American and Mexican-American children. *Psychological Reports,* 1976, *39,* 191–198.

Baldwin, A. *Theories of child development.* New York: Wiley, 1967.

Baldwin, C. P., & Baldwin, A. L. Children's judgments of kindness. *Child Development,* 1970, *41,* 29–47.

Baldwin, J. M. *Social and ethical interpretations in mental development: A study in social psychology.* New York: Macmillan, 1897.

Bandura, A. *Social learning theory.* Englewood Cliffs, N.J.: Prentice-Hall, 1977.

Bandura, A., & Walters, R. H. *Social learning and personality development.* New York: Holt, Rinehart & Winston, 1963.

Barash, D. P. *Sociobiology and behavior*. New York: Elsevier, 1977.

Barker, R. *Ecological psychology*. Stanford, Calif.: Stanford University Press, 1968.

Barnes, K. E. Preschool play norms: A replication. *Developmental Psychology*, 1971, *5*, 99–103.

Barnett, M. A., & Andrews, J. A. Sex differences in children's reward allocation under competitive and cooperative instructional sets. *Developmental Psychology*, 1977, *13*, 85–86.

Barnett, M. A., & Bryan, J. H. Effects of competition with outcome feedback on children's helping behavior. *Developmental Psychology*, 1974, *10*, 838–842.

Barnett, M. A., King, L. M., & Howard, J. A. Inducing affect about self or other: Effects on generosity in children. *Developmental Psychology*, 1979, *15*, 164–167.

Barnett, M. A., Matthews, K. A., & Howard, J. A. Relationship between competitiveness and empathy in 6- and 7-year-olds. *Developmental Psychology*, 1979, *15*, 221–222.

Barrett, D. E., & Yarrow, M. R. Prosocial behavior, social inferential ability, and assertiveness in children. *Child Development*, 1977, *48*, 475–481.

Barry, H., Bacon, M. K., & Child, I. L. A cross-cultural survey of some sex differences in socialization. *Journal of Abnormal and Social Psychology*, 1957, *55*, 327–332.

Bar-Tal, D. *Prosocial behavior: Theory and research*. New York: Wiley, 1976.

Bar-Tal, D., & Raviv, A. Consistency of helping-behavior measures. *Child Development*, 1979, *50*, 1235–1238.

Bar-Tal, D., Raviv, A., & Leiser, T. The development of altruistic behavior: Empirical evidence. *Developmental Psychology*, 1980, *16*, 516–524.

Bar-Tal, D., Raviv, A., & Shavit, N. *Motives for helping behavior expressed by kindergarten and school children in kibbutz and city*. Unpublished manuscript, 1980.

Bathurst, J. E. A study of sympathy and resistance (negativism) among children. *Psychological Bulletin*, 1933, *30*, 625–626.

Baumrind, D. Current patterns of parental authority. *Developmental Psychology Monograph*, 1971, *4*(1, Pt. 2).

Baumrind, D. Parental disciplinary patterns and social competence in children. *Youth and Society*, 1978, *9*, 239–276.

Baumrind, D. Reciprocity in the development of prosocial behavior. In J. L. Tapp, *Children's rights and the development of social responsibil-ity*. Symposium presented at the meeting of the American Psychological Association, New York, September 1979.

Baumrind, D. New directions in socialization research. *American Psychologist*, 1980, *35*, 639–652.

Bem, D. J., & Allen, A. On predicting some of the people some of the time: The search for cross-situational consistencies in behavior. *Psychological Review*, 1974, *81*, 506–520.

Berkowitz, L. A laboratory investigation of social class and national differences in helping behavior. *International Journal of Psychology*, 1966, *1*, 231–242.

Berkowitz, L., & Friedman, P. Some social class differences in helping behavior. *Journal of Personality and Social Psychology*, 1967, *5*, 217–225.

Berman, P. W. Are women predisposed to parenting? Developmental and situational determinants of sex differences in responsiveness to the young. *Psychological Bulletin*, 1980, *88*, 668–695.

Berman, P. W., Sloan, V. L., & Goodman, V. *Development of sex differences in response to an infant and to the caretaker role*. Paper presented at the meeting of the Society for Research in Child Development, San Francisco, March 1979.

Berndt, T. J. Effects of friendship on prosocial intentions and behavior. *Child Development*, 1981, *52*, 636–643.

Berne, E. An experimental investigation of social behavior patterns in young children. *University of Iowa Studies in Child Welfare*, 1930, *4* (No. 3).

Bethlehem, D. W. Cooperation, competition and altruism among schoolchildren in Zambia. *International Journal of Psychology*, 1973, *8*, 125–135.

Biron, A., Ramos, F., & Higa, W. R. Cooperation in children: Social and material rewards. *Psychological Reports*, 1977, *41*, 427–430.

Bizman, A., Yinon, Y., Mivtzari, E., & Shavit, R. Effects of the age structure of the kindergarten on altruistic behavior. *Journal of School Psychology*, 1978, *16*, 154–160.

Blanton, M. G. The behavior of the human infant during the first thirty days of life. *Psychological Review*, 1917, *24*, 456–483.

Blasi, A. Bridging moral cognition and moral action: A critical review of the literature. *Psychological Bulletin*, 1980, *88*, 1–45.

Block, J. *Lives through time*. Berkeley, Calif.:

Bancroft Books, 1971

Block, J. Recognizing the coherence of personality. In D. Magnusson & N. S. Endler (Eds.), *Personality at the crossroads: Current issues in interactional psychology*. Hillsdale, N.J.: Erlbaum, 1977.

Block, J. H. *Familial and environmental factors associated with the development of affective disorders in young children*. Paper presented at the National Institute of Mental Health Conference on Mood and Related Affective States, Washington, D.C., November 1976.

Block, J. H. *The child rearing practices report*, Berkeley: Institute of Human Development, University of California, 1965.

Block, J. H., Haan, N., & Smith, M. B. Socialization correlates of student activism. *Journal of Social Issues*, 1969, *25*, 143–178.

Bond, N. D., & Phillips, B. N. Personality traits associated with altruistic behavior of children. *Journal of School Psychology*, 1971, *9*, 24–34.

Borke, H. Interpersonal perception of young children: Egocentrism or empathy? *Developmental Psychology*, 1971, *5*, 263–269.

Borke, H. The development of empathy in Chinese and American children between three and six years of age: A cross-cultural study. *Developmental Psychology*, 1973, *9*, 102–108.

Bretherton, I., McNew, S., & Beeghly-Smith, M. Early person knowledge as expressed in gestural and verbal communications: When do infants acquire a ''theory of mind''? In M. E. Lamb & L. R. Sherrod (Eds.), *Infant social cognition*. Hillsdale, N.J.: Erlbaum, 1981.

Bridges, K. B. *The social and emotional development of the preschool child*. London: Kegan Paul, 1931.

Bridges, K. M. B. Emotional development in early infancy. *Child Development*, 1932, *3*, 324–341.

Brim, O. G., Jr., & Kagan, J. (Eds.). *Constancy and change in human development*. Cambridge: Harvard University Press, 1980.

Bronfenbrenner, U. The role of age, sex, class, and culture in studies of moral development. *Religious Education Research Supplement*, 1962, *57*, 3–17.

Bronfenbrenner, U. *The ecology of human development*. Cambridge: Harvard University Press, 1979.

Bryan, J. H. Children's reactions to helpers: Their money isn't where their mouths are. In J. R. Macaulay & L. Berkowitz (Eds.), *Altruism and helping behavior*. New York: Academic Press, 1970.

Bryan, J. H. Children's cooperation and helping behaviors. In E. M. Hetherington (Ed.), *Review of child development research* (Vol. 5). Chicago: University of Chicago Press, 1975.

Bryan, J. H., & London, P. Altruistic behavior by children. *Psychological Bulletin*, 1970, *73*, 200–211.

Bryan, J. H., & Walbek, N. H. The impact of words and deeds concerning altruism upon children. *Child Development*, 1970, *41*, 747–757. (a)

Bryan, J. H., & Walbek, N. H. Preaching and practicing generosity: Children's actions and reactions. *Child Development*, 1970, *41*, 329–353. (b)

Bryant, B. K., & Crockenberg, S. B. Correlates and dimensions of prosocial behavior: A study of female siblings with their mothers. *Child Development*, 1980, *51*, 529–544.

Bryant, B. K., & Hansen, B. K. The interpersonal context of success: Differing consequences of independent and dependent success on sharing behavior among boys and girls. *Representative Research in Social Psychology*, 1978, *9*, 103–113.

Buckley, N., Siegel, L. S., & Ness, S. Egocentrism, empathy, and altruistic behavior in young children. *Developmental Psychology*, 1979, *15*, 329–330.

Bühler, C. *The first year of life*. New York: John Day, 1930.

Bühler, C., & Hetzer, H. Das erste Verstandnis fur Ausdruck im ersten Lebensjahr. *Zeitschrift für Psychologie*, 1928, *107*, 50–61.

Burton, R. V. Honesty and dishonesty. In T. Lickona (Ed.), *Moral development and behavior: Theory, research, and social issues*. New York: Holt, Rinehart & Winston, 1976.

Cairns, R. B. Sociobiology: A new synthesis or an old cleavage? (Review of *Sociobiology: The new synthesis* by E. O. Wilson.) *Contemporary Psychology*, 1977, *22*, 1–3.

Cairns, R. B. *Social development: The origins and plasticity of interchanges*. San Francisco: W. H. Freeman, 1979.

Campbell, D. T. Ethnocentric and other altruistic motives. In D. Levine (Ed.), *Nebraska Symposium on Motivation* (Vol. 13). Lincoln: University of Nebraska Press, 1965.

Chan, W. *A source book in Chinese philosophy*. Princeton, N.J.: Princeton University Press, 1963.

Chandler, M., & Greenspan, S. Ersatz egocentrism: A reply to Borke. *Developmental Psychology*, 1972, *7*, 104–106.

Chapman, M. Listening to reason: Children's attentiveness and parental discipline. *Merrill-Palmer Quarterly*, 1979, *25*, 251–263.

Cialdini, R. B., & Kenrick, D. T. Altruism as hedonism: A social development perspective on the relationship of negative mood state and helping. *Journal of Personality and Social Psychology*, 1976, *34*, 907–914.

Coates, B., Pusser, H. E., & Goodman, I. The influence of "Sesame Street" and "Mister Rogers' Neighborhood" on children's social behavior in the preschool. *Child Development*, 1976, *47*, 138–144.

Cohen, T. B. Observations on school children in the Peoples' Republic of China. *Journal of the American Academy of Child Psychiatry*, 1977, *16*, 165–173.

Collins, W. A., & Getz, S. K. Children's social responses following modeled reactions to provocation: Prosocial effects of a television drama. *Journal of Personality*, 1976, *44*, 488–500.

Comte, A. *A system of positive polity*. New York: B. Franklin, 1968. (Originally published, 1875.)

Cook, H., & Stingle, S. Cooperative behavior in children. *Psychological Bulletin*, 1974, *81*, 918–933.

Cosgrove, J. M., & McIntyre, C. W. The impact of prosocial television on young children's behavior: The influence of "Mister Rogers' Neighborhood." *Southeastern Review*, 1977, *3*, 26–29.

Cox, N. Prior help, ego development, and helping behavior. *Child Development*, 1974, *45*, 594–604.

Crockenberg, S. B., & Bryant, B. K. Socialization: The "implicit curriculum" of learning environments. *Journal of Research and Development in Education*, 1978, *12*, 69–78.

Crockenberg, S. B., & Bryant, B. K. Individualized learning environments: Intra- and interpersonal consequences. *Journal of School Psychology*, 1979, *17*, 17–26.

Crockenberg, S. B., Bryant, B. K., & Wilce, L. S. The effects of cooperatively and competitively structured learning environments on inter- and intrapersonal behavior. *Child Development*, 1976, *47*, 386–396.

Damon, W. *The social world of the child*. San Francisco: Jossey-Bass, 1977.

Darley, J., & Latane, B. Bystander intervention in emergencies: Diffusion of responsibility. *Journal of Personality and Social Psychology*, 1968, *8*, 377–383.

Darwin, C. *On the origin of the species*. London: John Murray, 1859.

DePalma, D. Effects of social class, moral orientation, and severity of punishment on boys' moral responses to transgression and generosity. *Developmental Psychology*, 1974, *10*, 890–900.

DePalma, D. J., & Foley, J. M. (Eds.), *Moral development: Current theory and research*. Hillsdale, N.J.: Erlbaum, 1975.

Devereaux, E. C. The role of peer-group experience in moral development. In J. P. Hill (Ed.), *Minnesota Symposia on Child Psychology* (Vol. 4). Minneapolis: University of Minnesota Press, 1970.

DeVoe, M. W. Cooperation as a function of self-concept, sex and race. *Educational Research Quarterly*, 1977, *2*, 3–8.

Dienstbier, R. A., Hillman, D., Lehnhoff, J., Hillman, J., & Valkenaar, M. C. An emotion-attribution approach to moral behavior: Interfacing cognitive and avoidance theories of moral development. *Psychological Review*, 1975, *82*, 299–315.

Dlugokinski, E. L., & Firestone, I. J. Congruence among four methods of measuring other-centeredness. *Child Development*, 1973, *44*, 304–308.

Dlugokinski, E. L., & Firestone, I. J. Other centeredness and susceptibility to charitable appeals: Effects of perceived discipline. *Developmental Psychology*, 1974, *10*, 21–28.

Doland, D. J., & Adelberg, K. The learning of sharing behavior. *Child Development*, 1967, *38*, 695–700.

Drabman, R. S., & Thomas, M. H. Does TV violence breed indifference? *Journal of Communication*, 1975, *25*, 86–89.

Dreman, S. B. Sharing behavior in Israeli schoolchildren: Cognitive and social learning factors. *Child Development*, 1976, *47*, 186–194.

Dreman, S. B., & Greenbaum, C. W. Altruism or reciprocity: Sharing behavior in Israeli kindergarten children. *Child Development*, 1973, *44*, 61–68.

Dunn, J., & Kendrick, C. Interaction between young siblings in the context of family relationships. In M. Lewis & L. A. Rosenblum (Eds.), *The child and its family*. New York: Plenum, 1979.

Durkin, D. The specificity of children's moral judgments. *Journal of Genetic Psychology*, 1961, *98*, 3–13.

Dyson-Hudson, R., & Van Dusen, R. Food sharing among young children. *Ecology of food and nutrition*, 1972, *1*, 319–324.

Eckerman, C. O., Whatley, J. L., & Kutz, S. L.

Growth of social play with peers during the second year of life. *Developmental Psychology*, 1975, *11*, 42–49.

Eisenberg-Berg, N. Development of children's prosocial moral judgment. *Developmental Psychology*, 1979, *15*, 128–137.

Eisenberg-Berg, N., & Geisheker, E. Content of preachings and power of the model/preacher: The effect on children's generosity. *Developmental Psychology*, 1979, *15*, 168–175.

Eisenberg-Berg, N., & Hand, M. The relationship of preschoolers' reasoning about prosocial moral conflicts to prosocial behavior. *Child Development*, 1979, *50*, 356–363.

Eisenberg-Berg, N., & Lennon, R. Altruism and the assessment of empathy in the preschool years. *Child Development*, 1980, *51*, 552–557.

Eisenberg-Berg, N., & Mussen, P. H. Empathy and moral development in adolescence. *Developmental Psychology*, 1978, *14*, 185–186.

Eisenberg-Berg, N., & Neal, C. Children's moral reasoning about their own spontaneous prosocial behavior. *Developmental Psychology*, 1979, *15*, 228–229.

Ekstein, R. Psychoanalysis, sympathy, and altruism. In L. G. Wispe (Ed.), *Altruism, sympathy, and helping: Psychological and sociological principles*. New York: Academic Press, 1978.

Elliott, R., & Vasta, R. The modeling of sharing: Effects associated with vicarious reinforcement, symbolization, age, and generalization. *Journal of Experimental Child Psychology*, 1970, *10*, 8–15.

Emler, N. P., & Rushton, J. P. Cognitive-developmental factors in children's generosity. *British Journal of Sociology and Clinical Psychology*, 1974, *13*, 277–281.

Epstein, S. The stability of behavior: I. On predicting most of the people much of the time. *Journal of Personality and Social Psychology*, 1979, *37*, 1097–1126.

Fay, B. M. The relationships of cognitive moral judgment, generosity, and empathic behavior in six- and eight-year-old children (Doctoral dissertation, University of California, Los Angeles, 1970). *Dissertation Abstracts International*, 1971, *31*, 3951A. (University Microfilms No. 71-4868)

Feldman, S. S., & Nash, S. C. Changes in responsiveness to babies during adolescence. *Child Development*, 1979, *50*, 942–949.

Feldman, S. S., Nash, S. C., & Cutrona, C. The influence of age and sex on responsiveness to babies. *Developmental Psychology*, 1977, *13*, 675–676.

Feshbach, N. D. Empathy in children: Some theoretical and empirical considerations. *Counseling Psychologist*, 1975, *5*, 25–30. (a)

Feshbach, N. D. The relationship of child-rearing factors to children's aggression, empathy, and related positive and negative behaviors. In J. deWit & W. W. Hartup (Eds.), *Determinants and origins of aggressive behavior*. The Hague: Mouton, 1975. (b)

Feshbach, N. D. Studies of empathic behavior in children. In B. A. Maher (Ed.), *Progress in experimental personality research* (Vol. 8). New York: Academic Press, 1978.

Feshbach, N. D. Empathy training: A field study of affective education. In S. Feshbach & A. Fraazeh (Eds.) *Aggression and behavior change: Biological and social processes*. New York: Praeger, 1979, 234–249.

Feshbach, N. D., & Feshbach, S. The relationship between empathy and aggression in two age groups. *Developmental Psychology*, 1969, *1*, 102–107.

Feshbach, N. D., & Kuchenbecker, S. *A three-component model of empathy*. Symposium presented at the meeting of the American Psychological Association, New Orleans, September 1974.

Feshbach, N. D., & Roe, K. Empathy in six- and seven-year-olds. *Child Development*, 1968, *39*, 133–145.

Fincham, F. Recipient characteristics and sharing behavior in the learning disabled. *Journal of Genetic Psychology*, 1978, *133*, 143–144.

Fischer, W. F. Sharing in preschool children as a function of amount and type of reinforcement. *Genetic Psychology Monographs*, 1963, *68*, 215–245.

Floyd, J. *Effects of amount of reward and friendship status of the other on the frequency of sharing in children*. Unpublished doctoral dissertation, University of Minnesota, 1964.

Freud, A. *The ego and the mechanisms of defense* (C. Baines, trans.). New York: International Universities Press, 1946. (Originally published, 1936.)

Freud, A., & Dann, S. An experiment in group upbringing. *Psychoanalytic Study of the Child*, 1951, *6*, 127–168.

Freud, S. Civilization and its discontents. In J. Strachey (Ed. and trans.), *The standard edition of the complete psychological works of Sigmund Freud* (Vol. 21). London: Hogarth Press, 1953. (Originally published, 1930.)

Freud, S. Group psychology and the analysis of the

ego. In J. Strachey (Ed. and trans.), *The standard edition of the complete psychological works of Sigmund Freud* (Vol. 18). London: Hogarth Press, 1953. (Originally published, 1921.)

Freud, S. *The origins of psychoanalysis—letters to Wilhelm Fliess, drafts and notes: 1887 to 1902* (M. Bonaparte, A. Freud, & E. Kris, Eds.; E. Mosbacher & J. Strachey, trans.). New York: Basic Books, 1954.

Friedrich, L. K., & Stein, A. H. Aggressive and prosocial television programs and the natural behavior of preschool children. *Monographs of the Society for Research in Child Development*, 1973, *38*(4, Serial No. 151).

Friedrich, L. K., Stein, A. H., & Susman, E. J. The effects of prosocial television and environmental conditions on preschool children. In A. H. Stein, *Television in the development of socially desirable behavior*. Symposium presented at the meeting of the American Psychological Association, Chicago, September 1975.

Friedrich-Cofer, L. K., Huston-Stein, A., Kipnis, D. M., Susman, E. J., & Clewett, A. S. Environmental enhancement of prosocial television content: Effects on interpersonal behavior, imaginative play and self-regulation in a natural setting. *Developmental Psychology*, 1979, *15*, 637–646.

Froming, W. F., Allen, L. H., & Clawson-Marsh, L. A longitudinal investigation of donating behavior. *Proceedings of the Society for Research in Child Development*, 1981, *3*, 102.

Fukushima, O., & Kato, M. The effects of vicarious experiences on children's altruistic behavior. *Bulletin of Tokyo Gakugei University*, 1976, *27* (Series 1), 90–94.

Furman, W., Rahe, D. F., & Hartup, W. W. Rehabilitation of socially withdrawn children through mixed-aged and same-age socialization. *Child Development*, 1979, *50*, 915–922.

Gelfand, D. M., Hartmann, D. P., Cromer, C. C., Smith, C. L., & Page, B. C. The effects of instructional prompts and praise on children's donation rates. *Child Development*, 1975, *46*, 980–983.

Gergen, K. J., Gergen, M. M., & Meter, K. Individual orientations to prosocial behavior. *Journal of Social Issues*, 1972, *28*, 105–131.

Gesell, A., Halverson, H., Thompson, H., Ilg, F. L., Castner, B. M., Ames, L. B., & Amatruda, C. S. *The first five years of life: The preschool years*. New York: Harper, 1940.

Gilbert, D. C. The young child's awareness of affect. *Child Development*, 1969, *40*, 629–640.

Gnepp, J., Klayman, J., & Trabasso, T. A hierarchy of information sources for inferring emotional reactions. *Journal of Experimental Child Psychology*, 1982, *33*, 111–123.

Gottman, J. M., & Parkhurst, J. T. A developmental theory of friendship and acquaintanceship processes. In A. Collins (Ed.), *Minnesota Symposia on Child Psychology* (Vol. 13). Hillsdale, N.J.: Erlbaum, 1980.

Grant, J. E., Weiner, A., & Rushton, J. P. Moral judgment and generosity in children. *Psychological Reports*, 1976, *39*, 451–454.

Green, F. P., & Schneider, F. W. Age differences in the behavior of boys on three measures of altruism. *Child Development*, 1974, *45*, 248–251.

Greenberg, P. J. Competition in children: An experimental study. *American Journal of Psychology*, 1932, *44*, 221–248.

Grusec, J. E. Power and the internalization of self-denial. *Child Development*, 1971, *42*, 93–105.

Grusec, J. E. The socialization of altruism. In N. Eisenberg-Berg (Ed.), *The development of prosocial behavior*. New York: Academic Press, 1982.

Grusec, J. E., & Kuczynski, L. Directions of effect in socialization: A comparison of the parent's versus the child's behavior as determinants of disciplinary techniques. *Developmental Psychology*, 1980, *16*, 1–9.

Grusec, J. E., Kuczynski, L., Rushton, J. P., & Simutis, Z. M. Modeling, direct instruction, and attributions: Effects on altruism. *Developmental Psychology*, 1978, *14*, 51–57.

Grusec, J. E., Kuczynski, L., Rushton, J. P., & Simutis, Z. M. Learning resistance to temptation through observation. *Developmental Psychology*, 1979, *15*, 233–240.

Grusec, J. E., & Redler, E. Attribution, reinforcement, and altruism: A developmental analysis. *Developmental Psychology*, 1980, *16*, 525–534.

Grusec, J. E., Saas-Kortsaak, P., & Simutis, Z. M. The role of example and moral exhortation in the training of altruism. *Child Development*, 1978, *49*, 920–923.

Grusec, J. E., & Skubiski, S. L. Model nurturance, demand characteristics of the modeling experiment, and altruism. *Journal of Personality and Social Psychology*, 1970, *14*, 352–359.

Guillaume, P. *Imitation in children* (E. P. Halperin, trans.). Chicago: University of Chicago Press, 1968. (Originally published, 1926.)

Hamburg, B. A. Early adolescence: A special and stressful stage of the life cycle. In C. Coelho, D. Hamburg, & J. Adams (Eds.), *Coping and adaptation*. New York: Basic Books, 1974.

Hamilton, W. D. The genetical evolution of social behavior. I. *Journal of Theoretical Biology*, 1964, *7*, 1–16.

Hamilton, W. D. The genetical evolution of social behavior. II. *Journal of Theoretical Biology*, 1964, *7*, 17–52.

Hampson, R. B. *Peers, pathology, and helping: Some kids are more helpful than others.* Paper presented at the meeting of the Society for Research in Child Development, San Francisco, March 1979.

Handlon, B. J., & Gross, P. The development of sharing behavior. *Journal of Abnormal and Social Psychology*, 1959, *59*, 425–428.

Harford, T., & Cutter, H. S. G. Cooperation among negro and white boys and girls. *Psychological Reports*, 1966, *18*, 818.

Harlow, H. F. Induction and alleviation of depressive states in monkeys. In N. F. White (Ed.), *Ethology and psychiatry*. Toronto: University of Toronto Press, 1974.

Harris, L. A. A study of altruism. *Elementary School Journal*, 1967, *68*, 135–141.

Harris, M. B. Reciprocity and generosity: Some determinants of sharing in children. *Child Development*, 1970, *41*, 313–328.

Harris, M. B. Models, norms, and sharing. *Psychological Reports*, 1971, *29*, 147–153.

Harris, M. B. The effects of performing one altruistic act on the likelihood of performing another. *Journal of Social Psychology*, 1972, *88*, 65–73.

Harris, M. B., & Siebel, C. E. Affect, aggression, and altruism. *Developmental Psychology*, 1975, *11*, 623–627.

Harris, S., Mussen, P. H., & Rutherford, E. Some cognitive, behavioral, and personality correlates of maturity of moral judgment. *Journal of Genetic Psychology*, 1976, *128*, 123–135.

Hartmann, D. P., Gelfand, D. M., Smith, C. L., Paul, S. C., Cromer, C. C., Page, B. C., & Lebenta, D. V. Factors affecting the acquisition and elimination of children's donating behavior. *Journal of Experimental Child Psychology*, 1976, *21*, 328–338.

Hartshorne, H., May, M. A., & Maller, J. B. *Studies in the nature of character*, vol. 2, *Studies in service and self-control*. New York: Macmillan, 1929.

Hartup, W. W. Peer interactions and social organization. In P. H. Mussen (Ed.), *Carmichael's manual of child psychology* (Vol. 2, 3rd ed.). New York: Wiley, 1970.

Hartup, W. W., Glazer, J., & Charlesworth, R. Peer reinforcement and sociometric status. *Child Development*, 1967, *38*, 1017–1024.

Hartup, W. W., & Keller, E. D. Nurturance in preschool children and its relation to dependency. *Child Development*, 1960, *31*, 681–689.

Hay, D. F. Cooperative interactions and sharing between very young children and their parents. *Developmental Psychology*, 1979, *15*, 647–653.

Hay, D. F., Nash, A., & Pederson, J. Responses of six-month-olds to the distress of their peers. *Child Development*, 1981, *52*, 1071–1075.

Hay, D. F., & Rheingold, H. L. *The early appearance of some valued social behaviors.* Unpublished manuscript, State University of New York at Stony Brook, 1979.

Henry, R. M. A theoretical and empirical analysis of 'reasoning' in the socialization of young children. *Human Development*, 1980, *23*, 105–125.

Hobbes, T. *Leviathan*. In R. M. Hutchins (Ed.) *Great books of the Western world* (Vol. 23). Chicago: Encyclopaedia Britannica, 1952. (Originally published, 1651.)

Hoffman, M. L. Parent discipline and the child's consideration for others. *Child Development*, 1963, *34*, 573–588.

Hoffman, M. L. Moral development. In P. H. Mussen (Ed.), *Carmichael's manual of child psychology* (Vol. 2). New York: Wiley, 1970.

Hoffman, M. L. Altruistic behavior and the parent-child relationship. *Journal of Personality and Social Psychology*, 1975, *31*, 937–943. (a)

Hoffman, M. L. Developmental synthesis of affect and cognition and its implications for altruistic motivation. *Developmental Psychology*, 1975, *11*, 605–622. (b)

Hoffman, M. L. Empathy, role taking, guilt, and development of altruistic motives. In T. Lickona (Ed.), *Moral development and behavior: Theory, research, and social issues*. New York: Holt, Rinehart & Winston, 1976.

Hoffman, M. L. Empathy, its development and prosocial implications. In C. B. Keasey (Ed.), *Nebraska Symposium on Motivation* (Vol. 25). Lincoln: University of Nebraska Press, 1977. (a)

Hoffman, M. L. Sex differences in empathy and related behaviors. *Psychological Bulletin*, 1977, *84*, 712–722. (b)

Hoffman, M. L. Development of the motive to help others. In J. P. Rushton & R. M. Sorrentino (Eds.), *Altruism and helping behavior: Social, personality, and developmental perspectives*. Hillsdale, N.J.: Erlbaum, 1981.

Hoffman, M. L., & Levine, L. E. Early sex differences in empathy. *Developmental Psychology*, 1976, *12*, 557–558.

Hoffman, M. L., & Saltzstein, H. D. Parent discipline and the child's moral development. *Journal of Personality and Social Psychology*, 1967, *5*, 45–57.

Hogan, R. Moral conduct and moral character: A psychological perspective. *Psychological Bulletin*, 1973, *79*, 217–232.

Hornstein, H. A. Promotive tension: The basis of prosocial behavior from a Lewinian perspective. *Journal of Social Issues*, 1972, *28*, 191–218.

Hull, D., & Reuter, J. The development of charitable behavior in elementary school children. *Journal of Genetic Psychology*, 1977, *131*, 147–153.

Hume, D. *An inquiry concerning human understanding*. In R. M. Hutchins (Ed.), *Great books of the Western world* (Vol. 35). Chicago: Encyclopaedia Britannica, 1952. (Originally published, 1740.)

Hunt, J. McV. Psychological development: Early experience. In M. R. Rosenzweig & L. W. Porter (Eds.), *Annual Review of Psychology* (Vol. 30). Palo Alto, Calif.: Annual Reviews, 1979.

Hyman, H. H. Mass communication and socialization. *Public Opinion Quarterly*, 1973, *37*, 524–540.

Iannotti, R. J. *The many faces of empathy: An analysis of the definition and evaluation of empathy in children*. Paper presented at the meeting of the Society for Research in Child Development, Denver, April 1975.

Iannotti, R. J. Effect of role-taking experiences on role taking, empathy, altruism, and aggression. *Developmental Psychology*, 1978, *14*, 119–124.

Iannotti, R. J. *The elements of empathy: A reconceptualization of content and process*. Paper presented at the meeting of the Society for Research in Child Development, San Francisco, March 1979.

Isaacs, S. S. *Social development in young children: A study of beginnings*. London: Harcourt Brace, 1933.

Isen, A. M., Horn, N., & Rosenhan, D. L. Effects of success and failure on children's generosity. *Journal of Personality and Social Psychology*, 1973, *27*, 239–247.

Israely, Y., & Guttmann, J. *Children's sharing behavior as a function of exposure to puppet-show and story models*. Unpublished manuscript, Tel Aviv University, 1980.

Izard, C. E. *Human emotions*. New York: Plenum, 1977.

Jensen, R., & Moore, S. G. The effect of attribute statements on cooperativeness and competitiveness in school-age boys. *Child Development*, 1977, *48*, 305–307.

Jersild, A. T. *Child psychology*. New York: Prentice-Hall, 1933.

Jersild, A. T., & Markey, F. V. Conflicts between preschool children. *Child Development Monographs* (No. 21). New York: Teachers College, Columbia University, 1935.

Johnson, D. W. Affective perspective taking and cooperative predisposition. *Developmental Psychology*, 1975, *11*, 869–870. (a)

Johnson, D. W. Cooperativeness and social perspective taking. *Journal of Personality and Social Psychology*, 1975, *31*, 241–244. (b)

Johnson, D. W., & Johnston, R. T. Instructional goal structure: Cooperative, competitive, or individualistic. *Review of Education Research*, 1974, *44*, 213–240.

Kagan, S., & Knight, G. P. Cooperation-competition and self-esteem: A case of cultural relativism. *Journal of Cross-Cultural Psychology*, 1979, *10*, 457–467.

Kagan, S., & Madsen, M. C. Cooperation and competition of Mexican, Mexican-American, and Anglo-American children of two ages under four instructional sets. *Developmental Psychology*, 1971, *5*, 32–39.

Kagan, S., & Madsen, M. C. Experimental analyses of cooperation and competition of Anglo-American and Mexican children. *Developmental Psychology*, 1972, *6*, 49–59. (a)

Kagan, S., & Madsen, M. C. Rivalry in Anglo-American and Mexican children of two ages. *Journal of Personality and Social Psychology*, 1972, 24, 214–220. (b)

Kagan, S., Zahn, G. L., & Gealy, J. Competition and school achievement among Anglo-American and Mexican-American children. *Journal of Educational Psychology*, 1977, *69*, 432–441.

Kalhorn, J. Values and sources of authority among rural children. In K. Lewin, C. Myers, J. Kalhorn, M. Farber, & J. French (Eds.), *Authority and frustration. University of Iowa Studies in Child Welfare*, 1944, *20*.

Kanfer, F. H. Personal control, social control, and altruism: Can society survive the age of individualism? *American Psychologist*, 1979, *34*, 231–239.

Kant, I. *Fundamental principles of the metaphysics of morals*. In R. M. Hutchins (Ed.), *Great books of the Western world* (Vol. 42). Chicago: Encyclopaedia Britannica, 1952. (Originally published, 1785.)

Karylowski, J. Self-esteem, similarity, liking and helping. *Personality and Social Psychology Bul-*

letin, 1976, *2*, 71–74.

Keller, B. B., & Bell, R. Q. Child effects on adult's method of eliciting altruistic behavior. *Child Development*, 1979, *50*, 1004–1009.

Kessen, W. (Ed.). *Childhood in China*. New Haven, Conn.: Yale University Press, 1975.

Knight, G. P., & Kagan, S. Acculturation of prosocial and competitive behaviors among second- and third-generation Mexican-American children. *Journal of Cross-Cultural Psychology*, 1977, *8*, 273–284. (a)

Knight, G. P., & Kagan, S. Development of prosocial and competitive behaviors in Anglo-American and Mexican-American children. *Child Development*, 1977, *48*, 1385–1394. (b)

Kohlberg, L. Stage and sequence: The cognitive-developmental approach to socialization. In D. A. Goslin (Ed.), *Handbook of socialization theory and research*. New York: Rand McNally, 1969.

Kohn, M. L. *Class and conformity: A study in values* (2nd ed.). Chicago: University of Chicago Press, 1977. (Originally published, 1969.)

Kohn, M. L., & Schooler, C. Occupational experience and psychological functioning: An assessment of reciprocal effects. *American Sociological Review*, 1973, *38*, 97–118.

Krebs, D. Altruism: An examination of the concept and a review of the literature. *Psychological Bulletin*, 1970, *73*, 258–302.

Krebs, D., & Russell, C. Role-taking and altruism. In J. P. Rushton & R. M. Sorrentino (Eds.), *Altruism and helping behavior, social personality, and developmental perspectives*. Hillsdale, N.J.: Erlbaum, 1981.

Krebs, D., & Sturrup, B. Role-taking ability and altruistic behavior in elementary school children. *Personality and Social Psychology Bulletin*, 1974, *1*, 407–409.

Kreutzer, M. A., & Charlesworth, W. R. *Infants' reactions to different expressions of emotions*. Paper presented at the meeting of the Society for Research in Child Development, Philadelphia, March 1973.

Kuczynski, L. Intensity and orientation of reasoning: Motivational determinants of children's compliance to verbal rationales. *Journal of Experimental Child Psychology*, 1982, *34*, 357–370.

Kuczynski, L. Reasoning, prohibitions, and motivations for compliance. *Developmental Psychology*, 1983, *19*, 126–134.

Kurdek, L. A. Perspective taking as the cognitive basis of children's moral development: A review

of the literature. *Merrill-Palmer Quarterly*, 1978, *24*, 3–28. (a)

Kurdek, L. A. Relationship between cognitive perspective taking and teachers' ratings of children's classroom behavior in grades one through four. *Journal of Genetic Psychology*, 1978, *132*, 21–27. (b)

LaBarbera, J. D., Izard, C. E., Vietze, P., & Parisi, S. A. Four- and six-month-old infants' visual responses to joy, anger, and neutral expressions. *Child Development*, 1976, *47*, 535–538.

Ladd, G. W., Lange, G., & Stremmel, A. Personal and situational correlates of children's helping decisions and persistence. *Proceedings of the Society for Research in Child Development*, 1981, *3*, 159.

Ladd, G. W., & Oden, S. L. The relationship between children's ideas about helpfulness and peer acceptance. *Child Development*, 1979, *50*, 402–408.

Lasch, C. *The culture of narcissism*. New York: W. W. Norton, 1978.

Leiman, B. *Affective empathy and subsequent altruism in kindergartners and first graders*. Paper presented at the meeting of the American Psychological Association, Toronto, August 1978.

Lenrow, P. B. Studies of sympathy. In S. S. Tomkins & C. E. Izard (Eds.), *Affect, cognition, and personality: Empirical studies*. New York: Springer Publishing, 1965.

Leuba, C. An experimental study of rivalry in young children. *Journal of Comparative Psychology*, 1933, *16*, 367–378.

Leventhal, G. S., & Anderson, D. Self-interest and the maintenance of equity. *Journal of Personality and Social Psychology*, 1970, *15*, 57–62.

Levin, I., & Bekerman-Greenberg, R. Moral judgment and moral behavior in sharing: A developmental analysis. *Genetic Psychology Monographs*, 1980, *101*, 215–230.

Levine, L. E., & Hoffman, M. L. Empathy and cooperation in four-year-olds. *Developmental Psychology*, 1975, *11*, 533–534.

Lewin, K. Changes in social sensitivity in child and adult. *Childhood Education*, 1942, *19*, 53–57.

Lewin, K., Lippitt, R., & White, R. K. Patterns of aggressive behavior in experimentally created "social climates." *Journal of Social Psychology*, 1939, *10*, 271–299.

Lewis, C. E., Lewis, M. A., & Ifekwunigue, M. Informed consent by children and participation on an influenza vaccine trial. *American Journal of Public Health*, 1978, *68*, 1079–1082.

Lewis, H. B. *Shame and guilt in neurosis*. New

York: International Universities Press, 1971.

Lippitt, R. Popularity among preschool children. *Child Development*, 1941, *12*, 305–322.

Locke, J. *Concerning civil government, second essay*. In R. M. Hutchins (Ed.), *Great books of the Western world* (Vol. 35). Chicago: Encyclopaedia Britannica, 1952. (Originally published, 1690.)

Loevinger, J., & Wessler, R. *Measuring ego development* (Vol. 1). San Francisco: Jossey-Bass, 1970.

Londerville, S., & Main, M. Security of attachment, compliance, and maternal training methods in the second year of life. *Developmental Psychology*, 1981, *17*, 289–299.

London, P. The rescuers: Motivational hypotheses about Christians who saved Jews from the Nazis. In J. R. Macaulay & L. Berkowitz (Eds.), *Altruism and helping behavior*. New York: Academic Press, 1970.

Lorenz, K. *On aggression*. London: Methuen, 1966.

Lorr, M., More, W. W., & Harnett, C. *Personality determinants of prosocial behavior*. Unpublished manuscript, Catholic University, 1980.

Macaulay, J. R., & Berkowitz, L. (Eds.). *Altruism and helping behavior*. New York: Academic Press, 1970.

Maccoby, E. E., & Jacklin, C. N. *The psychology of sex differences*. Stanford, Calif.: Stanford University Press, 1974.

MacLean, P. D. A triune concept of the brain and behavior. In T. J. Boag & D. Campbell (Eds.), *The Clarence M. Hincks memorial lectures*. Toronto: University of Toronto Press, 1973.

Madsen, M. C. Cooperative and competitive motivation of children in three Mexican sub-cultures. *Psychological Reports*, 1967, *20*, 1307–1320.

Madsen, M. C. Developmental and cross-cultural differences in the cooperative and competitive behavior of young children. *Journal of Cross-Cultural Psychology*, 1971, *2*, 365–371.

Madsen, M. C., & Connor, C. Cooperative and competitive behavior of retarded and non-retarded children at two ages. *Child Development*, 1973, *44*, 175–178.

Madsen, M. C., & Shapira, A. Cooperative and competitive behavior of urban Afro-American, Anglo-American, Mexican-American, and Mexican village children. *Developmental Psychology*, 1970, *3*, 16–20.

Madsen, M. C., & Shapira, A. Cooperation and challenge in four cultures. *Journal of Social Psychology*, 1977, *102*, 189–195.

Madsen, M. C., & Yi, S. Cooperation and competition of urban and rural children in the Republic of South Korea. *International Journal of Psychology*, 1975, *10*, 269–274.

Mahler, M. S., Pine, F., & Bergman, A. *The psychological birth of the human infant*. New York: Basic Books, 1975.

Mander, J. *Four arguments for the elimination of television*. New York: William Morrow, 1978.

Mann, F. A. Sharing in kindergarten children as a function of friendship status and socio-economic status (Doctoral dissertation, University of Tennessee, 1973). *Dissertation Abstracts International*, 1974, *34*, 4050B (University Microfilms No. 74-3850).

Mannarino, A. P. Friendship patterns and altruistic behavior in preadolescent males. *Developmental Psychology*, 1976, *12*, 555–556.

Marcus, R. F., & Jenny, B. A naturalistic study of reciprocity in the helping behavior of young children. *Alberta Journal of Educational Research*, 1977, *23*, 195–206.

Marcus, R. F., & Roke, E. J. *The specificity of empathic responses in young children*. Paper presented at the meeting of the American Psychological Association, Montreal, September 1980.

Marcus, R. F., Telleen, S., & Roke, E. J. Relation between cooperation and empathy in young children. *Developmental Psychology*, 1979, *15*, 346–347.

Masters, J. C. Effects of social comparison upon children's self-reinforcement and altruism toward competitors and friends. *Developmental Psychology*, 1971, *5*, 64–72.

Masters, J. C., & Pisarowicz, P. A. Self-reinforcement and generosity following two types of altruistic behavior. *Child Development*, 1975, *46*, 313–318.

McClintock, C. G. Development of social motives in Anglo-American and Mexican-American children. *Journal of Personality and Social Psychology*, 1974, *29*, 348–354.

McClintock, C. G., & Nuttin, J. Development of competitive game behavior in children across two cultures. *Journal of Experimental Social Psychology*, 1969, *5*, 203–218.

McDougall, W. *An introduction to social psychology*. New York: Barnes & Noble, 1960. (Originally published, 1908.)

McKee, J. P., & Leader, F. B. The relationship of socio-economic status and aggression to the competitive behavior of preschool children.

Child Development, 1955, *26*, 135–142.

Mead, G. H. *Mind, self, and society*. Chicago: University of Chicago Press, 1974. (Originally published, 1934.)

Mead, M. (Ed.). *Cooperation and competition among primitive peoples*. Boston: Beacon Press, 1961. (Originally published, 1937.)

Meister, A. Perception and acceptance of power relations in children. *Group Psychotherapy*, 1956, *9*, 153–163.

Midlarsky, E., & Bryan, J. H. Training charity in children. *Journal of Personality and Social Psychology*, 1967, *5*, 408–415.

Midlarsky, E., & Bryan, J. H. Affect expressions and children's imitative altruism. *Journal of Experimental Research in Personality*, 1972, *6*, 195–203.

Midlarsky, E., Bryan, J. H., & Brickman, P. Aversive approval: Interactive effects of modeling and reinforcement on altruistic behavior. *Child Development*, 1973, *44*, 321–328.

Miller, A. G., & Thomas, R. Cooperation and competition among Blackfoot Indian and urban Canadian children. *Child Development*, 1972, *43*, 1104–1110.

Miller, R. L., Brickman, P., & Bolen, D. Attribution versus persuasion as a means for modifying behavior. *Journal of Personality and Social Psychology*, 1975, *31*, 430–441.

Miller, S. M. *Dependency, empathy, and altruism*. Paper presented at the meeting of the Society for Research in Child Development, New Orleans, March 1977.

Mischel, W. Continuity and change in personality. *American Psychologist*, 1969, *24*, 1012–1018.

Mischel, W., & Mischel, H. N. A cognitive social-learning approach to morality and self-regulation. In T. Lickona (Ed.), *Moral development and behavior: Theory, research, and social issues*. New York: Holt, Rinehart & Winston, 1976.

Mood, D. W., Johnson, J. E., & Shantz, C. U. Social comprehension and affect matching in young children. *Merrill-Palmer Quarterly*, 1978, *24*, 63–66.

Moore, B. S., Underwood, B., & Rosenhan, D. L. Affect and altruism. *Developmental Psychology*, 1973, *8*, 99–104.

Moore, S. G. Correlates of peer acceptance in nursery school children. In W. W. Hartup & N. Smothergill (Eds.), *The young child*. Washington, D.C.: National Association for the Education of Young Children, 1967.

Morris, W. N., Marshall, H. M., & Miller, R. S.

The effects of vicarious punishment on prosocial behavior in children. *Journal of Experimental Child Psychology*, 1973, *15*, 222–236.

Mowrer, O. H. *Learning theory and the symbolic processes*. New York: Wiley, 1960.

Munroe, R. L., & Munroe, R. H. Cooperation and competition among East African and American children. *Journal of Social Psychology*, 1977, *101*, 145–146.

Murchison, C., & Langer, S. (Eds. and trans.). Tiedemann's observations on the development of the mental faculties of children. *Pedagogical Seminary*, 1927, *34*, 205–230.

Murphy, G., Murphy, L. B., & Newcomb, T. M. *Experimental social psychology*. New York: Harper & Brothers, 1937.

Murphy, L. B. *Social behavior and child personality*. New York: Columbia University Press, 1937.

Murphy, L. B. Personal communication, May, 1980.

Murray, J. P., & Kippax, S. From the early window to the late night show: International trends in the study of television's impact on children and adults. In L. Berkowitz (Ed.), *Advances in experimental social psychology* (Vol. 12). New York: Academic Press, 1979.

Mussen, P. H. *Choices, regrets, and lousy models (with reference to prosocial development)*. Presidential address to Division 7 (Developmental Psychology), presented at the meeting of the American Psychological Association, San Francisco, September 1977.

Mussen, P. H., & Eisenberg-Berg, N. *Caring, sharing and helping*. San Francisco: W. H. Freeman, 1977.

Mussen, P. H., Harris, S., Rutherford, E., & Keasey, C. B. Honesty and altruism among preadolescents. *Developmental Psychology*, 1970, *3*, 169–194.

Muste, M. J., & Sharpe, D. F. Some influential factors in the determination of aggressive behavior in preschool children. *Child Development*, 1947, *18*, 11–28.

Nadler, A., Romek, E., Shapira-Friedman, A. Giving in the Kibbutz: Prosocial behavior of city and Kibbutz children as affected by social responsibility and social pressure. *Journal of Cross-Cultural Psychology*, 1979, *10*, 57–72.

Nelson, L., & Madsen, M. C. Cooperation and competition in four-year-olds as a function of reward contingency and subculture. *Developmental Psychology*, 1969, *1*, 340–344.

Novak, M. A., & Harlow, H. F. Social recovery of

monkeys isolated for the first year of life: 1. Rehabilitation and therapy. *Developmental Psychology,* 1975, *11,* 453–465.

O'Bryant, S. L., & Brophy, J. E. Sex differences in altruistic behavior. *Developmental Psychology,* 1976, *12,* 554.

O'Connor, M., Dollinger, S., Kennedy, S., & Pelletier-Smetko, P. Prosocial behavior and psychopathology in emotionally disturbed boys. *American Journal of Orthopsychiatry,* 1979, *49,* 301–310.

Olejnik, A. B. *Developmental changes and interrelationships among role-taking, moral judgments and children's sharing.* Paper presented at the meeting of the Society for Research in Child Development, Denver, April 1975.

Olejnik, A. B., & McKinney, J. P. Parental value orientation and generosity in children. *Developmental Psychology,* 1973, *8,* 311.

Olweus, D. The consistency issue in personality psychology revisited—with special reference to aggression. *British Journal of Social and Clinical Psychology,* 1980, *19,* 377–390. (a)

Olweus, D. Familial and temperamental determinants of aggressive behavior in adolescent boys: A causal analysis. *Developmental Psychology,* 1980, 16, 644–660. (b)

Parish, T. S. The enhancement of altruistic behaviors in children through the implementation of language conditioning procedures. *Behavioral Modification,* 1977, *1,* 395–404.

Parten, M. B. Social participation among preschool children. *Journal of Abnormal and Social Psychology,* 1932, *27,* 243–269.

Patterson, C. J., & Mischel, W. Effects of temptation: Inhibiting and task-facilitating plans on self-control. *Journal of Personality and Social Psychology,* 1976, *33,* 209–217.

Pearl, R. A. *Developmental and situational influences on children's understanding of prosocial behavior.* Paper presented at the meeting of the Society for Research in Child Development, San Francisco, March 1979.

Pepitone, E. A. Patterns of interdependence in cooperative work of elementary children. *Contemporary Educational Psychology,* 1977, *2,* 10–24.

Peterson, L., Hartmann, D. P., & Gelfand, D. M. Developmental changes in the effects of dependency and reciprocity cues on children's moral judgments and donation rates. *Child Development,* 1977, *48,* 1331–1339.

Piaget, J. *The moral judgment of the child.* Glencoe, Ill.: Free Press, 1965. (Originally published, 1932.)

Plato. *Phaedrus.* In R. M. Hutchins (Ed.), *Great books of the Western world* (Vol. 7). Chicago: Encyclopaedia Britannica, 1952.

Poulos, R. W., & Liebert, R. M. Influence of modeling, exhortative verbalization, and surveillance on children's sharing. *Developmental Psychology,* 1972, *6,* 402–408.

Presbie, R. J., & Coiteux, P. F. Learning to be generous or stingy: Imitation of sharing behavior as a function of model generosity and vicarious reinforcement. *Child Development,* 1971, *42,* 1033–1038.

Presbie, R. J., & Kanereff, V. T. Sharing in children as a function of the number of sharees and reciprocity. *Journal of Genetic Psychology,* 1970, *116,* 31–44.

Radke-Yarrow, M., & Zahn-Waxler, C. Roots, motives, and patterns in children's prosocial behavior. In J. Reykowski, J. Karylowski, D. Bar-Tal, & E. Staub (Eds.), *Origins and maintenance of prosocial behaviors.* New York: Plenum, in press.

Radke-Yarrow, M., Zahn-Waxler, C., Cummings, M., Strope, B., & Sebris, S. L. *Continuities and change in the prosocial and aggressive behavior of young children.* Paper presented at the meeting of the Society for Research in Child Development, Boston, April 1981.

Raviv, A., Bar-Tal, D., Ayalon, H., & Raviv, A. *Perception of giving and receiving help by group members.* Unpublished manuscript, Tel Aviv University, 1980.

Reykowski, J. Cognitive development and prosocial behavior. *Polish Psychological Bulletin,* 1977, *8,* 35–45.

Rheingold, H. L. *Helping by two-year-old children.* Paper presented at the meeting of the Society for Research in Child Development, San Francisco, March 1979.

Rheingold, H. L., & Hay, D. F. Prosocial behavior of the very young. In G. S. Stent (Ed.), *Morality as a biological phenomenon.* Berlin: Dahlem Konferenzen, 1978.

Rheingold, H. L., Hay, D. F., & West, M. J. Sharing in the second year of life. *Child Development,* 1976, *47,* 1148–1158.

Rice, M. E., & Grusec, J. E. Saying and doing: Effects on observer performance. *Journal of Personality and Social Psychology,* 1975, *32,* 584–593.

Richmond, B. O., & Weiner, G. P. Cooperation and competition among young children as a function of ethnic grouping, grade, sex, and reward condition. *Journal of Educational Psychology,*

1973, *64*, 329–334.

Roberts, D., & Bachen, C. Mass communication effects. In M. R. Rosenzweig & L. W. Porter (Eds.), *Annual Review of Psychology* (Vol. 32). Palo Alto, Calif.: Annual Reviews, 1981.

Roe, K. V. A study of empathy in young Greek and U.S. children. *Journal of Cross-Cultural Psychology*, 1977, *8*, 493–502.

Rogers-Warren, A., & Baer, D. M. Correspondence between saying and doing: Teaching children to share and praise. *Journal of Applied Behavior Analysis*, 1976, *9*, 335–354.

Rogers-Warren, A., Warren, S. F., & Baer, D. M. A component analysis-modeling, self-reporting, and reinforcement of self-reporting in the development of sharing. *Behavior Modification*, 1977, *1*, 307–322.

Rosenhan, D. L., Some origins of concern for others. In P. H. Mussen, J. Langer, & M. Covington (Eds.), *Trends and issues in developmental psychology*. New York: Holt, Rinehart & Winston, 1969.

Rosenhan, D. L., The natural socialization of altruistic autonomy. In J. R. Macaulay & L. Berkowitz (Eds.), *Altruism and helping behavior*. New York: Academic Press, 1970.

Rosenhan, D. L., Frederick, F., & Burrowes, A. Preaching and practicing: Effects of channel discrepancy on norm internalization. *Child Development*, 1968, *39*, 291–301.

Rosenhan, D. L., Underwood, B., & Moore, B. Affect moderates self-gratification and altruism. *Journal of Personality and Social Psychology*, 1974, *30*, 546–552.

Rosenhan, D. L., & White, G. M. Observation and rehearsal as determinants of prosocial behavior. *Journal of Personality and Social Psychology*, 1967, *5*, 424–431.

Rosenn, M. M. *The relation of moral reasoning to prosocial behavior: A developmental perspective*. Unpublished doctoral dissertation, University of California, Berkeley, 1976.

Rosenthal, T. L., & Zimmerman, B. J. *Social learning and cognition*. New York: Academic Press, 1978.

Ross, H. S., & Goldman, B. D. Establishing new social relations in infancy. In T. Alloway, L. Kramer, & P. Pliner (Eds.), *Advances in the study of communication and affect*, Vol. 3, *Attachment behavior*. New York: Plenum, 1977.

Rothenberg, B. B. Children's social sensitivity and the relationship to interpersonal competence, intrapersonal comfort, and intellectual level. *Developmental Psychology*, 1970, *2*, 335–350.

Rousseau, J. J. *On the origin of inequality*. In R. M. Hutchins (Ed.), *Great books of the Western world* (Vol. 38). Chicago: Encyclopaedia Brittanica, 1952. (Originally published, 1755.)

Rubin, K. H., & Schneider, F. W. The relationship between moral judgment, egocentrism, and altruistic behavior. *Child Development*, 1973, *44*, 661–665.

Rühle, O. *From the bourgeoisie to the proletarian revolution*. London: Socialist Reproduction, 1974. (Originally published, 1924.)

Rushton, J. P. Generosity in children: Immediate and long-term effects of modeling, preaching, and moral judgment. *Journal of Personality and Social Psychology*, 1975, *31*, 459–466.

Rushton, J. P. Socialization and the altruistic behavior of children. *Psychological Bulletin*, 1976, *83*, 898–913.

Rushton, J. P. Effects of prosocial television and film material on the behavior of viewers. In L. Berkowitz (Ed.), *Advances in experimental social psychology* (Vol. 12). New York: Academic Press, 1979.

Rushton, J. P. *Altruism, socialization, and society*. Englewood Cliffs, N.J.: Prentice-Hall, 1980.

Rushton, J. P., & Littlefield, C. The effects of age, amount of modeling and a success experience on seven to eleven-year-old children's generosity. *Journal of Moral Education*, 1979, *9*, 55–56.

Rushton, J. P. & Owen, D. Immediate and delayed effects of TV modeling and preaching on children's generosity. *British Journal of Social and Clinical Psychology*, 1975, *14*, 309–310.

Rushton, J. P., & Sorrentino, R. M. (Eds.). *Altruism and helping behavior: Social, personality, and developmental perspectives*. Hillsdale, N.J.: Erlbaum, 1981.

Rushton, J. P., & Teachman, G. The effects of positive reinforcement, attributions, and punishment on model induced altruism in children. *Personality and Social Psychology Bulletin*, 1978, *4*, 322–325.

Rushton, J. P., & Wiener, J. Altruism and cognitive development in children. *British Journal of Social and Clinical Psychology*, 1975, *14*, 341–349.

Rutherford, E., & Mussen, P. H. Generosity in nursery school boys. *Child Development*, 1968, *39*, 755–765.

Sagi, A., & Hoffman, M. L. Empathic distress in the newborn. *Developmental Psychology*, 1976, *12*, 175–176.

Sahlins, M. *The use and abuse of biology: An anthropological critique of sociobiology*. Ann Arbor: University of Michigan Press, 1977.

Sampson, E. Psychology and the American ideal. *Journal of Personality and Social Psychology,* 1977, *11,* 767–782.

Santrock, J. W. Moral structure: The interrelations of moral behavior, moral judgment, and moral affect. *Journal of Genetic Psychology, 1975, 127,* 201–213.

Sawin, D. B. Assessing empathy in children: A search for an elusive construct. In D. B. Sawin, *Empathy in children: Conceptual and methodological issues in current research.* Symposium presented at the meeting of the Society for Research in Child Development, San Francisco, March 1979.

Sawin, D. B. *A field study of children's reactions to distress in their peers.* Unpublished manuscript, University of Texas at Austin, 1980.

Sawin, D. B., & Parke, R. D. Development of self-verbalized control of resistance to deviation. *Developmental Psychology,* 1979, *15,* 120–127.

Scheler, M. *The nature of sympathy* (P. Heath, trans.). London: Routledge & Kegan Paul, 1954. (Originally published, 1923.)

Schopenhauer, A. *The world as will and representation* (Vol. 1) (E. J. J. Payne, trans.). New York: Dover, 1966. (Originally published, 1819.)

Sears, R. R., Maccoby, E. E., & Lewin, H. *Patterns of child rearing.* Evanston, Ill.: Row & Peterson, 1957.

Seegmiller, B. R., & Suter, B. Relations between cognitive and behavioral measures of prosocial development in children. *Journal of Genetic Psychology,* 1977, *131,* 161–162.

Shapira, A., & Lomranz, J. Cooperative and competitive behavior of rural Arab children in Israel. *Journal of Cross-Cultural Psychology,* 1972, *4,* 353–359.

Shapira, A., & Madsen, M. C. Cooperative and competitive behavior of kibbutz and urban children in Israel. *Child Development,* 1969, *40,* 609–617.

Shapira, A., & Madsen, M. C. Between and within-group cooperation and competition among kibbutz and nonkibbutz children. *Developmental Psychology,* 1974, *10,* 140–145.

Sharabany, R., & Hertz-Lazarowitz, R. Do friends share and communicate more than nonfriends? *International Journal of Behavior and Development,* 1981, *4,* 45–59.

Shigetomi, C. C., Hartmann, D. P., Gelfand, D. M., Cohen, E. A., & Montemayor, R. *Children's altruism: Sex differences in behavior and reputation.* Paper presented at the meeting of the Society for Research in Child Development, San Francisco, March 1979.

Sibley, B. A., Senn, S. K., & Epanchin, A. Race and sex of adolescents and cooperation in a mixed-motive game. *Psychonometric Science,* 1968, *13,* 123–124.

Silverman, L. T., & Sprafkin, J. N. *The effects of Sesame Street's prosocial spots on cooperative play between young children.* Paper presented at the meeting of the Society for Research in Child Development, San Francisco, March 1979.

Simner, M. L. Newborn's response to the cry of another infant. *Developmental Psychology,* 1971, *5,* 136–150.

Skarin, K., & Moely, B. E. Altruistic behavior: An analysis of age and sex differences. *Child Development,* 1976, *47,* 1159–1165.

Skinner, B. F. *Science and human behavior.* New York: Macmillan, 1953.

Skinner, B. F. *Beyond freedom and dignity.* New York: Knopf, 1971.

Slater, P. *The pursuit of loneliness.* Boston: Beacon Press, 1970.

Smith, A. *The wealth of nations.* In R. M. Hutchins (Ed.) *Great books of the Western world* (Vol. 39). Chicago: Encyclopaedia Britannica, 1952. (Originally published, 1776.)

Sociobiology Study Group of Science for the People. Sociobiology—Another biological determinism. *BioScience,* 1976, *26,* 182–186.

Sommerlad, E. A., & Bellingham, W. P. Cooperation-competition: A comparison of Australian European and aboriginal school children. *Journal of Cross-Cultural Psychology,* 1972, *3,* 149–157.

Sperling, O. C. A psychoanalytic study of social-mindedness. *Psychoanalytic Quarterly,* 1955, *24,* 256–269.

Spinoza, B. de. *Ethics.* In R. M. Hutchins (Ed.), *Great books of the Western world* (Vol. 31). Chicago: Encyclopaedia Britannica, 1952. (Originally published, 1677.)

Spivack, G., & Shure, M. B. *Social adjustment of young children: A cognitive approach to solving real-life problems.* San Francisco: Jossey-Bass, 1974.

Sprafkin, J. N., Liebert, R. M., & Poulos, R. W. Effects of a prosocial televised example on children's helping. *Journal of Experimental Child Psychology,* 1975, *20,* 119–126.

Sprafkin, J. N., & Rubinstein, E. A. Children's television viewing habits and prosocial behavior: A field study. *Journal of Broadcasting,* 1979, *23,* 265–276.

Stanjek, K. Das Uberreichen von Gaben: Funktion und Entwicklung in den ersten Lebensjahren. *Zeitschrift für Entwicklungspsychologie und Padagogische Psychologie,* 1978, *10,* 103–113.

Staub, E. *The effects of success and failure on children's sharing behavior.* Paper presented at the meeting of the Eastern Psychological Association, Washington, D.C., April 1968.

Staub, E. A child in distress: The effect of focusing responsibility on children on their attempts to help. *Developmental Psychology,* 1970, *2,* 152–153. (a)

Staub, E. A child in distress: The influence of age and number of witnesses on children's attempts to help. *Journal of Personality and Social Psychology,* 1970, *14,* 130–140. (b)

Staub, E. A child in distress: The influence of nurturance and modeling on children's attempts to help. *Developmental Psychology,* 1971, *5,* 124–132. (a)

Staub, E. Helping a person in distress: The influence of implicit and explicit "rules" of conduct on children and adults. *Journal of Personality and Social Psychology,* 1971, *17,* 137–144. (b)

Staub, E. The use of role playing and induction in children's learning of helping and sharing behavior. *Child Development,* 1971, *42,* 805–816. (c)

Staub, E. To rear a prosocial child: Reasoning, learning by doing, and learning by teaching others. In D. J. DePalma & J. M. Foley (Eds.), *Moral development: Current theory and research.* Hillsdale, N.J.: Erlbaum, 1975.

Staub, E. *Positive social behavior and morality: Social and personal influences* (Vol. 1). New York: Academic Press, 1978.

Staub, E. *Positive social behavior and morality: Socialization and development* (Vol. 2). New York: Academic Press, 1979.

Staub, E., & Fotta, M. *Participation in prosocial behavior and positive induction as means of children learning to be helpful.* Unpublished manuscript, University of Massachusetts, Amherst, 1978.

Staub, E., Leavy, R., & Shortsleeves, J. *Teaching others as a means of learning to be helpful.* Unpublished manuscript, University of Massachusetts, Amherst, 1975.

Staub, E., Sherk, L. Need for approval, children's sharing behavior, and reciprocity in sharing. *Child Development,* 1970, *41,* 243–252.

Stent, G. S. (Ed.). *Morality as a biological phenomenon.* Berlin: Dahlem Konferenzen, 1978.

Stern, W. *Psychology of early childhood.* New York: Holt, 1924

Stith, M., & Connor, R. Dependency and helpfulness in young children. *Child Development,* 1962, *33,* 15–20.

Strayer, F. F., Wareing, S., & Rushton, J. P. Social constraints on naturally occurring preschool altruism. *Ethology and Sociobiology,* 1979, *1,* 3–11.

Strayer, J. A naturalistic study of empathic behaviors and their relation to affective states and perspective-taking skills in preschool children. *Child Development,* 1980, *51,* 815–822.

Sullivan, H. S. *Conceptions of modern psychiatry.* London: Tavistock Press, 1940.

Sullivan, H. S. *The interpersonal theory of psychiatry.* New York: W. W. Norton, 1953.

Thomas, D. R. Cooperation and competition among Polynesian and European children. *Child Development,* 1975, *46,* 948–953.

Thompson, R. A., & Hoffman, M. L. Empathy and the development of guilt in children. *Developmental Psychology,* 1980, *16,* 155–156.

Thompson, W. C., Cowan, C. L., & Rosenhan, D. L. Focus of attention mediates the impact of negative affect on altruism. *Journal of Personality and Social Psychology,* 1980, *38,* 291–300.

Tomkins, S. S. *Affect, imagery, consciousness,* vol. 2, *The negative affects.* New York: Springer Publishing, 1963.

Trivers, R. L. The evolution of reciprocal altruism. *Quarterly Review of Biology,* 1971, *46,* 35–57.

Turner, W. D. Altruism and its measurement in children. *Journal of Abnormal Social Psychology,* 1948, *43,* 502–516.

Ugurel-Semin, R. Moral behavior and moral judgment of children. *Journal of Abnormal and Social Psychology,* 1952, *47,* 463–474.

Underwood, B., Froming, W. J., & Moore, B. S. Mood, attention, and altruism: A search for mediating variables. *Developmental Psychology,* 1977, *13,* 541–542.

Underwood, B., & Moore, B. S. The generality of altruism in children. In N. Eisenberg-Berg (Ed.), *The development of prosocial behavior.* New York: Academic Press, 1982.

Valentine, C. W. *The psychology of early childhood: A study of mental development in the first years of life.* London: Methuen, 1942.

Vance, J. J., & Richmond, B. O. Cooperative and competitive behavior as a function of self-esteem. *Journal of the Schools,* 1975, *12,* 225–259.

Wasik, B. H., Senn, S. K., & Epanchin, A. Cooperation and sharing behavior among culturally deprived preschool children. *Psychonomic Sci-*

ence, 1969, *17*, 371–372.

Waters, E., Wippman, J., & Sroufe, L. A. Attachment, positive affect, and competence in the peer group: Two studies in construct validation. *Child Development*, 1979, *50*, 821–829.

Weissbrod, C. S. Noncontingent warmth induction, cognitive style, and children's imitative donation and rescue effort behaviors. *Journal of Personality and Social Psychology*, 1976, *34*, 274–281.

Weston, D., & Main, M. *Infant responses to the crying of an adult actor in the laboratory: Stability and correlates of "concerned attention."* Paper presented at the meeting of the International Conference on Infant Studies, New Haven, Conn., April 1980.

White, G. M. Immediate and deferred effects of model observation and guided and unguided rehearsal on donating and stealing. *Journal of Personality and Social Psychology*, 1972, *21*, 139–148.

White, G. M., & Burnam, M. A. Socially cued altruism: Effects of modeling, instructions, and age on public and private donations. *Child Development*, 1975, *46*, 559–563.

Whiting, B. B., & Whiting, J. W. M. *Children of six cultures.* Cambridge: Harvard University Press, 1975.

Whiting, J. W. M., & Whiting, B. B. Altruistic and egoistic behavior in six cultures. In L. Nader & T. W. Maretzki (Eds.), *Cultural illness and health: Essays in human adaptation (Anthropological Studies, No. 9)*. Washington, D.C.: American Anthropological Association, 1973.

Wilcox, B. M., & Clayton, F. L. Infant visual fixation on motion pictures of the human face. *Journal of Experimental Child Psychology*, 1968, *6*, 22–32.

Willis, J. B., Feldman, N. S., & Ruble, D. N. Children's generosity as influenced by deservedness of reward and type of recipient. *Journal of Educational Psychology*, 1977, *69*, 33–35.

Wilson, E. O. *Sociobiology: The new synthesis.* Cambridge: Harvard University Press, 1975.

Wispe, L. G. Positive forms of social behavior: An overview. *Journal of Social Issues,* 1972, *28*, 1–19.

Wispe, L. G. (Ed.). *Altruism, sympathy, and helping: Psychological and sociological principles.* New York: Academic Press, 1978.

Wolff, P. H. The biology of morals from a psychological perspective. In G. S. Stent (Ed.), *Morality as a biological phenomenon*. Berlin: Dahlem

Konferenzen, 1978.

Wright, B. A. Altruism in children and the perceived conduct of others. *Journal of Abnormal Social Psychology*, 1942, *37*, 218–233.

Wynne-Edwards, V. C. *Animal dispersion in relation to social behavior.* Edinburgh: Oliver & Boyd, 1962.

Yarrow, M. R., & Scott, P. M. Imitation of nurturant and nonnurturant models. *Journal of Personality and Social Psychology*, 1972, *23*, 259–270.

Yarrow, M. R., Scott, P. M., & Waxler, C. Z. Learning concern for others. *Developmental Psychology*, 1973, *8*, 240–260.

Yarrow, M. R., & Waxler, C. Z. Dimensions and correlates of prosocial behavior in young children. *Child Development*, 1976, *47*, 118–125.

Yarrow, M. R., & Waxler, C. Z. The emergence and functions of prosocial behavior in young children. In M. S. Smart & R. C. Smart (Eds.), *Infants, development and relationships* (2nd ed.). New York: Macmillan, 1978.

Youniss, J. *Parents and peers in social development*. Chicago: University of Chicago Press, 1980.

Zahn-Waxler, C. *Workshop on infant reactions to emotional signals: 12–18 months. Young children's responses to the emotions of others.* Workshop presented at the meeting of the International Conference on Infant Studies, New Haven, Conn., April 1980.

Zahn-Waxler, C., & Chapman, M. Immediate antecedents of caretakers' methods of discipline. *Child Psychiatry and Human Development*, 1982, *12*, 179–192.

Zahn-Waxler, C., Friedman, S. L., & Cummings, E. M. Children's emotions and behaviors in response to infants' cries. *Child Development*, in press.

Zahn-Waxler, C., & Radke-Yarrow, M. The development of altruism: Alternative research strategies. In N. Eisenberg-Berg (Ed.), *The development of prosocial behavior*. New York: Academic Press, 1982.

Zahn-Waxler, C., Radke-Yarrow, M., & Brady-Smith, J. Perspective-taking and prosocial behavior. *Developmental Psychology*, 1977, *13*, 87–88.

Zahn-Waxler, C., Radke-Yarrow, M., & King, R. Child rearing and children's prosocial initiations toward victims of distress. *Child Development*, 1979, *50*, 319–330.

THE DEVELOPMENT OF AGGRESSION* | 7

ROSS D. PARKE, *University of Illinois*
RONALD G. SLABY, *Harvard University*

CHAPTER CONTENTS

*Preparation of this chapter was supported by NICHD Grant HEW PH5 05951, NICHD Training Grant HDO 7205–01, and the National Foundation March of Dimes. We are grateful to Steven Asher, Robert Emery, Kevin MacDonald, David Perry, and John Reid for helpful criticism of earlier drafts. Special thanks to Barbara R. Tinsley for her extensive feedback and support in the writing of this chapter. Finally, we thank Elaine Fleming, Jo Powell, and Sally Parsons for their assistance with the bibliography and in final manuscript preparation.

OVERVIEW

Few topics have attracted as much theoretical and empirical attention over the past century as the development and regulation of aggressive behavior. In this chapter, we present an overview of contemporary research in aggression. In the last decade, several themes have emerged that have significantly shaped the nature of research in social development in a general way and the study of aggression specifically. First, the active role of children in contributing to the development of their own aggression is recognized. Consistent with this view is the recognition of the bidirectional nature of the influence processes between the child and his or her environment in the development of aggression. Second, the development of aggression has been recognized to be influenced by multiple causes. Current views stress that biological-genetic factors as well as situational-environmental factors play an important role in shaping the development of aggression. Third, the child's aggressive behavior is best understood by recognition of the child's embeddedness in a variety of social systems and settings that mutually influence each other. These range from more immediate settings such as the family or peer group to larger contexts such as communities and cultures. The ways in which these various systems alter the development of children's aggression is an important theme.

Although multiple theories are evident in the study of aggression, the role of the child's cognitive development in mediating aggressive behavior has increasingly become a theoretical theme in the analysis of aggression. Moreover, multiple methodologies are currently more commonly employed

in the study of aggression. In recent years, under the influence of increased responsiveness to concerns about ecological validity, naturalistic observational strategies have been utilized to parallel laboratory investigations in this area.

Finally, although aggression remains a substantial social problem and, as yet, a poorly understood scientific phenomenon, the pace of research in this area has slowed in the past decade. In part, this circumstance reflects a shift toward an increased concern with children's prosocial development. A lessening of empirical interest in the development of aggression can also be traced to the difficulty of securing measures of aggression which are currently acceptable. Heightened sensitivity to the ethical issues involved in research with children may have drawn some researchers away from this area.

A related explanation of the state of research on aggression is that the area of social development, in general, has also shifted away from the study of specific traditional topics such as aggression and toward the study of broader topics, such as social relationships and children's competence. Much of our current research on children's aggression, in fact, comes from such studies, in which aggression is one of a number of dependent variables, which, in turn, are used to construct superordinate categories of behavior such as competence.

In this chapter, the following aspects of aggression are addressed: (1) problems of definition, (2) theories of aggression, (3) biological origins of aggression, (4) developmental and sex-related patterns of aggression, (5) social influences on aggression, including families, peers, and the mass media, (6) role of situational variables in aggression, and (7) techniques for the control and modification of aggression at the individual, group, and community levels.

DEFINITIONS OF AGGRESSION

Aggression has been defined, both theoretically and empirically, in a wide variety of ways, many of which are ambiguous and overlapping. These definitions include viewing aggression as a personality trait, a biological process, a stereotyped reflex, a learned habit, an instinct, and a class of observable physical and verbal responses. An objective and unambiguous definition of aggression has yet to be satisfactorily formulated despite numerous attempts. As Hartup and deWit (1978) usefully suggest, approaches to the definition of aggression have assumed three typical forms: (1) definitions that refer to some topographical or sequential feature of the response pattern, (2) definitions that refer to specific antecedent or eliciting conditions, and (3) definitions that refer to the consequences of the activity.

Topographical Definitions

A topographical approach assumes that careful scrutiny of the behavior patterns that result in flight or injury reveals the essential elements of an aggressive act. Under the influence of ethology, this approach has yielded impressive results for certain animal species in which the aggressive routines are highly specialized and ritualized (see Hinde, 1974, 1978; Immelmann, 1980). However, the application of this strategy for the study of aggression in children has been only partly successful. This limited success results from the fact that for humans "the range of their aggressions is much greater, the conditions of elicitation are less restricted, and the effects of experience are more pervasive than in the various nonhuman species" (Hartup & deWit, 1974, p. 597). Examples of these attempts can be found in the research of Blurton Jones (1967, 1972) and McGrew (1972). These investigators have attempted to define aggressive motor patterns such as "the beating movement" (Blurton Jones, 1967), but the fact that these movements occur with equal frequency in agonistic and nonagonistic play encounters casts doubt on the value of this approach.

Walters (1964) used a different approach to define aggression topographically. He argued that the high-magnitude nature of aggressive behavior was an important defining feature. While this approach had some utility for the study of physical aggression, the problem of scaling the intensity of verbal assaults and insults made this approach overly narrow. To date, a useful topographically-based definition has not been formulated for aggression in humans.

Antecedents Approach

Another approach to defining aggression focuses on the antecedent conditions surrounding the occurrence of the behavior. One of the most commonly accepted definitions of aggression, which was offered many years ago, states simply that "aggression is behavior for which the goal response is the injury of the person toward whom it is directed" (Dollard, Doob, Miller, Mowrer, & Sears, 1939). This definition focuses on the intentionality of the actor as a critical aspect of the definition. The introduction of intent into the definition raises a serious problem since "intentionality is not a property of behavior, but refers to antecedent conditions which frequently have to be inferred from the behavior of which they are supposedly an essential ingredient" (Bandura & Walters, 1963, p. 365). In other words, this definition involves more than an observable act or sequence of behavior that can be reliably measured, since the observer must also make judgments or inferences concerning the actor's intentions. In turn, this raises problems of the reliability and validity of judgments of the observer's intent.

"Antecedent-related conceptions" are somewhat more successful when specific conditions are referenced rather than the often subtle cues by which intentionality must be inferred. Thus, antecedent conditions such as crowding, mating, or hunger delimit meaningful subclasses of aggressive behavior among certain nonhuman species. The extent to which this strategy is useful in the study of human beings is limited since harm-doing in human adults is not as rigidly stimulus bound as harm-doing in animals. However, in some cases, there may be sufficiently narrow stimulus control of aggression, particularly among very young children, to warrant use of this strategy. For example, as much as 75% of the aggression displayed by nursery school children is elicited by loss of possessions (Dawe, 1934; Blurton Jones, 1967).

Outcome Approach

Aggression can be defined in terms of outcomes, thereby focusing attention on the harm or injuries associated with aggression. From this perspective, aggression could be defined as "behavior that results in injury of another individual." The advantage of this type of definition is that certain objectively quantifiable levels of injury could be established as standards for invoking the label of aggression, and inferences about the injuring agent's intent or motives could be minimized. Buss (1961) has advocated this approach to the definition of aggression. Although such a definition may be objective, it is too general since it would lead us to label many common behaviors of dentists, surgeons, and parents as aggressive. Similarly, children receiving accidental injuries would be grouped with those who are victims of intentionally inflicted injuries. Moreover, it is not clear that the problem of quantifying harm or injury is easily solved. For example, whose definition of harm is to be used—that of the victim, an observer, or the aggressor? Depending on the perspective of the defining agent, very different ratings of harm may be obtained, causing differences in whether or not a behavioral sequence would be defined as aggressive. A consideration of consequences alone has not proven to be a satisfactory approach to defining aggression.

Social Judgment Approach

Another approach to defining aggression recognizes that physical aggression is not a set of behaviors, but instead, a culturally determined label that is applied to particular behavior and injury patterns as an outcome of a social judgment on the part of the observer (Walters & Parke, 1964). Intention is merely one criterion that we typically employ in deciding whether an interpersonal exchange between two people is aggressive. In making this judgment, an observer takes into account a variety of factors, including the antecedents of the response, the form and intensity of the response, the extent of the injury, and the role and status of the agent and victim of the behavior. In short, an injurious act may be labeled aggressive in one situation or in one person or in one community, but the same injury may not be judged aggressive in another situation, in a different person, or in another community. For example, are injurious acts among family members less likely to be labeled aggressive than similarly injurious acts among strangers? Even an objective definition of aggression in terms of injuries must include standards concerning the severity of the outcome, which, in turn, are culturally defined. From this viewpoint, the definition of aggression varies with the social class and the cultural background of the defining individual. The aggression may be a community-defined phenomenon, which must be viewed in the context of community norms and standards that govern the appropriate conduct of people in their interactions with others. To date, insufficient

attention has been paid to the development of an empirically derived set of standards based on community consensus concerning the definition of aggression.

In summary, there is currently no single definition of aggression that simultaneously captures both the diversity of popular meanings and the variety of research strategies applied to the concept. The social judgment approach treats the very problem of definition as an opportunity to further our understanding of the social phenomenon of aggression. According to this approach, it is precisely the differing definitions and the judgmental processes that lead to such differences, that deserve further analyses and investigation, since social scientists' judgments of what constitutes "aggression" will heavily influence their research strategies and interpretations. Similarly, a clearer understanding of how judgments of "aggression" differ for children of different backgrounds, developmental levels, and sexes will help us to predict children's responses. These issues of social judgment will be discussed further in conjunction with the emerging social-cognitive perspective on aggression. For purposes of this chapter, aggression is defined in a minimal way as behavior that is aimed at harming or injuring another person or persons.

We next turn to an overview and evaluation of the major theories regarding the development of aggression in children.

THEORIES OF AGGRESSION

A large number of theories have been constructed to account for the acquisition, maintenance, and control of aggressive behavior. In this section, we focus our attention on modern theories of aggression that are currently influential in empirical research in this area, including drive theories, and ethological, social learning, and social-cognitive accounts of aggression. Historically, psychoanalytic theory has been extremely influential in this area, but there are few modern proponents of this theoretical approach to aggression (see Bandura, 1973a; Baron, 1977: Berkowitz, 1973; Feshbach, 1970; & Zillmann, 1978, for reviews of this position, as well as other reviews of aggression theories).

Ethological Approach to Aggression

Ethology is the comparative study of the biological bases of animal and human behavior. It derives from the theory that phylogenetic adaptations determine the behavior of animals. Ethologists contend that a basic repertoire of behavior patterns emerges as a function of maturational processes during the course of development, in contrast to a learning-environmental approach (Eibl-Eibesfeldt, 1970). The emergence and form of behavior patterns are determined by phylogenetically developed "blueprints;" consequently, they are often referred to as fixed action patterns.

One of the best-known ethological treatments of aggression has been offered by Konrad Lorenz, Nobel Prize winner and author of *On Aggression* (1966). Lorenz defines aggression as "the fighting instinct in beast and man." He views aggression as an instinctual system, the energy for which is generated within the organism independently of external stimuli. This aggressive energy, he explains, builds upon the organism and must periodically be discharged or released by an appropriate releasing stimulus. The elicitation of aggression is a joint function of the amount of accumulated aggressive energy and the presence and strength of specific aggression-releasing stimuli.

According to Lorenz, the adaptive species-preserving function of aggression, in combination with natural selection processes, accounts for the phylogenetic development of highly articulated and sophisticated mechanisms and weapons of aggression in both animals and humans. He describes three primary species-preserving functions of intraspecific aggression that have contributed to this phylogenetic development of aggressive behavior patterns in animals. The first is an ecological function. Fighting in defense of territory serves to balance the distribution of animals of the same species over the available supporting environment. Because of the limited sources of nutrition, shelter, and other essential life supports, the ecology of a given geographical area is capable of supporting only a limited number of organisms of the same species. The overpopulation of a territory by members of the same species exhausts the life-supporting resources and threatens the survival of both the individual organisms and the species. Innate tendencies of mutual repulsion acting on members of the same species effects a "spacing out" of the organisms that preserves a balanced ecology and thus serves individual survival and species preservation.

The second primary adaptive function of aggression described by Lorenz is the intraspecific combat that results in the selection of the best and strongest animals for reproduction. The dramatic and often violent fighting of rival males serves as a sexual selection process that contributes to the evolution of particularly well-adapted species members. In this way aggression leads to strong and effective defenders of family, herd, and territory.

The third positive function of aggression is brood defense: The selection process that derives from intraspecific combat associated with mating yields organisms that are adapted for extraspecific fighting as well as intraspecific contests. Lorenz states that the most important outcome of this process is the selection of an aggressive family defender. The protection of the young by the best defenders serves to assure the preservation of the species.

Three aspects of Lorenz' theory have been criticized by other behavioral scientists. The first is his extensive reliance on instinctual factors of aggression in animals and humans and the relatively minor role attributed to learning. Although experiments with animals have demonstrated that certain events are capable of eliciting aggressive responses without any prior learning, the demonstrations in numerous other studies that aggressive patterns of behavior are learned and modifiable belie a position which holds that aggression is determined *primarily* by innate biological factors derived through evolutionary processes. Based on considerations of a broad range of research on aggression, a more reasonable position is an intermediate one that asserts that both learning and innate determinants can coexist in humans and animals.

The second major criticism of Lorenz' theory of aggression centers around his use of an energy model of motivation. In a recent discussion of the origins and determinants of aggressive behavior, Hinde (1975) concludes that energy models are unnecessary and misleading. Not only are they too simplistic, but there is no neurophysiological evidence to support this type of model. Moreover, there are alternative explanations supported by factual evidence that better explain the behavior presumed to be mediated by aggressive energy. Instinct models of motivation are misleading because they imply that individuals deprived of aggression-eliciting stimuli will show a gradually increasing tendency to behave aggressively until they avidly seek an object to attack or dissipate the "energy" in some other way. Not only is this claim unfounded but this view leads to questionable recommendations for aggression control, such as sanctioned discharge of pent-up aggression directed toward alternative, "safe" targets. As we note later in this chapter, this type of safe outlet approach typically increases rather than decreases aggressive behavior.

Finally, Lorenz has been criticized for overgeneralizing his observations and interpretations of lower animal aggression to human aggression. He is guilty of "reverse" anthropomorphizing. His theorizing about human aggression neglects the vast differences in the complexity of behavior between human and subhuman species. Hinde (1975) warns that we must argue from one species to another only with the greatest caution because of the important differences in the level of cognitive functioning of which humans are capable, because of human value systems, because of the diversity of weapons at human command and the deviousness with which humans can operate, and perhaps, especially, because of the time span over which human behavior is organized. It is, in fact, the determination of phylogenetic differences, as opposed to similarities in aggressive behavior, that makes the comparative study of aggression so worthwhile and interesting.

In contrast to instinct theory as proposed by Lorenz, other ethological theorists have addressed some of these limitations and have stimulated interesting research on the development of human as well as animal aggression. There are several distinctive features that characterize post-Lorenzian ethological approaches to social behavior, such as aggression. Kummer (1971) notes four distinguishing features of the ethological framework for the analysis of behavior.

A common focus in all ethological research is the commitment to providing a sufficiently detailed description of behavioral patterns observed for all members of a given species. . . . A basic assumption is that qualitative differences in complex social phenomena cannot be understood without a detailed consideration of qualitative differences in individual action patterns which constitute social exchange between young children. (Strayer, 1980, p. 2)

Second, ethology focuses on immediate causation and immediate function of selected behavioral activity. In turn, this provides important information about the factors that influence and control the occurrence of behavioral phenomena. Such research "facilitates the refinement and reorganization of the ethogram for a species by showing either causal or functional similarities in morphologically distinct behavioral units" (Strayer, 1980, p. 3). Third, the historical context of behavior is emphasized, particularly the evolution of species-specific activity and the development of individual differences. Fourth, modern social ethology emphasizes the importance of the social ecology of the group as a primary influence on the individual. The description and analysis

of group organization and its role in regulating social behavior are some of the current concerns. In fact, recent studies of the relationship between the social organization of children's groups, especially social dominance, and social behavior such as aggression, have begun to build important bridges between psychological and ethological approaches. The construct of dominance has received a great deal of attention by animal researchers and especially primate social ethologists (Crook, 1970; Hinde, 1974; Jolly, 1972; Kummer, 1971). Only recently has the dominance concept been recognized as a way of understanding children's aggression. A series of studies by Strayer (1976, 1980), which are discussed in the section on peer influences on aggression, illustrate how ethological theory can lead to valuable insights into the role of group structure in mediating control of aggressive exchanges among preschool children.

In addition, ethology's emphases on the biological and evolutionary roots of aggression, as well as on the important role of descriptive studies in the understanding of aggression (e.g., McGrew, 1972), have been constructive. Ethology's emphasis on nonverbal behavior has been important in increasing our understanding of the ontogeny of emotions (Charlesworth, 1982); however, the overreliance on nonverbal cues to the exclusion of more cognitive strategies for the regulation of interpersonal behavior may be a limitation.

In fact, the limited attention to developmental issues to date and its failure to integrate seriously recent work on children's cognitive development into its framework are central shortcomings in the application of ethological theory to aggression. Investigation of children's understanding of seriation and its relationship to children's dominance rankings, however, represents a move in the cognitive direction (Edelman & Omark, 1973). For detailed reviews of modern ethological approaches to the study of social development, see Bateson and Hinde (1976), Hinde (1978), Immelmann (1980), McGrew (1972), and Strayer (1980).

Drive Theory: The Frustration-Aggression Hypothesis

One of the most long-standing and controversial explanations of aggressive behavior is a drive model of aggression, which assumes that individuals are motivated not by instincts but by internal drives instigated by external stimuli. The most influential version of this position, which has guided research for four decades, is the frustration-aggression hypothesis (Dollard et al., 1939). According to this position "the occurrence of aggressive behavior always presupposes the existence of frustration and contrariwise, the existence of frustration always leads to some form of aggression" (Dollard et al., 1939, p. 1). In a revision of the hypothesis, Miller (1941) recognized that other responses, in addition to aggression, may occur when frustration is present, but he continued to maintain that, whenever an aggressive response occurs, it is instigated by frustration. This theoretical modification of the frustration-aggression hypothesis resulted from research reports demonstrating that aggression is by no means an inevitable response to frustration. For example, in a landmark study, Barker, Dembo, and Lewin (1941) found that some children regressed when frustrated rather than showing the increase in aggression that the original frustration-aggression hypothesis predicted. In a later study, Davitz (1952) demonstrated that the response to frustration can be experimentally modified through training and that, while aggression is a highly probable response to frustration, it is not a necessary outcome. Davitz illustrated that alternative responses to frustration can be learned. In his study, Davitz engaged one group of children in prosocial training sessions in which they were rewarded for constructive and cooperative behavior. Other groups of children participated in training sessions in which they were rewarded with praise and approval for making competitive aggressive responses. Following this training, the children were subjected to a highly frustrating experience that involved interruption of an attractive film just at the climax of the story and the taking away of candy bars that the children had been given to eat during the movie. Immediately following this interruption, the children's prosocial and aggressive behaviors were recorded during a free-play session. The prefrustration training experiences significantly influenced the children's postfrustration behavior. Although aggression was the predominant response to frustration for the children previously rewarded for aggression, significantly, children who had been rewarded for constructive behavior played more cooperatively following frustration. The results of this study demonstrate that reactions to frustrating situations are a function of the response patterns that are currently dominant in a person's response hierarchy and that response hierarchies can be modified through training.

Other evidence indicates that frustration is not a unitary variable and that not all events subsumed under the "frustration" label are equally likely to produce aggressive acts. It is unlikely that attacks, insults, failure, competition, delay, or loss of valued objects—all potentially frustrating experiences—would have similar aggression-eliciting effects.

A study by Geen (1968) involving college students illustrates the necessity of refining the distinctions among different kinds of instigators of aggression. One group of subjects was presented with an insolvable jigsaw puzzle—a "task frustration" manipulation. A second group experienced "personal frustration" by which a peer prevented them from completing their assigned task, while a third group was verbally insulted by a peer confederate. All subjects, including a group of "no frustration" control subjects, then saw a boxing film. Aggression was measured by the intensity of the electric shock that the subject was willing to administer to the peer confederate (no shock, in fact, is delivered; see Buss, 1961, for a review of this procedure). Although the students in all frustration conditions delivered more intense shocks to their partners than the nonarousal controls, the insulted subjects were significantly more aggressive than the "task frustrated" or personally thwarted students. In addition to various forms of frustration, there are other events that are effective elicitors of aggressive reactions, including direct physical attack (O'Leary & Dengerink, 1973), physical pain (Pisano & Taylor, 1971), and threats to self-esteem (Toch, 1969). As Bandura (1973) notes, "frustration is only one—and not necessarily the most important—factor affecting the expression of aggression" (1973a, p. 33). Although it is clear that frustration does not always lead to aggression, and that all aggression is not caused by frustration, the shift away from an instinctual position to a recognition that external stimuli play a central role in aggression was a major theoretical advance prompted by the frustration-aggression position.

Another aspect of the drive position formulated by Dollard et al. merits mention. Since the theory assumes that frustration-elicited aggressive drives need to be reduced, considerable attention has been focused on the processes that control the reduction of aggressive drives. Aggression cannot always be directly expressed because of the threat of punishment (Dollard et al., 1939), but inhibition of aggression does not necessarily reduce the motivation to aggress. Instead, displacement may occur, which involves aggressing against a target associated with weaker threats of punishment (see Bandura, 1973a; Zillmann, 1978, for a discussion of this issue). In addition, aggression could be reduced by catharsis, a view which suggests that all acts of direct and vicarious aggression—regardless of their relationship to the original instigator—may reduce motivation to behave aggressively. As detailed later in this chapter, little support is evident for the vicarious version of this formulation, and only limited support for a highly modified version of the direct aspect of catharsis theory has been gathered.

An influential reformulation of the frustration-aggression hypothesis has been proposed by Berkowitz (1969, 1971, 1973, 1974). Berkowitz suggests that "frustration creates a readiness for aggressive acts," namely an arousal state of anger, but the presence of aggressive cues—stimuli associated with the present or previous anger instigators or with aggression in general—is necessary for aggression to occur. Berkowitz (1974) has proposed a classical conditioning theory to account for how cues acquire their aggression-evoking properties, and considerable evidence has been marshalled in support of the importance of aggressive cues in the elicitation of aggressive behavior. Data indicating that cues such as weapons (Berkowitz & LePage, 1967; Turner & Goldsmith, 1976) and aggressive models (Bandura, 1973a,b; Berkowitz, 1971) elicit aggressive behavior have been accumulated, and a number of these studies are reviewed later in this chapter.

Although the frustration-aggression hypothesis has generated a great deal of research, the impact on developmental psychology has not been extensive. In part, this is a result of: (1) the decline of Hullian and other behavioral analyses, (2) the shift away from internal drive states as useful theoretical constructs, and (3) the failure to offer specific developmental predictions that are amenable to empirical analyses. More support is available for two other approaches to aggression: social learning and social cognitive analyses.

Social Learning Theory

Bandura (1973a,b, 1977), the major proponent of the social learning theory of aggression, suggests that "a complete theory of aggression must explain how aggressive patterns of behavior are developed, what provokes people to behave aggressively and what maintains their aggressive actions" (Bandura, 1973a, p. 43). Figure 1 outlines the origins, instigators, and reinforcers of aggression according to social learning theory. In contrast to a drive or instinct view, which places emphasis on the inner factors that impel a person to act aggressively, social learning theory focuses on both environmental influences as well as cognitive and self-regulative influences.

Social learning theory recognizes that biological structures set limits on the type of aggressive responses that can be performed and that genetic endowment influences the rate at which learning progresses. However, this position assumes that humans are less constrained by biological determinants than are other species. Finally, in contrast to both instinct and drive theories, frustration or anger arousal is a facilitative but not a necessary condition for aggression. Prior learning histories and anticipated consequences determine the type of social behavior that will occur under conditions of emotional arousal (Davitz, 1952; Schachter, 1964). Figure 2 diagrams the motivational determinants of aggression in instinct, drive, and social learning theories of aggression.

In the acquisition process, observational learning is given a prominent position. This theory assumes that a great deal of aggressive behavior is acquired by the imitation of models such as parents and peers,

SOCIAL LEARNING ANALYSIS OF AGGRESSION

ORIGINS OF AGGRESSION	INSTIGATORS OF AGGRESSION	REINFORCERS OF AGGRESSION

OBSERVATIONAL LEARNING
 	
REINFORCED PERFORMANCE
 	
STRUCTURAL
	MODELING INFLUENCES
	  DISINHIBITORY
	  FACILITATIVE
	  AROUSING
	  STIMULUS ENHANCING
	AVERSIVE TREATMENT
	  PHYSICAL ASSAULTS
	  VERBAL THREATS AND INSULTS
	  ADVERSE REDUCTIONS IN REINFORCEMENT
	  THWARTING
	
	INCENTIVE INDUCEMENTS
	
	INSTRUCTIONAL CONTROL
	
	BIZARRE SYMBOLIC CONTROL
		EXTERNAL REINFORCEMENT
		  TANGIBLE REWARDS
		  SOCIAL AND STATUS REWARDS
		  EXPRESSIONS OF INJURY
		  ALLEVIATION OF AVERSIVE TREATMENT
		
		VICARIOUS REINFORCEMENT
		  OBSERVED REWARD
		  OBSERVED PUNISHMENT
		
		SELF—REINFORCEMENT
		  SELF—PUNISHMENT
		  SELF—REWARD
		  NEUTRALIZATION OF SELF—PUNISHMENT
		    MORAL JUSTIFICATION
		    SLIGHTING COMPARISON
		    DISPLACEMENT OF RESPONSIBILITY
		    DIFFUSION OF RESPONSIBILITY
		    DEHUMANIZATION OF VICTIMS
		    ATTRIBUTION OF BLAME TO VICTIMS
		    MISREPRESENTATION OF CONSEQUENCES

Figure 1. Schematic outline of the origins, instigators, and reinforcers of aggression in social learning theory. (From Bandura, 1973b, p. 211.)

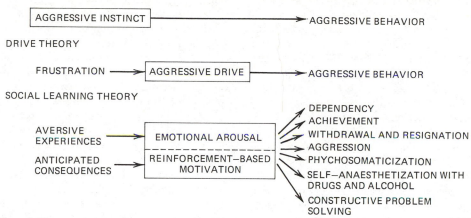

Figure 2. Diagrammatic representation of motivational determinants of aggression in instinct, reactive drive, and social learning theories. (From Bandura, 1973a, p. 54.)

as well as models from television and other media.

Bandura (1977) has proposed a series of four subprocesses that control the extent to which learning through observation will be effective. According to this view, one of the main component features of observational learning, consists of the attentional processes that determine the extent to which the observer closely attends to the model, the characteristics selected for attention, and the accuracy of the observer's perceptions. The second subprocess concerns retentions which generally involves symbolic coding of the observed behavior and mental rehearsal of the model's actions. The third subprocess—motor reproduction—involves behavioral enactment of the previously acquired behavior, which, in turn, is dependent on the previously acquired component skills and the requisite physical capacities. Finally, reinforcement and motivational processes are involved in observational learning, and these processes determine whether the previously acquired actions will be translated into actual behavior.

A large body of research (Bandura, 1973a) has documented the role of modeling in the acquisition and modification of aggressive behavior. This work will be reviewed, in detail, in later sections of the chapter. However, two limitations on the modeling theory of aggression should be noted here. First, although this is a cognitive-based theory, which assumes that developmental changes in the child's cognitive capacities will alter the efficacy of the child's learning of aggression through observation, there has been scant research attention paid to developmental changes in observational learning of social behavior including aggression. Evidence is available on increases in both attention to and retention of observationally presented information (e.g., McCall, Parke, & Kavanaugh, 1977; Yando, Seitz, & Zigler, 1978), but there is little demonstration of how these processes shift developmentally for different types of aggressive materials.

Second, although the original demonstrations of the utility of observational learning for the acquisition of aggression employed aggressive models (e.g., Bandura, Ross, & Ross, 1961, 1963a,b), with some exceptions (Bandura, Grusec, & Menlove, 1966), most of the demonstrations of the subprocesses involved in an observational learning analysis, such as rehearsal and retention, have involved nonsocial stimuli, such as sign language (Bandura & Jeffrey, 1973; Gerst, 1971). Greater attention needs to be paid to the uniqueness of social events, and an examination of the ways in which social and specifically aggressive events are coded in contrast to nonsocial events also needs to be undertaken (see Hoffman, 1981, and Gelman & Spelke, 1981, for discussions of the unique properties of social vs. nonsocial behaviors).

Social learning theory assumes that aggressive behaviors are shaped not only through modeling processes but also by direct feedback in the form of rewarding and punishing events. Numerous examples of this type of direct shaping process are provided in the following discussions. One unique feature of social learning theory is the emphasis on self-reinforcement processes. As Bandura notes:

"A great deal of human behavior is regulated by the self-evaluative consequences it produces. People set themselves certain standards of behavior and respond to their actions in self-approving or self-critical ways, in accordance with their self-prescribed demands" (Bandura, 1973b, p. 237). Several ways in which self-generated consequences enter into self-regulation of aggressive behavior can be distinguished. Individuals who have adopted a self-reinforcement system in which aggressive behavior is a source of self-esteem and pride act aggressively to experience the self-satisfaction that is associated with acting aggressively. In contrast, most individuals experience self-criticism after aggressive activities, and the anticipation of self-punishment often restrains individuals from injurious aggression. Finally, Bandura (1973a) notes that individuals often engage in a variety of neutralization strategies by which self-condemnation for aggression is minimized; these tactics include, for example, diffusion of responsibility, displacement of responsibility, justification of aggression in terms of higher principles, and dehumanization of victims (see Bandura, 1973a, for a fuller discussion of these strategies). The conditions under which children use these tactics and their relative effectiveness in different situations remain relatively unexplored. Finally, developmental analyses of these strategies, which would illuminate how children of different ages utilize these strategies, would be useful.

The Social-Cognitive Perspective

A growing number of research investigators have begun to develop further a social-cognitive model for the study of aggression. Although its theoretical framework has not yet been fully formulated, this model nevertheless brings a new set of research questions, conceptualizations, and interpretations to the area. The social-cognitive model of aggression has focused primarily on the following tasks: (1) identifying internal mediators of aggression (e.g., implicit rules of conduct, social judgments, attributions, justifications); (2) explaining how cognitive mediational processes may serve to regulate aggressive responses (e.g., decoding and interpreting social cues, as well as generating, evaluating, prioritizing, and enacting behavioral responses); (3) demonstrating how developmental and individual differences in aggressive response to a given social situation may be related to particular mediational patterns and abilities (e.g., inferring the motives of others' behavior, attributing stable dispositions to others); and (4) demonstrating how particular patterns of mediation may lead to relative consistency across situations and stability over time in an individual's aggressive behavior (e.g., goal setting, self-regulatory strategies).

The social-cognitive model draws on earlier work in a variety of areas, including Bandura's (1973a) formulation of self-regulatory mechanisms, Flavell's (1977) theory of cognitive development, Goldfried and d'Zurilla's (1969) model of problem solving, McFall's (1982) formulation of social skills, and Walters and Parke's (1964) perspective on social judgments. Major contributors to the current social-cognitive perspective on aggression include Dodge (1980, 1981; Dodge & Frame, 1982; Dodge & Newman, 1981), Feshbach (1974; Feshbach & Feshbach, 1981), Rule (1974; Ferguson & Rule, 1980; Rule, Nesdale, & McAra, 1974), and Spivack and Shure (1974).

Just as the social judgment approach recognizes that researchers make judgments in determining which interpersonal behaviors conform to a culturally determined label of aggression, the social-cognitive model assumes that the developing child also makes social interpretations about which interpersonal behaviors constitute aggressive provocation and retaliation. In both cases, the outcome of those judgments heavily influence the individual's future course of action. It should also be noted that the social-cognitive model may be well suited to address such issues as sex differences in aggression, developmental and individual differences in aggression, and stability of aggressive behavior. These issues are discussed in later sections.

To illustrate the social-cognitive perspective, a recent version of this approach outlined by Dodge (Dodge, 1981; Dodge & Frame, 1982; Dodge & Newman, 1981) is presented. An outline of the Dodge model is provided in Figure 3. According to this five-step model, a child must process cues in an orderly fashion and failure to do so increases the likelihood of deviant behavior occurring, such as aggression. According to Dodge (1981),

A child comes to a particular social situation or task with a data base (his memory store) and a set of programmed directives (goals), and he receives as input from the environment a set of social cues. That child's behavioral response to those cues occurs as a function of his progression through several cognitive steps. Each step is a necessary, but insufficient, part of competent responding. The steps are sequential in time, meaning that competent responding requires an orderly progression of cognitive steps. Effective or competent behavior occurs only following the successful completion of *all* steps.

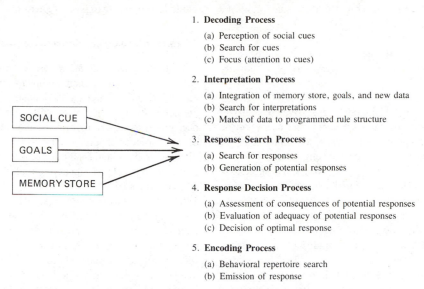

1. **Decoding Process**

    (a) Perception of social cues
    (b) Search for cues
    (c) Focus (attention to cues)

2. **Interpretation Process**

    (a) Integration of memory store, goals, and new data
    (b) Search for interpretations
    (c) Match of data to programmed rule structure

3. **Response Search Process**

    (a) Search for responses
    (b) Generation of potential responses

4. **Response Decision Process**

    (a) Assessment of consequences of potential responses
    (b) Evaluation of adequacy of potential responses
    (c) Decision of optimal response

5. **Encoding Process**

    (a) Behavioral repertoire search
    (b) Emission of response

Figure 3. A social information-processing model of aggression. (Adapted from Dodge, 1982.)

The first step is a decoding process. The child must accurately receive social cues from the environment through sensory processes and then perceive them. Relevant to this step of the process is the child's ability to search the environment for cues and to focus on, or attend to, appropriate cues. For example, in competently responding to a provocation by a peer, such as being hit in the back, the child must search for cues relevant to the peer's intention in committing the act, and then focus on those cues. This step is therefore an active process requiring skill.

The second step is an interpretation process. Once the child has perceived the cues in the situation, he must integrate them with his memory of past events and his goals for the task. He then searches for a possible interpretation of the social cues. The child who was hit by a peer must decide whether the peer was trying to be friendly or mean, or was acting accidentally. Finally, the child matches the environmental data and his memory with a programmed rule structure. For example, his rule might be: If the peer laughs after hitting me, then I know he meant to hurt me.

The third step is the response search process. Once the child has interpreted a situation, he must search for possible behavioral responses. The work of Spivack and Shure (1974) has demonstrated the importance of being able to generate many and varied responses, or solutions, to situations.* This skill is relevant to this step of the response process. Also important at this step is the child's application of response rules. For example, the child might acquire the following rule: if a peer intends to hurt me, then I can hit him back. Of course Piaget (1932) suggested that young children first acquire a different rule: if I get hurt, then I can hit back.

Beyond generating many responses, the child must begin to choose an optimal response, which takes place at the next step. In choosing a response, the child must first assess the probable consequences of each response that he has generated so that he or she can evaluate the adequacy of each response possibility. These skills require highly complex cognitive representations and may be a great source of difficulty for young or impulsive children. At some point, however, the child decides on an optimal behavioral response.

Finally, the child must proceed to act out the chosen behavioral response. This step is an encoding process. Motoric skills, acquired over time through practice, are critical here. The child who decides to respond to a peer's provocation

*Recent research suggests that the content as well as the number of social strategies may be important (Asher, Renshaw, & Geraci, 1980; Richard & Dodge, 1982).

with a verbal statement of displeasure and a request to stop the provocation must possess the verbal skills to accomplish this behavioral task. (Dodge, 1981, pp. 2–4)

Applying this general information-processing model to aggression, Dodge offers the following description:

According to the model, aggressive boys carry in their memory an expectancy that peers will be hostile toward them. When confronted with social cues from a peer, they engage in a decoding process. If, during this process, an aggressive boy fails to search for all available cues, or if he selectively attends to only hostile cues from a peer, then the probability is greatest that he will make interpretations that the peer is hostile. When this occurs, he is highly likely to behave aggressively toward the peer. This behavior is then likely to lead to retaliatory aggression from the peer, which serves to reinforce the aggressive boy's original expectancy that peers are hostile. The model describes a vicious circle. (Dodge, 1982)

In a later section data relevant to this model are presented. While the model is of potential importance for generating new ways of examining aggression, more attention to the developmental implications of the model is necessary. How do changes in information-processing skills across development alter children's ability to avoid aggressive encounters? Second, the model is adequate for describing differences in the skills of children who are already identified as aggressive, but the model offers only limited aid in determining how these children developed aggressive patterns at earlier ages. Third, competence in processing social information should be more clearly distinguished from performance deficits that particular groups of individuals may show under conditions that are not conducive to optimal cognitive functioning. To what extent do noncognitive factors, either situationally induced such as emotional arousal or more stable personality dispositions such as low frustration tolerance, impulsivity, or impatience disrupt an individuals' cognitive functioning in particular situations? Moreover, are the deficits in social information processing generalized across situations, targets, types of provocation, and so on? Or do some children fail to consider constructive solutions in peer conflicts but demonstrate competence in their social processing abilities in interaction with adults? Clearly many

issues remain, but this approach does appear to hold considerable promise and should serve as a useful guide to future research on aggression.

Toward an Ecological Model of Aggression

A limitation of all the theoretical models that have been outlined is their failure to give explicit recognition to the child's embeddedness in a variety of social systems, ranging from the family and the peer group to the community and the culture. Each of these sources of influence needs to be given explicit recognition and each must be viewed as a different but interrelated aspect of a multifactor social interactional analysis (Parke & Lewis, 1981; Parke, 1982). This viewpoint is compatible with those of Brim (1975) and Bronfenbrenner (1979) who have called for a macrostructural analysis in which a variety of immediate as well as larger social contexts are recognized as important ingredients for a complete analysis of aggression. As outlined in Figure 4, there is a bidirectional influence among various sources, and each source can influence another source either directly (e.g., culture to family, or community to culture) or indirectly through another source (e.g., culture to community to family). This is an important assumption, since it recognizes that children are able to be directly influenced by the community, for example, and not just through the mediation of the family unit. This model implies that children and adults have *direct* ties to cultural sources in a society, such as community services or television. This view is in contrast to a position that assumes that influences on individual children are necessarily mediated through the family, which acts as a buffer between community and cultural influences. Throughout this chapter, an attempt is made to illustrate the utility of expanding the range of contexts that may influence the development and regulation of aggression.

BIOLOGICAL DETERMINANTS OF AGGRESSION

Biological approaches to the development of aggression have addressed a wide range of factors as potential correlates of or influences on aggressive behavior, such as genetic factors, autonomic and central nervous system factors, and biochemical factors (Mednick, Pollock, Volavka, & Gabrielli, 1982). As is the case with any set of social behaviors such as aggression, biological factors interact with environmental agents in determining the extent to which aggression occurs. To illustrate this theme

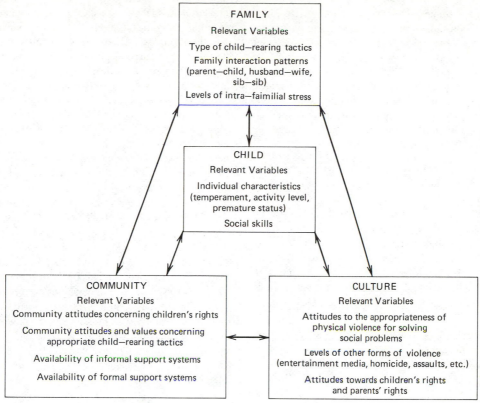

Figure 4. An ecological model of aggression. (Adapted from Parke, 1982).

selected examples of the role of biology in aggression are presented, including hormonal influences, as well as the impact of muscularity, physical appearance, and temperament on aggression.

Hormones and Aggression

The relationship between aggressive behavior and hormonal or other biochemical processes is a complex issue. Hormones have been suggested to serve two functions in the development of social behavior such as aggression (Young, 1961). First, hormones may have an organizing function. This hypothesis requires the assumption that there is a critical development period for each species during which the presence or absence of certain hormones permanently affects the structure of the biological system. Second, hormones may have an energizing or activating function: This hypothesis assumes that the level of certain hormonal agents may modify different classes of current behavior.

Two caveats are necessary: (1) These functions

are much more clearly demonstrated in lower animals than in humans, and (2) the influence between hormones and behavior is bidirectional. The evidence indicates that shifts in social circumstances can influence hormonal levels, just as changes in hormones can influence behavior. As Maccoby and Jacklin (1974) appropriately note "hormone levels constitute an open system. A testosterone level is not something that an individual 'has' independently of experience even though in a stable social situation a given individual's score is quite stable. At the present state of our knowledge, it would appear that a high testosterone level can be both a cause and a result of aggressive behavior" (1974, p. 246).

The evidence for the organizing function of hormones in lower animals is well established—at least for some species. For many animals, during the fetal period of gender differentiation, the presence of androgens are necessary for the normal development of the male fetus, and low levels of androgens result in reduced aggression at later ages. As Tieger (1980) recently summarized:

These studies show fairly reliably that critical periods for hormonal influence, measurable in terms of aggressive behavior tendencies in later life, do exist for various animal species. Male hormones can masculinize the behavior of genetic females, and their absence in genetic males (e.g., via castration) leads to a decrease in normal male patterns of behavior in agonistic encounters. Furthermore, female hormones reduce later fighting behavior in males.

The exact biophysical changes which may have occurred in the critical period due to these hormonal manipulations can only be inferred at this time. But clearly the anomalous hormones or their metabolites (Whalen, 1974) seem to sensitize certain central nervous system structures to allow for differences in the appearance of dimorphic sex-role behavior patterns when proper stimulus situations are present later in life (Levine, 1968). (Tieger, 1980, p. 948)

Is there any evidence for such an organizing effect in humans? A number of studies have been conducted by Ehrhardt and her colleagues (Ehrhardt & Baker, 1974; Ehrhardt, Grisanti, & Meyer-Bahlburg, 1977; Money & Ehrhardt, 1972). In one of the earliest investigations, Money and Ehrhardt (1972) studied genetic females with progestin-induced hermaphroditism and adrenogenital syndrome. It was anticipated that the inappropriate influx of fetal androgens in these children would produce masculinized behavior patterns in the same way that the animal studies had previously shown. Although the girls were rated as more masculinized in terms of physical energy, "tomboy" behavior, and playmate preferences, there were no differences between the progestin group and normal control females in aggressive behavior. In a later study (Ehrhardt & Baker, 1974), involving both boys and girls who were exposed to excessive levels of androgens, increases in activity level were found, but once again no differences in aggression were evident. Other later studies have yielded similarly inconclusive evidence for a link between hormones and aggression, and this evidence led Tieger to conclude that "the operation of hormones as an organizing function in humans does exist for some behaviors. However, hormones do not seem to be involved in organizing the central nervous system to predispose humans to act aggressively" (1980, p. 950).

More recently, Reinisch (1981) has rekindled interest in this issue by suggesting that Tieger's conclusions may have been premature. In her study, 17

females and 8 males who had been exposed during gestation to synthetic progestins were compared with their same-sex unexposed siblings. Although the timing and duration of the hormone treatment varied, treatment was initiated in all of the pregnancies during the first trimester—thus all of the subjects were exposed to the hormones during at least some portion of the period of gestation believed to be critical for hormonal differentiation of genital morphology and for central nervous system development in humans. It is important to note that no virilization of the genitalia was apparent in the progestin-exposed females. At the time of testing, the girls ranged in age from 6 to 17 years (mean age of 11½ years), while the boys ranged from 6 to 18 years (mean age of 11 years 4 months). To evaluate aggressive tendencies, all subjects were given the age-appropriate form of the Leifer-Roberts Response Hierarchy, a paper and pencil instrument designed to assess the potential for aggressive behavior by eliciting verbal estimates of the subjects' responses to a variety of common conflict situations. Choices of behavioral responses to each conflict are provided, including physical or verbal aggression, withdrawal, and nonaggressive coping with the frustrator.

Exposure to synthetic progestins during gestation led to differences in the subjects' Response Hierarchy Scores. Although males were higher overall than females in their physical aggression scores, both males and females who had been exposed to progestin, in comparison with their unexposed same-sex siblings, were higher in physical aggression. No difference in the number of verbal aggression responses was found. Neither age nor birth order showed any relationship to physical aggression scores. Although the reliance on the verbal report measure of aggression is a limitation of the study, earlier validation studies of the Leifer-Roberts Index increase our confidence in the generalizability of the results. However, further evaluation of this issue using direct behavioral observations would be helpful in isolating whether there is a general increase in the amount of initiating aggressive behavior or whether the effects are restricted to retaliatory reactions, as in the case of the effects of testosterone in aggression (Olweus, Mattsson, Schalling, & Low, 1980). More attention needs to be directed to the mediating factors that may account for these differences. Also a variety of physiognomic differences, which may be a by-product of the prenatal hormonal exposure and which, in turn, may lead to differential parental treatment, need to be examined as potential mediators of the exposure-aggression relationship. Finally, the developmental course of the relationship needs to be more carefully examined.

Next we examine the activating function of hormones. Is there a relationship between the level of certain hormonal agents and the amount or type of contemporaneous aggressive behavior? In animals, there is substantial evidence of a relationship between testosterone levels in circulating plasma and fighting behavior in males of a variety of species, including rodents (Suchowsky, Pegrassi, & Bonsignori, 1967) and nonhuman primates (Rose, Holaday, & Bernstein, 1971). Moreover, female primates who are given testosterone injections have been found to increase their aggressiveness (Joslyn, 1973). However, additional evidence indicating little or no relationship between testosterone and aggression (e.g., Eaton, 1976) underscores the important point that aggressive behavior is by no means solely dependent on hormonal control. Cairns (1979) notes a variety of reasons for this view:

> There appears, however, to be considerable day-to-day fluctuations in the level of testosterone in the blood, suggesting that this measure is sensitive to such factors as diurnal rhythm, nutrition, momentary states of arousal, as well as to chronic and stable individual differences in testosterone secretion. Cumulative indices of male hormone activity, such as the secondary characteristics of sex dimorphism (size, coat fullness and color) do appear to be correlated with dominance in primate societies. Ironically the less precise measures of testosterone activity (gross secondary sex characteristics as opposed to levels of testosterone in the blood) may prove to be the best predictors of social interchanges. (p. 178)

Is there any evidence of a link between testosterone and aggression in humans? The pioneering study in this area was undertaken by Persky, Smith, and Basu (1971). Levels of testosterone concentration and blood production rate of testosterone were significantly correlated with scores on the Buss-Durkee Hostile Inventory (a self-report measure of aggression) for younger (17–28 years of age) but not for older men (over 31 years of age).

In a later study, Kreuz and Rose (1972) examined testosterone levels in prisoners with a history of violent crime. Although there was no relationship between concurrent testosterone levels and aggression (self-reports of aggression or frequency of prison fights), those prisoners with a record of violent crimes in adolescence had significantly higher levels of testosterone in prison. In addition, these investigators found a significant and positive correlation between the age at which the aggressive crime first occurred and the current levels of testosterone.

However, recent tests of the relationship between plasma testosterone levels and aggressive and criminal behavior have yielded conflicting results. Positive relationships have been found in some studies between testosterone levels and some aggressive and criminal dimensions, while others have failed to show significant relationships.

For example, Olweus et al. (1980) failed to confirm the previously reported relationship between testosterone and antisocial behavior (Kreuz & Rose, 1972), at least for their normal sample of adolescents. Moreover, in their later study of juvenile delinquent boys, this group of investigators (Mattsson, Schalling, Olweus, & Low, 1982) failed to confirm the link between testosterone level and a history of violent crimes.

In spite of the lack of consistent support for the links between testosterone and criminal behavior, there appears to be more support for the relationship between testosterone and some types of aggression. Substantial support for the hypothesized relationship is provided by a recent study by Olweus et al. (1980). Using 16-year-old Swedish boys, these investigators found a significant relationship between plasma testosterone levels and self-reports of physical and verbal aggression, particularly aggressive responses to provocation and threat. In addition, these investigators found a smaller but significant correlation between testosterone and self-reports of frustration tolerance: Boys with higher levels of testosterone tended to be habitually more impatient and irritable than boys with lower testosterone levels. Other measures of aggression, such as aggressive attitude or impulses and unprovoked physical or verbal aggression, showed only weak relationships with levels of testosterone. Other research (Mattsson et al., 1982) involving institutionalized male delinquents is consistent with this earlier work and confirms that the strongest relationship of aggression to testosterone level involves aggressive responses to provocation. Finally, Scaramella and Brown (1978) reported a positive correlation between levels of testosterone and whose ratings of responsiveness to threat in a study of male hockey players. Together these studies underscore the necessity of distinguishing among various types of aggressive behavior in the search for underlying relationships between biochemical factors and aggression. In view of other research as well (see Hoyenga & Hoyenga, 1979, for a review), which shows that testosterone level in males rises rapidly at puberty and that aggression increases in some species (nonhuman primates) at that time, the relationship may be most evident in adolescence or at least among young men.

Are there comparable effects in women? There is some, albeit weak, evidence of a relationship between testosterone levels and aggression in women. Persky (1974) found a small but significant relationship between Buss-Durkee scores (a self-report hostility measure) and the average testosterone levels of women in the follicular phase of the menstrual cycle. However, although testosterone levels of women varied significantly over menstrual phases, the scores on the Buss-Durkee index did not. It may be that high levels of testosterone are evident only in women who view themselves as high in aggression—a reminder of the bidirectional nature of the influence. A more promising place to find links between hormonal shifts and aggressive behavior in women is during the premenstrual phase, where some researchers find that aggression is highest (e.g. Paige, 1971; Silbergeld, Brast, & Noble, 1971).

As Olweus et al. note, it is important to remember that "there is not a direct linear relationship between testosterone and antisocial behavior. If there is a systematic relationship between these two variables it is likely to be of a more complex and, perhaps, indirect nature" (1980, pp. 265–266). Finally, it is clear that there is no tyrannical control of aggressive behavior by hormones; instead, hormones should be viewed as part of a multivariate set of determinants rather than as sufficient causes of aggression.

Muscularity, Physical Appearance, and Aggression

There are other various biological factors that may play a role in aggression, such as muscularity, strength, and physical appearance. Muscularity and strength both are factors that could mediate some types of aggression, such as physical aggression, and, in turn, could account for individual differences within the sex as well as differences between boys and girls in aggression. Boys have larger and stronger muscles and seem to be more adapted to vigorous activity (Hoyenga & Hoyenga, 1979). Paralleling the sex difference in muscle tissue, the sex difference in strength increases from age 11 to age 17 (Tanner, 1970; Wilmore, 1975) and may even be present at birth (Korner, 1974).

Physical appearance is another biological factor that may be related indirectly to the development of aggression. Both adults and children form different expectations for the interpersonal behaviors of children of differing degrees of attractiveness. Children as young as age 3 to 5 can differentiate attractive from unattractive children and seem to judge these children on the basis of the same physical attributes as adults do (Dion, 1973; Styczynski & Langlois, 1977). Desirable characteristics are attributed by both children and adults more often to attractive than to unattractive children, even when unfamiliar children are assessed (Dion & Berscheid, 1974: Lerner & Lerner, 1977; Styczynski & Langlois, 1977). Aggressive, antisocial behavior and meanness are regarded as more characteristic of unattractive children, while positive behaviors such as independence and friendliness are attributed to attractive children (Langlois & Stephan, 1977).These negative views of unattractive children are not only impressions, but may have some basis in behavior as well. Langlois and Downs (1980) found no differences between the social behavior of attractive and unattractive 3-year-olds. However, unattractive, in contrast to attractive, 5-year-olds were more likely to be aggressive, hit peers, and play in an active, boisterous manner. According to Langlois and Stephan (1981):

> This finding suggests that differential behavioral expectations for attractive and unattractive children and a self-fulfilling prophecy work together: Unattractive children may be labeled as such and learn the stereotypes and behaviors associated with unattractiveness. Consequently, they may then exhibit aggressive behaviors consistent with this label and actually behave in accordance with others' expectations of them. (Langlois & Stephan, 1981, p. 167)

This research clearly illustrates the interplay among biological factors, social and cognitive expectations, and behavioral outcomes.

Temperament and Aggression

Finally, differences in temperament may be related indirectly to the development of aggressive behavior. As in the case of physical attractiveness, temperament may influence parental or peer reactions, which, in turn, could modify the likelihood of the emergence of aggressive or antisocial behavior patterns. Clear evidence of individual differences in temperament from infancy onward is available (Rothbart & Derryberry, 1981; St. Clair, 1978), as is evidence indicating that differences in temperament are associated with differential treatment by caregivers (Bates, 1982; Osofsky & Danzger, 1974). Other evidence (e.g., Thomas, Chess, & Birch, 1968) suggests that differences in temperament in interaction with parental treatment may result in long-term differences in developmental outcome. For example, Thomas et al. (1968) found that the children who developed behavior problems including aggressiveness had a particular temperamental pattern at earlier ages. They were more active, more irregular, had lower thresholds, were low on adaptability, and were rated high on intensity, persistence, and distractibility. In spite of the limitations in the research by Thomas et al., such as a heavy reliance on nonvalidated parental reports, the work does suggest the possible role of temperamental factors in mediating later aggressive patterns. However, aggression was part of a cluster of behavior problems, and the specific links between temperament and aggression per se cannot be discerned from this research.

Other evidence of the possible role of temperament as a mediating variable in the development of aggression comes from Olweus (1980). Based on mothers' reports of their adolescent boy's earlier temperament (a composite of the boy's general activity level and the intensity of his temperament, varying from calm to hot-tempered), Olweus found a positive relationship between temperament rated for what earlier age? and peer-rated aggression in adolescence. Again, methodological limitations, which are discussed in detail in the section titled *Parental child-rearing tactics*, limit the conclusions that can be drawn from this study concerning the relationship between temperament and aggression.

Recent work by Bates (1982) has overcome some of the limitations of the earlier studies by using both validated measures of temperament and direct observations of parent-infant interaction. As a result, this research permits some insight into how temperament may modify parent-child interaction patterns, which, in turn, may begin to account for differences in social behavior, including aggression. Difficult, in contrast to easy, infants (age 6 months to 3 years) were found to exhibit greater degrees of conflict in interaction with their mothers in control situations. Specifically, these mothers of difficult toddlers more frequently used several kinds of control, including prohibition/warning, repeat prohibition/warning, and restraint compared to other mothers. In turn, the difficult children responded differently to maternal control: They got into trouble again, failed to comply, or expressed negative affect. In summary, these toddlers with difficult temperaments show a "pattern of resistance to control which conceptually resembles the pattern of coercive counter-control that Patterson (1982) has seen in clinically aggressive grade school children's responses to their mothers' control efforts" (Bates, 1982, pp. 4–5). Moreover, difficultness measured at 6, 13, and 24 months appears to have implications for behavior problems at 3 years as rated by parents on the Preschool Behavior Questionnaire—a scale that includes measures of anxiety, hyperactivity, and—of greatest relevance—hostility. Both the overall scale and the individual factors were significantly related to earlier measures of difficultness. Although mere consistency in parental perception could explain the pattern of findings, the fact that the mother-toddler conflict sequences, associated with difficultness at age 24 months, also predict behavior problems as did directly observed gross-motor activity bursts in the 6-month-old infant, suggests that the parental bias does not account for this interesting pattern of results. A word of caution is necessary concerning the biological status of the types of measures usually termed "temperament." Since many of the dimensions are unable to be measured adequately until well after the newborn period, the relative contribution of environmental and biological factors is unclear.

As the research examples in this section indicate, biological contributions to aggression cannot be ignored and are again beginning to receive serious attention. Interactive models in which environmental conditions serve to both facilitate and restrain the expression of biological tendencies predominate (see Cairns, 1979; Hinde, 1978; for further discussion of biological approaches to aggression).

SEX DIFFERENCES IN AGGRESSION

The issue of sex differences in aggression has been of interest for many decades (Dawe, 1934; Green, 1933). Several reviews (Feshbach, 1970; Maccoby & Jacklin, 1974, 1980; Tieger, 1980) attest to both the continuing interest in and the controversy surrounding whether gender is a significant factor in determining children's level of aggression, their type of aggressive response and their susceptibility to various situational elicitors. The timing of the emergence of differences in aggressive behaviors of boys and girls is also of interest. Furthermore, the debate concerning the origins of sex differences in aggression is far from resolved (Maccoby & Jacklin, 1980; Tieger, 1980).

As Maccoby and Jacklin (1980) have recently demonstrated in their meta-analysis of observational studies of child-child aggression with children under 6 years of age, there are clear sex differences in aggression, with boys displaying more aggression than girls. Moreover, their analysis indicated that this sex difference was evident for *both* verbal and physical aggression; in fact, in the meta analysis of the 31 samples, the *z* scores for verbal and physical aggression were nearly identical. Their findings are not restricted to either the middle-class subculture or the American culture. In their analysis, Maccoby and Jacklin (1980) include a wide range of social classes, especially a substantial number of lower or lower middle-class children (e.g., Baumrind, 1971; Hartup, 1974), and there is no indication that sex differences in aggression vary with respect to social class. These findings reflect a compilation of many diverse studies of aggressive behavior in children, attesting to the robustness of the analysis, and the evidence clearly challenges such traditional assumptions that sex differences in aggression depend mainly on differences in the type of aggression displayed (e.g., physical vs. verbal aggression; as suggested by Feshbach, 1970).

Cross-cultural evidence, although not abundant, yields a similar picture of robust sex differences. In an extensive observational study of 15 English preschools, Smith and Green (1974) found greater amounts of aggression (verbal and/or physical) expressed by boys than girls. Omark and Edelman (1975) examined large samples of American, Swiss, and Ethiopian children. From preschool through third grade, males were significantly more aggressive (hitting or pushing) than females in all three cultures. A more complex story emerges from the studies of Whiting and Whiting (Whiting & Edwards, 1973; Whiting & Whiting, 1975) who observed children from 3 to 11 years of age in six different cultures for a 2-year period in a variety of natural settings. In all of the developing countries (e.g., Kenya, India, Phillipines, Mexico, Okinawa), boys were more verbally and physically aggressive than girls, especially the young children (3–6 years). Among the older children (7–11 years), males continued to show more frequent verbal aggression, but no clear sex differences in physical aggression emerged. In summary, there is clear evidence of a sex difference in aggression, but the evidence that this sex difference is restricted to either verbal or physical forms of aggression is less convincing, particularly for younger children.

For older children and adults, however, there are clear sex differences in some types of aggressive behavior (see Cairns, 1979). Using violent crime as an index, there are approximately five times as many adolescent boys as girls arrested for violent crimes (e.g., criminal homicide, robbery, aggravated assault), although there is a gradual increase in the amount and percentage of violent crime reported for females (Gibbons, 1976; Johnson, 1979).

Some researchers have argued that females express aggression indirectly. A study by Feshbach (1969) indicated that adolescent girls were more likely to use "indirect" aggression (ignoring, excluding, refusing, avoiding) in reaction to a newcomer to a group, while boys were more likely to use direct aggression (physical or verbal). While girls were more likely to perform these behaviors, the appropriateness of labeling these behaviors as indirect aggression has been questioned. As Maccoby and Jacklin (1974) note: "There is no evidence in the Feshbach work that the girls' initial avoidance or ignoring represented efforts to hurt or derogate the newcomers; on the other hand, it *may* have involved this quality" (1974, p. 235). Clearly, more attention needs to be addressed to describing the ontogeny of these sex differences in forms of aggressive expression.

Modifiers of Sex Differences in Aggression

There are various conditions that modify the extent to which sex differences are evident. One such modifier is the finding that boys and girls differ markedly in the extent to which they will retaliate after being attacked. In an observational study of 3½-year-old and 4½-year-old boys and girls, Darvill and Cheyne (1981) found clear sex differences in the amount of retaliatory aggression. Specifically, males were more likely than females to respond with counteraggression when being physically attacked, although the difference was mainly attributable to the older males. Males had only a 26% greater probability of initiating attacks than females, but males were approximately 116% more likely to respond to an attack on themselves with a counterattack than were females.

Whiting and Edwards (1973), in their cross-cultural studies, provide similar evidence of a clear sex difference in retaliatory aggression. However, these investigators found that only the older boys in their study (7–11 years of age) were more likely than girls to react with counteraggression after being attacked; in contrast to Darvill and Cheyne, among the younger children (3–6 years) there were no sex differences in retaliatory aggression. Further research on cultural norms with regard to the propriety of counteraggression for males and females and for children at different developmental levels will provide clues concerning the emergence of these sex differences across cultures. Finally, studies are needed that simultaneously assess children's understanding and endorsement of a counterattack principle, in combination with observations of aggression in these children. This type of research would begin to articulate the links between sex differences in type of aggression and the differential cognitive socialization of boys and girls.

Sex differences in aggressive behavior are modified by another situational factor, namely the sex of the partner. In their study of English nursery schools, Smith and Green (1974) found that aggressive interchanges were significantly higher in boy-boy dyads than in boy-girl pairs or in girl-girl dyads. Similarly, McGrew (1972) found that the frequency of agonistic interactions was higher in dyads involving boys (boy-boy or boy-girl) than in girl-girl dyads. Nor is this finding restricted to preschool age children. In a careful naturalistic observational study of 5- to 8-year-olds, Barrett (1979) found that when the target was male, boys showed higher rates of both physical and verbal aggression than girls. For female targets there was no sex difference in the frequency of aggressive acts. When nonaggressive behavior initiations directed to boys were controlled, boys had higher scores on physical aggression than did girls, but there were no sex differences in verbal aggression. In contrast, when the number of nonaggressive behavior initiations directed toward girls was controlled, boys had significantly higher scores than girls on both physical and verbal aggression. Retaliatory aggression also varied with sex of partner—especially for physical aggression. When provoked by males, boys were significantly more likely than girls to retaliate with physical aggression. When provoked by females, boys were less likely than girls to respond with physical aggression. Boys and girls did not differ in the likelihood of verbal retaliation to aggression, regardless of the sex of the provoking child.

As Barrett (1979) notes,

While the results do not necessarily contradict the hypothesis that learned inhibitions against aggression in females may be weakened if there is an explicit provocation, they do suggest another possible effect of provocation on children's aggressive behavior. If provocation were to increase the subject's awareness of his or her current behavior by arousing an anticipatory aggressive response, the subject might be more likely to refrain from socially unacceptable ag-

gressive behavior than if no such provocation had occurred. The tendency for boys to refrain from cross-sex physical retaliation would be consistent with this hypothesis. (1979, p. 201)

Finally, it should be noted that there are some situations in which females are equal to males in their aggressiveness. Recently, Brodzinsky, Messer, and Tew (1979) reported that fifth-grade boys were rated by peers and teachers as more directly physically and verbally aggressive than girls, but not more indirectly aggressive (e.g., taking or destroying things that belong to others or tattling on children). Others (Caplan, 1979; Frodi, Macauley, & Thome, 1977) have reported that adult women act just as aggressively as men in certain conditions, such as those involving low surveillance by others, in group contexts that permit diffusion of responsibility for individual aggressive action, or when some other individual explicitly assumes responsibility for their aggression. Frodi et al. argue that as a result of specific socialization experiences, females are more susceptible than males to guilt and anxiety over the expression of aggression, which under many but not all circumstances results in the inhibition of their aggression.

Consistent with the above view is the finding that girls experience more aggression control—an index of the extent to which an individual attempts to inhibit or modify the expression of aggression—when administered the TAT (Brodzinsky et al., 1979). Earlier, Sears (1961) found similar results; 12-year-old girls reported greater aggression anxiety than their male counterparts.

Under circumstances in which the negative emotions (e.g., guilt, anxiety, shame) associated with the expression of aggression are lessened, differences in male and female aggressiveness may be diminished.

Origins of Sex Differences in Aggressive Behavior

Attempts to account for sex differences in aggression have incorporated both biological and environmental factors. Concerning the biological case, Maccoby and Jacklin (1974) offer the following argument.

What are the implications of these consistencies across societies and across subcultures within societies for a possible biological contribution to sex differences in aggression? If societies varied more or less at random, with girls being more aggressive about as often as boys, a biological explanation would be fairly well ruled out. Cross-cultural universality would mean that a biological factor is possible, not that it is proven. And if there were a biological contribution, it might be something that does not act upon aggression itself but created aggressiveness in males, or nonaggressiveness in females, as a consequence of some other biological difference. If women's role in child-bearing and child rearing causes girls to be subject to closer surveillance by adults, or if it causes adults to train them in nurturance and teach them to inhibit aggression, it would not be surprising that girls would be universally less aggressive. The cause would be biological in that it stems from child-bearing, but the implications would be quite different than if there were a more direct biological influence on aspects of aggression itself (as in the case of hormonal sensitizing to certain eliciting stimuli). It is conceivable, but unlikely in our opinion, that cross-cultural universality could occur with no biological rootedness at all. (1974, p. 971)

Several pieces of evidence lend credence to a view in which biology serves as a setting condition for the development of sex differences in aggression. As noted earlier in this chapter, biologically based differences in individuals, for example, in terms of muscularity, strength, and temperament, may result in different reactions from socializing agents, which, in turn, may have consequences for the differential promotion of aggressive behavior patterns in males and females. Similarly, other sex differences—such as male newborns showing less sensitivity to pain than females (Lipsitt & Levy, 1959) and female newborns having more sensitive skin (Weller & Bell, 1965)—may result in both differential handling by parents and the male infants themselves tolerating more vigorous and rougher forms of stimulation than female infants.

Moreover, parents have clear cultural stereotypes concerning the qualities associated with infants of different sexes, which, in turn, could lead to differences in treatment. Rubin, Provenzano, and Luria (1974), for example, found that newborn sons were rated by parents, especially fathers, as firmer, better coordinated, more alert, stronger, and hardier while daughters were rated as softer, finer-featured, more awkward, weaker, and more delicate. As the authors note,

The central implication of the study, then, is that sex-typing and sex role socialization appear to have already begun their course at the time of the infant's birth, when information about the infant is minimal. The "Gestalt" parents develop, and the labels they ascribe to their newborn infant, may well affect subsequent expectations about the manner in which their infant ought to behave as well as parental behavior itself. (1974, pp. 518–519)

Furthermore, this sex stereotyping is not restricted to parents of newborn infants. In a study by Condry and Condry (1976), male and female college students rated a videotaped infant who was labeled either a "boy" or "girl." Observers rated the infant's emotional reaction to different stimuli (e.g., a jack-in-the-box) differently as a function of the sex label. The "boy" was rated as "angry," while the same reaction by an infant "girl" was labeled "fear." In addition, the "boy" was rated as more "active" and "potent" than the "girl" on semantic differential ratings. Together, these studies illustrate that socialization agents such as parents have clearly distinct expectations for males and females, which, if translated into differential treatment, could, in turn, possibly account for the different levels of aggression in boys and girls.

What are the paths by which this combination of constitutional differences and adult expectations results in the emergence of sex differences in aggression? An influential hypothesis was proposed by Kagan and Moss (1962) to account for sex differences in both the level of aggression typically displayed and the degree of long-term stability of aggression. These researchers argued that parents and other socialization agents provided differential reinforcement or at least tolerance of the aggressive behavior of boys and girls. They contend that, although girls may be allowed to engage in a limited degree of aggression, competitiveness, and "tomboyish" behavior during the preschool and elementary school years, they face strong socialization pressure during the adolescent years to suppress these tendencies in favor of traditionally feminine behavior, such as nurturance, dependency, and approval-seeking behavior. For boys, on the other hand, aggression may be consistently tolerated, or even explicitly encouraged and rewarded by socializing adults, since aggression is generally viewed as an integral component of traditional masculine behavior.

Although Mischel (1970) has appropriately questioned the adequacy of this hypothesis for explaining the differential stability of male and female aggression, the differential reinforcement argument could account for differences in the level of aggression of males and females. However, more recent evidence suggests that even this analysis is oversimplified. While some studies do indicate that aggression is either tolerated or explicitly encouraged more in boys than girls (Sears, Maccoby, & Levin, 1957), other studies find that boys are more severely reprimanded for aggression than girls (Lambert, Yackley, & Hein, 1971; Minton, Kagan, & Levine, 1971; Serbin, O'Leary, Kent, & Tonick, 1973). Moreover, other investigators report no differences in parental treatment of male and female aggression (Fagot, 1978; Newson & Newson, 1968).

However, there is a growing body of evidence that boys and girls are treated differently by their parents (Block, 1978) in a variety of other spheres such as child-rearing practices and attitudes toward toy choices and types of play activities. It is argued that such differential parental treatment of boys and girls in areas other than aggression may, indirectly, affect male and female development and expression of aggression. For example, parents are more likely to use physical punishment with sons than daughters and to use inductive techniques such as reasoning with daughters more often than with sons (Block, 1978; Hoffman, 1970). In view of experimental evidence (Gelfand, Hartmann, Lamb, Smith, Mahan, & Paul, 1974), which suggests that children will adopt the training tactics used by an adult in their own interactions with other children, these differences in child-rearing of boys and girls could, in fact, contribute to different levels of male and female aggression. Specifically, the investigators found that a child disciplined by an adult with punitive tactics was more likely to use similarly punitive techniques when given the opportunity to train another child (see the section on parental child-rearing tactics for a more detailed examination of this hypothesis). Parents select different toys for boys and girls (Rheingold & Cook, 1975) and encourage the two sexes to play with sex-typed toys (Fagot, 1978; Langlois & Downs, 1980). In view of the evidence that some male sex-typed toys, such as guns, may elicit aggressive activity (Turner & Goldsmith, 1976), these parental sex-typed activities assume importance in the differential socialization of male and female aggression. Moreover, parents engage in more physically active play with boys than girls not only in infancy (Power & Parke, 1982) but also in the preschool (MacDonald & Parke, 1982) and elementary school periods (Tauber, 1979). Moreover,

parents discourage rough-and-tumble games on the part of their daughters, and fathers discourage fighting on the part of their daughters more than their sons (Block, 1978). Other investigators (e.g., Tauber, 1979) found that fathers reacted more positively to physical activity by boys than by girls. Although the impact of these opportunities to engage in physical interaction on later aggression is not yet clearly established, evidence that choice of activities which emphasize physical skills, such as wrestling or judo, is related, for some children, to later patterns of aggression (Bullock & Merrill, 1980) suggests that these sex-typed opportunities provided by parents may, in fact, be important for aggression development (see the section on stability of aggressive behavior for a more detailed discussion of the Bullock & Merrill study).

Not incompatible with the above argument is an explanation of socialization influences on the development of sex-differential behavior patterns that emphasizes children's own "self-socialization" role in formulating social rules and standards that guide them in their display of relatively enduring and generalizable response patterns (Maccoby & Jacklin, 1974). There is ample opportunity for children to learn from a variety of sources that aggression is widely regarded as a masculine activity. Thus, boys and girls may develop sex-role-related cognitive standards for seeking, interpreting, and responding to aggressive stimulation. Recent evidence from longitudinal research, examining such internal cognitive standards, is consistent with the position that boys and girls may play a major role in defining their own socialization experiences related to aggression. In one study, it was found that children's aggressive behavior at the age of 5 years was independently related to both their viewing of television violence and their sex-role preferences, as measured 2 years earlier (Eron, 1980). For boys, aggression was related to a high preference for traditionally masculine activities and, for girls, aggression was related to a low preference for traditionally feminine activities.

In a second longitudinal study with older children, the viewing of television violence and sex-role preference were similarly found to be independent and stable predictors of aggression for boys, although not for girls (Eron, Lefkowitz, Walder, & Huesmann, 1974). Specifically, the preferences shown by 8-year-old boys for watching violent television programs and for avoiding traditionally feminine activities were found to be predictive of their peer-rated aggression, measured both at that time and 10 years later. The authors suggest that, for boys, the watching of television violence is likely to have both an immediate effect and a long-term cumulative effect on building aggressive habits. The overall pattern of the data further suggested that, by the time the boys had reached the age of 19 years, their aggressive behavior patterns were strongly established and no longer as responsive to the conditions that influenced the development of this behavior 10 years earlier.

In summary, it is argued that neither biological nor learning explanations alone can account for sex differences in aggression. Instead, biological differences in males and females may lead to differential opportunities to acquire aggressive behavior, although the mechanisms by which this learning occurs may often be indirect.

DEVELOPMENTAL PATTERNS IN AGGRESSION

Antecedents of Aggressive Behavior

In the search for the roots of aggressive behavior, researchers have examined the social encounters of infants and young children, especially social conflict. The study of social conflict in young children has been of interest for decades (Buhler, 1935; Dawe, 1934; Green, 1933; Maudry & Nekula, 1939; Shirley, 1933). Observational studies (Holmberg, 1977; Maudry & Nekula, 1939) indicate that approximately half of the interchanges among children 12 to 18 months old observed in a nursery school setting could be viewed as disruptive or conflictful. In contrast to prosocial actions, the proportion of aggressive actions tended to decrease with age. By 2 ½ years of age the proportion of disruptive interchanges with peers has decreased to 20%. In the nursery school setting, the children 12 to 42 months old showed few assertive behaviors directed toward adults (only 5%), and this proportion showed little change across age. These conflicts are most often disagreements concerning space and resources and have generally been viewed by researchers as neither aggressive nor hostile. In fact, some (Maudry & Nekula, 1939) have deemphasized the social nature of early conflicts and termed them ''socially blind,'' or in other words different from conflicts engaged in by older children and adults in which negative affect and hostile intent are more characteristic. This view has recently been challenged by Hay and Ross (1982) who argue that ''young children may be swayed by the *social significance* as well as the objective stimulus properties of the objects of dispute'' (1982, p. 106; italics added). Moreover, even though the early conflicts between infants and young

children may not possess all of the characteristics of the aggressive actions of older children and adults (e.g., such as specific intent to inflict harm), the precursors of social regulation of aggressive interchanges are most likely to be discovered in an examination of these early interchanges.

Evidence suggesting a relationship between early social interchanges and the development of aggression is provided by a recent study of the conflicts of 24 pairs of unacquainted 21-month-old children (Hay & Ross, 1982). Conflict was defined as ''the incompatibility of the behavior of two interacting children. A conflict began when the action of one child met with protest, resistance or retaliation'' (Hay & Ross, 1981, p. 11). Eighty-seven percent of the children participated in at least one conflict during the four 15-minute observation sessions in a laboratory playroom, although the relative amount of time spent in conflict was small (5.7% of their time or 205 seconds). Nor were the conflicts sustained; the average length of a conflict was 22.7 seconds. The brevity of the conflicting interchanges was not the result of adult intervention alone; mothers intervened 72 times, in 21% of the conflicts and for only 14 children. In 79% of the conflicts, the children terminated the exchange themselves, without adult intervention. The majority of the conflicts (72%) were concerned with object or possession struggles, while the remaining struggles were either exclusively interpersonal disputes, as when one child's actions were protested or resisted by the peer, or disputes involving both object-related and interpersonal themes. The most interesting findings from this study concerned the social qualities of early conflict. These data suggest that different types of actions by children were differentially effective in inducing peers to yield. For example, instrumental behaviors (e.g., tugging a toy; active resistance) were more likely than communicative actions (e.g., gesturing; verbally requesting) to lead to yielding. Moreover, this pattern suggests that children's actions within conflicts are not chosen randomly.

Detailed analysis revealed that these young children's verbalizations during disputes were often closely tailored to their socially directed actions. It was found that verbal statements were generally used in the object struggles as moves to gain access to the peer's object (49%) or to retain possession of one's own toy (33%). In contrast, negatives (''No,'' ''Don't'') and assertions of possession (''Me,'' ''Mine'') were used differentially in a manner appropriate to the speaker's role in the dispute: ''No'' was used in defense, to protest the peer's actions; the object's name was used when it would be most informative, that is, when the speaker had designs on a toy currently held by the peer rather than when defending a toy in his or her own possession.

Further evidence of the social or interpersonal nature of these conflicts comes from the observation that conflicts occurred over objects whose duplicates were readily available and because of the victor's failure to use objects that he or she had won. Clearly, one child's possession of an object increases the peer's interest in the object.

Together these findings underscore the social quality of early conflict and dispute claims that young children's conflicts are "socially blind." In addition to serving as a training ground for learning effective strategies for initiating and terminating conflicting aggressive interactions, "the experience of conflict with peers provides young children with information about the greater social order, including the important set of relations between members of society and their inanimate possessions" (Hay & Ross, 1982, p. 112).

Developmental Changes in Aggressive Behavior

It is surprising how little information is available concerning the developmental changes in the form and the elicitors of aggression in children, as well as their relationship to earlier behavioral antecedents. In the following discussion, the available data pertaining to these issues are presented.

Developmental Changes in the Form of Aggressive Behavior

There is a general trend across development showing that physical forms of aggression decrease and verbal aggression increases between 2 and 4 years of age (Goodenough, 1931; Jersild & Markey, 1935). Goodenough (1931), who used parental diaries as her data source, found that there was an increase in certain forms of physical aggression (e.g., stamping and hitting) until the third year, after which the frequency of physical aggression declined. Accompanying this drop in physical attack was an increase in verbally mediated aggression. Hartup (1974) has distinguished between hostile aggression (i.e., person-oriented aggression) and instrumental aggression (i.e., aggression that is aimed at the retrieval of an object, territory, or privilege) (see Buss, 1966; Feshbach, 1964; Rule, 1974). In his observational study of children at two age levels, 4 to 6 years old and 6 to 7 years old, Hartup (1974) evaluated developmental changes in these two forms of aggressive activity. Although younger children were more aggressive than older children, this age

difference was mainly the result of a higher rate of instrumental aggression among the younger children. In contrast, the older children used more hostile or person-oriented aggression than did the younger children. In part, these age differences were dependent on the type of eliciting stimulus, which is discussed below. Thus, there appears to be a relative decrease over the preschool period in instrumental aggression and an increase in person-directed, retaliatory aggression and hostile outbursts.

The Relationship Between Form and Elicitors of Aggression

How do the elicitors of aggressive behavior change across age? In her home-based analyses, Goodenough (1931) found that physical discomfort and need for attention were frequent elicitors of outbursts of anger in infancy, while "habit training" was often an elicitor in the second and third years. Conflicts among peers elicited angry outbursts in 4-year-olds. And in the Dawe (1934) study, quarrels over possessions were most common in the period from 18 to 65 months, with disagreements over possessions most often leading to quarrels among the younger children. Over this period, physical attack increased from 3 to 15% as an instigator of quarreling.

These trends have been confirmed in an observational study by Hartup (1974), who found that

> the prerequisites of hostile aggression (i.e., person-oriented aggression) include (a) frustration-produced stimuli which have ego-threatening properties, and (b) an inference by the subject that the agent of frustration has behaved intentionally. Other attributions may also be involved in eliciting other forms of aggression, but the literature emphasizes the linkage between hostile outbursts and frustrations which involve ego threats or threats to one's self-esteem. In contrast, instrumental aggression (i.e., aggression which is aimed at the retrieval of an object, territory or privilege) should be linked to simple goal blocking. (Hartup, 1974, p. 337)

As noted above, age modifies the effect of eliciting situations. Among older children in this study, derogations (negative social comparisons, tattling, criticism, ridicule) were highly likely (78%) to elicit some type of insult or reciprocated threat to self-esteem, but relatively unlikely to elicit hitting (only 22% of the time). In contrast, for younger children, derogation elicited reciprocated derogation threats and tattling only about half of the time (52%) and was nearly as likely to take the form of bodily injury, such as hitting (48%). A parallel age difference in types of hostile aggression was not found in the aggression elicited by blocking (involving possessions, space, and activity): About 25% of blocking-produced hostility involved derogation, rejection, tattling, and threats for each age group. Thus, while elementary school age children reciprocate an insult, preschoolers do not. In contrast, when either older or younger children's goals are blocked, the proportion of insulting, hostile reactions does not vary with age. Although it is assumed that there is a link between social-cognitive processes and age changes in children's aggression, no direct evidence of this covariation was presented. It is assumed, however, that this shift from instrumental to hostile aggression may be the result, in part, of the older child's ability to infer the intentions and motives of one's attacker. When children recognize that another person wants to hurt them, they are more likely to retaliate by a direct assault on the attacker rather than by an indirect attack on the aggressor's possessions. Moreover, as Hartup and deWit (1974) note, "there is no reason to assume that all types of physical aggression have common functions either within or across developmental stages" (1974, p. 293). Next we examine some recent social-cognitive studies that provide support for this analysis.

Developmental Shifts in Attribution of Aggressive Intent

A variety of studies have addressed how children's understanding of another person's intentions in interpersonal interchanges shifts across age. In this section, our focus is on children's cognitive understanding and, in a later section, the links between understanding and actual aggressive behavior will be addressed.

The assessment of developmental changes in children's reactions to intentional or accidental provocation was the aim of Shantz and Voydanoff (1973). In their study, boys 7, 9, and 12 years old reacted to a variety of hypothetical aggressive incidents, describing a boy attacking another either intentionally or accidentally with either verbal or physical aggression. Intensity of retaliatory aggression was measured by having the subject indicate which of seven wooden paddles he would hit the provoking boy with if the subject had been the target of the provocation. There were clear developmental changes: 9-year-olds and 12-year-olds responded less aggressively following accidental compared to intentional provocation, while 7-year-olds reacted

similarly to both types of provocation. In addition, although all age groups retaliated equally following intentional attacks, there was a general decrease in the intensity of aggression to an accidental provocation as children became older. Across age children show increasing differentiation in response to verbal and physical provocation: 12-year-olds responded less aggressively to intentional verbal than to intentional physical provocations, while 9-year-olds and 7-year-olds made no such differentiation. Clearly, children's ability to distinguish among underlying motives and forms of aggression alters their views concerning the intensity of retaliatory aggression that is appropriate.

Similarly, an age difference was found by Ferguson and Rule (1980) in a study comparing second- and eighth-grade children's evaluations of an aggressive act as presented in different stories involving varying levels of responsibility by the aggressor. Whereas second-grade children generally failed to vary their evaluations in accordance with different levels of aggressor responsibility, eighth-grade children made several distinctions. They viewed intended aggression as more reprehensible than foreseeable but unintentional aggression, and they judged foreseeable aggression as more reprehensible than either accidental or justified aggression.

As Feshbach (1971) has suggested, useful distinctions can be drawn among various types of intentional aggression. He proposed that aggression serving socially motivated purposes (i.e., aggressing in order to help the other person reach some goal) is evaluated differently from either aggression serving personally motivated purposes (i.e., aggressing to obtain a personal goal) or hostile aggression (i.e., aggressing to hurt the other person). Rule, Nesdale, and McAra (1974) assessed whether children of varying ages respond differently to the different types of intentions underlying aggressive responses. Children were asked to evaluate the "naughtiness" of same-sex children who aggressed for either personal (hostile or personal-instrumental) reasons or prosocial (social-instrumental) reasons. Boys at three age levels—6, 9, and 12—and girls of three age levels—5, 7, and 10—participated. Children of both sexes rated the aggression committed with prosocial intentions as "less bad" than aggression committed with either form of personal intention. Since Rule et al. (1974) did not include a condition involving nonintentional aggression, it is unclear whether children as young as 5 years of age can make the discrimination between intentional and accidental aggression.

As in many other areas (e.g., communicative competence; see Asher, 1978; Glucksberg, Krauss, & Higgins, 1975), the structuring of the task utilized by the researcher has an important impact on the apparent ability of children of differing ages. When the child is presented with unambiguous information about the intention underlying the aggressive act (Rule, Nesdale, & McAra, 1974), children as young as preschoolers are capable of altering their evaluative response to aggression based on the aggressor's intentions. However, in naturalistic settings, children are often faced with provocations for which the aggressor's intentions must be inferred from subtle cues and sophisticated knowledge of human motivation. Particularly in these circumstances, children's age-dependent level of social-cognitive functioning would be expected to be an important factor in determining how they would respond to provocation.

Not only are there increases across age in the extent to which children infer intentionality, but as children develop they are more likely to attribute stable individual dispositions to others. In a recent study, Rotenberg (1980) demonstrated that kindergarten children are unable to use intentionality as a cue for inferring dispositions about individuals, but that second and fourth graders possess this ability. Specifically, children heard a story in which a child either accidentally or intentionally inflicted harm. The older children (second and fourth graders) predicted that the child who acted intentionally would behave in an aggressive and unhelpful fashion in other situations in the future. In contrast, the kindergarten children appeared to be limited to utilizing as cues characteristics that do not have long-term behavioral implications for the actors. Support for this interpretation derives from the fact that the younger children (kindergarteners) judged the intentional actor as more mean and less likeable, but did not make differential attributions about future behavior. The implications for the development of negative reputations are interesting since they suggest that, as children develop reputations, other children's attitudes and behavior toward them may become more stable and less resistant to change. Rotenberg's study provides support for an earlier analysis (Jones & Davis, 1965) that suggested that the attribution of intentionality is a critical determinant of dispositional inferences. In Rotenberg's study, the failure of the youngest children to attribute dispositions to others is also consistent with earlier studies (Livesley & Bromley, 1973; Peevers & Secord, 1973).

In addressing the developmental issue of how children at different ages learn to recognize an event or situation as "aggressive," only limited attention has been paid to the role of nonverbal cues. Recent evidence indicates that infants and young children can recognize facial expressions of such emotions as happiness, sadness, anger, and fear (Izard, 1971; Sroufe, 1979). However, neither the developmental sequence of this recognition capacity nor the related issue of how infants and children learn to use different expressions for controlling social situations is well understood. An exception is the work of Camaras (1977, 1980) who has shown that children 5 to 6 years old can effectively use facial expressions to regulate a partner's behavior in a conflict situation.

The Relationship Between Perceived Intent and Aggressive Behavior

The studies reviewed in the previous section leave two central questions unanswered. First, do children modify their behavior in response to variations in perceived intent? Second, what accounts for children's ability to differentiate the intentions of others and their ability to integrate that intention information into their own behavior? Two explanations are plausible (Dodge, 1980). Children who persistently respond with aggression to a nonintentional negative outcome may be doing so because of a cue-utilization deficiency related to a lag in their ability to integrate intention information into their own behavior. An alternative explanation of persistent aggressive responses to nonintentional negative outcomes by children is that they may not be deficient in cue utilization but instead may engage in cue distortion. In short, children misperceive or distort the relevant social cues concerning the intentions of others.

To address these issues Dodge (1980) tested aggressive and nonaggressive boys in second, fourth, and sixth grades in a situation in which they were exposed to a frustrating negative outcome that was instigated by an unknown peer acting with either a hostile intent, a benign intent, or an ambiguous intent. Boys at all ages reacted with more aggression (as indexed by disassembling another's puzzle or by verbal hostility) to the hostile intent than to the benign intent. When the intent of the provoking peer was ambiguous, however, aggressive boys reacted as if the peer had acted with a hostile intent, while nonaggressive subjects reacted as if the peer had acted with a benign intent. These findings show that, when a peer's intention is stated clearly, aggressive boys alter their retaliatory behavior according to that intention as appropriately as do nonaggressive boys—a result that does not support the cue-utilization-deficiency hypothesis. Only under ambiguous conditions do aggressive and nonaggressive boys differ in their behavior toward others—a finding that supports the cue-distortion hypothesis that aggressive and nonaggressive boys may differ in their perceptions of the intentions of peers in ambiguous circumstances.

In a subsequent study using hypothetical episodes, Dodge (1980) found that aggressive and nonaggressive boys do, in fact, differ in their interpretation of ambiguous provocation situations; aggressive boys attribute hostile intentions more frequently than nonaggressive boys. Moreover, the subjects' interpretation of the situation is a predictor of their expectations of others' behavior since aggressive boys are also more likely to expect continued aggression from peers and to mistrust peers more compared to nonaggressive boys. In addition, Dodge found that the child's reputation was important in determining attributions made about his behavior and in determining how others will behave toward him. In contrast to nonaggressive children, boys who were known to be aggressive were more often attributed hostile intentions in ambiguous circumstances. Moreover, in these hypothetical situations, boys indicated that they would retaliate more against an aggressive boy, that they expected aggressive boys to continue to act in hostile ways, and that they would refuse to trust them.

Moreover, these effects are not restricted to hypothetical situations. In a later study, Dodge and Frame (1982) found that aggressive boys not only initiated more unprovoked aggressive acts but, more importantly, received more aggressive acts than nonaggressive boys. This suggests that "the biased attributions of aggressive status boys *may* have a basis in their experience. Their collective expectancy that peers will be biased in aggressing toward them is consistent with their experience" (1982, p. 28).

In a series of related studies, Dodge has examined various aspects of cognitive processing that affect this attributional bias displayed in aggressive boys. In one study, Dodge (1981) examined the role of deficits in the processing of those social cues that aid in decision making. On the assumption that highly aggressive boys expect hostility from peers and therefore are primed to perceive hostility, these boys may search for fewer cues than other boys prior to interpreting a situation. In turn, they may be more likely to make a hostile interpretation as a result of inadequate information. In addition, Dodge examined whether the attributional bias may be mediated by selective recall of hostile cues. A situation was

used in which aggressive and nonaggressive boys participated in a detective game in which the task was to accumulate evidence in order to determine whether a peer had acted with benevolence or hostility. Aggressive boys responded more quickly with less attention to available relevant social cues than nonaggressive boys and, in turn, overattributed hostile behavior to a peer.

In a subsequent study (Dodge & Frame, 1982), the amount of cue search in which a child could engage was held constant in order to examine the relationship between a child's *focus* of cue search and his or her interpretations about peers. Although aggressive boys do not differ from nonaggressive boys in their selective recall of hostile cues, selective recall of hostile cues is a significant determinant of an interpretation of peer hostility. Boys who recalled more hostile cues are more likely to attribute hostile intentions to a peer. In addition, these investigators found some interesting cognitive deficits in aggressive boys including a tendency to make intrusions into recall (i.e., make up a cue that had not occurred) and, during recognition tasks, a tendency to respond that a statement had previously occurred when actually it had not. Although younger subjects also made more recall intrusions that might suggest a developmental lag among aggressive boys, the overall pattern suggests that the cognitive deficit among aggressive boys is quite specific, since total recall patterns did not differ in aggressive and nonaggressive boys. Moreover, aggressive boys made only "false positives" in their recall intrusions, but not "false negatives" in recognition, unlike younger boys who made both types of recognition errors. Dodge interprets these data by suggesting a parallel between the cognitive deficit of the aggressive boys and the inhibition deficit in impulsive boys (Camp, 1977; Kendall & Finch, 1978). Both groups show an inability to inhibit responses appropriately in certain situations.

Dodge has hypothesized an intriguing cyclic interpretation of the relationship between attributions and aggressive behavior:

Given a negative outcome in the context of unclear intentions, an aggressive child may be likely to attribute a hostile intention to a peer who is responsible for this negative event. This attribution may confirm his general image of peers as hostile and may increase the likelihood of his interpreting future behavior by the peer as hostile. Consequently, he may retaliate against the peer with what he feels is justified aggression. Subsequently, the peer, who has become the recipient of a negative outcome, may attribute a hostile intention to the aggressive child. This attribution confirms the peer's view of the child as being inappropriately aggressive in general and increases the peer's likelihood of interpreting future behavior by the aggressive child as being hostile. Consequently, the peer may aggress against the aggressive child, which could start the cycle over again. Given a series of negative outcomes, which is inevitable, the cycle could turn into a self-perpetuating spiral of increased hostile attributions, aggressive behavior, and social rejection. (Dodge, 1980, p. 169)

Together, these studies provide considerable support for viewing aggressive behavior from an information-processing perspective. It is clear that children's abilities to infer motives about others' behavior influence their behavioral expression of aggression. The ways in which cognitive understanding and social behavior shift across development, however, remain relatively unexplored. Similarly, the antecedents—biological, social, or cognitive—of individual differences in children's social information-processing skills as investigated by Dodge and others are not yet determined. Finally, the extent to which cognitive models of aggression incorporate other dimensions such as affect will determine their ultimate usefulness; it is unlikely that simple cognitive models alone will suffice.

STABILITY OF AGGRESSIVE BEHAVIOR

Aggression varies developmentally with regard to form, function, and eliciting circumstances. A related but separate issue is the extent to which aggression is stable within individuals over time. A substantial amount of evidence indicates considerable stability. Since earlier studies indicated that the degree of stability varies with the sex of the child, evidence for males and females is reviewed separately.

Stability of Aggression in Males

In an extensive review of longitudinal studies of aggressive behavior in males, Olweus (1979) found impressive evidence of the stability of aggressive behavior in males and, in addition, systematically identified factors that attenuate the degree of the stability. Olweus examined 16 independent samples with subjects ranging from 2 to 18 years and follow-up evaluations to assess stability from 6 months to 21

years. The average interval covered was 5.7 years, although most studies of younger children covered intervals limited to 1½ years. With the older subjects, the intervals were more evenly distributed. Figure 5 summarizes the results of these studies. Of particular interest is that there are no obvious developmental patterns, but there is clear evidence that the size of the stability coefficient tends to decrease as the interval increases. As Figure 5 shows, the regression line is similar to the classic regression line for intelligence, suggesting that aggression may be as stable as IQ (Thorndike, 1933). This evidence is particularly impressive in view of the fact that studies using both ratings as well as direct observations were used. In spite of the argument that stability of individual behavior will more likely be found using ratings than from direct observation (Cairns & Green, 1979), Olweus found that the average stability correlation for the three studies using direct observation (Jersild & Markey, 1935; Martin, 1964; Patterson, Littman, & Bricker, 1967) was .81, which is similar to the .79 for three comparable studies using teacher ratings (Block, Block, & Harrington, 1974; Emmerich, 1966; Kohn & Rosman, 1973). Two factors may have accounted for the high level of stability in the observational studies: (1) the use of a large number of observations to estimate the level of aggression for individual children, and (2) the similarity of contexts in which the observations were made. Moreover, the degree of specificity of the behaviors used to index aggression may affect the size of the correlations obtained. Molecular measures, such as very specific types of physical or verbal aggression (e.g., low-frequency behaviors), may yield less stability than molar measures of aggression even when direct observation measures are employed. [For a more extensive discussion of this issue, see Cairns and Green (1979).]

Two recent studies that are consistent with this general pattern merit more detailed review. In one examination of the stability issue, Olweus (1977) conducted two short-term longitudinal studies of Swedish adolescent boys. In both studies a peer-rating scale was used. In the initial study, 85 boys were rated by their classmates at age 13 and again 1 year later, while in a second study 201 boys were rated at age 13 and again 3 years later at age 16. The stability correlations in the first study were .81 for starts fights and .79 for verbal protest (correlations corrected for attenuation were even higher: 1.00 and .96, respectively). In the second study (Olweus, 1977), which covered a longer interval, the correlations were .65 and .70, respectively (.77 and .81 for correlations corrected for attenuation). This

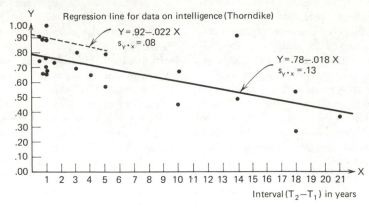

Figure 5. Comparative stability of aggression and intelligence. (From Olweus, 1979).

study provides impressive evidence of a substantial degree of stability in aggressive behavior, at least over modest periods of time.

Is there stability in male aggression over longer periods? This issue was addressed in an extensive longitudinal study conducted by Lefkowitz, Eron, Walder, and Huesmann (1977) who assessed the relationship between aggression measured at 8 years of age and again 10 years later: A peer nomination measure of aggression was used at the early age (Walder, Abelson, Eron, Banta, & Laulicht, 1961) and a modified version of this same instrument was used at the later age. In addition, Lefkowitz et al. utilized a self-report measure of aggression as well as two MMPI scales that are predictive of delinquent behavior. These analyses indicated a significant correlation between peer nomination of aggression in the third grade and the thirteenth grade for boys (r = .38). Similarly, peer-rated aggression in the third grade was predictive of potential delinquent behavior—as indexed by the MMPI—for boys 10 years later. For boys, aggression at the earlier age was also correlated with self-rated aggression at the later age. Similar evidence of long-term stability comes from Farrington (1978) who reported a significant relationship between teacher-rated aggression at 8 years of age and self-reported aggression at 18 years of age for a sample of English boys.

In a further analysis of this issue, Olweus (1982) has recently examined studies of the stability of conduct behavior problems on the assumption that aggressive behavior can be regarded as part of a more general antisocial reaction pattern. For example, he reports that in Rutter's Isle of Wight study (Rutter,

Tizard, & Whitmore, 1970) approximately 60% of the children with conduct disorders at age 10 were classified as having conduct problems 4 years later. Similarly, Robins (1966, 1978) found that a considerable portion of adolescent children referred to a child guidance clinic for a variety of antisocial behaviors such as fighting, theft, alcohol abuse, and truancy were exhibiting serious antisocial tendencies 30 years later (see Farrington, 1982, for a review of longitudinal analyses of more extreme forms of aggression, such as criminal violence). Olweus concludes that for males "aggressive and related 'acting-out' behavior shows a substantial degree of stability often over long periods of time. The degree of stability seems to vary inversely both with the length of the interval covered and the subject's age at the time of first assessment" (1982, p. 16). It is clear that males show a substantial degree of stability in aggression.

Stability of Aggression in Females

Do females exhibit similar stability in their aggressive behavior? Both empirical evidence as well as theoretical arguments have been offered to demonstrate that males show greater stability over time than females in their aggressive behavior. The cornerstone for the empirical basis of this view is the Kagan and Moss (1962) study, which found considerable stability for males but limited stability for females from early childhood to adulthood. Theoretically, it has been argued that sex-role standards dictate aggression as appropriate for males but not for females. Environmental supports, in the form of encouragement for aggression and opportunities to display aggression, are more abundant for males than females. However, in a recent evaluation of six studies on the stability of aggressive behavior in comparable male and female samples (up to age 19 years), Olweus (1982b) found substantial stability for females as well as males. In the studies in this analysis, the subjects' average age was 7 years, and they were followed for intervals varying from a half-year to 10 years, with the average follow-up interval being 2.8 years. The average correlation for males was .497, while for females the value was .439—a relatively small difference in stability. Olweus (1982b) concluded that

> In contrast to what is commonly believed there is a fairly high degree of stability in aggressive re-action patterns also in females, at least for inter-vals of 10 years up to age 19 . . . . The some-what lower stability in females as compared with males may partly reflect the fact that for whatever reason, there are far fewer highly aggressive girls than boys. This will result in lower variability in the female distributions, thereby reducing the size of the correlation coefficient. (Olweus, 1982b, p. 15)

However, the degree of stability for females may, in part, be the result of bias in the sample toward younger girls. In fact, Kagan and Moss found rea-sonable stability for girls between childhood and ad-olescence. It was only in adulthood that the level of female aggression was not related to levels of ag-gression in childhood and adolescence.

Other Issues in the Stability of Aggression

A general caution about the stability issue is in order. Although there is evidence of considerable stability, it is clear that there is also evidence of considerable instability or change in aggression over time. Impressive as a correlation of .40 or .50 may be, it is important to remember that 75% of the vari-ance remains unexplained. In our search for sta-bility, or the lack of stability, the openness to change that these correlations suggest should not be overlooked.

It is also important to note that the above discus-sion, although suggesting stability in aggression for both males and females, does not imply that a pre-diction of individual behavior patterns can be accu-rately achieved. Two types of errors are possible: (1) false positives, in which the predicted rates include many individuals who do not commit the expected

violent offense, and (2) false negatives, in which the prediction fails to include those who do actually commit the offense. Since violence is low in fre-quency among the population and multiply deter-mined, the prediction of adult interpersonal violence from measures collected at earlier ages is difficult. As illustrated by a study of 400 English boys, tracked from 10 to 21 years of age (Farrington, 1978), most children who are identified at an early age as aggressive do not become violent delin-quents. Even the prediction of recidivism among parolees with a history of interpersonal aggression is very difficult with estimates of false positive predic-tion being very high (Monahan, 1981; Monahan & Klassen, 1982). As Monahan (1973) concluded after a careful review of the violence prediction studies,

> Of those predicted to be dangerous, between 65% and 99% are false positives . . . violence is vastly overpredicted whether simple behavioral indicators are used or sophisticated multivariate analyses are employed and whether psychologi-cal tests are administered or thorough psychiatric examinations are performed . . . . The fact that even in these groups, with higher base rates for violence than the general population, violence cannot be validly predicted bodes very poorly for predicting violence among those who have not committed a criminal act. (1973, p. 8)

Since these studies were aimed at detecting criminal repeaters, it is assumed that the attempts to predict potentially violent, but currently nonviolent, indi-viduals may be even more difficult. Moreover, the impact of falsely labeling an individual as poten-tially violent has serious ethical problems and may negatively influence the individual's later develop-ment (Monahan, 1981; Parke, 1982).

Explanations of Stability and Instability of Aggression

Although measurement issues remain, the find-ings showing substantial stability in children's pat-terns of aggression require explanation. One view—the environmental feedback view—maintains that there is considerable similarity in the social domains or "social worlds" (e.g., family, peers) of child-hood; according to this view, long-term stability de-rives from the fact that a child's social worlds pro-vide relatively concordant, overlapping, or mutual supportive socialization influences (Hartup, 1979; Slaby & Roedell, 1982). Compatible with this view is the argument that within each domain there are significant sources of positive feedback that may often accrue to aggressive individuals. A variety of these sources can be noted, such as the achievement of instrumental goals; the gain of skills and prestige; the ability to dominate; popularity among certain peers; and, in the case of highly aggressive individuals, even the feedback of pain which accompanies aggressive encounters can be a source of reinforcement (Perry & Bussey, 1977).

A second interpretation, compatible with the first, is that children ultimately internalize relatively enduring and generalizable mediators of aggression—such as cognitive standards concerning aggression (e.g., Feshbach, 1974) or individual, differentiating reaction tendencies or motive systems (Olweus, 1979). In turn, these internal mediators may serve as guides in the selection of contexts, activities, and situations that are compatible with previously established patterns. A conceptualization in which trait and situational factors are considered as codeterminants of behavior is gaining increasing support (Bowers, 1973; Epstein, 1977; Wachtel, 1973). According to this view, "highly aggressive individuals actively select and create the kinds of situations in which they are often observed" (Olweus, 1979, p. 873). However, this view does not necessarily suggest that stability is inevitable; instead, individuals who wish to *change* their behavior patterns may choose settings that support their new behavioral preferences. A delinquent may choose a new peer group in order to facilitate a desire for a change toward a more law-abiding lifestyle.

Pertinent to this issue is a recent investigation of how children's choice of activity preferences and their level of aggression covary over time. Bullock and Merrill reasoned as follows:

> Children differ in their activity preferences. Such activity preferences should predict a child's pattern of time allocation across the behavior settings. . . . Some settings may be more likely than others to promote the adoption of aggressive behavior as tactics for securing desired outcomes . . . . If, over time, children maintain preferences for aggression-conducive settings, they can be expected to develop greater bias toward use of aggressive tactics. (Bullock & Merrill, 1980, p. 808)

To investigate this hypothesis, these investigators conducted a 1-year longitudinal study of 9-year-old children. Preferences for aggressive over nonaggressive activities and games (spear fishing vs. picking berries; learning kung-fu vs. learning to raise garden plants) were assessed at the start and end of the year. Aggression was measured by peer reports using a procedure similar to that used by Lefkowitz et al. (1977). The temporal stability of aggression was quite high ($r = .82$) and temporal stability of preference was moderately high ($r = .58$ for girls; $r = .51$ for boys). Although there were no significant relationships between preferences of aggression and aggressive activities for girls, for boys, the cross-lag analyses indicated that preference predicted levels of aggressiveness 1 year later, but only for boys who were at medium levels of aggression. For boys at either the low or high levels of aggression, activity preferences did not predict subsequent aggression. In fact, at the high levels of aggression, the boys' aggression level predicted activity preference, but not vice versa. In view of the high level of stability of aggression over time for the high-aggressive boys, these findings suggest that activity preferences can be a vehicle for maintaining aggressive behavior patterns. On the other hand, the data of the boys at the medium level of aggression suggest that activity preferences can serve as a mechanism for promoting change or stability.

Many questions remain, including what factors in either the self or the environment determine the preference choices that, in turn, are related to aggressive activity. Bullock and Merrill raise the issue of whether the changes attributed to preference should be viewed as a product of explicit attempts at self-control. To assess whether children are aware of the change-inducing value of different social activities would help clarify this issue. The Bullock and Merrill study provides a useful paradigm for assessing the determinants of stability and change and serves as a reminder that stability and change may, in part, be governed by some of the same mechanisms.

In summary, although there appears to be impressive stability in children's aggressive behavior over time, social behavior is modifiable throughout childhood as well as in adulthood. Individual children's aggressive behavior is subject to change initiated by the same mediators (e.g., cognitive standards, response patterns, and motivations) as may be responsible for the stability seen in children's aggression. Further research in this area is needed to specify the relative impact of such mediators on both the stability and changeability of children's aggression. Moreover, a better understanding of how these mediators interact with other environmental factors in either maintaining or altering behavior will be helpful in guiding those interested in the control of aggressive behavior.

SOCIAL DETERMINANTS OF AGGRESSION

Aggressive behavior patterns appear to be acquired from a variety of social environment sources. In this section, the roles played by (1) the family, (2) the peer group, and (3) television as socialization agents in the acquisition of aggressive behavior patterns are discussed. No single source can account for the socialization of aggression, nor is it yet possible to delineate the relative contributions of each of these sources in the development of aggressive behavior. Therefore, a theme in this section will be the interdependence of these various socializing forces in shaping children's aggressive behavior patterns. A second theme will be the shifting roles that each of these sources may play at different points in development. It is recognized that each of these socialization agents is important over the life span, but the relative impact of each may vary across development.

The Family as a Context for Acquiring Aggressive Behavior

Models of behavior acquisition within the family environment have recently been modified based on the assumption that theories that limit the learning of such behavior patterns as aggression to dyadic interactions or to only the direct effects of one individual on another are inadequate for understanding social interaction in families. Moreover, they do not allow full appreciation of the ways in which aggressive patterns develop (Belsky, 1981; Lewis, 1982; Parke, 1977, 1978a; Parke, Power, & Gottman, 1979). The complete family constellation, including parents as well as children, must be considered. Second, behaviors such as aggression may be affected by parent-child interaction indirectly as well as directly. Figure 6 outlines some of the indirect ways that aggression may develop in a three-person family (see Parke, Power, & Gottman, 1979, for a detailed

discussion of this model). In the direct or dyadic case (see Part A of Figure 6), the parent and child directly influence each other. However, as the model indicates in Part B of Figure 6, a parent (e.g., the father or mother) may influence a child not only directly, but through the mediation of another family member, such as the mother. For example, a father may verbally discipline a child, who, in turn, may provoke the mother to physically discipline the child. Alternatively, a wife may argue with her husband, who, in turn, may hit the child.

Another way in which one parent may indirectly influence the child's treatment by other agents is by modifying the child's behavior. Child behavior patterns that develop as a result of parent-child interaction may, consequently, affect the child's treatment by other social agents. For example, irritable infant patterns induced by an insensitive and impatient mother may make the infant more difficult for the father to handle and pacify. In short, patterns developed in interaction with one parent may alter interaction patterns with another caretaker. In larger families, siblings can play a mediating role similar to that of parents. Extended family members may also still be significant buffers in nuclear family interactions, despite modified proximity patterns (Tinsley & Parke, 1983).

Based on these expanded models of the processes involved in the socialization of such patterns of behavior as aggression in the family context, we now examine one well-researched area of the social learning of aggression: intrafamilial violence.

Levels and Forms of Intrafamilial Violence and Aggression

In recent years, increased attention has been given to studying the extent of intrafamilial violence. This documentation is of interest because it provides the basis for arguing that there are ample opportunities for the acquisition and practice of aggressive behaviors within the family setting. A description of the extent of familial violence is not adequate for a complete understanding of the ways in which a child learns to behave aggressively in this context. Therefore, after describing the amount and scope of familial violence that exist, we turn to an analysis of the processes involved in the development of aggression in the family environment.

Although a precise indication of the extent of intrafamilial violence in the United States is unavailable, Gelles and Straus (1979) have offered estimates across a number of spheres, including physical punishment, child abuse, murder, and assault. The use of physical force within the family is, ac-

Part A. Direct

1. F → I → F
2. M → I → M

Part B. Indirect

1. F → I ⇒ M → I
2. F → M ⇒ M → I
3. M → I ⇒ F → I
4. M → F ⇒ F → I

Figure 6. Model of direct and indirect effects in intrafamilial aggression. (Adapted from Parke and Lewis, 1981, p. 188.)

cording to these researchers, the most frequent and most carefully investigated. Between 84 and 97% of all parents use physical punishment at some point in the child's life (Erlanger, 1974; Stark & McEvoy, 1970). The use of physical punishment is not restricted to young children. In a series of studies (Steinmetz, 1971, 1977; Straus, 1971), it was found that about half of high school seniors had been hit or were threatened with being hit by their parents during their senior year (see Gelles & Straus, 1979, for a detailed review). The extreme use of physical punishment results in child abuse. Furthermore, intrafamilial violence in which the children are targets is not restricted to the use of physical punishment; research and intervention strategies with respect to child abuse have been expanded to include other forms of abuse (e.g., emotional, sexual) and neglect. Although the exact scope of child abuse is unknown, some investigators place the number who are abused annually at close to 500,000 children (Gil, 1970; see Kempe & Kempe, 1978).

In light of the expanded view of the family beyond simple consideration of the adult-child dyad, forms of aggression involving other family members, such as husband-wife aggression, are also relevant. The scope of husband-wife violence has recently been assessed in a nationally representative sample of 2143 couples by Straus, Gelles, & Steinmetz (1980). According to this survey, one or more incidents of husband-to-wife physical violence (hit, beat, threaten with or use gun or knife) occurred for 3.8% of the respondents during the previous year. For wife-to-husband violence, the percentage was 4.6. Extrapolation from these figures would suggest that among the approximately 47 million couples in the United States, about 1.8 million wives are beaten by their husbands. By using a less stringent index of violence (including pushing, slapping, grabbing, or throwing something at spouse), the figures are raised to 12.1% and 11.6% for husband-to-wife and wife-to-husband violence, respectively.

These rates of couple violence assume particular significance in light of evidence that other types of family violence involving children may be the result of husband-wife violence. Close examination of familial violence reveals striking degrees of interrelationship among marital conflict tactics, disciplinary techniques, and the methods employed by children in settling sibling conflicts. For example, Steinmetz (1977) found that families who use verbal and physically aggressive tactics for resolution of husband-wife disputes tend to use similar types of physical techniques in disciplining their children; the children, in turn, tend to duplicate these tactics in

their sib-sib relationships. Similarly Reid, Taplin, and Lorber (1981) found that the level of interspouse aggression was 15 to 20 times higher in child abusing families than in nonabusing control families.

Moreover, there is further evidence that child abuse may be a result of husband-wife violence. Particularly where there are strong norms limiting husband-wife violence, the child may become a victim. Aggression may also be directed toward the child when there are extreme dominant-submissive patterns in abusive families (Young, 1964). More recently, Pedersen, Anderson, and Cain (1977) reported that the level of negative affect between spouses was positively related to the amount of negative affect directed toward their 5-month-old infant; in short, husband-wife conflict was related to higher levels of parental expression of negative affect to their infant.

How prevalent is aggression between siblings? Steinmetz (1977), in an examination of physical violence between 88 pairs of siblings from 57 randomly selected families with two or more children between 3 and 17 years of age, found that high levels of aggression were employed by siblings to resolve conflicts. In families with children under 8 years of age, 70% of the children used physical aggression to settle disputes, which usually centered around possessions, a finding consistent with data on preschoolers' use of aggressive behavior reported elsewhere in this chapter (Hay & Ross, 1982). A nearly similar percentage (68%) of the families of adolescents (ages 9–13 years) reported physical aggression between siblings. Conflicts tended to revolve around personal space, boundaries, and touching. This finding is consistent with a marked increase in privacy demands among adolescents (Parke & Sawin, 1979). In the oldest group (14–17 years), whose fights were generally over responsibilities and social obligations, 63% used high levels of physical force on a sibling.

In a more recent study, Straus et al. (1980) found that of the 733 families who had two or more children between 3 and 17 years of age at home, 82% of the children were physically aggressive on one or more occasions to a sibling in the previous year. Developmental patterns are evident, with the rates of physically aggressive interchanges decreasing from 90% in the 3 to 4 year age group to 64% in the 15 to 17 year age group. This is consistent with general developmental shifts in physical aggression (Hartup, 1974). The overall rate of sib-sib aggression is much higher than the rate of aggression directed toward children by parents or husband-wife violence—using the same national survey data. According to the Straus et al. survey, sibling violence is the most frequent type of family aggression. However, it is likely that the degree of injury inflicted by siblings on each other is less than adult-initiated acts of physical aggression. Siblings are much less likely than adults to use extreme levels of aggression, involving a gun or knife. This fact, in turn, accounts for the higher rates of husband-wife and parent-child homicides compared to sibling homicides.

Sex differences in sibling-sibling aggression were also found. Girls are less aggressive than boys, but the differences were not very striking (83% for boys vs. 74% for girls). These differences are qualified by the sex composition of the sibling pairs. Families with all male offspring have the highest rates of sib-sib aggression, while all-girl families are lowest; mixed-sex families fall between these two extremes. Moreover, Straus et al. (1980) found that the difference between all-boy and all-girl families increases markedly as the children grow older. Few differences are present for children 3 to 4 years old but, by 10 years of age, the rate of intersib aggression for boys with only brothers is more than double the rate for boys with only sisters. These findings suggest that the presence of sisters may reduce the aggression of their brothers. Similarly, the presence of a male sib may increase the level of physical aggression displayed by a girl in her sibling interactions. This pattern is consistent with earlier studies of the effects of the sex of one's siblings on sex-role development (see Huston, vol. IV, chap. 5). For example, Brim (1958) found that boys with a sister were more feminine in their behavior than boys with a brother, and that girls with a brother were more masculine than girls with a sister.

Laboratory- and home-based observational analyses complement the above survey data by confirming that aggressive interchanges are not uncommon among siblings. In one study (Abramovitch, Corter, & Lando, 1979) of sibling pairs 2 to 5 years old interacting in the home, the investigators found that over 45% of the interactions between older and younger siblings were agonistic. These exchanges, which included physical aggression, object struggles, and verbal aggression (insult, threat), were generally initiated by the older sibling; the younger siblings initiated only about 10% of all agonistic behaviors. Although younger sibs are infrequent initiators of aggressive interchanges, they are often imitators of the actions of their older siblings (Dunn & Kendrick, 1982; Lamb, 1978). This pattern suggests that older siblings may, often inadvertently, be serving as aggressive models for their younger brothers and sisters. A parallel situation is evident in the ear-

lier work of Patterson et al. (1967), in which there was an increase in aggressive behavior as a result of exposure to aggressive peer encounters in a nursery school setting. These studies of siblings clearly indicate the necessity of viewing the family as a social system in order to understand the development of aggression.

According to Gelles and Straus (1979), there are various factors that may account for the high rates of violence within families, abusive as well as nonabusive. First, time at risk, or the amount of time spent interacting with other family members, may contribute to the high family violence. Second, a wide range of activities and interests are encompassed by the family, which means "that there are more 'events' over which a dispute or failure to meet expectations can occur" (Gelles & Straus, 1979, p. 552). Third, the intensity of involvement is higher in families in contrast to other groups. Fourth, the right to influence is a factor; membership in a family carries with it an implicit right to influence the behavior of others. Fifth, the right to privacy insulates many family interchanges from external monitoring as well as from controls and assistance in handling intrafamily conflict. Sixth, involuntary membership especially for young children as well as social expectations of stability for marital relationships makes leaving the situation a less likely alternative for resolution of conflict. A seventh factor "is the simple but important fact of de jure and de facto cultural norms legitimizing the use of violence between family members in situations which would make the use of physical force a serious moral or legal violation if it occurred between non-family members" (Gelles & Straus, 1979, p. 573). In summary, a variety of compelling reasons can explain the high level of intrafamilial violence. Clearly, in unraveling the aggression puzzle, the interaction patterns among all family members merit consideration. In a later section, the ways in which two other aspects of parental behavior, management and child-rearing tactics, contribute to the development of aggression is considered.

Parent as Manager

Traditionally, parents have been viewed as influencing the development of their children's aggression through their child-rearing practices. Although this continues to be a major focus, and as yet an unresolved issue, another perspective, namely the parent's role as a manager of the child's environment, is receiving increased attention.

Parents can indirectly influence their children's aggression through the ways in which they organize and arrange the home environment, set limits on the range of the home setting to which the young child has access, and, in the case of the older child and adolescent, the extrahome boundaries and the degree to which the parents monitor the child's out-of-home activities. Only recently have researchers begun to recognize this "management" function of parents and to appreciate the impact of variations in how this "managerial" function influences the child's social development (Hartup, 1979; Parke, 1978b). Even in infancy, the managerial role may be just as important as the parent's role as direct child-rearing agent since the amount of time that infants, for example, spend interacting with the inanimate environment far exceeds other interaction time with parents and other socializing agents. Here are some recent estimates based on extensive home observations by White and his colleagues (White, Kaban, Shapiro, & Attonucci, 1976):

> For 12-month-old to 15-month-old children, the figures were 89.7% for nonsocial tasks versus 10.3% for social tasks. By 18–21 months the figures are 83.8% nonsocial and 16.2% social; at 24–27 months 80.0% nonsocial and 20.0% social, and at 30–33 months they were 79.1% nonsocial and 20.9% social. (p. 125)

Others (Clarke-Stewart, 1973; Wenar, 1972) report similar findings. White et al. (1976) noted that over 85% of the time 12- to 33-month-old infants initiated their own activities. In infancy, the organization of the home—including access to different types of toys, such as aggressive toys (e.g., guns), or unmonitored access to television, including TV violence—may have an impact on the infant's aggressive behavior. As the child develops, a more important managerial function may be parental control over both selection of peers and opportunities for contact, as well as the degree of supervision exercised over peer-peer interaction. This is particularly important in view of the earlier finding of Wright (1967) that, between infancy and age 11, the amount of parent-child interaction decreased markedly and the amount of peer interaction increased. In a later section, the direct role that peers play in the development of aggression is reviewed.

One aspect of parental management that has received attention is monitoring, a measure of the extent to which parents are aware of the child's whereabouts, activities, and social contacts. A number of studies indicates that parents of delinquent children engage in less monitoring and supervision of their children's activities, especially with regard to the child's use of evening time, compared to parents of nondelinquent children (Belson, 1975; Pulkkinen, 1981; Wilson, 1980). Other researchers (Gold, 1963) have found that parents of delinquents report being less in control of their sons' choice of friends than parents of nondelinquents. Although earlier studies relied on single reports of either parents or children, a recent study by Patterson, Stouthamer-Loeber, and Loeber (1982), using multiple informants, found significant relationships between a lack of monitoring and court-reported delinquency, a measure of attacks against property, delinquent lifestyle, a measure of general rule-breaking outside the home, and a peer nomination index that measures a general antisocial disposition (e.g., fighting with peers, talks back to teachers, troublesome, breaking school rules). Monitoring varies across age; for a fourth-grade sample, there were no significant relationships, but at both the seventh and tenth grade the measure was a correlate of antisocial delinquent behavior. The study clearly underscores the value of broadening our conceptual view of the ways in which parents influence their children's aggressive development. Specification of the types of managerial functions, which are relevant for younger children, would be useful.

Parental Child-Rearing Tactics: Single-Variable Analyses

One of the most persistent searches for the determinants of aggressive behavior has focused on preferred disciplinary tactics used by parents for controlling their children's behavior in general and their children's aggressive behavior in particular. We have already reviewed one small aspect of this area: child abuse. In this section, the remaining areas of this widely researched and heavily reviewed body of literature is selectively highlighted. For other reviews of this literature, see Becker (1964), Feshbach (1970), Maccoby and J. Martin (*vol. IV, chap. 1*), and B. Martin (1975).

Various child-rearing factors have been isolated as contributors to aggressive behavior. Each of these factors is briefly discussed and then the combinations of practices most often associated with aggression is noted. Increasingly, as presented earlier, it is assumed that child-rearing antecedents of social behavior, including aggression, are best conceptualized as multivariate predictors rather than as single factors. In addition, neither mother-child nor father-child dyads alone are sufficient as units of analysis; instead, the family complex—in which the interactive behaviors of mother, father, and children are considered—is viewed more and more as the appropriate unit of analysis for a more complete understanding of the effects of child-rearing.

A number of child-rearing dimensions, including parental nonacceptance and parental permissiveness, have been isolated as correlates of aggressive behavior. In a large array of studies of delinquents, as well as preadolescent and preschool children, parental rejection is often correlated with child aggression (see Feshbach, 1970; Martin, 1975). As Martin notes,

> parental rejection may have some aggression-producing qualities because it is associated with frustrations—the rejecting parent may ignore the young child's expressions of discomfort and thwart his needs for nurturance. Also nonacceptance probably means that the parent is a poor source of positive reinforcements or rewards, which should result in the parent being less effective as a teacher of self-restraint, whether for the control of aggression or for any other socially disapproved behavior. And on the other side of the coin—aggressive, disobedient children—are not as "likeable" as more well-behaved children and are likely to elicit more critical reactions. (Martin, 1975, p. 511)

Another commonly found child-rearing correlate of aggression is permissiveness, which is often combined with parental inconsistency. Martin (1975) found clear evidence for this pattern among adolescent delinquents (e.g., Bandura & Walters, 1959) and fairly consistent support for this relationship among preadolescents (McCord, McCord, & Howard, 1961). A less consistent link between permissiveness and aggression was found at the preschool level, although some evidence exists that permissiveness, in combination with other parental characteristics such as low acceptance, low use of reasoning, and high punitiveness, is related to children's aggression (Baumrind, 1967, 1971).

Support for the potential role that inconsistent punishment may play in the development of aggression comes from both field and laboratory studies. Two types of inconsistent punishment merit distinction. Intraagent consistency refers to the extent to which a single agent treats violations in the same manner each time they occur or to the extent to which a parent or other socializing agent follows through on their threats of punishment. Interagent consistency, on the other hand, refers to the degree to which different socializing agents, such as two parents, respond in a similar fashion to rule violations. Although studies of the antecedents of delin-

quent and criminal behavior indicate that inconsistent discipline may be a factor in the development of antisocial aggressive behavior, the definition of inconsistency has shifted from study to study in the delinquency research, making evaluation and meaningful conclusions difficult. Gleuck and Gleuck (1950) found that parents of delinquent boys were more "erratic" in their disciplinary practices than were parents of nondelinquent boys. Similarly, McCord et al., (1961) found that erratic disciplinary procedures were correlated with high degrees of criminality. Inconsistent patterns involving a combination of love, laxity, and punitiveness, or a mixture of punitiveness and laxity alone, were particularly likely to be found in the background of their delinquent sample. Bandura and Walters (1959) obtained some evidence that parental disagreement concerning disciplinary practices was greater within families of aggressive boys than within families of nonaggressive boys.

Clearer evidence of the independent impact of interagent and intraagent inconsistent punishment comes from laboratory studies. It has been found that inconsistent punishment administered by a single agent (intraagent inconsistency) was less effective than consistent punishment in suppressing aggressive behavior (Katz, 1971; Parke & Deur, 1972). Similarly, interagent inconsistency in which two disciplinary agents are inconsistent (i.e., one punitive and the other rewarding) was less effective in inhibiting aggressive behavior than when the two agents were consistently punitive (Sawin & Parke, 1979).

Parents often use consistent punishment only after inconsistent punishment has failed to change the child's behavior. What is the impact of intraagent and interagent inconsistency on the persistence of aggressive behavior under conditions of consistent punishment? In their study of intra-agent inconsistency, Deur and Parke (1970) found that aggressive behavior (i.e., hitting response) was more persistent under conditions of either extinction or consistent punishment, following a period of inconsistent punishment. Similarly, in their study of interagent inconsistency, Sawin and Parke (1979) found that aggressive behavior during consistent verbal punishment from two disciplinary agents was greater following a period of inconsistent discipline than after either consistent approval or ignoring. These studies suggest that *both* intra-agent and interagent inconsistent punishment may increase subsequent resistance to control by disciplinary agents. These laboratory experimental studies, in combination with the field-correlational findings, lend support for the possible role of inconsistent discipline in the development of aggression.

Other evidence indicates that parental disagreement about child-rearing values is associated with the development of ego control, which, in turn, may mediate aggression. In a prospective longitudinal analysis, Block, Block, and Morrison (1981) found that parental disagreement measured when the child was 3 years of age was negatively related to ego control in boys over a 4-year range, from 3 to 7 years of age. These findings are consistent with earlier findings (Porter & O'Leary, 1980; Rutter, 1970; Wolkind & Rutter, 1973), which showed a positive relationship between family discord and disharmony and conduct disorders in boys.

Power-assertive disciplinary practices, which range from verbal rebukes to physical punishment, have often been associated with higher levels of aggression in children across a wide range of ages and samples, including delinquent male adolescents (Bandura & Walters, 1959; Hetherington, Stouwie, & Ridberg, 1971), delinquent female adolescents (Burt, 1929; Hetherington et al., 1971), preadolescent children (Martin & Hetherington, 1971; McCord et al., 1961), and preschool children (Baumrind, 1967, 1971; Hoffman, 1960; Sears et al., 1957).

More recent studies, however, have questioned whether power-assertive tactics, especially physical punishment, are necessarily antecedents of aggressive behavior. A longitudinal study by Eron and his colleagues (Eron, Walder, & Lefkowitz, 1971; Lefkowitz et al., 1977) provides a comprehensive examination of both the concurrent relationship between parental punitiveness and aggression as well as the predictive power of punitiveness for aggression in later childhood. In their first analysis, Eron et al. (1971) examined the relationship between parental disciplinary practices and peer ratings of aggression at a single point in time—when the children were in third grade. Using a sample of 875 third-grade children, these investigators found substantial correlations between parental use of physical punishment in the home and the aggressiveness of the child at school. However, the effects were qualified in important ways since punishment had different effects on different types of children. Punishment was negatively correlated with aggression in the case of low-aggressive children who had close identification with their parents. Punishment was positively correlated with aggression in high-aggressive children who identified moderately with their parents.

In a follow-up study 10 years later, Lefkowitz et al., (1977) reassessed both the current child-rearing practices as well as the levels of aggression in 427 children of the original sample. Peer ratings and parent ratings, as well as a self-report of aggression, were obtained at this later time. Although the correlation between punishment and contemporaneous aggression remains significant in the third grade for the peer-rating measure of aggression, using this reduced sample, and approaches significance in the thirteenth grade for boys, there was no significant relationship between earlier parental punitiveness and aggression 10 years later for children of either sex. Parental punishment alone was not a significant longitudinal predictor of aggression over the 10 year period.

The results of this study, in combination with the findings of other short-term longitudinal studies (Johannesson, 1974; Sears, 1961) which showed weak or nonexistent relationships between earlier parental punitiveness alone and later aggression, indicate that there is little basis for the assumption that parental punitiveness alone is a significant antecedent of later childhood aggression—at least at moderate levels.

Clearer support for the link between parental punitiveness and aggression comes from a recent study of the effects of child abuse on children's aggression, which suggests that the relationship may only be evident at high levels of intensity. In a careful observational analysis of children 1 to 3 years old, who either had or had not been physically abused by their parents, George and Main (1979) found that the abused children physically assaulted (hitting, kicking, pinching, spitting, slapping, or aggressively grabbing the body of another person) other toddlers twice as often as controls did. Moreover, fifty percent of the abused toddlers, but none of the control toddlers, assaulted or threatened to assault caregivers.

Further support is provided by Reid et al. (1981) who reported on the basis of extensive home observations that abused children showed higher rates of physical aggression and verbal threats than nonabused children. However, since child-abusing parents may differ from nonabusing controls in a variety of ways (Parke & Collmer, 1975; Parke & Lewis, 1981), in addition to their greater reliance on physical punishment, this study does not provide unambiguous support for the hypothesis that the relationship between punishment and aggression is evident only at extreme levels of punitiveness. Finally, the case for the long-term impact of abusive levels of physical punishment either on subsequent aggression or on later abusive child-rearing patterns remains unclear (Belsky, 1981; Parke & Lewis, 1981).

Parental Child-Rearing Tactics: Multivariate Analyses

Since child-rearing practices often tend to occur together in clusters or configurations, a more successful prediction of aggression will come from approaches that measure multiple dimensions rather than single indices of child-rearing. Although configurational approaches are not new, earlier studies (e.g., McCord, McCord, & Zola, 1959; Sears et al., 1957; Yarrow, Campbell, & Burton, 1968) were based on two, or at most three, variables. More recently, three other approaches have been employed: (1) clustering analyses, (2) multiple regression, and (3) path analyses. Examples of each of these multivariate approaches are discussed.

Martin and Hetherington (1971) performed a cluster-analytic procedure using 12 ratings obtained from interviews with fathers and mothers on a sample of 73 boys that was composed of subsamples of aggressive, withdrawn, mixed (aggressive and withdrawn), and nondeviant boys as determined by peer and teacher ratings. A four-group cluster solution yielded one group that was composed of 59% of the aggressive boys. This group, relative to the group in which the largest percentage of the nondeviant boys fell, (63%), was characterized by punitive punishment for both father and mother, low acceptance by mother only, and high reported aggression toward father, mother, and peers.

A further clustering led to a subdivision of this cluster into one that was characterized by fathers who were highly accepting and mothers who were low on rule enforcement (permissive), punitive and inconsistent in punishment, and nonaccepting. The boys in this cluster were reported to be highly aggressive toward the mother but not toward the father. This configuration suggests a family in which the mother-son dyad is largely involved in the maintenance of the son's aggression, perhaps with some general acceptance of aggressive behavior by a friendly father. In another cluster, both parents were clearly involved in the dynamics of aggressive interaction: Father and mother were both nonaccepting, punitive, and inconsistent in punishment, with the son being highly aggressive toward both parents. The potential value of this analytic approach is illustrated by these findings, since the single-variable analyses had failed to uncover differences in paternal acceptance between aggressive and nondeviant boys. The configural analyses suggest that low paternal acceptance is associated with aggression in some boys, while high paternal acceptance is associated with aggression in other boys. This latter possibility is consistent with the results of Winder and Rau (1962).

Further evidence of the value of multivariate approaches comes from the recent work of McCord (1979), who addressed the issue of whether child-rearing practices predict adult criminality. As part of a large-scale project involving children at risk for later delinquency, McCord examined the relationship of child-rearing practices, observed when the boys were between 5 and 13 years old, and the criminal behavior of these individuals 30 years later. Using court records, McCord determined that 71 of the 201 men included in the follow-up had been convicted of either a serious property crime (larceny, auto theft, breaking and entering, arson) or a serious personal crime (assault, attempted rape, rape, attempted murder, kidnapping, and murder). Six variables describing home atmosphere in childhood accounted for significant portions of the variance. Specifically, the following parental characteristics are best viewed as distinct from child-rearing practices: Parent aggressiveness (level of anger and interpersonal physical violence), paternal deviance (measure of alcoholism or criminality), and mother's lack of self confidence (low belief in her own abilities to control events) accounted for 5.9% of the variance, after controlling social status, in predicting total number of serious crimes. In addition, the child-rearing variables of supervision, parental conflict, and maternal affection—after controlling for both social status and parental characteristics—accounted for 26% of the variance in predicting adult criminality. Together, parental characteristics and child-rearing variables accounted for 36.3% of the variance in total crimes.

Discriminant function analyses based on the home-atmosphere cluster (parent characteristics and child-rearing variables) correctly identified 73.5% of the men as either subsequently criminal or noncriminal. Although this analysis includes juvenile crime, these home-atmosphere variables predict adult crime even better: 80% of the men were correctly distinguished as those convicted or those not convicted of serious crimes at later times. This set of predictions based on home atmosphere is significantly more accurate than predictions based on the individuals' juvenile criminal records. These analyses provide impressive evidence for the value of parental variables in predicting later criminality.

Olweus (1980) has moved the analyses of the child-rearing antecedents of aggression forward by a recent application of path analyses to the problem. Using samples of 13- and 16-year-old boys, Olweus assessed their habitual levels of aggression through peer ratings. Independent data were collected from both mothers and fathers concerning the early child-rearing conditions and temperamental characteristics of the boys. Four variables were included in the analysis. First, mother's negativism, which assessed the principal caretaker's basic emotional attitude to the boys during the first 4 to 5 years of life, was examined. This reflected either hostility or rejection as well as coldness or indifference. Second, the mother's permissiveness concerning aggression was rated, which reflected the caretaker's degree of permissiveness or laxness with regard to aggressive behavior directed to mother, to peers, and to siblings. Third, the mother's and father's use of power-assertive methods was scored. This variable indexed physical punishment as well as strong aggressive reactions, such as threats and violent outbursts. Finally, the boy's temperament was rated from interviews with the mother and father; this score was a composite of the boy's general level of activity and the intensity of his temperament (calm to hot-tempered) in early years (4–5 years).

Using prior theory and research as a guide, a path model was constructed, assigning primary importance to mother's negativism and boy's temperament—in part, based on the assumption that these two variables would be most important in the early years (4–5 years) of a boy's life. Methods of child-rearing, mother's permissiveness concerning aggression, and mother's and father's use of power-assertive methods are assumed to be predominant at later periods of the boy's rearing history and therefore were assigned a secondary role in the causal sequence (see Figure 7.). Although these assumptions are open to question in view of data which indicate that differences in child-care practices are evident in the preschool period (Baumrind, 1971; Sears et al., 1957), the results provide support for the general outlines of the model in both samples. Specifically, mother's negativism is directly related to boy's aggression; if the mother recalls being negative, rejecting, and indifferent to the boy from an early age, he is likely to be viewed by his peers as more aggressive and hostile. As the path diagram in Figure 7 illustrates, these same mothers tend to use power-assertive disciplinary practices, which, in turn, make a modest contribution to the level of aggression. As in earlier studies, the mother's degree of permissiveness for aggression—directed from the boy toward herself, peers, or siblings—is important. A highly accepting, tolerant, or lax attitude without clear limits for the boy's aggressive behavior contributes substantially to the development of an aggressive reaction pattern in the boy. Finally, the boy's temperament also had a direct causal effect on the boy's later aggression level. A boy with an active and "hot-headed" temperament, as manifested in early years, is more likely to develop aggressive modes of reaction than a calm and quiet boy. For the temperament variable there is also a marked indirect effect via the mother's permissiveness concerning aggression. Although interesting in view of the previously reported relationships between activity level and aggression (Patterson et al., 1967), perhaps this parental report could be viewed as another measure of the target variable—aggression. The role of temperament in the development of aggression awaits independent assessment of temperament and, one hopes, longitudinal analyses of the relationships between earlier measures of temperament and later aggressive behavior. (See Bates, 1982).

This type of analysis is useful for a number of reasons. First, it illustrates clearly that a multiple set

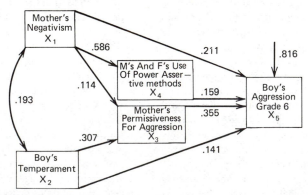

Figure 7. Path model relating, child-rearing variables to boy's aggression. (From Olweus, 1980, p. 650.)

of child-rearing variables needs to be considered in determining the development of aggression. Second, it suggests the relative importance of some child-care practices, especially maternal negativism. However, the reliance on retrospective reports is a serious limitation of this investigation (see Yarrow, Campbell, & Burton, 1968). Furthermore, although causal chains have been statistically demonstrated, the data were collected concurrently and any assumptions about temporal ordering of the order of co-occurrence of the behavior and child-rearing practices are only plausible, but not yet proven. A longitudinal study is necessary to establish the temporal sequence in a more conclusive fashion. Finally, the model is a useful hypothesis-generating device, but experimental manipulation is necessary to establish causal links between parental practices and children's behavior outcomes.

In summary, some support is available for demonstrating that certain child-rearing practices are significant antecedents of later aggression. Models that utilize multiple sets of predictors appear to show greater promise than single-factor models. Implicit in these studies of child-rearing correlates is the assumption that the direction of causality flows from parental behavior to child aggression. The analysis is basically unidirectional and noninteractive, and as such the focus is solely on the manner in which the parent influences a presumably passive and nonreactive child. However, unidirectional models of socialization have been seriously questioned over the past two decades (Bell, 1968; Bell & Harper, 1977), and current theories emphasize the role of the child in eliciting and modifying parents' child-rearing practices. In addition, reciprocal models which emphasize the ways in which the parent and child influence each other during the course of interaction are increasingly viewed as necessary for an adequate account of the way in which aggression develops. First, evidence of the role of the child in modifying disciplinary tactics is presented; then we turn to evidence for an interactional analysis of the development of aggression.

The Child as Contributor to Parental Child-Rearing Practices

Certain characteristics of the child as well as particular behaviors influence the parental choice of child-rearing practices, which, in turn, could account for the links between aggressive behavior and child-rearing practices.

Physical attractiveness can modify the disciplinary tactics that adults employ with children, as illustrated by Dion (1974). Female adults viewed a videotape of an interaction between another adult and an ostensibly attractive or unattractive 8-year-old child. When given the opportunity to penalize the child for incorrect responses on a picture-matching task, the adults penalized the unattractive boy more than the attractive boy. Berkowitz and Frodi (1978) found similar results. The degree of adult punitiveness, then, may in part be determined by the physical attractiveness of the victim and, by implication, may affect the child's likelihood of being punished.

In addition to physical attractiveness, certain behavior patterns may influence disciplinary choices as well. Activity level is one pattern examined by Stevens-Long (1973). Parents responded to videotapes of sequences depicting either an overactive, underactive, or an average-active child. The adults were required to select an appropriate disciplinary tactic (ranging from reward and affection to corporal punishment) when the child misbehaved at a number of points during the videotape sequence. More severe discipline was selected for the overactive child than for the underactive and average-active child. Thus, highly active children may elicit more extreme forms of discipline from their caretakers.

Another manner in which children may contribute to the selection of severe disciplinary tactics is, of course, by their own reactions to being disciplined. In one examination of this issue, Sawin, Parke, Harrison, and Kreling (1975) asked adults to monitor a child in a nearby room via a closed-circuit videotape arrangement. The adults were asked to discipline the child whenever the child misbehaved; the reaction of the child to the adult discipline was systematically varied in one of the following ways: (1) The child ignores the adult; (2) the child makes reparation; (3) the child pleads with the adult; or (4) the child behaves in a defiant manner. When the child misbehaved on a future occasion, the adult disciplinary choice was affected by the child's prior reaction to being disciplined. The children who had reacted with defiance received the harshest discipline, while those who had made a reparative response received less severe discipline. The implication of the study is clear: Children's reactions in a disciplinary context can clearly modify adult behavior and may serve to maintain, increase or decrease adult punitiveness.

Further evidence of the child's role in eliciting particular types of discipline is illustrated in a recent study by Grusec and Kuczynski (1980). Reports by mothers of elementary school children indicated that the type of discipline they were likely to use depended more on the particular form of misbehavior shown by the child than on the individual mother's general style of discipline. Mothers commonly chose to deal with children's physical aggression by using one of various power-assertive techniques (i.e., forcing compliance, withdrawing privileges, threatening, or punishing physically). However, other types of misbehavior, including property damage, disobedience, and self-harm, also elicited high levels of power-assertive tactics. In contrast, incidents involving psychological harm to another were dealt with exclusively by reasoning. These brief examples demonstrate a clear relationship between the child's characteristics and behavior and the adult's disciplinary tactics.

Toward a Social Interactional Model of Aggression: The Patterson Social Learning Project

Models that focus exclusively on either the child or the parent are both inadequate, as discussed earlier. It is clear that all family members must be considered in order to understand the development of aggression. Specifically, recognition of the reciprocal influences that the child, parents, and the siblings exert on each other during interaction is necessary if one is to understand the more specific problem of how child-rearing tactics contribute to childhood aggression.

The most systematic investigation of the familial determinants of aggression based on in situ observations of family interaction patterns is Patterson's continuing project (see Patterson, 1982, for a comprehensive review of this work).

Patterson views the family as a system of interacting members who develop particular patterns of behavior in the process of learning to respond to each other. Through detailed home observations of the sequences of behavior that frequently occur within both aggressive and nonaggressive families, Patterson and his colleagues have identified a particular coercive pattern that serves to elicit, maintain, and even increase aggression among all family members (e.g., Patterson, 1976, 1979; Patterson & Cobb, 1971, 1973; Patterson, Cobb, & Ray, 1973). According to the coercion process, when one person presents an aversive stimulus, the second is likely to respond with an aversive stimulus if the initial aversive stimulus appears alterable. The aversive interchange often continues, escalates in intensity, and may draw in other family members until one person withdraws the aversive stimulus; at this point, the other person withdraws as well, thereby breaking the cycle of aversive interchange for the moment. However, since the person who forces another family member to withdraw their aversive behavior first has

been encouraged by successfully stopping the aversive behavior of another person in the family, he or she will be even more likely to use highly aversive behaviors and to direct them at the submitting family member again in the future. Through this process of coercive interaction within families, children can quickly learn to become both initiators and victims of aggression while inadvertently training their parents to become highly punitive, since high-intensity aggressive responses by children may, in turn, elicit high-intensity disciplinary tactics from parents to suppress these behaviors. In the case of mothers, it is hypothesized

. . . that there are many grown women with no past history of Hitting who are shaped by interactions with infants and children to initiate physical assaults. Presumably, the shaping process is analogous to that provided by children, for children. The mother learns that hits terminate aversive child behavior. She may then be trained to display behavior of increasingly high amplitude as a function of contingencies supplied by children. We also suspect that many of the child homicides reported are in fact the outcome of such training programs. A young woman, unskilled in mothering, is trained by her own children to carry out assaults that result in bodily injury to her trainees. (Patterson & Cobb, 1971, p. 124)

Although coercive interchanges can occur in all families, they are particularly likely to be found in those families that are referred to clinics because of their problems with an aggressive child. Both parental child-rearing practices as well as characteristics of the aggressive children must be considered in accounting for the higher probability of coercive interaction cycles in the families of aggressive boys. The parents of the aggressive children are ineffective as punishing agents. Aggressive children have been found to be nearly twice as likely as nonaggressive children to respond to punishment from parents by either continuing or increasing their aversive behavior (Patterson, 1977). One reason for their persistence in misbehaving may be that the parents tend to be inconsistent punitive agents, which lowers their effectiveness as disciplinarians (Deur & Parke, 1970; Parke & Deur, 1972; Sawin & Parke, 1979). In addition, parents of socially aggressive children use ineffective forms of punishment. The Patterson group employ the term ''nattering'' to describe the often ineffective forms of scolding and nagging that mothers, in particular, use as punishment (Patterson, 1982).

On the child side, Patterson (1982) has suggested that there are characteristics of the antisocial aggressive child which, in turn, may make these children more difficult to control. Not only are these children noncompliant, but the antisocial aggressive child is characterized as displaying *arrested socialization*. These children seek to maximize short-term payoffs and to ignore long-term costs, while making frequent use of coercive means to gain their ends. Other research confirms the view that antisocial children showed less of a tendency to delay gratification and a greater likelihood for impulsive behavior (Quay, 1965; Riddle & Roberts, 1977; Weintraub, 1973). In Patterson's view, aggressors, like infants, are the original "here and now" people.

In addition, disruptions in the development of three interrelated mechanisms are posited as characteristics of the antisocial aggressive child. First, it is assumed that antisocial children are less responsive to social stimuli. Just as this type of child is significantly retarded in his or her learning of obedience, so is the child deficient in the development of learned responsiveness to social stimuli. The reduced responsiveness relates, in turn, to reduced responsiveness to social reinforcers and to threats and scolding. Finally, it is assumed that these deficiencies produce a failure to make subtle discriminations regarding the people with whom the child is interacting. Laboratory studies of responsivity to social reinforcers provide support for this hypothesis by showing that antisocial children show less responsivity to adult and peer social feedback than do normal children. However, antisocial children appear to be selectively hyporesponsive, since a number of researchers have found that antisocial children functioned as well as normals when material reinforcers (food, money) were used. Further evidence that is more ecologically valid comes from recent studies of the effectiveness of adult attention and approval for modifying prosocial behavior in the home (Herkert, Pinkston, Hayden, Sajwaj, Pinkston, Cordua, & Jackson, 1973) and in the classroom (Hops, Walker, & Greenwood, 1977). Antisocial children were *not* effectively modified by the use of these procedures alone. Moreover, as noted above, these children may be less responsive to control by parental disapproval as well (Patterson, 1982).

Two sources of this hyporesponsivity to social feedback have been suggested. First, these children may be constitutionally predisposed for hyporesponsiveness to both positive (Thomas, Chess, & Birch, 1968) and aversive stimuli (Mednick & Christensen,

1977; Patterson, 1982). Another alternative is the contingency hypothesis of Cairns (Paris & Cairns, 1972; Warren & Cairns, 1972), which suggests that when social reinforcers are initially used in a noncontingent fashion, their later effectiveness in controlling behavior will be reduced. On the aversive side, Seligman's work (1975) suggests that similar processes may be operative for aversive stimuli as well. Support for this possibility comes from research showing that mothers of antisocial children use fewer positive social reinforcers, such as approval, than mothers of normal children; moreover, mothers of problem children were shown by Sallows (1972) and Snyder (1977) to be significantly more likely to provide attention and other positive consequences for deviant behavior than were mothers of nonproblem children. In fact, the likelihood for positive consequences are similar for both deviant and prosocial behaviors in these families of antisocial children (Patterson, 1982). On the aversive side, mothers of aggressive children are more punitive than mothers of nonaggressive children. They punish not only a higher proportion of deviant behavior, but a higher proportion of prosocial behavior as well (Patterson, 1981; Sallows, 1972). Together, this pattern of indiscriminate use of positive and aversive feedback may reduce the effectiveness of social reinforcers for controlling the behavior of antisocial children.

Finally, Patterson (1982) suggests that antisocial children have skill deficits in the areas of work, peer relations, and academic achievement. Achenbach and Edelbrock (1981) found that children characterized as delinquent scored lower on a measure of social skills than normals did. In turn, Patterson (1981) finds that antisocial children are consistently rejected by their peers, which, in part, may be due to the high rates of coerciveness of these children—a characteristic behavior that has been identified as a determinant of peer rejection (see Hartup, Vol. IV, Chap. 2). In addition, the academic achievement and work patterns of these children are poor. It is interesting that antisocial children were less likely to be expected to do chores or to hold weekend or summer jobs.

The combination of ineffective parenting skills and certain child characteristics may make the development of coercive cycles more common in some families. However, longitudinal studies are clearly required to assess more adequately whether these differences in either parenting skills and/or child characteristics are producing these aggressive families or are themselves the outcome of the interaction patterns in these families. The directions of the causal arrows, in short, are still not fully understood.

Although parents were involved in 80% of the coercive episodes, it is not only parents who are involved in these episodes. Siblings, in fact, were involved in approximately 60% of the interchanges with problem children (Patterson, 1979), while both parents and siblings were involved in the same interchanges about 40% of the time. Patterson and Cobb (1971, 1973) have demonstrated clearly that younger siblings are often the initiators of coercive episodes for a problem child. In general, the Patterson data supports the general view that comes from the survey data (Strauss, Gelles, & Steinmetz, 1980) that social aggressors live in aggressive families.

As more family members adopt aversive behaviors as a method of coping with each other, the entire family system may become disrupted. Indeed, the coercive pattern of family interaction has often been found to be accompanied by a wide variety of disruptions in family interaction including: (a) avoidance of interaction among family members; (b) cessation of family recreational activities; (c) disruption in communication and problem-solving; (d) loss of self-esteem, particularly for mothers; and (e) development of marital conflicts. Patterson's (1982) analysis moves us forward significantly in identifying the processes that may lead to this disruption of the family system.

The Effect of Family Structure on Aggression

Does family structure affect the development of aggression? Most attention has been directed to the effects of single-parent families on the development of aggressive behavior patterns. Two approaches to this problem have been employed. The most common approach has been to examine the impact of father absence on children's aggression. A second and more recent approach involved examination of the effects of divorce on aggression in children.

The first approach has yielded a complex and somewhat inconsistent picture (Herzog & Sudia, 1973). Although a fatherless home is frequently cited as a major factor in delinquency (Gleuck & Gleuck, 1950; Gregory, 1965), it is unclear whether a father's absence directly contributes to juvenile delinquency. In their careful review, Herzog and Sudia (1973) conclude that the direct impact of father absence is "probably less than that of such factors as socioeconomic level and community traits" (p. 133). They point to various other factors that are associated with father absence as better candidates for explaining the link between father absence and delinquent behavior, namely,

stress and conflict within the home, inability of the mother to exercise adequate supervision, depressed income and living conditions (including exposure to unfavorable neighborhood influences), the mother's psychological and behavioral reaction to separation from the spouse as well as to the social and economic difficulties of her situation as a sole parent, and community attitudes toward the boy and the family. (Herzog & Sudia, 1973, p. 154)

Support for many of these factors as independent contributors is available (see Feshbach, 1970, for a review).

Does divorce affect aggressive behavior? In a longitudinal study of the impact of divorce, Hetherington, Cox, and Cox (1979, 1982) examined the social interactions, including aggressive behaviors, of 4-year-old children for a 2-year period after divorce. Mothers were awarded custody in all families in the study. Measures of social behavior were made at 2 months, 1 year, and 2 years following divorce across a wide range of situations including school. At 2 months, both boys and girls from divorced families showed a pattern of greater fantasy aggression and greater opposition and they more often sought help, attention, and proximity than did children from divorced families. Both boys and girls showed higher levels, physically and verbally, of hostile and instrumental aggression toward peers at both 2 months, and boys continued to show this pattern 1 year after divorce. However, by 2 years after divorce, boys from divorced families, in comparison to those from nondivorced families, were showing low physical aggression and high verbal aggression, a pattern more frequently found in girls. For girls, evidence of disruptive functioning had largely disappeared by 2 years. The verbal and physical aggression displayed by girls from divorced families at 2 months and by boys at 2 months and at 1 year tended to be immature, unprovoked, and ineffective. They were seldom successful in gaining their ends through instrumental aggression. Their aggression was often accompanied by, or followed by crying, dependency bids, or appeals to the teacher. This general pattern is consistent with peer ratings as well. At 2 months and at 1 year after divorce, boys from divorced families were viewed as more aggressive and less socially constructive than were boys from nondivorced families. They were still viewed by their peers as more aggressive at 2 years after divorce in spite of the observed decline in aggression. This suggests the possibility that the earlier aggressive behavior of boys in the first year after divorce was still being reacted to by their peers. The only differences in ratings between girls in divorced and nondivorced families were that girls in divorced families were rated as more aggressive at 2 months and more withdrawn, anxious, and dependent at all ages. The greater aggression displayed by boys than girls in divorced families closely parallels the generally negative and hostile interactions between boys and their mothers in the home situation. In turn, this may, in part, account for the considerable stability across situations in the behavior of children from divorced families, at least over the first year after divorce. Levels of aggression were stable across school and home contexts and between home and laboratory settings, although aggression was not significantly correlated for the laboratory and school observations. In addition, there was considerable congruence between parent and teacher ratings in the first year following divorce but not two years after divorce. For children in nondivorced families, there was generally much less stability across situations.

In summary, children, especially boys, who experience the process of parental divorce show disruption in their social behavior, including changes in the form and level of aggression. However, a variety of factors appears to affect how well children and parents cope with the divorce process and, in turn, may alter the child's social behavior, including aggression. These include the custodial parents' interaction with the child, attitudes between ex-spouses, the availability of social support systems, the custody arrangements (father vs. mother custody), and the developmental level of the child. (See Hetherington et al., 1982; Santrock, Warshak, & Elliott, 1982; Wallerstein & Kelly, 1980.) Of particular importance for future investigation is the impact of father versus mother custody, since some evidence (Santrock et al., 1982) indicates that boys adjust better in father-custody families rather than mother-custody families, although specific measures of peer-peer relationships including peer aggression are lacking in the research to date.

A final issue concerns the relative impact on children's social adjustment, including aggression, of living in a single-parent family or an intact conflict-ridden family (see Emery, 1982). Hetherington et al. (1982) compared divorced and intact families with high and low levels of family conflict. In the first year following divorce, children in the divorced families were functioning less well than those in either high- or low-discord nondivorced families; children of divorced families were more oppositional and aggressive and were more lacking in self-control. However, by 2 years following divorce the pattern of differences between children from stressed, nondivorced families and children from low-conflict, divorced families was reversed. At 2 years, more aggressive acting-out behavior, and less prosocial behavior, was found in boys from conflict-ridden nuclear families compared to low-conflict, divorced families. The boys from divorced families where high conflict persisted after the divorce showed the most problems, and both discord and divorce seem more pervasive and long-lasting for boys than girls. As Hetherington et al. note: "In the long run, marital discord may be associated with more adverse outcomes for children than is divorce" (1982, p. 262).

Thus, families play a central role in children's acquisition and maintenance of aggressive activity and, as we note later, in the control and modification of aggression as well. However, the family is only one of a variety of social influences that affect aggression, and familial influences are often modified by other socializing agents, such as peers and the mass media. Next we examine the role of the peer group in the development of aggression.

Peer Influence in the Development of Aggression

Families initiate the early socialization of aggression, but children's peers play an important role in the development, maintenance, and modification of aggressive behavior. Peers are active in the development of aggression by acting as reinforcing agents, elicitors of aggression, targets of hostility, and social models. Moreover, the ways in which children manage conflict in peer contexts have important consequences for their acceptance by their agemates, which, in turn, appears to affect long-term patterns of social adjustment.

Peers as Eliciting, Modeling, and Reinforcing Agents

Aggression between peers is a reciprocal process; just as is the case with aggression among family members, aggression in the peer context cannot be fully appreciated without considering the interdependence of the participants. The impact of the behavior of one member of a peer dyad in controlling the level of aggressive behavior of the other partner is well illustrated in a study by Hall (1973). On the basis of the assumption of reciprocal influence—that the acts of children tend to elicit similar acts from others—Hall argued that, in a dyad, the aggressive behavior of one child is a major determinant of the other child's aggressiveness. In this study, Hall "programmed" one member of each pair of boys, 6 to 7 years old, to behave aggressively, while the other member of the dyad was not trained. The results indicated that the active, aggressive partner was more effective in escalating the exchange than the passive partner was in de-escalating it. The reciprocal control of aggressive activity is clearly indicated by the high correlations between the behaviors of the two members of the pair. If one member of the pair performs no aggressive act, then the probability that the partner will perform one or no aggressive act is .86; in contrast, if the partner performs a high number of aggressive acts, then the probability of the partner performing more than one aggressive act is .75. Although reciprocal control is clearly demonstrated, the processes accounting for the effects are less clear. Whether the effect is the result of reciprocal modeling, or whether the partner elicited aggression, remains unknown.

Another illustration of dyadic control comes from research that demonstrated that peers can also serve as social models just as older siblings serve as models for their younger siblings. For example, Hicks (1965) showed that children will imitate film-mediated aggressive peer and adult models. The results of this study showed that male peer models were imitated more than either the female peer model or the adult models. This study is of particular interest since the children were brought back to the experimental setting after a 6-month period and were assessed for the amount of imitative aggressive behavior they displayed in a free-play session. In addition, the subjects were asked to recall and describe the actions of the aggressive model that they had previously observed. Although the amount of imitative aggressive behavior markedly decreased over time, there was still some evidence that exposure to a model had a lasting effect even up to 6 months after the initial viewing. The data also indicated that the effectiveness of a particular type of model may shift with time. The male adult model appeared to have the greatest long-term effect, even though the male peer model was most effective in the short run. These data suggest the interesting but untested hypothesis that peers may be more influential in the immediate situation, but that adults may have a more lasting influence in affecting children's aggressive behavior. Numerous other studies have demonstrated the impact of peer models on aggressive behavior, as we note in a later section on the effects of television on aggression (see also Bandura, 1973a).

Several studies have demonstrated that peers can serve as reinforcing agents for each other. Re-searchers employing either laboratory paradigms (Hartup, 1964) or trained confederates in naturalistic environments (Wahler, 1967) or observational assessments of naturalistic peer-peer interactions (Charlesworth & Hartup, 1967) have documented this finding. For example, in an observational study by Patterson et al. (1967) of peer reactions to aggressive behaviors among nursery school children, it was found that, when a child who was attacked responded by withdrawing, acquiescing, or crying, the attacker in later interactions was likely to perform the same type of aggressive act (pushing or grabbing toys) toward the same victim. In contrast, if the aggressive behavior was followed by negative reinforcement such as teacher intervention, attempts at recovery of property, or retaliation, there was a high probability that the aggressor would either choose a new victim or alter the form of his or her aggression. As Hartup (*Vol. IV, Chap. 2*) notes, caution is necessary in interpreting these data; since the observations were not continuous, "these data do not tell us that the victims' actions were associated with immediate repetition of the aggressive act."

Not only is aggression modified by peer feedback, but nonaggressive children may learn to behave aggressively within the peer context, particularly if they are frequently the victims of an aggressive attack. In the Patterson et al. study, children who were victimized by peers were provided with many opportunities to counterattack their aggressors. After experiencing frequent attacks, passive victims often counterattacked. As a result, the number of future attacks against them decreased. Patterson et al. found that, if a child counterattacked, there was a 68% probability that the counterattack successfully inhibited the attacker. Over repeated occasions, the victim's aggressive responses were therefore strengthened, thus making it more probable that the victim would initiate aggressive attacks in future situations. Over the period of the study, these investigators found a marked association among the frequency with which children were victimized by aggressive acts of peers, the frequency of their successful counterattacks, and increases in their aggressive behavior. This study suggests that peer reactions are important mediators of children's aggressive behaviors and that children may learn to behave aggressively by recognizing how to avoid being victimized. In combination with other work by Patterson (1982), which suggests that negative reinforcement rather than positive reinforcement plays a major role in coercive cycles of aggressive interaction in families, it seems likely that negative rather than positive feedback may play a more central role in aggression control in the peer context as well. Further analyses across situations and across age levels are necessary before any firm conclusions are possible.

Other Aspects of Peer-Peer Control: Victim and Attacker Behaviors

The above studies suggest that the behavior of the partner plays an important role in the elicitation and maintenance of aggression. Although the Patterson et al. study of nursery school children suggested that pain feedback from the victim had a reinforcing effect, this may be valid only for young children. A number of studies involving older children or adults suggests that pain feedback from a victim serves to inhibit the intensity of the aggressor's attack (Baron, 1971; Milgram, 1974). As Perry and Bussey suggest,

> pain cues curtail an aggressive attack, partly because pain cues arouse empathic distress and partly because the individual has learned that to prolong suffering in another person is wrong and worthy of blame from oneself and others. Furthermore, with age, an increasing number of aggressive episodes have as their goal the restoration of self-esteem (Feshbach, 1970; Hartup, 1974). Seeing the other suffer may "even the score," restore balance, and inform the aggressor that his or her goal has been achieved. (Perry & Bussey, 1983, p. 69)

The impact of pain feedback, however, varies not only with age but with the attacker's level of prior aggressiveness or the child's current level of anger. In a study of fifth-grade boys, Perry and Perry (1974) found that pain feedback was more effective in inhibiting aggression in low-aggressive than in high-aggressive boys. Similarly, individuals who are extremely angry may be less inhibited by pain feedback than nonangered individuals.

Pain is only one of a number of feedback cues that may control the intensity and length of aggressive interchanges. In a recent study Ginsburg, Pollman, and Wauson (1977) identified another effective inhibitor of human aggression, namely "making oneself smaller"—an appeasement gesture first suggested by Darwin (1872). In an observational analysis of male elementary school children, these investigators found that behaviors involving a diminution of body stature (kneeling, bowing, lying down) were found to precede the cessation of agonistic activity between children more frequently than

other forms of behavior exhibited by the child under attack (threat displays, face-to-face interaction, etc.). In short, these investigators have isolated another appeasement cue which appears to inhibit aggression in humans.

Nonverbal cues can serve not only to curtail aggressive attacks once an aggressive interchange is underway but may prevent the occurrence of aggressive behavior before it happens. Threat displays of nonhuman primates, for example, serve this function, and evidence indicates that children may also engage in nonverbal exchanges that serve a similar regulatory role in conflict situations. Camaras (1977) has identified facial expressions used by children to defend possessions in conflict situations. Children 5 and 6 years old were observed in a play situation involving an object with which only one child could play at a time. Through an examination of facial expressions used by the children while defending their possession, Camaras identified "aggressive" facial expressions—having such characteristics as a lowered brow, a stare, the face thrust forward, pressed together lips, a wrinkled nose—that the children used to retain the disputed object. Moreover, when the use of an aggressive expression was successful, the child was more likely to continue to resist the opponent in contrast to children who did not use "aggressive" expressions as a way of controlling their resources. The use of aggressive facial expressions also had a deterrent effect on the partner: The other child was more hesitant as reflected in longer waiting times before the next attempt if an aggressive as opposed to a nonaggressive expression was used. These findings suggest that facial expressions play an important role in conflict encounters between children. In terms of function, the aggressive expression—like threat displays of other species—is used in a process of conflict resolution, which seems to involve information transmission rather than physical fighting. "In terms of form, most of the aggressive expressions physically resemble threat displays described for other primates (Redican, 1975: Rowell, 1972; Van Hooff, 1967). These similarities of function and form suggest that there may be a phylogenetic relationship between the aggressive expressions observed in children and primate threat displays" (Camaras, 1977, p. 1434).

Dominance Hierarchies and Aggression Regulation in Peer Relationships

Another area of research on aggression within the peer context is the role of dominance hierarchies. In social settings such as nursery schools, playgrounds, or summer camps where children interact together over an extended period of time, children tend to form stable group structures in which the members are organized in some hierarchical arrangement. For many years ethologists (e.g., Crook, 1970) have been describing dominance hierarchies among non-human primates, which serve to regulate aggression in stable groups of animals. Two types of dominance—dyadic and group—have been distinguished.

> Dyadic dominance describes the relative balance of social power between two members of a group, while dominance hierarchies summarize the organization of such dyadic relations for all group members. Theoretically, the existence of dyadic dominance and maintenance of a stable dominance hierarchy function to minimize intragroup aggression by establishing a relatively stable sequence of individual prerogatives (Hinde, 1974). Having learned the power sequence for its social unit, each group member is able to anticipate, and thus to avoid immediate adverse consequences of social aggression. (Abramovitch & Strayer, 1978, p. 108)

Recently, a number of researchers have explored the existence and function of dominance hierarchies among human children.

In one study of 4-year-olds, Abramovitch and Strayer (1978) measured two types of conflict: aggressive interactions (attack-submission interchanges and threat-submission interchanges), and object/position struggles. Observation of these types of conflict among a group of preschool age children during free-play periods indicated stable dyadic dominance relationships and linear group status structures. According to a linear model, if individual A dominates B, and individual B dominates C, then A should also dominate C. There was considerable support for the model since 98% of exchanges between the children conformed to a linear model. In other studies (Abramovitch, 1976; Strayer, 1980) similar findings for separate samples of children have been reported. Further evidence suggests that dominance hierarchies based on the initiation of attacks and threats are as linear as hierarchies based on the outcomes of agonistic interactions (Sluckin and Smith, 1977).

Dominance hierarchies are not only of value in understanding aggressive control in established groups but may be useful in understanding how individuals react to aggression-eliciting stimuli. In one study, the reactions of delinquent boys to movie violence was related to their position in the dominance hierarchy (Leyens, Camino, Parke, & Berkowitz, 1975). Boys in the top third of the dominance hierarchy in a group of adolescent boys behaved more aggressively following the violent movies than the less dominant boys. More qualitative analysis indicated that the most dominant boys reacted immediately and powerfully, whereas the least dominant members delayed their reactions, which were notably weaker.

The behaviors by which dominance hierarchies are maintained among groups of peers change over development. As noted above, verbal forms of aggression become more common across age and physical aggression becomes less frequent; in maintaining positions in dominance hierarchies among adolescents, ridicule was more common than physical threats (Savin-Williams, 1979). Similarly, the criteria that determine rank or status may shift across development. While perceived toughness and physical prowess may play an important role among nursery school children, sexual maturity and athletic ability take on importance in early adolescence (Savin-Williams, 1979); however, by late adolescence, intelligence, creativity, and camp craft skills may predominate (Savin-Williams, 1980).

These studies not only further illustrate the value of ethological approaches, but begin to uncover some of the mechanisms by which animals and humans "short-circuit" or prevent the occurrence of harmful aggressive interchanges. A more complete developmental analysis of the emergence, stability, and regulatory basis of dominance hierarchies in peers of different ages would be valuable.

The Role of Peer Group Norms

Peers can function to either maintain, increase, or inhibit aggressive behavior, not only through direct interaction but also by setting norms that relate to the propriety of aggressive activities. Some groups and subcultures may promote aggressive and antisocial behavior. Among delinquent groups, status is often achieved by the skillful execution of antisocial actions (Miller, 1958). These patterns may vary across social class. Pope (1953) found that aggressive behavior was valued by the lower class boys in his study, while aggressive, domineering behaviors led to rejection among boys from high socioeconomic levels.

In turn, violation of peer group norms such as excessive aggression can have consequences for children's acceptance by other children. Numerous studies have found that children who are aggressive, especially inappropriately, are disliked more by their peers (Lesser, 1958; Moore, 1967). But these early studies merely indicate that aggressive behavior is a correlate of unpopularity or low sociometric status. Possibly, unpopular children behave aggressively because they are rejected by their peers. Several recent studies, however, suggest that aggressive behavior may, in fact, predict a child's unpopular status. In one study (Coie & Kupersmidt, 1981) fourth-grade boys of known sociometric status (rejected, neglected, popular, or average) formed groups. Half joined groups in which the children were unfamiliar with each other and the remaining children joined groups in which the children knew each other. Over 6 weeks, data indicated that children who were initially rated as rejected were found to be more possessive of toys, more verbally abusive, and more physically aggressive than popular children. Moreover, these previously rejected children were similarly rejected by their peers in the newly formed groups. Similar results were found by Dodge (1981), who also formed groups of children who were unfamiliar with one another. Again, over a period of eight play sessions, the children who engaged in physical aggression and in hostile verbalizations (insults, contentious statements, exclusion of peers from play) were rejected by their peers. In contrast, children who engaged in more cooperative play and social conversation were rated as more popular with their peers.

These studies inform us more about how aggressive behavior affects subsequent peer-peer interaction than they do about the processes that contribute to the emergence of these individual differences in aggressive behavior. The value of this type of research for the student of aggression, however, is its ability to isolate social skill deficits in aggressive children or differences between the social behavior of aggressive and nonaggressive children, which, in turn, could guide intervention strategies and provide some clues concerning the earlier antecedents of these problematic patterns. In addition, these studies suggest some of the conditions that may maintain these patterns. For example, to the extent that aggressive children are unpopular and rejected by peers, the amount of opportunity for peer-peer contact may decrease and, therefore, the opportunities for acquiring other more acceptable social skills through interaction with peers may decrease as well. Other research suggests that aggressive children may have a series of social skill deficits, which may take the form of inaccurate or limited knowledge of appropriate social behavior, poor impulse control, or biases in the ways in which they process social information. For example, recent research suggests that the unpopular children who have been identified as behaving aggressively may also lack knowledge of appropriate ways of resolving conflict. Asher and Renshaw (1982) found that these children were more likely to be inappropriately negative. In hypothetical situations concerning the management of conflict, unpopular children relied more on aggressive strategies than did popular children.

In summary, it is apparent that peers contribute substantially to the socialization of children's aggression. Further investigation of the processes involved in the impact of peers on the development of aggression is necessary, for both a better understanding of how peers function as elicitors and maintainers of aggressive behavior as well as for guidance in developing modification strategies for the regulation of children's aggression.

Next we examine the role of television in the development of aggression.

Television as a Socializer of Aggression

Scope of the Research

The role of television as a socialization agent in the development of aggression has been an issue of continuing public concern and research investigation for nearly three decades. Today the large body of accumulated research on TV violence attests to the responsiveness of social scientists to this issue of public concern. Still surrounded by public controversy over the proper application of the findings, the accumulated evidence nevertheless establishes a reliable link between children's experience of viewing televised violence and their tendency to increase both their own performance of aggression and their passive acceptance of aggression performed by others. In light of both the excessive amount of televised violence typically viewed by today's children and the strength of the accumulated evidence on the effects of such exposure, television clearly deserves its new-found status as a major contributor to the development of children's aggression. Indeed, any discussion of children's aggression must now be considered incomplete unless the role of television is not only included but also treated on a par with such traditional sources of socialization as families, peers, and schools.

The body of research on the effects of TV violence can be characterized by its distinctive combination of properties, including: (1) a condensed history; (2) an unusually close link to an issue of public concern; (3) a wide range of methodological perspectives applied to a single issue; and (4) an increasing concentration on specifying the nature of the causal relationship between TV violence and viewer aggression. In the last 30 years, this body of literature has grown to include over 630 scholarly papers and books, more than two-thirds of which were produced within the last 10 years. Data have been gathered from well over 30,000 individuals, primarily from children and youth. Although most of the research on TV violence has been conducted in the United States where many programs involving violence are produced and shown, significant empirical contributions have also come from a number of other countries, including: Australia (e.g., Edgar, 1977); Belgium (e.g., Leyens et al., 1975); Canada (e.g., Joy, Kimball, & Zabrack, 1977); Finland (Langerspetz, Wahlroos, & Wendelin, 1978); Great Britain (e.g., Belson, 1978); Japan (e.g., Furu, 1971); Mexico (e.g., Korzenny, 1976); Poland (Fraczek, 1980); Sweden (e.g., Linne, 1971); and West Germany (e.g., Schwartz, Eckert, & Bastine, 1971). One can safely say that the question of how TV violence influences viewer aggression has emerged as one of the major social science research issues of the latter half of the twentieth century.

Some recent reviews of the literature provide a comprehensive evaluation of our current knowledge concerning the role of TV violence in the development of aggression (e.g., Comstock, Chaffee, Katzman, McCombs, & Roberts, 1978; Howitt & Cumberbatch, 1975; Kaplan & Singer, 1976; Liebert & Schwartzberg, 1977; Murray & Kippax, 1979; Rubinstein, 1978; Slaby & Quarfoth, 1980: Stein & Friedrich, 1975). Most reviewers note that the strength of their conclusions is based on substantial convergence of empirical evidence that is derived from a wide range of data sources and complementary methodological techniques, including the use of laboratory experiments, correlational surveys, field experiments, and longitudinal studies. Recently the possibilities for surveying and evaluating the entire body of literature have been increased in several ways. Comprehensive bibliographies have been assembled (e.g., Comstock et al., 1978; Murray, 1980; Royal Commission on Violence in the Communications Industry, 1977); quantitative meta-analyses that combine the accumulated data from individual studies have been performed (e.g., Andison, 1977; Hearold, 1979); and an evaluation of the social significance and the future priorities of research on the effects of TV violence has been presented (e.g., Comstock et al., 1978; Ford Foundation Report, 1976; National Institute of Mental Health, 1982a,b; Palmer & Dorr, 1980).

Historical Perspective on the Social Issue of TV Violence

During the past three decades, social concern over the potentially harmful effects of televised violence has grown in close relationship with the available research evidence. The number of national organizations voicing concern has grown to include federal institutions, national scientific commissions, professional associations, and public citizen groups. More thorough documentation for the brief historical account that follows has been provided by Leibert, Sprafkin & Davidson (1982) and by Rubinstein (1980).

In 1951, the National Association of Educational Broadcasters surveyed TV programming in four major American cities and reported that crime and horror programs accounted for 10% of the programming time. Several years later the Senate Subcommittee on Juvenile Delinquency initiated the first in what was to become a long series of public inquiries into the effects of TV violence. Based on the testimony and data generated from these hearings, this subcommittee issued reports indicating that: (1) television could potentially be harmful to young children (1956); (2) the amount of TV violence had increased and much of it was shown during times when young children were typically viewing (1961, 1964); and (3) televised crime and violence were related to antisocial behavior among juvenile viewers (1965). In 1968, President Lyndon Johnson established a National Commission on the Causes and Prevention of Violence under the direction of Milton Eisenhower. Based on a large-scale content analysis of TV violence and a series of papers reviewing the scientific evidence, the Eisenhower Commission concluded that viewers of TV violence learned how to engage in violent behavior, and it presented recommendations (1969) for reducing the harmful effects of viewing TV violence.

Before the Eisenhower Commission had issued its final report, the Senate Subcommittee on Communications requested the U.S. Surgeon General to commission a series of original studies designed to establish definitively whether a causal connection exists between televised crime and violent or antisocial behavior of individuals, particularly children. As a result of this request, $1 million was made available through the National Institute of Mental Health to sponsor 23 independent research investigations and to convene a scientific advisory committee to review, evaluate, and develop conclusions concerning the findings (Surgeon General's Scientific Advisory Committee on Television and Social Behavior, 1972). Although the collective evidence generated by these empirical studies is generally regarded as a major scientific achievement, the advisory committee's summary and conclusions have been roundly criticized (e.g., Boffey & Walsh, 1970; Cater & Strickland, 1975; Liebert, Spraskin, Davidson, 1982; Rubinstein, 1980; Siegel, 1975). Critics begin by pointing out that the advisory committee members were selected through a political process that permitted noted scientists to be blackballed, while allowing participation by individuals with financial ties to the TV industry. Critics also fault the advisory committee for understating the strength and the scope of the relationship between televised violence and antisocial behavior.

In the 10 years following the Surgeon General's Committee Report in 1972, more than 2500 research publications have addressed the issue of influence of television on behavior, many of which focus on the effects of television on aggression. In recognition of the growing need for collection, review, synthesis, and assessment of this new literature, the National Institute of Mental Health was encouraged by the Surgeon General to prepare a report elucidating the interim research findings and their implications for public health and future research. The NIMH Report includes a summary on the 10 years of scientific research since the Surgeon General's Committee Report in 1972 (Vol. 1, 1982a), as well as 24 integrative reviews of the literature (Vol. 2, 1982b). This report indicates that a causal link between TV violence and aggressive behavior now seems obvious, and the major research question has moved from asking whether there is an effect to seeking explanations for the effect.

The Surgeon General's Commission Report in 1972 not only stimulated a rich "harvest" of new research on TV violence (Schramm, 1976), but it also served to spark new interest among many national professional associations and citizen groups. In the mid-1970s, major campaigns against TV violence were initiated by the American Medical Association, the National Council of Churches, and the National Parent Teachers Association. Many public citizen organizations were also formed to protest TV violence, including the National Correspondence Group, the National Citizens Committee for Broadcasting, and the National Coalition on Television Violence. A recent handbook of media organizations lists over 30 media action groups (Rivers, Thompson, & Nyhan, 1977). Many of these organi-

zations shar[...] awareness a[...] lence, prote[...] lence, and c[...] Meanwhile[...] regarding c[...] media viole[...] light of ma[...] cable televi[...] recording [...] video prog[...]

or no restrictions [...] and children pe[...] than their pa[...] Lyle & [...] 1975; [...]

Exposure to TV Violence

In spite of considerable individual variation in children's viewing patterns, virtually every American child today is exposed to a great deal of television violence, as the following set of observations indicates.

1. Television is readily accessible to almost every American child. Nearly every household has a television set (98%), and many households have at least one extra set (52%) (Nielsen Television Index, 1982). Extra television sets are often used primarily by children (Bower, 1973).

2. Children spend a great deal of time viewing television. American children between the ages of 2 and 18 years watch an average of well over 3 hours of programming per day (Nielsen Television Index, 1982). Considering that television watching continues during weekends, school holidays, and summer vacations, children spend more time watching television than they spend engaging in any other single waking activity, including attending school, interacting with family members, or playing with other children (Lyle, 1972).

3. Much of American TV programming contains violence as a common form of social interaction, and particularly high levels of violence are presented in programs designed specifically for children. Over 70% of prime-time dramatic fiction programs sampled from 1967 through 1979 were found to contain violence, and children's cartoon and weekend morning programs consistently contained the highest levels of violence among all categories of programming (Gerbner, Gross, Morgan, & Signorielli, 1980; Gerbner, Gross, Signorielli, Morgan, & Jackson-Beeck, 1979).

4. Most children are permitted to watch television with very few parental restrictions on either the amount or the content of their viewing. Despite substantial parental concern over the effects of TV viewing, parents generally report that they place few

on their children's TV viewing, ...ceive even fewer parental controls ...ents report (Bower, 1973; Lyle, 1972; ...offman, 1972a; Rossiter & Robertson, ...tein & Friedrich, 1972).

...oth the amount and the type of televised vio...nce that children view vary considerably depending on such factors as the children's age, sex, IQ, socioeconomic status, and ethnicity (Dorr & Kovaric, 1980). The predominant type of TV violence that children of various age levels view is typically quite different, since young children tend to watch cartoons and older children tend to watch action/adventure and crime drama programs (Lyle & Hoffman, 1972a; Schramm, Lyle, & Parker, 1961). Direct evidence is lacking, however, on the amount of TV violence viewed by children at various age levels. Boys have been found to watch more TV violence and to prefer it more than girls, and this sex difference has been reported for a wide range of age levels, including preschool (Lyle & Hoffman, 1972b; Stein & Friedrich, 1972), first through tenth grade (Atkin, Greenberg, Korzenny, & McDermott, 1979; Lyle & Hoffman, 1972a), and junior and senior high school (Chaffee & McLeod, 1972; Greenberg, 1975). Some studies have found no difference between boys and girls in the viewing of TV violence (e.g., Howitt, 1972b). Children with lower IQ scores have been found to watch more TV violence than children with higher IQ scores, a finding reported for preschool boys and girls (Stein & Friedrich, 1972) and for junior and senior high school boys and girls (Chaffee & McLeod, 1972).

A number of studies has also found socioeconomic status and ethnicity differences in children's viewing of TV violence, although at least one study has failed to find such differences for sixth- and tenth-grade children (Lyle & Hoffman, 1972a). From the preschool years through high school, lower class youth reliably report watching more televised violence than do middle-class youth (Chaffee & McLeod, 1972; Foulkes, Belvedere, & Brubaker, 1972; Greenberg, 1975; Howitt, 1972a,b; Stein & Friedrich, 1972). In the high school years, nonwhite children tend to watch more violent TV programs than white children, even when socioeconomic status is controlled (Greenberg, 1975; Lyle, 1972).

By far the most comprehensive program for monitoring televised violence has been developed by Gerbner and his colleagues (e.g., Gerbner et al., 1979, 1980). Extensive analyses of the amount and type of violence presented on television, as well as of the nature of the TV characters involved in violence, have been performed on week-long samples of prime-time and weekend daytime network dramatic programming broadcast from 1967 through 1979. For purposes of the analyses, violence is defined as "the overt expression of physical force (with or without a weapon, and against self or others) compelling action against one's will on pain of being hurt and/or killed or threatened to be so victimized as part of the plot (Gerbner et al., 1980, p. 11). Whereas idle threats, verbal abuse, or gestures without credible violent consequences are not coded as violence, both "accidental" violence and violence occurring in a fantasy or humorous context are included, together with violence occurring in a realistic or "serious" context. Although some critics representing the networks have proposed a narrower definition that excludes the accidental and fantasy violence often portrayed in cartoons (e.g., Heller, 1978), Gerbner defends their inclusion, pointing to substantial evidence that "fantasy and comedy are effective forms in which to convey serious lessons" (Gerbner et al., 1980, p. 12).

The evidence from Gerbner's monitoring program reveals that violence has been a frequent and consistent feature of American dramatic TV programming, and particularly children's programming. Over the entire 13-year monitoring period, approximately 80% of all monitored programs contained violence, and violent acts were presented at an overall rate of about 7.5 per hour. Weekend daytime programs that are typically designed for children contribute heavily to these overall averages. Approximately 93% of the weekend daytime programs contained violence, and violent acts were presented at a rate of about 17.6 per hour (Gerbner et al., 1979, 1980). In spite of popular claims to the contrary, these rates have remained remarkably stable over the last 13 years.

Besides presenting enormous amounts of violence, American TV programming generally portrays particular forms of stylized violence that regularly occur among characters representing particular age, sex, and social groups. Much of TV violence is presented as being clean, justified, effective, rewarded, and sometimes humorous (Slaby & Quarfoth, 1980). For example, TV violence is almost invariably clean violence, since network codes generally prohibit the presentation of such realistic negative consequences as blood, suffering, and agony. Painful consequences have been found to occur so infrequently that monitors could not rate them reliably (Gerbner, 1972). Network codes further specify that, when criminal acts are presented, the viewer must be shown that "crime does not pay." However, adherence to this code typically takes the form of presenting "good guys" who engage in justified, condoned, or even heroic violence as a means of punishing the "bad guys" for having committed a crime. On television the "good guys" perform as much violence as the bad guys, and they frequently break the law in the service of goals purported to be justifiable (Lange, Baker, & Ball, 1969).

In TV drama, the use of violence or illegal means is generally shown to be effective in attaining goals more frequently than the use of legal or socially approved means, and children's programs are particularly likely to depict violence as being effective (Larsen, Gray, & Fortis, 1968). When television's "good guys" use violence, they often gain not only the direct reward of attaining their goals but also such added rewards as praise, social advancement, and material advantage. It has been claimed that TV violence is rewarded at least as often as it is punished (Stein & Friedrich, 1975). Particularly in children's programming, TV violence is often presented as being humorous. For example, contrived adult laugh-tracks often accompany violent cartoon programming, cueing the viewing child to recognize that violence is to be considered funny.

Consistent patterns have emerged concerning the types of TV characters portrayed as the perpetrators and the victims of violence. About two-thirds of all male characters and nearly one-half of all female characters were found to be involved in violence over the past 11 years during which the types of characters involved in violence had been monitored (Gerbner et al., 1979, 1980). When involved, those characters found to be particularly likely perpetrators of violence were old men and women cast as "bad" characters. Those characters found to be particularly likely victims by violence were young men and women cast in minority roles (old or young women, upper or lower class women, and nonwhite women). Female victimization is currently particularly apparent in weekend children's programming (Gerbner et al., 1979). The consistent portrayal of these patterns of violence and victimization in American TV drama guarantees that the steady viewer will be repeatedly exposed to a number of societal lessons regarding which social groups have the power and status to force their will on others through acts of violence. Following a discussion of developmental changes in children's understanding of portrayed acts of violence, research on the effects of these societal lessons on the behavior of TV viewers is presented.

Developmental Changes in Viewer Understanding of Portrayed Violence

Children have been found to show developmental changes in their understanding of a variety of aspects of TV programming, many of which may be involved in any given portrayal of violence. For example, age-related changes have been found in the viewer's understanding of: (1) distinctions between true-to-life events and TV portrayals of fictional characters and programs (Greenberg & Reeves, 1976); (2) distinctions among human, puppet, and cartoon characters (Quarfoth, 1979); (3) central program content related to the plot, in contrast to peripheral program content (Collins, 1970; Collins, Wellman, Keniston, & Westby, 1978; Hale, Miller, & Stevenson, 1968; Hallahan, Kauffman, & Ball, 1974; Hawkins, 1973; Katzman, 1972; Ward, 1972); (4) sequences of events portrayed in TV programs (Leifer, Collins, Gross, Taylor, Andrews, & Blackmer, 1971); (5) interpretive links between separate scenes of a TV program (Collins, 1973; Collins, Berndt, & Hess, 1974); (6) motivations underlying behavior portrayed on television (Collins, 1973; Collins et al., 1974; Leifer et al., 1971; Leifer & Roberts, 1972); and (7) consequences of behavior portrayed on television (Collins, 1973; Collins et al., 1974; Leifer & Roberts, 1972). Although these findings strongly suggest that the viewer's understanding of TV violence may vary with the viewer's developmental level, relatively little research on the effects of televised violence has focused on developmental changes.

Available evidence on age-related differences indicates that younger children are more likely than older children to respond directly to violent acts, as though they were isolated events unconnected to the broader context of motivations and consequences that commonly accompanies a televised portrayal of violence. In one study of age-related changes in viewers' understanding and evaluation of televised violence, children of various ages were tested after they had viewed an edited version of an "action/adventure" program involving aggression (Collins et al., 1974). Children in kindergarten and second grade tended to remember either the aggressive act alone or the aggressive act and its consequences, whereas children in the fifth and eighth grades remembered both the motives and the consequences of a variety of behaviors, including aggression. The younger children also tended to evaluate aggressors solely in terms of the consequences of their actions, whereas the older children based their evaluations on a combination of aggressors' motives and consequences. The fact that the viewer's subsequent aggression may be mediated by his or her evaluation of the TV character's violent actions is demonstrated in a further study in which children's perceptions of televised violence were experimentally manipulated (Collins & Zimmermann, 1975). Children who saw a violent act portrayed in a context of consistently negative motives and consequences subsequently reduced their level of aggressive responses. On the other hand, children who saw the same violent acts portrayed in the context of a mixture of positive and negative motives and consequences subsequently increased their level of aggression.

In a complementary study of age-related changes in viewers' aggressive responses to televised violence, children were shown a program in which one scene portraying an aggressive act was both preceded by a scene depicting its hostile motivation and followed by a scene depicting its harmful consequences (Collins, 1973). Thus, for children who understood the links between scenes, the aggression would presumably be interpreted as an undesirable act to emulate. In one viewing condition, the three scenes were shown with no interruption, and in a second viewing condition the three scenes were separated by short commercial messages, as commonly occurs during the viewing of commercial TV programming. The results suggested that third-grade children failed to link the aggressive act with its motivation and its consequences when the three scenes were interrupted by commercials. Third-grade children subsequently made more aggressive choices in written responses to interpersonal conflict when the viewing conditions involved interruptions of the aggressive act from both its hostile intent and its harmful consequences compared to when the viewing condition involved no interruption. Older children were apparently able to make an interpretive link regardless of whether the scenes were interrupted.

Thus, young children appear to be less likely than older children to differentiate between various portrayed acts of violence, particularly when the interpretive context of motivation and consequences in which the violent act occurs is not portrayed immediately and explicitly. For this reason, an adult co-viewer may play a particularly important role with young children in helping them understand the implicit motives and consequences that accompany the portrayed acts of violence. The potential for an adult co-viewer to moderate the effects of televised violence on the young viewer, by making explanatory or evaluative comments at critical points during the program, is discussed later.

Effects on Viewer Aggression

Most reviewers have attempted to evaluate the cumulative weight of the research evidence, and their evaluations have led them to conclude that TV violence can and does increase subsequent aggression by the viewer (e.g., Bandura, 1973a; Comstock, 1975; Comstock et al., 1978; Liebert et al.,

1982; Rubinstein, 1978; Slaby & Quarfoth, 1980; Stein & Friedrich, 1975; Watt & Krull, 1977). Many of these reviewers have indicated that their confidence in this general conclusion is strengthened by the fact that complementary evidence converging on this conclusion derives from studies involving a wide range of viewing materials, types of viewers, viewing circumstances, measures of aggression, and methodological techniques. For example, portrayals of violence have been found to increase the likelihood or the amount of viewer aggression in the following conditions:

1. When violence is presented on a television set, a movie screen, or by live models (Bandura, 1965; Bandura et al., 1963a,b; Parke, Berkowitz, Leyens, West, & Sebastian, 1977; Stein & Friedrich, 1972).

2. When violent programs are presented just as they are televised or are specially constructed and edited for research purposes (Bandura, 1965; Stein & Friedrich, 1972).

3. With cartoon violence, fantasy violence, or realistically portrayed violence (Bandura, 1965; Bandura et al., 1961, 1963a,b; Ellis & Sekyra, 1972; Steuer, Applefield, & Smith, 1971).

4. With children, adolescents, or adults as viewers (Berkowitz, 1971; Liebert & Baron, 1972; Parke et al., 1977).

5. With viewers who have or have not experienced frustration prior to viewing violence (Hartmann, 1969; Liebert & Baron, 1972).

6. When viewers are with or without documented histories of unusually aggressive behavior (Hartmann, 1969; Parke et al., 1977).

7. In naturalistic or controlled laboratory viewing circumstances (Bandura, 1965; Steuer et al., 1971).

8. With individual or group viewing circumstances (Berkowitz, 1971; Parke et al., 1977).

9. With single or repeated exposure to violent programs (Bandura et al., 1963; Steuer et al., 1971).

10. When viewer aggressive responses are similar to, or different from, those portrayed (Bandura, 1965; Liebert & Baron, 1972; Stein & Friedrich, 1972).

11. When viewer aggressive responses are measured immediately following or with a long-term delay following exposure to violence (Lefkowitz, Eron, Walder, & Huesmann, 1972; Liebert & Baron, 1972).

In contrast to those reviewers who have attempted to evaluate the cumulative weight of the evidence, several reviewers have taken a different strategy for evaluating the evidence, and they have concluded that the case against TV violence has not been proven (Howitt & Cumberbatch, 1975; Kaplan & Singer, 1976). Rubinstein (1980) has pointed out that each of these dissenting reviewers has taken the strategy of discounting any importance that might be given to either the cumulative weight or the complementary nature of the evidence. They have focused instead on evaluating the ways in which each individual published study that purports to offer evidence may be held invalid because of serious flaws in methodology, measurement, statistical analyses, or interpretations.

The following discussion does not duplicate that of previous reviews by focusing on either an evaluation of the cumulative weight of the evidence or on a methodological critique of individual studies. Instead, this presentation highlights several key patterns in the findings that serve to advance our understanding of the relationship between televised violence and viewer aggression, as well as to raise some issues that deserve further attention. Following a discussion of empirical attempts to provide quantitative evaluation of the entire body of research evidence through meta-analyses, alternative perspectives on the issue are presented by discussing the nature of the evidence generated through the following methodological approaches: laboratory experiments, field experiments, correlational surveys, and longitudinal studies.

Meta-analyses. The large number of individual studies on the relationship between viewing violence and viewer aggression has made it possible to perform quantitative analyses on the set of outcomes. As the term implies, meta-analysis offers a formal quantitative method of analyzing the outcomes of a set of individual studies that address a common hypothesis. The simplest form of meta-analysis involves an overall headcount of studies, as well as various categorizations of the types of studies, that provide positive, negative, or neutral evidence with regard to the hypothesis, based on the simple criterion of presence or absence of a statistically significant effect. However, it is also possible to use statistical aspects of the degree of the effect found in individual studies as the basis for more complex metaanalyses performed on a set of outcomes (Glass, McGaw, & Smith, 1981). In an attempt to summarize the large body of evidence on the effects of viewing violence, one simple meta-analysis involving data from over 30,000 subjects (Andison, 1977) and one more complex meta-analysis involving data from more than 100,000 subjects (Hearold, 1979) have been performed.

Andison (1977) identified 67 studies that were conducted between 1956 and 1976 that dealt with the relationship between exposure to violent portrayal and aggressive behavior. Each study was scored according to its attributes and its outcome, thereby giving each an equal weight. With respect to the hypothesis that exposure to violence increases the viewer's aggression, 76% of the studies had positive outcomes, 19% had neutral outcomes, and less than 5% had negative outcomes. Most of the outcomes were positive regardless of age of the viewer (i.e., preschool, elementary school, high school, or college), time of the study, country of investigation, measure of aggression, or method of investigation. However, the findings were stronger for laboratory experiments, together with the measures they typically employ (87% positive), than for field experiments and surveys (70% positive). This difference presumably reflects the greater sensitivity and control that laboratory experiments often provide by eliminating many of the complexities of real-life events that are commonly included in field experiments and surveys.

Hearald (1979) used the more sensitive criterion of the statistical degree of the effect for the purpose of aggregating 230 studies that dealt with the effects of antisocial, neutral, or prosocial portrayals on antisocial and prosocial behavior. Overall, antisocial portrayals appeared to increase antisocial behavior, but they had little effect on prosocial behavior. Prosocial portrayals appeared to have the dual effect of increasing prosocial behavior and decreasing antisocial behavior. Antisocial portrayals had somewhat less influence on antisocial behavior than did prosocial portrayals on prosocial behavior. However, when only portrayals that resembled real-life TV or film programs were considered, antisocial portrayals were found to have the ability to affect a relatively wide range of nonportrayed antisocial behavior, including physical aggression, in contrast to the ability of prosocial portrayals, which affected a relatively narrow range of nonportrayed prosocial behavior. Finally, age trends for boys and girls appeared with regard to the strength of the effect of antisocial portrayals on overall antisocial behavior, and particularly on physical aggression. The strength of the effect was found to decline for both boys and girls from the preschool years through ages 9 to 13. Thereafter, the strength of the effect sharply increased for boys, while it continued to decrease for girls, indicating that during adolescence and adulthood antisocial portrayals had a greater elicitation effect on physical aggression for males than for females.

The fact that the age trends identified in Hearold's (1979) more sophisticated metaanalysis were not revealed in Andison's (1977) metaanalysis, which was based on the less sensitive criterion of simple presence or absence of an effect, illustrates the growing possibilities for metaanalyses to identify important patterns of findings as metaanalytic techniques are improved. Since metaanalyses can take account of psychological processes only as these are repeatedly represented in individual studies, they do not escape the biases that guide research questions to be formulated in particular ways (Comstock, 1980). Nevertheless, quantitative syntheses of a body of research evidence can provide new data by which to evaluate an issue, and this information may be particularly valuable when it is combined with qualitative information in the process of evaluating a body of research evidence (Light & Pillemer, 1982). Thus, our discussion of the quantitative findings of this research is augmented by a qualitative analysis of the complementarity of the research findings derived from different methodological techniques having dissimilar liabilities and assets.

Laboratory Experiments. Parallel groundbreaking experiments on the effects of viewing aggression on the viewer's subsequent aggressive behavior were initiated in the early 1960s by Bandura with child subjects and by Berkowitz with adolescent and adult subjects (e.g., Bandura, 1965; Bandura et al., 1961, 1963a,b; Bandura & Walters, 1963; Berkowitz, 1962; Berkowitz, Corwin, & Heironimus, 1963; Berkowitz & Rawlings, 1963). Although these initial laboratory experiments had little to do with TV effects, they served not only to establish a link between the observation of aggression and the subsequent aggressive behavior of the observer, but also to create a theoretical and methodological framework for experimentally testing the effects of television.

Laboratory experiments have provided the control necessary for examining the precise relationship among numerous variables related to the types of portrayals of aggression, the characteristics of the viewer, the circumstances of viewing, and the measurable effects on viewer aggression. Controlled experimentation has helped to identify not only the range of circumstances under which it is possible to find an effect on viewer aggression, but also the particular circumstances under which an effect is more probable. For example, Comstock (1980, p. 137) has summarized those aspects of portrayals that have been experimentally demonstrated to increase the likelihood of eliciting viewer aggression:

1. Reward or lack of punishment for the perpetrator (Bandura, 1965; Bandura et al., 1963b; Rosekrans & Hartup, 1967).

2. Depiction of the violence as justified (Berkowitz & Rawlings, 1963; Meyer, 1972).

3. Cues, such as attributes of a victim matching those in real life (Berkowitz & Geen, 1966).

4. Similarity of a perpetrator to a viewer (Rosekrans, 1967).

5. Depiction of violence as malevolent and injurious in intent (Berkowitz & Alioto, 1973; Geen & Stonner, 1972).

6. Violence labeled realistic rather than fictional (Feshbach, 1972).

7. Violence whose commission pleases the viewer (Ekman, Liebert, Friesen, Harrison, Zlatchin, Malmstrom, & Baron, 1972).

8. Highly exciting content, violent or not (Tannenbaum & Zillmann, 1975; Zillmann, 1971).

9. Violence that goes uncritized (Lefcourt, Barnes, Parke, & Schwartz, 1966).

As we have noted previously, many of these aspects of portrayed violence that often increase the probability of eliciting viewer aggression appear to be regular features of American TV programming commonly viewed by children.

The control provided by laboratory experiments is often gained at the potential sacrifice of altering the naturalistic conditions under which TV violence may have an effect in real life. Thus, attempts to generalize from the findings of the early laboratory experiments to conclusions about the real-life effects of TV violence were severely limited by the fact that these studies typically involved: (1) an experimenter-produced or selected portrayal of aggression; (2) a single exposure to the stimulus; (3) the nonnaturalistic circumstances of an individual viewing in a laboratory setting; (4) an assessment of the viewer's aggression immediately following viewing; and (5) an artificial measure of the viewer's aggression. Subsequent laboratory experiments have done much to remove major limitations to the generalizability of the findings that result from each of these factors. Moreover, field experiments have added an important perspective to this issue by attempting to maintain much of the rigor of laboratory experiments while preserving the ecological validity of both TV viewing and subsequent aggression as they occur in relatively natural environments, such as the preschool classroom or the living quarters of a residential institution.

Field Experiments. Although few in number, field experiments on the relationship between viewing violence and subsequent aggression have greatly advanced our understanding of the significance and the complexities of these effects in relatively naturalistic settings (Cameron & Janky, 1971; Feshbach & Singer, 1971; Granzberg & Steinbring, 1980; Joy et al., 1977; Leyens et al., 1975; Parke et al., 1977, includes two studies; Sawin, 1973; Stein & Friedrich, 1972; Steuer et al., 1971; Wells, 1973). While several of these field experiments have found either no effect (Sawin, 1973) or an effect of less aggression in the group that viewed violence compared to a group that viewed neutral films (Feshbach & Singer, 1971), the remaining majority of these field experiments has provided qualified evidence that the viewing of violence leads to an increase in viewer aggression. As a group, these field experiments have demonstrated the generalizability of previous laboratory findings to more naturalistic circumstances, and they have identified the importance of the viewer's prior history of aggression and past viewing of violence.

In direct response to criticisms of the limitations of previous laboratory experiments, field experiments have generally been designed to examine the effects of repeated exposure to a series of unedited violent films or TV programs on subjects who view in groups and subsequently engage in everyday interactions with one another in their preschool or residential institution. The naturalistic social context in which programs are viewed and subsequent observational measures are taken presents the possibility that children may be influenced by the program both directly by viewing it and indirectly by observing and responding to another viewer who has been directly influenced. It also permits children to show the full range of permissible social behaviors in a context in which retaliation for aggression is a realistic possibility.

Television programs found to elicit aggressive behavior in preschool children include aggressive cartoons such as "Batman" and "Superman" (Stein & Friedrich, 1972; Steuer et al., 1971). Films found to elicit aggressive behavior in teenage boys include *Bonnie and Clyde, Champion, The Dirty Dozen, Ride Beyond Vengence, The Wild One*, and *Zorro*. Behaviors found to increase in preschool boys as a result of viewing violence include physical assaults in the form of hitting, kicking, squeezing, holding down, choking, and throwing an object at another child (Steuer et al., 1971). Behaviors found to increase in teenage boys as a result of viewing violence include yelling, stamping feet, poking one another, moving chairs, and changing seats during the viewing session, as well as interpersonal and nonpersonal verbal and physical aggression following viewing (Leyens et al., 1975; Parke et al., 1977).

In addition to increasing the generalizability of the conclusions concerning the real-life effects of viewing violence, evidence from field experiments has highlighted the need to account for individual differences in viewers' responsiveness to violent portrayals. Several field experiments have found that those individual viewers whose baseline levels of aggression were higher than average among their group were more clearly influenced by the exposure to violence than viewers whose baseline levels of aggression were below average (Leyens et al., 1975; Parke et al., 1977, single exposure group in study 2 only; Stein & Friedrich, 1972; Wells, 1973). Although the elicitation-of-aggression effect is not limited to viewers who are highly aggressive prior to viewing violence, the individual viewer's predisposition toward aggression appears to play an important though poorly understood role in mediating this effect.

Correlational Surveys. Findings from correlational surveys, though not amenable to causal interpretation, have made an important contribution by demonstrating that the relationship between viewing televised violence and aggression occurs reliably in a wide variety of real-life contexts. Overall, the evidence is quite consistent in demonstrating a positive relationship between the viewing of televised violence and the viewer's aggressive behavior and attitudes. This positive correlation has been a reliable finding among preschool, grade school, high school, and adult subjects, as well as among grade school boys and girls in the United States, Australia, Finland, Poland (Eron, 1982), and Great Britain (Greenberg, 1975). As would be expected, this relationship has been most strong and clear in studies that measured the amount of violence viewed (e.g., Dominick & Greenberg, 1972; Greenberg & Atkin, 1977; Hartnagel, Teevan, & McIntyre, 1975; McCarthy, Langner, Gersten, Eisenberg, & Orzeck, 1975; McLeod, Atkin, & Chaffee, 1972a, 1972b; Singer & Singer, 1981). The relationship has been positive but generally less strong or less clear in studies that measured either preference for viewing violence (e.g., Chaffee, 1972; Chaffee & McLeod, 1972; Eron, 1963; Friedman & Johnson, 1972; Furu, 1962, 1971; Lovibond, 1967; McIntyre & Teevan, 1972; Robinson & Bachman, 1972) or number of hours of TV viewing (e.g., Schramm et al., 1961). No relationship was found in a study that simply recorded the presence or absence of a TV set in the home (Himmelweit, Oppenheim, & Vince, 1958).

It is certainly possible that both the propensity to view TV violence and the viewer's aggression may be found to result from some singular third variable or constellation of factors. However, the evidence indicates that this correlation has generally remained unchanged when a variety of factors are controlled, including family socioeconomic status, parental punishment, parental aggressiveness, parental aspirations for the child, child's IQ, and the number of hours of television watched by the child (e.g., Lefkowitz et al., 1972). Thus, contrary to popular belief, this correlation is a reliable finding among a wide range of viewers and real-life viewing circumstances, and its explanation does not readily derive from some peculiar factors exclusive to a narrow segment of the population who both watch violent television and behave aggressively.

Although the viewing of violence is commonly found to be a statistically significant predictor of current and subsequent levels of aggression in a large sample of subjects, it has rarely been found in survey studies to account for more than 10% of the variance among individuals on measures of aggression. An important task for future research is to identify those individual and developmental factors that may mediate stronger or weaker links between televised violence viewing and aggression, since identification of these factors may have important implications for intervention. Several promising social-cognitive factors have been identified as potentially important mediators of this relationship, including the extent to which the viewer identifies with the aggressive TV character, believes that television presents realistic portrayals of life, believes that violence is an acceptable way to achieve a goal, and fantasizes about aggressive activities (Eron, 1980, 1982; Hartnagel et al., 1975; Singer & Singer, 1981).

Longitudinal Studies. Evidence from longitudinal research has demonstrated that a long-term relationship clearly exists between the viewing of televised violence and the viewer's subsequent aggression (Belson, 1978; Eron, 1982; Granzberg & Steinbring, 1980; Joy et al., 1977; Lefkowitz et al., 1972; McCarthy et al., 1975; Singer & Singer, 1981, includes two studies). One major study sponsored by the National Broadcasting Association found cross-sectional but not longitudinal evidence of a positive relationship between the viewing of television violence and aggression (Milavsky, Kessler, Stipp, & Rubens, 1982). Longitudinal relationships lasting 1 year or more have been found to exist

among preschool age (Singer & Singer, 1981), elementary and secondary school age (McCarthy et al., 1975), and teenage viewers (Belson, 1978). One longitudinal relationship has been found to exist over a period as long as 10 years (Lefkowitz et al., 1972), and these data are currently being extended to cover a period of 20 years (Eron, 1982). Several longitudinal studies have combined methods of field experimentation with longitudinal assessment (Eron, 1982; Granzberg & Steinbring, 1980; Joy et al., 1977).

Although the existence of a long-term, as well as a short-term relationship between the viewing of violence and a viewer's subsequent level of aggression is no longer in doubt, numerous controversial methodological and statistical issues continue to be debated. In particular, the use of the time-lagged correlational method has provided a new and controversial approach to the problem of inferring causal relationships from correlational data. For example, Lefkowitz and his associates (1972) made use of this method to examine several possible interpretations of the pattern of simultaneous and time-lag correlations between preference for TV violence and aggressive behavior by boys during childhood and adolescence. The authors concluded that "The single most plausible causal hypothesis is that a preference for watching violent television in the third grade contributes to the development of aggressive habits" (Eron, Huesmann, Lefkowitz, & Walder, 1972, p. 258). This method and the conclusion deriving from its use have stirred a great deal of controversy (e.g., Becker, 1972; Howitt, 1972a,b; Kaplan, 1972; Kay, 1972). However, many of the methodological issues have been settled (e.g., Kenny, 1972; Neale, 1972), and the authors have refuted most of the remaining criticism (Huesmann, Eron, Lefkowitz, & Walder, 1973). Although data deriving from this method alone cannot offer definitive causal conclusions, longitudinal time-lagged correlations can offer a unique source of support favoring one causal hypothesis over others. Other approaches, such as causal modeling (e.g., Olweus, 1979), merit greater use in future studies in this area.

Longitudinal research has also addressed the issue of ecological validity by addressing specific naturalistic patterns of viewing, as well as socially significant aspects of aggression, such as aggressive behavior occurring during free-play period at day care centers (Singer & Singer, 1981) and serious acts of interpersonal violence in real-life settings (Belson, 1978). For example, in a study commissioned by the Columbia Broadcasting System, Belson (1978) found a long-term relationship between specific patterns of violence viewing by teenage boys residing in London and their subsequent frequency of involvement in serious violent behavior, such as: "I bashed a boy's head against a wall; I burned a boy on the chest with a cigarette while my mates held him down; I tried to force a girl to have sexual intercourse with me." Such acts of interpersonal violence were found to be positively related to prior long-term exposure to: (1) plays or films involving close personal relationships and featuring verbal or physical violence; (2) programs in which violence is included for its own sake or is unnecessary for plot development; (3) programs featuring fictional violence that is realistically presented; (4) programs in which violence is presented as justified by a good cause; and (5) violent Westerns. However, because the data derived primarily from retrospective accounts by the boys, Belson points out that even after employing solid control procedures it is still possible that all or part of this relationship may reflect the reverse hypothesis—that these boys showed a tendency to watch more violent programs simply because these boys are violent.

TV Violence and the Catharsis Issue. Although no single study nor single methodological perspective can provide conclusive evidence that the viewing of televised violence is one causal factor in the development of aggressive behavior, cumulative and complementary evidence derived from a variety of methodological perspectives strongly supports this conclusion.

It should be noted that this conclusion stands in opposition to one version of the catharsis doctrine that has achieved a great deal of popular support and research attention, particularly in the 1960s and early 1970s. According to this version of the catharsis hypothesis, the viewing of televised violence should reduce the likelihood that the viewer will engage in subsequent aggression, because the viewer is thought to discharge his or her pent-up anger, hostility, or frustration by identifying with the aggressive actor and experiencing violence vicariously. There is currently little research evidence to support the catharsis notion when applied to TV violence. One major field experiment offering support for the catharsis notion (Feshbach & Singer, 1971) has been seriously questioned on methodological grounds (e.g., Liebert, Davidson, & Sobol, 1972; Liebert, Sobol, & Davidson, 1972) to which the authors have replied (Feshbach & Singer, 1972a, 1972b). However, serious questions remain, particularly since an attempt to replicate the original finding has failed (Wells, 1973), and similar field experiments employing more stringent methodological controls

have provided evidence contrary to catharsis hypothesis (Leyens et al., 1975; Parke et al., 1977). Moreover, one of the original proponents of the catharsis hypothesis has recently repudiated the application of this concept to the question of the effects of media violence (Feshbach, 1980). In summary, there is little support for the vicarious version of the catharsis doctrine. Later in this chapter, the status of the direct version of this theory is addressed.

Effects on Viewer Apathy Toward Aggression

Exposure to televised violence has been shown not only to increase the viewer's own level of aggression, but also to decrease the viewer's behavioral and physiological responsiveness to aggression produced by others. In a series of laboratory studies, grade-school children's behavioral responsiveness to aggression was assessed following their viewing of either a violent or a nonviolent program (Drabman & Thomas, 1974, 1975, 1976; Thomas and Drabman, 1975). After viewing the television program, a child was left in charge of two younger children and told to notify the experimenter if anything went wrong. Thus, each child was held responsible for making a judgment about when something had gone wrong and for acting on that judgment. The child kept watch on a TV monitor while the two younger children, ostensibly playing in an adjacent room, began first to argue and then to fist-fight with one another. Replicated results indicated that, compared to children who had viewed an equally arousing nonviolent program, children who had previously viewed a violent TV program were significantly slower and less likely to attempt to stop the fight either by notifying the adult or by intervening themselves. Instead, these children who had just viewed a violent program showed relative indifference toward the aggression displayed by the children under their supervision.

Research investigators have commonly invoked the *emotional desensitization hypothesis* in an attempt to provide either an analog model or a direct account of the process by which viewers of violence may become behaviorally indifferent toward aggression (e.g., Thomas, Horton, Lippincott, & Drabman, 1977). According to this hypothesis, the experience of viewing televised violence serves to blunt the viewer's emotional sensitivity to subsequent experiences of aggression, including those in real life. It is commonly suggested that the process leading to diminished emotional responsiveness is either analogous to or directly linked to the diminished behavioral responsiveness effect demonstrated in the laboratory.

Investigation of the emotional desensitization hypothesis has focused almost exclusively on assessing the viewer's physiological responses to portrayals of violence and relating these responses to the viewer's prior history of viewing television. For example, grade-school children have been found to show greater skin conductance responses (Cline, Croft, & Courrier, 1973; Osborn & Endsley, 1971), greater blood volume pulse amplitude responses (Cline et al., 1973), and greater heart rate deceleration responses (Surbeck, 1973) to scenes of either human violence or cartoon violence compared to nonviolent scenes. Younger children showed greater heart rate deceleration responses to violent scenes than did older children (Surbeck, 1973). Furthermore, grade-school boys with histories of heavy TV viewing showed fewer skin conductance responses and smaller pulse amplitude responses to violent scenes than did boys with histories of light TV viewing (Cline et al., 1973).

Evidence that prior viewing of violence can lead to diminished physiological responsiveness toward depictions of "real-life" aggression has been generated in experimental circumstances that closely parallel those in which diminished behavioral responsiveness was similarly demonstrated (Thomas et al., 1977). Both grade-school children and adults who were previously shown a violent TV program segment (from the police series "S.W.A.T.") were found to show fewer skin conductance responses while watching "real-life" aggression on a TV monitor than did subjects who were previously shown an equally arousing but nonviolent sports program about a championship volleyball game. The fact that the violent and the nonviolent programs aroused equivalent skin conductance responses during viewing but differentially affected the viewer's skin conductance responses to the subsequent presentation of "real-life" aggression provides strong evidence that the critical factor involves certain aspects of the program's violent content rather than the program's potential to arouse the viewer. The "real-life" aggression shown to adults was the documentary TV coverage of violence between police and demonstrators during the 1968 Democratic National Convention in Chicago. The "real-life" aggression shown to children was the same videotape used to assess behavioral responsiveness in previous research (Thomas & Drabman, 1975). Children watched a videotape of two younger children, ostensibly in the next room, as their play developed first into an argument and then into a fist-fight with one another.

Although the evidence of diminished physiological responsiveness parallels the evidence of diminished behavioral responsiveness, the potential link between these two sets of findings has not been examined. It is not clear whether, nor under what conditions, diminished emotional reactivity to violence might contribute to diminished behavioral responsiveness. The fact that repeated exposure to televised violence may lead to habituation of physiological reactivity to similar portrayals of violence is not particularly surprising, but the simple process of habituation would not provide a complete explanation for complex behavioral responses such as those assessed in the laboratory test of behavioral apathy toward "real-life" aggression. It becomes clear that the explanatory potential of the concept of emotional arousal has been overextended when one attempts to use the viewer's level of emotion arousal as the singular explanation for both a decreased tendency to intervene in the aggression of others and an increased tendency to behave aggressively. This apparent contradiction disappears, however, when social-cognitive factors are used to explain both of these effects.

It seems likely that social-cognitive factors, perhaps in conjunction with emotional factors, play a major role in mediating both the behavioral apathy effect and the elicitation-of-aggression effect. Indeed, the laboratory test for behavioral apathy toward the aggression of others explicitly directs children to base their behavior on their judgment of when an escalating fight between other children should be considered sufficiently "wrong" to require intervention. Similarly, the elicitation-of-aggression effect appears to be heavily dependent on a variety of social-cognitive factors related to the viewer's interpretation of the televised violence. According to this social-cognitive perspective, the viewing of televised violence often stimulates viewers to alter their standards concerning the appropriate, acceptable, and prevalent uses of aggression in real-life situations. For example, youthful offenders have been found to increase their acceptance and approval of aggressive tactics for solving social conflict following repeated exposure to violent movies (Menzies, 1972).

Consistent with this perspective, individual viewers may be particularly likely to alter their own standards: (1) when they perceive violence to be relatively commonplace, effective, justified, rewarded, and realistic; (2) when they have a real-world environment that generally supports the TV portrayal of standards for the use of aggression; and (3) when they have relatively little real-world experience against which to weigh the TV portrayal of standards for the use of aggression. It is reasonable to expect developmental changes, as well as individual differences, in children's perceptions of televised violence, social environmental support for aggression, and level of real-world experiences with aggression.

Conclusion

Research has demonstrated that television must be considered one of the major socializers of children's aggressive behavior. Two major behavioral effects of heavy viewing of televised violence are: (1) an increase in children's level of aggression; and (2) an increase in children's passive acceptance of the use of aggression by others. Although the relationship between these two behaviors has not been investigated, it may be that children develop both of these response patterns simultaneously as a function of a single process of coming to adopt the TV portrayal of violence as one's own interpretative framework for initiating and responding to real-life aggression. Thus, children who view a great deal of TV violence may adopt an interpretive framework based on television's stylized portrayal of violent acts as relatively commonplace, effective, justified, and rewarded social actions. To the extent that this interpretive framework becomes a part of their daily lives, these children can be expected to show both an increased use of aggression and an increased acceptance of the use of aggression by others.

Only recently has television research moved from asking whether there are particular behavioral effects to seeking explanations for the demonstrated effects. One important direction for future research on television viewing involves the search to explain what appears to be relatively stable but individually and developmentally distinct patterns of responsiveness to televised violence. A second and perhaps related direction for future research on television viewing involves investigation of the interrelationship among family, peers, and television as sources of influence on the development of such aggressive patterns of behavior.

Toward a Multiinfluence Model of the Development of Aggression

In this section three sets of socialization agents have been discussed—family, peers, and television. It has often been implicitly assumed that various sources of influence operate independently in altering aggressive behavior. However, there is an increasing recognition of the interdependence among socialization agents in influencing social development (Hartup, 1979; Lewis, 1982). Families, as the initial socialization context for children, influence the ways in which peer-peer relationships develop. Both older studies as well as more recent evidence support this view. Over two decades ago, in a study of adolescent aggression, Bandura and Walters (1959) found that parents of aggressive boys were more inclined to actively encourage and condone aggression directed toward sibs and peers than were parents of nonaggressive boys. As more recent studies have demonstrated, parents may affect their children's aggression with peers by the extent to which they are active in their role as mediators in children's selection of friends and as monitors of peer activities (Patterson, 1982). Parents who are lax and unconcerned about a child's choice of peers could be indirectly contributing to the development of aggressive behavior if their children choose a deviant peer group. Research concerning the ways in which parents influence friendship choices would be a major contribution to our understanding of the socialization of both social and antisocial behavior.

As recent research has illustrated, parents may indirectly influence peer-peer relationships through the nature of their own relationships with their children. A series of studies of the links between early patterns of parent-infant attachment and later social interaction in peer-peer contexts shows this pattern very clearly (Easterbrooks & Lamb, 1979; Leiberman, 1977; Pastor, 1981; Waters, Wippman, & Sroufe, 1979). Infants who develop secure attachments to their parents in the first year of life appear to develop greater competence in their later peer relationships. However, further work is required to illuminate the nature of the parent-child interaction that can account for this relationship between early attachment patterns and later peer-peer interaction. Studies of the relationships between parent-infant play patterns and later peer-peer interaction (e.g., MacDonald & Parke, 1982) may illuminate these processes, since the opportunity for children to learn to regulate affect (both encoding and decoding) in the context of parent-infant interaction may be important for later success in peer-peer encounters.

Another example of the interdependence of socialization agents in the development of aggression is research linking the impact of children's TV viewing and family interaction. Several studies have demonstrated the modifying influence of co-observers on the impact of television on child viewers (Collins, Sobol, & Westby, 1981; Grusec, 1973; Hicks, 1968). Moreover, this influence is not unidirectional, since television can clearly affect family interaction patterns as well (see Parke, 1978b, for a review). Specifically, the amount of time family members spend together, the types of familial interactions, and the amount of family conflict may be influenced by patterns of TV viewing. Similarly, children's social patterns change as a result of television. Children spend more time at home when television is introduced into a community that has not had prior access to TV broadcasts; they also visit their playmates less frequently and will spend less time outdoors once television is in the home. This impact is especially substantial among younger children (Belson, 1959; Himmelweit et al., 1958).

Many questions remain. What is the relative influence of these different socialization agents? How do the patterns of influence change across development? Do different agents influence the development of different types of aggression? For example, are attitudes toward violence and actual aggressive behavior influenced by the same sources? What impact does the child's experience with aggression in one setting have on aggression in other settings populated by different socialization agents? Future research strategies should involve the simultaneous assessment of a variety of influence sources in order to begin to articulate the relative impact of various socialization agents and agencies on the development and maintenance of aggressive behavior.

PHYSICAL ENVIRONMENTAL INFLUENCES ON AGGRESSION

In addition to these types of interpersonal elicitors, certain environmental circumstances may increase the likelihood of aggression. Let us examine two factors: temperature and crowding.

Temperature and Aggression

Are people more aggressive when they are hot and uncomfortable during the summer months? Many authorities, including the U.S. Riot Commission, believe that individual and collective violence is more likely under heat wave conditions than under cooler circumstances. Baron and Lawton (1972) experimentally examined the effect of temperature on the modeling of aggression. One reason for this link between heat and social disorder is that our sensitivity to models is enhanced because of the heightened arousal produced by hot conditions. To test this proposition, Baron and Lawton exposed angered subjects to either an aggressive model or no model under cool (74°F) or hot (96–99°F) conditions. Subjects who saw the model in the hot room were more aggressive than subjects who saw no model, while the subjects who saw the model under "cool" con-

ditions were not affected by this exposure. In short, the high temperature increased the viewers' aggressive reaction to the model. Although parallel data on the effects of environmental temperature on aggression have not been collected with children, it is likely that the effects would be somewhat similar.

Crowding and Aggression

Another environmental condition that affects aggressive behavior is crowding. There are two methods of assessing the effects of crowding on behavior. Changing the *spatial density* conditions of a group involves placing the same size group of children in spaces of differing sizes. Changing the *social density* of a group involves changes in the numbers of children interacting in the same size space. Unfortunately, the links between aggression and either spatial or social density have not been unequivocally established and to date the literature is replete with contradictory or inconsistent findings. In one study, the influence of spatial density was assessed by observing the interactions of elementary school boys on large and small playgrounds (Ginsburg, 1975). On the small playground, children engaged in more frequent but shorter fights, and the fights generally involved more children than those occurring on the large playground. On the large playground, fights were more likely to last for longer periods of time, since other children were less likely to intervene. In contrast, in another study *less* aggression was found when a group of 4- and 5-year-old children was confined to a small indoor room than when the group was situated in a larger room (Loo, 1972). This apparently inconsistent finding may have resulted from the inclusion of play fighting in the definition of aggression. Several other studies have found that play chasing and play fighting are generally reduced under crowded conditions, which inhibit large motor activity (Smith, 1974a, 1974b).

The most systematic and extensive analysis of the impact of variations in space, group size, and physical resources (play equipment) is the Smith and Connolly (1980) project. While most variations in density yielded only small changes in aggressive behavior, extreme crowding (less than 15 square feet per child) was associated with increased aggression. However, rough-and-tumble play did *not* increase under crowded conditions.

In a study of social density involving groups of three sizes interacting in a hospital playroom, significantly more aggression was observed as group size increased (Hutt & Vaizey, 1966). When both social and spatial density conditions were varied in an English nursery school, the highest level of hitting was observed when the largest group was concentrated in the smallest space (McGrew, 1972). On the other hand, no effect of spatial or social density on aggression was found in a cross-cultural observational study of five different preschools in the United States and the Netherlands (Fagot, 1977). In fact, in the schools with the highest density, in the Netherlands, the only effect was that the Dutch children more often interacted positively and less often played alone in comparison to other schools. Fagot argues that the effects found in other studies might be the result of either making arbitrary changes in natural social groupings or changing the availability of play materials. It is also possible that the differing cultural contexts of the schools observed in this study outweighed any effects of differing densities.

The effect of changes in the amount of play equipment on aggression has also been examined in several studies. In one study at an elementary school, aggression increased when the amount of play equipment available at recess time was reduced (Johnson, 1935). A similar effect was found when the amount of indoor play equipment was varied in a preschool classroom (Smith, 1974a, 1974b). In the preschool studies, agonistic encounters most frequently occurred as a result of arguments over the possession of toys or use of an apparatus, and these conflicts increased when the number of toys was reduced. However, in addition to increased aggression, there were also increases in sharing under conditions of less equipment and in the size of groups playing together with similar toys. Aggression also increased when one or two new and desirable toys were added, particularly when they were toys that could be played with by one or two children at a time.

It has been noted that alterations in social density are often confounded with changes in the amount of play equipment per child (Smith, 1974b). To investigate this issue, Smith and Connolly (1980) systematically varied density and the amount of play material available for each child. Aggression did increase with greater social density, if there was no proportionate increase in physical resources; on the other hand, there was no change in aggression as social density increased if the resources also increased. This project underscores the necessity of viewing the effects of physical environment in a multivariate framework.

In summary, it appears that crowding large numbers of children in a small space can have the effect of increasing aggression, particularly if there is insufficient play equipment to keep all the children occupied. However, the effect of crowding on aggression does not always occur, and it is presumably affected by such variables as the guidance and response of teachers, the amount of play equipment, and the particular types of toys and activities available.

CONTROL AND MODIFICATION OF AGGRESSION

Individual Level

Catharsis

One of the most persistent beliefs about aggression is that opportunities for acting aggressively will reduce hostile and aggressive tendencies. According to the catharsis doctrine, aggressive urges build up in an organism and unless the reservoir of aggressive energies is drained, a violent outburst will occur. The control implications of this doctrine are clear: Provide individuals with a safe opportunity to behave aggressively, and the likelihood of antisocial aggression will be lessened. The term catharsis has also been used to refer to the reduction of aggression through vicarious exposure to violence. This issue has been reviewed in an earlier section and only the effect of directly acting aggressively on subsequent aggression will be discussed in this section.

This topic has had a long and controversial history (see Quanty, 1976, for a careful review). From the viewpoint of aggression control, two issues predominate: (1) whether the expression of aggression reduces subsequent aggression, and (2) the impact of the inanimate versus the animate aggressive targets on subsequent aggression reduction. First, the evidence in support of the prediction that engaging in physical aggression produces a catharsis, which lowers subsequent aggressive tendencies, is equivocal. Although some studies with college students have found that the opportunity to behave aggressively can lead to a reduction in aggression (Doob & Wood, 1972; Konecni & Doob, 1972), other studies have found an increase in subsequent aggression (Berkowitz, 1966). As Quanty (1976) notes, ''direct aggression can lead to reduced hostility, but, when it does, the effect may be interpreted in terms of increased restraints against aggression rather than true catharsis. When these restraints are minimized, expression of aggression seems to lead to increased rather than decreased hostility'' (1976, p. 123).

Does the opportunity to aggress against an inanimate object reduce aggression? One of the more adequate tests of this position was the study by Mallick and McCandless (1966). Half of a group of third-grade children were frustrated by a peer confederate who interfered with the subjects' task of building a block house in a short time and thereby caused them to lose a cash prize. The remaining boys were treated in a neutral fashion by the confederate. The boys then engaged in one of the following activities before being given the opportunity to aggress against the peer partner: (1) shooting a play gun at animated targets of a boy, a man, a woman, a dog, or a cat, (2) shooting at a bull's-eye target, or (3) solving arithmetic problems. The frustration manipulation proved effective; angered subjects more frequently administered uncomfortable shocks to the tormentor than the nonangered children did (in reality, no shocks were actually received by the other boy). However, *contrary* to catharsis theory, the type of intervening activity did not have a substantial impact on the children's aggressive behavior. Target shooting did not lower the aggressive behavior of the angered children any more than did a passive session of solving arithmetic problems. In contrast, a noncathartic technique *was* found to be effective in reducing hostility. Subjects who were provided with a reinterpretation of the frustrator's actions (e.g., "he was sleepy and upset") subsequently directed less aggression toward him. It appears, then, that aggressive retaliation can often be avoided if the angered protagonist adopts a sympathetic interpretation of his frustrator's thwarting behavior and that merely acting out aggressively toward an alternative target appears to be insufficient. Other evidence with adults indicates that vigorous physical exercise, such as pounding a rubber mallet (Ryan, 1970) or vigorously pedaling a bicycle (Zillmann, 1978), has no cathartic value and leads to no reduction in aggression. In summary, the catharsis position has not been well supported by empirical research, and it appears to be an ineffective control tactic for inhibiting aggressive behavior.

Elicitation of Incompatible Responses

Aggression can be reduced by eliciting responses that are incompatible with aggressive behavior. A number of techniques have been suggested including reinforcement of nonaggressive responses (such as cooperative behaviors), role playing, and modeling of nonaggressive behaviors. These approaches avoid some of the undesirable consequences usually associated with the use of punishment for suppressing aggression (Parke, 1972, 1977b). For instance, it is unlikely that the provision of alternate responses would lead to increases in aggressive behavior in situations different from the disciplinary context, as has been found when using punishment to control aggression.

The Use of Reinforcement in Reducing Aggression. An early study by Davitz (1952) illustrates the role of reinforcement in the aggression reduction process. In this experiment, children were reinforced for either nonangry cooperative responses or angry aggressive reactions. When they were subsequently frustrated by an adult, the children who had previously been reinforced for their nonangry cooperative behavior reacted with little anger and aggression relative to the other children who were encouraged for their angry responses. Clearly, reactions to frustration can be modified by reinforcement of alternative, nonangry responses. Using a related approach, Mahoney (1971) directly rewarded hyperaggressive boys for remaining calm and noncombative in the face of peer harassment. The magnitude of the rewards varied in relation to the length of time that the victim was able to maintain his composure and equanimity.

Brown and Elliot (1965) found a marked decrease in aggression by training teachers to ignore aggression and to attend to children only when they were engaged in cooperative behavior. This study illustrates not only the importance of reinforcement of prosocial behavior for controlling aggression, but also demonstrates the often paradoxical role played by teacher "attention." When the teachers were allowed to attend to the aggressive behaviors that were previously ignored as part of the treatment, the frequency of physical aggression increased. This increase may result, in part, from the fact that adult attention in the form of a mild rebuke or reprimand following an aggressive act usually increases the likelihood that the same act will occur again (Risley & Baer, 1973). Possibly, behaving aggressively is used by children as an attention-seeking tactic.

Other forms of adult intervention have proven more effective in reducing aggression without providing the reinforcement of teacher attention. One technique that has proven successful in reducing aggression is one in which the teacher steps between the children involved in an incident, while ignoring the aggressor but paying attention to the victim (Allen, Turner, & Everett, 1970; Pinkston, Reese, LeBlanc, & Baer, 1973). Attention to the victim might include comforting the hurt child, giving the victim something interesting to do, or suggesting to the victim assertive, nonaggressive ways of dealing with the aggressor. For example, the teacher can suggest that the victim use specific assertive phrases, such as "No hitting!" or "I'm playing with this now." There are several advantages to this technique. First, the aggressor receives no reward for the aggressive act, either in the form of teacher attention or victim submission. Second, the victim receives practice in coping assertively with conflict. Third, other children in the group observe that aggression is not a successful method of social interaction, that teachers will support nonviolent assertiveness, and that an appropriate response to a victim is a sympathetic one. These observations are likely to reduce aggression throughout the classroom and to increase both assertiveness and sympathetic behavior. Moreover, the behavior of an adult who has developed a nurturant relationship with children in a classroom can have a powerful modeling effect on the observing children (Yarrow, Scott, & Waxler, 1973).

In some cases, aggressive behavior may be so persistent that merely ignoring the behavior and attending to the victim will not be sufficient to reduce it. In these cases, it has been effective in many programs to use a "time-out" procedure contingent on the aggressive behavior (e.g., Green, Budd, Johnson, Lang, Pinkston, & Rudd, 1976; Porterfield, Herbert-Jackson, & Risley, 1976; Risley, & Baer, 1973; Tams & Eyberg, 1976). The purpose of time-out is to remove the child from all reinforcing stimuli for a designated short period of time (e.g., 1 to 10 minutes) *immediately* following a specific inappropriate behavior. Time-out for misbehavior will be most effective when paired with a great deal of adult attention and praise for cooperative helpful interactions (see review by Risley & Baer, 1973).

The regulation of aggressive behavior can be achieved by reinforcement of verbal responses as well. Several studies have shown that adult attention to either aggressive or cooperative speech can affect both future verbalizations and actual physical behaviors related to the verbalizations. Slaby and Crowley (1977) examined this issue using naturally occurring verbal statements in a nursery school setting. Preschool teachers were instructed to attend to children's verbal cooperative statements while ignoring both aggressive language and aggressive physical behavior. When teachers heard a cooperative statement, they were asked to say the child's name and then repeat the child's phrase, "I heard you say. . . ." After two weeks of applying these contingencies to verbal behavior, there was an increase in the amount of both verbal and physical cooperation in children's free play, while both verbal and physical aggression decreased. These shifts occurred in spite of the fact that the teachers were successful in attending to an average of only 14% of all cooperative statements observed to occur during this period.

Modeling and Coaching Strategies for Reducing Aggression. Responses that are incompatible with aggression may be elicited in other ways and not simply through direct reinforcement. Two other strategies are modeling and coaching. Although these are separate strategies, they are frequently employed in combination. In modeling, children are taught new social skills that are incompatible with aggressive behavior by exposure to social models enacting the appropriate behaviors. In coaching, the defining element is the provision of a general concept or strategy, either given orally or in writing. The learner is expected to use the concept to generate appropriate behavior in a variety of future situations.

Many years ago, Chittenden (1942) demonstrated that aggressive domineering behavior could be successfully modified by exposing nursery school children to a series of modeling displays in which aggressive solutions to conflicts were associated with negative outcomes, while cooperation was encouraged. In combination with discussion and practice of the positive prosocial activities, aggression was markedly reduced. More recently, similar success has been achieved in reducing aggression by employing a verbal coaching strategy involving verbal instruction and discussion (Zahavi & Asher, 1978). Using nursery school children, teachers emphasized in a one-to-one discussion both the negative consequences of aggression (e.g., that aggression hurts others, does not solve problems, and causes resentment) and at the same time taught the children alternative conflict-solving strategies. Children who received this intervention showed a decrease in aggressive behaviors and an increase in positive behaviors, such as cooperative play, compared to a control group of children. The improvements were maintained at the 2-week follow-up observations. As these studies indicate, modeling and coaching are effective procedures for teaching young children nonaggressive ways of solving conflict.

However, recent research suggests that simply increasing the number of responses available may not be a sufficient strategy for modifying the behavior of aggressive children. Richard and Dodge (1982) found that although aggressive boys do generate fewer solutions to interpersonal problems than popular boys, it is the inadequacy or ineffectiveness of their solutions that most clearly distinguishes popular and aggressive children. The initial solutions of both groups were rated as effective, but the adequacy of subsequent solutions varied with the boys' social status. Popular boys continued to generate effective solutions, whereas aggressive boys generated aggressive and ineffective solutions. In sum, when an initial solution fails, the aggressive child has fewer effective alternatives available for solving interpersonal problems. Retraining aggressive children should focus not simply on generating more responses but on generating more responses that are appropriate and effective. This study and other recent work (Asher, Renshaw, & Geraci, 1980) underscores the importance of focusing on not merely the number of strategies, but on the specific content of children's social strategies.

Another reasonable but as yet empirically unsupported suggestion for regulating young children's aggressive behavior is to increase children's exposure to prosocial TV programs. Viewing programs that stress themes of positive and socially valued interaction among people has been shown to result in increases in a wide range of children's prosocial behaviors, including helping, sharing, cooperating, showing nurturance, verbalizing feelings, showing empathy, and playing imaginatively (e.g., Murray & Kippax, 1979; Rushton, 1979; Slaby & Quarfoth, 1980; Stein & Friedrich, 1975). Since aggressive and prosocial behaviors frequently represent alternative choices for interpersonal interaction, it might be expected that aggressive and prosocial TV programs would have somewhat opposite effects on these behaviors. In one of the few studies assessing these potential effects, prosocial TV programming was found to have no effect on children's aggression in a preschool classroom when children's normal home-viewing experiences were supplemented with a daily viewing session of either aggressive, neutral, or prosocial programming for a 4-week period (Friedrich & Stein, 1973). Research is needed on the effects of children's viewing of TV diets that are designed to be *selective* with regard to prosocial and aggressive programming (Slaby & Roedell, 1982).

The Use of Humor in Regulating Aggression. Aggression can sometimes be inhibited by eliciting humor or feelings of amusement. Watching a humorous cartoon can decrease aggression in angered college students (Baron & Ball, 1974; Mueller & Donnerstein, 1977). Although these findings are consistent with the suggestion that humor is often incompatible with anger or overt aggression and may tend to inhibit such reactions, two cautions are in order (Baron, 1977).

First, not all forms of humor inhibit aggression. Exposure to hostile humor—in which some target is harmed, attacked, or humiliated—may enhance rather than inhibit aggressive actions (Berkowitz, 1970). Second, some evidence suggests that the inhibiting effects of nonhostile humor may not necessarily be the result of an induction of positive emotional states that are incompatible with aggression. Instead, humor-induced inhibition of aggression

may result from attentional shifts in which individuals are distracted away from past provocations (Mueller & Donnerstein, 1977). Both factors—incompatible and attentional-shift responses—may operate in mediating inhibition. However, most of this research on humor as a control technique has focused on college subjects and, to date, little attention has been devoted to the role of humor as a control tactic for aggressive behavior in children of different ages. Yet, there are interesting developmental analyses of humor (McGhee, 1980) that could serve as a guide for research on this neglected issue.

In summary, there is clear evidence that the elicitation of reactions incompatible with aggression is an effective technique for reducing aggression. The relative ease and effectiveness of eliciting different types of incompatible responses at different points in development merit further investigation.

Stress Inoculation: An Approach to Anger Control

Another approach to aggression control focuses on the emotional response of anger, which often accompanies aggression. By employing techniques that lessen anger in the face of potentially anger-eliciting stimuli, it is assumed that the likelihood of aggressive behavior is lessened. While many of the same techniques such as reinforcement, modeling, and coaching are often useful in teaching anger control, other techniques have been used as well, including stress inoculation and desensitization strategies.

Stress inoculation has been advocated by Meichenbaum (1975) and Novaco (1978). As a coping skills therapy, this approach is concerned with developing a client's competence to respond to stressful events so that disturbing emotions are reduced and behavioral adaptation is achieved.

> Inoculation is a medical metaphor. It refers to a process of exposing the client to manageable quantities of stressors that arouse, but do not overwhelm, the client's defenses. In conjunction with this exposure, the person is taught a variety of cognitive and behavioral coping skills intended to provide a means of managing the stress experience. (Novaco, 1978, p. 266)

The approach involves three phases: cognitive preparation, skill acquisition, and application training. Briefly, in the first phase, individuals receive information about anger arousal and its determinants—the cues that elicit anger and discrimination of adaptive and maladaptive occurrences of anger. Next, the person learns cognitive and behavioral coping skills through modeling and rehearsal. Finally, the person learns to practice the previously acquired methods of anger control during imaginal and role-play inductions of anger. In general, evaluations of this approach indicate its superiority over relaxation procedures alone (Novaco, 1978); in addition, the approach has been successfully applied in the treatment of adolescents with a history of having experienced verbal and physical abuse (Schrader, Long, Panzer, Gillet, & Kornblath, 1977).

The limits of the stress inoculation procedures for modifying the behavior of children of differing levels of cognitive development merit examination. In a more general sense, the comparative effectiveness of these various approaches for children of different ages needs to be explored.

Self-regulation of speech is another potential technique that may be employed in the modification of aggressive behavior. Self-directed speech has increasingly been shown to be an important aspect in the development of self-control (Meichenbaum, 1974; Mischel, 1973). The implications of this work for aggression have recently been explored by Camp (1977), who has shown that aggressive in comparison to nonaggressive boys differ in their verbal ability, in self-guided speech, in nonverbal IQ, in reading scores, in compulsivity, in ability to inhibit responses, and in response modulation following overt and covert commands. Aggressive boys showed a rapid response style and a failure to use mediational activity unless specifically requested. The aggressive boys exhibited a ''production deficiency'' since they were able to use self-guided speech effectively but failed to do so. In addition, Camp found evidence of a ''control deficiency'' in that the children produced verbal mediating responses but these responses failed to achieve or maintain functional control over behavior. Aggressive boys, for example, were unable to use covert verbalization to control their behavior effectively. In view of the effectiveness of training in the use of self-guiding verbalization to improve the cognitive performance of impulsive or hyperactive children (Meichenbaum & Goodman, 1971), it would be worthwhile to determine whether instruction in self-verbalization increases control of anger and aggressive behavior. Developmental analyses of this issue would be particularly worthwhile.

Another technique for anger control is desensitization by which the anger-evoking stimuli lose some of their anger-eliciting potency. Herrell (1971) successfully employed this technique in a chronically assaultive adult. By providing relaxation instruction while the person imagined the anger-eliciting scenes, the anger reactions were reduced. Similarly, O'Donnell and Worell (1973) reported successful reduction of anger using desensitization procedures.

Increasing Awareness of the Harmful Effects of Aggression

Another technique for controlling aggression involves increasing the attacker's awareness of the harmful consequences of the aggression for the victim. Baron (1971a) found that adults who heard expressions of pain and anguish from their victim were less aggressive than subjects not exposed to this type of feedback. Moreover, seeing your victim's suffering is even more inhibiting than merely hearing the distress that you have produced (Milgram, 1974). Similar kinds of effects have been found in film studies in which the anguish of the victim is graphically displayed. For example, Goranson (1970) showed college students a boxing film in which the loser of the match dies as a result of his injury. In a comparison group, the victim in the fight was not fatally injured. Subjects were then given the opportunity to administer electric shock to another student. Subjects who saw the film in which aggression had harmful consequences behaved less aggressively than the subjects who saw the other film. It is assumed that aggression is inhibited as a result of the arousal of empathetic reactions in the aggressor, which are caused by the victim's feedback; in turn, it is argued that these emotional responses are incompatible with the display of aggression (Feshbach & Feshbach, 1969).

However, not all individuals react to pain feedback by inhibiting aggression on all occasions. Some are either unaffected or react with increased rather than decreased aggression. Hartmann (1969) found that juvenile delinquents in contrast to nondelinquent adolescents responded with more, not less, aggression after exposure to a film emphasizing the victim's pain cues. For some children pain cues on the part of the victim may, in fact, be a source of reinforcement as a sign that the aggression is successful. This possibility was examined in a study of 12-year-old aggressive boys (Perry & Perry, 1974). Using a ''rigged'' procedure in which the boys thought that they were administering loud noxious noises to another child, the victim's reaction was varied. The victim signaled that either the noise ''hurt a lot'' or denied he was in any discomfort. When the victim denied that an aggressive attack caused any pain, high-aggressive boys escalated the intensity of their attacks. In the case of the low-aggressive boys, this denial of suffering did not increase the level of aggression. For the aggressive child, signs of pain and suffering may be an indication that the aggression is successful. Moreover, highly aggressive individuals often show little or no remorse after behaving aggressively, while low-aggressive boys show self-disapproval after harming another person (Perry & Bussey, 1977).

Clearly more research is needed to take into account individual differences and to explain how prior learning histories predispose or make some individuals more susceptible to certain kinds of models and eliciting cues, such as pain feedback.

Empathy and Role-Taking Training as Control Techniques

In view of the role that empathy is assumed to play in the regulation of aggression, increasing empathy is another approach to aggression control. This strategy is based on earlier research that showed an inverse relationship between empathy and aggression in first-grade children (Feshbach & Feshbach, 1969). More recently, Feshbach and Feshbach (1982) carried out a project to demonstrate experimentally that aggression could be effectively controlled by increasing empathy in children. Third- and fourth-grade children were assigned to either an empathy-training group, a problem-solving control activity group, or a control group. The empathy-training groups participated in activities that focused on the cognitive and affective components of empathy. Specifically, the children were encouraged to perceive situations from the perspective of other people, to discriminate and identify feelings, and to express feelings.

The exercises for the children in the problem-solving control condition entailed nonsocial content such as science projects. The children met in small groups three times a week for 10 weeks. Following the empathy-training experience, children had a more positive self-concept and displayed greater social sensitivity to feelings than children in the two control conditions. Empathy training in contrast to the two control conditions resulted in increases in prosocial behavior, such as cooperation, helping, and generosity. However, *both* the empathy-training group *and* the problem-solving control activity group declined in aggression relative to the nonparticipating controls, which suggests that the development of empathy is a sufficient but not necessary tactic for aggression control.

The problem-solving group experience probably required cooperative behavior, which, in turn, may have contributed to the reduction in aggressive behavior. Although this treatment may not have focused on empathy, strategies for conflict-resolution may inadvertently have been taught in this condition. Careful analyses of the specific components of the training conditions would be worthwhile. Finally, it should be noted that the training content did not focus on discouraging aggressive behavior. Possibly, a training program that involved a combination of empathy training and explicit discouragement of aggressive behavior would prove to be more effective than a group problem-solving experience.

Chandler (1973) conducted a closely related project that focused on the improvement of perspective-taking skills as a way of reducing antisocial behavior in juvenile delinquent boys, on the assumption that deficits in perspective-taking skills may, in fact, be responsible for aggressive behavior in some individuals. Chandler enrolled a group of 11- to 13-year-old delinquents in an experimental program that employed drama and the making of video films as vehicles for helping them to see themselves from the perspective of others and for providing remedial training in deficient role-taking skills. For three hours a week over a 10-week period, the boys developed skits, acted out various parts, consistently shifted roles in the plays and watched replays of the video recordings of their skits. All these features were designed to improve role-taking and perspective-taking skills. A second group made color cartoons and documentaries but had no opportunities to see themselves from the perspectives of others, nor did they receive special training in role-taking skills. A third group served as a nontreatment control. As a result, the special training was effective in improving the role-taking abilities of the boys, while the boys in the other two groups did not change. Of special interest is the impact on the subsequent aggressive delinquent behavior of the boys. The number of delinquent offenses committed during the 18-month period for the perspective-taking intervention group was significantly less than for the nonintervention groups. Modification of role-taking skills effectively improved the social behavior of these adolescents. These results, in combination with the Feshbach and Feshbach (1982) research, suggest that perspective-taking training, which, in turn, may improve empathetic skills, may be more important for populations such as delinquents who may have empathy deficits. For nondelinquent children this type of training may be unnecessary for inhibiting aggression. The issue of the effectiveness of various types of perspective-taking training for controlling aggression remains controversial. Not only have other studies (e.g., Iannotti, 1978) failed to find any shifts in aggression as a result of role-taking training, the processes that may account for the positive effects of role-taking behavior remain to be specified (see Shantz, *Vol. III, Chap. 8*). Finally, although differences across studies, including the age and characteristics of the samples, the type and duration of training, the measure of aggression, and the degree of similarity between training and evaluation may account for the discrepancies, more attention to mediating processes would be a helpful step in reconciling cross-investigation disparities.

Modifying Children's Understanding: Adults as Co-viewers of Televised Aggression

Adults can directly influence children's understanding and expression of aggression by participating in the evaluation and interpretation of televised violence. One effective method is for adults to co-view television with children and make specific comments on the program content. Variations of this procedure are commonly practiced in the home, but rarely in a systematic way. Family members frequently talk to each other while watching television, and many of their comments are related to the program content (Lyle, 1972; Lyle & Hoffman, 1972a,b). Several laboratory studies have assessed the influence on children's aggressive behavior of having the individual children co-view a violent TV program with an adult who systematically makes either approving, neutral, or disapproving comments about the observed violence (Grusec, 1973; Hicks, 1968). The findings of each of these studies indicate that negative adult evaluations of violence can successfully reduce the subsequent aggressive behavior of children, particularly, but not solely, in the presence of the adult co-viewer. Although these children have presumably learned the aggressive material presented on the program, they were also responding to the adult's implicit standards related to the inappropriateness of behaving in that way in the real world (Slaby & Roedell, 1982).

Reducing Exposure to Aggressive Cues

Aggression can be reduced by either removing cues or alternatively making nonaggressive cues salient. Several studies have shown that stimuli associated with aggression are capable of eliciting aggressive reactions from people who are set or ready to perform these responses. By minimizing encounters with aggression-evoking stimuli, aggression may be lessened. In a series of studies by Berkowitz (Berkowitz, 1973; Berkowitz & LePage, 1967), the researchers found that angered college students were more aggressive if guns rather than nonaggressive objects were present. Turner and Goldsmith (1976) found evidence for a similar effect in preschool children, who were observed during several free-play sessions with various kinds of toys. During some sessions, novel aggressive toy guns were made available and, in other sessions, nonaggressive toy airplanes were available. Children behaved more aggressively toward others during sessions with the toy guns than during sessions with their usual toys or with the novel nonaggressive toys.

Finally, aggression could be reduced by decreasing children's exposure to aggressive models. One suggestion for altering the effects of television on young children's aggression is to reduce the amount of violent programming they watch. Such a reduction might also be expected to stimulate a number of related alternative behaviors, such as self-control and tolerance of frustration (Stein & Friedrich, 1975). Although a great deal of research evidence indirectly supports this suggestion, it should be noted that there have been no specific experimental investigations designed to assess directly the effects of reducing children's viewing of violent programs (Slaby & Roedell, 1982).

Group Level

Provision of Superordinate Goals in Peer Groups

In a series of ambitious field experiments, Sherif (1956) examined another technique for controlling aggression and conflict: the provision of a superordinate goal that requires cooperation of rival groups in achieving the goal. To test the effectiveness of this approach, Sherif conducted the Robber's Cave experiment; and as one writer stated, "It was perhaps the first scientific war—because this was caused, conducted and concluded by behavioral scientists" (McNeil, 1962, p. 77). Sherif's plan was to study how conflict arises and then to establish effective ways of restoring harmony—all within the 2-week period of a summer camp program. On arrival at Robber's Cave, the 11-year-old boys were divided into two groups and for the first few days shared a variety of activities designed to produce strong feelings of pride and identification with their own group. To facilitate the development of this in-group feeling, the boys adopted names—the Rattlers and the Eagles. The working hypothesis guiding this aspect of the research was that "when two groups have conflicting aims—i.e., when one can achieve its ends only at the expense of the other—their members will become hostile to each other" (Sherif,

1956, p. 5). Sherif arranged a series of competitive games: baseball, tug-of-war, and a treasure hunt in order to produce hostility and friction between the groups. Competition was clearly effective in increasing hostility, rivalry, and conflict and, in addition, it enhanced in-group identification and strengthened group solidarity. To reduce the conflict that he so cleverly engineered, Sherif gave the members of the conflicting groups opportunities for noncompetitive, highly pleasant social contacts such as going to the movies or sharing the same dining room. The results were disastrous: The boys simply took advantage of these occasions to vent their hostilities against one another; if anything, the conflict was heightened rather than reduced by this approach. Sherif's next tactic, providing the groups with a series of tasks that required their cooperative efforts to solve, was much more successful. Working together on such projects as fixing a leak in the camp's water supply was effective in reducing the conflict and restoring harmony between the groups.

> What our limited experiments have shown is that the possibilities for achieving harmony are greatly enhanced when groups are brought together to work toward common ends. Then favorable information about a disliked group is seen in a new light, and leaders are in a position to take bolder steps toward cooperation. In short, hostility gives way when groups pull together to achieve overriding goals which are real and compelling to all concerned. (Sherif, 1956, p. 5)

Modification of Intrafamilial Aggression

Control of aggression through the resocialization of families can be viewed in both short- and long-term perspectives and as both preventive and corrective. Short-term control involves crisis intervention to prevent imminent cases of intrafamily aggression. Telephone hotlines, police intervention, crisis nurseries, and day care dropoff centers are examples of short-term control. Temporary removal of the aggressive family member or a victim of intrafamilial aggression from the home by the courts is yet another form of short-term control. But given the large amount of intrafamilial aggression, as discussed earlier, neither removal nor foster-care placement is an economically feasible solution. Long-term control tactics aimed at restructuring familial interaction patterns that may cause aggression or to modify child or parent attitudes, values, personality, or behaviors that are viewed as causative are more likely to be successful in reducing aggression in the long

run. The particular forms of either prevention or modification vary with the theoretical orientation of the intervention program. While some control tactics focus on changing the individual, other control programs aim to alter aggression rates by modifying social institutions and social conditions.

Intervention at the level of the individual family often focuses on the acquisition or modification of child-rearing skills. These strategies are based on the assumption that aggressive patterns develop as a result of dysfunctional interaction patterns among family members (e.g., Patterson, 1982).

The focus of such modification programs is to systematically restructure the interaction patterns among members of families demonstrating aggressive behavior patterns. Programs for altering family interaction patterns have a two-level goal. First, the parents themselves who are using ineffective child-rearing tactics need a new repertoire of training strategies that are effective in child control. Second, through the use of new techniques, child behaviors that may be eliciting ineffective parental reactions can be altered.

Patterson (1974, 1977, 1982) has developed a comprehensive program for the retraining of parents of aggressive children based on social learning principles, particularly operant conditioning concepts, in which the relationship between parental reactions and deviant behavior is the focus. By making parents aware of such a relationship and by providing the opportunity to learn and rehearse alternative techniques for dealing with their children, the deviant behavior can be modified. A few steps are involved. First, the parents are required to complete a programmed text on social learning-based child-management techniques, which emphasizes principles such as reinforcement, shaping, generalization, coercion, extinction, and punishment. In the next phase of the program, the parents are taught to carefully define, track, and record a series of targeted deviant or prosocial child behaviors. This involves defining in a precise fashion the exact behavior, noting the elicitors and consequences that accompany a response and, finally, recording the occurrences. During this phase they are monitored frequently by telephone. In the third stage, modeling and role-playing procedures are used to illustrate appropriate techniques. There are two aims in this phase: (1) to teach the parents to reinforce and encourage prosocial appropriate behaviors, and (2) to reduce the rate of occurrence of deviant behaviors. To accomplish the first aim, the parents are taught to recognize and reinforce in a consistent way instances of acceptable behavior. The complementary set of procedures involves the use of time-out for deviant behavior. Time-out is a procedure in which a child is removed for a specified period from the reinforcing environment and placed in isolation. This is an effective technique for reducing deviant behavior in children; moreover, the parent, who may use more severe punitive techniques, is provided with alternative and effective procedures for child control. These behavior management skills are directly modeled, and the novice parents engage in supervised role playing of these same skills. Usually 8 to 12 weekly sessions are sufficient. Where necessary, training sessions are conducted in the home with the experimenters modeling the appropriate parenting skills. Telephone monitoring of the parents' execution of these techniques is conducted as well. A final aspect of the program consists of learning to construct contracts that specify contingencies for a list of problem behaviors occurring at home. In addition, Patterson in some studies combines these procedures with a set of classroom interventions.

To assess the effectiveness of the program, detailed observations by trained observers of the interaction patterns between the parents and the deviant child are made in the home situation. A careful assessment of 27 families indicated that there was a significant decrease in deviant behavior from the baseline across the treatment phase. Follow-up assessments revealed that there was an increase in noxious behavior for half of the families during the month following the cessation of treatment; however, by providing families with a "booster shot" of approximately 2 hours of extra treatment, the deviant behavior was reduced. Most important, the results suggest that the effects induced by the training were relatively stable over 1 year. Finally, in contrast to long-term psychiatric therapy, this type of intervention program was relatively economical: The cost in terms of therapist contact time was 31.4 hours for the family training intervention.

The success of this program is impressive and clearly documents the feasibility of retraining parents to use disciplinary tactics that achieve both effective child control and a reduction in intrafamilial aggression. Part of the reason for the long-term stability of the changes is that, as the child's behavior improves, the relationship between parent and child may improve and the negative attitude to the child may diminish. The child may become a more attractive and valued family member and, as such, a less likely target for aggression.

More recently, Reid et al. (1981) reported that similar strategies have been successfully applied to the treatment of abusive families. For both mothers and children, the rate of aversive behavior was significantly lower following treatment. Follow-up studies by Reid et al. will reveal whether the retraining of abusive families does, in fact, reduce the rate of recidivism among these families.

Patterson's work should serve as a model for future intervention attempts in terms of the careful assessment, programmatic intervention, and detailed documentation of outcomes. Furthermore, this program illustrates the value of voluntary rehabilitation and nonpunitive procedures—in this case, for socializing children's deviant behaviors and resocializing abusive parent "offenders." [For examples of other similar programs, see Burgess and Conger (1977), Christophersen, Kuehn, Grinstead, Barnard, Rainey, and Kuehn (1976), Doctor and Singer (1978), and Wahler, House, and Stambaugh (1976).]

In summary, considerable progress has been made in the modification of aggression in families. However, families need to be viewed within their broader social context. Recognition of the embeddedness of the family in a community is necessary (Parke & Lewis, 1981). The ways in which families and communities mutually affect each other and the ways in which communities influence aggressive patterns are both important issues for an adequate theory of aggression control.

Community and Societal Levels

The extent to which individual and group social behaviors reflect the more general political and economic societal structures in which they are embedded has been a subject of interest not only to researchers of aggression but to scholars in various social sciences (Levine, 1977; McGranahan, 1946). In the case of aggression, for example, the political issue of children's rights has been demonstrated to affect the resolution of aggression-related juvenile crime cases (Worsfold, 1974).

For the most part, theoretical and empirical work relating aggression and community or societal values has focused on the embeddedness of families within communities and cultures. We are only beginning: (1) to articulate: the effects of these levels of social organization on family functioning, and (2) to explore the processes by which these effects are achieved. It should be noted that community influence, regardless of its form, can be either positive or negative; this view stands in contrast to the view that a high degree of connectedness with community resources is, ipso facto, necessarily positive. In addition, as stated above, it is assumed that the relationship between communities and families is bidirectional. Finally, it is assumed that both the ways in which communities and families are related and affect aggression will vary across the developmental span.

Similar theoretical models have been proposed by both Brim (1975) and Bronfenbrenner (1979) in which families function within larger social systems such as neighborhoods and communities. The functions of such extrafamilial systems are: (1) to educate members in culturally acceptable patterns of child-rearing, (2) to monitor these practices in order to maintain them within acceptable community boundaries, and (3) to provide relief from stress, since aggression may be the outcome of mounting stress. Next, we examine some of the mechanisms through which these extrafamilial influences operate to modify family interaction patterns.

Extrafamilial Support Systems for Modifying Aggression

To explore the mechanisms by which community influence is transmitted to the family, two kinds of support systems need to be distinguished: (1) informal and (2) formal. In times past, extended family members may have been more geographically available to monitor and, therefore, to reduce forms of individual and family violence than is often the case today. When living close by, they may have functioned in various ways to reduce levels of family tension and aggression. First, the stress often associated with child care may have been alleviated by other family members' assistance. Second, the novice mother may have had an experienced role model (e.g., her mother) available from whom to acquire mothering skills on a routine basis. At the same time, an older caretaker could modify disciplinary tactics that might contribute to intrafamily violence. Although extended family members still provide a significant amount of support (Tinsley & Parke, 1983), some of these roles have been subsumed by informal social support systems in communities (Parke & Tinsley, 1982).

Informal support systems include various neighborhood- or community-based organizations or groups that are not formally generated, controlled, or funded by local government officials. On the more structured side, these systems can include informal clubs organized by ethnic, recreational, or religious interest, "welcome wagon" organizations, and other newcomer groups. Less structured are neighborhood and family networks, including the acquaintance and interaction patterns among proximal and distal neighbors—and the number of

relatives in an extended family living within the target area. In the case of some types of families, such as abusive families, who are more frequently isolated from informal social support networks, formal community support systems in the legal, health, educational, and welfare areas take on an increasingly important role (Parke, 1977a).

Two types of formal support systems need to be distinguished: (1) general and (2) aggression specific. General support systems refer to the types of formal support systems that are available to all members of the community and are aimed at improving the general quality of life but are not targeted at a particular problem or subgroup. These include such government agencies as welfare service groups, educational and employment services, and recreational facilities.

Other formal support systems are specifically designed to reduce aggression and violence among children, adolescents, or families. For the most part, the availability of general and targeted types of formal support systems is probably highly correlated. In the case of family violence, specific support mechanisms include groups for parents concerned about intrafamily violence such as "Parents Anonymous," day care facilities, baby-sitting services, mother's helpers, homemaker and housekeeping services, dropoff centers and crisis nurseries, hotlines, and hospital-based courses in child care and child-rearing.

There is some recent evidence that demonstrates the role of formal and informal support systems in the regulation of aggression. Support for an ecological approach to child abuse comes from a series of studies by Garbarino. In one study, Garbarino (1976) demonstrated that child abuse rates were, in fact, clearly related to the availability of formal socioeconomic support systems. Specifically, he examined variations in abuse as a function of a number of socioeconomic and demographic variables. Using U.S. census data across 58 counties in New York State, Garbarino hypothesized that the socioeconomic support system for the family in each county is directly associated with the rate of child abuse or maltreatment: Where support systems are better and where the family has more human resources, the rate of child abuse or maltreatment is lower, and vice versa. Based on a multiple regression approach, which controlled the intercorrelation among the socioeconomic and demographic indices, Garbarino found that indexes including employment and income levels of mothers, educational opportunities for both mothers and preschool age children, and level of education accounted for an impressive

35% of the variance in child abuse across counties. Although the child abuse data were derived from public agency sources that potentially overrepresent lower socioeconomic classes, this study nevertheless suggests that environmental stress exacerbated by the lack of availability of socioecnomic resources—even within lower class groups—is related to child abuse.

In a more recent study, Garbarino and Crouter (1978) used more refined units of analysis—neighborhood areas and census tracts. Although economic level (above $15,000 or below $8000 annual income) accounted for the largest portion of the variance in child abuse and neglect, factors such as transience and the percentage of married women in the workforce with children also accounted for significant additional portions of variance in the neighborhood analyses. Together with economic status, these factors accounted for 81% of the variance in total maltreatment (abuse and neglect) rates. Such factors as transience may relate to abuse, in part, because of the disruption of social networks that may accompany moving. Census tract data showed similar trends but were less impressive. The Garbarino findings provide clear support for an ecological analysis of child abuse, with an emphasis on the need to recognize the family's position in the community as an important determinant of abuse.

Other evidence suggests that a family's pattern of interaction with others in the community may not only be related to the levels of intrafamily aggression, but may also determine the success of intervention programs aimed at modifying maladaptive interaction patterns. Wahler (1980), whose behavioral approach to modification of families of aggressive children, is related to Patterson's approach, found that the success of family intervention programs varied with the pattern of parental interactions outside the family. Specifically, the mothers who profited from the treatment had more interactions with extrafamilial individuals in the community than the mothers for whom treatment was unsuccessful. The mothers who were successful in treatment initiated most of their extrafamily interactions, spent most of their time with friends, and judged their contacts as either neutral or positive. In contrast, the social contacts of the mothers in the treatment failure group were usually initiated by other people (e.g., relatives and helping agencies) and were more often rated as aversive by these mothers. This study underscores the importance of considering cognitive factors such as parental perceptions of social support in assessing the impact of social supports on families.

These studies illustrate that social networks including both informal and formal support systems can play an important, but as yet only poorly documented, role in family violence and aggression. Further research is clearly needed to elucidate the processes that link such resources to specific aspects of family functioning. An understanding of these processes is necessary for an adequate theory of intrafamily violence and can illuminate the relationship among individual, group, and societal aggression.

Next, we examine the legal system, an institution that plays an important role in the regulation of aggression.

The Role of the Legal System in the Regulation and Prevention of Aggression

Aggression is not only a developmental and sociopsychological problem, but a legal one as well. In recent years, revised goals as well as revised roles for professionals within the legal systems have been evolving; these shifts involve a recognition that the legal system can play a rehabilitative as well as a punitive role in dealing with violence among children, adolescents, and families. In part, this shift represents an outcome determined by multiple factors: a changing legal philosophy (Worsfold, 1974); the limited success of the traditional adversary system in child abuse cases (Mesch, 1971); and the potential benefits of alternative therapeutic resocialization programs.

Two recent projects involving new roles for the police and the juvenile justice system illustrate possible ways in which the formal legal system can function as a support system in the control of intrafamily violence and in the reduction of juvenile delinquency. Although police are often the first formal authority to intervene in intrafamily conflict, little attention has been paid to their role in the prevention and control of child abuse and family violence. Parnas (1967) estimated that more police calls involve familyflict than all other types of criminal incidents. Police intervention often occurs before conflict has escalated to the abusive level, while medical authorities typically encounter the family only *after* the abusive incident. Unfortunately, police intervention itself frequently exaggerates rather than limits both individual violence (Toch, 1969) and collective aggression (Marx, 1970), perhaps because of serious differences in values between police and their clientele (Rokeach, Miller, & Snyder, 1977), or perhaps because of a lack of specific police training in handling familial violence (Bandura, 1973a; Bard, 1971).

Bard's work provides evidence that police can function effectively in settling intrafamily disputes and thereby may prevent the escalation of violence to abusive levels. A special "Family Crisis Unit" was trained to handle family disputes through such techniques as modeling, role playing, lectures, and discussion groups. Bard (1971, p. 152) noted that, although "40% of injuries sustained by police occur when they are intervening in family disputes . . . the 18-man unit, exposed for more than would ordinarily be the case to this dangerous event, sustained only one minor injury" during the 2-year project. The use of nonphysical tactics in interventions in family disputes, such as advice and mediation, not only defuses a short-term problem but also serves as a model of an alternative way of settling conflict.

The police officer's initial handling of the dispute affects later events. If an arrest is made, charging and labeling processes are activated that, in turn, may end up in a court hearing. But if an arrest is not made, costly legal procedures can be avoided, and social-service agency assistance can be invoked. Bard (1971) found that, in the untrained unit, family court was the referral choice in 95% of the cases, with no referrals to social and mental health agencies. In the trained (experimental) unit, 45% of the referrals were made to family court and 55% to social and mental health agencies. In addition, there were about 22% fewer arrests in the experimental unit. Bard concluded that

> The lower rate of arrests in the experimental precinct is suggestive of the greater use of referral resources and of mediation. . . . It is well known that upon reaching the courts, and long after the heated dispute has cooled, most complaints of this type are dropped anyway. Sophisticated police intervention can provide immediate mediation service but can also serve as a preliminary screening mechanism for final resolution of family disharmony. (1971, p. 160)

In summary, Bard's project shows that professionals within the legal system can effectively serve as facilitators of more constructive family functioning rather than merely as agents of law enforcement.

Another illustration of the role of the legal system in the control of aggression comes from recent studies of diversion tactics, which remove juvenile offenders from the justice system to examine the impact of these strategies on subsequent delinquency. Numerous critics have argued that "overcrowded courts and correctional facilities and the negative effect of the criminal justice system itself on those with whom it comes in contact (e.g., labeling ef-

fects, association of low risk persons with more hard-core criminal types)" justify the concept of diverting offenders from the criminal justice system into some alternative form of service or treatment (Kushler & Davidson, 1981, p. 386).

> The exact nature of the process used and the extent or nature of treatment provided vary greatly, but the underlying rationale is that the offender has certain needs for supervision, counseling and/or supplemental services which, if provided, will do more to prevent future crimes by that individual than will aversive stigmatizing formal correctional system handling. (Kushler & Davidson, 1981, p. 386)

A recent example of this approach is a field experimental study of diversion strategies for juvenile delinquents conducted by Seidman, Rappaport, and Davidson (1980). The model involves diverting adolescents from the legal system to a trained volunteer who works on a one-to-one basis with the youth in the youth's natural environment. With police cooperation, alleged adolescent offenders were assigned to the experimental program or a control group, which used ordinary processing of the alleged offender by juvenile court. Treatment strategies employed by the trained student volunteers involved a combination of relationship skills, behavioral contracting, and child advocacy. The contracting component involved the assessment and modification of the interpersonal contingencies in the life of the youths (e.g., with parents and teachers). The specific methods employed involved the establishment of written interpersonal agreements between the youth and significant others, as mediated by the students, according to the procedures outlined by Stuart (Stuart, 1971; Stuart & Tripodi, 1973). In addition to the enhancement of specific behavioral changes on the part of the youth and the significant others in his or her life, it was necessary in most cases to mobilize needed community resources for the youth to ensure durability of the desired change and to provide legitimate avenues for attainment of the youth's goals. The strategies used have recently been labeled "child advocacy" and involve the targeting of community resources such as educational, vocational, or recreational programs for change (Seidman et al., 1980, p. 107).

The program's success was indicated in the fewer police contacts, of lesser severity, and in the fewer petitions filed with the court for the experimental participants, compared to the control group, during the intervention and at 1-year and 2-year follow-up intervals. Follow-up research was aimed at separately examining the impact of the behavioral contracting and child advocacy components of the treatment. While both components made independent contributions, some evidence favors the value of the behavioral contracting over the advocacy component. Further research to fully examine the components of these two treatment approaches would be worthwhile in order to provide better guidelines for future intervention programs. Although both approaches focus on multiple life domains, the contracting group concentrated more on the family and the youth's behavior in school, while the advocacy group focused on employment, the youth's friends, and changes in the school per se. It is clear that we still understand little about the specific components of the child's and adolescent's social networks, which can be most effectively tapped for producing social change.

Closing Note

Finally, more attention needs to be given to the development of guidelines for choosing intervention strategies. Obviously, some strategies are more effective at some ages than others. Treatments that rely heavily on children's verbal and conceptual capacities, such as coaching techniques, are probably ineffective with very young children, while reinforcement strategies may be more appropriate at early points in development. Similarly, guidelines for the modification of different types of aggression are needed. Children who behave aggressively because they lack alternative and acceptable social skills would require a different intervention strategy than children who have adequate social skills but who have low frustration tolerance or who easily become angry. These suggestions underscore the importance of developing a more adequate taxonomy of aggressive behavior; without such a scheme, intervention and control strategies will often be less than optimally effective.

CONCLUSIONS

In closing this chapter, we would like to highlight some of the major themes that have emerged in our review as well as a number of issues that require more attention in future research. In the study of aggression, as in all areas of social development, cognition has assumed a major role. Although there have been an increasing number of studies in the cognitive tradition that have addressed children's knowledge and understanding of aggression-provoking situations, the links between understanding and behavior have not received an equivalent amount of attention. Describing the ways in which shifts in understanding and changes in behavior covary across development is an under-researched issue. In addition, the relative impact of modifying cognitive aspects of aggression such as attitudes and values on aggressive behavior, and vice versa, is another important, but poorly understood, aspect of the behavior-cognition problem.

Biological factors are being given more recognition in the development of children's aggression than in prior decades, but much more information about the biological basis of aggression is required. Not only are more detailed measures of hormonal changes across development necessary, but a variety of other possible biological contributions needs to be studied. Studies of the role of temperamental differences from infancy onward in the development of aggression appear to be promising.

Situational control has had a long and venerable history in the area of aggression research, and retaining a healthy commitment to understanding how aggressive behavior varies across contexts and settings is important. A wider range of contexts, however, needs to be examined in this regard. In this chapter, recognition of the embeddedness of children in a wide range of social contexts, both intrafamilial and extrafamilial, including communities and cultures, was advocated. The task of articulating how the extrafamilial social settings alter children's acquisition and display of aggressive behavior has hardly begun. Similarly, articulation of the processes that link children and families to informal and formal social networks in the community represents an important step in understanding the role of these social systems in the socialization of aggression.

These cognitive, biological, and social-contextual themes need to be pursued from a developmental perspective. In spite of a long, but sporadic, history of attention to the task of describing developmental changes, the developmental progression of aggressive behavior and related behaviors is still not well understood. The corresponding developmental changes in cognitive, biological, and social contexts need to be addressed in order to move the issue of developmental changes in aggression beyond description and toward a more process-based analysis of developmentally related shifts.

Certain developmental periods need special empirical and theoretical attention. While the preschool period has received a great deal of study, infancy and adolescence have not been sufficiently investigated with respect to aggression. The origins of aggression in infancy, in spite of the increased attention that this age period has received in the last two decades with regard to other social behaviors, are still not clearly articulated. Studies of early peer relations, particularly those involving conflict-resolution strategies among infant and toddler peers, hold particular promise, as do the recent studies of the impact of early infant-parent attachment relationships on later peer social relationships. Longitudinal studies of the relationship between peer-peer interaction patterns in infancy and later preschool interactive competence need to be executed.

Another issue that should be examined, which may provide important information on the early origins of aggression, is the development of both the recognition and production of emotions. The links between early manifestations of anger, for example, and later displays of overt aggressive action are still unknown. Similarly, the impact of early competence in decoding others' emotional states on later patterns of aggressive activity is unclear.

The adolescent period may be of particular value for the study of aggression, since this time provides a rich opportunity to examine the interplay among biological, social, and cognitive changes. Although studies of juvenile delinquency have been of interest for decades, studies of other forms of aggressive behavior in adolescence would be of interest as well. Studies that simultaneously examine these different domains (i.e., biological, social, cognitive) and their relationships across time will be particularly informative, not only for students of aggression but for social developmentalists in general. For example, the current interest of biologists and psychologists in the physical and hormonal changes associated with adolescence shows promise for elucidating related behavioral patterns such as aggression.

Multiple research strategies are necessary, since is likely that no single methodological approach will suffice in broadening our understanding of the development of aggression. Instead, a wide range of designs, data collections, and analyses strategies are necessary (Parke, 1978a, 1979). Naturalistic settings have become increasingly utilized in aggression research, in an effort to address the issue of ecological validity, and it is hoped that this trend will continue. Not only are more descriptive studies of actual aggressive interchanges needed to provide a more complete picture of the controlling events in interpersonal aggressive encounters, but greater use of field experimental strategies (e.g., Friedrich & Stein, 1973) would be of particular value. Combinations of laboratory and field methodological approaches, in which laboratory and field settings are used either for manipulation or measurement, merit more use. By measuring the impact of a laboratory-based intervention in a naturalistic setting, for example, the degree of generalization can be more adequately assessed (see Parke, 1979).

Different levels of analyses, such as microanalytic levels of observation as well as global or macroanalytic ratings of the same interchanges, may yield different information. Moreover, the relationships between these levels of analyses need to be assessed. It is not clear that the present focus on the fine-grained coding of interaction behaviors currently in vogue among social development researchers is necessary for studying all aspects of aggression. Although these methods have utility for examining immediate situational control, other levels of measurement may be more appropriate for investigating such problems as the long-term stability of aggression.

Social behavior, including aggression, is not independent of historical changes in societies or cultures. To date, there has been insufficient monitoring of the impact of secular changes on the levels and types of aggression. Some work has been conducted concerning the effects of changes in age distributions of the population on the levels of delinquency and violent crime (Turner, Fenn, & Cole, 1981), and systematic recording of the level of media violence has been carried out (Gerbner et al., 1980). A careful evaluation of the impact of shifts in media fare on children's aggression, however, has lagged behind this monitoring effort. Similarly, an analysis of the effects of societal changes—such as increases in divorce rates, shifts in mobility patterns, and modifications of the sex-role patterns of men and women at home and in the work sphere—on socialization patterns and on the development of aggression in children has hardly begun.

Implicit in our call for a multisystem analysis of aggression is the recognition that the understanding of aggression is a multidisciplinary endeavor. Awareness and utilization of research by sociologists, criminologists, biologists, and anthropologists, as well as collaborative efforts among researchers in these areas, are likely to be particularly helpful to developmental psychologists and others who wish to broaden their interpretive frameworks.

Finally, a recognition that aggression is a social as well as a scientific problem may not only help us select theoretically interesting issues for study, but may lead to the development of informed intervention programs and effective social policy as well.

REFERENCES

Abramovitch, R. The relation of attention and proximity to rank in preschool children. In M. Chance & R. Larsen (Eds.), *The social structure of attention*. London: Wiley, 1976.

Abramovitch, R., Corter, C., & Lando, B. Sibling interaction in the home. *Child Development*, 1979, *4*, 997–1003.

Abramovitch, R., & Strayer, F. F. Preschool social organization: Agonistic, spacing and attentional behaviors. In P. Pliner, T. Kramer, & T. Alloway (Eds.), *Recent advances in the study of communication and affect* (Vol. 6). New York: Plenum Press, 1978.

Achenbach, T. M., & Edelbrock, C. S. Behavioral problems and competencies reported by parents of normal and disturbed children aged 4 through 16. *Monographs of the Society for Research in Child Development*, 1981, Serial No. 188.

Allen, K. E., Turner, K. D., & Everett, P. M. A behavior modification classroom for head start children with problem behaviors. *Exceptional Children*, 1970, *37*, 119–127.

Andison, F. S. TV violence and viewer aggression: A cumulation of study results 1956–1976. *Public Opinion Quarterly*, 1977, *41*, 314–331.

Asher, S. R. Children's peer relations. In M. E. Lamb (Ed.), *Social and personality development*. New York: Holt, Rinehart and Winston, 1978.

Asher, S. R., & Renshaw, P. D. Social skills and social knowledge of high and low status kindergarten children. Unpublished manuscript, University of Illinois, 1982.

Asher, S. R., Renshaw, P. D., & Geraci, R. L. Children's friendships and social competence. *International Journal of Psycholinguistics*, 1980, *7*, 27–39.

Atkin, D., Greenberg, B., Korzenny, F., & McDermott, S. Selective exposure to televised violence. *Journal of Broadcasting*, 1979, *23*, 5–13.

Bandura, A. Influence of models' reinforcement contingencies on the acquisition of imitative responses. *Journal of Personality and Social Psychology*, 1965, *1*, 589–595.

Bandura, A. *Principles of behavior modification.* New York: Holt, Rinehart and Winston, 1969.

Bandura, A. *Aggression: A social learning analysis.* New York: Holt, 1973. (a)

Bandura, A. Social learning theory of aggression. In J. F. Knutson (Ed.), *Control of aggression: Implications from basic research.* Chicago: Aldine, 1973. (b)

Bandura, A. *Social learning theory.* Englewood Cliffs, N.J.: Prentice-Hall, 1977.

Bandura, A., Grusec, J. E., & Menlove, F. L. Observational learning as a function of symbolization and incentive set. *Child Development*, 1966, *37*, 499–506.

Bandura, A., & Jeffrey, R. W. Role of symbolic coding and rehearsal processes in observational learning. *Journal of Personality and Social Psychology*, 1973, *26*, 122–130.

Bandura, A., Ross, D., & Ross, S. A. Transmission of aggression through imitation of aggressive models. *Journal of Abnormal and Social Psychology*, 1961, *63*, 575–582.

Bandura, A., Ross, D., & Ross, S. A. Imitation of film-mediated aggressive models. *Journal of Abnormal and Social Psychology*, 1963, *66*, 3–11. (a)

Bandura, A., Ross, D., & Ross, S. A. Vicarious reinforcement and imitative learning. *Journal of Abnormal and Social Psychology*, 1963, *67*, 601–607. (b)

Bandura, A., & Walters, R. H. *Adolescent aggression.* New York: Ronald, 1959.

Bandura, A., & Walters, R. H. *Social learning and personality development.* New York: Holt, 1963.

Bard, M. The study and modification of intra-familial violence. In J. L. Singer (Ed.), *The control of aggression and violence.* New York: Academic Press, 1971.

Barker, R. G., Dembo, T., & Lewin, K. Frustration and regression: An experiment with young children. *University of Iowa Studies in Child Welfare*, 1941, *18*, No. 386.

Baron, R. A. Magnitude of victim's pain cues and level of prior anger arousal as determinants of adult aggressive behavior. *Journal of Experimental Social Psychology*, 1971, *2*, 343–355. (a)

Baron, R. A. Reducing the influence of an aggressive model: The restraining effects of discrepant modeling cues. *Journal of Personality and Social Psychology*, 1971, *20*, 240–245. (b)

Baron, R. A. *Human aggression.* New York: Plenum, 1977.

Baron, R. A., & Ball, R. L. The aggression-inhibiting influence of nonhostile humor. *Journal of Experimental Social Psychology*, 1974, *10*, 23–33.

Baron, R. A., & Lawton, S. F. Environmental influences on aggression: The facilitation of modeling effects by high ambient temperatures. *Psychonomic Science*, 1972, *26*, 80–83.

Barrett, D. E. A naturalistic study of sex differences in children's aggression. *Merrill-Palmer Quarterly*, 1979, *25*, 193–203.

Bates, J. E. Temperament as a part of social relationships: Implications of perceived infant difficultness. Paper presented at International Conference on Infant Studies, Austin, Texas, March, 1982.

Bateson, P. P. G., & Hinde, R. A. *Growing points in ethology*. Cambridge: Cambridge University Press, 1976.

Baumrind, D. Child care practices anteceding three patterns of preschool behavior. *Genetic Psychology Monographs*, 1967, *75*, 43–88.

Baumrind, D. Current patterns of parental authority. *Developmental Psychology*, 1971, *4*, 1–103.

Becker, G. Causal analysis in R-R studies: Television violence and aggression. *American Psychologist*, 1972, *27*, 967–968.

Becker, W. C. Consequences of different kinds of parental discipline. In M. L. Hoffman & L. W. Hoffman (Eds.), *Review of child development research* (Vol. 1). New York: Russell Sage Foundation, 1964.

Bell, R. Q. A reinterpretation of the direction of effects in studies of socialization. *Psychological Review*, 1968, *75*, 81–95.

Bell, R. Q., & Harper, L. V. *Child effects on adults*. Hillsdale, N.J.: Erlbaum, 1977.

Belsky, J. Early human experience: A family perspective. *Developmental Psychology*, 1981, *17*, 3–23.

Belson, W. A. *Television and the family*. London: British Broadcasting Corp., 1959.

Belson, W. A. *Juvenile theft: The causal factors*. London: Harper & Row, 1975.

Belson, W. A. *Television violence and the adolescent boy*. Westmead, England: Saxon House, 1978.

Berkowitz, L. *Aggression: A social psychological analysis*. New York: McGraw-Hill, 1962.

Berkowitz, L. On not being able to aggress. *British Journal of Social and Clinical Psychology*, 1966, *5*, 130–139.

Berkowitz, L. The frustration-aggression hypothesis revisited. In L. Berkowitz (Ed.), *Roots of aggression*. New York: Atherton Press, 1969.

Berkowitz, L. Aggressive humor as a stimulus to aggressive responses. *Journal of Personality and Social Psychology*, 1970, *16*, 710–717.

Berkowitz, L. The contagion of violence: An S-R mediational analysis of some effects of observed aggression. In W. J. Arnold & M. M. Page (Eds.), *Nebraska symposium on motivation* (Vol. 19). Lincoln: University of Nebraska Press, 1971.

Berkowitz, L. The case for bottling up rage. *Psychology Today*, 1973, *7*, 24–31.

Berkowitz, L. Some determinants of impulsive aggression: The role of mediated associations with reinforcements for aggression. *Psychological Review*, 1974, *81*, 165–176.

Berkowitz, L., & Alioto, J. T. The meaning of an observed event as a determinant of its aggressive consequences. *Journal of Personality and Social Psychology*, 1973, *28*, 206–217.

Berkowitz, L., Corwin, R., & Heironimus, M. Film violence and subsequent aggressive tendencies. *Public Opinion Quarterly*, 1963, *27*, 217–229.

Berkowitz, L., & Frodi, A. Reactions to a child's mistakes as affected by her/his looks and speech. Unpublished manuscript, University of Wisconsin, 1968.

Berkowitz, L., & Geen, R. G. Film violence and the cue properties of available targets. *Journal of Personality and Social Psychology*, 1966, *3*, 525–530.

Berkowitz, L., & LePage, A. Weapons as aggression-eliciting stimuli. *Journal of Personality and Social Psychology*, 1967, *7*, 202–207.

Berkowitz, L, & Rawlings, E. Effects of film violence on inhibitions against subsequent aggression. *Journal of Abnormal and Social Psychology*, 1963, *66*, 405–412.

Block, J., Block, J. H., & Harrington, D. M. Some misgivings about the Matching Familiar Figures Test as a measure of reflection-impulsivity. *Developmental Psychology*, 1974, *10*, 611–632.

Block, J. H. Another look at sex differentiation in the socialization behaviors of mothers and fathers. In J. Sherman & F. L. Denmark (Eds.), *The psychology of women: Future directions of research*. New York: Psychological Dimensions, 1978.

Block, J. H., Block, J., & Morrison, A. Parental agreement-disagreement on child-rearing orientations and gender-related personality correlates in children. *Child Development*, 1981, *52*, 965–974.

Blurton Jones, N. G. An ethological study of some aspects of social behavior of children in nursery school. In D. Morris (Ed.), *Primate ethology*. London: Weidenfeld and Nicolson, 1967.

Blurton Jones, N. G. (Ed.). *Ethological studies of child behavior*. Cambridge: Cambridge University Press, 1972.

Boffey, P. M., & Walsh, J. Study of TV violence: Seven top researchers blackballed from panel. *Science,* 1970, *168,* 949–952.

Bower, R. T. *Television and the public.* New York: Holt, 1973.

Bowers, K. S. Situationism in psychology: An analysis and critique. *Psychological Review,* 1973, *80,* 307–336.

Brim, O. G. Family structure and sex-role learning by children. *Sociometry,* 1958, *21,* 1–16.

Brim, O. G. Macro-structural influences on child development and the need for childhood social indicators. *American Journal of Orthopsychiatry,* 1975, *45,* 516–524.

Brodzinsky, D. M., Messer, S. M., & Tew, J. D. Sex differences in children's expression and control of fantasy and overt aggression. *Child Development,* 1979, *50,* 372–379.

Bronfenbrenner, U. *The ecology of human development.* Cambridge: Harvard University Press, 1979.

Brown, P., & Elliot, R. Control of aggression in a nursery school class. *Journal of Experimental Child Psychology,* 1965, *2,* 103–107.

Buhler, C. *From birth to maturity.* London: Routledge & Kegan Paul, 1935.

Bullock, D., & Merrill, L. The impact of personal preference on consistency through time: The case of childhood aggression. *Child Development,* 1980, *51,* 808–814.

Burgess, R. L., & Conger, R. D. Family interaction patterns related to child abuse and neglect: Some preliminary findings. *Child Abuse and Neglect: The International Journal,* 1977, *1,* 269–277.

Burt, C. H. *The young delinquent.* New York: Appleton, 1929.

Buss, A. H. *The psychology of aggression.* New York: Wiley, 1961.

Buss, A. H. Instrumentality of aggression, feedback, and frustration as determinants of physical aggression. *Journal of Personality and Social Psychology,* 1966, *3,* 153–162.

Cairns, R. B. *Social development.* San Francisco: W. H. Freeman, 1979.

Cairns, R. B., & Green, J. A. How to assess personality and social patterns: Observations or ratings? In R. B. Cairns (Ed.), *The analysis of social interactions.* Hillsdale, N.J.: Erlbaum, 1979.

Camaras, L. A. Facial expressions used by children in a conflict situation. *Child Development,* 1977, *48,* 1431–1435.

Camaras, L. A. Children's understanding of facial expressions used during conflict encounters. *Child Development,* 1980, *51,* 879–885.

Cameron, P., & Janky, C. The effects of TV violence upon children: A naturalistic experiment. *Proceedings of the 79th annual convention of the American Psychological Association.* Washington, D.C.: American Psychological Association, 1971.

Camp, B. W. Verbal mediation in young aggressive boys. *Journal of Abnormal Psychology,* 1977, *86,* 145–153.

Caplan, P. J. Beyond the box score: A boundary condition for sex differences in aggression and achievement striving. In B. A. Maher (Ed.), *Progress in experimental personality research* (Vol. 9). New York: Academic Press, 1979.

Cater, D., & Strickland, S. *TV violence and the child: The evolution and fate of the Surgeon General's Report.* New York: Russell Sage Foundation, 1975.

Chaffee, S. H. Television and adolescent aggressiveness. In G. A. Comstock & E. A. Rubinstein (Eds.), *Television and social behavior: III. Television and adolescent aggressiveness.* Washington, D.C.: U.S. Government Printing Office, 1972.

Chaffee, S. H., & McLeod, J. M. Adolescent television use in the family context. In G. A. Comstock & E. A. Rubinstein (Eds.), *Television and social behavior: III. Television and adolescent aggressiveness.* Washington, D.C.: U.S. Government Printing Office, 1972.

Chandler, M. J. Egocentrism and antisocial behavior: The assessment and training of social perspective taking skills. *Developmental Psychology,* 1973, *9,* 326–332.

Charlesworth, R., & Hartup, W. W. Positive social reinforcement in the nursery school peer group. *Child Development,* 1967, 38, 993–1002.

Charlesworth, W. R. An ethological approach to research on facial expressions. In C. E. Izard (Ed.), *Measuring emotions in infants and children.* New York: Cambridge, 1982.

Chittenden, G. E. An experimental study in measuring and modifying assertive behavior in young children. *Monographs of the Society for Research in Child Development,* 1942, 7(Serial No. 31).

Christophersen, E. R., Kuehn, B. S., Grinstead, J. D., Barnard, J. D., Rainey, S. K., & Kuehn, F. E. A family training program for abuse and neglect families. *Journal of Pediatric Psychology,* 1976, *1,* 90–94.

Clarke-Stewart, K. A. Interactions between mothers and their young children: Characteristics and consequences. *Monographs of the Society for*

Research in Child Development, 1973, *38*(6–7, Serial No. 153).

Cline, V. B., Croft, R. G., & Courrier, S. Desensitization of children to television violence. *Journal of Personality and Social Psychology*, 1973, *27*, 360–365.

Coie, J. D., & Kupersmidt, J. *A behavioral analysis of emerging social status in boys' groups.* Paper presented at the meeting of the Society for Research in Child Development, Boston, 1981.

Collins, W. A. Learning of media content: A developmental study. *Child Development*, 1970, *41*, 1133–1142.

Collins, W. A. Effect of temporal separation between motivation, aggression, and consequences: A developmental study. *Developmental Psychology*, 1973, *8*, 215–221.

Collins, W. A., Berndt, T. V., & Hess, V. L. Observational learning of motives and consequences for television aggression: A developmental study. *Child Development*, 1974, *65*, 799–802.

Collins, W. A., Sobol, B. J., & Westby, S. Effects of adult commentary on children's comprehension and inferences about a televised aggressive portrayal. *Child Development*, 1981, *52*, 158–163.

Collins, W. A., Wellman, H., Keniston, A. H., & Westby, S. D. Age-related aspects of comprehension and inference from a televised dramatic narrative. *Child Development*, 1978, *49*, 389–399.

Collins, W. A., & Zimmermann, S. A. Convergent and divergent social cues: Effects of televised aggression on children. *Communication Research*, 1975, *2*, 331–346.

Comstock, G. The effects of television on children and adolescents: The evidence so far. *Journal of Communication*, 1975, *25*(4), 25–34.

Comstock, G. New emphases in research on the effects of television and film violence. In E. L. Palmer & A. Dorr (Eds.), *Children and the faces of television: Teaching, violence, selling.* New York: Academic Press, 1980.

Comstock, G., Chaffee, S., Katzman, N., McCombs, M., & Roberts, D. *Television and human behavior.* New York: Columbia University Press, 1978.

Condry, J., & Condry, S. Sex differences: A study of the eye of the beholder. *Child Development*, 1976, *47*, 812–819.

Crook, J. H. Social organization and the environmental aspects of contemporary social ethology. *Animal Behavior*, 1970, *18*, 197–209.

Daniel, J. H., Newberger, E. H., Reed, R. B., & Kotelchuck, M. Child abuse screening: Implications of the limited predictive power of abuse discriminations from a controlled study of pediatric social illness. *Child Abuse and Neglect*, 1978, *2*, 247–259.

Darvill, D., & Cheyne, J. A. *Sequential analysis of responses to aggression: Age and sex effects.* Paper presented at the meeting of the Society for Research in Child Development, Boston, April 1981.

Darwin, C. R. *The expression of the emotions in man and animals.* New York: Appleton, 1872.

Davitz, J. R. The effects of previous training on postfrustration behavior. *Journal of Abnormal and Social Psychology*, 1952, *47*, 309–315.

Dawe, H. C. An analysis of two hundred quarrels of preschool children. *Child Development*, 1934, *5*, 139–157.

Deur, J. L., & Parke, R. D. The effects of inconsistent punishment on aggression in children. *Developmental Psychology*, 1970, *2*, 403–411.

Dion, K. K. Young children's stereotyping of facial attractiveness. *Developmental Psychology*, 1973, *9*, 183–188.

Dion, K. K. Children's physical attractiveness and sex as determinants of adult punitiveness. *Developmental Psychology*, 1974, *10*, 772–778.

Dion, K. K., & Berscheid, E. Physical attractiveness and peer perception among children. *Sociometry*, 1974, *37*, 1–12.

Doctor, R. M., & Singer, E. M. Behavioral intervention strategies with child abusive parents: A home intervention program. *Child Abuse and Neglect*, 1978, *2*, 57–68.

Dodge, K. A. Social cognition and children's aggressive behavior. *Child Development*, 1980, *51*, 162–170.

Dodge, K. A. *Behavioral antecedents of peer rejection and isolation.* Paper presented at the meeting of the Society for Research in Child Development, Boston, April 1981.

Dodge, K. A. Social information processing variables in the development of aggression and altruism in children. In C. Zahn-Waxler, M. Cummings, & M. Radke-Yarrow (Eds.), *The development of altruism and aggression: Social and sociobiological origins.* New York: Cambridge University Press, 1982.

Dodge, K. A., & Frame, C. L. Social cognitive biases and deficits in aggressive boys. *Child Development*, 1982, *53*, 620–635.

Dodge, K. A., & Newman, J. P. Biased decision-making processes in aggressive boys. *Journal of*

Abnormal Psychology, 1981, *90,* 375–379.

Dollard, J., Doob, L. W., Miller, N. E., Mowrer, O. H., & Sears, R. R. *Frustration and aggression.* New Haven: Yale University Press, 1939.

Dominick, J. R., & Greenberg, B. S. Attitudes toward violence: The interaction of television exposure, family attitudes. and social class. In G. A. Comstock & E. A. Rubinstein (Eds.), *Television and social behavior: III. Television and adolescent aggressiveness.* Washington, D.C.: U.S. Government Printing Office, 1972.

Doob, A. N., & Wood, L. E. Catharsis and aggression: Effects of annoyance and retaliation on aggressive behavior. *Journal of Personality and Social Psychology,* 1972, *22,* 156–162.

Dorr, A., & Kovaric, P. Some of the people some of the time—but which people? Televised violence and its effects. In E. L. Palmer & A. Dorr (Eds.), *Children and the faces of television: Teaching, violence, selling.* New York: Academic Press, 1980.

Drabman, R. S., & Thomas, M. H. Does media violence increase children's toleration of real-life aggression? *Developmental Psychology,* 1974, *10,* 418–421.

Drabman, R. S., & Thomas, M. H. Does TV violence breed indifference? *Journal of Communication,* 1975, *25,* 86–89.

Drabman, R. S.,& Thomas, M. H. Does watching violence on television cause apathy? *Pediatrics,* 1976, *57,* 329–331.

Dubanoski, R. A., Evans, I. M., & Higuchi, A. A. Analysis and treatment of child abuse: A set of behavioral propositions. *Child Abuse and Neglect,* 1978, *2,* 153–172.

Dunn, J., & Kendrick, C. *Siblings.* Cambridge: Harvard University Press, 1982.

Easterbrooks, M. A., & Lamb, M. E. The relationship between quality of infant-mother attachment and infant competence in initial encounters with peers. *Child Development,* 1979, *50,* 380–387.

Eaton, G. G. The social order of Japanese macaques. *Scientific American,* 1976, *235,* 97–106.

Edelman, M. S., & Omark, D. R. Dominance hierarchies in young children. *Social Science Information,* 1973, *12,* 1.

Edgar, P. *Children and screen violence.* St. Lucia: University of Queensland Press, 1977.

Ehrhardt, A. A., & Baker, S. W. Fetal androgens, human central nervous system differentiation and behavior sex differences. In R. Richart, R. Friedman, & R. VandeWiele (Eds.), *Sex differences in behavior.* New York: Wiley, 1974.

Ehrhardt, A. A., Grisanti, G. C., & Meyer-Bahlburg, H. F. L. Prenatal exposure to medroxyprogesterone acetate (MPA) in girls. *Psycho-neuroendocrinology,* 1977, *2,* 391–398.

Eibl-Eibesfeldt, I. *Ethology: The biology of behavior.* New York: Holt, Rinehart and Winston, 1970.

Ekman, P., Liebert, R. M., Friesen, W. V., Harrison, R., Zlatchin, C., Malmstrom, E. J., & Baron R. A. Facial expressions of emotion while watching televised violence as predictors of subsequent aggression. In G. A. Comstock, E. A. Rubinstein, & J. P. Murray (Eds.), *Television and social behavior:* V. *Television's effects: Further explorations.* Washington, D.C.: U.S. Government Printing Office, 1972.

Ellis, G. T., & Sekyra, F. The effect of aggressive cartoons on the behavior of first grade children. *Journal of Psychology,* 1972, *81,* 37–43.

Elmer, E., & Gregg, G. S. Developmental characteristics of abused children. *Pediatrics,* 1967, *40,* 596–602.

Emery, R. E. Interparental conflict and the children of discord and divorce. *Psychological Bulletin,* 1982, *92,* 310–330.

Emmerich, W. Continuity and stability in early social development. II: Teacher ratings. *Child Development,* 1966, *37,* 17–27.

Epstein, S. Traits are alive and well. In D. Magnusson & N. S. Endler (Eds.), *Personality at the cross-roads: Current issues in interactional psychology,* Hillsdale, N.J.: Erlbaum, 1977.

Erlanger, H. S. Social class differences in parents' use of physical punishment. In S. K. Steinmetz & M. A. Straus (Eds.), *Violence in the family.* New York: Dodd, Mead, 1974.

Eron, L. D. Relationship with TV viewing habits and aggressive behavior in children. *Journal of Abnormal and Social Psychology,* 1963, *67,* 193–196.

Eron, L. D. Prescription for reduction of aggression. *American Psychologist,* 1980, *35,* 244–252.

Eron, L. D. Parent-child interaction, television violence, and aggression of children. *American Psychologist,* 1982, *37,* 197–211.

Eron, L. D., Huesmann, L. R., Lefkowitz, M. M., & Walder, L. O. Does television violence cause aggression? *American Psychologist,* 1972, *27,* 253–263.

Eron, L. D., Lefkowitz, M. M., Walder, L. O., & Huesmann, L. R. Relation of learning in childhood to psychopathology and aggression in young adulthood. In A. Davids (Ed.), *Child personality and psychopathology: Current topics I.*

New York: Wiley, 1974.

Eron, L. D., Walder, L. O., & Lefkowitz, M. M. *Learning of aggression in children*. Boston: Little, Brown & Co., 1971.

Fagot, B. I. Variations in density: Effects on task and social behaviors of preschool children. *Developmental Psychology*, 1977, *13*, 166–167.

Fagot, B. I. The influence of sex of child on parental reactions to toddler children. *Child Development*, 1978, *49*, 30–36.

Farrington, D. P. The family backgrounds of aggressive youths. In L. Hersov, M. Berger, & D. Shaffer (Eds.), *Aggression and anti-social behavior in childhood and adolescence*. Oxford: Pergamon, 1978.

Farrington, D. P. Longitudinal analyses of criminal violence. In M. E. Wolfgang & N. A. Weiner (Eds.), *Criminal violence*. Beverly Hills, Calif.: Sage, 1982.

Ferguson, T. J., & Rule, B. G. Effects of inferential set, outcome severity, and basis of responsibility on children's evaluations of aggressive acts. *Developmental Psychology*, 1980, *16*, 141–146.

Feshbach, N. D. Sex differences in children's modes of aggressive responses toward outsiders. *Merrill Palmer Quarterly*, 1969, *15*, 249–258.

Feshbach, N. D. The relationship of child-rearing factors to children's aggression, empathy and related positive and negative social behaviors. In J. DeWit & W. W. Hartup (Eds.), *Determinants and origins of aggressive behavior*. The Hague: Mouton, 1974.

Feshbach, N. D., & Feshbach, S. The relationship between empathy and aggression in two age groups. *Developmental Psychology*, 1969, *1*, 102–107.

Feshbach, N. D., & Feshbach, S. Empathy training and the regulation of aggression: Potentialities and limitations. *Academic Psychology Bulletin*, 1982, *4*, 399–413.

Feshbach, S. The function of aggression and the regulation of aggressive drive. *Psychological Review*, 1964, *71*, 257–272.

Feshbach, S. Aggression. In P. H. Mussen (Ed.), *Carmichael's manual of child psychology* (Vol. 2; 3rd ed.). New York: Wiley, 1970.

Feshbach, S. The dynamics and morality of violence and aggression: Some psychological considerations. *American Psychologist*, 1971, *26*, 281–292.

Feshbach, S. Reality and fantasy in filmed violence. In J. P. Murray, E. A. Rubinstein, & G. A. Comstock (Eds.), *Television and social behavior: II. Television and social learning*. Washington,

D.C.: U.S. Government Printing Office, 1972.

Feshbach, S. The development and regulation of aggression: Some research gaps and a proposed cognitive approach. In W. W. Hartup & J. DeWit (Eds.), *Origins of aggression*. The Hague: Mouton, 1978.

Feshbach, S. Policy issues and alternatives: Television and children. In S. Feshbach (Chair), *Reducing the inequity between advertisers and children: A psycho-educational program*. Symposium presented at the meeting of the American Psychological Association, Montreal, August 1980.

Feshbach, S., & Singer, R. D. *Television and aggression: An experimental field study*. San Francisco: Jossey-Bass, 1971.

Feshbach, S., & Singer, R. D. Television and aggression: A reply to Liebert, Sobol, and Davidson. In G. A. Comstock, E. A. Rubinstein, & J. P. Murray (Eds.), *Television and social behavior: V. Television's effects: Further explorations*. Washington, D.C.: U.S. Government Printing Office, 1972. (a)

Feshbach, S., & Singer, R. D. Television and aggression: Some reactions to the Liebert, Davidson, & Sobol review and response. In G. A. Comstock, E. A. Rubinstein, & J. P. Murray (Eds.), *Television and social behavior: V. Televison's effects: Further explorations*. Washington, D.C.: U.S. Government Printing Office, 1972. (b)

Flavell, J. H. *Cognitive development*. Englewood Cliffs, N.J.: Prentice-Hall, 1977.

Ford Foundation. *Televison and children: Priorities for research*. New York: Ford Foundation, 1976.

Foulkes, D., Belvedere, E., & Brubaker, T. Televised violence and dream content. In G. A. Comstock, E. A. Rubinstein, & J. P. Murray (Eds.), *Televison and social behavior: V. Television's effects: Further explorations*. Washington, D.C.: U.S. Government Printing Office, 1972.

Fraczek, A. *Cross cultural study of media violence and aggression among children: Comments on assumptions and methodology*. Paper presented at the Twenty-second International Congress of Psychology, Leipzig, Germany, July 1980.

Friedman, H. L., & Johnson, R. L. Mass media use and aggression: A pilot study. In G. A. Comstock & E. A. Rubinstein (Eds.), *Television and social behavior: III. Television and adolescent aggressiveness*. Washington, D.C.: U.S. Government Printing Office, 1972.

Friedrich, L. K., & Stein, A. H. Aggressive and prosocial television programs and the natural behavior of preschool children. *Monographs of the Society for Research in Child Development*, 1973, *38*(4, Serial No. 151).

Frodi, A., Macauley, J., & Thome, P. R. Are women always less aggressive than men? A review of the experimental literature. *Psychological Bulletin*, 1977, *84*, 1634–1660.

Furu, T. *Television and children's life: A before-after study*. Tokyo: Japan Broadcasting Corporation, 1962.

Furu, T. *The function of television for children and adolescents*. Tokyo: Sophia University Press, 1971.

Garbarino, J. Some ecological correlates of child abuse: The impact of socioeconomic stress on mothers. *Child Development*, 1976, *47*, 178–185.

Garbarino, J. *The human ecology of child abuse and neglect: A conceptual model for research*. Paper presented at the meeting of the Society for Research in Child Development, New Orleans, March 1977.

Garbarino, J., & Crouter, A. Defining the community context for parent-child relations: The correlates of child maltreatment. *Child Development*, 1978, *49*, 604–616.

Geen, R. G. Effects of frustration, attack, and prior training in aggressiveness upon aggressive behavior. *Journal of Personality and Social Psychology*, 1968, *9*, 316–321.

Geen R. G., & Stonner, D. Context effects in observed violence. *Journal of Personality and Social Psychology*, 1972, *25*, 145–150.

Gelfand, D. M., Hartmann, D. P., Lamb, A. K., Smith, C. L., Mahan, M. A., & Paul, S. C. The effects of adult models and described alternatives on children's choice of behavior management techniques. *Child Development*, 1974, *45*, 585–593.

Gelles, R. J. The social construction of child abuse. *American Journal of Orthopsychiatry*, 1975, *45*, 363–371.

Gelles, R. J., & Straus, M. A. Determinants of violence in the family: Toward a theoretical integration. In W. Burr, R. Hill, F. I. Nye, & I. Reiss (Eds.), *Contemporary theories about the family*. New York: Free Press, 1979.

Gelman, R., & Spelke, E. The development of thoughts about animate and inanimate objects: Implications for research on social cognition. In J. H. Flavell & L. Ross (Eds.), *Social cognitive development*. New York: Cambridge University Press, 1981.

George, C., & Main, M. Social interactions of young abused children: Approach, avoidance and aggression. *Child Development*, 1979, *50*, 306–318.

Gerbner, G. Violence in television drama: Trends and symbolic functions. In G. A. Comstock & E. A. Rubinstein (Eds.), *Television and social behavior: I. Media content and control*. Washington, D.C.: U.S. Government Printing Office, 1972.

Gerbner, G., Gross, L., Morgan, M., & Signorielli, N. The mainstreaming of America. *Journal of Communication*, 1980, *30*, 12–29.

Gerbner, G., Gross, L., Signorielli, N., Morgan, M., & Jackson-Beeck, M. The demonstration of power: Violence profile no. 10. *Journal of Communication*, 1979, *29*, 177–196.

Gerst, M. S. Symbolic coding operations in observational learning. *Journal of Personality and Social Psychology*, 1971, *19*, 7–17.

Gibbons, D. C. *Delinquent behavior* (2nd ed.). Englewood Cliffs, N.J.: Prentice-Hall, 1976.

Gil, D. C. *Violence against children: Physical child abuse in the United States*. Cambridge: Harvard University Press, 1970.

Ginsburg, H. J. *Variations of aggressive interaction among male elementary school children as a function of spatial density*. Paper presented at the meeting of the Society for Research in Child Development, Denver, 1975.

Ginsburg, H. J., Pollman, V. A., & Wauson, M. S. An ethological analysis of nonverbal inhibitors of aggressive behavior in male elementary school children. *Developmental Psychology*, 1977, *13*, 417–418.

Gittelman, M. Behavior rehearsal as a technique in child treatment. *Journal of Child Psychology and Psychiatry*, 1965, *6*, 251–255.

Glass, G. V., McGaw, B., & Smith, M. L. *Meta-analysis of social research*. Beverly Hills, Calif.: Sage, 1981.

Gleuck, S., & Gleuck, E. *Unraveling juvenile delinquency*. Cambridge: Harvard University Press, 1950.

Glucksberg, S., Krauss, R., & Higgins, E. T. The development of referential communication skills. In F. D. Horowitz (Ed.), *Review of child development research* (Vol. 4). Chicago: University of Chicago Press, 1975.

Gold, M. *Status forces in delinquent boys*. Ann Arbor: University of Michigan Press, 1963.

Goldfried, M. R., & d'Zurilla, T. J. A behavioral-analytic model for assessing competence. In C. D. Speilberger (Ed.), *Current topics in clinical and community psychology* (Vol. 1). New York:

Academic Press, 1969.

Goodenough, F. L. *Anger in young children*. Minneapolis: University of Minnesota Press, 1931.

Goranson, R. E. Media violence and aggressive behavior: A review of experimental research. In L. Berkowitz (Ed.), *Advances in experimental social psychology* (Vol. 5). New York: Academic Press, 1970.

Granzberg, G., & Steinbring, J. *Television and the Canadian Indian* (Tech. Rep.). Manitoba, Canada: University of Winnipeg, Department of Anthropology, 1980.

Green, D. R., Budd, K., Johnson, M., Lang, S., Pinkston, E., & Rudd, S. Training parents to modify problem child behaviors. In E. J. Mash, L. C. Handy, & L. A. Hamerlynck (Eds.), *Behavior modification approaches to parenting*. New York: Brunner/Mazel, 1976.

Green, E. H. Friendships and quarrels among preschool children. *Child Development*, 1933, *4*, 236–252.

Greenberg, B. S. British children and televised violence. *Public Opinion Quarterly*, 1975, *38*, 531–547.

Greenberg, B. S., & Atkin, C. K. *Current trends in research on children and television: Social behavior content portrayals and effects in the family context*. Paper presented at the meeting of the International Communication Association, Berlin, 1977.

Greenberg, B. S., & Reeves, B. Children and perceived reality of television. *Journal of Social Issues*, 1976, *32*(4), 86–97.

Gregory, I. Anterospective data following childhood loss of a parent: I. Delinquency and high-school dropout. *Archives of General Psychiatry*, 1965, *13*, 99–109.

Grusec, J. E. Effects of co-observer evaluations on imitation: A developmental study. *Developmental Psychology*, 1973, *8*, 141.

Grusec, J. E., & Kuczynski, L. Direction of effect in socialization: A comparison of the parent's versus the child's behavior as determinants of disciplinary tactics. *Developmental Psychology*, 1980, *16*, 1–9.

Hale, G. A., Miller, L. K., & Stevenson, H. W. Incidental learning of film content: A developmental study. *Child Development*, 1968, *39*, 69–77.

Hall, W. M. *Observational and interactive determinants of aggressive behavior in boys*. Unpublished doctoral dissertation, Indiana University, 1973.

Hallahan, D. P., Kauffman, I. M., & Ball, D. W.

Developmental trends in recall of central and incidental auditory material. *Journal of Experimental Child Psychology*, 1974, *17*, 409–421.

Hartmann, D. P. Influence of symbolically modelled instrumental aggression and pain cues on aggressive behavior. *Journal of Personality and Social Psychology*, 1969, *11*, 280–288.

Hartnagel, T. F., Teevan, J. J., & McIntyre, J. J. Television violence and violent behavior. *Social Forces*, 1975, *54*, 341–351.

Hartup, W. W. Friendship status and the effectiveness of peers as reinforcing agents. *Journal of Experimental Child Psychology*, 1964, *1*, 154–162.

Hartup, W. W. Aggression in childhood: Developmental perspectives. *American Psychologist*, 1974, *29*, 336–341.

Hartup, W. W. The social worlds of childhood. *American Psychologist*, 1979, *34*, 944–950.

Hartup, W. W., & deWit, J. The development of aggression: Problems and perspectives. In J. deWit & W. W. Hartup (Eds.), *Determinants and origins of aggressive behavior*. The Hague: Mouton, 1974.

Hawkins, R. P. Learning of peripheral content in films: A developmental study. *Child Development*, 1973, *44*, 214–217.

Hay, D. F., & Ross, H. S. The social nature of early conflict. *Child Development*, 1982, *53*, 105–113.

Hearold, S. L. *Meta-analysis of the effects of television on social behavior*. Doctoral dissertation, University of Colorado, 1979.

Heller, M. S. *Broadcast standards editing*. New York: American Broadcasting Companies, 1978.

Herbert, E. W., Pinkston, E. M., Hayden, M. L., Sajwaj, T. E., Pinkston, S., Cordua, G., & Jackson, C. Adverse effects of differential parental attention. *Journal of Applied Behavior Analysis*, 1973, *6*, 15–30.

Herrell, J. M. Use of systematic desensitization to eliminate inappropriate anger. *Proceedings of the 79th annual convention of the American Psychological Association*. Washington, D.C.: American Psychological Association, 1971.

Herzog, E., & Sudia, C. E. Children in fatherless families. In B. Baldwell & H. Ricciuti (Eds.), *Review of Child Development Research* (Vol. 3). Chicago: University of Chicago Press, 1973.

Hetherington, E. M., Cox, M., & Cox, R. Play and social interaction in children following divorce. *Journal of Social Issues*, 1979, *35*, 26–49.

Hetherington, E. M., Cox, M., & Cox, R. Effects of

divorce on parents and children. In M. E. Lamb (Ed.), *Nontraditional families*. Hillsdale, N.J.: Erlbaum, 1982

Hetherington, E. M., Stouwie, R. J., & Ridberg, E. H. Patterns of family interaction and child-rearing attitudes related to three dimensions of juvenile delinquency. *Journal of Abnormal Psychology*, 1971, *78*, 160–176.

Hicks, D. J. Imitation and retention of film-mediated aggressive peer and adult models. *Journal of Personality and Social Psychology*, 1965, *2*, 97–100.

Hicks, D. J. Effects of co-observer's sanctions and adult presence on imitative aggression. *Child Development*, 1968, *39*, 303–309.

Himmelweit, H. T., Oppenheim, A. N., & Vince, P. *Television and the child: An empirical study of the effects of television on the young*. London: Oxford University Press, 1958.

Hinde, R. A. *Biological bases of social behavior*. New York: McGraw-Hill, 1974.

Hinde, R. A. *The bases of social behavior*. New York: McGraw-Hill, 1975.

Hinde, R. A. The study of aggression: Determinants, consequences, goals and functions. In W. W. Hartup & J. deWit (Eds.), *Origins of aggression*. The Hague: Mouton, 1978.

Hoffman, M. L. Power assertion by the parent and its impact on the child. *Child Development*, 1960, *31*, 129–143.

Hoffman, M. L. Moral development. In P. H. Mussen (Ed.), *Manual of child psychology*. New York: Wiley, 1970.

Hoffman, M. L. Perspectives on the difference between understanding people and understanding things: The role of affect. In J. H. Flavell & L. Ross (Eds.), *Social cognitive development*. New York: Cambridge University Press, 1981.

Holmberg, M. S. *The development of social interchange patterns from 12 to 42 months: Cross-sectional and short-term longitudinal analyses*. Doctoral dissertation, University of North Carolina at Chapel Hill, 1977.

Hops, H., Walker, H., & Greenwood, C. R. Peers—a program for remediating social withdrawal in the school setting: Aspects of a research development process. CORBEH *Report #33*, October 1977.

Howitt, D. Attitudes towards violence and mass media exposure. *Gazette*, 1972, *18*, 208–234. (a)

Howitt, D. Television and aggression: A counter argument. *American Psychologist*, 1972, *27*, 969–970. (b)

Howitt, D., & Cumberbatch, G. *Mass media violence and society*. New York: Halsted, 1975.

Hoyenga, K. B., & Hoyenga, K. T. *The question of sex differences: Psychological, cultural, and biological issues*. Boston: Little, Brown & Co., 1979.

Huesmann, L. R., Eron, L. D., Lefkowitz, M. M., & Walder, L. O. Television violence and aggression: The causal effect remains. *American Psychologist*, 1973, *28*, 617–620.

Hutt, C., & Vaizey, M. J. Differential effects of group density on social behavior. *Nature*, 1966, *209*, 1371–1372.

Iannotti, R. J. Effect of role-taking experiences on role-taking, empathy, altruism and aggression. *Developmental Psychology*, 1978, *14*, 119–124.

Immelmann, K. *Introduction to ethology*. New York: Plenum, 1980.

Izard, C. E. *The face of emotion*. New York: Appleton-Century-Crofts, 1971.

Jersild, A. T., & Markey, F. U. Conflicts between preschool children. *Child Development Monographs*, 1935, No. 21.

Johannesson, A. Aggressive behavior among school children related to maternal practices in early childhood. In J. deWit & W. W. Hartup (Eds.), *Determinants and origins of aggressive behavior*. The Hague: Mouton, 1974.

Johnson, M. W. The effect on behavior of variation in the amount of play equipment. *Child Development*, 1935, *6*, 56–68.

Johnson, R. E. *Juvenile delinquency and its origins*. New York: Cambridge University Press, 1979.

Jolly, A. *The evolution of primate behavior*. New York: Macmillan, 1972.

Jones, E. E., & Davis, K. E. From acts to dispositions: The attribution process in person perception. In L. Berkowitz (Ed.), *Advances in Experimental Social Psychology* (Vol. 2). New York: Academic Press, 1965.

Joslyn, W. D. Androgen-induced social dominance in infant female rhesus monkeys. *Journal of Child Psychology and Psychiatry*, 1973, *14*, 137–145.

Joy, L. A., Kimball, M, & Zabrack, M. L. Television exposure and children's aggressive behavior. In T. M. Williams (Chair), *The impact of television: A natural experiment involving three communities*. Symposium presented at the meeting of the Canadian Psychological Association, Vancouver, 1977.

Kagan, J., & Moss, H. A. *Birth to maturity*. New York: Wiley, 1962.

Kaplan, R. M. On television as a cause of aggression. *American Psychologist*, 1972, *27*,

968–969.

Kaplan, R. M., & Singer, R. D. Television violence and viewer aggression: A reexamination of the evidence. *Journal of Social Issues*, 1976, *32*, 35–70.

Katz, R. C. Interactions between the facilitative and inhibitory effects of a punishing stimulus in the control of children's hitting behavior. *Child Development*, 1971, *42*, 1433–1446.

Katzman, N. I. Violence and color television: What children of different ages learn. In G. A. Comstock, E. A. Rubinstein, & J. P. Murray (Eds.), *Television and social behavior: V. Television's effects: Further explorations*. Washington, D.C.: U.S. Government Printing Office, 1972.

Kay, H. Weakness in the television-causes-aggression analysis by Eron et al. *American Psychologist*, 1972, *27*, 970–973.

Kempe, R. S., & Kempe, C. H. *Child abuse*. Cambridge: Harvard University Press, 1978.

Kendall, P. C., & Finch, A. J. A cognitive-behavioral treatment for impulsivity: A group comparison study. *Journal of Consulting and Clinical Psychology*, 1978, *46*, 110–118.

Kenny, D. A. Threats to the internal validity of cross-lagged panel inference, as related to "Television violence and child aggression: A follow-up study." In G. A. Comstock & E. A. Rubinstein (Eds.), *Television and social behavior: III. Televison and adolescent aggressiveness*. Washington, D.C.: U.S. Government Printing Office, 1972.

Kohn, M., & Rosman, B. L. Cross-situational and longitudinal stability of social-emotional functioning in young children. *Child Development*, 1973, *44*, 721–727.

Konecni, V. J., & Doob, A. N. Catharsis through displacement of aggression. *Journal of Personality and Social Psychology*, 1972, *23*, 378–387.

Korner, A. F. Methodological considerations in studying sex differences in the behavioral functioning of newborns. In R. C. Friedman, R. M. Richart, & R. L. VandeWiele (Eds.), *Sex differences in behavior*. New York: Wiley, 1974.

Korzenny, F. The perceived reality of television and aggressive predispositions among children in Mexico. *Resources in Education*, 1976. (ERIC Document Reproduction Service No. ED 122 336)

Kreuz, I. E., & Rose, R. M. Assessment of aggressive behavior and plasma testosterone in a young criminal population. *Psychosomatic Medicine*, 1972, *34*, 321–332.

Kummer, H. *Primate societies: Group techniques in ecological adaptation*. Chicago: University of Chicago Press, 1971.

Kushler, M. G., & Davidson, N. S. Community and organizational level change. In A. P. Goldstein, E. G. Carr, W. S. Davidson, & P. Wehr (Eds.), *In response to aggression: Methods of control and prosocial alternatives*. New York: Pergamon Press, 1981.

Lamb, M. E. The development of sibling relationships in infancy: A short-term longitudinal study. *Child Development*, 1978, *49*, 1189–1196.

Lambert, W. E., Yackley, A., & Hein, R. Child training values of English, Canadian, & French Canadian parents. *Canadian Journal of Behavioral Sciences*, 1971, *3*, 217–236.

Lange, D. S., Baker, R. K., & Ball, S. J. *Mass media and violence: A report to the National Commission on the Causes and Prevention of Violence*. Washington, D.C.: U.S. Government Printing Office, 1969.

Langerspetz, K. N. J., Wahlroos, C., & Wendelin, C. Facial expressions of preschool children while watching televised violence. *Scandinavian Journal of Psychology*, 1978, *19*, 213–222.

Langlois, J. H., & Downs, A. C. Mothers, fathers and peers as socialization agents of sex-typed play behaviors in young children. *Child Development*, 1980, *51*, 1227–1247.

Langlois, J. H., & Stephan, C. The effects of physical attractiveness and ethnicity on children's behavioral attributions and peer preferences. *Child Development*, 1977, *48*, 1694–1698.

Langlois, J. H., & Stephan C. Beauty and the beast: The role of physical attractiveness in the development of peer relations and social behavior. In S. S. Brehm, S. M. Kassin, & F. X. Gibbons (Eds.), *Developmental Social Psychology*. New York: Oxford, 1981.

Larsen, O. N., Gray, L. N., & Fortis, J. G. Achieving goals through violence on television. In O. N. Larsen (Ed.), *Violence and the mass media*. New York: Harper & Row, 1968.

Lefcourt, H. M., Barnes, K., Parke, R. D., & Schwartz, F. Anticipated social censure and aggression-conflict as mediators of response to aggression induction. *Journal of Social Psychology*, 1966, *70*, 251–263.

Lefkowitz, M. M., Eron, L. D., Walder, L. O., & Huesmann, L. R. Television violence and child aggression: A followup study. In G. A. Comstock & E. A. Rubinstein (Eds.), *Television and social behavior: III. Television and adolescent aggressiveness*. Washington, D.C.: U.S. Government Printing Office, 1972.

Lefkowitz, M. M., Eron, L. D., Walder, L. O., & Huesmann, L. R. *Growing up to be violent: A longitudinal study of the development of aggression*. New York: Pergamon Press, 1977.

Leiberman, A. F. Preschoolers' competence with a peer: Relations with attachment and peer experience. *Child Development*, 1977, *48*, 1277–1287.

Leifer, A. D., Collins, W. A., Gross, B. M., Taylor, P. H., Andrews, L., & Blackmer, E. R. Developmental aspects of variables relevant to observational learning. *Child Development*, 1971, *42*, 1509–1516.

Leifer, A. D., & Roberts, D. F. Children's responses to television violence. In J. P. Murray, E. A. Rubinstein, & G. A. Comstock (Eds.), *Television and social behavior: II. Television and social learning*. Washington, D.C.: U.S. Government Printing Office, 1972.

LeMasters, E. E. Parenthood as crisis. *Marriage and Family Living*, 1957, *19*, 352–355.

Lerner, R. M., & Lerner, J. Effects of age, sex and physical attractiveness on child-peer relations, academic performance and elementary school adjustment. *Developmental Psychology*, 1977, *13*, 585–590.

Lesser, G. Conflict analysis of fantasy aggression. *Journal of Personality*, 1958, *26*, 29–41.

Levine, R. A. Child rearing as cultural adaptation. In P. H. Leiderman, S. R. Tulkin, & A. Rosenfeld (Eds.), *Culture and infancy: Variations in the human experience*. New York: Academic Press, 1977.

Lewis, M. The social network systems model: Toward a theory of social development. In T. M. Field, A. Huston, H. C. Quay, L. Troll, & G. E. Finley (Eds.), *Review of human development*. New York: Wiley, 1982.

Leyens, J. P., Camino, L., Parke, R. D., & Berkowitz, L. Effects of movie violence on aggression in a field setting as a function of group dominance and cohesion. *Journal of Personality and Social Psychology*, 1975, *32*, 346–360.

Liebert, R. M., & Baron, R. A. Short-term effects of televised aggression on children's aggressive behavior. In J. P. Murray, E. A. Rubinstein, & G. A. Comstock (Eds.), *Television and social behavior: II. Television and social learning*. Washington, D.C.: U.S. Government Printing Office, 1972.

Liebert, R. M., Davidson, E. S., & Sobol, M. P. Catharsis of aggression among institutionalized boys: Further discussion. In G. A. Comstock, E. A. Rubinstein, & J. P. Murray (Eds.), *Television*

and social behavior: V. Television's effects: Further explorations. Washington, D.C.: U.S. Government Printing Office, 1972.

Liebert, R. M., & Schwartzberg, N. S. Effects of mass media. *Annual Review of Psychology*, 1977, *28*, 141–173.

Liebert, R. M., Sobol, M. P., & Davidson, E. S. Catharsis of aggression among institutionalized boys: Fact or artifact? In G. A. Comstock, E. A. Rubinstein, & J. P. Murray (Eds.), *Television and social behavior: V. Television's effects: Further explorations*. Washington, D.C.: U.S. Government Printing Office, 1972.

Liebert, R. M., Sprafkin, J. N., & Davidson, E. S. *The early window: Effects of television on children and youth*. 2nd ed. New York: Pergamon Press, 1982.

Light, R. J. Abused and neglected children in America: A study of alternative policies. *Harvard Educational Review*, 1973, *43*, 556–598.

Light, R. J., & Pillemer, D. B. Numbers and narrative: Combining their strengths in research reviews. *Harvard Educational Review*, 1982, *52*, 1–26.

Linne, O. *Reactions of children to violence on TV*. Stockholm: Swedish Broadcasting Corporation, 1971.

Lipsitt, L. P., & Levy, N. Electroactual threshold in the neonate. *Child Development*, 1959, *30*, 547–554.

Livesley, W. J., & Bromley, D. B. *Person perception in childhood and adolescence*. London: Wiley, 1973.

Loo, C. M. Effects of spatial density on social behavior of children. *Journal of Applied Social Psychology*, 1972, *2*, 372.

Loo, C. M. Important issues in researching the effects of crowding on humans. *Representative Research in Social Psychology*, 1973, *4*, 219–227.

Lorenz, K. *On aggression*. New York: Harcourt, Brace & World, 1966.

Lovibond, S. H. The effects of media stressing crime and violence upon children's attitudes. *Social Problems*, 1967, *15*, 91–100.

Lyle, J. Television in daily life: Patterns of use. In E. A. Rubinstein, G. A. Comstock, & J. P. Murray (Eds.), *Television and social behavior: IV. Television in day-to-day life: Patterns of use*. Washington, D.C.: U.S. Government Printing Office, 1972.

Lyle, J., & Hoffman, H. Children's use of television and other media. In E. A. Rubinstein, G. A. Comstock, & J. P. Murray (Eds.), *Television and social behavior: IV. Television in day-to-day life: Patterns of use*. Washington, D.C.: U.S. Government Printing Office, 1972. (a)

Lyle, J., & Hoffman, H. Explorations in patterns of television viewing by preschool-age children. In E. A. Rubinstein, G. A. Comstock, & J. P. Murray (Eds.), *Television and social behavior: IV. Television in day-to-day life: Patterns of use*. Washington, D.C.: U.S. Government Printing Office, 1972. (b)

Maccoby, E. E., & Jacklin, C. N. *The psychology of sex differences*. Stanford, Calif.: Stanford University Press, 1974.

Maccoby, E. E., & Jacklin, C. N. Sex differences in aggression: A rejoinder and reprise. *Child Development*, 1980, *51*, 964–980.

MacDonald, K., & Parke, R. D. *The relationship between parent-child play patterns and peer-peer competence*. Unpublished manuscript, University of Illinois, 1982.

Mahoney, M. J. A. *A residential program in behavior modification*. Paper presented at the meeting of the Association for the Advancement of Behavior Therapy, Washington, D.C., 1971.

Mallick, S. K., & McCandless, B. R. A study of catharsis of aggression. *Journal of Personality and Social Psychology*, 1966, *4*, 591–596.

Martin, B. Parent-child relations. In F. D. Horowitz (Ed.), *Review of child development research* (Vol. 4). Chicago: University of Chicago Press, 1975.

Martin, B., & Hetherington, E. M. *Family interaction and aggression, withdrawal and nondeviancy in children* (Progress Report). University of Wisconsin, National Institute of Mental Health, 1971.

Martin, W. E. Singularity and stability of profiles of social behavior. In C. B. Stendler (Ed.), *Readings in child behavior and development*. New York: Harcourt, Brace & World, 1964.

Marton, P., Minde, K., & Perotta, M. The role of the father for the infant at risk. *American Journal of Orthopsychiatry*, 1981, *51*, 672–679.

Marx, G. T. Civil disorders and the agents of social control. *Journal of Social Issues*, 1970, *26*, 19–58.

Mattsson, A., Schalling, D., Olweus, D., & Low, H. Plasma testosterone, aggressive behavior and personality dimensions in young male delinquents. *Journal of the American Academy of Child Psychiatry*, in press.

Maudry, M., & Nekula, M. Social relations between children of the same age during the first two years of life. *Journal of Genetic Psychology*, 1939, *54*, 193–215.

McCall, R. B., Parke, R. D., & Kavanaugh, R. D. Imitation of live and televised models in children 1–3 years of age. *Monographs of the Society for Research in Child Development*, 1977, *42*(5, Serial No. 173).

McCarthy, E. D., Laugner, T. S., Gersten, J. C., Eisenberg, J. G., & Orzeck, L. Violence and behavior disorders. *Journal of Communication*, 1975, *25*, 71–85.

McCord, J. Some child-rearing antecedents of criminal behavior in adult men. *Journal of Personality and Social Psychology*, 1979, *37*, 1477–1486.

McCord, W., McCord, J., & Howard, A. Familial correlates of aggression in non-delinquent male children. *Journal of Abnormal and Social Psychology*, 1961, *62*, 79–93.

McCord, W., McCord, J., & Zola, I. K. *Origins of crime: A new evaluation of the Cambridge-Somerville Youth Study*. New York: Columbia University Press, 1959.

McFall, R. M. A review and reformulation of the concept of social skills. *Behavioral Assessment*, 1982, *4*, 1–33.

McGhee, P. *The development of children's humor*. New York: Academic, 1980.

McGranahan, D. V. A comparison of social attitudes among American and German youth. *Journal of Abnormal Social Psychology*, 1946, *41*, 245–257.

McGrew, W. C. *An ethological study of children's behavior*. New York: Academic Press, 1972

McIntyre, J. J., & Teevan, J. J., Jr. Television violence and deviant behavior. In G. A. Comstock & E. A. Rubinstein (Eds.), *Television and social behavior: III. Television and adolescent aggressiveness*. Washington, D.C.: U.S. Government Printing Office, 1972.

McLeod, J. M., Atkin, C. K., & Chaffee, S. H. Adolescents, parents, and television use: Adolescent self-report measures from Maryland and Wisconsin samples. In G. A. Comstock & E. A. Rubinstein (Eds.), *Television and social behavior: III. Television and adolescent aggressiveness*. Washington, D.C.: U.S. Government Printing Office, 1972. (a)

McLeod, J. M., Atkin, C. K., & Chaffee, S. H. Adolescents, parents, and television use: Self-report and other-report measures from the Wisconsin sample. In G. A. Comstock & E. A. Rubinstein (Eds.), *Television and social behavior: III. Television and adolescent aggressiveness*. Washington, D.C.: U.S. Government Printing Office, 1972. (b)

McNeil, E. B. Aggression in fantasy and behavior. *Journal of Consulting Psychology*, 1962, *26*, 232–240.

Meichenbaum, D. H. *Cognitive behavior modification*. Morristown, N.J.: General Learning Press, 1974.

Meichenbaum, D. H. A self-instructional approach to stress management: A proposal for stress inoculation training. In C. Spielberger & I. Sarason (Eds.), *Stress and anxiety* (Vol. 2). New York: Wiley, 1975.

Meichenbaum, D. H., & Goodman, J. Training impulsive children to talk to themselves: A means of developing self-control. *Journal of Abnormal Psychology*, 1971, *77*, 115–126.

Mednick, S., & Christiansen, K. O., *Biosocial bases of criminal behavior*. New York: Gardner Press, 1977.

Mednick, S. A., Pollock, V., Volavka, J., & Gabrielli, W. F. Biology and violence. In M. E. Wolfgang & N. A. Weiner (Eds.), *Criminal Violence*. Beverly Hills, Calif.: Sage, 1982.

Menzies, E. S. *Preferences in television content among violent prisoners*. Masters thesis, Florida State University, 1972.

Mesch, M. The role of the attorney. In A. Glacier (Ed.), *Child abuse: A community challenge*. Buffalo, N.Y.: Henry Stewart, 1971.

Meyer, T. P. Effects of viewing justified and unjustified real film violence on aggressive behavior. *Journal of Personality and Social Psychology*, 1972, *23*, 21–29.

Milavsky, J. R., Kessler, R., Stipp, H., & Rubens, W. S. Television and aggression: Results of a panel study. In D. Pearl (Ed.), *Television and behavior: Ten years of scientific progress and implications for the eighties: II. State of knowledge papers*. Washington, D.C.: U.S. Department of Health and Human Services, 1982.

Milgram, S. *Obedience to authority*. New York: Harper & Row, 1974.

Miller, N. E. The frustration-aggression hypothesis. *Psychological Review*, 1941, *48*, 337–342.

Miller, W. B. Lower class culture as a generating milieu of gang delinquency. *Journal of Social Issues*, 1958, *14*, 5–19.

Minton, C., Kagan, J., & Levine, J. A. Maternal control and obedience in the two year old. *Child Development*, 1971, *42*, 1873–1894.

Mischel, W. Sex typing and socialization. In P. H. Mussen (Ed.), *Carmichael's manual of child psychology* (Vol. 2; 3rd ed.). New York: Wiley, 1970.

Mischel, W. Toward a cognitive social learning reconceptualization of personality. *Psychological Review*, 1973, *80*, 252–283.

Monahan, J. The prediction and prevention of violence. *Proceedings of the Pacific Northwest Conference on Violence and Criminal Justice*. Issaquah, Washington, 1973.

Monahan, J. *Predicting violent behavior*. Beverly Hills, Calif.: Sage, 1981.

Monahan, J., & Klassen, D. Situational approaches to understanding and predicting individual violent behavior. In M. E. Wolfgang & N. A. Weiner (Eds.), *Criminal violence*. Beverly Hills, Calif.: Sage, 1982.

Money, J., & Ehrhardt, A. A. *Man and woman, boy and girl*. Baltimore: Johns Hopkins University Press, 1972.

Moore, S. G. Correlates of peer acceptance in nursery school children. In W. W. Hartup & N. L. Smothergill (Eds.), *The young child*. Washington, D.C.: National Association for the Education of Young Children, 1967.

Mueller, C., & Donnerstein, E. The effects of humor-induced arousal upon aggressive behavior. *Journal of Research in Personality*, 1977, *11*, 73–82.

Murray, J. P. *Television and youth: 25 years of research and controversy*. Stanford, Calif.: The Boys Town Center for the Study of Youth Development, 1980.

Murray, J. P., & Kippax, S. From the early window to the late night show: International trends in the study of television's impact on children and adults. In L. Berkowitz (Ed.), *Advances in experimental social psychology* (Vol. 12). New York: Academic Press, 1979.

National Institute of Mental Health. *Television and behavior: Ten years of scientific progress and implications for the eighties: I. Summary report*. Washington, D.C.: U.S. Department of Health and Human Services, 1982. (a)

National Institute of Mental Health. *Television and behavior: Ten years of scientific progress and implications for the eighties: II. State of knowledge papers*. Washington, D.C.: U.S. Department of Health and Human Services, 1982. (b)

Neale, J. M. Comment on television violence and child aggression: A follow-up study. In G. A. Comstock & E. A. Rubinstein (Eds.), *Television and social behavior: III. Television and adolescent aggressiveness*. Washington, D.C.: U.S. Government Printing Office, 1972.

Newson, J., & Newson, E. *Four year old in an urban community*. London: Allen & Unwin, 1968.

Nielsen Television Index. *National audience demographics report, 1982*. Northbrook, Ill.: A. C. Nielsen Co., 1982.

Novaco, R. Anger and coping with stress. In J. Foreyt & D. Rathjen (Eds.), *Cognitive behavior therapy, theory, research and procedures*. New York: Plenum, 1978.

O'Donnell, C. R., & Worell, L. Motor and cognitive relaxation in the desensitization of anger. *Behavior Research and Therapy*, 1973, *11*, 473–482.

O'Leary, M. R., & Dengerink, H. A. Aggression as a function of the intensity and pattern of attack. *Journal of Experimental Research in Personality*, 1973, *7*, 61–70.

Olweus, D. Aggression and peer acceptance in adolescent boys: Two short-term longitudinal studies of ratings. *Child Development*, 1977, *48*, 1301–1313.

Olweus, D. Stability and aggressive reaction patterns in males: A review. *Psychological Bulletin*, 1979, *86*, 852–875.

Olweus, D. Familial and temperamental determinants of aggressive behavior in adolescent boys: A causal analysis. *Developmental Psychology*, 1980, *16*, 644–666.

Olweus, D. Development of stable aggressive reaction patterns in males. In R. Blanchard & C. Blanchard (Eds.), *Advances in the study of aggression* (Vol. 1). New York: Academic Press, 1982. (a)

Olweus, D. Continuity in aggressive and inhibited, withdrawn behavior patterns. *Psychiatry and Social Science*, 1982. (b)

Olweus, D., Mattsson, A., Schalling, D., & Low, H. Testosterone, aggression, physical and personality dimensions on normal adolescent males. *Psychosomatic Medicine*, 1980, *42*, 253–269.

Omark, D. R., & Edelman, M. S. Formation of dominance hierarchies in young children: Attention and perception. In T. Williams (Ed.), *Psychological Anthropology*. The Hague: Mouton Press, 1975.

Osborn, D. K., & Endsley, R. C. Emotional reactions of young children to TV violence. *Child Development*, 1971, *42*, 321–331.

Osofsky, J. D., & Danzger, B. Relationships between neonatal characteristics and mother-infant characteristics. *Developmental Psychology*, 1974, *10*, 124–130.

Paige, K. E. Effects of oral contraceptives on affective fluctuations associated with the menstrual cycle. *Psychosomatic Medicine*, 1971, *33*, 515–537.

Palmer, E. L., & Dorr, A. (Eds.), *Children and the faces of television: Teaching, violence, selling*. New York: Academic Press, 1980.

Paris, S. G., & Cairns, R. B. An experimental and ethological analysis of social reinforcement with retarded children. *Child Development*, 1972, *43*, 717–729.

Parke, R. D. Some effects of punishment on children's behavior. In W. W. Hartup (Ed.), *The Young Child* (Vol. 2). Washington, D.C.: National Association for the Education of Young Children, 1972.

Parke, R. D. Socialization into child abuse: A social interactional perspective. In J. L. Tapp & F. J. Levine (Eds.), *Law, justice and the individual in society: Psychological and legal issue*. New York: Holt, Rinehart and Winston, 1977. (a)

Parke, R. D. Punishment in children: effects, side effects and alternative strategies. In H. Hom & P. Robinson (Eds.), *Psychological processes in early education*. New York: Academic, 1977. (b)

Parke, R. D. Parent-infant interaction: Progress, paradigms and problems. In G. P. Sackett & H. C. Haywood (Eds.), *Application of observational-ethological methods to the study of mental retardation*. Baltimore: University Park, 1978. (a)

Parke, R. D. Children's home environments. In I. Altman & J. F. Wohlwill (Eds.), *Children and the environment*. New York: Plenum, 1978. (b)

Parke, R. D. Interactional designs. In R. B. Cairns (Ed.), *The analysis of social interactions*. Hillsdale, N.J.: Erlbaum, 1979.

Parke, R. D. On prediction of child abuse: Theoretical considerations. In R. Starr (Ed.), *Prediction of abuse*. Philadelphia: Ballinger, 1982.

Parke, R. D., Berkowitz, L., Leyens, J. P., West, S. G., & Sebastian, R. J. Some effects of violent and nonviolent movies on the behavior of juvenile delinquents. In L. Berkowitz (Ed.), *Advances in experimental social psychology* (Vol. 10). New York: Academic Press, 1977.

Parke, R. D., & Collmer, C. W. Child abuse: An interdisciplinary analysis. In E. M. Hetherington (Ed.), *Review of Child Development Research* (Vol. 5). Chicago: University of Chicago Press, 1975.

Parke, R. D., & Deur, J. L. Schedule of punishment and inhibition of aggression in children. *Developmental Psychology*, 1972, *7*, 266–269.

Parke, R. D., & Lewis, N. G. The family in context: A multi-level interactional analysis of child abuse. In R. Henderson (Ed.), *Parent-child in-*

teraction. New York: Academic Press, 1981.

Parke, R. D., Power, T. G., & Gottman, J. M. Conceptualizing and quantifying influence patterns in the family triad. In M. E. Lamb, S. J. Suomi, & G. R. Stephenson (Eds.), *The study of social interaction: Methodological issues*. Madison: University of Wisconsin Press, 1979.

Parke, R. D., & Sawin, D. B. Children's privacy in the home: Developmental, ecological, and child-rearing determinants. *Environment and Behavior*, 1979, *11*, 87–104.

Parke, R. D., & Tinsley, B. R. The early environment of the at-risk infant: Expanding the social context. In D. Bricker (Ed.), *Intervention with at-risk and handicapped infants: From research to application*. Baltimore: University Park Press, 1982.

Parnas, R. I. The police response to the domestic disturbance. *Wisconsin Law Review*, 1967, 914–960.

Pastor, D. L. The quality of mother-infant attachment and its relationship to toddlers' initial sociability with peers. *Developmental Psychology*, 1981, *17*, 326–335.

Patterson, G. R. Interventions for boys with conduct problems: Multiple settings, treatments and criteria. *Journal of Consulting and Clinical Psychology*, 1974, *42*, 471–481.

Patterson, G. R. The aggressive child: Victim and architect of a coercive system. In E. J. Mash, L. A. Hamerlynck, & L. C. Handy (Eds.), *Behavior modification and families*. New York: Brunner/Mazel, 1976.

Patterson, G. R. A performance theory for coercive family interaction. In R. Cairns (Ed.), *Social interaction: Methods, analysis, and evaluations*. Hillsdale, N.J.: Erlbaum, 1979.

Patterson, G. R. Mothers: The unacknowledged victims. *Monographs of the Society for Research in Child Development*, 1981, *45*(5, Serial No. 186).

Patterson, G. R. *Coercive family processes*. Eugene, Oreg.: Castilia Press, 1982.

Patterson, G. R., & Cobb, J. A. A dyadic analysis of "aggressive" behavior. In J. P. Hill (Ed.), *Minnesota symposia on child psychology* (Vol. 5). Minneapolis: University of Minnesota Press, 1971.

Patterson, G. R., & Cobb, J. A. Stimulus control for classes of noxious behavior. In J. F. Knutson (Ed.), *The control of aggression: Implications from basic research*. Chicago: Aldine, 1973.

Patterson, G. R., Cobb, J. A., & Ray, R. S. A social engineering technology for retraining the families of aggressive boys. In H. E. Adams & I. P. Unikel (Eds.), *Issues and trends in behavior therapy*. Springfield, Ill.: Charles C. Thomas, 1973.

Patterson, G. R., Littman, R. A., & Bricker, W. Assertive behavior in children: A step toward a theory of aggression. *Monographs of the Society for Research in Child Development*, 1967, *32*(Serial No. 113).

Patterson, G. R., Stouthamer-Loeber, M., & Loeber, R. *Parental monitoring and antisocial child behavior*. Unpublished manuscript, Oregon Social Learning Center, 1982.

Pedersen, F. A., Anderson, B. J., & Cain, R. L. An approach to understanding linkages between the parent-infant and spouse relationships. Paper presented at the Society for Research in Child Development, New Orleans, March 1977.

Peevers, B. H., & Secord, P. F. Developmental changes in attribution of descriptive concepts to persons. *Journal of Personality and Social Psychology*, 1973, *27*, 120–128.

Perry, D. G., & Bussey, K. Self-reinforcement in high and low-aggressive boys following acts of aggression. *Child Development*, 1977, *48*, 653–657.

Perry, D. G., & Bussey, K. *Social Development*. Englewood Cliffs, N.J. Prentice-Hall, 1983.

Perry, D. G., & Perry, L. C. Denial of suffering in the victim as a stimulus to violence in aggressive boys. *Child Development*, 1974, *45*, 55–62.

Persky, H. Reproductive hormones, moods, and the menstrual cycle. In R. C. Friedman, R. M. Richart, & R. L. Vande Wiele (Eds.), *Sex differences in behavior*. New York: Wiley, 1974.

Persky, H., Smith, K. D., & Basu, G. K. Relation of psychological measures of aggression and hostility to testosterone production in man. *Psychosomatic Medicine*, 1971, *33*, 265–277.

Piaget, J. *The moral judgement of the child*. London: Kegan Paul, 1932.

Pinkston, E. M., Reese, N. M., LeBlanc, J. M., & Baer, D. M. Independent control of a preschool child's aggression and peer interaction by contingent teacher attention. *Journal of Applied Behavior Analysis*, 1973, *6*, 115–124.

Pisano, R., & Taylor, S. P. Reduction of physical aggression: The effects of four strategies. *Journal of Personality and Social Psychology*, 1971, *19*, 237–242.

Pope, B. Socio-economic contrasts in children's peer culture prestige values. *Genetic Psychology Monographs*, 1953, *48*, 157–220.

Porter, G., & O'Leary, D. K. Marital discord and

child behavior problems. *Journal of Abnormal Psychology*, 1980, *8*, 287–295.

Porterfield, J. K., Herbert-Jackson, E., & Risley, J. R. Contingent observation: An effective and acceptable procedure for reducing disruptive behavior. *Journal of Applied Behavior Analysis*, 1976, *9*, 55–64.

Poulos, R. W., Rubinstein, E. A., & Liebert, R. M. Positive social learning. *Journal of Communication*, 1975, *25*, 90–97.

Power, T. G., & Parke, R. D. Play as a context for early learning: Lab and home analyses. In I. E. Sigel & L. M. Laosa (Eds.), *The family as a learning environment*. New York: Plenum, 1982.

Pulkkinen, L. Search for alternatives to aggression in Finland. In A. P. Medstein & M. Segall (Eds.), *Aggression in global perspective*. New York: Pergamon Press, 1981.

Quarfoth, J. M. Children's understanding of the nature of television characters. *Journal of Communication*, 1979, *29*, 210–218.

Quanty, M. B. Aggression catharsis: Experimental investigations and implications. In R. G. Geen & E. C. O'Neal (Eds.), *Perspectives on Aggression*. New York: Academic Press, 1976.

Quay, H. C. Personality dimensions in delinquent males as inferred from factor analyses of behavior ratings. *Journal of Research in Crime and Delinquency*, 1964, *1*, 33–37.

Quay, H. C. Personality and delinquency. In H. C. Quay (Ed.), *Juvenile delinquency research and theory*. New York: Van Nostrand Reinhold, 1965.

Redican, W. K. Facial expressions in nonhuman primates. In L. A. Rosenblum (Ed.), *Primate behavior: Developments in field and laboratory research* (Vol. 4). New York: Academic Press, 1975.

Reid, J. B., Patterson, G. R., & Loeber, R. The abused child: Victim, instigator or innocent bystander. In J. Bernstein (Ed.), *Response Structure and Organization*. Lincoln: University of Nebraska Press, 1982.

Reid, J. B., Taplin, P. S., & Lorber, R. A social interactional approach to the treatment of abusive families. In R. B. Stuart (Ed.), *Violent behavior: Social learning approaches to prediction, management, and treatment*. New York: Brunner/Mazel, 1981.

Reinisch, J. M. Prenatal exposure to synthetic progestins increases potential for aggression in humans. *Science*, 1981, *211*, 1171–1173.

Rheingold, H. L., & Cook, K. V. The contents of boys' and girls' rooms as an index of parents' behavior. *Child Development*, 1975, *46*, 459–463.

Richard, B. A., & Dodge, K. A. Social maladjustment and problem solving in school-aged children. *Journal of Consulting and Clinical Psychology*, 1982, *50*, 226–233.

Riddle, M., & Roberts, A. Delinquency, delayed gratification, recidivism, and the Porteus maze test. *Psychological Bulletin*, 1977, *84*, 417–425.

Rimm, D. C., & Masters, J. C. *Behavior therapy: Techniques and empirical findings*. New York: Academic Press, 1974.

Risley, T. R., & Baer, D. M. Operant behavior modification: The deliberate development of behavior. In B. M. Caldwell & H. M. Ricciuti (Eds.), *Review of child development research* (Vol. 3). Chicago: University of Chicago Press, 1973.

Rivers, W. L., Thompson, W., & Nyhan, M. J. *Aspen handbook on the media: 1977–79 edition*. New York: Praeger, 1977.

Robins, L. N. *Deviant children grown up*. Baltimore: Williams & Wilkins, 1966.

Robins, L. N. Aetiological implications in studies of childhood histories relating to antisocial personality. In R. D. Hare & D. Schalling (Eds.), *Psychopathic behavior*. New York: Wiley, 1978.

Robinson, J. P., & Bachman, J. G. Television viewing habits and aggression. In G. A. Comstock & E. A. Rubinstein (Eds.), *Television and social behavior: III. Television and adolescent aggressiveness*. Washington, D.C.: U.S. Government Printing Office, 1972.

Rokeach, M., Miller, M. G., & Snyder, J. A. The value gap between police and policed. In J. L. Tapp & F. J. Levine (Eds.), *Law, Justice, and the Individual in Society*. New York: Holt, Rinehart and Winston, 1977.

Rose, R. M., Holaday, J. W., & Bernstein, I. S. Plasma testosterone, dominance rank and aggressive behavior in male rhesus monkeys. *Nature*, 1971, *231*, 366–368.

Rosekrans, M. A. Imitation in children as a function of perceived similarity to a social model and vicarious reinforcement. *Journal of Personality and Social Psychology*, 1967, *7*, 307–315.

Rosekrans, M. A., & Hartup, W. W. Imitative influences of consistent and inconsistent response consequences to a model on aggressive behavior in children. *Journal of Personality and Social Psychology*, 1967, *7*, 429–434.

Rossiter, J. R., & Robertson, T. S. Children's television viewing: An examination of parent child consensus. *Sociometry*, 1975, *38*, 308–326.

Rotenberg, K. J. Children's use of intentionality in judgements of character and disposition. *Child Development*, 1980, *51*, 282–284.

Rothbart, M. K., & Derryberry, D. Development of individual differences in temperament. In M. E. Lamb & A. L. Brown (Eds.), *Advances in Child Developmental Psychology*. Hillsdale, N.J.: Erlbaum, 1981.

Rowell, T. *The Social Behavior of Monkeys*. Harmondsworth, Middlesex, England: Penguin, 1972.

Royal Commission. *Report of the Royal Commission on violence in the communications industry: II. Violence and the media: A bibliography*. Toronto: Queen's Printer for Ontario, 1977.

Rubin, J. Z., Provenzano, F. J., & Luria, Z. The eye of the beholder: Parents' view on sex of newborns. *American Journal of Orthopsychiatry*, 1974, *43*, 720–731.

Rubinstein, E. A. Television and the young viewer. *American Scientist*, 1978, *66*, 685–693.

Rubinstein, E. A. Television violence: A historical perspective. In E. L. Palmer & A. Dorr (Eds.), *Children and the faces of television: Teaching, violence, selling*. New York: Academic Press, 1980.

Rule, B. G. The hostile and instrumental functions of human aggression. In J. deWit & W. W. Hartup (Eds.), *Determinants and origins of aggressive behaviors*. The Hague: Mouton, 1974.

Rule, B. G., Nesdale, A. R., & McAra, M. J. Children's reactions to information about the intentions underlying an aggressive act. *Child Development*, 1974, *45*, 794–798.

Rushton, J. P. Effects of prosocial television and film material on the behavior of viewers. In L. Berkowitz (Ed.), *Advances in Experimental Social Psychology* (Vol. 12). New York: Academic Press, 1979.

Rutter, M. Sex differences in children's responses to family stress. In E. J. Anthony & C. Koupernik (Eds.), *The child in the family*. New York: Wiley, 1970.

Rutter, M., Tizard, J., & Whitmore, K. *Education, Health and Behavior*. London: Longman, 1970.

Ryan, E. D. The cathartic effect of vigorous motor activity on aggressive behavior. *Research Quarterly*, 1970, *41*, 542–551.

Sallows, G. *Comparative responsiveness of normal and deviant children to naturally occurring consequences*. Unpublished doctoral dissertation, University of Oregon, 1972.

Sallows, G. *Responsiveness between aggressive behavior in children and parent perception of child behavior*. Paper presented at the meeting of the Midwestern Psychological Association, Chicago, May 1973.

Santrock, J. W., Warshak, R. A., & Elliott, G. L. Social development and parent-child interaction in father custody and stepmother families. In M. E. Lamb (Ed.), *Nontraditional Families*. Hillsdale, N.J.: Erlbaum, 1982.

Savin-Williams, R. C. Dominance hierarchies in groups of early adolescents. *Child Development*, 1979, *50*, 142–151.

Savin-Williams, R. C. Social interactions of adolescent females in natural groups. In H. C. Foot, A. J. Chapman, & J. R. Smith (Eds.), *Friendship and social relations in children*. New York: Wiley, 1980.

Sawin, D. B. *Aggressive behavior among children in small playgroup settings with violent television*. Doctoral dissertation, University of Minnesota, 1973.

Sawin, D. B., & Parke, R. D. The effects of interagent inconsistent discipline on children's aggressive behavior. *Journal of Experimental Child Psychology*, 1979, *28*, 525–538.

Sawin, D. B., Parke, R. D., Harrison, A. N., & Kreling, B. *The child's role in sparing the rod*. Paper presented at the American Psychological Association, Chicago, September 1975.

Scaramella, T. C., & Brown, W. A. Serum testosterone and aggressiveness in hockey players. *Psychosomatic Medicine*, 1978, *40*, 262–265.

Schachter, S. The interaction of cognitive and physiological determinants of emotional state. In L. Berkowitz (Ed.), *Advances in Experimental Social Psychology* (Vol. 1). New York: Academic Press, 1964.

Schrader, C., Long, J., Panzer, C., Gillet, D., & Kornblath, R. *An anger control package for adolescent drug abusers*. Paper presented at the annual convention of the Association for the Advancement of Behavior Therapy, Atlanta, Georgia, 1977.

Schramm, W. The second harvest of two research-producing events: The Surgeon General's inquiry and Sesame Street. *Proceedings of the National Academy of Education*, 1976, *3*, 151–219.

Schramm, W., Lyle, J., & Parker, E. B. *Television in the lives of our children*. Stanford, Calif.: Stanford University Press, 1961.

Schwartz, H. J., Eckert, J., & Bastine, R. Die Wirkung eines aggressiven films auf Jugendliche unter värlierten ausseren Bedingungen. (Effects of an aggressive film on adolescents under varying external conditions.) *Zeitschrift fur Entwicklungspsychologie und Pädagogische Psychologie,* 1971, *3,* 304–315.

Sears, R. R. Relation of early socialization experiences to aggression in middle childhood. *Journal of Abnormal & Social Psychology,* 1961, *63,* 466–492.

Sears, R. R., Maccoby, E. E., & Levin, H. *Patterns of child rearing.* Evanston, Ill.: Ron Peterson, 1957.

Seidman, E., Rappaport, J., & Davidson, W. S. Adolescents in legal jeopardy: Initial success and replication of an alternative to the criminal justice system. In R. Ross & P. Gendreau (Eds.), *Effective Correctional Treatment.* Toronto: Butterworths, 1980.

Seligman, M. E. P. *Helplessness.* San Francisco: Freeman & Co., 1975.

Serbin, L. A., O'Leary, K. D., Kent, R. N., & Tonick, I. J. A comparison of teacher response to the preacademic and problem behavior of boys and girls. *Child Development,* 1973, *44,* 796–804.

Shantz, C. Social cognition. In P. Mussen (Ed.), *Carmichael's Manual of Child Psychology,* (Vol. 3; 4th ed.). New York: Wiley, 1983.

Shantz, D. W., & Vogdanoff, D. A. Situational effects on retaliatory aggression at three age levels. *Child Development,* 1973, *44,* 149–153.

Sherif, M. Experiments in group conflict. *Scientific American,* 1956, 54–58.

Shirley, M. M. *The first two years: A Study of 25 Babies: II. Intellectual development.* Minneapolis: University of Minnesota Press, 1933.

Siegel, A. E. Communicating with the next generation. *Journal of Communication,* 1975, *25,* 14–24.

Silbergeld, S., Brast, N., & Noble, E. P. The menstrual cycle: A double-blind study of symptoms, mood and behavior, and biochemical variables using enovid and placebo. *Psychosomatic Medicine,* 1971, *33,* 411–428.

Singer, J. L., & Singer, D. G. *Television, imagination and aggression: A study of preschoolers' play.* Hillsdale, N.J.: Erlbaum, 1981.

Slaby, R. G., & Crowley, C. G. Modification of cooperation and aggression through teacher attention to children's speech. *Journal of Experimental Child Psychology,* 1977, *23,* 442–458.

Slaby, R. G., & Quarfoth, G. R. Effects of television on the developing child. In B. W. Camp (Ed.), *Advances in behavioral pediatrics* (Vol. 1). Greenwich, Conn.: JAI Press, 1980.

Slaby, R. G., & Roedell, W. C. The development and regulation of aggression in young children. In J. Worell (Ed.), *Psychological Development in the Elementary Years.* New York: Academic Press, 1982.

Sluckin, A., & Smith, P. Two approaches to the concept of dominance. *Child Development,* 1977, *48,* 917–923.

Smith, P. K. Temporal clusters and individual differences in the behavior of preschool children. In R. P. Michael & J. H. Crook (Eds.), *Comparative Ecology and Behavior of Primates.* New York: Academic Press, 1973.

Smith, P. K. Aggression in a preschool playgroup: Effects of varying physical resources. In J. deWit & W. W. Hartup (Eds.), *Determinants and Origins of Aggressive Behavior.* The Hague: Mouton, 1974. (a)

Smith, P. K. Aspects of the playgroup environment. In D. V. Canter & T. R. Lee (Eds.), *Psychology and the Built Environment.* London: Architectual Press, 1974. (b)

Smith, P. K., & Connolly, K. J. *The Ecology of Preschool Behaviour.* New York: Cambridge University Press, 1980.

Smith, P. K., & Green, M. Aggressive behavior in English nurseries and playgroups. Sex differences and response of adults. *Child Development,* 1974, *45,* 211–214.

Snyder, J. J. A reinforcement analysis of interaction in problem and nonproblem families. *Journal of Abnormal Psychology,* 1977, *86,* 528–535.

Spinetta, J. J., & Rigler, D. The child-abusing parent: A psychological review. *Psychological Bulletin,* 1972, *77,* 296–304.

Spivack, G., & Shure, M. B. *Social adjustment of young children: A cognitive approach to solving real life problems.* San Francisco: Jossey-Bass, 1974.

Sroufe, L. The coherence of individual development. *American Psychologist,* 1979, *34,* 834–841.

Stark, R., & McEvoy, J. Middle class violence. *Psychology Today,* 1970, *4,* 52–65.

St. Clair, K. L. Neonatal assessment procedures: A historical review. *Child Development,* 1978, *49,* 280–292.

Stein, A. H., & Friedrich, L. K. Television content and young children's behavior. In J. P. Murray, E. A. Rubinstein, & G. A. Comstock (Eds.), *Television and social behavior: II. Television and social learning.* Washington, D.C.: U.S. Government Printing Office, 1972.

Stein, A. H., & Friedrich, L. K. Impact of television on children and youth. In E. M. Hetherington

(Ed.), *Review of child development research* (Vol. 5). Chicago: University of Chicago Press, 1975.

Steinmetz, S. K. Occupation and physical punishment: A response to Straus. *Journal of Marriage and the Family*, 1971, *33*, 664–666.

Steinmetz, S. K. *The cycle of violence: Assertive, aggressive and abusive family interaction.* New York: Praeger, 1977.

Steuer, F. B., Applefield, J. M., & Smith, R. Televised aggression and the interpersonal aggression of preschool children. *Journal of Experimental Child Psychology*, 1971, *11*, 442–447.

Stevens-Long, J. The effect of behavioral context on some aspects of adult disciplinary practice and affect. *Child Development*, 1973, *44*, 476–484.

Straus, M. A. Some social antecedents of physical punishment: A linkage theory interpretation. *Journal of Marriage and the Family*, 1971, *33*, 658–663.

Straus, M. A., Gelles, R., & Steinmetz, S. *Behind Closed Doors.* New York: Doubleday, 1980.

Strayer, F. F. Learning and imitation as a function of social status in macaque monkeys. *Animal Behavior*, 1976, *24*, 832–848.

Strayer, F. F. Social ecology of the preschool peer group. In W. A. Collins (Ed.), *Development of cognition, affect and social relations. Minnesota Symposia on Child Psychology* (Vol. 13). Hillsdale, N.J.: Erlbaum, 1980.

Stuart, R. B. Behavioral contracting within the families of delinquents. *Journal of Behavior Therapy and Experimental Psychiatry*, 1971, *2*, 1–11.

Stuart, R. B., & Tripodi, T. Experimental evaluation of three time-constrained behavioral treatments for pre-delinquents and delinquents. In R. D. Rubin, J. P. Brady, & J. D. Henderson (Eds.), *Advances in behavior therapy* (Vol. 4). New York: Academic Press, 1973.

Styczynski, L. E., & Langlois, J. H. The effects of familiarity on behavioral stereotypes associated with physical attractiveness in young children. *Child Development*, 1977, *48*, 1137–1141.

Suchowsky, G. K., Pegrassi, L., & Bonsignori, A. The effect of steroids on aggressive behavior of mice. *Acta Endocrinologica*, 1967, *119*, 48 (Supplement).

Surbeck, E. *Young children's emotional reactions to TV violence: The effects on children's perceptions of reality.* Doctoral dissertation, University of Georgia, 1973.

Surgeon General's Scientific Advisory Committee on Television and Social Behavior. *Television and growing up: The impact of televised vio-*

lence. Washington, D.C.: U.S. Government Printing Office, 1972.

Tams, V., & Eyberg, S. A group treatment program for parents. In E. J. Mash, L. C. Handy, & L. A. Hamerlynck (Eds.), *Behavior modification approaches to parenting.* New York: Brunner/Mazel, 1976.

Tannenbaum, P. H., & Zillmann, D. Emotional arousel in the facilitation of aggression through communication. In L. Berkowitz (Ed.), *Advances in experimental social psychology* (Vol. 8). New York: Academic Press, 1975.

Tanner, J. M. Physical growth. In P. M. Mussen (Ed.), *Carmichael's manual of child psychology* (Vol. 1). New York: Wiley, 1970.

Tauber, M. Parental socialization techniques and sex differences in children's play. *Child Development*, 1979, *50*, 225–234.

Thomas, A., Chess, S., & Birch, H. *Temperament and behavior disorders in children.* New York: New York University Press, 1968.

Thomas, M. H., & Drabman, R. S. Toleration of real-life aggression as a function of exposure to televised violence and age of subject. *Merrill-Palmer Quarterly*, 1975, *21*, 227–232.

Thomas, M. H., Horton, R. W., Lippincott, E. C., & Drabman, R. S. Desensitization to portrayals of real-life aggression as a function of exposure to television violence. *Journal of Personality and Social Psychology*, 1977, *35*, 450–458.

Thorndike, R. L. The effect of interval between test and retest on the constancy of the IQ. *Journal of Educational Psychology*, 1933, *24*, 543–549.

Tieger, T. On the biological basis of sex differences in aggression. *Child Development*, 1980, *51*, 943–963.

Tinsley, B. R., & Parke, R. D., The contemporary impact of the extended family on the nuclear family: Grandparents as support and socialization agents. In M. Lewis (Ed.), *Beyond the dyad.* New York: Plenum Press, 1983.

Toch, H. *Violent Men: An Inquiry into the Psychology of Violence.* Chicago: Aldine, 1969.

Turner, C. W., Fenn, M. R., & Cole, A. M. A social psychological analysis of violent behavior. In R. B. Stuart (Ed.), *Violent behavior: Social learning approaches to prediction management and treatment.* New York: Brunner/Mazel, 1981.

Turner, C. W., & Goldsmith, D. Effects of toy guns and airplanes on children's antisocial free play behavior. *Journal of Experimental Child Psychology*, 1976, *21*, 303–315.

Van Hooff, J. A. The facial displays of the catarrhine monkeys and apes. In D. Morris (Ed.), *Primate ethology*. Chicago: Aldine, 1967.

Wachtel, P. L. Psychodynamics, behavior therapy and the implacable experimenter: An inquiry into the consistency of personality. *Journal of Abnormal Psychology*, 1973, *83*, 324–334.

Wahler, R. G. Child-child interactions in five field settings: Some experimental analyses. *Journal of Experimental Child Psychology*, 1967, *5*, 278–293.

Wahler, R. G. Parent insularity as a determinant of generalization success in family treatment. In S. Salzinger, J. Antrobus, & J. Glick (Eds.), *The ecosystem of the sick child*. New York: Academic Press, 1980.

Wahler, R. G., House, A. E., & Stambaugh, E. E. *Ecological assessment of child problem behavior*. New York: Pergamon, 1976.

Walder, L. O., Abelson, R., Eron, L. D., Banta, T. J., & Laulicht, J. H. Development of a peer-rating measure of aggression. *Psychological Reports*, 1961, *9*, 497–556.

Wallerstein, J. S., & Kelly, J. B. *Surviving the breakup: How children and parents cope with divorce*. New York: Basic Books, 1980.

Walters, R. H. On the high-magnitude theory of aggression. *Child Development*, 1964, *35*, 303–304.

Walters, R. H., & Parke, R. D. Social motivation, dependency, and susceptibility to social influence. In L. Berkowitz (Ed.), *Advances in Experimental Social Psychology* (Vol. 1). New York: Academic Press, 1964.

Ward, S. Effects of television advertising on children and adolescents. In E. A. Rubinstein, G. A. Comstock, & J. P. Murray (Eds.), *Television and social behavior: IV. Television in day-to-day life: Patterns of use*. Washington, D.C.: U.S. Government Printing Office, 1972.

Warren, V., & Cairns, R. B. Social reinforcement satiation: An outcome of frequency or ambiguity? *Journal of Experimental Child Psychology*, 1972, *13*, 249–260.

Waters, E. Wippman, J., & Sroufe, L. A. Attachment, positive affect and competence in the peer group. Two studies in construct validation. *Child Development*, 1979, *50*, 821–829.

Watt, J. H., & Krull, R. An examination of three models of television viewing and aggression. *Human Communication Research*, 1977, *3*, 99–112.

Weintraub, S. A. Self control as a correlate of an internalizing-externalizing symptom dimension.

Journal of Abnormal Child Psychology, 1973, *1*, 292–307.

Weller, G. M., & Bell, R. Q. Basal skin conductance and neonatal state. *Child Development*, 1965, *36*, 647–657.

Wells, W. D. *Television and aggression: Replication of an experimental field study*. Unpublished manuscript, University of Chicago, 1973.

Wenar, C. Executive competence and spontaneous social behavior in one year olds. *Child Development*, 1972, *43*, 256–260.

White, B. L., Kaban, B., Shapiro, B., & Attonucci, J. Competence and experience. In I. C. Uzgiris & F. Weizmann (Eds.), *The structuring of experience*. New York: Plenum Press, 1976.

Whiting, B. B., & Edwards, C. P. A cross-cultural analysis of the behavior of children aged 3–11. *Journal of Social Psychology*, 1973, *91*, 171–188.

Whiting, B. B., & Whiting, J. W. M. *Children of six cultures: A psychocultural analysis*. Cambridge: Harvard University Press, 1975.

Wilmore, J. H. Body composition and strength development. *Journal of Health, Physical Education and Recreation*, 1975, *January*, 38–40.

Wilson, H. Parental supervision: A neglected aspect of delinquency. *British Journal of Criminology*, 1980, *20*, 203–235.

Winder, C. L., & Rau, L. Parental attitudes associated with social deviance in preadolescent boys. *Journal of Abnormal and Social Psychology*, 1962, *64*, 418–424.

Wolfe, B. M., & Baron, R. A. Laboratory aggression related to aggression in naturalistic social situations: Effects of an aggressive model on the behavior of college student and prisoner observers. *Psychonomic Science*, 1971, *24*, 193–194.

Wolkind, S., & Rutter, M. Children who have been ''in care''—an epidemiological study. *Journal of Child Psychology and Psychiatry*, 1973, *14*, 97–105.

Worsfold, V. L. A philosophical justification for children's rights. *Harvard Educational Review*, 1974, *44*, 142–157.

Wright, H. F. *Recording and analyzing child behavior*. New York: Harper & Row, 1967.

Yando, R., Seitz, V., & Zigler, E. *Imitation: A developmental perspective*. Hillsdale, N.J.: Erlbaum, 1978.

Yarrow, M. R., Campbell, J. D., & Burton, R. V. *Child rearing*. San Francisco: Jossey-Bass, 1968.

Yarrow, M. R., Scott, P. M., & Waxler, C. Z.

Learning consideration for others. *Developmental Psychology*, 1973, *8*, 240–260.

Young, L. *Wednesday's children: A study of child neglect and abuse*. New York: McGraw-Hill, 1964.

Young, W. C. The hormones and mating behavior. In W. C. Young (Ed.), *Sex and internal secretions* (3rd ed.). Baltimore: Williams & Wilkins, 1961.

Zahavi, S., & Asher, S. R. The effect of verbal instructions on preschool children's aggressive behavior. *Journal of School Psychology*, 1978, *16*, 146–153.

Zillmann, D. Excitation transfer in communication-mediated aggressive behavior. *Journal of Experimental and Social Psychology*, 1971, *7*, 419–434.

Zillmann, D. *Hostility and aggression*. Hillsdale, N.J.: Erlbaum, 1978.

CAROL S. DWECK, *Harvard University*
ELAINE S. ELLIOTT, *Harvard University*

CHAPTER CONTENTS

INTRODUCTION: MOTIVATION AND ACHIEVEMENT MOTIVATION

This chapter deals with motivational factors that affect learning and performance. More specifically, it deals with the many factors other than ability that affect the acquisition and display of ability, particularly intellectual ability. Among these are factors that determine whether children seek or avoid tasks they can profit from most, whether children successfully display the skills we know they have, whether they succeed in acquiring new skills we know they can.

A few comments on our approach to this chapter. First, since much achievement research has been conducted with adult populations, we often include findings from the adult literature when they are consistent with those of the child literature and are germane to the issue at hand. Second, we have attempted always to give conceptual shape to the domains we address. In many cases, therefore, our proposed formulations are intended to be preliminary and, we hope, thought-provoking.

*The authors thank the many people who have contributed in various ways to this chapter. In particular, they would like to acknowledge: the valuable input of colleagues at Harvard University and the University of Illinois; the editorial wisdom of Mavis Hetherington; the superb technical assistance of Joan Dolamore, Terry Kovich, and Naomi Dinces; and the support of grant BNS 79-14252 from the National Science Foundation, grant MH 31667 from the National Institute of Mental Health, and a Research Scientist Development Award from the National Institute of Mental Health to the first author.

Determinants of Performance

Motivation Versus Competence

Intellectual performance and achievement have long been highly prized by our society, and psychologists have shared this enthusiasm. However, too often we have assumed that the key to understanding achievement lies in defining intelligence, assessing its level, and charting the course of its development. Yet it is clear to us that independent of ability, motivational factors exert a profound influence on children's intellectual performance and achievement, not only in the laboratory (see V. C. Crandall, 1967; Dweck & Goetz, 1978; Nicholls, 1981; Weiner, 1972, 1974; Wine, 1982), but in the classroom (see Brophy & Good, 1974; Covington, 1980; Licht & Dweck, 1981; Weinstein, 1976); not only in the school years (e.g., V. C. Crandall & Battle, 1970; Parsons, in press), but later on in their careers (Cohen, 1977; Jencks, 1979; McClelland, 1961). Motivational factors determine such critical things as whether children actually pursue and master skills that they are fully capable of mastering and that they themselves value. In many cases these motivational tendencies appear to be entirely independent of children's "actual" ability, as reflected in a broad range of measures from task-specific to general ones.[1] These measures include prior performance on the task at hand, grades in the area in question, and scores on general assessments of intellectual competence, such as IQ tests (V. C. Crandall, 1969; Dweck & Licht, 1980; Weiner, 1972). This means that even among children who are highly proficient in the very skills a task requires, there are those who are highly vulnerable to debilitation. Indeed, as we will see, among females it may sometimes be the most competent who are most susceptible to debilitation (V. C. Crandall, 1969; Licht & Dweck, 1981; in press; Stipek & Hoffman, 1980).

In light of this, how can we understand why motivational factors are sometimes underemphasized in the study of intellectual performance? Perhaps this is because motivational processes are so varied and complex. Achievement motivation consists of a varied and complex set of assumptions, assessments, predictions, inferences, values, standards, and affective reactions that may be irrational, inaccurate, and contradictory. The wealth of research brought together in this chapter, however, demonstrates that these processes are nonetheless amenable to precise, systematic analysis. As Gentner (1982) points out, murky, illogical processes need not inspire theory and research of the same nature.

The Study of Motivation Versus Cognition

If researchers of achievement motivation/motivational development and those of cognition/cognitive development are both interested in intellectual growth and performance, how might we characterize their differing foci? Although the contrast may be blurring (see, e.g., Kahneman & Tversky, 1973; Nisbett & Ross, 1980), we suggest that those who study cognition have generally examined such things as the reasoning processes, inference rules, and problem-solving strategies that individuals *can* use under what are designed to be optimal, clearly structured conditions. Granting the individual's cognitive capabilities, those who study achievement motivational processes would focus more on such things as the reasoning processes, inference rules, and problem-solving strategies that an individual *actually* uses—the cognitive skills an individual actually displays—under a variety of conditions, often, for example, under stressful or unstructured, ambiguous conditions. This distinction is relevant to our treatment of achievement motivation in several ways. First, there are the *assessments* (e.g., of one's skills) and *inferences* (e.g., about causes of outcomes) that constitute major components of the motivational process. Here we are often most interested in cases where children's self-assessments and inferences systematically depart from "reality," particularly when the same children appear fully capable of sophisticated, accurate reasoning with respect to these factors under other circumstances. Second, there are the *cognitive consequences* of motivational processes. That is, motivational factors affect the attention and effort children can or do deploy, which in turn affect the cognitive skills they can or do bring to bear on the task. Here again, we are often most interested in cases where children's learning and performance systematically differ, in a positive or negative direction, from what appear to be their capabilities. Third, there are *metacognitive skills*—the regulatory processes—that include such activities as task analysis, strategy planning, and performance monitoring. Here we will be most concerned with instances where children fail to use their skills appropriately and with the consequences of this failure for their motivation and performance.

For purposes of clarity, we will attempt to maintain the distinction we have drawn between intellectual skills and motivational processes. We will not offer a definition or theory of intelligence. Instead we will tend to focus on specific intellectual/cognitive skills and specific instances of intellectual performance. Only at the end will we return to a consideration of the nature of intelligence and the relationship between intelligence and motivation.

The Domain of Inquiry

We will lay the groundwork for our exploration of achievement motivation and its development by asking first: What are the questions for a theory of motivation? We will follow this by asking: What are the questions for a theory of achievement motivation, in particular? Third, we will ask: What are the questions for a developmental theory of achievement motivation? The remainder of the chapter will be devoted to integrating literature that is germane to these latter questions, and to generating a framework for future theory and research. Specifically, we will review past theoretical approaches to achievement motivation, pinpointing the aspects of the achievement process on which each has focused, and examining the motivational constructs used to account for the phenomena in question. We will then attempt to integrate research findings from the various approaches, and this will be done within the context of a proposed preliminary model of achievement motivation. Essentially, we will walk through the sequence of achievement processes from task choice to performance evaluation, and we will analyze the cognitive and affective mediators of behavior at each step in the process. Along the way, we will explore in detail the patterns of factors that tend to facilitate learning and performance and those that are associated with impaired learning and performance, linking these patterns to well-known individual differences where appropriate. In this context, we will examine questions of developmental change as the child moves from early mastery motivation to later forms of achievement motivation. Finally, we will address issues in the study of socialization practices that promote achievement-producing motivational tendencies.

Questions for a Theory of Motivation

Atkinson (1964), in framing the underlying question of motivation as "What causes a response?" has captured with great simplicity the great complexity of the task facing students of motivation. More specifically, in his view, motivation involves the contemporaneous factors that incite and direct behavior; that influence the direction, the vigor, and the persistence of an action (see also Atkinson, 1969; Beck, 1978; Melton, 1955; Weiner, 1972). In

attempting to define what is and is not motivation, many investigators have explicitly focused on the goal-directed nature of motivated activity (e.g., Beck, 1978; Dollard & Miller, 1950; Kagan, 1972; Veroff, 1969). Some have also highlighted the dynamic (variable, energizing) nature of motivational forces, as opposed to more static attributes (endowments, abilities) that can influence the quality of the activity but do not in and of themselves serve an energizing or directive function (e.g., Beck, 1978). Furthermore, with regard to the classes of phenomena on which motivational forces act, Kagan (1972) makes the important point that motivational forces can activate and maintain cognitive activity and need not eventuate in overt actions. In sum, "motivation" may be viewed as referring to the contemporaneous, dynamic psychological factors that influence such phenomena as the choice, initiation, direction, magnitude, persistence, resumption, and quality of goal-directed (including cognitive) activity. The task of a theory of motivation is to identify these factors and to illuminate the mechanisms through which they influence goal-directed activity.

Questions for a Theory of Achievement Motivation

Within the above definition of motivation, any specific type of motivation would involve goal-directed activity with respect to a particular class of goals. Achievement motivation may be viewed as involving goals relating to competence—increases in competence and judgments of competence (see, e.g., V. J. Crandall, Katkovsky, & Preston, 1962; Heckhausen, 1981; Maehr & Nicholls, 1980). Building on the analysis presented by Nicholls and Dweck (1979), we may identify three such goals. One we will call the "learning" goal: to increase competence. This involves seeking to acquire knowledge or skills, to master or understand something new. The two others we will call the "performance"[2] goals: to obtain favorable judgments of one's competence, and to avoid unfavorable judgments of one's competence (see Dweck & Elliott, 1981; Nicholls, 1981). As we will see, all three goals can coexist, but the presence of one is sufficient (also necessary) to define a situation as an achievement situation.

How does this view of achievement motivation mesh with previous views? Generally it appears to coordinate previously distinct approaches. For example, the learning goal is embodied in the definition of achievement motivation offered by Heckhausen (1967), whereas the performance goals are embodied in the definition offered by V. J. Crandall, Katkovsky, and Preston (1960). In a related vein, this definition allows for different anticipated sources of reward for achievement behavior. Surprisingly, with regard to this issue, previous investigators have sometimes defined essentially nonoverlapping domains. Some have specified the attainment of approval for competence (and the avoidance of disapproval) as the primary goal/reward of achievement activity (e.g., V. J. Crandall, Katkovsky, & Preston, 1960). Others in defining achievement situations have tended to exclude situations involving mainly such "extrinsic" factors, and to include situations in which the anticipated reward of achievement behavior is the more intrinsic satisfaction that derives directly from success or mastery (e.g., Atkinson & Feather, 1966; Kukla, 1978).

In our view, both types of rewards can serve as legitimate aims of achievement activity, (1) as long as the judgment or approval that is sought is for competence and not simply for such things as compliance, conduct, neatness, or effort, and (2) as long as the intrinsic pleasure that is sought is for competence and is not solely pleasure in the activity itself. Such additional goals or rewards (or any others) may be present in achievement situations and may indeed affect behavior, but they do not define what is or is not an achievement situation (see Nicholls & Dweck, 1979).

Central to most past treatments of achievement-motivated activity has been the notion that the product of such activity must be amenable to evaluation against a standard of excellence (e.g., Atkinson, 1964; V. J. Crandall, Katkovsky, & Preston, 1960; Maehr & Nicholls, 1980; Veroff, 1969). This view is highly compatible with the view of achievement activity proposed here, for the pursuit of competence-related goals implies criteria for determining or monitoring attainment of these goals, that is, standards of competence against which one's products or progress can be evaluated.

We would like to note that because achievement motivation involves a complex set of affective and cognitive factors that can vary in qualitative ways, and because it can involve qualitatively different achievement goals, we will not tend to treat achievement motivation as having a "level"; nor will we consider children to be high or low in achievement motivation. In examining motivational processes, we may speak of high or low expectancies and of high or low values attached to different goals; we may speak of achievement-producing patterns of motivational factors and achievement-inhibiting patterns, but not of high and low achievement motivation.

To summarize, one can explicitly identify two distinct types of achievement goals—those centered around learning and those centered around performance. One can then view the study of achievement motivation as the study of psychological factors (other than ability) that affect the adoption and pursuit of these goals—that affect whether an achievement goal is pursued, which achievement goal is pursued, how vigorously it is pursued, and how long it is pursued. These factors, along with the child's ability, will combine to determine the quality of that child's learning and performance.

In this chapter, we will utilize the literature on achievement motivation and behavior to attempt to identify these factors and to illuminate central parts of the process. The focal motivational factors will include cognitive factors, affective factors, and the in-between area of value-related factors. The treatment of cognitive factors will entail an examination of such variables as assessments, assumptions/beliefs, predictions, inferences, and standards. The analysis of affective factors will address their nature, their relationship to the cognitive factors, and their possible roles in goal choice and goal-oriented performance. Value-related factors will include valence of, interest in, and salience of both the achievement goals themselves and the spectrum of associated goal-oriented activities (i.e., attractiveness of the ends as well as the means). Moreover, we will employ the available literature to explore these motivational factors as both dependent and independent variables, asking what conditions affect them, as well as how they affect goal-oriented activity.

Questions for a Developmental Theory of Achievement Motivation

What are the additional tasks for a *developmental* theory of achievement motivation? In a general sense, these tasks would consist of characterizing the processes at different points in their development and accounting for the transformations (see Kessen, 1966). For example, critical among these are the tasks of characterizing early forms of mastery motivation (in terms of factors responsible for initiating, maintaining, and reinforcing competence-increasing activities), describing how these differ from later forms of achievement motivation, and proposing ways of understanding how the changes might come about. Indeed, much of the section on development will be devoted to comparing and contrasting early mastery motivation with later achievement motivation and to examining major cognitive changes and environmental shifts that are likely to spur or guide the transitions.

Having outlined the domain of inquiry, we are now in a position to examine the various theoretical approaches to achievement motivation and to determine what part of the domain each has addressed. Surprisingly (or not surprisingly), we will find that what are often considered to be rival approaches have, in fact, staked out different territory to explore (see Dweck & Wortman, 1982). Thus, we will find that the theories are in many ways complementary and that each could profit handsomely from the analytic tools of the others.

THEORETICAL APPROACHES TO ACHIEVEMENT MOTIVATION: CONSTRUCTS, MODELS, MECHANISMS, AND ORIGINS

In this section we will compare four major theoretical approaches to achievement motivation that have been influential over the last three decades: need achievement theory, test anxiety theory, social learning theory, and attribution/learned helplessness theory (in the context of what we might call the present social-cognitive developmental approach). For each approach we will ask: What are the major motivational factors, how are they believed to work, and how are they believed to develop?

More precisely, in each case we will examine (1) the central motivational constructs of the theory, and the manner in which they are operationalized/measured; (2) the guiding model of motivation, and the proposed mechanisms through which the motivational factors influence goal-oriented activity; (3) the dependent phenomena (goal-oriented activity) most reliably predicted by the theory, and (4) the explanation of the origins and development of the focal motivational factors.

Surveying the theory and research over the last thirty years, we can see a trend from theories centered around affect/drive constructs, to theories built on more cognitive constructs, to theories that are beginning the attempt to integrate affective and cognitive processes. We see a trend from an emphasis on global predictors of behavior, to a search for specific mediators of behavior, to an attempt to understand the impact of general dispositions in terms of specific mediators. We detect a trend from explanatory mechanisms based on conditioned responses that are elicited by external stimuli (e.g., anticipatory goal responses) or by internal stimuli (e.g., drive-

reducing responses), to mechanisms based on cognitive construal of past and future events, to the beginning search for mechanisms that reflect the complex interplay of affective and cognitive anticipations and reactions. Finally, there is a broadening view of motivational development from simply the learning of the motivational components via socialization practices, to a view that also places motivational development in the context of cognitive and affective development and thus seeks to understand the qualitative changes that mark the evolution of the motivational processes.

In our treatment of each theory we will concentrate chiefly on the original formulations developed by the major early proponents of the theory. In addition, because in many of the theories the formulations applied to adults and (older) children have been virtually identical, we will draw on both sources to explicate the theories. We should also note that although we will address many research-related issues in this section, we will reserve for later the wealth of empirical findings that each tradition has contributed.

Need Achievement Theory

The pioneering theory in terms of a general conception of achievement motivation is the theory built around the need for achievement (McClelland, Atkinson, Clark, & Lowell, 1953; see Atkinson, 1957, 1964; Atkinson & Feather, 1966; Heckhausen, 1967). Not only has it inspired many of the subsequent approaches, but we find that, despite its limitations, no subsequent theory has so directly addressed the critical question of what incites or energizes achievement-oriented activity.

Constructs and Measures. The central constructs in this theory are "motives": the *motive to achieve success* and the *motive to avoid failure*, and they represent the strength of the individual's anticipatory goal reactions to potential success and failure outcomes (Atkinson, 1964; McClelland et al., 1953). These motives are also viewed as dispositional variables reflecting the individual's capacity for experiencing pride in goal attainment or shame in nonattainment (Atkinson, 1964). They are assessed, respectively, by means of a projective measure and a questionnaire. That is, for an assessment of the motive to achieve success, subjects are given the Thematic Apperception Test (TAT) (Murray, 1936) or the Children's Apperception Test (CAT), a series of pictures about which they are asked to generate stories. The stories are then scored for a variety of achievement subcategories including, among other things, positive goal anticipation, an emphasis on instrumental activity as a means to success, the expressed need or desire to do a good job, and positive affect associated with achievement strivings. It is assumed that the degree to which these themes are elicited and projected in these fantasy measures indicates the degree to which they are elicited when individuals find themselves in comparable real-life situations. Thus the sum of these themes is taken to reflect an underlying need or disposition to achieve (McClelland et al., 1953; see Murray, 1938).

The motive to avoid failure is equated with anxiety about failure and is conceived of as *inhibiting* achievement activities, activities that may result in failure (Atkinson, 1964). In other words, the motive to avoid failure is not viewed as providing an additional impetus to strive for success, but rather as constituting an opposing force. To assess the motive to avoid failure, subjects are given the Test Anxiety Questionnaire (TAQ) (S. B. Sarason & Mandler, 1952) or the Test Anxiety Scale for Children (TASC) (S. B. Sarason, Davidson, Lighthall, Waite, & Ruebush, 1960). These are self-report scales that ask about the degree to which the individual typically experiences anxiety symptoms when in or thinking about evaluative situations, and the frequency with which he or she ruminates about negative outcomes or revelations of inadequacy in such situations.

Individuals are then classified on the basis of the strengths of their two motives, and predictions are made concerning their tendency to undertake various achievement-oriented activities.

Model and Mechanisms. The model of motivation is essentially an Expectancy × Value model, in which "motivation" is a function of the strength of the motives, the expectancy of success, and the incentive value of success and failure (the positive incentive value of success is assumed to increase with the difficulty of the task, whereas the negative value of failure is assumed to decrease with increases in task difficulty).

The theory assumes (see, e.g., Atkinson, 1964) that for all individuals, achievement situations arouse both motives, that is, both positive anticipatory goal responses resulting in excitatory approach tendencies, and negative anticipatory goal responses resulting in inhibitory avoidance tendencies. Thus every achievement situation inevitably provokes an approach-avoidance conflict, the resolution of which is dependent on the relative strengths of the two tendencies. Persons in whom the motive to achieve success is the stronger of the two motives will mostly tend to approach, particularly to approach challenging but feasible tasks (tasks of intermediate difficulty). In contrast, those in whom the motive to avoid failure predominates are predicted to avoid, and to avoid most strongly tasks of intermediate difficulty. Indeed, according to the theory, such individuals would never engage in achievement-oriented activity were it not for other extrinsic motives and incentives (e.g., those relating to affiliative needs). Since much of the theory involves predictions about task approach and avoidance, the dependent measure of choice has most often been a task-preference measure: level of aspiration or risk preference (e.g., Atkinson, 1957; Atkinson & Raynor, 1974; McClelland, 1958) and, more recently, changes in these preferences over time (e.g., Atkinson & Birch, 1970, 1974), although measures of persistence and performance have been examined as well (Atkinson & Litwin, 1960; Feather, 1961, 1962). In brief, then, achievement cues are seen as eliciting anticipatory goal reactions—affective states that energize and direct achievement-oriented activity.

Origins and Development. The achievement motives are viewed as arising from associative conditioning in achievement situations. That is, to the extent that a child experiences pride in accomplishment or shame of failure in these situations, achievement cues begin to elicit anticipatory pride or shame reactions. The more frequent or intense the experience, the stronger the related motive (McClelland, Atkinson, Clark, & Lowell, 1953).

We find many aspects of this theory to be compelling. For example, anticipatory affect undoubtedly plays an important role in determining those activities that an individual approaches and those he or she tends to avoid. However, as we will discuss later, we do not believe that the experience of or the capacity to anticipate negative affect need prompt avoidance behavior when individuals believe they can escape from or avoid the unpleasant state by means of active approach behavior. (As we note below, the TAQ and the TASC, by virtue of the questions they contain, are likely to predict mainly avoidance tendencies.) Moreover, we suggest later that in addition to anticipatory goal responses, anticipatory "means" responses (anticipatory pleasure or displeasure in activities necessary for goal attainment) may guide approach to or avoidance of achievement activities.

In the research guided by the theory, multidimensional, somewhat indirect, measures of the multifaceted motives are used to predict a range of subsequent behavior. The researchers do not tend to ask whether specific subcategories of the measures (reflecting variously goal expectancies, goal values, emphasis on effort, etc.) might best predict specific aspects of behavior, such as choice versus persistence; or, in a related vein, whether different mediators may come into play at different points in the achievement process (see C. I. Diener & Dweck, 1978). Finally, as Weiner (1972) suggests, there is little attention paid to mental events that, for example, might influence expectancy formation and expectancy shifts or might underlie affective reactions to outcomes.

In summary, one might call for greater clarity, directness, and specificity of the independent measures and clearer links to the dependent measures, as well as greater attention to cognitive variables. On the whole, however, we find much to value in this tradition and feel that in the recent, almost exclusive, focus on cognition, many have tended to overlook some of the field's most interesting insights.

Test Anxiety Theory

Another important theory based on the notion that acquired motives or drives can energize or interfere with productive achievement activity is the theory of test anxiety (Mandler & Sarason, 1952; S. B. Sarason, Davidson, Lighthall, Waite, & Ruebush, 1960; S. B. Sarason & Mandler, 1952; S. B. Sarason, Mandler, & Craighill, 1952), which was also elaborated first for adults (e.g., Mandler & Sarason, 1952) and then extended successfully to children (S. B. Sarason et al., 1960). It has spawned a long and productive research tradition, with even the earliest work foreshadowing more recent trends—for example, in the attention to cognitions that accompany and might influence performance (e.g., Doris & Sarason, 1955; Mandler & Sarason, 1952) or in the use of systematic experimentation to simulate and illuminate the workings of individual differences (e.g., Mandler & Watson, 1966; I. G. Sarason, 1958; S. B. Sarason et al., 1952). (For reviews of this literature see I. G. Sarason, 1982; Wine, 1971, 1982. For comparison and integration with other approaches see Dweck & Wortman, 1982; Hill, 1972.)

Constructs and Measures. The central construct of the theory is ''test anxiety,'' an acquired drive that is elicited by evaluative cues. This drive, in turn, elicits either task-relevant or task-irrelevant responses, and thereby enhances or interferes with performance. Individuals are believed to differ in the degree to which evaluative cues elicit the anxiety drive and in the degree to which anxiety elicits task-relevant versus task-irrelevant responses (Mandler & Sarason, 1952).

Despite this formulation of anxiety as potentially facilitating or debilitating, most of the theory and research has centered around its debilitating properties. Indeed, the measures that are typically employed as the sole measures of anxiety appear to address mainly debilitating tendencies, and, in fact, high scores are seen as predictive of debilitation. That is, as noted earlier, the Test Anxiety Questionnaire (TAQ) for adults (Mandler & Sarason, 1952) and the Test Anxiety Scale for Children (TASC) (S. B. Sarason et al., 1960) focus heavily on the individual's tendency to worry about failure and humiliation in evaluative situations and to experience unpleasant symptoms in those situations. (Alpert and Haber, 1960, in order to test more fully the implications of the theory, constructed a facilitating anxiety scale similar in structure to the TAQ. They report increased prediction of performance when the two scales are used in conjunction.)

Model and Mechanisms. The theory is based essentially on a Habit × Drive model of motivation, one in which drives are conceived of as strong internal stimuli which elicit responses that tend to reduce the drive (à la Miller & Dollard, 1941). In the view of Mandler and Sarason (1952), a variety of learned drives may be operative in achievement situations. For example, there are task drives (such as ''the need to achieve and finish the task'') that elicit and are reduced by responses leading to task completion. Working with or against such drives is the anxiety drive, which elicits responses of two sorts: (1) responses that are task-relevant, like those elicited by task drives, and that serve to reduce anxiety by leading to task completion, and (2) responses that are task-irrelevant, incompatible, or interfering. According to Mandler and Sarason (1952), these latter reactions may be manifested in a variety of ways, ways that appear to us to belong in conceptually distinct categories. Some of these manifestations appear to involve the manner in which the anxiety is experienced or interpreted (e.g., as feelings of inadequacy or helplessness), others involve expectations that are cued by (or that cue) the anxiety (e.g., anticipation of punishment or loss of esteem), others appear to involve concomitant physiological states (e.g., heightened somatic reactions), and others appear to involve resulting instrumental avoidance responses (e.g., implicit attempts to leave the test situation). It is only this final type of response that would seem to have drive-reducing consequences.

To continue, the theory predicts that increasing the anxiety drive will result in poorer performance for individuals who have task-irrelevant responses in their repertoire, but will lead to improved performance for those with predominantly task-relevant responses in their repertoire (S. B. Sarason, Mandler, & Craighill, 1952). Thus, the focal dependent measure in much anxiety research has been quality of performance, as a joint function of individual differences and situational factors that would influence anxiety level. In addition, because of predictions about the nature of the interfering anxiety reactions, dependent measures have been included that ask subjects to report on the cognitions that accompanied their performance or that directly monitor the occurrence of task-avoidant responses (e.g., see Nottelman & Hill, 1977).

Origins and Development. S. B. Sarason et al. (1960) proposed that debilitating anxiety reactions begin in early childhood when children who fail to meet the overly high standards set by their parents meet instead with negative evaluations of their adequacy. This pattern is thought to eventuate in a strong desire for approval and a strong fear of failure (see Hill & Sarason, 1966; Ruebush, 1963). However, as Wine (1982) points out, relatively little systematic research has been devoted to examining directly how differences in evaluation anxiety arise.

In summary, anxiety theory, growing out of the S-R drive tradition, may be seen as having helped pave the way for theories that examine achievement cognitions and affect-cognition linkages and for theories that strive to shed light on the precise way in which these factors influence moment-to-moment performance.

Social Learning Theory

In response to the fact that achievement motivation research neglected children and that child development research neglected achievement motivation, the Crandalls and their associates instituted their ground-breaking program of research on children's achievement motivation and its socialization (Battle, 1965, 1966; V. C. Crandall, 1967, 1969; V. C. Crandall, Katkovsky, & Crandall, 1965; V. J. Crandall, 1963; V. J. Crandall, Katkovsky, & Preston, 1960, 1962). The clarity of their concepts and the precision of their measures provided, from the beginning, findings that remain among our most reliable and important.

Constructs and Measures. Several beliefs guided the approach of this group and served to distinguish it from those of its predecessors. First, they did not conceive of achievement as a unitary domain, but rather as consisting of many skill areas (e.g., intellectual, physical, artistic), in each of which a child might hold different values or expectancies. Second, even within areas, they did not choose to construct a global index of achievement motivation, but rather focused on more specific concepts that they believed might increase predictive power and, in addition, might elucidate the relationships among the concepts themselves (V. J. Crandall, 1963; V. J. Crandall et al., 1960). Thus, in this Expectancy × Value theory, expectancies (of several types) and values were precisely defined, with specific scales constructed (V. C. Crandall, 1969; V. C. Crandall et al., 1965) and specific experimental measures devised to assess them (e.g., V. C. Crandall & McGhee, 1968).

Origins and Development. Individual differences were seen as having their roots in patterns of parent-child interaction. Thus, in the monumental Fels Longitudinal Study, parents' (mostly mothers') behavior and children's own emerging characteristics were regularly assessed over the subject's childhood years and into adulthood to illuminate the child-rearing antecedents of adaptive and maladaptive achievement tendencies (see V. C. Crandall & Battle, 1970; V. C. Crandall, Dewey, Katkovsky, and Preston, 1964, for reviews of the results of this research.)

In sum, the precise measurement of component motivational factors that is the hallmark of this tradition has allowed isolation of specific individual difference (e.g., sex differences in expectancy of success), as well as systematic sleuthing to discover the immediate and historical determinants of such differences.

Attribution and Learned Helplessness Approaches

The attributional approach (e.g., Weiner, 1972; Weiner, Frieze, Kukla, Reed, Rest, & Rosenbaum, 1971; Weiner & Kukla, 1970) and the learned helplessness approach (Dweck, 1975; Dweck & Reppucci, 1973; see Seligman, Maier, & Solomon, 1971) to achievement motivation are based on the assumption that individuals' beliefs about the outcomes they experience guide their subsequent behavior in that and analogous situations. Thus, the focus has been on the specific cognitions about success and failure that mediate persistence on achievement tasks. We believe that this narrowing of focus has had some extremely positive effects as well as some less desirable ones. On the positive side, putting a circumscribed portion of the achievement process under the microscope has allowed us to explore and manipulate that process with new precision. However, on the negative side, putting it under the microscope at times made it seem large enough to constitute the entire process. Happily, as we will see, the view is once again broadening, and connections to other parts of the process are being more widely examined.

Constructs, Measures, Model, and Mechanisms. The overriding emphasis of these approaches has been on the expectancy part of an Expectancy × Value model, with particular attention to changes in expectancy as a function of success and failure outcomes. It is assumed that the manner in which one interprets outcomes (in particular the cause to which one attributes them) guides hopes of subsequent success and thereby determines persistence. Different causal attributions are viewed as implying different probabilities of future success. For example, it is predicted that when an individual attributes a failure to a lack of ability, expectancies (and persistence) will decrease more rapidly than when failure is attributed to a more variable or controllable factor like effort (Dweck & Reppucci, 1973; McMahan, 1973; Weiner & Kukla, 1970).

Attributions have been assessed in actual performance situations through a great variety of means including forced choice measures, open-ended questions, and "talk-aloud" techniques (e.g., C. I. Diener & Dweck, 1978; Nicholls, 1975; Parsons, 1978; Weiner et al., 1971). Attributional dispositions have also been assessed by means of questionnaires (e.g., Dweck & Reppucci, 1973; Weiner & Kukla, 1970). Also, attributions have been manipulated directly and indirectly in a variety of ways, for example, through different types of instructions and feedback (e.g., Andrews & Debus, 1978; Chapin & Dyck, 1976; Dweck, 1975; Dweck, Davidson, Nelson, & Enna, 1978). The measured and manipulated attributions have then been related to concomitant changes in expectancies and persistence.

The learned helplessness approach may be said to differ from the general attributional approach in that its primary concern has been with understanding individual differences in the *pattern* of cognitions that accompany performance changes in the face of failure (differences that are independent of ability and goal value). Although much of the work has centered on attributions associated with facilitation or impairment, attention has been given as well to the occurrence, nature, and timing of various achievement cognitions (see C. I. Diener & Dweck, 1978).

Origins and Development. Because these approaches have highlighted specific, identifiable achievement beliefs involving specific, identifiable inference processes, they have fostered much developmental research. First, this characteristic has enabled researchers to generate and test detailed hypotheses about environmental factors (or about patterns of child-environment interactions) that favor particular inferences and thus might foster particular attributional styles (e.g., Ames, Ames, & Felker, 1977; Dweck, Davidson, Nelson, & Enna, 1978; Feldman & Bernstein, 1977). Second, these approaches appear to have provided useful analytic tools for other areas of developmental psychology, such as the study of peer relationships (Goetz & Dweck, 1980; Karniol & Ross, 1976). Third, the concern with inference processes and perceptions of causality has enabled achievement researchers to make contact with cognitive development and thus to be interested in such questions as: What information do children of different ages use and how do they use this information to make inferences? (e.g., Karabenick & Heller, 1976; Kun, 1977; Shultz & Butkowsky, 1977; Shultz & Mendelson, 1975; Surber, 1980). Although too often the observed differences have not been tied back into motivation (i.e., to show how or whether changes in cognitive processing influence relevant achievement motivational processes), this contact with cognitive developmental theory has marked an important new direction in achievement research. It has provided a framework for generating hypotheses about qualitative changes in achievement processes with age.

In sum, we feel that the attributional approach has opened truly important avenues of exploration and must constitute a major part of a comprehensive theory. However, even with recent attention to affective factors, it does not by itself constitute a comprehensive theory. That is, analysis of causal cognitions and consequent affect has illuminated critical mechanisms of persistence but has not provided all the factors (cognitive or affective) that incite, direct, and maintain achievement-oriented activity. For example, it has not explicitly addressed questions of the value of different goals and means (see Kruglanski, 1975; Nicholls, 1979b). Thus it has concentrated on why people expect to succeed, but not on why they want to succeed.

When these four approaches are viewed together, it becomes clear that a comprehensive theory of achievement motivation must ultimately integrate affect of various sorts and cognitions of various sorts, and must describe how they interact over time to determine the nature and quality of achievement activity. Indeed, a number of investigators have begun to propose achievement models (or models applicable to achievement) that incorporate affective and cognitive variables from a variety of traditions (e.g., A. Bandura, 1980; Harter & Connell, 1981; Parsons, in press; Weiner, 1982). In the next section we will draw on the range of theories and the research findings they have generated to spell out the affective and cognitive elements that might enter into a comprehensive theory, and to suggest ways in which these elements might work to influence achievement.

ACHIEVEMENT MOTIVATION: COMPONENTS AND PROCESSES

The integrative model we will propose draws on past theories to portray a dynamic set of cognitive, affective, and value-related variables that may guide children's choice and pursuit of achievement goals. In this preliminary formulation we attempt to maintain an emphasis on specific mediators and to suggest the flow of the process, while integrating questions, concerns, constructs, and findings from different traditions. As with most past achievement theories, the formulation is cast in expectancy-value terms. It is thus built around the subjective expectancies and values that children may attach to different achievement goals and activities.

The model is intended as an idealized representation of achievement motivational processes. We do not propose that children consider the variables in any systematic or exhaustive way, or that children enact the processes in any intentional or explicit way (see also Covington, 1980; Dweck & Wortman, 1982; Heckhausen, 1981). Rather, we suggest that available information is likely to be processed in a selective, subjective, less than conscious fashion, that the resulting expectancies, values, and goals tendencies are likely to be impressionistic blends of cognition and affect, and that the resulting behavior is often likely to be a response to these poorly articulated states. Thus, although we do not view affect and cognition as truly separable, for purposes of clarity we will treat them as somewhat distinct, interacting processes.

As we noted at the outset, we do not seek to explore children's capacity for engaging in systematic, rational, affect-free information processing when they are given a defined set of information; rather, we seek to examine what children tend to do in relatively unconstrained situations where they can select and organize the information that they perceive to be relevant to their concerns. Given the inevitability of biases and distortions, what becomes interesting is to consider the causes (personal and situational) and consequences of particular choices, whether they appear rational or not. Thus the model is a preliminary attempt to spell out many of the possible choices, to examine the factors that orient children toward particular choices, and to explore the consequences of those choices.

Overview of Cognitive and Affective Processes

Figure 1 represents an integration and elaboration of the motivational processes proposed by previous theories. Figure 2 takes what is a fundamental component in virtually every theory—goal expectancies—and depicts the factors potentially involved in the formation of expectancies.

More specifically, Figure 1 portrays the affective and cognitive processes potentially involved in the (1) instigation, (2) direction, (3) maintenance, and (4) reinforcement of achievement-oriented activity. Indeed, each successive line of the figure may be seen as bringing into sharper focus one of these phases. (Of course, they are by no means discrete phases, and there may be enormous carry-over or interplay among the processes in each phase.)

Essentially, we may conceive of the child as entering an achievement situation with particular cognitive sets (beliefs, theories, etc.) and with existing affective states, although these sets and states may be greatly influenced by situational cues. The cognitive sets, situational cues, and affective states are seen as influencing the salience of the different goals (and means to those goals), and as contributing to the expectancies and values attached to them.

How do the expectancies and values of the salient goals and means then influence the actual selection of goals and means? Or, how are expectancies and values represented and considered? It is possible, as implied by the more cognitive approaches, that they may sometimes simply and directly take the form of cognitions about what one can and wants to accomplish, with different goals being compared to each other in terms of some combination of "can" and "want." Or, we might combine and elaborate the views of Kagan (1972) and McClelland, Atkinson, Clark, and Lowell (1953) to suggest another possible mechanism. According to Kagan, motivation involves activating the cognitive representations of goals, and according to McClelland et al., motivation involves anticipatory affective responses to goals. Thus one might propose that given particular expectancies and values, the child may activate or generate cognitive representations of salient goals and, we would add, means (Goal/Means Represen-

Goal Formation:

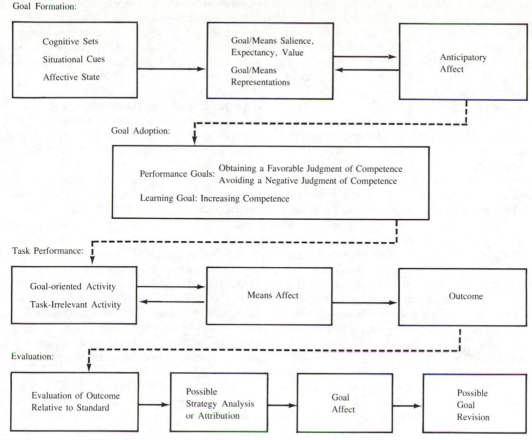

Figure 1. Achievement Motivation: Proposed Processes

tations). That is, a small, biased sampling of possible activities and outcomes may take place. The child may then experience or anticipate affective reactions in conjunction with each—for example, dread or excitement in task initiation, boredom or enjoyment of task activity, shame or pride in outcomes—and in this way may gain a sense of what courses of action will make him or her feel better or worse in the short or long run. (See Mischel, 1981, for a treatment of cognitive representations of goals and goal ideation that facilitate or interfere with goal attainment in situations requiring delay of gratification. See Parsons, in press, for a discussion of anticipatory affect.)

In any case, both cognitions about, and affective reactions to, likely or valued events may guide choice of achievement goals and goal-oriented activities. These, along with the positive or negative affect that derives from the activity (e.g., enjoyment or boredom), may then work to facilitate or interfere

with task performance. At some point, evaluation of the progress or product takes place. The evaluation may prompt a strategy analysis or an attribution, and depending on the conclusion, children may either maintain or alter their goals and goal-directed activity.

Using the wealth of findings from achievement research in the various traditions, we will now explore in detail specific parts of the process. Because achievement goals must lie at the heart of any analysis of achievement motivation, we will begin with an examination of the goals themselves and of the factors that may predispose children to focus on specific goals.

A Preliminary Model

Cognitive Sets and Achievement Goals

As we will see, the different achievement goals lead children to structure achievement situations in very different ways. That is, seeking to learn versus seeking to obtain competence judgments will lead children to process information differently: to define the variables differently, to judge them differently, to weight and combine them differently (see Nicholls, 1981). Table 1 outlines the two types of achievement goals and the different tendencies that they appear to foster.

But first we might ask: what orients children toward these different goals? In addition to the specific factors affecting goal value that we will discuss later, children may arrive in achievement situations with theories, hypotheses, or sets that orient them toward particular goals (Bruner, 1951; Epstein, 1973). One of these is the child's "theory of intelligence," which we have just begun to explore in our own work (M. Bandura & Dweck, 1981; Dweck & Elliott, 1981). (For related observations see Harari & Covington, 1981; Marshall, Weinstein, Middlestadt, & Brattesani, 1980; Surber, in press. For treatments of conceptions of mind and intelligence from a more cognitive point of view see Goodnow, 1980; Sternberg, Conway, Ketron, & Bernstein, 1981; Wellman, 1981.) We briefly present this work on children's theories of intelligence simply to illustrate how children's preexisting conceptions can affect their overall approach to achievement situations. Thus Table 1 also outlines the two general theories of intelligence that children tend to espouse and that appear to predict their choice of achievement goals (M. Bandura & Dweck, 1981; Dweck & Elliott, 1981).

Each theory embodies a very different conception of intellectual competence: intelligence as a fixed, general, judgable entity versus intelligence as an ever-growing repertoire of skills and knowledge. The first theory, which we term the "entity" theory of intelligence, involves the belief that intelligence is a rather stable, global trait that can be judged to be adequate or inadequate. That is, this trait or entity is displayed in one's performance, and the judgements of that performance can indicate whether one is or is not intelligent. The second theory, the "incremental" (or "instrumental") theory of intelligence, involves the belief that intellectual competence consists of a repertoire of skills that can be endlessly expanded through one's efforts. Within the entity view, then, the exertion of considerable effort may be seen as evidence of low intelligence, whereas within the incremental view high effort is more readily seen as the means of increasing intelligence.

By late grade school, virtually all children understand aspects of both views of intelligence (e.g., Harari & Covington, 1981; Heckhausen, 1981;

Marshall, et al., 1980; Rholes & Ruble, 1981; Surber, in press); however it appears that different children, independent of their actual ability, tend to favor different theories and that children who favor the different theories also favor different achievement goals when choices must be made (M. Bandura & Dweck, 1981; Dweck & Elliott, 1981). As would be predicted, entity theorists appear to prefer tasks that afford opportunities to avoid mistakes and to obtain competence judgments; incremental theorists appear to prefer tasks that afford them opportunities for learning.

As we noted above, once children are oriented toward different achievement goals, they will structure the "same" situation very differently (see also Nicholls, 1981, for an extensive discussion of the implications of different achievement goals). Indeed the meaning of many variables will be entirely altered within the context of learning and performance goals. Table 1 contains some of the contrasting views that are likely to be fostered by the two types of goals.[3] Most of these differential tendencies will be elaborated in later sections but provide here a good introduction to the critical impact of achievement goals on virtually every aspect of achievement processes.

As shown in Table 1, one may conceive of children with learning versus performance goals as confronting achievement tasks asking different questions: "How can I do it?" "What will I learn?" versus "Can I do it?" or "Will I look smart?" (see Langer & Dweck, 1973; Nicholls, 1979b). The former would orient children toward immersing themselves in the process of inquiry. The latter would orient them toward finding the "right answer" as rapidly as possible or avoiding tasks on which they might not find it rapidly enough to look smart (Bruner, 1961, 1965; Elliott & Dweck, 1981; Holt, 1964; Nicholls, 1981). Within a learning goal, errors or confusion would therefore be viewed as a natural, useful part of the inquiry process, whereas within performance goals, an error can more readily be viewed as failure—a failure to produce the right answer, a failure to look smart (e.g., Covington & Beery, 1976; Papert, 1980). In fact, in an experiment in which achievement goals and perceived ability were manipulated, Elliott and Dweck (1981) found no debilitation over a series of failure trials for children with learning goals (regardless of whether they believed themselves to have high or low ability). Children with performance goals who believed they had low ability, however, showed marked deterioration of performance under the same conditions.

For children seeking to learn something that they

Table 1.   Children's Theories of Intelligence and Achievement Goals

	Theories of Intelligence		
	Incremental	Entity	
Intelligence Is:	A repertoire of skills that increases through effort.	A global, stable entity whose adequacy is judged through performance.	
Effort Is:	An investment that increases intelligence.	A risk that may reveal low intelligence.	
	Goals		
	Learning Goal: Competence Increase	Performance Goal: Competence Judgment	Illustrative References
1. Entering Question:	How can I do it? What will I learn?	Can I do it? Will I look smart?	1. Langer & Dweck, 1973; Nicholls, 1979b.
2. Focus on:	Process	Outcome	2. Bruner, 1961, 1965.
3. Errors:	Natural, useful	Failure	3. Brophy & Good, 1974; Covington & Beery, 1976; Papert, 1980.
4. Uncertainty:	Challenging	Threatening	4. Dweck & Elliott, 1981; Holt, 1964.
5. Optimal Task:	Maximizes learning (becoming smarter)	Maximizes looking smart	5. Dweck & Elliott, 1981; Nicholls, 1981.
6. Seek:	Accurate information about ability	Flattering information	6. Atkinson & Feather, 1966; Janoff-Bulman & Brickman, 1981.
7. Standards:	Personal, long-term, flexible	Normative, immediate, rigid	7. E. Diener & Srull, 1979; Covington, 1980; Heckhausen, 1967; Nicholls, 1981.
8. Expectancy:	Emphasizes effort	Emphasizes present ability	8. Ames, Ames, & Felker, 1977; Elliott & Dweck, 1981; Nicholls, 1981.
9. Teacher:	Resource, guide	Judge, rewarder/punisher	9. Covington, 1980; Nicholls, 1981.
10. Goal Value:	"Intrinsic": value of skill, activity, progress	"Extrinsic": value of judgment	10. Elliott & Dweck, 1981; Nicholls, 1981; Parsons, 1982.

do not know, periods of uncertainty may be seen as inevitable and as stimulating or challenging, whereas for children seeking competence judgments, periods of true uncertainty might be seen as fraught with the peril of errors and failure. Thus children with learning goals would seek tasks that maximize learning, even if they are likely to make errors and thereby advertise their present lack of proficiency; children with performance goals would sacrifice learning tasks in favor of tasks that maximize competence judgments. (See Elliott & Dweck, 1981, for an experimental demonstration of this phenomenon.)

In order to facilitate learning, children with learning goals would seek accurate information about their abilities (cf. Atkinson & Feather, 1966; Janoff-Bulman & Brickman, 1981). This would help them structure proper instruction, plan strategies, set appropriate standards, and the like. In contrast, children seeking to obtain positive and avoid negative competence judgments are by definition seeking flattering information about their abilities and they may avoid diagnosing deficits even when this jeopardizes their future outcomes. One might say that children with learning goals are interested in results, not in excuses; children with performance goals may opt for the latter (see Covington, 1980; Dweck & Wortman, 1982).

Because learning goals involve competence increases, children's standards are more likely to be personal (increases judged with respect to their own initial level). In contrast, because performance goals involve looking smart, standards are more likely to be normative (see M. Bandura & Dweck, 1981; Nicholls, 1981). Performance goals are more likely to involve the immediate application of standards against which competence judgments are made. Learning goals are more likely to involve skill increases over longer periods of time and hence standards are more apt to be longer-term, more flexible ones. In addition, learning and performance standards carry different implications for nonattainment. Performance standards often have an all-or-nothing quality: if children fall short of their standards, they may well perceive themselves as having missed the boat. In contrast, for learning goals, partial attainment may have considerable value. That is, even if children fail to reach the standard they have set, they may still be pleased with their increased skill or knowledge. Thus, learning goals may be less tyrannical than performance goals in terms of whether and when they are attained.

Further, when one considers a child's expectancy of meeting personal, long-term, flexible learning standards, the expectancy depends in large part on how much time and effort the child is willing to exert. However, when one considers more normative, immediate, rigid performance standards, the child's expectancy depends to a greater extent on some assessment of his or her ability at the moment (Elliott & Dweck, 1981).

Given the differential emphasis on learning versus evaluation within the two types of goals, instructors may be viewed in different ways: as resources for and guides of the learning process versus judges or rewarders and punishers of performance outcomes (see, e.g., Covington, 1980; Nicholls, 1981).

Finally, different factors may enter into the determination of goal value. For learning goals, the personal value of the skill or activity will play a larger role, whereas for the performance goals the most critical factors will be those that affect the value of the competence judgment (see Nicholls, 1981; see also Elliott & Dweck, 1981).

In summary, children's cognitive sets, such as their theories about their intelligence, appear to guide their choice of achievement goals. Achievement goals, in turn, can lead children to conceptualize achievement situations in strikingly different ways and can affect essentially every part of the achievement process that we will now examine.

Expectancy Formation

In virtually every theory of achievement motivation, expectancy of goal attainment is a critical determinant of goal-directed activity. That is, which achievement activities children pursue—as well as the intensity, duration, and quality of that pursuit—is related to their confidence that they can realize their goals. In this section we will analyze the components that may go into the expectancies children form for each of the goals they are considering.

What makes this process particularly interesting is the fact that actual competence does not always clearly or directly translate into confidence. In fact, for girls, several investigators have found a *negative* relationship between measures of competence and confidence—bright girls showing unduly low expectancies relative to less bright ones (e.g., V. C. Crandall, 1969; Stipek & Hoffman, 1980). Bright girls' confidence in their ability also appears to be somewhat shakier (see Licht, 1980). It is by examining the process of expectancy formation (and of expectancy revision in light of performance outcomes) that we will begin to understand what leads some children to avoid or prematurely abandon valued goals that they are fully capable of attaining.

We begin this section by providing an overview of the factors potentially involved in expectancy formation. This context established, we turn to the literature for an examination of the general relationship between expectancies and achievement behavior, and then to a consideration of the characteristics of achievement-producing expectancies. This leads us back to a detailed analysis of how such expectancies may be formulated.

Figure 2 depicts the major variables involved in the (idealized) process of expectancy formation, variables that determine whether or not a given level of competence will lead the child to expect the desired competence increase or the desired competence judgments. These variables include the following:

1. *Perceived competence relative to task requirements.* The first steps involve children's assessment of what the task requires and an assessment of their competence or skills in relation to what the task requires. Whether these assessments are accurate or not, children may use them (a) to decide whether the task is well-suited for a particular goal (e.g., whether the difficulty level is a good one for obtaining a competence judgment), (b) to estimate the degree to which they possess the requisite skills to perform or learn the task, and (c) to gauge the amount of effort and time it would take to acquire or display the desired level of competence. These esti-

Performance Learning Expectancy:

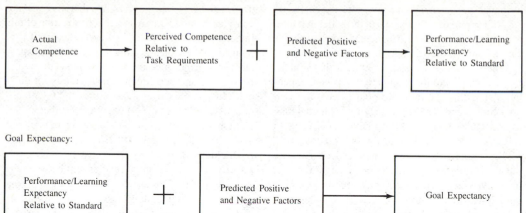

Goal Expectancy:

Figure 2. Goal Expectancy Formation

mates can then serve as the basis for predicting whether their performance or learning will reach their standards.

2. *Predicted positive and negative factors.* Before competence and task judgments are translated into performance expectancies, children can consider factors other than their skill that they believe will influence performance. They may then judge the extent to which they can exert control over these factors (to increase the impact of the desirable ones and decrease the impact of the undesirable ones). These factors may be personal characteristics of the child, such as work habits, or they may be external, environmental variables, such as available resources or quality of instruction—anything that can facilitate or interfere with acquiring or displaying competence.

3. *Performance/learning expectancy relative to standard.* The preceding assessments may then congeal to yield an impression of what level of performance or learning is likely, and of the degree to which this level will meet the child's standards. The standards represent the performance level the child believes is sufficient to obtain the desired judgment, to avoid the negative judgment, or to attain the desired skill increase. Whether any given performance/learning expectancy will become a high goal expectancy depends on the child's standards—all success or failure is defined relative to the standards.

4. *Predicted positive and negative factors.* As can be seen from Figure 2, "predicted positive and negative factors" can enter the process again between performance expectancy and goal expectancy. Here they would consist of factors that make it

more or less likely that a given level of performance would result in goal attainment. For example, the perceived characteristics of the agent making the competence judgment (his or her biases, thoroughness, judgment criteria) may lead children to expect that what they themselves consider good performance will go unrecognized or what they consider poor performance will be overrated by the evaluator.

5. *Goal expectancy.* This is the child's perceived probability of attaining the goal(s) under consideration—the likelihood of obtaining a judgment of high competence, avoiding a judgment of low competence, or increasing competence.

In this context, we would like to emphasize the distinction between the performance expectancy and the goal expectancy. (This is similar to the distinction A. Bandura, 1977, draws between the efficacy expectation and the outcome expectation, or that Weisz, 1981, makes between perceived competence and perceived contingency; see also V. C. Crandall, 1969, for a discussion of different types of expectancies.) The former consists of children's expected level of performance (relative to their standards); the latter consists of children's expectation that this level of performance, even if it reaches their standards, will result in goal attainment. For the learning goal, these two expectancies amount to the same thing: If children have reached their learning standard, then they have reached their goal. For the performance goal, however, the distinction is an important one, for, as we have just noted above, certain factors can lead children to expect judgments that may not be commensurate with their performance.

In such cases, for example, children with high performance expectancies but low goal expectancies may fail to pursue valued goals in the belief that they will ultimately be thwarted in their attempts to obtain the recognition they desire.

These, then, are the major classes of variables that can enter into the formulation of a goal expectancy (and that can influence goal value[4]) for each goal considered. The expectancy for each goal may then combine with the corresponding goal value to influence which goal or goals will predominate.

It is important to note that goal expectancies are not necessarily stable estimates but rather are subject to change whenever new variables become salient or already-considered ones are reassessed. This may occur even before the child begins to perform the task and to experience performance outcomes. For example, as the time to perform draws closer, new concerns may arise that can either undermine or strengthen the child's confidence (see, for example, Lawson, 1981). Furthermore, any change in expectancy for one achievement goal may spur a revision of expectancies for other goals. For example, if a child concludes that the chances of obtaining a positive competence judgment are poor, he or she may promptly recompute the chances of avoiding a judgment of incompetence. As we discuss in our section on performance evaluation, revision of expectancies plays a critical role in the maintenance or abandonment of achievement strivings. For example, the tendency to exhibit too-rapid expectancy decreases in the face of obstacles appears to be a key factor in certain maladaptive achievement patterns.

Moreover, how much care goes into formulating a preperformance expectancy may differ according to the achievement goal. If children are concerned about a fairly immediate competence judgment based on their initial performance, then prior to embarking on the task they may give a great deal of thought to the likelihood of obtaining a positive judgment. In contrast, if children are more concerned with what they can learn from the task, they may make some preliminary assessments but delay more precise ones (e.g., of their skill, of task difficulty, of what standards are appropriate) until they have tried out the task.

Relationship Between Expectancies and Achievement Activity. Our exploration of expectancies begins with the wealth of research that has examined the general correlates and consequences of high and low expectancies. As noted above, it is in this context that we will then undertake a more detailed examination of the process of expectancy formation.

The expectancy research to date has not typically observed distinctions between performance expectancies and goal expectancies. We therefore will not consider them separately in our consideration of this literature. On the whole, however, the results are rather consistent in indicating that the various expectancies, whether measured or manipulated, predict persistence and performance, particularly on difficult tasks and under evaluative pressure (A. Bandura, 1977, 1981; Battle, 1965, 1966; Feather, 1966; Halisch & Heckhausen, 1977; Parsons, in press; Todd, Terrell, & Frank, 1962; Tyler, 1958; Zajonc & Brickman, 1969).

In view of the general relationship between expectancy and performance, some of the most intriguing and puzzling findings have related to the sex differences in expectancy that occur in the absence of sex differences in prior or subsequent performance (see V. C. Crandall, 1969; Dweck, Goetz, & Strauss, 1980; Frieze, Fisher, Hanusa, McHugh, & Valle, 1978; Jackaway, 1974, Lenney, 1977; McMahan, 1972; Montanelli & Hill, 1969; Nicholls, 1975; Small, Nakamura, & Ruble, 1973). V. C. Crandall (1969), for example, reports a number of studies in which girls of different ages generated lower expectancies than boys, even on tasks where they outperformed the boys. The girls, it appeared, formed lower expectancies than were warranted by their past performance, whereas the boys formed higher ones than their past performance might suggest. Moreover, it was the *brightest* girls who underestimated the most. Indeed, in a recent study by Stipek and Hoffman (1980) the highest-achieving girls actually had lower expectancies of success than the average- or low-achieving girls. (For boys, the expected relationship was obtained, with the higher-achieving boys generating the higher expectancies.) If low expectancies do not appear to be related to poor performance in girls, why is this phenomenon of concern? First, as we will discuss later, there is much evidence to suggest that even when girls are performing as well as boys, their performance is more vulnerable to disruption by obstacles to success or by evaluative pressure than is boys' performance (e.g., Dweck & Gilliard, 1975; Dweck & Reppucci, 1975; Licht & Dweck, 1981; Nicholls, 1975). Moreover, it may tend to be brighter or better-performing girls whose performance is most disrupted (Licht & Dweck, 1981). Thus the lower expectancies may predict fragile performance rather than poor performance for girls. Second, even when girls' lower expectancies are not related to poorer performance compared with that of males, these expectancies may still predict more conservative task choices, which over the school years can result in girls' selection of less challenging courses and careers (see Parsons, in press). Third, the counter-intuitive relationship between girls' ability/achievement/performance and their expectancies can provide valuable insights into the process of expectancy formation. When and how do similar experiences yield different expectancies for boys and girls? How might superior performance yield lower expectancies for bright girls?

As Parsons (in press) points out, the sex difference in expectancy is more often found when there is greater ambiguity or uncertainty in the situation: When past performance feedback has been mixed or unclear, when the task is novel, or when the expectancy asked for is more general or global (see V. C. Crandall, 1969; Dweck, Goetz, & Strauss, 1980; Frieze, Fisher, Hanusa, McHugh, & Valle, 1978). Under these circumstances, girls tend to key on negative information, and boys on positive, in constructing expectancies. It is possible that this results from the greater tendency of girls (especially bright ones) to view negative outcomes as indicative of their ability (and thus of their future outcomes), and of boys to view positive ones as indicative of theirs (e.g., Bar Tal & Darom, 1979; Covington & Omelich, 1979a; Dweck & Bush, 1976; Dweck & Reppucci, 1973; Nicholls, 1975; Phillips, 1981; Weisz & McGuire, 1980). Thus different expectancies may grow out of the different data children use to compute them. Another, closely related, factor in the expectancy difference may be the tendency of girls to rate tasks (e.g., future courses) as being more difficult than boys rate them (see Foersterling, 1980; Parsons, in press), so that even if girls viewed their ability as high, they might still predict poorer performance than boys would. Finally, bright girls may have extremely high standards, so that even if they expected to attain a high level of performance, they might still view that as inadequate for goal attainment (see Stouwie, Hetherington, & Parke, 1970).

In short, expectancies appear to be generally related to measures of persistence, performance, and academic achievement. When lower expectancies are not associated with poorer performance, they may predict greater vulnerability to disruption by failure or threat of failure. These lower expectancies that occur despite equivalent performance may be related to differences in ability inferences, in perceived task difficulty, or in performance standards, factors we will now examine in greater detail. First, one might well ask, in view of these findings, whether high expectancies are always propitious, always breed fortitude in the face of obstacles and increased likelihood of mastery.

Recent research clarifies the distinction between the expectancies that are associated with productive problem-solving and those that are not. As we will see, most of the factors associated with achievement-producing expectancies are fostered by an incremental view of intelligence and a learning goal and are discouraged by an entity view of intelligence and a performance goal of avoiding incompetence judgments.

In sum, the literature endorses optimism, but optimism based on analysis, planning, and the patience born of a longer-term, learning perspective. Specifically, the research indicates that, regardless of children's actual competencies, the high expectancies associated with optimum performance on challenging tasks grow out of the following:

1. *Realistic task/skill analysis and strategy planning,* for which the child must have and apply the appropriate metacognitive skills (A. Bandura, 1979; Covington, 1980; deCharms, 1968, 1972; Meichenbaum & Asarnow, 1982). This is in contrast to either (a) the tendency to overestimate the difficulty of unfamiliar tasks and respond to them with a premature "I can't" (Parsons, in press; see also Holt, 1964) or (b) the tendency to engage in impulsive overoptimism (Bush & Dweck, 1975; Kagan & Kogan, 1970)—both of which may often reflect insufficient task analysis. Moreover, realistic analysis of the cognitive skills involved in effective performance fosters the maintenance of high expectancies in the face of subsequent obstacles (Schunk, 1979).

2. *High perceived ability* (A. Bandura, 1977, 1981; V. C. Crandall, 1969; Nicholls, 1981; Parsons, in press) and *high perceived control* (Covington, 1980; deCharms, 1968, 1972; Harter & Connell, 1981) based on (a) a knowledge of important causal factors (e.g., Harter & Connell, 1981) and (b) the belief that one can influence these factors (and outcomes) (Anderson, 1980; Covington, 1980; Harter & Connell, 1981). Particularly important is a belief that effort increases one's ability and control rather than that effort reveals low ability (see M. Bandura & Dweck, 1981; Covington, 1980; Dweck & Elliott, 1981; Harari & Covington, 1981; Nicholls, 1976a; Touhy & Villemez, 1980).

3. *Standards* that tend to be (a) personal rather than normative/competitive (see Ames, Ames, & Felker, 1977; Covington & Beery, 1976; Maehr & Stallings, 1972; Nicholls, 1979b, 1981; Veroff, 1969) and (b) flexible (M. Bandura & Dweck, 1981; Diggory, 1966; Masters, Furman, & Barden, 1977) versus rigid, overly high, and immediate (Martire, 1956; Sears, 1940). In the former case, success is defined in terms of a continuing process of which errors are an integral part (Bruner, 1961; C. I. Di-

ener & Dweck, 1978, 1980; Nicholls, 1981; Papert, 1980); in the latter case, a "sudden death" situation is created, in which the judgment of success or failure is likely to be made on the basis of immediate output.

This in broad outline is the picture conveyed by the literature. We will now turn to a more detailed look at expectancy formation. As we retrace our steps through the process, we will continue to emphasize how the different achievement goals impart different meaning and importance to the variables that go into expectancies, as well as how the different goals foster tendencies that facilitate or impair performance.

Perceived Competence Relative to Task Requirements. The first step in forming an expectancy involves an assessment of the task(s) at hand. The most productive approach appears to be for children to employ their metacognitive skills to the fullest: to formulate the problem in a way that is comprehensible and manageable, to analyze the skills (and effort) required by the task, then to evaluate the degree to which they have or can acquire the necessary skills, and to plan strategies for embarking on the task. (For the relevant research on metacognitive skills, see Brown & DeLoache, 1978; Flavell & Wellman, 1977; Markman, 1981). Not only is this general approach found to characterize successful students, but training in its use appears to encourage higher expectancies, greater perceived competence, increased persistence, improved performance, and the tackling of more challenging problems (see A. Bandura, 1981; Covington, 1980; deCharms, 1972; Dusek, Kermis, & Mergler, 1975; Meichenbaum & Asarnow, 1982; Olton & Crutchfield, 1969).

We suggest that children oriented toward learning goals and children oriented toward performance goals will perform somewhat different metacognitive analyses. As discussed above, children with learning goals can be viewed as asking the question: "How can I do it?" or "What will I learn?" Thus their task analysis may be aimed at formulating strategies and at evaluating whether the task is a good one for learning. Children with performance goals, on the other hand, may be viewed as asking: "Can I do it?" or "Will I look smart?" Thus their task analysis may focus more on evaluating the difficulty level of the task in order to determine whether it is a good one for performing well. Children oriented toward the goal of avoiding negative judgments may be particularly interested in making rapid decisions on this point in order to devise ways of avoiding such judgments when they appear likely.

The interesting question from a motivational point of view is why children who have the requisite skills to perform the metacognitive analysis fail to do so or to follow through on it. For example, it appears that highly anxious children under evaluative conditions fail to engage in a systematic task analysis, although they may do so under less pressured circumstances (see, e.g., Wine, 1982). In a related vein, C. I. Diener and Dweck (1978) found that in the face of failure problems, "helpless" children soon reduced or abandoned solution-oriented monitoring and planning, whereas "mastery-oriented" children intensified theirs. (Both types of children had shown equivalent levels of problem-solving strategies prior to the failure problems.) It is possible that those children whom we will see appear oriented toward the goal of avoiding negative judgments may react to threatened or actual negative outcomes with a premature "I can't." This belief may trigger interfering cognitions/affect that may disrupt attention (Kuhl, 1981; Wine, 1971, 1982) or may prompt reduced effort or defensive withdrawal from the task (Covington, 1980; Covington, Spratt, & Omelich, 1980; Frankl & Snyder, 1978; Nicholls, 1981). All of these reactions would impair the display of metacognitive skills just when they are needed most.

If it is the case that children who are oriented toward different goals are engaging in somewhat different sorts of analyses—are seeking answers to different questions—what are the answers they are hoping for? What are conclusions that would be most desirable given their goals? And, in light of this, what types of tasks would they *choose* if they were presented with tasks of varying characteristics?

Tasks most suitable for the learning goal and those most suitable for the positive performance goal provide an interesting contrast. Both goals are typically served by challenging tasks, but for different reasons: Challenging tasks often maximize favorable competence judgments, and they often maximize competence increases. Choosing tasks of intermediate difficulty has for many years been seen as the hallmark of achievement-producing motivational tendencies (e.g., Atkinson, 1964). Yet is is rarely made explicit that tasks of intermediate difficulty often happen to be optimum tasks for both the positive performance goal (cf. Trope & Brickman's, 1975, diagnosticity; Atkinson & Feather's, 1966, maximal incentive value of success) and the learning goal (cf. Berlyne's, 1960, or Hunt's, 1963, optimum degree of discrepancy). However, for theoretical as well as practical reasons it is important to distinguish between tasks that best serve the two different goals, even though the tasks often appear similarly challenging.

Toward this end, we would predict that when the performance goal predominates, if normative difficulty (e.g., how hard the task is considered to be for children of a certain age) and personal difficulty (how hard the task actually is for that child) are varied orthogonally, the child may well choose the task that at once appears most difficult to an evaluator and is actually easiest for him or her (i.e., allows the child to look smart with low effort). In other words, the best tasks for competence judgments from others may be those that are of greater than intermediate difficulty normatively, but less than intermediate difficulty personally. In contrast, we would predict that when the learning goal predominates, if task difficulty (personal or normative) and the degree to which a task fosters learning were varied independently, task difficulty would be relatively less important, and potential for learning would control task choice. Thus an easy task (e.g., a programmed learning task) or a very difficult task (e.g., one on which many errors are likely to be made) that better facilitated skill acquisition would be likely to be chosen over a task of intermediate difficulty that was more poorly suited to competence increases. Dweck and Elliott (1981) and Elliott and Dweck (1981) report recent findings that provide general support for this prediction of differential task choice for children holding learning and performance goals.

Tasks suitable for the two different performance goals also provide an interesting contrast. When a task is viewed as normatively difficult but personally easy, the child may form high expectancies both of obtaining favorable competence judgments and of avoiding unfavorable ones. However, the more a child's assessment shifts toward a view of the task as normatively easy but personally difficult, the more unsuitable the task becomes. Although this will be so for both of the performance goals, we suggest that focus on the goal of avoiding negative judgments, first, may render it more likely that this assessment will occur, and second, may make the potential consequences appear more aversive. Under these circumstances, then, children seeking to avoid negative judgments may find such effortful tasks that provide good tests of competence particularly unsuitable. If they are already involved in the task, some children may attempt to prevent or lessen a diagnosis of incompetence by (1) minimizing their effort (Covington, 1980; Covington, Spratt, &

Omelich, 1980; Frankl & Snyder, 1978; Nicholls, 1981), (2) redefining the tasks (inappropriately) into an easier one or a game (see Dweck & Elliott, 1981) or (3) switching to other, less diagnostic tasks, such as easy ones on which failure is less likely, or very difficult ones on which failure even after high effort is not as incriminating (Atkinson & Feather, 1966; deCharms & Carpenter, 1968; deCharms & Dave, 1965; Hill, 1972; Moulton, 1965; Raynor & Smith, 1966). It should be clear, however, that this strategy for making the task or situation more "suitable" for avoiding meaningful negative judgments also tends to eliminate chances for favorable judgments.

To summarize, formulating a goal expectancy involves an analysis of task requirements and of one's skills in relation to task requirements. Both the probability of a systematic analysis and the nature of the analysis that is undertaken are molded by the achievement goal on which the child is focusing.

Predicted Positive and Negative Factors. Before skill and task judgments are translated into expectancies, children may consider variables other than skill that can influence performance. These may be any personal or environmental factors that they believe will facilitate or interfere with desired outcomes. As we noted above, productive achievement behavior appears to be associated, first, with knowledge of causal factors or sources of control (Harter, 1981a; Harter & Connell, 1981) and second, with the perception that one is in control (A. Bandura, 1981; Clifford & Cleary, 1972; Covington, 1980; Covington & Omelich, 1979a; deCharms, 1972; Kennelly & Kinley, 1975). By high perceived control, we mean the belief that one can maximize the impact of positive factors and minimize the impact of, or compensate for, negative ones. It is likely that an incremental view of intelligence and a learning goal would foster greater perceived control (see Dweck & Elliott, 1981; Harter, 1981a; Nicholls, 1981) by virtue of promoting (1) systematic and sustained task analysis, (2) increased belief in the efficacy of effort for surmounting obstacles and compensating for deficiencies, and (3) decreased reliance on the tasks, rules, standards, and judgments of others.

Before examining possible causal factors and how they might influence expectancies, it is important to note that the same set of potential causal factors is available to enter the process at three points: as predictors of performance, as direct influences on actual performance, and still later as explanations of (attributions for) performance outcomes. That is, anything that can be a predicted influence before the fact (e.g., skill, task difficulty, other internal and external factors) can be a perceived influence after the fact, as well as, of course, an actual influence during the fact. It is critical, however, to keep these three points in the process conceptually distinct and to bear in mind, first, that a different subset of these factors may enter at each point. That is, the factors that are predicted to influence performance can be different from the factors that do influence performance, and both of these can be different from the factors that are later invoked to explain performance (cf. Covington & Omelich, 1979a; Fontaine, 1974). Second, as Surber (in press) cogently argues and compellingly illustrates, different causal schemes may be used for prediction and attribution; that is different combination rules may be used when one is considering factors that may cause future performance than when one is considering factors that may have caused past performance.

Nonetheless, because the set of causal factors from which predictions and attributions are drawn is the same, the same dimensions that have been used to analyze causal attributions can be applied to predicted causes: Specifically, causal factors can be viewed as varying on the dimensions of internality, stability, controllability, and globality (Weiner, 1982). Internality-externality refers to whether the causal factor resides in the child (i.e., his or her behavior or characteristics) or in the child's social or nonsocial environment. Stability reflects the degree to which the causal factor tends to vary, and controllability refers to the degree to which variations in the factor can be produced by the child. Globality reflects the generality or specificity of the factor (e.g., general ability versus specific skill) (see Abramson, Seligman, & Teasdale, 1978). These dimensions have implications for the level and stability of the child's expectancy. For example, the presence of positive factors that are perceived as stable, controllable, and global would encourage predictions of continuing success, whereas negative factors that are perceived as stable, uncontrollable, and global would contribute to predictions of consistently poor performance and would discourage the initiation and pursuit of challenging tasks (see e.g., Covington & Omelich, 1979a).[5]

Let us consider some factors other than skill level that children might predict would influence their performance. First, there are personal dispositions, characteristic preferences, and so on, that can influence the amount or quality of effort children are able or willing to exert. Knowledge of these factors might be considered the equivalent in the motivational domain of metacognitive skills—knowledge of one's own motivational processes (see Mischel, 1981).

For example, children may believe the level of *anxiety* they will experience will impair the quality of their performance. Another such factor would be children's level of *interest* in the activity: children who assess their interest as high may see themselves as more willing and perhaps more able to exert greater effort compared with children who assess their interest as low. Another, related, personal factor that children may see as relevant to performance is the degree of *self-control* they will be able to exercise (see Kanfer, 1977; Mischel, 1981). Indeed, as Harter (1981b) suggests, training programs aimed at increasing children's self-control (e.g., Meichenbaum, 1977, 1979) may serve to raise their perceived control over outcomes as well.

There are also environmental factors that children can believe will affect their performance or goal attainment. For example, the child may expect high- or low-quality instruction, adequate or inadequate amounts of help or resources, fair or unfair tasks or judgment criteria. (See, e.g., Dweck, Goetz, & Strauss, 1980, and Dweck & Licht, 1980, for a discussion of sex differences in perception of positive and negative factors; see Triandis, 1972, for a discussion of "eco-system distrust," the belief that the environment hinders attainment of goals.)

Learning/Performance Expectancy Relative to One's Standards.   According to the analysis, after children consider the contributing factors that seem relevant to them and arrive at a performance prediction, they ask whether this anticipated performance will meet the standards they hold. This comparison of predicted performance to standards will be done for each goal under consideration. For the performance goal of obtaining a favorable judgment of competence, the standard represents the performance level that the child believes must be reached or exceeded to obtain a favorable judgment. For the performance goal of avoiding a negative judgment of competence, the standard represents the performance level below which the child believes a negative judgment is likely. For the learning goal of increasing competence, the standard represents the level or rate of skill increase that the learner considers to be satisfactory.

As noted earlier, the research suggests that productive achievement efforts are best fostered by the setting of standards that are: (1) *Personal or autonomous* (defined with respect to the child's own former level or defined as the attainment of some absolute level of proficiency) as opposed to normative or competitive with others (see Ames, Ames, & Felker, 1977; Maehr & Stallings, 1972; Masters, Furman, & Barden, 1977; Nicholls, 1981; Veroff,

1969), for under the latter conditions a large number of children are prevented from succeeding; (2) *realistic,* that is, challenging, but reasonable considering the child's skill level (A. Bandura & Schunk, 1981; Battle, 1966; Covington, 1980; Kuhl, 1978; Martire, 1956); and, in a related vein, (3) *flexible,* usually escalating with increased knowledge of task or increased skill, as opposed to rigid and all-or-nothing with little leeway for improvement (M. Bandura & Dweck, 1981; Diggory, 1966; Masters, Furman, & Barden, 1977).

Yet another parameter of standards is related to who defines them and who judges them to be met (see V. J. Crandall, Katkovsky, & Preston, 1960), and the evidence here appears less abundant and less clear. Felixbrod and O'Leary (1974) and O'Leary and O'Leary (1976) found no difference in performance or productivity under self-determined or externally imposed standards. Although one would, of course, wish children to become increasingly able to set their own standards and judge their own performance, on any given occasion the source of a standard may be less important than the degree to which it is appropriately defined (i.e., personal, realistic, and flexible).

Through encouragement of personal, more realistic, longer-term, more flexible standards, learning goals may well foster higher goal expectancies, since, clearly, more things are ultimately learnable than immediately performable.

Value of Goals and Means

Having addressed issues of goal expectancy in the previous section, we will turn to an examination of factors that affect the salience and value of the different goals (and means). Then we will explore the goal tendencies that result when the expectancies and values combine. This will lead us into a more intensive examination of the expectancy-value patterns that facilitate or inhibit achievement, and we will link these to well-known individual differences. However, first we will review briefly some information about the three achievement goals and clarify some of the distinctions among them.

As we have suggested, many situations, even ones in which the task is determined, allow children a choice of achievement goals. That is, even when children are given something to learn, they may adopt performance goals and seek or avoid competence judgments (e.g., for their rate of acquisition). Conversely, even when children are given tests designed to evaluate existing skills or knowledge, they may adopt a learning goal and attempt to make use of the situation to increase their competence or to plan

future competence increases—for example, by diagnosing existing skills.

We might also reemphasize that all three achievement goals may be held simultaneously. That is, on a given task children may value and seek learning for its own sake but at the same time may seek positive and avoid negative competence judgments for their work. Some situations, however, may bring the goals into direct conflict, and it is important to understand the differences among the goals to appreciate when this might occur.

The two performance goals are distinguished by their orientations toward either seeking positive or avoiding negative judgments. It is important to realize that the goal of avoiding a negative judgment need not be associated with "avoidance" behavior. The presence of this goal can contribute to active approach and strivings in achievement situations when the child is confident of avoiding negative judgments. It is only when the child views negative judgments as likely that this goal will inhibit other approach tendencies or lead to attempts to avoid competence judgments entirely—for example, by choosing tasks that are not diagnostic of skill (such as chance tasks or tasks that are too easy or too hard) or by undermining the diagnosticity of tasks (e.g., by not trying). This is in contrast to Atkinson's (1964) "motive to avoid failure," which *is* conceptualized as an avoidance tendency. However, that motive is assessed by means of an anxiety scale, which is likely to reflect *both* a high value of avoiding a negative judgment and a high expectancy of receiving a negative judgment. (See Nicholls, 1976b, for a discussion of anxiety scales as measures of perceived ability.) This is not to say that active approach and striving prompted by the two performance goals are indistinguishable. It is likely that approach behavior fed by a goal of avoiding negative judgments is more tentative or fragile, characterized by less challenge-seeking, greater salience and impact of negative outcomes, and a greater likelihood of turning to escape or avoidance behavior in the face of obstacles.

When we compare the goal of obtaining a favorable competence judgment with the goal of increasing competence, we note that both goals tend to foster active pursuit of relatively challenging tasks. However, as we mentioned earlier and will develop later, tasks that maximize competence judgments may differ from tasks that maximize competence increases. Thus on some occasions children may feel they have to choose between looking smart and learning something new, if by choosing the latter they risk a display of ignorance.

Factors Affecting Goal Value.   By goal value, we mean the importance for the child of the competence increase or the competence judgment *per se*. Most investigators to date who have manipulated the value of achievement goals have manipulated the value of competence judgments. Specifically, they have varied the salience or importance of evaluation via: private versus public performance conditions (Carver & Scheier, 1978; Cox, 1966; Ganzer, 1968); relaxed versus test conditions (Entin & Raynor, 1973; Lekarczyk & Hill, 1969; McCoy, 1965; I. G. Sarason, 1958, 1972; S. B. Sarason, Davidson, Lighthall, Waite, & Ruebush, 1960); important skill versus unimportant skill conditions (Nicholls, 1975); self-focus versus task-focus conditions (Brockner, 1979; Brockner & Hulton, 1978); competitive versus noncompetitive reward structure (Ames, Ames, & Felker, 1977); important versus less important evaluator (Dweck & Bush, 1976; Halperin, 1977).

These studies tend to show that orienting children toward high-value performance goals, if they have low opinions of their competence, creates the conditions for performance debilitation (see Nicholls, 1981). However, orienting children toward high-value learning goals, regardless of how competent they believe themselves to be at that moment, creates conditions of mastery-oriented striving in the face of obstacles (e.g., Elliott & Dweck, 1981; see Nicholls, 1981). What then are factors that affect the salience or value of learning goals? First, the value or utility of the skill (or knowledge) in question will, naturally, contribute to the value of increasing that skill (see Elliott & Dweck, 1981; Nicholls, 1979b; Parsons, in press; Sorensen, 1976; see V. C. Crandall, 1969). Second, interest in the task or activity may also contribute to the value of increasing one's skill in that area (Nicholls, 1979b; Parsons, in press; see also Lepper, 1980). (Recall, however, that engaging in an activity solely because it is interesting does not constitute an achievement activity, even if an increase in skill occurs as a by-product.) A third factor involves the salience of the rewards inherent in skill acquisition. This is undoubtedly affected by the tendency to monitor one's own improvement— e.g., the attainment of "subgoals" (see A. Bandura & Schunk, 1981)—a practice that would be particularly important for intellectual activities that lack clear breakthroughs and in which gradual improvements may go unnoticed.

In short, when a skill is important, when exercising that skill is enjoyable, and when increases in that skill are salient, the learning goal is likely to assume greater value. In contrast to conditions that highlight performance goals, these are the conditions under which children will be more apt to perceive themselves as the producers and directors of meaningful intellectual activity (Covington, 1980; deCharms, 1968, 1972; Nicholls, 1979b).

One must also distinguish the salience or value attached to different outcomes within goals. That is, aside from the value attached to goal attainment ("success"), there may be separate values attached to nonattainment (see Parsons, in press). Furthermore, within the latter, separate values may be attached to nonattainment through nonpursuit (i.e., "nonsuccess") and nonattainment despite pursuit ("failure"). These three outcomes—attainment, passive nonattainment, and active nonattainment— may be differentially salient to and differentially valued by different individuals. For example, it is interesting to speculate that lower achievement in females versus males may sometimes be due to the greater salience of and greater acceptability (lower negative valence) of passive nonattainment for females. For males this option may be less salient and more negative. If this is true, then even in cases where the two sexes have equally low expectancies and equally strong negative values attached to failure, males might still be more likely than females to engage in active striving to avoid failure and attain success.

Means Value.   Although we have discussed the fact that interesting and enjoyable activities that serve as means to goals may contribute to goal expectancy and goal values, one might well consider "means value" as a variable in its own right (Kruglanski, 1975). Children may in fact key on "process" factors as well as "outcome" factors in choosing whether or not to pursue a particular goal. That is, quite apart from how valuable and attainable an achievement goal may be, an aversive route to the goal may discourage or disrupt the pursuit. At times children may have a choice of means and would be expected to choose among them on the basis of both the interest/enjoyment value and their suitability for attaining the goal in question (Nicholls, 1979b; Parsons, in press).

Goal Tendencies and Goal Choice

For each goal the child has considered, the expectancies and values may now coalesce to yield a "goal tendency" (see Atkinson & Feather, 1966). Regardless of how the expectancies and values may be combined and represented, goals with high salience, value, and expectancy (and with high-value means) are most likely to yield strong goal tendencies and to exert the greatest influence on behavior.

However, the absolute and relative strengths of goal tendencies can change continually as different information comes into focus, and hence behavior will vary accordingly (cf. Atkinson & Birch, 1970, 1974).

Of course, to predict accurately a child's achievement behavior in a given instance, one must consider together the various achievement and nonachievement goals that are salient to the child in that situation (e.g., see Atkinson, 1964; Parsons, in press). For example, if we considered only the fact that an achievement goal requiring much effort had very low value for a child, we might predict that any commerce with the activity in question would be halfhearted and would breed boredom. However, if we considered also the fact that the child's parents had instituted a harsh penalty for failure to perform well, we might wish to modify our prediction about the amount of effort the child would expend, as well as the intensity of the negative affect that would be generated. For clarity, however, we will focus on achievement goals in developing and illustrating our points.

As was suggested above, goal tendencies can act in concert vis-à-vis a given task when they are compatible (all approach or all avoidance) or may undermine each other or cause conflict when they are antagonistic (some approach, others avoidance) (see Atkinson, 1964; Dollard & Miller, 1950; Heckhausen, 1967). Nonachievement goals can combine with achievement goals in a similar manner. That is, nonachievement goals that are salient and valued may work with achievement goal tendencies or against them, overpowering avoidance tendencies, inhibiting approach tendencies, or posing unresolvable conflicts (Atkinson & Feather, 1966).

Task Performance

According to the model, the child finally does something. With the goal variables tentatively set, the child begins to perform the task. In this section we will examine the influence of different expectancy-value patterns (goal tendencies) on the quality of children's performance and its maintenance over time. Specifically, we will identify and contrast what we believe to be the major achievement-producing and achievement-inhibiting patterns.

Achievement-Producing Versus Effort-Producing Patterns. First we would like to clarify the distinction between achievement-producing patterns and effort-producing ones. By an achievement-producing pattern we mean one that optimizes productive learning and performance in a way that is consonant with the child's overall or long-term achievement goals. Although high and continued effort is a hallmark of much productive achievement behavior, there are clearly circumstances under which it is inappropriate or maladaptive. For example, continued effort can be considered maladaptive when it reflects rigid adherence to unpromising means and a failure to consider alternative means to the same goal (Janoff-Bulman & Brickman, 1981). Continued effort can also be considered unproductive when it represents excessive adherence to a "safe" avoidance strategy (for example, a too-difficult task intended to preclude incompetence judgments) and a failure to pursue an alternative, high-probability, high-value approach goal (see e.g., Atkinson & Feather, 1966). As a final example, high effort may be considered maladaptive when it represents an inordinate expenditure of time and energy aimed chiefly at eliminating any possibility of failure (see Covington & Beery, 1976).

It is important to distinguish here between maladaptive perseveration in an unpromising activity and an informed decision to pursue a highly valued but low-probability (or long-term, high-investment) goal. The latter is likely to be achievement-producing to the extent that (1) the goal expectancy and value are based on an objective, thorough consideration of available data and are revised appropriately in light of new data, and (2) the goal (or means) is considered in the context of other possible and existing goals (or means) and is reevaluated in this context over time. (See Janoff-Bulman & Brickman, 1981.) This would then constitute a "calculated risk" (Atkinson & Feather, 1966) as opposed to behavior driven by unrealistic hopes or self-defeating fears.

In short, effort-producing expectancy-value patterns will often generate productive striving. However, when they are based on distorted expectancies or inflated goal values, they may not. Viewed in this light, achievement-producing patterns would involve effort-producing patterns that are based on sound expectancies and values, and would thus involve the appropriate initiation, maintenance, and cessation of effort. In contrast, achievement-inhibiting patterns would be marked by an absence of soundly-based effort-producing patterns, and would thus involve inappropriate exertion or withholding of effort.

Achievement-Producing Versus Achievement-Inhibiting Patterns The chief achievement-inhibiting patterns appear to us to involve (1) unnecessarily low or shaky expectancies with respect to valued goals, (2) high expectancies that are ungrounded or unrevised in light of outcomes, (3) generally low value attached to achievement goals, (4) a tendency to focus on or inflate aversive aspects of means despite high expectancy and high value for goals, (5) a tendency to focus on negative consequences of attaining high-expectancy, high-value goals. Let us examine each in turn.

Unnecessarily Low or Shaky Expectancies with Respect to Valued Goals. In our discussion of expectancy formation we discussed factors that contribute to low expectancies, such as a tendency to focus on negative information in estimating competence and predicting performance, or the tendency to set high and rigid standards (tendencies that are fostered by performance goals). As we will see in the section *Performance Evaluation,* related factors contribute to rapid declines in expectancies in the face of negative or ambiguous outcomes (C. I. Diener & Dweck, 1978, 1980).

Here we would like to examine two of the major individual difference variables known to be associated with impaired performance: high-evaluation anxiety and learned helplessness. We will argue that at the time of impairment both represent a focus on avoidance of negative judgments along with low expectancies of avoiding those judgments through task performance. (For anxiety, see Nicholls, 1976b, 1981; Wine, 1982. For learned helplessness see C. I. Diener & Dweck, 1978, 1980; Dweck & Elliott, 1981; Dweck & Licht, 1980; Elliott & Dweck, 1981.) However, there remains an important difference. We suggest that anxiety represents chronically low expectancies in the presence of evaluative cues, whereas helplessness represents more of an acute response to negative outcomes, that is, plunging expectancies in the face of perceived failure. We will review the evidence for this distinction and then ask which pattern best characterizes girls, who have been shown to score higher on measures of both anxiety and helplessness.

First, the measures of anxiety and helplessness support this distinction. Anxiety scales, such as the Test Anxiety Scale for Children (S. B. Sarason, Davidson, Lighthall, Waite, & Ruebush, 1960), tend to tap children's self-evaluation, with high anxiety seeming to reflect low perceived ability (Nicholls, 1976b). In contrast, measures of helplessness, such as the Intellectual Achievement Responsibility Scale (V. C. Crandall, Katkovsky, & Crandall, 1965), tap, not expectation of negative outcomes, but rather interpretations of negative outcomes. As such, they would be expected to predict reaction to negative outcomes *when they occur.* There is much evidence documenting low expectancies and impaired performance on the part of highly anxious

students when they perform under evaluative conditions (see Hill, 1972; Nicholls, 1981; Wine, 1982). Under these conditions they often fail to formulate effective problem-solving strategies (see Dusek, Kermis, & Mergler, 1975; Meichenbaum, 1977; Wine, 1982) and to be overly attentive to cues from the evaluator (e.g., Nottelman & Hill, 1977). In contrast, helpless children under these conditions consistently show performance that is at least equivalent to their mastery-oriented counterparts—until they encounter obstacles (e.g., C. I. Diener & Dweck, 1978, 1980; Dweck & Reppucci, 1973). It is then that they appear to abandon effective strategies and to become more oriented toward the evaluator. A study by Licht (1980) afforded a direct comparison between anxious and helpless children in their acquisition of challenging new material. In line with our distinction, she found that anxiety predicted immediate impairment, whereas helplessness predicted impairment over time in the face of continued obstacles.

Thus, particularly in light of the evidence that highly anxious students show greatly diminished impairment under conditions that ease evaluative pressure (Hill, 1972; Nicholls, 1981; I. G. Sarason, 1958, 1972, 1978; S. B. Sarason, Davidson, Lighthall, Waite, & Ruebush, 1960; Wine, 1982) one can conceive of anxious children as simply having greater vulnerability to disruption: *shakier* expectancies than helpless children or a *greater* tendency to inflate the salience or value of incompetent judgments. In any case, the early and substantial impairment of highly anxious children is likely to be related to the fact that they have lower achievement test scores, I.Q. scores, and grades than children low in anxiety (see Hill, 1972; S. B. Sarason et al., 1960), for even if this difference were originally and entirely a result of anxiety (as opposed to a "truly" lower intelligence), the fact would remain that anxious children have a history of poorer performance. In contrast, helpless children do not show evidence of lower I.Q. or test scores in grade school (Licht, 1980). Indeed, Dweck, Davidson, Nelson, and Enna (1978) show how the circumstances that create helplessness need not involve more failure than those that foster mastery orientation (see Langer & Benevento, 1978, for an excellent discussion of nonfailure conditions that can lead to subsequent performance decrements).

Girls more often than boys show performance impairment in achievement situations with adult evaluators (see, e.g., Dweck & Bush, 1976). This may in part relate to the greater emphasis girls versus boys tend to place on adult evaluation and approval (Dweck & Bush, 1976; Harter, 1975; Maehr & Nicholls, 1980; Weisz & McGuire, 1980; Witryol, 1971); boys have been found to show greater impairment than girls under failure from peer evaluators (Dweck & Bush; 1976). The question for present purposes, however, is whether the pattern that girls display compared with that of boys is best conceptualized as an anxiety difference or helplessness difference. We suggest that it shares more of the characteristics of helplessness. Girls do consistently score higher than boys on anxiety scales (although Hill, 1972, suggests that much of this is due to the greater defensiveness of boys) and girls do often show the tendency toward lower expectancies. Yet unlike anxious children and like helpless ones, girls do not tend to have lower I.Q. scores, grades, or achievement test scores (until junior high school, when math achievement may decline) or lower self-esteem scores (see Licht, 1980). Moreover, girls seem most often to display equivalent performance to boys until the onset of failure, and the greater deterioration they may then evidence appears related to their tendency to view negative outcomes as indicative of their competence (i.e., the helpless attribution pattern).

Earlier in our discussion of expectancy formation, we suggested that even when girls' lower expectancies were not related to lower achievement, they reflected greater vulnerability to performance disruption. In the same vein, we would suggest that although the greater helplessness of girls is not related to lower achievement in the grade school years, it may pave the way for it in the future (see Dweck & Licht, 1980; Licht, 1980). An interesting question in the present context is whether in later years when females may indeed show lower achievement, lower self-esteem, and so on, we might then wish to say they have come more to resemble the high-anxiety pattern. We may also wonder, in line with an earlier discussion, whether in these later years lowered expectancies in the face of challenge may combine with greater acceptability of females' relinquishing challenging achievement goals to yield more conservative academic pursuits and career choices.

In the cases we have discussed, children are prevented from pursuing tasks they are capable of mastering because of inappropriately low expectancies. We turn now to goal tendencies that foster unproductive pursuit of goals because of inappropriately high expectancies.

High Expectancies that Are Ungrounded or Unrevised in Light of Outcomes. We have tended to emphasize the low expectancies that can result from failure to perform a systematic task/skill analysis. However, "impulsive," unwarrantedly high expec-

tancies can also result. As we will see, this pattern appears to occur in young children on cognitive tasks (e.g., Flavell & Wellman, 1977; Markman, 1981; Parsons, 1978; Stipek, 1981; Surber, in press) but may also typify older children who are characterized as impulsive (see Bush & Dweck, 1975; Kagan & Kogan, 1970; Meichenbaum, 1977; Zelniker & Jeffrey, 1976). Of course, high expectancies that arise in this way would not tend to have the salutary effects of high expectancies that accompany analysis and planning.

With regard to the issue of unshakably high expectancies, Janoff-Bulman and Brickman (1981) present an interesting analysis of overpersistence in the costly pursuit of tasks that show no signs of solution. They point out how disengagement may be made even more difficult by the inflated goal value stemming from the investment already made. We might note that this pattern may occur with either learning or performance goals and is most likely, as discussed earlier, when means and goals are not regularly evaluated in the context of other, more suitable alternatives.

In both the low-expectancy and high-expectancy achievement-inhibiting patterns, children are hindered in their attainment of goals they themselves value. In the low value pattern, children simply attach little importance to issues of intellectual competence.

Generally Low Value Attached to Achievement Goals. We wish to distinguish this apathy from the apparent apathy of much avoidance behavior that accompanies a low-expectancy/high-value goal of avoiding incompetence judgments. In the latter case, children may defensively devalue activities at which they are afraid of failing. In the cases in question, children simply place little emphasis on competence judgments or competence increases in the academic-intellectual arena. In the grade school years this may be more common among boys, who are less oriented than girls toward evaluations from adults but are more oriented toward peers (Dweck & Bush, 1976; Hollander & Marcia, 1970). Thus teachers' judgments may hold less allure for boys, and the peer group may emphasize competence judgments in domains other than the academic-intellectual. Indeed boys' peers may even directly discourage intellectual activity.

If this situation is combined with experiences that have undermined children's interest in intellectual activities and intellectual mastery experiences (see Lepper, 1980; Lepper & Greene, 1978; Sorensen, 1976, for discussions of the conditions under which reward practices may undermine intrinsic interest), they are left with little reason to initiate intellectual pursuits or to pursue with vigor the ones in which they must engage (see Nicholls, 1979b). Although we are not implying that intellectual activity should be prized above all else, we believe it should be highly prized and enjoyed and therefore regard the low-value pattern as maladaptive.

Inflating Aversive Aspects of Means. A child may typically have a high expectancy of attaining valued goals but also tend to view the initiation or execution of the means with aversion. Indeed this aversion may take on exaggerated proportions because these factors are temporally closer than the potential goal attainment down the road. In order to attain the goals, then, the child must choose to "feel worse" than he or she now does in order later to "feel better." These are circumstances that would appear to foster procrastination or task avoidance. It may be only when anticipated negative consequences of further avoidance come to overwhelm its positive consequences (e.g., as outcome time approaches) that the child will be catapulted into action—at which point any inherent pleasure the task might have offered earlier would be minimized. This counterproductive state of affairs might well be averted were the child able to focus at an earlier point on the more positive aspects of the means or the positive aspects of goal attainment, or were the child able to devise ways of modifying the aversive parts of the activity (see Mischel, 1981).

Focusing on Negative Consequences of Goal Attainment. Here again is a case in which children may have high expectancies and values for achievement goals but are deterred in their pursuit by a focus on negative factors. In this case, the focus is on possible undesirable consequences of goal attainment. This focus may result in what has been called a "fear of success" (Horner, 1972) and in attempts to limit, sabotage, or deny one's attainments (see Horner, 1972; Maracek & Mettee, 1972; Sigall & Gould, 1977). There are indeed many possible negative consequences of success and hence many possible fears of success. One may involve fear of the social repercussions (e.g., disapproval, rejection, rivalries, jealousy; see Horner, 1972; Veroff, 1969); another may involve a heightened fear of subsequent failure (i.e., of an inability to maintain or exceed this newly established standard of performance; see Maracek & Mettee, 1972); a third may involve fear of increased responsibility and loss of dependencies (i.e., the more that children learn to do for themselves, the fewer are the things that are done for them—learning to read may mean no longer being read to).

Much debate has centered around the question of whether fear of success is more prevalent among females than among males. This would be predicted from the notion that achievement is more in conflict with feminine sex role stereotypes and is thus more likely to incur disapproval. Evidence has been adduced to support various positions (see Zuckerman & Wheeler, 1975). It appears to us that given the range of possible fears involved in fear of success (rivalries, responsibilities, sacrifices, etc.), some may be more prevalent in one sex and some in the other (see Hoffman, 1974). Thus a more fine-grained analysis of the salience, expectancy, and value of various competing goals for the two sexes might be highly fruitful. In summary, the presence of conflicting goals, such as affiliative goals or future achievement goals, may create ambivalence about present achievement goals and interfere with the attainment of the latter or the enjoyment of attainment.

These, then, are some of the major expectancy-value patterns that influence learning and performance.

Performance Evaluation

At some point in their learning or performance attempt, children evaluate what they have done, or they receive evaluations of it. We will depict children as implicitly asking such questions as: What have I accomplished given my standards and goals? Is this satisfactory or unsatisfactory? What does this imply? What should I do? In this section we will examine the ways in which performance is affected by the kinds of evaluative questions children ask themselves, when they ask them, and how they answer them. We suggest that learning goals tend to orient children toward questions about progress and strategies, whereas performance goals orient them toward questions about performance relative to others and personal explanations for negative outcomes (see Dweck & Elliott, 1981; Elliott & Dweck, 1981; Nicholls, 1979b, 1981).

Perceived Performance and Goal Attainment. It should be noted that children's evaluation of their performance vis-à-vis their goals need not await any "real" performance outcome but may begin almost at once. That is, merely engaging in the task brings an immediate wealth of information, which may prompt a reevaluation of task difficulty, standards, and so on. Nonetheless, for purposes of clarity we will typically speak in terms of discrete, usually positive or negative, outcomes on discrete problems.

A first step in evaluating performance consists of

obtaining the raw data; for example, how many problems have been correctly solved. The next step consists of putting these data in a context that allows evaluation; for example, how many problems other children have correctly solved. The research suggests that children who display achievement-inhibiting patterns (i.e., learned helpless children, highly anxious children, and in some cases, girls) tend to have more negative perceptions of the raw data. For example, C. I. Diener and Dweck (1978) found that helpless children compared with mastery-oriented children (who experienced identical outcomes) estimated themselves to have solved significantly fewer problems correctly and significantly more problems incorrectly. (Specifically, they underestimated their successes and overestimated their failures.) (Cf. Alloy & Abramson, 1979; Lewinsohn, Mischel, Chaplain, & Barton, 1980, for related findings with depressed versus nondepressed adults.) As noted earlier, in situations where feedback is mixed, neutral, or ambiguous, girls tend to overestimate the negative and boys to overestimate the positive (e.g., V. C. Crandall, 1969). In a similar vein, Meunier and Rule (1967) found that highly anxious students responded to no-feedback trials as they did to negative feedback, whereas students low in anxiety responded to no-feedback as they did to positive feedback.

Subsequent transformations of the data provide further opportunity for such tendencies to operate. For example, C. I. Diener and Dweck (1978) found that when helpless and mastery-oriented children, after performing a task, were asked to estimate how other children had done on the same task, helpless children estimated that others had performed significantly better than mastery-oriented estimated others had. Thus, the normative contexts generated by the helpless and mastery-oriented children would make even the same perceived absolute performance levels appear relatively worse to the helpless child (see Ruble, in press, for a review of recent work on social comparison processes).

Once children have assessed their learning or performance in a way that allows a comparison with their standards, they may ask whether they have attained their goal (have "succeeded") or have made satisfactory progress (are "succeeding"). To the extent that errors are defined as failures (Covington, 1980; C. I. Diener & Dweck, 1978, 1980; Papert, 1980) or that "nonsuccess" is defined as failure (Holt, 1964), children are more likely to conclude that their performance is inadequate. To the extent that the initial stages of performance are viewed as the beginning of a learning process, there would be

less of a tendency to focus on and label past nonsolutions as failures and more of a focus on future success and strategies for bringing it about (see C. I. Diener & Dweck, 1978; Elliott & Dweck 1981).

Once children characterize their performance, they may draw implications from it—about their ability, about their strategy, about the task, and so on—that form the basis of their future actions (see Maehr, 1976, for a discussion of "continuing motivation").

Causal Inferences: Attributions and Strategy Analysis. Attributions are explanations for successes and failures, causal ascriptions for outcomes (see Weiner, 1972, 1974). We view them as being less often explicit explanations that result from careful causal analyses, and more often implicit, frequently habitual ways of understanding outcomes. That is, although a child may be quite capable of engaging in a sophisticated causal analysis, he or she may often react to outcomes in ambiguous situations by finding rather ready-made explanations (e.g., see Covington & Omelich, 1979a). Thus a child who has been performing well and who suddenly confronts an obstacle may react by quickly blaming his or her ability (C. I. Diener & Dweck, 1978).

One type of systematic analysis that many children do and should often engage in is a strategy analysis. That is, as they work on a task, they may continually monitor their strategies and plan new ones in light of outcomes. In a sense the child here is asking: Should I and how should I modify my task behavior in order to be successful in the future? In contrast, the attribution-seeking child may be portrayed as focusing on a failure and asking, in effect, whether or not there is a future on the task. In both cases, the child who confronts a negative outcome is asking: What does this mean? Yet the first child asks what this means for future solution-oriented strategies, whereas the second is more likely to be asking such questions as: What does this mean about me? Does it pay to continue, or is it hopeless, or too risky?

The evidence suggests that the tendency to focus on causal attributions is associated with achievement-inhibiting patterns and impaired performance in the face of obstacles (see C. I. Diener & Dweck, 1978, 1980; Elliott & Dweck, 1981; Heckhausen, 1981, 1982), whereas the tendency to focus on strategy or effort modification is associated with enhanced performance (see A. Bandura, 1979). Research carried out within the attributional framework has yielded findings that are consonant with these. Specifically, explanations for failure that emphasize strategy or effort are related to persistence or facilitation of learning and performance in the face of difficulty (Anderson & Jennings, 1980; Andrews & Debus, 1978; Chapin & Dyck, 1976; C. I. Diener & Dweck, 1978; Dweck, 1975; Dweck & Reppucci, 1973; Jennings, 1979; Licht & Dweck, 1981; Rhodes, 1977; Weiner, 1972, 1974), whereas explanations for failure that focus on one's ability or intelligence predict performance deterioration.

We suggest that these two processes of attribution and strategy analysis are best coordinated: If a child who has engaged in continual strategy analysis has reached an impasse, it may be wise to consider an array of causal factors; conversely, a child who is engaging in a causal analysis may wish to include a strategy analysis as part of this diagnostic process (see also Wong & Weiner, 1981).

We also suggest that more frequent analysis of *positive* outcomes may be beneficial. The research shows causal analysis to be more likely following negative outcomes than following positive ones (Lau & Russell, 1980; Pyszczynki & Greenberg, 1981; Wong & Weiner, 1981). This is not surprising in light of the fact that negative events (failure, disease, rejection) are typically viewed as calling for some coping action whereas positive events typically are not. Yet successes that are analyzed and understood may be more likely to be credited to one's ability, to be viewed as replicable, and thus to contribute to high and realistic future expectancies. Findings from much research support the notion that viewing successes as indicative of ability is associated with achievement-producing patterns (e.g., C. I. Diener & Dweck, 1980; Kukla, 1972, 1978; Parsons, in press; Weiner & Kukla, 1970), as opposed to viewing success as being a matter of chance, task ease, the beneficence of others, and the like.

Causal inferences have also been related to the affect that is experienced following outcomes (Sohn, 1977; Weiner, 1982; Weiner, Russell, & Lerman, 1978, 1979). Such outcome affect might positively reinforce (e.g., pride), negatively reinforce (e.g., relief), or punish (e.g., shame) the goal-oriented behavior. Thus, along with causal cognitions, outcome affect itself might influence the continuation or resumption of achievement activity.

If it is adaptive for children to think strategy in the face of difficulty, and to view successes rather than failures as indicative of their ability, what are some conditions that foster these tendencies? First, a number of studies have examined the effects of directly training children to focus on effort or strategy instead of insufficient ability when they are confronted with difficulty (Andrews & Debus, 1978; Chapin & Dyck, 1976; Dweck, 1975; Rhodes,

1977). These procedures have typically resulted in appreciably increased persistence under failure, and this persistence has tended to generalize to new tasks (e.g., Rhodes, 1977) and endure over substantial periods of time (e.g., Chapin & Dyck, 1976). Training programs that instruct children in strategic thinking and task/skills analysis are also likely to increase children's tendency to analyze their strategies when they encounter obstacles (see A. Bandura, 1981; Covington, 1980; deCharms, 1972; Meichenbaum, 1977).

Particular feedback patterns can promote the different types of inferences as well. For example, Dweck, Davidson, Nelson, and Enna (1978) demonstrated the manner in which teachers' classroom feedback may lead girls to view failures as indicative of ability but boys to view successes as indicative of theirs—even when girls are more positively regarded and more positively treated. Also contrary to the commonly held belief that praise bolsters confidence and promotes persistence are the results of Meyer, Bachman, Biermann, Hempelmann, Ploger, and Spiller (1979), who found that praise after success and neutral feedback after failure led to inferences of low ability. (See also Dweck, 1975, who found that "success" conditions, in which failure was eliminated or glossed over, led to no improvement, or even further impairment, in helpless children's ability to cope with subsequent failure.)

Simply orienting children toward learning versus performance goals may determine whether they think strategy or dwell on ability in the face of failure. Elliott and Dweck (1981) found that even when children believed they had low ability they nonetheless continued to focus on strategy and to persist under failure when they were experimentally oriented toward learning goals. In sharp contrast, when such children were oriented toward performance goals, they showed the typical helpless pattern of ability attributions and performance deterioration under failure.

Goal Revision

We have suggested that children differ in the salience or weight that negative and positive outcomes have for them, in their tendency to define themselves as succeeding or failing, and in the inferences they draw from their successes and failures. We would like to examine more closely the consequences of these inferences for their revision of their goals.

Specifically, in light of their outcomes children may reevaluate any of the variables that affect the expectancies or the values of their goals. For example, they may decide that they have more or less ability than they had previously believed, that the task is harder or easier, that the evaluator is more or less exacting, or that their standards were inappropriately high or low. As we suggested in our treatment of expectancy formulation, if children revise their estimates of factors that they believe to be stable, uncontrollable, and global, they will be most likely to revise their expectancies (Weiner, 1972, 1974, 1982; see also McMahan, 1973). We suggest that such expectancy revision, particularly downward revision, is most likely to occur with performance goals. First, performance goals are fostered by and, in turn, foster views of ability as a stable, uncontrollable, global factor (M. Bandura & Dweck, 1981; Dweck & Elliott, 1981; Nicholls, 1981). Moreover, since the performance goals entail judgments of this ability, lowering one's estimate of it would be likely to dampen one's expectancy of being judged competent or of avoiding a negative judgment through performance,[6] and escalating one's effort level in order to maintain the expected level of performance involves the risk of affirming the estimate of low ability (see Covington & Omelich, 1979b,c; Nicholls, 1976a). However, in the context of learning goals not only is ability more likely to be viewed as specific and acquirable, but learning goals encourage the view that "low ability" can be compensated for by additional effort. Thus children with learning goals who experience unanticipated difficulty and decide that they are not as adept at the task as they had suspected may simply conclude that more effort is now required for them to reach their standards.

Goal revision is a process that may continue well after discrete outcomes cease. As time passes, a child can re-evaluate both the nature of past outcomes and their meaning for future ones (Janoff-Bulman & Brickman, 1981). Again, learning goals may foster a view of "unsuccessful" past endeavors as having been ultimately worthwhile and as perhaps meriting further consideration.

In summary, in light of perceived outcomes and their implications, children may reenter the model from the top and emerge with different goal expectancies, different goal values, and perhaps different goals.

THE DEVELOPMENT OF ACHIEVEMENT MOTIVATION[7]

We know that children engage in competence-increasing activity as soon as they appear in our world, if not before. We also know that they do not yet engage in expectancy-value thinking but rather are more creatures of reflex, drive, and habit. Thus, we might look at the proposed model of "mature" achievement motivational processes depicted in Figure 1 and ask: What parts of this system might be sufficient to instigate, sustain, and reinforce competence-producing activity in a basically precognitive individual? Can we isolate portions that involve chiefly reflexive or simply associative mechanisms and sensory-motor/affective processes? And can we begin to understand, how, with development, they become elaborated into the processes we have just examined?

In this section, then, we will draw from the relevant literature on early motivational systems, on general developmental changes, and on specific changes in achievement-related variables in a preliminary attempt to chart the emergence of achievement motivation from early mastery or competence motivation. We will focus on two major periods: (1) the original appearance of achievement motivation, marked by the emergence of achievement goals and evaluative standards, and (2) the major changes that take place over the early school years with the emergence of new achievement goals and standards. We will propose that these changes reflect the emergence and evolution of the child's ideas about competence and are tied to the emergence and evolution of the "self" (see Kagan, 1978; Piaget & Inhelder, 1969). Indeed, children's striving to increase or document their competence can be seen as a means of self-definition and the way in which it is done as both reflecting and determining their self-concepts.

We suggest, as have psychobiologists studying motivational systems (Satinoff, 1982) and biologists studying cognitive development (Piaget, 1963, 1964), that when new, more advanced regulatory systems develop, the old, more primitive systems do not go out of business. Rather, they continue along, regulated by the fancier system. From an evolutionary perspective, it is quite adaptive to have multiple layers of systems helping to ensure the maintenance of life-sustaining activity. Thus as we chart the changes from early mastery motivation up to our model of "mature" achievement motivation, we will retain virtually all the instigating and maintaining forces that are present from the start.

However, we will also argue that the greater flexibility afforded by the more advanced regulatory system has dangers as well. To the extent that the motivational systems can be brought under cognitive control, maladaptive cognitions can distort (suppress, exaggerate, or pervert) the experience and expression of even the most basic drives. Many eating and sexual disorders, for example, can be found to have cognitive bases. In this vein, we suggest that as various cognitive structures for regulating achievement activity emerge, the basic "mastery urge" may be filtered through those structures with happy or unhappy consequences. Specifically, we suggest that dynamic, incremental views of competence may maintain the essence of mastery motivation, whereas static, entity views of competence are more likely to distort its experience and expression.

The Transition from Mastery Motivation to Achievement Motivation: Goals and Standards

Infants are said to display mastery (or competence, or effectance) motivation, basically conceived of as an urge to understand and manage the environment (see Donaldson, 1978; Harter, 1981a; R. W. White, 1959). These terms have been used to explain why even the youngest infants do what is good for them—why they seem naturally to do things that promote their own learning. Specifically, they appear to seek and be engaged by the kinds of tasks or stimulation that tend to maximize competence increases (Bruner, 1971; Elkind, 1972; Hunt, 1963, 1965; Izard, 1978; Piaget, 1954). Taking together the views of various investigators, we may see the mastery motivation "system" as involving a series of (affective?) states that instigate, maintain, and reinforce competence-producing activity (see Izard, 1978, 1979). Figure 3 depicts in broad outline the proposed processes involved in this system.

On the instigation side, some investigators have keyed on the types of stimulus situations that engage the child and incite action (e.g., Dember, 1960; Dember & Earl, 1957; Hunt, 1965; Piaget, 1954). It is generally proposed that a moderate degree of discrepancy between some external stimulus (or task or observed behavior, etc.) and the child's representa-

tion (expectations, schemata, present skills, etc.) provokes a state of arousal or internal disequilibrium. The child then works to bring the world and him- or herself into line (to resolve the discrepancy or incongruity, to reduce the uncertainty, to make the novel familiar, to match the standard) and regain the state of equilibrium. Other investigators have keyed on internal states (curiosity or exploratory "drives") that impel the child to seek or produce novelty or stimulus variability (e.g., Berlyne, 1960).

Once the mental or physical activity is initiated, the child appears to derive pleasure directly from engaging in it (Heckhausen, 1981; Hunt, 1965; Nuttin, 1973), and when mastery is attained, the child appears to experience satisfaction or joy (Izard, 1978; R. W. White, 1959). Both the pleasure inherent in the activity and that attending the outcome can reinforce the activity. They may come to be anticipated and thus serve increasingly to promote future initiation of such activities.

This system can be seen to require relatively little in the way of cognitive apparatus. The major thing that is needed along these lines is some way of registering discrepancy. Indeed the cognitive immaturity of the child—the lack of distinction between self and environment or the lack of dissociation between affect and sensory-motor activity (Piaget & Inhelder, 1969)—may be precisely what allows the discrepancies reliably to drive affect, and affect reliably to drive activity. In short, with the mastery motivation system the child need not plan, intend, or evaluate an outcome in order to set the wheels in motion and reach a satisfying destination.

Kagan (1978) proposes that the "self" be viewed as the psychological function that recognizes and evaluates alternative possibilities, both with respect to courses of action and outcomes (means and ends) and with respect to one's own personal qualities. Given that achievement motivation in-

Figure 3. Mastery Motivation: Proposed Processes

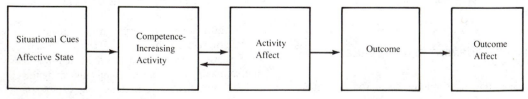

volves the purposeful pursuit of competence and the evaluation of competence, then the emergence of this function called "self" and the emergence of achievement motivation would seem to go hand in hand (see Heckhausen, 1981; Veroff, 1969). Although investigators differ in their estimates of when these functions emerge and crystallize, there is agreement that they are in full force by 3 years of age. By that age children can cognitively represent and react to self-related (e.g., competence) goals and can act in order to bring them about; they can evaluate the outcomes of these actions against standards of competence, view outcomes as reflecting on the self, and experience consequent positive or negative self-related affect (e.g., pride or shame) (Heckhausen, 1967, 1981; Kagan, 1978; Piaget, 1962; Veroff, 1969). Figure 4, a proposed representation of early achievement motivation, depicts these processes as they build on the mastery motivation system.

We note that despite our depiction of the competence-increasing activity as now being goal-oriented, we still depict only the learning goal. Although the groundwork has been laid for performance goals (e.g., in terms of self-related judgments and affect), and although, as we will see, performance goals can be induced, they are not yet likely to be in strong contention under ordinary circumstances. Among the major developments that remain in order to transform the model of early achievement motivation into the model of "mature" achievement motivation are new ways of defining and evaluating self and competence that, in certain environments, may bring performance goals into sharp focus.

The Transition to School: New Goals and Standards

In this section we will focus on the changes in achievement motivation that take place during the early years of school, when children confront in a serious and sustained fashion issues of learning and performance in the intellectual domain. As we have suggested and will discuss, before this time most children tend to display the characteristics of the learning-oriented, achievement-producing pattern—specifically, a more incremental view of abil-

Figure 4. Early Achievement Motivation: Proposed Basic Processes

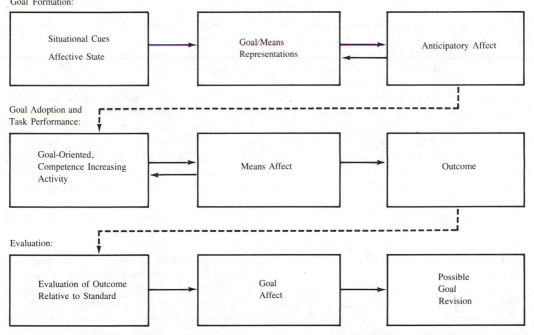

Note: cf. Figures 1 and 3.

ity, high perceived competence, high performance expectancies, personal standards, and continued optimism in the face of difficulty. We will suggest that with school, at least two major factors come into play that foster the adoption of performance goals: (1) children learn a new, entity, definition of ability that may lead them to seek normative or comparative competence judgments, and (2) they confront new tasks that differ in fundamental and critical ways and that may orient them more toward adults' judgments.

Let us first examine the major changes in children's achievement beliefs and behavior that occur in the early school years (see S. White, 1970, for a discussion of the widespread changes that take place at approximately 7 years of age).

Changes in Achievement Beliefs and Behavior

First, the concept of ability appears to undergo a transformation. Before the age of about 7, children seem to conceive of it more readily as the presence of a specific skill (i.e., the "ability" to do a task or produce a correct response) (see Frieze, Francis, & Hanusa, 1981; Heckhausen, 1981; Miscione, Marvin, O'Brien, & Greenberg, 1978; Veroff, 1969). After 7 they begin to be more able to conceive of ability as a more global, stable, psychological trait (see Heckhausen, 1981; Rholes & Ruble, 1981; Ruble, in press). This shift may be part of a more general developmental change in self-understanding from an emphasis on actions and physical attributes to an emphasis on psychological attributes (see Damon & Hart, 1982). (The latter, in turn, may be linked to increasing metacognitive skills, that is, increasing ability to take one's own mental processes as the objects of thought.) Ruble (in press) suggests that the great upsurge between the ages of 7 and 9 in the use of social comparison for self-evaluation of competence (see also Pepitone, 1972; Veroff, 1969) may well be related to the new tendency to look for personal traits. Although the requisite cognitive skills for engaging in social comparison seem to be present before that time, earlier social comparisons appear to be aimed more at gaining information about answers or strategies (Feldman & Ruble, 1977; Ruble, Boggiano, Feldman, & Lobel, 1980).

There has been some controversy over the developmental course of judgments of ability in relation to effort. Basically, in this research individuals of varying ages are given information about an actor's level of performance and effort and they are asked to judge the actor's level of ability. Individuals can judge ability to be unrelated to effort (and solely a

function of performance), they can judge it to be inversely related to effort (greater effort implies lower ability), or they can judge it to be positively related to effort (greater effort implies greater ability). It had been widely assumed that the most mature or correct view of ability involves perceiving it as inversely related to effort, and some of the earlier studies (with subjects ranging from kindergarten through college) appeared to provide support for a developmental progression from perceiving a positive relationship to an inverse one (e.g., Kun, 1977). However, others found the inverse relationship to predominate as early as first grade (Karabenick & Heller, 1976). An elegant series of recent studies by Surber (1980, 1981, in press), which included a reanalysis of Kun's (1977) data, appears to shed light on this issue. Although the results showed nonsignificant tendencies for the inverse relationship to increase over the grade school years, the strongest and most consistent finding was that children of all ages used the information in two distinct ways—some showing an inverse and others a positive relationship. Thus rather than reliable developmental differences in judgments, there appear to be individual differences in judgment. Moreover, even though college students have been shown to favor strongly the inverse relationship (Karabenick & Heller, 1976; Surber, 1980), Surber (in press) describes findings from a recent study with college students in which approximately half of the sample judged ability to increase as effort increased. In this study, subjects were given information about how hard hypothetical students had studied and how well they performed. We would like to suggest that perhaps when the information presented orients subjects toward an incremental view of ability or an acquisition process (studying increases knowledge or ability), the likelihood is increased that individuals of all ages will judge ability to be positively related to effort. Conversely, when the information orients subjects toward a view of ability as a more fixed quality (at least within the situation) or toward performance on a given occasion (e.g., Karabenick and Heller, 1976, described actors who "had to try very hard" or "didn't have to try at all" to solve a puzzle), the likelihood is increased that individuals of all ages will judge ability to be inversely related to effort. It may also be the case that the nonsignificant trends for older children to use the inverse rule more than younger children reflects a differential tendency that would be maximized when the stimulus situation was maximally ambiguous with respect to the implied view of ability. Or, to combine our immediately preceding discussion (of ability as a global, stable trait) with the present discussion, we might also propose that developmental differences may be more evident when children are asked to reason about general intellectual capacity (smartness or intelligence as in Nicholls, 1978) than about specific abilities (good at puzzles, as in Kun, 1977, or Karabenick & Heller, 1976) or physical ability (physical strength, as in Surber, 1980).

In summary, the developmental changes in the concept of competence in the early school years appear to involve a growing ability or tendency to view intellectual competence as a more global, stable personal characteristic. It has been suggested that this growing belief in the existence of stable psychological individual differences gives rise to a sharp increase in children's use of social comparison to evaluate their competence. Yet the ability to view intellectual competence as a global, stable quality does not imply that it will necessarily be used that way or even that it is generally most mature or correct to use this view as the basis for one's judgments. Instead, it is best seen as another view that is available for use in place of or in conjunction with a more dynamic view of ability. Indeed the most "mature" view of intelligence may well represent an integration of the two views, specifically a recognition of relative aptitude but an emphasis on individual growth (cf. Veroff, 1969).[8]

A similar picture emerges when we examine in more detail the kinds of standards (personal versus normative) children use to evaluate ability or define success. We noted above that young children (age 6 and below) appear to use correct task completion as a definition of success and evidence of ability (Frieze, Francis, & Hanusa, 1981; Heckhausen, 1981; Miscione et al., 1978; Veroff, 1969), but that then over the early school years normative or social standards come into frequent use (Pepitone, 1972; Ruble, in press; Ruhland & Feld, 1977; Veroff, 1969). However, during this time, individual standards continue to coexist (see Feld, Ruhland, & Gold, 1979) and in some cases may reemerge as a dominant tendency in later school years (post grade school) (see Heckhausen, 1981; Veroff, 1969). This reemergence may reflect what Veroff (1969) refers to as "autonomous achievement motivation integrated with social comparison strivings" and it overlaps in some ways with what we would refer to as a mature incremental theory of intelligence.

Next we consider the changes in level of perceived ability, perceived task difficulty, and performance expectancy that take place over the early school years. The evidence suggests that young children tend to view their ability as being extremely high, tend to underestimate task difficulty, and tend to hold and maintain high expectancies. The evidence suggests further that they are in fact capable of being as pessimistic as older children (e.g., when negative outcomes are made more salient) but are less apt to focus on negatives in more ambiguous situations.

It is a striking finding that in kindergarten and first grade most children rank themselves at or near the top of their class (Nicholls, 1979a; Marshall, Weinstein, Middlestadt, & Bratiesani, 1980; Stipek, 1981), although their ratings of other students may mirror the teachers' ratings (Stipek, 1981). From second grade on, however, children's self-perceptions move more into line with teacher ratings. On specific tasks as well, younger children may rate their abilities as being higher than older children rate their own (see Parsons, 1978; Ruble, 1975) and may also rate the task as being easier than older children do (Parsons, 1978). Younger children also tend to show higher performance expectancies even in the face of repeated failures (Parsons & Ruble, 1977; Ruble, Parsons, & Ross, 1976; Stipek, 1981; Weisz, 1981), although even preschoolers (4-year-olds) *can* show systematic declines under failure conditions when evaluation is heightened or outcomes are made salient (Stipek, 1981). (It is interesting that the tendency not to lower expectancies appreciably in the face of failure may depart sooner in females than males [Parsons & Ruble, 1977]. As Heckhausen, 1981, suggests, perhaps girls are in advance of boys in viewing ability as a cause of failure and therefore in showing lowered expectancies. It may also be the case that such patterns established early will tend to persist, especially when they continue to receive support from the environment [see Dweck, Davidson, Nelson, & Enna, 1978].)

In evaluating the pro's and con's of young children's optimism, we would ask (1) are their high expectancies "unrealistic," and (2) are they associated with achievement-producing behavior? We suggest that when the tasks are clearly comprehended, when the activity seems meaningful, and when the situation is seen as an achievement situation, the optimistic beliefs tend to be "realistic" and are associated with achievement-producing behavior.

With regard to the question of whether young children's high expectancies are unrealistic, it is clear that they sometimes are, particularly on cognitive tasks where the children have failed to analyze the task requirements or to reflect on their level of skill or understanding (see Flavell & Wellman, 1977; Markman, 1981). However, if young children tend to adopt a learning set when confronted with tasks (and if they do not expect adults to give them tasks they cannot learn), then it would not seem generally unrealistic of them to continue to believe, even in the face of difficulty, that they will improve, will gradually or suddenly catch on to how to do the task, and will ultimately succeed. Young children confront many difficult tasks on which sudden breakthroughs may be preceded by a long series of complete misses (e.g., learning to ride a bicycle, to swim, to tie a bow, to whistle). We would not consider their optimism to be misguided in these instances.

With regard to the question of whether young children tend to display achievement-producing behavior, again the picture is a bit complex. Do young children choose challenging tasks? Although a number of investigators have found that younger children are more likely than older ones to choose to repeat tasks at which they have been successful as opposed to ones at which they have not (e.g., Bialer, 1961; Bialer & Cromwell, 1960), Young and Egeland (1976) found no such tendency when task difficulty was matched to children's grade level. Moreover, from the perspective of a learning goal, "practicing" on an apparently easier version of the same type of task (after one has failed an apparently more difficult one) does not necessarily constitute an avoidance of a challenge. There is also evidence to suggest that when the information about task difficulty is presented to young children in concrete terms that they can comprehend (as opposed to normative ones that they cannot), when the task is familiar and meaningful to them (unlike many of the abstract, decontextualized intellectual tasks presented to them in experimental situations), and when they perceive the situation to be an achievement situation (as opposed to, for example, a play situation or a compliance situation), then they will more typically choose appropriately challenging tasks (see Nicholls, 1978, 1980; Schneider, 1981).

Do young children show mastery-oriented behavior on challenging tasks? A recent study by Rholes, Blackwell, Jordan, and Walters (1980) addressed this question directly. When children (grades K–5) were exposed to repeated failure on a hidden-figure task, young children proved to be less susceptible to learned helplessness, as reflected in measures of both persistence and performance (see also Weisz, 1981).

In sum, young children's optimism is often viewed as a sign of their immaturity and poor processing skills, and this may sometimes be the case. However, we suggest that it may also reflect a reasonable, coherent, and often adaptive orientation toward achievement situations. It may be, as implied earlier, that young children's achievement motivation can be seen as consisting of mastery motivation with a cognitive overlay that channels and regulates achievement strivings but that maintains the preeminence of competence-increasing activity. For older children, the additional cognitive, and metacognitive, overlay may grant them new power to choose, plan, execute, monitor, evaluate, revise, and sustain more generalized, long-term competence-increasing activity, but it may also generate greater self-consciousness, caution, and vulnerability in the realm of achievement. In attempts to understand environmental shifts that may contribute to these changes, it is often recognized that with entry into school, children do their learning in a social, perhaps competitive setting. Undoubtedly important as well, however, is the profound change in what they are now asked to learn (Bruner, 1965; Donaldson, 1979).

Changes from Physical to Intellectual Tasks

Prior to their attending school, children's experience with sustained effort and concentration in the service of skill acquisition has been centered around physical skills. With school there comes for many children the first major experience of deliberate, sustained (and required) effort aimed at the acquisition of intellectual skills. These two types of skills differ from each other in major ways, ways that may tend to make the acquisition of intellectual skills very much more an adult-defined and -judged enterprise, at least at the outset. First, many physical skills tend to be ones that children themselves value and choose to learn, or at least can easily grasp the value of. In contrast, many intellectual or conceptual skills, such as arithmetic, spelling or grammar, are ones that adults define as valuable but whose value may not be apparent to the child (and whose acquisition may appear tedious and laborious).

Second, on physical tasks, compared with intellectual ones, children can more easily launch, monitor, and guide the acquisition process and judge their own successes. This is because physical tasks usually have observable execution processes and observable outcomes whose adequacy can be readily judged by inspection (e.g., the child has or has not caught the ball, tied his or her shoes, ridden the bicycle). Moreover children need not have a deliberate, advance plan of attack, since they can experiment with observable process–outcome covariations. In the intellectual domain (e.g., solving arithmetic problems) the problem-solving process requires a planned, covert sequence of skills. Further, the process yields an answer (e.g., ''4'') whose quality or correctness is not self-evident from inspection (is not like the prespecified end state of a physical task) but must be subjected to further evaluation. Thus, before children have become metacognitive sophisticates an adult may be needed to teach the process, judge the products, and monitor progress.

In short, on intellectual tasks children may be less likely to know what they are aiming for, why they are aiming for it, how to get there, and when they have gotten there. Whereas on physical tasks the adult is chiefly a guide of the child's own learning process, on intellectual tasks the child may become a participant in the adult's teaching and evaluation process.

The Risks of Developmental Change

If we put the major points from our last section together, we gain a picture of children in transition—grappling with new kinds of tasks that may foster a greater orientation toward adults' evaluations, revising their concepts of competence and seeking information about this competence. Along with these changes appear to come declines in perceived ability and in confidence of success, as well as increased vulnerability to the effects of failure. In this context, it is interesting to note Harter's (1981a) finding of what seems to be a most dramatic decline over the grade school years in children's intrinsic interest in learning compared with their desire to perform to obtain teacher approval and good grades (see also Nicholls, 1981).

It is clear that developmental change can be a risky business. Greater cognitive capacity for self-reflection can provide the tools for new levels of mastery but can also result in greater inhibition of mastery attempts. In our own research with grade school children we have been continually impressed with how malleable the achievement tendencies of children this age are, how subject to influence by relatively subtle experimental manipulations (e.g., Dweck et al., 1978; Elliott & Dweck, 1981). We suspect, however, that in adolescence, when children form more coherent pictures of themselves and characterize themselves in terms of even more generalized and stable characteristics, some of these tendencies may become more resistant to change (Berzonsky & Barclay, 1981; Harari & Covington, 1981). Again, the ability to reason about abstract hypothetical entities opens many avenues of intellectual inquiry, but when the entity about which one

reasons is oneself there is potential for unflattering conclusions with undesirable consequences. Furthermore, this comes at a time when children may begin to make academic decisions that affect the course of their future pursuits.

It is indeed fortunate for our species that infants and young children seem naturally drawn to activities that promote mastery of the environment and that foster their development (Elkind, 1972; Hunt, 1965; R. W. White, 1959), for what would happen if infants learning to walk paused to reflect on the implications of errors for their general competence, for their futures as locomotors, or for the esteem in which they are held by others? If new capacities breed new vulnerabilities, how can we learn what socializing factors encourage enduring achievement-producing patterns? We will now turn to this question.

DIRECTIONS AND STRATEGIES FOR SOCIALIZATION RESEARCH

Given the growing understanding of achievement motivational processes, we believe that researchers can now investigate socialization issues with new clarity. Therefore, in this section we discuss several conceptual and methodological issues of importance for future socialization research, among them: (1) distinguishing clearly between achievement motivational patterns and achievement outcomes, such as grades; (2) distinguishing clearly among the different motivational patterns under study, especially those involving different achievement goals; (3) generating specific hypotheses, for example, about particular instructional feedback practices that foster particular motivational characteristics, and (4) utilizing research strategies that permit clearer causal inferences to be drawn. To illustrate these issues, we will examine some of the findings from past socialization research within the framework we have developed throughout the chapter. We will then generate hypotheses about cause–effect relationships and propose a three-stage research strategy for testing such hypotheses.

Achievement Motivational Patterns Versus Achievement Outcomes

In many ways socialization research has been hindered by the frequent failure to maintain a clear distinction between achievement motivational patterns and achievement outcomes, such as grades. That is, it has often been assumed, particularly in classroom research, that observing adult practices that relate to "high achievement" in children would reveal the practices that foster desirable achievement motivational patterns. Indeed, a frequent implication is that lower-achieving children are being discriminated against by not being given the same treatment as high achievers.

Yet, as our foregoing discussions have highlighted, high grades, high achievement test scores, or high I.Q. scores in the grade school years can by no means be equated with "optimal" motivational patterns. For example, among girls, the highest achievers may have motivational patterns that render them vulnerable to disruption. In addition, boys, who are on the whole poorer students than girls during these years, often appear to be the more challenge-seeking and resilient. Thus one might well hesitate to replicate with lower-achieving girls and with boys the factors that foster the motivational tendencies observed in high-achieving girls.

Moreover, the research on teacher–student interactions in the classroom has failed to reveal any consistent "facilitating" interaction style that teachers display toward high versus low achievers (see Brophy & Good, 1974; Brophy, 1979). In view of our analysis of achievement motivation, this is not surprising, for our analysis suggests many motivational routes to high or low achievement outcomes. For example, there are several achievement motivational patterns (e.g., expectancy-value-goal patterns) that we would predict to foster high grades and low ones. Specifically, high grades may be fostered by learning goals when the child holds a high value for the skills to be learned in school or has high interest in the tasks to be performed in school. High grades may also be fostered by both of the performance goals when there is high confidence in attaining those goals and when the child places high value on adults' judgments. Indeed, as noted earlier, a combination of the two performance goals may yield an excessively high-effort pattern aimed at eliminating any possibility of negative judgment. This may in fact be the predominant grade-producing pattern in many schools.

Low grades as well can be associated with either learning or performance goals, as for example, when children who tend to have learning goals find low value or interest in school activities, or when children who tend to have performance goals place low value on the teacher's evaluations (e.g., versus those of peers) or have low expectancies of obtaining positive evaluations and avoiding negative ones.

Given this analysis, it is interesting to note findings from the parent-child socialization literature: Parental practices associated with high grades in children appear similar to those practices associated with potentially debilitating motivational patterns. Specifically, the former, high grades, are found to be related to a high degree of parental dominance, pressure, evaluation, and criticism (G. W. Miller, 1970; Teichmann, Gollnitz, & Gohler, 1975; cf. V. C. Crandall & Battle, 1970). (Of course, such tactics would be expected to relate to high grades only when the child maintained a reasonably high expectancy of attaining those performance goals [see V. C. Crandall, 1966].) In a similar vein, the latter, debilitating motivational patterns, are often found to be related to unreasonable parental expectations for the child; overly direct, specific, intrusive help (versus general, facilitating assistance); criticism for errors (versus praise for progress), and the use of normative standards for judgment (Baumrind, 1971, 1973; Hermans, Ter-Laak, & Maes, 1972; Rosen & D'Andrade, 1959; S. B. Sarason, Davidson, Lighthall, Waite, & Ruebush, 1960; Trudewind & Husarek, reported in Heckhausen, 1981). These practices may well foster an entity view of intelligence and a concern with competence judgments from adults, particularly negative judgments.

In summary, it is critical in socialization research to distinguish achievement motivational patterns from achievement outcomes, for "desirable" patterns and "desirable" outcomes are not equivalent and, it appears, are often not related. Instead, research findings raise the unfortunate suspicion that motivational patterns often associated with good performance in our schools are not the patterns that are associated with independent initiation of challenges, persistence in the face of obstacles, or resilience after failure. This may suggest why those who are the stars in the grade years—girls—are often not the achievers later on.

Possible Determinants of Interaction Styles

What might determine adults' instructional interaction styles with particular children? First, there are the characteristics of the adult, such as the adult's theory of intelligence and his or her emphasis on learning or performance goals for the child. Teachers who favor incremental theories of intelligence and learning goals for children (as opposed to those with entity views and performance goals) would be predicted to act more as resources versus judges, to focus children more on process versus outcome, to react to errors as natural and useful versus as failures, to stress effort and personal standard versus ability and normative standards, to stimulate achievement through intrinsic versus extrinsic means (see Table 1). Furthermore, whereas teachers with an entity theory of intelligence may value "intelligence" (as they view it) and may favor "intelligent" children, teachers with an incremental theory may distribute the quantity and quality of their attention more equally, or may even devote more attention to fostering learning in less skilled children. Brophy and Good (1974) report individual differences among teachers in whether their instructional and feedback practices tend to favor high or low achievers. We propose that these differences may be related to teachers' theories and goals.

We do not wish to suggest that children are simply victims or beneficiaries of adults' practices, for we view children as often being accomplices, and sometimes even instigators. That is, children who act in particular ways may "pull" certain behavior from adults that, in turn, may promote and perpetuate certain motivational patterns. For example, when children become embarrassed or disoriented after making an error, teachers may, out of sympathy, turn to someone else for the answer or supply it themselves, instead of remaining with that child and teaching him or her to work out different solution-oriented strategies (see Brophy & Good, 1974). Or, children at particular points in development may crave different types of information about ability, such as social comparison information (Ruble, in press; Veroff, 1969). Teachers, in complying, may create a continuing overreliance on normative standards of success.

It is interesting to speculate whether the growing use of computers as instructors will minimize some of these problems by increasing the emphasis on process and strategy regardless of children's preexisting dispositions. Even so, computer programs can capitalize on motivational research to determine how best to do so. For example, achievement-producing patterns appear to be fostered not by eliminating errors from children's learning, but by teaching children how to use them constructively (Dweck, 1975; Papert, 1980).

Testing Hypotheses About Causal Relationships: A Three-Stage Research Strategy

Most of the research on the relationship between adult practices and children's motivational patterns has been correlational in nature, examining interactions with children who already display certain characteristics. Yet it is of course important to learn what specific beliefs and behaviors on the part of the socializer lead to what specific beliefs and behaviors on the part of the child. Toward this end we propose

and illustrate a three-stage research strategy consisting of: (1) field observation and correlation, (2) laboratory experimentation, and (3) field experimentation (see, e.g., Dweck, Davidson, Nelson, & Enna, 1978).

Basically, in order to test hypotheses about causal relationships, the first stage might involve measuring adults' (e.g., teachers') beliefs or observing their instructional practices and then determining whether these correlate with the achievement beliefs and behavior of target children (i.e., those children who are the objects of the different practices). For example, one hypothesis that can be drawn from the work of Brophy and Good (1974) is that the way teachers respond to children's errors during class recitations will affect children's perception of errors as failures, their attributions for failures, and their persistence in seeking solutions. Specifically, children who are typically given additional opportunities to supply the correct answer, along with clues and strategy suggestions, might be expected to be less likely to view errors as failures, more likely to view errors as indicating the need for effort or strategy variation, and more likely to show persistence. In contrast, children who are typically given little time or encouragement by the teacher to revise their errors (e.g., by the teacher's directly supplying the answer or calling on another child to supply it) might be expected to be more likely to view errors as failures, attribute them to a lack of ability, and show less persistence in the face of obstacles. Brophy and Good (1974) report that some teachers show the former, "facilitating" style more toward children they consider to be high achievers, some more toward children they consider to be low achievers. Some teachers do not discriminate between high and low achievers in this regard but differ from each other in the degree to which they employ one style or the other. Thus if one assessed and compared the relevant achievement beliefs and behaviors of children in the four types of classrooms (e.g., by individually administering measures and tasks designed to tap the predicted differences), one could perform a preliminary test of the hypothesized relationship between teachers' practices and children's motivational patterns.

If the results appear encouraging, the researcher may proceed to the next stage, in which the different teacher response styles are simulated in the laboratory. That is, the essence of each of the various feedback practices may be programmed in an experimental situation, where individual, randomly selected children receive experience with one type of feedback following errors on the experimental task. (Experiments may systematically assess different feedback dimensions, such as length of wait, type of clue, and so on, controlling, of course, for such variables as number of correct and incorrect answers by children in the various conditions.) Following the children's experience with a given feedback condition, their beliefs and reactions to errors in that situation may be assessed (see, e.g., Dweck et al., 1978).[9] In this way, the researcher can evaluate rather precisely specific aspects of adults' feedback practices that can directly influence children's motivational patterns.

If an accumulation of evidence consistently suggests that certain practices foster clearly desirable patterns in children, researchers may wish to verify this in the field. This stage may involve varying teachers' feedback practices (i.e., programming facilitating feedback) with specific children and monitoring changes in these children's achievement beliefs and behavior compared with those of control children.

In a similar fashion, one can test hypotheses about particular teacher beliefs that foster particular teacher practices: (1) by assessing the belief in question (e.g., teachers' theories of intelligence) and determining whether it is correlated with the predicted classroom practices; (2) by manipulating the beliefs in the laboratory and determining whether this produces the predicted practices (see, e.g., Swann & Snyder, 1980), and perhaps (3) by orienting teachers in the classroom toward particular beliefs and determining whether this promotes an increase in their facilitating practices.

In summary, past socialization research has given us many important observations and provides the basis for many potentially fruitful hypotheses. The task now is to test these hypotheses systematically and to begin to construct a coherent picture of the socialization processes at different points in children's development that lead to achievement-producing and achievement-inhibiting motivational patterns.

CONCLUSION: MOTIVATION VERSUS INTELLIGENCE RECONSIDERED

One theme that has clearly emerged throughout is the theme of vulnerability: individual differences in vulnerability, developmental differences in vulnerability, and situations that create vulnerability. By vulnerability we mean susceptibility to achievement-inhibiting patterns and to impairment of learning and performance. The individual differences consist in how readily these patterns are engaged.

Under nonthreatening conditions most children function rather effectively. When the situation becomes more evaluative, highly anxious children succumb. When actual negative outcomes are experienced, learned helpless children succumb. If the negative outcomes are made very salient, young children succumb. If children are given performance goals, low expectancies, and negative outcomes, most children succumb. We suggest, then, that children have the different patterns in their repertoire but that they differ in how likely the patterns are to be elicited. In a sense we might say that children differ in how readily they engage and disengage their intelligence—a point that returns us to the distinction between motivation and intelligence.

We began this chapter by insisting on a clear distinction between motivation and intelligence. However, if children differ so widely in how readily they become intelligent or unintelligent, doesn't the distinction begin to blur somewhat? Indeed, mightn't one begin to entertain the motivational definition of intelligence offered by Holt?

> The true test of intelligence is not how much we know how to do, but how we behave when we don't know what do do.

> The intelligent person, young or old, meeting a new situation or problem, opens himself up to it; . . . he thinks about it, instead of about himself or what it might cause to happen to him; he grapples with it boldly, imaginatively, resourcefully, and if not confidently at least hopefully; if he fails to master it, he looks without shame or fear at his mistakes and learns what he can from them. This is intelligence. (1964, p. 205)

NOTES

1. Even if measures of intelligence and facilitating motivational patterns were highly correlated, then as Nicholls (1979) points out, we would still wish to understand what fosters these patterns and then investigate the possibility of fostering them universally.

2. The word "performance" will be used in several ways, not only in connection with performance goals. We will use it also when we refer to the child's task activity (performance of a task) and to the product of that activity (level of performance). The meaning should be clear from the context.

3. We should point out that a number of tendencies we describe as fostered by performance goals

are fostered particularly by the performance goal of avoiding negative judgments, and particularly when negative judgments appear likely. Also, as will be explained later, a child may pursue learning and performance goals simultaneously; differential tendencies may become clear only when the two goals come into conflict.

4. Factors that influence goal expectancy may also influence goal value/salience. For example, perceiving oneself to have low skill in an important area may affect both the expectancy and the value of increasing that skill. We will, however, postpone detailed consideration of the factors affecting goal value.

5. Confusion often arises over a failure to distinguish between "internal" causal factors and "internal" control (over factors and over outcomes). Internal factors, such as effort or ability (or external factors, such as luck or task difficulty) may or may not be controllable and may or may not imply control over the outcome. For example, failure attributed to the internal factor of ability may imply that neither the factor nor the outcome is controllable. In contrast, attributing failure to luck, an external factor that is not controllable, may still imply that subsequent outcomes are controllable.

Confusion also arises over the distinction between trait attributions and causal attributions. Traits or characteristics may be ascribed to an individual without implying that they are causes of an outcome. For example, one may attribute high or low ability to a child or to oneself (trait attribution) without necessarily implying that this was the factor responsible for a success or failure (causal attribution).

6. See Dweck & Goetz (1978), Dweck, Goetz, & Strauss (1980), and Dweck & Licht (1980) for a discussion of how girls' lower expectancies in mathematics, and their avoidance of math courses, may be related to a tendency to infer a generalized, stable lack of ability from a failure on a specific task.

7. The authors would like to thank Ting Lei for his valuable contributions to this section.

8. It is interesting to think of entity and incremental theories as two alternative, qualitatively different forms (or aspects) of self-concept. Within the entity view, the self is essentially a static object with judgeable attributes or traits. Within the incremental view, the self is more of a dynamic process or a self-creating (energy) system that continually transforms itself through actions. Indeed, the various domains of endeavor or personal characteristics that are typically seen as entering into the self-concept (e.g., social, intellectual, artistic, and physical compe-

tence, morality, attractiveness, even health) may be conceived of in these alternative fashions—in terms of relatively unmalleable traits or as self-creative processes. A fascinating task for future research would be to examine the generality of entity versus incremental conceptions across domains within individuals (over the course of development) and to determine the extent to which such alternative conceptions may guide the choice and pursuit of goals in these different domains.

9. We have generally found children's achievement beliefs and behavior to be quite responsive to experimental manipulations within the research situation. In the Dweck, Davidson, Nelson, and Enna (1978) study, for example, the negative feedback teachers delivered to boys versus girls was observed in classrooms, and then programmed experimentally in the laboratory, in order to test hypotheses about possible causes of sex differences in attributions. Regardless of their actual sex, children showed attributions for failure that reflected the feedback they had received in the experimental situation.

REFERENCES

Abramson, L. Y., Seligman, M. E. P., & Teasdale, J. D. Learned helplessness in humans: Critique and reformulation. *Journal of Abnormal Psychology*, 1978, *87*, 49–74.

Alloy, L. B., & Abramson, L. Y. Judgment of contingency in depressed and nondepressed students: Sadder but wiser? *Journal of Experimental Psychology: General*, 1979, *108*, 441–485.

Alpert, R., & Haber, R. N. Anxiety in academic achievement situations. *Journal of Abnormal and Social Psychology*, 1960, *61*, 207–215.

Ames, C., Ames, R., & Felker, D. W. Effects of competitive reward structure and valence of outcome on children's achievement attributions. *Journal of Educational Psychology*, 1977, *69*, 1–8.

Anderson, C. A., & Jennings, D. L. When experiences of failure promote expectations of success: The impact of attributing failure to ineffective strategies. *Journal of Personality*, 1980, *48*, 393–407.

Andrews, G. R., & Debus, R. L. Persistence and the causal perception of failure: Modifying cognitive attributions. *Journal of Educational Psychology*, 1978, *70*, 154–166.

Atkinson, J. W. Motivational determinants of risk-taking behavior. *Psychological Review*, 1957, *64*, 359–372.

Atkinson, J. W. *An introduction to motivation.*

Princeton, N.J.: Van Nostrand, 1964.

Atkinson, J. W. Commentary. In C. P. Smith (Ed.), *Achievement-related motives in children*. New York: Russell Sage, 1969.

Atkinson, J. W., & Birch, D. *The dynamics of action*. New York: Wiley, 1970.

Atkinson, J. W., & Birch, D. The dynamics of achievement-oriented activity. In J. W. Atkinson & J. O. Raynor (Eds.), *Motivation and achievement*. Washington, D.C.: V. H. Winston, 1974.

Atkinson, J. W., & Feather, N. T. (Eds.). *A theory of achievement motivation*. New York: Wiley, 1966.

Atkinson, J. W., & Litwin, G. H. Achievement motive and test anxiety conceived as motive to approach success and motive to avoid failure. *Journal of Abnormal and Social Psychology*, 1960, *60*, 52–63.

Atkinson, J. W., & Raynor, J. O. (Eds.). *Motivation and achievement*. Washington, D.C.: V. H. Winston, 1974.

Bandura, A. Self-efficacy: Toward a unifying theory of behavioral change. *Psychological Review*, 1977, *84*, 191–215.

Bandura, A. The self and mechanisms of agency. In J. Suls (Ed.), *Social psychological perspectives on the self*. Hillsdale, N.J.: Erlbaum, 1980.

Bandura, A. Self-referent thought: The development of self-efficacy. In J. H. Flavell & L. D. Ross (Eds.), *Social Cognitive Development*, New York: Cambridge University Press, 1981.

Bandura, A., & Schunk, D. H. Cultivating competence, self-efficacy and intrinsic interest through proximal self-motivation. *Journal of Personality and Social Psychology*, 1981, *41*, 586–598.

Bandura, M., & Dweck, C. S. Children's theories of intelligence as predictors of achievement goals. Unpublished manuscript, Harvard University, 1981.

Bar Tal, D., & Darom, D. Pupils' attributions for success and failure. *Child Development*, 1979, *50*, 264–267.

Battle, E. S. Motivational determinants of academic task persistence. *Journal of Personality and Social Psychology*, 1965, *2*, 209–218.

Battle, E. S. Motivational determinants of academic competence. *Journal of Personality and Social Psychology*, 1966, *4*, 634–642.

Baumrind, D. Current patterns of parental authority. *Developmental Psychology Monographs*, 1971, *4*, 1–102.

Baumrind, D. The development of instrumental competence through socialization. In A. D. Pick (Ed.), *Minnesota Symposium on Child Psychol-*

ogy: VII. Minneapolis: University of Minnesota Press, 1973.

Beck, R. C. *Motivation: Theories and principles*. Englewood Cliffs, N.J.: Prentice-Hall, 1978.

Berlyne, D. E. *Conflict, arousal and curiosity*. New York: McGraw-Hill, 1960.

Berzonsky, M. D., & Barclay, C. R. Formal reasoning and identity formation: A reconceptualization. In J. A. Meacham & N. R. Santilli (Eds.), *Social development in youth: Structure and Content*. Basel: Karger, 1981.

Bialer, I. Conceptions of success and failure in mentally retarded and normal children. *Journal of Personality*, 1961, *29*, 303–320.

Bialer, I., & Cromwell, R. L. Task repetition in mental defectives as a function of chronological and mental age. *American Journal of Mental Deficiency*, 1960, *65*, 265–268.

Brockner, J. The effects of self-esteem, success–failure and self-consciousness on task performance. *Journal of Personality and Social Psychology*, 1979, *37*, 1732–1741.

Brockner, J., & Hulton, A. J. B. How to reverse the vicious cycle of low self-esteem: The importance of attentional focus. *Journal of Experimental Psychology*, 1978, *14*, 564–578.

Brophy, J. E. Teacher behavior and its effects. *Journal of Educational Psychology*, 1979, *71*, 733–750.

Brophy, J. E., & Good, T. *Teacher–student relationships: Causes and consequences*. New York: Holt, Rinehart & Winston, 1974.

Brown, A. L., & DeLoache, J. Skills, plans, and self-regulation. In R. Siegler (Ed.), *Children's thinking: What develops?* Hillsdale, N.J.: Erlbaum, 1978.

Bruner, J. S. Personality dynamics and the process of perceiving. In R. R. Blake & G. V. Ramsey (Eds.), *Perception: An approach to personality*. New York: Ronald Press, 1951.

Bruner, J. S. The act of discovery. *Harvard Educational Review*, 1961, *31*, 21–32.

Bruner, J. S. The growth of mind. *American Psychologist*, 1965, *20*, 1007–1017.

Bruner, J. S. Competence in infants. Paper presented at the meeting for the Society for Research in Child Development, Minneapolis, March 1971.

Bush, E. S., & Dweck, C. S. Reflections on conceptual tempo: Relationship between cognitive style and performance as a function of task characteristics. *Developmental Psychology*, 1975, *11*, 567–574.

Carver, C. S., & Scheier, M. F. Self-focusing effects of dispositional self-consciousness, mirror presence, and audience presence. *Journal of Personality and Social Psychology*, 1978, *36*, 324–332.

Chapin, M., & Dyck, D. G. Persistence in children's reading behavior as a function of *n* length and attribution retraining. *Journal of Abnormal Psychology*, 1976, *85*, 511–515.

Clifford, M. M., & Cleary, T. A. The relationship between children's academic performance and achievement accountability. *Child Development*, 1972, *43*, 647–655.

Cohen, D. K. Does IQ matter? In D. Rogers (Ed.), *Issues in child psychology*. Monterey, Cal.: Brooks/Cole, 1977.

Covington, M. V. Strategic thinking and fear of failure. Chapter for NIE-LRDC Proceedings, October 1980.

Covington, M. V., & Beery, R. *Self-worth and school learning*. New York: Holt, Rinehart & Winston, 1976.

Covington, M. V., & Omelich, C. L. Are causal attributions causal: A path analysis of the cognitive model of achievement motivation. *Journal of Personality and Social Psychology*, 1979, *37*, 1487–1504. (a)

Covington, M. V., & Omelich, C. L. Effort: The double-edged sword in school achievement. *Journal of Educational Psychology*, 1979, *71*, 169–182. (b)

Covington, M. V., & Omelich, C. L. It's best to be able and virtuous too: Student and teacher evaluative responses to successful effort. *Journal of Educational Psychology*, 1979, *71*, 688–700. (c)

Covington, M. V., Spratt, M. F., & Omelich, C. L. Is effort enough or does diligence count too? Student and teacher reactions to effort stability in failure. *Journal of Educational Psychology*, 1980, *72*, 717–729.

Cox, F. N. Some effects of test anxiety and the presence or absence of other persons on boys' performance on a repetitive motor task. *Journal of Experimental Child Psychology*, 1966, *3*, 100–112.

Crandall, V. C. Personality characteristics and social and achievement behaviors associated with children's social desirability response tendencies. *Journal of Personality and Social Psychology*, 1966, *4*, 477–486.

Crandall, V. C. Achievement behavior in the young child. In W. W. Hartup, (Ed.), *The young child: Reviews of research*. Washington, D.C.: National Association for the Education of Young Children, 1967.

Crandall, V. C. Sex differences in expectancy of intellectual and academic reinforcement. In C. P. Smith (Ed.), *Achievement-related motives in children*. New York: Russell Sage, 1969.

Crandall, V. C., & Battle, E. S. The antecedents and adult correlates of academic and intellectual achievement effort. In J. P. Hill (Ed.), *Minnesota symposium on child psychology, Vol. IX*. Minneapolis: University of Minnesota Press, 1970.

Crandall, V. C., Dewey, R., Katkovsky, W., & Preston, A. Parents' attitudes and behaviors and grade school children's academic achievements. *Journal of Genetic Psychology*, 1964, *104*, 53–66.

Crandall, V. C., Katkovsky, W., & Crandall, V. J. Children's beliefs in their own control of reinforcements in intellectual-academic situations. *Child Development*, 1965, *36*, 91–109.

Crandall, V. C., & McGhee, P. E. Expectancy of reinforcement and academic competence. *Journal of Personality*, 1968, *36*, 635–648.

Crandall, V. J. *Achievement*. In H. Stevenson (Ed.), *Child psychology: Sixty-second yearbook of the National Society for the Study of Education*. Chicago: University of Chicago Press, 1963.

Crandall, V. J., Katkovsky, W., & Preston, A. A conceptual formulation for some research on children's achievement development. *Child Development*, 1960, *31*, 787–797.

Crandall, V. J., Katkovsky, W., & Preston, A. Motivational and ability determinants of young children's intellectual achievement behaviors. *Child Development*, 1962, *33*, 643–661.

Damon, W., & Hart, D. The development of self-understanding from infancy through adolescence. *Child Development*, 1982, *53*, 841–864.

deCharms, R. *Personal Causation*. New York: Academic Press, 1968.

deCharms, R. Personal causation training in the schools. *Journal of Applied Social Psychology*, 1972, *2*, 95–113.

deCharms, R., & Carpenter, V. Measuring motivation in culturally disadvantaged school children. In H. J. Klausmeier & G. T. O'Hearn (Eds.), *Research and development toward the improvement of education*. Madison, Wis.: Dembar Education Services, 1968.

deCharms, R., & Dave, P. N. Hope of success, fear of failure, subjective probability, and risk-taking behavior. *Journal of Personality and Social Psychology*, 1965, *1*, 558–568.

Dember, W. N. *The psychology of perception*. New York: Holt, Rinehart & Winston, 1960.

Dember, W. N., & Earl, R. W. An analysis of exploratory, manipulative, and curiosity behaviors. *Psychological Review*, 1957, *64*, 91–96.

Diener, C. I., & Dweck, C. S. An analysis of learned helplessness: Continuous changes in performance, strategy, and achievement cognitions following failure. *Journal of Personality and Social Psychology*, 1978, *36*, 451–462.

Diener, C. I., & Dweck, C. S. An analysis of learned helplessness: II. The processing of success. *Journal of Personality and Social Psychology*, 1980, *39*, 940–952.

Diener, E., & Srull, T. K. Self-awareness, psychological perspective, and self-reinforcement in relation to personal and social standards. *Journal of Personality and Social Psychology*, 1979, *37*, 413–423.

Diggory, J. *Self-evaluation: Concepts and studies*. New York: Wiley, 1966.

Dollard, J., & Miller, N. E. *Personality and psychotherapy*. New York: McGraw-Hill, 1950.

Donaldson, M. *Children's minds*. New York: Norton, 1978.

Donaldson, M. The mismatch between school and children's minds. *Human Nature*, 1979, *2*, 60–67.

Doris, J., & Sarason, S. B. Test anxiety and blame assignment in a failure situation. *Journal of Abnormal Psychology*, 1955, *30*, 335–338.

Dusek, J. B., Kermis, M. D., & Mergler, N. L. Information processing in low- and high-test anxious children as a function of grade level and verbal labelling. *Developmental Psychology*, 1975, *11*, 651–652.

Dweck, C. S. The role of expectations and attributions in the alleviation of learned helplessness. *Journal of Personality and Social Psychology*, 1975, *31*, 674–685.

Dweck, C. S., & Bush, E. S. Sex differences in learned helplessness: I. Differential debilitation with peer and adult evaluators. *Developmental Psychology*, 1976, *12*, 147–156.

Dweck, C. S., Davidson, W., Nelson, S., & Enna, B. Sex differences in learned helplessness: II. The contingencies of evaluative feedback in the classroom, and III. An experimental analysis. *Developmental Psychology*, 1978, *14*, 268–276.

Dweck, C. S., & Elliott, E. S. A model of achievement motivation, a theory of its origins, and a framework for motivational development. Unpublished manuscript, Harvard University, 1981.

Dweck, C. S., & Gilliard, D. Expectancy statements as determinants of reactions to failure: Sex differences in persistence and expectancy change. *Journal of Personality and Social Psychology*, 1975, *32*, 1077–1084.

Dweck, C. S., & Goetz, T. E. Attributions and learned helplessness. In J. H. Harvey, W. Ickles, & R. F. Kidd (Eds.), *New directions in attribution research* (Vol. 2). Hillsdale, N.J.: Erlbaum, 1978.

Dweck, C. S., Goetz, T. E., & Strauss, N. L. Sex differences in learned helplessness: IV. An experimental and naturalistic study of failure generalization and its mediators. *Journal of Personality and Social Psychology*, 1980, *38*, 441–452.

Dweck, C. S., & Licht, B. G. Learned helplessness and intellectual achievement. In J. Garber & M. E. P. Seligman (Eds.), *Human helplessness: theory and applications*. New York: Academic Press, 1980.

Dweck, C. S., & Reppucci, N. D. Learned helplessness and reinforcement responsibility in children. *Journal of Personality and Social Psychology*, 1973, *25*, 109–116.

Dweck, C. S., & Wortman, C. B. Learned helplessness, anxiety, and achievement motivation: Neglected parallels in cognitive, affective, and coping responses. In H. W. Krohne & L. Laux (Eds.), *Achievement, stress, and anxiety*. Washington, D.C.: Hemisphere, 1982.

Elkind, D. Cognitive growth cycles in mental development. In J. K. Cole (Ed.), *Nebraska Symposium on Motivation, 1971*. Lincoln: University of Nebraska Press, 1972.

Elliott, E. S., & Dweck, C. S. Children's achievement goals as determinants of learned helpless and mastery-oriented achievement patterns: An experimental analysis. Unpublished manuscript, Harvard University, 1981.

Entin, E. E., & Raynor, J. O. Effects of contingent future orientation and achievement motivation on performance in two kinds of tasks. *Journal of Experimental Research in Personality*, 1973, *6*, 314–320.

Epstein, S. The self-concept revisited or a theory of a theory. *American Psychologist*, 1973, *28*, 405–416.

Feather, N. T. The relationship of persistence at a task to expectation of success and achievement related motives. *Journal of Abnormal and Social Psychology*, 1961, *63*, 552–561.

Feather, N. T. The study of persistence. *Psychological Bulletin*, 1962, *59*, 94–114.

Feather, N. T. Effects of prior success and failure on expectations of success and subsequent performance. *Journal of Personality and Social Psy-

chology, 1966, *3,* 287–298.

Feld, S., Ruhland, D., & Gold, M. Developmental changes in achievement motivation. *Merrill-Palmer Quarterly,* 1979, *25,* 43–60.

Feldman, N. S., & Ruble, D. N. Awareness of social comparison interest and motivations: A developmental study. *Journal of Educational Psychology,* 1977, *69,* 579–585.

Feldman, R. S., & Bernstein, A. G. Degree and sequence of success as determinants of self-attribution of ability. *Journal of Social Psychology,* 1977, *102,* 223–231.

Felixbrod, J. J., & O'Leary, K. D. Self-determination of academic standards by children: Toward freedom from external control. *Journal of Educational Psychology,* 1974, *66,* 845–850.

Flavell, J. H., & Wellman, H. M. Metamemory. In R. Kail & J. Hagan (Eds.), *Perspectives on the development of memory and cognition.* Hillsdale, N.J.: Erlbaum, 1977.

Foersterling, F. Sex differences in risk-taking: Effects of subjective and objective probability of success. *Personality and Social Psychology Bulletin,* 1980, *6,* 149–152.

Fontaine, G. Social comparison and some determinants of expected personal control and expected performance in a novel task situation. *Journal of Personality and Social Psychology,* 1974, *29,* 487–496.

Frankl, A., & Snyder, M. L. Poor performance following unsolvable problems: Learned helplessness or egotism? *Journal of Personality and Social Psychology,* 1978, *36,* 1415–1423.

Frieze, I. H., Fisher, J., Hanusa, B., McHugh, M. C., & Valle, V. A. Attributions of the causes of success and failure as internal and external barriers to achievement in women. In J. Sherman & F. Denmark (Eds.), *Psychology of women: Future directions for research.* New York: Psychological Dimensions, 1978.

Frieze, I. H., Francis, W. D., & Hanusa, B. H. Defining success in classroom settings. In J. Levine and M. Wang (Eds.), *Teacher and student perceptions: Implications for learning.* Hillsdale, N.J.: Erlbaum, 1981.

Ganzer, V. J. Effects of audience presence and test anxiety on learning and retention in a serial learning situation. *Journal of Personality and Social Psychology,* 1968, *8,* 194–199.

Gentner, D. Are scientific analogies metaphors? In D. S. Miall (Ed.), *Metaphor: Problems and perspectives.* Brighton, Sussex: Havester Press, 1982.

Goetz, T. E., & Dweck, C. S. Learned helplessness in social situations. *Journal of Personality and Social Psychology,* 1980, *39,* 246–255.

Goodnow, J. J. Concepts of intelligence and its development. In N. Warren (Ed.), *Studies in cross-cultural psychology* (Vol. 2). London: Pergamon, 1980.

Halisch, F., & Heckhausen, H. Search for feedback information and effort regulation during task performance. *Journal of Personality and Social Psychology,* 1977, *35,* 724–733.

Halperin, M. S. Sex differences in children's responses to adult pressure for achievement. *Journal of Educational Psychology,* 1977, *69,* 96–100.

Harari, O., & Covington, M. V. Reactions to achievement behavior from a teacher and student perspective: A developmental analysis. *American Educational Research Journal,* 1981, *18,* 15–28.

Harter, S. Developmental differences in the manifestation of mastery motivation on problem-solving tasks. *Child Development,* 1975, *46,* 370–378.

Harter, S. A model of intrinsic mastery motivation in children: Individual differences and developmental change. *Minnesota Symposium on Child Psychology* (Vol. 14), Hillsdale, N.J.: Erlbaum, 1981. (a)

Harter, S. One developmentalist's perspective on some parameters of the self-regulation process in children. In P. Karoly & F. Kanfer (Eds.), *The psychology of self-management: From theory to practice.* Elmsford, N.Y.: Pergamon Press, 1981. (b)

Harter, S., & Connell, J. P. A structural model of children's self perceptions of competence, control, and motivational orientation in the cognitive domain. Paper presented at the Meeting of the International Society for the Study of Behavioral Development, Toronto, August 1981.

Heckhausen, H. *The anatomy of achievement motivation.* New York: Academic Press, 1967.

Heckhausen, H. The development of achievement motivation. In W. W. Hartup (Ed.), *Review of Child Development Research* (Vol. 6). Chicago: University of Chicago Press, 1981.

Heckhausen, H. Task-irrelevant cognitions during an exam: Incidence and effects. In H. W. Krohne & L. Laux (Eds.), *Achievement, stress, and anxiety.* Washington, D.C.: Hemisphere, 1982.

Hermans, H. J., Ter-Laak, J. J., & Maes, P. C. Achievement motivation and fear of failure in family and school. *Developmental Psychology,* 1972, *6,* 520–528.

Hill, K. T. Anxiety in the evaluative context. In W. W. Hartup (Ed.), *The Young Child* (Vol. 2). Washington, D.C.: National Association for the Education of Young Children, 1972.

Hill, K. T., & Sarason, S. B. The relation of test anxiety and defensiveness to test and school performance over the elementary school years: A further longitudinal study. *Monographs of the Society for Research in Child Development*, 1966, *31*(2, Serial No. 104).

Hoffman, L. W. Fear of success in males and females: 1965 and 1972. *Journal of Consulting and Clinical Psychology*, 1974, *42*, 353–358.

Hollander, E. P., & Marcia, J. E. Parental determinants of peer-orientation and self-orientation among pre-adolescents. *Developmental Psychology*, 1970, *3*, 292–302.

Holt, J. *How children fail*. New York: Dell, 1964.

Horner, M. S. Toward an understanding of achievement-related conflicts in women. *Journal of Social Issues*, 1972, *28*, 157–175.

Hunt, J. McV. Motivation inherent in information processing and action. In O. J. Harvey (Ed.), *Motivation and social interaction: Cognitive determinants*. New York: Ronald Press, 1963.

Hunt, J. McV. Intrinsic motivation and its role in psychological development. In D. Levine (Ed.), *Nebraska Symposium on Motivation*. Lincoln: University of Nebraska Press, 1965.

Izard, C. E. On the development of emotions and emotion-cognition relationships in infancy. In M. Lewis & L. A. Rosenblum (Eds.), *The development of affect*. New York: Plenum, 1978.

Izard, C. E. Emotions as motivations: An evolutionary developmental perspective. In R. Dienstbier (Ed.), *Nebraska Symposium on Motivation, 1978*. Lincoln: University of Nebraska Press, 1979.

Jackaway, R. Sex difference in achievement motivation, behavior and attribution about success and failure. Unpublished doctoral dissertation, SUNY at Albany, 1974.

Janoff-Bulman, R., & Brickman, P. Expectations and what people learn from failure. In N. T. Feather (Ed.), *Expectancy, incentive, and action*. Hillsdale, N.J.: Erlbaum, 1981.

Jencks, C. *Who gets ahead? The determinants of economic success in America*. New York: Basic Books, 1979.

Jennings, D. L. Effects of attributing failure to ineffective strategies. Unpublished doctoral dissertation, Stanford University, 1979.

Kagan, J. Motives and development. *Journal of Personality and Social Psychology*, 1972, *22*, 51–66.

Kagan, J. On emotion and its development: A working paper. In M. Lewis & L. A. Rosenblum (Eds.), *The development of affect*. New York: Plenum, 1978.

Kagan, J., & Kogan, N. Individual variation in cognitive processes. In P. Mussen (Ed.), *Carmichael's manual of child psychology* (Vol. 1) (3rd ed.). New York: Wiley, 1970.

Kahneman, D., & Tversky, A. On the psychology of prediction. *Psychological Review*, 1973, *80*, 237–251.

Kanfer, F. H. The many faces of self-control, or behavior modification changes its focus. In R. B. Stuart (Ed.), *Behavioral self-management*. Brunner/Mazel, 1977.

Karabenick, J. D., & Heller, K. A. A developmental study of effort and ability attributions. *Developmental Psychology*, 1976, *12*, 559–560.

Karniol, R., & Ross, M. The development of causal attributions in social perception. *Journal of Personality and Social Psychology*, 1976, *34*, 455–464.

Kennelly, K., & Kinley, S. Perceived contingency of teacher administered reinforcements and academic performance of boys. *Psychology in the Schools*, 1975, *12*, 449–453.

Kessen, W. Questions for a theory of cognitive development. In H. W. Stevenson (Ed.), *Concept of Development. Monographs of the Society for Research in Child Development*, 1966, *31*(5, Serial No. 107).

Kruglanski, A. W. The endogenous-exogenous partition in attribution theory. *Psychological Review*, 1975, *82*, 387–406.

Kuhl, J. Standard-setting and risk preference: An elaboration of the theory of achievement motivation and an empirical test. *Psychological Review*, 1978, *85*, 239–248.

Kuhl, J. Motivational and functional helplessness: The moderating effect of state versus action orientation. *Journal of Personality and Social Psychology*, 1981, *40*, 155–170.

Kukla, A. Foundations of an attributional theory of performance. *Psychological Review*, 1972, *79*, 454–470.

Kukla, A. An attributional theory of choice. In L. Berkowitz (Ed.), *Advances in experimental social psychology* (Vol. 11). New York: Academic Press, 1978.

Kun, A. Development of the magnitude-covariation and compensation schemata in ability and effort attributions of performance. *Child Development*, 1977, *48*, 862–872.

Langer, E. J., & Benevento, A. Self-induced dependence. *Journal of Personality and Social Psychology*, 1978, *36*, 886–893.

Langer, E. J., & Dweck, C. S. *Personal Politics*. Englewood Cliffs, N.J.: Prentice-Hall, 1973.

Lau, R. R., & Russell, P. Attributions in the sports pages: A field test of some current hypotheses in attribution research. *Journal of Personality and Social Psychology*, 1980, *39*, 29–38.

Lawson, E. Changes in expectancy as a function of time to performance. Unpublished master's thesis, University of Sidney, 1981 (personal communication).

Lekarczyk, D. T., & Hill, K. T. Self-esteem, test anxiety, stress, and verbal learning. *Developmental Psychology*, 1969, *1*, 147–154.

Lenney, E. Women's self-confidence in achievement settings. *Psychological Bulletin*, 1977, *84*, 1–13.

Lepper, M. R. Intrinsic and extrinsic motivation in children: Detrimental effects of superfluous social controls. In W. A. Collins (Ed.), *Minnesota symposium on child psychology* (Vol. 14). Morristown, N.J.: Erlbaum, 1980.

Lepper, M. R., & Greene, D. (Eds.). *The hidden costs of reward: New perspectives on the psychology of human motivation*. Hillsdale, N.J.: Erlbaum, 1978.

Lewinsohn, P. M., Mischel, W., Chaplain, W., & Barton, R. Social competence and depression: The role of illusory self-perceptions. *Journal of Abnormal Psychology*, 1980, *89*, 203–212.

Licht, B. G. Determinants of academic achievement: The interaction of children's achievement orientations with task requirements. Unpublished doctoral dissertation, University of Illinois, 1980.

Licht, B. G., & Dweck, C. S. Determinants of academic achievement: The interaction of children's achievement orientations with skill area. Manuscript submitted for publication, 1981.

Licht, B. G., & Dweck, C. S. Sex differences in achievement orientations: Consequences for academic choices and attainments. In M. Marland (Ed.), *Sex differentiation and schooling*. London: Heinemann, in press.

Maehr, M. L. Continuing motivation: An analysis of a seldom considered educational outcome. *Review of Educational Research*, 1976, *46*, 443–462.

Maehr, M. L., & Nicholls, J. G. Culture and achievement motivation: A second look. In N. Warren (Ed.), *Studies in cross-cultural psychology* (Vol. 3). New York: Academic Press, 1980.

Maehr, M. L., & Stallings, W. M. Freedom from external evaluation. *Child Development*, 1972, *43*, 177–185.

Mandler, G., & Sarason, S. B. A study of anxiety and learning. *Journal of Abnormal and Social Psychology*, 1952, *47*, 166–173.

Mandler, G., & Watson, D. L. Anxiety and the interruption of behavior. In C. D. Spielberger (Ed.), *Anxiety and behavior*. New York: Academic Press, 1966.

Maracek, J., & Mettee, D. Avoidance of continued success as a function of self-esteem, level of esteem certainty, and responsibility for success. *Journal of Personality and Social Psychology*, 1972, *22*, 98–107.

Markman, E. M. Comprehension monitoring. In W. P. Dickson (Ed.), *Children's oral communication skills*. New York: Academic Press, 1981.

Marshall, H. H., Weinstein, R. S., Middlestadt, S. & Brattesani, K. A. "Everyone's smart in our class": Relationship between classroom characteristics and perceived differential teacher treatment. Paper presented at the American Educational Research Association, Boston, 1980.

Martire, J. G. Relationships between the self-concept and differences in the strength and generality of achievement motivation. *Journal of Personality*, 1956, *24*, 364–375.

Masters, J. C., Furman, W., & Barden, R. C. Effects of achievement standards, tangible rewards, and self-dispensed achievement evaluations on children's task mastery. *Child Development*, 1977, *48*, 217–224.

McClelland, D. C. Risk taking in children with high and low need for achievement. In J. W. Atkinson (Ed.), *Motives in fantasy, action, and society*. Princeton, N.J.: Van Nostrand, 1958.

McClelland, D. C. *The achieving society*. Princeton, N.J.: Van Nostrand, 1961.

McClelland, D. C., Atkinson, J. W., Clark, R. A., & Lowell, E. L. *The Achievement Motive*. New York: Appleton-Century-Crofts, 1953.

McCoy, N. Effects of test anxiety on children's performance as a function of instructions and type of task. *Journal of Personality and Social Psychology*, 1965, *2*, 634–641

McMahan, I. D. Sex differences in expectancy of success as a function of task. Paper presented at The Eastern Psychological Association, April 1972.

McMahan, I. D. Relationships between causal attributions and expectancy of success. *Journal of Personality and Social Psychology*, 1973, *28*, 108–114.

Meichenbaum, D. *Cognitive-behavior modification: An integrative approach*. New York: Plenum, 1977.

Meichenbaum, D. Teaching children self-control. In B. Lahey & A. Kazdin (Eds.), *Advances in child clinical psychology* (Vol. 2). New York: Plenum, 1979.

Meichenbaum, D., & Asarnow, J. Cognitive-behavior modification and metacognitive development: Implications for the classroom. In P. C. Kendall & S. D. Hollon (Eds.), *Cognitive-behavioral interventions: Theory, research, and procedures*. New York: Academic Press, 1982.

Melton, A. W. Motivation and learning. In D. C. McClelland (Ed.), *Studies in motivation*. New York: Appleton-Century-Crofts, 1955.

Meunier, C., & Rule, B. G. Anxiety, confidence and conformity. *Journal of Personality*, 1967, *35*, 498–504.

Meyer, W., Bachman, M., Biermann, U., Hempelmann, M., Ploger, F., & Spiller, H. The informational value of evaluative behavior: Influences of praise and blame on perceptions of ability. Unpublished manuscript, University of Bielefeld (Germany), 1979.

Miller, G. W. Factors in school achievement and social class. *Journal of Educational Psychology*, 1970, *61*, 260–269.

Miller, N. E., & Dollard, J. *Social learning and imitation*. New Haven: Yale University Press, 1941.

Mischel, W. Metacognition and the rules of delay. In J. H. Flavell & L. D. Ross (Eds.), *Social cognitive development: Frontiers and possible futures*. Cambridge New York: University Press, 1981.

Miscione, J. L., Marvin, R. S., O'Brien, R. G., & Greenberg, M. T. A developmental study of preschool children's understanding of the words "know" and "guess." *Child Development*, 1978, *49*, 1107–1113.

Montanelli, D. S., & Hill, K. T. Children's achievement expectations as a function of two consecutive, reinforcement experiences, sex of subject, and sex of experimenter. *Journal of Personality and Social Psychology*, 1969, *13*, 115–128.

Moulton, R. W. Effects of success and failure on level of aspiration as related to achievement motives. *Journal of Personality and Social Psychology*, 1965, *1*, 399–406.

Murray, H. A. Techniques for a systematic investigation of fantasy. *Journal of Psychology*, 1936, *3*, 115–143.

Murray, H. A. *Explorations in personality*. New York: Oxford University Press, 1938.

Nicholls, J. G. Causal attributions and other achievement related cognitions: Effects of task outcome, attainment value, and sex. *Journal of Personality and Social Psychology*, 1975, *31*, 379–389.

Nicholls, J. G. Effort is virtuous but it's better to have ability: Evaluative responses to perceptions of effort and ability. *Journal of Research in Personality*, 1976, *10*, 306–315. (a)

Nicholls, J. G. When a scale measures more than its name denotes: The case of the Test Anxiety Scale for Children. *Journal of Consulting and Clinical Psychology*, 1976, *44*, 976–985. (b)

Nicholls, J. G. The development of the concepts of effort and ability, perception of academic attainment, and the understanding that difficult tasks require more ability. *Child Development*, 1978, *49*, 800–814.

Nicholls, J. G. Development of perception of own attainment and causal attributions for success and failure in reading. *Journal of Educational Psychology*, 1979, *71*, 94–99. (a)

Nicholls, J. G. Quality and equality in intellectual development. *American Psychologist*, 1979, *34*, 1071–1084. (b)

Nicholls, J. G. The development of the concept of difficulty. *Merrill-Palmer Quarterly*, 1980, *26*, 271–281.

Nicholls, J. G. Striving to demonstrate and develop ability: A theory of achievement motivation. Unpublished manuscript, Purdue University, 1981.

Nicholls, J. G., & Dweck, C. S. A definition of achievement motivation. Unpublished manuscript, University of Illinois, 1979.

Nisbett, R. E., & Ross, L. *Human inference: Strategies and shortcomings of social judgment*. Englewood Cliffs, N.J.: Prentice-Hall, 1980.

Nottelman, E. D., & Hill, K. T. Test anxiety and off-task behavior in evaluative situations. *Child Development*, 1977, *48*, 225–231.

Nuttin, J. R. Pleasure and reward in human motivation and learning. In D. E. Berlyne & K. B. Madsen (Eds.), *Pleasure, reward, and preference*. New York: Academic Press, 1973.

O'Leary, S., & O'Leary, D. Behavior modification in the school. In H. Leitenberg (Ed.), *Handbook of behavior modification and behavior therapy*. Englewood Cliffs, N.J.: Prentice-Hall, 1976.

Olton, R. M., & Crutchfield, R. S. Developing the skills of productive thinking. In P. Mussen, J. Langer, & M. V. Covington (Eds.), *Trends and issues in developmental psychology*. New York: Holt, Rinehart and Winston, 1969.

Papert, S. *Mindstorms: Children, computers, and powerful ideas.* New York: Basic Books, 1980.

Parsons, J. E. The development of attributions, expectancies, and persistence. Unpublished manuscript, University of Michigan, 1978.

Parsons, J. E. Expectancies, values and academic behaviors. In J. T. Spence (Ed.), *Assessing achievement.* San Francisco: W. H. Freeman, in press.

Parsons, J. E., & Ruble, D. N. The development of achievement-related expectancies. *Child Development,* 1977, *48,* 1075–1079.

Pepitone, E. A. Comparison behavior in elementary school children. *American Educational Research Journal,* 1972, *9,* 45–63.

Phillips, D. A. High-achieving students with low academic self-concepts: Achievement motives and orientations. Unpublished doctoral dissertation, Yale University, 1981.

Piaget, J. *The construction of reality in the child.* (M. Cook, trans.). New York: Basic Books, 1954. (Originally published, 1937.)

Piaget, J. *Play, dreams, and imitation in childhood.* New York: Norton, 1962.

Piaget, J. *The origins of intelligence in children.* (M. Cook, trans.). New York: Norton, 1963. (Originally published, 1936.)

Piaget, J. Development and learning. In R. E. Ripple & V. N. Rockastle (Eds.), *Piaget rediscovered.* Ithaca, N.Y.: Cornell University Press, 1964.

Piaget, J., & Inhelder, B. *The psychology of the child.* (H. Weaver, trans.). New York: Basic Books, 1969.

Pyszcynki, T. A., & Greenberg, J. Role of disconfirmed expectancies in the instigation of attributional processing. *Journal of Personality and Social Psychology,* 1981, *40,* 31–38.

Raynor, J. O., & Smith, C. P. Achievement related motives and risk-taking in games of skill and chance. *Journal of Personality,* 1966, *34,* 176–198.

Rhodes, W. A. Generalization of attribution retraining. Unpublished doctoral dissertation, University of Illinois, 1977.

Rholes, W. S., Blackwell, J., Jordan, C., & Walters, C. A developmental study of learned helplessness. *Developmental Psychology,* 1980, *16,* 616–624.

Rholes, W. S., & Ruble, D. N. Children's understanding of dispositional characteristics of others. Manuscript submitted for publication, 1981.

Rosen, B. C., & D'Andrade, R. The psychosocial origins of achievement motivation. *Sociometry,* 1959, *22,* 185–218.

Ruble, D. N. Visual orientation and self-perceptions of children in an external cue-relevant or cue-irrelevant task situation. *Child Development,* 1975, *46,* 669–676.

Ruble, D. N. The development of social comparison processes and their role in achievement related self-socialization. In E. T. Higgins, D. N. Ruble, & W. W. Hartup (Eds.), *Social cognition and social behavior: Developmental issues.* New York: Cambridge University Press, in press.

Ruble, D. N., Boggiano, A. K., Feldman, N. S., & Loebl, J. H. A developmental analysis of the role of social comparison in self-evaluation. *Developmental Psychology,* 1980, *16,* 105–115.

Ruble, D. N., Parsons, J. E., & Ross, J. Self-evaluative responses of children in achievement settings. *Child Development,* 1976, *47,* 990–997.

Ruebush, B. K. Anxiety. In H. W. Stevenson, J. Kagan, & C. Spiker (Eds.), *Sixty-second yearbook of the National Society for the Study of Education: Part I.* Chicago: University of Chicago Press, 1963.

Ruhland, D., & Feld, S. The develpment of achievement motivation in black and white children, *Child Development,* 1977, *48,* 1362–1368.

Sarason, I. G. The effects of anxiety, reassurance, and meaningfulness of material to be learned on verbal learning, *Journal of Experimental Psychology,* 1958, *56,* 472–477.

Sarason, I. G. Experimental approaches to test anxiety: Attention and the uses of information. In C. D. Spielberger (Ed.), Anxiety and behavior: Current trends. In *Theory and research* (Vol. 2). New York: Academic Press, 1972.

Sarason, I. G. Anxiety and self-preoccupation. In I. G. Sarason & C. D. Spielberger (Eds.), *Stress and anxiety* (Vol. 2). Washington, D.C.: Hemisphere, 1975.

Sarason, I. G. *Test anxiety: Theory, research, and application.* Hillsdale, N.J.: Erlbaum, 1982.

Sarason, S. B., Davidson, K., Lighthall, F., Waite, F., & Ruebush, B. *Anxiety in elementary school children.* New York: Wiley, 1960.

Sarason, S. B., & Mandler, G. Some correlates of test anxiety. *Journal of Abnormal and Social Psychology,* 1952, *47,* 561–565.

Sarason, S. B., Mandler, G., & Craighill, P. G. The effect of differential instructions on anxiety and learning. *Journal of Abnormal and Social Psychology,* 1952, *47,* 561–565.

Satinoff, E. Are there similarities between thermoregulation and sexual behavior? In D. W. Pfaff (Ed.), *Physiological Mechanisms of Motivation.*

New York: Springer-Verlag, 1982.

Schneider, K. Subjective uncertainty, achievement orientation, and exploratory behavior. Paper presented at the Meeting of the International Society for the Study of Behavioral Development, Toronto, August 1981.

Schunk, D. Self-efficacy in achievement behavior. Unpublished doctoral dissertation, Stanford University, 1979.

Sears, P. S. Level of aspiration in academically successful and unsuccessful children. *Journal of Abnormal and Social Psychology*, 1940, *35*, 498–536.

Seligman, M. E. P., Maier, S. F., & Solomon, R. L. Unpredictable and uncontrollable aversive events. In F. R. Brush (Ed.), *Aversive conditioning and learning*. New York: Academic Press, 1971.

Shultz, T. R., & Butkowsky, I. Young children's use of the scheme for multiple sufficient causes in the attribution of real and hypothetical behavior. *Child Development*, 1977, *48*, 464–469.

Shultz, T. R., & Mendelson, R. The use of covariation as a principle of causal analysis. *Child Development*, 1975, *46*, 394–399.

Sigall, H., & Gould, R. The effects of self-esteem and evaluator demandingness on effort expenditure. *Journal of Personality and Social Psychology*, 1977, *35*, 12–20.

Small, A., Nakamura, C. Y., & Ruble, D. N. Sex differences in children's outer directedness and self-perceptions in a problem-solving situation. Unpublished manuscript, University of California at Los Angeles, 1973.

Sohn, D. Affect-generating powers of effort and ability self-attributions of academic success and failure. *Journal of Educational Psychology*, 1977, *69*, 500–505.

Sorensen, R. L. Attainment value and type of reinforcement: A hypothesized interaction effect. *Journal of Personality and Social Psychology*, 1976, *34*, 1155–1160.

Sternberg, R., Conway, B. E., Ketron, J. L., & Bernstein, M. People's conceptions of intelligence. *Journal of Personality and Social Psychology*, 1981, *41*, 37–55.

Stipek, D. J. Children's use of past performance information in ability and expectancy judgments for self and other. Paper presented by the Meeting of the International Society for the Study of Behavioral Development, Toronto, August 1981.

Stipek, D. J., & Hoffman, J. M. Children's achievement related expectancies as a function of aca-

demic performance histories and sex. *Journal of Educational Psychology*, 1980, *72*, 861–865.

Stouwie, R. J., Hetherington, E., & Parke, R. D. Some determinants of children's self-reward behavior after exposure to discrepant reward criteria. *Developmental Psychology*, 1970, *3*, 313–319.

Surber, C. F. The development of reversible operations in judgments of ability, effort and performance. *Child Development*, 1980, *51*, 1018–1029.

Surber, C. F. Effects of information reliability in predicting task performance using ability and effort. *Journal of Personality and Social Psychology*, 1981, *40*, 977–989.

Surber, C. F. The development of achievement-related judgment processes. In J. Nicholls (Ed.), *The development of achievement motivation*. Greenwich, Conn.: JAI Press, in press.

Swann, W. B., Jr., & Snyder, M. On translating beliefs into action: Theories of ability and their application in an instructional setting. *Journal of Personality and Social Psychology*, 1980, *38*, 879–888.

Teichmann, H., Gollnitz, G., & Gohler, I. The origin and effects on school children of high parental demands for achievement. *International Journal of Mental Health*, 1975, *4*, 83–106.

Todd, F. J., Terrell, G., & Frank, C. E. Differences between normal and underachievers of superior ability. *Journal of Applied Psychology*, 1962, *46*, 183–190.

Touhy, J. C., & Villemez, W. J. Ability attribution as a result of variable effort and achievement motivation. *Journal of Personality and Social Psychology*, 1980, *38*, 211–216.

Triandis, H. *The analysis of subjective culture*. New York: Wiley, 1972.

Trope, Y. Seeking information about one's own ability as a determinant of choice among tasks. *Journal of Personality and Social Psychology*, 1975, *32*, 1004–1013.

Trope, Y., & Brickman, P. Difficulty and diagnosticity as determinants of choice among tasks. *Journal of Personality and Social Psychology*, 1975, *31*, 918–926.

Trudewind, C., & Husarek, B. Reported in H. Heckhausen, The development of achievement motivation. In W. W. Hartup (Ed.), *Review of Child Development Research* (Vol. 6). Chicago: University of Chicago Press, 1981.

Tyler, B. B. Expectancy for eventual success as a factor in problem-solving behavior. *Journal of Educational Psychology*, 1958, *49*, 166–172.

Veroff, J. Social comparison and the development of achievement motivation. In C. P. Smith (Ed.), *Achievement-related motives in children.* New York: Russell Sage, 1969.

Weiner, B. *Theories of motivation: From mechanism to cognition.* Chicago: Markham, 1972.

Weiner, B. (Ed.). *Achievement and attribution theory.* Morristown, N.J.: General Learning Press, 1974.

Weiner, B. An attribution theory of motivation and emotion. In H. Krohne & L. Laux (Eds.), *Achievement, stress, and anxiety.* Washington, D.C.: Hemisphere, 1982.

Weiner, B., Frieze, I. H., Kukla, A., Reed, L., Rest, S., & Rosenbaum, R. M. *Perceiving the causes of success and failure.* Morristown, N.J.: General Learning Press, 1971.

Weiner, B., & Kukla, A. An attributional analysis of achievement behavior. *Journal of Personality and Social Psychology,* 1970, *15,* 1–20.

Weiner, B., Russell, D., & Lerman, D. Affective consequences of causal ascriptions. In J. H. Harvey, W. Ickes, & R. F. Kidd (Eds.), *New directions in attribution research* (Vol. 2). Hillsdale, N.J.: Erlbaum, 1978.

Weiner, B., Russell, D., & Lerman, D. The cognition-emotion process in achievement-related contexts. *Journal of Personality and Social Psychology,* 1979, *37,* 1211–1220.

Weinstein, R. S. Reading group membership in first grade: Teacher behaviors and pupil experience over time. *Journal of Educational Psychology,* 1976, *68,* 103–116.

Weisz, J. R. Achievement behavior, contingency judgments, and the perception of control. Paper presented at the Meetings of the International Society for the Study of Behavioral Development, Toronto, August 1981.

Weisz, J. R., & McGuire, M. Sex differences in the relation between attributions and learned helplessness in children. Unpublished manuscript, University of North Carolina at Chapel Hill, 1980.

Wellman, H. M. The child's theory of mind: The development of conceptions of cognition. In S.

R. Yussen (Ed.), *The growth of insight in the child.* New York: Academic Press, 1981.

White, R. W. Motivation reconsidered: The concept of competence. *Psychological Review,* 1959, *66,* 297–333.

White, S. Some general outlines of the matrix of developmental changes between five and seven years. *Bulletin of the Orton Society,* 1970, *20,* 41–57.

Williams, J. P., & Hill, K. T. Performance on achievement test problems as a function of optimizing test presentation instructions and test anxiety. Unpublished manuscript, University of Illinois, 1976.

Wine, J. D. Test anxiety and direction of attention. *Psychological Bulletin,* 1971, *76,* 92–104.

Wine, J. D. Evaluation anxiety: A cognitive-attentional construct. In H. W. Krohne & L. Laux (Eds.), *Achievement, stress, and anxiety.* Washington, D.C.: Hemisphere, 1982.

Witryol, S. I. Incentives and learning in children. In H. W. Reese (Ed.), *Advances in child development and behavior* (Vol. 6). New York: Academic Press, 1971.

Wong, P. T. P., & Weiner, B. When people ask "why" questions and the heuristics of attributional search. *Journal of Personality and Social Psychology,* 1981, *40,* 650–663.

Young, E., & Egeland, B. Repetition choice behavior as a function of chronological age, task difficulty and expectancy of success. *Child Development,* 1976, *47,* 682–689.

Zajonc, R. B., & Brickman, P. Expectancy and feedback as independent factors in task performance. *Journal of Personality and Social Psychology,* 1969, *11,* 148–156.

Zelniker, T., & Jeffrey, W. E. Reflective and impulsive children: Strategies of information processing underlying differences in problem solving. *Monographs of the Society for Research in Child Development,* 1976, *41*(5, Serial No. 168).

Zuckerman, M., & Wheeler, L. To dispel fantasies about the fantasy-based measure of fear of success. *Psychological Bulletin,* 1975, *82,* 932–946.

PLAY | 9

KENNETH H. RUBIN, *University of Waterloo*
GRETA G. FEIN, *University of Michigan*
BRIAN VANDENBERG, *University of Missouri—St. Louis*

CHAPTER CONTENTS

The study of children's play has proven enigmatic to developmental psychologists for some time. On the one hand, the phenomenon has been considered trivial or developmentally irrelevant (Montessori, 1973; Schlosberg, 1947). Yet, on the other hand, play has been widely proclaimed as a significant force in the development of tool use and problem solving (Bruner, 1972), of language and thinking (Vygotsky, 1967), of self-concept (Mead, 1934), and of personal adjustment (Erikson, 1950). Play has also proven difficult to define, and yet most everyone would agree that young children spend inordinately lengthy periods of time exploring their environments and engaging in make-believe activities. They revel in being silly and gleeful and in just plain having fun. Perhaps these conceptual jumps from the one hand to the other convinced editors of the previous *Handbooks* that play was not a topic worth reviewing. But in recent years, psychologists, anthropologists, and other behavioral scientists have been sufficiently impressed by their observations of children's playful activities so much so that they have seen fit to publish over 20 research-oriented books and countless articles on the topic of play in the late 1970s (Sutton-Smith, in press). The purpose of this chapter is to examine the rapidly accumulating psychological research pertaining to this pervasive childhood behavior.

Given that children do play, it is important to ask how and why they do so and whether such activity is fruitful for development. In this chapter we attempt to answer these and other recurring questions. Our examination of play begins with an overview of the nineteenth- and early twentieth-century classic theories that attempted to account for the existence of the phenomenon. In later sections we deal with the problem of defining play and then move to more recent theories concerning the significance of play for development. We also describe the development of different forms of play, as well as those social and nonsocial factors that influence play in childhood. Then we examine whether play is a causal agent in development. Finally, we conclude with a statement concerning future directions to be taken in the study of children's play.

EARLY THEORIES OF PLAY

Over the years, writers have been concerned with why members of the human species spend lengthy periods of time at play. Early theories of play appear to fall easily into four categories (Berlyne, 1969; Gilmore, 1971; Rubin, 1982a), labeled (1) the surplus energy theory of play, (2) the relaxation and recreation theory, (3) the practice theory, and (4) the recapitulation theory of play. In each case the particular classical theory predicts or explains why play exists and why it is a significant force in development.

Support for the classical theories of play remains mixed at best. Indeed, there have been few experimental attempts to *confirm* their validity. Alternatively, there have been attempts, largely philosophical, to *refute* a number of them. Given that for years practitioners and applied psychologists have accepted the tenets of particular classical theories at face value, it would appear appropriate to critically review these works.

The Surplus Energy Theory of Play

The most explicit early treatment of the theory that play is essentially "blowing off steam" is found in the writings of Friedrich von Schiller, an eighteenth-century poet and philosopher. Schiller's interest in play emanated from his primary concern with aesthetic education. In his writings, Schiller (1954) defined play as "The aimless expenditure of exuberant energy." His central hypothesis was that animals and people are driven to serious work by their primary, appetitive needs. Play, however, was viewed as the outcome of the *superfluous* energy that remained after the primary needs were satisfied. Young animals and children, because they are not responsible for their own survival, were thought to have a total energy "surplus." This surplus was worked off through play.

Schiller raised a number of contemporary issues in his writings. First, he considered play to be symbolic activity through which the participant could transform and transcend reality and thereby gain new symbolic representations of the world. From this early speculation, play enthusiasts can readily identify the seeds of thinking represented in the theories and research of Piaget (1962), Vygotsky (1967), and Singer (1973). Second, Schiller distinguished between different forms of play. *Material superfluity* purportedly resulted in physical play. *Aesthetic superfluity,* on the other hand, culminated in aesthetic or dramatic/symbolic play (J. N. Lieberman,

1977). The terms physical and symbolic play reappear in the twentieth-century play theories of Buhler (1928) and Piaget (1962).

Spencer (1873), a nineteenth-century British philosopher and psychologist, has been credited with the first psychological expression of the "surplus energy" theory of play. Spencer believed that there was a universal tendency for animals and humans to be active. He postulated that with mental and physical activity, nerve cells were torn down. He thought that these cells would repair and rebuild themselves gradually through quiescence. Furthermore, following replenishment, there was thought to be a renewed readiness for the organism to act. Since revitalized cells were viewed as being especially sensitive to stimulation, the result was an almost uncontrollable desire for action. The actions taken, however, were hypothesized to vary with the phylogenetic status of the organism. As phylogenetic status increased, proportionately less time and nervous energy was required to provide for the primary needs. Consequently, the "higher" animals had more energy to discharge on non-life-supporting endeavors than did the "lower" animals. These latter, "superfluous" activities, carried on without regard to ulterior benefit, were labeled "play."

Spencer was also an instinct theorist who viewed play as the unconscious product of such life-satisfying, inborn instincts as the desire for conquest and dominance. Thus, when there was little demand for the *literal activities of the instinctively based* behaviors in childhood, the young of the species produced nonliteral analogues, without necessarily having seen the literal behavior displayed by an adult. An example cited was the play fight or the rough-and-tumble play of young boys.

Perhaps Spencer's most interesting contribution to the study of play was his qualitative distinction between different forms of the phenomenon. In *Principles of Psychology* (1873), Spencer introduced (1) the superfluous activity of the sensory-motor apparatus, (2) artistic-aesthetic play, (3) the higher coordinating powers of games, and (4) mimicry. Each form resembles Buhler's (1928) and Piaget's (1962) conceptions of sensorimotor and symbolic representational play, games-with-rules, and imitation, respectively. These different forms of play were supposedly accounted for by various inborn instincts. As such, Spencer's theory shares much with the other classical theories that we will soon look at.

Although a number of twentieth-century psychologists have offered theoretical support for the surplus energy theory (e.g., Tolman, 1932), most contemporary accounts have been highly critical.

First, there is simply no empirical support for a hydraulic-energy model of functioning (Beach, 1945). Second, it has been observed that children will play to the point of exhaustion. Yet, with the introduction of novel and arousing stimuli, the players will resume their activities (Groos, 1901; Millar, 1968). Although intuitively promising, this latter criticism has yet to be supported experimentally.

Third, the surplus energy theory has been criticized because it contradicts the Darwinian and Spencerian doctrine of evolution (Ellis, 1973). This doctrine states that particular organismic behavioral attributes will persist and will be elaborated on from generation to generation only if they are advantageous to the species. Since surplus energy forces the organism to engage in superfluous, nonproductive enterprises, and since such exercises often are accompanied by relaxation and reduced vigilance, the behaviors would not appear to be sound in view of evolutionary theory. Of course, too much "steam," with no mechanism for its release, might also reduce a species' survival potential. Unfortunately, the doctrine of evolution rarely offers a conclusive basis for judging such matters.

Perhaps the most damning criticism of surplus energy theory is the circular, supportive logic offered by its proponents. The circular argument has best been described by Beach (1945, pp. 527–528).

> When a cat chases, catches and devours a mouse, a certain amount of energy is expended; but no one suggests that this is extra, or surplus energy. Now, when the same cat chases, catches or chews on a rubber ball, an equal energy loss may occur; but in this case it's said to be surplus energy which has been released . . . ball chasing must be play, whereas mouse chasing is not play . . . the decision as to whether or not the expended energy is surplus energy, depends upon the interpretation of the behavior as playful or serious. Therefore, to set up one criterion or explanation of play the condition that it involves the release of surplus energy is to do no more than complete the circle.

The Relaxation and Recreation Theories of Play

The second classical treatment of play suggested that the phenomenon derived from an energy deficit rather than from a surplus. Most contemporary writers attribute the "recreation theory" of play to Moritz Lazarus (1883), a nineteenth-century German philosopher. Lazarus suggested that arduous labor leaves humans mentally and physically spent. Such fatigue necessitates a certain amount of rest and sleep. However, full recuperation was only thought possible when a person engaged in activities that allowed a release from the reality-based constraints of work. Thus, Lazarus suggested that play or recreational activities could serve a restorative function.

Lazarus' recreation theory had little to say about children's play. Moreover, he failed to specify the sorts of playful activities that could serve a restorative purpose. Nevertheless, Lazarus' theory was extended by an early twentieth-century philosopher, G. T. W. Patrick (1916), who argued that play stemmed from a need for relaxation. According to Patrick, contemporary occupations required abstract reasoning, concentrated attention, and coordinated eye-hand activities, all of which were presumed to be recent evolutionary acquisitions. Because this work tapped recently acquired skills, it was considered more taxing than physical labor. Patrick suggested that relief from the fatigue caused by mentally straining work could be gained through play or the practice of "racially old" activities (e.g., hunting, fishing).

To Patrick, the play of children was motivated by "race habits" and "race memories." Primitive humans depended on wild and domesticated animals for sustenance, and this dependence was reflected in children's preoccupations with animal books, animal plays, and teddy bears (all, of course, manufactured for children by adults—a point missed somehow by Patrick). In addition, Patrick noted that the child's first musical instruments—the rattle, drum, and horn—were the first musical instruments of our primitive ancestors. In short, the theory incorporates notions of instinct and recapitulation theories commonly accepted at the turn of the century.

As with surplus energy theory, the recreation and relaxation theories of Lazarus and Patrick are open to a number of criticisms. First, the view that manual and physically arduous labors are less fatiguing than those requiring mental effort fails to explain why physical laborers play. Second, if play is indeed a function of a need for recuperation from the stresses of work, why do children play (Ellis, 1973)? The reason given by Patrick for the existence of children's play is simply that it is the "natural" and instinctively based activity of childhood. Since children's mental powers are not yet developed, they cannot work, and so all that is left to do is to play. Third, given that children lack mental skills, play is thought to lack either cognitive content or function. This, of course, is a position at variance with many contemporary writers (e.g., Bruner, 1976; Fein, 1979a,b) whose writings are based on empirical sources. Finally, there is simply no scientific evidence (nor could there be) for the existence of racial memory traces, a point which will be further discussed when we describe Hall's recapitulation theory.

The Practice (or Pre-exercise) Theory of Play

The most comprehensive and formidable early theory of play was articulated by Groos (1898; 1901). Groos, a neo-Darwinian, believed that play had to serve an adaptive purpose for it to have continued its existence over the years in various species. In fact, Groos suggested that the period of childhood (or immaturity) existed in order that the organism could play. Furthermore, he postulated that the length of the play period varied in direct accord with the organism's place in the phylogenetic domain; the more complex the organism, the longer its period of immaturity. These increasingly longer periods of immaturity were considered necessary for the more complex organisms to practice those instinctively based skills that were necessary for sustenance during adulthood. Thus, Groos presented the view that play existed to allow the practice of adult activities—a view that many contemporary psychologists have commonly come to accept (e.g., Bruner, 1972).

Of further contemporary interest was Groos' view that children's play was comprised of "don't have to" activities. He suggested that, while playing, children are more interested in the processes rather than in the products of the behavior. The more recent psychological speculations and experimental work concerned with effectance motivation (cf. Harter, *vol. IV, chap. 1*) can be traced back to Groos' early writings.

Groos (1901) also noted that the play of children changed with development. First, there was *experimental play,* which included sensory and motor practice play. Such sensorimotor play evolved into constructive play and the practice of the higher mental powers (a "games-with-rules" category). Second, there was *socionomic* play, which included fighting and chasing (rough-and-tumble play), and imitative, social, and family games (dramatic play). The purpose of experimental play was to aid in the development of self-control. Socionomic play served the purpose of developing interpersonal relationships.

According to Ellis (1973) the major problem with Groos' theory emanates from the necessity of imputing to particular play activities some preexisting knowledge of those responses that will be required during the serious period of adulthood. Needless to say, there is little evidence for such childhood prescience. Moreover, the theory is overdependent on the concept of instincts as the central driving force in development. Nevertheless, Groos has made several significant contributions to the study of play. He provided a provocative hypothesis that explained why play is found primarily in the young; he was the first to emphasize the role of practice in play (instincts notwithstanding); and he elaborated on the relationships among play, phylogeny, and intelligent behavior.

The Recapitulation Theory of Play

The fourth classical treatment of play emanated from the writings of G. S. Hall and Luther Gulick—two followers of nineteenth-century Darwinian theory. From Darwin's (1872) work concerning cross-species relations, philosophers and psychologists became interested in within-species explanations of evolution. Thus, children were viewed as the link in the evolutionary chain between animal and adult human being. For example, Hall (1920) noted that with embryonic growth the human appeared to pass through increasingly complex stages from protozoan to human. Hall further extended his phylogenetic beliefs by noting that during childhood the history of the human race was recaptured. More specifically, through play the motor habits and the spirits of the past could be progressively reenacted.

Cultural epochs in the history of humankind were postulated to be sequentially recapitulated as follows: the animal stage (as reflected in children's climbing and swinging); the savage stage (hunting, tag, hide-and-seek); the nomad stage (keeping pets); the agricultural/patriarchal stage (dolls, digging in sand); and the tribal stage (team games). Gulick (1898) also wrote that play was the ontogenetic rehearsal of the phylogenetic hierarchy. The games of modern humankind were viewed simply as reflections of earlier racial or epochal behaviors. For example, the hard running, accurate throwing, and club hitting in baseball were viewed as contemporary extensions of early hunting activities. Thus, as in the works of Groos and Patrick, play was linked to the expression of innate patterns of behavior.

It is important to note that the recapitulation theorists viewed children's play as serving a cathartic role in development. For example, Hall suggested that, in play, the racial instincts found outlets for expression. As a result, these instincts were weakened, thereby allowing the acquisition of higher, more complex forms of behavior that are seen in the adults of present-day society.

There are, of course, numerous criticisms of the recapitulation theory of play. For one, many "occupations" of earlier races are skipped and "reversions" or "regressions" occur from time to time in children's play. Second, there is no evidence for the invariant sequence of play activities suggested by Hall. Third, recapitulation theory is based partially on the Lamarkian assumption that skills learned in one generation can be inherited by the next—an assumption not supported by data. Finally, the theory fails to set limits on the course of evolution beyond which the play does not recapitulate activities of less complex species; nor does it explain play that involves highly technological materials such as bicycles and cars (Ellis, 1973).

In summary, despite their numerous shortcomings, the four classical theories of play have had major impacts on the field as it exists today. Contemporary views concerning the forms and functions of children's play can be traced readily to the classical theories. The connections will be elaborated further in our later section on twentieth-century play theories. We now turn to the contentious issue of defining play.

DEFINING PLAY

Problems in Defining Play

Almost every theoretical treatment of play includes a discussion of its definition (e.g., Bruner, 1972; Ellis, 1973; Garvey, 1977a; Neuman, 1971; Schwartzman, 1978; Sutton-Smith, in press; Vandenberg, 1978; Weisler & McCall, 1976). There are several reasons for this attention. First, a number of behavioral theorists have argued that it would be more parsimonious for researchers to dispense with the concept of play entirely (e.g., Schlosberg, 1947) in favor of narrower or broader categories (Berlyne, 1969). These critiques have sparked attempts to bring about definitional clarity and, more useful perhaps, to view the definitional problems in relation to those encountered in attempts to define other psychological or behavioral constructs (e.g., intelligence, language, aggression, altruism, and even drive, deprivation, and consumption). However, despite the lack of an agreed on definition (Buettner-Janusch, 1974; Weisler & McCall, 1976), the study of play continues to flourish.

A second reason why many theorists have attended to the definition of play appears to result from our cultural uneasiness about the phenomenon. The Puritan ethic dichotomized work and play, and passed evaluative judgment on these activities; work was considered to be an extension of God's work, while play was considered to be the province of the devil (e.g., "idle hands are the devil's workshop"; de Grazia, 1962). Although these attitudes are less pronounced today, they still influence the treatment of play as being the opposite of work, thereby contributing to the relative disregard of play as an important topic for scientific study.

Three general approaches to the definition of play have been attempted. In one, play is defined according to the psychological disposition or set presumed to mark its occurrence and to distinguish it from other types of behavior. In another, play is defined according to observable categories of behavior buttressed either by specified behavioral criteria or by a more intuitive identification process (e.g., Matthews & Matthews, 1982). In a third, play is defined according to the context likely to evoke the disposition or likely to yield one or more of the behaviors identified as play. Although these definitional approaches are not without problems, they reflect the widely shared notion that the entity "*play*" is *a behavioral disposition that occurs in describable and reproduceable contexts and is manifest in a variety of observable behaviors*. The dispositional, behavioral, and contextual markers of play, however, all will vary given the particular theoretical biases of an investigator.

To the degree that definitional differences stem from theoretical differences, a variety of paradigmatic approaches to the study of play is likely to emerge. Our task in this section is to review these varied paradigms and the information which they have yielded with the collective belief that no single paradigm adequately encompasses the range of plausible perspectives that continue to be germane to an intuitive meaning of play.

Play as a Disposition

Although there has not been universal agreement on a viable definition of play, there has been considerable convergence on a number of interrelated dispositional factors that might serve to characterize play. The six factors listed here serve to distinguish play according to its motivational source and according to the organism's orientation to goals, physical stimuli, rules, and nonplay behavior. Although these factors reflect different theoretical perspectives, each serves to express a somewhat different dispositional dimension and in so doing serves to exclude from play different aspects of behavior. In the following discussion, terms traditionally used to characterize play (e.g., that it is pleasurable, voluntary, or spontaneous) have been replaced by notions that more clearly specify the sense in which such characteristics might be understood.

1. A feature that is almost unanimously acknowledged to be the hallmark of play is that it is an *intrinsically motivated* behavior neither governed by appetitive drives (Berlyne, 1960; Bruner, 1972; Garvey, 1977a; Huizinga, 1955; Klinger, 1971; Koestler, 1964; Neuman, 1971; Schwartzman, 1978; Vandenberg, 1978; Weisler & McCall, 1976) nor by compliance with social demands or inducements external to the behavior itself (Klinger, 1971). The notion of play as intrinsically motivated thus permits a distinction between play and consummatory behavior, instrumental behavior leading to detectable consummatory behavior, or behavior leading to a goal external to the behavior. The notion is spiritually close to Spencer's early proposal that play expresses a particular type of neural state or mental condition rather than an appetitive one.

Recent theoretical formulations permit more refined statements concerning the intrinsic motivational properties of play. Some theorists posit that play results from the occurrence of a discrepancy or incongruity between incoming information and the organism's ability to process it. Play serves as the mechanism through which the discrepancy can be adjusted, thereby returning the organism to some optimal level of environment-organism balance. Other formulations refer to the positive effect associated with mastery (White, 1959) or to the exercise of attained skills or acquired functions (Piaget, 1962) as providing the impetus for play. Still others posit that an internal, pleasurable motivating state (e.g., arousal reduction) associated with neural functioning (Berlyne, 1966) serves to reinforce play.

2. A related feature, suggested by Piaget's view of play as assimilation, is that it is characterized by *attention to means* rather than ends (Bruner, 1972; Garvey, 1977a; Koestler, 1964; Miller, 1973; Piaget, 1962; Vandenberg, 1978). First, the goals of play behavior are self-imposed rather than imposed by others. Free from external sanction, goals can vary in importance or in salience according to the wishes of the player. In this sense, the behavior is spontaneous. A child might decide to build a block tower, a goal that may diminish in importance as different ways of stacking blocks become more important than the production of a standing structure. A simple activity of going down a slide may become deliberately complicated by new and varied ways of getting to the bottom. Free of the straight jacket of means-ends considerations, the individual is able to dismantle established instrumental behavioral sequences and to reassemble them in new ways (Bruner, 1972). This characteristic helps distinguish play from intrinsically motivated activities directed to the attainment of specific goals (enjoyable work)

as well as from those that seem aimless or unfocused.

Attention to means not only allows for the creation of new behavioral combinations, but the behaviors themselves lack the well-oiled efficiency of instrumental behaviors used to achieve a goal. Instead, play is characterized by a "galumphing" (Miller, 1973) or a lack of economy of movement (Loizos, 1967). Viewed within the framework of Piagetian notions, galumphing occurs after a skill or a means-end relation has been mastered (e.g., sliding down an inclined plane to get to the bottom), and this involves recombinations or reorganizations among familiar sensorimotor or representational schemes. Although much discussed, little empirical work has been addressed to clarifying the construct. For example, researchers have considered whether play facilitates problem solving, but few, if any, have considered whether problem solving facilitates play.

3. A third feature of play helps to distinguish it from exploratory behavior. According to investigators concerned with this distinction (e.g., Berlyne, 1960, 1966; Hutt, 1970; Weisler & McCall, 1976), *exploration is guided by the question*, "What is this object and what can it do?" Exploratory behavior is dominated by the stimulus insofar as it is oriented to obtaining information about its features. In contrast, *play is guided by the organism-dominated question*, "What can I do with this object?" Presumably exploration occurs when objects are unfamiliar or poorly understood. Exploratory behavior serves to reduce this uncertainty. Play, on the other hand, occurs when objects are familiar; it serves to produce stimulation and maintain a particular level of arousal. Thus play, unlike exploration, is organism rather than stimulus dominated.

Several suggestive implications follow from posing organism dominance as a characteristic of play (Fein, in press-a). One implication offered by Nunnally and Lemond (1973) is that play may temporally follow exploration. A second implication is that, in play, children impose meanings that are not given in the dimensions of actual physical or social stimulation (e.g., pretend substitutions are formulated by children). A final implication is that, in play, the child attributes to its own behavior an internal locus of control. "Whatever I wish" is thus the answer to the play question "What can I do with this object?"

4. A fourth characteristic held by some investigators to be a distinguishing marker of play is its *relation to instrumental behaviors*. Thus play behaviors are not serious renditions of the activities they resemble; the individual is not really fighting, but is play fighting (Aldis, 1975). Similarly, the usual instrumental meanings of objects can be dispensed with in play, and the individual can explore new potential meanings by treating the object as if it were something else; a chair is no longer used to sit on, but is used as if it were a horse. Thus, play has been said to be a nonliteral (Garvey, 1977a; 1977b), simulative (Reynolds, 1972) behavior that is characterized by an "as if" representational set (Sutton-Smith, 1966; 1967).

This feature restricts play to behaviors generally referred to as *pretense*. It eliminates a variety of sensorimotor activities (e.g., going down a slide in different ways, banging blocks together) that have no serious counterpart, but seem to be self-contained actions engaged in for their own sake. Going down a slide in different ways, chasing and being chased, banging blocks together *may* be viewed as play. But unless the child gives to these activities "as if" status—either by playing at sliding (but not really doing it) or by using the slide as an airplane runway—the activity is not viewed as pretense.

5. A fifth feature of play is its *freedom from externally imposed rules*. This criterion has been used to differentiate play from games, which "rule out" the flexibility said to characterize play (Bateson, 1955; Garvey, 1977a; Schwartzman, 1978). The distinction makes some heuristic sense and has been used to organize this chapter. However, there are several problems with the distinction.

First, games-with-rules have been shown to be developmentally related to earlier play behavior (Piaget, 1962). The developmental relationship between play and games-with-rules suggests that the latter may be a later developing form of play that emerges with the evolving cognitive sophistication of the individual. Classifying play and games as nonoverlapping phenomena obscures the genetic link that may exist between them. Second, sociodramatic play is also governed by rules that dictate how individuals are supposed to interact with each other (Garvey, 1977a). Although they do not have the character of the prescribed rules of a game, they may be the developmental precursors to games with rules (Vandenberg, 1981c), with the only difference being that the rules of play are less ironclad (for further discussion see the section *Games-with-Rules Versus Pretense Play*).

6. A sixth feature emphasized by some theorists is that play requires the participant to be *actively engaged* in an activity. This characteristic has been used to contrast play with daydreaming, lounging, and aimless loafing (Garvey, 1977a). The differentiation of play from passive states of boredom and inactivity is useful. However, the inclusion of

daydreaming with these other activities may be inappropriate and may reflect a bias toward defining play as the type of behavior engaged in by young children and nonhuman animals. Daydreaming, during which the individual "plays" with ideas, has been considered one of the developmental successors to the young child's active involvement with objects, action, and others (Freud, 1959; Klinger, 1971). Thus, it is important that we recognize the potential developmental kinship between the play of young children and the daydreaming of older children and adults.

These six features of play, although borrowed from different theoretical perspectives, do serve to incorporate or to exclude particular activities from a general definition of play. If applied additively, the features function to progressively restrict the domain of play. However, different theorists vary with reference to the definitional restrictions they impose. For Vygotsky (1967) play was synonymous with pretense, whereas for Piaget (1962) pretense was but one expression of a broader disposition.

As is evident from our preceding discussion, definitional efforts have traditionally drawn on metaphysical assumptions about the voluntaristic, spontaneous, pleasurable, or open-ended qualities of play that presumably distinguish it from nonplay behaviors. These formulations have had considerable heuristic value. More recent formulations, as discussed above, might provide a firmer base for serious theorizing, but even these fall considerably short of offering a guide to the *observation* of play behavior.

Play as Observable Behavior

Several investigators have offered taxonomies of behavior in which are described distinctive types of play (e.g., Garvey, 1974; Hutt, in press). A general and parsimonious developmental scheme offered by Piaget (1962) stresses three types of play in keeping with the notion of play as assimilation. (1) Practice play characterizes the play of infants; it appears after a sensorimotor skill has been acquired and it involves repetition with a "deliberate complication" of means when ends have receded in importance. (2) Symbolic play, emerging during the preoperational period, similarly involves the assimilative manipulation of symbols. (3) Games, emerging during the period of concrete operations, involve assimilative practice with rules. Piaget's taxonomy gives special emphasis to what a child can do at each developmental period. Other taxonomies involve the definition of behavioral categories such as play with language,

motion, interaction, or social materials (e.g., Garvey, 1977a). Hutt (in press) distinguishes between epistemic behavior (problem solving, exploration) and ludic behavior (symbolic or repetitive play that might be either innovative or perseverative). Another taxonomy developed by Rubin (Rubin, Maioni, & Hornung, 1976) involves the multiple classification of cognitive aspects of play and forms of social behavior.

There are several benefits to be gained by specifying particular types of play. First, at this level of analysis, the behavior is more easily rendered into observational criteria. Second, narrower categories might more convincingly demonstrate a particular aspect of play. For example, (1) pretend play illustrates the dominance of the organism over stimulus factors in the immediate environment; and (2) the contrast between functional and constructive play as defined by Rubin et al. (1976) may provide a basis for investigating variations in means-ends relations. Third, since there seems to be general agreement that play can manifest itself in these different ways, the minitheories likely to emerge from the investigation of such diverse manifestations might converge over time, permitting the formulation of a general theory, with factually interpreted symbols. Finally, and most important, these varied manifestations might have special implications for development that are obscured when play is viewed as a general behavioral disposition. At the very least, the notion of diverse and proper forms stresses the behavioral variability intrinsic to the concept of play.

Play as Context

Play as context expresses what adults of a given culture hold to be play, as well as the degree to which they believe that specific arrangements for play are necessary or desirable. The usefulness of a context definition depends, of course, on children sharing the adults' definition.

The context definition held by child psychologists is illustrated most clearly in the procedural sections of research reports. In numerous studies, participating children are brought by a friendly adult to an attractively equipped playroom and are invited to play. In others, they are observed during "free play" in a school classroom or playground. Although a given study may have little to do with play, these procedural formats reflect the belief that a describable and reproduceable set of environmental arrangements will evoke in children a set or inclination to play.

In contemporary research, these arrangements

tend to contain several components: (1) an array of familiar peers, toys, or other materials likely to engage children's interest; (2) an agreement between adults and children, expressed in word, gesture, or established by convention, that the children are free to choose from the array whatever they wish to do within whatever limits are required by the setting or the study; (3) adult behavior that is minimally intrusive or directive; (4) a friendly atmosphere designed to make children feel comfortable and safe; and (5) scheduling that reduces the likelihood of the children being tired, hungry, ill, or experiencing other types of bodily stress.

Depending on the particular arrangements, different types of play behavior may emerge, and, of course, some children will wander about aimlessly or watch rather than participate. For practical purposes then, play may be defined as a produceable context in which particular types of behavior occur, some of which may be play.

It is valuable to clarify the role of context issues in definitions of play since the phenomenon is so often discussed that it appears as if it is free of contextual assumptions or limitations (Sutton-Smith, in press). The adults of a nomadic desert tribe might define playthings as objects made by hand from natural materials. A child reared in such a group might be bewildered by the array of brightly colored plastic objects used by a Western psychologist in a cross-cultural study of play. A playroom, play areas in a school, or the suggestion of an adult may communicate "this is play" to children reared in Western cultures or in middle-class families, but not to those reared elsewhere. The important point, however, is that a general definition of play must include a description of the conditions under which play occurs, including statements about choice, interesting activities, protection from stress, and cultural sanction. If a general definition is to include behavioral manifestations of play, it must also include a description of the particular context in which each behavioral manifestation might occur.

Conclusion

Play poses a definitional dilemma familiar to psychologists. Play—like intelligence, language, aggression, or altruism—is easier to define behaviorally than theoretically. There seems to be agreement that play is a disposition and that there are different paradigms for specifying different dispositional features. Six of these were identified here. The notion of play as intrinsically motivated may draw on more than one theoretical framework (e.g.,

Berlyne, 1960; Hebb, 1948; White, 1959). By contrast, defining play with reference to adaptive goals draws on Piaget's theoretical distinction between assimilation and accommodation; play occurs when "assimilation is dissociated from accommodation"; it is "assimilation for the sake of assimilation with no need for new accommodation" (Piaget, 1962, p. 162). If play is to be defined with regard to the organism's relation to impinging stimulation, it can be viewed as behavior that is organism rather than stimulus dominated (e.g., Weisler & McCall, 1976). But, these are ways of expressing the issues by using theories, implying different but not necessarily conflicting paradigms. Whether rules or nonliteralness are also to be viewed as characteristics of play will depend again on theoretical considerations (e.g., these latter features exclude behaviors viewed as play from a Piagetian perspective).

Classifications of play also tend to reflect theoretical judgments. The scheme proposed by Hutt (in press) contrasts epistemic and ludic behavior (distinguished by informational orientation) and, within the ludic group, this taxonomy contrasts repetitive (with or without variations) and symbolic play. These distinctions resemble those of Piaget (1962), cast in the language of Berlyne's concept of arousal. The value of taxonomies is that play research can begin to focus on particular behaviors held to manifest one or more features of the more general disposition. If indeed these diverse and observable forms share central features, a general definition of play might be constructed inductively.

Procedures for bringing about play based on assumptions about the context or conditions for play abound in the research literature, although these have not been viewed as having definitional value. But by being tacit, the cultural as well as implicit theoretical assumptions are obscured. Play may be whatever is measured in particular circumstances. If so, circumstance as well as unit of measurement require explicit attention.

LIMITING THE SCOPE OF THE DISCUSSION

Drawing on the features of play already mentioned and given that authors of this volume of the *Handbook* review particular topics from a *psychological* perspective, we admit to limiting the scope of the remaining sections of this chapter. Hereafter our discussion will focus on children's play as the psychologist views it. As such, the anthropological, sociological, comparative, and recreational perspectives will purposely be given little attention. The reader is referred to Schwartzman (1978), Denzin

(1979), Bruner, Jolly, and Sylva (1976), and Levy (1977), respectively, for consideration of these viewpoints. Recent publications of the annual proceedings of the Association for the Anthropological Study of Play (e.g., Salter, 1978; Schwartzman, 1980) will also prove helpful in this respect.

We limit our discussion further by excluding much of the vast extant literature concerned with exploration, games (Avedon & Sutton-Smith, 1971; Opie & Opie, 1969), and play therapy (Axline, 1969; Jernberg, 1979). Finally, many psychologists include in their discussion of play all peer interaction that occurs in laboratory or natural settings. We concur with Parten's (1932) labeling of such activity as social participation and defer to Hartup (Chapter 2, this volume) concerning the description of this work. Thus, having specified our limited focus, we now turn to a number of twentieth-century theories concerned with the psychology of children's play.

TWENTIETH-CENTURY THEORIES OF PLAY

Early Twentieth-Century Theorists

Several psychologists dominated play theory in the first half of the twentieth century. Each of these psychologists made a mark in other areas of developmental psychology, thereby dealing with play as a secondary topic of interest. Interestingly, there are several common denominators found in these theories. They include speculations that (1) children play to express themselves via fantasy or pretense play and (2) that play results, in part, from wish fulfillment. Given these common denominators, it may be surprising to some that the theorists we will discuss include Freud, Piaget, and Vygotsky.

Freud

Freud never articulated a systematic theory of play. Instead, he made passing references to play at various points in his work and his speculations usually were embedded in a discussion of other issues that he considered more central to his theory, such as the repetition compulsion or the dynamics of humor. Nevertheless, his treatment of play is significant because of the way it subsequently was elaborated on by other psychoanalytic theorists.

Freud proposed that play provided children with an avenue for wish fulfillment and the mastery of traumatic events. In his early writings describing the properties of the id and the pleasure principle, Freud focused on the wish fulfillment aspects of play. According to Freud, "The opposite of play is not what is serious, but what is real" (Freud, 1959, p. 144). Play allowed the child to escape the constraints and sanctions of reality, thereby providing a safe context for venting unacceptable, usually aggressive impulses too dangerous to express in reality.

The mastery aspects of play were addressed in Freud's discussion of the repetition compulsion. According to Freud the repetition compulsion is a psychic mechanism that allows individuals to cope with a traumatic event. Individuals master traumatic events through a compulsive repetition of components of the disturbing events. In adulthood, the repetition compulsion occurs only in relatively rare instances of severe trauma. In childhood, however, individuals are more susceptible to trauma since the ego structure and psychic defenses are not sufficiently organized to ward off the destabilizing effects of anxiety-producing events. Consequently, the repetition compulsion is more common in childhood and is manifested in children's play. Thus, in play "children repeat everything that has made a great impression on them in real life, and that in so doing, they abreact the strength of the impressions and . . . make themselves masters of the situation" (Freud, 1961, p. 11). Therefore, play allows children to become the active masters of situations in which they were once passive victims.

As for the development of play, Freud believed the period during which children freely expressed their wishes through play was short-lived. It concluded with the onset of the rational thought processes associated with ego development. To Freud, "play is brought to an end by the strengthening of a factor that deserves to be described as the critical faculty or reasonableness" (Freud, 1960, p. 128).[1] With the development of the ego, the direct symbolic expression of the pleasurable, but unacceptable, wishes of the id is no longer possible. Instead, the ego engages in jests and jokes (Freud, 1960) or creative artistic activity (Freud, 1959) that seeks to express the same wishes and derive the same pleasures that were earlier derived in play. Play is thus replaced with more realistic and socially acceptable activities by the ego, but the dynamics of play live on in the unconscious motivations of these later activities.

In more recent years, psychoanalytic theorists have expanded on Freud's conceptualizations of play. Generally, these theorists have focused on either wish fulfillment or the mastery elements of his theory. A brief description of the psychoanalytic work follows.

[1]The idea that play is a characteristic feature of early childhood that disappears with the onset of rational thought is similar to that of Piaget. It was this notion that led to Sutton-Smith's (1966) critique of Piaget's theory.

Wish Fulfillment. Freud maintained that children are highly selective with regard to whom and what they imitate in their play. The choice of roles and contexts are supposedly based on the particular dynamics and motivations engendered by the play topics. Peller (1952) has provided an analysis of the particular roles and characters frequently selected by children in their play and has discussed the motivations behind these selections.

Peller noted that children's choices of roles often are based on feelings of love, admiration, fear, or anger for a particular person. Children will imitate those people, particularly adults, for whom they feel love and admiration, thereby fulfilling the wish to be like those people. People or things that evoke fear, on the other hand, prompt imitation in an attempt to master the anxiety associated with them. Other roles children are likely to play include those "beneath their dignity" (e.g., a baby, an animal, or a clown). These roles allow children to regress within the safe confines of play and to enjoy infantile pleasures that are no longer directly available to them.

Peller (1954) also described changes in the structure of children's play as they progressed through the psychosexual stages of development. In the first stages, children's anxieties are focused on the inadequacies and frustrated pleasures associated with their bodies. Their play reflects these anxieties; play is solitary and usually involves manipulation of body parts. With development, children enter the pre-Oedipal stage, which centers on the potential loss of the mother—the source of nurturance. Children in this stage play primarily with their mother, and the main theme of their play is "I can do to mother what she did to me" (Peller, 1954, p. 186). When children reach the stage of Oedipal conflict, they try to compensate for the powerless position vis-à-vis adults by taking on adult roles in their play. Post-Oedipal play consists of achieving independence from external superego figures through participation in games with peers. The games serve to create a self-contained social order, and scrupulous adherence to the rules of the game provides freedom from external superego figures.

Peller's discussion of how psychosexual developmental issues influence the structure of children's play greatly expands and enriches Freud's theory. However, as the reader will note in the sections on pretense that follow, examination of the roles and themes that children adopt in their play has been limited.

The belief that fantasy play is an index of wish fulfillment also has been espoused by Menninger (1942) who emphasized the carthartic, anxiety-reducing benefits of play. Menninger highlighted the value of play for relieving repressed aggressive impulses. This cartharsis view also was reformulated by drive theorists (e.g., Dollard, Doob, Miller, Mowrer, & Sears, 1939) who suggested that the aggression displaced in fantasy play serves to reduce the likelihood of aggressive expression in other contexts. The behavioral reformulation of the original Freudian tenets stimulated considerable research, much of which employed a doll play methodology (cf. Levin & Wardwell, 1962). The research basically exploited Freud's notion that children's intrapsychic dynamics are displayed in play. As such, doll play was used to investigate a host of topics, including the relation between classroom aggression and aggression in a fantasy situation (e.g., Sears, 1947), the reaction of children to racial and religious differences (e.g., Graham, 1955; Hartley & Swartz, 1951), and the effects of parental separation on children (e.g., Bach, 1946).

However, most of the questions addressed by this research were unrelated to the catharsis hypothesis, and those studies that did address this issue were methodologically flawed. Many of the studies failed to establish the reliability of their measures, and there were few attempts to determine what the relationship was between doll play activity and other behaviors. Did aggressive doll play reflect a propensity for aggression in other settings, or was it a reflection of repressed aggression (Fein, 1981; Levin & Wardwell, 1962)? Furthermore, the importance of play as a generative force in development was lost in the doll play studies. As originally conceived, play was a source of catharsis. The doll play studies, however, were not really concerned with play at all, but merely used it as a vehicle to study other, presumably more important, variables. While this may have been a useful research strategy, the conceptual consequence of the methodology was to change play from a causal agent in development to a passive container of other behaviors (Schwartzman, 1978).

The catharthis theory of play has been examined subsequently by Feshbach (1956), Bandura (1969), and others. Bandura's work in particular has generated a great deal of research interest. Although a review of this research is beyond the scope of this chapter, it should be noted that the results generally have not supported the psychoanalytic hypothesis. Indeed, Bandura's research has indicated that aggressive play may actually stimulate rather than reduce further aggression.

Mastery. Erikson (1940; 1963; 1977) is the principal theorist who has addressed the mastery aspect of Freud's theory of play. Erikson's theoretical emphasis is on understanding normal ego development, and this orientation is reflected in his treatment of play. According to Erikson (1963), cultural institutions and the evolving psychosexual stages, which give rise to the development of the individual, are like two gears moving as one. Together these forces give rise to the psychosocial stages of ego development. Adaptive resolutions of the psychosocial stages involve the successful integration of the social and biological spheres of functioning. Play aids this integration by creating "model situations in which aspects of the past are re-lived, the present represented and renewed, and the future anticipated" (Erikson, 1977, p. 44). Play creates an arena in which the uncertainties, anxieties, and hoped for solutions of the ego can be dramatized.

The form that play takes changes as the psychosocial issues and ego contexts change. Play with toys, for example, is an early behavior during which children explore their concerns about the budding issues of competence and sexuality. These issues are reflected in the space-time microsphere of the scenes constructed with toys. The adult form of play is creative imagination, which allows for the exploration of the boundaries and possibilities of cultural myth systems—be they in art, science, or "everyday life." In Erikson's words, "The growing child's play . . . is the training ground for the experience of a leeway of imaginative choices within an existence governed and guided by roles and visions" (Erikson, 1977, p. 78). Thus, play with the space-time microstructures of toys is the developmental precursor to creative play with its possibilities in the imaginative space-time microstructure of cultural myths and rituals.

Erikson (1940; 1941; 1951) has addressed empirically the way that psychosexual conflicts are reflected in the spatial configurations of children's toy play. In the best known study, Erikson (1951) found that young boys built vertical constructions that involved active themes, whereas girls' creations consisted of enclosures with static themes. Erikson indicated that children were facing the onset of sexual maturity, and the sex differences in their constructions reflected differences in their evolving sexual morphology. The girls' creations mirrored the passive, enclosed nature of female genitalia, whereas the boys' constructions reflected the intrusive, erect nature of the penis, with its active sperm cells.

The rigor of Erikson's research falls somewhere between the typical psychoanalytic case study and the statistical exactness of psychological research. Data from Erikson's original study were more systematically analyzed by Honzik (1951) who found

statistical support for the sex difference discussed above. Erikson's results have also been replicated by Cramer and Hogan (1975), which lends additional empirical credence to his findings.

Erikson's interpretations of the results, on the other hand, are indeed controversial. His assertions that behavioral differences in children's play are an outgrowth of the biological differences between the sexes has sparked considerable controversy (Janeway, 1971; Sherif, 1979; Sherman, 1971). Unfortunately, there have been few attempts to examine experimentally Erikson's theory of play, so the nature-nurture debate which he has spawned awaits further research.

While Erikson has made an important theoretical contribution to the mastery aspect of Freud's play theory, experimental examination of this aspect of play has been very limited. Nevertheless, his ideas have led to the development and use of play therapy to help children to cope with emotional difficulties. Although Freud never directly addressed the significance of play for therapy with children, he did hint at it in his treatment of Little Hans (Freud, 1955). Freud used the reported play activities of the child to assess the intrapsychic conflicts. Drawing on this example, Klein (1932: 1955) proposed that children could be treated in psychoanalysis similarly to adults. She noted that play productions rather than verbalizations could be used as the source of dynamic materials. While Klein has been criticized severely on particular aspects of her theory (e.g., A. Freud, 1964), play therapy with children has become nearly standard clinical practice. In addition, the use of play as a tool for assessment has become a highly accepted method for psychiatric diagnosis of children's emotional status (Goodman & Sours, 1967).

The belief that play can provide the opportunity to cope with traumatic events has led to a ground swell of support for providing hospitalized children with play experiences to help alleviate their anxieties associated with hospitalization (Harvey, 1975; Lindquist, Lind, & Harvey, 1977). Several researchers have found that hospitalized children play with more hospital-related toys than do non-hospitalized children (Erickson, 1958; Gips, 1950). Furthermore, Gilmore (1966) has found that the level of anxiety may influence whether hospitalized children will play with hospital-related toys; if children are too fearful, they are *not* likely to play with toys that are related to the source of their fears. It is now necessary for researchers to experimentally separate play *about* an anxiety-provoking event from play *during* an anxiety-provoking event (e.g., hospitalization). Moreover, researchers should now assess *post*play adjustment to determine if play does have therapeutic value.

In summary, although Freud's speculations about play constitute only a small aspect of his work, his impact has been widespread and profound. From a practical standpoint, the ubiquitous use of play in clinical settings can be directly traced to his influence. Theoretically, Freud has provided us with an understanding of the potential ways that play may aid the development of emotional stability and maturity. The many spin-offs from his theory, from Peller's elaborations to Erikson's reformulations, have enriched our understanding of play.

Piaget

Piaget's (1962) notion of play as assimilation is another example of a view of play derived from a theory addressed to other aspects of development. In the case of psychoanalytic theory described above, "play" is discussed in relation to wishes, anxieties, and ego processes; in the case of Berlyne's theory of intrinsic motivation described below, play is discussed in terms of mechanisms associated with exploratory behaviors and the regulation of arousal states. In these theories, and in Piaget's as well, statements about play represent extensions of theoretical constructs to a new domain and, as such, illustrate the contribution of theory in clarifying and integrating seemingly diverse phenomena.

As this kind of extension, Piaget's notion of play as assimilation is something of a tour de force (cf. Piaget, 1962). According to Piagetian theory, intellectual adaptations result from an equilibrium between the processes of assimilation and accommodation. In assimilation, children incorporate events, objects, or situations into existing ways of thinking. According to Piaget, play represents an imbalance or disequilibrium in which assimilation dominates accommodation. Not surprisingly, the behavior resulting from this assimilative orientation reflects the child's level of development. Piaget's categories (i.e., practice play, symbolic play, and games-with-rules) are therefore play counterparts of sensorimotor, preoperational, and concrete operational intelligence.[2]

In infancy, particular types of *practice play* emerge with the sequential development of primary, secondary, and tertiary circular reactions. But, since play is nonadaptive (as adaptation is defined in the theory), play as assimilation becomes the repetition

[2]It should be noted that Piaget's categorization of different play forms stems directly from Buhler (1928). Both schemes, however, are found earlier in Spencer (1873).

of already acquired modes of behavior detached from the functional focus under which the behavior was initially acquired. When Piaget's infant son, Laurent, discovers that he can see a toy by throwing his head back and then repeats the movement for its own sake, the behavior becomes play—that is, the exercise of an acquired schema detached from its initial adaptive purpose of bringing an interesting object into view. Play at the level of secondary circular reactions is illustrated by a child continuing to pull the string that makes a toy parrot move without seeming to be involved in the consequence as much as in the pulling. And, with relentless consistency, Piaget describes play at the level of tertiary circular reactions as the combination and repetition of different behaviors, again without attention to the impact of these variations on the environment. Instead, the child's attention is focused on combining for the sake of combining, on the production of "deliberate complications" that put obstacles in the way of accomplishing goals that may initially have served to organize the behavior. According to Piaget, the pleasure of practice play comes from the child's sense of control over self and environment. The skill was difficult to master; the problem was difficult to solve. But once mastered or solved, the child luxuriates in the feeling of growing competence and confidence when control is repeatedly demonstrated.

One psychological result of the practice is that the acquired skills become "consolidated." At first, the repetition is not mechanically exact; skills or problem solutions permit variations that might be less than optimally efficient, but nonetheless represent different ways of doing the same thing. For example, a child can go down a slide in numerous ways that do not alter substantially the physical and spatial relations of a body navigating an inclined plane. The slide can be navigated while rocking, kicking, or waving hands, by sitting, laying, standing, head first or feet first. These variations illustrate how a core set of physical-spatial relations might be varied while being preserved. Piaget's point is that this behavior differs from the intense, concentrated, and tentative behavior shown when the child first learned how to use the slide. In Piaget's terms, the initial learning is adaptation, but the subsequent exercise is play, serving to consolidate the initial learning by incorporating old skills into the new one, by smoothing out the new performance, or, perhaps, by separating the essential core of a skill from nonessential, elaborative variations.

In the Piagetian scheme, *symbolic play* reflects the appearance and development of the semiotic function, that is, the understanding that one thing (a signifier) can stand for something else (that which is signified). This form of play also reflects an assimilative orientation to the environment. In the previous sensorimotor period, these actions were exercised and elaborated for their functional value; now these actions are exercised for their representational value (cf. Fein, 1979a, for an examination of this aspect of Piaget's theory). In symbolic play, the child practices the method of relating signifier to that which is signified.[3] Symbolic play is one type of signification; words and images are others.

Symbolic actions have two characteristics: First, they are detached from the practical circumstances in which they were actually acquired, used, or practiced; second, they are recognized by the child as pertaining to those circumstances, though detached and different from them. Piaget's analysis of the shift from sensorimotor to symbolic play is nicely illustrated in the sleeping games of one of his children. First, the gestures associated with sleeping were practiced in the real-life context of bedroom, blanket, and pillow without any seeming need or intention of going to sleep. Thus, elements of the real-life behavior become identified as the salient characteristics of sleeping. As these elements are reproduced for their own sake, they are assimilated into the larger organization of affect and behavior, which together means "sleeping." With repetition, they become trimmed of superfluous gestures, ritualized or standardized, and increasingly differentiated from real-life sleeping behavior, while continuing to be assimilated into the affective-behavioral organization that constitutes the child's concept of sleeping. Soon these standardized gestures are produced in other contexts, with materials having little resemblance to those used at bedtime. But these gestures continue to be assimilated into the schema of sleeping; they are "motivated symbols" in the sense that they "mean" sleeping and "resemble" sleeping but are not sleeping. Put in non-Piagetian terms, the gestures were extracted from actual instances of sleeping and they are recognized by the child as belonging to that domain of activity. They are, however, a special type of instance insofar as they have been detached from the motivational and situational circumstances of the real activity. The meaning evoked in symbolic play is, in addition, informed by personal, idiosyncratic, and egocentric interpretations. The symbols of play have a cognitive core and an emotional penumbra.

The symbols of pretense also come from the deferred imitation of others. These observed and reproduced behaviors may not reflect the child's direct experience, but in play they are given a meaning that fits the child's understanding. Again, gestures and actions are interpreted through an assimilative process. The child pretending to be "father sleeping" (with closed eyes, head down, and snoring) or the child putting a doll to sleep (with bottle, blanket, and song) is generating expanded combinations that symbolize, or signify, expanded and refined meanings of sleeping, persons, and interpersonal relationships. As assimilation, the meanings of any moment may be charged with feelings, wishes, and memories beyond the purely cognitive aspects of the concept. Piaget draws close to psychoanalytic theory when he views pretense as a mechanism whereby areas of emotional discord can be ameliorated. The amelioration is achieved not by addressing or altering the real-life circumstances that produced the discord, but rather by altering (and thereby distorting) the meaning of these circumstances.

From a developmental perspective, play presupposes the differentiation of assimilation from accommodation. Piaget suggests that, in early infancy, these processes might be differentiated so poorly that play, as such, might not be possible. The possibility for play emerges as the infant begins to construct a notion of the environment as separate and independent of the self. Symbolic play depends especially on a degree of differentiation sufficient to permit the polarization of assimilation and accommodation as well as an extremity of disequilibrium sufficient to permit short-circuiting of the adaptive mechanism posited by Piaget that accounts for the development and exercise of intelligence. Therefore, pretend play illustrates a number of theoretical propositions. First, it illustrates one type of symbol making (one in which the signifier or symbolic vehicle bears some resemblance to that which is signified). Second, it illustrates differentiation along two dimensions, one being the differentiation of accommodation from assimilation, and another the differentiation of operative (i.e., action knowledge) from figurative (i.e., mechanisms for transforming the perceptual configuration of real-world events into mentally configured events) aspects of cognition (Piaget & Inhelder, 1971). Third, it illustrates that aspect of functioning whereby knowledge is "consolidated" rather than acquired.

In practice play, acquired adaptive behaviors are consolidated by repetition and reorganization. In pretend play, consolidation occurs at two levels. The first level is that of symbol making (i.e., the pretending child is practicing signification). The second,

---

[3]This relation is called "designation" by some theorists (e.g., Huttenlocher & Higgins, 1978) and "denotation" by others (e.g., Bateson, 1956).

more substantive level, involves the consolidation of particular life experiences by establishing what representations of these experiences will mean. In this sense the pretending child is achieving the symbolic assimilation and, therefore, the organization of important life experiences—a process that initially involves the construction of personal symbolic prototypes (e.g., behavioral elements that mean sleeping) and later the construction of collective symbolic prototypes.

In Piaget's scheme pretense (and play) is hypothesized to develop from the solitary to the social, when collective symbolization becomes possible. The development of overt pretense also is predicted to reflect an inverted U-shaped function; it is infrequent and ephemeral during the second year of life, increases in frequency and complexity during the third and fourth years, then decreases thereafter. Pretense is bounded at the early end by practice play, which decreases proportionally but appears whenever a new skill is acquired. It is bounded at the later end by the appearance of *games-with-rules*.

Since games-with-rules will not be discussed at length in this chapter, we merely note here that in Piaget's model of play games continue to express an assimilative orientation to reality. Rules result from the collective organization of ludic activities and thus carry with them a sense of social obligation. Games-with-rules are "games with sensory-motor combinations . . . or intellectual combinations . . . in which there is competition between individuals . . . and which are regulated either by a code handed down by earlier generations, or by temporary agreement" (Piaget, 1962, p. 144). But Piaget argued that a code cannot be worked out and applied without an effort at reasoning; games-with-rules call on aspects of intelligence available to the concrete operational child.

In symbolic play, individuals are rendered in concrete terms (witch, mother, father, monster, etc.). In games, individuals are rendered as more abstract units (in tag as "its" versus "non-its," or as more refined and restricted roles), specified in relation to spatial configurations, materials, moves, turns, sequences, and consequences. Notions such as one-to-one correspondence, classification, seriation, iteration, and equivalence are applied to pieces and people, configured in varied ways such that "winning" is defined intrinsically. But winning has meaning only if the underlying notions are applied in the manner agreed on by the players. A game of checkers or hide-and-seek can only be "won" if captured pieces or people are subtracted from the uncaptured group. The game makes sense only if capturing, and the relationships between those who

capture and those who are captured, are specified and honored. The intellectual complexity of the rules reflects the cognitive abilities of the concrete operational child, and the codification of social behavior reflects the child's ability to enter into regulated or rule-governed social relations.

Piaget (1962) insisted that his analysis of games-with-rules is not consistent with "the idea of assimilation of reality to the ego" but, instead, that this type of play "reconciles ludic assimilation with the demands of social reciprocity" (p. 168). Rules are needed to regulate competition between individuals. However, in these games, "there is still sensory-motor or intellectual satisfaction, and there is also the chance for victory over others, but these satisfactions are as it were made 'legitimate' by the rules of the game through which competition is controlled by a collective discipline with a code of honor and fair play."

Piaget's theory has stimulated numerous studies of developmental changes in forms of play, especially those emerging in the development of symbolic play. The appeal of Piaget's interpretation of symbolic play is that it offers a remarkably coherent analysis of play with respect to symbol making and of symbol making with respect to play. For investigators interested in play, Piaget's analysis indicates how play as assimilation functions with respect to progressively more mature expressions of intelligence (i.e., sensorimotor, symbolic, and rule systems). For investigators interested in representational forms, Piaget's analysis provides a vision of how varied modes of representation (e.g., imagery; linguistic and enactive modes) might develop from the child's discovery of signification.

In preparing this chapter, it soon became evident that infant play and games-with-rules have been slighted in the extant research, and that Piaget's contribution to a general theory of play has received less attention than his contribution to a theory of representational thought. If the former is to be pursued, it will be necessary to go beyond Piaget's provocative but fragmentary insights. A key, but underdeveloped, construct in Piaget's play theory is that of "consolidation" (Fein, 1979a; Fein & Apfel, 1979a; Rubin, 1980; Rubin & Pepler, in press). What happens when novel, adaptive constructions are consolidated? Put another way, what is the relationship between the old and the new, between the familiar and the novel in the application and development of thinking? For example, Saltz (1980) presented the case for consolidation as the organization of memory functions, whereas Fein (1979a) argued for consolidation as the organization of abstract concepts of objects and relationships. To date, Piaget's theory, for the most part, has stimulated descriptive studies rather than studies of process. The descriptive papers are discussed elsewhere in this chapter; the studies of process are yet to be conducted.

Vygotsky

Like Freud, Piaget, Berlyne, and other theorists discussed in this chapter, Vygotsky's view of play can be best appreciated in terms of the more general psychological problem he set out to address and the special presuppositions that guided this work (see Fein, 1979b, for a more exhaustive discussion). With respect to the problem, Vygotsky (1967) was concerned with the development and functioning of higher mental processes. His presuppositions were drawn from Marxist theory. According to the Marxist viewpoint, the higher mental processes are formed socially and are transmitted culturally in the life span of an individual; biological dispositions are superseded quickly by cultural forces. These forces become manifest in two ways. One is through the individual's active efforts to change the social and material environment; practical activity leads to the development of "tools of labor" and the ascendancy of man over nature. Another is through the system of social relationships within which practical activity occurs; understanding reflects a person's position in the system of social relationships and determines the form and purpose of such activity.

However, the task of constructing a Marxist theory of the relationship between society and the individual is not an easy matter. With respect to the origins of knowledge, Marxist theory rejects empiricism because it implies a passive individual. Rationalism is rejected because it implies a preformed, unchanging individual. Marxist theory thus requires an interactionist position of an especially elusive type, centered on a socially oriented individual who is (1) passive enough to acquire culturally organized knowledge, and yet (2) active enough to reject that knowledge when it yields intolerable contradictions. Vygotsky (1962) criticized Piaget's interactionist solution because it stressed the egocentric nature of early thinking. However, Vygotsky's attempt to embed the child in a social matrix was criticized subsequently by Soviet psychologists because it stressed the child's individual consciousness rather than consciousness determined by the child's changing social relationships (El'konin, 1968). Vygotsky did not live long enough to refine or to flesh out his distinctive solution to these problems. Much of the experimental work designed to examine his ideas either was not published or was not translated.

According to Vygotsky (1978), mental structures are constructed from the use of tools and signs. Tools develop from the individual's outward practical actions on the material environment. Activity is first organized around practical problems that involve direct actions on the material environment; gradually these direct actions are replaced by mediating technologies, that is, by objects used as tools to act on the environment in more efficient ways. But activity also is organized around practical problems in the social environment. This activity requires the development of *signs*, viewed by Vygotsky as a form of mediated activity that also acts indirectly on the environment. According to Vygotsky, the higher mental processes represent the fusion of tool use and sign use. First, the achievements of practical activity are represented by signs and, second, signs used initially to control or to communicate outwardly turn inward, becoming a mechanism whereby the individual is able to plan and regulate problem-solving behavior. As speech, signs function as tools with one important difference, namely that speech becomes a tool for controlling and organizing the use of objects as tools. The problem confronting Vygotsky was to demonstrate how practical activity comes to be represented by signs. This problem required that Vygotsky demonstrate how the individual's relationship to the environment changes from a direct (unmediated) one in which the immediate situation dominates the individual to an indirect one in which the individual dominates the immediate situation.

For Vygotsky, play provided the mechanism whereby this change was brought about. In keeping with the general theoretical problem of interest to Vygotsky, play was defined as the child's creation of an imaginary situation. Play originates, however, not from cognitive factors, but from affective-social pressures. Like Freud, Vygotsky held that play emerges from the tension between desires that can neither be forgotten by the child nor be fulfilled by society. To resolve the tension, the child enters an "imaginary, illusory world in which . . . unrealizable desires can be realized" (1967, p. 7). However, Vygotsky shunned the intellectualized, symbolist interpretation of specific play content pursued by psychoanalytic theorists. Instead, the imaginary situation was seen as being precipitated by more generalized affective needs or incentives, by long-term needs and desires that the child knows cannot be fulfilled but that, nonetheless, produce pressure for immediate realization. And so, play is "invented"; it is a "new formation." In terms of Marxist theory, play is a formation produced by contradictions that cannot be otherwise resolved. However, this new formation retains elements of real-life experiences (i.e., it is memory in action), especially the rules governing relationships in the original situation. As such, it is intrinsically linked to what the child knows about the real world. The new feature is that the child is liberated from the constraints of the immediate situation by virtue of creating a mental situation that supersedes the immediate one. The crucial feature of this new formation is its dependency on the child's willingness to subordinate behavior to rules extracted from previous experience and to renounce immediate impulses. Subordination and renunciation become means for maximizing the pleasure of play. Play is thus precipitated by negative and unpleasant tension; but it is maintained by positive and pleasant aftereffects produced by attempts to control tension.

Thus, for Vygotsky, play was viewed as a highly motivated behavioral formation. Like Freud, the motivation for play was regarded as deriving from real-life tension. However, unlike Freud, its maintenance stemmed less from the reduction of particular tensions than from the exercise of a more general system of controlling tension. Unlike Berlyne, whose theory is described next, the motivational force for play emanated from within the individual rather than from the level of immediate stimulation impinging on the person. And, unlike Piaget, Vygotsky did not consider play to be a natural byproduct or aberration of adaptive intelligence. Instead, it was viewed as an adaptive mechanism promoting cognitive growth during the preschool years (cf. Vygotsky, 1967; 1978).

According to Vygotsky, play brings into being the mediating role of signs. When children first begin to use words, the word is perceived as a property of the object rather than as a sign denoting the object. The child grasps the external structure of the word-object relationship earlier than the internal structure of the sign-referent relationship (Vygotsky, 1962). The fusion of word with object follows the more general fusion of action and object. In infancy, the child relates to things "as objects of action." For higher mental processes to develop, things must become "objects of thought" and practical actions must become mental operations (e.g., volitional choice). Play precipitates this emancipation of meaning from object and action.

The central event responsible for the emancipation is the use of one object (e.g., a stick) to substitute for another (a real horse), or the use of one action (stamping feet) to substitute for another (riding a horse). According to Vygotsky (1967, p. 15) "movement in a field of meaning" predominates in play. But the movement is possible only because substitute objects and actions serve as pivots to sever meaning (e.g., previous experience retained in memory) from immediate experience. In grasping the notion that a stick or a gesture can be given the meaning of horse, the child has taken a critical step toward understanding that a word can be given the same meaning. Words thus come to stand for functional behavioral systems. Of course, the separation is gradual. Early pivots resemble the objects for which they substitute, but with development the substitution of less prototypical objects become increasingly possible (Fein, 1975). More important, perhaps, this sign-referent relationship develops in the self-controlling rule-governed situation of play and thereby embodies, from the beginning, the directive, regulatory functions characteristic of mature thought.

As we discuss later, Vygotsky's influence has had its greatest impact on studies of the development of substitute object processes in symbolic play (e.g., Elder & Pederson, 1978; Fein, 1975; Watson & Fischer, 1977). Yet Vygotsky offered a strong theoretical basis for viewing pretend play as having a central role in the acquisition of language and problem solving, a position differing considerably from that advanced by Piaget for whom play served primarily expressive functions (Fein, 1979b). Vygotsky identified other aspects of pretense that merit further inquiry. One concerns the role of rules in play; according to Vygotsky, the covert rules of imaginary situations reflect the disciplined, self-controlling nature of play and provide the source of its pleasure (e.g., El'konin, 1969). Another concerns the relationship between children's level of development as expressed in play and as expressed in practical problem solving (cf. Rubin & Pepler, 1980). Vygotsky viewed play as creating the child's "zone of proximal development" (that is, the highest level of performance of which the child is capable), one comparable to that created by a teaching adult. In the instructional situation, the zone is created by an adult demonstrating the solution to a problem the child can manage with help but not independently. In play, the child spontaneously uses rules that in real life are condensed, compressed and employed by others. These very rules, narrowly demonstrated in instructional situations, are used more broadly and freely in play. One implication of Vygotsky's notions is that children given special encouragement to play socially should become more skillful in solving social problems that illustrate the rules of social relationships and social roles (e.g., Fink, 1976), especially if this social problem solving depends on the use of speech in the regulation of social behavior.

Recent Theorists

In recent years there have been three major threads of thought concerning play that have evolved from different points on the social science landscape. Berlyne (1960; 1966) has introduced an arousal theory of play based on behavioral learning theory. Bateson (1955; 1956) has proposed a theory of play that focuses on the communicative features of play using anthropological-systems theory. Finally, Sutton-Smith (1966; 1967; 1976) and Bruner (1972) have emphasized play as a source of behavioral variability based on a cognitive adaptation framework.

Berlyne

Play and curiosity have proved to be problematic behaviors for the drive theories of learning (e.g., Hull, 1943; 1952). The drive theorists proposed that learning was a consequence of the association of stimuli with responses which reduced basic drives, such as hunger and thirst. Such responses were viewed as necessary for the survival of the organism. Play and exploration were regarded as either epiphenomena or as unnecessary mentalistic fabrications (e.g., Schlosberg, 1947) and, consequently, were not considered worthy of scientific inquiry. These tidy solutions began to unravel in the face of research that indicated that, for rats, the need to explore a new environment was sometimes more powerful than the need to overcome hunger (Chance & Mead, 1955); that monkeys would solve puzzles apparently "just for the fun of it" (Harlow, Harlow, & Meyer, 1950); and that, for monkeys, viewing scenes outside their cage was a powerful form of reward (Butler, 1953; 1958). These findings led to the hypothesis of manipulatory and exploratory drives and to the distinction between internal and external motivation.

However, the concept of intrinsically motivated behavior undermined several fundamental assumptions of drive theory. The drives associated with hunger, thirst, and sex are physiological in origin, and behavior was viewed as an instrumental response for obtaining external rewards, which reduced these drives. Intrinsically motivated behaviors shared none of these characteristics; they were not associated directly with physiological needs, and the behavior was not a means to a reward, but was a reward in itself.

Berlyne (1960; 1964; 1966; 1969) proposed a potential solution for drive theorists. He suggested that externally motivated behavior is driven by tissue needs, while intrinsically motivated behavior serves central nervous system functions. The reward value of intrinsically motivated behaviors is not in their reduction of drives through the acquisition of external reinforcers, but in their direct effect on the level of arousal in central nervous system functioning. In this sense, then, they can be said to be self or intrinsically motivated behaviors.

According to Berlyne, the central nervous system of an organism seeks to maintain an optimal level of arousal (see also Hebb, 1948). When this level is elevated as a result of novelty, discrepancy, or an uncertainty, the organism seeks to reduce the arousal level of acquiring information. This is achieved by exploring those specific features of the environment that are the source of the arousal. These behaviors are collectively termed "specific exploration," and Berlyne has linked them to the orienting reflex (Pavlov, 1927). During the onset of this reflex, the organism is compelled neurologically to attend to novel or discrepant events in the environment.

When environmental stimulation falls below the optimum level, during which the organism is said to be "bored," the organism is thought to engage in stimulus-seeking activity. Berlyne labeled this type of activity "diverse exploration." Diverse exploration is aimed at decreasing arousal by producing stimulation rather than reducing it.

Berlyne has synthesized information from a wide range of sources into a systematic and clearly articulated theory that is consistent with learning theory. Of interest in the present chapter is the contribution of Berlyne's theory to an understanding of the motivating mechanisms of play.

In Berlyne's model of arousal, excessively high and excessively low levels of stimulation are aversive. The subjective states of uncertainty and boredom each represents an elevation of arousal above an optimum level. If play were identified with diverse exploration, it would function to *decrease* arousal by increasing stimulation. When arousal reached an optimum level, play would stop, only to begin again when the level of stimulation dropped and the arousal level increased. While setting out to revise drive theory, Berlyne retained one of its core assumptions—that behavior is motivated by aversive states that need to be alleviated.

An alternative to this view has been proposed by Ellis (1973). According to Ellis, arousal is high in the presence of stimulation and low in its absence. Play functions to produce stimulation that increases arousal toward optimum levels. In this model, the organism is pulled toward a positive state rather than away from a negative one. In Ellis' model, play is stimulus-seeking behavior. However, stimulus-seeking behavior appears in several forms; for example, the child going from one thing to another looking for something to do is one form of stimulus-seeking behavior that differs from that which is generally held to be play. The problem of equating play with diverse exploration is that the central distinction between responses that *produce* stimulation (Berlyne) and responses that *seek* it (Ellis) is not made.

Hutt (in press) attempted to resolve the dilemma in terms of temporal fluctuations in arousal potential. According to this model, environmental stimulation continuously cycles from too much to too little. Preserving Berlyne's notion that too much and too little each yields aversive increases in arousal, the organism escapes one extreme only to confront another, passing briefly through moderate levels along the way. Play appears at moderate levels as either epistemic (e.g., problem solving) or ludic (e.g., symbolic play) behaviors. In this model, the concept of an "optimum" level of arousal is replaced by the concept of a "moderate" level of arousal. One consequence of the replacement is that the notion of a regulatory function of an optimum state proposed by Ellis and implied by Berlyne is abandoned. Missing is a mechanism for holding the organism at a moderate level of arousal. In the absence of such a mechanism, play is merely a transitory state, an epiphenomenal by-product of the sweep from too much to too little. Play operates neither to reduce excessive stimulation, nor to thwart the onset of boredom.

A fourth model has been suggested by Fein (1981) and Shultz (1979). In this model, play serves to modulate arousal in familiar environments when pressing biological needs and social demands are absent. Play behaviors are viewed as *response oriented* in that they provide kinesthetic, perceptual, or ideational stimulation minimally constrained or dependent on a particular stimulus array. In play, the organism produces a novel event (e.g., by acting on an object, thereby changing its location, or by eliciting a sound or creating a different visual pattern) and arousal increases. If the arousal increase is within the boundaries of the optimum range, the increase is experienced as uncertainty accompanied by a mildly negative affect, followed by uncertainty reduction and positive affect. Berlyne (1960) described a boost/jag arousal mechanism similar to the above. But the mechanism presupposes that the organism controls the boosts that provide an affective after-image experienced as pleasurable. The mechanism offers a motivational account of some of the things children do in play. For example, a toddler might be clearly apprehensive about going down a slide; and yet the apprehension seems to have pleasurable elements, and the child repeats the activity again and again. After a while, ways of going down the slide are varied, and again each variation creates some uncertainty and opportunities for a reduction in uncertainty. The point is that the slide is not a "novel" object, and the child need not go down it. The uncertainty is produced by the child and reduced by the activity. Play stops when response variations are exhausted. The boost/jag mechanism might explain why forms of play become addictive, why a child might engage in the seemingly same activity day after day for long periods of time. Or, it might explain why children create pretend games about events that have been upsetting in real life. The mechanism also suits Piaget's analysis of play as assimilation insofar as it accounts for the appeal of practice and for the eventual shift from one play activity to another.

The boost/jag mechanism is also in keeping with the notion that some forms of adult activity culturally viewed as work might share the motivational features of play (Csikszentmihalyi, 1975; Csikszentmihalyi & Bennett, 1971). The doctor and writer, intrinsically bound up in their work, might be motivated more by the opportunity for controlled arousal modulation (i.e., uncertainty production-reduction) than by external rewards.

Bateson

Bateson (1955; 1956), drawing from the disciplines of both logic and number theory, has linked the metacommunicative features of play to those aspects of communication systems that allow for abstraction. According to Bateson, ambiguity and paradox are the results of abstraction. When there is a close correspondence between signal and referent, there can be mistakes, but no paradoxes. However, when it becomes possible to comment on comments or, as Bateson (1956) wrote, to metacommunicate, the result is paradox, confusion, and freedom. Bateson used Russell and Whitehead's theory of logical types to demonstrate how confusion arises from self-referent metacommunicative statements. In their theory of number, Russell and Whitehead made the distinction between classes of things and classes of classes (Hawkins, 1964). The types of mathematical paradoxes generated when this distinction is not made is analogous to the conceptual paradoxes that can arise when a statement comments on itself. For example, the statement "I am lying" poses a logical problem because, if it is true, it is false (Schwartzman, 1978).

Freedom and power also result from metacommunicative systems. The use of numbers, for example, allows us to transcend the concrete world of things, giving us the power to make calculations and construct elaborate mathematical systems independent of the world of things. Thus, abstract representational systems that involve metacommunication provide freedom and power and also, by necessity, generate paradoxes and confusion.

So what does all of this have to do with play? Bateson was interested in examining the particular ways that ambiguity and paradox creep into communicative systems by identifying sources of metacommunication. One source that Bateson (1955; 1956) identified was play. The message, "This is play," which is communicated in an interaction, is a metacommunication. In Bateson's words, the message "This is play" states that "these actions, in which we now engage, do not denote what would be denoted by those actions which these actions denote" (Bateson, 1955, p. 41). For example, in a play fight, "the playful nip denotes the bite, but it does not denote what would be denoted by the bite" (Bateson, 1955, p. 41).

The message "This is play" is a metacommunicative statement that creates the frame or context for interpreting and negating a set of communications that serves as the text. In order to make such statements, and to play, animals must be aware that they are communicating. This ability is similar to that associated with intentionality, and it has been suggested that to trace the phylogenetic history of play is to trace the evolution of consciousness among species (Vandenberg, 1978).

Another way of examining metacommunication is to note that the relationship between communication and metacommunication is analogous to the perceptual relationship between figure (text) and ground (context). The meaning of a perceptual image does not emerge from either the figure or the ground, but from their *relationship*. Similarly, symbolic "images" emerge from the relationship of text and context, of communication and metacommunication, of sense and nonsense, of "reality" and "fantasy." Play and make-believe provide the metacommunicative ground to the figure of "reality" that produces the cultural and personal images we live by (Miller, 1974). Metacommunicative representation frees us from the grim, monotonous, two-dimensional world of necessity, creating from the contrast of text and context a three-dimensional world of possibility.[4]

[4]See T. H. White (1958) for a graphic portrait of the playless, two-dimensional world of ants, whose only contrast is "done" and "not done."

This formulation offers a fresh perspective on the psychological research that has sought to identify how fantasy and play aid cognitive development. Much of this research has focused on identifying if and how fantasy play aids in the development of specific skills and abilities related to conservation, IQ tasks, or convergent and divergent problem solving. In this view, fantasy is a means to developing other, more culturally important skills. But as Bateson and other anthropologists point out (e.g., Miller, 1974), cultural reality is composed of a set of trusted myths that is shared by the members of the culture. This implies that play and fantasy are *the* skills required to enter the imaginary world of cultural symbols. Consequently, the developmental importance of play is not to be found in the skills that are indirectly and inadvertently elaborated on by it, but in the play itself.

Bateson (1956) emphasizes that the contribution of play to development is not to be found in the content of children's play. Children do not so much learn about the roles they are playing as they learn about the process of framing and reframing roles; they are not learning about a particular role, but about the concept of roles. Thus, play contributes to learning about learning or to "deutero-learning," as Bateson (1942) labeled it.

Bateson's analysis of play was only one component of his theoretical work, and his fertile ideas have spawned research on a wide variety of topics, ranging from cybernetics to schizophrenia. The research on play that has resulted from Bateson's work includes research on the ways in which nonhuman animals communicate "This is play," as in the "play face" made by chimpanzees (van Hooff, 1972). Anthropologists have examined the communicative aspects of play in several cultures (Geertz, 1972) and have elaborated Bateson's notions of text and contexts of play (Schwartzman, 1976a,b; 1978). Although Bateson's impact on psychologists has not been as extensive, threads of his ideas can be found in the work of Sutton-Smith (1976) and in the research of Garvey (Garvey, 1974; Garvey & Berndt, 1977), concerning the ways human children communicate "This is play."

Other Current Theorists

Sutton-Smith (1966; 1967; 1976) and Bruner (1972) have emphasized the importance of play for the generation of novelty and flexibility, which contributes to the adaptive plasticity of the organism. According to this view, play allows the individual to explore new combinations of behaviors and ideas within the safe confines of play. In so doing, the individual develops an array of new strategies, associations, and behavioral prototypes that subsequently may be used in more "serious" contexts.

Sutton-Smith (1966; 1967) has emphasized the importance of the "as if" nature of children's symbolic play, where children treat objects and people "as if" they were something else. A stick is played with "as if" it were a gun, or playmates are treated "as if" they are parents. Both the process of engaging in the "as if" posture and the products of "as if" thinking are important in development. The "as if" process helps the child learn how to break free from established meaning sets, or associations, and contributes to the development of divergent thinking abilities (Sutton-Smith, 1966; 1967). The "as if" process of play gives the individual the freedom to reframe, to do and undo, and to engage in role reversals (Sutton-Smith, 1976; 1978). These views are akin to those of Bateson. Sutton-Smith further suggests that play provides the opportunity to develop role flexibility as well as a sense of autonomy (Sutton-Smith, 1976).

In addition, Sutton-Smith (1976) has noted that play provides adaptive potentiation. According to this formulation, the innovative products of play create a storehouse of prototypes and associations that can be drawn on in time of adaptive need. So the novelty produced in play as well as the process of generating novelty contribute to development.

While Sutton-Smith has emphasized the importance of play for developing alternative symbolic constructions, Bruner (1972) has focused on play's contribution to the development of behavioral flexibility of motor skills. Bruner suggests that the safety of the play environment allows the organism to dispense with a concern over the consequences of behaviors, giving it opportunity to focus on the behaviors themselves; to attend to the means, and not to the ends of behavior. The organism plays with its own behaviors, creating novel combinations by splicing together behavioral subroutines that have functional utility in other contexts. In play, the organism is able to discover and practice new behavioral strategies with impunity. Bruner hypothesizes that the flexibility afforded by play makes possible the development of tool-using strategies.

The perspectives of Sutton-Smith and Bruner have been supplemented by other recent theorists. Vandenberg (1978) has discussed the attentional characteristics of play that aid in the development of tool-using strategies and has suggested that play is an aspect of a broader developmental rhythm including exploration and "application." Singer (1973; J. L. Singer & D. G. Singer, 1976) has proposed that fantasy play may serve to develop the capacity for using imagery, which is necessary for adaptive

thinking about the past (memory) and the future (imagination). Reynolds (1972) has suggested that play be considered as a simulative mode of experience, where new behavioral prototypes are generated and tested. Fagen (1976) has extended this idea by drawing an elaborate parallel between prototype simulation in aerospace engineering and the testing of behavioral prototypes in the safe confines of play. Fagen (1974; 1976) has indicated further that novel behaviors generated in play could be treated as the behavioral equivalent of genetic mutations in biological evolution. Vandenberg (1981c) has also used this analogy. He suggests that play, providing the behavioral diversity, and imitation, providing continuity, are crucial for the long-term survival of the human species, in a similar manner that genetic mutation and DNA provide biological diversity and continuity, respectively.

The psychological research that addresses if and how play develops novelty and flexibility has not been extensive and has generally stayed close to either Sutton-Smith's or Bruner's formulations. Dansky and Silverman (1973; 1975) and Dansky (1980a), drawing on Sutton-Smith (1968), have examined the importance of play for the development of associative fluency on tasks that tap divergent thinking. Bruner's work has spawned research that has examined the ways that play contributes to the development of novel tool-using abilities (Cheyne & Rubin, in press; Smith & Dutton, 1979; Sylva, Bruner, & Genova, 1976; Vandenberg, 1981b). This research offers some support that play contributes to the development of new, adaptive strategies.

The Future

Theories of play and, for that matter, most psychological theories generally have drawn from prevailing theories in biology. Spencer's surplus energy theory, Hall's recapitulation perspective, Freud's energy-instinct model, Piaget's assimilation-accommodation metaphor, Berlyne's neurological constructs, and the recent hypothesis of behavioral diversity as paralleling genetic mutations, all trace their roots to biology. It appears probable that future developments in theory and research on play will be influenced by the theoretical developments in biology.

Since Freud, there has been an increasing "cognification" of play by both psychoanalytic theorists, who have stressed the ego functions of play, and by others, who have focused on the rational, conceptual, symbolic, or adaptive benefits of play. This may be, in part, a reaction to Freud. Although these more rationalistic theories are useful and pleasing, Sutton-Smith (1977) points out that they overlook the passionate, the irrational, and the "bloody-mindedness" that are important aspects of play. Sutton-Smith (1978) and Schwartzman (1978) have recognized some of these aspects of play. We hope future conceptualizations will further explore the irrational aspects of play that have been neglected over the years.

THE CHANGING STRUCTURES OF PLAY

A number of theorists have suggested that the structural properties of play change with and reflect development (Peller, 1952; Piaget, 1962; Vygotsky, 1967). With this view in mind, we describe such changes as they occur within the periods of infancy and early and middle childhood. We also explore those features of the social and nonsocial environment that may affect structural growth in the play domain.

Infant Play

Descriptive Studies of Object Play

Whether the concept of play will contribute to an understanding of behavioral processes in infancy is an unresolved question. Much of the extant research has been descriptive and, as such, has yielded provocative information about the changing pattern of behaviors that infants produce in "free-play" settings.

In the typical study, infants are presented with a set of attractive toys and are invited to play. In some studies, children are observed in their own homes (e.g., Fein & Apfel, 1979a; Rosenblatt, 1977), and in others they are observed in a special playroom (e.g., Fein & Apfel, 1979b; Fenson, Kagan, Kearsley, & Zelazo, 1976; Inhelder, Lezine, Sinclair, & Stambak, 1972; Kagan, Kearsley, & Zelazo, 1978; McCall, 1974; Sinclair, 1970; Zelazo & Kearsley, 1980). The purpose of these studies has been to record the way children respond to these objects during the first and second years of life. Implicit in most studies, and explicit in some, is the notion that play with objects will reflect cognitive development during infancy.

Although investigators differ concerning their particular observational coding schemes, a number of common features have emerged. Most investigators, for example, distinguish between activities involving one object and those that involve two objects (Fein & Apfel, 1979b; Fenson et al., 1976; Inhelder et al., 1972; McCall, 1974; Rosenblatt, 1977). In most studies, object play is categorized as involving either (1) "appropriate" actions in keeping with the

specific functions and social usages for the object (e.g., "functional" or "symbolic" play drinking from an empty cup; putting a cup on a saucer) or (2) stereotyped or indiscriminate usages (e.g., banging a cup against a pail). The label "indiscriminate" has implied that a given sensorimotor action (e.g., banging) might be applied to a variety of objects regardless of their particular features (e.g., texture, shape) or that a variety of such actions (e.g., banging, waving, mouthing) might be applied to a given object seemingly without adjustments to the object's particular characteristics (Rosenblatt, 1977; Zelazo & Kearsley, 1980).

Differences in coding schemes lie largely with the inclusiveness of the behavioral categories. For example, with regard to two object actions, some investigators distinguish between appropriate combinations consisting of simple placements from those that represent social functions (e.g., Fein & Apfel, 1979a; Fenson et al., 1976; Rosenblatt, 1977). Others further impose a special category for symbolic or representational acts, distinguishing between those involving one or two objects (Belsky & Most, 1981; Fein, 1979b; Rosenblatt, 1977) or, in addition, between different levels or forms of symbolic activity (e.g., Belsky & Most, 1981; Fein & Apfel, 1979b; Fenson & Ramsay, 1980; Inhelder et al., 1972; Lowe, 1975). The categories used tend to reflect the age range of the infants participating in the study. For example, symbolic acts are likely to be included in studies of play during the second year of life. Developmental changes in aspects of symbolic play will be described in a later section. Of interest here are changes in less mature forms of play behavior, especially shifts in the patterns of play between 6 and 18 months of age.

First, there is considerable agreement that behaviors involving a single object decrease strikingly between 7 and 18 months of age, from about 90% in the observational period at 7 and 9 months to less than 20% by about 18 months (e.g., Fein & Apfel, 1979a; Fenson et al., 1976; Inhelder et al., 1972; Kagan et al., 1978; McCall, 1974; Rosenblatt, 1977; Zelazo & Kearsley, 1980). The downward trend, as well as the percentage of these behaviors produced at a given age level, is strikingly consistent across studies in which different toys and slightly different response definitions are used, and in which children from different cultural backgrounds are observed.

Moreover, this consistency holds even when investigators stress different conceptual views of play. Rosenblatt (1977), for example, stressed both a distinction between single versus multiple object play as well as a distinction among investigative, indiscriminate, and appropriate object usage. Investigative behaviors consisted of an exploration of specific object characteristics. Indiscriminate behaviors involved similar responses to objects differing in their characteristics. Appropriate behaviors were those during which the object was used according to its specific function. Rosenblatt not only found a general decrease in single object use from 9 to 24 months, but investigative and indiscriminate behaviors likewise decreased while appropriate actions increased over this age range. Since the younger infants were more likely to act on objects with little regard for their specific physical features, these sensorimotor behaviors may be viewed as oriented toward assimilation, or as organism rather than stimulus dominated.

Another consistent finding is that simple two-object combinations occur infrequently at any age, but that representational or symbolic acts show a striking increase between 15 and 18 months (e.g., Fein & Apfel, 1979a; Fenson et al., 1976; Inhelder et al., 1972; Kagan et al., 1978; Lowe, 1975; Rosenblatt, 1977). Those studies that use the term "appropriate" or "functional" for behaviors such as talking on a telephone or drinking from a cup similarly find a precipitous increase between 11 and 18 months (e.g., Rosenblatt, 1977; Zelazo & Kearsley, 1980). Again, the appearance and timing of these behaviors seems little affected by situational or cultural variations. These patterns have been observed in French children reared in a crèche (Inhelder et al., 1972), in Guatemalan children reared in an impoverished village (Kagan et al., 1978), and in American and English children from a variety of social class groups (e.g., Fein & Apfel, 1979b; Fenson et al., 1976; Rosenblatt, 1977).

In summary, infants' behaviors in relatively unstructured "free-play" situations seem to demonstrate systematic changes during the first two years of life. Moreover, the quality of the behavior seems in keeping with the notion that these behaviors initially are not dominated by the specific physical features of objects and, during the second year of life, show an abrupt shift toward behaviors that reflect the way objects are used in daily life, with concurrent elaborations in the pretend use of objects.

Adult-Infant Play

Recently, considerable attention has been paid to the games parents play with babies. These games have been defined as focused interactions, occurring within a bounded period of time, and characterized by temporal regularities, repetition, and the mutual interest of parent and child (Stern, 1974; 1977). However, although mothers tend to maintain a regular tempo and repeat vocal or gestural behaviors, there is variation within these aspects as well as variation in the stress, amplitude, and vigor of the mothers' behaviors (Stern, 1977). Turn-taking was viewed initially as a salient feature of such games, but recent evidence indicates considerable overlap and synchrony in these interactions (Stern, 1974; 1977). Infants' contributions to the play take the form of interactions, cooing, smiling, and laughter (Sroufe & Wunsche, 1972; Stern, 1977). But these games typically are initiated and organized by adults; as such, they differ in focus from the play described earlier in this section.

Several different game taxonomies have been suggested. Investigators may classify games according to whether they involve tactile or visual stimulation (Crawley, Rogers, Friedman, Iacobbo, Criticos, Richardson & Thompson, 1978; Power & Parke, 1980; Sroufe & Wunsche, 1972), limb or gross body movements (Crawley et al., 1978; Power & Parke, 1980), auditory stimulation (Sroufe & Wunsche, 1972), or toys (Power & Parke, 1980). The games adults play with infants are less likely to involve toys during the first few months of life than they are later (Stern, 1977). However, when responsive, inanimate objects are provided (even without an adult), infants as young as 2 months show positive affect and behave to maintain the stimulation (Watson & Ramey, 1972).

Investigators have suggested several ways in which these games might influence development. Some may facilitate the infant's ongoing activity through arousal or attention regulation, others might facilitate exploratory behavior, and still others seem to serve social-affective functions (Power & Parke, 1980). A popular view is that the game structure with its variable stimulation serves to keep infants in an optimal state of arousal that enhances the infants' exposure to social information, thereby facilitating bonding (Stern, 1977). Another position stresses the importance of the infant's control over stimulation provided by the contingencies of the social game situation and its implications for intellectual as well as social development (Watson & Ramey, 1972). We might add that the social-affective aspects of this play might be as important to the playing adult as they are to the playing child.

According to some investigators, adult-infant games during the first year of life contain structural elements of language and provide a context for language learning (Ratner & Bruner, 1978; Sachs, 1980; Snow, 1977). For example, play introduces the turn-taking rules of social conversation. Some games have a reciprocal role structure (e.g., peek-a-boo), others permit variations in the ordering of play elements (e.g., tickling games), and others provide a means by which a variety of behavioral or object elements can be used (e.g., playing peek-a-boo by covering eyes, using a screen, or hiding behind the baby). But the conversational turn-taking aspect of these playful encounters may have been exaggerated in early reports (Stern, 1977) and the level at which infants process game patterns has not been determined. Moreover, these games are not played by parents in all cultures, and there is considerable individual variability in cultures where they are played (Sachs, 1980; Stern, 1977). Thus, game playing may enhance the infant's attention to the social rather than the structural features of language.

Other investigators have noted that the study of adult-infant play might contribute to our understanding of the infant's capacity for processing information. Interestingly, adults seem to take the infant's capacity into account when playing (Crawley et al., 1978; Stern, 1974, 1977). To extend Piaget's notion of play as assimilation, the function of such games might be to facilitate the infant's consolidation of acquired interactive capacities rather than to promote the acquisition of new capacities.

Pretense Play in Infancy and Childhood

The Hypothesized Functions of Pretense Play

Having reviewed the literature concerning infant manipulative play and parent-infant games, we now turn to an area of study that has dominated the play literature during the past two decades—that is, pretense or nonliteral activities in infancy and early childhood.

A large number of psychologists and educators have proposed that the growing amount of time that pretense activities occupy, from the toddler to the early elementary school years, plays a significant role in children's lives. Thus, pretense has been viewed as partially responsible for the development of a plethora of skills.

As previously mentioned, Piaget (1962) suggested a consolidative role for pretend play. Vygotsky (1967) postulated that pretense served to separate meanings from objects and actions, thereby aiding in the development of symbolic representation. Freud (1959), of course, viewed pretense as a mechanism for alleviating anxieties and fears. Another early theorist, George Herbert Mead (1934), proposed that pretense was fundamental to the de-velopment of the self-concept. To establish a separate self-identity, Mead believed that the child must figuratively get "outside" the self and view the self from some other perspective. Fantasy activities allowed the child to take the role of others in play, thereby gaining a reflection of the self as different from, and yet related to, others.

More recently, pretense play has been hypothesized to foster the development of self-confidence and self-regulation (Singer, 1973), to alleviate boredom (Ellis, 1973), and to maintain an internally controlled optimal level of arousal (Fein, 1979a; 1981). Given that pretense is optimally arousing, it follows that children feel comfortable, relaxed, and secure during play (Bruner, 1972). This playful environment is felt to promote diversive exploration or the exploration of multiple object uses (Hutt, 1979). As such, another by-product of pretense is the development of creative and flexible thinking (J. N. Lieberman, 1977; Singer, 1973; Smilansky, 1968).

Singer also has suggested that make-believe activity is tightly linked to symbolic representation. Thus, other proposed outcomes of fantasy play include the development of (1) abstract thinking and "as if" metaphoric possibilities; (2) imagery; and (3) the learning of new words and phrases that emanate from the practice of imaginary roles in novel, interpersonal situations. In addition, Singer (1973) notes that young children can spend enormous amounts of time engaging in pretense activities. An obvious outcome of positively rewarding and lengthy bouts of play is the development of concentration, attention span, and a reflective mode of thought.

Another recent concern is the proposed benefit of *social* pretense. Garvey (1977a) has postulated that social pretense allows the practice and refinement of interactive "rules." Smilansky (1968), Saltz (1978; Saltz & Brodie, 1982; Saltz & Johnson, 1974), and Burns and Brainerd (1979), among others, have speculated that pretense activities in the company of peers allows the role-playing and role-taking experiences thought necessary to lessen the egocentric nature of preschool thought and to provide opportunities for the development of empathy and cooperation.

Taken together, many contemporary play theorists suggest that a number of developmental accomplishments are a direct result of pretense activity. Since many of these propositions have resulted in empirical research, it follows that one need only turn to the data to examine the proposed positive benefits of play. Such an examination will follow in a later section. At this time we will describe pretense play during the infancy, preschool, and kindergarten years to allow the reader to gain a better "feel" for those activities thought by many to be so important for growth and development.

The Beginnings of Pretend Play

The quality of children's play changes dramatically during the second year of life. From behavior dominated by sensorimotor schemes such as banging, mouthing, and waving, play shifts to behavior that seems to mimic real-life activities. Objects are used according to their social purposes (even though these purposes are not fulfilled), and behaviors associated with biological or social requirements are produced when these requirements are not present.

Researchers using strikingly different procedures and observing children from different cultures in various social circumstances seem to agree that pretend gestures first appear at about 12 or 13 months of age (Fein & Apfel, 1979a; Fenson et al., 1976; Inhelder et al., 1972; Jacobson, 1977; Kessen & Fein, 1975; Rosenblatt, 1977). Moreover, the appearance is quite abrupt. In a study of Guatemalan babies from impoverished villages, only 8% produced one or more pretend acts between 11 and 13 months, whereas 64% did so between 13 and 15 months. These findings are similar to those reported for middle-class American children by the same investigators (Fenson et al., 1976; Fenson & Ramsay, 1980; Kagan et al., 1978). In a longitudinal study of 25 advantaged American and Italian children, information from mothers' reports indicated a slightly earlier onset: 8% of the children produced at least one pretend gesture at 9½ months, 44% did so at 10½ months, 72% at 11½ months, and 96% at 12½ months (Bates, Benigni, Bretherton, Camaioni, & Volterra, 1977). Since pretend behaviors at these ages tend to be ephemeral, maternal reports may provide a better estimate of onset than brief, though systematic, observation. But it is difficult to establish the reliability of maternal reports, especially when the behavior is a topic of intensive probing in maternal interviews (Bates et al., 1977).

Developmental changes in the form of early pretend behaviors have been investigated in several studies. Since Piaget's (1962) work provided the impetus for these studies, play components that he identified provide a convenient framework for organizing research in this area (see Fein, 1978; 1979a; 1979b; 1981 for additional discussion of Piaget's contribution).

In Piaget's scheme, solitary pretense exhibits several levels reflecting increasing cognitive maturity. It is necessary to note that Piaget uses the term "stages" when discussing changes over wide developmental sweeps, and the term "levels" when describing changes within stages. Recently, researchers have confirmed Piaget's observation that these levels appear sequentially during the second and third years of life. However, individual children differ with respect to the age at which a particular level appears (Nicolich, 1977). The components of play embedded in Piaget's model have received explicit attention by investigators who have sought to provide a more detailed description of changes in solitary pretense during the early years. In the following discussion, these components are referred to as (1) decontextualized behavior, (2) self-other relationships, (3) object substitutions, and (4) sequential combinations.

Decontextualized Behavior

The earliest form of pretend behavior appears when the child produces a familiar behavior such as sleeping, drinking, or eating "in the void." The behavior is striking because the infant does not merely touch its head to a pillow, or its lips to a spoon or a cup. Instead, the behavior seems to replicate gesturally the details of such behavior in real life (e.g., eyes closed, stillness, curled position *as if* sleeping; or head tilted, cup tipped, synchronized in timing *as if* liquid was diminishing in volume). And yet the behavior is detached from the situational context in which it ordinarily occurs (e.g., bedtime, mealtime), from the outcome with which it is ordinarily associated (e.g., sleep, food consumption), and from the behavioral signs that ordinarily accompany a real need (e.g., crankiness for sleep, finger sucking for nourishment). In 12-month-olds, this behavior occurs with miniature replica objects (toy cups and spoons) as well as with adult-size objects (Fein & Apfel, 1979b; Fenson et al., 1976; Kagan et al., 1978; Lowe, 1975), provided that the objects resemble their real counterparts.

The possibility that this behavior reflects the infant's confusion or overgeneralization (Stern, 1924) is weakened by recent evidence that the behavior is selective, in keeping with social practices, and independent of appetitive needs (Fein & Apfel, 1979b; Fein & Moorin, in press). At 18 months, the child feeds a doll with empty bottles, and self-feeds with empty cups. At this age, the child's choices seem in keeping with social practices in which bottles are used with babies and cups are used with children. In addition, pretend feeding seems unrelated to a need or wish for food or drink. When the child is given a choice between a full bottle and an empty one, the full one is preferred; but when the choice is between a full cup and an empty one, the empty cup is preferred (Fein & Moorin, in press).

A key characteristic of pretense is that it is simulative or nonliteral behavior, which becomes especially interesting when viewed from the notion that social situations are cognitively organized or "framed" (Bateson, 1956; Garvey, 1974; Goffman, 1974). A similar idea is captured in recent conceptualizations of "scripts" as cognitive structures consisting of a set of rules (or roles) that govern an actor's relationship to objects and persons in a particular context (Schank & Abelson, 1977). Early pretense, in which action sequences are detached from immediate stimulation, might thereby reflect the beginning formation of such structures. For example, one script governing early pretense may pertain to events associated with "eating" and may contain slots for persons and eating utensils, which are elaborated on by rules identifying who gets fed with what.

Self-Other Relationships

A second component of early pretense involves the relationship between self and others. When pretense appears at about 12 months, it is self-referenced (e.g., the child feeds itself). In what appears to be a systematic developmental sequence, this behavior soon becomes other-referenced (Fein & Apfel, 1979b; Fenson & Ramsay, 1980; Inhelder et al., 1972; Lowe, 1975; Watson & Fischer, 1977). Researchers using widely different procedures suggest that the shift occurs roughly between 15 and 21 months of age. In the Fein and Apfel (1979b) study, 81% of the children who pretended at 12 months displayed self-referenced behavior, 31% displayed other-referenced behavior toward their mothers, and 19% displayed this behavior toward a doll. Generally, self-referenced pretend behavior declines between 12 and 30 months, whereas doll-referenced behavior increases (Belsky & Most, 1981; Fein & Apfel, 1979b; Inhelder et al., 1972; Lowe, 1975; Watson & Fischer, 1977). Other-referenced behavior toward a real person is fleeting and during the second year of life does not become an integral part of pretend activities (Fein & Apfel, 1979b; Lowe, 1975).

In the behavior discussed above, the child is the active agent and the "other" (e.g., the doll) is a passive recipient or object of the child's action. At a more advanced level, the child seems to step out of the situation and manipulate the "other" as if it were an active agent (Fenson & Ramsay, 1980; Heinicke, 1956; Inhelder et al., 1972; Lowe, 1975; Watson &

Fischer, 1977). The tendency to treat the "other" (e.g., a doll) as if it were acting on its own behalf increases dramatically from 12 to 30 months of age (Fenson & Ramsay, 1980; Lowe, 1975; Watson & Fischer, 1977). Watson and Fischer (1977), for example, demonstrated that the progression of self-referenced, other-referenced, and active other behavior appears in a predicted developmental sequence. Moreover, as new forms appear, less mature forms (i.e., self-referenced behavior) drop out of the child's repertoire.

At a descriptive level, these behaviors have been carefully studied, but their theoretical implications are unclear. At times, Piaget used the term "imitative" when describing such behavior (although a model is not immediately present) and, at other times, referred to the child's "identification" of his or her own body with that of another. Fenson and Ramsay (1980) discuss this shift in terms of the Piagetian concept of decentration.

According to Mead (1934), the child figuratively gets "outside" the self when acting *as if* she or he is another person. Certainly there is ample documentation that the development of pretense is characterized by a shift from self-referencing to other-referencing and, finally, to a type of role enactment in which the child retains a stable self-identity while performing other roles (Rubin & Pepler, 1980). Although these acts are initially single, isolated events, they soon become coordinated into sequences of behavior that increasingly resemble those of adults involved in activities such as caregiving, cooking, telephoning, or those actions associated with familial and occupational roles. As Sarbin and Allen (1969) note, the problem is to develop criteria for determining the relative appropriateness, propriety, and convincingness of these role enactments. Whether changes in these characteristics reflect changes in children's perceptions of themselves and others remains to be determined.

Substitute Objects

Piaget (1962) claimed that the child's ability to identify one object with another (a shell with a cup, hat, or boat) marked the transition to *Level 2* pretense. Interest in substitute objects comes from several sources. According to psychoanalytic theory, the substitute object has emotional meaning (Winnicott, 1971). In Piagetian theory, substitutional behavior reflects the development of representational thought; however, in and of itself, substitution serves no special role in the acquisition of operational processes (cf. Piaget, 1966; Piaget & Inhelder, 1971). By contrast, this behavior assumes a central importance in the formulations of Vygotsky (1967, 1978; Fein, 1979b) who viewed the development of substitution behavior as a factor in the development of language. Vygotsky suggested that, although the substitute object must resemble the real object initially, the requirement of resemblance is reduced as "meaning" becomes detached from immediate, external stimulation. The substitute object serves as a "pivot" object, precipitating the shift from "things as objects of action," to "things as objects of thought."

Several studies indicate that infants' use of realistic objects in pretense (e.g., a baby doll) increases between 14 and 19 months (Fein & Apfel, 1979b; Inhelder et al., 1972; Jackowitz & Watson, 1980; Lowe, 1975; Watson & Fischer, 1977). In contrast, the use of a substitute object (block for doll) is fleeting at 14 and 19 months, and increases between 19 and 24 months (Fein, 1975; Jackowitz & Watson, 1980; Ungerer, Zelazo, Kearsley, & O'Leary, 1981; Watson & Fischer, 1977). At 24 months, 75% of the children in the Watson and Fischer study demonstrated substitution behavior. These investigators employed only single substitutions (e.g., a cup used in "feeding" was always realistic when a block was substituted for the recipient of nourishment, a doll). In a study of substitution behavior at 24 months, Fein (1975) compared single and double substitutions (neither the cup nor the doll are realistic). When there was no substitution, 94% of the children pretended to feed a realistic toy horse. Under single substitution conditions, 70% of the children performed appropriately, a finding strikingly in line with Watson and Fischer. However, only 33% of the children were able to manage a double substitution. Subsequent research has clarified specific features of children's abilities to transform a present object into one that need not be present. Consider, for example, objects that the child acts on directly (e.g., a cup used in self-feeding). These objects can be dissimilar in form but similar in function (a canteen), they can be dissimilar in function but similar in form (a shell), or they can be dissimilar in both form and function (a car). When the sequence in which children acquire these transformational skills is examined, the results indicate that neither form nor function is especially important in facilitating transformational behavior. An object with an ambiguous function (a block) is easier to substitute than one with a clearly conflicting function (a car). The latter type of object is easier, in turn, to substitute than a condition in which no object is present (Jackowitz & Watson, 1980).

Experimental and observational studies of children in free-play settings confirm these age trends in the use of substitute objects. Between the ages of 18 and 26 months, children show higher levels of pretense with highly prototypical objects than with less prototypical objects (Fein & Robertson, 1975; Jeffree & McConkey, 1976). In older children, however, toy realism no longer is related to the frequency of pretense but is related to its diversity. Themes are more diverse when the materials are less realistic (Phillips, 1945; Pulaski, 1973).

Sequential Combinations

According to Piaget (1962) and Nicolich (1977), pretend acts become increasingly coordinated into sequences during the second and third years. At first, the child produces a single pretend gesture (drinking from a cup); later behavioral combinations appear. In a single-scheme combination, the child relates, in succession, the same act to itself and then to others (drinks from bottle, feeds doll from bottle). In a multischeme combination, the child coordinates different successive acts (pours food, feeds doll, puts it to bed). Finally, the child indicates that pretend sequences are planned before being executed. Evidence from a longitudinal study of children between the ages of 14 and 27 months indicates that these levels demonstrate the properties of an invariant sequence (Nicolich, 1977). Longitudinal and cross-sectional evidence of systematic changes with age have also been provided by Fenson and Ramsay (1980). Interestingly, most of the early multischeme combinations preserve the social logic of the situation (combing the mother's hair, then holding a mirror for her to look in). In the Fenson and Ramsay (1980) study, over 70% of the children produced ordered combinations by 20 months of age, whereas only 23% produced unordered combinations. This finding is in keeping with the notion that pretense, for all its flexibility, is a rule-governed behavior.

The Preschool and Kindergarten Years

From Solitary to Social Pretense

It has been suggested that the pretense play of children becomes more and more social with age, at least up to the early elementary school years. Piaget (1962), for example, viewed symbolic play as being exclusively solitary (Stage I) during the first two years of life. Social or interactive pretense (Stage II) was viewed as originating in the latter part of the third year. Piaget also suggested that by the concrete operational period (at around 7 years) pretense play declined only to be replaced by games-with-rules. In this section we review those studies in which researchers have explored the notion that (1) the play of children becomes increasingly dramatic at least until the early elementary school years; (2) that pretense play becomes increasingly social with age; and (3) that pretense play gradually declines.

The one common element among all of the studies reviewed here is that the methodological strategy involved observations of children during free play in naturalistic, familiar settings. Studies in which the researcher manipulated the environment or brought selected groups of acquainted or unacquainted children into small playrooms (e.g., Griffing, 1980; Matthews, 1977a, 1977b) have been excluded.

A typical observational procedure used by students of pretense play emanates from Rubin's (1977a; 1982b) nesting of the cognitive play categories of Smilansky (1968) within the social participation categories of Parten (1932). In most of the studies described here, it was first noted whether the activity observed was playful (thus, the observations included such categories of nonplay as onlooker, unoccupied, transitional, and reading behaviors). If the behavior was playful it was coded as (1) *functional or sensorimotor play*, which includes simple, repetitive muscular activities with or without objects (the term *functional* play must be distinguished from the use of the same term by Zelazo and Kearsley, 1977; 1980; these writers defined the category as functionally appropriate, object-specific play, for example, stirring a spoon in a tea cup, babbling into a toy telephone), (2) *constructive* play, (3) *dramatic* or *pretense* play and, finally, (4) *games-with-rules* in which the child accepts prearranged rules and adjusts his or her behaviors to them.

Once these four cognitive play categories were recorded, each was further subcategorized according to its social context. Did the play occur when the child was alone (*solitary*—functional play), when the child was in close proximity but not interacting with others (*parallel*—dramatic play), or when playing with others in joint activities (*group*—games-with-rules)? Typically, percentages of the total observations in which children engaged in any of the play or nonplay categories were computed by the researchers.

In general, the research on *middle-class* children from *intact* families supports the notion that the proportion of pretense to all play forms increases with age, from 3 years until approximately 6 or 7 years (Emmerich, 1977; Hetherington, Cox, & Cox, 1979; Johnson & Ershler, 1981; Rubin et al., 1976; Rubin, Watson, & Jambor, 1978; Sanders & Harper, 1976; Sponseller & Jaworski, 1979).

Few investigators have examined the hypothesis that the incidence of pretend play eventually declines in childhood. Eifermann (1971) indicated that the fantasy play of *disadvantaged* Israeli children reached a high point in the first and second grades and thereafter declined. For more affluent Israeli early elementary schoolers, pretend play occurred infrequently, presumably because the high point had been reached at an earlier age (Smilansky, 1968). Thus, it may be concluded tentatively that support exists for the inverted U-shape function proposed initially by Piaget (1962). Pretense rarely occurs before 1 year of age. However, between 1 and 5 or 6 years, the proportion of pretense to all other forms of play rises steadily, decreasing thereafter.

The above data, however, do not address the issue of whether play becomes increasingly *sociodramatic* with age. Nor do they address the question of the frequency of *sociodramatic* play relative to other (solitary, parallel) pretense activities. First, concerning sociodramatic play per se, it has been reported that interactive pretense does, indeed, increase with age from 3 to 6 years (Connolly, 1980; Hetherington et al., 1979; Iwanaga, 1973; Johnson & Ershler, 1981; Manwell & Mengert, 1934; Rubin & Krasnor, 1980; Rubin et al., 1978; Smilansky, 1968).

Solitary pretense shows little change during the preschool years. From 3 to 6 years, solitary pretense play hovers at about 1 to 5% of *all free play* (Hetherington et al., 1979; Johnson & Ershler, 1981; Rubin & Krasnor, 1980; Rubin et al., 1978). These data suggest that (1) solitary pretense does not occur often in classroom settings and (2) that such activity does not appear to reflect any strong developmental trends.

Although a reported increase does occur for social pretense activities, and although increases appear in the proportion of parallel dramatic play to all play from 3 to 5 years (Hetherington et al., 1979; Rubin et al., 1978), the quantitative relationships among these forms of activity remain unexplored. However, from a re-examination of those studies cited above, evidence concerning the proposed Piagetian shift from pretend play in Stage I (solitary) to pretend play in Stage II (social) can be assessed.

It would appear as if the proportion of group pretense play to *all pretense play* does, to some small degree, follow an inverted U developmental progression. Thus, it has been reported that group pretense constitutes 70% of all dramatic endeavors by 3-year-olds (Johnson & Ershler, 1981); between 74% and 80% of 4-year-old dramatic play (Hetherington et al., 1979; Johnson & Ershler, 1981; Rubin et al., 1976; Rubin et al., 1978); between 68% and 71% of 5-year-old dramatic play (Hetherington et al., 1979; Rubin et al., 1978); and 65% of 6-year-old dramatic play (Hetherington et al., 1979).

At 3 years, approximately 17% of *all pretense play* occurs when children are in close proximity to, but are not interacting in accord with, others (Johnson & Ershler, 1981). At 4 years, between 8% and 14% of pretense play is of a parallel fashion (Hetherington et al., 1979; Johnson & Ershler, 1981; Rubin et al., 1976; Rubin et al., 1978). By 5 years, the proportion of parallel dramatic play to *all dramatic play* appears to reach a high point, ranging between 21% (Hetherington et al., 1979) and 23% (Rubin et al., 1978). At 6 years, parallel dramatic play drops to 16% of *all pretense* play (Hetherington et al., 1979).

Perhaps most surprising is the finding that solitary play follows an upright U-shaped, developmental function. It has been observed that the proportion of solitary to all pretense play forms decreases steadily from a high of 13% at 3 years to a low of between 6% and 11% at 5 years (Hetherington et al., 1979; Johnson & Ershler, 1981; Rubin et al., 1976; Rubin et al., 1978; Rubin & Krasnor, 1980; Sanders & Harper, 1976). However, in the one study of 6-year-olds (Hetherington et al., 1979), solitary dramatic play consisted of 19% of all pretense activities.

In summary, researchers are now beginning to concern themselves with relative distributions of pretense play forms that differ with regard to the social context of the activity. The data offered above stem not only from cross-sectional (e.g., Rubin et al., 1978) but also from longitudinal (Hetherington et al., 1979; Rubin & Krasnor, 1980) sources. The data appear to suggest that interactive pretense play increases with age, dropping off during the late kindergarten and early elementary school years. It is important to note, however, that the magnitude of the decline is not very great and that there are, at present, no data to suggest that the incidence of social pretense decreases significantly from the early to middle childhood years. On the other hand, the frequency of solitary pretense decreases with age during the preschool years and appears to increase during the late kindergarten and early first grade years. Perhaps, the increase of solitary pretense activities in 6-year-olds is the result of the practice of social games-with-rules, which appear to emerge at this time. Thus, when away from the group, the child might practice and consolidate those skills necessary to participate effectively in group game situations (e.g., playing baseball, inning by inning, with the self as pitcher, batter, and all members of both teams). Such pretend "gaming" may explain the increase of solitary dramatic play following the preschool years. Of course, this explanation is merely speculative and necessitates an examination of the qualitative properties of pretense at different periods of childhood.

Structural Properties of Solitary Pretense Play

In the previous section we examined the social contexts within which pretense play occurs during the preschool and early elementary school years. There are, however, contextual, structural properties other than the degree of social participation that evince developmental change in pretense activities. In this section we review the structural properties of *solitary* pretense activities found in children ranging from 3 to approximately 6 years of age. From the outset, it should be noted that in most of the studies reviewed here the child played on his or her own, but in the company of an observant adult.

Much of the experimental research on pretense involves situations in which children are allowed to play with given materials on their own. The early work in this vein was heavily psychoanalytic in origin (cf. Fein, in press-a). Thus, solitary pretense was viewed as a means to assess information concerning the child's "inner person" (Sears, 1947), his or her anxieties and personal conflicts, and those experiences that produced them (Levin & Wardwell, 1962). For example, aggression during doll play supposedly allowed the researcher to infer that frustration and punishment are salient features of the home environment. However, as Fein and Apfel (1979b) have noted, clinical diagnoses based on solitary pretense activities were complicated by, among other factors, the transformations of the literal to the nonliteral during play. Thus, during pretense activities reality becomes distorted such that the actual occurrences in the home may be different and even opposite to those play activities that purportedly represent those occurrences. As such, direct links between home experiences and pretense activities become cloudy at best. Clinical psychologists may be better served by strengthening their data bases with other sources of information designed to allow inferences concerning how the child is feeling, what the child is thinking, and what it is that contributed to the child's mental status.

More recently, observations of pretend play in solitary, experimentally manipulated settings have been used to assess the symbolic maturity of children in the infant, toddler, and preschool years (e.g., Fein, 1975; Fein & Apfel, 1979b; Inhelder et al.,

1972; Lowe, 1975; Nicolich, 1977; Sinclair, 1970; Watson & Fischer, 1977). Much of this work is carried out within a Piagetian framework. As noted in the discussion of infant and toddler pretense play, Piaget (1962) believed that such activities are reflective of sequentially more complex cognitive competencies. Moreover, as previously described, studies of solitary pretense play between 1 and 3 years appear to demonstrate progressively sophisticated decontextualizations and object substitutions. These transformations continue to grow more complex during the early and middle years of childhood.

Overton and Jackson (1973), for example, asked children ranging in age from 3 to 8 years to pretend that they were using common objects in action sequences *appropriate* to the objects (e.g., given a real comb, "Pretend that you are combing your hair"). Subsequently, the children were asked to demonstrate the same action sequences but without physical props. At 3 and 4 years, the predominate strategy was to use a body part to designate the referent object (e.g., finger used as comb). At 6 years, the strategy of using a body part to represent an absent object was employed as often as the strategy of using symbolic, imaginary objects to carry out the designated action. At 8 years, the predominate strategy was to employ imaginary objects. This study revealed that object substitutions become more ideational with age. Moreover, the study indicated that even at 3 and 4 years, children could employ objects (body parts) *not* closely resembling the referent in pretense activities.

More recently, Elder and Pederson (1978), in a study of 2½- to 3½-year-olds, asked children to carry out pretense actions (e.g., "Pretend you are combing your hair.") with objects that had structural properties differing in degree of similarity to those being designated (a flat piece of wood would be similar to a *comb*, but a rubber ball would be dissimilar to a *comb*). In a third condition, no object was available for the specified pretense act. Elder and Pederson found that children younger than 3 years were most dependent on the presence of substitute objects that resembled their referents. Moreover, at 2½ years the children appeared to be *caught* by the physical properties of the object. Thus, they performed better in the no-object condition than in the dissimilar-object condition. The youngest children frequently used the dissimilar object according to *its own* appropriate use rather than pretending in the requested manner. By 3½ years, children performed equally well in all three conditions.

The results of numerous studies of children be-

tween the ages of 1½ and 8 years indicate that the ability to pretend with substitute objects begins at 19 months and increases through the preschool and early elementary school years (e.g., Copple, Cocking, & Matthews, 1980; Elder & Pederson, 1978; Golomb, 1977; Overton & Jackson, 1973). Moreover, in young children object substitution often is linked to prototypical objects that are good exemplars of given referents. The dependency on such exemplars appears to lead preschool age children to employ particular objects selectively as designative ("spoonlike" objects to serve as spoons), whereas older children appear to be less tied to perceived similarities between the pretense objects and the objects that they signify (Copple et al., 1980; Golomb, 1977). As such, the data may indicate that there are degrees of prototypicality, that a shift toward less prototypicality appears with development, and that such growth is reflected in the sophisticated object substitutions of elementary school age children (Copple et al., 1980; Phillips, 1945; Pulaski, 1973).

Structural Properties of Pretense Play in Naturalistic Settings

Decontextualizations and Object Substitutions

In addition to examining the growth of ideational substitutions and of decontextualizations during solitary pretense play, researchers have examined these phenomena in naturalistic settings in which groups of children are gathered. Typical of this line of research is a study of Matthews (1977b) in which 4-year-old children were invited to play in an attractive playroom with same-sex playmates. The results of her study indicated that approximately one-half of the pretend play initiated by the children (which occurred at the beginning of a fantasy episode) was ideational. That is, the pretense did not depend on the immediate presence of a physical object. McLoyd (1980), in analyzing *all* transformations that occurred in a play session, found that black 4-year-old children with lower socioeconomic status also produced ideational transformations, though somewhat less frequently.

It has been reported that preschoolers who are acquainted with one another engage in more fantasy play when in dyads than do previously unacquainted children (Doyle, Connolly, & Rivest, 1980; Matthews, 1978a). Moreover, with increased co-actor familiarity, it appears as if ideational transformations become facilitated. For example, from the first to the third (and final) dyadic play session between previously unacquainted preschoolers, Matthews (1977b) found that ideational transformations increased from 29% to 55% of all transformations.

In a more recent report, Gowen (1978) observed children 2 to 6 years of age during free play in a day care center. As in the earlier studies of solitary pretense, Gowen found that the younger 2- and 3-year-olds made greater use of concrete objects (toys) during pretense play than did the older, 4- to 6-year-olds. On the other hand, the older preschoolers were more likely to use imaginary, or ideational, signifiers than their younger counterparts. These data may be taken as supporting Vygotsky's (1967) position that very young children are less able than their older counterparts to sever thought from object and action and thus require concrete pivots or links to support their conceptualizations.

Ritualized Social Play

One structural feature of play that is found in group contexts concerns the role relationships between social partners. For example, Garvey (1974) has examined the nature of one early appearing form of interactive behavior—ritualized play. For the most part, Garvey's interest seems to center on the sociolinguistic rather than the pretense elements of these interactive sequences. Nevertheless, the activities are labeled as ritualistic pretense. Some examples follow.

X's turn	Y's turn
1. Bye, mommy. Bye, mommy.	**Bye, mommy. Bye, mommy.**
2. Hello, my name is Mr. Donkey. Hello, my name is Mr. Tiger.	**Hello, my name is Mr. Elephant. Hello, my name is Mr. Lion.**
3. I have to go to work. No I'm not.	**You're already at work.**
I have to go to school. No, I'm not.	**You're already at school.**

These examples, taken from Garvey (1974), indicate that ritualistic pretense is governed by the acceptance of what appear to be implicitly agreed on rules of turn-taking. The turns are characterized by their symmetry (examples 1, 2) or asymmetry (example 3) as well as by the sequential modifications apparent in the speakers' turns. In Garvey's research, the ritualistic pretense of previously acquainted preschool age dyads has been the focus of attention. Garvey has found that ritualized pretense sequences become increasingly complex with age. However, the *frequency of these simple role-play* sequences *decreases* with age. Presumably, older

preschoolers engage in pretense sequences in which the participants have more extensive role relationships (e.g., the playing of *Star Wars* or the acting out of a nursery story).

Interestingly, the ritual framework constructed by Garvey (1974) can be extended readily for use with toddlers and older children. For example, the ritualized games played by infants and toddlers appear to follow an analogous developmental course to the ritualized linguistic roles noted above. According to Mueller and his colleagues (Mueller & Lucas, 1975; Vandell & Mueller, 1980), in the first stage of infant social interaction, one play partner is likely to duplicate the physical effects produced by the other partner with toys or with objects. Several rounds of such symmetrical, identical behaviors may follow. As such, this early ritualized infant game (Ross, Goldman, & Hay, 1979) appears to have many of the structural properties of Garvey's least mature form of ritualized play (Example 1 above). It differs from Garvey's least mature play form in that preschoolers take on momentary pretense roles in their ritualistic language play.

During a later stage of toddler interaction (Mueller & Lucas, 1975), the participants appear to behave in particular ritualized ways in which the actions are intercoordinated. For example, in ball games one toddler may act as a thrower while the play partner acts as receiver. Subsequently, the participants may reverse roles (Ross, Goldman, & Hay, 1979). These intercoordinated and reciprocal games come close to those ritualized role interactions characterized by Example 3 above. As such, one can see precursors and analogues of early ritualized pretense play structures in the games of infants and toddlers.

One also can extend the concept of ritualized play patterns to the dramatic activities of kindergarten and elementary school age children. Although the research has yet to be done, it is conceivable that the extended, supposedly varied, and flexible dramatic endeavors of older children take on distinctively ritualistic overtones. For example, one may observe a group of three kindergarten children playing at *Star Wars*, each taking on different roles and carrying out what appear to be very creative actions. From subjective observations of his daughter at play, however, the first author has noted that, on returning to the kindergarten on a regular basis, the same groups of friends when playing at given fantasy themes tend to take the same roles and pursue similar, if not identical, actions. Thus, a "one-shot" view of the fantasy frames of 5- and 6-year-olds may give one the impression that their pretense is less repetitive and redundant than that of their younger counterparts. However, several observations of groups of friends at play may indicate the existence of more complex interactional modes of pretense that are, nevertheless, still ritualistic to some degree.

Role Adoptions

A third structural feature of social pretense concerns the types of roles adopted by the drama's participants. The major figure in this line of research is Garvey (1977a; Garvey & Berndt, 1977), who in a study of previously acquainted 3- to 5-year-olds examined children's techniques for indicating who they pretended to be, where the activity was to take place, and what the given objects in the environment represented. Garvey and Berndt identified four types of dramatic roles. First, there were *functional roles* defined as those organized by an object or activity (e.g., being the bus driver). Second, there were *relational roles,* identified as those familial roles that implied complementary relationships (mother-child, wife-husband). It is important to note that such relational roles could coincide with functional roles; for example, mother is usually the server in action formats of "dining" scripts or themes.

Third, Garvey and Berndt described *character roles*, which were based on stereotypic occupational or habitual activities (policeman, cowboy) or on fictional roles (characters with proper names, for example, Santa Claus, R2-D2). The latter fictional category included those characters whose source appeared to be stories, television, or oral tradition. Finally, *peripheral roles* were those that were discussed or addressed, but whose identity the child never assumed (e.g., real or imaginary friends).

According to Garvey and Berndt relational roles were acted most frequently. Similar findings were reported by Matthews (1977a). For the youngest group observed (3 years), the play activities associated with these roles closely approximated literal expectations. If one of the partners violated these expectations (child going to work), the play role was abandoned ("I'm not the baby anymore. I'm the Daddy.").

For the oldest group observed (5 years), relational roles extended beyond personal interactive experiences and incorporated relationships observed in others (e.g., wife in relation to husband). Moreover, with increasing age, pretense roles and their associated play themes were more elaborate, imaginary, and often involved imaginary third parties. For example, older children were more likely than younger children to play the contrasting roles of victim and defender with the latter actor chasing an imaginary villain.

Garvey and Berndt also indicated that the older, 5-year-old children were better able to accept departures from role-appropriate behaviors on the part of particular actors. However, the integrity of the role relationships was rarely violated (e.g., the mother never telephoned the baby). Unfortunately, the age differences cited in Garvey and Berndt's paper were not accompanied by supportive statistical data. Consequently, the structural framework of pretense role relationships remains useful, whereas conclusions regarding developmental differences remain somewhat speculative.

In another study concerned with the interpersonal structure of role-play, Iwanaga (1973) found that, when 3-year-olds engaged in group pretense in which differentiated roles were assigned (conductor and passengers), they were more likely than 5-year-olds to enact their roles independently (conductor stops the train and riders get off, but each develops his or her role without reference to one another). The older preschool children were more likely than their younger counterparts to develop integrative, complementary role relationships that linked the activities of the players through appropriate reciprocal behaviors. In keeping with the developmental pattern emerging from the preceding studies, Fein and Stork (in press) report a striking increase in behavior-stressing reciprocal relationships between 3 and 5 years.

Thematic Fantasy Play Versus Sociodramatic. Play

Another structural feature of social pretense concerns the recent distinction made between thematic fantasy play and sociodramatic play (Saltz & Brodie, 1982; Saltz, Dixon, & Johnson, 1977; Saltz & Johnson, 1974). Saltz and his colleagues have been most concerned with the tutorial benefits of imaginative play. Since one of the presumed benefits of pretense is that it allows children to free themselves from the control of the concrete, immediately present stimuli in the environment (Vygotsky, 1967), it was thought reasonable to assume that children would benefit most from pretense experiences that removed them furthest from concrete reality. As such, it was proposed that thematic fantasy play in which children played fantastic roles well removed from their everyday experiences (fairy tale, movie, and television characters) would place greater demands on imagery and symbolic representation than would sociodramatic play in which children played roles that were somewhat more familiar (playing house, school, police station). In many ways Saltz and his colleagues have implied that thematic fantasy play, because it places greater demands on the imagery process, is a more mature form of group pretense than is sociodramatic play. To the extent that the earliest forms of group pretense involve familial, relational roles (Garvey & Berndt, 1977; Matthews, 1977a) rather than fictional roles, the Saltz position is supported. It should be noted that, during the preschool years, children appear more likely to take on imitative, relational roles (Johnson & Ershler, 1981; Johnson, Ershler, & Bell, 1980). Both a developmental study of the relative distribution of sociodramatic versus group fantasy play, as well as an investigation of the relationships among these forms of social pretense and various social cognitive and imagery markers, would be worthwhile projects.

Structuring Play

The final structural property of social pretense concerns the preparation and the "framing" of the play itself. Perhaps the most influential author in this area has been Bateson (1955; 1956), who has written extensively on the topic of communicating about play by children. To Bateson (1956) and more recently to Sutton-Smith (1979a), Schwartzman (1976a; 1978), Fein (1979a), Garvey and Berndt (1977), and Rubin (1980), play is "framed," or surrounded by the preparations and negotiations that precede it and by the negations and conflicts that return the players to the world of "here and now" (Garvey & Berndt, 1977).

Prior to entering the play frame, there are negotiations among the potential co-actors that center on defining character roles (who is to play what role); on indicating what various objects represent; and where the play situation is to be taking place (Garvey, 1977a). As such, the negotiations set the *context* for the play situation while the play itself represents the *text* (Schwartzman, 1976a, 1978; Sutton-Smith, 1979a, in press).

Once within the play frame, it becomes essential that players communicate to their partners that the activity is "just pretend." These complex messages assuredly would be most difficult to decipher were they not accompanied by markers that make it quite clear that the actions should be interpreted as nonliteral exemplars of "real life." Thus, play is structured by such preparatory and accompanying markers or signals as attenuation or exaggeration of those behaviors that in nonplay (Garvey, 1974) would

have their primary form. In addition, smiles and laughter ease the inferential process that a given behavior is to be taken as playful or as "just pretend" (Bateson, 1956; Bruner, Jolly & Sylva, 1976; Garvey, 1974, 1977a; Schwartzman, 1978). Thus, an important structure of group fantasy or drama involves the negotiation and communication of pretense.

Although negotiations and communications about play roles have been reported to exist (and to play a causal accommodative role in development; Matthews, 1978a) in the interactions of children 4, 5, and 6 (Fein, 1979b; Matthews, 1978a; Sutton-Smith, 1971a), they do not appear in toddler and young 3-year-old conversations. Perhaps, then, one reason for the lack of spontaneous sociodramatic or group fantasy interactions in 2- and 3-year-olds results from the inability to produce and comprehend the message, "This is play" (Garvey & Berndt, 1977). Children of these young ages may simply not have grasped the notion that pretend play can be a social endeavor with shared rules about the production and communication of symbolic representations (Fein, 1979b). Given this position, it would be worthwhile for psychologists to consider examining the development of negotiations and communications concerning pretense.

When is it that children are able to distinguish literal from nonliteral events? When do they comprehend the rules and markers for communicating pretense in words and sentences? Certainly from the literature on rough-and-tumble play (Blurton-Jones, 1972; Smith & Connolly, 1972), during which children wrestle, hit, and chase each other and simultaneously display play faces and laugh, it would appear as if 4-year-olds have the skills to produce and to comprehend the messages that structure and frame pretense. Nevertheless, as Garvey (1977a) has noted, we know little about how spontaneous bouts of chasing or mock fighting are organized and little about how the roles and rules are negotiated. As a result, a worthwhile area for future work may well concern the development of "meta-play," or how children come to learn the structural features of play.

Other Forms of Play in Early and Middle Childhood

Having examined developmental issues concerned with quantitative and qualitative dimensions of pretense play in early childhood, we turn to other forms of play that exist during both this period and that of middle childhood. Drawing on Piaget's

(1962) and Smilansky's (1968) structural classifications of play forms, we consider the following: (1) functional play; (2) constructive play; and (3) games-with-rules.

Functional Play

Functional play consists of simple repetitive movements with or without objects.[5] This play also has been labeled sensorimotor exercise or practice play (Piaget, 1962). To Piaget, functional play exists simply for the pleasure of exercising already existing schemas without efforts of adaptation. The behavior has been mastered already and is not directed toward any goal except its performance. Behaviors typical of functional play include running around a room, rolling a toy vehicle back and forth repeatedly, and kneading Play-Dough repeatedly with no purpose to construct with it. According to Piaget (1962), Smilansky (1968), and others, functional play is the least mature form of ludic activity, preceding symbolic play and rule-governed games. Moreover, it is hypothesized to decline with age, being replaced by these more mature ludic activities.

Much of the evidence for the decline of functional play with age stems from observational studies of children engaged in this form of activity; percentages of total observations are computed. In both longitudinal (Hetherington et al., 1979; Rubin & Krasnor, 1980; Sponseller & Jaworski, 1979) and cross-sectional (Rubin et al., 1978) research, functional play has been demonstrated to decline with age. At 14 to 30 months, functional play constitutes 53% of all free activity (Sponseller & Jaworski, 1979). Between 3 and 4 years of age, it accounts for between 36% and 44% of all play (Johnson et al., 1980; Sponseller & Jaworski, 1979). This figure drops to between 17% and 33% from 4 to 5 years (Hetherington et al., 1979; Rubin et al., 1976, 1978). In the one study of 6- to 7-year-olds, Hetherington et al. (1979) reported that functional activities comprise 14% of all play. It should further be noted that practice play consistently has been shown to occur within solitary or parallel social contexts (Hetherington et al., 1979; Rubin et al., 1976, 1978).

Constructive Play

Piaget (1962) and Smilansky (1968) described constructive play as the manipulation of objects to construct or to create something. Although Piaget suggested that functional and symbolic play and games-with-rules were characterized by the three successive forms of intelligence (i.e., sensorimotor, representational, and reflective, respectively), he noted that constructive play did not fall within a given stage of intelligence. Instead, Piaget suggested that "constructive games" occupied a position halfway between play and adaptive intelligence. For example, Piaget (1962, p. 109) wrote:

> Making a house with plasticine or bricks involves both sensory-motor skill and symbolic representation, and, like drawing a house, is a move away from play in the strict sense, towards work, or at least towards spontaneous intelligent activity.

Those researchers who have centered on acts of self-regulated construction have been primarily interested in the relationship of such activity to the development of problem-solving skills (e.g., Cheyne & Rubin, in press; Forman & Hill, 1980; Pepler, 1979; Sylva, 1977). We deal with these purported relationships in a later section. Now we describe the relative frequency of constructive activities during early childhood.

It would be safe to say that constructive play is the most common form of activity in most preschool and kindergarten classrooms. In all studies examined for this section, the modal form of play was construction. Thus, the frequency of constructive play ranges from approximately 40% of all activity at 3½ years (Rubin et al., 1976) to approximately 51% at 4, 5, and 6 years (Hetherington et al., 1979; Rubin et al., 1976, 1978). Rubin and Krasnor (1980), in a short-term longitudinal study, did not find age changes in the frequency of constructive play for 3- and 4-year-olds. Since all of these studies were conducted in formal school settings, it may be that the materials made available to the children "pull for" educational forms of play. As such, the puzzles and art construction materials that normally are found in schools but not on playgrounds or in backyards may be somewhat responsible for the relatively high percentage figures noted above for constructive play. The possibility that the ecological setting can determine play behavior is examined in a later section.

Given the predominance of such activity in early childhood, it does not appear to fit well within the suggested hierarchy of Smilansky (1968). Indeed, Piaget (1962) had some difficulty in trying to place this category into the Buhler/Piaget scheme. Thus, it is recommended that those who use the cognitive

---

[5]This term has also been employed by Zelazo and his colleagues to denote functionally appropriate, object-specific play (Zelazo & Kearsley, 1977). This work was reviewed in the section on infant manipulative play and should not be confused with Smilansky's use of the term.

play hierarchy should attempt, in future years, to examine the relationships of practice play, pretense play, and games-with-rules to measures of sensorimotor, preoperational, and concrete operational intelligence, respectively. Constructive play might well be viewed as belonging to some other coding schemes.

Games-with-Rules

Piaget (1962) postulated that one resultant of increased cognitive competence was a corresponding increase in the complexity of play. This complexity was thought to involve the recognition, acceptance, and conformity to constraints or rules, imposed on ludic activity. Consequently, such complex behaviors were believed to occur rarely during the late preoperational years (6 to 7 years) and to "belong mainly to the third period (from 7 to 11 years)," that is, to concrete operations (Piaget, 1962).

In accord with the above suggestions, Piaget predicted that pretense activities would be replaced gradually by games because symbolic or pretend games themselves become increasingly social and rule governed with age. Since social pretense was recognized as necessitating elementary role and rule negotiations, it was natural to assume that such activities would evolve into formal, rule-governed, competitive games. Two basic criteria satisfied Piaget's definition of games-with-rules. First, at least two persons have to engage in competition with one another. Second, the participants' behaviors must be regulated by either a code handed down by earlier generations or by temporary agreement. Taken together, these criteria would exclude from the Piagetian category of games-with-rules all rule-governed behaviors that were not competitive.

Perhaps the best statement of the hierarchical relationship between functional (practice) and pretense play and games-with-rules is found in the following statement.

As the symbol replaces practice as soon as thought appears, the rule replaces the symbol and integrates practice as soon as social relations are formed. (Piaget, 1962, p. 163)

In this section we examine the Piagetian hypothesis that rules increasingly become a part of children's ludic exercises with age. In the following section we present a brief discussion of the distinctions drawn between play and games, particularly as they relate to the activities of elementary school children.

Drawing on the same cross-sectional and longitudinal data that allowed us to describe the relative frequencies of pretense, functional, and constructive play, it is evident that games-with-rules do increasingly become evident from the early to late preoperational years (Hetherington et al., 1979; Rubin & Krasnor, 1980; Rubin et al., 1976, 1978). In the one major psychological study concerned with the play of children in the concrete operational period, the Piagetian suggestion that pretense play declines while the frequency of games-with-rules increases was examined. Eifermann (1971) found that the sociodramatic endeavors of close to 14,000 Israeli children did decrease in both upper- and middle-class samples of youngsters in grades 3 to 8. Moreover, using Piaget's own strict definitive criterion that a game-with-rules must include competition, Eifermann found that participation in such activities increased from ages 6 through 10 and thereafter declined steadily, reaching a low point at 14 years.

It is important to note that Eifermann's data do indicate that once games-with-rules had peaked at about the fifth-grade level their occurrence did, in fact, decline thereafter. Perhaps, as Ellis (1973) speculates, competitive games, which are purported to decrease egocentric thought processes and to increase the capacities of children to deal with the realities of their social settings, have run their useful, accommodatory course by the end of the concrete operational period. However, prior to acceptance of the Eifermann finding and the various and sundry conclusions and explanations emanating from her report, it will be necessary to replicate her work in other settings and countries.

Games-with-Rules Versus Pretense Play: Some Conceptual Distinctions

It may be safely said that there has been far less *psychological* research concerning children's game-oriented behavior than that extant on children's play. Putting Eifermann's (1971) massive observational study and Piaget's (1962) examination of children's conceptions of game rules aside, the games literature emanates, for the most part, from anthropological and sociological sources (see Avedon & Sutton-Smith, 1971; Roberts, Arth, & Bush, 1959; Schwartzman, 1976a, b; for reviews of this work). Since we indicated earlier that we would consider children's play to the exclusion of games, it is necessary to make clear the distinction between the two phenomena. The purpose of excluding a lengthy consideration of the large literature on games is straightforward enough—we would have to review a nonpsychologically based literature, which is easily as voluminous as that which exists for children's play. In short, time and space constraints preclude a thorough examination of children's games. Given our arbitrary and yet practical decision not to review the work on games, it becomes necessary to distinguish it from play.

Both play and games appear to be rule governed to some degree. However, the nature and functions of the rules in games and play appear to differ. In play, rules exist to negotiate roles and to maintain the context of the make-believe world. However, the play themes and the roles adopted by the participants may change within brief spans of time. Thus, the sociodramatic or thematic fantasy "plots" can be altered at any given moment by the players themselves.

For games, on the other hand, structural modifications are not allowed *unless* mutual agreement among all participants has been reached *beforehand*. Game rules dictate what the players can or cannot do within their defined roles. Rules also determine, a priori, how the game is to be played. Consequently, game behavior is far more restricted and formalized than is play behavior. Given the flexibility of play and its specificity to given groups of children, it becomes unlikely (unless ritualized, Garvey, 1974) that themes, actions, and so on, would be replicated or passed on to later generations of other groups of children. However, given the rules of games, replication can easily occur. Play is further distinguished from games in that the latter phenomenon is goal oriented, whereas the former phenomenon is not. One plays for the satisfaction of playing. One engages in games to compete, to win, and to achieve some specified goal.

FACTORS INFLUENCING THE PLAY OF CHILDREN

Having described the structural features of play in infancy and childhood, it would now appear appropriate to discuss some of the factors that influence the ways in which children play. Psychologists have postulated that the play of children is influenced by (1) child-rearing and parental factors, (2) peer experiences, (3) the presence of particular materials within the physical environment, (4) the schools children attend, and (5) the media. We discuss the influence of each of these factors.

Child-Rearing Influences

It would appear obvious that some connection should exist between child-rearing patterns and the disposition to play in one way or another. Much of

the work in this regard is anthropological in nature and concerns the relationship between established cultural child-rearing patterns and the games (rather than the play) of children in various cultures (e.g., Roberts & Sutton-Smith, 1962). The psychological work concerned with child-rearing factors and play stems, for the most part, from those who espouse social learning theories. Theoretically, it has been suggested that parents contribute to their children's play by interacting with them in imaginative ways and by providing both the content and the modes for pretense (El'konin, 1968; Johnson, 1978; A. F. Lieberman, 1977; Singer, 1973). Singer (1973) has written that parents who engage their infants in make-believe, peek-a-boo, or find-the-hidden-object type games may call into play some early elements of imagery. As such, infants who are more likely to experience such interactions are predicted to develop fantasy and sociodramatic themes in their play earlier.

Singer (1973) also has indirectly proposed a possible relationship between infant security of attachment to the mother and later play dispositions. For example, he has written that the responsive, "non-smothering" mother is more likely than the "smothering" mother to have a child who practices independent exploration and play. This independence was thought to allow the child to internalize memories of the mother's activity and to access the desired parent via solitary fantasizing.

Research concerning this postulated relationship, albeit seemingly sound, has been surprisingly sparse. Much of the extant literature emanates from interview or questionnaire data and informs us little about the causal relationships between child-rearing and dispositions to fantasy play. Typical of such studies is that of Freyberg (1973). Based on interview data, Freyberg found that parents of kindergarten children who were high on fantasy predisposition were more likely than parents of low-fantasy, predisposed children to regard imaginative activities positively. However, the parents of the two groups of children (each group which numbered but six) did not report extraordinary differences in interactions with their children.

Similar clinically oriented interview/questionnaire studies have reported that elementary school age children predisposed to fantasy are more likely to enjoy close parental contact (Marshall, 1961; Singer, 1973). However, observational work has not generally supported the modeling or social learning approaches to the development of play. White and Carew-Watts (1973) and Dunn and Wooding (1977) reported that social pretense between parents and their young children was a rare event in their homes. Furthermore, Dunn and Wooding (1977) found that, when pretend episodes did occur in the home, they were more likely to be initiated by the child than by the mother, and although the mother may have acknowledged the pretense exercise, she was rarely found to have joined or extended it.

In perhaps the lone study that directly observed mother-child interaction and fantasy play, Johnson (1978) found that neither family member dominated the imaginative play episodes. He also found positive correlations between the percentages of mother and child imaginative behavior in the given play situation. Given the correlational nature of the study and given that both partners were equally likely to engage in fantasy play, any statement concerning the cause-effect relationship between parent and child behavior was unwarranted.

Given Singer's (1973) statements concerning the responsive parent, it indeed may be possible that the relationship between child-rearing and play is influenced *indirectly* by systems that facilitate or restrict children's behaviors in general. This suggestion receives initial empirical support from the longitudinal research of Sroufe, Waters, and their colleagues (Arend, Gove, & Sroufe, 1979; Matas, Arend, & Sroufe, 1978; Sroufe & Waters, 1977; Waters, Wippman, & Sroufe, 1979). For example, it has been found that securely attached infants at 18 months are more likely to explore their physical environment when in unfamiliar settings with their mothers than are their insecurely attached counterparts (Matas et al., 1978). Such findings, among others, conjure up the following developmental scenario.

Given feelings of comfort and security, produced in part by responsive, sensitive, and authoritative parenting (Bakeman & Brown, 1980; Blehar, Lieberman, & Ainsworth, 1977), the infant or toddler is more likely than his or her insecure age-mate to explore the physical environment when in the presence of his or her mother. This exploration allows the child to discover object properties (Hutt, 1970; Sutton-Smith, 1979a) and to use the objects in functional, literal ways (as in rolling a ball or pushing a truck along the floor). Once the child has learned what the object can do, she or he can proceed to discover what can be done with the object. Thus, as suggested by Hutt, object exploration may be followed by play. During play, the objects come to be used in "as if" pretense fashions. Taken together, the data would suggest that security of attachment, brought on in part by particular child-rearing patterns, may affect later object exploration and conse-

quently constructive play or problem solving with the objects (Pepler & Ross, 1981; Sylva, 1977; Vandenberg, 1980a, b). This suggestion has gained recent support in the literature (Arend et al., 1979; Matas et al., 1978). Moreover, Matas et al. (1978) have found that security of attachment at 18 months is predictive of fantasy play with objects at 24 months. Furthermore, Arend et al. (1979) have indicated that indexes of secure attachment at 18 months and of autonomous functioning at 2 years predicted curiosity and behavioral flexibility at 5 years.

As for the social side of play, security of attachment in children may lead to earlier exploration of the social environment in unfamiliar settings (e.g., day care) in comparison to insecure attachment in children. Researchers have revealed that securely attached children are more sociable than are their less secure counterparts (A. F. Lieberman, 1977). These early social encounters may invoke toddler "games" (Ross, Goldman, & Hay, 1979) that, in turn, ultimately may lead to social pretense endeavors during the preschool years. The prediction that securely attached infants should develop social pretense skills at an earlier age compared to insecurely attached children, however, has not been investigated.

To conclude, parents do provide role models for their children and, consequently, may influence role play via social learning. Perhaps, more importantly, parents may influence exploratory, functional, constructive, and pretense play indirectly by providing their children with responsive, sensitive, and secure bases that reduce stress and anxiety in unfamiliar settings.

Other Familial Influences

Although parents can be influential in promoting or modeling mature play forms for their children, recent data suggest that events within the home may have negative influences as well. For example, marital separation and the aftermath of divorce may prove particularly distressing to young children (Hetherington et al., 1979). It has been suggested that such disruptive forces which carry with them anxiety and emotional stress may elicit aberrations or regressions in children's normal play patterns (Hartup, 1976; Singer, 1977).

In the one major study of the effects of divorce on children's play, Hetherington et al. (1979) used an elaboration of the nested play observation scale developed by Rubin et al. (1976). These investigators followed two matched groups of preschoolers who varied from each other only insofar as one group was comprised of children with divorced parents whereas the other group consisted of children from intact nuclear families. The children were observed at 2 months, 1 year, and 2 years following divorce.

Hetherington et al. (1979) found that at 2 months after divorce, children produced more functional and less dramatic play than their matched age-mates from nuclear families. Whether these differences reflected a regression on the part of the first group could not be ascertained.

By 1 year following divorce, *females* evinced less group dramatic play than those children in the nuclear family. By 2 years after divorce, play differences between both female groups disappeared. For boys from divorced homes *at all three time periods*, there was significantly more solitary and parallel functional play and less sociodramatic play compared to their counterparts from two-parent homes. These data suggest that the effects of divorce on children's play may be more sustained in boys (Hetherington et al., 1979).

In an interesting examination of the quality of pretense play following divorce, Hetherington et al. (1979) indicated that children from nuclear families were less reliant on the presence of objects (i.e., more ideational) during pretense than were children from divorced homes at 2 months after divorce. Boys from divorced families were less able to make major or minor role transformations and were less flexible in their pretense themes at all three time periods than were their counterparts in nuclear families. In summary, it would appear as if the stressful experiences encountered by young children who reside in the homes of divorced parents are reflected in their less mature and less sophisticated play as exhibited in classroom settings. For boys the adjustment to divorce appears to be more difficult, at least as indicated by their continued lower levels of play over the full 2-year observational period. Perhaps the stress experienced by the boys was further exacerbated by a lack of sensitive and responsive same-sex role models. All children of divorced parents in the Hetherington et al. study resided with their mothers. Moreover, preschool, kindergarten, and first-grade teachers are more likely to be female than male—and perhaps more sympathetic to the plights of young girls than of boys. One reasonable study that could be carried out in the future would center on the possible ameliorative or compensatory effects of providing young boys from divorced homes with sensitive and responsive male teachers, for example, "Big Brothers."

Related to the issue of accessibility to adult males and females is the finding that fathers provide experiences different from those provided by the mothers. For one, fathers are generally more likely to play with their infants than are mothers (Lamb, 1977; Power & Parke, 1980; Smith & Daglish, 1977; Weinraub & Frankel, 1977). Furthermore, fathers play differently with their infants than do mothers. For example, fathers play more physical games, lifting and bouncing their children, whereas mothers play more watching games with their infants (Power & Parke, 1980). Fathers are also more likely to play these physical lifting games with their sons. Taken together, the above data suggest that fathers and mothers may make separate and unique contributions to the child-rearing process.

However, several questions remain to be answered. First, we do not know whether fathers or mothers are more likely to play with infants and children of one particular sex. Do fathers prefer to play with their sons and mothers with their daughters? If so, then the effects of divorce may be especially difficult for the little boys. Second, as we note below, boys and girls exhibit different play patterns. Does the greater frequency of rough-and-tumble behavior in boys and sedentary, constructive activities in girls emanate, in part, from different, sex-discriminative parental play styles and preferences? For example, the parent-infant play data do support the notion that boys are involved in more bouncing, lifting games than girls. Is this a precursor to rough-and-tumble play? Given these unanswered questions and given the relative lack of data concerning parent-child play during the toddler, preschool, and middle-childhood years, further documentation of parent-child play exchanges is warranted.

Peer Influences

Having noted the purported benefits of social fantasy or sociodramatic endeavors as well as the theoretical viewpoint that peer interaction and peer play, in general, may produce developmental changes (Piaget, 1962), it is somewhat surprising to find a dearth of literature concerning the influences of peers on play. Most of the related work focuses on social interaction (e.g., Mueller & Lucas, 1975) or social participation (e.g., Parten, 1932) rather than on play as defined here. Consequently, readers who are interested in the influences of variables such as peer familiarity or the presence of handicapped versus nonhandicapped peers, cross-age versus same-age peers, or opposite-sex versus same-sex peers on solitary, parallel, or cooperative forms of behavior can refer to Chapter 8 of this volume by Hartup.

Although few researchers have explored peer influences on play, their findings paint a fairly consistent picture. One variable that appears to play a critical role in determining behavior is that of *peer familiarity*. In a study of a small group of 19-month-old toddlers during free play at home, Rubenstein and Howes (1976) found that the quality of play was of a more sophisticated type when in the presence of a familiar peer than when alone. Thus, when in the company of a familiar age-mate, children were more likely to exploit unique properties of objects and to use objects in a nonliteral fashion than when alone. Rubenstein and Howes speculated that previously acquired skills with inanimate objects become elaborated or integrated at more complex levels of behavior in the context of imitating and being imitated by a peer and in the context of being reinforced by the shared pleasure of a shared activity.

In a recent study of 3-year-olds, Doyle, Connolly, and Rivest (1980) compared the play of children in the company of unfamiliar and familiar dyadic partners. The authors found that dramatic play was more likely to occur in the presence of familiar playmates. Moreover, the complexity of play when interacting with the partner was at a higher level with familiar than with unfamiliar playmates. For example, *group* pretense or sociodramatic activity occurred more frequently than group functional activity in familiar dyads, but not in unfamiliar dyads. As with Rubenstein and Howes (1976), Doyle et al. speculated that the same sense of shared meaning between familiar playmates led to the lesser likelihood of passive watching and solitary activity in familiar dyads and to the greater likelihood of verbal and physical exchange and pretense play.

Matthews (1977b; 1978a), in a study of previously unacquainted 4-year-olds, paired children into free-play dyads for three sessions. With increased co-actor familiarity, the proportion of time spent in fantasy play increased. Moreover, the frequency of ideational object transformations increased and material transformations decreased over time. Taken together, the literature on peer familiarity suggests that children play more, and at higher cognitive levels, when in the company of an acquaintance than when alone or with an unfamiliar child. Furthermore, with increased co-actor familiarity, there is a corresponding increase in the amount and in the complexity of pretense play.

A second peer influence on play is the *sex of the play partner*. Rabinowitz, Moely, Finkel, and McClinton (1975) found that preschoolers were more likely to explore a novel object and to spend less time with familiar toys when paired with a same-sex play partner than when paired with an opposite-sex playmate or when alone. However, no differences existed with regard to the frequency of diversive exploration (Hutt, 1970) in the three play partner conditions.

In a more recent study, Serbin, Conner, Burchardt, and Citron (1979) observed 3- and 4-year-olds at play when alone, when with a same-sex partner, and when with an opposite-sex partner. The authors found that play with "sex-inappropriate" toys was significantly lower in the presence of an opposite-sex peer than when in the solitary mode. Serbin et al. also found that the rate of play with opposite-sex-typed toys increased over the three successive sessions for the children.

Unlike research that centers on social interaction and peer relations per se (see Hartup, *vol. IV, chap. 8*), the play literature is, as yet, devoid of studies concerned with such peer influence as the age (younger, older, same age) or the social competence of the partner. Konner (1972), among others, has postulated that mixed-age play groupings serve to integrate the younger participants into their diverse environments and, at the same time, to enhance the communication skills of the older participants. Certainly it is conceivable that new roles and interactive rules may be learned from playing with more experienced and more socially adept partners. Older partners may be better able to initiate fantasy or constructive endeavors than younger play partners. Socially competent youngsters may be better able to organize and carry through sociodramatic or group constructive play themes than their less competent counterparts. Moreover, older or socially skilled play partners, in contrast to their counterparts may have the wherewithall to encourage exploration and more sophisticated levels of play from their playmates. Thus, the investigation of these play influences might prove to be a most fruitful endeavor in the future.

Ecological Influences

The social environment aside, it is conceivable that ecological factors, such as the types of materials available or the play venue, can affect how children play. That environmental factors can influence behavior is certainly not a novel idea. For example, in 1931 Lewin wrote:

> Objects are not neutral to the child but have an immediate psychologial effect on its behavior: many things *attract* the child to eating, to climbing, to grasping, to manipulating, to sucking, to

raging at them, etc. These imperative environmental facts—we shall call them valences—determine the direction of behavior. (Lewin, 1931, p. 6)

Lewin and his colleagues have had a strong influence on the study of ecological effects on behavior (see also Barker, 1968). Much of the developmental work in this area is concerned with the significance of physical environment in determining the incidence of such social interactive behaviors as cooperation, aggression, and altruism (see Hartup, *vol. IV, chap. 8*) and such cognitive facilitators as attention. For those interested in the effects of the ecological setting on behaviors other than play as defined here (e.g., social interaction), the reader is referred to an excellent recent review by Phyfe-Perkins (1980).

The Distinction Between Play and Exploration and the Effects of Stimulus Novelty on Play

It has been proposed that novel materials influence the child's play responses to them. This proposal emanates from the literature in which play has been distinguished from exploration (Berlyne, 1960, 1969; Hutt, 1970; Nunnally & Lemond, 1973). An overview of this literature is merited in order to understand better how and why novel objects appear to lead to different behaviors than do familiar objects.

The distinction between play and exploration, originally proposed by Berlyne (1960; 1969), has stimulated considerable discussion among investigators concerned with clarifying the sense in which play is intrinsically motivated behavior. As we indicated earlier, the distinction suggests a difference in the locus of control of the activity. In exploration external stimulation brought on by a novel object dictates the activity, while in play the individual is in control. In specific exploration, the individual is asking, "What does this object do?" In diversive exploration (play), the individual is asking, "Where can I find something to do?" In play, the question is, "What can I do with this object?" The answer given is, "Anything I wish." Some theorists have suggested that exploration transforms the novel into the familiar, while play transforms the familiar into the novel (Miller, 1974). Others have suggested that play, as an organism-dominated activity, both generates novelty and reduces it (Fein, 1981; Shultz, 1979).

The distinction between exploration and play and the temporal relationship between the two has been examined empirically by Hutt and her colleagues (Hughes, 1978; Hughes & Hutt, 1979; Hutt, 1966,

1967, 1970, 1979) as well as by others. Researchers have found that novel toys or objects first tend to elicit, both in infants and preschoolers, exploration (Hutt, 1979; Ross, Rheingold, & Eckerman, 1972; Scholtz & Ellis, 1975). Over time exploration decreases while the amount of time spent playing with the toy increases (Hutt, 1966). Thus, play is thought to occur once novelty effects wear off.

It is noteworthy that children are more resistant to interruption and that they have a less variable heartbeat during exploration than during play (Hughes & Hutt, 1979). Moreover, children's behaviors are more stereotypic and less flexible and relaxed during exploration than during play (Hughes, 1978). Hutt (1967) also discovered that the amount of time spent exploring a novel object is constant regardless of the temporal conditions of presentation (i.e., contiguous versus temporally spaced trials), while play is more susceptible to temporal differences in presentation. Hutt (1979) thus suggested that exploration is solely a function of the novelty and complexity of the object and the cognitive organization of the individual, while play is influenced more by subjective states. In addition, Hutt (1979) noted informally that, if a child failed to discover some of the particular properties of the toy in exploration, she or he would not likely discover these properties in play. Thus, Hutt concluded that play may actually preclude learning about the specific properties of an object, a point we return to in our discussion of the effects of play on development.

Although Hutt's work concerning exploration and play and the effects of novel stimulation are intriguing, it has several important limitations. First, in the early studies, reliability data for distinguishing exploration from play were not reported. Second, Hutt's studies were carried out in solitary situations within unfamiliar laboratory settings with unfamiliar adults directing the children to the "playroom." These less than naturalistic factors may have affected the results. Analysis of play and exploration in familiar and unfamiliar settings, with friends and strangers, alone and with others, would provide us with a more comprehensive understanding of the differences and relationships between play and exploration. For example, Hutt's original study might be inverted. Suppose children were observed playing in a nursery school or playroom with familiar toys and peers. Suppose that a novel object, or even new toys, were then introduced. This paradigm would permit an analysis of changes in behavior that occur when novel objects are added to an established play environment. Perhaps, more important, the paradigm would allow an analysis of how novel or new objects become incorporated into established behavioral repertoires. Indeed, in the analysis of exploration in relation to play, the difference between an object that is informationally novel and one that is simply new might have special interest.

Object or Materials Influences

Given that children are familiar with the set of materials available to them, it has been found that some objects are more likely to "pull for" some forms of play than others. For example, in an early observational study Van Alstyne (1932) revealed that by 4½ years, children tended to use blocks, clay, scissors, crayons, and colored cubes in constructive fashions while 3½-year-olds were less likely to do so. In a similar vein, Tizard, Philps, and Plewis (1976a) reported that the provision of creative activities such as collage, finger painting, and other art construction activities was negatively correlated with the amount of pretense play observed among the children. Presumably these materials better lent themselves to other play forms.

In a series of studies designed specifically to examine how particular preschool materials and activities "pull for" predictable play outcomes, children have been observed at free play in a number of preschool settings (Rubin, 1977a, 1977b; Rubin & Seibel, 1981; Shure, 1963; Vandenberg, 1981a). Briefly, it has been found that use of play-dough, plasticine, clay, and sand and water is most often associated with nonsocial (solitary and parallel) and functional (sensorimotor) play (Rubin, 1977a, 1977b). As with Van Alstyne, and perhaps as an explanation for the above mentioned findings by Tizard et al. (1976a), the use of art construction materials (paints, crayons, scissors) appears most likely to be accompanied by nonsocial but constructive play (Rubin, 1977a, 1977b; Shure, 1963). Those materials that best predict social pretense include dress-up materials and cars and vehicles.

In a longitudinal report, Rubin and Seibel (1981) replicated and extended the above findings. Their results further indicated that the forms of play associated with given classroom materials did not change, for the most part, over a 3-month period. Only the type of large-block play changed—the incidence of constructive play increased and functional play decreased over time. Moreover, it was discovered that, when children interacted with each other in the block corner, the play was most likely to be of a pretense nature. However, when alone in the block corner, the behavior was predominately constructive. The authors concluded that the degrees of freedom associated with "free play" are limited to a large extent by the materials set out for the children by their teachers. As such, educators might well set social or cognitive play curricular goals that are reached under the planned guise of a school opting for freedom of choice.

One of the major difficulties with these studies is that all were based on play situations in which the children were free to choose their own activities. In light of this, the effects of individual play preferences may have been confounded with the effects of the materials (Krasnor & Pepler, 1980). For example, the relatively high incidence of social pretense with dress-up materials reported by Rubin and his colleagues may better have reflected the characteristic behaviors of the children who selected the materials, thereby representing a finding in keeping with an explanation based on individual differences rather than an explanation based on the effects of materials. What appears to be called for is research in which there is controlled manipulation of the available set of materials (Krasnor & Pepler, 1980).

To this end, researchers recently have explored experimentally the effects of "toys" on children's play behaviors. Pepler (1979) for example, presented 3- and 4-year-olds with puzzle-type wooden materials (e.g., animals or vehicles) that could be fit into form board inserts or could be played with on their own. The children were presented with the materials in one of two ways. For one group of children the materials were presented with their accompanying form boards. The activity that followed could best be described as related to and including constructive play. That is, most children attempted to solve the puzzle. A second group of children received the materials minus the corresponding form boards. The activity that followed included not only construction, but also symbolic (i.e., replica) or dramatic play.

In another recent investigation, Bjorklund (1979) varied the quality of toys to examine their effects on play behaviors. Toys fell within three categories: (1) responsive toys designed to emit auditory or visual responses with manipulation (e.g., a squeak toy); (2) organizational toys designed for the orderly arrangement of related parts (e.g., a set of stacking rings on a stick); and (3) symbolic (i.e., replica) toys designed to be used in make-believe play. Equal numbers of toys within each category were given to children in each of three age groups, 12, 16, and 20 months. Bjorklund reported that children played longer and performed more relational acts with the organizational toys. Such acts were comprised of bringing into association two or more related objects (e.g., placing the rings of a stack ring toy on the stick). Symbolic acts were rare occurrences and were distributed equally across all three types of toys. This low occurrence of symbolic play might well be expected given the young ages of the children studied. Nonetheless, the study does represent further support for the notion that children's play behavior is influenced by the materials available to them.

In a study concerned specifically with imaginative play, Pulaski (1973) compared the influence of highly versus moderately structured materials on the play of kindergarten, first-, and second-grade children. The highly structured set consisted of costumes designating specific roles, toys, realistic play buildings, and realistic dolls. The moderately structured set contained bolts of fabric, blocks and cartons, and rag dolls. Pulaski found that play with the highly structured materials adhered to the content suggested by the materials, whereas play with the moderately structured set was more varied and inventive.

More recently, Fields (as reported in Fein, 1981; in press) presented preschoolers with two large play boxes that could be entered by the children. The boxes were identical in size, coloring, shape, and number and type of openings. The boxes differed in that one was painted to resemble a car, whereas the other was decorated in an abstract pattern. Fields found that more pretense occurred with the "car" box. As would be expected, much of the play associated with the car box took on a transportation theme. When such themes were excluded from the data base, the greater number of pretense elements became associated with the abstract patterned box. Nevertheless, Fields' findings concerning realistic versus abstract materials do not agree with those of Pulaski (1973). Fein (1981) speculates that the differences may have been a function of social class and age. Pulaski's children were older and came from middle-class backgrounds. Fields' children were disadvantaged preschoolers who may have better profited from the existence of realistic anchors for their pretense play.

Not only does the quality of available material appear to influence children's play, but so too does the quantity of the available set of materials. There is some evidence to suggest that social interaction is more likely to occur when there are few, if any, toys in the play setting (Bjorklund, 1979; Eckerman & Whatley, 1977). Pretense in young toddlers, however, would appear to be aided by the presence of realistic toys. Perhaps sociodramatic endeavors most likely would result when small numbers of large symbolic toys (e.g., a large toy bus complete

with steering wheel and passenger seats) are made available. Social constructive play may best be "pulled for" when limited numbers of materials are available to the children and when the activity is organized by an adult to avoid object conflicts (as in mural painting or in group construction of cardboard fire engines, buses, etc.). For older, elementary school children, the lack of toys in the environment may well "pull for" games-with-rules (Tizard, 1977).

Play Space Density

Related to the issue of numbers of materials made available to children is the question of the influence of social and material density on play. McGrew (1972) found that a reduction of play space while holding group size constant resulted in a decrease in running and an increase in physical contact. Increased social density also has been found to increase the incidence of both imaginative play and onlooker behavior (Peck & Goldman, 1978). Perhaps the increased density pulls not only for social contact, but also for a sharing of themes and dramatic interaction. The increase in onlooker behavior reported by Peck and Goldman may have been a function of the interest in nonparticipant observation of the ongoing dramatic plays by the less socially oriented children (Phyfe-Perkins, 1980).

Rough-and-tumble play also appears to be influenced by spatial density. Smith and Connolly (1976) have found that as the square footage available per preschooler in a play space decreased from 75 to 50 to 25, the incidence of rough-and-tumble play likewise decreased. In short, while studies of play space density are relatively rare in the literature, it would appear as if this variable is an important influence on play behavior. Certainly, further research that deals specifically with the influences of density on different forms of play is merited.

Indoor Versus Outdoor Play Space Influences

A fourth ecological influence on children's play is location. When given freedom of choice, older preschoolers spend relatively more time outdoors than do younger preschoolers (Sanders & Harper, 1976). Moreover, outdoor play is more likely to take on a pretense character for older preschoolers (Sanders & Harper, 1976).

The quality of outdoor play space also influences behavior. Campbell and Frost (1978) observed 7-year-olds on two types of playgrounds: a creative playground that had extensive varieties of mobile equipment and a traditional playground that had fixed, conventional equipment (e.g., swings, seesaws). The authors found that functional play was most likely to occur on the traditional playground. Imaginative play was observed more often on the creative playground. Constructive play was a rare occurrence on both playgrounds, thus speaking to the issue raised earlier regarding the common finding that this form of play is the most often occurring behavior found during *indoor* preschool and kindergarten free play. With changes in the available set of materials and in venue (outdoors vs. indoors), constructive play becomes but a minor character.

Cultural and Social Class Influences

Several psychologists have suggested that children's play varies across cultures and socioeconomic status (SES) groups. Studies of cultural differences in play stem from the assumption that play serves as an enculturative mechanism (see Schwartzman, 1976a, b, 1978, for critical reviews of the anthropological work concerning cultural differences in children's games and play). That is, through play children learn societal roles, rules, and values.

Closely related to the issue of cross-cultural differences in play is the belief that within given countries particular subgroups of the population produce differing forms of play. For example, it has been assumed that the play of children from lower SES backgrounds is less complex and sophisticated than that of children from more affluent homes. In the nineteenth century, Schiller (1954) noted that only after the bare necessities of life were taken care of could there be time for play. Since the "working classes" spent most, if not all, of their time satisfying their primary needs, there was little opportunity for play. Thus, to Schiller, play was seen as a prerogative of the more well-to-do in society. Schiller further noted that the purpose of play was to establish a sense of aesthetic appreciation. Thus, he concluded that only when humankind was not concerned with survival in the real world could it develop concerns for beauty and the symbolic.

In actuality, all four classical theories of play had an immediate, practical impact on educators and sociologists at the turn of the century (Bowen & Mitchell, 1924; Lee, 1915). According to Sutton-Smith (1980), the exigencies of the Industrial Revolution and the large-scale immigration to major cities in the Western world led to a need for the organization of children's activities. Organization was thought necessary both to educate and to keep impoverished, immigrant children out of mischief and off the streets. The prevailing view of impoverished children was that they simply did not play because of restrictive conditions and the lack of adequate space in poor and crowded urban communities (Gulick, 1898; Hetzer, 1929).

Drawing on the classical theories, those involved in the early recreation movement established formal play organizations to allow immigrant or impoverished children to profit from their play experiences. The prevailing view was that play experiences led to the development of problem-solving skills and aesthetic appreciation. Moreover, play allowed children to work through their primitive atavisms. Led by Joseph Lee and Luther Gulick, the organization of children's activities on special play spaces was advocated. Early playground enthusiasts proposed that such play spaces were ideal to organize activities and to indoctrinate young "vagrants" to the Protestant ethic deemed normative for the Western way of life. In short, the playground movement was initiated by those who believed that impoverished children did not play and thus their lot could be immeasurably improved through structured, play-oriented activities. The movement continues in intent but in a different fashion today in the work of those who advance *pretense* rather than physical activities for lower SES youngsters to help alleviate or to prevent social and cognitive deficits (Smilansky, 1968).

The impetus for designing compensatory curricula to teach lower SES children to play in a pretense fashion rests, of course, on the premise that there are, indeed, SES differences in children's play. Feitelson and Ross (1973) suggested that the emergence of pretense or thematic play depends in large part on the availability of (1) play props in unrestrictive familial conditions and (2) an ample amount of space in which to use the props without interference. These authors also noted that under certain environmental conditions (i.e., poverty) pretense play would emerge only to a limited extent.

The most often cited test of the position that children from lower SES backgrounds exhibit less fantasy play than their higher SES counterparts was conducted by Smilansky (1968). In a study of 36 classes of 3- to 6-year-olds, Smilansky found that Israeli children of North African and Middle-Eastern parents who lived in lower SES neighborhoods played in a sociodramatic fashion far less frequently than did their middle-class age-mates born of European parents. The middle-class group also revealed a greater diversity and variety of fantasy roles.

Similar findings concerning SES differences have been reported for kindergarten children residing in the United States (Griffing, 1980; Rosen, 1974) and in Great Britain (Smith & Dodsworth,

1978). For example, Griffing reported that verbal expression of make-believe was a far more frequent occurrence among black, middle-class kindergartners than among their black, lower-class counterparts. Smith and Dodsworth found that the fantasy play of middle-class children was more ideational and was more likely to consist of complex object transformations.

One of the major problems with all of these studies was that the children were observed in homogeneous SES classroom settings. As a result, the differences in imaginative play may have been the product of schools that offered different curricula or that had different materials available to the children. To rule this out, a number of researchers have observed lower- and middle-class preschoolers in the same preschool settings, and they have reported a higher incidence of sociodramatic play in the middle-class children (Fein & Stork, in press; Rubin et al., 1976). However, these differences are modest (Fein & Stork, in press) or only marginally significant (Rubin et al., 1976).

It should be pointed out, however, that the Smilansky (1968) position—that sociodramatic play will not develop in lower SES groups unless they are adult tutored—was forcefully challenged by Eifermann (1971). In another large-scale study of Israeli youngsters, Eifermann reported that for children ranging in age from 6 to 8 years sociodramatic activities were found more often in the lower rather than in the upper SES groups. Eifermann concluded that Smilansky's data reflected a lag rather than a deficit vis-à-vis the development of sociodramatic play. However, in the Fein and Stork (in press) study, social class differences did not appear in aspects of play that showed developmental changes between 3 and 5 years.

More recent studies have considered forms of play other than that of the sociodramatic ilk. For example, Rubin et al. (1976) reported that lower SES Canadian preschoolers were more likely to engage in solitary and parallel functional play and in less constructive play than their middle-class agemates. Interestingly, the total frequency of solitary plus parallel plus group *dramatic* play did not differ between the two groups. However, the middle-class children were more likely to produce group dramatic play than their counterparts. Tizard, Philps, and Plewis (1976b), in a study of 3- and 4-year-old British children, found that the middle-class group showed a higher frequency of symbolic play with materials and a lower frequency of partial use (functional play?) with materials than did the lower-class group.

Taken together, the data suggest that preschoolers and kindergarten age children from lower SES backgrounds play in a cognitively less mature fashion than do children from middle-class backgrounds. Although these studies have been limited to preschool classrooms, and little is known about the play of children in varied settings, psychologists who believe that pretense behaviors play a causal role in development have suggested that children from lower-class homes should be tutored in such activities. The extant training literature will be reviewed in a later section.

At this point, however, it is necessary to ask why the common findings of SES differences in play do occur. Feitelson and Ross (1973) suggest that pretense will not develop unless the home provides the necessary conditions—primarily the adequate access to materials and space. However, it is essential to note that all of the studies cited here have taken place in classroom settings or near schools. Researchers have not, for the most part, investigated the play of different SES groups in the familiar surroundings of their neighborhoods or homes (Schwartzman, 1979). We simply do not know what the play profiles of children would look like if we observed them on these more familiar grounds.

Given this perspective, the following scenario may explain the in-school play differences described above. Perhaps the children from lower SES homes are encountering the classroom materials for the first time. As a result, they may sequence their play as most children do in unfamiliar settings. First, the lower-class preschoolers may look around the environment (onlooker behavior is more frequent among these children than among middle-class groups; Rubin et al., 1976). Then, they may choose particular objects to explore (Hutt, 1970) and manipulate while alone or while surrounded by other like-playing youngsters (solitary and parallel functional play is reported as occurring more often in lower-class than middle-class SES preschoolers; Rubin et al., 1976). The middle-class children, being familiar with the materials do not need to engage in specific exploration (Hutt, 1970) and they may proceed directly to use the materials in nonliteral fashions. Moreover, since the materials are familiar, they may be less attractive to the children, thereby providing a motivational base for interacting with the other children rather than with the objects. In short, rather than being a play "deficit," reported SES differences in sociodramatic activities may be the result of unfamiliarity with the classroom materials.

An alternative scenario may be that children from lower SES backgrounds experience greater general anxiety than their middle-class age-mates when introduced to the novel preschool or kindergarten environment. Such anxiety is perpetrated not only by the unfamiliar materials but also by the presence of adult authority figures whose behaviors may be more "unfamiliar" to the lower SES children (Schwartzman, 1979). This greater "unfamiliarity" may result from differences in language used to communicate, differences in race, and so forth. Or, simply, it may be that lower-class children may not have experienced play opportunities in the presence of adult authority figures. In any case, the novel classroom paired with the unfamiliar adult may evoke inhibitory and perhaps regressive behaviors on the part of the lower SES children.

For all that has been written about SES differences, it is important to realize that the play of children varies considerably according to the place of observation (indoors versus outdoors) and the classroom structure (Huston-Stein, Friedrich-Cofer, & Susman, 1977; Tizard et al., 1976b). Given findings of considerable within SES groups variance dependent on ecological factors, and given a lack of control for intelligence in these studies, one is left with the unanswered question of whether SES differences exist at all in children's play. Thus, two courses for further research suggest themselves. First, if one can control the preschool or kindergarten experience and the exposure to classroom materials, another classroom study of SES differences may be merited. Second, observations of children in their natural habitats or in varying environments or curricula may be worthwhile carrying out.

In summary, studies of SES-related play differences are confounded, for the most part by variables such as cultural differences (Smilansky, 1968) or familial factors. Concerning the familial influences, Griffing (1980) has reported that, in a study in which children from different SES backgrounds were asked to "play mommies and daddies," 83% of the poor children came from single-parent families! Thus, it would appear that a clearer picture of possible SES differences in children's play will result when researchers provide adequate methodological controls for (1) cultural background, (2) familial background, (3) intelligence, (4) familiarity with school materials, (5) previous school experience, and (6) children's preferences for some settings over others.

Media and Curriculum Influences

In recent years researchers have begun to consider the possible effects of television viewing on the play of children. It has been suggested by some that a primary function of television is its contribution to fantasy behavior (Schramm, Lyle, & Parker, 1961). Others have noted that the result of television viewing is clearly dependent on program content (Salomon, 1977) and that some programs are "better for children" than others. Perhaps the most prolific contributors to the literature on television influences vis-à-vis play are D. G. Singer and J. L. Singer (1976, 1979; Tower, Singer, Singer, & Biggs, 1979). Given their beliefs that fantasy or pretense play is a major causal force in child development, the Singers have centered specifically on this particular ludic activity in their research. Their work indicates that children who watch a great deal of television play less imaginatively than their counterparts who watch less television (Singer & Singer, 1979). Sherrod and Singer (1977) explain these findings by suggesting that television interferes with the development of image manipulation processes. On the other hand, this medium may promote a more general attitude of compliance and passivity (Fein, in press-a).

Experimental studies in which the quality of television program viewing has been manipulated report that imaginary play can be affected differentially by varying content. For example, D. G. Singer and J. L. Singer (1976) exposed preschoolers to one of four conditions: (1) a tutorial or modeling condition in which an adult taught the youngsters make-believe games; (2) a television exposure to "Mr. Rogers' Neighborhood" with an adult mediator who focused the children on particular aspects of the program; (3) simple exposure to "Mr. Rogers' Neighborhood"; and (4) a no-treatment control condition. Pretest assessments and observations of children's imagination and imaginary play were contrasted with like posttest assessments. The results indicated that significant increases in imaginary activity were associated most highly with the adult tutorial condition. Less significant improvements were reported for the television plus adult catalyst condition, while nonsignificant pretest versus posttest differences were found for the remaining two conditions.

In a more recent study, Tower et al. (1979) found that children who initially were rated low in imagination at the outset of their experiment made significant gains in imaginative behaviors following a two-week exposure to either "Mr. Rogers' Neighborhood" or "Sesame Street" programs. The data are tempered by the additional finding that neutral television programming similarly increased the level of imaginative play in the preschoolers originally rated as low in imagination! Although the data indicate that the viewing of "Mr. Rogers' Neighborhood" best promoted the growth of imaginary play, follow-up multiple comparisons among the three treatment groups were not reported. Moreover, the "neutral" condition actually may have served a treatment rather than a control function. Given that the children were exposed to health and nature films, it may have been that these themes were later adopted in the preschoolers' play. A more appropriate control condition would simply have been nonexposure to television.

Given the Singers' experimental work which indicates that pretense activities may best be promoted via direct adult tuition or modeling, it is noteworthy that educational researchers have recently begun to consider the effects of particular curricula (as prepared or structured by an adult) on the quality of children's play. The results of these studies, however, are mixed.

Tizard et al. (1976b) examined the free play of children 3 to 5 years old who attended preschools oriented either toward structured language enrichment or health care. They found *less* symbolic play and more functional (or "appropriate") play in the school with the health care orientation than in the school with structured language enrichment. More recently, Johnson et al. (1980) observed the free play of preschoolers attending either a "formal," content-oriented or a "discovery," process-oriented center. One significant distinguishing feature was the presence of more teacher direction in the formal curriculum than in the discovery program. Children in the discovery center produced more functional play and less constructive play than their counterparts. Moreover, a greater number of pretense transformations was evinced by those who attended the "formal" school. The results of the Tizard et al. and the Johnson et al. studies indicate that greater classroom structure and teacher direction may encourage symbolic play and discourage or inhibit sensorimotor play.

However, in a recent report, Huston-Stein et al. (1977) indicated that classroom structure, as defined by the degree to which the program was prepared and directed by an adult, *negatively* related to the incidence of preschool pretense play. Finally, Bryant and Rubin (as cited in Rubin & Seibel, 1981) found that the play of preschoolers who attended a Montessori school was most often nonsocial and constructive. The children's play was rarely sociodramatic or dramatic in nature. The findings thus appear to support the ideological tenets of the Montessori program. These data were contrasted with the finding that children enrolled in a social problem-solving curriculum like that of Spivack and Shure's (1974) were more likely to engage in social-constructive, sociodramatic, and functional play than their Montessori counterparts. It is likely that both the Montessori "prepared environment" materials and the tutorial effects of role play in the Spivack and Shure curriculum "pulled for" the findings reported.

These studies appear to pose more questions than they answer. For example, Tizard et al. (1976b) and Johnson et al. (1980) allude to a greater incidence of dramatic play in adult-structured preschool environments, whereas Huston-Stein et al. (1977) suggest the reverse. Thus, one is left in a state of confusion concerning the impact of curriculum structure on play. As in earlier preschool research (see Clarke-Stewart & Fein, *vol. II, chap. 11*), a more formative, as opposed to summative, analytic methodology may be called for. For example, what *particular* aspects of given curricula are responsible for the behaviors displayed in their respective settings? The work reviewed earlier concerning the ecological determinants of play appears to be a step in the right direction. For example, Montessori-type schools make use of puzzle-type and constructive materials. Moreover, such schools draw on the Montessori notion that pretense activities encourage pathology; thus, materials that elicit pretense are not available for the children. These particular materials and other environmental factors (e.g., the use of floor mats on which children can "work" individually with their materials) clearly pull for particular forms of nonfantasy, nonsocial, but constructive play forms.

Given the equivocal findings for the adult-structured versus the less structured settings, it appears important to ask researchers who conduct such summative curriculum comparisons to consider the sorts of materials or activities made available during free play, the population density of respective classes, and the socioeconomic and sex mix of the students.

INDIVIDUAL DIFFERENCES IN CHILDREN'S PLAY

Are there individual differences in children's play? Do all same-age or same-stage children display characteristic play patterns? Over the years researchers have generated considerable information concerning individual differences in children's play. However, the focus of these endeavors has generally been on areas other than play. Thus, the play phenomenon often has been of marginal interest to researchers. The following discussion of individual differences is limited to those studies in which the primary focus was play.

Sex Differences

It should not be surprising that there are considerable and pervasive sex differences in various aspects of children's play. In general, the findings reflect traditional stereotypes concerning male-female differences. For example, almost all reports of sex differences in the level of physical activity in children's play indicate that boys are more vigorous and more physically active in their indoor and outdoor play than girls (DiPietro, 1981; Goldberg & Lewis, 1969; Halverson & Waldrop, 1973; Pederson & Bell, 1970; Pulaski, 1970, 1973; Smith & Daglish, 1977; Tauber, 1979). There is some evidence to suggest that sex differences emerge as early as the second year of life (Goldberg & Lewis, 1969; Smith & Daglish, 1977), although the data in this regard appear mixed (cf. Jacklin, Maccoby, & Dick, 1973; McCall, 1974).

These differences in activity level may well reflect the types of play young children engage in. For example, several writers have reported that during free-play periods in preschool and kindergarten settings, females are more likely to exhibit sedentary, constructive behaviors than males (Clark, Wyon, & Richards, 1969; Moore, Evertson, & Brophy, 1974; Rubin, 1977a; Rubin et al., 1976, 1978). Males, on the other hand, have been reported to display more gross motor and functional play (Freedman, 1971; Rubin et al., 1976).

Data concerning sex differences in the overall level of pretense play are equivocal. Fein and Robertson (1975) have reported differences favoring 2-year-old girls. Singer (1973) and Rubin et al. (1976) have reported differences in pretense activities favoring preschool boys. These discrepant findings may be a function of the availability of sex-typed materials or other ecological factors such as whether the children were observed indoors or outdoors (Enslein, 1979; Harper & Sanders, 1975).

Although the data concerning quantitative differences in pretense play are unclear, it does appear as if the quality of such activity varies with sex. Males appear more likely to enact fictional, superhero roles, while females are more likely to portray familial characters (Connolly, 1980; Cramer & Hogan, 1975; McLoyd, 1980; Pulaski, 1973). These data, derived from observations of children in preschool and kindergarten, are supported by the self-reported play interests of elementary school age children. Girls tend to list a preference for playing "house" and "school," whereas boys list "cowboys" and "soldiers" (Rosenberg & Sutton-Smith, 1959; Sutton-Smith, Rosenberg, & Morgan, 1963).

Given these reported differences in the themes of pretense play, it is not surprising to find that researchers have indicated a greater frequency of rough-and-tumble play in boys than girls (Aldis, 1975; Blurton-Jones, 1967; Brindley, Clarke, Hutt, Robinson, & Wethli, 1973; DiPietro, 1981; McGrew, 1972; Neill, 1976; Smith & Connolly, 1972). It would appear more likely that superhero, fictional themes would elicit more rough-and-tumble play than familial or scholastic themes (Pulaski, 1973; Tauber, 1979; Tizard et al., 1976).

Rough-and-tumble play is a cross-cultural phenomenon that may, at times, be independent of role-play activities. In this regard, Whiting and Edwards (1973), pooling their data from six cultures, found that boys between 3 and 11 years engaged in more rough-and-tumble play than girls. However, inspection of the results for each culture separately revealed that there were no significant sex differences in any one of the six cultures. In fact, in one culture, girls displayed more rough-and-tumble play than boys. Further evidence of the effects of cultural factors is provided by Konner's (1972) and Blurton-Jones and Konner's (1973) examination of the play of !Kung Bushmen. Sex differences were found in the rough-and-tumble play of the children in this culture, but the frequency of this type of play and the magnitude of the difference between the sexes was considerably less than that found in Western children.

Given the above data, one obvious question to ask is: "What factors contribute to sex differences in children's play?" Socialization and factors of toy choice appear to be significant explanatory variables. As previously mentioned, fathers of boys tend to play more physical, "lifting" games with their infants than do fathers of girls (Power & Parke, 1980). Such physical rough-housing in infancy may be a precursor to the more active, rough-and-tumble play typically found in boys. Concerning toy choice, parents of infants and young children provide their sons with more vehicles, construction materials, and sports equipment and with fewer dolls, doll houses, and domestic items than their daughters (Rheingold & Cook, 1975). Fein, Johnson, Kosson, Stork, and Wasserman (1975) noted that, prior to the age of 2 years, parents purchased sex-appropriate toys for their toddlers, although they were more likely to give "masculine" toys to girls than "feminine" toys to boys.

Children's toy preferences mirror these parental

purchasing patterns. There is considerable convergence across a wide array of studies that indicates that toddler and preschool boys prefer to play with vehicles, blocks, and construction materials, while girls prefer dolls and domestic materials in their play (Benjamin, 1932; Eisenberg, Murray, & Hite, 1981; Fagot, 1974; Farrell, 1957; Fein et al., 1975; Honzik, 1951; Sutton-Smith, 1979b, 1979c; Tauber, 1979; Tizard et al., 1976a). These differences apparently reflect strong cultural currents, since they have been noted as long ago as 1932 (Benjamin, 1932) and as recently as 1982 (Eisenberg et al., 1982). Ontogenetically, sex differences in children's toy preferences emerge quite early; in fact, a number of researchers have detected differences before 2 years of age (Fagot, 1974; Fein et al., 1975; Jacklin, Maccoby, & Dick, 1973; Smith & Daglish, 1977).

Not only are there sex differences in the types of toys preferred, but there are also differences in the breadth of preferences. Researchers consistently have found that girls' toy preferences are broader in scope and that they are more likely to play with masculine toys than boys are to play with feminine toys (Eisenberg et al., 1982; Fagot & Littman, 1975; Fling & Manosevitz, 1972; Sutton-Smith, 1979b; Tauber, 1979). Hartup, Moore, and Sager (1963) have also examined children's *avoidance* of sex-inappropriate toys. They found that older, grade-school boys avoid playing with feminine toys longer than preschool boys, but that there was no significant difference in avoidance of masculine toys for girls at these two ages. Analyses of the total time the children spent playing with sex-inappropriate toys indicated that the older children spent significantly less time playing with the sex-inappropriate toys than the younger children.

It is not surprising to find that girls do play differently from boys given the toy purchase and preference data as well as the research on ecological influences. The toys parents (and grandparents) buy for boys tend to "pull for" gross motor, functional activities (balls, vehicles) and for fictional character role enactments (laser guns, light sabers). The toys purchased for girls tend to elicit familial role enactments (dolls, carriages) and school-related pretense and constructive play themes (art construction materials). The above data are less interesting because of their match with cultural stereotypes than recent work that indicates sex differences in the degree to which children will demonstrate sex role flexibility. In children younger than 2 years of age, girls are more likely than boys to shift to opposite-sex toys when these have been modeled by adults (Fein et al.,

1975). Girls are more likely to engage in adventure (fictional) pretense themes than boys are to engage in domestic (familial) themes (Singer & Singer, 1980). Moreover, boys' imaginary playmates are usually male while, for girls, imaginary companions are as likely to be male as female (Manosevitz, Prentice, & Wilson, 1973).

Of further contemporary interest is the evidence that over the years (1926–1960) girls have expressed an increasing preference for boys' play activities (Rosenberg & Sutton-Smith, 1960). This preference may indicate changing attitudes toward females. The attitude changes may be accompanied by an increasing emphasis on the acquisition and utilization of information that requires cognitive rather than physical skills. Sutton-Smith (1979b), for example, has noted that boys' play has become less boisterous over the years and that toy manufacturers are emphasizing the use of materials designed to promote verbal, symbolic growth while indoors. Thus, although girls' play has become slightly more "masculine" than it was in the past, children's activities, in general, have moved closer to the types of play traditionally considered to be "feminine."

Playfulness and Imaginativeness as Individual Difference Variables

In relatively recent years psychologists have posited that *playfulness* may constitute a personality trait in children. Lieberman (1965), employing teacher ratings of kindergarten children's classroom behaviors found a high correlation between scores of physical, social, and cognitive spontaneity, manifest joy, and sense of humor. Lieberman concluded that these attributes are components of a playfulness factor in children. However, since these were essentially the only attributes rated by the teachers, it is conceivable that the results reflected a halo effect rather than a unique personality trait.

More recently, Lieberman's findings have received support from D. G. Singer and Rummo (1973). These latter investigators employed a teacher rating scale that required the assessment of a large number of behaviors. Subsequent factor analysis yielded three major factors, one of which was labeled "playfulness." The attributes which loaded significantly on this factor were similar to those suggested as definitive of playfulness by Lieberman— that is, imaginativeness, humorous and playful attitudes, emotional expressiveness, novelty-seeking activity, curiosity, openness, and communicativeness.

Both Lieberman (1965) and D. G. Singer and

Rummo (1973) also have investigated the relationship between playfulness and creativity, or divergent thinking. Intuitively, playfulness and creativity are sewn of the same fabric; both involve the creation of novelty from the commonplace within a permissive and relaxed psychological field. Lieberman initially indicated a strong positive relationship between playfulness and creativity. However, when the effects of intelligence were partialed out, the strength of the relationship was diminished severely (J. N. Lieberman, 1977). D. G. Singer and Rummo (1973), however, found a significant relationship only between the two variables for boys and not for girls. Explanations for this finding remain purely speculative.

The existence of a playfulness trait in children has recently been given further support by J. L. Singer and his colleagues (Singer & Singer, 1978; Singer, Singer, & Sherrod, 1980). Singer factor-analyzed behavioral data rather than teacher ratings and found that a playfulness factor could be identified. Children rated highly on this factor were characterized as having positive affect, being physically active, having a high degree of social and imaginative play, and being more verbal than their less playful preschool counterparts. Singer et al. (1980) also recorded the children's behaviors at several points in time, thereby allowing an examination of temporal stability. The playfulness factor was moderately, but significantly, stable over a 1-year period ($r = .29$).

Much of the research on playfulness has focused on young children. One of the few exceptions is the recent research of J. N. Lieberman (1977), who has extended her inquiry to the examination of playfulness in adolescents. Lieberman found that playfulness in adolescents is not as easily identifiable, or as homogeneous a trait, as it is in preschoolers. For the younger children, playfulness is a trait composed of a relatively small number of interrelated attributes. For adolescents, however, playfulness can take many forms, from horse-play and enthusiastic participation in social activities, to the use of hostile wit and taunting pranks directed toward others. Thus, playfulness in adolescents appears to include both positive and negative features.

Research by Cattell (1950; 1979) and others (e.g., Meehl, Lykken, Schofield, & Tellegen, 1971) has indicated that the features that have been found to be associated with playfulness in preschoolers may be distributed across several personality factors in adults. One of the factors is "surgency," which is comprised of attributes similar to the playfulness attributes found in preschoolers: cheerfulness, joyousness, sense of humor, wit, and energetic ac-

tivity. Another factor that incorporates some of the playfulness features is the "siza-affectia" factor (Cattell, 1979). This factor includes the attributes "good-natured," "laughs readily," and "likes to participate with people."

These results, in conjunction with Lieberman's, suggest that playfulness in adolescence and adulthood is not a homogeneous factor. The playfulness factor in preschoolers contains a variety of attributes and, with development, these attributes may be differentiated and integrated in various ways, creating different types of playful individuals. Unfortunately, longitudinal data in this area of development are lacking, and we can conclude only that playfulness in adolescents and adults appears to be a more heterogeneous factor than it is for preschoolers.

Individual differences in the *imaginativeness* of children's play have also been the focus of research. Interview questions and ratings of responses to ink blots have been developed by Singer (1973) to assess children's predispositions for imaginative play. Singer (1973) has used these measures to find that grade-school children with higher imaginative predispositions are less impatient, more creative in their storytelling, and spend more time with their parents.

Unfortunately, Singer's results must be interpreted with caution since the reliabilities of some of the variables are not reported. In addition, Singer's (Singer & Singer, 1978; Singer et al., 1980) most recent findings suggest that the measures of imaginative predisposition may not be consistent across environments for preschoolers. The results indicated that the measures of imaginative predisposition (e.g., interview data concerning imaginative play tendencies and parental reports of number and frequency of imaginary companions) loaded on a factor orthogonal to the factor on which children's fantasy play *behavior* loaded. Observed imaginative play behavior was found to load on the playfulness dimension mentioned earlier, while the measures of imaginative predisposition loaded together on a second factor. The data led Singer and his colleagues to distinguish between overt imaginative play behavior and individual, private forms of fantasy. This distinction may introduce potential interpretive difficulties. As Singer (1973) himself noted, the internalization of fantasy play as thought and imagery probably does not begin before the age of 6, when children begin to develop the cognitive (Piaget, 1970) and linguistic (Vygotsky, 1962) skills that are aspects of the internalization process. Since the study described above involves preschoolers who presumably have not yet begun to internalize images, it is unclear what the measures of imaginative predisposition are tapping. The loading of imaginative predisposition measures on a factor orthogonal to the free-play behavior may reflect a basic response style to adult questioning, as much as a separate dimension of fantasy.

Individual differences in *styles of symbolic play* have been the subject of an intensive, small-scale, longitudinal research project undertaken by researchers at Harvard's Project Zero (Shotwell, Wolf, & Gardner, 1979; Wolf & Gardner, 1978; Wolf & Grollman, 1982). The main focus of this project has been to track the development of children's symbolic abilities in a number of forms, including play. Preliminary results indicate that children proceed through invariant sequences in symbolic development, but do so at different rates, utilizing different styles.

Two types of players have been identified; those whose play is focused primarily on objects (''patterners''), and those whose play is focused primarily on people (''dramatists''). Patterners are children whose symbolic activity involves exploring the configural uses and physical properties of the play materials. These children are interested primarily in the object world and do not readily use play materials within a communicative, social context. Dramatists, on the other hand, use materials as props in the context of social interaction and are not as likely to investigate the physical properties of the materials. These two styles represent different, but equally valid, paths leading toward the development of symbolic skills. Analyses indicate that stylistic differences begin to emerge at about 12 months of age and, over the next year, become more pronounced. In the third year, children begin to utilize both styles of play and, although the children still maintain their preferences for one, they become proficient in using both play styles.

This project is one of the first to attempt to examine the evolution of symbolic abilities minutely within a longitudinal research framework. Because of the small sample size, the authors caution against bold conclusions. Nevertheless, their results provide important insights into uniformities and individual differences in the development of symbolic play. Furthermore, independent validation of the object-person difference in play styles has been provided by Jennings (1975), who found similar individual differences in preschoolers' play. So, although the conclusions drawn from Project Zero's current data must be considered tentative, the emergence of dimensions of individual differences in children's play merits further attention.

Play in Handicapped Children

The research on mental, emotional, and physical handicapped conditions has been influenced by our conceptualization of these conditions. Physical handicaps are seen as being a medical problem, mental retardation is viewed as a psychoeducational handicapping condition, and emotional disorders are seen as psychiatric conditions. Consequently, research on physical handicaps has been largely medical in orientation, research on mental retardation has been primarily directed toward learning methods or has been remedial in nature, and research on emotional handicaps has had an etiological or diagnostic thrust. Only recently has there been a broadening of concern for the psychological needs of the handicapped child.

Mental, emotional, and physical handicaps are not necessarily mutually exclusive. An individual may be multihandicapped, or particular conditions may involve impairments that cut across all of these areas. For example, autistic children frequently are mentally retarded, and it has been surmised that autism may be a result of some form of physical, organic impairment (Ornitz & Ritvo, 1976). This is further complicated by the fact that the nature, and even the existence, of some conditions, such as minimal brain dysfunction and hyperactivity, is the subject of heated debate.

A distinction among mental, emotional, and physical handicaps will be maintained in the following discussion with the realization that there are limitations to this classification scheme. While there is often a swirl of controversy surrounding many of the conditions that will be discussed, these contentious issues will be broached to the extent that they have a bearing on the research on play (see also Quinn & Rubin, in press, for a relevant review).

Mental Retardation

There is a general lack of research on the play of retarded children. Moreover, there has been an inconsistent line of investigation in this area. Topics as diverse as the effects of play therapy, the use of toys in play, mainstreaming, the training of social skills, and the use of play for assessment, all have been examined. This research has two foci: (1) those studies in which the free play of retarded children are examined, and (2) those studies in which interventions centering on play have been attempted.

Most observational studies of retarded children's play have been concerned with interactions with toys. Horne and Philleo (1942) found that nonretarded 7-year-olds preferred open-ended materials such as blocks and drawing materials, which purportedly lend themselves to symbolic activities (imaginative play and artistic endeavors, respectively). Older retarded children with mental ages of 7 years were found to prefer more structured puzzle and peg materials, which lend themselves to concrete construction.

Several investigators have examined how retarded children differ from nonretarded children in their play with toys. Tilton and Ottinger (1964) found that retarded children were less likely to combine toys together in their play than nonretarded children. These findings are echoed by Weiner and Weiner (1974), who found that retarded children with mental ages of 3 and 6 years of age made fewer toy combinations than nonretarded children of similar mental ages. Hulme and Lunzer (1966), however, failed to find differences in the complexity of constructive play in retarded and nonretarded children. The research described above thus suggests that normal and retarded children of similar ages differ in their object play. The reasons for this discrepancy are not immediately apparent. Zigler (1966) has shown that retarded children develop a sense of helplessness and dependency and come to rely on others for structure and guidance. They are not as likely as nonretarded children to take the opportunity to explore their environments actively. Their preference for more structured toys, and their failure to combine various toys in flexible manners, may be a consequence of this more fearful, dependent posture.

Although retarded and nonretarded children differ in some of the specific features of their object play, there is some convergence on the broader parameters of their play. Wing, Gould, Yeates, and Brierly (1977) discovered that a mental age of 20 months and competency in language development were significant prerequisites for the onset of symbolic play with objects by retarded children. The mental age of 20 months nicely coincides with that cited by Piaget (1962) for the development of symbolic thought in nonretarded children.

Another similar finding for the two groups of children was concerned with the effects of object complexity on play and exploration. Switzky, Ludwig, and Haywood (1979) found that both normal and retarded children showed a linear decline in exploration and a linear increase in play with repeated exposure to stimuli of varying complexity. They also found that there was a linear decrease in the time spent playing with objects of increasing complexity. Their results generally substantiate the predictions drawn by Berlyne (1960) and Hutt (1970) vis-à-vis the relationship of play, exploration, and object complexity.

The research comparing retarded and nonretarded children's play is often flawed both in regard to methodology as well as to developmental theory. For example, most of these studies have been limited to small sample sizes that include heterogeneous mixes of exceptional children. Mental retardation often is accompanied by cerebral palsy, language impairment, and epilepsy. Although mental age (MA) is often controlled for, these other factors are not.

Research on toy play also fails to control for sex differences. Given the relatively large body of research that points clearly to sex differences in the toy play of nonretarded children, this oversight is significant. Perhaps more significant is that developmental frameworks are not used for analyzing children's object play. This lack of a developmental perspective clearly is reflected by Weiner and Weiner (1974) who commented that, while they predicted and found differences between retarded and nonretarded children at 3 and 6 years of age (MA), they were surprised to find play differences between the nonretarded children at 3 and 6 years of age.

We believe that the growing body of research on the development of object play in nonretarded children could be applied fruitfully to studies of retarded children. For example, recent research has unearthed a sequence of developmental precursors to symbolic play with objects (e.g., Nicolich, 1977). Ungerer and Sigman (1981) have borrowed from the methodology and data of this research to examine the nature of object play in autistic children. Similar research with retarded children could shed considerable light on the relationship among mental age, retardation, and the development of symbolic representation.

There have been two types of intervention studies concerning the play of retarded children. One procedure has been to introduce children to play therapy in order to ameliorate developmental deficits. Other intervention procedures have been used to shape the "play behaviors" of retarded children. Regarding the former intervention procedures, several studies have reported the effects of group and individual, and directive and nondirective play therapy on the development of retarded children (Morrison & Newcomer, 1975; Newcomer & Morrison, 1974). The outcome measure of "development" often has been the Denver Developmental Screening Test. These studies have indicated that play therapy can affect various aspects of development, although the particular type of play therapy does not seem to matter. The results, however, are flawed by failures to report reliability coefficients for the dependent measure, as well as by a lack of adequate control groups.

Various behavioral techniques have been used to train children to acquire "play behaviors" (Wehman, 1975). These "play behaviors" can more accurately be described as peer interactive social behaviors, which may incidentally include such indexes of play as pretense. The typical intervention strategy has been to provide some form of training, whether it be modeling and reinforcement (Knapczyk & Yoppi, 1975; Morris & Dolker, 1974; Peck, Apolloni, Cooke, & Raver, 1978), or tutored sociodramatic intervention (Strain, 1975), and then to measure the effects of the training by analyzing the children's free play behaviors. However, since play is but an incidental feature of the outcome measures, the results of the studies are difficult to interpret. For example, Strain (1975) placed sociodramatic play and the giving of an object to another into the same behavioral category. As such, there is a loss of developmentally relevant information concerning the effect of training on the complexity of play (sociodramatic play is assuredly a more social, cognitively advanced mode of behavior than is giving objects to others). This example demonstrates the need for researchers to consider developmental issues in their analyses of retarded children's play.

Psychosis

Several factors have conspired to make play a relatively important area of interest for those working with autistic children. The peculiar play of autistic children has been noted by clinicians for some time (Bender, 1956) and has attracted attention because of its potential usefulness in supplementing other clinical procedures for the diagnosis of autism. Many autistic children are also mentally retarded, are frequently mute, and are severely impaired in their capacity to engage in even the most simple forms of social interaction (Rutter, 1974). This makes diagnostic testing nearly impossible. The overlay of mental retardation, coupled with the difficulty of using traditional assessment procedures, has forced clinicians and researchers to use children's play as an aid in diagnosing autism (Freeman & Ritvo, 1978; 1979).

There has been a convergence in opinion among clinicians (Bender, 1956; Jahoda & Goldfarb, 1957) and researchers (Demyer, Mann, Tilton, & Loew, 1967; Tilton & Ottinger, 1964; Weiner, Ottinger, & Tilton, 1969; Wing et al., 1977) on the characteristic features of autistic children's play. Generally, autistic children are thought to play in a stereotyped, manipulative way, frequently spinning or twirling various parts of toys in a repetitive way (Tilton & Ottinger, 1964). The prevailing belief is that autistic children do not use toys in a symbolic manner (Wing et al., 1977) and rarely combine one toy with another (Demyer et al., 1967; Tilton & Ottinger, 1964). They are thought to compulsively repeat manipulative sequences with parts of toys and not to use the toys in a meaningful way. For example, whereas normal and some mentally retarded children might drive a toy truck along the floor, or load blocks into it as cargo, autistic children are more likely to repetitively spin the wheels of the truck with their hands.

It has been hypothesized that autism involves an organically based impairment of symbolic functioning that hampers or impedes the acquisition of language and related symbolic abilities (Rutter, 1974). Many autistic children fail to acquire meaningful language, and those that do have pronounced linguistic idiosyncrasies (Rutter, 1978). Autistic children are also deficient in their ability to produce graphic representations (Demyer et al., 1967) and to pantomime (Curcio & Piserchia, 1978). This frequently cited failure to display symbolic play may be an aspect of a larger symbolic deficit in autistic children.

It should be noted, however, that few researchers have directly examined the relationship between language acquisition and development and the play of autistic children. Ungerer and Sigman (in press) appear to be the only investigators who have attempted to study this relationship from a developmental perspective. Ungerer and Sigman, drawing on data that indicate a relatively stable sequence of developmental precursors to symbolic play in normal children (Fenson et al., 1976; Fenson & Ramsay, 1980; Lowe, 1975; Nicolich, 1977), assessed the developmental sophistication of autistic children's play. They found a close correspondence between the level of play and children's receptive language skills. In addition, they found that autistic children failed to develop the ability to differentiate objects from their own actions on the objects in their play. This skill appears critical for the full emergence of symbolic play and the sophisticated use of symbols (Piaget, 1962). Thus, impairments in symbolic play and its precursors are related closely to linguistic deficits, supporting the hypothesis that autism involves a broadly based deficit in symbolic functioning.

Given the extant body of data on the play of autistic children, it is important that individual differences within this group are not dismissed. Tilton and Ottinger (1964), for example, found that 5 of the 13 autistic children they observed failed to display stereotyped, repetitive play. This suggests that stereotyped play may be an important aspect of the play of some autistic children, but that it is by no means a universal trait associated with autism. Furthermore, Black, Freeman, and Montgomery (1975) have demonstrated the existence of individual differences in the play of autistic children. These findings argue for caution in the exclusive use of play in diagnosing autism.

Much of this research represents an attempt to identify the specific features of play that would enable clinicians to diagnose autism more reliably and to differentiate it from mental retardation. While there is basic agreement on the behaviors that appear to characterize autistic children's play, none of the studies to date have controlled for or matched the mental ages of autistic and mentally retarded children. Since IQ has a significant impact on the symptomology of autism (Bartak & Rutter, 1976) few, if any, conclusions may be drawn about specific play behaviors that differentiate autistic from other children of the same mental age.

While it may be that autistic children with low IQs are difficult to distinguish from mentally retarded children, it is likewise the case that verbally expressive autistic children with high IQs are difficult to distinguish from child schizophrenics. The differentiation between childhood autism and schizophrenia has been a controversial topic (Ornitz & Ritvo, 1976) for a number of years. One of the features that has been said to differentiate the two groups is the fantasy content of the children's thought. Rutter (1972) suggested that children suffering from autism are rigid and concrete in thought and exhibit little fantasy, whereas schizophrenic children exhibit a florid fantasy and delusional system. These two styles may represent different responses to uncertainty regarding reality. For example, if a child is secure in his or her knowledge of what is "real," then playing with the "not-real" should be a source of pleasure. However, when the boundaries of the "real" and "not-real" are unclear, play within these boundaries may assume two forms: either the child will be frightened by the activity and will retreat or regress to ritualistic play, or he or she may be swept into the fantasy of play. Morison and Gardner (1978) recently demonstrated that normal children can make distinctions between fantasy and reality as early as kindergarten age. It would be fruitful to discover when and if autistic and schizophrenic children can make similar distinctions.

The play of autistic and schizophrenic children thus might prove to be a rich area of investigation, having both clinical and theoretical utility. Conceivably, it could yield a method for distinguishing autism from schizophrenia as well as provide a vision of what life is like when sense and nonsense cannot be differentiated.

Although there has been no research on the play of schizophrenic children per se, Nahme-Huang, Singer, Singer, and Wheaton (1977), drawing on the methodologies of Saltz, Dixon, and Johnson (1977), examined the effects of fantasy play training experiences on the cognitive and social functioning of emotionally disturbed children. The researchers were interested in discovering whether a fantasy play training procedure, which enhanced the cognitive and social abilities of disadvantaged preschoolers, would do likewise for a group of disturbed children. Nahme-Huang et al. found few lasting training effects. Their results suggest that such experiences may overstimulate emotionally disturbed children and actually may encourage overt aggression and decrease concentration. The authors noted that fantasy and play training for disturbed children may need to be more structured with a clearly delineated transition period between the play sessions and other classroom activities. Apparently, the adults must provide the reality boundaries that these children are unable to provide for themselves.

In much of the work concerned with emotional disturbance, children often are sampled from inpatient wards and day schools. As such, the exact nature of the emotional disturbance is frequently unknown. Given the possibility that play treatment experiences differentially may affect children with varying disorders, future research would benefit from carefully targeting homogeneous groups. It is a distinct possibility that certain forms of play training or therapy (e.g., fantasy play) may prove more harmful than beneficial for specific groups of emotionally disturbed children.

Physical Handicap

Studies of children with physical disabilities generally are carried out from a medical perspective. The discussion which follows centers on the few physically handicapping conditions that have received some attention in the play literature.

Several researchers have examined the play of children who are delayed or impaired in their *language development* but who are free of other intellectual, emotional, or neurological handicaps. It has been argued that the delay in language acquisition of these children reflects a more basic delay or impairment in the semiotic function described by Piaget (1962), which also should be manifest in the children's symbolic play (Leonard, 1979).

Williams (1980) has addressed this hypothesis by comparing the symbolic play of normal and language-impaired children between 2½ and 5½ years of age. She found that the language-impaired children had a significantly lower frequency of symbolic play than the normal children, leading to the conclusion that language-impaired children may suffer from a broader symbolic deficit. However, such a conclusion is premature. Differences in the *frequency* of symbolic play imply that the language-impaired children had the capacity for symbolic play, but displayed it less often. The differences between the groups may have been the result of a difference in symbolic performance rather than a disparity in symbolic competence. To fully test the original hypothesis, a more detailed assessment of the qualitative features of the children's symbolic play is required. Furthermore, researchers may benefit from differentiating between competence and performance in symbolic play. Lovell, Hoyle, and Siddall (1968) also have compared the symbolic play of normal and language-impaired preschoolers. They used a play scale developed by Lunzer (1959) to assess the symbolic features of play and did not find differences in the symbolic play of the two groups. However, the authors divided the ten children in each group into three subgroups by age and then tested their hypothesis on these subgroups. The very small numbers in these subgroups ($n = 3$ or 4) preclude detecting all but the most robust of differences between the normal and language-impaired groups.

In both of these experiments, children's intelligence was not tested formally. This is a critical oversight. Children with language problems frequently show signs of retardation. Without a formal assessment of intelligence, the results remain ambiguous. Furthermore, as will be discussed in more detail later, there are several important limitations to using only play to assess aspects of children's psychological functioning; play needs to be augmented with other assessment procedures to gain a valid appraisal of the phenomenon under scrutiny. Thus, although the above studies have identified an important area of investigation, methodological difficulties prevent us from drawing definitive conclusions.

A number of writers have commented on the paucity of play in *blind* children (Tait, 1972a, 1973; Wills, 1972). It has been noted that blind preschool and kindergarten children do not seem particularly interested in play, and that their intensity and personal involvement in play appears to be less when compared to children with sight. It also has been suggested that they are likely to seek tactile stimulation in their play by using objects in a repetitive, manipulative manner. Singer and Streiner (1966) offer some substantiation for these speculations. They found that fantasy play in blind, 8- to 12-year-old children tends to be more concrete and tends to lack the richness, variety, and flexibility of sighted children's play. Tait (1972b) also has found that blind children aged 4 to 9 years engage in more manipulative and less dramatic play than sighted age-mates. However, Tait's data do not support the notion of a pervasive inability to play, which some have attributed to blind children. Although Tait found detectable differences between the proportion of blind and sighted children who engaged in symbolic play, nearly two-thirds of the blind children did engage in some form of dramatic symbolic play. From our perspective, it would be productive for researchers to compare the play of blind and deaf children. This would allow psychologists to determine the effects of visual imagery and verbal communication on the development of play. Unfortunately, there have been few, if any, attempts to examine the play of deaf children.

Hyperactivity and minimal brain dysfunction (MBD) often are used synonomously to denote a disorder that allegedly has a neurological base. Therefore, this syndrome is included in the discussion of physically handicapping conditions. However, this disorder is unlike most other physical handicaps, in that its physical characteristics are, by definition, undetectable (e.g., minimal). Whether the condition actually exists is currently a contentious issue (Schmitt, 1975).

The arguments supporting the existence of MBD-hyperactivity have not been enhanced by the methods used to diagnose this disorder. Usually, assessment of MBD-hyperactivity consists of a short, informal play session in a psychiatrist's office, which is sometimes augmented by reports from teachers and parents (Rapoport, Abramson, Alexander, & Lott, 1971; Silvern, 1974). The methodological shortcomings of this procedure are numerous and obvious. Nevertheless, there has been no systematic attempt to develop a formalized play procedure to aid in the diagnosis of this disorder.

Several investigators, however, have examined the play of MBD-hyperactive and neurologically impaired children. Rapoport et al. (1971) compared the level of gross motor activity in the play of MBD-hyperactive children with parental and teacher reports of the child's activity level. Generally, significant relationships were not found. Kalverboer (1977) has used play observations to assess the level of organization of attention and behavior in children with minor neurological impairment. He noted the length of time the children spent in each particular play activity and also assessed the structure of children's play. His categories were roughly similar to those used by Ungerer and Sigman (1981) and included manipulative, relational functional, and symbolic play. Surprisingly, he found that boys with greater measured neurological impairment actually displayed a higher level of organization in their play than boys less impaired. These results raise questions about the measurement of MBD-hyperactivity as well as about the neurological instruments used to detect minor impairment. The failure to find a correspondence between the organization of play activity and other measures of MBD-hyperactivity also undermines the validity of using play in either a structured or informal way to assess potential minor neurological impairment.

Physically handicapping conditions not only deprive the individual of some particular form of sensory information or stimulation, but they also place children into a greater dependency relationship with their parents, peers, and other people. Although blind, deaf, language-impaired, and cerebral palsied children suffer from very different conditions, they share a common helplessness in negotiating the obstacles and challenges of their worlds. The dependency that results from this illness-imposed helplessness is particularly poignant in the formative years of infancy and childhood. Mogford (1977) notes that the condition places a great demand on parents to provide the special types of stimulating experiences and encouragements that are necessary to foster play in handicapped children. The present lack of appropriate play objects magnifies the problem of creating a stimulating environment. Thus, the reported delay and failure of blind children to engage in certain forms of play (Tait, 1972a; 1973) may be as much a consequence of their dependency and learned helplessness, as it is a function of their sensory impairment per se. Future research might focus profitably on both the unique features of the play of children with various physical handicaps, as well as on those common play features that may be tied to the psychological consequences of physically handicapping conditions.

Play also may prove to be a particularly potent therapeutic experience for coping with the problems of helplessness and dependency which physically handicapping conditions may foster. In play, the individual is actively initiating novel behaviors that intrinsically are interesting. It is an assertive activity and, as such, may be viewed as a means of overcoming helplessness. Thus, play may provide the opportunity for handicapped children to experience competency, efficacy, and delight. Families should also be encouraged to provide the safe, stimulating, and encouraging environments necessary for play. The resultant positive outcomes may alter the attitudes, expectancies, and behavioral strategies of families and how they approach their handicapped children. Furthermore, these children may develop self-confidence and independence outside of play contexts.

THE CORRELATES AND OUTCOMES OF PLAY

Play and Problem Solving

As the reader, no doubt, has gleaned from the preceding sections, many theorists, researchers, and educators strongly adhere to the belief that play of one form or another relates to and, indeed, causes growth in a variety of developmental domains. Insofar as the play and problem-solving research is concerned, Sylva (1977) and Sutton-Smith (1968), among others, identify playful object transformations as a variable in the development of the ability to produce a wide range of object uses, which provide a basis for subsequent problem-solving proficiency.

However, despite the relatively widespread belief that play contributes to learning and problem solving, surprisingly little research has addressed this issue directly. One recent approach to the study of the relationship between play and problem solving has been concerned with the effects of *pretense* play training programs. Another strategy has been to examine the effects of free-play exposure to specific materials that later must be used to solve given problems having a single solution. These single-solution tasks recently have been labeled as *convergent* problems (Pepler, 1979; Pepler & Ross, in press). The impetus for this work stems from earlier research with nonhuman primates (Birch, 1945; Kohler, 1925; Schiller, 1954).

Convergent Problem Solving

Sylva and her colleagues (Sylva, 1977; Sylva et al., 1976) recently have drawn on the methodologies employed in the earlier primate literature and on the notion that play provides the behavioral flexibility that makes tool use possible to examine empirically the relationship between play and convergent problem solving. Preschool children were seated in chairs and were asked to reach a distant lure without standing up. To solve the task the children had to clamp two long sticks together to reach the lure. Hints were provided by the experimenter whenever it was judged that the children were having difficulty with the problem. Prior to being presented with the problem, the children were assigned to one of three conditions. In the first condition, children were allowed to play freely with the materials that would later be used in the task. In the second condition, the children observed the experimenter perform the task that led to the solution. The third condition consisted of a control exposure to the material. Sylva's results indicated that play with materials was as potent an experience for subsequent convergent problem solving as was demonstration of the solution to the children. Both of the first two conditions produced more proficient problem solving than the third control condition. In addition, Sylva examined the process of task solution and found that the play group was more persistent and motivated to solve the task, and more likely to solve the task by piecing together the solution. Those who had been shown the solution, on the other hand, either solved the problem immediately or gave up. Sylva also concluded that the configural richness of the children's play affected their subsequent task performance. These findings have not only lent initial empirical credence to the hypothesis concerning the causal relationship between play and problem solving, but have spawned further research.

Vandenberg (1981b), using methods similar to Sylva's, attempted to extend the results by examining the effect of play across a wider age range (4 to 10 years) using several different convergent tasks. One task required the children to connect two long sticks together to reach a lure. The second task required the children to tie two pipe cleaners together to dislodge a small sponge that was stuck in a transparent tube. Hints similar to those used by Sylva were provided. Vandenberg compared a play experience with a condition in which the children were asked questions about the materials. The results indicated that the play experience was only influential in promoting successful solutions to the stick problem. Moreover, the play experience was found to be most beneficial for the 6- and 7-year-olds. Vandenberg also focused on *how* the play experience contributed to subsequent task performance. His results failed to yield a significant relationship between the "manipulative richness" of the children's play constructions and their problem-solving proficiency. Vandenberg further found that the more information contained in a task-specific behavior that could aid in the solution of the problem, the more likely it would aid in task solution. However, performance of task-specific behavior in play was not necessary for successful task completion; that is, children *were* able to solve both problems without having performed task-specific activity in their play.

Smith and Dutton (1979) recently have examined the effects of play on innovative problem solving. They used two tasks and compared the effects of a free-play exposure to task relevant materials with both a training (observation) condition and a nonexposure control condition. The tasks and methods were similar to Sylva's and Vandenberg's. On the first task, the children had to connect two sticks to reach a lure. On the second, "innovative" task, the children had to make a longer, three-stick tool to reach a lure, thereby using the same connective principles required in the first task. The results indicated that the play and training group performed equally well on the first task, and that both did better than the control group, which was not exposed to the materials prior to the problem solution phase. On the second task, the play group performed better than the training group, which in turn performed better than the no-exposure control group. The play group also proved to be more task oriented and motivated than the two other groups. Smith and Dutton concluded that play aids in the development of solutions to problems requiring innovation, and that it also enhances the motivation of the problem solvers.

These studies provide only mixed support for the hypothesis that play aids in problem solving. Moreover, there are several important limitations to this line of research. Only Smith and Dutton attempted to provide some control for the effects of exploration. This was done by providing children in the play and training (observe principle) conditions with a brief exposure to the materials prior to treatment. Given Hutt's (1979) cautionary notes concerning the relative contribution of play versus exploration to the acquisition of problem-solving skills, it is impossible to ascertain whether the Sylva and Vandenberg findings were attributable to one or the other phenomenon. It is important to note, however, that, while the opportunity for exploration was afforded the children assigned to the play and training conditions, Smith and Dutton did not actually examine the incidence of exploratory activity within this short, pretreatment period.

There are further methodological difficulties with the studies described here. For one, none of the studies have used double-blind procedures to ensure that the children could not respond to subtle reinforcement cues emitted by the experimenter (Cheyne, 1982). Second, in Sylva's (1977) study children in the play group were asked questions about their stick constructions during the play phase. It is thus possible that such queries (1) made the situation less playful and (2) presented the occasion for the ''nonblinded'' experimenter to make ''leading'' or possibly helpful comments vis-à-vis the problem. Although Vandenberg (1981b) did control for such a possibility, it is important to note that his play condition proved to be of significant benefit for children older than preschool age. Vandenberg explained these findings by noting that the task appeared too difficult for the youngest children and too simple for the older children. Those who gained optimally from play exposure were those whose interest and competency levels appeared commensurate with task difficulty.

In addition to these methodological difficulties, there are also some inconsistencies in the results that are puzzling. Smith and Dutton indicated that their second task required an innovative solution. However, the second task only required the reiterative use of principles that were necessary to solve the first task. The solution to the first task required the discovery of the principle of extention. This discovery would appear to require more ''innovation'' than the second task, which likewise necessitated the use of the same principle (but with three sticks instead of two). This clouds Smith and Dutton's conclusion that play is particularly helpful for *innovative* task solutions, since the play exposure effect was found for only the *second* task. Perhaps the findings may be explained by calling on Piaget's notion of consolidation. Children in the ''observe'' condition may have only learned the solution to the first problem. Children in the ''play'' condition, on the other hand, may have learned the *principle* required to solve the first problem. Having consolidated the principle, these latter children performed better than the ''observe'' group on the second task. Nevertheless, given that Sylva and Vandenberg found play to be helpful on tasks similar to Smith and Dutton's first task, it remains unclear why there would be a play effect for the former studies, but not for Smith and Dutton's first task.

In summary, the training research described in this section appears to suffer from sufficient methodological difficulties and unanswered questions, so much so that any firm statement concerning the causal relationship of play to *convergent* problem solving would be premature.

More recent research has been addressed to discovering those particular aspects of a given play experience that prove beneficial for solving a variety of different problems. Pepler (1979; Pepler & Ross, 1981) has examined the problem-solving performances of preschool children who experienced two different play conditions. In a convergent play condition, children were provided with puzzle pieces and their associated form boards and were instructed to play with them for a short period. In a divergent play condition, children were allowed to play with the puzzle pieces alone. Children in the convergent play condition spent almost two-thirds of their play time assembling the puzzles. Children in the divergent play condition were more likely to investigate the properties of the materials, to construct and group the materials, and to engage in symbolic play with the materials. Pepler found that the convergent play experience better enabled children to solve puzzle completion (convergent) problems using materials similar to those available during play than did the divergent play experience. However, the transfer of learning from the convergent play experience was specific and did not generalize to either convergent tasks involving form boards dissimilar to those available during play or to divergent tasks that required multiple solutions (e.g., How many ways could a given set of blocks be used?).

It is noteworthy that divergent play experience allowed better performance on tasks requiring divergent, creative thought (Pepler, 1979; Pepler & Ross, 1981). Moreover, children who experienced the divergent play condition demonstrated greater problem-solving flexibility in the convergent task (i.e., they tried more different strategies) than did children who had convergent play experiences. As such, the flexible problem-solving set engendered by the divergent play experience may have proven fruitful for the solution of divergent problems and yet have interfered somewhat with convergent problem solution.

These results suggest that the practice of behaviors conducive to particular types of problems during play does indeed aid in successful problem solving. Practicing puzzle assembly (Pepler, 1979) or using task-specific activity (Cheyne & Rubin, in press; Vandenberg, 1981b) during play does predict convergent problem-solving proficiency. Sylva (1977) and, more recently, Cheyne and Rubin (in press) have shown that configural richness or complexity of construction during play predicts convergent problem-solving skill. In the case of Cheyne and Rubin, the frequency with which children constructed figures having large numbers of sticks and connectors and having multidimensional features during play negatively correlated with the amount of time and the number of hints necessary to solve the stick-clamp problem (Cheyne & Rubin, in press).

As for Pepler's (1979) divergent tasks, successful performance could be predicted from both the opportunity to engage in divergent play and from the degree to which the children in the divergent group engaged in symbolic and representational play. These data support the contention that play, and in particular pretense, allows children to develop wide ranges of associations about play objects (Sutton-Smith, 1967).

Divergent Problem Solving

Original support for the notion that play in general, and pretense in particular, acts as a causal agent in the development of divergent problem-solving skills stemmed from Sutton-Smith's (1968) finding that preschoolers were able to generate more associations or usages for objects that they routinely played with than those that were not played with. However, his results were confounded by methodological weaknesses, including the lack of control for duration of exposure to the play materials.

Dansky and Silverman (1973) rectified this difficulty by assigning children to one of three conditions: (1) divergent play with novel materials, (2) imitation of the experimenter using the materials, and (3) observation of the experimenter's use of the materials. The children were exposed to the materials for equal amounts of time. They subsequently were administered the Alternative Uses Test (Wallach & Kogan, 1965) using the same materials. Although the results indicated that the play condition enhanced the number of unique responses given on this test of associative fluency, the specific mechanisms that led to this positive contribution remained unclear.

In a second experiment designed to answer the above question, Dansky and Silverman (1975) assigned children to either a divergent play, an observation, or a problem-solving condition, using one set of materials. However, the outcome measure was the extent to which children could provide uses for a second set of previously unseen materials. Dansky and Silverman reasoned that, if play contributes to subsequent problem solving by establishing a playful "set" or attitude toward the materials, then this playful set should transfer to any materials encountered subsequent to the play experience, regardless of the children's familiarity with the materials. If, on the other hand, play allows the child to acquire specific associations and information about the play materials, then this experience should not enhance children's associative fluency in relation to a novel set of materials. Dansky and Silverman found that divergent play experiences did enhance associative fluen-

cy with new materials. They thus inferred that the playful attitude or set toward the materials, resulting from the play experience, contributed significantly to subsequent divergent problem solving.

Dansky (1980a) has refined his earlier studies further by attempting to identify make-believe as *the* important element that aids in establishing the playful set. He reported that children identified as "pretend" players were more likely to produce make-believe behaviors with a given set of objects while in a dyad than were their nonpretend counterparts. The "pretend" group, if allowed to play, was also more likely to produce creative and unique uses for the given objects than "pretend" players not allowed to play, as well as more such uses than the nonpretend group. Dansky's (1980a) and Pepler's (1979) results thus indicate that play, and specifically pretense, may enhance performance on divergent problem-solving tasks.

Summary and Conclusions

Research on the causal relationship between play and problem solving is a relatively new area of investigation. While the different methodologies have proven useful for examining the hypothesized connection between play and problem solving, a number of issues remain to be addressed.

First, researchers have assumed that play is a unitary construct. Distinctions between exploration, and constructive play and pretense (both social and nonsocial) play often are not made by those who attempt to pursue the elusive causal variable in the problem-solving training studies. The suggestion (Pepler, 1979; 1982) that constructive activities may better foster convergent problem-solving skills whereas pretense activities may better enhance divergent problem-solving skills requires further attention.

Second, the research on play and problem solving has been limited to the study of young children. There have been few, if any, attempts to examine the developmental relationship between play and problem solving. A play experience prior to the presentation of a problem may aid the problem-solving efforts of young children. However, research by Hoffman, Burke, and Maier (1963) suggests that, for adults, play prior to the presentation of a problem may generate ideas that interfere with subsequent problem solving. Perhaps for older children and adults, play is more useful *after* the problem has been presented. Koestler has suggested that creative solutions to problems by adults occur through the "bisociation" of two seemingly irrelevant pieces of information. Such "bisociation" actually is hindered by thinking only in the plane of the presented problem, since the solution requires the association of other information that is outside the confines of the presented problem. Play after the problem has been presented may provide the opportunity to escape the plane of the problem and to explore seemingly irrelevant information. The presence of a problem in the individual's mind creates a tension that can transform a chance event, idly noticed in a relaxed setting (e.g., play), into a component of a creative solution. The "Eureka" experience of Archimedes is an example of this process (Koestler, 1964). This potential relationship between play and problem solving is different from the one discovered for younger children and suggests that a developmental perspective is needed to capture more fully the interrelationship between play and problem solving.

Pretense Play: Correlational Studies

As previously mentioned, fantasy or pretense activities have been hypothesized as contributing to a plethora of developmental virtues, including communicative and sex-role development, Piagetian operativity, cooperation, perspective-taking ability, creativity, and social and impersonal problem-solving skills. One common explanation for this hypothesized link is the belief that decentration skills, or the ability to consider multiple aspects of situations or things simultaneously (see Shantz, vol. III, chap. 8), are at least partially responsible for the emergence of the above skills as well as of dramatic play. For example, Piaget (1970) suggested that decentration was the basis not only for the abilities to communicate and to take the perspectives of others into account (indeed, Piaget believed that the former skill reflected the latter), but also for the ability to consider simultaneously the classificatory relationship between parts and the whole. As for dramatic play, writers have noted that it involves the ability to consider various roles simultaneously, to distinguish between literal and nonliteral roles and activities, and to perceive the relationship between play scripts and play frames (Johnson & Ershler, 1980b; Rubin & Pepler, 1980; Schwartzman, 1978).

Given the above speculations it is somewhat surprising to note the dearth of studies purporting to examine the relationship between spontaneously emitted play and indexes of decentration skill (or other abilities for that matter). Rubin and Maioni (1975) found significant positive correlations between the frequency of observed preschool dramatic play and scores on classification and spatial perspec-

tive-taking tasks. They further indicated that the frequency of functional sensorimotor play negatively correlated with the same cognitive variables.

Connolly (1980), in a recent study, observed preschool children at play. She also gathered data concerning the children's popularity, social competence, role-taking skills, and IQ. In reporting the results of multiple regression analyses, Connolly indicated that, with age, sex, IQ, and level of nonpretend social activity controlled for, social pretend play significantly predicted performance on measures of social competence, popularity, and role-taking activity. Connolly explained her results by noting that, in social pretend play, children must integrate disparate elements into meaningful sequences. Similarly, role-taking activity requires consideration of social situations from differing vantage points. Consequently, it was assumed that the common element of decentration skill partially could explain her results.

Psychologists do not only note a connection between decentration and the social cognitive domain, but they do so also in other areas in which children are called on to consider objects and events in divergent or alternative manners. For example, Johnson (1976) suggested that the underlying cognitive link among creativity, classification and role-taking skills, and play was decentration. He supported his argument by finding significant correlations between spontaneously produced sociodramatic play and a test of decentration, that is, divergent thinking. More recently, Emmerich, Cocking, and Sigel (1979) have found sociodramatic play to correlate significantly with a measure of conservation of continuous quantity.

Further correlational support for a positive link between fantasy play and creativity emanates from a series of recent studies. Dansky (1980a) identified children as either "players" or "nonplayers." The former group was observed to engage in make-believe activity during at least 28% of their free-play time. The nonplayer group played in a pretense fashion 5% or less of their free-play time. When brought into a dyadic play setting, the players were more likely to use a given set of objects in nonliteral fashions than were the nonplayers. Furthermore, when subsequently asked to suggest alternative uses for the given set of play objects, the players were significantly better able to do so. Thus, Dansky argued, the relationship between play opportunities and fluency of thought specifically depends on the occurrence of make-believe.

In a related study, Hutt and Bhavnani (1976) observed children at play with a novel toy. Then, they categorized children as being (1) nonexplorers, that is, those who looked at but did not explore the toy; (2) explorers, that is, those who explored the toy but did not play with it; and (3) inventive explorers, that is, those who not only investigated but also used the novel toy in imaginative ways. When a test of divergent thinking subsequently was administered, a positive correlation was found with inventive, imaginary play.

These latter data indicate that fantasy play and object transformations may enhance divergent rather than convergent problem solving. On the other hand, it may well be that convergent problem solving is more likely related to exploration and constructive play (Cheyne & Rubin, in press; Pepler, 1979; Sylva, 1977; Vandenberg, 1978). However, the correlational nature of these reviewed studies precludes acceptance of one form of play or another as the elusive causal variable in development. Recently, a number of researchers have carried out experimental play training studies in attempts to consider the directionality of the cognitive play, social cognitive, and social development relationship.

Pretense Play: Training Studies

Given the assumption that fantasy play is a significant commodity for the development of cognitive, social, and social cognitive skills, and given data that suggest that some groups of children are less likely than others to spontaneously produce pretense behaviors, it is not surprising that researchers have attempted recently to increase dramatic (and especially sociodramatic) activity via structured training. The most highly cited figure in the play training literature is Smilansky (1968), who, as Smith, Doglish, and Herzmark (in press) correctly noted, "pioneered the idea of 'play tutoring,' in which adults deliberately encourage sociodramatic play."

The prototypical play training paradigm thus may be drawn from Smilansky (1968). In her study, disadvantaged Israeli preschoolers and kindergartners were matched on several factors (family characteristics, age, and IQ) and were assigned to one of five groups. *Group A* made trips and visits to a medical clinic and to a grocery store. In the three-week period following each visit, the children were provided with toys and materials matched to the visitation theme during their free-play periods. *Group B* was actually "taught" how to engage in and sustain social pretense in the particular themes, for example, involving a medical clinic and a grocery store (this was done during the ongoing course of the

school day and the "tutorial" was delivered by a teacher to any given child who was seen as deficient in sociodramatic play). Smilansky's procedure actually deviates from most others in that more recent tutorials have advocated the use of structured periods of small group training (e.g., Saltz & Johnson, 1974). After the periods in which tutorials were offered, children were provided with toys and materials conducive to "playing at" the given themes. *Group C* was given both the visitation and tutorial experience. *Groups D* and *E* were both nontreatment controls. In the case of *Group D*, the children were matched to the treatment groups, whereas the *Group E* children came from more well-to-do familial backgrounds and had higher IQs.

It should be noted that the design employed by Smilansky is far more elaborate than those employed in most play training studies. The standard procedure is to examine the comparative effects of one play-trained group versus nontreatment controls, often with disregard to the possibility of Hawthorne effects (e.g., Lovinger, 1974). Insofar as outcome measures are concerned, researchers typically observe the frequency of imaginative play for a period prior to and immediately after intervention. Rarely are observations made of the children's play several months after the training session (one notable exception is the work of Saltz and his colleagues; see Saltz, 1978; Saltz & Brodie, 1982). Subsequently, the preplay and postplay training observations of the tutored and control (or comparison) groups are compared. Given the time and effort put into the tutorial work (often play training covers a period of several months), it is reassuring to discover that researchers do find increases in different types of imaginative play for the treatment but not for the control or comparison groups (e.g., Feitelson & Ross, 1973; Fink, 1976; Freyberg, 1973; Lovinger, 1974; Rosen, 1974; Saltz, Dixon, & Johnson, 1977; Saltz & Johnson, 1974; Smilansky, 1968; Smith et al., in press; Smith & Syddall, 1978).

When the effects of multiple treatment groups are compared, differential outcomes often are reported. For example, Smilansky (1968) reported that the most significant effect on gains in sociodramatic play was associated with her *Group C* trainees. Trips and visits, in and of themselves, had little effect on sociodramatic play, whereas play tutoring had some minor effects. Saltz et al. (1977) distinguished among several conditions: (1) play training in *thematic fantasy*, which involved the enactment of fairy tales (e.g., *The Three Billy Goats Gruff*); (2) *sociodramatic play training*, which consisted of trips to doctors' offices or grocery stores followed up by encouragement to enact these experiences; (3) *fantasy discussion,* during which the fairy tales enacted by the first group were read to children and subsequently discussed; and (4) a nonplay *control condition*. The authors found that play training in *thematic fantasy* resulted in considerably more spontaneous thematic fantasy play than did any of the other conditions. Similarly, *sociodramatic* play training appeared more effective than any other procedure used to produce spontaneous sociodramatic activity. Once again, it is reassuring to note that extensive play training does appear to produce its desired behavioral effects.

Given the relative successes of these training studies, and given the notion that pretense activities may play a causal role in social, cognitive, and social cognitive development, researchers with educational or other applied concerns have advocated the implementation of such structured play experiences in preschool and kindergarten programs (Saltz, 1978; Saltz & Brodie, 1982; Singer, 1973). An examination of the general utility of these tutorial procedures follows.

There is now a large body of literature that suggests that sociodramatic, dramatic, and thematic fantasy play training does have some impact in a wide variety of developmental areas. The theoretical tie that binds these studies appears to be the concept of *decentration* (see Fenson & Ramsay, 1980). Creativity, divergent thinking, social and spatial perspectivism, social cooperation, and quantitative invariance (conservation), all are purported to require the ability to consider flexibly and broadly that objects or social situations may be multidimensional and that these dimensions are interrelated. Pretense play purportedly allows children the opportunity to transform objects and situations while simultaneously understanding their original identities and states. Evidence of decentration appears in the early shift from self-directed to other-directed activities (Fenson & Ramsay, 1980). In play children establish an imaginary duality of object and role, of reality and appearance (Golomb & Cornelius, 1977). As such, pretense play may allow the practice of those decentration skills required for the development of the aforementioned abilities. The easy movement in and out of the play frame also has been cited as significant for the development of those abilities that require the operation of reversibility (e.g., conservation).

The play training paradigm employed in the literature is practically identical to that described for the goal of increasing pretense play. In the social, social cognitive, and cognitive consequences cited in the play literature, however, pretest and posttest assessments of the particular dependent measures of concern are also made. Much of the data clearly appear to reinforce the position that imaginative play is a significant causal force in the development of creativity (Dansky, 1980b; Feitelson & Ross, 1973), quantitative invariance (Golomb & Cornelius, 1977), sequential memory (Dansky, 1980b; Saltz et al., 1977), group cooperation (Rosen, 1974; Smith & Syddall, 1978), social participation (Smith et al., in press), language development or receptive vocabulary (Lovinger, 1974; Saltz et al., 1977), conceptions of kinship relationships (Fink, 1976), impulse control (Saltz et al., 1977), spatial perspective-taking skill (Burns & Brainerd, 1979; Matthews, Beebe, & Bopp, 1980; Rosen, 1974), affective perspective-taking skill (Burns & Brainerd, 1979; Saltz & Johnson, 1974), and cognitive perspective-taking skill (Burns & Brainerd, 1979; Rosen, 1974; Smith & Syddall, 1978).

However, it is important to realize that positive dramatic play effects do not appear to be stable from study to study. For example, in the areas of creativity (Feitelson & Ross, 1973), quantitative invariance (Brainerd, 1982; Fink, 1976; Golomb & Friedman, 1979; Guthrie & Hudson, 1979), language or communicative development (Marbach & Yawkey, in press; Marshall & Hahn, 1967), spatial perspective-taking skill (Brainerd, 1982; Fink, 1976), affective perspective-taking skill (Brainerd, 1982; Saltz et al., 1977), cognitive perspective-taking skill (Brainerd, 1982), all three forms of perspective-taking skill combined (Connolly, 1980), and social competence (Connolly, 1980), pretense play training effects were either not found or were not significantly different from those of comparative nonplay "treatments."

There are several possible explanations for the discrepancy in the play training results. For one, the training procedures employed by researchers do vary from study to study. In some cases the children receive sociodramatic play experiences (e.g., Burns & Brainerd, 1979; Lovinger, 1974), in others sociothematic play tutorials (e.g., Connolly, 1980; Saltz et al., 1977), and yet in others children meet individually with an adult to play "pretend roles" (e.g., Golomb & Cornelius, 1977). The length of the play training period also differs from one investigation to another. For example, in some studies, children meet with a play tutor for 1 to 3 sessions (Golomb & Cornelius, 1977; Marbach & Yawkey, in press), in others for 8 to 10 sessions (Brainerd, 1982; Burns & Brainerd, 1979; Connolly, 1980; Fink, 1976), and in others for weekly sessions over a period of 4 to 6 months (Lovinger, 1974; Saltz et al., 1977). Generally, the individual sessions are 15 to 20 minutes in duration.

Data interpretation is complicated further by the use of different outcome measures to assess the same phenomenon (e.g., different indexes of creativity or perspective-taking skill). In some cases, all or some of the outcome measures are suspect vis-à-vis their reliability and validity. This is a particular concern in those many studies in which perspective-taking skill has been a targeted outcome variable (Rubin, 1980). In some investigations, researchers have found improvements in one area of role-taking skill but not in others (e.g., in either cognitive or affective role-taking skill but not in both). These results reflect either the nonunitary nature of the perspective-taking construct or the psychometric weakness of some or all of the measures used (Rubin, 1978). In other studies different results have been obtained for multiple measures purporting to assess a single perspective-taking skill (e.g., affective perspective-taking skill; Burns & Brainerd, 1979; Saltz et al., 1977). Again, the use of particular outcome measures should be called into question rather than simply faulting the play curriculum for mixed findings (Brainerd, 1982; Rubin, 1980; Smith, 1977).

A further explanation for the lack of consistent findings may emanate from the different target groups offered training across the many extant studies. In some cases preschoolers receive play tutorials (Saltz et al., 1977), whereas in others kindergartners are the curriculum recipients (Rosen, 1974). In some cases lower SES children are targeted for special "compensatory" play treatment (Saltz et al., 1977; Saltz & Johnson, 1974; Smith et al., in press), whereas in others middle-class children who already display relatively high levels of social pretense play are tutored (Connolly, 1980). The sex and age composition of the tutored play groups is generally not described in the literature. Consequently, it is not known whether pretense play training better serves same or mixed SES groups, same or mixed age groups, or same or mixed sex groups. In short, it would appear that until long-term, consistent, and carefully planned programmatic research is carried out conclusive statements concerning the merits of play training cannot be made.

Furthermore, it is imperative that programmatic researchers employ greater methodological rigor than has generally been the case in these training projects. Most of the training studies have not employed appropriate "blinding" controls. Consequently, it has often been the case that the play trainers themselves collected the pretest and posttest data, a questionable methodological strategy. In ad-

dition, several researchers have not provided adequate control or nonplay treatment conditions. This methodological weakness is especially critical given that psychologists (e.g., Smith, 1977; Rubin, 1980) recently have begun to question whether it is the pretense play or the adult tuition that leads to gains in social and cognitive skills. Although some researchers have monitored and controlled the amount of time that children spend interacting with an adult (e.g., Rosen, 1974; Saltz et al., 1977), there are others who have not created such controls (e.g., Lovinger, 1974). Moreover, the quality of adult-child engagement in the control conditions rarely has been monitored and, when it has, the reader is left unaware of how it was done. Notable exceptions to this criticism include recent reports by Smith (Smith et al., in press; Smith & Syddall, 1978), in which the targeted groups were disadvantaged preschoolers, and those by Connolly (1980), who studied middle-class preschoolers. In Smith's studies, the children were assigned to either a tutored fantasy play group or a skills (games, puzzles) tutored group. Connolly added a nontreatment control group in her study. Records were kept concerning the occurrence of various adult-child interactive patterns. These observations generally indicated that, while specific types of interaction varied from one group to the other (e.g., there was more fantasy interaction in the play group; Connolly, 1980; Smith et al., in press), the overall amount of interaction remained the same.

Given the above controls, it is of some significance that Smith found the two tutoring groups, in both of his studies (Smith et al., in press; Smith & Syddall, 1978), to be equally effective in promoting gains in language development, attention span, and creativity. Although Smith and Syddall reported that the play group excelled on role-taking measures, Smith, in his more recent replication study using a larger sample size, found no such play versus skills tutoring differences. Connolly (1980), in her study of middle-class preschoolers who were evincing relatively high levels of pretense to begin with, not surprisingly found nonsignificant differences among her three comparison groups.

In summary, does fantasy play training make a difference at all? Until the methodological problems which have dominated the extant literature have been dealt with adequately, a conclusive answer cannot be offered. However, given reasonably adequate control procedures, two positive outcomes may be reported reliably. First, numerous studies indicate that fantasy tutorials lead to more group and fantasy activity in the classroom. Second, fantasy tutoring appears to produce relatively long-term (i.e., 2 months posttreatment) gains in social participation (Smith et al., in press). Given recent work that has suggested the significance of peer interaction for both social and cognitive growth (see Hartup, *vol. IV, chap. 8*), the finding may be an important one.

The Significance of Pretense Activities in Childhood

Although there are several studies that suggest a causal link between pretense play and various indexes of development, the issue is far from settled. For one, pretense behaviors do appear to reflect newly acquired cognitive and social cognitive abilities that become strengthened and consolidated through play. Golomb and Cornelius (1977) and Rubin (1980; Rubin & Pepler, 1980; in press) have suggested that the cognitive abilities reflected by the pretense play of young children include one-to-one correspondence, conservation, comprehension of the principles of transformation and identity, decentration, reversibility, seriation, classification, and perspective-taking skill. For example, young children are able to "conserve" the imaginary identities of play objects and play roles despite contraindicative stimuli.

Conservation of identity and reversibility appear to be indicated during role-play. The young 3- or 4-year-old who pretends to be Princess Leia (a *Star Wars* character) constantly is aware of her "real" identity and will revert to the role of self during the frequent occasions when she moves out of the play frame. Similarly, a play-dough hamburger, complete with all the play-dough fixings may be treated as if it were a Big Mac, but never really eaten. In both of these cases there is evidence of decentration as well as reversibility. Generic identity also may be inferred. That is, children, in their early pretense activities are (1) able to realize that they can play a role and be themselves simultaneously (decentration) and (2) can change to the self or the pretend identity at will (reversibility). As such, it may be the case that *elementary* cognitive forms of decentration, identity, and reversibility (Piaget, 1970) underlie the child's ability to distinguish fantasy from reality.

The above examples provide some evidence for the possible cognitive underpinnings of play. However, the position espoused here is that play may *reflect* rather than be constitutive of thought. This behavioral extension of the child's symbol system may allow practice of some recently acquired and as yet immature logical or concrete operations (see Fein & Apfel, 1979a; Sutton-Smith, in press). As such, play may be viewed as adaptive, serving not only to reflect the child's present level of conceptual skill but also to aid in the acquisition of further cognitive abilities through consolidation and practice. This is essentially Piaget's (1962) position and, yet, given the extant data base, it may well be the best interpretation of the significance of pretense. Since fantasy or sociodramatic training endeavors do increase the quantity of fantasy or sociodramatic activity in early childhood, the production of this pretense behavior may well allow consolidation and practice of the associated cognitive operations. If this is, in fact, the case, one might expect that the effects of play training would not become fully blown, at least insofar as laboratory measurement of decentration, conservation, or reversibility is concerned, until some time *after* tuition or some time after sustained playing. Thus, it might prove worthwhile to examine the *long-term* consequences of pretense tuition—a procedure decidedly at variance with the current crop of studies in which only the *immediate* effects of training are examined (see Fein, in press-b).

Pretense play also may contribute to development by providing the *context* for significant growth-oriented events. Consider the recent naturalistic work of Matthews (1977a) in which same-sex, same-age preschoolers were observed during dyadic free play. Matthews focused on the development of sex roles through spontaneous sociodramatic activities. She found that, when children agreed with each other about sex-typed behaviors, the social situation essentially was assimilative and socially redundant, thereby producing no new cognitive growth. For example, if two 4-year-old boys were playing house, one taking the role of "mother" and the other "father," and if they both agreed fully on the sex-role appropriateness of each others' behaviors, the children would learn nothing new about sex roles. On the other hand, Matthews found that, when preschoolers differed with regard to their sex-role expectancies within the play context, the situation became accommodatively and socially relevant. Take, for example, the following interchange between two 4-year-old boys who have adopted the roles of "mother" and "father" (from Rubin, 1980, p. 75).

Father:	"So long. I'll see ya later. It's time to go to work."
Mother:	"Hey, wait for me! I gotta go to work too!"
Father:	"Hey, my mom don't work . . . you stay here."

Mother: "Well my mom works . . . lotsa womens work ya know. My mom is a perfessor at the unibersity."

Father: "O.K. then, just hurry so we won't be late. Are you sure ya wanna work?"

Conflicts such as that described above appear to force the participants to step out of the play frame or text (Bateson, 1956) to discuss and negotiate their different perspectives. When the conflicts were resolved, the text or boundary of social fantasy became accessible again (Matthews, 1978b).

In summary, it would appear as if pretense activities provide opportunities for practice and consolidation of newly emerging cognitive and social skills. Such dramatic events may also set the stage for the role and rule peer conflicts that Piaget (1962) felt were significant for cognitive and social cognitive growth. The positive outcomes of play training studies are encouraging, but more refined designs and long-term follow-ups will be needed to clarify the relationship between pretense and cognitive or social developments.

FUTURE DIRECTIONS

A brief glance at the dates of the studies we have reviewed concerning the structural features, individual differences, and outcomes of play allows the inference that research in these areas has accelerated tremendously in quantity and has broadened in scope during the past decade. Accompanying this rapid growth are the inevitable critical questions concerning both content and methodology. In our review we have noted the criticisms and have suggested future research directions whenever possible. In this section we suggest yet additional areas meriting investigation in the near future.

Play and Assessment

We have suggested earlier that future work concerning the development of play *norms* be carried out with special emphasis on ecological and individual difference factors. The collection of normative data especially is important because play observations are widely used for clinical assessment and diagnosis. As previously discussed, play observations are used commonly to assess mental status and personality features, as well as to make differential diagnoses of various disorders (e.g., autism). There are both theoretical and practical reasons for using play in assessment. Theoretically, an important implication of both Freud's and Piaget's work is that play represents a window to the child's mind. Purportedly, a child's intrapsychic dynamics and mental structures are laid bare in play. Consequently, to assess socioemotional and intellectual status, one need only to look at the child's play. From a practical standpoint, play represents an important alternative to formal testing procedures that are often difficult to administer to very young or severely disturbed children.

Unfortunately, until recently, play assessment procedures have been informal or have lacked methodological attention to psychometric problems such as validity, reliability, or stability. However, several recent studies of observational play instruments have demonstrated temporal and intersituational reliability and stability, thereby offering encouragement for the notion that the assessment of different aspects of play might aspire to psychometric respectability (e.g., Enslein & Fein, 1981; Roper & Hinde, 1978). In addition to the psychometrics of assessment, there are other related problems inherent in the current use of play for assessment purposes.

First, there is the ubiquitous definition problem. Any assessment of a child's socioemotional or cognitive status through observations of play must necessarily be preceded by a definition and conceptualization of the phenomenon of interest. For example, it has been found that children are more anxious and display more exploratory behavior ("What is this environment about?") when brought to novel rather than familiar environments. Assessors should thus take into account the distinction between exploration and play when painting a picture of a child's developmental status. Moreover, distinctions between types and complexity of play should be made.

A second factor which presently complicates the assessment literature is the finding that children's play is especially sensitive to ecological or contextual variables. Thus, once definitions of the phenomenon of interest are produced, it would appear most important to derive norms within standardized settings equipped with specified sets of objects. This would allow replication of assessment procedures from one venue to another.

Another assessment difficulty concerns the interpretation of children's play content when psychologists attempt to make socioemotional diagnoses. For example, when a child is aggressive during the assessment trial, it remains unclear whether the play is imitative of observed behavior, reflective of a characteristic response style, or a cathartic release of impulses that the child has previously inhibited (Fein, in press-a). Interpretation might be aided by supplementing the assessment data with observations in natural settings, by maternal reports of children's play at home, or by interviewing the child and probing him or her concerning the rationale for play exhibited.

Play and Cognition

Another recent issue in the literature concerns the use of play observations to diagnose cognitive or intellectual status. Several researchers have standardized laboratory procedures for documenting the cognitive complexity of play (e.g., Belsky & Most, 1981; Fein, 1975; Nicolich, 1977; Rosenblatt, 1977; Watson & Fischer, 1977, 1980). These formal procedures have allowed investigators to infer the existence of cognitive competencies from play observations. Moreover, the use of play observations as cognitive assessment tools has allowed the reformulation of age norms typically associated with the onset of given cognitive competencies. For example, in addressing the relationship between play and social role and perspective conceptualizations, Rubin and Pepler (1980) have noted that those procedures used to measure the latter social cognitive phenomena often consist of lengthy, verbally loaded, hypothetical reflective tasks (e.g., Selman, 1976). Rubin and Pepler argued that such procedures may sorely underestimate the child's social cognitive competencies. They then attempted to demonstrate how different levels of perspective-taking skill could be inferred from observations of pretense play and games-with-rules.

Similarly, Watson and Fischer (1980) and Fischer (1980) have argued that the development of social role and perspective competencies would be better assessed by procedures that do not "overload" the child with complicated instructions and a heavy reliance on the verbal repertoire. Fischer and his colleagues have found that the complexity of children's social role conceptions is higher when measured through formal, structured, but simple, nonverbal play assessment procedures than when observed in spontaneous play. This performance discrepancy in measuring competence was found to widen as children developed a greater range of play skills such that, with age, children's spontaneous play became increasingly less likely to reflect their competencies (Hand, 1979; Watson & Fischer, 1980). Taken together, the above reports suggest that play may prove to be a fruitful mirror of social cognitive development especially when assessed in a formal, experimenter-manipulated fashion. Future research in which impersonal cognitive phenomena such as conservation, classification, or seriation

skills are measured through formal play observations may allow the reconceptualization of age norms typically associated with the onset of these skills.

Another new research direction is concerned with children's cognitions *about* play. Chaillé (1978), for example, recently asked children ranging in age from 5 to 11 years whether or not they could pretend to be a doctor, mother/father, teacher, friend, or the interviewer. At 5 years almost all children answered that they could enact the roles of doctor, parent, and teacher, but were less inclined to note that they could play friend or interviewer. Chaillé further found that the younger children made greater reference to the necessity of props (costumes, makeup) to enact roles, whereas the older children made greater reference to actions carried out by the pretense target. Finally, Chaillé found that younger elementary school children were more likely to insist that toys were necessary for pretense than their older counterparts.

Chaillé's results thus indicate a move from material to nonmaterial (ideational) conceptions of pretense with age, a finding in keeping with observational research. However, it is important to note that ideational forms of pretense (using nothing but air to denote a telephone) are found to exist in the play of familiar, *preschool* age dyads (Matthews, 1977b). Again, reliance on this form of verbal interview might distort the developmental picture of the growing complexity of pretense.

In a similar vein, Morison and Gardner (1978) found improvements with age in the use of fantasy classifications. When asked to sort 20 pictures into piles of "real" and "pretend" figures, kindergartners made more classification errors than did second-grade, fourth-grade, and sixth-grade counterparts. However, Morison and Gardner were quick to point out that their data may underestimate children's capacities to distinguish the realms of reality and fantasy. After all, preschoolers do appear to consider the signals of laughter and smiles when classifying rough-and-tumble activities as play rather than the "real thing" (Garvey, 1977a).

There are, however, no studies in which children's interpretations of others' behavior as play or nonplay have been examined. This would appear to be a worthwhile area of future study. For example, one could provide children of various ages with videotaped samples of dyadic interaction and then ask them to identify those events in which the participants engage in "make-believe" (as in the aforementioned paradigm case approach of Matthews & Matthews, 1982). Developmental norms concerning *conceptions* of pretense thus could be studied within a simple, nonverbal methodological framework. This would allow researchers to target children who cannot identify ''make-believe'' samples of behavior at an age when the norm is to be able to successfully distinguish nonliteral from literal behavior. Given current interest in social competence and peer rejection and their causal correlates (see Hartup, *vol. IV, chap. 8*), one might ask whether children who interpret events *too* literally are less popular and less likely to engage in productive social encounters (and sociodramatic play) than their more astute agemates.

Play and Language

Another recent issue deals with the relationship between symbolic play and language development. Although psychologists have assumed, over the years, that early pretense and early language have common characteristics or have some influence on one another (Piaget, 1962; Vygotsky, 1967; Werner & Kaplan, 1963), researchers have only recently begun to examine the relationship between the two. This research has been influenced by Piaget's notion that pretense marks the beginning of representational thinking and the emergence of a special capacity (e.g., the semiotic function) to endow arbitrary sound patterns, gestures, or images with meaning. As we indicated earlier, the implications of pretend play with respect to language development are central to the problems examined by Vygotsky (1967). However, for both Piaget and Vygotsky, the issue does not concern the development of speech as much as it concerns the child's understanding that one thing can signify something else, even when the something is not immediately present.

Up to now, studies of the relationship between play and language have stressed language production as reflected in communicative, imitative, or referential speech (Bates, Camaioni, & Volterra, 1975; Folger & Leonard, 1978; Ingram, 1977; Lodge, 1979; Lowe & Costello, 1976; McCune-Nicolich, 1981; McCune-Nicolich & Bruskin, 1982; Nicolich, 1977; Nicolich & Raph, 1978). These studies of production thus may not be consistent with the theoretical stress on comprehension. Generally, the findings suggest that particular phases in the development of symbolic play and language tend to occur together (Ingram, 1977; McCune-Nicolich, 1981; Nicolich & Raph, 1978), but when age is partialed out, the correlation between play and language is considerably reduced or entirely eliminated (Folger & Leonard, 1978; Lowe & Costello, 1976).

Symbolic play may be related to the expressive functions of language, but these relationships may reflect personal style rather than symbolic maturity (Bates et al., 1975; Fein, 1979b). Since theorists such as Piaget (1962) and Vygotsky (1967; 1978) stress the meaning or the control functions of language, rather than its productive quality or quantity, and since productive speech during the second year of life reflects stylistic as well as mastery differences, studies of language meaning (e.g., comprehension or mediation) might have more theoretical significance than studies of language production. In keeping with this notion, Fein (1979b) recently has examined the relationship between pretend play and independent measures of language comprehension and production. Language comprehension and not language production was related to more advanced levels of pretense play in children age 18 to 24 months. Given the suggestion that early markers of symbolic representation, such as the onset of pretense play and language comprehension, indeed are related, it would appear to be significant to examine those social and cognitive factors that contribute to development in this area.

Conclusion

In general, researchers have been unable to provide convincing evidence that pretend play is either a prerequisite for language or cognitive abilities, a concurrent achievement, or a consequence of having acquired such abilities. As Watson and Fischer (1977) have noted, precise correspondences between play and other developmental domains are unlikely since development does not proceed evenly across different task domains. More important, perhaps, is the likelihood that measurement within each domain offers only a moderately reliable and valid estimate of an individual child's level of skill or ability. Since the developmental model being tested presupposes ''best'' performance rather than ''typical'' performance, setting factors that optimize play become major issues. Moreover, the failure to demonstrate a precise correspondence between separate domains does not constitute evidence for the independence of these domains, for reasons other than measurement error. For example, the way in which a sequence manifests itself within each domain may vary as a function of the testing procedures (e.g., spontaneous or elicited play, productive or receptive language). Future investigation would thus do well to take into account methodological factors when examining the relationship between play and other developmental variables. The collection of normative play data, as suggested above, would certainly help in this regard.

In this chapter we have indicated that the play of children has long been a topic of considerable psychological interest. From the classical theories of the nineteenth century to the more recent speculations of Freud, Piaget, Vygotsky, Berlyne, and Bateson, we have attempted to describe the theoretical significance of play in development. Only recently, however, have researchers examined the verisimilitude of these earlier theoretical positions. Much of this research was conducted in the last decade and, consequently, there remains a plethora of unanswered questions concerning the study of play. However, after a dearth of research in the area, we appear to have turned the corner. Now, perhaps researchers can derive as much pleasure from their serious investigative efforts as children do from engaging in this mutual topic of interest—play!

REFERENCES

Aldis, O. *Play fighting*. New York: Academic Press, 1975.

Arend, R., Gove, F. L., & Sroufe, L. A. Continuity of individual adaptation from infancy to kindergarten: A predictive study of ego-resiliency and curiosity in preschoolers. *Child Development*, 1979, *50*, 950–959.

Avedon, E. M., & Sutton-Smith, B. (Eds.). *The study of games*. New York: Wiley, 1971.

Axline, V. *Play therapy*. New York: Ballantine, 1969.

Bach, G. R. Father-fantasies and father-typing in father-separated children. *Child Development*, 1946, *17*, 63–80.

Bakeman, R., & Brown, J. V. Early interaction: Consequences for social and mental development at three years. *Child Development*, 1980, *51*, 437–447.

Bandura, A. *Principles of behavior modification*. New York: Holt, Rinehart and Winston, 1969.

Barker, R. G. *Ecological psychology: Concepts and methods for studying the environment of human behavior*. Stanford, California: Stanford University Press, 1968.

Bartak, L., & Rutter, M. Differences between mentally retarded and normally intelligent autistic children. *Journal of Autism and Childhood Schizophrenia*, 1976, *6*, 109–120.

Bates, E., Benigni, L., Bretherton, I., Camaioni, L., & Volterra, J. From gesture to the first word: On cognitive and social prerequisites. In M. Lewis & L. A. Rosenblum (Eds.), *Interaction, conversation, and the development of language*. New York: Wiley, 1977.

Bates, E., Camaioni, L., & Volterra, V. The acquisition of performatives prior to speech. *Merrill-Palmer Quarterly*, 1975, *21*, 205–226.

Bateson, G. Social planning and the concept of deutero-learning. *Conference on Science, Philosophy and Religion, Second Symposium*. New York: Harper & Row, 1942.

Bateson, G. A theory of play and fantasy. *Psychiatric Research Reports*, 1955, *2*, 39–51.

Bateson, G. The message "This is play." In B. Schaffner (Ed.), *Group processes*. New York: Josiah Macy, 1956.

Beach, F. A. Current concepts of play in animals. *American Naturalist*, 1945, *79*, 523–541.

Bearison, D. J., & Cassel, T. Z. Cognitive decentration and social codes: Communicative effectiveness in young children from differing family contexts. *Developmental Psychology*, 1975, *11*, 29–36.

Belsky, J., & Most, R. From exploration to play: A cross-sectional study of infant free play behavior. *Developmental Psychology*, 1981, *17*, 630–639.

Bender, L. Schizophrenia in childhood: Its recognition, description and treatment. *American Journal of Orthopsychiatry*, 1956, *26*, 499.

Benjamin, H. Age and sex differences in toy preference of young children. *Journal of Genetic Psychology*, 1932, *41*, 417–429.

Berlyne, D. E. *Conflict, arousal and curiosity*. New York: McGraw-Hill, 1960.

Berlyne, D. E. Emotional aspects of learning. *Annual Review of Psychology*, 1964, *15*, 115–142.

Berlyne, D. E. Curiosity and exploration. *Science*, 1966, 153, 25–33.

Berlyne, D. E. Laughter, humor and play. In G. Lindzey & E. Aronson (Eds.), *The handbook of social psychology* (Vol. 3). Reading, Mass: Addison-Wesley, 1969.

Biblow, E. Imaginative play and the control of aggressive behavior. In J. L. Singer, *The child's world of make believe*. New York: Academic Press, 1973.

Birch, H. G. The relation of previous experience to insightful problem solving. *Journal of Comparative Psychology*, 1945, *38*, 267–283.

Bjorklund, G. *The effects of toy quantity and qualitative category on toddlers' play*. Paper presented at the meeting of The Society for Research in Child Development, San Francisco, March 1979.

Black, M., Freeman, B. J., & Montgomery, J. Systematic observation of play behavior in autistic children. *Journal of Autism and Childhood Schizophrenia*, 1975, *15*, 363–371.

Blehar, M. C., Lieberman, A. F., & Ainsworth, M. D. S. Early face-to-face interaction and its relation to later infant-mother attachment. *Child Development*, 1977, *48*, 182–194.

Blurton-Jones, N. G. An ethological study of some aspects of social behavior of children in nursery school. In D. Morris (Ed.), *Primate ethology*. London: Weidenfeld & Nicholson, 1967.

Blurton-Jones, N. G. Categories of child-child interaction. In N. G. Blurton-Jones (Ed.), *Ethological studies of child behavior*. Cambridge, England: Cambridge University Press, 1972.

Blurton-Jones, N., & Konner, M. J. Sex differences in behavior of London and Bushman children. In R. P. Michael & J. H. Crook (Eds.), *Comparative ecology and behaviour of primates*. London: Academic Press, 1973.

Borke, H. Interpersonal perception of young children: Egocentrism or empathy? *Developmental Psychology*, 1971, *5*, 263–269.

Bowen, W. P., & Mitchell, E. D. *The theory of organized play*. New York: Barnes, 1924.

Brainerd, C. J. Effects of group and individualized dramatic play on cognitive development. In D. J. Pepler & K. H. Rubin (Eds.), *The play of children: Current theory and research*. Basel, Switzerland: Karger AG, 1982.

Brindley, C., Clarke, P., Hutt, C., Robinson, I., & Wethli, E. Sex differences in the activities of social interactions of nursery school children. In R. P. Michael & J. H. Crook (Eds.), *Comparative ecology and behaviour of primates*. London: Academic Press, 1973.

Bruner, J. S. The nature and uses of immaturity. *American Psychologist*, 1972, *27*, 687–708.

Bruner, J. S. Introduction. In J. S. Bruner, A. Jolly, & K. Sylva (Eds.), *Play—Its role in development and evolution*. New York: Penguin, 1976.

Bruner, J. S., Jolly, A., & Sylva, K. (Eds.), *Play: Its role in development and evolution*. New York: Penguin, 1976.

Buettner-Janusch, J. Commentary. *Rice University Studies*, 1974, *60*, 93–94.

Buhler, C. *Kindheit und jugend*. Leipzig: Hirzel Verlag, 1928.

Burns, S. M., & Brainerd, C. J. Effects of constructive and dramatic play on perspective-taking in very young children. *Developmental Psychology*, 1979, *15*, 512–521.

Butler, R. A. Discrimination learning by rhesus monkeys to visual-exploration motivation. *Journal of Comparative and Physiological Psychology*, 1953, *46*, 95–98.

Butler, R. A. Exploratory and related behavior: A new trend in animal research. *Journal of Individual Psychology*, 1958, *14*, 111–120.

Caldeira, J., Singer, J. L., & Singer, D. G. *Imaginary playmates: Some relationships to preschoolers' spontaneous play, language and television viewing*. Paper presented at the Eastern Psychological Association, Washington, D.C., March 1978.

Campbell, S. D., & Frost, J. L. *The effects of playground type on the cognitive and social play behaviors of grade two children*. Paper presented at the Seventh World Congress of the International Playground Association, Ottawa, Canada, August 1978.

Cattell, R. B. *Personality*. New York: McGraw-Hill, 1950.

Cattell, R. B. *Personality and learning theory (Vol. 1). The structure of personality in its environment*. New York: Springer, 1979.

Chaillé, C. The child's conceptions of play, pretending and toys: Sequences and structural parallels. *Human Development*, 1978, *21*, 201–210.

Chance, M. R. A., & Mead, A. P. Competition between feeding and investigation in the rat. *Behaviour*, 1955, *8*, 174–182.

Chess, S. Childhood psychopathologies: A search for differentiation. *Journal of Autism and Childhood Schizophrenia*, 1972, *2*, 111–113.

Cheyne, J. A. Object play and problem-solving: Methodological problems and conceptual promise. In D. J. Pepler & K. H. Rubin (Eds.), *The play of children: Current theory and research*. Basel, Switzerland: Karger AG, 1982.

Cheyne, J. A., & Rubin, K. H. Playful precursors of problem-solving in preschoolers. *Developmental Psychology*, in press.

Clark, A. H., Wyon, S. M., & Richards, M. P. Free-play in nursery school children. *Journal of Child Psychology and Psychiatry*, 1969, *10*, 205–216.

Clarke-Stewart, A., & Fein, G. G. Intervention and social policy. In P. Mussen (Ed.), *Carmichael's manual of child psychology: Biology and infancy*. New York: Wiley, 1982.

Clune, C., Paolella, J. M., & Foley, J. M. Free-play behavior of atypical children: An approach to assessment. *Journal of Autism and Developmental Disorders, 9*, 61–72.

Connolly, J. *The relationship between social pretend play and social competence in preschoolers: Correlational and experimental studies*. Unpublished doctoral dissertation, Concordia University, 1980.

Copple, C. E., Cocking, R. R., & Matthews, W. S. *Awareness of object suitability in symbolic play*. Unpublished manuscript, Educational Testing Service, 1980.

Corter, C., Rheingold, H. L., & Eckerman, C. O. Toys delay the infant's following of his mother. *Developmental Psychology*, 1972, *6*, 138–145.

Cramer, P., & Hogan, K. A. Sex differences in verbal and play fantasy. *Developmental Psychology*, 1975, *11*, 145–154.

Crawley, S. B., Rogers, P., Friedman, S., Iacobbo, M., Criticos, A., Richardson, L., & Thompson, M. Developmental changes in the structure of mother-infant play. *Developmental Psychology*, 1978, *14*, 30–36.

Csikszentmihalyi, M. *Beyond boredom and anxiety*. San Francisco: Jossey-Bass, 1975.

Csikszentmihalyi, M., & Bennett, S. An exploratory model of play. *American Anthropologist*, 1971, *73*, 45–58.

Curcio, F., & Piserchia, E. Pantomimic representation in psychotic children. *Journal of Autism and Childhood Schizophrenia*, 1978, *8*, 181–189.

Dansky, J. L. Make believe: A mediator of the relationship between play and associative fluency. *Child Development*, 1980, *51*, 576–579. (a)

Dansky, J. L. Cognitive consequences of sociodramatic play and exploration training for economically disadvantaged preschoolers. *Journal of Child Psychology and Psychiatry*, 1980, *20*, 47–58. (b)

Dansky, J. L., & Silverman, I. W. Effects of play on associative fluency in preschool-aged children. *Developmental Psychology*, 1973, *9*, 38–43.

Dansky, J. L., & Silverman, I. W. Play: A general facilitator of associative fluency. *Developmental Psychology*, 1975, *11*, 104.

Darwin, C. R. *The expression of emotions in man and animals*. London: John Murray, 1872.

de Grazia, S. *Of time, work and leisure*. New York: Twentieth Century Fund, 1962.

Demyer, M. K., Mann, N. A., Tilton, J. R., & Loew, L. H. Toy-play behavior and use of body by autistic and normal children as reported by mothers. *Psychological Reports*, 1967, *21*, 975–981.

Denzin, N. K. *Childhood socialization*. San Francisco: Jossey-Bass, 1979.

DiPietro, J. Rough and tumble play: A function of gender. *Developmental Psychology*, 1981, *17*, 50–58.

Dollard, J., Doob, L., Miller, N., Mowrer, O., &

Sears, R. *Frustration and aggression*. New Haven: Yale University Press, 1939.

Doyle, A. B., Connolly, J., & Rivest, L. P. The effect of playmate familiarity on the social interactions of young children. *Child Development*, 1980, *51*, 217–223.

Dunn, J., & Wooding, C. Play in the home and its implications for learning. In B. Tizard & D. Harvey (Eds.), *Biology of play*. London: Heinemann, 1977.

Eckerman, C. O., & Whatley, J. L. Toys and social interaction between infant peers. *Child Development*, 1977, *48*, 1645–1656.

Eifermann, R. R. Social play in childhood. In R. E. Herron & B. Sutton-Smith (Eds.), *Child's play*. New York: Wiley, 1971.

Eisenberg, N., Murray, E., & Hite, T. Children's reasoning regarding sex-typed toy choices. *Child Development*, 1982, *53*, 81–86.

Elder, J., & Pederson, D. Preschool children's use of objects in symbolic play. *Child Development*, 1978, *49*, 500–504.

El'konin, D. B. Some results of the study of the psychological development of preschool-age children. In M. Cole & I. Maltzman (Eds.), *A handbook of contemporary Soviet psychology*. New York: Basic Books, 1969.

Ellis, M. J. *Why people play*. Englewood Cliffs, N.J.: Prentice-Hall, 1973.

Emmerich, W. Evaluating alternative models of development: An illustrative study of preschool personal-social behaviors. *Child Development*, 1977, *48*, 1401–1410.

Emmerich, W., Cocking, R. R., & Sigel, I. E. Relationships between cognitive and social functioning in preschool children. *Developmental Psychology*, 1979, *15*, 495–504.

Enslein, J. *An analysis of toy preference, social participation and play activity in preschool-aged children*. Unpublished masters thesis, The Merrill-Palmer Institute, 1979.

Enslein, J., & Fein, G. G. Temporal and cross-situational stability of children's social and play behavior. *Developmental Psychology*, 1981, *17*, 760–761.

Erickson, E. H. Studies in the interpretation of play: I. Clinical observations of play disruption in young children. *Genetic Psychology Monographs*, 1940, *22*, 557–671.

Erikson, E. H. Further explorations in play construction: Three spacial variables in their relation to sex and anxiety. *Psychological Bulletin*, 1941, *38*, 748.

Erikson, E. H. *Childhood and society*. New York:

Norton, 1950.

Erikson, E. H. Sex differences in the play configurations of American pre-adolescents. *American Journal of Orthopsychiatry*, 1951, *21*, 667–692.

Erickson, E. H. Play interviews for four year old hospitalized children. *Monographs for the Society for Research in Child Development*, 1958, *23* (4, Serial No. 64).

Erikson, E. H. *Childhood and society*. New York: Norton, 1963.

Erikson, E. H. *Toys and reasons*. New York: Norton, 1977.

Fagen, R. Selective and evolutionary aspects of animal play. *American Naturalist*, 1974, *108*, 850–858, 964.

Fagen, R. M. Modeling: How and why it works. In J. S. Bruner, A. Jolly, & K. Sylva (Eds.), *Play: Its role in development and evolution*. New York: Penguin, 1976.

Fagot, B. I. Sex differences in toddlers' behavior and parental reaction. *Developmental Psychology*, 1974, *10*, 554–558.

Fagot, B. I., & Littman, I. Stability of sex role and play interests from preschool to elementary school. *The Journal of Psychology*, 1975, *89*, 285–292.

Farrell, M. Sex differences in block play in early childhood education. *Journal of Educational Research*, 1957, *51*, 279–284.

Farrer, C. R. Play and inter-ethnic communication. In D. F. Lancy & B. A. Tindal (Eds.), *The anthropological study of play: Problems and prospects*. Cornwall, N.Y.: Leisure Press, 1976.

Fein, G. G. A transformational analysis of pretending. *Developmental Psychology*, 1975, *11*, 291–296.

Fein, G. G. Play revisited. In M. Lamb (Ed.), *Social and personality development*. New York: Holt, Rinehart and Winston, 1978.

Fein, G. G. Echoes from the nursery: Piaget, Vygotsky, and the relationship between language and play. In E. Winner & H. Gardner (Eds.), *Fact, fiction and fantasy in childhood (New directions in child development)*. San Francisco: Jossey-Bass, 1979. (a)

Fein, G. G. Play and the acquisition of symbols. In L. Katz (Ed.), *Current topics in early childhood education*. Norwood, N.J.: Ablex, 1979. (b)

Fein, G. G. Pretend play: An integrative review. *Child Development*, 1981, *52*, 1095–1118.

Fein, G. G. The physical environment: Stimulation or evocation? In R. Lerner and N. Busch (Eds.), *Individuals as producers of their development* (Vol. 1). New York: Academic Press, in press.

Fein, G. G., & Apfel, N. Some preliminary observations on knowing and pretending. In N. Smith & M. Franklin (Eds.), *Symbolic functioning in childhood*. Hillsdale, N.J.: Erlbaum, 1979. (a)

Fein, G. G., & Apfel, N. The development of play: Style, structure and situation. *Genetic Psychology Monographs*, 1979, *99*, 231–250. (b)

Fein, G. G., Johnson, D., Kosson, N., Stork, L., & Wasserman, L. Stereotypes and preferences in the toy choices of 20-month-old boys and girls. *Developmental Psychology*, 1975, *11*, 527–528.

Fein, G. G., & Moorin, E. R. Symbols, motives, and words. In K. Nelson (Ed.), *Children's language* (Vol. 5). New York: Gardner Press, in press.

Fein, G. G., & Robertson, A. R. Cognitive and social dimensions of pretending in two-year-olds. Detroit: Merrill-Palmer Institute, 1975. (ERIC Document Reproduction Service No. ED 119 806)

Fein, G. G., & Stork, L. Sociodramatic play: Social class effects in integrated preschool classrooms. *Journal of Applied Developmental Psychology*, in press.

Feitelson, D. Cross-cultural studies of representational play. In B. Tizard & D. Harvey (Eds.), *Biology of play*. London: Heinemann, 1977.

Feitelson, W., & Ross, G. S. The neglected factor—play. *Human Development*, 1973, *16*, 202–223.

Fenson, L., Kagan, J., Kearsley, R. B., & Zelazo, P. R. The developmental progression of manipulative play in the first two years. *Child Development*, 1976, *47*, 232–235.

Fenson, L., & Ramsay, D. Decentration and integration of the child's play in the second year. *Child Development*, 1980, *51*, 171–178.

Feshbach, S. The catharsis hypothesis and some consequences of interaction with aggressive and neutral play objects. *Journal of Personality*, 1956, *24*, 449–462.

Fields, W. *Imaginative play of four-year-old-children as a function of toy realism*. Unpublished masters thesis, The Merrill-Palmer Institute, 1979.

Fink, R. S. Role of imaginative play in cognitive development. *Psychological Reports*, 1976, *39*, 895–906.

Finley, G. E., & Layne, O. Play behavior in young children: A cross-cultural study. *The Journal of Genetic Psychology*, 1971, *119*, 203–210.

Fischer, K. A theory of cognitive development: The control and construction of hierarchies of skills. *Psychological Review*, 1980, *87*, 477–531.

Fling, S., & Manosevitz, M. Sex typing in nursery

school children's play interests. *Developmental Psychology*, 1972, *7*, 146–152.

Folger, K. M., & Leonard, L. B. Language and sensorimotor behavior during the early period of referential speech. *Journal of Speech and Hearing Research*, 1978, *21*, 519–527.

Forman, G. E., & Hill, F. *Constructive play: Applying Piaget in the preschool*. Monterey, Calif.: Brooks/Cole, 1980.

Freedman, D. G. *The development of social hierarchies*. Paper presented at the meeting of the World Health Organization on Society, Stress, and Disease: Childhood and Adolescence, Stockholm, Sweden, 1971.

Freud, A. *Psychoanalytic treatment of children*. New York: Schocken, 1964.

Freud, S. Analysis of phobia in a five year old boy. In J. Strackey (Ed.), *The standard edition of the complete works of Sigmund Freud* (Vol. X). London: Hogarth, 1955. (Originally published, 1909.)

Freud, S. Creative writers and daydreaming. In J. Strackey (Ed.), *The standard edition of the complete psychological works of Sigmund Freud* (Vol. IX). London: Hogarth, 1959. (Originally published, 1908.)

Freud, S. Jokes and their relation to the unconscious. In J. Strackey (Ed.), *The standard edition of the complete works of Sigmund Freud* (Vol. VIII). London: Hogarth, 1960. (Originally published, 1905.)

Freud, S. *Beyond the pleasure principle*. New York: Norton, 1961.

Freyberg, J. Increasing the imaginative play of urban disadvantaged kindergarten children through systematic training. In J. L. Singer (Ed.), *The child's world of make-believe*. New York: Academic Press, 1973.

Garvey, C. Some properties of social play. *Merrill-Palmer Quarterly*, 1974, *20*, 163–180.

Garvey, C. *Play*. Cambridge, Mass.: Harvard University Press, 1977. (a)

Garvey, C. Play with language. In B. Tizard & D. Harvey (Eds.), *Biology of play*. Philadelphia: Lippincott, 1977. (b)

Garvey, C., & Berndt, R. *Organization of pretend play*. Paper presented at the meeting of the American Psychological Association, Chicago, 1977.

Geertz, C. Deep play: Notes on the Balinese cockfight. *Daedalus*, 1972, *101*, 1–38.

Gilmore, J. B. The role of anxiety and cognitive factors in children's play behavior. *Child Development*, 1966, *37*, 397–416.

Gilmore, J. B. Play: A special behavior. In R. E.

Herron & B. Sutton-Smith (Eds.), *Child's play*. New York: Wiley, 1971.

Gips, C. D. A study of toys for hospitalized children. *Child Development*, 1950, *21*, 149–161.

Goffman, E. *Frame analysis: An essay on the organization of experience*. Cambridge, Mass.: Harvard University Press, 1974.

Goldberg, S., & Lewis, M. Play behavior in the year old infant: Early sex differences. *Child Development*, 1969, *40*, 21–32.

Golomb, C. Symbolic play: The role of substitutions in pretense and puzzle games. *British Journal of Educational Psychology*, 1977, *47*, 175–186.

Golomb, C., & Cornelius, C. B. Symbolic play and its cognitive significance. *Developmental Psychology*, 1977, *13*, 246–252.

Golomb, C., & Friedman, L. *Play and cognition: A study of pretense and conservation of quantity*. Unpublished manuscript, University of Massachusetts, 1979.

Goodman, J. D., & Sours, J. A. *The child mental status exam*. New York: Basic Books, 1967.

Gowen, J. *Structural elements of symbolic play of preschool children*. Paper presented at the meeting of the American Psychological Association, Toronto, August 1978.

Graham, M. Doll-play phantasies of negro and white primary-school children. *Journal of Clinical Psychology*, 1955, *11*, 29–33.

Griffing, P. The relationship between socioeconomic status and sociodramatic play among black kindergarten children. *Genetic Psychology Monographs*, 1980, *101*, 3–34.

Groos, K. *The play of animals*. New York: Appleton, 1898.

Groos, K. *The play of man*. New York: Appleton, 1901.

Gulick, L. H. *A philosophy of play*. New York: Scribners, 1898.

Guthrie, K., & Hudson, L. M. Training conservation through symbolic play: A second look. *Child Development*, 1979, *50*, 1269–1271.

Hall, G. S. *Youth*. New York: Appleton, 1920.

Halverson, C. F., & Waldrop, M. F. The relations of mechanically recorded activity level to varieties of preschool play behavior. *Child Development*, 1973, *44*, 678–681.

Hand, H. H. *The development of children's understanding of variations in behavior*. Paper presented at the meeting of the Society for Research in Child Development, San Francisco, April 1979.

Handelman, D. Play and ritual: Complementary frames of metacommunication. In A. J. Chapman and H. Foot (Eds.), *It's a funny thing, humor*. London: Pergamon, 1977.

Harlow, H. F., & Harlow, M. Learning to love. *American Scientist*, 1966, *3*, 244–272.

Harlow, H. F., Harlow, M. K., & Meyer, D. R. Learning motivated by a manipulation drive. *Journal of Experimental Psychology*, 1950, *40*, 228–234.

Harper, L. V., & Sanders, K. Preschool children's use of space: Sex differences in outdoor play. *Developmental Psychology*, 1975, *11*, 119.

Harter, S. The self system and self control. In E. M. Hetherington (Ed.), *Carmichael's manual of child psychology: Social development*. New York: Wiley, 1982.

Hartley, R. L., & Swartz, S. A pictorial doll-play approach for the study of childrens' intergroup attitudes. *International Journal of Opinion Attitude Research*, 1951, *5*, 261–270.

Hartup, W. W. Peer interaction and the behavioral development of the individual child. In E. Schopler & R. J. Reichler (Eds.), *Psychopathology and child-development*. New York: Plenum, 1976.

Hartup, W. W. The peer system. In E. M. Hetherington (Ed.), *Carmichael's manual of child psychology: Social development*. New York: Wiley, 1982.

Hartup, W. W., Moore, S. G., & Sager, G. Avoidance of inappropriate sex-typing by young children. *Journal of Consulting Psychology*, 1963, *27*, 467–473.

Harvey, S. Play for children in hospital. *International Journal of Early Childhood*, 1975, *7*, 185–187.

Hawkins, D. *The language of nature*. San Francisco: Freeman, 1964.

Hebb, D. O. *The organization of behavior*. New York: Wiley, 1948.

Heinicke, C. M. Some effects of separating two-year-old children from their parents: A comparative study. *Human Relations*, 1956, *9*, 105–176.

Hetherington, E. M., Cox, M., & Cox, R. Play and social interaction in children following divorce. *Journal of Social Issues*, 1979, *35*, 26–49.

Hetzer, H. *Kindbeit und armut*. Leipzig: Hirsch, 1929.

Hoffman, L. R., Burke, R. J., & Maier, N. R. F. Does training with differential reinforcement on similar problems help in solving a new problem? *Psychological Reports*, 1963, *12*, 147–154.

Honzik, M. P. Sex differences in the occurrence of materials in the play constructions of preadolescents. *Child Development*, 1951, *22*, 15–35.

Horne, B. M., & Philleo, C. P. A comparative study of the spontaneous play activities of normal and mentally defective children. *The Journal of Genetic Psychology*, 1942, *61*, 33–46.

Hughes, M. Sequential analysis of exploration and play. *International Journal of Behavioral Development*, 1978, *1*, 83–97.

Hughes, M., & Hutt, C. Heart-rate correlates of childhood activities: Play, exploration, problem-solving and day dreaming. *Biological Psychology*, 1979, *8*, 253–263.

Huizinga, J. *Homo ludens*. Boston: Beacon Press, 1955.

Hull, C. L. *Principles of behavior*. New Haven, Conn.: Yale University Press, 1943.

Hull, C. L. *A behavioral system*. New Haven, Conn.: Yale University Press, 1952.

Hulme, I., & Lunzer, E. A. Play, language and reasoning in subnormal children. *Journal of Child Psychology and Psychiatry*, 1966, *7*, 107–123.

Huston-Stein, A., Friedrich-Cofer, L., & Susman, E. J. The relation of classroom structure to social behavior, imaginative play, and self-regulation of economically disadvantaged children. *Child Development*, 1977, *48*, 908–916.

Hutt, C. Exploration and play in children. *Symposium of the Zoological Society of London*, 1966, *18*, 61–81.

Hutt, C. Temporal effects on response decrement and stimulus satiation in exploration. *British Journal of Psychology*, 1967, *58*, 365–373.

Hutt, C. Specific and diverse exploration. In H. Reese & L. Lipsett (Eds.), *Advances in child development and behavior*. New York: Academic Press, 1970.

Hutt, C. Exploration and play. In B. Sutton-Smith (Ed.), *Play and learning*. New York: Gardner Press, 1979.

Hutt, C. Towards a taxonomy and conceptual model of play. In S. J. Hutt, D. A. Rogers, & C. Hutt (Eds.), *Developmental processes in early childhood*. London: Routledge & Kegan Paul, in press.

Hutt, C., & Bhavnani, R. Predictions from play. In J. S. Bruner, A. Jolly, & K. Sylva (Eds.), *Play*. New York: Penguin, 1976.

Hutt, C., & Hutt, S. J. Heart rate variability—the adaptive consequences of individual differences and state changes. In N. Blurton-Jones & V. Reynolds (Eds.), *Human behavior and adaptation*. London: Taylor and Francis, 1977.

Huttenlocher, J., & Higgins, E. T. Issues in the study of symbolic development. In W. A. Collins (Ed.), *Minnesota symposia on child psychology*. New Jersey: Erlbaum, 1978.

Ingram, D. Sensorimotor intelligence and language development. In A. L. Lock (Ed.), *Action, gesture and symbol: The emergence of language*. New York: Academic Press, 1977.

Inhelder, B., Lezine, I., Sinclair, H., & Stambak, M. Les debut de la function symbolique. *Archives de psychologie*, 1972, *41*, 187–243.

Iwanaga, M. Development of interpersonal play structures in 3, 4 and 5-year-old children. *Journal of Research and Development in Education*, 1973, *6*, 71–82.

Jacklin, C. N., Maccoby, E., & Dick, A. E. Barrier behaviors and toy preference: Sex differences (and their absence) in the year old child. *Child Development*, 1973, *44*, 196–200.

Jackowitz, E. R., & Watson, M. W. The development of object transformations in early pretend play. *Developmental Psychology*, 1980, *16*, 543–549.

Jacobson, J. L. *The determinants of early peer interaction*. Unpublished doctoral dissertation, Harvard University, 1977.

Jahoda, H., & Goldfarb, W. Use of standard observation for the psychological evaluation of non-speaking children. *American Journal of Orthopsychiatry*, 1957, *27*, 745–753.

Janeway, E. *Man's world woman's place*. New York: Morrow, 1971.

Jeffree, D., & McConkey, R. An observation scheme for recording children's imaginative doll play. *Journal of Child Psychology and Psychiatry*, 1976, *17*, 189–197.

Jennings, K. D. People versus object orientation, social behavior, and intellectual abilities in preschool children. *Developmental Psychology*, 1975, *11*, 511–519.

Jernberg, A. M. *Theraplay*. San Francisco: Jossey-Bass, 1979.

Johnson, J. E. Relations of divergent thinking and intelligence tests scores with social and nonsocial make-believe play of preschool children. *Child Development*, 1976, *47*, 1200–1203.

Johnson, J. E. Mother-child interaction and imaginative behavior of preschool children. *The Journal of Psychology*, 1978, *100*, 123–129.

Johnson, J. E., & Ershler, J. *Developmental changes in imaginative play and cognitive ability of preschoolers*. Paper presented at the meeting of the American Psychological Association, Montreal, September 1980.

Johnson, J. E., & Ershler, J. Developmental trends in preschool play as a function of classroom setting and child gender. *Child Development*, 1981, *52*, 995–1004.

Johnson, J. E., Ershler, J., & Bell, C. Play behavior in a discovery-based and a formal education preschool program. *Child Development*, 1980, *51*, 271–274.

Kagan, J., Kearsley, R. B., & Zelazo, P. R. *Infancy: Its place in human development*. Cambridge, Mass.: Harvard University Press, 1978.

Kalverboer, A. F. Measurement of play: Clinical applications. In B. Tizard & D. Harvey (Eds.), *Biology of Play*. London: Heinemann, 1977.

Kearsley, R. B., & Zelazo, P. R. *Sex typed differences in the spontaneous play behavior of infants 9½ to 15½ months of age*. Paper presented at the meeting of the Society for Research in Child Development, San Francisco, 1979.

Kessen, W. & Fein, G. *Variations in home-based infant education*. Final report to the Office of Child Development, HEW, August 1975 (ERIC No. ED 118 233).

Klein, M. *The psychoanalysis of children*. London: Hogarth, 1932.

Klein, M. The psychoanalytic play technique. *American Journal of Orthopsychiatry*, 1955, *25*, 223–237.

Klinger, E. *The structure and functions of fantasy*. New York: Wiley-Interscience, 1971.

Knapczyk, D. R., & Yoppi, I. O. Development of cooperative and competitive play responses in developmentally disabled children. *American Journal of Mental Deficiency*, 1975, *80*, 245–255.

Koestler, A. *The act of creation*. New York: Dell, 1964.

Kohler, W. *The mentality of apes*. New York: Harcourt, Brace, 1925.

Konner, M. J. Aspects of the developmental ethology of a foraging people. In N. Blurton-Jones (Ed.), *Ethological studies of child behavior*. Cambridge, England: Cambridge University Press, 1972.

Krasnor, L. R., & Pepler, D. J. The study of children's play: Some suggested future directions. In K. H. Rubin (Ed.), *Children's play*. San Francisco: Jossey-Bass, 1980.

Lamb, M. E. Father-infant and mother-infant interaction in the first year of life. *Child Development*, 1977, *48*, 167–181.

Laosa, L., & Brophy, J. E. Effects of sex and birth order on sex-role development and intelligence among kindergarten children. *Developmental Psychology*, 1972, *6*, 409–415.

Lazarus, M. *Die reize des spiels*. Berlin: Ferd,

Dummlers Verlagsbuchhandlung, 1883.

Lee, J. P. *Play in education*. New York: MacMillan, 1915.

Leonard, L. B. Language impairment in children. *Merrill-Palmer Quarterly*, 1979, *25*, 205–232.

Levin, H., & Wardwell, E. The research uses of doll play. *Psychological Bulletin*, 1962, *59*, 27–56.

Levy, J. *Play behavior*. New York: Wiley, 1977.

Lewin, K. Environmental forces in child behavior and development. In C. Murchison (Ed.), *A handbook of child psychology*. Worcester, Mass.: Clark University Press, 1931.

Lieberman, A. F. Preschoolers' competence with a peer: Influence of attachment and social experience. *Child Development*, 1977, *48*, 1277–1287.

Lieberman, J. N. Playfulness and divergent thinking: An investigation of their relationship at the kindergarten level. *The Journal of Genetic Psychology*, 1965, *107*, 219–224.

Lieberman, J. N. *Playfulness: Its relationship to imagination and creativity*. New York: Academic Press, 1977.

Lindquist, I., Lind, J., & Harvey, D. Play in hospital. In B. Tizard & D. Harvey (Eds.), *Biology of play*. Philadelphia: Lippincott, 1977.

Lodge, K. R. The use of past tense in games of pretend. *Journal of Child Language*, 1979, *6*, 365–369.

Loizos, C. Play behavior in higher primates: A review. In D. Morris (Ed.), *Primate Ethology*, Chicago: Aldine Publishing Co., 1967.

Lovell, K., Hoyle, H. W., & Siddall, M. C. A study of some aspects of the play and language of young children with delayed speech. *Journal of Child Psychology and Psychiatry*, 1968, *9*, 41–50.

Lovinger, S. L. Sociodramatic play and language development in preschool disadvantaged children. *Psychology in the Schools*, 1974, *11*, 313–320.

Lowe, M. Trends in the development of representational play in infants from one to three years—An observational study. *Journal of Child Psychology and Psychiatry*, 1975, *16*, 33–47.

Lowe, M., & Costello, A. *Manual for the symbolic play test*. London: NFER, 1976.

Lunzer, E. A. Intellectual development in the play of young children. *Educational Review*, 1959, *11*, 205–217.

Maccoby, E. E., & Jacklin, C. N. *The Psychology of sex differences*. Stanford, Calif.: Stanford University Press, 1974.

Manosevitz, M., Prentice, N. M., & Wilson, F. Individual and family correlates of imaginary companions in preschool children. *Developmental Psychology*, 1973, *8*, 72–79.

Manwell, E. M., & Mengert, A. G. A study of the development of two and three-year-old children with respect to play activities. *University of Iowa Studies on Child Welfare*, 1934, *9*, 67–111.

Marbach, E. S., & Yawkey, T. D. The effect of imaginative play actions on language development in five-year-old children. *Psychology in the Schools*, in press.

Marshall, H. R. Relations between home experiences and childrens' use of language in play interactions with peers. *Psychological Monographs*, 1961, *75* (5, Whole No. 509).

Marshall, H., & Hahn, S. Experimental modification of dramatic. *Journal of Personality and Social Psychology*, 1967, *5*, 119–122.

Mason, W. A. The social development of monkeys and apes. In I. Devore (Ed.), *Primate behavior*. New York: Holt, Rinehart and Winston, 1965. (a)

Mason, W. A. Determinants of social behavior in young chimpanzees. In A. M. Schier, H. F. Harlow & F. Stollnitz (Eds.), *Behavior of nonhuman primates* (Vol. 2). New York: Academic Press, 1965. (b)

Matas, L., Arend, R. A., & Sroufe, L. A. Continuity of adaption in the second year: The relationship between quality of attachment and later competence. *Child Development*, 1978, *49*, 547–556.

Matthews, R. J., & Matthews, W. S. A paradigm case approach to the study of fantasy. In D. J. Pepler & K. H. Rubin (Eds.), *The play of children: Current theory and research*. Basel, Switzerland: Karger AG, 1982.

Matthews, W. S. *Sex role perception, portrayal, and preference in the fantasy play of young children*. Paper presented at the meeting of the Society for Research in Child Development, New Orleans, March 1977. (a)

Matthews, W. S. Modes of transformation in the initiation of fantasy play. *Developmental Psychology*, 1977, *13*, 212–216. (b)

Matthews, W. S. *Interruptions of fantasy play: A matter of breaking frame*. Paper presented at the meeting of the Eastern Psychological Association, Washington, D.C., March 1978. (a)

Matthews, W. S. *The facilitory affect of fantasy on the spatial perspective-taking ability of young children*. Paper presented at the meeting of the Eastern Psychological Association, Washington, D.C., March 1978. (b)

Matthews, W. S., Beebe, S., & Bopp, W. Spatial perspective-taking and pretend play. *Perceptual and Motor Skills,* 1980, *51*(1), 49–50.

McCall, R. B. Exploratory manipulation and play in the human infant. *Monographs of the Society for Research in Child Development,* 1974, *39* (Serial No. 155).

McCune-Nicolich, L. Toward symbolic functioning: Structure of early pretend games and potential parallels with language. *Child Development,* 1981, *52,* 785–797.

McCune-Nicolich, L., & Bruskin, C. Combinatorial competency in play and language. In D. J. Pepler & K. H. Rubin (Eds.), *The play of children: Current theory and research.* Basel, Switzerland: Karger AG, 1982.

McGraw, K. O. The detrimental effects of reward on performance: A literature review and a prediction model. In M. L. Lepper & D. Greene (Eds.), *The hidden costs of reward.* New York: Wiley, 1978.

McGrew, W. C. *An ethological study of children's behavior.* London: Academic Press, 1972.

McLoyd, V. C. Verbally expressed modes of transformation in the fantasy play of black preschool children. *Child Development,* 1980, *51,* 1133–1139.

Mead, G. H. *Mind, self and society.* Chicago: University of Chicago Press, 1934.

Meehl, P. E., Lykken, D. T., Schofield, W., & Tellegen, A. Recaptured-item technique (RIT): A method for reducing somewhat the subjective element in factor naming. *Journal of Experimental Research in Personality,* 1971, *5,* 171–190.

Melson, G. F. Sex differences in use of indoor space by preschool children. *Perceptual and Motor Skills,* 1977, *44,* 207–213.

Menninger, K. *Love against hate.* New York: Harcourt, 1942.

Mergen, B. From play to recreation: The acceptance of leisure in the United States. In P. Stevens (Ed.), *Studies in the anthropology of play.* New York: Leisure Press, 1977.

Millar, S. *The psychology of play.* Baltimore: Penguin, 1968.

Miller, S. N. Ends, means and galumphing: Some leitmotifs of play. *American Anthropologist,* 1973, *75,* 87–98.

Miller, S. N. The playful, the crazy and the nature of pretence. *Rice University Studies,* 1974, *60,* 31–51.

Mitchell, E. D., & Mason, B. S. *The theory of play.* Barnes, N.Y.: Ronald Press, 1948.

Mogford, K. The play of handicapped children. In B. Tizard & D. Harvey (Eds.), *The biology of play.* Philadelphia: Lippencott, 1977.

Montessori, M. *The Montessori method.* Cambridge, Mass.: Bentley, Inc., 1973.

Moore, N. V., Evertson, C. M., & Brophy, J. E. Solitary play: Some functional reconsiderations. *Developmental Psychology,* 1974, *10,* 830–834.

Morison, P., & Gardner, B. Dragons and dinosaurs: The child's capacity to differentiate fantasy from reality. *Child Development,* 1978, *49,* 642–648.

Morris, R. J., & Dolker, M. Developing cooperative play in socially withdrawn retarded children. *Mental Retardation,* 1974, *12,* 24–27.

Morrison, T. L., & Newcomer, B. L. Effects of directive vs. non-directive play therapy with institutionalized mentally retarded children. *American Journal of Mental Deficiency,* 1975, *79,* 666–669.

Mueller, E., & Lucas, T. A developmental analysis of peer interaction among toddlers. In M. Lewis & L. Rosenblum (Eds.), *Peer relations and friendship.* New York: Wiley, 1975.

Muste, M. J., & Sharpe, D. G. Some influential factors in the determination of aggressive behavior in preschool children. *Child Development,* 1947, *18,* 11–28.

Nahme-Huang, L., Singer, D. G., Singer, J. L., & Wheaton, A. Imaginative play and perceptual-motor intervention methods with emotionally-disturbed hospitalized children: An evaluation study. *American Journal of Orthopsychiatry,* 1977, *47,* 238–249.

Neill, S. R. Aggressive and non-aggressive fighting in twelve to thirteen-year-old preadolescent boys. *Journal of Child Psychology and Psychiatry,* 1976, *17,* 213–220.

Neuman, E. A. *The elements of play.* New York: MSS Information Corp., 1971.

Newcomer, B. L., & Morrison, T. L. Play therapy with institutionalized mentally retarded children. *American Journal of Mental Deficiency,* 1974, *78,* 727–733.

Nicolich, L. Beyond sensorimotor intelligence: Assessment of symbolic maturity through analysis of pretend play. *Merrill-Palmer Quarterly,* 1977, *23,* 89–99.

Nicolich, L., & Raph, J. B. Imitative language and symbolic maturity in the single-word period. *Journal of Psycholinguistic Research,* 1978, *7,* 401–447.

Norbeck, E. Anthropological views of play. *American Zoologist,* 1974, *14,* 43–55.

Nunnally, J. C., & Lemond, L. C. Exploratory behavior and human development. In H. Reese

(Ed.), *Advances in child development and behavior* (Vol. 8). New York: Academic Press, 1973.

Opie, I., & Opie, P. *Children's games in streets and playgrounds*. London: Clarendon Press, 1969.

Ornitz, E. M., & Ritvo, E. R. The syndrome of autism: A critical review. *American Journal of Psychiatry*, 1976, *133*, 609–621.

Overton, W. F., & Jackson, J. P. The representation of imagined objects in action sequences: A developmental study. *Child Development*, 1973, *44*, 309–314.

Parten, M. B. Social participation among preschool children. *Journal of Abnormal Psychology*, 1932, *27*, 243–269.

Patrick, G. T. W. *The psychology of relaxation*. Boston: Houghton-Mifflin, 1916.

Pavlov, I. P. *Conditioned reflexes*. Oxford: Clarendon Press, 1927.

Peck, C. A., Appoloni, T., Cooke, T. P., & Raver, S. A. Teaching retarded preschoolers to imitate the free play behavior of nonretarded classmates: Trained and generalized effects. *The Journal of Special Education*, 1978, *12*, 195–207.

Peck, J., & Goldman, R. *The behaviors of kindergarten children under selected conditions of the social and physical environment*. Paper presented at the meeting of the American Education Research Association, Toronto, March 1978.

Pederson, F. A., & Bell, R. Q. Sex differences in preschool children without histories of complications of pregnancy and delivery. *Developmental Psychology*, 1970, *3*, 10–15.

Peller, L. E. Models of children's play. *Mental Hygiene*, 1952, *36*, 66–83.

Peller, L. E. Libidinal phases, ego development and play. *Psychoanalytic Study of the Child*, 1954, *9*, 178–198.

Pepler, D. J. *Effects of convergent and divergent play experience on preschoolers' problem-solving behaviors*. Unpublished doctoral dissertation, University of Waterloo, 1979.

Pepler, D. J. Play and divergent thinking. In D. J. Pepler & K. H. Rubin (Eds.), *The play of children: Research and theory*. Basel, Switzerland: Karger AG, 1982.

Pepler, D. J., & Ross, H. S. The effects of play on convergent and divergent problem-solving. *Child Development*, 1981, *52*, 1202–1210.

Phillips, R. Doll play as a function of the realism of the materials and the length of the experimental session. *Child Development*, 1945, *16*, 145–166.

Phyfe-Perkins, E. Children's behavior in preschool settings—The influence of the physical environment. In L. G. Katz (Ed.), *Current topics in early childhood education* (Vol. 3). Norwood, N.J.: Ablex, 1980.

Piaget, J. *The moral judgment of the child*. New York: Free Press, 1932.

Piaget, J. *Play, dreams, and imitation in childhood*. New York: Norton, 1962.

Piaget, J. Response to Brian Sutton-Smith. *Psychological Review*, 1966, *73*, 111–112.

Piaget, J. Piaget's theory. In P. H. Mussen (Ed.), *Carmichael's Manual of Child Psychology* (Vol. 1). New York: Wiley, 1970.

Piaget, J., & Inhelder, B. *Mental imagery in the child*. New York: Basic Books, 1971.

Polanyi, M. *Personal knowledge*. Chicago: University of Chicago, 1958.

Polgar, S. K. The social context of games: Or when is play not play? *Sociology of Education*, 1976, *49*, 265–271.

Power, T. G., & Parke, R. D. Play as a context for early learning: Lab and home analyses. In I. E. Sigel & L. J. Laosa (Eds.), *The family as a learning environment*. New York: Plenum, 1980.

Pulaski, M. A. S. Play as a function of toy structure and fantasy predisposition. *Child Development*, 1970, *41*, 531–537.

Pulaski, M. A. Toys and imaginative play. In J. L. Singer, *The child world of make-believe*. New York: Academic Press, 1973.

Quinn, J., & Rubin, K. H. The play of handicapped children. In T. Yawkey & A. Pellegrini (Eds.), *Child's play: Developmental and applied*. Hillsdale, N.J.: Erlbaum, in press.

Rabinowitz, F. M., Moely, B. E., Finkel, N., & McClinton, S. The effects of toy novelty and social interaction on the exploratory behavior of preschool children. *Child Development*, 1975, *46*, 286–289.

Rapoport, J., Abramson, A., Alexander, D., & Lott, I. Playroom observations of hyperactive children on medication. *Journal of American Academy of Child Psychiatry*, 1971, *10*, 524–534.

Ratner, N., & Bruner, J. S. Games, social exchange, and the acquisition of language. *Journal of Child Language*, 1978, *5*, 391–402.

Reynolds, P. *Play language and evolution*. Paper presented at the meeting of the American Association for the Advancement of Science, Washington D.C., December 1972.

Rheingold, H. L., & Cook, K. V. The contents of boys' and girls' rooms as an index of parents behavior. *Child Development*, 1975, *46*, 459–463.

Rheingold, H. L., & Eckerman, C. O. The infant's free entry into a new environment. *Journal of Experimental Child Psychology*, 1969, *8*, 271–283.

Roberts, J. M., Arth, M. J., & Bush, R. R. Games in culture. *American Anthropologist*, 1959, *61*, 597–605.

Roberts, J. M., & Sutton-Smith, B. Child training and game involvement. *Ethnology*, 1962, *2*, 166–185.

Roper, R., & Hinde, R. A. Social behavior in a play group: Consistency and complexity. *Child Development*, 1978, *49*, 570–579.

Rosen, C. E. The effects of sociodramatic play on problem solving behavior among culturally disadvantaged children. *Child Development*, 1974, *45*, 920–927.

Rosenberg, B. G., & Sutton-Smith, B. The measurement of masculinity and femininity in children. *Child Development*, 1959, *30*, 373–380.

Rosenberg, B. G., & Sutton-Smith, B. A revised conception of masculine-feminine differences in play activities. *Journal of Genetic Psychology*, 1960, *96*, 165–170.

Rosenblatt, D. Developmental trends in infant play. In B. Tizard & D. Harvey (Eds.), *The biology of play*. Philadelphia: Lippincott, 1977.

Ross, H. S., Goldman, B. D., & Hay, D. F. Features and functions of infant games. In B. Sutton-Smith (Ed.), *Play and learning*. New York: Gardner Press, 1979.

Ross, H. S., Rheingold, H. L., & Eckerman, C. O. Approach and exploration of a novel alternative by 12-month-old infants. *Journal of Experimental Child Psychology*, 1972, *13*, 85–93.

Rubenstein, J. A concordance of visual and manipulative responsiveness to novel and familiar stimuli in six-month-old infants. *Child Development*, 1974, *45*, 194–198.

Rubenstein, J., & Howes, C. The effect of peers on toddlers interaction with mother and toys. *Child Development*, 1976, *47*, 597–605.

Rubin, K. H. The play behaviors of young children. *Young Children*, 1977, *32*, 16–24. (a)

Rubin, K. H. The social and cognitive value of preschool toys and activities. *Canadian Journal of Behavioural Science*, 1977, *9*, 382–385. (b)

Rubin, K. H. Roletaking in childhood: Some methodological considerations. *Child Development*, 1978, *49*, 534–536.

Rubin, K. H. Fantasy play: Its role in the development of social skills and social cognition. In K. H. Rubin (Ed.), *Children's Play*. San Francisco: Jossey-Bass, 1980.

Rubin, K. H. Early play theories revisited: Contributions to contemporary research and theory. In D. J. Pepler & K. H. Rubin (Eds.), *The play of children: Current theory and research*. Basel, Switzerland: Karger AG, 1982. (a)

Rubin, K. H. Nonsocial play in preschoolers: Necessarily evil? *Child Development*, 1982, *53*, 651–657. (b)

Rubin, K. H., & Krasnor, L. R. Changes in the play behaviors of preschoolers: A short-term longitudinal investigation. *Canadian Journal of Behavioral Science*, 1980, *12*, 278–282.

Rubin, K. H., & Maioni, T. Play preference and its relationship to egocentrism, popularity and classification skills in preschoolers. *Merrill-Palmer Quarterly*, 1975, *21*, 171–179.

Rubin, K. H., Maioni, T. L., & Hornung, M. Free play behaviors in middle and lower class preschoolers: Parten and Piaget revisited. *Child Development*, 1976, *47*, 414–419.

Rubin, K. H., & Pepler, D. J. The relationship of child's play to social-cognitive development. In H. Foot, T. Chapman, & J. Smith (Eds.), *Friendship and childhood relationships*. London: Wiley, 1980.

Rubin, K. H., & Pepler, D. J. A neo-Piagetian perspective of children's play. *Journal of Contemporary Educational Psychology*, in press.

Rubin, K. H., & Seibel, C. The effects of ecological setting on the cognitive and social play behaviors of preschoolers. *Proceedings of the Ninth Annual International Inter-disciplinary Conference on Piagetian Theory and the Helping Professions*, 1981.

Rubin, K. H., Watson, K., & Jambor, T. Free play behaviors in preschool and kindergarten children. *Child Development*, 1978, *49*, 534–536.

Rutter, M. Childhood schizophrenia reconsidered. *Journal of Autism and Childhood Schizophrenia*, 1972, *2*, 315–337.

Rutter, M. The development of infantile autism. *Psychological Medicine*, 1974, *4*, 147–163.

Rutter, M. Diagnosis and definition of childhood autism. *Journal of Autism and Childhood Schizophrenia*, 1978, *8*, 139–169.

Sachs, J. The role of adult-child play in language development. In K. H. Rubin (Ed.), *Children's play*. San Francisco: Jossey-Bass, 1980.

Salomon, G. *The language of media and the cultivation of mental skills*. Report of the Spencer Foundation, Chicago, 1977.

Salter, M. E. (Ed.). *Play: Anthropological perspectives*. West Point, N.Y.: Leisure Press, 1978.

Saltz, B. *Stimulating imaginative play: Some cogni-*

tive effects on preschoolers. Paper presented at the meeting of the American Psychological Association, Toronto, August 1978.

Saltz, E. *Pretend play: A complex of variables influencing development*. Paper presented at the meeting of the American Psychological Association, Montreal, September 1980.

Saltz, E., & Brodie, J. Pretend-play training in childhood: A review and critique. In D. J. Pepler & K. H. Rubin (Eds.), *The play of children: Current theory and research*. Basel, Switzerland: Karger AG, 1982.

Saltz, E., Dixon, D., & Johnson, J. Training disadvantaged preschoolers on various fantasy activities: Effects on cognitive functioning and impulse control. *Child Development*, 1977, *48*, 367–380.

Saltz, E., & Johnson, J. Training for thematic-fantasy play in culturally disadvantaged children: Preliminary results. *Journal of Educational Psychology*, 1974, *66*, 623–630.

Sanders, K. M., & Harper, L. V. Free play fantasy behavior in preschool children: Relations among gender, age, season and location. *Child Development*, 1976, *47*, 1182–1185.

Sarbin, T. R., & Allen, J. L. Role theory. In G. Lindzey & E. Aronson (Eds.), *The handbook of social psychology* (Vol. 5). Reading, Mass.: Addison-Wesley, 1969.

Schaffer, H. R., & Perry, M. H. Perceptual-motor behavior in infancy as a function of age and stimulus familiarity. *British Journal of Psychology*, 1969, *60*, 1–9.

Schank, R., & Abelson, R. Scripts, plans, and knowledge. In P. Johnson-Laird & P. Wason (Eds.), *Thinking: Readings in cognitive science*. New York: Cambridge University Press, 1977.

Schiller, F. *On the aesthetic education of man*. New Haven, Conn.: Yale University Press, 1954.

Schiller, P. H. Innate motor action as a basis of learning. In P. H. Schiller (Ed.), *Instinctive behavior*. New York: International Universities Press, 1957.

Schlosberg, H. The concept of play. *Psychological Review*, 1947, *54*, 229–231.

Schmitt, B. D. The minimal brain dysfunction myth. *American Journal of Diseases of Children*, 1975, *129*, 1313–1318.

Scholtz, G. J. L., & Ellis, M. J. Repeated exposure to objects and peers in a play setting. *Journal of Experimental Child Psychology*, 1975, *19*, 448–455.

Schramm, W., Lyle, J., & Parker, E. *Television in the lives of our children*. Stanford: Stanford University Press, 1961.

Schwartzman, H. B. The anthropological study of children's play. *Annual Review of Anthropology*, 1976, *5*, 289–328. (a)

Schwartzman, H. B. Children's play: A sideways glance at make believe. In D. F. Lancy & B. A. Tindall (Eds.), *The anthropological study of play: Problems and prospects*. Cornwall, N.Y.: Leisure Press, 1976. (b)

Schwartzman, H. B. *Transformations: The anthropology of children's play*. New York: Plenum, 1978.

Schwartzman, H. B. The sociocultural context of play. In B. Sutton-Smith (Ed.), *Play and learning*. New York: Gardner Press, 1979.

Schwartzman, H. B. (Ed.). *Play and culture*. West Point, N.Y.: Leisure Press, 1980.

Sears, R. R. Influence of methodological factors on doll-play performance. *Child Development*, 1947, *18*, 190–197.

Selman, R. L. Social-cognitive understanding: A guide to educational and clinical practice. In T. Lickona (Ed.), *Moral development and behavior*. New York: Holt, Rinehart and Winston, 1976.

Serbin, L. A., Conner, J. A., Burchardt, C. J., & Citron, C. C. Effects of peer presence on sex-typing of children's play behavior. *Journal of Experimental Child Psychology*, 1979, *27*, 303–309.

Shantz, C. U. Social cognition. In J. H. Flavell & E. Markman (Eds.), *Carmichael's manual of child psychology: Cognitive development*. New York: Wiley, 1982.

Sherif, C. W. Bias in psychology. In J. A. Sherman and E. T. Beck (Eds.), *The prism of sex*. Madison, Wis.: University of Wisconsin Press, 1979.

Sherman, J. A. *On the psychology of women*. Springfield, Ill.: Charles C. Thomas, 1971.

Sherrod, L., & Singer, J. L. The development of make-believe. In J. Goldstein (Ed.), *Sports, games, and play*. Hillsdale, N.J.: Erlbaum, 1977.

Shotwell, J. M., Wolf, D., & Gardner, H. Exploring early symbolization: Styles of achievement. In B. Sutton-Smith (Ed.), *Play and learning*. New York: Gardner Press, 1979.

Shultz, T. R. Play as arousal modulation. In B. Sutton-Smith (Ed.), *Play and learning*. New York: Gardner Press, 1979.

Shure, M. E. Psychological ecology of a nursery school child. *Child Development*, 1963, *34*, 979–994.

Silvern, L. B. *The playroom diagnostic evaluation*

of children with neurologically based learning disabilities. Paper presented at the meeting of the American Academy of Child Psychiatry, October 1974.

Sinclair, H. The transition from sensorimotor behavior to symbolic activity. *Interchange*, 1970, *1*, 119–125.

Singer, D. G., & Rummo, J. Ideational creativity and behavioral style in kindergarten aged children. *Developmental Psychology*, 1973, *8*, 154–161.

Singer, D. G., & Singer, J. L. Family television viewing habits and the spontaneous play of preschool children. *American Journal of Orthopsychiatry*, 1976, *46*, 496–502.

Singer, D. G., & Singer, J. L. *Some correlates of imaginative play in preschoolers*. Paper presented at the meeting of the American Psychological Association, Toronto, August 1978.

Singer, D. G., & Singer, J. L. *Television viewing and aggressive behavior in preschool children: A field study*. Paper presented at the Conference on Forensic Psychology, New York, N.Y., 1979.

Singer, J. L. (Ed.). *The child's world of make-believe: Experimental studies of imaginative play*. New York: Academic Press, 1973.

Singer, J. L. Imagination and make-believe play in early childhood: Some educational implications. *Journal of Mental Imagery*, 1977, *1*, 127–144.

Singer, J. L., & Singer, D. G. Imaginative play and pretending in early childhood. In A. Davids (Ed.), *Child personality and psychopathology*. New York: Wiley, 1976.

Singer, J. L., & Singer, D. G. *Imaginative play in preschoolers: Some research and theoretical implications*. Paper presented at the meeting of the American Psychological Association, Montreal, September 1980.

Singer, J. L., Singer, D. G., & Sherrod, L. R. A factor analytic study of preschooler's play behavior. *American Psychology Bulletin*, 1980, *2*, 143–156.

Singer, J. L., & Streiner, B. F. Imaginative content in the dreams and fantasy play of blind and sighted children. *Perceptual and Motor Skills*, 1966, *22*, 475–482.

Smilansky, S. *The effects of sociodramatic play on disadvantaged preschool children*. New York: Wiley, 1968.

Smith, P. K. Social and fantasy play in young children. In B. Tizard & D. Harvey (Eds.), *Biology of play*. London: Heinemann, 1977.

Smith, P. K., & Connolly, K. Patterns of play and social interaction in preschool children. In N.

Blurton-Jones (Ed.), *Ethological studies of child behaviour*. Cambridge: Cambridge University Press, 1972.

Smith, P. K., & Connolly, K. J. Social and aggressive behavior in preschool children as a function of crowding. *Social Science Information*, 1976, *16*, 601–620.

Smith, P. K., & Daglish, L. Sex differences in infant and parent behavior. *Child Development*, 1977, *48*, 1250–1254.

Smith, P. K., Daglish, M., & Herzmark, G. A comparison of fantasy play tutoring and skills tutoring in nursery classes. *International Journal of Behavioral Development*, in press.

Smith, P. K., & Dodsworth, C. Social class differences in the fantasy play of preschool children. *Journal of Genetic Psychology*, 1978, *133*, 183–190.

Smith, P. K., & Dutton, S. Play and training in direct and innovative problem solving. *Child Development*, 1979, *50*, 830–836.

Smith, P. K., & Syddall, S. Play and non-play tutoring in preschool children: Is it play or tutoring which matters? *British Journal of Educational Psychology*, 1978, *48*, 315–325.

Snow, C. E. The development of conversation between mothers and babies. *Journal of Child Language*, 1977, *4*, 1–22.

Spencer, H. *Principles of psychology* (Vol. 2; 3rd ed.). New York: Appleton, 1873.

Spivack, G., & Shure, M. B. *Social adjustment of young children*. San Francisco: Jossey-Bass, 1974.

Sponseller, D. B., & Jaworski, A. P. *Social and cognitive complexity in young children's play*. Paper presented at the meeting of the American Educational Research Association, San Francisco, April 1979.

Sroufe, L. A., & Waters, E. Attachment as an organizational construct. *Child Development*, 1977, *48*, 1184–1199.

Sroufe, L. A., & Wunsche, J. P. The development of laughter in the first year of life. *Child Development*, 1972, *43*, 1326–1344.

Stern, D. N. Mother and infant at play: The dyadic interaction involving facial, vocal, and gaze behaviors. In M. Lewis & L. Rosenblum (Eds.), *The effect of the infant on its caregiver*. New York: Wiley, 1974.

Stern, D. N. *The first relationship*. Cambridge, Mass.: Harvard University Press, 1977.

Stern, W. *Psychology of early childhood*. New York: Henry Holt, 1924.

Strain, P. Increasing social play of severely retarded

preschoolers with socio-dramatic activities. *Mental Retardation*, 1975, *13*, 7–9.

Sutton-Smith, B. Play preference and play behavior: A validity study. *Psychological Reports*, 1965, *16*, 65–66.

Sutton-Smith, B. Piaget on play: A critique. *Psychological Review*, 1966, *73*, 104–110.

Sutton-Smith, B. The role of play in cognitive development. *Young Children*, 1967, *22*, 361–370.

Sutton-Smith, B. Novel responses to toys. *Merrill-Palmer Quarterly*, 1968, *14*, 151–158.

Sutton-Smith, B. Boundaries. In R. E. Herron & B. Sutton-Smith (Eds.), *Child's play*. New York: Wiley, 1971. (a)

Sutton-Smith, B. A syntax for play and games. In R. E. Herron & B. Sutton-Smith (Eds.), *Child's play*. New York: Wiley, 1971. (b)

Sutton-Smith, B. Current research and theory on play, games and sports. In T. Craig (Ed.), *The humanistic and mental health aspects of sports, exercise and recreation*. Chicago: American Medical Association, 1976.

Sutton-Smith, B. Play as adaptive potentiation. In P. Stevens, Jr. (Ed.), *Studies in the antropology of play*. Cornwall, N.Y.: Leisure Press, 1977.

Sutton-Smith, B. *Die dialektik des spiele*. Schorndorf, Germany: Verlag Karl Holffman, 1978.

Sutton-Smith, B. (Ed.). *Play and learning*. New York: Gardner Press, 1979. (a)

Sutton-Smith, B. The play of girls. In C. B. Kopp and M. Kirkpatrick (Eds.), *Becoming female: Perspectives on development*. New York: Plenum, 1979. (b)

Sutton-Smith, B. Toys for object and role mastery. In K. Hewitt & L. Roomet (Eds.), *Educational toys in America: 1800 to the present*. Burlington, Vt.: Queen City, 1979. (c)

Sutton-Smith, B. Children's play: Some sources of play theorizing. In K. H. Rubin (Ed.), *Children's play*. San Francisco: Jossey-Bass, 1980.

Sutton-Smith, B. Piaget, play and cognition revisited. In W. Overton (Ed.), *The relationship between social and cognitive development*. New York: Erlbaum, in press.

Sutton-Smith, B., & Rosenberg, B. G. *The sibling*. New York: Wiley, 1970.

Sutton-Smith, B., Rosenberg, B. G., & Morgan, E. F. Development and sex differences in play choices during preadolescence. *Child Development*, 1963, *34*, 119–126.

Switzky, H. N., Ludwig, L., & Haywood, H. C. Exploration and play in retarded and nonretarded preschool children: Effects of object complexity and age. *American Journal of Mental Deficiency*, 1979, *83*, 637–644.

Sylva, K. Play and learning. In B. Tizard & D. Harvey (Eds.), *Biology of play*. London: Heinemann, 1977.

Sylva, K., Bruner, J., & Genova, P. The rule of play in the problem-solving of children 3–5 years old. In J. Bruner, A. Jolly, & K. Sylva (Eds.), *Play—Its role in development and evolution*. New York: Penguin, 1976.

Tait, P. The implications of play as it relates to the emotional development of the blind child. *Education of the Visually Handicapped*, 1972, *10*, 52–54. (a)

Tait, P. Behavior of young blind children in a controlled play session. *Perceptual and Motor Skills*, 1972, *34*, 963–969. (b)

Tait, P. Play and the intellectual development of blind children. *New Outlook for the Blind*, 1973, *66*, 361–369.

Tauber, M. A. Parental socialization techniques and sex differences in children's play. *Child Development*, 1979, *50*, 225–234.

Tilton, J. R., & Ottinger, D. R. Comparison of the toy play behavior of autistic, retarded and normal children. *Psychological Reports*, 1964, *15*, 967–975.

Tizard, B. Play: A child's way of learning? In B. Tizard & D. Harvey (Eds.), *Biology of play*. London: Heinemann, 1977.

Tizard, B., Philps, J., & Plewis, I. Play in preschool centres. I. Play measures and their relation to age, sex and IQ. *Journal of Child Psychology and Psychiatry*, 1976, *17*, 251–264. (a)

Tizard, B., Philps, J., & Plewis, I. Play in preschool centres. II. Effects on play of the child's social class and of the educational orientation of the centre. *Journal of Child Psychology and Psychiatry*. 1976, *17*, 265–274. (b)

Tolman, E. C. *Purposive behavior in animals and men*. New York: Century, 1932.

Tower, R. B., Singer, D. G., Singer, J. L., & Biggs, A. Differential effects of television programming on preschoolers' cognition, imagination, and social play. *American Journal of Orthopsychiatry*, 1979, *49*, 265–280; *60*, 53–92.

Ungerer, J., & Sigman, M. Symbolic play and language comprehension in autistic children. *Journal of the American Academy of Child Psychiatry*, 1981, *20*, 318–337.

Ungerer, J., Zelazo, P. R., Kearsley, R. B., & O'Leary, K. Developmental changes in the representation of objects in symbolic play from 18 to

34 months of age. *Child Development*, 1981, *52*, 186–195.

Van Alstyne, D. *Play behavior and choice of play materials of pre-school children*. Chicago: University of Chicago Press, 1932.

Vandell, D. L., & Mueller, E. C. Peer play and friendships during the first two years. In H. C. Foot, A. J. Chapman, & J. R. Smith (Eds.), *Friendship and social relations in children*. London: Wiley, 1980.

Vandenberg, B. Play and development from an ethological perspective. *American Psychologist*, 1978, *33*, 724–738.

Vandenberg, B. Play, problem-solving and creativity. In K. H. Rubin (Ed.), *Children's play: New directions for child development*. San Francisco: Jossey-Bass, 1980. (a)

Vandenberg, B. *Play: A causal agent in problem solving?* Paper presented at the meeting of the American Psychological Association, Montreal, August 1980. (b)

Vandenberg, B. Environmental and cognitive factors in social play. *Journal of Experimental Psychology*, 1981, *31*, 169–175. (a)

Vandenberg, B. The role of play in the development of insightful tool-using strategies. *Merrill-Palmer Quarterly*, 1981, *27*, 97–109. (b)

Vandenberg, B. Play: Dormant issues and new perspectives. *Human Development*, 1981, *24*, 357–365. (c)

van Hooff, J. A. R. A. M. A comparative approach to the phylogency of laughter and smiling. In R. A. Hinde (Ed.), *Non-verbal communication*. Cambridge, England: Cambridge University Press, 1972.

van Lawick-Goodall, J. The behavior of free living chimpanzees in the Gombe Stream Reserve. *Animal Behavior Monographs*, 1968, *1*.

Vygotsky, L. S. *Thought and language*. Cambridge, Mass.: M. I. T. Press, 1962.

Vygotsky, L. S. Play and its role in the mental development of the child. *Soviet Psychology*, 1967, *12*, 62–76.

Vygotsky, L. S. *Mind in society: The development of higher mental processes*. Cambridge, Mass: Harvard University Press, 1978.

Walker, R. N. Measuring masculinity and femininity by children's game choices. *Child Development*, 1964, *35*, 961–971.

Wallach, M. A., & Kogan, N. *Modes of thinking in young children: A study of the creativity intelligence distinction*. New York: Holt, 1965.

Waters, E., Vaughan, B. E., & Egeland, B. Individual differences in infant-mother attachment relationships at age one: Antecedents in neonatal behavior in an urban, economically disadvantaged sample. *Child Development*, 1980, *51*, 208–216.

Waters, E., Wippman, J., & Sroufe, L. A. Attachment, positive affect, and competence in the peer group: Two studies in construct validation. *Child Development*, 1979, *50*, 821–829.

Watson, J. S., & Ramey, C. T. Reactions to response-contingent stimulation in early infancy. *Merrill-Palmer Quarterly*, 1972, *18*, 219–227.

Watson, M. W., & Fischer, K. W. A developmental sequence of agent use in late infancy. *Child Development*, 1977, *48*, 828–836.

Watson, M. W., & Fischer, K. W. Development of social roles in elicited and spontaneous behavior during the preschool years. *Developmental Psychology*, 1980, *16*, 483–494.

Wehman, P. Establishing play behaviors in mentally retarded youth. *Rehabilitation Literature*, 1975, *36*, 238–246.

Weiner, B. J., Ottinger, D. R., & Tilton, J. R. Comparison of toy play behavior of autistic retarded and normal children: A reanalysis. *Psychological Reports*, 1969, *25*, 223–227.

Weiner, E. A., & Weiner, B. J. Differentiation of retarded and normal children through toy-play analysis. *Multivariate Behavioral Research*, 1974, *9*, 245–252.

Weinraub, M., & Frankel, J. Sex differences in parent-infant interaction during free play, departure, and separation. *Child Development*, 1977, *48*, 1240–1249.

Weisler, A., & McCall, R. Exploration and play. *American Psychologist*, 1976, *31*, 492–508.

Werner, H., & Kaplan, B. *Symbol formation*. New York: Wiley, 1963.

White, B. L., & Carew-Watts, J. *Experience and environment: Major influences on the development of the young child*. Englewood Cliffs, N.J.: Prentice-Hall, 1973.

White, R. W. Motivation reconsidered: The concept of competence. *Psychological Review*, 1959, *66*, 297–323.

White, T. H. *The once and future king*. New York: Putnam, 1958.

Whiting, B. B. *Six cultures: Studies of child rearing*. New York: Wiley, 1963.

Whiting, B., & Edwards, C. P. A cross-cultural analysis of sex differences in the behavior of children aged three through 11. *The Journal of Social Psychology*, 1973, *91*, 171–188.

Williams, R. *Symbolic play in young, language handicapped and normal speaking children*. Paper presented at the International Conference on Piaget and the Helping Professions, Los Angeles, February 1980.

Wills, D. M. Problems of play and mastery in the blind child. In E. P. Trapp & P. Himelstein (Eds.), *Readings on the exceptional child*. New York: Appleton-Century-Crofts, 1972.

Wilson, E. O. *Sociobiology*. Cambridge, Mass.: Belknap Press, 1975.

Wing, L., Gould, J., Yeates, S. R., & Brierly, L. M. Symbolic play in severely mentally retarded and in autistic children. *Journal of Child Psychology and Psychiatry*, 1977, *18*, 167–178.

Winnicott, D. *Playing and reality*. New York: Basic Books, 1971.

Wolf, D., & Gardner, H. Style and sequence in early symbolic play. In M. Franklin & N. Smith (Eds.), *Early symbolization*. Hillsdale, N.J.: Lawrence Erlbaum, 1978.

Wolf, D., & Grollman, S. H. Ways of playing: Indi-

vidual differences in imaginative style. In D. J. Pepler & K. H. Rubin (Eds.), *The play of children: Current theory and research*. Basel, Switzerland: Karger AG, 1982.

Young, W., Goy, R., & Phoenix, C. Hormones and sexual behavior. *Science*, 1964, *143*, 212–218.

Zelazo, P. R., & Kearsley, R. B. *Functional play: Evidence of cognitive metamorphosis in the year old infant*. Paper presented at the meeting of the Society for Research in Child Development, New Orleans, March 1977.

Zelazo, P. R., & Kearsley, R. B. The emergence of functional play in infants: Evidence for a major cognitive transition. *Journal of Applied Developmental Psychology*, 1980, *1*, 95–117.

Zigler, E. Mental retardation: Current issues and approaches. In L. W. Hoffman & M. L. Hoffman (Eds.), *Review of child development research* (Vol. 2). New York: Russell Sage Foundation, 1966.

DEVELOPMENTAL PSYCHOPATHOLOGY | 10

MICHAEL RUTTER, *University of London Institute of Psychiatry*
NORMAN GARMEZY, *University of Minnesota*

CHAPTER CONTENTS

INTRODUCTION

The title of this chapter emphasizes that its purpose is to consider some of the emotional, social, and conduct disorders of children from a developmental psychopathology perspective rather than in terms of psychological or psychiatric syndromes as such. As Eisenberg (1977) has argued persuasively, a concern for developmental issues constitutes one essential underlying concept in the psychiatry of both childhood and adulthood. The process of development constitutes the crucial link between genetic determinants and environmental variables, between physiogenic and psychogenic causes, and between the residues of prior maturation or earlier experiences and the modulations of behavior by the circumstances of the present. A developmental perspective requires us to take account of continuities *and* discontinuities between infancy, childhood, and adult life. The empirical data make clear that both occur (Rutter, in press-b). In our discussions of the

various types of emotional and social disturbance, we consider the longitudinal course of atypical development and, insofar as they are known, the links between childhood and adult life.

Although one of the key features of child psychopathology is its focus on a developing organism, it is a surprising and regrettable fact that, at least until very recently, research on child development and research on child psychiatric disorders have remained rather separate endeavors (Achenbach, 1978). Our task was to bring the two together by means of a developmental psychopathology approach.

Such an approach has several key features (Rutter, in press-d). The adjective developmental specifies a concern with the general course of psychosocial development, with the changes that take place with developmental progression, with the processes and mechanisms that underlie the developmental transitions, and with the implications that follow their occurrence. Thus, developmentalists question whether there are age-dependent variations in susceptibility to stress, whether the development of depression or delinquent activities at one age is dependent on prior occurrences at an earlier age, and whether there are points in development at which personality qualities become stabilized to the extent that, although behavior may change, no longer can it be totally transformed. However, developmental psychopathology differs from child development in its strong focus on individual differences. Much of developmental psychology has been based on the overriding perspective of the developmental progressions that occur in all normal children (Plomin, in press). Knowledge of these universals, of course, is fundamental to any understanding of the developmental process. Yet, the developmental psychopathologist will want to ask about the variations in that course and about individual differences in the developmental process. The distinction between the perspectives of individuality and universality is important because of the contrasts in the questions that they pose and because the two approaches require different methodologies and different research strategies (Plomin, in press; Rutter, 1982). In particular, the concern with individuality means the choice of measures that differentiate sensitively within broad domains of behavior, the use of epidemiological techniques to study quite large samples (to have a large enough number of children showing extreme variations), and, frequently, a recourse to a comparison of normal populations and samples that constitute high-risk groups for one reason or another.

A further characteristic of the developmental approach of the psychopathologist is the need to extend the perspective into adult life. Lifespan psychologists have emphasized that developmental tasks and crises occur in adult life as well as in childhood and that the ways in which early developmental issues are handled may influence the impact of later ones (Baltes & Brim, 1979). But the adult outcome of developmental processes in childhood may also throw light on the mechanisms of child development. Schizophrenia provides a case in point, and it is for this reason that we include a section on its behavioral precursors in childhood. The continuities over time indicate that nonpsychotic disturbances of attention, emotions, social behavior, and personal relationships represent the beginnings of the schizophrenic process. An understanding of the atypical development in childhood is dependent on a knowledge of the outcome in adult life. Similarly, an appreciation of *how* an institutional upbringing has an adverse effect on social functioning is aided by a knowledge of adult outcome and of the experiences

in adult life that may ameliorate the maladaptive consequences. Or, again, explanations of the rise in delinquent activities in early adolescence and in depressive feelings in later adolescence need to take account of the fact that there is a marked drop in delinquency in early adult life, whereas rates of adult depression remain well above those seen in early childhood. Any study of child development that stopped when physical maturity is reached would inevitably generate a peculiarly limited kind of developmental psychopathology.

The noun psychopathology in the title of the chapter emphasizes a rather different facet of the perspective to be followed. Developmental psychologists tend to assume an essential continuity in functioning so that, for example, severe depressive feelings are considered as on the same continuum as normal sadness or unhappiness, with both extending to equable mood and on to cheerfulness and happy feelings. Clinical psychiatrists, in contrast, tend to study conditions or disorders so that there is the implicit assumption of discontinuity, with illness on one side of the demarcation line and normality on the other. Of course, both viewpoints may be valid in different circumstances. Some disorders, such as autism and schizophrenia, concern behaviors that are abnormal at any development stage. Other aspects of atypical developmental represent handicapping exaggerations of normal developmental trends; some of the phobias of early childhood fall into that category. Some disorders constitute impairments or interference with the normal developmental process; the deficits and distortions in selective attachments associated with an institutional upbringing or with child abuse are examples. The use of the term psychopathology means that there is no prior assumption that there is either continuity or discontinuity. Instead, the central interest concerns both the connections *and* the lack of connections between normality and disorder. In this chapter, we focus on the parallels and discontinuities between the normal processes of adaptation and change on the one hand and abnormal responses to stress, trauma, or adversity on the other hand. So far as possible, we attempt to consider the nature of each disorder with this psychopathology perspective. To do so, occasional mention is made of some features of normal development, but for the most part, reference must be made to other chapters for a description and consideration of normal developmental changes.

A developmental psychopathology perspective serves another important purpose. The investigation of abnormality may shed light on the course of normal development because a focus on the unusual may be crucial in separating elements that ordinarily go together (Rutter, 1982). Thus, studies of institution-reared children show that the environmental features that most strongly influence social development are not the same as those that are crucial for intellectual growth (Rutter, 1981b). Similarly, the findings on autism point to the role of some, but not other, cognitive skills in the development of empathic relatedness (Rutter, in press-a). These implications for normal development are implicit throughout the chapter and, when the issues are central to the theme, they are made explicit.

Because psychopathology occurs throughout the lifespan, it is necessary also to consider whether the phenomena in childhood represent the same processes or mechanisms as those that apply to apparently similar phenomena in adult life. Where it seems that they may be comparable, we make occasional use of research findings on adults to highlight theoretical issues.

This discussion of developmental psychopathology has no single unifying theoretical perspective. That is not because we regard theories as unimportant in either research or clinical practice. To the contrary, they are essential as a means of ordering ideas and of making sense out of factual findings. Science cannot proceed by the mindless collection of factual information. Almost always, the strategies and tactics of research are guided by some theoretical construct, and, frequently, investigations are explicitly designed to test the comparative validity of various hypotheses. Also, it is not that the theories are necessarily wrong in what they propose. Rather, it is that no one theory even begins to approximate a complete explanation for the developmental processes—typical or atypical (Rutter, 1980). Moreover, many theories simply ignore or bypass some of the most striking empirical phenomena. Many pay little attention to individual differences; the major sex differences in some aspects of emotional development are left unexplained; and the timing of developmental changes after the infancy period is often ignored. For all these reasons, there is little point in restricting a consideration of atypical development to the single perspective of any one of the major theories. Equally, however, it would be foolish to ignore totally the ideas that have provided a powerful motivating force for much research in the fields of normal and abnormal development. We have, therefore, provided a brief critical examination of the relevant theoretical notions for most of the different types of atypical development we review. This is undertaken, not in terms of any testing of theoretical ideas as such, but rather to contrast the extent to which the theories successfully account for the major empirical findings that have been presented.

The topic of developmental psychopathology is a very broad one, and it has not proved possible to cover all types of disturbance within the confines of a single chapter, even a lengthy one. Our discussions are not strictly organized according to the traditional psychiatric categories, but it is obvious that several major topics are not considered at all. Some were omitted because they appear in other chapters in this volume—aggression, psychosexual development, peer relations, and therapeutic interventions are examples of this kind. Also, we have paid less attention to family variables than to other formative influences because these, too, are given extended discussion in a separate chapter. On the other hand, brain damage and the disputed concept of "minimal brain dysfunction" are given a lengthier discussion here because they are not considered elsewhere in this volume. The role of temperamental differences in development is discussed briefly in some sections of this chapter, but in view of the considerable recent upsurge in research on the topic (see, e.g., Plomin, in press; Porter & Collins, 1982), it warranted more extended discussion than we were able to give it in the space available. Other omissions include substance abuse and dependency, feeding and sleeping disturbances, and various important syndromes, such as anorexia nervosa, tics, enuresis, and encopresis. Our decision to exclude these topics was based in part on space restrictions, but, more positively, we wished to focus on the themes and issues that characterize developmental psychopathology as a whole rather than to provide a didactic text on the psychiatric disorders of childhood.

Of course, it was still necessary to decide on the extent to which we would follow the headings provided by the current systems of psychiatric classification as exemplified by ICD–9 (World Health Organization, 1978) or DSM–III (American Psychiatric Association, 1980). It will be apparent that, to a considerable extent, our broad headings coincide with the categories in these classification systems,[1] but we have not felt bound by the prevailing schema. Knowledge does not yet exist to justify most of the psychiatric diagnoses in common usage (Quay, 1979; Rutter, 1978c), and, in particular, there is a lack of empirical validation for the many finer subclassifications that clinicians tend to employ (Rutter & Shaffer, 1980). It is not that they are known to be invalid or inappropriate but rather that few of them have been put to the test in any adequate fashion. Accordingly, our usual course has been to discuss the evidence that is available and to note the nosological issues that are posed. However, where we thought that it was necessary to focus on important developmental issues, we have included discussions on behavioral constellations that are not generally recognized as psychiatric categories. The consideration of both deficits and distortions in selective attachments and of autistic psychopathy constitute examples of this kind.

A further point that taxed us in deciding how to structure the chapter was whether to follow a dimensional or categorical approach. Our compromise was to take a somewhat agnostic position by largely using categories to provide our headings while noting that, in most cases, there was a lack of evidence from which to determine the more effective approach.

All of these issues apply in force to the first of our major topics—abnormalities in social relationships.

ABNORMALITIES IN SOCIAL RELATIONSHIPS

Numerous investigations have documented the frequency with which psychiatric disorders of childhood involve serious problems in social relationships. Nevertheless—apart from infantile autism—there is no general recognition of specific syndromes with an abnormality in social relationships as their main or identifying feature, and there is a paucity of research into the origins of such social abnormalities. In recent years, there has been a growing appreciation of the importance of peer relationships in social development (see *Hartup, vol. IV, chap. 2*), and there is an increasing literature on the treatment of social isolation and of other social deficits and abnormalities (Furman, 1980). These are crucial matters in any consideration of developmental psychopathology but, as they are dealt with in some detail by Hartup (see *vol. IV, chap. 2*) and by Alexander and Malouf (see *vol. IV, chap. 11*), they will not be considered here. Instead, attention is focused on certain patterns or syndromes that represent social behaviors that seem to differ in kind as well as degree from normal social development. For this purpose, six categories have been selected for discussion as representative of the range of rather different sorts of social abnormalities that may occur: deficits and distortions in selective attachments, the abused child, elective mutism, infantile autism, autistic psychopathy/schizoid personality, and childhood precursors of adult schizophrenia.

Deficits and Distortions in Selective Attachments

Largely as a result of Bowlby's (1969, 1973, 1980) writings on the topic, the concept of selective attachments or bonds between infants and their parents has had a major influence on both empirical research and theorizing about the development of social relationships (see, e.g., Emde & Harmon, 1982; Parkes & Stevenson-Hinde, 1982; Rajecki, Lamb, & Obmascher, 1978; Rutter, 1981b; Sroufe, 1979). The terminology used has posed many problems, and investigators have varied in the conventions that they have followed. Nevertheless, general agreement has been obtained on several crucial distinctions. First, infants' ties to their parents are not synonymous with parents' ties to their infants, and the processes underlying the development of each may not be the same. For a time, Klaus and Kennell's (1976) hypothesis that parents became "bonded" to their infants as a result of physical contact during a brief sensitive period in the first 12 hr. after birth held sway. However, empirical findings have shown that this bonding model is invalid and should be abandoned (Herbert, Sluckin, & Sluckin, 1982; Lamb & Hwang, 1982; Svejda, Pannabecker, & Emde, 1982).

Second, a distinction is needed between a general tendency to seek the proximity of a familiar figure (attachment behavior) and selective attachments to a particular figure that persist over time, even during a period of no contact with that figure. Generalized attachment behavior is a universal phenomenon in the toddler-age period and is almost impossible to extinguish regardless of the rearing conditions. Selective attachments, on the other hand, are thought to be more dependent on environmental circumstances. Moreover, it is their development in the early years that is supposed to be important for later social development according to Bowlby's theory.

Third, it has become clear that the concept of attachment does not encompass all positive social interactions in young children. Thus, whereas social play is inhibited by anxiety, attachment is intensified. Children may prefer to play with peers or even with a stranger; nevertheless, they will choose to go to a parent for comfort. Also, the ways in which children play together are rather different from their style of interaction with parents. Clinging or hugging one another is unusual in peer play but common in parent-child relationships.

Fourth, the work of Ainsworth (1982) and Sroufe (1979) and their colleagues has done much to emphasize the importance of variations in the quality of attachments—with particular reference to the differences between secure and insecure attachments, as judged by responses during the strange-situation procedure. Securely attached infants explore their environments freely when with their mothers, but, following a brief separation, they tend to seek closeness and comfort. Anxiously attached infants appear less secure in their mothers' presence and are acutely distressed during brief separations, but they are angry, as well as seeking closeness, on reunion. Avoidant infants, in contrast, appear undisturbed during separations but avoid their mothers on reunion. The insecurity of their attachment is inferred from the infants' aggressive behavior toward their mothers in other situations.

Ainsworth and others (e.g., Main & Weston, 1982; Sroufe, 1979) have argued that secure attachments constitute the adaptive norm, with insecure attachments liable to lead to maladaptive outcomes. This may prove to be the case, but Hinde (1982) noted the problems in making that a basic postulate. Grossman and Grossman (1981) found avoidant responses more frequent than secure behavior in a study of German infants. Possibly, adaptiveness should be considered in terms of the needs in different social situations rather than as an absolute quality. In the earlier writings on the topic, there tended to be an implicit assumption that security/insecurity was a quality of the infant's attachment system. However, the empirical finding that the security of an infant's attachment with its mother is of little predictive value for the security of the attachment with its father (Lamb, 1978; Main & Weston, 1981) indicates that, rather than an infant characteristic, it is a variable describing a dyadic relationship. The quality of that relationship may well constitute an important predictor of the infant's later social development, but it cannot any longer be regarded as something within the child or part of the child's makeup.

Insecure Attachments and Peer Relationships

As a consequence of the last point made above, there are many difficulties in the conceptualization of the developmental processes underlying the apparent links between the quality of early selective attachments and later patterns of social relationships within the range of ordinary family childrearing environments. During the last few years, there have been several studies showing significant correlations between measures of the security of attachments in infancy and measures of various aspects of interactions with peers during the later preschool years (Arend, Gove, & Sroufe, 1979; Easterbrooks & Lamb, 1979; Lieberman, 1977; Matas, Arend, & Sroufe, 1978; Waters, Wippman, & Sroufe, 1979). Although the data do not indicate whether the correlations represent causal connections, the results do suggest some form of continuity between early parent-child attachments and later aspects of social functioning. But if the quality of an infant's attachment with one parent does not predict the quality of the attachment with the other parent, why should it predict to the rather different domain of peer relationships? Of course, the former concerns cross-situational consistency, whereas the latter refers to temporal consistency—two rather different concepts (Mischel, 1979). It may well be that the *quality* of security is strongly influenced by both the behavior of the particular parent and by the social context and degree of stress but that the *experience* of security in one or more relationships constitutes an important learning experience. Nevertheless, the question remains as to what developmental process underlies the links over time. Indeed, is there a developmental process at all? Perhaps the stability over time simply reflects stability in those environmental or temperamental factors that influence the quality of attachments.

This possibility raises the further question of why some children develop insecure attachments in the first place. Often it has tended to be assumed that the insecurity stems from the style or quality of parenting and, indeed, there is evidence that this is likely to be influential (Ainsworth, Blehar, Waters, & Wall, 1978). However, a number of recent studies have shown both that the mother-infant relationship may be adversely affected by the presence of external stresses (Vaughn, Egeland, Sroufe, & Waters, 1979) or the lack of social supports (Crockenberg, 1981) and that the security of attachment is also influenced by infant characteristics, such as neonatal difficulties (Waters, Vaughn, & Egeland, 1980) or infantile irritability (Crockenberg, 1981; Crockenberg & Smith, in press). The strong implication is that the whole process of bonding and attachment needs to be seen in transactional terms, with reciprocal effects from the infant to the parent and vice versa and with both infant and parent being influenced by the immediate and the wider social context (Belsky, 1981; Bronfenbrenner, 1979; Hinde, 1979).

Institutional Upbringing

For the most part, the studies of insecure attachments concern variations within the normal range (albeit at the extremes in some cases). However, Bowlby's initial interest in attachment derived from a study of a more abnormal group. In his clinical study of 44 thieves (Bowlby, 1946), he noted that some seemed to lack an ability to form enduring relationships (so-called "affectionless psychopathy") and that this lack was linked with multiple changes of a mother figure or a home during infancy or early childhood. A few years later, Goldfarb

(1955), in a study of children reared in an institution from infancy, found that those who remained in the institution until after 3 years of age were especially characterized by an inability to keep rules, a lack of guilt, a craving for affection, and an inability to make lasting relationships. The study is open to several criticisms, both in terms of the measures used and the uncertainty regarding the factors that determined whether the children stayed in institutions or were placed in foster homes. Nevertheless, the implication from these two studies considered together was that a failure to develop bonds in early childhood as a result of discontinuous parenting dispersed across a large number of caretakers might sometimes result in a persisting inability to make relationships.

This suggestion received circumstantial support from a variety of subsequent studies. For example, Pringle and Bossio (1958, 1960) found that "stable" children in long-term institutional care had remained with their mothers until well after the first year of life and, so, had had the opportunity of forming bonds prior to admission. Similarly, Wolkind (1974), in a study of 5- to 12-year-old children living in an institution, found that superficial overfriendliness and inappropriate social inhibition were largely confined to those admitted before the age of 2 years, whereas antisocial behavior was common in institutional children regardless of the age of admission. Trasler (1960), in his study of foster care, also noted that prolonged institutional care in early life was the factor most likely to lead to subsequent breakdown of fostering and, possibly, to affectionless detachment. The evidence pointed to the possibility that institutional rearing in the first few years of life might be responsible for later social incapacities. However, it seemed that the effect was apparent only if this rearing occurred in infancy, in that this picture of affectionless psychopathy was not found with older children placed in residential nurseries as a result of wartime evacuation (Maas, 1963) or in those admitted to TB sanatoria after the infancy period (Bowlby, Ainsworth, Boston, & Rosenbluth, 1956). Moreover, it seems that adverse development is not common if institutional rearing is restricted to the first year of life (Bohman & Sigvardsson, 1980).

The plausibility of this link between early parent-child bonding and later abilities to make and maintain friendships or heterosexual relationships was also shown by the rhesus monkey studies on the effects of social isolation in infancy (Harlow & Harlow, 1969; Ruppenthal, Arling, Harlow, Sackett, & Suomi, 1976). Isolation-reared rhesus monkeys failed to develop normal social relationships in adult life and showed severe abnormalities

in both sexual and parenting behavior. The importance of early relationships (not necessarily parent-infant) was shown by the fact that this deviant social outcome did not apply when the infant monkeys were separated from their parents but reared with peers; and the restriction of this effect to isolation experiences in the infancy period is suggested by the finding that it also did not apply when older, but still juvenile, animals were isolated. These studies provide a useful model for the human situation, but caution is needed in extrapolating across species in view of the finding that the effects of total social-isolation rearing vary markedly even between rhesus monkeys, pigtail macaques, and crab-eating macaques (Sackett, 1982).

Although a reasonable circumstantial case could be made for the adverse effects of institutional rearing in humans, the measures of social relationships in all the studies were rather limited and the links with early bonding rested on group comparisons in which many factors were left uncontrolled. Moreover, in most cases the children showed so many problems and had had so many different types of adverse experience that it was not possible to be sure whether specific experiences had specific effects. It was also clear that the concept of affectionless psychopathy was not at all well defined or validated and that it occurred in only some institution-reared children (Pringle & Bossio, 1958; Wolins, 1969; Wolkind, 1974).

There the matter rested until recently when more systematic evidence, provided by two follow-up studies of institution-reared children by Tizard and her colleagues (Tizard & Hodges, 1978; Tizard & Rees, 1974; Tizard & Tizard, 1971) and by Dixon (1983), became available. Most of the earlier studies had had to *assume* the lack of early bonding, but Tizard obtained contemporaneous measures at the appropriate times. At 2 years, the children were found to be both more clinging and more diffuse in their attachments than children brought up in ordinary families; at 4 years, too, they were still less likely than controls to show deep attachments. It seemed highly probable that this was a specific consequence of a lack of opportunity to form personal bonds in that, although the institutions were stimulating, interesting, and generally high quality in other respects, the children had experienced some 50 different caretakers during the preschool period.

The question, then, with respect to the later consequences of a lack of early bonding, is: What happened to these institutional children who failed to make selective attachments? Tizard found that at age 4, they had become attention seeking and overly friendly with strangers; at age 8, less than half of those still in institutions were closely attached to their housemothers and still sought affection more than other children. At school, they were more attention seeking, restless, disobedient, and unpopular. Tizard's data relied on interviews and questionnaires; Dixon's (1983) data from similar sources were closely comparable but also she employed systematic direct observations in the classroom, which confirmed the social/behavioral differences between institution-reared children and controls. The evidence pointed to a connection between a lack of early selective attachments and later difficulties in relationships as well as in social behavior more generally.

If the bonding hypothesis was to be tested rigorously, however, it was also necessary both to check that the link was indeed with the pattern of early caregiving rather than with some other background variable as well as that the effects endured after infancy, even when environmental circumstances changed. Dixon (1983) dealt with the first requirement by showing that institution-reared children differed from children fostered in individual families in spite of both groups having similarly severely disturbed parents. However, it should be added that some of the fostered children showed social problems similar to those of institution-reared children, but to a lesser degree. Tizard dealt with the second requirement by showing that the social abnormalities persisted at school for institution-reared children, even in those adopted into good homes after age 4 who developed deep relationships with their foster parents and seemed to behave normally at home.

The findings appear to suggest that a lack of early bonding in infancy may sometimes lead to later social deficits. However, so far, rather few children have been studied and the follow-up has extended only to age 8. It remains uncertain whether the social problems observed represent a deficit in the ability to make relationships or in the learning of styles of adaptation, which were adaptive in the institution but maladaptive outside it. It is also relevant that the behavior of the children in both the Tizard and Dixon studies, although different from controls, fell far short of the gross abnormalities first described under the label of affectionless psychopathy. Finally, it must be emphasized that the findings start from a group in which all had experienced institutional rearing and that it should not be assumed that an inability to form enduring relationships can only arise in that way. Although there is a paucity of good data, it is certainly clear from what is available that this cannot be the only cause of an affectionless character. H.

Lewis (1954), for example, in her study of 500 deprived children admitted into care, found that only 5 of the 19 children with this syndrome had suffered prolonged separation from their families.

The sometimes long-term effects of an institutional upbringing have been shown in Rutter, Quinton, and Liddle's (in press) follow-up into early adult life of institution-reared girls. Compared with controls (a general population sample brought up by their own parents in family settings), the institution group had a substantially worse outcome in terms of criminality, psychiatric disorder, and substantial difficulties in love relationships. Altogether, a third showed marked psychosocial problems in their mid-20s (compared with none of the controls) and only a fifth were free of problems (compared with two thirds of the controls). Of course, this relatively poor outcome could reflect the girls' often seriously adverse experiences before admission to the institution rather than an institutional upbringing per se. Nevertheless, the findings pointed to the importance of infantile experiences (the adult outcome was significantly associated with the qualities of rearing during the infancy period) and to the role of multiple caretaking in the institution (the girls admitted in infancy and who remained in the institution thereafter did particularly badly). On the other hand, the results cast serious doubt on the notion that a lack of stable parenting in the early years causes a lasting and irreversible distortion in social development. Some of the institution-reared women showed normal social functioning in adult life; the presence of a supportive nondeviant spouse proved to be a powerful ameliorating factor. Evidently, the capacity for changes in social relationships persists right into adult life. The overall pattern of findings suggest that, in some circumstances, infantile experiences can have long-term effects but that these effects tend to be indirect rather than direct (Rutter, in press-b).

In summary, children who experience institutional rearing during their preschool years have a substantially increased rate of later social difficulties. The investigation of the consequences of this form of upbringing may be informative concerning the factors associated with atypical social development and, hence, may throw light on the processes of normal development. The results, so far, run counter to many of the traditional theories, but we have some way to go before the mechanisms involved in the growth of socialization become fully understood.

The Abused Child

The social abnormalities considered under the

heading of deficiencies in bonding are thought to stem from a lack of appropriate parenting. A somewhat different set of abnormalities in early childhood have been reported to result from severe rejection, neglect, or actual physical abuse. These include the interrelated syndromes of a psychological failure to thrive in infancy, deprivation dwarfism, and physical abuse. Thus, Patton and Gardner (1963), in their account of growth failure in the context of maternal deprivation (so-called deprivation dwarfism),[2] described the infants as lethargic, apathetic and withdrawn, not smiling, and avoiding contact with people. Pollitt and Eichler (1976) found that failure-to-thrive children showed an increase in a wide range of problem behaviors as observed at home. Ounsted, Oppenheimer, and Lindsay (1974), in their report on physically abused children, noted what they called "frozen watchfulness," in which the toddlers stood silent, not playing, fixing their gaze on people who approached them but not smiling and not responding to them. In both cases, the parenting and family relationships were said to be severely discordant and disordered. However, other writers have emphasized somewhat different characteristics, and it is uncertain whether the behavior of abused, neglected, or rejected children constitutes a recognizable constellation of characteristics. For example, Krieger (1974), in his report on 10 children with deprivation dwarfism, noted their low frustration toleration. This resulted in severe temper tantrums, self-injury, and negativism that paradoxically coexisted with undue compliance, dependency, and seeking of affection. Of course, the parenting patterns may be equally variable and it should not be assumed that failure to thrive, deprivation dwarfism, and nonaccidental injury (the euphemism that has largely taken the place of battering or physical abuse) constitute the same groups, although it is evident that they overlap greatly (Cooper, 1978; Koel, 1969; Shaheen, Alexander, Truskowsky, & Barbero, 1968).

Most of the accounts of the behavior of abused children have been based on rather anecdotal clinical descriptions, but in recent years, there have been a few systematic studies of 1- to 3-year-olds with the use of appropriate control groups. Most have focused on the children's interactions with their parents, using some variant of the Ainsworth strange-situation procedure (Egeland & Sroufe, 1981; Gordon & Jameson, 1979; Hyman & Parr, 1978), standard tasks given to families in the laboratory (Egeland & Sroufe, 1981) or in their own homes (Burgess & Conger, 1978), or observations at day centers (George & Main, 1979; Herrenkohl & Herrenkohl, 1981; Lewis & Schaeffer, 1981). The studies have shown varied results in the extent to which the behavior of abused children differed from that of controls. However, the consistent trend shown has been toward an increase in insecure attachment and less positive interactions with mothers and more aggressive behavior toward parents or other caretakers. R. C. Herrenkohl and E. C. Herrenkohl (1981) found that abused children were more likely to respond to frustration with aggression; similarly, Egeland and Sroufe (1981) reported that their physical-abuse group had significantly higher scores on aggression, frustration, and noncompliance, with lower scores on positive affect. George and Main (1979) reported that abused children showed less positive responses to friendly overtures from caregivers in the day nursery and more avoidance of both other children and caregivers. The abused infants hit other infants twice as often as did the controls and only the abused children (5 of 10) hit or threatened to hit caregivers. Other studies have shown rather smaller differences in behavior with peers, and the extent to which the children's behavior is atypical in play situations away from their parents remains uncertain.

Gaensbauer (1982) used a modified strange-situation paradigm to examine the emotional expressions of 12 neglected or abused children from lower social-status families (who were compared with normal infants from middle-class homes). The abused/neglected group showed significantly less pleasure, more sadness, and less modulations in either distress or toy play. The findings suggest that differences in parenting resulted in less adaptive affective regulation by the infants; however, the failure to match the groups for social status means that it remains uncertain whether the group differences reflect economically depressed circumstances or neglect/abuse.

Altogether, the findings suggest a process of reciprocal interaction between parent and child (Parke & Lewis, 1981). This is not only a process in which the abused infants may be temperamentally more difficult to deal with before the abuse or may be reared in more difficult circumstances than their siblings (Lynch, 1975), but also one in which the abusive or neglectful parenting has important effects on the children's emotional expression and social interactions (Belsky, 1980). So far, the data are too sparse for any conclusions on the frequency and extent to which the children's behavior outside the family is altered by parental neglect or abuse, and it is not yet known if the social development of abused/neglected children follows a predictable course that is systematically different from that of other children.

In summary, parental rejection and maltreatment

are often associated with, and to a considerable extent result in, quite marked changes in infants' socioemotional behavior—an increase in insecure attachment and aggression, diminished positive affect, and, possibly, impaired modulation of emotional responses. These changes are most obvious in the presence of the parents, with many reports commenting on the great improvement that follows the child's admission to hospital or some other form of removal from home. But also it appears that more long-lasting alterations in social behavior can occur. Evidence is lacking on how often or under what circumstances this happens.

Elective Mutism

Elective mutism is the term coined by Tramer (1934) to describe children who are silent in most social circumstances but yet who speak with a small group of intimates in specific situations, usually in the child's own home (Kratochwill, 1981). There are a variety of reports of individual cases or a small series of children but only five studies of any size. One study was based on a questionnaire survey of children first beginning infants' school (Brown & Lloyd, 1975). This showed that some 8 weeks after starting school, about 7 children in every 1,000 were not speaking at all while at school (although they did so at home), but by the end of the school year nearly all were talking in all situations. The findings showed that a transient period of elective mutism is not particularly rare among young children in a new situation. On the other hand, clinic reports all emphasize the rarity of elective mutism as a persistent abnormality; the Newcastle epidemiological study (Fundudis, Kolvin, & Garside, 1979) showed a rate of just 0.8 per 1,000 at age 7 years.

One of the four series of studies of children attending clinics with persistent elective mutism had a comparison group drawn from the general population (Kolvin & Fundudis, 1981), whereas the other studies (Hayden, 1980; Parker, Olson, & Throdemorton, 1980; H. L. Wright, 1968) lacked controls. There is agreement that the condition is rather more common in girls than in boys (Hayden, 1980, found a very marked female preponderance, but the diagnostic criteria in that series were both wider and different from those generally employed). In four fifths of Kolvin and Fundudis's (1981) cases, there had been an insidiously increasing social shyness and withdrawal from the preschool years, but in a few instances, the children became shy and stopped speaking at the time of school entry.

All reports have noted that although they vary in personality, most electively mute children show quite widespread abnormalities in their social interactions. Kolvin and Fundudis (1981) report that all 24 children in their series were withdrawn in their peer relationships and that in two thirds of the cases severely so. Social withdrawal from adults was nearly as marked. This is not a necessary consequence of a failure to speak. Although severely deaf children show more social difficulties than hearing children, they may, nevertheless, engage in social interactions, communicating by gesture and physical contact rather than speech (Meadow, 1975). This type of social approach is much less usual in electively mute children. However, the character of the withdrawal differs from child to child. Some are apathetic, morose, unprepossessing, and withdrawn, whereas others are timid, tense, anxious, and fearful. Kolvin and Fundudis (1981) noted that a rather controlling aggressive style at home together with sulkiness with strangers was the predominant pattern found in half the children. About a quarter combined social shyness with an apparently submissive attitude at home, and a quarter appeared generally anxious, weepy, sensitive, and easily distressed in all situations. Wright (1968) stated that although some of the children studied were extremely shy outside the home, almost all were strong willed, negative, and difficult to manage in the family setting.

Most case reports have maintained that when the electively mute children do speak, their speech is normal. However, Wright (1968) noted that 5 of the 24 children he studied had speech problems, and Kolvin and Fundudis (1981) reported immaturities of speech or other speech difficulties in half their sample. Moreover, the mean age of gaining phrase speech was 6 months later in the elective mutism group than in the controls. Although the groups did not differ in motor milestones, the electively mute children included far more who wet or soiled. The mean nonverbal IQ was also 16 points lower, with a fifth intellectually retarded.

The long-term prognosis for elective mutism is generally said to be quite good; certainly it appears to be so for the younger children soon after school entry. But Kolvin and Fundudis (1981) report that after a follow-up period lasting 10 years, only half of their children improved; and only one showed improvement after the age of 10 years.

All the literature on the topic has emphasized the frequency of an abnormally strong tie between electively mute children and their mothers together with various abnormalities in parental personalities and parent-child interaction. However, systematic data on these points are lacking apart from Kolvin and

Fundudis's (1981) finding that twice as many of the parents in their elective mutism group as in their controls had had psychiatric treatment.

In summary, elective mutism constitutes an interesting condition that, at least in its severe and persistent form, seems rather different from the reluctance to speak as part of social shyness seen as a transient problem in some young children at the time they start school. Although mutism frequently occurs as an isolated social-communication problem, in a substantial minority of cases, it arises against a background of delayed development, especially in speech and language. The persistent form of mutism appears to involve quite widespread social problems and difficulties in interpersonal relationships. However, so far, the evidence is restricted to clinical observations of varying degrees of rigor; more detailed observational analyses of the children's social interactions would be valuable.

Both of the first two patterns considered—deficiencies in bonding and the atypical social interactions of the abused child—are thought primarily to be due to abnormalities in parenting, although child characteristics may act as predisposing factors. Elective mutism differs somewhat in the emphasis placed on temperamental factors, but usually it is supposed (with only rather weak supporting evidence) that it, too, is much influenced by patterns of upbringing. In contrast with the next three syndromes to be considered, constitutional factors are thought to be predominant in causation.

Infantile Autism

In 1943, Kanner described the clinical picture of a severe abnormality in social development that seemed to be qualitatively different from other forms of social impairment and from other types of psychiatric disorder. He emphasized the children's inability to relate as the fundamental feature, a feature which was present from infancy and which represented a failure of development rather than a withdrawal from social participation. This social deficit was associated with serious abnormalities in language, a lack of spontaneous play, and repetitive, stereotyped, and seemingly obsessive preoccupations and activities. Since Kanner's original observations, numerous clinical and research reports have confirmed the presence of this particular constellation of behaviors and have shown that the abnormalities are indeed distinctive (see DeMyer, Hingtgen & Jackson, 1981; Rutter, 1978b; & Werry, 1979, for a review of the evidence).

In keeping with Kanner's (1943) first report, subsequent studies have confirmed that autism is more frequent in boys—in a ratio of about 3 to 1 (Werry, 1979). Recent research (Tsai, Stewart, & August, 1981) suggests that autistic girls tend to be more seriously affected and more likely to have a family history of cognitive problems—a finding in keeping with a genetic transmission. The total population prevalence is approximately 2 to 4 per 10,000 (Brask, 1970; Lotter, 1966; Treffert, 1970), with the rate varying according to the strictness of the diagnostic criteria.

Behavioral Characteristics

Several studies, relying on observations and reports from parents and professionals, have drawn attention to those aspects of social impairment that seem to be particularly characteristic of the autistic syndrome (see Rutter, 1978b, for a summary of findings). During the first year, autistic infants may not take up an anticipatory posture or put up their arms to be picked up in the way that normal infants do. There is a lack of attachment behavior and a relative failure in specific bonding. Thus, unlike the normal toddler, autistic children tend not to follow their parents about the house or run to greet them when the parents return after having been out; they tend not to go to their parents for comfort when they are hurt or upset; and, frequently, they do not develop the bedtime kiss-and-cuddle routine followed by so many normal children. Lack of eye-to-eye gaze is usually said to be a feature of autism, but clinical observation suggests that it is not so much the amount of gaze that is abnormal but rather that it is the failure to use gaze to modulate social interactions that is unusual. In other words, autistic children tend not to look at people's faces when they want to gain their attention or when they are being spoken to, and they fail to use eye contact and gaze aversion to regulate the reciprocal to and fro that characterizes normal social contact. When older, there is a lack of cooperative group play with other children, a failure to make personal friendships, and an apparent lack of empathy and failure to perceive other people's feelings and responses.

Autistic children are usually markedly delayed in their acquisition of speech. But, more particularly, their pattern of language development and their usage of language is strikingly different from both normal children and children with other language disorders. Frequently, but not always, patterns of babble in infancy are impaired or abnormal (Bartak, Rutter, & Cox, 1975; Ricks, 1975). The children's understanding of spoken language is usually markedly reduced and remains so for a longer period than in dysphasic children with an initially comparable level of language retardation (Bartak et al., 1975; Cantwell, Baker, & Rutter, 1978). A lack of symbolic gesture or mime is equally characteristic. Most autistic children do not point, instead they tend to make their needs known by taking people by the wrist (not usually by the grasped hand). About half of autistic children, especially those who are also mentally retarded, never gain useful speech. In those who do learn to speak, there are a variety of characteristic abnormalities. I/you pronominal reversal, delayed and inappropriate echoing, and abnormal egocentric language usage tend to be particularly prominent (Bartak et al., 1975; Cantwell et al., 1978; Fay, 1979). In older autistic children, prosodic abnormalities, stereotyped utterances, and violations of semantic constraints have been noted (Simmons & Baltaxe, 1975). Cantwell's (1982) follow-up study of normally intelligent autistic children showed that abnormalities of speech rhythm, the use of neologisms, and idosyncratic word usage differentiated them from dysphasic children.

Perhaps most striking of all is the failure of autistic children to use speech for social communication. They do not chat, they lack the reciprocity of normal conversation—what they say tends not to constitute a response to what the other person has said—and they are poor at giving an account of happenings outside the immediate situation. In her study of autistic adolescents, Baltaxe (1977) found that they tended not to foreground and background their utterances. Similarly, Langdell (1980) noted that compared with mildly retarded children comparable in language level, autistic children were much worse at explaining things to someone else, tending not to adapt what they said to the needs of the situation. He suggested that the language problem is most appropriately viewed in terms of a defect in its pragmatics rather than its syntax or semantics. Certainly, although syntactical and semantical aspects of language development are usually delayed, autistic children's language deviance is not just a reflection of language impairment (Cantwell et al., 1978).

Stereotyped behaviors and routines constitute the third set of features that characterize autism (Black, Freeman, & Montgomery, 1975; Wing, Gould, Yeates, & Brierley, 1977). Typically, autistic children's play lacks variety and imagination so that much time may be spent endlessly lining up objects or making patterns. Autistic children rarely engage in make-believe games, and their use of toys is diminished and lacks symbolic or creative features (Riguet, Taylor, Benaroya, & Klein, 1981; Ungerer & Sigman, 1981). Typically, too, they are impaired in their ability to imitate (DeMyer, 1971) and to use abstract pantomime (Curcio & Piserchia, 1978). Often, they have intense specific attachments to unusual objects (Marchant, Howlin, Yule, & Rutter, 1974). Especially in middle or later childhood, many autistic children are preoccupied with routes, timetables, numbers, or patterns—interests that they pursue to the exclusion of other activities. Rigid routines are common and sometimes during adolescence these may develop into overt obsessions with touching compulsions and the like. Some, but not all, autistic children also show a marked resistance to changes in the environment so that they become distressed if, for example, ornaments or furniture at home are moved or changed.

These three areas of behavioral abnormality (social interaction, communication, and play) tend to be the ones that most clearly differentiate autistic children from those with other forms of psychiatric disorder but, in addition, motor stereotypies (especially hand and finger mannerisms), self-destructive behavior, and various nonspecific emotional and behavioral disturbances are all quite common.

Validity of the Syndrome

Several rather different issues arise with respect to the validity of the autistic syndrome. First, there is the question of whether children with these behavioral features differ in any meaningful way from children with other psychiatric conditions or with generalized developmental retardation. Numerous studies have shown that they do (see Rutter, 1978b). Thus, these children differ from mentally retarded children in outcome, in social background, and in pattern of cognitive deficits. Autism differs from schizophrenia in family history, evidence of cerebral dysfunction, symptom patterns, course of disorder, and level of intelligence. Moreover, the age of onset of severe psychiatric disorders of a kind usually termed psychoses follows a markedly bipolar distribution with one peak in infancy (autism) and another (schizophrenia) in adolescence. The pattern of cognitive and language disabilities differentiates autism from the developmental language disorders. Autism also differs in a host of ways from the social impairments associated with elective mutism, an institutional upbringing, or parental rejection. There can be no doubt that autism is meaningfully different from other psychiatric categories.

Second, there are queries on the boundaries of the syndrome. On the one hand, it is clear from the qualitatively abnormal behavior of autistic children that autism does *not* shade off into normal variations in social functioning. Moreover, the deviant (not merely delayed) pattern of autistic development indicates that autism cannot be viewed as just the social concomitant of intellectual impairment. This is also apparent from the fact that autism frequently accompanies some medical conditions giving rise to mental handicap but yet is quite rare with others. On the other hand, epidemiological studies have shown that many severely retarded (IQ < 50) children show some autistic features but not the full syndrome (Wing & Gould, 1979). Whereas the differentiation of autism from normal social oddities is a relatively straightforward matter with children whose IQ is in the normal or mildly retarded range (in spite of some difficulties with respect to "autistic psychopathy"), the distinctions are much less clearcut in the severely or profoundly retarded. As a consequence, it is in the below-50 IQ range that variations in diagnostic practice are greatest, with some investigators adopting a rather broad concept that includes up to half of all severely retarded children (Ritvo & Freeman, 1978; Schopler, Reichler, DeVellis, & Daly, 1980; Wing & Gould, 1979). More is known on the validity of the narrower concept (as described above), but the evidence is insufficient for any decision on just where the line should be drawn or, indeed, whether a categorical approach should be used at all.

Third, there is the related question of whether autism constitutes a single disease entity, a broad syndrome of biological impairment, or an unrelated collection of symptoms that may be due to a heterogeneous group of influences both biological and psychosocial (Newsom & Rincover, 1981; Rutter, 1978b). No entirely satisfactory answer to these questions is available. Certainly, it has been shown that autism can develop in children with quite different medical conditions, but it remains possible that there *may* be an etiologically homogeneous subgroup within the overall spectrum of autistic disorders (although there are no strong pointers that there is such a subgroup). At present, the balance of evidence suggests that autism probably represents the behavioral consequences of some form of organic brain disorder but that the syndrome may vary somewhat in both degree and form according to the extent and type of neuropathological impairment. However, the suggestion remains speculative and the issue is still open.

Language Impairment

The early recognition that language abnormalities constituted a particularly prominent feature in autism led to a research focus on their characteristics. One of the first issues was whether there was a true inability or incapacity in language as distinct from an emotional or social block to its usage. Three sets of data indicated that the autistic child's failure to use speech was not the result of a motivational problem (Rutter, in press-a). First, there was much evidence that when language developed, it was abnormal in many respects (DeMyer et al., 1981; Rutter, in press-a). Second, autistic children's pattern of IQ scores showed that they performed badly on cognitive tests that required verbal or sequencing skills, even when the test responses required no use of any kind of speech (Hoffman & Prior, 1982). Third, experimental studies showed cognitive deficits involving language, sequencing, and abstraction (Hermelin & O'Connor, 1970).

The next issue was whether the autistic child's language deficit might explain the other social and emotional deficits. The basic importance of language and cognition was shown by the universal finding that IQ and language constituted much the most powerful predictors of outcome (Lotter, 1978). The centrality of cognitive and language deficits was also shown by the finding that of all features, they were the most resistant to treatment (Howlin, 1981). On the other hand, there is a paucity of direct evidence on the functional relationship between language deviance and social impairment.

The third issue concerned the nature of the language abnormality in autism. Parallels had been drawn between autism and developmental dysphasia, but systematic comparison of the two types of disorder showed many differences (Bartak et al., 1975; Cantwell et al., 1978). It was found that autism was associated with language abnormalities and with a cognitive deficit that was more severe, more widespread, and somewhat different in pattern from that in dysphasia. Unlike dysphasic children, autistic children are impaired in inner language, in their use and understanding of gesture, in their social usage of speech, and in the presence of abnormal language features. Autistic children are often also generally retarded in the development of spoken language, but neither the form of their grammar nor the quality of their articulation constitute differentiating features (Bartolucci, Pierce, & Streiner, 1980; Boucher, 1976; Cantwell et al., 1978). It may be concluded that it is not a language *delay* as such that characterizes autism but rather language *deviance* associated with a deficit in cognitive functioning.

Cognitive Functioning

Although Kanner (1943) initially thought that the autistic child's poor cognitive performance was simply a secondary consequence of social withdrawal, several different types of evidence have shown that this is not so. It is now clear that there is a basic cognitive deficit that involves impaired language, sequencing, abstraction, and coding functions (De-Myer et al., 1981; Hermelin, 1976; Hermelin & O'Connor, 1970; Prior, 1979; Rutter, in press-a). All studies have shown that autistic children vary greatly in their intellectual performance, with IQ scores ranging from severely retarded to highly superior—but about three-quarters of autistic children show some degree of impaired general intellectual functioning. The IQ scores obtained by autistic children have the same properties as those obtained by other children. They predict later scholastic achievement, occupation, and social status; they show moderate consistency over time; they do not fluctuate markedly according to changes in psychiatric state. In addition, cognitive performance has been shown to vary with task difficulty and not to be explicable in terms of motivational factors. Also, a low IQ in early childhood is strongly related to the risk of epileptic seizures developing during adolescence. It may be concluded that many (but not all) autistic children also exhibit mental retardation. Moreover, evidence from home movies (Rosenthal, Massie, & Wulff, 1980) suggest that autistic children's sensorimotor intelligence is already impaired during the infancy period.

Research findings have indicated that the social and behavioral abnormalities found in autistic children are not explicable solely in terms of MA, in that autistic children consistently differ from MA matched controls in a host of ways. On the other hand, it could be that the autistic features are explicable in terms of some more specific cognitive deficit. Hermelin and O'Connor (1970), in a series of well-planned experiments, found that autistic children made relatively little use of meaning in their memory and thought processes. Fyffe and Prior (1978) confirmed this with lower functioning autistic children, but not with their higher functioning group. It has been found that even relatively intelligent autistic children are more impaired in their ability to process complex temporal sequences than apparently comparable codes that relate to the spatial framework (Hermelin, 1976). On the basis of these and other experiments, Hermelin has argued that the essential cognitive deficit seems to consist of an inability to reduce information through the appropriate extraction of crucial features, such as rules and redundancies.

At one time, it was hypothesized that overselective attention in multiple-cue situations might constitute the basis for autism (Lovaas, Schreibman, Koegel, & Rehm, 1971). But the initial studies failed to control for MA and IQ. When these controls were introduced, it was evident that the overselectivity was a function of low MA rather than autism (Schover & Newsom, 1976). It is now conceded that although overselectivity is a frequent characteristic in autism, it is not a feature specific to the syndrome (Lovaas, Koegel, & Schreibman, 1979).

Also, it has been suggested that extreme negativism might be responsible for the autistic child's intellectual deficits (Cowan, Hoddinott, & Wright, 1965). However, it has not been possible to replicate the experimental findings that gave rise to this suggestion (Clark & Rutter, 1977), and it is clear that autistic children's task performance is mainly a function of task difficulty (Clark & Rutter, 1979) or the nature of task demands (Volkmar & Cohen, 1982) without the need to invoke additional motivational factors. On the other hand, it has been found that the experience of repeated failure has a tendency greatly to reduce autistic children's motivation, with a consequent deleterious effect on their cognitive performance (Clark & Rutter, 1979; Koegel & Egel, 1979).

Ornitz & Ritvo (1968) have argued that "perceptual inconstancy" (meaning faulty modulation of sensory input) underlies autistic behavior and, indeed, behaviors thought to reflect perceptual disturbances are used by them as the main criteria for the syndrome (Ornitz, Guthrie, & Farley, 1977). However, corroborative evidence for this view is still needed (Prior, 1979). Nevertheless, it is likely that autism is associated with some kind of defect in information processing. That conclusion is no longer in serious dispute, although there is still some disagreement on the precise pattern (or patterns) of cognitive deficit specifically associated with autism (DeMyer et al., 1981; Rutter, in press-a). It is also generally agreed that a cognitive deficit underlies the language problems and many of the other abnormalities shown by autistic children. The two main issues still awaiting resolution are (1) the neurophysiological basis of the cognitive deficit and (2) how, if at all, the demonstrated cognitive disabilities relate to the social impairments of autistic children.

Analysis of Social Impairments

Although the abnormal pattern of social interaction in autism is striking and distinctively different from the forms of social impairment found in other conditions, it has been the subject of remarkably little systematic observational or experimental study—far less, for example, than that on cognition or language. As a consequence, little is known about the processes underlying autistic children's abnormal social interactions. E. A. Tinbergen and N. Tinbergen (1972) hypothesized that extreme social anxiety causes autistic children to withdraw when approached and, hence, that they are most likely to respond if the other person turns away. Richer (1978) confirmed that autistic children show far less social interaction than other children, in terms of both fewer initiations of social encounters and also more frequent withdrawal when approached. But the specific prediction that autistic children would show most social approach behavior when the other person turned away from them was not confirmed by the experimental findings—albeit in a rather unnatural social interaction (Richer & Richards, 1975).

The Tinbergens' (1972) hypothesis that social approaches by an adult will increase autistic withdrawal has been negated by several other sets of findings. Thus, Churchill and Bryson (1972) found that autistic children were more responsive when adults paid attention to them. Similarly, McHale, Simeonsson, Marcus, and Olley (1980) found that autistic children's social communication increased when a teacher interacted with them than when they were left to intiate their own activities. Clark and Rutter (1981), in an experimental study, observed that autistic children were most likely to make some sort of social response when the social demands made on them were increased. Behavior modification studies, too, have shown that deliberately increasing autistic children's social involvement by operant techniques or by social intrusion, far from increasing withdrawal, leads to social and behavioral improvement (Hemsley, Howlin, Berger, Hersov, Holbrook, Rutter, & Yule, 1978; Howlin, 1978; Schopler, Brehm, Kinsbourne, & Reichler, 1971). Taken as a whole, the evidence suggests that autistic children are most responsive when attempts are made actively to engage them in social interactions.

This has important implications for treatment, but it does not aid in the elucidation of the nature of the social disability. Probably, more than anything else, it is the reciprocity of social interchange that is missing in autism (Rutter, 1978b, in press-a). This observation is important if only because it forces any explanatory mechanism to an operation in the very early stages of development. Even in the first 6 months of life, normal babies will engage in responsive reciprocal social dialogues. However, it is also necessary to recognize that, to a very large extent, autistic individuals' lack of empathic relatedness persists right into adult life.

Piaget (1926) maintained that children's social behavior was constrained by an inability to appreci-ate and coordinate the perspectives of others (see *Shantz, vol. III, chap. 8,* for an account of cognitive factors in socialization). However, Hobson (in press), using an experimental design, found that autistic children were no more impaired in their recognition of visual-spatial perspectives than were normal or retarded children of comparable intellectual level. Hobson (1982) went on to argue that, instead, autistic children may lack the ability to experience empathy in that other people's expressions of emotions do not make the normal emotional impact. Using a picture-matching paradigm in connection with a series of short videotapes portraying emotions, people, or things in terms of visual stimuli, sound, movement, or context, he found that autistic children showed no deficits in their appreciation of things but that they were markedly impaired in their appreciation of emotions (i.e., the differentiation of happy, sad, frightened, etc.) and of people (i.e., the differentiation of man, woman, boy, girl). The findings suggest some form of cognitive deficit in the processing of stimuli relevant to affect and socialization. However, the nature of the deficit remains obscure. Langdell's (1978) analysis of autistic children's ability to recognize the faces of peers from isolated facial features and inverted photography provides a similar story. Both normal and mentally retarded subjects found the upper regions of the face most helpful in identification, whereas younger autistic children found the lower features most helpful. Older autistic children showed no specific reliance on any one area and made the least errors of all groups in recognition of the inverted face. The meaning of these differences remains rather obscure, but Langdell suggested that they point to a possible deficit in the processing of both verbal and nonverbal aspects of interpersonal communication.

In summary, it may be inferred that autistic children's social abnormalities probably stem from some kind of social-cognitive deficit in the processing of stimuli that carry social and emotional meaning (Rutter, in press-a). The precise nature of that deficit remains obscure, but it seems likely that the concepts and research methods concerned with the development of the self-system in normal children (see *Harter, vol. IV, chap. 4*) could be applied with benefit to the study of autism.

Course

Lotter (1978) has provided a comprehensive summary of the long-term follow-up findings. In adult life, some two thirds of autistic individuals are still severely handicapped and unable to look after themselves (with a majority of these in long-stay institutions); but about 5% to 17% are working, leading some kind of social life, and holding their own in the community. However, these figures convey a somewhat misleading picture of the variation in outcome, in that the prognosis is strongly influenced by the extent of the initial handicap, with IQ and language skills being much the most powerful predictors. Thus, if the child's IQ on performance tests is below about 50 or 60, it is almost certain that the child will remain severely handicapped throughout life. If the IQ is above that level but if there is gross language impairment that persists beyond age 5, the child may make a fair social adjustment, but a good outcome is quite unlikely. On the other hand, if the child has normal nonverbal intelligence *and* if there is a useful level of competence in spoken language by age 5 with no more than a mild comprehension deficit, there is about a 50/50 chance that the child will achieve a good level of social adjustment in adult life. However, even for the autistic child with the most favorable prognosis, there is only a very small chance of the child becoming completely normal (Rutter, 1970a).

One of the striking findings in the studies that have followed autistic children into adult life is the relative frequency with which epileptic seizures occur for the first time during adolescence—28% of cases in the Maudsley Hospital series (Rutter, 1970a). The most extensive data on this issue are provided by Deykin and MacMahon's (1979a) survey of 183 autistic children in Massachusetts. Their findings showed that approximately a fifth of autistic children developed seizures by age 18 years, with the peak period for onset being between 11 and 14 years. Not only was the rate of seizures in autistic children far above that in the general population but also the marked elevation in the onset of seizures during adolescence was quite different from the age pattern in nonautistic individuals (which showed a *decreasing* risk at that age). Deykin and MacMahon (1979a) conclude that the high incidence of seizures at puberty may be specific to children with autistic symptomatology and may represent a distinct pathological process associated with autism. However, it should be noted that the risk of seizures is several times higher in autistic children with severe mental retardation than in those of normal nonverbal intelligence (Rutter, in press-a).

A small proportion of autistic individuals (1 in 10 in the Maudsley study) show a deterioration in adolescence with a loss of language skills associated with inertia, decreasing activity, and sometimes an intellectual decline (Gillberg & Schaumann, 1981; Rutter, 1970a). Physical investigations have failed to provide any explanation for this atypical course and further follow-up (Le Couteur, 1982) has shown that generally the decline levels off and does not progress further after adolescence.

About half of autistic children gain useful speech. Usually, this occurs by age 5, but it can occur later. The pattern of speech development in those who improve is fairly consistent (Kanner, 1971; Kanner, Rodriguez, & Ashenden, 1972; Rutter, 1970a). The children first become more responsive to sounds and show improved understanding of spoken language. When the children begin to talk, there is usually a poverty in its use and a continuing lack of social communication. In the early stages of speech development (sometimes for much longer), much of the speech is echolalic with persisting pronominal reversal. Delayed·echoing, stereotyped phraseology, and idiosyncratic and unusual styles of language are characteristic. Even among those who achieve a normal or near-normal level of language competence, there are often continuing abnormalities in language usage and speech delivery. In some, there is a monotonous flat delivery with little lability or change of emphasis, whereas in others speech is staccato and lacking in cadence and inflection. Frequently, there is a formality of language with pedantic modes of expression. Until quite late in adolescence (sometimes always), many autistic children tend to converse mainly by a series of obsessive questions related to their particular preoccupation at the time. Difficulties with abstract concepts and (perhaps especially) a difficulty in using concepts of emotions or interpersonal feelings often persists.

About half of autistic children show improved interpersonal relationships as they grow older but, as the detailed descriptions of those who have progressed well indicate, social relationships usually remain abnormal (Bemporad, 1979; Kanner, 1971; Kanner et al., 1972; Rutter, 1970a). A few become somewhat outgoing in personality, although remaining shallow in affect and lacking in empathy; more usually, autistic individuals remain reserved and seemingly unaware of the feelings of others. In the least handicapped persons, some develop an interest in other people and a wish to make friendships, but they lack interpersonal skills and usually fail to proceed from acquaintance to friendship. There may be sexual drive, but usually there is a lack of heterosexual relationships, and it is quite exceptional for marriage to occur, although it has been reported (Des Lauriers, 1978). The characteristics are well exemplified in Bemporad's (1979) description of one 31-year-old man, originally diagnosed as autistic by

Kanner at age 4. He totally lacked small talk, and he tended to structure social encounters in a rigid fashion, in keeping with the general ritualization of his life. He could not emphasize with others and found other people's unpredictability (to him) unsettling and frightening; although he wanted to be included in social activities, he simply had no idea of how to set about making social contact. There was a striking lack of any inner fantasy life; he listened to other people, but he rarely initiated conversations; and he was painfully aware of being different from other people. The greatest social improvement tends to come in late adolescence together with an increasing self-awareness (Kanner et al., 1972). But in the great majority of cases, the emerging interest in people is not accompanied by the social reciprocity and response to other people's feelings that ordinarily form the basis of friendships.

The awkwardness and abnormality of autistic adults' social relationships are striking, but there has been no systematic observational study of just which features characterize their social ineptness. Moreover, it remains quite uncertain whether the abnormalities at maturity reflect a continuing social or affective incapacity, the persisting results of a lack of appropriate social experiences at a critical period in early childhood, or a failure to provide the appropriate remediation in adult life. The matter warrants investigation.

Family Characteristics

Although a host of environmental influences and psychogenic factors have been suggested as possible contributory factors in the causation of infantile autism, there is no satisfactory evidence that any kind of deviant family functioning leads to autism (see review by Cantwell et al., 1978). However, there are major methodological problems in assessing premorbid patterns of family interaction after the child is already handicapped with a severe disorder arising in infancy (if not already present at birth). Massie (1978) attempted to circumvent this difficulty by getting judges to rate home movies of 13 infants later diagnosed as having some form of childhood psychosis along with comparable home movies of 15 normal control infants. There was a tendency for the mothers of the psychotic children to receive lower ratings for holding, touching, eye gaze, and attachment and a lesser tendency for the infants to receive lower ratings on the same variables. Massie argued that the greater deviance in the mothers at a time when the infants were not yet showing psychotic features suggested that poor parenting may play a part in the genesis of autism. However, a later report

from the same study (Rosenthal et al., 1980) showed that many of the infants already showed cognitive abnormalities; the group studied was diagnostically heterogeneous with the number showing autism not specified; the ratings were of low reliability (0.31 to 0.67); there was great overlap between the groups; and few of the differences were statistically significant on two-tailed tests. In consequence, the results must be regarded as inconclusive.

Until recently, most clinic and general population studies have given rise to the puzzling finding that the syndrome is relatively more frequent in children born to middle-class parents (Werry, 1979). Two large clinic series failed to show this social-class association, but one series was atypical in its diagnostic criteria and in the excess of middle-class families in *both* autistic children and controls (Ritvo, Cantwell, Johnson, Clements, Benbrook, Slagle, Kelly, & Ritz, 1971); the other was unusual in including scarcely any autistic children of normal intelligence and in the fact that the autistic group included a higher proportion of black families than controls, which partially invalidates the social-class comparison (Schopler, Andrews, & Strupp, 1979). However, two recent epidemiological studies without these limitations, in London (Wing, 1980) and in Sweden (Gillberg & Schaumann, 1982), have also shown no social-class association. It is not clear why the findings should differ from Lotter's (1966, 1967) well-planned, large-scale general population survey (which did show a social-class effect). Nevertheless, it now seems more likely than hitherto that the social-class association in the earlier reports may have been the result of some type of referral or diagnostic artifact.

Most earlier reviews (including that of Rutter, 1967) argued that a genetic causation was unlikely on the grounds of the rarity of a family history of autism. However, this reasoning was fallacious, both because the almost universal failure of autistic individuals to give birth to children invalidates the family-history findings as a genetic index and because the rarity of a family history of autism must be assessed in relation to the rarity of autism (Curnow & Smith, 1975). On both these grounds, a strong family history would not be expected, even if autism was largely genetically determined. Moreover, in the last 5 years, positive evidence of hereditary influences has become available from several different lines of study. First, it is evident that although only about 2% of the siblings of autistic children suffer from the same condition, the rate is *50 times* that in the general population (Rutter, 1967). Second, although a family history of autism is very rare, a family history of speech delay is very much more common, being present in about a quarter of cases (Bartak et al., 1975; Rutter, Bartak, & Newman, 1971). Moreover, it has been shown (August, Stewart, & Tsai, 1981) that some 15% of the siblings of autistic children compared with 3% of the siblings of Down's syndrome individuals have language disorders, learning disabilities, or mental retardation. Also, Minton, Campbell, Green, Jennings, and Samit (1982) found that the siblings of autistic children had lower IQs than expected on the basis of demographic variables and that the intellectual deficits were more evident on verbal IQ than on performance IQ. Third, Folstein and Rutter's (1977) study of 21 same-sex twin pairs, in which one or both twins had autism, showed a 36% pairwise concordance rate for autism in monozygotic (MZ) pairs compared with 0% concordance in dizygotic (DZ) pairs. The concordance for cognitive abnormalities was 82% in MZ pairs and 10% in DZ pairs. The findings all indicate important genetic influences; they also suggest that (probably) it is not autism as such that is inherited but rather some broader predisposition to language and cognitive abnormalities, of which autism constitutes but one part. In addition, recent reports (Brown, Jenkins, Friedman, Brooks, Wisniewski, Raguthu, & French, 1982) indicate that some cases of autism are associated with the fragile-X syndrome, a condition in which there is a sex chromosome anomaly.

Neurophysiology

Neurophysiologic investigations have been undertaken using EEG techniques, contingent and noncontingent sensory-evoked responses, autonomic reactivity, and vestibular responses (James & Barry, 1980; Ornitz, 1978). Findings have been quite inconsistent and inconclusive, but various abnormalities have been reported. Thus, for example, some autistic children have been found to have increased brainstem transmission times as determined by auditory-evoked responses; this has been thought to indicate brainstem dysfunction (Fein, Skoff, & Mirsky, 1981; Rosenblum, Arick, Krug, Stubbs, Young, & Pelson, 1980; Skoff, Mirsky, & Turner, 1980). Other investigators have reported that brain potentials reflecting responses to random deletion of stimuli with a regular train of sensory (especially auditory) stimuli are reduced in autistic children compared with normals—suggesting defective information storage and, hence, abnormalities in the hippocampus or related structures (Novick, Kurtzberg, & Vaughn, 1979). Unfortunately, the interpretation of these (and other) neurophysiologic

findings is highly problematic because (1) many findings have been inconsistent or not replicated, (2) most studies have used normal rather than mentally retarded controls (with the consequence that it is unknown whether the results reflect low MA or brain abnormalities associated with global mental retardation rather than autism per se), and (3) little is known on the meaning of the neurophysiologic measures.

Other studies have focused on possible impairments in cerebral lateralization. Handedness investigations have failed to show a consistent pattern, but both autistic and retarded children have tended to show a slightly impaired establishment of lateral preferences compared with normals (McCann, 1981). Dawson, Warrenburg, & Fuller (1982) found (as judged from EEG measures of hemispheric activation) that 7 out of 10 autistic children had right-hemispheric dominance for both verbal and spatial functions—an atypical pattern previously found in children with developmental language disorders. Prior and Bradshaw (1979), using a dichotic-listening technique, found a significant excess of autistic children with a left-ear (right-hemispheric) advantage (LEA). Blackstock (1978) reported that autistic children tended to listen to music rather than songs and preferred their left ear for both—a result interpreted in terms of right-hemispheric processing. Although the findings are not unambiguous, they are consistent with a hypothesis that some cases of autism (in common with some other developmental disorders) are associated with abnormalities in hemispheric specialization.

Neuroanatomy

Various findings provide nonspecific pointers to some form of organic pathology. The strong association with epilepsy arising during adolescence (Deykin & MacMahon, 1979a) has already been noted; others include an increased incidence of EEG abnormalities (Small, 1975), the presence of growth retardation in some cases (Campbell, Petti, Green, Cohen, Genieser, & David, 1980), generalized ventricular dilatation as shown by air encephalography (Aarkrog, 1968), and a mixed bag of abnormalities on computerized brain tomography (Caparulo, Cohen, Rothman, Young, Katz, Shaywitz, & Shaywitz, 1981; Damasio, Maurer, Damasio, & Chui, 1980). However, the clinical significance of these findings remains uncertain, both because of doubts on their validity and meaning and because the abnormalities do not satisfactorily differentiate autism from other disorders. More specific findings were claimed by Hauser, DeLong, & Rosman (1975) who reported dilatations of the left temporal horn in 15 out of 18 children with retarded language development, many of whom also showed autistic features. But, again, the specificity of the finding remains in doubt in the absence of a comparison group with some other form of developmental disorder.

Hier, LeMay, & Rosenberger (1979), using computerized brain tomography, showed that a reversed pattern of cerebral asymmetry (i.e., the right parieto-occipital region wider than the left) was more frequently found in autistic than in mentally retarded patients. But this finding was only partially replicated by Damasio et al. (1980) and was not present at all in the study by Tsai, Jacoby, Stewart, & Beisler (1982). The meaning of reversed asymmetry is obscure, but the contradictory findings in autism together with the finding of the same reversal in dyslexic children (Hier, LeMay, Rosenberger, & Perlo, 1978) suggest that it has little, if any, specific diagnostic significance.

Neuropathology

Several studies have suggested the probable etiological importance of perinatal brain injury in some cases of autism. Thus, biological hazards known to carry an increased risk of brain damage (e.g., neonatal convulsions) differentiated the autistic from the nonautistic twin in 12 of the 17 discordant pairs in Folstein and Rutter's (1977) study. Also, unfavorable perinatal factors have been found to be more frequent in autistic children than in their siblings (Deykin & MacMahon, 1980; Finegan & Quadrington, 1979) or in controls (Gillberg & Gillberg, 1982; Torrey, Hersh, & McCabe, 1975). On the other hand, it appears that no single event or combination of events could reasonably account for a large number of cases of autism (Deykin & MacMahon, 1980). No evidence has been found to link autism with prenatal infections (Deykin & MacMahon, 1979b), with the possible exception of rubella and influenza that might account for some 5% of the cases.

It seems that, in some instances, adverse prenatal and perinatal factors may play a part in the genesis of autism. However, the obstetric factors found to be associated with autism have been rather heterogeneous in type and not consistent across studies so that the mechanisms have yet to be identified. Of course, too, it is obvious that with any of the prenatal and perinatal hazard studies, autism is one of the least common sequelae. Accordingly, it remains to be explained why, when it does result, autism rather than mental retardation or cerebral palsy is the consequence.

Apart from Williams, Hauser, Purpura, DeLong, & Swisher's (1980) recent study of four retarded persons with autistic behavior, there are very few systematic neuropathologic data on children dying from autism (Darby, 1976). Complete examinations of the brains by Williams and his colleagues (1980) failed to provide clues as to the cause or pathoanatomic substrate of autism. Nevertheless, autism has been associated with quite diverse medical conditions, such as congenital rubella (Chess, Fernandez, & Korn, 1978; Chess, Korn, & Fernandez, 1971), tuberous sclerosis (Creak, 1963; Lotter, 1974), infantile spasms with hypsarrhythmia (Riikonen & Amnell, 1981; Taft & Cohen, 1971), and cerebral lipoidosis (Creak, 1963). Although these conditions have no obvious features in common, it is likely that they *do* share some crucial feature because there is a fair degree of consistency in the medical conditions that are and are not associated with autism. Thus, within a mentally retarded population, the above mentioned disorders together with encephalitis in infancy tend to be more commonly linked with autism, whereas other disorders, such as cerebral palsy and especially Down's syndrome, only rarely give rise to autism (Wing & Gould, 1979). Identification of the crucial neuropathological features that differentiate those medical conditions associated with autism from those not associated might well provide important clues to the etiological processes.

Neurochemistry

There have been many attempts to find biochemical abnormalities that are specific to autism, but, so far, although some autistic children have been found to have biochemical anomalies, no specific associations have been found (Cohen, Caparulo, & Shaywitz, 1978; Coleman, 1976; Ritvo, Rabin, Yuwiler, Freeman, & Geller, 1978). Moreover, there have been many failures to replicate. For example, Coleman (1976) found serum zinc levels much elevated in autistic children, but there was not even a trend in that direction in the study by Jackson and Garrod (1978). Boullin, Coleman, O'Brien, and Rimland (1971) reported an association between autism and serotonin efflux. However, this was not found in the replication by Yuwiler and his colleagues (Yuwiler, Ritvo, Geller, Glossman, Schneiderman, & Matsuno, 1975), who used somewhat different criteria and a different laboratory technique, nor was it found in the collaborative study of Boullin and Yuwiler (Boullin, Freeman, Geller, Ritvo, Rutter, & Yuwiler, 1982), who used the techniques of both laboratories with the same set of autistic children. Several studies have found serotonin levels raised in about a third of autistic children, but they are also raised in about a third of nonautistic children with severe mental retardation (findings reviewed in the *British Medical Journal,* 1978). Because of this, it has seemed unlikely that serotonin has any specific role in the genesis of autism. However, Geller, Ritvo, Freeman, and Yuwiler (1982) have recently reported that the reduction of serotonin levels through the administration of fenfluramine hydrochloride in three autistic children was associated with significant cognitive and behavioral improvements, at least in the short term. The results are provocative in their implications but, as the authors point out, this pilot study could not determine whether the reduction in serotonin *caused* the improvement nor whether the benefits would persist.

Conclusions

In many respects, autism constitutes the clearest example of a disease entity in child psychiatry because of the evidence that it represents a qualitative departure from normality and that it is likely to be caused by some type of organic brain dysfunction. Nevertheless, it also provides a good example of a condition that requires a developmental psychopathology approach in its investigation. In the first place it is par excellence a developmental disorder, in that it arises in infancy and is associated with a serious and pervasive distortion of the developmental course that follows. Second, in terms of the prevailing hypothesis that it arises on the basis of some type of deficit in social cognition, it provides a most important opportunity to investigate the developmental interrelationships among cognition, conation, and affect (Rutter, in press-a). In that connection, the recent research into the basis of the social abnormalities in autism constitutes an important avenue that warrants much further exploration, which should make use of advances in techniques for the measurement of emotional responsiveness (Izard, 1982). Third, autism represents a key topic in the field of developmental neuropsychology and neuropsychiatry in terms of the opportunity it provides to study brain structure/brain function relationships and of the questions it raises with regard to age-related developmental differences in the effects of brain pathology. This, too, warrants further research of the type now possible as a result of methodological advances, such as those represented by positron emission tomography and by computer assisted EEG analyses of the changes in neurophysiological functioning during task performance (see *Behavioral Ef-*

fects of Brain Damage in Childhood). Last, autism is of interest in terms of the genetic evidence suggesting linkages between this severe and unusual syndrome and the broader range of developmental language and cognitive disabilities.

Autistic Psychopathy/Schizoid Personality

At about the same time as Kanner (1943) delineated the characteristics of infantile autism, Asperger (1944) outlined a syndrome that he termed autistic psychopathy. The children described by him had shown consistent social and emotional abnormalities from the second year onwards. Abnormalities of gaze, poverty of expression and gesture, a lack of feeling for others, solitariness, lack of humor, extreme egocentrism, unusual and constricted intellectual interests, and idiosyncratic attachments to objects were among the main phenomena said to be typical. All the patients with the syndrome were boys, and often one or more relatives showed somewhat similar personality features.

For a long time, little attention was paid to this concept, but in Europe there has been a resurgence of interest during recent years (Wing, 1981a). Although the validity of the syndrome remains in doubt, the topic is important for developmental psychopathology for several different reasons. First, it provides an hypothesized bridge between normality and disorders of psychotic severity. The supposition is that Asperger's syndrome represents an abnormality of development with characteristics similar to, but of milder degree than, those seen with autism or schizophrenia. As a consequence, it provides the opportunity for direct examination of the psychological features that supposedly constitute risk factors for these more serious conditions. Second, as shown by the two terms used for the syndrome (autistic psychopathy and schizoid personality), it appears to represent a possible link between autism and schizophrenia—two disorders that otherwise seem to have little in common (Rutter, 1972a). Third, it constitutes a set of features that are identifiable early in childhood and yet that show a remarkable degree of persistence into adult life.

Van Krevelen (Van Krevelen, 1971; Van Krevelen & Kuipers, 1962) noted both the parallels and contrasts with infantile autism. He suggested that the two conditions might be genetically linked but that autistic psychopathy differed from autism in two respects: (1) it constituted a personality trait rather than a psychotic process and (2) it was unassociated with organic brain dysfunction. Both Bosch (1962/1970) and Weber (1966), in describing their series of cases, considered that there was a substantial overlap between autism and autistic psychopathy.

In contrast, Wolff and her colleagues (Chick, Waterhouse, & Wolff, 1979; Wolff & Barlow, 1979; Wolff & Chick, 1980) have pointed to the links with schizophrenia. They noted the evidence that schizophrenia is genetically linked with abnormalities of personality, and they hypothesized that the childhood behavior pattern represented the earliest manifestations of that adult personality disorder. They reported that some 3% to 4% of new referrals to a general child psychiatry department conformed to the clinical picture described by Asperger (1944), but they preferred the term schizoid personality. The children were predominantly boys, in a 9 to 1 ratio, and they tended to come from middle-class families.

On a range of psychological tests, 17 schizoid children, 13 intelligent autistic children, and 8 controls were systematically compared. The schizoid children were similar to the autistic children in showing scatter in their cognitive test scores, in their relatively low scores on the visual retention and visual association subtests of the Illinois Test of Psycholinguistic Abilities, and in their relative failure to use meaning in their verbal recall. But in each instance, the schizoid children tended to be intermediate between the autistic and control groups; in some respects, they differed from the autistic children (the schizoid group were less perseverative than autistic children but used even fewer emotional constructs in describing people).

Some 10 years later, 22 boys with schizoid personality were followed up and compared with a matched control group with other diagnoses (unfortunately, the autism comparison was not retained). The schizoid group was differentiated in having fewer heterosexual relationships (none was married compared with 5 controls), in lacking empathy and showing increased emotional detachment (self-ratings), in more frequent single-minded pursuit of specific circumscribed interests, in unusual styles of communication, and in the increased frequency of suicidal thoughts and acts. One schizoid individual had developed a schizophrenic psychosis.

No systematic data are available on possible causal factors, but Wolff and Barlow (1979) commented that the children's life histories provided no adequate explanations for their difficulties. Both Asperger (1944) and Van Krevelen (1971) considered that genetic influences were likely to be operative. Wolff and Chick (1980) also noted that some schizoid children had developmental difficulties and

that a small number showed either intellectual retardation or evidence of cerebral dysfunction.

In summary, the follow-up findings clearly show the persistence into adult life of the features that differentiated the schizoid individuals in childhood, and, to that extent, the concept has been shown to identify a meaningful pattern. However, the homogeneity of the syndrome remains in doubt and its relationship with either autism or schizophrenia has still to be established. The parallels with autism are obvious in terms of the behavioral characteristics, sex ratio, and adult outcome. It seems likely that at least some cases of Asperger's syndrome are synonymous with mild cases of autism. On the other hand, the lack of early language delay in many cases of autistic psychopathy either suggests that these constitute a different disorder or that autism can develop in the absence of language abnormalities (a suggestion that would have important implications for concepts of the cognitive basis of autism). The relative frequency of Asperger's syndrome in Wolff's series also indicates that either the concept of autism as it occurs in children of normal intelligence needs to be greatly broadened or Asperger's syndrome is itself heterogeneous.

The parallels with schizophrenia are less striking in that the prepsychotic characteristics have generally been rather different. Schizophrenia does not show the huge male preponderance reported for Asperger's syndrome, and it is not more common in those from a middle-class background (as was the case for schizoid personalities in Wolff's series). On the other hand, 1 (or possibly 2) of Wolff's series of 22 developed schizophrenia and 3 of Wing's (1981a) series of 18 adults with Asperger's syndrome had psychotic episodes of a type that might have been schizophrenic. Moreover, there is no doubt that there are abnormalities of personality genetically linked with schizophrenia and that these have some similarities with some features of Asperger's syndrome.

It is apparent that the value of the concept of autistic psychopathy or schizoid personality does not lie in the knowledge that has accrued from its study (which is very little) but rather from the implication of the need for a more systematic study of the particular abnormalities in empathy and social relatedness said to characterize it. Such study, which would require both the experimental and naturalistic approaches of developmental psychology, should lead to a better understanding of the ways in which abnormalities of personality development may be associated with two serious psychiatric disorders, autism and schizophrenia.

Childhood Precursors of Adult Schizophrenia

Since the first reports by Bleuler and Kraepelin at the beginning of this century, it has been recognized that about half of all individuals who develop schizophrenic psychoses in adult life have shown abnormal (but nonpsychotic) patterns of behavior in childhood (Garmezy, 1974; Hanson, Gottesman, & Heston, 1976; Offord & Cross, 1969). During the last quarter of a century, there have been many attempts, using a variety of contrasting research strategies, to delineate the specific behavioral features of these childhood precursors of adult schizophrenia. The findings are most conveniently considered according to the three main research strategies that have been employed: (1) prospective studies of high-risk populations; (2) follow-back studies, using contemporaneous records, of adults with schizophrenia; (3) the follow-up of children with psychiatric disorders.

Prospective Studies of High-Risk Populations

The most frequently followed strategy over the last two decades has been the longitudinal study of individuals selected as having a high (genetic) risk of schizophrenia by virtue of having been born to a schizophrenic mother.[3] The one immense potential advantage of this strategy is that it enables precise and detailed measures to be taken in advance of the development of psychosis in people who will later become schizophrenic. However, so far, the advantage has been largely potential rather than actual, in that very few subjects have been followed long enough for the psychosis to appear. Instead, it has been necessary to rely on a high-risk (i.e., children born to a schizophrenic mother) versus low-risk (i.e., controls) comparison. This has produced a number of interesting findings, but their interpretation is bedeviled by the fact that: (1) only about 10% of the offspring of schizophrenics can be expected to become schizophrenics; (2) having a schizophrenic mother is likely to involve a greatly raised likelihood of the father being criminal and the child being separated from the family and admitted to an institution (Mednick, 1978)—factors that put the child at a much increased risk for disorders other than schizophrenia; and (3) only about 10% of schizophrenics are born to a schizophrenic parent (making it somewhat uncertain how far the findings in this special minority subgroup will apply to the other 90%).

A further problem in many of the studies is that schizophrenia was diagnosed using rather broader criteria than those now regarded as acceptable (Worland, Jones, & Anthony, in press). Currently, the data from a number of the high-risk studies are being reanalyzed according to the more stringent criteria of DSM–III (American Psychiatric Association, 1980). Until these data become available, there is the real possibility that some of the high-risk/low-risk differences reported here may have little to do with the specific childhood precursors of schizophrenia. The practical effects of this possibility have been indicated by several studies showing that many of the characteristics that differentiate the children of schizophrenics from normals do *not* clearly differentiate them from the children of mothers with other forms of psychiatric disorders. Most striking, this has applied to measures of aggression, emotional disturbance, and social maladaptation (see, e.g., Fisher, Kokes, Harder, & Jones, 1980; Rolf & Garmezy, 1974; Sameroff, Barocas, & Safer, in press; Weintraub & Neale, in press; Weintraub, Prinz, & Neale, 1978; Worland et al., in press) and to early temperamental features (McNeil & Kaij, in press). However, it has also been found with cognitive and attentional measures (Winters, Stone, Weintraub, & Neale, 1981).

Three main sets of variables have been investigated in the prospective high-risk studies: neurodevelopmental immaturities, autonomic functioning, and attentional deficits. Fish (1960, in press) reported that relatively poor motor and perceptual functioning was more often found in the offspring of schizophrenics than controls. However, Marcus, Auerbach, Wilkinson, & Burack (1981) showed that this applied to just a subgroup of infants, and the Lund study (McNeil & Kaij, in press), which included the necessary comparison group of children born to mothers with nonschizophrenic mental illnesses, showed only a slight trend for neurodevelopmental immaturities to be more frequent in the schizophrenic offspring group. Hanson et al. (1976) used data from the American Perinatal Collaborative Study to compare the offspring of 30 schizophrenic parents, 30 psychiatric patients with some other diagnosis, and 29 matched normals. The combination of poor motor skills *and* large cognitive test-score variance together with schizoid behavior at both 4 and 7 years proved the best differentiator; this combination *only* occurred in the children of schizophrenic parents (17% vs. 0% in the other groups).

The Copenhagen project (Mednick, 1978), which pioneered the prospective strategy, found that the autonomic functioning of the offspring of schizophrenics was characterized by hypersensitivity and fast responses. However, this was not replicated in the New York study (Erlenmeyer-Kimling, Kestenbaum, Bind, & Hilldoff, in press; Erlenmeyer-Kimling, Marcuse, Cornblatt, Friedman, Rainer, &

Rutschmann, in press). It seems that the probable explanation for the discrepant finding is that this particular autonomic feature applies only to men, to children in nonintact families and to those without a criminal father (Mednick, 1978; Mednick, Schulsinger, Teasdale, Schulsinger, Venables, & Rock, 1978). However, the very specialized circumstances in which the finding applies cast doubt on the likelihood of it playing a central role in the childhood precursors of schizophrenia.

Of all the variables differentiating the offspring of schizophrenics, perhaps the most consistent has been the presence of a particular type of attentional deficit involving poor signal/noise discrimination or sensitivity (Erlenmeyer-Kimling, Kestenbaum, Bind, & Hilldoff, in press; Erlenmeyer-Kimling, Marcuse, Cornblatt, Friedman, Rainer, & Rutschmann, in press; Nuechterlain; Phipps-Yonas, Driscoll, & Garmezy, in press; Rutschmann, Cornblatt, & Erlenmeyer-Kimling, 1977). Such a deficit has usually (but not always, see Winters et al., 1981) differentiated children of schizophrenics from children of depressives, and it also has differentiated them from hyperkinetic children, who tend to show a rather different type of attentional deficit (Nuechterlain et al., 1982).

The finding that the offspring of schizophrenics often show attentional difficulties does not, of course, necessarily mean that attentional deficits predispose to schizophrenia. The importance of this distinction is brought out in the Copenhagen project (Walker, Cudeck, Mednick, Schulsinger, in press). Their results showed that the verbal associative disturbances earlier found to differentiate children of schizophrenics from controls and to differentiate the more disturbed and less disturbed within schizophrenic offspring did *not* differentiate individuals who become schizophrenic from those who do not (Griffith, Mednick, Schulsinger, & Diderichsen, 1980). On the other hand, the finding that the attentional difficulties found in the away-fostered children of schizophrenics (Asarnow, Steffy, MacCrimmon, & Cleghorn, 1977) are similar to those found in remitted adult schizophrenics (Asarnow & MacCrimmon, 1978) suggests the plausibility of a specific link by which genetically determined attentional deficits are implicated in the origin of schizophrenia.

A marked sex difference in the factors that predicted schizophrenia was found in the Copenhagen project. In men, schizophrenia was predicted by perinatal complications, institutional care in infancy, and highly responsive, rapid autonomic responses (Mednick et al., 1978; Walker et al., in press). None of these except possibly perinatal complications (Parnas, Schulsinger, Teasdale, Schulsinger, Feldman, & Mednick, 1982), predicted schizophrenia in women. The findings are noncontributory to the identification of the *behavioral* precursors of schizophrenia, but they are valuable in emphasizing the need to examine sex differences.

The only other investigation with subjects coming into the schizophrenia age-group is Erlenmeyer-Kimling's New York study (Erlenmeyer-Kimling, Kestenbaum, Bind, & Hilldoff, in press; Erlenmeyer-Kimling, Marcuse, Cornblatt, Friedman, Rainer, & Rutschmann, in press; Rutschmann et al., 1977), one of the best planned and most thorough of all the prospective studies. So far, 8 subjects have been hospitalized and 15 have received psychiatric treatment (of these 23 subjects, 15 are the offspring of schizophrenics). It was found that this clinically deviant group differed from the remainder in having a lower verbal IQ, a poorer performance on the Bender-Gestalt test, more neurodevelopmental abnormalities, worse coordination, and greater attentional deficits. However, it should be noted that only a minority of these disorders were overtly schizophrenic, so, it remains to be determined whether these variables predict schizophrenia as distinct from other psychiatric disorders.

Follow-back Studies

The follow-back strategy relies on the use of contemporaneous records (usually school reports) to examine the childhood characteristics of people identified as schizophrenic in adult life. This approach provides a more representative group of schizophrenics than the high-risk approach but suffers from the severe constraints imposed by unstandardized reports designed for a quite different purpose. Nevertheless, this last limitation carries the corresponding advantage that the childhood data are necessarily free of any bias stemming from knowledge of adult outcome.

The most systematic and thorough investigation of this kind is that by Watt and his colleagues (Lewine, Watt, Prentky, & Fryer, 1980; Watt, 1974). The school records of 59 schizophrenics were compared with those of 40 patients with personality disorders, 29 neurotics, 14 psychotic depressives, and 141 matched controls. The schizophrenics differed from all other groups in showing a much lower level of interpersonal social competence; this applied to both males and females. The personality-disorder group showed the same pattern but to a lesser extent. Earlier findings from the same study had indicated that the differences were more marked during adolescence than earlier childhood and that although the boys who later became schizophrenics showed aggression and emotional instability, this was not so for the girls. The results are important in showing that childhood behavior differentiates schizophrenics both from normals and from individuals with other forms of psychiatric disorder in adult life. However, this applies to only about half of all schizophrenics, the other half appear indistinguishable from the general population during childhood. Also, the findings apply to a rather broader concept of schizophrenia than that now in use.

Follow-up of Children with Psychiatric Disorders

The classical study of the third type of research strategy is Robins' (1966) 30-year follow-up of children first seen in the 1920s at a St. Louis psychiatric clinic. Of the 436 clinic children followed up, 26 (6%) developed schizophrenia, a rate three times that of the controls. The childhood behavior of these 26 children was compared with the behavior of those who developed other forms of psychiatric disorder in adult life as well as those who were free of psychiatric disturbance. Although there was no delineation of a clear-cut preschizophrenic pattern, the childhood behavior of the adult schizophrenics was distinctive in three main respects: (1) antisocial behavior that tended to be restricted to the family and acquaintances, (2) a lack of activities with other delinquents, and (3) the presence of depressive, worrying, and overdependent behavior. In common with those who became alcoholic or sociopathic, the adult schizophrenics had lower levels of scholastic achievement than did those who showed no psychiatric condition in adult life. Children referred for shy, withdrawn, or hypersensitive behavior were *not* particularly likely to become schizophrenic.

The findings from other follow-up studies (see reviews by Garmezy, 1974; Offord & Cross, 1969) are in generally good agreement. Thus, it has been found that preschizophrenic social isolation is not associated with shyness or withdrawal but rather with active dislike by the peer group, who regard the child as odd or peculiar in some way (Roff, 1963); that emotional disturbance antedates schizophrenia in males but not females (Gardner, 1967), a finding that may mean that it is only when emotional disturbance is combined with antisocial behavior and poor peer relations (a pattern probably more common in males) that it predisposes to schizophrenia; and that preschizophrenic children tend also to show clumsiness and developmental delays (Nameche & Ricks, cited in Garmezy, 1974).

The main limitation of the follow-up strategy is that the findings apply only to individuals referred to psychiatric clinics during childhood. It may be that this overestimates the importance of items (such as aggression or antisocial behavior) that carry a high likelihood of referral and underestimates the importance of those (such as peculiarities in the style of social interaction or clumsiness) that are less likely to cause referral. However, this is not the same limitation as those that apply to the other two research strategies; perhaps the greatest weight should be placed on findings emerging in all three approaches.

Summary

Both the follow-up and follow-back strategies agree in showing that abnormalities in interpersonal relationships, represented by oddities and isolation rather than shyness or timidity, are characteristic. This was also apparent in the high-risk study of schizophrenics' offspring by Hanson et al. (1976). These social difficulties may often be accompanied in boys by antisocial behavior that differs from the general run of delinquency in tending to be both solitary and confined to the home setting. It is evident that these features are not sufficiently clearcut for the behavior of any individual child to be reliably diagnosed as preschizophrenic; nevertheless, the behavior does seem to be somewhat different from that associated with other forms of adult mental disorder.

Second, there are indications that schizophrenia may sometimes be associated with clumsiness and with other indications of neurodevelopmental immaturity in childhood. Obviously, this cannot be regarded as specific to schizophrenia as these features have been found in many other psychiatric conditions and in learning disabilities. Nevertheless, it seems that it may be a common enough finding in association with schizophrenia for it to be of some importance; moreover, it seems that neurodevelopmental immaturities are particularly characteristic of schizophrenia with onset in childhood (Quitkin, Rifkin, & Klein, 1976). With respect to neurodevelopmental abnormalities, it may be relevant that two independent computerized brain tomography studies (Johnstone, Crow, Frith, Husband, & Kreel, 1976; Weinberger, Torrey, Neophytides, & Wyatt, 1979), confirming earlier pneumoencephalographic investigations, have shown that a subgroup of adult schizophrenics show ventricular dilatation, a finding that suggests the probability of structural brain pathology. However, a recent study (Benes, Sunderland, Jones, LeMay, Cohen, & Lipinski, 1982) did not find enlarged ventricles in a small sample of young schizophrenics, and it remains uncertain whether the findings are associated with schizophrenia, with prolonged antipsychotic medication, or with chronic institutionalization.

The third feature of probable importance is the presence of an attentional deficit that involves poor signal/noise discrimination (Garmezy, 1978; Nuechterlain, in press). This has been noted only in the high-risk studies, but, of course, it could not be examined in either of the other two strategies. So far, it has been shown to be more frequent in the off-spring of schizophrenics and to predict later psychiatric disorder, but it has yet to be determined whether it predicts specifically schizophrenia. The suggestion of a specific link is plausible but, as yet, not proven.

It cannot be said that these findings as yet provide either a clear picture of the childhood precursors of adult schizophrenia or an understanding of the developmental processes underlying the disorder. Nevertheless, the results have been important in pointing to the probable role of cognitive and attentional deficits in the genesis of socioemotional abnormalities. Also, these findings have been crucial in their emphasis of the need to compare schizophrenia with other psychiatric disorders. Some of the precursors have turned out to be risk factors for a wide range of adverse outcomes, whereas others may constitute vulnerability factors with a greater specificity for schizophrenia. The better differentiation of general from specific precursors should throw light on both developmental issues and the nature of schizophrenia.

Overview of Disorders of Socialization

The study of social development has come to occupy an increasingly important place in developmental psychology (cf. Cairns, 1979; Maccoby, 1980). Also, it is clear that disturbances of socialization are common in many different types of psychiatric disorder. Poor peer relationships are predictive of later emotional and behavioral disorders (see *Hartup, vol. IV, chap. 2*) and family discord is strongly associated with the development of conduct disturbances in the children (see *Disturbances of Conduct*). Autism and schizophrenia, two of the most severe and persistent psychiatric conditions, are both characterized by serious distortions in interpersonal functioning. Our discussions of abnormalities in social relationships, therefore, has had to range over a rather diverse assortment of psychopathology. It will have been apparent that there is no agreed classification or categorization of disorders of socialization, no one overarching conceptualization to provide coherence, and no single theory that aims to explain the nature and origins of these disparate conditions. The demonstrated importance of abnormalities in social relationships as indicators of psychopathology stands in stark contrast to the relative lack of adequate concepts and measures to study these abnormalities. The need to develop this branch of developmental psychopathology is obvious.

EMOTIONAL DISTURBANCES

Our next topic, emotional disturbances, differs to the extent that disorders of emotions (usually under the term of neuroses) have had a prominent place in psychiatric classification for a long time. However, until recently, nearly all the research was with adults. It is only during the last few years that there has been much systematic study of the normal or abnormal development of emotions during childhood. Even so, conditions in which abnormally intense emotional states (such as anxiety, fear, or depression) comprise the main features constitute one of the two major groupings of psychiatric disorder in childhood. The other, conduct disorders (characterized by socially disapproved behavior) is discussed later.

Classification

Epidemiological studies based on detailed interviews with parents, children, and (sometimes) teachers have estimated the general population prevalence of emotional disturbance to be about 2% to 8%, with rates higher in adolescence than in early childhood and higher in city than in small-town or rural populations (Rutter, 1979; Yule, 1981).

Differentiation of Emotional and Conduct Disorders

The validity and utility of the differentiation between emotional disturbances and conduct disorders has been well demonstrated in a host of investigations (Rutter, 1978c). First, as summarized by Achenbach and Edelbrock (1978) and by Quay (1979), emotional disturbance (or anxiety/withdrawal reactions to use Quay's terminology) has constituted a major dimension of deviant behavior, separate from conduct disturbance, in almost all factor analytic and other multivariate statistical studies of children's behavior in both normal and clinic samples. Moreover, the distinction between patterns has been shown to have both interrater reliability and temporal stability. Second, whereas emotional disturbances in childhood have been found to have a roughly equal sex ratio with a tendency toward a slightly higher frequency in girls, conduct disorders consistently have been found to be considerably more frequent in boys (see *Disturbances of Conduct*). Third, whereas conduct disturbances have a quite strong association with reading difficulties, this has not been evident with emotional disorders (Clark, 1970; Rutter, Tizard, & Whitmore, 1970/1981). Fourth, conduct disturbances have shown a strong association with family discord and disharmony in all studies, but this association has been weaker and less consistent for emotional disorders (Bennett, 1960; Emery, in press; Rutter, 1971a; Rutter, Shaffer, & Shepherd, 1975; Wardle, 1961). Fifth, emotional disorders have been found to have a better short-term response to treatment (Cytryn, Gilbert, & Eisenberg, 1960; Lo, 1973), a better prognosis with respect to persistence of problems into adolescence (Graham & Rutter, 1973), a better long-term outcome (Hafner, Quast, & Shea, 1975; Robins, 1966, 1979), and a linkage with different types of adult psychiatric disorder (Hafner et al., 1975; Pritchard & Graham, 1966; Robins, 1966, 1979; Zeitlin, 1972, 1982). Also, twin and family-history findings indicate that the genetic background of emotional and conduct disorders is different (Shields, 1977).

Specific Types of Emotional Disorder

It is well established, then, that emotional disturbances and conduct disorders constitute rather different types of problems. Traditionally, psychiatrists have made a variety of finer differentiations within the overall group of emotional disorders. Thus, for example, DSM–III (American Psychiatric Association, 1980) includes categories, such as separation anxiety disorder, overanxious disorder, adjustment disorder with anxiety, and generalized anxiety disorders, all of which are supposed to be separate from each other as well as from phobic disorders, obsessive compulsive disorders, depression, and hypochondriasis. However, the validity of these differentiations lack adequate empirical support. To begin with, it has been found that most emotional disturbances in childhood involve a mixed picture that does not fit easily into any of the neat, well-circumscribed textbook categories. Moreover, it has been found that the interrater reliability on the specific subcategories of emotional disturbance is generally rather low (Cantwell, Russell, Mattison, & Will, 1979; Shaffer, Rutter, Sturge, & Nichols, 1979). Even in adults, family-history (Brown, 1942) and follow-up studies (Greer & Cawley, 1966) have indicated a considerable degree of overlap between different types of neurotic disorder in spite of some support for differentiation. The long-term links between emotional disorders in childhood and neurotic conditions in adult life have also proved to be more tenuous than once thought.

Most emotional disorders of childhood do *not* persist into adult life (Robins, 1966, 1979) and most neuroses of adult life do not begin in childhood (Lader & Marks, 1971; Marks, 1969; Zeitlin, 1982). Moreover, even in those cases where emotional disorders do persist into adult life or recur in childhood, there is only quite limited continuity in the form of the disorder or the specific type of symptomatology (Tyrer & Tyrer, 1974; Zeitlin, 1982). Nevertheless, there is the beginning of some empirical support for a limited degree of differentiation within the broad group of emotional disorders.

Depression stands out from other types of emotional disturbance in showing the most marked rise in prevalence during adolescence (Rutter, 1979; 1983d). It also differs fairly sharply in terms of the overlap with conduct disturbances. Whereas other types of emotional symptomatology (such as anxiety, phobias, and obsessions) are relatively infrequent in children with conduct disturbances, depression is as common as it is in those with pure emotional disorders (Rutter et al., 1970/1981). This difference is also brought out by the follow-up into adulthood which shows that depression is not separated from personality disorder in the way that other forms of emotional disturbance are (Zeitlin, 1982). It seems that whereas depression shows a change in sex ratio during the transition from childhood to adulthood—with an increasing female preponderance not seen in younger age groups (Carlson & Cantwell, 1980a, 1980b; Pearce, 1982)—this may not be evident with anxiety states (see *Theories of Anxiety and of Fear Formation*). Lastly, research with adults (Finlay-Jones & Brown, 1981) suggests that the life events associated with the onset of depression may not be of the same type as those linked with anxiety states; it is not known whether the same applies in childhood.

Fears differ from anxiety and worrying in terms of the presence of a definite focus; fears connate a differentiated unpleasant emotional response of agitation or fright in the actual or anticipated presence of a specific object or situation (Johnson & Melamed, 1979). Phobias are usually considered to be special sorts of fears that: (1) are out of proportion to the demands of the situation, (2) cannot be explained or reasoned away, (3) are beyond voluntary control, and (4) lead to avoidance of the feared situation (Marks, 1969). However, it is doubtful whether the distinction between fears and phobias has any real significance; in both cases, the response involves a physiological reaction, a subjective emotion, a cognitive appraisal, and avoidance (Johnson

& Melamed, 1979). Fears differ from nonspecific emotional disorders (with general anxiety and worrying) in terms of their developmental pattern; most fears are more prevalent in younger children than in older children or adolescents, and most diminish or cease within a relatively short period of time. Also, although the evidence is weaker (Graziano, De-Giovanni, & Garcia, 1979), it appears that the behavioral methods of treatment (desensitization, modeling, and flooding) that appear effective for phobias in adults (Marks, 1979)—and with less certainty in children (Johnson & Melamed, 1979)— may be unsuitable for generalized anxiety states or for depression.

Obsessions and compulsions, as abnormal phenomena, are usually defined in terms of thoughts or acts that: (1) are unwarranted, (2) involve a strong sense of pressure, (3) are felt to come from within, (4) are stereotyped and difficult to control, and (5) intrude into everyday activities (Rachman & Hodgson, 1980). Surveys of clinic patients (Adams, 1973) and of the general population (Rutter et al., 1970/1981) show that disorders mainly characterized by these phenomena are decidedly uncommon, constituting less than 1% of psychiatric outpatient referrals. It remains uncertain whether it is meaningful to regard obsessional disorders as a subcategory separate from other emotional disturbances. On the one hand, there is a considerable overlap between obsessional phenomena and phobias in terms of both their coexistence at the same time (Adams, 1973; Rachman & Hodgson, 1980) and their links over time, with some phobic children developing obsessions as they grow older (Berg, Butler, & Hall, 1976) and vice versa (W. Warren, 1965). There is also an association between obsessions and depression (Rachman & Hodgson, 1980). Within a group of patients showing psychiatric disorder in both childhood and adult life, obsessions were found to be associated with a diverse range of emotional disturbances at different times (Zeitlin, 1982). All these findings suggest a lack of syndrome specificity.

On the other hand, the few longitudinal data available suggest that emotional disturbances that include obsessions may tend to be somewhat more persistent than others (Hollingsworth, Tanguay, Grossman, & Pabat, 1980; J. Ross, 1964; W. Warren, 1965), particularly if they are not accompanied by marked depression. Moreover, when emotional disorders with obsessions in childhood do persist into adult life, there is a very strong tendency for the obsessions to continue. Zeitlin (1982) found that this temporal consistency in obsessive phenomenology was greater than for any other emotional item, which suggests that there is some specificity. The matter of syndrome definition and validity remains unresolved.

Of course, too, obsessivelike behaviors are part of normal development. Bedtime and dressing rituals (which often have a strong compulsive quality) are known to be very common in toddlers and preschoolers (Gessell, Ilg, & Ames, 1974; Newson & Newson, 1968). Similarly, slightly older children often feel impelled to touch certain objects or to avoid walking on the junctions between paving stones; also, there are widespread ritual elements in the games, chants, and songs of childhood (Opie & Opie, 1959). These forms of supposedly compulsive or obsessive behavior seem to be enjoyed, are not felt to be incongruous, and are not resisted by children (Judd, 1965). Preoccupations with specific ideas, interests, or activities persisting over months or even years are also relatively common (Bender & Schilder, 1940; Robinson & Vitale, 1954). It seems that for most children, all of these various obsessions prove to be a passing phase. However, information is lacking on age trends, on persistence, and on how often (if at all) these normal phenomena progress to or are connected with abnormal obsessional disorders of the kind that lead to clinic referral. In view of the lack of basic evidence on the developmental psychopathology of obsessions, the topic will not be considered further.

So-called conversion hysteria (in which somatic complaints *not* referrable to the autonomic nervous system are thought to be of emotional origin, such as psychogenic paralyses or blindness) stands out as most different in the one important respect—it is often a *mis*diagnosis in which an underlying organic disease has been overlooked (Caplan, 1970; Rivinus, Jamison, & Graham, 1975; Slater, 1965). This is so for both children and adults. Otherwise, the concept seems to have little unity, although true cases of psychogenic hysteria are well documented, if rather infrequent (Goodyer, 1981). Conversion hysteria will not be considered further in this chapter other than to note that there is a shift from a roughly equal sex ratio in childhood to a marked female preponderance in adult life. Epidemic hysteria differs from other emotional disorders in being far more common in girls and in being a group phenomenon rather than an individual disorder (Benaim, Horder, & Anderson, 1973; Moss & McEvedy, 1966). This, too, will not be discussed further in this chapter.

Because of the evidence that most emotionally

disturbed children do not become adult neurotics (Robins, 1966, 1979), the question has been raised as to whether emotional disturbances of childhood and adult neuroses involve the same conditions (Rutter, 1972b). There have been various attempts to differentiate between the two. Although, ultimately, it could prove to be a valid distinction, clinicians have not agreed on how to apply the differentiation to individual cases (Cantwell et al., 1979; Shaffer et al., 1979).

In summary, it is probably correct to say that there are distinct subvarieties of emotional disorder in childhood but that there is a paucity of empirical evidence to indicate how the subdivisions should be made and to validate those that have been proposed. For the present, however, it seems worthwhile to differentiate between nonspecific emotional disturbances, specific phobias, and depression. We will now consider these categories in greater detail.

Nonspecific Emotional Disturbances

As noted, most emotional disorders in childhood take the form of a nonspecific generalized disturbance in which anxiety and worrying are the most prominent features, but often in association with an admixture of obsessions, fears, and tics (Rutter et al., 1970/1981). Most epidemiological studies have relied on systematic standardized interviews with parents and with children for the assessment of emotional disturbance. Detailed accounts of the child's actual behavior are used to assess the extent to which the phenomena differ from normal in terms of severity, persistence, and interference with social functioning. Such measures have been shown to have satisfactory reliability and validity, with reasonable agreement between the accounts of parents and their children (Herjanic, Herjanic, Brown, & Wheatt, 1975; Hodges, Kline, Stern, Cytryn, & McKnew, 1982; Rutter et al., 1970/1981; Vikan, 1983). However, the agreement has tended to be lowest with specific emotional items, a problem that is even greater with questionnaire measures (Weissman, Orvaschel, & Padian, 1980). Numerous studies (reviewed by Johnson & Melamed, 1979) indicate that there are only quite modest correlations between anxiety as felt by the individual, anxious behavior as observed by others, and physiological measures of autonomic arousal. Measurement in several spheres seems indicated. Also, because of the heavy reliance on personal judgments regarding adjectives in most questionnaires (what is a lot of worry to one child may be a little to another), it seems desirable to include measures of social impairment either based on observations (Melamed & Siegel, 1975) or detailed interview accounts (Rutter et al., 1970/1981).

Epidemiological Features

So far as one can judge from the few available data, both individual emotional items and nonspecific emotional disorders show no consistent variation with age during childhood (Grant, 1958; Macfarlane, Allen, & Honzik, 1954; Shepherd, Oppenheim, & Mitchell, 1971), although there may be some tendency for a decrease in older age groups (Gersten, Langner, Eisenberg, Simcha-Fagan, & McCarthy, 1976; Werry & Quay, 1971). There is a roughly equal sex ratio throughout childhood but with a marginal tendency for a female preponderance (Richman, Stevenson, & Graham, 1982; Rutter et al., 1970/1981; Shepherd et al., 1971; Simon & Ward, 1982). During the later years of childhood and adolescence, girls tend to admit more worry and anxiety than boys (Maccoby & Jacklin, 1974). Also, whereas there is no sex difference in neuroticism up to age 10 years, thereafter there is an increasing sex differentiation because of increasing neuroticism in females but not in males (Eysenck & Eysenck, 1975).

The findings on sex differences in adult life are more difficult to interpret, in that general practice studies indicate that anxiety states are more common in women, whereas psychiatric clinic studies show no consistent sex difference (Lader & Marks, 1971). General population surveys have all shown neuroses to be more prevalent in women (Dohrenwend, Dohrenwend, Gould, Link, Neugebauer, & Wunsch-Hitzig, 1980) but few of these have considered anxiety states separately from other neurotic disorders.

The findings on the epidemiological correlates of emotional disturbance are disappointingly inconclusive (Graham, 1979). No consistent associations with either social class or educational attainment have been found, but disorders have tended to be somewhat more frequent in first-born children (Rutter et al., 1970/1981) and there is some association with parental mental disorder (Richman et al., 1982; Rutter, 1966). Studies of parent-child interaction (well reviewed by Hetherington & Martin, 1979) have shown various features of interest, but they have failed to indicate which family patterns are specifically associated with emotional disturbance. Some studies that have compared anxious children with antisocial children (e.g., Hewitt & Jenkins, 1946) have revealed clear differences, but the results have not indicated whether the families of anxious children differed in any significant way from those of normal children. Other studies (e.g., Ferreira & Winters, 1968; Murrell & Stachowiak, 1967) have dealt with disturbed children as a group without considering different types of disturbance, whereas still other studies have been concerned with essentially normal samples (e.g., Kagan & Moss, 1962). What are lacking, and much needed, are studies comparing families of anxious children with families of normal children. Without such data, no conclusions can be drawn regarding the family patterns associated with the development of emotional disturbance in childhood.

Longitudinal Course

The temporal consistency of personality variables has been reviewed by Moss and Sussman (1980), with the conclusion that the correlations from infancy to school age are generally very low and often near zero and that within the middle years of childhood, the correlations over time for emotional-type variables are still quite modest. Studies of abnormal anxious behavior also tend to show rather low temporal consistency, with most emotional disturbances tending to improve or remit completely with time (Kohlberg, LaCross, & Ricks, 1972). Thus, several epidemiological/longitudinal studies have shown that only about a third of children with an emotional disorder still have a disorder 4 or 5 years later (Richman et al., 1982; Rutter, 1977b, 1979). Clinic studies provide a similar picture (Gossett, Lewis, Lewis, & Phillips, 1973; Robins, 1979). On the other hand, there is substantial continuity in two respects. First, children who are extreme in terms of high anxiety rarely move to the opposite extreme of very low anxiety (Shepherd et al., 1971); this also applies to disturbed behavior generally in childhood (Ghodsian, Gofelman, Lambert, & Tibbenham, 1980). Second, there is high stability in the type of disturbance so that it is quite unusual for children with emotional disorders at one age to develop disturbances of conduct later.

Systematic data on the social and emotional functioning in adult life of individuals who showed emotional disturbance in childhood is provided by Robins' (1966) 30-year follow-up of St. Louis Child Guidance Clinic patients and controls and by the somewhat comparable Minnesota study by Hafner and colleagues (Hafner, Quast, & Shea, 1975; Shea, 1972). In Robins's (1966) study, those referred for nonantisocial behavior (a very mixed bag of emotional difficulties, learning problems, and temper tantrums) differed from controls in having a slightly higher overall rate of psychiatric problems (a lifetime prevalence up to the time of follow-up), but the rate of adult neurosis was only marginally higher than that in controls. The study is limited by the rather heterogeneous nature of the nonantisocial children studied, but the generally favorable long-term outcome for emotional disorders compared with that for conduct disturbances was also apparent in the Minnesota study which showed that internalizers had fewer psychosocial problems in adult life than externalizers. Also, whereas externalizers tended to show personality disorders with criminality and poor social functioning, internalizers more often had neurotic problems and achieved a social-status level as high as, or higher than, that of their parents. Other findings (Michael, Morris, & Soroker, 1957; Sundby & Kreyberg, 1968) are broadly comparable, apart from those of Waldron (1976) who, in a smaller scale follow-up of clinic children with neurotic disorders, found that 40% still showed disorder in early adult life compared with none of the controls. However, Waldron's study is based on small numbers and a younger age at follow-up; also, there must be doubts on the validity of the findings in view of the rather high proportion (45%) not followed into adult life.

Data are also available from the British National Survey (Douglas & Mann, 1979) on continuities between 16 years and 26 years on neuroticism as measured on the Eysenck scales. The overall correlation between the two ages was .32 with relatively few people having shifted from one extreme to the other.

The Pritchard and Graham (1966) and Zeitlin (1972, 1982) studies of individuals seen at a psychiatric clinic in *both* childhood and adult life showed that those with pure emotional disturbances rarely went on to develop either antisocial behavior or personality disorders. Instead, when they showed a psychiatric disorder in adult life, it usually took the form of a neurosis or depression. Zeitlin's (1982) study, like that of others (Lader & Marks, 1971), found that most anxiety states in adults began in early adult life rather than in childhood.

In summary, it is apparent that the evidence on continuities into adult life is both fragmentary and unsatisfactory. It is certainly clear that the continuities for emotional disturbances are substantially less than those for antisocial disorder; also, it is evident that most emotionally disturbed children do not become neurotic adults and (less certainly) that most neurotic adults did not exhibit emotional difficulties in childhood. However, conclusions are severely limited by the failure to differentiate between the various subcategories of emotional disturbances in childhood and by the failure to separate very young children from adolescents.

Specific Fears

Numerous studies have shown that most young children go through phases of fearing objects that involve no objective threat; in some cases, these fears may be temporarily incapacitating (Johnson &

Melamed, 1979). However, there are well-marked developmental trends.

Developmental Trends

There is a general tendency for specific fears to become less frequent as children grow older, as judged from parental reports (Coleman, Wolkind, & Ashley, 1977; Macfarlane et al., 1954), teacher reports (Cummings, 1944) and direct observations (Jersild & Holmes, 1935). During the elementary school years, children also come to include more mentalistic ideas in their concepts of emotion (Harris, Olthof, & Terwogt, 1981), although it is not known how this relates to changes in fears.

Against this background of a general diminution of fearfulness as children grow older, there are developmental patterns that vary according to the type of fear. At least four different groups are evident on the basis of age trends (Agras, Sylvester, & Oliveau, 1969; Angelino, Dollins, & Mech, 1956; Bauer, 1976, 1980; Hagman, 1932; Jersild & Holmes, 1935; Macfarlane et al., 1954; Miller, Barrett, & Hampe, 1974; Shepherd et al., 1971). First, there are those fears that are most characteristic of infancy and that are so common that they are most appropriately regarded as part of normal development, namely fears of noises, of falling, of strange objects, and of strange persons. These reach a peak before 2 years and decline rapidly during the preschool years. However, although these fears are almost universal in some degree in some contexts, it would be misleading to conclude, for example, that most infants inevitably become fearful of strangers during the third quarter of the first year of life (see reviews by Horner, 1980; Rheingold & Eckerman, 1973; Sroufe, 1977). Thus, there are marked individual differences in both the age of onset of fear and of its intensity. Also, at about the same time as infants become wary and fearful of strangers, they show a positive friendly interest in them. Moreover, infants' responses vary greatly according to situation and context, with six main variables shown to be important:

1. The presence or absence of the mother or some other attachment figure (less fear when she is present).

2. The strangeness of the overall situation (more fear shown in the laboratory than at home).

3. Previous social experiences (i.e., possibly less fear if there have been previous happy encounters with strangers).

4. Whether the stranger is an adult or a child (less fear toward a child).

5. Whether the stranger intrudes (more fear when the approach is rapid and intrusive).

6. The infant's control over the situation (less fear when a degree of control is possible).

Separation anxiety follows a broadly similar pattern (see review by Bowlby, 1973). Both naturalistic and experimental studies show that at about the age of 6 or 7 months, infants begin to show marked distress when their mother departs and leaves them alone, as indicated by increased crying, decreased exploration, following the mother, and calling for her return. This pattern, which is not present in the early months of life, reaches a peak at about 18 months and then gradually diminishes. As with stranger anxiety, there is considerable individual variation in the extent of separation anxiety and the emotional responses are much influenced by the context. Also, the timing of both seem to be quite strongly related to the child's developing cognitive capacities (Kagan, 1974; Kagan, Kearsley, & Selazo, 1978).

Second, there is a group of fears that are rare in infancy but that rise rapidly during the preschool years, only to fall again during middle childhood. Thus, fears of animals reach a peak at about 3 years, fears of the dark peak at 4 or 5, whereas fears of imaginary creatures intensify slightly later than that. Although basically part of normal development, in some children the fears may be severe and incapacitating, and in that sense abnormal. Similarly, they may be considered abnormal if they persist into later childhood or adulthood beyond the age when they ordinarily decline and then cease. Animal phobias may occur in adults, but when they do, they almost invariably began in early childhood (Marks & Gelder, 1966).

Third, there are fears that show a less consistent age trend. These include both specific fears that generally first arise in childhood but remain fairly common at all ages (such as a fear of snakes or storms) as well as those (such as a fear of meeting people) that are perhaps more closely associated with temperamental features involving generalized anxiety and timidity.

Fourth, there are a number of fears that are not part of normal development and that tend to arise later in childhood or adolescence (or even adult life). For these reasons together with their relative infrequency, these are generally considered intrinsically abnormal fears or phobias. They include a fear of closed or open spaces (agoraphobia), which begins at any time from late childhood to middle life, and possibly also certain social anxieties that generally arise at, or after, puberty. However, although agoraphobia rarely occurs in childhood, quite frequently it has been preceded by other types of phobic symptomatology or emotional disturbance (Berg, Marks, McGuire, & Lipsedge, 1974; Tyrer & Tyrer, 1974). Situational phobias can arise at any age. During adolescence there is also a marked rise in a state of fear that takes the form of school refusal (Rutter, 1979). The syndrome is complex, involving a variable admixture of separation anxiety, fear of school, depression, and other forms of widespread emotional disturbance (Hersov & Berg, 1980). Although it has some resemblance to the separation anxiety or fear of new situations that is a normal phenomenon in early childhood, often it shows no continuity with those early fears and appears to have rather different origins.

Last, there is one type of fear that stands out from all others in terms of its associated physiological response. Blood phobias in children and adults are accompanied by a sharp *fall* in pulse rate so that it is quite common for affected individuals to faint at the sight of blood (Connolly, Hallan, & Marks, 1976; Yule & Fernando, 1980). In contrast, exposure to the feared objects in other phobias is usually associated with a marked *rise* in pulse rate so that often palpitations are reported.

Sex Differences

In the early infancy period, there are no consistent sex differences in the frequency of crying or in fearfulness (Maccoby & Jacklin, 1974). During the nursery school period, sex differences are still not marked, but there is some trend for boys to be more likely to show distress in new situations or with strange objects (Smith, 1974). For example, Smith found that more boys than girls were distressed when first attending an experimental play group. Similarly, Gunnar-Vongnechten (1978) found that 1-year-old girls were not distressed by a novel toy monkey that clapped cymbals, whereas boys were frightened by it. In boys, but not girls, having control over the object changed it from being frightening to being pleasant.

During the preschool years fears seem to be about equally prevalent in boys and girls. In Jersild and Holmes' (1935) studies of 2- to 6-year-old children, this was evident both on maternal reports and in the observed responses to experimental situations (such as approaching a snake, remaining alone in an unfamiliar room, or going down a dark corridor). However, the fear responses shown by girls tended to be somewhat more intense.

At the time of first starting regular school at age 5, there is also little difference between boys and girls in their tendency to cry. However, among older children, there is an increasing disparity between the sexes. The evidence suggests that this is not because boys grow less likely to become emotionally distressed but rather because this form of emotional expression becomes less acceptable for boys. Thus, during the middle years of childhood, there is little difference between boys and girls in rates of various forms of emotional disturbance, although there is a slight tendency for these to be marginally more frequent in girls (Rutter et al., 1970/1981).

On the other hand, specific fears and phobias are substantially more frequent in girls, in a ratio of about 2 to 1 (Cummings, 1944; Lapouse & Monk, 1959; Rutter et al., 1970/1981; Simon & Ward, 1982). In adults, phobic disorders are considerably more frequent in women than in men (Marks, 1969), the sex difference being most marked in the case of agoraphobia and animal phobias (which, as already noted, differ sharply in their developmental pattern with agoraphobia usually beginning in adult life and animal phobias almost always starting in childhood). The findings on sex differences in anxiety and fearfulness may be summarized by stating that these are not apparent in very young children, that during the middle years of childhood *general* anxiety and fearfulness are only marginally more common in girls, that *specific* fears and phobias tend to be more frequent in girls at all ages from the time of starting school onwards, and that the differences between the sexes increase somewhat in the transition from childhood to adult life.

The explanation for these sex differences remains uncertain. The animal evidence is essentially noncontributory, in that the pattern of sex differences is not the same as in humans (Gray, 1979, 1982). The available data on physiological responses to stress also do not provide any satisfactory explanation (Rutter, 1970b). Although sex differences have been reported, they seem to vary according to the autonomic measure used; such differences (usually quite small) as have been found are difficult to interpret and provide no ready prediction regarding sex differences in emotional responses to stress. Altogether, it is not clear why specific fears should be more frequent in human females, nor why the sex difference is more marked for specific phobias than for generalized anxiety, nor why the sex difference increases after childhood.

Course and Outcome

As follows from the age trends in prevalence, most fears in young children prove to be quite transient. This is apparent both in children's fearful responses to new situations and in the outcome of more established phobias (Agras, Chapin, Jackson, & Oliveau, 1972; Cummings, 1944; Hampe et al., 1973; Minde & Minde, 1977; Slater, 1939). Treatment tends to hasten recovery, but it seems to make no difference to the eventual outcome. The outcome is better for children than for adults with improvement greatest in younger children. In most cases, the loss of the phobia (with or without treatment) is accompanied by a general improvement in psychic functioning without the appearance of other symptoms. On the other hand, some phobias do persist for many years and extend even into adult life (Berg et al., 1976; W. Warren, 1965). Not surprisingly, the prognosis has tended to be worse in the case of adolescents admitted to the hospital with severe disorders in which the phobia is accompanied by generalized emotional disturbance. However, even in this group some two fifths are free of emotional disturbance a few years later.

Although the statement is almost tautological, it is evident that the prognosis for fears that are part of normal developmental trends (and that are abnormal only in their intensity) is generally good. It is also apparent that when such isolated fears persist well beyond the age when they could be regarded as normal, the response to behavioral treatments is usually very good. Thus, animal phobias generally respond well to treatment at any age and so do cases of school phobia in young children (Rodriguez, Rodriguez, & Eisenberg, 1959). On the other hand, phobias that are abnormal at any age (such as agoraphobia) respond less well, as do those that are associated with more generalized emotional disturbance (Marks, 1974). This is exemplified by the poorest prognosis for school phobia when it arises during adolescence (Rodriguez et al., 1959).

Most phobic children develop into quite normal adults, but when individuals with phobias in childhood do show a psychiatric condition in adult life, it usually takes the form of some type of emotional disorder (Zeitlin, 1972, 1982). However, this need not necessarily involve phobic symptoms as such; indeed, in Zeitlin's study of people treated as both children and adults, only 42% of those with phobias in childhood exhibited that symptom as adults. On the other hand, Marks' (1971) four-year follow-up of adults with phobic disorder showed that the phenomenon generally did *not* change form; when the disorder did continue, they remained phobic in type. The follow-up studies within and between childhood and adult life are not truly comparable, but the implication is that the main change in symptomatology takes place at some time during the period of development rather than after reaching maturity.

Correlates and Background Factors

Studies of many different types of phobia have been consistent in showing that children's fears tend to be associated with both general anxiety and specific fears in the parents (Bandura & Menlove, 1968; Hagman, 1932; John, 1941; R. May, 1950; Solyom, Beck, Solyom, & Hugel, 1974). Also, fears are often associated with general anxiety and emotional disturbance. However, with those exceptions, there has been surprisingly little systematic research into the factors associated with phobias in children, other than school phobia, which in many respects constitutes a most atypical phobia (Hersov, 1977; Hersov & Berg, 1980). Although school refusal involves some form of emotional disturbance, it need not involve a fear of school as such. In many cases, separation anxiety is a prominent feature, whereas in other cases, there is a widespread disturbance marked by obsessional and effective problems. In many cases, the parents have emotional disorders, parental anxiety may be communicated to the child, often the parents appear overprotective and encouraging of dependency, and there may be various stresses present (including a change of school). Evidence is lacking on the extent to which these features apply to other types of childhood phobia.

Theories of Anxiety and of Fear Formation

Most theorists attribute some importance to personality features as one of the major variables predisposing to emotional disturbance. However, there is a scarcity of data to indicate their importance in childhood. Of course, there is no doubt that children differ markedly in their temperamental characteristics, and there is some evidence that these variations are associated with individual differences in vulnerability to emotional disturbance (Dunn, 1980; Plomin, 1982; Porter & Collins, 1982). Thus, for example, Dunn and Kendrick (1982) found that temperamental differences between firstborn children were associated with the pattern of their reactions to the birth of a sibling and also were linked to the persistence of anxious, worrying, and fearful behavior over the next year. Moreover, Torgersen (1981) has shown a substantial genetic component in these temperamental attributes. However, some of the attributes that predict emotional disturbance best seem to have a lower heritability than others; also, other genetic studies of personality attributes have produced rather contradictory and inconclusive findings

(Plomin, 1982). It should be added that there is little direct evidence of the extent to which personality features differentiate children showing either phobias or nonspecific emotional disturbances. Eysenck (1967) has postulated a model in which two supposedly constitutionally determined and stable dimensions of personality, neuroticism (N) and extraversion (E), predispose to emotional disturbance by means of an hypothesized mediating variable of "conditionability." Although there is evidence for some aspects of Eysenck's theory, there is a lack of empirical support for N and E as stable attributes in childhood (Eysenck & Eysenck, 1975) or as substantial correlates of emotional disturbance in childhood (MacMillan, Kolvin, Garside, Nicol, Leitch, 1980; Powell, 1977).

It is generally assumed that social learning in one form or other plays a major role in the acquisition of fears. Following Watson and Rayner's (1920) much quoted and misquoted (B. Harris, 1979; Samuelson, 1980) but nonreplicated (Bregman, 1934; English, 1929), study of little Albert, many behaviorists came to view conditioning as the main mechanism involved in the development of phobias (Eysenck & Rachman, 1965). However, although there is no doubt that fears can be both created and abolished through conditioning procedures, it is now obvious that the conditioning paradigm is quite inadequate as a general theory of fear acquisition.

Rachman (1977) notes six main problems for any such theory:

1. People frequently fail to acquire fears in what are theoretically fear-producing situations (such as air raids).
2. It has proved difficult to produce conditioned fear responses in human subjects in the laboratory.
3. The theory rests on the false assumption that all stimuli have an equal chance of being transformed into fear signals, whereas obviously they do not. As Rachman comments, fears of lambs and of pajamas are exceedingly rare, although fears of snakes and of the dark are very common!
4. It is unusual to find evidence of any traumatic precipitant for phobias, except perhaps for fear of dentists (Sermet, 1974).
5. There is good evidence that fears can be acquired vicariously and indirectly without contact with the feared object.
6. According to conditioning theory, unreinforced fear reactions should extinguish rapidly, whereas, in fact, some are remarkably persistent and resistant to treatment, whether this is attempted through extinction procedures or otherwise.

In addition, conditioning fails to account for the age trends in the onset of phobias (Gray, 1982), and there is a further difficulty (Öhman & Ursin, 1979) posed by the well-documented lack of synchrony between avoidance behavior, physiological responses, and verbal reports (Grey, Sartory, & Rachman, 1979; Lang, 1968, 1978).

To deal with the third point above, Eysenck (1979) now accepts that it is necessary to invoke notions of innate fear patterns together with some such concept as Seligman's (1971) preparedness; to deal with the sixth point above, he proposes an incubation mechanism by which conditioned stimuli acquire drive properties. However, the supporting evidence for this mechanism is rather weak (Bersh, 1980). We may conclude that learning processes are, indeed, likely to be important in the genesis of phobias, although whether Pavlovian conditioning is more important than modelling or vicarious learning may be questioned. However, all the specific learning theories that have been proposed beg many questions and fail to account for either major age trends or well-established sex differences.

Bowlby (1973) has put forward a rather different explanation. He recognizes the existence of constitutional factors in susceptibility to fear and includes both cognitive considerations and evolutionary notions in his theorizing. However, the most distinctive feature of his views resides in his argument that a person's tendency to respond with fear is determined in large part by the perceived availability of attachment figures. In this way, most fears are considered as derivatives of separation anxiety, with the persistence of fear mainly due to the individual having developed anxious insecure attachments in early childhood as a result of disturbed family interaction. Bowlby uses school refusal and agoraphobia as examples to illustrate how this may occur, but he claims that the same process applies to many (but not all) other phobic disorders. Although these ideas have not been empirically tested, the argument is certainly plausible as a partial explanation for *some* phobic conditions. However, as a general explanation it not only lacks empirical support but also fails to account for many features, such as the differing developmental patterns for different types of phobia and the rapid response that frequently follows behavioral treatments that are directed to the fear and not to family relationships or perceived attachments (Graziano et al., 1979).

Izard (1977, 1978), in keeping with developmental theorists, such as Kagan (Kagan, 1974; Kagan et al., 1978), has emphasized the close links between cognition and emotions. The need to invoke cognitive factors is obvious in relation to the changes in normal fears that take place during the infancy period. Thus, Kagan (1974) has interpreted separation anxiety and fear of strangers in terms of "an unassimilated discrepant event producing uncertainty." The general idea is that fear is brought about when there is a cognitive discrepancy (i.e., something unanticipated and unfamiliar) that infants try unsuccessfully to assimilate into their cognitive framework. This notion is in keeping with many of the empirical observations of infantile fears, but it is difficult to encompass them all in this explanation (Sroufe, 1977). With abnormal fears and phobias, too, it is likely that perceptual-appraisal processes and cognitive interpretative processes are important. However, the cognitive notions involved in these ideas remain too general to permit specific predictions about either individual differences or age trends after the early childhood years.

Psychoanalytic theories continue to influence many clinicians in their concepts of emotional development and of emotional disorders (Emde, 1980); certainly, anxiety occupies a central role in psychoanalytic views concerning development (Bowlby, 1973; Dare, 1977; Rapaport, 1953, 1960). However, psychoanalysts themselves are far from agreed on the basic concepts (Compton, 1972), and it is apparent that psychoanalytic ideas on anxiety lack both precision and relevance to many of the observed clinical features.

According to psychoanalytic theory, some infantile fears (such as those of darkness, of strangers, and of new situations) are archaic fears based on innate dispositions. True phobias are different, in that they are based on regression, conflict, or displacement that originates in the phallic phase of development (A. Freud, 1966). According to this view, the expressed fears are not truly related to the feared object; instead, they represent, in symbolic fashion, some unconscious process. Psychoanalytic concepts of phobias lack empirical support, fail to account for the developmental trends, and are inconsistent with the evidence that many phobias respond rapidly to behavioral methods of treatment without subsequent signs of symptom substitution (Graziano et al., 1979; Hampe, Noble, Miller, Barrett, 1973; Marks, 1969).

It is apparent that no one theory and no one postulated mechanism accounts for the empirical findings on fears in childhood. On the other hand, several theories have substantial empirical support as partial explanations, and it is likely that some combination of cognition, temperament, innate factors, and social learning will prove to be operative.

Depressive Disorders and Depressive Feelings

Although it remains a highly controversial topic, the concept of depressive disorder in childhood has recently come into prominence accompanied by a flurry of both empirical and review articles (see Costello, 1980; Graham, 1980; Kashani, Husain, Shekim, Hodges, Cytryn, & McKnew, 1981; Lefkowitz & Burton, 1978; Puig-Antich, 1980; Schulterbrandt & Raskin, 1977). The background to the present interest is as follows. For some time, clinicians have realized that manic-depressive psychosis is extremely rare before puberty (Anthony & Scott, 1960) and that suicide is equally rare in this age group (Shaffer, 1974). These observations together with theoretical views that suggested that depression could not occur at an immature stage of psychosexual development (Rochlin, 1959) made most psychiatrists skeptical about the possibility that depressive disorders as distinct conditions appeared before puberty. The result was a general lack of interest in the issue; depression was not included in most textbook accounts of child psychiatric disorders. Subsequently, several writers introduced the concept of masked depression or depressive equivalents, arguing that covert depression could appear during childhood in the form of somatic complaints, enuresis, hyperactivity, and aggression (see, e.g., Cytryn & McKnew, 1972; Glaser, 1967; Malmquist, 1971). The sometimes favorable response to antidepressant medication was seen as a validating feature (Frommer, 1968; Weinberg, Rutman, Sullivan, Penick, & Dietz, 1973). This led to claims that contrary to earlier views, depressive disorders were actually very common in children. Such claims, in turn, were followed by counterclaims that although unhappiness and misery might be common in childhood, this was not to be confused with a depressive illness because there was no evidence of a genetic or any other link with adult depression (Graham, 1974). Alternatively, it was argued that because depressive symptoms were so very common in children, they could not be considered statistically deviant and, hence, could not be used to support the concept of a depressive disorder (Lefkowitz & Burton, 1978). At the height of this conceptual dispute, various measures of depressive behavior designed for use with children became available (see Costello, 1980; Kazdin, 1981; Kazdin & Petti, 1982; Puig-Antich & Gittelman, 1982); empirical data then began to provide a better basis for the arguments.

Measurement

There are obvious difficulties in the assessment of depression in young children because of their limited ability to describe their subjective emotional state. This difficulty applies to any emotion with its essential components of feelings, cognition, and personal meaning. Some, however, such as fear, are easier for an outside observer to assess on the basis of the child's facial expression, behavior, and autonomic activity. Depression is particularly difficult to observe because it is generally held to involve not only misery and unhappiness (which may perhaps be observed) but also a lowering of vigor and energy, guilt, self-blame, a sense of rejection, and a negative self-image (Poznanski & Zrull, 1970; Sandler & Joffe, 1965). Empirical studies show that psychiatrists find it more difficult to agree on ratings of depression than on those of anxiety, especially with intellectually dull, unresponsive, or uncommunicative children (Rutter & Graham, 1968). Even with adolescents, it has been found that many parents and teachers fail to note depression when the young people themselves report quite severe depressive feelings during the course of a psychiatric interview (Rutter, 1979). Other studies (Leon, Kendall, & Garber, 1980; Weissman et al., 1980) have also reported weak associations between maternal measures and child measures of depression in the child. However, it has also been found that the various self-report and interview measures based on information provided by the child show only moderate intercorrelations (Kazdin & Petti, 1982). There has been considerable progress in the development of assessment techniques for childhood depression, but methodological problems remain and there is a paucity of data on the convergent and discriminant validity of measures (Kazdin, 1981; Kazdin & Petti, 1982).

Epidemiology and Developmental Trends

Epidemiological surveys of preadolescent children in the general population have shown that: (1) feelings of misery and unhappiness are relatively common, (2) feelings of misery and unhappiness are equally prevalent in boys and girls, (3) depressive phenomena frequently form part of other emotional and conduct disorders, and (4) clear-cut depressive conditions of the type seen in adult life are relatively rare. Thus, Rutter et al. (1970/1981) found that about 10% to 12% of 10-year-olds were described by parents and teachers as, "often appears miserable, unhappy, tearful or distressed"; interviews with the children themselves gave a similar figure for depressive feelings; and, on all measures, these were equally common in boys and girls. About two fifths of all children with an overt psychiatric disorder (some 6% of the population) gave evidence of a depressed mood. Strikingly, depressive features

(unlike anxiety) were as common in children with conduct disorders as in those with emotional disturbance. Although many children showed depressive feelings, only 3 out of 2,000 children were diagnosed as having a depressive disorder. In most cases, depression was not the predominant manifestation, and it was typically accompanied by a diverse range of apparently nondepressive features.

Extensive evidence (Rutter, in press-d) shows that major changes in affective disorders take place during adolescence—both depressive feelings and depressive disorders become much more frequent, there is a large shift in the sex ratio of depressive disorders (from being rather more common in boys to being much more prevalent in girls), suicidal feelings and acts show a huge rise in frequency, marked grief reactions become more common, and hypomania (disorders characterized by an unusual elevation of mood) begins to occur. At one time, it was thought that the much higher rate of depression in women compared with men might constitute an artifact of some kind, but the evidence is clearcut in showing that this is not the case (Amenson & Lewinsohn, 1981; Weissman & Klerman, 1977).

Thus, when the 10-year-olds in the Rutter et al. (1970/1981) survey were reassessed at 14 to 15 years of age, the rate of depressive feelings had risen from 1 in 10 of the general population to about 2 in 5 (Rutter, 1979). Self-ratings on a questionnaire indicated that such feelings were more frequent in the adolescents than in their parents, suggesting that the rate may fall slightly after the teenage years (this is not certain because the adult sample comprised parents rather than all adults). Depressive conditions at 14 to 15 years of age also were several times more frequent than they had been when the children were younger. The findings also showed that, at least in boys, the rise in depression was a function of puberty. Within a group of 14- to 15-year-olds, scarcely any of the prepubescent boys showed depressive feelings, whereas a third of the postpubertal boys did so.

The one clinic study (Pearce, 1978, 1982) with comparable data produced closely similar findings. Of prepubertal children attending a psychiatric clinic, 1 in 9 showed depressive symptomatology, whereas a quarter of postpubertal children did so—a more than twofold increase in rate. Moreover, among the prepubertal children, depressive symptoms were twice as common in boys, whereas after puberty they were twice as common in girls. Unfortunately, most other studies of depression in childhood either fail to report whether the sex ratio alters with age (Kuperman & Stewart, 1979) or describe changes in terms of age rather than sexual maturity (Carlson & Cantwell, 1980a, 1980b; Seligman & Peterson, in press). The latter limitation is particularly serious in studies of early adolescence (the most favored age group for study) as this is a time when most girls are likely to be postpubertal but most boys prepubertal because of the substantially later onset of puberty in boys. Even so, such evidence as there is (e.g., Albert & Beck, 1975; Carlson & Cantwell, 1980a) tends to support the finding of an increase in depressive disorders and a change in the sex ratio for such disorders. The evidence for depressive feelings is less consistent and also the extent to which depressive feelings show a change in sex ratio remains uncertain.

Although claims have been made that mania may be more frequent in childhood than usually thought (Weinberg & Brumback, 1976), most reports indicate that mania rarely occurs before puberty, although it becomes more frequent during the midteens (Anthony & Scott, 1960; Hassanyeh & Davison, 1980; Loranger & Levine, 1978; Lowe & Cohen, 1980). Mania is linked with depression, in that most individuals who experience mania also experience bouts of depression, but many people with depressive disorders never show mania. The evidence suggests that unipolar and bipolar affective disorders may constitute somewhat separate conditions (Depue & Monroe, 1978). Accordingly, three rather different explanations could be proposed for the rarity of mania in childhood: (1) bipolar disorders rarely arise before puberty; (2) bipolar disorders do occur in childhood but, before puberty, they take only the depressive form; or (3) mania does occur in early life, but it takes a different form that is not recognized as the same condition. The available data are inadequate to decide between these alternatives, but the few family-history findings that are available suggest that the first is most likely (Puig-Antich, in press).

Data on suicide may throw light on developmental trends in affective disturbance, in that most suicides occur in the context of depression, at least in adults (Barraclough, Bunch, Nelson, & Sainsbury, 1974). British (Shaffer, 1974), French (Haim, 1974), and American (Eisenberg, 1980; Shaffer & Fisher, 1981) statistics all show that suicide before age 12 years is excessively rare but that the rate rises rapidly during the mid teens—a hundredfold increase from below 10 years to 10-14 years of age and a further tenfold increase from 10-14 to 15-19 years of age. However, suicide is not an adolescent phenomenon. The rate continues to rise, reaching a peak in old age.

Attempted suicide also is relatively infrequent before puberty and shows a massive increase during middle and late adolescence (Hawton & Goldacre, 1982; Kreitman, 1977). However, it differs from completed suicide in three key respects: (1) the peak is at ages 15 to 19 and not in old age; (2) whereas suicide is much more frequent in males, attempted suicide is far commoner in females; and (3) a lower proportion of attempted suicides are associated with an overt depressive disorder (Hawton, O'Grady, Osborn, & Cole, 1982; Lumsden Walker, 1980).

Many writers have drawn parallels between grief and depression (Bowlby, 1980), and the few available data (Bowlby, 1980; Kliman, 1968; Rutter, 1966; van Eerdewegh, Bieri, Parilla, & Clayton, 1982) suggest that immediate grief reactions are both milder and of shorter duration in young children than in adolescents or adults.

Much less is known about depression during the preschool years. Spitz (1946), in an influential paper, described anaclitic depression as a common syndrome arising in institutionalized children aged 6 to 12 months and marked by weeping, withdrawal, apathy, weight loss, sleep disturbance, and a decrease in developmental quotient. The syndrome was attributed to the loss of a mother figure. However, four main areas of doubt surround the concept of infantile depression. First, it seems that it must be a rather infrequent occurrence. Although there have been a few isolated case reports over the last 30 years (Emde, Harmon, & Good, in press), there have been no substantial series of cases. Second, although Spitz (1946) suggested that infantile depression often caused death, it seems likely that malnutrition, physical disease, and maternal neglect all play a crucial role (Pinneau, 1955). Third, it appears that loss of a mother figure may not be a necessary precursor (Emde, Plak, & Spitz, 1965; Harmon, Wagonfeld, & Emde, 1982). Fourth, there is the query whether the clinical picture constitutes a depressive disorder. This last set of doubts arises because the behavior appears to be an understandable response to the loss of a loved person together with an absence of personal parenting (Robertson & Robertson, 1971) *and* because Spitz's (1946) descriptions indicate that in most (but not all) cases rapid recovery tends to follow return to the family. There is not the self-perpetuating autonomous course generally associated with a depressive condition. On the other hand, at least in some instances, the anaclitic depression syndrome does appear to represent a significant disorder that is not simply an immediate and transient reaction to environmental circumstances—although whether it is comparable with the depressive conditions that arise in adolescence or adult life is another matter.

Probably, anaclitic depression is a rather rare phenomenon. However, states of apparent misery in infancy are not particularly uncommon. Freud and Burlingham (1974), in their wartime studies of children in the Hampstead nurseries, reported the frequent grieving of young children for their absent mothers; the Robertsons and Bowlby have documented the protest-despair-detachment sequence seen in many toddlers admitted to hospital or to a residential nursery (see Bowlby, 1969, 1980). This response occurs most frequently in infants aged 6 months to 4 years of age. It appears likely that younger infants are relatively immune because they have not yet developed enduring selective attachments and, therefore, are not able to experience the separation anxiety thought to play a part in the genesis of the syndrome. Older children, on the other hand, may be less vulnerable because they have the cognitive skills needed to appreciate that separation does not necessarily mean abandonment and to understand better what is involved in admission to the hospital or other institutions (Rutter, 1981b). Again, though, there is the uncertainty as to whether this constitutes a depressive condition. Clearly, it represents a dysthymic reaction (one essential component of depression), but there is more doubt as to whether it involves the cognitive features of guilt, self-blame, and lowered self-esteem.

In summary, it is apparent that unhappiness or dysthymic mood can arise at any age but probably that feelings of depression (in which there are the cognitive components of self-devaluation and feelings of hopelessness) are less frequent in early childhood than in adolescence. The most striking major change in affective disturbance takes place during puberty—with depressive disorders and suicide becoming much more frequent, with the appearance of mania, and with a change in sex ratio for affective disorders.

Developmental Continuities and Discontinuities in Depressive Disorders

Seligman and Peterson (in press) showed high stability over 6 months ($r = .80$) for a self-report measure of depressive feelings in 9- to 13-year-olds. But little is known about the persistence (or nonpersistence) of depressive disorders, and there are no satisfactory data on the frequency with which depression in childhood leads to depression in adult life. However, it appears that most cases of adult depression are not preceded by any form of psychi-

atric disorder in childhood (Zeitlin, 1972, 1982). On the other hand, of those children with depressive syndromes who go on to have a psychiatric condition in adult life, the great majority show depression as part of their adult disorder. In Zeitlin's study, the strength of continuity from childhood to adulthood was stronger for depression than for any other constellation of items other than obsessive-compulsive phenomena. On the other hand, in both childhood and adult life, it was common for the depressed individuals to show other apparently nondepressive symptomatology so that in only a minority of cases was depression given as the primary diagnosis. The findings raise questions about the validity of a depressive syndrome and on the criteria to be used for its presence.

Concepts of Depressive Syndromes

The question of whether depression occurs in prepubescent children as a syndrome that is meaningfully different from other psychiatric conditions has been approached by means of several different strategies. Pearce (1978), using a discriminant functions analysis, showed that child and adolescent psychiatric patients with the symptom of depression differed from the rest of the patient group in terms of other symptoms. Those with depression had an increased likelihood of suicidal threats/attempts, ideas of reference or persecutory ideas, sleep disturbance, ruminations or obsessions, eating disturbance, and irritability. Numerous investigators went on to show that the research diagnostic criteria used to identify depressive disorders in adult life can be applied in childhood (Carlson & Cantwell, 1982; Puig-Antich, 1980, 1982b; Robbins, Alessi, Cook, Poznanski, & Yanchyshyn, 1982; Weinberg et al., 1973). The constellation of depressive symptomatology diagnosed as depressive disorders in adult life also occurs in childhood. Because of this consistent finding, the notion of masked depression has fallen into disuse even among those who previously supported the concept (Cytryn, McKnew, & Bunney, 1980).

On the other hand, the fact that certain depressive-type behaviors cluster together does not necessarily validate the concept of a syndrome. Three rather separate issues are involved here. First, there is the question of whether severe clinical depression (as diagnosed in psychiatric patients) differs from the much more frequent phenomenon of depression as seen in the general population (Tennant & Bebbington, 1978). Surveys of adults have produced prevalence rates for depressive conditions ranging from 2% to 25%, with the differences largely explicable in terms of variations in the criteria used to decide what is a case (Eastwood & Kramer, 1981). Some workers have chosen to differentiate between nonspecific distress or demoralization in general population samples and clinical depression in patient groups (Link & Dohrenwend, 1980; Dohrenwend, Shrout, Egri, & Mendelsohn, 1980). Others (Brown & Harris, 1978) have argued that these represent two ends of the same continuum. The matter is unresolved for both adults and children.

Second, there is the rather different question of whether syndromes characterized by depression differ in any fundamental way from other psychopathological syndromes. The issue has a particular importance because of the repeated finding that depression shows a very substantial overlap with conduct disturbance (Carlson & Cantwell, 1980c; Chiles, Miller, & Cox, 1980; Edelbrock & Achenbach, 1980; Puig-Antich, 1982a), with separation anxiety (Puig-Antich & Gittelman, 1982), and with poor peer relationships (Puig-Antich & Gittelman, 1982). One way to determine whether depression constitutes the core of these mixed syndromes is to find out whether the other behaviors abate when the children's mood returns to normal (Rutter, 1972b). Few data are available on this point, but it seems that improvements in mood tend to be accompanied by a reduction in conduct disturbance but not by any marked change in peer relationships (Puig-Antich, 1982a, 1982b; Puig-Antich & Gittelman, 1982). The matter needs further study.

There have been attempts to use response to antidepressant medication as a validating criterion (Frommer, 1968; Weinberg et al., 1973), but so far this has been unsuccessful. There is, at best, only contradictory evidence that depressive disorders in children do, in fact, respond to antidepressants (Kramer & Feiguine, 1981; Puig-Antich, in press; Puig-Antich & Gittelman, 1982). However, even if it could be shown that they did, this would not necessarily validate the concept of a depressive syndrome. First, antidepressants have a wide range of pharmacological effects; second, conditions as diverse as hyperkinesis and enuresis also respond to the most commonly used antidepressant drugs, namely, the tricyclics; third, it is not known whether depressive and nondepressive disorders differ in their response to antidepressant drugs; and fourth, as already noted, little is known about what happens to the other symptoms linked with depression when mood improves.

The third query is whether depressive syndromes in childhood constitute the same conditions as those in adult life. This has been examined by means of the psychobiological correlates of adult depression (reviewed by Puig-Antich, in press). It has been found that prepubertal children with a major depressive disorder are comparable to adult depressives in their response to the dexamethasone suppression test, fewer hypersecrete cortisol, but more show a depressed secretion of growth hormone following insulin induced hypoglycemia. The difficulties in drawing firm conclusions from these findings stem from both the mixture of similarities and dissimilarities and from the fact that, even in adults, only a proportion of depressed individuals show the characteristic neuroendocrine responses (Carroll, 1982; Checkley, 1980). Puig-Antich (in press) also found that depressed children differed from depressed adults in their sleep patterns, thus raising two very different alternatives: (1) that prepubertal and adult depressive disorders constitute different conditions or (2) that there is a maturational difference in the sleep correlates of the same disorder when it arises at different ages.

Cognitive features, too, have been compared. In adults, depressives are more likely than other individuals to expect that bad events will occur and that they will not have the power to avoid or to deal with them (Abramson, Seligman, & Teasdale, 1978). Recently, Seligman and Peterson (in press) have shown that this also applies to 9- to 13-year-old children with a high score on the Kovacs and Beck depression inventory.

Family-history data have also been used to compare prepubertal and adult depression. In both age groups, it is common to find a high rate of depression in first-degree relatives. In adults, there are grounds for concluding that this represents (at least in part) a hereditary component, although both the mode of inheritance and what is inherited remain matters of dispute and controversy (Baron, Klotz, Mendlewicz, & Rainer, 1981; Jakimow-Venulet, 1981; Kidd & Weissman, 1978). It seems likely that this also applies in childhood but the data are too limited to be confident. Also, it has been reported that many children of depressed parents appear depressed themselves (Cytryn & McKnew, in press; Orvaschel, Weissman, & Kidd, 1980; Welner, Welner, McCrary, & Leonard, 1977). However, in itself, this finding is essentially noncontributory to the question of whether depression in childhood and adult life constitute the same condition. This is because: (1) it is not known whether the link with depression in the child is specific to parental depression or whether it occurs with other forms of parental mental disorder (El-Guebaly, Offord, Sullivan, & Lynch, 1978; Orvaschel et al., 1980; Rutter, 1966) and (2) parental depression may predispose to disorder in the child by virtue of adverse effects on parenting rather than through any genetic link (Cooper, Leach, Storer, & Tonge, 1977; Mills & Puckering, 1982; Weissman, 1979; Radke-Yarrow & Kuczynski, in press).

In summary, a collation of available findings provides some limited support for the validity of a depressive syndrome in childhood, but many questions remain unanswered. Sound evidence is lacking on the proportion of childhood depressive disorders that are equivalent to adult depression (but clearly some are) as well as on the issue of whether the parallels, when they do exist, are primarily associated with bipolar affective disorders (a less likely hypothesis) or with the more frequent but less well-differentiated unipolar depressive disorders (a more likely one).

Theories of Depression

Obviously, the fact that the greatest change in affective disturbance occurs during adolescence raises the possibility that hormonal changes are responsible. There are various pointers suggesting that sex hormones may have an impact on mood—for example, the well-documented substantial increase in psychiatric disorder during the puerperium (Kendell, Rennie, Clarke, & Dean, 1981; Kendell, Wainwright, Hailey, & Shannon, 1976) and the irritability and depression experienced by some women during the premenstrual phase (Dalton, 1977; Sommer, 1978)—but, so far, the findings on hormonal effects do not lead to any clear-cut implications for affective disturbance.

Psychoanalytic theories on depression have changed somewhat over the years, but throughout there has been an emphasis on the early mother-child relationship, on orality, and on loss of a love object (Bowlby, 1980; Isenberg & Schatzberg, 1978; Mendelson, 1974; Rie, 1966). Many of the details of these views, especially the emphasis on the first year of life, do not stand up to critical scrutiny (Bowlby, 1980). Moreover, the insistence that depression cannot occur in childhood because the child's superego is not fully developed (Rochlin, 1959) is inconsistent with the evidence that depression does occur in childhood. However, although psychoanalytic theory as a whole provides an incomplete explanation for depression, its emphasis on the role of loss as an etiological factor has received empirical support and has also been generative in the development of alternative theories, many of which overlap a great deal in their postulates.

In recent years, cognitive explanations for depression have come to the fore. Thus, Beck (Beck, 1976; Kovacs & Beck, 1978) has argued that people become depressed because at an early stage in development they acquire cognitive schemata involving a devaluation of themselves and their experiences together with a hopelessness about the future. Similarly, Seligman and Peterson (in press) have postulated that depression arises when uncontrollable bad events occur to individuals with a cognitive style that cause them to attribute such events to internal, stable, and global causes.

Although both Beck (1976) and Seligman and Peterson (in press) hypothesize that cognitive sets develop in childhood, they have not focused on the developmental conditions that influence the type of set acquired. However, these do constitute essential elements in both Bowlby's (1980) and Brown and Harris' (1978) theories. Bowlby hypothesizes that insecure mother-infant attachments in early life, an upbringing that lacks love, or the actual loss of a parent during childhood lead to a negative cognitive set that causes the person to interpret later losses as yet another failure to establish or maintain an enduring affectionate relationship. Thus, early loss constitutes the basis for a depressive predisposition and later loss acts as the immediate precipitant for depression. Brown and Harris' (1978) views are somewhat similar, but loss is thought of in terms of a deprivation of sources of value or reward, which include roles and ideas as well as personal relationships.

Vulnerability factors that lead to a lack of a sense of self-esteem and mastery are thought to operate both during childhood (e.g., maternal loss) and during adult life (e.g., the lack of a close-confiding relationship or restriction to the home to care for young children on a full-time basis). As with Bowlby (1980), acute loss events are seen as the immediate precipitants of depression. Lewinsohn, Youngren, and Grosscup (1979), on the other hand, have placed greater emphasis on the lack of response-contingent positive reinforcement from pleasurable activities and interpersonal interactions as a circumstance leading to depression.

It is apparent that all these theories involve a rather complex set of interactions between vulnerability factors, cognitive sets, and precipitating stress events, any of which might affect the developmental trends in affective disturbance that have been found empirically. However, with respect to the cognitive formulations (for which there is some empirical support with respect to adult depression, although many questions remain—see Abramson et al., 1978; Blaney, 1977; Miller & Norman, 1979), clearly it is crucial to know whether there are changes with age in the cognitive functions that are supposed to predispose to depression. Presumably, if children are to show self-blame or experience a sense of failure, it is necessary for them to have self-awareness. In that connection, it is relevant that Kagan's (1981) data indicate that this does not develop until the latter half of the second year of life. These and other findings (Hoffman, 1975; Lewis & Brooks-Gunn, 1979) suggest that it is not until after age 2 or so that infants have the mental apparatus required to experience depression as seen in adults. Perhaps that is why depression is so uncommon in the very young.

Other explanations, however, are needed to account for the continuing low rate of depression in middle childhood and the marked rise during adolescence. Age changes in the mode of response to success or failure would be relevant in that connection, but there is a paucity of research on the topic (Masters, Felleman, & Barden, 1980). Nevertheless, there is some evidence suggesting that younger children are less likely to view failure as implying an enduring limitation on their performance. Rholes, Blackwell, Jordan, & Walters (1980) produced findings suggesting that helplessness was an unusual response to failure in younger children. The evidence from Dweck's research (Dweck & Bush, 1976; Dweck, Davidson, Nelson, & Enna, 1978) is also promising in terms of its possible explanation for the higher rate of depression in females after puberty. She found that girls are more likely to attribute their failure to their own perceived lack of ability and that one reason for this may be in the sex-differentiated pattern of feedback from adults. The study of developmental changes in cognitive attributional style has not yet provided any adequate explanation for the findings on age and sex differences in depression, but it is apparent that it constitutes an area worth further exploration.

There is very little direct evidence on the Bowlby (1980) and Brown and Harris (1978) hypotheses regarding the role of early loss or of insecure attachments as a cause of a negative attributional style. Brown and Harris's data suggest that early family disruptions may predispose to later depression, but other findings suggest that parental death (often taken as the prototype of early loss) has only a rather tenuous link with later depression (Crook & Eliot, 1980; Tennant, Bebbington, & Hurry, 1980). However, the link may be somewhat stronger than some of the negative reviews suggest (Brown, Harris, & Bifules, in press); moreover, most research has been concerned with *direct* links between early loss and depression, whereas the theories postulate *indirect* links mediated by a negative cognitive set. Studies of the attributional styles of children who experience early loss (or other family insecurities and adversities) are indicated.

If the developmental changes in depression are to be explained in terms of age-related alterations in stress, it must be hypothesized that loss events become more frequent as children grow older, with a major rise in adolescence that affects girls more than boys. Alternatively, it might be suggested that, during adolescence, there is a sex-linked change in people's perception of stress (Burke & Weir, 1979). Insufficient data are available to indicate whether or not that is the case.

In summary, the adult evidence indicates that genetic, neuroendocrine, cognitive, and psychosocial factors must all be taken into account in any adequate explanation of affective disturbance. Research into the operation of these variables in childhood is still in its infancy but it suggests that there are both similarities and dissimilarities between childhood and adult life with respect to affective disorders. There are pointers to possible developmental changes in cognitive set which may go some way toward an explanation of why depression is rare in infancy and increases greatly in frequency at puberty, but no firm conclusions are possible as yet.

DISTURBANCES OF CONDUCT

Disturbances of conduct represent the other major child psychiatric grouping apart from emotional disorders. General population surveys of school-age children (see Graham, 1979; Quay, 1979; Rutter & Giller, in press; Rutter et al., 1970/1981) and studies of clinic samples (Rutter et al., 1975) have been consistent in showing that disturbances of conduct (as indicated by fighting, temper tantrums, defiance, destructiveness, and generally uncooperative or inconsiderate behavior) constitute one of the most frequent causes of concern regarding children's behavior. Factor-analytic studies, using a variety of different measures, have usually shown that these features intercorrelate to constitute one of the main dimensions of behavior during childhood and adolescence (see reviews by Achenbach & Edelbrock, 1978; Quay, 1979).

The validity of the differentiation between emotional and conduct disorder is well substantiated (see *Emotional Disturbances*). However, there is a considerable overlap with overactive/inattentive behavior (see *Attention Deficit/Hyperkinetic Syndromes*), with aggression (see *Parke & Slaby, vol. IV, chap. 7*), and with delinquency. Not surprisingly, therefore, there is continuing dispute over whether conduct disorders can be validly subdivided and, if they can, over which dimensions to use in subclassification.

Classification

On the whole, clinicians tend to be agreed that disturbances of conduct are heterogeneous; the disagreement concerns how and on what basis this group of disturbances should be subdivided (Wolff, 1977). Nevertheless, it is not self-evident that the heterogeneity gives rise to useful replicable subcategories, and many of those studying delinquents have favored a single-category approach. West and Farrington (1977), in their detailed longitudinal study of London boys, noted that delinquents differed from nondelinquents in a wide range of lifestyle, characteristics of which aggressiveness, irregular work habits, immoderation in the pursuit of immediate pleasure, and lack of conventional social restraints are the most prominent. They argue that the findings vindicate the concept of the delinquent character and Farrington, Biron, & LeBlanc (1982) went on to claim that convicted juveniles and young adults were a relatively homogeneous group of thieves.

Robins and her colleagues (Robins, 1978; Robins & Ratcliff, 1980) have attempted to test the validity of the concept of a single syndrome of antisocial behavior, using data derived from three long-term longitudinal studies of very different populations. They suggest that the single-syndrome hypothesis is supported by four well-replicated findings: (1) that each *separate* type of childhood deviance is independently correlated with the *overall* level of adult deviance, (2) that each *separate* type of adult deviance is predicted by the *overall* level of childhood deviance, (3) that the *overall* level of deviant behavior in childhood is a better predictor of adult deviance than is any one particular child behavior, and (4) that these relationships do not depend on the continuation of the *same* behavior from childhood into adulthood. Indeed, as many other studies have shown (Rutter & Giller, in press), most offenders (with the partial exception of minor sex offenders) commit quite a varied range of offences with little evidence of specialization. It may be concluded that, as a group, delinquents of all types have many features in common and that little is to be gained by subdividing delinquency according to (legal definitions of) types of offences. However, it is clear that there are important differences between occasional minor delinquency—which is so common among boys, especially those in inner cities, as to be almost the norm and, thus, cannot be regarded as a conduct disturbance—and persistent, frequent delinquency, which is socially unacceptable in terms of victim involvement and personal space violation (Wadsworth, 1979; West & Farrington, 1973, 1977). It is largely the latter that is associated with abnormalities in psychological functioning and with a poor adult outcome (see *Continuity and Course of Antisocial Behavior*). Nevertheless, the question remains as to whether that group should be subdivided. Moreover, it is apparent that many children with manifest conduct disturbance (as shown by pervasive socially disapproved behavior and poor social relationships) do not appear before the courts and may not even commit officially delinquent acts.

Socialized and Unsocialized Patterns

On the basis of their factor-analytic study of clinic records many years ago, Hewitt and Jenkins (1946) suggested the importance of the distinction between unsocialized aggression (in which there are disturbed interpersonal relationships) and socialized delinquency (in which there are adequate social attachments). More recent statistical studies of symptom correlations both by Jenkins and his co-workers (Jenkins, 1973) and by others (Quay, 1979) have often, but far from always (Field, 1967), come up with similar groupings, and the socialized/unsocialized differentiation has now been included in the American Psychiatric Association's official diagnostic manual (DSM–III, 1980).

The main justification for the differentiation between the two hypothesized types of conduct disturbance comes from the evidence showing that they differ in terms of family background and of outcome. Unsocialized aggression tends to be associated with broken homes, family hostility, and maternal rejection; socialized delinquency with social disadvantage, parental neglect, and delinquent associates (Hetherington, Stouwie, & Ridberg, 1971; Hewitt & Jenkins, 1946; H. Lewis, 1954). The only outcome research utilizing this subclassification is that by Henn, Bardwell, & Jenkins (1980), whose 12-year follow-up study of institutionalized delinquents indicated that the socialized group had a significantly better prognosis in terms of adult convictions and imprisonment.

These findings provide some justification for the differentiation according to the presence/absence of stable personal relationships and loyalties, but three primary questions on validity remain. First, socialized conduct disturbance is sometimes equated with supposedly normal delinquency in boys from a socially disadvantaged background. This parallel is unjustified because (1) areas of social disadvantage tend also to be areas of increased family pathology and (2) delinquents from a socially deprived background are just as likely as others to show personal maladjustment and poor peer relationships (Conger & Miller, 1966; Stott, 1960, 1966; West & Farrington, 1973) as well as sociopathy in adult life, with a high rate of both social and psychiatric pathology (Robins, 1966, 1978). Second, by no means all factor-analytic studies show that socially disapproved behaviors fall into these two patterns (Achenbach & Edelbrock, 1978; Quay, 1979). Moreover, even those investigations that agree on the factors do not necessarily agree on the specific behaviors constituting the factors (Rutter & Giller, in press). Third, it is uncertain whether the differentiation concerns syndromes of conduct disturbance or general dimensions of personality functioning. Other research (Roff, Sells, & Golden, 1972; Sundby & Kreyberg, 1968) has shown that the quality of peer relationships predicts outcome in both delinquent and nondelinquent groups. Perhaps what matters is the degree of personality disturbance rather than the type of conduct disorder.

Aggression and Stealing

Many retrospective and prospective studies have shown that aggressive antisocial behavior in young children is associated with the later development of delinquency—both nonviolent and violent (Farrington, 1978; Robins, 1966; Wadsworth, 1979; West & Farrington, 1973; Wolfgang, Figlis, & Sellin, 1972)—and that there can be no doubt that there is a substantial and meaningful overlap between aggression and delinquency. However, this association could reflect the overlap between stealing and aggression in early childhood (before the youngsters could be officially adjudged delinquent), and it is important to ask what happens in the later development of young children who are aggressive but who do not steal and vice versa. The small study by Moore, Chamberlain, and Menkes (1979) of children referred for treatment provides the only data on this point. Only 13% of the children who showed manifest aggression at home (but no stealing) became delinquent by the time of follow-up at age 14 to 20 years of age, a rate no greater than the 15% in controls of the same age, but well below the 56% of children who stole (but were without a court record when first referred). Aggressive and nonaggressive

thieves had similar risks of court appearances. The implication is that stealing and aggression are frequently associated but that this association is evident from at least middle childhood and that aggression *on its own* at age 8 to 10 years may not carry any increased risk of delinquency. The finding requires replication, but also it refers to aggression mainly or only evident in the family. It is quite unclear whether the same findings would apply to children showing aggression with peers or with adults outside the home as well as in the family.

Findings on families in the same-treatment project (Patterson, 1981b, 1982) also suggest that stealing and pure aggression may constitute rather different syndromes. The two groups differed in parental characteristics (as assessed by MMPI profiles), in family patterns (the parents of boys who stole tended to show a distant, uninvolved pattern of interaction in contrast to the more actively hostile punitive environment of the families of aggressive boys), and in response to an intensive behaviorally oriented family-treatment program (those who stole were more likely to relapse). In short, there are slender pointers to the possibility that aggressive disorders, at least those confined within the family, may constitute a syndrome or dimension of behavior that is relatively separate from stealing and related delinquent activities.

Conduct Disorders with and Without Emotional Disturbance

Many children and adolescents with conduct disorders also show emotional disturbance, especially a depressive mood (Rutter et al., 1970/1981). It might be thought that the presence or absence of emotional disturbance would constitute an important differentiating feature within the broad group of conduct disorders. However, what little evidence there is suggests that it does not to any decisive extent (Graham & Rutter, 1973; Power, Benn, & Morris, 1972; Robins, 1966; Rutter et al., 1970/1981).

Autonomic Features, Stimulus Seeking, and Attention Deficits

Several studies (Borkovec, 1970; Davies & Maliphant, 1971a, 1971b; Siddle, Mednick, Nicol, & Foggitt, 1976; Siddle, Nicol, & Foggitt, 1973; West & Farrington, 1977) have shown that delinquents tend to have a reduced autonomic responsivity compared with normal boys and that this feature is most characteristic of the seriously antisocial. Also, one study (Davies & Maliphant, 1974) found that, when given electric shocks for mistakes, refractory adolescents made more errors in a learning task than normal boys. There is an obvious parallel with studies of psychopathic adults who have tended to show small sluggish skin responses to noxious stimuli, as well as impaired passive-avoidance learning (Hare, 1970; Hare & Schalling, 1978; Trasler, 1973). The implication is that conduct disturbances accompanied by psychopathic features (meaning broadly, poor personal relationships, lack of guilt and empathy, and impulsiveness) may differ from other varieties. However, the concept of psychopathy has proved elusive and difficult to define as well as difficult to measure (Hodgins, 1979; A. Lewis, 1974). Moreover, the psychophysiological findings to some extent parallel those for hyperkinetic children (Hastings & Barkley, 1978), and the links between hyperactivity, delinquency, and psychopathy within the broad domain of conduct disturbance remain quite uncertain.

Some years ago, Quay (1965, 1977a, 1977b) proposed that psychopaths were motivated by an abnormally great need for stimulation. Several studies with children and adolescents have attempted to test this hypothesis in relation to rather broader concepts of conduct disorder. The findings (DeMyer-Gapin & Scott, 1977; Orris, 1969; Whitehill, DeMyer-Gapin, & Scott, 1976) have been interpreted in terms of stimulus seeking, but, equally, it could be argued that the findings merely confirm that refractory boys tend to be restless, inattentive, and easily bored by externally imposed tasks.

Nevertheless, the consistent observations of inattentiveness among antisocial boys emphasizes the importance of considering measures of attention with respect to the possible subcategorization of conduct disturbances. There is an extensive literature on the attentional deficits associated with hyperkinetic syndromes (well reviewed by Douglas, in press, and Douglas & Peters, 1979), and it is apparent that the attentional features are closely similar to those thought to be characteristic of delinquents. Douglas concluded that hyperactive children are not particularly distractible but that they may perform better in stimulating environments (and, hence, may be said to be stimulus seeking) and that they do not show any abnormalities in selective attention but that they do show an important impairment in vigilance and sustained attention. Little is known as to whether these features meaningfully differentiate within the overall group of conduct disturbances, but there is some evidence that those who are hyperactive may be more seriously antisocial, have poorer school performance, and have a worse outcome (Offord, Poushinsky, & Sullivan, 1978; Schachar, Rutter, & Smith, 1981) than those who are not hyperactive.

It is obvious that there are major difficulties in drawing together these varied findings, which are based on different measures and differently defined (but overlapping) groups. Even so, there are findings to suggest that a subgroup of young people with conduct disturbance are characterized by diminished autonomic reactivity, impaired passive-avoidance learning, stimulus seeking, and impaired vigilance and sustained attention. Further research is needed to determine the extent of overlap between these four features, the proportion of children with conduct disturbance who show them, and whether the characteristics are associated with the degree or persistence of a conduct disturbance.

Personality Features

Eysenck (1977) has argued that what distinguishes the antisocial child is a failure of social learning, resulting from poor conditionability, which is associated with high extraversion (E) and high neuroticism (N). More recently, he has proposed that antisocial behavior is also closely linked with psychoticism (P). The empirical findings with children (Farrington et al., 1982; Feldman, 1977; Powell, 1977) show that antisocial behavior is quite strongly associated with P (a questionnaire dimension that itself is based on items reflecting conduct disturbance) and has some link with high N but no consistent association with E. The links with social learning remain rather tenuous, and there are conceptual criticisms of the disputed notion of any general characteristic of conditionability (Trasler, 1973). Whereas it seems likely that antisocial behavior is, indeed, linked with personality features, the value of these particular dimensions as a classifying characteristic within the group of conduct disturbances has not been established.

A quite different approach to personality assessment comes from the I–level or development of interpersonal maturity theory, which proposes that individuals can be meaningfully described in terms of seven successive levels of interpersonal maturity (Sullivan, Grant, & Grant, 1957; M. Q. Warren, 1977). There are problems in the construct validity of the classification (Austin, 1975), but the findings of the California Youth Authority's Community Treatment Project are provocative in their apparent indication that passive conformist, power-oriented, and neurotic delinquents differ in their responses to treatment (Palmer, 1974; M. Q. Warren, 1977). Little is known about the utility of this approach with children and adolescents, but other evidence (Rutter & Giller, in press) also suggests that variations in response to specific forms of treatment may be related to the personality feature of value in the subclassification of conduct disturbances. That possibility warrants further exploration, but, so far, this style of research has been severely limited by the lack of adequate personality measures for children.

Clinical Approaches

Finally, there are the more clinically oriented approaches to classification. Scott (1965) proposed a fourfold etiology-based subdivision: (1) well trained to the wrong standards, (2) reparative and avoidance patterns, (3) untrained, and (4) repetitive maladaptive delinquency. Rich (1956), on the other hand, suggested a motivational subdivision of types of stealing: (1) marauding offences with others, that is, stealing without planning when an opportunity is presented; (2) proving offences, such as stealing cars to demonstrate one's manhood; (3) comforting offences, involving stealing either as a substitute for loss of love or as an expression of resentment regarding wounded feelings; and (4) secondary offences with a clear idea of what can be stolen and with precautions taken against detection. Both classifications emphasize the variety of delinquent patterns, especially in relation to young people referred to psychiatric clinics. Although the categories appear to correspond to some of the types of conduct disturbance seen in clinics, their validity and utility remain untested.

In summary, current psychiatric and psychological classifications generally provide for some subdivision of conduct disorders, but evidence is lacking on their comparative merits. The empirical findings suggest that the quality of peer relationships, autonomic features, and attentional features as well as the distinction between pure aggression and stealing may all constitute useful means of differentiation.

Developmental Trends, Continuities, and Discontinuities

Age Trends

It is often considered that disorders in preschool children show a rather undifferentiated pattern so that the diagnostic categories used with older children are inapplicable (Earls, 1980; Richman et al., 1982). On the other hand, factor-analytic and statistical-clustering studies of both clinic and nonclinic

preschool children have shown much the same differentiation of emotional and conduct disorders as that found in older children (Behar & Stringfield, 1974; Kohn, 1977; Wolkind & Everitt, 1974). Although the most frequent problems among 3-year-olds in the general population concern enuresis and eating and sleeping difficulties (Earls, 1980; Richman et al., 1982), the commonest reason for psychiatric referral at that age is unmanageable behavior (Bentovim, 1973; Wolff, 1961).

The findings on age trends in conduct disturbances are somewhat contradictory and difficult to interpret because studies vary in their samples and measures. So far as temper outbursts are concerned, the best developmental data are still those provided by Goodenough's (1931) classical study of 2- to 7-year-old children using both detailed daily parental reports and direct observations. She found that anger outbursts reached their peak frequency for normal children during the second year. After age 2, there was a progressive shortening of the more violent initial stage of angry behavior but also a lengthening of such aftereffects as sulking, whining, or brooding. During all the preschool years (after the first), over half of the outbursts arose from some conflict with parental authority, and, not surprisingly, the content of the conflict tended to change with age—from issues over toileting and prohibited activities in the second year to refusal to put away toys and clashes over clothing in the fifth year. Other studies (Levy & Tulchin, 1923, 1925; Macfarlane et al., 1954), too, have suggested that negativism is most prevalent during the preschool years.

Disagreements with playmates were infrequent causes of temper outbursts in the first 3 years (Goodenough, 1931) but accounted for a fifth of outbursts during the fourth and fifth years. Dawe (1934) found that younger nursery school children started more quarrels but that the older children were more likely to become physically aggressive; Appel (1942) showed that among 2-year-olds quarrels tended to center around disputes over possessions, whereas in older children aggression arose over disputes concerning joint play; and Hartup (1974), in an observational study of 4- to 7-year-olds, found that the older children were less aggressive than the younger ones but also that their style varied. Most aggression in the younger subjects was instrumental, whereas in the older groups a higher proportion was hostile and most often it led to retaliation. It is apparent, of course, that these age trends reflect changing patterns of emotional expression and alterations in children's peer relationships (see *Hartup, vol. IV, chap.*

2) at least as much as they reflect developmental shifts in conduct disturbance.

For trends during middle childhood we have to rely on either questionnaire (Shepherd et al., 1971) or interview (Macfarlane et al., 1954) data rather than observations. However, the evidence is fairly consistent in showing that tantrums are at a peak about the age of 3 and diminish steadily thereafter. In the population as a whole, destructiveness, bullying, and lying also tend to diminish between 5 and 9 years of age (especially in girls), although age trends for the extremes are less consistent and there is little further change between 9 and 14 years of age (Macfarlane et al., 1954; Rutter & Yule, 1982; Shepherd et al., 1971).

All data (self-report, teacher report, and administrative statistics) are consistent in showing a marked increase in truanting, absconding, and other forms of unjustified absence during the high school years (Mortimore, 1978; Rutter, 1979; Rutter & Yule, 1982). This generally reaches a peak during the final year of compulsory schooling. Longitudinal studies using criminal statistics, such as those by the Gluecks (1940), the McCords (1959), Robins (1966), and Wolfgang, Figlio, and Sellin (1972) show that patterns of delinquent activities in the same individuals tend to change as they get older (Cline, 1980; West, 1982). In particular, theft and other property offences decline in frequency during the transition to adulthood, whereas violent crime increases during late adolescence—to reach a peak in the early 20s—and drunkenness only becomes a common problem during early adult life. Self-report data (Farrington, 1973; Shepherd, 1978) show a substantial increase during adolescence in the amount and range of delinquent activities, although, probably, there is less change in the number of individuals engaging in antisocial behavior.

Kohn (1977), in a longitudinal study of 400 children in six New York day centers, found that (according to teacher-questionnaire scores) conduct disturbance (based on items referring to anger, rebelliousness, cruelty, and disruptiveness) increased between first and third grades but diminished between third and fourth grades. Other data (Gersten et al., 1976; Rutter, 1979) show little change in the level of overall conduct disturbance between 6 and 18 years of age.

Although the rates of conduct disturbance may not change much during middle childhood and adolescence, both criminal statistics (Cline, 1980) and self-report data (Knight, Osborn, & West, 1977) show that delinquent acts as well as convictions tend

to diminish during early adult life to a substantial extent. Moreover, the reduction in delinquent activities during early adult life tends to be associated with a real relinquishment of antisocial behavior and a change to a nondeviant lifestyle (Osborn & West, 1980). Jessor's 7-year longitudinal study of American high school and college students similarly showed that early adult life was associated with a decrease in problem behavior, a reduction in drug taking, and a greater commitment to conventional values and behavior (Jessor, in press; Jessor & Jessor, 1977).

In summary, many forms of socially disapproved behavior tend to be at a peak during the preschool years, diminishing markedly during the early years of schooling. However, this early phase of negativism associated with a tendency to pull toys apart, write on walls, and take other people's belongings may not have the same meaning as the conduct disorders seen in older children. The latter show little change in overall prevalence between 8 and 18 years of age, although delinquent activities reach a peak in adolescence. However, there is a marked and real drop in antisocial behavior over the early years of adult life.

Continuity and Course of Antisocial Behavior

Given that the rates of conduct disturbance do not change greatly during the high school years (although they do in adult life), the next question is to what extent this is a function of continuities in antisocial behavior at an individual level. In other words, are the rates made up of the same individuals at each age or, instead, do a large number of children show conduct disturbances at some point in their development but with these rarely persisting for long? Although the answer depends to some extent on how conduct disturbances are assessed, the weight of evidence certainly suggests a substantial degree of continuity, at least during the school years.

Of course, as self-report data show, the majority of boys commit some form of delinquent act at some stage in their development so that, in itself, this can scarcely be regarded as indicative of a conduct disturbance. On the other hand, most of these acts are of a fairly trivial nature and more serious or persistent delinquency is decidedly less common (Belson, 1975; Farrington, 1973; Gold, 1970; Shepherd, 1978).

Nevertheless, although serious or frequent delinquent activities are shown by only a relatively small proportion of boys (and an even smaller proportion of girls), quite a substantial minority of young people appear in the courts and are found guilty of some offence. Most studies have shown that in British and American inner cities about one quarter to one third of boys and about 1 in 13 to 1 in 16 girls are officially declared delinquent (Farrington, 1979; Havighurst, Bowman, Liddle, Matthews, & Pierce, 1962; Ouston, in press; West & Farrington, 1973, 1977; Wolfgang et al., 1972). On the other hand, about half of delinquents have only one conviction before adult life and only about half go on to have an adult crime record (Farrington, 1979; West & Farrington, 1977).

Limited data are available on the continuities in disturbances of conduct in early childhood. Minde and Minde (1977) in a 9-month follow-up of children registered for junior kindergarten found that temper tantrums and difficulties in management at home showed an association with aggressiveness/hostility at school—an association that stood out in contrast to the generally low level of concordance between parent and teacher ratings. Richman et al. (1982), using similar measures, provide data on continuities between 3 and 8 years of age. Of the children with clinically significant disorders at age 3 years, 62% still showed disorders at age 8 compared with a rate of 22% among controls. In that the disorders were not classified according to type at age 3, it is not possible to determine persistence separately for disturbances of conduct. However, it was found that the factors associated with persistence included male sex, difficulties in management, and high activity level. Also, conduct disorders in boys at age 8 were those most likely to be associated with prior behavioral difficulties at age 3. Integrating the findings, it is evident that most of the boys with extreme restlessness and/or marked difficulties in management at age 3 or 4 showed conduct disorders at age 8. The same degree of persistence was not found for girls, with the consequence that tantrums and difficulties in management showed a male preponderance at 8 that had not been evident at 3. The findings are parallelled by those from the Fels Longitudinal Study (Kagan & Moss, 1962), which showed that, in the sample as a whole (as distinct from a problem group), aggression and behavioral disorganization (meaning destructive acts, rages, and tantrums) in the preschool years showed greater persistence into the middle childhood years for boys than for girls.

Further data on continuities in conduct disturbance in middle childhood come from Kohn's (1977) longitudinal study of New York daycare children. Pooled scores for grades 1 and 2 on the anger-defiance (conduct disturbance) factor correlated .60 with pooled scores on the same factor for grades 3 and 4. Even after partialling out the effects of both demographic variables and other aspects of behavior, the correlation was still highly significant ($p < .001$) and of moderate size (.36).

Olweus (1979) has reviewed the limited evidence on the temporal stability in early childhood of aggression in males, which indicates correlations of .48 to .72 over periods of 6 to 18 months for both direct observation data and teacher ratings. However, apart from the studies discussed above, no data are available on the strength of the links between the preschool years and middle or later childhood. Much more is known regarding the continuities in disturbance of conduct in older children. In his review, Olweus (1979) concluded that the correlation (corrected for attenuation) between two measures of aggression separated by time ranges from about .75 when the time interval is 1 year to about .4 when the time interval is 21 years. Of course, the use of correction factors is open to objection and may give rise to artificially high correlations; nevertheless, however assessed, it is clear that there is a substantial degree of consistency over time.

The same issue may be examined in a different way by determining the extent to which a varied range of measures of troublesome, difficult, or socially disapproved behaviors in elementary school or at home relate to delinquency as shown in adolescence or early adult life. Studies of this kind (Conger & Miller, 1966; Farrington, 1978; Havighurst et al., 1962; Mitchell & Rosa, 1981; Ouston, in press; Robins, 1978; West & Farrington, 1973, 1977; Wolfgang et al., 1972) show substantial continuities. For example, West and Farrington (1973), using a combination of teacher ratings at 8 and 10 years and peer ratings at 10 years found that of the most troublesome children, 27% became recidivist delinquents, in marked contrast to the rate of .7% among the least troublesome children. Expressed in reverse fashion, it is apparent that 68% of recidivists had been in the most troublesome group at primary school compared with 12% of nondelinquents.

However, this behavioral continuity is much greater with recidivism than with children who only receive one conviction. Thus, in the same West and Farrington (1973) study only 34% of one-time delinquents were in the most troublesome category at ages 8 to 10. Similarly, Ouston (in press) found that whereas 45% of boys with at least three convictions had shown deviant behavior on teacher ratings at age 10 (compared with 22% of nondelinquents), this held for only 23% of those with just one or two court appearances.

Interestingly, in contrast to the findings on conduct disturbance in the preschool period, delinquency in girls was more strongly associated with prior behavioral deviance than was the case with boys (Rutter, Maughan, Mortimore, & Ouston with Smith, 1979). Of the girls with low scores on the teachers' questionnaire at age 10 years, only 4% became delinquent compared with 21% among those with conduct-type deviance. Apparently, many boys without general problems of conduct disturbance become one-time delinquents (although far fewer become recidivists), whereas this is less often the case with girls. In girls, even a single conviction tends to have been often preceded by previous indications of troublesome, difficult, or disturbed behavior.

The course and outcome of children's conduct disturbances has been demonstrated in several longitudinal and follow-up studies, with highly consistent findings (Cline, 1980; Farrington, 1979; Robins, 1979). About half the youths who receive a conviction as juveniles do not appear in court again and (even among those with several convictions) a substantial proportion cease offending in early adult life. To that extent, the long-term outcome for delinquency must be regarded as fairly good in that their criminal career comes to an end with the taking up of an apparently normal pattern of social activities and personal relationships. However, no data are available on their functioning as adults after their early 20s, and other findings (Osborn & West, 1979) suggest that there is likely to be an increased risk of delinquency for their children. Whether this implies genetic transmission, the effects of labeling, or the continuation of some form of noncriminal personal deviance in the ex-delinquent parent that affects the upbringing of children remains quite uncertain. Be that as it may, it is clear that in many cases delinquency proves to be a transient phenomenon with few identifiable sequelae, at least in early adult life.

To a considerable extent, these transient delinquents appear different from recidivist delinquents (and more similar to nondelinquents) from the outset. Quite apart from the measures of troublesome behavior already discussed, one-time delinquents are less deviant than recidivists in their family background and characteristics, in their educational accomplishments, in the extent and nature of their self-reported antisocial activities, and in their social-life patterns (West & Farrington, 1973, 1977). It would be quite misleading to consider these one-time delinquents as unexceptional apart from the delinquent acts that led to their conviction because they do differ significantly from nondelinquents in a host of ways. Nevertheless, the differences are much less than those found with recidivists. Expressed another way, it is evident that the greater the weighting of

personal or family factors associated with delinquency, the greater the likelihood that the delinquency will be maintained (Osborn & West, 1978).

These findings help explain why the outcome for delinquency (as assessed from follow-up studies of children or adolescents appearing before the courts) appears rather better than the outcome either for conduct disorders in young people referred to psychiatric clinics or for those whose conduct disturbance is defined in terms of deviance on multiple indicators. Not only are these latter groups more likely to show a pervasive disturbance of personality functioning and more likely to come from a seriously disturbed family but also the follow-ups have usually been based on a much wider range of social indicators than just the presence or absence of further convictions. Research findings have been consistent in showing that clinic-referred children with conduct disorders are more likely than children with emotional disorders (and much more likely than those without disorders) to show persisting psychiatric and social impairment.

This has been apparent in follow-up studies from childhood to adolescence as in the Isle of Wight enquiries (Graham & Rutter, 1973) and in the comparable follow-up from ages 10 to 14 in inner London (Rutter, 1977b). It has been similarly shown in the follow-up studies from adolescence to early adult life (Annesley, 1961; Masterson, 1958, 1967; W. Warren, 1965) and also in the long-term follow-ups from childhood to adulthood (Mellsop, 1972; Michael, 1957; Michael, Morris, & Soroker, 1957; Morris, Escoll, & Wexler, 1956; Robins, 1966; Sundby & Kreyberg, 1968). It is clear that the prognosis for conduct disorders is generally worse than that for emotional disorders regardless of the age of ascertainment (in spite of the suggestion to the contrary by Gersten et al., 1976) and that within a child psychiatric clinic group it is antisocial symptoms and hyperactivity that predict criminality, alcoholism, and personality disorder in adult life (Nylander, 1979; Robins, 1966; Sundby & Kreyberg, 1968). Moreover, the same studies also show that the disorders tend to run true to form in that almost always adult antisocial personality disorders have been preceded by conduct disturbances in childhood (Robins, 1978). Emotional disorder in childhood or adolescence rarely leads to sociopathy or antisocial behavior in adult life. On the other hand, the reverse is not true. Conduct disorders tend to be followed by a wide range of emotional, social, and relationship problems in addition to antisocial behavior, hence, the use of the term sociopathy (Robins, 1966, 1978). As a consequence, conduct disorders may sometimes be followed by emotional disorders, at least for a time (Graham & Rutter, 1973). Of course, too, many youngsters with conduct disturbances also grow up to be reasonably well-functioning adults, none of the follow-up studies of antisocial children have shown rates of adult sociopathy in excess of 50% or so.

Comparable follow-ups of high-risk groups in the general population (Robins, 1978) have given rise to closely comparable findings so that it is clear that the conclusions are not restricted to clinic samples. Instead, they apply to any group of boys showing a wide variety of frequent antisocial activities. Robins has summarized the findings:

(1) adult antisocial behaviour virtually *requires* childhood antisocial behaviour; (2) most antisocial children do *not* become antisocial adults; (3) the variety of antisocial behaviour in childhood is a better predictor of adult antisocial behaviour than is any particular behaviour; (4) adult antisocial behaviour is better predicted by childhood *behaviour* than by family background or social class of rearing; (5) social class makes little contribution to the prediction of serious adult antisocial behaviour. (p. 611)

Hence, the interesting question becomes what family, social, or personal characteristics predict antisocial behavior in childhood, which is the beginning point.

These conclusions appear reasonably well supported so far as serious and persisting adult antisocial behavior as a whole is concerned. However, the West and Farrington (1977) longitudinal study of London boys showed that a minority of criminal men were free of significant conduct disturbance during childhood, as judged both by their own contemporaneous self-reports and by teacher ratings. It seems that criminal behavior can begin for the first time in adult life. Moreover, when it does, it is particularly associated with a family background of low social status and parental criminality; not so much with the measures of poor parental behavior and poor supervision associated with delinquency that begins in childhood and persists into adult life. Thus, although certainly there are substantial links between socially disapproved behavior in childhood and similar behavior in adult life, there are also important discontinuities.

The question remains, however, as to how far the links that do exist extend over time and, in particular, how far conduct disturbances in very early childhood lead to adult antisocial behavior. Although it is clear that the longer the duration of time the less strong the links, almost no data on children with disorders are available to link infancy with adulthood. The nearest approach is the Fels Longitudinal Study, which looked at the long-term predictive power of behavioral disorganization in the preschool years (Kagan & Moss, 1962). Very low correlations with adolescent and adult ratings were found. But the findings apply to ratings in a basically normal sample, and it cannot necessarily be assumed that the same would, or would not, apply to a much more deviant clinic sample.

The scope and value of different forms of therapeutic intervention are discussed in detail elsewhere (see *Alexander & Malouf, vol. IV, chap. 11*). Here it is necessary only to touch on the question of whether there are effective treatments and, if there are, whether they modify any of the conclusions above with regard to course and outcome. As the literature is extensive and has been thoroughly reviewed on several previous occasions (Clarke & Cornish, 1978; Patterson, 1982; Ross & Gendreau, 1980; Rutter & Giller, in press), only the conclusions relevant to issues of continuity will be briefly stated. Earlier reviews have generally concluded that all forms of intervention have proved ineffective, but recent work suggests that this is an unduly negative view. Nevertheless, it remains true that no form of treatment or of penal response has had sufficient effect to alter the general pattern of findings on course and continuity outlined earlier.

That raises, perhaps, the implications of the findings for general conclusions on continuities and discontinuities in personality development. Does the relative consistency in behavioral functioning (as evident with respect to disorders of conduct) together with the evidence on the very limited impact of therapeutic interventions imply that personality characteristics are established early in development and are very difficult to alter thereafter? There are many reasons why this would be a totally inappropriate conclusion (Rutter, in press; Rutter & Giller, in press). In the first place, the continuities found are of only moderate strength so that there is plenty of room for change at all stages of development. Second, it is helpful to differentiate between continuity, meaning that a person shows the same behavior across different time periods, and stability, meaning that an individual retains the same position over time relative to others on a behavioral dimension—to use Emmerich's (1964, 1968) terminology. The implication is that, relatively speaking, individuals may continue to be more antisocial than their peers but that in absolute terms their overall level of antisocial activity may nevertheless fall. Indeed, this is what the behavioral changes in early adult life reflect for many individuals.

Third, it is necessary to differentiate between stability in behavior over *time* and consistency in behavior over *space*. As Mischel (1979) puts it:

> No one seriously questions that lives have continuity and that we perceive ourselves and others as relatively stable individuals who have substantial identity and stability over time, even when our specific actions change across situations. But although. . . [this] is not in dispute, there is serious disagreement about the nature, degree and meaning of the cross-situational breadth of behaviors. (p. 742)

In fact, there is evidence of the importance of situational influences on the overall level of antisocial behavior in that context (Rutter, 1979; Rutter & Giller, in press). Such influences may not greatly alter the relative ranking of individuals with respect to antisocial behavior across the contexts, and the finding of situation effects does not invalidate the notion of personality traits (Eysenck & Eysenck, 1980). However, it may also be that individual predispositions help determine the style and extent of people's responses to different situations (Epstein, 1979). In the latter connection, it may be relevant to note that the greatest situational effects have usually been found with nondeviant samples rather than with the persistently antisocial individuals considered here.

Finally, it is important to recognize that, at least in part, the lack of lasting effects of the various forms of intervention is due to the presence, rather than the absence, of situational effects. As Clarke and Cornish (1978) and O'Donnell (1977) point out, it is not that residential treatments are without an impact on current behavior. To the contrary, institutional environments appear to have a marked influence on current behavior; it is just that the benefits do not persist when the young people return home to a totally different environment that maintains it delinquency-producing characteristics. These authors suggest that the implication is that efforts might be better directed toward changing the home environment rather than attempting to alter individual characteristics. The extent to which that is either practicable or useful remains to be determined. Nevertheless, the suggestion does underline the fact that we do not know to what extent the continuities

over time in antisocial behavior are mainly a function of the importance of individual personality features or a function of the effects of a relatively unchanging noxious environment.

Sex Differences

Few adequate data are available on sex differences in conduct disturbance during the preschool years, but one study showed that hyperactivity was more common in boys at age 3 years but that the male preponderance for difficulties in management did not appear until the age of 4 (Richman et al., 1982). However, with one exception (Leslie, 1974), epidemiological studies have been consistent in showing that disturbances of conduct are more common in boys than girls at all ages, extending from age 5 to adulthood (Graham & Rutter, 1973; Kastrup, 1977; Lavik, 1977; Remschmidt, Hohner, & Merschmann, 1977; Rutter et al., 1970/1981; Rutter et al., 1975; Shepherd et al., 1971; Werry & Quay, 1971). Both self-report data and criminal statistics show a similar strong male preponderance for delinquency. There can be no doubt that the sex difference is valid, in that it has been evident in a large number of studies conducted in a range of countries and cultures using a diversity of measures. Nevertheless, there is evidence that although the existence of the sex differences is an almost universal phenomenon, its extent varies across cultures and across time (Rutter & Giller, in press). The sex ratio tends to be less among blacks than whites in both the United Kingdom and the United States but perhaps greater among those from an Asian background. During the last 20 years, the sex ratio for official delinquency has been halved; whether this also applies to nondelinquent conduct disturbance is not known. The reasons for these cultural and temporal variations remain obscure.

Aggression, Hyperactivity, and Dishonesty

In seeking to account for the sex difference in conduct disturbance, it is appropriate to turn first to the evidence on the behavioral features with which it might be associated (Eme, 1979). The empirical evidence on this matter has been extensively reviewed by Maccoby and Jacklin (1974, 1980a, 1980b). Although their review has come under recent attack (Tieger, 1980), their reply (Maccoby & Jacklin, 1980b) adequately deals with the issues considered here.

Observational studies are generally consistent in showing that males are more aggressive in their verbal and physical interactions with their peers. The research findings suggest that, to an important extent, the greater aggression in boys has a biological basis because: (1) the sex difference is apparent from early childhood; (2) although the cross-cultural data are meager, the difference applies across the cultures studied; (3) it applies similarly to subhuman primates; (4) prenatal androgens have an organizing function that serves to influence aggression at a later age; and (5) alterations in circulatory testosterone levels in adolescence and adult life have an effect on aggression. In arguing for a biologically influenced sex difference in aggression, it should also be emphasized that there is substantial overlap between, and huge individual variation within, the sexes; aggression is much influenced by social learning and situational factors; and just as testosterone influences aggression, so also the expression of aggression influences hormone levels.

Undoubtedly, aggression constitutes the behavior with the best established and most marked sex difference that is (in part) biologically determined. However, there is somewhat less consistent evidence that high activity levels may be more characteristic of boys than girls (Levy, 1980). That this may have a biological component is suggested by the finding from the Bethesda study that the sex difference applied only to children who showed minor physical anomalies (Bell & Waldrop, 1982). The observation is unexpected in view of the rather conflicting findings on the association between such anomalies and hyperactivity (Krouse & Kauffman, 1982) and the rather minor sex differences usually found for activity level (Porter & Collins, 1982) or for temperamental differences generally in young children (Plomin & Foch, 1981b). The matter requires further study.

It seems probable that biologically influenced sex differences in aggression are relevant to the sex difference in conduct disturbance, but the extent of their importance remains quite uncertain. No conclusions are possible on the role of other temperamental attributes, but it seems unlikely that they account for a large part of the sex difference in overall disorders of conduct.

Other Constitutional Factors

The evidence of possible genetic factors in disturbances of conduct is very limited. It seems that although polygenic factors are of only minor importance in the broad spectrum of juvenile delinquency and conduct disorders, they probably play a significant (although not preponderant) role in antisocial personality disorders that continue into adult life (Rutter & Giller, in press). Cloninger, Christiansen,

Reich, and Gottesman (1978) suggest that genetic factors may be more important in female than in male crime in adults, but data are lacking to indicate whether or not this applies to disorder in childhood. However, there are some inconsistent indicators that female delinquency may be more likely to be associated with greater behavioral deviance (Rutter & Giller, in press). Also, it seems that in boys delinquency is more associated with family discord in intact homes, whereas in girls breakup of the home and changes in the parent figure appear more important (Caplan, Awad, Wilks, & White, 1980; Offord, 1982; Wadsworth, 1979).

Response to Family Discord

One of the early observations from British epidemiological studies (Rutter, 1970b, 1982) was the apparently greater vulnerability of boys to family stress and discord. It was found that whereas antisocial problems in boys were much more common when there was severe marital discord than when there was family harmony, this was not the case for girls except to a minor extent. The same sex difference was evident when total deviance was considered, so, it was clear that the finding was not an artifact of sex differences in diagnosis. This finding has now been replicated to a greater or lesser extent in further epidemiological studies in the United Kingdom (Rutter, 1979; Whitehead, 1979; Wolkind & Rutter, 1973), and, more important, in several American studies that use quite different sets of measures for both marital discord and conduct disturbances (Block, Block, & Morrison, 1981; Emery & O'Leary, 1982; Hetherington, Cox, & Cox, 1979a, 1979b, 1982; Porter & O'Leary, 1980).

Various possible explanations have been tentatively suggested for these findings. For example, Rutter (1970b) pointed to the lack of evidence for relevant sex differences in variables such as attachment, suggestibility, identification, conditionability, and physiologic responses to stress, that might be invoked as explanations. On the other hand, there was the possible parallel with the well-documented greater vulnerability of males to a wide range of physical stresses, which raised the possibility of a similar constitutionally determined male susceptibility to psychological stresses. Whitehead (1979) suggested that, at least with respect to divorce, the difference may be due to the children usually remaining with the mother so that boys are more likely to lack a positive role model. This may be a relevant factor with respect to children's responses to divorce, but it cannot account for the sex difference in response to discord in intact families. On the other hand, Hetherington, Cox, & Cox

(1978) found that warring parents were more likely to argue and quarrel in front of their sons than their daughters. Accordingly, at least in part, the sex difference could be a consequence of differences between boys and girls in the extent of their exposure to discord.

Block et al. (1981) put forward three other possible explanations. First, the salience of the two parents may differ for boys and girls; for girls, the lesser salience of the father—as suggested by Lamb (1976)—may attenuate the effects of parental disagreement. Second, it could be—as suggested by Gunnar-Vongnechten (1978)—that being able to control their environment is more important for boys than for girls and, hence, that the capricious environment of a discordant family is more disturbing for boys. Third, they (Block et al., 1981) suggest that the process of socialization has different implications for the two sexes, with the need to control aggression being greater for boys than for girls.

Emery and O'Leary (1982), in their empirical investigation, explored the possibility that boys and girls in discordant families would differ in their perceptions of parental discord or in their feelings of being accepted and loved, but neither hypothesis received support. Instead, Emery and O'Leary favored some form of differential-modeling explanation for the sex difference.

Yet a further possibility is that parents and teachers respond differently to disruptive behavior in boys than they do to similar behavior in girls. There are a variety of findings suggesting that, to some extent, this is the case both in general (see review by Maccoby & Jacklin, 1974) and following divorce (Hetherington, 1981).

The evidence, as a whole, suggests that the true picture is likely to reflect a complex two-way interaction in which the final outcome (for both children and their parents) is likely to be shaped by the fact that boys and girls respond differently to, and elicit different responses from, their parents in a host of ways that are separate from family discord and disruption. Thus, for example, Maccoby and Jacklin (in press) found that even at the early age of 12 to 18 months difficult boys can cause mothers to discontinue their efforts to apply socialization pressures (a backoff that, in turn, tends to increase their son's difficult behavior) and that whereas active girls elicit especially positive interactive behaviors from both mothers and fathers, this is not the case for active boys. The evidence so far is too fragmentary for drawing firm conclusions on the precise nature of the sex differences in parent-child interaction, on the reasons for the differences, or on the parents' role (if any) in the determination of sex differences in distur-

bances of conduct. Nevertheless, what is clear is that there are important questions here that require an answer and that further research should prove fruitful.

In summary, conduct disturbances are much more frequent in boys than girls. The reasons for this well-established sex difference are ill understood. The possible explanations include biologically influenced sex differences in temperamental features (especially aggression) that predispose to conduct disturbance, genetic factors, differences between boys and girls in their exposure to family discord and in their response to it, and variations in the ways parents respond to difficult behavior in their sons and daughters.

IQ and Scholastic Attainment

Although largely ignored by theorists, there is a very substantial body of empirical research that shows a consistent association between conduct disturbance and both lower IQ and below average educational attainment (see Hirschi & Hindelang, 1977; Rutter & Giller, in press). The associations, in both British and American studies, apply to self-report data, to teacher ratings of disruptive behavior, to measures of truancy, to convictions, and to clinical assessments of conduct disturbance. Moreover, the associations between IQ or reading and deviant behavior are maintained even after controlling for family size and social class. On the whole, the associations are stronger with reading than with IQ, and this is especially the case with the overall designation of conduct disorder in boys (based on information from parents, teachers, and the children themselves).

The delinquency findings indicate that the associations are much stronger with recidivism than with one-time delinquency and that, as with nondelinquent conduct disturbances, the negative correlations with IQ and educational attainment are maintained after controlling for race, social status, family size, and family income. The links are apparent early in schooling and do not increase later to any substantial extent. In large part, the association between IQ and delinquency is due to its prior association with troublesome behavior in the classroom when the children were much younger.

Meaning of Associations

The links, then, are well established, but what do they mean? The various possible alternatives have been explored by several different investigators with results that are both inconsistent and inconclusive. However, two possibilities can be ruled out—at least as major explanations. First, there is the suggestion that the association simply reflects the ability of the bright delinquent to avoid detection or prosecution (see, e.g., Doleschal & Klapmuts, 1973). This is contradicted both by the associations with self-reported delinquency and by the finding that the IQ/conviction association disappears once the IQ/troublesome-behavior association has been taken into account (West & Farrington, 1973). Second, there is the possibility that delinquency or disturbances of conduct cause poor intellectual performance, educational failure, and school dropout. Clearly, delinquency cannot be held responsible for the low IQ scores as the low scores antedate the delinquency. It is more difficult to test the possibility that disturbances of conduct so interfere with learning that they lower cognitive performance and scholastic attainment. However, several findings cast doubt on the hypothesis. Richman et al. (1982) showed that the IQ/behavioral-disturbance associations were already present as early as age 3 and did not increase over the next 5 years. Moreover, persistence of psychopathological problems (there was no separate analysis with respect to conduct disturbance) between 3 and 8 years of age was not accompanied by any intellectual deterioration; also, cognitive scores in the general population showed no significant correlation with behavioral measures taken during testing. Rutter, Tizard, Yule, Graham, & Whitmore (1976) also showed that changes in conduct disturbance were unassociated with changes in cognitive performance. Although it is possible that severe conduct disturbance may interfere with children's response to educational or intellectual tests, such a mechanism cannot account for the overall pattern of associations.

Of the possibilities that remain, there are two main contenders, each of which has some support in some populations. There is the hypothesis that educational failure leads to low self-esteem, emotional disturbance, and antagonism to school, which may contribute to the development of disturbances of conduct and delinquent activities (Cohen, 1956; Mangus, 1950; Rutter et al., 1970; Schonell, 1961). There are three different types of evidence supporting this suggestion. First, there is the comparison of children who show both reading difficulties and antisocial behavior with those showing pure reading difficulties and pure conduct disturbances. Both Rutter et al. (1970) on the Isle of Wight and Varlaam (1974) in London found that the combined group was most like the pure reading-difficulties group and rather dissimilar to the pure conduct-disturbance group. Because conduct disturbances in the combination group were linked with the characteristics associated with reading difficulties rather than those associated

with antisocial behavior, it was argued that the findings suggested that antisocial disorder in these cases may have arisen, in part, as a result of educational failure. On the other hand, Sturge's (1982) findings, using the same research strategy, were only partially supportive.

The second type of evidence comes from the very few investigations that show that the improvement of academic performance through behavior modification or other procedures may markedly reduce discipline problems in the classroom (Ayllon & Roberts, 1974; Gates & Bond, 1936).

Third, there is the observation that delinquency rates fall after children leave school (Phillips & Kelly, 1979). The possible importance of educational failure as a factor predisposing to delinquency is most strikingly shown in Elliott and Voss's (1974) longitudinal study of American high school students. The pupils who subsequently dropped out of school showed much higher self-report delinquency scores than those pupils who remained at school, but the delinquent activities of the dropouts markedly diminished after they left school, with the timing coincident with leaving school rather than with age. Elliott and Voss concluded that it was the combination of educational failure and the school's response to that failure that predisposed to delinquency. This interactionist view is supported by Robins and Hill's (1966) finding that educational failure is not characteristic of individuals whose delinquency begins in adult life and with the finding of Rutter (1979) that reading difficulties are not associated with conduct disturbance beginning in adolescence rather than in earlier childhood. On the other hand, West and Farrington (1977) found that low IQ was almost as frequent among men first convicted in early adult life as among those convicted as juveniles.

There are two types of contrary evidence against the educational-failure-causes-conduct-disturbance hypothesis. First, the finding that IQ and behavioral disturbance are already associated as early as age 3 or 4 years (Richman et al., 1982) is inconsistent with the hypothesis. Second, the one study to examine the sequential relationship of conduct disorders and reading difficulties (McMichael, 1979) showed that disturbances of conduct frequently preceded reading difficulties and that even at school entry conduct disturbances were already associated with poor performance on reading-readiness tests. At least within the 5- to 7-year age group studied, there was nothing to suggest that reading difficulties *caused* antisocial behavior.

Another possibility is that both cognitive deficits and conduct disturbance to some extent share a common etiology—either in terms of sociofamilial variables or temperamental characteristics. This explanation is favored by Offord et al. (1978) on the grounds that, in their study of boys on probation in Ottawa, delinquents did not differ significantly from their siblings in terms of either IQ or scholastic failure. On the other hand, although the difference fell short of significance, it was notable that whereas 51% of the delinquents showed poor school performance, only 33% of their brothers did so. Also, the delinquents whose antisocial behavior followed poor school performance differed from the primary delinquents (without scholastic difficulties) in showing more symptoms of a *non*antisocial type, which might be thought to suggest the possible role of emotional disturbance resulting from educational failure.

Richman et al. (1982) also favored a common etiology hypothesis on the basis of the presence or an IQ/behavior correlation as early as age 3. Of course, these data applied to a broader range of disorders than conduct disturbances and in many cases (as shown by their own data) conduct disturbances did not arise until later in childhood. Nevertheless, a common etiology is certainly suggested for those whose disorders were already apparent at age 3.

This raises the further question of what sort of etiology might be relevant. Offord et al. (1978) placed weight on family factors, but three different sorts of findings are inconsistent with this suggestion. First, in their own study, there were no family variables that differentiated children with either delinquency or school failure from those without both problems. That, of course, is a consequence of their within-family design. By the same token, it raises questions about their other negative findings on sib-sib comparisons on which they base their argument. Second, Richman et al. (1982) found that whereas cognitive and behavioral measures at 3 or 4 years of age were associated with persistence or disorders to age 8, family measures were not. Third, West and Farrington (1973) and Noblit (1976) found that IQ and educational attainment still correlated with delinquency, even after controlling for family variables. Of course, that is not to suggest that family variables are unimportant in the genesis of conduct disturbance and reading difficulties. To the contrary, there is good evidence that they are important. Nevertheless, it does seem that family variables may not account for the *association* between the two conditions. None of these studies have utilized measures of temperament and the possibility that these constitute the crucial common etiosocial variables remains open.

In summary, no single explanation for the IQ/conduct-disturbance association can be maintained.

Possibly, the main link may be found to lie in the temperamental features that predispose to both educational failure and antisocial behavior. However, most evidence on this suggestion comes from ruling out other explanations rather than from any data that provide direct support. In addition, it is possible that family factors play a subsidiary role and that, in some cases, educational failure may increase the predisposition to conduct disturbance.

School Factors

Several studies have documented large differences in delinquency rates between high schools serving much the same areas (Gath, Cooper, Gattoni, & Rockett, 1977; Power, Alderson, Phillipson, Schoenberg, & Morris, 1967; Power, Benn, & Morris, 1972; Reynolds, Jones, & St. Leger, 1976; Reynolds & Murgatroyd, 1977; Rutter et al., 1979), and similar differences between schools have also been found to be related to psychiatric referral rates (Gath et al., 1977) for truancy and for disruptive behavior in the classrooms of both primary and secondary schools (N. Goldman, 1961; Heal, 1978; Pablant & Baxter, 1975; Reynolds, Jones, & St. Leger, 1976; Reynolds, Jones, St. Leger, & Murgatroyd, 1980; Reynolds & Murgatroyd, 1977; Rutter, 1979). The authors of all these studies have drawn the implication that school factors may have played a part in influencing pupil's behavior in ways that affect the overall rates of conduct disturbance. However, before drawing that conclusion it is important to pay attention to possible noncausal interpretations and methodological artifacts (Rutter, in press-f).

Undoubtedly, the most serious potential source of bias is selective intake to the schools, that is, that some schools admit a far higher proportion of behaviorally difficult children and that the differences between schools in rates of conduct disturbance are simply a consequence of these differences in intake. Several studies have, indeed, shown that there *are* major variations between schools in their intakes (Farrington, 1972; Rutter et al., 1979). However, Rutter et al. (1979) found that the school variations in extent of disruptive behavior and in absenteeism were not solely due to the intake factors measured, although in the smaller Farrington (1972) study they were. Of course, this type of analysis is necessarily limited by the variables measured at intake, and it will always remain possible that the school variations were a consequence of some intake variable that was not measured. Accordingly, in testing the causal hypothesis, it is essential both to show that the school variations were not a result of intake factors and also to determine whether they were systematically associated with characteristics of the schools. This association was found in the detailed study by Rutter et al. (1979) of 12 London high schools. Measures of the social and organizational characteristics of schools, based on systematic time- and event-sampled observations in the classroom; interviews with teachers; and questionnaires from pupils all showed substantial correlations with measures of pupil behavior. The overall pattern of findings together with the evidence against other alternative explanations strongly suggested a possible causative influence of schools on children's behavior in that setting. Nevertheless, to test that hypothesis rigorously, intervention studies are needed to determine whether planned change of school practice is followed by the predicted changes in pupil behavior. Such studies have yet to be undertaken; thus, the causal hypothesis remains unproven in spite of circumstantial evidence in support of it.

However, assuming for the moment that the statistical associations do represent causative influences, it is important to consider what is being affected and which aspects of schooling are relevant in that connection. First, the Rutter et al. (1979) findings, in keeping with earlier studies concerned with school variations in scholastic attainment (Jencks, Smith, Acland, Bane, Cohen, Gintis, Heyns, & Michelson, 1972), indicated that school influences have a negligible impact on the extent of individual variation and, moreover, that compared with family variables, school factors account for only a small amount of population variance in children's behavior or scholastic attainment. Nevertheless, school variables do seem to have a considerable impact on the overall level of behavioral disturbance or scholastic attainment. In other words, in all schools, children vary greatly in their behavioral and cognitive features, but in some schools, there is a general tendency for the pupil group as a whole to be either better behaved or more generally disruptive. It is that general tendency that appears to be shaped by school characteristics.

Second, school factors have had a considerably greater effect on children's behavior in the classroom than on delinquent activities outside school. Also, the school features that are most important for each were not the same. The school processes associated with children's behavior in the school (as reflected in measures of items, such as disruptions in the classroom and the extent of graffiti and damage in the school) included styles and skill of classroom management, the models of behavior provided by teachers, the extent of rewards and encouragement, the granting of responsibility to pupils, the degree of academic emphasis, levels of expectations for the pupils, and the general quality of school conditions for pupils. On the other hand, although these school processes may have had some impact on delinquency, much the greater effect stemmed from the academic balance in the intake. Even after taking account of children's individual characteristics, it appeared that a child attending a school with a high proportion of intellectually less able children was more likely to become delinquent than a child of similar initial characteristics from a similar background who attended a school with a more even academic balance in the intake. In that academic balance did not have any substantial impact on teacher behavior (as measured), the inference is that the mechanism involved peer-group influences of some kind. Other studies, too, have emphasized this peer-group effect, both within- and between-schools (Hargreaves, 1967; Kratcoski & Kratcoski, 1977), and have shown that school differences in rates of delinquency are associated with differences in pupils' perceptions of the schools' emotional climate (Finlayson & Loughran, 1976).

In summary, the findings suggest that there are school influences on children's behavior in the classroom and on their delinquent activities outside the school. With the former, the effects are stronger and more closely related to the social ethos of the school. With the latter, it seems likely that peer-group influences may be more important.

Social Class

There is a somewhat inconsistent tendency for disturbances of conduct to be most prevalent in the lowest social-status groups and least prevalent in children and adolescents from a professional or managerial family background, but the association is very weak in the middle of the social-class distribution and is often not present at all. Possibly, the social trend may be slightly stronger with official convictions than with other measures, but this slight difference does not account for the inconsistencies in findings (Braithwaite, 1981; Rutter & Giller, in press; Tittle, Villemez, & Smith, 1978).

Given that there is some trend to explain, what does it mean? The evidence on this point is rather unsatisfactory, but it has usually been found that measures of family discord and disorganization show stronger associations with conduct disturbance than do social-class variables and that the social-class correlations either disappear or weaken once other family variables have been taken into account. For example, West and Farrington (1973) found that although criminality maintained a significant association with delinquency after controlling for family income, the reverse only applied in one out of three comparisons. Similarly, family income ceased to be associated with delinquency after controlling for the child's level of intelligence. Similarly, Robins (1978), in several studies, found that social class added little to the prediction of adult antisocial behavior once other family variables and the behavior in childhood were taken into account.

We may tentatively conclude that, to some extent, low social status probably increases the likelihood of various types of family problems and difficulty and that some of these family factors, in turn, predispose to disturbances of conduct. However, the associations between social status and family stress are rather weak, and, probably, social status has very little direct association (causal or otherwise) with disturbances of conduct.

Family Influences

A variety of studies have examined family variables by comparing institutionalized delinquents and controls, but these are open to the objection that any differences found may be a function of the judicial decision to commit the delinquent to an institution rather than anything to do with the development of disturbances of conduct or delinquent activities as such. Accordingly, for the most part, attention will be confined to studies of general population samples. The results are in good agreement in showing that the most important variables associated with both juvenile delinquency and adult criminality include parental criminality; poor parental supervision; cruel, passive, or neglecting attitudes; erratic or harsh discipline; marital conflict; and large family size. Much the same family variables are associated with nondelinquent disturbances of conduct (see reviews by Hetherington & Martin, 1979; Hinde, 1980; Rutter, in press-e; Rutter & Giller, in press).

The validity and wide applicability of these associations have been shown by the repeated finding that the family variables associated with conduct disturbance and with delinquency have been generally similar in different social and ethnic groups as well as in countries with rather different cultures and systems of social control (Friday, 1980; Rohner, 1975; Werner, 1979).

These family measures, usually based on inter-

view data, concern rather broad aspects of family functioning; observational studies of sequences of family interaction in the home have attempted to go further in delineating the actual processes of maladaptive interaction that are associated with disturbances of conduct (Patterson, 1981a, 1982). Although the associations are not very strong, it has been found that the parents of problem children differ from the parents of normal children in being more punitive (Patterson, 1982; Snyder, 1977), in issuing more commands (Delfini, Bernal, & Rosen, 1976; Forehand, King, Peed, & Yoder, 1975; Lobitz & Johnson, 1975b), in being more likely to provide attention and positive consequences following deviant behavior (Snyder, 1977), possibly in being less likely to perceive deviant behavior (Bogaard, 1976; Reid & Patterson, 1976), in being more likely to be involved in prolonged sequences of coercive negative interchanges with their children (Patterson, 1981a, 1982), in giving more vague commands (Forehand, Wells, & Sturgis, 1978), and in being less effective in stopping their children's deviant behavior (Patterson, 1981a, 1982). The causal nature of at least some of these family characteristics is shown by four different types of evidence. First, parents of normal children were able to make their children behave worse by issuing more commands (Lobitz & Johnson, 1975a). Second, the study of sequences of family interaction showed that hostile or coercive parent (or sib) actions were associated with an increased likelihood that the child's hostile or aggressive behavior would continue (Patterson, 1977). Third, behavioral interventions that focus on altering these patterns of coercive interchanges have proved successful in reducing the children's social aggression (Patterson, 1982). However, so far it has not been determined within the treated groups whether the degree of change in parental behavior is correlated with the degree of change in the children's conduct disturbance. Fourth, the family variables that are associated with delinquency are also predictive of recidivism within an already delinquent group (Rutter & Giller, in press).

Association with Delinquency or with Conviction

In spite of a strong consensus on the empirical findings relating family factors and conduct disorders, there is continuing disagreement on their meaning. Several rather different issues need to be considered. To begin with, there is the question of the degree to which they represent anything more than a methodological artifact. Thus, Farrington

(1979) has argued that most aspects of a stressful family environment produce convictions rather than delinquent behavior. He bases this argument on the Cambridge study findings showing that: (1) most family variables are associated with both self-reported delinquency and official convictions, (2) most of the associations with conviction remain significant after statistically partialling out the effects of self-reported delinquency, (3) many of the associations with self-reported delinquency cease to be significant after partialling out the effects of conviction. He inferred that this means that the associations with self-reported delinquency are, therefore, no more than secondary consequences of the more basic association between family influences and conviction. The empirical analyses undertaken by Farrington are both important and illuminating, but a review of the total body of empirical evidence indicates that the conclusions he draws rest on a very shaky base and are probably incorrect. First, as he himself points out, some family features (namely parental criminality and poor supervision) were significantly associated with self-reported delinquency even after partialling out the effects of conviction. Second, family variables showed much the strongest association with the combination of self-reported delinquency and conviction. If the family variables were causally linked only with conviction, there should be no familial differences between convicted delinquents who did and who did not report their own delinquencies, but this is not what was found. Indeed, in many instances the family difference associated with conviction was less than that associated with self-reported delinquency.

Third, it is legitimate to partial out the effects of conviction only when the conviction preceded the self-report. The point is that whereas the experience of being publicly labeled as delinquent may increase later delinquent activities (Farrington, 1977), it could not possibly increase previous delinquent activities. The appropriate analysis, therefore, would have been a contrast between the partial correlations according to whether the conviction preceded or followed the self-report. Unfortunately, this was not done.

Fourth, Farrington's (1979) conclusions are at variance with the several studies that show substantial associations between family variables and disturbances of conduct or antisocial behavior within groups of children either below the age at which they could be convicted or whose disorders were unassociated with conviction (Hetherington et al., 1982; Quinton, Rutter, & Rowlands, 1976; Richman et al., 1982; Rutter, 1979). However, Farrington's own data (West & Farrington, 1973) provide, perhaps, an even more interesting case in point. It was found that the various family variables that correlated significantly with delinquency ceased to show significant associations once the effects of troublesomeness had been taken into account. In contrast, troublesomeness continued to relate significantly to later delinquency regardless of which family variables were taken into account. The importance of these findings lies in the fact that the troublesomeness ratings were made when the boys were aged 8 and 10, years before they were first convicted. It follows from these analyses that the family variables were significantly associated with the boys' troublesome behavior. The implication is that family stresses lead to troublesome and disruptive behavior which then, in turn, predisposes to delinquency. In short, the family variables seem to be associated with conduct disturbance as a whole rather than with delinquency as such. As Farrington (1979) suggests, the adverse family factors also play a part in the decision to bring the delinquent boys to court, but the evidence indicates that this is in addition to, rather than in place of, its effect in the processes leading to delinquent activities.

Cause, Correlate, or Consequence?

The next issue is the meaning of the association between family variables and disturbances of conduct in terms of the implications regarding possible mechanisms. Several alternatives need to be considered (Rutter, in press-e). The associations may simply reflect a prior association with some third factor; they may represent genetic influences; they may be a consequence of the disturbing effect of the child's behavior on family functioning; or they may mean that family stresses or difficulties lead to delinquency through some kind of environmental effect.

The first possibility may be examined by determining both whether the association still holds up after controlling for other variables and whether changes in the one are associated with changes in the other. Of course, the decision as to which other variables to control for is crucial. However, it is clear from several studies that the family associations still hold up after taking into account social status and neighborhood and, indeed, that they predict well within populations that socially are fairly homogeneous (see, e.g., McCord, 1980; Robins, 1978; Rutter, 1979; West & Farrington, 1973, 1977; Wilson, 1980). It is also evident from the long-term follow-ups that the associations with adult antisocial behavior are mediated through antisocial behavior in the child. That is to say, early family stresses have long-term effects largely because they lead to forms of disturbance in the child that tend to persist rather than because there are delayed or sleeper effects (Robins, 1978; West & Farrington, 1973, 1977). The findings that changes for the better in family relationships are associated with a reduced risk of later conduct disturbance (Rutter, 1971a), that changes in the patterns of relationship after divorce (either for the better or worse) tend to be associated with parallel changes in the children's behavior (Hetherington et al., 1982; Wallerstein & Kelly, 1980), and that persistent family problems are associated with an increased risk of recidivism, even within a group of boys who are already delinquent (Osborn & West, 1978; Power, Ash, Schoenberg, & Sorey, 1974), make it unlikely that the association is merely an artifact of some prior association with a third variable.

The question of whether the mechanism is genetic or environmental is more difficult to answer. The evidence (Rutter & Giller, in press) that genetic influences are not very powerful in the case of juvenile delinquency (although they are more important with recidivist criminality extending into adult life) makes a purely genetic mechanism unlikely in the case of children. However, the matter may be investigated more directly by comparing the associations with biological and adoptive parental characteristics in early adopted groups. Few data of this kind are available, but the Cadoret and Cain (1980), Hutchings and Mednick (1974), and Crowe (1974) studies all showed associations with the adoptive family situation (psychiatric disorder or divorce in the adoptive family and institutional rearing in the first study, criminality in the adoptive parent in the second study, and adverse early life experiences in the third study) that point to an environmental effect (in addition to the genetic effect shown by the associations with criminality in the biological parent). Interestingly, in the latter two studies this environmental effect was evident only in the group that was genetically vulnerable by virtue of having biologically had a criminal parent. The suggestion (which needs replication) is that, in these circumstances, the genetic factor may operate, in part, by rendering the individual more susceptible to environmental hazards. (It should be noted that this does not seem to be the explanation in the case of schizophrenia where family-rearing variables seem to have most effect in the *absence* of a genetic predisposition [Rosenthal, Wender, Kety, Schulsinger, Welner, & Rieder, 1975].)

The possibility that some of the association is a result of the influence of the child on the parents rather than the other way round is difficult to test rigorously. Certainly, there is evidence that children can and do have effects on parents (Bell & Harper, 1977; Lerner & Spanier, 1978), and it may well be that the association, in part, reflects this direction of effect. On the other hand, some of the associations (such as that with parental criminality) cannot operate in that direction and others (e.g., large family size) are most unlikely to do so. In other cases, too, there is evidence that often the family discord and difficulties antedated the child's disturbance (Rutter, 1971a). Nevertheless, it has frequently not been possible to be sure which way the causal arrows run. The importance of the child's role in parent-child interactions is emphasized by the evidence that parental actions that are effective with normal children are not effective with socially aggressive children (Patterson, 1981b, 1982). It seems likely that the causal influences are bidirectional but that, at least with some of the family variables, the preponderant effect is likely to be from parent to child.

Which Environmental Mechanism?

Although we may reasonably conclude that family influences do, indeed, have some kind of environmental impact that plays a part in the process by which children develop disturbances of conduct, the precise mechanisms by which they operate remain rather obscure, although it has proved possible to rule out some. Thus, it is now clear that broken homes are associated with delinquency and conduct disturbances because of the discord associated with the break rather than because of the family breakup per se (Rutter, 1971a, 1982). The relevant evidence includes: (1) divorce and separation are associated with a much increased risk of delinquency, whereas parental death is not; (2) parental discord is associated with antisocial disorder in the children, even when the home is unbroken; (3) the extent of discord is associated with the likelihood of disorders in the children, even in groups in which all the homes are broken; and (4) children removed from home into institutions or foster care because of family difficulties or breakdown already show an excess of disturbed behavior before they were separated from their families. On all these grounds it is evident that it is the discord rather than the separation from the parents that is crucial. On the other hand, recent studies have made it abundantly clear that the notion that divorce necessarily brings family discord to an end is seriously mistaken (Hess & Camera, 1979; Hetherington et al., 1982; Wallerstein & Kelly, 1980). Discord sometimes continues long after the breakup, and the adaptations required by the divorce often bring new stresses for the family that may make things worse before they make them better. Furthermore, the conclusion that it is the discord that matters leaves wide open the question of *how* the discord operates.

Several possibilities have been suggested. First, it could be that it is the efficiency of parental supervision and discipline that matter and that the discord is important only insofar as it is associated with erratic, deviant, and inefficient methods of bringing up children (Wilson, 1974, 1980). Certainly, supervision has proved to be an important variable in nearly all studies examining associations with antisocial behavior, but the close links between the different types of family stress and difficulty make it very difficult to disentangle their separate effects (West & Farrington, 1973). Alternatively, it could be that modeling is important (Bandura, 1969) and that family discord is relevant because it provides children with a model of aggression, inconsistency, hostility, and antisocial behavior they then copy. A third alternative is that the discord constitutes the setting for sequences of coercive family interaction in which hostile or coercive behaviors serve to perpetuate aggressive encounters. Patterson's (1977, 1979, 1981a, 1982) careful and systematic moment-by-moment observational studies in the home strongly suggest that this does indeed occur, although it is not clear precisely what psychological mechanism these coercive sequences reflect. A fourth alternative is that children need loving relationships with their parents to develop appropriate social behavior later (Bowlby, 1969), and it is the difficulties in social relationships that constitute the basis of antisocial conduct. The ameliorating effect of a good relationship with one parent, even in the presence of general family discord (Rutter, 1971a), is consistent with this suggestion, but the finding is also open to a variety of different interpretations.

Similar issues apply with respect to other dimensions of family functioning (Rutter & Giller, in press). Thus, there is uncertainty on the mechanisms involved in the highly consistent association between parental criminality and conduct disturbances in children. The association is strongest when the parental crime is recidivist and extends into the period during which the children were reared (Osborn & West, 1979; Robins, West, & Herjanic, 1975). But in addition to parental criminality, persistent social difficulties (such as excessive drinking and a poor work record) and serious abnormalities of parental personality (Robins & Lewis, 1966; West & Farrington, 1973) are also associated. Probably, in part, the linkage represents a genetic factor, but (as noted) hereditary factors have a rather weak effect in conduct disturbances (Rutter & Giller, in press). It is unlikely to represent any direct imitation of parental crime since in many cases the criminal parents ceased offending when the children were quite young (West, 1982). Probably (at least in part), the association reflects linkages among such factors as parental criminality, family discord, and poor supervision.

Weak relationships with parents, too, have been associated with conduct disorders, as reflected in such items as lack of joint family leisure activities (West & Farrington, 1973), lack of intimate parent-child communication (Hirschi, 1969), lack of parental warmth (McCord & McCord, 1959; Rutter, 1971a; West & Farrington, 1973), and parental reports that they cannot get through to their children (Rutter et al., 1976) or that they do not feel attached to them (Patterson, 1982). Many of these measures are weak and inferential, but the possible importance of weak relationships is indicated by the finding of a raised rate of psychosocial problems (including conduct disorders) in girls reared in institutions from infancy (Rutter et al., in press).

There is rather weak evidence on the aspects of parental discipline and supervision that are most strongly associated with conduct disturbances. However, Patterson (1982) concludes that the findings suggest the importance of four main features:

1. A lack of house rules (no clearly predictable routines or expectations).
2. Lack of parental monitoring of children's behavior.
3. A lack of effective contingencies (inconsistent parental responses, with an inadequate differentiation between reactions to prosocial and to antisocial behavior.
4. A lack of techniques for dealing with family crises or problems.

Various explanations have been proposed for the association between large family size and conduct disturbance. The finding that the association is most evident in socially disadvantaged populations suggests that it may not be family size per se that is crucial but rather the disadvantages that tend to accompany it. However, Offord's (1982) data suggest that it may be some form of male contagion or potentiation of delinquent behavior that is important. He found that delinquency was associated with the number of brothers in the family but not with the number of sisters. When one boy in a family is delinquent, it is more likely that others in the family will also be affected (Robins et al., 1975).

In summary, there is continuing uncertainty about the environmental mechanisms involved in the mediation of family influences on the development of disorders of conduct. However, the key dimensions include family discord, deviant parental (and sibling) models, weak parent-child relationships, and poor discipline and supervision of the children's activities. If the psychological processes involved are to be identified more precisely, there will need to be studies of the effects of change and of planned therapeutic interventions (Conger, 1981) as well as more discriminating correlational studies within an epidemiological framework.

Area Influences

Over the last half century, since the pioneering studies by Shaw and McKay (1942), numerous investigations have shown that delinquency rates vary greatly according to geographical area, with rates tending to be highest in poor overcrowded areas of low social status in industrial cities and tending to be lowest in more affluent spacious rural areas (see Baldwin, 1979). This observation reflects two rather different sets of findings (namely urban/rural differences and intraurban differences) that may or may not reflect the same mechanisms.

Urban/Rural Differences

Official statistics indicate that delinquency rates are substantially higher in the cities than in small towns and higher in both of these than in rural areas (Clinard, 1968; McClintock & Avison, 1968). Self-report studies (Christie, Andenaes, & Skirbekk, 1965; Clark & Wenninger, 1962), too, show that delinquent activities are more common in urban areas; and psychiatric surveys based on detailed behavioral data from teachers and parents have demonstrated marked city/rural differences in rates of conduct disturbances, especially those with an early onset (Lavik, 1977; Rutter, 1979). However, it is important to note that this city/rural difference applies to a wide range of disorders, including emotional disturbances in both young people and their parents, reading difficulties, adult criminality, and various measures of family discord and adversity. These differences are not reporting artifacts, in that they are revealed by a wide variety of measures, and they hold up even when the same methods are applied by the same team of investigators in the differ-

ent areas. Also, they are not explicable in terms of disturbed families moving from the countryside into the cities because the differences are maintained even after comparisons are confined to those born and bred in the areas (Rutter, 1979; Rutter & Quinton, 1977). It seems likely that some aspect of the city environment may predispose to psychosocial disorder (including conduct disorders).

The hypothesis that the associations reflect a causal effect stemming from life in the inner city is supported by studies that have examined the effects of a move to a different neighborhood. Thus, Buikhuisen and Hoekstra (1974) found that delinquents who on discharge from a prison for juveniles moved away from an asocial environment had a lower reconviction rate than those who returned to their former address. A similar analysis was undertaken by West (1982) who found that delinquents who moved away from inner London had a lower reconviction rate than those who remained in the metropolis. West showed that this difference was not a function of the prior characteristics of those who moved; moreover, the move away from London was accompanied by a marked reduction in self-reported delinquency—there being no such reduction in those who remained in London. However, the move away from London was not followed by any changes on many of the antisocial lifestyle variables (e.g., aggressive attitudes or excessive drinking). The implication is that the diminution in delinquent activities was a consequence rather than a cause of the move away from London but that the effect had been largely on the committing of criminal acts, with little inpact on other aspects of conduct disturbance. However, this conclusion applies to youths who changed their place of residence but who remained with their family.

The question arises as to whether the area effect (whatever its nature and origin) operates directly on children or whether it operates through how it affects the family. In the one study that examined that question (Rutter & Quinton, 1977), the higher rate of child disorder in the city was almost entirely explicable in terms of the greater frequency of family adversity there (as shown by variables such as parental criminality and mental disorder, marital discord, and large family size). Of course, that only pushes the question back one stage further to ask why families in the inner city are more likely to be disadvantaged and what it was about life in the metropolis that predisposes to conduct disturbance and to family discord. A variety of possible explanations have been suggested (Baldwin & Bottoms, 1976; Quinton, 1980; Rutter, 1981b) without any very satisfactory answers. However, as similar issues apply to the intraurban differences, they will be discussed together.

Intraurban Differences

Many studies have shown that within cities, suburbs, and towns there are marked variations between geographical areas in rates of delinquency (Baldwin, 1979; Morris, 1957; Rutter, 1979; Rutter & Giller, in press). Delinquency rates have been shown to vary between boroughs, between wards in a borough, between enumerations districts within a ward, and even between streets in a small neighborhood so that the high-risk areas may be quite small as well as quite large. Moreover, the high-delinquency areas are often rather scattered, with no very obvious connection with recognizable neighborhoods. On the other hand, it has also been shown that the area differences in delinquency rates remain rather stable over quite long periods of time. As with city/rural differences, the variations apply to a wide range of psychological and social disturbances, including alcoholism and psychiatric disorder, suicide and attempted suicide.

The fact that the incoming residents to high-delinquency-rate estates have been shown to differ systematically from those moving into low-delinquency-rate estates (Baldwin & Bottoms, 1976) makes it essential to control for these prior differences when making area comparisons. Unfortunately, that has not been done satisfactorily in any of the area studies. The nearest approach has been to examine area differences in child guidance referral rates (Gath et al., 1977) or delinquency rates (Reiss & Rhodes, 1961) within social-class categories. These studies have shown that the area differences are not solely explicable in terms of the social class of the individuals in them and that, on the whole, the social status of the area may be as (or more) important than the social status of the individual. However, there are far too few studies for there to be much confidence in such a conclusion and, of course, social class is not the only, or indeed even the most relevant, variable to take into account. It seems that there may be an area effect that goes beyond individual characteristics and, therefore, that an ecological approach may be justified, but that is about as much as can be said.

Ecological Correlations and Explanations

In recent years, the most frequent statistical approach to area analyses has been to correlate census-tract variables with offender rates according to administratively defined geographical units (Baldwin, 1979). The results have usually shown that the high-

delinquency areas are those with a high proportion of low social-status individuals, a low proportion of owner-occupiers, a high proportion of overcrowded homes, and various features, such as shared accommodation, many single people, and many immigrants—features that in combination are thought to reflect social disorganization. In these respects, the findings are fairly consistent (although there are some differences in findings between studies). The problem lies in not knowing quite what they mean. Certainly, these ecological correlations do not mean that these associations apply at an individual level (Robinson, 1950). Nevertheless, it is important to consider whether any of them might operate through some direct effect on individuals.

The variables of population density, personal overcrowding, and high population turnover are, perhaps, the three most likely contenders in this connection. However, the results of empirical research are somewhat contradictory and inconclusive (Rutter & Giller, in press). A major limitation of most area studies stems from their use of administrative definitions of areas and their reliance on census data to define the characteristics of the areas. However, census tracts will rarely coincide with the areas felt to constitute neighborhoods or communities by the people living in them.

A useful, but rarely employed, alternative strategy is the comparison of high- and low-delinquency neighborhoods in terms of the social perceptions of the residents in them. Maccoby, Johnson, & Church (1968) did this with respect to two areas of Cambridge, Massachusetts, which were similar in socioeconomic status but which showed a threefold difference in delinquency rates and an eightfold difference in truancy rates. The two areas did not differ in terms of either population mobility or expressed attitudes to delinquency. But more residents in the high-delinquency area reported that they did not like the neighborhood, fewer knew more than five neighbors well enough to borrow something, and fewer felt that they shared the interests and ideas of other people in the area. The study was based on rather small numbers and was not very fully reported, but the findings suggest the possible relevance of feelings of social integration. Clinard and Abbott's (1973) comparison of slum areas in Kampala (Uganda) with high and low crime rates pointed to the same conclusion. The major difference seemed to apply to the quality of relationships—people in the low-delinquency area perceived a greater firmness and stability in heterosexual relationships, were more likely to participate in local community organizations, visited the homes of a greater range of people, and changed residence less often.

In both these studies, the findings leave unexplained why such differences developed. Quinton's (1980) data from the London/Isle of Wight study suggest that the availability of friends and kin is unlikely to constitute the explanation. Studies of the socially disadvantaged families of children with conduct disturbances have shown that, compared with other families, they tend to have less contact with friends and more aversive contact with social agencies—a pattern Wahler (Wahler, 1980; Wahler, Leske, & Rodgers, 1978) has described as insular. His research suggests that community influences may affect family functioning, but how they do so remains obscure. The potential importance of area influences on people's behavior has been shown, but surprisingly little is known of either the strength of the effect or the mechanisms involved.

Physical Environments and Situational Effects

There has been a recent upsurge of interest into the effects of the physical environment in regulating people's behavior and in possible situational influences on delinquent activities (Clarke, 1978, 1980). The impetus did not stem from ecological studies; instead, it came from a concern about the possibilities of effective prevention through situational measures (Clarke & Mayhew, 1981) and from architectural considerations (Newman, 1973), nevertheless, it carries the potential for increasing our understanding of ecological effects (Baldwin, 1979).

The most influential of the architectural reports was Newman's (1973) book, *Defensible Space,* which suggested that physical design features in housing estates could either predispose to, or protect against, crime. He argued that extensive semipublic areas in estates increased vandalism, both because the areas were not felt to belong to any particular group of residents (and, hence, were not looked after, or protected, by them) and because the nature of the design of the housing estates made surveillance difficult. In his own research, the crucial physical variables appeared to be the size of the housing project, the number of housing units sharing an entrance to a building, and a building's height. However, the characteristics of the residents were better predictors of crime and vandalism than were those physical design features (Newman, 1975, 1976).

Newman's ideas have been tested in London by Wilson and Herbert (1978), who confirmed that most damage did, indeed, occur in those semipublic areas that were out of general sight and that vandalism was particularly high both in building complexes with impersonal entrances used as throughways to other locations and in housing estates with little or no landscaping of the grounds. The implication is that a pleasant environment may make it less likely that people will want to damage it, in addition to the effect of public surveillance in reducing opportunities for vandalism. Research in other settings has shown similar reductions in delinquent activities either from physical controls (e.g., the marked reduction in car thefts as a result of steering-wheel locks and other antitheft devises) or from improved surveillance (shown by the evidence that vandalism on buses is greatest in areas of low supervision and on one-man operated buses without a conductor [Mayhew, Clarke, Sturman, & Hough, 1976]).

The operation of situational effects is also indicated by the various studies that show that institutions for delinquents have predictable effects on behavior (Rutter & Giller, in press). Quite wide differences between institutions in rates of absconding and of reconviction have been found. The between-institution variations remain after controlling for differences in intake and are systematically associated with institution characteristics. Both findings suggest a causal inference, but random allocation studies based on these differences have yet to be undertaken (those that have been carried out have compared therapeutic and custodial institutions that differed in other features found not to be relevant to outcome). The successful institutions are characterized by a combination of firmness, warmth, harmony, high expectations, good discipline, and a practical approach to training.

The findings from other studies (Clarke, 1980; Rutter, 1979) are in agreement in showing the importance of situational effects. Only a few children are completely honest and well behaved in all circumstances—most will be disruptive, or will cheat, or will steal given the right conditions. This effect, however, is by no means confined to disturbances of conduct. Mischel (1974, 1981) and his colleagues have shown the importance of situational factors in children's impulse control and delay of gratification. Also, there are close parallels with the effects of circumstances in relation to alcoholism, drug dependency, and suicide (Rutter, 1979).

Nevertheless, many questions remain regarding situational effects. Their strength is not known and there are few findings on the particular characteristics of the physical environment which increase or decrease the likelihood of disturbances of conduct. It also remains quite unclear how far the effects are a result of particular environments affecting people's *motivation* to behave in disruptive or delinquent ways and to what extent they are a consequence of limitations in the *opportunities* to behave in these ways. In addition, we remain ignorant of the extent to which situational factors truly reduce antisocial behavior rather than just displace it from one area to another or from one type of activity to another. As briefly noted, there are a variety of pointers to the probable importance of situational effects, and it is evident that their further study would be most worthwhile, but the existing knowledge on the topic is still very limited.

Social Change

The last set of variables to consider in relation to disturbances of conduct are those relating to social change. One of the most striking features of crime statistics in most European and North American countries is the steady rise in rates of delinquency since World War I. There are numerous methodological problems in determining how far this constitutes a real rise in the number of delinquent individuals, but it seems clear from a review of the evidence (Rutter & Giller, in press) that there has been a true increase, even though the extent may not be so great as the crime statistics suggest. The question as to why there has been a rise and what changes have caused it remains without any satisfactory answers. The research strategies that have been employed include international comparisons, as in Archer and Gartner's (1976) comparison of combatant and noncombatant nations regarding changes in homicide rates following wars; and both aggregated and individual time-series studies relating economic change to behavior disorders (see, e.g., Dooley & Catalano, 1980) or relating unemployment to delinquency in young males (Phillips, Votey, & Maxwell, 1972). Undoubtedly, the issue warrants further study as there have been major changes over time which require explanation and which might shed light on the causation of disturbances of conduct. However, perhaps the most striking feature to date is the contrast between the cross-sectional analyses and the secular-change analyses. Thus, the former show that delinquency is associated with poverty, low social status, and poor housing, but the latter show that delinquency rates have risen in spite of reductions in poverty and improvements in housing. The paradox remains unresolved.

Theories

Finally, with respect to conduct disturbance, it is necessary to consider theories regarding their origins. For several decades starting in the 1930s, the study of delinquency gave rise to a rich body of theorizing. Psychologists sought to explain individual differences in terms of personality factors and family influences; sociologists sought to relate social-group differences to theories of society and the social origins of human behavior. However, over recent years, there has been a move away from the monolithic grand theories and a general acceptance of the need for multifactorial explanations (Bahr, 1979; Elliott, Ageton, & Canter, 1979; Feldman, 1977; Johnson, 1979; Rutter & Giller, in press). Even so, a continuing limitation of most theoretical approaches is that they do not start with the empirical findings that require explanation; instead, they express views about society and human behavior that are then extended to disturbances of conduct. Accordingly, most fail to focus on the main phenomena considered in our discussion. For example, few consider the much higher rate of conduct disturbances in males, or the diminution in delinquent activities in early adult life, or the associations between cognitive performance and conduct disturbance, or the situational variations in delinquent behavior, or the marked rise in the crime rate over the last half century. This list of omissions highlights another feature, namely, that there are several quite different kinds of causal questions and explanations (Rutter, 1979; Rutter & Madge, 1976). For example, psychological theories have mainly focused on the *who* question—why one person shows a conduct disturbance, whereas another person does not. Sociological theories, in contrast, have tended to deal with the rather different issue of why the rate of delinquency in one social group differs from that in another. Developmental theories, on the other hand, have been more interested in why and how changes in behavior take place in relation to the maturational process. It is obvious that the causal mechanisms may be quite different for these disparate issues.

Most theories have been concerned with crime rather than with disturbances of conduct and, hence, they are of limited relevance for developmental psychopathology. Accordingly, our discussion is quite brief. Fuller considerations of theories are available elsewhere (Feldman, 1977; Glaser, 1979; Kornhauser, 1978; Rutter & Giller, in press; Trasler, 1973).

Sociological Theories of Delinquency

Unlike most psychological theories, almost all sociological explanations of delinquency start with the assumption that delinquency is not the result of any form of psychopathology. Instead, it is seen as a consequence of forces in society, although the various theories postulate rather different forces and different modes of operation. Anomie/strain theories have the premise that delinquent behavior is the result of the gap, or anomic disjunction, between cultural goals and the means available for those goals

(Merton, 1957). The two conditions in society thought to create anomie are: (1) greater emphasis on certain success goals than the means to reach them and (2) restriction in certain social groups of the legitimate means of achieving success. Thus, it is a class-based theory that assumes that most delinquent behavior is concentrated in the lower social strata. Accordingly, the major piece of disconfirming evidence is the weak and inconsistent association between social class and delinquency. In addition, high aspirations in working-class youths have not been found to be associated with delinquency (Hirschi, 1969; Elliott & Voss, 1974). Also, the fact that most delinquent boys become law-abiding adults constitutes a major source of difficulty for strain theories as the conditions of the model do not change on attainment of adulthood (Hirschi, 1969).

In its original form, anomie is untenable as a general theory of delinquency. However, several variations have been put forward, the most important of which is Cloward and Ohlin's (1960) attempted integration of anomie with Sutherland's (1939) theory of differential association. Its particular contribution lies in the attempt to explain why strain results in one form of deviance rather than another, in terms of the availability of illegitimate means and the opportunities for learning deviant roles. The ideas have been tested most systematically by Elliott and Voss (1974). They confirmed the importance of association with delinquent friends and of the link with educational retardation, but they found only weak relationships with perceived failure to achieve the culturally defined goals or with aspirations or attributions of blame. The strength of these theoretical developments lies in their emphasis on the known associations between educational failure and delinquency and on their recognition that much delinquency occurs within the context of the peer group. However, there are doubts on the particular mechanisms proposed to account for these features.

The subcultural approach shares the assumption that delinquency is concentrated in lower working-class groups, but it differs in that it postulates neither strains nor frustrations. Instead, it suggests that delinquency is simply normal behavior for the particular subculture and, hence, that it is learned in the same way as any form of social behavior (Mays, 1954). Its major value has been the recognition that some forms of minor delinquent behavior constitute an accepted part of the social activities of adolescents; indeed, it is clear from self-report studies that this is so in all strata of society. On the other hand, the consistent evidence that the victims of delinquent

acts tend to be poor people living in socially disadvantaged areas (Empey, 1978) and that slum dwellers are as condemnatory of most delinquent acts as anyone else (Kornhauser, 1978) runs completely counter to the suggestion that this constitutes a general explanation of delinquent behavior. The theory is also negated by the findings that social maladjustment is just as common in delinquents from a deprived background as in those from middle-class homes (Conger & Miller, 1966; Roff, Sells, & Golden, 1972; West & Farrington, 1973) and that the factors that predict delinquency in one social groups predict similarly in others (Robins, 1978).

In recent years, there has been an interest in theoretical approaches based on a labeling perspective that postulates that a person's view of himself is influenced by the reactions of others, that a stigmatizing label of delinquent is provided by legal processing, that this labeling adversely affects the labeled person's self-image, and that, as a consequence, the labeled person becomes more likely to engage in delinquent activities (Gibbs & Erickson, 1975). Empirical findings show that, as predicted, court appearances do make it more likely that boys will maintain antisocial attitudes and increase delinquent activities (see, e.g., Farrington, 1977; Farrington, Osborn, & West, 1978). On the other hand, the same findings also indicate that the effects of labeling are not as strong or as pervasive as sometimes assumed, that they do not necessarily operate through changes in self-image, and that the effects are most marked with first offenders and do not spiral as hypothesized (Bahr, 1979; Rutter & Giller, in press). The phenomenon has some validity, but reactions to labeling fail to account for most of the empirical findings on delinquency.

Many theories seek to explain why some people *do* commit delinquent acts; social control theories start from the opposite position. They assume that everyone has a delinquent predisposition, that there is no need for special motivational postulates, and that the crucial issue is how people learn not to offend (Hirschi, 1969). It is argued that delinquent acts result when an individual's bonds to society are weak or broken. The key elements in that bond are hypothesized to include attachment to other people, commitment to an organized society, involvement in conventional activities, and belief in a common value system. The empirical findings from studies designed to test this hypothesis provide support for the main social control postulates (Bahr, 1979; Hirschi, 1969), but the observation that associations with delinquent peers increases the risk of delinquency, even after controlling for parental attachment, is inconsistent, as is the evidence of the importance of parental criminality. Accordingly, it is now recognized that it is necessary to invoke additional concepts to take account of the social meaning of delinquent activities and of the rewards for delinquent behavior that are provided by particular social groups. Most of these recent developments of social control theories have argued for a combination with social learning perspectives (Elliott et al., 1979; Johnson, 1979).

Social Learning Theories of Conduct Disturbance

Most social learning theories do not postulate a single mechanism for disturbances of conduct and many include concepts of a biologically influenced individual predisposition and of social reaction, although they differ in the weights attached to these additional notions. What they have in common is the view that delinquent activities are not different in kind from other forms of behavior and that learning variables exert a major influence on the acquisition, performance, and maintenance of delinquent activities (Feldman, 1977). The hypothesized learning process involves both learning *not* to offend (as a result of training in socially acceptable behaviors, maintained by negative consequences for infractions and positive consequences for rule keeping) and learning *to* offend (maintained by intermittent positive consequences for offending). There is an abundance of evidence that both antisocial and prosocial activities are strongly influenced by learning, and the importance of these mechanisms can scarcely be in doubt. Moreover, social learning theories have the great merit of tackling the question of situational factors, an issue largely ignored by other theorists. Nevertheless, such theories overlook sex differences, age changes, and developmental factors; they lack specificity on just how antisocial behavior is acquired and, why there are such marked individual differences in behavior (Cairns, 1979). Also, there are difficulties in accounting for the observations that punishment is less effective with antisocial children and may actually increase their antisocial behavior, that coercive interchanges tend to be longer in the families of aggressive children, and that antisocial behavior diminishes so markedly in early adult life (Patterson, 1982).

Within the broad context of social learning perspectives, Patterson (1982) has put forward a performance theory of coercive family processes that seeks to account for these apparently discrepant features. He argues that the parents of children with conduct disturbances provide an inadequate and ineffective

set of conditions for social learning because there are no clear expectations or discriminatory contingencies (so that there is a lack of differentiation between prosocial and antisocial behaviors), poor monitoring of children's activities (so that the parents are in no position to respond effectively because they are relatively unaware of their children's behavior), and a lack of interest in the child combined with a paucity of problem solving (so that there is no constructive prosocial learning). This chaotic and confusing set of messages is accompanied by frequent coercive interchanges and a lack of pleasurable family interactions. It is hypothesized that the reinforcing value of parents is enhanced by the sharing of enjoyed activities and, hence, that parental influences are thereby reduced in families of children with conduct disorders. Patterson suggests that the prolonged coercive interchanges serve to convey affective information (irritation and anger) rather than a disciplinary request to the child to behave in any particular way. The negative interactions also serve to disrupt social problem solving.

It is too soon for any adequate assessment of the validity of these ideas, which, so far, have an empirical underpinning that is dependent on a small number of studies of selected samples. Nevertheless, the approach has the enormous strength of its derivation from detailed and systematic observations in the home rather than from a global view of human behavior. Perhaps, the major contributions of Patterson's approach are: (1) the demonstration of the affective component in parent-child interactions of a supposedly disciplinary character; (2) the translation of molar concepts, such as supervision or strictness of discipline, into observable and quantifiable processes of interaction; and (3) in common with other social learning theorists, the breaking down of the broad notion of conduct disturbance into hierarchies of interlinked behaviors.

Biological Theories

Most biological theories have focused on subgroups of conduct disturbance, usually those characterized by hyperkinetic, inattentive behavior (see *Attention Deficit/Hyperactivity Syndromes*) or psychopathic behavior. Quay (1977a, 1977b) hypothesized that those who ultimately manifest psychopathic behavior are born with a nervous system, cortical and/or autonomic, that is hyporeactive to stimulation. He suggests that the resulting combination of stimulus-seeking behavior and refractoriness to the effects of punishment creates difficult children who are likely to elicit punishment and become an aversive stimulus to their parents. The parents, faced with out-of-control children, then, understandably, retreat into hostility, rejection, and inconsistency. It is apparent that Quay's notions potentially offer some explanation of how the coercive patterns described by Patterson (1982) might arise. As discussed earlier, most of the research into these biological concepts has been undertaken with incarcerated adult criminals, and we do not know the extent to which the findings can be extended to children with disturbances of conduct. Nevertheless, Quay's hypotheses do give rise to several quite specific predictions readily subject to experimental verification or refutation. They warrant study, but there is likely to be difficulty in the designation of the psychopathic subgroup to which the theory is said to apply.

In summary, in spite of a lack of theoretical resolution, substantial progress has been made toward a conceptual integration of ideas on conduct disturbance. Both social control and social learning theories have received substantial empirical support, and ideas and findings on coercive family processes have provided important developments in this field. Until recently, less progress has been made in the elucidation of mechanisms underlying individual differences in predisposition to conduct disturbance. However, in part, this is because most research of that type has focused on the overlapping concept of attention deficit/hyperkinetic syndromes, which we consider next.

ATTENTION DEFICIT/HYPERACTIVITY SYNDROMES

Poor concentration, fidgetiness, and overactivity are three of the most frequent behaviors associated with both emotional and conduct disturbances. As such, they appear to constitute common but nonspecific accompaniments of a wide range of child psychiatric disorders. These same behaviors are among the most frequent complaints made by parents and teachers about supposedly normal children in the general population (Lapouse & Monk, 1958; Rutter et al., 1970; Werry & Quay, 1971). It is accepted that children, both normal and abnormal, may be inattentive and overactive for many different reasons. Nevertheless, in addition, it has been hypothesized that there is a specific syndrome characterized by inattention (shown by a failure to finish things, being easily distracted, not seeming to listen, and having difficulty concentrating), impulsivity (indicated by acting before thinking, undue shifting from one activity to another, difficulty in organizing work, needing a lot of supervision, frequently call-

ing out in class, and a difficulty in waiting one's turn in games), and hyperactivity (manifested by running about excessively, fidgeting, difficulty sitting still, and restlessness while asleep). These are often associated with poor peer relationships, aggression, disinhibition, and a lack of response to discipline (American Psychiatric Association, 1980; Barkley, 1981; Cantwell, 1975; Ross & Ross, 1976; Safer & Allen, 1976; Weiss & Hechtman, 1979; World Health Organization, 1978). Initially, the hypothesized disorder was called the hyperactivity (hyperkinetic) syndrome or minimal brain dysfunction (MBD) (Wender, 1971), but in the United States, the currently preferred term is attention deficit disorder. The change in term stems from the view that problems in attention may underly the other behaviors in the syndrome (Douglas & Peters, 1979) as well as both the recognition that some children who are hyperactive when young cease to be so when older (G. Weiss, in press) and an appreciation of the conceptual and empirical difficulties associated with the concept of MBD (Nichols & Chen, 1981; Rie & Rie, 1980; Rutter, in press-c). Even so, it is clear from the literature that these various terms are meant to refer to the same condition.

The constellation of behaviors said to constitute the attention deficit/hyperactivity syndrome sounds sufficiently striking for there to be little difficulty in diagnosis, but that has not proved to be the case. Several studies in the United States have shown relatively low levels of agreement among parents, teachers, and clinicians on which children should be regarded as showing the syndrome (Kenny, Clemmens, Hudson, Lentz, Cicci, & Nair, 1971; Lambert, Sandoval, & Sassone, 1978). Moreover, there are immense differences between countries in the frequency with which the diagnosis is made—from 1% to 2% of psychiatric clinic referrals in the United Kingdom (Rutter, Shaffer, & Shepherd, 1975; E. Taylor, 1980a) to 20% to 50% or even higher in the United States (Gross & Wilson, 1974; Safer & Allen, 1976; Stewart, Cummings, Singer, & De Blois, 1981; Wender, 1971)!

Research is needed to determine whether there are real differences between nations or cultures in the prevalence of the syndrome or the behaviors that it comprises. Nevertheless, it is clear that whether or not there are variations in prevalence, most of the variations must reflect differences in diagnostic practice. This is evident from the observation that scores on the hyperactivity factor of Conners's scale (which show good agreement with the diagnosis of the syndrome in the United States) do not vary between countries in the directions expected on the basis of frequency of the syndrome diagnosis (Rutter, in press-c; Sandberg, 1981). Although the diagnosis of attention deficit/hyperactivity syndrome is made only infrequently with children of normal intelligence in Great Britain, the behaviors that comprise the syndrome occur approximately as commonly as elsewhere. Possible explanations for the diagnostic differences need to be sought in the findings on the measurement and the concept of the syndrome.

Measurement of Hyperactivity

Four main approaches have been followed in the measurement of children's level of motor activity: mechanical devices, direct observations, interview ratings, and questionnaire scores (Rutter, in press-c; Sandberg, 1981; Sandoval, 1977). The devices used include actometers (self-winding watches modified to record the overall amount of limb movement), pedometers (that record overall amount of trunk movement), stabilimeters (special cushions that reflect the amount of body movement when sitting), and ultrasonic or photoelectric systems that record whenever a child's movement interrupts a beam. Observations have focused on such items as the amount of off-task behavior, getting up from the seat, the number of times children cross grid lines on the floor, fidgety movements, pencil tapping, and disruptive acts. It is apparent that observations have been concerned with the social appropriateness of the activity as well as its absolute level. The same has applied to both interview and questionnaire measures. On the whole, the reliability of all these measures has been satisfactory. Nevertheless, important methodological issues have arisen from the studies of variations across instruments and across settings.

Agreement Among Instruments

Although some questionnaires correlate well in their assessments of hyperactivity (Zentall & Barack, 1979), others do not (Sandberg, Wieselberg, & Shaffer, 1980). Two features appear important in this connection. First, there seem to be advantages in the use of more precise behavioral descriptions rather than judgmental items and in an admixture of positive and negative descriptors (Sandoval, 1981). Second, scales differ in the mixture of behaviors included in the hyperactivity factor. Thus, Conners's (1973) scale includes items on disruptive behavior (e.g., demands attention, disturbs other children, excitable, etc.), whereas Rutter's scale (Schachar et al., 1981) does not.

The general finding from all studies that have compared questionnaire and observation measures of hyperactivity has been of low, or at best moderate, levels of agreement (Abikoff, Gittelman-Klein, & Klein, 1977; Blunden, Spring, & Greenberg, 1974; Copeland & Weissbrod, 1978; Klein & Young, 1979; Rapoport & Benoit, 1975; Whalen, Collins, Henker, Alkus, Adams, & Stapp, 1978). It seems that the poor agreement across measures stems from three rather different sources. First, the measures do not deal with the same period of time—observation scores apply strictly to the hour or so of observation, whereas teacher and parent ratings are based on the children's behavior over many months or longer. Second, the measures do not deal with identical behaviors or concepts. Observations tend to refer to highly specific items, such as children leaving their chair, whereas questionnaires involve broader and more judgmental items, such as ratings on restlessness or attention-seeking behavior. Moreover, ratings by different people may use somewhat different concepts. Thus, Glow and Glow (1980) found that ratings of hyperactivity by peers loaded on an attention deficit factor, whereas teacher ratings loaded on an unsocialized behavior factor. As usually conceived, hyperactivity covers a variety of different behaviors (such as fidgetiness while stationary, rushing around vigorously when mobile, socially inappropriate activity, and socially disruptive behavior) that overlap but that are far from synonymous. At present, it is not clear which aspect is most relevant for diagnostic differentiation (Whalen et al., 1978) or, indeed, whether there are several different varieties of hyperactivity (Klein & Young, 1979). Third, different measures of hyperactivity may refer to different situations. The evidence of situational effects indicates that this is a crucial matter.

Situation Effects

Teacher and parent ratings of hyperactivity have been found to agree poorly (Campbell, Endman, & Bernfeld, 1977; Campbell, Schleifer, Weiss, & Perlman, 1977; Goyette, Connors, & Ulrich, 1978; Langhorne, Loney, Paternite, & Bechtoldt, 1976; Sandberg, 1981; Schachar et al., 1981). Thus, the correlations between the hyperactivity scores on the parent and teacher versions of Conners's scales have ranged from .18 to .36, with an across-study average of .26 (Sandberg, 1981). In part, this low level of agreement may reflect differing concepts and perceptions of hyperactivity as well as variations according to situation, but findings based on observations or mechanical devices indicate that the latter effect is large. Thus, several studies have shown near-zero correlations when the same measures have been repeated over the course of a few days (Klein & Young, 1979; Montagu, 1975).

Three rather different issues arise from this very low retest reliability for observational and mechanical measures of hyperactivity. First, if the aim is to pick out individuals with a *generally* raised level of activity it is necessary to sample behavior over several sessions and several situations (Epstein, 1979). Given an adequate range of sampling over occasions, measures of activity show substantial temporal stability (correlations of .4 to .7) over periods ranging from a few months to a couple of years (Buss, Block, & Block, 1980; Campbell, Endman, & Bernfeld, 1977; Campbell, Schleifer, Weiss, & Perlman, 1977; Plomin & Foch, 1981b). Second, strictly quantitative measures of activity level (such as actometer scores) vary markedly between different situations; also the children with high scores in one situation are not necessarily those with high scores in others (Barkley & Ullman, 1975; Schulman, Kaspar, & Throne, 1965; Stevens, Kupst, Suran, & Schulman, 1978). One result of this variation is that questionnaire ratings tend to show a substantial correlation with actometer counts of movements in the same setting but a much lower correlation with counts in other settings. Mothers' ratings correlate best with children's activity in unstructured rather than structured settings; the reverse applies to teachers' ratings. The difference probably reflects the differing circumstances in which each observe children. Third, some situations are better than others in differentiating children who, on clinical grounds, are regarded as showing an attention deficit/hyperkinetic disorder. On the whole, children with this syndrome differ most from normal children in their level of activity in familiar, structured, task-oriented settings, with least difference evident in informal classrooms, in after-school activities, or in those activities (such as physical education) in which high energy expenditure is expected (Jacob, O'Leary, & Rosenblad, 1978; Porrino, Rapoport, Behar, Sceery, Ismond, & Bunney, in press; Zentall, 1980). Accordingly, teachers' ratings are likely to provide a better differentiation than parental ratings. Nevertheless, using actometers that are worn continuously, hyperkinetic children have been found to differ from normals to some extent in all activities (including sleep) across the 24 hr. (Porrino et al., in press).

Measurement of Inattention

Much the same issues and conclusions as those concerning hyperactivity also apply to the measure-ment of inattention, a concept that is probably even more complex and multifaceted than activity (Berlyne, 1970; Douglas, in press; Douglas & Peters, 1979; Keogh & Margolis, 1976; E. Taylor, 1980b). Children need to direct and sustain their attention to tasks while maintaining appropriate vigilance; they also need to divide their attention selectively, responding to some cues but ignoring others. A variety of tests have been shown to have reasonable retest reliability and predictive validity. However, although the different measures tend to intercorrelate positively, they do so at quite a low level, with most correlations in the .1 to .5 range (Keogh & Margolis, 1976; Levy, 1980; Plomin & Foch, 1981b; Stores, Hart, & Piran, 1978). As discussed later, some measures of attention consistently differentiate hyperkinetic children from normals, whereas others do not. But, as with activity, situation effects are important also. Thus, Whalen et al. (1978, 1979) found that whereas hyperkinetic children differed from normals when given a difficult task at which they had to work at a pace set by the teacher rather than by themselves, they did not differ in a self-paced, easy-materials condition.

A further issue concerns the extent to which measures of activity and attention intercorrelate with each other. Several studies have shown surprisingly little overlap between overactivity and inattention (Barkley & Ullman, 1975; Ullman, Barkley, & Brown, 1978) in spite of the fact that most investigations have found that hyperactive children perform poorly on measures of attention (Douglas, in press; Douglas & Peters, 1979; Rosenthal & Allen, 1978). The findings serve to emphasize the heterogeneity in the concepts of inattention and hyperactivity.

Concepts of the Syndrome

In view of these methodological findings, it is obvious that there is room for huge variations in the ways in which the hypothesized attention deficit/hyperkinetic syndrome is diagnosed and in the concepts employed in the diagnostic process. A comparison of British and American practices brings out three key differences. First, from the outset British clinicians (Ingram, 1956; Ounsted, 1955) have tended to reserve the diagnosis for children who are markedly overactive and inattentive in nearly all situations whereas U.S. practice (American Psychiatric Association, 1980) has not demanded that the behaviors be pervasive across situations, although some writers have argued that this makes the definition too broad and overinclusive (Barkley, 1981).

Second, whereas in Britain many children diagnosed as showing the syndrome are mentally retarded (Rutter, Shaffer, & Shepherd, 1975; E. Taylor, 1980a), the usual practice in North America has been to exclude children with an IQ below 70 from the attention deficit disorder grouping. Third, when a child has both disturbances of conduct and overactivity/inattention, the tendency in the United States has been to give diagnostic precedence to the latter in diagnosis, whereas the reverse is the case in Britain. Thus, American writers report aggression and antisocial behavior in about three quarters of children with the attention deficit/hyperactivity syndrome (Barkley, 1981; Cantwell, 1975; Safer & Allen, 1976). Conversely, in Britain some three quarters of children with a conduct disorder show hyperactivity, and their scores on the hyperactivity factor of Conners' scale are almost identical to those diagnosed as hyperactive in the United States (E. Taylor, 1979). That this is, indeed, a matter of diagnostic practice rather than different conditions in the two countries is evident from the closely comparable findings of Stewart et al. (1981) on the overlap between hyperactivity and unsocialized aggression in an American sample in which both diagnoses were made according to behavioral criteria. In addition, in both the United Kingdom and the United States, there is ambiguity on the diagnostic practice to follow with respect to the overlap between hyperactivity and learning disorders (Silver, 1981).

Situational Versus Pervasive Hyperactivity

The first issue, then, is whether there is any utility in the distinction between children who are hyperactive/attentive in only some situations (situational hyperactivity) and those who are hyperactive in most settings (pervasive hyperactivity). Probably, Schleifer, Weiss, Cohen, Elman, Cvejic, and Kruger (1975) were the first investigators to make systematic use of this distinction; a 2-year follow-up study of the preschoolers in their project showed that the pervasively hyperactive children requested more feedback from their mothers, talked more in a problem-solving situation, and made more immature moral judgments (Campbell, Schleifer, Weiss, & Perlman, 1977). A further follow-up a year later (Campbell, Endman, & Bernfeld, 1977) confirmed the prognostic validity of the differentiation between situational and pervasive hyperactivity. Other classroom observations showed that the pervasive group were more often out of their seats and more often off-task than either situational hyperactives or classroom controls. Teacher ratings on Conners' scale showed no differences between the situational and pervasive hyperactivity groups on either the hyperactivity or conduct-problem factors, but the pervasive group was rated as significantly more inatten-

tive. In short, the results suggest that the pervasive hyperactivity group showed a significantly poorer prognosis and also that the difference was most striking with respect to the attention deficits assumed by many clinicians to be basic to the hyperkinetic syndrome.

The possible importance of the situational versus pervasive distinction was further investigated by Schachar et al. (1981), using data from a total population five-year follow-up study of children first seen at 10 years of age. Scores at age 10 years on the hyperactivity factors of Rutter's parent and teacher scales were used to divide the population into the 2% with pervasive hyperactivity (i.e., high scores on both), the 14% with situational hyperactivity (i.e., a high score on one only), and the remaining 86%. The results showed (1) that pervasive hyperactivity was strongly associated with cognitive deficits, whereas situational hyperactivity was not and (2) that the pervasive activity group had a worse prognosis in terms of behavioral disturbance 4 years later, again demonstrating the utility of the distinction. Situational hyperactivity did not differ from other forms of disturbance with respect to either cognitive correlates or prognosis, a finding that suggests that hyperactivity in only one situation may be of little diagnostic importance. It was possible that the pervasive/situational difference was one that applied to all types of disturbance rather than to hyperactivity as such. However, when this possibility was examined, it was found that the distinctive association with cognitive deficits and poor prognosis applied specifically to pervasive hyperkinesis and not to other pervasive forms of disturbed behavior.

Further support for the possible diagnostic importance of pervasive overactivity/inattention is provided by the findings on a very small subgroup of children in the clinic study of Sandberg, Rutter, and Taylor (1978) who showed overactivity both at home and at school as well as when systematically observed in a standard setting at the clinic. Even when matched with other clinic children for age and IQ, they showed significantly more anomalies on a neurodevelopmental examination, they made more errors on the Matching Familiar Figures Test, and they were significantly more likely to have been overactive from their preschool years.

Taylor (1980a) compared the few (5%) Maudsley Hospital child patients with gross hyperactivity (although not explicitly defined as such, this was probably equivalent to pervasive overactivity) with other psychiatric clinic attenders. Children in the grossly overactive group were significantly more likely to show intellectual retardation, clumsiness, specific developmental delays, and a long duration of symptoms (dissimilarities that still held when corrected for age and diagnostic differences).

Most recently, Howell and Huessy (1982) have reported on a long-term follow-up of children identified as hyperkinetic/inattentive on the basis of a rural community questionnaire survey. Children with deviant scores on at least two of three occasions when the questionnaire was administered in the second, fourth, and fifth grades differed markedly from controls in terms of poorer school performance and more conduct disturbance as a student and as a young adult. In contrast, those with deviant scores on only one of the three occasions differed little from controls.

In summary, although little research has been conducted so far into the situational versus pervasive distinction, the limited available evidence points to its usefulness. Hyperactivity/inattention that is pervasive over situations tends also to be persistent over time. Situation-specific hyperactivity seems to have little predictive validity, whereas disorders characterized by pervasive activity tend to differ from other psychiatric conditions in showing a stronger association with cognitive deficits and a worse long-term prognosis.

Hyperactivity, Inattention, and Conduct Disturbance

One of the central issues with respect to the validity of the attention deficit/hyperactivity syndrome concept is whether there is any meaningful differentiation between the syndrome and conduct disorders. Several distinct questions are involved here. The first is whether inattentive/overactive behaviors cluster together but are differentiated from aggressive and antisocial behaviors. Usually, this question has been examined by means of factor-analytic studies of ratings from questionnaires or clinic case records (Achenbach & Edelbrock, 1978; Quay, 1979). Most, but not all, studies have shown that hyperactivity emerges as a factor separate from conduct disturbance in both general population and clinic samples. On the whole, hyperactivity and inattention have formed part of the same factor (Glow, 1981; Loney, Langhorne, & Paternite, 1978; Milich, Loney, & Landau, 1982; Nuechterlain, Soli, Garmezy, Devine, & Schaefer, 1981; Schachar, Rutter, & Smith, 1981; Soli, Nuechterlain, Garmezy, Devine, & Schaefer, 1981; Taylor & Sandberg, 1982; Werry, Sprague, & Cohen, 1975) but sometimes they have constituted different factors (Goyette et al., 1978; Werry & Hawthorne, 1976). However, for several different reasons, these findings have little bearing on the separateness or otherwise of the behavioral dimensions. In the first place, the pat-

terns of intercorrelations found are strongly influenced by the wording of questionnaire items. If the items are expressed in terms that confound inattentiveness or overactivity with social disruption or inappropriateness, it is unlikely that distinct factors will emerge. Second, the factors found are likely to reflect the conceptions of the raters as much as the clustering of behaviors (especially in the case of judgmental items). Third, even when the factors are labeled hyperactivity or inattention, the items that load on the factor tend to include items describing disruptive or aggressive behavior. Fourth, although hyperactivity and conduct disturbance factors may be rotated to be orthogonal to one another in the scale construction, when the scale is applied to a new sample, substantial intercorrelations between the factor scores are found (Goyette et al., 1978; Sandberg et al., 1980; Taylor & Sandberg, 1982).

If the two behavioral dimensions are to be tested for independence, it is preferable to use observational data or mechanical measures. As already noted, it has proved possible to develop measures of activity and attention that are both conceptually and empirically distinct from measures of conduct disturbance. Moreover, the recent Milich et al. (1982) study showed that children identified as markedly overactive/inattentive on psychiatric chart data differed systematically on actometer scores and observation variables from those identified as aggressive. It seems that (provided adequate measures are used) it is possible to identify overactivity/inattention and conduct disturbance as separate dimensions of behavior. However, the choice of measures is crucial. It is clear, for example, that the intercorrelations between the hyperactivity and conduct-problem factors on Conners' scales are much too high for them to be regarded as independent dimensions. Accordingly, it is not surprising that classroom observations have not differentiated those factors (Lahey, Green, & Forehand, 1980).

The finding that there are separable dimensions of behavior does not necessarily mean that children who are extreme on one dimension will differ from those who are extreme on the other. Accordingly, the second question is whether there are meaningful differences among children who are purely overactive/inattentive, those who are purely aggressive or disruptive, and those who show both sets of problems. As we have seen, all studies have shown that this last overlap group is very large (Cantwell, 1980). Only a minority of children with conduct disturbances are not also hyperactive and (to a lesser extent) the reverse is true (Sandberg et al., 1978, 1980; Stewart et al., 1981).

The comparison of these groups has been made in

studies in Iowa by Loney and her colleagues (Lang-horne & Loney, 1979; Loney et al., 1978) and by Stewart and his collaborators (August & Stewart, 1982; Stewart, Cummings, Singer, & DeBlois, 1981) as well as in two British studies (Sandberg et al., 1978; Schachar et al., 1981). The results show: (1) that children with pure hyperactivity/inattention differ in having more cognitive and neurodevelop-mental difficulties, poorer school achievement, and, possibly, in being less likely to have fathers with alcoholism or antisocial personality problems; (2) that aggression (rather than hyperactivity) in early childhood predicts conduct disturbance when older; (3) that situational overactivity is of little predictive value; (4) that the children with pure conduct distur-bance differ little from those with both overactivity/ inattention and conduct disturbance; (5) that in many ways, the combined hyperactive/aggressive group constitutes a more extreme version of the pure ag-gressive group, but with a worse outcome.

In summary, the data are too limited for drawing firm conclusions, but the evidence points to the pos-sibility that there may be a pure hyperactivity/inat-tention syndrome that is somewhat distinctive in terms of its association with cognitive deficits and developmental delay. On the whole, the presence or absence of hyperactivity or inattention seems to pro-vide little differentiation within a group where all show disturbances of conduct. On the other hand, hyperactivity/inattention, especially if it is perva-sive, seems to denote a more severe disorder. It may be that this effect would be stronger with better mea-sures of pervasive attention deficits or hyperactivity.

Hyperactivity, Inattention, and Learning Disorders

Numerous studies attest to the considerable over-lap between attention deficit/hyperactivity syn-dromes and learning disabilities. This has been apparent from whichever syndrome the association is approached. Thus, children clinically identified as hyperactive/inattentive have been found to have rates of learning difficulties that are well above those of children in the general population (Cantwell & Satterfield, 1978; Lambert & Sandoval, 1980; Minde, Lewin, Weiss, Lavigueur, Douglas, & Sykes, 1971; Schachar et al., 1981). Conversely, children identified as having specific learning dis-abilities have been found to have increased rates of attentional deficits, hyperactive behavior, and im-pulsivity (Rutter & Yule, 1977), although whether the association is greater than with other measures of conduct disturbance is in doubt (Aman, 1979; De-lamater, Lahey, & Drake, 1981). The problems stemming from a confound between hyperactivity and learning difficulties are increased by the fact that many of the attentional and cognitive disabilities as-sociated with the one have also been found with the other, although there may be some differences (Douglas & Peters, 1979; A. O. Ross, 1976). Unfor-tunately, most published studies fail to indicate whether the children selected for one set of problems also had the other. As a result, it remains quite un-certain whether the features said to be associated with hyperactivity are a function of that behavior or rather of learning difficulties (Ross & Pelham, 1981). There is a need for systematic comparisons between children with hyperactive behavior alone, learning difficulties alone, and the two in combina-tion. Such research is beginning (Ackerman, Elar-do, & Dykman, 1979; Dykman, Ackerman, & Oglesby, 1979), but its findings have not yet indi-cated how the definitions of attention deficit/hyper-activity syndrome should deal with the overlap with learning disabilities.

Psychopathology

Any discussion of the psychopathological fea-tures associated with the hypothesized attention def-icit/hyperactivity syndrome is markedly handi-capped by the rather varied definitions used in different studies. It is obvious that many reports deal with broadly defined groups of children with an ad-mixture of overactivity, inattention, conduct distur-bance, and learning difficulties but that few give sufficient details for any assessment of com-parability across studies. Equally, studies vary in the extent to which pervasive hyperactivity is required for inclusion and in the use made of attentional defi-cits in diagnosis. Those limitations need to be borne in mind throughout our consideration of findings in the remainder of this discussion.

Activity Level

Most studies have found, on direct measurement, that hyperactive/inattentive children do, indeed, move somewhat more than do normal children, par-ticularly in formal structured situations in which they are expected to remain still, attentive, and en-gaged in tasks set by others (E. Taylor, in press-b). The few negative studies (Plomin & Foch, 1981a) tend to be based on loosely defined groups. Howev-er, in many cases, the between-group differences have been quite small and with considerable over-lap. Moreover, the differences between hyperactive children and children with other (supposedly non-hyperkinetic) disorders have been much less striking than those between hyperactive children and normals (Barkley & Ullman, 1975; Firestone & Martin, 1979; Sandberg et al., 1978). The only studies with a major clear differentiation from other psychiatric disorders concerned either brain-damaged children (Hutt & Hutt, 1964) or those diagnosed according to criteria demanding more severe abnormalities than those used in most North American studies (Luk, 1982). It appears that broadly defined attention deficit/hyperkinetic syndromes are associated with activity levels only slightly raised above those found in other psychiatric disorders, but more extreme groups with a markedly raised level of activity in quantitative as well as qualitative terms can be identified.

Social Interactions

Numerous studies, too, have shown that hyperactive children tend to be more likely than other children to show aggressive domineering non-compliant conflicting interactions with their peers (Campbell & Paulauskas, 1979; Milich & Landau, 1982; Pelham & Bender, 1982; Whalen & Henker, 1980; Whalen, Henker, Collins, McAuliffe, & Vaux, 1979). This has been evident in parent and teacher reports, peer ratings, self-reports, and observations. It seems that hyperkinetic children show more unprovoked aggression, are less liked and more often rejected by their peers, and have greater difficulty adapting their behavior to the demands of social situations. Similarly, in class, they are more disruptive and engage in more negative and socially inappropriate interactions with their teachers (Campbell, Endman, & Bernfeld, 1977; Campbell, Schlerfer, Weiss, & Perlman, 1977; Klein & Young, 1979). The basis for these maladaptive social interactions remains unclear. One study (Paulauskas & Campbell, 1979) showed no difference between hyperactive and control boys in social perspective-taking skills, although another (Whalen et al., 1979; Whalen, Henker, Datemato, & Vaux, 1981) had findings suggesting that hyperkinetic children were less efficient in their use of social communication. Other results (King & Young, 1981) suggest that hyperactive boys may have referential communication skills, although they seem unable to use them efficiently in all settings. The social problems appear generally similar to those associated with conduct disturbance and with learning disabilities (Bryan & Bryan, 1981; Serafica & Harway, 1979) and it is not known whether the social difficulties associated with hyperkinesis are in any way distinctive.

Attention

The extensive literature on attentional deficits in hyperkinetic children has been reviewed by Rosenthal and Allen (1978), Douglas and Peters (1979), and Douglas (in press). Of course, it is not surprising that attentional problems have been found because these form part of the definition of the syndrome. Instead, the interest lies in the particular pattern of attentional difficulties associated with the syndrome, whether the difficulties stem from production or mediation deficiencies, cognitive or motivational problems, and whether they are of a kind that are different from those found in other psychiatric syndromes. There are many findings related to the first of these issues, few as to the second, and scarcely any as to the third.

Although distractibility is included in most sets of defining criteria for the syndrome, the experimental evidence is reasonably consistent in showing that hyperkinetic children are not more disrupted in their behavior than are normal children by extraneous stimuli, provided that the intrinsic and extraneous stimuli are of equal interest (Douglas, in press; Douglas & Peters, 1979). However, all studies have found that hyperkinetic children rapidly lose interest in dull routine tasks, and it appears that they are prone to give attention to appealing distractors (Radosh & Gittelman, 1981; Rosenthal & Allen, 1980); they may also be poor at inhibiting responses to irrelevant stimuli (Douglas, in press).

Many studies have assessed children's performance on boring repetitive tasks requiring persistent vigilance in responding to some stimuli but not to others. The results show that hyperactive children more often fail to respond to correct stimuli, more often respond wrongly to incorrect stimuli, make more inappropriate responses, and show a slower reaction time (Douglas, in press; Douglas & Peters, 1979; Rosenthal & Allen, 1978). Whether these deficits are due to attentional, motivational, or impulsivity problems is not clear. It seems that the difficulties do not lie in failures in discrimination (Sykes, Douglas, & Morgenstern, 1973) and that they are reduced (but not eliminated) by the use of appropriate contingent rewards and punishments (Douglas, in press). On the other hand, noncontingent rewards have been found to increase inappropriate impulsive behavior (Douglas, in press; Douglas & Peters, 1979).

Investigations assessing perceptual- and logical-search strategies, as on the Matching Familiar Figures Test, have given rise to a similar picture (Douglas & Peters, 1979). Hyperkinetic children make more errors and make less efficient use of their looking time. They may be more impulsive, in that they seem to choose their answers hastily without thought, but, equally, they may be slower in that they waste more time looking around the room. However, it is not just off-task behavior that detracts from their performance, they also seem to notice or retain even less during the time they appear to be on-task.

Hypotheses concerning the role of psychophysiological processes have postulated underarousal (Satterfield & Dawson, 1971), overarousal (Zahn, Little, & Wender, 1978), and also poorly modulated arousal (Satterfield, Atoian, Brashears, Burleigh, & Dawson, 1974). In fact, different studies have reported all three conditions, although many investigations have found no consistent differences between hyperactive children and normal controls (see reviews by Hastings & Barkley, 1978; Ferguson & Pappas, 1979; Rosenthal & Allen, 1978). There are many difficulties in interpreting the inconsistent and contradictory findings, including differences in case definition, in the measures of arousal employed, and in test conditions. However, the weight of evidence is certainly against the notion of generally increased physiological arousal. Instead, it suggests that some hyperkinetic children may be characterized by cortical underarousal, particularly under conditions requiring attention and vigilance. Perhaps, it may be more appropriate to conclude that hyperactive children are less able than other children to maintain an optimal state of arousal, sometimes they are not sufficiently alert to the demands of a dull task and sometimes too excited to perform effectively (Douglas, in press).

In summary, the main phenomena associated with hyperactivity are: a vulnerability to reward-associated distractors, a failure to invest attention and effort in nonrewarding situations, a failure to modulate arousal levels in keeping with task demands, and impulsive behavior (Douglas, in press). In view of the rather diverse groups of children studied and the fact that many of the subjects had conduct disturbances and learning difficulties as well as hyperactivity, it would be premature to conclude that these (or any other) attentional deficits underlie overactivity. Nor can the findings serve to validate the syndrome; that would require comparisons with other disorders, a research strategy that has been rarely employed. However, the research has done much to increase our understanding of the complex set of behaviors involved in the general concept of attention and has pointed to the need to delineate further the ways in which abnormalities of attention may be associated with disturbances in social interactions in task-oriented behavior.

Course and Development

Gross motor activity, as measured by crossing lines between quadrants in a playroom or by parent ratings, decreases systematically between the ages of 3 and 9 years (Routh, Schroeder, & O'Tuama, 1974). Sustained attention and motor inhibition increase over the same age period (Levy, 1980). The main change with age is not in intensity of concentration (which may be considerable in young children) but rather an increase in the use of systematic logical strategies of exploration, in the ability to be flexible and selective in the approach to information, and in the power to maintain responsiveness for long periods (E. Taylor, 1980b). In some respects, hyperkinetic children resemble younger normal children (Routh & Schroeder, 1976); both show a decline in activity level with age (Abikoff et al., 1977). In preschool children, hyperactivity is associated with a lower IQ and some years later it is associated with clumsiness (Halverson & Waldrop, 1976). Thus, it appears that, in part, overactivity is a feature of developmental retardation.

However, there are marked individual differences in activity level that are not explicable in terms of developmental variations and which show substantial temporal stability from age 3 to 7 years, with correlations in the .2 to .6 range (Buss et al., 1980; Halverson & Waldrop, 1976). Follow-up studies of clinic samples or of deviant groups in the general population show similar consistency over time (Campbell, Endman, & Bernfeld, 1977; Campbell, Schleifer, Weiss, & Perlman, 1977; Richman et al., 1982). Moreover, the presence of overactive behavior in children with a more generalized disturbance has been found to be associated with a worse outcome in both early childhood (Richman et al., 1982) and adolescence (Nylander, 1979; Schachar et al., 1981; Sundby & Kreyberg, 1968).

Longitudinal or follow-up studies into middle childhood and early adolescence of children diagnosed as having hyperkinetic disorders show that difficulties tend to persist, with continuing behavioral and academic problems, although overactivity as such usually diminishes (Hoy, Weiss, Minde, & Cohen, 1978; Huessy & Cohen, 1976; Minde et al., 1971; Minde, Hackett, Killoa, & Silver, 1972; Riddle & Rapoport, 1976; Schachar et al., 1981; Weiss,

Minde, Werry, Douglas, & Nemeth, 1971). Attentional deficits and scholastic difficulties appear particularly prominent, but depressive affect is also relatively common. All these findings apply most markedly to hyperkinesis that is pervasive across settings (Schachar et al., 1981) and persistent over time during earlier childhood (Howell & Huessy, 1982; Huessy & Cohen, 1976).

There have been several long-term studies in which hyperactive children have been followed into adult life (reviewed by Helper, 1980; Milich & Loney, 1979; G. Weiss, in press). The most systematic and detailed is one undertaken by the Montreal group in which hyperactive subjects were first seen at 6 to 12 years of age and were reevaluated at ages 17 to 24 years and compared with controls matched for age, sex, IQ, and social class (Weiss, in press; Weiss, Hechtman, & Perlman, 1978; Weiss, Hechtman, Perlman, Hopkins, & Wener, 1979). Few hyperactive individuals were grossly disturbed at follow-up but, when compared with controls, their academic record was worse, more were delinquent, more showed impulsive and immature/dependent traits on psychiatric assessment, and more were lacking in self-esteem. No individual in either group became psychotic, although two hyperactives were diagnosed as borderline psychotic.

The Huessy study (Howell & Huessy, 1982; Huessy & Cohen, 1976) has the advantage that it was based on a survey of a total school population first studied in second grade. Compared with their peers, the individuals with hyperactive/attention deficit problems often associated with conduct disturbance (13% of the overall sample) differed in being less likely to continue in education beyond high school, more likely to be suspended from high school, more likely to have been arrested, and more likely to smoke marijuana daily. The follow-up by Loney and her colleagues (Loney, Kramer, & Milich, 1981; Loney, Whaley-Klahn, Kosier, & Conboy, 1981), although less satisfactory in its initial definition of groups, has the asset of comparing hyperkinetic boys with their nonhyperkinetic brothers. In the relatively small sample (22 pairs) followed to 21 years so far, twice as many (45% vs. 18%) of the hyperkinetic group met the criteria for antisocial personality, but there were many similarities in outcome. The best predictors of a poor outcome were low IQ, family pathology, and childhood aggression. Hyperactivity on its own was not a good predictor, but the measures of hyperactivity in childhood were weak and children with both hyperactivity and aggression did particularly poorly. In contrast, Schachar et al. (1981) found that pervasive

hyperactivity was an important predictor of persistence of behavioral disturbance, more so than a disorder of conduct or poor peer relations were in the absence of hyperactivity.

The one study with a rather different set of findings is that by Menkes, Rowe, & Menkes (1967), which showed that 4 of 18 hyperactive individuals became psychotic in adult life. The sample differed, in that many of them showed cognitive and neurodevelopmental problems. Controlled comparisons are lacking, but it may well be that the outcome is rather different when hyperactivity is associated with brain damage or serious deficits.

In summary, pervasive hyperactivity in early childhood shows a moderate temporal stability over periods of several years, in spite of a general tendency for activity levels to diminish and for attentional skills to increase as children grow older. Children with attention deficit/hyperactivity disorders tend to show persistent academic, social, and conduct problems that persist into at least early adult life. However, there is substantial individual variation in the course of the disorder, with family psychopathology, low IQ, and the combination of pervasive overactivity and conduct disturbance the most important predictors of a poor outcome. Children of normal intelligence from well-functioning families with overactivity/inattention but not aggression or conduct disturbance are quite likely to be functioning well during adolescence. So far, the follow-up findings do not validate the concept of a hyperkinetic syndrome that is separate from unsocialized disorders of conduct.

Genetic Factors

Twin studies (Scarr, 1966; Torgersen, 1981; Willerman, 1973) have shown a substantially greater concordance for activity level (usually assessed by parental interviews on questionnaires) within MZ pairs than within DZ pairs—suggesting a hereditary component to activity as a temperamental variable. Torgersen's (1981) data from her longitudinal study also indicate that the genetic components for activity, attention span, and intensity of mood were considerably stronger at 6 years than they had been in infancy. However, it is dubious whether these findings have relevance for the attention deficit syndrome because the twin data concern children's behavior at home rather than in the classroom (see *Measurement of Hyperactivity*).

Nevertheless, family-history data suggest that there may be a hereditary component to the syndrome as well. Safer (1973), for example, in a study of fostered children with MBD found that 50% of full siblings but only 14% of half siblings had histories suggestive of the same disorder. Similarly, in their analysis of the Collaborative Perinatal Project data, Nichols and Chen (1981) found a significantly increased risk for the siblings of children with severe overactivity; the risk for cousins was also in line with a genetic interpretation of the familial associations. However, the two key studies are those by Cantwell (1974) and Morrison and Stewart (1973), both of which showed an increase in hyperactivity, alcoholism, sociopathy, and hysteria in the biological, but not in the adoptive, parents of children with the hyperkinetic syndrome (as rather broadly defined). The data are suggestive of a genetic component, but they are inconclusive in the absence of information on the biological parents of adopted hyperkinetic children and on the adoptive parents of non-hyperkinetic children. The point is that the biological/adoptive difference could be an artifact resulting from the customary screening of adoptive parents to rule out those with mental disorders. Studies of adopted children (Bohman & Sigvardsson, 1980; Cunningham, Cadoret, Loftus, & Edwards, 1975) are inconclusive in their genetic implications, probably because of the unsatisfactory measures of hyperactivity/inattention used.

Taken as a whole, the evidence points to the probability, but not certainty, that genetic factors are of *some* importance. In itself, that is not very informative, in that hereditary influences are of some relevance for most human attributes. The key questions concern *what* is inherited, the mode of inheritance, and, especially, whether the genetic factors are different from those in other psychiatric syndromes. Wender (1971, 1978) has argued that the genetic data suggest that the attention deficit syndrome constitutes a distinct clinical entity, but the empirical findings do not support that claim. The family-history findings may differentiate broadly defined hyperkinetic disorders from schizophrenia and emotional disorders, as found by Morrison (1980) in a nonblind study. But the results of the investigations by Langhorne and Loney (1979) and by Stewart, DeBlois, and Cummings (1980) show that the links with parental alcoholism and sociopathy apply more strongly to conduct disturbances than to hyperkinetic syndromes when the two conditions are separated.

Environmental Factors

Because the prevailing view has been that the attention deficit/hyperkinetic disorder is a constitu-

tionally determined disorder, there has been little research into environmental factors. Nevertheless, there are some data suggesting that they may sometimes be contributory factors. Thus, both Tizard and Hodges (1978) and Dixon (1982) have shown that overactivity and inattention are particularly common in children reared from infancy in institutions, the rates of these behaviors being well above those in controls as well as above those in children from similar backgrounds fostered in ordinary families. The findings suggest that probably the institutional upbringing caused the overactive/inattentive behavior, but the data are not such as to allow any determination of whether the behavioral pattern meets the criteria for the syndrome. Rutter et al. (1979) showed that school variables were associated with the extent of inattentive, disruptive, off-task behavior in the classroom, but the data did not differentiate attentional deficits from socially disapproved behavior as a whole. Sandberg et al. (1980) noted an association between maternal depression and hyperactivity plus conduct disturbance in the children. Their data do not indicate whether this represents a causal relationship nor whether the link is with hyperactivity rather than with aggression.

Battle and Lacey (1972), using the Fels Longitudinal Study data, found that the mothers of hyperactive boys tended to be critical, disapproving, punitive, and lacking in affection. On these grounds, it was argued that parental responses were likely to exacerbate their sons' difficulties; this pattern did not hold for girls. Buss's (1981) observational data also showed that the parents of highly active children were more likely to intrude physically and to get into power struggles with their children. Cunningham and Barkley (1979) found that the mothers of hyperactive children were more likely than the mothers of normal children to ignore or respond negatively to their children's social overtures. However, none of these data indicate whether mother or child was the primary influencing agent.

Barkley (1981) has used stimulant drugs to investigate the direction of causal influences; this strategy is possible because it has been shown repeatedly that these drugs improve children's attention and reduce their overactivity. Using a double-blind, drug-placebo crossover design he observed (in free-play and task situations) the effects on mother-child interaction. The results showed that methylphenidate administration resulted in greater child compliance and less off-task behavior; this was accompanied by a reduction in the mothers' directive behavior and an increase in the mothers' positive attention to their children's compliance. The same effects were observed in a study of two hyperactive identical twins. Both sets of findings indicate that, at least in part, the mothers' behavior is responsive to that of their children.

Maccoby and Jacklin (in press) used a longitudinal design with observational measures when the infants were 12 and 18 months of age to examine the same issue. They found that when the mothers exerted considerable pressure on their sons to perform desired tasks at 12 months, the boys were less difficult (a temperamental measure based on diaries and questionnaires) at 18 months—a change that still held after partialling out the children's initial level of difficultness. However, the findings also showed that the mothers of boys who were difficult at 12 months tended to reduce their pressure by 18 months. The suggestion is of an escalating cycle in which difficult children create an interpersonal environment that serves to exacerbate their difficult temperament.

The findings are too sparse for firm conclusions, but it appears that the possibility that reciprocal influences operate between parents and their hyperkinetic children warrants further study.

Biological Validation of the Syndrome

As both Dubey (1976) and Ferguson and Rapoport (in press) point out in their systematic reviews of the topic, there are two separate issues involved in the possible biological validation of the hyperkinetic/attentional deficit syndrome: (1) whether there are any biological correlates and (2) whether there is specificity to any of the associations. The two issues are most conveniently considered together according to each of the various biological features that have been suggested as characteristic of the syndrome.

Drug Response

Almost all proponents of the biological uniqueness of the syndrome have pointed to the response to stimulant medication as one of the most consistent and distinctive defining features (Gross & Wilson, 1974; Wender, 1978; Wender, Reimherr, & Wood, 1981).

However, it seems that these claims are not supported by the empirical evidence. Several different points need to be considered. First, there is the question of whether hyperkinetic children respond favorably to stimulant medication. The answer from a host of well-controlled studies is that they do, at least in the short term (Barkley, 1977; Conners & Werry, 1979; Rapoport, in press; Sroufe, 1975). Attention

tends to be improved, impulsivity reduced, and overactivity diminished. Second, there is the question of whether stimulants affect the biological basis of the disorder rather than just provide symptomatic relief. This possibility is difficult to test adequately and the findings are inconclusive. Although improvement may continue over 1 or 2 years with a multimodality approach to treatment that includes the use of stimulants (Satterfield, Cantwell, & Satterfield, 1979; Satterfield, Satterfield, & Cantwell, 1981), many children continue to progress when stimulants are discontinued (Charles, Schain, & Guthrie, 1979; Sleator, von Neuman, & Sprague, 1974). Moreover, long-term follow-ups have shown no difference in outcome according to whether or not children continue on drugs (Blouin, Bornstein, & Trites, 1978; Charles & Schain, 1981; Weiss, Kruger, Danielson, & Ellman, 1975). However, none of these results are based on random allocation of children to long-term treatment.

A third issue is whether all the various drugs that are effective in the treatment of the hyperkinetic syndrome operate through the same biochemical mechanism (which might be predicted if the drugs provided a fundamental amelioration of the condition). In this connection, the leading hypothesis has been that the drugs act by influencing dopaminergic mechanisms (Shaywitz, Klopper, & Gordon, 1978; Shaywitz & Pearson, 1978; Wender, 1978). However, dopaminergic blocking agents, such as haloperidol or thioridazine, tend to be associated with improvement rather than the expected worsening of behavior (Gittelman-Klein, Klein, Katz, Saraf, & Pollack, 1976; Werry & Aman, 1975). Moreover, in spite of very different pharmacologic actions, it appears that amitriptyline and methylphenidate have somewhat comparable effects on hyperactivity (Rapoport, Quinn, Bradbard, Riddle, & Brooks, 1974; Winsberg, Bialer, Kupietz, & Tobias, 1972; Yepes, Balka, Winsberg, & Bialer, 1977). The drug response does not appear to be associated with changes in autonomic arousal, which constitutes another hypothesized specific mechanism (Barkley & Jackson, 1977). So far, the findings are inconclusive, in part because of the difficulty in determining whether children's responses to different drugs are truly comparable; some drugs could act as symptom suppressors, whereas others could affect underlying processes that are the basis of the disorder. To date, the findings neither substantiate nor rule out a biochemically specific drug response.

A fourth issue is whether the presence of a positive drug response identifies a clinically distinctive group of children. The balance of evidence suggests that it does not (Barkley, 1976), although improvements tend to be most marked in children with pervasive hyperactivity/inattention and least marked in highly anxious children (Langhorne & Loney, 1979; Taylor, in press-a). However, there are inconsistent pointers that a positive drug response may be more likely if there is an immediate effect on paired-associate learning (Swanson, Kinsbourne, Roberts, & Zucker, 1978) and if there are minor congenital anomalies (Ferguson & Trites, 1980), a history of perinatal complications (Loney et al., 1978), or signs of minor neurodevelopmental dysfunction (Satterfield et al., 1974).

The last issue, with respect to the use of drug response as a means of biological validation, is whether or not the nature of the drug response in children with the hyperkinetic/attentional deficit (or MBD) syndrome is qualitatively different from that in other children. It has often been supposed that the action of stimulants in hyperkinetic children is paradoxical because they reduce activity and improve concentration in formal task settings. However, these same actions are also apparent in the response of normal children (Rapoport, Buchsbaum, Zahn, Weingartner, Ludlow, & Mikkelsen, 1978; Rapoport, Buchsbaum, Weingartner, Zahn, Ludlow, Bartico, Mikkelsen, Langer, & Bunney, 1980) or enuretic children (Werry & Aman, 1979) and even normal adults (Rapoport et al., 1980). Moreover, in hyperkinetic children, activity in sports settings is increased by stimulants as it is in normal adults (Porrino, Rapoport, Behar, Ismond, & Bunney, in press). There does seem to be an age difference, in that stimulants are euphoriant in adults, whereas they do not seem to be so (and may even be dysphoriant) in children; however, in this respect, the affective responses of normal children and of hyperkinetic children are probably similar (Rapoport, in press).

In summary, there is much of interest to be learned from studying children's responses to stimulants but, so far, there is no evidence that the drug responses of children with the hyperkinetic/attentional deficit syndrome provide any type of biological validation of the syndrome.

Biochemical Influences

Both Wender (1971, 1978) and Shaywitz, Shaywitz, Cohen, and Young (in press) have argued that circumstantial evidence (from drug studies, analogies to encephalitis, genetic findings, and animal models) strongly suggests that MBD (by which is meant attention deficit disorder) is due to a bio-

chemical abnormality, probably of monoamine metabolism. However, so far the hypothesis has received little empirical support (Ferguson & Pappas, 1979; Rapoport & Ferguson, 1981; Shaywitz et al., 1978; Shaywitz & Pearson, 1978).

Various different approaches have been used in investigating the possibility of serotonin (5HT) dysfunction as the basis of hyperactivity/attentional deficit syndromes. Wender (1969) and Coleman (1971) reported reduced serotonin values in the blood of hyperactive children, but studies by other workers (Ferguson & Pappas, 1979; Goldman, Thibert, & Rourke, 1979; Rapoport et al., 1974) have not confirmed the finding. Moreover, Wender, Epstein, Kopin, and Gordon (1971) found no differences between hyperactive children and controls in the urinary excretion of 5-HIAA (a metabolite of serotonin), and two studies (Shaywitz, Cohen, & Bowers, 1977; Shetly & Chase, 1976) have failed to find any alteration in 5-HIAA in the cerebrospinal fluid of MBD children.

The possibility of an abnormality in catecholamine metabolism has been investigated through the assessment of urinary metabolites with both negative (Wender et al., 1971) and positive (Shekim, Dekirmenjian, & Chapel, 1977) findings. However, urinary metabolite levels did not predict drug response (Shekim, Dekirmenjian, Chapel, Javaid, & Davis, 1979), and the same findings have been found with autistic children (Young, Cohen, Caparulo, Brown, & Maas, 1979). Whatever the significance of the altered levels, it seems that they are not syndrome specific. Cerebrospinal fluid monoamine metabolites have been studied with both amphetamine administration (Shetly & Chase, 1976) and probenecid loading (Shaywitz et al., 1977). The findings were complex and ambiguous in their implications so that, although the results have been interpreted as support for a dopamine hypothesis, there are problems with this interpretation (Ferguson & Pappas, 1979; Shaywitz et al., 1978; Shaywitz & Pearson, 1978).

Several animal models have been used to study possible biochemical factors in MBD, including maturation-linked hyperactivity that is elicited in young rats isolated in an unfamiliar environment (Campbell & Randall, 1975; Campbell & Raskin, 1978), chronic lead ingestion (Goldberg & Silbergeld, 1977), ventral tegmental lesions (Grahame-Smith, 1978), and depletion of brain dopamine through the administration of a neurotoxin (Shaywitz, Yager, & Klopper, 1976; Shaywitz, Shaywitz, Cohen, & Young, in press). However, although hyperactivity can be induced in the rat by these various different means, it is very dubious how far the experimental states mimic the hyperkinetic/attentional deficit syndrome seen in humans and no very helpful conclusions on possible biochemical mechanisms are yet possible (Ferguson & Pappas, 1979; Shaywitz et al., 1978; Shaywitz & Pearson, 1978).

In summary, it would be wrong to conclude that biochemical abnormalities do not constitute the basis of the hyperkinetic syndrome, but it is evident that there is no good evidence as yet to assert that they do, and more importantly, there is no indication of any biochemical feature that is specific to the hyperkinetic syndrome (Dubey, 1976; Ferguson & Pappas, 1979; Rapoport & Ferguson, 1981; Rutter, in press c; Shaywitz et al., 1978; Shaywitz & Pearson, 1978).

Toxins and Allergies

On the basis of uncontrolled clinical studies, Feingold (1975) claimed that the ingestion of artificial food additives and naturally occurring salicylates in foods commonly resulted in hyperactivity and learning disabilities by virtue of a toxic effect. Others (Kittler & Baldwin, 1970) have postulated an allergic mechanism. These hypotheses have been tested through the double-blind assessment of diets, by comparing stimulants with diet, and by challenge studies (see Conners, 1980b; Mattes & Gittelman, 1981; B. Weiss, 1982). The findings show that the great majority of hyperactive/inattentive children do *not* show a consistent response to food additives, although a few individuals do. There has been one study (Swanson & Kinsbourne, 1980) that claimed that the food-additive response was specific to stimulant drug responders, but its data are open to different interpretations and other evidence provides no indication that the infrequently observed adverse reactions to food additives can be predicted on the basis of subject characteristics. The occasional idiosyncratic response to food additives is of toxicological interest, but it throws no light on attention deficit disorders.

During the 1970s, there were also claims that hyperactivity might be caused by fluorescent lighting and by raised lead levels. The first suggestion was negated in a controlled study by O'Leary and his colleagues (O'Leary, Rosenbaum, & Hughes, 1978). The evidence on the second is more contradictory, with some in support and some not (see *Behavioral Effects of Brain Damage in Childhood*).

Minor Congenital Anomalies

Minor congenital anomalies (such as epicanthic folds or low-set ears) have been found to be associated with hyperactivity, inattention, and aggression in boys but not in girls (Bell & Waldrop, 1982). However, the same anomalies also have been associated with socially inhibited behavior, infantile psychosis, speech and hearing difficulties, and learning problems (see *Behavioral Effects of Brain Damage in Childhood*). Within both clinic (Sandberg et al., 1978) and general population samples (Sandberg et al., 1980), it seems that the frequency of minor congenital anomalies is no more strongly associated with inattention/hyperkinesis than with conduct disturbance.

Other Biological Variables

Much the same conclusions apply to other biological variables, such as the presence of perinatal complications, EEG abnormalities, neurological soft signs, and delayed skeletal maturation (see Dubey, 1976; also see Nichols & Chen, 1981; Rie, Rie, Stewart, & Rettemnier, 1978; Sandberg et al., 1978, 1980; Schlager, Newman, Dunn, Chrichton, & Schulzer, 1979). In each case, there are weak and inconsistent associations with hyperkinesis and attentional deficits, but this is true of a wide variety of other developmental and psychiatric disorders. The links are in no way specific and do not provide any biological validation of the syndrome.

In summary, it is evident that a variety of biological factors are sometimes associated with hyperkinetic or attentional deficit disorders, but none of the associations seem specific to the syndrome and, hence, none provides a biological validation of the condition. On the other hand, most of the investigations have been concerned with rather heterogeneous groups of children, thus, it would be premature to reject the possibility that there may be biologically homogeneous subsets within those broad groups. If that possibility is to be adequately examined (as it should be), it is crucial that the methodological advances that are occurring in the study of biological variables be combined with a much more discriminating clinical analysis.

BEHAVIORAL EFFECTS OF BRAIN DAMAGE IN CHILDHOOD

For many years, hyperactivity/inattention was regarded as the prototypical behavioral response to brain injury in childhood; indeed, the terms brain damage syndrome and hyperkinetic syndrome came to be regarded as interchangeable (Birch, 1964; Rie & Rie, 1980; Rutter, in press-c). Because so few hyperkinetic children had any history of brain insult and so few had clinical signs of neurological dysfunction, that view gave way to a concept of minimal brain dysfunction, in which attention deficit syndromes were thought to be due to some genetically determined biochemical abnormality. As discussed earlier, that hypothesis lacks adequate empirical support. However, if brain-behavior relationships are to be understood, it is necessary to analyze the association from both ends. Accordingly, we turn to a consideration of the behavioral sequelae of known brain pathology.

It has long been recognized that brain disease or damage *may* impair intellectual functioning and *may* alter children's social behavior or emotional expression. However, it has proved more difficult to estimate the frequency with which this occurs with different types and degrees of brain pathology. It is equally difficult to determine the extent to which the sequelae are specific or distinctive in any way and to delineate the mechanisms that are involved in the genesis of emotional or social disorders consequent upon brain injury (see reviews by Boll & Barth, 1981; Rie & Rie, 1980; Rutter, in press-c; Shaffer, 1977; Werry, 1979).

The problems in resolving these questions arise from several different sources:

1. There has been the need for systematic, quantified, and objective measures of children's behavior. Unfortunately, much of the literature is comprised of unstandardized clinical observations which are open to a variety of biases; such observations are valuable in giving leads as to which ideas are worth exploring, but they are of no use in testing hypotheses; thus, little reference will be made to them in this chapter.

2. It is evident that psychopathological disorders have many causes, including psychosocial stresses as well as constitutional factors. Hence, the finding that some brain-damaged children show emotional/behavioral problems in no way indicates whether the two are meaningfully linked. Instead, it is essential to compare rates of disorder in brain-damaged groups with the rates in general population samples to determine whether the rates are above base level.

3. Many children with brain injury are also intellectually impaired, physically handicapped, or socially disadvantaged so that the psychological sequelae could stem from the cognitive handicap or the physical crippling or the psychosocial deprivation rather than from the brain lesions per se. Accordingly, comparative studies with the appropriate controls for possibly relevant variables are required.

4. Attention must be paid to the causes of brain injury because they could also constitute the cause of the psychological difficulties. Thus, disruptive children of limited intelligence from a socially disadvantaged background appear particularly prone to suffer road accidents resulting in head injury or to develop lead intoxication and encephalopathy as a result of pica. The need is for longitudinal studies of change following brain injury.

5. It is necessary to search for means by which to test the extent to which the observed statistical associations do or do not represent causal connections rather than noncausal correlates.

Risk of Psychopathological Disorder Following Brain Damage

Although no one study fully meets all these criteria, a reasonable appraisal of the extent to which brain damage increases the risk of emotional or social disorders may be obtained from a consideration of the systematic investigations of children with different forms of brain pathology.

Cerebral Palsy

Total population data for neuroepileptic conditions are available from the Isle of Wight epidemiological survey of school-age children (Rutter, Graham, & Yule, 1970). Children of normal intelligence who had an organic brain condition (in most cases, cerebral palsy) were twice as likely, as those with other physical handicaps (such as asthma, diabetes, or heart disease) to show behavioral deviance—as rated on parent and teacher questionnaires—and twice as likely to exhibit psychiatric disorder—as assessed from a standardized clinical interview of known reliability. The overall pattern of the findings, the fact that the two groups did not differ appreciably in terms of possibly relevant variables other than brain damage, and, especially, the observed association between psychiatric disorder and neurological features *within* the brain-damage group suggested that the increased psychiatric risk stemmed from organic pathology rather than from other factors. The possibility that visible crippling may have accounted for some of the association was eliminated in a further study (Seidel, Chadwick, & Rutter, 1975) using similar measures. In this study, normally intelligent school-age children with organic brain disorders (again, primarily cerebral palsy) were compared with children with handicapping disorders due to lesions below the brainstem (mainly paralyses following poliomyelitis). Psychiatric disorder was twice as frequent in the group whose handicap was attributable to brain damage. As the groups were comparable in other respects, including the presence of visible crippling, it could be inferred that it was likely that the brain damage had played a causal role in the behavioral disorders.

Head Injury

Several studies (reviewed by Rutter, Chadwick, & Shaffer, in press) have shown that children suffering head injuries exhibit higher rates of behavioral deviance than controls, but there are particular difficulties involved in any causal inference from these studies. In the first place, when head injuries are mild, it cannot be assumed that there is any significant brain damage. Second, there is evidence that children experiencing head injuries are more likely than other children to have been behaviorally deviant *prior* to the injury so that their impulsive, excitable, reckless behavior may have led to the accident rather than the reverse. Also, compared with the general population, children experiencing accidents tend more frequently to come from socially disadvantaged families with parental problems of various kinds. Clinical studies suggest that these preinjury behavioral characteristics and adverse family features may account for much of the postaccident psychopathological disorders, at least with respect to milder head injuries.

On the other hand, a prospective longitudinal study of children with head injuries, who were compared with a closely matched control group of children with orthopedic injuries (Rutter, Chadwick, & Shaffer, in press), provided strong evidence that brain damage played a crucial role in the etiology of the emotional/behavioral disorders ensuing after severe (but not after mild) head injuries. In the severe head-injury group, in which the posttraumatic amnesia (PTA) had lasted at least 1 week, the rate of disorder *before* the accident was closely similar to that in the control group; however, 4 months *after* the injury, the rate of disorder had greatly increased and remained well above that of controls during the remaining 2¼-years' follow-up. It is unlikely that these results were an artifact of any type of rating bias because the findings were based on blind ratings of systematic interview protocols by an investigator who was unaware of the group membership of each child. The strong probability that the brain-injury/psychopathological disorder represented a causal association was indicated by: (1) the change in behavior following the head injury in children who had been without disorders prior to the accident, a change that was two to three times as frequent as in the control group; and (2) the finding that the level of psychiatric risk was systematically associated with the severity of brain injury (as reflected in the dura-

tion of PTA). On the other hand, the observations that this association was of only moderate strength and consistency suggested that the effect was often indirect rather than direct and that factors other than brain injury played an important part in etiology.

Epilepsy

The Isle of Wight survey (Rutter et al., 1970) showed that psychopathological disorder as assessed from a standardized clinical interview was several times as frequent in children with uncomplicated epilepsy (i.e., epilepsy that was not part of some other neurological disorder) than in nonepileptic children in the general population. Parent and teacher questionnaires showed a similar increased rate of behavioral deviance. Stores (1978) has confirmed that disorders of behavior (as rated on a teacher questionnaire) are more frequent in epileptic children than in nonepileptic children of the same age and social background. However, unlike the Isle of Wight findings, the difference in that study applied only to boys and not to girls. As discussed by several writers (Bagley, 1971; Rutter et al., 1970; Sillanpaa, 1973), the increased psychiatric risk that accompanies epilepsy is likely to stem from a variety of factors separate from brain pathology, including community prejudice, social rejection, and family difficulties. However, the pattern of findings within groups of epileptic children indicates that organic brain dysfunction probably plays a crucial role. Thus, although the findings have not always been consistent across studies, there is some indication that the psychiatric risks may be greater when the seizures are frequent, when they are of the psychomotor type, or when there is a persistent left temporal spike discharge.

In summary, the research findings strongly indicate that severe brain damage does, indeed, create a substantially increased risk of emotional and behavioral problems. This is demonstrated by the increased risk of disorder that has been associated with the presence of brain injury in all the systematic comparative studies—an increase that is not explicable in terms of other variables; by the change in behavior following severe head injury; and by the pattern of associations between psychopathological disorder and neurological features within groups of children all of whom have some type of organic brain condition. However, this conclusion is well substantiated only in cases where the damage has been fairly severe or where there is active physiological disturbance (as in epilepsy). Although brain damage increases the psychiatric risk, most children with brain damage do not have any psychopathological condition and the majority follow a basically normal course of psychosocial development. Consequently, it is necessary to consider what is different about the types of brain damage or what is different about the children and their circumstances when emotional/behavioral disorders result. However, before turning to that basic issue, we must ask first whether brain pathology results in any specific type of disorder.

Types of Disorder Associated with Brain Damage

Research findings are consistent in showing a lack of specificity between brain damage and the type of psychopathological disorder. Organic brain dysfunction results in an increase in a wide range of behavioral, emotional, and social difficulties of a kind frequently found in children who show no evidence of brain damage or disease. Thus, Stores and his colleagues found that inattentiveness (Stores, Hart, & Piran, 1978), dependency (Stores & Piran, 1978), and anxiety, social isolation, and overactivity (Stores, 1977) were all more prevalent in epileptic children. The same overall nonspecificity of behavioral pattern was evident in the Isle of Wight and north London studies of neuroepileptic children (Rutter et al., 1970; Seidel et al., 1975) and in studies of children with both generalized and localized head injuries (Rutter, Chadwick, & Shaffer, in press). Moreover, the lack of specificity does not seem to be a function of limitations in interview or questionnaire measures as the same negative finding was evident in Shaffer's (Shaffer, McNamara, & Pincus, 1974) study of a clinic sample of children with neurological disorders in which he utilized finer, more objective measures of attention and activity.

However, there are a few minor exceptions to the general finding of lack of specificity to behavioral sequelae. Hyperactivity (Rutter et al., 1970; Schulman et al., 1965), distractibility (Schulman et al., 1965), perseveration (Chess, 1972), and social disinhibition (Rutter, Chadwick, & Shaffer, in press) have been found to be more characteristic of brain-damaged children than neurologically intact controls within samples of children with psychopathological disorders. Nevertheless, all these behaviors occur in only a minority of brain-damaged children, and the symptoms cannot be regarded as pathognomonic.

There may be a slight tendency for disorders attributable to brain injury to be more persistent than those in children without brain damage, but the differences found have been quite minor (Minde, 1978; Rutter, Chadwick, & Shaffer, in press). Almost nothing is known about the long-term outcome of

psychopathological disorders that arise as a result of brain damage in childhood. In particular, data are lacking on the extent to which such disorders lead to mental illness in adult life. Lindsay, Ounsted, and Richards (1979) have reported one of the few long-term follow-up studies. The findings apply, however, to a rather specialized group of hospitalized children with temporal lobe epilepsy often accompanied by low IQ (Ounsted, Lindsay, & Norman, 1966). Within this group (there were no controls), the rate of adult psychiatric disorder (30%) was strikingly lower than that found in the same individuals during childhood (85%). But, the course was influenced by the form of the childhood psychiatric condition, in that both severe hyperactivity and catastrophic rage were prognostic of a subsequent poor psychiatric and social outcome. A disordered home in childhood did not predict adult mental disorder, possibly suggesting that environmental variables were less important than brain damage (in this group with severe biological impairment); however, the environmental assessments were too limited in scope for substantial weight to be attached to that suggestion. Schizophrenialike psychoses developed in 10% of the sample and, in keeping with other evidence (D. Taylor, 1975), this outcome was particularly associated with an EEG focus in the left cerebral hemisphere.

In a 4- to 12-year follow-up study of 177 children who were 8 to 12 years old when originally seen at a clinic for learning difficulties, Peter and Spreen (1979) found that behavioral outcome was worse—according to parental accounts but not self-reports—for those with a definite neurological condition; this was so even after the effects of age, sex, and intelligence had been taken into account. Unfortunately, there were no data on the extent to which the groups differed behaviorally when first seen in middle childhood. The findings suggest that behavioral and emotional difficulties in brain-damaged children may persist into adult life, but they do not indicate whether the long-term prognosis is better or worse than for brain-damaged children with similar disorders.

Mediating Variables

Several rather different types of mediating variable may operate in the genesis of psychopathological disorders following brain pathology; these include neurological features, factors in the child, and environmental variables.

Severity of Brain Damage

As already noted, the severity of brain damage seems of some importance insofar as mild brain injuries do not appear to carry any substantial increase in psychopathological risk. On the other hand, within the range of damage that does result in an increased rate of psychiatric disorder, there is only a moderate and somewhat inconsistent association between the level of psychiatric risk and the extent of brain damage (as assessed by such variables as duration of PTA or coma following injury, whether the brain lesion is unilateral or bilateral, and by clinical signs of neurological abnormality) (Rutter, Chadwick, & Shaffer, in press; Rutter et al., 1970). In sharp contrast, these same measures of the severity of brain injury are strongly associated with the intensity of cognitive sequelae. It is clear that the severity of brain injury has a stronger and more consistent relationship with intellectual impairment than with behavioral disturbance.

Locus of Brain Injury

Less evidence is available on the possible relevance of the locus of brain injury for psychopathological sequelae. The lack of data is a consequence of the fact that rather few brain disorders in childhood result in strictly localized (or even strictly lateralized) lesions and of the inadequacy of the available neurological tools for accurately determining the site of pathology. However, the possible effects of locus constituted the major objective of Shaffer's study (Shaffer, Chadwick, & Rutter, 1975; Shaffer, Bijur, Chadwick, & Rutter, 1982; Shaffer, O'Conner, Shafer, & Prupis, in press) of 98 children with a localized cortical lesion caused by a unilateral compound depressed fracture of the skull with an associated dural tear in which gross damage to the underlying brain substance had been confirmed at operation. No association was found between the locus of injury and either the rate of psychiatric disorder or the degree or type of intellectual impairment (Chadwick, Rutter, Brown, Shaffer, & Traub, 1981). Apart from a suggestion that right frontal damage might be particularly associated with depressive symptoms (as found in adults by Lishman, 1968), little association was found between side of injury or locus of damage and type of symptomatology. However, because the temporal lobe tends to be relatively protected from external injuries, there were few cases of temporal lobe damage and no conclusions were possible regarding the effects of damage to that part of the brain.

The evidence from studies using EEG foci also does not suggest that there is any strong or consistent association between locus and type of symptomatology, although there may be some effect. Ritvo, Yuwiler, Geller, Ornitz, Saeger, and Plotkin (1970) in an investigation of the relationship between psy-

chiatric diagnosis and EEG findings in a double-blind study of 184 hospitalized children found no association. Neither did Waldo, Cohen, Caparulo, Young, Prichard, and Shaywitz (1978) in another clinic study, although they found a weak association between psychiatric diagnosis and other aspects of the EEG profile. On the other hand, in both studies there were too few children with a consistent EEG focus for much weight to be attached to the negative findings on focal abnormalities. Follow-up studies (e.g., Trojaborg, 1968) have shown the very high frequency with which EEG foci change their site and even the hemisphere; other studies (Kaufman, Harris, & Shaffer, 1980) have indicated the frequency with which there are multiple foci or a mixed EEG pattern so that no firm conclusions, positive or negative, are possible from investigations (such as that by Ritvo et al., 1970) that rely on single EEG measures. This criticism also applies to Nuffield's (1961) study of children attending a psychiatric clinic which showed an association between temporal lobe spikes and aggression. Stores' studies (Stores, 1978; Stores, Hart, & Piran, 1978; Stores & Piran, 1978), however, are not open to that objection, in that they were confined to children with a focus that persisted over repeated EEGs (although the criteria for a persistent focus were not as explicit as might be considered desirable). The numbers of children investigated were necessarily small, but it was found that a left temporal spike discharge was associated with a significantly higher rate of emotional and behavioral deviance, although not with any specific pattern of deviance. The finding is consistent with Aird and Yamamoto's (1966) observation that temporal lobe foci are those most strongly associated with psychopathological disorder (although, again, not with any specific type of disorder) and, perhaps, with the evidence that psychomotor seizures are those most likely to be associated with emotional/behavioral disturbance (Rutter et al., 1970). However, it should be appreciated that there are only rather modest associations between type of seizure and site of EEG focus and between both of these and locus of brain lesion.

Neither pneumoencephalographic findings (Aarkrog, 1968; Boeson & Aarkrog, 1967; Hauser et al., 1975) nor the results of computerized axial tomographic (CAT) brain scans (Caparulo et al., 1981) have shown links between the site of brain lesion and the type of mental disorder in childhood, although there has been a tendency for left-hemispheric abnormalities to be more often associated with psychopathologic disorder. The significance of this observation remains rather uncertain in the absence of adequate quantification of abnormalities and, especially, the lack of good data on pneumoencephalographic or CAT scan on normal children.

In adults, there is quite good evidence that seizures associated with a left-sided focus are those most likely to predispose to schizophrenialike psychoses (D. Taylor, 1975), and there is some evidence from studies of penetrating head injuries (Lishman, 1968, 1973) that affective disorders are most frequent after right-hemispheric lesions, particularly if these involve the frontal lobe. Other more indirect evidence (Flor-Henry, 1979; Wexler, 1980) generally supports the suggestion that right- and left-hemispheric lesions in adults have somewhat different psychiatric consequences. It remains uncertain whether such relationships also apply to children.

Left- and right-hemispheric lesions have different cognitive sequelae in adults, but it seems that they may not do so in childhood. Truly valid comparisons between children and adults are extremely problematic because the types of brain lesions tend to be different in different age groups (St. James-Roberts, 1979). Nevertheless, although, as in adults, there is a tendency for right-hemispheric lesions to be associated with impairment on visuospatial tasks and (to a lesser extent) left-hemispheric lesions to be accompanied by verbal deficits, the effects of site and laterality of lesion are probably less consistent and less marked in children than in adults (Boll & Barth, 1981; Chadwick et al., 1981).

Type of Brain Pathology

Although the differences in individual studies have not always reached statistical significance, there has been a general tendency for psychiatric disorders to be more frequent when brain lesions have been accompanied by active physiological disturbance (indicated by the occurrence of epileptic seizures) than when there has been just a loss of function (Rutter et al., 1970). Thus, in the Isle of Wight study (Rutter et al., 1970) the highest rate of disorder was found in children with structural disorders of the brain accompanied by seizures. Similarly, in Shaffer's localized head-injury study (Shaffer et al., 1975), disorder was most frequent among children with a late onset of seizures following the trauma. In adults, too, psychiatric disability is more likely to follow head injury when epileptic seizures occur (Lishman, 1968). Studies of temporal lobectomy in adults show a close relationship between a reduction in the number of fits and a decrease in aggressive behavior. In childhood, a similar phenomenon may be evident in the improvements in behavior and cognition that sometimes follow hemispherectomy for severe seizure disorders in hemiplegic children with grossly abnormal EEGs (Griffith & Davidson, 1966; Kohn & Dennis, 1974). Although the evidence is fragmentary and inconclusive, the available data suggest the likelihood that the behavioral consequences of abnormal brain function may often be greater than those of loss of brain function.

On the whole, in spite of a variety of widely held stereotypes for which there is only limited empirical support (e.g., that children with Down's syndrome are friendly and unaggressive and that hydrocephalic children are verbose and superficial), there is little indication that the particular type of medical condition associated with brain pathology has very specific behavioral consequences (Graham, in press; Rutter, 1971b).

But that conclusion should not be held to mean that there are no specific brain-behavior relationships and certainly not to mean that there are no mental disorders of a characteristically different type that have an organic basis (Rutter, in press-c). Autism constitutes the most obvious example of just such a condition (see *Infantile Autism*). The Lesch-Nyhan syndrome, an X-linked brain disorder associated with the overproduction of uric acid and dysfunction of brain neurotransmitters (Lloyd, Hornykiewicz, Davidson, Shannak, Garley, Goldstein, Shibuya, Kelley, & Fox, 1981) constitutes another. It is behaviorally quite distinctive in terms of a most unusual compulsive form of self-mutilation (Nyhan, 1976). This begins when teeth first erupt and characteristically it leads to loss of tissue about the lips and partial autoamputation of the fingers. The mechanisms remain ill understood; although the behavior is to some extent under environmental control (Anderson, Dancis, & Alpert, 1978), it does appear to represent a rather specific association between a medical condition and a particular form of behavior. Whether this is due to the type of brain lesion or to the abnormal circulating metabolites is not known. The Prader-Willi syndrome, a condition associated with deletion of chromosome 15 (Ledbetter, Riccardi, Airhart, Stickol, Keenan, & Crawford, 1981), may constitute another example of a specific brain-behavior association in terms of the occurrence of an unusually voracious appetite and consequent severe obesity.

The lesson is that if we are to make progress in elucidating specific brain-behavior relationships, we must approach the matter from both ends. That is, there is a need for research that has as its starting point established brain pathology of some kind. Equally, there is a need to study the processes underlying specific psychopathological disorders when it seems likely that they are due to some form of organic brain dysfunction.

Age at Injury

There are several good reasons for supposing that the behavioral sequelae of brain damage might vary according to the age of the child at the time of injury. The brain undergoes marked developmental changes during the infancy period (Ebels, 1980), and early animal studies have suggested that there is a general tendency for a greater sparing of function following lesions early in life. Human research, too, has shown that left-hemispheric damage in infancy is less likely to lead to permanent language impairment than similar damage occurring in later childhood or adult life (Lenneberg, 1967; Rutter et al., 1970). Accordingly, it came to be thought that the developing brain has greater plasticity than the mature brain (Chelune & Edwards, 1981). However, recent reviews of the evidence have included scathing attacks on both the hypothesis of better recovery with earlier brain lesions and the concept of plasticity (St. James-Roberts, 1979; Satz & Fletcher, 1981). Moreover, studies of children with head injuries have shown no marked age effects with respect to either the frequency or severity of cognitive or behavioral sequelae (Rutter, Chadwick, & Shaffer, in press).

Nevertheless, it would be wrong to suppose from these negative findings that developmental considerations are of no importance and that brain lesions have similar effects at all ages. There is evidence of age effects, but there can be no simple summary statement that brain lesions in early life have greater or lesser effects than similar lesions at an older age because age influences different brain mechanisms in different ways (Rutter, in press-c). In some respects, early damage is more serious in its consequences, but in others it is less so. To begin with, it appears that the effects of meningoencephalitis and therapeutic irradiation of the brain tend to be more damaging in early infancy than in later childhood. In part, at least, this reflects the general principle that immature organs are more susceptible to injury than mature ones and that organs tend to be most susceptible at the time of their most rapid growth (Dobbing, 1974). In the case of the brain, this embraces the prenatal period and the first 2 years or so after birth.

Second, there is evidence that the immature brain shows greater potential for interhemispheric transfer or take-up of functions so that it is more readily possible for the right hemisphere to take over language functions and, to a lesser extent, for the left hemisphere to take over visuospatial functions if the other hemisphere is damaged (Witelson, 1977). The phenomena are important and well demonstrated. Nevertheless, it is clear that they reflect many rather different mechanisms, some of which have little to do with plasticity (Geschwind, 1974; P. S. Goldman, 1974). The evidence mainly applies to interhemispheric effects and not to transfer of functions within one hemisphere. The extent of sparing varies with the site of lesion and with the specific function being examined (Nonneman & Isaacson, 1973; Teuber & Rudel, 1962); frequently, functional recovery is incomplete and achieved at some cost (Witelson, 1977). Although empirical data are lacking, it may well be that infants are just as vulnerable as older children to bilateral brain damage.

Third, lesions that are present in early life, at a stage when brain development is still occurring, however, may result in compensatory new growth of axons so that it may be supposed that the earlier the lesion, the greater the neural reorganization that is likely to occur (Lynch & Gall, 1979; Schneider, 1979; van Hof, 1981). But this regrowth and reorganization may be maladaptive as well as restorative in its effects (Schneider, 1979). Perhaps this is the explanation for the observation that late seizures are *more* frequent following head injury in infants than in older children, even though early seizures are *less* frequent (Black, Shepard, & Walker, 1975).

A fourth, and rather different, consideration is that insofar as brain damage impairs new learning (as first suggested by Hebb, 1942), it is likely to have greater practical effects in young children simply because they have more new learning (of cognitive and social skills) to accomplish, less accumulated knowledge, and less well-established patterns of adaptive behavior on which to rely.

Finally, in this connection, theoretical considerations would lead one to expect the greatest effects of age in modifying individual responses to brain injury to be apparent between infancy and later childhood or adult life rather than within the middle years of childhood, which is the period examined in most of the studies.

In summary, it would be premature to conclude that the child's age at the time of brain injury is of no consequence with respect to the type or frequency of emotional or social sequelae. There are too few empirical findings from which to draw firm conclusions, but it is also likely that the apparent lack of age effects is a result of age affecting different brain processes in opposite ways.

Individual Differences

Little evidence is available on the extent to which the children's characteristics prior to brain injury modify their response. However, in our prospective study of children with severe head injuries, we found that the children's preaccident behavior was important (Rutter, Chadwick, & Shaffer, in press). Within the group without preexisting psychiatric disorder, those with mild emotional or behavioral difficulties before their head injury were more likely to develop new or increased psychopathological problems during the following year than were those without any such difficulties.

In the general population, psychiatric disorder is more frequent among boys than girls (Rutter et al., 1970/1981), but this has not been found to be the case in several series of brain-damaged or epileptic children with psychopathological disturbances (Holdsworth & Whitmore, 1974; Rutter, Chadwick, & Shaffer, in press; Shaffer et al., 1975). The findings of all four studies cited suggest that brain damage may remove girls' relative invulnerability to psychopathological disorder, although why this occurs (if it does) remains obscure. On the other hand, Stores (1978) found that the behavioral difference between epileptic children and controls largely applied to boys rather than girls, a finding that runs counter to the other studies cited. The explanation for the contradictory results is not apparent.

Most studies have found that, to some extent, children with a lower IQ or with a lower level of educational attainment are more likely to develop emotional or social problems following brain damage (Rutter et al., 1970; Seidel et al., 1975; Shaffer et al., 1975). The implication is that one of the ways in which brain damage increases psychiatric risk is through its role in causing intellectual impairment which, in turn, predisposes to psychopathological disturbance—perhaps because it is associated with a limitation in problem-solving strategies.

Psychosocial Variables

All investigations that have examined the matter have been consistent in showing the importance of psychosocial variables in the genesis of psychopathological disturbances within brain-damaged groups. Thus, such disturbances are more likely to develop in brain-damaged or epileptic children from a broken or overcrowded home, whose mothers have emotional difficulties, or who are brought up in a discordant and quarrelsome family (Rutter, Chadwick, & Shaffer, in press; Rutter et al., 1970; Seidel et al., 1975; Shaffer et al., 1975). It is well demonstrated that, even in the presence of brain damage, psychosocial factors continue to play an important role in the genesis of emotional and social disorders.

Studies of children with a variety of chronic handicapping conditions have shown the personal adaptations that must be made by the disabled individual, and they have indicated how parent-child relationships and the style of family interaction may be influenced by the existence of a severe physical handicap and by the meaning and implications that it has for the child and the family (Barker, Wright, Myerson, & Gonick, 1953; Cummings, Bayley, & Rie, 1966; Dorner, 1976; Hewett, Newson, & Newson, 1970; Kogan, Tyler, & Turner, 1974; Minde, 1978; Minde et al., 1972; Pless & Pinkerton, 1975; B. A. Wright, 1960). Most investigations have been descriptive rather than comparative, and, hence, there is a lack of quantification of the relative importance of different factors in aiding or impeding children's adjustment. It appears that such factors include difficulties in coming to a realistic appreciation of the child's potential and limitations, the tendency to be overprotective of the child, the isolation that not only stems from attendance at a special school that prevents friendships with normal peers but also avoids competition with them, the effects of disfigurement in reducing social attractiveness, and the conflicts with normal siblings. It seems from interviews with handicapped persons themselves that, perhaps especially during adolescence, many worry and may become depressed over uncertainties regarding their own identity and capacity as a sexual partner and as a future parent. Nonhandicapped persons often report discomfort when interacting with handicapped individuals, and experimental studies with university students (Hastorf, Wildfogel, & Cassman, 1979) suggest that acknowledgment of the handicap by the disabled person may facilitate social interactions. Of course, most of these various factors apply to physical handicaps generally rather than to organic brain conditions specifically. However, these problems of adaptation are among those experienced by brain-damaged children and adolescents.

In summary, there is no doubt that brain damage substantially increases the risks of psychopathological disturbance; moreover, in part, it does so through various neurological mechanisms. But it is equally evident that, usually, the connection between brain damage and emotional/behavioral disorder is rather indirect, with psychosocial and temperamental influences also important. It might be supposed that brain damage would interact with these other variables, with the organic brain dysfunction increasing vulnerability to environmental stresses. However, although there is some suggestion that this may occur in some circumstances, on the whole the effects seem to be additive rather than interactive (Rutter, 1977a).

Concepts of Minimal Brain Dysfunction (MBD)

Quite apart from studies of the psychological sequelae of known brain damage in childhood, there is an extensive literature on hypothesized syndromes of MBD occurring in children who have neither a history of damage to the brain nor abnormal neurological signs (De la Cruz, Fox, & Roberts, 1973; Kalverboer, van Praag, & Mendlewicz, 1978; Bax & MacKeith, 1963; Rie & Rie, 1980; Rutter, in press-c). The term minimal brain dysfunction (MBD) has been used in a variety of ways and many of the concepts have been imprecise and confusing. Nevertheless, it appears that there are two main types of underlying hypotheses that reflect quite different postulates (Rutter, in press-c; Werry, 1979). The first suggests that MBD constitutes a lesser variant of gross traumatic or infective brain damage. Brain damage is thought of in quantitative terms as a relatively unitary continuous variable that produces a characteristic set of deficits.

Pasamanick and Knobloch's (1966) concept of a continuum of reproductive casualty constitutes one of the most cogently argued views of this type. They suggested that the effects of damage to the brain during the prenatal period and the birth process vary according to the severity of the damage, with mental retardation and cerebral palsy at one end of the continuum and learning disorders and behavioral difficulties at the other. The current concerns that subclinical lead intoxication may lead to impaired intelligence and hyperactive behavior in the absence of overt encephalopathy (Needleman, 1980; Rutter & Russell Jones, 1983) constitute an extension of that concept from prenatal and perinatal hazards to postnatal toxins.

The second type of concept of MBD is quite different in suggesting a discontinuity between MBD and overt brain disease or damage. According to this view, for which Wender (1971, 1978) is the foremost advocate, the organic origin of the condition lies in some form of genetic abnormality rather than in any form of injury to the brain. The two concepts are quite different in their implications and require assessment by different strategies. Here we will consider the former, continuum-type concept; the latter view was discussed earlier (see *Attention Deficit/ Hyperactivity Syndromes*).

The basic notion underlying the continuum concept is not an unreasonable one because there is good evidence that children can suffer overt and indisputable brain damage and yet still show no definite abnormalities on a carefully conducted, thorough clinical neurological examination. This has been shown, for example, by follow-up studies of children with neurological abnormalities in infancy (Solomons, Holden, Denhoff, 1963), with encephalitis (Meyer & Byers, 1952), or with a penetrating head injury (Shaffer et al., 1975). Moreover, it appears that these subclinical varieties of brain damage probably increase the risk of psychopathological disorder. Thus, in our study of children suffering severe head injuries, we found that there was a substantial rise in the rate of emotional/behavioral disturbance following head injury, even in the subgroup who were without neurological abnormalities at follow-up 2¼ years later (Rutter, Chadwick, & Shaffer, in press).

The general notion, then, of minimal damage is consistent with the empirical research findings. However, the same evidence also suggests that the threshold of severity of brain damage above which psychological sequelae can be detected is quite high. Thus, as already noted, children suffering head injuries show no identifiable sequelae with those giving rise to PTA of less than 1 week. The bulk of the evidence suggests, as Benton (1973) put it, that cerebral lesions in children must be either quite extensive or have specific disorganizing properties in order to produce important behavioral abnormalities. In that respect the adjective minimal in minimal brain dysfunction (MBD) seems misleading (Rutter, in press-c).

Nevertheless, even if that proves to be the case (and it must be said that more data are needed before conclusions on threshold can be at all firm), there remains the problem of how to diagnose MBD in children whose clinical neurological investigation reveals no definite abnormalities. Two general approaches have been followed: (1) the use of various measures of brain dysfunction and (2) a reliance on a history of physical risk factors.

Measures of Brain Dysfunction

The measures of brain dysfunction used include extensions of the neurological examination to provide a focus on so-called ''soft signs''; the identification of minor congenital physical anomalies; EEG studies and the more recent development of neurometric approaches; traditional medical tests, such as pneumoencephalography and brain scans; and psychometric evaluations.

Soft Signs. Clinicians have long been aware that children may show a variety of signs of atypical neurological function, including clumsiness, choreiform movements, impaired sensory integration, and delayed language development. Bender

(1947) was one of the first investigators to suggest that these constituted indications of cerebral dysfunction that could be utilized to pick out psychiatric disorders of organic etiology; during the last decade or so, a variety of systems of pediatric neurological examination have been devised for this purpose (e.g., Close, 1973; Holden, Tarnowski, & Prinz, 1982; Peters, Romine, & Dykman, 1975; Rutter et al., 1970; Touwen & Prechtl, 1970). These tend to include three rather different types of soft signs that involve different problems and have different implications (Rutter et al., 1970). First, there are slight abnormalities that are difficult to detect but that are of the same type as classical neurological signs, such as minor asymmetries of muscle tone or reflexes. Such signs tend to be unreliable as a direct consequence of the fact that they constitute minimal abnormalities. Nevertheless, if outside the normal range of variation and if repeatedly found on independent examinations, probably they have the same pathological significance as do more major forms of the same signs. Second, there are signs that sometimes indicate cerebral dysfunction but that also may be caused by nonneurological influences. Nystagmus and strabismus constitute examples of this type. Often, a careful delineation of the precise nature of the sign will allow a diagnosis of its cause. Third, there are developmental anomalies that represent deficits in functions characteristic of normal children at younger ages. These constitute the majority of soft signs in most examination batteries, and their interpretation is difficult for several rather different reasons.

In the first place, unlike the first two types of signs, they are not in themselves abnormal at all. Instead, their significance depends on the degree of atypicality (thus, some entirely normal children are much clumsier than others). Such significance can be assessed only in relation to the child's chronological and mental age because such signs are known to be systematically related to IQ and to developmental level (Camp, Bialer, Sverd, & Winsberg, 1978; Holden et al., 1982). Perhaps because this involves complex clinical judgments, some of the signs have been found to be rather inconsistent on serial examinations, particularly in children of low IQ (Hertzig, 1982; Holden et al., 1982; McMahon & Greenberg, 1977). Also, major differences have been found among clinicians in their threshold of recognition of such soft signs, thus, in the American perinatal collaborative study, 1.7% of children were diagnosed neurologically abnormal in one center, whereas in another center 16.5% were so diagnosed (Nichols & Chen, 1981)! On the other hand, with systematic

assessments, the judgments can be made reliable, especially if psychometric techniques are used to provide quantification (Rutter et al., 1970). Children with many soft signs on one testing still tend to have an increased number of signs some years later, although the particular signs that are abnormal may not be the same (Hertzig, 1982; Shaffer, 1982).

The second and larger problem concerns the interpretation of these developmental anomalies, even when they can be reliably demonstrated, because they may arise for a variety of quite different reasons, including extreme normal variation, specific maturational disorders, perhaps even poor cooperation, and organic brain disorders (Shafer, Shaffer, O'Conner, & Stokman, in press; Shaffer, O'Conner, Shafer, & Prupis, in press). Such signs are more frequent in children with structural brain disease. Even so, such signs have been found to be relatively frequent even in normal children drawn from the general population; often, they are absent in children with proven or suspected organic brain dysfunctions. Moreover, they do not correlate strongly at all with perinatal risk factors or with EEG abnormalities, and twin and family associations suggest that, in part, they may be genetically determined (Kennard, 1960; Nichols & Chen, 1981; Rutter et al., 1970). As a consequence, it is unwarranted to assume that these signs necessarily reflect any type of organic brain dysfunction, although in some cases they do. Hence, it is difficult to know how to interpret the rather contradictory and inconclusive evidence that soft signs tend to be frequent in children with behavioral or learning difficulties but yet are nonspecific in their behavioral and cognitive associations (Nichols & Chen, 1981; Shafer et al., in press; Shaffer et al., in press).

Minor Congenital Physical Anomalies. During recent years increasing attention has been paid to the presence of minor physical anomalies, such as epicanthic folds, low-set ears, high-steepled palate, and a furrowed tongue. These are of a type best known for their high incidence in people with Down's syndrome but that also occur in the general population with an average frequency of two to four anomalies per person (Waldrop & Halverson, 1971). It has been argued that these anomalies constitute developmental deviations resulting from either genetic transmission or some insult in early pregnancy that mimics genetic transmission (Rapoport & Quinn, 1975). Unfortunately, there is a paucity of empirical data on the biological significance or origin of these anomalies (Krouse & Kauffman, 1982). However, isolated studies have shown contradictory findings on their association with obstetric complications (Rapoport, Pandoni, Renfield, Lake, & Ziegler, 1977), a weak correlation with dopamine-beta-hydroxylase measurements in the newborn (Rapoport et al., 1977), and a zero correlation with a neurodevelopmental assessment (Sandberg et al., 1978). Accordingly, although the detection of anomalies has been shown to be both reliable and stable over time and although it seems reasonable to assume that they reflect some type of atypicality in physical development, their meaning with regard to organic brain dysfunction remains totally obscure. As a result, it is difficult to know what implications follow from the fact that some prospective studies have shown that minor physical anomalies identified at birth predict strongly to behavioral disturbance at age 3 years, whereas others have found much weaker and less consistent associations (Krouse & Kauffman, 1982).

Electroencephalographic (EEG) Measures and Neurometric Approaches. Although the EEG constitutes one of the traditional investigative tools of the neurologist, the presence of EEG abnormalities has proved to be a rather uncertain guide in attempts to diagnose organic brain dysfunction in the absence of frank neurological disease (Ellingson, 1954; R. Harris, 1977). Paroxysmal abnormalities and excessive slow-wave activity are both relatively common in normal children (Eeg-Olofsson, 1970) so that although EEG abnormalities tend to be somewhat more frequent when there is other evidence of organic brain disease (e.g., Caparulo et al., 1981; Gerson, Barnes, Mannino, Fanning, & Burns, 1972; Ritvo et al., 1970; Small, 1968), the association between clinical EEG abnormalities and brain pathology is rather weak and of limited value in the individual child. As a result and as with the other special investigations already considered, few conclusions can be drawn from the many (mostly uncontrolled) studies showing rather high rates of EEG abnormalities in children with one or another of a wide range of psychiatric disorders (R. Harris, 1977; Werry, 1979).

More recently, there have been developments in the use of evoked potentials to study the brain's response to standard sensory stimuli (e.g., Buchsbaum & Wender, 1973; Satterfield & Braley, 1977), in power spectra analyses (Maxwell, Fenwick, Fenton, & Dollimore, 1974; Montagu, 1975), and in the use of complex statistical analyses of neurometric EEG indices (John, Karmel, Corning, Easton, Brown, Ahn, John, Harmoney, Prichep, Toro, Gerson, Bartlett, Thatcher, Kaye, Valdes, & Schwartz, 1977; Prichep, John, Ahn, & Kaye, in press). Neurometric measures have been shown to

be reliable and moderately stable over time. The measures differentiate normal children from those with a neurological disorder and differentiate abnormalities in children with learning disabilities about as frequently as in neurological groups. Whether or not the latter finding validates or invalidates neurometric indices as a measure of organic brain dysfunction has been a matter of dispute (Ahn, Prichep, & John, 1982; McCauley & Ciesielski, 1982). Unquestionably, these approaches have considerable promise, but, as yet, it is too early to know just which brain functions they reflect (or whether neurometric indices are influenced by variables other than organic dysfunction). Most recently of all, neurometric techniques are being developed for the identification of dynamic spatiotemporal electrical patterns of the brain during purposive behaviors (Gevins, Doyle, Cutillo, Schaffer, Taunehill, Ghannem, Bilcrease, & Yeager, 1981). These techniques have the major advantage of studying the functioning of the brain in action, but, so far, they remain at the experimental stage, although their potential seems high.

Pneumoencephalographic and Brain-Scan Techniques. Both pneumoencephalography and CAT (brain scans) are, of course, well established as sound techniques for the identification and location of space-occupying brain lesions. However, in the field of minimal brain dysfunction they have been used to diagnose pathology on the basis of asymmetries, ventricular enlargements, and enlarged fissures or sulci. The two main difficulties here lie in the need to develop adequate means of quantifying measurements (see Johnstone et al., 1976; Weinberger, Bigelow, Kleinman, Klein, Rosenblatt, & Wyatt, 1980) and the need for data on the findings in normal children (a need that is difficult to meet in view of ethical considerations). The findings suggest raised rates of ventricular dilatation and asymmetry in children with psychopathological or developmental disorders, but doubts remain as to the placement of the threshold separating abnormality and normality. So far, there seems to be little diagnostic specificity to the findings (Boesen & Aarkrog, 1967; Caparulo et al., 1981), and these tools have not proved to be of much value in the study of children with mental retardation, learning difficulties, or other types of MBD (Lingham, Read, Holland, Wilson, Brett, & Hoare, 1982; Thompson, Ross, & Horwitz, 1980).

Powerful new experimental radiological techniques for the study of brain function and malfunction carry promise that they may provide some of the essential links required to elucidate brain-behavior relationships. Thus, the combination of positron computed tomography to measure the concentration of radioactivity in living brain tissues together with the use of physiologically active compounds labeled with positron-emitting isotopes and tracer kinetic models allows the measurement of focal neurochemical processes (Brownell, Budinger, Lauterbur, & McGeer, 1982). Already these techniques have been used to provide a metabolic mapping of the brain's response to visual stimulation and, presumably, carry the potential for studying other aspects of brain function as well.

Psychometric Evaluations. Last, there is the field of psychometric assessment, with the numerous attempts to use psychological tests to diagnose either the presence or locus of brain damage. The main points may be summarized briefly because the empirical evidence on the validity of tests of brain damage as well as the concepts underlying these approaches have been reviewed on several occasions with similar conclusions (Boll, 1981; Boll & Barth, 1981; Chadwick & Rutter, in press; Herbert, 1964; Reitan & Davison, 1974). Brain damage frequently leads to cognitive impairment; often, this is global in nature, but it may be selective and specific. On the whole, visuomotor and visuospatial skills tend to be more seriously affected than are language skills, but this may not apply in very early childhood. Scores on neuropsychological test batteries have been found to provide a reasonably good discrimination between brain-damaged and nonbrain-damaged groups, with groups thought to have questionable brain damage occupying an intermediate position. However, the extensive batteries provide a differentiation that is not much better than that offered by broad-range intelligence tests, such as the Wechsler scales, and there is no indication that the particular pattern of cognitive deficit can be used to diagnose brain damage in the individual child. This applies to both general and localized brain injuries. Psychological testing constitutes an essential part of the assessment of the child with possible or definite brain damage because the measures are invaluable in identifying both the severity and type of cognitive deficits that are present. However, they are of very little use in the determination of whether or not there is brain damage.

In summary, no measure of brain function provides an adequate means of identifyng minimal brain dysfunction of organic origin, although each contributes in a useful way to the overall assessment of any child having learning or behavior problems. The sum total of the findings may be used to provide a clinical estimate of the probability that a child has suffered some form of brain injury, but the degree of certainty is not such as to make the test findings suitable for the unequivocal diagnosis of covert brain damage in the absence of a history of some known brain disease or injury.

Physical Risk Factors

A recognition of the importance of identifiable physical risk factors has led investigators to extend studies of obvious causes of brain damage (such as severe head injury and encephalitis) to factors that are known to cause brain injury when present to a severe degree but that also might lead to minimal or covert cognitive or behavioral impairment when present in lesser degree. The findings with respect to two such risk factors—perinatal complications and lead intoxication—illustrate the issues posed as well as the strength of the overall effects that obtain.

Perinatal Complications

The extensive literature on the emotional and behavioral sequelae of pregnancy complications has been reviewed many times (see, e.g., Birch & Gussow, 1970; Sameroff & Chandler, 1975). As the data from the more recent systematic prospective studies (Drillien, Thomson, & Burgoyne, 1980; Neligan, Kolvin, Scott, & Garside, 1976; Nichols & Chen, 1981; Stewart, in press; Werner, Bierman, & French, 1977) are in substantial agreement with those from earlier investigations, the main conclusions can be stated briefly. It is clear that serious perinatal complications (especially low birthweight) substantially increase the risk of overt cerebral palsy and mental retardation. However, when these children with obvious handicaps are excluded, the cognitive and behavioral outcome for children suffering perinatal hazards is little different from that of other children from a comparable social background. The control for social variables is crucial, however, as low-birthweight babies are more likely to be born to women from a socially disadvantaged background.

Nevertheless, although the outcome for children born following perinatal complications is little different from controls in most studies, findings of marginal increments in temperamental difficulties or behavioral disorders have been reported by many investigators. Although it is quite clear that perinatal complications contribute little to the general population variance in either personality attributes or psychopathological disorder, it is necessary still to ask whether the small differences that have been found are valid and, if valid, what they mean with respect to the possible effects of ''minimal brain dysfunction.''

With respect to validity, there are at least four

major problems. First, because perinatal hazards and social disadvantage tend to be intercorrelated, it is necessary to consider whether the observed small differences are only an artifact due to a failure to control adequately for social variables. In view of the difficulty in obtaining good measures for the relevant psychosocial factors, this remains a real possibility that is difficult to exclude.

Second, the effect of perinatal hazards may have been underestimated because they do not lead directly to disorder but rather increase vulnerability to later stresses. Insofar as this is so, it might be expected that the differences would be greatest in socially disadvantaged groups and minimal in middle class populations—which is just what has been found in most investigations, at least with respect to IQ (see Sameroff & Chandler, 1975; also see Werner et al., 1977; Werner & Smith, 1982).

A third problem concerns the behavioral outcome measures that usually have consisted of relatively crude screening questionnaires that may be inadequate for the detection of subtle differences in personality functioning or in the ability to cope with stress. However, although this is a real problem, the more detailed investigations do not suggest that the limited range of measures accounts for the small differences found.

Fourth, false negative findings may have arisen in a different way as a consequence of the very few children with real brain injuries resulting from perinatal factors having been diluted by the much larger number who experienced perinatal hazards but who escaped cerebral damage. Various investigators have tried to meet this problem by focusing on infants who were thought to have suffered anoxia or asphyxia in the newborn period, by subdividing the group according to the presence of neurological malfunction in infancy, or by focusing on both (Corah, Anthony, Painter, Stern, & Thurston, 1965; Nichols & Chen, 1981; Stewart, in press). Of course, unless very severe, neonatal anoxia is a weak indication of brain damage and, as already discussed, minor neurological signs, too, are of uncertain significance. Both Corah et al. (1965) and Kalverboer (1979) have shown the very low correlations that exist between neurological soft signs in infancy and in middle childhood. However, it may be that special attention should be paid to those cases where there *is* consistency in signs of neurological dysfunction. It is noteworthy that Corah et al. (1965) found persistence of neurological signs between 3 and 7 years of age in only 7 of the 35 children who had abnormalities at age 3, but all seven were in their anoxic group. Nichols and Chen (1981) found that the risk of later hyperkinetic-impulsive behavior was in-

creased two-and-a-halffold when there were neurological soft signs in infancy *and* in later childhood—the increase being very much less when the signs were present at one age only. Drillien et al. (1980), in a follow-up of Edinburgh children, found that neurological dysfunction in infancy was associated with maladjustment (as judged from scores on the Bristol Social Adjustment Guide) at age 7 only in the group with a birthweight below 1,500 g.

In summary, it seems that the increase in emotional and behavioral difficulties applies mainly to the small subgroup of children who experienced perinatal hazards and who showed clinical evidence of persistent neurological dysfunction. Moreover, even in this subgroup, the increase in risk is only moderate and perhaps applies particularly to children who also experience psychosocial hazards. The suggestion is that perinatal hazards may sometimes lead to minor degrees of neurological dysfunction and that when this occurs (and it does so in only a minority of cases), it may somewhat increase the risk of later emotional or behavioral difficulties. In other words, the findings offer some rather weak support for the notion of minimal brain dysfunction as a risk factor, but they also indicate that it accounts for a tiny proportion of the population variance in personality functioning.

Lead Intoxication

The situation with regard to the behavioral effects of increased body lead burdens is somewhat comparable, in that lead is known to be a neurotoxin that in high dosage leads to encephalopathy and brain damage (U.S. Environmental Protection Agency, 1977). The implication is that lower levels of lead might lead to lesser degrees of organic brain dysfunction which, in turn, might predispose to emotional or behavioral disturbance. A substantial number of studies (reviewed in Rutter & Russell Jones, 1983; Yule & Rutter, in press) have set out to determine the extent to which this in fact occurs. The findings from the better studies are reasonably consistent in showing that persistently raised blood levels in the range above 35 μg/100 ml—and possibly below that as well—are associated with an average reduction of some 1 to 5 IQ points, even in children without clinical signs of encephalopathy. However, the data on behavioral effects are less satisfactory and more contradictory. The first large-scale epidemiological study to examine the effects of mild to moderate lead exposure (Needleman, Gunnol, Leviton, Reed, Peresie, Maher, & Banett, 1979) used dentine lead levels as an index of lead exposure. Teachers' ratings of inattentive behavior were found to show a consistent dose-response relationship with dentine lead, suggesting that the association may represent a causal effect. Unfortunately, it was not possible in that analysis to control for socioeconomic or other confounding variables. As a result, it remains uncertain how far the correlation with dentine lead was an artifact arising from psychosocial differences between the groups; because the dose-response relationship, too, may be related to such differences, it loses most of its power as a test of causal inference. Some subsequent studies have confirmed the association between raised lead levels and inattentive behavior, but others have not. So far, the reasons for the discrepant findings remain unclear (although it is apparent that difficulties in measurement play a part).

Many problems are involved in the difficult matter of determining how far moderately raised lead levels cause organic brain dysfunction, which then predisposes to behavioral disturbance (Rutter & Russell Jones, 1983). It is not that this hypothesized causal chain is an implausible one; indeed, there are claims that it has been experimentally induced in animals (although there are uncertainties on the analogues with human behavior). Nor is it doubted that lead can cause neurologic dysfunction in the absence of clinical signs of brain damage; both changes in motor nerve conduction velocities and quantitative EEG changes suggest that it can. Instead, the problems stem from two main features: (1) the effects are small and require large samples for their detection and (2) many of the subjects come from deprived or disadvantaged backgrounds so that it is difficult to determine whether it was the lead intoxication, the psychosocial deprivation, or an interaction between the two that caused their behavioral disturbance (or cognitive impairment). The psychosocial variables that can be measured and controlled statistically are not necessarily the most crucial.

A case for the possible role of moderately raised lead levels as an occasional clinically significant cause of minimal brain dysfunction has been made. There are indications that sometimes this may result in slight cognitive impairment and, with less certainty, that there may be behavioral sequelae. However, in both cases, the mechanisms are unknown, and it is unclear whether the brain dysfunction is due to structural damage or temporary impairment of function.

In summary, the evidence regarding the continuum concept of minimal brain dysfunction may be outlined as follows: (1) the postulate that there can be subclinical damage to the brain is valid; (2) in addition, there is evidence that such damage may sometimes give rise to behavioral and cognitive sequelae; (3) however, although the evidence is too limited for firm conclusions, it appears that fairly severe brain injuries are required for this to occur and that minimal brain dysfunction syndromes are relatively uncommon; (4) the psychological sequelae of subclinical brain damage do not constitute a homogeneous syndrome, and minimal brain dysfunction cannot be diagnosed on behavioral grounds; and (5) clinical and laboratory tools for brain functioning are being improved but, as yet, they are inadequate for the task of diagnosing minimal brain dysfunction in the individual child. In short, the general concept of minimal brain dysfunction has some limited validity, but in the absence of means to diagnose such a syndrome, it does not constitute a usable nosological category.

CONCLUSIONS

In this chapter, we have considered a diverse range of psychopathological issues. Indeed, at first sight, there is little in common between some of them, for example, child abuse, animal phobias, autism, head injury, and delinquency. Each of these topics has its own agenda and its own outstanding research questions; we have drawn attention to some of them in the course of our discussions of specific findings and specific concepts. But, also, there is an underlying unity to the variety of issues related to theory, content, and method raised by many of the studies we have considered. In this final section, we summarize and highlight those questions and issues arising from the investigation of psychopathology that have particular relevance for the understanding of the developmental process as a whole.

Normality and Psychopathology

One issue centers around the question of whether there are qualitative or quantitative differences between normality and psychopathology. The question does not allow a simple affirmative or negative response. There are some elements of behavior exhibited by disturbed children that are clearly qualitatively different from normality. The deviant language and social interactions of autistic children provide an obvious example. But, as we emphasized in our consideration of the syndrome of autism, even here, an adequate understanding of the psychopathological process demands knowledge of the normal course of development of empathic awareness together with detailed comparisons between normality and psychopathology. For the most part, such comparisons have yet to be undertaken.

Other behaviors seem to show essential continuity between normality and pathology. For example, the aggressive and socially disruptive behaviors of children with conduct disorders are more severe and pervasive than those shown by normal children, but they appear similar in kind. Severity also does not contravene an assumption of continuity. Often, factors that influence the degree and style of behavioral manifestations have been demonstrably similar in normal and psychopathological groups. Still, there may be differences in certain key respects. For example, we noted Patterson's (1982) observation that severely aggressive children's response to parental discipline is different from that of normal children. Does that imply that their behavior shows discontinuity with normality or, instead, that their cumulated experiences of parent-child interaction were sufficiently disparate from those of the ordinary child that the outcome was different, although the initial processes were similar? We do not know, but the issue is an important one that requires further study.

Also, it requires emphasis that the presence of some known organic deficit or disease does not necessarily mean that the process of sociopsychological development will take a fundamentally different course from that seen in normal children. Thus, for example, Cicchetti and Serafica (1981) found that attachment, affiliation, wariness, and exploration in Down's syndrome children showed a basically similar organization to that observed in normal children, although their development was delayed and slowed. However, there were some differences (Down's syndrome children were less distressed in an unfamiliar situation), emphasizing once more that there cannot be one general answer to the nature of the links between normality and psychopathology. Or again, children suffering brain damage remain vulnerable to the same psychosocial stresses and family adversities that have adverse effects on normal children (Rutter, 1977a). Neurological impairment is not a sufficient condition for predicting maladaptive behavior or an abnormal course of development (Eisenberg, 1977).

Classification and Measurement

Throughout the chapter, we have drawn attention to major outstanding questions on issues of classification and measurement. All too frequently findings have been inconclusive because the measures employed have been weak, nondiscriminating, or open to systematic bias. Similarly, comparisons between studies have often been vitiated because cases have

been defined differently, because the settings have been noncomparable, or because the measures have focused on different aspects of behavior. In these circumstances, the traditional plea is for the development of more reliable, more objective measures of observable behavior. These aims are indeed worthwhile, but reliability and objectivity are not sufficient criteria for sound measurement. The finding that neither observational nor mechanical measures of activity level provide a worthwhile level of prediction from one afternoon to the next morning or from one setting to another well illustrates this point. In their chapter on parent-child interaction, Maccoby and Martin (*vol. IV, chap. 1*) discuss the relative advantages and disadvantages of microanalytic methods and global macroscopic ratings. They make the point that the former may be better for the study of specific situational influences by that the latter may provide better measures of stable individual differences. The same applies to measures of normal and psychopathological behavior in children and, like Maccoby and Martin, we conclude that there is much to be said for multimethod approaches.

Whatever type of measure is employed, it is important to have a clear conceptualization of the behavioral dimensions to be studied and to devise measures that adequately reflect the concepts used. The confusion in the literature between overactivity, socially inappropriate activity, and disruptive behavior or the confusion between the multiple facets of attention and impulsivity underlines the importance of this matter. The burgeoning field of studies of depression in childhood carries the same need. If the course of development of affective expression is to be charted accurately, it will be essential to differentiate between the cognitive, affective, and behavioral components of depression. No one questions that infants show dysphoric mood, but there is more doubt about whether they experience the sense of self-blame, the feelings of hopelessness, and the negative self-attributions characteristic of depression in adult life. Measures that reflect these distinctions are required.

A differentiation between situational and pervasive behaviors also appears important. It is not just that there are both situational factors and personality traits together with an interaction between them. In addition, it seems to be the case that the developmental implications of pervasive behaviors may be different from those that vary across situations. Thus, hyperactivity that is pervasive over settings and circumstances is more likely to show persistence over time. In addition, it seems to carry a somewhat different meaning in terms of its stronger association with cognitive deficits. The further example of conduct disturbance suggests that pervasive and persistent antisocial behavior is more likely to be associated with abnormalities in personality functioning and with deviant family circumstances. Not surprisingly, it is also more likely to be followed by serious social impairment in adult life. The question of whether these differences reflect categorical distinctions or differences on a continuum of severity has no satisfactory answer as yet. As in the field of developmental psychopathology as a whole, it is important both to keep an open mind on the issue and also to find ways of testing which alternative best represents the true situation.

Another requirement concerns the appropriate choice of comparison groups. There are numerous examples in the literature of the assumption of specificity based on comparisons with normal samples, an assumption that turned out to be false when the appropriate comparisons were made. Thus, overselectivity was thought to be characteristic of autism until the necessary comparisons with mentally retarded groups were made; it now seems that overselectivity is more a function of low MA than of autism per se. Or again, recent comparisons between hyperactive and unsocialized aggressive groups have shown that some of the features thought to be specific to the attention deficit syndrome are just as commonly found in association with conduct disturbance. Similarly, some of the psychopathological characteristics thought to be specific to schizophrenia have been found to be associated with a much broader heterogeneous range of psychopathology. There are *both* specific and general risk factors, and a discriminating use of appropriate comparison groups is necessary to determine which is which.

Of course, that raises the basic issue of just how psychopathological disorders in childhood are to be subdivided and classified. Throughout the history of classification, investigators have included both lumpers and splitters. Child psychiatric classifications have moved from one extreme to the other over the last generation. From a single nondifferentiated category of behavior disorders of childhood, we have moved to schemes (such as DSM–III and ICD–9) with a proliferation of fine and subtle distinctions. It is clear that most of these distinctions lack empirical validation, but the answer is not necessarily a return to just a few broad groupings. The hopeful sign is that the new classification schemes have been accompanied by an increasing awareness that these are matters to be decided by empirical study—not by armchair theorizing, ex cathedra assertions, or even committee consensus.

Person-Situation Interactions

Research during the last decade has done much to resolve the differences between the proponents of situationism and personality trait theorists (Bem & Funder, 1978; Bowers, 1973; Endler, 1977; Epstein, 1979; Mischel, 1979). As a result, interactionist models of behavior have come to dominate the field (Magnusson & Endler, 1977). However, it is apparent that there are many different types of person-situation interaction, that it is no easy or straightforward matter to test for their occurrence, and that the conventional interaction term in multivariate statistics is not synonymous with many of the concepts of person-situation interaction that are included in contemporary theorizing (Rutter, in press-g).

There has been increasing interest during the last few years in gene-environment interactions by which the effects of environmental variables are increased in (or, even, are restricted to) genetically vulnerable individuals. In our discussion of conduct disturbance, we drew attention to the evidence (Crowe, 1974; Hutchings & Mednick, 1974), suggesting that, in part, the genetic factors associated with criminality operate by causing an increased vulnerability to environmental stressors. Recent findings on alcoholism (Cloninger, Bohman, & Sigvardsson, 1981) point to a similar effect. The findings begin to provide a possible explanation for the variations among studies in the strength of environmental effects according to the characteristics of the populations studied; more importantly, the findings throw much needed light on possible mechanisms involved in some genetic effects.

We also drew attention to the evidence showing that the effects of perinatal complications tend to be greater in children from a socially disadvantaged background. The same applies to the effects of malnutrition (Richardson, 1980). However, the mechanisms underlying the interaction remain ill understood. It may be that physical hazards increase children's biological vulnerability to adverse psychosocial influences, but there is also evidence that physically impaired children *elicit* different patterns of parent-child interaction (Chavez, Martinez, & Yaschine, 1974) and that improved patterns of interaction do much to reverse the intellectual impairments associated with severe malnutrition (Cravioto & Arrieta, in press).

But if further research is needed to elucidate the mechanisms underlying such interactions, so also is it required to explain the nonoccurrence of synergistic interactions. The findings on brain damage illustrate this point. They show (1) that both brain injury and psychosocial adversity operate at the same time; (2) for the most part, brain injury and psychosocial adversity give rise to the same kinds of disorders; and (3) the main effects of brain injury are likely to be indirect rather than direct. The obvious inference seems to be that brain injury operates by increasing children's susceptibility to life stresses and family problems. However, the data showed no such synergistic effect (Rutter, 1977a), leaving wide open the question of which mechanisms are involved in the process by which brain damage increases the risk of psychopathological disorder.

A further area in which person-situation interactions operate is that of sex differences. We noted the large sex differences seen with many types of disorder (autism and conduct disturbance constitute two striking, but very different, examples). The reasons for these sex differences remain ill understood, but the findings so far indicate the need to explore further both biological differences and sex-linked variations in patterns of family interaction.

Last, the evidence on the importance of situational influences indicates the need for using discriminating and sensitive measures of such situations. Traditionally, the main focus has been on mother-child interaction and considerable progress has been made in both the conceptualization and measurement of interaction patterns. During recent years, there has been an increasing awareness of the need to move from dyadic to triadic interactions as research findings began to show both the effects of fathers on infants and also the effects of the presence of one parent on the behavior of the other toward the children. As Bronfenbrenner (1979) has argued persuasively, an ecological perspective is needed. However, Dunn and Kendrick's (1982) study of the effects of the arrival of a second child in families has clearly shown that a triadic interaction model is too limiting. The birth of a second child affects the interaction of the first with its parents and introduces the possibility of effects from sib-sib interaction. The potential importance of this emphasis is indicated by the genetic data showing that for many personality variables the crucial environmental influences concern within-family variation rather than between-family differences (Rowe & Plomin, 1981). The implication is that the conventional between-groups comparison needs to be complemented by study of the variations in the ways in which parents interact with their children within the same family. Of course, as discussed in other chapters (*Hartup, vol. IV, chap. 2; Minuchin & Shapiro, vol. IV, chap. 3*), both peer group and school influences need to be studied as they, too, are responsible

for important situational effects that may influence the developmental process.

Situational and Temporal Consistency

In the early clashes between situationism and trait theories, there tended to be an implicit assumption that consistency across situations and consistency over time were reflections of the same phenomenon. Mischel (1979) has made clear that this was a mistaken assumption. It is quite possible to have marked variations across situations and yet substantial continuity over time. In part, the difference reflects the aggregation or nonaggregation of behaviors across occasions (Epstein, 1979), but Mischel's (in press) recent findings suggest that this may not be the whole explanation; apparently, even with aggregated measures, temporal stability far exceeds cross-situational consistency. That creates a paradox, if only because comparisons of behaviors over a span of several years *must* involve different situations. The settings in which a 3-year-old interacts with others are different from those for a 7-year-old; the meaning of the environment will have changed because of maturational (and other) changes in the child. Accordingly, why should temporal stability exceed situational consistency? What processes within the child or in person-situation interactions are involved? We noted this paradox when discussing insecurity of parent-child attachment. The quality of attachment to one parent is of little predictive value for the quality of attachment to the other, yet measures of the security/insecurity of attachment at one age predict peer relationships a few years later—a prediction across domains of relationships as well as over time. On the one hand, security/insecurity appears to be a measure of a dyadic interaction rather than any quality of the child as a person, but, on the other hand, it seems to predict later personality functioning. In some way, experiences of a particular type of interaction seem to have a relatively enduring effect in spite of marked situational variation. It may be that single experiences or even prolonged experiences with just one individual have little long-term impact but that the overall *pattern* of experiences across several relationships leads to a greater internalization of values or more established habits of behavior (see *Maccoby & Martin, vol. IV, chap. 1*).

Similar issues arise with the observation of the powerful impact of a supportive nondeviant spouse in leading to more adaptive social functioning among women at serious risk for maladaptive outcomes as a result of an institutional upbringing (Rutter, Quinton, & Liddle, in press). A good experience in early adult life apparently went a long way toward undoing the harm from bad experiences in childhood. But was this simply because a radically different environment created a "press" for a different sort of behavior or did the good experience lead to changes in personality functioning that would persist even if the situation changed? We do not know, but our inability to provide an answer underlines our ignorance of what changes in the child as a result of different experiences. Although we have a better understanding of the meaning of cross-situational consistency and temporal stability, we have only just begun to appreciate the psychological mechanisms involved in the differences between the two.

Developmental Transitions and Transformations

Throughout the study of normal and abnormal child development, much attention has been paid to the characteristics of major developmental transitions. Most research has focused on the changes that take place during the early years of childhood, but knowledge is accumulating on the transitions during adolescence. We have commented on the rise in the frequency and intensity of depressive feelings that is associated with the occurrence of puberty, a rise that to some extent persists into at least early adult life. Adolescence is also associated with a peaking in delinquent activities, a peak that is followed by a marked fall in early adult life and accompanied by a transition to more conventional attitudes and behavior.

Several issues arise from these observations. First, there is the crucial methodological point that the study of developmental transitions requires the *combination* of cross-sectional and longitudinal data if changes resulting from maturation are to be separated from generational differences or the effects of historical or cultural change. This requirement was first clearly demonstrated by Baltes and Schaie (1976) in relation to the effects of aging on intelligence, but it applies equally to other developmental transitions.

Second, it is essential to use the most appropriate biological marker for developmental level. Tanner (1960) showed this vividly with respect to puberty and physical growth. Because children reach puberty at such very different ages, the aggregation of data by chronological age greatly flattens the sharp growth spurt seen in all individuals. The lesson for those studying psychological development is obvious. If the developmental transitions of adoles-

cence are to be investigated it will be necessary to include measures of stage of puberty as well as chronological age (a need met in very few psychological studies of adolescence).

Third, there is the question of whether the developmental transitions of normal development are relevant for age changes in psychopathology. This matter has been little investigated so far, but it warrants more serious attention. We noted the parallels between the rise in depressive feelings during adolescence and the age changes in the pattern of affective disorders. It is clear that there is much to be gained from study of the links between normality and psychopathology regarding depression. But, there are numerous other parallels that could be drawn. For example, anorexia nervosa (a severe disorder with self-induced starvation that carries an appreciable mortality) is much more frequent among girls than boys, and, characteristically, it has its onset during adolescence. One cannot help being struck by the parallel with comparable changes in normal teenagers. Whereas, typically, girls put on fat when they reach puberty, boys do not (rather they gain in musculature); moreover, whereas most boys are pleased with their change in physique, many girls are not and seek to lose weight by dieting (Gross & Duke, in press; Rutter, 1979; Tobin-Richards, Boxer, & Peterson, 1982). A greater focus on possible normality-psychopathological links with respect to developmental transitions is indicated.

Further issues arise in relation to the possible psychological importance of individual differences in the timing of biological transitions in development. Thus, the early California longitudinal studies showed that early-maturing boys tended to be more relaxed, less dependent, more self-confident, and socially more attractive to other people than late-maturing boys (Clausen, 1975; Jones, 1965; McCandless, 1960). The findings for girls were less consistent and more recent research has suggested that girls who reach puberty much before their peers tend to develop a more negative self-image (Tobin-Richards et al., 1982). Again, the findings have both methodological and substantive implications for our understanding of the developmental process. First, it is evident that, if we are to study the effects of individual variation in the timing of developmental transitions, we must have measures before the onset of the transitions. The need for this was shown in the Isle of Wight study (Rutter, 1979) where the findings showed that psychiatric disorder was more frequent in late maturing boys (i.e., those still prepubescent at 15 years). In keeping with the personality data, the finding could be interpreted to mean that physically immature boys develop disorder in relation to worries and anxieties over their failure to reach puberty at a time when their peers have already had their growth spurt and are beginning to be sexually mature. However, this inference was shown to be wrong by the fact that the late-maturing boys had already shown an excess of psychopathology at age 10, before any boys had reached physical maturity.

Second, if the consequences of variations in the timing of transitions are to be delineated, it is equally necessary to continue data collection until after all individuals reach maturity. Magnusson and Stattin's (in press) data on alcohol consumption illustrate this point strikingly. At the age of 14 years, drunkenness was many times more frequent in those who had their menarche before 11 years than in those with a menarche after the age of 13. But, by the time the sample reached 25 years, there were no longer any differences. The onset of puberty determined when girls began to drink more heavily, but this increase occurred irrespective of whether the menarche was early or late, and there were no long-term consequences of an earlier onset to increased alcohol consumption.

Third, the occurrence of major developmental transitions does not necessarily mean that there is any change in the relative position of individuals on any behavioral dimension. Thus, Jessor (in press; Jessor & Jessor, 1977) showed that there was a substantial drop in problem behavior among college students followed from their freshman year to age 30; but, still, there was a correlation for males of .33 (or .67 when corrected for attenuation) over a 7-year time span. Last, the data on personality measures point to the importance of sex differences. Both boys and girls experience major biological transitions in development, but neither the character nor the meaning of the transitions are the same in the two sexes.

The question of possible transformations of behavior is also raised by studies of psychopathology. Most obviously, perhaps, this is seen with the developmental precursors of schizophrenia. The psychosis in adult life may be characterized by gross abnormalities, such as thought disorder, hallucinations, delusions, and paranoid ideation, but these have no phenotypic equivalent in the prepsychotic phase of development during childhood. Instead, the antecedents are to be found in subtle abnormalities in attentional processes and social functioning. There are developmental continuities, but they are accompanied by behavioral transformations. The phe-nomenon is dramatic with schizophrenia, but the issue is a general one with application to many spheres of behavior. Thus, as they grow older, children cease to be clinging to their parents, but usually it is supposed that early selective attachments in some way lead on to later love and social relationships. Conversely, there is no exact equivalent in early life of heterosexual behavior, of drug taking, or of religiosity—but that does not necessarily mean that these behaviors have no antecedents in childhood.

Developmental Continuities and Discontinuities

The whole question of continuities and discontinuities in development is complex and multi-faceted, as many reviewers have noted (e.g., Emmerich, 1964, 1968; Kagan, 1980; Magnusson & Endler, 1977; Rutter, in press-b; Wohlwill, 1980). Different commentators have come to startlingly different conclusions on the strengths of continuities. Some have emphasized the extent to which early life experiences are determinative of later behavior and development (Lipsitt, in press), whereas others have stressed the importance of discontinuities, with the development of new capacities that have little or no connection with past structures or past experiences (Kagan, 1981). For the most part, these variations in inference do not reflect disagreement on the empirical findings, instead, they represent different interpretations of what is meant by continuity together with a focus on different aspects of development.

As we have noted, the empirical findings show significant correlations between measures of behavioral functioning at different phases of development separated by some years, but the correlations are of modest to moderate strength so that behavior in early childhood provides but a weak prediction of functioning in adolescence or adult life. Moreover, although early life experiences may have enduring consequences for personality development, often they do not. Such findings give rise to several rather different implications. First, as we have noted, sometimes the strength of continuities is greater in psychopathological groups than in the normal population; this observation raises questions on whether the mechanisms that are involved are the same in the two cases. Second, even when there is gross psychopathology the concept of continuity implies meaningful links over the course of development rather than a lack of change. Third, we need to consider what is responsible for the continuities when they occur. Is it, as once thought, that early experiences fix personality development (a view that seems incompatible with the evidence) or is it that continuity comes from effects on habits, attitudes, and self-esteem (see *Harter, vol. IV, chap. 4*)? Or, perhaps, continuities in development reflect constancy in environmental forces. Fourth, the psychopathological data emphasize the importance of indirect, but nevertheless quite strong, links in the developmental process (Rutter, in press-b). Thus, one study showed links between early patterns of parenting and behavior in adult life (Rutter, Quinton, & Liddle, in press). But, the findings also showed that the continuities stemmed from a multitude of links over time; those included effects on behavior in childhood, the effects of one adverse experience in shutting down opportunities and in making other adverse experiences more likely, and effects on vulnerability to later stresses. Long-term effects are far from independent from intervening circumstances; because each link is incomplete, subject to marked individual variation and open to modification, there are many opportunities to break the chain. Research needs to be directed to a study of how these indirect continuities operate, a topic on which very little is known. Last, the large variations in outcome following adverse experiences emphasizes the need to determine the reasons for these variations.

The Role of Theory in Developmental Psychopathology

The limitations inherent in the current data base renders premature any effort to construct a global overarching theory of the psychopathological development of children. Although theory provides a unifying perspective, premature efforts at theory construction may prove to be not only disappointing but discouraging of research in the long run. In psychology, the era of great theoretical systems has come and gone. In psychiatry, the demise of psychoanalysis as an explanatory theory for normal and abnormal development heralds a similar message.

We are at present engaged in the slow accumulation of more solidly grouped empirical data, but there are many areas as yet unexplored and too few researchers to conduct the needed explorations. The needs are many: improvements in diagnosis and classification of childhood disorders; clinical and experimental sophistication combined in the same researcher; integrations of biological, psychological, sociological, and familial factors as these impinge on the developing child and impel the child along normal or abnormal pathways.

Yet, data gathering in the absence of hypotheses

can become an inconsequential exercise in gathering inconsequential facts. The value of theory as Kaplan (1964) notes ''Lies not only in the answers it gives but also in the new questions it raises. . . . New questions often arise, not only out of turning to new subject-matters, but also out of viewing old subject matters in a new light'' (p. 320).

The resolution of the paradox of vice accompanied by virtue in premature theory construction may lie in lowering our sights a bit. The goal may be one of settling for partials initially. Thus, the task for the developmental psychopathologist should be both the acquisition of facts, and the integration of such facts with existing data within more circumscribed areas of psychopathology, with the intent of forming hypotheses as to the possible lawful relationships that can bring coherence and an enhanced understanding of these areas of personality maldevelopment.

If the present foreshadows a failure to construct an overarching theory to explain all aspects of psychopathological development, it also seems to presage an opportunity to provide more coherent explanations for subsets of the phenomena we study. Disputes over such tentative explanations are both inevitable and healthy; theory is not designed to silence adversaries, but to allow resolution of differences in the open marketplace of ideas.

Finally, formulations of the origins and sources of maldevelopment are unlikely to stand independent of theoretical statements about normal development. Research that fosters an understanding of disordered behavior will ultimately enhance our comprehension of normal behavior as well. Therein lies the ultimate element of continuity, one that is inherent in the scientific enterprise itself.

NOTES

1. In recent years, concerns over the possible ill effects of labeling have led some people to doubt the value of any diagnosis or classification. We share the concern over the misuses of diagnosis and classification, but the plea to abandon classification is a counsel of despair. Classification as a means of ordering information and of grouping phenomena is basic to all forms of scientific enquiry. The error comes in equating the classification of behaviors or disorders with a classification of *people* (an error perpetuated in the very title of Hobbs', 1975, two-volume book on the subject). It is scientifically wrong to classify people because it assumes a persistence of psychiatric disorder and a fixity of per-

sonality that is completely out of keeping with what is known about development and about the course of disorders. Also, it is morally offensive because it is treating children as if they were no more than the vehicles of problems. Nevertheless, classifications are needed to provide a language with an agreed set of terms by which investigators can communicate with one another. However, it is important to emphasize that classifications have no necessary connection with concepts of disease. Categories and terms are needed to describe behaviors and behavioral constellations irrespective of whether they refer to disease states.

2. Although it was originally supposed that emotional deprivation might cause growth failure through a psychosomatic effect on endocrine function, it is now clear that undernutrition actually constitutes the immediate cause of the stunting of growth in the great majority of cases (see MacCarthy, 1981). Nevertheless, the term deprivation dwarfism still seems appropriate, in that the undernutrition stems from psychological factors—either in terms of the child being given insufficient food or through depression in the child that causes loss of appetite or impaired gastrointestinal function.

3. The question of the nature and causation of schizophrenia is beyond the scope of this chapter. The high-risk strategy used to identify the behavioral precurors is based on the extensive evidence of the importance of genetic factors (Gottesman & Shields, 1976). However, nongenetic factors also appear important (Wynne, Cromwell, & Matthysse, 1978) and research findings suggest that both environmental precipitants (Leff & Vaughn, 1980) and poor family communication combined with hostile or critical patterns of interactions may predispose to schizophrenia-spectrum disorders (Blakar, 1979; Doane, Goldstein, & Rodnick, 1983); Wynne, 1978). However, there is uncertainty on the extent to which family communication deviance is *specifically* associated with schizophrenia as currently diagnosed (Hirsch & Leff, 1975; Rutter, 1978c), on the direction of the causal effect (Blakar, 1979), and on whether the impact of family discord in the families with a schizophrenic parent is the same as in families with a depressive parent (Emery, Weintraub, & Neale, 1982). On the other hand, it is well established that patterns of affective expression in the family do predict the course of the disorder in young adults already schizophrenic (Leff & Vaughn, 1981; Vaughn & Leff, 1976). Moreover, the finding that social interventions designed to reduce critical overinvolvement significantly reduce the relapse rate (Leff, Kuipers, Berkowitz, Eberlein-Vries, &

Sturgeon, 1982) strongly suggests that this is a causal link. Whether the same family influences play a part in the initial genesis of schizophrenia is not known, but it is plausible that they might do so.

REFERENCES

Aarkrog, T. Organic factors in infantile and borderline psychoses: A retrospective study of 46 cases subject to pneumoencephalography. *Danish Medical Bulletin*, 1968, *15*, 283–288.

Abikoff, H., Gittelman-Klein, R., & Klein, D. F. Validation of a classroom observation code for hyperactive children. *Journal of Consulting and Clinical Psychology*, 1977, *45*, 772–783.

Abramson, L. Y., Seligman, M. E. P., & Teasdale, J. D. Learned helplessness in humans: Critique and reformulation. *Journal of Abnormal Psychology*, 1978, *87*, 49–74.

Achenbach, T. M. Psychopathology of childhood: Research problems and issues. *Journal of Consulting and Clinical Psychology*, 1978, *46*, 759–776.

Achenbach, T. M., & Edelbrock, C. S. The classification of child psychopathology: A review and analysis of empirical efforts. *Psychological Bulletin*, 1978, *85*, 1275–1301.

Ackerman, P. T., Elardo, P. T., & Dykman, R. A. A psychosocial study of hyperactive and learning-disabled boys. *Journal of Abnormal Child Psychology*, 1979, *7*, 91–99.

Adams, P. L. *Obsessive children*. New York: Penguin, 1973.

Agras, W. S., Chapin, H. N., Jackson, M. J., & Oliveau, D. C. The natural history of phobia: Course and prognosis. *Archives of General Psychiatry*, 1972, *26*, 315–317.

Agras, W. S., Sylvester, D., & Oliveau, D. C. The epidemiology of common fears and phobias. *Comprehensive Psychiatry*, 1969, *10*, 151–156.

Ahn, H., Prichep, L., & John, E. R. Electroencephalogram tests for brain dysfunction: A question of validity. *Science*, 1982, *217*, 82.

Ainsworth, M. D. S. Attachment: Retrospect and prospect. In C. M. Parkes & J. Stevenson-Hinde (Eds.), *The place of attachment in human behaviour*. London: Tavistock Press, 1982.

Ainsworth, M. D. S., Blehar, M. C., Waters, E., & Wall, S. *Patterns of attachment*. Hillsdale, N.J.: Erlbaum, 1978.

Aird, R. B., & Yamamoto, T. Behaviour disorders of childhood. *Electroencephalography and Clinical Neurophysiology*, 1966, *21*, 148–156.

Albert, N., & Beck, A. T. Incidence of depression in early adolescence: A preliminary study. *Journal of Youth and Adolescence*, 1975, *4*, 301–307.

Aman, M. G. Cognitive, social and other correlates of specific reading retardation. *Journal of Abnormal Child Psychology*, 1979, *7*, 153–168.

Amenson, C. S., & Lewinsohn, P. M. An investigation into the observed sex difference in the prevalence of unipolar depression. *Journal of Abnormal Psychology*, 1981, *90*, 1–13.

American Psychiatric Association. *Diagnostic and statistical manual of mental disorders—DSM–III* (3rd ed.). Washington, D.C.: American Psychiatric Association, 1980.

Anderson, L., Dancis, J., & Alpert, M. Behavioral contingencies and self-mutilation in Lesch-Nyhan disease. *Journal of Consulting and Clinical Psychology*, 1978, 529–536.

Angelino, H., Dollins, J., & Mech, E. Trends in the fears and worries of schoolchildren as related to socio-economic status and age. *Journal of Genetic Psychology*, 1956, *89*, 263–276.

Annesley, P. T. Psychiatric illness in adolescence: Presentation and prognosis. *Journal of Mental Science*, 1961, 107, 268–278.

Anthony, J., & Scott, P. D. Manic-depressive psychosis in childhood. *Journal of Child Psychology and Psychiatry*, 1960, *1*, 53–72.

Appel, M. H. Aggressive behaviour of nursery school children and adult procedures in dealing with such behaviour. *Journal of Experimental Education*, 1942, *11*, 185–199.

Archer, D., & Gartner, R. Violent acts and violent times: A comparative approach to postwar homicide rates. *American Sociological Review*, 1976, *41*, 937–963.

Arend, R. A., Gove, F. L., & Sroufe, L. A. Continuity of individual adaptation from infancy to kindergarten: A predictive study of ego-resiliency and curiosity in pre-schoolers. *Child Development*, 1979, *50*, 950–959.

Asarnow, R. F., & MacCrimmon, D. J. Residual performance deficit in chronically remitted schizophrenics: A marker of schizophrenia? *Journal of Abnormal Psychology*, 1978, *87*, 597–608.

Asarnow, R. F., Steffy, R. A., MacCrimmon, D. J., & Cleghorn, J. M. An attentional assessment of foster children at risk for schizophrenia. *Journal of Abnormal Psychology*, 1977, *86*, 267–275.

Asperger, H. Die autistischen Psychopathen im Kindesalter. *Archiv fur Psychiatrie und Nervenkrankheiten*, 1944, *117*, 76.

August, G. J., & Stewart, M. A. Is there a syndrome of pure hyperactivity? *British Journal of Psychiatry*, 1982, *140*, 305–311.

August, G. J., Stewart, M. A., & Tsai, L. The incidence of cognitive disabilities in the siblings of autistic children. *British Journal of Psychiatry*, 1981, *138*, 416–422.

Austin, R. L. Construct validity of I-level classification. *Criminal Justice and Behavior*, 1975, *2*, 113–129.

Ayllon, T., & Roberts, M. D. Eliminating discipline problems by strengthening academic performance. *Journal of Applied Behavior Analysis*, 1974, *7*, 71–76.

Bagley, C. Juvenile delinquency in Exeter. *Urban Studies*, 1965, *2*, 35–39.

Bagley, C. *The social psychology of the child with epilepsy*. London: Routledge & Kegan Paul, 1971.

Bahr, S. J. Family determinants and effects of deviance. In W. R. Burr, R. Hill, F. I. Nye, & I. L. Reiss (Eds.), *Contemporary theories about the family: Research-based theories* (Vol. 1). New York: Free Press, London: Collier-Macmillan, 1979.

Baldwin, J. British areal studies of crime: An assessment. *British Journal of Criminology*, 1975, *15*, 211–227.

Baldwin, J. Ecological and areal studies in Great Britain and the United States. In N. Morris & M. Tonry (Eds.), *Crime and justice: An annual review of research* (Vol. 1). Chicago & London: University of Chicago Press, 1979.

Baldwin, J., & Bottoms, A. E. *The urban criminal: A study in Sheffield*. London: Tavistock Press, 1976.

Baltaxe, C. Pragmatic deficits in the language of autistic adolescents. *Journal of Pediatric Psychology*, 1977, *2*, 176–180.

Baltes, P. B., & Brim, O. *Life-span development and behavior* (Vol. 2). New York: Academic Press, 1979.

Baltes, P. B., & Schaie, K. W. On the plasticity of intelligence in adulthood and old age: Where Horn and Donaldson fail. *American Psychologist*, 1976, *31*, 720–739.

Bandura, A. Social-learning theory of identificatory processes. In D. A. Goslin (Ed.), *Handbook of socialization theory and research*. New York: Rand McNally, 1969.

Bandura, A., & Menlove, F. Factors determining vicarious extinction of avoidance behavior through symbolic modeling. *Journal of Person-*

ality and Social Psychology, 1968, *8,* 99–108.

Barker, R. G., Wright, B. A., Myerson, L., & Gonick, M. R. Adjustment of physical handicap and illness: A survey of the social psychology of physique and disability. *Social Science Research Council Bulletin,* No. 55, 1953.

Barkley, R. A. Predicting the response of hyperkinetic children to stimulant drugs. *Journal of Abnormal Child Psychology,* 1976, *4,* 327–348.

Barkley, R. A. A review of stimulant drug research with hyperactive children. *Journal of Child Psychology and Psychiatry,* 1977, *18,* 137–166.

Barkley, R. A. *Hyperactive children: A handbook for diagnosis and treatment.* New York: Guilford Press, 1981.

Barkley, R. A., & Jackson, T. Hyperkinesis, autonomic nervous system activity and stimulant drug effects. *Journal of Child Psychology and Psychiatry,* 1977, *18,* 347–357.

Barkley, R. A., & Ullman, D. G. A comparison of objective measures of activity and distractibility in hyperactive and nonhyperactive children. *Journal of Abnormal Child Psychology,* 1975, *3,* 231–244.

Baron, M., Klotz, J., Mendlewicz, J., & Rainer, J. Multiple-threshold transmission of affective disorders. *Archives of General Psychiatry,* 1981, *38,* 79–84.

Barraclough, B., Bunch, J., Nelson, B., & Sainsbury, P. A hundred cases of suicide: Clinical aspects. *British Journal of Psychiatry,* 1974, *125,* 355–373.

Bartak, L., Rutter, M., & Cox, A. A comparative study of infantile autism and specific developmental receptive language disorder. I. The children. *British Journal of Psychiatry,* 1975, *126,* 127–145.

Bartolucci, G., Pierce, S. J., & Streiner, D. Cross-sectional studies of grammatical morphemes in autistic and mentally retarded children. *Journal of Autism and Developmental Disorders,* 1980, *10,* 39–50.

Battle, E. S., & Lacey, B. A context for hyperactivity in children over time. *Child Development,* 1972, *43,* 757–773.

Bauer, D. H. An exploratory study of developmental changes in children's fears. *Journal of Child Psychology and Psychiatry,* 1976, *17,* 69–74.

Bauer, D. H. Childhood fears in developmental perspective. In L. A. Hersov & I. Berg (Eds.), *Out of school: Modern perspectives in truancy and school refusal.* Chichester, Eng.: Wiley, 1980.

Bax, M., & MacKeith, R. (Eds.). *Minimal cerebral dysfunction* (Clinics in Developmental Medicine No. 10). London: Heinemann Medical/SIMP, 1963.

Beck, A. T. *Cognitive therapy and the emotional disorders.* New York: International Universities Press, 1976.

Behar, L., & Stringfield, S. A behavior rating scale for the preschool child. *Developmental Psychology,* 1974, *10,* 601–610.

Bell, R. Q., & Harper, L. V. *Child effects on adults.* Hillsdale, N.J.: Erlbaum, 1977.

Bell, R. Q., & Waldrop, M. F. Temperament and minor physical anomalies. In R. Porter & G. M. Collins (Eds.), *Temperamental differences in infants and young children* (Ciba Foundation Symposium No. 89). London: Pitman, 1982.

Belsky, J. Child maltreatment: An ecological integration. *American Psychologist,* 1980, *35,* 320–335.

Belsky, J. Early human experience: A family perspective. *Developmental Psychology,* 1981, *17,* 3–23.

Belson, W. A. *Juvenile theft: The causal factors.* London: Harper & Row, 1975.

Bem, D. J., & Funder, D. C. Predicting more of the people more of the time: Assessing the personality of situations. *Psychological Review,* 1978, *85,* 485–501.

Bemporad, J. R. Adult recollections of a formerly autistic child. *Journal of Autism and Developmental Disorders,* 1979, *9,* 179–198.

Benaim, S., Horder, J., & Anderson, J. Hysterical epidemic in a classroom. *Psychological Medicine,* 1973, *3,* 366–373.

Bender, L. Childhood schizophrenia: Clinical study of one hundred schizophrenic children. *American Journal of Orthopsychiatry,* 1947, *17,* 40–56.

Bender, L., & Schilder, P. Impulsions: A specific disorder of the behavior of children. *Archives of Neurological Psychiatry,* 1940, *44,* 990–1008.

Benes, F., Sunderland, P., Jones, B. D., LeMay, M., Cohen, B. M., & Lipinski, J. F. Normal ventricles in young schizophrenics. *British Journal of Psychiatry,* 1982, *141,* 90–93.

Bennett, I. *Delinquent and neurotic children: A comparative study.* New York: Basic Books, 1960.

Benton, A. L. Minimal brain dysfunction from a neuropsychological point of view. *Annals of the New York Academy of Science,* 1973, *205,* 29–37.

Bentovim, A. Disturbed and under five. *Special Education,* 1973, *62,* 31–35.

Berg, I., Butler, A., & Hall, G. The outcome of

adolescent school phobia. *British Journal of Psychiatry*, 1976, *128*, 80–85.

Berg, I., Marks, I., McGuire, R., & Lipsedge, M. School phobia and agoraphobia. *Psychological Medicine*, 1974, *4*, 428–434.

Berlyne, D. E. Attention as a problem in behavior therapy. In D. Mostofsky (Ed.), *Attention: Contemporary theory and analysis*. New York: Appleton-Century-Crofts, 1970.

Bersh, P. J. Eysenck's theory of incubation: A critical analysis. *Behaviour Research and Therapy*, 1980, *18*, 11–17.

Birch, H. G. The problems of "brain damage" in children. In H. G. Birch (Ed.), *Brain damage in children: The biological and social aspects*. Baltimore: Williams & Wilkins, 1964.

Birch, H. G., & Gussow, J. D. *Disadvantaged children: Health, nutrition and school failure*. New York: Grune & Stratton, 1970.

Black, M., Freeman, B. J., & Montgomery, J. Systematic observation of play behavior in autistic children. *Journal of Autism and Childhood Schizophrenia*, 1975, *5*, 363–372.

Black, P., Shepard, R. H., & Walker, A. E. Outcome of head trauma: Age and post-traumatic seizures. In R. Porter & D. W. FitzSimons (Eds.), *Outcome of severe damage to the central nervous system* (Ciba Foundation Symposium No. 34 [new series]). Amsterdam: Excerpta Medica, 1975.

Blackstock, E. Cerebral asymmetry and the development of early infantile autism. *Journal of Autism and Childhood Schizophrenia*, 1978, *8*, 339–353.

Blakar, R. M. *Studies of familial communication and psychopathology: A social-developmental approach to deviant behavior*. Oslo: Universitetsforlaget, 1979.

Blaney, P. H. Contemporary theories of depression: Critique and comparison. *Journal of Abnormal Psychology*, 1977, *86*, 203–223.

Block, J. H., Block, J., & Morrison, A. Parental agreement-disagreement on childrearing orientations and gender-related personality correlates in children. *Child Development*, 1981, *52*, 965–974.

Blouin, A. G. A., Bornstein, R. A., & Trites, R. L. Teenage alcohol use among hyperactive children: A five year follow-up study. *Journal of Pediatric Psychology*, 1978, *3*, 188–194.

Blunden, D., Spring, C., & Greenberg, L. M. Validation of the classroom behavior inventory. *Journal of Consulting and Clinical Psychology*, 1974, *42*, 84–88.

Boeson, V., & Aarkrog, T. Pneumoencephalography of patients in a child psychiatric department. *Danish Medical Bulletin*, 1967, *14*, 210–218.

Bogaard, C. *Relationship between aggressive behavior in children and parent perception of child behavior*. Unpublished doctoral dissertation, University of Oregon, 1976.

Bohman, M., & Sigvardsson, S. Long-term effects of early institutional care: A prospective longitudinal study. *Journal of Child Psychology and Psychiatry*, 1979, *20*, 111–118.

Bohman, M., & Sigvardsson, S. A prospective, longitudinal study of children registered for adoption: A 15 year follow-up. *Acta Psychiatrica Scandinavica*, 1980, *61*, 339–355.

Boll, T. J. The Halstead-Reitan neuropsychological battery. In S. B. Filskov & T. J. Boll (Eds.), *Handbook of clinical neuropsychology*. New York: Wiley, 1981.

Boll, T. J., & Barth, J. T. Neuropsychology of brain damage in children. In S. B. Filskov & T. J. Boll (Eds.), *Handbook of clinical neuropsychology*. New York: Wiley, 1981.

Borkovec, T. D. Autonomic reactivity to sensory stimulation in psychopathic, neurotic and normal juvenile delinquents. *Journal of Consulting and Clinical Psychology*, 1970, *35*, 217–222.

Bosch, G. (Ed.). *Infantile autism: A clinical and phenomenological-anthropological investigation taking language as the guide* (D. Jordan & I. Jordan, trans.). Berlin: Springer-Verlag. 1970. (Originally published, 1962.)

Boucher, J. Articulation in early childhood autism. *Journal of Autism and Childhood Schizophrenia*, 1976, *6*, 297–302.

Boullin, D., Coleman, M., O'Brien, R., & Rimland, B. Laboratory prediction of infantile autism based on 5-hydroxytryptamine efflux from blood platelets and their correlation with the Rimland E-2 score. *Journal of Autism and Childhood Schizophrenia*, 1971, *1*, 63–71.

Boullin, D., Freeman, B. J., Geller, E., Ritvo, E. R., Rutter, M., & Yuwiler, A. Towards the resolution of conflicting findings. *Journal of Autism and Developmental Disorder*, 1982, *12*, 97–98.

Bowers, K. S. Situationism in psychology: An analysis and a critique. *Psychological Review*, 1973, *80*, 307–336.

Bowlby, J. *Forty-four juvenile thieves: Their characters and home-life*. London: Baillere, Tindall & Cox, 1946.

Bowlby, J. *Attachment and loss*, vol. 1, *Attachment*. London: Hogarth Press, 1969.

Bowlby, J. *Attachment and loss*, vol. 2, *Separation*,

anxiety and anger. London: Hogarth Press, 1973.

Bowlby, J. *Attachment and loss*, vol. 3, *Loss, sadness and depression*. New York: Basic Books, 1980.

Bowlby, J., Ainsworth, M. D. S., Boston, M., & Rosenbluth, D. The effects of mother-child separation: A follow-up study. *British Journal of Medical Psychology*, 1956, *29*, 211–247.

Braithwaite, J. The myth of social class and criminality reconsidered. *American Sociological Review*, 1981, *46*, 36–57.

Brask, B. H. *A prevalence investigation of childhood psychosis*. Paper presented at the meeting of the Scandinavian Congress of Psychiatry, 1970.

Bregman, E. An attempt to modify the emotional attitudes of infants by the conditioned response technique. *Journal of Genetic Psychology*, 1934, *45*, 169–196.

British Medical Journal. Serotonin, platelets and autism, editorial. *British Medical Journal*, 1978, *1*, 1651–1652.

Bronfenbrenner, U. *The ecology of human development: Experiments by nature and design*. Cambridge: Harvard University Press, 1979.

Brown, B. J., & Lloyd, H. A controlled study of children not speaking at school. *Journal of the Association of Workers for Maladjusted Children*, 1975, *3*, 49–63.

Brown, F. W. Heredity in the psychoneuroses. *Proceedings of the Royal Society of Medicine*, 1942, *35*, 785–790.

Brown, G. W., & Harris, T. *Social origins of depression*. London: Tavistock Press, 1978.

Brown, G. W., Harris, T. O., & Bifulco, A. Long-term effect of early loss of parent. In M. Rutter, C. E. Izard, & P. Read (Eds.), *Depression in childhood: Developmental perspectives*. New York: Guilford Press, in press.

Brown, W. T., Jenkins, E. C., Friedman, E., Brooks, J., Wisniewski, K., Raguthu, S., & French, J. Autism is associated with the fragile-X syndrome. *Journal of Autism and Developmental Disorders*, 1982, *12*, 303–308.

Brownell, G. L., Budinger, T. F., Lauterbur, P. C., & McGeer, P. L. Positon tomography and nuclear magnetic resonance imagery. *Science*, 1982, *215*, 619–626.

Bryan, T., & Bryan, J. Some personal and social experiences of learning disabled children. In B. K. Keogh (Ed.), *Advances in special education*. Greenwich, Conn.: JAI Press, 1981.

Buchsbaum, M., & Wender, P. Averaged evoked responses in normal and minimally brain dysfunction children tested with amphetamine. *Archives of General Psychiatry*, 1973, *29*, 764–770.

Buikhuisen, W., & Hoekstra, H. A. Factors related to recidivism. *British Journal of Criminology*, 1974, *14*, 63–69.

Burgess, R. L., & Conger, R. D. Family interaction in abusive, neglectful and normal families. *Child Development*, 1978, *49*, 1163–1173.

Burke, R. J., & Weir, T. Sex differences in adolescent life stress, social support and well-being. *Journal of Psychology*, 1979, *98*, 277–288.

Buss, D. M. Predicting parent-child interaction from children's activity level. *Developmental Psychology*, 1981, *17*, 59–65.

Buss, D. M., Block, J. H., & Block, J. Preschool activity level: Personality correlates and developmental implications. *Child Development*, 1980, *51*, 401–408.

Cadoret, R. J., & Cain, C. Sex differences in predictors of antisocial behavior in adoptees. *Archives of General Psychiatry*, 1980, *37*, 1171–1175.

Cairns, R. B. *Social development: The origin and plasticity of interchanges*. San Francisco: W. H. Freeman, 1979.

Camp, J. A., Bialer, I., Sverd, J., & Winsberg, B. G. Clinical usefulness of the NIMNH physical and neurological examination for soft signs. *American Journal of Psychiatry*, 1978, *135*, 362–364.

Campbell, B. A., & Randall, P. K. Paradoxical effects of amphetamine on behavioral arousal in neonatal and adult rats: A possible animal model of the calming effect of amphetamine on hyperkinetic children. In N. R. Ellis (Ed.), *Aberrant development in infancy*. Hillsdale, N.J.: Erlbaum, 1975.

Campbell, B. A., & Raskin, L. A. Ontogeny of behavioral arousal: The role of environmental stimuli. *Journal of Comparative and Physiological Psychology*, 1978, *92*, 176–184.

Campbell, M., Petti, T. A., Green, W. H., Cohen, I. L., Genieser, N. B., & David, R. Some physical parameters of young autistic children. *Journal of the American Academy of Child Psychiatry*, 1980, *19*, 193–212.

Campbell, S. B. G., Endman, M. W., & Bernfeld, G. A three-year follow-up of hyperactive preschoolers into elementary school. *Journal of Child Psychology and Psychiatry*, 1977, *18*, 239–249.

Campbell, S. B. G., & Paulauskas, S. Peer relations in hyperactive children. *Journal of Child Psy-*

chology and Psychiatry, 1979, *20*, 233–246.

Campbell, S. B. G., Schleifer, M., Weiss, G., & Perlman, T. A two-year follow-up of hyperactive preschoolers. *American Journal of Orthopsychiatry*, 1977, *47*, 149–162.

Cantwell, D. P. Genetic studies of hyperactive children: psychiatric illness in biologic and adopting parents. In R. Fieve, D. Rosenthal & H. Brill (Eds.) *Genetic Research in Psychiatry*. Baltimore: Johns Hopkins University Press, 1974.

Cantwell, D. P. (Ed.). *The hyperactive child: Diagnosis, management, current research*. New York: Spectrum, 1975.

Cantwell, D. P. Hyperactivity and antisocial behavior revisited: A critical review of the literature. In D. Lewis (Ed.), *Biophysical vulnerabilities to delinquency*. New York: Spectrum, 1980.

Cantwell, D. P. Personal communication, August 1982.

Cantwell, D. P., Baker, L., & Rutter, M. Family factors. In M. Rutter & E. Schopler (Eds.), *Autism: A reappraisal of concepts and treatment*. New York: Plenum, 1978.

Cantwell, D. P., Russell, A. T., Mattison, R., & Will, L. A comparison of DSM–II and DSM–III in the diagnosis of childhood psychiatric disorders: I. Agreement with expected diagnosis. *Archives of General Psychiatry*, 1979, *36*, 1208–1213.

Cantwell, D. P., & Satterfield, J. H. The prevalence of academic underachievement in hyperactive children. *Journal of Pediatric Psychology*, 1978, *3*, 163–171.

Caparulo, B. K., Cohen, D. J., Rothman, S. L., Young, J. G., Katz, J. D., Shaywitz, S. E., & Shaywitz, B. A. Computed tomographic brain scanning in children with developmental neuropsychiatric disorders. *Journal of the American Academy of Child Psychiatry*, 1981, *20*, 338–357.

Caplan, H. L. Hysterical "conversion" symptoms in childhood. Unpublished master's thesis, University of London, 1970.

Caplan, P. J., Awad, G. A., Wilks, C., & White, G. Sex differences in a delinquent clinic population. *British Journal of Criminology*, 1980, *20*, 311–328.

Carlson, G. A., & Cantwell, D. P. A survey of depressive symptoms in a child and adolescent psychiatric population: interview data. *Journal of the American Academy of Child Psychiatry*, 1979, *18*, 587–599.

Carlson, G. A., & Cantwell, D. P. Personal communication, March 1980. (a)

Carlson, G. A., & Cantwell, D. P. A survey of depressive symptoms, syndrome and disorder in a child psychiatric population. *Journal of Child Psychology and Psychiatry*, 1980, *21*, 19–25. (b)

Carlson, G. A., & Cantwell, D. P. Unmasking masked depression. *American Journal of Psychiatry*, 1980, *137*, 445–449 (c)

Carlson, G. A., & Cantwell, D. P. Diagnosis of childhood depression: A comparison of the Weinberg and DSM–III criteria. *Journal of the American Academy of Child Psychiatry*, 1982, *21*, 247–250.

Carroll, B. J. The dexamethasone suppression test for melancholia. *British Journal of Psychiatry*, 1982, *140*, 292–304.

Chadwick, O., & Rutter, M. Neuropsychological assessment. In M. Rutter (Ed.), *Developmental neuropsychiatry*. New York: Guilford Press, in press.

Chadwick, O., Rutter, M., Brown, G., Shaffer, D., & Traub, M. A prospective study of children with head injuries. II. Cognitive sequelae. *Psychological Medicine*, 1981, *11*, 49–61.

Charles, L., & Schain, R. J. A four-year follow-up study of the effects of methylphenidate on the behavior and academic achievement of hyperactive children. *Journal of Abnormal Child Psychology*, 1981, *9*, 495–505.

Charles, L., Schain, R. J., & Guthrie, D. Long-term use and discontinuation of methylphenidate with hyperactive children. *Developmental Medicine and Child Neurology*, 1979, *6*, 758–764.

Chavez, A., Martinez, C., & Yaschine, T. The importance of nutrition and stimuli on child mental and social development. In J. Cravioto, L. Hambraeus, & B. Vahlquist (Eds.), *Early malnutrition and mental development* (Symposia of the Swedish Nutrition Foundation XII). Stockholm: Almqvist & Wiksell, 1974.

Checkley, S. A. Neuroendocrine tests of monoamine function in man: A review of basic theory and its application to the study of depressive illness. *Psychological Medicine*, 1980, *10*, 35–83.

Chelune, G. J., & Edwards, P. Early brain lesions: Ontogenic-environmental considerations. *Journal of Consulting and Clinical Psychology*, 1981, *49*, 777–790.

Chess, S. Neurological dysfunction and childhood behavioral pathology. *Journal of Autism and Childhood Schizophrenia*, 1972, *2*, 299–311.

Chess, S., Fernandez, P. B., & Korn, S. J. Behavioral consequences of congenital rubella. *Journal of Pediatrics*, 1978, *93*, 699–703.

Chess, S., Korn, S. J., & Fernandez, P. B. *Psychi-*

atric disorders of children with congenital rubella. New York: Brunner/Mazel, 1971.

Chick, J., Waterhouse, L., & Wolff, S. Psychological construing in schizoid children grown up. *British Journal of Psychiatry*, 1979, *135*, 425–430.

Chiles, J. A., Miller, M. L., & Cox, G. B. Depression in an adolescent delinquent population. *Archives of General Psychiatry*, 1980, *37*, 1179–1184.

Christie, N., Andenaes, J., & Skirbekk, S. A study of self-reported crime. *Scandinavian Studies in Criminology*, 1965, *1*, 86–116.

Churchill, D. W., & Bryson, C. Q. Looking and approach behavior of psychotic and normal children as a function of adult attention or preoccupation. *Comprehensive Psychiatry*, 1972, *13*, 171–177.

Cicchetti, D., & Serafica, F. C. Interplay among behavioral systems: Illustrations from the study of attachment, affiliation and wariness in young children with Down's syndrome. *Developmental Psychology*, 1981, *17*, 36–49.

Clark, J. P., & Wenninger, E. P. Socio-economic class and area as correlates of illegal behavior among juveniles. *American Sociological Review*, 1962, *27*, 826–834.

Clark, M. M. *Reading difficulties in school*. Harmondsworth, Eng.: Penguin, 1970.

Clark, P., & Rutter, M. Compliance and resistance in autistic children. *Journal of Autism and Childhood Schizophrenia*, 1977, *7*, 33–48.

Clark, P., & Rutter, M. Task difficulty and task performance in autistic children. *Journal of Child Psychology and Psychiatry*, 1979, *20*, 271–285.

Clark, P., & Rutter, M. Autistic children's responses to structure and to interpersonal demands. *Journal of Autism and Developmental Disorders*, 1981, *11*, 201–217.

Clarke, R. V. G. (Ed.). *Tackling vandalism* (Home Office Research Study No. 47). London: Her Majesty's Stationery Office, 1978.

Clarke, R. V. G. "Situational" crime prevention: Theory and practice. *British Journal of Criminology*, 1980, *20*, 136–147.

Clarke, R. V. G., & Cornish, D. B. The effectiveness of residential treatment. In L. A. Hersov & M. Berger with D. Shaffer (Eds.), *Aggression and antisocial behaviour in childhood and adolescence*. Oxford: Pergamon, 1978.

Clarke, R. V. G., & Mayhew, P. (Eds.), *Designing out crime*. London: Her Majesty's Stationery Office, 1981.

Clausen, J. A. The social meaning of differential physical and sexual maturation. In S. E. Dragastin & G. H. Elder, Jr. (Eds.), *Adolescence in the life cycle: Psychological change and social context*. Washington, D.C.: Hemisphere, 1975.

Clinard, M. B. *Sociology of deviant behavior* (3rd Ed.). New York: Holt, Rinehart & Winston, 1968.

Clinard, M. B., & Abbott, D. J. *Crime in developing countries: A comparative perspective*. New York: Wiley, 1973.

Cline, H. F. Criminal behavior over the life span. In O. G. Brim, Jr. & J. Kagan (Eds.), *Constancy and change in human development*. Cambridge: Harvard University Press, 1980.

Cloninger, C. R., Bohman, M., & Sigvardsson, S. Inheritance of alcohol abuse: Cross-fostering analysis of adopted men. *Archives of General Psychiatry*, 1981, *38*, 861–868.

Cloninger, C. R., Christiansen, K. O., Reich, T., & Gottesman, I. I. Implications of sex differences in the prevalences of antisocial personality, alcoholism, and criminality for familial transmission. *Archives of General Psychiatry*, 1978, *35*, 941–951.

Close, J., Scored neurological examination. *Psychopharmacology Bulletin*, 1973, 142–148. (Special issue: *Pharmacotherapy of children.*)

Cloward, R. A., & Ohlin, L. E. *Delinquency and opportunity*. Chicago: Free Press, 1960.

Cohen, A. K. *Delinquent boys: The culture of the gang*. London: Routledge & Kegan Paul, 1956.

Cohen, D. J., Caparulo, B. K., & Shaywitz, B. A. Neurochemical and developmental models in childhood autism. In G. Serban (Ed.), *Cognitive defects in the development of mental illness*. New York: Brunner/Mazel, 1978.

Coleman, J., Wolkind, S. N., & Ashley, L. Symptoms of behaviour disturbance and adjustment to school. *Journal of Child Psychology and Psychiatry*, 1977, *18*, 201–210.

Coleman, M. Serotonin concentration in whole blood of hyperactive children. *Journal of Pediatrics*, 1971, *78*, 985–990.

Coleman, M. (Ed.). *The autistic syndrome*. Amsterdam: North-Holland, 1976.

Compton, A. A study of the psychoanalytic theory of anxiety. *Journal of the American Psychoanalytic Association*, 1972, *20*, 3–44; 341–394.

Conger, J. J., & Miller, W. C. *Personality, social class and delinquency*. New York: Wiley, 1966.

Conger, R. P. The assessment of dysfunctional family systems. In B. B. Lahey & A. E. Kazdin (Eds.), *Advances in clinical child psychology*

(Vol. 4). New York: Plenum, 1981.

Conners, C. K. Rating scales for use in drug studies with children. *Psychopharmacology Bulletin,* 1973, 24–29. (Special issue: *Pharmacotherapy of children.*)

Conners, C. K. *Food additives and hyperactive children.* New York: Plenum, 1980.

Conners, C. K., & Werry, J. S. Pharmacotherapy. In H. C. Quay & J. S. Werry (Eds.), *Psychopathological disorders of childhood* (2nd ed.). New York: Wiley, 1979.

Connolly, J., Hallam, R. S., & Marks, I. M. Selective association of fainting with blood-illness-injury fear. *Behavior Therapy,* 1976, *7,* 8-13.

Cooper, C. E. Child abuse and neglect—medical aspects. In S. M. Smith (Ed.), *The maltreatment of children.* Lancaster, Eng.: MTP Press, 1978.

Cooper, S. F., Leach, C., Storer, D., & Tonge, W. L. The children of psychiatric patients: Clinical findings. *British Journal of Psychiatry,* 1977, *131,* 514–522.

Copeland, A. P., & Weissbrod, C. S. Behavioral correlates of the hyperactive factor of the Conners teacher questionnaire. *Journal of Abnormal Child Psychology,* 1978, *6,* 339–343.

Corah, N. L., Anthony, E. J., Painter, P., Stern, J. A., & Thurston, D. Effects of perinatal anoxia after seven years. *Psychological Monographs,* 1965, *79*(Whole No. 596).

Costello, G. C. Childhood depression: Three basic but questionable assumptions in the Lefkowitz and Burton critique. *Psychological Bulletin,* 1980, *87,* 185–190.

Cowan, P. A., Hoddinott, B. A., & Wright, B. A. Compliance and resistance in the conditioning of autistic children: An exploratory study. *Child Development,* 1965, *36,* 913–923.

Cravioto, J., & Arrieta, R. Malnutrition in childhood. In M. Rutter (Ed.), *Developmental neuropsychiatry.* New York: Guilford Press, in press.

Creak, M. Childhood psychosis: A review of 100 cases. *British Journal of Psychiatry,* 1963, *109,* 84–89.

Crockenberg, S. B. Infant irritability, mother responsiveness, and social support inferences on the security of infant-mother attachment. *Child Development,* 1981, *52,* 857–865.

Crockenberg, S. B., & Smith, P. Antecedents of mother-infant interaction and infant temperament in the first three months of life. *Infant Behavior and Development,* in press.

Crook, T., & Eliot, J. Parental death during childhood and adult depression: A critical review of the literature. *Psychological Bulletin,* 1980, *87,* 252–259.

Crowe, R. R. An adoption study of antisocial personality. *Archives of General Psychiatry,* 1974, *31,* 785–791.

Cummings, J. D. The incidence of emotional symptoms in school children. *British Journal of Educational Psychology,* 1944, *14,* 151–161.

Cummings, S. T., Bayley, H. C., & Rie, H. E. Effects of the child's deficiency on the mother: A study of mothers of mentally retarded, chronically ill and neurotic children. *American Journal of Orthopsychiatry,* 1966, *36,* 595–608.

Cunningham, C. E., & Barkley, R. A. The interactions of hyperactive and normal children with their mothers in free play and structured task. *Child Development,* 1979, *50,* 217–224.

Cunningham, L., Cadoret, R. J., Loftus, R., & Edwards, J. E. Studies of adoptees from psychiatrically disturbed biological parents: Psychiatric conditions in childhood and adolescence. *British Journal of Psychiatry,* 1975, *126,* 534–549.

Curcio, F., & Piserchia, E. A. Pantomimic representation in autistic children. *Journal of Autism and Childhood Schizophrenia,* 1978, *8,* 181–190.

Curnow, R. N., & Smith, C. Multifactorial models for familial diseases in man. *Journal of the Royal Statistical Society,* 1975, *138,* 131–169.

Cytryn, L., Gilbert, A., & Eisenberg, L. The effectiveness of tranquillizing drugs plus supportive psychotherapy in treating behavior disorders of children: A double-blind study of eighty outpatients. *American Journal of Orthopsychiatry,* 1960, *30,* 113–129.

Cytryn, L., & McKnew, D. H. Proposed classification of childhood depression. *American Journal of Psychiatry,* 1972, *129,* 149–155.

Cytryn, L., & McKnew, D. H. Developmental issues in risk research: The offspring of affectively ill parents. In M. Rutter, C. E. Izard, & P. Read (Eds.), *Depression in childhood: Developmental perspectives.* New York: Guilford Press, in press.

Cytryn, L., McKnew, D. H., & Bunney, W. T., Jr. Diagnosis of depression in children: A reassessment. *American Journal of Psychiatry,* 1980, *137,* 22–25.

Dalton, K. *The premenstrual syndrome and progesterone therapy.* London: Heinemann Medical, 1977.

Damasio, H., Maurer, R. G., Damasio, A. R., & Chui, H. C. Computerized tomographic scan findings in patients with autistic behavior. *Archives of Neurology*, 1980, *37*, 504–510.

Darby, J. K. Neuropathologic aspects of psychosis in children. *Journal of Autism and Childhood Schizophrenia*, 1976, *6*, 339–352.

Dare, C. Psychoanalytic theories. In M. Rutter & L. A. Hersov (Eds.), *Child psychiatry: Modern approaches*. Oxford: Blackwell Scientific, 1977.

Davies, J. G. V., & Maliphant, R. Autonomic responses of male adolescents exhibiting refractory behaviour in school. *Journal of Child Psychology and Psychiatry*, 1971, *12*, 115–128. (a)

Davies, J. G. V., & Maliphant, R. Refractory behaviour at school in normal adolescent males in relation to psychopathy and early experience. *Journal of Child Psychology and Psychiatry*, 1971, *12*, 35–42. (b)

Davies, J. G. V., & Maliphant, R. Refractory behaviour in school and avoidance learning. *Journal of Child Psychology and Psychiatry*, 1974, *15*, 23–32.

Dawe, H. C. An analysis of two hundred quarrels of preschool children. *Child Development*, 1934, *5*, 139–157.

Dawson, G., Warrenburg, S., & Fuller, P. Cerebral lateralization in individuals diagnosed as autistic in early childhood. *Brain and Language*, 1982, *15*, 353–368.

De la Cruz, F. F., Fox, B. H., & Roberts, R. H. (Eds.). Minimal brain dysfunction. *Annals of the New York Academy of Sciences*, 1973, *205*.

Delamater, A. M., Lahey, B. B., & Drake, L. Toward an empirical subclassification of "learning disabilities": A psychophysiological comparison of "hyperactive" and "nonhyperactive" subgroups. *Journal of Abnormal Child Psychology*, 1981, *9*, 65–77.

Delfini, L. F., Bernal, M. E., & Rosen, P. M. Comparison of deviant and normal boys in home settings. In E. J. Mash, L. A. Hamerlynck, & L. C. Handy (Eds.), *Behavior modification and families*. New York: Brunner/Mazel, 1976.

DeMyer, M. K. Perceptual limitations in autistic children and their relation to social and intellectual deficits. In M. Rutter (Ed.), *Infantile autism: Concepts, characteristics and treatment*. Edinburgh & London: Churchill Livingstone, 1971.

DeMyer, M. K., Hingtgen, J. N., & Jackson, R. K. Infantile autism reviewed: A decade of research. *Schizophrenia Bulletin*, 1981, *7*, 388–451.

DeMyer-Gapin, S., & Scott, T. J. Effect of stimulus novelty on stimulation seeking in antisocial and neurotic children. *Journal of Abnormal Psychology*, 1977, *86*, 96–98.

Depue, R. A., & Monroe, S. M. The unipolar-bipolar distinction in the depressive disorders. *Psychological Bulletin*, 1978, *85*, 1001–1029.

Des Lauriers, A. M. The cognitive-affective dilemma in early infantile autism: The case of Clarence. *Journal of Autism and Childhood Schizophrenia*, 1978, *8*, 219–229.

Deykin, E. Y., & MacMahon, B. The incidence of seizures among children with autistic symptoms. *American Journal of Psychiatry*, 1979, *136*, 1310–1312. (a)

Deykin, E. Y., & MacMahon, B. Viral exposure and autism. *American Journal of Epidemiology*, 1979, *109*, 628–638. (b)

Deykin, E. Y., & MacMahon, B. Pregnancy, delivery and neonatal complications among autistic children. *American Journal of Diseases of Childhood*, 1980, *134*, 860–864.

Dixon, P. Behavioural and social relationships of long-term fostered and institution reared children. Report in preparation, 1983.

Doane, J. A., Goldstein, M. J., & Rodnick, E. H. Parental patterns of affective style and the development of schizophrenia spectrum disorders. *Family Process*, 1981, *20*, 337–349.

Dobbing, J. The later development of the brain and its vulnerability. In J. A. Davis & J. Dobbing (Eds.), *Scientific foundations of paediatrics*. London: Heinemann Medical, 1974.

Dohrenwend, B. P., Dohrenwend, B. S., Gould, M. S., Link, B., Neugebauer, R., & Wunsch-Hitzig, R. *Mental illness in the United States: Epidemiological estimates*. New York: Praeger, 1980.

Dohrenwend, B. P., Shrout, P., Egri, G., & Mendelsohn, F. S. Non-specific psychological distress and other dimensions of psychopathology. *Archives of General Psychiatry*, 1980, *37*, 1229–1236.

Doleschal, E., & Klapmuts, N. Towards a new criminology. *Crime and Delinquency Literature*, 1973, *5*, 607–626.

Dooley, D., & Catalano, R. Economic change as a cause of behavioral disorder. *Psychological Bulletin*, 1980, *87*, 450–468.

Dorner, S. Adolescents with spina bifida: How they see their situation. *Archives of Disease in Childhood*, 1976, *51*, 439–444.

Douglas, J. W. B., & Mann, S. Personal communication, June 1979.

Douglas, V. I. Attentional and cognitive problems. In M. Rutter (Ed.), *Developmental neuro-*

psychiatry. New York: Guilford Press, in press.

Douglas, V. I., & Peters, K. G. Toward a clearer definition of the attentional deficit of hyperactive children. In G. A. Hale & M. Lewis (Eds.), *Attention and cognitive development*. New York: Plenum, 1979.

Drillien, C. M., Thomson, A. J. M., & Burgoyne, K. Low-birthweight children at early school age: A longitudinal study. *Developmental Medicine and Child Neurology*, 1980, *22*, 26–47.

Dubey, D. R. Organic factors in hyperkinesis: A critical evaluation. *American Journal of Orthopsychiatry*, 1976, *46*, 353–366.

Dunn, J. Individual difference in temperament. In M. Rutter (Ed.), *Scientific foundations of developmental psychiatry*. London: Heinemann Medical, 1980.

Dunn, J., & Kendrick, C. *Siblings: Love, envy and understanding*. Cambridge: Harvard University Press, 1982.

Dweck, C. S., & Bush, E. S. Sex differences in learned helplessness: I. Differential debilitation with peer and adult evaluators. *Developmental Psychology*, 1976, *12*, 147–156.

Dweck, C. S., Davidson, W., Nelson, S., & Enna, B. Sex differences in learned helplessness. II. The contingencies of evaluative feedback in the classroom, and III. An experimental analysis. *Developmental Psychology*, 1978, *14*, 268–276.

Dykman, R. A., Ackerman, P. T., & Oglesby, D. M. Selective and sustained attention in hyperactive, learning disabled and normal boys. *Journal of Nervous and Mental Diseases*, 1979, *167*, 288–297.

Earls, F. Prevalence of behavior problems in 3-year-old children: A cross-national replication. *Archives of General Psychiatry*, 1980, *37*, 1153–1157.

Easterbrooks, M. A., & Lamb, M. E. The relationship between quality of infant-mother attachment and infant competence in initial encounters with peers. *Child Development*, 1979, *50*, 380–387.

Eastwood, M. R., & Kramer, P. M. Epidemiology and depression. *Psychological Medicine*, 1981, *11*, 229–234.

Ebels, E. J. Maturation of the central nervous system. In M. Rutter (Ed.), *Scientific foundations of developmental psychiatry*. London: Heinemann Medical, 1980.

Edelbrock, C. S., & Achenbach, T. M. A typology of child behavior profile patterns: Distribution and correlates for disturbed children aged 6–16. *Journal of Abnormal Child Psychology*, 1980, *8*, 441–470.

Eeg-Olofsson, O. The development of the electroencephalogram in normal children and adolescents from the age of 1 through 21 years. *Acta Paediatrica Scandinavica*, Supplement No. 208, 1970.

Egeland, B. R., & Sroufe, L. A. Developmental sequelae of maltreatment in infancy. In R. Rizley & D. Cicchetti (Eds.), *Developmental perspectives on child maltreatment* (New Directions for Child Development No. 11). San Francisco: Jossey-Bass, 1981.

Eisenberg, L. Development as a unifying concept in psychiatry. *British Journal of Psychiatry*, 1977, *131*, 225–237.

Eisenberg, L. Adolescent suicide: On taking arms against a sea of troubles. *Pediatrics*, 1980, *66*, 315–320.

El-Guebaly, N., Offord, D. R., Sullivan, K. T., & Lynch, G. W. Psychosocial adjustment of the offspring of psychiatric inpatients: The effect of alcoholic, depressive and schizophrenic parentage. *Canadian Psychiatric Association Journal*, 1978, *23*, 281–290.

Ellingson, R. The incidence of EEG abnormality among patients with mental disorders of apparently non-organic origin: A critical review. *American Journal of Psychiatry*, 1954, *111*, 263–275.

Elliott, D. S., Ageton, S. S., & Canter, R. J. An integrated theoretical perspective on delinquent behaviors. *Journal of Research in Crime and Delinquency*, 1979, January, 3–27.

Elliott, D. S., & Voss, H. L. *Delinquency and dropout*. Toronto & London: Lexington Books, 1974.

Emde, R. N. Toward a psychoanalytic theory of affect. In S. I. Greenspan & G. H. Pollock (Eds.), *The course of life: Psychoanalytic contributions toward understanding personality development*, vol. 1, *Infancy and early childhood*. Washington, D.C.: National Institute of Mental Health, 1980.

Emde, R. N., & Harmon, R. J. (Eds.). *The development of attachment and affiliative systems*. New York: Plenum, 1982.

Emde, R. N., Harmon, R. J., & Good, W. V. Depressive feelings in children: A transactional model for research. In M. Rutter, C. E. Izard, & P. Read (Eds.), *Depression in childhood: Developmental perspectives*. New York: Guilford Press, in press.

Emde, R. N., Plak, P. R., & Spitz, R. A. Anaclitic depression in an infant raised in an institution. *Journal of the American Academy of Child Psychiatry*, 1965, *4*, 545–553.

Eme, R. F. Sex differences in childhood psychopathology: A review. *Psychological Bulletin,* 1979, *86,* 574–595.

Emery, R. E. Marital turmoil: Interparental conflict and the children of discord and divorce. *Psychological Bulletin,* in press.

Emery, R. E., & O'Leary, K. D. Children's perceptions of marital discord and behavior problems of boys and girls. *Journal of Abnormal Child Psychology,* 1982, *10,* 11–24.

Emery, R. E., Weintraub, S., & Neale, J. M. Effects of marital discord on the school behavior of children of schizophrenic, affectively disordered and normal parents. *Journal of Abnormal Child Psychology,* 1982, *10,* 215–228.

Emmerich, W. Continuity and stability in early social development. *Child Development,* 1964, *35,* 311–332.

Emmerich, W. Personality development and concepts of structure. *Child Development,* 1968, *39,* 671–690.

Empey, L. T. *American delinquency.* Homewood, Ill.: Dorsey Press, 1978.

Endler, N. S. The role of person-by-situation interactions in personality theory. In I. C. Uzgiris & F. Weizmann (Eds.), *The structuring of experience.* New York: Plenum, 1977.

English, H. B. Three cases of the "conditioned fear response." *Journal of Abnormal Social Psychology,* 1929, *24,* 221–225.

Epstein, S. The stability of behavior: I. On predicting most of the people much of the time. *Journal of Personality and Social Psychology,* 1979, *37,* 1097–1126.

Erlenmeyer-Kimling, L., Kestenbaum, C., Bind, H., & Hilldoff, U. Assessment of the New York high risk project subjects in a sample who are now clinically deviant. In N. F. Watt, E. J. Anthony, L. C. Wynne, & J. E. Rolf (Eds.), *Children at risk for schizophrenia: A longitudinal perspective.* New York: Cambridge University Press, in press.

Erlenmeyer-Kimling, L., Marcuse, Y., Cornblatt, B., Friedman, D., Rainer, J. D., & Rutschmann, J. The New York high risk project. In N. F. Watt, E. J. Anthony, L. C. Wynne, & J. E. Rolf (Eds.), *Children at risk for schizophrenia: A longitudinal perspective.* New York: Cambridge University Press, in press.

Eysenck, H. J. *The biological basis of personality.* Springfield, Ill.: Charles C. Thomas, 1967.

Eysenck, H. J. *Crime and personality.* London: Paladin, 1977.

Eysenck, H. J. The conditioning model of neurosis.

Behavioral and Brain Sciences, 1979, *2,* 155–199.

Eysenck, H. J., & Eysenck, S. B. G. *Manual of the Eysenck personality questionnaire: Junior and adults.* London: Hodder & Stoughton, 1975.

Eysenck, H. J., & Rachman, S. J. The application of learning theory to child psychiatry. In J. G. Howells (Ed.), *Modern perspectives in child psychiatry.* Edinburgh & London: Oliver & Boyd, 1965.

Eysenck, M. W., & Eysenck, H. J. Mischel and the concept of personality. *British Journal of Psychology,* 1980, *71,* 191–204.

Farrington, D. P. Delinquency begins at home. *New Society,* 1972, *21,* 495–497.

Farrington, D. P. Self-reports of deviant behavior: Predictive and stable? *Journal of Criminal Law and Criminology,* 1973, *64,* 99–110.

Farrington, D. P. The effects of public labelling. *British Journal of Criminology,* 1977, *17,* 112–125.

Farrington, D. P. The family backgrounds of aggressive youths. In L. A. Hersov & M. Berger with D. Shaffer (Eds.), *Aggression and antisocial behaviour in childhood and adolescence.* Oxford: Pergamon, 1978.

Farrington, D. P. Longitudinal research on crime and delinquency. In N. Morris & M. Tonry (Eds.), *Criminal justice: An annual review of research* (Vol. 1). Chicago & London: University of Chicago Press, 1979.

Farrington, D. P., Biron, L., & LeBlanc, M. Personality and delinquency in London and Montreal. In J. C. Gunn & D. P. Farrington (Eds.), *Advances in forensic psychiatry and psychology.* Chichester, Eng.: Wiley, 1982.

Farrington, D. P., Osborn, S. G., & West, D. J. The persistence of labelling effects. *British Journal of Criminology,* 1978, *18,* 277–284.

Fay, W. H. Personal pronouns and the autistic child. *Journal of Autism and Childhood Schizophrenia,* 1979, *9,* 247–260.

Fein, D., Skoff, B. F., & Mirsky, A. F. Clinical correlates of brainstem dysfunction in autistic children. *Journal of Autism and Developmental Disorders,* 1981, *11,* 303–316.

Feingold, B. F. *Why your child is hyperactive.* New York: Random House, 1975.

Feldman, M. P. *Criminal behaviour: A psychological analysis.* London: Wiley, 1977.

Ferguson, H. B., & Pappas, B. A. Evaluation of psycho-physiological, neurochemical, and animal models of hyperactivity. In R. L. Trites (Ed.), *Hyperactivity in children: Etiology, mea-*

surement, and treatment implications. Baltimore: University Park Press, 1979.

Ferguson, H. B., & Rapoport, J. Nosological issues and biological validation. In M. Rutter (Ed.), *Developmental neuropsychiatry.* New York: Guilford Press, in press.

Ferguson, H. B., & Trites, R. L. Predicting the response of hyperactive children to Ritalin: An empirical study. In R. M. Knights & D. J. Bakker (Eds.), *Treatment of hyperactive and learning disordered children: Current research.* Baltimore: University Park Press, 1980.

Ferreira, A. J., & Winters, W. D. Information exchange and silence in normal and abnormal families. *Family Process,* 1968, *7,* 251–276.

Field, E. *A validation of Hewitt and Jenkins' hypothesis* (Home Office Research Study in the Causes of Delinquency and the Treatment of Offenders No. 10). London: Her Majesty's Stationery Office, 1967.

Finegan, J., & Quadrington, B. Pre-, peri-, and neonatal factors and infantile autism. *Journal of Child Psychology and Psychiatry,* 1979, *20,* 119–128.

Finlay-Jones, R., & Brown, G. W. Types of stressful life event and the onset of anxiety and depressive disorders. *Psychological Medicine,* 1981, *11,* 803–816.

Finlayson, D. S., & Loughran, J. L. Pupils' perceptions in high and low delinquency schools. *Educational Research,* 1976, *18,* 138–145.

Firestone, P., & Martin, J. E. An analysis of the hyperactive syndrome: A comparison of hyperactive behavior problem, asthmatic and normal children. *Journal of Abnormal Child Psychology,* 1979, *7,* 261–273.

Fish, B. Involvement of the central nervous system in infants with schizophrenia. *Archives of Neurology,* 1960, *2,* 115–121.

Fish, B. Offspring of schizophrenics from birth to adulthood. In N. F. Watt, E. J. Anthony, L. C. Wynne, & J. E. Rolf (Eds.), *Children at risk for schizophrenia: A longitudinal perspective.* New York: Cambridge University Press, in press.

Fisher, L., Kokes, R. F., Harder, D. W., & Jones, J. E. Child competence and psychiatric risk. VI. Summary and integration of findings. *Journal of Nervous and Mental Disorders,* 1980, *168,* 353–355.

Flor-Henry, P. On certain aspects of localization of the cerebral systems regulating and determining emotions. *Biological Psychiatry,* 1979, *14,* 677–698.

Folstein, S., & Rutter, M. Infantile autism: A genet-

ic study of 21 twin pairs. *Journal of Child Psychology and Psychiatry,* 1977, *18,* 297–321.

Forehand, R., King, H., Peed, S., & Yoder, P. Mother-child interactions: Comparison of a noncompliant clinic group and a non-clinic group. *Behavior Research and Therapy,* 1975, *13,* 79–84.

Forehand, R., Wells, K. C., & Sturgis, E. T. Predictors of child noncompliant behavior in the home. *Journal of Consulting and Clinical Psychology,* 1978, *46,* 179.

Freud, A. *Normality and pathology in childhood.* London: Hogarth Press, 1966.

Freud, A., & Burlingham, D. *Infants without families and reports on the Hampstead nurseries, 1939–1945.* London: Hogarth Press, 1974.

Friday, P. C. International review of youth crime and delinquency. In G. Newman (Ed.), *Deviance and crime: International perspectives.* London: Sage Publications, 1980.

Frommer, E. A. Depressive illness in childhood. In A. J. Coppen & A. Walk (Eds.), *Recent developments in affective disorders* (British Journal of Psychiatry Special Publication No. 2). Ashford, Eng.: Headley Bros., 1968.

Fundudis, T., Kolvin, I., & Garside, R. (Eds.). *Speech retarded and deaf children: Their psychological development.* London: Academic Press, 1979.

Furman, W. Promoting social development: Developmental implications for treatment. In B. B. Lahey & A. E. Kazdin (Eds.), *Advances in clinical child psychology* (Vol. 3). New York: Plenum, 1980.

Fyffe, C., & Prior, M. R. Evidence of language recoding in autistic children: A re-examination. *British Journal of Psychiatry,* 1978, *69,* 393–403.

Gaensbauer, T. J. Regulation of emotional expression in infants from two contrasting caretaking environments. *Journal of the American Academy of Child Psychiatry,* 1982, *21,* 163–170.

Gardner, G. C. The relationship between childhood neurotic symptomatology and later schizophrenia in males and females. *Journal of Nervous and Mental Disease,* 1967, *144,* 97–100.

Garmezy, N. Children at risk: The search for the antecedents to schizophrenia. *Schizophrenia Bulletin,* 1974, *8,* 14–90; *9,* 55–125.

Garmezy, N. Attentional processes in adult schizophrenia and in children at risk. *Journal of Psychiatric Research,* 1978, *14,* 3–34.

Gates, A. I., & Bond, G. L. Failure in reading and

social maladjustment. *National Education Association Journal*, 1936, *25*, 205–206.

Gath, D., Cooper, B., Gattoni, F., & Rockett, D. *Child guidance and delinquency in a London borough* (Institute of Psychiatry Maudsley Monographs No. 24). London: Oxford University Press, 1977.

Geller, E., Ritvo, E. R., Freeman, B. J., & Yuwiler, A. Preliminary observations on the effect of fenfluramine on blood serotonin and symptoms in three autistic boys. *New England Journal of Medicine*, 1982, *307*, 165–169.

George, C., & Main, M. B. Social interactions of young abused children: Approach, avoidance, and aggression. *Child Development*, 1979, *50*, 306–318.

Gerson, I. M., Barnes, T. C., Mannino, A., Fanning, J. M., & Burns, J. J. EEG of children with various learning problems. Part I—Outpatient study. *Diseases of the Nervous System*, 1972, *33*, 170–177.

Gersten, J. C., Langner, T. W., Eisenberg, J. C., Simcha-Fagan, O., & McCarthy, E. D. Stability and change in types of behavioral disturbance of children and adolescents. *Journal of Abnormal Child Psychology*, 1976, *4*, 111–128.

Geschwind, N. Late changes in the nervous system: An overview. In D. G. Stein, J. J. Rosen, & N. Butters (Eds.), *Plasticity and recovery of function in the central nervous system*. New York: Academic Press, 1974.

Gesell, A., Ilg, F. L., & Ames, L. B. *Infant and child in the culture of today* (Rev. ed.). New York: Harper & Row, 1974.

Gevins, A. S., Doyle, J. C., Cutillo, B. A., Schaffer, R. E., Taunehill, R. S., Ghannem, J. H., Bilcrease, V. A., & Yeager, C. L. Electrical potentials in human brain during cognition: New method reveals dynamic patterns of correlations. *Science*, 1981, *213*, 918–922.

Ghodsian, M., Gofelman, K., Lambert, L., & Tibbenham, A. Changes in behaviour ratings of a national sample of children. *British Journal of Social and Clinical Psychology*, 1980, *19*, 247–256.

Gibbs, J. P., & Erickson, M. L. Major developments in the sociological study of deviance. *Annual Review of Sociology*, 1975, *1*, 21–42.

Gillberg, C., & Gillberg, I. C. Infantile autism: A total population study of non-optimal pre-, peri-, and neonatal conditions. *Journal of Autism and Developmental Disorders*, in press.

Gillberg, C., & Schaumann, H. Infantile autism and puberty. *Journal of Autism and Developmental Disorders*, 1981, *11*, 365–372.

Gillberg, C., & Schaumann, H. Social class and infantile autism. *Journal of Autism and Developmental Disorders*, 1982, *12*, 223–228.

Gittelman-Klein, R., Klein, D., Katz, S., Saraf, K., & Pollack, E. Comparative effects of methylphenidate and thioridazine in hyperkinetic children. *Archives of General Psychiatry*, 1976, *33*, 1217–1231.

Glaser, K. Masked depression in children and adolescents. *American Journal of Psychotherapy*, 1967, *19*, 228–240.

Glaser, K. A review of crime-causation theory and its application. In N. Morris & M. Tonry (Eds.), *Crime and justice: An annual review of research* (Vol. 1). Chicago & London: University of Chicago Press, 1979.

Glow, R. A. Cross-validity and normative data on the Conners' parent and teacher rating scales. In K. D. Gadow & J. Loney (Eds.), *Psychosocial aspects of drug treatment for hyperactivity*. Boulder, Colo.: Westview Press, 1981.

Glow, R. A., & Glow, P. H. Peer and self-rating: Children's perception of behavior relevant to hyperkinetic impulse disorder. *Journal of Abnormal Child Psychology*, 1980, *8*, 471–490.

Glueck, S., & Glueck, E. *Juvenile delinquents grown up*. New York: Commonwealth Fund, 1940.

Gold, M. *Delinquent behavior in an American city*. Belmont, Calif.: Brooks/Cole, 1970.

Goldberg, A. M., & Silbergeld, E. Animal models of hyperactivity. In I. Hanin & E. Usden (Eds.), *Animal models in psychiatry and neurology*. New York: Pergamon, 1977.

Goldfarb, W. Emotional and intellectual consequences of psychologic deprivation in infancy: A revaluation. In P. H. Hoch & J. Zubin (Eds.), *Psychopathology of childhood*. New York: Grune & Stratton, 1955.

Goldman, J. O., Thibert, R. J., & Rourke, B. P. Platelet serotonin levels in hyperactive children. *Journal of Pediatric Psychology*, 1979, *3*, 285–296.

Goldman, N. A socio-psychological study of school vandalism. *Crime and Delinquency*, 1961, *7*, 221–230.

Goldman, P. S. An alternative to developmental plasticity: Heterology of CNS structures in infants and adults. In D. G. Stein, J. J. Rosen, & N. Butters (Eds.), *Plasticity and recovery of function in the central nervous system*. New York: Academic Press, 1974.

Goodenough, F. L. *Anger in young children*. Minneapolis: University of Minnesota Press, 1931.

Goodyer, I. Hysterical conversion reactions in childhood. *Journal of Child Psychology and Psychiatry*, 1981, *22*, 179–188.

Gordon, A. H., & Jameson, J. C. Infant-mother attachment in patients with nonorganic failure to thrive syndrome. *Journal of the American Academy of Child Psychiatry*, 1979, *18*, 251–259.

Gossett, J. T., Lewis, S. B., Lewis, J., & Phillips, V. A. Follow-up of adolescents treated in a psychiatric hospital: I. *American Journal of Orthopsychiatry*, 1973, *43*, 602–610.

Gottesman, I. I., & Shields, J. A critical review of recent adoption, twin, and family studies of schizophrenia: Behavioral genetics perspective. *Schizophrenia Bulletin*, 1976, *2*, 360–400.

Goyette, C. H., Conners, C. K., & Ulrich, R. F. Normative data on revised Conners parent and teacher rating scales. *Journal of Abnormal Child Psychology*, 1978, *6*, 221–236.

Graham, P. J. Depression in prepubertal children. *Developmental Medicine and Child Neurology*, 1974, *16*, 340–349.

Graham, P. J. Epidemiological studies. In H. C. Quay & J. S. Werry (Eds.), *Psychopathological disorders of childhood* (2nd ed.). New York: Wiley, 1979.

Graham, P. J. Depressive disorders in children—a reconsideration. *Acta Paedopsychiatrica*, 1980, *46*, 285–296.

Graham, P. J. Specific medical syndromes. In M. Rutter (Eds.), *Developmental neuropsychiatry*. New York: Guilford Press, in press.

Graham, P. J., & Rutter, M. Psychiatric disorder in the young adolescent: A follow-up study. *Proceedings of the Royal Society of Medicine*, 1973, *66*, 1226–1229.

Grahame-Smith, D. G. Animal hyperactivity syndromes: Do they have any relevance to minimal brain dysfunction. In A. F. Kalverboer, H. M. van Praag, & J. Mendlewicz (Eds.), *Advances in biological psychiatry* (Vol. 1). Basel: S. Karger, 1978.

Grant, Q. A. F. R. *Age and sex trends in the symptomatology of disturbed children*. Unpublished DPM Dissertation, University of London, 1958.

Gray, J. A. Emotionality in male and female rodents: A reply to Archer. *British Journal of Psychology*, 1979, *70*, 425–440.

Gray, J. A. *The neuropsychology of anxiety*. Oxford: Clarendon, 1982.

Graziano, A. M., DeGiovanni, I. S., & Garcia, K. A. Behavioral treatment of children's fears: A review. *Psychological Bulletin*, 1979, *86*, 804–830.

Greer, H. S., & Cawley, R. H. *Some observations on the natural history of neurotic illness* (Mervyn Archdall Medical Monograph No. 3). Sydney: Australian Medical Association, 1966.

Grey, S., Sartory, G., & Rachman, S. J. Synchronous and desynchronous changes during fear reduction. *Behaviour Research and Therapy*, 1979, *17*, 137–147.

Griffith, H., & Davidson, M. Long-term changes in intellect and behaviour after hemispherectomy. *Journal of Neurology, Neurosurgery and Psychiatry*, 1966, *29*, 571–576.

Griffith, J. J., Mednick, S. A., Schulsinger, F., & Diderichsen, B. Verbal associative disturbances in children at high risk for schizophrenia. *Journal of Abnormal Psychology*, 1980, *89*, 125–131.

Gross, M. B., & Wilson, W. C. *Minimal brain dysfunction: A clinical study of incidence, diagnosis and treatment in over 1000 children*. New York: Brunner/Mazel, 1974.

Gross, R. T., & Duke, P. M. The effect of early versus late physical maturation on adolescent behavior. In M. D. Levine, A. C. Crocker, & R. T. Gross (Eds.), *Developmental-behavioral relations*. Philadelphia: W. B. Saunders, in press.

Grossman, K., & Grossman, K. Parent-infant attachment relationships in Bielefeld. A research note. In K. Immelmann, G. W. Barlow, L. Perronovich, & M. Main (Eds.), *Behavioral development. The Bielefeld interdisciplinary project*. New York: Cambridge University Press, 1981.

Gunnar-Vongnechten, M. R. Changing a frightening toy into a pleasant toy by allowing the infant to control its actions. *Developmental Psychology*, 1978, *14*, 157–162.

Hafner, A. J., Quast, W., & Shea, M. J. The adult adjustment of one thousand psychiatric and pediatric patients: Initial findings from a twenty-five years follow-up. In R. D. West, G. Winekur, & M. Roff (Eds.), *Life history research in psychopathology* (Vol. 4). Minneapolis: University of Minnesota Press, 1975.

Hagman, E. R. A study of fears of children of preschool age. *Journal of Experimental Education*, 1932, 1, 110–130.

Haim, A. *Adolescent suicide* (A. M. Sheridan Smith, trans.). London: Tavistock Press, 1974.

Halverson, C. F., Jr., & Waldrop, M. F. Relations between preschool activity and aspects of intellectual and social behavior at age 7½. *Develop-*

mental Psychology, 1976, *12*, 107–112.

Hampe, E., Noble, H., Miller, L. C., & Barrett, C. L. Phobic children one and two years post-treatment. *Journal of Abnormal Psychology*, 1973, *82*, 446–453.

Hanson, D. R., Gottesman, I. I., & Heston, L. L. Some possible childhood indicators of adult schizophrenia inferred from children of schizophrenics. *British Journal of Psychiatry*, 1976, *129*, 142–154.

Hare, R. D. *Psychopathy, theory and research.* New York: Wiley, 1970.

Hare, R. D., & Schalling, D. (Eds.). *Psychopathic behavior: Approaches to research.* New York: Wiley, 1978.

Hargreaves, D. *Social relations in a secondary school.* London: Routledge & Kegan Paul, 1967.

Harlow, H. F., & Harlow, M. K. Effects of various mother-infant relationships on rhesus monkey behaviours. In B. M. Foss (Ed.), *Determinants of infant behaviour* (Vol. 4). London: Methuen, 1969.

Harmon, R. J., Wagonfeld, S., & Emde, R. N. Anaclitic depression: A follow-up from infancy to puberty with observations and psychotherapy. *The Psychoanalytic Study of the Child*, 1982, *37*, 67–94.

Harris, B. Whatever happened to little Albert? *American Psychologist*, 1979, *34*, 151–160.

Harris, P. L., Olthof, T., & Terwogt, M. M. Children's knowledge of emotion. *Journal of Child Psychology and Psychiatry*, 1981, *22*, 247–261.

Harris, R. The EEG. In M. Rutter & L. A. Hersov (Eds.), *Child psychiatry: Modern approaches.* Oxford: Blackwell Scientific, 1977.

Hartup, W. W. Aggression in childhood: Developmental perspectives. *American Psychologist*, 1974, *29*, 336–341.

Hassanyeh, F., & Davison, K. Bipolar affective psychosis with onset before age 16 years: Report of 10 cases. *British Journal of Psychiatry*, 1980, *137*, 530–539.

Hastings, J. E., & Barkley, R. A. A review of psychophysiological research with hyperkinetic children. *Journal of Abnormal Child Psychology*, 1978, *6*, 413–448.

Hastorf, A., Wildfogel, J., & Cassman, T. Acknowledgement of handicap as a tactic in social interaction. *Journal of Personality and Social Psychology*, 1979, *37*, 1790–1797.

Hauser, S. L., DeLong, G. R., & Rosman, N. P. Pneumographic findings in the infantile autism syndrome: A correlation with temporal lobe disease. *Brain*, 1975, *98*, 667–688.

Havighurst, R. J., Bowman, P. H., Liddle, G. P., Matthews, C. V., & Pierce, J. V. *Growing up in River City.* New York & London: Wiley, 1962.

Hawton, K., & Goldacre, M. Hospital admissions for adverse effects of medicinal agents (mainly self-poisoning) among adolescents in the Oxford region. *British Journal of Psychiatry*, 1982, *141*, 166–170.

Hawton, K., O'Grady, J., Osborn, M., & Cole, D. Adolescents who take overdoses: Their characteristics, problems and contacts with helping agencies. *British Journal of Psychiatry*, 1982, *140*, 118–123.

Hayden, T. L. Classification of elective mutism. *Journal of the American Academy of Child Psychiatry*, 1980, *19*, 118–133.

Heal, K. H. Misbehaviour among school children: The role of the school in strategies for prevention. *Policy and Politics*, 1978, *6*, 321–322.

Hebb, D. O. The effect of early and late brain injury upon test scores, and the nature of normal adult intelligence. *Proceedings of the American Philosophical Society*, 1942, *85*, 275–292.

Helper, M. M. Follow-up of children with minimal brain dysfunctions: Outcomes and predictors. In H. E. Rie & E. D. Rie (Eds.), *Handbook of minimal brain dysfunction: A critical view.* New York: Wiley, 1980.

Hemsley, R., Howlin, P., Berger, M., Hersov, L. A., Holbrook, D., Rutter, M., & Yule, W. Training autistic children in a family context. In M. Rutter & E. Schopler (Eds.), *Autism: A reappraisal of concepts and treatment.* New York: Plenum, 1978.

Henn, F. A., Bardwell, R., & Jenkins, R. L. Juvenile delinquents revisited: Adult criminal activity. *Archives of General Psychiatry*, 1980, *37*, 1160–1163.

Herbert, M. The concept and testing of brain damage in children: A review. *Journal of Child Psychology and Psychiatry*, 1964, *5*, 197–216.

Herbert, M., Sluckin, W., & Sluckin, A. Mother-to-infant bonding. *Journal of Child Psychology and Psychiatry*, 1982, *23*, 205–222.

Herjanic, B. L., Herjanic, M., Brown, F., & Wheatt, T. Are children reliable reporters? *Journal of Abnormal Child Psychology*, 1975, *3*, 41–48.

Hermelin, B. Coding and the sense modalities. In L. Wing (Ed.), *Early childhood autism: Clinical, educational and social aspects* (2nd ed.). Oxford: Pergamon, 1976.

Hermelin, B., & O'Connor, N. *Psychological experiments with autistic children.* Oxford: Pergamon, 1970.

Herrenkohl, R. C., & Herrenkohl, E. C. Some antecedents and developmental consequences of child maltreatment. In R. Rizley & D. Cicchetti (Eds.), *Developmental perspectives on child maltreatment* (New Directions for Child Development No. 11). San Francisco: Jossey-Bass, 1981.

Hersov, L. A. School refusal. In M. Rutter & Hersov, L. A. (Eds.), *Child psychiatry: Modern approaches.* Oxford: Blackwell Scientific, 1977.

Hersov, L. A., & Berg, I. (Eds.). *Out of school: Modern perspectives in truancy and school refusal.* Chichester, Eng.: Wiley, 1980.

Hertzig, M. E. Stability and change in nonfocal neurological signs. *Journal of the American Academy of Child Psychiatry,* 1982, *21,* 231–236.

Hess, R. D., & Camera, K. A. Post-divorce family relationships as mediating factors in the consequences of divorce for children. *Journal of Social Issues,* 1979, *35,* 79–96.

Hetherington, E. M. Children and divorce. In R. W. Henderson (Ed.), *Parent-child interaction: Theory, research and prospects.* New York: Academic Press, 1981.

Hetherington, E. M., Cox, M., & Cox, R. The aftermath of divorce. In J. H. Stevens & M. Matthews (Eds.), *Mother-child father-child relations.* Washington, D.C.: National Association for the Education of Young Children, 1978.

Hetherington, E. M., Cox, M., & Cox, R. Family interaction and the social, emotional and cognitive development of children following divorce. In V. Vaughan & T. Brazelton (Eds.), *The family: Setting priorities.* New York: Science and Medicine, 1979. (a)

Hetherington, E. M., Cox, M., & Cox, R. Play and social interaction in children following divorce. *Journal of Social Issues,* 1979, *35,* 26–49. (b)

Hetherington, E. M., Cox, M., & Cox, R. Effects of divorce on parents and children. In M. E. Lamb (Ed.), *Non-traditional families.* Hillsdale, N.J.: Erlbaum, 1982.

Hetherington, E. M., & Martin, B. Family interaction. In H. C. Quay & J. S. Werry (Eds.), *Psychopathological disorders of childhood* (2nd ed.). New York: Wiley, 1979.

Hetherington, E. M., Stouwie, R., & Ridberg, E. H. Patterns of family interaction and child rearing attitudes related to three dimensions of juvenile delinquency. *Journal of Abnormal Psychology,* 1971, *77,* 160–176.

Hewett, S., Newson, J., & Newson, E. *The family and the handicapped child: A study of cerebral palsied children in their homes.* London: Allen & Unwin, 1970.

Hewitt, L. E., & Jenkins, R. L. *Fundamental patterns of maladjustment: The dynamics of their origin.* Springfield, Ill.: Charles C. Thomas, 1946.

Hier, D. B., LeMay, M., & Rosenberger, P. B. Autism and unfavorable left-right asymmetrics of the brain. *Journal of Autism and Developmental Disorders,* 1979, *9,* 153–159.

Hier, D. B., LeMay, M., Rosenberger, P. B., & Perlo, V. P. Developmental dyslexia: Evidence for a subgroup with a reversal of cerebral asymmetry. *Archives of Neurology,* 1978, *35,* 90–92.

Hinde, R. A. *Towards understanding relationships.* London: Academic Press, 1979.

Hinde, R. A. Family influences. In M. Rutter (Ed.), *Scientific foundations of developmental psychiatry.* London: Heinemann Medical, 1980.

Hinde, R. A. Attachment: Some conceptual and biological issues. In C. M. Parkes & J. Stevenson-Hinde (Eds.), *The place of attachment in human behaviour.* London: Tavistock Press, 1982.

Hirsch, S. R., & Leff, J. P. *Abnormalities in parents of schizophrenics* (Institute of Psychiatry Maudsley Monograph No. 22). London: Oxford University Press, 1975.

Hirschi, T. *Causes of delinquency.* Berkeley & Los Angeles: University of California Press, 1969.

Hirschi, T., & Hindelang, M. J. Intelligence and delinquency: A revisionist review. *American Sociological Review,* 1977, *42,* 571–587.

Hobbs, N. (Ed.). *Issues in the classification of children,* Vols. 1 & 2. San Francisco: Jossey-Bass, 1975.

Hobson, R. P. The autistic child's concept of persons. In D. Park (Ed.), *Proceedings of the 1981 International Conference on Autism, Boston.* Washington, D.C.: National Society for Children and Adults with Autism, 1982.

Hobson, R. P. Early childhood autism and the question of egocentrism. *Journal of Autism and Developmental Disorders,* in press.

Hodges, K. K., Kline, J., Stern, L., Cytryn, C., & McKnew, D. H. The development of a child assessment interview for research and clinical use. *Journal of Abnormal Child Psychology,* 1982, *10,* 173–190.

Hodgins, S. "Psychopathy": An examination of the psychophysiological findings. Paper presented at the meeting of the American Society of Criminology, Philadelphia, November 1979.

Hoffman, M. L. Developmental synthesis of affect and cognition and its implications for altruistic motivation. *Developmental Psychology*, 1975, *11*, 607–622.

Hoffman, W. L., & Prior, M. R. Neuropsychological dimensions of autism in children: A test of the hemispheric dysfunction hypothesis. *Journal of Clinical Neuropsychology*, 1982, *4*, 27–41.

Holden, E. W., Tarnowski, K. J., & Prinz, R. J. Reliability of neurobiological soft signs in children: Re-evaluation of the PANESS. *Journal of Abnormal Child Psychology*, 1982, *10*, 163–172.

Holdsworth, L., & Whitmore, K. A study of children with epilepsy attending ordinary schools. I. Their seizure patterns, progress and behaviour in school. *Developmental Medicine and Child Neurology*, 1974, *16*, 746–758.

Hollingsworth, C. E., Tanguay, P. E., Grossman, L., & Pabat, P. Long-term outcome of obsessive-compulsive disorder in childhood. *Journal of the American Academy of Child Psychiatry*, 1980, *19*, 134–144.

Horner, T. M. Two methods of studying stranger reactivity in infants: A review. *Journal of Child Psychology and Psychiatry*, 1980, *21*, 203–220.

Howell, D. C., & Huessy, H. R. Hyperkinetic behavior: Do early troubles predict future problems. Paper presented at the meeting of the International Association for Child and Adolescent Psychiatry and Allied Professions, Dublin, July 1982.

Howlin, P. The assessment of social behavior. In M. Rutter & E. Schopler (Eds.), *Autism: A reappraisal of concepts and treatment*. New York: Plenum, 1978.

Howlin, P. The effectiveness of operant language training with autistic children. *Journal of Autism and Developmental Disorders*, 1981, *11*, 89–106.

Hoy, E., Weiss, G., Minde, K., & Cohen, M. The hyperactive child at adolescence: cognitive, emotional and social functioning. *Journal of Abnormal Child Psychology*, 1978, *6*, 311–324.

Huessy, H. R., & Cohen, A. H. Hyperkinetic behaviors and learning disabilities followed over seven years. *Pediatrics*, 1976, *57*, 4–10.

Hutchings, B., & Mednick, S. A. Registered criminality in the adoptive and biological parents of registered male adoptees. In S. A. Mednick, F. Schulsinger, J. Higgins, & B. Bell (Eds.), *Genetics, environment and psychopathology*. Amsterdam: North-Holland, 1974.

Hutt, S. J., & Hutt, C. Hyperactivity in a group of epileptic (and some nonepileptic) brain damaged children. *Epilepsia*, 1964, *5*, 374–351.

Hyman, C. A., & Parr, R. A controlled video observational study of abused children. *Child Abuse and Neglect*, 1978, *2*, 217–222.

Ingram, T. T. S. A characteristic form of overactive behaviour in brain damaged children. *Journal of Mental Science*, 1956, *102*, 550–558.

Isenberg, P. I., & Schatzberg, A. F. Psychoanalytic contributions to a theory of depression. In J. O. Cole, A. F. Schatzberg, & S. H. Frazier (Eds.), *Depression: Biology, psychodynamics and treatment*. New York: Plenum, 1978.

Izard, C. E. *Human emotions*. New York: Plenum, 1977.

Izard, C. E. On the ontogenesis of emotions and emotion-cognitive relationships in infancy. In M. Lewis & L. A. Rosenblum (Eds.), *Genesis of behavior*, vol. 1, *The development of affect*. New York: Plenum, 1978.

Izard, C. E. *Measuring emotions in infants and children*. London: Cambridge University Press, 1982.

Jackson, M. J., & Garrod, P. J. Plasma zinc, copper, and amino acid levels in the blood of autistic children. *Journal of Autism and Childhood Schizophrenia*, 1978, *8*, 203–208.

Jacob, R. G., O'Leary, K. D., & Rosenblad, C. Formal and informal classroom settings: Effects on hyperactivity. *Journal of Abnormal Child Psychology*, 1978, *6*, 47–59.

Jakimow-Venulet, B. Hereditary factors in the pathogenesis of affective illness. *British Journal of Psychiatry*, 1981, *139*, 450–456.

James, A. L., & Barry, R. J. A review of psychophysiology in early onset psychosis. *Schizophrenia Bulletin*, 1980, *6*, 506–525.

Jencks, C., Smith, M., Acland, H., Bane, M. J., Cohen, D., Gintis, H., Heyns, B., & Michelson, S. *Inequality: A reassessment of the effects of family and schooling in America*. New York: Basic Books, 1972.

Jenkins, R. L. *Behavior disorders of childhood and adolescence*. Springfield, Ill.: Charles C. Thomas, 1973.

Jersild, A. T., & Holmes, F. G. *Children's fears*. New York: Teachers College, 1935.

Jessor, R. The stability of change: Psychosocial development from adolescent to young adulthood. In D. Magnusson & V. Allen (Eds.), *Human development: An interactional perspective*. London & New York: Academic Press, in press.

Jessor, R., & Jessor, S. L. *Problem behavior and psychosocial development: A longitudinal study of youth.* New York: Academic Press, 1977.

John, E. R. A study of the effects of evacuation and air raids on pre-school children. *British Journal of Educational Psychology,* 1941, *11,* 173–179.

John, E. R., Karmel, B. Z., Corning, W. C., Easton, P., Brown, D., Ahn, H., John, M., Harmoney, T., Prichep, L., Toro, A., Gerson, I. M., Bartlett, F., Thatcher, R., Kaye, H., Valdes, P., & Schwartz, E. Neurometrics: Numerical taxonomy identifies different profiles of brain functions within groups of behaviorally similar people. *Science,* 1977, *197,* 1393–1410.

Johnson, R. E. *Juvenile delinquency and its origins.* Cambridge: Cambridge University Press, 1979.

Johnson, S. B., & Melamed, B. G. The assessment and treatment of children's fears. In B. B. Lahey & A. E. Kazdin (Eds.), *Advances in clinical child psychology* (Vol. 2). New York: Plenum, 1979.

Johnstone, E. C., Crow, I. J., Frith, C. D., Husband, J., & Kreel, L. Cerebral ventricular size and cognition impairment in chronic schizophrenia. *Lancet,* 1976, *2,* 924–926.

Jones, M. C. Psychological correlates of somatic development. *Child Development,* 1965, *36,* 899–911.

Judd, L. Obsessive compulsive neurosis in children. *Archives of General Psychiatry,* 1965, *12,* 136–143.

Kagan, J. Discrepancy, temperament and infant distress. In M. Lewis & L. A. Rosenblum (Eds.), *The origins of fear.* New York: Wiley, 1974.

Kagan, J. Perspectives on continuity. In O. G. Brim, Jr. & J. Kagan (Eds.), *Constancy and change in human development.* Cambridge: Harvard University Press, 1980.

Kagan, J. *The second year: The emergence of self-awareness.* Cambridge: Harvard University Press, 1981.

Kagan, J., Kearsley, R. B., & Selazo, P. R. *Infancy: Its place in human development.* Cambridge: Harvard University Press, 1978.

Kagan, J., & Moss, H. A. *Birth to maturity.* New York: Wiley, 1962.

Kalverboer, A. F. MBD: Discussion of the concept. *Advances in Biological Psychiatry,* 1978, *1,* 5–17.

Kalverboer, A. F. Neurobehavioral findings in preschool and school-aged children in relation to pre- and perinatal complications. In D. Shaffer & J. Dunn (Eds.), *The first year of life: Psychological and medical implications of early experience.* Chichester, Eng., & New York: Wiley, 1979.

Kalverboer, A. F., van Praag, H. M., & Mendlewicz, J. (Eds.), Minimal brain dysfunction: Fact or fiction. In A. F. Kalverboer, H. M. van Praag, & J. Mendlewicz (Eds.), *Advances in biological psychiatry* (Vol. 1). Basel: S. Karger, 1978.

Kanner, L. Autistic disturbances of affective contact. *Nervous Child,* 1943, *2,* 217–250.

Kanner, L. Follow-up study of eleven autistic children originally reported in 1943. *Journal of Autism and Childhood Schizophrenia,* 1971, *1,* 119–145.

Kanner, L., Rodriguez, A., & Ashenden, B. How far can autistic children go in matters of social adaptation? *Journal of Autism and Childhood Schizophrenia,* 1972, *2,* 9–33.

Kaplan, A. *The conduct of inquiry.* San Francisco: Chandler, 1964.

Kashani, J. H., Husain, A., Shekim, W. O., Hodges, K. K., Cytryn, L., & McKnew, D. H. Current perspectives on childhood depression: An overview. *American Journal of Psychiatry,* 1981, *138,* 143–153.

Kastrup, M. Urban-rural differences in 6 year olds. In P. J. Graham (Ed.), *Epidemiological approaches in child psychiatry.* London: Academic Press, 1977.

Kaufman, K. R., Harris, R., & Shaffer, D. Problems in the categorization of child and adolescent EEG. *Journal of Child Psychology and Psychiatry,* 1980, *21,* 333–342.

Kazdin, A. E. Assessment techniques for childhood depression: A critical appraisal. *Journal of the American Academy of Child Psychiatry,* 1981, *20,* 358–375.

Kazdin, A. E., & Petti, J. A. Self-report and interview measures of childhood and adolescent depression. *Journal of Child Psychology and Psychiatry,* 1982, *23,* 437–458.

Kendell, R. E., Rennie, D., Clarke, J. A., & Dean, C. The social and obstetric correlates of psychiatric admission in the puerperium. *Psychological Medicine,* 1981, *11,* 341–350.

Kendell, R. E., Wainwright, S., Hailey, A., & Shannon, B. The influence of childbirth on psychiatric morbidity. *Psychological Medicine,* 1976, *6,* 297–302.

Kennard, M. Value of equivocal signs in neurologic diagnosis. *Neurology,* 1960, *10,* 753–764.

Kenny, T. J., Clemmens, R. L., Hudson, B. W., Lentz, G. A., Jr., Cicci, R., & Nair, P. Characteristics of children referred because of hyperactivity. *Journal of Pediatrics,* 1971, *79,* 618–622.

Keogh, B. K., & Margolis, J. S. A component

analysis of attentional problems of educationally handicapped boys. *Journal of Abnormal Child Psychology*, 1976, *4*, 349–359.

Kidd, K. K., & Weissman, M. M. Why we do not yet understand the genetics of affective disorders. In J. O. Cole, A. F. Schatzberg, & S. H. Frazier (Eds.), *Depression: Biology, psychodynamics and treatment*. New York: Plenum, 1978.

King, C. A., & Young, R. D. Peer popularity and peer communication patterns: Hyperactive versus active but normal boys. *Journal of Abnormal Child Psychology*, 1981, *9*, 465–482.

Kittler, F. J., & Baldwin, D. G. The role of allergic factors in the child with minimal brain dysfunction. *Annals of Allergy*, 1970, *23*, 203–206.

Klaus, M. H., & Kennell, J. H. *Maternal-infant bonding: The impact of early separation or loss on family development*. St. Louis: C. V. Mosby, 1976.

Klein, A. R., & Young, D. Hyperactive boys in their classroom: Assessment of teacher and peer perceptions, interactions, and classroom behaviors. *Journal of Abnormal Child Psychology*, 1979, *7*, 425–442.

Kliman, G. W. *Psychological emergencies of childhood*. New York: Grune & Stratton, 1968.

Knight, B. J., Osborn, S. G., & West, D. J. Early marriage and criminal tendency in males. *British Journal of Criminology*, 1977, *17*, 348–360.

Koegel, R. L., & Egel, A. L. Motivating autistic children. *Journal of Abnormal Psychology*, 1979, *85*, 418–426.

Koel, B. S. Failure to thrive and fatal injury as a continuum. *American Journal of Diseases of Children*, 1969, *118*, 565–567.

Kogan, K. L., Tyler, N., & Turner, P. The process of interpersonal adaptation between mothers and their cerebral palsied children. *Developmental Medicine and Child Neurology*, 1974, *16*, 518–527.

Kohlberg, L., LaCross, J., & Ricks, D. F. The predictability of adult mental health from childhood behavior. In B. A. Wolman (Ed.), *Manual of child psychopathology*. New York: McGraw-Hill, 1972.

Kohn, B., & Dennis, M. Patterns of hemisphere specialization after hemidecortication for infantile hemiplegia. In M. Kinsbourne & W. I. Smith (Eds.), *Hemispheric disconnection and cerebral function*. Springfield, Ill.: Charles C. Thomas, 1974.

Kohn, M. *Social competence, symptoms and underachievement in childhood: A longitudinal perspective*. London: Wiley, 1977.

Kolvin, I., & Fundudis, T. Elective mute children: Psychological development and background factors. *Journal of Child Psychology and Psychiatry*, 1981, *22*, 219–232.

Kornhauser, R. R. *Social sources of delinquency: An appraisal of analytic models*. Chicago & London: University of Chicago Press, 1978.

Kovacs, M., & Beck, A. T. Maladaptive cognitive structures in depression. *American Journal of Psychiatry*, 1978, *135*, 525–533.

Kramer, A. D., & Feiguine, R. J. Clinical effects of amitriptyline in adolescent depression: A pilot study. *Journal of the American Academy of Child Psychiatry*, 1981, *20*, 636–644.

Kratcoski, P. C., & Kratcoski, J. E. The balance of social status groupings within schools as an influencing variable on the frequency and character of delinquent behavior. In P. C. Friday & V. L. Stewart (Eds.), *Juvenile justice: International perspectives*. New York: Praeger, 1977.

Kratochwill, T. R. *Selective mutism: Implications for research and treatment*. London & Hillsdale, N.J.: Erlbaum, 1981.

Kreitman, N. (Ed.). *Parasuicide*. London: Wiley, 1977.

Krieger, I. Food restriction as a form of child abuse in ten cases of psychosocial deprivation dwarfism. *Clinical Pediatrics*, 1974, *13*, 127–133.

Krouse, J. P., & Kauffman, J. Minor physical anomalies in exceptional children: A review and critique of research. *Journal of Abnormal Child Psychology*, 1982, *10*, 247–264.

Kuperman, S., & Stewart, M. A. The diagnosis of depression in children. *Journal of Affective Disorders*, 1979, *1*, 213–217.

Lader, M., & Marks, I. M. *Clinical anxiety*. London: Heinemann Medical, 1971.

Lahey, B. B., Green, K. D., & Forehand, R. On the independence of ratings of hyperactivity, conduct problems, and attention deficits in children: A multiple regression analysis. *Journal of Consulting and Clinical Psychology*, 1980, *48*, 566–574.

Lamb, M. E. (Ed.). *The role of the father in child development*. New York: Wiley, 1976.

Lamb, M. E. Qualitative aspects of mother- and father-infant attachments. *Infant Behavior & Development*, 1978, *1*, 265–275.

Lamb, M. E., & Hwang, C.-P. Maternal attachment and mother-neonate bonding: A critical review. In M. E. Lamb & A. L. Brown (Eds.), *Advances in developmental psychology* (Vol. 2). Hillsdale, N.J.: Erlbaum, 1982.

Lambert, N. M., & Sandoval, J. The prevalence of learning disabilities in a sample of children considered hyperactive. *Journal of Abnormal Child Psychology*, 1980, *8*, 33–50.

Lambert, N. M., Sandoval, J., & Sassone, D. Prevalence of hyperactivity in elementary school children as a function of social system definers. *American Journal of Orthopsychiatry*, 1978, *48*, 446–463.

Lang, P. J. Fear reduction and fear behavior: Problems in treating a construct. In J. M. Shlien (Ed.), *Research in psychotherapy* (Vol. 3). Washington, D.C.: American Psychological Association, 1968.

Lang, P. J. Anxiety: Toward a psychobiological definition. In H. S. A-Kiskal & W. L. Webb (Eds.), *Psychiatric diagnosis: Exploration of biological predictors*. Jamaica, N.Y.: Spectrum, 1978.

Langdell, T. Recognition of faces: An approach to the study of autism. *Journal of Child Psychology and Psychiatry*, 1978, *19*, 255–268.

Langdell, T. Pragmatic aspects of autism: Or, why is "I" a normal word? Paper presented at the meeting of the Developmental Section of the British Psychological Society, September 1980.

Langhorne, J. E., Jr., & Loney, J. A four-fold model for subgrouping the hyperkinetic/MBD syndrome. *Child Psychiatry and Human Development*, 1979, *9*, 153–159.

Langhorne, J. E., Jr., Loney, J., Paternite, C. E., & Bechtoldt, H. P. Childhood hyperkinesis: A return to the source. *Journal of Abnormal Psychology*, 1976, *85*, 201–209.

Lapouse, R., & Monk, M. A. An epidemiologic study of behavior characteristics in children. *American Journal of Public Health*, 1958, *48*, 1134–1144.

Lapouse, R., & Monk, M. A. Fears and worries in a representative sample of children. *American Journal of Orthopsychiatry*, 1959, *29*, 803–818.

Lavik, N. J. Urban-rural differences in rates of disorder. A comparative psychiatric population study of Norwegian adolescents. In P. J. Graham (Ed.), *Epidemiological approaches in child psychiatry*. London: Academic Press, 1977.

Le Couteur, A. Unpublished data, July 1982.

Ledbetter, D. H., Riccardi, V. M., Airhart, S. D., Stickol, R. J., Keenan, B. S., & Crawford, J. D. Deletions of chromosome 15 as a cause of the Prader-Willi syndrome. *New England Journal of Medicine*, 1981, *304*, 325–329.

Leff, J. P., Kuipers, L., Berkowitz, R., Eberlein-Vries, R., & Sturgeon, D. A controlled trial of social intervention in the families of schizophrenic patients. *British Journal of Psychiatry*, 1982, *141*, 121–134.

Leff, J. P., & Vaughn, C. E. The interaction of life events and relatives' expressed emotions in schizophrenia and depressive neurosis. *British Journal of Psychiatry*, 1980, *136*, 146–153.

Leff, J. P., & Vaughn, C. E. The role of maintenance therapy and relatives' expressed emotion in relapse of schizophrenia: A two-year follow-up. *British Journal of Psychiatry*, 1981, *139*, 102–104.

Lefkowitz, M. M., & Burton, N. Childhood depression: A critique of the concept. *Psychological Bulletin*, 1978, *85*, 716–726.

Lenneberg, E. H. *Biological foundations of language*. New York: Wiley, 1967.

Leon, G. R., Kendall, P. C., & Garber, J. Depression in children's parent, teacher and child perspectives. *Journal of Abnormal Child Psychology*, 1980, 221–236.

Lerner, R. M., & Spanier, G. B. (Eds.). *Child influence on marital and family interaction: A life span perspective*. New York: Academic Press, 1978.

Leslie, S. A. Psychiatric disorder in the young adolescents of an industrial town. *British Journal of Psychiatry*, 1974, *125*, 113–124.

Levy, D. M., & Tulchin, S. H. The resistance of infants and children during mental tests. *Journal of Experimental Psychology*, 1923, *6*, 304–322.

Levy, D. M., & Tulchin, S. H. The response behavior of infants and children. II. *Journal of Experimental Psychology*, 1925, *8*, 209–224.

Levy, F. The development of sustained attention (vigilance) and inhibition in children: Some normative data. *Journal of Child Psychology and Psychiatry*, 1980, *21*, 77–84.

Lewine, R. R. J., Watt, N. F., Prentky, R. A., & Fryer, J. H. Childhood social competence in functionally disordered psychiatric patients and in normals. *Journal of Abnormal Psychology*, 1980, *89*, 132–138.

Lewinsohn, P. M., Youngren, M. A., & Grosscup, S. J. Reinforcement and depression. In R. A. Depue (Ed.), *The psychobiology of depressive disorders: Implications for the effects of stress*. New York: Academic Press, 1979.

Lewis, A. Psychopathic personality: A most elusive category. *Psychological Medicine*, 1974, *4*, 133–140.

Lewis, H. *Deprived Children*. London: Oxford University Press, 1954.

Lewis, M., & Brooks-Gunn, J. Toward a theory of social cognition: The development of the self. In

I. Uzgiris (Ed.), *Social interaction and communication during infancy* (New Directions for Child Development No. 4). San Francisco: Jossey-Bass, 1979.

Lewis, M., & Schaeffer, S. Peer behavior and mother-infant interaction in maltreated children. In M. Lewis & L. A. Rosenblum (Eds.), *The uncommon child: The genesis of behavior* (Vol. 3). New York: Plenum, 1981.

Lieberman, A. F. Preschoolers' competence with a peer: Relations with attachment and peer experience. *Child Development*, 1977, *48*, 1277–1287.

Lindsay, J., Ounsted, C., & Richards, P. Long-term outcome in children with temporal lobe seizures. III. Psychiatric aspects in childhood and adult life. *Developmental Medicine and Child Neurology*, 1979, *21*, 630–636.

Lingham, S., Read, S. Holland, I. M., Wilson, J., Brett, E. M., & Hoare, R. D. Value of computerized tomography in children with non-specific mental subnormality. *Archives of Disease in Childhood*, 1982, *57*, 381–383.

Link, B., & Dohrenwend, B. P. Formulation of hypotheses about the true prevalence of demoralization in the United States. In B. P. Dohrenwend, B. S. Dohrenwend, M. S. Gould, B. Link, R. Neugebauer, & R. Wunsch-Hitzig (Eds.), *Mental illness in the United States: Epidemiological estimates*. New York: Praeger, 1980.

Lipsitt, L. P. Stress in infancy: Toward understanding the origins of coping behavior. In N. Garmezy & M. Rutter (Eds.), *Stress, coping and development in children*. New York: McGraw-Hill, in press.

Lishman, W. A. Brain damage in relation to psychiatric disability after head injury. *British Journal of Psychiatry*, 1968, *114*, 373–410.

Lishman, W. A. The psychiatric sequelae of head injury: A review. *Psychological Medicine*, 1973, *3*, 304–318.

Lloyd, K. G., Hornykiewicz, O., Davidson, L., Shannak, K., Garley, I., Goldstein, M., Shibuya, M., Kelley, W. N., & Fox, I. H. Biochemical evidence of dysfunction of brain neurotransmitters in the Lesch-Nyhan syndrome. *New England Journal of Medicine*, 1981, *305*, 1106–1111.

Lo, W. H. A note on a follow-up study of childhood neurosis and behaviour disorder. *Journal of Child Psychology and Psychiatry*, 1973, *14*, 147–150.

Lobitz, G. K., & Johnson, S. M. Normal versus deviant children: A multi-method comparison. *Journal of Abnormal Child Psychology*, 1975, *3*, 353–374. (a)

Lobitz, G. K., & Johnson, S. M. Parental manipulation of the behavior of normal and deviant children. *Child Development*, 1975, *46*, 719–726. (b)

Loney, J., Kramer, J., & Milich, R. The hyperkinetic child grows up: Predictors of symptoms, delinquency, and achievement at follow-up. In K. D. Gadow & J. Loney (Eds.), *Psychosocial aspects of drug treatment for hyperactivity*. Boulder, Colo.: Westview Press, 1981.

Loney, J., Langhorne, J. E., Jr., & Paternite, C. E. An empirical basis for subgrouping the hyperkinetic/minimal brain dysfunction syndrome. *Journal of Abnormal Psychology*, 1978, *87*, 431–441.

Loney, J., Whaley-Klahn, M. A., Kosier, T., & Conboy, J. Hyperactive boys and their brothers at 21: Predictors of aggressive and antisocial outcomes. Paper presented at the meeting of the Society for Life History Research, Monterey, California, November 1981.

Loranger, A. W., & Levine, P. M. Age at onset of bipolar affective illness. *Archives of General Psychiatry*, 1978, *35*, 1345–1348.

Lotter, V. Epidemiology of autistic conditions in young children. I. Prevalence. *Social Psychiatry*, 1966, *1*, 124–137.

Lotter, V. Epidemiology of autistic conditions in young children. II. Some characteristics of the parents and children. *Social Psychiatry*, 1967, *1*, 163–173.

Lotter, V. Factors related to outcome in autistic children. *Journal of Autism and Childhood Schizophrenia*, 1974, *4*, 263–277.

Lotter, V. Follow-up studies. In M. Rutter & E. Schopler (Eds.), *Autism: A reappraisal of concepts and treatment*. New York: Plenum, 1978.

Lovaas, O. I., Koegel, R. L., & Schreibman, L. Stimulus overselectivity in autism: A review of research. *Psychological Bulletin*, 1979, *86*, 1236–1254.

Lovaas, O. I., Schreibman, L., Koegel, R. L., & Rehm, R. Selective responding by autistic children to multiple sensory input. *Journal of Abnormal Psychology*, 1971, *77*, 211–222.

Lowe, T. L., & Cohen, D. J. Mania in childhood and adolescence. In R. H. Belmaker & H. M. van Praag (Eds.), *Mania: An evolving concept*. New York: Spectrum, 1980.

Luk, S. L. *What are hyperactive behaviours?—A review of observational studies*. Unpublished manuscript, 1982.

Lumsden Walker, W. Intentional self-injury in school age children. *Journal of Adolescence,* 1980, *3,* 217–228.

Lynch, G. W., & Gall, C. Organization and reorganization in the central nervous system. In F. Falkner & J. M. Tanner (Eds.), *Human growth,* vol. 3, *Neurobiology and nutrition.* London: Balliere Tindall, 1979.

Lynch, M. A. Ill-health and child abuse. *Lancet,* 1975, *2,* 317–319.

Maas, H. S. The young adult adjustment of twenty wartime residential nursery children. *Child Welfare,* 1963, *42,* 55–72.

MacCarthy, D. The effects of emotional disturbance and deprivation on somatic growth. In J. A. Davis & J. Dobbing (Eds.), *Scientific foundations of paediatrics* (2nd ed.). London: Heinemann Medical, 1981.

Maccoby, E. E. *Social development: Psychological growth and the parent-child relationship.* New York: Harcourt Brace Jovanovich, 1980.

Maccoby, E. E., & Jacklin, C. N. *Psychology of sex differences.* Stanford, Calif.: Stanford University Press, 1974.

Maccoby, E. E., & Jacklin, C. N. Psychological sex differences. In M. Rutter (Ed.), *Scientific foundations of developmental psychiatry.* London: Heinemann Medical, 1980. (a)

Maccoby, E. E., & Jacklin, C. N. Sex differences in aggression: A rejoinder and reprise. *Child Development,* 1980, *51,* 964–980. (b)

Maccoby, E. E., & Jacklin, C. N. The "person" characteristics of children and the family as environment. In D. Magnusson & V. Allen (Eds.), *Human development: An interactional perspective.* London & New York: Academic Press, in press.

Maccoby, E. E., Johnson, J. P., & Church, R. M. Community integration and the social control of juvenile delinquency. In J. R. Stratton & R. M. Terry (Eds.), *Prevention of delinquency: Problems and programs.* New York: Macmillan, 1968.

Macfarlane, J. W., Allen, L., & Honzik, M. P. *Developmental study of the behavior problems of normal children between twenty-one months and fourteen years.* Berkeley: University of California Press, 1954.

Macmillan, A., Kolvin, I., Garside, R., Nicol, A. R., & Leitch, I. M. A multiple criterion screen for identifying secondary school children with psychiatric disorder: Characteristics and efficiency of screen. *Psychological Medicine,* 1980, *10,* 265–276.

Magnusson, D., & Endler, N. S. (Eds.). *Personality at the crossroads: Current issues in interactional psychology.* Hillsdale, N.J.: Erlbaum, 1977.

Magnusson, D., & Stattin, A. Short-term and long-term consistency: A methodological problem. In D. Magnusson & V. Allen (Eds.), *Human development: An interactional perspective.* London & New York: Academic Press, in press.

Main, M. B., & Weston, D. R. Security of attachment to mother and father: Related to conflict behavior and the readiness to establish new relationships. *Child Development,* 1981, *52,* 1064–1067.

Main, M. B., & Weston, D. R. Avoidance of the attachment figure in infancy: Descriptions and interpretations. In C. M. Parkes & J. Stevenson-Hinde (Eds.), *The place of attachment in human behaviour.* London: Tavistock Press, 1982.

Malmquist, C. P. Depression in childhood and adolescence. *New England Journal of Medicine,* 1971, *284,* 887–893; 955–961.

Mangus, A. R. Effect of mental and educational retardation on personality development of children. *American Journal of Mental Deficiency,* 1950, *55,* 208–212.

Marchant, R., Howlin, P., Yule, W., & Rutter, M. Graded change in the treatment of the behaviour of autistic children. *Journal of Child Psychology and Psychiatry,* 1974, *15,* 221–228.

Marcus, J., Auerbach, J., Wilkinson, L., & Burack, C. M. Infants at risk for schizophrenia: The Jerusalem infant development study. *Archives of General Psychiatry,* 1981, *38,* 703–713.

Marks, I. M. *Fears and phobias.* London: Heinemann, 1969.

Marks, I. M. Phobic disorders four years after treatment: A prospective follow-up. *British Journal of Psychiatry,* 1971, *118,* 683–688.

Marks, I. M. Research in neurosis: A selective review. 2. Treatment. *Psychological Medicine,* 1974, *4,* 89–100.

Marks, I. M. Cure and care of neurosis. *Psychological Medicine,* 1979, *9,* 629–660.

Marks, I. M., & Gelder, M. G. Different ages of onset in varieties of phobia. *American Journal of Psychiatry,* 1966, *123,* 218–221.

Massie, H. N. Blind ratings of mother-infant interaction in home movies of prepsychotic and normal infants. *American Journal of Psychiatry,* 1978, *135,* 1371–1374.

Masters, J. C., Felleman, E. S., & Barden, R. C. Experimental studies of affective states in children. In B. B. Lahey & A. E. Kazdin (Eds.), *Advances in clinical child psychology* (Vol. 4).

New York: Plenum, 1981.

Masterson, J. F. Prognosis in adolescent disorders. *American Journal of Psychiatry,* 1958, *114,* 1097–1103.

Masterson, J. F. *The psychiatric dilemma of adolescence.* London: Churchill, 1967.

Matas, L., Arend, R. A., & Sroufe, L. A. Continuity of adaptation in the second year: The relationship between quality of attachment and later competence. *Child Development,* 1978, *49,* 547–556.

Mattes, J. A., & Gittelman, R. Effects of artificial food colorings in children with hyperactive symptoms. *Archives of General Psychiatry,* 1981, *38,* 714–718.

Maxwell, A. E., Fenwick, P. B. C., Fenton, G. W., & Dollimore, J. Reading ability and brain function: A simple statistical model. *Psychological Medicine,* 1974, *4,* 274–280.

May, R. *The meaning of anxiety.* New York: Ronald Press, 1950.

Mayhew, P., Clarke, R. V. G., Sturman, A., & Hough, J. M. *Crime as opportunity* (Home Office Research Study No. 34). London: Her Majesty's Stationery Office, 1976.

Mays, J. B. *Growing up in the city.* Liverpool: Liverpool University Press, 1954.

McCandless, R. B. Rate of development, body building and personality. *Psychiatric Research Reports,* 1960, *13,* 42–57.

McCann, B. S. Hemispheric asymmetries and early infantile autism. *Journal of Autism and Developmental Disorders,* 1981, *11,* 401–412.

McCauley, C., & Ciesielski, J. Electroencephalogram tests for brain dysfunction: A question of validity. *Science,* 1982, *217,* 81–82.

McClintock, F. H., & Avison, N. H. *Crime in England and Wales.* London: Heinemann Educational, 1968.

McCord, J. Antecedents and correlates of vulnerability and resistance to psychopathology. In R. Zucker & A. Rabin (Eds.), *Further explorations in personality.* New York: Wiley, 1980.

McCord, W., & McCord, J. *Origins of crime: A new evaluation of the Cambridge-Somerville study.* New York: Columbia University Press, 1959.

McHale, S. M., Simeonsson, R. J., Marcus, L. M., & Olley, J. G. The social and symbolic quality of autistic children's communication. *Journal of Autism and Developmental Disorders,* 1980, *10,* 299–310.

McMahon, S. A., & Greenberg, L. M. Serial neurologic examination of hyperactive children. *Pediatrics,* 1977, *59,* 584–587.

McMichael, P. The hen or the egg? Which comes first—antisocial emotional disorders or reading disability. *British Journal of Educational Psychology,* 1979, *49,* 226–238.

McNeil, T. F., & Kaij, L. Offspring of women and nonorganic psychoses: Progress report, February 1980. In N. F. Watt., E. J. Anthony, L. C. Wynne, & J. E. Rolf (Eds.), *Children at risk for schizophrenia: A longitudinal perspective.* New York: Cambridge University Press, in press.

Meadow, K. P. The development of deaf children. In E. M. Hetherington (Ed.), *Review of child development research* (Vol. 5). Chicago: University of Chicago Press, 1975.

Mednick, S. A. Berkson's fallacy and high-risk research. In L. C. Wynne, R. L. Cromwell, & S. Matthysee (Eds.). *The nature of schizophrenia: New approaches to research and treatment.* New York: Wiley, 1978.

Mednick, S. A., Schulsinger, F., Teasdale, T. W., Schulsinger, H., Venables, P. H., & Rock, D. R. Schizophrenia in high risk children: Sex differences in predisposing factors. In G. Serban (Ed.), *Cognitive defects in the development of mental illness.* New York: Brunner/Mazel, 1978.

Melamed, B. G., & Siegel, L. Reduction of anxiety in children facing hospitalization and surgery by use of filmed modeling. *Journal of Consulting and Clinical Psychology,* 1975, *43,* 511–521.

Mellsop, G. W. Psychiatric patients seen as children and adults: Childhood predictors of adult illness. *Journal of Child Psychology and Psychiatry,* 1972, *13,* 91–101.

Mendelson, M. *Psychoanalytic concepts of depression* (2nd ed.). New York: Halstead Press, 1974.

Menkes, M., Rowe, J., & Menkes, J. A twenty-five year follow-up study on the hyperkinetic child with minimal brain dysfunction. *Pediatrics,* 1967, *39,* 393–399.

Merton, R. K. *Social theory and social structure.* New York: Free Press, 1957.

Meyer, E., & Byers, R. K. Measles encephalitis: A follow-up study of sixteen patients. *American Journal of Diseases of Children,* 1952, *84,* 543–579.

Michael, C. M. Relative incidence of criminal behavior in long term follow-up studies of shy children. *Dallas Medical Journal,* January, 1957.

Michael, C. M., Morris, D. R., & Soroker, E. Follow-up studies of shy withdrawn children: II. Relative incidence of schizophrenia. *American Journal of Orthopsychiatry,* 1957, *27,* 331–337.

Milich, R., & Landau, S. Socialization and peer

relations in hyperactive children. In K. D. Gadow & I. Bieler (Eds.), *Advances in learning and behavioral disabilities* (Vol. 1). Greenwich, Conn.: JAI Press, 1982.

Milich, R., & Loney, J. The role of hyperactive and aggressive symptomatology in predicting adolescent outcome among hyperactive children. *Journal of Pediatric Psychology*, 1979, *4*, 93–112.

Milich, R., Loney, J., & Landau, S. The independent dimensions of hyperactivity and aggression: A validation with playroom observation data. *Journal of Abnormal Psychology*, 1982, *91*, 183–198.

Miller, I. W., & Norman, W. H. Learned helplessness in humans: A review and attribution-theory model. *Psychological Bulletin*, 1979, *86*, 93–118.

Miller, L. C., Barrett, C. L., & Hampe, E. Phobias of childhood in a prescientific era. In A. Davis (Ed.), *Child personality and psychopathology: Current topics*. New York: Wiley, 1974.

Mills, M., & Puckering, C. What is it about depressed mothers that influences their children's functioning? Paper presented at the International Congress of the International Association for Child and Adolescent Psychiatry and Allied Professions, Dublin, July 1982.

Minde, K. Coping styles of 34 adolescents with cerebral palsy. *American Journal of Psychiatry*, 1978, *135*, 1344–1349.

Minde, K., Hackett, J., Killoa, D., & Silver, S. How they grow up: 41 physically handicapped children and their families. *American Journal of Psychiatry*, 1972, *128*, 1554–1560.

Minde, K., Lewin, D., Weiss, G., Lavigueur, H., Douglas, V. I., & Sykes, E. The hyperactive child in elementary school: A 5-year controlled follow-up. *Exceptional Children*, 1971, *38*, 215–221.

Minde, R., & Minde, K. Behavioural screening of pre-school children—A new approach to mental health? In P. J. Graham (Ed.), *Epidemiological approaches in child psychiatry*. London: Academic Press, 1977.

Minton, J., Campbell, M., Green, W. H., Jennings, S., & Samit, C. Cognitive assessment of siblings of autistic children. *Journal of the American Academy of Child Psychiatry*, 1982, *21*, 256–261.

Mischel, W. Processes in delay of gratification. In L. Berkowitz (Ed.), *Advances in experimental social psychology* (Vol. 7). New York: Academic Press, 1974.

Mischel, W. On the interface of cognition and personality: Beyond the person-situation debate. *American Psychologist*, 1979, *34*, 740–754.

Mischel, W. Metacognition and the rules of delay. In J. Flavell & L. Ross (Eds.), *Cognitive social development: Frontiers and possible failures*. New York: Cambridge University Press, 1981.

Mischel, W. Delay of gratification as process and as person variable in development. In D. Magnusson & V. Allen (Eds.), *Human development: An interactional perspective*. London & New York: Academic Press, in press.

Mitchell, S., & Rosa, P. Boyhood behaviour problems as precursors of criminality: A fifteen-year follow-up study. *Journal of Child Psychology and Psychiatry*, 1981, *22*, 19–34.

Montagu, J. D. The hyperkinetic child: A behavioural electrodermal and EEG investigation. *Developmental Medicine and Child Neurology*, 1975, *17*, 299–305.

Moore, D. R., Chamberlain, P., & Menkes, L. H. Children at risk for delinquency: A follow-up comparison of aggressive children and children who steal. *Journal of Abnormal Child Psychology*, 1979, *7*, 345–355.

Morris, H. H., Jr., Escoll, P. J., & Wexler, R. Aggressive behavior disorders of childhood: A follow-up study. *American Journal of Psychiatry*, 1956, *112*, 991–997.

Morris, T. *The criminal area*. London: Routledge & Kegan Paul, 1957.

Morrison, J. Adult psychiatric disorders in parents of hyperactive children. *American Journal of Psychiatry*, 1980, *137*, 845–847.

Morrison, J., & Stewart, M. A. The psychiatric status of the legal families of adopted hyperactive children. *Archives of General Psychiatry*, 1973, *28*, 888–891.

Mortimore, P. *Schools as institutions: A comparative study of secondary schools*. Unpublished doctoral dissertation, University of London, 1978.

Moss, H. A., & Sussman, E. J. Longitudinal study of personality development. In O. G. Brim, Jr. & J. Kagan (Eds.), *Constancy and change in human development*. Cambridge: Harvard University Press, 1980.

Moss, P. D., & McEvedy, C. An epidemic of over-breathing among schoolgirls. *British Medical Journal*, 1966, *2*, 1295–1300.

Murrell, S. A., & Stachowiak, J. G. Consistency, rigidity and power in the interaction patterns of clinic and non-clinic families. *Journal of Abnormal Psychology*, 1967, *72*, 265–272.

Nameche, G., & Ricks, D. F. Life patterns of children who become adult schizophrenics. Paper presented at the meeting of the American Orthopsychiatry Association, San Francisco, April 1966.

Needleman, H. L. (Ed.). *Low level lead exposure: The clinical implications of current research.* New York: Raven Press, 1980.

Needleman, H. L., Gunnoe, C., Leviton, A., Reed, M., Peresie, H., Maher, C., & Barrett, P. Deficits in psychological and classroom performance of children with elevated dentine lead levels. *New England Journal of Medicine,* 1979, *300,* 689–695.

Neligan, G. A., Kolvin, I., Scott, D. McI., & Garside, R. F. *Born too soon or born too small* (Clinics in Developmental Medicine No. 61). London: Heinemann Medical/SIMP, 1976.

Newman, O. *Defensible space.* London: Architectural Press, 1973.

Newman, O. Reactions to the "defensible space" study and some further findings. *International Journal of Mental Health,* 1975, *4,* 48–70.

Newman, O. *Design guidelines for creating defensible space.* Washington, D.C: U.S. Government Printing Office, 1976.

Newsom, C., & Rincover, A. Autism. In E. J. Mash & L. G. Terdal (Eds.), *Behavioral assessment of childhood disorders.* New York: Guilford Press, 1981.

Newson, J., & Newson, E. *Four years old in an urban community.* Harmondsworth, Eng.: Penguin, 1968.

Nichols, P. L., & Chen, T.-C. *Minimal brain dysfunction: A prospective study.* Hillsdale, N.J.: Erlbaum, 1981.

Noblit, G. The adolescent experience and delinquency. *Youth and Society,* 1976, *8,* 27–44.

Nonneman, A. J., & Isaacson, R. L. Task dependent recovery after early brain damage. *Behavioral Biology,* 1973, *8,* 143–172.

Novick, B., Kurtzberg, D., & Vaughn, H. G. An electrophysiologic indication of defective information storage in childhood autism. *Psychiatry Research,* 1979, *1,* 101–198.

Nuechterlain, K. H. Signal detection in vigilance tasks and behavioral attributes among offspring of schizophrenic mothers and among hyperactive children. *Journal of Abnormal Psychology,* in press.

Nuechterlain, K. H., Phipps-Yonas, S., Driscoll, R., & Garmezy, N. Attentional functioning among children vulnerable to adult schizophrenia: Vigilance, reaction time and incidental learning. In N. F. Watt, E. J. Anthony, L. C.

Wynne, & J. E. Rolf (Eds.), *Children at risk for schizophrenia: A longitudinal perspective.* New York: Cambridge University Press, in press.

Nuechterlain, K. H., Soli, S. D., Garmezy, N., Devine, V. T., & Schaefer, S. M. A classification system for research in childhood psychopathology: Part II. Validation research examining converging descriptions from the parent and from the child. In B. A. Maher (Ed.), *Progress in experimental personality research* (Vol. 10). New York: Academic Press, 1981.

Nuffield, E. Neurophysiology and behavior disorders in epileptic children. *Journal of Mental Science,* 1961, *107,* 438–458.

Nyhan, W. L. Behavior in the Lesch-Nyhan syndrome. *Journal of Autism and Childhood Schizophrenia,* 1976, *6,* 235–252.

Nylander, I. A 20-year prospective follow-up study of 2164 cases at the child guidance clinics in Stockholm. *Acta Paediatrica Scandinavica,* Supplement No. 276, 1979.

O'Donnell, C. R. Behavior modification in community settings. In M. Hersen, R. M. Eisler, & P. M. Miller (Eds.), *Progress in behavior modification* (Vol. 4). New York: Academic Press, 1977.

Offord, D. R. Family backgrounds of male and female delinquents. In J. C. Gunn & D. P. Farrington (Eds.), *Abnormal offenders, delinquency, and the criminal justice system.* Chichester, Eng.: Wiley, 1982.

Offord, D. R., & Cross, L. A. Behavioral antecedents of adult schizophrenia. *Archives of General Psychiatry,* 1969, *21,* 267–283.

Offord, D. R., Poushinsky, M. F., & Sullivan, K. School performance, IQ and delinquency. *British Journal of Criminology,* 1978, *18,* 110–127.

Öhman, A., & Ursin, H. Commentary on Eysenck's conditioning model of neurosis. *Behavioral and Brain Sciences,* 1979, *2,* 179–180.

O'Leary, K. D., Rosenbaum, A., & Hughes, P. C. Fluorescent lighting: A purported source of hyperactive behavior. *Journal of Abnormal Child Psychology,* 1978, *6,* 285–289.

Olweus, D. Stability of aggressive reaction patterns in males: A review. *Psychological Bulletin,* 1979, *86,* 852–875.

Opie, I., & Opie, P. *Lore and language of school children.* Oxford: Oxford University Press, 1959.

Ornitz, E. M. Neurophysiologic studies. In M. Rutter & E. Schopler (Eds.), *Autism: A reappraisal of concepts and treatment.* New York: Plenum, 1978.

Ornitz, E. M., Guthrie, D., & Farley, A. H. The

early development of autistic children. *Journal of Autism and Childhood Schizophrenia*, 1977, *7*, 207–230.

Ornitz, E. M., & Ritvo, E. R. Perceptual inconstancy in early infantile autism. *Archives of General Psychiatry*, 1968, *18*, 76–98.

Orris, J. B. Visual monitoring performance in three subgroups of male delinquents. *Journal of Abnormal Psychology*, 1969, *74*, 227–229.

Orvaschel, H., Weissman, M. M., & Kidd, K. K. Children and depression. *Journal of Affective Disorders*, 1980, *2*, 1–16.

Osborn, S. G., & West, D. J. The effectiveness of various predictors of criminal careers. *Journal of Adolescence*, 1978, *1*, 101–117.

Osborn, S. G., & West, D. J. Conviction records of fathers and sons compared. *British Journal of Criminology*, 1979, *19*, 120–133.

Osborn, S. G., & West, D. J. Do young delinquents really reform? *Journal of Adolescence*, 1980, *3*, 99–114.

Ounsted, C. The hyperkinetic syndrome in epileptic children. *Lancet*, 1955, *2*, 303–311.

Ounsted, C., Lindsay, J., & Norman, N. *Biological factors in temporal lobe epilepsy* (Clinics in Developmental Medicine No. 22). London: Heinemann Medical/SIMP, 1966.

Ounsted, C., Oppenheimer, R., & Lindsay, J. Aspects of bonding failure: The psychopathology and psychotherapeutic treatment of families of battered children. *Developmental Medicine and Child Neurology*, 1974, *16*, 447–456.

Ouston, J. Delinquency, family background and educational attainment. *British Journal of Criminology*, in press.

Pablant, P., & Baxter, J. C. Environmental correlates of school vandalism. *Journal of the American Institute of Planners*, 1975, *241*, 270–279.

Palmer, T. B. The youth authority's community treatment project. *Federal Probation*, 1974, *38*, 3–14.

Parke, R. D., & Lewis, N. G. The family in context: A multilevel interactional analysis of child abuse. In R. W. Henderson (Ed.), *Parent-child interaction: Theory, research and prospects*. New York: Academic Press, 1981.

Parker, E. B., Olson, T. F., & Throdemorton, M. D. Social casework with elementary school children who do not talk in school. *Social Work*, 1980, *5*, 64–70.

Parkes, C. M., & Stevenson-Hinde, J. (Eds.). *The place of attachment in human behaviour*. London: Tavistock Press, 1982.

Parnas, J., Schulsinger, F., Teasdale, T. W.,

Schulsinger, H., Feldman, P. M., & Mednick, S. A. Perinatal complications and clinical outcome within the schizophrenia spectrum. *British Journal of Psychiatry*, 1982, *140*, 416–420.

Pasamanick, B., & Knobloch, H. Retrospective studies on the epidemiology of reproductive casualty: Old and new. *Merrill-Palmer Quarterly*, 1966, *12*, 7–26.

Patterson, G. R. Accelerating stimuli for two classes of coercive behaviors. *Journal of Abnormal Child Psychology*, 1977, *5*, 335–350.

Patterson, G. R. A performance theory for coercive family interaction. In R. B. Cairns (Ed.), *The analysis of social interactions: Methods, issues, and illustrations*. Hillsdale, N.J.: Erlbaum, 1979.

Patterson, G. R. Mothers: The unacknowledged victims. *Monographs of the Society for Research in Child Development*, 1981, *46*(Whole No. 5). (a)

Patterson, G. R. Some speculations and data relating to children who steal. In T. Hirschi & M. Gottfredson (Eds.), *Theory and fact in contemporary criminology*. Beverley Hills, Calif.: Sage, 1981. (b)

Patterson, G. R. *Coercive family process*. Eugene, Ore.: Castalia Publications, 1982.

Patton, R. G., & Gardner, L. I. *Growth failure in maternal deprivation*. Springfield, Ill.: Charles C. Thomas, 1963.

Paulauskas, S. L., & Campbell, S. B. G. Social perspective-taking and teacher ratings of peer interaction in hyperactive boys. *Journal of Abnormal Child Psychology*, 1979, *7*, 483–494.

Pearce, J. The recognition of depressive disorder in children. *Journal of the Royal Society of Medicine*, 1978, *71*, 494–500.

Pearce, J. Personal communication, March 1982. (Data cited in Rutter, in press b.)

Pelham, W. E., & Bender, M. E. Peer relationships in hyperactive children: Description and treatment. In K. D. Gadow & I. Bieler (Eds.), *Advances in learning and behavioral disabilities* (Vol. 1). Greenwich, Conn.: JAI Press, 1982.

Peter, B. M., & Spreen, O. Behavior rating and personal adjustment scales of neurologically and learning handicapped children during adolescence and early adulthood: Results of a follow-up study. *Journal of Clinical Neuropsychology*, 1979, *1*, 75–92.

Peters, J. S., Romine, J. S., & Dykman, R. A. A special neurological examination of children with learning disabilities. *Developmental Medicine and Child Neurology*, 1975, *17*, 63–78.

Phillips, J. C., & Kelly, D. H. School failure and

delinquency: What causes which? *Criminology*, 1979, *17*, 194–207.

Phillips, L., Votey, H. L., & Maxwell, D. Crime, youth and the labour market. *Journal of Political Economy*, 1972, *80*, 491–504.

Piaget, J. *The language and thought of the child* (M. Gabian, trans.). London: Routledge & Kegan Paul, 1926.

Pinneau, S. R. The infantile disorders of hospitalism and anaclitic depression. *Psychological Bulletin*, 1955, *52*, 429–452.

Pless, B., & Pinkerton, P. *Chronic childhood disorder: Promoting patterns of adjustment*. London: Henry Kimpton, 1975.

Plomin, R. Behavioural genetics and temperament. In R. Porter & G. M. Collins (Eds.), *Temperamental differences in infants and young children* (Ciba Foundation Symposium No. 89). London: Pitman, 1982.

Plomin, R. Childhood temperament. In B. B. Lahey & A. E. Kazdin (Eds.), *Advances in clinical child psychology* (Vol. 6). New York: Plenum, in press.

Plomin, R., & Foch, T. T. Hyperactivity and pediatrician diagnoses, parental ratings, specific cognitive disabilities and laboratory measures. *Journal of Abnormal Child Psychology*, 1981, *9*, 55–64. (a)

Plomin, R., & Foch, T. T. Sex differences and individual differences. *Child Development*, 1981, *52*, 383–385. (b)

Pollitt, E., & Eichler, A. Behavioral disturbances among failure-to-thrive children. *American Journal of Diseases of Children*, 1976, *130*, 24–29.

Porrino, L. J., Rapoport, J. L., Behar, D., Ismond, D. R., & Bunney, W. E. A naturalistic assessment of the motor activity of hyperactive boys. II. Stimulant drug effects. *Archives of General Psychiatry*, in press.

Porrino, L. J., Rapoport, J. L., Behar, D., Sceery, W., Ismond, D. R., & Bunney, W. E. A naturalistic assessment of the motor activity of hyperactive boys. I. Comparison with normal controls. *Archives of General Psychiatry*, in press.

Porter B., & O'Leary, K. D. Marital discord and childhood behavior problems. *Journal of Abnormal Child Psychology*, 1980, *8*, 287–296.

Porter, R., & Collins, G. M. (Eds.). *Temperamental differences in infants and young children* (Ciba Foundation Symposium No. 89). London: Pitman, 1982.

Powell, G. E. Psychoticism and social deviancy in children. *Advances in Behavior Research and Therapy*, 1977, *1*, 27–56.

Power, M. J., Alderson, M. R., Phillipson, C. M., Schoenberg, E., & Morris, J. N. Delinquent schools? *New Society*, 1967, *10*, 542–543.

Power, M. J., Ash, P. M., Schoenberg, E., & Sorey, E. C. Delinquency and the family. *British Journal of Social Work*, 1974, *4*, 13–38.

Power, M. J., Benn, R. T., & Morris, J. N. Neighbourhood, school and juveniles before the courts. *British Journal of Criminology*, 1972, *12*, 111–132.

Poznanski, E. O., & Zrull, J. Childhood depression: Clinical characteristics of overtly depressed children. *Archives of General Psychiatry*, 1970, *23*, 8–15.

Prichep, L., John, E. R., Ahn, H., & Kaye, H. Neurometrics: Quantitative evaluation of brain damage in children. In M. Rutter (Ed.), *Developmental neuropsychiatry*. New York: Guilford Press, in press.

Pringle, M. L. K., & Bossio, V. Intellectual, emotional and social development of deprived children. *Vita Humana*, 1958, *1*, 66–92.

Pringle, M. L. K., & Bossio, V. Early prolonged separations and emotional adjustment. *Journal of Child Psychology and Psychiatry*, 1960, *1*, 37–48.

Prior, M. R. Cognitive abilities and disabilities in infantile autism: A review. *Journal of Abnormal Child Psychology*, 1979, *7*, 357–380.

Prior, M. R., & Bradshaw, J. L. Hemisphere functioning in autistic children. *Cortex*, 1979, *15*, 73–82.

Pritchard, M., & Graham, P. An investigation of a group of patients who have attended both the child and adult departments of the same psychiatric hospital. *British Journal of Psychiatry*, 1966, *112*, 603–612.

Puig-Antich, J. Affective disorder in childhood: A review and perspective. *Psychiatric Clinics of North America*, 1980, *3*, 403–424.

Puig-Antich, J. Major depression and conduct disorder in prepuberty. *Journal of the American Academy of Child Psychiatry*, 1982, *21*, 118–128. (a)

Puig-Antich, J. The use of RDC criteria for major depressive disorder in children and adolescents. *Journal of the American Academy of Child Psychiatry*, 1982, *21*, 291–293. (b)

Puig-Antich, J. Markers of major depressive disorders. In M. Rutter, C. E. Izard, & P. Read (Eds.), *Depression in childhood: Developmental perspectives*. New York: Guilford Press, in press.

Puig-Antich, J., & Gittelman, R. Depression in

childhood and adolescence. In E. S. Paykel (Ed.), *Handbook of affective disorders*. Edinburgh: Churchill Livingstone, 1982.

Quay, H. C. Psychopathic personality as pathological stimulation-seeking. *American Journal of Psychiatry*, 1965, *122*, 180–183.

Quay, H. C. Psychopathic behavior: Reflections on its nature, origins and treatment. In I. C. Uzgiris & F. Weizmann (Eds.), *The structuring of experience*. New York: Plenum, 1977. (a)

Quay, H. C. The three faces of evaluation: What can be expected to work. *Criminal Justice and Behavior*, 1977, *4*, 341–354. (b)

Quay, H. C. Classification. In H. C. Quay & J. S. Werry (Eds.), *Psychopathological disorders of childhood* (2nd ed.). New York: Wiley, 1979.

Quinton, D. Family life in the inner city: Myth and reality. In M. Marland (Ed.), *Education for the inner city*. London: Heinemann Educational, 1980.

Quinton, D., Rutter, M., and Rowlands, O. An evaluation of an interview assessment of marriage. *Psychological Medicine*, 1976, *6*, 577–586.

Quitkin, F., Rifkin, A., & Klein, D. F. Neurologic soft signs in schizophrenia and character disorders. *Archives of General Psychiatry*, 1976, *33*, 845–853.

Rachman, D. The conditioning theory of fear acquisition: A critical examination. *Behavior Research and Therapy*, 1977, *15*, 375–389.

Rachman, S. J., & Hodgson, R. J. *Obsessions and compulsions*. Englewood Cliffs, N.J.: Prentice-Hall, 1980.

Radke-Yarrow, M., & Kuczynski, L. Perspectives and strategies in child-rearing: Studies of rearing by normal and depressed mothers. In D. Magnusson & V. Allen (Eds.), *Human development: An interactional perspective*. New York & London: Academic Press, in press.

Radosh, A., & Gittelman, R. The effect of appealing distractors on the performance of hyperactive children. *Journal of Abnormal Child Psychology*, 1981, *9*, 179–190.

Rajecki, D. W., Lamb, M. E., & Obmascher, P. Toward a general theory of infantile attachment: A comparative review of aspects of the social bond. *Behavioral and Brain Sciences*, 1978, *3*, 417–464.

Rapaport, D. On the psychoanalytic theory of affects. *International Journal of Psychoanalysis*, 1953, *34*, 177–198.

Rapaport, D. On the psychoanalytic theory of motivation. In M. R. Jones (Ed.) *Nebraska Symposium on Motivation* (Vol. 8). Lincoln: University of Nebraska Press, 1960.

Rapoport, J. The use of drugs: Trends in research. In M. Rutter (Ed.), *Developmental neuropsychiatry*. New York: Guilford Press, in press.

Rapoport, J., & Benoit, M. The relation of direct home observations to the clinic evaluation of hyperactive school age boys. *Journal of Child Psychology and Psychiatry*, 1975, *16*, 141–147.

Rapoport, J., Buchsbaum, M., Weingartner, H., Zahn, T. P., Ludlow, C., Bartico, J., Mikkelsen, E. J., Langer, D. H., & Bunney, W. E., Jr. Dextroamphetamine: Cognitive and behavioral effects in normal and hyperactive boys and normal adult males. *Archives of General Psychiatry*, 1980, *37*, 933–946.

Rapoport, J., Buchsbaum, M., Zahn, T. P., Weingartner, H., Ludlow, C., & Mikkelsen, E. J. Dextroamphetamine: Cognitive and behavioral effects in normal prepubertal boys. *Science*, 1978, *199*, 560–563.

Rapoport, J., & Ferguson, H. B. Biological validation of the hyperkinetic syndrome. *Developmental Medicine and Child Neurology*, 1981, *23*, 667–682.

Rapoport, J., Pandoni, C., Renfield, M., Lake, C. R., & Ziegler, M. G. Newborn dopamine-b-hydroxylase, minor physical anomalies, and infant temperament. *American Journal of Psychiatry*, 1977, *134*, 676–679.

Rapoport, J., & Quinn, P. Minor physical anomalies (stigmata) and early developmental deviation: A major biological subgroup of "hyperactive children." *International Journal of Mental Health*, 1975, *4*, 29–44.

Rapoport, J., Quinn, P., Bradbard, G., Riddle, K., & Brooks, E. Imipramine and methylphenidate treatment of hyperactive boys: A double-blind comparison. *Archives of General Psychiatry*, 1974, *30*, 789–793.

Reid, J. B., & Patterson, G. R. Follow-up analyses of behavioral treatment program for boys with conduct problems: A reply to Kent. *Journal of Consulting and Clinical Psychology*, 1976, *44*, 299–302.

Reiss, A., & Rhodes, A. The distribution of juvenile delinquency in the social class structure. *American Sociological Review*, 1961, *26*, 730–732.

Reitan, R. M., & Davison, L. A. (Eds.). *Clinical neuropsychology: Current status and applications*. Washington, D.C.: Hemisphere, 1974.

Remschmidt, H., Hohner, G., & Merschmann, W. Epidemiology of delinquent behaviour in children. In P. J. Graham (Ed.), *Epidemiological* approaches in child psychiatry. London: Academic Press, 1977.

Reynolds, D., Jones, D., & St. Leger, S. Schools do make a difference. New Society, 1976, 37, 321.

Reynolds, D., Jones, D., St. Leger, S., & Murgatroyd, S. School factors and truancy. In L. A. Hersov & I. Berg (Eds.), Out of school: Modern perspectives in truancy and school refusal. Chichester, Eng.: Wiley, 1980.

Reynolds, D., & Murgatroyd, S. The sociology of schooling and the absent pupil: The school as a factor in the generation of truancy. In H. C. M. Carroll (Ed.), Absenteeism in South Wales: Studies of pupils, their homes and their secondary schools. Swansea, Wales: University of Swansea, Faculty of Education, 1977.

Rheingold, H., & Eckerman, C. Fear of the stranger: A critical examination. In H. Rease (Ed.), Advances in child development and behavior (Vol. 8). New York: Academic Press, 1973.

Rholes, W. S., Blackwell, J., Jordan, C., & Walters C. A developmental study of learned helplessness. Developmental Psychology, 1980, 16, 616–624.

Rich, J. Types of stealing. Lancet, 1956, 1, 496–498.

Richardson, S. A. The long range consequences of malnutrition in infancy: A study of children in Jamaica, West Indies. In B. Wharton (Ed.), Topics in paediatrics, vol. 2, Nutrition in childhood. London: Pitman Medical, 1980.

Richer, J. The partial noncommunication of culture to autistic children—an application of human ethology. In M. Rutter & E. Schopler (Eds.), Autism: A reappraisal of concepts and treatment. New York: Plenum, 1978.

Richer, J., & Richards, B. Reacting to autistic children: The danger of trying too hard. British Journal of Psychiatry, 1975, 127, 526–529.

Richman, N., Stevenson, J., & Graham, P. J. Preschool to school: A behavioural study. London: Academic Press, 1982.

Ricks, D. F. Vocal communication in pre-verbal normal and autistic children. In N. O'Connor (Ed.), Language, cognitive deficits and retardation. London: Butterworths, 1975.

Rie, E. D., Rie, H. E., Stewart, S., & Rettemnier, S. R. Analysis of neurological soft signs in children with learning problems. Brain and Language, 1978, 6, 32–46.

Rie, H. E. Depression in childhood: A survey of some pertinent contributions. Journal of the American Academy of Child Psychiatry, 1966, 5, 653–683.

Rie, H. E., & Rie, E. D. (Eds.). Handbook of minimal brain dysfunction: A critical view. New York: Wiley, 1980.

Riguet, C. B., Taylor, N. D., Benaroya, S., & Klein, L. S. Symbolic play in autistic, Down's, and normal children of equivalent mental age. Journal of Autism and Developmental Disorders, 1981, 11, 439–448.

Riikonen, R., & Amnell, G. Psychiatric disorders in children with earlier infantile spasms. Developmental Medicine and Child Neurology, 1981, 23, 747–760.

Ritvo, E. R., Cantwell, D. P., Johnson, E., Clements, M., Benbrook, F., Slagle, S., Kelly, P., & Ritz, M. Social class factors in autism. Journal of Autism and Childhood Schizophrenia, 1971, 1, 297–310.

Ritvo, E. R., & Freeman, B. J. National Society for Autistic Children definition of the syndrome of autism. Journal of Autism and Developmental Disorders, 1978, 8, 162–169.

Ritvo, E. R., Rabin, K., Yuwiler, A., Freeman, B. J., & Geller, E. Biochemical and hematologic studies: A critical review. In M. Rutter & E. Schopler (Eds.), Autism: A reappraisal of concepts and treatment. New York: Plenum, 1978.

Ritvo, E. R., Yuwiler, A., Geller, E., Ornitz, E. M., Saeger, K., & Plotkin, S. Increased blood serotonin and platelets in early infantile autism. Archives of General Psychiatry, 1970, 23, 566–572.

Rivinus, T. M., Jamison, D. L., & Graham, P. J. Childhood organic neurological disease presenting as psychiatric disorder. Archives of Disease in Childhood, 1975, 50, 115–119.

Robbins, D. R., Alessi, N. E., Cook, S. C., Poznanski, E. O., & Yanchyshyn, G. W. The use of the research diagnostic criteria (RDC) for depression in adolescent psychiatric inpatients. Journal of the American Academy of Child Psychiatry, 1982, 21, 251–255.

Robertson, J., & Robertson, J. Young children in brief separation: A fresh look. Psychoanalytic Study of the Child, 1971, 26, 264–315.

Robins, L. N. Deviant children grown up. Baltimore: Williams & Wilkins, 1966.

Robins, L. N. Sturdy childhood predictors of adult antisocial behavior: Replications from longitudinal studies. Psychological Medicine, 1978, 8, 611–622.

Robins, L. N. Follow-up studies. In H. C. Quay & J. S. Werry (Eds.), Psychopathological disorders of childhood (2nd ed.). New York: Wiley, 1979.

Robins, L. N., & Hill, S. Y. Assessing the contributions of family structure, class and peer groups to juvenile delinquency. *Journal of Criminal Law, Criminology and Police Science,* 1966, *57,* 325–334.

Robins, L. N., & Lewis, R. G. The role of the antisocial family in school completion and delinquency: A three-generation study. *Sociological Quarterly,* 1966, *7,* 500–514.

Robins, L. N., & Ratcliff, K. S. The long-term outcome of truancy. In L. A. Hersov & I. Berg (Eds.), *Out of school: Modern perspectives in truancy and school refusal.* Chichester, Eng.: Wiley, 1980.

Robins, L. N., West, P. A., & Herjanic, B. L. Arrests and delinquency in two generations: A study of black urban families and their children. *Journal of Child Psychology and Psychiatry,* 1975, *16,* 125–140.

Robinson, J. F., & Vitale, L. J. Children with circumscribed interest patterns. *American Journal of Orthopsychiatry,* 1954, *24,* 755–766.

Robinson, W. S. Ecological correlations and the behavior of individuals. *American Sociological Review,* 1950, *15,* 351–357.

Rochlin, G. The loss complex. *Journal of the American Psychoanalytic Association,* 1959, *7,* 299–316.

Rodriguez, A., Rodriguez, M., & Eisenberg, L. The outcome of school phobia: A follow-up study based on 41 cases. *American Journal of Psychiatry,* 1959, *116,* 540–544.

Roff, M. Childhood social interactions and young adult psychosis. *Journal of Clinical Psychology,* 1963, *19,* 152–157.

Roff, M., Sells, S. B., & Golden, M. M. *Social adjustment and personality development in children.* Minneapolis: University of Minnesota Press, 1972.

Rohner, R. P. *They love me, they love me not: A world-wide study of the effects of parental acceptance and rejection.* New Haven, Conn.: H.R.A.F. Press, 1975.

Rolf, J. E., & Garmezy, N. The school performance of children vulnerable to behavior pathology. In D. F. Ricks, T. Alexander, & M. Roff (Eds.), *Life history research in psychopathology* (Vol. 3). Minneapolis: University of Minnesota Press, 1974.

Rosenblum, S. M., Arick, J. R., Krug, D. A., Stubbs, E. G., Young, N. B., & Pelson, R. O. Auditory brainstem evoked responses in autistic children. *Journal of Autism and Developmental Disorders,* 1980, *10,* 215–226.

Rosenthal, D., Wender, P. H., Kety, S. S.,

Schulsinger, F., Welner, J., & Rieder, R. O. Parent-child relationships and psychopathological disorder in the child. *Archives of General Psychiatry,* 1975, *32,* 466–476.

Rosenthal, J., Massie, H. N., & Wulff, K. A comparison of cognitive development in normal and psychotic children in the first two years of life from home movies. *Journal of Autism and Developmental Disorders,* 1980, *10,* 433–444.

Rosenthal, R. H., & Allen, T. W. An examination of attention, arousal and learning dysfunctions of hyperkinetic children. *Psychological Bulletin,* 1978, *85,* 689–715.

Rosenthal, R. H., & Allen, T. W. Intratask distractibility in hyperkinetic and nonhyperkinetic children. *Journal of Abnormal Child Psychology,* 1980, *8,* 175–188.

Ross, A. O. *Psychological aspects of learning disabilities and reading disorders.* New York: McGraw-Hill, 1976.

Ross, A. O., & Pelham, W. E. Child psychopathology. *Annual Review of Psychology,* 1981, *32,* 243–278.

Ross, D. M., & Ross, S. A. *Hyperactivity: Research, theory and action.* New York: Wiley, 1976.

Ross, J. *A follow-up study of obsessional illness presenting in childhood and adolescence.* Unpublished DPM dissertation, University of London, 1964.

Ross, R. R., & Gendreau, P. (Eds.). *Effective correctional treatment.* Toronto: Butterworths, 1980.

Routh, D. K., & Schroeder, C. S. Standardized playroom measures as indices of hyperactivity. *Journal of Abnormal Child Psychology,* 1976, *4,* 199–207.

Routh, D. K., Schroeder, C. S., & O'Tuama, L. Development of activity level in children. *Developmental Psychology,* 1974, *10,* 163–168.

Rowe, D. C., & Plomin, R. The importance of nonshared (EI) environmental influences in behavioral development. *Developmental Psychology,* 1981, *17,* 517–531.

Ruppenthal, G. C., Arling, G. L., Harlow, H. F., Sackett, G. P., & Suomi, S. J. A 10-year perspective of motherless-mother monkey behavior. *Journal of Abnormal Psychology,* 1976, *85,* 341–349.

Rutschmann, J., Cornblatt, B., & Erlenmeyer-Kimling, L. Sustained attention in children at risk for schizophrenia. *Archives of General Psychiatry,* 1977, *34,* 571–575.

Rutter, M. *Children of sick parents: An environmen-*

tal and psychiatric study (Institute of Psychiatry Maudsley Monographs No. 16). London: Oxford University Press, 1966.

Rutter, M. Psychotic disorders in early childhood. In A. J. Coppen & A. Walk (Eds.), *Recent developments in schizophrenia*. Ashford, Eng.: Headley Bros., 1967.

Rutter, M. Autistic children: Infancy to adulthood. *Seminars in Psychiatry*, 1970, *2*, 435–450. (a)

Rutter, M. Sex differences in children's response to family stress. In E. J. Anthony & C. Koupernik (Eds.), *The child in his family*. New York: Wiley, 1970. (b)

Rutter, M. Parent-child separation: Psychological effects on the children. *Journal of Child Psychology and Psychiatry*, 1971, *12*, 233–260. (a)

Rutter, M. Psychiatry. In J. Wortis (Ed.), *Mental retardation: An annual review, III*. New York: Grune & Stratton, 1971. (b)

Rutter, M. Childhood schizophrenia reconsidered. *Journal of Autism and Childhood Schizophrenia*, 1972, *2*, 315–337. (a)

Rutter, M. Relationships between child and adult psychiatric disorder. *Acta Psychiatrica Scandinavica*, 1972, *48*, 3–21. (b)

Rutter, M. Brain damage syndromes in childhood: Concepts and findings. *Journal of Child Psychology and Psychiatry*, 1977, *18*, 1–21. (a)

Rutter, M. Prospective studies to investigate behavioral change. In J. S. Strauss, H. M. Babigian, & M. Roff (Eds.), *The origins and course of psychopathology*. New York: Plenum, 1977. (b)

Rutter, M. Communication deviance and diagnostic differences. In L. C. Wynne, R. L. Cromwell, & S. Matthysse (Eds.), *The nature of schizophrenia: New approaches to research and treatment*. New York: Wiley, 1978. (a)

Rutter, M. Diagnosis and definition. In M. Rutter & E. Schopler (Eds.), *Autism: A reappraisal of concepts and treatment*. New York: Plenum, 1978. (b)

Rutter, M. Diagnostic validity in child psychiatry. *Advances in Biological Psychiatry*, 1978, *2*, 2–22. (c)

Rutter, M. *Changing youth in a changing society*. London: Nuffield Provincial Hospitals Trust, 1979. (Cambridge: Harvard University Press, 1980).

Rutter, M. (Ed.). *Scientific foundations of developmental psychiatry*. London: Heinemann Medical, 1980.

Rutter, M. The city and the child. *American Journal of Orthopsychiatry*, 1981, *51*, 610–625. (a)

Rutter, M. *Maternal deprivation reassessed* (2nd ed.). Harmondsworth, Eng.: Penguin, 1981. (b)

Rutter, M. Epidemiological-longitudinal approaches to the study of development. In W. A. Collins (Ed.), *The concept of development*. Minnesota Symposia on Child Psychology (Vol. 15). Hillsdale, N.J.: Erlbaum, 1982.

Rutter, M. Cognitive deficits in the pathogenesis of autism. (The Kenneth Cameron memorial lecture). *Journal of Child Psychology and Psychiatry*, in press. (a)

Rutter, M. Continuities and discontinuities in socioemotional development: Empirical and conceptual perspectives. In R. N. Emde & R. J. Harmon (Eds.), *Continuities and discontinuities in development*. New York: Plenum, in press. (b)

Rutter, M. (Ed.). *Developmental neuropsychiatry*. New York: Guilford Press, in press. (c)

Rutter, M. The developmental psychopathology of depression: Issues and perspectives. In M. Rutter, C. E. Izard, & P. Read (Eds.), *Depression in childhood: Developmental perspectives*. New York: Guilford Press, in press. (d)

Rutter, M. Family and school influences: Meanings, mechanisms and implications. In A. R. Nicol (Ed.), *Practical lessons from longitudinal studies*. Chichester, Eng.: Wiley, in press. (e)

Rutter, M. School effects on pupil progress: Research findings and policy implications. *Child Development*, in press. (f)

Rutter, M. Statistical and personal interactions: Facets and perspectives. In D. Magnusson & V. Allen (Eds.), *Human development: An interactional perspective*. London & New York: Academic Press, in press. (g)

Rutter, M., Bartak, L., & Newman, S. Autism—a central disorder of cognition and language. In Rutter, M. (Ed.), *Infantile autism: Concepts, characteristics and treatment*. Edinburgh: Churchill Livingstone, 1971.

Rutter, M., Chadwick, O., & Shaffer, D. Head injury. In M. Rutter (Ed.), *Developmental neuropsychiatry*. New York: Guilford Press, in press.

Rutter, M., Cox, A., Tupling, C., Berger, M., & Yule, W. Attainment and adjustment in two geographical areas: I. The prevalence of psychiatric disorder. *British Journal of Psychiatry*, 1975, *126*, 493–509.

Rutter, M., & Giller, H. *Juvenile delinquency: Trends and perspectives*. Harmondsworth, Eng.: Penguin, in press.

Rutter, M., & Graham, P. The reliability and validity of the psychiatric assessment of the child. I. Interview with the child. *British Journal of Psychiatry*, 1968, *114*, 563–579.

Rutter, M., Graham, P. J., & Yule, W. *A neuropsychiatric study in childhood* (Clinics in Developmental Medicine No. 35/36). London: Heinemann Medical/SIMP, 1970.

Rutter, M., & Madge, N. *Cycles of disadvantage: A review of research*. London: Heinemann Educational, 1976.

Rutter, M., Maughan, B., Mortimore, P., & Ouston, J., with Smith, A. *Fifteen thousand hours: Secondary schools and their effects on children*. London: Open Books; Cambridge: Harvard University Press, 1979.

Rutter, M., & Quinton, D. Psychiatric disorder—ecological factors and concepts of causation. In H. McGurk (Ed.), *Ecological factors in human development*. Amsterdam: North-Holland, 1977.

Rutter, M., Quinton, D., & Liddle, C. Parenting in two generations: Looking backwards and looking forwards. In N. Madge (Ed.), *Families at risk*. London: Heinemann Educational, in press.

Rutter, M., & Russell Jones, R. *Lead versus health: Sources and effects of low level lead exposure*. Chichester, Eng.: Wiley, 1983.

Rutter, M., & Shaffer, D. DSM–III: A step forward or back in terms of the classification of child psychiatric disorder? *Journal of the American Academy of Child Psychiatry*, 1980, *19*, 371–394.

Rutter, M., Shaffer, D., & Shepherd, M. *A multiaxial classification of child psychiatric disorders*. Geneva: World Health Organization, 1975.

Rutter, M., Tizard, J., & Whitmore, K. (Eds.). *Education, health and behaviour*. Huntington, N.Y.: Krieger, 1981. (Originally published, 1970.)

Rutter, M., Tizard, J., Yule, W., Graham, P. J., & Whitmore, K. Research report: Isle of Wight studies 1964–1974. *Psychological Medicine*, 1976, *6*, 313–332.

Rutter, M., & Yule, W. Reading difficulties. In M. Rutter & L. A. Hersov (Eds.), *Child psychiatry: Modern approaches*. Oxford: Blackwell Scientific, 1977.

Rutter, M., & Yule, W. Unpublished data, 1982. (Described in Rutter & Giller, in press.)

Sackett, G. P. Can single processes explain effects of postnatal influences on primate development. In R. N. Emde & R. J. Harmon (Eds.), *The development of attachment and affiliative systems*. New York: Plenum, 1982.

Safer, D. J. A familial factor in minimal brain dysfunction. *Behavior Genetics*, 1973, *3*, 175–186.

Safer, D. J., & Allen, R. *Hyperactive children: Diagnosis and management*. Baltimore: University Park Press, 1976.

Sameroff, A. J., Barocas, R., & Safer, R. Rochester longitudinal study progress report. In N. F. Watt, E. J. Anthony, L. C. Wynne, & J. E. Rolf (Eds.), *Children at risk for schizophrenia: A longitudinal perspective*. New York: Cambridge University Press, in press.

Sameroff, A. J., & Chandler, M. J. Reproductive risk and the continuum of caretaking casualty. In F. D. Horowitz (Ed.), *Review of child development research* (Vol. 4). Chicago: University of Chicago Press, 1975.

Samuelson, F. J. B. Watson's little Albert, Cyril Burt's twins, and the need for a critical science. *American Psychologist*, 1980, *35*, 619–625.

Sandberg, S. On the overinclusiveness of the diagnosis of hyperkinetic syndrome. In M. Gittelman (Ed.), *Intervention strategies with hyperactive children*. New York: M. E. Sharpe, 1981.

Sandberg, S., Rutter, M., & Taylor, E. Hyperkinetic disorder in psychiatric clinic attenders. *Developmental Medicine and Child Neurology*, 1978, *20*, 279–299.

Sandberg, S., Wieselberg, M., & Shaffer, D. Hyperkinetic and conduct problem children in a primary school population: Some epidemiological considerations. *Journal of Child Psychology and Psychiatry*, 1980, *21*, 293–322.

Sandler, J., & Joffe, W. Notes on childhood depression. *International Journal of Psychoanalysis*, 1965, *46*, 88–96.

Sandoval, J. The measurement of the hyperactive syndrome in children. *Review of Educational Research*, 1977, *47*, 293–318.

Sandoval, J. Format effects in two teacher rating scales of hyperactivity. *Journal of Abnormal Child Psychology*, 1981, *9*, 202–213.

Satterfield, J. H., Atoian, G., Brashears, G. C., Burleigh, A. C., & Dawson, M. E. Electrodermal studies in minimal brain dysfunctioned children. In C. K. Conners (Ed.), *Clinical use of stimulant drugs in children*. Amsterdam: Excerpta Medica, 1974.

Satterfield, J. H., & Braley, B. W. Evoked potentials and brain maturation in hyperactive and normal children. *Electroencephalography and Clinical Neurophysiology*, 1977, *43*, 43–51.

Satterfield, J. H., Cantwell, D. P., & Satterfield, B. T. Multimodality treatment: A one-year follow-up of 84 hyperactive boys. *Archives of General Psychiatry*, 1979, *36*, 965–974.

Satterfield, J. H., & Dawson, M. E. Electrodermal correlates of hyperactivity in children. *Psychophysiology*, 1971, *8*, 191–197.

Satterfield, J. H., Satterfield, B. T., & Cantwell, D. P. Three-year multimodality treatment study of

100 hyperactive boys. *Journal of Pediatrics*, 1981, *98*, 650–655.

Satz, P., & Fletcher, J. M. Emergent trends in neuropsychology: An overview. *Journal of Consulting and Clinical Psychology*, 1981, *49*, 851–865.

Scarr, S. Genetic factors in activity motivation. *Child Development*, 1966, *37*, 663–673.

Schachar, R., Rutter, M., & Smith, A. The characteristics of situationally and pervasively hyperactive children: Implications for syndrome definition. *Journal of Child Psychology and Psychiatry*, 1981, *22*, 375–392.

Schlager, G., Newman, D. E., Dunn, H. G., Chrichton, J. U., & Schulzer, M. Bone age in children with minimal brain dysfunction. *Developmental Medicine and Child Neurology*, 1979, *21*, 41–51.

Schleifer, M., Weiss, G., Cohen, N., Elman, M., Cvejic, H., & Kruger, E. Hyperactivity in preschoolers and the effect of methylphenidate. *American Journal of Orthopsychiatry*, 1975, *45*, 38–50.

Schneider, G. E. Is it really better to have your brain lesion early? A revision of the "Kennard principle." *Neuropsychologia*, 1979, *17*, 557–583.

Schonell, F. J. *The psychology and teaching of reading*. Edinburgh: Oliver & Boyd, 1961.

Schopler, E., Andrews, C. E., & Strupp, K. Do autistic children come from upper-middle-class parents? *Journal of Autism and Developmental Disorders*, 1979, *9*, 139–152.

Schopler, E., Brehm, S. S., Kinsbourne, M., & Reichler, R. J. Effect of treatment structure on development in autistic children. *Archives of General Psychiatry*, 1971, *24*, 416–421.

Schopler, E., Reichler, R. J., De Vellis, R. F., & Daly, K. Toward objective classification of childhood autism: Childhood autism rating scale (CARS). *Journal of Autism and Developmental Disorders*, 1980, *10*, 91–103.

Schover, L. R., & Newsom, C. D. Overselectivity, developmental level, and overtraining in autistic and normal children. *Journal of Abnormal Child Psychology*, 1976, *4*, 289–298.

Schulman, J. L., Kaspar, J. C., & Throne, F. M. *Brain damage and behavior: A clinical experimental study*. Springfield, Ill.: Charles C. Thomas, 1965.

Schulterbrandt, J. G., & Raskin, A. (Eds.). *Depression in childhood: Diagnosis, treatment and conceptual models*. New York: Raven Press, 1977.

Scott, P. D. Delinquency. In J. G. Howells (Ed.), *Modern perspectives in child psychiatry*. Edinburgh & London: Oliver & Boyd, 1965.

Seidel, U. P., Chadwick, O. F. D., & Rutter, M. Psychological disorders in crippled children. A comparative study of children with and without brain damage. *Developmental Medicine and Child Neurology*, 1975, *17*, 563–573.

Seligman, M. E. P. Phobias and preparedness. *Behavior Therapy*, 1971, *2*, 307–320.

Seligman, M. E. P., & Peterson, C. A learned helplessness perspective on childhood depression: Theory and research. In M. Rutter, C. E. Izard, & P. Read (Eds.), *Depression in childhood: Developmental perspectives*. New York: Guilford Press, in press.

Serafica, F., & Harway, N. Social relations and self-esteem of children with learning disabilities. *Journal of Clinical Child Psychology*, 1979, *8*, 227–233.

Sermet, O. Emotional and medical factors in child dental anxiety. *Journal of Child Psychology and Psychiatry*, 1974, *15*, 313–322.

Shafer, S. Q., Shaffer, D., O'Connor, P. A., & Stokman, C. Hard thoughts on neurological soft signs. In M. Rutter (Ed.), *Developmental neuropsychiatry*. New York: Guilford Press, in press.

Shaffer, D. Suicide in childhood and early adolescence. *Journal of Child Psychology and Psychiatry*, 1974, *15*, 275–292.

Shaffer, D. Brain injury. In M. Rutter & L. A. Hersov (Eds.), *Child psychiatry: Modern approaches*. Oxford: Blackwell Scientific, 1977.

Shaffer, D. Personal communication, September 1982.

Shaffer, D., Bijur, P., Chadwick, O., Rutter, M. *Localized cortical injury and psychiatric symptoms in childhood*. Manuscript submitted for publication, 1982.

Shaffer, D., Chadwick, O., & Rutter, M. Psychiatric outcome of localized head injury in children. In R. Porter & D. W. FitzSimons (Eds.), *Outcome of severe damage to the central nervous system* (Ciba Foundation Symposium No. 34 [new series]). Amsterdam: Excerpta Medica, 1975.

Shaffer, D., & Fisher, P. The epidemiology of suicide in children and young adolescents. *Journal of the American Academy of Child Psychiatry*, 1981, *20*, 545–565.

Shaffer, D., McNamara, N., & Pincus, J. H. Controlled observations on patterns of activity, attention, and impulsivity in brain-damaged and psychiatrically disturbed boys. *Journal of Psychological Medicine*, 1974, *4*, 4–18.

Shaffer, D., O'Connor, P. A., Shafer, S. Q., & Prupis, S. Neurological soft signs: Their origins and significance for behavior. In M. Rutter (Ed.), *Developmental neuropsychiatry*. New York: Guilford Press, in press.

Shaffer, D., Rutter, M., Sturge, C., & Nichols, P. G. An examination of categories relating to child mental health in the International classification of diseases. Unpublished paper, American Academy of Child Psychiatry, Atlanta, Ga., 1979.

Shaheen, E., Alexander, D., Truskowsky, M., & Barbero, G. J. Failure to thrive—a retrospective profile. *Clinical Pediatrics*, 1968, *7*, 255–261.

Shaw, C. R., & McKay, H. D. *Juvenile delinquency and urban areas*. Chicago: University of Chicago Press, 1942.

Shaywitz, B. A., Cohen, D. J., & Bowers, M. B., Jr. CSF monoamine metabolites in children with minimal brain dysfunction—evidence for alteration of brain dopamine. *Journal of Pediatrics*, 1977, *90*, 67–71.

Shaywitz, B. A., Klopper, J. H., & Gordon, J. W. Methylphenidate in 6–hydroxydopamine treated developing rat pups. *Archives of Neurology*, 1978, *35*, 463–469.

Shaywitz, B. A., & Pearson, D. E. Effects of phenobarbital on activity and learning in 6–hydroxydopamine treated rat pups. *Pharmacology, Biochemistry and Behavior*, 1978, *9*, 153–179.

Shaywitz, B. A., Yager, R. D., & Klopper, J. H. Selective brain dopamine depletion in developing rats: An experimental model of minimal brain dysfunction. *Science*, 1976, *191*, 305–308.

Shaywitz, S. E., Shaywitz, B. A., Cohen, D. J., & Young, J. B. Monoaminergic mechanisms in hyperactivity. In M. Rutter (Ed.), *Developmental neuropsychiatry*. New York: Guilford Press, in press.

Shea, M. J. A follow-up study into adulthood of adolescent psychiatric patients in relation to internalizing and externalizing symptoms, MMPI configurations, social competence, and life history variables. (Doctoral dissertation, University of Minnesota, 1972.) *Dissertation Abstracts International*, 1972, *33*, 2822B–2823B. (University Microfilms No. 72–32,315.)

Shekim, W. O., Dekirmenjian, H., & Chapel, J. L. Urinary MHPG excretion in minimal brain dysfunction and its modification by *d*-amphetamine. *American Journal of Psychiatry*, 1977, *134*, 1276–1979.

Shekim, W. O., Dekirmenjian, H., Chapel, J. L., Javaid, J., & Davis, J. M. Norepinephrine metabolism and clinical response to dextroamphetamine in hyperactive boys. *Journal of Pediatrics*, 1979, *95*, 389–394.

Shepherd, M. Epidemiology and clinical psychiatry. *British Journal of Psychiatry*, 1978, *133*, 289–298.

Shepherd, M., Oppenheim, B., & Mitchell, S. (Eds.). *Childhood behaviour and mental health*. London: University of London Press, 1971.

Shetly, T., & Chase, T. N. Cerebral monoamines and hyperkinesis of childhood. *Neurology*, 1976, *26*, 1000–1002.

Shields, J. Polygenic influences. In M. Rutter & L. A. Hersov (Eds.), *Child psychiatry: Modern approaches*. Oxford: Blackwell Scientific, 1977.

Siddle, D. A. T., Mednick, S. A., Nicol, A. R., & Foggitt, R. H. Skin conductance recovery in anti-social adolescents. *British Journal of Social and Clinical Psychology*, 1976, *15*, 425–428.

Siddle, D. A. T., Nicol, A. R., & Foggitt, R. H. Habituation and over-extinction of the GSR component of the orienting response in anti-social adolescents. *British Journal of Social and Clinical Psychology*, 1973, *12*, 303–308.

Sillanpaa, M. Medico-social prognosis of children with epilepsy. *Acta Paediatrica Scandinavica*, Supplement No. 237, 1973.

Silver, L. A. The relationship between learning disabilities, hyperactivity, distractibility and behavioral problems: A clinical analysis. *Journal of the American Academy of Child Psychiatry*, 1981, *20*, 385–397.

Simmons, J. Q., & Baltaxe, C. Language patterns of adolescent autistics. *Journal of Autism and Childhood Schizophrenia*, 1975, *5*, 333–352.

Simon, A., & Ward, L. O. Sex-related patterns of worry in secondary school pupils. *British Journal of Clinical Psychology*, 1982, *21*, 63–64.

Skoff, B. F., Mirsky, A. F., & Turner, D. Prolonged brainstem transmission time in autism. *Psychiatry Research*, 1980, *2*, 157–166.

Slater, E. Short-distance prognosis of schizophrenia. *Journal of Neurology and Psychiatry*, 1939, *2*, 1–10.

Slater, E. Diagnosis of hysteria. *British Medical Journal*, 1965, *1*, 1395–1399.

Sleator, E. K., von Neuman, A., & Sprague, R. L. Hyperactive children: A continuous long-term placebo-controlled follow-up. *Journal of the American Medical Association*, 1974, *229*, 326–317.

Small, J. G. Epileptiform electroencephalographic studies in children presenting behavior disorders. *Journal of Nervous and Mental Disease*, 1968, *95*, 621–625.

Small, J. G. EEG and neurophysiological studies of early infantile autism. *Biological Psychiatry*,

1975, *10*, 385–423.

Smith, P. K. Social and situational determinants of fear in the playgroup. In M. Lewis & L. A. Rosenblum (Eds.), *The origins of fear*. New York: Wiley, 1974.

Snyder, J. J. A reinforcement analysis of interaction in problem and non-problem children. *Journal of Abnormal Psychology*, 1977, *86*, 528–535.

Soli, S. D., Nuechterlain, K. H., Garmezy, N., Devine, V. T., & Schaefer, S. M. A classification system for research in childhood psychopathology: Part I. An empirical approach using factor and cluster analyses and conjunctive decision rules. In B. A. Maher (Ed.), *Progress in experimental personality research* (Vol. 10). New York: Academic Press, 1981.

Solomons, G., Holden, R. H., & Denhoff, E. The changing picture of cerebral dysfunction in early childhood. *Journal of Pediatrics*, 1963, *63*, 113–120.

Solyom, I., Beck, P., Solyom, C., & Hugel, R. Some etiological factors in phobic neurosis. *Canadian Psychiatric Association Journal*, 1974, *19*, 69–78.

Sommer, B. B. Stress and menstrual distress. *Journal of Human Stress*, 1978, *4*, 5–10; 41–47.

Spitz, R. A. Anaclitic depression. *Psychoanalytic Study of the Child*, 1946, *2*, 313–342.

Sroufe, L. A. Drug treatment of children with behavior problems. In F. D. Horowitz (Ed.), *Review of child development research* (Vol. 4). Chicago: University of Chicago Press, 1975.

Sroufe, L. A. Wariness and the study of infant development. *Child Development*, 1977, *48*, 731–746.

Sroufe, L. A. The coherence of individual development: Early care, attachment and subsequent developmental issues. *American Psychologist*, 1979, *34*, 834–841.

Stevens, T. M., Kupst, M. J., Suran, B. G., & Schulman, J. L. Activity level: A comparison between actometer scores and observer ratings. *Journal of Abnormal Child Psychology*, 1978, *6*, 163–173.

Stewart, A. Severe perinatal hazards. In M. Rutter (Ed.), *Developmental neuropsychiatry*. New York: Guilford Press, in press.

Stewart, M. A., Cummings, C., Singer, S., & De Blois, C. S. The overlap between hyperactive and unsocialized aggressive children. *Journal of Child Psychology and Psychiatry*, 1981, *22*, 35–46.

Stewart, M. A., De Blois, C. S., & Cummings, C. Psychiatric disorder in the parents of hyperactive

boys and those with conduct disorder. *Journal of Child Psychology and Psychiatry*, 1980, *21*, 283–292.

St. James-Roberts, I. Neurological plasticity, recovery from brain insult and child development. In H. W. Reese & L. P. Lipsitt (Eds.), *Advances in child development and behavior* (Vol. 14). New York: Academic Press, 1979.

Stores, G. Behavior disturbance and type of epilepsy in children attending ordinary school. In J. K. Penry (Ed.), *Epilepsy: Proceedings of the eighth international symposium:* New York: Raven Press, 1977.

Stores, G. School children with epilepsy at risk for learning and behaviour problems. *Developmental Medicine and Child Neurology*, 1978, *20*, 502–508.

Stores, G., Hart, J., & Piran, N. Inattentiveness in schoolchildren with epilepsy. *Epilepsia*, 1978, *19*, 169–175.

Stores, G., & Piran, N. Dependency of different types in schoolchildren with epilepsy. *Psychological Medicine*, 1978, *8*, 441–445.

Stott, D. H. The prediction of delinquency from non-delinquent behaviour. *British Journal of Delinquency*, 1960, *10*, 195–210.

Stott, D. H. *Studies of troublesome children*. London: Tavistock Press, 1966.

Sturge, C. Reading retardation and antisocial behaviour. *Journal of Child Psychology and Psychiatry*, 1982, *23*, 21–31.

Sullivan, C., Grant, M. Q., & Grant, J. D. The development of interpersonal maturity: Applications to delinquency. *Psychiatry*, 1957, *20*, 373–385.

Sundby, H. S., & Kreyberg, P. C. *Prognosis in child psychiatry*. Baltimore: Williams & Wilkins, 1968.

Sutherland, E. H. *Principles of criminology*. Philadelphia: Lippincott, 1939.

Svejda, M. J., Pannabecker, B. J., & Emde, R. N. Parent-to-infant attachment: A critique of the early "bonding" model. In R. N. Emde & R. J. Harmon (Eds.), *The development of attachment and affiliative systems*. New York: Plenum, 1982.

Swanson, J. M., & Kinsbourne, M. Food dyes impair performance of hyperactive children on a laboratory learning test. *Science*, 1980, *207*, 1485–1486.

Swanson, J. M., Kinsbourne, M., Roberts, W., & Zucker, K. Time-response analysis of the effect of stimulant medication on the learning ability of children referred for hyperactivity. *Pediatrics*,

1978, *61*, 21–29.

Sykes, D. H., Douglas, V. I., & Morgenstern, G. Sustained attention in hyperactive children. *Journal of Child Psychology and Psychiatry*, 1973, *14*, 213–220.

Taft, L. T., & Cohen H. J. Hypsarrhythmia and infantile autism: A clinical report. *Journal of Autism and Childhood Schizophrenia*, 1971, *1*, 327–336.

Tanner, J. M. (Ed.). *Human growth*. London: Pergamon, 1960.

Taylor, D. Factors influencing the occurrence of schizophrenia-like psychosis in patients with temporal lobe epilepsy. *Psychological Medicine*, 1975, *5*, 249–254.

Taylor, E. Food additives, allergy and hyperkinesis. *Journal of Child Psychology and Psychiatry*, 1979, *20*, 357–363.

Taylor, E. Brain damage: Evidence from measures of neurological function in children with psychiatric disorder. In E. F. Purcell (Ed.), *Psychopathology of child and youth: A cross-cultural perspective*. New York: Josiah Macy, Jr., Foundation, 1980. (a)

Taylor, E. Development of attention. In M. Rutter (Ed.), *Scientific foundations of developmental psychiatry*. London: Heinemann Medical, 1980. (b)

Taylor, E. Drug response as a diagnostic feature. In M. Rutter (Ed.), *Developmental neuropsychiatry*. New York: Guilford Press, in press. (a)

Taylor, E. Overactivity and attention deficit. In M. Rutter & L. A. Hersov (Eds.), *Child psychiatry: Modern approaches* (2nd ed.). Oxford: Blackwell Scientific, in press. (b)

Taylor, E., & Sandberg, S. Classroom behaviour problems and hyperactivity: A questionnaire study in English schools. Manuscript submitted for publication, 1982.

Tennant, C., & Bebbington, P. The social causation of depression: A critique of the work of Brown and his colleagues. *Psychological Medicine*, 1978, *8*, 565–575.

Tennant, C., Bebbington, P., & Hurry, J. Parental death in childhood and risk of adult depressive disorders: A review. *Psychological Medicine*, 1980, *10*, 289–299.

Teuber, H.-L., & Rudel, R. G. Behaviour after cerebral lesions in children and adults. *Developmental Medicine and Child Neurology*, 1962, *4*, 3–20.

Thompson, J. S., Ross, R. J., & Horwitz, S. J. The role of computed axial tomography in the study of the child with minimal brain dysfunction.

Journal of Learning Disabilities, 1980, *13*, 48–51.

Tieger, T. On the biological basis of sex differences in aggression. *Child Development*, 1980, *51*, 943–963.

Tinbergen, E. A., & Tinbergen, N. Early childhood autism: An ethological approach. In *Advances in ethology* (Whole No. 10, Supplement, Journal of Comparative Ethology). Berlin: Verlag Paul Parry, 1972.

Tittle, C. R., Villemez, W. J., & Smith, D. A. The myth of social class and criminality: An empirical assessment of the empirical evidence. *American Sociological Review*, 1978, *43*, 643–656.

Tizard, B., & Hodges, J. The effect of early institutional rearing on the development of eight-year-old children. *Journal of Child Psychology and Psychiatry*, 1978, *19*, 99–118.

Tizard, B., & Rees, J. A comparison of the effects of adoption, restoration to the natural mother, and continued institutionalization on the cognitive development of four-year-old children. *Child Development*, 1974, *45*, 92–99.

Tizard, J., & Tizard, B. The social development of two-year-old children in residential nurseries. In H. R. Schaffer (Ed.), *The origins of human social relations*. London: Academic Press, 1971.

Tobin-Richards, M. H., Boxer, A. M. N., & Petersen, A. C. The psychological significance of pubertal change: Sex differences in perceptions of self during early adolescence. In J. Brooks-Gunn & A. C. Petersen (Eds.), *Girls at puberty: Biological and psychosocial perspectives*. New York: Plenum, 1982.

Torgersen, A. M. Genetic factors in temperamental individuality: A longitudinal study of same-sexed twins from two months to six years of age. *Journal of the American Academy of Child Psychiatry*, 1981, *20*, 702–711.

Torrey, E. F., Hersh, S. P., & McCabe, K. D. Early childhood psychosis and bleeding during pregnancy. *Journal of Autism and Childhood Schizophrenia*, 1975, *5*, 287–297.

Touwen, B. C. L., & Prechtl, H. F. R. *The neurological examination of the child with minor nervous dysfunction* (Clinics in Developmental Medicine No. 38). London: Heinemann/SIMP, 1970.

Tramer, M. Electiver mutismus kindern. *Zeitschrift Kinderpsychiatrie*, 1934, *1*, 30–35.

Trasler, G. *In place of parents: A study of foster care*. London: Routledge & Kegan Paul, 1960.

Trasler, G. Criminal behaviour. In H. J. Eysenck (Ed.), *Handbook of abnormal psychology* (2nd ed.). London: Pitman Medical, 1973.

Treffert, D. A. Epidemiology of infantile autism. *Archives of General Psychiatry*, 1970, *23*, 431–438.

Trojaborg, W. Changes of spike foci in children. In P. Kellaway & I. Petersen (Eds.), *Clinical electroencephalography in children*. New York: Grune & Stratton, 1968.

Tsai, L., Jacoby, C. G., Stewart, M. A., & Beisler, J. M. Unfavorable left-right asymmetries of the brain and autism: A question of methodology. *British Journal of Psychiatry*, 1982, *140*, 312–319.

Tsai, L., Stewart, M. A., & August, G. J. Implication of sex differences in the familial transmission of infantile autism. *Journal of Autism and Developmental Disorders*, 1981, *11*, 165–173.

Tyrer, P., & Tyrer, S. School refusal, truancy and adult neurotic illness. *Psychological Medicine*, 1974, *4*, 416–421.

Ullman, D. G., Barkley, R. A., & Brown, H. W. The behavioral symptoms of hyperkinetic children who successfully responded to stimulant drug treatment. *American Journal of Orthopsychiatry*, 1978, *48*, 425–437.

Ungerer, J. A., & Sigman, M. Symbolic play and language comprehension in autistic children. *Journal of the American Academy of Child Psychiatry*, 1981, *20*, 318–337.

U.S. Environmental Protection Agency. *Air quality criteria for lead*. Washington, D.C.: U.S. Government Printing Office, 1977.

van Eerdewegh, M. M., Bieri, M. D., Parilla, R. H., & Clayton, P. The bereaved child. *British Journal of Psychiatry*, 1982, *140*, 23–29.

van Hof, M. W. Development and recovery from brain damage. In K. Connolly & H. F. R. Prechtl (Eds.), *Maturation and development: Biological and psychological perspectives* (Clinics in Developmental Medicine No. 77/78). London: Heinemann Medical/SIMP, 1981.

Van Krevelen, D. A. Early infantile autism and autistic psychopathy. *Journal of Autism and Childhood Schizophrenia*, 1971, *1*, 82–86.

Van Krevelen, D. A., & Kuipers, C. The psychopathology of autistic psychopaths. *Acta Paedopsychiatrica*, 1962, *29*, 22–31.

Varlaam, A. Educational attainment and behaviour at school. *Greater London Intelligence Quarterly*, No. 29, December 1974, 29–37.

Vaughn, B. E., Egeland, B. R., Sroufe, L. A., & Waters, E. Individual differences in infant-mother attachment at 12 and 18 months: Stability and change in families under stress. *Child Develop-*

ment, 1979, *50*, 971–975.

Vaughn, C. E., & Leff, J. P. The influence of family and social factors on the course of psychiatric illness. A comparison of schizophrenic and depressed neurotic patients. *British Journal of Psychiatry*, 1976, *129*, 125–137.

Vikan, A. *Psychiatric epidemiology in a sample of 1510 10-year-old children. I. Prevalence.* Manuscript submitted for publication, 1983.

Volkmar, F. R., & Cohen, D. J. A hierarchical analysis of patterns of non-compliance in autistic and behavior-disturbed children. *Journal of Autism and Developmental Disorders*, 1982, *12*, 35–42.

Wadsworth, M. *Roots of delinquency: Infancy, adolescence and crime*. Oxford: Martin Robinson, 1979.

Wahler, R. G. The insular mother: Her problems in parent-child treatment. *Journal of Applied Behavior Analysis*, 1980, *13*, 207–219.

Wahler, R. G., Leske, G., & Rodgers, E. S. The insular family: A deviant support system for oppositional children. In L. A. Hamerlynck (Ed.), *Behavioral systems for the developmentally disabled*, vol. 1, *School and family environments*. New York: Brunner/Mazel., 1978.

Waldo, M. C., Cohen, D. J., Caparulo, B. K., Young, J. G., Prichard, J. W., & Shaywitz, B. A. EEG profiles of neuropsychiatrically disturbed children. *Journal of the American Academy of Child Psychiatry*, 1978, *17*, 656–670.

Waldron, S. The significance of childhood neurosis for adult mental health. *American Journal of Psychiatry*, 1976, *133*, 532–538.

Waldrop, M. F., & Halverson, C. F., Jr., Minor physical anomalies and hyperactive behavior in young children. In J. Hellmuth (Ed.), *The exceptional infant* (Vol. 2). New York: Brunner/Mazel, 1971.

Walker, E. F., Cudeck, R., Mednick, S. A., & Schulsinger, F. Effects of parental absence and institutionalization on the development of clinical symptoms in high risk children. In N. F. Watt, E. J. Anthony, L. C. Wynne, & J. E. Rolf (Eds.), *Children at risk for schizophrenia: A longitudinal perspective*. New York: Cambridge University Press, in press.

Wallerstein, J. S., & Kelly, J. B. *Surviving the breakup: How children and parents cope with divorce*. London: Grant McIntyre, 1980.

Wardle, C. J. Two generations of broken homes in the genesis of conduct and behaviour disorders in childhood. *British Medical Journal*, 1961, *2*, 349–354.

Warren, M. Q. Correctional treatment and coercion:

The differential effectiveness perspective. *Criminal Justice and Behavior*, 1977, *4*, 355–376.

Warren, W. A study of adolescent psychiatric inpatients and the outcome six or more years later. II. The follow-up study. *Journal of Child Psychology and Psychiatry*, 1965, *6*, 141–160.

Waters, E., Vaughn, B. E., & Egeland, B. R. Individual differences in infant-mother attachment relationships at age one: Antecedents in neonatal behavior in an urban, economically disadvantaged sample. *Child Development*, 1980, *51*, 208–216.

Waters, E., Wippman, J., & Sroufe, L. A. Attachment, positive affect and competence in the peer group: Two studies in construct validation. *Child Development*, 1979, *50*, 831–839.

Watson, J. B., & Rayner, R. Conditioned emotional reactions. *Journal of Experimental Psychology*, 1920, *3*, 1–14.

Watt, N. F. Childhood roots of schizophrenia. In D. F. Ricks., A. Thomas, & M. Roff (Eds.), *Life history research in psychopathology* (Vol. 3). Minneapolis: University of Minnesota Press, 1974.

Weber, D. Zur Atiologie autistischer Syndromes des Kindesalters. *Praxis der Kinderpsychologie und Kinderpsychiatrie*, 1966, *15*, 12–18.

Weinberg, W. A., & Brumback, R. A. Mania in childhood: Case studies and literature review. *American Journal of Diseases of Children*, 1976, *130*, 380–385.

Weinberg, W. A., Rutman, J., Sullivan, L., Penick, E. C., & Dietz, S. G. Depression in children referred to an educational diagnostic center: Diagnosis and treatment. *Journal of Pediatrics*, 1973, *86*, 1065–1072.

Weinberger, D. R., Bigelow, L. B., Kleinman, J. E., Klein, S. T., Rosenblatt, J. E., & Wyatt, R. J. Cerebral ventricular enlargement in chronic schizophrenia: An association with poor response to treatment. *Archives of General Psychiatry*, 1980, *37*, 11–13.

Weinberger, D. R., Torrey, E. F., Neophytides, A. N., & Wyatt, R. J. Structural abnormalities in the cerebral cortex of chronic schizophrenic patients. *Archives of General Psychiatry*, 1979, *36*, 935–939.

Weintraub, S., & Neale, J. M. The Stony Brook high-risk project. In N. F. Watt, E. J. Anthony, L. C. Wynne, & J. E. Rolf (Eds.), *Children at risk for schizophrenia: A longitudinal perspective*. New York: Cambridge University Press, in press.

Weintraub, S., Prinz, R. J., & Neale, J. M. Peer evaluations of the competence of children vulnerable to psychopathology. *Journal of Abnormal Child Psychology*, 1978, *6*, 461–474.

Weiss, B. Food additives and environmental chemicals as sources of childhood behavior disorder. *Journal of the American Academy of Child Psychiatry*, 1982, *21*, 144–152.

Weiss, G. Long term outcome: Findings, concepts, and practical implications. In M. Rutter (Ed.), *Developmental neuropsychiatry*. New York: Guilford Press, in press.

Weiss, G., & Hechtman, L. The hyperactive child syndrome. *Science*, 1979, *205*, 1348–1354.

Weiss, G., Hechtman, L., & Perlman, T. Hyperactives as young adults: School, employer, and self-rating scales obtained during ten-year follow-up evaluation. *American Journal of Orthopsychiatry*, 1978, *48*, 438–445.

Weiss, G., Hechtman, L., Perlman, T., Hopkins, J., & Wener, A. Hyperactives as young adults. *Archives of General Psychiatry*, 1979, *36*, 675–682.

Weiss, G., Kruger, E., Danielson, U., & Ellman, M. Effect of long-term treatment of hyperactive children with methylphenidate. *Canadian Medical Association Journal*, 1975, *112*, 159–165.

Weiss, G., Minde, K., Werry, J. S., Douglas, V. I., & Nemeth, E. Studies on the hyperactive child. VIII. Five-year follow-up. *Archives of General Psychiatry*, 1971, *24*, 409–414.

Weissman, M. M. Depressed parents and their children: Implications for prevention. In I. N. Berlin & L. A. Stone (Eds.), *Basic handbook of child psychiatry*, vol. 4, *Prevention and current issues*. New York: Basic Books, 1979.

Weissman, M. M., & Klerman, G. L. Sex differences and the epidemiology of depression. *Archives of General Psychiatry*, 1977, *34*, 98–111.

Weissman, M. M., Orvaschel, H., & Padian, N. Children's symptom and social functioning self-report scales: Comparison of mothers' and children's reports. *Journal of Nervous and Mental Disorders*, 1980, *168*, 736–740.

Welner, Z., Welner, A., McCrary, D., & Leonard, M. A. Psychopathology in children of inpatients with depression: A controlled study. *Journal of Nervous and Mental Disorders*, 1977, *164*, 408–413.

Wender, P. Platelet serotonin level in children with "minimal brain dysfunction." *Lancet*, 1969, *2*, 1012.

Wender, P. *Minimal brain dysfunction in children*. New York: Wiley-Interscience, 1971.

Wender, P. Minimal brain dysfunction: An overview. In M. A. Lipton, A. DiMascio, & K. F. Killam (Eds.), *Psychopharmacology: A generation of progress.* New York: Raven Press, 1978.

Wender, P., Epstein, R., Kopin, I., & Gordon, E. Urinary monoamine metabolites in children with minimal brain dysfunction. *American Journal of Psychiatry,* 1971, *127,* 1411–1415.

Wender, P., Reimherr, F. W., & Wood, D. R. Attention deficit disorder (minimal brain dysfunction) in adults: A replication study of diagnosis and drug treatment. *Archives of General Psychiatry,* 1981, *38,* 449–456.

Werner, E. E. *Cross-cultural child development: A view from the Planet Earth.* Monterey, Calif.: Brooks/Cole, 1979.

Werner, E. E., Bierman, J. M., & French, F. E. *The children of Kauai.* Honolulu: University Press of Hawaii, 1977.

Werner, E. E., & Smith, R. S. *Vulnerable but invincible: A study of resilient children.* New York: McGraw-Hill, 1982.

Werry, J. S. The childhood psychoses. In H. C. Quay & J. S. Werry (Eds.), *Psychopathological disorders of childhood* (2nd ed.). New York: Wiley, 1979.

Werry, J. S., & Aman, M. G. Methylphenidate in hyperactive and enuretic children. In B. Shopsin & L. Greenhill (Eds.), *The psychobiology of childhood: Profile of current issues.* Jamaica, N.Y.: Spectrum, 1979.

Werry, J. S., & Hawthorne, D. Conners' teacher questionnaire—norms and validity. *Australian and New Zealand Journal of Psychiatry,* 1976, *10,* 259–262.

Werry, J. S., & Quay, H. C. The prevalence of behavior symptoms in younger elementary school children. *American Journal of Orthopsychiatry,* 1971, *41,* 136–143.

Werry, J. S., Sprague, R. L., & Cohen, M. N. Conners' teacher rating scale for use in drug studies with children: An empirical study. *Journal of Abnormal Child Psychology,* 1975, *3,* 217–229.

West, D. J. *Delinquency: Its roots, careers and prospects.* London: Heinemann Educational, 1982.

West, D. J., & Farrington, D. P. *Who becomes delinquent?* London: Heinemann Educational, 1973.

West, D. J., & Farrington, D. P. *The delinquent way of life.* London: Heinemann Educational, 1977.

Wexler, B. E. Cerebral laterality and psychiatry: A review of the literature. *American Journal of Psychiatry,* 1980, *137,* 279–291.

Whalen, C. H., Collins, B. E., Henker, B., Alkus, S. R., Adams, D., and Stapp, J. Behavior observations of hyperactive children and methylphenidate (Ritalin) effects in systematically structured classroom environments: Now you see them, now you don't. *Journal of Pediatric Psychology,* 1978, *3,* 177–187.

Whalen, C. H., & Henker, B. (Eds.). *Hyperactive children: The social ecology of identification and treatment.* New York: Academic Press, 1980.

Whalen, C. H., Henker, B., Collins, B. E., McAuliffe, S., & Vaux, A. Peer interaction in a structured communication task: Comparisons of normal and hyperactive boys and of methylphenidate (Ritalin) and placebo effects. *Child Development,* 1979, *50,* 388–401.

Whalen, C. H., Henker, B., Datemato, S., & Vaux, A. Hyperactivity and methylphenidate: Peer interaction styles. In K. D. Gadow & J. Loney (Eds.), *Psychosocial aspects of drug treatment for hyperactivity.* Boulder, Colo.: Westview Press, 1981.

Whitehead, L. Sex differences in children's responses to family stress: A reevaluation. *Journal of Child Psychology and Psychiatry,* 1979, *20,* 247–254.

Whitehill, D., DeMyer-Gapin, S., & Scott, T. J. Stimulation seeking in antisocial preadolescent children. *Journal of Abnormal Psychology,* 1976, *85,* 101–104.

Willerman, L. Activity level and hyperactivity in twins. *Child Development,* 1973, *44,* 288–293.

Williams, R. S., Hauser, S. L., Purpura, D., DeLong, G. R., & Swisher, C. N. Autism and mental retardation: Neuropathological studies performed in four retarded persons with autistic behavior. *Archives of Neurology,* 1980, *37,* 749–753.

Wilson, H. Parenting in poverty. *British Journal of Social Work,* 1974, *4,* 241–254.

Wilson, H. Parental supervision: A neglected aspect of delinquency. British Journal of Criminology, 1980, *20,* 203–235.

Wilson, H., & Herbert, G. W. *Parents and child in the inner city.* London: Routledge & Kegan Paul, 1978.

Wing, L. Childhood autism and social class: A question of selection. *British Journal of Psychiatry,* 1980, *137,* 410–417.

Wing, L. Asperger's syndrome: A clinical account. *Psychological Medicine,* 1981, *11,* 115–130. (a)

Wing, L. Sex ratios in early childhood autism and related conditions. *Psychiatry Research,* 1981, *5,* 129–137. (b)

Wing, L., & Gould, J. Severe impairments of social

interaction and associated abnormalities in children: Epidemiology and classification. *Journal of Autism and Developmental Disorders*, 1979, *9*, 11–30.

Wing, L., Gould, J., Yeates, S. R., & Brierley, L. M. Symbolic play in severely mentally retarded and in autistic children. *Journal of Child Psychology and Psychiatry*, 1977, *18*, 167–178.

Winsberg, B. G., Bialer, I., Kupietz, S., & Tobias, J. Effects of imipramine and dextroamphetamine on behavior of neuropsychiatrically impaired children. *American Journal of Psychiatry*, 1972, *128*, 1425–1431.

Winters, K. C., Stone, A. A., Weintraub, S., & Neale, J. M. Cognitive and attentional deficits in children vulnerable to psychopathology. *Journal of Abnormal Child Psychology*, 1981, *9*, 435–454.

Witelson, S. F. Early hemispheric specialization and inter-hemispheric plasticity: An empirical and theoretical review. In S. J. Segalowitz & F. A. Gruber (Eds.), *Language development and neurological theory*. London: Academic Press, 1977.

Wohlwill, J. F. Cognitive development in childhood. In O. G. Brim, Jr., & J. Kagan (Eds.), *Constancy and change in human development*. Cambridge: Harvard University Press, 1980.

Wolff, S. Symptomatology and outcomes of preschool children with behaviour disorders attending a child guidance clinic. *Journal of Child Psychology and Psychiatry*, 1961, *2*, 269–276.

Wolff, S. Nondelinquent disturbances of conduct. In M. Rutter & L. A. Hersov (Eds.), *Child psychiatry: Modern approaches*. Oxford: Blackwell Scientific, 1977.

Wolff, S., & Barlow, A. Schizoid personality in childhood: A comparative study of schizoid, autistic and normal children. *Journal of Child Psychology and Psychiatry*, 1979, *20*, 19–46.

Wolff, S., & Chick, J. Schizoid personality in childhood: A controlled follow-up study. *Psychological Medicine*, 1980, *10*, 85–100.

Wolfgang, M. E., Figlio, R. M., & Sellin, T. *Delinquency in a birth cohort*. Chicago: University of Chicago Press, 1972.

Wolins, M. Young children in institutions. *Developmental Psychology*, 1969, *2*, 99–109.

Wolkind, S. N. The components of "affectionless psychopathy" in institutionalized children. *Journal of Child Psychology and Psychiatry*, 1974, *15*, 215–220.

Wolkind, S. N., & Everitt, B. A cluster analysis of the behavioural items in the preschool child. *Psy-*

chological Medicine, 1974, *4*, 422–427.

Wolkind, S. N., & Rutter, M. Children who have been "in care"—an epidemiological study. *Journal of Child Psychology and Psychiatry*, 1973, *14*, 97–105.

Worland, J., Janes, C. L., & Anthony, E. J. St. Louis risk research project: Experimental studies. In N. F. Watt, E. J. Anthony, L. C. Wynne, & J. E. Rolf (Eds.), *Children at risk for schizophrenia: A longitudinal perspective*. New York: Cambridge University Press, in press.

World Health Organization. *International classification of diseases* (9th rev.). Geneva: World Health Organization, 1978.

Wright, B. A. *Physical disability: A psychological approach*. New York: Harper & Row, 1960.

Wright, H. L. A clinical study of children who refuse to talk. *Journal of the American Academy of Child Psychiatry*, 1968, *7*, 607–617.

Wynne, L. C. Concluding comments. In L. C. Wynne, R. L. Cromwell, & S. Matthysse (Eds.), *The nature of schizophrenia: New approaches to research and treatment*. New York: Wiley, 1978.

Wynne, L. C., Cromwell, R. L., & Matthysse, S. (Eds.). *The nature of schizophrenia: New approaches to research and treatment*. New York: Wiley, 1978.

Yepes, L. E., Balka, E. B., Winsberg, B. G., & Bialer, I. Amitriptyline and methylphenidate treatment of behaviourally disordered children. *Journal of Child Psychology and Psychiatry*, 1977, *18*, 39–52.

Young, J. G., Cohen, D. J., Caparulo, B. E., Brown, S. L., & Maas, J. W. Decreased 24-hour urinary MHPG in childhood autism. *American Journal of Psychiatry*, 1979, *136*, 1055–1057.

Yule, W. The epidemiology of child psychopathology. In B. B. Lahey & A. E. Kazdin (Eds.), *Advances in clinical child psychology* (Vol. 4). New York: Plenum, 1981.

Yule, W., & Fernando, P. Blood phobia—beware. *Behavior Research and Therapy*, 1980, *18*, 587–590.

Yule, W., & Rutter, M. Effects of lead on children's behavior and cognitive performance: A critical review. In K. R. Makaffey (Ed.), *Health implications of typical levels of lead exposure: Dietary and environmental sources*. Amsterdam: Elsevier, in press.

Yuwiler, A., Ritvo, E. R., Geller, E., Glossman, R., Schneiderman, G., & Matsuno, D. Uptake and efflux of serotonin from platelets of autistic and nonautistic children. *Journal of Autism and*

Childhood Schizophrenia, 1975, *5,* 83–98.

Zahn, T. P., Little, B. C., & Wender, P. H. Pupillary and heart rate reactivity in children with minimal brain dysfunction. *Journal of Abnormal Child Psychology,* 1978, *6,* 135–147.

Zeitlin, H. A study of patients who attended the children's department and later the adults' department of the same psychiatric hospital. Unpublished master's thesis, University of London, 1972.

Zeitlin, H. The natural history of psychiatric disorder in children. Unpublished M.D. thesis, University of London, 1982.

Zentall, S. S. Behavioral comparisons of hyperactive and normally active children in natural settings. *Journal of Abnormal Child Psychology,* 1980, *8,* 93–109.

Zentall, S. S., & Barack, R. S. Rating scales for hyperactivity: Concurrent validity, reliability and decisions to label for the Conners and Davids abbreviated scales. *Journal of Abnormal Child Psychology,* 1979, *7,* 179–190.

INTERVENTION WITH CHILDREN EXPERIENCING PROBLEMS IN PERSONALITY AND SOCIAL DEVELOPMENT | 11

JAMES F. ALEXANDER and ROBERTA E. MALOUF, *University of Utah*

CHAPTER CONTENTS

It is probably safe to say that all professionals in the field of child mental health have experienced a situation in which friends, relatives, or acquaintances have described some problem they are experiencing with a child, coupled with the question: "What should I do?" When the professional inevitably responds with some form of "Well, it depends," the questioner feels somewhat disconcerted that the expert did not provide an easy answer. What friends and acquaintances find even more disconcerting is the fact that professionals apparently become more, not less, uncertain as they become more experienced. Whereas the novice may offer such apparently simple solutions as "Put the child in 'time out' when he does it," or "There's a new drug that will settle her right down," the more experienced clinicians seem hesitant to provide such apparently simple solutions until they receive additional information, such as the meaning of the behavior to everyone involved, the nature of the circumstances in which the behavior occurs, the reaction others have to it, the resources available for dealing with it, and the capacities (physical, intellectual, etc.) of the child as well of the parent(s).

In other words, professionals are aware that even apparently simple problems can often involve a complex set of variables that must be known, or at least guessed at, when planning intervention. These variables must then become direct targets of intervention or at least be taken into account in order to produce change successfully. To use the example of encopresis, is the child who soiled 1 year old, 2 years old, or 5 years old? Do the parents find soiling disgusting or merely troublesome? Does the soiling occur at random times, or does it seem related to other, especially stressful, circumstances in the family? Has the child never been toilet trained, or has the problem arisen after training appeared to have been accomplished successfully? Have there been changes in diet or any clues regarding changing physical status? Is there a new younger sibling who receives considerable nurturance or a disproportionate share of parent resources in general? Does the child live in a cultural-social-religious milieu that values neatness and control, or independence and spontaneity? Is this a situation in which a single, isolated mother receives attention and support from her social system only in the context of having problems?

These questions can be, but are not always, relevant to the course and outcome of intervention. They cannot be ignored, because with different answers they can imply dramatically different interventions. And as complicated a meaning that a soiling problem can have, it seems mundane when compared to the complexity associated with treating multiproblem children with long individual and generational histories of maladaptive behavior patterns, difficult living environments, or both. In the face of this complexity, clinicians must make numerous decisions, decisions that may be irreversible in their effects or implications. These decisions are not simple, nor are they made in a vacuum. They reflect the interaction of a number of sometimes formal and sometimes intuitive considerations that are based on a conceptual model or strategy of intervention. These decisions are also based on the knowledge that comes from experience, coupled with the contributions of researchers, theorists, and clinicians in the field.

We cannot portray the essence of experience in a written chapter. We can, however, describe and discuss the knowledge that has been generated through the experience of researchers, theorists, and clinicians. To do so in a coherent fashion, we will present this knowledge in the organizational framework of the major models of clinical intervention that have provided the basis for the field's accumulated knowledge. Clinical models represent the basic organizational units of this chapter because models are the primary context or background within which

clinical and basic research questions are asked, data interpreted, intervention strategies developed, and techniques applied. Without a model, data developed through clinical and research experience would be little more than a conglomerate of observations having no inherent significance for each other or for new data that will be collected (Kaplan, 1964).

Whereas clinical models provide a context for organizing and interpreting events, they are also influenced by events. Clinical models have evolved in content and have waxed and waned in popularity over the years. These changes in content and popularity derive in part from the research and clinical data that accumulate as the models are applied. The changes have also derived from ideological, economic, and political forces that have often had little to do with the models per se. Finally, some models have developed in part out of clinicians' and researchers' disenchantment with previously developed models.

So just as clinicians do not make decisions in a vacuum, models do not exist in a vacuum. An appreciation of the contexts in which the major clinical models have developed will help us understand how they currently affect clinical decision making. More importantly, this appreciation can help us forecast the future impact of the models, and perhaps even suggest how we can influence the very models that will in turn influence us. Subsequent sections thus describe the various clinical models from two perspectives: how they provide a basis for clinical decision making, and how they are influenced by larger contexts and each other. The immense scope of the field precludes an exhaustive review of each and every clinical and research application of each model. Instead, representative examples of traditional as well as innovative or otherwise promising applications of the models will be presented, and relevant reviews on specific topics will be cited for the interested reader.

Although some variation exists in their clarity and explicitness, the major models of intervention all posit a logical and sometimes empirically demonstrated relationship between the hypothesized causes of deviant behavior, the goals of intervention, and the levels at which intervention occurs. The levels of intervention represent the primary medium targeted by the therapist in order to produce change. They include (1) intraindividual physiological systems; (2) psychological-cognitive processing mechanisms; (3) external behavior classes; (4) interactional-relational systems; and (5) sociocultural contexts. There exists a rough, though not complete, correspondence between each of these levels of intervention and the major therapeutic models, as follows: Biological models have dealt primarily with intraindividual physiological systems; personality and internal-dynamic models have focused primarily on psychological-cognitive processing mechanisms; the behavioral model has historically focused on external behavior classes, though recent trends have developed toward cognitive-processing mechanisms and interactional-relational systems; systems and communication therapies have primarily focused on the level of interactional-relational systems; and community approaches have focused primarily on sociocultural contexts. Because of these differences in primary level of intervention, each major model has prompted unique sets of questions, data, intervention strategies, and implications as to the use of these intervention strategies. These unique sets of knowledge have sometimes been integrated to provide a comprehensive and multimodel knowledge base for the clinician. Unfortunately, they have also often confronted the clinician with jarring inconsistency and incompatibility, a problem to be addressed in the last section of this chapter.

BIOLOGICAL MODELS

Biological approaches as discussed here are, very broadly, those interventions that seek to correct or modify an intraindividual process that is seen as causing or mediating a dysfunction. The most widely used and widely researched subset of biological approaches is drug therapies, and, as a result, they will be the principal focus of this discussion. The goal of this section is not to provide an exhaustive review of the psychopharmacological literature on children. That literature is enormous and, to the credit of workers in those areas, rapidly changing. Instead, the purpose is to provide nonmedical interventionists a basic understanding of the historical and clinical contexts within which biological interventions are selected and employed. A second purpose is to provide a basic understanding of the biological interventions that currently enjoy wide application and some basic research findings as to their effectiveness.

The biological approaches to treating children's dysfunctional behavior have been predominantly based on the hypothesis that biochemical or neurological aberrations directly cause deviant behavior, or directly or indirectly produce conditions in a child that make normal development and learning difficult if not impossible. An example of a direct effect is the finding that the effects of phe-

nylketonuria can be prevented if dietary modifications are instituted early enough in the life of the child (Altrocchi, 1980). An example of an indirect effect is extending the short attention span of a hyperactive child who, when calmed down through the use of drugs, can more likely learn to read and write.

Most biological interventions for children have been developed for specific brain disorders and other organic pathology, and systemic disorders such as hormone imbalances. Although these pathological processes in children are manifested in disturbed behavior, enough is known about these pathologies in terms of their causes or the disease processes themselves that therapy is directed toward eliminating or controlling the diseases rather than targeting the symptoms. With some forms of diabetes, for example, dietary or drug therapy or both, directed to control of the disease process, can result in a relatively symptom-free existence. Anticonvulsants can correct atypical brain functioning, leaving the child free of symptoms, and systemic diseases such as thyroid deficiencies can be corrected directly through the use of medications. Directly treating an illness rather than the symptom has been the goal of basic epidemiological research on disease processes. Nevertheless, there is currently an array of disorders such as autism, hyperactivity, anxiety, and depression for which underlying disease processes, if any, have not yet been agreed on, and are thus regarded as functional disorders. In contrast to organic and systemic disorders, functional disorders are treated with biological approaches by targeting the symptom (Chess, 1969). Thus medications or specific diets or other biological interventions are evaluated in terms of their effectiveness in abating the severity of symptoms rather than in terms of their effects in eliminating or arresting the underlying disease process. As a result, developments of biological interventions have been historically empirical, which for some practitioners is the same as saying trial and error. Regardless of the label for the chronology of these therapies, however, the fact remains that the development and use of many biological interventions have not been based on deductive scientific approaches. The process of demonstrating causal mechanisms through a priori testing for hypothesized effects, followed by outcome testing in applied research and program evaluation, is not much in evidence in this intervention literature. Instead, many of the *apparently* beneficial effects of drugs are initially identified, often serendipitously, as side effects of drugs administered in a different context for a different problem. In addition, although they are popular in clinical settings (Rapoport, 1977), chemical interventions with children have not received the well-controlled experimental and longitudinal scrutiny necessary to demonstrate their potential effects, both positive and negative (Campbell, 1978). Instead, the clinical literature is characterized by descriptions, often relying on a case study methodology, of therapy application and effects, with few examples of the controlled experimental studies necessary to identify underlying causes. At the same time, psychological and pharmacological research is characterized by experimental studies, but these have been criticized as lacking in methodological rigor as well (Campbell, 1978). These methodological issues will be addressed at the end of this section of the chapter.

Because of such concerns, most biological approaches and psychoactive drug therapies in particular are viewed primarily as short-term adjuncts to treatment of children and adolescents. Practitioners are warned that all psychoactive agents may cause untoward effects (Campbell & Small, 1978) in terms of both short-term toxicity and possible long-range threats to normal maturation. Whereas short-term effects can be regulated through reduction of dosages and institution of drug holidays, information regarding long-term effects is limited if not absent. For example, the effects of long-term drug use on growth, intelligence, the central nervous system, endocrine systems, and other aspects of development are not known (Campbell, 1978).

Perhaps as a result of warnings issued by researchers, public alarm over potential or real abuses of drug therapies has increased in the last decade. Sprague (1977), for example, pointed out that although they are not as numerous as represented in the popular media, the number of school-age children in the United States receiving medications primarily for the diagnosis of hyperactivity is substantial, about 500,000 to 600,000. O'Leary in 1980 estimated that number to have increased to as high as 700,000. He further estimated that the proportion of the institutionalized retarded receiving these medications is between 60 and 65%.

The mixed or sometimes contradictory findings and the unanswered questions in the area of chemotherapy with children have produced a confusing situation for professionals in the field. Though some of the inconsistency undoubtedly stems from methodological and statistical problems, it also stems from a paucity of clearly articulated and testable theoretical propositions. A "shotgun" approach to evaluating new types of drugs, as well as parametric studies evaluating the impact of varying dosages, represent highly inefficient means of advancing knowledge. So, too, does exclusive reliance on comparative studies in which chemotherapy is contrasted with nondrug treatments, or different drugs against each other. In addition to producing inconsistent data, such studies alone can at best only help clinicians to decide between two or more incompletely effective interventions and to opt responsibly for clinical conservatism as a result of not knowing all the medical, psychological, and social implications of one treatment alone or of several types of treatment in combination.

Clearly basic researchers, pharmacological researchers, and practitioners alike recognize the need to support and engage in carefully conducted research on the etiology of symptoms and specific drug effects. In addition, conceptual frameworks along with supporting empirical findings must be generated to shed light on the factors that mediate and influence the target symptoms. One refreshing and potentially rewarding example of such an approach can be found in the work of Whalen and her associates. In focusing specifically on hyperactivity, Whalen and Henker (1976) argue that symptoms associated with hyperactivity and their responses to chemotherapy (principally psychostimulants) represent a complex set of interactions. The expression of the various components of hyperactivity and the nature of the drug response both depend considerably on a number of individual and contextual factors that, if not actually ignored, are seldom conceptualized as formal aspects of a model of hyperactivity and its treatment. Whalen and Henker have demonstrated how an apparently simple intervention at one level (physiological) represents in reality numerous levels of intervention. Psychostimulant medication appears to effect an intraindividual physiological response system. Although the specific nature or cause of this effect has not been agreed on, it is this process that is regarded as a vehicle for change. Unfortunately it is often viewed as a vehicle for change in the absence of explicit appreciation or identification of the cognitive and social contexts that surround and interpret not only subsequent behavior from the child but also the very meaning of psychotropic drug use. Whalen and Henker make the point that chemical intervention launches "the child into a new and highly complex ecological system" (Whalen & Henker, 1976, p. 1122). The process of instituting a medical regimen has immediate effects on children's self-perceptions as well as the attributional frameworks of others. Thus in addition to influencing internal physiological states, drug intervention also influences and interacts with cognitive processing and with social systems (e.g., the overt behaviors and attributional activities of family members, teachers, and others). In the traditional literature these other levels are occasionally acknowledged, but are often seen as tangential or "nuisance" factors. Whalen and Henker, however, suggest that such sociocognitive factors may be both more pervasive and less reversible than the direct chemical effects of the drugs themselves.

In order to provide empirical support for this view, Bugental, Whalen, and Henker (1977) contrasted external social reinforcement and instruction in self-controlling speech with hyperactive boys, half of whom were receiving methylphenidate (a widely used stimulant) and the other half no medication. The authors found significant interactions between the two interventions that were dependent on (1) whether or not the children were on medication, and (2) the "attributional style" with respect to high versus low personal causality. Nonmedicated children and those with attributions of high personal causality (i.e., a sense of personally being able to influence grades) were significantly more responsive to self-control training. In contrast, external social reinforcement tended to produce greater positive effects with medicated children and those with perceptions of low personal causality. This investigation demonstrates that chemical intervention is not merely an intraindividual physiological event, any more than social reinforcement and self-control techniques only involve simple learning processes. Instead, these interventions interact with attributional processes that can mediate, if not determine, how these interventions produce change. Studies such as this serve to define a *model* that Whalen and her associates provide for moving beyond the pedantry, dogmatism, and inconsistencies that often characterize the field of intervention with children. Whereas most research and conceptual articles argue for the superiority of one versus another type of intervention (e.g., internal-dynamic vs. biochemical vs. behavioral), Whalen and colleagues present a framework that conceptually separates levels but then identifies how they may be inextricably intertwined. Unlike simple eclecticism, such a view does not "pick, choose, and mix" models, techniques, and levels of intervention. Instead, Whalen and her co-workers demonstrate how the main components of different processes (such as biological and cognitive) interface and mutually change the effects of each other. Biological and cognitive processes are not simply parallel, and interventions cannot be expected to change just one in order to produce *automatically* a particular change in another. Instead, all levels contribute to an ecological or interactive reality that must be understood in its entirety if we are to develop the most efficient and effective interventions. This, of course, requires no small effort, but the availability of an empirically based model is an important beginning. Conceptualizing drug therapies as sociocognitive as well as physiological phenomena opens up new avenues for reinterpreting inconsistent and confusing findings in the literature and suggests the direction of large, integrated research programs.

Clearly the importance of this type of multilevel framework extends beyond the drug therapies. As described elsewhere, many traditional models are struggling with new approaches to intervention, as in the case of behaviorism, which is becoming both more cognitive and more interactive. Whereas such movements have the potential of only creating a new set of contradictory mini-models, Whalen's work demonstrates how it is possible for new frameworks to integrate multiple sets of variables so as to increase knowledge rather than simply add to the existing data potpourri.

Drug Intervention with Major Clinical Syndromes

As mentioned earlier, drug therapies are by far the most widely used of the physiological therapies. They have been used since the 1930s when anticonvulsants and hypnotics (sleep producers) were used in the management of psychomotor excitement in psychotic children (Campbell, 1978). Since then a variety of psychopharmacological agents have been discovered and developed for use with both children and adults, and although they have been used to treat symptoms rather than to cure, their impact on intervention has been no less great. The hopes that chlorpromazine (Thorazine), for example, might offer a cure for schizophrenia have not been realized. Nevertheless, its impact on the mental health field has probably not been equaled by any other modern advance. Currently there are a number of disorders that are rarely treated without some reliance on psychoactive drugs. Hyperactivity, autism, schizophrenia, and certain habit disorders, for example, are characterized by behaviors found to be responsive to drug treatment. Because these therapies target symptoms, more specific discussion of these drugs will be organized around those symptom categories.

Hyperactivity

The hyperactivity syndrome and its treatment have been the subject of considerable study and debate in the last decade (O'Leary, 1980). A variety of labels have been used in discussing the problem, such as hyperkinetic syndrome, minimal brain damage, or minimal cerebral dysfunction. No one cause for the syndrome has been identified, but there is agreement in defining it as an impairment manifested by a lack of goal directedness and distraction from task behavior (and not necessarily sheer amounts of motor activity) (Dykman, Ackerman, Peters, & McGrew, 1974). Estimates of the prevalence of diagnosed hyperactivity range from 3 to 7% of all children (Huessy, Marshall, & Gendron, 1974; Sprague & Sleator, 1973). Thomas, Chess, and Birch (1968) found that 15% of newborn babies are "difficult" and suggested that (1) this may be a result of cerebral dysfunction, and that (2) many or most of those children will eventually manifest behavioral symptoms of hyperactivity. Behavioral problems associated with hyperactivity (short attention span, impulsiveness, daydreaming) have been argued to account for 80% of the problems reported in an elementary school population of over 1100 (Huessy et al., 1974). Given even conservative estimates of the incidence of hyperactivity, then, the attention it has received in the drug literature since it was first described.as treatable with drugs (Bradley & Green, 1940) is not surprising.

Drug treatment of hyperactivity has been directed toward the elimination of symptoms thought to make the learning of adaptive responses such as reading and writing difficult. Though they differ somewhat in frequency of administration and side effects, the drugs dextroamphetamine, methylphenidate, and magnesium pemoline (Dexedrine, Ritalin, and Cylert, respectively) have been cited as significantly reducing components of hyperactivity such as psychomotor restlessness, short attention span, daydreaming, verbal impulsiveness, and aggressiveness (Barkley, 1977; Cerny, Kucerova, & Sturma, 1975; Cohen, Douglas, & Morgenstern, 1971; Conners, Eisenberg, & Barcai, 1967; Rapoport, Quinn, Bradbard, Riddle, & Brooks, 1974). In addition to symptom reduction, it has also been suggested that stimulant drug intervention with hyperactive children can have secondarily preventive effects in reducing the likelihood of subsequent delinquency in adolescence and criminality in adulthood (Satterfield & Cantwell, 1975).

There appears to be little argument that stimulant drug intervention with hyperkinetic children results in a reduction in children's hyperactive behavior within just a few days (Barkley, 1977). The serious question regarding the utility of such an intervention, however, relates to the subsequent academic and interpersonal gains made by those children whose problematic behaviors have been reduced.

The indirect gains in such realms resulting from stimulant chemotherapy are less impressive than the reduction of symptoms per se. For example, Barkley and Cunningham (1979), in a well-controlled observational study of interactions among mothers and their hyperactive male children, reported that methylphenidate use increased the compliance of the children to maternal commands, but decreased the level of directiveness (commands and questions) of mothers and increased mothers' focus on compliance. At the same time that the boys were more compliant, however, their rate of social initiations declined. Thus the children became more manageable, but it was not clear that alternative and more desirable responses such as social initiations were necessarily forthcoming or even likely, given the effects of the drugs.

Because hyperactivity has been even more closely associated with academic difficulties, a substantial number of studies have been focused on the effects of stimulants on hyperactive children's learning (e.g., Blacklidge, & Ekblad, 1971; Comly, 1971; Conners & Rothschild, 1968; Sleator, Von Neumann, & Sprague, 1974). Researchers who have relied on teacher ratings have consistently reported an improved academic achievement on the parts of the treated children. More recently, however, failures in short- and long-term gains have been reported. In a review of this literature, Barkley and Cunningham (1978) argued that reported gains can be attributed almost entirely to increased attention spans during testing and to decreased levels of activity (i.e., manageability). Thus reports of achievement gains may be nothing more than additional support for the impact of stimulants on symptom reduction. Barkley and Cunningham also pointed out that few benefits in learning have been attributable to drug intervention in studies using more objective measures of academic performance. They recommended adjunctive and independently evaluated use of stimulants but not without additional educational intervention to enhance school performance. Thus stimulants may have documented benefits for the teachers who must manage large numbers of children simultaneously, but such drug intervention with hyperactive children without intensified nonbiological interventions may be more an environmental, quality-of-life intervention for care-giving adults than they are a method by which a biologically based anomaly can be arrested so development and learning can occur "naturally." The danger, aside from potential long-term and irreversible direct effects of the drugs themselves, is not that the drugs will fail to produce a reduction in problematic behavior, but that in having those effects they may render the children more invisible (i.e., manageable) and thus less likely to receive the intensified and specialized education they need.

In the context of mixed outcome data, many researchers and writers argue against excessive enthusiasm and widespread acceptance of this form of intervention. Some of the arguments represent passionate and almost bitter indictment of chemotherapy as directly harmful (e.g., Schrag & Divoky, 1975), or indirectly harmful by virtue of interfering with other aspects of treatment (Adams, 1973). Other arguments represent a more moderate urging of caution with emphasis on potential side effects, the need for much additional research, and the importance of evaluating chemotherapy in the context of other interventions or theoretical principles (Campbell & Small, 1978; Fish, 1971; O'Leary, 1980; Whalen & Henker, 1976). For example, not only are the definitions of hyperactivity inconsistent (O'Leary, 1980), but the mechanisms responsible for hyperactivity are unknown (Whalen & Henker, 1976), as are the modes of drug action (Campbell & Small, 1978). In addition there are numerous reports of untoward side effects of a somatic nature (e.g., blood pressure increases, headaches, and nausea), of a behavioral-affective nature (e.g., irritability, depression, and tearfulness), and of a cognitive nature (e.g., hallucinations) (Aman & Werry, 1975; Ney, 1967; Page, Bernstein, Janicki, & Michelli, 1974). Other deleterious side effects such as impaired growth rate have also been reported (Safer & Allen, 1975), though not consistently supported (McNutt, Boileau, & Cohen, 1977; Page et al., 1974). Finally, there is growing evidence that alternative and less potentially dangerous interventions such as behavioral therapy can produce effects that are at least as beneficial as chemotherapy (O'Leary, 1980). Unfortunately, long-term studies of this alternative are generally unavailable or disappointing (O'Leary, 1980), and some studies continue to demonstrate superiority of chemotherapy over behavior therapy (Gittleman-Klein, Klein, Abikoff, Katz, Gloisten, & Kates, 1976).

Perhaps in reaction to alarm over short-term and possible long-term side effects of stimulant drug use, some interest has been directed toward alternative biological and additional biological interventions. For example, one biological nondrug intervention that has seen considerable application is diet therapy. On the basis of the hypothesis that symptomatic behaviors may be allergic reactions to particular aspects of a child's diet, Feingold (1975) has described a diet that excludes or at least reduces the additives and salicylates in a child's diet. At least one well-controlled test of this intervention (Conners, Goyette, Southwick, Lees, & Andrulonis, 1976) revealed an improvement in teachers' ratings of manageability but no changes in parents' ratings. Conners et al. noted that the failure to find differences may have been an artifact of the dependent variables used. Nevertheless, before the utility of the Feingold or any other diet can be justified, well-controlled outcome studies need to be conducted.

A second biological intervention proposed as an alternative to stimulant drug use is megavitamins (Cott, 1972; Rimland, 1973). However, the use of large doses of vitamins and controlled glucose levels has not been demonstrated as an effective strategy for reducing problematic behaviors and increasing attention span, nor has visuomotor training (Getman, 1965), a nonbiological intervention proposed as an alternative to psychoactive drug use.

Thus stimulant drug therapy with hyperkinetic children represents the most clinically popular, but nevertheless highly controversial, biological intervention. The data suggest both optimism and caution, and because of this numerous authors (e.g., Barkley & Cunningham, 1978; Campbell & Small, 1978; Fish, 1971) suggest that chemotherapy should usually only be initiated in conjunction with other forms of intervention. For example, advantages of methylphenidate in combination with behavior therapy have been argued by Satterfield, Cantwell, and Satterfield (1979) and Conners, Denkhoff, Millichap, and O'Leary (1978). Similarly, Pelham, Schnedler, Bologna, and Contreras (1980) have demonstrated that the administration of methylphenidate significantly enhanced the already positive effects of behavior therapy, and in combination the two interventions were superior to either alone. Unfortunately, the benefits of methylphenidate administration were only temporary, failing to continue after the medication was discontinued (Pelham, Schnedler, Miller, Ronnei, Paluchowski, Budrow, Marks, Nilsson, & Bender, 1979).

Psychosis

A second class of behavioral symptoms that have been widely treated with drug therapies are those associated with autism and schizophrenia. Drug treatment of psychotic children has been used since the 1930s (Campbell, 1978). It has been argued that this class of disorders should be divided into categories based on the age of onset of symptoms. Fish (1975), for example, has advocated such a basis for dimensionalizing these disorders on the assumption that psychoses are neurologically involved and that onset may thus be related to the level of that involvement such that the earlier the onset the more globally the child may be affected. In turn, the greater the level of involvement, the more severe the disturbed behavior, the more pronounced the related retardation, and the poorer the prognosis (Bender & Faretra, 1972; Kolvin, 1971). This conceptualization is used to explain and predict the range of responses that children and adolescents make to antipsychotic medications, but it also implies a neurological basis for the disorders and thus also justifies the use of psychoactive drugs.

This theoretical justification is necessary because, in contrast with hyperactivity, the effects of drug treatments with psychotic children have not been demonstrated. The utility of neuroleptics (antipsychotic sedatives) with adults has, for most practitioners, been established (Group for the Advancement of Psychiatry, 1975), and drug treatment for adult psychotics sees universal application. However, parallel outcome demonstrations are far from the case in the treatment of children diagnosed as manifesting some type of psychosis. Because of the nature of the target population, demonstrations of the utility of neuroleptics must necessarily be more stringent. Specifically, intervention with children and adolescents must not only be shown to produce symptom reduction but also to enhance or at least not constrain normal development. Such criteria are not as strongly emphasized as part of the burden of proof that antipsychotics with adults must pass. Despite these problems, use of the drugs, especially of neuroleptics, in the treatment of psychosis in children is very common (Chess, 1969).

By far the most widely used drug group in the treatment of children diagnosed as psychotic are sedative types of phenothiazines (chlorpromazine and thioridazine) (Campbell, 1978). These drugs are major tranquilizers and have the general effect of reducing levels of reactivity. As a result their use is limited to those children who display high rates of agitation, self-destructive behaviors, and stereotypic movements. Their sedative effects are considered undesirable for those children who are apathetic, anergic, and lacking in motor initiative.

Fish (1960) found chlorpromazine (Thorazine) to be effective in reducing levels of agitation in children although it tended to depress less active children. In some of the few double-blind studies in this literature, Fish and Shapiro (1965) and Korein, Fish, Shapiro, Gerner, and Levidow (1971) found that the more severely disturbed children improved in their symptomatic behavior when they received chlorpromazine. At the same time, however, these researchers found that chlorpromazine use with autistic preschool children did not produce significant improvements and was even associated with sedation, irritability, insomnia, and worsening of psychotic symptoms such as catatonic-like states. Fish and her associates have also examined the effects of trifluoperazine (Stelazine) on autistic preschoolers because this drug has been found to have fewer sedative effects on adults. They found that only their most severely affected subjects benefited from this treatment in the form of increased alertness, social responsiveness, and motor and language production. Similar outcomes have also been reported by Wolpert, Hagamen, and Merlis (1967). They found that trifluoperazine proved effective with school-age schizophrenics in improving appetites and reducing withdrawal and stereotypic behaviors. Although this was a double-blind study, dependent measures were confined to global ratings and changes in nonobjective instruments (Bender Gestalt and Human Figure drawings).

Another of the phenothiazines that has seen wide use is fluphenazine (Permitil). Engelhardt, Polizos, Waizer, and Hoffman (1973) found it to be effective with 93% of their child subjects in significantly modifying rates of self-awareness, constructive play, compulsive behavior, and self-mutilation. Similar findings have been reported by Faretra, Dooher, and Dowling (1970), who found that the drug primarily affected anxiety levels in 5- to 12-year-old children. A final drug that enjoys wide use in the treatment of psychotic children is thioridazine (Mellaril). Campbell and Small (1978) report that it is a recommended treatment for children with histories of seizure disorders and can be used without many of the untoward side effects associated with neuroleptic use such as extrapyramidal symptoms (e.g., drooling, tremors, wrist twisting, or cogwheeling).

The phenothiazines represent the class of neuroleptics that are most widely used in the treatment of psychotic symptoms in children. There are, in addition to this group of drugs, four other groups of neuroleptics: thioxanthenes (Navane and Taractan), butyrophenones (Haldol), dihydroindolones (Moban), and an experimental drug, tricyclic dibenzoxazepine. Very generally, these drugs tend to be recommended for older children (over 12), and each has proved effective in modifying target symptoms (Campbell & Small, 1978). Each has also been associated with reduced likelihood of some untoward effects but increased likelihood of others, and attempts to demonstrate relative advantages of one over another in symptom change have not proved successful (e.g., Pool, Bloom, Mielke, Roniger, & Gallant, 1976).

A range of drugs that are not neuroleptics have also been utilized and evaluated to some extent. For example, LSD was at one time offered as a promising alternative to antipsychotics (Mogar & Aldrich, 1969; Rhead, 1977). However, studies testing the effects have been poorly controlled and have revealed doubtful therapeutic benefits (Simmons, Benor, & Daniel, 1972; Simmons, Leiken, Lovaas, Schaeffer, & Perloff, 1966). In addition, unknown side effects of long-term use made LSD-25 a poor choice for psychotic children (Gelfand, Jensen, & Drew, 1981). Lithium carbonate has been tested with children diagnosed as infantile autistics (ages 8–22). Gram and Rafaelsen (1972) reported lithium to be effective in reducing hyperactivity, aggressiveness, and stereotypies, but other investigators (Campbell, Fish, Korein, Shapiro, Collins, & Koh, 1972) found that it did not produce significant pre-post changes and it was not more effective than chlorpromazine. Finally, drugs such as amphetamines (Campbell, Fish, David, Shapiro, Collins, & Koh, 1972), antidepressants (Kurtis, 1966), and megavitamins (Greenbaum, 1970) have seen varying levels of use, but outcome data have not been produced, or the drugs are associated with behavior deterioration, or they are associated with serious untoward effects.

In sum, drug intervention has been widely applied with psychotic children. Its use has dramatically changed intervention with adults, and is not likely to be abandoned in the treatment of children awaiting further basic and outcome research. To date this intervention approach is in a primitive state (Campbell, 1978). Though it boasts a burgeoning literature, the research represented is notably lacking in double-blind designs, nonreactive measures, behaviorally specific outcome measures, and control groups. As reviewed by Campbell and Small (1978), untoward immediate and short-term effects include such problems as sleepiness, irritability, parkinson-like symptoms, dyskinetic symptoms (tremors, excessive salivation), abnormal movements of face, neck, and tongue and associated muscles, convulsive seizures, and ocular changes (McAndrew, Case, & Treffert, 1972). Knowledge about long-term untoward effects is more limited, but psychoactive drugs, because of their site of action (neurotransmitters) do affect the secretion of neurohormones. This can pose potential hazards particularly to prepubertal children whose hormonal functioning has not yet been established. Menstrual irregularities and sterility in males have also been associated with long-term use of neuroleptics (Campbell, 1978). McAndrew et al. (1972) have reported deleterious effects on IQ as a result of prolonged use of phenothiazines. Finally, withdrawal from phenothiazines has been associated with temporary symptoms resembling tardive dyskinesia (a motor syndrome involving involuntary movements) in adults (McAndrew et al., 1972; Polizos, Engelhardt, Hoffman, & Waizer, 1973; Schiele, Gallant, Simpson, Gardner, & Cole, 1973). These involuntary movements, primarily in the arms, head, and upper trunk, can take as long as 6 months to disappear and do not seem to be diminished by gradual rather than sudden drug withdrawal. Their relationship to the permanent disorder seen in adults has also not been established.

Though progress has been made in adjusting dosages or instituting additional drugs to reduce these side effects, major reviewers continue to urge extreme caution, discontinuing drug treatment if it interferes with educational opportunities and physical development (Campbell, 1975, 1976). Further, drug therapy cannot represent a solitary modality for positive change. Instead, its purpose is to help the child become more amenable to other educational and social treatments (Campbell, 1976; Fish, 1976). Studies reporting success in using drugs in this way are available and often describe the effects of combining antipsychotic drugs with various forms of psychotherapy such as individual and group (Rock, 1974) or therapeutic communities (Murphy & Elder, 1974). Unfortunately, no formal conceptual models have been developed and researched that integrate psychopharmacological and psychosocial therapeutic treatment. As a result, the effects of the widespread practice of combining these two treatment modalities remains for the most part unknown.

Neurotic or Habit Disorders

Although the principal targets of biological interventions with children and adolescents have been hyperactivity and psychoses, the utility of drug interventions has also been evaluated in use with a variety of other disorders including phobias (Gittleman-Klein & Klein, 1973; Kelly, Guirguis, Frommer, Mitchell-Heggs, & Sargant, 1970), depression (Anneil, 1969; Ossofsky, 1974), enuresis and sleepwalking (Meadow, 1974; Pesikoff & Davis, 1971), and Gilles de la Tourette syndrome (Chapel, Brown, & Jenkins, 1964). Polák, Molčan, and Škoricová (1975) found imipramine (an antidepressant) superior to psychostimulants, vitamins, and behavioral training in treating enuresis.

Though beneficial effects are often reported,

fears of potential abuses of drugs are voiced (Petit & Biggs, 1977). In part because of such concerns, drug therapies with nonpsychotic and nonhyperactive children have neither received widespread and programmatic empirical scrutiny nor become a focal point for theory and conceptual model building. Because other therapeutic approaches primarily treat and sometimes demonstrate effectiveness with such "neurotic" and habit disorders, the drug therapies have not attained the same popularity that they have enjoyed in the treatment of psychotic and hyperkinetic children. In fact, respected researchers and reviewers such as Campbell and Small (1978) have argued that in cases of phobic reactions and depression, drug treatment should be avoided until it is clear that alternative psychosocial therapies have failed. Similarly, chemical intervention "should not be used in mild disorders where environmental factors are prominent, if not causative, except where the purpose of drug administration is to break a vicious cycle" (Campbell & Small, 1978, p. 13).

Methodological Issues

Biological, and in particular drug interventions, may be seen by the nonmedical practitioner as an exacting aspect of treatment for children. Quite to the contrary, the research in this area of intervention suffers from the same methodological flaws as nonbiological intervention research. Experienced researchers and practitioners alike in this area are keenly aware of the experimental nature of these therapies, advise caution in their practice, and urge improvements in the research of these interventions (Campbell & Small, 1978; Conners, 1973). The purpose of this section is to outline some of the principal methodological issues that should guide future research in this area and that should serve as a basis for evaluating existing research.

As pointed out by Campbell (1978), a fundamental issue in drug research with children (although it is shared by research on children in general) is thorough descriptions of target populations. Characteristics of children such as age, IQ, gender, family health histories (including pregnancy histories) are generally lacking in whole or in part in the published literature. In an area in which idiosyncratic responses to treatment may account for significant amounts of data variation, detailing aspects of the individual child subject becomes critical in the interpretation of data and the planning of future studies. In addition to systematic description of treatment subjects, drug studies should also include a drug vacation for subjects prior to onset of the ex-

perimental manipulation. During this time, the effects of previous drug treatment may wash out, and contextual (e.g., family) responses to drug-free states can be evaluated.

With regard to study design, there is a notable lack of rigorous experimental methodology including such features as use of control groups, random assignment of subjects to control and treatment conditions, control for unsystematic environment manipulations (e.g., responses of teachers and parents), and control for concurrent nonbiological interventions such as parent counseling, special education for children, and family therapy.

With regard to dependent variable selection, drug research has been notably lacking in objective behavior-rating instruments used by independent observers. Behavioral ratings, when they are used, are often reported without controlling for or documenting the conditions in which the ratings were made (Gleser, 1968); this is critical because environmental characteristics play an important role in mediating children's responses. Also lacking in the drug literature is the use of natural contexts within which children are evaluated. Finally, drug studies on children should include controls for separating drug effects from maturational changes (Eisenberg & Conners, 1971; Sprague & Werry, 1971). The sometimes rapid and relatively poorly documented pace of various aspects of children's maturation undoubtedly accounts for a great deal of the unexplained variance in all intervention research. Drug researchers especially need to attend to these normal developmental shifts because drug interventions have been justified on the grounds that they can be useful to the extent that they free children from problematic symptoms that may block the course of normal development.

INTERNAL-DYNAMIC APPROACHES

Basic Assumptions

At the time of the previous publication of *Carmichael's Manual of Child Psychology* (Mussen, 1970), Anthony indicated in his chapter entitled "The Behavior Disorders of Childhood" that individual psychotherapy had for decades been the treatment of choice for children with problems in social and personality development. This individual approach was developed primarily from the psychoanalytic model, which retained considerable preeminence in the field even as derivative (e.g., ego psychology) and competitive (e.g., existential-humanistic-client centered) internal-dynamic models evolved. Taken together, these intrapsychic approaches assume the actual or metaphorical existence of internal processes or states that produce symptomatic behavior on the part of the child. The goal of these therapies is to modify these internal states so that children will both eliminate the symptomatic behavior and continue normal developmental growth.

The internal-dynamic approaches discussed here are analytic therapies and humanistic-Gestalt therapies. Although this may not be an exhaustive listing of internal-dynamic approaches, these two groups of therapies provide the roots of all dynamic approaches. Variations occur primarily in the metaphor used to conceptualize normal versus atypical functioning and in the vocabulary used to describe the intervention process.

Analytic Therapies

In the analytic therapies, the problematic internal processes are hypothesized to derive primarily from an inherent conflict between a child's basic instinctual drives and the demands of parents and society. Although these conflicts are assumed to continue throughout life, they can be dealt with in adaptive and nonsymptomatic ways. Development is satisfactory as long as the child can experience (rather than defend against) life conflicts and develop adequate (ego) coping mechanisms for appropriately interpreting and responding to life experiences. The major therapeutic goal for the child is the conscious experiencing of conflicts and feelings, primarily through the vehicle of therapist interpretation. However, because children are less capable than adults of conceptualizing their experiences and articulating them verbally, the literature on child-analytic approaches has deemphasized traditional verbally mediated processes such as free association. Instead, analytic therapists generally rely on a play therapy approach (Scharfman, 1978).

In play therapy, therapists provide a range of materials such as toys, dolls, crayons, or paint and paper. These materials provide the child with means to express various behaviors and feelings directly and indirectly, as well as verbally and nonverbally. Therapists use both verbal and nonverbal expressions as a base for interpreting symbolic content, reflecting affect, and pointing out defensive operations such as rationalization. With seriously disturbed children in particular, the early phases of intervention reflect little of the esoteric content and processes characteristic of dynamic insight-oriented therapy with adults. Instead, therapists emphasize very basic activities such as pointing out and labeling people and objects. Therapists point out and la-

bel affect responses and discharge behaviors such as aggression (Gilpin, 1976; Holter & Ruttenberg, 1971), and pay special attention to developing a stable treatment context (Tustin, 1973) and establishing a strong client-therapist relationship (Holter & Ruttenberg, 1971).

Rather than creating an ambiguous structure to elicit free association and emphasizing the symbolic nature of associations with seriously disturbed children, therapists are more likely to identify feelings currently expressed by the children and to engage in overt and consistent relationship-building behaviors. Further, ego development in children is believed to be incomplete, and children are directly and intensely involved with the parental relationship at the same time they are in therapy. As a result, transference to the therapist and the play therapy materials becomes confounded with displacements from present relationships. That is, children tend to act out *current* conflicts in therapy, whereas adults act out *previously developed* conflicts. In adult-oriented psychoanalytic psychotherapy it is assumed that reactions to the environment, including reactions made to the essentially neutral therapist, are manifestations of previously developed (and usually unconscious) conflicts and learned response patterns. In contrast, children are often still in the process of learning how to respond, and in the process of actively struggling with the processes that produce internal conflicts. Their physical and psychological boundaries are still not well established, and their ability to interpret reality is incompletely developed. Thus rather than becoming a transference object for past conflicts as in adult psychoanalytic therapy, the therapist often becomes more of an "auxiliary ego" (Gilpin, 1976). As such, the therapist represents a stable adult whom the child can trust and depend on for reality testing, the establishment of self-boundaries, and the labeling of cause-effect relationships.

Humanistic Therapies

The client-centered humanistic, existential, and Gestalt therapies also rely heavily on play and other forms of expression such as dance and art, and similarly emphasize the experiencing of feelings as a vehicle for positive change. They reflect, however, a more "positive" view of child development than does analytic therapy, in that they emphasize the inherent tendencies for children to move toward growth, creativity, and fulfillment (Rogers, 1974). For example, the Gestalt approach assumes that "deviant" behavior is the way children communicate what they need and want to those around them when natural self-expression has been repeatedly or traumatically interrupted or brings no satisfaction. Through interaction with the parents, children learn how and when they can express themselves, and they discover which behaviors bring desired parental responses. Sometimes deviant ways of expression are actually encouraged by one or the other of the parents, either implicitly or explicitly.

The goal of working with children in Gestalt therapy is to help them achieve more "normal" and "acceptable" self-expression. Because disturbed children are seen as having "disowned" their feelings and behaviors, it is necessary to reacquaint children with themselves. Only then can they come to behave in ways that stem from their true feelings and be undistorted by the anticipated reactions of others. Contact with and awareness of self go hand in hand with contact with and awareness of others. Thus each therapeutic intervention is designed to foster the child's awareness, expression, and contact both in terms of himself and in terms of the therapist. Therapists encourage children to perform and to take responsibility for the deviant behavior that has frequently been disowned and unacknowledged by them. With a so-called compulsive swearer, for instance, the therapist might say "do it more," "exaggerate," "say it into the tape recorder," or "spell it."

Additional frequently used techniques include fantasy, storytelling, and drama (see Lederman, 1969; Oaklander, 1978). Rather than relying on such techniques to provide material for symbolic interpretation, Gestalt therapists emphasize the use of these techniques as a means of creating accepting relationship conditions and a sense of personal responsibility in the child. These contexts will facilitate the expression, recognition, and acceptance of the child's underlying feelings. Once this is accomplished, and assuring a benign environment, the child will be able to rely on basic strengths in order to develop adaptively.

Internal-dynamic interventions have been described as useful for a wide range of childhood neuroses including obsessiveness (Adams, 1973), anger inhibition problems (Gardner, 1971), suicide attempts (Aleksandrowicz, 1975), depression (Mosse, 1974), withdrawn behavior (Smith, 1976), separation anxiety (LeRoy & Derdeyn, 1976), eczema, and asthma (Bentley, 1975). With seriously disturbed children, reported outcomes vary widely, as in the case of Kestenbaum (1978), who reports outcomes ranging from presumably extraordinary achievement (college professorship) to institutionalization (see also Rolphe, 1973).

Therapy Outcomes

The absence of systematic outcome evaluation of psychodynamic therapies has led to repeated criticism in the psychotherapy literature (Heinicke & Strassmann, 1975; Levitt, 1971). This absence, however, cannot fairly be attributed to merely an antiempirical attitude. Instead, it reflects an emphasis on diagnostic differences, clinical creativity, and flexibility, which represents both a great strength and great weakness in the psychodynamic approaches. For example, writers have given considerable attention to sometimes quite subtle distinctions between various forms of childhood psychosis. Kestenbaum (1978), for example, cites such diagnostic categories as nuclear schizophrenia versus early infantile autism versus symbiotic psychoses versus unusual sensitivity versus borderline psychoses versus atypical development. Unfortunately, the reliability and validity of these distinctions and the methods used to determine them are often questioned in the literature (Kestenbaum, 1978; Magnussen, 1979), as are more general assumptions about etiology (e.g., Behrens & Goldfarb, 1958; Miller, 1975). Further, these diagnostic and etiological distinctions do not translate in the literature into unique and well-defined treatment strategies for each diagnostic group. Instead, recurrent themes in the literature include an emphasis on creativity and flexibility on the part of therapists, and research as a vehicle for model refinement rather than model testing. Kestenbaum (1978), for example, uses the characteristic case study format to emphasize the striking differences among four psychotic children, each involving different therapeutic processes and quite different outcomes.

The emphasis on subtle diagnostic differences, clinical creativity, and flexibility often strikes a responsive chord in clinicians, who must frequently make important clinical decisions based on a perceived mixture of gross and very subtle individual differences. Unfortunately, this heavy idiosyncratic emphasis also creates difficulty for researchers who want to initiate a careful and programmatic evaluation of the model. Certainly the traditional group designs used in much outcome research are not useful, because group heterogeneity makes comparisons of group means inappropriate. Single-subject designs, so informative in the behavioral literature, are theoretically inappropriate because immediate cause-effect relationships between behavior and environment (with possibilities for multiple base-line and reversal designs) are not hypothesized in the dynamic models, nor are some treatment goals conceptualized as being observable or measurable behavior. As a result, the traditional one-to-one dynamically oriented approaches to treating children have received very little systematic research evaluation, and are difficult if not impossible to evaluate in terms of effectiveness (Gelfand et al., 1981).

As competing intervention models grow in influence, as mental health budgets decrease, and as accountability becomes an even greater issue in service delivery, greater pressure will be brought to bear on practitioners to demonstrate and justify the use of methods that are time-consuming and thus expensive. Centers in which these forms of intervention are regarded as the ''real'' cures for dysfunction may be asked why so relatively few children receive these cures. The very difficulty of defining obtainable dependent measures and of then evaluating treatment process and outcome may contribute significantly to the decline in use of and support for these interventions. Their value, if it cannot be identified, may make their use too costly. Though efforts at outcome research have appeared in the literature (Heinicke, 1969; Luborsky & Spence, 1978; Miller, Barrett, Hampe, & Noble, 1972), the volume of outcome research is not as great as would be expected given the wide use of internal-dynamic approaches.

Current Contributions

It is not appropriate, however, to conclude that the internal-dynamic models will soon be written off as institutional anachronisms. Innovations in theoretical derivations, intervention techniques, and training-supervision formats are emerging. These new directions are important not only for the internal-dynamic approaches, but for other models as well. For example, one often-repeated injunction in the literature concerns the need to place the child in the appropriate developmental context, the idea being that treatment should be varied as a function of the developmental stage of the child (Heinicke & Strassmann, 1975; Magnussen, 1979; Scharfman, 1978). Behavioral, interactional, and community models have emphasized intervention principles, paradigms, and techniques, but have rarely done much more than make offhand references to unique aspects of different developmental stages and capacities. In contrast, the internal-dynamic models have made great strides in integrating treatment techniques and developmental theory. The literature is replete with specific descriptions of deviations from traditional psychoanalytic principles that are necessary when treating children (Vandersall, 1978), as

well as the different expectations that the therapist must hold. Scharfman (1978) not only discusses the developmental capacities of children in the stages of prelatency, latency, and adolescence; he also describes specific techniques that are necessary and appropriate to initiate and terminate therapy in each of these developmental stages. In addition, he offers a rationale for how the traditional psychoanalytic processes of free association, therapeutic alliance, and transference must be conceptualized and relied on in different ways with children and youth. For example, prelatency children tend to experience relatively little subjective distress from their symptoms and tend to externalize their conflict more than older children and adults. Thus the therapist must be quite patient and more understanding than interpretive.

The latency-age child, in contrast, would appear to be a better candidate for interpretation-based insight. The latency-age child tends to be less aggressive or destructive in play activities, is more logical, and has a more consolidated superego with attendant guilt. Also, transference reactions often occur. However, powerful operations (such as repression of recent oedipal conflicts) do not necessarily make the latency child easier to treat than the prelatency child. Whereas play is a less relevant context for developing therapeutic content, free association and other forms of significant disclosure do not come easily. Because of this, regular contacts with the parent(s) is recommended in order to (1) supplement information, (2) educate the parent(s) regarding expectations and the meaning of changes, (3) assess the parent(s) in order to understand the child's environment more fully, and (4) deal with parental concern about the child's attachment to the therapist (Sharfman, 1978).

For the adolescent patient the therapist can represent a new adult about whom the adolescent is curious. However, the adolescent can also view the therapist as a representative of the parents' generation. Thus in early phases the therapist must attempt to provide cues that he or she understands the adolescent and that the therapist will be neither too distant nor too close. In addition, because separation from parents is so often a central concern for the adolescent, many therapists avoid contact with parents, or interact with them more carefully in terms of sharing information that has emerged in analysis.

Coming from a more humanistic perspective, Bratter (1975) emphasizes that with suicidal adolescents, therapists need to provide limits more systematically than is usually stressed in the literature. They cannot follow the usual permissive, nondirective psychotherapeutic orientation based on the ideas of relationship democracy and freedom of choice. Another deviation from traditional one-to-one relationship therapy with both neurotic and psychotic children includes the use of therapeutic groups (Kraft, 1972; Plenk, 1978; Ross & Bernstein, 1976), which are designed to help children express their feelings and problems in ways that cannot be expressed individually with an adult therapist (Coolidge & Grunebaum, 1964; Gratton & Rizzo, 1969). Troester and Darby (1976) have additionally used a "mini-meal" context in which food is used as a therapeutic tool in a group of children. Group approaches such as these are designed to facilitate verbal problem solving, identification of and acting out of family problems, and the development of group cohesion (Troester & Darby, 1976).

The modifications of traditional analytic techniques represent not just pragmatic changes derived from clinical experiences, but often result from careful integration of therapeutic principles with various aspects of developmental theory (see Lamb, 1978; Sandler, 1975; Ulrici & Jurkovic, 1979). This type of integration of therapeutic goals, intervention technology, and knowledge of developmental aspects of children and families has been noticeably absent in the general body of intervention literature (Heinicke & Strassmann, 1975). Nevertheless, for decision-making strategies and treatment approaches to become more effective and efficient, all intervention models must better articulate the relationship between client characteristics (such as developmental capacities), the goals of intervention, and specific techniques.

It is also noteworthy that despite their focus on individual processes, the internal-dynamic approaches often emphasize that parents must be involved in conjunction with the one-to-one child contacts. Parental involvement has been encouraged either in the form of consultation and collaboration, or direct therapy (Ack, Beale, & Ware, 1975; Adams, 1973; Awad & Harrison, 1976; Levitt, 1971; Reinhart, Kenna, & Succop, 1972; Schneiderman & Evans, 1975; Szurek, 1973). Although this parental involvement has been frequently mentioned, several theorists have formally expanded the internal-dynamic model to include larger family relationships (Ackerman, 1966) and even multigenerational influences on the child's behavior (Bowen, 1976). These theoretical expansions have brought the internal-dynamic models into the realm of communication and systems theories, and hold the promise of producing new levels of formal theoretical integration and clinical intervention.

For example, Nathan Ackerman, who is widely considered the "grandfather" of family therapy, was one of the first psychoanalysts to assert that successes in individual therapy often broke down when the patient returned to the family context. He therefore suggested that therapists should treat the whole family, emphasizing three distinct phases of therapy: (1) reeducation of the family through guidance, (2) reorganization through a change in the patterns of family communication, and (3) resolution of pathogenic conflict and induction of change and growth by means of a dynamic in-depth approach to the affective currents of family life (Ackerman, 1966). Key goals in Ackerman's approach include reestablishing role complementarity, helping the family renegotiate more flexible rules, and developing clearer communication. Murray Bowen has evolved a more elaborate theory of family functioning and change based essentially on a psychoanalytic perspective. His recent theory (Bowen, 1976) states that a person begins life as part of an undifferentiated family ego mass, and over time must learn to differentiate a self. The truly mature person is one who can stay in emotional contact with his or her family without becoming fused or joined to them. Therapy helps the patient to identify rationally the patterns in the family system that tend to "hook" emotions and that can often be traced back over many generations. The therapist facilitates this process by acting as a "coach." In this role the therapist encourages people to study their families and develop strategies for differentiating themselves from other family members, for gaining the ability to respond rather than to react to feelings (i.e., replace "automatic" affect responses with rationality) and for avoiding triangulation. *Triangulation* is a process that involves a dyad (e.g., husband and wife) who are experiencing a conflict they can neither solve nor ignore. In order to gain an advantage, one or both members will draw in a third person (e.g., the child). In such a situation, the child is very powerful (often holding the balance of power), but also very vulnerable. According to many family theories, children who have been triangulated cannot develop individualized and rational modes of interpreting and responding to their environments, because their safety and importance in the family depends on viewing the world the way their "triangulators" do. Thus in the Bowen model the basic conflict dealt within therapy is between the instinctual force toward togetherness and the force toward differentiation. Successful intervention lasts for 1 year or more, and is attained when emotional bonds within the family remain but specific reactions are no longer linked to historical family patterns.

An additional contribution of the dynamic therapies consists of the prominent place historically given to the relationship between the therapist and the client (Langs, 1973; Menninger & Holtzman, 1973). This prominence has led quite naturally to emphasis on therapist training and supervision, as well as an emphasis on therapist characteristics (Parloff, Waskow, & Wolfe, 1978). Whereas theorists such as Bowen (1976) have developed elaborate concepts and techniques regarding the complexities of therapists' training and involvement with families, adherents of the systems and behavioral models have only recently begun formally to conceptualize, dimensionalize, and evaluate this crucial component of intervention (e.g., Alexander, Barton, Schiavo, & Parsons, 1976). In the biological model this issue has been essentially ignored.

Thus although scientific scrutiny has not persuasively demonstrated that the dynamic approaches are effective and efficient in producing positive behavior change, the nature and quality of therapists' conceptual, technical, and interpersonal skills emphasized in the dynamic approaches will continue to be a critical component of therapeutic success with children. By emphasizing both the developmental capacities of children and the various aspects of the therapist's involvement, the internal-dynamic models continue to have an important impact on the entire field of intervention with children.

BEHAVIORAL MODELS

The behavioral approach to understanding and treating problematic behavior emerged in the 1950s as a powerful alternative to the internal causality assumptions of both the dynamic and the biological therapies. This approach gained considerable momentum in the 1960s, and by 1970 had "begun to enter the practice of some clinics, replacing, though still to a very small extent, the explicit assumption that the main therapeutic task is to resolve conflicts" (Anthony, 1970, p. 745). In retrospect a decade later, this modest appraisal seems grossly understated. Though not without conflict and controversy, this model has become the principal component of intervention strategies employed and promoted by numerous clinics, training programs, academic departments, professional journals, and professional societies. A major goal among workers in this model has been not only to demonstrate desired therapeutic outcomes, but in doing so, also to demonstrate, expand, and articulate conceptual principles and intervention technologies. In the process, adherents of the behavioral model have so emphasized research

and evaluation that the collection of data as an ongoing part of the clinical intervention is seen as essential to the conduct of intervention and to the continued growth of the model (Barlow, 1980). The resulting wealth of empirical data has enhanced considerably the quality, scientific legitimacy, and persuasiveness of the model.

In its early stages of development, the behavioral model provided a strong contrast to the predominant internal-dynamic approach by emphasizing not only the need for defining overt observable external events but also by identifying and documenting achievement of therapeutic goals in terms of specific changes in those observable target behaviors. Receiving particular emphasis was the therapeutic manipulation of antecedent and consequent stimuli as the basis of behavior rate acceleration and deceleration techniques, the activation of desired target behaviors, and the identification of therapeutic goals exclusively in behavioral terms.

In developing the majority of these behavior-control techniques, the behavioral model adopted an assumption of external and unidirectional control, in which the variables maintaining the behavior were assumed to reside outside the individual child. The behavioral model included the assumption that regulations of those environmental features would result in behavioral changes on the part of the target individual (Bijou & Baer, 1961, 1965). Thus the modification of the external social environment became the major vehicle for change.

Because the variables that maintained behavior were assumed to be external to the child and because these variables could presumably be identified in a relatively straightforward and simple fashion, sophisticated and extensive training of change agents was not seen as necessary to the extent it was in the internal-dynamic models. Training instead was focused on the application of change techniques, research evaluation, and data analysis so that therapists could competently evaluate therapy outcome as well as add to the development of intervention technology. Thus technology, almost independent of the therapist, was formally identified as the major active ingredient of intervention.

This trend in the development of the behavioral model has not, however, occurred free of criticism. Staats (1975), for example, has criticized this view as being too limited, arguing that the majority of clinical behavioral theories have not formally addressed the learning theory-based social interaction principles pertaining to the client-therapist relationship. According to Staats, behavioral clinicians must understand these social interaction principles to understand the process of therapy. He has also criticized the frequent lack of integration between the two major types of conditioning: instrumental and classical. Instrumental conditioning is the general paradigm used in *behavior modification,* and generally involves the use of reinforcement principles to increase or decrease the incidence of an instrumental behavior. *Behavior therapy,* in contrast, has relied on classical conditioning procedures for modifying "the emotional value of stimuli" (i.e., the extent to which these stimuli elicit emotional responses such as fear) (Staats, 1975). *Modeling* (Bandura, 1969) is a third type of learning in which subjects seem to learn or at least perform previously unexpressed instrumental or emotional behaviors after watching a model perform these behaviors. Though dispute exists about the theoretical reasons for this change in performance in the absence of direct instrumental or classical conditioning, modeling is an important technical component of many clinical interventions with children. According to Staats, the various learning principles have rarely been integrated into a basic learning theory that conceptualizes how these principles interact. His A-R-D (attitude-reinforcer-directive) model involves such an integration, and readers are urged to review his treatment of numerous clinical and developmental issues (Staats, 1975).

Despite Staats's argument, the current chapter will begin the review of behavioral approaches by describing relatively straightforward clinical applications of each of the three forms of learning. Then several issues pertaining to application effectiveness will be raised, and the field's attempts to respond to them will be described. The reader should keep in mind that whereas the behavioral approaches can be described as technology oriented, theorists and researchers such as Staats, Bandura, and others to be cited later have engaged in considerable model scrutiny and conceptual elaboration. And though it is true that clinicians often need not struggle with many of the conceptual issues to be able to apply specific techniques, without these struggles the field would not have experienced the impressive growth and continuing development that has characterized it thus far.

Basic Techniques

A review of clinical behavioral principles can be organized in several ways, including grouping by technique and by problem classification (e.g., enuresis, aggressive behavior). The latter approach provides a more accurate representation of clinical

behaviorism, because in order to deal with children's problems clinicians often use a variety of techniques based on either pragmatic or theoretical (see Staats, 1975) reasons. Lazarus (1973), for example, argued that behavioral therapists must remain flexible and not restrict themselves to particular techniques or even particular theories. Because many clients experience more than one isolated problem, Lazarus's Multimodal Therapy systematically evaluates six client modalities (behavior, affect, sensation, imagery, cognition, and interpersonal relationships), and specific treatments are proposed for some or sometimes all of these modalities.

Unfortunately, this clinical breadth and flexibility can confuse the student, and just as discussed in the context of the dynamic models (see *Internal-Dynamic Approaches*), it can make precise evaluation of specific techniques difficult. Additional potential problems with a flexible (eclectic) approach to clinical intervention will be discussed in the last section of this chapter, *The Application of Knowledge.* For the purposes of clarity and simplicity, the next three sections of this chapter will focus on specific classes of techniques. It should be noted that the review is intended to be representative, not exhaustive. Some studies are included not because they represent well-documented and replicated interventions, but because they exemplify the range of current application of learning principles.

Operant Approaches

The most widely applied learning paradigm has been operant conditioning. In this paradigm, assessment involves (1) a careful analysis of antecedent or contextual conditions, (2) a clear description of the properties of the response in question, (3) an analysis of the consequent events, and (4) a clear statement of alternative behaviors deemed to be more appropriate and acceptable. Based on an understanding of these events, behavior therapists rearrange the antecedent and consequent events so that the response is modified or replaced. This approach is exemplified in a number of single-case and small-sample studies. In a classic description of the treatment of feeding difficulties (refusal to eat solid food), Palmer, Thompson, and Linscheid (1975) applied the Premack principle (making desired activities and objects contingent on performance of less desired responses; see Premack, 1965) with a 6-year-old child by making a bite of preferred (pureed) food contingent on taking a bite of solid food. Whining was extinguished by the therapist's turning away (extinction). Munford and Liberman (1978) eliminated high-rate coughing behavior in a 13-year-old boy. Hypothesizing that in-the-home coughing was being reinforced by parental attention, the therapists hospitalized the boy and instituted a differential attention program in which the cough was completely ignored and age-appropriate behavior was lavishly praised and rewarded with points. Positive benefits were generalized to the home through parental consultation and the development of contingency contracts involving a range of social, personal, and educational activities. A similar program was reported involving a 17-year-old girl whose hysterical coughing and mutism were treated by such techniques as shaping verbal behaviors and extensive work with the family (Munford, Reardon, Liberman, & Allen, 1976). Matson and Ollendick (1976) eliminated biting in 18-month to 3½-year-old children by administering mouthwash (a mild punishment) after biting attempts. Salvin, Routh, Foster, and Lovejoy (1977) trained sign language in a mute child by reinforcing imitation with food.

Two widely reported and researched techniques that have employed operant principles have been two forms of overcorrection: restitution and positive practice (Ollendick & Matson, 1978). In *restitution overcorrection,* the child "is required to 'perform restitution' for his inappropriate reactions by correcting the situation and restoring the environment to an improved state" (Ollendick & Matson, 1978, p. 830). For example, "accidents" during toilet training require changing soiled clothing, putting them in a predesignated place, cleaning the area in which the soiling occurred (Azrin & Foxx, 1974), and after hours making up schoolwork missed as a result of soiling (Ferinden & Van Handel, 1970). *Positive practice overcorrection* involves the extensive performance of behaviors that are incompatible with the unwanted behavior. With inappropriate self-stimulatory behaviors such as head-weaving and hand-clapping, for example, Foxx and Azrin (1973b) developed a program in which children were guided through a series of functional head and hand movements. For six aggressive-disruptive boys, Azrin and Powers (1975) reported successful reductions and maintenance of treatment effects in the classroom when the boys were required to extensively practice appropriate procedures for talking in class and leaving their seats. With the appropriate duration of practice and immediate feedback on performance, overcorrection appears to be a powerful treatment technique with positive long-term effects (Ollendick & Matson, 1978).

Various aspects of verbal behavior such as mutism, echolalia, and stuttering have also been treated with operant techniques. In the general paradigm, children are prompted to emit appropriate sounds or approximations, then positive consequences of a verbal (i.e., praise) or physical (e.g., tokens, points, food) nature are provided (Carlsson, 1971; Freeman, Rivto, & Miller, 1975; Nelson & Evans, 1968; Rosenbaum & Kellman, 1973; Stevens-Long, Schwarz & Bliss, 1976). Children's awareness of the response contingency, the reinforcement of easily identified behaviors, and the selection of rewards by the children represent three conditions that seem to enhance particularly the effectiveness of this form of verbal training (Manning, Trutna, & Shaw, 1976).

Working with excessively loud children, Michelson and DiLorenzo (1979) designed a voice-activated buzzer that sounded contingently when voice volume exceeded 75 decibels. With an 11-year-old "hyperactive" and loud boy, the contingent application of the buzzer dramatically reduced voice volume. Michelson, DiLorenzo, Calpin, and Williamson (1981) replicated these findings with a group of 14 institutionalized 6- to 14-year-olds, and included additional measures that demonstrated significant improvements in positive behaviors.

Operant techniques have also been applied in group contexts. In a general review of intervention with large intact groups of schoolchildren, O'Leary and Drabman (1971) concluded that contingent reinforcement in the form of teacher attention or tokens can be highly successful in modifying such problematic behaviors as disruptive behavior, nonattention, and lack of sharing (Barton & Ascione, 1979). Patterns of extreme shyness and social withdrawal in both moderately and severely disturbed children have also been successfully treated in a group context in which the contingent reinforcement of social behavior with food and social reinforcements significantly increased social play (Clement & Milne, 1967; Kerr & Strain, 1978; Romanczyk, Diament, Goren, Trunnell, & Harris, 1975). Graziano (1970) reported similarly positive effects with autistic children, in which nonprofessional staff (with professional supervision) used a blend of operant and respondent procedures to elicit and then reinforce a range of adaptive behaviors or their approximations.

The successful treatment of enuresis has been demonstrated using operant principles (Doleys, 1977). Foxx and Azrin (1973a) describe detailed procedures that included (1) providing extra liquid intake to increase urination rate, (2) immediate reinforcement (social as well as desired edibles) of all components as well as the final act of urinating, (3) verbal instruction and guiding, (4) prompted practice trials, (5) contingent verbal reprimands and positive practice of appropriate behaviors in the case of accidents, (6) fading of prompts and reinforcers, and (7) ensuring generalization by having the parents continue, then fade, the program. With 34 nondisturbed normal children this procedure averaged 4 hours in duration and resulted in almost complete success. Success has also been reported with retention training (Kimmel & Kimmel, 1970) in which the child is reinforced (e.g., cookies) for "holding it" for increasingly longer periods of time after first reporting the urge to urinate. Even greater benefits have been reported when retention training is coupled with "response shaping" (child sets the alarm at increasingly longer periods to awaken self for purposes of getting up to urinate) and "responsibility reinforcement," wherein the child maintains his own records and monitors progress. When successful, this self-monitoring is assumed to be reinforcing in and of itself. Encopresis has been similarly treated, using discrimination training plus social and material reinforcers (Ashkenazi, 1975), and verbal instructions plus positive reinforcement for successful retention (Allyon, Simon, & Wildman, 1975; Keehn, 1965; Young & Goldsmith, 1972). Edelman (1971) reported success when a condition of punishment (isolation) for soiling was added to positive reinforcement for retention in the treatment of a 12-year-old encopretic girl.

Respondent Conditioning

Learning theorists have successfully applied techniques derived from the classical (or respondent) conditioning model with "emotional" or direct anxiety symptoms such as phobias. Wolpe (1969) developed the technique of *systematic desensitization*, which he described as involving the creation or use of "internal" responses such as physiological relaxation. In this physiologically relaxed state, graded stimuli (either "real" or "imaginal") that were previously related to anxiety are presented. When paired repeatedly with the relaxed state, which is antagonistic to arousal, these stimuli eventually no longer elicit anxiety responses; that is, they are counterconditioned. Though Wolpe's explanation of this process is controversial, the technique has been widely used. Successful treatment has been reported in such diverse areas as insomnia (Weil & Goldfried, 1973) and trichotillomania (self-injurious hair pulling) with the addition of a response-cost condition contingent on the unwanted behavior (McLaughlin & Nay, 1975). Croghan and Musante (1975) attained a nonanxious physiological state with game-playing, and coupled in vivo desensitization in the form of playing the games near a tall

building in order to eliminate a phobia about high buildings. In another variation, Kissel (1972) used the client-therapist relationship to produce a nonanxious physiological state, and in that context presented pictures of previously feared stimuli in order to countercondition the phobic responses. Tasto (1969) successfully treated a 4-year-old boy with a phobia for loud noises by training him in muscle relaxation (Wolpe & Lazarus, 1966) as a first step in systematic desensitization. However, because the use of imagined stimuli, which were paired with the relaxed state, did not generalize to real-stimulus situations, Tasto presented hierarchically ordered in vivo stimuli either directly or at home via parental presentation.

Examples of more direct counterconditioning include Jones's classic study (1924), and Wish, Hasazi, and Jurgela's (1973) self-administered pairing of increasingly loud sounds (the phobia of an 11-year-old boy) with relaxation plus music that the child enjoyed and found relaxing. Weil and Goldfried (1973) used in vivo self-relaxation to remediate insomnia in an 11-year-old girl. In this procedure they first used a live therapist, then tape recordings of the therapist's relaxation instructions, then finally nothing other than self-relaxation. In a more comprehensive program, O'Rourke (1977) worked with both academic and social development behaviors of 16 severely emotionally disturbed schoolchildren. Teachers designed success-oriented experiences in a school day program that relied heavily on relaxation and body-awakening experiences.

Implosion therapy represents a variation of the counterconditioning model. Rather than trying to avoid eliciting the anxiety response as in systematic desensitization, in the implosion therapy approach a stimulus or scene is presented that elicits anxiety. In the context of therapist support, the modeling of "nonanxious" responses, and the absence of untoward consequences, the child's anxiety is expected to disappear quickly. This form of intervention has been reported to be successful with such problems as anxiety-related compulsive behaviors (Hersen, 1968) and nightmares (Handler, 1972). This approach has also been used by Yule, Sacks, and Hersof (1974), who repeatedly busted balloons in front of an 11-year-old with a noise phobia. After repeated exposures, the child not only experienced an extinction of the fear reaction, but was described as enjoying breaking the balloons himself. Despite reports of success using implosion techniques, however, some have argued that the effectiveness of the procedure, with adults at least, is approximately equal to that of client-centered therapies (Glass &

Smith, 1976). Gottman and Markman (1978) have concluded that as a technique the magnitude of treatment effect is substantially lower than systematic desensitization.

Interventions based on the counterconditioning model are not targeted exclusively at the physiological response level, because they usually involve additional cognitive or external behavioral-change techniques (e.g., modeling, shaping, social reinforcement, contingency management) that provide new coping skills around which the child develops alternative appropriate behaviors. Though there has been substantial debate as to the mechanisms underlying systematic desensitization (Murray & Jacobson, 1978) and similar covert techniques (Mahoney & Arnkoff, 1978), the techniques are well defined and are derived from a formal theoretical model. Further, Lazarus (1973) has emphasized that many social and personality problems involve cognitive-attributional components, physiological reactions, and overt behavioral and interactive manifestations. Because counterconditioning techniques formally involve emotional responses, cognitive operations, and instrumental behaviors (usually avoidance), they represent interventions that encompass many of these modalities. Such treatments, which simultaneously target several levels of intervention, provide an example of more integrative and multimodal interventions, which can in the future generate more widely applicable intervention models.

Modeling

Modeling is the third major learning paradigm that has been employed in the treatment of behavioral and emotional disorders. In general, the technique involves in vivo or filmed presentations of adaptive behaviors in the stimulus context that is problematic for the target child. Albert Bandura (1971) is the best known proponent of modeling, having demonstrated its effectiveness in numerous contexts. Bandura and Menlove (1968), for example, had dog phobic children watch a fearless model engage in several interactions with a friendly dog. After viewing these interactions, the children significantly increased their willingness to approach and interact with a dog. Johnson and Thompson (1974) reported the successful elimination of enuresis in a 5-year-old boy when he observed his mother reinforcing the successful toilet experiences of a younger sibling. Impulsiveness in first- and fourth-graders has been reduced when teachers modeled reflective behaviors (Bower & Mercer, 1975) or peers modeled covert self-instructions (Goodwin & Mahoney, 1975). Such avoidance behaviors as snake phobias

have been successfully eliminated through modeling of both peers and adults (Kornhaber & Schroeder, 1975) as has extreme social withdrawal (O'Connor, 1969, 1972; Ross, Ross, & Evans, 1971). Treatment effects of modeling have been shown to be durable in the treatment of excessive shyness (O'Connor, 1972), although Keller and Carlson (1974) have noted that the maintenance of these effects depends on opportunities to practice and the continued availability of positive reinforcement.

In a similar vein, Hewett (1965) used imitation training of speech as a first step in the treatment of an autistic child. Bornstein and Quevillon (1976) had therapists verbally model a self-instruction program directed at children (e.g., "What does the teacher want me to do? Oh, that's right, I'm supposed to copy that picture.") They also verbally modeled mistakes so as to try to give children a coping response to mistakes.

Designing for Generalization Across Behaviors, Settings, and Time

The early development of behavioral approaches primarily involved the straightforward demonstration and refinement of behavior-change technology. Operant, classical, and modeling paradigms have served as the basis for a variety of creative environmental manipulation techniques that have been utilized in treating a broad range of behavioral excesses and deficits. In the course of demonstrating the effectiveness of these techniques, behavioral researchers have been critical of their own work in terms of one principal problem: generalization of treatment effects. As a result, generalization has increasingly become a focus of interest and systematic study.

Despite being in a competitive situation requiring that adherents establish the behavioral model as an alternative to the older and more established intervention models, many behavioral theorists and researchers have consistently called for critical self-scrutiny and empirical demonstrations of the mechanisms and effectiveness of behavioral interventions. They have emphasized the importance of reliable evaluations of intervention components and have expressed concern regarding such problematic issues as the generalization or maintenance of treatment effects across time, behaviors, and other settings. Wahler, Berland, and Coe (1979) describe both the pragmatic and conceptual issues relevant to the problems of generalization that have both plagued and challenged the behavioral approaches to intervention with children. Generalization across behaviors refers to the degree to which behaviors other than the direct target of intervention reflect change. Because many referred children experience a range of behavioral problems, interventions that affect only one behavioral class at a time will of necessity be quite lengthy and expensive to implement. Even more problematic is the possibility that improvements in one behavior class will be associated with deterioration in other behavior classes (Wahler, 1975; Williams, 1974). Generalization across settings is also a problematic and crucial issue. Considerable evidence demonstrates that intervention programs successfully implemented in one setting often fail to generalize to other settings (Miller & Sloane, 1976; Wahler, Berland, & Coe, 1979). Of even greater concern are suggestions that behaviors in settings other than those directly the focus of an intervention program may deteriorate in appropriateness (Walker, Hops, & Johnson, 1975; Wahler, 1975; Wahler, Berland, & Coe, 1979). To anticipate and evaluate such potential effects, as well as to design programs that will enhance positive generalization effects and decrease negative generalization effects, Wahler, Berland, and Coe (1979) argue that intervention programs must be designed to focus on more than one isolated response class and more than one setting (Stokes & Baer, 1977). For example, Koegel and Rincover (1974) trained attending behavior, imitation behavior, and basic speech skills to eight autistic children. This training occurred on a one-to-one (1:1) basis between each child and a behavior therapist. Children then interacted with the teacher in the context of groups of varying sizes. The children initially showed only variable success at generalizing their learned skills from the 1:1 context to the group (classroom) context. However, classroom behavior improved considerably when stimulus elements of both contexts were faded in, reinforcement schedules gradually thinned, and group size increased.

Finally, generalization across time represents the extent to which treatment effects endure beyond the treatment phase per se. In the early behavioral literature, it was often the case that although powerful positive treatment effects could be demonstrated, once the formal intervention conditions were removed the beneficial effects disappeared (Graziano, 1978). In fact, Forehand and Atkeson (1977) argue that there is evidence that the rigor of follow-up assessment and evidence of long-term positive treatment effects are inversely related!

To the credit of behavioral researchers and theorists, these issues have been self-identified and aggressively examined. In order to deal with them,

behavioral interventions have been developed so as to increase response generalization, increase generalization across settings, render feasible direct interventions in settings other than the clinic, and maintain treatment effects over time. In general, these efforts have taken the form of programs that employ change agents in the natural environment and programs that target generalized adaptive response patterns.

Modifying the Natural Environment: Training Teachers and Peers

For educationally related goals the behavioral model has seen extensive use for quite some time. As reviewed by Graziano (1978), the technology of teaching machines (Skinner, 1954) and programmed instruction (Gray, 1932) have enjoyed considerable popularity. For clinical problems in the schools, however, the popularity of behavioral principles has come only recently, and not without controversy. Nevertheless, as demonstrations of the direct positive effects of operant, respondent, and modeling principles have accumulated, behavior therapists have begun to develop intervention programs that include training teachers to apply learning principles in order to produce positive change. The use of teachers in the natural environment has been defended in terms of the generalization issues. It has been argued that at least for school-related behavior problems, (1) generalization of positive treatment effects from the clinic are obviated, because treatment occurs directly in the context where the problems occur; (2) generalization across behaviors is less of a problem, for once the teachers learn the various principles of the behavior management they can apply them to as wide a range of behaviors as necessary; and (3) generalization across time—that is, maintenance issues—is less of a problem because when the behavior therapists are no longer available, teachers can still be there to carry on.

The development of this technology has not involved any new or different principles; instead, behavior therapists merely set out to train teachers to apply the same sort of operant, respondent, and modeling techniques that the behavior therapists themselves have directly applied with success. Representative examples of such teacher training include an operant program designed to increase verbal rate in an electively mute child (Griffith, Schnelle, McNees, Bissinger, & Huff, 1975). They found both immediate and long-term (3 months follow-up) effects when the teacher was instructed to give positive reinforcement (with points) for spontaneous speech.

In addition to the delivery of positive reinforcers, withdrawal of occasions for positive reinforcement (time out) has also seen wide application. Sachs (1973) describes a standard format involving (1) clear statement by the teacher to the class as to the unacceptable behaviors, (2) clear statement that performance of such behaviors will immediately result in being taken to the time-out room, and (3) clear statement to the student when transgressions occur as to why he or she is being sent to the time-out room and as to the time period involved. In a variation with normal children, Porterfield, Herbert-Jackson, and Risley (1976) used disruptive behaviors as an occasion for care givers to instruct the child in appropriate alternatives, then institute a brief time-out condition wherein the child was removed from activity and had to observe play activities of the other children before being asked to rejoin. In another variation designed to eliminate high-rate obscene verbalizations, Lahey, McNees, and McNees (1973) instructed the teacher of a 10-year-old student to have the child engage in negative practice (rapidly repeat an obscene word for four 15-minute sessions daily), and to confine the child to a bare time-out room when an instance of cursing occurred (except during the negative practice time, of course).

With socially withdrawn children, Hops (1981) reviewed a wide range of studies that included standard reinforcement for social behavior (e.g., teacher attention, primary reinforcers such as candy, or tokens/points that could be turned in for privileges or other reinforcers), modeling of appropriate social behavior plus reinforcement, and various forms of skill training. Unfortunately, the degree of generalization across time and other settings has "not been overly impressive," though theoretically one would not expect generalization unless it was specifically programmed. Strain and Wiegerink (1975), for example, report an intervention involving multiple base lines (social play across four tasks) with reversals. Contingent teacher attention (verbal praise) produced dramatic increases in social play, and reversals (removal of contingent attention) produced dramatic decreases though not a return to original base-line rates. Modeling of appropriate sociointeractional behavior has produced inconsistent results when used alone (Hops, 1981). However, when combined with prompting and powerful back-up reinforcements (e.g., points both for the target child *and* for the peer contingent on increases in the target child's rate of social interaction), dramatic improvement has been noted (Walker & Hops, 1973).

Consistent generalization across time and contexts cannot be expected unless subsequent settings are carefully programmed for it and environmental agents such as teachers are, in turn, reinforced for consistently applying contingent reinforcement. The apparently obvious assumption that teachers (or parents for that matter) will maintain a regimen of appropriate contingent reinforcement simply because the accruing positive changes in child behavior are "inherently reinforcing" is no longer defensible in light of considerable data demonstrating the absence of long-term positive follow-up effects (Wahler, Berland, & Coe, 1979).

As demonstrated in the Walker and Hops (1973) study, peers have also been used as change agents in the natural environment. J. A. Ross (1974) has trained peers to reinforce positively a chronic thumb sucker for not sucking, and to deliver verbal reminders if they caught him sucking his thumb. In another study, Ross and Levine (1972) used a reversal design to demonstrate that reinforcing classmates contingently on a child's not sucking his thumb significantly reduced the rate of thumb-sucking. In a similar vein, "normal" siblings have been trained to act as change agents for their behavior-problem siblings, resulting in positive benefits not only for the target child but the sibling as well (Miller & Cantwell, 1976). Strain and his associates (Ragland, Kerr, & Strain, 1978; Strain, 1977; Strain, Kerr, & Ragland, 1979) report on the training of intelligent preschool peers either to emit social initiations or to prompt and reinforce play behaviors in autistic peers. Not only did both these conditions produce a greater rate of prosocial responding in the autistic children when they were directly experiencing the intervention, but they also produced spillover effects on autistic children when they were not under direct intervention (Strain, Shore, & Kerr, 1976). Unfortunately, once again the positive benefits of intervention failed to generalize over time or settings.

Modifying the Natural Environment: Training Parents

Gerald Patterson has called the period from the mid-1960s to 1970s the "whoopie" phase in the development of parent-training procedures (Patterson, 1980). Although all three previously described learning paradigms have been employed, operant techniques have received by far the greatest attention. A review of parent-training programs demonstrates that initial emphasis was placed on demonstrating that parents could be taught the same change techniques that are used by behavior therapists in modifying clinical problems in children. For example, Bernal (1972) trained a mother to use shaping and reinforcement principles with her 4-year-old girl who would eat only strained foods. The main element of the program involved making preferred foods and activities (such as television viewing) contingent on eating new foods. After 32 weeks the child had gained weight, was eating well, and had added about 50 new foods to her diet. Kauffman and Scranton (1974) instructed the mother of a 2-year-old thumb sucker to engage in a reading activity with the child and positively reinforce the child (praise and stickers that could be accumulated for a party) for not sucking. Stickers were then faded, and social praise interspersed at other times during the day. A 30-day follow-up revealed no evidence of continued thumb sucking. In cases of enuresis (Samaan, 1972) and encopresis (Davis, Mitchell, & Marks, 1976), parents were instructed to help their children become more sensitive to elimination cues and to provide positive reinforcement for appropriate toilet performance in the form of praise and tangible rewards. In a variation, Wright (1973) instructed parents to begin by administering suppositories or, if necessary, an enema to facilitate predictable defecation, and then to produce positive reinforcement for success (e.g., by game-playing) as well as to punish soiling. External aids were then systematically faded, and successful training was accomplished after an average of 15–20 weeks.

Parent training for socially aggressive and predelinquent children has been the main focus of several major clinical and research programs. Most prominent has been the work of Patterson and his colleagues, who have developed and evaluated parent-training techniques for children aged 5–12 and have conducted considerable basic research. Although the interventions were initially designed to be applied directly by the therapist (Patterson & Brodsky, 1966), concerns about temporal and setting generalizability led to a treatment program involving all elements of a natural environment, particularly the parents. A series of parent-training projects (Patterson, Cobb, & Ray, 1973) and replications (e.g., Fleischman & Szykula, 1981; Weinrott, Bauske, & Patterson, 1979) involved the basic elements of (1) assigning a programmed learning text on social learning principles (Patterson, 1971; Patterson & Gullion, 1968); (2) training parents to define, monitor, and record a range of deviant and acceptable prosocial behavior; and (3) participating in a parent-training group involving instruction, modeling, and role-playing of parenting skills and contract negotiations. Because many referral families were unmotivated, parenting salary

contingencies were introduced. This significantly increased parental cooperation, especially for families of lower socioeconomic status (SES) (Fleischman, 1979). Large-scale studies and replications demonstrate significant improvements after training in such family-process measures as rates of aversive behavior from mothers and siblings (fewer), coercive sequences (fewer and shorter), and positive parental consequences for deviant behavior (fewer) (Patterson & Fleischman, 1979). Outcome measures consisting of parent global ratings and attitudes showed significant improvements often ranging up to 100% (Patterson & Reid, 1973). Similar parent-training programs using global parent-rating scores have reported similar success rates (e.g., Walter & Gilmore, 1973).

Whereas "hard" data such as direct observation and parents' daily reports also demonstrate improvement, the rates of success are more modest than those indicated by global parent-report measures (e.g., Patterson, 1974). In fact, some studies have reported improvement in parental global perceptions whereas more direct measures of a child's behavior reflect no change or even a worsening of performance (e.g., Clement & Milne, 1967; Schelle, 1974; Walter & Gilmore, 1973). These findings represent at best a mixed blessing for adherents of a traditional learning-theory perspective. The model's emphasis on overt behavior requires that modest behavioral improvements are interpreted to mean only modest program success. Yet if the consumers (parents) are quite pleased, and if their perceptions and global ratings reflect reality for them, then at a phenomenological level the interventions are quite successful. Adherents of both dynamic and interactional models are less disturbed than are behaviorists by an apparent discrepancy between objective rates of behavior and global attitudes and perceptions. In the dynamic and interactional models, behavior rates per se do not represent the essence of deviance or normality. Instead, overt behavior is relevant only in terms of its phenomenological representation and meaning, or in terms of its relational impact. Of course, this fact has made it more difficult for the dynamic and interactional models to develop unambiguous measures of therapeutic success, and they have not been able to attain the degree of scientific credibility enjoyed by behaviorists. This fact, among others, has contributed to the continuing schisms to be discussed later in this chapter.

Nevertheless, despite the occasional disparity between global parent reports and directly observed behavior, numerous replications show the learning-based approaches to treating children with high rates of aggressive behavior in the home to be a most promising intervention, because roughly "two-thirds to three-fourths" of these very troubled families have experienced significant improvement (Weinrott et al., 1979). Further, total cost is often fewer than 30 and as low as 10 professional hours. The careful and programmatic work of Forehand and his co-workers with noncompliant children has provided considerable refinement of knowledge about the elements of successful parent training and its generality of effects. In addition to demonstrating the global "social validity" (measured in terms of improvements and compliance, parental perception of the child's adjustment, and parental depression) in the parent-training program (Forehand, Wells, & Griest, 1980; Peed, Roberts, & Forehand, 1977), these investigators have specified and evaluated numerous aspects of the parent-training process. McMahon, Forehand, and Griest (1979) demonstrated that specific training in learning-theory principles, in addition to the usual behavioral skill training, enhanced program effectiveness (including temporal and setting generality) and consumer satisfaction. Bean and Roberts (1981) demonstrated that parent-established time-out release (behavioral and temporal; for example, "Come out when you have sat without moving or talking for 5 minutes") produced significantly greater child compliance than did child-determined time-out release (e.g., "Come out when you are ready to behave"), which was in turn superior to controls. Roberts, McMahon, Forehand, and Humphreys (1978) demonstrated that training parents to manipulate antecedents (e.g., commands for compliance) as well as consequences (e.g., time out) resulted in even greater program success. Moreover, Wells, Forehand, and Griest (1980) demonstrated successful response generalization of program effects to untreated behavior. However, Roberts and Hatzenbuehler (1981) warn that generalization will be restricted to those untreated response classes that are functionally related to the targeted behavior, a conclusion similar to that of Wahler, Berland, and Coe (1979).

Follow-up studies of parent-training programs have produced mixed results. Though the Patterson studies generally lack control groups, 12-month follow-up data (Patterson & Fleischman, 1979) showed that 76% of the treated families who were available for follow-up had total deviance scores within the normal range. Ferber, Keeley, and Schemberg (1974) reported follow-up rates of deviant behavior to be comparable to preintervention base lines. However, the program had demonstrated only minimal effects at termination, so lack of follow-up effects are not surprising. Patterson (1980) concludes that for those programs that demonstrate strong effects during treatment, follow-up data are generally positive.

Programs Designed to Change General or Stylistic Ways of Behaving

Proponents of the traditional learning-theory perspective have emphasized situational specificity and the environmental control of behavior, including the previously described one-way directionality of behavior causation and maintenance. As a result, most learning theory-based interventions with children and youth have involved the direct manipulation of antecedent and consequent environmental events by therapists, parents, or other change agents. However, several programs have developed alternative strategies, including (1) removing the child or youth from the natural environment and (2) training in generalized social skills and self-control strategies.

Alternative Treatment Environments

Social learning principles, particularly contingency management and token economy systems, seem particularly well suited for institutional contexts that have the potential for a high degree of structure and control. With delinquent and predelinquent youth, the logic of institutional approaches to behavior change is that in a controlled and structured context, antecedent and consequent conditions can be reliably arranged so that previously maladaptive response patterns will be extinguished and new, more adaptive patterns learned (Burchard & Barrera, 1972; Cohen & Filipczak, 1971; Jesnes, DeRisis, McCormick, & Quedge, 1972; Karachi, Schmidt, & Cairor, 1972).

As an alternative to traditional approaches to institutionalization, community-based residential living settings (e.g., group homes) have also been developed. The most completely described and evaluated example of such an alternative is the Achievement Place Project, which has been disseminated to over 140 cities across the United States (Phillips, Phillips, Fixsen, & Wolf, 1971, 1972). Consisting primarily of predelinquents, each group home consists of six to eight adolescents and a set of intensively trained houseparents. Each youth lives in a "real home" environment under an individualized token economy system. The youths attend regular schools, often earn weekend visits to their natural homes, and participate in group home meetings concerning governance issues. Teaching parents are carefully selected and trained to monitor each youth's behavior, as well as to guide, prompt, model, and reinforce adaptive academic social, interpersonal, and independent living skills. Self-report and less reactive delinquency data show that during the treatment period, Achievement Place youths experience a marked reduction in delinquency, coupled with increases in school performance when compared to base line and to comparison group homes not based on the social learning, teaching-parent model.

Unfortunately, the follow-up data also suggest that after leaving the Achievement Place Program, earlier gains are essentially lost and delinquency rates approximate comparison programs (Kirigin, Wolf, Braukmann, Fixsen, & Phillips, 1979). This finding is consistent with the often-encountered long-term outcomes of institutional and alternative living environment programs that remove delinquent youth from their natural environments and then return them: impressive control and demonstration of improvement during the period of removal, then a deterioration of positive effects after reentry into the natural environment (Patterson, 1980). However, the general absence of randomly generated no-treatment controls leaves open the question whether or not this deterioration is less than, equal to, or worse than no treatment at all.

These results, of course, are quite predictable given the social learning theory emphasis on current environmental influences on behavior and in light of these programs' consistent failure to plan *carefully* for generalization (Wahler, Berland, & Coe, 1979). Though parents and caretakers in the natural environment are "educated" after a fashion, none of the institutional and alternative living programs have developed formal interventions that have been shown to produce the kinds of enduring environmental (especially family) changes necessary to maintain adaptive behavior styles of the youth when they return to the natural environment. Until such reentry components have been developed, it appears that even though institutions and alternative environments can impressively change behavior, these gains will not be maintained.

The Achievement Place Program has recently made great strides in struggling with this issue by attempting to identify variables within and subsequent to the treatment experience that relate to both short- and long-term positive effects. Recently, for example, Bedlington, Braukmann, Kirigin, & Wolf (1979) and Solnick, Braukmann, Bedlington, Kirigin, & Wolf (1979) found strong inverse correlations between self-reported delinquency and the amount of time youths talked to ($r = -.95$) and were

in proximity to ($r = -.81$) the group home parents. Youth ($r = -.65$) and teacher ($r = -.56$) measures of subjective evaluation of program effectiveness were similarly negatively correlated with self-reported delinquency. These findings suggest important relationships between delinquency and the environmental milieu experienced by the youth, relationships that could well be relevant to the reentry process. The precise and programmatic nature of Achievement Place researchers' continuing investigations promises to unravel many of the necessary ingredients for treatment programs operating as alternatives to the natural environment.

Cognitive Self-Management Approaches

To this point the present chapter has been focused on two predominant levels of intervention with children. The biological and internal-dynamic models have targeted internal (physiological and psychic) processes and mechanisms, whereas the majority of the behavioral approaches have focused on specific overt behavioral events. This chapter has also implied that among the psychosocial therapies the upsurge in popularity of the behavioral approaches during the 1960s and 1970s has reflected a major evolution from an emphasis on internal events to one on external events. This, however, is not entirely the case. Staats (1975), for example, articulated principles and techniques that targeted language and cognitive operations. He and others described below have suggested that overt behavior is not the sole, or always appropriate, target for intervention.

These cognitive approaches contrast with traditional behavioral therapies in that the targets of intervention are not overt behaviors but instead are processes that are assumed to underlie overt behavior. An assumption follows that if the cognitive strategies that underlie behavior can be changed, then behavior will change as well. In traditional behavior therapy the surrounding environment is manipulated; things are done *to* the child's surroundings. In cognitive therapies, the child's thinking is manipulated and then the *child* does things to his behavior (Kazdin, 1979). This strategy identifies the child as a primary change agent, a portable therapist. This view of the child is shared to some extent by dynamic therapy approaches as well. Even though the focus is on presumed internal processes, however, the newer cognitive approaches rest on different principles than do psychodynamic views in that the former point out that cognitive intervention deals with thinking rather than with the more nebulous "feeling" domain of the dynamic writers (Urbain & Kendall, 1980).

Much of the intervention technology per se employed by cognitive interventionists is reapplication of basic classical and operant paradigms and is thus characteristically "behavioral." Techniques such as the viewing of models, programmed instruction and coaching, and sequential rehearsal are borrowed from the behavioral literature. Thus it is not the technology but rather the target (i.e., cognition) of these approaches that distinguishes them.

Aside from the nature of their intervention strategies, cognitive therapists reflect a return to a relatively individual focus with an emphasis on internal operations that are assumed to mediate, create, and maintain problematic "external" behavior styles. The basic research and language of workers in this area have resulted in part from an attempt to generate useful analogies for theory building and for predicting complex internal processes and overt human behavior (Enright, 1976; Henker, Whalen, & Hinshaw, 1980; Meichenbaum & Asarnow, 1979; Wollersheim, 1981). Questions such as the nature of self-control, attribution of meaning, cognitive restructuring, and coping, to name a few, have prompted the sort of theorizing decried by applied behaviorists for years. In terms of theory building and systematic hypothesis testing, however, the cognitive literature can be described as still being in a stage of infancy. There has yet to emerge a unifying model for identifying and classifying dimensions that may mediate the effects of specific interventions and information processing in general. Nevertheless, though the strategies, range of targets, and dimensions relevant to the cognitive perspective have been diverse, several assumptions have been identified as being common to the various research and intervention reports appearing in the literature. These are as follows (see Mahoney & Arnkoff, 1978):

1. Human behavior patterns are developed through cognitive processes.

2. These processes can be initiated or modified using procedures identified and described in learning research.

3. Intervention is a process whereby target individuals learn or relearn cognitive processes, which will then alter the overt behaviors that are related to the targeted cognitive processes.

Cognitive therapies still reflect a commitment to social learning theory and research such that intervention is intended to modify skills or to establish new and more effective skills. Nevertheless, they differ from traditional behavioral approaches in that the training, which is presumed to be the active ingredient in these therapies, is directed at cognitive processes. These processes, in turn, are believed to mediate behavior across time and settings. Thus the modification of cognitions is hypothesized to have a "built-in" generalization component. The potential for these approaches to effect change across a wide array of problems and settings for the individual child is an important basis of the appeal of the cognitive approaches. As will be seen, targeting cognitions has not offered an easy solution to the problem of generalization, but these disappointments have prompted the current focus in that literature on the identification of variables, internal and external, that may mediate generalization of training effects.

Several early studies focusing on cognitive processes raised hopes as to the potential advantages of cognitive intervention with children. Meichenbaum and Goodman (1971) taught strategies for self-verbalization as a means for young, impulsive children to increase their levels of self-control. Their results demonstrated treatment effects in subsequent tests of cognitive reflectivity. Unfortunately no generalization was observed in the classroom in terms of overt behavior. Similarly, Goodwin and Mahoney (1975) used a procedure in which aggressive boys were exposed to a model self-administering instructions and maintaining impulse control. Subjects were then placed in the same situation as the model and coached in the procedure. Generalization was reported to the classroom, as reflected by rates of observed disruptive behavior, but the absence of a control group limited interpretation of the data. Studies performed since this work have begun to deal with some of the questions raised by these early efforts, including issues such as the generalization of effects across measures, tasks, and settings, the nature of the change agent, and the effects of combining cognitive and behavioral procedures.

Measures, Tasks, and Settings

In terms of generalization across settings and tasks, the status of self-control intervention is not clear. Gottman, Gonso, and Schuler (1976), for example, used self-instruction to teach social skills to two isolated elementary schoolgirls. The girls observed a filmed model who verbalized a stepwise procedure as to how to anticipate, plan, initiate, and engage in a social interaction. This was followed by actual rehearsal and coaching of the procedure with an adult coach. Nine weeks after intervention the two girls continued to show an improvement in their peer-rated social status, but no improvement relative to an untreated control group was observed in the number of peer contacts. So although some generalization over time (9 weeks) was documented, generalization was not observed to occur with respect to the desired treatment goal (decreased social isolation). In contrast, Dougles, Parry, Marton, and Garson (1976) used a self-instruction procedure to train children on noninterpersonal academic tasks, and did report generalization to tasks that were similar to training tasks. Kendall and Finch (1975, 1978) have also reported generalization to impulse-control training across rooms, games, and therapists (1976), and from training-task performance to improved teacher ratings (1978). Another program reporting success in generalization across measures was that described by Camp, Blom, Hebert, and van Doorninck (1977). In their "Think Aloud" program they used modeling and verbal-mediation skills training to target both identified cognitive and interpersonal problems of aggressive second-grade boys. They reported improved teacher ratings on aggression for both experimental and control subjects, but experimental subjects showed significantly greater improvement in terms of number of prosocial behaviors. In addition, they described changes in test score patterns, with experimental subjects more closely resembling "normals" on posttest scores. However, Urbain and Kendall (1980) reported a lack of change in teacher ratings of impulsive-aggressive behavior despite demonstrated shifts in sociocognitive measures of problem solving and perspective taking. Even when generalization is reported, attempts at replication have failed. Bornstein and Quevillon (1976) reported success in the use of self-instruction to increase on-task behavior of an overactive child, but a subsequent modified attempt to replicate those findings was unsuccessful (Friedling & O'Leary, 1979).

Change Agent

In an attempt to improve generalization across settings as well as to target behaviors not accessible in the classroom or clinic, some attention has been given to the nature of change agents, as well as the question of who functions effectively as a change agent. Glenwick and Barocas (1979) used the procedure described by Meichenbaum and Goodman (1971) for acquisition of verbal self-regulation skills. They trained teachers and parents to teach fifth- and sixth-grade children the skills, but after 4 weeks of training found only slight differences when parents and teachers each or jointly conducted training as compared with an experimenter. In addition, most gains were obtained on measures relating to academic achievement, with no classroom gains being reported. Somewhat related is a study reported by Wells, Forehand, and Griest (1980), in which mothers of noncompliant children received self-control training in which they were trained to self-monitor their performance of new parenting skills. As compared with the children of a group of mothers who received only parenting training, the children of the self-monitoring mothers were more compliant and less deviant. These gains were maintained at follow-up (approximately 70 days).

A number of studies have been focused on the effects of self-reinforcement and self-monitoring versus teacher reinforcement and monitoring. Using a multiple-base line procedure, Edgar and Clement (1980) compared the effects of teacher-controlled with self-controlled reinforcement and found the self-controlled procedure to be more effective in increasing academic behaviors (looking, talking, writing, and reading). Generalization from academic behaviors to academic achievement was inconsistent, with only one of four scores (correct answers to reading questions) showing a significant gain. Related to the question as to what kinds of change agents are effective and who they should ideally be is the question as to what aspect of self-administered therapy is effective. Clement, Anderson, Arnold, Butman, Fantuzzo, and Mays (1978) and Argast and Clement (1980) have compared the effectiveness of self-observation with self-reinforcement in changing rates of covert behaviors (e.g., attending, out of seat, aggression, vocalizing), and have found self-reinforcement to be superior to self-observation.

Treatment Combinations

It could be argued that all the efforts described thus far represent a combining of cognitive and behavioral techniques (modeling and behavioral rehearsal). Some workers, principally Kendall and his co-workers, have considered the question as to what the active ingredient of these intervention techniques might be. They have combined cognitive and behavior components of training (Kendall & Finch, 1979) and have varied the nature of the cognitive training (Kendall & Wilcox, 1980). Combining a response-cost contingency program and cognitive self-instructional training, they treated 20 impulsive, emotionally disturbed children. Of six verbal codes used, differences between treated and untreated groups were significant for one measure: on-task verbalizations. This finding was interpreted as support for the efficacy of the combined treatments in changing verbal behavior. In contrast with a focus on verbal measures, Kendall and Wilcox (1980) have combined a response-cost contingency with self-instruction training and varied the type of self-instruction: concrete (task-specific) versus conceptual (generally applicable) self-instructions. They found no changes in self-report data, but blind teacher ratings of both self-control and hyperactivity indicated change in the desired direction for both the concrete group and the conceptual group, with the differences between concrete and control groups being nonsignificant. The nature of the relationship between verbal and nonverbal behavior has still not been identified, but given the importance assigned to this relationship in the cognitive approaches (Mahoney & Arnkoff, 1978), further study of this issue is pivotal to the continued development of these intervention approaches.

The promise of cognitive self-control approaches as a solution to the problem of generalization has not been realized, and, though the subject of generalization remains central to writers in this area (Kendall, 1979; Meichenbaum & Asarnow, 1979; Wahler, Berland, & Coe, 1979), research findings have not been encouraging. Of course, concern with generalization is central to the development of any intervention approach, but inasmuch as it is the precipitating event to the emergence of the cognitive approach, it is preeminent. Paradoxically, however, focus on the generalization issue may be having the effect of making efforts in this area seem "helter-skelter." Current work seems less grounded in basic and existing applied research than it seems to represent stopgap efforts to find the key to the temple of generalization. As a result, the development of these approaches has been unsystematic.

Despite the importance of generalization, attention to this issue may be somewhat premature in light of the fact that the outcome data have been no more impressive than the findings on generalization. They are, in fact, quite modest. Given the meagerness of outcomes, one is not surprised to discover limited generalization inasmuch as there are frequently very few cognitive or behavioral shifts *to* generalize. At this stage in their development, either these approaches must be established as effective in producing more than "promising" outcomes, or focus should be given to testing the utility of the technology and the assumptions that underlie their use (see Wahler, Berland, & Coe, 1979). What began as a responsive attempt to deal with the thorny problem of generalization has developed into, at worst, a grab bag of studies with inconsistent and marginal findings and, at best, a vehicle for asking important and basic questions as to the relationship between cognition and behavior. This is potentially no small contribution. In the intervention literature writers are more often considering the importance of perception

and causal labeling as processes that define the meaning of behavior not only to the child but to the child's surrounding interpersonal milieu as well (Henker et al., 1980).

The salience of cognitive variables such as attribution is underlined by the findings of workers such as Griest, Wells, and Forehand (1979) that overt behavioral acts may be less useful in discriminating problem behavior from non-problem behavior than are the labels given those events. The implication that intervention is a relabeling process (i.e., a cognitive one) makes the development of programmatic research in the area of cognitive self-management an important facet of the intervention field in general.

To summarize, the cognitive therapies emphasize that children should not be seen as passive reactors to external environmental manipulation, but they should instead be seen as interpreters of their own experiences and as influencers of their environments (Bandura, 1971). Their behaviors are, in part, a product of that interpretation, and that interpretation varies with the developmental status of each child as well as with individual learning history. The formal consideration of children's cognitive and interactive contributions to adaptive and maladaptive behaviors has had a powerful impact on both behavioral theory and technology.

Discussion of behaviorally based interactional approaches will be deferred (see *Family-Interactional Models*), but it is important to note here that these approaches represent a point in the development of behavioral approaches as they have been increasingly influenced by research in areas such as cognition and communication. At this point, it is difficult to determine whether or not these and other trends represent a movement to new levels of integrated behavioral theory, or movement to a set of (at times) contradictory "mini-models" that will contribute toward splintering the field.

FAMILY-INTERACTIONAL MODELS

In the early history of intervention approaches to children with social and personality problems, interactional models experienced relatively little impact and popularity. Currently, however, they experience wide popularity to the point that they have been described as being a part of the third major revolution in mental health (Hobbs, 1964). The popularity of interactional approaches in general, and family therapy in particular, has resulted in large part from growing disenchantment with the "traditional" dynamic and behavioral treatment approaches. Clinicians have experienced this growing disenchantment with directly treating an individual child in a traditional one-to-one (1:1) format when, in so many instances, others in the child's environment could so easily influence or undermine intervention (Bell, 1963; Satir, 1967). Studies demonstrating the superiority of family therapy over individual therapy (Wellish, Vincent, & Ro-Trock, 1976), as well as the previously discussed data on behaviorally oriented parent-training approaches that question the generalization of treatment effects across settings and time, have also led more and more clinicians to search for models that formally define and develop techniques for treating entire families rather than a single child and one or two of the parents (Haley, 1963, 1973; Lutzker, 1980; Wahler, 1969; Wahler, Berland, Coe, & Leske, 1977). Thus, whereas a decade ago family therapy was seen as an adjunct to "real" (i.e., 1:1 insight-oriented) psychotherapy, by the end of the 1970s it was increasingly seen as *the* treatment of choice for a wide range of problems. Stanton (1980b) provides an impressive list of various disorders that are described as having been successfully treated in a family-systems modality.

Contributions to Current Interactional Approaches

Statistical and Methodological Advances

One of the most important bases underlying advances in the development and application of family-interactional models has been the development of statistical tools that accommodate the interdependency of interacting units. Because psychology has traditionally adopted a one-way cause-effect paradigm (i.e., independent and dependent variables), most traditional statistical models require statistical independence between subjects. However, the main tenet of interactional models is that members are mutually interdependent and influence one another in a reciprocal or circular fashion. Even with limited statistical and methodological tools, the early systems and interactional researchers developed numerous large-scale research projects to understand the interaction processes in family systems (e.g., Bateson, Jackson, Haley, & Weakland, 1956; Cheek, 1965; Farina & Dunham, 1963; Ferreira & Winter, 1965, 1968; Fontana, 1965; Framo, 1965; Goldstein, Judd, Rodnick, Alkire, & Gould, 1968; Haley, 1967a,b; Handel, 1965; Hetherington, Stouwis, & Ridderg, 1971; Hill, 1964; Jackson, 1959; Levinger, 1963; Mishler & Waxler, 1968, 1970; Murrell & Stachowiak, 1967; Olson, 1969, 1972; Rabkin, 1965; Reiss, 1971; Riskin & Faunce,

1972; Ryder, 1968; Ryder & Goodrich, 1966; Straus, 1968; Strodtbeck, 1951, 1954, 1958; Watzlawick, Beavin, & Jacksin, 1967; Waxler & Mishler, 1970; Weakland, 1960; Winter & Ferreira, 1969; Wynne & Singer, 1963). Unfortunately, methodological and statistical tools were insufficiently developed to keep pace with the conceptual advances being made. Thus many of the major theorists switched their commitment from basic research to the dissemination of therapeutic models and techniques. This process enhanced the clinical popularity of family-interactional models but left the empirical bases of interaction theory somewhat in abeyance.

Recently, however, with the advance of computer technology and such statistical tools as time-series analyses (Holtzman, 1963) and nested-hierarchical designs (Kirk, 1968), the statistical dependency that exists within interacting units such as families has changed the status of dependency from a statistical nuisance to a phenomenon of direct interest (Gottman, 1979). As a result, systems researchers have been able to begin asking questions directly pertaining to these mutual dependencies, rather than having to examine individuals arbitrarily in statistical isolation. This has facilitated the demonstration of interactional model assumptions and principles that were previously too abstract or complex to be available for empirical scrutiny.

Intrafamilial reciprocal influences have been defined by Bell (1979) as "a moving bidirectional system in which the responses of each participant serve not only as the stimuli for the other but also change as a result of the same stimulus exchanges, leading to the possibility of altered response on the part of the other" (Bell, 1979, p. 822). This conceptualization, though clinically very persuasive, has created difficult methodological, statistical, and technical problems for researchers and clinicians. The traditional paradigm in all of psychology has involved a unidirectional cause-effect sequence, in which independent ("causal") variables are manipulated or evaluated to determine their impact on dependent ("effect") variables. The concept of circular causality (or reciprocal influences or bidirectionality), however, renders this traditional cause-and-effect framework meaningless, along with most of the experimental and statistical stratagems that have evolved in the field. In the interactional context, a response is no longer simply a dependent variable, or simply an independent variable (i.e., stimulus for a subsequent response). Instead, a response both sets the stage for a subsequent response *and* alters the nature of subsequent stimuli that in turn will alter future responses. To use Patterson's words (1975), children and parents alike are *both* victims *and* architects of their interactions with each other.

Additional impetus to the growing popularity of family-interactional approaches derives from technical advances that allow for more rigorous experimental demonstration of the basic concepts as well as the therapeutic efficiency of such approaches. For example, Minuchin, Rosman, and Baker (1978) used physiological measures of free fatty acid levels to demonstrate a direct link between certain conflicted family-interaction patterns and direct antecedents of dangerous blood sugar levels in diabetic children. By demonstrating the direct link between these measures across family members and totally different response systems, Minuchin et al. provided persuasive evidence for an interdependency of processes that formerly was only a hypothesis based primarily on clinical folklore and only incompletely developed theory. In a similar manner, Alexander (1973) and Barton and Alexander (1979) developed system-based interaction measures to demonstrate links between family attributional sets, maladaptive and reciprocally dependent interaction patterns, and adolescent delinquency. Attributional sets were manipulated by the researchers to approximate relevant variations in the ways that family members interpret behavior and evaluate the nature and goals of their interaction. In the Barton and Alexander (1979) study, families were placed in a cooperative or competitive situation. In the competitive as opposed to the cooperative situation, nondelinquent family members expressed a modestly higher rate of defensive interactions (e.g., sarcasm, blaming, complaining, belittling) with one another. Delinquent families, in contrast, demonstrated a considerably higher rate of defensive interactions in the competitive versus cooperative set condition. These data suggest that the problematic interactions found in delinquent families (Alexander, 1973) are not ubiquitous, but are instead considerably influenced by the attributional sets family members possess as they interact. Further, family-interactional therapies based on such empirically demonstrated processes have been shown to be more effective with juvenile delinquent populations than dynamic and client-centered approaches (Alexander & Parsons, 1973; Klein, Alexander, & Parsons, 1977), as well as more effective than behaviorally based treatments that focus primarily on the delinquent rather than on the entire family system (Shostak, 1977).

Extensions of Social Learning Theory

A second major contribution of current interactional approaches to treating children is represented in the recent conceptual extensions of social learning theory into the realms of family interaction and therapy as well as larger community networks. Whereas the early behavioral literature focused on one-way cause-effect assumptions involved in developing parent-control techniques, more recent research and clinical efforts have focused more on the interactive nature of families and the bidirectionality of mutual influence.

Patterson and Reid's coercion hypothesis (1970) describes a situation in which a child (for example) emits a high rate of aversive stimulation (such as whining) in a certain context (e.g., shopping with mother). If the mother provides a positive reinforcer (e.g., cookie), the whining ceases at least for a while, and both interactants are reinforced: the mother by the cessation of whining, the child by the receipt of the cookie. This hypothesis represents a model for a wide range of relational interactions, both within and external to the family. The coercion hypothesis represents a well-researched and documented phenomenon with families of aggressive children, and easily translates into several alternatives for clinical intervention. It suggests clearly and objectively defined measures of therapeutic impact, and it goes beyond a specific class of behaviors and instead defines and conceptualizes a relatively common but nevertheless problematic relationship form.

At least as important, however, the coercion hypothesis conceptualizes the interlocking and bidirectional influences of behavior that are increasingly emphasized in the recent theoretical, research, and applied literature. To understand the phenomenon of bidirectionality in relationships, Bell (1979) argues: "We must do more than simply shift perspectives in order to identify reciprocal influences. We cannot climb by cliches" (Bell, 1979, p. 823). That is, reciprocal influences are not simply an additive function of two people interacting. Rather, each provides a context for the other. In addition they are also together in a larger context that has important yet still largely unspecified effects on the quality and outcome of the interaction (Bronfenbrenner, 1979; Minuchin, 1974). For example, such phenomena as the mere presence or absence of a spouse, or the continued support of a mother's role as parent by an ex-husband significantly influence both the quantity and quality of parent-child and mother-child interaction (Hetherington, 1979; Hetherington, Cox, & Cox, 1976, 1978; Parke, 1978).

Wahler and his associates have extended social learning concepts to include relationships existing even beyond the family (Wahler, Leske, & Rogers, 1979). They have described the "insular mothers" who, even with careful and initially successful parent training, are unable to perpetuate the attitudes and parent-control techniques necessary to maintain continuing adaptive behavior patterns in their children. A notable characteristic of these mothers is the fact that they demonstrate a clearly lower rate of extrafamilial relationship contacts than do normal mothers or mothers who are able to maintain therapeutic gains. Further, when contacts do occur outside the home for these insular mothers, they are generally perceived as negative. The phenomenon of insularity, though not measured until recently, represents a potentially useful concept, and may represent a major factor in many of the parent-training studies that report successful intervention but lack of maintenance of treatment effects over time. The insularity hypothesis and similar concepts can lead to conceptual and technical advances in the parent-training treatment literature. Of equal importance is the fact that concepts such as reciprocity and coercion, coupled with Wahler's work on generalization and insularity, represent an orderly, scholarly, and clinically relevant extension of the social learning model into the interactional realm. This extension of behavioral principles not only has added specific knowledge, but has also brought a new commitment to scientific rigor that was present in the early family-systems research but that had waned during the mid-1970s. This reemergence of a commitment to basic knowledge and scientific rigor has profoundly enhanced the legitimacy of family-oriented treatment approaches, which were in danger of becoming clinically popular but losing their credibility within the scientific community. These concepts also reflect an evolution from a primarily technological (e.g., skill-training) focus to one that conceptualizes intervention as a contextually dependent process. Whereas contextual dependency has always represented a main tenet of interactional approaches, it is being increasingly adopted by other models such as social learning theory and the biological approaches described earlier (Whalen & Henker, 1976).

Two recently developed behaviorally oriented family-treatment programs reflect the evolution from a traditional parent-training approach to one dealing with the entire family. Designed primarily for in-home problems of children and youth, these programs are designed for use with both one- and two-parent families, and emphasize techniques that are specifically designed to enhance generalization to the home environment.

Family Problem Solving (Blechman, 1977, 1980) involves the family's participation in the Family Contract Game (Blechman & Olson, 1976) in order to practice, on a step-by-step basis, the processes of effective problem solving. The game uses specific and clear directives involving the basic steps in interpersonal problem solving in order to help the family learn how to identify displeasing behavior, then develop, monitor, and reward desired alternative behaviors (Blechman & Olson, 1976). The problem-solving strategies that are learned can then be used at home to resolve major complaints. The Family Contract Game is ''self-contained'' and employs therapist introduction and monitoring, but therapists do not directly participate on a moment-to-moment basis. One major impetus behind the Family Problem-Solving approach is the failure reported in the literature of many contracting programs, in terms of either participants' failure to comply with contracts (Stuart & Lott, 1972) or high dropout rates (Weathers & Liberman, 1975). Consistent with Stuart and Lott's conclusions, Family Problem Solving is based on the premise that the technological aspects of contracting (i.e., the elements of a contract) may not be as salient for successful intervention as is helping the family learn the *processes* of developing contracts and solving problems. The program's goal is the facilitation of democratic family process, in which interactions are based on a quid pro quo (something for something) principle (Jackson, 1965), and in which the children are directly involved. Initial evaluations demonstrate that the Family Contract Game can facilitate adaptive problem-solving behaviors and the attainment of high-quality contracts during treatment, and that families report the maintenance of positive effects in 6- and 9-month follow-ups (Blechman, 1980).

Robin and his associates (Robin, 1980; Robin, Kent, O'Leary, Foster, & Prinz, 1977) have adopted a somewhat similar strategy in which families of adolescents experiencing parent-adolescent conflict are treated with Problem-Solving/Communication Training. Therapists employ modeling, behavior rehearsal, and feedback techniques to teach problem-solving and communication skills to families in the context of attempting to resolve a family-generated issue. Families are also assigned homework involving the implementation of negotiated solutions and the use of problem-solving and communication skills in everyday activities.

Problem-Solving/Communication Training involves the resolution of specific disputes by (1) defining the problem in nonaccusatory terms; (2) brainstorming alternative solutions; (3) evaluating the benefits and detriments of each solution, resulting in a negotiated agreement; and (4) planning to implement the solution. In the process of being trained to follow these procedures, families are helped to replace negative communication styles (e.g., verbal hostility, inattention, overgeneralization) with positive communication skills such as active listening and I-messages. With random assignment to conditions, preliminary data suggest the clear superiority of Problem-Solving/Communication Training over waiting-list controls, and the possible superiority of Problem-Solving/Communication Training over other forms of family therapy on some process and outcome measures, including parent satisfaction (Robin, 1980). Unfortunately, the degree of generalization to the home is questionable (Robin et al., 1977), suggesting program improvements are necessary.

Nevertheless, the Problem-Solving/Communication Training approach and Blechman's Family Contract Game represent two promising and inexpensive programs for dealing with parent-child conflict problems. They differ from traditional behavioral parent-training programs in terms of not only the technical aspects of training but also the underlying conceptual framework. "Traditional" social learning-based parent-training programs emphasize parent control (or lack of it) of their child's behavior, with the child's influence almost seen as a nuisance factor or "error" variance in the statistical sense. The Family Problem Solving and Problem-Solving/Communication Training approaches, in contrast, legitimize, measure, and often enhance components of the child's influence potential. Parents are still seen as "the leaders," but they are directed to be democratic, not authoritarian or permissive, types of leaders (Blechman, 1980). This recognition and formal inclusion of child influences in family-treatment programs is particularly relevant and important as a developmental issue. Adolescents, compared to younger children, possess considerably more power vis-à-vis their parents, as well as alternative contexts for reinforcement outside the family (Morton, Alexander, & Altman, 1976). Thus simple contingency-management systems are not functional for older children and adolescents (Lutzker, 1980). This developmental reality forces family-treatment programs with older children and youth to incorporate more reciprocal and symmetrical concepts and techniques. Because traditional social learning programs have generally been more successful with younger children than with adolescents, the conceptual and technical extensions represented in the Family Problem Solving and Problem-Solving/Communication Training approaches are most promising and reflect a nice matching of technology with developmental theory.

Systems Therapies

Whereas the social learning extensions represent relatively new and significant contributions to interactional approaches, the backbone of family-interactional approaches has consisted of the "systems therapies," which can roughly be grouped into the strategic family therapies (Haley, 1973, 1976; Palazzoli-Salvini, Boscolo, Cecchin, & Prata, 1978; Watzlawick, Weakland, & Fisch, 1974; Weakland, Fisch, Watzlawick, & Bodin, 1974), structural family therapies (Minuchin, 1974; Minuchin et al., 1978), triadic-based "Go-Between" family therapies (Zuk, 1966, 1971), and Functional Family Therapy (Alexander & Barton, 1980; Alexander & Parsons, 1982; Barton & Alexander, 1980). Though they occasionally differ in terms of the specific concepts and techniques, the systems therapies taken together share several themes and assumptions.

The behaviors constituting the "referral problem" per se are not as important as are family structures, processes, and relationships. In fact, families are often quite capricious in the labeling of a family member as deviant (Lutzker, 1980). Patterson (1975), for example, has shown that siblings are often no more or less aggressive in their in-home behavior than are children referred for aggressiveness. The systems therapies thus posit that problem or deviant behaviors have meaning only in terms of the *functions* they serve in the family system (Stanton, 1980a) or the relationship configurations they reflect both within and without the home.

As emphasized by Wahler, Leske, & Rogers (1979), a referral for an apparently clear-cut problem such as oppositional behavior in a child often involves more complex problems within the family (e.g., with siblings and with parents), as well as possible problems the parents are experiencing as adults outside the home or in the marriage. Unfortunately these problems, functions, and relationship configurations are often not immediately evident during the direct expressions of the problematic behavior. For example, in a single-mother family, a child's fire-setting or encopresis may result in a grandmother's "parenting" involvement during mother's working hours. In addition to providing increased adult contact for the child, the problem behavior in this instance also functions to create a support source that may be otherwise unavailable for mother. To the family-systems therapist, the problem behavior is thus not as relevant as are the relationships involved: a three-generational configuration of potentially blurred parenting responsibilities, a set of conflicting relationship demands on mother (e.g., work vs. parenting vs. her own social relationships), and perhaps a lack of resolution of the mother-grandmother relationship (e.g., grandmother is forced into a developmentally inappropriate role of caretaker vis-à-vis her own daughter). In two-parent families, a child's deviant behavior is similarly often a "side effect" of inappropriate interactions between the mother and father (Mealiea, 1976). Thus systems therapists conceptualize problematic family relationships in terms of triads (see earlier discussion on triangulation under *Current Contributions* in the section on *Internal-Dynamic Approaches*) and larger units. Behavior expressed by one family member to another is often a function of more than just that other person's behavior (Berland, 1976), requiring a focus beyond a particular apparently problematic interchange in order to achieve efficient understanding and change. For the family-systems therapist, it is such structural and functional relationship configurations that provide the basis for specific treatment strategies. Particular care must be taken to ensure that therapeutically imposed changes and contingencies are not inconsistent with the organization and functional relationships in the child's natural environment (Williams, 1974). Treatments attempting to change the behavior per se without taking into account its relationship context will encounter resistance, dropouts, and failure of families to maintain treatment effects over time.

Family-systems therapists also share a developmental or family life-cycle perspective (Morton et al., 1976) such that deviant behaviors are often seen as resulting from natural changes initiated within (e.g., the biological and other changes of adolescence) or outside of the family (e.g., the child begins school, mother or father encounter additional career responsibilities). These changes impose modifications on family structure and process, modifications to which one or more family members cannot or will not respond in adaptive ways. For example, schizophrenia in youth reflects not a child's "problem," but the difficulty the family has in allowing or facilitating the child's process of leaving home (Haley, 1973). Intervention is conceptualized more in terms of reestablishing adaptive developmental processes rather than "curing disease." The therapist helps the family learn new interactional sequences that substitute for the problematic ones they are experiencing (Weakland et al., 1974). When the developmental processes involve extrafamilial systems such as schools, family-systems therapists endeavor to work directly with all relevant systems, both to enhance generalization and to ensure that the systems are not working toward conflicting goals, or operating according to incompatible processes.

Therapeutically, family-systems therapists emphasize three major components of intervention: entering or joining the family (Minuchin, 1974);

therapeutically modifying the family's sets, attributions, and expectations; and educating the family in order to change their behavior sequences (Alexander & Parsons, 1982; Barton & Alexander, 1980; Haley, 1976). Therapists enter the family system in specific ways in order to initiate the process of change, assess the current nature of family functioning, and assess the family's response to initial change attempts (Haley, 1963, 1976; Minuchin, 1974). Emphasis is on the "here-and-now" and reflects the systems notion that current redundant interactions are responsible for the problematic behaviors being expressed. Therapeutic characteristics and style are critically important, as therapists must be able to change the family's view of reality without so violating the family's values and expectations that they reject the process of intervention. To accomplish this, family therapists must possess sufficient cognitive ability to understand the family's values, structure, and dynamics. They must also possess the technical skills to produce change and the interpersonal qualities that mediate the expression of their conceptual and technical operations. The therapist's interpersonal skills include two orthogonal classes of behavior: structuring skills and relationship skills (Alexander, Barton, Schiavo, & Parsons, 1976).

Structuring skills include such attributes as directiveness, clarity, and self-confidence, all of which are necessary for the therapist to "take charge" of the therapeutic encounter, provide the family with a sense of hope and direction, and direct them in ways that produce lasting change (Alexander & Parsons, 1982; Haley, 1976). Relationship skills include sensitivity to affect, an ability to relate family members' experiential reality and affect to overt behavior, and sufficient warmth and humor that family members can feel less trapped by their existing circular and problematic interactions (Alexander & Parsons, 1982).

The "therapy" component of intervention involves changing the attributional sets, perceptions, and expectations of all family members through relabeling (Alexander & Parsons, 1982; Minuchin, 1974). *Relabeling* involves a reattribution about the meaning of a family member's behavior (Barton & Alexander, 1980) in terms of motives or context. The overcontrolling mother is relabeled as "concerned" (Minuchin, 1974); the oppositional adolescent as "struggling for identity," and so on. Related to relabeling is *nonblaming,* or "positive connotation" (Palozzoli-Selvini, Boscolo, Cecchin, & Prata, 1978). This technique involves ascribing positive motives to family members' behaviors and interactions. Family-systems therapists avoid negative labeling or blaming of any family member's behavior or motives. Family members are characterized as doing the best they can, and as being trapped by circumstances, their past histories, biology, and so on. This positive emphasis enhances family motivation and dramatically reduces the resistance so often lamented by clinicians (Alexander & Parsons, 1982; Stanton, 1980a). Relabels must also be plausible to family members, and must be tied to subsequent educational techniques that will help the family members maintain a more benign form of behavior, because reattributions not supported by subsequent behavior changes will not be maintained.

In the context of ascription of positive motives, the *educational* component of family-systems therapy involves therapists directly changing behavior. The specific activities designed to change behavior may include re-creating communication channels and manipulating space (Minuchin, 1974), giving directives (Haley, 1976) or assigning homework tasks, training in communication and problem solving, and engaging in contingency contracting (Alexander & Parsons, 1982). Haley (1976) uses directives as a major tool, designing directives to change the family's subjective experiences to help them behave differently, to intensify the family's relationship with the therapist, and to gather information. An example of a directive is this: ''A father who is siding with his small daugher against the wife may be required to wash the sheets when the daugher wets the bed. This task will tend to disengage daughter and father or cure the bedwetting'' (Haley, 1976, p. 60). There are two types of directives: those designed to get people to do something the therapist wants them to do, and those in which the therapist tells the family to do something when the therapist does not want them to do it. This latter form of directive is designed to elicit rebelling in such a way that the family changes. For example, a therapist might tell the family to behave in ''old'' (i.e., problematic) ways, suggesting that he or she fears the family is unable to behave differently. In this paradoxical context, many resistant families rebel against the directive, behaving in a more beneficial manner (Haley, 1976).

Taken together, these various educational techniques provide families with new ways of interacting, solving problems, and maintaining adaptive relationship forms. Again, the focus of these approaches is away from the internal dynamics of individuals or the topographical features of individuals' behaviors, and is instead directed to the relationships among those individuals. As such these approaches can be said to focus on relationships as the sites of problems and as the entities that should be changed for the benefit of the relationship participants.

Current Status of Interactional Approaches

Whereas during the early 1970s interactional approaches were centered around a few major theorists such as Haley (1963), Minuchin (1974), and Satir (1967), as of the beginning of the 1980s these approaches are undergoing tremendous growth, diversification, and dissemination. The extension of social learning principles into the interactional realm has considerably enhanced the scientific credibility of interactional approaches, and has provided not only a new set of carefully implemented therapeutic techniques, but also new technologies for observing, recording, and statistically analyzing interactional phenomena. In addition, after a period of relatively low rates of basic and applied research, systems therapists have begun systematic evaluation of the basic concepts of the theory as well as the therapeutic effectiveness of the techniques.

Empirical demonstrations of the efficacy of systems therapies with children are woefully few (Stanton, 1980a), but recent efforts involving systematic research programs are promising. Such programs are necessary in order for the systems approaches to avoid repeating the experience of traditional psychodynamic approaches, in which the popularity of the model in the applied professional community was quite disparate from its representation and legitimacy in formal academic training contexts. Examples of such promising programs include the work of Minuchin et al. (1978) with anorexia nervosa. Using what they call Structural Family Therapy, and including follow-up periods of 1½ to 7 years, Minuchin et al. report an 86% complete recovery rate, defined in terms of both the cessation of anorectic behavior, and the amelioration of psychological variables associated with it. Though control groups were not present in the study, this success rate compares very favorably with the usual success rates of 40–60% reported for anorectics (Stanton, 1980a). In their major review of over 200 outcome studies of family and marital therapy, Gurman and Kniskern (1978) note the promise of Structural Family Therapy with psychophysiological disorders in general. Though not involving well-controlled designs, ''the use of highly objective change measures (e.g., weight gain, blood sugar levels, respiratory functioning) constitute, to us, compelling evidence of major clinical changes in conditions universally acknowledged to have extremely poor prognoses when untreated or treated by standard medical regimens" (Gurman & Kniskern, 1978, p. 832).

Zuk's "Go-Between" family therapy for emotionally disturbed children has been carefully evaluated by Garrigan and Bambrick (1975, 1979). In a well-controlled study involving both male and female youths (aged 11–17), families were randomly assigned to one of two treatment conditions: family therapy or a program involving parent group discussions and seminars. Unfortunately, data are not reported describing the extent to which families in the group discussions and seminar programs (controls) actually used services; a potential confound thus exists because the family-therapy group may have received more professional attention. However, the data are impressive in demonstrating the superiority of the brief family-therapy program, both in the contexts of school and home, as well as at a 1- to 2-year follow-up interval (data available on 85% of the cases).

In a comprehensive and programmatic series of well-controlled studies with delinquent youth, Alexander and his associates have provided an empirical base for and evaluation of Functional Family Therapy. Based on a literature review of interaction studies and a research project examining the different interaction patterns of delinquent and nondelinquent families (Alexander 1973), the Functional Family Therapy model was developed, which integrated the interactional framework and many of the techniques of "traditional" systems therapies and the behavior-change technologies of social learning therapies (Alexander & Parsons, 1982; Barton & Alexander, 1980). Functional Family Therapy is a short-term conjoint family approach that involves also direct intervention with associated systems such as schools, vocational training programs, extended family networks, and peers. Intervention consists of the two previously described major (and usually sequential) phases of *therapy*, (especially relabeling, nonblaming, and a relational focus) and *education* (communication training, contracting and negotiation, and task assignments designed to enhance generalizability).

A critical component of the model is the assessment of the interpersonal functions maintained by the maladaptive interactions. Intervention is designed to legitimize, not change, these functions. Family members are first motivated (through therapy), then helped (through education) to learn new and acceptable ways to maintain their interpersonal functions. For example, a youth who creates interpersonal distance through withdrawal learns alternative ways to distance (e.g., via negotiating), just as a parent who creates contact via smothering learns new ways to create contact. The creative aspect of the program involves providing family members with behaviors that integrate apparently incompatible functions such as distance versus contact. The therapy phase involving reattributions is critical to this process.

The functional family model has undergone several evaluations and replications with probation officers, graduate students, and practicing clinicians as therapists. With random assignment of families to treatment conditions, it was demonstrated that Functional Family Therapy alone and combined with individual therapy were superior to individual therapy and no treatment (Klein, Barton, & Alexander, 1980). However, because treatment conditions differed in the amount of professional attention involved, a potential confound existed that could jeopardize the conclusion of the superiority of Functional Family Therapy. Thus a second major study was instituted, involving delinquents diverted from the juvenile justice system who were randomly assigned to one of the following: Functional Family Therapy; either of two alternative treatment programs (a "client-centered" family-therapy program and an "eclectic-dynamic" treatment program); or a no-treatment control group. Additional control groups were generated by yoking, on a post hoc basis, untreated families to those treated with Functional Family Therapy. These controls consisted of youth referred at the same time, and for the same offense, as the experimental treatment and control group subjects. However, because case loads were too great for all delinquents to receive formal treatment, their progress was merely monitored by court personnel. Several measures of family process, including talk time and positive interruptions, demonstrated the clear superiority of Functional Family Therapy over the alternative treatments and no treatment (Parsons & Alexander, 1973). Outcome data, consisting of recidivism rates measured 6–18 months after treatment, again demonstrated a significant treatment effect, with Functional Family Therapy (26% recidivism) superior to the alternative treatments (49 and 73% recidivism) and the no-treatment control (51% recidivism) (Alexander & Parsons, 1973). An additional follow-up measure, which represents an indirect evaluation of generalization effects, was reported by Klein et al. (1977). This measure consisted of the percentage of families in each treatment condition who experienced a subsequent delinquent offense by a sibling of the originally referred delinquent. These delinquency rates, measured (on the average) 3 years after therapeutic intervention, again reflected the superiority of Functional Family Therapy, which was associated with delinquency rates that were only one-third to one-half of those found in the comparison conditions.

Subsequent replications of the Functional Family Therapy model with similar and more serious delinquent populations demonstrate considerable stability of the treatment impact of the Functional Family Therapy model (Alexander et al., 1976).

Conclusions

The recent trends in the dissemination of interactional therapies, expansion of conceptual principles, and availability of basic and applied research data suggest that interactional models of intervention will continue to grow in importance and application. The interactional approach is still not central to many psychology training programs, partly because circular or bidirectional causality is not a traditional concept in psychology. However, with more than 300 independent family-therapy training institutes now in existence and growing popularity in academic training programs, the family-interactional approaches promise to play an increasing role in the treatment of children with personality and social problems (Framo, 1979). It is not likely that the interactional therapies represent a panacea, and they may not be appropriate for all types of childhood problems (Blechman, 1981). At this point, adherents of interactional approaches have only begun to provide the conceptual and empirical bases that will allow consumers to know the scope and limitations of such approaches. However, the upsurge in recent activities along such lines has been considerable. In addition, other intervention models are expanding their focus to include an interactional perspective in clinical assessment and intervention. All these factors suggest that the interactional models will continue to grow in popularity and impact.

COMMUNITY APPROACHES

The models of deviant behavior and its treatment reviewed to this point have reflected several common correlated dimensions. Though not always the case, the biological, dynamic, behavioral, and interactional models have each been characterized by a unique set of goals, levels of intervention, and assessment and intervention technologies. To know, for example, that a clinician relies heavily on personality tests is also to be reasonably certain that the clinician adopts a dynamic model, uses some form of "talking cure," and emphasizes some form of

insight or emotional experience such as acknowledging and expressing certain feelings as the major vehicle for change. Similarly, the use of the techniques of modeling and shaping usually implies behavioral assessment and adoption of the behavioral model. Further, interpersonal evaluation and family therapy generally implies an interactional-systems model, just as medication implies the biological model.

Community approaches do not reflect the same type of confound of conceptual model with unique intervention technologies. Instead, community approaches are characterized by a particular intervention *philosophy* and a focus on particular *populations*, especially those felt to be underserved, inefficiently served, or inappropriately served. The specific intervention techniques employed by community interventionists have been developed in other models, so the community literature pays relatively little attention to the development of techniques per se. Instead, primary attention is given to the political and social implications of therapeutic goals and technologies, as well as such "meta-therapy" issues as how to identify appropriate intervention targets, how to identify their needs, and how to bring the appropriate therapeutic resources to bear.

Because of these characteristics, the techniques of many of the specific community intervention programs could be classified under previously described models. They are classified under community approaches because they represent a particular philosophy of intervention and a particular set of goals. Thus this section of the chapter will devote considerable attention to that particular philosophy, programs guided by that philosophy, and some issues raised by the community movement.

The Community Philosophy and Its Evolution

Community intervention approaches reflect an even broader look at environmental contexts than do interactionist approaches. They emphasize that intervention must focus on larger environmental and interpersonal systems and must use more of the resources that a targeted system already has. The reasons for this are partly pragmatic and partly sociological, but intuitively compelling: A community approach is more cost effective in that it capitalizes on existing resources, and it is more positive in that it emphasizes existing strengths and supports existing community norms. In actual practice this orientation often leads community writers to encourage the use of paraprofessionals who are members of targeted communities and to argue the need for community assessments, which include not only needs assessment but descriptions of local values, assets, and goals as well.

Community intervention was born during the 1960s, a time when existing institutions of every kind were vulnerable to attack. During the "Great Society" administration of President Lyndon Johnson all manner of social issues gained visibility, with the "system" being identified as a facilitator (if not the cause) of social and psychological ills. Health delivery systems, including mental health, were criticized for their failures to serve adequately the high-risk groups of society: ethnic minorities, poor, aged, and children. By the early 1970s substantial numbers of lay and professional critics had switched their focus away from the shortcomings of existing technology and were instead critical of the professional groups and agencies that trained students in that technology and that implemented intervention programs. To varying extents, service delivery and training sites came to be viewed not only as behind the times but as active culprits in the promotion and maintenance of an antiquated system that ignored and subjugated many members of the communities whom the agencies and professionals were mandated to serve. In the contexts of a mood for social reform, of public and institutional demands for accountability and self-evaluation, and of professional frustration with arriving too late with too little, a substantial number of professionals began to argue that traditional ideas of intervention ought to be reexamined, modified, and even replaced with a focus on community prevention programs. With respect to children, criticisms have included arguments that mental health professionals see too few children, do not work to change the environments that surround children, and lack abilities to relate to the problems experienced in particular communities.

Thus in the community literature the criticisms of more "conventional" programs concern not the intervention technologies those programs have developed, but the mechanics of service delivery or of their application. For example, in discussing the place of community approaches in the service delivery spectrum, Cowen and Gesten (1978) argue that existing service systems fail in that they serve too late, fail to identify high-risk groups currently or eventually in need of service, and lack resources in a form useable to the target group (e.g., their services require behaviors that are incompatible with the value system, physical capabilities, or economic conditions of the population they are attempting to serve).

The community philosophy rests on the assumption that technology, no matter how refined, is of limited use if it is applied inappropriately or at a point in the development of dysfunction at which only partial gains can be attained. This community-oriented zeitgeist has had an impact on all health delivery programs. It has forced a broadened definition of just what qualifies as intervention, the role of the intervenor (and, importantly, the limits and impact of that role), the settings in which intervention technology can be brought to bear, and even models of health. Community interventionists have articulated an ideology regarding social, environmental, and political bases of dysfunction, the role of the intervenor, and appropriate targets of the intervention itself. They have challenged long-held assumptions guiding the application of technology (e.g., Adams, 1976; Donofrio, 1976) and views of the role of professionals as intervenors (Rappaport, 1977). The community philosophy underlines the importance of the environment as causing or maintaining social and personality dysfunction, defines the environment rather than the individual as being the appropriate target of intervention, and casts the professional in the role of an active interventionist rather than a passive source of expertise. As will be seen, it is this orientation that can also serve as a basis for evaluating the extent to which community programs approximate their goals, or succumb instead to the same pitfalls of service development and delivery against which the community approaches developed in the first place.

The boundaries between community approaches and more conventional modes of intervention are not easy to identify, for the differences do not exist in terms of theory and technology. Very broadly, however, community approaches have extended psychological intervention from a more or less one-to-one basis in the practitioner's office to active involvement with a surrounding community or a specific context (e.g., a school, hospital, work environment). They attempt modifications of the environment that will increase the chances of successful functioning of the individual within that system, regardless of how long the individual is expected to be a member of that system. For example, some community interventionists have focused on relatively "normal" milestone events in children's lives such as entry into school (Newton & Brown, 1967), hospitalization and surgery (Melamed & Siegel, 1975), or even such aspects of day-to-day functioning as real-time conversation (Jewett & Clark, 1979) as appropriate targets of intervention. The goal here is prevention of trauma that might easily become a serious problem but that could perhaps be avoided by educating children as to what they can expect to see and experience. Projects aimed at longer term needs but that are also consistent with the idea of making shifts in the environment in accommodation to special needs include activities such as recreation programs for adolescents (e.g., Cohen, 1976), in which youths engage in socially approved activities rather than delinquent acts. Regardless of their specifics, these programs reflect a commitment to seek intervention targets actively and to identify potentially high-risk and already existing at-risk populations rather than to wait passively and deliver services only when called on or compelled to do so (Cowen & Gesten, 1978; Rappaport, 1977).

Another important element of the community philosophy is that of person-environment fit. It is widely accepted in the community literature that there are differences across individuals and settings, that these differences should be respected (Gesten, de Apodaca, Rains, Weissberg, & Cowen, 1979; Rappaport, 1977), and that health is a condition that exists *relative* to the environmental context. Models of ideal health are rejected as too narrowly defining what constitutes health and as ignoring individual differences. Instead, community writers have urged the adoption of criterion-based models of health that would be sensitive to the fact that behavior norms vary across environments and that what may appear to be deviant behavior may more accurately reflect an adaptation to a particular setting. Implicit to criterion-based models of health is the idea that the critical predictor of dysfunction is the interplay or fit between the individual and the environment (Kelly, 1966; Rappaport, 1977; Zax & Specter, 1974). Individuals who deviate from surrounding social norms, who are particularly dependent on their surroundings (e.g., young, aged, poor, ethnic minorities), or who are encountering unusual or potentially stressful circumstances are the populations on whom community workers focus their energy (Bolman, 1969). Those groups have one thing in common: They are seen as likely to suffer poor "fits" with larger environments, either chronically or acutely. Person-environment fit is a basis on which community intervenors have worked to develop assessment technology useful in the detection of target groups (e.g., Cowen, Trost, Lorion, Dorr, Izzo, & Isaacson, 1975).

Definitions of Prevention

In addition to articulating the community philosophy, community interventionists have devoted effort to the development of a scheme for dimensionalizing and categorizing community-type programs. Such a scheme would presumably be useful for comparing and contrasting community programs among themselves, as well as for identifying boundaries between community intervention and clinical intervention (jurisdictional disputes occur over ideas as well). A number of dimensions have been proposed as being useful in discussing the community literature (Bolman, 1969; Heller & Monahan, 1977; Jason, 1981). These schemes vary considerably in their complexity, and therefore probably in their ultimate utility as well, but these efforts at dimensionalizing this literature are indicative of how difficult it is to identify the boundaries of the community literature. For the purposes of this chapter, community literature will be discussed on the basis of a basic definition of community intervention. Heller and Monahan (1977) have noted that "*a population perspective and a preventive* orientation toward psychological dysfunction perhaps most sharply distinguish between community and clinical perspectives" (Heller & Monahan, 1977, p. 111). *Population perspective* refers to the practice of seeking out and identifying high-risk groups in their natural settings and of understanding the relationships among a population, community, mental health needs, and social ecology in general. One facet of this population perspective that will be a focus in this chapter is community programs for children with social and personality disorders in typical natural settings of home, school, and neighborhood.

The essence of the orientation noted by Heller and Monahan (1977) is that the timing of intervention mediates how effective the technology will be and what particular intervention strategy would be most useful. Herein lies the basis for the important status the community literature has given to needs-assessment technology and dimensions of prevention.

A variety of definitions of prevention have appeared (Bolman, 1969; Caplan, 1964; Jason, 1981; Klein et al., 1977), with distinctions having been made in terms of *levels* of prevention: primary, secondary, and tertiary. Only primary prevention refers to the actual prevention of a problematic event or behavior. Definitions of secondary and tertiary prevention vary somewhat, and some attention has been given to whether or not either should be labeled prevention at all (Heller & Monahan, 1977). Nevertheless, Bolman's definition (1969) of the two has found general acceptance. Secondary prevention is defined as either a decrease in the chances of a *reoccurrence,* or a *reduction* in the severity, of a disorder already identified. Most interventions, including community programs, fall within this category. Cowen (1973) has noted that the term secondary prevention has been used in varying ways: One way refers to the age of the target of intervention (treating young children to forestall further development of a disorder), and the other refers to the stage of the disorder at which intervention occurs (early intervention with acute episodes). The former use of the term secondary prevention has seen greater acceptance than the latter (Heller & Monahan, 1977). Tertiary prevention is defined as a reduction in the impact of an impairment or a reduction in the chronicity of a disorder. Community programs of a tertiary nature for high-risk groups are more likely to be for adults because children and adolescents are not likely to be diagnosed as chronic. Also, tertiary programs such as removal of handicap barriers are not identified as existing specifically for children, but are communitywide.

The commitment to primary prevention (prevention of initial occurrence) and, at the same time, the focus on identification and intervention with high-risk groups may seem to represent a logical inconsistency in the community approaches. The resolution to the problem of trying to identify and correct a problem before it exists is to assume a relatedness of various facets of human functioning to each other and a relationship of early experience to later difficulties (Murphy & Chandler, 1972). For example, preschool enrichment programs for poverty groups have typically been justified on the assumption that disadvantaged environments are also stimulus-deprived environments, and that early cognitive deprivation is predictive of later academic problems, school dropout, and delinquency. Unfortunately, this relationship is largely an assumed one rather than an established one, as there is an acknowledged lack of basic research as to the causal relatedness of early difficulties to later difficulties (Cowen & Gesten, 1978). Nevertheless, programs of primary prevention with high-risk children rest on the assumptions that (1) there are etiological relationships between program targets and aspects of subsequent social and personality adjustment, and that (2) early adjustment difficulties necessarily portend later problems. Though long-term follow-up and basic longitudinal studies that can establish empirical links between immediate secondary targets and long-range primary objectives are for the most part lacking (an exception is Weikart, 1979), community interventionists nevertheless argue the merits of their programs on the basis of the (at times) intuitive appeal that those links do in fact exist.

In the present chapter attention will be given to primary and secondary prevention programs designed for high-risk children—that is, children identified as suffering personality and social disorders, and the family and school systems that most strongly influence their lives. Because of the visibility and relatively greater accessibility of schools, they have been the primary sites for community intervention with children. As will be seen, the sites of programs for adolescents are somewhat more varied, reflecting the expanded interpersonal environments of adolescents relative to children. The aspects of children's functioning most likely to be targeted are their academic skills and their social skills, but the boundary between these two targets is not always clear. Indeed, one is often seen as requisite to the other such that mastery of academic skills (e.g., reading) is often expected to generalize to improve nonacademic experiences. That is, the long-range goal may be to teach children to be successful, happy, and creative in their particular environments, and the development of academic skills is seen as relevant to that end because they are skills associated with success.

Intervention with Preschool and Elementary Schoolchildren

Examples of Programs

Young children have been popular targets for community interventionists because of their conviction that the younger the children, the more flexible and easily changed they are (Cowen & Gesten, 1978), and thus the more cost effective the intervention will be. If early experience in fact "weighs" more in predicting subsequent health, intervention and prevention programs for the very young would seem to be well worth the effort.

Certainly the best known of the community-based preschool intervention programs is Head Start. The initial popularity and later controversy surrounding the usefulness of Head Start parallels the experience of many subsequent community-based preschool programs. Head Start was developed out of the zeitgeist of the 1960s that widespread and sweeping intervention with disadvantaged groups was feasible and desirable, and that intervention with a preventative orientation would ameliorate the problems (e.g., academic failure, poor self-concepts, lack of social skills) thought to underlie major social ills such as poverty. Head Start programs became operational in 1965 (Rappaport, 1977), and by 1970 many studies of their effectiveness had been reported (Cicirelli, Evans, & Schiller, 1970). The evaluation issues of primary interest were immediate social and educational benefits of

Head Start interventions (Campbell & Eriebacher, 1970; Cicirelli et al., 1970; Smith & Bissel, 1970; Westinghouse Learning Corporation, 1969) and the generalizability of those effects over time. The programs varied substantially in terms not only of orientations and curricula employed, but also of how easily they could be evaluated and how successful they were. Thus it is not surprising that the findings from the various outcome evaluations were mixed. With some exceptions, however, it appeared that the positive gains reported were often temporary and frequently modest. The Head Start experience helped, however, to force attention to the need for improved program evaluations and the need for greater rigor in the description and execution of any action program.

Programs for preschoolers and elementary children during and since Head Start follow a basic formula: identification of children who are likely to become in some way of dysfunctional by virtue of their group membership (e.g., poor blacks and Hispanics) or by virtue of individual differences (e.g., lacking the skills necessary to do well in a classroom environment). Considerable effort has been devoted to the generation of needs-assessment devices and to the measurement of social and academic skills that are related to good classroom adjustment. The long-range goal of this research is to establish etiological links between classroom behaviors and subsequent adjustment. The immediate goal of the applied aspects of these programs is to socialize children in ways that it is hoped will lead to successful child and adult functioning. These short- and long-range goals are apparent in those programs that not only focus on intervention, but also include concurrent efforts in early detection. Development of an early-detection technology is necessary so that interventionists can actively seek out at-risk children who might otherwise go without specialized services (Rae-Grant & Stringer, 1969). The percentage of such children who are at risk (Brownbridge & Van Vleet, 1969) has been estimated to be from 30% (Glidewell & Swallow, 1969) to as high as 70% (Kellam, Branch, Agrawal, & Ensminger, 1975).

Early-detection efforts have taken the form of using various measures (e.g., intelligence test scores, personality test scores, parent interview data, teacher ratings, grades) to identify those children from a given school population who appear to be dysfunctional in some way. Not surprisingly, these detection programs are generally tied to intervention programs because, as Cowen and Gesten have stated, "What . . . would be the value of lung X-ray procedures that accurately detected [TB] if there were no meaningful follow-through?" (Cowen & Gesten, 1978, p. 107). Although attempts have been made to establish empirical links between secondary prevention programs and primary prevention of later dysfunction (Cowen, Pederson, Babigian, Izzo, & Trost, 1973; Zax, Cowen, Rappaport, Beach, & Laird, 1968), most work on early detection has been devoted to identifying aspects of children's functioning that may be problematic to their ongoing success in an educational setting (e.g., sociability, tolerance for frustration, ability to follow rules), and that then become the targets of the intervention. For example, LeBlanc, Etzel, and Domash (1978) described a preschool intervention curriculum that was based on those behaviors identified via observations of elementary schoolteachers as well as through direct observations as representing differences between preschool and elementary school settings (e.g., seeking attention appropriately, taking turns, sharing materials). Those behaviors (in this case, attention) were selected as targets because they were thought to be important to successful academic and social functioning in the elementary school classroom. The relevant curriculum goals then became the teaching of those skills that were defined as needed by children in order to adjust to and function successfully in elementary school.

There is some disagreement within this literature as to the most useful orientation of intervention with children. That is, do at-risk children profit more from a specialized academic program, or is it more profitable to emphasize social and personal skills training? There are numerous examples of each for both preschool children and elementary schoolchildren (see Rappaport, 1977), but it is still not clear whether one strategy is superior to the other, or if that dimension of the intervention is relevant at all.

Some programs have been focused on children's intellectual and academic growth. For example, Bereiter and Englemann (1966) argued that the basis of the risk of disadvantaged children is not social or emotional deprivation, but inappropriate or inadequate cognitive stimulation (e.g., poor language models to interact with and emulate) and exercise. On that basis they implemented a preschool curriculum for disadvantaged children based on the idea that children of the poor lack the cognitive experience necessary for them to be ready for the school classroom. To help these children "catch up," the curriculum was designed to be content enriched and language based so as to help target children improve their use of language in the various modes of verbal reasoning, self-monitoring, and receiving and giving information. Subsequent to the early description of the program, Englemann (1970) reported greater short-term and long-term (1 year) gains for children in the experimental program as compared with a more traditional preschool (Montessori) that emphasized self-image and play. These data on the effect of structured instruction with preschool children are similar to those reported by Karnes, Teska, and Hodgins (1970), who also compared a structured, language-based preschool program with more traditional preschool programs (again, Montessori-type programs). They found, at the end of 7–8 months, larger (but not significant) gains in IQ scores for children in the language-based program. One program with impressive follow-up efforts was created for low-income black families as described by Gray and Klaus (1970). In this program preschool children were assigned to a program of either 2 or 3 years, consisting of summer preschool sessions and weekly home meetings throughout a year with a trained home visitor. A third and a fourth group were no-treatment controls drawn locally and from a nearby community. The goals of the program were to overcome assumed deficits in cognitive and language skills, increase tolerance for delay of gratification, establish habits of follow-through and persistence on the part of parents, and change attitudes about the importance of academic achievement. The program, a combination of systematic application of learning technology and materials, plus consistent home visits, parent instruction, and classroom follow-through, achieved significant IQ gains relative to no-treatment controls. Although in follow-up testing the initial IQ gains declined, treatment subjects still showed statistically significant but probably not meaningful differences. In addition, follow-up data were collected at the end of 4 academic years, and at least on achievement test scores the differences between treated and untreated children had disappeared by the end of the fourth year. The experience of this outcome evaluation is reminiscent of the comment made by Forehand and Atkeson (1977) regarding generalization of effects of present training programs. They offer that the better the study's design, the less likely that evaluations will find generalization of effects over time.

Other programs that have targeted mothers as part of the intervention effort have produced findings similar to those described by Gray and Klaus. Programs employing mothers to serve as teachers to their own children in their own homes (Karnes, Teska, Hodgins, & Badger, 1970; Levinstein, 1969), programs using home tutors (Schaefer & Aronson, 1970, cited in Zax and Specter, 1974), and

programs designed to intervene conjointly with high-risk parents and high-risk children (Goodman, 1979), have all reported significant gains relative to no-treatment controls. Unfortunately, few if any follow-up data are reported for these types of programs, raising the issue of lack of generalization over time of home teaching. One of these studies helps also to underline yet another generalization issue: generalization over contexts. Karnes, Teska, Hodgins, and Badger (1970) used, in part, siblings of experimental subjects as no-treatment controls. The use of siblings as no-treatment controls may be reflective of the expectation that treatment effects (e.g., teaching mothers to teach and stimulate their children) will not generalize beyond the target context, in this case a particular child.

Generally then, academically oriented preschool programs are able to achieve initial gains on those measures that reflect the focus of the program (e.g., vocabulary, perceptuomotor skills, concept formation). However, preschool projects for which follow-up data are reported cannot boast many long-term residual effects on dimensions such as subsequent grades, teacher ratings, or test scores. This is similar to the general findings regarding the effects of Head Start programs—that is, early gains that disappear over time. Remembering the aspirations of the Head Start concept as the elimination of problematic characteristics of the poor, the long-term academic gains achieved by community preschool programs require examination. Some argument has been made that these preschool programs for the disadvantaged have failed to produce gains because the schools that children attend after the specialized preschool experience are themselves disadvantaged in some way. McAfee (1972) and Plant and Southern (1972) have attributed failure of preschool programs for Hispanic and native American children to the orientation of teachers. They argue that, as a result of their own teacher education, teachers are more concerned with those aspects of children's school adjustment that make for a smoother running classroom than with the needs of individual children from varying cultural contexts. Bereiter (1972) has argued, in addition, that the lack of generalization over time is a result of the failure of teachers to follow through and employ the instructional methods and curriculum content demonstrated to be effective with preschoolers.

Another skills-training target of cognitive-based programs has been problem-solving training and "causal teaching." In the causal teaching approach, children are taught that all behaviors (events) have causes and that one's responses to those events should be based as much on the causes as on the possible future consequence of the event. This concept is taught through the academic content of the curriculum, and it contrasts with an approach of teaching children facts that should not be questioned. The goal of causal teaching, through generalization of causal principles learned via academic lessons, is to reduce children's punitiveness toward themselves and others and to reduce anxiety in the classroom. Such an outcome is assumed to be more likely to occur because once children better understand the importance of knowing *why* a behavior occurred (e.g., teacher discipline), they may be less likely to react maladaptively. Although the concept of causal teaching has enjoyed some popularity (e.g., Griggs & Bonney, 1970; Ojemann, Levitt, Lyle, & Whiteside, 1955), its utility in helping to ameliorate or prevent academic or socioemotional problems has been challenged (Levine & Graziano, 1972).

In contrast with programs that target children's cognitive development are school-based programs that have been focused on social aspects of children's functioning. Implicit in these programs is the notion that schools prepare children for many aspects of adult functioning, including such non-academic realms as individual problem-solving and social skills. For example, Spivack and Schure (1974) have argued that successful school adjustment is related more to children's *social* problem-solving skills than to their academic prowess. They have further argued that social problem solving may require skills different from those useful in meeting academic material, and that interpersonal skills would more easily generalize across settings and time than would academic skills. With a population of 4-year-old children, they initiated a 10- to 12-week program using Head Start teachers to implement the social interaction curriculum (e.g., listening, causal thinking, and identification of alternatives). Both in a posttest and in a 6-month follow-up in kindergarten classes, experimental children received superior teaching ratings for classroom adjustment and problem-solving skills, with children initially being diagnosed as maladjusted showing the greater gains. Cowen and Gesten (1978) cited a program described by Stamps in which behavioral technology was used to train elementary school children to set more appropriate goals and to self-reinforce. They described this program as being successful in increasing self-awareness and self-acceptance, and in reducing behavior problems. According to Cowen and Gesten, gains made by targeted children were maintained as measured in a 2-year follow-up.

A variant of causal teaching in which interpersonal content rather than academic content has been emphasized is problem-solving training. Problem-solving techniques thought to be useful to the resolution of interpersonal and personal problems have been incorporated into intervention program curricula using personal rather than academic material to illustrate the importance of causal relationships. Lessons in problem solving are presented in gamelike scripts in which students and teachers act out and discuss among themselves the stories (e.g., a student finds something belonging to someone else) in terms of planning future actions and identifying alternative solutions. Larcen, Selinger, Lochman, Chinsky, & Allen (1974) used a problem-solving curriculum with third- and fourth-graders that was based on one developed for preschool children (Spivak & Schure, 1974). Griggs and Bonney (1970) and researchers describing similar approaches to such problems (e.g., Allen, Chinsky, Larcen, Lochman, & Selinger, 1976) have also reported gains on posttest measures.

Interest in skills training as an important content feature of secondary prevention programs has remained high. More recent work in the development of skills-training curricula has been focused less on the content of the program (academic vs. interpersonal material) and more on the *technology* employed to produce changes in targeted behaviors. Allen et al. (1976), for example, reported success in working with acting-out children and shy, withdrawn children when they used teachers and aides to conduct skills-training sessions during which children observed video models, discussed story problems, and practiced solutions. Durlak (1977) and Durlak and Mannarino (1977) have also described successful behavioral programs designed for children identified as having socioemotional problems. They applied token reinforcement programs to increase rates of behaviors incompatible with children's dysfunctional classroom behaviors (e.g., acting out, withdrawal, low rates of learning). Likewise, Clark, Caldwell, and Christian (1979) and Whitehill, Hersen, and Bellack (1979) have used behavioral technology to improve conversational skills and social competence among children diagnosed as having behavioral and emotional problems or as being socially isolated. Finally, Michelson and Wood (1980) have employed an assertion-training program for undiagnosed elementary school children on the premise that effective assertion skills are necessary life skills for all citizens and that all children could benefit to some extent. Whereas behavioral technology is most often the model of choice among practitioners who are developing school-based programs for dysfunctional children and children in general, other relationship-oriented programs (e.g., Rickel & Smith, 1979) are appearing in the literature and may gain in visibility commensurate with increased use of the interaction model.

Issues in Programs for Children

In justifying continued financial and ideological support for schools and home-based intervention programs for young children, community writers are faced principally with two issues: generalizability of treatment effects, and the presence or absence of a relationship between the targets of secondary prevention and long-range primary objectives. An examination of community-based programs for young children suggests that the Head Start experience was not unique. Programs that have appeared in the literature generally accomplish desired gains in the short run, but either these gains disappear over time as reflected in follow-up data, or follow-up evaluations are not performed. The problem of poor generalizability in these programs has been responded to in a way consistent with community philosophy, but not in a way conducive to the rigorous testing of technology and its specific applications. That is, program developers point out larger system influences that mediate and even circumvent program short- and long-term successes (e.g., Bereiter, 1972; McAfee, 1972; Plant & Southern, 1972). Whereas sensitivity to the social, economic, and political forces that shape intervention application and outcome may represent the major contribution of community approaches, community programs themselves are lacking in a unified model that can aid in specifying and modifying these important and powerful influences. Consequently, community programs for children end up having less impact because they deal with these forces as explanations of program failure rather than as the most appropriate targets of community intervention.

At least one attempt to begin the formal study of some of these system variables is work reported by Weikart (1972). He challenged the underlying premise of the Head Start philosophy by asking if, indeed, preschool programs matter; and, if they matter, what variables mediate their success. Generating a two-dimensional model based on differing assumptions as to the role of teachers and children as responders or initiators, Weikart evaluated three types of programs suggested by his dimensional scheme. He found that the specific type of curriculum or teaching method was less relevant in achieving and maintaining gains in children than was staff enthusiasm for the program. He concluded that although curricula and technology may be important as means by which teachers structure materials and organize time, it is the enthusiasm of teachers and their support of individual children that are the critical elements in achieving and maintaining good academic and social adjustment. Indeed, the artifact of reactivity (i.e., teacher enthusiasm), which exists as a threat to the validity of outcome data of many preschool and school-based mental health intervention programs, may actually be the active ingredient of the programs reviewed here. That possibility is consistent with the community philosophy that conventional interventionists have not given sufficient attention to the sites of application and the range of people who could usefully perform those interventions. Unfortunately, community programs themselves do not seem to be attending *systematically* to those variables. They instead are primarily focusing on demonstrating the efficacy of particular intervention strategies and models. The result is that the community philosophy remains a tempting source of many promises, but it has yet to be developed formally as a model of intervention that guides the selection of appropriate targets for reasons dictated by the model.

The second issue related to the success or failure of these programs is the relationship between target behaviors and good adjustment. In general, community interventionists have not addressed themselves systematically to questions of the stability of those behaviors targeted by intervention programs. Although it could be argued that this issue is the bailiwick of basic researchers, the utility of early intervention with children hangs on this sort of epidemiological research, and the fact remains that many of the etiological or even correlational relationships discussed in this literature have not been empirically established. It is not clear which aspects of children's elementary classroom behaviors are related to later functioning, or which of the adjustment problems children frequently experience (e.g., phobic reactions) can be expected to dissipate developmentally without special intervention.

A second potential pitfall in preventative intervention with children is that the intervention itself may increase a child's risk of the trauma the intervention was designed to prevent (e.g., see Melamed & Siegel, 1975). It is also not always clear how changes in targeted behaviors relate to treatment goals. For example, though it may be possible to increase the rates of behaviors thought to be related to friendship formations, one must consider the fact that those children who are targets of those interventions may not show any change in the number of friendships they have (Whitehill, Hersen, & Bellack, 1979). Whereas on the one hand it may be unethical not to deliver services to those identified as being at risk, it may be imprudent to deliver services to those children who may not need them, or to ignore the possibility that the intervention itself may increase children's risk of dysfunction. It may also be imprudent to intervene before researchers establish what constitutes a clinical need, what is developmentally and sociologically transitory, or what is environmentally adaptive. Failure to make these distinctions renders community programs vulnerable to the same criticism that is leveled by community writers at more conventional modes of application. That is, a model of health and dysfunction useful to the development of intervention strategies for one group may be inappropriate with another. Because social systems do not affect people in a uniform way, interventionists must "match" person-environment combinations (Cowen & Gesten, 1978). To be consistent with the community philosophy, then, the concern of community workers would appropriately be more with basic investigations of adaptive functioning, normal development, and life quality (Zautra & Goodhart, 1979), so that community workers would have clearer objectives and criteria for what to focus on, the reasons for that focus, and what the criteria for good outcome might be.

In actual practice, however, community workers have seemed in the past decade to be less inclined to direct their efforts toward making those matches through changes in larger social systems than they have been to applying and contributing to existing intervention technology. Reasons for this may involve several factors. Needs for professional visibility are real, and these needs may more easily be met if an interventionist devotes energies to work that is based on models that have already been demonstrated to produce verifiable and publishable results. The model development that must take place in order to generate and test appropriate dependent variables is time-consuming and thus not an activity many professionals seeking grant funds may regard as attractive. In addition to what may in the short run be a professionally unrewarded activity, community workers are also faced with the difficult challenge of generating programs that can maintain the enthusiasm of staff and participants and, at the same time, satisfy demands for methodological rigor.

It may seem to community workers that methodological rigor is antithetical to program flexibility and spontaneity. Indeed, complaints from community workers have been voiced that stringent demands for rigorous program and variable descriptions, and for outcome and follow-up evaluations, have resulted in boundaries around these programs, stifling creative and unique mental health programs (Goodman, 1979). Of course, packaging a program so as to maintain community and worker support, and at the same time to deliver an effective and needed service, is no mean task. Nevertheless, community intervention boasts a philosophy that can be used as a guide to identifying outcome goals and measures for documenting movement toward those goals. Selection of outcome variables can occur as part of the natural process of specifying goals and targets of intervention, and should be responsive to the active elements of the intervention. If a community endorses the goals and mission of a program, it would also endorse the outcome measures selected by the program's workers. The danger of not being able to show a community systematically what advantages a given program offers is that the impressions given by the program are likely to be based on extreme examples, hearsay, and political whimsy. Those forces are no less stifling of creativity and worker enthusiasm than are requirements for reliable program evaluation. In fact, the reverse is more likely to be the case.

Intervention with Youth

Examples of Programs

According to Weiner (1970), adolescents are the largest users of mental health clinics in the United States, though only about one third of them actually receive treatment. He argues that youth represent a vast underserved population that could be helped by preventative intervention. In this context, community-based programs for youth have, for the most part, targeted adolescents in school or in settings that are near the target population either physically or in terms of "on-call" availability of staff (e.g., big brother programs). These programs also tend to be directed at youths with already identified social problems, notably delinquency. As with programs for younger children, community youth programs are generally focused on the individual such that interventions are designed to upgrade or shift the nature of a youth's experience through specialized academic and interpersonal guidance, structured social skills training, and job training. In contrast with programs for children, however, adolescent programs implicitly or explicitly include the element that intervention may be for the benefit of the youth but it must also offer benefits for other members of society as well. For example, programs for teenage mothers may be designed to improve their job skills, or personal relationships, or health, but they are also expected to benefit indirectly the children of these mothers (Lipsitz, 1977). Likewise, programs for delinquents are evaluated in terms of the extent to which adolescents cease to be a danger to people and property about them.

The group of adolescents most likely to be recognized as at risk and therefore in need of some sort of preventative program are status offenders and index offenders. *Status offenses* are those crimes that are unique to minors in the sense that they are not adult crimes (e.g., truancy, ungovernable, smoking, runaway). *Index offenses* are those that would be criminal acts regardless of the age of the offender. Even though it is not clear as to which status offenders will become index delinquents and, later still, adult criminal offenders, secondary prevention programs are frequently focused on status youths. At the same time, programs for index offenders, though often defined as secondary prevention, are often actually tertiary prevention programs. For example, Cotton and Fein (1976) described a community program for index delinquents with records of aggressive and antisocial acting out. Their outcome recidivism measure was not so much the reduced *rate* of recidivism (secondary prevention) as a shift in reason for the recidivism from physically aggressive acts to less violent ones.

Youth programs identified as community oriented find their roots in a theory-based social policy that was popular in the 1960s, to the effect that delinquency was caused by the interruption of or absence of social and economic opportunity (Clark & Hopkins, 1969). This attitude pervaded early community action programs designed for youth. Consistent with the view of delinquency as being rooted in social and economic poverty, early community-based youth programs were focused on job training, job-maintenance skills training, and job identification. Fishman, Denham, Levine, and Schatz (1969) described the Howard University program implemented in the 1960s for the purposes of identifying and intervening with youth and young adults who lacked skills, education, and self-esteem, and who had police records. The goal of this program reflected the broad-spectrum social activism popular at that time, including primarily the conversion of individuals who were social liabilities into productive citizens. Program features included actual job-skills training and resocialization-type groups. The goal of these groups was to teach the values and expectations of the work world so as to increase the chances that trainees, once they were hired, would

stay employed. Outcome data on job placement and longevity were impressive, with 87% of participants being employed as of the time of the first follow-up (as early as 6 months after completion). Unfortunately, one criticism of the program is that virtually all of the participants who were working were employed in the human services field (e.g., day care, welfare, recreation). Thus although the program succeeded in converting nonworkers to workers, they were located in jobs in which they served as helpers to individuals with many of the same difficulties. The capacity of human services agencies, which are generally government funded, to absorb these trainees is limited. This limit has been acknowledged in granting criteria for federal money. For example, CETA funding criteria stressed that the program be designated to place workers in private businesses rather than other government-supported agencies.

At about the same time as the Howard University program, another well-known program for disadvantaged youth appeared. This program, described by Goldenberg (1971), was called the Residential Youth Center (RYC), and was designed to intervene with economically disadvantaged youth and their families without removing participants from their natural environments. With almost a 1:1 participant to intervenor ratio, helpers were assigned a student and family with whom the helper maintained very close contact. The goal of the program was to establish new kinds of relationships between the target population and the institutional and political systems (e.g., school, police, social service agencies) that directly and indirectly affect these youths in substantial ways. Unfortunately, either the program fell short of its goals or the program evaluation included measures inappropriate to the goals of the program. With the exception of work attendance scores, no significant experimental group versus control group differences were obtained on behavioral and attitudinal measures. Efforts in the program to change the kind of relationships that existed between the population and existing institutional authorities also did not prove to be as successful as hoped, and served to underline the difficulty of carrying out the community mission of influencing large systems and policy.

Since the time of the RYC program, community youth programs have been characterized by greater precision and less ambitious goals. Fo and O'Donnell (1974), for example, conducted an experimental study in which they tested the efficacy of unconditional friends or ''buddies'' on the social and academic problems of youth. They randomly assigned subjects to one of three treatment conditions: friendship development, friendship plus contingent social approval for desired behavior, and friendship with contingent approval and contingent monetary rewards. They found friendship to be no better than no treatment at all, a significant advantage of contingent over noncontingent groups, and equal effectiveness of contingent social rewards and contingent monetary rewards. Another example of experimental community intervention research is a study reported by Chandler (1973). Operating from a "role-taking" deficit model of delinquency, Chandler held a filmmaking workshop at a youth center. Experimental subjects were asked to portray real-life situations followed by a subsequent discussion of the film among the participants and staff. A placebo group made films, receiving equal attention from staff in that activity, but received no role-taking training or opportunity to view and discuss the films. Experimentals scored higher in a subsequent role-taking test, and after 18 months showed a lower recidivism rate relative to the placebo group.

Advocacy programs for youth have also continued in the 1970s, but with a narrower focus as compared with the earlier broad-based programs described by Fishman, Denham, Levine, and Schatz (1969) and Goldenberg (1971). The aim of the youth advocacy generally is to help youth learn how to use existing community resources in ways that increase the chances that those resources will prove helpful. Davidson, Seidman, Rappaport, Berck, Rapp, Rhodes, and Herring (1977) described an advocacy program for youths designed to provide an alternative to police reliance on court referrals for youth. Advocates who were college volunteers were trained to work with the youths' families, schools, and legal system with the goal of reintegrating the youths in their natural environments as quickly and smoothly as possible. Although they did report lower recidivism rates among participants at a 1-year follow-up, that, unfortunately, was the only variable that was influenced by the program. School attendance and participation with families did not improve, but the program did accomplish its short-range goal of reducing the number of juvenile court referrals. This program illustrates the specific nature of the changes accompanied in a narrowly defined intervention program and the need to identify carefully a priori those aspects of functioning that should most usefully be the targets of intervention. In addition to this point, this advocacy program illustrates the potential pitfalls of using unpaid volunteers whose commitment is almost certainly short term. Short-term staff cannot be shaped and trained over long periods of time, thus allowing for program refinement.

This represents a drawback of many community programs in that they exist no longer than does the enthusiasm of their originators and their volunteers who staff them. The uncertainty that exists when one's basis of support is short-term soft money and college credit earned by volunteers undoubtedly has some effect on the momentum of programs and the incentives to improve them. Given this problem, the primary benefit of some of these programs may be less the service they deliver to the target population than the social skills training that accrues to the volunteers who staff the program. Kushler, Emshoff, Blakely, and Davidson (1979), for example, describe a variety of skills necessary to be a competent advocate ranging from speaking with employees about hiring a delinquent youth to pursuading parents to change unfair rules. Competent mastery of the skills necessary to be successful in those endeavors is nothing short of impressive, and specifying the training the advocates received would in itself constitute an important contribution to the literature.

Issues in Programs for Youth

The current trend in community youth intervention is a shift away from broad-spectrum programs that are designed to provide economic and social opportunities. Instead there is increased reliance on formal models of individual functioning with the attending intervention technologies and evaluation philosophies. Despite this increased emphasis on clearer and more narrow program descriptions and outcome evaluations, intervention programs for youth in the United States have not been characterized by good program description and evaluation (Dixon & Wright, 1974). Program particulars (e.g., big brother advocacy, the redirection of adolescent energies into rewarding activities) are not clearly defined, and the lack of methodology and data collection necessary to evaluate individual aspects of multifaceted programs make further program conceptualization and development very difficult. More recently described programs have tended to rely on operant technology and behavioral-cognitive models of functioning. However, this impression may be based on artifact. That is, these sorts of programs are more likely to be carefully described and evaluated and therefore published, than others based on alternative models of intervention that do not share the same emphasis on replicability.

More specifically, the assumption underlying programs for youth is much the same as that witnessed in the literature concerned with young children. Later and more serious difficulties can be avoided or reduced in severity if early remedial action is taken to correct and amplify the learning contexts of the at-risk adolescent. Unfortunately, evaluation of these secondary prevention programs is, in general, limited and often not performed at all. Dixon and Wright (1974), in a review of over 6,600 programs, including 200 on-site reviews, concluded that little quality evaluation is being performed on prevention programs, with 57% of federally funded programs receiving no evaluation at all. Further, of those programs in which evaluations were being performed, they considered only 8% to have been methodologically sound. Methodological flaws and a lack of statistical assessments aside, Dixon and Wright nevertheless recommended discarding recreation programs, guided group-interaction programs (e.g., peer support and problem-solving groups), and certain types of worker-training projects on the basis of failure to demonstrate results when applied to delinquents. More generally, Lemert (1971) has argued that preventative programs fail because they have not accurately identified target groups, program facets are too diffuse and focused unsystematically on too many aspects of functioning, programs are not evaluated, and programs do not become part of stable institutions but instead last only as long as the enthusiasm of program developers and staff. If one of the ultimate goals of community intervention is to affect public policy in the direction of improving the environments of citizens, then short-lived programs are especially inadvisable. Programs that come and go relatively quickly are not likely to become crystallized as part of the identity of a community or to have a beneficial impact on future planning decisions occurring within that community. They may instead have a negative impact on citizens by way of appearing to be unreliable and fickle, and therefore nothing on which the members can depend. Ironically, one of the very tenets of the community philosophy, the avoidance of system crystallization, may be operating to reduce the potential effectiveness of community-type intervention programs.

A second issue that was discussed earlier as pertinent to detection and intervention programs with young children may raise more profound social and ethical questions with respect to youth programs. This is the issue of the number of false positives identified in the course of detecting at-risk youth, a phenomenon called "overprediction" (Heller & Monahan, 1977). Efforts to predict who a target group or individual should be are requisite to the implementation of primary prevention and many secondary prevention programs. As pointed out by Lemert (1971), however, there exists no accurate way of predicting who will become a delinquent and who will not. In the case of young children it might be argued that enrichment programs can only do good (assuming that one can count on a positive halo or pygmalion effect) regardless of their ultimate bearing on subsequent social dysfunction in adolescence and adulthood. However, the same may not be true for prevention programs for youth. Actually, the methods and events by which youth are typically identified may raise more serious implications as to the legal and ethical rights of youth to privacy. As argued by Shah (1973), efforts to identify and prevent social dysfunctions such as delinquency using detection technology of questionable predictive validity raises important constitutional questions as to the right of government to intervene in peoples' lives before they display those behaviors that would make them visible to judicial and mental health authorities. This may be a serious issue, particularly in light of the fact that simply contact with the juvenile justice system may directly increase the chances of deviant conduct on the part of the juvenile (Schur, 1973). Whether these serious issues are among the tasks individual interventionists can systematically consider, they certainly seem to be an important part of action programs and are suggestive of where this intervention approach would best direct its energies.

Goldenberg (1971) argued the merits of focusing on the institutional and psychological sources of poverty and dysfunction rather than on individual symptoms. It would seem that this message has been the primary promise of the community approach. Unfortunately there is a gulf between the philosophy of social activism and social change and the actual community work that has been reported in the last decade. For some, what was initially a credible call to activism and reform may be on the verge of sounding like empty rhetoric filled with promises of how things should be, but lacking a formal model that could be useful in dictating the program specifics necessary to produce change where community advocates see it as most wanting—not in individual children but in the physical and interpersonal contexts that surround them.

THE APPLICATION OF KNOWLEDGE

The voluminous literature represented in this review reflects the tremendous expansion of intervention models, research data, training programs, and popular as well as scientific literature during the decade of the 1970s. This expansion has produced many effects, one of which is an increase of potentially available treatment resources. However, positive trends in prevention and amelioration are not evident for children with social and personality problems. Rates of childhood problems such as suicidal behavior (McIntire & Angle, 1971), runaway rates (Justice & Duncan, 1976), drug and alcohol abuse (Sorosiak, Thomas, & Balet, 1976), delinquency rates (*FBI Uniform Crime Reports,* 1979), and the like seem to be increasing. Although bookshelves bulge with a large number of journals and books, and graduate students have more and more information to learn, there are no approaches that are generally agreed on by professionals or consumers that will produce a child who is "mentally healthier" today than 10 years ago.

How can this be? Certainly the number of drugs potentially available to treat problems has increased dramatically. So, too, have the number of formally trained therapists, technical aides, therapeutic and educational techniques, treatment models, and treatment contexts. As of the end of 1979, the International Year of the Child, the literature contained descriptions of every imaginable form of therapeutic intervention for every conceivable childhood problem. Any single professional, treating any given child for any given problem or teaching parents how to avoid having certain problems, could find up to hundreds of literature references on how to treat that problem.

Unfortunately, this apparent wealth of information and technology produces a misleading picture of the current nature and status of intervention with children, often leaving the consumer with a sense of "starving in the midst of plenty." Greater intervention effectiveness and efficiency requires more than knowledge about models, drugs, techniques, data, and the like. They also require better understanding of the contextual influences and constraints that operate at the various points of clinical decision making and intervention. Understanding these contextual influences can sometimes allow the clinician to modify them directly in ways that enhance treatment effectiveness and efficiency. When such modification is impossible, understanding these contextual influences and constraints can at least allow the clinican to anticipate their impact more effectively, thereby enhancing the quality of clinical decision making and service delivery.

The Contexts of Knowledge Generation and Application

As stated in the introductory section of this chapter, the generation, dissemination, and application of knowledge do not occur in a vacuum. The very nature of childhood problems that confronts the clinician is heavily influenced, if not determined, by a large number of contexts in which the clinician and child exist. To cite but one example, the apparent contributors to delinquency, as well as the specific behaviors that it entails, may differ widely between two locations. The contributions of such factors as poverty and crowding to delinquency in a ghetto appear to be powerful but may be irrelevant in a rural setting or an affluent neighborhood. Delinquency occurs in all three environments, but often in different forms and for different reasons. Further, the clinician trained or experienced in treating delinquency in one environment may encounter great difficulty when applying those skills in a different environment.

Of the numerous contexts that influence the generation and application of knowledge relevant to intervention with childhood problems, the most salient include the social, political, and economic zeitgeists that influence (1) the nature and quality of basic and applied research and the knowledge that accrues from them; (2) the treatment goals implicitly and explicitly adopted by the clinician and the child/family/caretaker/community; (3) the nature and quality of training and the range of techniques available to the clinician; and (4) the resources available to the clinician and the child/family/caretaker/community. For example, in some locales a vast (and, to the consumer, often confusing) array of resources appear to be available. Unfortunately, these treatment resources often present conflicting goals and compete, sometimes savagely, for funds that seemed plentiful earlier in the decade of the 1970s but that are increasingly difficult to obtain. A collection of related political and economic realities are operating in the direction of increased fiscal and professional conservatism. The more liberal social and economic policies of the Kennedy and Johnson presidential administrations have passed, and with them have passed widespread support of social reform. The end of the 1970s and the beginning of the 1980s have been years of increased cynicism as to the effectiveness and value of intervention technology to solve social problems, coupled with an increased conservatism even as to the responsibility of public institutions to solve those problems. Interest in and willingness to invest public monies in youth-oriented problems has leveled off, and as the mean age of the general population increases, the commitment to serve children may continue to decline.

In the face of public demands for tax limitations and decreased government spending, legislatures are dramatically modifying funding priorities by paring down social service expenditures. In response to reduced budgets but, at the same time, increased service demands, public service agencies are shifting their staffing policies to increased hiring of paraprofessionals and ''new'' professionals who do not require the same salary expenditures as senior professionals. Related to increased competition for available funds are professional jealousies and jurisdictional conflicts among agencies, which often preclude effective case management and collaboration. In large part as a result of economic competition and the political zeitgeist of professional autonomy across the mental health professions, practitioners from different disciplines are competing for the status of independent service providers and thus are active in defining and expanding their respective service boundaries (Malouf & Alexander, 1976b).

A general picture of too many resources but too few funds is not, however, an accurate view of the entire reality of human services delivery. In many locales, primarily rural or poor, competition among service providers is negligible because few services are available. Many areas of geographic or relative cultural isolation receive so few clinical resources that the National Institute of Mental Health currently has the policy of supporting specifically those training programs that target unserved and underserved populations or problems. Although these pressures may eventually have considerable impact on the nature of training, in large part they currently seem to be creating confusion, resistance, and as yet only slight improvement in the quality of services available to children.

In a related vein, the funding priorities of research-supporting agencies influence the nature and extent of research on pathology and intervention. The goals reflected in many of the applied research projects in the 1970s have defined the limits of the development of the knowledge necessary to enhance the quality of intervention. Basic research is often funded by agencies that are separate from applied-research funding agencies. Many of the basic research questions asked, and the variables studied, are not in a form that can be readily used by applied researchers. The applied researchers, on the other hand, are rarely funded for projects that will provide the kinds of basic knowledge that is necessary as a foundation for intervention programs. Instead, both applied researchers and the agencies providing their funding exist in a context that demands relatively short-term payoffs (''bang for the buck'' was a popular buzzword during the 1970s), reflecting the emphasis on higher rates of demonstrated effectiveness for relatively lower amounts of funding. Thus many

program developers are forced to put together multi-component treatment packages that can demonstrate effectiveness, ending up with programs in which the variables responsible for the obtained effects are impossible to separate. Further, when funding sources learn that a particular form of intervention is ''superior'' to others, they generally begin to demand service, but often fail to continue providing the basic research money (not tied to service delivery) that is necessary to perform component evaluation and extend parametric research. With the present shift from federal to local control of economic resources, this situation is likely to be exacerbated.

Applied researchers often add to this problem by incompletely describing the specific operations involved (Blechman, 1981; O'Dell, 1974). Quite often the literature contains such descriptions as ''the parents were persuaded'' (Alexander & Barton, 1980), which are too vague to be replicated or systematically and objectively evaluated.

An additional factor that has served to inhibit implementation of the wealth of *apparently* useful technology is the quality and nature of applied and program evaluation research. It has become routine for reviewers to lament the quality of research investigation, both generally and with respect to childhood intervention in particular. In a narrow sense, the criticisms refer to such basic issues as the inadequate use of controls and sampling methods, poor criterion selection, reactivity of measures, lack of follow-up data, poor replicability, poor reliability, multiple treatment interference, and the confounding effects of maturation (e.g., Bergin & Lambert, 1978; Heinicke & Strassman, 1975; Levitt, 1971; Malouf & Alexander, 1976a). Beyond these inadequacies, there is a widespread distrust of empirically based approaches to intervention. Whereas the great majority of professionals agree that careful research is necessary to understand, evaluate, and improve the nature of technology, many are hesitant to rely solely on interventions that have received careful research scrutiny and support. This hesitation results from the fact that because of statistical and conceptual limitations, only a limited array of problems and techniques amenable to current statistical treatment have been researched. To the extent that these problems and techniques are not comprehensive, this acceptance of only currently supported interventions can stifle the applied community. To use but one example, in the mid-1960s Frank (1965), among others, concluded that no solid evidence supporting the efficacy of family intervention, or even family involvement in deviant behavior, could be found. The fact of the matter was that prior to the time of those reviews, statistical models were simply not readily available that could handle the interdependencies and bidirectional effects that were (and are) cornerstones of family-therapy and research models. Since that time, of course, methodological technologies such as reliable interaction codes (e.g., Alexander, 1973; Haley, 1967a,b; Patterson et al., 1973; Waxler & Mishler, 1965), as well as statistical technologies such as nested ANOVA designs (Kirk, 1968), and time-series analysis (Holtzman, 1963), have allowed researchers to demonstrate much more conclusively the nature of family effect on deviant behavior, as well as the utility of family intervention (Alexander & Parsons, 1973). However, if during the mid-1960s everyone in the field of child deviance had simply accepted the early reviews as "truth," then these impressive gains could not have been realized. As long as basic knowledge is incomplete and methodologies and statistical tools inadequate, divergent intervention models and techniques without strong empirical support will continue to exist.

An inadequate empirical support base, however, is not the only reason for contradiction and inefficiency. The fact is that a great deal of the information that is available is contradictory. There exist very few, if any, phenomena for which a given intervention is agreed on as most effective *by the field as a whole*. For example, a clinician trying to select a strategy for treating a severely disturbed child will find articles that argue the potential virtues of a given drug such as LSD (e.g., Mogar & Aldrich, 1969), articles that warn against the use of that drug (e.g., Simmons, Benor, & Daniel, 1972) but support alternative drugs (e.g., Campbell, Fish, David, Shapiro, Collins, & Koh, 1972; Campbell, Fish, Korein, Shapiro, Collins, & Koe. 1972), and still others that argue the advantages of entirely different forms of intervention (e.g., Fenichel, 1974; Kahn & Arbib, 1973).

Magnifying the content contradictions are the ideological battles that still characterize areas within the intervention literature. This fact reduces the potential impact of techniques, models, and resources. It is not surprising, given the amount of contradiction and didactic infighting that exists within and across treatment categories, to find that they have been interpreted by the consumer as incompetence or indifference. Clinical intervention will always be a sociocultural phenomenon, and as such will be highly influenced by the goals and values of both the clinical practitioners who perform it and the context in which it occurs. Some interventions, although potentially quite effective in producing certain desired changes, are simply unacceptable to society or at least to powerful and important components of it. Some uses of aversive physical stimulation, such as electric shock or spanking, as well as certain time-out procedures, have been targets of critical social and professional discussion (Bachman, 1972; Burchard & Barrera, 1972). Other less obvious forms of influence that may reduce effective application include phenomena such as the considerable community resistance in some locales toward the development and operation of day-care and similar programs (Baxandall, 1977). There are private citizen groups that have organized as private lobbies at least in part for the purposes of reducing what they perceive to be overinvolvement of state and federal governments in the family. What is assistance for some is for others active and dangerous interference with the private family and erosion of parents' power.

Within the scientific and professional communities considerable disagreement also exists with respect to the appropriateness of particular interventions. Consider, for example, a situation in which a given child exhibits excessive and inappropriate anxiety as defined by the environment. It is conceivable that uncontroversial scientific support could be rallied in order to argue that a particular intervention (e.g., therapeutic drug) could reliably and inexpensively reduce anxiety in this type of child when given under specific conditions. Yet despite the fact that this therapeutic effect could be reliably demonstrated and agreed on by all to exist, it could create continued conflict among professionals, and only minimal adoption by clinicians as a treatment of choice. The reasons for this consequence would be the same as those that the field has already experienced in many forms. For example, one professional group would undoubtedly argue that the beneficial effects of drug administration represent only symptomatic treatment, which according to them would be inappropriate and potentially quite harmful because underlying problems would likely be ignored. Other groups might argue that the demonstrated changes could not be positively valued unless they were found to be maintained in a long-term follow-up and unless they had no adverse side effects such as interfering with the learning of appropriate coping responses. Yet another group might argue that the direct treatment of anxiety is inappropriate, as the anxiety represents "an appropriate response to an inappropriate situation," in which case the situation, not the individual response to it, requires changing. Finally, another group might question the entire procedure in terms of the protection of children's rights, because even if the child did give permission for treatment, she or he was too young or too disturbed to understand fully the implications of the procedure.

Numerous additional examples of responses to an empirically demonstrated intervention can be presented. The main point is that even when data are available, their implications are often disputed if not overtly rejected. Clear, concise, and responsible scholarship alone cannot move the field from being in an ever-expanding quagmire into a state of unanimity. Nor will the development of elegant conceptual models and powerfully effective intervention techniques alone solve the problem. In both the professional literature and the larger social context, fundamental and powerful disagreements exist with respect to the nature of the causes of social and personality problems, as well as to what *should* be the goals and the appropriate modalities of intervention.

In fact, it may be the case that basic and irreconcilable forces present in society and culture will prevent consensus as to the nature of the child, what is and should be the function of the child in society, and what are the ideal "end points" of both effective socialization and (in the case of deviancy) clinical intervention. At least one force that exists to prevent consensus is the idea of the private child in the context of a public society. The social and economic factors underlying the development and growing popularity of the concept of the private child have been discussed widely by historians and economists (Ariès, 1962; Zaretsky, 1976). It remains that the idea of private experience and free expression as a personal birthright of children has become thematic of American culture and historically underpins the view of the child as following a natural course of healthy development, of the world as being harsh and impersonal, and of the family as ideally being a place of retreat and sanctuary (Demos, 1975). Prior to the emergence of the concept of the private child, children were evaluated on the basis of whether or not they fulfilled the demands of their public roles, with virtually all aspects of their lives being public events rather than private (Ariès, 1962). With the concept of the private child, issues of the self came into existence. It was no longer enough to know and competently perform one's role within the public sphere. New questions became relevant and these questions pertained to the importance of the child's happiness, opportunities for self-development, and the boundaries of the private versus the public self (Demos, 1975).

At the same time that the popularity of "private experience" grew, however, there remained the need to maintain social organization and conformity as a goal of socialization. Successful socialization of new members had always included the expectation that children become committed and competent members of the society (Elkind & Handel, 1978). However, with a commitment to the private child added to a commitment to the need for social appropriateness, the task of socialization has become more complex and potentially more problematic. Children are not only expected to become good citizens but personally autonomous and happy as well.

Thus the theme of modern socialization may have become one of contradiction: Socializing agents place limits on children's behavior, but at the same time they also make demands that children function more and more autonomously with increasing age. Demands for individuality and, at same time, demands for conformity may amount to a behavior paradox or bind for children (Coser, 1974), making more likely those social and personality problems that involve issues of individual choice versus environmental control. The implications of this socialization paradox are apparent in the intervention literature as well. Behavioral engineers, for example, have struggled for some time with the ethics of controls being imposed on one person by another, and with the potential hazards of a misuse of behavior-modification technology (Ross, 1978). Even at the level of defining and categorizing deviant behavior in children, the considerable debate over the criteria for dysfunction in the development of the DSM-III (Foltz, 1980) reflects contradictory and ambivalent views among professionals.

One resolution to this conflict is to focus on only half of it, and that, intentionally or unintentionally, is what seems to have happened in the course of developing intervention models and technology. If one focuses on the "public" or conformity aspect of existence, one is led quite naturally to technology based on ideas of impulse-taming and social engineering. If one focuses on the importance of the "private" aspects of existence, then one is more likely to generate technology designed to focus on the search for personal growth and experience in the face of difficult external circumstances. Unfortunately, this selective attention maintains the schisms and inconsistencies currently plaguing the field, but these inconsistencies are not unlike the conflict within the larger society as to the boundaries between the rights of personal happiness and the need for social conformity.

Implications

In the early stages of its explosive growth, the field of intervention with children experienced considerable excitement and enthusiasm, but fragmentation and inefficiency as well. Many who defined themselves primarily as clinicians harbored a distrust of the motives and methods of those identifying themselves primarily as scientists, and vice versa. Among themselves, clinicians and scientists alike also experienced considerable disagreement. Adherents of different theoretical positions either actively competed with each other or rejected each other out of hand. For every attempt at rapprochement there were counterattempts at separation in the form of more exclusionary and doctrinaire professional organizations, journals, and the like. Models and data proliferated in such divergent directions that it became impossible to characterize the field as having any clearly defined center of gravity. The clash of ideologies burgeoned to the point that in the parking lots of child treatment facilities one could see such bumper stickers as "Better Living Through Behaviorism," "Big Brothers Are for You," "Have You Hugged Your Kid Today?" and various forms of "Family Unity" slogans. Researchers and theorists adhering to particular models tended to retain a relatively narrow conceptual focus, struggling only with research questions that were amenable to their research methodologies and restricting client populations to those most responsive to their particular interventions. Through the mid-1970s therapists and researchers primarily focused on technical development of traditional models, asking questions in the form of "How can we apply and demonstrate the effectiveness of a given technique or approach on a given clinical problem?"

Many professionals dealing with problems that they felt spanned more than one narrow ideology rejected these trends toward ideological narrowness and "purity," and have supported instead conceptual and technical diversity. Experiencing increased pressures around the issues of service costs and accountability, and being increasingly aware of the unique and sometimes contradictory value system of different client populations, these professionals have called for flexible clinical problem solving and a reexamination of traditional conceptual models.

Unfortunately, these trends could evolve into a period of "wild eclecticism," in which professionals "pick and choose" from among the array of available intervention technologies, many of which are mutually exclusive. In the process, these clinicians could end up sabotaging their own efforts by sequentially or concurrently adopting incompatible techniques. To use but one oversimplified example, it is impossible to create an unconditionally accepting relationship required by some play therapies while at the same time employing a strategy involv-ing systematic differential attention coupled with time out to shape desired behaviors. *Both* approaches may be useful and have empirical support, but they cannot be used simultaneously. Without a comprehensive conceptual model to guide decision making, such problems of incompatibility are not unlikely. Shotgun approaches to treatment can also have the effect of driving treatment costs still higher. Practitioners who add treatment facets without a sense of their independent and cumulative effects may be reducing their own efficiency and effectiveness in the long run.

A second problem with eclecticism is that whereas it can lead to greater flexibility, it can tend also to have a deleterious effect on the generation of new knowledge. Because decisions are often intuitive and post hoc, programmatic evaluation is almost impossible. Because eclectics can differ so widely both when compared to themselves across time and when compared to each other, there is no way to initiate systematic component analyses to help refine our understanding of which components of intervention work and which ones do not. Of course, each therapist could be evaluated with nonreactive and independently obtained outcome measures, but very few clinicians are able or willing to do this in such a way (i.e., using such essential methods as random assignment, matched groups, multiple base lines) that they can know how well they are doing. It is only through precise understanding as to the impact of specific program components and the nature of a specific dysfunction that knowledge can be meaningfully generated and decision-making strategies articulated (Achenbach, 1978). Knowledge will suffer if anecdote, experience, and intuition remain the primary bases for clinical decision making and intervention. Stated in somewhat pessimistic terms, the field could at best become one of flexible and intuitive technicians who can add nothing to the field beyond the quality of service they directly offer to clients, and this quality could be impossible to assess.

Fortunately such dire outcomes are not inevitable. Recently, adherents of many intervention models have moved toward expanding the scope of their concepts and techniques, asking the general question, "How must our conceptual model and techniques be expanded or modified to better handle the difficulties we experience in treating different kinds of children with different kinds of problems?" To reiterate but two previously discussed examples, psychoanalytic authors have developed new conceptual frameworks and modified such historically basic processes as free association and transference (Scharfman, 1978). Similarly, some behavioral researchers have questioned the generally assumed uniformity of positive effects of differential social attention (Wahler, Berland, & Coe, 1979). As clinicians, researchers, and theorists continue to struggle with phenomena that "don't fit" the previously narrow ideologies, the field will experience growth in the sophistication of intervention models. Rather than being disheartened and constrained by inconsistent data, both eclectics and adherents of specific models can suggest not only a greater range of techniques but a more comprehensive conceptual framework for decision making.

Thus the problems previously described as characteristic of the field need not preclude strong positive movement during the decade of the 1980s. Although inconsistent data, competing ideologies, and political and social forces could impede growth, they could also provide momentum to produce major advances. For this to occur, the field must recognize how these various factors operate, and how they can be used in ways that facilitate, rather than stunt, the development of more comprehensive, efficient, and effective intervention models and techniques for use with children. In addition, we in the field must recognize that scholarship and scientific inquiry cannot alone define what the goals of intervention should be. Scholarship and scientific inquiry can identify the outcomes that particular intervention strategies and techniques will produce, both in terms of specific changes and theoretical implications. They can bring to light relationships between particular assumptions regarding the nature and meaning of behavior, the dynamics of dysfunction, and the mechanisms of change. They can identify the effectiveness, efficiency, and indirect effects of particular combinations of theory and technique. Scholarship and scientific inquiry can even tell us why society, clients, and practitioners value particular goals, and why they make certain choices in the context of these goals. However, it is society, clients, and individual practitioners who will decide both the *meaning* and the *importance* of this knowledge, as well as whether or not it is appropriate in terms of the context in which it might be applied. Society, not science, will determine what the goals of intervention should be. Whether or not this determination facilitates the generation and application of knowledge depends on how well we in the field recognize and respond to this and the other contexts that so heavily influence us.

REFERENCES

Achenbach, T. M. Psychopathology of childhood: Research problems and issues. *Journal of Con-* *sulting and Clinical Psychology*, 1978, *46*, 759–776.

Ack, M., Beale, E., & Ware, L. Parent guidance: Psychotherapy of the young child via the parent. *Bulletin of the Menninger Clinic*, 1975, *39*, 436–447.

Ackerman, N. W. *Treating the troubled family*. New York: Basic Books, 1966.

Adams, P. L. Psychotherapy with obsessive children. *International Journal of Child Psychotherapy*, 1973, *2*, 471–491.

Adams, P. L. Local community change for service to children. *Child Psychiatry and Human Development*, 1976, *7*, 22–30.

Aleksandrowicz, M. K. The biological strangers: An attempted suicide of a seven-and-a-half-year-old girl. *Bulletin of the Menninger Clinic*, 1975, *39*, 163–176.

Alexander, J. F. Defensive and supportive communications in normal and deviant families. *Journal of Consulting and Clinical Psychology*, 1973, *40*, 223–231.

Alexander, J. F., & Barton, C. Systems-behavioral intervention with delinquent families. In J. Vincent (Ed.), *Advances in family intervention, assessment and theory*. Greenwich, Conn.: JAI Press, 1980.

Alexander, J. F., Barton, C., Schiavo, R. S., & Parsons, B. V. Behavioral intervention with families of delinquents: Therapist characteristics and outcome. *Journal of Consulting and Clinical Psychology*, 1976, *44*, 656–664.

Alexander, J. F., & Parsons, B. V. Short-term behavioral intervention with delinquent families: Impact on family process and recidivism. *Journal of Abnormal Psychology*, 1973, *81*, 219–225.

Alexander, J. F., & Parsons, B. V. *Functional family therapy*. Carmel, Calif.: Brooks/Cole, 1982.

Allen, G. J., Chinsky, J. M., Larcen, S. W., Lochman, J. E., & Selinger, H. V. *Community psychology and the schools: A behaviorally oriented multi-level preventive approach*. Hillsdale, N.J.: Erlbaum, 1976.

Allyon, T., Simon, S. J., & Wildman, R. W. Instructions and reinforcement in the elimination of encopresis. *Journal of Behavior Therapy and Experimental Psychiatry*, 1975, *6*, 235–238.

Altrocchi, J. *Abnormal behavior*. New York: Harcourt Brace Jovanovich, 1980.

Aman, M. G., & Werry, J. S. Methylphenidate in children: Effects upon cardio-respiratory function on exertion. In C. K. Conners (Ed.), *Clinical use of stimulant drugs in children*. Amsterdam: Excerpta Medica, 1975.

Anneil, A. L. Manic-depressive illness in children and effect of treatment with lithium carbonate. *Acta Paedopsychiatrica,* 1969, *36,* 292–301.

Anthony, E. J. The behavior disorders of childhood. In P. H. Mussen (Ed.), *Carmichael's manual of child psychology.* New York: Wiley, 1970.

Argast, T. L., & Clement, P. W. *Reducing deviant classroom behavior by self-orientation and self-reinforcement.* Paper presented at the convention of the Western Psychological Association, Honolulu, May 1980.

Ariès, P. *Centuries of childhood: A social history of family life.* New York: Random House, 1962.

Ashkenazi, Z. The treatment of encopresis using a discriminative stimulus and positive reinforcement. *Journal of Behavior Therapy and Experimental Psychiatry,* 1975, *6,* 155–157.

Awad, G. A., & Harrison, S. I. A female fire-setter: A case report. *Journal of Nervous and Mental Disease,* 1976, *163,* 432–437.

Azrin, N. H., & Foxx, R. M. *Toilet training in less than a day.* New York: Simon & Schuster, 1974.

Azrin, N. H., & Powers, M. A. Eliminating classroom disturbances of emotionally disturbed children by positive practice procedures. *Behavior Therapy,* 1975, *6,* 525–534.

Bachman, J. A. Self-injurious behavior: A behavioral analysis. *Journal of Abnormal Psychology,* 1972, *80,* 211–224.

Bandura, A. *Principles of behavior modification.* New York: Holt, Rinehart & Winston, 1969.

Bandura, A. Vicarious and self-reinforcement processes. In R. Glaser (Ed.), *The nature of reinforcement.* New York: Academic Press, 1971.

Bandura, A., & Menlove, F. L. Factors determining vicarious extinction of avoidance behavior through symbolic modeling. *Journal of Personality and Social Psychology,* 1968, *8,* 99–108.

Bandura, A., & Walters, R. H. *Social learning and personality development.* New York: Holt, Rinehart & Winston, 1963.

Barkley, R. A. The effects of methylphenidate on various types of activity level and attention in hyperkinetic children. *Journal of Abnormal Child Psychology,* 1977, *5,* 351–369.

Barkley, R. A., & Cunningham, C. E. Do stimulant drugs improve the academic performance of hyperkinetic children? *Clinical Pediatrics,* 1978, *17,* 85–92.

Barkley, R. A., & Cunningham, C. E. The effects of methylphenidate on the mother-child interactions of hyperactive children. *Archives of General Psychiatry,* 1979, *36,* 201–208.

Barlow, D. H. Behavioral therapy: The next decade. *Behavior Therapy,* 1980, *11,* 315–328.

Barton, C., & Alexander, J. F. *The effects of competitive and cooperative sets on normal and delinquent families.* Paper presented at the convention of the American Psychological Association, New York, September 1979.

Barton, C., & Alexander, J. F. Functional family therapy. In A. S. Gurman & D. P. Kniskern (Eds.), *Handbook of family therapy.* New York: Brunner-Mazel, 1980.

Barton, E. J., & Ascione, F. R. Sharing in preschool children: Facilitation, stimulus generalization, response generalization, and maintenance. *Journal of Applied Behavior Analysis,* 1979, *3,* 81–94.

Bateson, G., Jackson, D. D., Haley, J., & Weakland, J. Toward a theory of schizophrenia. *Behavioral Science,* 1956, *1,* 251–264.

Baxandall, R. F. Who shall care for our children? In A. S. Skolnick & J. H. Skolnick (Eds.), *Family in transition: Rethinking marriage, sexuality, child rearing, and family organization.* Boston: Little, Brown & Co., 1977.

Bean, A. W., & Roberts, M. W. The effect of time-out release contingencies on changes in child non-compliance. *Journal of Abnormal Child Psychology,* 1981, *9,* 95–105.

Bedlington, M. M., Braukmann, C. J., Kirigin, K. A., & Wolf, M. M. *Treatment interactions, delinquency, and youth satisfaction.* Paper presented in symposium at the convention of the Association for the Advancement of Behavior Therapy, San Francisco, December 1979.

Behrens, M., & Goldfarb, W. A study of patterns of interaction of families of schizophrenic children in residential treatment. *American Journal of Orthopsychiatry,* 1958, *28,* 300–312.

Bell, J. E. A theoretical position for family group therapy. *Family Process,* 1963, *2,* 1–14.

Bell, R. Q. Parent, child, and reciprocal influences. *American Psychologist,* 1979, *34,* 821–826.

Bender, L., & Faretra, G. The relationship between childhood schizophrenia and adult schizophrenia. In A. R. Kaplan (Ed.), *Genetic factors in "schizophrenia,"* Springfield, Ill.: Charles C. Thomas, 1972.

Bentley, J. Psychotherapeutic treatment of a boy with eczema and asthma. *Journal of Asthma Research,* 1975, *12,* 207–214.

Bereiter, C. An academic preschool for disadvantaged children: Conclusions from evaluation studies. In J. C. Stanley (Ed.), *Preschool programs for the disadvantaged: Five experimental approaches to early childhood education.* Baltimore: Johns Hopkins University Press, 1972.

Bereiter, C., & Englemann, S. *Teaching disadvan-*

taged children in the preschool. Englewood Cliffs, N.J.: Prentice-Hall, 1966.

Bergin, A. E., & Lambert, M. J. The evaluation of therapeutic outcomes. In S. L. Garfield & A. E. Bergin (Eds.), Handbook of psychotherapy and behavior change: An empirical analysis. New York: Wiley, 1978.

Berland, R. M. The family social system and child deviancy: A comparison of deviant and nondeviant families. Unpublished doctoral dissertation, University of Tennessee, Knoxville, 1976.

Bernal, M. E. Behavioral treatment of a child's eating problems. Journal of Behavior Therapy and Experimental Psychiatry, 1972, 3, 43–50.

Bijou, S. W., & Baer, D. M. Child development: A systematic and empirical theory (Vol. 1). New York: Appleton-Century-Crofts, 1961.

Bijou, S. W., & Baer, D. M. Child development: Universal stage of infancy (Vol. 2). New York: Appleton-Century-Crofts, 1965.

Blacklidge, V. Y., & Ekblad, R. L. The effectiveness of methylphenidate hydrochloride (Ritalin) on learning and behavior in public school educable mentally retarded children. Pediatrics, 1971, 47, 923–926.

Blechman, E. A. Objectives and procedures believed necessary for the success of a contractual approach to family intervention. Behavior Therapy, 1977, 8, 275–277.

Blechman, E. A. Family problem-solving training. American Journal of Family Therapy, 1980, 8, 3–22.

Blechman, E. A. Toward comprehensive behavioral family intervention: An algorithm for matching families and interventions. Behavior Modification, 1981, 5, 221–236.

Blechman, E. A., & Olson, D. H. L. The family contract game: Description and effectiveness. In D. H. L. Olson (Ed.), Treating relationships. Lake Mills, Iowa: Graphic Publishing Co., 1976.

Bolman, W. M. Preventive psychiatry for the family: Theory, approaches, and programs. American Journal of Psychiatry, 1969, 125, 458–472.

Bornstein, P., & Quevillon, R. Effects of a self-instructional package on overactive preschool boys. Journal of Applied Behavior Analysis, 1976, 9, 179–188.

Bowen, M. Theory in the practice of psychotherapy. In P. Guerin (Ed.), Family therapy. New York: Gardner Press, 1976.

Bower, K. B., & Mercer, C. D. Hyperactivity: Etiology and intervention techniques. The Journal of School Health, 1975, 45, 195–202.

Bradley, C., & Green, E. Psychometric performance of children receiving amphetamine (benzedrine) sulfate. American Journal of Psychiatry, 1940, 97, 388–394.

Bratter, T. E. Responsible therapeutic eros: The psychotherapist who cares enough to define and enforce behavior limits with potentially suicidal adolescents. Counseling Psychologist, 1975, 5, 97–104.

Bronfenbrenner, U. Contexts of child rearing. American Psychologist, 1979, 34, 844–850.

Brownbridge, R., & Van Vleet, P. Investments in prevention: The prevention of learning and behavior problems in young children. San Francisco: Pace ID Center, 1969.

Bugental, D. B., Whalen, C. K., & Henker, B. Causal attributions of hyperactive children and motivational assumptions of two behavior-change approaches: Evidence for an interactionist perspective. Child Development, 1977, 48, 874–884.

Burchard, J., & Barerra, F. An analysis of time-out and response cost in a programmed environment. Journal of Applied Behavior Analysis, 1972, 5, 271–282.

Camp, B. W., Blom, G. E., Hebert, F., & van Doorninck, W. J. "Think aloud:" A program for developing self-control in young aggressive boys. Journal of Abnormal Child Psychology, 1977, 5, 157–169.

Campbell, D. T., & Eriebacher, A. How regression artifacts in quasi-experimental evaluation can mistakenly make compensatory education look harmful. In J. Hellmuth (Ed.), Compensatory education: A national debate, vol. 3, The disadvantaged child. New York: Brunner-Mazel, 1970.

Campbell, M. Psychopharmacology in childhood psychosis. International Journal of Mental Health, 1975, 4, 238–254.

Campbell, M. Biological intervention in psychosis of childhood. In E. Schopler & R. Reichler (Eds.), Psychotherapy and child development. New York: Plenum, 1976.

Campbell, M. Pharmacotherapy. In M. Rutter & E. Schopler (Eds.), Autism: A reappraisal of concepts and treatment. New York: Plenum, 1978.

Campbell, M., Fish, B., David, R., Shapiro, T., Collins, P., & Koh, C. Response to triiodothyronine and dextro-amphetamine: A study of preschool schizophrenic children. Journal of Autism and Childhood Schizophrenia, 1972, 2, 343–358.

Campbell, M., Fish, B., Korein, J., Shapiro, T.,

Collins, P., & Koh, C. Lithium-chlorpromazine: A controlled crossover study of hyperactive severely disturbed young children. *Journal of Autism and Childhood Schizophrenia*, 1972, *2*, 234–263.

Campbell, M., & Small, A. M. Chemotherapy. In B. B. Wolman, J. Egan, & A. O. Ross (Eds.), *Handbook of treatment of mental disorders in childhood and adolescence*. Englewood Cliffs, N.J.: Prentice-Hall, 1978.

Caplan, G. *Principles of preventive psychiatry*. New York: Basic Books, 1964.

Carlsson, B. Operant conditioning techniques with autistic children. *Nordisk Psykologie*, 1971, *23*, 200–210.

Cerny, L., Kucerova, Z., & Sturma, J. Pemoline in comparison with amphetamine and placebo in pedopsychiatric practice. *Activitas Nervosa Superior*, 1975, *17*, 300–301.

Chandler, M. J. Egocentrism and antisocial behavior: The assessment and training of social perspective-taking skills. *Developmental Psychology*, 1973, *9*, 326–332.

Chapel, J. L., Brown, N., & Jenkins, R. L. Tourette's disease: Symptomatic relief with haloperidol. *American Journal of Psychiatry*, 1964, *121*, 608–610.

Cheek, F. E. Family interaction patterns and convalescent adjustment of the schizophrenic. *Archives of General Psychiatry*, 1965, *13*, 138–147.

Chess, S. *An introduction to child psychiatry*. New York: Grune & Stratton, 1969.

Cicirelli, V. G., Evans, J. W., & Schiller, J. S. The impact of Head Start: A reply to the report analysis. *Harvard Educational Review*, 1970, *40*, 105–131.

Clark, H. B., Caldwell, C. P., & Christian, W. P. Classroom training of conversational skills and remote programming for the practice of these skills in another setting. *Child Behavior Therapy*, 1979, *1*, 139–160.

Clark, K. B., & Hopkins, J. *A relevant war against poverty: A study of community action programs and observable social change*. New York: Harper & Row, 1969.

Clement, P. W., Anderson, E., Arnold, J., Butman, R., Fantuzzo, J., & Mays, R. Self-observation and self-reinforcement as sources of self-control in children. *Biofeedback and Self-Regulation*, 1978, *3*, 247–267.

Clement, P. W., & Milne, D. C. Group play therapy and tangible reinforcers used to modify the behavior of eight-year-old boys. *Behavior Re-

search and Therapy*, 1967, *5*, 301–312.

Cohen, N. J., Douglas, V. I., & Morgenstern, C. The effect of methylphenidate on attentive behavior and autonomic activity in hyperactive children. *Psychopharmacologia*, 1971, *22*, 282.

Cohen, R. L. BPLAY: A community support system, phase one. In E. Ribes-Inesta & A. Bandura (Eds.), *Analysis of delinquency and aggression*. Hillsdale, N.J.: Erlbaum, 1976.

Cohen, R. L., & Filipczak, J. *A new learning environment*. San Francisco: Jossey-Bass, 1971.

Comly, H. H. Cerebral stimulants for children with learning disorders? *Journal of Learning Disabilities*, 1971, *4*, 484–490.

Conners, C. K. Deanol and behavior disorders in children: A critical review of the literature and recommended future studies for determining efficacy. In Pharmacotherapy of children (Special Issue), *Psychopharmacology Bulletin*, 1973.

Conners, C. K., Denkhoff, E., Millichap, J. G., & O'Leary, S. G. Decisions for action in hyperkinesis. *Patient Care*, 1978, *12*, 94–154.

Conners, C. K., Eisenberg, L., & Bercai, A. Effect of dextroamphetamine on children. *Archives of General Psychiatry*, 1967, *17*, 478–485.

Conners, C. K., Goyette, C. H., Southwick, D. A., Lees, J. M., & Andrulonis, P. A. Food additives and hyperkinesis. A controlled double blind experiment. *Pediatrics*, 1976, *58*, 154–166.

Conners, C. K., & Rothschild, G. Drugs and learning in children. In J. Hellmuth (Ed.), *Learning disorders* (Vol. 3). Seattle, Wash.: Special Child Publications, 1968.

Coolidge, J. C., & Grunebaum, M. G. Individual and group therapy of a latency-age child. *International Journal of Group Psychotherapy*, 1964, *14*, 84–96.

Coser, R. L. Authority and structural ambivalence in the middle-class family. In R. L. Coser (Ed.), *The family: Its structures and functions*. New York: St. Martin's Press, 1974.

Cott, A. Megavitamins: The orthomolecular approach to behavioral disorders and learning disabilities. *Academic Therapy*, 1972, *7*, 245–258.

Cotton, M., & Fein, D. Effectiveness of a community based treatment program in modifying aggressiveness of delinquent behavior. *Corrective and Social Psychiatry and Journal of Behavior Technology, Methods and Therapy*, 1976, *22*, 35–38.

Cowen, E. L. Social and community intervention. *Annual Review of Psychology*, 1973, *24*, 423–472.

Cowen, E. L., & Gesten, E. L. Community approaches to intervention. In B. B. Wolman, J. Egan, & A. O. Ross (Eds.), *Handbook of treatment of mental disorders in childhood and adolescence*. Englewood Cliffs, N.J., Prentice-Hall, 1978.

Cowen, E. L., Pederson, A., Babigian, H., Izzo, L. E., & Trost, M. A. Long-term follow-up of early detected vulnerable children. *Journal of Consulting and Clinical Psychology*, 1973, *41*, 438–446.

Cowen, E. L., Trost, M. A., Lorion, R. P., Dorr, D., Izzo, L. D., & Isaacson, R. V. *New ways in school mental health: Early detection and presentation of school maladaption*. New York: Human Sciences Press, 1975.

Croghan, L., & Musante, G. J. The elimination of a boy's high building phobia by in vivo desensitization and game playing. *Journal of Behavior Therapy and Experimental Psychiatry*, 1975, *6*, 87–88.

Davidson, W. S., Seidman, E., Rappaport, J., Berck, P., Rapp, N., Rhodes, W., & Herring, J. Diversion program for juvenile offenders. *Social Work*, 1977, *13*, 40–49.

Davis, H., Mitchell, W. S., & Marks, F. A behavioural programme for the modification of encopresis. *Child Care, Health, and Development*, 1976, *2*, 273–282.

Demos, J. Myths and realities in the history of American family-life. In H. Gruenbaum & J. Christ (Eds.), *Contemporary marriage: Structure, dynamics and therapy*. Boston: Little Brown & Co., 1975.

Dixon, M., & Wright, W. E. *Juvenile delinquency prevention programs*. Paper presented at the Institute on Youth and Social Development, the John F. Kennedy Center for Research on Education and Human Development, George Peabody College for Teachers, Nashville, Tenn., October 1974.

Doleys, D. M. Behavioral treatments for nocturnal enuresis in children: A review of the recent literature. *Psychological Bulletin*, 1977, *84*, 30–54.

Donofrio, A. F. Parent education vs. child psychotherapy. *Psychology in the Schools*, 1976, *13*, 175–180.

Dougles, V., Parry, P., Marton, P., & Garson, C. Assessment of a cognitive training program for hyperactive children. *Journal of Abnormal Child Psychology*, 1976, *4*, 389–410.

Durlak, J. A. Description and evaluation of a behaviorally oriented school-based preventive mental health program. *Journal of Consulting and Clinical Psychology*, 1977, *45*, 27–33.

Durlak, J. A., & Mannarino, A. P. The social skills development program: Description of a school-based preventive mental health program for high risk youth. *Journal of Clinical Child Psychology*, 1977, *6*, 48–52.

Dykman, R. A., Ackerman, P. T., Peters, J. E., & McGrew, J. Psychological tests. In C. K. Conners (Ed.), *Clinical use of stimulant drugs in children*. New York: American Elsevier, 1974.

Edelman, R. I. Operant conditioning treatment of encopresis. *Journal of Behavior Therapy and Experimental Psychiatry*, 1971, *2*, 71–73.

Edgar, R., & Clement, P. W. *Teacher-controlled and self-controlled reinforcement with under-achieving, Black children*. Paper presented at the convention of the Western Psychological Association, Honolulu, May 1980.

Eisenberg, L., & Conners, C. K. Psychopharmacology in childhood. In N. B. Tabot, J. Kagan, & L. Eisenberg (Eds.), *Behavioral science in pediatric medicine*. Philadelphia: W.B. Saunders Co., 1971.

Elkind, F., & Handel, G. *The child and society: The process of socialization*. New York: Random House, 1978.

Engelhardt, D. M., Polizos, A., Waizer, J., & Hoffman, S. P. A double-blind comparison of fluphenazine and haloperidol in outpatient schizophrenic children. *Journal of Autism and Childhood Schizophrenia*, 1973, *3*, 128–137.

Englemann, S. The effectiveness of direct instruction on IQ performance and achievement in reading and arithmetic. In J. Hellmuth (Ed.), *Compensatory education: A national debate*, vol. 3, *The disadvantaged child*. New York: Brunner-Mazel, 1970.

Enright, R. D. Social cognition in children: A model for intervention. *Counseling Psychologist*, 1976, *6*, 65–69.

Erickson, M. H., & Rossi, E. L. *Hypnotherapy: An exploratory casebook*. New York: Irvington, 1979.

Faretra, G., Dooher, L., & Dowling, J. Comparison of haloperidol and fluphenazine in disturbed children. *American Journal of Psychiatry*, 1970, *126*, 1670–1673.

Farina, A., & Dunham, R. M. Measurement of family relationships and their effects. *Archives of General Psychiatry*, 1963, *9*, 64–73.

FBI Uniform Crime Reports. Crime in the United States 1978. Washington, D.C.: U.S. Government Printing Office, 1979.

Feingold, B. F. *Why your child is hyperactive*. New York: Random House, 1975.

Fenichel, C. Special education as the basic therapeutic tool in treatment of severely disturbed children. *Journal of Autism and Childhood Schizophrenia*, 1974, *4*, 177–186.

Ferber, H., Keeley, S. N., & Schemberg, K. M. Training parents in behavior modification: Outcome of and problems encountered in a program after Patterson's work. *Behavior Therapy*, 1974, *5*, 415–419.

Ferinden, W., & Van Handel, D. Elimination of soiling behavior in an elementary school child through the application of aversive techniques. *Journal of School Psychology*, 1970, *8*, 267–269.

Ferreira, A. J., & Winter, W. D. Family interaction and decision-making. *Archives of General Psychiatry*, 1965, *12*, 214–233.

Ferreira, A. J., & Winter, W. D. Decision making in normal and abnormal two-child families. *Family Process*, 1968, *7*, 17–26.

Fish, B. Drug therapy in child psychiatry: Pharmacological aspects. *Comprehensive Psychiatry*, 1960, *1*, 212–227.

Fish, B. The "one child, one drug" myth of stimulants in hyperkinesis: Importance of diagnostic categories in evaluating treatment. *Archives of General Psychiatry*, 1971, *25*, 193–203.

Fish, B. Biological antecedents of psychosis in children. In D. X. Freedman (Ed.), *The biology of the major psychoses: A comparative analysis.* New York: Raven Press, 1975.

Fish, B. Pharmacotherapy for autistic and schizophrenic children. In E. R. Ritvo, B. J. Freeman, E. M. Ornitz, & P. E. Tanguay (Eds.), *Autism: Diagnosis, current research and management.* New York: Spectrum Publications, 1976.

Fish, B., & Shapiro, T. A typology of children's psychiatric disorders: I. Its application to a controlled evaluation of treatment. *Journal of the American Academy of Child Psychiatry*, 1965, *4*, 32–52.

Fishman, J. R., Denham, W. H., Levine, M., & Schatz, E. O. *New careers for the disadvantaged in human service: Report of a social experiment.* Washington, D.C.: Howard University Institute for Youth Studies, 1969.

Fleischman, M. J. The effects of a parenting salary to control attrition and cooperation in therapy. *Behavior Therapy*, 1979, *10*, 111–116.

Fleischman, M. J., & Szykula, S. A. A community setting replication of a social learning treatment for aggressive children. *Behavior Therapy*, 1981, *12*, 115–122.

Fo, W. S. O., & O'Donnell, C. R. The buddy system: Relationship and contingency conditions in a community intervention program for youth with professionals as behavior change agents. *Journal of Consulting and Clinical Psychology*, 1974, *42*, 163–169.

Foltz, D. Judgment withheld on DSM-III, new child classification pushed. *APA Monitor*, January 1980, p. 1.

Fontana, A. F. Familial etiology of schizophrenia: Is a scientific methodology possible? *Psychological Bulletin*, 1965, *66*, 214–227.

Forehand, R., & Atkeson, B. M. Generality of treatment effects with parents as therapists: A review of assessment and implementation procedures. *Behavior Therapy*, 1977, *8*, 575–593.

Forehand, R., Wells, K. C., & Griest, D. L. An examination of the social validity of a parent training program. *Behavior Therapy*, 1980, *11*, 488–502.

Foxx, R. M., & Azrin, N. H. Dry pants: A rapid method of toilet training children. *Behavior Research and Therapy*, 1973, *11*, 435–442. (a)

Foxx, R. M., & Azrin, N. H. The elimination of autistic self-stimulatory behavior by overcorrection. *Journal of Applied Behavior Analysis*, 1973, *6*, 1–14. (b)

Framo, J. L. Systematic research on family dynamics. In I. Boszormenyi-Nagy & J. L. Framo (Eds.), *Intensive family therapy*. New York: Hoeber/Harper & Row, 1965.

Framo, J. L. Family theory and therapy. *American Psychologist*, 1979, *34*, 988–992.

Frank, G. H. The role of the family in the development of psychopathology. *Psychological Bulletin*, 1965, *64*, 191–205.

Freeman, B. J., Rivto, E., & Miller, R. An operant procedure to teach an echolalic, autistic child to answer questions appropriately. *Journal of Autism and Childhood Schizophrenia*, 1975, *5*, 169–176.

Friedling, C., & O'Leary, S. G. Effects of self-instructional training on second- and third-grade hyperactive children: A failure to replicate. *Journal of Applied Behavior Analysis*, 1979, *12*, 211–219.

Gardner, R. A. The mutual storytelling techniques in the treatment of anger inhibition problems. *International Journal of Child Psychotherapy*, 1971, *1*, 34–64.

Garrigan, J. J., & Bambrick, A. F. Short-term family therapy with emotionally disturbed children. *Journal of Marriage and Family Counseling*, 1975, *1*, 379–385.

Garrigan, J. J., & Bambrick, A. F. New findings in

research on the go-between process. *International Journal of Family Therapy*, 1979, *1*, 76–85.

Gelfand, D. W., Jensen, R., & Drew, C. J. *Understanding children's behavior disorders*. New York: Holt, Rinehart & Winston, 1981.

Gesten, E. L., de Apodaca, R., Rains, R., Weissberg, R. P., & Cowen, E. L. Promoting peer related social competence in schools. In M. W. Kent & J. E. Rolf (Eds.), *The primary prevention of psychopathology*, vol. 3, *Social competence in children*. Hanover, N.H.: University Press of New England, 1979.

Getman, G. The visuomotor complex in the acquisition of learning skills. *Learning Disorders*, 1965, *1*, 1949.

Gilpin, D. C. Psychotherapy of borderline psychotic children. *American Journal of Psychotherapy*, 1976, *30*, 483–496.

Gittleman-Klein, R., & Klein, D. F. School phobia: Diagnostic considerations in the light of Imipramine effects. *The Journal of Nervous and Mental Disease*, 1973, *156*, 199–215.

Gittleman-Klein, R., Klein, D. F., Abikoff, H., Katz, S., Gloisten, A. C., & Kates, W. Relative efficacy of methylphenidate and behavior modification in hyperkinetic children: An interim report. *Journal of Abnormal Child Psychology*, 1976, *4*, 361–379.

Glass, G. V., & Smith, M. L. *Meta-analysis of psychotherapy outcome studies*. Paper presented at meeting of the Society for Psychotherapy Research, San Diego, June 1976.

Glenwick, D. S., & Barocas, R. Training impulsive children in verbal self-control by use of natural change agents. *Journal of Special Education*, 1979, *13*, 387–398.

Gleser, G. C. Psychometric contributions to the assessment of patients. In D. H. Efron, J. O. Cole, J. Levine, & J. R. Wittenhorn (Eds.), *Psychopharmacology, a review of progress, 1956–1967*. (U.S. Public Health Service Publication No. 1836). Washington, D.C.: U.S. Government Printing Office, 1968.

Glidewell, J. C., & Swallow, C. S. *The prevalence of maladjustment in elementary schools: A report prepared for the Joint Commission on the mental health of children*. Chicago: University of Chicago Press, 1969.

Goldenberg, I. I. *Build me a mountain: Youth poverty and the creation of new settings*. Cambridge, Mass.: MIT Press, 1971.

Goldstein, M. J., Judd, L. L., Rodnick, E. H., Alkire, A. A., & Gould, E. A method for studying social influence and coping patterns within families of disturbed adolescents. *Journal of Nervous and Mental Disorders*, 1968, *147*, 233–251.

Goodman, C. *Developing natural support systems in a day hospital program for parents of high risk children*. Paper presented at the convention of the American Psychological Association, New York, September 1979.

Goodwin, S., & Mahoney, M. Modification of aggression through modeling: An experimental probe. *Journal of Behavior Therapy and Experimental Psychiatry*, 1975, *6*, 200–202.

Gottman, J. M. *Marital interaction: Experimental investigations*. New York: Academic Press, 1979.

Gottman, J., Gonso, J., & Schuler, P. Teaching social skills to isolated children. *Journal of Abnormal Child Psychology*, 1976, *4*, 179–197.

Gottman, J. M., & Markman, H. J. Experimental designs in psychotherapy research. In S. L. Garfield & A. E. Bergin (Eds.), *Handbook of psychotherapy and behavior change: An empirical analysis*. New York: Wiley, 1978.

Gram, L. F., & Rafaelsen, O. J. Lithium treatment of psychotic children. A controlled clinical trial. In A. L. Annell (Ed.), *Depressive states in childhood and adolescence*. Stockholm: Almquist and Wiksell, 1972.

Gratton, L., & Rizzo, A. E. Group therapy with young psychotic children. *International Journal of Group Psychotherapy*, 1969, *19*, 63–71.

Gray, J. S. A biological view of behavior modification. *Journal of Educational Psychology*, 1932, *23*, 611–620.

Gray, S. W., & Klaus, R. A. The early training project: A seventh year report. *Child Development*, 1970, *41*, 909–924.

Graziano, A. M. A group treatment approach to multiple problem behaviors of autistic children. *Exceptional Children*, 1970, *36*, 765–770.

Graziano, A. M. Behavior therapy. In B. B. Wolman, J. Egan, & A. O. Ross (Eds.), *Handbook of treatment of mental disorders in childhood and adolescence*. Englewood Cliffs, N.J.: Prentice-Hall, 1978.

Greenbaum, G. H. An evaluation of niacinamide in the treatment of childhood schizophrenia. *American Journal of Psychiatry*, 1970, *127*, 129–132.

Griest, D., Wells, K. C., & Forehand, R. An examination of predictors of maternal perceptions of maladjustment in clinic-referred children. *Journal of Abnormal Psychology*, 1979, *88*, 277–281.

Griffith, E. E., Schnelle, J. R., McNees, M. P.,

Bissinger, C., & Huff, T. M. Elective mutism in a first-grader: The remediation of a complex behavioral problem. *Journal of Abnormal Child Psychology*, 1975, *3*, 127–134.

Griggs, J. W., & Bonney, M. E. Relationship between "causal" orientation and acceptance of others, "self-ideal self" congruency and mental health changes for fourth and fifth grade children. *Journal of Educational Research*, 1970, *63*, 471–477.

Group for the Advancement of Psychiatry (GAP). *Pharmacotherapy and psychotherapy: Paradoxes, problems and progress*, 1975, *9*, Report No. 93.

Gurman, A. S., & Kniskern, D. P. Research on marital and family therapy: Progress, perspective, and prospect. In S. L. Garfield & A. E. Bergin (Eds.), *Handbook of psychotherapy and behavior change: An empirical analysis*. New York: Wiley, 1978.

Haley, J. *Strategies of psychotherapy*. New York: Grune & Stratton, 1963.

Haley, J. Experiments with abnormal families. *Archives of General Psychiatry*, 1967, *17*, 53–63. (a)

Haley, J. Speech sequences of normal and abnormal families with two children present. *Family Process*, 1967, *6*, 81–97. (b)

Haley, J. *Uncommon therapy*. New York: Norton, 1973.

Haley, J. *Problem-solving therapy*. San Francisco: Jossey-Bass, 1976.

Handel, G. The psychological study of whole families. *Psychological Bulletin*, 1965, *63*, 19–41.

Handler, L. The amelioration of nightmares in children. *Psychotherapy: Theory, Research, and Practice*, 1972, *9*, 54–56.

Heinicke, C. M. Frequency of psychotherapeutic session as a factor affecting outcome: Analysis of clinical ratings and test results. *Journal of Abnormal Psychology*, 1969, *74*, 533–560.

Heinicke, C. M., & Strassmann, L. H. Toward more effective research on child psychotherapy. *American Academy of Child Psychiatry*, 1975, *14*, 561–588.

Heller, K., & Monahan, J. *Psychology and community change*. Homewood, Ill.: Dorsey Press, 1977.

Henker, B., Whalen, C. K., & Hinshaw, S. P. The attributional contexts of cognitive intervention strategies. *Exceptional Education*, 1980, *1*, 17–30.

Hersen, M. Treatment of a compulsive and phobic disorder through a total behavior therapy program: A case study. *Psychotherapy: Theory, Research, and Practice*, 1968, *5*, 220–225.

Hetherington, E. M. Divorce: A child's perspective. *American Psychologist*, 1979, *34*, 851–858.

Hetherington, E. M., Cox, M., & Cox, R. Divorced fathers. *Family Coordinator*, 1976, *25*, 417–428.

Hetherington, E. M., Cox, M., & Cox, R. The aftermath of divorce. In J. H. Stevens, Jr., & M. Mathews (Eds.), *Mother-child, father-child relations*. Washington, D.C.: National Association for the Education of Young Children, 1978.

Hetherington, E. M., Stouwis, R. J., & Ridderg, E. H. Patterns of family interaction and child-rearing attitudes related to three dimensions of juvenile delinquency. *Journal of Abnormal Psychology*, 1971, *78*, 160–176.

Hewett, F. M. Teaching speech to an autistic child through operant conditioning. *American Journal of Orthopsychiatry*, 1965, *35*, 927–936.

Hill, R. Methodological issues in family development research. *Family Process*, 1964, *3*, 186–206.

Hobbs, N. Mental health's third revolution. *American Journal of Orthopsychiatry*, 1964, *34*, 822–833.

Holter, F. R., & Ruttenberg, B. A. Initial interventions in psychotherapeutic treatment of autistic children. *Journal of Autism and Childhood Schizophrenia*, 1971, *1*, 206–214.

Holtzman, W. H. Statistical models for the study of change in the single case. In C. W. Harris (Ed.), *Problems in measuring change*. Madison: University of Wisconsin Press, 1963.

Hops, H. Social skills training for socially withdrawn/isolated children. In P. Karoly & J. Steffen (Eds.), *Advances in child behavior analysis and therapy*, vol. 2, *Intellectual and social deficiencies*. New York: Gardner Press, 1981.

Huessy, H. R., Marshall, C. D., & Gendron, R. A. Five hundred children followed from grade two through grade five for the prevalence of behavior disorder. In C. K. Conners (Ed.), *Clinical use of stimulant drugs in children*. New York: American Elsevier, 1974.

Jackson, D. D. Family interaction, family homeostasis and some implications for conjoint family psychotherapy. In J. Masserman (Ed.), *Individual and family dynamics*. New York: Grune & Stratton, 1959.

Jackson, D. D. Family rules. *Archives of General Psychiatry*, 1965, *12*, 589–594.

Jason, L. A. Behavioral approaches to prevention in the schools. In R. Price, J. Monahan, B. C.

Bader, & R. F. Ketterer (Eds.), *Prevention in community mental health: Research, policy and practice.* New York: Russell Sage Foundation, 1981.

Jesnes, C. F., DeRisis, W. J., McCormick, P. M., & Quedge, R. F. *The youth center research project.* Sacramento, Calif.: American Justice Institute, 1972.

Jewett, J., & Clark, H. B. Teaching preschoolers to use appropriate dinnertime conversation: An analysis of generalization from school to home. *Behavior Therapy,* 1979, *10,* 589–605.

Johnson, J. H., & Thompson, D. J. Modeling in the treatment of enuresis: A case study. *Journal of Behavior Therapy and Experimental Psychiatry,* 1974, *5,* 93–94.

Jones, M. C. A laboratory study of fear: The case of Peter. *Pedagogical Seminary,* 1924, *31,* 308–315.

Justice, B., & Duncan, D. F. Running away: An epidemic problem of adolescence. *Adolescence,* 1976, *11,* 365–371.

Kahn, R. M., & Arbib, M. A. A cybernetic approach to childhood psychosis. *Journal of Autism and Childhood Schizophrenia,* 1973, *3,* 261–273.

Kaplan, A. *The conduct of inquiry: Methodology for behavioral science.* New York: Thomas Y. Crowell, 1964.

Karachi, L., Schmidt, A., & Cairor, H. *Follow-up of Kennedy Youth Center releases.* Kennedy Youth Center, Charleston, West Virginia, 1972.

Karnes, M. B., Teska, J. A., & Hodgins, A. S. The effects of four programs of classroom intervention on the intellectual and language development of 4-year-old disadvantaged children. *American Journal of Orthopsychiatry,* 1970, *40,* 58–76.

Karnes, M. B., Teska, J. A., Hodgins, A. S., & Badger, I. D. Educational intervention at home by mothers of disadvantaged infants. *Child Development,* 1970, *41,* 925–935.

Kauffman, J. M., & Scranton, T. R. Parent control of thumb sucking in their home. *Child Study Journal,* 1974, *4,* 1–10.

Kazdin, A. E. Advances in child behavior therapy: Applications and implications. *American Psychologist,* 1979, *34,* 981–987.

Keehn, J. D. Brief case report: Reinforcement therapy for incontinence. *Behavior Research and Therapy,* 1965, *2,* 239.

Kellam, S. G., Branch, J. D., Agrawal, K. C., & Ensminger, M. E. *Mental health and going to school: The Woodlawn program of assessment,* early intervention, and evaluation. Chicago: University of Chicago Press, 1975.

Keller, M. F., & Carlson, P. M. The use of symbolic modeling to promote social skills in preschool children with low levels of social responsiveness. *Child Development,* 1974, *45,* 912–919.

Kelly, D., Guirguis, W., Frommer, E., Mitchell-Heggs, N., & Sargant, W. Treatment of phobic states with antidepressants: A retrospective study of 246 patients. *British Journal of Psychiatry,* 1970, *116,* 387–398.

Kelly, J. G. Ecological constraints on mental health services. *American Psychologist,* 1966, *21,* 535–539.

Kendall, P. C. *Self-instructions with children: An analysis of the inconsistent evidence for treatment generalization.* Paper presented at the convention of the American Association for Behavior Therapy, San Francisco, December 1979.

Kendall, P. C., & Finch, A. J., Jr. A cognitive-behavioral treatment for impulse control: A case study. *Journal of Consulting and Clinical Psychology,* 1976, *44,* 852–857.

Kendall, P. C., & Finch, A. J., Jr. A cognitive-behavioral treatment for impulsivity: A group comparison study. *Journal of Consulting and Clinical Psychology,* 1978, *46,* 110–118.

Kendall, P. C., & Finch, A. J., Jr. Analyses of changes in verbal behavior following a cognitive-behavioral treatment for impulsivity. *Journal of Abnormal Child Psychology,* 1979, *7,* 455–463.

Kendall, P. C., & Wilcox, L. E. Cognitive-behavioral treatment for impulsivity: Concrete versus conceptual training in non-self-controlled problem children. *Journal of Consulting and Clinical Psychology,* 1980, *48,* 80–91.

Kerr, M. M., & Strain, P. S. *The use of peer social initiation strategies to improve the social skills of withdrawn children.* Paper presented at the First World Congress on Future Special Education, Stirling, Scotland, June 1978.

Kestenbaum, C. J. Childhood psychosis: Psychotherapy. In B. B. Wolman, J. Egan, & A. Q. Ross (Eds.), *Handbook of treatment of mental disorders in childhood and adolescence.* Englewood Cliffs, N.J.: Prentice-Hall, 1978.

Kimmel, H. D., & Kimmel, E. An instrumental conditioning method for the treatment of enuresis. *Journal of Behavior Therapy and Experimental Psychiatry,* 1970, *1,* 121–123.

Kirigin, K. A., Wolf, M. M., Braukmann, C. J., Fixsen, D. L., & Phillips, E. L. Achievement place: A preliminary outcome evaluation. In J. S.

Stumphauzer (Ed.), *Progress and behavior therapy with delinquents*. Springfield, Ill.: Charles C. Thomas, 1979.

Kirk, R. E. *Experimental design: Procedures for the behavioral sciences*. Belmont, Calif.: Brooks/Cole, 1968.

Kissel, S. Systematic desensitization therapy with children: A case study and some suggested modifications. *Professional Psychology*, 1972, *3*, 164–168.

Klein, N. C., Alexander, J. F., & Parsons, B. V. Impact of family systems intervention on recidivism and sibling delinquency: A model of primary prevention and program evaluation. *Journal of Consulting and Clinical Psychology*, 1977, *45*, 469–474.

Klein, N. C., Barton, C., & Alexander, J. F. Intervention and action in family settings. In R. Price & P. Politsen (Eds.), *Evaluation and action in the community context*. New York: Academic Press, 1980.

Koegel, R. L., & Rincover, A. Treatment of psychotic children in classroom environment: I. Learning in a larger group. *Journal of Applied Behavior Analysis*, 1974, *7*, 45–59.

Kolvin, I. Psychoses in childhood: A comparative study. In M. Rutler (Ed.), *Infantile autism: Concepts, characteristics, and treatment*. Edinburgh: Churchill Livingstone, 1971.

Korein, J., Fish, B., Shapiro, T., Gerner, E. W., & Levidow, L. EEG and behavioral effects of drug therapy in children. Chlorpromazine and diphenhydramine. *Archives of General Psychiatry*, 1971, *24*, 552–563.

Kornhaber, R. C., & Schroeder, H. E. Importance of model similarity on extinction of avoidance behavior in children. *Journal of Consulting and Clinical Psychology*, 1975, *43*, 601–607.

Kraft, I. A. Child and adolescent group therapy. In H. I. Kaplan & B. J. Sadock (Eds.), *Group treatment of mental illness*. New York: E. P. Dutton, 1972.

Kurtis, L. B. Clinical study of the response to nortriptyline on autistic children. *International Journal of Neuropsychiatry*, 1966, *2*, 298–301.

Kushler, M. G., Emshoff, J. G., Blakely, C. H., & Davidson, W. S. *Youth advocacy: A strategy for service to troubled youth*. Paper presented at the convention of the American Psychological Association, New York, September 1979.

Lahey, B. B., McNees, M. P., & McNees, M. C. Control of an obscene ''verbal tick'' through time-out in an elementary school classroom. *Journal of Applied Behavior Analysis*, 1973, *6*, 101–104.

Lamb, D. *Psychotherapy with adolescent girls*. San Francisco: Jossey-Bass, 1978.

Langs, R. *The technique of psychoanalytic psychotherapy*. New York: Jason Aronson, 1973.

Larcen, S. W., Selinger, H. V., Lochman, J. E., Chinsky, J. M., & Allen, G. J. *Implementation and evaluation of a multilevel preventive mental health program in a school system*. Paper presented at the convention of the American Psychological Association, New Orleans, August 1974.

Lazarus, A. A. Multimodal behavior therapy: Treating the BASIC ID. *Journal of Nervous Mental Disease*, 1973, *156*, 404–411.

LeBlanc, J. M., Etzel, B. C., & Domash, M. A. A functional curriculum for early intervention. In K. E. Allen, V. A. Holm, & R. L. Schiefelbusch (Eds.), *Early intervention: A team approach*. Baltimore: University Park Press, 1978.

Lederman, J. *Anger and the rocking chair*. New York: McGraw-Hill, 1969.

Lemert, E. M. *Instead of court: Diversion in juvenile justice. Crime and delinquency issues*. Rockville, Md.: National Institute of Mental Health, Center for Studies of Crime and Delinquency, 1971.

LeRoy, J. B., & Derdeyn, A. Drawings as a therapeutic medium. The treatment of separation anxiety in a four-year-old boy. *Child Psychiatry and Human Development*, 1976, *6*, 155–169.

Levine, M., & Graziano, A. M. Intervention programs in elementary schools. In S. E. Golann & C. Eisdorfer (Eds.), *Handbook of community mental health*. New York: Appleton-Century-Crofts, 1972.

Levinger, G. Supplementary methods in family research. *Family Process*, 1963, *2*, 357–366.

Levinstein, P. *Cognitive growth in preschoolers through stimulation of verbal interaction with mothers*. Paper presented at the convention of the American Orthopsychiatric Association, New York, March 1969.

Levitt, E. E. Research on psychotherapy with children. In A. E. Bergin & S. L. Garfield (Eds.), *Handbook of psychotherapy and behavior change: An empirical analysis*. New York: Wiley, 1971.

Lipsitz, J. *Growing up forgotten: A review of research and programs concerning early adolescence*. Lexington, Mass.: Lexington Books, 1977.

Luborsky, L., & Spence, D. P. Quantitative research on psychoanalytic therapy. In S. L. Garfield & A. E. Bergin (Eds.), *Handbook of psy-*

chotherapy and behavior change: An empirical analysis. New York: Wiley, 1978.

Lutzker, J. R. Deviant family systems. In B. B. Lahey & A. E. Kazdin (Eds.), *Advances in clinical child psychology* (Vol. 3). New York: Plenum, 1980.

Magnussen, M. G. Psychometric and projective techniques. In J. D. Call, J. D. Noshpitz, R. L. Cohen, & I. N. Berlin (Eds.), *Basic handbook of child psychiatry,* vol. 1, *Development.* New York: Basic Books, 1979.

Mahoney, M. J., & Arnkoff, D. B. Cognitive and self-control therapies. In S. L. Garfield & A. E. Bergin (Eds.), *Handbook of psychotherapy and behavior change: An empirical analysis.* New York: Wiley, 1978.

Malouf, J. L., & Alexander, J. F. Family therapy research in applied community settings. *Community Mental Health Journal,* 1976, *12,* 61–71. (a)

Malouf, R. E., & Alexander, J. F. *Peer review for psychologists.* Paper presented at the convention of the Western Psychological Association, Los Angeles, April 1976. (b)

Manning, W. H., Trutna, P. A., & Shaw, C. K. Verbal versus tangible reward for children who stutter. *Journal of Speech and Hearing Disorders,* 1976, *41,* 52–62.

Matson, J. L., & Ollendick, T. H. Elimination of low frequency biting. *Behavior Therapy,* 1976, *7,* 410–412.

McAfee, O. An integrated approach to early childhood education. In J. C. Stanley (Ed.), *Preschool programs for the disadvantaged: Five experimental approaches to early childhood education.* Baltimore: Johns Hopkins University Press, 1972.

McAndrew, J. B., Case, Q., & Treffert, D. A. Effects of prolonged phenothiazine intake on psychotic and other hospitalized children. *Journal of Autism and Childhood Schizophrenia,* 1972, *2,* 75–91.

McIntire, M., & Angle, C. Suicide as seen in Poison Control Centers. *Pediatrics,* 1971, *48,* 914–922.

McLaughlin, J. G., & Nay, W. R. Treatment of trichotillomania using positive coverants and response cost: A case study. *Behavior Therapy,* 1975, *6,* 87–91.

McMahon, R. J., Forehand, R., & Griest, D. C. *Effects of knowledge of social learning principles on enhancing treatment outcome and generalization in a parent training program.* Paper presented at the convention of the Association for the Advancement of Behavior Therapy, San Francisco, December 1979.

McNutt, B. A., Boileau, R. A., & Cohen, M. The effects of long-term stimulant medication on the growth and body composition of hyperactive children. *Psychopharmacology Bulletin,* 1977, *13,* 36–38.

Meadow, R. Drugs for bed-wetting. *Archives of Disease in Childhood,* 1974, *49,* 257–258.

Mealiea, W. L. Conjoint-behavior therapy: The modification of family constellations. In E. J. Mash, L. C. Handy, & L. A. Hamerlynck (Eds.), *Behavior modification approaches to parenting.* New York: Brunner-Mazel, 1976.

Meichenbaum, D., & Asarnow, J. Cognitive behavior modification and metacognitive development: Implications for the classroom. In P. C. Kendall & S. D. Hollon (Eds.), *Cognitive-behavioral interventions: Theory, research, and procedures.* New York: Academic Press, 1979.

Meichenbaum, D. H., & Goodman, J. Training impulsive children to talk to themselves: A means of developing self-control. *Journal of Abnormal Psychology,* 1971, *77,* 115–126.

Melamed, B. G., & Siegel, L. J. Reduction of anxiety in children facing hospitalization and surgery by use of filmed modeling. *Journal of Consulting and Clinical Psychology,* 1975, *43,* 511–521.

Menninger, K. A., & Holtzman, P. S. *Theory of psychoanalytic techniques.* New York: Basic Books, 1973.

Michelson, L., & DiLorenzo, T. M. The effect of audio feedback on reducing excessively loud voice volume. *Behavioral Engineering,* 1979, *5,* 141–145.

Michelson, L., DiLorenzo, T. M., Caplin, J. P., & Williamson, D. A. Modifying excessive lunchroom noise: Omission training with audio feedback and group contingent reinforcement. *Behavior Modification,* 1981, *5,* 553–564.

Michelson, L., & Wood, R. A group assertive training program for elementary school children. *Child Behavior Therapy,* 1980, *2,* 1–9.

Miller, L. C., Barrett, C. L., Hampe, E., & Noble, H. Comparison of reciprocal inhibition, psychotherapy and waiting list control for phobic children. *Journal of Abnormal Psychology,* 1972, *79,* 269–279.

Miller, N. B., & Cantwell, D. P. Siblings as therapists: A behavioral approach. *American Journal of Psychiatry,* 1976, *133,* 447–450.

Miller, R. Childhood schizophrenia: A review of selected literature. *International Journal of Mental Health,* 1975, *3,* 3–46.

Miller, S. J., & Sloane, H. N. The generalization effects of parent training across stimulus settings. *Journal of Applied Behavior Analysis,* 1976, *9,* 355–370.

Minuchin, S. *Families and family therapy.* Cambridge, Mass.: Harvard University Press, 1974.

Minuchin, S., Rosman, B., & Baker, L. *Psychosomatic families: Anorexia nervosa in context.* Cambridge, Mass.: Harvard University Press, 1978.

Mishler, E. G., & Waxler, N. E. *An experimental study of family processes and schizophrenia.* New York: Wiley, 1968.

Mishler, E. G., & Waxler, N. E. Functions of hesitations in the speech of normal families and the families of schizophrenic patients. *Language and Speech,* 1970, *13,* 102–117.

Mogar, R. E., & Aldrich, R. W. The use of psychedelic agents with autistic schizophrenic children. *Psychedelic Review,* 1969, *10,* 5–13.

Morton, T. L., Alexander, J. F., & Altman, I. Communication and relationship definition. In G. R. Miller (Ed.), *Annual review of communication research, vol. 5, Interpersonal communication.* Beverly Hills, Calif.: Sage Publications, 1976.

Mosse, H. L. The psychotherapeutic management of children with masked depression. In S. Lesse (Ed.), *Masked depression.* New York: Jason Aronson, 1974.

Munford, P. R., & Liberman, R. P. Differential attention in the treatment of operant cough. *Journal of Behavioral Medicine,* 1978, *1,* 289–295.

Munford, P. R., Reardon, D., Liberman, R. P., & Allen, L. Behavioral treatment of hysterical coughing and mutism: A case study. *Journal of Consulting and Clinical Psychology,* 1976, *44,* 1008–1014.

Murphy, I. C., & Elder, R. Treatment of a psychotic non-autistic. *Acta Paedopsychiatrica,* 1974, *40,* 190–195.

Murphy, L. B., & Chandler, C. A. Building foundations for strength in the preschool years: Preventing developmental disturbances. In S. E. Golann & C. Eisdorfer (Eds.), *Handbook of community mental health.* New York: Appleton-Century-Crofts, 1972.

Murray, E. J., & Jacobson, L. I. Cognition and learning in traditional and behavioral therapy. In S. L. Garfield & A. E. Bergin (Eds.), *Handbook of psychotherapy and behavior change: An empirical analysis.* New York: Wiley, 1978.

Murrell, S. A., & Stachowiak, J. G. Consistency, rigidity, and power in the interaction patterns of clinic and non-clinic families. *Journal of Abnormal Psychology,* 1967, *72,* 265–272.

Mussen, P. H. *Carmichael's manual of child psychology.* New York: Wiley, 1970.

Nelson, R. D., & Evans, I. M. The combinations of learning principles and speech therapy techniques in the treatment of non-communicating children. *Journal of Child Psychology and Psychiatry and Allied Disciplines,* 1968, *9,* 111–124.

Newton, M. R., & Brown, R. D. A preventive approach to developmental problems in school children. In E. M. Bower & W. G. Hollister (Eds.), *Behavioral science frontiers in education.* New York: Wiley, 1967.

Ney, P. G. Psychosis in a child, associated with amphetamine administration. *Canadian Medical Association Journal,* 1967, *97,* 1026–1029.

Oaklander, V. *Windows to our children.* Moab, Utah: Real People Press, 1978.

O'Connor, R. D. Modification of social withdrawal through symbolic modeling. *Journal of Applied Behavior Analysis,* 1969, *2,* 15–22.

O'Connor, R. D. Relative efficacy of modeling, shaping, and the combined procedures for modification of social withdrawal. *Journal of Abnormal Psychology,* 1972, *79,* 327–334.

O'Dell, S. Training parents in behavior modification: A review. *Psychological Bulletin,* 1974, *81,* 418–433.

Ojemann, R. H., Levitt, E. E., Lyle, W. H., & Whiteside, M. F. The effects of a "causal" teacher-training program and certain curricular changes on grade school children. *Journal of Experimental Education,* 1955, *24,* 95–114.

O'Leary, K. D. Pills or skills for hyperactive children. *Journal of Applied Behavior Analysis,* 1980, *13,* 191–204.

O'Leary, K. D., & Drabman, R. S. Token reinforcement programs in the classroom: A review. *Psychological Bulletin,* 1971, *75,* 379–398.

Ollendick, T. H., & Matson, J. L. Over-correction: An overview. *Behavior Therapy,* 1978, *9,* 830–842.

Olson, D. H. The measurement of power using self-report and behavioral methods. *Journal of Marriage and the Family,* 1969, *31,* 545–550.

Olson, D. H. Empirically unbinding the double bind: Review of research and conceptual reformulations. *Family Process,* 1972, *11,* 69–94.

O'Rourke, R. D. Troubled children: A new design for learning. *Teaching Exceptional Children,* 1977, *9,* 34–35.

Ossofsky, H. J. Endogenous depression in infancy

and childhood. *Comprehensive Psychiatry*, 1974, *15*, 19–25.

Page, J. G., Bernstein, J. E., Janicki, R. S., & Michelli, F. A. A multiclinical trial of pemoline in childhood hyperkinesis. In C. K. Conners (Ed.), *Clinical use of stimulant drugs in children*. New York: American Elsevier, 1974.

Palazzoli-Selvini, M., Boscolo, L., Cecchin, G., & Prata, G. *Paradox and counterparadox: A new model in the therapy of the family in schizophrenic transaction*. New York: Jason Aronson, 1978.

Palmer, S., Thompson, R. J., & Linscheid, T. R. Applied behavior analysis in the treatment of childhood feeding problems. *Developmental Medicine and Child Neurology*, 1975, *17*, 333–339.

Parke, R. D. Interactional design and experimental manipulation: The field lab interface. In R. B. Cairns (Ed.), *Social interaction: Methods, analysis and illustration*. Hillsdale, N.J.: Erlbaum, 1978.

Parloff, M. B., Waskow, I. E., & Wolfe, B. E. Research on therapist variables in relation to process and outcome. In S. L. Garfield & A. E. Bergin (Eds.), *Handbook of psychotherapy and behavior change: An empirical analysis*. New York: Wiley, 1978.

Parsons, B. V., & Alexander, J. F. Short term family intervention: A therapy outcome study. *Journal of Consulting and Clinical Psychology*, 1973, *41*, 195–201.

Patterson, G. R. *Families: Applications of social learning to family life*. Champaign, Ill.: Research Press, 1971.

Patterson, G. R. Interventions for boys with conduct problems: Multiple settings, treatments, and criteria. *Journal of Consulting and Clinical Psychology*, 1974, *42*, 471–481.

Patterson, G. R. The aggressive child: Victim or architect of a coercive system. In L. A. Hamerlynck, L. C. Handy, & E. J. Mash (Eds.), *Behavior modification and families: I. Theory and research*. New York: Brunner-Mazel, 1975.

Patterson, G. R. Treatment for children with conduct problems: A review of outcome studies. In S. Feshbach & A. Fraczek (Eds.), *Aggression and behavior change*. New York: Praeger, 1980.

Patterson, G. R., & Brodsky, G. A behavior modification programme for a child with multiple problem behaviors. *Journal of Child Psychology and Psychiatry*, 1966, *7*, 277–295.

Patterson, G. R., Cobb, J. A., & Ray, R. S. A social engineering technology for retraining the families of aggressive boys. In H. E. Adams & I. P. Unikel (Eds.), *Issues and trends in behavior therapy*. Springfield, Ill.: Charles C. Thomas, 1973.

Patterson, G. R., & Fleischman, M. J. Maintenance of treatment effects: Some considerations concerning family systems and follow-up data. *Behavior Therapy*, 1979, *10*, 168–185.

Patterson, G. R., & Guillion, M. E. *Living with children: New methods for parents and teachers*. Champaign, Ill.: Research Press, 1968.

Patterson, G. R., & Reid, J. B. Reciprocity and coercion: Two facets of social systems. In C. Neuringer & J. Michael (Eds.), *Behavior modification in clinical psychology*. New York: Appleton-Century-Crofts, 1970.

Patterson, G. R., & Reid, J. B. Intervention for families of aggressive boys: A replication study. *Behavior Research and Therapy*, 1973, *11*, 383–394.

Peed, R., Roberts, M., & Forehand, R. An evaluation of the effectiveness of a standardized parent training program and altering the interaction of mothers and their noncompliant children. *Behavior Modification*, 1977, *1*, 323–350.

Pelham, W. E., Schnedler, R. W., Bologna, N. C., & Contreras, J. A. Behavioral and stimulant treatment of hyperactive children: A therapy study with methylphenidate probes in a within-subject design. *Journal of Applied Behavior Analysis*, 1980, *13*, 221–236.

Pelham, W. E., Schnedler, R. W., Miller, J., Ronnei, M., Paluchowski, C., Budrow, M. S., Marks, D. A., Nilsson, D., & Bender, M. E. *The combination of behavior therapy and psychostimulant medication in the treatment of hyperactive children: A therapy outcome study*. Paper presented at the meeting of the Association for the Advancement of Behavior Therapy, San Francisco, December 1979.

Pesikoff, R. B., & Davis, P. C. Treatment of pavor nocturnus and somnambulism in children. *American Journal of Psychiatry*, 1971, *128*, 778–781.

Petit, J. M., & Biggs, J. T. Tricyclic antidepressant overdoses in adolescent patients. *Pediatrics*, 1977, *59*, 283–287.

Phillips, E. L., Phillips, E. A., Fixsen, D. L., & Wolf, M. M. Achievement place: Modification of the behavior of pre-delinquent boys within a token economy period. *Journal of Applied Behavior Analysis*, 1971, *4*, 45–59.

Phillips, E. L., Phillips, E. A., Fixsen, D. L., & Wolf, M. M. *The teaching family handbook*. Lawrence, Kansas: University of Kansas Printing Service, 1972.

Plant, W. T., & Southern, M. L. The intellectual and achievement effects of preschool cognitive stimulation of poverty Mexican-American children. *Genetic Psychology Monographs*, 1972, *86*, 141–173.

Plenk, A. M. Activity group therapy for emotionally disturbed preschool children. *Behavior Disorders*, 1978, *3*, 210–218.

Polák, L., Molčan, J., & Škoricová, M. Comparison of three types of therapy in enuresis. *Activitas Nervosa Superior*, 1975, *17*, 238.

Polizos, P., Engelhardt, D. M., Hoffman, S. P., & Waizer, J. Neurological consequences of psychotropic drug withdrawal in schizophrenic children. *Journal of Autism and Childhood Schizophrenia*, 1973, *3*, 247–253.

Pool, D., Bloom, W., Mielke, D. H., Roniger, J. J., & Gallant, D. M. A controlled evaluation of Loxitane in seventy-five adolescent schizophrenic patients. *Current Therapeutic Research*, 1976, *19*, 99–104.

Porterfield, J. K., Herbert-Jackson, E., & Risley, T. R. Contingent observation: An effective and acceptable procedure for reducing disruptive behavior of young children in a group setting. *Journal of Applied Behavior Analysis*, 1976, *9*, 55–64.

Premack, D. Reinforcement theory. In D. Levine (Ed.), *Nebraska symposium on motivation*. Lincoln, Neb.: University of Nebraska Press, 1965.

Rabkin, L. Y. The patient's family: Research methods. *Family Process*, 1965, *4*, 105–132.

Rae-Grant, O., & Stringer, L. A. Mental health programs in schools. In M. F. Shore & F. V. Mannino (Eds.), *Mental health and the community: Problems, programs and strategies*. New York: Behavioral Publications, 1969.

Ragland, E. U., Kerr, M. M., & Strain, P. S. Behavior of withdrawn autistic children: Effects of peer social initiations. *Behavior Modification*, 1978, *2*, 565–578.

Rapoport, J. L. Pediatric psychopharmacology and childhood depression. In J. Schulterbrandt & A. Taskin (Eds.), *Depression in childhood: Diagnosis, treatment, and conceptual models*. New York: Raven Press, 1977.

Rapoport, J. L., Quinn, P. O., Bradbard, G., Riddle, D., & Brooks, E. Imipramine and methylphenidate treatments of hyperactive boys. *Archives of General Psychiatry*, 1974, *30*, 789–793.

Rappaport, J. *Community psychology: Values, research, and action*. New York: Holt, Rinehart &

Winston, 1977.

Reinhart, J. B., Kenna, M. D., & Succop, R. A. Anorexia nervosa in children: Outpatient management. *Journal of the American Academy of Child Psychiatry*, 1972, *11*, 114–131.

Reiss, D. Intimacy and problem solving: An automated procedure for testing a theory of consensual experiences in families. *Archives of General Psychiatry*, 1971, *25*, 442–455.

Rhead, J. C. The use of psychedelic drugs in the treatment of severely disturbed children: A review. *Journal of Psychedelic Drugs*, 1977, *9*, 93–101.

Rickel, A. U., & Smith, R. L. Maladapting preschool children: Identification, diagnosis and remediation. *American Journal of Community Psychology*, 1979, *7*, 197–208.

Rimland, B. High dosage levels of certain vitamins in the treatment of children with severe mental disorders. In D. Hawkins & L. Pauling (Eds.), *Orthomolecular psychiatry*. San Francisco: W. H. Freeman & Co., 1973.

Riskin, J., & Faunce, E. E. An evaluative review of family interaction research. *Family Process*, 1972, *11*, 365–455.

Roberts, M. W., & Hatzenbuehler, L. C. Parent treatment of command elicited negative verbalizations: A question of persistence. *Journal of Clinical Child Psychology*, 1981, *10*, 107–113.

Roberts, M. W., McMahon, R. J., Forehand, R., & Humphreys, L. The effect of parent instruction-giving on child compliance. *Behavior Therapy*, 1978, *9*, 973–978.

Robin, A. L. Parent-adolescent conflict: A skill training approach. In D. P. Rathjen & J. P. Foreyt (Eds.), *Social competence: Interventions for children and adults*. New York: Pergamon, 1980.

Robin, A. L., Kent, R. M., O'Leary, K. D., Foster, S., & Prinz, R. J. An approach to teaching parents and adolescents problem-solving communication skills: A preliminary report. *Behavior Therapy*, 1977, *8*, 639–643.

Rock, N. L. Childhood psychosis and long-term chemo- and psychotherapy. *Diseases of the Nervous System*, 1974, *35*, 303–308.

Rogers, C. In retrospect: Forty-six years. *American Psychologist*, 1974, *29*, 115–123.

Roiphe, H. Some thoughts on childhood psychosis: Self and object. *Psychoanalytic Study of the Child*, 1973, *28*, 131–145.

Romanczyk, R. G., Diament, C., Goren, E. R., Trunnell, G., & Harris, S. L. Increasing isolate and social play in severely disturbed children:

Intervention and post-intervention effectiveness. *Journal of Autism and Childhood Schizophrenia*, 1975, *5*, 57–70.

Rosenbaum, E., & Kellman, M. Treatment of a selectively mute third-grade child. *Journal of School Psychology*, 1973, *11*, 26–29.

Ross, A. L., & Bernstein, N. D. A framework for the therapeutic use of group activities. *Child Welfare*, 1976, *55*, 627–640.

Ross, A. O. Behavior therapy with children. In S. L. Garfield & A. E. Bergin (Eds.), *Handbook of psychotherapy and behavior change: An empirical analysis*. New York: Wiley, 1978.

Ross, D. M., Ross, S. A., & Evans, T. A. The modification of extreme social withdrawal by modeling with guided participation. *Journal of Behavior Therapy and Experimental Psychiatry*, 1971, *2*, 275–279.

Ross, J. A. Use of teacher and peers to control classroom thumb-sucking. *Psychological Reports*, 1974, *34*, 327–330.

Ross, J. A., & Levine, B. A. Control of thumb-sucking in the classroom, case study. *Perceptual and Motor Skills*, 1972, *34*, 584–586.

Ryder, R. G. Husband-wife dyads versus married strangers. *Family Process*, 1968, *7*, 233–238.

Ryder, R. G., & Goodrich, D. W. Married couples' responses to disagreement. *Family Process*, 1966, *5*, 30–42.

Sachs, D. A. The efficacy of time-out procedures in a variety of behavior problems. *Journal of Behavior Therapy and Experimental Psychiatry*, 1973, *4*, 237–242.

Safer, D. J., & Allen, R. P. Side effects from long-term use of stimulants in children. In R. Gittlemen-Klein (Ed.), Recent advances in child psychopharmacology. *International Journal of Mental Health*, 1975, *4*, 105–118.

Salvin, A., Routh, D. K., Foster, R. E., & Lovejoy, K. M. Acquisition of modified American sign language by a mute child. *Journal of Autism and Childhood Schizophrenia*, 1977, *7*, 359–371.

Samaan, M. The control of nocturnal enuresis by operant conditioning. *Journal of Behavior Therapy and Experimental Psychiatry*, 1972, *3*, 103–105.

Sandler, A. Comments on the significance of Piaget's work for psychoanalysis. *International Review of Psychoanalysis*, 1975, *2*, 365–377.

Satir, V. *Conjoint family therapy*. Palo Alto, Calif.: Science & Behavior Books, 1967.

Satterfield, J. H., & Cantwell, D. P. Psychopharmacology in the prevention of antisocial and delinquent behavior. *International Journal of Mental Health*, 1975, *4*, 227–237.

Satterfield, J. H., Cantwell, D. P., & Satterfield, B. T. Multimodality treatment. *Archives of General Psychiatry*, 1979, *36*, 965–974.

Scharfman, M. A. Psychoanalytic treatment. In B. B. Wolman, J. Egan, & A. O. Ross (Eds.), *Handbook of treatment of mental disorders in childhood and adolescence*. Englewood Cliffs, N.J.: Prentice-Hall, 1978.

Schelle, J. A brief report on invalidity of parent evaluations of behavior change. *Journal of Applied Behavior Analysis*, 1974, *7*, 341–343.

Schiele, B. C., Gallant, D., Simpson, G., Gardner, E. A., & Cole, J. O. Tardive dyskinesia. *American Journal of Orthopsychiatry*, 1973, *43*, 506.

Schneiderman, G., & Evans, H. An approach to families of acting-out adolescents: A case study. *Adolescence*, 1975, *10*, 495–498.

Schrag, P., & Divoky, D. *The myth of the hyperactive child*. New York: Pantheon, 1975.

Schur, E. *Radical non-intervention: Rethinking the delinquency problem*. Englewood Cliffs, N.J.: Prentice-Hall, 1973.

Shah, S. A. Perspectives and directions in juvenile corrections. *Psychiatric Quarterly*, 1973, *47*, 12–36.

Shostak, D. A. *Family versus individual oriented behavior therapy as treatment approaches to juvenile delinquency*. Unpublished doctoral dissertation, University of Virginia, 1977.

Simmons, J. Q., Benor, D., & Daniel, D. The variable effects of LSD-25 on the behavior of a heterogeneous group of childhood schizophrenics. *Behavioral Neuropsychiatry*, 1972, *4*, 10–16.

Simmons, J. Q., III, Leiken, S. J., Lovaas, O. I., Schaeffer, B., & Perloff, B. Modification of autistic behavior with LSD-25. *American Journal of Psychiatry*, 1966, *122*, 1201–1211.

Skinner, B. F. The science of learning and art of teaching. *Harvard Educational Review*, 1954, *24*, 86–97.

Sleator, E. K., Von Neumann, A., & Sprague, R. L. Hyperactive children: A continuous long-term placebo-controlled follow-up. *Journal of the American Medical Association*, 1974, *229*, 316–317.

Smith, J. Innovation in preventive psychotherapy with children. *American Journal of Psychoanalysis*, 1976, *36*, 355–360.

Smith, M. B., & Bissell, J. S. Report analysis: The impact of Head Start. *Harvard Educational Review*, 1970, *40*, 51–104.

Solnick, J. D., Braukmann, C. J., Bedlington, M. M., Kirigin, K. A., & Wolf, M. M. *The relation-*

ship between parents-youth interaction and delinquency in group homes. Paper presented in symposium at the convention of the American Psychological Association, New York, September 1979.

Sorosiak, F. M., Thomas, L. E., & Balet, F. N. Adolescent drug use: An analysis. *Psychological Reports,* 1976, *38,* 211–221.

Spivack, G., & Schure, M. B. *Social adjustment of young children.* San Francisco: Jossey-Bass, 1974.

Sprague, R. L. Psychopharmacotherapy in children. In M. F. McMillan & S. Henao (Eds.), *Child psychiatry: Treatment and research.* New York: Brunner-Mazel, 1977.

Sprague, R. L., & Sleator, E. K. Effects of psychopharmacologic agents on learning disorders. *Pediatric Clinics of North America,* 1973, *20,* 719–735.

Sprague, R. L., & Werry, J. S. Methodology of psychopharmacological studies with the retarded. In N. R. Ellis (Ed.), *International review of research in mental retardation.* New York: Academic Press, 1971.

Staats, A. W. *Social behaviorism.* Homewood, Ill.: Dorsey Press, 1975.

Stanton, M. D. Family therapy: Systems approaches. In G. P. Sholevar, R. M. Benson, & B. J. Blinder (Eds.), *Handbook of emotional disorders in children and adolescents: Medical and psychological approaches to treatment.* Jamaica, N.Y.: Medical and Scientific Books, Spectrum Publications, 1980. (a)

Stanton, M. D. Strategic approaches to family therapy. In A. S. Gurman & D. P. Kniskern (Eds.), *Handbook of family therapy.* New York: Brunner-Mazel, 1980. (b)

Stevens-Long, J., Schwarz, J. L., & Bliss, D. The acquisition and generalization of compound sentence structure in an autistic child. *Behavior Therapy,* 1976, *7,* 397–404.

Stokes, T. F., & Baer, D. M. An implicit technology of generalization. *Journal of Applied Behavior Analysis,* 1977, *10,* 349–367.

Strain, P. S. An experimental analysis of peer social initiations on the behavior of withdrawn preschool children: Some training and generalization effects. *Journal of Abnormal Child Psychology,* 1977, *5,* 445–455.

Strain, P. S., Kerr, M. M., & Ragland, E. U. Effects of peer-mediated social initiations and prompting-reinforcement procedures on the social behavior of autistic children. *Journal of Autism and Developmental Disorders,* 1979, *9,* 41–54.

Strain, P. S., Shore, R. E., & Kerr, M. M. An experimental analysis of "spill-over" effects on the social interaction of behaviorally handicapped preschool children. *Journal of Applied Behavior Analysis,* 1976, *9,* 31–40.

Strain, P. S., & Wiegerink, R. The school play of two behaviorally disordered preschool children during four activities. *Journal of Abnormal Child Psychology,* 1975, *3,* 61–69.

Straus, M. A. Communication, creativity and problem-solving ability of middle- and working-class families in three societies. *American Journal of Sociology,* 1968, *73,* 417–430.

Strodtbeck, F. L. Husband-wife interaction over revealed differences. *American Sociological Review,* 1951, *16,* 468–473.

Strodtbeck, F. L. The family as a three-person group. *American Sociological Review,* 1954, *19,* 23–29.

Strodtbeck, F. L. Family interaction, values and achievement. In D. C. McClelland (Ed.), *Talent and society.* New York: Van Nostrand, 1958.

Stuart, R. B., & Lott, L. A., Jr. Behavioral contracting with delinquents: A cautionary note. *Journal of Behavior Therapy and Experimental Psychiatry,* 1972, *3,* 161–169.

Szurek, S. A. Attachment and psychotic treatment. In S. A. Szurek & I. N. Berlin (Eds.), *Clinical studies in childhood psychosis.* New York: Brunner-Mazel, 1973.

Tasto, D. L. Systematic desensitization, muscle relaxation and visual imagery in the counter-conditioning of a four-year-old phobic child. *Behavior Research and Therapy,* 1969, *7,* 409–411.

Thomas, R., Chess, S., & Birch, H. G. *Temperament and behavior disorders in children.* New York: New York University Press, 1968.

Troester, J. D., & Darby, J. A. The role of the mini-meal in therapeutic play group. *Social Casework,* 1976, *57,* 97–103.

Tustin, F. Therapeutic communication between psychotherapist and psychotic child. *International Journal of Child Psychotherapy,* 1973, *2,* 440–450.

Ulrici, D. K., & Jurkovic, G. J. *Role of insight in child psychotherapy, reconsidered: A developmental analysis.* Paper presented at the convention of the American Psychological Association, New York, September 1979.

Urbain, E. S., & Kendall, P. C. Review of social-cognitive problem-solving interventions with children. *Psychological Bulletin,* 1980, *88,* 109–143.

Vandersall, T. A. Ulcerative colitis. In B. B. Wolman, J. Egan, & A. O. Ross (Eds.), *Handbook of treatment of mental disorders in childhood and adolescence*. Englewood Cliffs, N.J.: Prentice-Hall, 1978.

Wahler, R. G. Setting generality. Some specific and general effects of child behavior therapy. *Journal of Applied Behavior Analysis*, 1969, *2*, 239–246.

Wahler, R. G. Some structural aspects of deviant child behavior. *Journal of Applied Behavior Analysis*, 1975, *8*, 27–42.

Wahler, R. G., Berland, R. M., & Coe, T. D. Generalization processes in child behavior change. In B. B. Lahey, & A. E. Kazdin (Eds.), *Advances in clinical child psychology* (Vol. 2). New York: Plenum, 1979.

Wahler, R. G., Berland, R. M., Coe, T. D., & Leske, G. Social systems analysis: Implementing an alternative behavioral model. In A. R. Warren & S. F. Warren (Eds.), *Ecological perspectives in behavior analysis*. Baltimore: University Park Press, 1977.

Wahler, R. G., Leske, G., & Rogers, E. S. The insular family: A deviance support system for oppositional children. In L. A. Hammerlynck (Ed.), *Behavioral systems for the developmentally disabled: I. School and family environments*. New York: Brunner-Mazel, 1979.

Walker, H. M., & Hops, H. The use of group and individual reinforcement contingencies in the modification of social withdrawal. In L. A. Hamerlynck, L. C. Handy, & E. J. Mash (Eds.), *Behavior change: Methodology, concepts, and practice*. Champaign, Ill.: Research Press, 1973.

Walker, H. M., Hops, H., & Johnson, S. M. Generalization and maintenance of classroom treatment effects. *Behavior Therapy*, 1975, *6*, 188–200.

Walter, H. I., & Gilmore, S. K. Placebo vs. social learning effects in parent training procedures designed to alter the behavior of aggressive boys. *Behavior Research and Therapy*, 1973, *4*, 361–377.

Watzlawick, P., Beavin, J. H., & Jackson, D. D. *Pragmatics of human communication*. New York: Norton, 1967.

Watzlawick, P., Weakland, J., & Fisch, R. *Change: Principles of problem formation and problem resolution*. New York: Norton, 1974.

Waxler, N. E., & Mishler, E. G. Scoring and reliability problems in interaction process analysis: A methodological note. *Sociometry*, 1965, *29*, 32–49.

Waxler, N. E., & Mishler, E. G. Experimental studies of families. *Advances in Experimental Social Psychology*, 1970, *5*, 249–304.

Weakland, J. H. The "double bind" hypothesis of schizophrenia and three-party interaction. In D. D. Jackson (Ed.), *The etiology of schizophrenia*. New York: Basic Books, 1960.

Weakland, J. H., Fisch, R., Watzlawick, P., & Bodin, A. M. Brief therapy: Focused problem resolution. *Family Process*, 1974, *13*, 141–168.

Weathers, L., & Liberman, R. P. Contingency contracting with families of delinquent adolescents. *Behavior Therapy*, 1975, *6*, 356–366.

Weikart, D. P. Relationship of curriculum, teaching, and learning in preschool education. In J. C. Stanley (Ed.), *Preschool programs for the disadvantaged: Five experimental approaches to early childhood education*. Baltimore: Johns Hopkins University Press, 1972.

Weikart, D. P. *The impact of early childhood intervention on the development of juvenile delinquency*. Paper presented at the convention of the American Psychological Association, New York, September 1979.

Weil, G., & Goldfried, M. R. Treatment of insomnia in an eleven-year-old child through self-relaxation. *Behavior Therapy*, 1973, *4*, 282–284.

Weiner, I. B. *Psychological disturbance in adolescence*. New York: Wiley, 1970.

Weinrott, M. R., Bauske, B. W., & Patterson, G. R. Systematic replication of a social learning approach to parent training. In P. O. Sjoden, S. Bates, & W. S. Dockens (Eds.), *Trends in behavior therapy*. New York: Academic Press, 1979.

Wellish, D. K., Vincent, J., & Ro-Trock, G. K. Family therapy versus individual therapy: A study of adolescents and their parents. In D. H. L. Olson (Ed.), *Treating relationships*. Lake Mill, Iowa: Graphic Publishing Co., 1976.

Wells, K. C., Forehand, R., & Griest, D. L. Generality of treatment effects from treated to untreated behaviors resulting from a parent training program. *Journal of Clinical Child Psychology*, 1980, *9*, 217–219.

Westinghouse Learning Corporation/Ohio University. *The impact of Head Start: An evaluation of the effects of Head Start on children's cognitive and affective development*. Springfield, Va.: U.S. Department of Commerce (No. PB 184329), 1969.

Whalen, C. K., & Henker, B. Psychostimulants and children: A review and analysis. *Psychological Bulletin*, 1976, *83*, 1113–1130.

Whitehill, M. B., Hersen, M., & Bellack, A. S. *Conversation skills training for socially isolated children*. Paper presented at the convention of the American Psychological Association, New York, September 1979.

Williams, E. P. Behavioral technology and behavioral ecology. *Journal of Applied Behavior Analysis*, 1974, *7*, 151–160.

Winter, W. D., & Ferreira, A. J. *Research in family interaction: Readings and commentary*. Palo Alto, Calif.: Science & Behavior Books, 1969.

Wish, P. A., Hasazi, J. E., & Jurgela, A. R. Automated direct deconditioning of a childhood phobia. *Journal of Behavior Therapy and Experimental Psychology*, 1973, *4*, 279–283.

Wollersheim, J. P. Direct cognitive therapies: Distinguishing features and implication for psychology. In H. E. Wilson (Chair), *Direct cognitive therapist: Psychological and philosophical foundations and implications*. Symposium presented at the meeting of the Rocky Mountain Psychological Association, Tucson, Arizona, April 1981.

Wolpe, J. The practice of behavior therapy. Elmsford, N.Y.: Pergamon, 1969.

Wolpe, J., & Lazarus, A. A. *Behavior therapy techniques*. Oxford: Pergamon, 1966.

Wolpert, A., Hagamen, H. B., & Merlis, S. A comparative study of thiothixene and trifluoperazine in childhood schizophrenia. *Current Therapeutic Research*, 1967, *9*, 482–485.

Wright, L. Handling the encopretic child. *Professional Psychology*, 1973, *4*, 137–144.

Wynne, L. C., & Singer, M. T. Thought disorder and family relations of schizophrenics: I. A research strategy. II. A classification of forms of thinking. *Archives of General Psychiatry*, 1963, *9*, 191–206.

Young, I. L., & Goldsmith, A. O. Treatment of encopresis in a day treatment program. *Psychotherapy: Theory, Research, and Practice*, 1972, *9*, 231–235.

Yule, W., Sacks, B., & Hersof, L. Successful flooding treatment of a noise phobia in an eleven-year-old. *Journal of Behavior Therapy and Experimental Psychiatry*, 1974, *5*, 209–211.

Zaretsky, E. *Capitalism, the family and personal life*. New York: Harper & Row, 1976.

Zautra, A., & Goodhart, D. Quality of life: A review of the literature. *Community Mental Health Review*, 1979, *4*, 1–10.

Zax, M., Cowen, E. L., Rappaport, J., Beach, D. R., & Laird, J. D. Follow-up study of children identified early as emotionally disturbed. *Journal of Consulting and Clinical Psychology*, 1968, *32*, 369–374.

Zax, M., & Specter, G. A. *An introduction to community psychology*. New York: Wiley, 1974.

Zuk, G. H. The go-between process in family therapy. *Family Process*, 1966, *5*, 162–168.

Zuk, G. H. *Family therapy: A triadic-based approach*. New York: Behavioral Publications, 1971.

AUTHOR INDEX

SUBJECT INDEX